OAS-L	OAS's definition of Latin America (*see* SALA, 24-1000)	P10I	per ten thous...
OECD	Organization for Economic Cooperation and Development	PTP	percent of to...
		R-GAP	relative gap
OECS	Organization of Eastern Caribbean States (*see* SALA, 24-1000)	SDRs	Special Drawi...
		SNA	system of natio... accounts
OPEC	Organization of Petroleum Exporting Countries	T	Thousand (i.e., 000 omitted)
p (pp)	page(s)	TJ	Terajoules
PC	percentage change	U	unit
PHI	per hundred inhabitants	UN	United Nations
PHTI	per hundred thousand inhabitants	US	U.S. currency
PI	per inhabitant	U.S. or USA	United States of America
PIB	*producto interno bruto* (English = GDP)	WDC	Washington, D.C.
PMI	per million inhabitants	YA	yearly arithmetic mean
PTI	per thousand inhabitants	YE	year end

Sources

Sources frequently cited. (Abbreviation generally shows agency followed by title of publication or series).
Other sources appear in tables throughout.

ADEMA	*See* ECLA	IASI-C	*Características de la Estructura Demográfica*
AE	Anuario Estadístico	IBRD	International Bank for Reconstruction and Development. (*see* WB)
AR	Annual Report		
BDM	Banco de México	ICAO	International Civil Aviation Organization
BID	Banco Interamericano de Desarrollo (*see* IDB)	ICAO-DS-B	Digest of Statistics, *Bulletin*
C/CAA	Caribbean/Central American Action, *Caribbean Data Book*	ICAO-DS-T	Digest of Statistics, *Traffic: Commercial Air Carriers*
CELADE	Centro Latinoamericano de Demografía (Santiago)	ICAO-DS-AT	Digest of Statistics, *Airport Traffic*
		IDB	Inter-American Development Bank (WDC)
CELADE-BD	*Boletín Demográfico*	IDB-AR	*Annual Report*
CEPAL	Comisión Económica para América Latina (*see* ECLA)	IDB-SPTF	Social Progress Trust Fund, *Socio-Economic Progress in Latin America* (1961-71) and *Econimic and Social Progress in Latin America* (1972)
COHA	Council on Hemispheric Affairs, *Washington Report on the Hemisphere*		
		ILO	International Labour Office (Geneva)
Colombia-DANE	Departamento Administrativo Nacional	ILO-YLS	*Yearbook of Labor Statistics*
Cuba-CEE	Comité Estatal de Estadística	IMF	International Monetary Fund (WDC)
DGE	Dirección General de Estadística	IMF-BPS	*Balance of Payment Statistics*
DGEC	Dirección General de Estadística y Censos	IMF-BPS-Y	*Balance of Payment Statistics Yearbook*
ECLA	Economic Commission for Latin America (Santiago)	IMF-DOT	*Direction of Trade Statistics*
		IMF-DOT-Y	*Yearbook*
ECLA-ADEMA	*Agua, Desarrollo y Medio Ambiente* (1977)	IMF-GFSY	*Government Finance Statistics Yearbook*
ECLA-AE	*Anuario Estadístico de América Latina*	IMF-IFS	*International Financial Statistics*
ECLA-BPAL	*Balance de Pagos 1950-77*	IMF-IFS-S	*IFS Supplement* (No. 1, 1981–). (*See also* IFS-Y)
ECLA-CC	*Cuadernos de la CEPAL*		
ECLA-CEC	*Cuadernos Estadísticos de la CEPAL*	IMF-IFS-Y	*Yearbook* (entitled IFS-S from 1961 through 1978)
ECLA-D	Document		
ECLA-EIC	*Estudios e Informes de la CEPAL*	INE	Instituto Nacional de Estadística
ECLA-N	*Notas sobre la Economía y el Desarrollo*	INEC	Instituto Nacionale de Estadística y Censos
ECLA-S	*Economic Survey of Latin America*	JLP	José López Portillo (Mexico City)
ECLA-SHCAL	*Series Históricas del Crecimiento 1900-76 (1978)*	JLP-AE-H	*Anexo Estadístico Histórico*
ECLA-SP	Preliminary version of ECLA-S	JLP-AP-E	*Anexo de Política Económica*
ECLA-SY	*Statistical Yearbook (see ECLA-AE)*	Mexico-	
EYB	*Europa Year Book*	BANAMEX	Banco Nacional de México
FAO	UN, Food and Agriculture Organization (Rome)	BANAMEX-	
		RESM	Review of the Economic Situation of Mexico
FAO-FY	*Fertilizer Yearbook*	Mexico-BDM	Banco de México
FAO-PY	*Production Yearbook* (1958-)	BDM-IE	*Indicadores Económicos*
FAO-SFA	*State of Food and Agriculture*	BDM-IE-AH	*Indicadores Económicos, Acervo Histórico*
FAO-TY	*Trade Yearbook* (1958-)	Mexico-BNCE	Banco Nacional de Comercio Exterior
FAO-YFP	*Yearbook of Forestry Products*	BNCE-CE	*Comercio Exterior*
FAO-YFS	*Yearbook of Fishery Statistics*	Mexico-INEGI	Instituto Nacional de Estadística, Geografía e Informática
FAO-YFSCL	*Catches and Landings*		
FAO-YFSFC	*Fishery Commodities*	INEGI-EHM	Estadísticas Históricas de México
IASI	OAS, Inter-American Statistical Institute	Mexico-NAFINSA	Nacional Financiera, S.A.
IASI-AC	*América en Cifras*	NAFINSA-EMC	*La Economía Mexicana en Cifras*
IASI-BE	*Boletín Estadístico*	NAFINSA-MV	*Mercado de Valores*

Continued on back endsheet.

STATISTICAL ABSTRACT OF LATIN AMERICA

Series editor

JAMES W. WILKIE

SALA PUBLICATION HISTORY

Edition	Editors	Year of Publication
1 (1955)	[Robert N. Burr and Russell H. Fitzgibbon], 8 tables	1956
2 (1956)	[John D. Rees], 10 tables	1957
3 (1957)	[Berl Golomb], 18 tables	1959
4 (1960)	[Berl Golomb], 20 tables	1960
5 (1961)	[Berl Golomb], 23 tables	1961
6 (1962)	Berl Golomb and Ronald H. Dolkart, 51 tables	1963
7 (1963)	Donald S. Castro, Berl Golomb, and C. Breyer, 59 tables	1963
8 (1964)	Juan Gómez-Quiñones, 78 tables	1965
9 (1965)	Norris B. Lyle and Richard A. Calman, 102 tables	1966
10 (1966)	C. Paul Roberts and Takako Kohda, 81 tables	1967
11 (1967)	C. Paul Roberts and Takako Kohda, 95 tables	1968
12 (1968)	C. Paul Roberts and Takako Kohda Karplus, 102 tables	1969
13 (1969)	Kenneth Ruddle and Mukhtar Hamour, 131 tables	1970
14 (1970)	Kenneth Ruddle and Mukhtar Hamour, 200 tables	1971
15 (1971)	Kenneth Ruddle and Donald Odermann, 195 tables	1973
16 (1972)	Kenneth Ruddle and Kathleen Barrows, 282 tables	1974
17*	James W. Wilkie and Paul Turovsky, 303 tables	1976
18	James W. Wilkie and Peter Reich, 415 tables	1977
19	James W. Wilkie and Peter Reich, 439 tables	1978
20	James W. Wilkie and Peter Reich, 684 tables	1980
21	James W. Wilkie and Stephen Haber, 666 tables	1981
22	James W. Wilkie and Stephen Haber, 752 tables	1983
23	James W. Wilkie and Adam Perkal, 892 tables	1984
24	James W. Wilkie and Adam Perkal, 982 tables	1985
25	James W. Wilkie and David E. Lorey, 1063 tables	1987
26	James W. Wilkie, David E. Lorey, and Enrique Ochoa, 1077 tables	1988

*Beginning with volume 17, designation by volume number rather than year of edition.

STATISTICAL ABSTRACT OF LATIN AMERICA

Volume 26

JAMES W. WILKIE
Editor

DAVID E. LOREY
and
ENRIQUE OCHOA
Co-Editors

UCLA Latin American Center Publications
University of California • Los Angeles

Citation

James W. Wilkie, David E. Lorey, and Enrique Ochoa eds., *Statistical Abstract of Latin America*, Volume 26 (Los Angeles: UCLA Latin American Center Publications, University of California, 1988).

Other Library Entries

1. Statistical Abstract of Latin America.

2. California. University, Los Angeles. Latin American Center. Statistical Abstract of Latin America.

3. [Earlier name] . California. Univeristy, Los Angeles. Committee on Latin American Studies. Statistical Abstract of Latin America.

4. University of California. Los Angeles. Latin American Center. *Statistical Abstract of Latin America*.

Statistical Abstract of Latin America Volume 26
UCLA Latin American Center Publications
Los Angeles, California 90024-1447

ISBN (cloth): 0-87903-248-0

Library of Congress Card Number: 56-63569

Printed In the United States of America

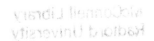

CONTENTS

PART X. NATIONAL ACCOUNTS, GOVERNMENT
POLICY AND FINANCE, AND PRICES

PART XI. DEVELOPMENT OF DATA

PREFACE
The Parameters of SALA

Goals of the Statistical Abstract

The goals of the *Statistical Abstract of Latin America* (SALA) are ten:

1. To provide a yearly one-volume selection of important statistics culled from more than 200 sources.
2. To offer the latest figures available on a timely basis for the 20 countries of Latin America, defined below.
3. To provide a context for present and future-oriented statistics by presenting whenever possible the data in series covering several decades or years.
4. To generate through research new data not published elsewhere.
5. To develop new types of data and/or to provide new analytical treatment of statistical series through SALA-sponsored research.
6. To guide the user of this volume to the wide variety of statistical material and sources available.
7. To suggest kinds of data that may be found in other sources as well as where to look for more complete coverage than can be abstracted here.
8. To present maps and graphs so that statistics take on greater meaning than would otherwise be possible to achieve.
9. To provide a SALA Supplement Series which offers interpretation, longitudinal data, and cartographic analysis of statistics on Latin America.
10. To coordinate presentation of statistics in SALA with the theory and model presented in James W. Wilkie, *Statistics and National Policy*, Statistical Abstract of Latin America, Supplement 3 (1974).

Organization

In order to accomplish these goals, SALA is organized in the following ways:

1. Historical statistics are presented across time. As new statistics become available, they can be traced back in time from volume to volume generating a long-term profile of Latin America's past and present as well as providing baselines for projecting into the future.
2. Explicit sources and qualifying notes are given for all data presented. Sources are given at the end of each table, not at the end of chapters where difficulty of use would be increased manyfold.
3. Source abbreviations and symbols are standardized. A key to sources is included for convenient reference.

4. A section on "Explanation of Terms" lists the abbreviations used. This information is repeated in the front endsheets for easy use.
5. The "Note on Statistical Definitions" gives weight and measure equivalencies and explains alternative methods for calculating rate of change over time.
6. Data are cross-referenced from one table to another throughout the volume.
7. Each volume is fully indexed to help readers find topics and related subjects.
8. A "Guide to Data" section in some volumes leads the user to additional sources and supplemental bibliographic aids.
9. The "Development of Data" section contains analysis of concepts, problems, and methods in organizing new topics or chapters included in SALA.
10. A carefully selected international advisory board guides the research and compilation for SALA and its Supplements.

Thus, SALA is intended to be the standard source for statistical information on Latin America and to encourage the use of data by scholars, researchers, business, and governments.

Cautions in Use of Statistics

Readers are cautioned that all data for any topic vary according to definition, parameters, methods of compilation and calculation, and completeness of coverage as well as data gathered, and/or date adjusted. Indeed, readers are reminded that statistics do not reveal "truth," but rather serve as proxy to interpret reality, and alternative statistics are available for most data series. Although such data as import statistics are often suspect because they do not take into account the extensive smuggling of goods, such figures are important because national and international policy decisions are made on the basis of the data recorded, data which interact with events to help change the course of "history." In this manner, "statistical reality" becomes quite as important as "reality" itself.

Presentation of Data

To help make the SALA series more useful to readers, beginning with Volume 24, we have included alternative data in the form of partial tables from previous issues going back to Volume 17. Previously we included in a cumulative index references to tables not reprinted from volume to volume. Such an index, however, created a problem for investigators who had to consult each back issue in order to determine whether or not (regardless of title) the table format carried the information (or additional data) actually sought.

For example, the method of presenting a partial table showing subheadings and data for one country among the twenty permits the reader to see at a glance the relevance of the type of information given, hence eliminating searches in earlier issues.

Elimination of the cumulative index also has two added advantages:

1. Data and references (to full data in the partial tables) on similar topics are now grouped together and not separated between the chapters and the index.
2. No cumulative index is necessary—the cumulative index often led readers to the same table (with no new information) reprinted in more than one volume for persons who might not have a complete set of SALA.

Latin America Defined

The concept of Latin America used in SALA utilizes the standard definition involving 20 countries. This standard definition is used for two reasons. First, Latin America's own self-identification of the 20 countries is critical, as discussed below. Second, data are not consistently available for the various other definitions of Latin America, some of which include units (such as Martinique and French Guiana) that are not independent bodies but rather colonies of Europe, legally as well as in economic and financial flows. Although SALA focuses on the standard list of 20 countries of Latin America, at times comparative data are given for bodies considered part of the region when it is defined in extended terms, that is, as Extended Latin America (ELA).

The 20 countries of Latin America (coded A through T) are presented in table 1, which presents Latin America as perceived by itself. According to Latin America's self-identification, the region is traditionally united by core language, religion, culture, bureaucratic outlook, and timing of the post-independence experience based upon nineteenth-century liberalism and free trade. Haiti is included not because of its Latin-based French language but because of its interaction with the Dominican Republic (which it ruled between 1822 and 1844) and its historic identification with Latin American affairs. Former non-Spanish colonies of the Caribbean and South America are excluded because they have had little or no interaction in dialogue and events in Latin America. Puerto Rico is excluded from Latin America, of course, because it has never been independent, belonging until 1898 to Spain and subsequently to the United States.

Problems in the definition of Latin America have come from several directions. After 1910 the 20 traditional Latin American republics (plus the United States) made up the Pan

Table 1

THE 20 COUNTRIES OF LATIN AMERICA

A. ARGENTINA	K. GUATEMALA
B. BOLIVIA	L. HAITI
C. BRAZIL	M. HONDURAS
D. CHILE	N. MEXICO
E. COLOMBIA	O. NICARAGUA
F. COSTA RICA	P. PANAMA
G. CUBA	Q. PARAGUAY
H. DOMINICAN REPUBLIC	R. PERU
I. ECUADOR	S. URUGUAY
J. EL SALVADOR	T. VENEZUELA

Source: See table 1001.

American Union, known since 1948 as the Organization of American States (OAS). Cuba was expelled from the OAS in 1962, reducing the number of Latin American members to 19. In 1967 the former English colonies of Barbados and Trinidad-Tobago joined the OAS as did Jamaica in 1969; and thus, in the minds of those who equate the Latin American region with the OAS, the number of countries south of the U.S. border rose to 22. Statistical publications of the OAS in the 1970s began to compare total figures for the 22 countries with data for the United States, with the total reaching 31 in the 1980s. Further problems of definition come from some geographically minded observers who have sought to delimit the world neatly into physical regions regardless of cultural ties and other historical patterns. For those observers "Latin America" includes all of the islands of the Caribbean and the three South American mainland Guianas (see table 3) even though they are oriented toward Europe. Latin America sees its own regional groupings in table 2.

With regard to cartographic representation, which shows the size of countries according to population rather than according to geographical area, several views help in understanding the relationships of Latin America's 20 countries. The situation in 1980 is shown in figure 6:1 (see Chapter 6). The cartographic view in 1972 of Latin America's 20 countries (figure 1) is compared to that view for Extended Latin America (ELA) based on 30 political units (figure 2). In 1972 Latin America had an estimated population of 283,822,140 compared with ELA's 291,646,708. The difference of 7.8 million meant that Latin America had 97 percent of ELA's population. Of ELA's 19 metropolitan areas of one million persons or more in 1972, 18 were in Latin America. San Juan, Puerto Rico, was the only major city in ELA outside of Latin America proper.

Various definitions of Extended Latin America are given in table 3, with concepts differing according to agency. ELA contains up to 25 more bodies than the 20 standard Latin

Table 2

REGIONAL GROUPINGS IN LATIN AMERICA

LAIA   *Latin American Integration Association*
(Latin American Free Trade Association [LAFTA]
from 1960–80)

Member	Date of Entry
ARGENTINA	Jan. 1981
BOLIVIA	Mar. 1982
BRAZIL	Nov. 1981
CHILE	May 1981
COLOMBIA	May 1981
ECUADOR	Mar. 1982
MEXICO	Feb. 1981
PARAGUAY	Dec. 1980
PERU	Nov. 1981
URUGUAY	Mar. 1981
VENEZUELA	Mar. 1982

AG   *Cartagena Agreement, Andean Group*

Member	Date of Entry
BOLIVIA	Nov. 1969
CHILE	Sept. 1969[a]
COLOMBIA	Sept. 1969
ECUADOR	Nov. 1969
PERU	Oct. 1969
VENEZUELA	Nov. 1973

CACM   *Central American Common Market*

Member	Date of Entry
COSTA RICA	Sept. 1963
EL SALVADOR	May 1961
GUATEMALA	May 1961
HONDURAS	Apr. 1962[b]
NICARAGUA	May 1961

a. Withdrew Oct. 1976.
b. Withdrew Jan. 1971.

American countries. Table 3 expands Latin America to ELA on the basis of the "Caribbean" units defined by the Caribbean/Central American Action (C/CAA). Because C/CAA is oriented toward the U.S. legislative concept called the Caribbean Basin Initiative, C/CAA considers as belonging to the Caribbean 25 political units in addition to the Central American countries (including even El Salvador, which borders the Pacific Ocean, not the Caribbean). The FAO definition is almost as inclusive as that of the C/CAA, omitting only Bermuda. The OAS has 31 members, the Latin American countries plus the 11 included in table 3. (Since 1962 Cuba has been suspended from activities but not membership; Guyana has observer status but not membership.)

Figures 3 and 4 present a geographical view and a political view of ELA, respectively. Some small Caribbean islands appear as dots on these maps, but are better represented in figure 2 which portrays the population relationship.

The comparative land area of Latin America proper is detailed in table 4. Comparisons are made not only among the 20 countries but with states in the United States and with three small countries which have achieved major roles on the world stage—Israel, Japan, and Switzerland. Comparisons of the size of Latin American countries vary according to observers; for example, in England Guatemala is often compared to Greece but in Guatemala the comparison is to Holland, Belgium, and Switzerland. Latin America constitutes 97 percent of ELA, as can be calculated from table 6.

Rankings of the 20 Latin American countries are given in table 5. The countries with the first and third largest land area (Brazil and Mexico) contain 52.4 percent of the region's territory (see table 4). The countries with the first and second largest populations (Brazil and Mexico) contained 53.4 percent of the region's population in 1972—see figure 1. (In 1980 these two countries reached 54.3 percent of the total Latin American population, as can be calculated from figure 6:1.) The country with the smallest land area (El Salvador) was the highest in density even though it ranked 14 in population size. The country with the smallest population (Panama) ranked 16 in area and 11 in density. The country of median rank (10) in area is Ecuador, which in the 1970s ranked 9 in population and 13 in density.

For expanded discussion defining Latin America, see the Preface to SALA 23 and SALA 25.

Analysis of New Trends in Latin America or in Meaning of Statistical Data

In addition to organizing and presenting data, SALA often seeks through its Preface to assess new trends in the Latin American situation as well as types of data becoming available (or decreasing in availability). Previous issues of SALA contain discussion of the following topics in the Preface:

"On the Accuracy of Statistics and Development of Time-Series Data" (vol. 19)

"On Defining the Concepts of Latin America, the Caribbean, and Economically Questionable Nations (EQNs)" (vol. 23)

"Views of Latin America's Reality," (vol. 25).

Development of Data

To develop new statistical series on Latin America, SALA and the SALA Supplement Series carry articles analyzing sources, methods, and findings. Articles appearing to date in SALA and Supplement 6 (*Quantitative Latin American Studies*, 1977), Supplement 7 (*Money and Politics in Latin America*, 1977), and Supplement 10 (*Society and Economy*

Figure 1

POPULATION CARTOGRAM OF LATIN AMERICA

(1972)

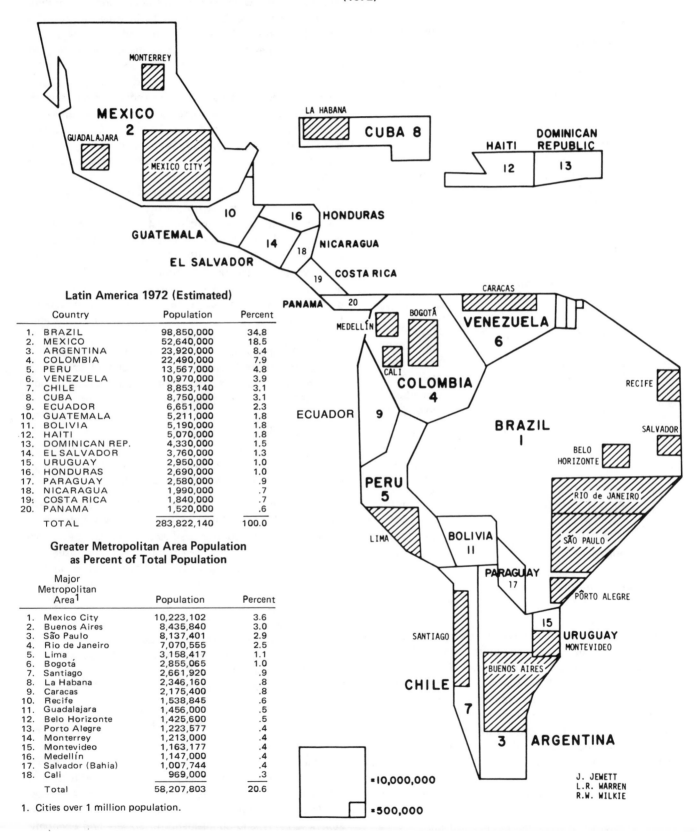

Latin America 1972 (Estimated)

	Country	Population	Percent
1.	BRAZIL	98,850,000	34.8
2.	MEXICO	52,640,000	18.5
3.	ARGENTINA	23,920,000	8.4
4.	COLOMBIA	22,490,000	7.9
5.	PERU	13,567,000	4.8
6.	VENEZUELA	10,970,000	3.9
7.	CHILE	8,853,140	3.1
8.	CUBA	8,750,000	3.1
9.	ECUADOR	6,651,000	2.3
10.	GUATEMALA	5,211,000	1.8
11.	BOLIVIA	5,190,000	1.8
12.	HAITI	5,070,000	1.8
13.	DOMINICAN REP.	4,330,000	1.5
14.	EL SALVADOR	3,760,000	1.3
15.	URUGUAY	2,950,000	1.0
16.	HONDURAS	2,690,000	1.0
17.	PARAGUAY	2,580,000	.9
18.	NICARAGUA	1,990,000	.7
19.	COSTA RICA	1,840,000	.7
20.	PANAMA	1,520,000	.6
	TOTAL	283,822,140	100.0

Greater Metropolitan Area Population as Percent of Total Population

	Major Metropolitan Area[1]	Population	Percent
1.	Mexico City	10,223,102	3.6
2.	Buenos Aires	8,435,840	3.0
3.	São Paulo	8,137,401	2.9
4.	Rio de Janeiro	7,070,555	2.5
5.	Lima	3,158,417	1.1
6.	Bogotá	2,855,065	1.0
7.	Santiago	2,661,920	.9
8.	La Habana	2,346,160	.8
9.	Caracas	2,175,400	.8
10.	Recife	1,538,845	.6
11.	Guadalajara	1,456,000	.5
12.	Belo Horizonte	1,425,600	.5
13.	Porto Alegre	1,223,577	.4
14.	Monterrey	1,213,000	.4
15.	Montevideo	1,163,177	.4
16.	Medellín	1,147,000	.4
17.	Salvador (Bahia)	1,007,744	.4
18.	Cali	969,000	.3
	Total	58,207,803	20.6

1. Cities over 1 million population.

J. JEWETT
L.R. WARREN
R.W. WILKIE

Figure 2

CARTOGRAM OF EXTENDED LATIN AMERICA (ELA)

(1972)

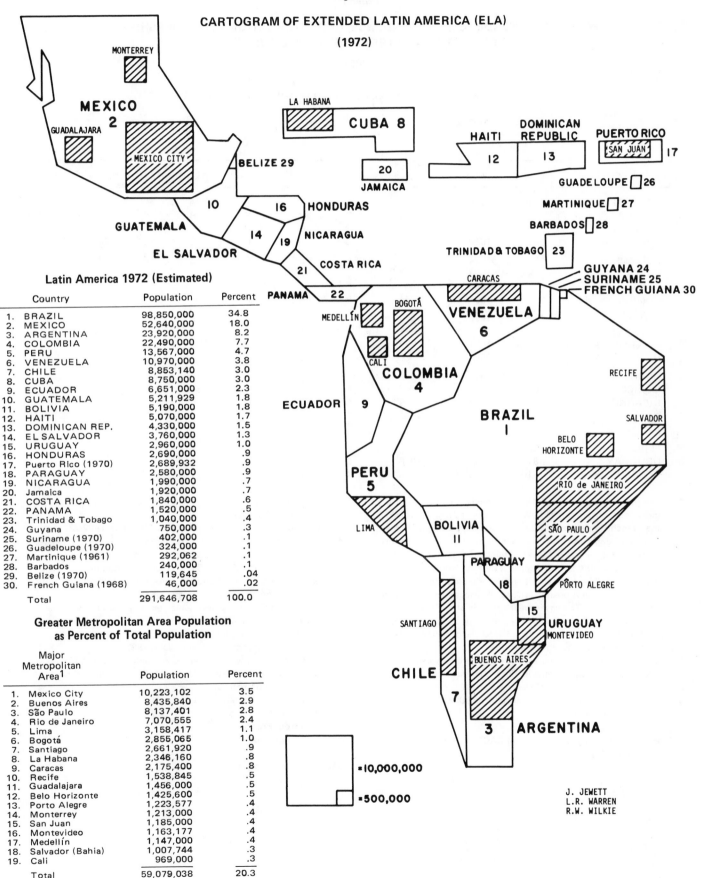

Latin America 1972 (Estimated)

	Country	Population	Percent
1.	BRAZIL	98,850,000	34.8
2.	MEXICO	52,640,000	18.0
3.	ARGENTINA	23,920,000	8.2
4.	COLOMBIA	22,490,000	7.7
5.	PERU	13,567,000	4.7
6.	VENEZUELA	10,970,000	3.8
7.	CHILE	8,853,140	3.0
8.	CUBA	8,750,000	3.0
9.	ECUADOR	6,651,000	2.3
10.	GUATEMALA	5,211,929	1.8
11.	BOLIVIA	5,190,000	1.8
12.	HAITI	5,070,000	1.7
13.	DOMINICAN REP.	4,330,000	1.5
14.	EL SALVADOR	3,760,000	1.3
15.	URUGUAY	2,960,000	1.0
16.	HONDURAS	2,690,000	.9
17.	Puerto Rico (1970)	2,689,932	.9
18.	PARAGUAY	2,580,000	.9
19.	NICARAGUA	1,990,000	.7
20.	Jamaica	1,920,000	.7
21.	COSTA RICA	1,840,000	.6
22.	PANAMA	1,520,000	.5
23.	Trinidad & Tobago	1,040,000	.4
24.	Guyana	750,000	.3
25.	Suriname (1970)	402,000	.1
26.	Guadeloupe (1970)	324,000	.1
27.	Martinique (1961)	292,062	.1
28.	Barbados	240,000	.1
29.	Belize (1970)	119,645	.04
30.	French Guiana (1968)	46,000	.02
	Total	291,646,708	100.0

Greater Metropolitan Area Population as Percent of Total Population

	Major Metropolitan Area[1]	Population	Percent
1.	Mexico City	10,223,102	3.5
2.	Buenos Aires	8,435,840	2.9
3.	São Paulo	8,137,401	2.8
4.	Rio de Janeiro	7,070,555	2.4
5.	Lima	3,158,417	1.1
6.	Bogotá	2,855,065	1.0
7.	Santiago	2,661,920	.9
8.	La Habana	2,346,160	.8
9.	Caracas	2,175,400	.8
10.	Recife	1,538,845	.5
11.	Guadalajara	1,456,000	.5
12.	Belo Horizonte	1,425,600	.5
13.	Porto Alegre	1,223,577	.4
14.	Monterrey	1,213,000	.4
15.	San Juan	1,185,000	.4
16.	Montevideo	1,163,177	.4
17.	Medellín	1,147,000	.4
18.	Salvador (Bahia)	1,007,744	.3
19.	Cali	969,000	.3
	Total	59,079,038	20.3

1. Cities over 1 million population.

J. JEWETT
L.R. WARREN
R.W. WILKIE

Table 3

POLITICAL DEPENDENCE, INDEPENDENCE, AND INTERNATIONAL MEMBERSHIPS OF COUNTRIES AND TERRITORIES, 20 L AND 45 ELA

(1983)

PART I. TRADITIONALLY DEFINED LATIN AMERICA

Independent Countries[1]	As Result of			Memberships						
	War[2]		Special Circumstances	OAS	IDB:L	ECLA:L	ALADI	AG	CACM	CBI-IB
	Declared	Won								
A. ARGENTINA	1810	1816[a]		A	A	A	A			
B. BOLIVIA	1809	1825[a]		B	B	B	B	B		
C. BRAZIL			1822[b]	C	C	C	C			
D. CHILE	1810	1818[a]		D	D	D	D	D[5]		
E. COLOMBIA	1810	1824[a]	1830[e]	E	E	E	E	E		
F. COSTA RICA		1821[c]	1838[d]	F	F	F			F	F
G. CUBA		1898[a]	1902[i]	G[4]		G				
H. DOMINICAN REP.[3]		1821[a]	1844[h]	H	H	H				H
I. ECUADOR[7]	1809	1822[a]	1830[e]	I	I	I	I	I		
J. EL SALVADOR		1821[c]	1841[d]	J	J	J			J	J
K. GUATEMALA		1821[c]	1839[d]	K	K	K			K	K
L. HAITI	1791	1804[k]		L	L	L				L
M. HONDURAS		1821[c]	1838[d]	M	M	M			M[6]	M
N. MEXICO	1810	1821[a]		N	N	N	N			
O. NICARAGUA		1821[c]	1838[d]	O	O	O			O	O
P. PANAMA			1903[j]	P	P	P				P
Q. PARAGUAY			1811[a]	Q	Q	Q	Q			
R. PERU	1821	1824[a,f]		R	R	R	R	I		
S. URUGUAY	1811	1814[a]	1828[l]	S	S	S	S			
T. VENEZUELA[7]	1810	1821[a,g]	1829[e]	T	T	T	T	T		

1. The three events that provided the immediate stimulation for independence were the U.S. War for Independence (1776-81); the French Revolution of 1789 proclaiming the Rights of Man and abolishing slavery for France but not its colonies—the most prosperous of which was Saint Domingue (the future Haiti); and the capture of the Spanish monarch by Napoleon Bonaparte, Spain's "ally," who placed his brother Joseph on the throne of Spain in 1808, thus breaking strong allegiances between Spain and its colonies. (The latter event occurred after France had passed through Spain, driving the monarchy of Portugal to Brazil in 1807, laying the basis for Brazil's independence once the monarchy returned to Portugal in 1821.)
2. Excludes precursor movements such as that by Tiradentes in 1788 (Brazil) or by Miranda in 1806 (Venezuela).
3. France ceded to Spain in 1795.
4. Since 1962 Cuba has been suspended from OAS activities but not membership.
5. Chile withdrew from AG in 1976.
6. Honduras partially withdrew from CACM in 1971.
7. Member of OPEC.

a. Won from Spain.
b. Won from Portugal.
c. Won from Spain and became part of Mexico in 1822-23.
d. Breakup of United Provinces of Central America, which existed to unite Costa Rica, El Salvador, Guatemala, Honduras, and Nicaragua from 1823 to 1841. For all practical purposes the breakup came by 1838 and attempts to revive union were militarily defeated by 1842.
e. Breakup of Gran Colombia, which existed to unite Colombia, Ecuador, and Venezuela from 1819 to 1830.
f. Last Spanish troops left Peru in 1826.
g. Last Spanish troops left Venezuela in 1823.
h. Won from Haiti, which governed Hispaniola or Santo Domingo (future Dominican Republic) from 1822 to 1844. Spain reoccupied from 1861 to 1865.
i. Won from the United States.
j. Won from Colombia.
k. Won from France.
l. Won from Brazil.

SOURCE: SALA, 23-1.

Table 3 (Continued)

POLITICAL DEPENDENCE, INDEPENDENCE, AND INTERNATIONAL MEMBERSHIPS OF COUNTRIES AND TERRITORIES, 20 L AND 45 ELA

(1983)

PART II. NON-TRADITIONALLY DEFINED LATIN AMERICA ADDS:

Independent Countries	Year of Independence	From	OAS	IDB:L	ECLA:L	CARICOM[1]	ECCM	OECS	CBI-IB	FAO[4]
1. Antigua-Barbuda	1981	Gr. Britain	1			1	1	1	1	1
2. Bahamas	1973	Gr. Britain	2	2	2				2	2
3. Barbados	1966	Gr. Britain	3	3	3	3			3	3
4. Belize	1981	Gr. Britain				4			4	4
5. Dominica	1978	Gr. Britain	5			5	5	5	5	5
6. Grenada	1974	Gr. Britain	6		6	6	6	6	6	6
7. Guyana	1966	Gr. Britain		7	7	7			7	7
8. Jamaica	1962	Gr. Britain	8	8	8	8			8	8
9. St. Kitts-Nevis[2]	1983	Gr. Britain	9			9	9	9	9	9
10. St. Lucia	1977	Gr. Britain	10			10	10	10	10	10
11. St. Vincent-Grenadines	1979	Gr. Britain	11			11	11	11	11	11
12. Suriname	1975	Netherlands	12	12	12				12	12
13. Trinidad and Tobago	1962	Gr. Britain	13	13	13	13				

Dependent Countries	Belonging to	OAS	IDB:L	ICLA:L	CARICOM[1]	ECCM	OECS	CBI-IB	FAO
T1. Anguilla	Great Britain					T1			T1
T2. Bermuda	Great Britain[3]								
T3. British Virgin Islands	Great Britain							T3	T3
T4. Cayman Islands	Great Britain							T4	T4
T5. French Guiana	France								T5
T6. Guadeloupe	France								T6
T7. Martinique	France								T7
T8. Montserrat	Great Britain				T8	T8	T8	T8	T8
T9. Netherlands Antilles	Netherlands							T9	T9
T10. Puerto Rico	United States								T10
T11. Turks and Caicos	Great Britain							T11	T11
T12. U.S. Virgin Islands	United States								T12

1. The Caribbean Community and Common Market (CARICOM) was established in 1973 to replace the Caribbean Free Trade Association (CARIFTA), founded in 1967.
2. St. Kitts is officially known as St. Christopher.
3. Bermuda has been self-governing since 1968. Although under Great Britain, it claims Bermudian nationality.
4. Includes Falkland Islands.

SOURCE: Various, including especially C/CAA, 1983; COHA, May 4, 1982, p. 4; WA, 1987, p. 640.

Table 4

LAND AREA OF LATIN AMERICA, 20 LRC

Country	% of Latin America	Sq Mi. (T)	Equals Approximate Foreign Area as Coded	
Latin American Total	100.0	7.686	ASA	2 X the 50 U.S. States[6]
A. ARGENTINA[1,2]	14.0	1,072	ASA	4 X Texas
B. BOLIVIA[4]	5.5	423	SLT	California and Texas
C. BRAZIL[2]	42.5	3,265	ASA	9% larger than continental U.S.[7]
D. CHILE[1,2]	3.8	292	ASA	Texas and West Virginia
E. COLOMBIA[2]	5.7	440	SLT	California, Texas, Maryland and Connecticut
F. COSTA RICA	.3	20	ASA	5 X Los Angeles County
G. CUBA	.6	44	SLT	Pennsylvania
H. DOMINICAN REP.	.2	19	ASA	Vermant and New Hampshire
I. ECUADOR[2]	1.4	104	ASA	Colorado
J. EL SALVADOR	.1	8	ASA	2 X Los Angeles County
K. GUATEMALA	.5	42	ASA	Tennessee
L. HAITI	.1	11	ASA	Maryland
M. HONDURAS	.6	43	MT	Tennessee
N. MEXICO[3]	9.9	760	SLT	3 X Texas
O. NICARAGUA[8]	.6	46	SLT	Mississippi
P. PANAMA[5]	.4	30	SLT	South Carolina
Q. PARAGUAY	2.0	157	SLT	California
R. PERU[2,9]	6.4	494	SLT	2 X Texas
S. URUGUAY	.9	69	MT	Washington State
T. VENEZUELA[2,10]	4.5	347	MT	2 X California
Israel	**	8	ASA	2 X Los Angeles County
Japan	**	144	SLT	California
Switzerland	**	16	ASA	4 X Los Angeles County

Code: ASA = about same as . . .
       MT = more than . . .
       SLT = slightly less than . . .

1. Excludes Argentina's South Atlantic islands and Antarctica (482,000 sq. mi.) and Chile's Antarctica (483,000 sq. mi.).
2. Excludes areas in litigation.
3. Excludes islands.
4. Excludes 1,424 sq. mi. of Bolivia's part of Lake Titicaca.
5. Includes Panama Canal Zone (568 sq. mi).
6. Fifty U.S. states = 3,540 sq. mi., excluding lakes.
7. Forty-eight continental states = 2,968 sq. mi., excluding lakes.
8. Excludes 3,474 sq. mi. of Nicaragua's lakes.
9. Excludes 1,917 sq. mi. of Peru's part of Lake Titicaca.
10. Excludes 5,113 sq. mi. of Venezuela's Lake Maracaibo and Lake Valencia.

SOURCE: Calculated from SALA, 21–300 and 21–301; IASI-AC, 1972, table 101–04 and IASC-AC, 1974, table 201–01. Bolivia is from Jorge Muñoz Reyes, *Geografía de Bolivia* (La Paz: Academia Nacional de Ciencias de Bolivia, 1977), p. 2; United States is from USBC-SA, 1978, p. 6. Israel, Japan, and Switzerland is from WA, 1984, pp. 509, 512, 541. For area in square kilometers, including each country's lakes and inland waters, see table 100, below.

Table 5

LATIN AMERICAN COUNTRIES RANKED ACCORDING TO AREA, POPULATION SIZE, AND DENSITY[1]

Country (Largest Area to Smallest)	Area (Excluding Lakes)[2]	Population (Highest = 1) (1972)	Density[3] (Lowest = 1) (1970s)[4]
BRAZIL	1	1	5
ARGENTINA	2	3	3
MEXICO	3	2	14
PERU	4	5	4
COLOMBIA	5	4	10
BOLIVIA	6	11	1
VENEZUELA	7	6	8
CHILE	8	7	7
PARAGUAY	9	17	2
ECUADOR	10	9	13
URUGUAY	11	15	9
NICARAGUA	12	18	6
CUBA	13	8	17
HONDURAS	14	16	12
GUATEMALA	15	10	16
PANAMA	16	20	11
COSTA RICA	17	19	15
DOMINICAN REP.	18	13	18
HAITI	19	12	19
EL SALVADOR	20	14	20

1. For discussion, see SALA 25, pp. xxii–xxvi.
2. Excluding lakes and inland waters; for these inclusions, see table 100 below.
3. Persons per km^2 (population divided by area).
4. Varying years from 1971 to 1982; according to data in tables 627–648.

SOURCE: SALA 25, p. xxiii.

in Mexico, forthcoming 1988) include the following (arranged by area and topic):

Latin America

"The Rapid Expansion of Voter Participation in Latin America: Presidential Elections, 1845–1986," by Enrique C. Ochoa (vol. 25)

"On Measuring Political Conflict in Latin America, 1948–1967," by Manual Moreno-Ibáñez (vol. 20)

"Survey Research in Authoritarian Regimes: Brazil and the Southern Cone of Latin America Since 1970," by Brian H. Smith and Frederick C. Turner (vol. 23)

"Democratic versus Dictatorial Budgeting: The Case of Cuba with Reference to Venezuela and Mexico," by Enrique A. Baloyra (Supp. 7)

"Measuring the Scholarly Image of Latin American Democracy, 1945–1970," by Kenneth F. Johnson (vol. 17)

"Research Perspectives on the Revised Fitzgibbon-Johnson Index of the Image of Political Democracy in Latin America, 1945–1975," by Kenneth F. Johnson (Supp. 6)

"Measuring U.S. Government Perception of the 'Communist Menace' in Latin America, 1947–1976," by Peter Reich (vol. 19)

"Alternative Interpretations of Time-Series Data on the Growth of the Latin American Film Industry, 1926–1970," by Daniel I. Geffner (vol. 19)

"Religious Data History, [1956–1974]," by Peter Reich (vol. 18)

"Protestant Church Growth in Twentieth-Century Central America and the Caribbean," by T. D. Proffitt III (vol. 22)

"Exchange Rate History, 1937–1974," by Bridget Reynolds (vol. 17)

"Labor's Real Wages in Latin America Since 1940," by John L. Martin (vol. 18)

"Problems of Measuring Housing and Shelter in Latin America, 1940–1980," by Manual Moreno-Ibáñez (vol. 22)

Figure 3

MAP OF EXTENDED LATIN AMERICA (ELA)

(Mercator Projection)

SOURCE: SALA-SNP, p. xxvi.

Figure 4

POLITICAL MAP OF EXTENDED LATIN AMERICA (ELA)

Table 6

LATIN AMERICA LAND AREA IN ELA AND THE WORLD

Category	Area (k^2)	Explanation
World	132,495,836	
A. ELA[1]	20,447,284	A = B + G
B. Latin America	19,907,626	Included in A
C. CACM[2]	411,170	Included in B
D. ALADI[3]	19,228,658	Included in B
E. Andean Group	5,443,818	Included in D
F. CLA[4]	267,798	Included in B
G. CNLA[5]	539,658	Included in A
H. CARICOM[6]	257,384	Included in G

1. Extended Latin America.
2. Central American Common Market.
3. Latin American Integration Association.
4. Caribbean Latin America.
5. Caribbean Not Latin America.
6. Caribbean Community and Common Market.

SOURCE: Adapted in summary form from SALA, 23-2.

"Projecting the HEC (Health, Education, and Communication) Index for Latin America Back to 1940," by James W. Wilkie and Maj-Britt Nilsson (Supp. 6)

"Educational Enrollment History, [1880–1929]," by José Casimiro Ortal (vol. 18)

"Food Production in Latin America Since 1942," by James W. Wilkie and Manual Moreno-Ibáñez (vol. 23)

"Latin American Fisheries: National Resources and Expanded Jurisdiction, 1938–1978," by Manual Moreno-Ibáñez (vol. 21)

"Problems in Comparative Crime Statistics for Latin America and the English-Speaking Caribbean, 1973–1978," by Luis P. Salas and Raymond Surette (vol. 23)

"Determining the Population in the Largest City of Each Latin American Country, 1900–1970," by Marshall C. Eakin (vol. 19)

"The Populations of Mexico and Argentina in 1980: Preliminary Data and Some Comparisons," by Richard W. Wilkie (vol. 21)

Argentina

"The Rural Population of Argentina to 1970," by Richard W. Wilkie (vol. 20)

"Losses and Lessons of the 1982 War for the Falklands," by Adam Perkal (vol. 23)

"Financing Argentine Industrial Corporate Development in the Aftermath of the First Perón Period," by David K. Eiteman (Supp. 7)

Bolivia

"Bolivia: Ironies in the National Revolutionary Process," by James W. Wilkie (vol. 25)

"U.S. Foreign Policy and Economic Assistance in Bolivia, 1948–1976," by James W. Wilkie (vol. 22)

"Bolivian Public Expenditure and the Role of Decentralized Agencies: A Test of the Wilkie View," by Thomas M. Millington (vol. 21)

Cuba

"An Index of Cuban Industrial Output, 1930–1958," By Jorge F. Pérez-López (Supp. 6)

El Salvador

"The Demographics of Land Reform in El Salvador Since 1980," by Roy L. Prosterman (vol. 22)

Mexico

"Six Ideological Phases: Mexico's 'Permanent Social and Economic Revolution' Since 1910," by James W. Wilkie (Supp. 10)

"Trends in Mexico's Socioeconomic and Political Structure," by James W. Wilkie (vol. 26)

"Charting Mexico's Capacity to Modernize: The Development of an Engineering Base Since 1929," by David E. Lorey (Supp. 10)

"Professional Expertise and Mexican Modernization: Sources, Methods, and Preliminary Findings," by David E. Lorey (vol. 26)

"Complexities of Measuring the Food Situation in Mexico: Supply of Basic Grains, 1925–1986," by Aída Mostkoff and Enrique Ochoa (Supp. 10)

"Mexican Community Studies in a Historical Framework, 1930–1970," by Stephen Haber (vol. 21)

"Modernization and Change in Mexican Communities, 1930–1970," by Stephen Haber (vol. 22)

"Changes in Mexico Since 1895: Central Government Revenue, Public Expenditure, and National Economic Growth," by James W. Wilkie (vol. 24)

"Mexico's 'New' Financial Crisis of 1982 in Historical Perspective," by James W. Wilkie (vol. 22)

"The Dramatic Growth of Mexico's Economy and the Rise of Statist Government Power, 1910–1982," by James W. Wilkie (Supp. 10)

"Borrowing as Revenue: The Case of Mexico," by James W. Wilkie (Supp. 10)

"Sources of Investment Capital in Twentieth-Century Mexico," by Dale Story (vol. 23)

"Las Distintas Caras de la Deuda del Sector Público Mexicano, 1970–1976," by Samuel Schmidt (vol. 22)

"Revisando la Deuda Pública en México, 1970–1982," by Samuel Schmidt (vol. 23)

"Quantifying the Class Structure of Mexico, 1895–1970," by James W. Wilkie and Paul D. Wilkins (vol. 21)

"Class Structure in Mexico, 1895–1980," by Stephanie Granato and Aída Mostkoff (Supp. 10)

"Mexican Demographic History of the Nineteenth Century: Evidence and Approaches," by John E. Kicza (vol. 21)

"Employment and Lack of Employment in Mexico, 1900–1970," by Donald B. Keesing (Supp. 6)

"Losers in Mexican Politics: A Comparative Study of Official Party Precandidates for Gubernatorial Elections, 1970–1975," by Roderic A. Camp (Supp. 6)

"Mexican Military Leadership in Statistical Perspective Since the 1930s," by Roderic A. Camp (vol. 20)

"Federal Expenditures and 'Personalism' in the Mexican 'Institutional' Revolution," by James A. Hanson (Supp. 7)

"Mexico in the U.S. Press: A Quantitative Study, 1972–1978," by Thomas Michael Laichas (vol. 20)

Guides to Statistical Data for Research

To assess research on Latin American statistics, SALA and the SALA Supplement Series publish articles on issues and publications. Articles to date include the following:

"The Management and Mismanagement of National and International Statistics," by James W. Wilkie (vol. 22)

"The Status of Quantitative Research on Latin America," by James W. Wilkie (vol. 19)

"A Social Census Questionnaire for Latin American Countries," by James W. Wilkie, John C. Super, and Edna Monzón de Wilkie (vol. 18)

"Quantitative Research on Latin America: An Inventory of Data Sets," by Carl W. Deal (vol. 17)

"Quantitative Data Sets on Latin America: The Second Survey by the Latin American Studies Association," by Carl W. Deal (vol. 21)

"File Inventory of the Latin American Data Bank, University of Florida, Gainesville," by M. J. Carvajal and J. E. Uquillas (vol. 17)

"Latin American Official Statistical Series on Microfiche, 1860–1974," compiled by Valerie Bloomfield (vol. 20)

Special SALA Supplements

In addition to the above listed 50 articles on development of statistical series and 7 articles on guides to data (all published in SALA and SALA Supplements 6, 7, and 10), 7 supplements have been published to treat specially focused topics.

Urbanization

Latin American Population and Urbanization Analysis: Maps and Statistics, 1950–1982, No. 8 (1984; reprint 1988, forthcoming), by Richard W. Wilkie

Urbanization in 19th Century Latin America: Statistics and Sources, No. 4 (1973), by Richard E. Boyer and Keith A. Davies

Society and Economy

Statistical Abstract of the United States–Mexico Borderlands, No. 9 (1984), edited by Peter L. Reich

Measuring Land Reform: Bolivia, Venezuela, and Latin America, No. 5 (1974), by James W. Wilkie

Cuba 1968, No. 1 (1970), edited by C. Paul Roberts and Mukhtar Hamour

Policy and Politics

Statistics and National Policy, No. 3 (1974), by James
W. Wilkie

Latin American Political Statistics, No. 2 (1972), edited
by Kenneth Ruddle and Philip Gillette

SALA Supplements are published periodically, and are
not correlated with any particular edition of SALA.

Request for User Assistance

SALA welcomes comments and suggestions for improve-
ment in presentation of statistics as well as notice of clarifi-
cations and corrections needed. We would very much like to
receive statistics that we might publish in SALA and will give
appropriate credit.

El Paso, Texas   J.W.W.
December 1987

TABLES

Detailed data in tables may not equal totals because of rounding

PART I. GEOGRAPHY AND LAND TENURE

PART IV: POLITICS, RELIGION, AND THE MILITARY

Chapter 10 Political Statistics

Chapter 11 Religion

Chapter 12 The Military

PART V: WORKING CONDITIONS, MIGRATION, AND HOUSING

Chapter 13 Labor Force, EAP, Unemployment, Class Structure, and Crime

PART VI: INDUSTRY, MINING, AND ENERGY

PART VII. SEA AND LAND HARVESTS

Chapter 25 Structure and Terms of Trade

PART IX: FINANCIAL FLOWS

Chapter 33 Gross Product

FIGURES

EXPLANATION OF TERMS

Cautions

1. All data for any topic vary according to definition, parameters, methods of compilation and calculation, and completeness of coverage as well as date gathered, date prepared, and/or date adjusted.

2. Totals for the "Latin American region" and for the "world" vary according to the definition used by the different international statistical agencies.

Symbols

‡	Preliminary, provisional, or unofficial	* *	Data not applicable
0 or #	Zero or negligible (less than half of unit employed, e.g., less than .05 or 500,000)	$	U.S. dollars
		† or x	Estimate by or in source
~	Data not available in source	@	Estimate made herein
- -	Source does not specify whether data are recorded separately, not applicable, zero or negligible	***	Obviously erroneous data
		*	Link (splice) in series or technical change
1965/66	Split year, e.g., fiscal or crop year	( )	Subtotal within tabular data

Abbreviations

A	arithmetic mean	EVN	Economically Viable Nation
AA	average annual change	FAO	UN, Food and Agriculture Organization
AA-EC	AA, exponential (see p. xxxvi)	FOB or fob	free on board
AA-GA	AA, geometric approximation (see p. xxxvi)	FY	fiscal year
AA-GR	AA, Growth rate in source	G	grams
ADCs	advanced developing countries	GA	Grupo Andino (see p. xxxv and SALA 24-1000)
AG	Andean Group (see p. xxxv and SALA, 24-1000)	GDP	gross domestic product (Spanish = PIB)
A-GAP	absolute gap	GDP/C	GDP per capita
ALALC	Asociación Latinoamericano de Libre Comercio (see p. xxxv and SALA, 24-1000)	GNP	gross national product
		H	hundred
ALADI	Latin American Integration Association (see p. xxxv)	Ha	hectare(s)
		IDB	Inter-American Development Bank
APGR	average of PC (see p. xxxvi)	IDB-L	IDB's definition of Latin America (see SALA, 24-1000)
B	billion (i.e., 000,000,000 omitted)		
BDM-DGE	Banco de México-Dirección General de Estadística	kg	kilogram(s)
C	per capita (e.g., GDP/C)	km, km^2	kilometer(s), square kilometers
ca.	about	Kw	kilowatt(s)
CA	Central America	KWH	kilowatt hours
CACM	Central American Common Market (see p. xxxv and SALA, 24-1000)	L or LA	Latin American countries (cf. EL; see SALA, 23, pp. vii-xxv)
CARICOM	Caribbean Common Market (see SALA, 24-1000)	LAFTA	Latin American Free Trade Association (see p. xxxv)
CARIFTA	Caribbean Free Trade Association (see SALA, SALA, 23, pp. vii-xxv)	LAIA	Latin American Integration Association (see p. xxxv and SALA, 24-1000)
CBI	Caribbean Basin Initiative (U.S. legislation) (see SALA, 23, pp. vii-xxv)	LC	Latin American countries and comparisons (e.g., to USA)
CBI-IB	Caribbean Basin Initiative—Intended Beneficiaries (see SALA, 24-1000 and SALA, 23, pp. vii-xxv)	LDCs	Less Developed Countries
		LR	Latin American countries and their regional totals
CIF or cif	cost, insurance, and freight	LRC	20 Latin American countries, regional total, and comparison (e.g., USA)
CLA	Caribbean Latin America (cf. CNLA, ECR; see SALA, 23, vii-xxv)	M	million (i.e., 000,000 omitted)
CNLA	Caribbean Not Latin America (e.g., Grenada; cf. CLA). See SALA, 23, pp. vii-xxv	M_1	currency outside of banks plus private sector demand deposits
CSOR	Caribbean Sea Oriented Region (includes CBI-IB and Cuba; cf. ECR; see SALA, 23, pp. vii-xxv)	M_2	M_1 plus time, savings, and foreign currency deposits
		Me^2	square meters
EAP	economically active population	Me^3	cubic meters
ECCM	Eastern Caribbean Common Market (see SALA 24-1000)	MERCOMUN	Mercado Común Centroamericano (see p. xxxv and SALA, 24-1000)
ECLA	Economic Commission for Latin America	MET	metric tons
ECLA-L	ECLA definition of L (see SALA 24-1000)	Mw	megawatts
ECR	Extended Caribbean Region (cf. CSOR; see SALA, 23, pp. vii-xxv)	N	number
		NC	national currency
EEC	European Economic Community	nes	not elsewhere shown
EFTA	European Free Trade Area	NIC	newly industrializing country
EL or ELA	Extended Latin America (cf. L; see SALA, 23, pp. vii-xxv)	nie	not included elsewhere
		NYC	New York City
EQN	Economically Questionable Nation	OAS	Organization of American States (see SALA, 24-1000)

I **Explanation of Terms**

OAS-L	OAS's definition of Latin America (*see* SALA, 24-1000)		P10I	per ten thousand inhabitants
OECD	Organization for Economic Cooperation and Development		PTP	percent of total population
			R-GAP	relative gap
OECS	Organization of Eastern Caribbean States (*see* SALA, 24-1000)		SDRs	Special Drawing Rights (IMF's currency)
			SNA	system of national accounts
OPEC	Organization of Petroleum Exporting Countries		T	Thousand (i.e., 000 omitted)
p (pp)	page(s)		TJ	Terajoules
PC	percentage change		U	unit
PHI	per hundred inhabitants		UN	United Nations
PHTI	per hundred thousand inhabitants		US	U.S. currency
PI	per inhabitant		U.S. or USA	United States of America
PIB	*producto interno bruto* (English = GDP)		WDC	Washington, D.C.
PMI	per million inhabitants		YA	yearly arithmetic mean
PTI	per thousand inhabitants		YE	year end

Sources

Sources frequently cited. (Abbreviation generally shows agency followed by title of publication or series).
Other sources appear in tables throughout.

ADEMA	*See* ECLA		IASI-C	*Características de la Estructura Demográfica*
AE	Anuario Estadístico		IBRD	International Bank for Reconstruction and Development. (*see* WB)
AR	Annual Report			
BDM	Banco de México		ICAO	International Civil Aviation Organization
BID	Banco Interamericano de Desarrollo (*see* IDB)		ICAO-DS-B	Digest of Statistics, *Bulletin*
C/CAA	Caribbean/Central American Action, *Caribbean Data Book*		ICAO-DS-T	Digest of Statistics, *Traffic: Commercial Air Carriers*
			ICAO-DS-AT	Digest of Statistics, *Airport Traffic*
CELADE	Centro Latinoamericano de Demografía (Santiago)		IDB	Inter-American Development Bank (WDC)
CELADE-BD	*Boletín Demográfico*		IDB-AR	*Annual Report*
CEPAL	Comisión Económica para América Latina (*see* ECLA)		IDB-SPTF	Social Progress Trust Fund, *Socio-Economic Progress in Latin America* (1961-71) and *Econimic and Social Progress in Latin America* (1972)
COHA	Council on Hemispheric Affairs, *Washington Report on the Hemisphere*		ILO	International Labour Office (Geneva)
Colombia-DANE	Departamento Administrativo Nacional		ILO-YLS	*Yearbook of Labor Statistics*
Cuba-CEE	Comité Estatal de Estadística		IMF	International Monetary Fund (WDC)
DGE	Dirección General de Estadística		IMF-BPS	*Balance of Payment Statistics*
DGEC	Dirección General de Estadística y Censos		IMF-BPS-Y	*Balance of Payment Statistics Yearbook*
ECLA	Economic Commission for Latin America (Santiago)		IMF-DOT	*Direction of Trade Statistics*
			IMF-DOT-Y	*Yearbook*
ECLA-ADEMA	*Agua, Desarrollo y Medio Ambiente* (1977)		IMF-GFSY	*Government Finance Statistics Yearbook*
ECLA-AE	*Anuario Estadístico de América Latina*		IMF-IFS	*International Financial Statistics*
ECLA-BPAL	*Balance de Pagos 1950-77*		IMF-IFS-S	*IFS Supplement* (No. 1, 1981-). (*See also* IFS-Y)
ECLA-CC	Cuadernos de la CEPAL		IMF-IFS-Y	*Yearbook* (entitled IFS-S from 1961 through 1978)
ECLA-CEC	Cuadernos Estadísticos de la CEPAL			
ECLA-D	Document		INE	Instituto Nacional de Estadística
ECLA-EIC	*Estudios e Informes de la CEPAL*		INEC	Instituto Nacionale de Estadística y Censos
ECLA-N	*Notas sobre la Economía y el Desarrollo*		JLP	José López Portillo (Mexico City)
ECLA-S	*Economic Survey of Latin America*		JLP-AE-H	*Anexo Estadístico Histórico*
ECLA-SHCAL	*Series Históricas del Crecimiento 1900-76 (1978)*		JLP-AP-E	*Anexo de Política Económica*
ECLA-SP	Preliminary version of ECLA-S		Mexico-	
ECLA-SY	*Statistical Yearbook (see ECLA-AE)*		BANAMEX	Banco Nacional de México
EYB	*Europa Year Book*		BANAMEX-	
FAO	UN, Food and Agriculture Organization (Rome)		RESM	Review of the Economic Situation of Mexico
FAO-FY	*Fertilizer Yearbook*		Mexico-BDM	Banco de México
FAO-PY	*Production Yearbook* (1958-)		BDM-IE	*Indicadores Económicos*
FAO-SFA	*State of Food and Agriculture*		BDM-IE-AH	*Indicadores Económicos, Acervo Histórico*
FAO-TY	*Trade Yearbook* (1958-)		Mexico-BNCE	Banco Nacional de Comercio Exterior
FAO-YFP	*Yearbook of Forestry Products*		BNCE-CE	*Comercio Exterior*
FAO-YFS	*Yearbook of Fishery Statistics*		Mexico-INEGI	Instituto Nacional de Estadística, Geografía e Informática
FAO-YFSCL	*Catches and Landings*			
FAO-YFSFC	*Fishery Commodities*		INEGI-EHM	Estadísticas Históricas de México
IASI	OAS, Inter-American Statistical Institute		Mexico-NAFINSA	Nacional Financiera, S.A.
IASI-AC	*América en Cifras*		NAFINSA-EMC	*La Economía Mexicana en Cifras*
IASI-BE	*Boletín Estadístico*		NAFINSA-MV	*Mercado de Valores*

OAS	Organization of American States (WDC)
OAS-A	*Latin America's Development and the Alliance for Progress* (1973)
OAS-DB	*Datos Básicos de Población*
OASL	OAS's definition of L (*see* SALA, 24-1000)
OAS-SB	*Statistical Bulletin*
PAHO	Pan American Health Organization (WDC)
PAHO-F	*Facts on Health Progress*
PAHO-HC	*Health Conditions in the Americas*
PC	Population Council (NYC)
PC-PFP	*Population and Family Planning*
PC-RPFP	*Report on Population/Family Planning*
SA	*South American Handbook*
SALA	*Statistical Abstract of Latin America*
SALA, 23:1	Volume 23, figure 1 (sample reference)
SALA, 23-100	Volume 23, table 100 (sample reference)
SALA-Cuba	Supplement 1: *Cuba 1968*
SALA LAPUA	Supplement 8: *Latin American Population and Urbanization Analysis*
SALA-MB	Supplement 9: *Statistical Abstract of the United States—Mexico Borderlands*
SALA-MLR	Supplement 5: *Measuring Land Reform*
SALA-SEM	Supplement 10: *Society and Economy in Mexico*
SALA-SNP	Supplement 3: *Statistics and National Policy*
SALA-TNG	Supplement forthcoming: *The Narrowing Gap*
Schroeder	Susan Schroeder, *Cuba: A Handbook of Historical Statistics* (Boston: G. K. Hall, 1982)
SELA	Sistema Económico para Latinoamérica
SIPRI-Y	Stockholm International Peace Research Institute, *Yearbook*
SY	Statistical Yearbook
UN	United Nations (NYC)
UN-CSS	*Compendium of Social Statistics*
UN-DY	*Demographic Yearbook*
UN-MB	*Monthly Bulletin of Statistics*
UN-SP	*Statistical Papers*
UN-SP-A	*Series A, Population and Vital Statistics*
UN-SP-J	*Series J, World Energy Supplies*
UN-SP:T	*Series T, Direction of International Trade*
UN-SY	*Statistical Yearbook*
UN-YCS	*Yearbook of Construction Statistics*
UN-YIS	*Yearbook of Industrial Statistics*
UN-YITS	*Yearbook of International Trade Statistics*
UN-YNAS	*Yearbook of National Account Statistics*
UN-YWES	*Yearbook of World Energy Statistics*
UNESCO	UN Educational and Scientific Organization (NYC)
UNESCO-SY	*Statistical Yearbook*
U.S.	United States (WDC)
USAID	U.S. Agency for International Development
USAID-OLG	*U.S. Overseas Loans and Grants Assistance from International Organizations*
USBC	U.S. Bureau of the Census
USBC-HS	*Historical Statistics of the United States*
USBC-SA	*Statistical Abstract of the United States*
USBG	U.S. Board of Governors, Federal Reserve System
USBG-FRB	*Federal Reserve Bulletin*
USBOM	U.S. Bureau of the Mines
USBOM-MCP	*Mineral Commodity Profiles*
USBOM-MIS	*Mineral Industry Surveys*
USBOM-MY	*Minerals Yearbook*
USCIA	U.S. Central Intelligence Agency
USDA	U.S. Department of Agriculture
USDA-AT	*Agricultural Trade of the Western Hemisphere*
USDA-ERS	Economic Research Service
USDA-FAT	*Foreign Agricultural Trade*
USDC-SCB	U.S. Dept. of Commerce, *Survey of Current Business*
USDOD	U.S. Department of Defense
USDOD-FMSA	*Foreign Military Sales Assistance*
USEX-IM	U.S. Export-Import Bank
USINS	U.S. Immigration and Naturalization Service
USINS-AR	*Annual Report*
USINS-SY	*Statistical Yearbook*
USNCC	U.S. National Climatic Center
USNCC-MCDW	*Monthly Climatic Data of the World*
WA	*World Almanac*
WB	World Bank (formerly IBRD)
WB-EDC	*Energy in Developing Countries*
WB-WDR	*World Development Report*
WB-WT	*World Bank Tables*, published by Johns Hopkins University Press, 1976, 1980
WCE	*World Christian Encyclopedia*
WHO	World Health Organization
WHO-WHSA	*World Health Statistics Annual*
Wilkie	See SALA
WTO	World Tourism Organization (Madrid)
WTO-WTS	*World Tourism Statistics*
YC	Yearbook Compendium

NOTE ON STATISTICAL DEFINITIONS

Weights and Measures

Length		
	1 kilometer	.6213712 mile
	1.609344 kilometers	1 mile
	1 yard	.914 meter
	1 meter	1.093 yard
	1 foot	.3048 meters
	1 meter	3.2808 feet
	1 inch	25.4 millimeter
	1 inch	2.54 centimeter
	1 millimeter	.03937 inch
	1 centimeter	.3937 inch

Area		
	1 Hectare (10,000 sq. meters)	2.471054 acres
	.4046856 hectares	1 acre
	1 square kilometer	.3861022 square mile
	2.589988 square kilometers	1 square mile

Volume		
	1 cubic meter	35.31467 cubic feet
		1.307951 cubic yards
	.02831685 cubic meter	1 cubic foot

Liquid measure		
	1 liter	1.056688 U.S. quarts
		.26417200 U.S. gallon
	1 U.S. quart	.9463529 liter
	1 U.S. gallon	3.785412 liters

Weight		
	1 kilogram	35.27396 avoirdupois ounces
		32.15075 troy ounces
	.45359237 kilogram	1 avoirdupois pound
	1 metric ton	1.1023113 short tons
		.9842065 long ton
	.9071847 metric ton	1 short ton (2,000 pounds)
	1.0160469 metric tons	1 long ton (2,240 pounds)

Ship tonnage		
	1 register ton (110 cubic feet)	2.83 cubic meters
	1 deadweight ton (1 long ton)	1.016047 metric tons

Rail traffic		
	1 metric ton-kilometer	.684945 short ton-mile
		.611558 long ton-mile
	1 short ton-mile	1.459972 ton-kilometers
	1 long ton-mile	1.635169 ton-kilometers

Lumber		
	1 cubic meter	220.75 board feet
	1,000 board feet	4.53 cubic meters

Agricultural products		Bales per metric ton
Wheat, pulses, and root crops	Bushel (60 lbs.)	36.744
Maize	Bushel (56 lbs.)	39.638
Coffee	Bags (132.28 lbs.)	16.67
Coffee (El Salvador)	Bags (152.12 lbs.)	14.493
Cotton	Gross Bales (500 lbs.)	4.409
	Net Bales (480 lbs.)	4.593

Coal equivalence	Metric tons of coal equivalent
Bituminous coal briquettes (1 metric ton)	1.00
Lignite briquettes (1 metric ton)	.67
Pitch coal and black lignite (1 metric ton)	.67
Lignite and brown coal (1 metric ton)	.33
Coke (1 metric ton)	.90
Crude petroleum and shale oil (1 metric ton)	1.30
Gasoline and fuel oil (1 metric ton)	1.50
Natural gas (1,000 cubic meters)	1.33
Manufactured gas (1,000 cubic meters)	.60
Refinery gas (1,000 cubic meters)	1.67
Electric energy (1,000 kilowatt hours)	.125

Energy equivalence

Terajoule $1 \text{ TJ} = 7 \times 10^6/.0293076$ Kilo. calories

Temperature Equivalence
   See table 305

Other conversions

For other conversions used to obtain standard measures of international comparability, see appendices to U.N., *Statistical Yearbook*; F.A.O., *Production Yearbook*; F.A.O., *World Forestry Inventory 1963*; and especially, U.N., Statistical Papers, Series M, No. 21, *World Weights and Measures*, 1955.

Mathematical Calculation of "Average" Rates of Change Over Time

Example data for calculating rate of change in a country according to four methods

Elapsed Time	Date	Absolute Data
0.00	March 26, 1937	15,920,694
10.00	March 26, 1947	18,966,767
13.49	Sept. 20, 1960	26,085,326

Methods of Calculating Average Annual (AA) Change[1] in Example Data

Category	Linear	Non-Linear		
	1. APGR Average of Percent Change	2. AA-EC Exponential Change	3. AA-GA Geometric Approximation	4. Geometric Change
Formula[2]	$r = \dfrac{\left(\dfrac{P_n}{P_o}\right) - 1}{n}$	$r = \dfrac{\log \dfrac{P_n}{P_o}}{n \log e}$	$r = \dfrac{2(P_n - P_o)}{n(P_n + P_o)}$	$r = \dfrac{\log\left(\dfrac{P_n}{P_o}\right)}{n}$
Rate 1937-47	1.91	1.75	1.75	1.77
Rate 1947-60	2.78	2.36	2.34	2.39
Analysis	$\dfrac{PC}{n}$	Continuous compounding	Annual compounding; adequate for periods of 5 years or longer	Annual compounding
Short-cut Method	**	Calculate P_n/P_o and look up corresponding value of x in U.S. National Bureau of Standards, *Tables of the Exponential Function e^x*, Applied Mathematics Series 14 (1951), "values of the ascending exponential," pp. 18 and 32. Divide result by elapsed time in example data (10.00 and 13.49).	**	**

---

[1] For further analysis of methodology, see U.S. Bureau of the Census, *The Methods and Materials of Demography*, 2 vols. (Washington, D.C.: Government Printing Office, 1971), II, pp. 377-380, from which the presentation of methods 2, 3, and 4 is adapted. Cf. *SNP*, p. 184.

[2] P_o the initial population

P_n the population at the end of period (in years)
n, the time in years
b, the annual amount of change
e, a mathematical constant (logarithm to the base 10 = .4342945)
PC, percentage change

Part I: Geography and Land Tenure

CHAPTER 1

GEOGRAPHY

Figure 1:1

POLITICAL MAP OF EXTENDED LATIN AMERICA (ELA)

NOTE: See SALA 23, pp. vii-xxv, for additional maps and analysis.

Figure 1:2

POLITICAL MAP OF EXTENDED CARIBBEAN REGION (ECR)

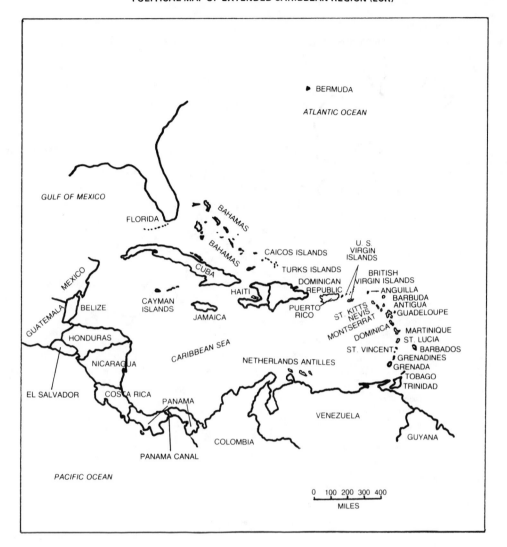

NOTE: See SALA 23, pp. vii-xxv, for additional maps and analysis.

Figure 1:3

CENTRAL AMERICA AND THE CARIBBEAN: HYDROGRAPHIC REGIONS

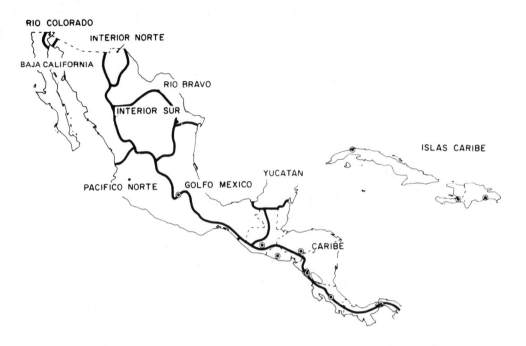

LEGEND FOR FIGURES 1:3 AND 1:4

- - -   International boundary

◉   Capital of country

•   City of over 1 million inhabitants

〰   Boundary of major hydrographic regions

SOURCE: ADEMA, 1977.

Figure 1:4

SOUTH AMERICA: HYDROGRAPHIC REGIONS

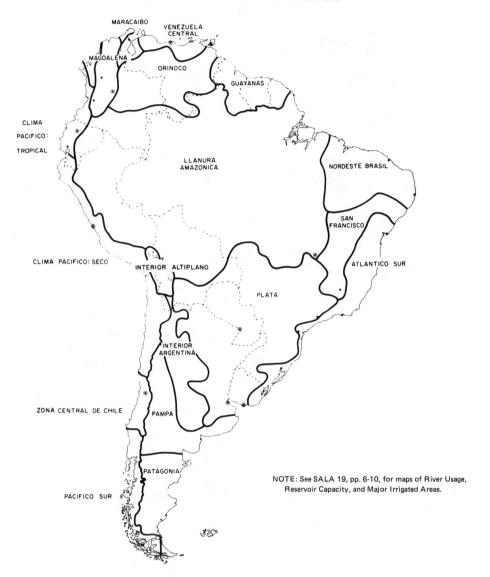

NOTE: See SALA 19, pp. 6-10, for maps of River Usage,
Reservoir Capacity, and Major Irrigated Areas.

Figure 1:5

RIVER SYSTEMS AND ELECTRIC PLANT LOCATIONS, SOUTH AMERICA

(ca. 1977)

LEGEND

●   Thermal plants

▲   Hydroelectric plants

- - -   International boundary

⊙   Capital of country

━━━   Navigable rivers for ocean-going vessels

───   Navigable rivers except for ocean-going vessels

R   River

Table 100

ECONOMIC REGIONS: AREA, POPULATION, AND DENSITY, 20 LRC

Country	Area (km²)	Population 1981 M	%	Density[a]
A. World				
Total	135,830,000	4,508	100.0	32.5
Africa	30,319,000	484	10.6	15.5
Asia	27,580,000	2,625	58.0	92.7
Europe	4,937,000	486	11.0	98.2
Oceania	8,510,000	23	.5	2.7
USSR	22,402,000	267	6.0	11.9
Americas	42,082,000	622	13.9	14.6
B. Americas				
Total	42,082,000	622	100.0	14.6
United States[1]	9,363,123	230	37.1	24.4
Latin America	20,003,443	368	59.0	18.1
Canada	9,976,139	24	3.9	2.4
Other	2,739,295	#	#	#
C. Latin American Economic Regional Groupings				
CACM	425,718	21	100.0	39.9
Costa Rica	50,700	2	9.5	39.4
El Salvador	21,041	5	23.8	237.6
Guatemala	108,889	7	33.3	64.3
Honduras	112,088	4	19.0	36.7
Nicaragua	133,000	3	14.3	22.6
ALADI	13,834,368	312	100.0	22.6
Argentina	2,766,889	28	8.7	9.8
Bolivia	1,098,581	6	1.9	5.5
Brazil	8,511,965	123[b]	39.4	14.5
Chile‡	756,945	11	3.5	14.5
Colombia	1,138,914	27	8.6	23.7
Ecuador	283,561	8	2.5	28.2
Mexico	1,972,547	72	23.1	36.5
Paraguay	406,742	3	1.0	7.4
Peru‡	1,285,216	18	5.8	14.0
Uruguay	176,215	3	1.0	17.0
Venezuela	912,050	14	4.5	15.4
AG	5,475,267	73	100.0	13.3
Bolivia	1,098,581	6	8.2	5.5
Colombia	1,138,914	27	37.0	23.7
Ecuador	283,561	8	11.0	28.2
Peru‡	1,285,216	18	24.6	14.0
Venezuela	912,050	14	19.2	15.4
Other				
Total	268,090	22	100.0	82.1
Cuba	114,524	10	45.5	87.3
Dominican Rep.	48,734	5	22.7	102.6
Haiti	27,750	5	22.7	180.2
Panama	75,650	2	9.1	26.4
Panama Canal Zone‡	1,432	~	~	~

1. De jure population, but excluding civilian citizens absent from the country for an extended period of time estimated at 764,701 at the time of the 1960 census.

a. Population divided by area.
b. 1980 data.

SOURCE: Area data from IASI-AC, 1974, table 201-01; population data from UNESCO-SY, 1983, table 1.1; density calculated.

Table 101

ARGENTINA MAJOR CIVIL DIVISIONS: AREA
AND PERCENTAGE

(1980)

| Division[1] | Area[2] | |
	km^2	%
Total	2,794,948	100.0
Capital Federal	200	#
Provinces		
Buenos Aires	310,440	11.1
Catamarca	103,859	3.7
Córdoba	171,982	6.2
Corrientes	94,493	3.4
Chaco	100,199	3.6
Chubut	263,116	9.4
Entre Ríos	75,693	2.7
Formosa	73,972	2.6
Jujuy	51,251	1.8
La Pampa	208,260	7.4
La Rioja	82,109	2.9
Mendoza	149,529	5.3
Misiones	29,449	1.1
Neuquén	81,283	2.9
Río Negro	191,677	6.9
Salta	165,718	5.9
San Juan	93,195	3.3
San Luis	71,472	2.6
Santa Cruz	229,882	8.2
Santa Fé	129,766	4.6
Santiago del Estero	148,730	5.3
Tucumán	22,620	.8
Tierra del Fuego and territories	29,392	1.1

1. For number of civil subdivisions during previous years, see SALA, 23-310.
2. Totals may not add up due to rounding.

SOURCE: Calculated from census data included in SALA, 23-626.

Table 102

BOLIVIA MAJOR CIVIL DIVISIONS: AREA
AND PERCENTAGE

(1976)[‡]

| Division[1] | Area[2] | |
	km^2	%
Total	1,161,954	100.0
Departments		
Bení	167,969	14.4
Chuquisaca	59,541	5.1
Cochabamba	56,181	4.8
La Paz	134,923	11.6
Oruro	51,874	4.5
Pando	34,409	3.0
Potosí	109,786	9.4
Santa Cruz	357,536	30.8
Tarija	37,731	3.2

1. For number of civil subdivisions during previous years, see SALA, 23-301.
2. Totals may not add up due to rounding.

SOURCE: Calculated from census data included in SALA, 23-627.

Table 103

BRAZIL MAJOR CIVIL DIVISIONS: AREA AND PERCENTAGE (1980)‡

Division[1]	Area[2] km^2	%
Total	8,650,935	100.0
Distrito Federal	5,810	.1
States		
Acre	153,458	1.8
Alagoas	27,561	.3
Amapá	180,078	2.1
Amazonas	1,447,373	16.7
Bahía	564,334	6.5
Ceará	149,442	1.7
Espírito Santo	45,858	.5
Fernando de Noronha	26	#
Goiás	661,217	7.6
Maranhão	315,178	3.6
Mato Grosso[3]	1,169,287	13.5
Mato Grosso do Sul[3]	349,867	4.0
Minas Gerais	593,212	6.9
Pará	1,168,864	13.5
Paraíba	56,200	.6
Paraná	198,706	2.3
Pernambuco	97,513	1.1
Piauí	243,128	2.8
Rio de Janeiro[4]	44,194	.5
Rio Grande do Norte	52,247	.6
Rio Grande do Sul	1,985,512	23.0
Randônia	251,530	2.9
Roraima	20,474	.2
Santa Catarina	97,044	1.1
São Paulo	248,610	2.9
Sergipe	21,834	.3

1. For number of civil subdivisions during previous years, see SALA, 23-301.
2. Totals may not add up due to rounding.
3. Mato Grosso and Mato Grosso do Sul are new states created by dividing the old state of Mato Grosso.
4. Guanabara and Rio de Janeiro states were combined to create the new state of Rio de Janeiro.

SOURCE: Calculated from census data included in SALA, 23-628.

Table 104

CHILE MAJOR CIVIL DIVISIONS: AREA AND PERCENTAGE (1982)

Division[1]	Area[2] km^2	%
Total	751,696	100.0
Regions		
Antofagasta	113,734	15.1
Araucanía	31,497	4.2
Atacama	91,536	12.2
Aysén del General Carlos Ibáñez del Campo	109,130	14.5
Bío Bío	36,989	4.9
Coquimbo	41,918	5.6
Libertador General Bernardo O'Higgins	16,250	2.2
Los Lagos	64,879	8.6
Magallanes y la Antártica Chilena	132,333	17.6
Maule	30,134	4.0
Metropolitana de Santiago	15,505	2.1
Tarapacá	54,685	7.3
Valparaíso	16,063	2.1

1. For number of civil subdivisions during previous years, see SALA, 23-301.
2. Totals may not add up due to rounding.

SOURCE:Calculated from census data included in SALA, 23-629.

Table 105

COLOMBIA MAJOR CIVIL DIVISIONS: AREA
AND PERCENTAGE
(1973)

Division[1]	Area[2] km^2	%
Total	1,170,562	100.0
Bogotá, D.E.	1,587	.1
Departments		
Antioquia	63,322	5.4
Atlántico	3,272	.3
Bolívar	29,719	2.5
Boyacá	67,798	5.8
Caldas	7,302	.6
Cauca	30,195	2.6
César	24,275	2.1
Córdobo	24,826	2.1
Cundinamarca (excludes Bogotá, D.E.)	22,133	1.9
Chocó	50,479	4.3
Huila	19,576	1.7
La Guajira	20,058	1.7
Magdalena	23,310	2.0
Meta	81,725	7.0
Nariño	31,043	2.7
Norte de Santander	21,009	1.8
Quindío	1,828	.2
Risaralda	3,970	.3
Santander	30,567	2.6
Sucre	10,424	.9
Tolima	23,167	1.9
Valle del Cauca	21,199	1.8
Intendencias[3]		
Aracuca	23,196	1.9
Caquetá	83,343	7.1
Putumayo	27,584	2.4
San Andrés y Providencia	44	#
Comisarías[3]		
Amazonas	112,025	9.6
Guainía	70,160	6.0
Vaupés[4]	82,610	7.1
Vichada	107,800	9.2

1. For number of civil subdivisions during previous years, see SALA, 23-301.
2. Totals may not add up due to rounding.
3. Four *intendencias* and four *comisarías* have been estimated from the known total for all growth between 1964 and 1968 published in the *Diccionario Geográfico de Colombia* (1970), p. 334.
4. In 1982 a new political unit, Guaviare, was created by dividing Vaupés. The capital is San José del Guaviare.

SOURCE: Calculated from census data included in SALA, 23-630.

Table 106

COSTA RICA MAJOR CIVIL DIVISIONS: AREA
AND PERCENTAGE
(1973)

Division[1]	Area[2] km^2	%
Total	50,589	100.0
Provinces		
Alajuela	9,589	18.9
Cartago	2,591	5.1
Guanacaste	10,511	20.7
Heredia	2,910	5.7
Limón	9,595	18.9
Puntarenas	10,910	21.5
San José	5,188	10.3

1. For number of civil subdivisions during previous years, see SALA, 23-301.
2. Totals may not add up due to rounding.

SOURCE: Calculated from census data included in SALA, 23-631.

Table 107

CUBA MAJOR CIVIL DIVISIONS: AREA
AND PERCENTAGE
(1981)[‡]

Division[1]	Area[2]	
	km[2]	%
Total	110,300	100.0
Ciudad de la Habana	741	.7
Provinces		
Camagüey	14,140	12.8
Ciego de Avila	6,550	5.9
Cienfuegos	4,132	3.7
Granma	8,498	7.7
Guantánamo	6,392	5.8
Holquín	8,932	8.1
Isla de la Juventud	2,226	2.0
La Habana	741	.7
Las Tunas	6,417	5.8
Matanzas	11,617	10.5
Pinar del Río	10,860	9.8
Sancti Spíritus	6,775	6.1
Santiago de Cuba	6,360	5.8
Villa Clara	8,050	7.3

1. For number of civil subdivisions during previous years, see SALA, 23-301.
2. Totals may not add up due to rounding.

SOURCE: Calculated from census data included in SALA, 23-632.

Table 108

DOMINICAN REPUBLIC MAJOR CIVIL DIVISIONS: AREA
AND PERCENTAGE
(1980)[‡]

Division[1]	Area[2]	
	km[2]	%
Total	48,465	100.0
Distrito Nacional	1,477	3.0
Provinces		
Azúa	2,434	5.0
Bahoruco	1,377	2.8
Barahona	2,540	5.2
Dajabón	902	1.8
Duarte	1,294	2.6
El Seibo	3,033	6.2
Espaillat	974	2.0
Independencia	1,903	3.9
La Altagracia	2,781	5.7
La Estrelleta	3,871	7.9
La Romana	3,785	7.8
La Vega	3,455	7.1
María Trinidad Sánchez	1,324	2.7
Montecristi	2,034	4.2
Pedernales	1,032	2.1
Peravia	1,631	3.3
Puerto Plata	1,895	3.9
Salcedo	493	1.0
Samaná	983	2.0
San Cristóbal	3,739	7.7
San Juan	3,582	7.4
San Pedro de Macorís	1,162	2.4
Sánchez Ramírez	1,170	2.4
Santiago	3,100	6.4
Santiago Rodríguez	1,026	2.1
Valverde	580	1.2

1. For number of civil subdivisions during previous years, see SALA, 23-301.
2. Totals may not add up due to rounding.

SOURCE: Calculated from census data included in SALA, 23-633.

Table 109

ECUADOR MAJOR CIVIL DIVISIONS: AREA
AND PERCENTAGE
(1982)‡

Division[1]	Area[2]	
	km²	%
Total	277,699	100.0
Provinces		
Archipiélago de Colón	6,201	2.2
Azuay	9,374	3.3
Bolívar	4,004	1.4
Cañar	4,507	1.6
Carchi	4,418	1.6
Cotopaxi	5,825	2.1
Chimborazo	6,469	2.3
El Oro	6,581	2.3
Esmeraldas	17,705	6.3
Guayas	18,674	6.7
Imbabura	5,684	2.0
Loja	12,364	4.4
Los Ríos	6,633	2.4
Manabí	20,829	7.5
Morona/Santiago	22,365	8.1
Napo	56,521	20.3
Pastaza	32,536	11.7
Pichincha	17,113	6.2
Tungurahua	3,490	1.3
Zamora Chinchipe	22,421	8.1

1. For number of civil subdivisions during previous years, see SALA, 23-301.
2. Totals may not add up due to rounding.

SOURCE: Calculated from census data included in SALA, 23-634.

Table 110

EL SALVADOR MAJOR CIVIL DIVISIONS: AREA
AND PERCENTAGE
(1971)‡

Division[1]	Area[2]	
	km²	%
Total	20,878	100.0
Departments		
Ahuachapán	1,175	5.6
Cabañas	1,025	4.9
Cuscatlán	739	3.5
Chalatenango	1,509	7.2
La Libertad	1,644	7.8
La Paz	1,205	5.7
La Unión	2,472	11.8
Morazán	1,386	6.6
San Miguel	2,139	10.2
San Salvador	868	4.1
San Vicente	1,202	5.7
Santa Ana	2,043	9.7
Sonsonate	1,391	6.6
Usulután	2,125	10.1

1. For number of civil subdivisions during previous years, see SALA, 23-301.
2. Totals may not add up due to rounding.

SOURCE: Calculated from census data included in SALA, 23-635.

Table 111

GUATEMALA MAJOR CIVIL DIVISIONS: AREA
AND PERCENTAGE
(1981)

Division[1]	Area[2] km^2	%
Total	107,921	100.0
Departments		
Alta Verapaz	8,706	8.0
Baja Verapaz	3,114	2.8
Chimaltenango	1,972	1.8
Chiquimula	2,386	2.2
El Progreso	1,931	1.7
Escuintla	4,376	4.0
Guatemala	2,125	1.9
Huehuetenango	7,404	6.8
Izabal	9,236	8.5
Jalapa	2,051	1.9
Jutiapa	3,226	2.9
Petén	32,771	30.3
Quezaltenango	1,949	1.8
Quiché	8,363	7.7
Retalhuleu	1,853	1.7
Sacatepéquez	465	.4
San Marcos	3,798	3.5
Santa Rosa	2,953	2.7
Sololá	1,061	.9
Suchitepéquez	2,500	2.3
Totonicapán	1,060	.9
Zacapa	2,693	2.4

1. For number of civil subdivisions during previous years, see SALA, 23-301.
2. Totals may not add up due to rounding.

SOURCE: Calculated from census data included in SALA, 23-636.

Table 112

HAITI MAJOR CIVIL DIVISIONS: AREA
AND PERCENTAGE
(1971)

Division[1]	Area[2] km^2	%
Total	27,756	100.0
Departments		
Artibonite	6,171	22.2
Nord	4,221	15.2
Nord-Ouest	2,364	8.5
Ouest	8,435	30.3
Sud	6,642	23.9

1. For number of civil subdivisions during previous years, see SALA, 23-301.
2. Totals may not add up due to rounding.

SOURCE: Calculated from census data included in SALA, 23-637.

Table 113

HONDURAS MAJOR CIVIL DIVISIONS: AREA
AND PERCENTAGE
(1974)

Division[1]	Area[2]	
	km[2]	%
Total	110,577	100.0
Departments		
Atlántida	4,241	3.8
Colón	8,582	7.7
Comayagua	5,209	4.7
Copán	3,219	2.9
Cortes	3,932	3.5
Choluteca	4,177	3.7
El Paraíso	7,042	6.3
Francisco Morazán	7,925	7.1
Gracias a Dios	21,079	19.0
Intibucá	3,025	2.7
Islas de la Bahía	259	.2
La Paz	2,335	2.1
Lempira	4,248	3.8
Ocotepeque	1,650	1.4
Olancho	25,320	22.8
Santa Bárbara	5,143	4.6
Valle	1,568	1.4
Yoro	7,798	7.0

1. For number of civil subdivisions during previous years, see SALA, 23-301.
2. Totals may not add up due to rounding.

SOURCE: Calculated from census data included in SALA, 23-638.

Table 114

MEXICO MAJOR CIVIL DIVISIONS: AREA
AND PERCENTAGE
(1980)[‡]

Division[1]	Area[2]	
	km[2]	%
Total	1,981,853	100.0
Federal District	1,479	.1
States		
Aguascalientes	5,471	.2
Baja California	68,079	3.4
Baja California Sur	73,796	3.7
Campeche	53,175	2.6
Chiapas	74,886	3.7
Chihuahua	241,732	12.1
Coahuila	155,840	7.8
Colima	5,218	.2
Durango	128,910	6.5
Guanajuato	30,444	1.5
Guerrero	63,945	3.2
Hidalgo	20,774	1.0
Jalisco	81,010	4.0
México	21,375	1.1
Michoacán	59,778	3.0
Morelos	4,955	.2
Nayarit	27,037	1.3
Nuevo León	64,823	3.2
Oaxaca	93,265	4.7
Puebla	33,814	1.7
Querétaro	11,524	.6
Quintana Roo	52,464	2.6
San Luis Potosí	64,255	3.2
Sinaloa	58,753	3.0
Sonora	187,366	9.4
Tabasco	24,994	1.3
Tamaulipas	80,205	4.0
Tlaxcala	4,024	.2
Veracruz	72,117	3.6
Yucatán	38,320	1.9
Zacatecas	71,582	3.6

1. For number of civil subdivisions during previous years, see SALA, 23-301.
2. Totals may not add up due to rounding.

SOURCE: Calculated from census data included in SALA, 23-639.

Table 115

**NICARAGUA MAJOR CIVIL DIVISIONS: AREA
AND PERCENTAGE
(1971)**

Division[1]	Area[2]	
	km[2]	%
Total	135,335	100.0
Departments		
Boaco	5,060	3.7
Carazo	1,025	.7
Chinandega	4,653	3.4
Chontales	4,966	3.7
Estelí	4,966	3.6
Granada	962	.7
Jinotega	9,234	6.8
León	5,196	3.8
Madriz	1,727	1.2
Managua	3,628	2.6
Masaya	541	.4
Matagalpa	6,887	5.0
Nueva Segovia	3,332	2.4
Río San Juan	6,750	4.9
Rivas	2,160	1.6
Zelaya	49,610	3.6

1. For number of civil subdivisions during previous years, see SALA, 23-301.
2. Totals may not add up due to rounding.

SOURCE: Calculated from census data included in SALA, 23-640.

Table 116

**PANAMA MAJOR CIVIL DIVISIONS: AREA
AND PERCENTAGE
(1980)**

Division[1]	Area[2]	
	km[2]	%
Total	77,772	100.0
Provinces		
Bocas del Toro	8,736	11.2
Chiriquí	8,679	11.1
Coclé	5,018	6.4
Colón[3]	7,506	9.6
Darién	13,123	16.8
Herrera	2,408	3.1
Los Santos	3,904	5.0
Panamá	11,274	14.4
Veraguas	10,804	13.8

1. For number of civil subdivisions during previous years, see SALA, 23-301.
2. Totals may not add up due to rounding.
3. Includes San Blas territory.

SOURCE: Calculated from census data included in SALA, 23-641.

Table 117

PARAGUAY MAJOR CIVIL DIVISIONS: AREA
AND PERCENTAGE
(1972)

| Division[1] | Area[2] | |
	km^2	%
Total	392,345	100.0
Departments		
Alto Paraná	15,607	4.0
Amambay	13,105	3.3
Boquerón	130,710	33.3
Caaguazú	23,706	6.0
Caazapá	9,364	2.4
Asunción	200	#
Central	2,650	.7
Concepción	18,033	4.6
De la Cordillera	4,984	1.3
Guairá	3,201	.8
Itapuá	16,815	4.3
Misiones	7,702	2.0
Ñeembucú	145,956	3.7
Olimpo	17,893	4.6
Paraguarí	8,142	2.1
Presidente Hayes	38,515	9.8
San Pedro	19,727	5.0

1. For number of civil subdivisions during previous years, see SALA, 23-301.
2. Totals may not add up due to rounding.

SOURCE: Calculated from census data included in SALA, 23-642.

Table 118

PERU MAJOR CIVIL DIVISIONS: AREA
AND PERCENTAGE
(1981)

| Division[1] | Area[2] | |
	km^2	%
Total	1,288,274	100.0
Departments		
Amazonas	41,058	3.2
Ancash	36,368	2.8
Apurimac	20,595	1.6
Arequipa	63,656	4.9
Ayacucho	44,157	3.4
Cajamarca	35,443	2.8
Callao (Provincia Constitucional)	148	#
Cuzco	76,377	5.9
Huancavelica	21.146	1.6
Huánuco	35,385	2.7
ICA	21,269	1.7
Junín	43,482	3.4
La Libertad	23,260	1.8
Lambayeque	13,250	1.0
Lima	33,827	2.6
Loreto	342,591	26.6
Madre de Dios	85,518	6.4
Moquegua	16,129	1.3
Pasco	21,747	1.7
Piura	36,435	2.8
Puno	72,379	5.6
San Martín	53,292	4.1
Tacna	14,751	1.1
Tumbes	4,742	.4
Ucayali[3]	167,224	12.9

1. For number of civil subdivisions during previous years, see SALA, 23-301.
2. Totals may not add up due to rounding.
3. The department of Ucayali was created on June 18, 1980, and is formed by the provinces of Ucayali and Coronel Portillo.

SOURCE: Calculated from census data included in SALA, 23-643.

Table 119

URUGUAY MAJOR CIVIL DIVISIONS: AREA
AND PERCENTAGE
(1975)

Division[1]	Area[2] km[2]	%
Total	173,111	100.0
Departments		
Artigas	11,486	6.6
Canelones	4,595	2.7
Cerro Largo	14,739	8.5
Colonia	6,104	3.5
Durazno	10,939	6.3
Flores	4,937	2.9
Florida	11,046	6.4
Lavalleja	10,870	6.3
Maldonado	4,727	2.7
Montevideo	543	.3
Paysandú	14,128	8.2
Río Negro	9,993	5.8
Rivera	9,108	5.3
Rocha	9,893	5.7
Salto	14,700	8.5
San José	4,967	2.9
Soriano	10,038	5.8
Tacuarembó	16,966	9.8
Treinta y Tres	9,136	5.3

1. For number of civil subdivisions during previous years, see SALA, 23-301.
2. Totals may not add up due to rounding.

SOURCE: Calculated from census data included in SALA, 23-644.

Table 120

VENEZUELA MAJOR CIVIL DIVISIONS: AREA
AND PERCENTAGE
(1981)[‡]

Division[1]	Area[2] km[2]	%
Total	912,655	100.0
Distrito Federal	1,929	.2
States		
Anzoátegui	43,097	4.7
Apure	65,602	7.2
Aragua	6,944	.8
Barinas	35,378	3.9
Bolívar	222,121	24.3
Carabobo	43,736	.5
Cojedes	15,064	1.7
Falcón	25,395	2.8
Guárico	61,903	6.8
Lara	19,767	2.2
Mérida	11,314	1.2
Miranda	7,934	.9
Monagas	30,009	3.3
Nueva Esparta	1,152	.1
Portuguesa	14,947	1.6
Sucre	11,834	1.3
Táchira	11,126	1.2
Trujillo	7,370	.8
Yaracuy	7,115	.8
Zulia	50,936	5.6
Territories		
Amazonas	152,000	1.7
Delta Amacuro	34,629	3.8

1. For number of civil subdivisions during previous years, see SALA, 23-301.
2. Totals may not add up due to rounding.

SOURCE: Calculated from census data included in SALA, 23-645.

Table 121

ALTITUDE OF PRINCIPAL MOUNTAINS, 20 L

Country	Peak or Volcano	Cordillera	Major Political Division	Altitude Above Sea Level	
				Meters	Feet
A. ARGENTINA	Aconcagua	Andes	Mendoza	6,960[a]	22,835

Continued in SALA, 23-302.

Table 122

HIGH PEAKS OF LATIN AMERICA
(In Descending Order of Altitude)

Peak	Mountain Range	Country	Meters	Peak	Mountain Range	Country	Meters
Aconcagua	Andes	Argentina-Chile	7,040[a]	Huila	Andes	Colombia	5,750

Continued in SALA, 23-303.

Table 123

VOLCANOES OF LATIN AMERICA
(In Descending Order of Altitude)

Volcano (Last Eruption)	Place	Meters
North America		
Colima (1982)	Mexico	4,268
El Chichoń (1983)	Mexico	2,225
Citlaltepec (Orizaba)	Mexico	5,676
Popocatépetl (1920)	Mexico	5,452
Colima (1975)	Mexico	3,960
Paricutín (1952)	Mexico	3,170
Central America—Carribean		
Tajumulco	Guatemala	4,220
Tacana	Guatemala	4,092
Acatenango (1972)	Guatemala	3,976
Santiaguito (Santa María) (1982)	Guatemala	3,772
Fuego (1980)	Guatemala	3,736
Atitlán	Guatemala	3,537
Irazú (1967)	Costa Rica	3,432
Poás (1982)	Costa Rica	2,704
Pacaya (1983)	Guatemala	2,552
San Miguel (1976)	El Salvador	2,130
Izalco (1966)	El Salvador	1,965
Rincon de la Vieja (1968)	Costa Rica	1,806
El Viejo (San Cristóbal) (1981)	Nicaragua	1,745
Ometepe (Concepcion) (1982)	Nicaragua	1,610
Arenal (1982)	Costa Rica	1,552
Conchagua (1947)	El Salvador	1,250
Momotombo (1982)	Nicaragua	1,191
Telica (1982)	Nicaragua	1,010
Masaya (1978)	Nicaragua	635
South America		
Guallatiri (1960)	Chile	6,060
Cotopaxi (1975)	Ecuador	5,897
El Misti	Peru	5,825
Ubinas (1969)	Peru	5,672
Lascar (1968)	Chile	5,641
Tupungatito (1980)	Chile	5,640
Tolima (1943)	Colombia	5,525
Sangay (1976)	Ecuador	5,230
Tungurahua (1944)	Ecuador	5,016
Pichincha (1982)	Ecuador	4,787
Nevada del Ruiz (1985)	Colombia	4,724
Purace (1977)	Colombia	4,600
Reventador (1976)	Ecuador	3,485
Lautaro (1960)	Chile	3,380
Llaima (1979)	Chile	3,124
Villarrica (1980)	Chile	2,840
Hudson (1973)	Chile	2,600
Rinihue	Chile	2,430
Puyhue (1960)	Chile	2,240
Calbuco (1961)	Chile	2,015
Fernandina (1977)	Galapagos Is.	1,546
Alcedo (1970)	Galapagos Is.	1,127

SOURCE: WA, 1980, p. 437; *National Geographic Magazine*, Jan. 1981, pp. 7ff; WA, 1980, p. 437; WA, 1984, p. 593.

Table 124

MAJOR EARTHQUAKES IN LATIN AMERICA, 1797–1986

Date	Place	Deaths	Magnitude[a]
1797 Feb 4	Quito, Ecuador	41,000	~
1868 Aug 13-15	Peru and Ecuador	40,000	~
1875 May 16	Venezuela and Colombia	16,000	~
1906 Aug 16	Valparaiso, Chile	20,000	8.6
1939 Jan 24	Chillan, Chile	28,000	8.3
1949 Aug 5	Pelileo, Ecuador	6,000	6.8
1960 May 21-30	Southern Chile	5,000	8.3
1970 May 31	Northern Peru	66,794	7.7
1972 Dec 23	Nicaragua	5,000	6.2
1976 Feb 4	Guatemala	22,778	7.5
1979 Dec 12	Colombia and Ecuador	800	7.9
1983 Mar 31	Southern Colombia	250	5.5
1983 Apr 3	Southwest Costa Rica	~	7.2
1983 June 7	Southern Mexico	~	7.0, 6.7
1983 June 19	El Salvador	~	7.0
1983 Nov 19	Central Peru	~	6.5
1983 Dec 16	Western Cuba	~	4.4
1985 Sept 19	Central Mexico	10,000[b]	7.8
1986 Oct 10	El Salvador	890[c]	5.4

a. Each higher number represents a tenfold increase in energy measured in ground motion.

b. Mexican government estimate.

c. El Salvador government estimate.

SOURCE: WA, 1984, pp. 593, 698.

Table 125

RIVERS

Part I: Principal Rivers of the World

River	Continent	Length (Miles)	Drainage Area (T Sq. Mi.)	Flow[1]
Nile	Africa	4,132	1,293	110
Amazon	South America	3,915	2,722	4,200
Mississippi-Missouri	North America	3,892	1,243.7	620
Yangtze	Asia	3,434	756.5	770
Congo	Africa	2,900	1,425	2,000
Amur	Asia	2,900	711	390
Lena	Asia	2,650	963	530
Yenisei	Asia	2,566	1,003	614
La Plata-Paraná	South America	2,450	1,198	2,800
Ob	Asia	2,287	1,431	441

Part II: Principal Rivers of Latin America

River	Continent	Length (Miles)	Drainage Area (T Sq. Mi.)	Flow[1]
Amazon	South America	3,915	2,722	4,200
Araguaia	South America	1,367	~	~
La Plata-Paraná	South America	2,450	1,198	2,800
Madeira	South America	2,013	~	600
Orinoco	South America	1,700	350	600
Paraguay	South America	1,584	~	160
Paraná	South America	2,796	1,198	550
Purus	South America	1,995	~	~
Río Grande	North America	1,885	172	3
São Francisco	South America	1,811	252	120
Tocantins	South America	1,677	~	~

1. Thousands of cubic feet per second.

SOURCE: U. S. National Oceanic and Atmospheric Administration, *Principal Rivers and Lakes of the World* (Rockville, Md.: U.S. Department of Commerce, 1971).

Table 126

PRINCIPAL NATURAL LAKES OF LATIN AMERICA

Lake	Continent	Depth (Feet)	Sq. Mile Area	Length (Miles)
Maracaibo	South America	115	5,127	96
Nicaragua	North America	230	3,100	102
Titicaca	South America	922	3,200	122

SOURCE: See table 125.

Table 127

PRINCIPAL DESERTS OF LATIN AMERICA

Desert	Place	Sq. Mile Area
Atacama	Northern Chile	70,000
Bolsón de Mapimi	North Central Mexico	50,000
Olmos	Northwestern Peru	1,000
Morrope	Northwestern Peru	1,500
Sechura	Northwestern Peru	2,000
Vizcaino	Northwestern Mexico	6,000

SOURCE: See table 125.

Table 128

TEMPERATURE AND RAINFALL BY GEOGRAPHIC LOCATION, 20 L

$$\left(\frac{\text{Temp., } ^\circ F}{\text{Rain, inches}} \right)$$

Station	Years Covered	Elev.	Lat.	Long.	Jan.	Feb.	Mar.	Apr.	May	June	July	Aug.	Sept.	Oct.	Nov.	Dec.	Annual
A. ARGENTINA					58.5	57.2	53.1	48.0	42.1	38.1	36.7	37.0	41.0	46.4	50.4	54.3	46.9
SAN CARLOS DE BARILOCHE	30	2,798	41.09	71.18	1.16	1.42	2.40	2.97	5.66	7.95	6.65	5.17	3.08	1.75	1.82	1.75	41.78

Continued in SALA, 23-309 to 23-328. For centigrade conversions, see SALA, 22-305.

Table 129

HIGH AND LOW TEMPERATURE — MONTHLY AVERAGES IN CAPITAL CITY,[1] 20 L

(Fahrenheit)[2]

Country		Jan.	Feb.	March	Apr.	May	June	July	Aug.	Sept.	Oct.	Nov.	Dec.
A. ARGENTINA	High	83	83	79	72	64	57	57	60	64	69	76	82
	Low	63	63	60	53	47	41	42	43	46	50	56	61

Continued in SALA, 23-329. For centigrade conversions, see SALA, 22-305.

Table 130

AVERAGE NUMBER OF DAYS WITHOUT RAIN EACH MONTH, 20 L

(Capital Cities)

Country	Jan.	Feb.	March	April	May	June	July	Aug.	Sept.	Oct.	Nov.	Dec.
A. ARGENTINA	24	22	24	22	24	23	23	22	22	22	21	23

Continued in SALA, 23-330.

CHAPTER 2

LAND USE

Table 200

FAO LAND USE DATA, 20 LRC

(T Ha. 1984[a])

	Country	Surface		Agricultural			Nonagricultural	
		Total Area[1]	Land Area[2]	Arable Land[3]	Land under Permanent Crops[4]	Permanent Meadows and Pastures[5]	Forests and Woodlands[6]	Other Uses
A.	ARGENTINA[7]	276,689	273,669	25,850[t]	9,750[t]	142,800[t]	59,800[t]	35,469
B.	BOLIVIA	109,858	108,439	3,260[t]	125[t]	26,900[t]	55,950[t]	22,204
C.	BRAZIL	851,197	845,651	63,500[t]	11,750[t]	165,000[t]	565,280[t]	40,121
D.	CHILE	75,695	74,880	5,330	198	11,900	15,480	41,972
E.	COLOMBIA	113,891	103,870	4,050[t]	1,645[t]	30,000[t]	49,900[t]	18,275
F.	COSTA RICA	5,070	5,066	283[t]	354[t]	2,167[t]	1,560[t]	702
G.	CUBA	11,452	11,452	2,560[t]	676[t]	2,480[t]	1,940[t]	3,430
H.	DOMINICAN REP.	4,873	4,838	1,120[t]	350[t]	2,092[t]	627[t]	649
I.	ECUADOR	28,356	27,684	1,580[t]	930[t]	4,700[t]	14,150[t]	6,324
J.	EL SALVADOR	2,104	2,072	560[t]	165[t]	610[t]	116[t]	621
K.	GUATEMALA	10,889	10,843	1,330[t]	485[t]	1,334[t]	4,230[t]	3,464
L.	HAITI	2,775	2,756	555[t]	349[t]	500[t]	54[t]	1,298
M.	HONDURAS	11,209	11,189	1,575[t]	202[t]	3,400[t]	3,740[t]	2,272
N.	MEXICO	197,255	192,304	23,150[t]	1,550[t]	74,500[t]	45,700[t]	47,404
O.	NICARAGUA	13,000	11,875	1,095[t]	172[t]	5,100[t]	4,040[t]	1,468
P.	PANAMA[8]	7,708	7,599	438[t]	126[t]	1,161[t]	4,050[t]	1,824
Q.	PARAGUAY	40,675	39,730	1,640[t]	300[t]	15,500[t]	20,400[t]	1,890
R.	PERU	128,522	128,000	3,200[t]	317[t]	27,120[t]	69,900[t]	27,463
S.	URUGUAY	17,662	17,362	1,400[t]	46[t]	13,632[t]	630[t]	1,654
T.	VENEZUELA	91,205	88,205	3,080[t]	678[t]	17,400[t]	31,915[t]	35,132
	LATIN AMERICA	2,000,045	1,967,484	145,556[@]	30,168[@]	548,296[@]	949,462[@]	293,636
	UNITED STATES	936,312	912,680	187,881[t]	2,034[t]	241,467[t]	265,188[t]	220,090

1. Refers to total area of country, including area under inland water bodies. Definition of such bodies usually embraces major rivers and lakes.
2. Refers to total area excluding that beneath water bodies.
3. Land under temporary crops, temporary meadows for mowing or pasture, truck gardens or temporarily fallow or idle. Areas double cropped are counted only once.
4. Refers to long-lived perennial crops. Trees for timber production are excluded.
5. Land under permanent (5 or more years) herbaceous forage crops, both cultivated and natural.
6. Land under natural or planted stand of trees, whether productive or not.
7. Continental sector only.
8. Excludes Canal Zone.

a. For previous years see SALA, 18-400; SALA, 19-400; SALA, 20-400; SALA, 21-400; SALA, 22-400; SALA, 23-400; SALA, 24-200.

SOURCE: FAO-PY, 1985, table 1.

Table 201

IDB LAND USE DATA BY REGION
(km^2 1970)

Region	Arable Land		Pastures		Forests		Other	
	Area	%	Area	%	Area	%	Area	%
Mexico	232,200	12.1	744,990	38.7	707,000	36.8	238.850	12.4
Central America[1]	60,580	11.9	96.140	18.9	271,130	53.3	80,850	15.0
Caribbean[2]	60,620	25.9	54,030	23.1	47,220	20.2	71,700	30.7
South America								
Andean[3]	226,690	5.0	908,000	19.9	2,700,100	59.2	728,270	15.9
Atlantic[4]	740,369	7.9	1,821,140	19.6	5,373,382	57.8	1,358,550	14.6
Southern Cone[5]	427,380	11.6	1,700,500	46.3	809,068	22.0	734,340	20.0
Latin America and the Caribbean	1,747,839	8.5	5,324,800	26.3	9,907,900	49.1	3,212,560	15.9

1. Belize, Costa Rica, El Salvador, Guatemala, Honduras, Nicaragua, and Panama.
2. Cuba, Haiti, and the Dominican Republic plus thirteen smaller island republics and possessions.
3. Bolivia, Colombia, Ecuador, Peru, and Venezuela.
4. Brazil, French Guiana, Guyana, Paraguay, and Suriname.
5. Argentina, Chile, and Uruguay.

SOURCE: IDB-SPTF, 1983, table II-1.

Table 202

IDB AGRICULTURAL LAND USE DATA BY REGION
(km^2 1977)

Region	Arable	Cultivated	Irrigated	
			Area	% of Cultivated Land
Mexico	232,200	151,900	50,000	32.9
Central America	60,580	43,979	3,210	7.3
Caribbean	60,620	55,175	10,070	18.3
South America				
Andean	226,690	108,850	24,500	22.5
Atlantic	740,369	471,590	12,070	2.6
Southern Cone	427,380	310.360	28,700	9.2
Latin America and the Caribbean	1,747,839	1,141,854	128,550	11.3

SOURCE: IDB-SPTF, 1983, table II-2.

Table 203

CULTIVATED LAND, 20 LR, 1959–74

	Country	T Ha.					Indexes (1959-61 = 100)			
		1959-1961	1964-1966	1970	1973	1974	1964-1966	1970	1973	1974
A.	ARGENTINA	14,498	14,745	15,232	15,687	15,655	101.7	106.1	108.2	108.0
B.	BOLIVIA	613	680	771	771	888	110.9	125.8	125.8	144.9
C.	BRAZIL	25,152	29,441	33,906	36,662	40,971	117.1	134.8	145.8	162.9
D.	CHILE	1,544	1,424	1,425	1,200	1,312	92.2	92.3	77.7	85.0
E.	COLOMBIA	3,192	3,546	3,580	3,804	3,997	111.1	112.2	119.2	125.2
F.	COSTA RICA	321	401	352	351	358	124.9	109.7	109.3	111.5
G.	CUBA	1,710	1,679	2,026	1,810	1,817	98.2	118.5	105.8	106.3
H.	DOMINICAN REP.	625	618	667	671	676	98.9	106.7	107.4	108.2
I.	ECUADOR	1,024	1,425	1,678	1,662	1,644	139.2	163.9	162.3	160.5
J.	EL SALVADOR	585	708	614	709	689	121.0	105.0	121.2	117.8
K.	GUATEMALA	1,257	1,523	1,491	1,759	1,809	121.2	118.6	139.9	143.9
L.	HAITI	867	917	931	956	957	105.8	107.4	110.3	110.4
M.	HONDURAS	618	617	599	660	682	99.8	96.9	106.8	110.4
N.	MEXICO	11,458	14,225	13,971	14,570	14,632	124.1	121.9	127.2	127.7
O.	NICARAGUA	518	819	705	708	715	158.1	136.1	136.7	138.0
P.	PANAMA	371	332	449	458	478	89.5	121.0	123.5	128.8
Q.	PARAGUAY	336	497	622	618	742	147.9	185.1	183.9	220.8
R.	PERU	1,612	1,727	1,894	1,749	1,809	107.1	117.5	108.5	112.2
S.	URUGUAY	1,415	1,231	1,035	989	1,073	87.0	73.1	69.9	75.8
T.	VENEZUELA	1,250	1,332	1,727	1,534	1,659	106.6	138.2	122.7	132.7
	LATIN AMERICA[1]	69,257	78,292	84,023	87,677	92,913	111.9	121.3	126.6	134.2

1. Includes Barbados, Guyana, Jamaica, Trinidad and Tobago.

SOURCE: ECLA, *El Desarrollo Latinoamericano y la Coyuntura Económica Internacional, Tercera Parte*, 1975, p. 253.

Table 204

FAO IRRIGATED LAND DATA, 20 LRC, 1961–84
(T Ha.)

	Country	1961-65	1966	1970	1975	1976	1977	1978	1979[†]	1980	1982	1984
A.	ARGENTINA	1,046[†]	1,650[†]	1,700[†]	1,800[†]	1,477[†]	1,510[†]	1,540[†]	1,560	1,580	1,620[†]	1,660[†]
B.	BOLIVIA	74[†]	75[†]	80[‡]	120[†]	120[†]	120[†]	125[†]	125	140	150[†]	155[†]
C.	BRAZIL	546[†]	640[†]	796	950[†]	1,400[†]	1,000[†]	1,050[†]	1,700	1,800[†]	2,000[†]	2,200[†]
D.	CHILE	1,084	1,100[†]	1,180[†]	1,260[†]	1,245[†]	1,300[†]	1,320[†]	1,252	1,255[†]	1,259[†]	1,257
E.	COLOMBIA	231	240[†]	250[†]	280[†]	285[†]	290[†]	295[†]	305	310[†]	318[†]	322[†]
F.	COSTA RICA	26	26[‡]	26[‡]	26[‡]	26[‡]	26[‡]	26[‡]	26	61[†]	74	84[†]
G.	CUBA	280	500[†]	520[†]	535[†]	650[†]	700	720[†]	900	962	1,000[†]	1,030[†]
H.	DOMINICAN REP.	113	120[†]	125	135	135[†]	140[†]	140[†]	145	145[†]	176	180[†]
I.	ECUADOR	446[†]	463[‡]	470[†]	500[†]	510[†]	510[†]	520[†]	520	520[†]	530[†]	537[†]
J.	EL SALVADOR	18	20[‡]	20[‡]	33	30	50	50	102	110[†]	110	110[†]
K.	GUATEMALA	38	45[†]	56	60[‡]	62[†]	64[†]	64[†]	66	68[†]	72[†]	75[†]
L.	HAITI	38[†]	42	60[†]	70	70[‡]	70[‡]	70[‡]	70	70[‡]	70[†]	70[†]
M.	HONDURAS	60	66[‡]	70[†]	80[†]	80[†]	80[†]	80[†]	80	82[†]	84[†]	85[†]
N.	MEXICO	2,900[†]	3,750[†]	3,950[†]	4,479	4,816	5,000[†]	5,000[†]	5,100	5,100[†]	5,053	5,100[†]
O.	NICARAGUA	18	18[‡]	29[‡]	32	70	74	76[†]	78	80[†]	82[†]	83[†]
P.	PANAMA	15	18[†]	20[†]	23[†]	23[†]	25[†]	26[†]	28	28[†]	28[†]	30[†]
Q.	PARAGUAY	30[†]	40[†]	40[†]	55[†]	55[†]	55[†]	55[†]	55	60[†]	62[†]	62[†]
R.	PERU	1,041	1,078	1,106	1,130[†]	1,150[†]	1,180[†]	1,180[†]	1,180	1,190[†]	1,180[†]	1,200[†]
S.	URUGUAY	32	42	52	57[†]	58[†]	60[†]	64[†]	70	80[†]	88[†]	92[†]
T.	VENEZUELA	218	255[‡]	284[‡]	314[‡]	303[†]	350[†]	360[†]	310	315[†]	317[†]	322[†]
	LATIN AMERICA	8,254	9,725[@]	10,364[@]	11,439[@]	12,565[@]	12,604[@]	12,761[@]	13,672[@]	13,921[@]	14,273[@]	14,654[@]
	UNITED STATES	14,659	15,300[†]	15,900[†]	16,500[†]	16,694[†]	17,200[†]	16,700[†]	16,697	20,582	19,831	19,831[†]

SOURCE: FAO-PY, 1976-81, table 2; FAO-PY, 1983, table 2; FAO-PY, 1985, table 2.

Table 205

IDB ARABLE AND IRRIGATED LAND DATA

(T Ha., ca. 1978)

	Country	Land		Under Irrigation/Arable (%)
		Arable[1]	Under Irrigation[2]	
A.	ARGENTINA	34,420	1,400	4.1
B.	BOLIVIA	1,100	100	9.1
C.	BRAZIL	38,803	851	2.2
D.	CHILE	5,742	1,244	21.7
E.	COLOMBIA	5,090	270	5.3
F.	COSTA RICA	622	66	10.6
H.	DOMINICAN REP.	995	130	13.1
I.	ECUADOR	4,324	190	4.4
J.	EL SALVADOR	733	26	3.5
K.	GUATEMALA	1,700	60	3.5
L.	HAITI	908	70	7.7
M.	HONDURAS	870	44	5.1
N.	MEXICO	27,390	5,000	18.3
O.	NICARAGUA	960	29	3.0
P.	PANAMA	555	30	5.4
Q.	PARAGUAY	970	50	5.2
R.	PERU	2,880	1,120	38.9
S.	URUGUAY	2,252	45	2.0
T.	VENEZUELA	5,214	235	4.5
	LATIN AMERICA[3]	135,528	10,960	8.1

1. Includes annual and perennial crops, cultivated prairies, and fallow lands.
2. Includes all land irrigated by means of canals, deposits, common and artesian wells, and machinery for drip irrigation, whether it is subject to irrigation all year or only during the dry season.
3. Includes Guyana, Jamaica, Trinidad and Tobago.

SOURCE: IDB-SPTF, 1983, table III-4.

Table 206

U.N. ARABLE LAND AND CROPLAND, 20 LC

(Ha. per Capita and per Person Agriculturally Employed, 1970)

	Country	Arable Land PI	Cropland	
			PI	Agricultural Population
A.	ARGENTINA	1.43	1.07	7.03
B.	BOLIVIA	.47	.63	1.08
C.	BRAZIL	.36	.32	.73
D.	CHILE	.55	.47	1.86
E.	COLOMBIA	.23	.25	.55
F.	COSTA RICA	.28	~	~
G.	CUBA	.42	.43	1.30
H.	DOMINICAN REP.	.23	~	~
I.	ECUADOR	.63	~	~
J.	EL SALVADOR	.18	~	~
K.	GUATEMALA	.30	.29	.46
L.	HAITI	.21	.08	.10
M.	HONDURAS	.33	~	~
N.	MEXICO	.55	.47	1.01
O.	NICARAGUA	.46	~	~
P.	PANAMA	.37	~	~
Q.	PARAGUAY	.43	~	~
R.	PERU	.21	.21	.46
S.	URUGUAY	.63	.67	4.04
T.	VENEZUELA	.48	.47	1.81
	UNITED STATES	.94	.86	21.48

SOURCE: UN-CSS, 1977, pp. 150-152, 1157.

Table 207

TROPICAL LAND DEVELOPMENT PROJECTS, 8 L

Level of Government Participation and Project	Country	Date of Project Initiation	Gross Area (ha)[1]	No. of Farms[1]	Rural and Urban Population in Project Area[1]	Ecological Zone[2]
Directed Colonization						
Nuevo Ixcatlán	Mexico	1955	13,400	703	3,000	Sw
Cihualtepec	Mexico	1957	18,600	476	1,700	Sm
La Joya	Mexico	1956	8,000	285	1,400	Sm
La Chontalpa	Mexico	1965	83,000	4,900	22,000	Tm
Bataan	Costa Rica	1964	10,500	265	1,300	Tw
Alto Beni I	Bolivia	1959	7,000	520	2,500	Tm
Alto Beni II	Bolivia	1963	36,000	1,400	6,500	Tm
Chimoré	Bolivia	1963	120,000	700	3,400	Tr
Yacapani	Bolivia	1963	110,000	1,900	9,500	Sm
Semidirected Colonization[3]						
Santo Domingo de los Colorados	Ecuador	1964	210,000	5,200	40,000	S/Tm
Valle del Upano	Ecuador	1964	170,000	1,400	7,150	Sr
Tingo María-Tocache	Peru	1966	127,500	2,150	30,000	Sw
Puerto Presidenta Stroessner	Paraguay	1963	45,000	900	4,500	Sm
Spontaneous Colonization[3]						
Caranavi	Bolivia	1945	500,000	8,250	39,000	Sm
Chapare	Bolivia	1920	185,000	5,460	18,600	Tr
Caquetá	Colombia	1932	1,050,000	22,000	175,000	Tw
Puyo-Tena	Ecuador	1940	220,000	4,000	30,000	Sr
Private Subdivision and Development						
Ivinheima (SOMECO)	Brazil	1958	1,000,000	1,600	28,000	Sm
Cia. Melhoramentos Norte do Paraná	Brazil	1930	1,250,000	39,000	1,700,000	Sm
Gleba Arinos (CONOMALI)	Brazil	1954	200,000	120	600	Tw
Tournavista	Peru	1954	410,000	100	600	Tw
Foreign Colonization						
San Juan	Bolivia	1957	35,000	280	1,580	Sm
Okinawa	Bolivia	1957	55,000	600	4,000	Sm
Filadelfia	Paraguay	1927	500,000	1,500	20,000	Sd

1. Data are for 1967–68.
2. T = tropical, S = subtropical, r = rainy, w = wet, m = moist, d = dry.
3. Projects involving provision of services in areas already occupied by spontaneous settlers.

SOURCE: SPTF, 1985.

Table 208

HUMID TROPICAL LAND RESOURCES OF SOUTH AMERICA, 8 LR

(M Ha.)

Soil Areas According to Suitability

| | Country | | Cropping | | | | | Pasture or Plantations[6] | Forestry or Reserve | Total |
		Alluvial[1]	Hydromorphic[2]	Good Upland[3]	Marginal-low Fertility[4]	Marginal-shallow or Steep[5]	Total			
A.	ARGENTINA	2.7	2.3	3.1	5.7	1.7	15.5	15.2	6.5	37.2
B.	BOLIVIA	.7	10.8	.6	12.3	2.2	26.6	52.2 ←	→	78.8
C.	BRAZIL	3.2	25.4	21.8	174.4	18.5	243.3	333.3	170.1	746.7
E.	COLOMBIA	3.6	6.3	1.5	20.2	.4	32.0	69.4 ←	→	101.4
I.	ECUADOR	.1	.6	.4	4.8	.1	6.0	15.3 ←	→	21.3
Q.	PARAGUAY	.7	2.8	4.2	7.1	.7	15.5	14.8	10.4	40.7
R.	PERU	.1	2.7	1.6	17.2	.4	22.0	55.1 ←	→	77.1
T.	VENEZUELA	.2	5.7	2.3	17.1	5.0	30.3	6.1	18.7	55.1
	Total	11.3	56.6	35.5	258.8	29.0	391.2	767.1 ←	→	1,158.3

1. Soils developed from recent deposits and located in floodplains or deltas. Characteristics of the soils depend on their parent material.
2. These soils are found on flat or depressed landscapes with little or no runoff where drainage presents a problem.
3. These soils occur on undulating or level topography, are well drained, are not susceptible to serious erosion, and have medium-high natural fertility.
4. These soils are of the upland type but with very low natural fertility. With appropriate crops and fertilizer, reasonable yields may be expected.

5. These soils pose special problems for agricultural use due to shallowness or slope, heavy texture or sandiness. They occur primarily in highland areas and are susceptible to severe erosion.
6. These soils are unsuited to normal crop production because of major limiting factors such as steep topography, poor drainage, low fertility, sandiness, heavy texture, and rock outcrops or stones.

SOURCE: Adapted from Michael Nelson, *The Development of Tropical Lowlands: Policy Issues in Latin America* (Baltimore: John Hopkins University Press, 1973), table 2.

Table 209

PROJECTED NEW LAND DEVELOPMENT AND INVESTMENTS IN SOUTH AMERICA, 7 LR, 1962–85

(M Ha.)

| | Country | Irrigated | Dry Land | Dry and Irrigated Cropland[1] | | | Pasture From Forest | Total Forest Clearing | Total Investment[3] |
				From Pasture[2]	From Forest	Total			
B.	BOLIVIA	.3	#	.15	.15	.3[a]	4.15	4.3	120
C.	BRAZIL	.4	9.4	4.9	4.9	9.8	12.2	17.1	2,120
E.	COLOMBIA	.3	1.7	1.0	1.0	2.0[a]	6.6	7.6	440
I.	ECUADOR	.1	.6	.35	.35	.7	.85	1.2	93
Q.	PARAGUAY	#	.4	.2	.2	.4	3.7	3.9	147
R.	PERU	.3[b]	.8	.4	.4	.8	.7	1.1	70
T.	VENEZUELA	.3	.1	.2	.2	.4[a]	3.8	4.0	270
	TOTAL	1.7	13.0	7.2	7.2	14.4	31.7	39.2[c]	3,260

1. Irrigated land derived 50 percent from pasture and 50 percent from dryland crop area. For table on humid land tropical resources, see SALA, 18-403.
2. Assumption that 50 percent of new cropland will be derived from existing pasture.
3. Investment in development of new lands not associated with irrigation, drainage, or flood control, at 1962 prices.

a. Total area in nonirrigated crops in Colombia is projected to increase by 1.7 million ha. The additional .3 million compensate for projected irrigation of currently nonirrigated pasture and croplands. Increases of .3 million ha. are made for both Bolivia and Venezuela in similar compensation.
b. Irrigated land derived from desert.
c. Annual rate of forest clearing would be 1.75 million ha.

SOURCE: FAO, *Indicative World Plan for Agricultural Development to 1975 and 1985, South America*, vol. 1 (Rome, 1968). Cf. table 2300.

Table 210

FERTILIZER CONSUMPTION,[1] 20 LRC, 1971–85[a]

(T MET)

	Country	1970/71	1973/74	1974/75	1975/76	1976/77	1977/78	1978/79	1979/80	1980/81	1981/82	1982/83	1983/84	1984/85
A.	ARGENTINA	87	83	75‡	60‡	78	74	107	130	113	96	113	131‡	156‡
B.	BOLIVIA	2	5	6‡	3‡	3‡	4	5	3	3	7	3‡	8	5
C.	BRAZIL	1,002	1,673	1,825	1,978	2,528	3,209	3,216	3,563	4,201	2,753	2,729	2,272	3,428
D.	CHILE	153	201	167	99	121	103	129	121	116	113	105	137	181
E.	COLOMBIA	144	256	250	215	246	282‡	276	294	312‡	280‡	325‡	318‡	363‡
F.	COSTA RICA	49	64	73‡	66‡	56	67‡	80‡	79‡	74	72‡	72‡	88‡	95‡
G.	CUBA	396	277	302	331	356	418‡	451	464	530	607	555	528	593
H.	DOMINICAN REP.	38	76	98	73‡	76‡	50‡	57	72	52	58‡	51‡	42‡	59‡
I.	ECUADOR	34	52	41	33	81	86	71	79	73	70‡	72	74‡	84‡
J.	EL SALVADOR	65	110‡	99‡	94‡	102	106	112	75‡	65	88	60	82	55
K.	GUATEMALA	46	50	65	55‡	95	103	95	100‡	86‡	89	89	68	90‡
L.	HAITI	~	1‡	2	2‡	~	3‡	4‡	4‡	~	6‡	5‡	3‡	4‡
M.	HONDURAS	24‡	24‡	19‡	20‡	25‡	28‡	23‡	20‡	29‡	28‡	24	28‡	35‡
N.	MEXICO	538	780	864	1,073	1,120	1,068	1,067	1,134	1,238	1,561	1,825	1,486‡	1,661‡
O.	NICARAGUA	26	55‡	35‡	19‡	48	48	48	23‡	54	60‡	23‡	71	49
P.	PANAMA	21	22	28	25	23‡	23	23‡	30‡	31	30‡	27‡	23‡	28‡
Q.	PARAGUAY	9	3	2	1	1‡	1‡	3‡	6	6	9	8	9‡	9‡
R.	PERU	84‡	98	142	94	117	131	126	110	110	132	93	79	78
S.	URUGUAY	69	77	68	47	74	63	58	92	81	64‡	49‡	42‡	53‡
T.	VENEZUELA	59	91	129	140	161	176	197	222	241	146	153‡	154‡	268‡
	LATIN AMERICA	2,846@	3,998@	4,290@	4,428@	5,311@	6,046@	6,144@	6,621@	7,415@	6,365	6,451	5,727	7,385
	UNITED STATES	15,535	17,516	15,941	18,914	20,059	18,676	20,471	20,941	21,274	19,439	16,416	19,768	19,646
	WORLD	69,068	84,369	82,365	90,404	96,658	101,217	108,832	112,403	116,089	114,937	114,698	125,428	130,671

1. Includes nitrogenous, phosphate, and potash fertilizers.

a. For 1961–70 data, see SALA, 23-1519.

SOURCE: FAO-FY, 1979 and 1981, table 33; FAO-FY, 1983, table 32; FAO-FY, 1985, table 32.

Table 211

FERTILIZER CONSUMPTION[1] PER HECTARE OF ARABLE LAND AND PER INHABITANT, 20 LC, 1970–84[a]

(H G)

		Per Ha. Arable Land and Permanent Crops						PI					
	Country	1970	1975	1979	1980	1982	1984	1970	1975	1979	1980	1982	1984
A.	ARGENTINA	26	16	37	32	31	37	37	22	49	42	41	44
B.	BOLIVIA	7	10	12	9	8	25	3	6	7	5	5	14
C.	BRAZIL	283	523	576	678	365	304	101	174	288	343	213	175
D.	CHILE	285	162	246	210	189	249	158	92	125	105	91	118
E.	COLOMBIA	284	421	525	537	538	558	65	83	112	118	113	115
F.	COSTA RICA	1,001	1,353	1,614	1,500	1,134	1,391	284	344	366	332	310	357
G.	CUBA	1,517	1,071	1,557	1,653	1,726	1,642	463	351	505	543	564	533
H.	DOMINICAN REP.	393	843	585	421	353	288	87	164	124	87	82	70
I.	ECUADOR	89	91	358	277	277	297	57	55	120	90	85	83
J.	SALVADOR	1,043	1,442	1,052	892	830	1,132	185	229	160	135	118	157
K.	GUATEMALA	300	285	587	507	498	375	87	81	151	128	115	90
L.	HAITI	4	24	44	4	51	36	1	5	7	1	8	5
M.	HONDURAS	286	226	111	139	137	159	94	66	55	66	61	69
N.	MEXICO	216	393	481	517	778	602	118	186	169	173	247	198
O.	NICARAGUA	283	200	152	358	186	557	131	83	86	198	80	231
P.	PANAMA	387	455	523	533	469	411	144	152	157	159	135	111
Q.	PARAGUAY	95	11	29	33	39	46	39	4	11	20	23	26
R.	PERU	300	297	321	325	266	224	64	63	64	63	50	42
S.	URUGUAY	273	231	481	424	376	292	171	139	316	277	184	142
T.	VENEZUELA	113	262	599	642	408	411	56	114	154	154	92	94
	UNITED STATES	809	900	1,106	1,116	867	1,041	758	881	945	934	712	843
	WORLD	217	287	~	799	779	853	88	109	~	262	250	268

1. Includes nitrogenous, phosphate, and potash fertilizers.

a. For 1961–65 data, see SALA, 23-1520.

SOURCE: FAO, Annual Fertilizer Review, 1976, table 12; FAO-FY, 1979-81, table 11; FAO-FY, 1983, table 10; FAO-FY, 1985, table 10.

Table 212

TRACTORS IN USE, 20 LRC, 1961–84

(N)

	Country	1961-65	1969-71	1974	1977	1978	1979†	1980†	1981	1982	1983	1984
A.	ARGENTINA	139,000	171,450	184,000	195,000†	173,000	171,400	166,700	158,900	203,700	201,800	203,700
B.	BOLIVIA	220	355	720†	665	726	750	750	740†	750†	750†	750†
C.	BRAZIL	97,200	168,257	236,000†	280,000†	300,000†	320,000	330,000	340,000†	655,000†	710,000†	765,000†
D.	CHILE	21,061	21,523	28,000†	20,700†	34,500†	34,550	34,600	34,650†	34,700†	34,730†	34,760†
E.	COLOMBIA	24,290	22,780	31,000†	25,594	26,500†	27,500	28,423	28,500†	28,600†	28,700†	28,800†
F.	COSTA RICA	4,311	5,100	5,500†	5,750†	5,850†	5,900	5,950	6,000†	6,050†	6,100†	6,150†
G.	CUBA	19,800	48,434	52,700	64,423	66,349	70,374	68,300	64,500	66,509	66,262	66,000†
H.	DOMINIAN REP.	2,330	2,510	5,500†	2,930†	3,000†	3,050	3,150	3,220†	3,250†	3,270†	3,300†
I.	ECUADOR	1,689	3,133	3,400†	5,440	5,564	5,650	5,750	6,844	7,186	7,400†	7,600†
J.	EL SALVADOR	1,800	2,514	2,850†	3,050†	3,150†	3,250	3,300	3,320†	3,340†	3,360†	3,380†
K.	GUATEMALA	2,250	3,167	3,600†	3,800†	3,900†	3,950	4,000	4,020†	4,040†	4,060†	4,080†
L.	HAITI	271	363	420†	460†	480†	500	520	530†	540†	550†	560†
M.	HONDURAS	331	1,693	950†	3,100†	3,080	3,160	3,250	3,280†	3,300†	3,310†	3,330†
N.	MEXICO	72,000	91,318	135,000†	101,611	108,259	114,000	120,000	143,078	146,083	152,319†	155,000†
O.	NICARAGUA	450	500	768	1,636	1,900†	2,100	2,200	2,250†	2,300†	2,350†	2,400†
P.	PANAMA	789	2,414	3,500†	3,850†	3,900†	3,950	4,000	4,050†	4,100†	4,150†	4,180†
Q.	PARAGUAY	1,500	2,200	2,600†	2,900†	3,000†	3,100	3,200	3,300†	8,000†	8,500†	9,000†
R.	PERU	7,707	10,902	12,000†	13,000†	13,300†	13,600	13,900	14,300†	16,500†	17,300†	17,800†
S.	URUGUAY	23,812	26,659	27,400†	27,700†	27,900†	28,000	28,200	33,470†	33,550†	33,490†	33,500†
T.	VENEZUELA	13,086	19,200	23,460	33,888	35,000†	37,000	38,000	39,000†	40,000†	41,500†	42,500†
	LATIN AMERICA	433,447	604,472	765,200@	795,497@	819,358@	851,784@	864,193@	893,952@	1,267,498@	1,329,901@	1,391,790@
	UNITED STATES	4,751,600	4,584,000	4,273,000	4,370,000	4,839,000	4,810,000	4,775,000	4,655,000	4,669,000	4,671,000	4,657,000†

SOURCE: FAO-PY, 1976-81, table 109; FAO-PY, 1983, table 117; FAO-PY, 1985, table 117.

Table 213

AGRICULTURAL TECHNOLOGY, 8 LR

(1980)

		Cereal Yield/ Hectare	Cereals		% Irrigated Area	Fertilizers		Tractor (units)	
			Agricultural EAP	Tractors		Tons/1,000 Arable Hectares	1,000 Agricultural EAP	1,000/Arable Hectares	1,000 Agricultural EAP
	UNITED STATES	4,162	135.6	.06	10.8	54.2	4,639.5	25.0	2,142.0
	BULGARIA	3,854	5.3	.13	28.6	100.6	272.0	14.8	40.0
	JAPAN	5,272	2.2	.01	66.6	159.2	117.5	224.5	165.7
	NETHERLANDS	5,688	4.4	.01	31.9	504.6	1,659.1	206.7	607.5
A.	ARGENTINA	2,204	13.0	.09	4.5	1.7	43.4	5.8	150.0
C.	BRAZIL	1,329	1.8	.08	2.9	12.7	52.0	5.2	21.2
E.	COLOMBIA	2,390	1.3	.11	5.5	26.9	68.4	4.9	18.0
F.	COSTA RICA	2,207	1.0	.04	~	80.4	152.7	9.9	22.0
J.	EL SALVADOR	1,737	.8	.18	~	71.3	68.3	4.6	4.4
K.	GUATEMALA	1,524	.9	.26	3.8	32.1	48.8	2.2	3.3
N.	MEXICO	1,918	1.6	.10	22.0	35.6	114.6	4.9	15.8
T.	VENEZUELA	1,882	1.8	.04	8.5	26.1	118.3	6.3	4.0
	LATIN AMERICA		1.8	.09	8.3	15.0	61.6	5.1	21.0

SOURCE: CEPAL *Review* 24 (1984).

CHAPTER 3

LAND TENURE

Table 300

SYSTEMS OF LAND TENURE, ABSOLUTE DATA, 18 LC

(N and Ha.)

Country	Year	Unit	Total	Operated Under Single Tenurial Systems		Rented from Others							Operated Under Other Simple Systems	Operated Under Mixed Systems
				Total	Operated by Owner	Total	Payment in Cash/Kind	Partnerships or Similar Forms	Payment by Services	Other Arrangements	Occupied Without Title	Operated Under Collective System		
A. ARGENTINA[1,2]	1960	N	457,173	457,173	~	~	~	~	#	~	#	#	~	#
		Ha.	175,142,497	175,142,497	103,219,103	29,592,386	22,679,273	2,095,770[a]	#	4,817,343[b]	#	#	42,331,008[c]	#
B. BOLIVIA[3]	1950[v]	N	86,377	86,377	64,396[d]	17,248	13,598	3,033	617[e]	#	#	3,779[f]	9549	#
		Ha.	32,749,850	32,749,850	22,227,498[d]	2,471,306	1,983,765	382,115	105,426[e]	#	#	7,178,448[f]	872,598[9]	#
C. BRAZIL	1970	N	4,924,019	4,793,215	2,975,572	1,006,505	~	~	~	~	811,338	~	~	130,804
		Ha.	294,145,466	252,020,808	242,873,710	17,949,833	~	~	~	~	21,197,265	~	~	12,124,658
D. CHILE[6]	1965	N	253,532	225,572	119,704	99,746	12,312	18,009	53,922	15,503[n]	6,122	#	#	27,960
		Ha.	30,644,131	27,513,587	22,669,238	4,354,313	3,523,319	261,673	94,607	474,714[n]	490,037	#	#	3,130,543
E. COLOMBIA[4]	1960	N	1,209,672	1,110,316	755,318	282,347	~	~	~	~	46,961	#	25,690	99,356
		Ha.	27,337,826	25,660,351	19,779,585	2,009,274	~	~	~	~	3,314,076	#	557,416	1,677,475
F. COSTA RICA	1973	N	81,562	81,562	69,660	3,821[b]	1,474	359	~	244	-.[Q]	7,909	172	::
		Ha.	3,122,457	3,122,457	2,836,060	37,993[b]	24,926	3,563	~	2,712	-.[Q]	243,495	4,909	::
H. DOMINICAN REP.	1960	N	447,098	~	262,979	137,865	16,474	30,782	8,716[f]	81,893[pp]	39,596[j]	~	6,658	~
		Ha.	2,069,156[t]	~	1,512,375	427,241	92,549	86,561	35,840[f]	212,291[pp]	109,281[j]	~	20,259	~
I. ECUADOR	1954	N	344,234	313,582	233,900	50,121	17,038	13,336[o]	19,747[p]	#	#	5,778[f]	23,783[q]	30,652
		Ha.	5,999,700	5,668,800	4,889,400	551,700	426,200	64,700[o]	60,800[p]	#	#	25,700[f]	202,000[q]	330,900
J. EL SALVADOR	1961	N	226,896	197,091	89,918	99,226	43,457	~	55,769[i]	~	#	#	7,947	29,805[i]
		Ha.	1,581,428	1,458,110	1,225,221	122,954	78,877	~	44,077[i]	~	#	#	109,935	123,900[i]
EL SALVADOR	1971	N	272,432	233,999	107,450	126,549	80,547	~	~	~	#	#	46,002[s]	38,433[i]
		Ha.	1,463,859	1,326,162	1,118,080	208,082	108,841	~	~	~	#	#	99,241[s]	137,697[i]
K. GUATEMALA	1964	N	417,344	371,039	241,541	95,631	47,026	~[w]	48,605[r]	~	~[q]	20,593[f]	13,274[y]	46,305
		Ha.	3,448,736	2,983,292	2,670,962	195,380	106,712	~[w]	88,668[r]	~	~[q]	59,328[f]	57,622[y]	465,445
M. HONDURAS	1966	N	178,361	148,564	39,991	60,142	40,053	~	~	20,089[z]	4,308	44,123[aa]	#	29,797
		Ha.	2,417,053	1,869,402	1,106,907	363,710	122,760	~	~	240,950[z]	30,114	368,671[aa]	#	547,651
N. MEXICO[7]	1970	N	1,020,016	997,324	931,476	52,433	27,277	25,156[bb]	~	~[cc]	20,375[dd]	~[ee]	38,324	22,692
		Ha.	139,868,191	70,144,089	62,243,958	3,669,841	3,047,110	622,731[bb]	~	~[cc]	1,747,805[dd]	~[ee]	2,482,486	69,724,102
O. NICARAGUA	1963	N	102,201	88,223	39,445	12,872	4,799	2,906	1,215	3,952	16,049	8,170[aa]	11,687[ff]	13,978
		Ha.	3,822,813	3,822,813	2,550,113	98,300	53,135	13,542	4,354	27,269	735,846	311,343[aa]	127,211[ff]	~99
P. PANAMA	1971	N	105,272	92,971	12,906	4,671	~	~	~	~	75,394	::	::	12,301
		Ha.	2,098,062	1,552,489	545,414	73,961	~	~	~	~	933,144	::	::	545,573

Table 300 (Continued)
SYSTEMS OF LAND TENURE, ABSOLUTE DATA, 18 LC
(N and Ha.)

| Country | Year | Total | Operated by Owner | Operated Under Single Tenurial Systems | | | | | | | | | |
| | | | | Rented from Others | | | | | Occupied Without Title | Operated Under Collective System | Operated Under Other Simple Systems | Operated Under Mixed Systems |
				Total	Payment in Cash/Kind	Partnerships or Similar Forms	Payment by Services	Other Arrangements				
q. PARAGUAY[5]	1961											
N		160,777	59,994	12,000	12,000	#	#	#	66,653	#	#	22,130
Ha.		17,473,474	14,200,935	726,799	726,799	#	#	#	1,235,656	#	#	1,310,084
R. PERU	1961											
N		869,945[hh]	574,560	132,647	84,139	48,508[ii]	#	#	#	45,235[jj]	28,678	88,825
Ha.		17,722,044	11,875,859	2,465,253	2,256,939	2,208,314[ii]	#	#	#	1,933,939[jj]	540,887	906,106
S. URUGUAY[8]	1966											
N		79,193	43,656	22,068	19,201	2,867[k]	#	#	4,147	#	2,090	7,232
Ha.		16,533,556	8,198,667	3,845,625	3,688,187	157,438[k]	#	#	167,936	#	503,314	3,818,014
URUGUAY[8]	1970											
N		77,163	45,205	17,398	15,086	2,312[k]	#	#	4,233	#	2,662	7,665
Ha.		16,517,730	8,700,215	3,081,084	2,933,699	147,385[k]	#	#	174,984	#	606,670	3,954,777
T. VENEZUELA	1961[n]											
N		320,094[m]	125,627	41,189	25,966	15,223	#	#	124,119	#	#	24,542
Ha.		26,004,862[x]	21,187,669	613,631	494,950	118,681	#	#	2,832,834	#	#	1,370,728
UNITED STATES	1969											
N		2,730,250	1,705,720	352,923	~	~[u]	~	~	..	~	~[h]	671,607[i]
Ha.		430,336,324	151,799,714	55,688,760	~	~[u]	~	~	..	~	~[h]	222,847,850[i]

1. Details on the number of holdings were not obtained.
2. Excluding 14,583 holdings, the area of which is unknown.
3. For data on Bolivian and Venezuelan land reform, see James W. Wilkie, *Measuring Land Reform*, Supplement 5 (1974).
4. Excluding *Intendencias* and *Comisarías*.
5. Data obtained by sampling.
6. Excluding 5,125 properties without lands.
7. The data refer to the type of producer for 997,324 of total number.
8. Excluding holdings with an area of less than 1 ha.

a. "*Medieros y Tanteros.*"
b. Free occupancy.
c. Comprises 29,477,389 ha. operated in the *Tierras Fiscales* and 12,883,619 ha. operated under "Other Forms of Tenancy."
d. Comprises holdings worked by proprietors alone, properties with settlers, day laborers, etc.
e. "*Tolerados.*"
f. Communal lands.
g. Comprises 818 properties (439,264 ha.) operated by possessors of *Tierras Fiscales* and 136 properties (433,334 ha.) operated by *Granjas Cooperativas y Sociedades Agrícolas.*
h. Holdings operated by administrators.
i. Holdings operated by proprietors lessees.
j. Concessionaire.
k. Holdings operated by "*Medianeros.*"
l. Holdings operated illegally.
m. Including 4,617 holdings without agricultural land.

n. For data on Venezuelan land reform, see Wilkie, *Measuring Land Reform.*
o. Holdings operated by "*Partidarios.*"
p. Holdings operated by "*Huasipungueros.*"
q. Data obtained by sampling.
r. Properties operated by settlers.
s. Holdings operated by "*Colonos.*"
t. Excluding 188,544 ha. in sugar cane.
u. Holdings operated by sharecroppers and livestock sharers.
v. See note 3.
w. Excluding 14,583 holdings, the area of which is unknown.
x. See note 3.
y. Comprises those lands not included in preceding categories. Such lands include those in legal usufruct at time of census; those continuously and pacifically occupied without owners' permission by squatters who do not pay rent; lands in judicial process of transfer.
z. Agricultural holdings in National Lands.
aa. Agricultural holdings in Ejidal Lands.
bb. "*Aparcero*" only.
cc. "*Arrendatario.*"
dd. "*Ocupantes.*"
ee. Property overseen by ejidal president.
ff. Including 7,543 properties (93,716 ha.) operated by usufructuaries.
gg. Farms operated under mixed tenure systems are included in the category of those operated under single systems.
hh. Including 26,663 holdings without land.
ii. Comprises partnership and bound-service by Amerinds (*Yanaconaje*).
jj. Including communal lands.

SOURCE: IASI-AC, 1974, table 311-03; IASI-AC, 1977, table 311-03.

Table 301

SYSTEMS OF LAND TENURE, PERCENTAGE DATA, 18 LC

(N and Ha.)

	Country	Year	Total	Operated Under Single Tenurial Systems			Rented from Others				Occupied Without Title	Operated Under Collective System	Operated Under Other Simple Systems	Operated Under Mixed Systems
				Total	Operated by Owner	Total	Payment in Cash/Kind	Partnerships or Similar Forms	Payment by Services	Other Arrangements				
A.	ARGENTINA[1,2]	1960												
	N		100.0	100.0	~	~	~	~	#	~	#	#	~	#
	Ha.		100.0	100.0	58.9	16.9	12.9	1.2[a]	#	2.8[b]	#	#	24.2[c]	#
B.	BOLIVIA[3]	1950[u]												
	N		100.0	100.0	74.6[d]	20.0	15.8	3.5	.7[e]	#	#	4.4[f]	1.1[g]	#
	Ha.		100.0	100.0	67.9[d]	7.5	6.0	1.2	.3[e]	#	#	21.9[f]	2.7[g]	#
C.	BRAZIL	1970												
	N		100.0	97.3	60.4	20.4	~	~	~	~	16.5	~	~	2.7
	Ha.		100.0	95.9	82.6	6.1	~	~	~	~	7.2	~	~	4.1
D.	CHILE[6]	1965												
	N		100.0	89.0	47.2	41.8	4.9	7.1	21.3	6.1	2.4	#	#	11.0
	Ha.		100.0	89.8	74.0	14.2	11.5	.9	.3	1.5	1.6	#	#	10.2
E.	COLOMBIA[4]	1960												
	N		100.0	91.8	62.4	23.3	~	~	~	~	3.9	#	2.1	8.2
	Ha.		100.0	93.9	72.4	7.3	~	~	~	~	12.1	#	2.0	6.1
F.	COSTA RICA[5]	1973												
	N		100.0	90.1	85.4	4.7[b]	1.8	.4[j]	- -	.3[k]	-.[l]	9.7	.2	- -
	Ha.		100.0	92.0	90.8	1.2[b]	.8	.1[j]	- -	.1[k]	-.[l]	7.8	.2	- -
H.	DOMINICAN REP.	1960												
	N		100.0	~	58.8	30.8	3.7	6.9	1.9[r]	18.3[jj]	8.9[jj]	~	1.5	~
	Ha.		100.0[ii]	~	73.1	20.6	4.5	4.2	1.7[r]	10.3[jj]	5.3[jj]	~	1.0	~
I.	ECUADOR	1954												
	N		100.0	91.1	67.9	14.6	5.0	3.9[n]	5.7[o]	#	#	1.7[f]	6.9[p]	8.9
	Ha.		100.0	94.5	81.5	9.2	7.1	1.1[n]	1.0[o]	#	#	.4[f]	3.4[p]	5.5
J.	EL SALVADOR	1961												
	N		100.0	86.9	39.6	43.7	19.2	~	24.6[q]	~	#	#	3.5	13.1[i]
	Ha.		100.0	92.2	77.5	7.8	5.0	~	2.8[q]	~	#	#	7.0	7.8[i]
	EL SALVADOR	1971												
	N		100.0	85.9	39.4	46.5	29.6	~	~	~	#	#	16.9[r]	14.1[i]
	Ha.		100.0	90.6	76.4	14.2	7.4	~	~	~	#	#	6.8[r]	9.4[i]
K.	GUATEMALA	1964												
	N		100.0	88.9	57.9	22.9	11.3	~[v]	11.6[q]	#	~	4.9[f]	3.2[x]	11.1
	Ha.		100.0	86.5	77.4	5.7	3.1	~[v]	2.6[q]	#	~	1.7[f]	1.7[x]	13.5
M.	HONDURAS	1966												
	N		100.0	83.3	22.4	33.8	22.5	~	~	11.3[y]	2.4	24.7[aa]	#	16.7
	Ha.		100.0	77.3	45.8	15.0	5.1	~	~	10.0[y]	1.2	15.3[aa]	#	22.7
N.	MEXICO N[7]	1970												
	N		100.0	97.8	~	~	~	~[bb]	~	~[cc]	~[dd]	~	~	2.2
	Ha.		100.0	50.2	44.5	2.6	2.2	.4[bb]	~	~[cc]	1.2[dd]	~	1.8	49.8
O.	NICARAGUA	1963												
	N		100.0	86.3	38.6	12.6	4.7	2.8	1.2	3.9	15.7	8.0[aa]	11.4[ee]	13.7
	Ha.		100.0	100.0	66.7	2.6	1.4	.4	.1	.7	19.2	8.1[aa]	3.3[ee]	~[ff]
P.	PANAMA[8]	1971												
	N		100.0	88.3	12.3	4.4	~	~	~	~	71.6	- -	- -	11.7
	Ha.		100.0	74.0	26.0	3.5	~	~	~	~	44.5	- -	- -	26.0
Q.	PARAGUAY[9]	1961												
	N		100.0	86.2	37.3	7.5	7.5	#	#	#	41.5	#	#	13.8
	Ha.		100.0	92.5	81.3	4.2	4.2	#	#	#	7.1	#	#	7.5
R.	PERU	1961												
	N		100.0[ii]	89.8	66.0	15.2	9.7	5.6[gg]	#	#	#	5.2[hh]	3.3	10.2
	Ha.		100.0	94.9	67.0	13.9	12.7	1.2[gg]	#	#	#	10.9[hh]	3.1	5.1
S.	URUGUAY[8]	1966												
	N		100.0	90.9	55.1	27.9	24.2	3.6[2]	#	#	5.2	#	2.6	9.1
	Ha.		100.0	76.9	49.6	23.3	22.3	1.0[2]	#	#	1.0	#	3.0	23.1
	URUGUAY[8]	1970												
	N		100.0	90.1	58.6	22.6	19.6	3.0[2]	#	#	5.5	#	3.4	9.9
	Ha.		100.0	76.1	52.7	18.6	17.7	.9[2]	#	#	1.1	#	3.7	23.9
T.	VENEZUELA	1961[w]												
	N		100.0[s]	90.9	39.2	12.9	8.1	4.8	#	#	38.8	#	#	7.7
	Ha.		100.0[m]	94.7	81.5	2.4	1.9	.5	#	#	10.9	#	#	5.3
	UNITED STATES	1969												
	N		100.0	75.4	62.5	12.9	~	~[t]	~	~	- -	- -	-.[h]	24.6[i]
	Ha.		100.0	48.2	35.3	12.9	~	~[t]	~	~	- -	- -	-.[h]	51.8[i]

Table 301 (Continued)

SYSTEMS OF LAND TENURE, PERCENTAGE DATA, 18 LC

(N and Ha.)

1. Details on the number of holdings were not obtained.
2. Excluding 14,583 holdings, the area of which is unknown.
3. For data on Bolivian and Venezuelan land reform, see James W. Wilkie, *Measuring Land Reform,* Supplement 5 (1974).
4. Excluding *Intendencias and Comisarías.*
5. Data obtained by sampling.
6. Excluding 5,125 properties without lands.
7. The data refer to the type of producer.
8. Excluding holdings with an area of less than 1 ha.

a. *"Medieros y Tanteros."*
b. Free occupancy.
c. Comprises 29,477,389 ha. operated in the *Tierras Fiscales* and 12,833,619 ha. operated under "Other Forms of Tenancy."
d. Comprises holdings worked by proprietors alone, properties with settlers, day laborers, etc.
e. *"Tolerados."*
f. Communal lands.
g. Comprises 818 properties (439,264 ha.) operated by possessors of *Tierras Fiscales* and 136 properties (433,334 ha.) operated by *Granjas Cooperativas y Sociedades Agrícolas.*
h. Holdings operated by administrators.
i. Holdings operated by proprietors lessees.
j. Product-sharing arrangements.
k. Holdings operated without payment.
l. Holdings operated illegally.
m. For data on Venezuelan land reform, see Wilkie, *Measuring Land Reform.*
n. Holdings operated by *"Partidarios."*
o. Holdings operated by *"Huasipungueros."*

p. Data obtained by sampling.
q. Properties operated by settlers.
r. Holdings operated by *"Colonos."*
s. Including 4,617 holdings without agricultural land.
t. Holdings operated by sharecroppers and livestock-sharers.
u. See note 3.
v. Excluding 14,583 holdings, the area of which is unknown.
w. See note 3.
x. Comprises those lands not included in preceding categories. Such lands include those in legal usufruct at time of census; those continuously and pacifically occupied without owner's permission by squatters who do not pay rent; lands in judicial process of transfer.
y. Agricultural holdings in National Lands.
z. Holdings operated by *"Medianeros."*
aa. Agricultural holdings in Ejidal Lands.
bb. *"Aparcero"* only.
cc. *"Arrendatario."*
dd. *"Ocupantes."*
ee. Including 7,543 properties (93,716 ha.) operated by usufructuaries.
ff. Farms operated under mixed tenure systems are included in the category of those operated under single systems.
gg. Comprises partnership and bound-service by Amerinds (*Yanaconaje*).
hh. Including communal lands.
ii. Excluding 188,544 ha. in sugar cane.
jj. Concessionaire.

SOURCE: IASI-AC, 1974, table 311-03; IASI-AC, 1977, table 311-03.

Table 302

AGRICULTURAL LANDHOLDINGS:[1] NUMBER AND AREA BY SIZE AND CLASS, 20 L

(T Ha.)

Country		Total	Under 1 Ha. N	%	1 to 5 Ha. N	%	5 to 10 Ha. N	%	10 to 20 Ha. N	%	20 to 50 Ha. N	%	50 to 100 Ha. N	%	100 to 200 Ha. N	%	200 to 500 Ha. N	%	500 to 1,000 Ha. N	%	1,000 to 2,500 Ha. N	%	Over 2,500 Ha. N	%
A. ARGENTINA (1960)[2,3]	N	457,173	71,814	15.7	109,590		↑		↑	24.0	127,463		↑	27.9	58,795	12.9	38,277	8.4	24,876	5.4	14,899	3.3	11,459	2.5
	Ha.	175,142	201	.1	1,559		↑		↑	.9	7,710		↑	4.4	8,778	5.0	10,290	6.2	15,625	8.9	25,774	14.7	104,576	59.7
B. BOLIVIA (1950)[4]	N	86,377	24,756	28.7	26,472	30.6	8,760	10.1	5,881	6.8	4,837	5.6	2,776	3.2	2,239	2.6	2,443	2.8	1,540	1.8	2,140	2.5	3,272	3.8
	Ha.	32,750	11	#	63	.2	63	.2	82	.3	142	.4	183	.6	295	.9	756	2.3	1,051	3.2	3,295	10.1	26,803	81.8
C. BRAZIL (1970)[5,10]	N	4,905,642	396,846	8.1	1,403,397	18.7	719,387	14.7	768,448	15.7	824,090	16.7	341,854	7.0	215,329	4.4	151,514	3.1	47,903	1.0	36,847		↑	.8
	Ha.	294,145	236	.1	3,661	1.2	5,186	1.8	10,743	3.7	25,425	8.6	23,902	8.1	29,700	10.1	45,958	15.6	33,084	11.3	116,250		↑	29.5
D. CHILE (1965)[6,7]	N	253,532	45,233	17.8	78,460	30.9	33,076	13.0	29,976	11.8	29,360	11.6	14,785	5.8	9,164	3.6	6,998	2.8	3,156	1.2	3,324		↑	1.3
	Ha.	30,644	22	.1	184	.6	230	.8	414	1.4	912	3.0	1,023	3.3	1,262	4.1	2,168	7.1	2,144	7.0	22,285		↑	72.7
E. COLOMBIA (1971)[10]	N	1,176,811	268,705	22.9	431,520	36.7	159,659	13.6	117,863	10.0	100,010	8.5	47,763	4.1	26,553	2.2	16,344	1.4	4,927	.4	3,467		↑	.3
	Ha.	30,993	127	.4	1,020	3.3	1,088	3.5	1,599	5.2	3,054	9.9	3,198	10.3	3,552	11.4	4,700	15.2	3,229	10.4	9,426		↑	30.4
F. COSTA RICA (1973)[8,9,10]	N	81,562	14,413	17.1	20,830	25.7	9,095	11.0	8,777	11.0	12,436	14.6	5,801	7.3	2,922	3.7	1,929	2.5	495	.6	300		↑	.4
	Ha.	3,123	6	.2	53	1.7	65	2.1	123	3.9	387	12.4	396	12.7	392	12.6	577	18.4	339	10.9	785		↑	25.1
G. CUBA (1952)	N	100,965	2,912	2.9	11,146	11.0	12,480	12.4	30,045	29.8	20,427	20.2	11,282	11.2	10,158		↑	10.1	1,638	1.6	877		↑	.9
	Ha.	7,790	~	~	~	~	~	~	~	~	~	~	~	~	~		↑	~	~	~	~		↑	~
H. DOMINICAN REP. (1971)[10]	N	304,820	97,981	32.1	136,962	44.9	33,803	11.1	16,909	5.6	12,078	3.9	3,974	1.3	1,791	.7	884	.3	222	.1	216	.1	↑	#
	Ha.	2,736	41	1.5	311	11.3	231	8.4	231	8.5	357	13.1	268	9.8	249	9.1	268	9.8	148	5.4	632		↑	23.1
I. ECUADOR (1974)[9,10]	N	519,111	134,684	26.0	201,297	38.7	54,935	10.6	41,425	7.9	42,537	8.1	22,276	4.2	5,760	1.2	3,897	.8	825	.2	609		↑	.2
	Ha.	7,949	63	.8	476	6.0	378	4.8	558	7.0	1,312	16.5	1,353	17.0	682	8.6	994	12.5	544	6.8	1,589		↑	20.0
J. EL SALVADOR (1971)[9,10]	N	318,041	132,464	41.8	102,477	32.1	15,598	5.0	9,164	2.8	6,986	2.2	2,238	.6	1,103	.3	636	.2	139	.1	63	.1	↑	#
	Ha.	1,452	70	4.8	213	14.7	111	7.6	127	8.8	215	14.8	154	10.6	152	10.5	191	13.2	95	6.5	124		↑	8.5
K. GUATEMALA (1964)[8]	N	417,344	364,879		↑	87.4	37,025		↑	8.9	6,631	1.6	7,859		↑		↑	1.9	561	.1	294	.1	95	#
	Ha.	3,449	642		↑	18.7	447		↑	13.0	204	5.9	915		↑		↑	26.5	346	10.0	387	11.2	509	14.8
L. HAITI (1971)[10]	N	616,710	361,985	58.7	231,340	37.4	18,550	3.1	3,945	.6	890		↑		↑		↑		↑		↑		↑	.2
	Ha.	864	185	21.4	485	56.1	121	14.0	49	5.7	24		↑		↑		↑		↑		↑		↑	2.8
M. HONDURAS (1974)[10]	N	195,341	33,771	17.5	91,010	46.7	28,264	14.4	19,220	9.7	15,170	7.7	4,433	2.1	1,971	1.0	1,057	.5	276	.2	169	.1	↑	.1
	Ha.	2,630	22	.8	218	8.3	201	7.6	268	10.2	461	17.5	301	11.5	267	10.2	313	11.9	184	7.0	395		↑	15.0
N. MEXICO (1970)[9,10]	N	1,020,016	255,020	25.0	266,757	26.2	101,922	10.0	78,984	7.8	83,232	8.1	49,119	4.8	33,530	3.3	28,036	2.7	13,780	1.4	22,479		↑	2.2
	Ha.	139,868	145	.1	736	.5	778	.6	1,198	.9	2,783	2.0	3,714	2.6	4,916	3.5	9,148	6.5	10,023	7.2	106,427		↑	76.1
O. NICARAGUA (1963)[8,11]	N	102,201	51,936		↑	50.8	13,273	13.0	25,652		↑	25.1	6,291	6.2	3,554		↑	3.5	920	.9	405	.4	170	.2
	Ha.	3,823	133		↑	3.5	122	3.2	783		↑	20.5	538	14.1	673		↑	17.6	409	10.7	394	10.3	771	20.2

Table 302 (Continued)

AGRICULTURAL LANDHOLDINGS:[1] NUMBER AND AREA BY SIZE AND CLASS, 20 L

(T Ha.)

Country	Total	Under 1 Ha. N	%	1 to 5 Ha. N	%	5 to 10 Ha. N	%	10 to 20 Ha. N	%	20 to 50 Ha. N	%	50 to 100 Ha. N	%	100 to 200 Ha. N	%	200 to 500 Ha. N	%	500 to 1,000 Ha. N	%	1,000 2,500 Ha. N	%	Over 2,500 Ha. N	%
P. PANAMA (1971)[9,10]																							
N	115,364	20,032	17.4	34,368	29.5	13,937	12.2	14,179	12.2	14,138	12.2	5,526	5.2	1,920	1.7	853	.9	211	.2	108	#	↑	16.3
Ha	2,098	5	.3	72	3.4	90	2.6	183	4.3	415	19.8	363	17.3	252	12.0	238	11.3	139	6.6	341	16.3		
Q. PARAGUAY (1961)[12]																							
N	160,777	7,937	4.9	66,622	41.4	37,735	23.5	26,451	16.5	13,700	8.5	3,053	1.9	1,699	1.1	1,310	.8	641	.4	720	.4	909	.6
Ha	17,473	?	?	?	?	?	?	?	?	?	?	?	?	?	?	?	?	?	?	?	?	?	.6
R. PERU (1972)[10]																							
N	1,390,877	483,939	33.1	600,425	43.2	153,141	11.0	78,699	5.7	46,648	3.3	12,944	.9	7,034	.5	4,245	.3	1,615	.1	2,187	.1	↑	61.7
Ha	23,545	185	.8	1,375	5.8	1,011	4.3	1,026	4.3	1,339	5.7	843	3.6	908	3.9	1,243	5.3	1,087	4.6	14,528	61.7	↑	
S. URUGUAY (1970)[13]																							
N	77,163			22,982	↑	↑	29.8	12,259	15.9	13,071	16.9	7,927	10.3	6,603	8.6	6,734	8.7	3,626	4.7	2,784	3.6	1,177	1.5
Ha	16,518			110	↑	↑	1.7	169	1.0	411	2.5	559	3.4	931	5.6	2,133	12.9	2,561	15.5	4,305	26.1	5,339	32.3
T. VENEZUELA (1971)[9,10]																							
N	287,919	13,134	4.5	108,644	37.9	49,345	17.0	41,358	14.2	32,414	11.4	14,308	4.9	8,340	2.8	7,903	2.8	3,883	1.4	4,904		↑	1.7
Ha	26,470	6	#	246	.9	315	1.2	512	1.9	918	3.5	920	3.5	1,051	4.0	2,291	8.7	2,534	9.6	17,667		↑	66.7

1. Economic units of land used for the production of agricultural crops or of livestock. These units are worked or administered by one person, with or without the aid of others; they may consist of either one or of several parcels of land separated one from another so long as they form part of the same economic or management unit.
2. Excluding 14,583 holdings for unknown areas.
3. Actual sizes are: 5–25; 200–400; 400–1,000
4. Including 1,127 (1.4%) holdings (8.747 equals .03% ha.) not distributed for extension.
5. Excluding 18,377 holdings of size not reported.
6. Excluding 5,162 holdings without area.
7. Actual sizes are: 1,000–2,000; 2,000 and over.
8. Original figures presented in manzanas. A manzana is equal to .7 ha. Sixty-four manzanas equal one caballeria.
9. Total number of holdings includes holdings without land.
10. Actual sizes are: 1–2; 2–5; 1,000 and over.
11. Actual sizes are: 0–6.99; 7.00–13.99; 14.00–69.99; 70.00–139.99; 140.00–349.99; 350.00–699.99; 700.00–1,749.99; 1,750.00 and over.
12. Data obtained by sampling.
13. Excluding holdings less than 1 ha.

SOURCE: Adapted from IASI-AC, 1972, table 311-04. FAO Preliminary Results of the 1960 World Census of Agriculture, 5th, 19th and 21st Issues. IASI-AC, 1974, table 311-04; FAO 1970 World Census of Agriculture, tables 2.2, 2.3, 3.2, and 3.3.

Table 303

SIZE OF AGRICULTURAL HOLDINGS, 15 LC, 1950-70
(Area in T Ha.)

A. ARGENTINA[1]

Size of Holding	Number 1970	Number 1960	Number 1950	Area 1970	Area 1960	Area 1950
Total	527,314‡	457,173	441,431	142,445‡	175,142	173,448
To 5.0	?	71,814	59,616	?	201	?
5.1-25.0	?	109,590	101,836	?	1,559	?
25.1-100.0	?	127,463	128,285	?	7,710	?
100.1-200.0	?	58,795	63,025	?	8,778	?
200.1-400.0	?	38,277	62,976	?	10,920	?
400.1-1,000.0	?	24,876		?	15,625	?
1,000.1-2,500.0	?	14,899	20,151	?	25,774	?
2,500.1-5,000.0	?	5,798		?	22,240	?
5,000.1-10,000.0	?	3,110	3,393	?	23,929	?
10,000.1+	?	2,551	2,149	?	58,407	?

C. BRAZIL[2]

Size of Holding	Number 1970	Number 1960	Number 1950	Area 1970	Area 1960	Area 1950
Total	4,905,642	3,333,746	2,064,278	294,145	249,862	232,211
To 10	2,519,630	1,495,020	710,934	9,083	5,952	3,025
10 to less than 100	1,934,392	1,491,415	1,052,557	60,070	47,566	35,563
100 to less than 1,000	414,746	314,831	268,159	108,742	86,029	75,521
1,000 to less than 10,000	36,847	30,883	31,017	116,250	71,421	73,093
10,000+		1,597	1,611		38,893	45,009

D. CHILE[3]

Size of Holding	Number 1970	Number 1960	Number 1950	Area 1970	Area 1960	Area 1950
Total	258,657	253,532	159,959	30,644	30,644	27,712
Less than 1.0	?	45,233	28,246	?	22	8
1.0-4.9	?	78,460	27,515	?	184	70
5.0-9.9	?	33,076	19,866	?	230	139
10.0-19.9	?	29,976	19,225	?	414	272
20.0-49.9	?	14,785	12,346	?	1,023	857
50.0-99.9	?	9,164	8,474	?	1,262	1,164
100.0-199.9	?	6,998	6,766	?	2,168	2,100
200.0-499.9	?	3,156	3,076	?	2,144	2,101
500.0-999.9	?	1,533	1,555	?	2,115	2,112
1,000.0-1,999.9	?	1,061	999	?	3,315	3,020
2,000.0-4,999.9	?	730	696	?	16,855	15,165
5,000.0+	?			?		

E. COLOMBIA[4]

Size of Holding	Number 1970	Number 1960	Number 1950	Area 1970	Area 1960	Area 1950
Total	1,176,811	1,209,672	919,000	30,993	27,338	27,748
Less than .5	268,705	165,652	161,778	127	38	84
.5 to less than 1		132,419			94	
1 to less than 2		191,347			270	
2 to less than 3	431,550	117,005	342,788ᵃ	1,020	276	843ᵃ
3 to less than 4		92,001			309	
4 to less than 5		58,181			252	
5 to less than 10	159,659	169,145	143,549	1,088	1,165	983
10 to less than 20	117,863	114,231	101,275	1,599	1,572	1,376
20 to less than 30		44,049			1,044	
30 to less than 40	100,010	26,500	85,371ᵇ	3,054	890	2,594ᵇ
40 to less than 50		16,240			705	
50 to less than 100	47,763	39,990	37,814	3,198	2,680	2,586
100 to less than 200	26,553	22,317	22,969	3,552	2,996	3,432
200 to less than 500	16,344	13,693	15,366	4,700	3,994	4,686
500 to less than 1,000	4,927	4,141	4,912	3,229	2,731	3,749
1,000 to less than 2,500	3,467	1,975	2,541	9,426	2,808	4,037
2,500+		786	637		5,513	3,378

F. COSTA RICA[5]

Size of Holding	Number 1970	Number 1960	Number 1950	Area 1970	Area 1960	Area 1950
Total	81,562	64,621	47,286	3,123	2,671	1,854
0.70-1.04	?	3,661	2,940	?	3	2
1.05-4.89	?	19,572	10,693	?	49	21
4.90-6.99	?	4,692	7,362	?	26	35
7.00-10.49	?	6,113	4,580	?	51	38
10.50-13.99	?	3,429	2,468	?	40	29
14.00-20.99	?	5,732	4,231	?	95	70
21.00-34.99	?	7,435	5,614	?	195	147
35.00-69.99	?	7,240	5,061	?	342	238
70.00-101.49	?	2,522	1,725	?	205	139
101.50-121.49	?	745	480	?	82	52
122.50-174.99	?	1,174	704	?	169	101
175.00-199.49	?	318	183	?	58	34
199.50-349.99	?	973	634	?	247	160
350.00-699.99	?	596	359	?	276	164
700.00-1,000.99	?	177	92	?	144	74
1,001.00-1,049.99	?	14	13	?	14	14
1,050.00-2,449.99	?	169	97	?	244	147
2,450.00+	?	59	50	?	431	388

J. EL SALVADOR[6]

Size of Holding	Number 1970	Number 1960	Number 1950	Area 1970	Area 1960	Area 1950
Total	318,041	226,896	174,204	1,452	1,581	1,530
To .99	132,464	107,054	70,416	70	61	35
1.00-1.99		48,501	35,189		68	48
2.00-2.99		22,038	19,882		54	48
3.00-3.99	102,477	8,527	7,760	213	31	27
4.00-4.99		7,178	7,226		33	32
5.00-9.99	15,598	14,001	14,064	111	99	99
10.00-19.99	9,164	8,824	8,874	127	117	122
20.00-49.99	6,986	6,711	6,660	215	209	206
50.00-99.99	2,238	2,214	2,107	154	155	148
100.00-199.99	1,103	1,121	1,059	152	158	146
200.00-499.99	636	713	654	191	219	198
500.00-999.99	139	189	168	95	128	115
1,000.00-2,499.99	63	91	110	124	132	172
2,500.00+		34	35		117	133

K. GUATEMALA[7]

Size of Holding	Number 1970	Number 1960	Number 1950	Area 1970	Area 1960	Area 1950
Total	?	417,344	348,687	?	3,449	3,721
To .69	?	85,083	74,269	?	33	29
0.70-1.39	?	98,658	91,581	?	95	95
1.40-3.49	?	129,116	99,779	?	271	212
3.50-6.99	?	52,023	42,444	?	243	198
7.00-22.39	?	37,025	26,916	?	447	311
22.40-44.71	?	6,631	6,125	?	204	190
44.72-447.19	?	7,859	6,488	?	915	813
447.20-894.39	?	561	569	?	346	354
894.40-2,235.99	?	293	358	?	387	496
2,236.00-4,471.99	?	56	104	?	170	328
4,472.00-8,943.99	?	30	32	?	178	196
8,944.00+	?	9	22	?	161	500

Table 303 (Continued)

SIZE OF AGRICULTURAL HOLDINGS, 15 LC, 1950-70

(Area in T Ha.)

Size of Holding	Number 1970	Number 1960	Number 1950	Area 1970	Area 1960	Area 1950
L. HAITI[8]						
Total	616,710	~	~	864	~	~
To .10	16,820	~	~	1	~	~
.11-.20	36,050	~	~	6	~	~
.20-.32	107,480	~	~	35	~	~
.33-.49	28,485	~	~	13	~	~
.50-.64	104,890	~	~	66	~	~
.65-1.00	68,260	~	~	64	~	~
1.01-1.29	76,010	~	~	96	~	~
1.30-1.99	65,920	~	~	116	~	~
2.00-2.58	44.340	~	~	110	~	~
2.59-3.00	9,260	~	~	27	~	~
3.01-3.87	27,370	~	~	97	~	~
3.88-4.99	8,440	~	~	39	~	~
5.00-5.16	4,300	~	~	22	~	~
5.17-6.45	7.810	~	~	48	~	~
6.46-9.99	6,440	~	~	51	~	~
10.00-12.90	2,660	~	~	29	~	~
12.91-19.99	1.285	~	~	20	~	~
20.00-25.80	590	~	~	13	~	~
25.81 +	300	~	~	11	~	~
M. HONDURAS[9]						
Total	195,341	178,361	156,135	2,630	2,417	2,507
To .69	~	26,719	~	~	19	~
.70-3.49	~	57,409	~	~	113	~
3.50-6.99	~	36,313	~	~	168	~
7.00-13.99	~	27,112	~	~	252	~
14.00-34.99	~	19,977	~	~	412	~
35.00-69.99	~	6,429	~	~	298	~
70.00-139.99	~	2,449	~	~	226	~
140.00-349.99	~	1,286	~	~	265	~
350.00-699.99	~	398	~	~	190	~
700.00-1,749.99	~	196	~	~	202	~
1.750.00 +	~	73	~	~	272	~
N. MEXICO[10]						
Total	1,020,016	1,365,141	1,383,212	139,868	169.084	145,517
Less than 1	255,020	899,108 (Less than 1 and 1-5)	499,399	145	1,328 (Less than 1 and 1-5)	182
1-5	266,757		506,440	736		1,180
5-10	101,922	94,319	90,216	778	679	703
10-25	162,216 (10-25 and 25-50)	132,335	101,143	3,981 (10-25 and 25-50)	2,105	1,708
25-50		70,250	59,605		2,490	2,237
5 50-100	49,119	59,091	43,568	3,714	4,169	3,304
100-200	33,530	42,264	28,585	4,916	5,846	4,212
200-500	28,036	30,382	24,247	9,148	9,492	8,057
500-1,000	13,780	14,749	11,469	10,023	10,436	8,359
1,000-5,000	22,479 (1,000-5,000 to 10,000 +)	17,036	14,802	106,427 (1,000-5,000 to 10,000 +)	39,905	33,757
5,000-10,000		5,564 (5,000-10,000 and 10,000 +)	2,564		92,635 (5,000-10,000 and 10,000 +)	18,110
10,000 +			2,174			63,706

Size of Holding	Number 1970	Number 1960	Number 1950	Area 1970	Area 1960	Area 1950
O. NICARAGUA[11]						
Total	~	102,201	51,581	~	3,823	2,372
To .69	~	2,258	~	~	1	~
.70-3.49	~	33,948	10,214	~	58	18
3.50-6.99	~	15,730	7,729	~	74	36
7.00-13.99	~	13,273	8,621	~	122	79
14.00-34.99	~	14.703	10,687	~	308	224
35.00-69.99	~	10.949	7,829	~	475	344
70.00-139.99	~	6,291	3,782	~	538	321
140.00-349.99	~	3,554	1,874	~	673	356
350.00-699.99	~	920	483	~	409	215
700.00-1,749.99	~	405	256	~	394	249
1.750.00 +	~	170	106	~	771	529
P. PANAMA[12]						
Total	115,364	95,505	85,473	2,098	1,806	1,159
.5 to less than 1	20,032	4,959	44,442 (.5 to less than 1 and 1-5)	5	3	96 (.5 to less than 1 and 1-5)
1-5	34,368	38,733		72	93	
5-10	13,937	18,086	16,847	90	118	106
10-20	14,179	14,897	12,235	183	192	153
20-50	14,138	12,038	8,231	415	355	237
50-100	5,526	4,329	2,407	363	284	156
100-200	1,920	1,574	809	250	201	103
200-500	853	665	348	238	189	100
500-1,000	211	133	96	139	87	67
1,000 +	108	91	58	341	284	141
Q. PARAGUAY[13]						
Total	~	160,777	149,614	~	17,473	16,817
.1-.4	~	2,192	1,593	~	~	~
.5-.9	~	5,745	4,829	~	~	3
1.0-1.9	~	18,870	17,549	~	~	22
2.0-2.9	~	18,977	17,793	~	~	40
3.0-3.9	~	15,575	15,253	~	~	49
4.0-4.9	~	13,200	11,697	~	~	49
5.0-9.9	~	37,735	34,949	~	~	230
10.0-19.9	~	26,451	25,192	~	~	317
20.0-49.9	~	13,700	12,982	~	~	341
50.0-99.9	~	3,053	2,837	~	~	183
100.0-199.9	~	1,699	1,568	~	~	224
200.0-499.9	~	1,310	1,234	~	~	375
500.0-999.9	~	641	589	~	~	399
1,000-1,999.9	~ (1,000-1,999.9 and 2,000-4,999.9)	720	1,015 (1,000-1,999.9 and 2,000-4,999.9)	~ (1,000-1,999.9 and 2,000-4,999.9)	~ (1,000-1,999.9 and 2,000-4,999.9)	2,220 (1,000-1,999.9 and 2,000-4,999.9)
2,000-4,999.9		361				
5,000-9,999.9	~	270	259	~	~	1,795
10,000-19,999.9	~	132	130	~	~	1,787
20,000 +	~	146	145	~	~	8,783

Table 303 (Continued)

SIZE OF AGRICULTURAL HOLDINGS, 15 LC, 1950-70
(Area in T Ha.)

Size of Holding	Number 1970	Number 1960	Number 1950	Area 1970	Area 1960	Area 1950
S. URUGUAY[14]						
Total	77,163	86,928	85,258	16,518	16,988	16,974
1-4	11,085	12,769	10,953	30	34	29
5-9	11,897	13,028	11,117	80	89	77
10-19	12,259	14,032	13,771	169	197	193
20-49	13,071	15,715	16,910	411	495	535
50-99	7,927	9,490	10,375	559	674	732
100-199	6,603	7,387	7,814	931	1,042	1,104
200-499	6,734	6,986	7,241	2,133	2,174	2,272
500-999	3,626	3,712	3,475	2,561	2,609	2,444
1,000-2,499	2,784	2,587	2,452	4,305	3,994	3,810
2,500-4,999	869	891	763	2,963	3,043	2,584
5,000-9,999	253	280	316	1,644	1,857	2,065
10,000 +	55	51	71	732	780	1,130
T. VENEZUELA[15]						
Total	287,910	315,477	234,730	26,470	26,005	22,127
Less than .5	13,134	5,068	14,274	6	1	7
.5-.9		12,666			8	
1.0-1.9		40,920			49	
2.0-2.9	108,644	42,449	111,716	246	94	260
3.0-3.9		29,899			98	
4.0-4.9		24,615			107	
5.0-5.9		19,083			103	
6.0-6.9		14,703			95	
7.0-7.9	49,395	8,874	42,014	315	65	276
8.0-8.9		10,392			88	
9.0-9.9		4,750			45	

Size of Holding	Number 1970	Number 1960	Number 1950	Area 1970	Area 1960	Area 1950
T. VENEZUELA (Cont'd)						
10.0-14.9	41,358	29,535	27,551	512	316	363
15.0-19.9		11,852			191	
20.0-29.9	32,414	15,920	18,900	918	345	546
30.0-39.9		7,646			251	
40.0-49.9		5,034			220	
50.0-99.9	14,308	11,567	7,123	920	719	464
100.0-199.9	8,340	7,332	4,284	1,051	943	541
200.0-499.9	7,903	6,147	3,582	2,291	1,766	1,044
500.0-999.9	3,883	2,802	1,864	2,534	1,844	1,221
1,000.0-2,499.9	4,904	2,335	1,669	17,667	3,456	2,468
2,500.0 +		~1,888	1,753		15,199	14,936
UNITED STATES[16]						
Total	2,730,250	3,157,857	3,710,503	430,321	449,293	454,631
to 4.04	~	182,581	244,328	~	315	431
4.05-20.23	~	637,434	813,216	~	7,012	8,896
20.24-40.46	~	542,430	657,990	~	16,022	19,397
40.47-56.65	~	324,652	394,505	~	15,333	18,624
56.66-72.84	~	308,288	378,003	~	19,711	24,155
72.85-89.02	~	191,254	225,576	~	15,299	18,035
89.03-105.21	~	164,188	188,899	~	15,805	18,166
105.22-202.34	~	451,301	471,547	~	64,589	67,051
202.35-404.69	~	210,437	200,012	~	58,519	55,444
404.70 +	~	145,292	136,427	~	236,688	224,432

1. 1960 = Census of September, 1960; 1950: 1950 = Census of April, 1947.
2. 1970 = Census of December, 1970; 1960: 1970 = Census of September, 1960; 1950 = Census of July, 1950.
3. 1960 = Census of April, 1965; 1950 = Census of April 1955.
4. 1960 - Census of 1960; 1950 = Census of June, 1954; 1970 = Census of 1971.
5. 1960 = Census of April, 1963; 1950 = Census of March, 1955.
6. 1970 = Census of July 1971; 1960 = Census of June, 1961; 1960 = Census of October, 1950.
7. 1960 = Census of April, 1964; 1950 = Census of April, 1950.
8. 1970 = Census of September, 1971.
9. 1960 = Census of March, 1966; 1950 = Census of March, 1952.
10. 1960 = Census of May, 1960; 1950 = Census of May, 1950; 1970 = Census of 1970.

11. 1960 = Census of May, 1963; 1950 = Census of May, 1952.
12. 1970 = Census of May, 1971; 1960 = Census of April, 1961; 1950 = Census of December, 1950.
13. 1960 = Census of August, 1961; 1950 = Census of September, 1956.
14. 1970 = Census of 1970; 1960 = Census of May, 1961; 1950 = Census of May, 1951.
15. 1960 = Census of February, 1961; 1950 = Census of November, 1950; 1970 = Census of 1971.
16. 1960 = Census of October, 1964; 1950 = Census of October, 1959.

a. 1-5 Ha.
b. 21-50 Ha.

SOURCE: IASI-AC, 1974, table 311-04; FAQ-PY, 1975, table 3; FAO 1970 World Census of Agriculture, tables 2.2 and 3.2.

Table 304

CUMULATIVE LAND REFORM DATA[1], 15 L
(Through 1969)

Country	Initiation of Program	Number of Families Benefitted	Number of Hectares Distributed or Confirmed
B. BOLIVIA	1955	208,181	9,740,681
C. BRAZIL	1964	46,457	957,106
D. CHILE	1965	15,800	2,093,300
E. COLOMBIA	1961	91,937	2,832,312
F. COSTA RICA	1963	3,889	60,055
H. DOMINICAN REPUBLIC	1963	9,717	46,082
I. ECUADOR	1964	27,857	152,115
K. GUATEMALA	1955	26,500	166,734
M. HONDURAS	1963	5,843	90,642
N. MEXICO	1916	2,525,811	59,413,656
O. NICARAGUA	1964	8,117	357,989
P. PANAMA	1963	2,594	37,339
Q. PARAGUAY	1963	#	#
R. PERU	1961	31,600	850,522
T. VENEZUELA	1959	117,286	4,605,594

1. Excludes colonization and land settlement.

SOURCE: James W. Wilkie, *Measuring Land Reform*, Statistical Abstract of Latin
America, Supplement 5 (Los Angeles: UCLA Latin American Center Publications,
University of California, 1974), p. 3, from which this table is adapted.

Table 305

AGRARIAN REFORM AND NUMBER OF
PEASANT FAMILIES BENEFITED, 9 L
(Through 1982)

Country	Agriculture and Forest Surface Distributed[1] (T Ha)			Number of Recipients		
	Total	Assigned	%	Total[2]	Benefited	%
B. BOLIVIA	3,275.0[a]	2,740.0[d]	83.4	516,200	384,560[d]	74.5
D. CHILE	28,759.0[j]	2,940.0[e]	10.2	412,000	38,000[e]	9.2
F. COSTA RICA	3,122.4[b]	221.6[b]	7.1	155,200	8,349[b]	5.4
H. DOMINICAN REP.	2,676.7[c]	374.6[c]	14.0	697,800	59,411[c]	8.5
I. ECUADOR	7,949.0[j]	718.1[l]	9.0	749,000	78,088[l]	10.4
N. MEXICO	139,868.0[j]	60,724.0[f]	43.4	4,629,000	1,986,000[f]	42.9
P. PANAMA	2,253.9[k]	493.2[g]	21.9	132,800	17,703[g]	13.3
R. PERU	23,545.0[j]	9,255.6[h]	39.3	1,419,400	431,982[h]	30.4
T. VENEZUELA	26,470.0[j]	5,118.7[i]	19.3	561,800	171,861[i]	30.6

1. Total surface of exploitations.
2. Based on FAO data.

a. 1950 data.
b. Corresponds to the peasant settlements created by the Instituto de Tierras y Colonización
through 1980.
c. 1983 data.
d. Through 1976.
e. Through 1981.
f. 1970 data.
g. 1977 data.
h. Through 1981.
i. Through 1978.
j. As of 1981.
k. Undated.
l. Through 1982.

SOURCE: IDB-SPTF, 1986, p. 130.

Table 306

NICARAGUA DISTRIBUTION OF LAND UNDER LAND
REFORM PROGRAM BY REGION,[1] 1981–86

Region	1981–86	1986
Region 1		
Co-ops[2]	102,391	5,489
Individuals[3]	24,153	18,132
Families[4]	598	470
Region 2		
Co-ops	165,891	31,065
Individuals	28,832	24,720
Families	8,179	1,071
Region 3		
Co-ops	59,839	9,312
Individuals	5,123	1,481
Families	205	152
Region 4		
Co-ops	154,291	35,633
Individuals	7,793	15,158
Families	1,310	1,200
Region 5		
Co-ops	148,826	80,379
Individuals	46,543	15,311
Families	793	~
Region 6		
Co-ops	132,205	24,329
individuals	42,960	30,420
Families	2,316	2,187
Special Zone 1		
Co-ops	22,767	0
Individuals	0	0
Families	~	0
Special Zone 2		
Co-ops	24,411	6,800
Individuals	14,350	14,350
Families	91	91
Special Zone 3		
Co-ops	73,164	6,250
Individuals	34,178	18,726
Families	552	~
Total		
Co-ops	899,137	199,207
Individuals	203,932	138,298
Total land	1,103,069	337,505
Total families	60,282	14,276

1. As of 1982, Nicaragua was divided into the following regions:
   Region 1, Departments of Esteli and Nueva Segovia
   Region 2, Department of León
   Region 3, Department of Managua
   Region 4, Departments of Granada, Masaya, and Rivas
   Region 5, Departments of Chontales, Boaco, and Zelaya
   Region 6, Departments of Matagalpa and Jinotega
   Special Zone 1, Northern Zelaya
   Special Zone 2, Southern Zelaya
   Special Zone 3, Department of Rio San Juan.
2. Co-ops: Amount of land distributed to Sandinista Agricultural Cooperatives in hectares.
3. Individuals: Amount of land distributed to individual farmers, in hectares.
4. Families: Number of families benefiting under land reform.

SOURCE: *Central American Report*, April 10, 1987.

Part II: Transportation and Communication

CHAPTER 4

TRANSPORTATION

Figure 4:1

MAJOR HIGHWAYS OF SOUTH AMERICA

Source: IDB-SPTF, 1984, p. 82.

Table 400

CITY TO CITY DISTANCES BY NONSTOP AIR SERVICE
(Miles)

From/To	Country[1]	City Code/ Miles	From/To	Country[1]	City Code/ Miles	From/To	Country[1]	City Code/ Miles
ACAPULCO	**MEX**	**ACA**	SANTA MARTA	COL	42	MANAUS	BRAZ	1,119
ATLANTA GA	USA	1,507	SANTO DOMINGO	D R	619	MANIZALES	COL	109
CHICAGO ILL	USA	1,879	VALLEDUPAR	COL	109	MARACAIBO	VEN	447
DALLAS TEX	USA	1,124				MEDELLIN	COL	145
GUADALAJARA	MEX	346	**BELEM**	**BRAZ**	**BEL**	MEXICO CITY	MEX	1,961
HOUSTON TEX	USA	934	BELO HORIZONTE	BRAZ	1,382	MIAMI FLA	USA	1,513
LIMA	PERU	2,527	BRASILIA	BRAZ	1,001	NEIVA	COL	145
LOS ANGELES CAL	USA	1,654	CAMPO GRANDE	BRAZ	1,545	NEW YORK NY	USA	2,487
MEXICO CITY	MEX	191	CAYENNE	F GU	506	OCANA	COL	250
MONTREAL QUE	CAN	2,487	CONCEICAO	BRAZ	480	PANAMA CITY	PAN	470
NEW YORK NY	USA	2,260	CUIABA	BRAZ	1,567	PEREIRA	COL	112
OAXACA	MEX	204	CURITIBA	BRAZ	1,674	POINTE A PITRE	GUAD	1,171
PAPEETE	F POL	4,138	FLORIANOPOLIS	BRAZ	1,828	QUITO	ECUA	450
PUERTO VALLARTA	MEX	448	FORTALEZA	BRAZ	710	RIO DE JANEIRO	BRAZ	2,827
SAN ANTONIO TEX	USA	886	GOIANIA	BRAZ	1,102	SAN ANDRES	COL	749
TORONTO ONT	CAN	2,202	IMPERATRIZ	BRAZ	400	SAN JUAN	P R	1,096
			LISBON	PORT	3,733	SANTA MARTA	COL	444

Continued in SALA, 23-308.

Table 401

AIR PASSENGER KILOMETERS OF SCHEDULED SERVICE,[1] 20 LC, 1975-85[a]

(M)

	Country	Total[3]					International Flights[4]				
		1975	1980	1983[c]	1984	1985	1975	1980	1983[c]	1984	1985
A.	ARGENTINA	4,373	8,031	6,034	7,405	7,521[‡]	2,128	4,413	2,741	3,504	3,877[‡]
B.	BOLIVIA	331	944	787	877	894[‡]	163	570	406	482	513[‡]
C.	BRAZIL	9,787	15,573	16,738	17,175	18,494	4,503	6,008	6,103	6,928	7,370
D.	CHILE	1,276	1,875	1,493	1,624[‡]	1,802[‡]	892	1,364	893	969[‡]	1,150[‡]
E.	COLOMBIA	2,778	4,161	4,986	4,481	4,242[‡]	1,384	2,203	2,360	2,209	1,959
F.	COSTA RICA	306	495	505	546	579[‡]	279	485	493	541	567
G.	CUBA	517	932	1,136	1,289[‡]	1,801[‡]	264	666	783	927[‡]	1,459[‡]
H.	DOMINICAN REP.	319	550	429	479	606[‡]	319	550	429	479	606[‡]
I.	ECUADOR	301	861	762	893[‡]	969[‡]	220	851	552	681[‡]	754[‡]
J.	EL SALVADOR	185	289	282	360[‡]	575[‡]	185	289	282	360[‡]	575[‡]
K.	GUATEMALA	139	159	156	168	156[‡]	139	159	156	159	150[‡]
L.	HAITI[‡]	~	~	~	~	~	~	~	~	~	~
M.	HONDURAS	240	387[b]	348	408	782[‡]	225	369	327	387	759[‡]
N.	MEXICO	6,710	13,870	15,875	17,197[‡]	17,777	2,889	6,594	7,083	8,414	7,853
Q.	NICARAGUA	83	~	~	110[‡]	115[‡]	~	~	~	110[‡]	115[‡]
P.	PANAMA	405	409	419	482	534	376	395	419	482	534
Q.	PARAGUAY	76	~	~	524[‡]	675[‡]	~	~	~	510[‡]	620[‡]
R.	PERU	1,222	1,974	1,699	1,664	1,598	387	822	751	737	704
S.	URUGUAY	79	178	325	322	389	60	160	310	307	373
T.	VENEZUELA	2,269	4,367	3,747	3,602[‡]	4,370[‡]	1,558	2,670	1,990	1,964[‡]	2,139[‡]
	UNITED STATES[2]	262,013	409,063	443,136	479,340	525,751	43,404	82,639	91,541	102,240	107,197

1. Regularly scheduled domestic and international services of the registered airlines, including flights occasioned by excess traffic.
2. Since 1965 flights to U.S. territories have been considered domestic.
3. Includes scheduled domestic and international services of the registered domestic and international airlines.

4. Includes international flights from international scheduled, registered airlines.
a. For earlier years, see SALA, 23–2200.
b. Data for one or more months missing.
c. Data from UN-SY, 1983/84, table 176.

SOURCE: Calculated from ICAO-DS-T, 1969–73, no. 33, vol. 2, tables 9 and 14; ICAO-DS-T, 1975–79, no. 39, parts B and C; ICAO-DS-T, 1978–82, parts A, B, and C; ICAO Bulletin, July 1984; ICAO, Advance 1983 Statistics for Scheduled Services; data for 1984 from ICAO Bulletin, July 1985; UN-SY, 1983/84, table 176; *Civil Aviation Statistics of the World, 1985*, ICAO, 1986.

Table 402

KILOMETERS[1] FLOWN OF SCHEDULED SERVICE,[2] 20 LC, 1975-85[a]

(T)

	Country	1975	1980	1981	1982	1983[c]	1984	1985
A.	ARGENTINA	63,700	93,800	90,300	75,900	76,200	74,700	84,100[‡]
B.	BOLIVIA	6,000	13,500	12,600	10,500	9,700	11,000	11,300[‡]
C.	BRAZIL	170,200	203,400	116,900	169,400	202,700	225,000	228,100
D.	CHILE	21,000	24,700	28,800	26,300	22,500	22,700[‡]	22,900[‡]
E.	COLOMBIA	43,300	42,900	48,900	61,300	71,500	63,000	59,700[‡]
F.	COSTA RICA	6,000	8,400[c]	7,600	7,500	7,600	7,100	8,100[‡]
G.	CUBA	8,400	14,700[c]	6,800[b]	~	15,400	14,500[‡]	18,200[‡]
H.	DOMINICAN REP.	4,000	5,700[c]	3,200[b]	5,500	4,800	4,400	4,900[‡]
I.	ECUADOR	10,400[c]	20,800[c]	~	~	17,400	17,500[‡]	16,900[‡]
J.	EL SALVADOR	6,500[c]	6,100	6,200	6,400	4,600	4,600[‡]	7,100[‡]
K.	GUATEMALA	3,800	3,700	3,500	3,500	2,500	2,300	2,600[‡]
L.	HAITI	~	~	~	~	~	700[‡]	700[‡]
M.	HONDURAS	5,700	7,300	5,900	4,300[b]	4,900	5,100	9,800[‡]
N.	MEXICO	89,200	157,400[c]	160,200	72,200	163,900	182,000[‡]	185,900[‡]
O.	NICARAGUA	~	~	~	~	~	1,800[‡]	1,700[‡]
P.	PANAMA	8,700	6,600	6,800	5,000[b]	6,400	6,200	6,300
Q.	PARAGUAY	~	~	~	~	~	7,600[‡]	7,900[‡]
R.	PERU	21,800	24,600	24,400	12,900[b]	26,600	24,300	22,500
S.	URUGUAY	2,700	4,300[c]	2,000[b]	3,100[b]	5,500	5,200	5,300
T.	VENEZUELA	37,200	61,000	41,800[b]	24,000[b]	56,900	53,200[‡]	44,000[‡]
	UNITED STATES	3,605,400	4,413,400	4,331,300[b]	4,252,700[b]	4,373,700	4,839,100	5,102,100

1. Some figures may be rounded.
2. Regularly scheduled domestic and international services of the registered airlines, including flights occasioned by excess traffic.

a. For previous years, see SALA, 23–2201.
b. Data for one or more months missing.
c. Data from UN-SY, 1983/84 and 1986, table 176.

SOURCE: ICAO-DS-T, 1969–73, no. 33, vol. 2, table 4; ICAO-DS-T, 1975–79, no. 39, parts B and C; ICAO-DS-T, 1978–82, parts A, B, and C; ICAO-DST, Advance 1983 Statistics for Scheduled Services at International Airlines; UN-SY, 1983/84, 1986, table 176; *Civil Aviation Statistics of the World, 1985*, ICAO, 1986.

Table 403

AIR PASSENGERS TRANSPORTED,[1] 18 LRC, 1970-85

(T)

	1970			1980			1983[b]			1984			1985		
Country	Total	Domestic	International	Total	Domestic	International	Total	Domestic	International	Total	Domestic	International	Total	Domestic	International
A. ARGENTINA	2,332	1,201	1,131	5,589	4,289	1,300	4,400	3,675	725	5,164	4,287	877	4,797‡	3,885‡	912‡
B. BOLIVIA	244	204†	40	1,342	1,074	268	1,299	1,094	205	1,359	1,104	255	1,343‡	1,072‡	271‡
C. BRAZIL	3,340	2,811	529	13,008	11,678	1,330	12,606	11,487	1,119	12,948	11,649	1,299	13,403	12,106	1,297
D. CHILE	575	430	145	669	370	299	652	446	206	731‡	497	234‡	776‡	507‡	269‡
E. COLOMBIA	3,011	2,726	285	4,728	3,976	752	6,584	5,816	768	5,737	5,119	618	5,737‡	5,121‡	616
F. COSTA RICA	256	159	97	393	99	294a	380	79	301	323	39	284	380‡	93‡	287
G. CUBA	874	844	30	296	232	64a	839	673	166	839‡	666‡	173‡	894‡	668‡	226‡
H. DOMINICAN REP.	129†	1	128†	764a	372a	392a	477	~	477	605	~	605	734‡	~	734‡
I. ECUADOR	419	347†	72	255	~	255	618	450	168	634‡	454‡	180	665‡	459‡	206‡
J. EL SALVADOR	138†	~	138	4	~	4	266	~	266	360‡	~	360‡	395‡	~	395‡
K. GUATEMALA	113†	47†	66	119	#	119	100	~	100	124	32	92	108‡	23‡	85‡
M. HONDURAS	296	160	136	508	139	369	436	134	302	439	134	305	713‡	143	570‡
N. MEXICO	2,966	2,282†	684	11,189	8,396	2,793	13,923	10,974	2,948	14,440‡	10,947	3,493	15,372	12,044	3,328
P. PANAMA	307†	194†	113	355	48	307	323	~	323	372	~	372	390	~	390‡
Q. PARAGUAY	81†	14†	67	~	~	~	~	~	~	179‡	18‡	161‡	212‡	22‡	190‡
R. PERU	392	230†	161	1,098	877	221	1,698	1,490	208	1,617	1,398	219	1,564	1,340	224
S. URUGUAY	219	6	213	89	~	89	310	37	273	338	39	299	329‡	42	287
T. VENEZUELA	757	501	226	5,133	4,173	960	5,000	4,367	633	4,571‡	3,987	584‡	4,967‡	4,372	595‡
LATIN AMERICA	16,448	12,157	4,291	45,539	35,723	9,816	49,588	40,722	9,188	50,780	40,370	10,410	52,779	41,897	10,882
UNITED STATES	163,449	148,174	15,275	294,186	268,463	25,723	309,836	282,788	27,048	333,057	303,918	29,139	362,794	333,359	29,435

1. Regularly scheduled domestic and international services of the airlines registered in each country, including flights occasioned by excess traffic.

a. Data for one or more months missing.
b. Data calculated from UN-SY, 1983/84 and 1986, table 176.

SOURCE: 1970-82 calculated from ICAO-DS-T, 1969-73, no. 33, vol. 2, tables 4, 9, and 14; ICAO-DS-T, 1975-79, no. 39, parts B and C; ICAO-DS-T, 1978-82, parts A, B, and C; ICAO-DS-T, Advance 1983 Statistics for Scheduled Services of International Airlines; UN-SY, 1983/84, 1986, table 176; Civil Aviation Statistics of the World, 1985, ICAO, 1986.

Table 404

UTILIZATION OF AIRLINE CAPACITY, PASSENGER LOAD FACTOR,[1] 20 LC, 1970–85[a]

(%)

	Country	1970	1974	1975	1978	1979	1980	1981	1982	1983[‡,c]	1984	1985
A.	ARGENTINA	53	66	64	59	62	60	50	48	47[b]	61	55
B.	BOLIVIA	43[†]	72	64	59	55	61	60	59	~	65	65
C.	BRAZIL	59	56	57	58	68	63	60	63	59[b]	60	64
D.	CHILE	55	58	57	62	61	64	63	57	53[b]	58	60
E.	COLOMBIA	54	58	61	59	61	63	59	66	50[b]	63	64
F.	COSTA RICA	61	61	64	69	72	69[b]	64	59	53	57	61
G.	CUBA	86	76	73	75	74	69[b]	69[b]	~	~	84	78
H.	DOMINICAN REP.	48[†]	66	72	73	74	78[b]	68[b]	68	78[b]	73	75
I.	ECUADOR	57	51	52	53	58	62	~	~	~[b]	56	63
J.	EL SALVADOR	52[†]	55	56	64	68	70	65	57	60[b]	72	67
K.	GUATEMALA	53[†]	48	48	46	47	41	43	42	55[b]	70	64
L.	HAITI	54[†]	~	~	~	~	~	~	~	~	~	~
M.	HONDURAS	49	56	50	57	58	57	59	57[b]	67[b]	71	68
N.	MEXICO	51	57	57	68	70	66[b]	65	60	~	60	60
O.	NICARAGUA	49[†]	38	38	40	51	~	~	~	~	52	55
P.	PANAMA	52[†]	54	47	52	54	57	58	57[b]	58[b]	59	62
Q.	PARAGUAY	54[†]	52	53	48	50	~	~	~	~	52	55
R.	PERU	52	63	58	59	62	61	55	57[b]	55[b]	56	57
S.	URUGUAY	39	66	70	50	51	~	52[b]	48[b]	59[b]	55	64
T.	VENEZUELA	44	49	51	52	54	46	63[b]	60[b]	45[b]	51	56
	UNITED STATES	49	55	54	62	63	59[b]	58[b]	58[b]	62[b]	59	61

1. Obtained by dividing actual passengers/km by available seats/km of the regularly
   scheduled domestic and international services of the registered airlines, including
   flights occasioned by excess traffic.

a. Data for the years 1972-77 are from SALA, 22-2103.
b. Data for one or more months missing.
c. Advance 1983 statistics, based on data received up to 14 March 1984.

SOURCE: ICAO-DS-T, 1969-73, no. 33, vol. 2, table 4; ICAO-DS-T, 1975-79, vol. 39;
   1980-82 calculated from ICAO-DS-T, 1978-82, parts B and C; ICAO-DS-T, Advance
   1983 Statistics for Scheduled Services of International Airlines, *Civil Aviation
   Statistics of the World, 1985*, ICAO, 1986.

Table 405

AIR TRANSPORT IN TON KILOMETERS,[1] 19 LC, 1970–85

(M)

Country	Total[3] 1970	1983[a]	1984	1985	International Flights[4] 1970	1983[a]	1984	1985
A. ARGENTINA								
Freight	47.9	174.3	179.8	177.4‡	35.9	145.6	144.7	139.1‡
Mail	6.0	19.8	19.9	~	4.5	6.4	7.2	~
Total[2]	277.0	728.0	855.0	804.0‡	177.0	416.0	488.0	518.0‡
B. BOLIVIA								
Freight	1.5	17.2	33.0	41.5‡	.6	14.5	34.9	38.0‡
Mail	~	1.0	1.9	~	~	.9	1.8	~
Total[2]	12.0	85.0	115.0	120.0‡	5.0	52.0	81.0	86.0‡
C. BRAZIL								
Freight	164.1	692.1	831.7	909.2‡	129.8	402.6	504.6	513.1
Mail	9.3	25.2	30.1	~	6.2	14.8	16.4	~
Total[2]	538.0	2,150.0	2,350.0	2,547.0‡	340.0	992.0	1,177.0	1,233.0
D. CHILE								
Freight	41.1	120.3	105.4	112.1	18.6	103.0	88.4‡	98.4‡
Mail	1.1	2.0	2.5	~	.8	1.7	1.9	~
Total[2]	117.0	257.0	254.0‡	277.0‡	59.0	185.0	178.0‡	204.0‡
E. COLOMBIA								
Freight	74.7	292.5	381.2	341.7‡	31.0	245.4	337.2	296.0‡
Mail	4.1	5.1	4.5	~	3.2	4.3	3.8	~
Total[2]	260.0	747.0	784.0	723.0‡	116.0	473.0	550.0	485.0‡
F. COSTA RICA								
Freight	9.3	21.0	24.0	25.4‡	7.8	21.0	23.6	25.3
Mail	.2	.7	.7	~	.2	.7	.7	~
Total[2]	25.0	76.0	86.0	90.0‡	21.0	74.0	85.0	89.0
G. CUBA								
Freight	9.1	15.8	15.5‡	17.1‡	5.7	13.9	13.5‡	14.9‡
Mail	2.1	1.9	3.1	~	1.8	1.7	2.9	~
Total[2]	53.0	116.0	135.0‡	179.0‡	24.0	86.0	100.0‡	150.0‡
H. DOMINICAN REP.								
Freight	~	7.1	9.7‡	8.5‡	~	7.1	9.7‡	8.5‡
Mail	~	~	~	~	~	~	~	~
Total[2]	~	46.0	53.0	63.0‡	~	46.0	53.0‡	63.0‡
I. ECUADOR								
Freight	9.3	33.0	42.5‡	50.7‡	1.7	25.5	34.5	42.7‡
Mail	.3	1.5	1.5	~	.3	1.4	2.4	~
Total[2]	34.0	104.0	125.0‡	147.0‡	19.0	78.0	98.0	120.0‡
J. EL SALVADOR								
Freight	11.4	7.3	4.0‡	~	11.4	7.3	4.0‡	0‡
Mail	#	~	~	~	#	~	~	~
Total[2]	26.0	33.0	36.0‡	49.0‡	26.0	33.0	36.0‡	49.0‡
K. GUATEMALA								
Freight	6.3	6.3	8.1	9.0‡	5.5	6.3	8.0	8.9‡
Mail	.2	~	~	~	.1	~	~	~
Total[2]	16.0	20.0	23.0	23.0‡	14.0	20.0	22.0	22.0‡
M. HONDURAS‡								
Freight	3.6	1.9	2.2	1.0‡	2.7	1.8	2.1	1.0‡
Mail	~	.5	.3	~	~	.5	.2	~
Total[2]	18.0	35.0	41.0	69.0‡	15.0	33.0	39.0	67.0‡
N. MEXICO								
Freight	36.7	109.2	145.8‡	171.0	17.1	58.9	78.7	92.9
Mail	3.7	3.7	~	~	1.9	2.1	2.3	~
Total[2]	288.0	1,584.0	1,623.0‡	1,700.0	138.0	734.0	816.0	773.0
O. NICARAGUA‡								
Freight	.8	~	1.3‡	1.4‡	.5	~	1.3‡	1.4‡
Mail	.1	~	~	~	.1	~	~	~
Total[2]	8.0	~	11.0‡	12.0‡	7.0	~	11.0‡	12.0‡
P. PANAMA								
Freight	4.2	1.8	3.9	4.3	3.9	1.8	3.9	4.3
Mail	~	.6	~	~	~	.6	.7	~
Total[2]	16.0	40.0	49.0	54.0	13.0	40.0	49.0	54.0
Q. PARAGUAY								
Freight	.7	~	3.0‡	3.1‡	.1	~	2.3‡	2.4‡
Mail	#	~	~	~	#	~	~	~
Total[2]	8.0	~	50.0‡	60.0‡	6.0	~	48.0‡	58.0‡
R. PERU								
Freight	22.4	75.7	61.0‡	47.4‡	16.1	38.7	26.5‡	18.2‡
Mail	2.2	.8	~	~	2.1	.4	.2	~
Total[2]	99.0	229.0	212.0	192.0	83.0	107.0	93.0	82.0

Table 405 (Continued)

AIR TRANSPORT IN TON KILOMETERS,[1] 19 LC, 1970-85

(M)

Country	Total[3]				International Flights[4]			
	1970	1983[a]	1984	1985	1970	1983[a]	1984	1985
S. URUGUAY								
Freight	.3	1.5	2.0	1.9	.3	1.5	1.9	1.8
Mail	~	.3	.2	~	~	.3	.2	~
Total[2]	5.0	31.0	30.0	37.0	5.0	29.0	29.0	36.0
T. VENEZUELA								
Freight	58.6	103.3	107.1‡	91.7‡	54.1	102.2	106.1‡	90.4‡
Mail	2.1	2.4	~	~	2.0	2.3	2.9	~
Total[2]	166.0	438.0	429.0‡	483.0‡	132.0	287.0	288.0‡	288.0‡
UNITED STATES								
Freight	5,151.2	9,143.9	10,112.3	9,472.2	7,714.3	3,776.3	4,265.0	4,137.2
Mail	2,154.8	2,141.4	~	~	990.1	586.9	667.0	~
Total[2]	26,537.0	51,473.0	55,967.0	59,566.0	6,198.0	12,659.0	14,209.0	14,498.0

1. To convert to long ton miles, multiply by coefficient of .6611558. Ton kilometers obtained by multiplying the number of tons of freight transported by number of kilometers traveled.
2. Includes freight, mail, and passengers.
3. Includes domestic and international scheduled, registered airlines.
4. International flights from international scheduled, registered airlines.

a. For years between 1970 and 1973, see SALA, 25–405.

SOURCE: UN-SY, 1979/80, table 151; UN-SY, 1983/84, 1986, table 176; *Civil Aviation Statistics of the World, 1985*, ICAO, 1986.

Table 406

LENGTH OF RAILWAY NETWORK, 17 LR, 1970–83

(km)

Country	1970	1975	1977	1978	1979	1980	1981	1982	1983
A. ARGENTINA	39,905	39,787	36,996	34,393	34,350	34,077	34,172	34,098	34,127
B. BOLIVIA	3,284	3,269	3,373	3,473	3,473	3,328	3,628	3,628	3,628
C. BRAZIL	30,445[a]	29,788	28,756	28,972	29,061	28,671	28,310	28,237	28,228
D. CHILE	6,475	6,606	6,372	6,366	6,365	6,302	6,300	6,236	6,236
E. COLOMBIA	3,436	3,431	3,403	2,884	3,403	3,403	3,403	2,710	3,400
G. CUBA	5,286	5,342	4,214	4,382	4,382	4,382	4,382	4,382	4,382
I. ECUADOR	~	1,008	990	965	965	965	965	966	966
J. EL SALVADOR	620	161***	602	602	602	602	602	602	602
K. GUATEMALA	~	775	775	775	927	927	927	927	927
M. HONDURAS	~	~	205	205	205	205	205	205	205
N. MEXICO	19,868	19,960	19,999	20,000	20,031	20,058	19,953	19,955	20,000
O. NICARAGUA	318	320	345	345	345	345	345	331	331
P. PANAMA	- -	- -	- -	- -	- -	118	118	118	109
Q. PARAGUAY[1]	441	441	441	441	441	441	441	441	441
R. PERU	2,242	1,875	1,875	1,875	1,882	2,099	2,159	2,159	2,159
S. URUGUAY	2,975	2,975	2,988	2,998	3,005	3,005	3,005	3,010	3,001
T. VENEZUELA[2]	226	226	284	264	268	268	268	268	280
LATIN AMERICA[3]	115,521	115,964	111,618	108,940	109,705	109,496	109,183	108,273	109,022

1. President Carlos A. López railway only.
2. Excluding the 145 km Orinoco Mining Company railway.
3. Does not include Costa Rica, Dominican Republic, Haiti.

a. 1969.

SOURCE: ECLA-AE, 1984, table 343; 1985, table 343.

Table 407

RAILWAY ROLLING STOCK, 20 LC

	Country	Year	Rolling Stock		
			Locomotives	Coaches	Cars
A.	ARGENTINA	1976[‡]	3,104	3,837	60,275
B.	BOLIVIA	1972	156	236	2,005
C.	BRAZIL	1976[‡]	1,970	3,042	63,770
D.	CHILE	1976[‡]	672	709	10,046
E.	COLOMBIA	1975[‡]	208	316	5,719
F.	COSTA RICA	1975[‡]	94	225	2,821
G.	CUBA	~	~	~	~
H.	DOMINICAN REP.	1973[‡]	2	2	15
I.	ECUADOR[1]	1971	60	50	518
J.	EL SALVADOR	1971	55	96	747
K.	GUATEMALA	1972	92	106	2,121
L.	HAITI	~	~	~	~
M.	HONDURAS	1972	66	90	2,846
N.	MEXICO	1976[‡]	1,293	1,634	39,240
O.	NICARAGUA	1972	8	35	231
P.	PANAMA	1972	42	70	1,473
Q.	PARAGUAY[2]	1973	17	9	151
R.	PERU[3]	1972	158	233	4,806
S.	URUGUAY[4]	1976[‡]	157	117	2,438
T.	VENEZUELA[5]	1972	13	19	265
	UNITED STATES	1976[‡]	27,573	5,478	1,269,602

1. Data for Empresa de Ferrocarriles del Estado.
2. Data for Ferrocarril Central del Paraguay.
3. Including 286 km of lines used exclusively for industrial and agricultural purposes.
4. Data for Los Ferrocarriles del Estado only.
5. Data for El Instituto Autónomo de Administración de Ferrocarriles del Estado only.

a. Only government railroads.

SOURCE: IASI-AC, 1970, 1972 and 1974, tables 333-01-03; UN-SY, 1977, table 158.

Table 408

RAILROAD PASSENGERS KILOMETERS,[1] 18 LC, 1970–86

(M)

	Country	1970	1975	1978	1979	1980	1981	1982	1983	1984	1985[a]	1986[a]
A.	ARGENTINA	12,828	14,384	12,241	12,032	12,706	11,261	10,153	10,260	10,524	10,464	~
B.	BOLIVIA	271	310	398	363	529	482	551	771[f]	~	~	~
C.	BRAZIL	12,070	10,621	11,923	11,404	12,376	13,133	13,266	13,797	~	~	~
D.	CHILE	2,338	2,103	2,126	1,732	1,431	1,582	1,506	1,575	1,424	1,524	1,272
E.	COLOMBIA	249	523	342	322	315	230	158	175	193	228	180
F.	COSTA RICA[5]	55	~	~	~	~	~	152	152[f]	~	~	~
G.	CUBA	1,130	695	1,572	1,636	1,802	1,916	2,073	2,144	2,352	2,258	2,208
I.	ECUADOR	85	65	65	69	70	58	50	~	~	~	~
J.	EL SALVADOR	33	23	36	36	25	14	6	4	5	0	~
K.	GUATEMALA	106	127	~	~	~	~	~	~	~	~	~
M.	HONDURAS	- -	- -	8	8	8	8	8	8[f]	~	~	~
N.	MEXICO	4,534	4,123	5,326	5,253	5,296	5,305	5,261	5,630	5,950	5,940	~
O.	NICARAGUA	30	18	17	15	19	20	25	45	60	~	~
P.	PANAMA	544	~	~	~	38	38	38	22[f]	~	~	~
Q.	PARAGUAY[2]	24	23	1	2	4	1	2	2	~	~	~
R.	PERU	248	455	473	534	586	494	458	454	486	~	~
S.	URUGUAY	529	362	494	476	418	339	274	312[f]	~	~	~
T.	VENEZUELA[3]	36	40	40	25	28	10	19	22	12	~	~
	UNITED STATES[4]	17,284	15,715	16,452	18,025	17,695	29,451	28,164	28,807	29,773	~	~

1. To convert to passenger miles, multiply by coefficient .62137. Passenger kilometers obtained by multiplying the number of passengers by the number of kilometers traveled.
2. Presidente Carlos A. López railway only.
3. Excluding the 145 km Orinoco Mining Company railway.
4. Beginning 1967, Class 1 railway only.
5. Incomplete coverage.

a. Data for Empresa de Ferrocarriles del Estado.
b. Data for Ferrocarril Central del Paraguay.
c. Including 286 km of lines used exclusively for industrial and agricultrual purposes.
d. Dat for Los Ferrocarriles del Estado only.
e. Data for El Instituto Autónomo de Administración de Ferrocarriles del Estado only.
f. Data from ECLA-AE, 1985, table 344.
g. Calculated from monthly averages.

SOURCE: IASI-AC, 1970 and 1972, tables 333-01-03; ECLA-AE, 1983, table 349.
U.S. data: UN-SY, 1981, table 189; U.S. data: UN-SY, 1982, table 174; UN-SY, 1983/84, table 171; ECLA-SY, 1985, table 344; UN-MB, August 1987, table 52.

Table 409

RAILROAD FREIGHT IN TON KILOMETERS,[1] 18 LC, 1965-86

(M)

Country	1965	1976	1979	1980	1981	1982	1983[g]	1984[h]	1985[i]	1986[i]
A. ARGENTINA	14,027	11,107	10,978	9,492	9,260	11,498	13,391	11,244	9,504	~
B. BOLIVIA	301	523	602	658	632	493	590	~	~	~
C. BRAZIL	18,815[a]	27,744	33,642	40,603	37,981	38,980	36,187	~	~	~
D. CHILE	2,621	1,657	1,345	1,445	1,300	1,327	1,792	2,315	2,352	2,484
E. COLOMBIA	934	1,157	1,105	862	625	553	642	726	780	696
F. COSTA RICA[4]	31	16	~	~	~	~	~	~	~	~
G. CUBA	1,326	1,848[h]	1,899[h]	2,358[h]	2,885[h]	2,669[h]	2,724[h]	2,814	2,796	2,172
I. ECUADOR	84[b]	35	32	32	32	12	~	~	~	~
J. EL SALVADOR	72	48	78	55	31	32	31[h]	24	24	~
K. GUATEMALA	129	117	91	91	91	91	~	~	~	~
M. HONDURAS	~	~	29	29	29	29	~	~	~	~
N. MEXICO	18,332	33,666	37,275	41,831	43,802	38,960	42,586	44,590	45,444	~
O. NICARAGUA	13	12	6	6	6	8	2[h]	5	~	~
P. PANAMA	19,070	~	~	10	10	10	~	~	~	~
Q. PARAGUAY[2]	19[c]	13	28	29	23	33	19	~	~	~
R. PERU	464[d]	621	571	742	687	682	529	1,014	~	~
S. URUGUAY	332[e]	311	296	253	221	188	220	~	~	~
T. VENEZUELA[3]	32[f]	14	18	21	14	29	22[h]	11	~	~
UNITED STATES[5]	1,029,585	1,112,689	1,334,417	1,341,717	1,359,582	1,191,844	1,237,428[h]	1,377,264	1,310,388	~

1. To convert to long ton miles, multiply by coefficient of .6611558. Ton kilometers obtained by multiplying the number of tons of freight transported by the number of kilometers traveled.
2. Presidente CArlos A. López railway only.
3. Excluding the 145 km Orinoco Mining Company railway.
4. Incomplete coverage.
5. Class 1 railways only.

a. Including service traffic.

b. Data for Empresa de Ferrocarriles del Estado.
c. Data for Ferrocarril Central del Paraguay.
d. Including 286 km of lines used exclusively for industrial and agricultural purposes.
e. Data for Los Ferrocarriles del Estado only.
f. Data for El Instituto Autoónomo de Administración de Ferrocarriles del Estado only.
g. Data from ECLA-AE, 1985, table 344, unless otherwise noted.
h. Data from UN-SY, 1985, table 171.
i. Calculated from monthly averages.

SOURCE: IASI-AC, 1970 and 1972, tables 333-01-03; ECLA-AE, 1983, table 349; U.S. data; UN-SY, 1981, table 189; ECLA-AE, 1984, table 344; U.S. data; UN-SY, 1982, table 174; UN-SY, 1983/84, table 176, ECLA-AE, 1985, table 344; UN-MB, August 1987, table 52.

Table 410

LENGTH OF ROADS, 20 LR

(ca. 1983)

Country	Year	Total (km)	Percentage Paved
A. ARGENTINA	1984	212,305	26
B. BOLIVIA	1983	40,969	4
C. BRAZIL	1984	1,437,574	8
D. CHILE	1984	79,010	11
E. COLOMBIA	~	~	~
F. COSTA RICA	1984	29,094	10
G. CUBA	~	~	~
H. DOMINICAN REP.	1982	17,362	29
I. ECUADOR	1984	35,718	16
J. EL SALVADOR	1984	12,149	14
K. GUATEMALA	~	~	~
L. HAITI	1983	3,688	18
M. HONDURAS	1984	12,058	16
N. MEXICO	1982	214,403	46
O. NICARAGUA[1]	~	~	~
P. PANAMA	~	~	~
Q. PARAGUAY[2]	1983	11,320	19
R. PERU	~	~	~
S. URUGUAY	1981	49,813	20
T. VENEZUELA	1984	63,050	38
LATIN AMERICA	1983[b]	143,166	20

1. Excluding urban roads.
2. National only.

a. Ca. 1980.
b. Ca. 1983

SOURCE: ECLA-AE, 1984, table 342.

Table 411

COMMERCIAL MOTOR VEHICLE REGISTRATION,[1] 20 LC, 1960-84

(T)

	Country	1960	1975	1978	1979	1980	1981	1982	1983	1984
A.	ARGENTINA	389.7	1,062.3	1,203.4	1,256.4	1,333.4	~	~	~	1,388.0
B.	BOLIVIA	~	21.3	29.4	20.7	32.5	52.6	59.1	63.5	~
C.	BRAZIL	~	1,150.2	1,574.6	1,935.5	1,569.8	1,677.7	1,758.9	1,825.7	~
D.	CHILE[2,3]	68.8	168.7	191.2	203.3	219.6	259.2	256.5	248.8	237.2
E.	COLOMBIA[4]	82.9	88.4	256.3	275.5	294.9	328.2	353.9	368.3	~
F.	COSTA RICA[2]	9.7	40.7	58.9	58.1	65.9	65.6	65.9	65.7	~
G.	CUBA	65.3‡	~	107.2	117.8	132.6	142.8	152.4	158.9	164.5
H.	DOMINICAN REP.[5]	6.3	35.6	46.2	50.9	46.9	57.6	60.6	62.3	59.1
I.	ECUADOR	19.0	77.2	114.9	131.1	112.2	161.6	~	~	~
J.	EL SALVADOR	9.0	~	46.4	58.2	71.4	~	67.8	~	~
K.	GUATEMALA	14.7	40.1	56.0	73.1	81.5	~	~	~	~
L.	HAITI	3.7	2.5	6.5	8.3	11.2	12.4	~	~	~
M.	HONDURAS[2,7]	5.2	25.7	33.5	40.9	45.4	47.1	49.9	49.0	~
N.	MEXICO	315.0	887.9	1,352.0	1,513.8	1,574.8	1,792.1	1,872.6	2,038.2	~
O.	NICARAGUA	5.5	22.7	25.5	28.1	27.7	~	~	~	~
P.	PANAMA	6.6	19.6	24.7	30.3	32.5	35.6	38.3	39.8	~
Q.	PARAGUAY	2.5	13.0	30.8	30.8	17.7	15.5	12.6	23.6	~
R.	PERU	65.2	145.0	167.2	169.6	176.6	191.0	204.6	212.9	217.0
S.	URUGUAY	76.0	~	41.0	42.0	42.7	49.8	52.5	49.3	~
T.	VENEZUELA	100.7	369.4	560.8	640.0	718.3	795.9	891.1	951.4	~
	UNITED STATES[6]	11,466.9	26,242.8	32,203.0	31,841.2	33,410.6	34,995.0	35,852.0	37,133.0	~

1. Including trucks, buses, tractor and semitractor combinations; but excluding trailers and farm tractors.
2. Including vehicles operated by police and government security organizations.
3. Including special-purpose vehicles.
4. Including vehicles no longer in circulation.
5. Excluding jeeps beginning 1978.
6. Excluding Alaska and Hawaii.
7. Excluding tractors and semi-trailer combinations.

SOURCE: UN-SY, 1972, table 150; 1974, table 153; 1981, table 190; 1982, table 175; 1983/84, table 172.

Table 412

PASSENGER MOTOR VEHICLE REGISTRATION,[1,4] 20 LC, 1960-84

(T)

	Country	1960	1975	1978	1979	1980	1981	1982	1983	1984
A.	ARGENTINA	473.5	2,305.9	2,683.7	2,818.9	3,024.4	3,193.0	~	~	3,685.0
B.	BOLIVIA	9.7	29.6	38.6	43.1	50.2	63.3	66.6	72.6	~
C.	BRAZIL	~	4,833.6	7,123.9	7,537.1	8,004.6	8,478.5	8,909.5	9,378.9	~
D.	CHILE	57.6	255.7	335.8	386.0	448.5	573.8	605.6	618.7	629.3
E.	COLOMBIA[2]	89.6	376.1	434.7	478.0	522.7	599.3	669.9	723.4	~
F.	COSTA RICA[3]	16.0	59.8	79.6	78.0	88.1	89.1	91.4	101.3	~
G.	CUBA	179.6‡	~	160.4	152.6	159.4	171.4	182.2	190.4	200.1
H.	DOMINICAN REP.	11.0	71.5	90.6	89.8	94.4	105.0	97.2	87.6	116.2
I.	ECUADOR	9.3	51.3	61.0	69.8	65.1	95.1	~	~	~
J.	EL SALVADOR	20.2	~	69.9	78.8	72.5	~	72.5	~	~
K.	GUATEMALA	26.1	76.1	156.4	147.5	166.9	~	~	~	~
L.	HAITI	8.2	17.9	24.3	24.9	21.8	21.8	~	~	~
M.	HONDURAS[3]	5.5	18.2	24.1	23.5	25.6	27.3	28.9	28.7	~
N.	MEXICO	476.4	2,400.9	3,359.9	3,762.2	4,241.4	4,727.2	4,759.8	4,853.9	~
O.	NICARAGUA	8.6	36.5	41.0	37.5	37.8	~	~	~	~
P.	PANAMA	17.6	66.2	75.4	90.2	98.0	104.3	110.2	115.9	~
Q.	PARAGUAY	3.8	11.6	24.8	33.2	58.5	57.5	62.9	78.7	~
R.	PERU	79.4	256.7	302.0	302.6	309.5	330.9	359.7	371.7	374.1
S.	URUGUAY	99.8	~	207.7	219.8	220.4	281.3	298.4	291.8	~
T.	VENEZUELA	268.7	955.2	1,277.3	1,390.0	1,501.8	1,643.3	1,814.0	1,955.4	~
	UNITED STATES	61,430.9	106,075.9	116,575.0	116,573.4	118,458.7	123,461.0	123,698.0	126,728.0	~

1. Motor cars seating less than eight persons, including taxis, jeeps, and station-wagons.
2. Including vehicles no longer in circulation.
3. Including vehicles operated by police and government security organizations.
4. Official estimates of vehicles in use. Unless otherwise stated, special-purpose vehicles are not included.

SOURCE: UN-SY, 1972, table 153; 1974, table 153; 1981, table 190; 1982, table 175, 1983/84, table 172.

Table 413

MERCHANT FLEETS,[1] 20 L, 1982 and 1984

(Tons)

	Country	Year	Overseas					Coastal				Inland Waterways
			Cargo Vessels	Bulk Carriers	Refrigerated Vessels	Tankers	Others	Cargo Vessels	Refrigerated Vessels	Tankers	Others	
A.	ARGENTINA	1982	626,554	434,465	43,754	~	~	29,454	~	709,847	13,779	172,374
		1984	608,598	485,126	43,754	11,773	~	29,454	~	656,797	~	164,661
B.	BOLIVIA	1982	10,915	~	~	~	~	~	~	~	~	~
		1984	10,915	~	~	~	~	~	~	~	~	~
C.	BRAZIL	1982	803,638	1,135,788	13,478	2,304,159	~	190,527	~	437,277	178,005	86,256
		1984	816,021	1,329,043	13,478	2,305,937	~	209,691	~	444,570	16,929	91,323
D.	CHILE	1982	99,354	87,853	~	204,434	~	17,693	~	26,966	10,842	~
		1984	122,391	70,889	~	204,434	~	4,950	~	41,245	13,959	~
E.	COLOMBIA	1982	270,123	36,056	~	~	~	1,544	~	25,271	11,234	~
		1984	253,107	36,056	~	~	~	1,544	~	25,271	11,234	~
F.	COSTA RICA	1982	~	5,940	~	~	~	~	~	~	2,509	~
		1984	5,940	~	~	~	~	~	~	~	2,509	~
G.	CUBA	1982	463,907	62,576	71,472	3,600	2,333	52,376	~	62,217	21,658	~
		1984	464,147	62,576	71,472	3,600	2,333	59,124	~	62,217	21,658	~
H.	DOMINICAN REP.	1982	18,462	12,002	~	~	~	~	~	~	~	~
		1984	24,217	1,599	~	~	~	~	~	~	~	~
I.	ECUADOR	1982	113,964	11,153	81,031	82,613	~	1,132	~	83,684	3,845	~
		1984	99,484	11,153	109,916	82,613	~	1,132	~	83,684	3,845	~
J.	EL SALVADOR	1982	~	~	~	~	~	~	~	~	~	~
		1984	~	~	~	~	~	~	~	~	~	~
K.	GUATEMALA	1982	12,091	3,527	~	~	~	~	~	~	~	~
		1984	12,179	3,527	~	~	~	~	~	~	~	~
L.	HAITI	1982	~	~	~	~	~	~	~	~	~	~
		1984	~	~	~	~	~	~	~	~	~	~
M.	HONDURAS	1982	- -	- -	- -	- -	- -	~	~	~	~	~
		1984	~	~	~	~	~	~	~	~	~	~
N.	MEXICO	1982	- -	- -	- -	- -	- -	8,432	4,695	266,082	84,854	~
		1984	125,351	209,830	~	647,616	~	18,531	~	266,082	72,746	~
O.	NICARAGUA	1982	9,650	2,353	~	~	~	~	~	~	~	~
		1984	12,003	~	~	~	~	~	~	~	~	~
P.	PANAMA	1982	~	~	~	~	~	~	~	~	~	~
		1984	~	~	~	~	~	~	~	~	~	~
Q.	PARAGUAY	1982	12,714	~	~	~	~	~	~	~	~	17,857
		1984	19,726	~	~	~	~	~	~	~	~	~
R.	PERU	1982	279,982	201,057	1,544	35,823	~	~	~	119,184	~	10,955
		1984	270,374	159,883	1,544	35,823	~	~	~	135,817	~	10,955
S.	URUGUAY	1982	54,708	13,203	4,172	88,617	~	1,110	~	2,516	~	3,749
		1984	47,790	13,203	4,172	88,617	~	1,110	~	3,956	~	3,749
T.	VENEZUELA	1982	208,701	56,784	6,682	11,065	~	4,896	~	443,666	91,629	1,325
		1984	216,465	57,400	~	15,870	~	1,355	~	499,905	67,671	1,325

1. Gross registered tons for vessels of 1,000 tons and over.

SOURCE: ECLA-AE, 1984, table 345; 1985, table 345.

Table 414

INTERNATIONAL SEABORNE SHIPPING,[1] 20 LC, 1975-85

(Vessels in T Net Registered Tons; Goods in T MET)

Country		1975	1976	1977	1978‡	1979	1980	1981	1982	1983	1984	1985
A. ARGENTINA[14]												
Vessels:[2]	entered	12,859	13,178	15,394	17,745	17,433	16,560	21,538	18,870	23,204	?	?
	cleared	?	?	?	?	?	?	?	?	?	?	?
Goods:[3,5,18]	loaded	11,770	15,299	23,807	23,352	28,500‡	20,000	30,047	26,490	35,203	31,608	37,728
	unloaded	12,220	9,154	10,619	8,375	12,616‡	10,568	8,816	6,599	5,579	6,278	5,376
B. BOLIVIA		?	?	?	?	?	?	?	?	?	?	?
C. BRAZIL												
Vessels:[2,4]	entered	143,172	165,681	146,249	152,149	169,234	178,791	178,088	167,552	167,343	?	?
	cleared	?	?	?	?	?	?	?	?	?	?	?
Goods[5,6,18]	loaded	92,985	89,689	81,856	87,517	98,010	107,596	122,599	119,095	117,847	141,732	146,364
	unloaded	55,605	61,652	62,067	69,790	75,328	71,855	64,066	60,718	55,056	53,856	48,864
D. CHILE												
Vessels:	entered	?	?	?	?	?	?	?	?	?	?	?
	cleared	?	?	?	?	?	?	?	?	?	?	?
Goods[3,5,7,18,20]	loaded	12,361	15,155	13,043	12,230	12,723	12,590	9,323	11,542	10,698	11,832	12,636
	unloaded	5,925	6,848	7,288	8,541	8,894	8,792	7,720	5,208	5,258	5,268	4,476
E. COLOMBIA												
Vessels:[2]	entered	10,943	10,731	11,302	10,942	11,230	11,200	12,663	15,883	15,112	?	?
	cleared	?	?	?	?	?	?	?	?	?	?	?
Goods:[5,18]	loaded	3,374	2,342	1,954	2,671	4,918	6,038‡	5,414	5,408	6,672	7,128	7,416
	unloaded	2,101	2,182	3,663	4,012	4,938	7,276	7,151	7,107	7,623	6,638	6,912
F. COSTA RICA												
Vessels:	entered	3,736	?	?	?	?	?	1,421	1,366	1,326	?	?
	cleared		?	?	?							
Goods:[18]	loaded	1,448	1,410	?	?	1,554	1,284	1,626	1,405	1,406	?	?
	unloaded	1,216	1,401	?	?	2,009	1,862	1,457	1,333	1,542	?	?
G. CUBA												
Vessels:	entered	?	?	?	?	?	?	?	?	?	?	?
	cleared	?	?	?	?	?	?	?	?	?	?	?
Goods:[18]	loaded	5,943	6,091	7,248	8,532	9,500	7,500	8,900	8,800	8,200	2,208	2,280
	unloaded	13,302	13,131	14,352	14,448	15,500	16,900	17,900	16,900	17,000	2,712	3,048
H. DOMINICAN REP.												
Vessels:[2]	entered	?	?	4,950	5,045	7,747	8,904	8,405	7,446	?	?	?
	cleared:			2,723	3,040	2,782						
Goods:[15,18]	loaded	2,596	2,395	2,445	2,704	2,732	2,411	2,355	2,058	1,750‡	?	?
	unloaded	3,065	2,996	3,294	3,072	3,269	1,457‡	1,606	1,346	1,566	?	?
I. ECUADOR												
Vessels:	entered	13,244	13,256	12,894	12,994	13,036	11,491	12,143	12,391	?	?	?
	cleared	?	?	?	?	?	?	?	?	?	?	?
Goods:[8,18]	loaded	9,557	10,616	9,372	?	8,969‡	8,371	7,894	7,303	9,924	?	?
	unloaded	3,140	3,175	3,823	?	2,745	2,282	2,725	2,424	2,541‡	?	?
J. EL SALVADOR												
Vessels:	entered	2,291	2,390	3,308	3,172	3,226	2,741	2,774	2,304	2,381	?	?
	cleared	?	?	?	?	?	?	?	?	?	?	?
Goods:[18]	loaded	490	599	558	540[c]	538	361	347	309	425	300	384
	unloaded	1,281	1,590	2,063	1,848[c]	1,705	1,482	1,391	1,128	1,486	1,476	1,488
K. GUATEMALA												
Vessels:[2]	entered	?	?	?	?	?	?	?	?	?	?	?
	cleared	?	?	?	?	?	?	?	?	?	?	?
Goods:[18]	loaded	771	1,173	1,651	?	1,442‡	1,022	964‡	1,140‡	2,821‡	?	?
	unloaded	1,201	1,408	1,689	?	2,592‡	2,405	1,943‡	1,713‡	1,998‡	?	?

Table 414 (Continued)

INTERNATIONAL SEABORNE SHIPPING,[1] 20 LC, 1975-85
(Vessels in T Net Registered Tons; Goods in T MET)

Country		1975	1976	1977	1978[‡]	1979	1980	1981	1982	1983	1984	1985
L. HAITI												
Vessels:[2]	entered	~	~	~	~	~	~	~	~	~	~	~
	cleared	~	~	~	~	~	~	~	~	~	~	~
Goods:[18]	loaded	632	855	850	~	750[‡]	620[‡]	264	374	328	~	~
	unloaded	461	485	645	~	669[‡]	521[‡]	506	662	886	~	~
M. HONDURAS												
Vessels:[2]	entered	~	~	~	~	~	~	~	~	~	~	~
	cleared	~	~	~	~	~	~	~	~	~	~	~
Goods:[5,18]	loaded	1,256	1,331	~	~	1,550[‡]	1,597[‡]	1,452[‡]	1,600[‡]	1,400	~	~
	unloaded	1,163	917	~	~	1,320[‡]	1,252[‡]	1,146[‡]	971[‡]	1,215	~	~
N. MEXICO												
Vessels:[2]	entered	10,102	9,300	~	11,626	11,797	13,190	14,008	12,952	~	~	~
	cleared	12,058	11,480	~	18,673	22,162	27,582	35,141				
Goods:[18]	loaded	13,980	14,278	20,450	22,455	36,945	50,430	62,556	73,600	77,508	72,108	69,540
	unloaded	9,300	7,166	8,353	11,654	11,898	14,557	15,656	12,816	11,448	10,932	10,956
O. NICARAGUA												
Vessels:[2]	entered	~	~	~	~	~	~	~	~	~	~	~
	cleared	~	~	~	~	~	~	~	~	~	~	~
Goods:[5]	loaded	765[‡]	829	725	710	685	382	470	343	453	~	~
	unloaded	1,475[‡]	1,096	1,423	1,458	820	1,283	1,281	1,039	1,286	~	~
P. PANAMA												
Vessels:	entered	~	~	~	~	~	~	~	~	~	~	~
	cleared	~	~	~	~	~	~	~	~	~	~	~
Goods:	loaded	1,770	1,089	1,183	1,250	1,300[‡]	977	1,025	916	1,021	~	~
	unloaded	4,793	3,751	3,419	2,882	2,900[‡]	2,647	2,313	2,335	2,381	~	~
(FORMER) CANAL ZONE												
Vessels:[14,18]	entered	~	~	~	~	~	~	~	~	~	~	~
	cleared	~	~	~	~	~	~	~	~	~	~	~
Goods:	loaded	85,440[a]	67,054[a]	70,648[a,*]	69,197[a]	80,268[a,c]	90,756	98,112	89,244	79,512	75,336	73,764
	unloaded	56,904[b]	52,039[b]	54,304[b,*]	75,608[b]	76,380[b,c]	83,220	90,324	58,692	63,204	65,472	68,304
Q. PARAGUAY		~	~	~	~	~	~	~	~	~	~	~
R. PERU												
Vessels:[2]	entered	19,982	17,783	19,012	19,601	~	~	~	~	~	~	~
	cleared											
Goods:[9]	loaded	9,173	9,745	10,356	10,287	10,000[‡]	9,277	10,692	11,755	10,750[‡]	~	~
	unloaded	8,043	7,068	5,787	2,693	3,000[‡]	3,831	3,671	3,170	3,230	~	~
S. URUGUAY												
Vessels:[2]	entered	~	~	~	~	~	~	~	~	~	~	~
	cleared	~	~	~	~	~	~	~	~	~	~	~
Goods:[17]	loaded	947	608	473	430	364	457	977	570	859	~	~
	unloaded	2,595	2,458	2,437	1,451	1,476	888	770	454	401	~	~
T. VENEZUELA												
Vessels:[5,11]	entered	~	~	~	~	~	~	~	~	~	~	~
	cleared	~	~	~	~	~	~	~	~	~	~	~
Goods:[5,11]	loaded	6,707	~	8,676	8,568	110,528[‡]	110,452[‡]	105,685[‡]	89,134[‡]	87,237[‡]	~	~
	unloaded					12,788[‡]	11,966	12,505	11,145	9,646	~	~

Table 414 (Continued)

INTERNATIONAL SEABORNE SHIPPING,[1] 20 LC, 1975-85

(Vessels in T Net Registered Tons; Goods in T MET)

Country	1975	1976	1977	1978[‡]	1979	1980	1981	1982	1983	1984	1985
UNITED STATES											
Vessels:[11,18]											
entered	254,346	296,910	338,300	346,535	360,572	320,684	307,355	264,732	273,720	304,170	?
cleared	188,845	196,876	199,737	215,162	249,833	269,660	274,475	278,530	267,045	273,505	?
Goods:[12,19]											
loaded	246,311[‡]	258,168[‡]	250,198	274,988	347,588	366,348	369,572	365,744	329,028	339,888	317,460
unloaded	435,970[‡]	516,221[‡]	568,138	549,283	578,449	468,909	421,426	359,504	346,116	374,664	357,648

1. Vessels: Unless otherwise stated, the data for vessels entered and cleared represent the sum of the net registered tonnage of sea-going foreign and domestic merchant vessels entered with cargo, from or cleared with cargo to a foreign port. They refer to only one entrance of clearance for each foreign voyage. Where possible the data exclude vessels "in ballast."
   Goods: The data for goods loaded and unloaded represent the weight of goods (including packaging) in external trade loaded onto and unloaded from sea-going vessels of all flags at the ports of the country in question. Goods excluded are: bunker, ships' stores, ballast, and transshipment.
2. Includes vessels in ballast.
3. Excluding packing and reexports before 1979; after 1983, except for Chile.
4. All entrances counted.
5. Excluding transit traffic and packing until 1978; Colombia, transit traffic only.
6. Including mail, passengers' baggage until 1979, and a small amount of goods imported and exported other than by sea before 1979 and after 1983.
7. Including mail, passengers' baggage, bullion, and bunkers before 1979.
8. Excluding transit traffic, packing, and certain government goods; including goods imported and exported other than by sea until 1978.
9. Excluding transit traffic, packing, reexports, and certain government goods until 1978.

10. Including mail, passengers' baggage, and bullion.
11. Including Great Lakes International traffic. For goods 1965 and after 1983.
12. Including transshipments until 1978.
13. Thousand manifest tons until 1966.
14. Data are for former Canal Zone only. Prior to 1977, 12 months ending June 30. From 1977, 12 months beginning October 1. Goods in transit for 1965, 1970, and 1973-78.
15. Including goods imported and exported other than by sea until 1978.
16. Excluding traffic with United States Virgin Islands.
17. Port of Montevideo only after 1978.
18. Calculated from monthly averages, for goods only.
19. Including Puerto Rico and the Virgin Islands, except for 1965 for the Virgin Islands.
20. Including ships' stores until 1978.

   a.   Traffic from Atlantic to Pacific.
   b.   Traffic from Pacific to Atlantic.
   c.   Calculated from monthly averages.

SOURCE: UN-SY, 1974, table 157; 1977, table 162; 1979, table 150; 1982, tables 177 and 178; 1983/84, tables 174 and 175; UN-MB, August 1987, table 53.

Table 415

INTERNATIONAL SEABORNE GOODS LOADED AND UNLOADED, 18 LC, 1979-83[a]

(T MET)

			Goods Loaded				Goods Unloaded			
				Petroleum		Dry		Petroleum		Dry
Country		Year	Total	Crude	Products	Cargo	Total	Crude	Products	Cargo
A.	ARGENTINA	1979	28,500‡	~	500	28,000‡	12,616‡	341‡	3,475‡	8,800‡
		1980	20,500	~	1,373‡	19,127‡	10,568	2,255‡	481‡	7,832‡
		1981	30,047	~	2,777‡	27,270‡	8,816	1,622‡	522‡	6,672‡
		1982	26,490	~	2,600‡	23,890‡	6,599	541‡	152‡	5,906‡
		1983	35,203	~	1,728‡	33,475‡	5,579	~	88‡	5,491‡
C.	BRAZIL	1979	98,010	~	1,012	96,998	75,328	50,158	477	24,693
		1980	107,596	59	1,172	106,365	71,855	43,590	1,645	26,620
		1981	122,599	607	3,183	118,809	64,066	42,209	1,146	20,711
		1982	119,095	1,087	4,209	113,799	60,718	39,766	1,930	19,022
		1983	117,847	49	4,509	113,289	55,056	36,452	918	17,686
D.	CHILE	1979	12,723	100‡	23‡	12,600‡	8,894	3,294‡	~	5,600†
		1980	12,590	~	125‡	12,465‡	8,792	2,899‡	299‡	5,594†
		1981	9,323	~	30‡	9,293‡	7,720	2,223‡	577‡	4,920‡
		1982	11,942	~	10‡	11,932‡	5,208	1,063‡	320‡	3,825‡
		1983	10,698	~	80‡	10,618‡	5,258	1,881‡	67‡	3,310‡
E.	COLOMBIA	1979	4,918	258‡	1,352‡	3,308	4,938	1,049†	824†	3,065‡
		1980	6,038‡	34‡	490‡	5,514‡	7,276	657‡	1,118‡	5,461‡
		1981	5,414	~	565‡	4,849‡	7,151	1,191‡	1,243‡	4,717‡
		1982	5,408	~	1,678‡	3,730‡	7,107	850‡	1,285‡	4,972‡
		1983	6,672	~	2,334‡	4,338‡	7,623	2,034	976‡	4,613‡
F.	COSTA RICA	1979	1,554	~	~	1,554	2,009	366	471	1,170
		1980	1,284	~	~	1,284	1,862	485	349	1,028
		1981	1,626	~	~	1,626	1,457	478	217	762
		1982	1,405	~	~	1,405	1,333	420‡	232‡	681‡
		1983	1,406	~	~	1,406	1,542	500‡	150‡	892‡
G.	CUBA	1979	9,500	~	150†	9,350†	15,500	8,800	2,100	4,600
		1980	7,500	~	~	7,350†	16,900	5,900	2,900	8,100
		1981	8,900	~	94†	8,806†	17,900	6,200	3,200	8,500
		1982	8,800	~	177†	8,623†	16,900	6,000	3,600	7,300
		1983	8,200	~	200‡	8,000‡	12,000	5,600	4,000	7,400
H.	DOMINICAN REP.	1979	2,732	~	~	2,732	3,269	1,400†	564†	1,305†
		1980	2,411	~	~	2,411	3,714	1,457†	215‡	2,042‡
		1981	2,355	~	~	2,355	3,063	1,606	513‡	944‡
		1982	2,058	~	~	2,058	3,192	1,346	498‡	1,348‡
		1983	1,750‡	~	~	1,750‡	3,500‡	1,566	675‡	1,259‡
I.	ECUADOR	1979	8,969‡	6,242‡	1,170†	1,557‡	2,745	~	323‡	2,422‡
		1980	8,371	5,690	1,180‡	1,501‡	2,282	~	65‡	2,217‡
		1981	7,894	6,256	825‡	813‡	2,725	11‡	622‡	2,092‡
		1982	7,303	5,940	833‡	530‡	2,424	~	230‡	2,194‡
		1983	9,924	8,234	633‡	1,057‡	2,541‡	~	441‡	2,100‡
J.	EL SALVADOR	1979	538	~	23	515‡	1,705	885†	70‡	750
		1980	361	~	1	360	1,482	615‡	17‡	850
		1981	347	~	45	302	1,391	581‡	15‡	785
		1982	309	~	47	262	1,128	603‡	10‡	515
		1983	425	~	51	374	1,486	622‡	14‡	850
K.	GUATEMALA	1979	1,442‡	~	~	1,442‡	2,592‡	850‡	510‡	1,232‡
		1980	1,022	~	~	1,022	2,405	710‡	671‡	1,024‡
		1981	964‡	~	~	964‡	1,943‡	500‡	440‡	1,003‡
		1982	1,140‡	~	~	1,140‡	1,713‡	496‡	420‡	797‡
		1983	2,821‡	~	~	2,821‡	1,998‡	550‡	400‡	1,048‡
L.	HAITI	1979	750†	~	12‡	738†	669†	~	269‡	400‡
		1980	620‡	~	~	620‡	521‡	~	82‡	439‡
		1981	264	~	~	264	506	~	90‡	416‡
		1982	374	~	~	374	662	~	86‡	576‡
		1983	328	~	~	328	886	~	64‡	822‡
M.	HONDURAS	1979	1,550‡	~	30‡	1,520‡	1,320‡	250‡	300‡	770‡
		1980	1,597‡	~	22‡	1,575‡	1,252‡	459‡	110‡	683‡
		1981	1,452‡	~	12‡	1,440‡	1,146‡	260‡	226‡	660‡
		1982	1,600‡	~	~	1,600‡	971‡	105‡	296‡	570‡
		1983	1,400‡	~	19‡	1,381‡	1,215‡	387‡	263‡	565‡
N.	MEXICO	1979	36,945	27,426	608	8,911	11,898	~	1,459	10,439
		1980	50,430	41,309	2,366	6,755	14,557	~	1,468	13,089
		1981	62,556	54,796	3,968	3,792	15,656	~	1,277	14,379
		1982	73,600	64,462‡	2,875	6,263	12,816	~	1,094	11,722
		1983	77,508	67,488‡	4,020‡	6,000‡	11,448	~	680‡	10,768

Table 415 (Continued)

INTERNATIONAL SEABORNE GOODS LOADED AND UNLOADED, 18 LC, 1979-83[a]
(T MET)

| | | Goods Loaded | | | | Goods Unloaded | | | |
| | | | Petroleum | | | | Petroleum | | |
Country	Year	Total	Crude	Products	Dry Cargo	Total	Crude	Products	Dry Cargo
O. NICARAGUA	1979	685	~	4[‡]	681[‡]	820	500	150[‡]	170[‡]
	1980	382	~	~	382	1,283	617[‡]	11	655[‡]
	1981	470	~	~	470	1,281	628	29	624[‡]
	1982	343	~	~	343	1,039	561	53	425[‡]
	1983	453	~	~	453	1,286	523	147	616[‡]
P. PANAMA	1979	1,380[‡]	~	660[‡]	720[‡]	2,900[‡]	1,977[‡]	200[‡]	723[‡]
	1980	977	~	376	601	2,647	1,926	671[‡]	50[‡]
	1981	1,025	~	243	782	2,313	1,487	493[‡]	333[‡]
	1982	916	~	109	807	2,335	1,636	530[‡]	169
	1983	1,021	~	57	964	2,381	1,638	554[‡]	189
R. PERU	1979	10,000[‡]	1,270[‡]	230[‡]	8,500[‡]	3,000[‡]	15[‡]	185[‡]	2,800[‡]
	1980	9,277	2,390[‡]	460[‡]	6,427[‡]	3,831[‡]	~	44[‡]	3,787[‡]
	1981	10,692	1,936[‡]	460[‡]	8,296	3,671[‡]	~	53[‡]	3,618[‡]
	1982	11,755	1,999[‡]	890[‡]	8,866	3,170[‡]	~	25[‡]	3,145[‡]
	1983	10,750[‡]	1,500[‡]	250[‡]	8,500[‡]	3,230[‡]	~	30[‡]	3,200[‡]
S. URUGUAY[b]	1979	364	50	6	308	1,476	330	246	900
	1980	457	~	1	456	888	12	161	715
	1981	977	~	99	878	770	23	142	605
	1982	570	~	36[‡]	534[‡]	454	35[‡]	11[‡]	408[‡]
	1983	859	~	48[‡]	811[‡]	401	25[‡]	38[‡]	338[‡]
T. VENEZUELA	1979	110,528[‡]	63,801[‡]	31,888[‡]	14,839[‡]	12,788[‡]	10[‡]	220[‡]	12,558[‡]
	1980	110,452[‡]	68,556[‡]	28,830[‡]	13,066[‡]	11,966	391[‡]	81[‡]	11,494
	1981	105,685[‡]	66,837[‡]	24,821[‡]	14,027[‡]	12,505	154[‡]	131[‡]	12,220
	1982	89,134[‡]	55,994[‡]	24,979[‡]	8,161[‡]	11,145	62[‡]	101[‡]	10,982
	1983	87,237[‡]	51,132[‡]	27,102[‡]	9,003[‡]	9,646	~	10[‡]	9,636

a. For years 1976, 1977 see SALA, 22-2213.
b. Port of Montevideo only.

SOURCE: UN-SY, 1982, table 177; 1983/84, table 174.

Table 416

PRINCIPAL MERCHANT MARINES OF THE WORLD,[1] 6 LC, 1985
(T Tons)

Country	World Rank	Number of Vessels	Gross Registered Tons	Gross Freight Tons	% of Gross Freight Tons
A. ARGENTINA	34	196	2,054	3,111	.5
C. BRAZIL	19	415	5,594	9,251	1.5
G. CUBA	49	116	804	1,098	.2
N. MEXICO	40	103	1,285	2,055	.3
P. PANAMA[2]	3	3,873	35,107	59,637	9.4
T. VENEZUELA	50	100	804	1,199	.2
WORLD		34,177	365,932	617,021	96.6

1. Vessels of 300 or more gross registered tons.
2. Pavillion of open registration or flag of convenience.

SOURCE: *Los Conceptos Básicos del Transporte Marítimo y la Situación de la Actividad en América Latina* (Santiago: Cuadernos de la CEPAL, 1986), pp. 32-33.

Table 417

NATIONAL MERCHANT MARINES, 16 L

(1985)

Country	State Sector					Private Sector					Total				
	Units	Gross Registered Tons	Gross Freight Tons	Average Age	% According to Gross Freight Tons	Units	Gross Registered Tons	Gross Freight Tons	Average Age	% According to Gross Freight Tons	Units	Gross Registered Tons	Gross Freight Tons	Average Age	% According to Gross Freight Tons
A. ARGENTINA	82	915,833	1,352,272	8.4	43	86	1,103,165	1,766,362	16.5	57	168	2,018,998	3,118,634	12.8	15.8
B. BOLIVIA	1	10,915	12,544	20.0	100	~	~	~	~	~	1	10,915	12,544	20.0	.1
C. BRAZIL	126	3,795,796	6,635,850	7.6	73	208	1,673,599	2,471,415	7.4	27	334	5,469,395	9,107,265	7.5	46.1
D. CHILE	5	147,871	299,278	11.6	39	26	309,997	461,107	15.2	61	31	457,868	760,385	14.1	3.8
E. COLOMBIA	5	11,234	10,858	14.6	3	31	315,978	417,347	12.6	97	36	327,212	428,205	12.7	2.2
F. COSTA RICA	2	2,509	1,108	26.5	11	1	5,940	9,289	15.0	89	3	8,499	10,397	18.4	.0
G. CUBA	102	747,127	1,024,017	12.2	100	~	~	~	~	~	102	747,127	1,024,017	12.2	5.2
H. DOMINICAN REP.	~	~	~	~	~	10	25,816	44,559	14.3	100	10	25,816	44,559	14.3	.2
I. ECUADOR	17	225,478	355,157	6.3	63	34	166,349	207,441	19.0	37	51	391,827	562,598	11.7	2.8
K. GUATEMALA	2	7,962	12,700	28.0	53	2	7,744	11,337	18.3	47	4	15,706	24,037	23.2	.1
N. MEXICO	58	753,483	1,120,076	10.0	53	39	588,265	992,947	15.2	47	97	1,341,748	2,113,023	12.3	10.7
O. NICARAGUA	2	12,003	17,122	12.8	100	~	~	~	~	~	2	12,003	17,122	12.8	.1
Q. PARAGUAY	16	23,688	24,186	14.9	55	7	12,808	19,972	22.0	45	23	36,496	44,158	17.4	.2
R. PERU	33	303,873	451,126	11.6	47	26	310,523	515,017	15.4	53	59	614,396	966,143	13.5	4.9
S. URUGUAY	4	93,260	169,279	11.2	63	11	69,337	98,152	21.0	37	15	162,597	267,431	15.4	1.4
T. VENEZUELA	35	703,711	1,070,332	5.7	85	33	156,284	184,748	16.2	15	68	859,995	1,255,080	7.6	6.4
TOTAL	490	7,754,743	12,555,905	8.5	64	514	4,745,805	7,199,693	12.9	36	1,004	12,500,548	19,755,598	10.2	100.0

SOURCE: *Los Conceptos Básicos del Transporte Marítimo y la Situación de la Actividad en América Latina* (Santiago: Cuadernos de la CEPEL, 1986).

Table 418

EVOLUTION OF ALADI MERCHANT MARINES, 11 LR, 1961-85[a]

Country	Year	Units	Gross Registered Tons (T)	% Variation 1961-85	Gross Freight Tons (T)	Average Age
A. ARGENTINA	1961	151	664		1,274	20.0
	1970	185	1,090		1,425	19.5
	1985	168	2,019	204	3,119	12.8
B. BOLIVIA	1961	~	~		~	~
	1970	~	~		~	~
	1985	1	11		13	20.0
C. BRAZIL	1961	227	1,006	~	1,433	19.0
	1970	201	1,212		1,748	11.8
	1985	324	5,469	444	9,107	7.5
D. CHILE	1961	48	224		299	14.0
	1970	43	273		273	12.3
	1985	31	458	104	760	14.1
E. COLOMBIA	1961	24	92		134	9.0
	1970	33	199		269	9.6
	1985	36	327	255	428	12.7
I. ECUADOR	1961	8	24		34	10.0
	1970	8	40		46	8.5
	1985	51	392	1,533	563	11.7
N. MEXICO	1961	30	160		232	22.0
	1970	37	309		477	6.5
	1985	97	1,342	739	2,113	12.3
Q. PARAGUAY	1961	7	8		7	1.0
	1970	15	17		15	8.1
	1985	21	36	350	44	17.4
R. PERU	1961	26	102		155	14.0
	1970	38	284		395	11.9
	1985	59	614	502	966	13.5
S. URUGUAY	1961	15	67		101	17.0
	1970	15	110		172	17.3
	1985	15	163	143	267	15.4
T. VENEZUELA	1961	42	318		485	10.0
	1970	38	327		472	13.4
	1985	68	860	170	1,255	7.6
Total ALADI	1961	578	2,965		4,154	17.0
	1970	613	3,864		5,384	13.9
	1985	883	11,691		18,635	10.2
Percent Variation	1961–					
	1985	53		294	349	–60.0

a. Vessels of 1,000 or more gross registered tons.

SOURCE: *Los Conceptos Básicos del Transporte Marítimo y la Situación de la Actividad en América Latina* (Santiago: Cuadernos de la CEPAL, 1986).

CHAPTER 5

COMMUNICATION

Table 500

DAILY NEWSPAPERS, CIRCULATION, AND NEWSPRINT CONSUMPTION PER INHABITANT, 20 LC, 1965–84

	Newspapers Published[1] (N)								Circulation (PTI)								Newsprint Consumption[2] (kg/PI)								
Country	1965	1970	1975	1977	1978	1979	1982	1984	1965	1970	1975	1977	1978	1979	1982	1984	1965	1970	1975	1977	1978	1979	1980	1982	1983
A. ARGENTINA	171	179	164	~	141	133	191	~	149	~	~	~	~	~	~	~	10.1	11.6	5.7	4.6	7.5	7.9	9.6	5.0	6.3
B. BOLIVIA	9	21	14	~	14	14	12	13	22	~	35	45	37	39	46	46	.7	1.1	1.0	.9	1.5	1.3	1.1	1.2	1.1
C. BRAZIL	~	~	299	318	328	328	~	322	~	~	45	45	44	44	~	~	2.1	2.2	2.2	1.5	2.2	1.9	2.4	2.4	2.0
D. CHILE	~	~	47	42	37	37	37	~	~	~	90	~	84	87	~	~	4.8	4.9	4.0	4.1	5.2	5.4	6.1	6.0	5.4
E. COLOMBIA	39	~	40	~	39	38	28	31	~	~	~	~	48[b]	48[b]	~	~	2.4	2.8	1.9	1.7	2.4	2.6	2.8	3.5	2.8
F. COSTA RICA	~	8	6	~	4	4	4	5	~	103	89	~	72	70	77	72	4.1	6.4	5.7	5.4	7.1	6.9	5.3	3.0	4.6
G. CUBA	~	16	15	~	9	9	17	18	~	~	6	~	93	91	118	144	2.4	2.7	2.9	2.4	2.8	3.3	3.3	3.4	3.9
H. DOMINICAN REP.	7	~	10	~	7	7	9	7	28	~	42	~	49	42	~	30	.2	1.0	1.3	.5	1.7	1.8	2.2	2.4	2.4
I. ECUADOR	23	25	29	37	37	38	18	16	47	42	49	46	45	49	64	~	2.6	2.3	1.5	1.5	3.9	3.9	4.0	3.7	3.6
J. EL SALVADOR	~	13	12	~	12	12	6	6	~	~	~	~	~	~	~	~	3.0	3.6	2.5	2.3	3.1	3.0	3.1	2.6	2.4
K. GUATEMALA	~	8	10	~	9	9	9	5	~	28	41	~	~	~	~	~	1.2	1.6	1.3	1.2	1.0	1.7	2.5	1.5	1.4
L. HAITI	6	7	7	~	7	4	4	4	6	19	20	~	~	7	4	~	.1	.2	.2	.2	.1	.1	.1	.1	.1
M. HONDURAS	~	~	8	~	7	7	6	6	~	~	32	~	~	63	61	~	.7	1.0	.7	.7	1.3	1.3	1.8	1.5	1.0
N. MEXICO	220	200	256	352	~	~	374	312	116	~	~	~	~	~	~	120	2.6	3.1	3.6	3.9	2.7	3.0	3.3	6.4	3.0
O. NICARAGUA	6	~	7	~	6	8	3	3	50	~	78	~	49	69	50	47	1.7	1.8	1.7	1.6	1.1	1.0	1.1	1.4	1.2
P. PANAMA	10	7	6	~	6	6	5	6	82	91	~	~	81	79	61	~	2.8	3.9	1.9	1.9	2.8	2.4	1.3	1.4	2.7
Q. PARAGUAY	~	11	8	~	5	5	5	5	~	~	~	~	~	~	~	~	.7	1.8	1.2	1.1	2.2	2.1	2.5	1.5	.1
R. PERU	69	85	49	30	57	59	68	~	~	~	89	51	~	~	~	~	3.5	3.7	3.4	1.7	2.2	.1	2.1	8.0	2.6
S. URUGUAY	~	~	30	26	29	28	24	21	~	~	~	~	~	~	~	~	6.4	7.4	3.7	4.0	4.4	4.7	5.2	7.4	2.9
T. VENEZUELA	33	~	49	54	55	69	36	~	70	~	89	178	101	176	~	~	4.8	7.9	6.8	7.7	9.4	9.4	9.4	8.4	10.1
UNITED STATES	1,751[a]	1,763[a]	1,775[a]	1,829[a]	1,774[a]	1,787[a]	1,710	1,687	311	303	287	287	284	282	269	268	39.3	44.0	39.4	41.6	45.4	45.1	46.9	44.1	45.7

1. A daily newspaper is defined as a publication devoted primarily to recording news of current events in public affairs, international affairs, politics, etc., and which is published at least four times a week.

2. Newsprint consumption represents apparent consumption (i.e., domestic production plus imports, minus exports, or simply annual imports). For a few countries, where information is available, fluctuation in stocks has been taken into account, and this is indicated in a footnote. Data cover newsprint for both daily and non-daily newspapers.

a. English-language papers only.

b. Circulation figures refer to 33 dailies only.

SOURCE: UNESCO-SY, 1977, tables 12.1, 13.1; UNESCO-SY, 1981, tables 8.16, 8.19; UNESCO-SY, 1982, tables 8.16, 8.19; UNESCO-SY, 1984, tables 7.20, 7.23; UNESCO-SY, 1986, table 7.22.

Table 501

NEWSPRINT: VOLUME OF IMPORTS, 20 LC, 1965–84

(T MET)

	Country	1965	1970	1975	1976	1977	1978	1979	1980	1981	1982	1983	1984
A.	ARGENTINA	220	274	149	110	160	161	117	174	137	49	49†	28†
B.	BOLIVIA	3‡	5	5	5†	6†	6‡	7‡	6‡	7‡	7‡	7‡	7†
C.	BRAZIL	54	149	116‡	143	174	172‡	219‡	167‡	170‡	161	158‡	164
D.	CHILE	5	1	#	#	#	#	#	#	#	#	~	~
E.	COLOMBIA	45	59	44	36‡	44‡	60‡	67‡	71‡	95‡	95	78	78†
F.	COSTA RICA	6	11	11	11	12	15	12	12‡	8‡	7	8	10‡
G.	CUBA	19	23‡	27‡	25‡	28‡	32	32	32	32‡	35‡	39	39†
H.	DOMINICAN REP.	1	4	7	7	9	9	10	12		17‡	14	14†
I.	ECUADOR	13	14	11	22‡	28	29	31	33	37‡	28‡	32	32
J.	EL SALVADOR	9	13	10	10	14	15‡	15‡	15‡	15	12‡	13	13†
K.	GUATEMALA	6	8	8	7	7	15	11‡	17	10	11	11	13
L.	HAITI	~	1†	1‡	1‡	1	1†	1‡	~	1‡	1‡	1†	1†
M.	HONDURAS	2	3	2	3	2	5	5	7‡	6‡	5‡	4	5†
N.	MEXICO	91	119	186	191	297	55‡	110‡	110‡	230‡	148	67	67†
O.	NICARAGUA	3	4	4	3	3†	5‡	2‡	3‡	5‡	3‡	4†	4†
P.	PANAMA	4	6	3	3†	4	5	5	3	5	3	6	6
Q.	PARAGUAY	1	4	3†	4	7	7	6	8	5	10	3‡	6
R.	PERU	40	49	51	29	56	41	7	7	32	48‡	38‡	38†
S.	URUGUAY	18	21	11	11	12	13	14	15	22	13	9	9†
T.	VENEZUELA	43	84	86	91	107†	131‡	132‡	141‡	168‡	151	167	156‡
	UNITED STATES	5,736	6,019	5,305	5,959	5,950	6,787	6,552	6,594	6,330	5,924	6,277	7,161

SOURCE: FAO-YFP, 1973, p. 275; FAO-YFP, 1975, p. 264; FAO-YFP, 1976, p. 264;
FAO-YFP, 1980, p. 324; FAO-YFP, 1981, p. 317; FAO-YFP, 1982, p. 317; FAO-YFP,
1983, p. 316, FAO-YFP, 1984, p. 309.

Table 502

NEWSPRINT: VALUE OF IMPORTS, 20 LC, 1965–84

(T US)

	Country	1965	1970	1975	1978	1979	1980	1981	1982	1983	1984
A.	ARGENTINA	36,345	47,870	73,990	76,291	59,552	98,724	83,637	30,843	16,019	16,019†
B.	BOLIVIA	319‡	950	950†	2,172†	2,600†	2,200	3,000†	3,000†	2,900†	2,900†
C.	BRAZIL	10,259	27,950	40,252†	65,500†,a	83,000†	98,000†	106,400†	98,938†	68,800	67,354
D.	CHILE	872	88	#	#	#	#	#	#	#	#
E.	COLOMBIA	7,349	9,947	16,608	22,700‡	27,600	26,379	48,567	58,530	45,205	45,205†
F.	COSTA RICA	843	1,918	4,262	6,294	4,898	5,400†	4,600†	4,294	6,454	5,600†
G.	CUBA	3,015	3,370‡	4,500†	8,249	9,058	11,679	11,300†	11,727	15,926	15,926†
H.	DOMNICAN REP.	100	607	2,100‡	4,634‡	4,023	4,957	7,168	6,606	6,901	6,901†
I.	ECUADOR	1,867	2,306	7,600	10,215	12,146	17,227	19,000‡	12,605	17,965	16,877
J.	EL SALVADOR	1,360	2,171	4,000	6,300†	6,870†	6,900	7,200	6,800	6,970	6,970†
K.	GUATEMALA	888	1,352	2,722	5,790†	5,065	9,016	5,609	6,447	5,601	1,543
L.	HAITI	80‡	123†	190†	312†	267†	139†	373†	285†	285†	285†
M.	HONDURAS	280	472	801	1,950	2,900†	2,595	3,400†	3,186	2,376	2,500†
N.	MEXICO	13,644	19,016	59,687	22,700†	22,750†	64,200†	144,200†	89,000†	31,667	31,667†
O.	NICARAGUA	443	635	1,607†	2,707	1,087	1,600†	2,600	2,331	2,331†	2,331†
P.	PANAMA	457	818	1,130	1,990	1,914	1,079	2,388	1,385	2,739	2,887
Q.	PARAGUAY	199	636	1,366†	2,513	2,790	3,877	2,624	5,400†	1,315	2,106
R.	PERU	5,940	7,171	18,182	12,188	2,597	3,450	20,281	30,400†	24,000†	24,000†
S.	URUGUAY	3,213	3,347	4,805	5,488	6,502	8,635	11,686	8,484	4,603	4,603†
T.	VENEZUELA	6,008	12,180	25,284†	51,088	51,900†	54,000†	65,200†	94,561	87,749	81,900†
	UNITED STATES	789,604	929,626	1,456,915	2,140,814	2,379,109	2,637,857	2,824,777	3,748,652	2,817,193	3,369,904†

a. Revised datum for 1977 is 64,554.

SOURCE: FAO-YFP, 1973, p. 277; FAO-YFP, 1977; FAO-YFP, 1980, p. 326;
FAO-YFP, 1981, p. 319; FAO-YFP, 1982, p. 319; FAO-YFP, 1983, p. 319;
FAO-YFP, 1984, p. 311.

Table 503

BOOK PRODUCTION: TITLES BY SUBJECT, 11 L

Country/Year

Subject	A. ARGENTINA (1983)	B. BOLIVIA (1982)	C. BRAZIL (1982)	D. CHILE (1983)	E. COLOMBIA (1983)	F. COSTA RICA (1984)	G. CUBA (1983)	N. MEXICO (1984)	O. NICARAGUA (1984)	R. PERU (1984)	S. URUGUAY (1984)
1. Generalities	189	8	1,160	30	1,078	38	339	569	4	12	21
2. Philosophy, Psychology	536	1	732	24	239	47	28	276	1	16	22
3. Religion, Theology	~[b]	13	2,251	112	352	82	2	114	2	7	42
4. Sociology, Statistics	337	14	327	73	205	89	6	292	#	26	46
5. Political Science	~[c]	15	447	172	413	197	44	341	1	71	69
6. Law, Public Administration	342	23	1,551	125	1,025	191	20	182	#	54	112
7. Military Art	#	2	22	9	89	1	10	13	#	#	11
8. Education, Leisure	243	16	2,679	180	517	88	404	338	#	29	76
9. Trade, Transport	#	2	96	38	340	3	5	19	#	10	84
10. Ethnography, Folklore	#	21	361	9	195	7	1	17	1	12	3
11. Linguistics, Philology	~[a]	11	606	28	290	69	114	129	#	10	6
12. Mathematics	179	1	613	15	530	77	72	119	#	17	50
13. Natural Sciences	20	10	849	53	568	77	85	238	#	16	27
14. Medical Sciences	131	3	772	47	4,787	18	221	269	#	25	52
15. Engineering, Crafts	492	2	902	56	365	60	161	67	#	22	79
16. Agriculture	36	3	280	38	570	185	47	37	#	9	59
17. Domestic Science	#	#	86	7	150	4	9	11	#	11	4
18. Management, Administration	#	4	197	12	195	24	8	74	#	40	37
19. Planning, Architecture	7	1	52	12	135	20	8	24	#	1	24
20. Plastic Arts	639	9	1,239	7	205	6	10	50	#	1	15
21. Performing Arts	~[d]	13	#	19	332	3	59	46	#	7	21
22. Games, Sports	56	4	633	11	325	3	36	31	#	7	16
23. Literature											
(A) History and Criticism	58	64	2,588	7	340	150	200	971	1	15	36
(B) Literary Texts	934	~[a]	~[a]	336	1,161	190	99	[a]	14	68	169
24. Geography, Travel	17	14	202	19	290	49	24	56	#	19	45
25. History, Biography	[a]	47	533	76	345	81	57	222	2	41	80
26. Total	4,216	301	19,179	1,653	15,041	1,759	2,069	4,505	26	546	1,206

a. Included in History Criticism.
b. Included in Philosophy, Psychology.
c. Included in Sociology, Statistics.
d. Included in Plastic Arts.

SOURCE: UNESCO-SY, 1986, table 7.8.

Table 504

MAIL TRAFFIC,[1] 16 LC, 1970–78

(M items sent or received)

Country	Code[2]	1970	1971	1972	1973	1974	1975	1976	1977	1978
A. ARGENTINA	A	833	903	885	960	870	737	620	~	~
	B	124	103	87	88	89	79	70	~	~
	C	55	61	55	54	58	56	50	~	~

Continued in SALA, 23-1205.

1. The figure covers letters (airmail, ordinary mail, and registered), postcards, printed matter, merchandise samples, small packets, and phonopost packets. Includes mail carried without charge, but excludes ordinary parcels, and insured letters and boxes.
2. Code: A = Domestic: items mailed for distribution within the national territory.
   B = Foreign-received: items received from or mail from places outside the national territory. Mail in transit is not included.
   C = Foreign-sent: items sent or mailed for distribution outside the national territory. Mail in transit is not included.

Table 505

TELEGRAPH SERVICE, BY NUMBER OF TELEGRAMS, 12 L, 1970–81[a]

(T)

Country		1970	1973	1975	1976	1977	1978	1979	1980	1981
A. ARGENTINA	Domestic	14,645	17,409	14,340	12,400	12,710	11,193	12,255	13,435	15,509
	Foreign	689	564	515	342	364	376	382	421	420

Continued in SALA, 25-506.

Table 506

U.N. DATA ON TELEPHONES, 19 L, 1975–84[a]

Country	T								PHI							
	1975	1978	1979	1980	1981	1982	1983	1984	1975	1978	1979	1980	1981	1982	1983	1984
A. ARGENTINA	1,996	2,404	2,491	2,588	2,767	3,235	3,108	~	7.8	9.1	9.2	9.3	9.8	11.2	10.4	~
C. BRAZIL	3,372	5,525	6,494	7,496	8,536	9,126	9,856	10,570	3.0	4.5	5.1	6.3	7.2	7.3	7.7	8.0
D. CHILE	434	514	536	551	595	584	629	680	4.1	4.8	4.8	5.0	5.2	5.2	5.4	5.7
E. COLOMBIA	1,227	1,493	1,587	1,718	1,842	1,866	1,894	1,978	5.2	5.8	6.0	6.4	6.5	6.5	6.5	6.6
F. COSTA RICA	122	185	200	236	256	283	292	304	6.3	8.8	9.3	10.7	10.9	11.8	11.8	12.1
G. CUBA	~	341	362	~	406	~	~	493	~	3.5	3.7	~	4.2	~	~	4.9
H. DOMINICAN REP.	108	~	155	165	175	~	~	~	2.4	~	2.9	2.9	3.0	~	~	~
I. ECUADOR	182	240	260	272	290	312	318	332	2.7	3.0	3.2	3.3	3.3	3.9	4.0	3.6
J. EL SALVADOR	60	80	83	86	100	100	116	124	1.5	1.8	1.9	1.9	2.2	2.1	2.3	2.4
K. GUATEMALA	~	~	~	~	~	~	~	~	~	~	~	~	~	~	~	~
L. HAITI	~	~	~	~	~	~	~	~	~	~	~	~	~	~	~	~
M. HONDURAS	20	21	27	~	~	~	35	46	.7	.7	.8	~	~	~	.9	1.1
N. MEXICO	2,915	4,140	4,533	4,992	5,511	5,961	6,414	6,796	5.0	6.4	6.8	7.2	7.7	8.1	8.9	9.1
O. NICARAGUA	36	~	58	~	33	~	~	50	1.6	~	2.2	~	1.1	~	~	1.6
P. PANAMA	142	152	164	173	185	213	220	227	8.4	8.3	8.7	9.5	9.5	10.7	10.5	10.4
Q. PARAGUAY	37	48	55	59	64	71	78	83	1.4	1.6	1.8	1.8	1.9	2.3	2.2	2.6
R. PERU	369	420	437	475	~	520	543	571	2.5	2.5	2.5	2.7	~	3.0	2.9	3.1
S. URUGUAY	250	270	279	287	294	~	332	338	9.0	9.6	9.9	9.9	10.1	~	10.3	11.3
T. VENEZUELA	650	678	789	~	~	1,378	1,021	1,311	5.3	5.1	5.8	~	~	9.4	6.7	7.8

a. For pre-1975 data see SALA, 21-1207.

SOURCE: UN-SY, 1977, p. 620; UN-SY, 1978, p. 628; UN-SY, 1979, table 154; UN-SY, 1981, table 188; UN-SY, 1982, table 181; UN-SY, 1983, table 117; UN-SY, 1984, table 117.

Table 507

AMERICAN TELEPHONE AND TELEGRAPH DATA ON TELEPHONES,
20 LC, 1960–81

	Country	T Telephones[1]						PHI[1]					
		1960	1970	1975	1979	1980	1981	1960	1970	1975	1979	1980	1981
A.	ARGENTINA	1,244	1,668	2,374	2,660	2,760	2,881	6.0	6.9	9.4	10.1	10.3[†]	10.4
B.	BOLIVIA	21	38	~	126	~	135	.6	.8	~	2.6	~	2.6

Continued in SALA, 24-508.

Table 508

TELEPHONES BY CONTINENTAL AREA, 1960–81

Category	1960	1965	1970	1975	1979	1980	1981
Absolute Total (Million)	133.6	182.5	255.2	358.6	448.3	472.1	508.3
Percentage Total	100.0	100.0	100.0	100.0	100.0	100.0	100.0
Latin America[1]	3.1	3.0	3.1	3.5	5.0	4.0	3.9
North America	56.9	52.3	48.6	43.5	41.1	40.5	41.0
Europe	30.2	31.5	32.8	34.6	37.2	37.6	37.4
Africa	1.4	1.3	1.2	1.2	1.1	1.0	1.0
Asia	6.1	9.7	12.2	15.2	14.8	14.9	14.7
Oceania	2.3	2.2	2.1	2.0	1.8	2.0	2.0

1. Includes non-Latin American Caribbean and mainland countries and dependencies.

SOURCE: American Telephone and Telegraph Overseas Administration, *World's Telephones*, 1960, 1965, 1969, 1970, 1971, 1974, 1977, 1978, 1979, 1980, and 1981.

Table 509

RADIO AND TELEVISION TRANSMITTERS, 19 LC

	Country	Radio[1]					Television[2]				
		Year	Total	Governmental	Public	Commercial	Year	Total	Governmental	Public	Commercial
A.	ARGENTINA	1979	202	42	16	144	1977	75	8	2	65
B.	BOLIVIA	1981	184	5	25	154	~	~	~	~	~
C.	BRAZIL	1983	1,818	27	15	1,776	1983	137	2	12	123
D.	CHILE	1979	109	24	12	73	~	~	~	~	~
E.	COLOMBIA	~	~	~	~	~	1983	49	#	49	#
F.	COSTA RICA	1981	123	3	17	103	~	~	~	~	~
G.	CUBA	1983	150	150	#	#	1983	58	58	#	#
H.	DOMINICAN REP.	1979	188	#	#	188	~	~	~	~	~
J.	EL SALVADOR	1979	75	#	7	68	~	~	~	~	~
K.	GUATEMALA	1979	115	#	#	115	~	~	~	~	~
L.	HAITI	1979	48	#	#	48	~	~	~	~	~
M.	HONDURAS	1979	153	#	#	153	~	~	~	~	~
N.	MEXICO	1983	872	51	#	821	1983	405	230	#	175
O.	NICARAGUA	1979	87	#	5	82	~	~	~	~	~
P.	PANAMA	1977	93	10	~	83	1977	10	~	~	10
Q.	PARAGUAY	1979	56	3	#	53	~	~	~	~	~
R.	PERU	1977	189	35	~	154	~	~	~	~	~
S.	URUGUAY	1981	94	4	~	90	1983	33	12	#	21
T.	VENEZUELA	1977	210	11	3	196	~	~	~	~	~
	UNITED STATES	1977	8,359	414	531	7,414	1977	972[a]	184	71	717

1. Figures relate to low=, medium=, super=high frequency transmitters in service used for
   domestic radio broadcasts to the general public.
2. Figures relate to very-high and ultra-high frequency transmitters operating on a regular
   basis and used for broadcasting to the general public.

a. Does not include relay transmitters.

SOURCE: UNESCO-SY, 1987.

Table 510

RADIO RECEIVERS,[1] 20 LC, 1965–83

	Country	T						PTI					
		1965	1970	1975	1980	1982	1983	1965	1970	1975	1980	1982	1983
A.	ARGENTINA	6,600	9,000	9,890	12,000	21,200	16,000	298	379	386	433	727	540
B.	BOLIVIA	~	402	1,150	2,800	3,380	3,500	~	82	235	500	571	575
C.	BRAZIL	~	11,800	16,980	35,000	45,000	50,000	~	128	162	284	355	386
D.	CHILE	~	1,400	1,700	3,250	3,450	3,550	~	149	167	293	300	304
E.	COLOMBIA	1,600	2,217	2,808	3,250	3,550	3,650	89	108	119	120	122	133
F.	COSTA RICA	~	130	151	180	195	205	~	75	77	80	84	86
G.	CUBA	~	1,330	1,805	2,914	3,100	3,121	~	156	194	299	317	316
H.	DOMNICAN REP.	~	164	160	220	250	1,200	~	~	160	165	44	201
I.	ECUADOR	540	1,700	~	2,650	2,850	2,950	107	285	~	317	319	319
J.	EL SALVADOR	396	583	1,400	1,550	1,680	1,900	135	165	350	326	336	362
K.	GUATEMALA	~	220	262	310	330	340	~	42	42	43	43	43
L.	HAITI	63	76	93	101	110	120	~	43	46	48	21	49
M.	HONDURAS	135	108	142	176	190	200	~	43	46	48	48	49
N.	MEXICO	8,600	14,005	~	19,000	21,300	21,800	208	~	~	274	292	290
O.	NICARAGUA	100	137	~	700	800	850	62	75	~	256	274	278
P.	PANAMA	~	215	260	300	325	335	~	150	155	158	159	160
Q.	PARAGUAY	~	~	180	224	250	260	~	~	67	71	74	75
R.	PERU	~	1,748	2,050	2,750	2,950	3,000	~	132	135	159	161	160
S.	URUGUAY	900	1,000	1,500	1,630	1,700	1,700	331	347	530	560	577	573
T.	VENEZUELA	~	~	4,775	5,600	6,000	6,650	~	~	398	403	408	405
	UNITED STATES	240,000	290,000	401,000	453,000	495,000	479,000	1,235	1,415	1,934	2,099	2,133	2,043

1. Estimated number of receivers in use.

SOURCE: UNESCO-SY, 1983, table 9.2; UNESCO-SY, 1984, table 9.2; UNESCO-SY, 1986, table 10.2.

Table 511

TELEVISION SETS,[1] 20 LC, 1965–83

	Country	T						PTI					
		1965	1970	1975	1980	1982	1983	1965	1970	1975	1980	1982	1983
A.	ARGENTINA	1,600	3,500	4,000	5,140	5,900	5,910	72	147	156	185	202	199
B.	BOLIVIA	~	~	45	300	350	386	~	~	9	54	59	64
C.	BRAZIL	~	6,100	~	15,000	15,500	16,500	~	66	~	126	122	127
D.	CHILE	~	500	700	1,225	1,300	1,350	~	53	69	110	113	116
E.	COLOMBIA	350	810	1,600	2,250	2,600	2,700	19	39	68	83	89	98
F.	COSTA RICA	50	100	128	162	200	181	34	58	65	72	86	76
G.	CUBA	~	~	595	1,273	1,600	1,658	~	~	64	131	164	168
H.	DOMINICAN REP.	50	100	180	400	450	550	14	25	37	73	78	92
I.	ECUADOR	42	150	252	500	550	570	8	25	36	60	61	62
J.	EL SALVADOR	35	92	135	300	320	330	12	26	34	63	64	63
K.	GUATEMALA	55	72	110	175	200	202	12	14	18	24	26	25
L.	HAITI	~	11	13	16	18	19	~	3	3	3	4	4
M.	HONDURAS	2	22	34	49	50	52	1	8	11	13	13	13
N.	MEXICO	1,200	3,000	~	7,500	8,000	8,300	30	59	~	108	111	111
O.	NICARAGUA	16	55	83	175	195	200	10	30	39	64	67	65
P.	PANAMA	70	~	185	220	245	255	57	~	110	116	120	122
Q.	PARAGUAY	~	~	54	68	80	81	~	~	20	21	24	23
R.	PERU	210	395	610	850	910	920	18	30	40	49	50	49
S.	URUGUAY	200	~	351	363	370	376	74	~	124	125	126	126
T.	VENEZUELA	650	~	1,284	1,710	1,850	2,050	75	~	107	123	126	126
	UNITED STATES	70,350	84,600	125,060	142,000	150,000	185,300	362	413	560	684	646	790

1. Estimated number of television sets in use.

SOURCE: UNESCO-SY, 1983, table 9.4; UNESCO-SY, 1984, table 9.4; UNESCO-SY, 1985, table 10.4.

Table 512

CINEMA ATTENDANCE, 20 LC, 1955-83

Country	1955 Attendance (M)	1955 Per Capita Visits	1960 Attendance (M)	1960 Per Capita Visits	1965 Attendance (M)	1965 Per Capita Visits	1970 Attendance (M)	1970 Per Capita Visits	1975 Attendance (M)	1975 Per Capita Visits	1980 Attendance (M)	1980 Per Capita Visits	1983 Attendance (M)	1983 Per Capita Visits
A. ARGENTINA	120[a]	6.3[a]	145	7.0	344[b]	15.5[b]	53	2.2	82	3.2	44[m]	.2[m]	49.9	1.7
B. BOLIVIA	~	~	~	~	3[c]	.7[c]	~	~	~	~	31[n]	5.7[n]	~	~
C. BRAZIL	312[d]	5.0[d]	316	4.5	314[e]	3.8[e]	234[b]	2.5[b]	276	2.6	138[m]	~	137.5[m]	~[m]
D. CHILE	28	4.2	~	~	61	7.1	47[f]	4.8[f]	23	2.3	15[m]	1.3[m]	12.2	1.0
E. COLOMBIA	56[g]	4.1[g]	67[h]	5.8[h]	80	4.3	92[i]	4.2[i]	96	4.1	68[m]	2.4[m]	66.0	2.4
F. COSTA RICA	~	~	49[j]	8.4[j]	~	~	~	~	~	~	~	~	~	~
G. CUBA	~	~	~	~	~	~	~	~	124[q]	14.2[q]	50[m]	9.2[m]	49.7	8.7
H. DOMINICAN REP.	4	1.5	~	~	~	~	~	~	~	~	~	~	~	~
I. ECUADOR	8	2.2	~	~	15	2.9	22	3.7	39	5.6	16[t]	~	~	~
J. EL SALVADOR	9	4.1	15	8.1	~	~	10[f]	2.9[f]	14[r]	3.5[r]	10[n]	1.4[n]	~	~
K. GUATEMALA	9	2.6	10	3.6	~	~	9[f]	1.7[f]	15[s]	2.8[t,s]	10[n]	1.4[n]	7.9[u]	1.0[u]
L. HAITI	1	..	1[k]	1.3[k]	1[c]	..	~	~	6[o]	1.3[o]	6[o]	1.3[o]	2.1[m]	.4[m]
M. HONDURAS	2	1.2	~	~	~	~	~	~	~	~	~	~	~	~
N. MEXICO	362	11.7	374[j]	10.7[j]	346	8.0	251	4.9	251	4.2	264[p]	3.7[p]	211.5	2.8
O. NICARAGUA	5[l]	3.9[l]	6	5.7	7	4.1	5[i]	3.6[i]	~	~	5[m]	1.9[m]	.5[m]	1.9[m]
P. PANAMA	~	~	~	~	~	~	~	~	.3[r]	6.5[f]	~	~	~	~
Q. PARAGUAY	~	~	~	~	~	~	~	~	~	~	~	~	~	~
R. PERU	~	~	67[j]	6.7[j]	~	~	~	~	~	~	33[p]	1.9[p]	~	~
S. URUGUAY	~	~	25[h]	9.8[h]	16[e]	5.7[e]	~	~	33[o]	2.6[o]	6.2[m]	2.1[m]	6.2[m]	2.1[m]
T. VENEZUELA	42	7.0	60[h]	7.8[h]	~	~	37[f]	3.5[f]	~	~	67.6[m]	4.7[m]	67.5[m]	4.7[m]
UNITED STATES	2,000	12.1	2,165[j]	12.0[j]	2,288	11.8	920	4.5	1,565[t,o]	7.2[o]	1,067[m]	4.6[m]	1,053.3	5.1

a. 1953.
b. 1967.
c. 1964.
d. 1954.
e. 1963.
f. 1971.
g. 1956.
h. 1959.
i. 1968.
j. 1961
k. 1958.
l. 1952.
m. 1981.
n. 1979.
o. 1977.
p. 1980.
q. 1972.
r. 1974.
s. 1973.
t. 1976.
u. 1982.

SOURCE: For years 1955-70, Daniel I. Geffner, "Alternative Interpretations of Time-Series Data on the Growth of Latin American Film Industry, 1926-1970," SALA, 19-3601. For subsequent years see UNESCO-SY, 1977, table 14.3; UNESCO-SY, 1980, table 9.3; UNESCO-SY, 1983, table 8.3; UNESCO-SY, 1984, table 8.3; UNESCO-SY, 1986.

Table 513

MOTION PICTURE THEATERS,[1] 20 LC, 1926–83

(N)

Country	1926	1930	1940	1950	1955	1960	1965	1970	1975	1980	1983
A. ARGENTINA	200	975	1,208	1,881	2,063	2,228	1,587[a,b]	1,637[c]	1,420	1,018[n]	921
B. BOLIVIA	16	20	38	60	47	82	120[d]	~	~	226[q]	225[q]
C. BRAZIL	200	1,600	1,300	1,736	3,301	3,284	3,261[e]	3,194[a]	2,910	2,264[n]	2,237[n]
D. CHILE	200	221	263	300	410	336	336	368[f]	291	172[n]	161
E. COLOMBIA	200	218	274	500	641	819[g]	895	726[h]	700	393[n]	323
F. COSTA RICA	8	21	42	100	100	136[i]	~	~	~	~	~
G. CUBA	350	457	375	516	555	481[i,k]	~	439[l,c]	888[s]	1,322[n]	1,405
H. DOMINICAN REP.	~	31	28	55	74	84	~	80[f,c]	~	~	~
I. ECUADOR	25	25	37	71	240	122	164	164	255[t]	~	~
J. EL SALVADOR	33	~	41	32	34	55[i]	~	57[f]	72[t]	~	~
K. GUATEMALA	20	39	28	25	99	105	~	105[f,c]	131[u]	126[q]	140[v]
L. HAITI	6	9	7	24	21	26[m,i]	20[d,b]	~	~	23[p]	~
M. HONDURAS	6	27	23	28	30	60[i]	~	~	~	~	~
N. MEXICO	700	701	829	1,726	2,062	2,000[j,k]	1,555[b]	1,765[c]	2,505	2,831[o]	3,026
O. NICARAGUA	11	24	27	~	50	98	104[e,i]	~	~	128[n]	127[n]
P. PANAMA	30	38	54	60	60	62	~	23[h,c]	6[t]	~	~
Q. PARAGUAY	~	9	8	~	30	55	~	~	~	~	~
R. PERU	60	70	212	~	243	319[j]	~	276[l,c]	388[p]	425[o]	425[o]
S. URUGUAY	101	125	181	177	220	223[g,i]	386[e]	180[a]	~	120[n]	120[n]
T. VENEZUELA	18	123	177	350	575	744[g,k]	~	436[f,c]	588[p]	555[n]	535[n]
LATIN AMERICA	~	~	5,162	~	10,855	11,319	~	~	~	9,603[r]	~
UNITED STATES	~	23,000	17,003	20,239	19,000	15,105[j,k]	9,805[b]	10,520[c]	15,000	18,040[n]	16,032

1. Includes mobile and fixed units.

a. 1967.
b. Does not include drive-in cinemas or their capacity (in parentheses) for cars:
Argentina 1; Haiti, 1 (450); Mexico, 5 (3,200); United States, 3,600.
c. Does not include drive-in cinemas or their capacity (in parentheses) for cars:
Argentina, 8 (5,150); Cuba, 1 (550); Dominican Republic, 2 (420);
Guatemala, 1 (544); Mexico, 3 (1,970); Panama, 1 (330); Peru, 1 (100);
Venezuela, 20 (4,030); United States, 3,900.
d. 1964.
e. 1963.
f. 1971.
g. 1959.
h. 1968.
i. It was not indicated if the cinemas concerned were equipped to exhibit 35 mm or 16 mm films.
j. 1961.

k. Does not include drive-in cinemas or their capacity (in parentheses) for cars:
Cuba, 2 (1,366); Mexico, 5 (2,500); Venezuela, 3 (900); United States, 6,000 (2,400,000).
l. 1972.
m. 1958.
n. 1981.
o. 1980.
p. 1977.
q. 1979.
r. Indicates the number of fixed cinemas for 1981.
s. 1972.
t. 1974.
u. 1976.
v. 1982.

SOURCE: For years 1926-70, same as table 513. For subsequent years see UNESCO-SY,
1977, table 14.3; UNESCO-SY, 1978-79, table 17.3; UNESCO-SY, 1983, table 8.3;
UNESCO-SY, 1984, table 8.3; UNESCO-SY, 1986, table 9.3.

Table 514

ADVERTISING EXPENDITURES, 6 LC

(1977 M US)

	Country	Total	Print	Television	Radio
A.	ARGENTINA	382.2	181.6	120.9	51.3
C.	BRAZIL	1610.9	483.8	697.1	337.6
E.	COLOMBIA[1]	167.8	36.4	91.0	29.0
H.	DOMINICAN REP.	41.1	12.3	18.8	6.3
N.	MEXICO	298.3	37.3	202.0	46.6
T.	VENEZUELA	280.2	108.7	92.7	48.8
	UNITED STATES[2]	25,269.0	14,605.0	7,612.0	2,634.0

1. Data are for 1978.
2. Expenditure for cinema not reported.

SOURCE: World Press Encyclopedia, 1984.

Table 515

INSTALLED COMPUTERS IN BRAZIL, 1970–81

Class[1]	1970	1973	1975	1977	1979	1981	Growth Rates		
							1970–75	1977–81	1973–81
Micro	~	586	2,143	3,846	4,791	8,576	~	20.1	33.5
Mini	~	19	173	356	1,015	2,719	~	50.8	62.1
Small	378	639	1,057	1,296	1,494	1,858	25.7	9.0	15.9
Medium	122	250	327	353	377	408	24.7	3.6	12.1
Large	2	45	82	122	226	374	92.8	28.0	52.3
Very Large	4	33	61	87	97	134	68.1	10.8	35.1
Total	506	1,572	3,843	6,060	8,000	14,069	50.7	21.1	33.8

1. The class sizes are generally based on the size of the equipment, as well as upon prices and technical parameters (CPU speed, memory, and input/output capacity).

SOURCE: Alexandra Pou, "The Brazilian Informática Sector." Master's Thesis, University of California, Los Angeles, 1985.

Part III: Population, Health, and Education

CHAPTER 6

DEMOGRAPHY

Note: This volume contains statistics from numerous sources. Alternative data on many topics are presented. Variations in statistics can be attributed to differences in definition, parameters, coverage, methodology, as well as date gathered, prepared, or adjusted. See also Editor's Note on Methodology.

Figure 6:1

POPULATION CARTOGRAM OF LATIN AMERICA, 1980

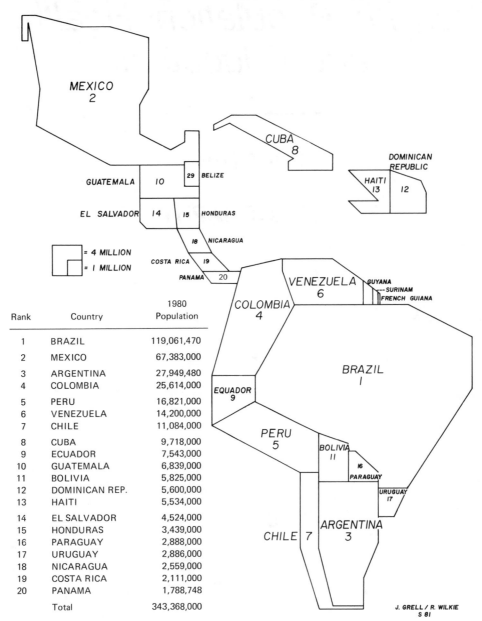

Rank	Country	1980 Population
1	BRAZIL	119,061,470
2	MEXICO	67,383,000
3	ARGENTINA	27,949,480
4	COLOMBIA	25,614,000
5	PERU	16,821,000
6	VENEZUELA	14,200,000
7	CHILE	11,084,000
8	CUBA	9,718,000
9	ECUADOR	7,543,000
10	GUATEMALA	6,839,000
11	BOLIVIA	5,825,000
12	DOMINICAN REP.	5,600,000
13	HAITI	5,534,000
14	EL SALVADOR	4,524,000
15	HONDURAS	3,439,000
16	PARAGUAY	2,888,000
17	URUGUAY	2,886,000
18	NICARAGUA	2,559,000
19	COSTA RICA	2,111,000
20	PANAMA	1,788,748
	Total	343,368,000

SOURCE: SALA LAPUA, pp. 30, 33.

Table 600

WORLD POPULATION (MID-1980) AND AVERAGE ANNUAL GROWTH RATES AND RANKS, 20 LRC, 1960-80

(126 Countries with Populations of 1 Million or More)

Population Rank	Country	Population (T)	AA-GR (%) 1960-73	AA-GR (%) 1970-79	AA-GR (%) 1970-80
1	China	979,600	1.7a	1.9a	1.5
2	India	674,984	2.3	2.1	2.1
3	USSR	265,542	1.0	.9	.9
4	United States[1]	227,658	1.0	.9	1.0
5	Indonesia	146,345	2.1	2.3	2.4
6	**Brazil**	**118,332**	**2.9**	**2.3**	**2.1**
7	Japan	116,782	1.2	1.2	1.2
8	Bangladesh	88,513	2.4	3.0	2.5
9	Nigeria	84,732	2.5	2.5	2.5
10	Pakistan	82,061	2.9	3.1	3.1
11	**Mexico**	**69,393**	**3.5**	**3.0**	**3.1**
12	Germany, Federal Republic of	61,561	.6	#	#
13	Italy	56,159	.7	.5b	.5
14	United Kingdom[2]	55,944	.4b	.1b	.1
15	Viet Nam	54,175	2.6	2.9	2.9
16	France[3]	53,713	.8	.6	.5
17	Phillippines	48,300	3.0	2.7	2.7
18	Thailand	46,950	3.0	2.5	2.6
19	Turkey	44,438	2.4	2.5	2.3
20	Egypt, Arab Republic of	42,289	2.5	2.0	2.4
21	Iran, Islamic Republic of	38,829	3.2	3.0	3.1
22	Korea, Republic of	38,198	1.9	1.9	1.7
23	Spain	37,430	1.1	1.1	1.1
24	Poland	35,578	.8	.9	.9
25	Burma	33,313	2.2	2.2	2.1
26	Ethiopia	31,065	2.4	2.2	2.0
27	Zaire	28,893	2.7	2.7	3.0
28	South Africa	28,723	3.2	2.7	2.8
29	**Argentina**	**27,740**	**1.5**	**1.6**	**1.6**
30	**Colombia**	**25,892**	**1.8**	**2.3**	**1.9**
31	Canada	23,941	1.4	1.1	1.2
32	Yugoslavia	22,344	.9	.9	.9
33	Romania	22,201	1.2	.9	.9
34	Morocco	20,182	2.4	3.0	3.0
35	Algeria	18,919	3.4	3.4	3.2
36	Sudan	18,681	2.8	2.7	3.1
37	Korea, Democratic People's Republic of	18,270	2.8	2.6	2.6
38	Tanzania	18,141	2.8c	3.4c	3.4
39	German Democratic Republic	16,737	#	-.2	-.2
40	Kenya	16,642	3.2	3.5	4.0
41	**Peru**	**16,610**	**2.9**	**2.7**	**2.6**
42	Afghanistan	15,940	2.2	2.6	2.6
43	Czechoslovakia	15,272	.3	.7	.7
44	**Venezuela**	**14,930**	**3.4**	**3.4**	**3.4**
45	Sri Lanka	14,738	2.3	1.7	1.7
46	Nepal	14,640	1.9	2.4	2.6
47	Australia	14,616	1.9	1.5	1.4
48	Nethlands, The[4]	14,144	1.1	.8	.8
49	Malaysia	13,871	2.6	2.3	2.5
50	Iraq	13,072	3.2	3.4	3.4
51	Uganda	12,630	2.8	3.0	2.6
52	Mozambique	12,084	2.0	2.5	4.1
53	Ghana	11,500	2.6	3.1	3.0
54	**Chile**	**11,104**	**2.2**	**1.7**	**1.7**
55	Hungary	10,711	.3	.4	.4
56	Belgium	9,859	.5	.2	.2
57	Portugal[5]	9,752	#	1.4	1.2
58	Greece	9,599	.5	.6	.9
59	**Cuba**	**9,579**	**2.0**	**1.4**	**1.1**
60	Syrian Arab Republic	8,979	3.3	3.6	3.7
61	Saudi Arabia	8,960	1.7	4.6	4.6
62	Bulgaria	8,862	.7	.6	.5
63	Madagascar	8,714	2.0	2.5	2.5
64	Cameroon	8,444	2.0	2.2	2.2
65	**Ecuador**	**8,354**	**3.4**	**3.3**	**3.4**
66	Sweden	8,311	.7	.3	.3
67	Ivory Coast	8,262	3.8	5.7	5.1
68	Angola	7,581	1.3	2.4	2.5
69	Austria	7,546	.5	.1	.1
70	**Guatemala**	**7,262**	**2.4**	**2.9**	**3.1**
71	Yemen Arab Republic	7,039	2.4	1.8	3.0
72	Kampuchea, Democratic				
73	Zimbabwe	6,934	~	3.3	3.2
74	Mali	6,894	3.3	3.3	3.2
75	Tunisia	6,699	2.1	2.6	2.6
76	Switzerland	6,369	1.3	.3	#
77	Upper Volta	6,349	2.1	1.6	2.0
78	Malawi	6,161	2.6	2.9	2.9
79	Senegal	6,037	2.1	2.6	2.7
80	Zambia	5,703	2.9	3.1	3.1
81	**Bolivia**	**5,570**	**2.6**	**2.6**	**2.6**
82	Niger	5,532	2.7	2.8	3.3
83	**Dominican Republic**	**5,431**	**2.9**	**3.0**	**3.0**
84	Guinea	5,425	2.8	2.9	2.9
85	Rwanda	5,168	3.4	2.8	3.4
86	Denmark[6]	5,123	.7	.4	.4
87	Hong Kong	5,068	3.3	2.6	2.3
88	**Haiti**	**5,009**	**1.7**	**1.7**	**1.7**
89	Finland	4,779	.3	.6	.4
90	**El Salvador**	**4,540**	**3.5**	**2.9**	**2.9**
91	Chad	4,455	1.8	2.0	2.0
92	Somalia	4,272	2.4	2.3	2.8
93	Burundi	4,114	2.0	2.0	2.2
94	Norway	4,086	.8	.5	.5
95	Israel	3,871	3.1	2.7	2.6
96	**Honduras**	**3,691**	**3.2**	**3.4**	**3.4**
97	Benin	3,479	2.2	2.9	2.7
98	Sierra Leone	3,474	2.2	2.6	2.6
99	Puerto Rico	3,438	1.0	3.0	2.6
100	Lao People's Democratic Republic	3,426	2.4	1.3	1.9
101	Ireland	3,307	.5	1.2	1.2
102	New Zealand[7]	3,268	1.6	1.6	1.6
103	Jordan	3,244	3.3	3.5	3.5
104	Papua New Guinea	3,007	2.4	2.3	2.2
105	**Paraguay**	**2,982**	**2.6**	**2.9**	**2.6**
106	Libya	2,978	3.7	4.2	4.2
107	**Uruguay**	**2,908**	**1.3**	**.3**	**.4**
108	Albania	2,734	2.8	2.5	2.5
109	**Nicaragua**	**2,672**	**2.6**	**3.3**	**3.9**
110	Lebanon	2,658	2.6	-1.0	.7
111	Togo	2,578	2.7	2.4	2.5
112	Singapore	2,415	2.1	1.4	1.5
113	Central African Republic	2,330	2.2	2.3	2.3
114	**Costa Rica**	**2,279**	**3.1**	**2.5**	**2.8**
115	Jamaica	2,172	1.6	1.6	1.5
116	Yemen, People's Democratic Republic of	1,907	~	2.4	2.5
117	Liberia	1,873	3.1	3.3	3.4
118	**Panama**	**1,835**	**3.1**	**2.3**	**2.3**
119	Mongolia	1,663	2.7	3.0	2.9
120	Congo, People's Republic of the	1,605	2.7	2.9	2.9
121	Mauritania	1,523	2.1	2.7	2.5
122	Kuwait	1,372	~	6.2	6.3
123	Lesotho	1,341	2.2	2.4	2.4
124	Bhutan	1,273	2.3	2.2	2.0
125	Trinidad and Tobago	1,168	1.7	1.2	1.3
126	United Arab Emirates	1,000	~	~	17.7
	Latin American 20-Country Average[8]	**17,306**	**2.7**	**2.3**	**2.5**

1. Excluding data for Puerto Rico, the Trust Territory of the Pacific Islands, and its unorganized and unincorporated territories.
2. Excluding data for its colonies, dependencies, and associated states.
3. Excluding data for its overseas departments and territories.
4. Excluding data for the overseas portion of the Netherlands realm.
5. Excluding data for its overseas administred territory.
6. Excluding data for the overseas integral parts with home rule of the Danish realm.
7. Excluding data for its overseas territory and self-governing associated states.
8. Regardless of size.

a. Includes data for Taiwan, China, which are as follows: population, mid-1979: 17,307,000; growth rate, 1970-79: 2.0%.
b. Excludes Puerto Rico, the Trust Territory of the Pacific Islands, and its unorganized and unincorporated territories.
c. Mainland Tanzania.

SOURCE: Adapted from the following: World Bank, Atlas, 1975; World Bank, Atlas, 1980; World Bank, Atlas, 1981; and World Bank, Atlas, 1983.

Table 601

ARGENTINA POPULATION ESTIMATE AND INDEX, 1900–86[a]

Year	M	1970 = 100	Year	M	1970 = 100
1900	4.61	19	1950	17.07	72
1901	4.74	20	1951	17.48	74
1902	4.87	21	1952*	17.70	75
1903	4.98	21	1953	17.96	76
1904	5.10	22	1954	18.24	77
1905	5.29	22	1955	18.53	78
1906	5.52	23	1956	18.80	79
1907	5.82	25	1957	19.10	80
1908	6.15	26	1958	19.38	82
1909	6.43	27	1959	19.66	83
1910	6.80	29	1960	19.92	84
1911	7.07	30	1961	20.24	85
1912	7.47	31	1962	20.54	86
1913	7.84	33	1963	20.85	88
1914	8.00	34	1964	21.17	89
1915	8.15	34	1965	22.18	93
1916	8.30	35	1966	22.49	95
1917	8.45	36	1967	22.80	96
1918	8.60	36	1968	23.11	97
1919	8.75	37	1969	23.43	99
1920	8.97	38	1970	23.75	100
1921	9.22	39	1971	24.07	101
1922	9.52	40	1972	24.39	103
1923	9.89	42	1973	24.82	105
1924	10.22	43	1974	25.22	106
1925	10.50	44	1975	26.05	110
1926	10.80	45	1976	26.48	112
1927	11.13	47	1977	26.91	113
1928	11.44	48	1978	27.35	115
1929	11.75	49	1979	27.79	117
1930	12.05	51	1980	28.24	119
1931	12.29	52	1981	28.69	121
1932	12.52	53	1982	29.16	123
1933	12.73	54	1983	29.63	125
1934	12.94	54	1984	30.10	127
1935	13.15	55	1985	30.56‡	129
1936	13.37	56	1986	31.03	131
1937	13.61	57			
1938	13.84	58			
1939	14.06	59			
1940	14.17	60			
1941	14.40	62			
1942	14.64	62			
1943	14.88	63			
1944	15.13	64			
1945	15.40	65			
1946	15.65	66			
1947	15.93	67			
1948	16.27	69			
1949	16.66	70			

a. Mid-year estimates.

SOURCE: 1900-51 data from SALA-SNP, pp. 173–183; since 1952, data from IMF-IFS-Y, 1980, 1986 and UN-MB, June 1987; cf. SALA, 26–600, 624, and 626.

Table 602

BOLIVIA POPULATION ESTIMATE AND INDEX, 1900–86[a]

Year	M	1970 = 100	Year	M	1970 = 100
1900	1.77	39	1950	3.01	66
1901	1.79	39	1951	3.07	67
1902	1.80	39	1952*	3.13	68
1903	1.82	40	1953	3.19	70
1904	1.84	40	1954	3.26	71
1905	1.86	41	1955	3.34	73
1906	1.88	41	1956	3.42	75
1907	1.90	41	1957	3.50	76
1908	1.91	42	1958	3.59	78
1909	1.93	42	1959	3.70	81
1910	1.95	43	1960	3.82	83
1911	1.97	43	1961	3.92	86
1912	1.98	43	1962	4.02	88
1913	2.01	44	1963	4.12	90
1914	2.03	44	1964	4.23	92
1915	2.04	45	1965	4.33	95
1916	2.06	45	1966	4.45	97
1917	2.08	45	1967	4.48‡	98
1918	2.10	46	1968	4.51‡	98
1919	2.12	46	1969	4.55‡	99
1920	2.14	47	1970	4.58‡	100
1921	2.16	47	1971	4.62‡	101
1922	2.19	48	1972	4.64‡	101
1923	2.21	48	1973	4.67‡	102
1924	2.24	49	1974	4.75‡	104
1925	2.26	49	1975*	4.89	107
1926	2.29	50	1976	5.03	110
1927	2.32	51	1977	5.16	113
1928	2.34	51	1978	5.30	116
1929	2.37	52	1979	5.45	119
1930	2.40	52	1980	5.60	122
1931	2.43	53	1981	5.76	126
1932	2.45	53	1982	5.92	129
1933	2.48	54	1983	6.08	133
1934	2.51	55	1984	6.25	136
1935	2.54	55	1985	6.43‡	140
1936	2.57	56	1986	6.55	143
1937	2.60	57			
1938	2.63	57			
1939	2.66	58			
1940	2.70	59			
1941	2.72	59			
1942	2.75	60			
1943	2.79	61			
1944	2.82	62			
1945	2.85	62			
1946	2.88	63			
1947	2.92	64			
1948	2.95	64			
1949	2.96	65			

a. Mid-year estimates.

SOURCE: 1900-51 data from SALA-SNP, pp. 173–183; since 1952, data from IMF-IFS-Y, 1980, 1986 and UN-MB, June 1987; cf. SALA, 26–600, 624, and 626.

Table 603

BRAZIL POPULATION ESTIMATE AND INDEX, 1900-86[a]

Year	M	1970 = 100	Year	M	1970 = 100
1900	17.98	19	1950	52.18	56
1901	18.39	20	1951	53.68	58
1902	18.78	22	1952	55.10	60
1903	19.18	21	1953	56.74	61
1904	19.58	21	1954	58.44	63
1905	20.00	22	1955	60.18	65
1906	20.43	22	1956	61.98	67
1907	20.86	23	1957	63.83	69
1908	21.30	23	1958	65.74	71
1909	21.75	24	1959	67.70	73
1910	22.22	24	1960*	69.72	75
1911	22.69	25	1961	71.94	78
1912	23.17	25	1962	74.17	80
1913	23.66	26	1963	76.53	83
1914	24.16	26	1964	78.73	85
1915	24.67	27	1965	81.01	88
1916	25.20	27	1966	82.93	90
1917	25.73	28	1967	85.24	92
1918	26.28	28	1968	87.62	95
1919	26.84	29	1969	90.07	97
1920	27.40	30	1970	92.52	100
1921	27.97	30	1971	95.17	103
1922	28.54	31	1972	97.85	106
1923	29.13	31	1973	99.92	108
1924	29.72	32	1974	102.40	111
1925	30.33	33	1975	104.94	113
1926	30.95	33	1976	107.54	116
1927	31.59	34	1977	110.21	119
1928	32.23	35	1978	112.94	122
1929	32.90	36	1979*	115.74	125
1930	33.57	36	1980	121.27	131
1931	34.26	37	1981	124.02	134
1932	34.96	38	1982	126.81	137
1933	35.67	39	1983	129.66	140
1934	36.40	39	1984	132.58	143
1935	37.15	40	1985	135.56‡	146
1936	37.91	41	1986	138.49	150
1937	38.69	42			
1938	39.48	43			
1939	40.29	44			
1940	41.11	44			
1941	42.07	45			
1942	43.06	47			
1943	43.99	48			
1944	44.84	48			
1945	45.86	50			
1946	46.97	51			
1947	48.16	52			
1948	49.42	53			
1949	50.76	55			

a. Mid-year estimates.

SOURCE: 1900-51 data from SALA-SNP, pp. 173-183; since 1952, data from IMF-IFS-Y, 1980, 1986 and UN-MB, June 1987; cf. SALA, 26–600, 624 and 626.

Table 604

CHILE POPULATION ESTIMATE AND INDEX, 1900-86[a]

Year	M	1970 = 100	Year	M	1970 = 100
1900	2.96	32	1950	6.07	65
1901	2.99	32	1951	6.21	65
1902	3.03	32	1952*	6.30*	67
1903	3.07	33	1953	6.46	69
1904	3.10	33	1954	6.62	71
1905	3.14	34	1955	6.79	72
1906	3.18	34	1956	6.96	74
1907	3.21	34	1957	7.14	76
1908	3.25	35	1958	7.32	78
1909	3.29	35	1959	7.49	80
1910	3.34	36	1960	7.58	81
1911	3.38	36	1961	7.76	83
1912	3.42	36	1962	7.95	85
1913	3.47	37	1963	8.14	87
1914	3.51	37	1964	8.33	89
1915	3.55	38	1965	8.51	91
1916	3.60	38	1966	8.68	93
1917	3.64	39	1967	8.85	94
1918	3.69	39	1968	9.03	96
1919	3.74	40	1969	9.20	98
1920	3.79	40	1970	9.37	100
1921	3.85	41	1971	9.53	102
1922	3.91	42	1972	9.70	104
1923	3.96	42	1973	9.86	105
1924	4.02	43	1974	10.03	107
1925	4.07	43	1975	10.20	109
1926	4.13	44	1976	10.37	111
1927	4.19	45	1977	10.55	113
1928	4.25	45	1978	10.73	115
1929	4.31	46	1979	10.92	117
1930	4.37	47	1980	11.10	118
1931	4.43	47	1981	11.29	120
1932	4.50	48	1982	11.49	123
1933	4.56	49	1983	11.68	125
1934	4.63	49	1984	11.88	127
1935	4.70	50	1985	12.07‡	129
1936	4.77	51	1986	12.33	132
1937	4.84	52			
1938	4.91	52			
1939	4.99	53			
1940	5.06	54			
1941	5.15	55			
1942	5.24	56			
1943	5.34	57			
1944	5.44	58			
1945	5.54	59			
1946	5.64	60			
1947	5.75	61			
1948	5.85	62			
1949	5.96	64			

a. Mid-year estimates.

SOURCE: 1900-51 data from SALA-SNP, pp. 173–183; since 1952, data from IMF-IFS-Y, 1980, 1986 and UN-MB, June 1987; cf. SALA, 26–600, 624, and 626.

Table 605

COLOMBIA POPULATION ESTIMATE AND INDEX, 1900–86[a]

Year	M	1970 = 100	Year	M	1970 = 100
1900	3.89	19	1950	11.33	56
1901	3.94	19	1951	11.62	57
1902	3.99	19	1952*	11.81	58
1903	4.04	20	1953	12.07	59
1904	4.09	20	1954	12.34	61
1905	4.14	20	1955	12.97	64
1906	4.28	21	1956	13.59	67
1907	4.41	21	1957	14.03	69
1908	4.54	22	1958	14.48	71
1909	4.67	23	1959	14.94	73
1910	4.81	23	1960	15.42	76
1911	4.94	24	1961	15.91	78
1912	5.07	25	1962	16.42	80
1913	5.19	25	1963	16.94	83
1914	5.32	26	1964	17.48	86
1915	5.45	27	1965	18.04	88
1916	5.58	27	1966	18.47	90
1917	5.72	28	1967	18.96	93
1918	5.86	29	1968	19.46	95
1919	6.03	29	1969	19.98	98
1920	6.09	30	1970	20.53	100
1921	6.21	30	1971	21.09	103
1922	6.37	31	1972	21.67	106
1923	6.46	31	1973	22.34	109
1924	6.59	32	1974	22.98	112
1925	6.72	33	1975	23.64	115
1926	6.86	33	1976	24.33	119
1927	7.00	34	1977	25.05	122
1928	7.14	35	1978	25.64	125
1929	7.28	35	1979	26.36	128
1930	7.43	36	1980	27.09	132
1931	7.57	37	1981	26.73*	130
1932	7.73	38	1982	27.19‡	132
1933	7.88	38	1983	27.52‡	134
1934	8.03	39	1984	28.22‡	137
1935	8.20	40	1985	28.62‡	139
1936	8.36	41	1986	29.19	142
1937	8.53	42			
1938	8.70	42			
1939	8.90	43			
1940	9.10	44			
1941	9.32	45			
1942	9.54	47			
1943	9.77	48			
1944	10.02	49			
1945	10.27	50			
1946	10.53	52			
1947	10.80	53			
1948*	10.85	53			
1949	11.09	54			

a. Mid-year estimates.

SOURCE: 1900-51 data from SALA-SNP, pp. 173-183; since 1952, data from IMF-IFS-Y, 1980, 1986 and UN-MB, June 1987; cf. SALA, 26–600, 624, and 626.

Table 606

COSTA RICA POPULATION ESTIMATE AND INDEX, 1900–86[a]

Year	M	1970 = 100	Year	M	1970 = 100
1900	.31	18	1950	.80	47
1901	.31	18	1951	.83	48
1902	.32	19	1952*	.92	54
1903	.32	19	1953	.95	55
1904	.33	19	1954	.99	58
1905	.34	20	1955	1.03	60
1906	.34	20	1956	1.07	62
1907	.35	21	1957	1.11	65
1908	.35	21	1958	1.15	67
1909	.36	21	1959	1.19	69
1910	.36	21	1960	1.25	75
1911	.37	22	1961	1.30	76
1912	.38	22	1962	1.35	78
1913	.38	22	1963	1.39	81
1914	.39	23	1964	1.44	84
1915	.39	23	1965	1.49	87
1916	.40	24	1966	1.54	89
1917	.40	24	1967	1.59	92
1918	.41	24	1968	1.63	95
1919	.42	25	1969	1.69	98
1920	.42	25	1970	1.73	100
1921	.43	25	1971	1.80	104
1922	.43	25	1972	1.84	107
1923	.44	26	1973	1.87	108
1924	.45	26	1974	1.92	111
1925	.46	27	1975	1.96	113
1926	.47	28	1976	2.01	116
1927	.47	28	1977	2.07	120
1928	.48	28	1978	2.12	123
1929	.49	29	1979	2.17	125
1930	.50	29	1980	2.25	130
1931	.51	30	1981	2.27	131
1932	.52	30	1982	2.32	134
1933	.53	31	1983	2.38	138
1934	.54	32	1984*	2.42	140
1935	.55	32	1985	2.49	144
1936	.56	33	1986	~	~
1937	.58	34			
1938	.59	35			
1939	.61	36			
1940	.62	36			
1941	.63	36			
1942	.65	37			
1943	.66	39			
1944	.68	40			
1945	.70	41			
1946	.71	41			
1947	.73	43			
1948	.75	44			
1949	.77	45			

a. Mid-year estimates.

SOURCE: 1900-51 data from SALA-SNP, pp. 173-183; since 1952, data from IMF-IFS-Y, 1980, 1986 and UN-MB, June 1987; cf. SALA, 26–600, 624 and 626.

Table 607

CUBA POPULATION ESTIMATE AND INDEX, 1900–86[a]

Year	M	1970 = 100	Year	M	1970 = 100
1900	1.60	19	1950	5.51	65
1901	1.68	20	1951	5.62	66
1902	1.76	21	1952	5.73	67
1903	1.84	22	1953*	6.04	71
1904	1.88	22	1954	6.16	72
1905	1.93	23	1955	6.28	73
1906	1.98	24	1956	6.41	75
1907	2.03	24	1957	6.54	76
1908	2.09	25	1958	6.76	79
1909	2.15	20	1959	6.90	81
1910	2.22	20	1960	7.03	83
1911	2.29	27	1961	7.13	84
1912	2.36	40	1962	7.25	85
1913	2.41	29	1963	7.41	87
1914	2.51	30	1964	7.61	89
1915	2.59	31	1965	7.81	92
1916	2.66	32	1966	7.99	94
1917	2.75	33	1967	8.14	96
1918	2.83	45	1968	8.28	97
1919	2.91	34	1969	8.42	99
1920	3.00	35	1970	8.55	100
1921	3.08	36	1971	8.69	102
1922	3.17	37	1972	8.86	104
1923	3.26	39	1973	9.04	106
1924	3.35	40	1974	9.19	108
1925	3.43	41	1975*	8.55	100
1926	3.52	42	1976	9.43	110
1927	3.61	43	1977	9.55	112
1928	3.51	41	1978	9.64	113
1929	3.58	42	1979	9.72	114
1930	3.65	43	1980	9.72	114
1931	3.96	47	1981	9.72	114
1932	3.96	47	1982	9.80	115
1933	3.96	47	1983	9.90	116
1934	4.04	48	1984	9.99	117
1935	4.07	48	1985	10.10	118
1936	4.11	48	1986	10.19	119
1937	4.17	49			
1938	4.23	50			
1939	4.25	50			
1940	4.29	51			
1941	4.33	51			
1942	4.37	52			
1943	4.78	56			
1944	4.85	57			
1945	4.93	58			
1946	5.04	59			
1947	5.15	61			
1948	5.27	62			
1949	5.39	63			

SOURCE: 1900-52 data from SALA-SNP, p. 176; 1953-74 data from Cuba, JUCEPLAN, AE, 1972, 1974, and 1975; since 1975, data from UN-MB, March 1985 and June 1987; cf. SALA, 26–600, 624, and 626.

Table 608

DOMINICAN REPUBLIC POPULATION ESTIMATE AND INDEX, 1900–86[a]

Year	M	1970 = 100	Year	M	1970 = 100
1900	.60	15	1950	2.24	55
1901	.61	15	1951	2.31	57
1902	.63	16	1952*	2.29	56
1903	.64	16	1953	2.37	58
1904	.66	17	1954	2.45	60
1905	.67	17	1955	2.54	63
1906	.68	17	1956	2.63	65
1907	.70	18	1957	2.73	67
1908	.71	18	1958	2.83	70
1909	.73	18	1959	2.93	72
1910	.74	19	1960	3.04	75
1911	.75	19	1961	3.12	77
1912	.77	19	1962	3.21	79
1913	.78	20	1963	3.31	82
1914	.80	20	1964	3.41	84
1915	.81	20	1965	3.51	87
1916	.82	21	1966	3.62	90
1917	.84	21	1967	3.72	92
1918	.85	21	1968	3.83	95
1919	.87	22	1969	3.95	98
1920	.88	22	1970	4.06	100
1921	.91	23	1971	4.18	103
1922	.95	24	1972	4.30	106
1923	.98	25	1973	4.43	110
1924	1.02	26	1974	4.56	113
1925	1.05	26	1975	4.70	116
1926	1.09	27	1976	4.89	120
1927	1.13	28	1977	5.03	124
1928	1.17	29	1978	5.17	127
1929	1.21	30	1979	5.30	131
1930	1.26	31	1980	5.44	134
1931	1.30	32	1981	5.58	137
1932	1.35	34	1982	5.74	141
1933	1.39	35	1983	5.96	147
1934	1.44	36	1984	6.10	150
1935	1.48	37	1985	6.24	154
1936	1.52	38	1986	6.42	158
1937	1.56	39			
1938	1.60	40			
1939	1.63	41			
1940	1.76	44			
1941	1.80	45			
1942	1.84	46			
1943	1.89	47			
1944	1.93	48			
1945	1.98	49			
1946	2.03	50			
1947	2.08	52			
1948	2.13	53			
1949	2.19	54			

a. Mid-year estimates.

SOURCE: 1900-51 data from SALA-SNP, pp. 173-183; since 1952, data from IMF-IFS-Y, 1980, 1986 and UM-MB, June 1987; cf. SALA, 26–600, 624, and 626.

Table 609

ECUADOR POPULATION ESTIMATE AND INDEX, 1900–86[a]

Year	M	1970 = 100	Year	M	1970 = 100
1900	1.30	22	1950	3.20	54
1901	1.31	22	1951	3.25	55
1902	1.32	22	1952*	3.43	58
1903	1.34	22	1953	3.53	59
1904	1.35	23	1954	3.64	61
1905	1.36	23	1955	3.75	63
1906	1.37	23	1956	3.87	65
1907	1.38	23	1957	3.98	67
1908	1.40	23	1958	4.11	69
1909	1.41	24	1959	4.23	71
1910	1.42	24	1960	4.36	73
1911	1.43	24	1961	4.50	76
1912	1.45	24	1962*	4.65	78
1913	1.46	24	1963	4.78	80
1914	1.47	25	1964	4.93	83
1915	1.48	25	1965	5.07	85
1916	1.49	25	1966	5.22	88
1917	1.51	25	1967	5.40	91
1918	1.52	26	1968	5.58	94
1919	1.53	26	1969	5.77	97
1920	1.54	26	1970	5.96	100
1921	1.57	26	1971	6.17	104
1922	1.61	27	1972	6.38	107
1923	1.65	28	1973	6.60	111
1924	1.69	28	1974	6.83	115
1925	1.72	29	1975	7.03‡	118
1926	1.76	30	1976	7.24	121
1927	1.80	30	1977	7.45	125
1928	1.84	31	1978	7.67	129
1929	1.90	32	1979	7.89	132
1930	1.94	33	1980	8.12	136
1931	2.00	34	1981	8.36	140
1932	2.05	34	1982	8.61	144
1933	2.10	35	1983	8.86	149
1934	2.14	36	1984	9.11	153
1935	2.20	37	1985	9.38	157
1936	2.25	38	1986	9.65	162
1937	2.30	39			
1938	2.36	40			
1939	2.41	40			
1940	2.47	41			
1941	2.52	42			
1942	2.58	43			
1943	2.64	44			
1944	2.71	45			
1945	2.78	47			
1946	2.85	48			
1947	2.94	49			
1948	3.02	51			
1949	3.10	52			

a. Mid-year estimates.

SOURCE: 1900-51 data from SALA-SNP, pp. 173-183; since 1952, data from IMF-IFS-Y, 1980, 1986 and UM-MB, June 1987; cf. SALA, 26–600, 624, and 626.

Table 610

EL SALVADOR POPULATION ESTIMATE AND INDEX, 1900–86[a]

Year	M	1970 = 100	Year	M	1970 = 100
1900	.80	24	1950	1.86	54
1901	.82	24	1951	1.90	56
1902	.84	25	1952*	1.97*	58
1903	.86	25	1953	2.02	59
1904	.87	26	1954	2.08	61
1905	.89	26	1955	2.14	63
1906	.91	27	1956	2.20	64
1907	.93	27	1957	2.26	66
1908	.95	28	1958	2.32	68
1909	.97	29	1959	2.39	70
1910	.99	29	1960	2.45	72
1911	1.00	29	1961*	2.51	73
1912	1.02	30	1962†	2.63	77
1913	1.04	31	1963†	2.72	79
1914	1.06	31	1964†	2.82	82
1915	1.07	32	1965†	2.93	86
1916	1.10	32	1966†	3.04	89
1917	1.11	33	1967†	3.15	92
1918	1.13	33	1968†	3.27	95
1919	1.15	34	1969†	3.36	98
1920	1.17	34	1970†	3.44	100
1921	1.19	35	1971†	3.55	104
1922	1.22	36	1972*	3.67	107
1923	1.24	36	1973	3.77	107
1924	1.27	37	1974	3.89	113
1925	1.30	38	1975	4.01	117
1926	1.33	39	1976	4.12	120
1927	1.35	40	1977	4.26	124
1928	1.39	41	1978	4.35	126
1929	1.41	41	1979	4.44	129
1930	1.44	42	1980	4.75	138
1931	1.46	43	1981	4.87	142
1932	1.47	43	1982	5.00	145
1933	1.49	44	1983	5.23‡	152
1934	1.51	44	1984	4.78	140
1935	1.53	45	1985	4.82	140
1936	1.55	45	1986	4.91	143
1937	1.				
1938	1.59	47			
1939	1.61	47			
1940	1.63	48			
1941	1.65	48			
1942	1.68	48			
1943	1.69	50			
1944	1.72	50			
1945	1.74	51			
1946	1.76	52			
1947	1.78	52			
1948	1.81	53			
1949	1.84	54			

a. Mid-year estimates.

SOURCE: 1900-51 data from SALA-SNP, pp. 173-183; since 1952, data from IMF-IFS-Y, 1980, 1986 and UN-MB, June 1987, cf. SALA, 26–600, 624, and 626.

Table 611

GUATEMALA POPULATION ESTIMATE AND INDEX, 1900–86[a]

Year	M	1970 = 100	Year	M	1970 = 100
1900	.89	19	1950*	2.81	58
1901	.91	19	1951	2.89	60
1902	.94	20	1952	2.98	61
1903	.96	21	1953	3.07	63
1904	.99	21	1954	3.18	66
1905	1.01	21	1955	3.29	68
1906	1.03	22	1956	3.39	70
1907	1.05	22	1957	3.49	72
1908	1.06	22	1958	3.61	74
1909	1.08	23	1959	3.72	77
1910	1.10	23	1960	3.83	79
1911	1.12	23	1961	3.95	81
1912	1.14	24	1962	4.06	84
1913	1.17	24	1963	4.19	86
1914	1.18	25	1964*	4.31	89
1915	1.20	25	1965[†]	4.41	91
1916	1.21	25	1966[†]	4.50	93
1917	1.23	26	1967[†]	4.70	95
1918	1.24	26	1968[†]	4.84	97
1919	1.26	26	1969	5.02	99
1920	1.27	26	1970	5.27	100
1921	1.32	27	1971	5.42	102
1922	1.37	28	1972	5.58	106
1923	1.42	29	1973	5.74	109
1924	1.47	31	1974*	6.05	115
1925	1.51	31	1975	6.24	118
1926	1.56	32	1976	6.43	122
1927	1.60	33	1977	6.63	126
1928	1.66	34	1978	6.84	130
1929	1.71	35	1979	7.05	134
1930	1.76	36	1980	7.26	138
1931	1.81	37	1981	7.48	142
1932	1.86	39	1982	7.70	146
1933	1.91	40	1983	7.46*	142
1934	1.94	40	1984	7.60	144
1935	1.98	40	1985	7.96	151
1936	2.02	42	1986	8.19	155
1937	2.07	43			
1938	2.11	44			
1939	2.15	44			
1940	2.20	45			
1941	2.25	47			
1942	2.30	47			
1943	2.34	48			
1944	2.39	49			
1945	2.44	50			
1946	2.50	52			
1947	2.57	53			
1948	2.64	54			
1949	2.72	56			

a. Mid-year estimates.

SOURCE: 1900-51 data from SALA-SNP, pp. 173-183; since 1952, data from IMF-IFS-Y, 1980, 1986, and UN-MB, June 1987; cf. SALA, 26–600, 624, and 626.

Table 612

HAITI POPULATION ESTIMATE AND INDEX, 1900–86[a]

Year	M	1970 = 100	Year	M	1970 = 100
1900	1.25	30	1950	3.39	80
1901	1.29	31	1951	3.44	82
1902	1.34	32	1952	3.51	83
1903	1.38	33	1953	3.58	84
1904	1.43	34	1954	3.65	86
1905	1.47	35	1955	3.72	88
1906	1.51	36	1956	3.80	90
1907	1.56	37	1957*,[a]	3.75	88
1908	1.56	37	1958[a]	3.70	87
1909	1.64	39	1959[a]	3.67	87
1910	1.69	40	1960*	3.62	85
1911	1.73	41	1961	3.68	87
1912	1.77	42	1962	3.74	88
1913	1.82	43	1963	3.79	89
1914	1.86	44	1964	3.85	91
1915	1.91	45	1965	3.91	92
1916	1.95	46	1966	3.97	94
1917	1.99	47	1967	4.03	95
1918	2.04	49	1968	4.10	97
1919	2.08	49	1969	4.16	99
1920	2.12	50	1970	4.24	100
1921	2.15	51	1971	4.31	103
1922	2.18	52	1972	4.37	103
1923	2.21	53	1973	4.44	105
1924	2.23	53	1974	4.51	107
1925	2.26	54	1975	4.58	108
1926	2.29	54	1976	4.67	110
1927	2.33	55	1977	4.75	112
1928	2.36	56	1978	4.83	114
1929	2.39	57	1979	4.92	116
1930	2.42	58	1980	5.01	118
1931	2.46	58	1981	5.10	120
1932	2.50	59	1982	5.05*	119
1933	2.54	60	1983	5.12[‡]	121
1934	2.57	61	1984	5.18[‡]	122
1935	2.61	62	1985	5.27[‡]	124
1936	2.65	63	1986	5.36	126
1937	2.70	64			
1938	2.74	65			
1939	2.79	66			
1940	2.83	67			
1941	2.88	68			
1942	2.94	70			
1943	2.98	71			
1944	3.03	72			
1945	3.09	73			
1946	3.14	74			
1947	3.20	76			
1948	3.26	77			
1949	3.32	79			

a. Mid-year estimates.

SOURCE: 1900–56 data from SALA-SNP, p. 179; 157–59, estimated by SALA with assumed impact of Duvalier's rise to power; since 1960, data from IMF-IFS-Y, 1986 and UN-MB, June 1987; cf. SALA, 26–600, 624, and 626.

Table 613

HONDURAS POPULATION ESTIMATE AND INDEX, 1900-86[a]

Year	M	1970 = 100	Year	M	1970 = 100
1900	.42	16	1950	1.43	54
1901	.44	17	1951	1.47	56
1902	.45	17	1952*	1.53*	58
1903	.47	18	1953	1.57	59
1904	.48	18	1954	1.62	61
1905	.50	19	1955	1.65	63
1906	.51	19	1956	1.68	64
1907	.52	20	1957	1.71	65
1908	.53	20	1958	1.75	66
1909	.54	20	1959	1.80	68
1910	.55	21	1960	1.85	70
1911	.56	21	1961	1.91	72
1912	.57	22	1962	1.97	75
1913	.58	22	1963	2.04	77
1914	.59	22	1964	2.11	80
1915	.60	23	1965	2.18	83
1916	.61	23	1966	2.26	86
1917	.63	24	1967	2.28	86
1918	.66	25	1968	2.31	88
1919	.69	26	1969	2.45	93
1920	.72	27	1970	2.64	100
1921	.74	28	1971	2.72	103
1922	.77	29	1972	2.81	106
1923	.80	30	1973	2.90	110
1924	.82	31	1974	2.99	113
1925	.85	32	1975	3.09	117
1926	.88	33	1976	3.20	121
1927	.89	34	1977	3.32	126
1928	.91	34	1978	3.44	130
1929	.93	35	1979	3.56	135
1930	.95	36	1980	3.69	140
1931	.97	37	1981	3.83	145
1932	.99	38	1982	3.96	150
1933	1.01	38	1983	4.09	155
1934	1.02	39	1984	4.23	160
1935	1.04	39	1985	4.37	165
1936	1.06	40	1986	~	~
1937	1.08	41			
1938	1.10	42			
1939	1.12	42			
1940	1.15	44			
1941	1.17	44			
1942	1.20	45			
1943	1.21	46			
1944	1.24	47			
1945	1.26	48			
1946	1.29	49			
1947	1.32	50			
1948	1.35	51			
1949	1.39	53			

a. Mid-year estimates.

SOURCE: 1900-51 data from SALA-SNP, pp. 173-183; since 1952, data from IMF-IFS-Y, 1980, 1986, and UN-MB, June 1987; cf. SALA, 26–600, 624 and 626.

Table 614

MEXICO POPULATION ESTIMATE AND INDEX, 1900-86[a]

Year	M	1970 = 100	Year	M	1970 = 100
1900	13.61	27	1950	25.79	51
1901	13.76	27	1951	25.59	50
1902	13.91	27	1952	27.85*	55
1903	14.07	28	1953	28.70	57
1904	14.21	28	1954	29.61	58
1905	14.36	28	1955	30.56	60
1906	14.52	29	1956	31.56	62
1907	14.68	29	1957	32.61	64
1908	14.84	29	1958	33.70	66
1909	15.00	30	1959	34.86	69
1910	15.16	30	1960	36.05	71
1911	15.33	30	1961	37.27	74
1912	15.51	31	1962	38.54	76
1913	15.37	30	1963	39.87	79
1914	15.09	30	1964	41.25	81
1915	14.64	29	1965	42.69	84
1916	14.03	28	1966	44.14	87
1917	13.90	27	1967	45.67	90
1918	14.00	28	1968	47.27	93
1919	14.15	28	1969	48.93	97
1920	14.15	28	1970	50.69	100
1921	14.34	28	1971	52.45	103
1922	14.44	28	1972	54.27	107
1923	14.69	29	1973	56.16	111
1924	14.95	29	1974	58.12	115
1925	15.20	30	1975	60.15	119
1926	15.47	31	1976	62.33	123
1927	15.74	31	1977	64.59	127
1928	16.01	32	1978*	65.43	129
1929	16.93	33	1979	67.42	133
1930	16.55	33	1980	69.35	137
1931	16.88	33	1981	71.19	140
1932	17.17	34	1982	73.01	144
1933	17.47	34	1983	75.10[‡]	148
1934	17.78	35	1984	76.79[‡]	151
1935	18.09	36	1985	78.52[‡]	155
1936	18.41	36	1986	79.56	157
1937	18.76	37			
1938	19.07	38			
1939	19.41	38			
1940	19.65	39			
1941	20.21	40			
1942	20.66	41			
1943	21.17	42			
1944	21.67	43			
1945	22.23	44			
1946	22.78	45			
1947	23.44	46			
1948	24.13	48			
1949	24.83	49			

a. Mid-year estimates.

SOURCE: 1900-51 data from SALA-SNP, pp. 173-183; since 1952, data from IMF-IFS-Y, 1980, 1986 and UN-MB, June 1987; cf. SALA, 26–600, 624, and 626.

Table 615

NICARAGUA POPULATION ESTIMATE AND INDEX, 1900–86[a]

Year	M	1970 = 100	Year	M	1970 = 100
1900	.42	23	1950	1.06	58
1901	.43	24	1951	1.09	60
1902	.45	25	1952*	1.12*	62
1903	.46	26	1953	1.15	63
1904	.48	27	1954	1.18	65
1905	.49	27	1955	1.22	67
1906	.51	28	1956	1.26	69
1907	.52	29	1957	1.29	71
1908	.52	29	1958	1.33	73
1909	.53	29	1959	1.37	75
1910	.54	30	1960	1.41	77
1911	.55	30	1961	1.45	80
1912	.56	31	1962	1.50	82
1913	.57	32	1963	1.54	85
1914	.58	32	1964	1.58	87
1915	.59	33	1965	1.62	89
1916	.60	33	1966	1.66	91
1917	.61	34	1967	1.70	93
1918	.62	34	1968	1.74	95
1919	.63	35	1969	1.79	98
1920	.64	35	1970	1.83	100
1921	.64	35	1971	1.89	104
1922	.65	36	1972	1.95	107
1923	.65	36	1973	2.01	110
1924	66	36	1974	2.08	114
1925	.66	36	1975	2.16	118
1926	.67	37	1976	2.24	122
1927	.67	37	1977	2.32	127
1928	.67	37	1978	2.41	132
1929	.68	38	1979	2.54	144
1930	.68	38	1980	2.73	149
1931	.69	38	1981	2.86	156
1932	.69	38	1982	2.96	162
1933	.70	39	1983	3.06	167
1934	.71	39	1984	3.16‡	173
1935	.73	40	1985	3.27‡	177
1936	.75	41	1986	~	~
1937	.77	42			
1938	.78	43			
1939	.81	45			
1940	.83	46			
1941	.84	46			
1942	.86	47			
1943	.88	48			
1944	.90	50			
1945	.92	51			
1946	.95	52			
1947	.98	54			
1948	1.00	55			
1949	1.03	57			

a. Mid-year estimates.

SOURCE: 1900-51 data from SALA-SNP, pp. 173-183; since 1952, data from IMF-IFS-Y, 1980, 1986, and UN-MB, June 1987; cf. SALA, 26–600, 624, and 626.

Table 616

PANAMA POPULATION ESTIMATE AND INDEX, 1900–86[a]

Year	M	1970 = 100	Year	M	1970 = 100
1900	.26	19	1950	.80	56
1901	.27	19	1951	.82	58
1902	.28	20	1952*	.84*	59
1903	.28	20	1953	.87	61
1904	.29	21	1954	.89	63
1905	.30	21	1955	.92	65
1906	.30	21	1956	.95	67
1907	.31	22	1957	.97	68
1908	.32	23	1958	1.00	70
1909	.33	23	1959	1.03	72
1910	.33	23	1960	1.06	75
1911	.34	24	1961	1.09	77
1912	.35	25	1962	1.13	79
1913	.36	26	1963	1.17	82
1914	.38	27	1964	1.20	84
1915	.39	28	1965	1.24	87
1916	.40	28	1966	1.27	89
1917	.41	29	1967	1.31	92
1918	.43	30	1968	1.35	95
1919	.44	31	1969	1.39	98
1920	.45	32	1970	1.43	100
1921	.45	32	1971	1.48	104
1922	.45	32	1972	1.52	107
1923	.45	32	1973	1.57	110
1924	.46	33	1974	1.62	114
1925	.46	33	1975	1.68	117
1926	.46	33	1976	1.72	120
1927	.46	33	1977	1.77	124
1928	.46	33	1978	1.81	127
1929	.47	33	1979	1.85	129
1930	.47	33	1980	1.90	133
1931	.49	35	1981	1.94	136
1932	.50	35	1982	2.04	143
1933	.52	37	1983	2.09	146
1934	.53	37	1984	2.13	149
1935	.55	39	1985	2.18	152
1936	.56	40	1986	2.23	156
1937	.58	41			
1938	.59	42			
1939	.61	43			
1940	.62	44			
1941	.64	45			
1942	.65	46			
1943	.67	47			
1944	.69	49			
1945	.70	49			
1946	.72	51			
1947	.74	52			
1948	.76	54			
1949	.78	55			

a. Mid-year estimates.

SOURCE: 1900-51 data from SALA-SNP, pp. 173-183; since 1952, data from IMF-IFS-Y, 1980, 1986 and UN-MB, June 1987; cf. SALA, 26–600, 624, and 626.

Table 617

PARAGUAY POPULATION ESTIMATE AND INDEX, 1900-86[a]

Year	M	1970 = 100	Year	M	1970 = 100
1900	.49	22	1950	1.40	61
1901	.51	23	1951	1.43	63
1902	.52	23	1952*	1.46	64
1903	.54	24	1953	1.50	66
1904	.56	25	1954	1.53	67
1905	.57	25	1955	1.57	69
1906	.58	26	1956	1.61	70
1907	.59	26	1957	1.68[‡]	73
1908	.60	26	1958	1.68[‡]	73
1909	.61	27	1959	1.71[‡]	74
1910	.62	27	1960	1.75	76
1911	.63	28	1961	1.80	78
1912	.64	28	1962	1.85	80
1913	.65	29	1963	1.91	83
1914	.66	29	1964	1.97	86
1915	.66	29	1965	2.03	88
1916	.67	30	1966	2.07	90
1917	.68	30	1967	2.13	93
1918	.69	30	1968	2.18	95
1919	.69	30	1969	2.24	97
1920	.70	31	1970	2.30	100
1921	.72	32	1971	2.36	103
1922	.73	32	1972	2.43	106
1923	.75	33	1973*	2.50	109
1924	.77	34	1974	2.57	112
1925	.79	35	1975	2.69	117
1926	.80	35	1976	2.78	121
1927	.82	36	1977	2.87	125
1928	.84	37	1978	2.97	129
1929	.86	38	1979	3.07	133
1930	.88	39	1980	3.17	138
1931	.90	40	1981	3.27	142
1932	.92	40	1982	3.37	147
1933	.94	41	1983	3.47	151
1934	.97	43	1984	3.28*	143
1935	.99	43	1985	3.68*	160
1936	1.01	44	1986	3.81	166
1937	1.04	46			
1938	1.06	46			
1939	1.09	48			
1940	1.11	49			
1941	1.14	50			
1942	1.16	51			
1943	1.19	52			
1944	1.22	53			
1945	1.25	55			
1946	1.28	56			
1947	1.31	57			
1948	1.34	59			
1949	1.37	60			

a. Mid-year estimates.

SOURCE: 1900–51 data from SALA-SNP, pp. 173–183; since 1952 data from IMF-IFS-Y, 1980, 1986 and UN-MB, June 1987; cf. SALA, 26–600, 624, and 626.

Table 618

PERU POPULATION ESTIMATE AND INDEX, 1900-86[a]

Year	M	1970 = 100	Year	M	1970 = 100
1900	3.00	23	1950	7.97	60
1901	3.10	23	1951	8.12	61
1902	3.20	24	1952*	8.27	62
1903	3.30	25	1953	8.43	63
1904	3.40	26	1954	8.60	64
1905	3.50	26	1955	8.79	65
1906	3.60	27	1956	9.00	67
1907	3.70	28	1957	9.23	69
1908	3.80	29	1958	9.48	70
1909	3.90	29	1959	9.75	72
1910	4.00	30	1960	10.02	74
1911	4.10	31	1961	10.32	77
1912	4.19	32	1962	10.63	79
1913	4.27	32	1963	10.96	82
1914	4.35	33	1964	11.30	84
1915	4.43	33	1965	11.65	87
1916	4.51	34	1966	12.01	90
1917	4.59	35	1967	12.31	92
1918	4.67	35	1968	12.67	94
1919	4.75	36	1969	13.05	97
1920	4.83	36	1970	13.45	100
1921	4.91	37	1971	13.59	101
1922	4.99	38	1972	13.95	104
1923	5.07	38	1973	14.35	107
1924	5.15	39	1974	15.16	113
1925	5.23	39	1975	15.47	115
1926	5.31	40	1976	15.57	116
1927	5.40	41	1977	15.99	119
1928	5.48	41	1978	16.41	122
1929	5.57	42	1979	16.85	125
1930	5.65	42	1980	17.30	129
1931	5.74	43	1981	17.75	132
1932	5.84	44	1982	18.23	136
1933	5.94	45	1983	18.71	139
1934	6.04	45	1984	19.20	143
1935	6.13	46	1985	19.70[‡]	146
1936	6.24	47	1986	20.21	150
1937	6.35	48			
1938	6.46	48			
1939	6.57	49			
1940	6.68	50			
1941	6.80	51			
1942	6.92	52			
1943	7.04	53			
1944	7.16	54			
1945	7.29	55			
1946	7.42	56			
1947	7.55	57			
1948	7.68	58			
1949	7.82	59			

a. Mid-year estimates.

SOURCE: 1900–51 data from SALA-SNP, pp. 173–183; since 1952, data from IMF-IFS-Y, 1980, 1986 and UN-MB, June 1987; cf. SALA, 26–600, 624, and 626.

Table 619

URUGUAY POPULATION ESTIMATE AND INDEX, 1900-86[a]

Year	M	1970 = 100	Year	M	1970 = 100
1900	.96	35	1950	2.20	81
1901	.97	36	1951	2.22	81
1902	.90	33	1952*	2.26*	83
1903	1.02	37	1953	2.30	84
1904	1.04	38	1954	2.33	85
1905	1.07	39	1955	2.36	86
1906	1.10	40	1956	2.40	88
1907	1.14	42	1957	2.43	89
1908	1.05	38	1958	2.46	90
1909	1.10	40	1959	2.50	92
1910	1.13	41	1960	2.54	93
1911	1.18	43	1961	2.58	95
1912	1.23	45	1962	2.61	96
1913	1.28	47	1963	2.65	97
1914	1.32	48	1964	2.68	98
1915	1.35	49	1965	2.71	99
1916	1.38	51	1966	2.75	101
1917	1.41	52	1967	2.69[‡]	99
1918	1.43	52	1968	2.70[‡]	99
1919	1.46	53	1969	2.71[‡]	99
1920	1.48	54	1970	2.73[‡]	100
1921	1.50	55	1971	2.74[‡]	100
1922	1.52	56	1972	2.75[‡]	101
1923	1.54	56	1973	2.76[‡]	101
1924	1.55	57	1974	2.77[‡]	101
1925	1.57	58	1975*	2.83	104
1926	1.60	59	1976	2.85	104
1927	1.63	60	1977	2.86	105
1928	1.67	61	1978	2.88	105
1929	1.70	62	1979	2.89	106
1930	1.73	63	1980	2.91	107
1931	1.76	64	1981	2.93	107
1932	1.79	66	1982	2.95	108
1933	1.82	67	1983	2.97	109
1934	1.84	67	1984	2.99	109
1935	1.87	68	1985	3.01[‡]	110
1936	1.89	69	1986	2.98	109
1937	1.91	70			
1938	1.93	71			
1939	1.95	71			
1940	1.97	72			
1941	1.99	73			
1942	2.01	74			
1943	2.03	74			
1944	2.06	75			
1945	2.08	76			
1946	2.10	77			
1947	2.12	78			
1948	2.14	78			
1949	2.17	79			

a. Mid-year estimates.

SOURCE: 1900-51 data from SALA-PNP, pp. 173-183; since 1952, dated from IMF-IFS-Y, 1980, 1986 and UN-MB, June 1987; cf. SALA, 26-600, 624, and 626.

Table 620

VENEZUELA POPULATION ESTIMATE AND INDEX, 1900-86[a]

Year	M	1970 = 100	Year	M	1970 = 100
1900	2.45	24	1950	4.97	48
1901	2.45	24	1951	5.14	50
1902	2.46	24	1952*	5.39	52
1903	2.47	24	1953	5.62	55
1904	2.47	24	1954	5.85	57
1905	2.49	24	1955	6.09	59
1906	2.51	24	1956	6.33	62
1907	2.53	25	1957	6.57	64
1908	2.55	25	1958	6.83	66
1909	2.57	25	1959	7.09	69
1910	2.60	25	1960	7.35	71
1911	2.61	25	1961	7.61	74
1912	2.64	26	1962	7.86[‡]	76
1913	2.66	26	1963	8.12	79
1914	2.68	26	1964	8.40	82
1915	2.71	26	1965	8.71	85
1916	2.73	27	1966	9.03	88
1917	2.75	27	1967	9.31	91
1918	2.77	27	1968	9.62	94
1919	2.79	27	1969	9.94	97
1920	2.82	27	1970	10.28	100
1912	2.84	28	1971	10.61	103
1922	2.87	28	1972	10.94	106
1923	2.90	28	1973	11.28	110
1924	2.93	29	1974	11.63	113
1925	2.95	29	1975*	12.67	123
1926	2.98	29	1976	13.12	128
1927	3.01	29	1977	13.59	132
1928	3.04	30	1978	14.07	137
1929	3.08	30	1979	14.55	142
1930	3.12	30	1980	15.02	146
1931	3.15	31	1981	15.48	151
1932	3.19	31	1982	15.94	155
1933	3.23	31	1983	16.39	159
1934	3.26	32	1984	16.85	164
1935	3.30	32	1985	17.32	168
1936	3.38	33	1986	17.79	173
1937	3.46	34			
1938	3.55	35			
1939	3.63	35			
1940	3.71	36			
1941	3.80	37			
1942	3.91	38			
1943	4.03	39			
1944	4.15	40			
1945	4.27	42			
1946	4.39	43			
1947	4.55	44			
1948	4.69	46			
1949	4.83	47			

a. Mid-year estimates.

SOURCE: 1900-51 data from SALA-PNP, pp. 173-183; since 1952, data from IMF-IFS-Y, 1980, 1986 and UN-MB, June 1987; cf. SALA, 26-600, 624, and 626.

Table 621

UNITED STATES POPULATION ESTIMATE
AND INDEX, 1900–86[a]

Year	M	1970 = 100	Year	M	1970 = 100
1900	76.09	37	1950	152.27	74
1901	77.59	38	1951	154.88	76
1902	79.16	39	1952*	157.55	77
1903	80.63	39	1953	160.18	78
1904	82.17	40	1954	163.03	80
1905	83.82	41	1955	165.93	81
1906	84.44	41	1956	168.90	82
1907	87.00	42	1957	171.98	84
1908	88.71	43	1958	174.88	85
1909	90.49	44	1959	177.83	87
1910	92.40	45	1960*	180.68	88
1911	93.87	46	1961	183.69	90
1912	95.33	46	1962	186.54	91
1913	97.23	47	1963	189.24	92
1914	99.12	48	1964	191.89	94
1915	100.55	49	1965	194.30	95
1916	101.97	50	1966	196.56	96
1917	103.27	50	1967	198.71	97
1918	103.20	50	1968	200.71	98
1919	104.51	51	1969	202.68	99
1920	106.47	52	1970	205.05	100
1921	108.54	53	1971	207.66	101
1922	110.95	54	1972	209.90	102
1923	111.95	55	1973	211.91	103
1924	114.11	56	1974	213.85	104
1925	115.83	56	1975	215.97	105
1926	117.40	57	1976	218.04	106
1927	119.04	58	1977	220.24	107
1928	120.50	59	1978	222.59	109
1929	121.77	59	1979	225.06	110
1930	123.07	60	1980	227.66	111
1931	124.84	61	1981	229.81	112
1932	124.84	61	1982	232.06	113
1933	125.58	61	1983	234.50	114
1934	126.37	62	1984	236.68	115
1935	127.25	62	1985	239.28	117
1936	128.05	62	1986	241.60	118
1937	128.83	63			
1938	129.83	63			
1939	130.88	64			
1940	132.59	65			
1941	133.89	65			
1942	135.36	66			
1943	137.25	67			
1944	138.92	68			
1945	140.47	69			
1946	141.94	69			
1947	144.70	71			
1948	147.21	72			
1949	149.77	73			

a. Mid-year estimates.

SOURCE: 1900–51 data from SALA-SNP, pp. 173–183; since 1952, data from
    IMF-IFS-Y, 1980, 1986 and UN-MB, June 1987; cf. SALA, 26–600, 624, and 626.

Table 622

INDEX OF ESTIMATED POPULATION, 20 LRC, 1900–80

(1970 = 100)

	Country	1900	1910	1920	1930	1940	1950	1960	1970	1980
A.	ARGENTINA	19	29	38	51	60	72	84	100	119
B.	BOLIVIA	39	43	47	52	59	66	83	100	122
C.	BRAZIL	19	24	30	36	44	56	75	100	131
D.	CHILE	32	36	40	47	54	65	81	100	118
E.	COLOMBIA	19	23	30	36	44	56	76	100	132
F.	COSTA RICA	18	21	25	29	36	47	75	100	130
G.	CUBA	19	20	35	43	51	65	83	100	114
H.	DOMINICAN REP.	15	19	22	31	44	56	75	100	134
I.	ECUADOR	22	24	26	33	41	54	73	100	140
J.	EL SALVADOR	24	29	34	42	48	54	72	100	138
K.	GUATEMALA	19	23	26	36	45	58	79	100	149
L.	HAITI	30	40	50	58	67	80	85	100	118
M.	HONDURAS	16	21	27	36	44	54	70	100	140
N.	MEXICO	27	30	28	33	39	51	71	100	137
O.	NICARAGUA	23	30	35	38	46	58	77	100	149
P.	PANAMA	19	23	32	33	44	56	75	100	133
Q.	PARAGUAY	22	27	31	39	49	61	76	100	138
R.	PERU	23	30	36	42	50	60	74	100	129
S.	URUGUAY	35	41	54	63	72	81	93	100	107
T.	VENEZUELA	24	25	27	30	36	48	71	100	146
	LATIN AMERICA	24	28	34	40	49	60	77	100	131
	UNITED STATES	37	45	52	60	65	74	88	100	111

SOURCE: SALA, 26–601 through 621; cf. SALA, 26–600, 624, and 626.

Table 623

POPULATION ESTIMATES BY DECADE, 20 LRC, 1900–80

(M)

	Country	1900	1910	1920	1930	1940	1950	1960	1970	1980
A.	ARGENTINA	4.61	6.80	8.97	12.05	14.17	17.07	19.92	23.75	28.24
B.	BOLIVIA	1.77	1.95	2.14	2.40	2.70	3.01	3.82	4.58	5.60
C.	BRAZIL	17.98	22.22	27.40	33.57	41.11	52.18	69.72	92.52	121.27
D.	CHILE	2.96	3.34	3.79	4.37	5.06	6.07	7.58	9.37	11.10
E.	COLOMBIA	3.89	4.81	6.09	7.43	9.10	11.33	15.42	20.53	27.09
F.	COSTA RICA	.31	.36	.42	.50	.62	.80	1.25	1.73	2.25
G.	CUBA	1.60	2.22	3.00	3.65	4.29	5.51	7.03	8.55	9.72
H.	DOMINICAN REP.	.60	.74	.88	1.26	1.76	2.24	3.04	4.06	5.44
I.	ECUADOR	1.30	1.42	1.54	1.94	2.47	3.20	4.36	5.96	8.35
J.	EL SALVADOR	.80	.99	1.17	1.44	1.63	1.86	2.45	3.44	4.75
K.	GUATEMALA	.89	1.10	1.27	1.76	2.20	2.81	3.83	4.88	7.26
L.	HAITI	1.25	1.69	2.12	2.42	2.83	3.39	3.62	4.24	5.01
M.	HONDURAS	.42	.55	.72	.95	1.15	1.43	1.85	2.64	3.69
N.	MEXICO	13.61	15.16	14.15	16.55	19.65	25.79	36.05	50.69	69.35
O.	NICARAGUA	.42	.54	.64	.68	.83	1.06	1.41	1.83	2.73
P.	PANAMA	.26	.33	.45	.47	.62	.80	1.06	1.43	1.90
Q.	PARAGUAY	.49	.62	.70	.88	1.11	1.40	1.75	2.30	3.17
R.	PERU	3.00	4.00	4.83	5.65	6.68	7.97	10.02	13.45	17.30
S.	URUGUAY	.96	1.13	1.48	1.73	1.97	2.20	2.54	2.73	2.91
T.	VENEZUELA	2.45	2.60	2.82	3.12	3.71	4.97	7.35	10.28	15.02
	LATIN AMERICA	59.56	72.56	84.58	102.82	123.66	155.09	204.07	268.96	352.15
	UNITED STATES	76.09	92.40	106.47	123.07	132.59	152.27	180.68	205.05	227.66

SOURCE: SALA, 26–601 through 621; cf. SALA, 26–600, 624, and 626.

Table 624

CELADE POPULATION ESTIMATES AND PROJECTIONS BY DECADE, 20 LRC, 1920–2020

(M)

	Country	1920	1930	1940	1950	1960	1970	1980	1990	2000	2010	2020
A.	ARGENTINA	8,861	11,896	14,169	17,150	20,616	23,962	28,237	32,880	37,197	41,507	45,564
B.	BOLIVIA	1,918	2,153	2,508	2,766	3,428	4,325	5,570	7,314	9,724	12,820	16,401
C.	BRAZIL	27,404	33,568	41,233	53,444	72,594	95,847	121,286	150,368	179,487	207,454	233,817
D.	CHILE	3,783	4,424	5,147	6,091	7,609	9,456	11,127	12,987	14,792	16,348	17,724
E.	COLOMBIA	6,057	7,350	9,077	11,597	15,538	20,803	25,794	31,820	37,999	43,840	49,259
F.	COSTA RICA	421	499	619	858	1,236	1,732	2,279	2,937	3,596	4,239	4,837
G.	CUBA	2,950	3,837	4,566	5,858	7,029	8,572	9,732	10,540	11,718	12,584	13,307
H.	DOMINICAN REP.	1,140	1,400	1,759	2,409	3,224	4,289	5,558	6,971	8,407	9,945	11,465
I.	ECUADOR	1,898	2,160	2,586	3,310	4,413	6,051	8,123	10,782	13,939	17,403	21,064
J.	EL SALVADOR	1,168	1,443	1,633	1,940	2,574	3,582	4,797	6,484	8,708	11,188	13,769
K.	GUATEMALA	1,450	1,771	2,201	2,969	3,964	5,246	6,917	9,197	12,222	15,827	19,706
L.	HAITI	2,124	2,422	2,825	3,097	3,723	4,605	5,809	7,509	9,860	12,868	16,438
M.	HONDURAS	783	948	1,119	1,401	1,943	2,639	3,691	5,105	6,978	9,394	11,972
N.	MEXICO	14,500	16,589	19,815	27,376	37,073	51,176	69,393	89,012	109,180	128,241	145,956
O.	NICARAGUA	639	742	893	1,098	1,493	2,053	2,771	3,871	5,261	6,824	8,435
P.	PANAMA	429	502	595	839	1,105	1,487	1,956	2,418	2,893	3,324	3,701
Q.	PARAGUAY	699	880	1,111	1,371	1,778	2,290	3,168	4,231	5,405	6,653	7,930
R.	PERU	4,862	5,651	6,681	7,632	9,931	13,193	17,295	22,332	27,952	33,479	38,647
S.	URUGUAY	1,391	1,704	1,947	2,239	2,538	2,808	2,908	3,128	3,364	3.581	3,782
T.	VENEZUELA	2,408	2,950	3,710	5,009	7,502	10,604	15,024	19,735	24,715	30,006	35,394
	LATIN AMERICA	84,885	102,889	124,194	158,454	209,311	274,720	351,435	439,621	533,397	627,525	719,169
	UNITED STATES	106,470	123,070	132,590	152,270	180,680	205,050	227,660	244,000	260,000	275,000	290,000

SOURCE: CELADE-BD, 23 (1979); and CELADE-BD, 35 (1985). For higher range
estimates, see CELADE data quoted in SALA, 22–624 and 625. U.S. data are from
SALA, 26–621 through 1980, then from USBC-SA, 1978, p. 7.

Table 625

IDB TOTAL POPULATION AND AVERAGE ANNUAL GROWTH RATES, 19 L, 1960–85[a]

	Country	Population (T)						AA–GR (%)		
		1960	1970	1980	1983	1984	1985[†]	1961–70	1971–80	1981–85
A.	ARGENTINA	20,611	23,748	27,127	29,627	30,097	30,564	1.4	1.7	1.7
B.	BOLIVIA	3,294	4,295	5,600	6,082	6,253	6,429	2.7	2.7	2.8
C.	BRAZIL	72,325	92,771	118,998	128,226	131,185	134,500	2.5	2.5	2.5
D.	CHILE	7,596	9,363	11,104	11,682	11,878	12,081	2.1	1.7	1.7
E.	COLOMBIA	17,213	21,202	26,199	27,880	26,199	26,526	2.1	1.8	1.2
F.	COSTA RICA	1,320	1,713	2,217	2,378	2,460	2,523	2.6	2.5	2.6
H.	DOMINICAN REP.	3,441	4,276	5,546	6,016	6,102	6,257	2.2	2.6	2.4
I.	ECUADOR	4,429	5,960	8,051	8,836	9,115	9,378	3.0	3.1	3.1
J.	EL SALVADOR	2,661	3,539	4,513	4,627	4,756	4,857	2.9	2.5	1.5
K.	GUATEMALA	3,921	5,206	6,913	7,527	7,740	7,963	2.9	2.9	2.9
L.	HAITI	3,575	4,231	5,016	5,268	5,403	5,498	1.7	1.7	1.9
M.	HONDURAS	1,988	2,709	3,707	4,092	4,232	4,369	3.1	3.2	3.3
N.	MEXICO	37,073	51,176	68,544	74,824	77,043	79,327	3.3	3.0	3.0
O.	NICARAGUA	1,503	1,970	2,767	3,058	3,163	3,272	2.7	3.5	3.4
P.	PANAMA	1,220	1,497	1,955	2,034	2,134	2,183	2.1	2.4	2.2
Q.	PARAGUAY	1,959	2,290	3,168	3,472	3,576	3,691	1.6	3.3	3.1
R.	PERU	10,385	13,413	17,325	18,707	19,198	19,696	2.6	2.6	2.6
S.	URUGUAY	2,617	2,765	2,859	2,961	2,931	2,931	.6	.6	.5
T.	VENEZUELA	7,963	11,148	15,024	16,400	16,851	17,355	3.4	3.0	2.9

a. Data have been revised in accordance with the information furnished by the countries,
including results of recent censuses.

SOURCE: Adapted from IDB-SPTF, 1986, table 1, p. 389.

Table 626

POPULATION PROJECTIONS, 20 L, 1985–2025

(T)

	Country	Total Population			Population Age 15–24		
		1985	2000	2025	1985	2000	2025
A.	ARGENTINA	30,564	37,197	47,421	4,770	6,635	7,395
B.	BOLIVIA	6,371	9,742	18,294	1,207	1,890	3,686
C.	BRAZIL	135,564	179,487	245,809	27,566	33,671	38,854
D.	CHILE	12,038	14,792	18,301	2,455	2,380	2,639
E.	COLOMBIA	28,714	37,999	51,718	6,261	7,192	8,259
F.	COSTA RICA	2,600	3,596	5,099	561	676	812
G.	CUBA	10,038	11,718	13,575	2,251	1,555	1,750
H.	DOMINICAN REP.	6,243	8,407	12,154	1,388	1,621	1,957
I.	ECUADOR	9,378	13,939	22,910	1,913	2,695	4,017
J.	EL SALVADOR	5,552	8,708	15,048	1,105	1,738	2,799
K.	GUATEMALA	7,963	12,222	21,668	1,541	2,479	4,228
L.	HAITI	6,585	9,860	18,312	1,293	1,929	3,677
M.	HONDURAS	4,372	6,978	13,293	864	1,433	2,680
N.	MEXICO	78,996	109,180	154,085	16,552	22,095	24,666
O.	NICARAGUA	3,272	5,261	9,219	656	1,066	1,752
P.	PANAMA	2,180	2,893	3,862	460	536	593
Q.	PARAGUAY	3,681	5,405	8,552	750	1,074	1,519
R.	PERU	19,698	27,952	41,006	3,989	5,454	6,828
S.	URUGUAY	3,012	3,364	3,875	486	536	563
T.	VENEZUELA	17,317	24,715	37,999	3,550	4,794	6,407

SOURCE: *Population Bulletin*, vol. 41, no. 3, July 1986, p. 45.

Table 627

NATIONAL POPULATION CENSUS SERIES, 20 L, 1774-1984[a]

A. ARGENTINA		G. CUBA		N. MEXICO	
1869	1,737,076	1774	171,620	1895	12,632,427
1895	3,954,911	1792	272,300	1900	13,607,259
1914	7,885,237	1817	572,363	1910	15,160,369
1947	15,897,127	1827	704,487	1921	14,334,780
1960	20,010,539	1841	1,007,624	1930	16,552,722
1970	23,362,204[‡]	1861	1,396,530	1940	19,653,552
1980	27,947,446	1877	1,509,291	1950	25,791,017
		1887	1,631,687	1960	34,923,129
B. BOLIVIA[1]		1899	1,572,797	1970	48,225,238
1831	1,018,900	1907	2,048,980	1980	66,846,833
1835	992,700	1919	2,889,004		
1845	1,031,500	1931	3,962,344	O. NICARAGUA	
1854	1,544,300	1943	4,778,583	1778	106,926
1882	1,097,600	1953	5,829,029	1867	257,000
1900	1,696,400	1970	8,569,121[e]	1906	505,377
1950	3,019,031	1981	9,723,605	1920	638,119
1976	4,613,486			1940	983,000
		H. DOMINICAN REP.		1950	1,057,023
C. BRAZIL		1920	894,665	1963	1,535,588
1872	10,112,061	1935	1,479,417	1971	1,877,952[e]
1890	14,333,915	1950	2,135,872		
1900	17,318,556	1960	3,047,070	P. PANAMA[2]	
1920	30,635,605	1970	4,006,405	1911	336,742
1940	41,236,315	1981	5,647,977[‡]	1920	446,098
1950	51,944,397			1930	467,459
1960	70,119,071	I. ECUADOR		1940	622,576
1970	92,341,556[a]	1950	3,202,757	1950	805,285
1980	118,674,604	1962	4,476,000	1960	1,075,541
		1974	6,521,710	1970	1,428,082[d]
D. CHILE		1982	8,050,630[f]	1980	1,824,796[j]
1835	1,010,336				
1843	1,083,801	J. EL SALVADOR		Q. PARAGUAY	
1854	1,439,120	1930	1,434,361	1936	931,799
1865	1,819,223	1950	1,855,917	1950	1,328,452
1875	2,075,971	1961	2,510,984	1962	1,819,103
1885	2,507,005	1971	3,554,648	1972	2,357,955
1895	2,695,625			1982	3,029,830
1907	3,231,022	K. GUATEMALA			
1920	3,730,235	1880	1,224,602	R. PERU	
1930	4,287,445	1893	1,364,678	1836	1,373,736
1940	5,023,539	1921	2,004,900 ***	1850	2,001,203
1952	5,932,995	1930	1,771,000	1862	2,460,684[c]
1960	7,374,115	1935	1,996,000	1876	2,651,840[c]
1970	8,884,768	1940	2,222,000	1940	6,208,000
1982	11,275,440	1950	2,790,686	1961	9,906,746
		1964	4,284,473	1972	14,121,564[h,]
E. COLOMBIA		1973	5,160,221[e]	1981	17,005,210[g]
1825	1,223,598	1981	6,054,227[‡,e]		
1835	1,686,038			S. URUGUAY	
1843	1,955,264	L. HAITI		1852	131,969
1851	2,243,730	1918	1,631,260	1860	229,480
1864	2,694,487	1950	3,097,220	1908	1,042,686
1870	2,391,984	1971	4,329,991	1963	2,595,510
1905	4,143,632	1982	5,053,792[‡,e]	1975	2,788,429
1912	5,072,604				
1918	5,855,077	M. HONDURAS		T. VENEZUELA	
1928	7,851,000[b]	1791	93,505	1873	1,784,194
1938	8,701,816	1801	130,000	1881	2,075,545
1951	11,548,172	1881	307,289	1891	2,323,527
1964	17,484,508	1887	331,917	1920	2,365,098
1973	22,551,811	1905	500,136	1926	2,890,631
		1910	553,446	1936	3,491,159
F. COSTA RICA		1916	605,997	1941	3,850,771
1864	120,499	1926	700,811	1950	5,034,838
1883	182,073	1930	854,184	1961	7,523,999
1892	243,205	1935	962,000	1971	10,721,522
1927	471,524	1940	1,107,859	1981	14,516,735
1950	800,875	1945	1,200,542		
1963	1,336,274	1950	1,368,605		
1973	1,871,780[e]	1961	1,884,765		
1984	2,416,809[e]	1974	2,656,948[e]		

1. Territorial variations have been taken into account — the figures refer to the population within the present boundaries of the country.
2. Includes the indigenous population.

a. Territorial changes have not necessarily been taken into account.
b. This census was not accepted by the National Congress because it was believed that the figures for certain civil divisions were inflated.
c. Excludes the population of the province of Arica and the department of Tarapaca.
d. Excludes former U.S. Canal Zone.
e. Dejure population.
f. Excluding nomadic Indian tribes.

g. Excluding Indian jungle population.
h. Adjusted census total.
i. Excluding Indian jungle population estimated at 39,800 in 1972.
j. Census data have not been adjusted for underenumeration estimated at 6.6%.

SOURCE: Since 1900, SALA-SNP, table VIII-1; BE, 96, 109, 114, 122; IASI-AC, 1974; Cuban, El Salvadoran, Guatemalan, Mexican, and Venezuelan statistical agencies. Before 1900, IASI, *Noticiero*, January 3, 1965. Data for the 1970s and 1980s revised with figures from UN-DY, 1979–1985, table 3, except Chile from SALA-LAPUA, p. 178 and p. 430; Mexico data from Instituto Nacional de Estadística, *Resumen General Abreviado* (1984); and Peru data from SALA, 25–645.

Table 628

ARGENTINA POPULATION CENSUS AND DENSITY
OF MAJOR CIVIL DIVISIONS
(1980)

Division	Population	%	Density Per km²
Total	27,949,480	100.0	10
Capital Federal	2,922,829	10.4	14,614
Provinces			
Buenos Aires	10,865,408	38.9	35
Catamarca	207,717	.7	2

Continued in SALA, 23–626.

Table 629

BOLIVIA POPULATION CENSUS AND DENSITY
OF MAJOR CIVIL DIVISIONS
(1976‡)

Division	Population	%	Density Per km²
Total	4,647,816	100.0	4
Departments			
Beni	167,969	3.6	1
Chuquisaca	357,244	7.7	6

Continued in SALA, 23–627.

Table 630

BRAZIL POPULATION CENSUS AND DENSITY
OF MAJOR CIVIL DIVISIONS[1]
(1980‡)

Division	Population	%	Density Per km²
Total	121,113,084	100.0	14
Distrito Federal	1,202,683	1.0	207
States			
Acre	306,916	.2	2
Alagoas	2,011,956	1.7	73

Continued in SALA, 24–628.

Table 631

CHILE POPULATION CENSUS AND DENSITY
OF MAJOR CIVIL DIVISIONS
(1982)

Division	Population	%	Density Per km^2
Total	11,275,440	100.0	15
Regions			
Antofagasta	341,203	3.0	3
Araucanía	692,924	6.1	22

Continued in SALA, 23–629.

Table 632

COLOMBIA POPULATION CENSUS AND DENSITY
OF MAJOR CIVIL DIVISIONS
(1973)

Division	Population	%	Density Per km^2
Total	21,070,115	100.0	18
Bogotá, D.E.	2,855,065	13.6	1,799
Departments			
Antioquia	2,976,153	14.1	47
Atlántico	958,560	4.5	293

Continued in SALA, 23–630.

Table 633

COSTA RICA POPULATION BY PROVINCE, 1864, 1883, 1892, 1927

Province	1864 Population	%	1883 Population	%	1892 Population	%	1927 Population	%
San José	37,206	30.88	56,162	30.85	76,718	31.54	153,183	32.49
Cartago	22,519	18.69	30,428	16.71	37,973	15.61	70,198	14.89
Heredia	17,791	14.76	25,818	14.18	31,611	13.00	38,407	8.15
Alajuela	27,171	22.55	45,205	24.83	57,203	23.52	96,577	20.48
Puntarenas	4,836	4.01	7,700	4.23	12,167	5.00	28,739	6.09
Guanacaste	10,431	8.66	14,902	8.18	20,049	8.24	51,142	10.85
Limón	545[a]	.45	1,858	1.02	7,484	3.08	32,278	6.85
Total	120,499	100.00	182,073	100.00	243,205	100.00	471,524	100.00

a. The population of the Atlantic Coast can be found under Cartago in the 1864 census.

SOURCE: DGEC, *Censos de población* 1864, 1883, 1892, 1927.

Table 634

COSTA RICA POPULATION CENSUS AND DENSITY
OF MAJOR CIVIL DIVISIONS
(1982)

Division	Population	%	Density Per km^2
Total	2,403,781	100.0	47.0
Provinces			
San José	890,443	37.0	17.5
Alajuela	413,765	17.2	8.1
Cartago	259,916	10.8	5.1
Heredia	171,688	7.1	3.4
Guanacaste	228,249	9.5	4.5
Puntarenas	286,082	11.9	5.6
Limón	153,638	6.4	3.2

SOURCE: Costa Rica, DGEC, AE, 1984.

Table 635

CUBA POPULATION CENSUS AND DENSITY
OF MAJOR CIVIL DIVISIONS
(1981‡)

Division	Population	%	Density Per km^2
Total	9,706,369	100.0	88
Ciudad de la Habana	1,924,886	19.8	2,598
Provinces			
Camagüey	664,566	6.9	47
Ciego de Avila	320,961	3.3	49

Continued in SALA, 23–632. For projections to 1985 by province, see SALA, 22–627.

Table 636

DOMINICAN REPUBLIC POPULATION CENSUS AND DENSITY
OF MAJOR CIVIL DIVISIONS
(1980‡)

Division	Population	%	Density Per km^2
Total	5,621,985	100.0	116
Distrito Nacional	1,555,739	27.7	1,053
Provinces			
Azúa	143,628	2.6	59
Baoruco	78,508	1.4	57

Continued in SALA, 23–633.

Table 637

ECUADOR POPULATION CENSUS AND DENSITY OF MAJOR CIVIL DIVISIONS
(1982)

Division	Population	%	Density Per km^2
Total	8,018,556	100.0	29.6
Provinces			
Azuay	442,019	5.5	1.6
Bolívan	145,949	1.8	.5

Continued in SALA, 25-636.

Table 638

EL SALVADOR POPULATION CENSUS AND DENSITY OF MAJOR CIVIL DIVISIONS
(1971[‡])

Division	Population	%	Density Per km^2
Total	3,549,260	100.0	170
Departments			
Ahuachapán	179,820	5.1	153
Cabañas	129,199	3.6	126

Continued in SALA, 23-635.

Table 639

GUATEMALA POPULATION CENSUS AND DENSITY OF MAJOR CIVIL DIVISIONS
(1981)

Division	Population	%	Density Per km^2
Total	6,043,559	100.0	56
Departments			
Alta Verapaz	322,132	5.3	37
Baja Verapaz	115,206	1.9	37

Continued in SALA, 23-636.

Table 640

HAITI POPULATION CENSUS AND DENSITY OF MAJOR CIVIL DIVISIONS
(1971)

Division	Population	%	Density Per km^2
Total	4,329,991	100.0	156
Departments			
Artibonite	765,228	17.7	124
Nord	700,725	16.2	166
Nord-Quest	217,489	5.0	92
Quest	1,670,140	38.6	198
Sud	976,409	22.5	147

1. Unless otherwise indicated the data refer to the defacto population. For the size of each political unit see SALA, 23-301. Population density is calculated by dividing the population figure by km^2.

SOURCE: SALA-LAPUA, table 16-1.

Table 641

HONDURAS POPULATION CENSUS AND DENSITY
OF MAJOR CIVIL DIVISIONS[1]

(1985)

Division	Population	%	Density Per km^2
Total	4,372,487	100.0	39.0
Departments			
Atlántida	262,227	6.0	2.3
Colón	138,473	3.2	1.2
Comayagua	226,259	5.2	2.0

Continued in SALA, 25-640.

Table 642

MEXICO POPULATION CENSUS AND DENSITY
OF MAJOR CIVIL DIVISIONS

(1980‡)

Division	Population	%	Density Per km^2
Total	67,383,000	100.0	34
Distrito Federal	9,373,958	13.9	6,337
States			
Aguas Calientes	503,410	.7	92
Baja California	1,225,436	1.8	18

Continued in SALA, 23–639.

Table 643

NICARAGUA POPULATION CENSUS AND DENSITY
OF MAJOR CIVIL DIVISIONS

(1971)

Division	Population	%	Density Per km^2
Total	1,894,690	100.0	14
Departments			
Boaco	70,850	3.7	14
Carazo	71,810	3.8	70

Continued in SALA, 24–640.

Table 644

PANAMA POPULATION CENSUS AND DENSITY
OF MAJOR CIVIL DIVISIONS

(1980)

Division	Population	%	Density Per km^2
Total	1,788,748	100.0	23
Provinces			
Bocas del Toro	52,416	2.9	6
Chiriquí	286,416	16.0	33

Continued in SALA, 24–641.

Table 645

PARAGUAY POPULATION CENSUS AND DENSITY
OF MAJOR CIVIL DIVISIONS
(1979‡)

Division	Population	%	Density Per km^2
Total	3,068.4	100.0	7.5
Departments			
Asunción	497.1	16.2	1.2
Concepción	126.2	4.1	.3

Continued in SALA, 25-644.

Table 646

PERU POPULATION CENSUS AND DENSITY
OF MAJOR CIVIL DIVISIONS
(1981)

Division	Population	%	Density Per km^2
Total	17,005,210	100.0	13.2
Departments			
Amazonas	254,560	1.5	6.2
Ancash	818,289	4.8	22.5

Continued in SALA, 23–643.

Table 647

URUGUAY POPULATION CENSUS AND DENSITY
OF MAJOR CIVIL DIVISIONS
(1975)

Division	Population	%	Density Per km^2
Total	2,769,781	100.0	16
Departments			
Artigas	57,432	2.1	5
Canelones	321,662	11.6	70

Continued in SALA, 23–644.

Table 648

VENEZUELA POPULATION CENSUS AND DENSITY
OF MAJOR CIVIL DIVISIONS
(1981‡)

Division	Population	%	Density Per km^2
Total	14,602,480	100.0	16
Distrito Federal	2,074,203	14.2	1075
Dependencias Federales[2]	~	~	~
States			
Anzoátegui	689,555	4.7	16
Apure	196,808	1.3	3

Continued in SALA, 23–645.

Table 649

EXTENDED CARIBBEAN REGION (ECR) POPULATION, 28 CSOR, 6 CA,
AND 3 TANGENTIAL COUNTRIES, 1960–79

Category	1960	1979	Change	PC
I. Caribbean Sea Oriented Region (CSOR)				
Anguilla	6@	6@	0	0
Antigua-Barbuda[1]	55	74	19	34.5
Bahamas[1]	112	236	124	110.7
Barbados[1]	232	279	47	20.3
Belize[1]	92	152	60	65.2
Bermuda	45	72	27	60.0
British Virgin Islands[1]	7	12	5	71.4
Cayman Islands[1]	8	17	9	112.5
G. Cuba	7,027	9,824	2,797	39.6
Dominica[1]	60	78	18	30.0
H. Dominican Republic[1]	3,159	5,551	2,392	75.7
French Guiana	32	63	31	96.9
Grenada[1]	90	106	16	17.8
Guadeloupe	273	312	39	14.3
Guyana[1]	571	832	261	45.7
L. Haiti[1]	3,723	5,670	1,947	52.3
Jamaica[1]	1,632	2,215	583	35.7
Martinique	283	310	27	9.5
Montserrat[1]	12	11	–1	–.8
Netherlands Antilles[1]	194	240	46	23.7
Puerto Rico	2,358	3,395	1,037	44.0
St. Kitts-Nevis[1]	51	51	0	0
St. Lucia[1]	88	121	33	37.5
St. Vincent and Grenadines[1]	81	111	30	37.0
Suriname[1]	285	404	119	41.8
Trinidad and Tobago[1]	840	1,150	310	36.9
Turks and Caicos[1]	6	7	1	16.7
U.S. Virgin Islands	33	99	66	200.0
Total CSOR	(21,355)	(31,398)	(10,043)	(47.0)
II. Central America (CA)				
F. Costa Rica[1]	1,248	2,184	936	75.0
J. El Salvador[1]	2,574	4,662	2,088	81.1
K. Guatemala[1]	3,969	6,849	2,880	72.5
M. Honduras[1]	1,952	3,645	1,693	86.7
O. Nicaragua[1]	1,438	2,365	927	64.5
P. Panama[1]	1,112	1,876	764	68.7
Total CA	(12,293)	(21,581)	(9,288)	75.6
III. Mainland Tangential Countries				
E. Colombia	15,953	26,205	10,252	64.3
N. Mexico	36,182	65,770	29,588	81.8
T. Venezuela	7,632	14,539	6,907	90.5
Total Tangential	(59,767)	(106,514)	(46,747)	78.2
Total ECR	93,415	159,493	66,078	70.7
Subtotal CBI-IB[2]	(23,591)	(38,898)	(15,307)	(64.9)

1. CBI-IB.
2. CBI-IB includes CA and CSOR, except Anguilla, Bermuda, Cuba,
   French Guiana, Guadeloupe, Martinique, Puerto Rico, U.S.
   Virgin Islands.

SOURCE: SALA, 24–646.

Table 650

POPULATION OF LARGEST CITY, 20 L, 1900-84

(T)

Country/Largest City	1900	1920	1930	1940	1950	1960	1970	Ca. 1984
A. ARGENTINA (Buenos Aires)[1]	756	1,576	~	2,410	5,213	7,000	9,400	9,928
B. BOLIVIA (La Paz)[1]	54	~	~	~	300	400	500	881[t,l,n]
C. BRAZIL (Rio de Janeiro except Sao Paulo in 1970 and 1984)[1]	683	1,158	~	1,519	3,025	4,692	8,213	10,099[‡,p]
D. CHILE (Santiago)[1]	307	507	713	952	1,275	1,907	2,600	4,067[t,l]
E. COLOMBIA (Bogotá)	101	144[a]	260	356[b]	607	1,241	2,500	4,169[t,l]
F. COSTA RICA (San José)[1]	28	39	89[c]	~	140	257	435	395[m,p,o]
G. CUBA (Havana)[1]	209	466[d]	721[e]	936[f]	1,081	1,549	1,700	1,992[t]
H. DOMINICAN REP. (Santo Domingo)	15	31	~	71[g]	182	367	650	818
I. ECUADOR (Guayaquil)	79	~	~	~	259	450	800	1,388[t,l]
J. EL SALVADOR (San Salvador)[1]	49	81	89	103	162	239	375	336[l]
K. GUATEMALA (Guatemala City)[1]	41	112[h]	~	186	294	474	770	754
L. HAITI (Port-au-Prince)	56	~	~	~	134	240	400	738[t]
M. HONDURAS (Tegucigalpa)[1]	12	~	~	56[i]	72	159	281	539[t,l]
N. MEXICO (Mexico City)[2]	381	615	1,049	1,560	2,872	4,910	8,567	14,750[t]
O. NICARAGUA (Managua)[1]	24	28	~	63	109	197	350	608[t,l]
P. PANAMA (Panama City)[1]	- -	~	74	112	128	273	440	424[t,q]
Q. PARAGUAY (Asunción)[1]	42	~	~	~	219	311	445	719[t]
R. PERU (Lima-Callao)[1]	78	255	~	~	947	1,519	2,500	5,008[‡,r]
S. URUGUAY (Montevideo)	290	393	482	537	609	962	1,530	1,173[l]
T. VENEZUELA (Caracas)[1]	80	92	259[j]	354[k]	694	1,280	2,147	2,944[s]

1. Beginning in 1950, figures are for city proper and adjacent urban area.
2. All figures are for city proper and adjacent urban area.

a. 1918.
b. 1938.
c. 1927.
d. 1919, Greater Havana.
e. 1931, Greater Havana.
f. 1943.
g. 1935.
h. 1921.
i. 1945.
j. 1936, metropolitan area.
k. 1941, metropolitan area.
l. For city proper area only.
m. Metropolitan area.
n. La Paz is the actual capital and the seat of the government, but Sucre is the legal capital and the seat of the judiciary.
o. For July 1, 1970.
p. De jure population.
q. Including corregimientos of Bella Vista, Betania, Calidonia, Curundú, El Chorillo, Juan Diaz, Parque Lefevre, Pedregal, Pueblo Nuevo, Río Abajo, San Felipe, San Francisco, and Santa Ana.
r. "Metropolitan Area" (Gran Lima).
s. For June 30, 1980. "Metropolitan Area" comprising Caracas proper (the urban parishes of Department of Libertador) and a part of district of Sucre in state of Miranda.
t. "Metropolitan Area," comprising Asunción proper and localities of Trinidad, Zeballos Cué, Campo Grande, and Lambaré.

SOURCE: 1900–1970: Marshal C. Eakin, "Determining the Population in the Largest City of Each Latin American Country, 1920–1970," SALA, 19–3500 and 19–3503; 1984 data from UN-DY, 1985, table 8.

Table 651

PERCENTAGE OF POPULATION OF LARGEST CITY, 20 L, 1900–84

Country/Largest City	1900	1920	1930	1940	1950	1960	1970	Ca. 1984
A. ARGENTINA (Buenos Aires)	16.4	17.6	~	17.0	30.5	35.1	39.6	32.9
B. BOLIVIA (La Paz)	3.1	~	~	8.5	10.0	10.8	10.7	14.6
C. BRAZIL (Rio de Janeiro except								
São Paulo for 1970 and 1984)	3.8	4.2	~	3.7	5.8	6.7	8.9	7.4
D. CHILE (Santiago)	10.4	13.4	16.3	18.8	21.0	25.2	27.7	34.2
E. COLOMBIA (Bogotá)	2.6	2.5[a]	3.5	4.1[b]	5.4	8.0	12.2	14.8
F. COSTA RICA (San José)	9.3	9.3	18.9[c]	10.6	17.5	20.6	25.1	19.5
G. CUBA (Havana)	13.1	16.0[d]	18.2[e]	19.6[f]	19.6	22.0	19.9	19.9
H. DOMINICAN REP. (Santo Domingo)	2.5	3.5	~	4.8[g]	8.1	12.1	16.0	13.6
I. ECUADOR (Quito, except								
Guayaquil since 1940)	6.1	~	~	5.2	8.1	10.3	13.7	15.2
J. EL SALVADOR (San Salvador)	6.2	6.9	6.2	6.3	8.7	9.8	10.9	6.8
K. GUATEMALA (Guatemala City)	4.7	8.5[h]	~	8.5	10.5	12.4	15.8	9.8
L. HAITI (Port-au-Prince)	4.5	~	~	4.0	4.0	6.2	9.4	18.0
M. HONDURAS (Tegucigalpa)	3.0	~	~	4.4[i]	5.0	8.6	11.2	12.3
N. MEXICO (Mexico City)	2.8	4.3	6.3	7.9	11.1	14.1	17.8	20.1
O. NICARAGUA (Managua)	5.9	4.4	~	7.6	10.3	14.0	19.1	20.0
P. PANAMA (Panama City)	~	14.4[j]	15.7	18.1	16.0	25.8	30.8	19.9
Q. PARAGUAY (Asunción)	8.7	~	~	8.7	15.6	17.6	19.3	15.3
R. PERU (Lima-Callao)	2.6	5.3	~	7.4	11.9	15.1	18.6	26.1
S. URUGUAY (Montevideo)	30.3	26.6	27.9	27.3	27.7	37.9	52.9	40.0
T. VENEZUELA (Caracas)	3.3	3.3	7.7[k]	9.3[l]	14.0	17.4	20.6	18.1

a. 1918	g. 1935.
b. 1938.	h. 1921.
c. 1927.	i. 1945.
d. 1919.	j. 1919.
e. 1931.	k. 1936.
f. 1943.	l. 1941.

SOURCE: 1900–70 data from SALA, 19–3501; 1983 data calculated from SALA, 26–601
    through 620 and 649.

Table 652

POPULATION OF PRINCIPAL CITIES, ACCORDING TO RECENT CENSUSES,[1] 20 L

A. ARGENTINA (Census of X-22-1980)

Buenos Aires	9,967,826
Rosario, Santa Fé	957,301
Córdoba, Córdoba	983,969
La Plata, Buenos Aires	564,750
Mendoza, Mendoza	605,623
San Miguel de Tucumán, Tucumán	498,579
Mar del Plata, Buenos Aires	414,696[f]
Santa Fé, Santa Fé	291,966
San Juan, San Juan	291,707
Bahía Blanca	223,818
Salta	260,744[f]
Corrientes	180,612[f]
Paraná	161,638[f]
Santiago del Estero	148,758[f]

B. BOLIVIA (Estimated VII-I, 1982)[f]

La Paz, La Paz[2]	881,404[a]
Santa Cruz, Santa Cruz	376,912[a]
Cochabamba, Cochabamba	281,962[a]
Oruro, Oruro	162,213[a]
Sucre, Chuquisaca[2]	63,625[n]
Potosí, Potosí	103,183[a]

C. BRAZIL (Estimated VII-1, 1985)[‡,o]

São Paulo, São Paulo	10,099,086
Rio de Janeiro, Guanabara	5,615,149
Belo Horizonte, Minas Gerais	2,122,073
Recife, Pernambuco	1,289,627
Salvador, Bahia	1,811,367
Porto Alegre, Rio Grande do Sul	1,275,483
Belém, Pará	1,120,777
Fortaleza, Ceará	1,588,709
Curitiba, Paraná	1,285,027
Santo André, São Paulo	637,010
Gioania, Goiás	928,046
Nova Iguacú, Rio de Janeiro	1,324,639
Campinas, São Paulo	845,057
Santos, São Paulo	461,096
Niterói, Rio de Janeiro	442,706
Manaus, Amazonas	834,541
Osasco, São Paulo	594,249
Brasília, Distrito Federal	1,576,657
Duque de Caxias, Rio de Janeiro	666,128
Natal, Rio Grande do Notre	512,241
Maceló, Alagoas	484,094
Guarulhos, São Paulo	717,723
Juiz de Fora, Minas Gerais	350,687
João Pessoa, Paraíba	397,715
Ribeirão Prêto, São Paulo	384,604
Olinda, Pernambuco	335,889
Teresina, Pisuí	476,102
Aracaju, Sergipe	361,544
São Luis, Maranhão	564,434
Sorocaba, São Paulo	328,787
São João de Meriti, Rio de Janeiro	459,103
Campina Grande, Paraíba	280,665
São Gonçalo, Rio de Janeiro	731,061
Londrina, Paraná	347,707
Campos, Rio de Janeiro	367,134
Ponta Grossa, Paraná	223,989
Pelotas, Rio Grande do Sul	278,427
São Caetano do Sul	171,187
Canoas, Rio Grande do Sul	262,156
Jundiaí, São Paulo	314,909
Campo Grande, Mato Grosso	386,520
Nilópolis, Rio de Janeiro	166,324
Feira de Santana, Bahia	356,660
Piracicaba, São Paulo	252,945

C. BRAZIL (Continued)

Governado Valadares, Espírito Santo	217,434
Vitória, Espírito Santo	325,448
Montes Claros, Minas Gerais	215,323
Santa María, Rio Grande do Sul	197,177
Volta Redonda, Rio de Janeiro	220,084
Bauru, São Paulo	220,871
Rio Grande, Rio Grande do Sul	164,636
Petrópolis, Rio de Janeiro	275,076
Florianópolis, Santa Catarina	218,853
Maringá, Paraná	197,527
Santarém, Pará	227,412
Mogi das Cruzes, São Paulo	234,937
Caxias do Sul, Rio Grande do Sul	267,869
Marília, Sao Päulo	136,518
Caruaru, Pernambuco	136,212

D. CHILE (Estimated VII-1, 1985)[‡,f]

Santiago, Santiago[3]	4,067,047
Valparaíso, Valparaíso	273,006
Concepción, Concepción	278,398
Vina del Mar Valparaíso	258,439
Talcahuano	215,082
Antofagasta	200,319
Temuco	166,165
Talca	136,222
Arica	155,455
Rancagua	155,161
Chillán	125,379
Valdivia	104,453

E. COLOMBIA A

	(Census of X-24-1973)	Estimated 1985
Bogotá D.E., Cundinamarca	2,855,065	4,208,000
Medellín, Antioquia	1,159,194	2,069,000
Cali, Valle de Cauca	990,304	1,654,000
Barranquilla, Atlántico	691,728	1,120,000
Bucaramanga, Santander	322,883	545,000
Cartegena, Bolívar	354,735	530,000[f]
Cúcuta, Norte de Santander	278,933	441,000
Pereira, Risaralda	226,888	390,000
Manizales, Coldas	231,888	328,000[f,d]
Ibagué, Tolima	233,112	285,000[f]
Bello, Antioquia	122,780	~
Montería, Córdoba	172,407	~
Armenia, Quinidio	160,345	239,000[f]
Valledupar, Magdalena	160,654	301,000
Palmirá Valle del Cauca	184,970	~
Pasto, Narino	158,533	245,000[f]
Buenaventura, Valle del Cauca	136,308	193,000[f]
Neiva, Huila	128,784	193,000[f]
Santa Marta, Magdalena	150,987	216,000[f]

F. COSTA RICA (Estimate of VII-1-1983)

San José, San José	395,401[c,j,m]
Limón, Limón	35,000[p]
Puntarenas, Punterenas	30,000[p]
Alajuela, Alajuela	28,000[p]
Heredia, Heredia	22,000[p]
Cartago, Cartago	21,000[p]

G. CUBA (Estimate of X11-31-1984)[f]

La Habana, Habana	1,992,620
Santiago de Cuba, Oriente	356,033
Camagüey, Carnagüey	287,392
Santa Clara, Las Villas	176,917
Guantánamo, Oriente	172,491
Matanzas, Matanzas	104,583
Holquín	194,113
Bayamo	104,363
Cienfuegos	172,491

Table 652 (Continued)

POPULATION OF PRINCIPAL CITIES, ACCORDING TO RECENT CENSUSES,[1] 20 L

H. DOMINICAN REP. (XII-12-1981)[f]

Santo Domingo, Distrito Nacional	1,313,172
Santo de los Caballers, Santiago	278,638
La Romana, La Romana	91,571
San Pedro de Macorís, San Pedro de Macorís	78,562
San Francisco de Macorís, Duarte	64,906
Concepción de la Vega	52,432

I. ECUADOR (Estimate of VI-30-1984)[f]

Guayaquil, Guayas	1,387,819
Quito, Pichincha	1,003,875
Machaía	123,966
Portoviejo	120,896
Cuenca	176,865
Manta	117,461
Ambato	114,493
Esmeraldas	105,153

J. EL SALVADOR (Census of VI-28-1971)

San Salvador, San Salvador	335,930[f]
Santa Ana, Santa Ana	168,047[l]
San Miguel, San Miguel	107,658[l]
Nueva San Salvador, La Libertad	36,000[k]
Villa Delgado, San Salvador	30,000[k]

K. GUATEMALA (Census of 1981)

Ciudad de Guatemala, Guatemala	754,243
Escuintla, Escuintla	75,442
Quezaltenango, Quezaltenango	72,922
Puerto Barrios, Izabel	46,882
Retalhulev	46,652

L. HAITI (Estimate of VII-I-1984)[c]

Port-au-Prince, Ouest	738,342[a]
Cap-Haitien, Nord	46,000[q]
Gonaives, Artibonite	29,000[q]
Les Cayes, Sud	22,000[q]

M. HONDURAS (Estimate of VI-30-1985)

Tegucigalpa, D.C., Francisco Morazán	539,042[f]
San Pedro Sula, Cortés	335,029[f]
La Ceiba, Atlántida	103,600[f]
Choluteca	50,700
El Progreso, Yoro	50,000

N. MEXICO (Estimate of VI-30-1979)[a,g]

Ciudad de México, Distrito Federal	14,750,182
Guadalajara, Jalisco	2,467,657
Monterrey, Nuevo León	2,018,625
León, Guanajuato	624,816
Puebla de Zaragoza, Puebla	710,833
Ciudad Juárez, Chihuahua	625,040
Mexicali, Baja California	348,528
Chihuahua, Chihuahua	385,953
Culiacán, Sinoloa	324,292
Tijuana, Baja California	566,344
San Luis Potosí, San Luis Potosí	327,333
Terreón, Coahuila	407,271

N. MEXICO (Continued)

Mérida, Yucatán	269,582
Veracruz, Veracruz	306,843
Aguascalientes, Aguascalientes	257,179
Morelia, Michoacán	251,011
Hermosillo, Sonora	319,257
Tampico, Tamaulipas	389,940
Durango, Durango	228,686
Saltillo, Coahuila	258,492
Matamoros, Tamaulipas	193,305
Villa de Guadalupe, Hidalgo (part of Federal District)	124,573[b]
Nuevo Laredo, Tamaulipas	223,606

O. NICARAGUA (Estimate of VII-1-1979)

Managua, D.N., Managua	608,020[f]
León, León	58,000[f]
Granada, Granada	36,000[f]
Masaya, Masaya	30,000[f]
Chinandega, Chinandega	30,000[f]

P. PANAMA (Estimate of VII-1-1984)[f]

Panamá, Panamá	424,204[i]
San Miguelito	200,584

Q. PARAGUAY (Census of 1982)

Asunción	457,210[f]
San Lorenzo	74,359
Fernando de la Mora	66,810
Lambaré	65,145

R. PERU (Estimate of XII-30-1985)[‡,f]

Lima, Lima	5,008,400[h]
Callao, Provincia Constitucional de Callao	515,200
Arequipa, Arequipa	545,165
Trujillo, La Libertad	421,345
Chiclayo, Lemayeque	349,249
Cuzco, Cuzco	235,857
Chimbote	255,078
Huancayo	190,226
Iquitos	229,557
Piura	265,866
Tacna	125,848

S. URUGUAY (Census of 1975)

Montevideo	1,229,748
Salto	71,000
Pay Sandú	61,000
Las Piedras	53,000

T. VENEZUELA A (Census of X-20-1981)

Caracas, Distrito Federal	2,944,000[a,e]
Maracaibo, Zulia	888,824
Valencia, Carabobo	616,037
Barquismeto, Lara	496,684
Maracay, Araqua	440,098
San Cristóbal, Táchira	198,578
Cabimas, Zulia	138,529
Ciudad Bolívar, Bolívar	181,864

---

1. Unless otherwise indicated, data refer to "Urban Agglomeration." Each city is followed by the name of the major territorial division (department, state, province, etc.) to which it belongs.
2. La Paz is the actual capital and seat of government, but Sucre is the legal capital and seat of the judiciary.
3. "Metropolitan Area" (Gran Santiago).

a. Estimate of questionable reliability.
b. Villa de Guadalupe, 1973.
c. De jure population.
d. Includes population of Villamaría.
e. "Metropolitan Area," comprising Caracas proper (the urban parishes of the department of Libertador) and a part of the district of Sucre in the state of Miranda.
f. Data refer to city proper.
g. Data refer to city proper with the exception of Mexico City, Guadalajara, Monterrey, Tampico, and Torreón.

h. Data refer to "Metropolitan Area" (Gran Lima).
i. Data refer to city proper and include the *corregimientos* of Bella Vista, Betania, Calidonia, Curundo, El Chorillo, Juan Diaz, Parque Lefevre, Pedregal, Pueblo Nuevo, Río Abajo, San Felipe, San Francisco, and Santa Ana.
j. "Metropolitan area" comprising *cantón central* of San José (including San José city), cantones Curridabat, Escazú, Montes de Oca, and Tibá, and parts of cantones of Alajuelita, Desamparados, Goicoechea, and Moravia.
k. 1961 estimate.
l. 1969 estimate.
m. For July 1, 1970.
n. For September 29, 1976.
o. Data refer to "urban agglomeration" and "city proper."
p. 1973 estimate.
q. 1971 estimate.

SOURCE: Colombia estimates from *Colombia Today, 21:3* (1986); Dominican Rep., Guatemala, Paraguay, and Uruguay estimates from *South America, Central America, and the Caribbean* (London: Europa Publications Limited, 1986); Costa Rica, El Salvador, Haiti and Nicaragua estimates from IASI-AC, 1970 and 1973, table 201–07 and UN-DY, 1984, table 8; and UN-DY, 1985, table 8.

Table 653

POPULATION PROJECTIONS AND RANKS FOR THE LARGEST METROPOLITAN AREAS, 7 L, 1950–2000

(T)

	1950	Population Rank	1985	Population Rank	2000	Population Rank
A. ARGENTINA						
Buenos Aires	5,250	1	10,880	3	13,180	4
C. BRAZIL						
Belo Horizonte	480	10	3,250	9	5,110	8
Porto Alegre	670	9	2,740	11	4,020	11
Rio de Janeiro	3,480	2	10,370	4	13,260	3
São Paulo	2,760	4	15,880	2	23,970	2
D. CHILE						
Santiago	1,430	5	4,160	7	5,260	7
E. COLOMBIA						
Bogotá	700	7	4,490	6	6,530	6
N. MEXICO						
Guadalajara	430	11	2,770	10	4,110	10
Mexico City	3,050	3	17,300	1	25,820	1
Monterrey	380	12	2,530	12	3,970	12
R. PERU						
Lima	1,050	6	5,680	5	9,140	5
T. VENEZUELA						
Caracas	680	8	3,740	8	5,030	9

SOURCE: Adapted from *Population Bulletin*, vol. 41, no. 3, July 1986, p. 25.

Table 654

CELADE URBAN POPULATION PERCENTAGES, NON-STANDARD TERMS,[1] 20 LR, 1970–2025

(%)

Country	1970	1975	1980	1985	1990	1995	2000	2005	2010	2015	2020	2025
A. ARGENTINA	78.48	80.16	81.62	82.96	84.10	85.15	86.05	86.85	87.55	88.20	88.70	89.14
B. BOLIVIA	38.19	41.30	44.68	50.54	51.45	54.28	56.58	58.15	60.53	62.85	65.30	67.65

Continued in SALA 24, 653.

Table 655

POPULATION OF CAPITAL CITY URBAN AREAS,
ACCORDING TO RECENT CENSUSES,[1] 20 LC

	Country	Date of Estimate	Date of Census[2]	Capital City	City Proper	Urban Agglomeration
A.	ARGENTINA	**	X-22-1980	Buenos Aires	2,922,829	9,967,826
B.	BOLIVIA	VII-I-1982	**	LaPaz[6]	881,404[b]	~
C.	BRAZIL[‡]	VII-I-1985	**	Brasilia, D.F.	1,576,657[g]	~
D.	CHILE[‡]	VII-I-1985	**	Santiago	4,067,047[h]	~
E.	COLOMBIA	X-24-1983	**	Bogota	4,169,000	~
F.	COSTA RICA[3]	VII-I-1983	**	San José	274,832	395,401[a,e]
G.	CUBA	XII-31-1984	**	La Habana	1,992,620	~
H.	DOMINICAN REP.	**	I-9-1970	Santo Domingo	673,470	817,645
I.	ECUADOR	VI-30-1984	**	Quito	1,003,875	~
J.	EL SALVADOR	**	VI-28-1971	San Salvador	335,930	~
K.	GUATEMALA	III-23-1981	**	Guatemala, Ciudad de	754,243	~
L.	HAITI[‡,3]	VII-I-1984	**	Port-Au-Prince	461,464[b]	738,342
M.	HONDURAS	VII-I-1985	**	Tegucigalpa	539,042	~
N.	MEXICO	VI-30-1979	**	México, Ciudad de	9,191,295[b]	14,750,182[b]
O.	NICARAGUA	VII-I-1979	**	Managua	608,020	~
P.	PANAMA	VII-I-1984	**	Panamá	424,204[c]	~
Q.	PARAGUAY	**	VII-II-1982	Asunción	457,210	718,690[d]
R.	PERU[‡]	VI-30-1985	**	Lima	5,008,400	~
S.	URUGUAY	**	V-21-1975	Montevideo	1,173,254	~
T.	VENEZUELA	**	X-20-1981	Caracas	1,816,901	2,944,000[f]
	UNITED STATES[4,5]	VII-I-1984	**	Washington, D.C.	622,800	3,369,600

1. Definition of cities varies from country to country. Urban agglomeration includes the suburban fringe or thickly settled territory lying outside of, but adjacent to, the city boundaries.
2. Data are the result of a national or municipal census.
3. Based on de jure population.
4. De jure population, but excluding armed forces overseas and civilian citizens absent from the country for an extended period of time.
5. Urban agglomeration data refer to "Standard Metropolitan Statistical Area."
6. La Paz is the actual capital and seat of government, but Sucre is the legal capital and the seat of the judiciary.

a. "Metropolitan Area," comprising canto central of San José (including San José city), cantones Curridabat, Escazú, Montes de Oca, and Tibás, and parts of cantones of Alajuelita, Desamparados, Goicoechea, and Moravia.
b. Estimate of questionable reliability.
c. Including corregimientos of Bella Vista, Betania, Calidonia, Curundú, El Chorillo, Juan Díaz, Parque Levevre, Pedregal, Pueblo Nuevo, Río Abajo, San Felipe, San Francisco, and Santa Ana.
d. "Metropolitan Area," comprising Asunción proper and localities of Trinidad, Zeballos, Cué, Campo Grande, and Lambaré.
e. For VII-I-1970.
f. For June 30, 1980; "Metropolitan Area," comprising Caracas proper (the urban parishes of Department of Libertador) and part of the district of Sucre in the State of Miranda.
g. Includes urban population.
h. "Metropolitan Area" (Gran Santiago).

SOURCE: UN-DY, 1984 and 1985, table 8.

Table 656

PERSONS BY AGE UP TO 15 YEARS, 20 LC

(N)

	Country	Year	Code	Under 1 Year	1-4 Years	5-9 Years	10-14 Years
				Age			
A.	ARGENTINA[+,4]	1985	E	3,472,635[a]	~[a]	3,223,845	2,776,709
B.	BOLIVIA[3,9]	1982	E	1,010,300[+,a]	~[a]	826,391	709,582
C.	BRAZIL[+,2]	1985	E	18,072,000[a]	~[a]	16,368,000	14,926,000
D.	CHILE[3]	1984	E	274,896	1,065,475	1,235,286	1,156,192
E.	COLOMBIA[+,4]	1985	E	800,000	2,959,000	3,277,000	3,263,000
F.	COSTA RICA[+,1,11]	1984	E	~[b]	~[b]	701,566[b]	193,881[c]
G.	CUBA	1984	E	164,148	582,648	800,906	1,116,251
H.	DOMINICAN REP.[9]	1980	E	183,719	736,468	890,819	774,522
I.	ECUADOR[4,5,9]	1984	E	1,444,948	~[a]	1,255,783	1,135,082
J.	EL SALVADOR[+]	1985	E	789,501	~[a]	755,434	652,566
K.	GUATEMALA[+]	1985	E	1,433,545	~[a]	1,213,315	1,008,947
L.	HAITI[+,9,10]	1984	E	150,890	602,499	686,616	577,469
M.	HONDURAS[+,9]	1985	E	169,918	630,851	680,714	569,777
N.	MEXICO[+,1,4,9]	1985	E	11,280,453[a]	~[a]	11,037,365	10,541,500
O.	NICARAGUA[9]	1980	E	466,640[a]	~[a]	455,852	387,061
P.	PANAMA[9]	1984	E	57,435	222,011	270,343	264,083
Q.	PARAGUAY[+]	1982	C	102,850	362,100	399,760	381,470
R.	PERU[3,6,9]	1985	E	2,999,691[a]	~[a]	2,602,421	2,368,746
S.	URUGUAY[9]	1980	E	274,427[a]	~[a]	267,110	245,206
T.	VENEZUELA[+,7,9]	1984	E	2,513,382[a]	~[a]	2,218,003	1,966,329
	UNITED STATES[+,4,8,10]	1985	E	3,742,000	14,295,000	16,822,000	17,103,000

Code:　C = census data; E = estimate.

1. De jure population.
2. Excluding Indian jungle population.
3. Data have been adjusted for underenumeration at latest census.
4. Because of rounding, totals are not in all cases the sum of the parts.
5. Excluding nomadic Indian tribes.
6. Excluding Indian jungle population estimated at 39,800 in 1972.
7. Excluding Indian jungle population estimated at 31,800 in 1961.
8. De jure population, but excluding civilian citizens absent from country for extended period of time.
9. Estimates are unreliable.
10. Excluding armed forces overseas.
11. Excluding transients afloat and non-locally domiciled military and civilian services personnel and their dependents and visitors, numbering 5,553, 5,187, and 8,985 respectively at 1980 census.

a. Figures for under one year category include 1-4 years population.
b. Figures for 5 to 9 years of age include persons under 12 years of age.
c. Includes persons 12 to 14 years of age.

SOURCE: Adapted from UN-DY, 1985, table 7.

Table 657

CELADE MALE AND FEMALE POPULATION PROJECTIONS, 20 LR, 1970–2000

(T)

PART I. TOTALS

	Country	1970			1980			1990			2000		
		Total	Male	Female	Total	Male	Female	Total	Male	Female	Total	Male	Female
A.	ARGENTINA	23,962	12,019	11,943	28,237	14,045	14,192	32,879	16,285	16,594	37,197	18,391	18,806
B.	BOLIVIA	4,325	2,134	2,191	5,570	2,744	2,826	7,314	3,605	3,709	9,724	4,800	4,924
C.	BRAZIL	95,847	47,984	47,863	121,286	60,607	60,679	150,368	74,992	75,376	179,487	89,323	90,164

Continued in SALA, 25-655.

Table 658

ESTIMATES OF FEMALE POPULATION 15–49 YEARS OF AGE,
20 LRC, 1950–2010

(%)

Country	1950	1960	1970	1980	1990	2000	2010
A. ARGENTINA	54.1	51.2	49.8	48.3	48.4	49.6	49.2
B. BOLIVIA	46.8	47.4	45.8	45.4	46.4	47.6	47.7
C. BRAZIL	47.9	46.2	46.5	47.1	48.2	49.7	52.9

Continued in SALA, 25-656.

Table 659

SALA RURAL POPULATION PERCENTAGES ACCORDING TO NATIONAL SELF-PERCEPTION, 20 LRC,
1940–80[a]

(Non-Standard Definition)

Country	Data Years	ca. 1940	ca. 1950	ca. 1960	ca. 1970	ca. 1980	Rural Defined as Population Clusters Which Are:
A. ARGENTINA	1947, 1960, 1970, 1980	~	38	26	21	17	Less than 2,000 persons
B. BOLIVIA	1950, 1960, 1970, 1980	~	74	76	72	67	Less than 2,000 persons
C. BRAZIL	1940, 1950, 1960, 1970, 1980	69	64	54	44	36	Non-administrative centers
D. CHILE	1940, 1952, 1960, 1970, 1980	48	40	32	24	19	Lack of certain public services
E. COLOMBIA	1938, 1951, 1964, 1973, 1980	71	61	47	40	32	Less than 1,500 persons
F. COSTA RICA	1950, 1963, 1973, 1980	~	67	65	59	54	Non-administrative centers
G. CUBA	1943, 1953, 1960, 1970, 1980	54	49	45	40	35	Less than 2,000 persons (adjusted by source)
H. DOMINICAN REP.	1935, 1950, 1960, 1970, 1980	82	76	70	60	53	Non-administrative centers
I. ECUADOR	1950, 1962, 1974, 1980	~	72	64	59	56	Non-administrative centers
J. EL SALVADOR	1930, 1950, 1961, 1971, 1980	62	64	61	60	56	Lightly populated
K. GUATEMALA	1940, 1950, 1964, 1973, 1980	74	75	66	66	62	Varies[1]
L. HAITI	1950, 1960, 1971, 1980	~	88	85[†]	80	75	Non-administrative centers
M. HONDURAS	1950, 1960, 1974, 1980	~	82[†]	77	69	51	Less than 1,000-2,000 persons
N. MEXICO	1940, 1950, 1960, 1970, 1980	65	57	49	42	34	Less than 2,500 persons
O. NICARAGUA	1950, 1963, 1971, 1980	~	65	59	52	46	Non-administrative centers
P. PANAMA	1940, 1950, 1960, 1970, 1980	63	64	58	52	46	Less than 1,500 persons
Q. PARAGUAY	1950, 1962, 1972, 1980	~	65	64	62	58	Non-administrative centers
R. PERU	1940, 1950, 1961, 1972, 1980	65	59[†]	53	40	35	Non-administrative centers and/or lack of certain public services
S. URUGUAY	1950, 1960, 1970, 1980	~	43[†]	28[†]	16[†]	15	Not cities[2]
T. VENEZUELA	1941, 1950, 1961, 1971, 1980	69	52	37	25	21	Less than 2,500 persons
LATIN AMERICA	20 countries	67[b]	63	56	42	36	Average of above, weighted by population
UNITED STATES	1940, 1950, 1960, 1970, 1980	39	36	30	27	23	"Current Definition"[3]

1. In 1940: hamlets, small settlements, and farms; since 1950: less than 2,000 except 1,500 if running water.
2. In 1963 census definition gave 19%.
3. Less than 2,500 persons except for urbanized unincorporated areas; data for 1940 adjusted for consistency.

a. Self-definitions vary according to national circumstances.
b. Calculated from population-weighted data for 11 countries which had 80% of Latin America's population.

SOURCE: See SALA, 24–658.

Table 660

SALA URBAN POPULATION PERCENTAGES ACCORDING TO NATIONAL SELF-PERCEPTION, 20 LRC, 1940-80

(Non-Standard Definition)[1]

	Country	Ca. 1940	Ca. 1950	Ca. 1960	Ca. 1970	Ca. 1980
				%		
A.	ARGENTINA	~	62	74	79	83
B.	BOLIVIA	~	26	24	28	33
C.	BRAZIL	31	36	46	56	64
D.	CHILE	52	60	68	76	81
E.	COLOMBIA	29	39	53	60	68
F.	COSTA RICA	~	33	35	41	46
G.	CUBA	46	51	55	60	65
H.	DOMINICAN REP.	18	24	30	40	47
I.	ECUADOR	~	28	36	41	44
J.	EL SALVADOR	38	36	39	40	44
K.	GUATEMALA	26	25	34	34	38
L.	HAITI	~	12	15	20	25
M.	HONDURAS	~	18	23	31	49
N.	MEXICO	35	43	51	58	66
O.	NICARAGUA	~	35	41	48	54
P.	PANAMA	37	36	42	48	54
Q.	PARAGUAY	~	35	36	38	42
R.	PERU	35	41	47	60	65
S.	URUGUAY	~	57	72	84	85
T.	VENEZUELA	31	48	63	75	79
	LATIN AMERICA	33	37	44	58	64
	UNITED STATES	61	64	70	73	77

1. For national definitions, cf. SALA, 25-657.

SOURCE:

1940: U.N., *Demographic Yearbook* (1948), pp. 213-216.

1950: SALA, 3-2.

1960: IASI-AC, 1970, table 201-08.

1970: IASI-AC, 1977, table 201-08.

1980: ECLA, *Latin American Development Projections for the 1980s* (Santiago, 1982) p. 19. Exceptions: Data for Haiti in 1960, Peru for 1950, and Uruguay for 1950-1960 are from Kingsley Davis, *World Urbanization, 1950-1970*; 2 vols. (Berkeley: Population Monograph Series, University of California, 1969), 1, pp. 54-68. Figure for Colombia in 1950 is from AC, 1977, table 201-08. Bolivian data for 1950 are from *Human Resources in Bolivia* (Columbus: Center for Human Resource Research, Ohio State University, 1971), p. 55 and for 1960 and 1970 from WB-WBT, 1980, p. 439. Mexican data are from the Mexican Statistical Agency. Cuban data for 1943 and 1953 are from UCLA-Cuba, p. 24 and 1960 from WB-BDR, 1982, p. 149. Venezuelan data are from DGE, *Censo de Población*, 1961, A, p. 11; and *idem, Censo General de Población y Vivienda*, 1971: *Resultados Comparativos*, table 2. U.S. Data are from USBC-SA, p. 17, the figure for 1940 being adjusted here (splice of "previous" and "current" series). Bolivia, Cuba, and United States for 1980 are from WB-WDR, 1982, pp. 148-149. Cf. SALA-SNP, p. 483.

Table 661

CELADE URBAN AND RURAL POPULATION ESTIMATES,
NON-STANDARD TERMS,[1] 20 LR, 1970–2020

(T)

Country	1970	1980	1990	2000	2010	2020
A. ARGENTINA						
Total	23,748	27,036	30,277	33,222	35,843	38,101
Urban	18,637	22,066	25,463	28,586	31,380	33,795
Rural	5,111	4,970	4,814	4,636	4,463	4,306

1. For each of the countries involved, the definition adopted for an urban population is
   the one appearing in the last population census of the corresponding country. Cf.
   SALA, 25–657.

Continued in SALA, 23–654.

Table 662

ECLA URBAN AND RURAL POPULATION ESTIMATES, BY AGE GROUP,
NON-STANDARD DEFINITION,[1] 20 L, 1975–2025

(% and T)

Country/Age Group	1975		1980		2000		2025	
	Urban	Rural	Urban	Rural	Urban	Rural	Urban	Rural
A. ARGENTINA								
0-14 (%)	26.38	36.42	26.05	36.12	24.07	33.95	20.96	30.46
15-59	60.85	54.87	60.45	54.67	60.65	55.52	61.02	56.74
60-	12.77	8.71	13.50	9.21	15.28	10.53	18.02	12.80
Total (T)	20,343	5,035	22,066	4,970	28,586	4,636	34,816	4,241

1. Rural and urban defined according to national self-perception as defined in
   SALA, 25–657.

Continued in SALA, 23-656.

Table 663

URBAN POPULATION IN NON-STANDARD AND STANDARD TERMS, 20 LR, 1960–80

| | | Density Per km² | | | Non-Standard Terms[1] | | | | | | Standard Terms | | | | | |
| | | | | | T | | | % | | | % over 20,000 | | | % over 100,000 | | |
	Country	1960	1970	1980	1960	1970	1980	1960	1970	1980	1960	1970	1980	1960	1970	1980
A.	ARGENTINA	7.4	8.6	10.2	15,112	18,810	23,041	73.3	78.5	81.6	59.0	66.3	70.2	50.6	55.6	57.7
B.	BOLIVIA	3.1	3.9	5.1	1,035	1,652	2,490	30.2	38.2	44.7	22.9	27.2	34.0	15.3	20.9	29.2
C.	BRAZIL	8.6	11.3	14.3	33,538	53,483	76,168	46.2	55.8	62.8	27.0	36.2	45.7	25.2	32.5	38.0
D.	CHILE	10.1	12.5	14.7	5,144	7,111	8,756	67.6	75.2	78.7	50.6	60.6	67.9	32.9	41.7	52.0
E.	COLOMBIA	13.6	18.3	22.6	7,551	12,336	17,101	48.6	59.3	66.3	33.5	43.9	54.3	27.5	35.7	42.5
F.	COSTA RICA	24.3	34.0	44.8	421	672	1,042	34.1	38.8	45.7	18.5	26.0	30.1	18.5	20.9	22.2
G.	CUBA	63.4	77.2	87.7	3,803	5,109	6,520	54.1	59.6	67.0	38.9	43.4	47.5	24.5	30.8	33.2
H.	DOMINICAN REP.	66.6	89.4	114.7	935	1,690	2,601	29.0	19.4	45.8	18.7	30.2	40.8	12.1	20.7	27.5
I.	ECUADOR	17.0	22.9	30.8	1,406	2,359	3,585	31.8	39.6	44.7	26.5	33.0	39.5	18.6	22.0	28.7
J.	EL SALVADOR	123.0	170.6	229.1	808	1,415	2,120	31.4	39.5	44.2	17.7	20.5	24.9	13.3	15.7	17.8
K.	GUATEMALA	36.4	49.1	66.7	1,214	1,841	2,651	30.6	34.4	36.5	14.5	15.9	18.9	13.2	13.7	14.3
L.	HAITI	134.6	164.5	209.9	484	912	1,342	13.0	18.2	23.1	9.5	13.4	16.5	7.9	11.1	14.7
M.	HONDURAS	17.3	23.6	32.9	464	876	1,432	23.9	33.2	38.8	11.1	17.7	23.8	6.9	13.3	17.9
N.	MEXICO	18.8	26.0	35.3	19,204	30,143	45,452	51.8	58.9	65.5	29.6	34.8	42.5	13.6	23.3	29.8
O.	NICARAGUA	12.6	17.4	23.4	596	965	1,491	39.9	47.0	53.8	20.3	30.5	36.9	14.1	20.5	24.4
P.	PANAMA	14.6	19.6	25.9	454	711	1,082	41.1	47.8	55.3	33.1	39.4	40.9	25.4	30.3	30.6
Q.	PARAGUAY	4.4	5.6	7.8	558	847	1,223	31.4	37.0	38.6	22.1	27.3	32.2	22.1	24.2	25.9
R.	PERU	7.7	10.3	13.5	4,419	7,652	10,965	44.5	58.0	63.4	27.4	38.5	47.2	18.3	28.0	38.0
S.	URUGUAY	13.6	15.0	15.6	1,972	2,303	2,437	77.7	82.0	83.8	60.0	63.3	66.1	40.4	44.7	41.5
T.	VENEZUELA	8.4	11.8	16.7	4,719	7,645	11,448	62.9	72.1	76.2	47.0	59.4	67.0	25.8	38.0	52.7
	LATIN AMERICA	10.5	13.8	17.6	103,837	158,532	222,947	49.6	57.7	63.3	32.4	39.9	47.3	25.3	31.5	36.4

1. Urban defined according to national definitions; Cf. SALA, 25–657.

SOURCE: ECLA-N, No. 397/8 (July, 1984), p. 5.

Table 664

NUMBER AND POPULATION OF PLACES WITH 20,000 INHABITANTS AND OVER,
ACCORDING TO CENSUSES, 20 L, ca. 1950, 1960, 1970

| | | | 1950 | | 1960 | | 1970 | |
	Country	Number of Inhabitants	Number of Localities	Population	Number of Localities	Population	Number of Localities	Population
A.	ARGENTINA	Total 20,000+	42	7,934,082	57	11,804,276	79	15,479,372
		1,000,000 and more	1	4,927,919	1	6,807,236	1	8,435,840
		500,000 – 999,999	≠	≠	2	1,260,736	2	1,597,450
		100,000 – 499,999	7	1,694,032	10	2,059,161	12	2,951,313
		50,000 – 99,999	8	552,643	7	475,009	16	1,057,550
		20,000 – 49,999	26	759,488	37	1,202,134	48	1,437,219

Continued in SALA, 24–658.

Table 665

INDICES OF URBANIZATION AND URBAN CONCENTRATION,[1] 20 LR, 1950 AND 1975

Country	Year	% Total Population in Urban Areas of			% Urban Population in Urban Areas of	
		20,000 Inhabitants or More	100,000 Inhabitants or More	Most Populated City[2]	100,000 Inhabitants or More	Most Populated City[3]
A. ARGENTINA	1950	52.4	44.0	32.0	84.0	61.1
	1975	69.8	57.9	37.0	83.0	53.0

Continued in SALA, 21-635.

Table 666

VANHANEN URBAN AND RURAL POPULATION PERCENTAGE ESTIMATES, 20 LRC, 1900–70
(Urban = Clusters of Population 20,000 and Over)

PART I. URBAN

(%)

Country	1900	1910	1920	1930	1940	1950	1960	1970
A. ARGENTINA	24.9	28.4	37.0	38.0	41.0	49.91	58.98	66.25
B. BOLIVIA	6.6	9.2	9.4[a]	13.1[b]	18.7[c]	19.36	22.93	27.22

PART II. RURAL

(%)

Country	1900	1910	1920	1930	1940	1950	1960	1970
A. ARGENTINA	75.1	71.6	63.0	62.0	59.0	50.1	41.0	33.8
B. BOLIVIA	93.4	90.8	90.6[a]	86.9[b]	81.3[c]	80.1	77.1	72.8

Continued in SALA, 24–657.

Table 667

AGE STRUCTURE, 20 LC, 1960–80

(%)

	Country	0-14 Years			15-64 Years			65 Years and Over		
		1960	1970	1980	1960	1970	1980	1960	1970	1980
A.	ARGENTINA	31.0	29.0	28.1	63.0	63.0	63.2	6.0	8.0	8.6
B.	BOLIVIA	42.0	42.0	43.9	54.0	55.0	52.7	4.0	3.0	3.4

Continued in SALA, 24–661.

Table 668

DISTRIBUTION OF POPULATION BY SEX AND AGE, 18 LC

(%, 1980)

	Country	All Ages		Under 5 Years		5-14 Years		15-24 Years		25-44 Years		45-64 Years		65 Years and Over	
		M	F	M	F	M	F	M	F	M	F	M	F	M	F
A.	ARGENTINA	49.9	50.1	5.1	4.9	9.2	8.9	8.5	8.2	13.5	13.2	9.7	10.1	3.8	4.8
B.	BOLIVIA	49.3	50.7	8.5	8.4	13.5	13.5	9.4	9.6	11.0	11.5	5.3	5.9	1.5	1.9

Continued in SALA, 24–662.

Table 669

U. S. POPULATION CENSUS DATA ON HISPANICS
(1980)

PART I. STATE

Rank	State	Hispanic Population	Hispanic Percentage of Population	Percentage of U.S. Hispanic State Population	Hispanics in State Elected Offices
1	California	4,543,770	19.2	31.1	10/120[a]
2	Texas	2,985,643	21.0	20.4	22/181[b]
3	New York	1,659,245	9.5	11.4	7/210
4	Florida	857,898	8.8	5.9	1/170
5	Illinois	635,525	5.6	4.4	0/236
6	New Jersey	491,867	6.7	3.4	0/120
7	New Mexico	476,089	36.6	3.3	33/112**
8	Arizona	440,915	16.2	3.0	12/90
9	Colorado	339,300	11.7	2.3	9/100
10	Michigan	162,388	1.8	1.1	2/148
11	Pennsylvania	154,004	1.3	1.1	0/252
12	Massachusetts	141,043	2.5	1.0	0/199
13	Connecticut	124,499	4.0	.9	0/187
14	Washington	119,986	2.9	.8	0/147
15	Ohio	119,880	1.1	.8	0/132

PART II. CITY

Rank	City	Hispanic Population	Percentage of Total Population	Hispanics on Elected Council[1]
1	New York City	1,405,957	19.9	3/43
2	Los Angeles	815,989	27.5	1/15[c]
3	Chicago	422,061	14.0	1/50
4	San Antonio[2]	421,774	53.7	4/9
5	Houston	281,224	17.6	1/14
6	El Paso	265,819	62.5	2/6
7	Miami[2]	194,087	55.8	2/4
8	San Jose	140,574	22.1	1/6
9	San Diego	130,610	14.9	1/8
10	Phoenix	115,572	15.1	0/6
11	Albuquerque	112,084	33.8	3/9
12	Dallas	111,082	12.3	1/10
13	Corpus Christi	108,175	46.6	0/6
14	Hialeah[2]	107,908	74.3	2/7
15	Denver	91,937	18.7	2/13
16	Santa Ana	90,646	39.3	2/7
17	Laredo[2]	85,076	93.0	8/8
18	San Francisco	83,373	12.3	0/11
19	Tucson	82,189	24.9	2/6
20	Brownsville[2]	71,139	83.7	3/4

1. Column shows the number of Hispanics and the total membership of the city council or comparable elected body. For example, of New York City's 43 council members, 3 are Hispanic.
2. City has a Hispanic mayor.
a. These figures include both houses of state legislatures.
b. Figures adjusted after November 1982 elections.
c. As of 1985.

SOURCE: *Los Angeles Herald Examiner,* Nov. 21, 1982.

Table 670

POPULATION PERCENTAGE UNDER 15 YEARS
20 LRC, 1950–2010

(%)

Country	1950	1960	1970	1980	1990	2000	2010
A. ARGENTINA	30.6	30.7	29.2	28.2	27.3	25.0	27.2
B. BOLIVIA	42.5	41.9	43.7	43.8	42.5	41.2	42.6
C. BRAZIL	42.4	43.5	42.7	41.5	39.9	37.3	28.7
D. CHILE	38.2	39.1	38.1	32.5	30.6	28.1	26.0
E. COLOMBIA	43.3	46.8	46.1	40.4	38.4	35.2	28.9
F. COSTA RICA	43.5	47.5	46.1	37.9	34.1	31.7	28.1
G. CUBA	36.2	34.4	37.1	32.0	25.9	25.1	21.3
H. DOMINICAN REP.	44.8	47.8	49.0	44.8	38.8	35.5	28.9
I. ECUADOR	41.7	44.4	45.3	44.4	43.9	41.3	37.8
J. EL SALVADOR	42.2	45.1	46.1	45.1	43.4	40.6	37.3
K. GUATEMALA	44.3	46.2	45.7	44.1	41.8	39.5	36.6
L. HAITI	39.5	40.9	42.9	43.6	43.6	43.4	42.4
M. HONDURAS	44.7	45.7	47.5	47.8	45.2	42.3	41.4
N. MEXICO	42.9	45.6	46.5	45.3	44.8	42.3	30.0
O. NICARAGUA	44.1	47.8	48.5	48.0	46.5	44.0	38.4
P. PANAMA	41.6	44.0	43.3	39.8	34.7	31.5	27.8
Q. PARAGUAY	42.4	45.9	46.0	44.3	42.7	39.7	34.2
R. PERU	41.1	43.6	44.3	42.5	40.8	38.0	31.1
S. URUGUAY	28.2	28.5	28.2	27.2	26.7	26.1	24.5
T. VENEZUELA	42.3	46.2	46.4	41.6	39.9	35.6	32.4
LATIN AMERICA[1]	40.6	42.5	42.7	40.9	39.5	37.1	30.5
Caribbean	39.1	40.2	41.7	37.5	33.3	31.7	30.3[a]
Continental Middle America	43.0	45.8	46.4	45.2	44.1	41.7	36.7[b]
Temperate South America	32.2	32.7	31.4	29.4	28.1	26.0	28.5[c]
Tropical South America	42.4	44.3	43.7	41.7	40.1	37.3	31.9[d]
UNITED STATES	26.9	31.1	28.3	22.5	22.7	21.9	~

1. Includes Barbados, Guadeloupe, Guyana, Jamaica, Martinique, Puerto Rico, Suriname,
   Trinidad and Tobago, and the Windward Islands for decades 1950 to 2010.

a. Includes Mexico, Cuba, Dominican Republic, and Haiti.
b. Includes Costa Rica, El Salvador, Guatemala, Honduras, Nicaragua, and Panama.
c. Includes Argentina, Brazil, Paraguay, and Uruguay.
d. Includes Bolivia, Chile, Colombia, Ecuador, Peru, and Venezuela.

SOURCE: PAHO-HC, table 1-5; 2010 data calculated from CELADE-BD, 32 (1983).

Table 671

CELADE RATES OF DEMOGRAPHIC GROWTH, 20 LR, 1920-2000[a]

(AA-GR)

	Country	1920-25	1925-30	1930-35	1935-40	1940-45	1945-50	1950-55	1955-60	1960-65	1965-70
A.	ARGENTINA	3.17	2.81	1.86	1.67	1.67	2.11	2.05	1.98	1.58	1.56
B.	BOLIVIA	1.06	1.26	1.45	1.62	1.78	1.92	1.97	2.16	2.29	2.41
C.	BRAZIL	2.05	2.05	2.05	2.11	2.27	2.55	2.97	3.03	2.86	2.87
D.	CHILE	1.54	1.61	1.55	1.50	1.54	1.74	2.41	2.40	2.50	2.26
E.	COLOMBIA	1.94	1.96	2.03	2.19	2.36	2.65	3.05	3.27	3.32	3.46
F.	COSTA RICA	1.61	1.82	2.00	2.35	2.98	3.44	3.74	4.13	3.65	3.05
G.	CUBA	2.66	2.67	1.93	1.58	1.55	2.28	2.13	2.14	2.07	2.00
H.	DOMINICAN REP.	1.99	2.16	2.28	2.34	2.62	2.84	3.02	3.20	3.25	3.44
I.	ECUADOR	1.14	1.46	1.71	1.91	2.06	2.41	2.83	3.11	3.35	3.41
J.	EL SALVADOR	2.18	2.09	1.19	1.30	1.23	2.05	2.51	2.90	3.04	3.36
K.	GUATEMALA	1.11	2.94	2.42	1.97	3.36	3.10	2.67	2.82	2.98	2.89
L.	HAITI	1.25	1.39	1.51	1.60	1.78	1.84	1.95	2.15	2.28	2.45
M.	HONDURAS	1.94	1.92	1.61	1.73	2.01	2.36	2.62	3.18	3.37	3.43
N.	MEXICO	.95	1.76	1.75	1.84	2.88	3.12	2.94	3.20	3.45	3.50
O.	NICARAGUA	1.46	1.55	1.74	2.00	2.27	2.55	2.66	3.04	3.06	2.98
P.	PANAMA	1.58	1.59	.86	2.57	2.55	2.53	2.89	2.97	3.23	3.27
Q.	PARAGUAY	2.35	2.31	2.34	2.37	1.82	2.01	2.60	2.78	3.24	3.46
R.	PERU	1.47	1.56	1.65	1.72	1.75	1.81	1.98	2.66	3.05	3.12
S.	URUGUAY	2.06	2.04	1.50	1.18	1.13	1.30	1.48	1.44	1.35	1.23
T.	VENEZUELA	1.93	2.17	2.27	2.37	2.84	3.11	3.99	3.92	3.31	3.37
	LATIN AMERICA	1.86	2.03	1.89	1.91	2.22	2.54	2.73	2.85	2.85	2.91

	Country	1970-75	1975-80	1980-85	1985-90	1990-95	1995-2000
A.	ARGENTINA	1.3	1.3	1.2	1.1	9.7***	8.8***
B.	BOLIVIA	2.5	2.6	2.7	2.8	2.8	2.9
C.	BRAZIL	2.6	2.4	2.3	2.2	2.1	2.0
D.	CHILE	1.7	1.7	1.7	1.6	1.4	1.3
E.	COLOMBIA	2.2	2.1	2.1	2.1	1.9	1.7
F.	COSTA RICA	2.5	2.4	2.3	2.2	2.1	1.9
G.	CUBA	1.7	.8	.6	1.0	1.1	1.0
H.	DOMINICAN REP.	2.9	2.6	2.4	2.3	2.2	2.1
I.	ECUADOR	2.9	3.0	3.1	3.1	3.0	2.8
J.	EL SALVADOR	2.9	2.9	2.9	3.1	3.0	2.9
K.	GUATEMALA	3.1	3.0	2.9	2.8	2.8	2.7
L.	HAITI	2.3	2.4	2.5	2.6	2.7	2.7
M.	HONDURAS	3.2	3.5	3.4	3.1	3.1	3.2
N.	MEXICO	3.2	3.0	2.9	2.7	2.4	2.2
O.	NICARAGUA	3.3	3.3	3.3	3.2	3.1	3.1
P.	PANAMA	2.7	2.5	2.2	2.1	1.9	1.8
Q.	PARAGUAY	3.2	3.3	3.0	2.8	2.6	2.3
R.	PERU	2.7	2.7	2.8	2.8	2.8	2.7
S.	URUGUAY	.1	.5	.7	.7	.7	.7
T.	VENEZUELA	3.6	3.5	3.3	2.9	2.6	2.3
	LATIN AMERICA	2.6	2.5	2.4	2.3	2.2	2.0

a. 1920-70 estimated in 1972; 1970-80 estimated in 1981.

SOURCE: CELADE-BD, 10 (1972); CELADE-BD, 28 (1981); CELADE-BD, 30 (1982).

Table 672

CELADE GROWTH RATES FOR TOTAL, URBAN, AND RURAL POPULATION, 20 LR, 1970-2000

(AA-GR for Non-Standard Definition)[1]

		Period					
	Country	1970-75	1975-80	1980-85	1985-90	1990-95	1995-2000
A.	ARGENTINA						
	Total	1.3	1.3	1.2	1.1	9.7	8.8
	Urban	1.8	1.6	1.5	1.4	1.2	1.1
	Rural	−.3	−.3	−.3	−.3	−.4	−.4

Continued in SALA, 23-655 (based upon CELADE-BD, 30 [1982]).

Table 673

ESTIMATED AMERIND POPULATION, 16 L, MID–1950s

	Country	Date	Total Population	Amerind Population	%	Geographic Distribution of Principal Amerind Groups
A.	ARGENTINA	1960	20,956,039	130,000	.6	a. Northern or Chaqueña region (30,000). Chulupíes, Chorotes, Matacos, Tobas, Pilagas.
						b. Northwest or Andean regions and Central (18,000). Coyas, Tobas, Mocobies.
						c. Pampeana region and South (18,000). Araucanos, Onas, Yaganes, Alacalufes.

Continued in SALA, 17-610.

Table 674

AMERIND POPULATION ESTIMATES,[1] 16 LC, LATE 1970s
(1978)

Category	Indigenous Population (T)	% of National Population
Countries with High Percentage of Indigenous Peasant Population		
B. BOLIVIA	3,526	59.2
I. ECUADOR	2,564	33.9
K. GUATEMALA	3,739	59.7
N. MEXICO	8,042	12.4
R. PERU	6,025	36.8
Countries with Principally Tribal Indigenous Population		
C. BRAZIL	243	.2
E. COLOMBIA	547	2.2
P. PANAMA	121	6.8
Q. PARAGUAY	67	2.3
T. VENEZUELA	202	1.5
Countries with Indigenous Minorities		
A. ARGENTINA	398	1.5
D. CHILE	616	5.7
F. COSTA RICA	10	.6
J. EL SALVADOR[2]	100	2.3
M. HONDURAS[2]	107	3.2
O. NICARAGUA[2]	43	1.8
UNITED STATES[3]	1,568	.7
TOTAL	27,927	

1. Indigenous peoples are those who still maintain specific social ties that give them an identity of their own as indigenous in the local context and are, in turn, recognized as such by the nonindigenous people of the countries, although they might have undergone substantial changes since their first contacts with the European colonizers.
2. Unreliable information.
3. The 1980 census gave a total of 1,418,195 who identified themselves as Indian, including American Indians, Eskimos, and Aleuts.

SOURCE: Inter-American Indian Institute, "La Población Indígena en América en 1978," *América Indígena* 39:2 (1979), quoted in *Intercom*, The International Population News Magazine of the Population Reference Bureau 9:6(1981), 4.

CHAPTER 7
VITAL STATISTICS AND DISEASE

Table 700

LIFE EXPECTANCY,[1] 20 LC

PART I. AGES 0-80

		0		1		5		10		15		20		25		30	
Country	Years[2]	Male	Female	Male	Female	Male	Female	Male	Female	Male	Female	Male	Female	Male	Female	Male	Female
A. ARGENTINA	1975-80	65.4	72.1	67.5	73.9	64.0	70.4	59.2	65.6	54.3	60.7	49.6	55.9	45.1	51.2	40.5	46.5
B. BOLIVIA	1975-80	46.5	50.9	53.5	57.3	55.7	58.6	52.0	54.7	47.7	50.3	43.6	46.1	39.8	42.1	36.0	38.1
C. BRAZIL	1975-80	59.5	64.3	64.5	67.7	62.9	65.4	58.5	60.8	53.8	56.1	49.3	51.4	44.9	46.9	40.7	42.5
D. CHILE	1975-80	64.6	70.8	66.7	72.8	63.2	69.2	58.4	64.4	53.6	59.5	48.9	54.7	44.4	50.0	39.9	45.3
E. COLOMBIA	1975-80	60.0	64.5	63.2	67.0	61.8	65.1	57.4	60.7	52.9	56.1	48.4	51.6	44.2	47.2	39.8	43.8
F. COSTA RICA	1975-80	69.0	74.0	70.4	74.9	66.8	71.4	62.0	66.5	57.2	61.6	52.5	56.8	48.0	52.0	43.4	47.2
G. CUBA	1975-80	71.2	74.5	72.4	75.1	69.0	71.6	64.2	66.7	59.3	61.9	54.6	57.0	49.9	52.2	45.2	47.4
H. DOMINICAN REP.	1975-80	58.4	62.2	62.3	65.4	60.7	63.7	56.4	59.4	51.9	54.8	47.5	50.5	43.3	46.2	39.1	42.0
I. ECUADOR	1975-80	58.0	62.0	62.9	65.8	61.7	64.0	57.3	59.5	52.8	54.8	48.5	50.4	44.4	46.1	40.2	41.8
J. EL SALVADOR	1975-80	60.0	64.5	64.7	68.8	63.2	67.0	59.2	63.0	54.5	58.2	50.0	53.7	45.6	49.1	41.3	44.8
K. GUATEMALA	1975-80	56.9	58.8	61.2	62.2	60.9	62.3	57.0	58.3	52.5	53.9	48.0	49.4	43.8	45.1	39.7	40.9
L. HAITI	1975-80	49.2	52.2	55.5	57.7	55.4	57.0	51.3	52.8	47.0	48.4	43.0	44.3	39.2	40.4	35.4	36.5
M. HONDURAS	1975-80	55.4	58.9	61.2	62.9	61.0	62.5	57.0	58.3	52.5	53.8	48.1	49.3	43.9	45.0	39.8	40.7
N. MEXICO	1975-80	61.9	66.3	65.3	69.2	63.2	67.1	58.7	62.6	54.0	57.8	49.5	53.2	45.0	48.6	40.7	44.2
O. NICARAGUA	1975-80	55.3	57.3	60.3	61.7	59.7	60.8	55.4	56.6	50.0	52.1	46.9	47.8	42.9	43.8	38.9	39.8
P. PANAMA	1975-80	67.6	70.9	69.0	72.0	66.1	69.1	61.5	64.5	56.8	59.7	52.3	55.0	47.8	50.3	43.4	45.7
Q. PARAGUAY	1975-80	61.9	66.4	64.5	68.3	62.5	65.9	58.0	61.3	53.3	56.5	48.9	51.8	44.6	47.4	40.3	42.9
R. PERU	1975-80	55.2	58.7	61.0	64.2	60.7	63.8	56.4	59.5	51.9	55.0	47.4	50.5	43.2	46.2	39.0	41.9
S. URUGUAY	1975-80	66.4	73.0	68.7	74.7	65.0	71.0	60.2	66.1	55.3	61.2	50.6	56.4	45.9	51.6	41.3	46.8
T. VENEZUELA	1975-80	64.9	70.7	67.1	72.5	64.0	69.5	59.3	64.7	54.6	59.8	50.0	55.1	45.5	50.3	41.1	45.6
UNITED STATES‡	1983	71.0	78.3	70.9	78.0	67.0	74.2	62.1	69.2	57.3	64.3	52.6	59.5	48.0	54.6	43.4	49.8

		35		40		45		50		55		60		65		70		75		80	
Country	Years[2]	Male	Female	Male	Female	Male	Female	Male	Female	Male	Female	Male	Female	Male	Female	Male	Female	Male	Female	Male	Female
A. ARGENTINA	1975-80	35.9	41.9	31.5	37.3	27.3	32.8	23.3	28.4	19.6	24.2	16.2	20.0	13.1	16.1	10.3	12.6	7.8	9.3	5.4	6.6
B. BOLIVIA	1975-80	32.1	34.1	28.3	30.1	24.5	26.1	20.8	22.3	17.2	18.5	13.9	15.0	10.9	11.8	8.3	9.0	6.2	6.7	4.7	5.0
C. BRAZIL	1975-80	36.5	38.1	32.5	33.9	28.5	29.8	24.7	25.8	21.0	22.0	17.5	18.3	14.3	14.9	11.3	11.8	8.6	9.0	6.3	6.6
D. CHILE	1975-80	35.5	40.6	31.2	36.0	27.0	31.6	23.1	27.3	19.5	23.2	16.2	19.4	13.2	15.9	10.6	12.7	8.4	10.0	6.8	7.7
E. COLOMBIA	1975-80	35.5	38.5	31.3	34.1	27.1	29.8	23.1	25.6	19.3	21.4	15.7	17.4	12.3	13.8	9.4	10.5	6.9	7.7	5.0	5.7
F. COSTA RICA	1975-80	38.8	42.4	34.3	37.7	29.9	33.1	25.6	28.6	21.5	24.2	17.5	19.9	14.0	16.0	10.8	12.4	8.0	9.2	5.6	6.5
G. CUBA	1975-80	40.6	42.7	36.0	38.0	31.5	33.4	27.1	28.9	22.9	24.6	18.9	20.4	15.2	16.5	11.8	12.9	8.9	9.5	6.6	7.0
H. DOMINICAN REP.	1975-80	35.0	37.8	30.9	33.7	27.0	29.6	23.2	25.6	19.6	21.8	16.3	18.2	13.4	14.9	10.6	11.8	8.5	9.3	6.3	6.9
I. ECUADOR	1975-80	36.0	37.5	31.9	33.3	27.9	29.1	24.0	25.1	20.2	21.2	16.7	17.5	13.4	14.0	10.4	10.9	7.9	8.2	5.8	6.0
J. EL SALVADOR	1975-80	37.1	40.5	32.8	36.2	28.7	32.0	24.7	27.8	21.0	23.8	17.4	19.9	14.2	16.0	11.3	12.4	8.9	9.5	6.9	7.0
K. GUATEMALA	1975-80	35.6	36.8	31.6	32.7	27.6	28.7	23.8	24.7	20.2	20.9	16.8	17.2	13.6	14.0	11.0	11.0	8.3	8.5	6.1	6.3
L. HAITI	1975-80	31.6	32.5	27.9	28.7	24.2	24.9	20.7	21.3	17.4	17.9	14.3	14.7	11.5	11.8	9.0	9.2	7.0	7.1	5.5	5.5
M. HONDURAS	1975-80	35.7	36.6	31.7	32.5	27.7	28.5	23.8	24.5	20.0	20.6	16.5	17.0	13.4	13.8	10.5	10.8	7.9	8.1	5.3	5.5
N. MEXICO	1975-80	36.5	39.8	32.4	35.4	28.4	31.2	24.6	27.0	21.0	23.0	17.6	19.2	14.4	15.7	11.6	12.6	9.1	9.9	6.8	7.4
O. NICARAGUA	1975-80	34.9	35.7	30.9	31.6	26.9	27.5	23.1	23.6	19.4	19.8	15.9	16.2	12.7	13.0	9.8	10.0	7.5	7.7	5.7	5.8
P. PANAMA	1975-80	38.9	41.1	34.4	36.6	30.1	32.2	25.9	27.8	21.9	23.6	18.1	19.6	14.7	15.9	11.7	12.6	8.9	9.7	6.7	7.2
Q. PARAGUAY	1975-80	36.0	38.4	31.8	34.1	27.7	29.9	23.7	25.7	19.9	21.7	16.2	17.9	13.0	14.3	10.0	11.1	7.7	8.4	5.9	6.4
R. PERU	1975-80	34.7	37.6	30.5	33.3	26.4	29.0	22.5	24.8	18.7	20.7	15.2	16.7	11.9	13.1	9.0	9.9	6.6	7.3	4.8	5.2
S. URUGUAY	1975-80	36.6	42.0	32.1	37.4	27.7	32.8	23.6	28.4	19.7	24.1	16.2	20.1	13.0	16.3	10.3	12.8	7.9	9.8	6.0	7.3
T. VENEZUELA	1975-80	36.7	41.0	32.4	36.4	28.2	31.9	24.3	27.6	20.5	23.5	16.9	19.7	13.8	16.2	11.2	13.1	8.9	10.4	7.1	8.1
UNITED STATES‡	1983	38.7	45.0	34.1	40.2	29.7	35.5	25.4	31.0	21.4	26.7	17.8	22.6	14.5	18.8	11.5	15.2	9.0	11.9	6.9	9.0

1. The life expectancy represents average number of years of life remaining to persons surviving to exact age specified if subject to mortality conditions of period indicated, i.e., the average number of years a person of the age specified may be expected to live if the age specific mortality rates of the indicated period do not change in the future.
2. For previous years, see SALA, 23-700.

SOURCE: CELADE-BD, 33, 1984, tables 2-21, except data for U.S. from UN-DY, 1985, table 34.

Table 700 (Continued)

LIFE EXPECTANCY,[1] 20 LC

PART II. ESTIMATES AND PROJECTIONS, 1950–2000

		1950-55			1980-85			1995-2000			2020-25		
	Country	M	F	T	M	F	T	M	F	T	M	F	T
A.	ARGENTINA	60.4	65.1	62.7	66.7	73.3	69.9	68.1	74.5	71.2	68.6	75.5	72.0
B.	BOLIVIA	38.5	42.5	40.4	48.6	53.0	50.7	57.0	62.0	59.4	64.5	70.0	67.2
C.	BRAZIL	49.8	52.2	51.0	61.6	65.4	63.5	65.2	69.7	67.4	69.1	74.8	71.9
D.	CHILE	52.3	56.0	54.1	63.8	70.4	67.0	67.4	73.9	70.6	68.5	75.5	71.9
E.	COLOMBIA	48.8	52.6	50.6	61.4	66.0	63.6	64.7	69.3	66.9	69.0	73.8	71.3
F.	COSTA RICA	56.0	58.6	57.3	68.7	73.3	70.9	70.4	75.4	72.8	71.4	76.6	73.9
G.	CUBA	56.7	61.0	58.8	71.8	75.2	73.4	72.7	76.7	74.7	73.0	77.4	75.1
H.	DOMINICAN REP.	43.6	46.7	45.1	60.7	64.6	62.6	66.1	70.2	68.1	70.4	74.6	72.4
I.	ECUADOR	46.0	47.9	46.9	60.6	64.7	62.6	67.0	71.0	69.0	69.3	73.8	71.5
J.	EL SALVADOR	44.1	46.5	45.3	62.6	67.1	64.8	69.4	73.3	71.3	71.1	75.1	73.1
K.	GUATEMALA	42.1	43.3	42.7	59.7	61.8	60.7	66.8	69.3	68.0	70.2	74.3	72.2
L.	HAITI	36.3	38.9	37.6	51.2	54.4	52.7	56.7	60.2	58.4	63.8	68.4	66.0
M.	HONDURAS	40.9	43.5	42.2	58.2	61.7	59.9	66.0	69.7	67.8	70.2	74.3	72.2
N.	MEXICO	50.3	53.3	51.8	63.9	68.2	66.0	68.0	72.3	70.1	70.6	75.0	72.7
O.	NICARAGUA	41.5	44.6	43.0	55.8	59.5	57.6	62.8	66.8	64.7	67.8	72.5	70.1
P.	PANAMA	57.6	60.1	58.8	68.5	73.0	70.7	70.4	75.4	72.8	70.5	76.6	73.5
Q.	PARAGUAY	50.0	54.0	51.9	62.8	67.5	65.1	65.3	70.5	67.8	69.0	74.5	71.7
R.	PERU	42.6	44.8	43.7	57.6	60.7	59.1	62.7	66.1	64.4	69.5	73.0	71.2
S.	URUGUAY	63.3	69.4	66.3	67.1	73.7	70.3	69.5	76.0	72.7	70.1	77.1	73.6
T.	VENEZUELA	50.3	54.4	52.3	65.1	70.6	67.8	68.1	73.8	70.9	71.0	77.0	73.9

SOURCE: CEPAL, *Informe de la Reunión Regional Latinoamericana Preparatoria de la Asamblea Mundial sobre el Envejecimiento*, San José, March 31, 1982, pp. 30-31.

Table 701

LIVE BIRTHS BY AGE OF MOTHER, 20 L

(N)

				Age of Mother									
	Country	Year	Total Births	Under 15	15–19	20–24	25–29	30–34	35–39	40–44	45–49	50+	Unknown
A.	ARGENTINA	1981	680,292	2,922	88,691	187,303	185,183	124,166	61,075	18,502	2,342	871	9,237
B.	BOLIVIA	1977	142,277	106	14,779	39,220	36,251	24,989	16,778	6,804	2,443	907	- -
C.	BRAZIL[4]	1984	2,559,038	5,192	349,591	824,723	693,071	392,968	184,884	63,807	9,017	974	34,811
D.	CHILE[9]	1983	243,712	707	36,077	81,213	65,236	37,506	17,532	4,929	441	71	- -
E.	COLOMBIA[4,5]	1969	691,000	382	66,073	170,675	152,191	99,683	75,909	23,292	6,266	~	96,634
F.	COSTA RICA	1983	72,953	290	12,335	24,368	18,459	10,331	4,768	1,286	755	#	361
G.	CUBA[2]	1983	165,284	1,390	51,482	58,592	30,652	15,642	5,532	1,020	147	108	719
H.	DOMINICAN REP.[1]	1976	169,161	388	17,685	42,314	34,607	25,388	19,336	10,728	5,396	5,491	7,828
I.	ECUADOR[4,6]	1981	223,182	332	29,340	67,914	54,151	36,584	22,356	10,082	1,734	371	318
J.	EL SALVADOR	1984	142,202	395	27,537	45,359	30,355	18,092	10,743	4,434	864	136	4,287
K.	GUATEMALA	1979	295,972	883	51,682	86,604	68,542	46,347	28,721	10,602	1,762	470	359
L.	HAITI[4]	1972	137,621	- -	12,659	32,519	33,873	23,917	23,493	7,703	3,457	~	- -
M.	HONDURAS[1,4]	1983	158,419	1,471	22,206	55,190	32,281	20,268	12,476	4,945	1,063	#	8,519
N.	MEXICO[4]	1982	2,392,849	6,382	372,963	747,839	561,223	336,589	201,508	75,836	18,177	20,824	51,508
O.	NICARAGUA[1,4]	1967	78,141	51	10,521	19,780	17,338	9,581	6,634	1,982	533	~	11,721
P.	PANAMA	1984	56,659	322	10,943	18,637	13,603	7,504	3,356	1,030	131	26	1,107
Q.	PARAGUAY[1,4]	1971	21,317	30	2,376	5,530	4,795	3,415	2,068	1,018	343	~	1,742
R.	PERU[4,8]	1978	465,503	677	61,155	137,181	115,714	73,163	51,408	18,042	3,645	247	4,271
S.	URUGUAY[1]	1981	53,923	268	7,585	15,733	14,153	9,154	4,843	1,643	79‡	79‡	465
T.	VENEZUELA[7]	1981	497,270	3,843	80,111	157,896	126,862	76,689	36,010	13,411	2,169	253	26

1. Data tabulated by year of registration, not of occurrences.
2. Data are births recorded in National Register of Consumers.
3. Excluding the Canal Zone.
4. Data incomplete.
5. Data based on baptismal records of the Roman Catholic Church.
6. Excluding nomadic Indian tribes.
7. Excluding Indian jungle population, estimated at 31,800 in 1961.
8. Excluding Indian jungle population, estimated at 39,800 in 1972.
9. Excluding adjustment for under-registration.

SOURCE: UN-DY, 1975, table 23; 1976, 1983–85, table 10.

Table 702

CRUDE BIRTH RATES, 20 LC, 1960–85[a]

(PTI)[1]

Country	Code	1960	1965	1970	1975	1980	1981	1982	1983	1984	1985
A. ARGENTINA	C	22.8[‡]	21.7	22.9	~	24.7	23.7	~	23.9	~	~
B. BOLIVIA[9,10]	U	25.6[‡,c]	46.1	45.6	46.6	44.8	~	~	~	~	~
C. BRAZIL[10]	U	~	42.1	38.8	35.8	33.3	30.6[‡]	30.6[‡]	30.6[‡]	30.6[‡]	30.6[‡]
D. CHILE[8]	C	35.7	33.2	27.6	24.6	22.2	23.4	23.9	22.3	22.3	~
E. COLOMBIA[10]	U	42.4[c,d]	44.6	39.6	33.3	32.0	31.0[‡]	31.0[‡]	31.0[‡]	31.0[‡]	31.0[‡]
F. COSTA RICA	C	48.4	42.3	33.4	29.5	29.4	29.8	30.7	30.0	32.7	~
G. CUBA[2,4,11]	C	29.8	33.8	27.6	20.7	14.1	14.0	16.3	16.7	16.6	18.0[‡]
H. DOMINICAN REP.[2,10]	C	36.8[c]	42.7	~	~	34.6[‡]	33.1[‡]	33.1[‡]	33.1[‡]	33.1[‡]	33.1[‡]
I. ECUADOR[3,10]	U	47.7[c]	46.1	44.2	42.2	41.6	36.8[‡]	36.8[‡]	36.8[‡]	36.8[‡]	36.8[‡]
J. EL SALVADOR	C	46.5	46.9	40.0	39.9	35.8	35.6	33.6	30.5	29.8	~
K. GUATEMALA	C	49.5	45.3	40.2	39.9	41.8	43.3	42.6	38.3	~	~
L. HAITI[10]	U	~	44.4	43.7	42.7	41.8	41.3[‡]	41.3[‡]	41.3[‡]	41.3[‡]	41.3[‡]
M. HONDURAS[2,10]	U	44.7[c,d]	50.9	50.0	48.6	47.1	43.9[‡]	43.9[‡]	43.9[‡]	43.9[‡]	43.9[‡]
N. MEXICO[2,10]	U	46.0[b,d]	44.6	43.9	41.8	37.6	33.9[‡]	33.9[‡]	33.9[‡]	33.9[‡]	33.9[‡]
O. NICARAGUA[2,10]	U	45.2[c,d]	50.0	48.6	48.3	46.6	44.2[‡]	44.2[‡]	44.2[‡]	44.2[‡]	44.2[‡]
P. PANAMA[6]	C	40.8	38.4	36.4	33.2	26.9	26.9	26.7	26.4	26.5	~
Q. PARAGUAY[3,10]	U	~	42.2	40.4	37.5	36.7	36.0[‡]	36.0[‡]	36.0[‡]	36.0[‡]	36.0[‡]
R. PERU[2,7,10]	U	38.9[c,d]	46.4	44.5	40.0	38.0	41.5	35.7	36.8	36.4	35.5
S. URUGUAY[2]	C	21.4[‡,c,d]	22.4	19.5	20.9	18.6	18.4	18.5	~	~	~
T. VENEZUELA[5,10]	U	45.9[c,d]	45.2	40.9	37.5	36.9	33.0[‡]	33.0[‡]	33.0[‡]	33.0[‡]	33.0[‡]
UNITED STATES	C	23.7	19.4	18.2	14.6	15.9	15.8	15.8	15.4[‡]	15.6[‡]	15.7[‡]

Code: C = Data estimated to be virtually complete, representing at least 90% of the events
occurring each year.

U = Data estimated to be incomplete, representing less than 90% of the events
occurring each year.

1. Crude birth rates are determined by the number of live births per thousand, mid-year
population.
2. Data tabulated by year of registration rather than year of occurrence.
3. Excluding nomadic Amerind tribes.
4. For 1960, data estimates based on analysis of 1943 and 1953 census returns plus an
assumed rate of growth.
5. Excluding Indian jungle population estimated at 31,800 in 1961.
6. Excluding Canal Zone.
7. Excluding Indian jungle population.
8. For 1960, data are births tabulated by year of occurrence.
9. Data for 1975 were based on a national sample survey.
10. U.N. Population Division estimate for years 1965–85.
11. Based on births registered in National Consumer Register.

a. For 1930-59 data, see SALA, 21-705.
b. Data considered complete.
c. Data considered incomplete.
d. Data tabulated by year of registration.

SOURCE: UN-DY, 1964, 1981 and 1985, tables 16, Special Topic Table 21, and 9 respectively.

Table 703

AGE-SPECIFIC FERTILITY RATES, CRUDE BIRTH RATE (CBR),
TOTAL FERTILITY RATE (TFR), AND GROSS
REPRODUCTION RATE (GRR), 20 LC,
1975–80

Country	Age of Mother							CBR	TFR	GRR
	15-19	20-24	25-29	30-34	35-39	40-44	45-49			
A. ARGENTINA	57.2	149.1	158.5	115.4	66.8	21.9	5.4	21.24	2.87	1.40

Continued in SALA, 23-702.

Table 704

TOTAL FERTILITY RATES,[1] 20 L, 1950–85

| | | Period | | | % Change | |
	Country	1950–55	1960–65	1980–85	1950–55 to 1960–65	1960–65 to 1980–85
A.	ARGENTINA	3.2	3.1	3.4	-2.6	9.9
B.	BOLIVIA	6.7	6.6	6.3	-1.8	-5.6
C.	BRAZIL	6.2	6.2	3.8	0	-38.0
D.	CHILE	4.9	5.1	2.6	4.2	-49.4
E.	COLOMBIA	6.7	6.7	3.9	0	-41.5
F.	COSTA RICA	6.7	6.9	3.5	3.4	-49.6
G.	CUBA	4.0	4.7	2.0	16.4	-57.7
H.	DOMINICAN REP.	7.5	7.3	4.2	-2.5	-42.9
I.	ECUADOR	6.9	6.9	5.0	0	-27.6
J.	EL SALVADOR	6.5	6.8	5.6	6.0	-18.9
K.	GUATEMALA	7.1	6.8	6.1	-3.5	-10.5
L.	HAITI	6.2	6.2	5.7	0	-6.7
M.	HONDURAS	7.1	7.4	6.5	4.4	-11.7
N.	MEXICO	6.7	6.7	4.6	0	-31.6
O.	NICARAGUA	7.3	7.3	5.9	0	-19.0
P.	PANAMA	5.7	5.9	3.5	4.3	-41.5
Q.	PARAGUAY	6.6	6.6	4.9	0	-26.6
R.	PERU	6.9	6.9	5.0	0	-27.2
S.	URUGUAY	2.7	2.9	2.8	6.0	-4.3
T.	VENEZUELA	6.5	6.5	4.1	0	-36.5

1.   Average number of lifetime births per woman at current age-specific fertility rates.

SOURCE: *Population Bulletin* (July 1986), vol. 41, no. 3, p. 16.

Table 705

TOTAL FERTILITY RATES,[1] 4 L, 1970–2000

(N)

	Country	1970	1975	1980	1985	1990	1995	2000
C.	BRAZIL	5.33	4.54	4.42	4.06	3.74	3.45	3.20
E.	COLOMBIA	~	4.44	3.60	3.22	2.90	2.57	2.25
N.	MEXICO	6.83	~	4.57	4.05	3.59	3.20	2.85
R.	PERU	6.28	5.69	5.19	4.74	4.23	3.74	3.30

1.   Average number of children born per woman.

SOURCE: Adapted from USBC, *World Population Profile: 1985* (Washington, D.C.: U.S. Government Printing Office, 1986), p. 47.

Table 706

FERTILITY RATES, BY AGE OF MOTHER, 4 LC, 1985

(Births per 1,000 Women)

	Country		Under 20	20–24	25–29	30–34	35–39	40–44	45+
						Age of Mother			
C.	BRAZIL		74.7	198.8	210.8	160.5	108.3	48.8	10.0
E.	COLOMBIA		52.8	168.3	158.4	124.4	85.9	46.5	7.2
M.	HONDURAS		121.2	281.8	255.7	225.1	158.8	77.5	21.9
N.	MEXICO		93.8	205.4	194.4	162.1	105.4	42.6	7.0
	UNITED STATES		53.3	115.3	115.4	66.2	20.9	4.0	.2

SOURCE: Adapted from USBC, *World Population Profile: 1985* (Washington D.C.:
U.S. Government Printing Office, 1986), p. 48.

Figure 7:1

FERTILITY RATES,[1] BY AGE OF MOTHER, 4 LC, 1985

(Births per 1,000 Women)

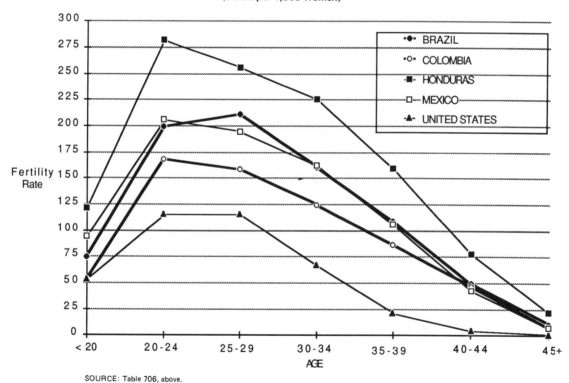

SOURCE: Table 706, above.

Table 707

PERCENT OF MARRIED WOMEN[1] USING CONTRACEPTION, 18 LC, 1977-85
(%)

	Country	Year	% of Women
A.	ARGENTINA	1977	2
B.	BOLIVIA	1983	24
C.	BRAZIL	1980	56
D.	CHILE	1978	43
E.	COLOMBIA	1984	55
F.	COSTA RICA	1984	65
H.	DOMINICAN REP.	1983	36
I.	ECUADOR	1982	40
J.	EL SALVADOR	1985	48
K.	GUATEMALA	1983	25
L.	HAITI	1977	19
M.	HONDURAS	1981	27
N.	MEXICO	1982	48
O.	NICARAGUA	1977	9
P.	PANAMA	1979	61
Q.	PARAGUAY	1979	39
R.	PERU	1981	41
T.	VENEZUELA	1977	60
	UNITED STATES	1982	68

1. Ages 15 to 44.

SOURCE: Adapted from USBC, *World Population Profile: 1985* (Washington, D.C.: U.S. Government Printing Office, 1986), p. 46.

Table 708

ANNUAL BIRTH AND DEATH RATES, 20 L, 1930–85
(AA, PTI)

	Country	1930–35		1945–49		1960–65		1980–85	
		Birth	Death	Birth	Death	Birth	Death	Birth	Death
A.	ARGENTINA	28.9	11.6	25.2	9.6	23.2	8.8	24.6	8.7
B.	BOLIVIA	~	~	47.1[a]	24.1[a]	46.1	21.5	44.0	13.9
C.	BRAZIL	~	~	44.6[a]	15.1[a]	42.1	12.3	30.6	8.4
D.	CHILE	40.2	24.5	37.0	17.5	36.4	11.8	22.7	6.7
E.	COLOMBIA	43.3	22.5	43.4	20.8	44.6	12.2	31.0	7.7
F.	COSTA RICA	44.6	21.5	42.7	13.2	45.3	9.1	30.5	4.2
G.	CUBA	31.3	13.3	30.0	8.7	35.3	8.8	16.9	6.4
H.	DOMINICAN REP.	~	~	49.1[a]	21.8[a]	47.7	15.4	33.1	8.0
I.	ECUADOR	48.5	25.7	45.9	20.0	45.6	14.3	36.8	8.1
J.	EL SALVADOR	46.5	32.7	44.8	22.8	47.4	15.3	40.2	8.1
K.	GUATEMALA	46.2	31.7	49.1	26.5	47.8	18.3	42.7	10.5
L.	HAITI	~	~	45.5[a]	26.8[a]	44.4	21.6	41.3	14.2
M.	HONDURAS	42.0	21.7	44.5	19.0	50.9	17.7	43.9	10.1
N.	MEXICO	44.1	26.7	44.5	17.8	44.9	11.3	33.9	7.1
O.	NICARAGUA	~	~	54.1[a]	22.7[a]	50.3	17.1	44.2	9.7
P.	PANAMA	37.4	15.1	38.3	10.8	40.8	9.6	28.0	5.4
Q.	PARAGUAY	~	~	45.5[a]	15.5[a]	42.2	11.9	36.0	7.2
R.	PERU	~	~	44.9	24.7	46.3	17.6	36.7	10.7
S.	URUGUAY	22.3	11.6	19.7	9.1	21.9	9.6	19.5	10.2
T.	VENEZUELA	39.9	21.9	43.6	16.1	44.2	9.1	33.0	5.5

a. Data are for 1950–55 from UN, 1984 Assessment.

SOURCE: *Population Bulletin* (July 1986), vol. 41, no. 3, p. 8.

Table 709

FETAL MORTALITY RATES,[1] 16 LC, 1960-83[a]

(Deaths per 1,000 Live Births)

	Country	1960	1965	1970	1975	1977	1978	1979	1980	1981	1982	1983
A.	ARGENTINA	24.3	23.9	20.6	~	~	~	17.8	12.7	12.3	~	~
C.	BRAZIL[2]	28.5	~	~	~	29.4	19.0	18.5	17.2	17.0	16.0	16.1
D.	CHILE[3,4]	26.5	24.2	18.6	15.5	12.7	11.0	10.1	9.1	7.7	7.3	5.9
E.	COLOMBIA[3,5]	11.3	15.6	~	12.3	~	~	~	~	~	~	~
F.	COSTA RICA[3,8]	17.2	17.2	15.7	~	~	~	~	~	~	~	~
G.	CUBA[3,6]	26.8	20.5	15.0	11.3[b]	11.7	11.5	13.1	12.4	12.1	11.8	11.6
H.	DOMINICAN REP.[3]	27.7	23.2	25.4	19.7[b]	~	~	~	~	~	~	~
I.	ECUADOR[7]	22.4	21.0	19.6	22.2	24.9	25.6	24.0	22.4	19.3	~	~
J.	EL SALVADOR	8.5	9.5	10.2	8.0	7.5	6.6	6.6	6.2	~	~	~
K.	GUATEMALA	30.1	29.5	28.7	27.1	21.8	23.8	23.2	23.2	21.9	19.7	~
N.	MEXICO[3]	17.2	17.3	16.6	~	13.8	11.8	12.2	10.4	10.0	9.3	~
O.	NICARAGUA	2.0	8.5	~	~	~	~	~	~	~	~	~
P.	PANAMA[10]	24.1	24.8	21.0	~	~	~	~	~	~	~	~
R.	PERU[3,7,9]	11.2	10.8	~	~	~	~	~	~	~	~	~
S.	URUGUAY	~	14.9	13.2	~	~	~	~	~	~	~	~
T.	VENEZUELA[3,7]	19.9	17.8	15.9	16.2	15.6	14.6	14.7	14.2	~	~	~
	UNITED STATES	12.7	12.6	14.2	8.3	8.1	7.7	7.4	7.2	6.8	~	~

1. Deaths after more than 20-28 weeks gestation. Reliability and comparability of data known to be greatly affected by incomplete or irregular registration of fetal deths, and/or live births, and by variations in definitions.
2. 1960 data for state of Guanabara only.
3. Data tabulated by year of registration rather than of occurrence.
4. Rates for 1960 computed on live births which have been adjusted or under-registration.
5. Based on burial permits but computed on number of baptisms recorded in Roman Catholic Church registers.
6. 1960 data computed on births which are estimated based on analysis of 1943 and 1953 census returns and application of an assumed rate of growth.
7. Excluding tropical forest Amerinds.
8. Ratios for 1951-65 computed on live births registered during the period 1951-65 tabulated by year of occurrence.
9. Ratios are based on burial permits, estimated to be 50% complete.
10. Excluding Canal Zone and tribal Amerind population.

a. Includes fetuses of less than 5 months gestation; for 1950-59 data, see SALA, 23-704.
b. Data tabulated by year of occurrence.

SOURCE: IN-DY, 1966, 1974, and 1981, tables 10, 17, and Special Topic table 38 respectively; 1982 and 1983, table 12; 1985, table 17.

Table 710

INFANT MORTALITY RATES, 19 LC, 1960-85[a]
(Deaths per 1,000 Live Births)[1]

	Country	Code	1960	1965	1970	1975	1980	1981	1982	1983	1984	1985
A.	ARGENTINA[11]	C	62.4	56.9	58.9	~	33.2	33.6	~	35.3	~	~
B.	BOLIVIA[11]	**	~	76.5	~	~	138.2‡	124.4‡	124.4‡	124.4‡	124.4‡	124.4‡
C.	BRAZIL[2,11]	U	~	~	~	~	78.8‡	70.6‡	70.6‡	70.6‡	70.6‡	70.6‡
D.	CHILE[6,11]	C	125.1	107.1	78.8	56.4	33.0	27.0	23.6	21.9	19.6	~
E.	COLOMBIA[2,3,7,11]		99.8	82.4	~	46.7	55.0‡	50.0‡	50.0‡	50.0‡	50.0‡	50.0‡
F.	COSTA RICA[12]	C	70.8	71.8	61.5	38.2	20.2	19.1	19.3	18.6	~	~
G.	CUBA[2,5,9]	C	35.4^c	38.4	35.9	27.3‡	19.6	18.5	17.3	16.8	15.0‡	16.5‡
H.	DOMINICAN REP.[11]	U	100.6^d	72.7	50.1	43.5	84.3‡	74.5‡	74.5‡	74.5‡	74.5‡	74.5‡
I.	ECUADOR[8,11,12]	U	100.0	93.0	76.6	65.8	82.4‡	69.5‡	69.5‡	69.5‡	69.5‡	69.5‡
J.	EL SALVADOR	C	76.3	70.6	66.6	58.1	42.0	44.0	42.2	~	35.1	~
K.	GUATEMALA	C	91.9	92.6	87.1	81.4	65.5	63.9	62.5	71.5	~	~
M.	HONDURAS[2,11]	U	52.0	41.2	33.2	33.7	94.7‡	81.5‡	81.5‡	81.5‡	81.5‡	81.5‡
N.	MEXICO[2,11,13]	U	74.2^b	60.7	68.5	52.8	60.0‡	53.0‡	53.0‡	53.0‡	53.0‡	53.0‡
O.	NICARAGUA[2,11]	U	70.2	51.6^d	~	~	93.0‡	76.4‡	76.4‡	76.4‡	76.4‡	76.4‡
P.	PANAMA[4,11]	U	56.9	44.7	40.5	31.6	31.6‡	25.6‡	25.6‡	25.6‡	25.6‡	25.6‡
Q.	PARAGUAY[2,11]	U	~	41.5	33.3	~	48.6‡	45.0‡	45.0‡	45.0‡	45.0‡	45.0‡
R.	PERU[10,11,2]	U	92.1	90.7	~	~	104.9‡	98.6‡	98.6‡	98.6‡	98.6‡	98.6‡
S.	URUGUAY[2]	C	47.4‡,c	49.8	42.6	48.8^d	37.6	33.4	29.4	30.0	~	~
T.	VENEZUELA[8,11]	U	53.9	47.7	49.3	43.7^d	43.3‡	27.7‡	27.7‡	27.7‡	27.7‡	27.7‡
	UNITED STATES	C	26.0	24.7	20.0	16.1	12.6	11.9	11.5	10.9‡	10.6‡	10.5‡

Code: C = Data estimated to be virtually complete, representing at least 90% of the
events occurring each year.
U = Data estimated to be virtually incomplete, representing less than 90% of the
events occurring each year.

1. Number of deaths of infants of less than 1 year, per 1,000 live births.
2. Data tabulated by year of registration rather than of occurrence.
3. Prior to 1951 tabulated by year of registration rather than of occurrence.
4. Excluding the former Canal Zone.
5. Prior to 1957 rates excluded those dying within 24 hours of birth. Beginning in
1957 rates computed on births which are in turn estimates based on analysis of
1943 and 1953 census and the application of an assumed rate of growth.
6. Prior to 1968 rates computed on live births with an upward adjustment for
undernumeration.
7. Rates computed on number of baptisms recorded in Roman Catholic Church
registers, for years 1960, 1965, and 1970 while 1975 data are based on burial
permits.
8. Excluding tropical forest Amerinds.
9. Rates for 1965-85 computed on live births recorded in the National Register of
Consumers established December 31, 1964.
10. Excluding Indian jungle population estimated at 100,830 in 1961.
11. Estimate for 1975-85 prepared by the Population Division of the United Nations.
12. Rates for 1960 and 1965 were computed on live births registered during the period
1951-65 tabulated by year of occurrence.
13. Rates computed by date of occurrence for years 1975-85.

a. For 1930-59, see SALA, 23-705.
b. Data considered complete.
c. Data considered incomplete.
d. Data tabulated by year of occurrence.

SOURCE: UN-DY, 1966, 1974, tables 14 and 20 respectively; 1979 and 1983, table 15;
1985, table 20.

Table 711

DEATHS OF CHILDREN UNDER 5 YEARS BY PRINCIPAL CAUSE,[1] 20 LC

(N, PHTI, and %)

	Country	Date	Total		Childhood Diseases[8]			Gastritis, Enteritis, etc.[9]			Influenza, and Pneumonia		
			Number	Rate	Number	Rate	%	Number	Rate	%	Number	Rate	%
A.	ARGENTINA	1981	26,904	3,588.2	4,516	400.9	16.7	1,812	236.2	6.7	2,012	260.7	7.4
B.	BOLIVIA	1965	14,706	~	4,451	~	30.3	798	~	5.4	315	~	2.1
C.	BRAZIL	1962	45,134	2,219.0	12,344	606.9	27.3	7,885	387.6	17.5	5,351	263.1	11.9
D.	CHILE[2]	1983	6,963	2,331.8	776	267.5	11.1	338	115.9	-4.7	903	303.4	12.9
E.	COLOMBIA[6]	1967	83,935	2,398.2	17,752	507.2	21.1	18,930	540.9	22.6	9,177	262.2	10.9
F.	COSTA RICA	1983	1,624	2,226.1	255	349.5	15.7	199	272.8	12.3	111	152.2	6.8
G.	CUBA	1983	3,248	1,960.8	525	316.9	16.2	212	127.9	6.5	293	176.9	9.0
H.	DOMINICAN REP.[2]	1982	8,256	3,468.1	2,621	1,001.9	31.7	1,190	497.0	19.6	415	153.1	5.0
I.	ECUADOR[7]	1980	22,464	1,005.8	8,939	4,002.2	39.8	5,589	2,502.3	24.9	2,341	1,048.1	10.4
J.	EL SALVADOR[3]	1984	7,031	4,944.4	1,996	1,403.6	28.4	1,229	864.3	17.5	288	202.5	4.1
K.	GUATEMALA[2]	1981	28,436	6,634.9	14,377	2,946.9	50.5	7,115	1,520.4	25.0	5,002	1,158.6	17.5
L.	HAITI	~	~	~	~	~	~	~	~	~	~	~	~
M.	HONDURAS[4]	1981	6,226	3,866.6	2,601	1,615.3	41.8	1,501	932.2	24.1	374	232.3	6.0
N.	MEXICO	1982	100,278	4,190.8	31,693	1,324.5	31.6	24,328	1,016.7	24.3	16,442	687.1	16.4
O.	NICARAGUA[2]	1966	5,405	1,753.9	1,370	444.6	25.3	1,267	411.1	23.4	318	103.2	5.9
P.	PANAMA[2,5]	1984	1,473	2,599.7	238	420.0	16.2	112	197.7	7.6	95	167.7	6.4
Q.	PARAGUAY	1984	3,928	6,966.3	1,230	2,181.4	31.3	678	1,202.4	17.3	511	906.3	13.0
R.	PERU	1982	32,462	4,780.8	11,215	1,651.7	34.5	5,674	835.6	17.5	6,685	984.5	20.6
S.	URUGUAY	1984	1,805	3,014.5	332	554.5	18.4	148	247.2	8.2	73	121.9	4.0
T.	VENEZUELA[7]	1983	17,544	3,410.7	5,418	1,053.3	30.9	3,338	648.9	19.0	1,484	288.5	8.5
	UNITED STATES	1983	48,428	1,340.1	1,550	42.9	3.2	1,011	27.9	2.1	1,001	27.7	2.1

1. Unless otherwise stated, the causes of death have been classified according to the ninth revision of the International Classification of Diseases. The data refer to the number of deaths of children under 5 years of age with the national boundaries indicated. Fetal deaths are excluded as, in some cases, are those which occurred before the respective births or within 24 hours of birth.
2. Causes of death classified according to the eighth revision of the International Classification of Diseases.
3. Includes deaths of residents living abroad.

4. Data tabulated by year of record and not of death.
5. Excluding Canal Zone.
6. Data based on burial permits.
7. Excluding Selvatic Amerinds.
8. Includes infectious and parasitic diseases, measles, protein-caloric malnutrition, and meningitis except in the cases of Bolivia, Brazil, Colombia, Haiti, and Nicaragua.
9. Corresponds to the classification: Other intestinal infectious diseases.

SOURCE: AC, 1974, table 207-28; adapted from WHO-WHSA, 1985 and 1986, tables 13 and 11 respectively.

Figure 7:2

FERTILITY, LITERACY, AND CONTRACEPTIVE USE, 3 LC, 1980–84

PART I. CONTRACEPTIVE USE AND TOTAL FERTILITY RATE

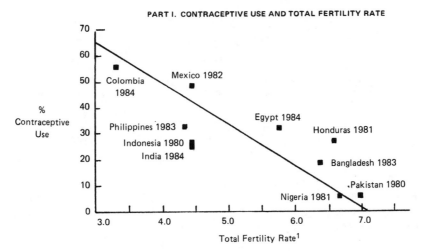

1. Average number of children born to women ages 15 to 44.

PART II. LEVEL OF LITERACY AND CONTRACEPTIVE USE

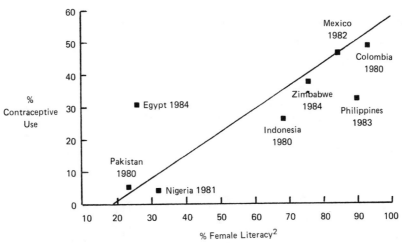

2. Women ages 15 to 44.

SOURCE: Adapted from USBC, *World Population Profile: 1985* (Washington, D.C.:
U.S. Government Printing Office, 1986), p. 46.

Table 712

MATERNAL DEATH RATES,[1] 16 LC, 1970–84

(Deaths PHT Live Births)

Country	1970	1975	1977	1978	1979	1980	1981	1982	1983	1984
A. ARGENTINA[10]	~	~	91.5	84.5	84.6*	69.5	69.4	~	~	~
C. BRAZIL[3,4]	~	~	~	~	96.8	92.1	~	~	~	~
D. CHILE[10]	125.7	122.2	107.8	94.7	74.9	74.9*	43.8	52.5	40.3	~
E. COLOMBIA[2,4]	~	~	133.5[b]	~	~	~	~	~	~	~
F. COSTA RICA[9,10]	105.6	70.5	53.0	39.5[a]	44.3[a]	24.2*,[a]	36.9[a]	29.5[a]	26.0[a]	~
G. CUBA[10]	48.0[c]	38.9[c]	49.1[c]	45.2[c]	~	59.9*	51.4	55.7	45.4	~
I. ECUADOR[2,4,5]	220.3	231.9	198.5	216.3	~	~	185.9	~	~	~
J. EL SALVADOR[3]	~	~	~	~	~	70.6	61.8	84.8	74.2	69.6
K. GUATEMALA[10]	142.8	~	120.8	119.8	150.3*	91.0	105.8	~	~	~
N. MEXICO[10]	135.3	113.5	~	100.4	108.3*	93.9	86.9	~	~	~
P. PANAMA[4,6,9,10]	118.2	94.7	68.3	90.5	69.9*	72.2	61.3	89.9	59.8	49.4[a]
R. PERU[4,7,10]	198.5[c]	~	171.5[c]	148.2	69.9*	108.2	91.9	~	~	~
S. URUGUAY[2]	44.8[a]	69.3	58.6	55.9	~	~	~	~	~	~
T. VENEZUELA[4,8,10]	~	68.4	74.8	65.2	64.7*	~	~	~	~	~
UNITED STATES[10]	18.1	12.9	11.2	9.6	9.6*	9.2	8.5	7.9	~	~

1. Deaths due to complications of pregnancy, childbirth, and the puerperium. For an
    alternative series, 1965–75, see SALA, 21-711.
2. All data classified by 1965 Revision.
3. All data classified by 1975 Revision.
4. Data from incomplete civil registers.
5. Excluding nomadic Indian tribes.
6. Prior to 1980, excluding former Canal Zone.
7. Excluding Indian jungle population estimated at 100,831 in 1961 and 39,800 in 1972.
8. Excluding Indian jungle population estimated at 31,800 in 1961.
9. Data for 1970 were classified by 1965 Revision.
10. Separates data classified by 8th and 9th Revisions of the Abbreviated List of
    Causes for Tabulation of Mortality in the International Classification of Diseases.

a. Rates based on 30 or fewer maternal deaths.
b. Based on burial permits.
c. Data tabulated by date of registration rather than date of occurrence.

SOURCE: UN–DY, 1979 and 1985, tables 17 and 24, respectively.

Table 713

FIRST FIVE PRINCIPAL CAUSES OF DEATH AND RATE BY SEX, 18 LC

(All Ages)

Principal Cause of Death	Total				Male				Female			
	Rank Order	N	Rate PHTI	%	Rank Order	N	Rate PHTI	%	Rank Order	N	Rate PHTI	%
A. ARGENTINA (1981)												
All causes	**	241,904	843.2	100.0	**	138,504	802.2	100.0	**	103,400	905.0	100.0
Diseases of the heart[2]	1	77,483	269.2	31.9	1	43,194	250.0	31.3	1	34,115	300.0	33.1
Malignant neoplasms	2	42,700	148.8	17.6	2	24,693	143.0	17.8	2	18,007	157.6	17.5
Cerebrovascular disease	3	23,044	80.3	9.5	3	11,981	69.4	8.7	3	11,063	96.8	10.7
Accidents and adverse effects	4	12,293	42.8	5.1	4	8,767	50.8	6.3	5	3,526	30.9	3.4
Causes of perinatal mortality	5	10,348	36.1	4.3	5	5,926	34.3	4.3	4	4,422	38.7	4.3
C. BRAZIL (1979)[3]												
All causes	**	710,702	577.7	100.0	**	409,211	668.0	100.0	**	301,491	488.1	100.0
Diseases of the heart[2]	1	104,677	85.1	14.7	1	57,580	94.0	14.1	1	47,097	76.2	15.6
Infectious, parasitic, and intestinal diseases	2	72,990	59.3	10.3	2	41,965	68.5	10.3	2	31,025	50.2	10.3
Cerebrovascular disease	3	58,162	47.3	8.2	4	30,116	49.2	7.4	3	28,046	45.4	9.3
Malignant neoplasms	4	56,296	45.8	7.9	3	30,920	50.5	7.6	4	25,376	41.1	8.4
Causes of perinatal mortality	5	50,113	40.7	7.1	5	28,783	47.0	7.0	5	21,330	34.5	7.1
D. CHILE (1983)												
All causes	**	74,428	637.1	100.0	**	42,135	728.4	100.0	**	32,293	547.6	100.0
Malignant neoplasms	1	11,969	102.5	16.1	2	6,030	104.2	14.3	1	5,939	100.7	18.4
Diseases of the heart[2]	2	12,235	104.6	16.4	1	6,360	110.0	15.1	2	15,875	99.6	18.2
Cerebrovascular disease	3	6,899	59.1	9.3	3	3,253	56.2	7.7	3	3,646	61.8	11.3
Influenza and pneumonia	4	9,355	37.7	5.9	5	2,407	41.6	5.7	4	1,948	33.0	6.0
Accidents and adverse effects	5	3,571	30.6	4.8	4	2,568	44.4	6.1	**	1,003	17.0	3.1
Causes of perinatal mortality	**	2,104	18.0	2.8	**	1,181	20.4	2.8	5	923	15.7	2.9
E. COLOMBIA (1977)												
All causes	**	145,426	580.6	100.0	**	78,948	640.7	100.0	**	33,059	599.9	100.0
Diseases of the heart	1	23,739	94.8	16.3	1	12,293	99.8	15.6	1	11,446	89.9	17.2
Malignant neoplasms	2	13,020	52.0	9.0	4	5,996	48.7	7.6	2	7,024	55.2	10.6
Enteritis and other diarrheal diseases	4	11,375	45.4	7.8	3	6,010	48.8	7.6	3	5,365	42.2	8.1
Accidents	3	11,400	45.5	7.8	2	8,440	68.5	10.7	**	2,960	23.3	4.5
Influenza and pneumonia	5	10,308	41.2	7.1	5	5,343	43.4	6.8	4	4,965	39.0	7.5
Cerebrovascular disease	**	8,625	34.4	5.9	**	3,935	31.9	5.0	5	4,690	36.9	7.1
F. COSTA RICA (1983)												
All causes	**	9,432	396.5	100.0	**	5,313	448.6	100.0	**	4,119	344.9	100.0
Malignant neoplasms	2	1,853	77.9	19.6	2	1,032	87.1	19.4	2	821	68.7	19.9
Diseases of the heart[2]	1	1,959	82.4	20.8	1	1,073	90.6	20.2	1	886	74.2	21.5
Accidents and adverse effects	4	644	27.1	6.8	3	486	41.0	9.1	5	158	13.2	3.8
Cerebrovascular disease	3	678	28.5	7.2	5	321	27.1	6.0	3	357	29.9	8.7
Causes of perinatal mortality	5	603	25.4	6.4	4	370	31.2	7.0	4	233	19.5	5.7
G. CUBA (1983)												
All causes	**	58,348	589.4	100.0	**	33,161	656.9	100.0	**	25,187	519.6	100.0
Diseases of the heart[2]	1	19,514	197.1	33.4	1	11,000	217.9	33.2	1	8,514	175.5	33.8
Malignant neoplasms	2	11,202	113.2	19.2	2	6,675	732.2	20.1	2	4,527	93.3	17.9
Accidents[4]	3	6,628	66.9	11.4	3	4,328	85.7	13.1	4	2,300	47.4	9.1
Cerebrovascular disease	4	5,597	56.5	9.6	4	2,859	56.6	8.6	3	2,738	56.4	10.9
Influenza and pneumonia	5	3,744	37.8	6.4	5	2,096	41.5	6.3	5	1,648	34.0	6.5
H. DOMINICAN REP. (1982)												
All causes	**	26,589	462.9	100.0	**	14,796	516.3	100.0	**	11,793	409.8	100.0
Diseases of the heart	1	3,284	57.2	12.3	1	1,776	42.0	8.1	1	1,498	52.3	12.8
Enteritis and other diarrheal diseases	3	1,408	24.5	5.3	4	770	26.9	5.2	3	638	22.2	5.4
Causes of perinatal mortality	2	2,601	45.3	9.8	3	1,480	51.6	10.0	2	1,121	39.0	9.5
Malignant neoplasms	5	1,590	27.7	6.0	5	790	27.6	5.4	4	800	27.8	6.8
Cerebrovascular disease	**	1,236	21.5	4.6	**	617	21.5	4.2	5	619	21.5	5.3
Accidents	4	1,241	21.6	4.7	2	937	32.7	6.3	**	304	10.6	2.6
I. ECUADOR (1980)												
All causes	**	57,020	682.6	100.0	**	30,663	728.3	100.0	**	26,357	636.2	100.0
Infectious and parasitic diseases	1	9,920	118.8	17.4	1	5,203	123.6	16.9	1	4,717	113.9	17.9
Influenza and pneumonia	4	4,290	51.4	7.5	4	2,181	51.8	7.1	3	2,109	50.9	8.0
Diseases of the heart[2]	2	5,128	61.4	9.0	3	2,576	61.2	8.4	2	2,552	61.6	9.7
Accidents	3	4,874	58.4	8.5	2	3,670	87.2	11.9	**	1,204	29.1	4.6
Bronchitis, emphysema, and asthma	**	2,849	34.1	5.0	**	1,479	35.1	4.8	5	1,370	33.1	5.2
Malignant neoplasms	5	3,387	40.5	5.9	5	1,585	37.6	5.2	4	1,802	43.5	6.8

Table 713 (Continued)

FIRST FIVE PRINCIPAL CAUSES OF DEATH AND RATE BY SEX, 18 LC

(All Ages)

	Total				Male				Female			
Principal Cause of Death	Rank Order	N	Rate PHTI	%	Rank Order	N	Rate PHTI	%	Rank Order	N	Rate PHTI	%
J. EL SALVADOR (1984)												
All causes	**	28,870	535.8	100.0	**	17,320	640.0	100.0	**	11,550	430.6	100.0
Infectious and parasitic diseases	1	2,870	53.3	9.9	4	1,578	58.3	9.1	2	1,292	48.2	11.2
Accidents	4	2,174	40.3	7.5	2	1,696	62.7	9.8	1	478	17.8	4.1
Causes of perinatal mortality	2	2,861	53.1	9.9	3	1,613	59.6	9.3	3	1,248	46.5	10.8
Homicide, legal intervention, and operations of war	5	1,929	35.8	6.7	1	1,783	65.9	10.3	**	146	5.4	1.3
Malignant neoplasms	**	1,033	19.2	3.6	**	421	15.6	2.4	5	612	22.8	5.3
Bronchitis, emphysema, asthma	**	742	13.8	2.6	**	398	14.7	2.4	**	344	12.8	3.0
Diseases of the heart[2]	3	2,186	40.6	7.6	5	1,195	44.2	6.9	4	991	36.9	8.6
K. GUATEMALA (1981)												
All causes	**	71,748	959.1	100.0	**	42,997	1,133.9	100.0	**	28,751	779.2	100.0
Infectious, parasitic, and intestinal diseases	1	29,768	397.9	41.4	1	15,960	411.3	36.3	1	13,808	374.3	48.0
Influenza, pneumonia	2	8,415	112.5	11.7	2	4,453	117.5	10.4	2	3,962	107.4	13.8
Causes of perinatal mortality	3	3,429	1,112.0	11.7	3	1,923	122.9	10.8	3	1,506	99.1	12.7
Homicide	4	8,079	108.0	11.2	4	7,454	196.6	17.3	**	625	16.9	2.2
Diseases of the heart[2]	5	2,811	37.7	3.9	**	1,501	39.6	3.5	4	1,310	35.1	4.5
Malignant neoplasms	**	2,004	26.8	2.8	**	892	23.5	2.1	5	1,112	30.1	3.4
Accidents and adverse effects	**	1,780	23.8	2.5	5	1,344	35.4	3.1	**	436	11.8	1.5
M. HONDURAS (1981)												
All causes	**	18,313	479.3	100.0	**	10,239	534.5	100.0	**	8,074	423.7	100.0
Infectious, parasitic and intestinal diseases	1	3,091	80.9	16.9	2	1,715	89.5	16.7	1	1,376	72.2	17.0
Diseases of the heart[2]	3	1,532	40.1	8.4	3	803	41.9	7.8	2	729	38.3	9.0
Injury and poisoning	2	2,061	53.9	11.3	1	1,756	91.7	17.2	4	305	16.0	3.8
Influenza and pneumonia	5	557	14.6	3.0	4	28.7	15.0	2.8	5	270	14.2	3.3
Malignant neoplasms	4	569	14.9	3.1	5	208	10.9	2.0	3	361	18.9	4.5
N. MEXICO (1982)												
All causes	**	409,777	560.4	100.0	**	236,592	646.2	100.0	**	173,185	474.4	100.0
Influenza and pneumonia	5	28,130	38.5	6.7	4	15,174	41.4	6.4	4	12,956	35.5	7.5
Infectious and parasitic diseases	3	49,911	68.3	12.2	3	26,643	72.8	11.3	2	23,268	63.7	13.4
Diseases of the heart[2]	1	53,006	73.3	13.1	2	27,285	74.5	11.5	1	26,321	72.1	15.2
Accidents	2	52,360	71.6	12.8	1	41,653	113.8	17.6	5	10,707	29.3	6.2
Malignant neoplasms	4	29,415	40.2	7.2	**	13,265	36.2	5.6	3	16,150	44.2	9.3
Causes of perinatal mortality	**	24,221	33.1	5.9	5	14,292	39.0	6.0	**	9,929	27.2	5.7
O. NICARAGUA (1979)												
All causes	**	12,492	504.3	100.0	**	7,012	618.2	100.0	**	5,480	465.1	100.0
Diseases of the heart	2	1,404	60.7	11.2	3	681	60.1	9.7	2	723	61.4	13.2
Enteritis and other diarrheal diseases	1	1,702	73.6	13.6	1	973	85.8	13.9	1	729	61.9	13.3
Accidents	3	932	40.3	7.5	2	755	66.6	10.8	**	177	15.0	3.2
Malignant neoplasms	**	395	17.1	3.2	**	133	11.7	1.9	3	262	22.2	4.8
Homicide, legal intervention, and operations of war	4	693	30.0	5.5	4	606	53.5	8.6	**	87	7.4	1.6
Influenza and pneumonia	5	506	21.9	4.1	5	279	24.6	4.0	4	227	19.3	4.1
Cerebrovascular disease	**	441	19.1	3.5	**	214	18.9	3.1	4	227	19.3	4.1
P. PANAMA (1984)												
All causes	**	8,250	386.6	100.0	**	4,674	429.5	100.0	**	3,576	341.9	100.0
Diseases of the heart[2]	1	1,581	74.1	19.2	1	839	77.1	17.9	1	742	70.9	20.7
Accidents	3	764	35.8	9.2	2	588	54.0	12.6	5	176	16.8	4.9
Malignant neoplasms	2	1,065	49.9	12.9	3	575	52.8	12.3	2	490	46.9	13.7
Cerebrovascular disease	4	668	31.3	8.1	4	313	28.8	6.7	3	355	33.9	9.9
Causes of perinatal mortality	5	500	23.4	6.0	5	274	25.2	5.9	4	225	21.6	6.3

Table 713 (Continued)

FIRST FIVE PRINCIPAL CAUSES OF DEATH AND RATE BY SEX, 18 LC[1]

(All Ages)

	Total				Male				Female			
Principal Cause of Death	Rank Order	N	Rate PHTI	%	Rank Order	N	Rate PHTI	%	Rank Order	N	Rate PHTI	%
Q. PARAGUAY (1984)												
All causes	**	14,106	621.4	100.0	**	7,368	647.5	100.0	**	6,738	595.8	100.0
Diseases of the heart[2]	1	2,232	98.3	15.8	1	1,144	100.5	15.5	1	1,088	96.2	16.1
Infectious, and parasitic diseases	2	1,450	63.9	10.3	2	779	68.5	10.6	2	671	59.3	9.9
Cerebrovascular disease	3	1,190	52.4	8.4	3	559	49.1	7.6	3	631	55.8	9.4
Malignant neoplasms	4	914	40.3	6.5	5	423	37.2	5.7	4	491	43.4	7.3
Influenza and pneumonia	5	776	34.2	5.5	**	399	35.1	5.4	5	377	33.3	5.6
Accidents	**	627	27.6	4.4	4	444	39.0	6.0	**	183	16.2	2.7
R. PERU (1982)												
All causes	**	85,441	468.7	100.0	**	44,841	488.2	100.0	**	40,600	448.9	100.0
Influenza and pneumonia	2	12,901	77.8	15.1	2	6,528	71.1	14.6	2	6,373	70.5	15.7
Infectious and parasitic diseases	1	16,078	88.2	18.8	1	8,472	92.2	18.9	1	7,606	84.1	18.7
Malignant neoplasms	4	6,102	33.5	7.1	4	2,702	29.4	6.0	4	3,400	37.6	8.4
Diseases of the heart[2]	3	7,853	43.1	9.2	3	3,834	41.7	8.6	3	4,019	44.4	9.9
Cerebrovascular disease	5	2,708	14.9	3.2	**	1,362	14.8	3.0	5	1,346	14.9	3.3
Bronchitis, emphysema, asthma, and tuberculosis	**	2,683	14.7	3.1	5	1,420	15.5	3.2	**	1,263	14.0	3.1
S. URUGUAY (1984)												
All causes	**	29,990	1,003.0	100.0	**	16,589	1,128.4	100.0	**	13,401	881.8	100.0
Disease of the heart[2]	1	8,760	292.9	29.2	1	4,684	318.6	28.2	1	4,076	268.2	30.4
Malignant neoplasms	2	6,372	213.1	21.2	2	3,738	254.3	22.5	2	2,634	173.3	19.7
Cerebrovascular disease	3	3,784	126.6	12.6	3	1,652	112.4	9.9	3	2,132	140.3	15.9
Accidents	4	1,169	39.1	3.9	4	783	53.3	4.7	4	386	25.4	2.9
Causes of perinatal mortality	5	638	21.3	2.1	5	359	24.4	2.2	5	279	18.4	2.1
T. VENEZUELA (1983)												
All causes	**	76,725	468.0	100.0	**	44,101	537.6	100.0	**	32,624	398.3	100.0
Diseases of the heart[2]	1	16,675	101.7	21.7	1	9,205	112.2	20.9	1	7,470	91.2	22.9
Accidents	2	8,876	53.6	11.5	2	6,894	84.0	15.6	5	1,892	23.1	5.8
Malignant neoplasms	3	8,901	54.3	11.6	3	4,281	52.2	9.7	2	4,620	56.4	14.2
Causes of perinatal mortality	4	5,392	32.9	7.0	4	3,149	38.4	7.1	4	2,243	27.4	6.9
Cerebrovascular disease	5	4,961	30.3	6.5	5	2,391	29.1	5.4	3	2,570	31.4	7.8
Influenza and pneumonia	**	3,429	20.9	4.5	**	1,710	20.8	3.9	**	1,719	20.9	5.3
UNITED STATES (1983)												
All causes	**	2,019,201	863.0	100.0	**	1,071,923	942.9	100.0	**	947,278	787.5	100.0
Diseases of the heart[2]	1	830,534	354.9	41.1	1	431,994	379.9	40.3	1	398,540	331.3	42.1
Malignant neoplasms	2	442,986	189.3	21.9	2	238,383	209.7	22.2	2	204,603	170.1	21.6
Cerebrovascular disease	3	155,398	66.5	7.7	4	62,847	55.3	5.9	3	92,751	77.1	9.8
Accidents and adverse effects	4	92,488	39.5	4.6	3	63,902	56.2	5.9	4	28,586	23.8	3.0
Influenza and pneumonia	5	55,584	23.9	2.8	5	28,007	24.6	2.6	5	27,847	23.2	2.9

1. For deaths by all causes in previous years, see SALA, 24-708.
2. Includes chronic rheumatic heart disease, acute myocardial infarction, other ischaemic heart diseases, diseases of pulmonary circulation, and other forms of heart disease and atherosclerosis.
3. Rates based on 1980 population figures.
4. Includes injuries and poisonings.

SOURCE: PAHO-HC, 1977-80, p. 270; adapted from WHO-WHSA, 1982,1983, 1985, and 1986, tables 7A, 8, 9A, 13 and 11 respectively.

Table 714

REPORTED CASES AND DEATHS FROM DIPHTHERIA, 20 LC, 1973-76

| | | Cases | | | | | | | | Deaths | | | | | | | |
| | | N | | | | PHTI | | | | N | | | | PHTI | | | |
Country	1973	1974	1975	1976	1973	1974	1975	1976	1973	1974	1975	1976	1973	1974	1975	1976
A. ARGENTINA	325	290	148	183	1.3	1.2	.6	.7	~	~	~	~	~	~	~	~

Continued in SALA, 24-709.

Table 715

REPORTED CASES AND RATES OF AMEBIASIS AND BACILLARY DYSENTERY, 17 LC, 1973-76

| | | Amebiasis | | | | | | | | Bacillary Dysentery | | | | | | | |
| | | N | | | | PHTI | | | | N | | | | PHTI | | | |
Country	1973	1974	1975	1976	1973	1974	1975	1976	1973	1974	1975	1976	1973	1974	1975	1976
A. ARGENTINA[a]	~	~	~	~	~	~	~	~	139,439	144,811	~	~	564.1	578.1	~	~

Continued in SALA, 24-710.

Table 716

WESTERN HEMISPHERE RANKING OF TOTAL
CONFIRMED CASES OF AIDS, 19 LC
(December 31, 1986)

Ranking	Country	Cases	Deaths
1	UNITED STATES	29,003	16,301
2	Canada	926	436
3	BRAZIL[a]	921	497
4	HAITI[b]	507	111
5	MEXICO[c]	316	100
6	Trinidad and Tobago	134	93
7	DOMINICAN REP.	96	35
8	Bahamas	85	29
9	VENEZUELA	69	54
9	ARGENTINA	69	37
11	French Guiana	58	41
12	Bermuda	48	29
13	Guadeloupe	40	23
14	COLOMBIA	30	15
15	CHILE	22	14
16	Martinique	16	10
16	COSTA RICA	16	11
18	GUATEMALA	15	8
18	Barbados	15	9
20	HONDURAS	13	7
21	PANAMA[d]	12	9
22	PERU[b]	9	6
23	URUGUAY	8	5
24	ECUADOR[b]	7	4
25	Jamaica	6	6
25	EL SALVADOR	6	3
27	St. Lucia[b]	3	2
27	St. Vincent[b]	3	2
27	Grenada	3	3
30	Suriname[b]	2	2
30	Antigua and Barbuda	2	2
30	Turks and Caicos	2	2
33	PARAGUAY	1	1
33	BOLIVIA[b]	1	1
33	CUBA[b]	1	1
33	Caymans	1	1
33	St. Chris/Nevis[b]	1	0
33	Belize	1	0

a. As of November 20, 1986.
b. As of June 31, 1986.
c. As of January 15, 1987.
d. As of September 30, 1986.

SOURCE: *Times of the Americas*, May 6, 1987.

Table 717

RANKING OF AMERICAN COUNTRIES
BY CASES OF AIDS, 19 LC
(PHTI, December 31, 1986)

Ranking	Country	Number
1	BERMUDA	84.73
2	FRENCH GUIANA	79.43
3	BAHAMAS	37.28
4	TURKS AND CAICOS	26.90
5	GUADELOUPE	12.82
6	TRINIDAD AND TOBAGO	12.42
7	UNITED STATES	12.08
8	HAITI[a]	8.83
9	Barbados	5.98
10	Caymans	5.33
11	Martinique	5.28
12	Canada	3.69
13	Grenada	3.26
14	Antigua and Barbuda	2.52
15	St. Lucia[a]	2.42
16	St. Vincent[a]	2.35
17	St. Chris/Nevis[a]	2.25
18	DOMINICAN REP.	1.71
19	BRAZIL[b]	.65
19	Belize	.65
21	COSTA RICA	.62
22	PANAMA[c]	.60
23	Suriname[a]	.50
24	VENEZUELA	.47
25	MEXICO[d]	.40
26	HONDURAS	.30
27	URUGUAY	.27
28	Jamaica	.26
29	ARGENTINA	.23
30	GUATEMALA	.19
31	CHILE	.18
32	EL SALVADOR	.12
33	COLOMBIA	.11
34	ECUADOR[a]	.8
35	PERU[a]	.5
36	PARAGUAY	.3
37	BOLIVIA[a]	.2
38	CUBA[a]	.1

a. As of June 31, 1986.
b. As of November 20, 1986.
c. As of September 30, 1986.
d. As of January 15, 1987.

SOURCE: *Times of the Americas*, May 6, 1987.

Table 718

MARRIAGES, 19 LC, 1965–85

N

Country	Code	1965	1970	1975	1980	1981	1982	1983	1984	1985
A. ARGENTINA	C	152,625	174,137	?	?	?	?	177,010+	?	?
B. BOLIVIA	U	20,838	?	24,315	26,990	?	?	?	?	?
C. BRAZIL[6]	U	?	109,027	840,614	948,164	933,522	994,246	866,190	936,070	?
D. CHILE[1]	C	64,922	71,631	76,205	86,001	90,564	80,115	82,483	87,261	?
E. COLOMBIA[1,4]	U	86,722	110,704	72,370	?	?	?	?	?	?
F. COSTA RICA	C	8,562	11,024	14,683	17,527	16,654	18,542	19,171	20,558	?
G. CUBA	C	67,323	110,982	65,416+	68,941	72,824	80,295	76,365+	75,254+	80,193+
H. DOMINICAN REP.[1]	C	12,712	16,987	20,411	26,862	?	28,874	?	?	?
I. ECUADOR[5]	U	30,362	35,558	37,858	48,305	49,936	?	49,571	54,038	?
J. EL SALVADOR	C	10,315	11,763	16,628	22,763	21,260	20,387	?	16,727	?
K. GUATEMALA	C	15,112	18,150	24,354	29,519	32,155	31,233	30,422	?	?
M. HONDURAS[1]	C	7,611	9,704	11,254	?	15,437	16,051	19,875	?	?
N. MEXICO[1]	C	293,227	356,658	472,091	495,996	477,474	528,963	?	?	?
O. NICARAGUA[1]	C	6,224	?	?	17,174	?	?	?	?	?
P. PANAMA[2]	C	4,710	7,324	8,042	10,252	10,315	11,321	11,346	12,253	?
Q. PARAGUAY[1]	U	8,065	13,103	14,313	17,259	15,131	13,053	?	?	?
R. PERU[1,7]	C	45,160	50,810	?	?	?	109,200	?	?	?
S. URUGUAY[3]	C	20,976	23,668	24,404	22,448	22,542	20,068	?	?	?
T. VENEZUELA[8]	?	49,523	60,128	85,662	92,608	91,492	?	91,397+	?	?
UNITED STATES	C	1,800,207	2,158,802	2,127,000+	2,390,252	2,422,145	2,495,000+	2,444,000+	2,487,000+	2,425,000+

Rate PTI

Country	1965	1970	1975	1980	1981	1982	1983	1984	1985
A. ARGENTINA	6.8	7.3	?	?	?	?	6.0	?	?
B. BOLIVIA	4.8	?	4.3	4.8	?	?	?	?	?
C. BRAZIL[6]	?	1.2	?	7.8	7.5	7.8	6.7	7.1	?
D. CHILE[1]	7.5	7.7	7.4	7.7	8.0	7.0	7.1	7.3	?
E. COLOMBIA[1,4]	4.8	5.2	3.1	?	?	?	?	?	?
F. COSTA RICA	5.7	6.4	7.5	7.8	7.3	8.0	7.9	8.5	?
G. CUBA	8.8	13.1	7.0+	7.1	7.5	8.2	7.7+	7.5+	7.9+
H. DOMINICAN REP.[1]	3.5	4.2	4.4	4.9	?	5.0	?	?	?
I. ECUADOR[5]	5.9	5.8	5.4	5.8	6.0	?	5.6	5.9	?
J. EL SALVADOR	3.5	3.3	4.2	4.8	4.6	4.4	?	3.5	?
K. GUATEMALA	3.4	3.6	4.0	4.1	4.5	4.3	4.0	?	?
M. HONDURAS[1]	3.5	3.9	3.6	?	4.0	4.1	4.9	?	?
N. MEXICO[1]	6.9	7.0	7.8	7.2	6.7	7.2	?	?	?
O. NICARAGUA[1]	3.8	?	?	6.3	?	?	?	?	?
P. PANAMA[2]	4.0	5.1	4.8	5.2	5.2	5.5	5.4	5.7	?
Q. PARAGUAY[1]	4.0	5.7	5.4	5.4	4.6	4.3	?	?	?
R. PERU[1,7]	3.9	3.7	?	2.7	?	6.0	?	?	?
S. URUGUAY[3]	7.7	8.2	8.7	7.7	7.7	6.8	?	?	?
T. VENEZUELA[8]	5.7	5.9	7.1	6.7	5.9	?	5.6+	?	?
UNITED STATES	9.3	10.5	10.0+	10.5	10.5	10.7+	10.4+	10.5+	10.1+

Code: C = Data estimated to be virtually complete, representing at least 90% of the events
occurring each year.

U = Data estimated to be incomplete, representing less than 90% of the events
occurring each year.

1. Data tabulated according to year of registration rather than year of marriage.
2. Excludes marriages in Canal Zone and indigenous villages.
3. Data for years 1965 and 1970 are considered incomplete.
4. Except for Bogotá, data are only for marriages recorded in Roman Catholic Church
registers.
5. Excludes marriages in indigenous jungle population.
6. For state capitals only except for the 1965 data.
7. Excludes marriages in indigenous jungle population, estimated at 39,800 in 1972.
8. Excludes marriages in indigenous jungle population, estimated at 31,800 in 1961.

SOURCE: UN-DY, 1969, 1974, tables 47 and 11 respectively; 1979 and 1983, table 23;
1985, table 12.

Table 719

DIVORCES, 19 LC, 1965-85

N

	Country	Code	1965	1970	1975	1980	1981	1982	1983	1984	1985
A.	ARGENTINA[1]	~	**	**	**	**	**	**	**	**	**
B.	BOLIVIA[1]	~	**	**	**	**	**	**	**	**	**
C.	BRAZIL[1]	~	**	**	**	**	~	27,266	31,521	30,847	~
D.	CHILE[1]	~	**	**	**	**	**	**	**	**	**
E.	COLOMBIA[1]	~	**	**	**	**	**	**	**	**	**
F.	COSTA RICA	C	181	226	318	1,733	2,010	2,371	~	~	~
G.	CUBA[7]	C	8,937	24,813	22,819‡	24,487	28,091	31,343	29,249‡	~	29,182‡
H.	DOMINICAN REP.[2]	C	1,199	3,754	9,292	~	~	~	~	~	~
I.	ECUADOR[6]	~	1,300	1,291	1,679	2,737	3,010	2,967	3,133	3,546	~
J.	EL SALVADOR	C	671	847	1,286	1,549	1,589	1,738	~	1,549	~
K.	GUATEMALA[2]	C	436	674	912	~	1,368‡	1,126‡	1,328‡	~	~
M.	HONDURAS[2]	C	363	454	672	~	885	970	1,520	~	~
N.	MEXICO[2]	C	24,705	28,779	16,791	21,674	22,989	25,901	~	~	~
O.	NICARAGUA[1]	~	292	~	~	759	~	~	~	~	~
P.	PANAMA[3]	C	579	574	949	1,116	1,039	1,156	1,172	1,361	~
Q.	PARAGUAY[1]	~	**	**	**	**	**	**	**	**	**
R.	PERU[4]	~	1,803	~	~	~	~	~	~	~	~
S.	URUGUAY[2,8,9]	C	2,500	2,927	3,430	4,298	4,297	3,706	~	~	~
T.	VENEZUELA[4]	~	2,292	2,467	4,377	~	5,653	~	~	~	~
	UNITED STATES[5]	U	479,000	708,000	1,026,000	1,189,000	1,213,000	1,170,000	1,179,000‡	1,155,000‡	1,187,000‡

Rate PTI

	Country	Code	1965	1970	1975	1980	1981	1982	1983	1984	1985
A.	ARGENTINA[1]	~	**	**	**	**	**	**	**	**	**
B.	BOLIVIA[1]	~	**	**	**	**	**	**	**	**	**
C.	BRAZIL[1]	~	**	**	**	**	~	.21	.24	.23	~
D.	CHILE[1]	~	**	**	**	**	**	**	**	**	**
E.	COLOMBIA[1]	~	**	**	**	**	**	**	**	**	**
F.	COSTA RICA	C	.12	.13	.16	.77	.88	1.02	~	~	~
G.	CUBA[7]	C	1.17	2.92	2.45‡	2.52	2.89	3.20	2.96‡	~	2.89‡
H.	DOMINICAN REP.[2]	C	.33	.92	1.98	~	~	~	~	~	~
I.	ECUADOR[6]	~	.25	.21	.24	.33	.36	.34	.35	.39	~
J.	EL SALVADOR	C	.23	.24	.32	.33	.35	.37	~	.32	~
K.	GUATEMALA[2]	C	.10	.13	.15	~	.19‡	.15‡	.18‡	~	~
M.	HONDURAS[2]	C	.17	.18	.24	~	.23	.24	.37	~	~
N.	MEXICO[2]	C	.58	.57	.28	.31	.32	.35	~	~	~
O.	NICARAGUA[1]	~	.18	**	**	.28	~	~	~	~	~
P.	PANAMA[3]	C	.49	.40	.57	.57	.52	.56	.56	.64	~
Q.	PARAGUAY[1]	~	**	**	**	**	**	**	**	**	**
R.	PERU[4]	~	.15	~	~	~	~	~	~	~	~
S.	URUGUAY[2,8,9]	C	.92	1.01	1.22	1.48	1.44	1.26	~	~	~
T.	VENEZUELA[4]	~	.26	.24	.37	~	.36	~	~	~	~
	UNITED STATES[5]	U	2.47	3.47	4.82	5.22	5.27	5.03	5.03‡	4.88‡	4.96‡

Code: C = Data estimated to be virtually complete, representing at least 90% of the events
           occurring each year.
       U = Data estimated to be incomplete, representing less than 90% of the events
           occurring each year.

1. There are no legal provisions for "divorce."
2. Data tabulated according to year of registration and not year of divorce.
3. Excludes divorces in the Canal Zone and among indigenous tribal Indian population
   numbering 62,187 in 1960.
4. Excludes indigenous jungle population.
5. Estimates based on incomplete data for some states; includes annulments.
6. Excludes nomadic Indian tribes.
7. Data for years 1965 and 1970 are considered incomplete.
8. Includes annulments since 1970.
9. Data for 1965 are considered incomplete.

SOURCE: UN-DY, 1969, 1974, tables 49 and 13 respectively; 1979 and 1983, table 25;
   1985, table 14.

CHAPTER 8

HEALTH, NUTRITION, FAMILY PLANNING, AND WELFARE

Table 800

SUMMARY OF HEALTH, EDUCATION, AND COMMUNICATION (HEC)
INDICATORS, 1940–80

PART I: HEC COMPONENTS

Health (H), 5 items

> Life expectancy at birth—LIFE
> Infant mortality rate (deaths under one year of age per 1,000 live births)—INFANT
> Persons per hospital bed—BEDS
> Population per physician—DOCTORS
> Persons per dentist—DENTISTS

Education (E), 4 items

> Literacy percentage for population age 15 and over—Literate
> Percentage of school-age population 7-14 enrolled in primary school—Primary
> Students enrolled in secondary school as a percentage of school-age population 13-18—Secondary
> College enrollment (including, professional, technical, and vocational schools) as a percentage of
>   primary school enrollment—College

Communication (C), 3 items

> Newspaper circulation, copies per 1,000 persons—News
> Number of telephones per 100 persons—Telephone
> Number of persons per motor vehicle (autos, buses, trucks) in use—Motor

PART II: HEC INDEXES[1] AND INDEX REDUCTION RATES (IRR) FOR LATIN AMERICA
(0% = EQUALITY)

Health Indexes

Year	LIFE	INFANT	BEDS	DOCTORS	DENTISTS	Subtotals and Total Indexes[2]	IRR[3]
1940	39.5	67.8	81.5	73.0	81.9	68.7	- -
1950	26.5	73.6	82.8	77.4	82.7	68.6	−.1
1960	18.6	70.5	79.1	73.5	80.6	64.5	−6.0
1970	14.1	74.4	70.7	69.6	69.9	59.7	−7.4
1980	12.2	80.3	64.3	64.1	64.0	57.0	−4.5

Education Indexes

Year	LITERATE	PRIMARY	SECONDARY	COLLEGE		
1940	48.5	44.4	89.0	90.7	68.2	- -
1950	43.3	49.0	90.4	85.0	66.9	−1.9
1960	32.7	36.0	83.3	80.9	58.2	−13.0
1970	26.3	22.2	69.9	82.2	50.2	−13.7
1980	19.2	16.2	58.8	82.5	44.2	−12.0

Communication Indexes

Year	NEWS	TELEPHONE	MOTOR		
1940	78.4	93.7	98.4	90.2	- -
1950	82.2	95.0	97.9	91.7	1.7
1960	76.4	95.0	97.1	89.5	−2.4
1970	74.3	94.9	95.6	88.3	−1.3
1980	70.2	92.7	91.7	84.9	−3.6

Total Index

Year		IRR
1940	73.9	- -
1950	73.8	−.1
1960	68.6	−7.0
1970	63.7	−7.1
1980	59.7	−6.3

1. The indexes (weighted by population in each Latin American country) presented here
    are calculated as the scaled percentage decrease necessary in each year to bring the
    United States and Latin America to equality. (The scale occurs in the process of calcu-
    lating the percentage decrease between high and low absolute numbers because there is
    a ceiling of 100% on possible changes.) At .0 equality will exist. In 1940 the total index
    was 73.9, closing to 63.7 in 1970. If during the 1970s to 1990s the Index Reduction
    Rate (IRR) closes linearly at the same rate as during the 1950s and 1960s, the index
    will stand at about 59.2 by 1980 and 51.1 by the year 2000.
2. Arithmetic mean for 5 Health items, 4 Education items, 3 Communication items, and
    12 HEC items in each decade. Each item is equally weighted, thus giving Health an
    implicit weight of 42% in the total index, Education 33%, and Communication 25%.
3. The IRR is calculated here as the rate of change in the subtotals and totals, summary
    index scores from decade to decade. A minus sign (–) indicates that the index is
    improving, i.e., the gap is narrowing between Latin America and United States.

SOURCE: James W. Wilkie, *The Narrowing Gap: Primary Social Change in the Americas
    since 1940*. Statistical Abstract of Latin America Supplement Series (Los Angeles: UCLA
    Latin American Center Publications, forthcoming).

Table 801

HEC TOTAL INDEX BY COUNTRY,[1] 20 LRC, 1940–80

(Average for 12 indicators; 0 = U.S. Equality with Latin America)

	Country	1940	1950	1960	1970	1980
A.	ARGENTINA	46.1	46.4	39.9	34.0	38.2
B.	BOLIVIA	83.9	79.8	76.1	70.6	67.8
C.	BRAZIL	74.7	73.9	68.5	61.5	56.4
D.	CHILE	63.5	61.8	57.9	54.1	55.1
E.	COLOMBIA	77.3	73.8	69.7	65.6	61.7
F.	COSTA RICA	69.3	65.8	60.9	57.2	49.9
G.	CUBA	58.7	57.5	55.2	54.3	40.3
H.	DOMINICAN REP.	80.4	77.5	70.2	66.7	67.2
I.	ECUADOR	80.2	76.3	71.2	67.7	60.6
J.	EL SALVADOR	79.9	78.8	74.1	69.7	69.9
K.	GUATEMALA	83.8	81.2	79.1	77.0	76.1
L.	HAITI	88.3	89.7	86.7	86.2	83.9
M.	HONDURAS	82.9	81.0	77.2	71.7	73.1
N.	MEXICO	74.1	75.5	70.1	63.8	54.9
O.	NICARAGUA	80.3	76.9	73.3	68.9	66.8
P.	PANAMA	66.9	61.9	60.3	56.6	48.0
Q.	PARAGUAY	77.0	71.8	67.9	67.3	63.8
R.	PERU	77.5	75.5	67.6	61.2	56.8
S.	URUGUAY	44.2	42.3	40.6	40.4	34.9
T.	VENEZUELA	75.2	69.9	61.2	55.8	49.2
	LATIN AMERICA[2]	73.9	73.8	68.6	63.7	59.7

1. The index presented here is calculated as the scaled percentage decrease necessary to bring the United States and Latin America to equality. (The scale occurs in the process of calculating the percentage decrease between high and low absolute numbers because there is a ceiling of 100% on possible changes.) At .0 no index gap will exist. In 1940 the 12-item average was 73.9 closing to 63.7 in 1970.
2. Data are weighted by the population of each Latin American country.

SOURCE: See table 800.

Table 802

ADJUSTED PHYSICAL QUALITY OF LIFE INDEX (PQLI),[1] 20 LRC, 1950 TO MID 1970s

(Zero = No Gap with U.S. Best Performance Expected by the Year 2000 for Arithmetic Average of Three Equally Weighted Items)[2]

	Country	1950	1960	1970[a]	Mid-1970s
A.	ARGENTINA	12	9	8.	10
B.	BOLIVIA	~	~	~	56
C.	BRAZIL	36	28	27	29
D.	CHILE	27	26	16	16
E.	COLOMBIA	42	27[g]	20	23
F.	COSTA RICA	22	13[f]	7[j]	10
G.	CUBA	~	~	~	10
H.	DOMINICAN REP.	42[k]	29	30	31
I.	ECUADOR	41[b]	31[c]	26	26
J.	EL SALVADOR	38	30[e]	29[j]	31
K.	GUATEMALA	53	47[e]	41	41
L.	HAITI	~	68	56	55
M.	HONDURAS	~	~	~	42
N.	MEXICO	34[k]	26[d]	22	20
O.	NICARAGUA	47	38[f]	~	40
P.	PANAMA	21	18	12[i]	16
Q.	PARAGUAY	~	~	~	20
R.	PERU	~	33[e]	27	30
S.	URUGUAY	~	6[h]	~	9
T.	VENEZUELA	31	22[e]	14[i]	16
	LATIN AMERICA[3]	~	~	~	25

1. Converted here from "100 = no gap" to "0 = no gap" according to the following formula: (100) minus (unadjusted PQLI) minus (U.S. figure).
2. The PQLI includes 3 items: life expectancy at age 1, infant mortality, literacy of persons age 15 and over.

   a. Compared to United States in 1971.
   b. 1952.   d. 1959.   f. 1963.   h. 1966.   j. 1973.
   c. 1962.   e. 1961.   g. 1964.   i. 1971.   k. 1951.
3. Data are weighted by the population of each Latin American country.

SOURCE: 1950-70 data adapted from Morris David Morris, *Measuring the Condition of the World's Poor: The Physical Quality of Life Index* (New York: Pergamon, 1979), pp. 150-152; and *The United States and World Development: Agenda 1979* (New York: Praeger, 1979), pp. 169-171. Mid-1970s data adapted from *Agenda 1979*, pp. 158-166, except total here calculated with population weights for each country.

Table 803

PHYSICIANS, NURSES, AND NURSING AUXILIARIES, 20 LRC

(Ca. 1979)

| | | | Physicians | | | Nursing Personnel | | | |
| | | | | | | Nurses | | Nursing Auxiliaries | |
Country	Year	N	PTI	Year	N	PTI	N	PTI
A. ARGENTINA	1979	71,253	26.7	1977	18,658	7.2	22,153	8.5
B. BOLIVIA	1974	2,583	4.7	1980	955	1.7	2,498	4.5
C. BRAZIL	1980	106,479	8.7	1980	22,895	1.9	153,214	12.6
D. CHILE	1979	5,671	5.2	1980	3,596	3.2	22,961	20.7
E. COLOMBIA	1977	12,720	5.1	1980	3,010	1.1	27,760	10.2
F. COSTA RICA	1979	1,506	6.9	1980	1,226	5.5	4,884	21.9
G. CUBA[1]	1979	13,531	13.8	1980	14,156	14.3	13,037	13.2
H. DOMINICAN REP.[1]	1976	1,230	2.5	1980	500	.9	3,981	7.3
I. ECUADOR[‡]	1977	4,660	6.2	1980	2,200	2.6	10,000	12.0
J. EL SALVADOR	1980	1,491	3.1	1980	1,715	3.8	3,521	7.7
K. GUATEMALA[1]	1979	819	1.2	1980	811	1.1	4,088	5.6
L. HAITI[1]	1979	600	1.2	1980	771	1.5	1,128	2.3
M. HONDURAS	1979	1,141	3.2	1980	545	1.5	3,000	8.1
N. MEXICO	1974	46,473	8.0	1980	39,189	5.4	58,877	8.2
O. NICARAGUA[1]	1980	1,212	4.5	1980	1,017	3.7	4,306	15.7
P. PANAMA	1978	1,550	8.5	1980	2,132	11.0	3,524	18.2
Q. PARAGUAY	1979	1,700	5.7	1980	521	1.7	1,421	4.6
R. PERU	1979	11,682	6.8	1980	8,350	4.6	3,524	1.9
S. URUGUAY	1979	5,400	18.8	1979	15,200	52.8	~	~
T. VENEZUELA	1978	14,777	11.3	1978	9,077	6.9	28,984	22.1
LATIN AMERICA	**[a]	306,455	9.2	**[a]	146,524	6.0	372,861	15.3
UNITED STATES	1980	414,916	18.2	1980	1,164,000	51.1	~	~

1. Physicians in government services.

a. Total for the 20 countries for years given.

SOURCE: PAHO-HC, 1977-80, table IV-15; WHO-WHSA, 1983, table 18.

Table 804

POPULATION PER PHYSICIAN, 20 L, 1960–80

Country	1960	1969	1970	1971	1972	1973	1974	1975	1976	1977	1978	1979	1980
A. ARGENTINA	680	518	~	~	495	~	~	521	~	~	~	383	~
B. BOLIVIA	5,756	~	2,231	~	2,342	~	2,117	~	~	~	~	~	~
C. BRAZIL	2,181	1,958	~	~	2,025	2,025	1,648	~	~	~	~	~	~
D. CHILE	1,661	1,842	~	~	~	1,836	~	~	2,117	1,636	2,069[b]	1,935	~
E. COLOMBIA	2,632	~	2,331	~	2,282	2,184	~	1,818	~	1,969	~	~	~
F. COSTA RICA	2,729	1,805	~	~	2,663	1,413	~	1,524	~	1,396[d]	2,044	1,441	~
G. CUBA	1,021[a]	1,395	1,392	1,408	1,360	~	1,121	~	~	~	673[b]	722	~
H. DOMINICAN REP.	7,149	~	2,244	2,189	2,088	1,866	~	~	402[b]	~	~	~	~
I. ECUADOR	2,609	2,930	2,900	~	~	2,165	~	2,017	~	1,622	~	~	~
J. EL SALVADOR	5,232	5,218	4,065	4,477	3,934	4,063	~	3,592	3,745	3,685	3,640	3,491	3,179
K. GUATEMALA	4,644	~	~	4,515	~	4,338	~	~	~	~	~	8,608[b]	~
L. HAITI	34,325	14,055	15,666	~	13,264	~	~	~	~	5,936[b]	~	8,198[b]	~
M. HONDURAS	5,132	4,046	3,668	~	3,503	~	3,352	2,992	~	3,297	3,176	3,120	~
N. MEXICO	1,798	~	1,480	~	1,385	~	1,251	~	~	~	~	~	~
O. NICARAGUA	2,809	1,963	1,727	~	1,516	1,437	1,713	1,543	1,592	~	~	2,579[c]	2,228[b]
P. PANAMA	2,701	1,787	1,701	1,491	1,441	1,339	1,234	1,335	~	1,262	1,129	~	~
Q. PARAGUAY	1,996	1,800	2,529	~	2,270	~	1,875	1,189	2,196	~	~	1,747	~
R. PERU	1,975	1,872	~	~	1,751	~	~	~	~	1,556	1,525	1,480	~
S. URUGUAY	821	~	~	921	911	~	~	700	~	~	~	533	~
T. VENEZUELA	1,513	1,100	1,053	1,065	997	866	~	915	870	875	888	~	~

a. 1958.

b. Physicians in government services.

c. Physicians in hospitals and other health establishments.

d. Registered physicians.

SOURCE: SALA, 19-800; WHO-WHSA, 1983, table 18.

Table 805

PROFESSIONAL AND AUXILIARY HEALTH PERSONNEL, 20 LC
(Ca. 1979)

PART I.

			Pharmacy		Radiology		Midwifery			Community Health	
	Country	Year	Pharma-cists	Auxil-iaries	Radiol-ogists	X-Ray Techni-cians[1]	Nurse Midwives	Assistant Midwives	Tradition-al Birth Attendants	Health Educa-tors	Health Promo-ters
A.	ARGENTINA	1979	919	692	~	3,447	~	~	~	25	1,789

PART II.

			Environmental Health		Nutrition	Data Management		Rehabilitation	Health Institution Support Personnel		Animal Health
	Country	Year	Sanitary Engineers	Sanitary Inspectors	Nutritionists and Dieticians	Statistical Personnel	Medical Re-cord Personnel	Therapy Personnel	Health Admin-istrators[1]	Laboratory Personnel	Veterinarians
A.	ARGENTINA	1979	~	61	508	1,283	~	~	~	3,142	~

Continued in SALA, 24-805.

Table 806

DENTISTS AND DENTAL AUXILIARIES, 20 LC
(Ca. 1979)

			Dentists		Dental Auxiliaries[1]
	Country	Year	N	PTI	N
A.	ARGENTINA	1979	7,415	2.8	1,068

Continued in SALA, 24-806.

Table 807

NURSES BY MAJOR FUNCTION, 18 LC
(Ca. 1980)

	Country	Practicing Nurses	Hospital Nurses	Nursing Faculty	Providers of Direct Com-munity Care	Community Health Supervisors	Trainers of Community Health Workers	Private Sector	Other
A.	ARGENTINA	18,658	12,607	310	~	~	380	5,361	#

Continued in SALA, 23–809.

Table 808

HOSPITALS BY TYPE, 20 LRC

Country	Year	Total	Short-Stay Hospitals				Other Hospitals					
			Total	General[2]	Maternity	Pediatrics	Total	Tuberculosis	Mental Diseases	Leprosy	Cancer	Other[3]
A. ARGENTINA	1973	2,864	2,733	2,486	216	31	131	31	57	7	6	30

Continued in SALA, 24-808.

Table 809

HOSPITALS: NUMBER, PERCENTAGE, AND OWNERSHIP, 20 LRC

Country	Year	Total	Government		Private Non-Profit		Private Profit	
			N	%	N	%	N	%
A. ARGENTINA	1969	2,864	1.294[c]	45.2[c]	~	~	1,570	54.8

Continued in SALA, 24-809.

Table 810

SHORT-STAY HOSPITALS[1]: INDICES OF UTILIZATION
BY ALL TYPES OF OWNERSHIP, 19 LRC
(Ca. 1978)

Country	Year	Beds	Discharges	Patient Days	Turnover Rate	Average Days of Stay	Occupancy Rate (%)
A. ARGENTINA	1973	72,221	1,174,415	18,314,265	16.3	15.6	69.5

Continued in SALA, 24-810.

Table 811

HOSPITAL BEDS AND RATE, IN THE CAPITAL
AND REST OF COUNTRY, 20 LC

Country	Year	Total	Capital and Major Cities		Rest of Country	
		Hospital/ Beds	Beds	Rate PTI	Beds	Rate PTI
A. ARGENTINA	1971	46,149	32,129[g]	2.5[g]	14,020	1.3

Continued in SALA, 20-810.

Figure 8:1

A. ARGENTINA 1955–BASED INDEX OF FOOD/C PRODUCTION, 20 LRC, 1952–81
(1955 = 100)

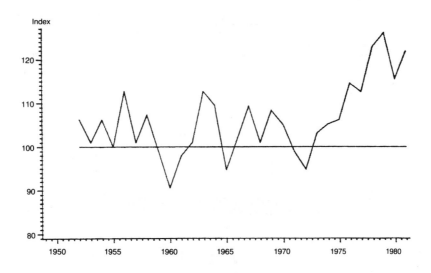

Continued in SALA, 23-35:23 through 35:44.

Figure 8:2

A. ARGENTINA PC IN FOOD/C PRODUCTION, 20 LRC, 1953–81
(0 = Equilibrium between Food Production and Population)

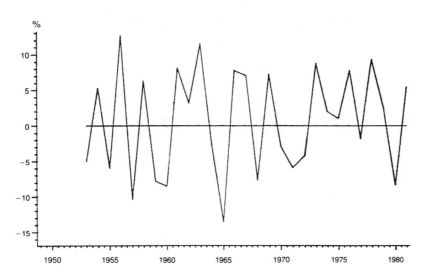

Continued in SALA, 23-35:1 through 35:22.

Table 812

HOSPITAL BEDS: NUMBER, PERCENTAGE, AND OWNERSHIP, 20 LRC

(Ca. 1978)

Country	Year	Total	Government		Private Non-Profit		Private Profit	
			N	%	N	%	N	%
A. ARGENTINA	1969	133,847	103,752[a]	77.5[a]	~	~	30,095	22.5

Continued in SALA, 24-812.

Table 813

HEALTH ESTABLISHMENTS WITH
OUTPATIENT SERVICES, 15 L

(Ca. 1979)

Country	Year	Total	Health Centers	Clinics and Dispensaries	Other
C. BRAZIL	1980	8,646	4,370	4,276	#

Continued in SALA, 23-804.

Table 814

URBAN AND RURAL HEALTH ESTABLISHMENTS
WITH OUTPATIENT SERVICES, 8 L

(Ca. 1979)

Country	Year	Total	Localities of 20,000 or More				Localities of 19,999 or Less			
			Total				Total			
			N	%	Hospitals	Other	N	%	Hospitals	Other
J. EL SALVADOR	1979	330	125	37.9	25	100	205	62.1	7	198

Continued in SALA, 23-805.

Table 815

MENTAL HEALTH CLINICS, REHABILITATION
CENTERS, AND DENTAL CLINICS, 11 LC
(Ca. 1972 and 1978)

Country	Mental Health Clinics		Rehabilitation Centers		Dental Clinics	
	1972	1978	1972	1978	1972	1978
D. CHILE	2	4	24	~	1	50

Continued in SALA, 23-806.

Table 816

CHILD HEALTH SERVICES, 8 L
(Ca. 1979)

Country	Year	Children Attended					Visits		
		Centers with Information	Under 1 Year	Per 100 Live Births	1-4 Years	Ratio[1]	Centers with Information	Under 1 Year	1-4 Years
E. COLOMBIA	1976	~	502,431	68.7	703,915	20.6	~	1,011,195	1,373,960

Continued in SALA, 23-812.

Table 817

CHILDREN UNDER ONE YEAR RECEIVING BCG, DPT, MEASLES,
AND POLIOMYELITIS VACCINES, 20 L
(%)

Country	BCG	DPT		Measles	Polio	
		First Dose	Third Dose		First Dose	Third Dose
A. ARGENTINA	64	67	42	60	100	96

Continued in SALA, 23-813.

Table 818

TOTAL FOOD PRODUCTION INDEX,[1] 20 LC, 1974–85

(1979–81 = 100)

	Country	1974	1975	1976	1977	1978	1979	1980	1981	1982	1983	1984	1985
A.	ARGENTINA	87.71	85.96	92.95	91.76	97.28	101.81	95.69	102.50	107.55	103.75	107.08	104.18
B.	BOLIVIA	88.05	95.26	98.57	93.43	93.95	94.55	99.65	105.80	109.95	81.63	99.86	103.65
C.	BRAZIL	80.10	83.85	89.37	93.87	89.00	92.92	102.77	104.31	113.07	109.10	111.77	121.36
D.	CHILE	87.07	91.30	89.28	97.89	91.71	96.73	97.13	106.14	104.86	103.04	107.39	111.97
E.	COLOMBIA	76.20	81.86	88.50	88.38	93.25	97.94	99.03	103.03	100.11	101.38	105.18	106.22
F.	COSTA RICA	84.48	94.30	97.19	98.85	99.34	101.94	98.96	99.10	93.75	99.81	103.09	100.14
G.	CUBA	79.04	78.40	79.53	85.12	94.55	100.89	95.78	103.34	107.66	104.74	112.44	109.02
H.	DOMINICAN REP.	94.36	90.23	95.84	98.15	101.45	100.88	98.59	100.52	108.04	113.34	112.60	114.23
I.	ECUADOR	88.45	90.30	91.68	93.60	91.91	93.62	101.83	104.55	107.29	93.47	100.05	114.02
J.	EL SALVADOR	80.61	90.72	90.24	91.52	103.64	105.43	99.48	95.10	91.63	96.81	106.12	104.70
K.	GUATEMALA	79.18	84.86	87.78	90.79	91.58	93.93	99.18	106.89	108.35	104.31	103.47	108.74
L.	HAITI	92.85	92.98	95.36	91.91	97.92	101.27	98.76	99.97	100.07	101.88	105.03	99.09
M.	HONDURAS	80.96	74.79	82.51	89.70	96.40	91.30	101.31	107.39	101.52	98.29	105.20	108.14
N.	MEXICO	78.68	81.78	80.99	88.60	98.77	94.74	99.54	105.72	100.69	106.34	103.94	108.91
O.	NICARAGUA	87.77	98.78	102.31	105.90	116.31	122.86	85.75	91.39	91.68	97.77	91.01	95.31
P.	PANAMA	85.50	89.29	88.28	95.33	98.36	99.51	96.84	103.65	99.49	102.05	101.72	103.15
Q.	PARAGUAY	77.97	77.29	81.37	88.99	88.08	97.06	99.67	103.27	105.75	104.07	100.70	106.85
R.	PERU	105.98	103.90	105.65	106.18	103.53	104.25	93.89	101.85	110.37	105.04	114.09	112.85
S.	URUGUAY	98.39	97.65	110.27	92.02	89.96	89.74	95.22	115.04	111.14	113.92	110.95	109.73
T.	VENEZUELA	81.69	91.96	87.41	89.36	95.88	99.70	99.61	100.70	99.74	99.56	96.98	99.90
	UNITED STATES	83.38	90.00	92.24	95.73	94.41	99.11	95.86	105.03	104.84	89.81	102.22	107.62

1. Food Production Index is included in Index of Total Agricultural Production, table 2100.

SOURCE: FAO-PY, 1985, table 4.

Table 819

PER CAPITA FOOD PRODUCTION INDEX,[1] 20 LC, 1974–85

(1979–81 = 100)[a,b]

	Country	1974	1975	1976	1977	1978	1979	1980	1981	1982	1983	1984	1985
A.	ARGENTINA	96.67	93.17	99.10	96.27	100.44	103.45	95.68	100.87	104.15	98.89	100.47	96.24
B.	BOLIVIA	102.82	108.52	109.46	101.12	99.09	97.15	99.74	103.11	104.35	75.42	89.79	90.70
C.	BRAZIL	92.16	94.19	98.07	100.64	93.23	95.13	102.83	102.04	108.14	102.05	102.26	108.64
D.	CHILE	95.48	98.35	94.77	102.39	94.53	98.25	97.20	104.55	101.68	98.36	100.92	103.58
E.	COLOMBIA	86.68	91.12	96.45	94.29	97.38	100.09	99.05	100.85	95.91	95.06	96.54	95.44
F.	COSTA RICA	100.27	109.25	109.42	108.03	105.29	104.86	98.85	96.29	88.71	91.99	92.61	87.68
G.	CUBA	83.83	81.75	81.98	86.92	95.80	101.52	95.77	102.71	106.40	102.91	109.78	105.68
H.	DOMINICAN REP.	109.11	101.40	105.05	105.08	106.15	103.21	98.58	98.21	103.11	105.66	102.56	101.68
I.	ECUADOR	105.34	104.35	102.94	102.11	97.42	96.42	101.91	101.67	101.38	85.82	89.26	98.84
J.	EL SALVADOR	95.96	104.90	101.36	99.83	109.74	108.40	99.34	92.25	86.37	88.64	94.35	90.34
K.	GUATEMALA	93.58	97.56	98.17	98.75	96.91	96.68	99.29	104.03	102.52	95.97	92.55	94.56
L.	HAITI	106.95	104.71	104.91	98.76	102.74	103.75	98.73	97.51	95.23	94.55	95.03	87.40
M.	HONDURAS	100.01	89.37	95.24	99.91	103.63	94.71	101.45	103.84	94.82	88.75	91.87	91.41
N.	MEXICO	93.80	94.40	90.72	96.38	104.43	97.42	99.60	102.98	95.33	98.32	93.68	95.73
O.	NICARAGUA	103.99	113.34	114.11	114.92	122.84	126.19	85.50	88.32	85.72	88.39	79.52	80.48
P.	PANAMA	98.29	99.94	96.49	101.87	102.80	101.73	96.87	101.40	95.23	95.59	93.27	92.58
Q.	PARAGUAY	94.94	91.17	92.80	98.17	93.99	100.23	99.68	100.09	99.42	94.97	89.22	91.97
R.	PERU	124.26	118.48	117.28	114.79	109.04	106.97	93.86	99.18	104.69	97.08	102.74	99.04
S.	URUGUAY	101.35	100.44	113.02	93.86	91.22	90.34	95.28	114.32	109.70	111.66	107.98	106.01
T.	VENEZUELA	100.19	108.86	99.99	98.78	102.44	102.94	99.39	97.66	94.03	91.22	86.37	86.49
	UNITED STATES	88.75	94.86	96.30	98.94	96.55	100.25	95.82	103.93	102.72	87.17	98.32	102.57

1. Per Capita Food Production Index is included in Index of Per Capita Agricultural
    Production, table 2101. For a long-term data, cf. SALA, 23, Ch. 35.

a. These index numbers are calculated by FAO on a uniform basis employing regionally
    constant weights. They differ from national index numbers produced by the coun-
    tries themselves because of differences in concepts of production, coverage, weights,
    time reference of the production data, and method of calculation. They are not
    substitutes for National Index numbers. Whenever revised basic data are reported,
    the index numbers previously published are revised accordingly.
b. For previous years, see SALA, 24-819, and SALA, 25-819.

SOURCE: FAO-PY, 1985, table 9.

Table 820

DAILY CALORIC INTAKE, 20 LRC, 1965–83

(PI)

YA

	Country	1965	1966–68	1969–71	1975–77	1978–80	1980–82	1981–83
A.	ARGENTINA	2,868	3,252	3,358	3,362	3,386	3,368	3,195
B.	BOLIVIA	1,731	1,915	1,976	2,041	2,086	2,116	2,061
C.	BRAZIL	2,541	2,487	2,493	2,493	2,517	2,574	2,564
D.	CHILE	2,523	2,742	2,696	2,616	2,738	2,706	2,662
E.	COLOMBIA	2,220	~	~	~	2,473	2,536	2,543
F.	COSTA RICA	2,223	2,313	2,415	2,480	2,635	2,638	2,548
G.	CUBA	2,665	2,381	2,579	2,678	2,717	2,917	2,874
H.	DOMINICAN REP.	2,004	1,919	1,952	2,117	2,133	2,147	2,330
I.	ECUADOR	1,848	1.924	1,987	2,087	2,092	2,081	2,052
J.	EL SALVADOR	1,877	1,840	1,840	2,076	2,163	~	~
K.	GUATEMALA	1,952	1,971	2,049	2,035	2,064	2,111	2,189
L.	HAITI	1,904	1,855	1,873	1,793	1,882	1,906	1,901
M.	HONDURAS	1,930	2,059	2,115	2,081	2,175	2,170	2,143
N.	MEXICO	2,623	2,685	2,701	2,756	2,803	2,930	2,966
O.	NICARAGUA	2,253	2,523	2,470	2,445	2,284	~	~
P.	PANAMA	2,317	2,425	2,500	2,398	2,290	2,388	2,305
Q.	PARAGUAY	2,732	2,658	2,752	2,774	2,902	2,824	2,817
R.	PERU	2,255	2,225	2,254	2,209	2,166	2,141	2,150
S.	URUGUAY	3,039	2,837	3,027	2,918	2,868	2,809	2,706
T.	VENEZUELA	2,392	2,316	2,389	2,538	2,649	2,557	2,664
	LATIN AMERICA[1]	2,295	2,333	2,391	2,416	2,449	2,467	2,481
	UNITED STATES	3,393[a]	3,380	3,462	3,552	3,652	3,630	3,647

1. Unweighted average.

a. 1966-68.

SOURCE: Derived from Mexico — BNCE — CE, March 1981; FAO-PY, 1982, table 103;
    1984, table 105; 1985, table 105.

Table 821

PERCENT OF MINIMUM DAILY CALORIC REQUIREMENTS,
19 LR, 1961-77

	Country	1961–63	1975–77
A.	ARGENTINA	137.9	143.1

Continued in SALA, 23-108.

TABLE 822

FISH CONSUMPTION,[1] 11 LC, 1949–74

(kg PI)

	Country	1949-51	1970	1974
A.	ARGENTINA	4.0	4.8	6.9

Continued in SALA, 23-3510.

Table 823

FATS CONSUMED DAILY,[1] 19 LRC, 1966–83

(PI)

Country	YA (G)					
	1966–68	1969–71	1975–77	1978–80	1979–81	1981–83
A. ARGENTINA	111.7	114.0	117.2	119.1	120.6	112.2
B. BOLIVIA	36.8	38.0	42.1	44.6	43.5	44.3
C. BRAZIL	48.4	48.9	50.9	51.5	50.3	51.1
D. CHILE	58.4	59.5	51.7	55.7	57.1	58.0
F. COSTA RICA	53.7	55.1	62.1	65.8	67.4	58.6
G. CUBA	52.6	55.8	56.3	58.8	60.9	62.4
H. DOMINICAN REP.	45.9	47.5	50.3	49.9	50.7	58.1
I. ECUADOR	43.5	45.6	50.3	54.1	54.0	53.1
J. EL SALVADOR	40.0	38.5	46.0	46.7	46.1	~
K. GUATEMALA	35.5	36.0	37.6	39.3	41.2	41.3
L. HAITI	28.1	28.6	28.0	30.2	30.2	30.5
M. HONDURAS	38.4	39.2	39.3	41.6	41.8	45.3
N. MEXICO	55.6	56.8	59.7	62.7	69.9	74.5
O. NICARAGUA	51.6	53.4	56.2	51.5	42.0	~
P. PANAMA	51.1	53.9	55.5	55.7	56.9	59.0
Q. PARAGUAY	72.8	75.0	73.5	78.9	77.7	73.8
R. PERU	45.8	46.2	44.3	44.0	42.3	40.6
S. URUGUAY	104.7	111.9	108.4	104.7	102.9	101.9
T. VENEZUELA	57.6	59.4	66.5	69.4	68.4	72.8
LATIN AMERICA	54.3	56.0	57.7	59.1	60.4	57.6
UNITED STATES	154.8	160.8	161.5	169.2	168.4	167.3

1. Total grams per day includes vegetable and animal products.

SOURCE: FAO-PY, 1982, table 105; 1983, table 107; 1985, table 107.

Table 824

PER CAPITA PRIVATE FOOD CONSUMPTION CHANGE, 19 LR, 1960–75

(AAGR)

Country	Previous Decade		1970	1971	1972	1973	1974	1975
	Decade	Second Half of Decade						
A. ARGENTINA	3.1	2.4	2.8	2.0	1.4	2.8	6.3	1.9

Continued in SALA, 21-107.

Table 825

PROTEIN CONSUMPTION, 20 LRC, 1965–83

	Animal Proteins — Daily G PI						Vegetable Proteins — Daily G PI						Total Proteins — Daily G PI					
Country	1965	1966–68	1969–71	1975–77	1980–82	1981–83	1965	1966–68	1969–71	1975–77	1980–82	1983–83	1965	1966–68	1969–71	1975–77	1980–82	1981–83
A. ARGENTINA	51.7	66.8	66.7	72.2	75.1	65.9	36.8	38.2	39.4	37.5	37.7	37.6	88.5	104.9	106.1	109.8	112.8	103.4
B. BOLIVIA	12.1	13.3	13.7	15.8	17.6	17.1	33.0	36.6	36.5	36.7	38.5	37.2	45.1	50.0	50.1	52.5	56.1	54.2
C. BRAZIL	22.4	20.9	21.1	22.8	21.4	22.4	41.5	43.0	41.3	37.1	39.0	38.2	63.9	63.6	62.3	60.0	60.4	60.6
D. CHILE	25.1	26.2	25.9	23.5	27.2	27.7	40.2	47.3	45.0	46.3	45.8	45.4	65.3	73.5	70.9	70.0	73.1	73.1
E. COLOMBIA	22.7	22.3	22.5	22.4	23.9	23.9	30.5	26.5	26.4	28.6	32.3	32.5	53.2	48.9	48.9	51.1	56.1	56.4
F. COSTA RICA	24.6	21.0	23.9	26.6	28.8	26.6	32.1	34.9	34.2	30.7	32.5	33.8	56.7	55.9	57.9	57.4	62.2	60.4
G. CUBA	27.3	29.2	33.6	33.9	37.6	37.1	35.2	33.2	35.9	37.4	40.3	38.6	62.5	62.4	69.5	71.2	77.8	75.7
H. DOMINICAN REP.	17.3	15.5	16.1	15.3	17.4	19.0	27.5	25.8	25.8	28.7	28.8	31.4	44.8	41.4	41.9	44.0	46.3	50.4
I. ECUADOR	16.2	19.1	19.8	20.7	22.9	23.0	30.5	31.1	30.2	27.5	24.4	23.8	46.7	50.2	50.0	48.1	47.3	46.9
J. EL SALVADOR	30.0	15.4	14.7	16.8	~	~	32.9	35.2	35.0	37.6	~	~	62.9	50.5	49.8	54.3	~	~
K. GUATEMALA	11.9	12.3	12.6	12.4	14.0	13.5	37.3	42.0	44.0	41.3	43.1	44.7	49.2	54.4	56.6	53.7	57.1	58.1
L. HAITI	4.7	6.5	7.0	7.9	6.9	7.0	42.1	38.1	38.0	34.0	38.0	38.4	46.8	44.6	45.1	41.8	44.9	45.4
M. HONDURAS	13.1	12.9	13.4	12.3	16.3	14.6	35.5	40.6	40.4	38.0	38.8	38.1	48.6	53.4	53.8	50.3	55.1	52.8
N. MEXICO	14.2	17.9	18.5	20.7	24.7	24.4	52.3	50.7	50.8	49.0	51.9	51.8	66.5	68.6	69.3	69.7	76.6	76.2
O. NICARAGUA	19.8	25.4	27.6	30.1	~	~	40.9	47.5	46.0	39.7	~	~	60.7	72.9	73.5	69.9	~	~
P. PANAMA	24.9	22.3	24.8	26.6	33.2	31.4	37.6	37.2	36.2	31.9	29.9	29.2	62.5	59.2	60.9	58.6	63.1	60.6
Q. PARAGUAY	29.8	35.1	33.8	30.1	32.2	30.5	38.3	38.6	40.5	46.0	47.3	48.2	68.1	73.7	74.3	76.1	79.4	78.6
R. PERU	20.2	21.1	20.2	19.5	22.0	21.3	38.3	39.8	39.9	37.2	36.6	36.9	58.5	61.0	60.1	56.7	58.6	58.2
S. URUGUAY	71.7	55.0	59.2	55.4	54.8	54.3	33.7	30.2	31.8	31.3	29.7	29.2	105.4	85.2	91.0	86.7	84.5	83.5
T. VENEZUELA	26.6	25.5	27.2	32.3	35.9	36.9	34.5	33.4	33.6	34.4	33.7	36.0	61.1	58.9	60.8	66.7	69.6	73.0
LATIN AMERICA[1]	24.3	24.2	25.2	26.1	25.6	27.6	36.5	38.1	38.1	37.0	37.1	37.3	60.8	62.3	63.4	63.0	65.6	64.9
UNITED STATES	71.1[a]	70.7	71.9	72.2	71.3	70.9	33.0[a]	33.0	32.8	34.5	34.1	34.9	104.1[a]	103.7	104.8	106.7	105.4	105.8

1. Unweighted average.

a. 1966–68.

SOURCE: Derived from Mexico-BNCE-CE, March 1981; FAO-PY, 1982, table 104; 1984, table 104; 1985, table 106.

Table 826

AVERAGE YEARLY PC IN FOOD/C PRODUCTION
BY PERIOD, 20 LRC, 1953–81

	Country	1953–59 (7 years)	1960–69 (10 years)	1970–79 (10 years)	1980–81 (2 years)	Total (29 years)
A.	ARGENTINA	–.7	1.3	1.7	–1.5	.7
B.	BOLIVIA	4.8	1.1	.7	–1.9	1.7
C.	BRAZIL	2.0	1.3	2.2	3.8	1.9
D.	CHILE	.4	–.4	.1	1.1	.1
E.	COLOMBIA	–.8	–.4	2.5	.5	.6
F.	COSTA RICA	–1.5	.8	1.9	–3.1	.4
G.	CUBA	–2.8	–1.1	4.6	–3.8	.3
H.	DOMINICAN REP.	–.1	–1.5	.2	1.0	–.4
I.	ECUADOR	6.9	–.1	–.7	3.8	1.6
J.	EL SALVADOR	–3.7[a]	–.4	1.2	–6.9	–.6[b]
K.	GUATEMALA	–.1	.8	1.7	0	.8
L.	HAITI	–2.0[a]	0	–.9	–3.8	–1.0[b]
M.	HONDURAS	–.3	1.7	–2.0	0	–.2
N.	MEXICO	3.4	1.0	.4	3.4	1.5
O.	NICARAGUA	1.1[a]	1.7	.7	–12.9	–.1[b]
P.	PANAMA	1.7	2.0	–.5	2.5	1.1
Q.	PARAGUAY	–.1	–.4	1.6	.2	.4
R.	PERU	.1	.8	–1.2	1.1	0
S.	URUGUAY	–3.7	2.6	–.4	11.2	.6
T.	VENEZUELA	1.3	3.1	1.0	–5.2	1.4
	LATIN AMERICA[1]	.2	.2	.9	1.0	.5
	UNITED STATES	.2	.5	1.7	1.9	.9

1. ELA.

a. 1955–59.

b. 27 years.

SOURCE: SALA, 23-3502.

Table 827

ACCEPTORS OF GOVERNMENT FAMILY PLANNING SERVICES BY METHOD AND
YEAR OF ACCEPTANCE,[1] 12 L, 1971 AND 1975

(T)

	Country	All Program Methods		IUD		Oral Contraceptives		Sterilization		Other Program Methods	
		1971	1975	1971	1975	1971	1975	1971	1975	1971	1975
B.	BOLIVIA	~	7.6	~	5.6	~	1.2	~	- -	~	.8

Continued in SALA, 20-802.

Table 828

ACCEPTORS OF GOVERNMENT FAMILY PLANNING SERVICES BY METHOD
AND AGE OF WIFE,[1] 7 L

	Country	Year	Method	N (T)	% in Wife's Age Group							Wife's Median Age
					Under 20	20-24	25-29	30-34	35-39	40+	Unknown	
C.	BRAZIL	1974	All	15.4	13.1	32.0	25.6	15.6	9.1	4.1	.5	25.9
			IUD	1.0	3.6	22.5	31.5	22.5	12.6	6.8	.5	28.7
			Oral	13.6	14.0	32.8	25.3	15.0	8.8	3.7	.4	25.5

Continued in SALA, 20-803.

Table 829

ACCEPTORS OF GOVERNMENT FAMILY PLANNING SERVICES
BY METHOD AND NUMBER OF LIVING CHILDREN,[1] 7 L

Country	Year	Method	N (T)	% by Number of Living Children						Unknown	Median Number of Living Children
				0-1	2	3	4	5	6+		
C. BRAZIL	1974	All	15.4	33.5	21.3	13.4	27.2 ←———————————┤			4.6	2.2
		IUD	1.0	19.7	23.3	17.9	37.2 ←———————————┤			1.9	2.8
		Oral	13.6	34.4	21.5	13.2	26.5 ←———————————┤			4.4	2.1

Continued in SALA, 20-804.

Table 830

USERS OF BIRTH CONTROL METHODS BY PUBLIC AND PRIVATE SOURCE,[1] 6 L

Country	Year[2]	Method	All Sources		National Program Supplies and Services		Private Sector Supplies and Services	
			N (T)	Users as % of Married Women Age 15-44	N (T)	Users as % of Married Women Age 15-44	N (T)	Users as % of Married Women Age 15-44
F. COSTA RICA	1976	All	78.8	33.7	~	~	~	~
		IUD	8.1	3.5	~	~	~	~
		Oral	53.7	23.0	~	~	~	~
		Condoms	9.0	3.8	~	~	~	~
		Other	8.1	3.4	~	~	~	~

Continued in SALA, 20-805.

Table 831

RELATIVE AGE DISTRIBUTION OF FAMILY PLANNING
PARTICIPANTS AT ENTRY INTO PROGRAM, 14 L

Country	Year	Relative Age Distribution						Median Age
		15-19	20-24	25-29	30-34	35-39	40+	
B. BOLIVIA	1973	5.5	26.5	32.0	23.1	11.6	1.3	28.1

Continued in SALA, 20-807.

Table 832

WOMEN PARTICIPATING IN FAMILY PLANNING PROGRAMS, BY BIRTH CONTROL METHOD, 19 LR, 1970–73

Country and Years	Total		Method Adopted									
			IUD		Oral		Sterilization		Other		Not Specified	
	N	%	N	%	N	%	N	%	N	%	N	%
A. ARGENTINA	27,003	100.0	7,627	28.2	18,187	67.4	—	—	1,189	4.4	—	—
1970	11,162	100.0	2,582	23.1	8,209	73.6	—	—	371	3.3	—	—

Continued in SALA, 20-808.

Table 833

COST OF SOCIAL SECURITY, 18 L, 1965 and 1977

		Revenue and Expenditure as % of GDP					
		Revenue		Expenditure			
				Total		Benefits	
	Country	1965	1977	1965	1977	1965	1977
A.	ARGENTINA	3.8	8.0[a]	3.2	7.3[a]	~	7.0[a]
B.	BOLIVIA	4.3[b]	3.5[c]	3.6[b]	3.1[c]	3.0[b]	2.8[c]
C.	BRAZIL	4.5	6.2	4.3	6.2	3.4	5.3
D.	CHILE[1]	14.1	13.2	12.2	10.1	10.0	9.4
E.	COLOMBIA	1.1	4.5	1.1	3.7	1.0	3.3
F.	COSTA RICA	3.8	7.4	2.3	5.8	1.9	5.3
G.	CUBA	8.3	9.2[d]	~	~	8.3	9.2[d]
H.	DOMINICAN REP.	2.9[e]	2.6	2.7[b]	2.5	1.8[e]	2.4
I.	ECUADOR	4.1	4.5[‡]	2.9	3.0[‡]	2.5	2.8[‡]
J.	EL SALVADOR	2.4	3.4	2.2	2.9	2.1	2.0
K.	GUATEMALA	2.0	2.1	2.0	1.6	1.8	1.5
L.	HAITI	~	.9	~	.8	~	.7
N.	MEXICO	2.8	3.9[f]	2.6	3.4[f]	2.2	2.9[f]
O.	NICARAGUA	2.6	2.8	2.1	2.3	1.9	2.1
P.	PANAMA	7.3	9.9	6.0	7.9	5.6	7.0
R.	PERU	2.3	~	2.9	~	~	~
S.	URUGUAY	10.1[g]	11.3	14.5[g]	10.3	8.7[g]	9.1
T.	VENEQUELA	3.0	4.5	3.1	4.1	3.0	3.8

1. In 1971 the percentages increased to unprecedented levels of 19.4, 17.2, and 15.6.

a. 1975.
b. 1961.
c. 1976.
d. 1978.
e. 1970.
f. 1974.
g. 1969.

SOURCE: Carmelo Mesa-Lago, *El Desarrollo de la Seguridad Social en América Latina* (Santiago, 1985).

Table 834

FINANCING OF SOCIAL SECURITY, BY SOURCE, 20 L, LATE 1970s

	Country	Legal Contribution as % of Salary (Ca. 1980)			Distribution of Benefits of Social Security				
		Insured	Employer	Government	Insured	Employer	Government	Investment	Other
A.	ARGENTINA	14.0–15.0	21.5	15.3	27.3	57.2	6.8	6.8	1.9
B.	BOLIVIA	3.5	20.0	1.5	28.5	47.6	11.8	0	12.1
C.	BRAZIL	8.6	14.7	~[a]	~	~	~	~	~
D.	CHILE	19.56–27.84	2.85	~[a]	17.5	45.6	30.7	2.5	3.7
E.	COLOMBIA	3.8–5.5	14.67–18.0	~[a]	12.3	31.3	35.0	2.7	18.7
F.	COSTA RICA	8.0	22.6	1.5	23.4	44.2	22.3	5.9	4.2
G.	CUBA	0	10.0	~[a]	0	10.0	→	0	0
H.	DOMINICAN REP.	2.5	9.5	2.5	~	~	67.6	~	~
I.	ECUADOR	9.0	9.5	~[a]	30.2[b]	32.2	20.4	16.3	.9
J.	EL SALVADOR	3.5	8.25	.5[a]	11.0	32.6	52.8	3.1	.5
K.	GUATEMALA	4.5	10.0	3.0[a]	26.1	41.1	31.7	0	1.1
L.	HAITI	3.5	6.0–9.0	1.2	26.6	→	69.9	3.5	0
M.	HONDURAS	4.0–9.0	5.0	3.5	~	~	~	~	~
N.	MEXICO	3.75	12.42	1.88	24.0[b]	50.3	19.7	2.5	3.5
O.	NICARAGUA	4.0	11.0	.5	14.8	36.3	45.5	3.1	.3
P.	PANAMA	7.25	15.22	.8[a]	23.8	49.7	18.3	7.2	1.0
Q.	PARAGUAY	9.25	16.5	1.5	~	~	~	~	~
R.	PERU	5.0	14.0	2.0[a]	~	~	~	~	~
S.	URUGUAY	12.0–16.0	19.0–29.0	~[a]	24.6	49.4	18.5	2.3	5.2
T.	VENEZUELA	4.0	7.0–9.0	1.5	9.2	18.4	67.8	4.6	0

a. Taxes, covering of the deficit, and other subsidies.
b. Distribution in 1974.

SOURCE: Carmelo Mesa-Lago, *El Desarrollo de la Seguridad Social en América Latina* (Santiago, 1985).

Table 835

TOTAL POPULATION AND EAP COVERED BY SOCIAL SECURITY, 20 LR, 1980

Country	Total Population (T)	Total Insured[1] (T)	Coverage	Distribution (%)	EAP (T)	Active Insured[2] (T)	Coverage	Distribution (%)
A. ARGENTINA	28,237	22,278	78.9	10.3	10,690	7,391	69.1	10.5
B. BOLIVIA	5,570	1,412	25.4	.7	1,754	324	18.5	.5
C. BRAZIL	121,286	116,800	96.3	54.1	40,292	38,523	95.6	54.6
D. CHILE	11,104	7,418	67.3	3.5	3,788	2,337	61.7	3.3
E. COLOMBIA[3,4]	25,247	2,925	11.6	1.4	8,477	1,900	22,4	2.7
F. COSTA RICA	2,279	1,733	76.0	.8	770	526	68.3	.7
G. CUBA[5]	9,724	9,724[†]	100.0[†]	4.5	3,618	3,364[†]	93.0[†]	4.8
H. DOMINICAN REP.	5,558	440[a]	7.9	.2	2,019	283[a]	14.0	.4
I. ECUADOR	8,021	636	7.9	.3	2,393	555	23.2	.8
J. EL SALVADOR	4,797	300	6.2	.1	1,611	187	11.6	.3
K. GUATEMALA[5]	7,480	1,064	14.2	.5	2,314	767	33.1	1.1
L. HAITI	5,809	44	.8	~	2,815	44[a]	1.6	.1
M. HONDURAS[6]	3,955	288	7.3	.1	1,172	156	14.4	.2
N. MEXICO	69,393	37,056	53.4	17.2	19,423	8,158	42.0	11.6
O. NICARAGUA	2,771	253	9.1	.1	773	146	18.9	.2
P. PANAMA	1,956	985	50.3	.4	701	319	45.6	.4
Q. PARAGUAY[4]	3,168	575	18.2	.3	1,077	151	14.0	.2
R. PERU	17,295	3,016	17.4	1.4	5,719	2,142	37.4	3.0
S. URUGUAY	2,908	1,993	68.5	1.0	1,123	912	81.2	1.3
T. VENEZUELA	15,024	6,790	45.2	3.1	4,723	2,350	49.8	3.3
LATIN AMERICA	352,774	215,730	61.2	100.0	115,252	70,535	61.2	100.0
Excluding Brazil	231,488	98,930	42.7	45.9	74,960	32,012	42.7	45.4

1. Program of sickness and maternity leave.
2. Pension program.
3. 1979.
4. Excludes various groups of insured people.
5. 1981.
6. 1982.

a. Estimates based on legal coverage.

SOURCE: Carmelo Mesa-Lago, *El Desarrollo de la Seguridad Social en América Latina* (Santiago, 1985).

Table 836

CHILE REAL VALUE OF ANNUAL PENSIONS, 1964–80[a]

Year	Pensions (M Pesos)	Persons with Pension (T)	Average Pension PI (Pesos)	Index (1970 = 100) Nominal Pension	Index (1970 = 100) Inflation[1]	Index (1970 = 100) Real Pension
1964	.5	380	1.4	16	24	66.7
1965	.8	436	1.9	23	31	74.2
1966	1.2	484	2.5	30	38	78.9
1967	1.6	514	3.2	39	45	86.7
1968	2.3	545	4.2	51	51	89.5
1969	3.1	591	5.3	64	74	86.5
1970	5.1	614	8.3	100	100	100.0
1971	9.3	643	14.5	175	127	138.0
1972	15.4	689	23.3	281	264	106.6
1973	51.0	713	71.6	864	1,428	60.5
1974	345.0	750	459.3	5,537	8,535	64.8
1975	1,526.0	810	1,885.0	22,725	40,899	55.5
1976	5,816.0	862	6,747.6	81,345	136,111	59.8
1977	14,459.0	916	15,791.7	190,376	291,006	65.4
1978	24,085.0	975	24,690.9	297,659	436,509	68.2
1979	38,962.0	1,023	38,094.3	459,244	595,398	77.1
1980	58,100.0	1,070	54,265.6	654,197	794,261	82.4

1. Average annual variation for 1964–70; data adjusted for 1970–80.

a. Pre-1975 data have been converted from escudos to pesos (1,000 escudos = 1 peso); includes all pensions.

SOURCE: Carmelo Mesa-Lago, *El Desarrollo de la Seguridad Social en América Latina* (Santiago, 1985).

Table 837

COSTA RICA SOCIAL SECURITY LEGISLATION, BY RISKS PROTECTED AND GROUPS COVERED, 1886–1983

Year[1]	Risks Protected[2]	Groups Covered
1886, 1958	VIS	Education
1918	VIS	Communication
1923	VIS	Public Workers
1924, 1951	RP	All Workers in Private Companies
1935	VIS	Musicians
1939	VIS	Judicial Powers
1941	VIS	Municipalities
1941, 1961, 1971	VIS, EM	General Systems (CCSS), But Limited to Capital City and Provincial Capitals
1943	VIS	Legislative Powers and Treasury
1944	VIS	Public Works and Transportation
1955, 1965	EM	Extension of General Systems to the Dependents of the Insured
1973, 1978	EM	Transference of All Public Hospitals to the CCSS
1974	EM, VIS	Indigents (through Family Assignment)
1974, 1976	EM	Workers, People on Pension, and Their Dependents

1. The first date corresponds to the first law and subsequent dates to modifications and amplifications.
2. VIS: pensions for elderly, invalids, and surviving relatives
   EM: medical and maternity
   RP: occupational hazards.

SOURCE: Carmelo Mesa-Lago, *El Desarrollo de la Seguridad Social en América Latina* (Santiago, 1985).

Table 838

COSTA RICA COST OF SOCIAL SECURITY, 1960–80

(M Colones and %)

Year	GNP	Total Expenditure of the Central Government	Expenditure on Social Security[1]		
			Total	% of GNP	% of Government Expenditure
1961	2,929	419	56	1.9	13.4
1965	3,928	649	90	2.3	13.9
1970	6,524	1,192	349	5.3	29.3
1975	16,805	3,544	1,104	6.6	31.2
1979	34,584	8,658	2,764	8.0	31.9
1980	41,405	10,436	3,716	9.0	35.6

1. Includes expenditure of CCSS and the Ministry of Health; excludes expenditure on occupational hazards.

SOURCE: Carmelo Mesa-Lago, *El Desarrollo de la Seguridad Social en América Latina* (Santiago, 1985).

Table 839

CUBA SOCIAL SECURITY LEGISLATION, BY RISKS PROTECTED
AND GROUPS COVERED, 1913–83

Year[1]	Risks Protected[2]	Groups Covered
1913, 1934	VIS	Armed Forces
1915	VIS	Communications
1916, 1933	RP	Salaried Employees of Public and Private Sectors
1917, 1927	VIS	Judicial Powers
1919	VIS	Public Employees, Scholastic[3]
1920, 1936	VIS	Police
1921, 1923	VIS	Railroad, Telephone[3]
1927	VIS	Maritime
1929	VIS	Notaries, Transportation[3]
1934, 1937	M	Salaried Employees of Public Sector
1935	VIS	Journalists
1938	VIS	Banking
1939	VIS	Registered Merchants
1943	VIS	Doctors, Sugar Producers[3]
1945	VIS	Lawyers, Textile Workers[3]
1946	VIS	Solicitors, Graphic Artists, State Workers, Barbers, Tobacco Growers
1947	VIS	Pharmacists
1948	VIS	Tax Collector, Electricity
1949	VIS	Dentists, Veterinarians, Architects, Businessmen, Flour[3]
1950	VIS	Members of Congress
1951	VIS	Petroleum, Radio[3]
1952	VIS	Securities and Finances, Nurses[3]
1953	VIS	Brewers
1954	VIS	Civil Engineers, Stenographers, Health Sector, Construction, Cattlemen[3]
1955	VIS	Agronomists, Private School Teachers, Educators, Agriculture Teachers[3]
1956	VIS	Governors, Mayors, and Council Members
1957	VIS	Chauffeurs
1959	VIS	Unification of Salaried Workers of Private Sector
1960–61	VIS	Unification and Regulation of Private Sector Workers
1962	VIS	Unification of Professional Institutions
1963	VIS, PT, E	Unification of the Social Security System, Regulation and Extension of Monetary Loans to All Salaried Workers, Creation of Medical Insurance for Everyone, Integration of Social Assistance
1964	VIS, PT	Special Treatment for Independent Workers
1974	M	New Program for Maternity
1976	VIS, PT	Special Program for the Armed Forces
1977	RP	Regulation of the Prevention of Occupational Hazards and Hygiene of Working Conditions
1979	VIS, PT	New Social Security System
1983	VIS, PT	Special Program for Agricultural Cooperative Members

1. The first date corresponds to the initial law and subsequent dates to modifications and
   amplifications.
2. VIS: pensions for elderly, invalids, and surviving spouses
   E: sickness
   M: maternity
   PT: temporary loans
   RP: occupational hazards.
3. Established by separate laws.

SOURCE: Carmelo-Mesa Lago, *El Desarrollo de la Seguridad Social en América Latina*
(Santiago, 1985).

Table 840

CUBA REAL VALUE OF ANNUAL PENSIONS, 1962–81[a]

Year	Pensions (M Pesos)	Persons with Pensions (T)	Average Pension PI (Pesos)	Index (1970 = 100)		
				Nominal Pension	Inflation	Real Pension
1962	152	213	713	90.2	79.2	114.0
1965	208	298	699	88.4	93.4	94.6
1970	286	363	790	100.0	100.0	100.0
1971	311	394	790	100.0	106.1	94.3
1972	344	432	796	100.7	112.5	89.5
1973	383	470	816	103.2	119.4	86.4
1974	417	507	823	104.1	126.6	82.3
1975	448	544	824	104.3	134.3	77.7
1976	473	581	814	103.1	135.1	76.3
1977	492	629	781	98.8	134.3	73.7
1978	508	652	778	98.5	139.3	70.7
1979	523	671[†]	779	98.6	140.1	70.4
1980	542	690	785	99.4	141.1	70.4
1981	553	710[†]	779	98.6	156.4	63.0

a. Old age pensions, pensions for invalids and surviving spouses.

SOURCE: Carmelo Mesa-Lago, *El Desarrollo de la Seguridad Social en América Latina* (Santiago, 1985).

Table 841

CUBA DIFFERENCES IN LOANS AND HEALTH
SERVICES, BY PROVINCE, 1982

Province	Expenditure of Monetary Loans (Pesos) (PI)	Doctors (P10I)	Hospital Beds (PTI)
Pinar del Río	66.81	11.8	4.6
La Habana	99.85	14.0	2.6
Ciudad de La Habana	120.48	41.2	11.2
Matanzas	95.47	16.9	5.4
Villa Clara	93.05	11.7	4.2
Cienfuegos	86.09	12.5	4.8
Sancti Spíritus	85.62	10.1	4.5
Ciego de Avila	79.78	11.4	3.5
Camagüey	79.35	13.5	6.3
Las Tunas	65.30	8.9	4.6
Holguín	58.02	8.6	3.9
Granma	50.34	7.2	4.1
Santiago de Cuba	58.74	12.8	5.5
Guantánamo	52.83	8.9	5.1
Isla de la Juventud	47.69	16.4	7.2
Total	82.20	17.3	5.9

SOURCE: Carmelo Mesa-Lago, *El Desarrollo de la Seguridad Social en América Latina* (Santiago, 1985).

Table 842

MEXICO SOCIAL SECURITY LEGISLATION, BY RISKS PROTECTED AND GROUPS COVERED, 1925–83

Year[1]	Risks Protected[2]	Groups Covered
1925, 1959	VIS, EM	Public Federal Workers
1983	RP	Public Federal Workers
1926, 1946	VIS, RP	Armed Forces
1928	VIS, EM, RP	Public Teachers
1931	RP	Private Employees and Workers
1935, 1966–70	VIS, RP	Petroleum Workers
1936–38, 1948	VIS, EM	Railroad
1966–70	RP	Railroad
1941, 1966–70	VIS, EM, RP	Electricity
1943	VIS, EM, RP	Private Employees and Workers[3]
1954–55	VIS, EM, RP	Permanent Rural Workers, Ejidatarios, Coop-erative Members, Small Farmers
1960	VIS, EM, RP	Rural Seasonal Workers and Temporary Urban Workers
1963	VIS, EM, RP	Sugar Workers
1970	VIS, EM, RP	All Workers in Dependent Relationships
1971–73	VIS, EM, RP	Henequen and Tobacco Workers
1973	VIS, EM, RP	Domestic Service,[3] Independent Workers, and Employers[3]
1974	VIS, EM, RP	Coffee and Palm Workers
1962, 1973	Nurseries	All under the IMSS
1973–74	EM	Marginal Groups
1979–83	EM	Rural Population

1. The first date corresponds with the initial law, and subsequent dates to modifications and amplifications.
2. VIS: pensions for elderly, invalids, and surviving spouses
   EM: medical and maternity
   RP: occupational hazards.
3. The date of incorporation was postponed.

SOURCE: Carmelo Mesa-Lago, *El Desarrollo de la Seguridad Social en América Latina* (Santiago, 1985).

Table 843

MEXICO REAL VALUE OF ANNUAL PENSIONS, 1960–81[a]

Year	Pensions (M Pesos)	Persons with Pensions (T)	Average Pension PI (Pesos)	Index (1970 = 100) Nominal Pension	Inflation[1]	Real Pension
1960	66	49	1,347	47.5	80.0	59.4
1961	85	58	1,466	51.7	80.7	64.1
1962	112	70	1,600	56.4	82.2	68.6
1963	144	77	1,870	66.0	82.6	79.9
1964	180	92	1,956	69.0	86.1	80.1
1965	211	105	2,009	70.9	87.8	80.8
1966	257	121	2,124	74.9	88.9	84.2
1967	315	143	2,203	77.7	91.5	84.9
1968	397	163	2,436	85.9	93.3	92.1
1969	507	184	2,755	97.2	95.4	101.9
1970	618	218	2,835	100.0	100.0	100.0
1971	778	234	3,325	117.3	105.5	111.2
1972	915	253	3,617	127.6	110.8	115.2
1973	1,195	265	4,509	159.0	124.2	128.0
1974	1,613	300	5,377	189.6	153.6	123.4
1975	2,492	327	7,621	268.8	176.6	152.2
1976	3,184	364	8,747	308.5	204.6	150.8
1977	4,444	402	11,055	389.9	264.1	147.6
1978	5,447	443	12,296	433.7	310.3	139.8
1979	7,108	489	14,536	512.7	366.8	139.8
1980	9,994	536	18,646	657.6	463.2	142.0
1981	13,781	584	23,598	832.3	592.5	140.5

1. 1970–81: annual average variation of consumer prices; January to December, wholesale prices.

a. Includes pensions for elderly, invalids, surviving spouses, and occupational hazards.

SOURCE: Carmelo Mesa-Lago, *El Desarrollo de la Seguridad Social en América Latina* (Santiago, 1985).

Table 844

MEXICO COST OF SOCIAL SECURITY, 1961–80

(B Pesos and %)

Year	GNP	Total Expenditure of Central Government	Expenditure of Social Security		
			Total	% of	
				GNP	Government Expenditure
1961	163.8	20.4[a]	3.2	2.0	15.7
1965	252.0	36.7[a]	6.5	2.6	17.7
1970	418.7	52.7[a]	12.7	3.0	24.1
1975	998.3	161.6	46.7	4.7	28.9
1980	4,276.5	750.2	137.6	3.2	18.2

a. According to the federal budget, excluding expenditure of decentralized agencies and state companies.

SOURCE: Carmelo Mesa-Lago, *El Desarrollo de la Seguridad Social en América Latina* (Santiago, 1985).

Table 845

MEXICO SOCIAL SECURITY COVERAGE, BY STATE, 1980

(T and %)

State	Total Population	Total Insured[1]	% Coverage
Distrito Federal	9,640	9,682	100.4
Aguas Calientes	521	261	50.1
Baja California	1,262	743	58.9
Baja California Sur	228	141	61.8
Campeche	382	162	42.4
Coahuila	1,607	1,143	71.1
Colima	350	180	51.4
Chiapas	2,158	429	19.9
Chihuahua	1,991	974	48.9
Durango	1,193	510	42.7
Guanajuato	3,135	962	30.7
Guerrero	2,236	523	23.4
Hidalgo	1,559	372	23.9
Jalisco	4,419	1,837	41.6
México[2]	7,768	420	5.4
Michoacán	3,137	621	19.8
Morelos	960	394	41.0
Nayarit	750	287	38.2
Nueva León	2,536	1,872	73.8
Oaxaca	2,586	444	17.2
Puebla	3,378	947	28.0
Querétaro	753	373	49.5
Quintana Roo	217	142	65.4
San Luis Potosí	1,719	499	29.0
Sinaloa	1,938	916	47.3
Sonora	1,541	1,027	66.6
Tabasco	1,183	418	35.3
Tamaulipas	1,978	1,020	51.6
Tlaxcala	564	39	6.9
Veracruz	5,415	2,107	38.9
Yucatán	1,063	576	54.2
Zacatecas	1,178	214	18.2
Total	69,347	30,243[a]	43.6

1. Includes IMSS, IMSS-COPLAMAR, ISSSTE, PEMEX, and Armed Forces.
2. Excludes the Federal District.

a. Includes 5,460 insured persons living in foreign countries.

SOURCE: Carmelo Mesa-Lago, *El Desarrollo de la Seguridad Social en América Latina* (Santiago, 1985).

Table 846

PERU SOCIAL SECURITY LEGISLATION, BY RISKS PROTECTED AND GROUPS COVERED, 1850–1983

Year[1]	Risks Protected[2]	Groups Covered
1850, 1910, 1923	VIS, D	Armed Forces
1850, 1936, 1941, 1950, 1960	VIS, D	Public Employees
1911, 1935	RP	Workers
1934	VIS	Stevedores in Callao
1936	EM	Workers
1946	A	Private Employees
1947	VIS	Jockeys
1948	EM	Public and Private Employees
1950	EM	Armed Forces
1961	VIS	Workers
1961–62	VIS	Public and Private Employees
1965	VIS	Congress, Judiciary, Public Inspector, Public Teachers
1965, 1978	D, EM	Fishermen
1966–68	VIS	Independent Chauffeurs (Taxi Owners)
1970	VIS	Domestic Service
1972	VIS	Fishermen
1972	VIS	Uniform System of the Armed Forces
1973–74	VIS	Unified and Uniform the System of Workers
1979	EM	Unified and Uniform the System of Workers and Private and Public Employees
1980	All	New System Unified and Uniform (excluding Armed Forces)

1. The first data corresponds to the initial law and the subsequent dates to modifications and amplifications.
2. VIS: pensions for the elderly, invalids, and surviving spouses
    EM: medical and maternity
    RP: occupational hazards
    D: compensation or unemployment pay
    A: old-age pension.

SOURCE: Carmelo Mesa-Lago, *El Desarrollo de la Seguridad Social en América Latina* (Santiago, 1985).

Table 847

URUGUAY COST OF SOCIAL SECURITY, 1965–82

(M New Pesos and %)[1]

			Expenditure on Social Security		
		Total Expenditure of Central Government		% of	
Year	GNP		Total	GNP	Federal Expenditure
1965	52	13	8	14.5	61.5
1969	499	118	70	14.2	59.3
1975	7,108	1,878	872	12.3	46.4
1980	81,429	20,812	6,797	8.3	32.6
1981	106,384	30,969	12,192	11.4	39.4
1982	112,564	41,274	14,398	12.8	34.9

1. Billions of old pesos in 1965 and 1969; new peso = 1,000 old pesos.
2. Excludes expenditure on occupational hazards and lesser programs.

SOURCE: Carmelo Mesa-Lago, *El Desarrollo de la Seguridad Social en América Latina* (Santiago, 1985).

Table 848

URUGUAY REAL VALUE OF ANNUAL PENSIONS, 1963–82[a]

| Year | Pensions (M New Pesos)[1] | Persons with Pension (T) | Average Pension PI (New Pesos)[2] | Index (1970 = 100)[2] | | |
				Nominal Pension	Inflation[3]	Real Pension
1963	2.1	328	6.4	7.0	5.4	129.6
1964	2.7	346	7.9	8.7	7.5	116.0
1965	3.4	358	9.6	10.6	11.8	89.8
1966	5.4	368	14.6	16.1	18.2	88.5
1967	9.9	408	24.2	26.6	42.8	62.1
1968	17.4	426	40.8	44.9	71.0	63.2
1969	34.0	451	75.4	83.1	85.2	97.5
1970	40.5	447	90.7	100.0	100.0	100.0
1971	56.7	464	122.3	134.7	135.7	99.3
1972	86.9	489	177.8	195.9	239.5	81.8
1973	155.0	500	309.9	341.5	469.4	72.8
1974	285.2	508	561.5	618.7	831.8	74.4
1975	492.9	494	997.7	1,099.4	1,509.0	72.9
1976	770.6	502	1,535.1	1,691.6	2,272.5	74.4
1977	1,180.5	529	2,231.6	2,459.2	3,595.1	68.4
1978	1,777.4	547	3,255.3	3,587.3	5,194.9	69.1
1979	2,798.0	567	4,934.7	5,438.0	8,665.1	62.8
1980	4,972.3	596	8,342.8	9,193.8	14,167.5	64.9
1981	9,439.1	616	15,323.3	16,886.3	18,984.5	88.9
1982	12,093.8	634	19,075.4	21,021.1	22,591.5	93.0

1. Ratio of old peso to new peso, 1000:1.
2. Calculation of average pensions and index of pensions corresponds to 1963–69 and is based on total pesos.
3. 1963–68, 1971, variation is from December to December; remainder is calculated by annual average.

a. Includes pensions for elderly, invalids, surviving spouses; excludes armed forces, since 1970.

SOURCE: Carmelo Mesa-Lago, *El Desarrollo de la Seguridad Social en América Latina* (Santiago, 1985).

Table 849

SOCIAL SECURITY: PERCENT SERVED OF ECONOMICALLY ACTIVE POPULATION, 20 LR, 1960 and 1970

Country	1960	1970
A. ARGENTINA	53.8	67.4

Continued in SALA, 17-810.

Table 850

INSURED POPULATION IN RELATION TO TOTAL AND ECONOMICALLY ACTIVE POPULATION, 5 L, 1960–71

A. ARGENTINA

| Year | Total Population[1] (T) (1) | Economically Active Population[1,2] (T) (2) | Insured Population[3] | | | | Percent of EAP Insured (3)/(2) | Percent of Total Population Insured (6)/(1) | Ratio of Active to Passive (3)/(4) |
			Active[4] (3)	Passive[5] (4)	Dependents (5)	Total (6)			
1960	20,850	7,270	4,011	745	4,412	9,168	55.2	44.0	5.4
1961	21,203	7,334	4,031	812	4,407	9,250	55.0	43.6	5.0

Continued in SALA, 24-834 through 24-838.

CHAPTER 9

EDUCATION AND SCIENCE

Table 900

ILLITERACY, AGE 15 AND OVER, BY URBAN AND RURAL AREAS AND BY SEX, 20 L

	Country	Year	Illiterate Population			% of Total Population		
			Total (T)	Male (T)	Female (T)	Total	Male	Female
A.	ARGENTINA[1]	1985	934	406	528	4.5	4.0	5.0
B.	BOLIVIA	1985	925	282	643	25.8	16.2	34.9
C.	BRAZIL	1985	19,085	9,047	10,038	22.3	21.0	23.5
D.	CHILE	1983	~	~	~	5.6	~	~
E.	COLOMBIA	1985	2,149	984	1,165	11.9	10.9	12.9
F.	COSTA RICA	1985	103	49	55	6.4	6.0	6.8
G.	CUBA	1979	218	101	117	4.6	4.3	4.9
H.	DOMINICAN REP.[2]	1985	893	441	452	22.7	22.3	23.2
I.	ECUADOR	1985	923	312	531	17.6	15.0	20.2
J.	EL SALVADOR[3]	1985	858	383	475	27.9	25.0	30.7
K.	GUATEMALA	1985	2,154	904	1,250	45.0	37.4	52.9
L.	HAITI	1985	2,318	1,080	1,238	62.4	59.9	64.7
M.	HONDURAS	1985	~	~	~	40.5	39.3	41.6
N.	MEXICO	1985	4,400	1,700	2,700	9.7	7.7	11.7
O.	NICARAGUA[4]	1980	186	~	~	13.0	~	~
P.	PANAMA	1985	~	~	~	11.8	11.0	12.3
Q.	PARAGUAY	1985	253	94	159	11.8	8.8	14.6
R.	PERU	1985	1,800	506	1,294	15.2	8.5	21.9
S.	URUGUAY	1975	125	65	60	6.1	6.6	5.7
T.	VENEZUELA	1985	1,416	623	793	13.1	11.6	14.5

1. Data refer to age 18 and over.
2. Excluding 8% of the population unspecified as to literacy or illiteracy.
3. Data refer to age 10 and over.
4. In 1980, after the National Literacy Campaign, the Ministry of Education estimated that
   of the 722,431 illiterates identified in the census of October, 1979, 130,372 were "analfabetos inaptos" and 406,056 were made literate, leaving only 186,003 "analfabetos aptos"
   (or 12.96% of the population of 10 years and over). Data for 1985 refer to age 10 and over.

SOURCE: UNESCO-SY, 1980, 1986, table 1.3.

Table 901

ILLITERACY AND HIGHER EDUCATION, 20 L

Country	Gross Rate of Schooling (to 1980)		Illiterates Age 15 and Over (%)		Illiterates Age 15–24
	Universities and Similar Institutions	Tertiary Level	1950	1980	1970
Rapid Modernization Countries					
A. ARGENTINA	18.0	22.2	13.6	6.7	4.2
D. CHILE	10.9	13.2	19.8	7.5	4.7
F. COSTA RICA	21.5	25.8	20.6	7.0	5.2
G. CUBA	19.5	19.5	22.1	3.9	~
P. PANAMA	22.2	22.2	30.0	15.3	12.4
S. URUGUAY	16.1	16.1[b]	9.5	6.1	~
T. VENEZUELA	17.9	20.2	50.5	17.7	12.0
TOTAL	17.1	19.7[c]	26.1	9.7	7.7
Big Countries with Rapid Unbalanced Modernization					
C. BRAZIL	11.7	11.7	50.5	26.0	24.5
E. COLOMBIA	10.5	10.9	37.7	13.7	11.5
N. MEXICO	12.2	14.0	43.2	16.0	16.4
TOTAL	11.7	12.3[c]	43.8	18.6	17.5
Medium-Sized and Small Countries with Partial Modernization					
H. DOMINICAN REP.	7.5	7.5	57.1	26.4	21.1
I. ECUADOR	36.6	36.6	44.3	18.7	14.2
Q. PARAGUAY	6.7	6.8	34.2	14.3	9.6
R. PERU	15.4	19.2[b]	38.9	18.5	13.5
TOTAL	18.0	19.9	45.2	19.8	14.6
Countries with Incipient Modernization					
B. BOLIVIA	9.3	9.3	67.9	36.7	17.3
J. EL SALVADOR	2.9	3.9[d]	60.6	35.3	28.8
K. GUATEMALA	6.7	7.2	70.7	47.3	45.4
L. HAITI	.8	.8[b]	89.5	71.3	~
M. HONDURAS	7.6	8.2	64.8	31.4	27.1
O. NICARAGUA	13.7	14.1	61.6	33.5	35.1
TOTAL	6.2	6.6[c]	65.1	36.8	30.7

a. Calculated as the ratio of graduates to the population aged 20 to 24.
b. These countries were excluded to establish the averages of the country categories.
c. Arithmetical averages.
d. In 1979 the figures for El Salvador were 7.4 and 8.1 respectively.

SOURCE: Henry Kirsch, "University Youth As Social Protagonist in Latin America," *Cepal Review* No. 29 (Santiago, 1986).

Table 902

DROPOUT AND GRADE REPETITION AT THE PRIMARY LEVEL, 8 LR, 1970–84

(%)

Country	1970		1979		1980		1981		1982		1983		1984	
	Repeat	Dropout	Repeat	Dropout	Repeat	Dropout	Repeat	Dropout	Repeat	Dropout	Repeat	Dropout	Repeat	Dropout
F. COSTA RICA	10.3	4.4	7.6	4.2	7.9	4.2	7.4	3.8	7.1	4.2	11.6	3.0	11.2	2.0
H. DOMINICAN REP.	12.7	9.8	13.7	8.5	11.9	5.9	11.1	4.8	10.4	4.2	9.7	4.1	9.0	3.0
J. EL SALVADOR	16.6	~	7.6	8.6	10.6	10.5	8.9	8.7	~	~	~	~	~	~
K. GUATEMALA	15.8	10.6	11.1	12.4	12.7	11.9	10.0	17.4	14.8	8.7	15.4	8.3	~	8.4
L. HAITI	~	~	~	~	~	~	31.0[†]	13.0[†]	~	~	~	~	~	~
M. HONDURAS	~	15.0	17.0	5.0	17.0	4.0	16.0	5.0	16.0	6.0	~	5.2	~	4.8
O. NICARAGUA	12.8	~	~	~	16.6	23.3	16.6	23.3	15.3	15.1	~	~	~	~
P. PANAMA	15.4	1.9	12.9	3.5	13.0	2.3	12.8	3.7	12.6	2.9	12.0	2.5	~	3.2
LATIN AMERICA AND CARIBBEAN	15.5	~	~	~	14.7	~	~	~	~	~	~	~	~	~

SOURCE: *Educación en América e Informaciones Estadísticas: Centroamérica, República Dominicana y Haiti* (Washington, D.C.: Departamento de Asuntos Educativos, Organización de los Estados Americanos, 1986).

Table 903

STUDENTS ENROLLED AS SHARE OF ELIGIBLE AGES, 20 LR,
1960 AND 1980

(%)

	Country	6 to 11 Years		12 to 17 Years		18 to 23 Years	
		1960	1980	1960	1980	1960	1980
A.	ARGENTINA	91.2	99.9	48.1	72.7	13.2	36.7
B.	BOLIVIA	45.1	76.6	29.0	54.2	5.0	17.1
C.	BRAZIL	47.7	76.2	29.6	58.6	4.7	32.0
D.	CHILE	76.4	100.0	54.7	86.5	7.2	22.2
E.	COLOMBIA	47.9	70.0	28.8	63.8	4.4	32.9
F.	COSTA RICA	74.4	97.5	35.7	54.7	8.0	21.4
G.	CUBA	77.7	100.0	43.0	83.4	6.6	29.9
H.	DOMINICAN REP.	66.8	82.2	39.4	64.4	3.7	20.6
I.	ECUADOR	66.3	80.0	30.3	60.8	5.1	28.5
J.	EL SALVADOR	48.7	69.2	40.3	58.1	8.5	18.9
K.	GUATEMALA	32.0	53.3	17.7	33.8	3.6	10.1
L.	HAITI	33.6	41.4	16.4	21.9	1.9	4.3
M.	HONDURAS	49.5	71.3	24.6	44.7	3.2	14.8
N.	MEXICO	58.4	94.2	37.4	67.3	4.7	18.2
O.	NICARAGUA	42.9	60.8	29.7	53.7	3.6	18.6
P.	PANAMA	68.3	95.7	50.3	83.2	12.7	43.3
Q.	PARAGUAY	69.7	80.0	44.8	51.9	5.8	13.3
R.	PERU	56.7	83.9	43.2	84.0	13.0	32.6
S.	URUGUAY	89.9	~	53.2	67.2	14.1	24.3
T.	VENEZUELA	68.8	83.2	49.0	60.9	8.6	24.0
	LATIN AMERICA[1]	57.3	82.3	35.4	63.3	6.3	26.1

1. Includes Barbados, Guyana, Jamaica, and Trinidad and Tobago.

SOURCE: ECLA-D, "Informe del Secretario Ejecutivo al Décimonoveno Período de
Sesiones de la Comisión," July 27, 1981.

Table 904

**ENROLLMENT RATIOS FOR THE FIRST, SECOND, AND
THIRD LEVELS OF EDUCATION, 20 LC**

Country	School Year Beginning	Sex	First Level Gross	First Level Net	Second Level Gross	Second Level Net	First and Second Levels Gross	Third Level Gross
A. ARGENTINA[2]	1983	MF	107	~	60	~	89	25.2
		F	11	~	62	~	90	27.4
		M	11	~	57	~	89	23.1
B. BOLIVIA[3]	1983	MF	87	~	35	~	72	~
		F	81	~	32	~	67	~
		M	94	~	38	~	78	~
C. BRAZIL[4]	1983	MF	102	~	42	~	87	~
		F	99	~	~	~	~	~
		M	106	~	~	~	~	~
D. CHILE[3]	1984	MF	111	~	65	~	96	~
E. COLOMBIA[5]	1984	MF	120	77	49	~	82	~
		F	122	~	49	~	83	~
		M	119	~	48	~	81	~
F. COSTA RICA[6]	1983	MF	102	~	44	~	75	26.3
		F	100	~	46	~	76	~
		M	103	~	41	~	75	~
G. CUBA[7]	1983	MF	108	97	74	~	90	~
		F	105	~	77	~	90	~
		M	111	~	71	~	89	~
H. DOMINICAN REP.[8]	1983	MF	98	~	45	~	73	~
I. ECUADOR[9]	1983	MF	115	~	53	~	87	~
		F	114	~	54	~	86	~
		M	117	~	53	~	88	~
J. EL SALVADOR[10]	1983	MF	69	64	24	~	60	11.9
		F	~	~	~	~	~	~
		M	69	64	23	~	59	13.5
K. GUATEMALA[8]	1984	MF	74	~	16	~	48	~
L. HAITI[8]	1981	MF	69	40	13	~	44	~
		F	64	38	12	~	41	~
		M	74	42	13	~	46	~
M. HONDURAS[11]	1983	MF	101	86	33	24	73	9.7
		F	100	86	34	26	73	8.3
		M	101	86	31	23	73	11.1
N. MEXICO[9]	1983	MF	119	~	55	~	79	15.2
		F	112	~	53	~	87	11.1
		M	120	~	56	~	91	19.3
O. NICARAGUA[11]	1984	MF	99	~	43	~	76	~
P. PANAMA[7]	1984	MF	104	~	59	~	82	~
Q. PARAGUAY[8]	1982	MF	103	90	36	~	71	~
		F	99	89	35	~	69	~
		M	107	92	37	~	74	~
R. PERU[6]	1982	MF	116	~	61	~	92	21.5
		F	112	~	57	~	88	15.6
		M	120	~	64	~	96	27.4
S. URUGUAY[9]	1983	MF	109	75	67	~	89	20.8
		F	107	~	~	~	~	23.8
		M	110	~	~	~	~	17.8
T. VENEZUELA[8]	1983	MF	105	~	43	~	76	21.7
UNITED STATES[12]	1982	MF	~	~	~	~	98	56.4
		F	~	~	~	~	98	59.2
		M	~	~	~	~	99	53.8

1. The gross enrollment ratio is the total enrollment of all ages divided by the population of the specific age groups which correspond to the age groups of primary and secondary schooling. The net enrollment ratio has been calculated by using only that part of the enrollment which corresponds to the age groups of primary and secondary schooling.

   These ratios have been calculated taking into account the differing national systems of education and the duration of schooling at the first and second levels. At the third level, the figures for the population age 20-24 have been used throughout.

   First level = primary school; second level = high school, teacher training, or vocational school; third level = university and other institutions of higher learning. See table 1005.
2. The age brackets are: 1st level 6-12, 2nd level 13-17, combined 1st and 2nd levels 6-17, and 3rd level 20-24.
3. The age brackets are: 1st level 6-13, 2nd level 14-17, combined 1st and 2nd levels 6-17, and 3rd level 20-24.
4. The age brackets are: 1st level 7-14, 2nd level 15-17, combined 1st and 2nd levels 7-17, and 3rd level 20-24.
5. The age brackets are: 1st level 6-10, 2nd level 11-16, combined 1st and 2nd levels 6-16, and 3rd level 20-24.
6. The age brackets are: 1st level 6-11, 2nd level 12-16, combined 1st and 2nd levels 6-16, and 3rd level 20-24.
7. The age brackets are: 1st level 6-11, 2nd level 12-17, combined 1st and 2nd levels 6-17, and 3rd level 20-24.
8. The age brackets are: 1st level 7-12, 2nd level 13-18, combined 1st and 2nd levels 7-18, and 3rd level 20-24.
9. The age brackets are: 1st level 6-11, 2nd level 12-17, combined 1st and 2nd levels 6-17, and 3rd level 20-24.
10. The age brackets are: 1st level 7-15, 2nd level 16-18, combined 1st and 2nd levels 7-18, and 3rd level 20-24.
11. The age brackets are: 1st level 7-12, 2nd level 13-17, combined 1st and 2nd levels 7-17, and 3rd level 20-24.
12. The age brackets are: 1st level 6-12, 2nd level 13-17, combined 1st and 2nd levels 6-17 and 3rd level 20-24.

SOURCE: UNESCO-SY, 1986, table 3.2.

Table 905

COMPULSORY EDUCATION, ENTRANCE AGES, AND DURATION OF SCHOOLING AT FIRST AND SECOND LEVELS, 20 LC

	Country	Compulsory Education		Pre-Primary Entrance Age	First Level		Second Level	
		Age Limits	Duration (Years)		Entrance Age	Duration (Years)	Entrance Age	Duration (Years)
A.	ARGENTINA	6-14	7	3	6	7	13	3 + 2
B.	BOLIVIA	6-14	8	4	6	8	14	4
C.	BRAZIL	7-14	8	4	7	8	15	3
D.	CHILE	6-13	8	4	6	8	14	4
E.	COLOMBIA	6-12	5	5	6	5	11	4 + 2
F.	COSTA RICA	6-15	9	5	6	6	12	3 + 2
G.	CUBA	6-11	6	5	6	6	12	3 + 3
H.	DOMINICAN REP.	7-14	6	3	7	6	13	2 + 4
I.	ECUADOR	6-14	6	4	6	6	12	3 + 3
J.	EL SALVADOR	7-15	9	4	7	9	16	3
K.	GUATEMALA	7-14	6	4	7	6	13	3 + 3
L.	HAITI	6-14	6	2	7	6	13	3 + 3
M.	HONDURAS	7-13	6	4	7	6	13	3 + 2
N.	MEXICO	6-11	6	4	6	6	12	3 + 3
O.	NICARAGUA	7-12	6	3	7	6	13	3 + 2
P.	PANAMA	6-15	9	4	6	6	12	3 + 3
Q.	PARAGUAY	7-14	6	5	7	6	13	3 + 3
R.	PERU	6-11	6	3	6	6	12	3 + 2
S.	URUGUAY	6-15	9	3	6	6	12	3 + 3
T.	VENEZUELA	7-14	6	4	7	6	13	3 + 3
	UNITED STATES	6-16	11	3	6	8	14	4

SOURCE: UNESCO-SY, 1986, table 3.1.

Table 906

EDUCATIONAL ATTAINMENT, BY URBAN AND RURAL AREAS, AGE, AND SEX, 19 LC

| | | | | | | Highest Level Attained[1] (%) | | | | |
| | | | | | | First Level | | Entered Second Level | | |
Country and Category	Year	Sex	Age Group	Total Population	No Schooling	Incompleted	Completed	First Cycle	Second Cycle	Post-Secondary
A. ARGENTINA										
Total Population	1980	MF	25+	14,913,575	6.0	32.0	34.6	20.5 ⊢→		6.9
		F	25+	7,711,356	6.7	32.1	35.2	20.1 ⊢→		5.8
B. BOLIVIA										
Total Population	1976	MF	25+	1,759,432	48.6	28.5 ⊢→		10.8	7.1	5.0
		F	25+	918,709	62.2	20.7 ⊢→		8.2	5.6	3.3
Urban Population		MF	25†	690,374	23.2	30.6 ⊢→		19.7	15.6	10.9
		F	25†	368,977	34.3	28.6 ⊢→		17.0	13.0	7.2
Rural Population		MF	25†	1,069,058	65.0	27.2 ⊢→		5.1	1.5	1.3
		F	25†	549,732	80.8	15.4 ⊢→		2.3	.7	.7
C. BRAZIL										
Total Population	1980	MF	25+	48,310,722	32.9	50.4	4.3	6.9 ⊢→		5.0
		F	25+	25,576,023	35.2	48.8	4.6	7.2 ⊢→		4.1
Urban Population	1976	MF	25†	34,355,258	22.8	54.7	6.5	9.2 ⊢→		6.8
		F	25†	17,928,564	25.9	53.1	6.0	9.4 ⊢→		5.6
Rural Population	1976	MF	25†	13,955,464	57.7	40.0	.9	1.0 ⊢→		.4
		F	25†	6,647,459	60.5	37.3	.9	1.1 ⊢→		.3
D. CHILE										
Total Population	1970	MF	25+	3,721,125	12.4	57.2 ⊢→		26.6 ⊢→		3.8
		F	25+	1,945,921	13.3	57.7 ⊢→		26.5 ⊢→		2.5
Urban Population		MF	25+	2,712,020	8.3	34.1	26.0	27.0 ⊢→		4.8
Rural Population		MF	25+	792,400	29.8	54.2	10.0	5.4 ⊢→		.6
E. COLOMBIA										
Total Population	1973	MF	20+	8,478,100	22.4	55.9 ⊢→		18.4 ⊢→		3.3
		F	20+	4,483,086	23.7	56.0 ⊢→		18.5 ⊢→		1.8
Urban Population		MF	20+	5,593,002	14.2	54.8 ⊢→		26.1 ⊢→		4.9
		F	20+	3,108,408	16.1	56.2 ⊢→		25.1 ⊢→		2.6
Rural Population		MF	20+	2,885,098	38.4	58.0 ⊢→		3.5 ⊢→		.2
		F	20+	1,374,677	40.8	55.6 ⊢→		3.5 ⊢→		.1
F. COSTA RICA										
Total Population	1973	MF	25+	657,543	16.1	49.1	17.8	6.3	4.9	5.8
		F	25+	331,240	16.0	49.8	17.7	6.5	4.5	5.4
Urban Population		MF	25+	297,887	7.2	37.4	24.8	10.9	9.0	10.6
		F	25+	161,996	8.1	39.3	24.4	10.9	8.1	9.3
Rural Population		MF	25+	359,656	23.6	58.8	12.1	2.4	1.4	1.8
		F	25+	169,244	23.6	59.8	11.4	2.3	1.1	1.7
H. DOMINICAN REP.										
Total Population	1970	MF	25+	1,145,090	40.1	41.6	4.3	9.6	2.5	1.9
		F	25+	563,150	42.8	40.9	3.9	8.7	2.4	1.3
Urban Population		MF	25+	487,675	22.9	42.1	7.4	18.3	5.2	4.1
Rural Population		MF	25+	657,415	52.8	41.2	2.0	3.2	.5	.3
I. ECUADOR										
Total Population	1982	MF	25+	2,887,330	25.4	17.0	34.1	8.1	7.9	7.6
		F	25+	1,457,435	29.6	16.8	31.1	8.3	8.7	5.6
Urban Population	1974	MF	25+	958,110	13.0	56.7 ⊢→		12.1	11.2	7.0
		F	25+	508,630	16.4	56.3 ⊢→		11.9	11.9	3.5
Rural Population	1974	MF	25+	1,338,172	45.4	51.5 ⊢→		1.5	1.1	.4
		F	25+	652,265	52.8	44.7 ⊢→		1.3	1.1	.2
J. EL SALVADOR										
Total Population	1980	MF	10†	3,132,400	30.2	60.7 ⊢→		6.9 ⊢→		2.3
		F	10†	1,635,100	33.1	58.3		6.6 ⊢→		1.9
Urban Population		MF	10†	1,405,000	15.5	66.2 ⊢→		13.5 ⊢→		4.8
		F	10†	776,200	19.6	64.0 ⊢→		12.5		3.9
Rural Population		MF	10†	1,727,400	42.2	56.2 ⊢→		1.4 ⊢→		.2
		F	10†	858,900	45.4	53.7 ⊢→		1.3 ⊢→		.2
K. GUATEMALA										
Total Population	1973	MF	25+	1,785,720	93.9 ⊢→	⊢→		4.9 ⊢→		1.2
		F	25+	897,960	94.7 ⊢→	⊢→		4.8 ⊢→		.5
Urban Population		MF	25+	639,780	85.2 ⊢→	⊢→		11.8 ⊢→		2.9
Rural Population		MF	25+	1,145,940	98.7 ⊢→	⊢→		1.1 ⊢→		.2
L. HAITI[2]										
Total Population	1982	MF	25+	2,103,124	77.0	15.2 ⊢→		7.2 ⊢→		.7
		F	25+	1,093,992	81.3	12.3 ⊢→		5.9 ⊢→		.4
Urban Population	1971	MF	25+	325,778	50.3	24.5	6.5	7.8	9.4	1.5
		F	25+	192,574	59.2	22.0	6.0	6.0	5.9	.9
Rural Population	1971	MF	25+	1,400,330	91.2	7.4	.7	.4	.3	.0
		F	25+	723,070	95.7	3.7	.3	.2	.1	.0

Table 906 (Continued)

EDUCATIONAL ATTAINMENT, BY URBAN AND RURAL AREAS, AGE, AND SEX, 19 LC

Country and Category	Year	Sex	Age Group	Total Population	No Schooling	First Level Incompleted	First Level Completed	Entered Second Level First Cycle	Entered Second Level Second Cycle	Post-Secondary
M. HONDURAS										
Total Population	1974	MF	25+	858,459	53.1	34.5	6.0	1.5	3.8	1.0
		F	25+	440,453	56.3	32.1	6.0	1.4	3.8	.4
Urban Population		MF	25+	279,554	29.5	41.1	12.5	3.9	10.0	3.0
		F	25+	152,135	33.7	40.2	12.0	3.5	9.5	1.1
Rural Population		MF	25+	578,905	64.5	31.4	2.9	.4	.8	.1
		F	25+	288,318	68.3	27.8	2.8	.3	.8	#
N. MEXICO										
Total Population	1970	MF	20+	20,797,757	35.0	39.4	15.3	4.1	3.7	2.6
O. NICARAGUA										
Total Population	1971	MF	25+	593,100	53.9	41.8 ⟶	⟶		4.4 ⟶	
P. PANAMA	1980	MF	25+	718,509	17.4	27.3	23.4	11.7	11.8	8.4
		F	25†	355,390	18.3	26.5	23.3	11.7	12.3	7.8
Q. PARAGUAY										
Total Population	1972	MF	25+	842,223	19.6	57.7	10.3	5.9	4.6	2.0
		F	25+	438,419	25.4	53.8	10.6	5.1	4.0	1.2
Urban Population		MF	25+	346,870	11.3	46.8	16.5	11.0	9.8	4.6
		F	25+	192,086	15.4	47.0	17.5	9.5	8.0	2.5
Rural Population		MF	25+	495,353	25.5	65.3	5.9	2.2	.9	.2
		F	25+	246,333	33.2	59.1	5.1	1.6	.8	.1
R. PERU[3]										
Total Population	1981	MF	25+	6,532,002	21.6	27.3	17.4	33.7	~	~
		F	25+	3,322,482	30.6	25.2	15.9	28.3	~	~
Urban Population		MF	5+	7,073,800	23.7	31.1	17.6	12.8	10.1	4.8
		F	5+	3,545,100	28.4	31.2	16.8	11.0	9.0	3.6
Rural Population		MF	5+	4,689,400	57.7	32.8	6.3	2.0	.9	.3
		F	5+	2,334,600	70.3	24.3	3.6	1.1	.5	.2
S. URUGUAY										
Total Population	1975	MF	25+	1,590,200	9.9	36.7	29.6	17.4 ⟶		6.3
		F	25+	824,700	10.4	34.9	31.2	16.6 ⟶		6.8
T. VENEZUELA[4]										
Total Population	1981	MF	25+	5,542,852	23.5	47.2 ⟶		22.3 ⟶		7.0
		F	25+	2,802,602	26.4	46.2 ⟶		21.9 ⟶		5.5
UNITED STATES										
Total Population	1981	MF	25+	132,899,000	3.3 ⟶		64.6	⟶		32.2
		F	25+	70,390,000	3.1 ⟶		68.8	⟶		28.0

1. For definition of levels, see table 1003, above.
2. "No Schooling" includes illiteracy data.
3. "No Schooling" includes persons who did not state their level of education.
4. The number and percentage within the total population of persons whose educational level is unknown was: MF 25+ 426,614 (15.3%); F 25+ 194,484 (14.2%).

SOURCE: UNESCO-SY, 1986, table 1.4.

Table 907

TEACHERS PER 10,000 PERSONS AGES 7–14, 20 LR, 1960–75

Country	1960	1965	1970	1975
A. ARGENTINA	343.4	388.4	470.1	525.3
B. BOLIVIA	145.8	164.8	187.7	239.9
C. BRAZIL	125.8	170.3	220.4	288.4
D. CHILE	170.0	173.8	188.0[a]	248.7
E. COLOMBIA	124.2	137.0	152.0	197.1
F. COSTA RICA	223.4	222.2	228.0	250.7
G. CUBA	143.7	199.1	275.2	365.5
H. DOMINICAN REP.	98.2	104.4	113.8	121.4
I. ECUADOR	138.8	159.9	187.8	230.7
J. EL SALVADOR	144.6	139.7	128.1	152.6
K. GUATEMALA	103.7	101.9	100.5	107.6
L. HAITI	46.2	44.7	46.1[b]	~
M. HONDURAS	109.1	119.1	149.2[b]	~
N. MEXICO	113.3	129.3	153.5[a]	169.5
O. NICARAGUA	104.7	111.6	122.9	119.7
P. PANAMA	193.5	221.7	240.0	296.8
Q. PARAGUAY	210.0	204.5	209.7	225.8
R. PERU	166.2	180.0	204.6	221.5
S. URUGUAY	288.1	270.3	328.1[b]	~
T. VENEZUELA	177.2	176.0	188.4	223.8
LATIN AMERICA	150.7	176.8	208.2	253.5

a. 1969.
b. 1968.

SOURCE: ECLA: *Indicators of Social and Economic Development in Latin America*, (Santiago), p. 32.

Table 908

TEACHERS AND SCHOOL ENROLLMENT, BY LEVEL AND TYPE, 20 L

Country	Level and Type of Education[1]	Year	Teaching Staff		Students Enrolled	
			Total	Females	Total	Females
A. ARGENTINA	Pre-primary	1983	29,597	29,531	602,226	302,809
	Primary	1983	212,932	197,029	4,315,752	2,123,487
	Intermediate	1983	79,728	60,223	614,615	382,721
	Higher	1983	56,089	25,728	580,626	311,772
B. BOLIVIA	Pre-primary	1983	~	~	116,614	36,262
	Primary	1983	45,024	~	1,105,922	512,116
	Intermediate	1983	7,143[a]	~[a]	182,760	83,506
	Higher	1976	~	~	51,585[‡]	~
C. BRAZIL	Pre-primary	1983	671,038	50,038	1,625,177	595,747
	Primary	1983	208,663	934,282	24,304,875	11,724,670
	Intermediate	1983	221,710	96,426	3,481,804	1,358,213
	Higher	1982	121,954	~	1,436,287	~
D. CHILE	Pre-primary	1984	~	~	148,311	67,675
	Primary	1984	62,746	~	2,102,356	1,016,101
	Intermediate	1984	27,207[d]	14,220[d]	613,546	317,818
	Higher	1983	10,097	1,916	127,353	50,985
E. COLOMBIA	Pre-primary	1984	9,506	5,694	259,845	129,663
	Primary	1984	132,675	104,813	4,054,891	2,027,040
	Intermediate	1984	93,121	39,380	1,889,023	942,622
	Higher	1983	41,006	8,232	378,999	182,011
F. COSTA RICA	Pre-primary	1983	~	~	31,008	15,324
	Primary	1983	10,784	~	343,800	166,507
	Intermediate	1983	6,540	~	122,836	64,308
	Higher	1980	~	~	60,990	~
G. CUBA	Pre-primary	1983	4,898	4,881	107,660	52,201
	Primary	1983	83,424	64,105	1,282,989	610,778
	Intermediate	1983	89,826	42,285	1,024,113	522,487
	Higher	1982	12,222	4,843	173,403	90,758
H. DOMINICAN REP.	Pre-primary	1983	~	~	43,365	~
	Primary	1983	20,607	~	980,808	565,266
	Intermediate	1983	4,668[b]	2,644[b]	379,998	~
	Higher	1978	~	~	42,412	19,196
I. ECUADOR	Pre-primary	1983	2,777	2,645	66,809	33,663
	Primary	1983	50,347	32,526	1,677,364	823,800
	Intermediate	1983	39,909	~	650,278	325,313
	Higher	1981	11,877	~	264,353	98,174
J. EL SALVADOR	Pre-primary	1983	1,100	1,068	60,805	31,417
	Primary	1983	17,633	11,902	851,895	120,212
	Intermediate	1983	3,390	1,001	81,318	42,049
	Higher	1983	2,888	846	57,374	24,635
K. GUATEMALA	Pre-primary	1984	2,278	1,869	61,897	29,730
	Primary	1984	26,963	16,052	979,888	421,460
	Intermediate	1984	12,023	4,269	174,653	79,062
	Higher	1980	2,845	~	50,890	~
L. HAITI	Pre-primary	~	~	~	~	~
	Primary	1981	14,927	~	658,102	304,103
	Intermediate	1981	4,392[e]	~	101,519	~
	Higher	1978	493	50	4,186	979
M. HONDURAS	Pre-primary	1983	1,224	1,224	46,228	23,599
	Primary	1983	18,966	14,046	703,608	349,021
	Intermediate	1983	5,342	2,553	156,665	81,308
	Higher	1983	2,269	~	34,468	~
N. MEXICO	Pre-primary	1983	60,937	60,937	1,893,643	947,049
	Primary	1983	428,029	~	15,376,153	7,439,855
	Intermediate	1983	337,914	~	6,064,264	2,887,320
	Higher	1983	99,127	~	1,071,676	385,710
O. NICARAGUA	Pre-primary	1984	1,701	1,203	60,617	20,219
	Primary	1984	17,969	~	534,317	~
	Intermediate	1984	6,014	~	161,745	~
	Higher	1985	2,526	~	29,001	16,355
P. PANAMA	Pre-primary	1983	1,016	961	25,843	12,637
	Primary	1983	12,912	10,234	335,651	160,805
	Intermediate	1983	9,184	4,937	176,441	92,077
	Higher	1983	3,492	~	46,273	26,024

Table 908 (Continued)

TEACHERS AND SCHOOL ENROLLMENT, BY LEVEL AND TYPE, 20 L

Country	Level and Type of Education[1]	Year	Teaching Staff		Students Enrolled	
			Total	Females	Total	Females
Q. PARAGUAY	Pre-primary	1982	~	~	13,590	6,994
	Primary	1982	20,746	~	539,889	256,952
	Intermediate	1982	~	~	164,464	~
	Higher	1978	~	~	20,812	9,037
R. PERU	Pre-primary	1982	8,076	7,973	279,504	140,099
	Primary	1982	89,370	~	3,343,631	1,582,518
	Intermediate	1980	37,383	~	1,203,116	547,393
	Higher	1980	17,853	~	306,353	107,980
S. URUGUAY	Pre-primary	1983	1,026	~	53,999	~
	Primary	1983	17,036	~	350,178	170,094
	Intermediate	1983	~	~	197,890	~
	Higher	1983	4,349	1,141[e]	50,151	28,389
T. VENEZUELA	Pre-primary	1984	16,683	16,393	591,524	230,274
	Primary	1982	100,681	83,611	2,660,440	1,305,833
	Intermediate	1982	63,303	22,808[c]	939,678	512,613
	Higher	1982	28,892	~	349,773	~

1. For definition of levels, see table 903 above; intermediate is defined as "Secondary" level.

a. 1975 data.
b. 1970 data.
c. 1979 data.
d. 1978 data.
e. 1980 data.

SOURCE: UNESCO-SY, 1984, 1986, tables 3.3, 3.4, 3.7, 3.11.

Table 909

PRE-PRIMARY SCHOOLS, TEACHERS, AND PUPILS, 19 LC

Country	School Year Beginning	Number of Institutions	Teaching Staff			Pupils Enrolled			
			Total	Female	%	Total	Female	%	% Private
A. ARGENTINA	1983	7,280	29,597	29,531	100	602,226	302,809	50	32
B. BOLIVIA	1983	~	~	~	~	116,614	~	55	12
C. BRAZIL	1983	17,899	71,038	~	98	1,625,177	~	50	47
D. CHILE	1983	~	~	~	~	146,369	72,284	49	39
E. COLOMBIA	1984	4,681	9,506	5,694	60	259,845	129,663	50	62
F. COSTA RICA	1983	483	483	~	~	31,008	15,324	49	11
G. CUBA	1983	~	4,898	4,881	100	107,660	52,201	49	#
H. DOMINICAN REP.	1983	292	~	~	~	43,365	~	~	60
I. ECUADOR	1983	1,235	2,777	2,645	95	66,809	33,663	50	52
J. EL SALVADOR	1983	550	1,100	1,068	97	60,805	31,417	52	25
K. GUATEMALA	1984	889	2,278	~	~	61,897	~	~	44
M. HONDURAS	1983	615	1,224	1,224	100	46,228	23,599	51	15
N. MEXICO	1983	28,245	60,937	60,937	100	1,893,643	947,049	50	7
O. NICARAGUA	1984	646	1,701	~	99	60,617	~	53	30
P. PANAMA	1983	608	1,016	1,011	100	25,843	12,637	49	30
Q. PARAGUAY	1982	32	~	~	~	13,590	6,994	52	63
R. PERU	1982	3,886	8,076	7,973	99	279,504	140,099	50	29
S. URUGUAY	1983	928	1,026	~	~	53,999	~	~	23
T. VENEZUELA	1982	1,164	18,181	~	~	499,093	~	~	16
UNITED STATES	1981	~	~	~	~	5,219,000	2,469,000	47	37

SOURCE: UNESCO-SY, 1984, 1986, table 3.3.

Table 910

PRIMARY SCHOOLS,[1] TEACHERS, AND PUPILS, 20 LC

	Country	School Year Beginning	Number of Institutions (A)	Teaching Staff Total (B)	Teaching Staff Female (C)	Teaching Staff % Female (D)	Pupils Enrolled Total (E)	Pupils Enrolled Female (F)	Pupils Enrolled % Female (G)	Pupil/Teacher Ratio (H)
A.	ARGENTINA	1983	20,339	212,932	179,027	93	4,315,752	2,123,487	49	20
B.	BOLIVIA	1983	~	45,024	~	~	1,105,922	512,116	46	23
C.	BRAZIL	1983	208,663	934,282	~	~	24,304,875	11,724,670	48	26
D.	CHILE	1983	8,479	~	~	~	2,085,128	1,015,518	49	33
E.	COLOMBIA	1984	33,996	132,675	104,813	79	4,054,891	2,027,040	50	31
F.	COSTA RICA	1983	2,993	~	~	~	343,800	166,507	48	30
G.	CUBA	1983	10,866	83,424	64,105	77	1,282,989	610,778	48	15
H.	DOMINICAN REP.[2]	1983	4,846	20,067	~	~	980,808	~	~	46
I.	ECUADOR[3]	1983	13,011	50,347	32,526	65	1,677,364	823,800	49	33
J.	EL SALVADOR[4]	1983	2,464	17,633	11,902	68	851,895	420,212	49	48
K.	GUATEMALA	1984	7,820	26,963	~	~	979,888	~	~	36
L.	HAITI	1981	3,321	14,927	~	~	658,102	304,103	46	44
M.	HONDURAS	1983	6,205	18,966	14,046	74	703,608	349,021	50	37
N.	MEXICO	1983	78,903	428,029	~	~	15,376,153	7,439,855	48	36
O.	NICARAGUA[6]	1984	~	17,969	~	~	534,317	~	~	35
P.	PANAMA	1983	2,378	12,912	10,264	80	335,651	160,805	48	26
Q.	PARAGUAY[4]	1982	3,613	20,746	~	~	539,889	256,952	48	30[†]
R.	PERU	1982	21,335	89,370	~	~	3,343,631	1,582,518	47	37
S.	URUGUAY	1983	2,295	17,036	~	~	350,178	170,094	49	21
T.	VENEZUELA	1982	12,990	100,681	83,611	83	2,660,440	1,305,833	49	26
	UNITED STATES[5]	1982	~	1,352,000	~	~	27,411,000	13,310,000	49	20

1. For primary levels see table 903.
2. Columns F and G refer to public education only.
3. Except for column E, includes evening schools.
4. Includes evening schools.
5. Includes special education.
6. Data in columns A, B, C, D, and H include pre-school.

SOURCE: UNESCO-SY, 1984, 1986, table 3.4.

Table 911

HIGHER EDUCATION: [1] TEACHERS AND STUDENTS, BY TYPE OF INSTITUTION, 20 LC

Country	School Year Beginning	All Institutions		Universities and Equivalent Institutions		Other Non-University Institutions	
		Total	Female	Total	Female	Total	Female
A. ARGENTINA							
Teachers	1985	70,699	32,694	44,038	14,222	26,661	18,472
Students	1985	846,145	444,636	664,200	302,509	181,945	142,127
B. BOLIVIA							
Teachers	1982	~	~	3,480	~	~	~
Students	1982	~	~	56,632	~	~	~
C. BRAZIL							
Teachers	1983	122,697	52,935	122,697	52,935	#	#
Students	1983	1,479,397	740,327	1,479,397	740,327	#	#
D. CHILE							
Teachers	1984	15,131	3,350	11,603	2,209	3,528	1,141
Students	1984	188,665	80,652	132,254	52,565	56,411	28,087
E. COLOMBIA							
Teachers	1985	42,344	9,819	36,335	8,090	6,009	1,729
Students	1984	378,588	180,909	331,758	153,612	46,828	27,297
F. COSTA RICA							
Teachers	1982	~	~	4,343	~	~	~
Students	1984	60,288	~	54,456	~	5,832	~
G. CUBA							
Teachers	1984	17,717	7,043	17,717	7,043	#	#
Students	1984	212,155	113,956	212,155	113,956	#	#
H. DOMINICAN REP.							
Teachers	1975	~	~	1,435	~	~	~
Students	1978	~	~	42,412	~	~	~
I. ECUADOR							
Teachers	1981	11,877	~	11,679	~	198	68
Students	1981	264,353	98,174	258,054	93,623	6,299	4,551
J. EL SALVADOR							
Teachers	1983	2,888	846	2,202	499	686	347
Students	1983	57,374	24,635	46,941	19,692	10,433	4,943
K. GUATEMALA[2]							
Teachers	1978	2,845	~	2,845	~	#	#
Students	1982	47,433[†]	~	~	~	47,433[†]	~
L. HAITI							
Teachers	1980	690	75	523	66	167	9
Students	1982	5,300	~	3,618	~	1,682	517
M. HONDURAS							
Teachers	1983	2,269	~	1,940	~	329	97
Students	1983	34,468	~	30,119	12,127	4,349	~
N. MEXICO							
Teachers	1983	99,127	~	92,926	~	6,201	~
Students	1983	1,071,676	385,710	939,513	317,276	132,163	68,434
O. NICARAGUA							
Teachers	1984	1,887	613	1,450	486	437	127
Students	1985	29,001	16,355	24,430	14,009	4,571	2,364
P. PANAMA							
Teachers	1984	3,272	~	3,272	~	#	#
Students	1984	52,224	29,246	52,224	29,246	#	#
Q. PARAGUAY							
Teachers	1978	~	~	~	441	~	~
Students	1978	20,812	9,037	20,496	8,791	316	246
R. PERU							
Teachers	1980	17,853	~	16,913[a]	2,991[a]	3,126	~
Students	1980	306,353	107,980	305,390[a]	105,968[a]	59,843	24,189
S. URUGUAY							
Teachers	1984	4,537	~	4,537	~	#	#
Students	1983	50,151	28,389	50,151	28,389	#	#
T. VENEZUELA							
Teachers	1984	30,122	~	23,570	~	5,790	~
Students	1984	381,575	~	318,727	~	62,848	~
UNITED STATES							
Teachers	1982	391,594	105,545	301,943	72,352	89,651	33,193
Students	1982	12,425,780	6,394,396	7,654,074	3,792,852	4,771,706	2,601,544

1. For pre-higher education levels, see table 903.
2. University of San Carlos only.

a. Data for 1982.

SOURCE: UNESCO-SY, 1984 and 1986.

Table 912

HIGHER EDUCATION:[1] DISTRIBUTION OF STUDENTS, BY SEX AND FIELD OF STUDY, 17 L, 1980–84

Country and Field of Study	1980 MF	1980 F	1983 MF	1983 F	1984 MF	1984 F
A. ARGENTINA[2]						
Total	491,473	247,656	403,978	175,392	~	~
Education Science and Teacher Training	84,727	74,588	7,681	6,622	~	~
Humanities, Religion, and Theology	24,738	18,746	26,178	19,487	~	~
Fine and Applied Arts	7,214	5,372	4,194	2,940	~	~
Law	60,981	28,416	59,165	27,296	~	~
Social and Behavioral Science	10,749	7,690	10,075	7,245	~	~
Commercial and Business Administration	74,963	25,606	78,646	30,768	~	~
Mass Communication and Documentation	1,788	1,062	#	#	~	~
Home Economics (Domestic Science)	#	#	#	#	~	~
Service Trades	#	#	#	#	~	~
Natural Science	18,877	11,473	22,969	13,495	~	~
Mathematics and Computer Science	20,022	13,874	20,849	14,151	~	~
Medical Science and Health-Related	57,460	31,583	51,112	26,683	~	~
Engineering	68,861	8,235	69,323	7,730	~	~
Architecture and Town Planning	29,920	12,206	30,320	12,515	~	~
Trade, Craft, and Industrial Programs	6,139	2,028	#	#	~	~
Transport and Communications	#	#	#	#	~	~
Agriculture, Forestry, and Fishery	25,034	6,777	23,466	6,460	~	~
Other and Not Specified	#	#	#	#	~	~
B. BOLIVIA[3],[4]						
Total	~	~	56,632	~	~	~
Education Science and Teacher Training	~	~	366	~	~	~
Humanities, Religion, and Theology	~	~	1,543	~	~	~
Fine and Applied Arts	~	~	77	~	~	~
Law	~	~	6,239	~	~	~
Social and Behavioral Science	~	~	1,107	~	~	~
Commercial and Business Administration	~	~	16,529	~	~	~
Mass Communication and Documentation	~	~	98	~	~	~
Home Economics (Domestic Science)	~	~	#	#	~	~
Service Trades	~	~	#	#	~	~
Natural Science	~	~	720	~	~	~
Mathematics and Computer Science	~	~	564	~	~	~
Medical Science and Health-Related	~	~	11,146	~	~	~
Engineering	~	~	12,179	~	~	~
Architecture and Town Planning	~	~	3,058	~	~	~
Trade, Craft, and Industrial Programs	~	~	#	#	~	~
Transport and Communications	~	~	#	#	~	~
Agriculture, Forestry, and Fishery	~	~	3,006	~	~	~
Other and Not Specified	~	~	#	#	~	~
C. BRAZIL[5]						
Total	1,409,243	~	1,479,397	740,327	~	~
Education Science and Teacher Training	403,949	~	113,294	~	~	~
Humanities, Religion, and Theology	77,696	~	149,302	108,377	~	~
Fine and Applied Arts	13,849	~	30,664	22,483	~	~
Law	137,373	~	139,870	53,868	~	~
Social and Behavioral Science	87,696	~	177,713	103,023	~	~
Commercial and Business Administration	208,620	~	220,067	74,325	~	~
Mass Communication and Documentation	34,486	~	40,527	25,230	~	~
Home Economics (Domestic Science)	1,956	~	1,948	1,805	~	~
Service Trades	6,331	~	4,494	3,422	~	~
Natural Science	51,374	~	120,903	~	~	~
Mathematics and Computer Science	12,710	~	38,197	15,979	~	~
Medical Science and Health-Related	110,123	~	132,094	81,216	~	~
Engineering	156,726	~	164,607	20,290	~	~
Architecture and Town Planning	24,287	~	24,801	13,146	~	~
Trade, Craft, and Industrial Programs	13,891	~	13,357	1,942	~	~
Transport and Communications	#	#	#	#	~	~
Agriculture, Forestry, and Fishery	33,162	~	40,616	8,965	~	~
Other and Not Specified	35,014	~	66,943	43,300	~	~

Table 912 (Continued)

HIGHER EDUCATION:[1] DISTRIBUTION OF STUDENTS, BY SEX AND FIELD OF STUDY, 17 L, 1980–84

Country and Field of Study	1980 MF	1980 F	1983 MF	1983 F	1984 MF	1984 F
D. CHILE						
Total	145,497	62,804	178,332	75,492	188,665	80,652
Education Science and Teacher Training	11,732	9,538	16,137	11,957	19,278	15,222
Humanities, Religion, and Theology	12,097	7,361	15,460	8,999	13,961	8,725
Fine and Applied Arts	5,738	3,176	7,317	4,153	7,614	4,335
Law	2,757	838	3,921	1,028	4,314	1,235
Social and Behavioral Science	1,743	916	4,477	2,139	5,087	2,714
Commercial and Business Administration	17,188	5,929	34,272	14,991	36,430	14,701
Mass Communication and Documentation	2,825	1,996	631	413	652	428
Home Economics (Domestic Science)	756	573	531	432	528	440
Service Trades	7,176	4,468	295	208	298	213
Natural Science	9,015	4,335	9,583	4,680	9,535	4,623
Mathematics and Computer Science	8,674	3,793	7,444	1,782	8,051	3,017
Medical Science and Health-Related	14,531	8,701	14,862	8,448	15,485	8,729
Engineering	33,508	4,175	50,480	10,155	54,412	11,211
Architecture and Town Planning	2,797	737	2,463	717	2,554	741
Trade, Craft, and Industrial Programs	3,391	938	1,020	77	1,575	441
Transport and Communications	1,594	901	#	#	#	#
Agriculture, Forestry, and Fishery	3,023	1,090	4,574	1,776	3,888	1,288
Other and Not Specified	6,952	3,339	4,865	2,537	5,003	2,589
E. COLOMBIA[6]						
Total	271,630	~	378,586	180,909	389,075	~
Education Science and Teacher Training	44,379	~	69,952	43,371	76,374	~
Humanities, Religion, and Theology	2,755	~	2,860	1,372	2,675	~
Fine and Applied Arts	~	~	8,047	5,230	8,389	~
Law	25,646	~	42,918	20,601	46,425	~
Social and Behavioral Science	14,069	~	~	~	~	~
Commercial and Business Administration	88,192	~	104,542	50,486	102,384	~
Mass Communication and Documentation	~	~	~	~	~	~
Home Economics (Domestic Science)	~	~	~	~	~	~
Service Trades	~	~	~	~	~	~
Natural Science	5,830	~	5,936	1,781	6,367	~
Mathematics and Computer Science	~	~	~	~	~	~
Medical Science and Health-Related	25,934	~	45,124	22,358	40,662	~
Engineering	36,657	~	88,944	32,631	95,630	~
Architecture and Town Planning	17,805	~	~	~	~	~
Trade, Craft, and Industrial Programs	~	~	~	~	~	~
Transport and Communications	~	~	~	~	~	~
Agriculture, Forestry, and Fishery	10,363	~	10,263	3,079	10,169	~
Other and Not Specified	#	#	#	#	#	#
F. COSTA RICA[7]						
Total	50,812	~	54,257	~	54,456	~
Education Science and Teacher Training	6,838	~	5,570	~	5,738	~
Humanities, Religion, and Theology	7,947	~	15,318	~	11,152	~
Fine and Applied Arts	924	~	1,036	~	1,227	~
Law	2,428	~	2,613	~	3,153	~
Social and Behavioral Science	4,622	~	4,471	~	5,830	~
Commercial and Business Administration	5,778	~	4,950	~	6,053	~
Mass Communication and Documentation	636	~	1,071	~	1,208	~
Home Economics (Domestic Science)	#	#	#	#	#	#
Service Trades	#	#	115	~	188	~
Natural Science	1,952	~	1,578	~	1,530	~
Mathematics and Computer Science	2,065	~	2,119	~	2,440	~
Medical Science and Health-Related	2,824	~	2,886	~	3,323	~
Engineering	4,319	~	4,361	~	4,799	~
Architecture and Town Planning	1,161	~	1,038	~	984	~
Trade, Craft, and Industrial Programs	- -	#	#	#	#	#
Transport and Communications	- -	#	#	#	#	#
Agriculture, Forestry, and Fishery	3,169	~	2,328	~	2,296	~
Other and Not Specified	6,149	~	4,803	~	4,535	~

Table 912 (Continued)

HIGHER EDUCATION:[1] DISTRIBUTION OF STUDENTS,
BY SEX AND FIELD OF STUDY, 17 L, 1980–84

Country and Field of Study	1980 MF	1980 F	1983 MF	1983 F	1984 MF	1984 F
G. CUBA[8]						
Total	151,733	~	192,958	101,711	212,155	113,956
Education Science and Teacher Training	60,942	~	82,567	52,032	92,535	58,196
Humanities, Religion, and Theology	2,795	~	3,371	2,381	2,815	2,678
Fine and Applied Arts	902	~	615	261	1,222	627
Law	3,175	~	3,047	1,687	2,898	1,738
Social and Behavioral Science	1,727	~	14,281	7,588	13,385	6,310
Commercial and Business Administration	15,340	~	5,717	3,421	8,166	5,300
Mass Communication and Documentation	1,222	~	1,542	833	1,443	847
Home Economics (Domestic Science)	#	#	#	#	#	#
Service Trades	#	#	#	#	#	#
Natural Science	3,791	~	2,570	1,574	2,715	1,715
Mathematics and Computer Science	1,475	~	1,588	891	1,619	901
Medical Science and Health-Related	15,559	~	22,689	13,609	25,793	15,321
Engineering	18,893	~	28,101	8,682	24,177	7,651
Architecture and Town Planning	4,876	~	1,910	991	6,606	2,990
Trade, Craft, and Industrial Programs	~	~	339	244	351	254
Transport and Communications	1,987	~	2,730	414	2,988	484
Agriculture, Forestry, and Fishery	14,538	~	14,336	5,440	16,790	7,032
Other and Not Specified	4,511	~	7,555	1,663	8,652	1,912
I. ECUADOR[9]						
Total	269,775	97,350	266,222	~	280,594	~
Education Science and Teacher Training	59,426	30,497	50,659	~	53,520	~
Humanities, Religion, and Theology	13,379	8,210	14,076	~	14,264	~
Fine and Applied Arts	1,394	406	2,798	~	2,634	~
Law	13,394	4,004	13,238	~	13,803	~
Social and Behavioral Science	21,219	8,526	19,915	~	21,116	~
Commercial and Business Administration	35,307	15,791	38,527	~	41,993	~
Mass Communication and Documentation	1,377	523	1,812	~	1,882	~
Home Economics (Domestic Science)	225	223	389	~	389	~
Service Trades	357	221	392	~	314	~
Natural Science	6,194	2,270	7,263	~	8,797	~
Mathematics and Computer Science	4,679	409	8,215	~	5,255	~
Medical Science and Health-Related	30,233	12,556	27,304	~	28,824	~
Engineering	47,244	5,194	50,787	~	54,876	~
Architecture and Town Planning	10,456	2,527	10,345	~	10,672	~
Trade, Craft, and Industrial Programs	1,800	483	900	~	900	~
Transport and Communications	#	#	#	#	#	#
Agriculture, Forestry, and Fishery	16,584	2,898	5,197	~	4,043	~
Other and Not Specified	6,507	2,612	14,405	~	17,312	~
J. EL SALVADOR[10]						
Total	16,838	5,202	57,374	24,635	~	~
Education Science and Teacher Training	698	236	9,074	5,342	~	~
Humanities, Religion, and Theology	158	44	1,025	567	~	~
Fine and Applied Arts	339	240	357	241	~	~
Law	592	250	3,261	1,170	~	~
Social and Behavioral Science	1,959	952	4,371	2,221	~	~
Commercial and Business Administration	4,198	1,277	14,284	5,847	~	~
Mass Communication and Documentation	#	#	467	329	~	~
Home Economics (Domestic Science)	#	#	74	69	~	~
Service Trades	99	75	117	65	~	~
Natural Science	29	8	344	157	~	~
Mathematics and Computer Science	#	#	205	68	~	~
Medical Science and Health-Related	479	479	6,679	3,930	~	~
Engineering	6,308	1,156	10,682	1,448	~	~
Architecture and Town Planning	945	398	2,259	1,168	~	~
Trade, Craft, and Industrial Programs	551	87	195	120	~	~
Transport and Communications	#	#	#	#	~	~
Agriculture, Forestry, and Fishery	483	#	1,940	183	~	~
Other and Not Specified	#	#	2,040	1,710	~	~

Table 912 (Continued)

HIGHER EDUCATION:[1] DISTRIBUTION OF STUDENTS, BY SEX AND FIELD OF STUDY, 17 L, 1980–84

Country and Field of Study	1980 MF	1980 F	1983 MF	1983 F	1984 MF	1984 F
L. HAITI[11]						
Total	4,671	1,410	6,289	2,119	~	~
Education Science and Teacher Training	324	79	1,016	623	~	~
Humanities, Religion, and Theology	~	~	226	30	~	~
Fine and Applied Arts	#	#	#	#	~	~
Law	1,039	432	958	222	~	~
Social and Behavioral Science	769	209	731	224	~	~
Commercial and Business Administration	#	#	1,313	555	~	~
Mass Communication and Documentation	#	#	#	#	~	~
Home Economics (Domestic Science)	#	#	#	#	~	~
Service Trades	#	#	#	#	~	~
Natural Science	175	20	159	4	~	~
Mathematics and Computer Science	~	~	~	~	~	~
Medical Science and Health-Related	1,112	506	767	323	~	~
Engineering	908	68	896	108	~	~
Architecture and Town Planning	#	#	#	#	~	~
Trade, Craft, and Industrial Programs	#	#	#	#	~	~
Transport and Communications	#	#	#	#	~	~
Agriculture, Forestry, and Fishery	174	24	223	30	~	~
Other and Not Specified	170	72	#	#	~	~
M. HONDURAS						
Total	25,825	9,736	34,468	~	33,742	~
Education Science and Teacher Training	491	343	4,220	~	3,407	~
Humanities, Religion, and Theology	204	114	178	~	211	~
Fine and Applied Arts	16	3	31	~	21	~
Law	2,222	766	3,087	~	2,978	~
Social and Behavioral Science	3,345	1,575	4,000	~	3,850	~
Commercial and Business Administration	6,171	2,626	6,894	~	6,216	~
Mass Communication and Documentation	147	56	339	~	340	~
Home Economics (Domestic Science)	61	61	#	#	#	#
Service Trades	#	#	#	#	#	#
Natural Science	232	120	287	~	1,891	~
Mathematics and Computer Science	215	107	111	~	92	~
Medical Science and Health-Related	4,432	2,300	5,307	~	4,239	~
Engineering	6,389	1,009	6,319	~	6,364	~
Architecture and Town Planning	#	#	484	~	323	~
Trade, Craft, and Industrial Programs	#	#	#	#	#	#
Transport and Communications	#	#	#	#	#	#
Agriculture, Forestry, and Fishery	707	#	3,133	~	2,850	~
Other and Not Specified	1,193	656	78	~	960	
N. MEXICO[3]						
Total	785,419	239,791	939,513	317,276	~	~
Education Science and Teacher Training	10,528	5,308	11,505	7,939	~	~
Humanities, Religion, and Theology	9,894	5,115	10,632	5,853	~	~
Fine and Applied Arts	5,825	2,922	8,647	4,536	~	~
Law	65,726	19,892	101,280	32,423	~	~
Social and Behavioral Science	55,600	29,026	83,728	45,663	~	~
Commercial and Business Administration	162,402	61,600	181,465	76,738	~	~
Mass Communication and Documentation	13,188	7,270	19,291	11,748	~	~
Home Economics (Domestic Science)	#	#	#	#	~	~
Service Trades	7,394	4,712	11,409	7,643	~	~
Natural Science	21,024	7,095	24,242	9,937	~	~
Mathematics and Computer Science	7,855	1,871	12,917	5,341	~	~
Medical Science and Health-Related	155,100	66,839	133,685	63,384	~	~
Engineering	160,522	14,586	257,537	28,484	~	~
Architecture and Town Planning	31,409	5,735	39,298	8,692	~	~
Trade, Craft, and Industrial Programs	2,268	818	#	#	~	~
Transport and Communications	467	33	274	#	~	~
Agriculture, Forestry, and Fishery	75,038	6,763	39,049	7,828	~	~
Other and Not Specified	1,179	206	4,554	1,067	~	~

Table 912 (Continued)

HIGHER EDUCATION:[1] DISTRIBUTION OF STUDENTS,
BY SEX AND FIELD OF STUDY, 17 L, 1980–84

Country and Field of Study	1980 MF	1980 F	1983 MF	1983 F	1984 MF	1984 F
O. NICARAGUA						
Total	35,268	~	31,725	15,115	29,001	16,355
Education Science and Teacher Training	2,253	~	5,696	3,935	5,856	4,150
Humanities, Religion, and Theology	675	~	1,342	1,044	112	105
Fine and Applied Arts	#	#	#	#	142	105
Law	1,145	~	606	285	446	235
Social and Behavioral Science	2,957	~	~	~	2,760	1,650
Commercial and Business Administration	3,871	~	7,438	3,456	3,528	2,068
Mass Communication and Documentation	346	~	~	~	360	294
Home Economics (Domestic Science)	129	~	~	~	244	239
Service Trades	#	#	#	#	#	#
Natural Science	1,239	~	1,184	764	712	486
Mathematics and Computer Science	759	~	162	81	395	255
Medical Science and Health-Related	1,987	~	4,273	2,540	4,339	2,728
Engineering	3,538	~	5,208	1,138	4,013	1,290
Architecture and Town Planning	497	~	535	254	404	246
Trade, Craft, and Industrial Programs	66	~	#	#	69	57
Transport and Communications	#	#	#	#	46	4
Agriculture, Forestry, and Fishery	933	~	5,281	1,618	4,477	2,039
Other and Not Specified	14,873	~	#	#	1,098	404
P. PANAMA[12]						
Total	31,277	16,852	44,568	26,131	52,224	29,229
Education Science and Teacher Training	1,210	996	2,367	1,885	3,033	2,346
Humanities, Religion, and Theology	1,293	966	2,210	1,689	2,029	1,494
Fine and Applied Arts	553	257	429	265	409	254
Law	1,739	641	2,047	801	2,163	858
Social and Behavioral Science	3,156	1,653	3,399	1,880	3,672	2,008
Commercial and Business Administration	8,968	5,368	14,804	9,575	17,228	10,808
Mass Communication and Documentation	968	620	1,168	802	1,514	976
Home Economics (Domestic Science)	319	319	239	239	253	253
Service Trades	#	#	#	#	16	4
Natural Science	2,278	914	1,303	606	1,329	659
Mathematics and Computer Science	284	141	1,019	521	1,106	562
Medical Science and Health-Related	3,200	2,296	3,482	2,720	3,609	2,842
Engineering	1,747	401	6,865	1,894	9,607	2,489
Architecture and Town Planning	764	205	778	293	830	250
Trade, Craft, and Industrial Programs	1,984	326	324	150	509	242
Transport and Communications	#	#	#	#	#	#
Agriculture, Forestry, and Fishery	457	110	229	68	332	61
Other and Not Specified	2,357	1,639	3,905	2,743	4,585	3,123
R. PERU[13]						
Total	306,353	~	305,390	105,968	~	~
Education Science and Teacher Training	23,314	~	24,034	15,535	~	~
Humanities, Religion, and Theology	3,513	~	4,367	2,278	~	~
Fine and Applied Arts	441	~	275	159	~	~
Law	14,534	~	20,614	5,659	~	~
Social and Behavioral Science	37,388	~	46,572	15,471	~	~
Commercial and Business Administration	76,026	~	57,657	20,335	~	~
Mass Communication and Documentation	5,670	~	6,169	3,020	~	~
Home Economics (Domestic Science)	1,425	~	611	477	~	~
Service Trades	403	~	1,283	1,038	~	~
Natural Science	8,373	~	10,484	4,196	~	~
Mathematics and Computer Science	4,201	~	5,680	1,484	~	~
Medical Science and Health-Related	23,781	~	27,913	15,302	~	~
Engineering	53,338	~	57,718	5,500	~	~
Architecture and Town Planning	5,049	~	5,253	1,611	~	~
Trade, Craft, and Industrial Programs	10,523	~	#	#	~	~
Transport and Communications	#	#	#	#	~	~
Agriculture, Forestry, and Fishery	24,018	~	20,736	3,529	~	~
Other and Not Specified	14,356	~	16,094	10,374	~	~

Table 912 (Continued)

HIGHER EDUCATION:[1] DISTRIBUTION OF STUDENTS, BY SEX AND FIELD OF STUDY, 17 L, 1980–84

Country and Field of Study	1980 MF	1980 F	1983 MF	1983 F	1984 MF	1984 F
S. URUGUAY[6]						
Total	36,298	19,236	63,734	~	77,480	~
Education Science and Teacher Training	253	199	681	540	1,048	834
Humanities, Religion, and Theology	582	435	1,894	1,339	2,704	1,877
Fine and Applied Arts	312	175	264	137	1,677	~
Law	10,812	6,641	13,871	9,570	15,840	~
Social and Behavioral Science	1,310	1,018	5,530	4,084	7,823	~
Commercial and Business Administration	4,183	2,055	11,784	6,338	12,902	~
Mass Communication and Documentation	156	145	380	346	816	~
Home Economics (Domestic Science)	#	#	#	#	151	~
Service Trades	#	#	#	#	#	#
Natural Science	627	348	3,749	1,968	2,423	1,255
Mathematics and Computer Science	496	178	2,141	777	3,058	~
Medical Science and Health-Related	10,324	5,788	11,768	7,609	15,723	~
Engineering	1,303	116	3,544	408	4,121	~
Architecture and Town Planning	1,850	712	2,791	~	3,316	~
Trade, Craft, and Industrial Programs	74	#	179	#	278	#
Transport and Communications	#	#	#	#	#	#
Agriculture, Forestry, and Fishery	3,600	1,042	4,511	1,491	4,792	~
Other and Not Specified	416	384	647	587	808	~
T. VENEZUELA						
Total	307,133	~	349,773	~	381,575	~
Education Science and Teacher Training	44,875	~	51,373	~	55,416	~
Humanities, Religion, and Theology	3,478	~	3,897	~	5,051	~
Fine and Applied Arts	410	~	516	~	679	~
Law	18,975	~	23,395	~	32,060	~
Social and Behavioral Science	21,699	~	28,095	~	51,730	~
Commercial and Business Administration	42,286	~	49,673	~	64,304	~
Mass Communication and Documentation	3,667	~	4,060	~	4,317	~
Home Economics (Domestic Science)	#	#	#	#	#	#
Service Trades	1,419	~	1,105	~	#	#
Natural Science	5,912	~	6,401	~	6,899	~
Mathematics and Computer Science	6,221	~	7,528	~	11,731	~
Medical Science and Health-Related	35,650	~	40,585	~	40,879	~
Engineering	51,306	~	62,074	~	65,068	~
Architecture and Town Planning	5,858	~	6,210	~	6,397	~
Trade, Craft, and Industrial Programs	1,175	~	673	~	#	#
Transport and Communications	#	#	#	#	#	#
Agriculture, Forestry, and Fishery	12,813	~	14,740	~	14,868	~
Other and Not Specified	51,389	~	49,448	~	22,052	~

1. Includes awards not equivalent to a first university degree, first university degrees, and post-graduate university degrees.
2. Data for 1983 refer to 1981 and to universities and equivalent degree-granting institutions.
3. Data refer to universities and degree-granting institutions only.
4. Excludes Universidad Católica Boliviano.
5. For 1980 data on education science and teacher training include part of natural science, and of humanities, religion, and theology.
6. Data for 1983 and 1984 refer respectively to 1984 and 1985.
7. Data refer to universities only.
8. For 1980 engineering includes trade, craft, and industrial programs.
9. For 1980 data on female students refer to universities and equivalent degree-granting institutions only.
10. 1980 data exclude figures for the National University which was closed in 1979.
11. Natural science includes mathematics and computer science. Law includes economics. In 1980 education science and teacher training includes humanities, religion, and theology.
12. For 1980 data exclude regional centers.
13. For 1982 data refer to universities only.

SOURCE: UNESCO-SY, 1986, table 3.12.

Table 913

HIGHER EDUCATION: GRADUATES, BY LEVEL[1] AND FIELD OF STUDY, 16 LC

Country and Field of Study	All Levels		Level 5		Level 6		Level 7	
	MF	F	MF	F	MF	F	MF	F
B.　BOLIVIA (1981)[2,3]								
Total	1,272	~	~	~	~	~	~	~
Education Science and Teacher Training	~	~	~	~	~	~	~	~
Humanities, Religion, and Theology	139	~	~	~	~	~	~	~
Fine and Applied Arts	#	#	~	~	~	~	~	~
Law	192	~	~	~	~	~	~	~
Social and Behavioral Science	222	~	~	~	~	~	~	~
Commercial and Business Administration	#	#	~	~	~	~	~	~
Mass Communication and Documentation	#	#	~	~	~	~	~	~
Home Economics (Domestic Science)	#	#	~	~	~	~	~	~
Service Trades	#	#	~	~	~	~	~	~
Natural Science	51	~	~	~	~	~	~	~
Mathematics and Computer Science	#	#	~	~	~	~	~	~
Medical Science and Health-Related	359	~	~	~	~	~	~	~
Engineering	235	~	~	~	~	~	~	~
Architecture and Town Planning	23	~	~	~	~	~	~	~
Trade, Craft, and Industrial Programs	13	~	~	~	~	~	~	~
Transport and Communications	#	#	~	~	~	~	~	~
Agriculture, Forestry, and Fishery	38	~	~	~	~	~	~	~
Other and Not Specified	#	#	~	~	~	~	~	~
C.　BRAZIL (1982)								
Total	253,553	151,391	#	#	244,639	147,501	8,914	3,890
Education Science and Teacher Training	48,932	41,170	#	#	48,208	40,632	724	538
Humanities, Religion, and Theology	20,621	17,944	#	#	19,865	16,993	756	951
Fine and Applied Arts	6,890	5,567	#	#	6,871	5,556	19	11
Law	21,983	8,723	#	#	21,287	8,470	696	253
Social and Behavioral Science	34,499	24,314	#	#	33,598	24,188	901	126
Commercial and Business Administration	32,596	12,087	#	#	32,322	12,035	274	52
Mass Communication and Documentation	7,173	5,015	#	#	7,033	4,958	140	57
Home Economics (Domestic Science)	253	246	#	#	253	246	#	#
Service Trades	624	504	#	#	624	504	#	#
Natural Science	7,726	4,127	#	#	5,927	3,376	1,799	751
Mathematics and Computer Science	4,369	2,311	#	#	4,020	2,192	349	119
Medical Science and Health-Related	23,528	14,470	#	#	22,222	13,895	1,306	575
Engineering	21,025	2,678	#	#	19,992	2,498	1,033	180
Architecture and Town Planning	2,954	1,695	#	#	2,873	1,661	81	34
Trade, Craft, and Industrial Programs	1,716	225	#	#	1,716	225	#	#
Transport and Communications	#	#	#	#	#	#	#	#
Agriculture, Forestry, and Fishery	6,832	1,374	#	#	6,033	1,142	799	232
Other and Not Specified	11,832	8,941	#	#	11,795	8,930	37	11
D.　CHILE (1984)								
Total	20,256	9,945	1,462	350	18,581	9,505	213	90
Education Science and Teacher Training	4,391	3,238	#	#	4,367	3,225	24	13
Humanities, Religion, and Theology	2,038	1,314	34	30	1,996	1,280	8	4
Fine and Applied Arts	770	437	#	#	770	437	#	#
Law	377	149	1	1	360	144	16	4
Social and Behavioral Science	591	298	#	#	580	294	11	4
Commercial and Business Administration	1,897	506	92	42	1,803	463	2	1
Mass Communication and Documentation	153	79	38	14	115	65	#	#
Home Economics (Domestic Science)	142	111	#	#	109	86	33	25
Service Trades	36	29	36	29	#	#	#	#
Natural Science	1,197	605	38	22	1,127	577	32	6
Mathematics and Computer Science	625	271	41	17	565	249	19	5
Medical Science and Health-Related	2,704	1,602	#	#	2,668	1,579	36	23
Engineering	3,580	612	779	88	2,790	522	11	2
Architecture and Town Planning	330	83	12	3	312	79	6	1
Trade, Craft, and Industrial Programs	330	94	330	94	#	#	#	#
Transport and Communications	#	#	#	#	#	#	#	#
Agriculture, Forestry, and Fishery	357	105	61	10	282	93	14	2
Other and Not Specified	738	412	#	#	737	412	1	#

Table 913 (Continued)

HIGHER EDUCATION: GRADUATES, BY LEVEL[1] AND FIELD OF STUDY, 16 LC

Country and Field of Study	All Levels		Level 5		Level 6		Level 7	
	MF	F	MF	F	MF	F	MF	F
E. COLOMBIA (1984)[4]								
Total	42,006	21,657	11,086	6,939	29,062	13,962	1,858	756
Education Science and Teacher Training	7,206	4,297	1,073	777	5,840	3,362	293	158
Humanities, Religion, and Theology	319	189	36	28	219	135	64	26
Fine and Applied Arts	1,261	1,045	1,012	858	249	187	#	#
Law	5,896	2,979	236	183	5,402	2,693	258	103
Social and Behavioral Science	~	~	~	~	~	~	~	~
Commercial and Business Administration	13,143	7,689	5,082	3,882	7,180	3,446	881	361
Mass Communication and Documentation	~	~	~	~	~	~	~	~
Home Economics (Domestic Science)	~	~	~	~	~	~	~	~
Service Trades	~	~	~	~	~	~	~	~
Natural Science	666	247	233	114	346	111	87	22
Mathematics and Computer Science	~	~	~	~	~	~	~	~
Medical Science and Health-Related	4,608	2,520	418	284	3,993	2,173	197	63
Engineering	7,988	2,311	2,709	623	5,211	1,668	68	20
Architecture and Town Planning	~	~	~	~	~	~	~	~
Trade, Craft, and Industrial Programs	~	~	~	~	~	~	~	~
Transport and Communications	~	~	~	~	~	~	~	~
Agriculture, Forestry, and Fishery	919	380	287	190	622	187	10	3
Other and Not Specified	#	#	#	#	#	#	#	#
F. COSTA RICA (1984)[5,6]								
Total	3,054	~	168	~	2,670	~	216	#
Education Science and Teacher Training	237	~	#	#	237	~	#	#
Humanities, Religion, and Theology	139	~	19	~	120	~	#	#
Fine and Applied Arts	162	~	14	~	148	~	#	#
Law	212	~	#	#	212	~	#	#
Social and Behavioral Science	231	~	#	#	231	~	#	#
Commercial and Business Administration	344	~	22	~	322	~	#	#
Mass Communication and Documentation	83	~	#	#	82	~	1	#
Home Economics (Domestic Science)	#	#	#	#	#	#	#	#
Service Trades	#	#	#	#	#	#	#	#
Natural Science	92	~	#	#	92	~	#	#
Mathematics and Computer Science	76	~	#	#	76	~	#	#
Medical Science and Health-Related	592	~	44	~	488	~	60	#
Engineering	276	~	10	~	266	~	#	#
Architecture and Town Planning	63	~	#	~	63	~	#	#
Trade, Craft, and Industrial Programs	#	#	#	#	#	#	#	#
Transport and Communications	#	#	#	#	#	#	#	#
Agriculture, Forestry, and Fishery	234	~	~	~	234	~	#	#
Other and Not Specified	313	~	59	~	99	~	155	#
G. CUBA (1983)								
Total	19,429	~	#	#	19,429	~	#	#
Education Science and Teacher Training	6,806	~	#	#	6,806	~	#	#
Humanities, Religion, and Theology	487	~	#	#	487	~	#	#
Fine and Applied Arts	85	~	#	#	85	~	#	#
Law	723	~	#	#	723	~	#	#
Social and Behavioral Science	1,104	~	#	#	1,104	~	#	#
Commercial and Business Administration	703	~	#	#	703	~	#	#
Mass Communication and Documentation	206	~	#	#	206	~	#	#
Home Economics (Domestic Science)	#	#	#	#	#	#	#	#
Service Trades	#	#	#	#	#	#	#	#
Natural Science	244	~	#	#	244	~	#	#
Mathematics and Computer Science	163	~	#	#	163	~	#	#
Medical Science and Health-Related	2,582	~	#	#	2,582	~	#	#
Engineering	3,039	~	#	#	3,039	~	#	#
Architecture and Town Planning	207	~	#	#	207	~	#	#
Trade, Craft, and Industrial Programs	28	~	#	#	28	~	#	#
Transport and Communications	290	~	#	#	290	~	#	#
Agriculture, Forestry, and Fishery	1,871	~	#	#	1,871	~	#	#
Other and Not Specified	891	~	#	#	891	~	#	#

Table 913 (Continued)

HIGHER EDUCATION: GRADUATES, BY LEVEL[1] AND FIELD OF STUDY, 16 LC

Country and Field of Study	All Levels		Level 5		Level 6		Level 7	
	MF	F	MF	F	MF	F	MF	F
I. ECUADOR (1981)								
Total	15,441	6,262	~	~	~	~	~	~
Education Science and Teacher Training	6,892	3,603	~	~	~	~	~	~
Humanities, Religion, and Theology	179	92	~	~	~	~	~	~
Fine and Applied Arts	86	43	~	~	~	~	~	~
Law	858	225	~	~	~	~	~	~
Social and Behavioral Science	1,445	603	~	~	~	~	~	~
Commercial and Business Administration	991	350	~	~	~	~	~	~
Mass Communication and Documentation	93	32	~	~	~	~	~	~
Home Economics (Domestic Science)	61	61	~	~	~	~	~	~
Service Trades	#	#	~	~	~	~	~	~
Natural Science	#	#	~	~	~	~	~	~
Mathematics and Computer Science	#	#	~	~	~	~	~	~
Medical Science and Health-Related	2,077	883	~	~	~	~	~	~
Engineering	1,074	100	~	~	~	~	~	~
Architecture and Town Planning	397	71	~	~	~	~	~	~
Trade, Craft, and Industrial Programs	~	~	~	~	~	~	~	~
Transport and Communications	#	#	~	~	~	~	~	~
Agriculture, Forestry, and Fishery	1,252	187	~	~	~	~	~	~
Other and Not Specified	36	12	~	~	~	~	~	~
J. EL SALVADOR (1983)								
Total	5,083	2,382	3,872	1,839	1,211	543	#	#
Education Science and Teacher Training	2,117	1,175	1,952	1,044	165	131	#	#
Humanities, Religion, and Theology	20	11	#	#	20	11	#	#
Fine and Applied Arts	#	#	#	#	#	#	#	#
Law	83	27	#	#	83	27	#	#
Social and Behavioral Science	104	57	#	#	104	57	#	#
Commercial and Business Administration	579	221	321	102	258	119	#	#
Mass Communication and Documentation	2	1	#	#	2	1	#	#
Home Economics (Domestic Science)	#	#	#	#	#	#	#	#
Service Trades	43	30	43	30	#	#	#	#
Natural Science	23	16	#	#	23	16	#	#
Mathematics and Computer Science	5	1	#	#	5	1	#	#
Medical Science and Health-Related	330	281	217	207	113	74	#	#
Engineering	779	99	475	43	304	56	#	#
Architecture and Town Planning	137	59	61	22	76	37	#	#
Trade, Craft, and Industrial Programs	52	32	49	30	3	2	#	#
Transport and Communications	#	#	#	#	#	#	#	#
Agriculture, Forestry, and Fishery	387	18	340	12	47	6	#	#
Other and Not Specified	422	354	414	349	8	5	#	#
L. HAITI (1982)								
Total	831	276	~	~	~	~	~	~
Education Science and Teacher Training	68	20	~	~	~	~	~	~
Humanities, Religion, and Theology	~	~	~	~	~	~	~	~
Fine and Applied Arts	#	#	~	~	~	~	~	~
Law	108	25	~	~	~	~	~	~
Social and Behavioral Science	116	34	~	~	~	~	~	~
Commercial and Business Administration	#	#	~	~	~	~	~	~
Mass Communication and Documentation	#	#	~	~	~	~	~	~
Home Economics (Domestic Science)	#	#	~	~	~	~	~	~
Service Trades	#	#	~	~	~	~	~	~
Natural Science	33	10	~	~	~	~	~	~
Mathematics and Computer Science	~	~	~	~	~	~	~	~
Medical Science and Health-Related	264	166	~	~	~	~	~	~
Engineering	200	13	~	~	~	~	~	~
Architecture and Town Planning	#	#	~	~	~	~	~	~
Trade, Craft, and Industrial Programs	#	#	~	~	~	~	~	~
Transport and Communications	#	#	~	~	~	~	~	~
Agriculture, Forestry, and Fishery	42	8	~	~	~	~	~	~
Other and Not Specified	#	#	~	~	~	~	~	~

Table 913 (Continued)

HIGHER EDUCATION: GRADUATES, BY LEVEL[1] AND FIELD OF STUDY, 16 LC

Country and Field of Study	All Levels		Level 5		Level 6		Level 7	
	MF	F	MF	F	MF	F	MF	F
M. HONDURAS (1983)								
Total	1,350	~	~	~	~	~	~	~
Education Science and Teacher Training	136	~	~	~	~	~	~	~
Humanities, Religion, and Theology	15	8	~	~	~	~	~	~
Fine and Applied Arts	2	1	~	~	~	~	~	~
Law	87	25	~	~	~	~	~	~
Social and Behavioral Science	260	150	~	~	~	~	~	~
Commercial and Business Administration	174	~	~	~	~	~	~	~
Mass Communication and Documentation	1	~	~	~	~	~	~	~
Home Economics (Domestic Science)	#	#	~	~	~	~	~	~
Service Trades	#	#	~	~	~	~	~	~
Natural Science	5	1	~	~	~	~	~	~
Mathematics and Computer Science	16	1	~	~	~	~	~	~
Medical Science and Health-Related	262	170	~	~	~	~	~	~
Engineering	119	33	~	~	~	~	~	~
Architecture and Town Planning	#	#	~	~	~	~	~	~
Trade, Craft, and Industrial Programs	#	#	~	~	~	~	~	~
Transport and Communications	#	#	~	~	~	~	~	~
Agriculture, Forestry, and Fishery	273	~	~	~	~	~	~	~
Other and Not Specified	#	#	~	~	~	~	~	~
N. MEXICO (1982)[2]								
Total	96,572	~	#	#	96,572	~	#	#
Education Science and Teacher Training	1,758	~	#	#	1,758	~	#	#
Humanities, Religion, and Theology	907	~	#	#	907	~	#	#
Fine and Applied Arts	829	~	#	#	829	~	#	#
Law	8,342	~	#	#	8,342	~	#	#
Social and Behavioral Science	8,148	~	#	#	8,148	~	#	#
Commercial and Business Administration	19,499	~	#	#	19,499	~	#	#
Mass Communication and Documentation	2,053	~	#	#	2,053	~	#	#
Home Economics (Domestic Science)	#	#	#	#	#	#	#	#
Service Trades	1,264	~	#	#	1,264	~	#	#
Natural Science	2,142	~	#	#	2,142	~	#	#
Mathematics and Computer Science	760	~	#	#	760	~	#	#
Medical Science and Health-Related	19,761	~	#	#	19,761	~	#	#
Engineering	23,866	~	#	#	23,866	~	#	#
Architecture and Town Planning	3,047	~	#	#	3,047	~	#	#
Trade, Craft, and Industrial Programs	#	#	#	#	#	#	#	#
Transport and Communications	92	~	#	#	92	~	#	#
Agriculture, Forestry, and Fishery	3,452	~	#	#	3,452	~	#	#
Other and Not Specified	652	~	#	#	652	~	#	#
O. NICARAGUA (1985)								
Total	1,636	810	635	226	1,001	584	#	#
Education Science and Teacher Training	214	139	#	#	214	139	#	#
Humanities, Religion, and Theology	29	19	#	#	29	19	#	#
Fine and Applied Arts	3	2	#	#	3	2	#	#
Law	86	30	#	#	86	30	#	#
Social and Behavioral Science	122	80	#	#	122	80	#	#
Commercial and Business Administration	218	142	4	2	214	140	#	#
Mass Communication and Documentation	15	9	#	#	15	9	#	#
Home Economics (Domestic Science)	32	21	32	21	#	#	#	#
Service Trades	#	#	#	#	#	#	#	#
Natural Science	96	62	#	#	96	62	#	#
Mathematics and Computer Science	16	10	5	3	11	7	#	#
Medical Science and Health-Related	265	208	163	152	102	56	#	#
Engineering	217	76	120	42	97	34	#	#
Architecture and Town Planning	10	4	#	#	10	4	#	#
Trade, Craft, and Industrial Programs	#	#	#	#	#	#	#	#
Transport and Communications	#	#	#	#	#	#	#	#
Agriculture, Forestry, and Fishery	311	7	309	5	2	2	#	#
Other and Not Specified	2	1	2	1	#	#	#	#

Table 913 (Continued)

HIGHER EDUCATION: GRADUATES, BY LEVEL[1] AND FIELD OF STUDY, 16 LC

Country and Field of Study	All Levels		Level 5		Level 6		Level 7	
	MF	F	MF	F	MF	F	MF	F
P. PANAMA (1984)								
Total	3,284	1,841	1,088	674	1,905	1,004	291	163
Education Science and Teacher Training	279	244	172	160	95	78	12	6
Humanities, Religion, and Theology	151	116	#	#	132	101	19	15
Fine and Applied Arts	52	31	39	18	13	13	#	#
Law	128	51	#	#	120	46	8	5
Social and Behavioral Science	247	132	#	#	203	112	44	20
Commercial and Business Administration	799	502	176	133	572	339	51	30
Mass Communication and Documentation	47	28	4	4	35	21	8	3
Home Economics (Domestic Science)	20	20	#	#	19	19	1	1
Service Trades	#	#	#	#	#	#	#	#
Natural Science	139	60	8	5	89	36	42	19
Mathematics and Computer Science	92	48	#	#	34	15	58	33
Medical Science and Health-Related	381	323	231	227	140	89	10	7
Engineering	614	139	415	101	199	38	#	#
Architecture and Town Planning	78	31	13	8	64	23	1	#
Trade, Craft, and Industrial Programs	22	16	19	14	3	2	#	#
Transport and Communications	#	#	#	#	#	#	#	#
Agriculture, Forestry, and Fishery	109	27	11	4	88	19	10	4
Other and Not Specified	126	73	#	#	99	53	27	20
R. PERU (1982)								
Total	10,449	4,197	~	~	~	~	~	~
Education Science and Teacher Training	1,973	1,213	~	~	~	~	~	~
Humanities, Religion, and Theology	17	8	~	~	~	~	~	~
Fine and Applied Arts	2	1	~	~	~	~	~	~
Law	898	193	~	~	~	~	~	~
Social and Behavioral Science	754	323	~	~	~	~	~	~
Commercial and Business Administration	1,815	566	~	~	~	~	~	~
Mass Communication and Documentation	47	26	~	~	~	~	~	~
Home Economics (Domestic Science)	1	1	~	~	~	~	~	~
Service Trades	#	#	~	~	~	~	~	~
Natural Science	179	75	~	~	~	~	~	~
Mathematics and Computer Science	52	12	~	~	~	~	~	~
Medical Science and Health-Related	2,177	1,148	~	~	~	~	~	~
Engineering	947	86	~	~	~	~	~	~
Architecture and Town Planning	180	52	~	~	~	~	~	~
Trade, Craft, and Industrial Programs	#	#	~	~	~	~	~	~
Transport and Communications	#	#	~	~	~	~	~	~
Agriculture, Forestry, and Fishery	788	63	~	~	~	~	~	~
Other and Not Specified	619	430	~	~	~	~	~	~
S. URUGUAY (1985)								
Total	2,628	1,479	644	519	1,976	956	8	4
Education Science and Teacher Training	11	6	#	#	11	6	#	#
Humanities, Religion, and Theology	45	37	33	30	12	7	#	#
Fine and Applied Arts	4	3	#	#	4	3	#	#
Law	422	275	#	#	422	275	#	#
Social and Behavioral Science	146	114	125	104	21	10	#	#
Commercial and Business Administration	276	129	#	#	276	129	#	#
Mass Communication and Documentation	40	40	40	40	#	#	#	#
Home Economics (Domestic Science)	23	23	23	23	#	#	#	#
Service Trades	#	#	#	#	#	#	#	#
Natural Science	27	13	#	#	27	13	#	#
Mathematics and Computer Science	92	37	77	35	15	2	#	#
Medical Science and Health-Related	1,008	638	295	250	705	384	8	4
Engineering	134	13	#	#	134	13	#	#
Architecture and Town Planning	98	49	#	#	98	49	#	#
Trade, Craft, and Industrial Programs	8	#	8	#	#	#	#	#
Transport and Communications	#	#	#	#	#	#	#	#
Agriculture, Forestry, and Fishery	251	65	#	#	251	65	#	#
Other and Not Specified	43	37	43	37	#	#	#	#

Table 913 (Continued)

HIGHER EDUCATION: GRADUATES, BY LEVEL[1] AND FIELD OF STUDY, 16 LC

Country and Field of Study	All Levels MF	All Levels F	Level 5 MF	Level 5 F	Level 6 MF	Level 6 F	Level 7 MF	Level 7 F
T. VENEZUELA (1983)[6]								
Total	24,147	~	5,082	~	19,065	~	#	#
Education Science and Teacher Training	6,719	~	306	~	6,413	~	#	#
Humanities, Religion, and Theology	272	~	#	#	272	~	#	#
Fine and Applied Arts	30	~	#	#	30	~	#	#
Law	1,104	~	#	#	1,104	~	#	#
Social and Behavioral Science	1,602	~	255	~	1,347	~	#	#
Commercial and Business Administration	3,547	~	1,841	~	1,706	~	#	#
Mass Communication and Documentation	311	~	48	~	263	~	#	#
Home Economics (Domestic Science)	#	#	#	#	#	#	#	#
Service Trades	183	~	183	~	#	#	#	#
Natural Science	404	~	#	#	404	~	#	#
Mathematics and Computer Science	688	~	415	~	273	~	#	#
Medical Science and Health-Related	2,770	~	57	~	2,713	~	#	#
Engineering	4,316	~	1,071	~	3,245	~	#	#
Architecture and Town Planning	469	~	#	#	469	~	#	#
Trade, Craft, and Industrial Programs	151	~	151	~	#	#	#	#
Transport and Communications	#	#	#	#	#	#	#	#
Agriculture, Forestry, and Fishery	1,400	~	687	~	713	~	#	#
Other and Not Specified	181	~	68	~	113	~	#	#
UNITED STATES (1982)								
Total	1,810,732	911,518	445,390	243,225	969,510	490,370	395,832	177,923
Education Science and Teacher Training	197,915	144,898	7,520	5,169	97,991	74,321	92,404	65,408
Humanities, Religion, and Theology	73,448	41,371	1,809	942	54,964	32,531	16,675	7,898
Fine and Applied Arts	55,050	33,643	6,365	3,965	39,251	24,659	9,434	5,019
Law	78,140	24,448	1,742	1,475	1,099	642	75,229	22,331
Social and Behavioral Science	168,680	85,787	3,749	2,087	138,423	71,510	26,508	12,190
Commercial and Business Administration	409,300	187,722	116,279	73,549	226,893	95,175	66,128	18,998
Mass Communication and Documentation	50,761	29,873	4,052	1,920	38,860	22,647	7,849	5,306
Home Economics (Domestic Science)	28,410	24,885	9,044	6,779	16,705	15,751	2,661	2,355
Service Trades	#	#	#	#	#	#	#	#
Natural Science	85,067	31,553	4,084	1,598	63,387	24,807	17,596	5,148
Mathematics and Computer Science	56,528	22,182	10,447	5,183	36,963	14,362	9,118	2,637
Medical Science and Health-Related	148,586	125,857	65,749	58,105	64,614	54,410	18,223	13,342
Engineering	160,991	17,854	49,611	4,981	89,199	10,951	22,181	1,922
Architecture and Town Planning	14,731	5,720	1,454	1,144	9,823	3,420	3,454	1,156
Trade, Craft, and Industrial Programs	#	#	#	#	#	#	#	#
Transport and Communications	#	#	#	#	#	#	#	#
Agriculture, Forestry, and Fishery	33,957	10,572	7,645	2,478	20,909	6,824	5,403	1,270
Other and Not Specified	249,168	125,153	155,840	73,850	70,429	38,360	22,899	12,943

1. Level 5: Programs leading to an award not equivalent to a first university degree. Programs of this type are usually vocational.
   Level 6: Programs leading to a first university degree or equivalent qualification. These include bachelor's degrees and doctorates awarded after completion of studies in medicine, engineering, law, etc.
   Level 7: Programs leading to a post-graduate university degree or equivalent qualification.
2. Data refer to universities and equivalent degree-granting institutes only.
3. Data exclude Universidad Católica Boliviana.
4. Law includes Social and Behavioral Science. Commercial and Business Administration includes Mass Communication and Documentation, Home Economics, and Service Trades. Natural Science includes Mathematics and Computer Science. Engineering includes Architecture and Town Planning, Trade, Craft, and Industrial Programs, and Transport and Communications.
5. Data refer to universities only.
6. Programs of level 5 and 6 are combined.

SOURCE: UNESCO-SY, 1986, table 3.13.

Table 914

PERCENTAGE OF "LEFTIST" STUDENTS IN SAMPLE[1] BY FATHER'S RELIGION AND UNIVERSITY, 4 L

Country	Father's Religion		
	Practicing Catholic	Non-practicing Catholic	Non-Catholic, Atheist, Agnostic
E. COLOMBIA Los Andes[2]	9	21	13

Continued in SALA, 24-913.

Table 915

ACADEMIC STUDENTS STUDYING IN COMMUNIST COUNTRIES, 10 L
(December 1978)

Country	Total	USSR	Eastern Europe
B. BOLIVIA	170	110	60

Continued in SALA, 24-914.

Table 916

SCHOOL ENROLLMENT, 20 L, 1880–1929

A. ARGENTINA

Year	Total	Primary	Secondary	Higher	Year	Total	Primary	Secondary	Higher
1880	~	~	~	~	1905	~	543,881	~	~
1881	~	~	1,616	~	1906	~	659,460[†]	16,852[†,i]	~
1882	101,027	97,756[a]	2,270	1,001	1907	~	~	~	~
1883	~	107,961	~	~	1908	~	~	~	~
1884	~	~	5,198[†,b]	904[c]	1909	~	668,534	~	10,289

Continued in SALA, 18-1024 through 1043.

Table 917

ADULT EDUCATION: TEACHERS AND STUDENT ENROLLMENT, 20 L

Country	Number of Teachers				Number of Students Enrolled				Ratio of Students to Teachers
	Year	Total	Male	Female	Year	Total	Male	Female	
A. ARGENTINA[1]	1973[‡]	19,204	~	~	1973[‡]	518,752	~	~	27.0

Continued in SALA, 18-1022.

Table 918

SPECIAL EDUCATION: ESTABLISHMENTS, TEACHERS, AND STUDENT ENROLLMENT, 20 L

Country	Year	Type of Establishment (N)					Teachers	Students Enrolled		
		Total	Blind	Deaf and Dumb	Mentally Retarded	Others		Total	Male	Female
A. ARGENTINA	1971	316	17	16	283	- -	5,675	22,668	14,043	8,625

Continued in SALA, 18-1023.

Table 919

UNIVERSITY LIBRARY COLLECTIONS, BORROWERS, WORKS LOANED, CURRENT EXPENDITURE, AND PERSONNEL, 13 LC

		Collections							Current Expenditures		Library Employees		
Country	Year	Number of Administrative Units	Number of Service Units	Meters of Shelving	Number of Volumes (T)	Annual Additions (Volumes)	Number of Registered Borrowers	Works Loaned (Volumes)	Amount (T)	Staff (%)	Total	Holding a Diploma	Trained on the Job
A. ARGENTINA	1977	1,528	1,528	317,723	9,532	~	4,201,244	9,552,904	~	~	~	~	~
B. BOLIVIA	1980	~	99	33,622	125	599	1,119,618	~	9,664	~	110	1	54
C. BRAZIL	1982	3,600	~	~	18,106	~	2,919,155	7,728,684	~	~	10,533	82	4
D. CHILE	1983	179	~	~	783	~	18,345	4,292,364	66,141	84	476	~	~
F. COSTA RICA	1977	18	18	~	~	~	~	4,275,200	~	~	1,146	448	~
G. CUBA	1983	296	2,713	~	3,711	517,918	553,111	10,298,200	~	~	1,420	992	428
H. DOMINICAN REP.	1980	68	~	~	~	~	532,852	645,886	~	~	~	~	~
K. GUATEMALA	1977	1	36	2,000	27	3,000	~	~	~	~	10	2	1
M. HONDURAS	1980	1	1	~	~	~	~	19,931	~	~	~	~	~
N. MEXICO	1983	557	557	~	3,720	~	8,492,000	13,040,000	103,920	35	1,933	~	~
P. PANAMA	1980	18	18	~	26	450	56,550	56,550	~	~	37	~	~
R. PERU	1983	557	~	~	1,950	~	~	2,293,846	~	~	~	6	577
T. VENEZUELA	1980	23	373	31,315	977	87,120	66,250	2,374,219	13,072	44	1,102	29	1,073
UNITED STATES	1978	8,456	~	5,679,317	439,486	26,007,296	~	986,714,576	1,467,891	54	93,335	27,900	~

SOURCE: UNESCO-SY, 1984, 1986, table 7.3.

Table 920

LIBRARIES BY CATEGORY, 16 LC

	Country	Year	Category of Libraries	Number of Libraries	Collections		Annual Additions (Volumes)	Number of Registered Borrowers
					Number of Volumes (T)	Metres of Shelving		
A.	ARGENTINA	1984	Special	63	~	1,645	~	654,288
B.	BOLIVIA	1980	National	2	1,200	135	600	~
		1980	Public	~	33,622	125	599	1,119,618
		1983	Higher Education	17	~	220	3,000	~
		1982	Non-Specialized	13	6,220	220	1,890	~
C.	BRAZIL	1982	Public	3,600	~	18,106	~	2,919,155
		1979	Higher Education	1,029	~	11,496	1,176,253	1,115,408
		1982	School	9,169	~	26,048	~	4,038,811
		1982	Special	1,494	~	12,854	~	424,425
		1982	Non-Specialized	763	~	2,175	~	276,169
D.	CHILE	1984	National	1	~	2,766	8,380	1,694
		1983	Public	179	~	783	~	18,345
		1981	School	~	~	1,458	~	~
E.	COLOMBIA	1980	National	1	18,000	540	26,027	~
F.	COSTA RICA	1983	Higher Education	1	6,826	227	10,687	17,000
G.	CUBA	1983	National	1	~	1,396	158,626	30,259
		1983	Public	296	~	3,711	517,918	553,111
		1982	Higher Education	56	~	1,438	69,827	204,568
		1982	School	2,432	~	11,508	113,859	~
H.	DOMINICAN REP.	1980	Public	68	~	~	~	532,852
I.	ECUADOR	1983	Special	1	60	2	330	230
J.	EL SALVADOR	1980	National	1	2,442	80	1,000	22,780
K.	GUATEMALA	1981	Higher Education	1	818	120	~	45,000
N.	MEXICO[‡]	1983	National	2	~	1,548	~	~
		1983	Public	557	~	3,720	~	8,492,000
		1981	Higher Education	263	~	2,698	~	8,427,513
		1981	School	1,880	~	5,403	~	15,932,421
		1983	Special	171	~	2,300	~	2,829,264
P.	PANAMA	1980	National	~	6,784	221	13,572	49,794
		1980	Public	18	~	26	450	~
		1983	Special	1	~	55	1,500	530
R.	PERU	1983	National	1	19,507	2,690	69,155	39,672
		1983	Public	557	~	1,950	~	~
		1982	Higher Education	3	~	58	2,888	~
		1981	School	292	~	516	102,500	447,000
S.	URUGUAY	1983	National	1	25,356	879	17,451	~
		1984	Non-Specialized	1	2,700	115	~	~
T.	VENEZUELA	1980	National	1	3,830	765	7,077	~
		1980	Public	23	31,315	977	87,120	66,250
		1978	School	46	~	105	8,187	~
	UNITED STATES	1978	National	3	~	20,799	359,656	~
		1978	Public	8,456	5,679,317	439,486	26,007,296	~
		1979	Higher Education	3,122	~	519,895	21,608,010	~
		1978	School	85,096	24,646,328	591,261	32,717,838	~
		1978	Non-Specialized	1,877	~	36,348	1,591,752	~

SOURCE: UNESCO-SY, 1986, table 7.1.

Table 921

SCHOOL AND FINANCIAL YEARS, 20 LC

	Country	School Year Beginning	School Year End	Financial Year Beginning
A.	ARGENTINA	March	November	January
B.	BOLIVIA	February	October	January
C.	BRAZIL	February	November	January
D.	CHILE	March	December	January
E.	COLOMBIA	February	November	January
F.	COSTA RICA	March	November	January
G.	CUBA	September	June	January
H.	DOMINICAN REP.	September	June	January
I.	ECUADOR	October	July	January
J.	EL SALVADOR	January	November	January
K.	GUATEMALA	January	October	January
L.	HAITI	October	June	October
M.	HONDURAS	February	November	January
N.	MEXICO	September	June	January
O.	NICARAGUA	February	November	January
P.	PANAMA	April	December	January
Q.	PARAGUAY	March	November	January
R.	PERU	April	December	January
S.	URUGUAY	March	December	January
T.	VENEZUELA	October	July	January
	UNITED STATES	September	May	October

SOURCE: UNESCO-SY, 1986, Appendix B.

Table 922

TOTAL PUBLIC EDUCATIONAL EXPENDITURE, 20 LC
(Current and Capital Funds)

	Country	Year	Total Ed. Amount (T NC)	As % of GNP	As % of Total Govt Exp	Current Amount (T NC)	As % of Total	As % of GNP	As % of Current Govt Exp	Capital Expenditure (T NC)
A.	ARGENTINA	1982	10,211,808	2.5	14.5	3,155,062	89.7	2.2	18.2	362,647
B.	BOLIVIA	1981	5,109,345	3.0	25.8	3,517,710	100.0	3.0	~	2,931
C.	BRAZIL	1981	963,546,000	3.2	18.4	10,214,739	~	~	~	~
D.	CHILE	1982	65,336,340	5.8	~	3,709,515	~	~	~	~
E.	COLOMBIA	1983	83,436,200	3.0	21.5	86,528,000	96.4	2.9	27.7	3,091,800
F.	COSTA RICA	1983	5,853,136	6.0	~	6,462,562	90.6	5.4	~	609,426
G.	CUBA	1982	1,457,000	6.3	~	1,457,100	95.8	6.0	~	61,100
H.	DOMINICAN REP.	1983	165,477	2.1	16.0	175,853	~	2.0	19.0	10,376
I.	ECUADOR	1980	15,579,992	5.6	33.3	14,649,139	94.0	5.2	36.0	930,853
J.	EL SALVADOR	1982	322,158	3.7	8.5	333,863	96.5	3.6	10.8	11,705
K.	GUATEMALA	1983	153,750	1.8	12.4	162,884	94.4	1.7	17.1	9,134
L.	HAITI	1983	92,943	1.1	9.5	94,799	98.0	1.1	13.6	1,856
M.	HONDURAS	1982	206,880	4.3	16.9	224,921	92.0	4.0	24.0	18,041
N.	MEXICO	1983	416,192,879	2.7	6.4	443,829,058	93.8	2.6	~	27,636,179
O.	NICARAGUA	1982	1,079,240	4.0	10.3	1,146,547	94.1	3.8	~	67,307
P.	PANAMA	1983	198,413	5.5	17.5	216,126	91.8	5.0	17.7	17,713
Q.	PARAGUAY	1979	5,627,500	1.3	12.4	~	~	~	~	
R.	PERU	1983	873,165	3.3	14.7	888,229	98.3	3.2	17.3	15,064
S.	URUGUAY	1981	2,951,337	2.5	12.8	2,771,237	93.7	2.3	13.7	187,100
T.	VENEZUELA	1982	18,007,971	6.5	21.2	18,985,128	94.9	6.2	29.3	977,157
	UNITED STATES	1981	199,800	6.8	~	~	~	~	~	~

SOURCE: UNESCO-SY, 1984, 1985, table 4.1.

Table 923

PUBLIC CURRENT EDUCATIONAL EXPENDITURE,[1] BY LEVEL, 20 LC

Country	Year	Total Expenditure (T NC)	Total = 100%					
			Pre-school	First Level	Second Level	Third Level	Other Types of Education	Expenditure Not Allocated by Level
A. ARGENTINA	1970[a]	1,620[e]	1.4	29.0	30.3	21.0	2.2	16.2
	1984	180,530,252	. .[b]	37.7	27.4	19.2	.7	15.0
B. BOLIVIA	1970	396,056	1.9	60.2	12.8	10.9	2.0	12.3
	1982	10,211,808	. .[b]	71.9	13.0	3.2	3.3	8.5
C. BRAZIL[2]	1975	25,194,300	. .	62.7[c]	. .	26.1	2.3	9.0
	1983	3,709,515	. .[b]	44.2	7.2	19.9	1.3	27.4
D. CHILE	1975	1,321,482	. .[b]	34.9	13.5	25.2	4.1	22.4
	1984	81,651,572	. .[b]	54.5	16.7	24.3	#	4.5
E. COLOMBIA	1970[a]	1,545,185	.1	36.5	16.9	23.9	1.4	21.2
	1980	108,896,000	. .[b]	43.1	29.3	21.2	1.1	5.3
F. COSTA RICA	1970	318,500	. .[b]	51.2	18.9	10.5	#	19.4
	1983	5,853,136	. .[b]	26.6	18.9	25.8	.9	27.9
G. CUBA	1982	1,396,000	5.7	22.8	43.3	10.6	5.0	12.6
H. DOMINICAN REP.	1970	39,306	#	41.1	18.3	20.7	7.6	12.5
	1984	170,322	.4	44.6	19.6	18.8	10.2	6.3
I. ECUADOR	1970	1,133,523	. .[b]	45.9	41.0	9.9	1.1	2.0
	1980	14,649,139	. .[b]	20.6	18.5	15.6	2.5	42.7
J. EL SALVADOR	1970	69,621	#	57.9	11.8	21.4	2.5	6.4
	1981	321,814	#	60.3	6.0	15.7	1.9	16.2
K. GUATEMALA	1970	32,566	2.8	55.2	16.9	13.1	4.5	7.4
	1982	129,226	1.8	38.2	17.2	19.7	14.2	8.9
L. HAITI	1970	25,098	#	65.1	17.8	9.1	. .[d]	8.0
	1983	92,943	#	63.2	15.8	9.4	5.6	5.9
M. HONDURAS	1970	41,660	#	64.2	15.4	12.2	1.7	6.5
	1982	206,880	#	54.0	18.2	26.5	1.0	.3
N. MEXICO	1970[a]	7,148,000	3.1	47.7	27.2	10.4	#	11.5
	1983	416,192,879	4.1	30.8	15.7	28.8	6.3	14.4
O. NICARAGUA	1970	120,901	#	57.9	17.6	10.0	9.7	4.8
	1984	2,458,200	1.9	31.5	14.4	18.3	8.6	25.3
P. PANAMA[3]	1970	50,824	#	38.9	18.7	10.8	18.4	13.2
	1984	210,998	#	39.8	25.4	19.4	3.0	12.3
Q. PARAGUAY	1984	12,629,900	#	41.5	25.3	22.2	4.0	7.0
R. PERU	1970	8,730,500	1.1	39.8	20.8	. .[e]	4.8	33.5
	1983	873,165	3.3	36.5	23.2	1.9	4.8	30.4
S. URUGUAY	1980	1,926,769	#	48.4	33.2	16.1	2.3	#
T. VENEZUELA	1970	2,220,651	. .[b]	38.3	20.6	25.5	8.5	7.0
	1983	16,758,800	5.9	28.2	10.0	42.6	4.8	8.4
UNITED STATES	1970	56,000[e]	. .[b]	70.5	. .[b]	29.5	#	#
	1981	199,800	. .[b]	63.4	. .[b]	36.6	#	#

1. Current expenditure includes expenditure on administration, emoluments of teachers and supporting teaching staff, school books and other teaching materials, scholarships, welfare services and maintenance of school buildings. It differs from capital expenditure which includes expenditure on land, buildings, construction, equipment, and loan transactions.
2. Data refer to current and capital expenditure incurred by the Federal Government and by the Federal States. Expenditure of municipalities is not included.
3. Does not include Canal Zone.

a. Expenditure of the Ministry of Education only.
b. Included in First Level.
c. Includes pre-primary, first and second levels and also special education and ensino supletivo.
d. Included in Expenditure Not Allocated by Level.
e. In millions.

SOURCE: UNESCO-SY, 1984, 1986, table 4.3.

Table 924

SCIENTISTS AND ENGINEERS ENGAGED IN RESEARCH AND DEVELOPMENT (R AND D), BY FIELD OF SCIENCE, 14 L

| | | | | Scientists and Engineers | | | | | |
| | | | | Field of Science | | | | | |
Country	Year	Code[1]	Total	Natural Sciences	Engineering and Technology	Medical Sciences	Agriculture	Social Sciences and Humanities	Other
A. ARGENTINA	1982	FTE	10,486	4,024	1,971	856	1,835	1,076	724
		FPT	6,705	3,107	452	797	645	1,275	429
C. BRAZIL[2]	1977	FTE	13,678	4,363	2,581	1,817	2,693	2,224	#
D. CHILE	1975	FTE	5,948	1,885	1,367	1,562	411	723	#
E. COLOMBIA[3]	1982	FT	831	288	49	21	334	139	#
		PT	3,938	1,238	544	1,088	358	710	#
		FTE	1,083	341	150	299	98	195	#
G. CUBA	1983	FT	6,903	666	1,773	1,187	1,741	1,209	327
		PT	5,387	29	885	513	518	253	3,198
		FTE	8,247	686	1,938	1,379	1,896	1,310	1,038
		FPT	5,089	298	969	650	789	808	1,575
I. ECUADOR[4]	1976	FT	378	88	33	#	242	15	#
		PT	239	26	26	#	180	7	#
		FTE	469	100	45	#	304	20	#
J. EL SALVADOR[5]	1974	FT	674	190	71	153	78	182	#
		PT	255	#	98	60	14	83	#
		FTE	802	190	120	183	85	224	#
K. GUATEMALA	1974	FT	250	34	79	16	49	72	#
		PT	134	18	42	9	27	38	#
		FTE	310	43	98	20	61	88	#
M. HONDURAS[6]	1974	FT	5	#	5	#	#	#	#
N. MEXICO[7]	1974	FT	2,227	631	422	216	375	519	#
		PT	6,219	1,379	1,232	919	594	1,772	#
		FTE	5,896	1,523	1,170	648	765	1,535	#
P. PANAMA[7]	1975	FT	193	39	41	31	33	28	#
		PT	34	1	2	21	#	#	#
		FTE	204	39	41	40	33	28	#
R. PERU[7,8]	1970	FT	1,522	445	76	267	494	151	#
		PT	318	100	13	125	24	54	#
		FTE	1,686	496	83	330	507	180	#
S. URUGUAY[7,9]	1971	FPT	1,537‡	184‡	356‡	359‡	253‡	160‡	#
		FTE	1,150‡	142‡	285‡	239‡	253‡	109‡	#
T. VENEZUELA[7]	1983	FTE	2,175	786	300	204	437	388	60
		FPT	6,047	1,895	861	860	1,045	1,177	209

1. FT = Full-Time; PT = Part-time; FPT = Full-time plus part-time; FTE = Full-time equivalent.
2. Data refer to post-graduate fundamental research and post-graduate teaching in the higher education sector only.
3. Excludes data for law, humanities, and education.
4. Data refer to research and development in the agricultural sciences only.
5. Data refer to 28 institutions out of a total of 41 which perform research and development.
6. Data relate to one research institute only.
7. Total data include scientists and engineers for whom a distribution by field of science is unknown.
8. Excludes humanities and education.
9. Data refer to the year 1971/72.

SOURCE: UNESCO-SY, 1977, table 7.3; 1978, table 7.3; 1980, table 5.3; 1984, table 5.3; 1986, table 5.5.

Table 925

RESEARCH AND DEVELOPMENT (R AND D) PERSONNEL, BY SECTOR OF PERFORMANCE, 15 LC

Country	Year	Type of Personnel[1]	(A) All Sectors	(B) Integrated R&D	(C) Non-integrated R&D	(D) Higher Education	(E) General Service
A. ARGENTINA[2,9]	1982	% by Sector	100	4.5	23.5	33.3	38.6
		Scientists & Engineers	10,486	476	2,466	3,497	4,047
C. BRAZIL	1978	Total in R&D	~	43,056	→	~	~
		Scientists & Engineers	~	8,497	→	15,518	~
		Technicians	~	5,392	→	~	~
		Auxiliary	~	29,167	→	~	~
D. CHILE	1983	% by Sector	100	1.1	24.8	69.8	4.3
		Total in R&D	2,005	22	497	1,399	87
E. COLOMBIA[3,4]	1982	Total in R&D	3,709	91	~	1,474	2,144
		% by Sector	100	2.5	~	39.7	57.8
		Scientists & Engineers	1,083	33	~	687	363
		Technicians	1,024	34	~	388	602
		Auxiliary	1,602	24	~	399	1,179
G. CUBA	1984	Total in R&D	32,937	341	17,386	2,621	12,589
		% by Sector	100	1.0	52.8	8.0	38.2
		Scientists & Engineers	9,548	135	4,011	1,821	3,581
		Technicians	8,843	115	4,456	281	3,991
		Auxiliary	14,546	91	8,919	519	5,017
I. ECUADOR[5]	1979	Total in R&D	5,297	270	→	1,202	3,825
		% by Sector	100	5.1	→	22.7	72.2
		Scientists & Engineers	2,049	52	→	599	1,398
		Technicians	1,252	44	→	283	925
		Auxiliary	1,996	174	→	320	1,502
J. EL SALVADOR	1981	Total in R&D	2,535	1,656	~	454	425
		% by Sector	100	65.3	~	17.9	16.8
		Scientists & Engineers	564	42.1	~	115	28
		Technicians	1,971	1,235	~	339	397
K. GUATEMALA[9]	1974	Total in R&D	749	#	290	113	346
		% by Sector	**	#	38.7	15.1	46.2
		Scientists & Engineers	310	#	166	43	101
		Technicians	439	#	124	70	245
M. HONDURAS[6]	1974	Total in R&D	7	#	#	#	7
		% by Sector	**	#	#	#	100
		Scientists & Engineers	5	#	#	#	5
		Technicians	1	#	#	#	1
		Auxiliary	1	#	#	#	1
N. MEXICO	1974	% by Sector	**	11.9	21.6	33.4	33.2
		Scientists & Engineers	5,896	701	1,272	1,968	1,955
P. PANAMA	1975	Total in R&D	982	#	600	249	133
		% by Sector	100	#	61.1	25.4	13.5
		Scientists & Engineers	204	#	116	62	26
		Technicians	301	#	194	80	27
		Auxiliary	477	#	290	107	80
Q. PARAGUAY	1971	% by Sector	**	28.4	→	36.6	35.1
		Scientists & Engineers	134	38	→	49	47
R. PERU	1981	Total in R&D	12,528	1,269	→	4,753	6,506
		% by Sector	100	10.1	→	37.9	51.9
		Scientists & Engineers	7,464	896	→	3,600	2,968
		Technicians	5,064	373	→	1,153	3,538
		Auxiliary	~	~	~	~	~
S. URUGUAY[7]	1971	Total in R&D	3,033‡	385‡	758‡	1,068‡	822‡
		% by Sector	**	12.7‡	25.0‡	35.2‡	27.1‡
		Scientists & Engineers	1,150‡	114‡	280‡	537‡	219‡
		Technicians	1,087‡	138‡	241‡	336‡	372‡
		Auxiliary	796‡	133‡	237‡	195‡	231‡
T. VENEZUELA[3,10]	1983	Total in R&D	10,687	903	337	5,913	3,534
		% by Sector	100	8.4	3.2	55.3	33.1
		Scientists & Engineers	4,568	347	117	2,921	1,183
		Technicians	2,692	97	126	1,297	1,172
		Auxiliary	3,427	459	94	1,695	1,179
UNITED STATES[4,8]	1983	% by Sector	100	73.5	→	13.7	12.8
		Scientists & Engineers	728,600	535,600	→	100,000	93,000

1. Scientists and engineers engaged in research and development are given in full-time equivalent (FTE).
2. Data are in net man-years.
3. Data for scientists and engineers refer to full-time plus part-time.
4. Excludes law, humanities, and education.
5. Data refer to research and development in the agricultural sciences only.
6. Data relate to one research institute only.
7. Data refer to 1971-72.
8. The general service sector includes data referring to private non-profit organizations.
9. Excludes auxiliary personnel.
10. Data concern 167 institutes out of a total of 406 which perform R&D.

SOURCE: UNESCO-SY, 1984, table 5.4; 1986, table 5.6.

Table 926

INDICATORS OF SCIENTIFIC AND TECHNOLOGICAL DEVELOPMENT, 17 LC

Country	Year	Qualified Manpower		Personnel Engaged in R&D			Expenditure for R&D		
		Scientists and Engineers (PMI)	Technicians (PMI)	Scientists and Engineers (FTE)[1] (PMI)	Technicians (PMI)	Number of Technicians per Scientists and Engineers	% of GNP	Per Capita (NC)	Annual Average per R&D Scientists and Engineers (NC)
A. ARGENTINA[2,3]	1982	18,970	60,077	360	~	~	.4	80,959.4	221,431,600
B. BOLIVIA	1976	11,562	~	~	~	~	~	~	~
C. BRAZIL[3]	1982	11,231	25,348	256	~	~	.6‡	2,407.1‡	9,397,700‡
D. CHILE	1983	~	~	172	⟶	~	.3	388.9	~
E. COLOMBIA	1982	~	~	40	38	.9	.1	102.1	2,543,200
F. COSTA RICA	1982	~	~	171	~	~	.1	33.8	197,900
G. CUBA[4]	1984	14,349	~	955	855	.9	.6	16.4	17,200
I. ECUADOR	1979	~	~	259	158	.6	.4	108.3	417,800
J. EL SALVADOR	1984	~	~	397	⟶	~	.9	18.0	~
K. GUATEMALA[5]	1984	~	~	348	⟶	~	.5	5.9	~
M. HONDURAS	1974	22.5[a]	10.6[a]	.02[a]	~	.2	~	~	~
N. MEXICO[6]	1974	69.1‡,[a]	150.0[a]	1.0[a]	~	~	.2	22.7	216,700‡
O. NICARAGUA	1971	~	~	~	~	~	.1‡	4.2	~
P. PANAMA[7,8]	1976	3,150	8,058	121	179	1.5	.2	1.5	16,200
Q. PARAGUAY	1981	~	~	247	⟶	~	.2	70.7	1,248,200
R. PERU[9]	1981	16,426	78,690	420	285	.7	.3	8,282.2	~
S. URUGUAY[10]	1975	19,939	~	~	~	~	.2	.6	1,620‡
T. VENEZUELA[9,11]	1983	21,819	96,456	279	165	.6	.4	80.9	298,100‡
UNITED STATES	1983	14,777	~	3,111	~	~	2.7	376.1	120,900

1. Code: FTE = Full-time equivalent.
2. Data for Expenditure for R & D refer to 1981.
3. Data for Qualified Manpower refer to 1980.
4. Data for Qualified Manpower refer to 1981.
5. Data for Expenditure for R & D refer to 1983.
6. Data for Qualified Manpower refer to 1969. Expenditure for R & D refer to 1973.
7. Data for Personnel Engaged in R & D refer to 1975.
8. Data for Expenditure for R & D refer to 1975.
9. Data for Expenditure for R & D refer to 1984.
10. Data for Expenditure for R & D refer to 1972.
11. Data for Qualified Manpower refer to 1982.

a. Data expressed in P10TI.

SOURCE: UNEXCO-SY, 1984, table 5.14 and table 5.15; 1986, table 5.18 and 5.19.

Part IV: Politics, Religion, and the Military

CHAPTER 10

POLITICAL STATISTICS

Note: This volume contains statistics from numerous sources. Alternative data on many topics are presented. Variations in statistics can be attributed to differences in definition, parameters, coverage, methodology, as well as date gathered, prepared, or adjusted. See also Editor's Note on Methodology.

Table 1000

LOS ANGELES TIMES VIEW OF EMERGING DEMOCRACY IN LATIN AMERICA, 20 L

(1986)

	Country	Type of Rule	Year of Newly Established Democracy[2]	Years of Previous Military Rule
A.	ARGENTINA	Democratic	1983	7
B.	BOLIVIA	Democratic	1982	18
C.	BRAZIL	Democratic	1985	20
D.	CHILE	Military	**	**
E.	COLOMBIA	Democratic	1958[a]	~
F.	COSTA RICA	Democratic	1949[b]	~
G.	CUBA	Military	**	**
H.	DOMINICAN REP.	Democratic	1966	30
I.	ECUADOR	Democratic	1979	16
J.	EL SALVADOR	Democratic	1980	20
K.	GUATEMALA	Democratic	1986	~
L.	HAITI	Military	**	**
M.	HONDURAS	Democratic	1981	18
N.	MEXICO	Democratic***	1928	~
O.	NICARAGUA	Military	**	**
P.	PANAMA	Democratic[1]	1978	~
Q.	PARAGUAY	Military	**	**
R.	PERU	Democratic	1980	12
S.	URUGUAY	Democratic	1985	12
T.	VENEZUELA	Democratic	1958	~[c]

1. Since 1978, the presidency has been under the control of the military.
2. The latest year in which democratic rule has been instituted.

a. Democratic rule has been instituted since the early twentieth century; however, a military dictatorship occurred in 1953-57, and the country is under frequent state of siege.
b. The democratic process has been interrupted only twice this century, in 1917 and 1948.
c. Under military rulers this century except 1945-48.

SOURCE: Adapted from *Los Angeles Times*, June 15, 1986.

Table 1001

POLITICAL DEPENDENCE, INDEPENDENCE, AND INTERNATIONAL MEMBERSHIPS OF COUNTRIES AND TERRITORIES, 20 L AND 45 ELA

(1983)

PART I. TRADITIONALLY DEFINED LATIN AMERICA

Independent Countries[1]	As Result of			Memberships						
	War[2]		Special Circumstances	OAS	IDB:L	ECLA:L	ALADI	AG	CACM	CBI-IB
	Declared	Won								
A. ARGENTINA	1810	1816[a]		A	A	A	A			
B. BOLIVIA	1809	1825[a]		B	B	B	B	B		
C. BRAZIL			1822[b]	C	C	C	C			
D. CHILE	1810	1818[a]		D	D	D	D	D[5]		
E. COLOMBIA	1810	1824[a]	1830[e]	E	E	E	E	E		
F. COSTA RICA		1821[c]	1838[d]	F	F	F			F	F
G. CUBA		1898[a]	1902[i]	G[4]		G				
H. DOMINICAN REP.[3]		1821[a]	1844[h]	H	H	H				H
I. ECUADOR[7]	1809	1822[a]	1830[e]	I	I	I	I	I		
J. EL SALVADOR		1821[c]	1841[d]	J	J	J			J	J
K. GUATEMALA		1821[c]	1839[d]	K	K	K			K	K
L. HAITI	1791	1804[k]		L	L	L				L
M. HONDURAS		1821[c]	1838[d]	M	M	M			M[6]	M
N. MEXICO	1810	1821[a]		N	N	N	N			
O. NICARAGUA		1821[c]	1838[d]	O	O	O			O	O
P. PANAMA			1903[j]	P	P	P				P
Q. PARAGUAY			1811[a]	Q	Q	Q	Q			
R. PERU	1821	1824[a,f]		R	R	R	R	I		
S. URUGUAY	1811	1814[a]	1828[l]	S	S	S	S			
T. VENEZUELA[7]	1810	1821[a,g]	1829[e]	T	T	T	T	T		

1. The three events that provided the immediate stimulation for independence were the U.S. War for Independence (1776-81); the French Revolution of 1789 proclaiming the Rights of Man and abolishing slavery for France but not its colonies—the most prosperous of which was Saint Domingue (the future Haiti); and the capture of the Spanish monarch by Napoleon Bonaparte, Spain's "ally," who placed his brother Joseph on the throne of Spain in 1808, thus breaking strong allegiances between Spain and its colonies. (The latter event occurred after France had passed through Spain, driving the monarchy of Portugal to Brazil in 1807, laying the basis for Brazil's independence once the monarchy returned to Portugal in 1821.)
2. Excludes precursor movements such as that by Tiradentes in 1788 (Brazil) or by Miranda in 1806 (Venezuela).
3. France ceded to Spain in 1795.
4. Since 1962 Cuba has been suspended from OAS activities but not membership.
5. Chile withdrew from AG in 1976.
6. Honduras partially withdrew from CACM in 1971.
7. Member of OPEC.

a. Won from Spain.
b. Won from Portugal.
c. Won from Spain and became part of Mexico in 1822-23.
d. Breakup of United Provinces of Central America, which existed to unite Costa Rica, El Salvador, Guatemala, Honduras, and Nicaragua from 1823 to 1841. For all practical purposes the breakup came by 1838 and attempts to revive union were militarily defeated by 1842.
e. Breakup of Gran Colombia, which existed to unite Colombia, Ecuador, and Venezuela from 1819 to 1830.
f. Last Spanish troops left Peru in 1826.
g. Last Spanish troops left Venezuela in 1823.
h. Won from Haiti, which governed Hispaniola or Santo Domingo (future Dominican Republic) from 1822 to 1844. Spain reoccupied from 1861 to 1865.
i. Won from the United States.
j. Won from Colombia.
k. Won from France.
l. Won from Brazil.

SOURCE: SALA, 23-1.

Table 1001 (Continued)

POLITICAL DEPENDENCE, INDEPENDENCE, AND INTERNATIONAL MEMBERSHIPS
OF COUNTRIES AND TERRITORIES, 20 L AND 45 ELA

(1983)

PART II. NON-TRADITIONALLY DEFINED LATIN AMERICA ADDS:

Independent Countries	Year of Independence	From	Organization by Country							
			OAS	IDB:L	ECLA:L	CARICOM[1]	ECCM	OECS	CIB-IB	FAO[4]
1. Antigua-Barbuda	1981	Gr. Britain	1			1	1	1	1	1
2. Bahamas	1973	Gr. Britain	2	2	2				2	2
3. Barbados	1966	Gr. Britain	3	3	3	3			3	3
4. Belize	1981	Gr. Britain				4			4	4
5. Dominica	1978	Gr. Britain	5			5	5	5	5	5
6. Grenada	1974	Gr. Britain	6		6	6	6	6	6	6
7. Guyana	1966	Gr. Britain		7	7	7			7	7
8. Jamaica	1962	Gr. Britain	8	8	8	8			8	8
9. St. Kitts-Nevis[2]	1983	Gr. Britain	9			9	9	9	9	9
10. St. Lucia	1977	Gr. Britain	10			10	10	10	10	10
11. St. Vincent-Grenadines	1979	Gr. Britain	11			11	11	11	11	11
12. Suriname	1975	Netherlands	12	12	12				12	12
13. Trinidad and Tobago	1962	Gr. Britain	13	13	13	13				

Dependent Countries	Belonging to	OAS	IDB:L	ICLA:L	CARICOM[1]	ECCM	OECS	CIB-IB	FAO
T1. Anguilla	Great Britain					T1			T1
T2. Bermuda	Great Britain[3]								
T3. British Virgin Islands	Great Britain							T3	T3
T4. Cayman Islands	Great Britain							T4	T4
T5. French Guiana	France								T5
T6. Guadeloupe	France								T6
T7. Martinique	France								T7
T8. Montserrat	Great Britain				T8	T8	T8	T8	T8
T9. Netherlands Antilles	Netherlands							T9	T9
T10. Puerto Rico	United States								T10
T11. Turks and Caicos	Great Britain							T11	T11
T12. U.S. Virgin Islands	United States								T12

1. The Caribbean Community and Common Market (CARICOM)
was established in 1973 to replace the Caribbean Free Trade
Association (CARIFTA), founded in 1967.
2. St. Kitts is officially known as St. Christopher.
3. Bermuda has been self-governing since 1968. Although under
Great Britain, it claims Bermudian nationality.
4. Includes Falkland Islands.

SOURCE: SALA, 23-1; and WA, 1987, p. 640.

Table 1002

SHARE OF ADULT POPULATION VOTING, 12 LC

	Country	Year	Type of Election[1]	Total Vote (T)	% Adult Population Voting[2]
A.	ARGENTINA	1983	P, L	15,180	89
C.	BRAZIL	1982	L	48,440	81
E.	COLOMBIA	1982	P	6,816	68
F.	COSTA RICA	1982	P, L	992	87
I.	ECUADOR	1984	L	2,204	53
J.	EL SALVADOR	1984	P	1,524	69
K.	GUATEMALA	1984	CA	1,856	57
M.	HONDURAS	1981	P, L	1,171	79
N.	MEXICO	1982	P, L	22,523	75
O.	NICARAGUA	1984	P, CA	1,170	91
R.	PERU	1980	P, L	4,030	49
T.	VENEZUELA	1983	P, L	6,741	90
	UNITED STATES	1984	P, L	92,000	53

1. P = Presidential, L = Legislative, CA = Constituent Assembly.
2. Estimates based on votes cast as a percentage of total population age 20 or over.

SOURCE: *LASA Forum* (Latin American Studies Association), Winter, 1985, p. 25.

Table 1003

POLITICAL AND CIVIL RIGHTS,[1] 20 LC, 1972–86

(1+ = Best Score; 7– = Worst Score)

Country	Year	Political Rights[2]	Civil Rights[3]	Country	Year	Political Rights[2]	Civil Rights[3]
A. ARGENTINA	1972	6	3	F. COSTA RICA	1972	1	1
	1973	2	2		1973	1	2
	1974	2	4–		1974	1	1
	1975	2	4		1975	1	1
	1976	6–	5–		1976	1	1
	1977	6	6–[a]		1977	1	1
	1978	6	5+		1978	1	1
	1979	6	5		1979	1	1
	1980	6	5		1980	1	1
	1981	6	5		1981	1	1
	1982	6	5		1982	1	1
	1983	3+	3+		1983	1	1
	1984	2+	2+		1984	1	1
	1985	2	2		1985	1	1
	1986	2	1+		1986	1	1
B. BOLIVIA	1972	5	4	G. CUBA	1972	7	7
	1973	5	4		1973	7	7
	1974	6–	5–		1974	7	7
	1975	6	5		1975	7	7
	1976	6	4[a]		1976	7	6[a]
	1977	6	4		1977	7	6
	1978	5+	3+		1978	6[a]	6
	1979	3+	3		1979	6	6
	1980	7–	5–		1980	6	6
	1981	7	5		1981	6	6
	1982	2+	3+		1982	6	6
	1983	2	3		1983	6	6
	1984	2	3		1984	6	6
	1985	2	3		1985	6	6
	1986	2	3		1986	6	6
C. BRAZIL	1972	5	5	H. DOMINICAN REP.	1972	3	2
	1973	5	5		1973	3	2
	1974	4+	4+		1974	4	2
	1975	4	5–		1975	4	2
	1976	4	5		1976	4	3[a]
	1977	4	5		1977	4	2+[a]
	1978	4	4+		1978	2+	2
	1979	4	3+		1979	2	3–
	1980	4	3		1980	2	3
	1981	4	3		1981	2	3
	1982	3+	3		1982	1+	2+
	1983	3	3		1983	1	2
	1984	3	3		1984	1	3–
	1985	3	2+		1985	1	3
	1986	2+	2		1986	1	3
D. CHILE	1972	1	2	I. ECUADOR	1972	7	3
	1973	7[b]	5[b]		1973	7	4[a]
	1974	7	5		1974	7	4
	1975	7	5		1975	7	4
	1976	7	5		1976	6[a]	4
	1977	7	5		1977	6	4
	1978	6+	5		1978	5+	3+
	1979	6	5		1979	2+	2+
	1980	6	5		1980	2	2
	1981	6	5		1981	2	2
	1982	6	5		1982	2	2
	1983	6	5		1983	2	2
	1984	6	5		1984	2	2
	1985	6	5		1985	2	3
	1986	6	5		1986	2	3
E. COLOMBIA	1972	2	2	J. EL SALVADOR	1972	2	3
	1973	2	2		1973	2	3
	1974	2	2		1974	2	3
	1975	2	3–		1975	2	3
	1976	2	3		1976	3–	3
	1977	2	3		1777	3	3
	1978	2	3		1978	4–	4–
	1979	2	3		1979	5[a]	3+
	1980	2	3		1980	6–	4–
	1981	2	3		1981	5	5–
	1982	2	3		1982	4+	5
	1983	2	3		1983	4	5
	1984	2	3		1984	3+	5
	1985	2	3		1985	2+	4+
	1986	2	3		1986	3	4

Table 1003 (Continued)

POLITICAL AND CIVIL RIGHTS,[1] 20 LC, 1972–86
(1+ = Best Score; 7– = Worst Score)

Country	Year	Political Rights[2]	Civil Rights[3]	Country	Year	Political Rights[2]	Civil Rights[3]
K. GUATEMALA	1972	2	3	P. PANAMA	1972	7	6
	1973	2	2		1973	7	6
	1974	4	3		1974	7	6
	1975	4	3		1975	7	6
	1976	4	3		1976	7	6
	1977	4	4[a]		1977	6+	5+
	1978	3+	4		1978	5+	5
	1979	3	5[a]		1979	5	5
	1980	5–	6–		1980	4+	4+
	1981	6–	6		1981	4	4
	1982	6	6		1982	5–	5–
	1983	6	6		1983	5	4+
	1984	5+	6		1984	4+	3+
	1985	4+	4+		1985	6–	3
	1986	3+	3+		1986	6	3
L. HAITI	1972	7	6	Q. PARAGUAY	1972	4	6
	1973	6	6		1973	5	5
	1974	6	6		1974	5	5
	1975	6	6		1975	5	5
	1976	6	6		1976	5	6–
	1977	7[a]	6		1977	5	6
	1978	7	6		1978	5+	5
	1979	6+	5+		1979	5	5
	1980	6	6–		1980	5	5
	1981	7–	6		1981	5	5
	1982	7	6		1982	5	5
	1983	7	6		1983	5	5
	1984	7	6		1984	5	5
	1985	7	6		1985	5	5
	1986	5+	4+		1986	5	6–
M. HONDURAS	1972	7	3	R. PERU	1972	7	5
	1973	6	3		1973	7	5
	1974	6	3		1974	6[a]	6–
	1975	6	3		1975	6	4+
	1976	6	3		1976	6	4
	1977	6	3		1977	6	4
	1978	6	3		1978	5+	4
	1979	6	3		1979	5	4
	1980	4+	3		1980	2+	3+
	1981	3+	3		1981	2	3
	1982	2+	3		1982	2	3
	1983	3–	3		1983	2	3
	1984	2+	3		1984	2	3
	1985	2	3		1985	2	3
	1986	2	3		1986	2	3
N. MEXICO	1972	5	3	S. URUGUAY	1972	3	4
	1973	4[b]	3		1973	5[b]	5[b]
	1974	4	3		1974	5	5
	1975	4	3		1975	5	5
	1976	4	4–		1976	6–	6–[a]
	1977	4	4		1977	6	6
	1978	4	4		1978	6	6
	1979	3+	3+		1979	6	6
	1980	3	4		1980	5+	5+
	1981	3	4		1981	5	5
	1982	3	4		1982	5	4+
	1983	3	4		1983	5	4
	1984	3	4		1984	5	4
	1985	4–	4		1985	2+	2+
	1986	4	4		1986	2	2
O. NICARAGUA	1972	4	3	T. VENEZUELA	1972	2	2
	1973	5	4[b]		1973	2	2
	1974	5	4		1974	2	2
	1975	5	4		1975	2	2
	1976	5	5[a]		1976	1[a]	2
	1977	5	5		1977	1	2
	1978	5	5		1978	1	2
	1979	5	5		1979	1	2
	1980	5	5		1980	1	2
	1981	6–	5		1981	1	2
	1982	6	5		1982	1	2
	1983	6	5		1983	1	2
	1984	5+	5		1984	1	2
	1985	5	5		1985	1	2
	1986	5	6–		1986	1	2

Table 1003 (Continued)

POLITICAL AND CIVIL RIGHTS,[1] 20 LC, 1972–86

(1+ = Best Score; 7– = Worst Score)

Country	Year	Political Rights[2]	Civil Rights[3]
UNITED STATES	1972	1	1
	1973	1	1
	1974	1	1
	1975	1	1
	1976	1	1
	1977	1	1
	1978	1	1
	1979	1	1
	1980	1	1
	1981	1	1
	1982	1	1
	1983	1	1
	1984	1	1
	1985	1	1
	1986	1	1

1. This "freedom" survey, conducted annually by Freedom House, defines freedom in terms of both civil and political freedoms as these have been traditionally understood in the constitutional democratic states.

2. The score for *political rights* is determined by the degree to which a given country satisfies the following requirements: (a) that leaders are chosen in decisions made on the basis of an open voting process, (b) that significant opposition is allowed to compete in this process, (c) that there are multiple political parties and candidates not selected by the government, (d) that polling and counting of votes is conducted without coercion or fraud, (e) that a significant share of political power is exercised by elected representatives, (f) that all regions, even the most remote, are included in the political process, and (g) that the country is free of foreign or military control or influence. Countries assigned a rank of 1 most closely satisfy these requirements and those assigned a rank of 7 most seriously violate them.

3. The score for *civil rights* is determined by the degree of liberty a given country grants its news media and individual citizens, primarily as it applies to political expression. The survey looks at censorship applied to the press or radio. It also assesses the rights granted any individual to openly express ideas, to belong to an organization free of government supervision, and the individual's right to a free trial, i.e., the degree to which the judiciary is independent of administrative control. Also important is the number of political prisoners held in a country, the use of torture or brutality, and the degree to which the state security forces respect individual rights. Countries assigned the rank of 1 grant the greatest degree of civil liberties and those assigned the rank of 7 most seriously violate them.

a. Change in status since the previous year owing to reevaluation by the author. This does not imply any change in the country.

b. Change in status since the previous year owing to events in the country.

SOURCE: Freedom House — *Freedom at Issue*, Jan.-Feb., 1973–87.

Figure 10:1

APPROXIMATION OF GUATEMALAN POLITICAL VIOLENCE,
MAY 1983–DECEMBER 1984[a]

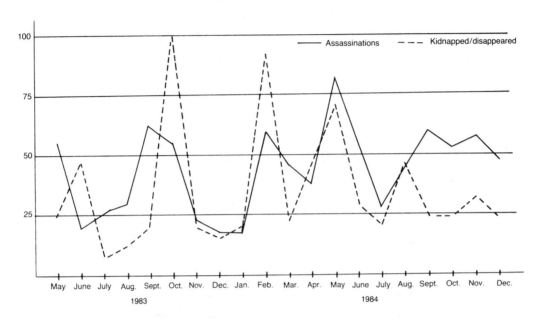

a. These cases have been selected exclusively from the local press for their probable
    political links. All cases that appeared to be common crime, or which were directly
    related to military-guerrilla encounters or guerrilla actions, were excluded. Apparent
    political motivations were determined on the basis of the victim's personal data
    (university student or professor, police officer, political leader, union activist) com-
    bined with the circumstances (abduction by "heavily armed men," signs of torture,
    machine-gun wounds, decapitation). When a kidnapped or missing person was later
    found dead in the same calendar month he or she was abducted, it was counted only
    as an assassination. Of course, there may be some cases in which a victim of a com-
    mon crime was mistakenly included, or in which a non-obvious political killing or
    abduction was mistakenly excluded.

SOURCE: *Central American Report*, Feb. 1, 1985.

Table 1004

U.N. SUPPORT FOR U.S. POLICY,
20 LC, 1985
(% Voting with U.S.)

PART I. AMERICAN NATIONS

	Country	%		Country	%
	Antigua & Barbuda	25.0	K.	GUATEMALA	25.2
A.	ARGENTINA	16.4		Guyana	13.9
	Bahamas	18.6	L.	HAITI	23.8
	Barbadoes	20.3	M.	HONDURAS	29.8
	Belize	37.8		Jamaica	22.7
B.	BOLIVIA	18.5	N.	MEXICO	14.5
C.	BRAZIL	16.0	O.	NICARAGUA	8.4
	Canada	69.8	P.	PANAMA	19.7
D.	CHILE	31.4	Q.	PARAGUAY	35.4
E.	COLOMBIA	27.9	R.	PERU	17.8
F.	COSTA RICA	29.1		St. Christopher & Nevis	50.0
G.	CUBA	6.2		St. Lucia	26.2
	Dominica	24.2		St. Vincent & Grenadines	32.7
H.	DOMINICAN REPUBLIC	25.0		Suriname	16.2
I.	ECUADOR	24.6		Trinidad & Tobago	17.9
J.	EL SALVADOR	30.2	S.	URUGUAY	18.1
	Grenada	71.7	T.	VENEZUELA	19.0

PART II. OTHER WORLD REGIONS

Region/Country	%
Europe	
Britain	86.6
Africa	
Ivory Coast	27.3
Asia	
Japan	66.3
Eastern Europe	
Poland	14.8

SOURCE: *New York Times*, July 4, 1986.

Table 1005

REVISED FITZGIBBON-JOHNSON INDEX RANKINGS: U.S. VIEW OF POLITICAL
DEMOCRACY, FIVE KEY CRITERIA,[1] 20 L, 1945-85

(Most Democratic = #1)

	Country	1945	1950	1955	1960	1965	1970	1975	1980	1985
A.	ARGENTINA	9	15[a]	15	4	7	14	5	15	4
B.	BOLIVIA	16	13	12	15	16	15	15	17	15
C.	BRAZIL	12[a]	5	4	6	10	17	16	11	12
D.	CHILE	3[a]	2	3	3	2[a]	2	18	18	19
E.	COLOMBIA	3[a]	6	9	5	5	5	3	3	3
F.	COSTA RICA	2	4	2	2	1	1	1	1	1
G.	CUBA	5	3	10	16	19	19	14	12	16
H.	DOMINICAN REP	20	20	20	20	14[a]	10	6	6	8
I.	ECUADOR	12[a]	7	6	9	12	7	10	7	7
J.	EL SALVADOR	14	14	8	13	11	8	8	14[c]	14
K.	GUATEMALA	11	11	13	12	13	9	9	13	17
L.	HAITI	19	17	14	18	20	20	20	20	20
M.	HONDURAS	17	8	11	14	14[a]	12	12	10	13
N.	MEXICO	7	9	5	7	6	6	4	4	5
O.	NICARAGUA	15	18	19	17	17	16	17	8[b]	11
P.	PANAMA	6	10	7	11	9	11	11	9[b]	10
Q.	PARAGUAY	18	19	18	19	18	18	19	19	18
R.	PERU	8	15[a]	17	10	8	13	13	5	6
S.	URUGUAY	1	1	1	1	2[a]	3	7	16	9
T.	VENEZUELA	10	12	10	8	4	4	2	2	2

1. The five criteria are:
    1. Free speech
    2. Free elections
    3. Free party organization
    4. Independent judiciary
    5. Civilian supremacy

a. Tie ranking.
b. Johnson reports that corrected raw score is 992.
c. Corrected raw score is 688.

SOURCE: Kenneth F. Johnson, "Research Perspectives on the Revised Fitzgibbon-Johnson
Index of the Image of Political Democracy in Latin America, 1945-75," in
James W. Wilkie and Kenneth Ruddle, eds. *Quantitative Latin American Studies*,
Statistical Abstract of Latin America Supplement 6 (Los Angeles: UCLA Latin
American Center Publications, 1977), pp. 87-91; table is from p. 89. Data for 1980 are
from *Latin American Research Review* 17:3 (1982), p. 198. Unpublished 1985 data
provided by Kenneth F. Johnson and Philip L. Kelly, "Political Democracy in Latin
America 1985: Partial Results of the Image-Index Survey," Emporia State University,
Emporia, Kansas, 1985.

Table 1006

ARGENTINA PRESIDENTIAL AND CONGRESSIONAL FINAL ELECTION RESULTS,
BY POLITICAL PARTY

(Oct. 30, 1983)

Party	Presidential/Vice Presidential			Congressional		
	Votes	As % of Total Votes Received	Electoral Votes	Votes	As % of Total Votes Received	Electoral Votes
Alianza Demócrata Socialista	47,736	.32	0	121,889	.82	0
Demócrata Progresista	2,183	.01	0	2,907	.02	0
Socialista Democrático	269	.00	0	293	#	0

Continued in SALA, 24-1004.

Table 1007

POPULATION VOTING IN PRESIDENTIAL ELECTIONS, 20 LC, 1853–1983

(%)

A. ARGENTINA

Year	Number of Voters (A)	Total Population (T) (B)	Percentage of Population Voting (A/B)	Person Elected President
1853[a]	106	640	1.0	Justo José de Urquiza
1859	~	1,280	1.0	Santiago Derqui
1862	133	1,400	1.0	Bartolomé Mitre
1868	127	1,688	1.0	Domingo Faustino Sarmiento
1874	224	2,154	1.2	Nicolás Avellaneda
1880	225	2,640	2.0	Julio A. Roca
1886	213	3,094	2.0	Miguel Juárez Celman
1892	215	3,858	2.0	Luis Sáenz Peña
1898	256	4,462	2.0	Julio A. Roca
1904	295	5,716	2.5	Manual Quintana
1910	265	7,092	2.8	Roque Sáenz Peña
1916	723,909	8,300	8.8	Hipólito Irigoyen
1922	823,380	9,368	8.8	Marcelo T. de Alvear
1928	1,461,671	11,282	12.9	Hipólito Irigoyen
1931	1,355,954	12,167	11.1	Agustín P. Justo
1937	1,913,154	13,490	14.2	Roberto M. Ortiz
1946	2,690,333	15,654	17.2	Juan Domingo Perón
1951	7,461,555	17,635	42.3	Juan Domingo Perón
1958	9,063,498	19,250	47.1	Arturo Frondizi
1963	9,325,997	21,688	43.0	Arturo Illía
1973	12,077,422	24,820	48.6	Juan Domingo Perón
1983	15,374,769	29,630	52.0	Raul Alfonsín

a. For 1853 through 1910 the number of electors is given. The percentage is equal to the number of people who voted for the electors.

Continued in SALA, 25-3400 through 3420.

Figure 10:2

POPULATION VOTING IN PRESIDENTIAL ELECTIONS, 20 LC, 1853–1983

(%)

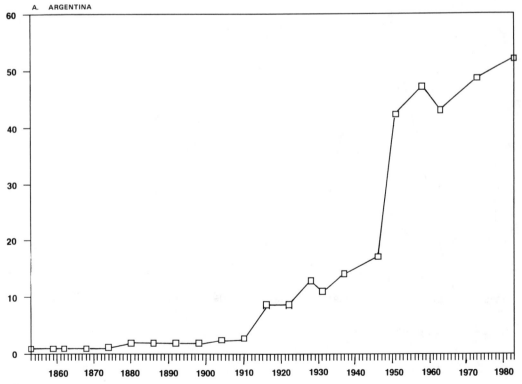

Continued in SALA, 25, figures 34:1–34:19.

Table 1008

REGISTERED VOTERS VOTING IN PRESIDENTIAL ELECTIONS, 4 L

A.   ARGENTINA

Year	Number of Voters A	Number Registered B	Percentage of Registered Who Voted[1] A/B
1916	723,909	1,189,254	60.9
1922	823,380	1,586,366	52.0
1928	1,461,671	1,807,566	80.9
1931	1,355,954	2,116,552	64.1
1937	1,913,154	2,672,750	71.6
1946	2,690,333	3,405,173	79.0
1951	7,461,555	8,623,998	86.5
1958	9,063,498	10,002,327	90.6
1963	9,325,997	11,356,240	82.1
1973	12,077,422	14,334,253	84.3
1983	15,374,769	17,890,000	85.9

1.   After 1951 null and blank votes included.

Continued in SALA, 25 — 3427 through 3430.

Figure 10:3

REGISTERED VOTERS VOTING IN PRESIDENTIAL ELECTIONS, 4 L

A.   ARGENTINA

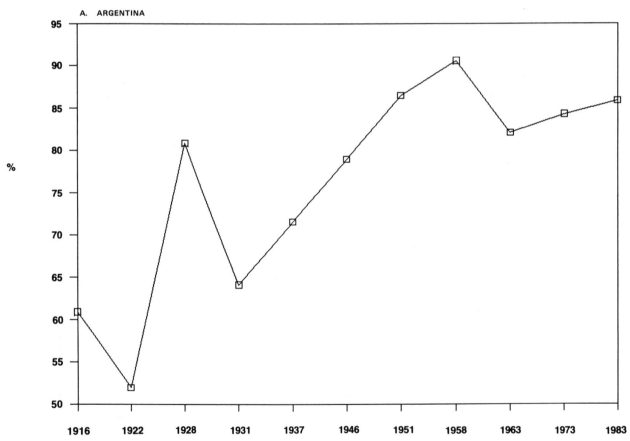

Continued in SALA, 25, figures 34:24 — 34:27.

Table 1009

IMPACT OF WOMEN'S SUFFRAGE ON VOTER PARTICIPATION, 20 LC

Country	Year of Women's Suffrage A	PC in Voter Participation After Women's Suffrage B
A. ARGENTINA	1947	+146.0
B. BOLIVIA	1952	+705.0
C. BRAZIL	1932	+509.0[a]
D. CHILE	1949	+77.6
E. COLOMBIA	1957	+108.7
F. COSTA RICA	1949	+63.1
G. CUBA	1934	+126.3
H. DOMINICAN REP.	1942	+63.1
I. ECAUDOR	1929	−50.0[a]
J. EL SALVADOR	1939	+258.0
K. GUATEMALA	1945	+31.1
L. HAITI	1950	+443.5
M. HONDURAS	1955	+46.1[a]
N. MEXICO	1953	+69.5
O. NICARAGUA	1955	+61.8
P. PANAMA	1945	+29.5[a]
Q. PARAGUAY	1961	−9.3
R. PERU	1955	+113.0
S. URUGUAY	1932	−73.9
T. VENEZUELA	1947	+53.8[a]
Latin America Average[b]		+138.6
UNITED STATES	1920	+36.4

a. Elections where zero percent of the population voted were not used; the next election in which at least 1 percent voted, was used.
b. Unweighted by population.

SOURCE: A. Elsa Chaney, *Supermadres*, p. 169.
              B. Calculated from SALA, 25-3400 through 3420.

Table 1010

LATIN AMERICA PRESIDENTIAL ELECTIONS, BY DECADE, 1840–1986

Decade	Number of Elections
1841–1850	12
1851–1860	39
1861–1870	35
1871–1880	45
1881–1890	40
1891–1900	42
1901–1910	40
1911–1920	45
1921–1930	41
1931–1940	43
1941–1950	39
1951–1960	38
1961–1970	35[a]
1971–1980	14[a]
1981–1986	21[a]

a. Brazilian elections are not included from 1964 through 1984, because the president was chosen by congress.

SOURCE: Calculated from SALA, 25-3400 through 3419.

Table 1011

POLITICAL STATUS, 19 LC, 1964–79

Country Ruled by Military	Years	Country in Which Electoral Process Remained in Tact	Country with "Rigged Elections
A. ARGENTINA	1966–1973	E. COLOMBIA	K. GUATEMALA[2]
	1976–1983	F. COSTA RICA	L. HAITI[2]
B. BOLIVIA	1964–1980	N. MEXICO	O. NICARAGUA[2]
C. BRAZIL	1964–1985	T. VENEZUELA	Q. PARAGUAY[2]
D. CHILE	1973–		
H. DOMINICAN REP.[1]	1964–1965		
I. ECUADOR	1972–1979		
J. EL SALVADOR	1973-1984		
M. HONDURAS	1972–1981		
P. PANAMA	1968–		
R. PERU	1968–1980		
S. URUGUAY	1973–1984		

1. The Dominican Republic was occupied by the United States.
2. These countries, although they may have been controlled by dictators, still held
   presidential elections. In the case of Haiti, the last presidential election was in 1961,
   when Duvalier was elected president for life. Cuba is not listed since it does not fall
   in either category.

SOURCE: Vanhanen; *The Cambridge Encyclopedia of Latin America and the Caribbean*.

Table 1012

ARGENTINA PRESIDENTIAL ELECTION RESULTS, BY POLITICAL PARTY AND PROVINCE
(OCTOBER 30, 1983)

Political Party
(% of Total Vote)

Province	Alianza Demócrata Socialista	Alianza Federal	Comunista	Demócrata Cristiano	Frente de Izquierda Popular	Intransigente	Justicialista	Movimiento al Socialismo	Movimiento de Integración y Desarrollo	Obrero	Socialista Popular	Unión Cívica Radical	Unión del Centro Democrático	Positive Votes	Null Votes	Blank Votes	Participation as % of Eligible Voters
Federal Capital	.32	.72	#	.18	.05	4.48	27.36	.40	.73	.13	.09	64.26	1.28	98.34	.62	1.05	85.78
Buenos Aires	.25	.59	#	.23	.07	3.24	42.23	.44	.84	.11	.09	51.41	.44	97.23	.38	2.39	87.69
Catamarca	**	**	#	.47	.11	.58	43.50	.09	.77	~	.13	46.73	**	95.00	.95	4.06	82.90
Córdoba	.19	**	#	.37	.08	.87	39.92	.17	.93	.05	.18	56.22	**	97.68	.33	1.99	88.35

Continued in SALA, 24-1005.

Table 1013

ARGENTINA CONGRESSIONAL ELECTION RESULTS
BY POLITICAL PARTY

(NOV. 3, 1985)

	Chamber of Deputies		
	1983	1985	
Party	Seats Won	Seats Won	Votes Cast
Unión Cívica Radical	129	130	43.5
Movimiento Nacionalista Justicialista	111	103	34.5
Partido Intransigenta	3	6	6.0
Uníon del Centro Democrática	2	3	3.0
Partido Demócrata Cristiano	1	~	~
Other	8	12	13.0
Total	254	254	100.0

SOURCE: *Keesing's Contemporary Archives: Record of World Events* (Oct. 1986), vol. 32, p. 34666.

Table 1014

BOLIVIA CONGRESSIONAL ELECTION RESULTS, BY
POLITICAL PARTY AND CANDIDATE

(June 29, 1980)

Party	Candidate	Seats Won
Unión Democrática Popular [1]	Hernán Siles Zuazo	57
Movimiento Nacionalista Revolucionario Histórico	Víctor Paz Estenssoro	44
Acción Democrática Nacionalista	Hugo Bánzer Suárez	30
Partido Socialista–Uno	Marcelo Quiroga Santa Cruz	11
Others	– –	15
Total	**	157[a]

1. Alliance with Movimiento Nacionalista Revolucionario de Izquierda, Movimiento de la Izquierda Revolucionario, and Partido.

a. Comprising 27 senators and 130 members of the Chamber of Deputies.

SOURCE: *South America, Central America and the Caribbean* (London: Europa Publications Limited 1986), p. 152.

Table 1015

BOLIVIA PRESIDENTIAL AND CONGRESSIONAL ELECTION RESULTS, BY POLITICAL PARTY AND CANDIDATE
(July 14, 1985)

Party	Candidate	As % of Total Votes Cost	Votes Received	Congressional Seats Won
Acción Democrática Nacionalista	Hugo Bánzer Suárez	28.6	493,735	51
Movimiento Nacionalista Revolucionario Histórico	Víctor Paz Estenssoro[1]	26.4	456,704	59
Movimiento de la Izquierda Revolucionaria	Jaime Paz Zamora	8.8	153,143	16
Movimiento Nacionalista Revolucionario de la Izquierda	Roberto Jordán Pando	4.8	82,418	8
Movimiento Nacionalista Revolucionario de Vanguardia	Carlos Serrate Reich	4.2	72,197	6
Portido Socialista–Uno	Ramiro Velasco	2.2	38,782	5
Frente Pueblo Unido	Antonio Araníbar Quiroga	2.2	38,124	4
Movimiento Revolucionario Tupaj Katari–Liberación	Flores Santos	1.8	31,678	2
Partido Demócrata Cristiana	Luis Ossio Sanjines	1.4	24,079	3
Falange Socialista Boliviana	David Añez Pedraza	1.2	19,985	3
	Total	81.6	1,410,845	157[a]

1. Since no candidate attained absolute majority, as required by the constitution, Victor Paz Estenssoro was finally elected president after winning a clear majority vote from the new congress.

a. Consists of 130 deputies and 27 senators.

SOURCE: *Keesing's Contemporary Archives: Record of World Events* (Oct. 1985), vol. 31, p. 33905.

Table 1016

BRAZIL CONGRESSIONAL ELECTION RESULTS, BY POLITICAL PARTY
(November 15, 1982)

Party	Seats Won	
	Federal Senate[1]	Chamber of Deputies
Partido Democrático Social	46	235
Partido do Movimiento Democrático Brasileiro	21	200
Partido Democrático Trabalhista	1	24
Partido Trabalhista Brasileiro	1	14
Partido dos Trabalhadores	—	6
Total	69	479

1. Elections for one-third of senate seats were held on Nov. 15, 1982.

SOURCE: *South America, Central America and the Caribbean* (London: Europa Publications Limited, 1986), p. 174.

Table 1017

CHILE ELECTORAL INTENTIONS IN SANTIAGO PLEBISCITE
(%, September 1980)

Response	Aug. 25	Aug. 29	Sept. 3	Sept. 5	Sept. 7	Sept. 9
Yes	50.0	45.3	51.0	52.4	58.7	58.4
No	32.1	31.4	32.5	28.4	19.5	19.4
No answer	18.9	23.3	16.5	19.2	21.8	22.2
	(483)	(468)	(433)	(487)	(491)	(448)

SOURCE: SALA, 23-3701.

Table 1018

CHILE COMPARISON OF GALLUP PREDICTIONS WITH ACTUAL
VOTE IN SANTIAGO PLEBISCITE
(%, September 1980)

Response	Gallup Forecast	Official Vote in Santiago	Difference
Yes	61.5	62.1	-.6
No	34.8	35.6	-.8
Null	3.6	2.2	+1.4

SOURCE: SALA, 23-3702.

Table 1019

COLOMBIA PRESIDENTIAL WINNING PERCENTAGES,
BY POLITICAL PARTY AND CANDIDATE
(1986)

Party	Candidate	Votes Cast[‡]	As % of Total Votes Cast
Partido Conservador	Alvaro Laureano Gómez-Hurtado	2,535,953	35.84
Partido Demócrata Cristiano	Luis Enrique Agudelo-Pino[1]	1,027	#
Partido Humanista	Juan David Pérez–Garciá	438	#
Partido Liberal	Virgilio Barco-Vargas	4,123,716	58.29
Movimiento Metapolítico	Regina Bentancourt-de-Liska	49,745	.70
Unión Patriótica	Jaime Pardo–Leal	312,494	4.42
Blank and Null Votes[2]	~	51,353	.73
Total	**	7,074,726[a]	100.00

1. Withdrew before elections.
2. Includes votes from non-registered candidates and abroad.

a. There were 13 million eligible voters.

SOURCE: Adapted from *El Espectador* (Bogotá), May 22 and 27, 1986.

Table 1020

COLOMBIA PRESIDENTS, 1930-86

Year	President	Political Orientation
1930	Enrique Olaya–Herrera	Liberal
1934	Alfonso López–Pumarejo	Liberal
1938	Eduardo Santos	Liberal
1942	Alfonso López–Pumarejo[1]	Liberal
1945	Alberto Lleras–Camargo	Liberal
1946	Mariano Ospina–Pérez	Conservative
1950	Laureano Gómez[2]	Conservative
1953	Roberto Urdaneta–Arbeláez	Conservative
1953	Gustavo Rojas–Pinilla	Military
1957	Military Junta[3]	Military
1958	Alberto Lleras Camargo	Liberal
1962	Guillermo León–Valencia	Conservative
1966	Carlos Lleras Restrepo	Liberal
1970	Misael Pastrana–Borrero	Conservative
1974	Alfonso López–Michelsen	Liberal
1978	Julio Cesar Turbay–Ayala	Liberal
1982	Belisano Betancur	Conservative
1986	Virgilio Barco–Vargas	Liberal

1. Resigned and was succeeded by Vice President, Alberto Lleras Camargo.
2. Resigned and was succeeded by Vice President, Roberto Urdaneta–Arbeláez.
3. Functioned as interim government following the overthrow of Rojas-Pínilla.

SOURCE: 1930–82 data from *Colombia Today*, 21:3 (1986); and 1986 data from *El Espectador* (Bogotá), May 27, 1986.

Table 1021

COLOMBIA PRESIDENTIAL ELECTION RESULTS,[‡] BY DEPARTMENT AND POLITICAL PARTY CANDIDATES (1986)

Department	PC[1] Alvaro Laureano Gómez Hurtado	PDC[2,7] Luis Enrique Agudelo-Pino	PH[3] Juan David Pérez-Gracía	PL[4] Virgilio Barco-Vargos	MM[5] Regina Betancourt-de-Liska	UP[6] Jaime Pardo-Leal	Total Voting Tables	Tables Tabulated	% of Tabulated Tables	Non-Registered Candidates	Blank Votes	Null Votes	Total Votes
Antioquia	321,185	890	29	441,271	9,298	32,097	5,194	5,003	99.3	205	5,826	729	811,530
Atlántico	87,066	71	14	185,362	495	9,003	2,033	2,013	99.0	3	1,603	266	283,883

Continued in SALA, 25-1014.

Table 1022

COLOMBIAN PRESIDENTIAL ELECTION RESULTS, 1978 AND 1982[a]

(T)

Regions and Departments	Conservatives		Liberals		"New Liberalism"
	1978	1982	1978	1982	1982
Total	2,357	3,155	2,504	2,749	751
Eastern Region[1]	590	703	564	582	144

Continued in SALA, 24-1009.

Table 1023

COSTA RICA PRESIDENTIAL WINNING PERCENTAGES, 1953-86[a]

Year	President	%
1953	José Figueres	64.70
1958	Mario Echandi	46.42
1962	Francisco J. Orlich	50.29
1966	José Joaquín Trejos	50.47
1970	José Figueres	54.78
1974	Daniel Oduber	43.44
1978	Rodrigo Carazo	50.51
1982	Luis Alberto Monge	58.60
1986	Oscar Arias Sánchez	52.33[a]

a. Refers to valid votes.

SOURCE: Adapted from the following: *La Nación* (San José), Feb. 9, 1982, p. 12A; and *La Nación* (San José), Feb. 13, 1986.

Table 1024

COSTA RICA COMPARATIVE PRESIDENTIAL WINNING PERCENTAGES BETWEEN MAJOR POLITICAL PARTIES, 1982 AND 1986

Province	Liberación Nacionál				Unidad Social Christiana			
	1982		1986		1982		1986	
	Valid Votes	%	Valid Votes	%	Valid Votes	%	Valid Votes	%
San José	230,958	58.3	256,781	54.4	128,623	32.5	207,615	43.8
Alajuela	102,324	59.5	112,298	53.0	61,026	35.5	97,560	45.7
Cartago	65,676	61.9	71,977	54.1	34,806	32.8	58,969	44.3
Heredia	45,976	57.0	53,687	52.8	29,288	36.3	45,972	45.2
Guanacaste	50,215	60.7	46,301	50.0	27,202	34.6	45,011	48.7
Puntarenas	50,215	58.3	51,200	48.2	28,208	32.8	52,319	49.2
Limón	25,526	53.9	27,440	42.4	16,034	33.8	34,988	54.0
Total	568,374	58.8	620,314	52.3	325,187	33.6	542,434	45.8

SOURCE: *La Nación* (San José), Feb. 2, 1986.

Table 1025

COSTA RICA PRESIDENTIAL ELECTION RESULTS, BY PROVINCE AND POLITICAL PARTY

(February 2, 1986)

Province	Registered Voters	Partido Alianza Nacional Cristiana	Partido Inde-pendiente	Partido Liberación Nacional[1]	Partido Unidad Social Cristiana[2]	Alianza Popular (Coalición)	Pueblo Unido (Coalición)	Valid Votes
San José	590,640	2,407	477	256,781	207,615	3,943	2,640	473,863
Alajuela	257,699	721	123	112,928	97,560	1,044	850	213,226
Cartago	161,467	695	140	71,977	58,969	667	538	132,986
Heredia	122,123	503	74	53,687	45,972	778	644	101,658
Guanacaste	114,457	289	117	46,301	45,011	304	440	92,462
Puntarenas	145,609	583	125	51,200	52,319	1,294	757	106,278
Limón	94,479	449	73	27,440	34,988	1,069	730	64,749
Total	1,486,474	5,647	1,129	620,314	542,434	9,099	6,599	1,185,222[a]

1. Oscar Arias Sánchez was the candidate.
2. Rafael Angel Calderón was the candidate.

a. Excludes 26,090 null votes as reported by the U.S. Embassy, Costa Rica.

SOURCE: Adapted from *La Nación* (San José), February 2, 1986.

Table 1026

COSTA RICA PRESIDENTIAL WINNING PERCENTAGES, BY POLITICAL PARTY

(February 2, 1986)

Party	Valid Votes	As % of Registered Voters[1]	As % of Total Valid Votes[2]
Partido Alianza Nacional Cristiana	5,647	.37	.48
Partido Independiente	1,129	.08	.10
Partido Liberación Nacional	620,314	41.73	52.33
Partido Unidad Social Cristiana	542,434	36.49	45.76
Alianza Popular (Coalición)	9,099	.60	.77
Pueblo Unido (Coalición)	6,599	.44	.56
Total	1,185,222	79.71[a]	100.00

1. There were 1,486,474 registered voters.
2. Excludes blank and null votes.

a. This implies an abstention rate, including blank and null ballots, of approximately 20.29%.

SOURCE: Derived from table 1018.

Table 1027

DOMINICAN REPUBLIC PRESIDENTIAL AND CONGRESSIONAL ELECTION RESULTS, BY POLITICAL PARTY AND CANDIDATE

(May 16, 1982)

Party	Candidate	Votes	As % of Total Votes	Congressional Seats Won Senate	Congressional Seats Won Chamber of Deputies
Partido Revolucionario Dominicano	Salvador Jorge Blanco	854,868	50.17	17	62
Partido Reformista	Joaquín Balaguer	669,176	39.27	10	50
Partido de la Liberación Dominicana	Juan Bosch	179,849	10.56	—	7
Partido Acción Constitucionalista	--	--	--	--	1
Total		1,703,893	100.00	27	120

SOURCE: Adapted from *South America, Central America and the Caribbean* (London: Europa Publications Limited, 1986), p. 284.

Table 1028

DOMINICAN REPUBLIC PRESIDENTIAL ELECTION RESULTS, BY POLITICAL PARTY

(May 16, 1986)

Party	Votes	As % of Valid Votes	As % of Registered Votes
Partido Reformista Social Cristiano	855,565	40.51	28.15
Partido Revolucionario Dominicano	706,588	33.46	23.25
Partido Liberación Dominicana	387,881	18.37	12.76
La Estructura	112,617	5.33	3.71

Continued in SALA, 25-1021.

Table 1029

ECUADOR PRESIDENTIAL ELECTIONS, FINAL RESULTS, BY PROVINCE AND POLITICAL PARTY

(June 1984)

Province	FRN[1] Votes	FRN[1] %	CID[2] Votes	CID[2] %	Null Votes Votes	Null Votes %	Blank Votes Votes	Blank Votes %	Total Votes	Total Voters	Total %
Azuay	47,662	31.97	87,596	58.76	10,809	7.25	2,998	2.01	149,065	191,995	77.64

Continued in SALA, 24-1010.

Table 1030

ECUADOR ABSENTEEISM IN ELECTIONS, BY PROVINCE, 1978 AND 1984

Province	1978 Registered N	1978 Participated N	1978 Absentee N	1978 Absentee %	1984 Registered[1] N	1984 Participated N	1984 Absentee N	1984 Absentee %
Carchi	43,117	36,501	6,616	15.34	63,981	47,748	16,233	25.37

Continued in SALA, 24-1011.

Table 1031

ECUADOR ELECTIONS FOR PROVINCIAL DEPUTIES, BY POLITICAL PARTY
(June 1984)

Province	PCE[1]	LRE[2]	PD[3]	CFP[4]	DP[5]	SC[6]	PCD[7]	CID[8]	FADI[9]	PRE[10]	PNR[11]	ID[12]	APRE[13]	FRA[14]	MPD[15]	Nacional Velazquista	Socialista Ecuatoriano	Valid Votes	Null Votes	Blank Votes	Total
Pichincha	14,158	44,809	70,661	10,127	20,221	71,820	6,521	5,588	27,869	11,333	3,958	108,950	210	24,166	30,576	1,611	5,133	457,521	45,700	48,963	530,184

Continued in SALA, 24-1012.

Table 1032

EL SALVADOR FIRST ROUND PROVISIONAL ELECTION RESULTS,
BY DEPARTMENT AND POLITICAL PARTY
(March 25, 1984)

Department	Party								Valid Votes	Null Votes	Factors				Total
	Arena[1]	PDC[2]	PCN[3]	Mercen[4]	PAISA[5]	PPS[6]	AD[7]	POP[8]			Abstentions	Contested Votes	Not Used	Lost Ballots	
San Salvador	101,834	205,381	44,701	3,066	4,239	6,237	19,196	1,677	386,331	29,606	3,261	1,506	363,536	1,760	791,000

Continued in SALA, 24-1013.

Table 1033

EL SALVADOR ELECTION RESULTS FOR
THE CONSTITUENT ASSEMBLY BY
POLITICAL PARTY
(March 31, 1985)[a]

Party	Seats Won
Partido Democrático Cristiano	33
Partido Alianza Republicana Nacionalista	13
Partido de Conciliación Nacional	12
Partido Acción Democrática	1
Partido Auténtico Institucional Salvadoreño	1
Total	60

a. For assembly of 1982, see SALA, 23-3403.

SOURCE: *South America, Central America and the Caribbean*
(London: Europa Publications Limited, 1986), pp. 319-320.

Table 1034

EL SALVADOR SECOND ROUND PROVISIONAL ELECTION RESULTS,
BY DEPARTMENT AND POLITICAL PARTY
(May 6, 1984)

Department	Arena[1]	PDC[2]	Valid Votes	Null Votes	Abstentions	Contested Votes	Not Used	Lost Ballots	Total
San Salvador	156,460	278,786	435,246	25,678	6,840	1,917	319,312	1,513	790,506

Continued in SALA, 24-1014.

Table 1035

GUATEMALA PRESIDENTIAL ELECTION RESULTS[1] BY
POLITICAL PARTY AND CANDIDATE
(March 7, 1982)

Candidate	Political Party	Votes Received	As % of Total Votes
Angel Aníbal Guevara	Coalition with Partido Institucional, Partido Revolucionario, and Frente de Unidad Nacional	379,051	38.9
Mario Sandoval Alarcón	Movimiento de Liberación Nacional	275,487	28.2
Alejandro Maldonado Aguirre	Coalition with Partido Democracia Guatemalteca and Partido Nacionalista Renovador	221,810	22.7
Gustavo Anzueto Vielman	Central Auténtica Nacionalista	99,047	10.2
Total	**	975,395	100.0

1. No candidate achieved the required overall majority; the final decision was made by
the National Congress, which endorsed Angel Aníbal Guevara as President on
March 13, 1982. He was then deposed by a military coup on March 23, 1982.

SOURCE: *South America, Central America and the Caribbean* (London: Europa Publications Limited, 1986), p. 340.

Table 1036

GUATEMALA CONGRESSIONAL ELECTION RESULTS, BY POLITICAL PARTY
(July 1, 1984)

Party	Seats Won
Movimiento de Liberación Nacional and Central Auténtica Nacionalista Coalition	23
Unión del Centro Nacional	21
Partido Democracia Cristiana Guatemalteca	20
Partido Revolucionario	10
Partido Nacionalista Renovador	5
Others	9
Total	88

SOURCE: *South America, Central America and the Caribbean*
(London: Europa Publications Limited, 1986), p. 340.

Table 1037

GUATEMALA PRESIDENTIAL AND CONGRESSIONAL ELECTION RESULTS, BY POLITICAL PARTY AND CANDIDATE
(November 3, 1985)

Party	Candidate	As % of Total Votes Cast[1]	Congressional Seats Won
Partido Democracia Cristiana Guatemalteca	Vinicio Cerezo[a]	38.7	51
Unión del Centro Nacional	Jorge Carpio Nicolle	20.2	22
Partido Revolucionario and Partido de Cooperación Democrática Nacional Coalition	Jorge Serrano Elias	13.8	11
Movimiento de Liberación Nacional	Mario Sandóval Alarcón	6.3	6
Partido Institucional Democrático	Mario Sandoval Alarcón	6.3	6
Central Auténtica Nacionalista	Mario David García	6.3	1
Alliance between: Partido Socialista Democrático, Movimiento 20 de Octubre, Movimiento Humanista de Integración Demócrata, and Fuerza Nueva	Mario Solórzano Martínez	3.4	2
Partido Nacionalista Renovador	Alejandro Maldonado Aguirre	3.2	1
Alliance between: Partido de Unificación Anticomunista, Frente de Unidad Nacional, and Movimiento Emergente de Concordia	Leonel Sisniega Otero	1.9	0
Total		100.0	100

1. There were 2,750,000 eligible voters and a 73% voter turnout. Blank and null votes were at 6%.

a. Since no candidate attained absolute majority, Vinicio Cerezo was finally elected president after a run-off election held on Dec. 8, 1985.

SOURCE: *Keesing's Contemporary Archives: Record of World Events* (April 1986), Vol. 32, p. 34285.

Table 1038

HONDURAS PRESIDENTIAL ELECTION RESULTS

(1981)

Department	PDCH[1]	PINU[2]	PL[3]	PN[4]	Total Valid Votes	Blank Votes	Null Votes	Total Votes
Atlántida	701	2,031	33,900	21,879	58,511	885	1,102	60,498

Continued in SALA, 23–3411.

Table 1039

HONDURAS REGISTERED POLITICAL PARTIES

(November 1985)

Party	Leader	Political Inclination
Partido Demócrata Cristiano	Efraín Díaz Arrivillaga	Moderate left
Partido de Innovación y Unidad	Miguel Andonie Fernández	Moderate
Partido Liberal	Juan de la Cruz Avelar	Moderate
Partido Nacional	Juan Alberto Melgar	Conservative right

SOURCE: Adapted from U.S. Department of State, *Resource Book, The 1985 Honduras Elections: Presidential, Congressional and Municipal*, November 1985, pp. 7–11.

Table 1040

HONDURAS CURRENT AND AMENDED CONGRESSIONAL
APPORTIONMENT, BY DEPARTMENT AND POLITICAL
PARTY, 1981–85

(N)

Department	PDCH[1]	PINU[2]	PL[3]	PN[4]	1981 Total	1985 Total
Atlántida	--	--	2	3	4	8
Colón	--	--	1	1	2	4
Comayagua	--	--	2	2	4	7
Copán	--	--	2	2	4	7
Cortés	--	1	7	3	11	20
Choluteca	--	1	3	3	7	9
El Paraíso	--	--	3	2	5	6
Francisco Morazán	1	1	7	5	14	23
Gracias a Dios	--	--	--	1	1	1
Intibucá	--	--	1	1	2	3
Islas de la Bahía	--	--	1	--	1	1
La Paz	--	--	1	1	2	3
Lempira	--	--	2	3	5	5
Octotepeque	--	--	1	1	2	2
Olancho	--	--	2	2	4	7
Santa Bárbara	--	--	3	2	5	9
Valle	--	--	2	1	3	4
Yoro	--	--	4	2	6	9
Total	1	3	44	34	82	128[5]

1. Partido Demócrata Cristiano de Honduras, led by Efraín Díaz Arrivillaga.
2. Partido de Innovación y Unidad, led by Miguel Andonie Fernández.
3. Partido Liberal, led by Juan de la Cruz Avelar.
4. Partido Nacional, led by Juan Alberto Melgar.
5. A total of 132 deputies will be elected. Four seats, in addition to the 128, will be distributed according to a complex formula to provide for fully proportional representation on a nationwide basis.

SOURCE: Adapted from U.S. Department of State, *Resource Book, The 1985 Honduras Elections: Presidential, Congressional and Municipal*, November 1985, p. 11.

Table 1041

HONDURAS PRESIDENTIAL WINNING PERCENTAGES, BY POLITICAL PARTY AND CANDIDATE

(1985)

Party	Candidate	Valid Votes	As % of Total Valid Votes
Partido Demócrata Cristiano de Honduras	Hernán Corrales Padilla	30,173	1.9
Partido de Innovación y Unidad	Enrique Aguilar Paz	23,705	1.5
Partido Liberal	Oscar Mejía Arellano	250,519	15.7
	Efraín Bu Girón	64,230	4.0
	José Azcona del Hoyo	424,358	26.5
	Carlos Roberto Reina	43,373	2.7
	~	4,114[a]	.3
Partido Nacional	Rafael Leonardo Callejas	656,882	41.1
	Fernando Larrizábal	22,163	1.4
	Juan Pablo Urrútia	20,121	1.3
	~	2,240[a]	.1
Blank and Null Votes	~	55,963	3.5
Total	**	1,597,841	100.0

a. Additional party votes.

SOURCE: U.S. Embassy, Tegucigalpa.

Table 1042

HONDURAS PRESIDENTIAL ELECTION RESULTS, BY DEPARTMENT AND POLITICAL PARTY CANDIDATES

(1985)

Department	PDCH[1] Hernán Corrales Padilla	PINU[2] Enrique Aguilar Paz	PL[3] Oscar Mejía Arellano	Efraín By Girón	José Azcona del Hoyo	Carlos Roberto Reina	PN[4] Rafael Leonardo Callejas	Fernando Lardizábal	Juan Pablo Urrutia
Atlántida	1,110	1,273	6,633	3,876	27,825	2,869	31,102	886	1,498
Colón	1,032	587	9,861	1,103	11,391	1,212	16,441	431	178
Comayagua	1,213	879	21,109	2,315	18,070	1,253	34,523	1,583	1,490
Copán	2,041	1,296	15,301	2,908	19,391	708	37,285	1,585	1,257
Cortés	4,022	4,803	22,989	4,054	90,477	9,096	96,002	1,253	1,374
Choluteca	2,764	1,536	20,137	5,042	23,032	1,519	52,067	1,878	1,641
El Paraíso	1,019	789	20,088	1,577	28,739	1,734	30,941	825	1,831
Francisco Morazán	4,099	4,454	37,986	3,765	92,152	12,373	138,212	1,771	2,283
Gracias a Dios	166	83	783	236	1,972	69	4,403	140	810
Intibucá	1,183	572	12,327	2,527	2,439	480	19,231	1,494	489
Islas de la Bahía	105	82	2,147	32	1,041	29	3,479	37	15
La Paz	608	575	16,334	475	4,295	250	14,405	256	801
Lempira	1,645	1,400	11,420	2,428	10,082	372	25,827	1,857	2,179
Octotepeque	1,579	533	6,920	1,958	6,389	319	10,910	1,589	197
Olancho	2,140	1,761	15,949	2,051	24,022	1,063	35,780	2,132	1,332
Santa Bárbara	2,619	1,475	5,737	24,711	14,791	4,788	42,599	2,338	284
Valle	1,070	484	5,708	1,325	13,911	885	21,260	945	232
Yoro	1,758	1,122	19,090	3,847	34,338	4,354	42,415	1,163	2,230
Total	30,173	23,705	250,519	64,230	424,358	43,373	656,882	22,163	20,121

1. Partido Demócrata Cristiano de Honduras, led by Efraín Díaz Arrivillaga.
2. Partido de Innovación y Unidad, led by Miguel Andonie Fernández.
3. Partido Liberal, led by Juan de la Cruz Avelar.
4. Partido Nacional, led by Juan Alberto Melgar.

SOURCE: U.S. Embassy, Tegucigalpa.

Table 1043

HONDURAS PRESIDENTIAL ELECTION RESULTS, BY DEPARTMENT AND POLITICAL PARTY

(1985)

Department	PDCH[1]	PINU[2]	PL[3]	PN[4]	Blank Votes	Null Votes	Total Valid Votes[5]	Other[6]	Total Votes[7]
Atlántida	1,110	1,273	41,499	33,595	1,394	1,279	80,150	7,526	98,579
Colón	1,032	587	23,719	17,147	921	911	44,317	~	55,818
Comayagua	1,213	879	42,747	37,709	1,571	1,343	85,675	1,989	101,116
Copán	2,041	1,296	38,502	40,237	1,555	1,836	85,467	1,982	96,667
Cortés	4,022	4,803	127,285	98,916	3,916	3,603	242,545	2,193	295,413
Choluteca	2,764	1,536	49,915	55,723	2,407	2,076	114,421	304	131,775
El Paraíso	1,019	789	52,388	33,668	1,792	1,489	91,145	1,441	112,797
Francisco Morazán	4,099	4,454	146,929	142,595	4,417	4,866	307,360	10,538	369,887
Gracias a Dios	166	83	3,187	5,485	235	219	9,375	~	11,286
Intibucá	1,183	572	17,782	21,273	909	883	42,652	942	47,477
Islas de la Bahía	105	82	3,307	3,559	79	60	7,192	~	9,270
La Paz	608	575	21,446	15,483	770	939	39,822	847	44,435
Lempira	1,645	1,400	24,424	29,968	1,182	1,331	59,955	2,399	69,238
Octotepeque	1,579	533	15,632	12,721	380	451	31,296	101	34,817
Olancho	2,140	1,761	43,263	39,363	1,565	1,722	89,813	1,396	107,348
Santa Bárbara	2,619	1,475	50,360	45,326	1,840	1,734	103,404	314	119,084
Valle	1,070	484	21,922	22,629	917	807	47,829	2,762	56,490
Yoro	1,758	1,122	62,020	45,959	2,380	2,184	115,423	~	140,260
Total	30,173	23,705	786,594	701,406	28,230	27,733	1,597,841	34,734	1,901,757

1. Partido Demócrata Cristiano de Honduras, led by Efráin Díaz Arrivillaga.
2. Partido de Innovación y Unidad, led by Miguel Andonie Fernández.
3. Partido Liberal, led by Juan de la Cruz Avelar.
4. Partido Nacional, led by Juan Alberto Melgar.
5. Includes blank and null votes.
6. Reported as excess votes.
7. Includes additional votes.

SOURCE: U.S. Embassy, Tegucigalpa.

Table 1044

MEXICO PRESIDENTIAL ELECTION RESULTS, BY PARTY AND STATE

(July 4, 1982)

State	PAN[1]	PRI[2]	PPS[3]	PARM[4]	PDM[5]	PSUM[6]	PST[7]	PRT[8]	PSD[9]	Other[10]	Total[11]	Null
Aguascalientes	31,576	137,847	1,379	770	3,112	1,879	4,809	1,306	345	38	200,023	16,967
Baja California Norte	147,092	271,899	12,264	3,510	6,298	16,456	11,047	12,403	1,149	385	533,499	50,996
Baja California Sur	13,852	64,573	996	479	537	2,336	763	3,444	124	23	90,744	3,617
Campeche	8,052	103,193	993	230	401	898	419	333	52	29	124,231	9,631
Coahuila	86,155	224,753	2,499	1,435	996	4,770	6,581	2,334	351	292	334,972	4,805
Colima	7,126	136,139	965	267	2,009	1,331	1,788	737	82	15	153,993	3,534
Chiapas	21,103	679,429	6,691	5,862	1,463	7,745	8,848	4,998	1,109	762	753,144	15,200
Chihuahua	153,709	362,027	7,184	3,062	4,729	13,139	5,683	2,811	739	67	600,770	47,620
Distrito Federal	906,753	1,796,431	71,798	33,097	86,929	284,796	72,639	195,348	17,369	2,836	3,759,299	291,303
Durango	67,159	280,606	4,620	3,584	2,732	7,619	2,453	2,080	413	13	379,331	8,052
Guanajuato	178,468	518,412	8,232	6,039	61,135	10,755	12,194	3,053	1,154	76	887,274	27,756
Guerrero	22,392	422,905	3,516	4,419	5,667	20,798	15,583	6,522	594	17	517,568	15,155
Hidalgo	50,641	487,739	8,977	2,407	2,998	8,876	10,289	4,806	537	107	595,775	18,398
Jalisco	360,192	814,470	15,354	11,863	49,243	89,842	12,208	8,694	2,301	115	1,438,001	75,519
Mexico	606,871	1,490,682	58,957	25,067	67,432	140,745	40,001	91,490	7,669	383	2,710,762	180,965
Michoacán	88,330	599,259	7,563	4,280	35,121	16,771	7,825	5,078	692	63	794,567	29,585
Morelos	33,673	249,769	3,968	2,326	4,754	8,587	6,514	15,142	644	44	337,447	12,026
Nayarit	6,883	157,242	3,184	1,135	2,013	22,577	1,106	708	160	48	205,159	10,103
Nuevo León	213,919	635,010	4,128	4,696	2,460	4,447	3,633	3,975	843	12	888,019	14,896
Oaxaca	46,185	638,965	27,896	14,549	2,296	20,908	4,467	4,948	580	64	766,915	11,057
Puebla	135,372	1,050,921	13,346	5,837	8,443	25,393	9,061	10,714	1,172	98	1,303,271	42,919
Querétaro	40,518	197,152	1,350	1,616	4,543	3,439	1,429	1,267	467	18	263,021	11,222
Quintana Roo	3,513	87,798	1,344	221	247	896	845	300	65	15	96,587	1,343
San Luis Potosí	41,171	411,796	2,020	2,035	21,249	3,909	4,139	2,391	710	49	499,790	10,321
Sinaloa	65,035	475,275	9,267	4,739	2,713	31,947	4,596	5,374	827	142	615,027	15,112
Sonora	113,166	422,712	2,686	1,250	1,688	6,759	1,215	4,759	742	152	576,464	21,335
Tabasco	11,706	309,194	5,186	960	645	2,129	2,921	1,045	207	9	339,082	5,080
Tamaulipas	60,620	463,612	5,011	45,579	6,234	8,255	3,986	3,319	961	2,695	620,648	20,376
Tlaxcala	23,890	187,790	2,001	963	10,035	3,897	836	1,028	139	35	236,372	5,758
Veracruz	70,630	1,705,902	71,740	45,103	29,185	43,783	73,689	13,995	4,565	14,217	2,116,943	44,564
Yucatán	59,275	270,002	1,352	490	389	3,022	411	536	141	19	347,499	11,862
Zacatecas	39,859	347,836	1,958	1,192	2,707	6,903	1,587	1,435	176	25	412,196	8,518
Total	3,714,886	16,061,340	363,025	239,063	430,376	825,607	333,565	414,333	47,079	23,388	23,498,393	1,045,731

1. Partido Acción National (Pablo Emilio Madero).
2. Partido Revolucionario Institucional (Miguel de la Madrid).
3. Partido Popular Socialista (Miguel de la Madrid).
4. Partido Auténtico de la Revolución Mexicana (Miguel de la Madrid).
5. Partido Demócrata Mexicano (Ignacio González Gollaz).
6. Partido Socialista Unificado de México (Arnoldo Martínez Verdugo).
7. Partido Socialista de los Trabajadores (Cándido Díaz Cenecedo).
8. Partido Revolucionario de los Trabajadores (Rosario Ibarra de la Piedra).
9. Partido Social Demócrata (Manuel Moreno Sánchez).
10. Unregistered.
11. Includes null votes.

SOURCE: Secretaría General y Presidencia del Comité Técnico y de Vigilancia del
Registro Nacional de Electores. México, D.F., August 18, 1982.

Table 1045

MEXICO RESULTS OF LOCAL ELECTIONS BY POLITICAL PARTY, 1985-86

(% of Registered Voters)

				Type of Election				
				Congress				
	Governor		Relative Majority		Proportional Representation		Local Officials	
Political Party	1985	1986	1985	1986	1985	1986	1985	1986
Registered Voters	100.0	100.0	100.0	100.0	100.0	100.0	100.0	100.0
Total Votes Cast	51.6	53.3	45.6	50.9	46.4	51.9	42.5	49.0
Valid Votes[1]	51.0	52.1	45.2	49.2	45.5	50.7	41.8	46.8
PAN	8.4	6.1	7.8	6.6	7.5	4.9	4.9	8.3
PRI	37.2	42.0	32.3	37.3	33.4	38.0	33.4	34.4
PPS	.8	.7	.5	.9	.6	1.7	.4	.4
PDM	2.5	.4	2.0	.5	1.6	.6	1.1	.4
PSUM	.4	.9	.5	1.1	.5	1.7	.5	.9
PST	1.2	1.1	1.1	1.3	1.2	2.0	.8	.8
PRT	.2	.2	.1	.3	.2	.2	.1	.3
PARM	.2	.6	.8	1.0	.5	1.3	.2	1.0
PMT	#	.1	.1	.2	#	.2	.2	.1
Not Registered	.1	~	~	~	~	~	.2	.2
Null Votes	.6	1.2	.4	1.7	.9	1.2	.7	2.2
Abstentions	48.4	46.7	54.4	49.1	53.6	48.1	57.5	51.0
Number of Elections Held	7	12	10	14	9	14	14	10

1. Party names:
   PAN (Partido Acción Nacional)
   PRI (Partido Revolucionario Institucional)
   PPS (Partido Popular Socialista)
   PDM (Partido Demócrata Mexicano)
   PSUM (Partido Socialista Unificado de México)
   PST (Partido Socialista de los Trabajadores)
   PRT (Partido Revolucionario de los Trabajadores)
   PARM (Partido Auténtico de la Revolución Mexicana)
   PMT (Partido Mexicano de los Trabajadores)

SOURCE: *El Mercado de Valores* (Mexico), no. 19, May 11, 1987.

Table 1046

MEXICO NATIONAL ELECTION RESULTS FOR THE CHAMBER OF DEPUTIES, BY POLITICAL PARTY, 1961-85

| | As % of Votes Case | | | | | | | | | Seats Won[‡] | | | |
| | | | | | | | | | | 1982 | | 1985 | |
Party	1961	1964	1967	1970	1973	1976	1979	1982	1985	First Allotment[1]	Second Allotment[2]	First Allotment[1]	Second Allotment[2]
Partido Acción Nacional	7.6	11.5	12.4	13.9	14.7	8.5	10.8	17.5	15.5	1	50	8	32
Partido Revolucionario Institucional	90.2	86.3	83.3	80.1	69.7	80.1	69.7	69.3	65.0	299	- -	290	- -
Partido Popular Socialista	1.0	1.4	2.8	1.4	3.6	3.0	2.6	1.9	2.0	- -	10	- -	11
Partido Autentico de la Revolución Mexicana	.5	.7	1.3	.8	1.9	2.5	1.8	1.4	1.7	- -	0	2	9
Partido Demócrata Mexicano	- -	- -	- -	- -	- -	- -	2.1	2.2	2.7	- -	12	- -	12
Partido Socialista Unificado de México	- -	- -	- -	- -	- -	- -	4.9	4.4	3.2	- -	17	- -	12
Partido Socialista de los Trabajadores	- -	- -	- -	- -	- -	- -	2.7	1.8	2.5	- -	11	- -	12
Partido Revolucionario de los Trabajadores	- -	- -	- -	- -	- -	- -	- -	1.3	1.3	- -	0	- -	6
Partido Mexicano de los Trabajadores	- -	- -	- -	- -	- -	- -	- -	- -	1.5	- -	0	- -	6
Null	- -	- -	- -	3.9	10.0	5.7	5.9	#	4.6	**	**	**	**
Abstention	31.7	33.4	37.7	35.8	39.7	38.0	50.7	34.3	49.5	**	**	**	**
Total										300	100	300	100

1. Based on the percentage of votes case.
2. Based on winning a minimum of 1.5% of the vote nationwide. Allows opposing parties to have proportional representation.

SOURCE: Adapted from *LASA Forum* (Latin American Studies Association), Fall, 1985, tables 1 and 3.

Table 1047

NICARAGUA ELECTION RESULTS
(1984)

Party	Presidential Votes	% of Valid Votes Cast	Seats Won in Assembly
FSLN[1]	735,967	67.0***	61
PCD[2]	154,327	14.0	14
PLI[3]	105,560	9.6	9
PPSC[4]	61,199	5.6	6
PCdeN[5]	16,034	1.5	2
PSN[6]	14,494	1.3	2
MAP–ML[7]	11,352	1.0	2
Null	71,209	- -	- -
Total	1,170,142	100.0	96

1. Frente Sandinista de Liberación Nacional.
2. Partido Conservador Demócrata de Nicaragua.
3. Partido Liberal Independiente.
4. Partico Popular Social Cristiano.
5. Partido Comunista de Nicaragua.
6. Partido Socialista Nicaragüense.
7. Movimiento de Acción Popular Marxista Leninista.

SOURCE: *LASA Forum* (Latin American Studies Association), Winter, 1985, p. 24.

Table 1048

PANAMA PRESIDENTIAL ELECTION RESULTS,
BY POLITICAL PARTY
(May 20, 1984)

Party	Votes
Unión Nacional Democrática[1]	266,533
Alianza de Oposición[2]	299,035[a]
Partido del Pueblo	4,598
Acción Popular	13,782
Partido Nacionalista Popular	15,976
Partido Socialista de los Trabajadores	2,085
Partido Revolucionario de los Trabajadores	3,969

1. Formed by the Partido Liberal (28,568 votes), Partido Revolucionario Democrático (175,722 votes), Frampo (5,280 votes), Partido Laborista (45,384 votes), and Partido Panameñista (11,579 votes), led by Nicolás Ardito Barletta.
2. Formed by Partido Demócrata Cristiano (46,963 votes), Molinena (30,737 votes), and Partido Panameñista Auténtico (221,335 votes), led by Arnulfo Arias.

a. The military did not allow Arias to take office; Barletta assumed the office.

SOURCE: Information provided by the U.S. Embassy, Panama.

Table 1049

PARAGUAY PRESIDENTIAL AND CONGRESSIONAL ELECTION RESULTS, BY
POLITICAL PARTY AND CANDIDATE

(February 6, 1983)

Party	Candidate	Votes	% As of Total Votes	Congressional Seats Won	
				Senate	Chamber of Deputies
Partido Colorado	Alfredo Stroessner	919,533	90.0***	20	40
Partido Liberal Radical	Enzo Doldán	58,076	5.7	6	13
Partido Liberal	Hugo Fulvio Celaudro	32,935	3.2	4	7
Null Votes	**	11,053	1.1	**	**
Total	**	1,021,597	100.0	30	60

SOURCE: Adapted from *South America, Central America and the Caribbean* (London:
Europa Publications Limited, 1986), p. 484.

Table 1050

PERU PRESIDENTIAL AND CONGRESSIONAL ELECTION RESULTS, BY
POLITICAL PARTY AND CANDIDATE

(April 14, 1985)

Party	Candidate	Votes	% As of Total Votes	Congressional Seats Won	
				Senate	Chamber of Deputies[1]
Alianza Popular Revolucionaria Americana	Alan García Pérez	3,457,030	45.7	32	107
Izquierda Unida	Alfonso Barrantes Lingán	1,606,914	21.3	15	48
Convergencia Democrática[2]	Luis Bedoya Reyes	773,705	10.2	7	12
Acción Popular	Javier Alva Orlandini	472,627	6.3	5	10
Izquierda Nacionalista	--	--	--	1	1
Others[2]	--	1,246,906[a]	16.5	--	2
Total	**	7,557,182	100.0	60	180

1. Elections were held on May 18, 1980.
2. An alliance between the Partido Popular Cristiano and Movimiento Bases Hayistas.
3. Includes Independents.

a. Includes invalid votes.

SOURCE: Adapted from *South America, Central America and the Caribbean* (London:
Europa Publications Limited, 1986), pp. 501–502.

Table 1051

PERU PRESIDENTIAL ELECTION RESULTS, BY PARTY
(1985)

Party[1]	Number of Votes	Party[1]	Number of Votes
APRA	3,457,030	FDUN	54,560
IU	1,606,914	PAN	26,757
AP	472,627	PST	15,607
CODE	773,705	7 of June Movement	10,020
IN	91,986		
		Total	7,557,182

1. Party names and presidential candidates:
   APRA (Alianza Popular Revolucionaria de América), Alan García Pérez
   IU (Alianza Izquierda Unida), Alfonso Barrantes Lingan
   AP (Acción Popular), Javier Alva Orlandini
   CODE (Convergencia Democrática), Luis Bedoya Reyes
   IN (Izquierda Nacionalista), Roger Cáceres Velásquez
   FDUN (Frente Democrática para la Unión Nacional), Francisco Morales Bermúdez Cerruti
   PAN (Partido Adelantamiento Nacional), Miguel Campos Arredondo
   PST (Partido Socialista Trabajador), Ricardo Napuri Schapiro
   7 Junio (Movimiento Cívica Nacional del 7 de Junio), Peter Uculmana Suárez

SOURCE: *Diario de la República* (Lima), June 1985.

Table 1052

PERU PRESIDENTIAL ELECTION RESULTS, BY DEPARTMENT AND POLITICAL PARTY
(1985)

Department	Party[1] (%)					Null Votes	Blank Votes (%)	Abstentions
	APRA	IU	AP	CODE	Other			
Amazonas	57.14	16.62	18.67	5.57	2.00	10.64	8.44	9.28
Ancash	64.00	22.58	6.92	4.77	1.72	11.69	11.28	8.65
Apurimac	50.19	33.77	6.95	4.46	4.63	17.73	17.82	17.90
Arequipa	33.23	38.49	6.57	17.37	4.34	5.50	5.40	7.57
Ayacucho	61.84	24.19	5.13	3.78	5.06	15.38	14.62	1.04
Cajamarca	61.80	17.69	16.31	2.75	1.44	11.23	10.96	12.51
Cuzco	44.07	36.55	6.38	5.59	7.41	11.35	12.29	12.85
Huancavelica	41.28	43.14	5.80	5.95	3.83	16.98	18.85	21.69
Huanuco	60.06	23.91	5.00	8.15	2.88	10.65	15.98	14.49
Ica	55.65	23.30	7.67	11.35	2.03	6.09	5.26	5.06
Junín	43.41	39.86	5.53	7.98	3.22	7.35	9.55	9.81
La Libertad	77.77	10.95	6.11	4.05	1.12	6.78	5.15	6.46
Lambayeque	64.30	20.02	7.25	7.30	1.13	6.87	3.64	7.70
Lima	51.22	23.61	4.84	18.35	1.98	4.21	2.65	7.83
Loreto	48.09	17.12	26.35	6.70	1.74	7.02	5.42	12.83
Madre de Dios	45.83	30.18	14.51	4.52	4.96	6.90	7.76	16.61
Moquegua	46.40	30.40	7.84	11.28	4.08	5.62	4.48	7.41
Pasco	52.80	30.64	8.46	5.41	2.69	8.21	8.24	13.06
Piura	55.87	25.40	10.26	6.93	1.55	.35	.82	21.91
Puno	40.53	30.31	8.49	3.41	17.26	13.00	11.50	9.01
San Martín	56.28	14.45	24.24	3.68	1.36	6.07	5.43	14.52
Tacna	32.95	32.98	6.50	17.86	9.71	5.40	4.19	6.27
Tumbes	49.80	22.88	16.53	9.01	1.77	6.73	4.87	4.39
Ucayali	64.44	15.81	10.44	6.97	2.34	6.11	6.90	14.05
Callao	60.89	18.01	4.22	15.08	1.80	4.09	2.10	5.95
Total Average	45.74	21.26	6.25	10.23	3.68	8.5	6.5	8.84

1. For code, see table 1044.

SOURCE: *Diario de la República* (Lima), June 1985.

Table 1053

PERU LEGISLATIVE SEATS WON, BY PARTY[1]

PART I. SENATE

Party	Number of Seats	Party	Number of Seats
APRA	32	CODE	6
IU	18	AP	4
		Total	60

PART II. CHAMBER OF DEPUTIES

	Party (Number of Seats)				
Department	APRA	IU	CODE	AP	Ind.
Amazonas	3				
Ancash	7	1			
Apurimac	2	1			
Arequipa	3	3	1	1	1
Ayacucho	2	2			
Cajamarca	7	2		1	
Callao	5	1	1		
Cuzco	4	4			
Huancavelica	1	2			
Huanuco	3	1			
Ica	4	1	1		
Junín	4	4	1	1	
La Libertad	10	1			
Lambayeque	6	2			
Lima (Metro)	21	10	7	2	
Lima (Provincial)	5	2	1	1	
Loreto	3	1		1	
Madre de Dios					1
Moquegua		1			
Pasco	1	1			
Piura	7	3	1		
Puno	3	3	1	1	
San Martín	2	1			
Tacna	1	1			
Tumbes	1				
Ucayali	2				

1. For political party names, see table 1051, note.

SOURCE: U.S. Embassy, Lima (May 1987).

Table 1054

URUGUAY PRESIDENTIAL AND CONGRESSIONAL ELECTION RESULTS, BY POLITICAL PARTY AND CANDIDATE
(November 25, 1984)

Party	Candidate	Votes	% As of Total Votes	Congressional Seats Won	
				Senate	Chamber of Deputies
Partido Colorado	Julio María Sornguinetti	744,999	38.63	13	41
Partido Nacional	Alberto Sáenz de Zumarán	634,166	32.88	11	35
Frente Amplio	Juan José Crottogini	393,949	20.43	6	21
Unión Cívica	--	--	--	--	2
Others	--	~	8.06	--	--
Total		1,773,114	100.00	30	99

SOURCE: Adapted from *South America, Central America and the Caribbean* (London: Europa Publications Limited, 1986), p. 553.

Table 1055

VENEZUELAN PRESIDENTIAL ELECTION RESULTS,
1947–83

Year	Candidate	Votes	%
1947	Rómulo Gallegos	871,752	74.34
	Rafael Caldera	262,204	22.36
	Gustavo Machado	38,587	3.29
	Total	1,172,543	
1958	Rómulo Betancourt	1,284,092	49.18
	Wolfgang Larrazábal	903,479	34.60
	Rafael Caldera	423,262	16.21
	Total	2,610,833	
1963	Raúl Leoni	957,574	32.84
	Rafael Caldera	589,177	20.21
	Jóvito Villalba	510,975	17.50
	Arturo Uslar Pietri	469,363	16.08
	Wolfgang Larrazábal	275,325	9.43
	Raúl Ramos Giménez	66,880	2.29
	Germán Borregeles	9,292	.31
	Total	2,878,586	
1968	Rafael Caldera	1,083,712	29.13
	Gonzalo Barrios	1,050,806	28.24
	Miguel Angel Burelli	826,758	22.22
	Luis Beltrán Prieto	719,461	19.34
	Alejandro Hernández	27,336	.73
	Germán Borregales	12,587	.34
	Total	3,720,660	
1973	Carlos Andrés Pérez	2,130,743	48.70
	Lorenzo Fernández	1,605,628	36.70
	Jesús A. Paz Galarraga	221,827	5.07
	José Vicente Rangel	186,255	4.26
	Jóvito Villalba	134,478	3.07
	Miguel Angel Burelli	33,977	.77
	Pedro Tinoco	29,399	.66
	Martín Garcia Villasmil	11,965	.27
	Germán Borregales	9,331	.21
	Pedro Segnini La Cruz	6,176	.14
	Raimundo Verde Rojas	3,754	.08
	Alberto Solano	1,736	.03
	Total	4,375,269	
1978	Luis Herrera Campíns	2,469,042	46.63
	Luis Piñerua Ordaz	2,295,052	43.34
	José Vicente Rangel	272,595	5.15
	Diego Arria	90,379	1.71
	Luis Alberto Prieto	58,723	1.11
	Américo Martin	51,972	.98
	Héctor Mújica	28,835	.54
	Leonardo Montiel Ortega	13,754	.26
	Alejandro Gómez Silva	8,583	.16
	Pablo Salas Castillo	5,990	.11
	Total	5,294,925	
1983	Jaime Lusinchi	3,733,220	57.17
	Rafael Caldera Rodríguez	2,271,269	34.78
	Teodoro Petkoff	274,197	4.19
	José Vicente Rangel	219,368	3.35
	Jorge Olavarria	31,099	.47
	Total	6,529,153[a]	

a. There were eight other candidates.

SOURCE: Armando Veloz Mancera, *Manual Electoral: 1946, 1947, 1952, 1957, 1958,*
1963, 1968, 1973, 1978, 2nd ed.. [Caracas: COPEI[?] , 1978] , pp. 69, 89; *El Nacional*
(Caracas), Dec. 11, 1979; and *South America, Central America and the Caribbean*
(London: Europa Publications Limited, 1986), p. 572.

Table 1056

VENEZUELA CONGRESSIONAL ELECTION RESULTS, BY POLITICAL PARTY

(December 4, 1983)

	Seats Won	
Party	Senate	Chamber of Deputies
Acción Democrática	27	109
Partido Social-Cristiano	16	60
Movimiento al Socialismo	2	10
Unión Republicana Democrática	2	8
Opinión Nacional	--	3
Movimiento de Izquierda Revolucionaria	--	2
Partido Comunista de Venezuela	--	2
Movimiento de Integración Nacional	--	1
Nueva Alternativa	--	1
Total	47	196

SOURCE: Adapted from *South America, Central America and the Caribbean* (London: Europa Publications Limited, 1986), pp. 572-573.

CHAPTER 11

RELIGION

Table 1100

CATHOLIC CHURCH HIERARCHY AND INSTITUTIONS, 20 L, 1981-84[a]

Country	Year	Cardinals	Archbishops	Bishops	Priests	Seminarians	Brothers	Sisters	Missionary Personnel[1]	Pontifical Universities	Catholic % of Total Population
A. ARGENTINA	1981	3	10	66	5,450	1,373	1,179	12,446	~	1	92.1
	1982	3	10	65	5,482	1,655	1,188	12,552	~	1	92.8
	1984	3	14	69	5,496	1,940	1,159	12,709	~	1	92.8
B. BOLIVIA	1981	1	4	19	929	167	233	1,682	236	~	93.7
	1982	1	5	17	872	165	232	1,680	229	~	94.0
	1984	1	7	20	828	176	200	1,732	217	~	94.6
C. BRAZIL	1981	7	37	239	13,169	4,283	2,701	37,024	457	4	90.1
	1982	6	35	237	13,443	4,606	2,638	36,983	454	4	90.1
	1984	6	47	305	~	5,661	2,339	36,772	456	5	90.1
D. CHILE	1981	1	4	24	2,020	663	467	5,088	175	2	85.5
	1982	1	3	24	2,046	895	445	5,091	178	2	85.5
	1984	1	4	29	2,163	999	446	4,994	173	2	85.0
E. COLOMBIA	1981	1	11	49	5,254	1,857	1,025	17,654	~	2	95.5
	1982	2	12	49	5,196	2,174	939	18,304	~	2	95.5
	1984	2	15	57	5,355	2,443	889	18,171	~	2	94.8
F. COSTA RICA	1981	0	1	5	434	189	31	867	~	~	93.5
	1982	0	1	5	452	226	29	1,001	~	~	92.7
	1984	0	2	5	461	294	48	898	~	~	92.3
G. CUBA	1981	0	2	5	200	50	22	214	~	1	41.2
	1982	0	2	5	221	47	20	218	~	1	41.2
	1984	0	2	6	205	47	25	240	~	1	41.0
H. DOMINICAN REP.	1981	1	2	8	505	286	90	1,496	~	~	94.8
	1982	1	2	8	550	283	82	1,320	~	~	94.8
	1984	1	1	9	484	263	84	1,322	~	~	93.7
I. ECUADOR	1981	1	3	19	1,513	185	367	4,151	~	1	90.2
	1982	1	3	18	1,524	180	367	4,133	~	1	91.0
	1984	1	3	24	1,537	293	329	4,112	~	1	92.0
J. EL SALVADOR	1981	0	0	5	361	105	88	836	~	~	90.4
	1982	0	1	6	347	110	76	852	~	~	90.9
	1984	0	1	6	391	129	60	890	~	~	91.7
K. GUATEMALA	1981	1	0	14	699	244	136	1,191	179	1	83.6
	1982	0	0	13	652	251	124	1,181	169	1	83.3
	1984	0	0	15	655	310	127	1,094	159	1	84.0
L. HAITI	1981	0	1	6	405	139	239	900	43	~	83.4
	1982	0	1	6	420	149	218	917	45	~	86.5
	1984	0	1	6	427	165	205	905	42	~	86.0
M. HONDURAS	1981	0	1	6	236	26	22	359	~	~	95.8
	1982	0	1	7	249	29	16	341	~	~	96.0
	1984	0	1	7	240	46	12	308	~	~	96.0
N. MEXICO	1981	3	10	74	10,087	2,947	1,127	25,598	215	~	92.8
	1982	3	10	74	10,235	3,385	1,155	25,468	212	~	96.4
	1984	3	10	75	10,110	4,217	1,423	24,207	211	~	95.0
O. NICARAGUA	1981	0	1	7	340	49	100	692	~	~	91.6
	1982	0	1	7	341	52	95	701	~	~	90.7
	1984	1[b]	0	9	327	46	61	651	~	~	86.8
P. PANAMA	1981	0	1	6	290	52	46	457	~	1	88.8
	1982	0	1	6	302	105	39	490	~	1	89.0
	1984	0	1	6	280	130	39	454	~	1	88.1
Q. PARAGUAY	1981	0	1	15	543	151	106	932	~	1	91.2
	1982	0	1	14	554	172	96	977	~	1	91.4
	1984	0	1	15	536	249	103	997	~	1	91.9
R. PERU	1981	1	6	42	2,233	693	443	4,732	438	1	92.1
	1982	1	5	44	2,198	787	427	4,944	429	1	92.4
	1984	1	6	44	2,258	895	461	4,910	459	1	92.4
S. URUGUAY	1981	0	1	10	587	67	149	1,621	~	~	78.6
	1982	0	1	11	586	89	148	1,595	~	~	78.6
	1984	0	1	11	552	124	148	1,641	~	~	79.0
T. VENEZUELA	1981	1	6	29	1,995	371	326	4,345	~	1	92.2
	1982	2	5	31	2,022	383	229	4,270	~	1	92.4
	1984	2	4	33	1,975	496	234	3,862	~	1	91.0

1. Field distribution.

a. The source supplies 1984 data that are identical to those for 1983. For years 1956–80, see SALA, 23-1100.

SOURCE: *Catholic Almanac*, 1982–87.

Table 1101

INHABITANTS PER CATHOLIC PRIEST, 20 L, 1912–84[a]

(T)

Country	1912	1945	1950	1955	1960	1966	1970	1975	1980	1981	1982	1984
A. ARGENTINA	4.5	5.1	4.3	4.3	4.3	4.3	4.2	5.0	5.5	5.2	5.3	5.4
B. BOLIVIA	2.8	5.8	6.1	5.1	4.9	4.8	4.3	6.9	6.8	6.6	6.9	7.3
C. BRAZIL	5.7	6.8	6.9	6.8	6.4	7.1	7.8	8.6	8.5	9.2	9.4	9.7
D. CHILE	2.1	3.2	3.3	3.5	3.1	3.6	3.6	4.7	5.7	5.5	5.6	5.4
E. COLOMBIA	3.8	3.8	3.7	3.7	3.6	3.3	3.6	5.0	5.4	5.1	5.2	5.1
F. COSTA RICA	2.5	4.7	4.8	4.1	4.6	4.2	3.7	5.4	5.7	5.0	5.1	5.0
G. CUBA	6.1	9.5	10.8	8.8	9.4	34.4	39.8	48.4	50.1	43.9	49.7	48.3
H. DOMINICAN REP.	10.0	17.3	13.5	10.5	11.0	9.7	9.0	10.7	11.4	10.1	11.8	12.3
I. ECUADOR	2.2	3.1	3.2	3.3	3.3	3.4	4.2	5.3	6.2	5.5	5.6	5.8
J. EL SALVADOR	7.0	8.7	8.7	9.1	9.2	8.4	9.0	10.2	13.8	14.0	14.4	13.4
K. GUATEMALA	9.4	20.7	21.2	13.5	12.3	9.5	10.2	9.3	10.8	11.5	11.8	11.4
L. HAITI	10.5	12.5	9.3	8.4	7.8	10.7	10.5	15.0	13.1	12.1	12.5	11.9
M. HONDURAS	5.0	12.3	11.9	13.0	11.5	12.0	10.6	14.9	9.7	15.3	15.9	17.0
N. MEXICO	2.6	5.3	5.8	5.3	5.3	5.8	5.7	6.4	6.9	6.9	7.1	7.4
O. NICARAGUA	~	~	~	~	~	~	6.3	7.2	8.5	8.4	9.5	9.4
P. PANAMA	6.4	7.8	6.7	6.2	6.2	6.0	5.6	6.0	6.5	6.4	6.8	7.5
Q. PARAGUAY	7.2	6.1	6.3	5.7	4.9	4.5	6.6	5.7	6.2	5.9	6.1	6.5
R. PERU	3.6	5.8	6.0	5.9	5.7	5.3	5.9	6.8	7.8	8.1	8.3	8.3
S. URUGUAY	4.8	3.6	3.7	4.3	4.1	4.2	4.1	5.0	5.2	5.0	5.0	5.4
T. VENEZUELA	4.4	6.4	6.4	5.3	5.2	5.1	5.5	5.7	7.0	7.7	7.9	8.3

a. The source supplies 1984 data that are identical to those of 1983.

SOURCE: Data 1912–60 from Yvan Labelle and Adriana Estrada (Comp.), *Latin America in Maps, Charts, Tables; No. 2: Socio-Religious Data (Catholicism)* (Mexico, D.F.: Center of Intercultural Formation, 1964); data for 1966 from *Atlas Hier-archicus,* 1968; and data for 1970–84 calculated from number of priests in *Catholic Almanac,* 1973–87 and SALA, 25–601 through 621.

Table 1102

JEHOVAH'S WITNESSES PUBLISHERS AND MEMBERS, 20 LC

(1986)[a]

	Country	Publishers[1] (N)	Population per Publisher	Persons Baptized (N)	Congregations (N)	Memorial Attendance (N)
A.	ARGENTINA	59,348	505	5,587	877	149,905
B.	BOLIVIA	4,467	1,455	642	86	21,674
C.	BRAZIL	196,948	748	19,878	3,056	533,400
D.	CHILE	27,585	445	3,052	316	90,290
E.	COLOMBIA	27,587	1,010	3,831	365	121,358
F.	COSTA RICA	9,433	273	641	178	25,990
G.	CUBA	~	~	~	~	~
H.	DOMINICAN REP.	9,307	607	718	143	35,374
I.	ECUADOR	10,013	909	1,011	147	49,967
J.	EL SALVADOR	14,546	361	1,363	281	51,151
K.	GUATEMALA	8,401	923	811	130	29,720
L.	HAITI	4,220	1,422	699	79	22,530
M.	HONDURAS	4,161	1,054	370	73	20,080
N.	MEXICO	186,291	428	22,054	5,878	838,467
O.	NICARAGUA	~	~	~	~	~
P.	PANAMA	4,480	497	384	96	17,466
Q.	PARAGUAY	2,251	1,496	157	35	5,696
R.	PERU	21,471	931	2,580	432	95,062
S.	URUGUAY	5,596	522	654	92	16,828
T.	VENEZUELA	31,691	584	4,008	307	128,627
	UNITED STATES	710,344	334	41,697	8,336	1,691,297

1. Local printers or distributors who are Jehovah's Witnesses.

a. Average for year.

SOURCE: *Yearbook of Jehovah's Witnesses*, 1987.

Table 1103

ESTIMATED JEWISH POPULATION,[1] 20 LC, 1965–84

(N)

	Country	1965	1970	1975	1978	1979	1980	1982	1984
A.	ARGENTINA[2]	450,000	500,000	300,000	300,000	300,000	242,000	233,000	228,000
B.	BOLIVIA	4,000	2,000	2,000	2,000	750	1,000	1,000	600
C.	BRAZIL	130,000	150,000	165,000	150,000[b]	150,000[c]	110,000	100,000	100,000
D.	CHILE	30,000	35,000	27,000	28,000	30,000[c]	25,000	20,000	17,000
E.	COLOMBIA	10,000	10,000	12,000[d]	14,000	12,000	7,000	7,000	7,000
F.	COSTA RICA	1,500	1,500	1,500	2,500[b]	2,500	2,500	2,200	2,500
G.	CUBA	2,400	1,700	1,500	1,500	1,500	1,000	700	700
H.	DOMINICAN REP.	400	350	200[d]	250	200	200	100	100
I.	ECUADOR	2,000	2,000	1,000	1,000	1,000	1,000	1,000	1,000
J.	EL SALVADOR	300	300	310[d]	350[b]	350	350	~	~
K.	GUATEMALA	1,200	1,900	1,900	2,000	2,000	1,100	900	800
L.	HAITI	150	150	150	150	150	200	100	100
M.	HONDURAS	150	150	200[d]	200	200[c]	~	~	~
N.	MEXICO	30,000	35,000[a]	37,500[d]	37,500	37,500	35,000	35,000	35,000
O.	NICARAGUA	200	200	200	200	200	~	~	~
P.	PANAMA	2,000	2,000	2,000	2,000	2,000	2,000	3,500	3,800
Q.	PARAGUAY	1,200	1,200	1,200	1,200	1,200	700	700	900
R.	PERU	4,000	5,300	6,000	5,200[b]	5,200	5,000	5,000	5,000
S.	URUGUAY	50,000	50,000	50,000	50,000	50,000[c]	40,000	30,000	27,000
T.	VENEZUELA	85,000	12,000	15,000	17,000	15,000	17,000	20,000	20,000
	UNITED STATES	5,720,000	5,870,000	5,840,000	5,860,900	5,920,890	5,690,000	5,705,000	5,705,000

1. Prepared by AJY staff from questionnaires sent to local Jewish community leaders.
2. Decline after 1972 reflects revision of estimate rather than mass exodus.

a. 49,181 according to 1970 Mexican census.
b. Reply to 1977 inquiry.
c. Reply to 1980 inquiry.
d. Reply to 1974 inquiry.

SOURCE: *American Jewish Yearbook*, 1966, 1971, 1977, 1978, 1980, 1981, 1983 and 1984.

Table 1104

WORLD CHRISTIAN ENCYCLOPEDIA (WCE) SCHEME[1] FOR CATEGORIZING RELIGIOUS (INCLUDING PROTESTANT) AND NON-RELIGIOUS PERSONS, 1900–80

(Guide to table 1105)

Category[2] (A + G = 100.0%)	Definition
A. Christians	Total of all Christian adherents of all kinds (professing and crypto-Christians, which is by definition equal to nominal plus affiliated).
B. Professing (C + D)	Those publicly professing (declaring, stating, confessing, self-identifying) their preference or adherence in a government census or public opinion poll, hence known to the state or society or the public.
(Crypto-Christians)	Secret believers in Christ not professing publicly nor enumerated or known in government census or public opinion poll, hence known to the state or the public or society (but usually affiliated and known to churches), of the following seven varieties: (1) unorganized individuals in legal churches, (2) political prisoners or exiles, (3) organized believers in unregistered denominations or congregations, (4) members of deliberately clandestine illegal underground churches, (5) members of anti-state minority churches or sects, (6) organized believers in Christ rejecting the label Christian (anti-church believers), and (7) isolated radio or radiophonic or correspondence-course believers in small groups or cells in non-Christian or anti-Christian areas.

Continued in SALA, 25-1104.

Table 1105

RELIGIOUS (INCLUDING PROTESTANT) AND NON-RELIGIOUS PERSONS, 20 LC, 1900–80

(A + G = 100.0%)

A. ARGENTINA	1900		1970		AA–GR	1980	
Category	N	%	N	%	1970-80	N	%
A. Christians	4,126,500	98.3	22,757,300	95.8	1.28	25,871,100	95.6
B. Professing (C + D)	4,126,500	98.3	22,757,300	95.8	1.28	25,871,100	95.6
C. Roman Catholics	4,092,100	97.4	21,962,300	92.5	1.21	24,802,600	91.6
Christo-pagans	50,000	(1.2)	200,000	(.8)	(1.31)	228,000	(.8)
D. { Protestants	29,000	.7	500,000	2.1	3.03	676,600	2.5
Argentinian indigenous	0	.0	120,000	.5	4.56	189,500	.7
Orthodox	3,000	.1	100,000	.4	1.31	114,000	.4
Marginal Protestants	1,000	.0	45,000	.2	1.84	54,000	.2
Catholics (non-Roman)	0	.0	20,000	.1	1.40	23,000	.1
Anglicans	1,000	.0	10,000	.0	1.31	11,400	.0
E. Nominal	21,000	.5	337,000	1.4	2.46	430,940	1.6
F. Affiliated (B − E) = (1 to 8)	4,105,000	97.8	22,419,000	94.4	1.26	25,440,160	94.0
1. Doubly-affiliated	−72,000	−1.7	−975,000	−4.1	2.86	−1,291,380	−4.8
2. Roman Catholics	4,132,000	98.4	22,301,530	93.9	1.26	25,304,840	93.5
3. Protestants	40,000	1.0	593,000	2.5	2.80	784,900	2.9
4. Argentinian Indigenous	0	.0	251,400	.9	3.60	351,800	1.3
5. Orthodox	3,000	.1	122,000	.5	1.23	138,000	.5
6. Marginal Protestants	1,000	.0	63,774	.3	2.25	80,000	.4
7. Catholics (non-Roman)	0	.0	50,000	.2	1.32	57,000	.2
8. Anglicans	1,000	.0	13,200	.1	1.28	15,000	.1
G. { Jews	6,500	.2	475,000	2.0	1.28	540,000	2.0
Non-religious	5,000	.1	210,000	.9	3.20	290,000	1.1
Atheists	5,000	.1	140,000	.6	1.94	170,000	.6
Muslims	4,000	.1	50,000	.2	1.31	57,000	.2
Spiritists[1]	1,000	.0	50,000	.2	1.48	58,000	.2
Tribal religionists[2]	50,000	1.2	30,000	.1	−4.00	20,000	.1
Buddhists	1,000	.0	10,000	.0	.95	11,000	.0
Baha'is	0	.0	5,700	.0	1.90	6,900	.0
Other religionists	1,000	.0	20,000	.1	6.67	40,000	.1
Country Population	4,200,000	100.0	23,748,000	100.0	1.31	27,064,000	100.0

1. Spiritists: Organized under the Confederación Espiritista Argentina. A number of
lapsed Catholics and Protestants become spiritists each year, and by 1976 spiritism
was recognized as a growing phenomenon.
2. Tribal Religionists: Of the 170,000 tribal lowland Amerindians (or Aborigines) in
1970, mostly along the Paraguayan border, a proportion are still shamanists or
animists, including a majority of the 20,000 Chiriguano (Guarani) and the other 8
Aboriginal groups: Chane (Guana), Chorote, Chulupi, Mataco (population 12,000),
Mbya, Mocovi, Pilaca and some Toba (17,060). Guarani shamans in particular occupy
a respected healing role in society, and Guarani mysticism remains the main agent for
social cohesion.

DEFINITIONS: See table 1104.

Continued in SALA, 23-1115 through 1134.

Table 1106

PRACTICING AND NON-PRACTICING CHRISTIANS,
20 LC, 1900-80
(Total = 100.0%)

	Country	Practicing[1]			Non-Practicing[2]		
		1900	1970	1980	1900	1970	1980
A.	ARGENTINA	90	70	70	10	30	30
B.	BOLIVIA	85	71	69	15	29	31
C.	BRAZIL	80	62	60	20	38	40
D.	CHILE	80	75	65	20	25	35
E.	COLOMBIA	96	92	92	4	8	8
F.	COSTA RICA	95	85	85	5	15	15
G.	CUBA	90	40	60	10	60	40
H.	DOMINICAN REP.	90	70	70	10	30	30
I.	ECUADOR	90	80	80	10	20	20
J.	EL SALVADOR	95	85	85	5	15	15
K.	GUATEMALA	90	75	75	10	25	25
I.	HAITI	95	85	85	5	15	15
M.	HONDURAS	90	80	80	10	20	20
N.	MEXICO	80	65	65	20	35	35
O.	NICARAGUA	95	85	85	5	15	15
P.	PANAMA	90	80	80	10	20	20
Q.	PARAGUAY	70	45	45	30	55	55
R.	PERU	95	80	80	5	20	20
S.	URUGUAY	80	70	70	20	30	30
T.	VENEZUELA	85	70	70	15	30	30
	UNITED STATES	95	90	88	5	10	12

1. Practicing: Total affiliated of all denominations who attend public worship at least once a year, or who fulfill their churches' minimum annual attendance requirements, or who are radio/TV-service listeners (% here = % of affiliated, not % of total population); church attenders (daily, weekly, fortnightly, monthly, occasional, on festivals only, or annual), excluding civic attenders, private attenders, attending non-members, and attending non-Christians; active Christians, committed Christians, militant Christians.

2. Non-Practicing: Affiliated but inactive, non-attending (dominant Christians) (% = % of affiliated).

SOURCE: See table 1104.

Table 1107

ORGANIZED BIBLE DISTRIBUTION PER YEAR, 20 LC, 1900–75

(N)

	Country	Free					Subsidized					Commercial
		1900	1950	1960	1970	1975	1900	1950	1960	1970	1975	1975
A.	ARGENTINA	0	0	0	0	0	13,000	37,579	73,640	67,191	44,159	60.000
B.	BOLIVIA	0	0	0	0	0	0	8,016	10,434	15,894	39,401	10,000
C.	BRAZIL	0	0	0	260	0	17,782	77,387	297,546	204,943	189,005	486,975
D.	CHILE	0	0	0	0	0	500	13,934	31,338	34,964	28,736	4,000
E.	COLOMBIA	0	0	0	0	0	0	2,721	25,736	47,660	37,964	50,000
F.	COSTA RICA	0	0	0	0	0	400	832	3,695	8,886	14,222	20,000
G.	CUBA	0	0	0	0	0	1,360	12,206	40,532	0	2,000	0
H.	DOMINICAN REPUBLIC	0	0	0	60	200	300	5,510	5,396	17,302	22,124	10,000
I.	ECUADOR	0	0	0	0	0	10	2,868	4,052	15,972	21,878	30,000
J.	EL SALVADOR	0	0	0	0	0	400	2,274	6,103	9,328	16,513	20,000
K.	GUATEMALA	0	0	0	0	0	100	4,661	11,096	24,944	31,925	50,000
L.	HAITI	0	0	0	0	0	200	7,944	3,846	24,776	35,475	5,000
M.	HONDURAS	0	0	0	0	1,000	50	1,606	3,666	9,054	21,807	30,000
N.	MEXICO	0	0	0	0	10,000	6,544	27,130	38,579	93,501	149,164	100,000
O.	NICARAGUA	0	0	0	0		400	992	3,540	6,761	13,709	2,000
P.	PANAMA	0	0	0	200	0	200	2,174	3,210	10,627	11,419	5,000
	Panama Canal Zone	0	0	0	0	0	200	1,710	1,100	2,000	3,000	500
Q.	PARAGUAY	0	0	0	0	0	50	3,177	3,676	3,117	7,027	5,000
R.	PERU	0	0	0	0	0	49	13,344	22,117	46,557	79,390	60,000
S.	URUGUAY	0	0	0	0	0	50	4,547	8,736	14,974	10,490	5,000
T.	VENEZUELA	0	0	0	0	0	0	5,835	20,998	45,663	45,233	60,000

SOURCE: See table 1104.

Table 1108

CATHOLIC BAPTISMS PER 1,000 CATHOLICS, 20 L, 1972-84[a]

	Country	1972	1973	1974	1975	1980	1981	1982	1984
A.	ARGENTINA	21.7	21.2	22.0	21.7	24.8	23.4	23.4	22.1
B.	BOLIVIA	25.7	26.9	23.0	25.5	31.0	32.6	32.6	33.6
C.	BRAZIL	27.8	27.9	26.1	26.1	25.1	24.9	24.9	24.3
D.	CHILE	17.9	17.0	18.4	18.0	19.4	19.2	19.2	19.5
E.	COLOMBIA	32.1	29.8	18.4	18.0	27.7	26.7	26.7	29.2
F.	COSTA RICA	31.6	29.6	28.8	27.9	25.8	29.2	28.9	30.6
G.	CUBA	16.5	13.1	10.9	10.2	4.9	4.9	5.3	5.4
H.	DOMINICAN REP.	21.1	21.1	19.6	18.9	18.3	16.6	16.3	15.9
I.	ECUADOR	30.2	31.8	32.8	32.8	27.3	25.8	25.8	23.7
J.	EL SALVADOR	30.0	29.6	29.8	28.8	17.9	23.5	23.5	17.4
K.	GUATEMALA	30.9	31.9	37.5	35.9	29.6	29.9	29.9	26.8
L.	HAITI	23.7	24.4	23.3	21.8	21.0	22.9	21.0	21.7
M.	HONDURAS	32.4	32.5	30.2	27.5	30.7	26.5	26.5	23.6
N.	MEXICO	37.0	34.2	34.8	35.6	30.4	27.7	27.7	28.6
O.	NICARAGUA	31.6	32.3	34.4	31.8	27.5	25.2	25.0	27.2
P.	PANANA	26.3	24.9	26.4	25.3	20.7	20.4	20.4	~
Q.	PARAGUAY	27.2	28.7	30.6	28.6	32.1	30.3	30.3	31.7
R.	PERU	26.9	22.8	25.0	23.5	25.8	26.5	26.5	24.9
S.	URUGUAY	15.2	14.9	14.5	14.6	18.3	17.7	17.7	17.1
T.	VENEZUELA	27.1	26.4	26.0	25.8	27.2	26.5	26.5	21.7

a. The source supplies 1984 data that are identical to those for 1983. Data for 1980–83 represent figures as of December 31 for each corresponding year.

SOURCE: Data from 1972–75 from Consejo Episcopal Latinoamericano (CELAM), *Iglesia y América Latina Cifras,* 1978, p. 6; and 1980–83 data adapted from *Catholic Almanac,* 1983–87.

Table 1109

PROTESTANT SECTS AND MISSIONARIES,[1] 20 LC

(1968)

	Country	Places of Worship	Protestant Population	Native Personnel		Foreign Missionaries		Seminaries and Bible Schools
				Ordained	Laymen	Ordained	Laymen	
A.	ARGENTINA	2,412	529,657	695	506	401	112	15

Continued in SALA, 21-1108.

CHAPTER 12

THE MILITARY

Table 1200

U.S. DATA ON MILITARY EXPENDITURES, ARMED FORCES, GNP, AND CENTRAL GOVERNMENT EXPENDITURES, 20 LRC, 1974–84[a]

Country	Year	Military Expenditures (ME) (M US) Current	Constant 1983	Armed Forces (T)	GNP (M US) Current	Constant 1983	Central Government Expenditures (CGE) (M US) Constant 1983	ME GNP (%)	ME CGE (%)	ME Per Capita (Constant 1983 Dollars)	Armed Forces (PTI)	GNP Per Capita (Constant 1983 Dollars)
A. ARGENTINA	1974	552	1,049	150	33,410	63,550	14,440	1.7	7.3	41	5.9	2,480
	1975	781	1,357	160	36,440	63,260	13,570	2.1	10.0	52	6.1	2,428
	1976	1,218	1,989	155	38,500	62,890	12,410	3.2	16.0	75	5.8	2,373
	1977	1,398	2,155	155	43,390	66,900	11,460	3.2	18.8	80	5.8	2,483
	1978	1,369	1,952	155	45,330	64,630	12,630	3.0	15.5	71	5.7	2,359
	1979	1,694	2,237	155	52,180	68,890	13,560	3.2	16.5	80	5.6	2,473
	1980	2,036	2,463	155	57,100	69,090	14,560	3.6	16.9	87	5.5	2,440
	1981	2,120	2,374	155	56,130	62,850	16,060	3.8	14.8	82	5.4	2,183
	1982	3,461	3,620	175	55,970	58,540	13,980	6.2	25.9	124	6.0	2,001
	1983	2,745	2,745	175	59,740	59,740	18,360	4.6	14.9	92	5.9	2,009
	1984	2,327	2,250	174	63,300	61,190	13,050	3.7	17.2	74	5.8	2,024
B. BOLIVIA	1974	49	92	18	2,893	5,502	614	1.7	15.1	20	3.8	1,172
	1975	70	122	20	3,396	5,894	691	2.1	17.6	25	4.2	1,226
	1976	80	131	22	3,826	6,250	815	2.1	16.1	27	4.5	1,268
	1977	82	126	20	4,184	6,451	854	2.0	14.7	25	4.0	1,277
	1978	104	148	20	4,656	6,637	917	2.2	16.1	28	3.9	1,281
	1979	114	150	20	4,958	6,545	903	2.3	16.6	28	3.8	1,232
	1980	145	176	24	5,287	6,398	977	2.7	18.0	32	4.4	1,174
	1981	188	210	26	5,672	6,351	927	3.3	22.7	38	4.7	1,136
	1982	100	105	26	5,223	5,463	1,418	1.9	7.4	18	4.5	953
	1982	74	74	27	5,437	5,437	694	1.4	10.7	13	4.6	924
	1984	120	116	28	5,576	5,390	2,157	2.2	5.4	19	4.6	893
C. BRAZIL	1974	954	1,814	435	76,660	145,800	27,080	1.2	6.7	17	4.1	1,375
	1975	994	1,726	455	88,130	153,000	31,010	1.1	5.6	16	4.2	1,408
	1976	1,222	1,996	450	102,700	167,700	34,150	1.2	5.8	18	4.0	1,506
	1977	1,097	1,692	450	114,800	177,000	42,400	1.0	4.0	15	3.9	1,552
	1978	1,092	1,556	450	130,200	185,700	45,100	.8	3.5	13	3.8	1,588
	1979	1,075	1,419	450	149,200	197,000	44,750	.7	3.2	12	3.8	1,643
	1980	1,191	1,441	450	173,600	210,100	51,020	.7	2.8	12	3.7	1,708
	1981	1,272	1,424	450	183,000	204,900	55,550	.7	2.6	11	3.6	1,623
	1982	1,833	1,917	460	195,600	204,600	59,650	.9	3.2	15	3.6	1,579
	1983	1,726	1,726	460	196,600	196,600	61,420	.9	2.8	13	3.5	1,479
	1984	1,778	1,719	459	212,300	205,200	60,570	.8	2.8	13	3.4	1,505
D. CHILE	1974	441	838	90	9,047	17,210	5,895	4.9	14.2	83	9.0	1,713
	1975	404	700	110	8,427	14,630	5,334	4.8	13.1	69	10.8	1,432
	1976	380	620	111	9,332	15,240	4,812	4.1	12.9	60	10.7	1,468
	1977	441	680	111	10,930	16,860	5,699	4.0	11.9	64	10.5	1,598
	1978	537	766	111	12,780	18,220	6,069	4.2	12.6	72	10.4	1,703
	1979	540	713	111	14,870	19,640	5,944	3.6	12.0	66	10.2	1,810
	1980	625	757	116	17,420	21,080	6,268	3.6	12.1	69	10.5	1,914
	1981	739	828	116	19,640	21,990	6,977	3.8	11.9	74	10.4	1,964
	1982	742	776	116	17,360	18,160	6,192	4.3	12.5	68	10.2	1,594
	1983	759	759	126	18,120	18,120	6,000	4.2	12.7	65	10.9	1,563
	1984	817	790	123	19,520	18,870	6,659	4.2	11.9	67	10.4	1,597
E. COLOMBIA	1974	146	277	50	14,400	27,380	3,305	1.0	8.4	12	2.1	1,161
	1975	195	338	50	16,080	27,910	3,670	1.2	9.2	14	2.1	1,158
	1976	167	273	60	17,870	29,190	3,261	.9	8.4	11	2.4	1,187
	1977	144	223	60	19,850	30,610	3,450	.7	6.5	9	2.4	1,221
	1978	171	244	60	23,320	33,240	3,879	.7	6.3	10	2.4	1,304
	1979	258	341	60	26,640	35,170	4,478	1.0	7.6	13	2.3	1,355
	1980	325	394	60	30,350	36,720	5,119	1.1	7.7	15	2.3	1,387
	1981	340	380	65	33,360	37,350	5,494	1.0	6.9	14	2.4	1,383
	1982	438[†]	458[†]	70	35,720	37,370	5,746	1.2	8.0	17	2.5	1,355
	1983	505	505	70	37,810	37,810	5,453	1.3	9.3	18	2.5	1,343
	1984	574	555	70	39,980	38,650	5,569	1.4	10.0	19	2.4	1,344
F. COSTA RICA	1974	7	14	2	1,307	2,485	489	.6	2.8	7	1.0	1,282
	1975	9	16	2	1,447	2,511	524	.6	3.0	8	1.0	1,259
	1976	11	18	3	1,615	2,638	572	.7	3.2	9	1.5	1,285
	1977	15	23	5	1,869	2,882	584	.8	3.9	11	2.4	1,364
	1978	15	21	5	2,131	3,039	753	.7	2.8	10	2.3	1,396
	1979	17	22	6	2,395	3,162	822	.7	2.7	10	2.6	1,371
	1980	17	21	6	2,599	3,146	833	.7	2.5	9	2.6	1,370
	1981	17	19	6	2,686	3,007	703	.6	2.7	8	2.5	1,273
	1982	17	17	6	2,557	2,675	588	.6	3.0	7	2.5	1,102
	1983	23	23	7	2,814	2,814	747	.8	3.0	9	2.8	1,126
	1984	33	32	8	3,151	3,046	792	1.0	4.0	12	3.1	1,185

Table 1200 (Continued)

U.S. DATA ON MILITARY EXPENDITURES, ARMED FORCES, GNP, AND CENTRAL GOVERNMENT EXPENDITURES, 20 LRC, 1974–84[a]

Country	Year	Military Expenditures (ME) (M US) Current	Constant 1983	Armed Forces (T)	GNP (M US) Current	Constant 1983	Central Government Expenditures (CGE) (M US) Constant 1983	ME GNP (%)	ME CGE (%)	ME Per Capita (Constant 1983 Dollars)	Armed Forces (PTI)	GNP Per Capita (Constant 1983 Dollars)
G. CUBA[1,2]	1974	340	647	140	9,240[†]	17,570[†]	~	3.7	~	71	15.3	1,920
	1975	393	682	120	10,650[†]	18,490[†]	~	3.7	~	73	12.9	1,989
	1976	~	~	125	11,700[†]	19,110[†]	~	~	~	~	13.3	2,028
	1977	~	~	200	12,960[†]	19,980[†]	~	~	~	~	21.0	2,094
	1978	1,040	1,483	210	14,830[†]	21,140[†]	~	7.0	~	154	21.8	2,194
	1979	1,160	1,531	210	16,600[†]	21,920[†]	~	7.0	~	158	21.6	2,256
	1980	1,140	1,380	220	17,630[†]	21,330[†]	~	6.5	~	143	22.8	2,209
	1981	1,200	1,344	225	20,840[†]	23,330[†]	~	5.8	~	138	23.2	2,401
	1982	1,330	1,391	230	22,750[†]	23,800[†]	~	5.8	~	142	23.5	2,431
	1983	1,470	1,470	250	25,220[†]	25,220[†]	~	5.8	~	149	25.3	2,550
	1984	1,600	1,547	297	26,920[†]	26,020[†]	~	5.9	~	155	29.7	2,604
H. DOMINICAN REP.	1974	51	97	18	2,997	5,700	1,116	1.7	8.7	20	3.7	1,157
	1975	55	95	18	3,450	5,989	1,097	1.6	8.6	19	3.6	1,182
	1976	65	106	19	3,912	6,390	1,057	1.7	10.1	20	3.6	1,226
	1977	71	109	19	4,365	6,729	1,022	1.6	10.7	20	3.5	1,256
	1978	91	129	19	4,831	6,887	1,148	1.9	11.3	24	3.5	1,251
	1979	103	136	19	5,426	7,163	1,428	1.9	9.5	24	3.4	1,267
	1980	86	104	24	5,811	7,031	1,331	1.5	7.8	18	4.1	1,211
	1981	104	116	24	6,460	7,233	1,311	1.6	8.9	19	4.0	1,213
	1982	104	109	25	7,093	7,419	1,105	1.5	9.8	18	4.1	1,212
	1983	105	105	23	7,744	7,744	1,217	1.4	8.7	17	3.7	1,233
	1984	94	91	22	7,896	7,633	1,090	1.2	8.3	14	3.4	1,184
I. ECUADOR[1]	1974	91	173	20	4,242	8,069	1,055	2.1	16.4	25	2.9	1,181
	1975	123	214	20	5,107	8,865	1,100	2.4	19.5	30	2.8	1,260
	1976	144	235	24	5,881	9,607	1,254	2.4	18.7	32	3.3	1,326
	1977	153	236	30	6,663	10,270	1,412	2.3	16.7	32	4.0	1,378
	1978	218	310	35	7,665	10,930	1,256	2.8	24.7	40	4.6	1,425
	1979	204	269	35	8,594	11,350	1,246	2.4	21.6	34	4.4	1,437
	1980	219	265	35	9,764	11,820	1,766	2.2	15.0	33	4.3	1,454
	1981	245	274	34	10,930	12,240	2,080	2.2	13.2	33	4.1	1,464
	1982	235[†]	245[†]	36	11,570	12,100	2,028	2.0	12.1	29	4.2	1,406
	1983	200	200	39	11,750	11,750	1,683	1.7	11.9	23	4.4	1,327
	1984	204	197	39	12,380	11,960	1,737	1.6	11.3	22	4.3	1,313
J. EL SALVADOR	1974	27	51	8	2,156	4,100	539	1.2	9.4	13	2.0	1,019
	1975	29	51	8	2,491	4,323	620	1.2	8.2	12	1.9	1,044
	1976	33	54	8	2,782	4,544	667	1.2	8.0	13	1.9	1,067
	1977	36	56	8	3,099	4,778	729	1.2	7.7	13	1.8	1,090
	1978	58[†]	82[†]	11	3,545	5,055	747	1.6	11.0	18	2.3	1,121
	1979	82[†]	109[†]	14	3,802	5,020	749	2.2	14.5	23	3.0	1,084
	1980	101[†]	123[†]	16	3,761	4,551	791	2.7	15.5	26	3.4	965
	1981	131[†]	147[†]	23	3,720	4,165	850	3.5	17.3	32	5.0	908
	1982	154[†]	161[†]	28	3,729	3,901	788	4.1	20.4	34	6.0	835
	1983	160[†]	160[†]	32	3,922	3,922	703	4.1	22.8	33	6.7	821
	1984	251[†]	243[†]	45	4,120	3,982	793	6.1	30.6	50	9.2	817
K. GUATEMALA	1974	32	61	13	3,689	7,017	733	.9	8.3	10	2.2	1,185
	1975	72	126	13	5,889	10,220	1,023	1.2	12.3	21	2.1	1,677
	1976	49	80	14	4,696	7,671	924	1.0	8.6	13	2.2	1,223
	1977	68	105	14	5,430	8,372	986	1.2	10.6	16	2.2	1,295
	1978	74	106	14	6,165	8,789	1,063	1.2	10.0	16	2.1	1,316
	1979	83	109	21	6,974	9,207	1,087	1.2	10.1	16	3.0	1,334
	1980	109	132	21	7,842	9,490	1,448	1.4	9.1	19	2.9	1,331
	1981	114	128	27	8,503	9,520	1,605	1.3	8.0	17	3.6	1,283
	1982	167	175	30	8,762	9,165	1,384	1.9	12.6	23	3.9	1,198
	1983	185	185	40	8,937	8,937	1,192	2.1	15.5	23	5.1	1,137
	1984	179[†]	173[†]	40	9,215	8,908	1,159[†]	1.9	14.9	21	4.9	1,100
L. HAITI	1974	10	18	6	701	1,332	173	1.4	10.4	4	1.2	274
	1975	11	19	6	752	1,306	232	1.5	8.2	4	1.2	265
	1976	11	18	6	868	1,418	266	1.3	6.7	4	1.2	284
	1977	11	17	7	920	1,418	290	1.2	5.9	3	1.4	280
	1978	13	19	7	1,041	1,484	274	1.3	6.8	4	1.4	289
	1979	15	20	7	1,214	1,603	304	1.2	6.6	4	1.3	308
	1980	23	28	7	1,422	1,721	302	1.6	9.3	5	1.3	326
	1981	29	32	8	1,489	1,668	335	1.9	9.6	6	1.5	311
	1982	28	29	8	1,539	1,609	297	1.8	9.9	5	1.5	295
	1983	25	25	8	1,616	1,616	284	1.6	8.9	5	1.4	291
	1984	27	27	6	1,716	1,659	299	1.6	8.9	5	1.1	293

Table 1200 (Continued)

U.S. DATA ON MILITARY EXPENDITURES, ARMED FORCES, GNP, AND CENTRAL GOVERNMENT EXPENDITURES, 20 LRC, 1974–84[a]

Country	Year	Military Expenditures (ME) (M US) Current	Constant 1983	Armed Forces (T)	GNP (M US) Current	Constant 1983	Central Government Expenditures (CGE) (M US) Constant 1983	ME GNP (%)	ME CGE (%)	ME Per Capita (Constant 1983 Dollars)	Armed Forces (PTI)	GNP Per Capita (Constant 1983 Dollars)
M. HONDURAS	1974	18	35	10	1,123	2,136	303	1.6	11.4	11	3.3	697
	1975	23	40	12	1,180	2,048	349	2.0	11.5	13	3.8	646
	1976	25	41	12	1,334	2,179	392	1.9	10.4	12	3.7	664
	1977	31	48	12	1,569	2,418	424[†]	2.0	11.4	14	3.5	712
	1978	43	61	14	1,815	2,588	544[†]	2.4	11.2	17	3.8	735
	1979	50	65	14	2,084	2,751	574[†]	2.4	11.4	18	3.8	755
	1980	51[†]	62	14	2,322	2,810	686[†]	2.2	9.1	16	3.7	744
	1981	46[†]	51	17	2,557	2,863	657[†]	1.8	7.8	13	4.3	728
	1982	56[†]	58	17	2,641	2,763	710[†]	2.1	8.2	14	4.2	679
	1983	80[†]	80	19	3,809	2,809	605[†]	2.8	13.2	19	4.5	668
	1984	124[†]	120	20	2,981	2,882	733[†]	4.2	16.4	28	4.6	662
N. MEXICO	1974	313	595	85	50,000	95,110	13,390	.6	4.3	10	1.4	1,592
	1975	444	771	95	57,840	100,400	17,360	.8	4.4	13	1.5	1,634
	1976	434	709	100	63,810	104,200	18,070	.7	3.9	11	1.6	1,650
	1977	451	695	100	70,060	108,000	18,030	.6	3.9	11	1.5	1,664
	1978	393	561	120	82,000	116,900	19,710	.5	2.8	8	1.8	1,754
	1979	465	614	120	96,280	127,100	22,960	.5	2.7	9	1.8	1,859
	1980	471	570	120	112,400	136,100	26,600	.4	2.1	8	1.7	1,941
	1981	676	757	125	130,100	145,600	33,230	.5	2.3	11	1.7	2,025
	1982	693	725	130	133,500	139,700	47,500	.5	1.5	10	1.8	1,893
	1983	726	726	130	133,100	133,100	38,180	.5	1.9	10	1.7	1,759
	1984	966	934	129	144,200	139,400	35,370	.7	2.6	12	1.7	1,795
O. NICARAGUA	1974	29	56	6	1,934	3,679	757	1.5	7.4	24	2.6	1,575
	1975	39	68	5	2,205	3,828	768	1.8	8.9	28	2.1	1,590
	1976	51	83	5	2,440	3,985	723	2.1	11.5	34	2.0	1,605
	1977	66	102	6	2,603	4,014	863	2.5	11.9	40	2.3	1,567
	1978	89	126	6	2,580	3,679	752	3.4	16.8	48	2.3	1,397
	1979	69	92	6	2,131	2,814	629	3.3	14.6	36	2.3	1,097
	1980	151[†]	183[†]	24	2,593	3,138	977	5.8	18.8	67	8.7	1,139
	1981	204[†]	228[†]	39	2,997	3,355	1,293	6.8	17.6	80	13.6	1,174
	1982	330[†]	345[†]	41	3,132	3,276	1,612	10.5	21.4	117	13.9	1,110
	1983	348[†]	348[†]	46	3,367	3,367	2,107	10.3	16.5	115	15.2	1,110
	1984	473[†]	457[†]	67	3,520	3,403	2,666[†]	13.4	17.1	146	21.4	1,086
P. PANAMA	1974	12	23	8	1,461	2,779	888	.8	2.5	13	4.7	1,629
	1975	14	24	8	1,656	2,875	950	.8	2.5	14	4.6	1,645
	1976	14	23	8	1,768	2,888	976	.8	2.3	13	4.5	1,614
	1977	14	22	8	1,892	2,917	966	.7	2.3	12	4.3	1,586
	1978	26[†]	38[†]	8	2,265	3,229	1,017	1.2	3.7	20	4.3	1,724
	1979	28[†]	37[†]	8	2,544	3,358	1,318	1.1	2.8	19	4.2	1,754
	1980	~	~	8	3,062	3,706	1,294	~	~	~	4.1	1,894
	1981	41[†]	46[†]	9	3,474	3,889	1,450	1.2	3.2	23	4.5	1,945
	1982	58[†]	61[†]	10	3,884	4,062	1,296[†]	1.5	4.7	30	4.9	1,988
	1983	88[†]	88[†]	10	4,050	4,050	1,878[†]	2.2	4.7	42	4.8	1,939
	1984	98[†]	95[†]	11	4,147	4,009	2,476[†]	2.4	3.8	44	5.2	1,878
Q. PARAGUAY	1974	24	46	15	1,841	3,502	352	1.3	13.1	17	5.4	1,263
	1975	40	70	15	2,154	3,740	431	1.9	16.2	24	5.2	1,308
	1976	44	72	15	2,445	3,994	492	1.8	14.7	25	5.1	1,353
	1977	51	79	15	2,944	4,539	516	1.7	15.3	26	4.9	1,487
	1978	57	81	15	3,489	4,974	589	1.6	13.7	26	4.8	1,576
	1979	62	82	15	4,225	5,578	611	1.5	13.4	25	4.6	1,708
	1980	74	90	15	5,095	6,166	674	1.5	13.3	27	4.4	1,825
	1981	93	105	15	6,015	6,735	791	1.6	13.2	30	4.3	1,928
	1982	115[†]	120[†]	16	6,396	6,691	749	1.8	16.0	33	4.4	1,852
	1983	163[†]	163[†]	16	6,482	6,482	728	2.5	22.4	44	4.3	1,736
	1984	118[†]	114[†]	17	7,002	6,769	791	1.7	14.5	30	4.4	1,753
R. PERU	1974	299	569	90	9,610	18,280	2,808	3.1	20.3	39	6.1	1,239
	1975	436	757	95	10,880	18,890	3,172	4.0	23.9	50	6.3	1,246
	1976	540	882	100	11,670	10,070	3,352	4.6	26.3	57	6.4	1,224
	1977	837	1,291	125	12,350	19,040	3,282	6.8	39.3	81	7.8	1,191
	1978	680	969	125	12,390	17,670	3,026	5.5	32.0	59	7.6	1,076
	1979	470	621	125	14,790	19,530	2,903	3.2	21.4	37	7.4	1,159
	1980	851[†]	1,030[†]	151	17,250	20,870	3,811	4.9	27.0	60	8.7	1,207
	1981	826[†]	924[†]	157	19,460	21,790	3,899	4.2	23.7	52	8.8	1,227
	1982	970[†]	1,015[†]	164	20,890	21,850	3,363	4.6	30.2	56	9.0	1,199
	1983	921[†]	921[†]	167	18,850	18,850	3,069	4.9	30.0	49	8.9	1,008
	1984	1,450[†]	1,402[†]	135	20,280	19,600	2,962	7.1	47.3	73	7.0	1,021

Table 1200 (Continued)

U.S. DATA ON MILITARY EXPENDITURES, ARMED FORCES, GNP, AND CENTRAL GOVERNMENT EXPENDITURES, 20 LRC, 1974–84[a]

Country	Year	Military Expenditures (ME) (M US) Current	Constant 1983	Armed Forces (T)	GNP (M US) Current	Constant 1983	Central Government Expenditures (CGE) (M US) Constant 1983	ME GNP (%)	ME CGE (%)	ME Per Capita (Constant 1983 Dollars)	Armed Forces (PTI)	GNP Per Capita (Constant 1983 Dollars)
S. URUGUAY	1974	69	132	25	2,426	4,614	1,122	2.9	11.8	46	8.8	1,625
	1975	76	133	25	2,799	5,858	1,144	2.7	11.6	47	8.8	1,709
	1976	68	112	28	3,092	5,051	1,248	2.2	8.9	39	9.8	1,772
	1977	79	121	28	3,323	5,123	1,255	2.4	9.7	43	9.8	1,797
	1978	86	123	28	3,779	5,388	1,274	2.3	9.7	43	9.8	1,878
	1979	104	137	28	4,361	5,758	1,228	2.4	11.2	48	9.7	2,001
	1980	148	180	28	5,030	6,087	1,366	2.9	13.1	62	9.7	2,108
	1981	218	244	28	5,569	6,235	1,584	3.9	15.4	84	9.7	2,153
	1982	218	228	29	5,323	5,568	1,727	4.1	13.2	79	10.0	1,916
	1983	170	170	30	5,070	5,070	1,373	3.4	12.4	58	10.3	1,739
	1984	144	139	30	5,034	4,866	1,280	2.9	10.9	48	10.3	1,663
T. VENEZUELA	1974	519	987	50	29,300	55,740	20,360	1.8	4.8	81	4.1	4,558
	1975	675	1,172	55	34,880	60,550	20,710	1.9	5.7	93	4.3	4,781
	1976	568	928	55	40,130	65,560	21,270	1.4	4.4	71	4.2	4,997
	1977	705	1,087	55	45,280	69,820	22,330	1.6	4.9	80	4.0	5,137
	1978	793	1,131	55	50,390	71,840	21.060	1.6	5.4	80	3.9	5,105
	1979	785	1,036	55	54,830	72,380	16,320	1.4	6.3	71	3.8	4,974
	1980	747	903	55	58,280	70,530	18,590	1.3	4.9	60	3.7	4,694
	1981	721	807	55	62,490	69,970	25,150	1.2	3.2	52	3.6	4,519
	1982	1,143	1,196	56	66,090	69,120	23,470	1.7	5.1	75	3.5	4,337
	1983	995	995	56	65,310	65,310	19,150	1.5	5.2	61	3.4	3,984
	1984	1,067	1,031	64	66,620	64,400	18,170	1.6	5.7	61	3.8	3,822
LATIN AMERICA[3]	1974	4.0	7.6	1,248	264	502	109.8	1.5	7.0	25	4.0	1,613
	1975	4.9	8.6	1,297	303	525	118.3	1.6	7.2	27	4.1	1,645
	1976	5.9	9.6	1,328	338	552	122.8	1.7	7.8	29	4.1	1,687
	1977	6.7	10.3	1,438	376	580	133.3	1.8	7.8	31	4.3	1,734
	1978	7.0	10.0	1,478	424	605	139.2	1.7	7.2	29	4.3	1,766
	1979	7.5	9.9	1,491	484	639	139.5	1.5	7.1	28	4.3	1,822
	1980	8.6	10.5	1,561	550	666	156.5	1.6	6.7	29	4.3	1,854
	1981	9.5	10.6	1,617	598	669	178.5	1.6	5.9	29	4.4	1,820
	1982	12.4	13.0	1,687	623	652	193.1	2.0	6.7	35	4.5	1,732
	1983	11.8	11.8	1,746	632	632	185.5	1.9	6.4	31	4.5	1,640
	1984	12.7	12.3	1,798	673	650	176.8	1.9	6.9	31	4.6	1,647
UNITED STATES	1974	85,910	163,400	2,146	1,473,000	2,801,000	539,100	5.8	30.3	764	10.0	13,100
	1975	90,950	157,900	2,098	1,598,800	2,775,000	601,700	5.7	26.2	731	9.7	12,850
	1976	91,010	148,700	2,075	1,783,000	2,912,000	630,800	5.1	23.6	682	9.5	13,360
	1977	100,900	155,600	2,060	1,990,000	3,069,000	653,300	5.1	23.8	707	9.4	13,930
	1978	109,200	155,800	2,033	2,250,000	3,207,000	678,200	4.9	23.0	700	9.1	14,410
	1979	122,300	161,400	2,050	2,508,000	3,311,000	692,700	4.9	23.3	717	9.1	14,710
	1980	144,000	174,200	2,101	2,732,000	3,306,000	753,000	5.3	23.1	765	9.2	14,520
	1981	169,900	190,200	2,168	3,053,000	3,418,000	804,600	5.6	23.6	827	9.4	14,860
	1982	196,400	205,400	2,201	3,166,000	3,312,000	821,700	6.2	25.0	884	9.5	14,250
	1983	217,200	217,200	2,222	3,406,000	3,406,000	856,000	6.4	25.4	926	9.5	14,520
	1984	237,100	229,200	2,244	3,765,000	3,640,000	866,900	6.3	26.4	968	9.5	15,380
WORLD[3]	1974	319.9	608.5	25,900	5,503	10,470	2,570.7	5.8	23.7	152	6.5	2,622
	1975	362.9	630.0	25,930	6,091	10,570	2,803.1	6.0	22.5	155	6.4	2,602
	1976	392.2	640.6	16,160	6,786	11,090	2,943.4	5.8	21.8	154	6.3	2,665
	1977	422.1	650.8	26,180	7,492	11,550	3,136.7	5.6	20.7	154	6.2	2,729
	1978	465.7	663.9	26,740	8,399	11,970	3,212.5	5.5	20.7	154	6.2	2,782
	1979	514.4	679.1	27,120	9,389	12,400	3,373.1	5.5	20.1	155	6.2	2,830
	1980	583.6	706.2	27,280	10,460	12,660	3,596.9	5.6	19.6	159	6.1	2,841
	1981	654.6	732.9	27,870	11,520	12,900	3.763.9	5.7	19.5	162	6.1	2,847
	1982	734.9	768.7	27,890	12,310	12,880	3,872.7	6.0	19.8	167	6.0	2,792
	1983	789.1	789.1	28,080	13,110	13,110	3,962.4	6.0	19.9	168	6.0	2,795
	1984	835.7	807.8	29,020	14,110	13,640	4,019.2	5.9	20.1	169	6.1	2,861

1. This series probably excludes most capital expenditures or arms acquisitions.
2. For years 1973–83 GNP is an estimate based on partial or uncertain data.
3. Latin America and World totals are expressed in billions of dollars instead of millions of dollars. In order to reduce distortions in trends caused by data gaps, the totals for World and Latin America include rough approximations for those countries and years in which data or estimates are unavailable.

a. For 1963–73, see SALA, 17-2302.

SOURCE: U.S. Arms Control and Disarmament Agency, *World Military Expenditures and Arms Transfers, 1973–1984* (Washington, D.C., 1986), table 1.

Table 1201

U.S. DATA ON VALUE OF ARMS TRANSFERS AND TOTAL IMPORTS AND EXPORTS, BY REGION, ORGANIZATION, AND COUNTRY, 20 LRC, 1975–85[a]

Country	Year	Arms Imports[1] (M US) Current	Arms Imports[1] (M US) Constant 1983	Arms Exports[1] (M US) Current	Arms Exports[1] (M US) Constant 1983	Total Imports[2] (M US) Current	Total Imports[2] (M US) Constant 1983	Total Exports[2] (M US) Current	Total Exports[2] (M US) Constant 1983	Arms Imports Total Imports (%)	Arms Exports Total Exports (%)
A. ARGENTINA	1975	30	52	0	0	3,947	6,851	2,961	5,140	.8	.0
	1976	50	82	0	0	3,033	4,955	3,916	6,397	1.6	.0
	1977	40	62	5	8	4,162	6,417	5,652	8,714	1.0	.1
	1978	370	528	0	0	3,834	5,466	6,400	9,125	9.7	.0
	1979	500	660	10	13	6,700	8,845	7,810	10,310	7.5	.1
	1980	210	254	5	6	10,540	12,760	8,021	9,706	2.0	.1
	1981	500	560	10	11	9,430	10,560	9,143	10,240	5.3	.1
	1982	290	303	0	0	5,337	5,582	7,625	7,976	5.4	.0
	1983	975	975	20	20	4,504	4,504	7,836	7,836	21.6	.3
	1984	450	435	80	77	4,585	4,432	8,107	7,837	9.8	1.0
	1985	150	140	0	0	3,814	3,568	8,396	7,854	3.9	.0
B. BOLIVIA	1975	10	17	0	0	575	998	444	771	1.7	.0
	1976	5	8	0	0	594	970	568	928	.8	.0
	1977	10	15	0	0	591	911	632	974	1.7	.0
	1978	20	29	0	0	769	1,096	629	897	2.6	.0
	1979	80	106	0	0	980	1,294	760	1,003	8.2	.0
	1980	40	48	0	0	678	820	942	1,140	5.9	.0
	1981	70	78	0	0	975	1,092	912	1,021	7.2	.0
	1982	0	0	0	0	578	605	828	866	.0	.0
	1983	0	0	0	0	545	545	755	755	.0	.0
	1984	10	10	0	0	474	458	724	700	2.1	.0
	1985	0	0	0	0	582	544	673	630	.0	.0
C. BRAZIL	1975	100	174	60	104	13,590	23,590	8,670	15,050	.7	.7
	1976	140	229	70	114	13,730	22,420	10,130	16,540	1.0	.7
	1977	90	139	80	123	13,260	20,440	12,120	18,690	.7	.7
	1978	200	285	100	143	15,050	21,460	12,660	18,050	1.3	.8
	1979	240	317	110	145	19,800	26,150	15,240	20,130	1.2	.7
	1980	130	157	140	169	24,960	30,210	20,130	24,360	.5	.7
	1981	60	67	170	190	24,080	26,960	23,290	26,080	.2	.7
	1982	30	31	320	335	21,070	22,040	20,170	21,100	.1	1.6
	1983	40	40	130	130	16,800	16,800	21,900	21,900	.2	.6
	1984	140	135	500	483	15,210	14,700	27,000	26,110	.9	1.9
	1985	20	19	60	56	13,680	12,800	25,640	23,980	.1	.2
D. CHILE	1975	20	35	0	0	1,338	2,323	1,552	2,694	1.5	.0
	1976	130	212	0	0	1,643	2,684	2,083	3,403	7.9	.0
	1977	60	93	0	0	2,259	3,483	2,190	3,376	2.7	.0
	1978	60	86	0	0	3,002	4,280	2,478	3,533	2.0	.0
	1979	190	251	0	0	4,218	5,569	3,894	5,141	4.5	.0
	1980	250	303	0	0	5,124	6,201	4,671	5,652	4.9	.0
	1981	310	347	5	6	6,364	7,125	3,906	4,373	4.9	.1
	1982	280	293	0	0	3,528	3,690	3,710	3,881	7.9	.0
	1983	90	90	0	0	2,969	2,969	3,836	3,836	3.0	.0
	1984	160	155	20	19	3,191	3,085	3,657	3,535	5.0	.5
	1985	20	19	20	19	2,743	2,566	3,823	3,576	.7	.5
E. COLOMBIA	1975	40	69	0	0	1,495	2,595	1,465	2,543	2.7	.0
	1976	0	0	0	0	1,708	2,790	1,745	2,851	.0	.0
	1977	10	15	0	0	2,028	3,127	2,443	3,767	.5	.0
	1978	10	14	0	0	2,836	4,043	3,003	4,281	.4	.0
	1979	20	26	0	0	3,233	4,268	3,300	4,357	.6	.0
	1980	70	85	0	0	4,663	5,643	3,945	4,774	1.5	.0
	1981	40	45	0	0	5,199	5,821	2,956	3,310	.8	.0
	1982	130	136	0	0	5,478	5,730	3,095	3,237	2.4	.0
	1983	20	20	0	0	4,968	4,968	3,081	3,081	.4	.0
	1984	675	653	0	0	4,498	4,348	3,462	3,347	15.0	.0
	1985	10	9	0	0	4,141	3,874	3,552	3,323	.2	.0
F. COSTA RICA	1975	0	0	0	0	694	1,205	493	856	.0	.0
	1976	0	0	0	0	770	1,258	593	969	.0	.0
	1977	0	0	0	0	1,021	1,574	828	1,277	.0	.0
	1978	0	0	0	0	1,166	1,662	865	1,233	.0	.0
	1979	0	0	0	0	1,397	1,844	934	1,233	.0	.0
	1980	0	0	0	0	1,540	1,864	1,002	1,213	.0	.0
	1981	0	0	0	0	1,209	1,354	1,008	1,129	.0	.0
	1982	0	0	0	0	889	930	870	910	.0	.0
	1983	0	0	0	0	988	988	882	882	.0	.0
	1984	5	5	0	0	1,087	1,051	967	935	.5	.0
	1985	20	19	0	0	1,098	1,027	962	900	1.8	.0

Table 1201 (Continued)

U.S. DATA ON VALUE OF ARMS TRANSFERS AND TOTAL IMPORTS AND EXPORTS, BY REGION, ORGANIZATION, AND COUNTRY, 20 LRC, 1975-85[a]

Country	Year	Arms Imports[1] (M US) Current	Constant 1983	Arms Exports[1] (M US) Current	Constant 1983	Total Imports[2] (M US) Current	Constant 1983	Total Exports[2] (M US) Current	Constant 1983	Arms Imports / Total Imports (%)	Arms Exports / Total Exports (%)
G. CUBA	1975	70	122	30	52	3,767	6,539	3,572	6,200	1.9	.8
	1976	130	212	120	196	3,879	6,337	3,284	5,365	3.4	3.7
	1977	100	154	10	15	4,362	6,725	3,669	5,657	2.3	.3
	1978	550	784	0	0	4,751	6,774	4,575	6,523	11.6	.0
	1979	400	528	0	0	5,089	6,719	4,829	6,375	7.9	.0
	1980	330	399	0	0	6,409	7,756	5,593	6,768	5.1	.0
	1981	850	952	10	11	6,546	7,329	5,406	6,053	13.0	.2
	1982	1,000	1,046	20	21	6,645	6,951	5,928	6,201	15.0	.3
	1983	700	700	40	40	7,219	7,219	6,416	6,416	9.7	.6
	1984	700	677	10	10	8,145	7,874	6,174	5,968	8.6	.2
	1985	800	748	0	0	8,616	8,060	6,521	6,100	9.3	.0
H. DOMINICAN REP.	1975	0	0	0	0	889	1,543	894	1,552	.0	.0
	1976	0	0	0	0	878	1,434	716	1,170	.0	.0
	1977	0	0	0	0	975	1,503	780	1,203	.0	.0
	1978	0	0	0	0	987	1,407	676	964	.0	.0
	1979	0	0	0	0	1,213	1,601	869	1,147	.0	.0
	1980	10	12	0	0	1,640	1,985	962	1,164	.6	.0
	1981	0	0	0	0	1,668	1,868	1,188	1,330	.0	.0
	1982	10	10	0	0	1,444	1,510	768	803	.7	.0
	1983	5	5	0	0	1,471	1,471	785	785	.3	.0
	1984	10	10	0	0	1,446	1,398	868	839	.7	.0
	1985	5	5	0	0	1,487	1,391	735	688	.3	.0
I. ECUADOR	1975	60	104	0	0	987	1,713	974	1,691	6.1	.0
	1976	90	147	0	0	958	1,565	1,258	2,055	9.4	.0
	1977	160	247	0	0	1,189	1,833	1,436	2,214	13.5	.0
	1978	90	128	0	0	1,505	2,146	1,558	2,221	6.0	.0
	1979	180	238	0	0	1,600	2,112	2,104	2,778	11.3	.0
	1980	180	218	0	0	2,253	2,726	2,481	3,002	8.0	.0
	1981	100	112	0	0	2,246	2,515	2,542	2,846	4.5	.0
	1982	280	293	0	0	1,989	2,080	2,140	2,238	14.1	.0
	1983	180	180	0	0	1,465	1,465	2,223	2,223	12.3	.0
	1984	160	155	0	0	1,716	1,659	2,583	2,497	9.3	.0
	1985	20	19	0	0	1,606	1,502	2,905	2,717	1.2	.0
J. EL SALVADOR	1975	5	9	0	0	598	1,038	531	922	.8	.0
	1976	5	8	0	0	735	1,201	743	1,214	.7	.0
	1977	0	0	0	0	929	1,432	972	1,499	.0	.0
	1978	5	7	0	0	1,027	1,464	801	1,142	.5	.0
	1979	30	40	0	0	1,039	1,372	1,131	1,493	2.9	.0
	1980	0	0	0	0	962	1,164	1,074	1,300	.0	.0
	1981	10	11	0	0	985	1,103	797	892	1.0	.0
	1982	40	42	0	0	857	896	699	731	4.7	.0
	1983	50	50	0	0	891	891	735	735	5.6	.0
	1984	90	87	0	0	977	944	725	701	9.2	.0
	1985	90	84	0	0	961	899	676	632	9.4	.0
K. GUATEMALA	1975	10	17	0	0	733	1,272	641	1,113	1.4	.0
	1976	20	33	0	0	839	1,371	782	1,277	2.4	.0
	1977	5	8	0	0	1,053	1,623	1,225	1,889	.5	.0
	1978	10	14	0	0	1,286	1,833	1,113	1,587	.8	.0
	1979	10	13	0	0	1,504	1,986	1,270	1,677	.7	.0
	1980	10	12	0	0	1,598	1,934	1,557	1,884	.6	.0
	1981	0	0	0	0	1,674	1,874	1,254	1,404	.0	.0
	1982	40	42	0	0	1,388	1,452	1,153	1,206	2.9	.0
	1983	5	5	0	0	1,135	1,135	1,180	1,180	.4	.0
	1984	40	39	0	0	1,277	1,234	1,127	1,089	3.1	.0
	1985	10	9	0	0	1,174	1,098	~	~	.9	~
L. HAITI	1975	0	0	0	0	149	259	80	139	.0	.0
	1976	0	0	0	0	207	338	124	203	.0	.0
	1977	0	0	0	0	213	328	149	230	.0	.0
	1978	0	0	0	0	233	332	155	221	.0	.0
	1979	0	0	0	0	272	359	185	244	.0	.0
	1980	0	0	0	0	375	454	195	236	.0	.0
	1981	10	11	0	0	461	516	154	172	2.2	.0
	1982	0	0	0	0	284	297	178	186	.0	.0
	1983	5	5	0	0	~	~	166	166	~	.0
	1984	0	0	0	0	~	~	~	~	~	~
	1985	20	19	0	0	~	~	~	~	~	~

Table 1201 (Continued)

U.S. DATA ON VALUE OF ARMS TRANSFERS AND TOTAL IMPORTS AND EXPORTS, BY REGION, ORGANIZATION, AND COUNTRY, 20 LRC, 1975–85[a]

Country	Year	Arms Imports[2] (M US) Current	Constant 1983	Arms Exports[2] (M US) Current	Constant 1983	Total Imports[3] (M US) Current	Constant 1983	Total Exports[3] (M US) Current	Constant 1983	Arms Imports / Total Imports (%)	Arms Exports / Total Exports (%)
M. HONDURAS	1975	0	0	0	0	404	701	303	526	.0	.0
	1976	40	65	0	0	453	740	397	649	8.8	.0
	1977	5	8	0	0	579	893	519	800	.9	.0
	1978	5	7	0	0	699	997	613	874	.7	.0
	1979	10	13	0	0	826	1,091	734	969	1.2	.0
	1980	0	0	0	0	1,009	1,221	829	1,003	.0	.0
	1981	10	11	0	0	949	1,063	761	852	1.1	.0
	1982	0	0	0	0	701	733	660	690	.0	.0
	1983	10	10	0	0	700	700	~	~	1.4	~
	1984	90	87	0	0	~	~	~	~	~	~
	1985	20	19	0	0	~	~	~	~	~	~
N. MEXICO	1975	20	35	0	0	6,570	11,400	2,904	5,041	.3	.0
	1976	20	33	0	0	6,028	9,847	3,417	5,582	.3	.0
	1977	10	15	0	0	5,883	9,070	4,518	6,966	.2	.0
	1978	10	14	0	0	7,555	10,770	5,958	8,494	.1	.0
	1979	10	13	0	0	12,090	15,960	8,982	11,860	.1	.0
	1980	20	24	0	0	19,460	23,550	15,570	18,840	.1	.0
	1981	50	56	0	0	24,070	26,950	19,650	22,000	.2	.0
	1982	200	209	0	0	15,130	15,820	21,210	22,190	1.3	.0
	1983	50	50	0	0	8,023	8,023	21,820	21,820	.6	.0
	1984	30	29	0	0	11,790	11,400	24,410	23,590	.3	.0
	1985	30	28	0	0	13,990	13,090	22,110	20,680	.2	.0
O. NICARAGUA	1975	0	0	0	0	517	897	375	651	.0	.0
	1976	0	0	0	0	532	869	542	885	.0	.0
	1977	10	15	0	0	762	1,175	637	982	1.3	.0
	1978	10	14	0	0	596	850	646	921	1.7	.0
	1979	5	7	0	0	360	475	567	749	1.4	.0
	1980	10	12	0	0	887	1,073	451	546	1.1	.0
	1981	40	45	0	0	999	1,119	508	569	4.0	.0
	1982	100	105	0	0	776	812	406	425	12.9	.0
	1983	140	140	0	0	772	772	414	414	18.1	.0
	1984	250	242	0	0	808	781	393	380	30.9	.0
	1985	120	112	0	0	850	795	320	299	14.1	.0
P. PANAMA	1975	5	9	0	0	892	1,548	286	496	.6	.0
	1976	0	0	0	0	848	1,385	238	389	.0	.0
	1977	5	8	0	0	861	1,327	251	387	.6	.0
	1978	0	0	0	0	942	1,343	256	365	.0	.0
	1979	0	0	0	0	1,184	1,563	303	400	.0	.0
	1980	30	36	0	0	1,449	1,753	360	436	2.1	.0
	1981	5	6	0	0	1,540	1,724	328	367	.3	.0
	1982	10	10	0	0	1,569	1,641	375	392	.6	.0
	1983	0	0	0	0	1,412	1,412	321	321	.0	.0
	1984	5	5	0	0	1,423	1,376	276	267	.4	.0
	1985	10	9	0	0	~	~	~	~	~	~
Q. PARAGUAY	1975	0	0	0	0	206	358	177	307	.0	.0
	1976	5	8	0	0	220	359	182	297	2.3	.0
	1977	0	0	0	0	308	475	279	430	.0	.0
	1978	10	14	0	0	383	546	257	366	2.6	.0
	1979	10	13	0	0	521	688	305	403	1.9	.0
	1980	40	48	0	0	615	744	310	375	6.5	.0
	1981	5	6	0	0	600	672	296	331	.8	.0
	1982	0	0	0	0	672	703	330	345	.0	.0
	1983	0	0	0	0	546	546	269	269	.0	.0
	1984	30	29	0	0	675	653	381	368	4.4	.0
	1985	10	9	0	0	816	763	403	377	1.2	.0
R. PERU	1975	120	208	0	0	2,551	4,428	1,291	2,241	4.7	.0
	1976	260	425	0	0	2,037	3,328	1,360	2,222	12.8	.0
	1977	430	663	0	0	1,911	2,946	1,726	2,661	22.5	.0
	1978	310	442	0	0	1,959	2,793	1,941	2,767	15.8	.0
	1979	110	145	0	0	1,820	2,403	3,491	4,609	6.0	.0
	1980	260	315	0	0	2,500	3,025	3,898	4,717	10.4	.0
	1981	290	325	0	0	3,447	3,859	3,255	3,644	8.4	.0
	1982	370	387	60	63	3,601	3,767	3,293	3,444	10.3	1.8
	1983	190	190	0	0	2,548	2,548	3,015	3,015	7.5	.0
	1984	210	203	0	0	2,212	2,138	3,147	3,042	9.5	.0
	1985	80	75	0	0	1,835	1,717	2,966	2,775	4.4	.0

Table 1201 (Continued)

U.S. DATA ON VALUE OF ARMS TRANSFERS AND TOTAL IMPORTS AND EXPORTS, BY REGION, ORGANIZATION, AND COUNTRY, 20 LRC, 1975-85[a]

Country	Year	Arms Imports[1] (M US) Current	Constant 1983	Arms Exports[1] (M US) Current	Constant 1983	Total Imports[2] (M US) Current	Constant 1983	Total Exports[2] (M US) Current	Constant 1983	Arms Imports / Total Imports (%)	Arms Exports / Total Exports (%)
S. URUGUAY	1975	5	9	0	0	556	965	384	667	.9	.0
	1976	5	8	0	0	587	959	546	892	.9	.0
	1977	20	31	0	0	730	1,125	608	937	2.7	.0
	1978	5	7	0	0	757	1,079	686	978	.7	.0
	1979	5	7	0	0	1,206	1,592	788	1,040	.4	.0
	1980	40	48	0	0	1,680	2,033	1,059	1,282	2.4	.0
	1981	60	67	0	0	1,641	1,837	1,215	1,360	3.7	.0
	1982	20	21	0	0	1,110	1,161	1,023	1,070	1.8	.0
	1983	10	10	0	0	788	788	1,045	1,045	1.3	.0
	1984	0	0	0	0	777	751	925	894	.0	.0
	1985	0	0	0	0	708	662	855	800	.0	.0
T. VENEZUELA	1975	90	156	0	0	6,006	10,430	8,800	15,280	1.5	.0
	1976	60	98	0	0	7,663	12,520	9,299	15,190	.8	.0
	1977	100	154	0	0	10,950	16,880	9,551	14,370	.9	.0
	1978	30	43	0	0	11,790	16,810	9,188	13,100	.3	.0
	1979	40	53	0	0	10,690	14,110	14,320	18,900	.4	.0
	1980	130	157	0	0	11,840	14,330	19,220	23,260	1.1	.0
	1981	290	325	0	0	13,110	14,680	20,120	22,530	2.2	.0
	1982	250	261	0	0	12,950	13,550	16,500	17,260	1.9	.0
	1983	50	50	0	0	8,715	8,715	15,160	15,160	.6	.0
	1984	360	348	0	0	7,373	7,127	13,420	12,970	4.9	.0
	1985	330	309	0	0	8,178	7,650	12,270	11,480	4.0	.0
LATIN AMERICA	1975	585	1,015	90	156	50	87	40	70	1.2	.2
	1976	960	1,568	190	310	51	84	45	74	1.9	.4
	1977	1,055	1,627	95	146	58	89	54	83	1.8	.2
	1978	1,695	2,417	100	143	65	93	58	83	2.6	.2
	1979	1,840	2,429	120	158	80	106	76	101	2.3	.2
	1980	1,790	2,166	145	175	106	128	98	119	1.7	.1
	1981	2,710	3,034	195	218	113	127	104	117	2.4	.2
	1982	3,060	3,201	400	418	92	97	96	100	3.3	.4
	1983	2,530	2,530	190	190	72	72	96	96	3.5	.2
	1984	3,435	3,321	610	590	73	70	103	99	4.7	.6
	1985	1,780	1,665	80	75	72	68	98	92	2.5	.1
UNITED STATES	1975	140	243	4,900	8,505	105,900	183,800	108,100	187,700	.1	4.5
	1976	110	180	5,900	9,638	132,500	216,400	115,400	188,500	.1	5.1
	1977	120	185	6,700	10,330	160,400	247,300	121,200	186,900	.1	5.5
	1978	120	171	6,500	9,267	186,000	265,200	143,800	205,000	.1	4.5
	1979	130	172	6,100	8,053	222,200	293,400	182,000	240,300	.1	3.4
	1980	140	169	6,500	7,866	257,000	311,000	220,800	267,200	.1	2.9
	1981	210	235	8,600	9,629	273,400	306,100	233,700	261,700	.1	3.7
	1982	430	450	9,300	9,728	254,900	266,600	212,300	222,000	.2	4.4
	1983	500	500	11,800	11,800	269,900	269,900	200,500	200,500	.2	5.9
	1984	480	464	10,200	9,860	341,200	329,800	217,900	210,600	.1	4.7
	1985	575	538	9,400	8,793	361,600	338,300	213,100	199,400	.2	4.4
WORLD	1975	13,180	22,890	13,270	23,030	890	1,545	870	1,510	1.5	1.5
	1976	17,290	28,250	17,310	28,280	1,002	1,637	983	1,607	1.7	1.8
	1977	20,270	31,250	20,280	31,270	1,146	1,768	1,122	1,730	1.8	1.8
	1978	24,380	34,770	24,440	34,840	1,332	1,900	1,296	1,847	1.8	1.9
	1979	28,190	37,220	28,200	37,230	1,661	2,193	1,633	2,156	1.7	1.7
	1980	30,260	36,620	30,240	36,600	2,027	2,453	1,985	2,402	1.5	1.5
	1981	37,460	41,950	37,570	42,070	2,008	2,248	1,961	2,196	1.9	1.9
	1982	40,150	42,000	39,910	41,740	1,908	1,996	1,850	1,935	2.1	2.2
	1983	39,800	39,800	40,040	40,040	1,863	1,863	1,810	1,810	2.1	2.2
	1984	41,670	40,290	41,460	40,080	1,966	1,900	1,902	1,839	2.1	2.2
	1985	28,850	26,990	28,900	27,030	2,012	1,882	1,935	1,810	1.4	1.5

1. Total imports and exports are total trade figures as reported by individual countries. The extent to which arms are included may differ from country to country. Country imports are reported "cif" (includes the costs of shipping, insurance, and freight) and country exports are reported "fob" (excludes these costs). For these reasons and because of divergent sources, world totals for imports and exports are not equal.
2. Latin America and World Totals are expressed in billions of dollars instead of millions of dollars. In order to reduce distortions in trends caused by data gaps, the totals for World and Latin America include rough approximations for those countries and years in which data or estimates are unavailable.

a. To avoid the appearance of excessive accuracy, arms transfer data have been independently rounded, with greater severity for large numbers. Because of this rounding and the fact that they are obtained from different sources, world arms exports do not equal world arms imports.

SOURCE: U.S. Arms Control and Disarmament Agency, *World Military Expenditures and Arms Transfers, 1973-1984* (Washington, D.C., 1986), table II.

Table 1202

U.S. DATA ON WORLD ARMS TRADE: RECIPIENT COUNTRIES BY MAJOR SUPPLIERS, 20 LR, CUMULATIVE 1981-85[a]

(M US)

						Supplier					
Recipient	Total	Soviet Union	United States	France	United Kingdom	West Germany	China	Italy	Poland	Czecho-slovakia	Others
A. ARGENTINA	2,400	#	40	230	90	1,400	#	110	40	165	2,845
B. BOLIVIA	85	#	#	5	#	#	#	#	#	#	80
C. BRAZIL	280	#	90	60	10	#	#	70	#	#	50
D. CHILE	870	#	#	460	60	130	#	#	#	#	220
E. COLOMBIA	865	#	70	#	10	675	#	#	#	#	110
F. COSTA RICA	20	#	20	#	#	#	#	#	#	#	#
G. CUBA	4,010	3,500	#	#	#	#	#	#	40	160	310
H. DOMINICAN REP.	30	#	10	20	#	#	#	#	#	#	#
I. ECUADOR	750	#	50	120	60	#	#	260	#	#	260
J. EL SALVADOR	285	#	250	#	#	#	#	#	#	#	35
K. GUATEMALA	95	#	5	#	#	#	#	#	#	#	90
L. HAITI	25	#	5	#	#	#	#	10	#	#	10
M. HONDURAS	130	#	50	#	10	#	#	#	#	#	70
N. MEXICO	360	#	130	40	#	10	#	#	#	#	180
O. NICARAGUA	645	250	#	10	#	#	#	#	#	5	380
P. PANAMA	35	#	10	10	#	#	#	#	#	#	15
Q. PARAGUAY	45	#	#	#	#	#	#	#	#	#	45
R. PERU	1,150	390	110	210	#	230	#	100	#	#	110
S. URUGUAY	100	#	5	50	#	5	#	#	#	#	40
T. VENEZUELA	1,275	#	470	30	#	5	#	500	#	#	270
LATIN AMERICA	13,530	4,150	1,325	1,245	255	2,455	#	1,050	40	165	2,845

a. For previous years, see SALA, 18-2802.

SOURCE: U.S. Arms Control and Disarmament Agency, *World Military Expenditures and Arms Transfers, 1975–1985* (Washington, D. C., 1986), pp. 145–146.

Table 1203

IISS DATA ON ARMED FORCES EXPENDITURE, PERSONNEL, VESSELS, AND AIRCRAFT, 20 L,

(1984)

	Country	Defense Expenditure (MUS)	Total Armed Forces (N)	Army (N)	Army Reserves (N)	Navy (N)	Naval[1] Vessels (N)	Air Force (N)	Combat Aircraft (N)	Para-Military (N)
A.	ARGENTINA	1.889[a,c]	73,000	40,000	~	21,000[d]	47	15,000	43	45,000
B.	BOLIVIA	216.076	23,600	20,000	~	3,600[d]	46	4,000	29	14,000
C.	BRAZIL	1.055[b]	283,400	182,900	~	49,800[e]	162	50,700	180	240,000
D.	CHILE	1.622[†]	101,000	57,000	~	29,500[e]	40	15,000	105	27,000
E.	COLOMBIA	426.5	66,200	53,000	100,000	9,000[d]	35	4,200	43	87,500
F.	COSTA RICA	20.21[f]	~	~	~	~	~	~	~	9,500
G.	CUBA	1.357[a,b]	162,000	130,000	120,000[†]	13,500	119	18,500	250	1,368,500[g]
H.	DOMINICAN REP.	56.48[c]	21,300	13,000	~	4,000[h]	32	4,300	28	1,000
I.	ECUADOR	223.871[†]	42,000	35,000	~	4,000[d]	28	3,000	60	200
J.	EL SALVADOR	252[i,†]	42,640	38,650	~	1,290[e]	20	2,700	24	18,600[j]
K.	GUATEMALA	179.8[b]	32,000	30,300	~	1,000[d]	59	700	12	911,600[j]
L.	HAITI	30[†]	6,900	6,400	~	300[k]	14	200	7	~
M.	HONDURAS	90[b]	19,200	17,000	~	700	11	1,500	28	5,000
N.	MEXICO	1.168[a,l]	259,500	105,000	60,000[†]	28,000[e]	114	6,500	87	120,000
O.	NICARAGUA	598.04[†]	72,000	69,000	34,000	1,000	25	2,000	14	57,000
P.	PANAMA	96.469[b]	12,000	11,500	~	300	12	200	0	0
Q.	PARAGUAY	76.375[c]	15,970	12,500	~	2,500[d]	16	970	5	6,000
R.	PERU	1.327[b]	127,000	85,000	175,000[†]	27,000[c]	51	15,000	96	51,600
S.	URUGUAY	147.963	31,900	22,300	~	6,600[m]	18	3,000	30	2,670
T.	VENEZUELA	1.069[a,†]	71,000	34,000	~	10,000[e]	21	5,000	102	22,000

1. Naval vessels may include submarines, aircraft carriers, destroyers, corvettes, patrol
   ships, patrol vessels, fast attack craft, anti-mine vessels, frigates, river ships, tankers,
   amphibious craft, hospital ships, oceanographic vessels, submarine support vessels,
   gunboats, landing craft, intelligence collectors, replenishment ships, minesweepers,
   cargo.

a. B US.
b. Defense budget.
c. Defense budget 1985.
d. Includes marines.
e. Includes navel air force and marines.
f. Figures for public security and civil guard.
g. Includes territorial militia, youth labor, army, frontier guards, civil defense force,
   state security.
h. Includes naval infantry.
i. Defense expenditure 1985.
j. Includes territorial defense force.
k. Coast guard.
l. 1985 expenditure.
m. Naval air and naval infantry.

SOURCE: International Institute for Strategic Studies (IISS), *The Military Balance*, 1986–
1987, pp. 174–197.

Table 1204

IISS DATA ON DEFENSE EXPENDITURE PER MILITARY MAN AND AS PERCENTAGE OF
TOTAL GOVERNMENT SPENDING PER MILITARY MAN, 19 LC, 1975–83

(T)

	Country	Per Military Man (US)							% of Government Spending						
		1975	1976	1978	1980	1981	1982	1983	1975	1976	1978	1980	1981	1982	1983
A.	ARGENTINA	41	49	102	157	305	504	431	9.7	11.6	16.8	18.3	23.1	27.1	~
B.	BOLIVIA	~	~	20	25	33	35	32	~	~	16.5	16.8	23.2	29.3	~
C.	BRAZIL	12	16	16	17	15	22	10	9.3	9.7	9.3	9.7	8.2	11.0	7.5
D.	CHILE	~	~	94	185	186	117	141	~	~	25.2	22.1	31.4	13.1	18.4
E.	COLOMBIA	~	5	11	11	13	15	17	~	9.2	7.0	8.7	9.5	9.3	10.9
F.	COSTA RICA	~	~	~	20	~	10	12	~	~	~	4.4	~	5.5	5.5
G.	CUBA	~	~	120	111	131	128	130	~	~	5.6	5.7	5.4	6.9	7.2
H.	DOMINICAN REP.	~	~	20	30	21	36	36	~	~	10.7	15.5	10.8	19.8	17.8
I.	ECUADOR	~	~	23	23	31	26	23	~	~	15.8	10.2	10.6	9.4	~
J.	EL SALVADOR	~	~	15	15	24	28	32	~	~	10.3	10.7	15.6	25.2	24.5
K.	GUATEMALA	~	~	15	15	17	21	21	~	~	13.4	9.7	9.4	14.5	16.3
L.	HAITI	~	~	~	3	~	5	~	~	~	~	5.3	~	~	~
M.	HONDURAS	~	~	~	16	~	15	17	~	~	~	6.5	~	5.0	5.4
N.	MEXICO	10	9	9	12	20	13	8	2.4	4.4	2.2	2.5	2.8	1.9	~
O.	NICARAGUA	~	~	~	23	~	96	114	~	~	~	9.1	~	23.2	~
Q.	PARAGUAY	~	~	15	22	27	33	27	~	~	17.4	27.3	21.6	22.1	14.4
R.	PERU	24	~	31	50	49	89	75	5.3	~	20.6	21.6	19.3	30.7	19.8
S.	URUGUAY	~	~	64	89	133	134	~	~	~	17.6	15.9	19.7	18.3	~
T.	VENEZUELA	41	34	52	57	57	72	58	5.4	5.5	5.6	6.5	3.5	5.8	5.5
	UNITED STATES	417	423	491	632	739	846	1,023	23.8	23.8	23.7	24.0	25.8	26.3	29.6

SOURCE: International Institute for Strategic Studies (IISS), *The Military Balance*,
1978–79, pp. 88–89; 1983–84, pp. 126–127; 1984–85, pp. 140–142; 1985–86,
pp. 170–173.

Table 1205

MILITARY EXPENDITURE AS PERCENTAGE OF GDP, 20 LC, 1962-85[a]

	Country	1962	1963	1964	1965	1966	1967	1968	1969	1970	1971	1972	1973	1974	1975	1976	1977	1978	1979	1980	1981	1982	1983	1984	1985
A.	ARGENTINA	2.2	2.1	1.7	1.8	2.1	2.3	1.9	1.9	1.9	1.7	1.6	1.6	1.7	2.0	2.4	2.4	2.7	2.5	2.6	2.9	5.9†	3.9†	3.3	~
B.	BOLIVIA	1.1	2.4	2.3	2.5	2.2	2.0	1.6	1.3	1.6	1.4	1.6	1.6	1.8	2.4	3.8	3.3	3.5	3.5	3.7†	4.9†	4.8†	3.8†	4.0†	~
C.	BRAZIL	1.7	1.6	1.7	2.5	2.2	2.9	2.6	2.6	1.9	1.5	1.4	2.1	1.3	1.3	1.3	1.1	.9	.8	.5	.6	.6	.8†	.7†	.8†
D.	CHILE	2.4	2.1	1.9	1.9	2.1	2.0	2.0	2.0	2.5	2.3	2.5	5.9	6.7	5.7	6.7	6.9	6.4	6.2	7.4	6.5	8.7	9.5†	8.8†	~
E.	COLOMBIA	1.9	2.2	2.0	2.0	2.0	2.0	2.3	1.3	1.4	2.5	1.2	1.0	.9	1.0	1.2†	~	1.6†	1.8†	2.0	1.8	1.8	2.2	2.0	~
F.	COSTA RICA	1.1	1.0	.9	.9	1.0	.9	1.1	1.1	.5	.6	.5	.5	.5	.6	.7	.8	.7	.7	.7	.7	.8	.8	.8†	~
G.	CUBA	6.6	6.2	5.3	5.1	5.3	6.1	6.9	6.0	6.9	4.9	4.1	3.7	3.6	3.7†	3.7†	8.3	8.3	8.5	7.8	8.0	9.2	8.6	9.8	~
H.	DOMINICAN REP.	3.7	3.4	3.4	3.7	3.1	2.8	2.8	2.3	2.1	1.9	1.7	1.6	1.6	1.6	1.7	1.7	1.8	2.0	1.5	1.7†	1.6†	1.5	1.5†	~
I.	ECUADOR	2.0	1.8	1.9	1.9	1.7	1.7	1.8	2.2	2.2	1.8	2.0	2.0	1.9	2.3	2.2	3.1	2.1	2.0	1.9	1.9†	1.6†	1.7†	1.8†	~
J.	EL SALVADOR	1.4	1.4	1.2	1.2	1.1	1.1	1.3	3.0	1.0	1.1	1.1	1.5	1.7	1.6	1.7	2.0	2.1	2.0†	2.8	3.7	4.4	4.4	4.9	~
K.	GUATEMALA	.8	.8	1.0	1.1	1.1	1.1	1.0	.9	1.5	.9	1.1	.8	.9	1.2	1.5	1.5	1.7	1.7	1.8	1.9	2.4†	2.6†	2.9†	4.0†
L.	HAITI	2.6	2.4	2.3	2.1	1.9	1.9	1.9	1.8	1.7	1.6	1.6	1.2	1.4	1.7	1.2	1.2	1.3	1.4	1.4	1.5	1.6	1.7	~	~
M.	HONDURAS	1.9	1.9	1.3	1.2	1.3	1.3	1.0	2.2	1.2	1.5	1.8	1.7	1.6	1.9	1.8	1.9	2.3	2.3	3.5	4.5†	5.0†	5.7†	6.0†	~
N.	MEXICO	.7	.7	.7	.7	.7	.7	.7	.7	.7	.6	.7	.5	.5	.5	.6	.6	.5	.5	.6	.6	.6	.7†	.6†	~
O.	NICARAGUA	1.9	1.8	1.5	1.4	1.6	1.6	1.5	1.4	1.6	1.5	1.8	1.4	1.5	1.7	2.1	2.5	3.2	3.1†	4.4	5.0†	5.9†	9.6†	11.7†	~
P.	PANAMA	.5	.5	.4	.5	.4	.5	.5	.7	.8	1.2	.7	.7	.7	.8	1.7	1.5†	1.5†	1.5†	1.2†	1.2†	1.3†	1.4†	~	~
Q.	PARAGUAY	1.7†	1.8†	1.6†	1.7†	1.9	2.0	2.0	2.0	2.0	2.2	2.0	1.7	1.5	1.7	1.7	1.6	1.5	1.3	1.4	1.5	1.6†	1.5†	~	~
R.	PERU	2.4†	3.2	2.9	2.9	2.6	3.2	3.2	3.2	3.7	3.6	3.2	3.8	3.5	4.6	5.0	7.3	5.5	3.9	5.7†	7.2†	7.2†	8.6†	8.2†	~
S.	URUGUAY	1.2	1.6	1.6	1.7	1.5	1.9	1.5	1.8	1.9	2.6	2.5	2.4	2.8	2.6	2.2	2.3	2.6	2.9†	2.6	3.4	4.3†	~	~	~
T.	VENEZUELA	1.7	1.9	1.8	2.0	2.0	2.1	2.0	1.9	1.7	1.9	2.1	1.7	1.5	1.5	2.2	2.2	2.1	2.4	2.7	3.1	3.4	2.9	3.1†	~
	UNITED STATES	9.2	8.7	8.0	7.5	8.4	9.4	9.3	8.7	8.0	7.1	6.6	6.0	6.1	5.9	5.4	5.3	5.1	5.1	5.6	5.8	6.5	6.7	6.5	6.6

a. For previous years, see SALA, 25-1205.

SOURCE: SIPRI-Y, 1977, pp. 222-225, 242-245; 1979, pp. 36-37, 54-57; 1980, pp. 29-33;
1981, pp. 166-169; 1982, pp. 150-153; 1983, pp. 171-174; 1984, pp. 127-131; 1986,
pp. 243-246.

Table 1206

USDOD DATA ON U.S. MILITARY SALES AGREEMENTS, 20 LR, 1977-86[a]

(T US)

	Country	1977	1978	1979	1980	1981	1982	1983	1984	1985	1986	1950-86
A.	ARGENTINA	18,393	5,061	- -	- -	- -	- -	- -	64	5,724	219	197,414
B.	BOLIVIA	140	- -	42	19	- -	- -	- -	4	2,959	437	5,454
C.	BRAZIL	10,940	10,549	311	2,506	3,527	12,713	31,270	8,525	19,337	6,022	356,328
D.	CHILE	235	- -	- -	- -	- -	- -	- -	- -	- -	673	179,540
E.	COLOMBIA	3,368	6,934	4,341	8,869	8,523	12,317	15,180	2	789	6,268	89,844
F.	COSTA RICA	7	- -	316	- -	- -	- -	4,165	2,556	15,845	5,926	30,008
G.	CUBA	- -	- -	- -	- -	- -	- -	- -	- -	- -	- -	4,510
H.	DOMINICAN REP.	#	- -	112	#	3	3,453	586	6,699	4,258	7,309	24,599
I.	ECUADOR	22,463	30,315	13,402	2,190	11,093	617	1,793	26,490	1,389	4,887	137,098
J.	EL SALVADOR	146	9	#	2,291	10,022	16,117	66,011	127,082	134,442	122,040	481,179
K.	GUATEMALA	5,662	3,618	1,903	10	4	- -	71	2,809	1,786	5,133	42,236
L.	HAITI	190	- -	241	12	- -	- -	- -	99	481	1,125	3,009
M.	HONDURAS	760	641	203	2,297	4,193	9,115	26,768	34,895	93,151	79,392	259,295
N.	MEXICO	156	1,973	88	15	94,313	5,347	2,027	3,117	6,078	5,493	137,468
O.	NICARAGUA	652	2	- -	1	- -	- -	- -	- -	- -	- -	5,205
P.	PANAMA	173	116	123	244	382	472	178	803	17,322	3,605	28,038
Q.	PARAGUAY	248	40	9	90	23	122	7	- -	- -	- -	971
R.	PERU	9,737	10,578	4,976	3,783	5,112	2,516	2,049	2,853	666	8,883	185,391
S.	URUGUAY	605	44	2	624	626	1,447	434	346	122	1,003	22,015
T.	VENEZUELA	1,958	3,840	1,436	2,827	56,974	617,809	3,520	5,784	10,862	42,360	976,560
	LATIN AMERICA	76,961	75,453	28,707	26,419	208,600	683,601	168,588	244,837	348,400		

a. For 1950-74, see SALA, 23-1103; for 1975-76, see SALA, 24-1206.

SOURCE: USDOD-FMSA, Sept. 1983, pp. 5-7; Sept. 1985, pp. 6-7; Sept. 1986, pp. 6-7.

Table 1207

USDOD DATA ON U.S. MILITARY SALES DELIVERIES, 20 LR, 1977-86[a]

(T US)

	Country	1977	1978	1979	1980	1981	1982	1983	1984	1985	1986	1950-86
A.	ARGENTINA	6,815	9,426	6,635	14,423	6,426	4,244	1,769	1,195	770	1,032	190,731
B.	BOLIVIA	24	90	23	186	- -	- -	- -	- -	10	2,562	4,627
C.	BRAZIL	8,531	6,324	7,591	7,213	5,307	4,269	8,924	9,748	10,269	25,531	325,496
D.	CHILE	56,026	10,993	7,794	4,797	- -	- -	- -	- -	- -	- -	177,564
E.	COLOMBIA	944	1,917	5,018	3,689	8,959	14,434	6,994	10,575	2,475	3,854	80,278
F.	COSTA RICA	- -	21	266	123	- -	9	814	2,712	8,305	8,360	21,670
G.	CUBA	---	- -	- -	- -	- -	- -	- -	- -	- -	- -	4,510
H.	DOMINICAN REP.	2	71	8	137	- -	3,176	329	3,598	2,104	2,971	14,466
I.	ECUADOR	9,051	7,798	7,971	9,951	5,859	11,816	28,622	5,215	2,856	8,742	107,786
J.	EL SALVADOR	257	594	21	1,109	1,953	16,715	28,096	82,793	111,892	103,279	348,926
K.	GUATEMALA	2,167	2,410	3,374	1,884	462	631	668	546	1,064	920	33,686
L.	HAITI	102	314	251	79	12	- -	5	- -	35	459	1,800
M.	HONDURAS	384	461	899	581	1,319	1,426	12,106	19,488	26,412	59,075	129,514
N.	MEXICO	3,612	467	362	2,015	1,325	70,845	16,001	2,888	3,618	5,521	120,971
O.	NICARAGUA	354	768	43	18	- -	- -	- -	- -	- -	- -	5,205
P.	PANAMA	243	148	246	187	154	360	481	546	2,124	12,488	21,058
Q.	PARAGUAY	219	43	2	48	41	182	9	- -	1	2	971
R.	PERU	25,911	13,345	11,835	13,951	5,907	5,534	3,195	2,432	1,608	3,558	170,758
S.	URUGUAY	5,088	1,171	202	717	689	445	679	295	664	753	20,870
T.	VENEZUELA	42,451	3,894	4,767	5,838	13,809	19,039	32,778	136,501	243,637	80,919	759,172
	LATIN AMERICA	162,179	60,263	57,309	67,078	52,237	153,146	141,759	281,708	428,640	325,243	2,559,813

a. For 1950-74, see SALA, 23-1104; for 1975-76, see SALA, 24-1207.

SOURCE: USDOD-FMSA, Sept. 1983, pp. 13-15; Sept. 1985, pp. 14-15; Sept. 1986, pp. 14-15.

Table 1208

USDOD DATA ON STUDENTS TRAINED UNDER U.S. INTERNATIONAL MILITARY EDUCATION AND TRAINING PROGRAM, 20 LR, 1977-86[a]

(N)

	Country	1977	1978	1979	1980	1981	1982	1983	1984	1985	1986	1950-86
A.	ARGENTINA	140	- -	- -	- -	- -	- -	- -	- -	- -	- -	4,082
B.	BOLIVIA	183	227	211	36	- -	- -	- -	29	70	23	5,039
C.	BRAZIL	- -	- -	- -	- -	- -	- -	- -	- -	- -	- -	8,726
D.	CHILE	- -	- -	- -	- -	- -	- -	- -	- -	- -	- -	6,917
E.	COLOMBIA	350	257	408	444	539	642	910	665	720	813	12,650
F.	COSTA RICA	- -	- -	- -	- -	37	55	79	36	71	76	1,065
G.	CUBA	- -	- -	- -	- -	- -	- -	- -	- -	- -	- -	523
H.	DOMINICAN REP.	73	90	113	47	163	129	153	168	168	130	5,176
I.	ECUADOR	288	421	451	385	217	252	381	146	108	146	7,708
J.	EL SALVADOR	47	- -	- -	125	256	736	1,223	104	276	369	5,077
K.	GUATEMALA	127	- -	- -	- -	- -	- -	- -	- -	123	95	3,578
L.	HAITI	12	14	17	10	27	25	29	64	45	20	852
M.	HONDURAS	116	219	226	166	261	328	332	326	321	350	5,527
N.	MEXICO	37	39	54	43	107	63	28	33	76	19	1,391
O.	NICARAGUA	234	275	6	- -	- -	- -	- -	- -	- -	- -	5,740
P.	PANAMA	234	83	219	202	293	219	301	260	183	167	6,584
Q.	PARAGUAY	99	145	- -	- -	- -	8	14	16	19	19	2,131
R.	PERU	677	56	72	195	178	369	284	88	160	64	9,379
S.	URUGUAY	- -	- -	- -	- -	- -	1	15	45	18	19	2,927
T.	VENEZUELA	13	30	- -	- -	18	22	52	46	49	63	5,834
	LATIN AMERICA	2,630	1,856	1,778	1,671	2,144	2,923	3,954	2,193	2,743	2,587	101,868

a. For 1950-74, see SALA, 23-1105; for 1975-76, see SALA, 24-1208.

SOURCE: USDOD-FMSA, Sept. 1983, pp. 92-93; Sept. 1985, pp. 88-91; Sept. 1986, pp. 88-91.

Table 1209

USDOD DATA ON U.S. EXPENDITURE FOR INTERNATIONAL MILITARY EDUCATION AND TRAINING PROGRAM, 20 LR, 1977-86[a]

(T US)

	Country	1977	1978	1979	1980	1981	1982	1983	1984	1985	1986	1950-86
A.	ARGENTINA	721	- -	- -	- -	- -	- -	- -	- -	- -	- -	12,796
B.	BOLIVIA	581	628	367	144	- -	- -	- -	125	347	143	14,835
C.	BRAZIL	46	- -	- -	- -	- -	- -	- -	- -	- -	- -	16,353
D.	CHILE	- -	- -	- -	- -	- -	- -	- -	- -	- -	- -	16,847
E.	COLOMBIA	697	1,122	455	258	246	345	665	751	816	1,005	19,322
F.	COSTA RICA	- -	- -	- -	- -	31	46	123	134	230	222	1,687
G.	CUBA	- -	- -	- -	- -	- -	- -	- -	- -	- -	- -	2,023
H.	DOMINICAN REP.	527	610	443	239	345	430	574	682	706	688	14,159
I.	ECUADOR	393	703	453	222	296	477	532	698	678	709	16,179
J.	EL SALVADOR	565	- -	- -	244	1,157	5,250	4,984	3,326	1,810	1,441	24,059
K.	GUATEMALA	490	- -	- -	- -	- -	- -	- -	- -	451	357	8,310
L.	HAITI	93	130	173	116	110	212	341	715	388	233	3,378
M.	HONDURAS	631	692	240	435	537	1,223	782	910	1,096	1,047	14,496
N.	MEXICO	118	115	173	121	101	82	61	160	217	190	3,585
O.	NICARAGUA	658	384	7	- -	- -	- -	- -	- -	- -	- -	11,583
P.	PANAMA	456	439	392	270	328	359	466	453	575	507	7,709
Q.	PARAGUAY	359	587	- -	- -	- -	8	55	75	95	99	6,997
R.	PERU	986	779	398	289	278	453	486	686	528	611	22,723
S.	URUGUAY	- -	- -	- -	- -	- -	5	58	98	81	100	6,944
T.	VENEZUELA	73	101	- -	- -	8	23	42	45	95	100	14,178
	LATIN AMERICA	7,395	6,291	3,106	2,384	3,529	9,107	9,532	9,430	8,964	8,310	241,159

a. For 1950-74, see SALA, 23-1106; for 1975-76, see SALA, 24-1209.

SOURCE: USDOD-FMSA, Sept. 1983, pp. 86-87; Sept. 1985, pp. 80-83; Sept. 1986, pp. 80-83.

Table 1210

USDOD DATA ON TOTAL VALUE OF U.S. ARMS TRANSFERS,[1]
20 L, FY 1970-85

(T US)

	Country	1970[a]	1975	1976[b]	1977	1978	1979	1980	1981	1982	1983	1984	1985
A.	ARGENTINA	10,730	10,287	11,898	13,129	22,684	36,131	21,916	10,979	9,244	4,683	9,061	4,763
B.	BOLIVIA	345	779	1,014	732	884	1,427	386	9	700	21	29	155
C.	BRAZIL	2,458	46,478	88,990	14,586	11,117	15,765	14,788	15,208	14,269	26,335	30,730	15,617
D.	CHILE	6,982	12,824	40,581	57,383	10,993	7,794	4,797	- -	- -	- -	11	964
E.	COLOMBIA	1,317	1,842	2,324	8,015	4,500	7,099	5,108	11,664	19,435	21,391	14,362	8,851
F.	COSTA RICA	#	123	231	132	187	470	325	57	159	970	2,968	18,156
G.	CUBA	#	- -	- -	- -	- -	- -	- -	- -	- -	- -	- -	- -
H.	DOMINICAN REP.	222	283	73	841	891	204	443	101	4,339	1,040	5,227	2,331
I.	ECUADOR	770	2,485	6,468	9,694	24,356	8,580	10,307	7,295	12,889	37,984	10,243	5,275
J.	EL SALVADOR	35	1,727	611	486	864	172	1,316	1,970	17,045	32,152	84,485	114,531
K.	GUATEMALA	701	3,849	3,386	3,189	2,960	4,242	2,343	469	1,381	671	583	1,212
L.	HAITI	#	270	245	553	710	268	79	18	200	1,308	290	3,203
M.	HONDURAS	26	916	4,910	486	1,563	2,758	1,247	2,242	1,926	13,212	23,525	27,989
N.	MEXICO	12	963	1,780	5,998	3,077	1,746	3,750	4,928	75,417	28,014	7,799	10,306
O.	NICARAGUA	423	724	1,591	1,960	1,365	44	18	5	50	- -	1	1
P.	PANAMA	206	1,903	2,069	2,823	1,124	1,074	29,428	906	1,360	1,985	2,346	2,721
Q.	PARAGUAY	151	342	1,792	672	255	279	688	218	482	204	63	61
R.	PERU	2,185	9,288	32,616	31,279	17,830	13,502	14,869	9,917	10,573	21,297	5,858	4,192
S.	URUGUAY	2,375	2,159	1,735	5,483	1,238	316	976	1,280	695	1,123	454	1,004
T.	VENEZUELA	738	42,360	12,647	51,433	9,784	13,485	19,224	21,809	29,040	52,853	149,139	257,508

1. Includes foreign military sales deliveries, commercial exports licensed under arms
   export control act, and military assistance program excess defense articles program
   acquisition act.

a. Data on commercial export licensed under arms control act not available prior to
   1971.

b. Fiscal year 1976 includes transitional quarter.

SOURCE: USDOD-FMSA, Dec. 1979, pp. 2, 3, 16, 22; 2; Sept. 1983, pp. 12-13, 42-43,
   66-67; Sept. 1985, pp. 14-15, 42-45, 68-69.

Table 1211

ARGENTINA AND GREAT BRITAIN (GB) HUMAN LOSSES IN THE 1982 FALKLANDS WAR

PART I. ARGENTINA

Category	Freedman			GB Official	Gaceta Marinera			Press[1]	
	Engaged	Killed	Injured	Prisoners	Engaged	Killed	Injured	Killed	Prisoners
Navy								**	~
Regular	~	~	~	~	~	244[a]	~	**	~
Conscripted	~	~	~	~	~	124[a]	~	**	~
Total	~	~	~	~	~	368[a]	~	**	~
Air Force	~	~	~	~	~	~	~	**	~
Army	~	50	~	~	~	~	~	**	~
Belgrano Incident	~	360	~	~	1,042	321	~	**	~
Total	12,000	800-1,000	~	11,400	~	~	~	1,000	11,845

PART II. GREAT BRITAIN

Category	Freedman			GB Official			Gaceta Marinera			Press[1]	
	Engaged	Killed	Injured	Engaged	Killed	Injured	Engaged	Killed	Injured	Killed	Injured
Marines	3,000	~	~	~	~	~	~	~	~	**	**
Air Force	~	~	~	~	~	~	~	~	~	**	**
Army	6,000	~	~	~	~	~	~	~	~	**	**
Total	~	~	~	28,000	255	777	~	~	~	250+	**
Remaining Garrison	~	**	**	3,000-4,000[b]	**	**	~	**	**	**	**

1. Ongoing casualty reports by the press are not considered applicable since they were often drastically inaccurate. The totals cited are from "Surrender in the Falklands," *Newsweek*, June 28, 1982, pp. 33-37.

a. To date there have been no official reports on Argentine war losses. The data presented are for those men given distinction and honors by the Argentine navy for death in combat. It appears that none of these medals were given to victims of the *General Belgrano* sinking.

b. Based upon press reports outlined by the British Consul General (letter to the author, January 14, 1983).

SOURCE: Adam Perkal, "Losses and Lessons of the 1982 War for the Falklands," SALA, 23, Chapter 38.

Part V: Working Conditions, Migration, and Housing

CHAPTER 13

LABOR FORCE, EAP, UNEMPLOYMENT, CLASS STRUCTURE, AND CRIME

Note: This volume contains statistics from numerous sources. Alternative data on many topics are presented. Variations in statistics can be attributed to differences in definition, parameters, coverage, methodology, as well as date gathered, prepared, or adjusted. See also Editor's Note on Methodology.

Table 1300

TOTAL PARTICIPATION RATES,[1] 9 L, 1970–85

(AA)

	Country	1970	1976	1980	1981	1982	1983	1984	1985[‡]
B.	BOLIVIA[10]	47.3	48.1	49.6	49.2	49.1	49.0	48.9	48.7
C.	BRAZIL[2]	58.8	58.1	61.0	62.0	61.9	60.5	61.3	60.7
D.	CHILE[3]	51.8	50.3	50.7	51.7	51.7	52.2	52.5	52.3
E.	COLOMBIA[4]	~	49.8	54.4	52.3	53.0	54.6	56.2	56.6
F.	COSTA RICA[5]	44.9	50.2	50.2	49.3	50.9	48.7	48.7	49.3
N.	MEXICO[5,6]	~	50.9	50.1	50.1	49.5	49.1	49.4	52.6
P.	PANAMA[7]	~	55.0	52.0	~	53.7	56.1	55.9	56.8
S.	URUGUAY[8]	48.5	52.8	56.4	54.6	56.6	56.9	57.9	58.5
T.	VENEZUELA[7,9]	43.4	~	55.0	54.7	54.4	54.2	55.3	56.1

1. Economically active population as a percentage of population of working age, according to household survey data.
2. Metropolitan areas of Rio de Janeiro, São Paulo, Belo Horizonte, Porto Alegre, Salvador, and Recife with a lower age limit of 15 years.
3. Greater Santiago with a lower age limit of 14 years for March, June, September, and December.
4. Barranquilla, Bogotá, Cali, and Medellín with a lower age limit of 12 years for March, June, September, and December.
5. Lower age limit of 12 years.
6. Metropolitan areas of Mexico City, Guadalajara, and Monterrey.
7. Lower age limit of 15 years.
8. Lower age limit of 14 years for four quarters.
9. Data for two quarters.
10. Lower age limit of 10 years.

SOURCE: ECLA-S, 1985, vol. 1, p. 25.

Table 1301

LABOR FORCE PARTICIPATION BY SEX, 17 L, 1950–80

(%)

	Country	1950			1960			1970			1980		
		Total	M	F	Total	M	F	Total	M	F	Total	M	F
A.	ARGENTINA	51.36	79.14	21.71	50.18	77.69	21.78	48.36	72.59	23.98	48.16	71.28	25.30
B.	BOLIVIA	71.94	84.78	59.33	50.42	79.08	22.56	47.29	75.09	20.59	46.75	73.17	21.61
C.	BRAZIL	48.41	81.23	15.12	46.96	77.05	16.32	45.53	70.85	19.93	45.56	70.85	19.93
D.	COLOMBIA	48.81	81.05	17.50	45.93	74.49	17.29	44.89	68.49	21.69	46.01	68.36	23.87
E.	COSTA RICA	49.08	83.85	14.28	47.12	78.74	15.33	44.87	73.21	16.28	46.46	73.77	18.84
F.	CHILE	49.19	77.19	20.06	45.73	72.73	19.56	41.66	66.03	18.07	42.97	66.92	19.80
H.	DOMINICAN REP.	50.09	80.35	17.65	48.97	76.39	20.54	47.12	69.63	24.09	46.49	68.10	24.52
I.	ECUADOR	49.49	85.21	15.58	48.64	82.38	15.70	47.84	77.77	18.20	47.71	75.88	20.05
J.	EL SALVADOR	50.57	85.19	16.08	49.15	81.77	16.56	47.23	77.12	17.16	47.15	75.20	18.82
K.	GUATEMALA	49.37	85.69	12.33	47.36	81.99	12.03	45.36	78.11	11.84	45.76	77.43	13.27
M.	HONDURAS	49.42	86.72	11.64	48.18	84.19	11.93	45.88	78.72	12.98	45.45	75.36	15.46
N.	MEXICO	47.09	82.30	12.13	45.55	77.83	13.80	43.29	71.78	15.05	43.97	71.41	16.46
O.	NICARAGUA	49.58	85.82	13.83	48.17	80.79	16.19	46.29	75.69	18.30	47.04	74.56	20.36
P.	PANAMA	49.31	77.81	19.48	48.37	74.51	20.98	49.76	72.19	26.27	50.30	71.04	28.74
R.	PERU	56.82	80.16	34.65	51.54	73.91	29.72	47.21	68.14	26.47	46.72	66.69	26.80
S.	URUGUAY	47.80	73.39	21.74	47.96	73.39	22.67	48.21	71.69	25.28	47.65	69.73	26.39
T.	VENEZUELA	49.10	80.17	17.09	47.35	75.73	17.46	43.39	67.88	18.46	44.65	68.15	21.26
	LATIN AMERICA	49.74	81.02	18.23	47.49	77.04	17.84	45.44	71.65	19.20	45.58	70.53	20.59

SOURCE: ILO, *Mercado de Trabajo en Cifras, 1950-1980*, 1982, table I-1.

Table 1302

ESTIMATED GROWTH OF LABOR FORCE BY SEX, 19 L, 1975–2000

(AA-GR)

	Country	1975-80 Total	M	F	1980-85 Total	M	F	1985-90 Total	M	F	1990-95 Total	M	F	1995-2000 Total	M	F
A.	ARGENTINA	1.10	.87	1.76	1.09	.89	1.65	1.08	.87	1.66	1.12	.95	1.54	1.08	.94	1.42
B.	BOLIVIA	2.40	2.19	3.20	2.54	2.25	3.60	2.63	2.32	3.69	2.84	2.42	4.16	2.84	2.42	4.06
C.	BRAZIL	2.81	2.50	3.91	2.93	2.54	4.20	2.92	2.52	4.13	3.03	2.59	4.26	2.96	2.55	4.03
D.	CHILE	2.66	2.28	3.84	2.48	2.19	3.34	2.13	1.89	2.81	1.93	1.73	2.46	1.88	1.67	2.41
E.	COLOMBIA	3.25	3.25	3.24	3.40	3.31	3.67	3.28	3.20	3.52	3.33	3.17	3.80	3.17	3.01	3.61
F.	COSTA RICA	3.59	3.26	4.91	3.27	2.92	4.55	2.86	2.56	3.91	2.79	2.44	3.93	2.67	2.32	3.73
H.	DOMINICAN REP.	3.27	3.12	4.35	3.42	3.24	4.68	3.50	3.32	4.67	3.61	3.38	5.00	3.62	3.39	4.89
I.	ECUADOR	3.34	3.07	4.37	3.46	3.12	4.67	3.38	3.05	4.52	3.39	3.00	4.63	3.28	2.88	4.43
J.	EL SALVADOR	3.38	3.12	4.44	3.36	3.06	4.53	3.25	2.96	4.30	3.33	2.95	4.60	3.31	2.93	4.52
K.	GUATEMALA	2.87	2.74	3.73	2.90	2.72	3.95	2.90	2.71	3.98	2.95	2.71	4.24	2.91	2.66	4.13
L.	HAITI	1.49	1.62	1.34	1.51	1.71	1.27	1.54	1.77	1.28	1.72	1.98	1.40	1.80	2.08	1.46
M.	HONDURAS	3.19	3.07	3.91	3.36	3.20	4.37	3.42	3.24	4.47	3.40	3.19	4.54	3.34	3.14	4.35
N.	MEXICO	3.39	3.13	4.49	3.49	3.18	4.71	3.43	3.12	4.59	3.58	3.21	4.86	3.59	3.21	4.78
O.	NICARAGUA	3.26	3.00	4.23	3.44	3.10	4.61	3.54	3.18	4.65	3.72	3.27	5.02	3.67	3.24	4.83
P.	PANAMA	2.78	2.77	2.82	2.82	2.75	3.03	2.66	2.62	2.78	2.78	2.61	3.26	2.73	2.55	3.21
Q.	PARAGUAY	3.12	2.86	4.01	3.18	2.83	4.28	3.15	2.79	4.22	3.23	2.78	4.45	3.91	2.76	4.30
R.	PERU	3.12	2.82	4.14	3.28	2.91	4.48	3.31	2.94	4.42	3.35	2.96	4.44	3.27	2.89	4.26
S.	URUGUAY	1.00	.75	1.61	1.19	.97	1.73	1.03	.81	1.54	1.05	.88	1.42	.97	.80	1.32
T.	VENEZUELA	3.73	3.34	5.02	3.59	3.24	4.67	3.25	2.93	4.17	3.08	2.84	3.72	3.02	2.78	3.63

SOURCE: ILO, *Labor Force Estimates and Projections, 1950-2000*, 1977.

Table 1303

CHILDREN IN THE LABOR FORCE,[1] 20 LC, 1960–2000

	Country	T 1960	1970	1975	2000	PTI 1960	1970	1975	2000
A.	ARGENTINA	211	192	167	107	10.2	8.1	6.6	3.3

Continued in SALA, 21-1310.

Table 1304

COMPOSITION OF LABOR FORCE, 20 LC, 1965–2000

(%)

	Country	Working Age Population (15–64 Years) 1965	1985	Agriculture 1965	1980	Industry 1965	1980	Services 1965	1980	AA–GR of Labor Force 1965–80	1980–85	1985–2000
A.	ARGENTINA	63	60	18	13	34	34	48	53	1.1	1.1	1.5
B.	BOLIVIA	53	53	54	46	20	20	26	34	2.0	2.7	2.7
C.	BRAZIL	53	59	49	31	20	27	31	42	3.3	2.3	2.1
D.	CHILE	56	63	27	17	29	25	44	58	2.2	2.6	1.7
E.	COLOMBIA	49	59	45	34	21	24	34	42	2.6	2.8	2.3
F.	COSTA RICA	49	59	47	31	19	23	34	46	3.8	3.1	2.4
G.	CUBA	~	~	~	~	~	~	~	~	~	~	~
H.	DOMINICAN REP.	47	53	59	46	14	15	27	39	2.8	3.5	2.9
I.	ECUADOR	50	53	55	39	19	20	26	42	2.7	3.1	2.9
J.	EL SALVADOR	50	60	59	43	16	19	26	37	3.3	2.9	3.3
K.	GUATEMALA	50	53	64	57	15	17	21	26	2.3	2.8	3.3
L.	HAITI	52	51	77	70	7	8	16	22	1.0	2.0	2.2
M.	HONDURAS	50	50	68	61	12	16	20	23	2.8	3.9	3.9
N.	MEXICO	49	54	50	37	22	29	29	35	3.9	3.2	3.0
O.	NICARAGUA	48	50	57	47	16	16	28	38	2.9	3.8	3.9
P.	PANAMA	51	58	46	32	16	18	38	50	2.7	3.0	2.6
Q.	PARAGUAY	49	51	55	49	20	21	26	31	3.2	3.1	2.8
R.	PERU	51	56	50	40	19	18	32	42	2.9	2.9	2.8
S.	URUGUAY	63	63	20	16	29	29	51	55	.4	.6	.9
T.	VENEZUELA	49	56	30	16	24	28	47	56	4.2	3.5	3.0
	UNITED STATES	60	66	5	4	35	31	60	66	2.2	1.2	.8

SOURCE: *World Development Report*, 1987, table 32.

Table 1305

LABOR FORCE STRUCTURE, 20 LC, 1960–2000

Country	% of Population of Working Age (15–64 Years)				% Agriculture				% Industry				% Services				AA–GR			
	1960	1965	1982	1984	1960	1965	1980	1981	1960	1965	1980	1981	1960	1965	1980	1981	1960–70	1965–73	1973–84	1980–2000
A. ARGENTINA	64	63	63	61	44	18	13	13	29	34	34	28	27	48	53	59	.4	1.4	1.1	1.5
B. BOLIVIA	55	53	53	53	61	54	46	50	18	20	20	24	21	26	34	26	1.7	1.8	2.5	2.9
C. BRAZIL	54	53	55	58	52	48	31	30	15	20	27	24	33	31	42	46	2.7	2.5	3.0	2.3
D. CHILE	57	56	62	63	31	27	16	19	20	29	25	19	50	44	58	62	1.4	1.3	2.5	2.1
E. COLOMBIA	50	49	60	59	51	45	34	26	19	21	24	21	29	34	42	53	3.0	3.1	2.8	2.5
F. COSTA RICA	50	49	59	59	51	47	31	29	19	19	23	23	30	34	46	48	3.5	3.7	3.8	2.8
G. CUBA	61	59	61	65	39	33	24	23	22	25	29	31	39	41	48	46	.8	1.0	2.2	1.7
H. DOMINICAN REP.	49	48	53	55	67	59	46	49	12	13	16	18	21	27	39	33	2.2	2.7	3.3	3.0
I. ECUADOR	52	50	52	53	57	55	39	52	19	19	20	17	23	26	42	31	2.9	3.1	2.9	3.0
J. EL SALVADOR	52	50	52	51	62	59	56	50	17	16	14	22	21	25	30	28	2.6	3.2	2.9	3.4
K. GUATEMALA	51	50	54	53	67	64	57	55	14	15	17	21	19	21	25	24	2.8	2.7	2.8	2.9
L. HAITI	55	54	53	55	80	77	70	74	6	7	8	7	14	16	22	19	.6	.7	1.6	2.0
M. HONDURAS	52	50	50	50	70	68	61	63	11	12	16	20	19	20	23	17	2.5	2.4	3.3	3.4
N. MEXICO	51	49	52	53	55	50	37	36	20	22	29	26	25	29	34	38	2.8	3.1	3.2	3.2
O. NICARAGUA	50	48	50	50	62	57	47	39	16	16	16	14	22	27	38	47	2.3	3.0	3.2	3.7
P. PANAMA	52	51	56	57	51	46	32	33	14	16	18	18	35	38	50	49	3.4	3.3	2.6	2.2
Q. PARAGUAY	51	50	53	55	56	55	49	49	19	20	21	19	25	26	31	32	2.3	2.5	3.3	3.0
R. PERU	52	51	54	56	52	50	40	40	20	19	18	19	28	31	42	41	2.1	2.4	2.9	2.9
S. URUGUAY	64	63	63	63	21	20	16	11	30	29	29	32	50	51	55	57	.8	.3	.5	.9
T. VENEZUELA	51	49	55	55	35	30	16	18	22	24	28	27	43	47	56	55	2.8	3.5	3.9	3.4
UNITED STATES	60	60	66	66	7	5	4	2	36	35	31	32	57	60	66	66	1.8	1.9	1.6	.9

SOURCE: WB-WDR, 1984 and 1986, table 30.

Table 1306

SECTORAL DISTRIBUTION OF THE LABOR FORCE,[1]
19 LC, 1960–80
(%)

	Country	Agriculture 1960	Agriculture 1980	Industry 1960	Industry 1980	Services 1960	Services 1980
1.	Capitalist industrial countries	18	6	38	38	44	56
2.	Socialist industrial countries	41	16	31	45	28	39
3.	Latin American countries	47	31	20	24	33	45
N.	MEXICO	55	36	20	26	25	38
K.	GUATEMALA	67	55	14	21	19	24
J.	EL SALVADOR	65	58	17	22	21	27
M.	HONDURAS	70	63	11	15	19	22
O.	NICARAGUA	62	39	16	14	22	47
F.	COSTA RICA	51	29	19	23	30	48
P.	PANAMA	51	27	14	18	35	55
T.	VENEZUELA	35	18	22	27	43	55
E.	COLOMBIA	51	26	19	21	30	53
I.	ECUADOR	58	52	19	17	23	31
R.	PERU	52	40	20	19	28	41
B.	BOLIVIA	61	50	18	24	21	26
Q.	PARAGUAY	56	49	19	19	25	32
D.	CHILE	30	19	20	19	50	62
A.	ARGENTINA	20	13	36	28	44	59
S.	URUGUAY	21	11	29	32	50	57
C.	BRAZIL	52	30	15	24	33	46
G.	CUBA	39	23	22	31	39	46
H.	DOMINICAN REP.	67	49	12	18	21	33

1. Order corresponds to that in Figure 13:1, above.
2. The Agricultural sector includes crop and stock farming, forestry, hunting and fishing. The Industrial sector includes mining, manufacturing, construction and public utilities (electricity, water, and gas). All other branches of economic activity are included in the Services category.

SOURCE: Aníbal Pinto, "Metropolization and Tertiarization," *Cepal Review* 24, (Santiago, 1984).

Table 1307

AGRICULTURAL LABOR FORCE,[1] 26 ECLA:L,[2] 1950–75

	Country	1950	1955	1960	1965	1970	1975*	1950–60	1960–70	1970–75	1950–75
		T						AA–GR			
A.	ARGENTINA	4,318	4,270	4,118	4,023	3,883	3,142	–.5	–.6	–.7	–.6
	Bahamas	23	26	30	33	35	34	2.7	1.6	–.6	1.5
	Barbados	61	62	62	54	47	41	.2	–2.7	–2.7	–1.5
B.	BOLIVIA	1,855	2,067	2,307	2,470	2,655	2,869	2.2	1.4	1.6	1.8

Continued in SALA, 24–1305.

Table 1308

AGRICULTURAL POPULATION AS SHARE
OF TOTAL POPULATION,[1]
26 ECLA:L,[2] 1950–75

	Country	1950	1960	1970	1975*
A.	ARGENTINA	25.2	20.0	16.4	14.7
	Bahamas	28.9	26.8	19.7	16.7
	Barbados	28.9	26.8	19.7	16.7
B.	BOLIVIA	61.4	61.0	55.5	53.0

Continued in SALA, 24–1306.

Figure 13:1

AGRICULTURAL SECTOR SHARE IN PRODUCT
AND EMPLOYMENT, 17 LR, 1980

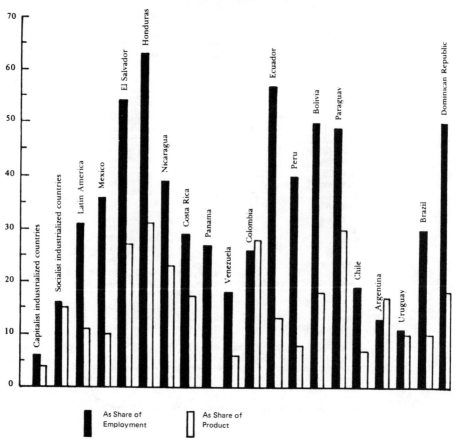

SOURCE: *Cepal Review* 24 (Santiago, 1984).

Table 1309

AGRICULTURAL POPULATION AND ECONOMICALLY ACTIVE POPULATION IN AGRICULTURE, 20 LC, 1980-85[a]

Country	1980					1985				
	Total Population (T)	Agricultural Population (T)	EAP Total (T)	EAP In Agriculture (T)	% Agriculture	Total Population (T)	Agricultural Population (T)	EAP Total (T)	EAP In Agriculture (T)	% Agriculture
A. ARGENTINA	28,237	3,660	10,792	1,399	13.0	30,564	3,588	10,884	1,278	11.7
B. BOLIVIA	5,570	2,784	1,819	909	50.0	6,371	2,780	1,987	867	43.6
C. BRAZIL	121,286	46,319	38,157	14,572	38.2	135,564	34,186	49,642	12,519	25.2
D. CHILE	11,104	2,099	3,673	678	18.4	12,038	1,691	4,276	586	13.7
E. COLOMBIA	25,794	7,062	2,692	2,106	27.4	28,714	9,140	9,195	2,927	31.8
F. COSTA RICA	2,279	799	764	268	35.1	2,600	666	904	232	25.6
G. CUBA	9,732	2,267	2,971	692	23.3	10,038	2,102	3,987	835	20.9
H. DOMINICAN REP.	5,558	3,118	1,461	820	56.1	6,243	2,574	1,862	768	41.2
I. ECUADOR	8,021	3,565	2,553	1,135	44.4	9,378	3,089	2,839	935	32.9
J. EL SALVADOR	4,797	2,465	1,495	754	50.4	5,552	2,095	1,832	677	37.0
K. GUATEMALA	7,262	3,985	2,207	1,211	54.9	7,963	4,346	2,261	1,234	54.6
L. HAITI	5,809	3,870	2,902	1,933	66.6	6,585	4,455	2,822	1,909	67.6
M. HONDURAS	3,691	2,310	1,087	680	62.6	4,372	2,545	1,303	758	58.2
N. MEXICO	69,393	24,995	19,999	7,204	36.0	78,996	26,036	26,080	8,596	33.0
O. NICARAGUA	3,056	1,199	911	366	42.8	3,272	1,407	993	438	44.1
P. PANAMA	1,956	674	657	226	34.5	2,180	598	760	208	27.4
Q. PARAGUAY	3,168	1,549	1,019	498	48.9	3,681	1,713	1,223	569	46.5
R. PERU	17,625	6,976	5,189	1,937	37.3	19,698	7,680	6,204	2,273	36.6
S. URUGUAY	2,908	345	1,151	126	11.9	3,012	436	1,171	169	14.5
T. VENEZUELA	15,620	2,804	4,166	857	18.0	17,817	2,140	5,871	725	12.4
UNITED STATES	227,700	4,896	103,672	2,229	2.2	238,840	7,418	117,203	3,640	3.1

a. For 1965, 1981, and 1983, see SALA, 24–1307; for 1970 and 1975, see SALA, 25–1307.

SOURCE: FAO-PY, 1985, table 3.

Table 1310

ECONOMICALLY ACTIVE POPULATION (EAP),[1] 20 LC

Country	Year[4]	Code[2]	Total Population	Economically Active Population N	%	Males	Active Males As % of Total Male Population	Females	Active Females As % of Total Female Population
A. ARGENTINA[3]	1985	F	30,563,835	11,452,444	37.5	8,380,179	55.3	3,072,265	19.9
B. BOLIVIA[‡]	1985	F	6,429,226	1,996,459	31.1	1,528,385	48.1	468,074	14.4
C. BRAZIL[14]	1980	C	119,070,865	43,796,763	36.8	31,757,833	53.7	12,038,930	20.1
D. CHILE[6]	1984	D	11,774,800	3,890,100	33.0	2,694,000	46.8	1,195,500	19.9
E. COLOMBIA[‡]	1980	E	26,806,866	8,467,000	31.6	6,247,000	50.0	2,220,000	15.5
F. COSTA RICA[5]	1985	E	2,489,212	887,456	35.7	655,762	53.2	231,694	18.5
G. CUBA	1981	A	9,723,605	3,617,620	37.2	2,479,733	50.5	1,137,887	23.7
H. DOMINICAN REP.[‡]	1981	A	5,647,977	1,915,388	33.9	1,361,109	48.1	554,279	19.7
I. ECUADOR[5],[‡]	1982	A	8,060,712	2,346,063	29.1	1,861,652	46.3	484,411	12.0
J. EL SALVADOR	1980	E	4,497,257	1,593,353	35.4	1,039,446	47.5	553,907	24.0
K. GUATEMALA[12]	1981	A	6,054,227	1,696,464	28.0	1,449,058	48.0	247,406	8.1
L. HAITI	1982	F	5,118,936	2,263,832	44.2	1,292,177	52.1	971,655	36.9
M. HONDURAS[10]	1984	F	3,955,116[a]	1,256,349	~	1,046,415	~	209,934	~
N. MEXICO	1980	A	66,846,833	22,066,084	33.0	15,924,806	48.2	6,141,278	18.2
O. NICARAGUA[9]	1980	F	2,703,147	863,925	32.0	681,089	51.4	182,836	13.3
P. PANAMA[7]	1984	D	1,701,921[b]	682,732	~	472,007	~	210,725	~
Q. PARAGUAY[5]	1982	A	3,029,830	1,039,258	34.3	834,308	54.8	204,950	13.6
R. PERU[13]	1981	A	17,005,210	5,281,714	31.1	3,937,696	46.6	1,344,018	15.7
S. URUGUAY[3]	1984	D	2,565,100	1,077,900	42.0	637,700	53.6	440,200	32.0
T. VENEZUELA	1985	E	17,209,388	5,827,650	33.9	4,238,847	48.8	1,588,803	18.7
UNITED STATES[8],[11]	1985	D	238,740,000[c]	117,167,000	49.1	65,967,000	56.8	51,200,000	41.8

1. "Economically active" includes all persons engaged or seeking to be engaged in productive work in some branch of economic activity. Comparability of data is limited by the various differing minimum age limits, seasonal fluctuations in some economies, and international differences in the concepts and definitions of the term "labor force."

2. Codes: A, complete count, final data;
    B, sample tabulation, size not specified;
    C, sample tabulation, size specified;
    D, labor force sample survey;
    E, household survey;
    F, official estimates.

3. Economically active population figures relate to persons 14 years of age and over.

4. May or may not coincide with year of population census.

5. Economically active population figures relate to persons 12 years of age and over.

6. Figures rounded to the nearest hundred.

7. Includes 12,796 male and 3,093 female workers in the Canal Zone.

8. Economically active population figures relate to persons 16 years of age and over.

9. Excludes unemployed.

10. Data exclude unemployed persons not previously employed.

11. Economically active population figures include 1,706,000 resident members of the armed forces. Figures are rounded to the nearest thousand.

12. Excludes institutional households.

13. Economically active population figures relate to persons 6 years of age and over.

14. Based on a 1% sample tabulation of census returns.

a. 1982 estimate.

b. 1980 estimate.

c. Mid-year estimates.

SOURCE: ILO-YLS, 1983–86, table 1.

Table 1311
EAP BY INDUSTRY, 20 LC

	Country	Year	Code[1]	EAP	Agriculture Forestry, Hunting, and Fishing		Mining and Quarrying		Manufacturing		Construction		Electricity Gas, and Water		Wholesale/Retail Trade, Restaurants, and Hotels	
					N	%	N	%	N	%	N	%	N	%	N	%
A.	ARGENTINA[2]	1980	A	10,033,798	1,200,992	12.0	47,171	.4	1,985,995	19.8	1,003,175	10.0	103,256	1.1	1,702,080	16.9
B.	BOLIVIA	1976	A	1,501,391	693,049	46.2	60,599	4.0	145,404	9.7	82,447	5.5	2,143	.1	106,862	7.1
C.	BRAZIL[3]	1980	C	43,796,763	13,109,415	29.9	7,523,883[o]	17.2[o]	~[k]	~[k]	3,151,094	7.2	~[k]	~[k]	4,111,307	9.4
D.	CHILE[10]	1984	D	3,887,600	567,400	14.6	71,000	1.8	540,000	13.9	173,500	4.5	28,600	.7	697,600	18.0
E.	COLOMBIA‡	1980	E	8,467,000	2,412,413	28.4	49,740	.6	1,136,735	13.4	242,191	2.9	44,233	.5	1,261,633	14.9
F.	COSTA RICA[4]	1985	E	887,456	238,207	26.8	142,187[f]	16.1[f]	~[k]	~[k]	47,465	5.3	~[j]	~[j]	164,863	18.6
G.	CUBA	1981	A	3,540,692	790,869	22.3	668,340[o]	18.9[o]	~[k]	~[k]	313,240	8.9	~[k]	~[k]	305,630	8.6
H.	DOMINICAN REP.‡	1981	A	1,915,388	420,463	22.0	4,743	.2	224,437	11.7	80,850	4.3	13,891	.7	192,181	10.0
I.	ECUADOR[4]	1982	A	2,346,063	786,972	33.5	7,406	.4	286,530	12.2	158,009	6.8	13,183	.5	271,914	11.6
J.	EL SALVADOR	1980	E	1,593,353	636,617	40.0	4,394	.2	247,621	15.6	80,089	5.0	9,681	.6	256,086	16.1
K.	GUATEMALA[5]	1981	A	1,696,464	908,513	53.6	2,348	.1	177,494	10.5	86,191	5.1	7,714	.4	147,120	8.7
L.	HAITI[9]	1983	F	2,263,832	1,299,440	57.4	20,374	.9	129,038	5.7	22,638	1.0	2,264	.1	303,353	13.4
M.	HONDURAS[6]	1984	F	1,256,349	718,505	57.2	3,895	.3	167,597	13.3	43,470	3.5	5,151	.4	107,292	8.5
N.	MEXICO	1980	A	22,066,084	5,699,971	25.8	477,017	2.2	2,575,124	11.7	1,296,337	5.9	115,932	.5	1,729,296	7.8
O.	NICARAGUA[7]	1980	F	863,925	391,963	45.4	6,566	.7	91,403	10.6	37,322	4.3	6,652	.8	105,053	12.2
P.	PANAMA	1984	E	682,732	177,783	26.0	856	.2	65,969	9.6	36,854	5.4	8,608	1.3	98,585	14.4
Q.	PARAGUAY[4]	1982	A	1,039,258	445,518	42.9	1,406	.1	124,658	12.0	69,900	6.8	2,605	.2	85,956	8.2
R.	PERU[11],‡	1981	A	5,281,734	1,844,434	34.9	94,211	1.8	543,698	10.3	187,112	3.6	17,719	.3	629,636	11.9
S.	URUGUAY	1975	A	1,094,599	174,871	16.0	2,159	.2	205,943	18.8	59,428	5.4	16,206	1.5	134,509	12.3
T.	VENEZUELA	1984	E	5,716,207	825,777	14.4	81,412	1.5	874,215	15.3	482,535	8.5	73,293	1.2	1,065,876	18.6
	UNITED STATES[8,12]	1985	D	117,167,000	3,603,000	3.1	1,036,000	.9	22,587,000	19.2	7,848,000	6.7	1,529,000[m]	1.3[m]	24,027,000	20.5

Table 1311 (Continued)
EAP BY INDUSTRY, 20 LC

	Country	Year	Code[1]	Transport, Storage, and Communication		Financing, Insurance, Real Estate, and Business Services		Community Social, and Personal Services		Activities Not Adequately Defined		Other[13]	
				N	%	N	%	N	%	N	%	N	%
A.	ARGENTINA[2]	1980	A	460,476	4.6	395,704	4.0	2,399,039	23.9	691,302	6.9	44,608	.4
B.	BOLIVIA	1976	A	55,972	3.8	12,941	.8	281,911	18.8	53,600	3.6	6,463	.4
C.	BRAZIL[3]	1980	C	1,815,541	4.1	7,089,709	16.2	4,857,061[e]	11.1[e]	1,255,815	2.9	882,938	2.0
D.	CHILE[10]	1984	D	235,700	6.0	124,300	3.2	1,327,800	34.2	2,100	#	119,600	3.1
E.	COLOMBIA‡	1980	E	352,623	4.2	278,210	3.2	1,998,460	23.6	690,762[i]	8.2[i]	~	~
F.	COSTA RICA[4]	1985	E	53,421[d]	6.0[d]	~[q]	~[q]	222,845	25.1	6,942	.8	11,526	1.3
G.	CUBA	1981	A	248,644	7.0	~[q]	~[q]	1,086,052[a]	30.7[a]	127,917[g]	3.6[g]	~	~
H.	DOMINICAN REP.‡	1980	A	40,470	2.1	22,369	1.2	363,125	18.9	421,628	22.0	131,231	6.9
I.	ECUADOR[4]	1982	A	101,321	4.3	44,116	1.9	554,915	23.6	38,594	1.7	83,103	3.5
J.	EL SALVADOR	1980	E	65,593	4.1	15,863	1.0	250,158	15.7	224	#	27,027	1.7
K.	GUATEMALA[5]	1981	A	43,255	2.5	21,159	1.3	214,981	12.6	75,053	4.5	12,636	.7
L.	HAITI[9]	1983	F	18,111	.8	4,528	.2	133,566	5.9	54,332	2.4	276,188	12.2
M.	HONDURAS[6]	1984	F	37,565	3.0	12,438	1.0	160,436	12.8	~	~	~	.6
N.	MEXICO	1980	A	672,111	3.0	405,754	1.9	2,418,114	10.9	6,552,037	29.7	124,391	~
O.	NICARAGUA[7]	1980	F	30,064	3.4	16,761	2.0	158,789	18.4	19,352	2.2	~	~
P.	PANAMA	1984	E	38,770	5.7	24,126	3.5	185,720	27.2	15,889[p]	2.4	29,572	4.3
Q.	PARAGUAY[4]	1982	A	30,524	3.0	18,019	1.7	174,228	16.8	79,568	7.6	6,876	.7
R.	PERU[11],‡	1981	A	203,903	3.9	120,591	2.2	1,011,737	19.2	272,992	5.2	355,701	6.7
S.	URUGUAY	1975	A	53,728	4.9	29,461	2.7	316,078	28.9	85,085	7.7	17,131[b]	1.6[b]
T.	VENEZUELA	1984	E	384,111	6.8	295,175	4.8	1,517,971	26.5	27,820[h]	.5[h]	108,022	1.9
	UNITED STATES[8,12]	1985	D	6,387,000	5.5	11,562,000	9.9	35,790,000[j]	30.5[j]	1,706,000[c]	1.5[c]	1,093,000[n]	~[n]

1. Code: A, complete count, final data; ;
   B, sample tabulation, size not specified.
   C, sample tabulation, size specified;
   D, labor force sample survey;
   E, household survey;
   F, official estimates.

2. Figures relate to persons 14 years of age and over.
3. Figures based on 1% sample of census returns.
4. Figures relate to persons 12 years of age and over.
5. Excludes institutional households.
6. Data exclude unemployed persons not previously employed.
7. Excludes unemployed.
8. Economically active population figures refer to persons 16 years of age and over.
9. Figures based on a 2.5% sample tabulation of census returns.
10. Figures rounded to the nearest hundred.
11. Economically active population figures relate to persons 10 to 69 years of age.
12. Figures rounded to the nearest thousand.
13. Data refer to persons seeking first job.

a. Includes financing, insurance, real estate, and business services.
b. Includes storage and personal services.
c. Data refer to members of the armed forces.
d. Includes electricity, gas, water, and sanitary services.
e. Includes restaurants and hotels.
f. Includes manufacturing.
g. Data refer to members of producers' co-operatives.
h. Data refer to the unemployed.
i. Includes persons seeking first job.
j. Includes hotels.
k. Included in mining and quarrying industries.
l. Included in transport, storage, and communication.
m. Includes sanitary services.
n. Includes 52,000 persons whose last job was in armed forces.
o. Includes manufacturing, electricity, gas, and water.
p. Includes 15,889 Canal Zone workers.
q. Not recommended separately.

SOURCE: ILO-YLS, 1977 and 1981–86, table 2A.

Table 1312
EAP BY MAJOR OCCUPATIONS, 20 LC

Country	Year	Code[1]	Total EAP[1]	Professional, Technical, and Related Workers (0-1) N	%	Administrative and Managerial Workers (2) N	%	Clerical and Related Workers (3) N	%	Sales Workers (4) N	%	Service Workers (5) N	%	Agriculture, Animal Husbandry, and Forestry Workers, Fishermen and Hunters (6) N	%	Production and Related Workers, Transport Equipment Operators and Laborers (7-9) N	%	Workers Not Classifiable by Occupation (X) N	%	Person Seeking First Job N	%
A. ARGENTINA	1970	B	9,011,450	677,500	7.5	137,850	1.5	1,025,400	11.4	1,072,800	11.9	1,136,550[b]	12.6[b]	1,296,100	14.4	3,091,350	34.3	573,900	6.4	~	~
B. BOLIVIA	1976	A	1,501,391	85,500	5.7	9,092	.6	59,609	4.0	91,385	6.1	128,595[h]	8.5[h]	1,067,675[c]	71.1[c]	~	~	53,072	3.6	6,463	.4
C. BRAZIL[4]	1970	C	29,557,224	1,410,746	4.8	497,079	1.7	1,561,678	5.3	2,193,661	7.4	3,404,014[h]	11.6[h]	13,039,149	44.0	6,263,571	21.2	1,187,308	4.0	~	~
D. CHILE[6]	1984	E	3,887,200	252,900	6.5	108,400	2.8	452,200	11.6	476,900	11.3	471,600	12.1	572,000	14.7	1,394,200	35.9	39,400	1.0	119,600	3.1
E. COLOMBIA[5],‡	1980	E	8,467,000	138,813	1.6	87,590	1.1	501,582	5.9	1,044,854	12.3	1,619,334	19.2	2,405,538	28.4	1,978,527	23.3	690,762	8.2	~[d]	~[d]
F. COSTA RICA[12]	1985	E	887,456	83,006	9.4	108,521[f]	12.2[f]	~[f]	~[f]	132,092	14.6	136,173	5.4	414,034[g]	46.6[g]	~	~[g]	4,104	.5	11,526	1.3
G. CUBA[10,7]	1970	~	2,633,309	220,298	8.4	112,745	4.3	136,185	5.2	564,403[e]	21.4[e]	~[e]	~[e]	708,165	26.9	857,089	32.5	34,424	1.3	~	~
H. DOMINICAN REP.‡	1981	A	1,915,388	77,573	4.0	20,364	1.1	96,592	5.1	133,153	6.9	207,645	10.8	428,045	22.4	345,525	18.0	475,260	24.8	131,231	6.9
I. ECUADOR[12]	1982	A	2,346,063	183,579	7.8	11,123	.5	131,925	5.6	209,380	8.9	179,444	7.7	784,767	33.4	601,374	25.7	161,368[j]	6.9[j]	83,103	3.5
J. EL SALVADOR	1980	E	1,593,353	67,411	4.2	8,476	.6	85,929	5.4	225,438	14.1	128,413	8.1	629,345	39.5	421,090	26.4	224	#	27,027	1.7
K. GUATEMALA[13]	1981	A	1,696,464	81,237	4.8	20,117	1.2	56,568	3.3	99,516	5.9	109,848	6.5	911,256	53.7	349,943	20.6	55,342	3.3	12,636	.7
L. HAITI	1983	F	2,263,832	45,277	2.0	13,583	.6	9,055	.4	210,536	9.3	49,804	2.2	1,129,652	49.9	151,677	6.7	378,060	16.7	276,188	12.2
M. HONDURAS	1974	~	762,795	30,982	4.1	7,012	.9	31,784	4.2	43,907	5.8	49,674	6.5	453,113	59.4	131,408	17.2	7,744	1.0	7,171	.9
N. MEXICO	1980	A	22,066,084	1,451,200	6.6	20,853	.1	2,202,272	10.0	1,603,985	7.2	1,928,758	8.8	5,532,680	25.0	4,813,513	21.8	4,388,432	19.9	124,391	.6
O. NICARAGUA	1971	~	504,240	26,040	5.2	4,750	.9	21,080	4.2	35,840	7.1	55,130	10.9	235,120	46.7	110,500	21.9	15,780	3.1	~	~
P. PANAMA[3,13]	1984	D	682,732	70,809	10.4	30,912	4.5	68,565	10.0	49,167	7.2	107,176	15.7	169,086	24.8	156,635	22.9	810	.2	29,572	4.3
Q. PARAGUAY[12]	1982	A	1,039,258	53,820	5.2	53,720[a]	5.1[a]	~[k]	~[k]	66,690	6.5	87,710	8.5	445,650	43.3	246,970	24.0	66,770	6.5	6,130	.6
R. PERU[15],‡	1981	A	5,281,734	392,593	7.4	24,329	.5	514,363	9.7	523,921	10.0	375,804	7.1	1,817,407	34.4	992,653	18.8	284,963	5.4	355,701	6.7
S. URUGUAY[2]	1984	D	1,077,900	109,500	10.2	18,900	1.7	158,100	14.7	137,400	12.7	200,600	18.6	34,900	3.3	357,300	33.1	23,800	2.2	37,400	3.5
T. VENEZUELA[7,9]	1985	E	5,827,650	583,598	10.0	222,174	3.8	588,397	10.1	751,997	12.9	795,109	13.7	842,003	14.4	1,894,851	32.5	44,843	.8	104,678	1.8
UNITED STATES[8,11,14]	1985	D	117,167,000	17,311,000	14.8	12,550,000	10.7	18,191,000	15.5	13,369,000	11.4	15,827,000	13.5	3,785,000	3.3	33,335,000	28.4	1,758,000[b],[j]	1.5[b],[j]	1,041,000	.9

1. Code: A, Complete count, final data;
   B, Sample tabulation, size not specified;
   C, Sample tabulation, size specified;
   D, Labor force sample survey;
   E, Household survey;
   F, Official estimates.

2. Includes persons 14 years of age and over.
3. Excludes persons working in the Canal Zone.
4. De jure population. EAP figures based on a 25% sample tabulation of census returns.
5. Figures include persons seeking work for the first time.
6. Figures rounded to nearest hundred.
7. Figures rounded to nearest ten.
8. Figures based on the 1980 census occupational classification system.
9. The group not classifiable by status refers to unemployed.
10. Does not include domestic servants.
11. Includes persons 16 years of age and over.
12. Includes persons 12 years of age and over.
13. Figures related to persons 12 years of age and over.
Figures exclude institutional household, ds.

14. Figures rounded to nearest thousand.
15. Economically active population figures relate to persons 10 to 69 years of age.

a. Figures include clerical and related workers.
b. Figures include members of the armed forces.
c. Figures include miners and quarrymen.
d. Not recorded separately.
e. Figures for service workers are included under sales workers.
f. Administrative and managerial workers includes clerical and related workers.
g. Figures in category 6 include workers from categories 7-9.
h. Service workers includes clerical and related workers.
i. Includes 52,000 persons whose last job was in armed forces.
j. Includes 39,363 unemployed persons previously employed.
k. Included in category 2.

SOURCE: ILO-YLS, 1977, 1980, and 1982–86, table 2B.

Table 1313

OCCUPATIONAL CATEGORIES, BY SEX, 20 LC
(%)

	Country	Year	Code[1]	N (M)		Professional, Technical, and Related Workers (0-1)		Administrative and Managerial Workers (2)		Clerical and Related Workers (3)		Sales Workers (4)		Service Workers (5)		Agriculture, Animal Husbandry, and Forestry Workers, Fishermen and Hunters (6)		Production and Related Workers, Transport Equipment Operators and Laborers (7-9)		Workers Not Classifiable by Occupation (X)		Other (Y)	
				M	F	M	F	M	F	M	F	M	F	M	F	M	F	M	F	M	F	M	F
A.	ARGENTINA	1970	~	6.7	2.3	4.5	1.6	1.9	.4	9.8	15.9	12.1	11.2	6.7	30.0	18.1	3.4	41.0	15.2	5.9	7.6	~	~
B.	BOLIVIA	1976	A	1.2	.3	4.3	10.5	.6	.4	3.5	3.5	3.5	14.9	4.9[a]	21.2[a]	52.2	26.5	26.6[b]	18.0[b]	3.8	2.6	.6	.4
C.	BRAZIL	1970	~	23.4	6.2	2.5	13.5	1.9	1.0	4.4	8.5	8.0	5.2	3.7	35.6	50.4	20.4	23.7	11.4	3.9	4.4	1.5[a]	#
D.	CHILE[2]	1984	D	2.7	1.2	2.9	3.6	2.3	.5	6.6	5.1	7.6	4.7	3.4	8.7	13.9	.8	30.0	5.8	1.0	#	1.6	1.5
E.	COLOMBIA[8]	1973	~	6.0	↓	4.5	↓	.7	↓	5.9	↓	7.4	↓	10.0	↓	26.8	↓	20.6	↓	9.8	↓	14.3[c]	↓
F.	COSTA RICA[9]	1985	E	.6	.2	5.0	4.4	10.9[e]	1.3[e]	~[f]	~	8.4	6.2	7.1	8.3	41.3[h]	5.3[h]	~[i]	~	.4	#	.7[d]	.6[d]
G.	CUBA[8]	1970	~	2.2	↓	8.4	↓	4.3	↓	5.2	↓	21.4[e]	↓	…	↓	26.9	↓	32.5	↓	1.3	↓	7.1[d]	↓
H.	DOMINICAN REP.‡	1981	A	1.4	.5	2.9	6.9	1.2	.8	3.9	7.9	7.2	6.4	4.2	27.3	28.4	7.4	21.8	8.8	23.5	28.2		6.3[d]
I.	ECUADOR[9]	1982	A	1.9	.5	4.5	3.3	.4	#	3.1	2.5	6.3	2.8	3.0	4.6	30.9	2.5	22.8	2.9	5.8	1.1	2.7[d]	.9[d]
J.	EL SALVADOR	1980	E	1.0	.6	3.6	5.4	.7	.2	4.8	6.5	6.3	28.9	3.6	16.5	49.5	20.8	30.7	18.4	.0	.0	.8	.3
K.	GUATEMALA[3,10]	1981	D	1.4	.2	3.4	12.9	1.2	1.3	2.3	9.5	4.6	13.5	2.6	29.3	61.9	8.4	21.3	17.7	2.6	7.3	~	~
L.	HAITI[11]	1982	B	1.3	.8	2.1	1.9	.6	.4	.3	.5	1.6	20.5	1.3	3.6	63.0	30.9	7.8	5.2	12.1	23.2	11.2[c]	13.6[c]
M.	HONDURAS	1974	~	.6	.1	2.6	12.2	.8	1.3	3.5	7.8	4.3	13.5	2.1	30.3	69.6	5.0	15.2	28.0	1.0	1.0	.9[d]	.9[d]
N.	MEXICO	1980	A	15.9	6.1	5.4	9.7	.1	.1	8.1	14.8	6.8	8.4	6.6	14.4	30.5	11.0	25.1	13.2	16.8	27.9	.5[d]	.6[d]
O.	NICARAGUA	1971	D	.4	.1	3.7	10.2	1.0	.9	3.4	7.0	4.5	16.3	3.0	39.1	57.8	6.4	23.6	15.7	2.7	4.6	~	~
P.	PANAMA[4]	1984	D	.5	.2	4.7	5.6	3.6		3.0	7.0	4.1	3.1	6.8	8.9	24.1	.7	20.4	2.5	.1	~	2.2[d]	2.1[d]
Q.	PARAGUAY[7]	1982	C	.8	.2	2.8	10.6	.8	.6	4.4	9.8	4.9	12.3	3.8	27.3	51.4	11.3	24.9	20.4	6.3	7.3	.6[d]	.5[d]
R.	PERU[12,‡]	1981	A	3.9	1.3	6.3	10.8	.6	.1	8.5	13.4	8.7	13.6	4.6	14.5	39.6	19.1	22.4	8.3	4.0	9.5	5.4[c]	10.7[c]
S.	URUGUAY[13]	1984	D	.6	.4	4.2	6.0	1.6	.2	8.0	6.7	7.8	5.0	5.5	13.1	3.0	.2	25.6	7.6	2.1	#	1.4[d]	2.1[d]
T.	VENEZUELA‡	1985	E	4.2	1.6	4.5	5.5	3.3	.5	4.2	5.8	9.2	3.6	6.3	7.3	14.0	.4	29.4	3.1	.7	#	.9[d]	.9[d]
	UNITED STATES[5,6]	1985	D	65.9	51.2	7.6	7.2	6.9	3.8	3.1	12.4	5.8	5.6	5.3	8.2	2.7	.5	23.1	5.3	.4[d]	.5[d]	1.4[a,c]	.1[a,c]

1. Code: A, Complete count, final data;
   B, Sample tabulation, size not specified;
   C, Sample tabulation size specified;
   D, Labor force sample survey;
   E, Household survey;
   F, Official estimates.
2. Figures rounded to the nearest hundred.
3. Excludes institutional households.
4. Includes 15,889 persons working in the Canal Zone (12,796 males and 3,093 females).
5. Economically active population figures relate to persons 16 years of age and over.
6. All figures rounded to nearest thousand; consequently, the totals shown may differ from the sum of the component parts.
7. Based on a 10% sample tabulation.
8. Figures for female workers are included in the male category.
9. Figures relate to persons 12 years of age and over.

10. Figures relate to persons 10 to 79 years of age and over.
11. Figures based on a 2.5% sample tabulation of census returns.
12. Figures relate to persons 10 to 69 years of age.
13. Persons aged 14 years and over.

a. Includes members of the armed forces.
b. Figures include miners, quarrymen, and related workers.
c. Figures refer to persons seeking work for the first time.
d. Figures relate to persons 10 to 69 years of age.
e. Includes clerical and related workers.
f. Included in administrative and managerial workers.
g. Included in administrative and managerial workers.
h. Included in agriculture, animal husbandry and forestry workers, fishermen, and hunters.
i. Included in production and related workers, transport equipment operators, and laborers.

SOURCE: ILO-YLS, 1976, 1977, 1979–82, 1984, 1985, and 1986, table 2B.

Table 1314

OCCUPATIONAL STRATA,[1] 9 L, 1960–73

(%)

Category	A. ARGENTINA		C. BRAZIL		D. CHILE		F. COSTA RICA	
	1960	1970	1960	1972	1960	1970	1963	1970
1. Medium and High Strata (except the occupations of the primary sector)	31.4	32.2	15.0	23.3	20.3	27.8	33.6	46.2
a. Employees	8.2	4.3	1.9	4.1	1.5	2.4	3.0	6.0
b. Self-Employed, Owners of Commercial Establishments	2.4	4.4	.2	1.6	3.7	4.9	4.4	3.1

	J. ECUADOR		P. PANAMA		Q. PARAGUAY		S. URUGUAY		T. VENEZUELA	
	1962	1968	1960	1970	1962	1972	1963	1970	1960	1973
	25.0	39.8	16.4	21.8	11.8	13.9	50.9	45.8	23.9	36.8
	1.7	4.1	1.3	1.0	1.2	1.4	8.4	5.6	1.8	3.6
	9.1	12.1	.9	1.3	2.7	3.1	3.0	3.8	5.4	7.0

Continued in SALA, 21-1304.

Table 1315

ECONOMICALLY ACTIVE POPULATION ESTIMATED BY AGE GROUP, 20 LR, 1970–2000

Country	Age Groups	1970	1975	1980	1985	1990	1995	2000
A. ARGENTINA	Total	9,429,603	10,139,106	10,726,912	11,452,423	12,304,794	13,363,746	14,611,885
	10-14	203,219	191,983	181,811	194,872	214,161	217,129	210,275
	15-19	1,082,636	1,068,007	1,006,875	1,031,474	1,141,226	1,291,981	1,354,283
	20-24	1,286,940	1,431,032	1,477,305	1,554,659	1,679,103	1,955,616	2,331,904
	25-29	1,163,412	1,329,935	1,462,758	1,554,482	1,630,617	1,754,440	2,036,065
	30-34	1,058,637	1,162,099	1,321,442	1,474,883	1,556,897	1,621,853	1,733,485
	35-39	1,015,080	1,056,883	1,157,263	1,310,830	1,448,328	1,513,083	1,560,043
	40-44	968,658	1,005,217	1,043,096	1,125,520	1,271,948	1,401,679	1,460,507
	45-49	850,743	935,959	960,269	978,816	1,058,121	1,197,551	1,321,603

Continued in SALA, 25-1313.

Table 1316

EAP BY ACTIVITY,[1] 14 L, 1950–80

(%)

Country	Year	Urban			Agricultural				Coverage of the Underemployed
		Formal (1)	Informal[a] (2)	Total (3)	Modern (4)	Traditional (5)	Total (6)	Mining (7)	(2+5) (8)
A. ARGENTINA	1950	56.8	15.2	72.0	19.9	7.6	27.5	.5	22.8
	1970	66.0	15.6	81.6	11.2	6.7	17.9	.5	22.3
	1980[b]	65.0	19.4	84.4	8.8	6.3	15.1	.5	25.7

Continued in SALA, 24–1314.

Table 1317

POPULATION EMPLOYED BY SECTOR, 13 L, 1960 AND 1970

(N)

Country	Agricultural Sector		Basic Services		And Other Services	
	1960	1970	1960	1970	1960	1970
A. ARGENTINA	19.1	15.2	38.0	37.0	42.9	47.8

Continued in SALA, 21-1305.

Table 1318

EMPLOYMENT IN MANUFACTURING, 18 LC, 1970-85[a]

(T)

Country	Code[1]	1970	1971	1972	1973	1974	1975	1976	1977	1978	1979	1980	1981	1982	1983	1984	1985
A. ARGENTINA	C	**	**	**	**	**	**	223.1	217.6	199.7	193.8	180.6	160.9	143.8	149.3	156.9	~
B. BOLIVIA[12,15,18,20]	D[19]	103.9	108.2	112.6	117.1	121.8	**	152.3	160.5	166.1	172.7	177.7	168.4	155.5	150.2	149.3	~
C. BRAZIL[2,15,23]	A[19]	2,499[b]	2,599[b]	2,830[b]	3,230[b]	3,720[b]	**	6,266	6,510	7,099	7,288	~	7,562	7,790	~	~	~
E. COLOMBIA[4]	C	100.0	102.3	106.2	111.7	116.4	117.9	120.6	122.3	124.5	127.2	100.0	95.4	90.5	84.5	83.6	~
F. COSTA RICA[5,14,15,24]	A	**	**	**	**	**	**	78.4	85.8	87.9	94.5	95.9	88.1	89.5	98.3	101.7[d]	100.0
G. CUBA[6,26,27]	C[25]	**	440.5	438.5	453.2	466.7	472.2	514.1	550.5	558.7	559.9	565.7	564.9	596.6	639.2	674.8	695.1
H. DOMINICAN REP.	C	110.7	113.9	124.2	137.7	139.4	122.3	110.8	112.6	113.3							
I. ECUADOR[7]	C	..	123.4	125.4	132.1	139.2	147.6	158.7	154.1	165.3	173.2	174.5	177.4	189.4	181.0	~	~
J. EL SALVADOR[16]	C	**	**	**	**	**	49.5	54.2	56.4	57.7	58.8	54.3	50.6	47.8	50.6	49.9	48.9[‡]
K. GUATEMALA[3]	C	**	37.7	40.9	41.6	37.4	32.8	32.4	36.8	38.6	46.5	41.3	40.3	35.9	32.9	~	~
L. HAITI[2,8]	D	118.7	119.4	121.6	120.9	121.5	122.3	115.9	116.6	117.2	117.8	132.2	134.2	121.2	121.7	~	~
M. HONDURAS	D	..	..	..	..	..	**	98.3	103.7	109.4	115.5	121.9	128.6				
N. MEXICO[12,17,22]	C	~		346.7	362.2	403.2[e]	413.5	491.2[f]	487.2	510.1	547.6	587.2	619.3	605.1	548.2	537.9	554.3
O. NICARAGUA[10,12]	B	22.2	22.2	23.6	22.4	25.0	26.6	28.2	30.5	29.2	24.8	27.9	~				
P. PANAMA[11,14,28]	A	**	**	**	~	37.4[c]	33.7[c]	34.2	37.9[c]	39.9	42.7	~	~	44.8	49.6	47.4	~
R. PERU[2]	D	574.0	601.3	627.4	658.4	694.7	727.9	744.0	741.2	772.3	803.9	812.5	808.4				
S. URUGUAY[9,29]	A	..	..	..	..	..	~	130.2	139.6	139.9	140.7	130.7[a]	145.5	120.7	110.5[h]	115.6	123.0
T. VENEZUELA[13,16,21]	C	61.4	62.1	62.9	65.5	70.1	289.7	392.8	419.6	455.2	404.6	477.1	412.6	449.5	453.5	421.9	~
UNITED STATES[21]	C	19,367	18,263	19,151	20,154	20,077	18,323	18,997	19,682	20,505	21,040	20,285	20,170	18,781	18,434	19,378	19,314

1. The series refer, in general, to salaried employees and wage earners in manufacturing[g] (excluding public utilities, building, and other construction). Workers on paid or unpaid holiday or vacation are generally included, but employers, self-employed, and workers on strike, or temporary military leave or temporarily laid off are generally excluded. Code A, Labor force sample surveys, B, Social insurance statistics; C, Statistics of establishments; D, Official estimates.
2. Civilian labor force employed.
3. Wage earners after 1974.
4. Base: 1980 = 100, prior to 1980: July 1970 — June 1971 = 100.
5. July of each year after 1974.
6. Prior to 1977. Includes mining and quarrying, electricity, gas, and water; state sector.
7. Base: 1965 = 100.
8. Year beginning in July of each year indicated.
9. Montevideo.
10. Eight main cities of the country.
11. August of each year.
12. Employees after 1974.
13. Second semester of each year, prior to 1975.
14. Wage earners and salaried employees.
15. Includes mining and quarrying after 1974.
16. After 1974, includes establishments with five or more persons employed.
17. Last week of October of each year.

18. July 1st of each year after 1975.
19. Prior to 1975, statistics of establishments.
20. Prior to 1975, civilian labor force employed.
21. Registered employees prior to 1975.
22. Prior to 1975, include 57 industrial groups of the national classification.
23. Persons 10 years and over.
24. Persons 12 years and over.
25. Prior to 1976, official estimates.
26. State sector employees.
27. Includes fishing, gas, mining and quarrying, and water.
28. After 1975, persons 15 years and over.
29. Includes professional army and excludes compulsory military service.

a. For employment indices data, 1964-79, see SALA, 22-1304.
b. December.
c. October.
d. November.
e. Not strictly comparable.
f. Prior to 1975: 54 industrial groups.
g. First quarter.
h. Prior to 1983: First semester of each year.

SOURCE: Data for 1970-74 from ILO-YLS, 1980, table 6A; 1975-85 data from ILO-YLS, 1985 and 1986, table 5A.

Table 1319

EMPLOYMENT INDEX FOR MANUFACTURING, 9 L, 1977–83[a]

(1980 = 100)

Country	1977	1978	1979	1980	1981	1982	1983	% Change[3] 1977	1978	1979	1980	1981	1982	1983
A. ARGENTINA[1]	109.7	99.3	97.2	100.0	78.4	74.2	76.7	−6.2	−9.7	−2.1	2.9	−21.6	−5.4	3.3
C. BRAZIL[1]	91.8	93.7	96.9	100.0	92.6	86.5	80.1	1.0	2.1	3.4	3.2	−7.4	−6.7	−7.4
D. CHILE[2]	91.4	92.7	93.1	100.0	102.2	80.9	78.8	2.2	1.4	.5	7.4	2.2	−20.8	−2.6
E. COLOMBIA[1]	96.9	98.6	100.8	100.0	95.5	90.7	85.1	1.5	1.8	2.2	−.8	−4.5	−5.0	−7.2
F. COSTA RICA[2]	98.7	99.2	99.5	100.0	100.4	102.1	101.8	7.0	.5	.4	.5	.4	1.7	−2.0
I. ECUADOR[1]	89.2	94.5	97.3	100.0	107.1	109.6	104.0	6.0	6.0	2.9	2.8	7.1	2.3	−3.4
N. MEXICO[1]	82.5	86.6	93.2	100.0	105.6	103.0	94.4	.9	4.9	7.6	7.3	5.6	−2.4	−8.3
R. PERU[1]	98.6	97.9	97.9	100.0	101.1	94.7	94.3	.7	−.7	#	2.1	1.1	−1.4	−5.4
T. VENEZUELA[2]	91.7	99.6	99.1	100.0	101.8	100.8	94.5	6.2	8.6	−.5	1.0	1.8	−1.0	−6.1

1. Personnel employed in manufacturing, according to periodic sample surveys of enterprises.
2. Personnel employed in manufacturing, according to household surveys.
3. In relation to the same period in the preceding year.

a. For ILO-YLS employment indices data, 1964–79, see SALA, 22–1304.

SOURCE: ECLA-CC, 1985, vol. 49, table 7.

Table 1320

HOURS OF WORK IN MANUFACTURING, 12 LC, 1964–85

(Actual Hours of Work per Week per Worker)[1]

Country	1964	1970	1975	1976	1977	1978	1979	1980	1981	1982	1983	1984	1985
A. ARGENTINA[8,9]	- -	- -	**	**	**	**	191.4	186.7	180.4	181.3	177.9	178.4	179.7
B. BOLIVIA[7]	- -	- -	43.1	46.1	46.9	47.7	~	46.8	46.3	~	~	~	44.9
E. COLOMBIA	50.0	- -	- -	- -	- -	- -	- -	- -	- -	- -	- -	- -	- -
F. COSTA RICA[10,11,12]	- -	- -	**	**	48.9	48.3	49.5	49.8	48.5	48.0	49.3	42.5[a]	43.0
G. CUBA[13,14,15]	**	**	**	**	**	43.1	42.1	42.4	42.2	41.8	43.1	43.2	43.4
I. ECUADOR	45.0	48.0	51.0	50.0	51.0	53.0	47.0	45.0	45.0	45.0	~	~	~
J. EL SALVADOR[2,3]	49.5	48.0	44.3	44.3	44.3	44.6	44.6	44.6	44.5	44.2	44.0	44.0	44.0
K. GUATEMALA[4]	45.7	45.9	47.2	47.3	48.5	47.5	47.4	45.1	46.1	45.7	46.5	~	~
N. MEXICO[5]	45.6	44.9	45.6	45.6	45.5	46.4	46.5	46.6	46.0	45.6	45.8	46.4	~
P. PANAMA	44.6	42.3	45.5	45.9	45.9	45.4	46.0	~	45.5	~	46.1	~	~
R. PERU[5,6]	47.3	**	46.1	48.1	45.4	45.8	45.7	45.6*	45.0	45.4	47.8	45.9	~
T. VENEZUELA	~	44.4	42.3	43.1	43.7	43.9	44.9	44.2	45.4	~	~	~	~
UNITED STATES[16]	40.7	39.8	39.5	40.1	40.3	40.4	40.2	39.7	39.8	38.9	40.1	40.7	40.5

1. The series generally represent the average hours actually worked by wage earners. In a few cases the data refer to hours paid for, or to normal hours, rather than to actual hours worked. Where possible, annual data are averages of twelve monthly figures.
2. San Salvador.
3. Males only.
4. Prior to 1974, Guatemala City.
5. October of each year.
6. Lima, May of each year; prior to 1980, June of each year.
7. Employees.
8. Per month.
9. Averages: April and October of each year.

10. Includes mining and quarrying.
11. July of each year.
12. Civilian labor force employed.
13. Includes fishing, mining and quarrying, water, and gas.
14. State sector.
15. Wage earners.
16. Hours paid for.

a. November figures.

SOURCE ILO-YLS 1974, 1980, table 13A; and 1985 and 1986, table 12A.

Table 1321
GOVERNMENT EMPLOYEES BY LEVEL, 6 LC

Country	Year	Central Government		State and Local Government		Nonfinancial Public Enterprises		General Government		Public Sector	
		T	PHI	T	PHI	T	PHI	T	PHI	T	PHI
A. ARGENTINA	1981	573.5	2.12	703.0	2.60	313.8	1.16	1,276.5	4.72	1,590.3	5.88
I. ECUADOR	1980	163.3	1.96	~	~	~	~	~	~	~	~
J. EL SALVADOR	1982	111.5	2.32	~	~	13.9	.29	~	~	~	~
K. GUATEMALA	1981	105.0	1.45	18.8	.26	7.3	.10	123.8	1.71	13.1	1.81
M. HONDURAS	1981	27.0	.73	~	~	~	~	~	~	~	~
P. PANAMA	1979	63.7	3.39	4.1	.22	38.5	2.05	71.7	3.81	110.2	5.86

SOURCE: IMF, Occasional Paper 24, October 1983, tables 20 and 21.

Table 1322
CENTRAL GOVERNMENT EMPLOYEES BY FUNCTIONAL SECTOR[1], 6 LC
(PHI)

Country	Year	Administration	Education	Health	Defense	Police	Finance and Planning	Agriculture	Mining, Manufacturing and Construction	Utilities	Transport and Communication	Posts	Labor and Social Security	Other
A. ARGENTINA	1981	.09	1.83	.36	.43	.72	.07	.03	.07	.01	.07	~	.05	.11
I. ECUADOR	1980	.06	.74	.19	.43	.20	.06	.10	.01	.01	.11	~	.03	~
J. EL SALVADOR	1982	.11	.64	.34	.23	.07	.09	.11	.03	~	.50	~	.16	.01
K. GUATEMALA	1981	.08	.54	.17	.19	.15	.07	.05	.08	~	~	~	.09	.01
P. PANAMA	1979	.26	1.38	.50	~	.60	.14	.18	.31	~	.08	.08	.07	.09
S. URUGUAY	1979	~	~	~	1.03	~	~	~	~	~	~	~	~	~
UNITED STATES	1981	.07	2.33	.67	1.38	.36	.06	.05	.01	+	.27	~	.21	.18

1. The number of employees in the police, health, and education sectors has been augmented by the number of such employees at the state and local government levels.

SOURCE: IMF, Occasional Paper 24, October 1983, table 30.

Ch. 13, Labor Force, EAP, Unemployment, Class Structure, and Crime   269

Table 1323

CENTRAL GOVERNMENT EMPLOYEES BY FUNCTIONAL SECTOR AS A SHARE OF TOTAL CENTRAL GOVERNMENT EMPLOYMENT,[1] 5 LC

(%)

Country	Year	Administration	Education	Health	Defense	Police	Finance and Planning	Agriculture	Mining, Manufacturing, and Construction	Utilities	Transport and Communication	Posts	Labor and Social Security	Other
A. ARGENTINA	1981	2.40	47.80	9.32	11.25	18.74	1.75	.80	1.72	.38	1.75	~	1.31	2.80
I. ECUADOR	1980	3.18	37.66	9.74	22.23	10.29	3.00	5.27	.61	.73	5.88	~	1.35	~
J. EL SALVADOR	1982	4.75	27.44	14.80	9.87	3.14	4.04	4.84	1.43	~	21.61	~	6.82	.36
K. GUATEMALA	1981	5.71	37.52	11.81	13.33	10.57	4.86	3.62	5.62	~	~	~	6.10	.67
P. PANAMA	1979	7.69	40.66	14.76	~	17.74	4.24	5.18	9.11	~	2.35	2.35	2.04	2.51
UNITED STATES	1981	1.26	41.58	12.01	24.72	6.48	1.03	.89	.14	.06	4.81	~	3.75	3.27

SOURCE: IMF, Occasional Paper 24, October 1983, table 3I.

Table 1324

UNDERUTILIZATION OF LABOR, 6 L

(Ca. 1970)

Country	EAP			Open Unemployment		Equivalent Unemployment in Agriculture[1]		Nonagricultural Underemployment[2]		Equivalent Nonagricultural Employment		Total Underutilization of Labor	
	N	Agricultural	Nonagricultural	Thousands	Rate[3]	Thousands	Rate[3]	Thousands	Rate[3]	Thousands	Rate[3]	Thousands	Rate[3]
A. ARGENTINA	8,823	1,318	7,505	168	1.9	132	10	2,086	27.8	901	12.0	1,201	13.6

Continued in SALA, 21-1309.

Table 1325

UNDEREMPLOYMENT TOPICS COVERED IN HOUSEHOLD SURVEYS, 13 L

Country	Hours Worked	Average Workday	Reasons for Not Working Longer Hours	Desire to Work Longer Hours	Job Stability	Method of Payment	Reasons for Not Having Worked	Job Search	Reasons for Search
A. ARGENTINA	Yes	No	No	Yes	Yes	No	Yes	Yes	Yes

Continued in SALA, 23-1310.

Table 1326

UNEMPLOYMENT TOPICS COVERED IN HOUSEHOLD SURVEYS, 13 L

					Characteristics of Last Employment				
Country	Length of Search for Employment	Means of Search	Part-time or Full-time Search	Type of Employment Sought	Date of Last Employment	Occupation	Economic Activity	Employment Category	Size of Establishment	Reasons for Leaving
A. ARGENTINA	Yes	No	No	Yes	Yes	Yes	Yes	Yes	Yes	Yes

Continued in SALA, 23-1311.

Table 1327

MINIMUM AGE FROM WHICH ECONOMIC CHARACTERISTICS WERE INVESTIGATED IN POPULATION CENSUSES AND NATIONAL HOUSEHOLD SURVEYS IN THE 1970s, 20 L

	Country	Population Censuses	Household Surveys
A.	ARGENTINA	10 years and over	- -
B.	BOLIVIA	7 years and over	- -
C.	BRAZIL	10 years and over	10 years and over
D.	CHILE	12 years and over	12 years and over
E.	COLOMBIA	10 years and over	12 years and over
F.	COSTA RICA	12 years and over	12 years and over
G.	CUBA	10 years and over	- -
H.	DOMINICAN REP.	10 years and over	- -
I.	ECUADOR	12 years and over	- -
J.	EL SALVADOR	10 years and over	10 years and over
K.	GUATEMALA	10 years and over	- -
L.	HAITI	5 years and over	- -
M.	HONDURAS	10 years and over	- -
N.	MEXICO	12 years and over	12 years and over
O.	NICARAGUA	10 years and over	- -
P.	PANAMA	10 years and over	15 years and over
Q.	PARAGUAY	12 years and over	- -
R.	PERU	6 years and over	14 years and over
S.	URUGUAY	12 years and over	14 years and over
T.	VENEZUELA	15 years and over	10 years and over

SOURCE: ECLA-CC, Nov. 1983, table III.3, p. 157.

Table 1328

DECLARATION PERIOD AND MINIMUM TIME OF EMPLOYMENT FOR DETERMINING ACTIVITY STATUS, POPULATION CENSUS 1970, 20 L

Country	Criteria Used in Determining Activity Status (type)		Additional Criteria Concerning Minimum Time of Employment Required for Inclusion in the Category of:	
	Period of Declaration	Minimum Time Employed	Work	Unpaid Family Worker
A. ARGENTINA	Preceding week	Majority of week, i.e. 4 normal working days	Not specified	Not specified
B. BOLIVIA	Preceding week	Majority of week	Not specified	Not specified
C. BRAZIL	Time of the census	Not specified	Not specified	Not specified
D. CHILE	Preceding week	More than half of the week	1 day	1/3 normal working day
E. COLOMBIA	Preceding week	Not specified	1 hour	15 hours
F. COSTA RICA	Preceding week	Not specified	1 hour	Not Specified
G. CUBA	Preceding week	Not specified	1 day	1/3 normal working day
H. DOMINICAN REP.	Preceding week	More than half of the week	Not specified	Not specified
I. ECUADOR	Preceding week	More than half of the week	Not specified	Not specified
J. EL SALVADOR	Preceding week	Not specified	Not specified	Not specified
K. GUATEMALA	Preceding week	Not specified	1 day	15 hours
L. HAITI	Preceding six months	More than half of time covered	Not specified	1/3 normal working day
M. HONDURAS	Preceding week	Not specified	1 day	15 hours
N. MEXICO	Preceding week	Not specified	1 hour	15 hours
O. NICARAGUA	Preceding week	More than half of the week	Not specified	1/3 normal working day
P. PANAMA	Preceding week	Not specified	Not specified	1/3 normal working day
Q. PARAGUAY	Preceding week	More than half of the week	Not specified	2 days
R. PERU	Preceding week	Not specified	Not specified	15 hours
S. URUGUAY	Preceding week	Not specified	Not specified	Not specified
T. VENEZUELA	Preceding week	More than half of the week	Not specified	15 hours

SOURCE: ECLA-CC, 1983, table III.4, p. 158.

Table 1329

UNEMPLOYMENT,[1] 14 LC, 1979–85[f]

Country	Code[2]	1979 T	1979 %	1980 T	1980 %	1981 T	1981 %	1982 T	1982 %	1983 T	1983 %	1984 T	1984 %	1985 T	1985 %
A. ARGENTINA[3,11]	A	69.5	2.0	82.2	2.3	174.8	4.5	183.6	4.8	159.4	4.2	152.1	3.8	231.6[e]	5.7[e]
B. BOLIVIA	C	99.5	5.6	105.9	5.8	180.5	9.7	200.7	10.5	277.6	14.2	303.2	15.1	370.9	18.0
C. BRAZIL[4]	A	1,210.0	2.8	~	~	2,023.0	4.3	2,533.0	~	~	~	~	~	~	~
D. CHILE[5,12]	A	169.4	13.4	152.4	12.0	121.3	9.0	272.1	20.0	248.9	17.1	281.8	18.5	241.4	15.3
E. COLOMBIA[6,13,14]	A	292.9	8.8	320.8	9.1	266.2	8.1	311.6	9.2	406.5	11.2	503.5	13.0	~	~
F. COSTA RICA[14,15]	A	36.9	4.9	45.6	5.9	69.6	8.7	78.6	9.4	76.2	9.0	44.4[a]	5.0[a]	60.8	6.8
K. GUATEMALA[7]	B	.2	~	.2	~	.3	~	.3	~	.3	~	.4	~	~	~
M. HONDURAS	C	112.8	~	117.0	~	113.5	~	128.3	~	254.2	~	~	~	~	~
N. MEXICO[10]	A	~	5.7	~	4.5	~	4.2	~	4.2	~	6.7	~	6.0	~	~
O. NICARAGUA	~	~	~	~	~	~	~	~	~	~	~	~	~	~	~
P. PANAMA[12]	A	50.7[b]	8.8[b]	~	~	~	~	51.5[b]	8.4[b]	64.2[b]	9.7[b]	68.8[b]	10.1[b]	84.6[b]	11.8[b]
R. PERU[8]	A	387.6	7.1	394.5	7.0	392.0	6.8	417.1	7.0	564.6	9.2	691.4	10.9	~	~
S. URUGUAY[9,16]	A	43.2	8.4	40.0	7.3	37.0	6.6	60.9[c]	11.0[c]	89.7	15.4	83.7	13.9	77.9	13.0
T. VENEZUELA[12]	A	231.4	5.4	263.4	6.0	287.7	6.2	333.3[c]	7.1[c]	469.0[c]	9.8[c]	706.3[c]	13.4[c]	816.6[c]	14.0[c]
UNITED STATES[17]	A	6,137.0	5.8	7.637.0	7.0	8.273.0	7.5	10,678.0	9.5	10,717.0	9.5	8,539.0	7.4	8,312.0	7.1

1. The series generally represent the total number of persons wholly unemployed and temporarily laid off. The nature of Latin American economies makes gathering, reporting, and interpretation of unemployment somewhat difficult. Thus cautious use of the few data available is recommended.
2. Code: A, Labor force sample surveys and general household sample surveys:
        B, Employment office statistics;
        C, Office estimates.
3. Greater Buenos Aires.
4. Data for 1965 relate to Rio de Janeiro, Sao Paulo, and other areas varying according to the surveys. Data exclude rural areas of Rondaná, Acre, Amazonas, Roraima, Pará, Amapa, Mato Grosso, and Goiás.
5. Greater Santiago.
6. Bogotá, Barranquilla, Bucaramanga, Cali, Manizales, Medellín, and Pasto for September of each year.
7. Guatemala City, Quetzaitenango, Escuintla, and Puerto Barrios; prior to 1973 Guatemala City only.

8. Urban areas, for 1965 data.
9. Montevideo.
10. Metropolitan areas of Mexico City, Monterrey, and Guadalajara.
11. After 1975, averages: April and Oct. of each year.
12. Persons 15 years and over.
13. After 1975, Sept. of each year.
14. Persons 12 years and over.
15. After 1975, July of each year.
16. Persons 14 years and over.
17. Persons 16 years and over.

a. Nov.
b. August.
c. First semester.
d. Second semester.
e. April.

SOURCE: ILO-YLS, 1975, 1980, table 10; 1985 and 1986, table 9A. For 1963, 1968, and 1971–77 data, see SALA, 24-1326; for 1965–78 data, see SALA, 25-1327.

Table 1330

UNEMPLOYMENT ACCORDING TO PREVIOUS JOB EXPERIENCE, 8 LC, 1975–85

(T)

Country	Category[1]	1975	1976	1977	1978	1979	1980	1981	1982	1983	1984	1985
A. ARGENTINA[2,3]	A. Total	75.8	125.4	89.9	82.3	57.9	68.4	145.4	150.9	119.5	117.3	169.8[e]
	B. Total	21.2	33.7	13.4	19.3	11.5	10.3	22.3	29.6	32.2	23.9	34.8[e]
D. CHILE[3,8]	A. Total	308.2	264.9	259.9	343.5	336.1	273.9	321.3	563.7	437.2	411.1	404.1*
	B. Total	159.4	140.9	118.6	151.8	138.1	104.4	95.7	153.9	114.8	119.3	112.6*
E. COLOMBIA[3,4]	A. Total	161.95	175.70	164.52	157.59	194.33	217.78	187.80	221.43	292.68	358.77	~
	Male	95.09	112.86	93.37	89.35	106.24	122.76	~	~	~	~	~
	Female	66.86	62.83	71.15	68.24	88.09	95.01	~	~	~	~	~
	B. Total	91.17	93.34	96.48	86.05	98.56	103.02	78.41	90.17	113.84	144.71	~
	Male	41.97	42.43	39.58	37.10	38.53	39.01	~	~	~	~	~
	Female	49.21	50.91	56.89	48.95	60.03	64.01	~	~	~	~	~
F. COSTA RICA[3,5]	A. Total	~	23.54	22.59	23.64	25.60	35.35	58.54	62.66	59.80	34.89[b]	49.23
	B. Total	~	18.01	9.21	9.55	11.27	10.21	11.08	15.91	16.64	9.49[b]	11.53
P. PANAMA[3,9,11]	A. Total	24.40[b]	24.60	24.47[a]	21.17	30.12	~	~	29.06	39.63	39.22	51.39
	Male	13.70[b]	15.49	15.75[a]	12.21	17.36	~	~	16.19	23.11	23.79	29.10
	Female	10.70[b]	9.11	8.72[a]	8.96	12.76	~	~	12.87	16.53	15.43	22.29
	B. Total	7.20[b]	9.10	20.53[a]	22.61	20.61	~	~	22.44	20.49	29.57	33.16
	Male	3.50[b]	3.55	10.72[a]	11.20	9.56	~	~	10.49	12.51	15.13	15.62
	Female	3.70[b]	5.55	9.81[a]	11.41	11.50	~	~	11.95	12.08	14.44	17.54
R. PERU[3]	A. Total	~	~	~	~	~	~	~	~	~	~	~
	B. Total	~	~	~	~	~	~	~	~	~	~	~
S. URUGUAY[3,6,12]	A. Total	~	46.1	42.5	32.2	29.0	27.3[c]	24.5	48.7	73.0	61.7	56.8
	B. Total	~	22.1	21.6	17.8	13.4	12.7[c]	12.5	12.2	16.7	22.0	21.1
T. VENEZUELA[3,7,10,11,13]	A. Total	207.84	192.03	157.21	151.57	207.85	239.56[c]	280.78*	321.70	454.23	599.76	711.94
	Male	~	154.92	122.65	125.78	170.34	196.74[c]	230.12*	269.60	373.34	483.67	558.44
	Female	~	37.11	34.56	25.78	37.41	42.81[c]	30.66*	52.10	80.89	116.09	153.50
	B. Total	33.91	29.55	28.20	28.79	36.79	32.80[c]	44.14*	52.53	82.03	106.50	104.68
	Male	~	14.79	15.84	16.09	20.42	19.29[c]	24.37*	30.62	48.18	61.09	54.36
	Female	~	14.76	12.36	12.70	16.38	13.51[c]	19.77*	21.91	33.85	45.41	50.32
UNITED STATES[3,14]	A. Total	7,101	6,508	6,036	5,316	5,319	6,764	7,291	9,488	9,498	7,425	7,271
	Male	4,063	3,609	3,225	2,748	2,767	3,861	4,105	5,612	5,670	4,215	4,033
	Female	3,037	2,898	2,811	2,569	2,553	2,903	3,186	3,876	3,828	3,210	3,238
	B. Total	828	898	955	886	818	873	982	1,190	1,219	1,114	1,041
	Male	379	427	442	394	353	406	472	567	590	529	488
	Female	449	471	513	492	465	467	510	623	629	585	553

1. Category A refers to those with previous job experience. Category B refers to those seeking their first job.
2. Greater Buenos Aires.
3. Labor force sample survey or general household sample survey.
4. September of each year and includes seven main cities.
5. July of each year.
6. Montevideo.
7. Second semester.
8. Prior to 1982: persons 12 years and over, while 1982 figures and beyond relate to persons 15 years and over.
9. Data for 1976, 1978, 1979, and 1982–84 represent August figures.

10. Data for 1980–83 represent first semester figures.
11. Persons 15 years and over.
12. Persons 14 years and over.
13. Data for 1982–85 represent first semester figures.
14. Persons 16 years and over.

a. October
b. November.
c. First semester.
d. Mean of the observation: August 1974 – February 1975.
e. April.

SOURCE: ILO-YLS, 1981, 1985, and 1986, table 10A.

Table 1331

EVOLUTION OF URBAN UNEMPLOYMENT, 16 L, 1975–86

(AA)

	Country	1975	1977	1978	1979	1980	1981	1982	1983	1984	1985	1986[‡]
A.	ARGENTINA[1]	3.7	2.8	2.8	2.0	2.3	4.5	4.7	4.2	3.8	5.3	4.8[a]
B.	BOLIVIA[2]	~	~	~	~	5.8	9.7	10.9	13.0	15.5	18.0	20.0
C.	BRAZIL[3]	~	~	6.8	6.4	6.3[d]	7.9	6.3	6.7	7.1	5.3	3.8[b]
D.	CHILE[6]	15.0	13.9	13.7	13.4	11.8	9.0	20.0	18.9[c]	18.5	17.2	13.4
E.	COLOMBIA[4]	11.0	9.0	9.0	8.9	9.7	8.2	9.3	11.8	13.5	14.1	14.2[e]
F.	COSTA RICA[5]	~	5.1	5.8	5.3	6.0	9.1	9.9	8.6	6.6[f]	6.7	6.7[f]
I.	ECUADOR[†]	**	~	~	5.4	5.7	6.0	6.3	6.7	10.6	10.4	12.0
K.	GUATEMALA[†]	**	~	~	~	2.2	2.7	4.7	7.6	9.7	12.9	~
M.	HONDURAS[†]	**	~	~	~	8.8	9.0	9.2	9.5	10.7	11.7	~
N.	MEXICO[7]	7.2	8.3	6.9	5.7	4.5	4.2	4.1	6.7	6.0	4.8[g]	~
O.	NICARAGUA[8]	~	~	~	~	22.4	19.0	19.9	18.9	21.1	22.3	21.7
P.	PANAMA[12]	8.6	~	9.6	11.6	9.8[h]	11.8[i]	10.3	11.5	11.0	11.8	9.0
Q.	PARAGUAY[8,9]	~	3.7	3.1	2.6	2.1	4.6	9.4	15.0	12.5	8.0	8.0
R.	PERU[13]	~	9.4	10.4	11.2	10.9	10.4	10.6	9.2	10.9	11.8	10.6
S.	URUGUAY[10]	~	11.8	10.1	8.3	7.4	6.7[k]	11.9[k]	15.5[k]	14.0[k]	13.1[k]	11.0[j]
T.	VENEZUELA[11]	8.3	5.5	5.1	5.8	6.6	6.8	7.8	10.5	14.3	14.3	11.8[l]

1. Includes Federal Capital and Greater Buenos Aires and the average for April and October.
2. National data.
3. Metropolitan areas of Rio de Janeiro, São Paulo, Belo Horizonte, Porto Alegre, Salvador, and Recife.
4. Data for March, June, September, and December for the areas of Bogotá, Barranquilla, Medellín, and Cali.
5. Includes urban data for March, July, and November.
6. Greater Santiago data for four quarters.
7. Data for four quarters in metropolitan areas of Mexico City, Guadalajara, and Monterrey.
8. National averages.
9. Data for areas of Asunción, Fernando de la Mora, Lambaré, Lugue, and San Lorenzo.
10. Montevideo data for two semesters.
11. Data for two semesters.
12. August of each year.
13. Non-agricultural activities.

a. June.
b. January through October.
c. Metropolitan region of Santiago.
d. June through December.
e. April, June and September.
f. March, and July.
g. January through August.
h. Unemployment in urban area for February.
i. Metropolitan areas.
j. January through November.
k. Average for four quarters.
l. First semester.

SOURCE: ECLA-N, Dec. 1985 and 1986, pp. 12 and 15 respectively.

Table 1332

EVOLUTION OF UNEMPLOYMENT RATE IN PRINCIPAL CITIES, 11 L, 1979–1985

(%)

Country/City	1979	1980	1981	1982	1983	1984	1985[‡]
A. ARGENTINA[1]							
Buenos Aires[2]	2.0	2.3	4.5	4.7	4.2	3.8	5.3
Córdoba	2.2	2.4	3.8	4.4	5.0	4.8	5.0
Mendoza	3.1	2.3	4.8	4.1	4.5	3.5	3.7
Rosario	2.9	3.4	5.8	8.4	6.3	6.5	10.7
B. BOLIVIA							
La Paz	7.6[a]	7.5[b]	~	9.4[c]	12.8[c]	12.6	~
C. BRAZIL[3]							
Rio de Janeiro	~	7.5	8.6	6.6	6.2	6.8	4.9
São Paulo	~	5.6	7.3	6.0	6.8	6.8	5.0
Recife	~	6.8	8.6	7.5	8.0	9.0	7.2
Porto Alegre	~	4.6	5.8	5.2	6.7	7.0	5.4
D. CHILE[4]							
Santiago	13.6	11.8	11.1	22.1	22.2	19.3	16.3
E. COLOMBIA[4]							
Bogotá	6.6	7.9	5.5	7.4	9.4	12.2	12.8
Barranquilla	6.3	8.1	11.1	10.4	13.8	13.8	15.7
Medellín	14.3	14.7	13.1	13.3	17.0	16.4	16.0
Cali	10.7	10.0	9.0	9.6	11.6	13.3	14.0
F. COSTA RICA[5]							
San José	4.5	5.6	9.3	10.5	8.5	6.6	6.5
N. MEXICO[3]							
Mexico City	5.7	4.3	3.9	4.0	6.3	5.8	4.9
Guadalajara	5.7	5.0	5.8	5.0	7.4	6.1	3.4
Monterrey	5.9	5.2	4.2	4.9	9.8	7.5	5.4
Q. PARAGUAY[6]							
Asunción	5.9	3.9	2.2	5.6	8.4	7.4	5.2
R. PERU							
Lima	6.5[d]	7.1[e]	6.8[f]	6.6	9.0	8.9	10.1
S. URUGUAY							
Montevideo	8.4	7.4	6.6	11.9	15.5	14.0	13.1
T. VENEZUELA[7]							
Caracas	~	6.7	5.7	7.0	10.5	11.3[g]	13.2

1. April and October figures.
2. Includes surroudning areas.
3. Quarter figures.
4. March, June, September, and December figures.
5. March, July, and November figures.
6. Including Fernando de la Mora, Lambaré, and the urban areas of Luque and San Lorenzo.
7. Metropolitan area.

a. Two semesters.
b. May through October.
c. June and December.
d. September.
e. April.
f. June.
g. First semester.

SOURCE: Adapted from ECLA-S, 1984 and 1985, vol. 1, p. 24.

Table 1333

EVOLUTION OF URBAN UNEMPLOYMENT IN SECTORS OF ECONOMIC ACTIVITY,
6 L, 1982–85

(AA)

	Country	Business				Manufacturing				Construction			
		1982	1983	1984	1985[‡]	1982	1983	1984	1985[‡]	1982	1983	1984	1985[‡]
A.	ARGENTINA[1]	3.2	3.3	3.2	~	4.6	2.8	3.2	~	11.2	9.3	10.1	~
C.	BRAZIL[2]	~	6.8	6.5	5.6	~	6.4	7.1	5.2	~	11.7	12.8	7.7
D.	CHILE[3]	14.5	16.0	13.1	11.1	26.7	25.9	19.5	14.9	49.4	49.0	34.9	27.9
F.	COSTA RICA[4]	8.8	~	6.6	6.3	10.0	~	6.4	4.7	15.0	~	14.0	8.4
S.	URUGUAY[5]	7.7	13.3	11.3	11.1	13.0	16.6	13.3	12.3	9.7	16.6	17.5	13.3
T.	VENEZUELA[6]	5.1	7.8	10.3	10.7	7.8	11.7	13.0	13.2	13.3	21.4	29.3	30.2

1. Greater Buenos Aires for April through October.
2. Metropolitan areas of Rio de Janeiro, São Paulo, Belo Horizonte, Porto Alegre,
   Salvador, and Recife.
3. Greater Santiago for March, June, September, and December.
4. San José metropolitan area data for March.
5. Data for Montevideo for four quarters.
6. Data for two quarters.

SOURCE: ECLA-S, 1984 and 1985, vol. 1, pp. 28 and 27, respectively.

Table 1334

URBAN OPEN UNEMPLOYMENT, 12 LR, 1970–82

(%)

	Country	1970	1978	1979	1980	1981	1982
A.	ARGENTINA	4.9	2.8	2.0	2.3	4.5	5.7

Continued in SALA, 23-1315.

Table 1335

MIDDLE AND UPPER CLASSES, 18 L, 1950–70

(%)

	Country	1950	1960	1970
A.	ARGENTINA	35.9	36.6	38.2
B.	BOLIVIA	~	~	~
C.	BRAZIL	15.2	15.3	18.6
D.	CHILE	21.4	22.1	29.0
E.	COLOMBIA	21.9	23.6	26.8
F.	COSTA RICA	22.3	22.1	24.1
H.	DOMINICAN REP.	~	13.6	18.2
I.	EQUADOR	10.5	15.0	18.7
J.	EL SALVADOR	10.5	12.2	13.6
K.	GUATEMALA	7.7	12.3	11.8
M.	HONDURAS	5.1	10.9	20.6
N.	MEXICO	~	21.1	24.4
O.	NICARAGUA	~	14.7	19.2
P.	PANAMA	15.2	20.4	23.4
Q.	PARAGUAY	14.2	14.3	15.7
R.	PERU	~	18.1	23.2
S.	URUGUAY	~	35.8	35.0
T.	VENEZUELA	18.2	24.8	31.3

SOURCE: Carlos Filgueira and Carlo Genelitti, *Estratificación y Movilidad Ocupacional
en América Latina*, ECLA-CC, E/CEPAL/G. 1122, Oct. 1981, p. 53.

Figure 13:2

EVOLUTION OF URBAN UNEMPLOYMENT, 15 L, 1976–86[a]

(AA)

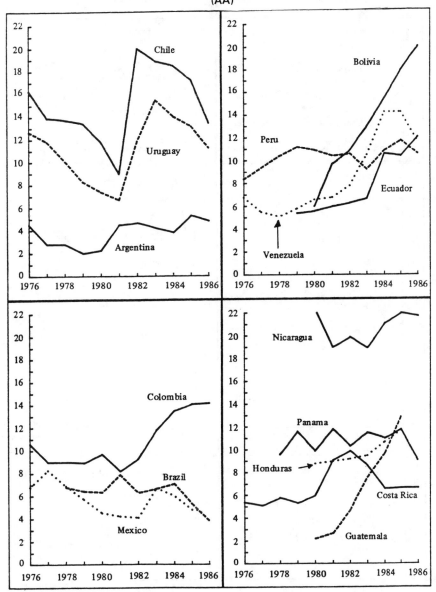

a. For 1975–85, see SALA 25, 13:1.

SOURCE: ECLA-N, Dec. 1986, p. 26.

Figure 13:3

EVOLUTION OF URBAN EMPLOYMENT IN PRINCIPAL CITIES, 8 L, 1982–86[a]

(AA)

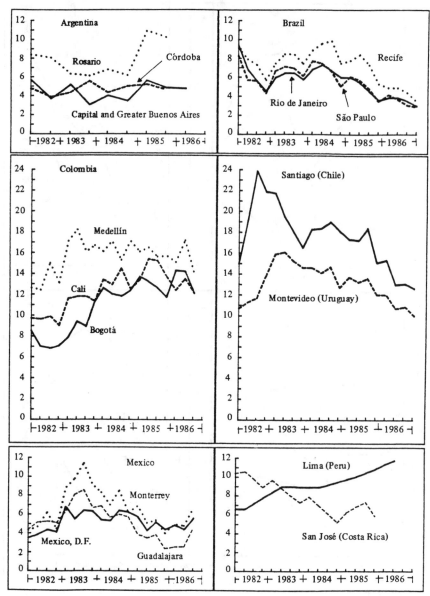

a. For 1981–85. see SALA 25, 13:2.

SOURCE: ECLA-N, Dec. 1986, p. 27.

Figure 13:4

THE MIDDLE CLASS, 17 L, 1950–70

(% of EAP)

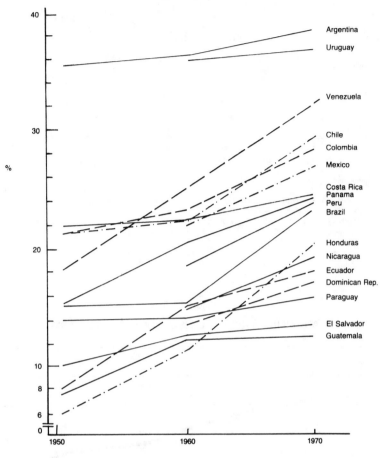

SOURCE: Table 1335, above.

Table 1336

MEXICO CLASS STRUCTURE, REVISED, 1950–80

(%)

Class and Subclass	1950			1960			1970			1980		
	Income[1]	Occupation	Combined[1]	Income[1]	Occupation	Combined[1]	Income	Occupation	Combined[1]	Income	Occupation	Combined[1]
Upper	1.8	1.6	1.7	5.6	2.0	3.8	7.0	4.4	5.7	6.7	3.6	6.2
Leisure	.2	.8	.5	1.0	.8	.9	1.5	2.5	2.0	2.4	1.2	1.8
Semi-leisure	1.6	.8	1.2	4.6	1.2	2.9	5.9	1.9	3.7	4.3	2.4	3.4
Middle	19.4	16.6	18.0	21.8	20.2	21.0	32.5	23.4	27.9	36.3	25.9	31.1
Stable	3.2	6.6	4.9	4.8	8.5	6.6	7.9	10.0	8.9	11.1	11.7	11.4
Marginal	16.2	10.0	13.1	17.0	11.7	14.4	24.6	13.4	19.0	25.2	14.2	19.7
Lower	78.8	81.8	80.3	72.6	77.8	75.2	60.5	72.2	66.4	67.0	70.5	63.7
Transitional	25.4	20.0	22.7	15.8	20.9	18.4	12.4	24.8	18.6	12.0	24.7	18.3
Popular	53.4	61.8	57.6	56.8	56.9	56.8	48.1	47.4	47.8	45.0	45.8	45.4
Total	100.0	100.0	100.0	100.0	100.0	100.0	100.0	100.0	100.0	100.0	100.0	100.0

1. Arithmetic average of the data for incomes and occupations.

SOURCE: Stephanie Granato and Aída Mostkoff, "The Class Structure of Mexico, 1895–1980," in James W. Wilkie, ed., *Society and Economy in Mexico*, Statistical Abstract of Latin America Supplement 10 (Los Angeles: UCLA Latin American Center Publications, forthcoming).

Figure 13:5

CHANGES IN MEXICAN CLASS STRUCTURE, 1895–1980[a]

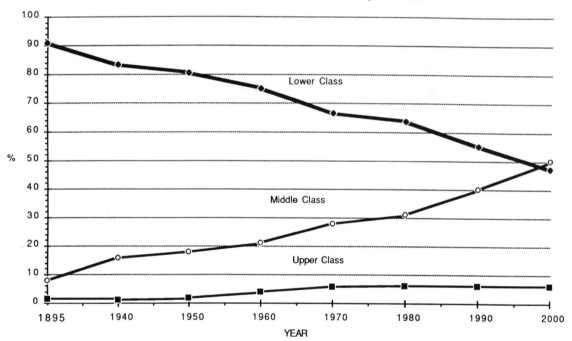

a. Indications after 1980 are projections.

SOURCE: Stephanie Granato and Aída Mostkoff, "The Class Structure of Mexico, 1895–1980," in James W. Wilkie, ed., *Society and Economy in Mexico*, Statistical Abstract of Latin America Supplement 10 (Los Angeles: UCLA Latin American Center Publications, forthcoming).

Table 1337

MEXICO SOCIAL MODERNIZATION INDEX (SMI),[1] 1930–70
(Zero Indicates Complete Modernization)[2]

Category[3]	1930[e]	1940	1950	1960	1970
Selected Rural[a]	69.1	67.7	61.1	54.6	46.2
Selected Semiurban[b]	34.0	30.8	25.6	20.7	16.5
Selected Urban[c]	10.5	7.2	5.9	6.1	5.2
National Average[d]	52.6	48.6	40.7	33.5	24.1

1. Nonmodern persons live in social isolation (are [1] illiterate, [2] speak Indian and Spanish, or [3] do not speak Spanish) and geographic isolation (definition as [4] living in localities of less than 2,500 persons), eat a nonmodern diet (measured by [5] share of persons who habitually consume tortillas instead of wheat bread), and have traditional dress patterns (those who [6] go barefoot or who [7] wear sandals instead of shoes). These seven items in the SMI are averaged with equal weight because there is no theoretical reason to assume that any one component is more important than the others as a measure of modernization.
2. The SMI divides the total of seven components by five values instead of seven because non-Spanish speakers and bilingual persons are both part of a larger category of Indian speakers, and barefoot persons and sandal-wearers are subcategories of the larger category of shoeless persons.
3. Represents 103 sample municipios from the 2,367 Mexican municipios including the municipio in each state which had the highest percentage of illiterates in 1940, the capital of each of the 32 Mexican states, and 40 municipios represented in the community-study literature.
   a. Municipios which in 1930 had more than 50% of the population living in localities of less than 2,500 persons.
   b. Municipios not included in "Rural" or "Urban."
   c. Mexico City, Guadalajara, and Monterrey.
   d. Includes all of Mexico's population in 2,367 municipios.
   e. Variance between seven-item average (seven items, five values) and four-item average (four items, three values) in 1940 is used to link the 1930 index to make it comparable to the post-1940 index.

SOURCE: Stephen Haber, "Modernization and Change in Mexican Communities, 1930–1970," SALA, 22, ch. 40.

Figure 13:6

MEXICO SMI FOR RURAL, SEMIURBAN, AND URBAN CATEGORIES, 1930–70
(100 = Nonmodern Characteristics)

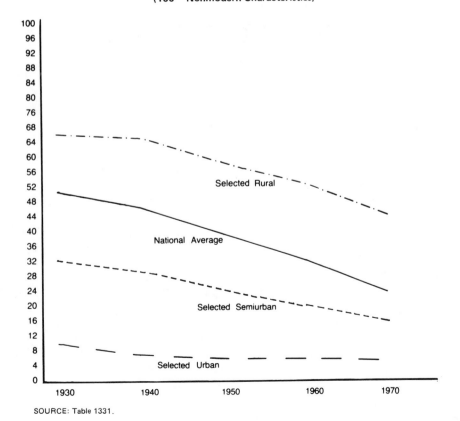

SOURCE: Table 1331.

Figure 13:7

SOCIAL POVERTY INDEX FOR MEXICO, 1910–70

(%)

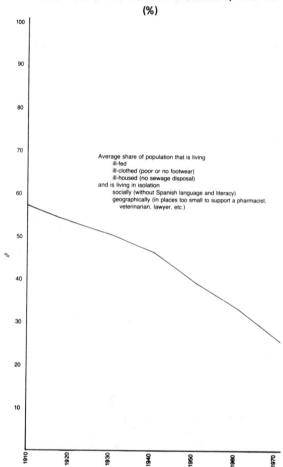

SOURCE: James W. Wilkie, *La Revolución Mexicana (1910-1976): Gasto Público y Cambio Social* (México, D.F.: Fondo de Cultura Económica, 1978), p. 384.

Table 1338

CALCULATIONS OF POVERTY, 20 LR, 1970–80

		% Undernourished			Rural % of Under- nourished	Life Expectancy at Birth 1970	Infant Mortality 1980	GDP/C 1980	% Under- employed 1980	% Employed in Agriculture 1980	% Rural Population 1980	Share of Poorest 40%	Productivity of Agricultural Labor 1980
	Country	Total	Rural	Urban									
A.	ARGENTINA	8	19	5	51	70	45	2,390	27.7	13	18	14.1	7,343
B.	BOLIVIA	~	~	~	~	50	131	570	74.1	50	67	~	730
C.	BRAZIL	49	73	35	59	63	77	2,050	44.5	30	32	7.0	1,172
D.	CHILE	17	25	12	59	67	43	2,150	28.9	19	29	13.4	1,512
E.	COLOMBIA	45	54	38	49	63	56	1,180	41.0	26	30	~	1,971
F.	COSTA RICA	24	34	14	83	70	24	1,730	27.2	29	57	12.0	2,060
G.	CUBA	~	~	~	~	73	21	~	~	23	27	~	~
H.	DOMINICAN REP.	~	~	~	~	61	68	1,160	~	49	49	~	916
I.	ECUADOR	~	~	~	~	61	82	1,270	63.3	52	55	~	672
J.	EL SALVADOR	68	76	61	66	63	78	660	49.0	50	59	~	832
K.	GUATEMALA	79	82	75	67	59	70	1,080	50.9	55	61	~	1,047
L.	HAITI	90	4	71	68	53	115	270	~	74	72	~	312
M.	HONDURAS	61	75	40	80	58	88	560	~	63	64	~	628
N.	MEXICO	34	45	20	69	65	56	2,090	40.4	36	33	9.9	1,302
O.	NICARAGUA	64	80	50	67	56	91	740	~	39	47	~	975
P.	PANAMA	35	~	~	~	70	22	1,730	45.5	27	46	~	1,807
Q.	PARAGUAY	~	~	~	~	65	47	1,300	~	49	61	7.2	1,669
R.	PERU	50	61	35	67	58	88	930	55.8	40	33	7.0	405
S.	URUGUAY	~	~	10	~	71	40	2,810	27.0	11	16	~	4,215
T.	VENEZUELA	25	36	20	56	67	42	3,630	31.5	18	17	~	2,401
	LATIN AMERICA	40	62	26	60	64	~	2,174	42.0	35	41	~	1,417

SOURCE: Alberto Couriel, "Poverty and Underemployment in Latin America," *Cepal Review* 24 (Santiago, 1984).

Table 1339

ABSOLUTE POVERTY ESTIMATES, 10 LR

(%, Ca. 1970)

	Households Below the Poverty Line			Households Below the Extreme Poverty Line		
Country	Urban	Rural	National	Urban	Rural	National
A. ARGENTINA	5	19	8	1	1	1
C. BRAZIL	35	73	49	15	42	25

Continued in SALA, 24–1332.

Table 1340

AVAILABILITY OF CRIMINAL STATISTICS FOR LATIN AMERICA AND THE ENGLISH-SPEAKING CARIBBEAN

Country	Data Year Utilized in 1978 Survey			
	Crimes	Arrests	Sentenced	Inmates
A. ARGENTINA	~	1975	1976	1975
Bahamas	1973	~	1973	1973
Barbados	1973	~	1973	1973

Continued in SALA, 24–1333.

Table 1341

PERSONS ARRESTED, 5 L, 1965-70

	Country	1965	1966	1967	1968	1969	1970
C.	BRAZIL	47,094	49,606	50,323	62,721	69,809	~
D.	CHILE	548,944	610,729	614,049	647,048	~	~
J.	EL SALVADOR	47,599	55,999	54,875	50,817	46,892	43,550
K.	GUATEMALA	85,609	69,566	~	~	~	~
P.	PANAMA	27,584	28,440	33,671	35,926	36,320	36,206

SOURCE: IASI-AC, 1967 and 1972, table 603-01.

Table 1342

PRISON POPULATION, 4 L, 1965-70

	Country	1965	1966	1967	1968	1969	1970
C.	BRAZIL	23,385	24,219	22,534	24,767	27,521	28,538
E.	COLOMBIA	32,088	31,816	~	~	~	~
J.	EL SALVADOR	11,043	5,148	5,541	5,745	5,729	5,425
T.	VENEZUELA	9,025	10,519	10,858	11,492	11,278	11,144

SOURCE: IASI-AC, 1967 and 1972, table 603-01.

CHAPTER 14

WAGES AND INCOME DISTRIBUTION

Table 1400

COMPENSATION OF EMPLOYEES AND NATIONAL INCOME,[1] 15 LC, 1962–75

(M of NC)

Country	Code[2]	1962	1965	1967	1968	1969	1970	1971	1972	1973	1974	1975
A. ARGENTINA	A	~	~	58,700	67,900	79,600	93,800	124,451	209,460	350,376	469,022	1,289,312
	B	~	~	24,200	27,300	31,500	38,500	55,928	85,813	156,638	208,963	579,370
	C	~	~	41.2	40.2	39.6	41.0	44.9	41.0	44.7	44.6	44.9

Continued in SALA, 21–1404.

Table 1401

WAGES IN NONAGRICULATURAL ACTIVITIES,[1] 8 LC, 1965–85

Country	1965	1970	1975	1980	1981	1982	1983	1984	1985
B. BOLIVIA[2,3]	~	1,015	2,171	5,540	6,681	14,714	61,089	501,964[†]	~
F. COSTA RICA[4]	~	~	1,339	2,728	3,293	4,995	7,337	8,813	11,090
G. CUBA[3,4,15,16]	~	~	~	154	172	179	183	188	190
M. HONDURAS[3,5,6]	~	~	43.21	93.52	130.28	197.84	139.79	167.92	227.80
O. NICARAGUA[3,7,8]	~	3.55	5.92	11.23	~	~	~	~	~
R. PERU[9,10]	72.60	115.12	260	1,432[a]	2,428	3,979	6,837	12,134	~
S. URUGUAY[11,12,13]	~	100	1,593	9,860	14,424	17,054	20,361	29,880	60,267
T. VENEZUELA[4,14]	~	1,201	1,523	2,733	2,956	~	~	~	~
UNITED STATES[7]	2.45	3.23	4.53	6.66	7.25	7.68	8.02	8.32	8.57

1. The wage series shown in this table cover the following divisions of economic activity: mining and quarrying; manufacturing; electricity, gas, and water; construction; whole-sale and retail trade, restaurants, and hotels; transports, storage, and communication; financing, insurance, real estate, and business services; community, social, and personal services. In some cases, however, these divisions are only represented by certain of the groups composing them.
2. Rates per month.
3. Includes salaried employees.
4. Earnings per month.
5. Establishments with ten or more persons employed.
6. Earnings per week.
7. Earnings per hour.
8. Excluding electricity, gas, water, wholesale and retail trade, restaurants, hotels, financing, insurance, real estate, business services, and community, social, and personal services.
9. Excluding mining, quarrying, electricity, gas and water.
10. Earnings per day for Lima only during May of each year.
11. For Montevideo only.
12. Excluding mining and quarrying.
13. For private sector employees with an index of average monthly earnings (1968 = 100).
14. Excluding construction and transport.
15. Including fishing.
16. State sector (civilian).

a. Prior to 1980, data were taken at June of each year.

SOURCE: ILO-YLS, 1975 and 1980, tables 18 and 17 respectively; 1985 and 1986, table 16.

Table 1402

WAGES IN MANUFACTURING,[1] 18 LC, 1965–85

(NC)

Total		Specification	1965	1970	1975	1980	1981	1982	1983	1984	1985
A.	ARGENTINA[2,17]	Australes/hour	69.30	1.65[a]	20	.15	.35	1.01	6.32	51.1	.40
B.	BOLIVIA[3]	Pesos/month	~	902	1,709	5,182	6,145	9,984	50,328	399,353[†]	~
C.	BRAZIL[3,4]	Cruzeiros/month	~	535	1,938	~	~	~	~	~	~
D.	CHILE[10,11]	Pesos/month	212.14	1,041.63	206	10,890	14,727	16,432	31,717	38,867	~
E.	COLOMBIA[3]	Index: 1980 = 100	3.65	* *	13.18	100.0	130.2	167.9	212.5	262.4	~
F.	COSTA RICA[14,18]	Colones/month	~	~	1,123	2,335	2,779	4,450	6,634	6,920	9,038
G.	CUBA[3,15]	Pesos/month	~	~	141	156	178	183	188	192	193
H.	DOMINICAN REP.[3]	Pesos/month	76.59	72.06	120.25	155.62	166.78	184.34	~	~	~
I.	ECUADOR	Sucres/hour	3.22	6.10	13.20	35.8	39.9	42.8	55.4	~	~
J.	EL SALVADOR[5]	Colones/hour	.81	.94	1.14	2.61	2.76	2.81	3.27	3.31	3.56
K.	GUATEMALA	Quetzales/hour	37.3	43.30	.46	.91	1.02	1.07	1.17	~	~
M.	HONDURAS[3,16]	Lempiras/week	~	* *	41.30	70.35	83.94	174.42	272.29	97.00	107.10
N.	MEXICO	Pesos/month	1,324	1,703	3,412	9,147	11,989	18,792	27,853	44,453	70,068
O.	NICARAGUA[3]	Córdobas/hour	2.08	3.24	5.54	10.90	~	~	~	~	~
P.	PANAMA	Balboas/hour	.65	.80	1.07	~	1.50	~	2.59	~	~
R.	PERU[6,7,12,13]	Soles/day	75.54	120.50	255	1,477*	2,470	4,115	7,099	12,556	~
S.	URUGUAY[8,9]	Index: 1968 = 100	~	100	1,492	8,844	12,653	14,604	17,286	26,203	54,945
T.	VENEZUELA	Bolívares/month	793.0	960	1,473	2,621	2,955	~	~	~	~
	UNITED STATES	Dollars/hours	2.61	3.35	4.83	7.27	7.99	8.50	8.83	9.19	9.53

1. The figures generally relate to average earnings of all wage-earners. They normally include bonuses, cost of living allowances, taxes, social insurance contributions payable by the employed person and, in some cases, payment in kind. They normally exclude social insurance contributions payable by the employers, family allowances, and other social security benefits. Unless otherwise indicated, figures relate to earnings of both male and female wage-earners.
2. Minimum earnings; unskilled workers.
3. Including salaried employees.
4. 1964-65, production workers.
5. Metropolitan area. Figures are for male wage-earners only. Data for female wage-earners are as follows: 1965 — .57; 1970 — .77; 1975 — 1.03; 1976 — 1.25; 1977 — 1.26; 1978 — 1.39; 1979 — 1.50; 1980 — 2.12; 1981 — 2.37; 1982 — 2.51; 1983 — 2.51; 1984 — 2.77; 1985 — 2.90.
6. Lima and Callao.
7. May of each year.
8. Montevideo only.
9. Private sector; employees; index of average monthly earnings.
10. Including the value of payments in kind.
11. April of each year.
12. Lima only after 1975.
13. Prior to 1980; June of each year.
14. Insured persons since 1975.
15. Including mining and quarrying, electricity, gas, and water for the years 1975-77.
16. Includes establishments with ten or more persons employed.
17. Prior to 1985; pesos: 1 Austral = 1,000 pesos.
18. Including electricity, gas, and water.

a. New currency introduced in January 1970: 1 new peso = 100 old pesos.

SOURCE: ILO-YLS 1975 and 1980, tables 19 and 18A respectively; 1985 and 1986, table 17A.

Table 1403

WAGES IN CONSTRUCTION,[1] 15 LC 1965-85

(NC)

	Country	Specification	1965	1970	1975	1980	1981	1982	1983	1984	1985
A.	ARGENTINA[2,3,4]	Pesos/hour	76.44	1.79	~	~	~	~	~	~	~
B.	BOLIVIA[6]	Pesos/month	~	775	1,609	5,476	6,806	7,513	25,887	230,671[‡]	~
C.	BRAZIL	Cruzeiros/hour	~	~	~	~	~	~	~	~	~
F.	COSTA RICA[12]	Colones/month	~	~	883	1,857	2,237	3,362	5,452	6,466	8,210
G.	CUBA[6]	Pesos/month	~	~	157	164	187	186	195	205	202
J.	EL SALVADOR[7]	Colones/hour	.70	.69	~	~	~	~	~	~	~
K.	GUATEMALA	Quetzales/week	~	~	~	~	~	~	~	~	~
M.	HONDURAS[5,6]	Lempiras/week	~	~	36.52	77.59	168.54	241.50	256.44	126.00	135.00
N.	MEXICO[8]	Pesos/hour	3.40	5.31	11.51	29.13	34.92	66.32	92.92	158.95	~
O.	NICARAGUA[6]	Córdobas/hour	~	3.39	5.40	9.94	~	~	~	~	~
P.	PANAMA	Balboas/week	~	~	~	~	~	~	~	~	~
Q.	PARAGUAY	Guaraníes/month	~	~	~	~	~	~	~	~	~
R.	PERU[9]	Soles/day	81.16	117.25	289	1,414*	2,300	4,211	7,059	11,951	~
S.	URUGUAY[10]	1970 = 100	~	100.0	2,064	12,320	18,707	21,404	24,538	32,563	58,040
T.	VENEZUELA[11]	Bolívares/day	~	~	~	~	~	~	~	~	~
	UNITED STATES	Dollars/hour	3.55	5.24	7.31	9.94	10.82	11.63	11.94	12.13	12.31

1. Unless otherwise indicated the data pertain to the average nominal gross wages (i.e., before tax deductions and the workers' social security contribution) of construction workers.
2. Minimum earnings.
3. Unskilled workers.
4. To make the series uniform, wages to 1969 were converted to new pesos which equal 100 of the former pesos.
5. Establishments with ten or more persons employed.
6. Including salaried employees.
7. Males only: metropolitan area of San Salvador.
8. October of each year.
9. Lima, mean of the observation: May of each year; prior to 1980, June of each year.
10. Montevideo; private sector only and including salaried employees; index of average monthly wage rates.
11. The data refer to the average nominal wages of electricians in Caracas during the fourth trimester of the year indicated.
12. Insured persons.

SOURCE: ILO-YLS, 1975 and 1980, tables 21 and 20 respectively; 1985 and 1986, table 19.

Table 1404

WAGES IN TRANSPORT, STORAGE, AND COMMUNICATION,[1] 13 LC, 1965-85

(NC)

Country	Specification	1965	1970	1975	1980	1981	1982	1983	1984	1985
A. ARGENTINA[2,3]	Road Haulage/hour	58.88	1.67[a]	~	~	~	~	~	~	~
B. BOLIVIA[5]	Transports/month	~	982	1,717	6,947	8,498	16,031	59,303	531,966[†]	~
C. BRAZIL[4]	Per month	~	~	~	~	~	~	~	~	
F. COSTA RICA[10]	Per month	~	~	1,289	2,320	2,868	4,414	6,861	9,098	10,390
G. CUBA[5]	Transports/month	~	~	162	177	196	202	208	212	211
M. HONDURAS[5,9]	Per week	~	~	109.10	74.30	172.80	253.26	176.32	139.00	154.50
N. MEXICO[6]	Transports/hour	8.00	8.09	~	~	~	~	~	~	~
O. NICARAGUA[5]	Per hour	~	3.80	5.60	11.17	~	~	~	~	~
P. PANAMA	Per week	~	~	~	~	~	~	~	~	~
Q. PARAGUAY	Per month	~	~	~	~	~	~	~	~	~
R. PERU[7]	Transport/day	95.34	115.76	299	1,787*	3,087	5,062	9,021	17,050	~
S. URUGUAY[5,8]	Index: 1970 = 100	~	100	1,333	8,030	11,655	14,909	17,837	26,721	54,341
T. VENEZUELA	Bus Drivers/day	~	~	~	~	~	~	~	~	~
UNITED STATES	Principal Railways/hour	3.00	3.89	6.05	9.92	10.65	11.50	12.84	13.33	13.64

1. Unless otherwise indicated, the data pertain to the average nominal gross wages (i.e., before income tax deduction and the workers' social security contribution) in national currency of workers in transport, storage, and communications. Details concerning the type of work and earnings are included under the column "specifications." Due to the use of different data sources, not all specifications are equally detailed for every country.
2. Minimum earnings: unskilled workers.
3. To make the series uniform wages for 1963 to 1969 were converted to new pesos which equal 100 of the former pesos.
4. Includes workers in maritime transport.
5. Data include salaried employees.
6. October of each year.
7. Lima area; May of each year; prior to 1980, June of each year.
8. Montevideo; private sector only.
9. Establishments with ten or more persons employed.
10. Insured persons.

a. New currency Jan. 1970; 1 new peso = 100 old pesos.

SOURCE: ILO-YLS, 1975 and 1980, tables 22 and 21 respectively; 1985 and 1986, table 20.

Table 1405

WAGES IN AGRICULTURE,[1] 15 LC, 1965–85

(NC)

Country/Specification	Code	1965	1970	1975	1976	1977	1978	1979	1980	1981	1982	1983	1984	1985
A. ARGENTINA[2]														
Unskilled Workers	M-I-H	43.99	1.14c	16.83	50.29	106.32	~	~	~	~	~	~	~	~
C. BRAZIL[3]														
Workers in Rice Production	H	~	~	~	~	~	~	~	~	~	~	~	~	~
D. CHILE[3,4]	M-I-D	3.26	12.00	4.35b	17.81	41.44	60.45	79.97	108.25	155.44	172.86	177.18	181.50	~
E. COLOMBIA	M-I-D	11.95	19.30	~	~	~	~	~	~	~	~	~	~	~
	F-I-D	9.55	14.75	~	~	~	~	~	~	~	~	~	~	~
	MF-I-D	~	~	~	61.75	92.13	119.13	147.63	181.50	~	~	~	~	~
F. COSTA RICA[3]														
General Farm Hands:														
Coffee Plantations[9]	MF-III-H	1.28	1.34	2.52	3.00	3.39	4.00	4.48	5.27	6.55	12.00	18.42	~	~
Agriculture and Livestock	MF-III-H	1.15	1.21	~	~	~	~	~	~	~	~	~	~	~
G. CUBA[5]	MF-I-Mo	~	**	**	132	112	114	119	127	160	167	167	175	179
J. EL SALVADOR[6]	M-I-D	~	2.25	3.10	3.75	3.75	4.25	5.20	5.20	~	~	~	~	~
Permanent Workers	F-I-D	~	1.75	2.50	3.15	3.15	3.65	4.60	4.60	~	~	~	~	~
M. HONDURAS[7]														
Establishments with Ten or More Persons Employed	W	~	~	**	**	30.69	28.70	39.72	108.72	183.72	91.83	~	157.89	224.94
N. MEXICO[3,10]														
Regular Day Laborers	M-II-D	13.47	21.20	46.10	69.55	76.48	88.50	106.81	134.16	178.87	311.51	548.18	702.10	918.75
O. NICARAGUA	W	~	~	238	266	310	330	402	593	~	~	~	~	~
P. PANAMA														
Agriculture, Silviculture, Hunting and Fishing	W	~	~	~	~	~	~	~	~	~	~	~	~	~
Q. PARAGUAY	Mo	~	~	~	~	~	~	~	~	~	~	~	~	~
R. PERU														
General Farm Hands	MF-I-D	~	~	~	~	~	~	~	~	~	~	~	~	~
S. URUGUAY[8]														
General Farm Hands	MF-I-Mo	920	17,315	206a	262	460	662	1,049	1,500	1,832	2,015	2,787	5,425	9,586
	MF-II-Mo	530	12,070	140a	178	260	374	593	848	1,035	1,139	1,575	3,250	5,685
T. VENEZUELA														
Agricultural Workers	D	~	~	~	~	~	~	~	~	~	~	~	~	~
General Farm Hands	D	~	~	~	~	~	~	~	~	~	~	~	~	~
UNITED STATES	MF-I-H	~	~	2.60	2.81	3.06	3.22	3.58	3.82	~	~	~	~	~
	MF-I+III-H	~	~	2.43	2.66	2.87	3.09	3.39	3.66	~	~	~	~	~

1. The statistics of agricultural wages presented in this table refer in most cases to wages paid in national currency to general farm laborers. A distinction is made between permanent workers, seasonal workers, and day workers; in the last mentioned group, regular day laborers and casual day laborers are distinguished. These distinctions as well as any further details are included under Specifications. The methods of payment and the types of labor contracts and arrangements in agriculture are often quite different from those in other activities. To indicate the sex of the laborer and the nature of the wage statistics, special notations have been adopted under Code. The key to this Code is as follows:

   M — Male laborer
   F — Female laborer
   MF — Both male and female
   I — Complete Wage — workers remunerated wholly in cash
   II — Cash part only of remuneration — where received partly in cash and partly in kind.
   III — Cash part of remuneration — where received partly in cash and partly in kind — as well as the estimated value of payments in kind for board and lodging.
   H — Hourly earnings
   D — Daily earnings

W — Weekly earnings
Mo — Monthly earnings
Owing to the use of different data sources, not all details of labor arrangements are available in every country.

2. To make the series uniform, wages from 1963 to 1969 were converted to new pesos which equal 100 of the former pesos.
3. Minimum wages.
4. Adults only.
5. Excludes fishing.
6. Department of San Salvador.
7. Includes salaried employees.
8. December of each year.
9. Includes livestock beginning with 1975 data.
10. January of each year figures.

a. New currency July 1975: 1 peso = 1,000 old pesos.
b. New currency September 1975: 1 peso = 1,000 old escudos.
c. New currency January 1970: 1 new peso = 100 old pesos.

SOURCE: ILO-YLS, 1975 and 1980, tables 23 and 23 respectively; 1985 and 1986, table 21.

Table 1406

MINIMUM URBAN WAGES AND AGRICULTURAL,
INDUSTRIAL, AND CONSTRUCTION WAGES, 18 L, 1965–80

(NC, Monthly)

A. ARGENTINA

| | Nominal Wages | | | | | | Real Wages (1970 Prices) | | | | |
| | Manufacturing | | Construction (Laborer) MA | Agriculture (Laborer) NA | Urban Minimum MA | Consumer Price Index (1970=100) MA | Manufacturing | | Construction (Laborer) MA | Agriculture (Laborer) NA | Urban Minimum MA |
Year	Base MA[1]	Paid NA[2]					Base MA[1]	Paid NA[2]			
1965	139	#	153	88	116	41	339	#	373	215	283
1966	189	#	201	117	158	55	344	#	365	213	287
1967	245	#	262	153	158	70	350	#	374	219	226

Continued in SALA, 23–1406 through 1423.

Table 1407

METROPOLITAN LEGAL MINIMUM WAGES, 18 L, 1965–80

(NC, Monthly)

| | A. | B. | C. | D. | E. | F. | H. | I | J. |
Year	ARGENTINA	BOLIVIA	BRAZIL	COLOMBIA	CHILE	COSTA RICA	DOMINICAN REP.	ECUADOR	EL SALVADOR
1965	116	#	62	364	.21	310	55.1	#	~
1966	158	#	81	364	.26	310	55.1	#	~

Continued in SALA, 24–1411.

Table 1408

EVOLUTION OF VALUE, URBAN REAL MINIMUM WAGE, 18 L, 1976–85
(1980 = 100)

PART I. INDEXES

	Country	1976	1977	1978	1979	1980	1981	1982	1983	1984	1985[†]
A.	ARGENTINA[1]	104.0	99.7	81.0	85.3	100.0	97.8	97.8	136.9	167.7	117.1
C.	BRAZIL[2]	~	~	97.7	97.5	100.0	104.4	104.9	93.0	86.0	88.8
D.	CHILE[16]	67.5	79.6	100.7	99.8	100.0	115.9	116.6	93.9	80.3	76.1
E.	COLOMBIA[3]	75.1	77.9	89.5	97.5	100.0	98.9	103.2	107.6	113.3	109.1
F.	COSTA RICA[1]	79.5	86.2	96.0	98.5	100.0	90.4	85.9	99.3	104.4	112.2
H.	DOMINICAN REP.[1]	~	~	94.7	105.0	100.0	93.0	86.4	80.8	82.0	80.2
I.	ECUADOR[4]	60.5	53.8	48.1	60.4	100.0	86.2	75.9	63.6	62.8	60.8
J.	EL SALVADOR[5]	100.8	90.3	40.3	87.7	100.0	96.8	86.6	76.5	76.8	66.3
K.	GUATEMALA[1]	85.0	77.6	70.0	62.5	100.0	89.8	89.6	85.5	82.8	69.8
L.	HAITI[6]	~	74.3	94.1	85.8	100.0	96.3	100.8	94.0	87.1	~
M.	HONDURAS[7]	112.3	104.6	100.0	109.2	100.0	105.6	104.5	96.6	92.1	88.8
N.	MEXICO[8]	113.5	112.5	108.6	107.2	100.0	101.9	92.7	76.6	72.3	71.7
O.	NICARAGUA[9]	116.1	118.1	119.8	112.7	100.0	90.2	74.4	56.7	63.6	45.1
P.	PANAMA[10]	126.0	120.5	115.7	113.6	100.0	116.5	111.8	129.2	127.2	125.7
Q.	PARAGUAY[11]	100.6	92.0	94.8	92.4	100.0	103.6	101.4	93.9	93.7	100.1
R.	PERU[12]	107.3	94.2	72.3	80.8	100.0	83.4	77.1	79.0	61.1	53.4
S.	URUGUAY[13]	171.5	114.7	113.6	104.8	100.0	103.4	104.6	89.6	89.9	94.1
T.	VENEZUELA[14]	78.9	73.2	68.2	60.7	100.0	83.7	76.0	71.0	61.8	80.3

PART II. % VARIATION[15]

	Country	1976	1977	1978	1979	1980	1981	1982	1983	1984	1985[†]
A.	ARGENTINA[1]	−48.2	−4.1	−18.8	13.7	17.3	−2.2	.1	39.9	22.5	−30.2
C.	BRAZIL[2]	~	~	~	−.2	2.6	4.4	.4	−11.3	−7.5	3.3
D.	CHILE[16]	10.8	17.9	26.5	−.8	.2	15.9	.7	−19.5	−14.6	−5.1
E.	COLOMBIA[3]	−6.2	3.7	13.1	10.7	2.5	−1.1	4.3	4.3	5.3	−3.7
F.	COSTA RICA[1]	14.8	8.4	11.4	2.6	1.4	−9.6	−5.1	15.7	5.2	7.4
H.	DOMINICAN REP.[1]	~	~	~	9.7	−4.8	−7.0	−7.1	−6.5	1.5	−2.2
I.	ECUADOR[4]	~	−11.2	−10.6	25.7	65.5	−13.8	−11.9	−16.2	−1.3	−3.2
J.	EL SALVADOR[5]	9.5	−10.7	#	−2.9	8.6	−3.2	−10.5	−11.7	.4	−13.6
K.	GUATEMALA[1]	−10.6	−8.7	−9.7	−10.7	59.9	−10.2	−.2	−4.6	−3.2	−15.7
L.	HAITI[6]	~	~	26.6	−8.8	16.5	−3.7	4.7	−6.7	−7.3	~
M.	HONDURAS[7]	−4.7	−6.9	−4.4	11.5	−8.3	5.0	−.5	−7.7	−4.5	−3.3
N.	MEXICO[8]	11.6	−.9	−3.4	−1.3	−6.7	1.9	−9.0	−17.4	−5.6	−.9
O.	NICARAGUA[9]	3.1	1.7	1.4	−5.9	−11.3	−9.8	−17.5	−23.8	12.1	−29.1
P.	PANAMA[10]	−3.8	−4.4	−4.0	−1.8	−12.0	16.5	−4.0	15.6	−1.6	−1.0
Q.	PARAGUAY[11]	~	−8.3	3.1	−2.5	8.0	3.6	−2.0	−7.5	−.2	6.9
R.	PERU[12]	~	−12.2	−23.2	11.7	27.8	−16.6	−7.6	2.4	−22.6	−12.5
S.	URUGUAY[13]	−3.1	−33.5	−.5	−7.7	−4.6	3.4	1.2	−14.3	.3	4.7
T.	VENEZUELA[14]	−7.1	−7.2	−6.8	−11.0	64.7	−16.3	−9.2	−6.6	−13.0	30.0

1. National figures.
2. Rio de Janeiro, deflated by the corresponding consumer price index.
3. For upper urban sectors.
4. Includes legal supplementary benefits.
5. Non-agricultural sectors in San Salvador.
6. Industry in general.
7. Central Disctrict and San Pedro Sula for manufacturing.
8. Mexico City, deflated by the corresponding consumer price index.
9. Department of Managua industry.
10. Excluding construction.
11. Asunción and Puerto Stroesner.
12. Lima for non-agricultural activities.
13. National figures for workers over 18 years of age.
14. National figures excluding agricultural and cattle-raising activities.
15. Compared with the same period in the preceding year.
16. Minimum Income.

SOURCE: ECLA-S, 1985, Vol. 1, p. 34.

Table 1409

EVOLUTION OF REAL WAGES, BY SECTOR, 10 LR, 1978-82

(1970 = 100)

Country	Minimum Real Salaries					Real Industrial Salaries					Real Construction Salaries				
	1978	1979	1980	1981	1982	1978	1979	1980	1981	1982	1978	1979	1980	1981	1982
A. ARGENTINA[1]	50.5	46.8	55.0	53.6	49.1	72.3	83.1	92.9	82.9	73.8	60.6	59.2	63.7	58.7	~

Continued in SALA, 24-1406.

Table 1410

REAL WAGE INDEXES,[1] 18 L, 1965-80

(1970 = 100)

Country	Code	1965	1966	1967	1968	1969	1970	1971	1972	1973	1974	1975	1976	1977	1978	1979	1980
A. ARGENTINA	Sm	128.6	130.5	102.7	87.7	103.2	100.0	106.8	95.0	111.8	136.4	101.8	52.7	50.9	50.5	46.8	55.0
	Si(1)	102.7	104.2	106.1	93.9	96.4	100.0	101.8	94.2	103.0	106.7	104.8	60.3	54.5	47.3	47.9	56.7
	Si(2)	#	#	#	#	#	100.0	103.4	98.3	104.4	117.9	111.7	74.2	81.4	79.7	90.4	~
	Sc(m)	104.2	102.0	104.5	95.3	97.2	100.0	101.1	93.0	103.1	110.1	137.4	73.2	72.1	60.6	~	~
	Sa(m)	94.3	93.4	96.1	87.3	90.8	100.0	113.6	103.1	115.4	132.5	122.8	67.5	61.8	54.4	~	~

Continued in SALA, 24-1407.

Table 1411

EVOLUTION OF REAL AVERAGE WAGES, 11 L, 1979–85[a]

(1976 = 100)

PART I. INDEXES

Country	1979	1980	1981	1982	1983	1984	1985[a][†]
A. ARGENTINA[1]	89.5	100.0	89.4	80.1	103.6	131.0	113.4
C. BRAZIL[2]	95.0	100.0	105.5	113.3	101.9	103.0	109.7
D. CHILE[3]	91.8	100.0	109.1	108.7	97.1	97.4	93.0
E. COLOMBIA[1]	99.3	100.0	101.4	105.2	110.4	118.7	114.9
F. COSTA RICA[4]	99.2	100.0	88.3	70.8	78.5	84.7	92.2
N. MEXICO[1]	102.9	100.0	103.6	104.4	80.7	75.7	76.6
O. NICARAGUA[4]	122.7	100.0	101.3	91.8	84.5	75.8	60.4
P. PANAMA	104.8	100.0	98.6	100.4	104.6	108.1	~
Q. PARAGUAY[5]	99.4	100.0	105.3	102.4	95.2	91.8	89.9
R. PERU[6]	88.9	100.0	98.2	100.4	83.6	70.8	59.6
S. URUGUAY[7]	100.4	100.0	107.5	107.1	84.9	77.1	88.0

PART II. % VARIATION[8]

Country	1979	1980	1981	1982	1983	1984	1985[a][†]
A. ARGENTINA[1]	14.3	11.8	−10.6	−10.4	29.3	26.4	−13.4
C. BRAZIL[2]	3.3	5.3	5.5	7.4	−10.1	1.1	6.5
D. CHILE[3]	8.3	9.0	9.1	−.4	−10.6	.3	−4.5
E. COLOMBIA[1]	6.5	.8	1.4	3.7	5.0	7.5	−3.2
F. COSTA RICA[4]	4.8	.8	−11.7	−19.8	10.9	7.8	8.9
N. MEXICO[1]	−1.4	−2.9	3.6	.8	−22.7	−6.2	1.2
O. NICARAGUA[4]	−14.3	−18.5	1.3	−9.4	−7.8	−10.3	−17.5
P. PANAMA	−.1	−4.6	−1.4	1.8	4.1	3.4	~
Q. PARAGUAY[5]	−6.5	.7	5.3	−2.7	−7.1	−3.5	−2.1
R. PERU[6]	−6.3	12.4	−1.8	2.2	−16.7	−15.3	−15.8
S. URUGUAY[7]	−8.1	−.4	7.5	−.3	−20.7	−9.2	14.1

1. Manufacturing.
2. Industry in general.
3. Non-agricultural sectors, excluding large-scale copper mining and pulp and paper
   industries.
4. Affiliates of the Social Security System.
5. General wages for Asunción.
6. Private sector in the metropolitan area of Lima.
7. Private and public sectors in Montevideo and the interior.
8. Compared with the same period of the preceding year.
a. For previous years, see SALA, 25–1413.

SOURCE: ECLA-S, 1985, Vol. 1, p. 39.

Table 1412

REAL AVERAGE WAGES, SELECTED LATIN AMERICAN COUNTRIES
AND PACIFIC RIM COMPETITORS, 1975–85[a]

(US 1980)

Country	1975	1976	1977	1978	1979	1980	1981	1982	1983	1984	1985
A. ARGENTINA	1.1	.8	.8	.7	.9	1.0	.9	.7	.7	.9	1.1
C. BRAZIL	.8	.8	.8	.8	.9	.9	1.0	1.1	1.0	1.0	1.1
F. COSTA RICA	.9	.9	.9	.9	1.0	1.0	1.0	1.1	1.2	1.4	.6
N. MEXICO	1.7	1.8	1.9	1.8	1.8	1.7	1.7	1.9	1.5	1.1	.7
R. PERU	1.2	1.3	1.1	1.0	.9	1.0	.9	.9	1.8	.6	.3
JAPAN	4.5	4.7	4.7	4.8	5.0	4.9	5.0	5.1	5.1	5.3	~
KOREA	.6	.7	.9	1.1	1.2	1.1	.9	1.2	1.3	1.3	~
UNITED STATES	7.4	7.5	7.7	7.8	7.6	7.3	7.2	7.3	7.3	7.3	7.3

a. Manufacturing.

SOURCE: *El Cotidiano* 3(12):61.

Figure 14:1

EVOLUTION OF REAL AVERAGE WAGES, 11 L, 1970–85[a]

(AA, 1980 = 100)

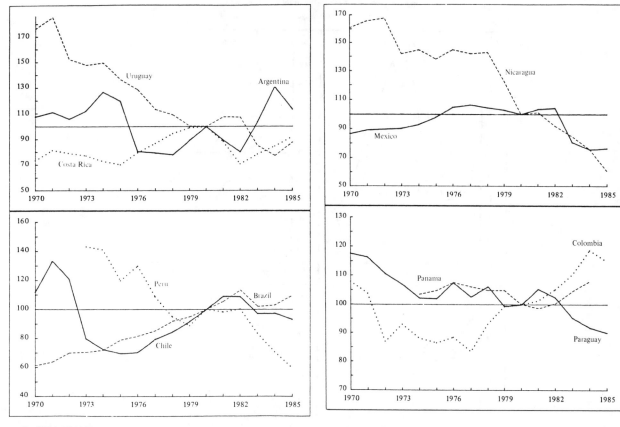

a. See SALA, 26-1411.
SOURCE: ECLA-S, 1985, vol. 1, pp. 36–37.

Figure 14:2

VARIATION IN REAL AVERAGE WAGES, 6 L, 1981–85[a]

—————— Average wage in the manufacturing sector
– – – – – Minimum urban wage

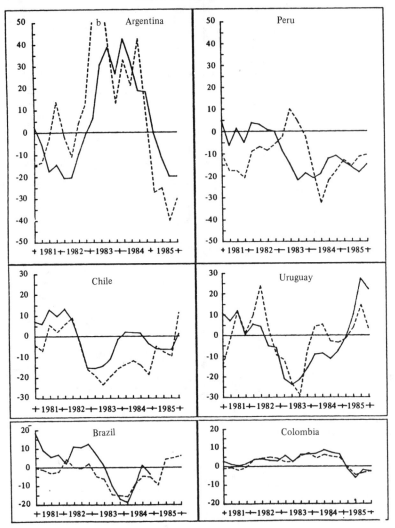

a. See SALA, 26–1411, Part II.
b. In the second trimester of 1983, the variation was 73.5%.

SOURCE: ECLA-S, 1985, vol. 1, p. 42.

Table 1413

REAL INDUSTRIAL WAGE INDEX (RIWI) FOR MEXICO CITY, 1934–76

Year	(A) Worker Cost of Living[1] Index (WCL)	(B) Annual Average Percentage Change	(C) New WCL (BXC)[2]	(D) Industrial Wage Index (IWI)	(E) Annual Average Percentage Change	(F) New IWI (EXF)[2]	(G) RIWI (F/C)	(H) Annual Average Percentage Change
1934	100	**	63.7	.28	**	44.5	70	**
1935	108	8.0	68.8	.30[a]	7.1	47.6	69	−1.4
1936	114	5.6	72.6	.33	10.0	52.4	72	4.3

Continued in SALA, 21-1405.

Table 1414

REAL INDUSTRIAL WAGE INDEX, 18 LC, 1940–73

A. ARGENTINA

Year	(A) Consumer Price Index (CPI)	(B) Percentage Change	(C) New CPI (A x B)	(D) Industrial Wage Index (IWI)	(E) Percentage Change	(F) New IWI (D x E)	(G) RIWI (F/C)	(H) Percentage Change
1940	91.2	~	100	88	~	100	100	~
1941	93.6	2.6	103	91	3.4	103	101	1.0
1942	98.9	5.7	108	96	5.5	109	101	#

Continued in SALA, 18-1411 through 1429.

Table 1415

INDUSTRIAL DISPUTES,[1] 16 LC, 1965–85

Country	Code[2]	1965	1970	1975	1980	1981	1982	1983	1984	1985
A. ARGENTINA[6]	A[4,5]	32	5	~	~	~	~	~	~	~
	B[3]	203,596	2,912	~	~	~	~	~	~	~
	C	590,511	32,849	~	~	~	~	~	~	~
B. BOLIVIA	A	**	**	**	**	31	301	261	300	319
C. BRAZIL	A	**	**	**	81	79	126	312	~	~
D. CHILE	A[4]	723	1,819	~	89[b]	~	~	41	38	42
	B	182,359	656,170	~	29,400[b]	25,000[b]	2,400[b]	4,400	3,600	8,500
	C	~	2,814,517	~	428,400[b]	676,200[b]	~	~	~	~
E. COLOMBIA	A	~	~	~	261	219	149	146	147	87
	B	~	~	~	30,915	22,560	60,119	54,391	30,624	10,481
	C	~	~	~	~	~	~	2,305	925	461
F. COSTA RICA	A	~	~	18	61	6	14	15	15	10
	B	~	~	11,500	24,750	7,380	13,387	8,248	13,780	10,915
	C	~	~	47,252	427,350	166,580	285,930	34,049	265,090	239,010
I. ECUADOR	A	~	~	61	75	99	86	97	96	72
	B	~	~	11,913	16,065	12,255	15,776	13,913	13,866	9,617
	C	~	~	418,226	508,170	368,910	431,980	467,540	372,730	266,860
J. EL SALVADOR	A	~	~	14	42[c]	15	4	15	36	~
	B	~	~	2,902	12,110[c]	5,324	373	2,680	26,311	~
	C	~	~	39,059	44,217[c]	138,490	4,975	92,732	233,490	~
K. GUATEMALA	A	~	36	7	51	3	#	#	**	**
	B[3]	~	27,067	8,336	68,683	1,350	#	#	**	**
	C	~	50,934	53,476	817,300	37,070	#	#	**	**
L. HAITI	A	~	~	~	2,946	2,728	2,642	2,161	1,845	1,653
	B	~	~	~	3,688	3,686	3,464	2,808	2,644	3,030
	C	~	~	~	21,954	21,565	24,074	~	~	~
M. HONDURAS	A	1	~	~	37	49	~	~	28	14
	B	135	~	~	34,431	9,273	13,387	~	3,643	744
	C	13,770	~	~	~	~	~	~	~	~
N. MEXICO	A[4]	67	206	236	1,339	1,066	1,925	~	~	~
	B[3]	610	14,329	9,680	42,774	31,512	25,173	~	~	~
P. PANAMA	A	~	6	6	18	16	7	9[d]	12[d]	7
	B	~	17,510	~	2,438	7,835	1,333	6,677	755	795
	C[7]	~	13,148	~	158,740	248,280	5,463	635,660	15,942	19,867[‡]
Q. PARAGUAY	A	3	~	~	~	~	~	~	~	~
	B	780	~	~	~	~	~	~	~	~
	C	540	~	~	~	~	~	~	~	~
R. PERU	A	397	345	779	739	871	809	643	509	~
	B	135,582	110,990	617,120	481,480	856,910	572,260	785,540	696,820	~
	C[7]	802,576	722,732	2,533,676	2,239,900	2,496,700	2,843,900	2,537,500	1,712,200	~
T. VENEZUELA	A	24	64	100	195	129	102	67	73	99
	B	4,690	23,934	25,752	67,960	29,560	14,870	17,420	12,130	12,945
	C[7]	17,800	234,349	100,662	315,310	255,920	329,600	418,170	108,300	95,800
UNITED STATES[5,8]	A	3,963	5,716	235*	187	145	96	81	62	54
	B	1,550,000	3,305,200	964,600*	795,300	728,900	855,800	909,400	376,000	323,900
	C	23,300,000	66,413,800	17,563,000*	20,844,000	16,908,000	9,061,200	17,461,000	8,498,800	7,079,100

1. This table shows the total number of industrial disputes which resulted in a stoppage of work, and the numbers of workers involved and working days lost. No differentiation between strikes and lockouts has been possible, since in most countries the distinction is not observed in the compilations. In a few cases, however, the data relate to strikes only. Disputes of small importance and political strikes are frequently not included in the statistics. In some cases the data do not cover workers "indirectly affected," i.e., workers who, though not parties in the dispute, are thrown out of work within the establishment directly affected by the stoppage of work. As far as possible such cases are indicated by footnotes. Various methods are used for calculating the number of working days lost, and these data, as well as the statistics of workers involved, are often approximations only. Nevertheless, the statistics indicate in a general way the extent of industrial disputes in the different countries.
2. Code: A — number of disputes;
    B — number of workers involved;
    C — number of working days lost.

3. Excluding workers indirectly affected.
4. Strikes only.
5. Excluding disputes involving less than 1,000 workers and those lasting less than a full day or shift.
6. Buenos Aires.
7. Computed on the basis of eight-hour working days.
8. Disputes can extend to many divisions.

a. Includes 57 disputes for which data relating to workers involved and working days lost are not available.
b. Includes data from Sept. 1979 to Dec. 1980.
c. Includes data from Jan. to June.
d. Excluding illegal strikes.

SOURCE: ILO-YLS, 1975, table 27; 1985 and 1986, table 30A.

Table 1416

INCOME DISTRIBUTION AMONG INCOME GROUPS AND INDICATORS IN INEQUALITY, 13 L

					Percentiles of Recipients (%)						
			Q_1	Q_2	Q_3	Q_4	D_9	D_{10}		Gini	Theil
Country	Year	Incomes Recipient Unit	0–20	21–40	41–60	61–80	81–90	91–95	96–100	Coefficient	Index
A. ARGENTINA	1961	Economically active person	5.2	8.3	13.1	18.3	13.2	10.7	31.2	.478	.475
	1961	Household	7.0	10.3	13.1	17.6	12.9	9.7	29.4	.425	.398
C. BRAZIL	1960	Economically active person	4.0	7.0	10.0	20.4	18.0	11.6	29.0	.520	.510
	1970	Household	4.0	8.0	12.0	18.0	18.0	13.0	27.0	.500	.467
D. CHILE	1968	Household	4.0	8.0	13.0	17.5	15.0	12.1	30.4	.503	.499
E. COLOMBIA	1964	Economically active person	2.9	6.0	10.2	18.3	14.8	12.0	35.8	.572	.655
	1974	Household	4.0	6.5	13.0	18.0	15.0	12.0	31.5	.520	.533
F. COSTA RICA	1971	Household	6.0	8.5	12.0	18.4	15.1	11.0	29.0	.466	.437
I. ECUADOR	1970	Economically active person	2.9	4.7	6.4	16.5	18.0	14.0	37.5	.625	.777
J. EL SALVADOR	1961	Economically active person	5.5	6.5	8.8	17.8	15.8	12.6	33.0	.532	.574
M. HONDURAS	1967–68	Household	3.2	4.1	7.7	17.5	16.9	14.6	36.0	.612	.735
N. MEXICO	1969	Household	4.0	6.5	9.5	16.0	13.0	15.0	36.0	.567	.666
P. PANAMA	1970	Economically active person	2.5	5.7	12.3	18.9	15.4	11.8	33.4	.558	.608
R. PERU	1961	Economically active person	2.5	5.5	10.2	17.4	15.2	10.2	39.0	.591	.712
S. URUGUAY	1967	Household	3.8	9.0	14.0	23.0	17.0	11.0	22.5	.449	.363
T. VENEZUELA	1962	Household	3.3	6.3	11.2	20.2	17.8	14.0	27.2	.531	.512
	1976	Economically active person	3.5	6.0	11.0	20.0	17.0	13.0	29.5	.540	.539

SOURCE: Jacques Lecaillon et al., *Income Distribution and Economic Development*
(Geneva: International Labour Office, 1984).

Table 1417

INCOME DISTRIBUTION,[1] 9 LC

(% Share of Household Income by Percentile Groups of Households[2])

	Country	Year	Lowest 20%	Second Quintile	Third Quintile	Fourth Quintile	Highest 20%	Highest 10%
A.	ARGENTINA	1970	4.4	9.7	14.1	21.5	50.3	35.2
C.	BRAZIL	1972	2.0	5.0	9.4	17.0	66.6	50.6
D.	CHILE	1968	4.4	9.0	13.8	21.4	51.4	34.8
E.	COSTA RICA	1971	3.3	8.7	13.3	19.9	54.8	39.5
J.	EL SALVADOR	1976–77	5.5	10.0	14.8	22.4	47.3	29.5
N.	MEXICO	1977	2.9	7.0	12.0	20.4	57.7	40.6
P.	PANAMA	1970	2.0	5.2	11.0	20.0	61.8	44.2
R.	PERU	1972	1.9	5.1	11.0	21.0	61.0	42.9
T.	VENEZUELA	1970	3.0	7.3	12.9	22.8	54.0	35.7
	UNITED STATES	1980	5.3	11.9	17.9	25.0	39.9	23.3

1. These estimates should be treated with caution because the collection of data on income distribution has not been systematically organized and integrated with the official statistical system in many countries; estimates were typically derived from surveys designed for other purposes, most often consumer expenditure surveys, which also collect some information or income. These surveys use a variety of income concepts and sample designs. Furthermore, the coverage of many of these surveys is too limited to provide reliable nationwide estimates of income distribution. Thus, although the estimates shown are considered the best available, they do not avoid all these problems and should be interpreted with extreme caution.
   The scope of the indicator is similarly limited. Because households vary in size, a distribution in which households are ranked according to per capita household income, not according to their total household income, is superior for many purposes. The distinction is important because households with low per capita incomes frequently are large households, whose total income may be relatively high.
2. Data refer to distribution of total disposable household income accruing to percentile groups of households ranked by total household income. The distributions cover rural and urban areas.

SOURCE: WB-WDR, 1986, table 24.

Table 1418

INCOME DISTRIBUTION: LATIN AMERICA AVERAGE,[1] 1960 AND 1970

Stratum	Share of Each Stratum in the Total Income		Per Capita Income in 1960 Dollars[a]		Increase in Per Capita Income		Total Increase	Percentage of the Total Increase Represented by the Increase in Each Stratum
	1960	1970	1960	1970	Percentage	1960 Dollars		
20% poorest	3.1	2.5	53	55	3.8	2	107.6	.4
30% following	10.3	11.4	118	167	41.5	49	3,919	15.4
20% following	14.1	13.9	243	306	25.9	63	3,359	13.2
20% before the highest 10%	24.6	28.0	424	616	45.3	192	10,237	40.3
10% highest	47.9	44.2	1,643	1,945	17.7	292	7,785	30.7
(5% highest)[b]	(33.4)	(29.9)	(2,305)	(2,630)	(14.1)	(325)	(4,332)	(17.1)
Total	100.0	100.0	345	440	27.5	95	25,406	100.0

1. The average distribution in Latin America in 1970 has been estimated on the basis of information provided by Argentina, Brazil, Chile, Colombia, Mexico, Paraguay, Honduras, and Venezuela.

a. Corresponds to the concept of personal per capita income.
b. Subtotal within 10% highest.

SOURCE: ECLA, *Long-Term Trends and Projections of Economic Development of Latin America*, Spanish edition, 1977, table 1.

Table 1419

DISTRIBUTION OF INCOME: CHRONOLOGICAL
SERIES, 3 LC, 1953-62

	Country	Year	Unit[1]	Income PI, (US)[2]	Coefficients		D.S. Log
					Gini	Variation	
A.	ARGENTINA	1953	H	786	.41	1.09	.64
		1959	H	832	.45	1.29	.70
		1961	H	927	.42	1.18	.67

Continued in SALA, 25-1418.

Table 1420

DISTRIBUTION OF AVERAGE PER INHABITANT INCOME,
BY INCOME GROUPS, 5 L, 1965

Country	Average PI Personal Income[1]	Average Income by Group				
		Poorest 20%	30% Below the Median	30% Above the Median	15% Below the Top	Top 5%
C. BRAZIL	260	45	100	200	380	2,055
Rio de Janeiro	805	200	405	780	1,425	3,880
São Paulo	775	225	390	675	1,280	4,340

Continued in SALA, 25-1419.

Table 1421

INCOME GROUPS, PERCENTAGE SHARES, 5 L, 1965

	Country	Lowest 20%	30% Below the Median	30% Above the Median	15% Below the Median	Top 5%
A.	ARGENTINA	5.2	15.3	25.4	22.9	31.2
F.	COSTA RICA	5.5	12.5	22.0	25.0	35.0
J.	EL SALVADOR	5.5	10.5	22.2	28.4	32.9
N.	MEXICO	3.6	11.8	26.1	29.5	29.0
T.	VENEZUELA	3.0	11.3	27.7	31.5	26.5

SOURCE: SALA, 16-16 (p. 26).

Table 1422

NATIONAL DISTRIBUTION OF TOTAL HOUSEHOLD INCOME, BY INCOME GROUPS, 10 L

Country	Year	Per Capita GDP (Dollars at 1970 Prices)	Household Percentile Groups (Percentage Shares in Total Income)						Coefficients of Concentration	
			0-20	21-40	41-60	61-80	81-90	91-100	Gini	Theil
A. ARGENTINA	1970	1,208	4.4	9.7	14.1	21.5	15.1	35.2	.44	.15

Continued in SALA 24, 1418.

Table 1423

URBAN DISTRIBUTION OF HOUSEHOLD INCOME, BY INCOME GROUPS, 11 L

Country	Year	Non-Agricultural GDP (Dollars at 1970 Prices)	Household Percentile Groups (Percentage Shares in Total Income)						Coefficients of Concentration	
			0-20	21-40	41-60	61-80	81-90	91-100	Gini	Theil
A. ARGENTINA	1970	1,254	4.3	9.3	14.2	21.3	15.1	35.8	.45	.15

Continued in SALA 24, 1419.

Table 1424

NUMBER OF COOPERATIVES AND MEMBERSHIP, 20 L, 1962 AND 1969

Country	Cooperatives			Membership		
	1962	1969	PC	1962	1969	PC
A. ARGENTINA	3,220	3,654	13	2,088,000	3,453,947	65

Continued in SALA 24, 1420.

CHAPTER 15

MIGRATION AND TOURISM

Table 1500

POPULATION IN UNITED STATES REPORTING LATIN AMERICAN ANCESTRY[1]
(Number of Persons Reporting in 1980)

PART I. TOTAL NUMBER OF PERSONS REPORTING

	Nation of Ancestry	Type of Ancestry				Location in the U.S.			
		Single[2] Ancestry	Multiple[3] Ancestry	Reported[4] Ancestry	Percent of[5] Total	Northeast	North Central	South	West
A.	ARGENTINA	28,109	9,800	37,909	.02	15,357	2,439	7,915	12,198
B.	BOLIVIA	12,585	3,463	16,048	.01	3,516	1,853	5,402	5,277
C.	BRAZIL	18,750	8,890	27,640	.01	12,035	3,128	6,387	6,090
D.	CHILE	24,410	7,433	31,843	.02	10,711	2,829	7,678	10,625
E.	COLOMBIA	137,162	19,114	156,276	.08	84,307	10,793	40,214	20,962
F.	COSTA RICA	21,121	5,871	26,992	.01	9,623	1,828	5,009	10,532
G.	CUBA	500,564	97,138	597,702	.32	143,036	24,625	373,695	56,346
H.	DOMINICAN REP.	155,930	14,768	170,698	.09	156,053	2,054	9,939	2,652
I.	ECUADOR	77,247	10,726	87,973	.05	56,392	5,961	9,804	15,816
J.	EL SALVADOR	77,384	7,373	84,757	.05	10,992	2,286	7,917	63,562
K.	GUATEMALA	54,674	7,424	62,098	.03	10,508	7,507	7,897	36,186
L.	HAITI	81,509	8,714	90,223	.05	65,246	3,505	19,346	2,126
M.	HONDURAS	45,294	10,271	55,565	.03	19,986	4,297	18,568	12,714
N.	MEXICO	6,992,476	700,143	7,692,619	4.09	62,116	705,349	2,663,868	4,261,286
O.	NICARAGUA	37,845	7,232	45,077	.02	6,239	1,543	12,257	25,038
P.	PANAMA	33,546	11,208	44,754	.02	21,557	3,376	10,669	9,152
R.	PERU	44,884	13,054	57,938	.03	24,360	4,538	11,237	17,803
S.	URUGUAY	7,240	1,350	8,590	#	4,876	543	1,842	1,329
T.	VENEZUELA	25,548	7,481	33,029	.02	10,355	3,536	14,031	5,107
	PUERTO RICO	1,270,420	173,442	1,443,862	.77	1,057,461	157,857	120,394	108,150
	SPANISH/ HISPANIC[6]	1,685,151	1,001,529	2,686,680	1.43	613,844	205,758	705,594	1,161,484
	OTHER SPANISH[7]	52,774	12,421	65,195	.03	14,992	4,887	27,199	18,117

1. The source provides "ethnic data on persons regardless of the number of generations removed from their country of origin." The ancestry question was based on self-identification. About 83% of the population reported at least one specific ancestry.
2. Persons reporting only one ancestry group.
3. Persons reporting more than one ancestry group. Double origin ancestry reports were coded; 17 triple-origin ancestries expected to be frequently reported were also coded. A person reporting double origin will appear twice in the table.
4. Reported at least one specific ancestry. Sum of single and multiple ancestry. The total of the column will add to more than the total reporting a Latin American ancestry due to double counting (see note 3 above).
5. Percent of total population reporting at least one specific ancestry. Numbers and percents by ancestry group do not add to totals due to persons with multiple ancestry being included in more than one group.
6. This category represents a general type of response, which may encompass several ancestry groups.
7. Other Spanish not elsewhere considered. Since the "Spaniard" entry excludes Basques they may appear here. However, Latin America appears under the general heading "Spanish" so a clear distinction is lacking.

SOURCE: US-BC, 1980 Supplementary Report, PC 80-SI-10, April 1983, table 3.

Table 1500 (Continued)

POPULATION IN UNITED STATES REPORTING LATIN AMERICAN ANCESTRY[1]

(Number of Persons Reporting in 1980)

PART II. NUMBER OF PERSONS REPORTING AT LEAST ONE SPECIFIC ANCESTRY GROUP

Nation of Ancestry	New England	Middle Atlantic	East North Central	West North Central	South Atlantic	East South Central	West South Central	Mountain	Pacific
A. ARGENTINA	1,629	13,728	1,990	449	6,254	242	1,419	1,027	11,171
B. BOLIVIA	412	3,104	1,442	411	4,041	152	1,209	630	4,647
C. BRAZIL	2,683	9,352	2,549	579	4,677	426	1,284	1,020	5,070
D. CHILE	1,306	9,405	2,209	620	6,171	213	1,294	1,186	9,439
E. COLOMBIA	7,961	76,346	9,104	1,689	33,072	635	6,507	1,732	19,230
F. COSTA RICA	1,829	7,794	1,600	228	3,189	197	1,623	533	9,999
G. CUBA	10,603	132,433	21,965	2,660	355,950	2,123	15,622	5,972	50,374
H. DOMINICAN REP.	7,360	148,493	1,861	193	8,747	172	1,020	590	2,062
I. ECUADOR	2,102	54,290	5,336	625	7,899	154	1,751	668	15,148
J. EL SALVADOR	874	10,118	1,948	338	5,371	253	2,293	947	62,615
K. GUATEMALA	2,028	8,480	7,127	380	4,984	217	2,696	862	35,324
L. HAITI	6,004	59,242	3,132	373	18,446	184	716	198	1,928
M. HONDURAS	1,919	18,067	3,638	659	8,499	775	9,294	690	12,024
N. MEXICO	10,849	51,267	579,234	126,115	98,860	17,891	2,547,117	781,190	3,480,096
O. NICARAGUA	312	5,927	1,150	393	8,945	252	3,060	421	24,617
P. PANAMA	1,129	20,428	2,570	806	6,886	670	3,113	1,102	8,050
R. PERU	2,538	21,822	3,904	634	8,349	342	2,546	1,274	16,529
S. URUGUAY	469	4,407	471	72	1,452	48	342	109	1,220
T. VENEZUELA	2,209	8,146	2,574	962	9,131	823	4,077	1,020	4,087
PUERTO RICO	118,833	938,628	151,896	5,961	92,515	5,493	22,386	11,018	97,132
SPANISH/HISPANIC[2]	81,976	531,868	158,219	47,539	352,533	32,078	320,983	548,787	612,697
OTHER SPANISH[3]	1,065	13,927	4,382	505	6,245	456	20,498	1,272	16,845

1. The source provides "ethnic data on persons regardless of the number of generations removed from their country of origin." The ancestry question was based on self-identification. About 83% of the population reported at least one specific ancestry. Some individuals reported a single ancestry group; others reported more than one group. All single- and double-ancestry responses were coded. In addition, 17 triple-origin ancestries expected to be frequently reported were coded; only the first two ancestries were coded for all other responses of three or more ancestries. Since persons who reported multiple ancestries were included in more than one group, the sum of persons reporting the ancestry group is greater than the total.
2. This category represents a general type of response, which may encompass several ancestry groups.
3. Other Spanish not elsewhere considered. Since the "Spaniard" entry excludes Basques they may appear here. However, Latin America appears under the general heading "Spanish" so a clear distinction is lacking.

SOURCE: US-BC, 1980 Supplementary Report, PC 80-SI-10, April 1983, table 3.

Table 1501

IMMIGRANTS ADMITTED TO THE UNITED STATES,[1] 20 LC, 1976–85[a]

(N)

Country	1976	1977	1978	1979	1980	1981	1982	1983	1984	1985
A. ARGENTINA	2,267	2,787	3,732	2,856	2,815	2,236	2,065	2,029	2,141	1,844
B. BOLIVIA	522	699	1,030	751	730	820	750	823	918	1,006
C. BRAZIL	1,038	1,513	1,923	1,450	1,570	1,616	1,475	1,503	1,847	2,272
D. CHILE	1,266	2,596	3,122	2,289	2,569	2,048	1,911	1,970	1,912	1,992
E. COLOMBIA	5,742	8,272	11,032	10,637	11,289	10,335	8,608	9,658	11,020	11,982
F. COSTA RICA	1,137	1,664	1,575	1,467	1,535	1,359	1,272	1,182	1,473	1,281
G. CUBA	29,233	69,708	29,754	15,585	15,054	10,858	8,209	8,978	10,599	20,334
H. DOMINICAN REP.	12,526	11,655	19,458	17,519	17,245	18,220	17,451	22,058	23,147	23,787
I. ECUADOR	4,504	5,302	5,732	4,383	6,133	5,129	4,127	4,243	4,164	4,482
J. EL SALVADOR	2,363	4,426	5,826	4,479	6,101	8,210	7,107	8,596	8,787	10,156
K. GUATEMALA	1,970	3,599	3,996	2,583	3,751	3,928	3,633	4,090	3,937	4,389
L. HAITI	5,410	5,441	6,470	6,433	6,540	6,683	8,779	8,424	9,839	10,165
M. HONDURAS	1,310	1,626	2,727	2,545	2,552	2,358	3,186	3,619	3,405	3,726
N. MEXICO	57,863	44,079	92,367	52,096	56,680	101,268	56,106	59,079	57,557	61,077
O. NICARAGUA	934	1,850	1,888	1,938	2,337	2,752	3,077	2,983	2,718	2,786
P. PANAMA[4]	1,699	2,389	3,108	3,472	3,572	4,613	3,320	2,546	2,276	2,611
Q. PARAGUAY	110	216	202	175	181	153	161	187	167	170
R. PERU	2,640	3,903	5,243	4,135	4,021	4,664	4,151	4,384	4,368	4,181
S. URUGUAY	676	1,156	1,052	754	887	972	707	681	712	790
T. VENEZUELA	191	736	990	841	1,010	1,104	1,336	1,508	1,721	1,714
LATIN AMERICA[2]	133,000	172,900	200,000	125,700	~	182,643	137,431	~	~	~
ALL COUNTRIES[3]	398,613	462,315	601,442	460,348	530,639	596,600	594,131	559,763	543,903	570,009

1. Countries indicated are those of birth rather than those of last permanent residence.
2. Excludes Bolivia and Paraguay. In addition, the total figures for 1951–60, 1961–70, and 1971–80 exclude Chile, Costa Rica, Honduras, Nicaragua, Uruguay, and Venezuela.
3. Includes Latin America.
4. Historical data for the Canal Zone are included in Panama.

a. For prior years since 1951, see SALA, 25–1501.

SOURCE: USBC-SA, 1984, table 126; USINS-SY, 1979/80, table 13; USINS-SY, 1982, IMM 1.3; USINS-SY, 1983/84; USINS-SY, 1984/85, table IMM 1.3.

Table 1502

IMMIGRANTS ADMITTED TO THE UNITED STATES, BY OCCUPATION, 10 L

(1985)[a]

Country or Region of Birth	Total	Occupations								
		Total	Professional Specialty	Executive, Administrative, and Managerial	Sales	Administrative Support	Precision Production, Craft, and Repair	Operators, Fabricators, and Laborers	Farming, Forestry, Fishing	Service	No Occupation
A. ARGENTINA	1,844	746	211	98	67	53	104	80	3	130	1,098
B. BOLIVIA	1,006	423	94	36	17	64	37	46	1	128	583
C. BRAZIL	2,272	759	208	69	52	100	51	79	6	194	1,513
D. CHILE	1,992	742	170	60	60	98	120	80	6	148	1,250
E. COLOMBIA	11,982	3,787	445	276	274	301	602	943	32	914	8,195
I. ECUADOR	4,482	1,535	160	71	112	179	286	387	25	315	2,947
Q. PARAGUAY	170	70	13	5	4	4	13	10	4	17	100
R. PERU	4,181	1,733	243	168	92	274	201	356	16	383	2,448
S. URUGUAY	790	376	45	33	19	32	67	73	1	106	414
T. VENEZUELA	1,714	520	206	68	40	61	24	33	~	88	1,194

a. For prior years, 1973–78, see SALA, 25–1502.

SOURCE: USINS-SY, 1985, table IMM 6.1.

Table 1503

IMMIGRANTS ADMITTED TO THE UNITED STATES, BY CLASSIFICATION, 20 L

(1980)

Country	Total Admitted (1+2)	Immigrants Subject to Numerical Limitation (1)	Immigrants Admitted Without Numerical Limitation (2=3+4+5+6+7+8+9+10)	Parents of U.S. Citizens (3)	Spouses of U.S. Citizens (4)	Children of U.S. Citizens[1] (5)	Special Immigrants (6)	Spouse Child[2] (7)	Children Born Abroad to Aliens[3] (8)	Refugee and Exile (9)	Other (10)
A. ARGENTINA	2,815	1,824	891	150	566	74	33	28	14	25	1

Continued in SALA, 24-1503.

Table 1504

U.S. NATURALIZATION, BY COUNTRY OF ORIGIN AND YEAR OF ENTRY, 20 L, 1965–80

(N)

Country	1965	1970	1971	1972	1973	1974	1975	1976	1977	1978	1979	1980[a]
A. ARGENTINA	151	85	51	91	103	117	28	26	8	3	3	~

Continued in SALA, 24-1504.

Table 1505

"DEPORTABLE ALIENS" LOCATED IN THE UNITED STATES, FY 1966–85

(N)

Year	Total	Mexican	Mexicans as % of Total
1966	138,520[a]	89,751	65
1967	161,608[a]	108,327	67
1968	212,057[a]	151,705	72
1969	283,557[a]	201,636	71
1970	231,116*	219,254*	94*
1971	302,517	290,152	95
1972	369,495	355,099	96
1973	498,123	480,588	96
1974	634,777	616,630	97
1975	596,796	579,448	97
1976	871,189	848,130	97
1977	812,541	792,613	97
1978	862,217	841,525	97
1979	888,729	866,761	97
1980[b]	910,361	817,479	90
1981	975,780	874,433	90
1982	970,246	887,481	91
1983	1,246,491	1,172,297	94
1984	1,246,977	1,170,769	94
1985	1,348,749	1,266,999	94

a. Includes "involuntary" deportation given in table 1509.
b. Year ended Sept. 30, 1980.

SOURCE: USINS-AR, various years; USINS-SY, 1984/85, p. 177.

Table 1506

TEMPORARY WORKERS ADMITTED TO THE UNITED STATES, 19 L, 1984 AND 1985

(N)

	Country	1984				1985			
		Total	Workers of Distinguished Merit and Ability	Other Temporary Workers	Industrial Trainees	Total	Workers of Distinguished Merit and Ability	Other Temporary Workers	Industrial Trainees
A.	ARGENTINA	2,033	421	27	33	2,554	660	29	20
B.	BOLIVIA	299	37	#	1	379	29	1	#
C.	BRAZIL	3,316	389	27	46	3,837	554	24	100
D.	CHILE	1,095	144	49	11	1,148	171	40	3
E.	COLOMBIA	1,949	418	34	45	1,963	416	36	24
F.	COSTA RICA	551	88	45	8	743	110	51	11
H.	DOMINICAN REP.	2,079	1,196	431	28	1,828	977	338	18
I.	ECUADOR	538	46	22	19	454	36	#	9
J.	EL SALVADOR	907	115	51	7	1,199	118	21	6
K.	GUATEMALA	648	51	7	3	1,030	126	14	2
L.	HAITI	224	66	39	2	210	88	21	3
M.	HONDURAS	377	34	11	3	628	45	12	2
N.	MEXICO	9,622	2,391	2,412	71	10,081	2,761	2,212	80
O.	NICARAGUA	306	96	1	6	262	73	1	1
P.	PANAMA	547	70	52	1	711	63	42	3
Q.	PARAGUAY	99	5	#	#	117	1	#	#
R.	PERU	1,069	152	139	8	1,199	200	186	10
S.	URUGUAY	385	90	3	4	390	46	8	9
T.	VENEZUELA	3,056	468	88	19	2,851	480	97	25

SOURCE: USINS-SY, 1948, p. 140; 1985, p. 136.

Table 1507

MEXICAN IMMIGRATION TO THE UNITED STATES,[1,2] 1900–85

(N)

Year	N	Year	N	Year	N	Year	N
1900	237	1922	19,551	1944	6,598	1966	45,163
1901	347	1923	63,768	1945	6,702	1967	42,371
1902	709	1924	89,336	1946	7,146	1968	43,563
1903	528	1925	32,964	1947	7,558	1969	44,623
1904	1,009	1926	43,316	1948	8,384	1970	44,469
1905	2,637	1927	67,721	1949	8,083	1971	50,103
1906	1,997	1928	59,016	1950	6,744	1972	64,040
1907	1,406	1929	40,154	1951	6,153	1973	70,141
1908	6,067	1930	12,703	1952	9,079	1974	71,586
1909	16,251	1931	3,333	1953	17,183	1975	62,205
1910	18,691	1932	2,171	1954	30,645	1976	57,863
1911	19,889	1933	1,936	1955	43,702	1977	44,079
1912	23,238	1934	1,801	1956	61,320	1978	92,400
1913	11,926	1935	1,560	1957	49,321	1979	52,100
1914	14,614	1936	1,716	1958	26,791	1980[a]	56,680
1915	12,340	1937	2,347	1959	22,909	1981	101,268
1916	18,425	1938	2,502	1960	32,708	1982	56,106
1917	17,869	1939	2,640	1961	41,476	1983	59,079
1918	18,524	1940	2,313	1962	55,805	1984	57,557
1919	29,818	1941	2,824	1963	55,986	1985	61,077
1920	52,361	1942	2,378	1964	34,448		
1921	30,758	1943	4,172	1965*	37,969		

1. Immigration data to 1907 refer only to seaport arrivals.
2. Excludes undocumented or illegal immigrants.

a. Year ended Sept. 30, 1980.

SOURCE: 1900-64: USBC-HS, 1976; 1965-77: USINS-AR, 1965-77, yearly. USINS-AR, 1966-77, yearly: USINS-SY, 1977/80; 1983/84; 1984/85, table IMM 1.3.

Table 1508

MEXICAN "ILLEGAL" ALIENS REPORTED,[1] 1924–85

(N)

Year	Total	Year	Total	Year	Total
1924	4,614	1945	63,602	1966	89,751
1925	2,961	1946	91,456	1967	108,327
1926	4,047	1947	182,986	1968	151,705
1927	4,495	1948	179,385	1969	201,636
1928	5,529	1949	278,538	1970	277,377
1929	8,538	1950	458,215	1971	348,178
1930	18,319	1951	500,000	1972	430,213
1931	8,409	1952	543,538	1973	576,823
1932	7,116	1953	865,318	1974	709,959
1933	15,875	1954	1,075,168	1975	680,392
1934	8,910	1955	242,608	1976	781,474
1935	9,139	1956	72,442	1977	954,778
1936	9,534	1957	44,451	1978	976,667
1937	9,535	1958	37,242	1979	866,761
1938	8,684	1959	30,196	1980	817,479
1939	9,376	1960	29,651	1981	874,433
1940	8,051	1961	29,817	1982	887,481
1941	6,082	1962	30,272	1983	1,172,297
1942	~	1963	39,124	1984	1,170,769
1943	8,189	1964	43,844	1985	1,266,999
1944	26,689	1965	55,349		

1. Includes deportations, voluntary departures, and forced departures.

SOURCE: Julian Samora, *Los Mojados: The Wetbacks* (South Bend, Ind.: University of Notre Dame Press, 1971); USINS-AR, 1966-78, yearly; USINS-SY, various years.

Table 1509

U.S. IMMIGRATION AND NATURALIZATION SERVICE MAN-HOURS PER DEPORTABLE UNDOCUMENTED LOCATED, 1978–82[a]

(N)

Year	Border Patrol[1]		Investigations[2]	
------	Mexican Undocumenteds	All Undocumenteds	Mexican Undocumenteds	All Undocumenteds
1978	7.03	6.86	21.38	15.58
1979	7.22	7.04	22.17	16.20
1980	8.26	7.99	33.70	19.53
1981	7.94	7.68	34.62	20.60
1982	8.12	7.88	25.48	16.44

1. Includes line watch, patrol, farm-ranch check, traffic check, city patrol, boat patrol, crewman-stowaway, aircraft operations, liaison, intelligence, litigation, identification, special programs, and headquarters staff sections.
2. Includes subversive, criminal, fraud, general, and area control sections.

a. Productive and support hours divided by number of undocumenteds located inside the United States.

SOURCE: SALA-MB, table 404.

Table 1510

MEXICAN UNDOCUMENTED ALIENS COUNTED[†] IN THE 1980 U.S. CENSUS, BY PERIOD OF ENTRY, 1960-80[a]

Period of Entry	Mexican Undocumenteds (T)	As % of Western Hemisphere Undocumenteds in U.S.	As % of Total Undocumenteds in U.S.
Total Entered Since 1960[1]	931	64.1	45.5
Entered 1960-69	138	42.3	24.2
Entered 1970-74	280	64.7	50.8
Entered 1975-80	292	72.3	53.5

1. Includes 36,000 Mexican undocumenteds who entered before 1960 (only figure available for pre-1960 undocumenteds).

a. Estimates based on differences between 1980 census alien population as modified and 1980 alien registration (I-53) data adjusted for underregistration.

SOURCE: SALA-MB, table 405.

Table 1511

KNOWN EXCLUDABLE HAITIAN ARRIVALS, MIAMI, FLORIDA,[1] 1979-82

(N)

1979	1980	1981	1982
2,522	15,093	8,069	~

1. Low illegal entry figures for the period beginning October 1981 and ending June 1982 are the result of an Interdiction Program jointly conducted by the INS and the Coast Guard. Initiated in October 1981, after a joint U.S.–Haitian deportation agreement was signed, the program proved to be a deterrent to unauthorized traffic to U.S. shores.

SOURCE: USINS-AR, 1982, p. 8.

Table 1512

KNOWN IMMIGRANTS TO AND EMIGRANTS FROM CUBA, 1959-77

(N)

Year	Immigrants	Emigrants	Balance
1959	86,069	73,724	12,345
1960	56,557	118,936	−62,379

Continued in SALA, 25–1512.

Table 1513

IMMIGRANTS ADMITTED TO RECIPIENT COUNTRY, BY EDUCATIONAL LEVEL AND OCCUPATION,[1] 4L

(%)

Recipient Country	Code[2]	Population with More than 10 Years of Schooling	Agricultural and Service Workers		Nonagricultural Workers	
			Observed	Estimated	Observed	Estimated
A. ARGENTINA	A	7	31	53	52	22
	B	9	29	49	57	24
	C	7	30	53	53	22
	D	6	54	55	27	21
	E	22	19	21	39	36
F. COSTA RICA	H	8	57	51	22	23
Q. PARAGUAY	D	3	82	62	10	18
	F	14	54	38	22	28
T. VENEZUELA	G	7	50	53	21	22

1. Statistics derived from national census data. The dates of the census are as follows:
   Argentina, 1970; Bolivia, 1976; Brazil, 1970; Colombia, 1973; Costa Ricka, 1973;
   Chile, 1970; Nicaragua, 1971; Paraguay, 1971; Uruguay, 1975; Venezuela, 1971.
2. Code: A, Chileans; B. Bolivians; C, Paraguayans; D, Brazilians; E, Uruguayans;
   F, Argentines; G, Colombians; H, Nicaraguans.

SOURCE: ECLA-N, no. 346, Aug. 1981.

Table 1514

REFUGEES "IN NEED," 1983–85

(N)

Country of Asylum	Source Country/Area	Total		
		1983	1984	1985
A. ARGENTINA	Europe, Latin America, SE Asia	12,300	12,000[‡]	11,500[‡]
C. BRAZIL	Europe, other	5,400	5,000[‡]	5,300[‡]
D. CHILE	Europe	1,500	3,000	2,500
F. COSTA RICA	Latin America	15,000[a]	17,000[a]	18,800
H. DOMINICAN REP.	Haiti	5,000	5,000	6,000[‡]
K. GUATEMALA	El Salvador	70,000	70,000[‡]	70,000[‡]
M. HONDURAS	Latin America	33,300[b]	38,000[e]	62,500[‡,g]
N. MEXICO	Latin America	140,000[c]	170,000[‡,f]	175,000[‡,h]
P. PANAMA	Latin America	1,500[d]	2,000[d]	4,700[i]
R. PERU	Europe, Latin America	500	500[‡]	600
T. VENEZUELA	Europe, Latin America	500	1,000	1,400

a. 10,000 from El Salvador.
b. 20,000 from El Salvador; 12,000 from Nicaragua.
c. 120,000 from El Salvador; 20,000 from Guatemala.
d. 1,000 from El Salvador.
e. 19,000 from Nicaragua; 18,000 from El Salvador.
f. 120,000 from El Salvador; 40,000 from Guatemala.
g. 32,000 from Nicaragua; 30,000 from El Salvador.
h. 120,000 from El Salvador.
i. 1,200 from El Salvador.

SOURCE: U.S. Committee for Refugees, New York, *World Refugee Survey*, 1983, 1984,
   1985.

Table 1515

U. S. BORDER PATROL APPREHENSIONS ALONG U. S.–MEXICAN BORDER, 1981–85

(N)

Year	Number
1981	750,559
1982	743,830
1983	1,034,142
1984	1,056,907
1985	1,185,795

SOURCE: USINS.

Table 1516

"ILLEGAL" ALIENS APPREHENDED IN THE UNITED STATES, 1951–85

(N)

Year	Number	Year	Number
1951	509,040	1969	283,557
1952	543,535	1970	345,353
1953	885,587	1971	420,126
1954	1,089,583	1972	505,949
1955	254,096	1973	655,968
1956	87,696	1974	788,145
1957	59,918	1975	766,600
1958	53,474	1976	875,915
1959	45,336	1977	1,042,215
1960	70,684	1978	1,057,977
1961	88,823	1979	1,076,418
1962	92,758	1980	910,361
1963	88,712	1981	975,780
1964	86,597	1982	970,246
1965	110,371	1983	1,251,357
1966	138,520	1984	1,241,489
1967	161,608	1985	1,320,000[†]
1968	212,057		

SOURCE: USINS.

Table 1517

APPLICATIONS FOR REFUGEE STATUS,[1] BY GEOGRAPHIC AREA
AND COUNTRY OF CHARGEABILITY, 6 LC, FY 1982–85

Country of Chargeability	Applications Pending Beginning of FY	Applications Filed During FY	Applications Approved During FY	Applications Denied During FY	Applications Otherwise Closed During FY	Applications Pending End of FY
N FY 1982						
D. CHILE	6	7	- -	7	- -	- -
G. CUBA	49	984	580	311	67	26
J. EL SALVADOR	16	16	- -	- -	- -	16
L. HAITI	- -	2	- -	- -	- -	2
M. HONDURAS	- -	2	- -	- -	- -	2
O. NICARAGUA	8	15	- -	7	- -	8
LATIN AMERICA	79	1,026	580	325	67	54
N FY 1983						
A. ARGENTINA	- -	1	- -	1	- -	- -
D. CHILE	- -	4	- -	4	- -	- -
G. CUBA	26	944	710	206	5	23
J. EL SALVADOR	16	20	- -	- -	10	10
L. HAITI	2	2	- -	- -	2	- -
M. HONDURAS	2	3	- -	1	2	- -
O. NICARAGUA	8	11	- -	2	6	3
LATIN AMERICA	54	965	710	214	25	36
N FY 1984						
E. COLOMBIA	- -	3	- -	3	- -	- -
G. CUBA	23	140	57	49	- -	34
J. EL SALVADOR	10	129	96	21	- -	12
N. MEXICO	- -	2	- -	2	- -	- -
O. NICARAGUA	3	58	3	55	- -	- -
LATIN AMERICA	36	332	156	130	- -	46
N FY 1985						
D. CHILE	- -	4	- -	- -	- -	4
G. CUBA	34	2,104	1,865	149	38	54
J. EL SALVADOR	12	12	- -	11	- -	1
O. NICARAGUA	- -	11	3	8	- -	- -
LATIN AMERICA	46	2,131	1,868	168	36	59

1. Refers to applications under U.S. Code, Section 207, PL96–212.

SOURCE: USINS-SY, 1982, Ref. 1.3; 1983, p. 73; 1984, p. 71; 1985.

Table 1518

ALIENS DEPORTED, BY COUNTRY AND CAUSE, 20 LC, FY 1981–85

(N)

Country to Which Deported	Total					Criminal					Violation of Narcotics Laws				
	1981	1982	1983	1984	1985	1981	1982	1983	1984	1985	1981	1982	1983	1984	1985
A. ARGENTINA	28	23	17	43	27	1	~	~	2	2	2	~	~	4	3
B. BOLIVIA	13	20	28	48	55	~	~	~	~	1	3	4	5	18	22
C. BRAZIL	15	28	22	36	21	1	~	~	~	1	~	1	1	3	3
D. CHILE	30	26	36	25	21	~	~	~	~	~	1	4	2	2	~
E. COLOMBIA	368	428	460	624	817	1	~	5	2	10	11	24	53	115	111
F. COSTA RICA	23	24	58	53	49	~	~	~	1	1	1	~	1	~	2
G. CUBA	~	2	1	2	18	~	~	~	1	1	~	~	~	~	2
H. DOMINICAN REP.	307	146	166	300	184	8	7	8	11	10	1	2	2	9	18
I. ECUADOR	96	143	116	150	139	~	1	2	4	~	~	2	~	7	4
J. EL SALVADOR	2,333	2,118	3,104	2,585	3,078	2	3	13	15	23	~	1	6	5	22
K. GUATEMALA	557	587	917	880	1,649	2	2	4	2	6	~	2	1	3	8
L. HAITI	12	13	14	35	60	~	~	1	1	1	1	1	~	~	1
M. HONDURAS	487	211	471	469	771	~	~	~	4	2	~	~	~	4	2
N. MEXICO	10,452	8,387	9,327	10,510	11,284	96	68	390	388	527	70	64	144	204	339
O. NICARAGUA	40	60	43	41	134	~	~	~	2	~	~	~	1	~	1
P. PANAMA	44	45	38	25	33	1	2	1	1	1	4	3	3	3	5
Q. PARAGUAY	1	2	1	3	8	~	~	~	~	~	~	~	~	~	~
R. PERU	87	98	89	81	118	~	~	2	21	3	5	6	5	12	10
S. URUGUAY	17	9	12	7	18	~	~	~	~	~	~	~	~	~	1
T. VENEZUELA	18	15	30	41	40	~	3	3	1	~	4	1	2	7	~

Country to Which Deported	Previously Excluded or Deported					Entered Without Proper Documents					Failed to Comply with Conditions of Nonimmigrant Status				
	1981	1982	1983	1984	1985	1981	1982	1983	1984	1985	1981	1982	1983	1984	1985
A. ARGENTINA	~	~	~	~	~	1	~	~	1	~	17	15	16	24	11
B. BOLIVIA	1	~	~	~	~	~	~	~	1	~	7	14	20	18	22
C. BRAZIL	1	~	~	~	~	~	~	~	1	~	8	17	14	23	13
D. CHILE	3	~	1	~	~	1	~	~	~	1	14	14	20	12	9
E. COLOMBIA	5	3	1	3	3	8	3	6	7	7	72	106	109	136	149
F. COSTA RICA	~	~	~	1	~	~	~	3	1	~	10	10	22	13	13
G. CUBA	~	~	~	~	~	~	~	~	~	1	~	~	1	~	1
H. DOMINICAN REP.	9	12	13	4	6	14	9	27	14	8	32	35	27	37	40
I. ECUADOR	~	~	1	3	~	~	4	4	4	~	33	32	36	53	35
J. EL SALVADOR	4	~	8	4	8	24	12	23	7	14	29	24	28	17	18
K. GUATEMALA	3	2	3	4	3	10	6	8	6	3	25	23	33	24	36
L. HAITI	~	~	~	~	1	1	~	~	5	1	9	5	3	13	14
M. HONDURAS	~	~	2	2	4	3	2	3	3	~	369	27	22	30	51
N. MEXICO	55	38	57	68	96	318	268	296	246	301	138	153	201	194	231
O. NICARAGUA	~	~	~	~	~	3	~	~	~	~	3	8	8	7	11
P. PANAMA	~	2	~	~	~	6	2	~	~	3	11	16	20	9	19
Q. PARAGUAY	~	~	~	~	~	~	~	~	~	~	1	1	1	2	~
R. PERU	~	~	~	1	~	4	1	2	3	1	37	48	56	25	38
S. URUGUAY	~	~	2	~	1	~	~	~	~	~	4	4	7	5	8
T. VENEZUELA	~	~	2	~	1	~	~	~	~	~	10	7	20	25	14

Country to Which Deported	Entered Without Inspection or by False Statements				
	1981	1982	1983	1984	1985
A. ARGENTINA	8	7	1	12	11
B. BOLIVIA	2	2	3	11	10
C. BRAZIL	5	9	6	9	4
D. CHILE	11	6	13	11	11
E. COLOMBIA	270	289	286	361	537
F. COSTA RICA	12	14	29	37	33
G. CUBA	~	2	~	1	13
H. DOMINICAN REP.	243	80	89	225	102
I. ECUADOR	63	104	73	79	35
J. EL SALVADOR	2,274	2,078	3,007	2,536	2,992
K. GUATEMALA	517	551	858	841	1,592
L. HAITI	1	7	10	16	41
M. HONDURAS	114	182	441	425	712
N. MEXICO	9,765	7,767	8,073	9,362	9,782
O. NICARAGUA	34	52	34	32	122
P. PANAMA	19	20	14	12	25
Q. PARAGUAY	~	1	~	1	8
R. PERU	41	42	24	37	65
S. URUGUAY	13	5	5	2	8
T. VENEZUELA	4	2	2	8	11

SOURCE: USINS unpublished data; USINS-SY, 1985, p. 198.

Table 1519

EXIT OF NATIONAL TOURISTS, 14 LC, 1970-76

(N)

Country	1970	1971	1972	1973	1974	1975	1976
B. BOLIVIA	42,948	55,022	68,261	76,859	87,220	~	~

Continued in SALA, 20-3209.

Table 1520

RECEIPTS FROM TOURISM,[1] 19 LC, 1965-84

(M US)

Country	1965	1970	1975	1976	1979	1980	1981	1982	1983	1984
A. ARGENTINA	~	74.0	154	180	279	345	510	516	651[‡]	~
B. BOLIVIA	2	2.6	19	25	37	40	36	30	35[‡]	~
C. BRAZIL	30	30.0	72	56	132	1,794	1,727	1,608[a]	1,533	1,512
D. CHILE	45	50.0	83	96	127	166	192	118	85	104
E. COLOMBIA	28	54.0	164	146	358	357	384	231	235	209
F. COSTA RICA	~	22.1	52	49	71	87	94	131	131	117
H. DOMINICAN REP.	3	16.4	61	91	131	168	~	~	260	277
I. ECUADOR	7	8.5	29	31	80	91	~	~	120	120
J. EL SALVADOR	~	8.5	18	32	14	7	4	7	4	5
K. GUATEMALA	6	12.1	78	85	201	183	131	87	62	57
L. HAITI[3]	1	8.7	22	28	63	65	~	~	~	~
M. HONDURAS	~	4.1	11	12	29	27[†]	~	~	45	~
N. MEXICO	782	1,454.0	2,171	822	1,443	1,671	1,760	1,406	1,625	3,282
O. NICARAGUA	~	13.2	26	28	18	22	23	20	5	~
P. PANAMA	~	78.1	133	124	164	167	171	169	171	186
Q. PARAGUAY	~	14.2	10	14	69	91	80	54	49	96
R. PERU	25	52.0	91	118	202	334	257	257	253	258
S. URUGUAY	~	40.8	57	68	223	298	283[b]	149[b]	47	107
T. VENEZUELA	15	50.0	180	214	265	246	251	264[‡]	257[‡]	~
UNITED STATES[2]	1,380	2,330.0	4,842	5,808	8,335	10,058	12,163	11,293	11,187	11,386

1. Travel receipts are defined by the International Monetary Fund to include receipts for goods and services provided to foreigners visiting the reporting country, including transportation within that country. Includes funds spent by tourists, business travelers, students, patients undergoing medical treatment, military personnel on leave, and traveling government officials. In many cases, comparable data for a national series are not available throughout the period covered by the table, and also close comparisons between countries are often rendered difficult by the lack of uniformity in definitions and scope.

2. For all countries figures cover the following categories of travelers who are formally admitted into the United States as non-immigrant aliens: temporary visitors for pleasure, students, temporary visitors for business, foreign government officials and their employees and families, treaty traders and investors, representatives to international organizations, and miscellaneous minor groups. These figures do not include less formally admitted visitors arriving from Mexico for less than three days.

3. Fiscal year ending September 30.

a. International tourism receipts for 1982 have been estimated by EMBRATUR through sample survey based parameters.

b. Calculated on the basis of the average rate of the dollar in Dec. 1982.

SOURCE: UN-SY, 1972 and 1973, table 153; UN-SY, 1975, table 164; UN-SY, 1976, table 161; UN-SY, 1977, table 163; UN-SY, 1978, table 162; WTO-WTS, 1978/79, table 20; WTO-WTS, 1979/80, payments section. WTO-WTS, 1981/82, table 15; *World Travel and Tourism Statistics*, Vol. 38, 1983–84; UN-SY, 1983/84, table 169.

Table 1521

ENTRY OF TOURISTS,[1] 19 LC, 1970–83

(N)

Country Entered	1970	1975	1977	1978	1979	1980	1981	1982	1983
A. ARGENTINA	694,940	1,200,000†	1,104,923	1,198,407	1,019,439	1,120,000‡	1,145,000‡	1,040,000	1,312,952
B. BOLIVIA	22,248[b]	156,600[d]	101,637	202,903	159,417	155,412	155,000‡	150,000	176,000
C. BRAZIL	194,186	517,967	634,595	784,316	1,081,799	913,878	1,357,879	1,146,881	1,420,481
D. CHILE	198,824	250,000†	296,964	267,239	285,000†	320,000	405,000	263,250	275,000
E. COLOMBIA	161,668	443,264	~	826,276	1,151,284	1,228,000	1,059,630	1,127,662	506,884
F. COSTA RICA	154,867	297,207	327,548	340,442	317,724	345,470	333,102	371,582	326,142
H. DOMINICAN REP.[4]	67,566[a]	221,795	309,459	257,107[a]	286,573[a]	566,000	613,000‡	656,000‡	668,000‡
I. ECUADOR	57,548	172,945	201,897	228,917	239,802	243,485	245,000‡	245,000‡	247,000‡
J. EL SALVADOR	137,804	266,016	278,761	293,080	230,889	118,000	81,847	98,981	106,090
K. GUATEMALA[3]	173,652	454,436	444,843	415,580	503,908	466,041	328,878	233,881	235,166
L. HAITI	62,304	77,322	95,036	112,018	134,118	138,000	158,484	158,000	167,000‡
M. HONDURAS	45,800	167,100	~	~	134,507	122,000‡	126,000‡	126,000‡	126,000‡
N. MEXICO[2]	2,250,159	3,217,878	3,247,246	3,754,348	4,141,801	4,144,576	4,031,432	3,767,600	4,749,000
O. NICARAGUA	132,000	189,070	~	~	~	~	~	~	~
P. PANAMA	125,237	282,728	362,666	388,045	389,877	335,000	363,000	352,570	327,000
Q. PARAGUAY	119,239	93,113	~	201,919[c]	301,906[c]	302,056	267,089	184,914	147,830
R. PERU	133,546[c]	256,210	265,191	269,659	338,468	372,790	335,000	317,000	273,324
S. URUGUAY	615,000‡	602,506[c]	690,143[c]	713,653[c]	1,103,857[c]	1,066,692	927,666	621,732	622,000‡
T. VENEZUELA	116,962[d]	436,182	652,845	783,670	269,569	215,042	200,000	210,000	205,000‡
UNITED STATES	13,264,380[c]	15,698,118	18,609,794	19,816,380	20,310,000	22,500,000	23,080,000‡	21,916,000	20,441,020

1. Unless otherwise indicated refers to foreign nationals staying for more than 24 hours and less than 90 days. Not included are day visitors at border points or from cruise ships; also excludes passengers in transit.
2. Excludes Mexican nationals residing in other countries and who entered as tourists.
3. Includes visitors from neighboring countries entering with a "local pass."
4. Includes tourists from the Dominican Republic residing abroad.

a. Excludes Dominican Republic tourists residing abroad.
b. Arrivals to La Paz only.
c. Refers to visitors.
d. Arrival of passengers.

SOURCE: IASI-AC, 1977, table 334-01; WTO-WTS, 1975, 1976, 1977, 1978/79, 1979/80, 1981/82, World Travel and Tourism Statistics, Vol. 38, 1983–84; UN-SY, 1983/84.

Table 1522

TOURIST ENTRY,[1] BY MEANS OF TRANSPORTATION, 18 LC, 1970-83

(%)

Recipient Country	Means	1970	1975	1977	1978	1979	1980	1981	1982	1983
A. ARGENTINA	Air	45.0	40.9[†]	69.0[†]	68.3[†]	69.8	~	~	40.4	27.69
	Land	15.4	17.3[†]	~[†]	~	~	~	~	38.8	33.07
	Sea	1.3	.7[†]	24.9[†]	25.4	24.1	~	~	20.8	39.24
	Other	38.4[b]	41.1[b,†]	6.1	6.3[†]	6.1	~	~	#	#

Continued in SALA, 25–1522.

Table 1523

LODGING ESTABLISHMENTS CAPACITY,[1] 16 LC, 1982-84

(N)

	Country	1982		1983		1984	
		Rooms	Beds	Rooms	Beds	Rooms	Beds
A.	ARGENTINA	~	~	109,269	256,670	~	~
B.	BOLIVIA	~	~	3,424	6,300	3,405	6,437
C.	BRAZIL[2]	99,854	199,708	105,342	210,684	110,872	221,744
D.	CHILE	14,293	31,913	14,494	15,010	32,450	32,595
E.	COLOMBIA[2]	15,439	41,840	13,922	30,869	14,230	31,512
F.	COSTA RICA	3,804	7,608	~	~	~	~
G.	CUBA	~	~	14,061	27,422	13,335	29,359
I.	ECUADOR	~	~	23,585	41,795	22,793	40,639
J.	EL SALVADOR	1,740	2,585	1,701	2,597	1,742	2,678
K.	GUATEMALA[2]	7,514	15,028	7,615	15,742	7,871	15,230
M.	HONDURAS	~	~	~	~	4,441	8,077
N.	MEXICO	~	~	216,831	~	~	~
P.	PANAMA[2]	2,916	5,213	2,793	5,586	2,842	5,684
Q.	PARAGUAY	2,786	6,135	2,899	6,460	3,005	6,271
R.	PERU	~	~	40,573	71,595	42,316	74,512
S.	URUGUAY[2]	11,293	25,114	11,293	25,104	9,166	22,131
	UNITED STATES[2]	~	~	2,500,000	~	5,000,000	~

1. Unless otherwise indicated, figures refer to lodging establishments called hotels and motels.
2. Hotels only.

SOURCE: *World Travel and Tourism Statistics*, Vol. 38, 1983–84.

Table 1524

TOURIST ARRIVALS TO CUBA, 1950-76[a]

(T)

Year	N	Year	N
1950	168.0	1957	272.3

Continued in SALA, 23-3315.

CHAPTER 16

CONSTRUCTION, HOUSING, AND UTILITIES

DEFINITIONS OF TERMS

STAGES OF CONSTRUCTION

Construction Authorized. Building projects for the carrying out of which a permit has been issued.

Construction Completed. It is considered that the work is completed when the building or other structure is physically ready to be occupied or to be put into use.

TYPE OF BUILDING ACTIVITY

Building. A building is any independent structure comprising one or more rooms or other spaces, covered by a roof, enclosed with external walls or dividing walls, which extend from the foundation to the roof and intended for residential, industrial, commercial, educational, or other purposes.

Residential building. A building should be regarded as residential when the major part of the building (i.e., more than half of its floor area) is used for dwelling purposes.

One- or two-dwelling buildings. Detached, semi-detached, row, and terraced buildings with one or two dwellings on one or more floors.

Multi-dwelling buildings. All residential buildings other than one- or two-dwelling buildings.

Non-residential buildings. A building should be regarded as non-residential when less than half of its floor area is used for dwelling purposes.

 Industrial buildings. All buildings which are used to house the production, assembly, and warehousing activities of industrial establishments, i.e., factories, plants, work-shops, etc.

 Commercial buildings. Office buildings and all buildings which are intended for use primarily in wholesale, retail, and service trades, i.e., hotels, restaurants, shops, ware-houses, public garages, etc.

 Educational buildings. All buildings which are intended for use directly in instructional activities, furnishing academic and technical courses, i.e., schools, universities, etc., as well as museums, art galleries, libraries, etc.

 Health buildings. All buildings which are primarily engaged in providing hospital and institutional care, i.e., hospitals, infirmaries, sanitariums, etc.

Other Buildings. Buildings which are not included in any of the above classifications, i.e., non-residential farm buildings, stadiums, recreational buildings, etc.

FLOOR AREA OF BUILDINGS

The sum of the area of each floor of the building measured to the outer surface of the outer walls including the area of lobbies, cellars, elevator shafts, and in multi-dwelling buildings all the common spaces. Areas of balconies are excluded.

DWELLING

A dwelling is a room or a suite of rooms and its accessories in a permanent building or a structurally separated part which is intended for private habitation. It should have a separate access to a street or to a common space within the buildings. Detached rooms for habitation which are clearly built to be used as a part of the dwelling should be counted as part of the dwelling.

Table 1600

NEW BUILDING CONSTRUCTION AUTHORIZED AND NEW BUILDINGS COMPLETED, 17 LC, 1973–83

(N)

Country	Code[1]	1973	1975	1976	1977	1978	1979	1980	1981	1982	1983
A. ARGENTINA	I[a]	101,593	143,483	107,943	54,198	35,095	33,863	33,335	30,379	25,716	2,800[w]
	II=										
C. BRAZIL	I[b,c]	108,154	112,169	135,535	116,555	139,048	137,615	162,217	132,222	170,716	122,036
	II[b]	60,019	63,086	70,178	64,479	87,296	89,567	90,026	88,910	107,590	98,135
D. CHILE	I[i,q,u]	1,350.9	1,353.9	1,243	1,244.6	1,932.8	2,975.3	4,031.7	4,935.2	1,941.2	2,292.5
	II[v]	1,247.7	363.4	1,354.9	953	484.5	198.6	311.9	279.4	186.6	155.3
E. COLOMBIA	I[c]	17,706	13,768	14,167	16,040	17,052	14,984	15,194	16,183	15,575	16,872
	II=										
F. COSTA RICA	I[d,e]	11,027	14,316	16,421	13,878	14,852	15,269	15,958	11,385	11,614	11,334
	II=										
G. CUBA	I=										
	II=										
H. DOMINICAN REP.	I[f]	3,059	5,331	3,625	4,656	7,065	1,558	1,568	1,204	876	1,009
	II=						8,286	9,577	12,940	27,568	23,724
I. ECUADOR	I[c,g]	5,869	7,699	8,072	8,824	12,181	9,726	9,612	10,494	11,585	11,978
	II=										
J. EL SALVADOR	I[c,h]	2,016	2,463	1,976	1,521	2,058	4,124	4,762	10,957	17,337	12,672
	II[i]	2,851	2,744	2,299	4,203	3,014	5,073	2,977	2,976		
K. GUATEMALA	I[e]	1,618	1,701	2,668	2,432	2,269	1,904	1,529	1,222	1,793	
	II[e]	975	1,034	1,091	950	818	1,008	750	877	851	
L. HAITI	I[c,j]	369	320	304	445	462	428	364	310	250	117
	II[e,j]	408	398	370	527	571	553	620	597	358	
M. HONDURAS[2]	I[k]	1,143	1,683	1,948	1,727	1,515	1,593	2,271			
	II=	1,219	1,683	1,948	1,727	1,515	1,593				
O. NICARAGUA	I[t]	478	1,789	2,333	1,162	747	168	356	1,017	1,259	419
	II[t]							2,271	2,858	5,122	1,643
P. PANAMA	I[j,s]	1,621	506	618	872	871	1,184	952	878	1,094	841
	II=										
Q. PARAGUAY	I=										
	II=										
S. URUGUAY	I[m]	514	515	429	1,120			1,629	1,900	1,565	
	II=										
T. VENEZUELA	I[c,n]	5,229	5,512	6,653	5,778	5,428	4,495	5,661	4,687	3,678	2,807
	II=										
UNITED STATES	I[o,p,q]	1,402.4[r]	1,052.9[r]	1,333.6[r]	1,602.1[r]	1,719.5[r]	1,494.4[r]	1,137.3[r]	986.5[r]	979.8	1,402.7
	II=										

1. Code: I = New building construction authorized.
   II = New buildings completed.
2. Data on construction authorized and completed refer to private construction in Tegucigalpa, San Pedro Sola, and La Ceiba.

a. Beginning 1977 data refer to the capital and Greater Buenos Aires.
b. Including reconstruction and alterations.
c. Data refer to buildings for which a building permit has been issued.
d. Data based on building permits issued by the municipalities.
e. Number of works.
f. Data cover only the urban areas of the country.
g. Including reconstructions.
h. Permits issued by the municipalities to private enterprises and individuals. Construction work done by the Instituto de Vivienda Urbana and the Instituto de Colonización Rural are excluded.
i. Data provided by the Dirección General de Servicios Eléctricos.
j. Data relating to construction authorized and completed cover the municipalities of Port-au-Prince and Petion Ville.
k. Year ending 30 September of the year stated.
l. New construction excluding extensions.

m. Data obtained from the Intendencia Municipal de Montevideo and refer to new construction, restoration, and conversion in the capital.
n. Data refer to private building construction.
o. Data do not include buildings constructed in areas not requiring building permits and represent, therefore, only about 85% of the actual number of all buildings stated. Prior to 1978, construction authorized in building permit–issuing places were based on a universe of 14,000 places. Beginning 1978, the universe was increased to 16,000, accounting for an increase of about 7% in total new building construction authorized.
p. Excluding publicly owned structures.
q. Excluding extensions.
r. Thousands.
s. Data based on permits supplied by the Oficina de Seguridad and refer to new private construction in Panama City.
t. Data on construction authorized refer to building activity in Managua only.
u. Data refer to private holding projects in 80 communes, approved by the Dirección de Obras Municipales. Prior to 1975, data refer to 60 communes.
v. New construction started by the public sector, excluding extensions.
w. Federal capital.

SOURCE: UN-YCS, 1973-83. For previous years, see SALA, 20-900.

SOURCE: UN-YCS, 1973-83. For previous years, see SALA, 20-900.

Table 1601

ARGENTINA NEW BUILDING CONSTRUCTION AUTHORIZED,[1] 1973–83

Category	Unit	1973	1975	1976	1977	1978	1979	1980	1981	1982	1983
All Buildings											
Number	N	101,593	143,483	107,943	54,198	35,095	33,863	33,335	30,379	25,716	2,800[a]
Floor Area	T Me^2	13,177	18,251	15,063	12,093	8,055	4,115	4,308	4,041	3,406	781[a]

1. Beginning in 1977 data refer to the capital and Greater Buenos Aires.

a. Federal capital.

SOURCE: UN-YCS, 1973–80; 1974–83.

Table 1602

BRAZIL NEW BUILDING CONSTRUCTION AUTHORIZED AND NEW BUILDINGS COMPLETED, 1973–83

Category	Unit	1973	1975	1976	1977	1978	1979	1980	1981	1982	1983
I. New Building Construction Authorized[1,2]											
All Buildings											
Number	N	108,154	112,169	135,535	116,555	139,048	137,615	162,217	132,222	170,716	122,036
Floor Area	T Me^2	30,813	26,683	31,487	27,199	28,510	30,327	43,592	34,145	39,254	30,754
Tender Value	T NC	15,639	19,291	25,622	25,649	~	~	~	~	~	~
Residential											
Number	N	~	~	~	~	~	129,272	153,444	125,234	163,584	114,453
Floor Area	T Me^2	21,163	17,757	22,792	20,338	21,345	23,251	35,369	28,973	33,155	24,836
Non-Residential											
Number	N	~	~	~	~	~	8,343	8,773	6,988	7,132	7,583
Floor Area	T Me^2	9,650	8,926	8,695	6,861	7,165	7,076	8,223	5,172	6,099	5,918
Industrial											
Number	N	~	~	~	~	~	1,244	1,261	815	720	669
Floor Area	T Me^2	3,596	3,022	2,352	1,735	2,004	1,978	2,460	1,205	897	813
Commercial											
Number	N	~	~	~	~	~	5,734	6,102	4,962	5,065	5,444
Floor Area	T Me^2	4,722	4,303	4,499	3,646	3,635	3,801	4,320	2,886	3,920	3,903
Educational											
Number	N	~	~	~	~	~	204	169	144	173	180
Floor Area	T Me^2	~	~	~	~	~	314	294	253	217	220
Health											
Number	N	~	~	~	~	~	75	100	60	55	54
Floor Area	T Me^2	~	~	~	~	~	182	151	163	130	75
Other[3]											
Number	N	~	~	~	~	~	1,086	1,141	1,007	1,119	1,236
Floor Area	T Me^2	1,332	1,601	1,844	1,480	1,526	801	998	665	935	907
II. New Buildings Completed[1,4]											
All Buildings											
Number	N	60,019	63,086	70,178	64,479	87,296	89,567	90,026	88,910	107,590	98,135
Floor Area	T Me^2	16,539	15,297	17,671	18,627	18,394	19,451	19,432	19,590	23,917	20,993
Value	T NC	7,180	10,819	14,846	17,626	~	~	~	~	~	~
Residential											
Number	N	~	~	~	~	~	84,118	85,127	84,674	103,469	93,936
Floor Area	T Me^2	12,298	11,253	12,388	13,082	13,710	14,573	15,500	16,111	20,404	17,628
Non-Residential											
Number	N	~	~	~	~	~	5,449	4,899	4,236	4,121	4,199
Floor Area	T Me^2	4,241	4,044	5,283	5,545	4,684	4,879	3,932	3,479	3,513	3,365
Industrial											
Number	N	~	~	~	~	~	872	717	566	507	444
Floor Area	T Me^2	1,609	1,498	1,907	1,883	1,245	1,317	992	885	678	584
Commercial											
Number	N	~	~	~	~	~	3,831	3,577	3,129	2,978	3,035
Floor Area	T Me^2	1,924	2,065	2,513	2,749	2,564	2,487	2,151	2,036	2,350	2,225
Educational											
Number	N	~	~	~	~	~	95	100	77	97	134
Floor Area	T Me^2	~	~	~	~	~	234	179	94	140	192
Health											
Number	N	~	~	~	~	~	40	31	21	36	31
Floor Area	T Me^2	~	~	~	~	~	102	109	33	40	32
Other[3]											
Number	N	~	~	~	~	~	611	474	443	503	555
Floor Area	T Me^2	708	481	863	913	875	741	501	431	305	332

1. Including reconstruction and alterations.
2. Data for construction authorized refer to buildings for which a building permit has been issued.
3. Prior to 1979 including educational and health buildings.
4. Information covers buildings for which occupancy permits have been issued, although in some cities occupancy permits are not required after completion.

SOURCE: UN-YCS, 1973-80; 1974-83.

Table 1603

CHILE NEW BUILDING CONSTRUCTION AUTHORIZED AND NEW BUILDINGS COMPLETED, 1973–83

Category	Unit	1973	1975	1976	1977	1978	1979	1980	1981	1982	1983
I. New Building Construction Authorized[1,2]											
All Buildings											
Floor Area	T Me^2	1,350.9	1,353.9	1,243	1,244.6	1,932.8	2,975.3	4,031.7	4,935.2	1,941.2	2,292.5
Tender Value	M NC	11.4	258.7	930.7	2,817.8	6,412.1	13,155.5	26,697	42,079.1	14,518.8	19,504
Residential											
Floor Area	T Me^2	1,098.9	1,050.7	868	776.1	1,276.7	2,173.2	2,932.8	3,660.8	1,308.9	1,770.3
Tender Value	M NC	10	209.9	638.9	1,799.4	4,470.9	9,841.9	19,573.9	31,956.7	9,810.1	15,570
Non-Residential											
Floor Area	T Me^2	252	303.2	375	468.5	656.1	802.1	1,093.9	1,274.4	632.3	522.2
Tender Value	M NC	1.4	48.8	291.8	1,018.4	1,941.2	3,313.6	7,123.1	10,122.4	4,708.7	3,934
Industrial[3]											
Floor Area	T Me^2	206.7	261.9	316.8	414.4	584.9	699.6	929.4	1,064.6	453.9	363.4
Tender Value	M NC	1	43	235.9	902.8	1,699.7	2,818.6	5,960.4	8,278.7	3,033.5	2,387
Other[4]											
Floor Area	T Me^2	45.3	41.3	58.2	54.1	71.2	102.5	169.5	209.8	178.4	158.8
Tender Value	M NC	.4	5.8	55.9	115.6	241.5	495	1,162.7	1,843.7	1,675.2	1,547
II. New Buildings Completed[5]											
All Buildings											
Floor Area	T Me^2	1,247.7	363.4	1,354.9	953	484.5	198.6	311.9	279.4	186.6	155.3
Value	M NC	12.5	110.3	1,207.4	1,764.1	2,054.7	1,426.8	2,697.7	4,068.2	2,185.8	1,725
Residential											
Floor Area	T Me^2	1,057.5	239	1,220.6	823.4	259.3	23.5	134.8	46.4	25.4	62.0
Value	M NC	11.1	81.7	1,051.5	1,408.4	998	101.1	883.1	411.3	234.1	615
Non-Residential											
Floor Area	T Me^2	190.2	124.4	134.3	129.6	225.2	175.1	177.1	233.0	161.2	93.3
Value	M NC	1.4	28.6	155.9	355.7	1,056.7	1,325.7	1,8146	3,656.9	1,951.7	1,110
Industrial[3]											
Floor Area	T Me^2	2.4	38.3	12.5	35	31	11.9	5.3	1.7	11.7	2.6
Value	M NC	~	5.2	11.1	61.2	82	55.6	37.3	12.9	92.0	27
Other[4]											
Floor Area	T Me^2	187.8	86.1	121.8	94.6	194.2	163.2	171.8	231.3	149.5	90.7
Value	M NC	1.4	23.4	144.8	294.5	974.7	1,270.1	1,777.3	3,644.0	1,859.7	1,083

1. Private new construction projects, excluding extensions.
2. Data refer to private holding projects in 80 communes, approved by the Dirección de Obras Municipales. Prior to 1975, data refer to 60 communes.
3. Including commercial buildings.
4. Including educational and health buildings.
5. New construction started by the public sector, excluding extensions.

SOURCE: UN—YCS, 1973-80; 1974-83.

Table 1604

COLOMBIA NEW BUILDING CONSTRUCTION AUTHORIZED,[1] 1973–83

Category	Unit	1973	1975	1976	1977	1978	1979	1980	1981	1982	1983
All Buildings											
Number of Permits	N	17,706	13,768	14,167	16,040	17,052	14,984	15,194	16,183	15,575	16,872
Floor Area	T Me^2	6,072.8	4,842.5	5,127.9	6,404.5	7,126.6	6,093.7	5,942.9	6,294.6	6,327.9	8,572.5
Tender Value	M NC	4,361.7	5,478.5	7,634.1	12,940.2	17,364.8	17,930.8	27,870.3	35,772.9	43,836.3	56,764
Residential											
Number of Permits	N	16,740	12,600	12,985	14,737	15,817	13,813	14,086	15,077	14,403	15,649
Floor Area	T Me^2	4,948.6	3,637	3,928.2	5,011.4	5,941.3	4,717.7	4,633.6	5,150.2	4,929.9	7,293.6
Tender Value	M NC	3,362.3	3,975.5	5,748.6	9,775.3	14,447.4	13,201.7	20,726.2	27,531.5	32,614.7	44,974.5
One, Two-Dwelling											
Number of Permits	N	13,572	9,615	10,889	12,784	12,222	10,057	10,644	9,531	8,879	7,480
Multi-Dwelling											
Number of Permits	N	3,168	2,985	2,096	1,953	3,595	3,756	3,442	5,546	5,524	8,169
Non-Residential											
Number of Permits	N	966	1,168	1,182	1,303	1,235	1,171	1,108	1,106	1,172	1,223
Floor Area	T Me^2	1,124.2	1,205.5	1,199.7	1,393.1	1,185.3	1,376	1,308.3	1,144.4	1,398.0	1,278.9
Tender Value	M NC	999.4	1,503	1,885.5	3,164.9	2,917.4	4,729.1	7,144.1	8,241.4	11,221.6	11,789.5
Industrial											
Number of Permits	N	140	182	160	173	169	140	121	86	106	107
Floor Area	T Me^2	181.9	290.3	260	223.4	210.8	246.2	175.1	102.1	175.4	129.9
Tender Value	M NC	126.9	347.3	355.9	389.4	372	893.9	950.7	677.1	1,176.4	1,085.5
Commercial											
Number of Permits	N	650	765	783	877	772	797	744	783	792	794
Floor Area	T Me^2	718.8	696.1	714.5	934.6	755.5	919.7	781.1	774.8	768.9	754.8
Tender Value	M NC	647.6	832.7	1,195.5	2,256.8	2,064.5	3,136.8	4,567.3	6,326.2	6,983.4	7,610.8
Educational											
Number of Permits	N	44	64	65	60	63	51	42	44	52	74
Floor Area	T Me^2	78	61.9	87.7	68.5	85.3	70.7	132.8	69.2	72.7	122.0
Tender Value	M NC	61.9	73.6	144.1	137.6	153.6	240.8	250.5	359.3	473.0	862.9
Health											
Number of Permits	N	22	30	18	24	19	23	19	21	41	16
Floor Area	T Me^2	21.7	32.6	15.2	59.1	32.3	43.4	29.6	21.2	203.5	30.6
Tender Value	M NC	20.7	33.6	17.9	173.5	85.7	110.6	294.2	135.6	1,288.8	142.3
Other											
Number of Permits	N	110	127	156	169	212	160	182	172	181	232
Floor Area	T Me^2	123.9	124.4	122.3	107.6	101.4	96	189.8	177.1	177.5	241.6
Tender Value	M NC	142.3	215.8	172.1	207.6	241.6	347	1,081.4	743.2	1,300.0	2,088

1. Data are derived from information supplied to local authorities by enterprises and
   collected by the Departamento Administrativo Nacional de Estadística.

SOURCE: UN-YCS, 1973-80; 1974-83.

Table 1605

COSTA RICA NEW BUILDING CONSTRUCTION AUTHORIZED,[1] 1973–83

Category	Unit	1973	1975	1976	1977	1978	1979	1980	1981	1982	1983
All Buildings											
Number of Works	N	11,027	14,316	16,421	13,878	14,852	15,269	15,958	11,385	11,614	11,334
Floor Area	T Me^2	1,160	2,221	3,246	2,079	2,902	1,793	3,291	1,854	875	792
Tender Value	M NC	423.2	806.2	820.8	877.9	1,134.7	1,480.7	1,533.9	1,506.8	1,534.9	4,286.6
Residential											
Number of Permits	N	9,921	11,918	13,273	11,163	12,208	12,229	12,439	10,473	8,317	8,180
Floor Area	T Me^2	832	736	751	853	986	1,075	1,016	805	702	664
Tender Value	M NC	301.1	535	507.6	639.9	834.9	1,101.9	1,151	1,207.9	1,022.4	3,068.8
Non-Residential											
Number of Permits	N	1,106	2,398	3,142	2,715	2,644	3,040	3,519	912	3,297	3,154
Floor Area	T Me^2	328	1,485	2,495	1,220	1,915	718	2,275	1,049	173	128
Tender Value	M NC	122.1	271.2	313.2	238	299.8	378.8	382.9	298.9	512.5	1,217.8
Industrial											
Number of Permits	N	134	157	156	115	120	85	82	42	75	82
Floor Area	T Me^2	83	66	73	48	69	49	44	20	23	21
Tender Value	M NC	26.6	51	57.5	45.5	56	51.1	42.1	24.3	53.6	79.1
Commercial											
Number of Permits	N	773	1,278	795	478	478	533	469	372	335	412
Floor Area	T Me^2	195	236	122	110	113	146	97	96	68	86
Tender Value	M NC	71.8	179.3	105	108.7	99.1	123.3	145.7	169.6	202.9	550.2
Educational											
Number of Permits	N	11	23	16	12	12	16	27	15	14	19
Floor Area	T Me^2	4	6	8	7	5	5	7	4	4	10
Tender Value	M NC	1.6	4.6	7.1	8.5	5.3	5.8	6.7	6.4	15.6	82.8
Health											
Number of Permits	N	6	5	1	2	1	~	1	2	#	#
Floor Area	T Me^2	3	1	#	1	#	#	2	#	#	#
Tender Value	M NC	2.1	.6	.2	.4	#	#	2	.1	#	#
Other											
Number of Permits	N	182	935	2,174	2,108	2,033	2,406	2,940	481	2,873	2,641
Floor Area	T Me^2	43	1,176	2,292	1,055	1,728	518	2,125	929	78	11
Tender Value	M NC	20	35.7	143.4	74.9	139.4	198.6	186.4	98.5	240.4	505.7

1. Data based on building permits issued by the municipalities.

SOURCE: UN–YCS, 1973-80; 1974-83.

Table 1606

CUBA NEW BUILDINGS COMPLETED,[1] 1979–83

Category	Unit	1979	1980	1981	1982	1983
All Buildings						
Number	N	1,558	1,568	1,204	876	1,009
Floor Area	T ME^2	~	~	~	2,928.7	3,425.4
Tender Value	M NC	427.3	450.7	353.4	3,520	402.1
Residential						
Number	N	552	755	744	647	753
Floor Area	T ME^2	1,092	1,372	1,856	830	2,036
Tender Value	M NC	64.9	104.6	88.2	79.1	108.4
Non-Residential						
Number	N	1,006	813	460	476	256
Floor Area	T ME^2	~	~	~	4,445	1,389.5
Tender Value	M NC	362.4	346.1	266.2	277.0	293.7
Industrial						
Number	N	226	228	179	106	133
Floor Area	T ME^2	~	~	~	1,774	1,173
Tender Value	M NC	80.5	111.2	87.0	157.6	176
Commercial						
Number	N	6	16	9	15	7
Floor Area	T ME^2	~	~	~	9.8	9.8
Tender Value	M NC	.8	1.7	1.2	2.1	4.4
Educational						
Number	N	181	120	73	26	24
Floor Area	T ME^2	~	~	~	64.3	93.7
Tender Value	M NC	113.3	70.5	44.5	15.1	27.7
Health						
Number	N	15	23	15	22	21
Floor Area	T ME^2	~	~	~	147.6	34.6
Tender Value	M NC	18.6	39.0	26.7	46.3	7.9
Other						
Number	N	578	426	184	60	71
Floor Area	T ME^2	~	~	~	102.8	78.3
Tender Value	M NC	148.2	123.7	106.8	51.8	77.7

1. Data refer to the activities of the construction sector, local administrations,
   the people at their own expense, and cooperatives.

SOURCE: UN-YCS, 1983.

Table 1607

DOMINICAN REPUBLIC NEW BUILDING CONSTRUCTION AUTHORIZED,[1] 1973–83

Category	Unit	1973	1975	1976	1977	1978	1979	1980	1981	1982	1983
All Buildings											
Number of Permits	N	3,059	5,331	3,625	4,656	7,065	8,286	9,577	12,940	27,568	23,724
Floor Area	T Me^2	964	1,191	1,172	1,156	1,385	1,048	1,179	869	968	1,175
Tender Value	M NC	72.3	132.3	140	150.5	171.5	189.7	235	227.5	408.8	412.6
Residential											
Number of Permits	N	2,547	4,861	3,173	4,041	6,388	7,563	8,926	12,434	27,073	23,077
Floor Area	T Me^2	540	879	799	781	980	798	881	659	727	777
Tender Value	M NC	40.9	99.3	94.7	100.5	121.5	144.2	190.2	185.1	356.6	347.9
One, Two-Dwelling											
Number of Permits	N	2,539	4,199	2,777	3,820	6,201	7,272	8,704	12,220	26,934	22,980
Multi-Dwelling											
Number	N	8	662	396	221	187	291	222	214	139	97
Non-Residential											
Number of Permits	N	512	470	452	615	677	723	651	506	495	647
Floor Area	T Me^2	424	312	373	375	405	250	298	210	241	398
Tender Value	M NC	31.4	33	45.3	50	50	40.5	44.8	37.6	52.2	64.7
Industrial											
Number of Permits	N	21	19	25	15	20	13	21	20	9	15
Floor Area	T Me^2	41	64	110	24	25	17	31	22	5	12
Tender Value	M NC	2.5	6.5	11.9	1.9	2.8	2.1	3.4	3.2	1.1	2.0
Commercial											
Number of Permits	N	102	84	73	108	81	88	130	112	132	106
Floor Area	T Me^2	57	34	36	77	62	28	50	37	39	56
Tender Value	M NC	3.7	3.3	4.1	9.6	7.3	3.5	7.1	6.1	7.6	8.4
Educational											
Number of Permits	N	30	35	32	51	104	136	30	16	5	17
Floor Area	T Me^2	37	37	41	55	71	40	21	11	5	16
Tender Value	M NC	2.7	3.3	4.8	5.2	7.7	5.2	2.9	1.9	1.6	3.1
Health											
Number of Permits	N	8	3	3	24	5	33	8	8	3	7
Floor Area	T Me^2	10	6	14	10	2	14	12	3	3	9
Tender Value	M NC	.8	.9	2	1.1	.2	2.5	2.3	.6	1.0	1.9
Other											
Number of Permits	N	351	329	319	417	467	453	462	350	346	502
Floor Area	T Me^2	279	171	172	209	245	151	184	137	189	305
Tender Value	M NC	21.7	19	22.5	32.2	32	27.2	29.1	25.8	40.9	49.3

1. Data cover only the urban areas of the country.

SOURCE: UN-YCS, 1973-80; 1974-83.

Table 1608

ECUADOR NEW BUILDING CONSTRUCTION AUTHORIZED, 1973–84

I. New Building Construction Authorized[1]

Category	Unit	1973	1974	1975	1976	1977	1978	1979	1980	1981	1982	1983	1984
All Buildings													
Number of Permits	N	5,869	8,340	7,699	8,072	8,824	12,181	9,726	9,612	10,494	11,585	11,978	18,103
Floor Area	T Me²	1,401.9	1,888.3	1,931.5	2,172.6	2,326.4	2,763	2,398.7	2,320.4	2,468.2	2,671.3	2,628	2,913.5
Tender Value	M NC	1,567.9	2,734.5	3,256.1	4,510.8	5,521.5	6,947.8	6,965.4	7,545.8	9,152	12,228.1	14,155.3	20,179
Residential													
Number of Permits	N	5,530	7,920	7,240	7.564	8,268	11,580	9,149	9,009	9,880	10,945	11,439	16,989
Floor Area	T Me²	~	~	~	~	~	1,865.8	1,656.4	1,529.8	1,711.1	2,077.5	2,110.1	2,355.2
Tender Value	M NC	1,276.2	2,172	2,586	3,531.2	4,125.4	5,417.5	4,918	5,715.9	6,645.1	10,233.3	12,235.3	17,268.9
One, Two-Dwelling													
Number of Permits	N	4,219	6,489	5,196	5,480	6,015	9,030	6,764	6,083	7,395	7,190	7,563	13,323
Multi-Dwelling													
Number of Permits	N	1,311	1,431	2,044	2,084	2,253	2,550	2,385	2,926	2,485	3,755	3,876	3,666
Non-Residential													
Number of Permits	N	339	420	459	508	556	601	577	603	614	640	539	1,114
Floor Area	T Me²	~	~	~	~	~	897.2	742.3	790.6	757.1	593.8	517.9	558.3
Tender Value	M NC	291.7	562.5	670.1	979.6	1,396.1	1,530.3	2,047.4	1,829.9	2,506.7	1,994.8	1,920	2,910.1
Industrial													
Number of Permits	N	~	~	~	152	165	143	119	119	111	95	64	65
Tender Value	M NC	~	~	~	~	~	382.9	384.4	314.5	321.3	408	250.5	530
Commercial													
Number of Permits	N	~	~	~	249	295	320	333	344	363	417	358	925
Tender Value	M NC	~	~	~	~	~	915.5	1,194.1	1,055.4	1,838	1,179.6	1,157.6	1,665.4
Educational													
Number of Permits	N	~	~	~	26	33	30	23	35	24	34	25	37
Tender Value	M NC	~	~	~	~	~	80.9	63.2	131.3	100.7	108.5	103.3	219.6
Health													
Number of Permits	N	~	~	~	4	12	9	7	13	8	8	16	10
Tender Value	M NC	~	~	~	~	~	15.9	17.5	65	20.8	39	41.3	141.5
Other													
Number of Permits	N	~	~	~	77	51	99	95	92	108	86	76	77
Tender Value	M NC	~	~	~	~	~	135.1	388.2	263.7	226.1	259.7	367.3	353.6

1. Includes reconstructions.

SOURCE: UN-YCS, 1973-80; 1974-84.

Table 1609

EL SALVADOR NEW BUILDING CONSTRUCTION AUTHORIZED AND NEW BUILDINGS COMPLETED, 1973-84

I. New Building Construction Authorized[1]

Category	Unit	1973	1974	1975	1976	1977	1978	1979	1980	1981	1982	1983	1984
All Buildings													
Number of Permits	N	2,016	2,819	2,463	1,976	1,521	2,058	4,124	4,762	10,957	17,337	12,672	4,267
Floor Area	T Me^2	412.8	603.4	383	~	440.9	572.8	567.2	427.2	504.3	706.6	588.2	223.3
Tender Value	M NC	63.4	98.7	86.9	100	177.8	224.9	215.9	156.3	167.1	265.6	204.6	105.5
Residential													
Number of Permits	N	1,864	2,679	2,357	1,805	1,375	1,738	3,879	4,646	10,922	17,256	12,620	4,232
Floor Area	T Me^2	297.4	405.2	241.7	291.2	295.2	378.9	379.4	332.9	483.5	684.3	566	200.3
Tender Value	M NC	43.4	63.2	47	65.3	132.8	147.3	132.8	115.1	158.7	255.8	196.6	84.1
One, Two-Dwelling													
Number of Permits	N	1,848	2,673	2,355	1,799	1,364	1,475	3,845	4,616	10,840	17,112	12,482	4,232
Multi-Dwelling													
Number of Permits	N	16	6	2	6	11	263	34	30	82	144	138	~
Non-Residential													
Number of Permits	N	152	140	106	171	146	320	245	116	35	81	52	35
Floor Area	T Me^2	115.4	198.2	141.3	~	145.7	193.9	187.8	94.2	20.8	22.3	22.2	23
Tender Value	M NC	20	35.4	39.9	34.7	45	77.6	83.1	41.2	8.4	9.8	8	24.1
Industrial													
Number of Permits	N	24	37	18	44	10	22	14	14	3	2	6	2
Floor Area	T Me^2	31	71.2	19.3	~	13.8	10.6	33.2	31.3	3	.9	4.9	2.2
Tender Value	M NC	2.7	7.5	3.2	8.3	2.6	1.9	8.3	9.4	1.1	.3	1.5	1.1
Commercial[2]													
Number of Permits	N	128	103	88	127	136	298	231	102	32	79	46	33
Floor Area	T Me^2	84.4	127	122	89.8	131.9	183.3	154.6	62.9	17.8	21.4	17.3	20.8
Tender Value	M NC	17.3	27.9	36.7	26.4	42.4	75.7	74.8	31.8	7.3	9.5	6.5	20.3

II. New Buildings Completed[3]

Category	Unit	1973	1974	1975	1976	1977	1978	1979	1980	1981	1982	1983	1984
All Buildings													
Number	N	2,851	2,217	2,744	2,299	4,203	3,015	5,264	3,183	3,031	7,227	8,649	9,091
Floor Area	T Me^2	291.7	279.8	256.8	181.6	371.2	300.7	375	182.3	185.3	290.3	345.2	384.3
Value	M NC	40	45.3	50.7	37.2	93.3	96.9	127.7	624	70.3	107.2	134.5	155.7
Residential													
Number	N	2,776	2,155	2,730	2,272	4,131	2,926	5,216	3,178	3,028	7,227	8,647	9,081
Floor Area	T Me^2	263.9	245.6	245.5	173	340	274.1	352.8	177.7	183.7	290.3	348.2	383.6
Value	M NC	36.3	41.3	48.9	35.6	86	87.4	119.0	59.4	68.8	107.2	134.5	155.1
One, Two-Dwelling													
Number	N	2,775	2,151	2,728	2,271	4,131	2,926	5,016	2,972	2,901	7,187	8,628	8,963
Multi-Dwelling													
Number	N	1	4	2	1	#	#	9	~	72	40	19	118
Non-Residential													
Number	N	75	62	14	27	72	89	48	5	3	#	2	10
Floor Area	T Me^2	27.9	34.3	11.3	8.7	31.2	26.6	22.2	4.6	1.6	#	#	.7
Value	M NC	3.7	4	1.8	1.6	7.3	9.5	8.7	3	1.5	#	#	.6
Industrial													
Number	N	11	7	1	#	3	1	3	1	#	#	#	#
Floor Area	T Me^2	6.2	4.2	1.2	#	1.8	2.4	2.3	.2	#	#	#	#
Value	M NC	.5	.6	.1	#	.3	.3	.3	#	#	#	#	#
Commercial[2]													
Number	N	64	55	13	27	69	88	45	4	3	#	2	?
Floor Area	T ME^2	21.7	30.1	10.1	8.7	29.4	24.2	19.9	4.5	1.6	#	#	?
Value	M NC	3.2	3.4	1.7	1.6	7	9.2	8.4	3	1.5	#	#	?

1. Permits issued by the municipalities to private enterprises and individuals. Construction work done by the Instituto de Vivienda Urbana and the Instituto de Colonización Rural is excluded.

2. Including educational, health, and other buildings.

3. Data provided by the Dirección General de Servicios Eléctricos.

SOURCE: UN-YCS, 1973-80, 1974-84.

Table 1610

GUATEMALA NEW BUILDING CONSTRUCTION AUTHORIZED AND NEW BUILDINGS COMPLETED,[1] 1973–83

Category	Unit	1973	1975	1976	1977	1978	1979	1980	1981	1982	1983
I. New Building Construction Authorized											
All Buildings											
Number of Construction Works	N	1,618	1,701	2,668	2,432	2,269	1,904	1,529	1,222	~	~
Floor Area[2]	T Me^2	365.5	423.2	451.3	519.4	633.4	997.2	228.2	151.0	377.7	343.5
Tender Value	M NC	20.7	27.7	29.4	36.8	46.7	40.4	23	18.9	42.5	41.4
Residential											
Floor Area[2]	T Me^2	211	208.4	270.2	281.3	278.5	229.4	128.5	86.9	268.7	222.7
Tender Value	M NC	11.9	13.5	18.4	20.4	18	20.2	13.9	11.4	33.2	29.4
Non-Residential											
Floor Area[2]	T Me^2	154.5	214.8	181.1	238.1	354.9	767.8	99.7	64.1	109.0	120.8
Tender Value	M NC	8.8	14.2	11	16.4	28.7	20.2	9.1	7.5	9.3	12.0
Industrial											
Floor Area[2]	T Me^2	25.8	17.8	8.6	21.3	16.2	112.9	6	5.0	14.0	15.2
Tender Value	M NC	1	.7	.4	1.5	.9	1.8	.4	0.3	1.7	1.8
Commercial											
Floor Area[2]	T Me^2	60.6	142.9	87.8	103.6	227	530.1	64.5	30.7	21.7	37.7
Tender Value	M NC	3.5	10.6	5.7	7.6	24.7	16.2	7.1	4.4	3.0	5.7
Other[3]											
Floor Area[2]	T Me^2	68.1	54.1	84.7	113.2	111.7	124.8	29.2	63.6	73.3	67.9
Tender Value	M NC	4.3	2.9	4.9	7.3	3.1	2.2	1.6	7.3	4.6	4.5
II. New Buildings Completed											
All Buildings											
Number of Construction Works	N	975	1,034	1,091	950	818	1,008	750	877	851	~
Floor Area[2]	T Me^2	176.9	173.1	184.2	139.6	124	248.2	205.0	351.2	170.2	~
Value	M NC	9.5	10.4	11.3	8.9	8.3	18.7	16.0	31.7	21.4	~

1. Data on authorized and completed construction refer to private building activity in
   Guatemala City.
2. Area covered by the building.
3. Including educational and health buildings.

SOURCE: UN-YCS, 1973-80; 1974–83.

Table 1611

HAITI NEW BUILDING CONSTRUCTION AUTHORIZED AND NEW BUILDINGS COMPLETED,[1] 1973–83

Category	Unit	1973	1974	1975	1976	1977	1978	1979	1980	1981	1982	1983
I. New Building Construction Authorized												
Residential												
Number of Permits	N	369	325	320	304	445	462	428	364	310	250	117
II. New Buildings Completed												
All Buildings												
Number of Works	N	408	438	398	370	527	571	553	620	597	358	~

1. Data relating to construction authorized and completed cover the municipalities of
   Port-au-Prince and Petion-Ville.

SOURCE: UN-YCS, 1973-80; 1974-83.

Table 1612

HONDURAS NEW BUILDING CONSTRUCTION AUTHORIZED AND NEW BUILDINGS COMPLETED,[1] 1973–83

Category	Unit	1973	1975	1976	1977	1978	1979	1980	1981	1982	1983
I. New Building Construction Authorized[2]											
All Buildings											
Number	N	1,143	1,683	1,948	1,727	1,515	~	~	~	~	~
Floor Area	T Me^2	223	224.6	297.5	263.8	287.0	~	~	~	~	~
Tender Value	M NC	27.2	31.8	41.3	39.4	50.9	~	~	~	~	~
Residential[3]											
Number	N	985	1,452	1,741	1,513	~	~	~	~	~	~
Floor Area	T Me^2	131.6	123.3	199.2	174	~	~	~	~	~	~
Tender Value	M NC	18.3	17.6	28.6	30.2	32.6	~	~	~	~	~
Non-Residential											
Number	N	158	231	207	214	~	~	~	~	~	~
Floor Area	T Me^2	91.4	101.3	98.3	89.8	~	~	~	~	~	~
Tender Value	M NC	8.9	14.3	14.2	11.2	21.2	~	~	~	~	~
Industrial											
Number	N	25	16	28	7	~	~	~	~	~	~
Floor Area	T Me^2	27.3	14.6	27	7.9	~	~	~	~	~	~
Tender Value	M NC	2	1.5	1.9	.8	5.5	~	~	~	~	~
Commercial											
Number	N	114	202	156	161	~	~	~	~	~	~
Floor Area	T Me^2	57.6	82	62	66.6	~	~	~	~	~	~
Tender Value	M NC	6.2	12.3	11.1	9.1	13.8	~	~	~	~	~
Other[4]											
Number	N	19	13	23	46	~	~	~	~	~	~
Floor Area	T Me^2	6.5	4.7	9.3	15.3	~	~	~	~	~	~
Tender Value	M NC	.7	1.4	1.2	1.3	1.9	~	~	~	~	~
II. New Buildings Completed[2]											
All Buildings											
Number	N	1,219	1,683	1,948	1,727	1,515	1,593	2,271	2,858	5,122	1,643
Floor Are	T Me^2	243.1	224.6	297.6	263.8	287	354.9	304.6	233.6	313.6	189.5
Value	M NC	26.3	31.8	41.3	39.4	50.9	85.5	70.3	61.8	75.3	50.5
Residential[3]											
Number	N	1,061	1,443	1,739	1,513	1,314	1,381	2,090	2,214	4,795	1,549
Floor Area	T Me^2	136.5	129.7	186	178.9	169.6	222.8	220.2	175.0	254.1	145.7
Value	M NC	16.8	17.6	27	28.1	29.7	52.9	52.4	45.8	60.2	40.8
Non-Residential											
Number	N	158	240	209	208	201	212	181	117	106	94
Floor Area	T Me^2	106.6	94.9	111.6	84.9	117.4	132.1	84.4	58.6	59.5	43.8
Value	M NC	9.5	14.2	14.3	11.3	21.2	32.6	17.9	16.0	15.1	9.7
Industrial											
Number	N	25	16	31	7	23	29	15	13	9	8
Floor Area	T Me^2	35.3	13.1	29.9	7.5	43.6	37.6	20.3	9.6	11.4	12.3
Value	M NC	2.6	1.5	1.9	.8	5.5	8.6	3.3	1.9	1.8	2.1
Commercial											
Number	N	115	209	155	162	146	156	150	77	79	74
Floor Area	T Me^2	67.8	78.5	72.5	63.7	64.3	86.2	57.7	36.2	42.7	23.5
Value	M NC	6.5	12.2	11.2	9.2	13.8	22.2	13	10.7	11.9	5.0
Other[4]											
Number	N	18	15	23	39	32	27	16	27	18	12
Floor Area	T Me^2	3.5	3.3	9.2	13.7	9.5	8.3	6.4	12.8	5.4	8.0
Value	M NC	.4	.5	1.2	1.3	1.9	1.8	1.6	3.4	1.4	2.6

1. Data on construction authorized and completed refer to private construction in Tegucigalpa, San Pedro Sala, and La Ceiba.
2. 1981: 11 months ending Aug. 30. All other years: Fiscal year ending Sep. 30 of the year stated.
3. Dwellings or one-family houses.
4. Includes educational and health buildings.

SOURCE: UN-YCS, 1973-80; 1974–83.

Table 1613

NICARAGUA NEW BUILDING CONSTRUCTION AUTHORIZED, 1973–84

Category	Unit	1973	1974	1975	1976	1977	1978	1979	1980	1981	1982	1983	1984
					I. New Building Construction Authorized								
All Buildings													
Number	N	478	1,472	1,789	2,333	1,162	747	168	356	1,017	1,259	419	870
Floor Area	T Me²	79.6	322.5	270.2	251.6	217.8	90.2	17.1	19.6	54.7	62.5	47.1	62.8
Tender Value	M NC	32.2	221.6	236.5	213.9	204.3	81.5	13.8	12.5	42.9	60.6	77.9	157.7
Residential													
Number	N	404	1,314	1,694	2,236	1,068	708	153	339	987	1,234	366	892
Floor Area	T Me²	50	164.7	176.5	140.5	128.9	58.8	8.5	16.6	45.4	57.3	20.3	43.2
Tender Value	M NC	18.1	110.9	145.2	110.7	118.1	53.6	5.5	10.4	30.8	49.7	18.5	64.1
Non-Residential													
Number	N	74	158	95	97	94	39	15	17	30	25	53	28
Floor Area	T Me²	29.6	157.8	93.7	111.1	88.9	31.4	8.6	3	9.2	5.2	26.8	19.6
Tender Value	M NC	14.1	110.7	91.3	103.2	86.2	27.9	8.4	2.1	12.1	10.9	59.4	93.6
Industrial[1]													
Number	N	4	7	2	4	2	1	4	3	6	8	7	2
Floor Area	T Me²	.6	9.6	6.3	8.1	4.7	.1	2.7	.4	1.8	2.4	7.1	.3
Tender Value	M NC	.2	5.9	3.2	4	3.3	.1	1.5	.2	1.8	7.2	25.3	1.4
Commercial[1]													
Number	N	17	30	16	6	12	3	2	5	10	6	10	4
Floor Area	T Me²	7.1	52.6	13.4	11	13.2	3.5	1	.6	3	.9	3.1	1.9
Tender Value	M NC	2.4	38.7	15.1	12.3	17.3	3.4	1	.2	2.7	1.2	3.4	18.6
Educational[1]													
Number	N	11	10	10	8	6	2	2	#	1	3	5	#
Floor Area	T Me²	7.2	19.6	15.3	17.2	5.8	2	.5	#	.1	1.1	5.3	#
Tender Value	M NC	3.1	9.6	8.4	17	4.6	2.2	.3	#	.1	1.6	3.8	#
Other[1,2]													
Number	N	42	111	67	79	74	33	7	9	13	8	31	22
Floor Area	T Me²	14.7	76	58.7	74.8	65.2	25.8	3.4	2	4.3	.8	11.3	17.4
Tender Value	M NC	8.4	56.5	64.6	69.9	61	22.2	5.6	1.7	7.5	.9	26.9	73.6

1. Extensions to all non-residential buildings are included in other buildings.
2. Includes health buildings.

SOURCE: UN-YCS, 1973-80; 1974-84.

Table 1614

PANAMA NEW BUILDING CONSTRUCTION AUTHORIZED,[1,2] 1973–83

Category	Unit	1973	1975	1976	1977	1978	1979	1980	1981	1982	1983
All Buildings											
Number	N	1,621	506	618	872	871	1,184	952	878	1,094	841
Floor Area	T Me^2	807.7	175.8	172.1	131.9	205.5	411.3	400.9	369.5	574.4	323.1
Tender Value	M NC	77.5	20.2	20.2	16.7	27.5	57.9	68.3	73.5	112.4	65.0
Residential											
Number	N	1,530	449	571	835	824	1,121	886	807	964	762
Floor Area	T Me^2	593	94	101.2	99.1	131.6	203	208.2	259.6	304.4	175.2
Tender Value	M NC	60.5	9.9	12	13.3	18.4	29.2	39.4	52.7	67.3	37.9
One, Two-Dwelling[3]											
Number	N	1,281	414	519	810	809	1,068	815	734	879	667
Multi-Dwelling[3]											
Number	N	249	35	52	25	15	53	71	73	85	95
Non-Residential											
Number	N	91	57	47	37	47	63	66	71	85	79
Floor Area	T Me^2	214.7	81.8	70.9	32.8	73.9	208.3	192.7	136.9	270.0	147.9
Tender Value	M NC	17	10.3	8.2	3.4	9.1	28.7	28.9	20.7	45.1	27.1
Industrial											
Number	N	23	6	11	13	7	15	14	6	18	7
Floor Area	T Me^2	25.4	3.5	17.9	7.5	26.9	40.5	22	9.1	19.6	8.1
Tender Value	M NC	1.1	.4	1.6	1	3.5	3	3.3	1.0	2.0	.6
Commercial											
Number	N	55	45	27	20	38	40	37	53	93	63
Floor Area	T Me^2	158.6	56.9	42.1	23.2	45.5	161.6	136.6	90.3	226.3	128.5
Tender Value	M NC	14.1	5.8	4.2	2.1	5.3	24.8	22.9	14.3	40.4	24.2
Educational											
Number	N	~	1	1	1	#	2	3	5	2	~
Floor Area	T Me^2	~	.2	.1	.1	.1	1.4	6.1	10.2	2.2	~
Tender Value	M NC	~	.3	.1	.2	#	.2	.7	2.6	.3	~
Other[4]											
Number	N	13	5	8	3	2	6	12	7	15	9[a.]
Floor Area	T Me^2	30.7	21.2	10.8	2	1.4	4.8	28	27.3	16.6	11.3
Tender Value	M NC	1.8	3.8	2.3	.1	.3	.7	2	2.8	1.8	2.3

1. Data based on permits supplied by the Oficina de Seguridad and refer to new private
   construction in Panama City.
2. New construction excluding extensions.
3. Buildings with two dwellings are included with multi-dwelling buildings; prior to 1982
   data include health buildings.
4. Including health buildings.

a. Including health buildings; also 1983 data include educational buildings.

SOURCE: UN-YCS, 1973-80; 1974-83.

Table 1615

PARAGUAY NEW BUILDINGS COMPLETED,[1] 1978–82

Category	Unit	1978	1979	1980	1981	1982
All Buildings						
Number	N	~	~	1,629	1,900	1,565
Floor Area[2]	T Me^2	483	572	468	451	327
Value	M NC	10,586..0	8,171.8	8,812.1	9,297.0	6,693.1
Residential Buildings						
Number	N	~	~	736	638	451
Floor Area[2]	T Me^2	267	319	275	193	117
Value	M NC	8,627.5	4,785.9	5,800.7	4,770.9	2,751.2
One, Two Dwelling Buildings[3]	N	~	~	673	589	418
Multi-Dwelling Buildings[3]	N	~	~	63	49	33
Non-Residential Buildings						
Number	N	~	~	893	1,262	1,114
Floor Area[2]	T Me^2	261	253	3,011	4,526	3,942
Industrial						
Number	N	~	~	66	41	31
Floor Area[2]	T ME^2	1	2	38	17	17
Value	M NC	~	16.0	270.4	163.8	98.3
Commercial						
Number	N	~	~	205	189	123
Floor Area[2]	T Me^2	84	119	98	129	74
Value	M NC	1,303.4	1,784.0	1,594.3	2,183.1	1,517.7
Educational						
Number	N	~	~	3	4	5
Floor Area[2]	T Me^2	1	11	.5	2	3
Value	M NC	11.5	222.4	7.3	18.2	33.3
Health						
Number	N	~	~	3	2	4
Floor Area[2]	T Me^2	~	12	2	1	4
Value	M NC	~	143.2	43.8	32.1	212.9
Other[4]						
Number	N	~	~	616	1,026	951
Floor Area[2]	T Me^2	130	110	55	110	112.3
Value	M NC	643.6	1,220.3	1,095.6	2,128.9	2,079.7

1. Data are from the Dirección de Obras Particulares de la Municipalidad de la Capital and refer to private building activity in the municipality of Asuncion.
2. Area occupied by the buildings.
3. Two-dwelling buildings are included with multi-dwelling buildings.
4. Extensions and reconstruction of all types of buildings are included with other buildings.

SOURCE: UN-YCS, 1982.

Table 1616

URUGUAY NEW BUILDING CONSTRUCTION AUTHORIZED AND NEW BUILDINGS COMPLETED, 1973–83

Category	Unit	1973	1975	1976	1977	1978	1979	1980	1981	1982	1983
I. New Building Construction Authorized[1]											
All Buildings											
Number	N	514	515	429	1,120	~	~	~	~	~	~
Floor Area	T Me^2	120.6	303.8	333	482.9	649.1	913.2	1,237.2	862.8	574.5	202.4
Tender Value	M NC	144.7	182.5	229.4	569.4	517.9	~	~	~	~	~
Residential											
Floor Area[3]	T Me^2	84	194.9	229	353.3	471.2	667.7	911.9	626.2	427.1	126.8
Non-Residential											
Floor Area[4]	T Me^2	36.6	108.9	104	129.6	177.9	245.5	325.8	236.6	147.4	75.6
II. New Buildings Completed[1,2]											
All Buildings											
Floor Area	T Me^2	335.5	375.4	380.5	353.7	415.2	667.1	1,013.4	1267.8	990	478.9
Value	M NC	39	131.7	183.8	238.8	390.4	1,044.4	2,636.1	4,399.6	3,928	2,752.6
Residential											
Floor Area	T Me^2	280.6	318.5	303.8	257.3	310	437.6	678.7	914.4	720.5	345.5
Non-Residential											
Floor Area	T Me^2	54.9	56.9	76.7	96.4	105.2	229.5	334.7	353.4	278.5	133.4

1. Construction in Montevideo.
2. Private construction.
3. Residential area of all buildings.
4. Non-residential area of all buildings.

SOURCE: UN-YCS, 1973-80; 1974-83.

Table 1617

VENEZUELA NEW BUILDING CONSTRUCTION AUTHORIZED,[1] 1973–83

Category	Unit	1973	1975	1976	1977	1978	1979	1980	1981	1982	1983
All Buildings											
Number of Permits	N	5,229	5,512	6,653	5,778	5,428	4,495	5,661	4,687	3,678	2,807
Floor Area	T Me^2	5,194.1	6,403.4	8,053.8	8,572	8,652	8,609	7,254	5,929.6	6,473.0	3,677.1
Tender Value	M NC	1,778.7	2,990.1	4,714.7	5,959.7	8,315	8,180	9,541	8,275.6	9,594.4	5,350.1
Residential											
Number of Permits	N	4,549	4,726	5,829	4,854	4,683	3,752	4,690	3,893	2,875	2,172
Floor Area	T Me^2	3,548.1	4,462.4	5,697.3	5,913	6,694	6,897	5,015	4,556.2	5,083.1	2,574.5
Tender Value	M NC	1,337.8	2,122.3	3,449.9	4,336.7	6,482	6,492	6,605	6,665.5	8,072.1	4,076.0
One, Two-Dwelling											
Number of Permits	N	3,446	3,673	4,635	3,658	3,563	2,675	4,000	3,297	2.375	1,826
Multi-Dwelling[2]											
Number of Permits	N	1,103	1,053	1,194	1,196	1,120	1,077	690	596	500	346
Non-Residential											
Number of Permits	N	680	786	824	924	745	743	971	794	803	635
Floor Area	T Me^2	1,646	1,941	2,356.5	2,659	1,958	1,712	2,239	1,373.4	1,389.9	1,102.6
Tender Value	M NC	440.9	867.8	1,264.8	1,623	1,833	1,688	2,936	1,610.1	1,522.4	1,274.1
Industrial[3]											
Number of Permits	N	525	664	649	694	644	593	~	183	196	114
Floor Area	T Me^2	1,394.2	1,663.1	1,846.8	2,032	1,717	1,311	~	523.9	511.3	362.1
Tender Value	M NC	341.1	675.7	843.2	1,254	1,611	1,298	~	390.1	373.5	295.0
Commercial											
Number	N	~	~	~	~	~	~	~	542	558	470
Floor Area	T Me^2	~	~	~	~	~	~	~	726.6	781.5	633.1
Tender Value	M NC	~	~	~	~	~	~	~	1,040.1	1,041.3	833
Educational											
Number	N	~	~	~	~	~	~	~	20	19	13
Floor Area	T Me^2	~	~	~	~	~	~	~	32.0	25.9	28
Tender Value	M NC	~	~	~	~	~	~	~	40.1	31.9	35.6
Health											
Number	N	~	~	~	~	~	~	~	10	4	6
Floor Area	T Me^2	~	~	~	~	~	~	~	26.9	19.2	35.5
Tender Value	M NC	~	~	~	~	~	~	~	32.8	31.6	57.5
Other[4]											
Number	N	155	122	175	230	101	150	~	39	26	32
Floor Area	T Me^2	251.8	277.9	509.7	627	241	401	~	58.1	39.6	43.9
Tender Value	M NC	99.8	192.1	421.6	369	222	390	~	107.0	44.1	53.0

1. Data refer to private building construction.
2. Prior to 1980, two-dwelling buildings are included in multi-dwelling buildings.
3. Prior to 1980, includes commercial buildings.
4. Prior to 1980, includes educational and health buildings.

SOURCE: UN-YCS, 1973-80; 1974-83.

Table 1618

INDEX OF CONSTRUCTION ACTIVITY, 20 LC, 1975–82[a]

(1980 = 100)

	Country	1975	1976	1977	1978	1979	1980	1981	1982	1983
A.	ARGENTINA	72	93	104	99	98	100	86	69	64
B.	BOLIVIA	96	100	111	114	113	100	65	39	~
C.	BRAZIL	~	78	84	90	93	~	96	96	~
D.	CHILE	72	61	60	65	81	100	121	86	86
E.	COLOMBIA	98	83	90	87	87	100	108	115	~
F.	COSTA RICA	64	99	98	96	100	100	105	94	93
G.	CUBA	80	77	80	85	101	100	78	53	~
H.	DOMINICAN REP.	77	78	85	88	93	100	101	~	~
I.	ECUADOR	86	93	95	100	99	100	106	104	92
J.	EL SALVADOR	131	104	141	132	130	100	85	83	~
K.	GUATEMALA	45	78	88	90	96	100	118	105	~
L.	HAITI[b]	73	78	81	88	97	100	104	94	99
M.	HONDURAS	70	73	83	87	94	100	92	88	~
N.	MEXICO	71	74	70	79	89	100	112	106	~
O.	NICARAGUA	44	44	46	49	76	100	114	126	155
P.	PANAMA	77	80	59	82	82	100	103	124	86
Q.	PARAGUAY	30	35	46	61	79	100	117	110	103
R.	PERU	101	105	97	81	84	100	111	114	89
S.	URUGUAY	57	64	66	86	96	100	103	89	66
T.	VENEZUELA	79	96	120	133	120	100	98	90	78
	UNITED STATES	62	60	72	84	88	100	106	108	~

a. For previous years, see SALA, 21-901.
b. Year ending Sept. 30.

SOURCE: UN-YCS, 1974–82, pp. 234–236, 1983, p. 239.

Table 1619

POPULATION WITH WATER SUPPLY AND SEWERAGE SERVICES, 19 L

(As of December 31, 1980)

	Country	Total				Urban				Rural			
		Total	With Water (T)	(%)	With Sewerage (T)	(%)	Total	With Water (T)	(%)	With Sewerage (T)	(%)	Total	With Water (T)	(%)	With Sewerage (T)	(%)

	Country	Total	With Water (T)	(%)	With Sewerage (T)	(%)	Total	With Water (T)	(%)	With Sewerage (T)	(%)	Total	With Water (T)	(%)	With Sewerage (T)	(%)
A.	ARGENTINA	27,863	16,141	58	12,560	45	22,359	14,636	65	8,060	36	5,504	1,505	27	4,500[b]	82

Continued in SALA, 24-1617.

Table 1620

WATER SERVICES IN 26 CITIES, 13 L, 1975

	Drinking Water		Sewerage	Recipient Water Body			Flow Me³/sec.		Estimated Outflow of Sewage Me³/sec.
City	Coverage[1] (%)	Quantity[1] (L/I/D)[2]	Coverage[1] (%)	Name (R = Rio)	Type[3]		Annual minimum	Annual average	
A. ARGENTINA									
Buenos Aires	885-91	852[a]	52.4	R. de la Plata and Affluents	II		~	20,425	96
Cordova	65	460	~	R. Primero	I		2.52	9.44	4

Continued in SALA, 20-910.

Table 1621

HOUSING ACCESS TO WATER SUPPLY, 18 L

(%)

			Piped System					Self-Supply				
Country	Area	Year	Inside House	Within Lot but Outside House	Less than 100 Meters from House	More than 100 Meters from House	Subtotal[a]	Well	Rainwater	River	Other Means	Subtotal[a]
A. ARGENTINA	Total	1960	43.5	3.6	4.4	~	51.5	41.8	~	~	6.7	48.5
	Urban	1960	54.5	3.9	4.5	←——⊢	62.9	33.5	~	~	3.6	37.1
	Rural	1960	7.4	2.3	4.4	←——⊢	14.1	68.9	~	~	16.9	85.9

Continued in SALA, 24-1619.

Table 1622

HOUSING SANITARY FACILITIES, 18 LC

(%)

			Water Closet				
County	Area	Year	Sewerage	Septic Tank	Subtotal[a]	Latrine[a]	None or Unknown[a]
A. ARGENTINA	Total	1960	~	~	61.5	25.2	13.3
	Urban	1960	~	~	73.8	19.3	6.9
	Rural	1960	~	~	21.1	44.7	34.2

Continued in SALA, 24-1620.

Table 1623

ESTIMATED PROVISION OF WATER SUPPLY
AND EXCRETA DISPOSAL,[1] 20 LC

(Late 1970s, % of Population)

Country	Water Supply[2]		Sewerage[2]		Other Excreta[2] Disposal Devices[2]
	Urban	Rural	Urban	Rural	Rural
A. ARGENTINA[a]	70	14	33	~	66
B. BOLIVIA[b]	30	2	31	#	4
C. BRAZIL[c]	66	10	65	9	31
D. CHILE[b]	92	13	69	9	81
E. COLOMBIA[b]	80	29	76	7	81
F. COSTA RICA[d]	95	60	42	4	79
G. CUBA[d,e]	91	10	46	6	~
H. DOMINICAN REP.[d]	66	12	27	~	40
I. ECUADOR[b]	73	6	63	3	7
J. EL SALVADOR[d]	54	3	34	~	21
K. GUATEMALA[b]	58	6	40	~	17
L. HAITI[d]	17	#	#	#	5
M. HONDURAS[b]	75	13	43	1	10
N. MEXICO[d]	70	32	41	#	35
O. NICARAGUA[d]	65	9	38	#	18
P. PANAMA[b]	92	12	74	6	41
Q. PARAGUAY[b]	27	#	38	#	92
R. PERU[b]	55	3	42	1	1
S. URUGUAY[b]	75	24	54	21	55
T. VENEZUELA[b]	65	31	65	15	73

1. This table is based upon various sources including censuses and PAHO Surveys. The most significant source is indicated for each country and entry.
2. Water supply is taken to be a connection to a centralized piped system either in the house or lot. Sewerage is connection to a sewerage system or a septic tank. Other excreta disposal devices are mainly latrines.

a. Argentina, Secretaría de Estado de Transporte y Obras Públicas, Subsecretaría de Recursos Hídricos, Instituto Nacional de Ciencia y Técnica Hídricas, *La demanda de agua en la República Argentina* (Mendoza, 1976).
b. Most recent census of population or housing.
c. IBRD, Brazil, *Human Resources Special Report*.
d. Pan American Health Organization, *Health Conditions in the Americas*, 1977.
e. In the case of Cuba, the government has adopted a policy of concentration of the rural population and the provision of sewerage. In consequence, the use of other sanitary devices is not relevant to future policies and no estimate of the population currently so served has been made.

SOURCE: U.N., CEPAL, *Drinking Water Supply and Sanitation in Latin America 1981–1990* (Santaigo, 1983), p. 81.

Table 1624

ELECTRICALLY LIGHTED OCCUPIED HOUSING UNITS, 13 LC

Country	Year	Area	Number of Occupied Housing Units				
			Total	With Electric Lighting	Lacking Electric Lighting		
					Total	Kerosene	Other
B. BOLIVIA[1]	1976[†]	Total	989,055	326,287	662,768	~	~

Continued in SALA, 20-907.

Table 1625

POPULATION WITH ELECTRIC LIGHTING, 20 LR, 1960-73

(%)

Country	1960	1970	1973
A. ARGENTINA	69.0	76.0	78.5

Continued in SALA, 21-902.

Table 1626

HOUSING DEFICIT, 20 L, 1960-69

(N)

	Housing Unit Deficit			Housing Units Constructed by Public Sector			
Country	Ca. 1960	Ca. 1965	Ca. 1969	1960-69	Annual Average 1960-65	Annual Average 1960-69	% Increase in Average
A. ARGENTINA	1,500,000	2,000,000	2,630,000	240,323	21,187	28,300	33.6

Continued in SALA, 18-903.

Table 1627

OCCUPIED HOUSING UNITS BY NUMBER OF ROOMS, 15 LC

				Room					
Country	Year	Area	Total	1	2	3	4	5	6 and Over
B. BOLIVIA	1976[1,2]	Total	989,055[a]	441,388	115,458	41,066	12,425	4,414	2,132

Continued in SALA, 20-904.

Table 1628

TENANCY OF OCCUPIED HOUSING UNITS, 19 LC, 1970-76

			Total		Urban Areas		Rural Areas	
Country	Year	Code	N	%	N	%	N	%
A. ARGENTINA	1970	A[1]	6,056,100	100.0	~	~	~	~
		B	3,553,250	58.7	~	~	~	~
		C	1,380,950	22.8	~	~	~	~
		D	1,121,900	18.5	~	~	~	~

Continued in SALA, 20-905.

Table 1629

INHABITANTS BY SIZE OF HOUSEHOLD,[1] 20 LC

| Country | Year | Total | Size of Household | | | | |
			1 Person	2 Persons	3-4 Persons	5-8 Persons	9 and Over
A. ARGENTINA[2,‡]	1970	22,961,500	615,900	2,250,500	8,711,800	9,661,100	1,722,200

Continued in SALA, 20-903.

Table 1630

STATUS OF PERSONS RESIDING IN PRIVATE HOUSEHOLDS, 14 L

Country	Year of Census	Total	Heads of Household	Spouses	Children	Other Relatives	Guests	Servants	Other Persons
A. ARGENTINA	1960	19,227,447	4,418,791	3,252,791	7,820,735	2,325,279	772,271	239,576	398,776

Continued in SALA, 18-902.

Table 1631

MEXICO: GEOGRAPHIC DISTRIBUTION OF CONSTRUCTION ACCORDING TO THE INTERNAL CONSUMPTION OF CEMENT, 1970–79
(Each Year = 100.0%)

State	1970	1971	1972	1973	1974	1975	1976	1977	1978	1979
Aguascalientes	1.0	1.0	.8	.8	.9	.9	.9	.9	1.0	.9

Continued in SALA, 23-904.

Part VI: Industry, Mining, and Energy

CHAPTER 17

INDUSTRIAL PRODUCTION

Table 1700

INDUSTRIAL PRODUCTION INDEX, 18 LC, 1970–83

(1975 = 100)

Country	1970	1975	1976	1977	1978	1979	1980	1981	1982	1983
A. ARGENTINA										
General[†]	79	100	96	100	91	100	97	83	79	87
Mining	100	100	102	111	114	121	125	126	128	130
Manufacturing	78	100	96	100	89	98	94	79	76	83
Electricity, gas, and water	67	100	103	109	114	130	141	138	142	153
Construction	~	100	112	128	128	131	139	128	86	80

Continued in SALA, 24-1700.

Table 1701

AUTOMOBILE PRODUCTION, ALADI COUNTRIES,[1] 10 LR, 1977-82

(N)

Country	1977	1978	1979	1980	1981	1982[‡]
A. ARGENTINA	235,350	179,160	253,217	281,793	172,363	132,116

Continued in SALA, 24-1701.

Table 1702

BUTTER PRODUCTION, 20 LC, 1959–84

(T MET)

	Country	1959	1970	1975	1977	1978	1979	1980	1981	1982	1983	1984
A.	ARGENTINA	61	28	40	30	29	33	29	32	37	34	31[‡]
B.	BOLIVIA	~	#	#	#	1	#	1[†]	1[†]	~	~	~
C.	BRAZIL	29	45[†]	63[‡]	69[‡]	90[‡]	90[‡]	90[‡]	95[‡]	70[‡]	70[‡]	70[‡]
D.	CHILE[1]	7	8[‡]	7	5	4	4	4[‡]	5	3	4	3[‡]
E.	COLOMBIA	~	11[†]	11[†]	11[†]	12[†]	12[†]	12[†]	12[†]	13[†]	13[†]	13[†]
F.	COSTA RICA	~	3[†]	3[†]	3[†]	3[†]	3[†]	3[†]	3[†]	4[†]	4[†]	4[†]
G.	CUBA	~	#	8	6	11	11	10	9	10	10	11
H.	DOMINICAN REP.	~	#	1	1	1	1	1	1[†]	1[†]	1	1[†]
I.	ECUADOR	~	4[†]	5[†]	6[†]	6[†]	4[†]	4[†]	4[†]	4[†]	4[†]	4[†]
J.	EL SALVADOR	~	5[†]	5[†]	5[†]	5[†]	6[†]	6[†]	6[†]	6[†]	6[†]	6[†]
K.	GUATEMALA	~	4[†]	4[†]	4[†]	4[†]	4[†]	4[†]	5[†]	5[†]	5[†]	4[†]
L.	HAITI	~	~	~	~	~	~	~	~	~	~	~
M.	HONDURAS	~	4[†]	4[†]	4[†]	4[†]	4[†]	4[†]	4[†]	4[†]	4[†]	4[†]
N.	MEXICO	~	18[†]	23[†]	24[†]	25[†]	24[‡]	21[‡]	21[‡]	23[‡]	24[‡]	25[‡]
O.	NICARAGUA	~	3[†]	4[†]	4[†]	4[†]	4[†]	2[†]	2[†]	2[†]	2[†]	2[†]
P.	PANAMA	~	#[†]	#[†]	#[†]	#[†]	#[†]	#[†]	#[†]	~	~	~
Q.	PARAGUAY	~	~	~	~	~	~	~	~	~	~	~
R.	PERU	3	5	6	5[‡]	4[‡]	5[‡]	5[‡]	4[‡]	4[‡]	3[†]	3[†]
S.	URUGUAY	5	7	6[‡]	6[†]	6[†]	6	8[‡]	8[‡]	8[‡]	12	12[†]
T.	VENEZUELA	4	5	6	7	7	10[‡]	10[‡]	10[‡]	10[‡]	8[‡]	10[‡]
	UNITED STATES	640	518	446	493	451	447	519	557	570	589	508

1. Twelve months beginning in April of year stated.

SOURCE: SALA, 22-1904; UN-SY, 1982, table 116; UN-SY, 1983–84, table 110.

Table 1703

CEMENT PRODUCTION,[1] 20 LC, 1953–83

(T MET)

PART I. UN-SY SERIES

	Country	1953	1970	1976	1977	1978	1979	1980	1981	1982	1983
A.	ARGENTINA	1,655	4,770	5,707	6,030	6,322	6,698	7,289	6,913	5,818	5,882
B.	BOLIVIA	34	116	220	267	257	253	318	388	325[‡]	327[‡]
C.	BRAZIL	1,655	9,002	18,675	20,545	22,348	23,683	25,880	24,886	25,440	20,586
C.	CHILE	762	1,349	968	1,140	1,203	1,357	1,583	1,863	1,131	1,255
E.	COLOMBIA	875	1,757	3,612	3,298	4,153	4,257	4,356	4,610	4,572	4,740
F.	COSTA RICA	~	187	362	406	490	528	554	460	424	386
G.	CUBA	405	742	2,501	2,656	2,712	2,613	2,831	3,292	3,163	3,231
H.	DOMINICAN REP.	130	493	654	862	839	862	928	960	959	1,047
I.	ECUADOR	91	458	608	623	834	1,099	1,389	1,451	1,400	1,420
J.	EL SALVADOR	30	167	322	334	520	571	519	459	276	320
K.	GUATEMALA	67[a]	231	445	491	515	574	569	568[‡]	613	491
L.	HAITI	26[b]	65	246	268	247	195	243	241[‡]	213	216
M.	HONDURAS	~	161	234	184	206	205	232	184	165	300
N.	MEXICO	1,754	7,267	12,691	13,328	14,150	15,352	16,398	18,173	19,343	17,363
O.	NICARAGUA	24	98	226	226	199	86	154[‡]	100[‡]	100[‡]	298
P.	PANAMA	80	181	282	271	300	510	565	520	350	350
Q.	PARAGUAY	3	63	155	200	166	155	177	156	111	155
R.	PERU	449	1,144	1,966	1,968	2,047	2,428	2,758	3,080[‡]	2,477	1,972[‡]
S.	URUGUAY	297	497	676	682	674	680	684	604	550	401
T.	VENEZUELA	982	2,318	3,538	3,136	3,426	3,973	4,842	4,900	5,594	4,147
	UNITED STATES	45,001	67,682	67,581	72,629	77,546	76,648	68,241	65,054	57,475	63,883

1. The figures cover, as far as possible, all hydraulic cements used for construction
   (portland, metallurgic, aluminous, natural, etc.).

a. Refers to volume of sales only.
b. 1954.

SOURCE: UN-SY, 1967, table 125; UN-SY, 1978, table 124; UN-SY, 1979/80, table 112;
UN-SY, 1981, table 152; UN-SY, 1982, table 140; UN-SY, 1983–84, table 134.

Table 1704

CHEESE PRODUCTION, 20 LC, 1959–84

(T MET)

	Country	1959	1970	1975	1978	1979	1980	1981	1982	1983	1984
A.	ARGENTINA	116	167	226	245	248	248	229	232	248	210[‡]
B.	BOLIVIA[1]	~	6[†]	7[†]	7[†]	7[†]	7[†]	7[†]	7[†]	8[†]	8[†]
C.	BRAZIL[2,3]	31	50[†]	53[†]	56[†]	58[†]	58[†]	58[†]	59[†]	59[†]	59[†]
D.	CHILE[1]	~	23	14	19	17	18	19	22	19	18
E.	COLOMBIA[1]	~	39[†]	38[†]	43[†]	44[†]	44[†]	45[†]	47[†]	47[†]	48[†]
F.	COSTA RICA[1]	~	4	5[†]	5[†]	6[†]	6	5	6[†]	6[†]	6[†]
G.	CUBA[1]	~	1	7	9	10	11	12	10	11	14
H.	DOMINICAN REP.[1]	1	1	1	2	2	2	2	3	3	3[†]
I.	ECUADOR[1,2]	~	10[†]	13[†]	15[†]	13[†]	12[†]	12[†]	13[†]	13[†]	13[†]
J.	EL SALVADOR[1]	~	15[†]	16[†]	17[†]	18[†]	18[†]	18[†]	18[†]	18[†]	18[†]
K.	GUATEMALA[1]	~	12[†]	13[†]	14[†]	14[†]	14[†]	15[†]	15[†]	15[†]	15[†]
L.	HAITI[3]	~	1[†]	2[†]	2[†]	2[†]	2[†]	2[†]	2[†]	2[†]	2[†]
M.	HONDURAS[1]	~	7[†]	8[†]	8[†]	8[†]	8[†]	8[†]	8[†]	8[†]	8[†]
N.	MEXICO[1,3]	~	78[†]	89	96	96[†]	97[†]	99[†]	101[†]	100[†]	100[†]
O.	NICARAGUA[1]	~	14[†]	16[†]	16[†]	15[†]	7[†]	8[†]	8[†]	8[†]	8[†]
P.	PANAMA	~	1	#	#[†]	#[†]	#[†]	#[†]	~	~	~
Q.	PARAGUAY	~	~	~	~	~	~	~	~	~	~
R.	PERU[1,3]	9	35	37	39	34	34	33	33	25	29
S.	URUGUAY[1]	7	9	8[†]	8[†]	11[‡]	12	12	15	10[‡]	10[†]
T.	VENEZUELA[1]	15	27	39	29	28[‡]	28[‡]	28[‡]	28[‡]	29[‡]	29[‡]
	UNITED STATES[1]	~	1,330	1,593	1,909	1,989	2,109	2,234	2,345	2,471	2,402

1. Cheese from whole and partly skimmed milk of cows or buffalo.
2. Cheese from sheep milk.
3. Cheese from goat milk.

SOURCE: SALA, 22-1904; UN-SY, 1981, table 126; UN-SY, 1982, table 117; UN-SY, 1983–84, table 111.

Table 1705

CIGARETTE PRODUCTION, 20 LC, 1953–83

(M)[1]

	Country	1953	1963	1970	1975	1979	1980	1981	1982	1983
A.	ARGENTINA	21,675	24,619	30,220	38,621	33,368	34,680	29,085	26,930	28,241
B.	BOLIVIA	443	496	730	1,500	1,260	1,265	1,155	624	1,200[‡]
C.	BRAZIL[3]	41,599	59,964	70,703	101,741	137,000	142,300[‡]	135,000	133,200[‡]	129,200[‡]
D.	CHILE	5,382	6,315	6,590	8,149	9,988	10,510	9,201	7,609	7,680
E.	COLOMBIA	12,089	17,753	19,080	16,972	20,600	21,200	19,800	20,440	21,700[‡]
F.	COSTA RICA	~	1,265	1,420	2,154	2,403	2,252	2,320	1,976	2,200
G.	CUBA	7,743	15,346	19,806	15,366	17,377	15,109	15,409	17,044	16,802
H.	DOMINICAN REP.	896	1,722	2,125	3,023	3,364	3,375	3,493	3,612	3,604
I.	ECUADOR	743	729	1,295	2,085	4,090	3,858	4,227	5,149	5,000
J.	EL SALVADOR	799	1,076	1,441	1,779	2,481	2,570	2,328	2,291	2,500[‡]
K.	GUATEMALA	1,550	1,997	2,986	2,360	3,615	2,699	2,162	2,273	2,156
L.	HAITI	259	336	421	674	988	1,094	1,061	921	909
M.	HONDURAS	801	1,214	1,266	1,804	2,311	2,475	2,160	2,281[‡]	2,300[‡]
N.	MEXICO	26,434	33,659	40,633	46,763	52,791	54,520	54,660	54,979	46,798
O.	NICARAGUA	654	891	1,260	1,588	1,904	2,228	2,117	2,200	1,919
P.	PANAMA	~	742	1,011	1,045	1,057	1,083	1,050	1,001	981
Q.	PARAGUAY	660	528	458	834	808	648	752	758	931
R.	PERU	2,280	1,938	2,904	3,722	3,650	4,034	3,965	3,812	3,181
S.	URUGUAY		2,455	3,121	3,349[‡]	3,863[‡]	3,914	4,242[‡]	3,700[‡]	3,750[‡]
T.	VENEZUELA	2,725	8,256	10,463	16,486	22,000	21,300	19,800	20,000	20,200[‡]
	UNITED STATES[2]	423,070	543,687	562,153	626,760	706,974	697,000	740,000	732,082	710,565

1. Where production of cigarettes was reported by weight, a conversion rate of one million
   cigarettes per metric ton has been used.
2. Twelve months ending June 30 of year stated.
3. Production by main establishments only.

SOURCE: UN-SY, 1968, table 95; UN-SY, 1978, table 92; UN-SY, 1979/80, table 86;
   UN-SY, 1981, table 132; UN-SY, 1982, table 123; UN-SY, 1983–84, table 117.

Table 1706

COPPER (REFINED) PRODUCTION, 4 LC, 1970–83

(T MET)

	Country	1970	1975	1980	1981	1982	1983
C.	BRAZIL	18.6[a]	74.8	63.0	45.0	61.8	103.0
D.	CHILE	461.3	535.2	810.7	775.5	729.1	692.7
N.	MEXICO	53.9	73.6	85.6	61.3	61.3	80.9
R.	PERU	36.2	53.8	230.6	209.1	224.9	190.6
	UNITED STATES	2,065.7	1,621.9	1,725.9	2,037.6	1,694.6	1,583.7

a. Primary metal only.

SOURCE: UN-SY, 1977, table 129; UN-SY, 1982, table 143; UN-SY, 1983–84, table 137.

Table 1707

COTTON (WOVEN) FABRIC PRODUCTION,[1] 16 LC, 1953-83
(Measure Varies)[3,4,7]

	Country	Code[2]	1953	1963	1970	1975	1978	1979	1980	1981	1982	1983
A.	ARGENTINA[3]	A + B	72	63	76	70	~	~	~	~	5‡	8‡
B.	BOLIVIA[7]	A	6	10	12	10	12	12	13	7		
C.	BRAZIL[4]	A + B	~	231	784ᵃ	864ᵃ	~	~	~	~	~	~
D.	CHILE[4,5]	A + B	81	89	100	53	69	67	53	36	27	28
E.	COLOMBIA[4,6]	A	181	299	~	~	~	~	~	~	~	- -
G.	CUBA[7]	A	~	91	76	138	154	149	157	149	138	156
H.	DOMINICAN REP.[4,8]	A + B	2	8	7	8	12	17	15	8	8	10
I.	ECUADOR[4,9]	A + B	17	31	29	28	35	~	9	4	2	~
J.	EL SALVADOR[4,6]	A	13	36	37	23	22	18	16	15	~	~
L.	HAITI[4]	A	2	3	3	1	1	1	1	1	1	1
M.	HONDURAS[4,6]	A	1	2	11	15	14	8	8	~	~	~
N.	MEXICO[3]	A + B	36	99	119	123	67	68	67	71	66	66
O.	NICARAGUA[4]	A	4	11	16	~	~	4.8	7.4	8.8	14	16
Q.	PARAGUAY[4]	A	2	15	20	16	21	20	17	16	9	6
R.	PERU[4]	A	~	85	~	126	~	~	~	~	~	- -
T.	VENEZUELA[4,6]	A + B	18	59	80	~	~	~	~	~	~	- -
	UNITED STATES[4]	A + B	9,330	8,009	5,711	3,744	3,664	3,527	4,355	2,864	2,668	2,940‡

1. The data refer, in general, to the total production of woven cotton fabrics (including mixed fabrics where indicated) before undergoing finishing processes such as bleaching, dyeing, printing, mercerizing, glazing, etc.
2. Code: A = pure; B = mixed.
3. Thousand metric tons.
4. Million meters.
5. Incomplete coverage.
6. Including finished fabrics.

7. Million square meters.
8. Including a small amount of rayon fabrics.
9. After undergoing finishing processes.

a. Incomplete coverage.

SOURCE: UN-SY, 1968, table 99; UN-SY, 1978, table 94; UN-SY, 1979/80, table 88; UN-SY, 1981, table 133; UN-SY, 1982, table 124; UN-SY, 1983–84, table 118.

Table 1708

COTTON (YARN) FABRIC PRODUCTION,[1] 13 LC, 1953-83
(T MET)

	Country	Code[4]	1953	1963	1970	1978	1979	1980	1981	1982	1983
A.	ARGENTINA	A	76.2	72.8	89.6	83.6	92.4	74.9	61.3	68.4	8.3
B.	BOLIVIA	A	.2	.3	1.2	1	1	.8	.7	4.5‡	~
C.	BRAZIL[2]	A + B	71.1	110.9	118.0	~	~	~	~	~	~
D.	CHILE[3]	A	3.9	23.4	26.8	~	3.8	4.8	4.0	4.6	3.6
E.	COLOMBIA	A + B	.6	5.4	1.3	47.8	55.5	~	14.1	15.0‡	~
G.	CUBA	A	~	14.2	11.8	24.3	21.7	25	26.2	23.9	26.4
H.	DOMINICAN REP.	B	.2	~	#	1.1	.8	.8	.4	.5	.5
I.	ECUADOR	A + B	.3	.9	1.7	~	~	2.2	.8	1.5	~
J.	EL SALVADOR	A	.7	3.1	3.7	6.1	3.6	3.9	2.9	3	~
N.	MEXICO	A	~	103.7	132.0	~	~	~	~	~	~
Q.	PARAGUAY	A	12.0	12.9	11.6	90.7	73.3	74.9	105.9	90.8	77.2
R.	PERU	A + B	~	17.5	~	~	~	~	~	~	~
T.	VENEZUELA	A + B	4.2	13.6	13.0	~	~	~	~	~	~
	UNITED STATES	A + B	1,695.0	1,761.4	1,525	1,096	1,112‡	1,114	989.9	932.0	1,063.8

1. The data refer to the total weight of pure cotton yarn spun (including mixed yarns where indicated), whether for sale, on commission, or for further processing. Yarn spun from cotton waste is included. Unless otherwise stated, tire cord yarn is excluded.
2. Production in Sao Paulo only.
3. Estimated on the basis of mill consumption data supplied by the international Cotton Advisory Committee, allowing an average waste rate of about 8%.
4. Code: A = pure; B = mixed.

SOURCE: UN-SY, 1968, table 98; UN-SY, 1978, table 93; UN-SY, 1979/80, table 87; UN-SY, 1981, table 134; UN-SY, 1982, table 125; UN-SY, 1983–84, table 119.

Table 1709

FERTILIZER (NITROGENOUS) PRODUCTION, 19 LC, 1948–84[a]

(T MET)

Country	1948/49–1952/53	1952/53–1956/57	1965/66	1969/70	1978/79	1979/80	1980/81	1981/82	1982/83	1983/84
A. ARGENTINA	2.3[b]	1.1	4.0[‡]	20.4	27.9	25.4	30.4	25.1	29.0[‡]	32.2[‡]
B. BOLIVIA	#	#	#	#	~	~	~	~	~	~
C. BRAZIL[1]	.5	1.4	14.4	6.5	273.1	288.0	384.5[‡]	349.4[‡]	396.8	533.0[‡]
D. CHILE[1]	237.3	215.0	183.0[‡]	120.3[‡]	89.2	93.9	100.7	108.5	92.1	98.1[‡]
E. COLOMBIA[1]	~	~	39.0[‡]	49.5[‡]	59.4	56.7	41.9[‡]	42.2[‡]	48.3[‡]	56.4[‡]
F. COSTA RICA	~	~	10.0[‡]	12.4	33.1[‡]	36.0[‡]	40[‡]	42[‡]	46.0[‡]	36.0[‡]
G. CUBA[1]	~	~	~	~	34.3[‡]	131.5	111.9	142.2	96.0	73.6
H. DOMINICAN REP.	#	#	#	#	#	~	~	~	~	~
I. ECUADOR	~	~	~	2.8	1.6[‡]	2.5	2.4[‡]	2.5[‡]	3.0[‡]	2.6[‡]
J. EL SALVADOR	~	~	4.0[‡]	8.0[‡]	24.4	15.0[‡]	~	~	~	~
K. GUATEMALA	~	~	~	~	6.6	2.0[‡]	11.4[‡]	8.9[‡]	12.4[‡]	8.0[‡]
L. HAITI	#	#	#	#	#	#	~	~	~	~
M. HONDURAS	#	#	#	#	#	#	~	~	~	~
N. MEXICO	8.8	13.7	155.0[‡]	362.3	593.4	642.0	739.5	877.2	1,067.2	1,044.5
O. NICARAGUA	#	#	#	#	#	#	~	~	~	~
P. PANAMA	#	#	#	#	#	#	~	~	~	~
Q. PARAGUAY	#	#	#	#	#	#	~	~	~	~
R. PERU[1]	33.3[d]	39.5[d]	43.4[d]	32.9[c]	70.7	66.9	73.8	86.1	73.5	33.0[‡]
T. VENEZUELA	~	~	24.2[‡]	14.0	61.7	102.6	144.7[‡]	165.3[‡]	208.3[‡]	206.9[‡]
UNITED STATES[2,3]	~	~	~	7,562.0	10,076.0	11,180.0	11,825	10,513	9,000.0	9,277.0

1. Calendar year referring to the first part of the split year.
2. Excluding sodium nitrate.
3. Including data for Puerto Rico.

a. Cf. SALA, 22-1521.
b. 1952/53.
c. Production of guano only.
d. Includes guano.

SOURCE: SALA, 16-224; UN-SY, 1974, table 117 UN-SY, 1978, table 117; UN-SY, 1979/80, table 105; UN-SY, 1981, table 148; UN-SY, 1982, table 136; UN-SY, 1983–84, table 130.

Table 1710

IRON (PIG AND FERROALLOY) PRODUCTION, 7 LC, 1970–83

(T MET)

Country	1970	1975	1979	1980	1981	1982	1983
A. ARGENTINA[1]	847	1,094	1,195	1,095	964	1,074	957
C. BRAZIL	4,339	7,393	12,203	14,774	12,859	12,916	13,356
D. CHILE[1]	481	432	668	707	620	509	547
E. COLOMBIA	229	293	240	279	263	246	242
N. MEXICO	2,353	3,082	5,026	5,330	5,555	5,223	5,161
R. PERU[1]	86	1,216	257	851	225	162	113
T. VENEZUELA[1]	510	572	1,332	2,450	2,288	2,440	2,298
UNITED STATES	85,303	74,253	80,630	63,748	68,121	40,033	44,898

1. Excluding ferro-alloys.

SOURCE: UN-SY, 1977, table 125; UN-SY, 1978, table 125; UN-SY, 1979/80, table 113; UN-SY, 1981, table 153; UN-SY, 1982, table 141; UN-SY, 1983–84, table 135.

Table 1711

MEAT PRODUCTION,[1] 19 LC, 1961–84

(T MET)

	Country	1961-65	1970	1975	1976	1979	1980	1981	1982	1983	1984[‡]
A.	ARGENTINA	2,569	3,021	2,825	3,204	3,486	3,220	3,353	2,977	2,764	2,919
B.	BOLIVIA	70	90	113	121	139	145	147	150	153	155
C.	BRAZIL	2,026	2,669	2,981	3,025	3,066	3,115	3,147	3,418	3,362	3,205
D.	CHILE	202	249	273	277	232	232	261	272	285	275
E.	COLOMBIA	447	495	577	558	703	698	747	709	742	754
F.	COSTA RICA	36	52	74	72	93	86	90	77	65	70
G.	CUBA	190	237	171	195	207	206	222	225	225	235
H.	DOMINICAN REP.	33	43	57	63	69	61	47	55	59	63
I.	ECUADOR	81	99	115	112	154	164	158	161	161	181
K.	GUATEMALA	55	72	75	81	96	99	115	95	83	85
L.	HAITI	33	47	56	47	58	51	47	43	45	46
M.	HONDURAS	27	40	48	57	74	65	64	80	77	76
N.	MEXICO	705	708	923	944	1,015	1,145	1,151	1,172	1,269	1,318
O.	NICARAGUA	40	76	82	92	98	66	56	74	75	74
P.	PANAMA	29	39	50	53	44	48	57	60	60	59
Q.	PARAGUAY	139	172	156	162	190	198	202	187	180	178
R.	PERU	175	190	188	189	189	185	194	199	216	203
S.	URUGUAY	381	488	407	459	318	384	471	449	490	414
T.	VENEZUELA	182	253	357	369	432	435	434	430	436	446
	UNITED STATES	13,826	16,448	16,675	17,966	17,066	17,680	17,707	17,045	17,812	17,818

1. Beef, veal, pork, mutton, and lamb.

SOURCE: UN-SY, 1976, table 80; UN-SY, 1978, table 80; UN-SY, 1979/80, table 75; UN-SY, 1981, table 124; UN-SY, 1982, table 115; UN-SY, 1983–84, table 109.

Table 1712

METAL (SHEET) PRODUCTION, ALADI COUNTRIES, 9 LR, 1977–85

(T MET)

	Country	1977	1980	1982	1983	1984	1985
A.	ARGENTINA	2,282	2,127	2,345	2,492	2,365	1,054
C.	BRAZIL	8,815	12,850	11,462	12,457	14,705	7,835
D.	CHILE	383	571	390	~	~	~
E.	COLOMBIA	295	320	314	377	408	250
I.	ECUADOR	74	116	127	~	~	~
N.	MEXICO	4,151	5,876	5,568	5,364	5,950	3,446
R.	PERU	312	285	218	~	~	~
S.	URUGUAY	15	34	40	~	~	~
T.	VENEZUELA	1,140	1,698	2,061	2,030	2,236	1,452
	ANDEAN GROUP	~	2,418	2,718	2,709	2,994	1,928
	LATIN AMERICA	17,467	23,877	22,525	25,429	28,658	15,965

SOURCE: Mexico-NAFINSA-MV, May 9, 1983; Mexico-NAFINSA-MV, Jan. 13, 1986.

Table 1713

SHIPS (MERCHANT VESSELS) UNDER
CONSTRUCTION IN ARGENTINA,
1975-83

(T Gross Tons Registered)

Year	Amount
1975	97
1976	136
1977	117
1978	170
1979	143
1980	127
1981	155
1982	78
1983	82

SOURCE: UN-MB, Jan. 1983, special table A, p. xv; Oct. 1984, special table A, p. xiv.

Table 1714

STEEL (CRUDE) PRODUCTION, 10 LR, 1950-85[a]

(T MET)

PART I. MV SERIES

	Country	1950	1965	1980	1981	1982	1983	1984	1985
A.	ARGENTINA	100	1,300	2,702	2,517	2,913	2,925	2,614	1,563
C.	BRAZIL	800	3,000	15,203	13,106	12,924	14,609	18,390	11,475
D.	CHILE	100	500	695	625	484	~	~	~
E.	COLOMBIA	#	200	402	395	408	464	499	277
I.	ECUADOR	~	~	15	26	27	~	~	~
N.	MEXICO	400	2,500	6,982	7,673	7,048	6,962	7,542	4,189
R.	PERU	~	~	470	357	275	~	~	~
S.	URUGUAY	~	~	16	13	19	~	~	~
T.	VENEZUELA	#	600	1,975	2,030	2,216	2,410	2,721	1,786
	ANDEAN GROUP	~	~	2,862	2,807	2,926	3,153	3,567	2,293
	LATIN AMERICA[1]	1,400	8,100	28,443	26,675	26,665	30,523	35,333	21,583

1. Total from above.

a. Steel and hot sheet metal production.

SOURCE: Mexico-NAFINSA-MV, May 9, 1983; for 1950 and 1965 data, Jan. 7, 1985; NAFINSA-MV, Jan. 13, 1986.

PART II. UN-SY SERIES

	Country	1969	1970	1975	1976	1979	1980	1981	1982	1983
A.	ARGENTINA	1,720	1,859	2,043	2,244	3,090	2,556	2,389	2,752	2,828
C.	BRAZIL	4,925	5,390	7,829	9,169	10,039	10,232	8,410	7,660	8,166
D.	CHILE	601	547	458	448	642	695	625	429	618
E.	COLOMBIA	206	239	266	252	234	263	262	215	272
G.	CUBA	119	140	298	261	328	304	330	301	364
N.	MEXICO	3,470	3,846	5,196	5,243	7,023	7,003	7,448	6,926	6,747
R.	PERU	194	94	432	349	426	447	364	274	289
T.	VENEZUELA	840	927	919	752	1,480	1,784	1,817	2,296	2,246
	UNITED STATES	128,152	119,309	105,817	116,121	123,695	101,456	109,614	67,656	76,762

SOURCE: UN-SY, 1979/80, table 114; UN-SY, 1981, table 153; UN-SY, 1982, table 141; UN-SY, 1983-84, table 135.

Table 1715

SUGAR (RAW) PRODUCTION, 20 LC, 1850–1984

1950-81
(M MET)

Year	World[1]	Cuba	
		Plan	Actual
1950	29.2		5.6
1951	33.6		5.8
1952	36.1		7.3
1953	35.0		5.2
1954	38.8		5.0
1955	38.4		4.6
1956	39.7		4.8
1957	41.6		5.7
1958	44.4		5.9
1959	49.6		6.0
1960	52.1		5.9
1961	54.7		6.9
1962	51.6		4.9
1963	52.6		3.9
1964	60.1		4.5
1965	65.1	6.0[b]	6.2
1966	64.2	6.5	4.5
1967	66.7	7.5	6.2
1968	66.9	8.0	5.2
1969	70.0	9.0	4.5
1970	71.1	10.0	7.6
1971	74.0	7.0	5.9
1972	75.7	- -	4.3
1973	75.8	5.5	5.3
1974	76.4	- -	5.9
1975	78.8	- -	6.3
1976	82.4	- -	6.2
1977	90.4	- -	6.5
1978	90.6	7.3	7.4
1979	89.2	- -	8.0
1980	84.6	- -	6.7
1981	92.6	- -	7.4
1982[‡]	100.7	- -	8.0
1983	96.9	- -	7.4
1984	99.2	- -	7.8

1. Cane and beet.

a. Excludes India and some Far Eastern production prior to 1900.

b. No plan prior to 1965.

SOURCE: 1850-1949, adapted from Hugh Thomas, *Cuba: The Pursuit of Freedom* (New York: Harper and Row, 1971), pp. 1561-1564; and from Noel Deere, *The History of Sugar*, 2 vols. (London: Chapman and Hall, 1949), I. p. 133 and II, pp. 490-491.

1950-69, compiled from *Los Angeles Times, New York Times, Wall Street Journal*, USDA, FAO, and ECLA sources. World data are from Deere, *History of Sugar*.

1970-82, UN-SY, 1981, table 128, and Cuba, CEE, *Anuario Estadístico*, 1983, p. 109; UN-SY, 1982, table 119; UN-SY, 1983–84, table 113.

Table 1715 (Continued)

SUGAR (RAW) PRODUCTION, 20 LC, 1950–1984

PART II. 19 LC[1]

	Country	1953	1970	1975	1978	1979	1980	1981	1982	1983	1984
A.	ARGENTINA	740	976	1,353	1,397	1,411	1,716	1,624	1,623	1,624	1,545
B.	BOLIVIA	3	131	213	285	288	262	260	228	197	201[‡]
C.	BRAZIL[2]	2,002	5,019[a]	6,299	7,913	7,362	8,270	8,726	8,941	9,555	9,259
D.	CHILE	~	228	219	129	97	60	235	132	229	360
E.	COLOMBIA	190	676	970	1,014	1,107	1,247	1,212	1,318	1,340	1,177
F.	COSTA RICA	31	150	205	227	204	220	190	206	245[‡]
H.	DOMINICAN REP.	552	1,014[‡]	1,170	1,199	1,200	1,013	1,108	1,285	1,209	1,133
I.	ECUADOR[3]	61	235[‡]	292	347	355	368	330	246	164	329
J.	EL SALVADOR	30	117	244	279	274	217	182	199	259	242
K.	GUATEMALA	37	185	384	446	415	452	474	580	614	555
L.	HAITI	55	66	69	57	60	65	50	55	43	41
M.	HONDURAS	8	53[‡]	75[‡]	131	164	191	196	217	221	207
N.	MEXICO	868	2,402	2,636	3,131	3,095	2,719	2,642	2,739	3,076	3,308
O.	NICARAGUA	33	141	210[‡]	222	202	190	214	247	249	267
P.	PANAMA	17	76	135[‡]	187	226	200	186	239	215[‡]	176
Q.	PARAGUAY	14	52	59	69	76	89	77	85	92	92[‡]
R.	PERU	602	771	964[a]	881	715	553	492	623	452	645[‡]
S.	URUGUAY	21	53	95[‡]	91	84	102	97	103	104	100[‡]
T.	VENEZUELA	78	455	508	403	347	358	303	382	377	390[‡]
	UNITED STATES	3,148	5,327	5,680	5,133[b]	5,435[b]	5,313[b]	5,789[b]	5,418[b]	5,215[b]	5,342[b]

1. Covers the production of centrifugal sugar from both beet and cane, and the figures are expressed, as far as possible, in terms of raw sugar. Where exact information about polarization or grades is lacking, qualities are expressed in terms of sugar "Tel quel".

2. "Tel quel" sugar indicates lack of exact information about polarization of grades.

3. Crop year, except 1967.

a. "Tel quel" (see note 2).

b. Includes data for Puerto Rico.

SOURCE: UN-SY, 1968, table 89; UN-SY, 1978, table 86; UN-SY, 1979/80, table 81; UN-SY, 1981, table 128; UN-SY, 1982, table 119; UN-SY, 1983–84, table 113.

Table 1716

WHEAT FLOUR PRODUCTION,[1] 19 LC, 1953–83

(T MET)

	Country	1953	1963	1967	1970	1975	1979	1980	1981	1982	1983
A.	ARGENTINA	2,013	2,163	2,161	2,347	2,483	2,482	2,438	2,456	2,550	2,678
B.	BOLIVIA	~	10	20	39	60	~	225	207	180[‡]	200[‡]
C.	BRAZIL	1,475	1,607	1,865	2,393	2,053[a]	4,698	5,154	4,666	4,647	4,540
D.	CHILE	585	653	762	808	479	~	874	914	894	913
E.	COLOMBIA	56	170	180	231	215	300	329	353	350[‡]	376
G.	CUBA	~	133	131	160	176	170	271	354	386	428
H.	DOMINICAN REP.	~	44	53	55	85	107	115	108	117	127
I.	ECUADOR[3,4]	31	64	68	91	156	~	164	191	181	~
J.	EL SALVADOR	~	27	41	43	56	~	82	80	50	84[‡]
K.	GUATEMALA	15	58	71	72	86	~	~	110	95	97
L.	HAITI	~	44	42	28	67	75	117	114	104	139[‡]
M.	HONDURAS	5	15	23	33	35	43	40	65	60[‡]	75[‡]
N.	MEXICO	368	1,040	1,142	1,331	1,580	1,951	2,147	2,422	2,484	2,544
O.	NICARAGUA	~	~	24	29	~	33	40	45	55	47
P.	PANAMA[5]	~	~	~	32	38	43	45	45	46	~
Q.	PARAGUAY	34	85	60	70	38	82	82	101	97	100
R.	PERU[2]	265	364	417	500	587	~	733	760	766	761
S.	URUGUAY	~	239	249	251	~	~	240	118	242[‡]	260[‡]
T.	VENEZUELA	~	257	322	388	457	~	540	550	600	600
	UNITED STATES	10,078	11,794	11,124	11,504	11,747	12,884	12,821	12,880	13,195	14,133

1. Sifted (bolted) flours from soft and hard wheat and from spelt. Bran and offal, wheat groats, meal, and flour obtained by milling cereals other than wheat are excluded.
2. Incomplete coverage. Data for main establishments only.
3. Twelve months ending June 30.
4. Including flour from other grains.
5. Including groats.

a. Incomplete coverage. Data for main establishments only.

SOURCE: IASI-AC, 1970, table 323-05; UN-SY, 1968, table 88; UN-SY, 1978, table 85; UN-SY, 1979/80, table 80; UN-SY, 1981, table 127; UN-SY, 1982, table 118; UN-SY, 1983–84, table 112.

Table 1717

MAQUILADORA EMPLOYMENT AND INDUSTRY
BY BORDER MUNICIPALITY, MEXICO
(July 1984)

City	Plants		Employees		Direct Employees		Technicians and Administrators	
	Number	%	Number	%	Number	%	Number	%
Tijuana	144	21.5	23,779	11.30	19,977	11.4	3,802	10.80
Mexicali	67	10.0	10,692	5.10	8,995	5.15	1,697	4.82
Nogales	46	6.80	17,570	8.40	14,569	8.30	3,001	8.52
Ciudad Juárez	157	23.40	75,334	35.90	61,943	35.50	13,391	38.10
Matamoros	38	5.7	20,159	9.6	17,302	9.90	2,857	8.11
Reynosa y Rio Bravo	22	3.3	15,358	7.30	12,497	7.20	2,861	8.13
Other Border Municipalities	154	22.9	36,672	17.5	31,365	18.00	5,380	15.39
Municipalities of the Interior	43	6.4	10,184	4.8	7,981	4.60	2,203	6.30
National Total	671	100.0	209,748	100.0	174,629	100.0	35,192	100.0

SOURCE: MEXICO-BNCE-CE, Jan. 1986.

Table 1718

PLANNED STRIKES AND ACTUAL STRIKES IN MAQUILADORA
INDUSTRY, MEXICO, 1967–83

(N)

Year	Planned Strikes			Actual Strikes		
	Tijuana	Ciudad Juárez	Matamoros	Tijuana	Ciudad Juárez	Matamoros
1967	3	- -	- -	- -	- -	- -
1968	- -	- -	- -	- -	- -	- -
1969	- -	1	- -	- -	- -	- -
1970	2	- -	- -	- -	- -	- -
1971	- -	- -	- -	- -	- -	- -
1972	4	5	- -	- -	- -	- -
1973	10	14	11	5	1	- -
1974	7	10	13	1	1	- -
1975	7	8	17	1	1	1
1976	5	10	18	- -	- -	- -
1977	3	8	26	- -	- -	- -
1978	9	15	12	1	1	- -
1979	16	14	12	1	1	- -
1980	11	12	17	- -	2	- -
1981	14	14	16	- -	2	- -
1982	24	38	53	- -	- -	1
1983	20	21	25	1	1	- -

SOURCE: MEXICO-BNCE-CE, Jan. 1986.

CHAPTER 18

MINING PRODUCTION

Table 1800

ANTIMONY MINE PRODUCTION, 7 LC, 1977–85

(Short Tons)

	Country	1977	1978	1979	1980[‡]	1981	1982	1983[‡]	1984	1985
B.	BOLIVIA	18,012	14,702	14,351	17,047	16,866	15,408	10,969	10,231	9,500
C.	BRAZIL	289	216	80	51	297	298	330	~	~
K.	GUATEMALA	1,010	254	728	613	563	550[†]	500	100[†]	220
M.	HONDURAS	77	86	51	25	22[†]	11[†]	11	350[†]	440[†]
N.	MEXICO[1]	2,974	2,708	3,166	2,399	1,984	1,725	2,777	3,377	3,300
R.	PERU[3]	903	821	602	379	755	814	786	741	720
	UNITED STATES[2]	610	798	722	343	646	503	838	557	~

1. Antimony content of ores for export plus antimony content of antimonial lead
    and other smelter products produced.
2. Production from antimony mines; excludes a small amount produced as a byproduct
    of domestic lead ores.
3. Recoverable.

SOURCE: USBOM-MY, 1981, Volume I; USBOM-MIS, *Antimony in 1982*, p. 3; 1983, p. 3;
    USBOM-MY, 1983, Volume 1; USBOM-MY, 1984, Volume 1; USBOM-MY, 1985, Volume 1.

Table 1801

BAUXITE MINE PRODUCTION, 3 LC, 1977–85[1]

(T MET)

	Country	1977	1978	1979	1980	1981	1982	1983	1984[‡]	1985[†]
C.	BRAZIL	1,120[†]	1,160[†]	2,388	5,538	5,770	6,289	7,199	6,433	6,650
H.	DOMINICAN REP.[1]	576	568	635	606	457	141	~	~	~
L.	HAITI[1,2]	588	580	584	312	427	377	~	~	~
	UNITED STATES[1]	2,013	1,669	1,821	1,559	1,510	732	679	856	674

1. Dry Bauxite equivalent of Crude Ore.
2. Shipment.

a. Data available through July 8, 1986.

SOURCE: USBOM-MY, 1981, Volume I; USBOM-MIS, *Bauxite in 1982*, p. 5; 1983, p.3;
    USBOM-MY, 1984, Volume 1; USBOM-MY, 1985, Volume 1.

Table 1802

CHROMITE MINE PRODUCTION, 3 L, 1977–85[a]

(T Short Tons)

	Country	1977	1978	1979	1980	1981	1982	1983	1984[‡]	1985[†]
C.	BRAZIL[1]	342	297	375	345	261	304	171	282	303
E.	COLOMBIA[†]	6	6	6	6	6	~	~	~	~
G.	CUBA[2]	22	32	31	35	23	30	37	41	44

1. Figures are sum of (1) crude ore sold directly for use and (2) concentrate output, both
    as reported in Brazilian sources. Data for 1979 and 1980 may include 45,000 to 55,000
    short tons annually of run-of-mine ore that required benefication. Total run-of-mine crude
    ore production (not comparable to data for other countries) was as follows, in thousand
    short tons: 1979–983; 1981–1,021; 1982–736, and 1983–740 (estimated).
2. Production of marketable product (direct-shipping lump ore plus concentrates and
    foundry sand).

a. Date available through July 1, 1986.

SOURCE: USBOM-MY, 1981, Volume I; 1983, p. 3; USBOM-MY, 1984, Volume 1;
    USBOM-MY, 1985, Volume 1.

Table 1803

COPPER MINE PRODUCTION, 12 LC, 1977–85

(T MET)

	Country	1977	1978	1979	1980	1981	1982	1983	1984[‡]	1985[†]
A.	ARGENTINA	.2	.3	.1	.2	.1	#[a]	.3	.3	.3
B.	BOLIVIA	3.2	2.9	1.8	1.9	2.6	2.3	2.0	1.6	1.5
C.	BRAZIL	#	#	5.3	1.4	11.8	24.4	40.0	44.4	32.0
D.	CHILE[3]	1,056.2	1,035.5	1,062.7	1,067.9	1,081.1	1,242.2	1,257.5	1,290.7	1,356.4[b]
E.	COLOMBIA	#	.1	.1	.1	.5	.5	.4	.8	.8
G.	CUBA	2.6	2.8	2.8	3.3	2.9	2.6	2.7	2.7	3.1
I.	ECUADOR	1.0	.8	.7	.9	.8	#[a]	#[a]	.2[†]	.1
K.	GUATEMALA	2.5	2.1	1.8	.8	.7	.7[†]	#	#	~
M.	HONDURAS	.5	.6	1.4	.3	.5	.5	.6	.7[†]	.8
N.	MEXICO[3]	89.7	87.2	107.1	175.4	232.9	229.2	196.0	303.5	290.0
O.	NICARAGUA[1]	3	.1[†]	- -	- -	- -	~	~	~	~[b]
R.	PERU[3]	338.1	366.4	390.7	366.8	342.1	356.6	322.2	375.1	397.2[b]
	UNITED STATES[2,4]	1,364.4	1,357.6	1,446.6	1,281.1	1,538.2	1,147.0	1,038.1	1,072.6	1,105.8

1. Copper content of concentrates produced.
2. Recoverable.
3. Copper content by analysis of concentrates for export plus nonduplicative total of copper content of all metal and metal products produced indigenously from domestic ores and concentrates.
4. By concentration, and leaching (electrowon).

a. Less than 50 tons.
b. Reported figure.

SOURCE: USBOM-MY, 1981, Volume I; USBOM-MIS, *Copper in 1982*, p. 3; 1983, p. 3; USBOM-MY, 1984, Volume 1; USBOM-MY, 1985, Volume 1.

Table 1804

FLUORSPAR PRODUCTION,[1,2] 5 LC, 1977–85

(Short Tons)

	Country	1977	1978	1979	1980	1981	1982	1983	1984[‡]	1985[†]
A.	ARGENTINA	48,272	29,482	41,972	17,050	22,878	26,155	31,950	25,526	27,500
B.	BOLIVIA	75,598	68,123	57,866	61,144	66,000		56,218	76,059	82,600[†]	89,300
C.	BRAZIL[4]	127,824	139,147	57,760	61,034	59,116				
N.	MEXICO	727,621	1,057,980	964,759	1,219,155	1,230,177	810,198	666,897	770,989	803,156
S.	URUGUAY[†]	83	125	85[†]	89	#	#	#	#	~
	UNITED STATES[3]	169,489	129,428	109,299	92,635	115,404	77,017	61,000[†]	72,000[†]	66,000

1. Data available through May 13, 1986.
2. Total for all grades.
3. Shipments.
4. Series revised. Data presented are marketable concentrates (1979–83).

SOURCE: USBOM-MY, 1981, Volume I; USBOM-MIS, *Fluorspar in 1982*, p. 3; USBOM-MCP, *Fluorspar, 1982*, p. 5; 1983, p. 3; USBOM-MY, 1984, Volume 1; USBOM-MY, 1985, Volume 1.

Table 1805

GOLD MINE PRODUCTION, 14 LC, 1977–85

(Troy Ounces)

	Country	1977	1978	1979	1980	1981	1982	1983	1984[‡]	1985[†]
A.	ARGENTINA	5,509	5,600	10,140	10,622	14,757	20,319	23,374	22,120	22,500
B.	BOLIVIA	24,293	24,660	30,319	52,075	66,372	40,146	49,217	40,827	30,000
C.	BRAZIL[1,†]	279,520	300,898	319,258	1,300,000	1,200,000	1,446,782	1,750,000	1,768,305	2,000,000
D.	CHILE	116,376	102,287	111,405	219,773	400,478	543,569	570,971	541,051	554,281
E.	COLOMBIA	257,070	246,446	269,369	510,439	529,214	472,674	438,579	799,899	1,142,830
F.	COSTA RICA[†]	12,200	15,900	16,700	18,000	20,000	27,000	30,000	35,000	~
H.	DOMINICAN REP.	342,755	342,830	352,982	369,603	407,813	380,254	348,065	330,000	~
I.	ECUADOR	8,124	2,734	2,251	225	2,347	2,300	643	1,000	~
J.	EL SALVADOR	2,156	3,619	2,720	2,492	3,883	3,300	650	650	~
M.	HONDURAS	2,481	2,500	1,501	2,027	1,579	1,711	2,151	2,200	~
N.	MEXICO[2]	212,709	202,003	190,364	176,089	198,594	214,349	198,177	270,998	297,000
O.	NICARAGUA	65,764	73,947	61,086	59,984	61,913	54,384	46,428	34,000	~
R.	PERU	104,393	103,069	141,656	142,041	161,590	157,667	165,576	198,691	223,447[a]
T.	VENEZUELA	17,403	13,384	14,989	13,565	27,810	27,993	33,200	50,885	72,919
	UNITED STATES	1,100,347	998,832	964,390	969,782	1,379,161	1,465,686	2,002,256	2,084,615	2,475,436

1. All figures except those for 1978 differ substantially from those appearing in latest
   available official Brazilian sources owing to the inclusion here of estimates for
   unreported production by small mines (garimpos).
2. Production series for Mexico revised since 1980 to reflect mine output data published
   for each state and municipality.

a. Reported figure.

SOURCE: USBOM-MY, 1981, Volume 3; USBOM-MIS, *Gold in 1982*, p. 3;
USBOM-MCP, *Gold*, 1982, p. 4; 1983, p. 3; USBOM-MY, 1984, Volume 1;
USBOM-MY, 1985, Volume 1.

Table 1806

GYPSUM MINE PRODUCTION, 16 LC, 1977–85

(T Short Tons)

	Country	1977	1978	1979	1980	1981	1982	1983	1984	1985
A.	ARGENTINA	603	674	648	1,028	739	679	637	625	585
B.	BOLIVIA	1[†]	1[†]	1[†]	1	1	1	1[†]	1[†]	1
C.	BRAZIL[1]	599	523	512	668	659	750	613	544	610
D.	CHILE	162	192	179	300	262	99	73	185	216
E.	COLOMBIA	231	281	283	289	328	309	247	287	300
G.	CUBA[†]	100	105	100	134	143	140	145	145	145
H.	DOMINICAN REP.	249	190	193	259	225[a]	230[†]	230[†]	230[†]	255
I.	ECUADOR	46	38	7	7	2[a]	2[†]	2[†]	2[†]	2
J.	EL SALVADOR	8	8	8	10	7[†]	6[†]	5[†]	5[†]	4[†]
K.	GUATEMALA	35	42	28	37	32	31	43	28	27
M.	HONDURAS[†]	20	25	25	25	22	22	25	25	25
N.	MEXICO	1,649	1,938	2,228	2,393	2,635	2,251	3,261	2,347	3,100
O.	NICARAGUA[†]	40	40	40	44	33[†]	22	13	10[†]	9[a]
Q.	PARAGUAY	15	10	12[†]	13	11	7	4	7	6
R.	PERU	157	186	240	309	386[a]	400[†]	400[†]	400[†]	400
T.	VENEZUELA	184	206	287	129	241	175	226	158	147[a]
	UNITED STATES[2]	13,390	14,891	14,630	12,376	11,497	10,538	12,884	14,319	14,726[a]

a. Reported figure.

SOURCE: USBOM-MY, 1981, Volume I; USBOM-MIS, *Gypsum in 1982*, p. 3; 1983, p. 3;
USBOM-MY, 1984, Volume 1; USBOM-MY, 1985, Volume 1.

Table 1807

IRON ORE PRODUCTION,[1,2] 8 LC, 1977–85

(T Long Tons)

	Country	1977	1978	1979	1980	1981	1982	1983	1984[‡]	1985[†]
A.	ARGENTINA	1,014	895	601	430	392	578	599	618	620
B.	BOLIVIA	7	55	25	6	6	8	11	~	~
C.	BRAZIL	80,706	83,643	102,440	112,920	97,928	91,687	87,315	110,287	118,100
D.	CHILE	7,535	6,695	7,006	8,451	8,380	6,368	5,880	7,004	6,407[a]
E.	COLOMBIA	497	489	391	498	426	463	449	434	490
N.	MEXICO[3]	5,296	5,249	5,965	7,510	8,573	8,026	7,913	8,186	7,700
R.	PERU	6,184	4,844	5,358	5,614	5,973	5,683	4,289	4,012	5,023[a]
T.	VENEZUELA	13,467	13,302	15,019	15,848	15,286	11,023	9,562	12,848	15,240
	UNITED STATES[4]	55,750	81,583	85,716	69,613	73,174	35,433	37,562	51,269	48,751

1. Data available through Sept. 5, 1986.
2. Gross weight: insofar as availability of sources permits, gross weight data represent the nonduplicative sum of marketable direct-shipping iron ores, iron ore concentrates, and iron ore agglomerates produced by each of the listed countries. Concentrates and agglomerates produced from imported iron ores have been excluded, under the assumption that the ore from which such materials are produced has been credited as marketable ore in the country where it was mined.
3. Gross weight calculated from reported iron content based on grade of 66% Fe.
4. Includes byproduct ore.

a. Reported figure.

SOURCE: USBOM-MY, 1981, Volume I; USBOM-MIS, *Iron in 1982*, p. 3; 1983, p. 3; USBOM-MY, 1984, Volume 1; USBOM-MY, 1985, Volume 1.

Table 1808

LEAD MINE PRODUCTION,[1] 11 LC, 1977–85

(T MET)

	Country	1977	1978	1979	1980	1981	1982	1984	1984	1985
A.	ARGENTINA	33.6	30.3	31.8	32.6	32.7	30.1	31.7	28.5	29.0
B.	BOLIVIA	18.9	18.0	15.4	17.7	16.8	12.4	11.8	7.4	7.5
C.	BRAZIL	24.0	31.2	27.9	21.8	21.7	19.4	18.8	16.7	19.0
D.	CHILE	.1	.4	.3	.3	.2	1.6	1.7	4.3	2.5[b]
E.	COLOMBIA	.2	.1	.2	.3	.2	.2	.2	.1	.1
I.	ECUADOR	.2	.2	.2	.2	.2	.2	.2	.2	.2
K.	GUATEMALA[†]	.1	.1	.1	.1	#[a]	#[a]	~	~	~
M.	HONDURAS	20.6	21.8	16.4	13.3	12.6	15.1	19.3	20.5	21.3
N.	MEXICO[2,4]	163.5	170.6	173.5	147.2	148.9	170.2	184.3	202.6	200.0
O.	NICARAGUA	1.0	.4	- -	- -	- -	- -	~	~	~
R.	PERU[3]	175.7	182.7	174.0	189.1	192.7	175.8	212.6	205.3	209.9
	UNITED STATES	537.5	529.7	525.6	573.1	459.0	530.3	465.6	334.5	424.4[b]

1. Data available through June 24, 1986.
2. Recoverable metal content of lead in concentrates for export plus lead content of domestic smelter products (refined lead, antimonial lead, mixed bars, and other unspecified items).
3. Recoverable metal content of lead in concentrates for export plus lead content of domestic smelter products (refined lead, antimonial lead, and bizmuth-lead bars).
4. Production series modified according to data on mine output per municipality and state.

a. Revised to zero.
b. Reported figure.

SOURCE: USBOM-MY, 1981, Volume I; USBOM-MIS, *Lead in 1982*, p. 3; 1983, p. 3; USBOM-MY, 1984, Volume 1; USBOM-MY, 1985, Volume 1.

Table 1809

MANGANESE ORE PRODUCTION, 4 L, 1980-85

(T Short Tons Unless Otherwise Specified)

	Country	1980	1981	1982	1983	1984[‡]	1985[†]
B.	BOLIVIA[1,2]	5[‡]	- -	- -	- -	- -	~
C.	BRAZIL[1,2]	2,515[a]	2,251[a]	2,580[a]	2,306[a]	2,969	2,976
D.	CHILE	31	30[†]	~	~	~	~
N.	MEXICO	493[†]	637[†]	561[†]	386[†]	525[†]	511

1. Gross weight reported; metal content estimated.
2. Calculated metal content includes allowance for assumed moisture content.

a. Figures are the sum of (1) sales of direct-shipping manganese ore and (2) productioned
    beneficiated ore, both as reported in Anuário Mineral Brasiliero.

SOURCE: USBOM-MY, 1985, Volume 1; for years 1977, 1978, 1979 see SALA, 24-1809.

Table 1810

MERCURY MINE PRODUCTION, 3 LC, 1977-85

(Flasks)

	Country	1977	1978	1979	1980	1981	1982	1983	1984	1985
D.	CHILE	20	- -	- -	- -	- -	~	~	~	~
H.	DOMINICAN REP.	495	500	128	159	77	49	40[†]	30[†]	20
N.	MEXICO	9,660	2,205	1,973	4,206	6,962	8,558	6,411	11,140	10,000
	UNITED STATES	28,244	24,163	29,519	30,657	27,904	25,760	25,070	19,048	16,530[a]

a. Reported figure.

SOURCE: USBOM-MY, 1981, Volume I; USBOM-MIS, Mercury in 1982, p. 3; 1983, p. 3;
    USBOM-MY, 1984, Volume 1; USBOM-MY, 1985, Volume 1.

Table 1811

MOLYBDENUM MINE PRODUCTION, 3 LC, 1977-85

(T Pounds Contained Molybdenum)

	Country	1977	1978	1979	1980	1981	1982	1983	1984[‡]	1985[†]
D.	CHILE	24,112	29,092	29,895	30,133	33,863	44,198	33,651	37,172	40,543[a]
N.	MEXICO	2	24	105	163	994	11,442	12,932	8,938	8,150[a]
R.	PERU	1,005	1,607	2,637	5,926	5,485	6,378	5,794	6,788	8,439[a]
	UNITED STATES	122,408	131,843	143,967	150,686	139,900	84,381	33,593	103,664	108,409[a]

a. Reported figure.

SOURCE: USBOM-MY, 1981, Volume I; USBOM-MIS, Molybdenum in 1982, p. 3; 1983, p. 3;
    USBOM-MY, 1984, Volume 1; USBOM-MY, 1985, Volume 1.

Table 1812

NICKEL MINE PRODUCTION,[1] 5 LC, 1977–85

(Short Tons)

	Country	1977	1978	1979	1980[‡]	1981	1982	1983	1984[‡]	1985[†]
C.	BRAZIL[2]	4,675	3,968	3,267	2,504	7,239	15,929	17,153	23,887	26,000
G.	CUBA[3]	40,510	38,346	34,275	40,338	42,489	39,790	41,487	35,087	35,700
H.	DOMINICAN REP.	27,446	15,765	27,680	18,019	20,601	5,926	21,552	26,371	29,000
K.	GUATEMALA	328	1,189	6,833	7,434	~	~	~	~	~
N.	MEXICO[2]	37	24	1	- -	- -	~	~	~	~
	UNITED STATES[4]	14,347	13,509	15,065	14,653	12,099	3,203	400	14,540	6,127[a]

1. Data available through May 13, 1986.
2. Content of ore.
3. Content of oxide, sinter, and sulfide.
4. Content of ore shipped.

a. Reported figure.

SOURCE: USBOM-MY, 1981, Volume I; USBOM-MIS, *Nickel in 1982*, p. 3; USBOM-MCP,
     Nickel, 1982, p. 6; 1983, p. 6; USBOM-MY, 1984, Volume 1, USBOM-MY, 1985, Volume 1.

Table 1813

PHOSPHATE ROCK MINE PRODUCTION,[1] 5 LC, 1977–85

(T MET)

	Country	1977	1978	1979	1980	1981	1982	1983	1984[‡]	1985[†]
C.	BRAZIL[2]	676	1,096	1,628	2,612	3,238	2,732	3,208	3,855	4,214
E.	COLOMBIA	6	1	6	6	17	20	17	28	23
N.	MEXICO	285	322	274	397	252	379	389	375	350
R.	PERU	~	~	5	14	12	29	3	13	12
T.	VENEZUELA	139	109	- -	- -	- -	~	~	~	~
	UNITED STATES	47,256	50,037	51,611	54,415	53,624	37,414	42,573	49,197	50,835[a]

1. Data derived from International Fertilizer Industry Association and official sources
   where available.
2. Figure represents total of direct sales of run-of-mine product plus output of marketable
   concentrate. Direct sales of run-of-mine product were as follows, in thousand metric
   tons: 1977, 26; 1978, 27; 1979, 39; 1980, 40; 1981, 40 (estimated). Total output of
   crude ore reported in Brazilian sources is far higher than figures presented here, but
   such figures are not equivalent to data shown for other countries.

a. Reported figure.

SOURCE: USBOM-MY, 1981, Volume I; USBOM-MY, 1984, Volume 1, USBOM-MY, 1985,
     Volume 1.

Table 1814

SALT PRODUCTION,[1] 15 LC, 1977–85

(T Short Tons)

	Country	1977	1978	1979	1980	1981	1982	1983	1984[‡]	1985[†]
A.	ARGENTINA[2]	2	1	1	1	1,034	656	747	1,034	881
C.	BRAZIL[3]	323	631	759	877	3,974	4,105	4,615[a]	4,990	5,130
D.	CHILE	467	434	650	486	320	743	788	690	831[b]
E.	COLOMBIA[3]	383	416	422	383	789	554	614	817[†]	720
F.	COSTA RICA[4,†]	30	38	51	44	43	121[b]	120	120	120
G.	CUBA	142	144	134	144	177	218	198	203	200
H.	DOMINICAN REP.[†]	38	42	42	61	70	70	70	70	70
J.	EL SALVADOR[†]	30[‡]	30[‡]	30[‡]	2	2	2	2	2	3
K.	GUATEMALA	12	12	16	11	15	15[†]	17	18[b]	18
M.	HONDURAS[†]	35	35	35	35	35	35	35	35	35
N.	MEXICO	5,400	6,212	6,800	7,248	8,767	6,130	6,287	6,787	6,600
O.	NICARAGUA[†]	18[†]	20	20	22	20	20	20	17	17
P.	PANAMA[5]	23	17	21	20	35	27	94	100[†]	100
R.	PERU	350	384	440	504	558	535	540[†]	550[†]	550
T.	VENEZUELA	266	174	170[†]	268	275[†]	375	342	360[b,†]	390
	UNITED STATES[2,6]	43,412	42,869	45,793	40,351	38,915	37,910	34,605	39,256	39,266

1. Data available through June 24, 1986.
2. Rock salt plus other salt.
3. Rock salt plus marine salt.
4. Marine salt.
5. Crude.
6. Including Puerto Rico (sold or used by producers).

a. Data represents sales.
b. Reported figure.

SOURCE: USBOM-MY, 1981, Volume I; USBOM-MIS, *Salt in 1982*, p. 3; 1983, p. 3;
     USBOM-MY, 1984, Volume 1; US BOM-MY, 1984, Volume 1.

Table 1815

SILVER MINE PRODUCTION,[1] 14 LC, 1977–85

(T Troy Ounces)

	Country	1977	1978	1979	1980	1981	1982	1983	1984[‡]	1985[†]
A.	ARGENTINA	2,450	2,164	2,209	2,357	2,518	2,684	2,500	1,662	1,600
B.	BOLIVIA	5,813	6,285	5,742	5,099	6,394	5,472	6,025	4,560	4,000
C.	BRAZIL[3]	372	506	1,065	784	765	760	486	829	850
D.	CHILE	8,461	8,210	8,740	9,598	11,610	12,288	15,055	15,766	16,633[a]
E.	COLOMBIA[2]	91	77	99	152	143	136	99	130	200
F.	COSTA RICA[†]	1	2	2	2	2	2	2	2	2
H.	COMINICAN REP.	1,852	1,848	2,276	1,623	2,034	2,198	1,329	1,207	1,560[a]
I.	ECUADOR	57	29	44	29	32	10[†]	3	2	2
J.	EL SALVADOR	112	185	152	146	137	86	22	22	20
K.	GUATEMALA[†]	~	10	10	10	8	3	#[b]	#[b]	~
M.	HONDURAS	2,819	2,788	2,434	1,766	1,823	2,100	2,587	2,650[†]	2,678[a]
N.	MEXICO	47,030	50,779	49,408	50,052	52,916	59,175	63,607	75,340	69,000
O.	NICARAGUA	167	482	389	164	140	76	63	50[†]	30[†]
R.	PERU	39,731	37,022	29,248	44,419	46,940	53,479	55,878	56,523	60,395[a]
	UNITED STATES	38,166	39,385	37,896	32,329	40,683	40,248	43,431	44,592	39,357[a]

1. Data available through July 1, 1986.
2. Smelter and/or refinery production.
3. Partially revised officially reported output; of total production, the following
   quantities in thousand troy ounces, are identified as placer silter (the balance
   being silver content of other ores and concentrates); 1980–47; 1981–144;
   1982–123; 1983–247; and 1984– not available.

a. Reported figure.
b. Revised to zero.

SOURCE: USBOM-MY, 1981, Volume 1; USBOM-MIS, *Gold and Silter in 1982*, p. 5; 1983, p. 5;
     USBOM-MY, 1984, Volume 1; USBOM-MY, 1985, Volume 1.

Table 1816

SULFUR PRODUCTION,[1,2] 11 LC, 1977–85
(T MET)

	Country	1977	1978	1979	1980	1981	1982	1983	1984[‡]	1985[†]
A.	ARGENTINA[†]	47	38	20	~	10	~	~	#	~
B.	BOLIVIA[3]	6[a]	14[a]	15[a]	11	10	6	3	2	2
C.	BRAZIL[4]	44	57	92	156	163	184	316	316[†]	337
D.	CHILE[3]	61	52	104	115	143	137	131	86	109[c]
E.	COLOMBIA[3]	29	38	18	27	28	35	34	39	38
G.	CUBA[5,†]	42[†]	31[†]	20[†]	30	22	28	13	8	8
I.	ECUADOR[3,†]	13[†]	15[†]	15[†]	14	12	15	15	15	14
N.	MEXICO[6,†]	1,936[†]	1,918[†]	2,125[†]	2,217	2,178	1,916	1,702	1,985	2,190
R.	PERU[3]	20	28	20	20	20	58	65	70	70
S.	URUGUAY[7,†]	2	2	2	2	2	2	2	2	2
T.	VENEZUELA[8,†]	95	95	85	85	85	85	85	86	88
	UNITED STATES[9]	10,727	11,175	12,101	11,866	12,145	9,787	9,290	10,652	11,609

1. Data available through June 3, 1986.
2. In all forms.
3. Data are for native sulfur. May, however, produce limited quantities of byproduct sulfur from crude oil and natural gas and/or from petroleum refining. May also produce limited quantities of byproduct sulfur from metallurgical operations and/or coal processing.
4. By product, petroleum, metallurgy.
5. Pyrites, By product, petroleum.
6. Frasch, By product, metallurgy, petroleum.
7. By product, petroleum.
8. By product, petroleum and natural gas.
9. Frasch, pyrites, By product, metallurgy, natural gas, petroleum and unspecified.

a. Exports regarded as tantamount to production, owing to minimal domestic consumption levels.

SOURCE: USBOM-MY, 1981, Volume I; USBOM-MY, 1984, Volume 1; USBOM-MY, 1985, Volume 1.

Table 1817

TIN MINE PRODUCTION,[1,2] 5 L, 1977–85
(MET)

	Country	1977	1978	1979	1980	1981	1982	1983	1984	1985
A.	ARGENTINA	537	362	386	351	413	304	291	274	270
B.	BOLIVIA	33,740	30,881	27,648	27,291	29,830	26,773	25,278	19,911	18,000
C.	BRAZIL	6,287	6,341	7,005	6,377	8,297	8,218	13,275	19,957	22,000
N.	MEXICO	220	73	23	60	28	27	334	416	400
R.	PERU	329	458	870	1,077	1,519	1,672	2,368	2,991	3,807[a]

1. Data available through June 17, 1986.
2. Data derived in part from the monthly Statistical Bulletin of the International Tin Council.

a. Reported figure.

SOURCE: USBOM-MY, 1981, Volume I; USBOM-MIS, *Tin in 1982*, p. 3; 1983, p. 3; USBOM-MY, 1984, Volume 1; USBOM-MY, 1985, Volume 1.

Table 1818

TUNGSTEN CONCENTRATE PRODUCTION,[1] 5 LC, 1977–85
(T Pounds of Contained Tungsten)

	Country	1977	1978	1979	1980[a]	1981	1982	1983	1984[‡]	1985[†]
A.	ARGENTINA	154	214	130	44	11	17	41	37	36
B.	BOLIVIA	5,355	5,373	5,445	2,732	2,779	2,534	2,449	1,893	1,551
C.	BRAZIL	2,672	2,568	2,595	1,116	1,576	1,524	1,026	1,037	1,175
N.	MEXICO	421	516	556	266	263	194	186	274	291
R.	PERU	1,160	1,283	1,243	581	521	692	723	754	870
	UNITED STATES	6,008	6,896	6,643	2,754	3,605	1,521	980	1,203	996

1. Data available through August 8, 1986.

a. 1980 and subsequent years measured in metric tons of tungsten content.

SOURCE: USBOM-MY, 1981, Volume I; USBOM-MIS, *Tungsten in 1982*, p. 3; 1983, p. 3; USBOM-MY, 1984, Volume 1; USBOM-MY, 1985, Volume 1.

Table 1819

ZINC MINE PRODUCTION,[1] 11 LC, 1977–85
(T MET)

	Country	1977	1978	1979	1980	1981	1982	1983	1984[‡]	1985[†]
A.	ARGENTINA	39.2	36.6	37.5	33.4	35.2	36.4	36.6	35.9	36.0
B.	BOLIVIA	61.4	53.9	51.6	50.3	47.0	45.7	47.1	37.8	41.0
C.	BRAZIL	57.6	58.7	89.9	67.0	95.2	110.6	118.6	103.2	110.0
D.	CHILE	3.9	1.8	1.8	1.1	1.5	5.7	6.0	19.2	18.0
E.	COLOMBIA	- -	- -	- -	.3	.3	#	#	~	1.0[†]
I.	ECUADOR	2.0	1.3	1.6	.6	.7	#	#	.1[†]	.1
K.	GUATEMALA	1.0	1.0	1.0[†]	~	3.0	1.0	~	~	~
M.	HONDURAS	26.5	24.3	22.0	16.0	16.2	24.6	38.0	41.5	44.0[a]
N.	MEXICO	265.5	244.9	245.5	235.8	206.6	242.3	266.3	303.6	280.0
O.	NICARAGUA	11.2	3.6	- -	- -	- -	~	~	~	~
R.	PERU	405.3	402.6	432	487.6	498.9	507.1	576.4	558.5	588.6[a]
	UNITED STATES	407.9	302.7	267.3	348.0	343.0	326.5	296.7	277.5	251.9[a]

1. Data available through July 15, 1986.

a. Reported figure.

SOURCE: USBOM-MY, 1981, Volume I; USBOM-MIS, *Zinc in 1982*, p. 3; 1983, p. 3; USBOM-MY, 1984, Volume 1; USBOM-MY, 1985, Volume 1.

Table 1820

INDICATORS FOR THE ECONOMIC CONTRIBUTION OF MINING
(%)

| | | | Share of the Mining Sector in: | | |
| | | | Exports | | |
Country	GDP	Employment	Non-Fuel Minerals[1]	Petroleum[2]	Public Revenues
	1981	Various, 1970-76	Average, 1978-80		Year Varies
Mining Economies					
B. BOLIVIA	6.8	3.9	41.2	3.4	90.0

Continued in SALA, 24–1820.

Table 1821

PRODUCTION AND RESERVES OF NON-FUEL MINERALS, BY MAJOR PRODUCERS
(%, 1982)

	Share of Major Producers In	
Mineral and Major Producer	World Production	World Reserves[1]
Ferrous Metals		
Colombium (Brazil)	85.8[a]	93.4[a]

Continued in SALA, 24–1821.

CHAPTER 19

ENERGY RESOURCES: PRODUCTION, CONSUMPTION, AND RESERVES

Table 1900

TOTAL ENERGY RESERVES AND PRODUCTION POTENTIAL, 19 LR

(M Tons of Oil Equivalent, 1982)

	Country	Petroleum	R/P[1]	Natural Gas	R/P[1]	Coal[2]	R/P	Hydroelectric	R/P[3]	Geothermal	Uranium	Bituminous Coal	Unrefined Petroleum	Biomass	Solar
A.	ARGENTINA	362	15	518	45	2,359	100[a]	493	6.6	#[b]	74	#[b]	..	..	..
B.	BOLIVIA	22	15	93	45	..	~	..	..	..	..	..	..	..	..
C.	BRAZIL	167	21	31	21	8,129	100[a]	232	1.3	~	1	..	..	..	..
D.	CHILE	55	..	~	..	2,984	100[a]	3,083	9.5	~	284	84	..	..	..
E.	COLOMBIA	97	16	112	30	5,778	100[a]	229	5.6	#[b]	10	..	..	..	..
F.	COSTA RICA	..	..	..	..	#[b]	~	774	5.3	~	102	..	#[b]	..	..
H.	DOMINICAN REP.	..	..	..	..	#[b]	~	~	~	~	~	~	~	~	~
I.	ECUADOR	151	13	31	..	98	100[a]	98	4.7	#[b]	..	..	..	..	..
J.	EL SALVADOR	..	..	..	..	..	~	388	.6	#[b]	..	..	#[b]	..	..
K.	GUATEMALA	2	..	..	..	..	~	12	18.9	#[b]	..	..	..	..	..
L.	HAITI	..	..	..	..	#[b]	~	186	..	..	..	..	..	..	..
M.	HONDURAS	..	..	..	..	..	~	10	2.9	~	..	..	..	..	..
N.	MEXICO	3,900	59	1,480	64	2,108	100[a]	6	5.1	~	..	..	..	..	..
O.	NICARAGUA	..	..	..	..	..	~	444	25	#[b]	21	..	..	..	..
P.	PANAMA	..	..	..	..	..	~	46	2.3	#[b]	..	..	..	..	..
Q.	PARAGUAY	..	..	..	..	..	~	31	10.7	#[b]	..	..	..	..	..
R.	PERU	90	12	29	15	573	100[a]	77	2.3	~	..	..	..	..	..
S.	URUGUAY	..	..	..	..	..	~	25	16.5	..	..	..	..	..	..
T.	VENEZUELA	2,448	23	1,065	34	5,394	100[a]	784	4.8	~	..	..	20,000	..	..
	LATIN AMERICA	7,294	~	3,359	~	27,423	~	6,918	~	~	492	84	20,000	~	~

1. Reserves in relation to production. Indicates number of years reserves will last at present rate of production or generation of energy.
2. Includes "turba," lignite and anthracite.
3. Percentage of utilization of the existent capacity.

a. More than 100 years.
b. It is known to exist.

SOURCE: Mexico-NAFINSA-MV, Oct. 11, 1982, table 5.

Table 1901

BIOMASS PARTICIPATION IN THE TOTAL
ENERGY SUPPLY, 13 L

(T Tons of Oil Equivalent, 1980)

	Country	Biomass[1]	Total Consumption	% Participation
B.	BOLIVIA	20,403	88,039	23
E.	COLOMBIA	3,280	13,358	25
F.	COSTA RICA	558	1,406	40
H.	DOMINICAN REP.	1,130	2,999	38
J.	EL SALVADOR	1,407	2,031	69
K.	GUATEMALA	2,078	3,312	63
L.	HAITI	1,249	1,718	73
M.	HONDURAS	1,211	1,822	67
N.	MEXICO	12,830	67,080	19
O.	NICARAGUA	692	1,224	57
P.	PANAMA	421	1,114	38
R.	PERU	3,061	9,197	33
S.	URUGUAY	575	2,144	27

1. Plant and animal material that can be converted into energy. Includes trees, shrubs, other woody vegetation, grasses, other herbaceous plants, energy crops, algae, aquatic plants, agricultural and animal residues.

SOURCE: IDB-SPTF, 1983, table IV-7.

Table 1902

ANNUAL GROWTH IN COMMERCIAL ENERGY PRODUCTION AND CONSUMPTION, 20 LC, 1965–85

	Country	Average Annual Energy Growth Rate % Production 1965–80	Production 1980–85	Consumption 1965–80	Consumption 1980–85	Energy Consumption/C (kg) 1965	Energy Consumption/C (kg) 1985	Energy Imports as % of Merchandise Imports 1965	Energy Imports as % of Merchandise Imports 1985
A.	ARGENTINA	4.5	3.6	4.3	2.2	975	1,468	8	6
B.	BOLIVIA	9.4	–7	7.7	–1.5	156	263	1	1[a]
C.	BRAZIL	8.6	12.6	10	3.2	286	781	14	37
D.	CHILE	1.8	3	3.1	–1.2	657	726	5	16[a]
E.	COLOMBIA	1	5.4	6.1	2.4	413	755	1	14[a]
F.	COSTA RICA	8.2	7.1	8.8	.6	269	534	8	14[a]
G.	CUBA	~	~	~	~	~	~	~	~
H.	DOMINICAN REP.	10.9	–5	11.5	3.3	130	372	7	71[a]
I.	ECUADOR	35	7.8	11.6	11.1	162	720	11	1[a]
J.	EL SALVADOR	9	3.1	7	.9	140	186	5	~
K.	GUATEMALA	12.5	7.2	6.8	–2.7	150	176	9	17
L.	HAITI	~	4.1	8.4	1.9	25	55	~	~
M.	HONDURAS	14	2.5	7.6	1.7	111	201	5	28
N.	MEXICO	9.7	4.8	7.9	1.2	622	1,290	4	1[a]
O.	NICARAGUA	2.6	1	6.5	.3	172	259	6	21
P.	PANAMA	6.9	11.1	5.9	.5	576	634	~	~
Q.	PARAGUAY	~	15.1	9.9	6.1	86	281	14	57[a]
R.	PERU	6.7	–0.3	5.1	.7	403	543	3	4[a]
S.	URUGUAY	3.7	20.8	1.3	–3.1	765	745	13	30[a]
T.	VENEZUELA	–3.1	–3.6	4.7	1.7	2,319	2,409	#	1[a]
	UNITED STATES	1.1	.2	2.3	–.4	6,535	7,278	8	26

a. Figures are for years other than those specified.

SOURCE: *World Development Report 1987*, table 9.

Table 1903

TOTAL COMMERCIAL ENERGY PRODUCTION,[1] 20 LC, 1950–84
(M MET Coal Equivalent)

	Country	1950	1955	1960	1970	1975	1980	1981	1982	1983	1984
A.	ARGENTINA	5.00	7.00	15.22	37.29	41.13	51.13	52.41	53.99	56.77	57.14
B.	BOLIVIA	.14	.49	.74	1.76	4.87	4.66	4.98	5.29	5.02	4.83
C.	BRAZIL	2.60	4.04	9.02	18.69	24.47	34.50	37.22	42.53	50.16	62.71
D.	CHILE	2.10	2.99	3.20	6.11	5.94	5.77	6.62	6.66	6.74	6.98
E.	COLOMBIA	8.72	9.36	14.55	21.81	19.32	21.90	22.99	24.58	25.90	27.57
F.	COSTA RICA	.02	.03	.05	.12	.16	.26	.28	.29	.34	.37
G.	CUBA	.03	.07	.02	.24	.36	.43	.39	.81	1.10	1.13
H.	DOMINICAN REP.	~	~	.01	.01	.01	.07	.10	.09	.10	.06
I.	ECUADOR	.54	.64	.57	.38	12.02	15.32	15.83	15.88	17.98	19.46
J.	EL SALVADOR	.01	.02	.03	.06	.06	.18	.16	.17	.18	.19
K.	GUATEMALA	.01	.02	.02	.04	.05	.33	.35	.52	.61	.42
L.	HAITI	~	- -	~	~	.02	.03	.03	.03	.03	.03
M.	HONDURAS	#	~	#	.02	.05	.10	.10	.11	.11	.11
N.	MEXICO	16.18	21.50	29.04	53.81	82.05	198.10	232.02	266.23	261.50	264.29
O.	NICARAGUA	#	~	#	.04	.05	.06	.06	.05	.04	.06
P.	PANAMA	#	~	#	.01	.01	.15	.16	.13	.11	.18
Q.	PARAGUAY	~	~	~	.02	.07	.07	.09	.08	.10	1.1
R.	PERU	3.43	3.44	4.34	6.43	6.89	16.57	16.6	16.6	14.7	15.92
S.	URUGUAY	.07	.08	.08	.15	.14	.43	.31	.30	.44	.43
T.	VENEZUELA	114.88	153.92	224.94	298.49	199.39	193.94	189.48	174.57	165.5	168.69
	UNITED STATES	1,156.42	1,269.88	1,414.50	2,103.70	1,963.02	2,045.68	2,032.15	2,004.37	1,908.02	2,054.1

1. Based on the production of coal, lignite, crude petroleum, natural gas, and hydro and nuclear electricity. Where peat used as fuel is important, it is included with coal and lignite.

SOURCE: UN-SP: J, 19 (1976), tables 1 and 2; UN-YWES, 1979–85, table 1; 1984, table 1.

Table 1904

PC OF TOTAL COMMERCIAL ENERGY PRODUCTION, 20 LC, 1955–84
(APGR)

	Country	1955	1960	1970	1975	1980	1981	1982	1983	1984
A.	ARGENTINA	80.0	24.56	10.9	2.1	5.2	2.5	3.0	5.1	.7
B.	BOLIVIA	50.0	10.2	28.2	35.3	.4	4.7	6.2	−5.1	−3.8
C.	BRAZIL	7.4	26.3	11.9	6.2	11.6	8.1	14.3	17.9	25.0
D.	CHILE	8.5	8.5	−1.5	−.6	8.1	14.7	.6	1.2	3.6
E.	COLOMBIA	3.3	11.5	4.2	−2.3	8.5	5.5	6.9	5.4	6.4
F.	COSTA RICA	10.0	13.3	14.3	6.7	30.0	7.7	3.6	17.2	8.8
G.	CUBA	26.7	−14.3	40.0	10.0	−6.5	−9.3	107.7	35.8	2.7
H.	DOMINICAN REP.	~	~	0	0	600.0	42.9	−10.0	11.1	−40.0
I.	ECUADOR	3.7	−2.2	−5.9	612.6	−4.8	3.3	.3	13.2	8.2
J.	EL SALVADOR	20.0	10.0	4.0	0	0	−11.1	6.3	5.9	5.6
K.	GUATEMALA	20.0	0	60.0	5.0	120.0	3.0	48.6	17.3	−31.1
L.	HAITI	~	~	~	~	0	0	0	0	0
M.	HONDURAS	~	~	20.0	30.0	42.9	0	10.0	0	0
N.	MEXICO	4.5	8.8	5.6	10.5	30.5	17.1	14.7	−1.8	1.1
O.	NICARAGUA	~	~	6.7	5.0	20.0	0	−16.7	−20.0	50.0
P.	PANAMA	~	~	~	0	50.0	33.3	−18.8	−15.4	63.6
Q.	PARAGUAY	~	~	~	50.0	−22.2	14.3	−11.1	25.0	1,000.0
R.	PERU	−2.5	8.3	4.8	1.4	5.7	−.1	0	−10.8	7.6
S.	URUGUAY	2.9	0	17.5	−1.3	230.8	9.3	−3.2	46.7	−2.3
T.	VENEZUELA	6.5	9.4	4.2	−6.6	−5.9	−2.3	−7.9	−5.2	1.9
	UNITED STATES	1.8	2.6	5.8	−1.3	−1.4	−.83	−1.4	−4.8	7.6

SOURCE: SALA calculations from table 1903.

Table 1905

INDEX OF TOTAL PRODUCTION OF COMMERCIAL ENERGY,[1] 20 LC, 1970–84
(1975 = 100)

	Country	1970	1980	1981	1982	1983	1984
A.	ARGENTINA	91	124	127	131	138	139
B.	BOLIVIA	36	101	102	109	103	99
C.	BRAZIL	76	141	152	174	205	256
D.	CHILE	103	97	111	112	113	118
E.	COLOMBIA	113	109	119	127	134	143
F.	COSTA RICA	72	164	175	181	213	231
G.	CUBA	68	121	108	225	306	314
H.	DOMINICAN REP.	157	89	1,000	900	1,000	600
I.	ECUADOR	3	128	132	132	150	162
J.	EL SALVADOR	100	302	267	283	300	317
K.	GUATEMALA	86	723	700	1,040	1,220	840
L.	HAITI	~	179	150	150	150	150
M.	HONDURAS	47	152	200	220	220	220
N.	MEXICO	66	228	283	324	319	322
O.	NICARAGUA	86	139	120	100	80	120
P.	PANAMA	84	1,265	1,600	1,300	1,100	1,800
Q.	PARAGUAY	29	161	129	114	143	1,571
R.	PERU	93	233	241	241	215	231
S.	URUGUAY	110	201	221	214	314	307
T.	VENEZUELA	150	97	95	88	83	85
	UNITED STATES	107	107	104	102	97	105

1. Includes all types of solid, liquid, and gaseous fuels, plus electricity production.

SOURCE: SALA calculations from table 1903.

Table 1906

TOTAL COMMERCIAL ENERGY PRODUCTION BY RESOURCE CLASSIFICATION, 20 LC, 1980–84

Country/Year	T MET Coal Equivalent					(%)				
	Total	Solids[1]	Liquids[2]	Gas[3]	Electricity[4]	Total[5]	Solids	Liquids	Gas	Electricity
A. ARGENTINA										
1980	51,183	329	37,499	11,555	2,151	100	.6	73.3	21.8	4.2
1981	52,405	420	38,229	11,606	2,150	100	1.0	73.0	22.1	4.1
1982	53,986	434	37,756	13,403	2,393	100	1.0	70.0	24.8	4.4
1983	56,774	410	38,103	15,577	2,684	100	1.0	67.1	27.4	4.7
1984	57,141	429	37,381	16,315	3,015	100	.8	65.4	28.5	5.3
B. BOLIVIA										
1980	4,662	**	1,805	2,724	133	100	0	38.7	58.4	2.9
1981	4,976	**	1,763	3,071	142	100	0	35.4	61.7	2.9
1982	5,292	**	1,959	3,185	148	100	0	37.0	60.8	2.8
1983	5,016	**	1,812	3,060	144	100	0	36.1	61.0	2.9
1984	4,828	~	1,684	2,997	147	100	0	34.9	62.1	3.0
C. BRAZIL										
1980	34,499	3,744	13,494	1,406	15,856	100	10.9	39.1	4.1	45.9
1981	37,221	4,003	15,868	1,265	16,084	100	10.8	42.6	3.4	43.2
1982	42,530	4,424	19,283	1,464	17,359	100	10.4	45.4	3.4	40.8
1983	50,066	4,684	24,599	2,151	18,631	100	9.4	49.1	4.3	37.2
1984	62,714	5,170	34,442	2,756	20,346	100	8.3	54.9	4.4	32.4
D. CHILE										
1980	5,765	978	2,960	924	903	100	17.0	51.3	16.0	15.7
1981	6,620	1,104	3,443	1,139	933	100	16.7	52.0	17.2	14.1
1982	6,655	994	3,443	1,177	1,040	100	14.8	50.3	18.6	16.3
1983	6,742	999	3,393	1,251	1,099	100	17.1	48.5	18.0	16.4
1984	6,979	1,191	3,386	1,256	1,147					
E. COLOMBIA										
1980	21,901	4,947	9,761	5,137	2,056	100	22.6	44.6	23.5	9.4
1981	22,998	4,870	10,357	5,600	2,170	100	21.8	44.8	24.0	9.4
1982	24,575	5,374	10,911	6,008	2,282	100	22.5	44.2	24.0	9.2
1983	25,901	5,810	11,429	6,251	2,411	100	22.8	44.5	23.5	9.2
1984	27,568	5,907	12,791	6,386	2,485	100	21.4	46.4	23.2	9.0
F. COSTA RICA										
1980	262	**	**	**	262	100	0	0	0	100
1981	277	**	**	**	277	100	0	0	0	100
1982	293	**	**	**	293	100	0	0	0	100
1983	342	**	**	**	342	100	0	0	0	100
1984	366	**	**	**	366	100	0	0	0	100
G. CUBA										
1980	434	**	398	24	12	100	0	91.7	5.5	2.8
1981	387	**	368	12	7	100	0	95.0	3.1	1.8
1982	806	**	787	14	5	100	0	97.6	1.7	.6
1983	1,098	**	1,079	11	8	100	0	98.3	1.0	.7
1984	1,133	**	1,120	4	9	100	0	98.9	.4	.8
H. DOMINICAN REP.										
1980	71	**	**	**	71	100	0	0	0	100
1981	101	**	**	**	101	100	0	0	0	100
1982	93	**	**	**	93	100	0	0	0	100
1983	96	**	**	**	96	100	0	0	0	100
1984	63	**	**	**	63	100	0	0	0	100
I. ECUADOR										
1980	15,322	**	15,162	51	109	100	0	99.0	#	.7
1981	15,828	**	15,640	91	97	100	0	98.8	.6	.6
1982	15,881	**	15,649	121	111	100	0	98.5	.8	.7
1983	17,982	**	17,628	140	213	100	0	98.0	.8	1.2
1984	19,457	**	19,116	126	215	100	0	98.2	.7	1.1
J. EL SALVADOR										
1980	177	**	**	**	177	100	0	0	0	100
1981	164	**	**	**	164	100	0	0	0	100
1982	171	**	**	**	171	100	0	0	0	100
1983	183	**	**	**	183	100	0	0	0	100
1984	192	**	**	**	192	100	0	0	0	100
K. GUATEMALA										
1980	335	**	301	**	34	100	0	89.9	0	10.1
1981	345	**	302	**	42	100	0	87.7	0	12.3
1982	520	**	461	**	59	100	0	88.7	0	11.3
1983	608	**	509	**	99	100	0	83.7	0	16.3
1984	419	**	345	**	74	100	0	82.3	0	17.7
L. HAITI										
1980	27	**	**	**	27	100	0	0	0	100
1981	28	**	**	**	28	100	0	0	0	100
1982	31	**	**	**	31	100	0	0	0	100
1983	32	**	**	**	32	100	0	0	0	100
1984	32	**	**	**	32	100	0	0	0	100

Table 1906 (Continued)

TOTAL COMMERCIAL ENERGY PRODUCTION BY RESOURCE CLASSIFICATION, 20 LC, 1980–84

Country/Year	T MET Coal Equivalent					(%)				
	Total	Solids[1]	Liquids[2]	Gas[3]	Electricity[4]	Total[5]	Solids	Liquids	Gas	Electricity
M. HONDURAS										
1980	96	**	**	**	96	100	0	0	0	100
1981	101	**	**	**	101	100	0	0	0	100
1982	107	**	**	**	107	100	0	0	0	100
1983	111	**	**	**	111	100	0	0	0	100
1984	108	**	**	**	108	100	0	0	0	100
N. MEXICO										
1980	198,100	5,007	155,561	35,339	2,192	100	2.5	78.5	17.8	11.1
1981	232,017	5,776	187,847	35,247	3,147	100	2.5	81.0	15.2	1.4
1982	266,231	5,612	221,346	36,453	2,977	100	2.1	83.0	13.7	1.1
1983	261,500	5,571	217,439	35,772	2,718	100	2.1	83.2	13.7	1.0
1984	264,287	5,571	222,245	33,349	3,122	100	2.1	84.1	12.6	1.2
O. NICARAGUA										
1980	63	**	**	**	63	100	0	0	0	100
1981	61	**	**	**	61	100	0	0	0	100
1982	52	**	**	**	52	100	0	0	0	100
1983	39	**	**	**	39	100	0	0	0	100
1984	62	**	**	**	62	100	0	0	0	100
P. PANAMA										
1980	145	**	**	**	145	100	0	0	0	100
1981	164	**	**	**	164	100	0	0	0	100
1982	132	**	**	**	132	100	0	0	0	100
1983	107	**	**	**	107	100	0	0	0	100
1984	183	**	**	**	183	100	0	0	0	100
Q. PARAGUAY										
1980	71	**	**	**	71	100	0	0	0	100
1981	87	**	**	**	87	100	0	0	0	100
1982	80	**	**	**	80	100	0	0	0	100
1983	96	**	**	**	96	100	0	0	0	100
1984	109	**	**	**	109	100	0	0	0	100
R. PERU										
1980	16,565	56	14,081	1,491	938	100	#	85.0	9.0	5.7
1981	16,611	69	13,899	1,660	984	100	#	83.7	10.0	5.9
1982	16,639	65	14,048	1,494	1,033	100	#	84.4	9.0	6.2
1983	14,760	58	12,330	1,374	998	100	#	83.5	9.3	6.8
1984	15,917	55	13,308	1,483	1,071	100	#	83.6	9.3	6.7
S. URUGUAY										
1980	428	**	**	**	428	100	0	0	0	100
1981	313	**	**	**	313	100	0	0	0	100
1982	301	**	**	**	301	100	0	0	0	100
1983	435	**	**	**	435	100	0	0	0	100
1984	430	**	**	**	430	100	0	0	0	100
T. VENEZUELA										
1980	193,944	44	170,194	21,938	1,763	100	#	87.8	11.3	.9
1981	189,477	46	165,505	22,070	1,856	100	#	87.3	11.6	1.0
1982	174,575	47	149,275	23,286	1,968	100	#	85.5	13.4	1.2
1983	165,506	39	140,508	22,782	2,177	100	#	84.9	13.8	1.3
1984	168,685	51	141,062	25,153	2,419	100	#	83.6	14.9	1.4
UNITED STATES										
1980	2,045,682	626,451	696,522	657,039	65,671	100	30.6	47.4	32.1	3.2
1981	2,032,150	621,064	694,353	650,233	66,500	100	30.6	34.2	32.0	3.3
1982	2,004,373	631,957	696,400	602,418	73,598	100	31.5	34.7	30.1	3.7
1983	1,908,824	586,244	699,243	545,440	77,898	100	30.7	36.6	28.6	4.1
1984	2,054,071	668,387	718,435	586,214	81,035	100	32.5	35.0	28.5	3.9

1. Comprised of hard coal, lignite-brown coal, peat and oil shale.
2. Comprised of crude petroleum and natural gas liquids.
3. Comprised of natural gas.
4. Comprised of electricity generation from hydro, nuclear and geothermal sources.
5. May not total due to rounding.

SOURCE: UN-YWES, 1984, table 1; percentages calculated by SALA.

Table 1907

TOTAL COMMERCIAL ENERGY CONSUMPTION,[1] 20 LC, 1929-84[a,b,c]

(M MET Coal Equivalent and Kg PI)

Year	A. ARGENTINA		B. BOLIVIA		C. BRAZIL		D. CHILE		E. COLOMBIA		F. COSTA RICA		G. CUBA		H. DOMINICAN REP.		I. ECUADOR		J. EL SALVADOR		K. GUATEMALA	
	Total	Per Capita	Total	Per Capita	Total	Per Capita	Total	Per Capita	Total	Per Capita	Total	Per Capita	Total	Per Capita	Total	Per Capita	Total	Per Capita	Total	Per Capita	Total	Per Capita
1929	7.58	680	.10	30	4.13	100	3.09	740	.60	70	.08	150	2.11	590	.10	40	.04	20	.08	40	.13	60
1937	9.22	650	.13	40	5.02	130	3.21	670	1.18	140	.09	150	1.49	340	.07	40	.11	40	.06	40	.12	60
1950	12.52	730	.25	89	9.60	180	3.64	597	3.04	264	.16	182	2.51	429	.15	61	.34	103	.13	68	.30	97
1960	22.3	1,057	.5	150	22.16	305	5.29	697	7.6*	487	.3	222	6.06	862	.5	142	.8	186	.3	117	.63	158
1970	37.9	1,581	1.0	225	41.7	435	10.8	1,152	12.7	609	.7	374	8.5	997	1.4	318	1.7	282	.7	192	1.0	191
1971	40.4	1,678	1.1	230	46.4	488	11.8	1,239	13.0	617	.8	437	9.1	1,046	1.7	396	1.9	301	.7	197	1.1	204
1972	41.4	1,698	1.2	251	52.0	532	11.5	1,187	13.3	615	.9	469	9.4	1,059	2.2	509	1.9	299	.7	199	1.2	217
1973	44.3	1,793	1.2	259	59.5	591	11.6	1,177	14.6	655	1.0	534	10.0	1,102	2.7	566	2.1	313	.9	241	1.3	228
1974	44.0	1,756	.4	298	66.7	649	11.3	1,124	15.2	660	1.0	500	10.1	1,096	2.8	622	2.4	355	.9	234	1.4	233
1975	43.1	1,654	1.6	333	71.2	659	9.8	956	16.0	688	1.0	524	11.8	1,261	2.7	549	2.8	409	1.0	230	1.5	239
1976	44.2	1,720	1.8	357	77.7	712	9.6	933	16.6	684	1.0	483	10.7	1,126	2.6	537	3.2	433	1.0	251	1.4	217
1977	46.1	1,769	2.1	410	82.0	731	10.1	956	17.9	713	1.2	582	12.4	1,297	2.6	520	3.2	418	1.1	259	1.6	226
1978	44.9	1,746	2.2	427	87.8	777	10.4	972	19.3	754	1.4	645	12.7	1,312	2.4	465	4.3	543	1.1	260	1.8	263
1979	48.6	1,831	2.3	430	91.2	788	10.9	1,002	19.8	749	1.2	572	13.2	1,346	2.2	410	5.0	621	1.2	261	2.1	291
1980	49.3	1,746	2.1	383	92.5	763	11.4	1,025	23.8	923	1.2	547	13.6	1,394	2.8	501	5.6	708	1.0	199	1.9	267
1981	47.7	1,663	2.4	412	86.8	700	11.4	1,006	22.1	840	1.2	523	14.0	1,436	2.7	474	6.0	728	.9	186	1.7	226
1982	48.6	1,666	2.4	410	86.7	683	10.5	912	23.0	854	1.1	469	15.0	1,522	2.6	443	6.2	724	.9	177	1.6	202
1983	51.6	1,742	2.4	396	85.1	656	10.6	909	23.7	860	1.1	456	13.8	1,395	3.5	585	5.9	671	1.0	185	1.4	181
1984	51.7	1,718	2.1	338	87.1	656	10.9	920	24.1	857	1.1	452	14.6	1,467	3.0	490	6.2	677	.9	174	1.6	194

Table 1907 (Continued)

TOTAL COMMERCIAL ENERGY CONSUMPTION,[1] 20 LC, 1929–84[a,b,c]

(M MET Coal Equivalent and Kg PI)

Year	L. HAITI Total	Per Capita	M. HONDURAS Total	Per Capita	N. MEXICO Total	Per Capita	O. NICARAGUA Total	Per Capita	P. PANAMA Total	Per Capita	Q. PARAGUAY Total	Per Capita	R. PERU Total	Per Capita	S. URUGUAY Total	Per Capita	T. VENEZUELA Total	Per Capita	UNITED STATES Total	Per Capita	WORLD Total	Per Capita
1929	.02	10	.22	236	4.82	300	0.3	40	..	..	..	..	.86	140	.82	440	.70	230	803.40	6,570	1,857.4	975
1937	.02	10	.18	167	8.19	440	.05	60	..	..	.01	10	.85	130	.83	400	1.04	300	759.30	5,890	2,002.2	1,001
1950	.06	17	.14	102	13.2	481	.09	81	.24	300	.03	22	2.05	268	1.0	445	5.0	953	1,138.07	7,474	2,391.9	955
1960	.1	34	.3	147	26.6	717	.25	165	.5	493	.14	80	4.0	396	2.1	788	13.8	1,824	1,454.0	8,047	3,924.2	1,302
1970	.2	37	.6	227	53.1	1,038	.7	320	.9	629	.3	142	8.0	608	2.5	887	24.6	2,242	2,216.9	10,811	6,439.6	1,748
1971	.2	42	.6	207	57.6	1,098	.7	366	1.1	768	.3	130	8.3	600	2.6	889	25.1	2,369	2,258.8	10,909	6,770.8	1,817
1972	.2	41	.6	226	61.2	1,128	.8	397	1.2	818	.3	134	8.3	583	2.8	944	27.1	2,478	2,376.6	11,380	7,078.7	1,868
1973	.2	42	.7	230	65.9	1,174	.8	415	1.3	846	.4	154	8.6	589	2.7	955	31.8	2,817	2,437.7	11,504	7,438.1	1,923
1974	.2	36	.7	223	71.9	1,238	.9	429	1.3	799	.4	162	9.0	596	2.6	947	32.1	2,760	2,345.6	11,070	7,471.3	1,899
1975	.2	40	.7	232	73.7	1,226	.9	375	1.4	856	.4	149	10.2	674	2.6	931	33.5	2,558	2,260.8	10,468	7,439.7	1,825
1976	.2	40	.8	247	77.6	1,247	1.0	442	1.4	842	.5	169	10.1	634	2.9	1,030	35.8	2,975	2,378.3	11,054	7,872.2	1,930
1977	.2	48	.9	275	84.3	1,290	1.2	505	1.4	809	.6	198	10.1	619	2.8	946	37.9	2,952	2,406.2	11,095	8,075.5	1,946
1978	.3	67	.8	229	93.5	1,397	1.1	456	1.4	760	.7	233	10.2	612	2.7	931	40.0	3,046	2,489.8	11,186	8,369.7	1,967
1979	.3	67	.8	231	106.6	1,536	.8	296	1.5	817	.6	210	10.8	626	2.8	981	45.6	3,372	2,502.5	11,120	8,653.5	2,000
1980	.3	56	.8	245	118.6	1,709	.9	330	1.6	849	.7	233	12.0	693	2.8	957	49.0	3,140	2,364.5	10,386	8,544.3	1,919
1981	.3	56	.9	218	129.8	1,821	1.0	359	1.6	763	.7	225	12.4	697	2.6	878	50.2	3,109	2,302.0	10,018	8,457.4	1,867
1982	.3	53	.9	219	131.4	1,796	1.0	345	1.4	703	.7	214	12.0	661	2.4	822	51.8	3,101	2,196.4	9,476	8,428.1	1,830
1983	.3	54	.9	223	130.4	1,736	1.0	322	1.3	615	.8	219	11.7	634	2.1	698	50.6	2,938	2,177.5	9,316	8,549.7	1,825
1984	.3	53	1.0	225	130.2	1,826	.9	279	1.6	740	.8	231	12.3	640	1.9	633	55.2	3,100	2,257.1	9,577	8,855.7	1,859

1. Includes solid and liquid fuels; natural and imported gas, hydro, nuclear, and imported electricity.

a. Change in terminology: "gross commercial consumption" through 1950; "gross consumption" through 1954; "aggregate consumption" since 1955.

b. Prior to 1960 total data given to two decimal places, and per capita data for 1951–54 calculated with population statistics in SALA-SNP, chapter VIII. Per capita data for 1929 and 1937 calculated with population statistics in WA, 1929 and 1937.

c. For yearly data in 1940s and 1950s, see SALA, 24-1906.

SOURCE: SALA-SNP, XI-1; UN-SP: J, 1 (1952); J, 17 (1974); J, 19 (1976), table 2; WA, 1929 and 1973; UN-SP: J, 20 (1977), table J, 21 (1978), table 2; UN-YWES, yearly, 1979–84, table 1.

Table 1908

INDEX OF TOTAL CONSUMPTION OF COMMERCIAL ENERGY,[1] 20 LC, 1970–84

(1975 = 100)

	Country	1970	1972	1973	1974	1976	1977	1978	1979	1980	1981	1982	1983	1984
A.	ARGENTINA	88	96	103	102	103	107	107	114	115	111	113	120	120
B.	BOLIVIA	60	70	74	87	110	130	139	143	131	150	150	150	131
C.	BRAZIL	59	73	84	94	110	116	123	128	132	122	122	120	122
D.	CHILE	109	118	117	116	99	103	105	110	116	116	107	108	111
E.	COLOMBIA	77	86	94	98	107	114	124	127	133	138	144	148	151
F.	COSTA RICA	65	88	97	98	99	123	132	120	120	120	110	110	110
G.	CUBA	73	89	85	96	101	118	108	112	117	119	127	117	124
H.	DOMINICAN REP.	50	~	~	~	~	~	~	~	102	100	96	130	111
I.	ECUADOR	60	67	73	86	112	112	152	178	198	214	221	211	221
J.	EL SALVADOR	72	~	~	~	~	~	~	~	100	90	90	100	90
K.	GUATEMALA	69	80	88	91	95	109	120	137	130	113	107	93	107
L.	HAITI	82	~	~	~	~	~	~	~	158	150	150	150	150
M.	HONDURAS	83	88	93	93	110	127	110	115	116	129	129	129	143
N.	MEXICO	73	83	90	97	105	113	128	146	160	176	178	177	177
O.	NICARAGUA	73	86	93	99	110	130	122	87	97	111	111	111	100
P.	PANAMA	64	87	94	94	90	101	100	96	105	132	114	100	93	114
Q.	PARAGUAY	81	82	97	104	115	139	103	161	148	175	175	200	200
R.	PERU	78	81	84	88	99	99	101	106	109	122	118	117	121
S.	URUGUAY	95	102	101	96	107	99	101	107	105	100	92	81	73
T.	VENEZUELA	73	83	95	99	110	116	119	136	146	150	155	151	165
	UNITED STATES	98	104	108	103	105	107	110	111	107	102	97	96	100
	WORLD	~	~	~	~	~	~	~	~	~	114	113	115	119

1. Includes all types of solid, liquid, and gaseous fuels, plus electricity production.

SOURCE: UN-YWES, 1979, table 7; 1981, table 2; 1983, table 2; 1984, table 2.

Table 1909

CRUDE OIL PRODUCTION, 11 LC AND 10 L, 1955–85

PART I: M MET

	Country	1955	1960	1965	1970	1973	1975	1976	1977	1978	1979	1980	1981	1982	1983	1984
A.	ARGENTINA	4.37	9.17	13.81	20.02	21.48	20.77	20.81	22.17	23.24	24.28	25.28	25.53	25.19	25.20	24.63
B.	BOLIVIA	.35	.41	.44	1.12	2.20	1.87	1.89	1.61	1.51	1.29	1.11	1.03	1.13	1.03	.962‡
C.	BRAZIL	.28	3.87	4.49	7.98	8.28	8.35	8.12	7.81	7.79	8.04	9.08	10.66	12.98	16.60	23.13
D.	CHILE	.35	.96	1.71	1.47	1.28	.99	.94	.93	.78	1.01	1.60	1.95	2.00	1.91	1.88
E.	COLOMBIA	5.49	7.71	10.17	11.33	9.49	8.10	7.55	7.11	6.76	6.41	6.50	6.97	7.33	7.68	8.61
G.	CUBA	.05	.01	.06	.16	.14	.23	.23	.24†	.29	.29	.27	.25	.54	.74	.77
I.	ECUADOR	.48	.38	.39	.19	10.62	8.16	9.49	9.28	10.22	10.87	10.42	10.75	10.75	12.01	13.01
K.	GUATEMALA	~	~	~	~	~	~	~	~	~	~	.21	.21	.32	.35	.24
N.	MEXICO	13.02	15.75	18.54	21.51	23.26	36.89	41.34	49.28	63.33	75.48	96.85	115.41	142.78	139.76	143.35
R.	PERU	2.41	2.64	3.19	3.55	3.48	3.55	3.78	4.50	7.44	9.45	9.65	9.52	9.62	8.44	9.10
T.	VENEZUELA	115.54	152.86	182.84	194.31	175.78	122.40	120.15	117.01	113.63	124.03	114.79	111.69	100.39	94.47	94.85
	UNITED STATES	352.12	364.34	405.36	475.29	454.19	413.09	401.25	405.71	428.49	420.82	424.20	421.80	425.59	427.52	438.13
	WORLD	791.65	1,076.29	1,539.04	2,275.0	2,779.94	2,643.66	2,870.19	2,984.87	3,010.12	3,126.08	2,978.66	2,794.85	2,674.40	2,652.49	2,708.51

SOURCE: SALA-SNP, p. 223; UN-SP: J, 17 (1974); UN-SP: J, 19 (1976); J 20 (1977),
p. 64; J 21 (1978), table 6; J, 22 (1979), table 10; UN-YWES, yearly, 1978–81,
table 16; 1983, table 14;1984, table 14.

PART II: T BARRELS

	Country	1960	1973	1975	1976	1977	1978	1979	1980	1981	1982	1983	1984	1985‡
A.	ARGENTINA	63,860	153,537	144,465	145,591	157,528	165,119	172,354	179,680	181,316	179,071	179,120	175,102	167,848
B.	BOLIVIA	3,111	17,261	14,732	14,856	12,695	11,845	10,200	8,704	8,091	8,918	8,100	7,624	7,248
C.	BRAZIL	29,614	62,397	62,700	62,934	58,685	58,528	60,434	66,435	80,321	91,980	114,975	173,010	205,495
D.	CHILE	7,231	11,430	8,946	8,371	7,120	6,291	7,572	12,140	15,104	14,965	14,365	14,069	13,048
E.	COLOMBIA	55,770	66,657	57,318	53,376	50,221	47,245	44,979	45,629	48,852	51,765	55,530	61,154	64,409
I.	ECUADOR	2,807	76,358	58,753	68,362	67,002	73,896	78,320	74,769	77,028	77,090	86,691	93,880	102,416
K.	GUATEMALA	#	#	#	#	#	221	571	1,513	1,494	2,292	2,549	1,715	1,068
N.	MEXICO	99,049	164,909	294,254	326,390	358,090	442,607	536,926	708,593	844,241	1,003,093	981,229	1,024,324	1,020,905
R.	PERU	19,272	25,767	26,294	28,101	33,271	55,071	69,952	71,356	70,431	71,197	62,454	67,374	68,788
T.	VENEZUELA	1,041,675	1,228,594	856,364	839,738	816,870	790,590	863,590	793,488	769,055	691,687	657,365	656,635	612,105

SOURCE: IDB-SPTF, yearly, 1978–86, table 66.

Table 1910

PC OF CRUDE OIL PRODUCTION, 11 LC, 1973–84

	Country	1973	1974	1975	1976	1977	1978	1979	1980	1981	1982	1983	1984
A.	ARGENTINA	-2.9	-1.6	-1.8	.2	6.5	4.8	4.5	4.1	1.0	-1.3	#	-2.3
B.	BOLIVIA	8.4	-4.1	-11.4	1.1	-14.8	-6.2	-14.6	-14.0	-7.2	9.7	-9.7	-6.6
C.	BRAZIL	1.7	4.1	-3.1	-2.8	-3.8	-.3	3.2	9.9	17.3	21.8	21.8	39.3
D.	CHILE	-9.9	-13.3	-10.8	-5.1	889.4	-16.1	38.4	58.4	16.9	2.6	-4.7	-1.6
E.	COLOMBIA	-6.3	-8.4	-6.8	-6.8	-5.8	-4.9	-5.1	1.4	6.6	6.1	4.6	12.1
G.	CUBA	27.3	21.4	35.3	0	4.3	20.8	0	-6.9	3.7	116.0	27.0	4.1
I.	ECUADOR	164.8	-15.3	-9.3	16.3	-2.2	10.1	6.4	-4.1	3.0	#	10.5	8.3
K.	GUATEMALA	~	~	~	~	~	~	~	~	#	52.4	8.6	-31.4
N.	MEXICO	5.0	27.2	24.7	12.1	19.2	28.5	19.2	28.3	19.2	23.7	-2.2	2.6
R.	PERU	9.1	9.8	-7.1	6.5	19.0	65.3	27.0	2.1	-1.0	-10.1	-6.3	.4
T.	VENEZUELA	4.6	-11.2	-21.6	-1.8	-2.6	-2.9	9.2	-7.2	-3.1	-10.1	-6.3	.4
	UNITED STATES	-2.7	-4.7	-4.6	-2.9	1.1	5.6	-1.8	.2	#	.9	.5	2.5
	WORLD	9.1	.3	-5.2	8.6	4.0	.8	3.9	-4.8	-6.2	-4.3	-.8	2.1

SOURCE: SALA calculations from table 1908, part I.

Table 1911

OFFSHORE PRODUCTION OF CRUDE PETROLEUM, 6 LC, 1970–84
(T MET)

	Country	1970	1973	1974	1975	1976	1977	1978	1979	1980	1981	1982	1983	1984
A.	ARGENTINA	95[†]	90[†]	94	90[†]	90[†]	90[†]	90[†]	90[†]	95[†]	95[†]	95[†]	95[†]	95[†]
C.	BRAZIL	396	661	1,190	1,340	1,584	1,864	2,104	2,763	3,738	5,009	6,854	9,919	15,926
D.	CHILE	~	~	~	~	~	~	~	~	~	1,511	1,610	1,300	1,200[†]
N.	MEXICO	1,991	1,777	2,341	2,665	2,242	2,283	2,199	4,914	34,669	56,277	84,085	87,021	90,600
R.	PERU	1,000[†]	1,544	1,676	1,500[†]	1,600	1,900[†]	1,427[†]	1,437[†]	1,380	1,320	1,363	1,204	1,325
T.	VENEZUELA	128,050	140,543	108,437	85,000[†]	85,000[†]	85,000[†]	56,852[†]	55,302[†]	58,013[†]	56,000[†]	50,300[†]	47,700[†]	48,002[†]
	UNITED STATES	77,786	79,690	73,466	67,200	62,351	57,848	55,914	52,500	51,033	50,895	54,640	58,848	63,295

SOURCE: UN-YWES, yearly, 1979–81, table 16; 1983, table 14; 1984, table 14.

Table 1912

REFINED OIL PRODUCTION, 18 L, 1973–85
(T Barrels)

	Country	1973	1975	1976	1977	1978	1979	1980	1981	1982	1983	1984	1985[‡]
A.	ARGENTINA	162,548	157,931	165,768	175,224	117,283	182,400	189,624	189,771	183,217	175,857	170,441	164,990
B.	BOLIVIA	9,308	7,365	8,568	9,283	8,400	10,044	9,618	8,651	8,810	7,925	7,898	7,847
C.	BRAZIL	205,100	336,150	344,157	343,950	385,577	401,931	405,101	397,922	394,958	386,462	408,070	404,420
D.	CHILE	36,559	31,783	34,212	35,180	34,442	37,278	35,805	35,455	27,729	30,583	31,046	30,918
E.	COLOMBIA	59,713	57,685	59,127	60,174	57,461	59,247	58,699	62,343	63,291	69,199	69,063	69,279
F.	COSTA RICA	3,358	1,941	1,902	2,535	3,054	2,981	3,690	3,488	2,923	2,412	2,709	3,077
H.	DOMINICAN REP.	5,465	8,545	8,885	9,009	9,422	9,147	9,384	9,447	8,804	9,679	10,413	10,117
I.	ECUADOR	11,023	14,643	15,571	31,724	30,063	31,931	34,122	32,562	34,009	27,493	32,498	31,438
J.	EL SALVADOR	4,199	4,491	4,680	4,962	5,254	5,288	4,588	4,304	3,994	4,220	4,420	4,491[†]
K.	GUATEMALA	7,132	4,855	4,443	4,615	5,959	5,767	5,381	5,345	4,508	4,306	5,009	5,017
M.	HONDURAS	3,439	3,459	3,004	3,090	3,107	3,383	3,639	1,900	678	2,329	2,973	2,569
N.	MEXICO	206,108	232,839	258,282	300,635	320,220	349,920	417,138	459,973	451,651	455,666	462,271	462,000[†]
O.	NICARAGUA	3,869	4,728	5,006	5,376	4,459	1,364	4,709	4,621	4,237	3,911	3,097	3,590
P.	PANAMA	25,974	~	18,207	20,451	17,013	15,731	13,653	10,543	11,807	11,720	10,653	8,919
Q.	PARAGUAY	1,480	1,662	2,121	1,863	2,278	2,186	1,960	1,913	1,610	1,583	1,116	1,370
R.	PERU	36,624	41,157	41,511	43,328	44,399	53,282	53,692	56,281	57,801	54,864	60,871	61,709
S.	URUGUAY	11,667	12,465	12,452	12,767	13,490	12,964	12,377	11,603	12,031	9,179	9,173	8,266
T.	VENEZUELA	376,836	317,044	360,885	353,065	358,940	360,255	377,452	313,535	316,090	327,770	303,315	331,185

SOURCE: IDB-SPTF, 1978, p. 470; 1979, p. 455; 1980, p. 451; 1983, p. 395; 1985, table 66,
p. 437; 1986, table 66, p. 443.

Table 1913

PC OF REFINED OIL PRODUCTION, 18 L, 1974-85

	Country	1974	1975	1976	1977	1978	1979	1980	1981	1982	1983	1984	1985
A.	ARGENTINA	-3.7	.9	5.0	5.7	1.2	2.8	4.0	.1	-3.5	-4.0	-3.1	-3.2
B.	BOLIVIA	7.2	24.2	16.3	8.3	-9.5	19.6	-4.2	-10.1	1.8	-10.0	-.3	-.6
C.	BRAZIL	49.9	9.4	2.4	.1	12.1	4.2	.8	-1.8	-.7	-2.2	5.6	-.9
D.	CHILE	4.8	-17.0	7.6	2.8	-2.1	8.2	-4.0	-1.0	-21.8	10.3	1.5	-.4
E.	COLOMBIA	1.5	-4.8	2.5	1.8	-4.5	3.1	-9.2	6.2	1.5	9.3	-.2	.3
F.	COSTA RICA	-18.5	-29.1	-2.0	33.3	20.4	-2.4	23.8	-5.5	-16.2	-17.5	11.9	14.0
H.	DOMINICAN REP.	21.1	29.1	4.0	1.4	4.6	-2.9	2.6	1.0	-7.1	9.9	7.6	-2.3
I.	ECUADOR	15.7	14.8	6.3	103.7	-5.2	6.2	6.9	4.6	4.4	-19.2	18.2	-3.3
J.	EL SALVADOR	-4.5	11.9	4.2	6.0	5.9	.6	-13.2	-6.2	-7.2	5.7	4.7	1.6
K.	GUATEMALA	-8.4	-25.7	-8.5	3.9	29.1	-3.2	-6.7	-.7	-15.7	-4.5	16.3	.2
M.	HONDURAS	-3.8	4.5	-13.2	2.9	.6	8.9	7.6	-47.8	-64.3	243.5	27.7	-13.6
N.	MEXICO	8.4	4.3	10.9	16.4	6.5	9.3	19.2	10.3	-1.8	.9	1.4	-.1
O.	NICARAGUA	14.5	6.7	5.9	7.4	-17.1	-69.4	245.2	-1.9	-8.3	-7.7	-20.8	15.9
P.	PANAMA	~	~	~	12.3	-16.8	-7.5	-13.2	-22.8	12.0	-.7	-9.1	-16.3
Q.	PARAGUAY	13.5	-1.1	27.6	-12.2	22.3	-4.0	-10.3	-2.4	-15.8	-1.7	-29.5	40.7
R.	PERU	8.5	3.6	.9	4.4	2.5	20.0	.1	4.8	2.7	-5.1	10.9	1.4
S.	URUGUAY	-2.5	7.3	-.1	2.5	5.7	-3.9	-4.5	-6.3	3.7	-23.7	-.1	-9.9
T.	VENEZUELA	15.8	-27.4	13.8	-2.2	1.7	.4	-6.0	-16.9	.8	3.7	-7.5	9.4

SOURCE: SALA calculations from table 1911.

Table 1914

PETROLEUM REFINERY DISTILLATION CAPACITY, 19 LC, 1975-84

(T MET)

	Country	1970	1975	1977	1978	1979	1980	1981	1982	1983	1984
A.	ARGENTINA	23,980	31,310	33,205	33,786	34,235	34,500[†]	34,604	34,600	34,600	34,600
B.	BOLIVIA	1,180	1,290	1,930	1,955	3,715[†]	3,725	2,800[†]	2,800[†]	3,200[†]	3,000[†]
C.	BRAZIL	27,300	51,700	57,500	62,300	62,300[†]	72,200	72,260	76,350	76,780	76,780
D.	CHILE	3,850	6,000	6,000	6,000	6,000[†]	6,000[†]	6,000[†]	6,000[†]	6,000	6,000
E.	COLOMBIA	7,000[†]	8,670	8,670	8,670	8,670[†]	9,680	10,250	10,675	10,810	10,810[†]
F.	COSTA RICA	470	470	470[†]	470[†]	470[†]	550[†]	678	678	678	678
G.	CUBA	4,340	6,000[†]	6,450[†]	6,450[†]	6,450[†]	7,970	7,970	7,970	7,970	7,970
H.	DOMINICAN REP.	~	1,500	1,550	2,350[†]	2,350[†]	2,350[†]	2,350[†]	2,350[†]	2,350[†]	2,350[†]
I.	ECUADOR	1,740	2,190	5,040	5,040	4,800	4,800[†]	4,800[†]	4,800	4,800	4,800[†]
J.	EL SALVADOR	650	750	750[†]	800[†]	800[†]	800[†]	800[†]	800[†]	800[†]	800[†]
K.	GUATEMALA	1,250	1,250	1,250[†]	1,250[†]	1,250[†]	1,250[†]	1,250[†]	1,250[†]	1,250[†]	1,250
M.	HONDURAS	700	700	700	700[†]	700[†]	700[†]	700[†]	700[†]	700[†]	700[†]
N.	MEXICO	29,600	39,250	48,650	49,322	66,910	66,025[†]	66,025[†]	66,025[†]	67,586	68,000[†]
O.	NICARAGUA	650	750	750	750[†]	750[†]	750[†]	750[†]	750[†]	750[†]	750[†]
P.	PANAMA	4,000	5,000	10,000	5,000[†]	5,000[†]	5,000[†]	5,000[†]	5,000[†]	5,000[†]	5,000[†]
Q.	PARAGUAY	500[†]	500[†]	500[†]	500[†]	500[†]	500[†]	350[†]	375[†]	375[†]	375
R.	PERU	4,680	5,540	9,060	9,060	9,060[†]	8,900	8,000[†]	8,400[†]	8,400[†]	8,780[†]
S.	URUGUAY	2,250	2,450	2,450	2,232	2,232	2,232	2,408	2,408	2,408	2,408
T.	VENEZUELA	68,200	77,750	80,220	75,500	75,500	71,645	71,456	70,090	69,407	69,900
	UNITED STATES	643,000	760,000	793,100	839,700	885,200	890,730	792,450	829,642	804,184	770,563

SOURCE: UN-YWES, 1979, table 26; 1981, table 21; 1983; table 16; 1984, table 16.

Table 1915

INDEX OF TOTAL PRODUCTION OF CRUDE PETROLEUM, 10 LC, 1970–84

(1975 = 100)

	Country	1970	1974	1976	1977	1978	1979	1980	1981	1982	1983	1984
A.	ARGENTINA	96	102	100	107	112	117	122	123	121	121	119
B.	BOLIVIA	60	113	101	86	80	69	59	55	61	55	51
C.	BRAZIL	96	103	97	94	93	96	106	128	155	199	277
D.	CHILE	148	112	94	93	78	102	161	196	202	193	189
E.	COLOMBIA	140	107	93	88	83	79	80	85	90	95	106
G.	CUBA	70	74	104	104	127	127	121	112	239	328	341
I.	ECUADOR	~	~	~	~	~	~	128	132	132	148	160
N.	MEXICO	58	80	112	134	172	205	271	326	387	379	389
R.	PERU	100	107	106	127	209	266	271	268	271	238	256
T.	VENEZUELA	159	128	98	96	93	101	94	91	82	77	77
	UNITED STATES	115	105	97	98	104	102	103	102	103	103	106
	WORLD	86	105	109	113	114	118	113	106	101	100	102

SOURCE: UN-YWES, 1979, table 23; 1981, table 18; 1983, table 14; 1984, table 14.

Table 1916

INDEX OF TOTAL CONSUMPTION OF CRUDE PETROLEUM, 19 LC, 1970–84

(1975 = 100)

	Country	1970	1974	1976	1977	1978	1979	1980	1981	1982	1983	1984
A.	ARGENTINA	96	105	104	112	113	115	122	119	115	110	108
B.	BOLIVIA	62	107	101	86	133	149	133	109	111	101	104
C.	BRAZIL	59	100	97	94	122	128	121	121	120	123	129
D.	CHILE	92	125	94	93	121	140	127	117	88	97	98
E.	COLOMBIA	88	107	93	88	98	96	94	99	104	115	120
F.	COSTA RICA	113	147	94	124	148	144	194	175	153	118	147
G.	CUBA	72	93	103	105	108	107	105	111	114	115	116
H.	DOMINICAN REP.	~	76	107	108	112	105	115	119	108	137	127
I.	ECUADOR	54	83	101	94	195	206	221	249	285	268	324
J.	EL SALVADOR	27	87	108	134	118	116	107	92	88	95	97
K.	GUATEMALA	78	98	78	76	87	89	90	87	75	66	79
M.	HONDURAS	112	97	82	85	65	78	78	36	15	42	41
N.	MEXICO	72	98	113	125	131	139	187	207	208	195	206
O.	NICARAGUA	70	92	106	113	99	75	93	102	95	85	68
P.	PANAMA	94	92	69	73	61	54	49	44	46	44	47
Q.	PARAGUAY	91	112	112	111	156	139	155	132	114	105	73
R.	PERU	72	~	~	~	~	~	129	136	142	134	142
S.	URUGUAY	97	93	99	99	100	98	99	92	88	69	67
T.	VENEZUELA	149	141	109	106	109	110	103	98	99	97	96
	UNITED STATES	88	98	108	117	119	118	108	100	95	94	96
	WORLD	86	104	107	113	115	118	113	107	104	103	105

SOURCE: UN-YWES, 1979, table 23; 1981, table 18; 1983, table 14; 1984, table 14.

Table 1917

REFINED PETROLEUM PRODUCTS PRODUCTION,[1] 20 LC, 1950–84

(T MET)

Country	1950	1955	1960	1965	1970	1975	1977	1978	1979	1980	1981	1982	1983	1984
A. ARGENTINA														
Liquefied Petrol. Gas	30	51	74	323	548	677	779	715	718	765	883	900	1,173	1,203
Motor Spirit	1,525	1,681	1,951	32,000	3,978	3,841	4,318	4,475	4,621	5,157	5,121	5,146	5,137	5,005
Kerosene	586	844	1,124	1,057	886	853	796	654	524	591	425	437	527	456
Jet Fuel	3†	4	19	122	301	463	516	578	625	782	786	661	608	661
Distillate Fuel Oils	763	1,170	1,623	3,092	4,829	5,512	6,318	6,418	6,775	7,621	7,778	7,752	7,793	7,823
Residual Fuel Oils	2,573	3,716	6,264	7,990	8,502	7,749	8,584	8,277	8,421	8,134	8,129	7,231	6,539	5,697
Lubricating Oils	85	109	145	140	144	244	294	243	307	277	268	282	282	286
Bitumen (Asphalt)	~	~	263	374	695	429	545	572	677	640†	623	487	393	367
Petroleum Coke	~	~	84	356	663	666	746	896	810	710†	869	970	983	944
B. BOLIVIA														
Liquefied Petrol. Gas	~	6	6	~	3	27	47	66	84	103	148	183	172	171
Motor Spirit	39	108	106	139	220	377	502	497	526	406	324	385	332	340
Kerosene	9	19	52	66	103	143	135	151	133	129	92	90	83	87
Jet Fuel	~	~	~	2	13	43	62	78	70	92	91	68	73	76
Distillate Fuel Oils	6	32	48	73	89	159	232	255	253	261	272	235	214	230
Residual Fuel Oils	25	113	82	124	143	191	226	230	210	151	124	128	140	101
Lubricating Oils	~	~	~	~	7	14	16	14	22	25	19	21	15	16
C. BRAZIL														
Liquefied Petrol. Gas	~	47	242	562	972	1,940	2,100	2,259	2,274	2,342	2,432	2,291	2,588	2,860
Motor Spirit	19	1,323	2,514	4,310	7,067	10,472	10,077	10,781	9,959	10,419	10,531	11,533	11,455	12,814
Kerosene	7	12	519	531	629	830	591	646	700	530	510	518	576	487
Jet Fuel	24	298	~	~	663	1,413	1,448	1,700	1,911	2,170	2,503	2,573	2,260	2,905
Distillate Fuel Oils	14	~	1,378	3,831	5,766	10,316	13,495	14,869	15,350	16,986	16,013	16,889	16,817	17,675
Residual Fuel Oils	~	1,560	3,561	5,282	8,439	14,762	15,207	16,896	17,100	16,515	15,517	13,644	12,238	12,431
Lubricating Oils	~	~	~	5	11	218	331	288	485	556	546	659	675†	675
Bitumen (Asphalt)	3†	40†	207	300	702	807	974	1,269	1,316	1,028	888	973	800†	774
Petroleum Coke	~	~	~	~	#	116	~	~	~	182	212	210	225†	271
D. CHILE														
Liquefied Petrol. Gas	~	7	29	46	226	457	471	509	481	479	483	403	443	448
Motor Spirit	~	213	527	751	1,137	899	926	1,003	1,010	990	1,052	856	947	956
Kerosene	~	15	142	240	354	322	344	311	260	227	215	164	172	111
Jet Fuel	~	~	~	~	62	95	135	164	165	158	195	147	145	164
Distillate Fuel Oils	~	99	264	418	607	824	876	1,053	1,207	1,211	1,089	850	1,048	1,107
Residual Fuel Oils	~	251	378	679a	1,090	1,332	1,575	1,649	1,645	1,629	1,430	1,008	1,065	1,005
Lubricating Oils	~	~	~	~	~	~	~	~	~	~	~	~	~	~
Bitumen (Asphalt)	~	~	~	~	7	6	~	~	~	6†	31	23	8	7
E. COLOMBIA														
Liquefied Petrol. Gas	~	~	46	95	292	320	309	290	285	260	281	263	344	354
Motor Spirit	227	556	1,022	1,410	1,810	2,311	2,426	1,963	1,797	2,138	2,438	2,434	2,456	2,765
Kerosene	50	145	232	250	457	432	403	395	413	352	336	291	293	263
Jet Fuel	~	~	6	31	167	315	371	406	453	453	502	539	541	450
Distillate Fuel Oils	76	201	460	636	920	916	1,039	1,101	1,074	1,187	1,337	1,335	1,430	1,436
Residual Fuel Oils	926	834	1,450	1,515	2,470	2,643	2,783	2,862	2,304	2,566	2,462	2,691	2,943	2,912
Lubricating Oils	11	9	10	60	68	9	5	7	10†	10†	6†	5†	10†	15†
Bitumen (Asphalt)	~	~	28	30	116	92	76	99	117	156	187	184	148	159
Petroleum Coke	~	~	98	109	158	148	151	155†	175†	150†	140†	90†	100†	175†
F. COSTA RICA														
Liquefied Petrol. Gas	~	~	~	~	1	5	7	9	8	8	7	7	3	4
Motor Spirit	~	~	~	~	57	60	65	74	70	87	85	87	69	74
Kerosene	~	~	~	~	18	22	22	24	24	20	12	11	10	12
Jet Fuel	~	~	~	~	~	~	~	~	~	~	~	~	~	~
Distillate Fuel Oils	~	~	~	~	116	63	75	96	85	151	143	116	75	104
Residual Fuel Oils	~	~	~	~	112	113	162	172	181	216	212	176	144	183
Bitumen (Asphalt)	~	~	~	~	~	5	~	~	~	12†	11	9	12	12

Table 1917 (Continued)

REFINED PETROLEUM PRODUCTS PRODUCTION,[1] 20 LC, 1950–84
(T MET)

Country	1950	1955	1960	1965	1970	1975	1977	1978	1979	1980	1981	1982	1983	1984
G. CUBA														
Liquefied Petrol. Gas	~	~	~	52	57	83	96	102	92	106	104	112	106	116
Motor Spirit	84	118	710	810	745	947	828	885	872	1,898	2,143	2,286	2,285	2,488
Kerosene	59	107	130	202	401	447	436	427	415	438	429	456	494	506
Jet Fuel	~	~	~	~	~	~	~	~	~	39	57	76	66	89
Distillate Fuel Oils	54	129	606	643	583	1,084	1,020	1,083	1,094	1,098	1,118	1,117	1,060	1,020
Residual Fuel Oils	38	81	1,654	1,899	2,367	2,821	3,209	3,101	3,213	3,026	3,130	3,198	3,414	3,437
Lubricating Oils	~	~	~	67	95	151	170†	126	133	130	115	137	138	125
Bitumen (Asphalt)	~	~	~	10	63	148	157†	202	173	196	210	198	223	234
Petroleum Coke	~	~	~	~	9	17	~	~	~	20	18	18	20	24
H. DOMINICAN REP.														
Liquefied Petrol. Gas	~	~	~	~	~	47	53	62	67	53	42	45	45	43
Motor Spirit	~	~	~	~	~	322	322	321	301	289	267	240	260	295
Kerosene	~	~	~	~	~	17	14	19	27	69	71	72	81	93
Jet Fuel	~	~	~	~	~	34	32	36	40	42	45	17	19	20
Distillate Fuel Oils	~	~	~	~	~	370	369	357	347	393	374	351	476	407
Residual Fuel Oils	~	~	~	~	~	369	399	427	353	536	659	457	815	537
I. ECUADOR														
Liquefied Petrol. Gas	1	1	1	1	5	5	14	46	70	75	65	78	55	93
Motor Spirit	62	78	204	254	365	668	581	858	958	968	918	890	720	926
Kerosene	16	25	39	57	65	184	245	350	322	292	284	325	265	293
Jet Fuel	~	~	4	23	79	60	48	127	146	139	148	137	117	135
Distillate Fuel Oils	33	47	96	133	255	436	285	625	711	785	694	723	605	749
Residual Fuel Oils	104	117	194	224	352	541	748	1,966	2,096	2,260	2,163	2,189	1,886	2,110
Lubricating Oils	1	1	13	16	9	19	28	33	37	42	43	46	32	39
Bitumen (Asphalt)	~	~	~	~	#	#	~	~	~	52	48	49	42	55†
J. EL SALVADOR														
Liquefied Petrol. Gas	~	~	~	3	4	18	23	26	28	26	24	22	25	27
Motor Spirit	~	~	~	104	36	115	142	155	153	128	115	107	120	127
Kerosene	~	~	~	52	15	32	47	40	42	27	23	27	20	26
Jet Fuel	~	~	~	27	6	14	11	9	9	17	17	17	20	18
Distillate Fuel Oils	~	~	~	140	43	206	219	232	240	194	182	171	185	181
Residual Fuel Oils	~	~	~	105	68	220	251	227	213	191	193	182	190	196
Bitumen (Asphalt)	~	~	~	~	~	21	22	22	18	16	20†	20†	22†	21†
K. GUATEMALA														
Liquefied Petrol. Gas	~	~	~	3	9	6	4	4	3	2	2	2	3	5
Motor Spirit	~	~	~	105	163	209	131	144	132	108	109	100	104	122
Kerosene	~	~	~	27	49	51	30	31	35	37	35	29	32	33
Jet Fuel	~	~	~	16	31	39	34	41	46	32	27	25	28	29
Distillate Fuel Oils	~	~	~	98	215	225	204	261	259	242	222	204	200	232
Residual Fuel Oils	~	~	~	155	257	360	303	326	307	313	334	246	209	251
L. HAITI				~	~	~	~	~	~	~	~	~	~	~
M. HONDURAS														
Liquefied Petrol. Gas	~	~	~	~	4	8	7	4	3	3	4	3	4	4
Motor Spirit	~	~	~	~	106	84	104	90	86	81	42	26	50	55
Kerosene	~	~	~	~	30	32	40†	37	40	40	8	0	5	8
Jet Fuel	~	~	~	~	6	11	17	15	19	20	18	10	10	12
Distillate Fuel Oils	~	~	~	~	214	172	235	171	190	202	58	12	89	90
Residual Fuel Oils	~	~	~	~	348	313	130	99	118	141	56	32	87	90

Table 1917 (Continued)

REFINED PETROLEUM PRODUCTS PRODUCTION,[1] 20 LC, 1950–84

(T MET)

Country	1950	1955	1960	1965	1970	1975	1977	1978	1979	1980	1981	1982	1983	1984
N. MEXICO[2]														
Liquefied Petrol. Gas	50	101	334	503	1,134	1,620	2,650	2,320	2,838	3,763	4,258	4,726	4,854	4,479
Motor Spirit	1,298	1,831	3,090	4,514	5,913	7,839	8,513	10,233	11,878	13,983	15,360	14,736	15,117	15,000
Kerosene	547	888	1,413	1,567	1,461	1,666	1,715	1,783	1,893	1,953	1,938	2,130	1,835	1,800
Jet Fuel	~	~	23	138	397	718	973	952	1,179	1,299	1,360	1,439	1,288	1,275
Distillate Fuel Oils	735	680	1,649	2,908	4,206	7,626	9,113	9,792	10,619	12,364	13,629	11,652	11,309	11,848
Residual Fuel Oils	4,883	7,221	6,354	6,325	7,195	9,853	12,283	13,355	13,143	17,053	19,131	19,279	19,306	20,956
Lubricating Oils	27	81	151	195	276	423	391	413	400	404	494	408	345	375
Bitumen (Asphalt)	32	178	299	249	1,076	342	298	440	351	1,017	1,100	1,205	1,023	1,311
Petroleum Coke	~	~	~	~	54	71	20	100	89	30	46	93	86	85†
O. NICARAGUA														
Liquefied Petrol. Gas	~	~	~	2	9	13	16	16	13	16	17	16	16	14
Motor Spirit	~	~	~	79	109	141	167	136	121	134	133	107	90	61
Kerosene[3]	~	~	~	25	27	17	15	16	13	14	17	19	20	27
Jet Fuel	~	~	~	65	129	159	172	181	131	174	198	168	160	127
Distillate Fuel Oils	~	~	~	47	158	243	284†	184	117	160	217	228	221	180
Residual Fuel Oils	~	~	~	~	~	31	32†	16	15†	15†	13	6	4	3
Bitumen (Asphalt)														
P. PANAMA														
Liquefied Petrol. Gas	~	~	~	314	19	35	31	27	23	22	20	25	20	25
Motor Spirit	~	~	~	95	386	342	289	305	277	240	220	210	220	225
Kerosene	~	~	~	44	54	16	25	11	10	10	12	15	16	15
Jet Fuel	~	~	~	702	318	337	238	148	135	125	100	100	100	100
Distillate Fuel Oils	~	~	~	1,210	725	662	607	632	576	462	400	400	400	450
Residual Fuel Oils	~	~	~	~	2,048	2,366	1,590	1,191	1,021	1,001	900	940	875	900
Bitumen (Asphalt)	~	~	~	~	90	10†	15†	20†	20†	18†	20†	25†	20†	25†
Q. PARAGUAY														
Liquefied Petrol. Gas	~	~	~	~	3	4	4	4	4	2	3	6	7	3
Motor Spirit	~	~	~	~	77	51	76	94	85	106	63	64	58	46
Kerosene	~	~	~	~	19	14	19	17	20	16	12	8	10	11
Jet Fuel	~	~	~	~	5	6	9	10	10	13	14	13	11	2
Distillate Fuel Oils	~	~	~	~	34	80	70	110	95	115	112	99	97	71
Residual Fuel Oils	~	~	~	~	33	41	50	56	50	56	59	35	30	22
Bitumen (Asphalt)	~	~	~	~	3	4†	5†	2	2†	2†	2†	2†	1†	~
R. PERU														
Liquefied Petrol. Gas	4	6	7	22[d]	27	167	112	110	122	106	129	139	133	140
Motor Spirit	454	551	576	711	1,116	1,525	1,410	1,306	1,540	1,533	1,642	1,600	1,400	1,550
Kerosene	153	327	470	423	510	605	646	713	793	868	902	916	775	800
Jet Fuel	~	~	32	102	198	238	171	233	342	387	425	371	315	345
Distillate Fuel Oils	194	547	705	865	929	1,006	1,009	1,348	1,653	1,712	1,801	1,676	1,475	1,600
Residual Fuel Oils'	832	473	372	820	1,231	1,931	2,333	2,194	2,335	2,511	2,564	2,848	3,000	3,035
Lubricating Oils	11	12	10	12[c]	11	12	19†	20	20	12	15†	21	15†	20†
Bitumen (Asphalt)	11	30	9	33	47	38	40†	35	30	39	42	52	50†	55†
S. URUGUAY														
Liquefied Petrol. Gas	~	~	~	17	31	29	26	38	37	40	36	44	41	47
Motor Spirit	173	239	243	268	244	268	227	238	225	207	185	204	164	173
Kerosene	153	327	470	166	168	160	154†	149	133	124	96	88	80	66
Jet Fuel	~	~	7	14	23	23	35	28	41	28	26	28	19	9
Distillate Fuel Oils	63	167	205	307	361	423	464	513	460	473	468	492	432	444
Residual Fuel Oils	376	581	651	751	785	816	815†	763	788	845	788	701	437	392
Lubricating Oils	~	~	2	1	#	#†	5†	1†	8	7	6	7	6†	6†
Bitumen (Asphalt)	~	~	11	19	41†	39†	35	48	59	51	37	54	40	37
Petroleum Coke	~	~	~	~	11	9	~	~	~	15	12	12	12	11

Table 1917 (Continued)

REFINED PETROLEUM PRODUCTS PRODUCTION,[1] 20 LC, 1950–84

(T MET)

Country	1950	1955	1960	1965	1970	1975	1977	1978	1979	1980	1981	1982	1983	1984
VENEZUELA														
Liquefied Petrol. Gas	111	316	640	489	1,295	1,842	2,125	1,667	1,957	1,647	1,429	1,505	1,298	1,535
Motor Spirit[4]	620†	1,215†	1,755†	2,247	3,138	4,674	5,560	6,095	6,774	6,772	7,009	8,095	9,200	9,196
Kerosene	282	984	1,223	1,038	554	421	845	492	482	560	678	473	572	729
Jet Fuel	~	~	473	2,206	3,494	1,062	1,379	1,441	1,391	1,498	1,457	1,850	2,486	1,834
Distillate Fuel Oils	2,378	5,727	7,671	9,584	7,628	6,908	6,922	7,129	7,737	8,809	8,562	8,679	9,338	10,633
Residual Fuel Oils	7,879	15,832	28,613	40,917	44,939	26,953	30,242	31,139	30,764	25,653	22,220	21,153	16,424	16,000
Lubricating Oils	523	143	209	527	551	497	400	411	439	469	392	355	343	333
Bitumen (Asphalt)	109	163	1,047	912	849	564	709	917	1,219	1,135	1,531	1,540	1,432	1,408
Petroleum Coke	#	~	#	~	160	120†	~	~	~	125†	149†	99†	132†	125†
UNITED STATES														
Liquefied Petrol. Gas	7,530	13,015	20,045	26,433	45,123	47,859	49,073	48,169	48,765	48,229	49,225	47,865	51,442	53,310
Motor Spirit	108,835	143,274	166,192	193,554	245,377	279,999	302,009	307,850	294,223	280,194	275,053	272,153	272,257	277,887
Kerosene	15,262	7,169	15,085	11,996	12,321	7,170	8,064	7,254	8,601	6,447	5,613	5,406	5,153	5,385
Jet Fuel	~	~	15,150†	27,516	38,883	40,950	45,722	45,580	47,548	47,081	45,487	45,974	48,055	53,356
Distillate Fuel Oils	55,177	83,344	92,266	105,824	124,085	133,983	165,470	159,910	159,173	134,743	131,932	131,579	124,006	135,722
Residual Fuel Oils	64,224	63,486	50,167	40,564	38,894	68,113	96,685	91,927	92,976	87,364	72,814	58,962	46,952	49,267
Lubricating Oils	7,403	7,990	8,498	9,004	9,470	8,045	9,227	9,940	10,157	9,318	8,666	7,389	7,699	8,335
Bitumen (Asphalt)	10,698	15,051	17,236	21,449	24,190	23,744	28,588	28,588	27,908	23,339	20,412	19,743	22,431	23,370
Petroleum Coke	3,122	5,141	10,877	15,594	19,551	23,449	24,447	24,418	24,907	24,580	25,842	27,132	27,816	29,118
WORLD														
Liquefied Petrol. Gas	8,072	15,321	26,182	45,029	81,477	99,925	105,568	111,322	119,926	118,931	120,488	125,752	130,332	136,031
Motor Spirit	148,543	213,861	273,626	365,848	478,095	585,457	635,270	657,426	655,723	650,077	643,643	642,584	649,506	664,104
Kerosene	30,937	41,421	55,921	64,546	91,796	104,865	124,672	122,599	129,077	110,491	108,634	109,595	111,559	115,205
Jet Fuel	472	12,414	25,338	50,700	81,373	89,900	96,661	99,362	105,789	106,422	104,894	106,241	109,362	115,865
Distillate Fuel Oils	94,942	157,588	219,722	322,560	482,643	589,398	681,875	699,278	727,867	722,837	695,204	693,208	692,518	720,144
Residual Fuel Oils	175,429	235,150	330,798	513,241	798,319	880,417	957,639	956,250	974,154	904,535	829,239	765,109	728,156	722,101
Lubricating Oils	10,016	12,181	14,631	18,335	28,721	31,228	35,120	36,788	39,469	41,241	39,282	37,411	38,485	40,280
Bitumen (Asphalt)	13,654	21,833	30,668	42,688	75,457	85,721	92,372	98,485	102,009	100,389	95,854	95,164	98,743	100,112
Petroleum Coke	3,142	5,535	12,017	17,186	22,534	27,052	29,152	30,647	31,449	31,458	32,636	34,846	35,919	37,478

1. The figures in this table refer to the liquid fuels, lubricant oils, and solid and semisolid products obtained by distillation of domestic and imported crude petroleum, shale oil, or unfinished petroleum products. So far as possible, the figures include fuels consumed in refining but exclude oils obtained from natural gas, coal, lignite, and their derivatives.

Liquefied petroleum gas. A hydrocarbon fraction of the paraffin series lighter than gasoline derived from the distillation of crude petroleum only (excluding LPG from natural gas or liquefied natural gas and also unliquefied gases). It is presented in the liquid state by compression or absorption process to facilitate storage, transport, and handling. It mainly consists of butanes (normal butane and isobutane) and propane or a mixture of them, and is used in domestic heating, as fuel and as solvent.

Motor spirit. Blended light petroleum fuel. Commonly known as petrol or gasoline, suitable as a fuel in spark-ignition internal-combustion engines.

Aviation gasoline. Any of the specially blended grades of gasoline, with high antiknock value, high stability, a high volatility, and low freezing point, intended for use in aviation piston power unit only.

Kerosene. A refined crude petroleum fuel, in volatility between motor spirit and gas oil, free of gasolines and heavy hydrocarbons such as gas oil and lubricating oil. It is used as an illuminant and as a fuel in certain types of spark-ignition engines such as those used for agricultural tractors and stationary engines. The data cover those products commonly termed as burning oil, vaporizing oil, power kerosene illuminating oil, and also white spirit (used commonly as a paint thinner).

Jet fuels. Fuel meeting the required properties for use in jet engines and aircraft turbine engines, mainly refined from kerosene; gasoline-type jet fuel is included.

Distillate fuel oils. A fuel oil which is a crude petroleum distillate, having a viscosity and distillation range between those of kerosene and lubricating oil; used as a fuel for internal combustion in diesel engines, as a burner fuel in heating installations such as furnaces, and for enriching water gas to increase its luminosity. The data cover those products commonly termed as diesel fuel (diesel oil) or gas oil, solar oil, etc.

Residual fuel oil. A fuel oil which is crude petroleum residues, such as viscous residuum, obtained by the refinery operations of crude petroleum after gasoline, kerosene, and sometimes heavier distillates (such as gas oil or diesel oil) have been removed. It is commonly used by ships and industrial, large-scale heating installations as a fuel in furnace or boilers firing to produce heat and power (known as mazout).

Lubricating oils. A heavy liquid distillate obtained by refining crude petroleum, used for lubricating purposes. It may be produced either from petroleum distillates or residues at refineries. Solid lubricants (e.g., grease) are excluded.

Bitumen. Brown or black solid or semisolid material, obtained as a residue in the distillation of crude petroleum; used mainly for asphalt paving in road construction. Excluding that which may be obtained from natural occurrence.

Petroleum coke. A solid residue consisting mainly of carbon, obtained by the distillation of heavier petroleum oils, used mainly in metallurgical processes (excluding those solid residues obtained from carbonization of coal).

2. Including aviation spirit.
3. Including jet fuel.
4. Including naphtha prior to 1968.
a. Excluding quantities used at refineries and lost.
b. Data not strictly comparable with those of previous years.
c. Including grease.
d. Including liquefied petroleum gas made from natural gas.
e. Including aviation spirit.

SOURCE: SALA, 16-226; UN-SP: J, 14-16 (1970-1973), tables 9, 11, 12, 13, 14, J, 19 (1976), tables 9, 11, 12, 13, 14; J, 20 (1977), tables 9, 11, 12, 13, 14; J, 21 (1978), tables 9, 11, 12, 13, 14; J, 22 (1979), tables 13, 15, 16, 17, 18; UN-YWES, 1979, tables 28 and 30; UN-SP: J, 19 (1950-74), tables 9, 11, 12, 13 and 14; UN-YWES, 1981, tables 22 through 28 and 30; 1982, tables 19, 21, 22–25, 27; 1983, tables 17, 19, 20–23, 25; 1984, tables 17, 19, 20–23, 25.

Table 1918

CONSUMPTION OF PETROLEUM AND DERIVATIVES, 19 L, 1960–84

(T Barrels)

	Country	1960	1973	1978	1979	1980	1981	1982	1983	1984[‡]
A.	ARGENTINA	95,285	167,766	138,113	177,285	168,266	173,777	168,240	142,465	139,095
B.	BOLIVIA	1,819	4,526	7,625	7,261	8,690	8,689	9,720	8,445	~
C.	BRAZIL	96,106	281,654	385,368	411,237	413,882	372,715	373,709	350,927	363,279
D.	CHILE	16,179	37,376	36,736	37,258	36,941	39,057	36,376	34,562	34,718
E.	COLOMBIA	21,179	47,270	53,206	59,814	60,375	56,420	56,474	60,890	61,897
F.	COSTA RICA	1,304	3,797	6,927	5,957	5,343	4,549	3,789	3,810	3,962
H.	DOMINICAN REP.	2,835	12,331	14,879	15,879	15,123	14,892	14,277	16,256	17,667
I.	ECUADOR	3,806	10,795	22,786	25,526	28,020	30,194	30,322	27,741	29,337
J.	EL SALVADOR	1,588	3,972	5,067	4,761	3,909	3,572	3,971	3,987	4,004
K.	GUATEMALA	3,523	7,014	10,702	11,575	11,422	10,177	9,199	8,308	9,023
L.	HAITI	620	971	1,697	1,775	1,674	1,670	1,528	~	~
M.	HONDURAS	1,495	3,283	3,792	4,711	5,019	3,723	4,000[†]	2,945	3,043
N.	MEXICO	104,100	175,930	334,340	376,315	455,520	531,440	523,775	520,125	544,215
O.	NICARAGUA	1,418	4,107	6,226	4,302	5,000	4,730	4,649	4,652	4,573
P.	PANAMA	2,845	6,405	7,266	7,098	7,200[†]	~	~	~	6,249
Q.	PARAGUAY	673	1,750	3,100	3,032	3,215	3,107	3,553	3,300	3,712
R.	PERU	18,514	39,085	43,300	44,700	48,253	48,180	46,927	40,626	41,623
S.	URUGUAY	9,888	12,509	12,850	12,052	13,597	12,245	11,981	9,161	8,605
T.	VENEZUELA	46,683	92,548	109,183	120,251	133,900	142,100	143,100	143,300	131,600

SOURCE: IDB-SPTF, yearly, 1978–85, table 69.

Table 1919

ACTUAL AND POTENTIAL PROVEN RESERVES AND PRODUCTION OF CRUDE PETROLEUM
AND NATURAL GAS, 19 L, 1960–82

PART I: 1960 AND 1975

		Crude Petroleum						Natural Gas					
		Reserves (M Barrels)		Production (M Barrels)		Production Potential[1] (Years)		Reserves (B Cubic Feet)		Production (B Cubic Feet)		Production Potential[1] (Years)	
	Country	1960	1975	1960	1975	1960	1975	1961	1975	1961	1975	1961	1975
A.	ARGENTINA	1,550	2,465	63.9	144.4	24.2	17.1	6,004	7,200	156.3	276.0	38.4	26.1
B.	BOLIVIA	125	235	3.1	14.7	40.1	16.0	250	10,800	5.8	137.4	53.1	78.6

Continued in SALA, 24–1918.

Table 1920

NATURAL GAS PRODUCTION,[1] 20 LC, 1970–84
(T TJ)

	Country	1970	1975	1979	1980	1981	1982	1983	1984
A.	ARGENTINA	209.0	265.5	302.9	326.9	340.2	392.8	456.5	478.2
B.	BOLIVIA	1.3	59.1	74.1	79.8	90.0	93.3	89.7	87.8
C.	BRAZIL	3.3	24.6	38.1	41.2	37.1	42.9	63.0	80.8
D.	CHILE	48.1	45.8	40.7	27.1	33.4	34.5	36.7	36.8
E.	COLOMBIA	55.2	73.2	117.1	150.6	164.1	176.1	183.2	187.1
F.	COSTA RICA	#	#	#	#	#	#	#	#
G.	CUBA	~	.7	.7	.7	.4	.4	.3	.1
H.	DOMINICAN REP.	#	#	#	#	#	#	#	#
I.	ECUADOR	.7	1.5	1.7	1.5	2.6	3.5	4.1	3.7
J.	EL SALVADOR	* #	#	#	#	#	#	#	#
K.	GUATEMALA	#	#	#	#	#	#	#	#
L.	HAITI	#	#	#	#	#	#	#	#
M.	HONDURAS	#	#	#	#	#	#	#	#
N.	MEXICO	450.9	523.5	802.5	1,036	1,033	1,068	1,048	977.4
O.	NICARAGUA	#	#	#	#	#	#	#	#
P.	PANAMA	#	#	#	#	#	#	#	#
Q.	PARAGUAY	#	#	#	#	#	#	#	#
R.	PERU	16.0	27.4	29.4	43.7	48.6	43.8	40.3	43.5
S.	URUGUAY	#	#	#	#	#	#	#	#
T.	VENEZUELA	381.9	480.4	600.2	643.0	646.8	682.4	667.7	737.2
	UNITED STATES	22,860	20,723	21,275	19,256	19,057	17,655	15,986	17,181
	WORLD	38,440	46,232	59,376	53,938	54,471	54,079	54,586	58,294

1. Natural gas comprises any combustible gas of natural origin from underground sources
   consisting primarily of hydrocarbons.

SOURCE: UN-YWES, 1981, table 35; 1983, table 28; 1984, table 28.

Table 1921

HARD COAL PRODUCTION,[1] 20 LC, 1970–84
(T MET)

	Country	1970	1975	1979	1980	1981	1982	1983	1984
A.	ARGENTINA	616	502	727	390	498	515	486	509
B.	BOLIVIA	#	#	#	#	#	#	#	#
C.	BRAZIL	2,361	2,817	4,643[†]	5,240	5,689	6,346	6,737	7,461
D.	CHILE	1,351	1,461	926	968	1,099	985	990	1,184
E.	COLOMBIA	2,268	3,447	4,885	4,947	5,030	5,550	6,000[†]	6,100[†]
F.	COSTA RICA	#	#	#	#	#	#	#	#
G.	CUBA	#	#	#	#	#	#	#	#
H.	DOMINICAN REP.	#	#	#	#	#	#	#	#
I.	ECUADOR	#	#	#	#	#	#	#	#
J.	EL SALVADOR	#	#	#	#	#	#	#	#
K.	GUATEMALA	#	#	#	#	#	#	#	#
L.	HAITI	#	#	#	#	#	#	#	#
M.	HONDURAS	#	#	#	#	#	#	#	#
N.	MEXICO	2,959	5,193	7,357	7,010	8,086	7,637	7,800[†]	7,800[†]
O.	NICARAGUA	#	#	#	#	#	#	#	#
P.	PANAMA	#	#	#	#	#	#	#	#
Q.	PARAGUAY	#	#	#	#	#	#	#	#
R.	PERU	156	23	51	56[†]	106[†]	100[†]	90[†]	85[†]
S.	URUGUAY	#	#	#	#	#	#	#	#
T.	VENEZUELA	40	60	55	44	46	47	39	51
	UNITED STATES	550,388	575,901	670,483	710,384	700,845	712,777	656,568	750,262
	WORLD	824,911	992,116	1,166,881	2,728,475	2,728,259	2,828,905	2,824,571	2,941,782

1. Hard coal comprises all grades of anthracite and bituminous coal with a gross calorific
   value over 5,700 calories per gram. Includes lignite, brown coal, and peat.

SOURCE: UN-YWES, 1981, table 7; 1983, table 6; 1984, table 6.

Table 1922

BITUMINOUS COAL/ANTHRACITE RESOURCES, 6 LC
(M MET)

	Country	Year	Total	Proven Reserves In Place	Proven Reserves Recoverable	Additional Resources
C.	BRAZIL	1978	1,717	270	189	1,447
D.	CHILE	1979	522	231	27	291
E.	COLOMBIA	1979	9,225	2,025	1,010	7,200
N.	MEXICO	1981	2,800[b]	1,623	1,295	1,960
R.	PERU	1981	960[b]	28	~	856
T.	VENEZUELA	1981	4,861[b]	161[b]	275	1,000
	UNITED STATES	1979	1,286,366[a]	223,725	125,353	472,103

a. 1974 estimate.
b. 1979 estimate.

SOURCE: UN-YWES, 1979 and 1980, table 56; UN-YES, 1983, table 38.

Table 1923

SUB-BITUMINOUS COAL/LIGNITE RESOURCES 10 LC
(M MET)

	Country	Year	Total	Proven Reserves In Place	Proven Reserves Recoverable	Additional Resources
A.	ARGENTINA	1981	9,900[b]	195	130	7,735
C.	BRAZIL	1981	14,090[b]	23,000	13,000	12,770
D.	CHILE	1979	5,285	1,150	1,150	4,135
E.	COLOMBIA	1979	~	48	25	790
I.	ECUADOR	1981	36[c]	#	18	6
L.	HAITI	1979	40	13	~	27
M.	HONDURAS	1979	21	~	~	~
N.	MEXICO	1981	980[c]	620	496	400
R.	PERU	1979	~	~	~	100
T.	VENEZUELA	1981	4,317[c]	17[c]	34	14,058
	UNITED STATES	1979	2,313,291[a]	205,113	131,750	669,321

a. 1974 estimate.
b. 1978 estimate.
c. 1979 estimate.

SOURCE: UN-YWES, 1979 and 1980, table 56; UN-YES, 1983, table 38.

Table 1924

GEOTHERMAL ENERGY INSTALLED
CAPACITY, 5 LC, 1980–2000
(T Kw)

	Country	1980	1985	1990	1995	2000
D.	CHILE	#	#	15	15[a]	15[a]
F.	COSTA RICA	#	#	80	380	380
J.	EL SALVADOR	95	150	260	425	535
N.	MEXICO	150	620	1,000	2,000	4,000
O.	NICARAGUA	#	#	35	35	100
	UNITED STATES	923	1,674	4,374	4,974	5,284

a. Minimum estimate.

SOURCE: Mexico-NAFINSA-MV, August 17, 1981, p. 863.

Table 1925

ELECTRICAL ENERGY PRODUCTION,[1] 20 LC, 1975-84[a]

(M KWH)

	1975		1980		1981		1982		1983		1984	
Country	Total	Hydro-Electric	Total	Hydro-Electric	Total	Hydro-Electric	Total	Hydro-Electric	Total	Hydro-Electric	Total	Hydro-Electric
A. ARGENTINA	29,468	5,197	39,676	15,148	38,838	14,665	39,804	17,586	42,998	18,419	44,914	19,874
B. BOLIVIA	1,057	800	1,564	1,080	1,677	1,155	1,677	1,205	1,698	1,169	1,695	1,195
C. BRAZIL[2]	78,936	72,287	139,485	128,907	142,198	130,765	151,999	141,132	161,969	151,475	175,710	165,414
D. CHILE	8,732	6,135	11,751	7,343	11,979	7,589	11,872	8,459	12,624	8,933	13,490	9,325
E. COLOMBIA	14,025	9,851	22,935	16,717	24,195	17,642	25,605	18,553	27,100	19,600	27,800	20,200
F. COSTA RICA	1,531	1,301	2,227	2,130	2,355	2,253	2,464	2,380	2,869	2,783	3,067	2,975
G. CUBA	6,583	62	9,896	97	10,559	60	11,070	43	11,551	63	12,292	70
H. DOMINICAN REP.[2]	2,556	54	3,317	578	3,582	818	3,206	757	3,400	780	4,009	514
I. ECUADOR	1,650	647	3,352	887	3,730	791	4,118	899	4,289	1,730	4,400	1,750
J. EL SALVADOR	1,059	404	1,544	1,078	1,474	763	1,489	800	1,600	850	1,684	890
K. GUATEMALA	1,167	382	1,617	278	1,593	343	1,552	479	1,560	805	1,625	601
L. HAITI	158	123	315	220	325	225	360	250	373	260	375	260
M. HONDURAS	545	419	928	783	1,014	821	1,090	870	1,150	900	1,060	874
N. MEXICO	43,329	15,140	66,954	16,910	73,559	24,618	80,589	22,924	82,343	20,741	87,083	23,583
O. NICARAGUA	932	371	1,049	515	1,106	496	1,054	425	941	252	973	235
P. PANAMA	1,447	98	2,454	1,182	2,037	1,334	2,238	1,074	2,389	866	2,360	1,491
Q. PARAGUAY	598	538	700	575	785	708	832	647	978	783	1,095	886
R. PERU	7,486	5,470	9,805	7,622	10,757	7,997	11,351	8,401	10,675	8,111	11,769	8,704
S. URUGUAY	2,444	1,132	4,559	3,477	3,588	2,546	3,592	2,445	3,691	3,538	3,637	3,500
T. VENEZUELA	19,591	8,898	35,932	14,337	37,542	15,090	39,964	16,000	42,000	17,700	44,370	19,665
UNITED STATES[2]	2,003,002	303,153	2,354,384	277,721	2,359,258	262,295	2,302,287	310,739	2,367,637	333,564	2,472,304	322,550
WORLD	6,518,535	1,456,368	8,247,331	1,755,010	8,383,918	1,775,735	8,473,725	1,820,550	8,820,705	1,902,451	9,267,420	1,952,633

1. Unless otherwise indicated, the data refer to the production of generating centers and therefore include station use and transmission loss. "Total" refers to all. "Total" minus "Hydroelectric" production generally equals "Thermal" (not given), except for data on the United States. Unless stated otherwise, production includes electrical energy produced for both public and industrial purposes.

2. Production of industrial establishments nil or negligible.

a. For data prior to 1975 see SALA, 21-2008.

SOURCE: UN-YWES, 1979, tables 49 and 50; 1981, table 42; 1983, table 34; 1984, table 34.

Table 1926

ELECTRICITY CONSUMPTION,[1] 20 LC, 1929–84[a]

(Total = B Kw, Per Capita = KWH)

Year	A. ARGENTINA Total	Per Capita	B. BOLIVIA Total	Per Capita	C. BRAZIL Total	Per Capita	D. CHILE Total	Per Capita	E. COLOMBIA Total	Per Capita	F. COSTA RICA Total	Per Capita	G. CUBA Total	Per Capita	H. DOMINICAN REP. Total	Per Capita	I. ECUADOR Total	Per Capita	J. EL SALVADOR Total	Per Capita	K. GUATEMALA Total	Per Capita	UNITED STATES Total	Per Capita	WORLD Total	Per Capita
1929	1.67	143	.02	8	.74	22	.68	158	.15	21	.03	61	.20	56	.01	8	.04	21	.02	14	.02	12	92.18	756	255.9	134
1937	2.20	162	.05	19	2.03	52	1.45	302	.29	34	.06	104	.26	62	.02	13	.05	22	.03	19	.03	14	118.91	922	411.4	205
1950	4.43	259	.20	67	4.70	90	3.00	492	.71	61	.10	125	.76	138	.08	36	.13	41	.08	42	.07	25	329.14	2,164	959.2	386
1960	10.5	510	.5	135	22.9	328	4.6	597	3.8	265	.4	374	2.7	399	.4	116	.4	90	.3	103	.3	75	848.8	4,698	2,300.9	772
1970	21.7	915	.8	184	45.4	491	7.6	806	8.8	426	1.0	595	4.9	570	1.0	247	.9	159	.7	190	.8	144	1,642.0	8,008	4,953.8	1,393
1971	23.6	981	.8	189	51.0	535	8.5	893	9.5	450	1.1	638	5.0	578	1.0	253	1.0	170	.7	204	.8	158	1,721.1	8,312	5,269.2	1,413
1972	25.3	1,037	.9	193	64.7	582	8.9	919	11.0	508	1.3	687	5.3	594	1.2	279	1.1	175	.8	228	.9	169	1,861.1	8,911	5,398.7	1,501
1973	26.7	1,081	.9	198	64.8	664	8.8	889	12.6	564	1.3	719	5.7	631	2.3	509	1.3	190	.9	242	1.0	178	1,979.1	9,339	6,127.7	1,584
1974	28.0	1,119	1.0	208	80.3	701	9.3	923	13.2	575	1.4	764	6.0	655	2.4	527	1.4	209	1.0	254	1.1	187	1,980.0	9,344	6,313.8	1,604
1975	29.5	1,164	1.1	216	79.0	744	8.7	857	14.0	594	1.5	778	6.6	705	2.6	544	1.7	234	1.1	264	1.2	187	2,009.2	9,303	6,516.7	1,626
1976	30.4	1,184	1.1	225	90.1	812	9.3	888	15.5	637	1.6	818	7.2	761	2.6	534	1.9	258	1.2	291	1.3	198	2,417.4	9,901	6,983.4	1,711
1977	32.6	1,249	1.3	244	100.9	890	9.8	918	16.1	643	1.7	850	7.7	802	3.1	615	2.2	299	1.4	318	1.6	236	2,528.2	10,299	7,296.0	1,759
1978	33.5	1,270	1.4	256	112.4	995	10.4	965	18.1	707	1.9	911	8.5	875	3.2	629	2.6	326	1.5	342	1.7	252	2,305.2	10,357	7,686.8	1,806
1979	37.7	1,406	1.4	264	126.0	1,089	11.1	1,020	19.9	754	2.0	917	9.4	962	3.1	590	2.7	331	1.6	358	1.9	272	2,348.4	10,435	7,998.0	1,848
1980	39.7	1,467	1.6	281	139.2	1,148	11.8	1,058	22.9	890	2.2	977	9.9	1,017	3.4	597	3.4	420	1.5	325	1.6	223	2,354.4	10,459	8,247.3	1,851
1981	39.0	1,361	1.7	294	142.0	1,144	12.0	1,061	24.3	921	2.4	1,055	10.6	1,079	3.6	630	3.7	452	1.5	299	1.6	213	2,392.9	10,414	8,384.2	1,851
1982	39.8	1,367	1.7	286	151.6	1,195	11.9	1,034	25.6	950	2.5	1,024	11.1	1,124	3.2	551	4.1	484	1.5	293	1.6	201	2,333.0	10,065	8,473.4	1,839
1983	42.9	1,451	1.7	277	161.7	1,246	12.6	1,081	27.1	984	2.4	964	11.6	1,166	3.4	570	4.3	489	1.6	306	1.6	197	2,402.8	10,280	8,819.0	1,883
1984	44.9	1,492	1.7	274	175.6	1,324	13.5	1,136	27.8	989	2.4	954	12.3	1,233	4.0	657	4.4	486	1.7	313	1.6	199	2,512.0	10,658	9,264.1	1,945

Year	L. HAITI Total	Per Capita	M. HONDURAS Total	Per Capita	N. MEXICO Total	Per Capita	O. NICARAGUA Total	Per Capita	P. PANAMA Total	Per Capita	Q. PARAGUAY Total	Per Capita	R. PERU Total	Per Capita	S. URUGUAY Total	Per Capita	T. VENEZUELA Total	Per Capita
1929	.01	4	.01	11	1.46	86	.01	15	.02	43	.01	1	.20	36	.13	76	.10	32
1937	.01	4	.02	18	2.48	132	.01	13	.03	52	.01	10	.32	50	.20	105	.07	20
1950	.02	6	.05	36	4.42	171	.03	27	.09	113	.03	21	.80	100	.60	273	.52	104
1960	.1	23	.1	48	11.2	320	.2	131	.2	223	.1	55	2.7	268	1.2	512	4.7	632
1970	.1	28	.3	119	28.9	569	.6	342	.8	573	.2	95	5.5	411	2.2	811	12.7	1,237
1971	.1	28	.3	136	31.5	600	.7	348	1.0	669	.2	104	5.9	430	2.4	820	13.4	1,261
1972	.1	30	.3	146	34.7	640	.8	386	1.1	724	.3	112	6.3	442	2.4	825	14.8	1,356
1973	.1	32	.4	151	37.4	667	.7	354	1.3	811	.3	120	6.7	455	2.5	913	16.1	1,425
1974	.1	32	.5	183	41.1	707	.9	419	1.4	877	.3	133	7.3	484	2.4	860	18.2	1,567
1975	.2	34	.5	176	43.6	725	.9	432	1.5	868	.4	163	7.5	484	2.5	875	19.6	1,632
1976	.2	45	.6	187	46.5	747	1.1	476	1.5	898	.4	143	7.9	497	2.6	973	21.0	1,701
1977	.2	45	.7	209	50.7	784	1.2	516	1.5	864	.5	170	8.6	527	2.8	1,001	23.0	1,808
1978	.2	51	.8	226	57.3	855	1.2	489	1.6	876	.5	178	8.8	521	3.1	1,074	25.6	1,951
1979	.3	57	.9	240	62.9	906	1.0	373	1.8	961	.6	211	9.3	535	2.7	955	28.4	2,100
1980	.3	54	.9	250	67.0	972	1.1	380	2.5	1,255	.7	213	9.8	567	4.6	1,182	35.9	2,298
1981	.3	55	1.0	264	73.8	1,036	1.1	388	2.0	1,019	1.0	304	10.8	606	3.6	1,238	37.5	2,319
1982	.4	59	1.1	274	80.5	1,100	1.2	391	2.2	1,095	1.1	335	11.4	623	3.6	1,226	40.0	2,394
1983	.4	60	1.1	280	82.3	1,095	1.3	416	2.4	1,144	1.2	346	10.7	571	3.7	1,249	42.0	2,435
1984	.4	58	1.2	290	87.0	1,129	1.2	392	2.4	1,106	1.3	361	11.8	613	3.6	1,220	44.3	2,487

1. Prior to 1950 data are for production, in Latin America essentially the same as consumption. For further notes and methods, see SALA-SNP, especially with regard to calculation per capita data through 1954 and rounding of data after 1960.

a. For yearly data in 1950s and 1960s, see SALA, 24-1926.

SOURCE: SALA-SNP, XI-9, updated with WA, 1929, 1937, and 1949; UN-SP: J, 17 (1974): J, 19 (1976), table 21: J, 20 (1977), table 21: J, 21 (1978), table 21: J, 22 (1979), table 25; UN-YWES, 1979, table 50: 1981, table 43: 1983, table 35: 1984, table 35.

Table 1927

INDEX OF TOTAL PRODUCTION OF ELECTRICITY, 20 LC, 1970–84

(1975 = 100)

	Country	1970	1976	1977	1978	1979	1980	1981	1982	1983	1984
A.	ARGENTINA	74	103	110	113	128	135	132	135	146	152
B.	BOLIVIA	74	107	119	128	135	148	159	159	161	160
C.	BRAZIL	58	114	128	143	160	177	180	193	205	223
D.	CHILE	86	106	112	119	127	135	137	136	145	154
E.	COLOMBIA	62	110	115	129	142	172	181	192	203	208
F.	COSTA RICA	67	108	115	126	130	202	154	161	187	200
G.	CUBA	74	109	117	129	143	150	160	168	175	187
H.	DOMINICAN REP.	39	101	120	126	122	107	140	125	133	157
I.	ECUADOR	58	114	137	156	162	187	226	250	260	267
J.	EL SALVADOR	63	93	113	128	141	146	139	141	151	159
K.	GUATEMALA	65	109	134	148	164	139	137	133	134	139
L.	HAITI	75	132	136	156	177	199	206	228	236	237
M.	HONDURAS	58	110	127	143	158	170	186	200	211	194
N.	MEXICO	66	107	116	132	145	155	170	186	190	201
O.	NICARAGUA	67	114	128	127	106	113	119	113	101	104
P.	PANAMA	66	106	105	108	131	170	141	155	165	163
Q.	PARAGUAY	36	89	109	112	129	156	131	139	164	183
R.	PERU	74	106	115	117	124	131	144	152	143	157
S.	URUGUAY	90	108	116	125	111	187	147	147	151	149
T.	VENEZUELA	65	107	118	131	145	183	192	204	214	226
	UNITED STATES	82	106	110	114	116	118	118	115	118	123
	WORLD	76	107	112	118	123	126	128	130	135	142

SOURCE: UN-YWES, 1979, table 51; 1981, table 44; 1983; table 35; 1984, table 35.

Table 1928

INDEX OF TOTAL CONSUMPTION OF ELECTRICITY, 20 LC, 1970–84

(1975 = 100)

	Country	1970	1976	1977	1978	1979	1980	1981	1982	1983	1984
A.	ARGENTINA	74	103	110	113	128	134	132	135	146	152
B.	BOLIVIA	74	107	119	128	135	148	159	159	158	161
C.	BRAZIL	58	114	128	142	160	176	180	192	205	222
D.	CHILE	86	106	112	119	127	135	137	136	145	154
E.	COLOMBIA	62	110	115	129	142	172	182	191	203	208
F.	COSTA RICA	67	108	115	126	130	145	154	161	156	158
G.	CUBA	74	109	117	129	143	150	160	168	175	187
H.	DOMINICAN REP.	39	101	120	126	122	107	140	125	133	157
I.	ECUADOR	58	114	137	156	162	188	227	250	261	268
J.	EL SALVADOR	63	113	128	141	150	146	139	141	151	159
K.	GUATEMALA	65	109	134	148	164	139	137	133	134	139
L.	HAITI	75	132	136	156	177	199	206	228	236	239
M.	HONDURAS	58	110	127	143	157	170	185	199	210	225
N.	MEXICO	66	107	116	131	144	155	169	185	189	199
O.	NICARAGUA	67	114	128	127	106	113	119	124	136	133
P.	PANAMA	58	106	105	109	122	169	140	154	164	162
Q.	PARAGUAY	50	89	109	121	148	194	227	258	274	295
R.	PERU	74	106	115	117	124	131	144	152	143	157
S.	URUGUAY	90	108	116	125	111	186	147	146	150	148
T.	VENEZUELA	65	107	118	131	145	183	191	204	215	226
	UNITED STATES	82	106	111	115	117	119	119	116	120	125
	WORLD	76	107	112	118	123	128	128	130	135	142

SOURCE: UN-YWES, 1979, table 51; 1981, table 44;,1983, table 35; 1984, table 35.

Table 1929

ELECTRICAL ENERGY INSTALLED CAPACITY,[1] 20 LC, 1975–84[a]

(Mw)

Country	1975 Total	1975 Hydro-Electric	1980 Total	1980 Hydro-Electric	1981 Total	1981 Hydro-Electric	1982 Total	1982 Hydro-Electric	1983 Total	1983 Hydro-Electric	1984 Total	1984 Hydro-Electric
A. ARGENTINA	9,260	1,531	11,988	3,626	12,296	4,180	13,480	4,646	14,872	4,844	15,280	5,384
B. BOLIVIA	376	242	489	265	508	283	517	283	562	301	566	304
C. BRAZIL	19,569	16,184	33,293	27,522	36,947	31,037	38,904	32,892	40,097	34,035	41,662	35,524
D. CHILE	2,620	1,462	2,940	1,470	3,210	1,771	3,358	1,772	3,345	1,775	3,355	1,780
E. COLOMBIA	3,504	2,297	5,130	3,470	5,500	3,775	5,820	4,025	6,150	4,300	6,150	4,300
F. COSTA RICA	404	239	646	457	640	455	817	629	819	631	819	631
G. CUBA[2]	1,677	44	2,673	46	2,756	46	2,975	46	3,000	46	3,115	45
H. DOMINICAN REP.	732	150	970	180	960	165	960	165	960	165	960	165
I. ECUADOR	525	139	1,080	226	1,194	240	1,335	240	1,833	742	1,837	742
J. EL SALVADOR	314	109	501	233	499	232	500	233	500	223	500	233
K. GUATEMALA	327	121	410	99	488	189	475	188	695	408	775	488
L. HAITI	89	47	121	50	126	50	126	50	126	50	126	50
M. HONDURAS	159	69	234	109	239	109	258	131	258	131	285	130
N. MEXICO	11,328	4,120	16,985	6,063	19,895	6,621	21,574	6,621	22,218	6,603	23,386	6,621
O. NICARAGUA	252	107	356	103	365	103	364	103	395	103	394	103
P. PANAMA	346	16	748	298	566	251	564	251	585	251	879	551
Q. PARAGUAY[3]	191	122	210	150	274	190	349	190	349	190	349	190
R. PERU	2,357	1,396	3,192	1,861	3,300	1,900	3,237	1,917	3,167	1,917	3,167	1,917
S. URUGUAY	705	252	1,075	611	944	461	1,364	881	1,339	881	1,321	881
T. VENEZUELA	4,570	1,735	8,471	2,728	9,225	2,682	10,125	2,682	10,541	2,704	12,499	4,426
UNITED STATES	527,346	66,553	630,111	76,651	651,108	77,445	667,043	78,428	674,947	79,268	688,430	82,182
WORLD	1,606,428	371,495	2,024,160	467,258	2,114,345	488,041	2,193,785	508,295	2,258,364	522,201	2,332,245	541,976

1. Unless otherwise indicated, the data refer to production for generating centers and therefore station losses. "Total" refers to all. "Total" minus "Hydraulic" production generally equals "Thermal" (not given), except for data from the United States. Unless otherwise stated, production is for both public and industrial purposes.

2. On June 30 of year.

3. Beginning 1960 Asunción only.

a. For data prior to 1975 see SALA, 21–2009.

SOURCE: UN-YWES, 1979, table 46; 1981, table 40; 1983, table 32; 1984, table 32.

Table 1930

ELECTRICAL ENERGY INSTALLED CAPACITY AND PROJECTIONS, 11 L,[a] 1979 AND 2000

(Mw)

A. ARGENTINA

	Capacity in Place, 1979			Projected Increases, 1980–2000		
Firm	Hydro-Electric	Thermo-Electric	Total	Hydro-Electric	Thermo-Electric	Total
Public Service[5]						
AyE[1]	1,237.1	2,071.6	3,308.7	14,098.0	780.0	14,878.0
SEGBA	#	2,224.1	2,224.1	#	660.0	660.0
ASE Ex-CIAE	#	579.0	579.0	#	#	#
DEBA	#	452.6	452.6	1,200.0	620.0	1,820.0
EPEC	6.5	411.1	417.6	15.0	203.0	218.0
HIDRONOR	1,650.0	#	1,650.0	4,730.0	#	4.730.0
CNEA	#	370.0	370.0	#	2,622.0	2,622.0
CTMSG[2]	225.0	#	225.0	#	#	#
EMSA[3]	#	#	#	120.0	#	120.0
Cooperatives	0.5	160.6	161.1	#	#	#
Binationals	#	#	#	5,252.0	#	5,252.0
Other	25.9	157.0	182.9[b]	31.0	#	31.0[c]
Total Public Service	3,145.0	6,426.0	9,571.0	25,446.0	4,885.0	30,331.0
Self-Production[4]	24.0	1,903.0	1,927.0	~	~	~
Total	3,169.0	8,329.0	11,498.0	~	~	~

1. For "Projected Additions," joint projects with the province of Santa Cruz are included.
2. Appropriation of capacity according to 1947 resolution.
3. See "Other"and footnote a.
4. Refers to firms producing energy for their own use. Data on projects for expansion are unknown.
5. Code: AyE Agua y Energía Eléctrica, Sociedad Anónima del Estado. Coordinated by Secretería de Estado de Energía.
    SEGBA   Servicios Eléctricos del Gran Buenos Aires, Sociedad Anónima. State owned. Coordinated directly by Secretaría de Estado de Energía.
    CTMSG   Comisión Técnica Mixta de Salto Grande. Binational entity Argentina-Uruguay.
    HIDRONOR Hidroeléctrica Nor Patagónica, Sociedad Anónima. State owned. Coordinated directly by Secretaría de Estado de Energía.
    EBY   Ente Binacional Yacireta. Binational entity Argentina-Paraguay.
    CNEA   Comisión Nacional de Energía Atómica. Controlled directly by Presidencia de la República.
    EPEC   Impresa Provincial de Energía de la Provincia de Buenos Aires. Property of the provincial government.
    EMSA   Electricidad de Misiones Sociedad Anónima. Property of the provincial government.
    ASE Ex-CIAE Administración Servicios Eléctricos, Ex-Compañía Italo-Argentina de Electricidad. State owned. Coordinated directly by the Secretaría de Estado de Energía.

a. For Bolivia, Brazil, Chile, Colombia, Ecuador, Mexico, Paraguay, Peru, Uruguay, and Venezuela, see SALA, 24–1931 through 1940.
b. Includes EMSA and other provincial and municipal firms.
c. Corresponds to project Uruguay I, firm owner of project is unknown.

SOURCE: ECLA-CC, E/CEPAL/G. 1241, June 1983, pp. 30–32.

Table 1931

URANIUM PRODUCTION,[1] 3 LC, 1970–84

(MET)

	Country	1970	1973	1975	1978	1979	1980	1981	1982	1983	1984
A.	ARGENTINA	45	24	22	126	134	187	187	123	155	179
C.	BRAZIL	#	#	#	#	103	#	#	4	242	189
N.	MEXICO	~	~	#	#	90[t]	~	~	~	~	~
	UNITED STATES	9,900	10,200	8,900	14,200	14,400	16,800	16,800	14,793	10,331	8,135
	WORLD	18,289	19,773	19,068	33,891	38,303	43,093	43,093	42,897	41,256	36,670

1. Uranium content.

SOURCE: UN-YWES, 1981, table 46; 1983, table 37; 1984, table 37.

Part VII: Sea and Land Harvests

CHAPTER 20

FISHERIES PRODUCTION

STATISTICAL NOTES

This chapter presents annual time-series statistics on Latin American fisheries production. The data include statistics on the nominal catches of fish, crustaceans, molluscs, and other types of acquatic animals and plants which have been killed, caught, trapped, collected, bred, or cultivated for all kinds of commercial, industrial, and subsistence purposes. The nominal catch data include quantities taken by all types and classes of fishing units operating in both fresh and marine fishing areas, with the exception of quantities taken in recreational facilities by sports fishermen.

The statistical category *nominal catches* refers to the landings converted to a live weight basis. The term *landings* refers to the weight of fish and fish products brought ashore, i.e., the actual weight of the quantities landed. The nominal catch data include quantities caught during the calendar year (January–December) although landed in the subsequent year. Nominal catch data for Argentina, Chile, Mexico, Peru, Uruguay, and the United States exclude the production of acquatic plants.

For a related discussion of Latin American fisheries resources and fishery statistics between 1938 and 1970 see M. Moreno Ibáñez, "Latin American Fisheries: Natural Resources and Expanded Jurisdiction, 1938-1978," SALA, 21.

Note: This volume contains statistics from numerous sources. Alternative data on many topics are presented. Variations in statistics can be attributed to differences in definition, parameters, coverage, methodology, as well as date gathered, prepared, or adjusted. See also Editor's Note on Methodology.

Table 2000

TOTAL NOMINAL CATCHES BY MAJOR FISHING AREA,[1] 20 LC, 1970-84[a]
(MET)

Country	Code[2]	1970	1974	1975	1976	1977	1978	1979	1980	1981	1982	1983	1984
A. ARGENTINA	03	5,400	10,181	15,068	9,846	10,436	15,077	16,082	8,407	9,689	15,395	14,594	9,287
	34	600	#	#	#	#	#	#	#	#	#	#	#
	41	208,800	286,180	213,830	255,931	359,281	504,138	550,266	376,865	351,857	459,648	401,771	304,901
	Total	214,800	296,361	228,898	265,777	369,717	519,215	566,348	385,272	361,546	475,043	416,365	314,188
B. BOLIVIA	03	1,600	1,800	1,800	2,000	2,300	1,550	3,650	4,379	5,617	5,617	5,617†	5,617
	Total	1,600	1,800	1,800	2,000	2,300	1,550	3,650	4,379	5,617	5,617†	5,617†	5,617
C. BRAZIL	03	93,500	168,145	173,455	144,829	168,444	170,645	126,701	187,594	197,340	207,919	205,345	201,000†
	41	434,800	572,177	598,691	508,202	580,031	631,983	728,418	632,239	631,316	621,008	670,103	745,000†
	Total	528,300	740,322	772,146	653,031	748,475	802,628	855,119	819,833	828,656	828,927	875,448	946,000†
D. CHILE	03	#	#	#	#	#	35	35	92	52	257	253	386
	87	1,181,400	1,157,053	929,464	1,378,600	1,318,950	1,929,091	2,632,216	2,816,614	3,385,346	3,672,740	3,977,825	4,497,227
	Total	1,181,400	1,157,053	929,464	1,378,600	1,318,950	1,929,091	2,632,251	2,816,706	3,385,398	3,672,997	3,978,078	4,497,613
E. COLOMBIA	03	33,200	37,234	42,075	51,437	42,174	56,612	48,535	46,903	47,719	49,000	45,343	53,354
	31	13,600	12,758	11,600	5,880	7,621	5,837	5,320	5,155	9,363	6,367	3,058	7,491
	77	7,700	12,426	12,900	17,790	14,170	17,129	9,538	24,139	37,608	16,014	9,136	17,669
	Total	54,500	62,418	66,575	75,107	63,965	79,578	63,393	76,197	94,690	71,381	57,537	78,514
F. COSTA RICA	02	#	40	50	60	61	61	100	350	400	455	523	213
	31	100	134	423	456	254	342	110	132	141	228	254	549
	77	7,000	13,316	13,591	12,376	12,781	16,919	20,649	14,405	14,482	10,219	8,464	11,214
	Total	7,100	13,490	14,064	12,892	13,096	17,322	20,859	14,887	15,023	10,902	9,241	11,976
G. CUBA	02	500	2,200	1,700	1,800	1,900	3,200	5,400	6,339	10,314	13,629	14,121	16,189
	21	#	#	7,495	29,871	18,282	13,124	12,482	9,255	6,668	18,565	14,786	20,521
	31	61,800	73,000	58,900	79,200	72,300	71,077	66,100	68,424	59,846	68,483	73,749	76,503
	34	22,100	10,700	6,600	6,400	20,700	7,200	7,500	9,258	9,016	7,109	7,357	18,049
	47	21,400	53,579	44,630	33,219	29,300	63,569	42,917	4,555	#	689	32,799	34,163
	87	#	25,500	24,000	43,600	42,700	55,000	19,400	88,650	78,791	86,771	55,639	34,131
	Total	105,800	164,979	143,325	194,090	185,182	213,170	153,799	186,481	164,815	195,246	198,451	199,622
H. DOMINICAN REP.	02	200	367	585	618	359	513	1,040	2,459	2,836	1,721	1,721†	1,721†
	31	5,000	8,025	6,467	6,435	4,235	4,573	6,845	8,199	9,167	11,448	11,448†	11,448†
	Total	5,200	8,392	7,052	7,053	4,594	5,086	7,885	10,658	12,003	13,169	13,169†	13,169†
I. ECUADOR	03	91,400	174,400	263,400	298,268	433,950	616,550	607,835	671,310†	731,024	654,111	307,288	867,496
	77	#	#	#	#	#	#	#	#	#	#	#	#
	Total	91,400	174,400	263,400	298,268	433,950	616,550	607,835	671,310†	731,024	654,111	307,288	867,496
J. EL SALVADOR	02	800	1,552	2,689	3,072	1,624	1,512	1,719	1,818	983	551	795	1,705
	77	10,300	8,110	7,861	6,058	4,744	8,028	11,019	12,140	19,271	12,966	6,808	10,484
	Total	11,100	9,662	10,550	9,130	6,368	9,540	12,738	13,958	20,254	13,517	7,603	12,189
K. GUATEMALA	02	1,400	528	550	574	600	580	615	400	410	721	40	54
	31	100	100	100	100	100	100	100	50	50	150	150	150
	77	3,500	3,253	3,880	2,979	2,374	4,824	4,183	3,057	3,805	3,413	3,413	2,759
	Total	5,000	3,881	4,530	3,653	3,074	5,504	4,898	3,507	4,265	4,284	4,284	2,963
L. HAITI	02	300†	300†	300†	300†	300†	300†	300†	300†	300†	300†	300†	300†
	31	2,200†	2,200†	3,700†	3,700†	3,700†	3,700†	3,700†	3,700†	3,700†	3,800†	3,900†	4,100†
	Total	2,500†	2,500†	4,000†	4,000†	4,000†	4,000†	4,000†	4,000†	4,000†	4,100†	4,200	4,400†
M. HONDURAS	02	100	172	170	170	97	114	110	83	238	74	65	113
	31	3,700	2,674	3,066	2,928	4,953	5,478	6,333	5,031	4,550	3,906	7,621	6,113
	77	#	21	26	56	782	783	859	1,295	1,512	1,043	746	2,155
	Total	3,800	2,867	3,262	3,154	5,832	6,375	7,302	6,409	6,300	5,023	8,432	8,381

Table 2000 (Continued)

TOTAL NOMINAL CATCHES BY MAJOR FISHING AREA,[1] 20 LC, 1970-84[a]
(MET)

Country	Code[2]	1970	1974	1975	1976	1977	1978	1979	1980	1981	1982	1983	1984
N. MEXICO	02	7,500	14,176	17,826	18,023	18,971	18,865	28,653	9,809	19,614	12,473	100,527	116,922
	21	1,400	#	#	#	#	3,954	8,085	4,697	#	6,584	13,321	9,037
	31	114,200	124,770	117,454	122,944	124,886	147,499	163,687	222,330	290,377	282,835	288,691	294,872
	77	267,700	303,096	364,064	385,364	466,909	532,315	676,554	985,614	1,226,199	1,018,866	661,754	682,827
	Total	390,800	442,042	499,344	526,331	610,766	702,633	876,979	1,222,450	1,536,190	1,321,028	1,064,293	1,103,658
O. NICARAGUA	02	1,300	3,100	3,500	4,467	4,043	178	126	79	193	486	378	113
	31	6,200	9,000	9,900	10,062	12,889	7,676	5,637	5,025	3,385	2,701	3,018	2,767
	77	2,300	4,600	5,000	3,352	5,429	2,306	1,478	1,892	2,366	1,813	1,152	1,454
	Total	9,800	16,700	18,400	17,881	22,361	10,160	7,241	6,996	5,944	5,000	4,548	4,339
P. PANAMA	02	#		~	~	~	#	~	#	~	#	~	#
	31	~	7,346	~	~	~	~	~	3,558†	1,445	4,972	547	2,995
	34		~	~	~	~	~	~	7,392†	3,323	4,163	6,587	4,010
	77	53,200	81,045	81,085	152,368	207,798	109,958	147,072	205,418†	144,700	107,416†	162,265†	131,235†
	Total	53,200	88,391	81,055	152,368	207,798	109,958	147,072	216,368†	149,468	116,551†	169,399†	138,240†
Q. PARAGUAY	03	1,800†	2,700†	2,700†	2,700†	2,700†	2,700†	2,700†	3,300†	3,350†	3,400†	3,500	5,000
	Total	1,800†	2,700†	2,700†	2,700†	2,700†	2,700†	2,700†	3,300†	3,350†	3,400†	3,500	5,000
R. PERU	03	2,000†	5,514	6,777	6,280	9,015	14,064	15,217	12,538	16,077	17,358	24,610	24,543
	87	12,532,900	4,139,344	3,440,713	4,338,005	2,525,388	3,458,341	3,666,969	2,722,356	2,725,104	3,511,252	1,543,717	2,972,441
	Total	12,534,900	4,144,858	3,447,490	4,344,285	2,534,403	3,472,405	3,682,186	2,734,894	2,741,181	3,528,610	1,568,327	2,996,984
S. URUGUAY	03	#	300	245	179	321	472	578	312	321	186	57	435
	41	13,200	15,700	26,088	33,425	47,953	73,751	107,555	120,087	146,652	118,892	144,074	133,588
	Total	13,200	16,000	26,333	33,604	48,274	74,223	108,133	120,399	146,973	119,078	144,131	134,023
T. VENEZUELA	03	12,300	9,198	7,657	6,626	8,021	11,260	12,456	15,933	13,346	14,998	20,009	21,073
	31	114,100	140,887	145,750	139,105	137,898	154,858	113,573	161,640	161,687	180,692	196,992	233,370
	77	~	~	~	~	~	~	~	9,000	16,898	18,000	9,868	10,567
	Total	126,400	150,085	153,407	145,731	145,919	166,118	126,029	186,573	191,931	213,690	226,869	265,010
UNITED STATES	02	78,000	84,516	77,267	76,368	71,831	80,416	65,684	69,572	65,197	73,433	75,753	74,632
	21	972,500	992,437	930,879	979,955	1,076,037	1,117,140	1,196,504	1,298,798	1,236,253	1,205,930	1,236,464	1,251,780
	27												
	31	1,016,300	1,041,819	1,024,947	1,080,706	940,874	1,332,572	1,281,468	1,216,251	1,259,201	1,490,374	1,556,757	1,846,681
	34	~	~	~	3,402	10,616	5,789	2,764	2,650	3,904	1,067	19	~
	47									498			
	67	397,200	360,829	352,602	442,890	477,662	516,175	593,307	653,674	806,594	845,010	1,017,703	1,270,603
	71								3,759	26,728	41,265	36,494	155,733
	77	312,400	449,198	533,071	458,777	398,536	364,107	367,883	369,493	353,945	325,253	215,312	209,553
	81								7,218	3,529	1,857	4,044	5,313
	87	#	#	1,172	8,380	4,740	1,360	3,244	13,111	11,584	4,118	~	~
	Total	2,776,400	2,928,799	2,919,938	3,050,478	2,980,296	3,417,559	3,510,854	3,634,526	3,767,433	3,988,307	4,142,546	4,814,295

1. Includes marine and inland catches.
2. Code: 02, America, North–Inland Waters; 03, American, South–Inland Waters; 21, Atlantic, Northwest; 31, Atlantic, Western Central; 34, Atlantic, Eastern Central; 41, Atlantic, Southwest; 47, Atlantic, Southeast; 67, Pacific, Northeast; 77, Pacific, Eastern Central; 87, Pacific, Southeast. See map of FAO fishing areas on following page.
a. For 1964–69 and 1971–73 data see SALA, 21-3815.

SOURCE: FAO-YFSCL, 1976–84, tables A-2, D-2, and D-3.

Figure 20:1

FAO FISHING AREA CODES

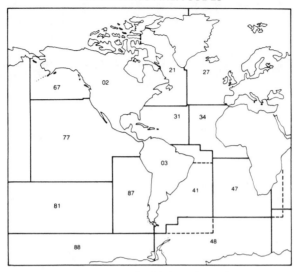

FAO fishing areas. 02, America, North—Inland Waters; 03, America, South—Inland Waters; 21, Atlantic,
Northwest; 27, Atlantic, Northeast; 31, Atlantic, Western Central; 34, Atlantic, Eastern Central; 41,
Atlantic, Southwest; 47, Atlantic, Southeast; 48, Atlantic, Antarctic; 67, Pacific Northeast; 77, Pacific,
Eastern Central; 81, Pacific Southwest; 87, Pacific, Southeast; 88, Pacific, Antarctic.
SOURCE: Adapted from FAO map of major fishing areas for statistical purposes.

Table 2001

NOMINAL CATCHES, MARINE AREAS, 18 LRC, 1971–84
(MET)

	Country	1971	1972	1973	1974	1975	1976	1977
A.	ARGENTINA	201,400	211,100	270,000	266,380	199,068	256,206	369,430
C.	BRAZIL	493,800	523,800	614,600	557,775	579,536	508,202	580,031
D.	CHILE	1,491,600	795,300	667,700	1,127,772	899,458	1,378,600	1,318,950
E.	COLOMBIA	18,400	27,900	32,200	25,184	24,500	23,670	21,791
F.	COSTA RICA	7,200	10,800	10,700	13,450	14,052	12,832	13,037
G.	CUBA	125,400	138,600	148,900	162,779	141,625	192,290	183,282
H.	DOMINICAN REP.	4,100	4,600	8,900	8,025	5,309	6,435	4,235
I.	ECUADOR	106,700	108,200	153,900	174,400	223,738	299,668	433,050
J.	EL SALVADOR	9,900	9,600	11,000	8,110	7,861	6,058	4,744
K.	GUATEMALA	2,800	2,700	3,200	3,353	3,980	3,079	2,474
L.	HAITI	2,500[†]	2,900[†]	3,300[†]	3,700[†]	3,700[†]	3,700[†]	3,850
M.	HONDURAS	6,600	5,100	3,700	3,403	4,484	4,290	5,735
N.	MEXICO	390,200	414,900	433,400	387,506	449,677	476,465	513,854
O.	NICARAGUA	8,100	10,000	11,300	8,229	10,419	9,205	10,161
P.	PANAMA	72,500	63,400	92,300	89,392[†]	117,071[†]	184,196[†]	239,526
R.	PERU	10,526,100	4,722,300	2,323,200	4,139,395	3,439,804	4,336,816	2,536,698
S.	URUGUAY	14,400	20,600	17,500	15,700	26,003	33,425	47,953
T.	VENEZUELA	133,400	145,700	153,700	135,774	145,176	139,184	143,033
	LATIN AMERICA	13,615,100	7,217,500	4,959,500	7,130,327	6,294,827	6,632,181	6,432,563
	UNITED STATES	2,797,700	2,686,300	2,712,200	2,762,078	2,764,803	2,974,100	2,910,167
	WORLD	59,678,800	55,451,400	55,891,800	59,103,900	58,752,300	62,300,100	61,108,400

	Country	1978	1979	1980	1981	1982	1983	1984
A.	ARGENTINA	503,654	551,594	376,865	351,857	459,648	401,771	304,901
C.	BRAZIL	631,983	728,418	632,239	631,316	621,008	670,103	745,000
D.	CHILE	1,929,090	2,631,915	2,816,614	3,853,346	3,672,740	3,981,577	4,498,876
E.	COLOMBIA	22,966	14,858	29,294	46,971	22,381	12,194	25,160
F.	COSTA RICA	17,261	20,759	17,293	14,623	10,447	8,718	11,763
G.	CUBA	209,970	148,399	180,142	154,501	181,617	184,330	183,423
H.	DOMINICAN REP.	4,573	6,845	8,199	9,167	11,448	11,448[†]	11,448[†]
I.	ECUADOR	616,550	609,101	643,476	731,024	654,111	307,288	367,496
J.	EL SALVADOR	8,028	11,019	12,140	19,271	12,966	6,808	10,484
K.	GUATEMALA	4,924	4,283	3,107	3,855	3,563	2,336	2,909
L.	HAITI	3,700[†]	3,750[†]	3,800[†]	3,800[†]	3,900[†]	4,000[†]	4,100[†]
M.	HONDURAS	6,261	7,192	6,326	6,062	4,949	8,367	8,268
N.	MEXICO	775,519	948,422	1,212,641	1,516,576	1,308,285	963,766	986,736
O.	NICARAGUA	9,982	7,115	6,917	5,751	4,514	4,170	4,221
P.	PANAMA	139,470	165,069	216,368	149,468	116,551[†]	169,355[†]	138,240[†]
R.	PERU	3,458,752	3,666,731	2,726,057	2,725,104	3,511,252	1,543,717	2,972,441
S.	URUGUAY	73,751	107,555	120,087	146,652	118,892	144,074	133,588
T.	VENEZUELA	164,009	164,421	170,640	178,585	198,692	206,860	243,937
	LATIN AMERICA[1]	8,580,443	9,832,300	9,175,648	10,544,492	10,870,297	8,603,606	11,152,991
	UNITED STATES	3,337,153	3,445,170	3,564,954	3,702,236	3,914,874	4,066,793	4,739,663
	WORLD	63,112,500	63,774,000	64,393,200	66,712,400	68,139,300	67,714,400	73,053,600

1. Latin American total computed by SALA.

SOURCE: FAO-YFSCL, 1979–84, table A-4.

Table 2002

DISTRIBUTION OF MARINE AREA NOMINAL CATCHES, 18 LR, 1971-84

(%)

	Country	1971	1973	1974	1975	1976	1977	1978	1979	1980	1981	1982	1983	1984
A.	ARGENTINA	1.5	5.4	3.7	3.1	3.9	5.7	5.9	5.6	4.1	3.3	4.2	4.7	2.7
C.	BRAZIL	3.6	12.4	7.8	9.2	6.4	8.9	7.4	7.4	6.9	6.0	5.7	7.5†	6.7
D.	CHILE	11.0	13.5	15.9	14.3	17.5	20.5	22.8	26.8	30.5	36.5	33.8	46.2	40.3
E.	COLOMBIA	.1	.6	.3	.3	.3	.3	.2	.1	.3	.4	.2	.1	.2
F.	COSTA RICA	.1	.2	.1	.2	.1	.2	.2	.2	.1	.1	.1	.1†	.1
G.	CUBA	.9	3.0	2.2	2.2	2.4	2.8	2.4	1.5	1.9	1.5	.8	2.1	1.6
H.	DOMINICAN REP.	0	.2	.1	0	0	0	0	0	0	0	.1	.1†	.1
I.	ECUADOR	.8	3.1	2.4	3.6	3.5	6.7	7.2	6.2	7.0	6.9	6.0	3.6	7.8
J.	EL SALVADOR	.1	.2	.1	.1	0	0	0	.1	.1	.1	.1	.1	0
K.	GUATEMALA	0	.1	0	0	0	0	0	0	0	0	0	0†	0
L.	HAITI	0	.1	0	0	0	0	0	0	0	0	0	0	0†
M.	HONDURAS	0	.1	0	0	0	0	0	0	0	0	0	.1	0
N.	MEXICO	2.9	8.7	5.5	7.1	7.2	8.0	9.0	9.6	13.2	14.4	12.0	12.2	8.8
O.	NICARAGUA	.1	.2	.1	.1	0	0	0	0	0	0	0	0	0†
P.	PANAMA	.5	1.9	1.2†	2.8†	2.8†	3.7†	1.6†	1.7†	2.4†	1.4†	1.0†	1.9†	1.2
R.	PERU	77.8	46.8	58.2	56.4	65.4	39.4	40.3	37.3	29.7	25.8	32.3	18.6	26.7
S.	URUGUAY	.1	.4	.2	.4	.4	.7	.8	1.1	1.3	1.4	1.1	1.7	1.2
T.	VENEZUELA	1.0	3.2	1.9	2.3	2.1	2.2	1.9	1.7	1.9	1.7	1.8	2.4	2.2
	LATIN AMERICA	100.0	100.0	100.0	100.0	100.0	100.0	100.0	100.0	100.0	100.0	100.0	100.0	100.0

SOURCE: Calculated from table 2001.

Table 2003

PC OF NOMINAL CATCHES IN MARINE AREAS, 18 LRC, 1971-84

	Country	1971	1973	1974	1975	1976	1977	1978	1979	1980	1981	1982	1983	1984
A.	ARGENTINA	8.2	27.9	-1.3	-25.3	28.7	30.6	36.3	9.5	-31.7	-6.6	30.6	-12.6	-31.8
C.	BRAZIL	14.1	17.3	-9.2	3.9	-12.3	14.1	9.0	15.3	-13.2	-.2	-1.6	7.3	10.1
D.	CHILE	24.3	-16.0	68.9	-25.4	53.3	-4.5	46.3	26.7	7.0	36.8	-4.7	7.8	11.5
E.	COLOMBIA	-13.6	15.4	-21.8	-2.7	-3.4	-7.9	5.4	-35.3	97.2	60.3	-52.3	-45.5	51.5
F.	COSTA RICA	2.9	-.9	25.7	4.5	-8.7	1.6	32.4	20.3	-20.0	-15.3	-14.1	-19.8	25.9
G.	CUBA	19.1	7.4	9.3	-13.0	35.8	-4.7	14.6	-29.3	21.4	-14.2	-47.2	125.9	-.5
H.	DOMINICAN REP.	-18.0	93.5	-9.8	-51.2	-.5	-34.2	8.0	49.7	19.8	11.8	14.9	0†	0
I.	ECUADOR	16.7	42.2	13.3	22.1	25.3	30.8	42.1	-1.2	5.6	13.6	-10.5	-53.0	64.6
J.	EL SALVADOR	-3.9	14.6	-26.3	-3.1	-22.9	-21.7	69.2	37.3	10.2	58.7	-32.7	-47.5	35.1
K.	GUATEMALA	-6.7	18.5	4.8	18.7	-22.6	-19.6	99.0	-13.0	-27.5	24.1	-7.6	-52.5	19.7
L.	HAITI	13.6	13.8	12.1	0	0	3.9	0	0	0†	0†	0†	0†	2.4
M.	HONDURAS	78.4	-27.5	-8.0	31.8	-4.3	33.7	9.2	14.9	-12.0	-4.2	-18.4	69.1	-1.2
N.	MEXICO	13.4	4.5	-10.6	16.0	6.0	7.8	50.9	22.3	27.9	25.1	-13.6	-20.0†	2.3
O.	NICARAGUA	-4.7	13.0	-27.2	26.6	-11.7	10.4	-1.8	-28.7	-2.8	-16.9	-21.5	-7.6	1.2
P.	PANAMA	0	45.6	-3.1†	31.0†	57.3†	30.0†	-41.8†	18.3†	31.1†	-30.9†	-28.2	31.2	-22.5
R.	PERU	-16.0	-50.8	78.2	-16.9	26.1	-71.0	36.3	5.7	-34.5	0	22.4	-127.5	48.1
S.	URUGUAY	9.1	-15.0	-10.3	65.6	28.5	43.5	53.8	45.8	11.7	22.1	-23.3	21.2	-7.8
T.	VENEZUELA	8.8	5.5	-11.7	6.5	-4.1	2.8	14.7	.2	3.8	4.7	10.6	4.8	15.2
	LATIN AMERICA	90.2	-15.0	43.8	-11.7	5.4	-30.1	33.4	14.6	-6.7	14.9	3.1	-20.8	22.9
	UNITED STATES	2.5	1.0	1.8	.1	7.6	-2.2	12.8	3.1	3.4	3.7	5.4	3.7	14.2
	WORLD	.3	.8	5.7	5.8	5.7	-1.9	3.2	1.0	1.0	3.5	2.1	-.6	7.3

SOURCE: Calculated from table 2001.

Table 2004
NOMINAL CATCHES, INLAND WATERS, 18 LRC, 1971–84
(MET)

Country	1971	1973	1974	1975	1976	1977	1978	1979	1980	1981	1982	1983	1984
A. ARGENTINA	5,700	7,600	10,181	15,068	9,846	10,436	15,077	16,082	8,407	9,689	15,395	14,594	9,287
B. BOLIVIA	1,900	1,500	1,050	1,050	1,250	1,550	1,550	3,650	4,379	5,617	5,617†	5,617†	5,617
C. BRAZIL	87,900	84,100	168,145	173,455	144,829	168,444	170,645	126,701	187,594	197,340	207,919	205,345	201,000†
D. CHILE	#	#	#	#	#	#		35	92	52	257	253	386
E. COLOMBIA	19,300	73,100	37,234	42,075	51,437	42,174	56,612	48,535	46,903	47,719	49,000	45,343	53,354
F. COSTA RICA	..	..	40	50	60	61	61	100	350	400	455	523	213
G. CUBA	600	1,000	2,200	1,700	1,800	1,900	3,200	5,400	6,339	10,314	13,629	14,121	16,199
H. DOMINICAN REP.	500	300	367	585	618	359	513	1,040	2,459	2,836	1,721	1,721†	1,721†
J. EL SALVADOR	800	900	1,514	869	1,143	1,624	1,512	1,719	1,818	983	551	795	1,705
K. GUATEMALA	500	500	528	550	574	600	580	615	400	410	721†	40	54
L. HAITI	300†	300†	300†	300†	300†	300†	300†	300†	300†	300†	300†	300†	300†
M. HONDURAS	100	100	172	170	170	97	114	110	83	238	74	65	113
N. MEXICO	7,900	15,000	14,164	17,826	2,277	2,699	6,253	6,464	9,809	19,614	12,743	100,527	116,992
O. NICARAGUA	1,300	2,600	460	359	458	393	178	126	79	193	486	378	118
Q. PARAGUAY	2,200†	2,700	2,700†	2,800†	2,900†	3,000†	3,100†	3,200†	3,300†	3,350†	3,400†	3,500	5,000
R. PERU	2,500	5,400	5,514	6,671	6,280	12,597	14,064	14,426	12,538	16,077	17,358	24,610	24,543
S. URUGUAY	..	..	300	245	179	321	472	578	312	321	186	57	435
T. VENEZUELA	5,700	8,600	9,198	7,657	6,626	8,021	11,260	6,934	15,933	13,346	14,998	20,009	21,073
LATIN AMERICA	137,200	203,700	254,067	278,160	230,747	254,576	285,491	236,015	300,815	328,799	344,548	351,707	458,110
UNITED STATES	77,500	83,800	84,516	77,267	76,368	71,831	80,416	65,684	69,572	65,197	73,433	75,753	74,632
WORLD	6,382,000	6,770,900	6,841,900	6,961,000	6,890,100	7,105,800	7,034,900	7,238,600	7,603,100	8,138,000	8,454,800	9,131,500	9,716,200

SOURCE: FAO-YFSCL, 1979–84, table A-3.

Table 2005

DISTRIBUTION OF NOMINAL CATCHES IN INLAND WATERS, 18 LR, 1971–84

(%)

	Country	1971	1973	1974	1975	1976	1977	1978	1979	1980	1981	1982	1983	1984
A.	ARGENTINA	4.2	3.7	4.0	5.6	4.0	3.9	5.0	6.1	2.7	3.0	4.5	4.1	2.0
B.	BOLIVIA	1.4	.7	.4	.4	.5	.6	.5	1.4	1.4	1.5	1.6	1.6	1.2
C.	BRAZIL	64.1	41.3	66.2	63.9	58.8	63.1	57.3	48.0	62.4	60.0	60.3	58.4	43.9[†]
D.	CHILE	0	0	0	0	0	0	0	0	0	0	0	0	0
E.	COLOMBIA	14.1	35.9	14.7	15.5	20.9	15.8	19.0	18.4	15.1	12.4	14.2	12.9	11.6
F.	COSTA RICA	0	0	0	0	0	0	0	0	.1	.1	.1	.1	0
G.	CUBA	.4	.5	.9	.6	.7	.7	1.1	2.0	2.0	2.7	4.0	4.0	3.5[†]
H.	DOMINICAN REP.	.4	.1	.1	.2	.2	.1	.2	.4	.8	.7	.5	.5[†]	.4
J.	EL SALVADOR	.6	.4	.6	1.0	1.2	1.1	.5	.7	.6	.3	.2	.2	.4
K.	GUATEMALA	.4	.2	.2	.2	.2	.2	.2	.2	..1	.1	.2[†]	0	0[†]
L.	HAITI	.2	.1	.1	.1	.1	.1	.1	.1	0	0	0[†]	0[†]	0
M.	HONDURAS	.1	0	.1	.1	.1	0	0	0	0	0	0	0	0
N.	MEXICO	5.8	7.3	5.6	6.4	1.0	1.1	2.2	2.7	3.3	6.0	3.7	28.6	25.5
O.	NICARAGUA	.9	1.3	.2	.1	.2	.1	.1	0	0	0	.1	.1	0
Q.	PARAGUAY	1.6	1.3	1.0	1.0[†]	1.3[†]	1.2[†]	1.1[†]	1.4[†]	1.1[†]	1.0[†]	1.0[†]	1.0	1.1
R.	PERU	1.8	2.7	2.2	2.4	2.5	5.0	4.7	6.1	4.2	4.9	5.0	7.0	5.4
S.	URUGUAY	0	0	.1	.1	.1	.1	.2	.2	.1	0	0	0	0
T.	VENEZUELA	4.2	4.2	3.6	2.8	2.6	2.9	3.8	2.9	5.3	3.5	4.3	5.7	4.6
	LATIN AMERICA	100.0	100.0	100.0	100.0	100.0	100.0	100.0	100.0	100.0	100.0	100.0	100.0	100.0

SOURCE: Calculated from table 2004.

Table 2006

PC OF NOMINAL CATCHES IN INLAND WATERS, 18 LRC, 1971–84

	Country	1971	1973	1974	1975	1976	1977	1978	1979	1980	1981	1982	1983	1984
A.	ARGENTINA	5.6	20.6	34.0	48.0	-34.7	6.0	44.5	6.7	-47.7	15.3	58.2	-5.0	-36.4
B.	BOLIVIA	18.8	0	-30.0	0	19.0	24.0	0	135.5	20.0	28.3	0	0	-1.0
C.	BRAZIL	-6.0	8.1	99.9	3.2	-16.5	16.3	1.3	-25.8	48.0	5.2	5.3	-4.5[†]	-2.1
D.	CHILE	0	0	0	0	0	0	0	**	162.9	-43.5	39.4	-1.6	52.6
E.	COLOMBIA	-41.9	-11.7	-49.1	13.0	22.3	-18.0	34.2	-14.3	-3.7	1.7	2.7	-7.5	23.1
F.	COSTA RICA	~	~	~	25.0	20.0	1.7	0	63.9	25.0	14.3	13.8	0[†]	-59.3
G.	CUBA	50.0	0	120.0	-22.7	5.9	5.6	68.4	68.8	17.3	62.7	32.1	3.6	14.7
H.	DOMINICAN REP.	150.0	-70.0	22.3	59.4	5.6	-41.9	42.9	102.7	136.4	15.3	-39.3	0[†]	
J.	EL SALVADOR	0	12.5	68.2	-42.6	31.5	42.1	-6.9	13.7	5.8	-45.9	-43.9	44.3	114.5
K.	GUATEMALA	25.0	25.0	5.6	4.2	4.4	4.5	-3.3	6.0	-35.0	2.5	75.9	0[†]	35.0
L.	HAITI	0[†]	0[†]	0[†]	0[†]	0[†]	0[†]	0[†]	0[†]	0[†]	0[†]	0[†]	0[†]	0
M.	HONDURAS	0	~	72.0	-1.2	0	-42.9	17.5	-3.5	-24.5	186.7	-68.9	-12.1	73.8
N.	MEXICO	9.7	35.1	-5.6	25.9	-87.2	18.5	131.7	3.4	51.8	100.0	-35.0	62.4[†]	10.9
O.	NICARAGUA	0	116.7	-82.3	-22.0	27.6	-14.2	-54.7	-29.2	-37.3	144.3	151.8	-22.2	-68.8
Q.	PARAGUAY	22.2	8.0	0[†]	3.7	3.6	3.4	3.3	3.2	3.1	1.5	1.5	2.9	42.9
R.	PERU	25.0	80.0	2.1	22.9	-7.3	100.6	56.0	2.6	-13.1	28.2	6.7	43.4	-.3
S.	URUGUAY	~	~	~	-18.3	-26.9	79.3	47.0	22.5	-46.0	2.9	-42.1	-69.3	663.2
T.	VENEZUELA	50.0	32.3	7.0	-16.8	-13.5	21.1	40.4	-38.4	129.8	-15.9	12.4	33.4	5.3
	LATIN AMERICA	-9.7	3.8	24.7	9.5	-17.0	10.3	12.1	-17.3	27.5	9.3	4.8	2.1	30.3
	UNITED STATES	-4.0	14.2	.9	-8.6	-1.2	-5.9	12.0	-18.3	5.9	-6.3	12.6	3.2	-1.5
	WORLD	4.8	3.6	1.1	2.1	.7	3.4	-1.0	3.0	5.0	6.8	3.5	5.1	6.4

SOURCE: Calculated from table 2004.

Table 2007

PRODUCTION OF SEAWEEDS,[1] 5 LC, 1970–84

(MET)

	Country	1970	1974	1975	1976	1977	1978	1979	1980	1981	1982	1983	1984
A.	ARGENTINA	23,300	19,400	18,073	15,675	22,856	23,161	15,299	14,739	13,231	13,072	11,699	7,522
D.	CHILE	28,000	30,000	30,000	30,000	30,000	30,000	65,000	74,523	109,631	173,375	190,371	174,756
N.	MEXICO	35,200	40,372	31,841	45,955	45,553	36,739	48,039	34,698	29,275	35,277	11,254	30,934
R.	PERU	#	228	193	292	265	326	286	361	91	136	103	305
S.	URUGUAY	#	#	85	200	100	76	37	#	#	#	#	#
	UNITED STATES	117,100	156,907	157,853	158,468	160,810	160,761	160,624	162,809	48,703	78,475	4,781[a]	39,000
	WORLD	1,633,400	2,614,600	2,480,500	2,492,400	3,080,300	3,224,400	3,187,100	3,348,700	3,060,900	3,096,500	3,251,600	3,544,300

1. Includes production of seaweeds and other aquatic plants through both culture and harvesting of wild stocks.

a. Questionable data.

SOURCE: FAO-YFSCL, 1979–84, table A-6.

CHAPTER 21

AGRICULTURAL PRODUCTION

Table 2100

INDEX OF TOTAL AGRICULTURAL PRODUCTION,[1] 20 LC, 1974–85
(1979–81 = 100)[a]

	Country	1974	1975	1976	1977	1978	1979	1980	1981	1982	1983	1984	1985
A.	ARGENTINA	88.28	86.95	93.67	93.02	98.04	102.30	95.87	101.83	107.62	103.67	107.15	103.99
B.	BOLIVIA	90.43	96.58	98.35	94.19	95.15	95.62	99.11	105.27	108.82	82.18	98.59	102.35
C.	BRAZIL	84.03	84.74	83.46	91.93	88.98	93.03	99.97	107.00	108.56	108.63	110.06	122.60
D.	CHILE	86.87	91.13	89.15	97.61	91.77	96.65	97.23	106.11	104.86	103.08	107.41	111.92
E.	COLOMBIA	75.85	81.49	86.43	89.84	93.37	97.58	99.09	103.34	100.78	101.88	105.35	103.45
F.	COSTA RICA	82.87	89.14	91.99	95.50	97.55	99.62	99.22	101.16	97.23	103.23	112.42	103.27
G.	CUBA	80.54	79.69	81.67	85.94	94.71	101.14	94.40	104.46	108.50	104.63	112.76	109.76
H.	DOMINICAN REP.	93.81	89.92	96.72	98.59	98.68	101.68	99.20	99.12	107.58	113.02	112.93	112.85
I.	ECUADOR	88.67	90.10	92.56	93.96	91.74	94.65	100.79	104.56	106.37	93.12	100.21	113.83
J.	EL SALVADOR	89.01	93.64	84.66	88.76	97.75	105.99	103.08	90.93	86.09	90.96	95.64	93.29
K.	GUATEMALA	83.23	83.82	87.87	93.41	95.03	96.66	99.51	103.84	105.10	96.42	94.52	100.26
L.	HAITI	94.40	94.88	95.75	92.15	97.26	102.36	98.25	99.39	101.70	103.72	105.71	100.37
M.	HONDURAS	76.27	72.50	78.26	85.00	94.36	94.74	98.64	106.62	101.44	99.46	105.02	110.42
N.	MEXICO	81.79	82.02	81.16	89.28	99.21	94.97	99.80	105.23	99.01	105.84	103.44	107.32
O.	NICARAGUA	96.91	103.89	106.89	110.02	121.26	121.22	82.95	95.83	97.53	95.66	93.58	94.09
P.	PANAMA	84.42	88.30	87.38	94.66	97.93	99.07	97.09	103.84	100.09	102.79	103.57	107.48
Q.	PARAGUAY	74.08	74.43	78.81	90.62	90.89	96.19	97.97	105.84	105.52	102.72	102.35	116.64
R.	PERU	102.98	100.00	101.65	103.17	101.97	104.16	94.51	101.33	105.07	102.87	111.43	110.67
S.	URUGUAY	96.95	96.57	107.96	92.17	89.54	90.11	95.93	113.95	111.08	113.98	111.48	108.44
T.	VENEZUELA	82.58	94.14	87.36	90.42	96.53	100.13	99.55	100.32	99.42	99.80	97.05	100.40
	UNITED STATES	84.14	89.74	92.33	96.36	94.32	99.03	95.39	105.58	104.31	88.29	101.76	106.72

1. The index numbers of total agricultural production cover all of the items included in food production (cereals, starchy roots, sugar, pulses, edible oil crops, nuts, fruit, vegetables, wine, cocoa, livestock and livestock products) and, in addition, industrial oilseeds, tobacco, fibres (vegetable and animal), rubber, coffee and tea. Agricultural commodities used in the agricultural production process are deducted from total production. The deduction items include amounts used for seed (or, in the case of eggs, used for hatching), and for livestock feed, i.e., agricultural products fed as such and semi-processed feed such as oilcakes and grain as well as imported feed, to the extent that adequate estimates are possible.

a. For subindex of food production, see SALA, 24-818.

SOURCE: FAO-PY, 1985, table 5.

Table 2101

INDEX OF PER CAPITA AGRICULTURAL PRODUCTION,[1] 20 LC, 1974–85
(1979–81 = 100)[a]

	Country	1974	1975	1976	1977	1978	1979	1980	1981	1982	1983	1984	1985
A.	ARGENTINA	97.29	94.24	99.86	97.58	101.22	103.94	95.86	100.20	104.21	98.80	100.53	96.07
B.	BOLIVIA	105.58	110.01	109.20	101.93	100.33	98.23	99.18	102.59	103.27	75.91	88.64	89.55
C.	BRAZIL	96.71	95.21	91.61	98.58	93.24	95.26	100.05	104.69	103.85	101.62	100.72	109.78
D.	CHILE	95.26	98.17	94.63	102.10	94.59	98.16	97.31	104.53	101.68	98.40	100.93	103.53
E.	COLOMBIA	86.29	90.72	94.20	95.84	97.50	99.72	99.11	101.17	96.56	95.54	96.69	92.96
F.	COSTA RICA	98.40	103.32	103.62	104.41	103.43	102.52	99.15	98.33	92.03	95.18	101.03	90.46
G.	CUBA	85.42	83.09	84.19	87.76	95.96	101.78	94.39	103.84	107.24	102.82	110.10	106.41
H.	DOMINICAN REP.	108.45	101.04	106.00	105.53	103.24	104.00	99.17	96.83	102.65	105.35	102.85	100.44
I.	ECUADOR	105.60	104.11	103.92	102.50	97.24	97.47	100.86	101.66	100.50	85.49	89.40	98.66
J.	EL SALVADOR	105.92	108.23	95.05	96.77	103.46	108.93	102.90	88.18	81.11	83.25	85.00	80.46
K.	GUATEMALA	98.32	96.31	98.22	101.55	100.51	99.43	99.56	101.01	99.40	88.66	84.50	87.14
L.	HAITI	108.73	106.83	105.33	99.00	102.04	104.85	98.22	96.94	96.77	96.24	95.63	88.51
M.	HONDURAS	94.17	86.60	90.29	94.63	101.39	98.22	98.72	103.05	94.70	89.77	91.67	93.30
N.	MEXICO	97.50	94.67	90.90	97.11	104.89	97.65	99.85	102.50	93.93	97.84	93.23	94.32
O.	NICARAGUA	114.88	119.27	119.30	119.47	128.15	124.58	82.76	92.67	91.25	86.54	81.82	79.50
P.	PANAMA	97.05	98.84	95.52	101.15	102.36	101.28	97.12	101.60	95.81	96.28	94.97	96.47
Q.	PARAGUAY	90.24	87.83	89.91	100.00	97.02	99.37	98.02	102.61	99.24	93.77	90.71	100.43
R.	PERU	120.73	114.03	112.84	111.54	107.39	106.87	94.47	98.66	99.67	95.07	100.34	97.12
S.	URUGUAY	99.86	99.32	110.65	94.01	90.78	90.76	95.99	113.25	109.64	111.71	108.49	104.76
T.	VENEZUELA	101.28	111.42	99.93	99.96	103.13	103.38	99.33	97.29	93.72	91.44	86.43	86.91
	UNITED STATES	89.57	94.58	96.40	99.60	96.46	100.17	95.35	104.48	102.20	85.69	97.87	101.72

1. For alternative data from 1971 to 1977, see SALA, 21–1517.

a. For subindex of per capita food production, see SALA, 24–819.

SOURCE: FAO-PY, 1985, table 10.

Table 2102

BARLEY PRODUCTION, 10 LC, 1982–85[a]
(Area = T Ha.; Production = T MET; Yield = kg/Ha.)

	Country	1982			1983			1984			1985		
		Area[1]	Production	Yield[2]	Area[1]	Production	Yield[2]	Area[1]	Production	Yield[2]	Area[1]	Production	Yield[2]
A.	ARGENTINA	119	211	1,778	96	166	1,724	137	238	1,741	135[‡]	215[‡]	1,593
B.	BOLIVIA	84	61	726	46	30	507	90	72	799	94	75	800
C.	BRAZIL	167	99	590	121	125	1,033	73	78	1,059	110	161	1,437
D.	CHILE	57	118	2,050	38	73	1,919	33	74	2,217	35	85	2,425
E.	COLOMBIA	35	56	1,593	18	28	3,011	17[‡]	28	1,588	19	31	1,679
I.	ECUADOR	34	35	1,045	30	30	994	33[‡]	33	943	33	36	1,097
K.	GUATEMALA	~	1[†]	1,486	~	1[†]	1,500	~	1[†]	1,500	~	1[†]	1,505
N.	MEXICO	281	396	1,407	303	557	1,837	321	635	1,980	292	629	2,154
R.	PERU	90	100	1,112	81	72	891	91	96	1,081	95	108	1,133
S.	URUGUAY	26	45	1,741	52	90[‡]	1,562	82	90[†]	1,566	90[‡]	140[‡]	1,556
	UNITED STATES	3,647	11,233	3,080	3,938	11,080	2,814	4,545	3.046	2,870	4,675	12,828	2,744

1. Area harvested.
2. Yield may not equal kg/Ha. due to rounding of area and production data.

a. For prior years, see SALA, 23–1501 and SALA, 24–2102.

SOURCE: FAO-PY, 1980–81, table 12; 1985, table 18.

Table 2103

BANANA PRODUCTION, 17 LC, 1970–85[a]
(T MET)

	Country	1970	1975	1978	1979	1980	1981	1982	1983	1984	1985
A.	ARGENTINA	223	374	129	144	146	180[†]	89	126	161	110
B.	BOLIVIA	212	252	152	203	216	220[†]	152	154	160[†]	260[‡]
C.	BRAZIL	6,408[†]	5,311	6,240	6,133	6,736	6,696[‡]	6,818	6,566	7,062	7,505
E.	COLOMBIA	780	1,050[†]	1,100[†]	1,040[†]	1,030[‡]	1,155[‡]	1,147	1,173	1,350[†]	1,200[†]
F.	COSTA RICA	1,146[‡]	1,121	1,149	1,078	1,092	1,144	1,136	1,153	1,161	1,100[†]
G.	CUBA	47	92[‡]	150	147	145	155[†]	192	200	221	220[†]
H.	DOMINICAN REP	275	318	315[‡]	275	301	320[‡]	320[‡]	320[‡]	320[†]	320[†]
I.	ECUADOR	2,700[‡]	2,544	2,152	2,032	2,269	2,275[‡]	1,999	1,642	1,524[‡]	1,705[‡]
J.	EL SALVADOR	45	53[†]	53[†]	52[†]	52[†]	53[†]	54[†]	54[†]	55[†]	55[†]
K.	GUATEMALA	487	520[†]	550[†]	556[†]	650[†]	650[†]	655[†]	675[†]	680[†]	704[†]
L.	HAITI	176[†]	51[†]	195[‡]	210	200[†]	210[†]	230[†]	230[†]	235[†]	235[†]
M.	HONDURAS	1,200[†]	852	1,267	1,300[‡]	1,330[†]	1,330[†]	1,425	1,186	1,250[†]	1,300[†]
N.	MEXICO	1,136	1,194	1,384	1,553	1,515	1,562[†]	1,572	1,640	1,500[†]	1,500[†]
O.	NICARAGUA[1]	217	153	157[†]	170[†]	171[†]	170[†]	157[†]	128	128	127
P.	PANAMA	947	989	1,056	1,000[†]	1,050[†]	1,082[†]	1,057	1,045	1,056	1,100[†]
Q.	PARAGUAY	249	260[†]	254	306	300[†]	305[†]	314[‡]	315[†]	325[†]	325[†]
T.	VENEZUELA	968	860	900	961	983	980	917	934	965	989[‡]
	UNITED STATES	3	3	3	3	2	3	3	2	4	3

1. Refers to exports.

a. For prior years, see SALA, 23–1512 and SALA, 24–2103.

SOURCE: FAO-PY, 1972, table 76; 1976–77 and 1979–81, table 65; 1985, table 73.

Table 2104

BEAN PRODUCTION,[1] 20 LC, 1982–85[a]

(Area = T Ha.; Production = T MET; Yield = kg/Ha.)

Country	1982 Area[2]	1982 Production	1982 Yield[3]	1983 Area[2]	1983 Production	1983 Yield[3]	1984 Area[2]	1984 Production	1984 Yield[3]	1985 Area[2]	1985 Production	1985 Yield[3]
A. ARGENTINA	230	254	1,106	200	217	1,083	210‡	235‡	1,119	185‡	200‡	1,081
B. BOLIVIA	4†	4†	1,053	5	4	868	7	10	1,388	9	13	1,388
C. BRAZIL	5,926	2,903	490	4,064	1,581	390	5,320	2,626	494	5,317	2,547	479
D. CHILE	122	162	1,337	86	84	977	85	94	1,113	83	101	1,212
E. COLOMBIA	112	73	650	113	82	727	110	80	732	110	83	751
F. COSTA RICA	38	16	424	42	14	374	43	20	513	43	25	577
G. CUBA	35†	27†	757	35†	27†	771	35†	27†	771	35†	27†	771
H. DOMINICAN REP.	55‡	58	1,056	62	61	992	66†	67	1,019	69†	70†	1,014
I. ECUADOR	51	29	560	37	20	550	58‡	34‡	579	48	31	646
J. EL SALVADOR	56	38	687	56	42	750	58	49	841	58‡	48‡	828
K. GUATEMALA	97‡	84‡	866	167	104	626	167	111	668	166†	115†	691
L. HAITI	90†	50†	556	90†	50†	556	95†	52†	547	95†	52†	547
M. HONDURAS	51	31	600	51	31	603	84	52	624	80†	48†	600
N. MEXICO	1,712	1,093	638	1,996	1,282	642	2,158	1,270	589	2,032	1,085	534
O. NICARAGUA	68	47	684	93	57	613	72	44	613	86	57	662
P. PANAMA	9	3	358	9	4	451	8	3†	349	10†	3†	300
Q. PARAGUAY	80	60	750	80	60	750	80‡	60‡	750	80†	60†	750
R. PERU	50	43	868	46	35	772	53	45	853	64	57	892
S. URUGUAY	5†	3†	587	5†	3†	609	5†	3†	617	5†	3†	617
T. VENEZUELA	63	30	477	63	30	480	51	24	459	73‡	37‡	507
UNITED STATES	719	1,160	1,612	461	704	1,527	591	956	1,617	602	1,010	1,679

1. Includes *Phaseolus vulgaris*, *P. lunatus*, *P. aureus*, and *p. mungo*.
2. Area harvested.
3. Yield may not equal kg/Ha. due to rounding of area and production data.

a. For prior years, see SALA, 23–1509 and SALA, 24–2104.

SOURCE: FAO-PY, 1984 and 1985, table 31.

Table 2105

CASSAVA PRODUCTION, 18 L, 1982–85[a]

(Area = T Ha.; Production = T MET; Yield = kg/Ha.)

Country	1982 Area[1]	1982 Production	1982 Yield[2]	1983 Area[1]	1983 Production	1983 Yield[2]	1984 Area[1]	1984 Production	1984 Yield[2]	1985 Area[1]	1985 Production	1985 Yield[2]
A. ARGENTINA	24	216	9,076	16	139	8,688	16†	140†	8,750	16†	140†	8,750
B. BOLIVIA	21	271	12,868	15	179	12,082	33	280	8,471	41	376	9,142
C. BRAZIL	2,122	24,072	11,344	2,061	21,848	10,600	1,816	21,466	11,824	1,866	23,073	12,366
E. COLOMBIA	207	2,000	9,662	173‡	1,155	9,002	183	1,675	9,150	190	1,729	9,099
F. COSTA RICA	5	17	3,131	5	21	4,667	5†	18	3,576	5†	20†	4,000
G. CUBA	49†	330‡	6,735	46†	300‡	6,522	46†	300‡	6,522	46†	300†	6,522
H. DOMINICAN REP.	13	68	5,105	17	102	6,083	20†	129	5,496	23	125	5,496
I. ECUADOR	20	184	9,231	20	195	9,690	27‡	243‡	9,000	26‡	234‡	9,000
J. EL SALVADOR	2	23	11,829	2	23	12,814	2†	28	14,644	2†	23†	12,778
K. GUATEMALA	3†	9†	3,600	3†	9†	3,680	3†	9†	3,680	3†	9†	3,760
L. HAITI	64†	260‡	4,063	65†	265†	4,077	65†	265†	4,077	65†	265†	4,077
M. HONDURAS	2†	8†	5,000	2†	7	18,619	~	7†	17,500	~	7†	17,500
N. MEXICO	2‡	43‡	17,660	2†	43†	17,551	2†	43†	17,551	2†	43†	17,555
O. NICARAGUA	7†	27†	4,015	7†	27†	4,030	7†	27†	4,030	7†	27†	4,030
P. PANAMA	5†	35	7,277	5†	34	7,056	5†	34	7,012	5†	35†	7,143
Q. PARAGUAY	141‡	2,111‡	14,972	145†	2,100†	14,483	150†	2,200†	14,667	150†	2,200†	14,667
R. PERU	30	324	10,997	33	361	10,912	33	356	10,883	32	337	10,489
T. VENEZUELA	39	301	7,701	41	325	8,013	41	331	8,008	39‡	310‡	7,949

1. Area harvested.
2. Yield may not equal kg/Ha. due to rounding of area and production data.

a. For prior years, see SALA, 23–1509 and SALA, 24–2105.

SOURCE: FAO-PY, 1984 and 1985, table 27.

Table 2106

COCOA BEAN PRODUCTION, 16 L, 1982–85[a]

(Area = T Ha.; Production = T MET; Yield = kg/Ha.)

	Country	1982 Area[1]	1982 Production	1982 Yield[2]	1983 Area[1]	1983 Production	1983 Yield[2]	1984 Area[1]	1984 Production	1984 Yield[2]	1985 Area[1]	1985 Production	1985 Yield[2]
B.	BOLIVIA	5†	3‡	556	5†	3‡	667	5†	3‡	667	5†	3†	667
C.	BRAZIL	533	351	658	591	380	644	609	345	567	638	419	657
E.	COLOMBIA	77	39	510	75‡	37	493	84	39	463	87	43	496
F.	COSTA RICA	12	5	453	9	2	237	12‡	3‡	284	11	5	425
G.	CUBA	2	2	708	3†	2	723	4†	3	750	5†	4‡	769
H.	DOMINICAN REP.	135†	43	321	140†	45	322	125‡	35‡	276	140‡	41‡	295
I.	ECUADOR	277	97	350	270	45	167	263‡	55‡	209	269‡	128‡	479
J.	EL SALVADOR	~	~	1,000	~	~	1,000	~	~	1,000	~	~	1,000
K.	GUATEMALA	3†	2†	500	3†	2†	500	3†	2†	500	3†	2†	500
L.	HAITI	2	3‡	2,000	2†	3‡	2,000	2†	3‡	2,000	2†	3†	2,000
M.	HONDURAS	1†	1†	1,000	1†	1†	1,000	1†	1†	1,000	1†	1†	1,000
N.	MEXICO	82	38	466	59	33	567	82‡	38‡	463	82‡	40‡	488
O.	NICARAGUA	3†	~	143	2†	~	150	2	~	150	2†	~	150
P.	PANAMA	6†	2	311	4†	1	335	4†	1	365	4†	1‡	250
R.	PERU	15†	9‡	600	11†	7	611	11†	7	620	11†	6	543
T.	VENEZUELA	64	13	208	68	14	206	61	12	201	62‡	11‡	177

1. Area harvested.
2. Yield may not equal kg/Ha. due to rounding of area and production data.

a. For prior years, see SALA, 23–1507 and SALA, 24–2106.

SOURCE: FAO-PY, 1984 and 1985, table 78.

Table 2107

COFFEE PRODUCTION, 17 LC, 1982–85[a]

(Area = T Ha.; Production = T MET; Yield = kg/Ha.)

	Country	1982 Area[1]	1982 Production	1982 Yield[2]	1983 Area[1]	1983 Production	1983 Yield[2]	1984 Area[1]	1984 Production	1984 Yield[2]	1985 Area[1]	1985 Production	1985 Yield[2]
B.	BOLIVIA	24	21	900	24	21	899	24†	18†	729	25†	18†	720
C.	BRAZIL	1,895	958	505	2,279	1,665	731	2,452‡	1,339‡	546	2,483	1,877‡	756
E.	COLOMBIA	1,087‡	861‡	792	955‡	816	845	945‡	780‡	825	900†	660‡	733
F.	COSTA RICA	85‡	115	1,354	87	123	1,412	90	151	1,678	85	121	1,424
G.	CUBA	50†	29	574	50†	18	368	50†	19‡	380	50†	23‡	450
H.	DOMINICAN REP.	160†	63	397	160†	68	425	170†	72	424	162‡	68†	420
I.	ECUADOR	322	84	261	339	81	239	330‡	90‡	273	335‡	96	287
J.	EL SALVADOR	161‡	146	908	186‡	155	833	186‡	162	872	188‡	156‡	830
K.	GUATEMALA	257‡	159‡	619	260‡	153‡	587	260‡	140‡	540	260‡	152‡	585
L.	HAITI	35†	39‡	1,114	31†	40‡	1,277	34†	38‡	1,121	34†	39‡	1,147
M.	HONDURAS	123	85	688	122	74	606	123	73	593	133‡	84	632
N.	MEXICO	420	231	550	581	313	538	415‡	262‡	632	410†	269‡	656
O.	NICARAGUA	100	71	713	97	45	461	92	50	544	93	50	538
P.	PANAMA	24	8	339	26	9	336	24‡	11	448	35†	16‡	446
Q.	PARAGUAY	16‡	16‡	1,016	14	17	1,200	14‡	18‡	1,286	14†	18‡	1,286
R.	PERU	142†	90	633	143‡	91	635	143‡	87	623	125‡	91	724
T.	VENEZUELA	254	58	229	255	59	231	256	61	238	269‡	64‡	238
	UNITED STATES	1	~	468	1	1	1,392	1	1	920	1	1	894

1. Area harvested.
2. Yield may not equal kg/Ha. due to rounding of area and production data.

a. For prior years, see SALA, 23–1506 and SALA, 24–2107.

SOURCE: FAO-PY, 1984 and 1985, table 77.

Table 2108

COPRA PRODUCTION, 11 L, 1970–85[a]
(T MET)

Country	1970	1975	1980	1982	1983	1984	1985
C. BRAZIL	2.2	2†	2†	7†	3†	3†	3†
E. COLOMBIA	2.2†	~	~	~	~	~	~
F. COSTA RICA	1.2	2†	2†	2†	2†	2†	2†
H. DOMINICAN REP.	7.5	9†	12†	11†	13‡	14†	14†
I. ECUADOR	2.2†	4†	14†	13†	11†	13†	14†
J. EL SALVADOR	3.0†	5‡	3‡	3†	3†	3†	3‡
M. HONDURAS	2.4†	3†	3†	2†	2†	2†	2†
N. MEXICO	137.4	145‡	140‡	147	143	120	120
O. NICARAGUA	.2†	~	~	~	~	~	~
P. PANAMA	.6	1†	1†	1	1†	1†	~
T. VENEZUELA	16.9	18	12	16‡	16‡	12‡	9‡

a. For prior years, see SALA, 23–1516.

SOURCE: FAO-PY, 1974, table 57; 1977–81, table 38; 1985, table 46.

Table 2109

COTTON LINT PRODUCTION, 18 LC, 1970–85[a]
(T MET)

Country	1970	1975	1980	1982	1983	1984	1985
A. ARGENTINA	145	171	146	153	111	174	165‡
B. BOLIVIA	5	22	7	4	3	1	2‡
C. BRAZIL	672	515	572‡	639	552	723	926‡
E. COLOMBIA	128	121	116‡	33‡	77‡	126‡	114‡
F. COSTA RICA	1†	1	4‡	5†	2	2	3
G. CUBA	1†	1‡	1‡	1‡	1‡	1‡	1‡
H. DOMINICAN REP.	1†	1†	2‡	2‡	1‡	2‡	2†
I. ECUADOR	4‡	11	15‡	9‡	1‡	4‡	11‡
J. EL SALVADOR	46	78	65	40	41	30	31
K. GUATEMALA	57	105‡	156	71	55	59	67‡
L. HAITI	1†	1†	1†	2†	2†	2†	2†
M. HONDURAS	3	5‡	7‡	4‡	6‡	5‡	4‡
N. MEXICO	312	197	329‡	166	229	291	196‡
O. NICARAGUA	67	123	21‡	63	80	85	69
Q. PARAGUAY	13	33‡	75	91	77	90	160‡
R. PERU	92	60‡	90‡	36‡	76‡	87‡	97‡
S. URUGUAY	- -	1	~	~	~	~	~
T. VENEZUELA	13	31	18	6	15‡	15‡	15‡
UNITED STATES	2,213	1,807	2,422	2,605	1,692	2,894	2,947

a. For prior years, see SALA, 23–1504.

SOURCE: FAO-PY, 1971, table 96; 1976–81, table 78; 1985, table 86.

Table 2110

COTTONSEED PRODUCTION, 18 LC, 1970–85[a]

(T MET)

	Country	1970	1975	1980	1982	1983	1984	1985
A.	ARGENTINA	249	541	276	270	202	316	290†
B.	BOLIVIA	10	61‡	12	8‡	6‡	2‡	3‡
C.	BRAZIL	1,227	1,751	1,125‡	1,238‡	995‡	1,338‡	1,750†
E.	COLOMBIA	231	385	216‡	66‡	130	243	217‡
F.	COSTA RICA	2	2‡	8‡	9†	3†	4†	6†
G.	CUBA	2†	3†	2‡	2‡	2‡	2‡	2†
H.	DOMINICAN REP.	3	2†	4‡	4‡	4‡	4‡	4†
I.	ECUADOR	10‡	30	24‡	15‡	2	6‡	18†
J.	EL SALVADOR	76	210	109	63	60	45†	45‡
K.	GUATEMALA	92	280‡	251	115	76		92
L.	HAITI	1†	3†	2†	3†	3†	3†	3†
M.	HONDURAS	6	15‡	15‡	5	10†	7‡	7‡
N.	MEXICO	550	544	538	289	355	395	335†
O.	NICARAGUA	112	330‡	37‡	95	119	126	98
Q.	PARAGUAY	25	94‡	146‡	185‡	150‡	174‡	310‡
R.	PERU	153	180‡	172‡	61‡	140‡	165†	170†
S.	URUGUAY	#	2‡	~	~	~	~	~
T.	VENEZUELA	23	88	32‡	10‡	26‡	25‡	25†
	UNITED STATES	3,690	4,556	4,056	4,304	2,791	4,671	4,872

a. For prior years, see SALA, 23–1505.

SOURCE: FAO-PY, 1971, table 80; 1976–81, table 37; 1984 and 1985, table 45.

Table 2111

MAIZE PRODUCTION, 20 LC, 1982–85[a]

(Area = T Ha.; Production = T MET; Yield = kg/Ha.)

	Country	1982 Area[1]	1982 Production	1982 Yield[2]	1983 Area[1]	1983 Production	1983 Yield[2]	1984 Area[1]	1984 Production	1984 Yield[2]	1985 Area[1]	1985 Production	1985 Yield[2]
A.	ARGENTINA	3,170	9,600	3,028	2,970	9,000	3,030	3,025	9,500	3,141	3,498	12,600	3,603
B.	BOLIVIA	286	450	1,572	261	337	1,293	322‡	489‡	1,519	349	554	1,588
C.	BRAZIL	12,620	21,842	1,731	10,706	18,731	1,750	12,018	21,164	1,761	11,802	22,017	1,866
D.	CHILE	115	425	3,696	118	512	4,337	138	721	5,213	131	772	5,913
E.	COLOMBIA	636	899	1,413	582	864	1,483	593	864	1,458	598	882	1,476
F.	COSTA RICA	54	85	1,579	62	105	1,697	61	103	1,680	61	107	1,754
G.	CUBA	77†	96†	1,247	77†	96†	1,247	77†	97†	1,260	77†	97†	1,260
H.	DOMINICAN REP.	21	28	1,299	27	42	1,559	58	76	1,321	38	68	1,779
I.	ECUADOR	217	324	1,496	206	229	1,115	220‡	292‡	1,326	200‡	250†	1,250
J.	EL SALVADOR	239	414	1,734	242	443	1,835	243	527	2,166	243‡	521‡	2,144
K.	GUATEMALA	669	1,100	1,645	800	1,046	1,308	760‡	1,038	1,366	770‡	1,102‡	1,431
L.	HAITI	186	176‡	945	171	171‡	999	200‡	180‡	900	100‡	90‡	900
M.	HONDURAS	272	366	1,345	308	458	1,485	402	552	1,373	350‡	550‡	1,571
N.	MEXICO	5,704	10,030	1,759	7,421	13,061	1,760	8,864	13,222	1,492	8,418	15,013	1,783
O.	NICARAGUA	164	164	997	183	218	1,190	141	187	1,325	161	234	1,452
P.	PANAMA	69	62	900	71	69	969	63	71	1,119	70‡	70‡	1,000
Q.	PARAGUAY	420	510	1,214	370	420	1,135	400‡	500‡	1,250	400†	500†	1,250
R.	PERU	218	631	2,900	340	585	1,720	380	776	2,041	371	708	1,910
S.	URUGUAY	95	97	1,025	93	104	1,114	86	112	1,300	89	108	1,207
T.	VENEZUELA	305	501	1,643	310	488	1,573	313	1,749	547	480‡	900‡	1,875
	UNITED STATES	29,428	209,180	7,108	20,834	106,041	5,090	29,013	194,928	6,719	30,406	225,180	7,406

1. Area harvested.
2. Yield may not equal kg/Ha. due to rounding of area and production data.

a. For prior years, see SALA, 23–1502 and SALA, 24–2111.

SOURCE: FAO-PY, 1984 and 1985, table 19.

Table 2112

ORANGE AND TANGERINE PRODUCTION, 20 LC, 1970–85[a]

(T MET)

Country	1970	1975	1980	1982	1983	1984	1985
A. ARGENTINA	1,092	959	918	861	853	805‡	850‡
B. BOLIVIA	68	87	109	119†	120†	120†	63†
C. BRAZIL	3,343	6,643†	9,327‡	9,836	10,047‡	13,902‡	14,649†
D. CHILE[1]	42‡	43	49‡	65	67	69	76
E. COLOMBIA[1]	..	..	225‡	231‡	250	253‡	260‡
F. COSTA RICA[1]	59	68†	75†	77†	78†	78†	80†
G. CUBA	138	142	328	358	431	395	433‡
H. DOMINICAN REP.[1]	60†	68†	71	73†	74†	75†	75†
I. ECUADOR	197†	303	564	535	384	380†	380†
J. EL SALVADOR[2]	41	45†	101†	107†	101†	102†	100†
K. GUATEMALA	~	~	~	~	~	~	~
L. HAITI	6†,b	32†	38†	39†	40†	41†	41†
M. HONDURAS[1]	48	25†	27†	45	46†	47†	47†
N. MEXICO	1,555b	2,478‡	1,810‡	2,139	2,197	1,730†	2,123†
O. NICARAGUA[1]	45	50†	52†	54†	55†	55†	55†
P. PANAMA[1]	42	62	66	66	34	34	34
Q. PARAGUAY	225†	154†	272†	272‡	283‡	283‡	289†
R. PERU	261	241†	170†	174†	176†	177†	169†
S. URUGUAY	59b	77†	85‡	105	85	80	103†
T. VENEZUELA[1]	184	245	433	372	384	362	370‡
UNITED STATES	7,761	9,913	11,490	7,426	9,190	7,012	6,501

1. Oranges only.
2. Includes tangerines beginning in 1982.

a. For prior years, see SALA, 23–1513.

SOURCE: FAO-PY, 1971, table 65; 1976–77 and 1979–81, table 62; 1985, table 70.

Table 2113

POTATO PRODUCTION, 20 LC, 1982–85[a]

(Area = T Ha.; Production = T MET; Yield = kg/Ha.)

		1982			1983			1984			1985		
	Country	Area[1]	Production	Yield[2]	Area[1]	Production	Yield[2]	Area[1]	Production	Yield[2]	Area[1]	Production	Yield[2]
A.	ARGENTINA	102	1,817	17,775	108	2,013	18,617	114	2,118	18,607	114†	2,000†	17,544
B.	BOLIVIA	159	900	5,648	108	316	2,926	143	668	4,689	198	721	3,635
C.	BRAZIL	183	2,155	11,807	169	1,827	10,804	173	2,171	12,577	157	1,989	12,641
D.	CHILE	77	842	10,871	67	684	10,179	81	1,036	12,734	63	909	14,453
E.	COLOMBIA	165	2,149	13,008	161	2,187	13,624	160	2,463	15,422	146	2,017	13,825
F.	COSTA RICA	3†	22	7,097	4†	42	12,000	2	30	14,006	3	39	14,502
G.	CUBA	15	258	17,035	13	207	16,256	17	259	15,589	15†	230†	15,333
H.	DOMINICAN REP.	1	12	10,632	2	19	11,254	1	14	12,438	1	11	13,427
I.	ECUADOR	35	416	11,863	27	314	11,742	33‡	363‡	11,000	35‡	385‡	11,000
J.	EL SALVADOR	~	6†	19,375	~	6†	19,091	~	7†	18,571	~	7†	18,571
K.	GUATEMALA	6‡	28‡	4,667	6‡	30‡	5,000	6†	30†	5,000	6†	30†	5,085
L.	HAITI	1†	9†	15,000	1†	9†	15,000	1†	9†	15,000	1†	9†	15,000
M.	HONDURAS	1	8	11,571	1†	9†	12,143	1†	9†	12,000	1†	9†	12,000
N.	MEXICO	68	941	13,842	74	835	11,225	70†	830†	11,857	70†	840†	12,000
O.	NICARAGUA	~	2†	4,268	~	2†	4,286	~	2†	4,186	~	2†	4,186
P.	PANAMA	2‡	17	11,545	2‡	16	10,913	2†	16	10,943	2†	15†	10,000
Q.	PARAGUAY	1†	9‡	9,000	1†	9†	9,000	1†	10†	9,091	1†	10†	9,091
R.	PERU	217	1,800	8,296	156	1,200	7,683	172	1,463	8,510	189	1,590	8,432
S.	URUGUAY	21	149	7,075	19	109	5,845	20†	144	7,500	20†	150†	7,500
T.	VENEZUELA	17	217	12,799	17	225	13,533	19	245	12,601	14‡	191‡	13,643
	UNITED STATES	516	16,109	31,248	503	15,146	30,123	527	16,448	31,240	550	18,331	33,356

1. Area harvest.
2. Yield may not equal kg/Ha. due to rounding of area and production data.

a. For prior years, see SALA, 23–1510 and SALA, 24–2113.

SOURCE: FAO-PY, 1984 and 1985, table 25.

Table 2114

RICE PADDY PRODUCTION, 20 LC, 1982–85[a]

(Area = T Ha.; Production = T MET; Yield = kg/Ha.)

		1982			1983			1984			1985		
	Country	Area[1]	Production	Yield[2]	Area[1]	Production	Yield[2]	Area[1]	Production	Yield[2]	Area[1]	Production	Yield[2]
A.	ARGENTINA	114	437	3,849	81	277	3,422	129	476[‡]	3,679	117	400	3,419
B.	BOLIVIA	54	87	1,596	44	62	1,417	121[‡]	194[‡]	1,605	120	184	1,540
C.	BRAZIL	6,025	9,735	1,616	5,108	7,741	1,516	5,351	9,027	1,687	4,752	9,019	1,898
D.	CHILE	37	131	3,549	30	116	3,798	40	165	4,138	39	157	4,066
E.	COLOMBIA	446	2,018	4,526	397	1,780	4,489	304	1,606	5,280	328	5,385	1,764
F.	COSTA RICA	77	146	1,896	88	281	3,185	72	223	3,079	69	219	3,173
G.	CUBA	143	520	3,632	150	518	3,461	151	555	3,665	155	524	3,372
H.	DOMINICAN REP.	93	447	4,809	119	355	2,999	118	507	4,296	110	438[‡]	3,971
I.	ECUADOR	132	384	2,918	93	270	2,898	136	414	3,043	120[†]	300[†]	2,500
J.	EL SALVADOR	11	35	3,166	13	43	3,435	15	63	4,132	17	69	3,988
K.	GUATEMALA	17	49	2,823	12	46	3,713	16	45	2,788	22	62	2,789
L.	HAITI	50[‡]	116[‡]	2,316	50[‡]	113[‡]	2,268	55[‡]	124[‡]	2,255	60[†]	120[†]	2,083
M.	HONDURAS	23	38	1,641	22	46	2,127	22	53	2,416	39[†]	56[‡]	1,436
N.	MEXICO	156	511	3,270	133	416	3,118	156	511	3,270	276	988	3,580
O.	NICARAGUA	43	176	4,137	44	171	3,891	41	162	3,937	41	156[‡]	3,813
P.	PANAMA	106	176	1,662	107	199	1,872	93	175	1,877	105[‡]	199[‡]	1,895
Q.	PARAGUAY	26	54	2,113	34	75	2,206	32[‡]	65[‡]	2,031	32[†]	70[†]	2,188
R.	PERU	169	776	4,578	195	798	4,086	249	1,156	4,651	218	973	4,456
S.	URUGUAY	69	419	6,031	70	323	4,606	79	340	4,313	85	423	4,984
T.	VENEZUELA	227	609	2,676	164	449	2,734	151	408	2,700	148[‡]	472[‡]	3,189
	UNITED STATES	1,320	6,969	5,279	878	4,523	5,153	1,134	6,296	5,552	1,113	6,171	6,095

1. Area harvested.
2. Yield may not equal kg/Ha. due to rounding of area and production data.

a. For prior years, see SALA, 23–1503 and SALA, 24–2114.

SOURCE: FAO-PY, 1984 and 1985, table 17.

Table 2115

SUGAR CANE PRODUCTION, 19 LC, 1982–85[a]

(Area = T Ha.; Production = T MET; Yield = kg/Ha.)

		1982			1983			1984			1985		
	Country	Area[1]	Production	Yield[2]	Area[1]	Production	Yield[2]	Area[1]	Production	Yield[2]	Area[1]	Production	Yield[2]
A.	ARGENTINA	309	15,046	48,771	313	15,070	48,086	319	15,468	48,565	200[†]	11,000[†]	55,000
B.	BOLIVIA	70	3,103	44,540	71	2,649	37,455	70	2,315[†]	33,063	78	2,000[†]	25,734
C.	BRAZIL	3,084	186,647	60,515	3,479	216,037	62,101	3,656	222,318	60,812	3,854	245,904	63,846
E.	COLOMBIA	274	23,500[†]	85,735	280	24,200[†]	86,429	275[†]	23,500[†]	85,455	290[†]	25,000[†]	86,207
F.	COSTA RICA	51[‡]	2,446	47,965	36	2,618	72,732	44	2,936	67,502	60[†]	2,800[†]	46,667
G.	CUBA	1,327	73,100	55,074	1,200	69,700	58,069	1,500[†]	75,000[†]	50,000	1,400[‡]	73,000[‡]	52,143
H.	DOMINCAN REP.	188[‡]	11,805	62,793	188[‡]	11,520	61,277	188[‡]	10,271	54,633	185[‡]	10,200[‡]	55,135
I.	ECUADOR	92	5,421	58,757	80	5,620	70,327	80[†]	6,100[†]	76,250	80[†]	5,800[†]	72,500
J.	EL SALVADOR	32[‡]	2,372[‡]	74,803	41	2,984	72,992	42	3,200[†]	77,090	50[†]	3,400[†]	68,000
K.	GUATEMALA	78[‡]	6,080[‡]	77,949	90[‡]	7,400	82,222	89[‡]	6,600[‡]	74,157	90[†]	7,500[†]	83,519
L.	HAITI	80[†]	3,000[‡]	37,500	80[†]	3,000[‡]	37,500	80[†]	3,000[‡]	37,500	80[†]	3,000[†]	37,500
M.	HONDURAS	95[†]	3,096	32,585	95[†]	3,195	33,627	95[†]	3,250[†]	34,211	95[†]	3,300[†]	34,737
N.	MEXICO	526	34,066	64,766	505	34,109	67,591	525[†]	36,500[†]	69,524	550[†]	37,800[†]	68,727
O.	NICARAGUA	44	2,827	64,053	46	2,911	63,969	47	2,545	54,355	46	2,831	60,916
P.	PANAMA	50	2,094	41,512	38	2,134	56,674	38	1,821	47,808	37[‡]	2,000[†]	54,054
Q.	PARAGUAY	40	1,500	37,500	40	1,700	42,500	40[‡]	1,700[‡]	42,500	40[†]	1,700[†]	42,500
R.	PERU	46	6,509	140,481	45	6,380	140,645	53	6,988	131,615	54[†]	7,425	137,493
S.	URUGUAY	10	480	47,241	10	551	55,639	10[‡]	552	53,181	10	552	53,181
T.	VENEZUELA	81	5,372	66,407	79	4,861	61,119	82	4,966	60,662	87[‡]	5,673[‡]	65,207
	UNITED STATES	300	27,002	89,978	311	25,547	82,232	302	24,802	82,165	310	25,390	82,036

1. Area harvested.
2. Yield may not equal kg/Ha. due to rounding of area and production data.

a. For prior years, see SALA, 23–1514 and SALA, 24–2115.

SOURCE: FAO-PY, 1984 and 1985, table 66.

Table 2116

TOBACCO LEAF PRODUCTION, 20 LC, 1982–85[a]

(Area = T Ha.; Production = T MET; Yield = kg/Ha.)

	Country	1982 Area[1]	1982 Production	1982 Yield[2]	1983 Area[1]	1983 Production	1983 Yield[2]	1984 Area[1]	1984 Production	1984 Yield[2]	1985 Area[1]	1985 Production	1985 Yield[2]
A.	ARGENTINA	55	69	1,245	60	74	1,242	61	75	1,229	50[†]	61	1,210
B.	BOLIVIA	2[‡]	2[‡]	1,000	1[‡]	1[‡]	1,000	2[†]	2[†]	1,000	2[†]	2[†]	1,000
C.	BRAZIL	317[‡]	420[‡]	1,325	312	393	1,259	282	414	1,466	269	411	1,530
D.	CHILE	2[‡]	6[‡]	2,900	2	6	3,096	3	8	3,250	3	8	2,795
E.	COLOMBIA	26[†]	41	1,569	29	48	1,660	26	43	1,650	25	42[‡]	1,667
F.	COSTA RICA	1	2	1,392	2	2	1,289	2	2	1,425	1[‡]	2[‡]	1,296
G.	CUBA	65[‡]	45	696	51[‡]	30	597	66[‡]	45	677	66[‡]	46[‡]	697
H.	DOMINICAN REP.	35[‡]	34	963	30[‡]	34	1,123	29[‡]	28	978	21	23	1,125
I.	ECUADOR	2	3	1,890	1	2	1,546	2[‡]	3[‡]	1,667	2[‡]	3[‡]	1,667
J.	EL SALVADOR	2[‡]	4[‡]	1,781	3	5	1,853	3[†]	5[†]	1,800	3[†]	5[†]	1,800
K.	GUATEMALA	5[‡]	10[‡]	1,877	4[‡]	7[‡]	1,851	4[‡]	7[‡]	1,839	5[‡]	9[‡]	1,800
L.	HAITI	1[‡]	1[‡]	941	1[‡]	1[‡]	1,122	1[‡]	1[‡]	1,214	1[†]	1[†]	1,250
M.	HONDURAS	10	7	745	10	7	750	8[‡]	12[‡]	1,523	8[†]	10[†]	1,250
N.	MEXICO	39	67	1,709	37	53	1,431	35[‡]	55[‡]	1,562	36[‡]	56[‡]	1,584
O.	NICARAGUA	2	3	1,776	2	5	1,886	2	4	1,804	2[‡]	4[‡]	1,782
P.	PANAMA	1	2	1,542	1	1	1,648	1	1	1,743	1[‡]	1[‡]	1,708
Q.	PARAGUAY	9[‡]	12[‡]	1,333	12[‡]	18[‡]	1,500	15[‡]	20[‡]	1,333	15[†]	20[†]	1,333
R.	PERU	3[‡]	4[‡]	1,404	2[‡]	3[‡]	1,242	2[‡]	3[‡]	1,242	3[‡]	3[‡]	1,240
S.	URUGUAY	1[‡]	1[‡]	1,649	1	1	1,684	1[†]	1[†]	1,750	1[†]	1[†]	1,750
T.	VENEZUELA	10	16	1,598	10	16	1,641	7[‡]	11[‡]	1,574	9[‡]	15[‡]	1,667
	UNITED STATES	369	905	2,449	319	648	2,029	320	784	2,447	284	702	2,474

1. Area harvested.
2. Yield may not equal kg/Ha. due to rounding of area and production data.

a. For prior years, see SALA, 23–1515 and SALA, 24–2116.

SOURCE: FAO-PY, 1984 and 1985, table 81.

Table 2117

WHEAT PRODUCTION, 13 LC, 1982–85[a]

(Area = T Ha.; Production = T MET; Yield = kg/Ha.)

	Country	1982 Area[1]	1982 Production	1982 Yield[2]	1983 Area[1]	1983 Production	1983 Yield[2]	1984 Area[1]	1984 Production	1984 Yield[2]	1985 Area[1]	1985 Production	1985 Yield[2]
A.	ARGENTINA	7,320	15,000	2,049	6,880	12,300	1,788	5,901	12,300	2,237	5,296[‡]	8,500[†]	1,605
B.	BOLIVIA	96	66	684	71	40	572	89	68	771	93	68	727
C.	BRAZIL	2,828	1,827	646	1,879	2,237	1,190	1,742	1,983	1,139	2,658	4,247	1,598
D.	CHILE	374	650	1,739	359	586	1,631	471	988	2,097	506	1,165	2,301
E.	COLOMBIA	45	71	1,561	46	78	1,680	43[‡]	59[‡]	1,382	45[‡]	79[‡]	1,776
I.	ECUADOR	33	39	1,166	26	27	1,045	20[‡]	23[‡]	1,150	18[‡]	19[‡]	1,056
K.	GUATEMALA	37	49	1,303	41	31	754	36[‡]	32	882	31[‡]	44[‡]	1,419
M.	HONDURAS	1	1	636	1[†]	1[†]	636	1[†]	1[†]	682	1[†]	1[†]	682
N.	MEXICO	1,013	4,468	4,409	857	3,460	4,037	1,089	4,542	4,170	1,242	5,228	4,209
Q.	PARAGUAY	60	65	1,083	75	107	1,427	80[‡]	100[‡]	1,250	80[†]	105[†]	1,313
R.	PERU	84	101	1,195	81	76	931	79	84	1,060	81	90	1,116
S.	URUGUAY	240	363	1,512	255	419	1,639	226	349	1,544	300[‡]	440[‡]	1,467
T.	VENEZUELA	1	~	373	1	~	380	1	~	365	1[‡]	1[‡]	500
	UNITED STATES	31,540	75,251	2,386	24,843	65,858	2,651	27,085	70,618	2,607	26,197	65,992	2,519

1. Area harvested.
2. Yield may not equal kg/Ha. due to rounding of area and production data.

a. For prior years, see SALA, 23–1500 and SALA, 24–2117.

SOURCE: FAO-PY, 1984 and 1985, table 16.

Table 2118

SWEET POTATO AND YAM PRODUCTION, 17 LC, 1982–85[a]

(Area = T Ha.; Production = T MET; Yield = kg/Ha.)

	Country	1982 Area[1]	1982 Production	1982 Yield[2]	1983 Area[1]	1983 Production	1983 Yield[2]	1984 Area[1]	1984 Production	1984 Yield[2]	1985 Area[1]	1985 Production	1985 Yield[2]
A.	ARGENTINA[3]	32	368	11,536	28	310	11,151	31	325	10,552	31†	325†	10,484
B.	BOLIVIA[3]	2	9	5,714	1	5	3,914	2	8	4,131	2	7	3,813
C.	BRAZIL[4]	103†	931†	18,075	105†	930†	17,824	105†	930†	17,824	100†	930†	18,375
D.	CHILE[3]	1†	7†	7,000	1†	7†	7,000	1†	7†	7,000	1†	7†	7,000
E.	COLOMBIA[5]	13	96	7,385	13†	96	7,408	14†	120†	8,571	15	106	7,303
G.	CUBA[3]	82†	330†	4,024	83†	332†	4,000	84†	335†	4,012	83†	330†	4,000
H.	DOMINICAN REP.[4]	5	24	10,826	6	44	13,569	12†	74	12,942	9	59	13,193
I.	ECUADOR[3]	1	5	5,441	1	7	5,118	1†	6†	6,000	1†	6†	6,000
J.	EL SALVADOR[3]	~	~	5,000	~	~	5,000	~	~	5,000	~	~	5,000
L.	HAITI[4]	100†	428†	8,101	106†	466†	8,276	106†	470†	8,333	106†	470†	8,333
M.	HONDURAS[3]	~	1	3,560	~	2	3,333	~	2	3,478	~	2	3,478
N.	MEXICO[3]	3	51	15,969	3	51	17,818	3†	50†	16,667	3†	50†	16,667
P.	PANAMA[5]	2†	11	5,728	2†	11†	5,500	2†	11†	5,500	2†	18†	9,000
Q.	PARAGUAY[3]	15†	119‡	7,933	15†	120†	8,000	15†	120†	8,000	15†	120†	8,000
R.	PERU[3]	7	93	13,640	11	127	11,575	10	141	13,522	7	100	14,827
S.	URUGUAY	15‡	60‡	4,000	15†	60†	4,000	15†	60†	4,000	15†	60†	4,000
T.	VENEZUELA[4]	6	34	8,725	7	40	9,831	7	41	10,517	7†	40†	10,272
	UNITED STATES[3]	47	673	14,407	41	548	13,226	42	589	14,057	43	654	15,388

1. Area harvested.
2. Yield may not equal kg/Ha. due to rounding of area and production data.
3. Sweet potatoes only.
4. Sweet potatoes and yams.
5. Yams only.

a. For prior years, see SALA, 23–1511 and SALA, 24–2118.

SOURCE: FAO-PY, 1984 and 1985, tables 26 and 28.

Table 2119

FERTILIZER PRODUCTION,[1] 13 LC, 1970-85[a]

(T MET)

Country	1970/71	1971/72	1972/73	1973/74	1974/75	1975/76	1976/77	1977/78	1978/79	1979/90	1980/81	1981/82	1982/83	1983/84	1984/85
A. ARGENTINA	35	44	43	34	30+	25+	29+	28	29	26	31	25	29+	32	34+
B. BRAZIL	225	346	422	515	628	755	1,126	1,354	1,459	1,594	1,967	1,536	1,512	1,588+	2,154
D. CHILE	140	162	155	156	153	146	123	113	100	118	112	100	92	98	114
E. COLOMBIA	88	96	117	155	156	101	99	122+	110	102	88+	92+	79+	93+	100
F. COSTA RICA	12	17	16	27+	30+	30+	31	32	33+	36+	40+	42+	46+	36+	41+
G. CUBA	5+	7	9+	29+	49+	91	80	60	48+	139	117+	148+	100	76	171
I. ECUADOR	6+	~	7+	4+	6+	7	7	6	9+	10+	9+	10+	13+	3+	~
J. EL SALVADOR	10+	9+	6+	11+	9+	8	8	17	28	17+	~	~	~	~	~
K. GUATEMALA	~	~	~	~	2	5+	12+	12+	11	4+	17+	16+	23+	17+	19+
N. MEXICO	580	627	700	782	817	864	856	893	820	869	940	1,114	1,320	1,303	1,420
R. PERU	26+	29+	26+	24	26+	35	57+	70	72	69	78	90+	77	35	20+
S. URUGUAY	27	43+	36+	52	62+	35	17+	24+	20	41	30+	20+	17+	6+	10+
T. VENEZUELA	18	12	29	26+	69	75	92+	93+	76	105	168+	179	247+	237+	308+
UNITED STATES	15,789	15,899	16,669	17,753	17,117	18,221	19,202	18,950	20,918	22,508	23,377	19,250	17,983	19,356	22,079
WORLD	72,945	77,891	84,045	88,838	93,319	94,348	100,770	107,263	114,354	119,045	124,717	119,610	119,945	130,257	140,069

1. Includes nitrogenous, phosphate, and potash fertilizers.

a. For 1961-70 data, see SALA, 23-1521.

SOURCE: FAO-FY, 1979 and 1981, table 30; 1985, table 29.

CHAPTER 22

RANCH PRODUCTION

Table 2200

CATTLE POPULATION, 20 LRC, 1947–85

(T)

	Country	Average 1947/48– 1951/52	Average 1961-65	1975	1980	1981	1982	1983	1984	1985
A.	ARGENTINA	42,320[†]	43,096	59,600[‡]	55,761	54,235	52,717	53,937	54,594	54,800
B.	BOLIVIA	1,450[b]	1,930	2,877	4,000[‡]	4,100[†]	4,100[†]	5,500[†]	5,985	5,851
C.	BRAZIL	51,305	59,770	92,480[‡]	91,000[‡]	93,000[‡]	93,000[‡]	124,186	132,801[‡]	134,500[†]
D.	CHILE	2,293	2,850	3,606	3,664	3,745	3,800	3,865	3,650	3,400
E.	COLOMBIA	13,750	16,281	23,888[‡]	23,945	24,251	24,499	24,000[‡]	22,441[‡]	21,935[‡]
F.	COSTA RICA	601	1,074	1,843	2,181	2,275	2,276	2,365	2,550[‡]	2,553[‡]
G.	CUBA	4,333[‡]	5,591	5,450[†]	5,900[†]	5,900[†]	6,200[†]	6,300[†]	6,400[†]	6,400[†]
H.	DOMINICAN REP.	711	899	1,900	2,153[‡]	2,155[‡]	1,949	2,154	2,326	2,420
I.	ECUADOR	1,467[d]	1,816	2,800	2,916	3,032	3,200[†]	3,270	3,324[‡]	3,378[‡]
J.	EL SALVADOR	795	1,158	1,031	1,440	1,211	1,055	954	937	929
K.	GUATEMALA	977[c]	1,216	2,148[‡]	1,653	1,730	2,280[‡]	2,185	2,605[‡]	2,587[‡]
L.	HAITI	582[a]	685	742[†]	1,100[‡]	1,200[‡]	1,200[‡]	1,300[‡]	1,350[†]	1,350[†]
M.	HONDURAS	884	1,447	1,689[†]	2,262	2,336	2,499	2,086	2,434[‡]	2,508[‡]
N.	MEXICO	12,980	20,658	27,863	31,094	31,784[†]	36,839	37,522	37,845	37,450[†]
O.	NICARAGUA	1,068	1,672	2,500[†]	2,401[‡]	2,301[‡]	2,379	2,116[‡]	2,000[†]	1,890[‡]
P.	PANAMA	567	860	1,348	1,525[‡]	1,604[‡]	1,456	1,459	1,452	1,423[‡]
Q.	PARAGUAY	4,600[‡]	5,348	4,836	5,300[†]	5,400[†]	5,152	6,400[‡]	6,400[†]	6,400[†]
R.	PERU	2,830	3,358	4,200[‡]	3,837	3,895	4,152	4,000	3,950[‡]	3,900[‡]
S.	URUGUAY	7,981	8,630	11,362[†]	10,952	10,971[‡]	10,959	9,704	9,491[‡]	9,948[‡]
T.	VENEZUELA	5,768	6,769	9,089	10,607	10,840	9,112	11,575	12,286[‡]	12,486[‡]
	LATIN AMERICA	157,262	185,468	261,252	263,691	265,965	267,188	306,389	316,316	317,608
	UNITED STATES	80,569	103,785	131,826	111,192	114,321	115,604	115,001	113,700	109,749

a. 1950/51.
b. 1949/50.
c. Four-year average.
d. Three-year average.

SOURCE: FAO-PY, 1971, table 107; FAO-PY, 1976–81, table 80; FAO-PY, 1983–85, table 88.

Table 2201

HORSE POPULATION, 20 LRC, 1947–85

(T)

	Country	Average 1947/48– 1951/52	Average 1961-65	1975	1980	1981	1982	1983	1984	1985
A.	ARGENTINA	7,265[b]	3,696	3,400[‡]	3,000[‡]	3,000[‡]	3,000[‡]	3,050[†]	3,050[†]	3,100[†]
B.	BOLIVIA	158[c]	197	340[†]	400[†]	410[†]	410[†]	300[†]	293	311
C.	BRAZIL	6,942[d]	8,693	5,215	6,300[‡]	6,300[‡]	5,100[†]	5,289	5,200[†]	5,200[†]
D.	CHILE	523[c]	503	450[‡]	450[‡]	450[†]	430[†]	450[†]	500[†]	500[†]
E.	COLOMBIA	1,208[a]	937	1,435	1,696	1,710[‡]	1,710[‡]	1,779[‡]	1,815[‡]	1,906[‡]
F.	COSTA RICA	76[a]	100	112[‡]	113	113	113[†]	113[†]	113[†]	113[†]
G.	CUBA	410[c]	488	804	812	829[†]	820	781	759	749
H.	DOMINICAN REP.	137	213	201[‡]	204[‡]	204[‡]	204[‡]	204[‡]	204[†]	204[†]
I.	ECUADOR	111[c]	218	285[†]	314	299[‡]	322	327	306[†]	31[†]
J.	EL SALVADOR	130[c]	73	81[†]	88[‡]	88[‡]	89[†]	90[†]	90[†]	90[†]
K.	GUATEMALA	166[a]	159	125[†]	100[†]	100	100[†]	100[†]	100[†]	100[†]
L.	HAITI	253[d]	282	379[†]	410[†]	415[†]	420[†]	425[†]	425[†]	425[†]
M.	HONDURAS	178[a]	262	278[†]	150[†]	151[†]	152[†]	167[†]	168[†]	168[†]
N.	MEXICO	3,181[d]	4,323	6,376	6,300	6,502[†]	5,635[†]	6,634	6,134	6,135
O.	NICARAGUA	150[c]	172	164[†]	275[‡]	270[‡]	275[†]	270[†]	270[†]	270[†]
P.	PANAMA	138[c]	162	164[†]	165[†]	166[†]	166[†]	167[†]	168[†]	168[†]
Q.	PARAGUAY	302[d]	555	325	330[†]	330[†]	330[†]	330[†]	330[†]	330[†]
R.	PERU	496	579	637[‡]	650[‡]	653[‡]	653[‡]	653[‡]	655[†]	655[†]
S.	URUGUAY	667[b]	473	470[†]	530[‡]	530[‡]	495	453	500[†]	500[†]
T.	VENEZUELA	344[b]	402	454	478[‡]	482[‡]	481[‡]	412[‡]	491[‡]	495[‡]
	LATIN AMERICA	22,835	22,490	21,695	22,765	23,002	20,905	21,535	21,613	21,771
	UNITED STATES	7,757	4,579	8,600[†]	9,662[†]	9,928[†]	10,155[†]	10,500[†]	10,500[†]	10,580[†]

a. Three-year average.
b. 1950/51.
c. Two-year average.
d. Four-year average.

SOURCE: FAO-PY, 1971, table 106; FAO-PY, 1976-81, table 79; FAO-PY, 1983–85, table 87.

Table 2202

SHEEP POPULATION, 19 LRC, 1947–85

(T)

Country	Average 1947/48– 1951/52	Average 1961-65	1975	1980	1981	1982	1983	1984	1985
A. ARGENTINA	52,940[†]	48,023	34,000[‡]	33,000	30,000[‡]	30,401	30,000	30,000[†]	29,000[†]
B. BOLIVIA	7,224[b]	6,136	7,694	8,750[‡]	8,900[†]	9,200[‡]	9,200[†]	9,287	9,413
C. BRAZIL	14,427	19,996	17,400[‡]	18,000[‡]	18,000[‡]	18,000	18,121	17,500[†]	17,500[†]
D. CHILE	5,789	6,356	5,644	6,064	6,185	6,000	6,200	6,000	5,800
E. COLOMBIA	1,153[c]	1,506	1,921	2,413	2,427	2,249	2,660*	2,689[†]	2,714[†]
F. COSTA RICA	1[†]	1	2[†]	2[†]	2[†]	3[†]	3[†]	3[†]	3[†]
G. CUBA	177[†]	229	330[†]	355[†]	365[†]	365[†]	370[†]	375[†]	378[†]
H. DOMINICAN REP.	27	38	50[†]	54[†]	55[†]	55[†]	76	78[†]	80[†]
I. ECUADOR	1,720[d]	1,699	2,105	2,980	3,034	2,391[†]	2,303*	2,311*	2,086[‡]
J. EL SALVADOR	5[e]	3	4[‡]	4[‡]	4[‡]	4[†]	4	4[†]	4[†]
K. GUATEMALA	735[c]	743	540[‡]	679	734	500[†]	615	657	660[†]
L. HAITI	52[a]	58	79[†]	89[†]	90[†]	91[†]	89	92[†]	92[†]
M. HONDURAS	8	8	5[‡]	5[‡]	5[‡]	5[†]	5	5[†]	5[†]
N. MEXICO	5,041	5,886	7,825	7,318	7,990[‡]	6,657[†]	6,270	6,837	6,500[†]
O. NICARAGUA	1[†]	1	2[‡]	3[‡]	3[‡]	3[†]	3[†]	3[†]	3[†]
Q. PARAGUAY	207	413	366	430[†]	430[†]	435[†]	440[†]	445[†]	445[†]
R. PERU	17,515	14,311	15,400	14,473	14,671[†]	14,500[†]	14,650	13,500[†]	13,500[†]
S. URUGUAY	21,935	21,818	15,062[‡]	20,034	20,429[‡]	20,307[†]	20,447	21,120	20,600[†]
T. VENEZUELA	101[a]	88	101	306[‡]	321[‡]	382[‡]	356[‡]	379[‡]	410[‡]
LATIN AMERICA	46,545	54,166	67,977	73,868	71,980	111,498	112,936	112,379	110,313
UNITED STATES	31,565	29,144	14,515	12,687	12,936	12,966	12,140	11,487	10,443

a. 1950/51.
b. 1949/50.
c. Four-year average.
d. Three-year average.
e. Two-year average.

SOURCE: FAO-PY, 1971, table 110; FAO-PY, 1976-82, table 81; FAO-PY, 1983-85, table 89.

Table 2203

SWINE POPULATION, 20 LRC, 1947–85

(T)

Country	Average 1947/48– 1951/52	Average 1961-65	1975	1980	1981	1982	1983	1984	1985
A. ARGENTINA	3,250	3,476	4,200[‡]	3,800	3,900[‡]	3,900[‡]	3,800[‡]	3,800[‡]	3,800[†]
B. BOLIVIA	509[b]	650	1,158	1,450[‡]	1,500[†]	1,650[†]	1,200[†]	1,136	1,112
C. BRAZIL	24,879	26,500	34,192	36,500[‡]	35,000[†]	33,500[‡]	31,678	30,000[‡]	30,000[‡]
D. CHILE	710	945	701	1,068	1,150	1,150	1,100	1,070	1,100
E. COLOMBIA	2,368[c]	1,649	1,877	2,078	2,245	2,179	2,244	2,337[‡]	2,378[‡]
F. COSTA RICA	111[a]	146	225[‡]	223[‡]	240[‡]	243[‡]	236[‡]	223[‡]	220[‡]
G. CUBA	1,315[†]	1,296	1,450[‡]	1,950[‡]	1,950[†]	2,000[†]	2,100[†]	2,300[†]	2,400[†]
H. DOMINICAN REP.	739	706	700[‡]	250[‡]	50[†]	85	375	1,000	1,850
I. ECUADOR	547[b]	1,461	2,543	3,549	3,721	3,250	3,735	4,007[‡]	4,230[‡]
J. EL SALVADOR	335[†]	392	420[‡]	421	386	400	400	379	375
K. GUATEMALA	408[c]	595	659	792	835	850[†]	806	810[†]	832[†]
L. HAITI	1,137[a]	1,264	1,735[†]	1,100[‡]	600[‡]	600[†]	500[†]	500[†]	500[†]
M. HONDURAS	445	748	511[‡]	534	580[‡]	409	409[†]	410[†]	410[†]
N. MEXICO	6,340[b]	9,168	11,466	13,222	12,900[‡]	18,373	19,364	19,930	19,000[†]
O. NICARAGUA	243[b]	423	650[‡]	500[‡]	510[‡]	520[‡]	540[‡]	540[†]	540[†]
P. PANAMA	196[a]	201	166	195[‡]	202[‡]	206	197	195	215[‡]
Q. PARAGUAY	340[c]	635	975	1,300[†]	1,310[†]	1,330[†]	1,350[†]	1,350[†]	1,400[†]
R. PERU	960	1,813	2,135	2,150	2,100[†]	2,050[‡]	2,105	2,052[‡]	2,050[‡]
S. URUGUAY	259[a]	414	418[‡]	450[‡]	450[‡]	430[‡]	440[‡]	450[†]	450[†]
T. VENEZUELA	1,454[a]	1,696	1,795	2,230	2,351[‡]	2 303	2,459	2,985[‡]	3,152[‡]
LATIN AMERICA	46,545	54,172	67,977	73,768	71,980	75,428	75,958	76,417	76,972
UNITED STATES	58,895	55,610	54,693	67,353	64,512	58,688	54,534	56,694	54,073

a. 1950/51.
b. Two-year average.
c. Four-year average.

SOURCE: FAO-PY, 1971, table 109; FAO-PY, 1976-81, table 81; FAO-PY, 1983-85, table 89.

Table 2204

COW MILK PRODUCTION,[1] 20 LRC, 1948–85

(T MET)

Country	Average 1948-52	Average 1961-65	1970	1975	1980	1983	1984	1985
A. ARGENTINA	3,758	4,294	4,189	5,650	5,307	5,692‡	5,200‡	5,600‡
B. BOLIVIA	18†	23	25†	53	57‡	78†	80†	80†
C. BRAZIL	2,581	5,870	7,300‡	9,971	10,265‡	11,818	10,117	10,722
D. CHILE	683	779	950‡	986	1,080	900	880	1,040*
E. COLOMBIA	1,540†	1,843	2,250	2,096	2,419	2,702	2,769	2,800†
F. COSTA RICA	138ᵃ	131	242‡	259	318	327	346	371
G. CUBA	180†	394	300†	612	1,188†	1,109	1,100†	1,000†
H. DOMINICAN REP.	140†	186	283	320	431	460*	495†	498†
I. ECUADOR	174ᵇ	376	530†	773	758‡	981	946‡	988*
J. EL SALVADOR	107ᵇ	156	177†	235	291	283†	288†	288†
K. GUATEMALA	78ᵇ	194	262‡	310†	320†	320*	330†	333†
L. HAITI	15†	23	20†	40†	19†	21†	22†	22†
M. HONDURAS	99	128	175‡	180†	205†	281†	280†	280†
N. MEXICO	1,539	2,305ᵃ	3,053	4,980	6,750‡	7,171	7,227	6,920‡
O. NICARAGUA	92†	158	200‡	246‡	165‡	125†	125†	125†
P. PANAMA	34ᵇ	56	73	73	95†	88	92	90*
Q. PARAGUAY	80ᵃ	81	92†	121	165†	160†	165†	170†
R. PERU	229ᶜ	515	825	814†	780	752	780	809
S. URUGUAY	449	764	763	745	838‡	866	851	850†
T. VENEZUELA	203ᵃ	548	830	1,224	1,318	1,511	1,487	1,532‡
LATIN AMERICA	12,137	18,824	22,539	29,688	32,769	36,165	34,072	35,021
UNITED STATES	52,349	56,998	53,268	52,314	58,298	63,488	61,734	64,954

1. Intended to represent the total production for consumption fresh or for conversion into dairy products. The figures generally exclude milk sucked by young animals, but include milk fed to them.

a. Three-year average.
b. Two-year average.
c. Four-year average.

SOURCE: FAO-PY, 1971, table 123; FAO-PY, 1973, table 111; FAO-PY, 1976-81, table 90; FAO-PY, 1983-85, table 98.

Table 2205

MILK YIELD PER THOUSAND MILKING COWS PER ANNUM, 20 LC, 1948–85

(kg)

Country	Average 1948-52	Average 1961-65	1970	1975	1980	1983	1984	1985
A. ARGENTINA	1,624†	1,836	1,920†	1,883	1,698	1,897	1,751	1,898
B. BOLIVIA	1,760ᵇ	1,200	~	1,403	1,295	1,418	1,418	1,418
C. BRAZIL	502†	746	800†	767	752	726	688	729
D. CHILE	2,360†	1,787	2,720†	1,340	1,470	1,324	1,375	1,576
E. COLOMBIA	462	707	1,090†	937	985	982	989	982
F. COSTA RICA	~	920	1,175‡	1,043	1,077	1,168	1,281	1,279
G. CUBA	524ᶜ	733	840†	986	1,398	1,459	1,571	1,471
H. DOMINICAN REP.	950	917	~	1,391	1,760	2,009	1,996	2,000
I. ECUADOR	1,129ᵈ	1,301	1,300†	1,311	1,217	1,376	1,313	1,372
J. EL SALVADOR	795ᵉ	769	850‡	925	960	959	958	958
K. GUATEMALA	980	866	900‡	912	913	797	825	825
L. HAITI	382	232	~	357	190	233	238	238
M. HONDURAS	380ᵃ	480	543‡	545	606	652	651	651
N. MEXICO	933†	948	1,100†	1,360	763	815	812	814
O. NICARAGUA	700‡	549	550‡	654	825	625	625	625
P. PANAMA	610†	872	747†	910	1,001	977	1,025	1,000
Q. PARAGUAY	180†	188	220†	201	1,919	1,905	1,897	1,889
R. PERU	509†	1,019	1,320†	1,291	1,068	1,140	1,156	1,172
S. URUGUAY	1,332†	1,397	1,550†	1,702	1,612	1,634	1,605	1,604
T. VENEZUELA	400ᶜ	540	720†	1,106	1,097	1,090	1,070	1,087
UNITED STATES	2,389	3,519	4,258	4,695	5,393	5,709	5,677	5,844

a. Four-year average.
b. 1950.
c. 1949.
d. Two-year average.
e. 1952.

SOURCE: FAO-PY, 1971, table 123; FAO-PY, 1973, table 111; FAO-PY, 1976-81, table 90; FAO-PY, 1983-85, table 98.

Table 2206

WOOL OUTPUT, 10 LRC, 1974–85[a]

(MT)

	Country	Code[1]	Average 1974–76	1981	1982	1983	1984	1985
A.	ARGENTINA	I	157,000	150,155	151,941	155,000[‡]	153,000[‡]	160,000[‡]
		II	85,006	95,845	101,620	103,500[†]	103,500[‡]	96,500[†]
B.	BOLIVIA	I	7,729	9,060[†]	9,200[†]	9,200[†]	9,287[†]	9,313[†]
		II	4,100	4,800[†]	5,000[†]	5,000[†]	5,000[†]	5,000[†]
C.	BRAZIL	I	31,486	32,636	30,000[‡]	30,563	30,000[†]	30,000[†]
		II	19,833	19,000[‡]	19,200[‡]	19,000[‡]	19,000[†]	19,000[†]
D.	CHILE	I	18,530	21,400	22,000	21,400	21,300[‡]	22,000[‡]
		II	9,265	10,700	11,000	10,700	10,650[‡]	11,000[‡]
E.	COLOMBIA	I	1,100	1,570[†]	1,650[†]	1,500[†]	1,500[†]	1,600[†]
		II	658	940[†]	990[†]	900[†]	900[†]	900[†]
I.	ECUADOR	I	1,627	3,082[‡]	3,089[‡]	3,300[†]	3,350[†]	2,920[†]
		II	813	1,540[†]	1,550[†]	1,600[†]	1,650[†]	1,650[†]
N.	MEXICO	I	7,367	8,600	8,700[†]	6,415	6,840[†]	6,500[†]
		II	3,684	4,300[†]	4,350[†]	3,200	3,420[†]	3,250[†]
Q.	PARAGUAY	I	390	470[†]	480[†]	490[†]	500[†]	500[†]
		II	208	250[†]	250[†]	250[†]	260[†]	260[†]
R.	PERU	I	11,465	10,000	12,000	11,400	11,000	11,300
		II	5,733	5,000	5,500[‡]	5,500[‡]	6,000[‡]	6,000[‡]
S.	URUGUAY	I	60,530	74,603	78,377	82,000	81,676	71,000[†]
		II	33,664	44,000[‡]	46,000[‡]	47,000[†]	47,000[†]	50,000[†]
	LATIN AMERICA	I	297,224	311,576	317,437	323,546	320,557	317,390
		II	162,964	186,375	195,460	198,050	198,769	195,109
	UNITED STATES	I	56,201	49,754	47,612	45,479	50,300[‡]	53,000[‡]
		II	30,725	26,270	25,139	24,640	22,260	28,620

1. Wool Code: I = greasy; II = clean.

a. For previous years since 1948, see SALA, 24-2206.

SOURCE: FAO-PY, 1983-85, table 103.

Table 2207

ANNUAL AVERAGE APPARENT CONSUMPTION OF
FRESH COW'S MILK, 20L, 1964–66 AND 1975–77

(Kilograms/C)

	Country	1964-66	1975-77
A.	ARGENTINA	75.5	67.9
B.	BOLIVIA	2.9	6.7
C.	BRAZIL	65.5	58.8
D.	CHILE	48.4	36.9
E.	COLOMBIA	**	55.2
F.	COSTA RICA	74.3	87.1
G.	CUBA	24.9	29.6
H.	DOMINICAN REP.	46.5	54.1
I.	ECUADOR	56.8	72.4
J.	EL SALVADOR	21.1	27.7
K.	GUATEMALA	25.4	28.9
L.	HAITI	3.9	8.4
M.	HONDURAS	26.4	29.3
N.	MEXICO	35.8	61.8
O.	NICARAGUA	42.7	45.9
P.	PANAMA	20.3	15.1
Q.	PARAGUAY	39.4	43.3
R.	PERU	17.0	19.2
S.	URUGUAY	187.2	154.4
T.	VENEZUELA	21.7	27.0

SOURCE: Lowell S. Jarvis, *Livestock Development in Latin America*,(Washington, D.C.,
The World Bank, 1986).

Table 2208

TRADE IN DRIED MILK, 19L, 1966-70, 1976-80, AND 1981

(T Tons)

	Country	Exports			Imports			Net Imports or Exports (–)		
		1966-70	1976-80	1981	1960-70	1976-80	1981	1966-70	1976-80	1981
A.	ARGENTINA	1	11	10	3	12	4	2	1	–6
B.	BOLIVIA	#	#	#	3	7	8	3	7	8
C.	BRAZIL	1	1	1	20	30	15	19	29	14
D.	CHILE	#	1	#	11	13	13	11	12	13
E.	COLOMBIA	1	#	#	10	11	7	9	11	7
F.	COSTA RICA	1	1	#	1	3	2	#	2	2
G.	CUBA	#	#	#	37	41	30	37	41	30
H.	DOMINICAN REP.	#	#	#	7	6	8	7	6	8
I.	ECUADOR	#	#	#	2	6	6	2	6	6
J.	EL SALVADOR	1	1	#	5	10	13	4	9	13
K.	GUATEMALA	1	1	#	3	6	8	2	5	8
M.	HONDURAS	#	1	#	3	4	6	3	3	6
N.	MEXICO	1	1	#	26	90	154	25	89	154
O.	NICARGUA	1	4	#	2	2	6	1	–2	6
P.	PANAMA	#	#	#	2	4	3	2	4	3
Q.	PARAGUAY	#	#	#	1	1	1	1	1	1
R.	PERU	#	#	#	14	25	30	14	25	30
S.	URUGUAY	#	3	#	1	1	1	1	–2	1
T.	VENEZUELA	#	#	#	23	90	94	23	90	94

SOURCE: Lovell S. Jarvis, *Livestock Development in Latin America*, (Washington, D.C.:
The World Bank, 1986).

Table 2209

TRADE IN FRESH BEEF AND VEAL, 19 LC, 1966-70, 1976-80, AND 1981

(T Tons)

	Country	Exports			Imports			Net Imports or Exports (–)		
		1966-70	1976-80	1981	1960-70	1976-80	1981	1966-70	1976-80	1981
A.	ARGENTINA	359	270	220	#	#	#	359	270	220
B.	BOLIVIA	1	1	#	#	#	#	1	1	#
C.	BRAZIL	50	13	47	1	68	61	49	–55	–14
D.	CHILE	1	1	#	13	6	8	–12	–5	–8
E.	COLOMBIA	5	16	19	1	1	#	4	15	19
F.	COSTA RICA	14	31	34	1	1	#	13	30	34
G.	CUBA	5	#	#	#	3	#	5	–3	#
H.	DOMINICAN REP.	4	3	4	1	1	1	3	2	3
J.	EL SALVADOR	1	5	1	1	1	1	#	4	#
K.	GUATEMALA	10	14	13	1	1	1	9	13	12
L.	HAITI	1	1	2	1	1	1	#	#	1
M.	HONDURAS	9	24	23	#	1	#	9	23	23
N.	MEXICO	31	21	2	1	1	2	30	20	#
O.	NICARAGUA	18	29	15	1	1	#	17	28	15
P.	PANAMA	2	2	3	1	1	1	1	1	2
Q.	PARAGUAY	3	3	1	0	0	#	3	3	1
R.	PERU	#	#	#	9	4	11	–9	–4	–11
S.	URUGUAY	90	101	140	#	#	#	90	101	140
T.	VENEZUELA	#	#	#	1	17	12	–1	–17	–12
	LATIN AMERICA	607	538	525	42	124	112	565	414	413

SOURCE: Lovell S. Jarvis, *Livestock Development in Latin America* (Washington, D.C.:
The World Bank, 1986).

Table 2210

TRADE IN CANNED MEAT, 18 LC, 1966–70, 1976–80, AND 1981

(T Tons)

	Country	Exports			Imports			Net Imports or Exports (−)		
		1966-70	1976-80	1981	1960-70	1976-80	1981	I966-70	1976-80	1981
A.	ARGENTINA	113	132	65	1	2	2	112	130	63
B.	BOLIVIA	#	#	#	1	1	1	−1	−1	−1
C.	BRAZIL	14	64	101	1	1	1	13	63	100
E.	COLOMBIA	1	1	#	1	1	1	#	#	1
F.	COSTA RICA	1	2	3	1	2	2	#	#	1
G.	CUBA	#	#	#	21	30	33	−21	−30	−33
H.	DOMINICAN REP.	#	1	1	1	1	1	−1	#	#
I.	ECUADOR	#	1	#	1	1	1	−1	#	−1
J.	EL SALVADOR	1	1	1	1	2	2	#	−1	−1
K.	GUATEMALA	1	3	1	1	1	1	#	2	#
L.	HAITI	#	#	#	1	1	1	−1	−1	−1
M.	HONDURAS	1	1	#	1	1	2	#	#	−2
N.	MEXICO	1	1	#	2	2	2	−1	−1	−2
O.	NICARAGUA	1	1	#	1	1	1	#	#	−1
P.	PANAMA	#	1	#	2	3	3	−2	−2	−3
Q.	PARAGUAY	17	7	#	1	#	#	16	7	#
R.	PERU	#	1	#	1	1	1	−1	#	−1
S.	URUGUAY	4	4	3	#	1	1	4	3	2
	LATIN AMERICA	159	227	177	51	60	70	108	167	107

SOURCE: Lovell S. Jarvis, *Livestock Development in Latin America* (Washington, D.C.:
The World Bank, 1986).

CHAPTER 23

FORESTRY PRODUCTION

Table 2300

WORLD RANKING OF ANNUAL LOSS OF TROPICAL FORESTS, 14 LC, 1981–85

(T Acres)

Rank	Country	Acres	Rank	Country	Acres	Rank	Country	Acres
1.	BRAZIL	3,656	21.	BOLIVIA	215	41.	Tanzania	24
2.	COLOMBIA	2,025	22.	Nepal	207	42.	Uganda	24
3.	Indonesia	1,482	23.	Cameroon	198	43.	Belize	22
4.	MEXICO	1,470	24.	COSTA RICA	161	44.	Bangladesh	20
5.	Nigeria	741	25.	Vietnam	161	45.	Ethiopia	20
6.	Ivory Coast	716	26.	Sri Lanka	143	46.	Pakistan	17
7.	PERU	667	27.	Liberia	114	47.	Sierra Leone	15
8.	Malaysia	630	28.	Angola	109	48.	Brunei	12
9.	Thailand	622	29.	Zambia	99	49.	Central African	
10.	PARAGUAY	469	30.	Guinea	89		Republic	12
11.	Zaire	450	31.	PANAMA	89	50.	EL SALVADOR	12
12.	Madagascar	370	32.	ECUADOR	84			
13.	India	363	33.	Cambodia	62			
14.	VENEZUELA	309	34.	Congo	54			
15.	NICARAGUA	299	35.	Ghana	54			
16.	Burma	259	36.	Papua New Guinea	54			
17.	Laos	247	37.	Kenya	47			
18.	Philippines	225	38.	Guinea-Bissau	42			
19.	GUATEMALA	222	39.	Gabon	37			
20.	HONDURAS	222	40.	Mozambique	24			

SOURCE: *Los Angeles Times*, June 14, 1987.

Table 2301

YEARLY RATE OF MAJOR DEFORESTATION AREAS, 7 LC, 1981–85

(%)

Country	%
Ivory Coast	5.9
PARAGUAY	4.6
Nigeria	4.0
COSTA RICA	3.9
Nepal	3.9
HAITI	3.1
EL SALVADOR	2.9
Gambia	2.8
Benin	2.6
Guinea-Bissau	2.6
NICARAGUA	2.7
HONDURAS	2.4
Thailand	2.4
ECUADOR	2.3
Liberia	2.2

SOURCE: *Los Angeles Times*, June 14, 1987.

Table 2302

ESTIMATED FOREST AREA, NATURAL FORESTS, AND INDUSTRIAL PLANTATIONS
(T Ha. 1980)

Subregion	Total Land Area	Total Forest Area	% of Land Area	Natural Forest			Forest Plantations			
				Productive Coniferous	Share Broadleaf	Annual Deforestation	Total Forest Plantation	Industrial Plantations		Annual Planting Area
								Coniferous	Broadleaf	
Latin America	2,014,786	719,735	35.7	15,794	531,147	3,983	5,913.6	2,367.5	1,327.3	297.8[a]
MEXICO	197,255	46,250	23.5	11,720	12,580	530	159.0	37.0	35.0	7.8
Central America	50,862	18,679	36.7	2,512	11,682	382	25.4	15.8	9.6	3.9
Caribbean[1]	56,435	44,511	78.9	277	34,960	21	48.8	26.1	16.0	8.1
BRAZIL	851,196	357,480	42.0	280	300,910	1,360	3,855.0	1,232.0	741.0	158.0
Andean	446,311	206,210	46.2	185	142,975	1,535	372.4	181.8	115.6	26.8
Southern Cone	412,727	46,605	11.3	820	28,040	155	1,453.0	874.8	410.1	93.2

1. Includes Suriname, French Guiana, and Guyana. They account for the large share of forest area in this category.

a. Of which 211.0 are softwoods and 86.8 are hardwoods.

SOURCE: IDB-SPTF, 1983, table IV-5.

Table 2303

TOTAL ROUNDWOOD PRODUCTION,[1,2] 20 LRC, 1970–84
(T Me^3)

	Country	1970*	1975	1977	1978	1979	1980	1981	1982	1983	1984
A.	ARGENTINA	8,915	8,770	9,434	10,144	10,311	9,866	8,889	10,478	10,520	13,375
B.	BOLIVIA	4,279	1,175	1,166	1,326	1,490	1,474	1,451	1,322	1,272	1,282
C.	BRAZIL	155,568	164,608	177,699[†]	188,151[†]	199,040[†]	207,654[†]	211,213[†]	214,823[†]	218,482[†]	222,177[†]
D.	CHILE	8,269	10,331	11,351	12,079	13,855	20,052	13,849	12,751	12,849	14,971
E.	COLOMBIA	34,295	14,726	15,246	15,521	16,094	16,132	16,316	16,312	16,553[†]	16,916[†]
F.	COSTA RICA	2,362	2,863	2,960	2,968	2,970	2,732	2,614	2,627	2,631	3,395
G.	CUBA	2,064	2,490	2,070	2,367	3,216	3,151	3,179	3,193	3,193	3,132
H.	DOMINICAN REP.	136	453	466	477	486	900	936	944	957	969
I.	ECUADOR	4,944	5,641[†]	6,107[†]	6,080	7,364	7,553	8,249	7,632	7,908	8,228
J.	EL SALVADOR	2,374	3,564	3,774[†]	3,880[†]	4,010[†]	4,137[†]	4,279[†]	4,395[†]	4,494[†]	4,620[†]
K.	GUATEMALA	8,937	5,780	6,049	6,200	6,141	6,247	6,474	6,652	6,806	7,000
L.	HAITI	4,056[†]	4,676	4,881[†]	4,999[†]	5,115[†]	5,235[†]	5,360[†]	5,487[†]	5,624[†]	5,761[†]
M.	HONDURAS	4,752	4,080[†]	4,619	4,714	4,762	4,943	5,033	5,069	4,793	4,937[†]
N.	MEXICO	10,115	17,155	18,178	16,589	17,864	18,508	18,742	19,321	19,707	20,762
O.	NICARAGUA	2,123	2,795	2,982	3,040	3,101	3,168	3,241	3,319	3,404[†]	3,491[†]
P.	PANAMA	1,366	1,577	1,629	1,632	1,677	2,010	2,047[†]	2,047[†]	2,047[†]	2,047[†]
Q.	PARAGUAY	3,969	4,935	5,180	5,660	6,219	6,720	6,762	6,792[†]	6,822[†]	6,852[†]
R.	PERU	3,326	6,862	7,418	7,358	7,635	8,152	7,833	7,769	7,775	7,775[†]
S.	URUGUAY	1,406	1,750	2,063	2,117	2,299	1,564	1,716	2,978	2,975	2,975
T.	VENEZUELA	6,893	1,140	1,177[†]	1,197	1,217	1,237	1,258	1,279	1,300	1,322[†]
	LATIN AMERICA	169,654	265,548	285,205	297,580	316,258	332,738	330,534	336,702	331,859	353,182
	UNITED STATES	327,945	304,723	349,438	391,381	419,134	415,453	416,016	393,896	437,762	438,058

1. Wood in the rough. Wood in its natural state as felled, or otherwise harvested, with or without bark, round, split, roughly squared or other forms (e.g., roots, stumps, burls, etc.). It may also be impregnated (e.g., telegraph poles) or roughly shaped or pointed. It comprises all wood obtained from removals, i.e., the quantities removed from forests and from trees outside the forest, including wood recovered from natural, felling and logging losses during the period—calendar year or forest year. Commodities included are saw-logs and veneer logs, pitprops, pulpwood, other industrial roundwood, and fuelwood.

2. For coniferous and non-coniferous, see SALA, 23-1800 and 1801.

SOURCE: FAO-YFP, 1981–84, p. 64.

Table 2304

INDUSTRIAL ROUNDWOOD PRODUCTION,[1] 20 LC, 1970–84

(T Me^3)

	Country	1970*	1975	1977	1978	1979	1980	1981	1982	1983	1984
A.	ARGENTINA	3,072	3,628	4,029	3,644	4,787	4,070	3,894	3,864	3,864	4,967
B.	BOLIVIA	231[‡]	300	229	355	488	433	323	226	149	149
C.	BRAZIL	23,823	30,597	37,319	44,479	52,026	57,240	57,345	57,499	57,561	57,670
D.	CHILE	4,625	5,178	6,022	6,656	8,342	14,449	8,154	6,951	6,951	8,979
E.	COLOMBIA	2,851	3,002	3,002	3,002	3,301	3,054	2,954	2,673	2,673[†]	2,673
F.	COSTA RICA	838	1,335	1,491	1,495[†]	1,495[†]	1,257	1,139	1,146	1,150	906
G.	CUBA	382[†]	385[†]	385[†]	385[†]	385[†]	385[†]	385[†]	385	385	385
H.	DOMINICAN REP.	1	13	10[†]	10	9	9	9	9	9	6
I.	ECUADOR	1,506	1,659	1,878[†]	1,720[†]	1,868[†]	2,029[†]	2,693	2,052	2,149	2,232
J.	EL SALVADOR	79	78	79[†]	78[†]	91[†]	100[†]	127[†]	120[†]	90[†]	90[†]
K.	GUATEMALA	530	546	486	466	231	159	202	194	158	156
L.	HAITI	239[†]	239[†]	239[†]	239[†]	239[†]	239[†]	239[†]	239[†]	239[†]	239[†]
M.	HONDURAS	800	868[†]	1,175	1,146	1,064	1,112	1,066	962	544	544
N.	MEXICO	5,302	6,613	6,995	5,082	6,030	6,345	6,253	6,498	6,547	7,261
O.	NICARAGUA	445	880	880[†]	880[†]	880[†]	880[†]	880[†]	880[†]	880[†]	880[†]
P.	PANAMA	98	117	86	44	44	339	339[†]	339[†]	339[†]	339[†]
Q.	PARAGUAY	806	1,155	1,128	1,522	1,989	2,412	2,412[†]	2,412[†]	2,412[†]	2,412
R.	PERU	1,087	1,475	1,738	1,518	1,636	1,988	1,498	1,256	1,256	1,256[†]
S.	URUGUAY	148	290	347	345	427	242	319	222	213	213
T.	VENEZUELA	558	636	636[†]	636[†]	636[†]	636[†]	636[†]	636[†]	636[†]	636[†]
	UNITED STATES	312,653	288,581	320,441	346,919	354,707	327,095	317,094	294,974	334,993	336,136
	WORLD	1,277,638	1,285,956	1,375,008	1,415,419	1,443,840	1,439,928	1,404,962	1,357,857	1,443,161	1,455,641

1. All wood as defined in "Total Roundwood" with the exception of fuelwood and
charcoal.

SOURCE: FAO-YFP, 1981–83, p. 96; 1984, p. 97.

Table 2305

INDUSTRIAL WOOD AS A PERCENTAGE OF TOTAL ROUNDWOOD PRODUCTION,[1] 20 LC, 1970–84

(%)

	Country	1970*	1975	1977	1978	1979	1980	1981	1982	1983	1984
A.	ARGENTINA	34.5	41.4	42.7	35.9	46.4	41.3	43.8	36.9	36.7	37.1
B.	BOLIVIA	5.4	25.5	19.6	26.8	32.8	29.4	22.3	23.1	11.7	11.6
C.	BRAZIL	15.4	18.6	21.8	23.5	25.9	27.4	26.9	26.6	26.6	25.9
D.	CHILE	55.7	50.1	53.1	55.1	60.2	72.1	58.9	54.5	54.1	59.9
E.	COLOMBIA	8.3	20.4	19.7	19.3	20.5	18.9	18.1	16.4	16.1	15.8
F.	COSTA RICA	35.5	46.6	50.4	50.4	50.3	46.0	43.6	43.6	43.7	26.7
G.	CUBA	18.5	15.5	18.6	16.3	11.9	12.2	12.1	12.1	12.1	12.3
H.	DOMINICAN REP.	.7	2.7	1.9	1.9	1.7	1.7	1.6	1.6	1.6	.6
I.	ECUADOR	30.5	29.4	30.8	28.3	25.4	26.9	28.0	27.8	27.6	27.1
J.	EL SALVADOR	3.3	2.2	2.1	2.0	2.3	2.4	2.9	2.7	2.0	1.9
K.	GUATEMALA	5.9	9.5	8.0	7.5	3.8	2.5	3.1	2.9	2.3	3.4
L.	HAITI	5.7	5.1	4.8	4.8	4.7	4.6	4.5	4.4	4.2	4.1
M.	HONDURAS	16.8	21.3	25.4	24.3	22.3	22.5	21.2	18.9	18.5	11.0
N.	MEXICO	52.4	38.6	38.5	30.6	33.7	34.2	33.2	33.4	32.7	34.9
O.	NICARAGUA	20.9	31.5	30.1	29.4	28.7	28.0	27.4	26.7	26.1	25.2
P.	PANAMA	7.2	7.4	5.3	2.7	2.7	16.9	16.6	16.6	16.6	16.6
Q.	PARAGUAY	20.3	23.4	21.8	26.9	31.9	35.9	35.8	35.5	35.4	35.2
R.	PERU	32.7	21.5	23.4	20.6	21.4	24.4	19.1	16.2	16.2	16.2
S.	URUGUAY	10.5	16.6	16.8	16.3	18.8	15.5	14.6	14.5	7.2	7.2
T.	VENEZUELA	8.1	55.8	54.0	53.2	52.3	51.5	50.6	49.8	48.9	48.1
	UNITED STATES	95.3	94.7	91.7	88.6	84.6	78.7	76.2	74.9	76.7	76.7
	WORLD	48.4	49.1	50.0	49.9	49.5	48.5	47.2	45.9	46.3	47.6

1. Industrial roundwood is comprised of all of those woods included in table 2301, above,
with the exception of fuelwoods and charcoal. This table thus demonstrates the amount
of wood produced for industry rather than fuel. For fuelwood, coal, and bagasse
production see Chapter 19, above.

SOURCE: Calculated from tables 2301 and 2302 above.

Table 2306

TOTAL SAWNWOOD AND SLEEPER PRODUCTION,[1,2] 19 LC, 1970–84

(T Me^3)

	Country	1970	1975	1977	1978	1979	1980	1981	1982	1983	1984
A.	ARGENTINA	736	480	859	640	908	883	1,047	947	1,163	1,237[†]
B.	BOLIVIA	72	140	109	167	233	220	172	117	97	97
C.	BRAZIL	8,035	10,129	12,643	13,337	14,070	14,881	15,852	15,852	15,852	15,852
D.	CHILE	1,075	1,320	1,267	1,717	2,371	2,186	1,735	1,176	1,610	2,001
E.	COLOMBIA	1,100	954	934[†]	934[†]	983	970	1,006	721	721[†]	721[†]
F.	COSTA RICA	369	612	689	689[†]	364	524	534	378	306[†]	412
G.	CUBA	96[†]	105[†]	105[†]	105[†]	101	112	108	108[†]	107	107[†]
I.	ECUADOR	704	747	852	752	830	905	986	980	1,142	1,212
J.	EL SALVADOR	20	38	34	33[†]	37	37	47	45	39	39[†]
K.	GUATEMALA	204	222	353	346	138	93	136	130	104	103
L.	HAITI	13	14[†]	14[†]	14[†]	14[†]	14[†]	14[†]	14[†]	14[†]	14[†]
M.	HONDURAS	457	551	628	633	624	560	560	489	468	427
N.	MEXICO	1,572	1,986	2,259	2,299	2,109	1,991	1,928	1,669	1,827	1,711
O.	NICARAGUA	197	402	402[†]	402[†]	402[†]	402[†]	402[†]	402[†]	222[†]	222[†]
P.	PANAMA	44	50	33	12	12[†]	53	53[†]	53[†]	53[†]	53[†]
Q.	PARAGUAY	214	340	314	380	524	655	655[†]	655[†]	655[†]	655[†]
R.	PERU	351	516	476	486	546	611	653	577	577[†]	577[†]
S.	URUGUAY	73	105	107	104	99	99[†]	100	47	16	16[†]
T.	VENEZUELA	328	349	349[†]	349[†]	349[†]	349[†]	349[†]	220	210	210[†]
	UNITED STATES	81,854	75,903	88,593	88,932	87,678	74,955	70,048	63,836	78,110	87,880
	WORLD	415,009	405,042	445,558	451,854	452,811	411,350	422,918	413,203	451,388	453,487

1. Sawnwood, unplaned, planed, grooved, tongued, etc., sawn lengthwise, or produced
   by a profile-chipping process (e.g., planks, beams, joists, boards, rafters, scantlings,
   laths, boxboards, "lumber," etc.) and planed wood which may also be finger jointed,
   tongued or grooved, chamfered, rabbeted, V-jointed, beaded, etc. Wood flooring is
   excluded. With few exceptions, sawnwood exceeds 5 mm in thickness. Pieces of
   wood of more or less rectangular section laid transversely on the railway road-bed to
   support the rails. Sleepers may be sawn or hewn.
2. For coniferous and non-coniferous, see SALA, 23-1802 and 1803.

SOURCE: FAO-YFP, 1982–84, p. 172.

Table 2307

TOTAL WOOD-BASED PANEL PRODUCTION,[1] 17 LC, 1970–84[a]

(T Me^3)

	Country	1970	1975	1977	1978	1979	1980	1981	1982	1983	1984
A.	ARGENTINA	193	331	280	302	367	414	357	341	341[†]	390[†]
B.	BOLIVIA	1	2	21	17	23	28	28	23	23[†]	23[†]
C.	BRAZIL	819	1,725	2,139	2,218[†]	2,236	2,482	2,576	2,398	2,523	2,523[†]
D.	CHILE	57	44	74	95	113	115	142	99	113	183
E.	COLOMBIA	77	80	112	112[†]	103	111	106	123	123[†]	124[†]
F.	COSTA RICA	25	45	73	61	67	68	57	52	39	43
G.	CUBA	70	6	6	6	6	6	6	50	54	54[†]
I.	ECUADOR	20	39	51	66	75	87	95	117	98	100
K.	GUATEMALA	5	21	11	9	11	9	6	6	6	6
M.	HONDURAS	6	10	13	14	14	11	11	5	6	8
N.	MEXICO	174	253	362	404	442	604	683	761	696	732
O.	NICARAGUA	16	10	10[†]	10[†]	16	14	14[†]	22	14	14[†]
P.	PANAMA	4	9	14	14[†]	14[†]	14[†]	14[†]	14[†]	14[†]	14[†]
Q.	PARAGUAY	15	17	19	27[†]	43[†]	69[†]	69[†]	69[†]	69[†]	69[†]
R.	PERU	54	60	64	48	66	84	78	57	57	57
S.	URUGUAY	18	15	14	15	17	16	17	10	12	12
T.	VENEZUELA	59	81	74	69	101	136	151	101	129	129[†]
	UNITED STATES	23,026	25,005	32,464	32,023	31,519	26,224	27,498	23,000	28,400	29,611
	WORLD	69,591	84,271	101,217	103,911	105,656	100,773	100,546	95,008	103,654	107,693

1. Includes veneer sheets, plywood, particle board, and fiberboard.

a. For 1962-69 data see SALA, 21-1704.

SOURCE: FAO-YFP, 1981–83, p. 206; 1984, p. 198.

Table 2308

FIBERBOARD PRODUCTION,[1] 8 LC, 1970–84

$(T ME^3)$

	Country	1970	1975	1977	1978	1979	1980	1981	1982	1983	1984
A.	ARGENTINA	24	51	52	68	59	90	86	80	95	95[†]
C.	BRAZIL	269	504	710[†]	765[†]	724[‡]	780	780[†]	602[‡]	727[‡]	727[†]
D.	CHILE	20	14	28	33	44	45	44	44	42	40
E.	COLOMBIA	11	15	13	13[†]	17	19	17	18	19	19[†]
G.	CUBA	~	~	~	~	~	~	~	44	48	48[†]
N.	MEXICO	21	14	30	26	26	26	26	26	67	65
S.	URUGUAY	4	3	3	3	3	2	4	3	3	3
T.	VENEZUELA	2	6[†]	10[†]	12[†]	16	16	16[†]	4	4[‡]	4[†]
	UNITED STATES	5,821	6,236	7,343	7,170	7,187	5,098	5,098	4,500	4,790	4,704

1. A panel manufacture from fibers of wood or other ligno-cellulosic materials with the primary bond deriving from the felting of the fibers and their inherent adhesive properties. Bonding materials and/or additives may be added. It is usually flat pressed but may be moulded.

SOURCE: FAO-YFP, 1982–83, p. 242; 1984, p. 234.

Table 2309

PARTICLE BOARD PRODUCTION,[1] 14 LC, 1970–84

$(T Me^3)$

	Country	1970	1975	1977	1978	1979	1980	1981	1982	1983	1984
A.	ARGENTINA	117	209	176	185	248	268	217	215	241	241[†]
C.	BRAZIL	112[‡]	407	541	541[†]	550	660	660[†]	660[†]	660[†]	660[†]
D.	CHILE	22	16	32	42	46	43	72	37	72	114[†]
E.	COLOMBIA	9	12[†]	20[‡]	20[†]	30[‡]	31	42	50	50[†]	50[†]
F.	COSTA RICA	#	#	24	28	31	32	23	11	11[†]	11[†]
G.	CUBA	4	4[†]	4[†]	4[†]	4[†]	4[†]	4[†]	4[†]	4[†]	4[†]
I.	ECUADOR	#	#	8	14	19	26	28	49	30	32[†]
K.	GUATEMALA	4	16[†]	6	3	4	3	3	4	4	4
N.	MEXICO	56	125	155	162	194	316	339	412	335	379
P.	PANAMA	#	2[†]	2[†]	2[†]	2[†]	2[†]	2[†]	2[†]	2[†]	2[†]
Q.	PARAGUAY	1[†]	2[†]	2	2[†]	2[†]	2[†]	2[†]	2[†]	2[†]	2[†]
R.	PERU	7	8	#	1	#	#	#	#	#	#
S.	URUGUAY	2	6	6	6	7	7[†]	6	4	5	5[†]
T.	VENEZUELA	24	35	35[†]	35[†]	35[†]	65	66	60	78	78[†]
	UNITED STATES	3,127	4,190	7,140	7,797	7,204	6,269	6,100	5,200	6,520	6,923
	WORLD	19,144	30,713	38,210	40,251	41,303	41,332	40,050	38,464	40,820	43,467

1. A sheet material manufactured from small pieces of wood or other ligno-cellulosic materials (e.g., chip, flakes, splinters, strands, shreds, shives, etc.) agglomerated by use of an organic binder together with one or more of the following agents: heat, pressure, humidity, a catalyst, etc. (Flaxboard is included. Wood wool and other particle boards, with inorganic binders, are excluded.)

SOURCE: FAO-YFP, 1981–83, p. 234; 1984, p. 226.

Table 2310

PLYWOOD PRODUCTION,[1] 17 LC, 1970–84

(T Me^3)

	Country	1970	1975	1977	1978	1979	1980	1981	1982	1983	1984
A.	ARGENTINA	48	61	50	47	53	53	50	45	45[†]	48[†]
B.	BOLIVIA	1[‡]	2	3	1	4	6	6	1	1[†]	1[†]
C.	BRAZIL	342[‡]	660	698[†]	722[†]	762	826	902	902[†]	902[†]	902[†]
D.	CHILE	13	13	9	13	16	20	18	10	15	20
E.	COLOMBIA	52	50[†]	75	75[†]	52	52	40	48	48[†]	48[†]
F.	COSTA RICA	22	40	44	30	31	31	26	33	23[†]	25
G.	CUBA	2	2[†]	2	2[†]	2[†]	2[†]	2[†]	2[†]	2[†]	2[†]
I.	ECUADOR	20	38	40	50	55	59	65	65	65[†]	65[†]
K.	GUATEMALA	1	4	4	4	4	4	3	1	1	1[†]
M.	HONDURAS	6	10	13	14	14	11	11	5	6	8
N.	MEXICO	96	110	171	188	206	254	304	313	286	286
O.	NICARAGUA	16	10	10[†]	10[†]	16	14	14[†]	22	14	14[†]
P.	PANAMA	4	7	12	12[†]	12[†]	12[†]	12[†]	12[†]	12[†]	12[†]
Q.	PARAGUAY	7	8	3[†]	3[†]	4[†]	4[†]	4[†]	4[†]	4[†]	4[†]
R.	PERU	33	49	39	24	38	49	40	37	37[†]	37[†]
S.	URUGUAY	12	6	5	6	7	7	7	3	4	4[†]
T.	VENEZUELA	33	40	29	22	50	55	69	37	47	47[†]
	UNITED STATES	14,078	14,579	17,981	17,056	17,128	14,857	16,300	13,300	17,000	17,984
	WORLD	33,174	34,288	41,303	41,859	42,331	39,275	40,006	37,075	42,452	43,960

1. Plywood, veneer plywood, core plywood including veneered wood, blockboard, laminboard, and battenboard. Other plywood such as cellular board and composite plywood.

SOURCE: FAO-YFP, 1981–83, 224; 1984, p. 216.

Table 2311

VENEER SHEET PRODUCTION,[1] 11 LC, 1970–84

(T Me^3)

	Country	1970	1975	1977	1978	1979	1980	1981	1982	1983	1984
A.	ARGENTINA	4	10	2	2	7	3	4	5	6	6[†]
B.	BOLIVIA	#	#	18[†]	16[†]	19[†]	22[†]	22[†]	22[†]	22[†]	22[†]
C.	BRAZIL	96[‡]	154	190[‡]	190[†]	200	216	234	234[†]	234[†]	234[†]
D.	CHILE	2[†]	2	5	6	7	7	8	8	9	9
E.	COLOMBIA	5[†]	4[†]	4	4[†]	4	9	7	7	7[†]	7[†]
F.	COSTA RICA	3	5	5	3	5	5[†]	8	8[†]	5	7
I.	ECUADOR	#	1	3	2	2	2	2	3	3[†]	3[†]
K.	GUATEMALA	#	2[†]	1[†]	2[†]	2	2[†]	1	1	1	1
N.	MEXICO	1	4[†]	6	28	16	8	14	10	8	2
Q.	PARAGUAY	8	8[†]	14	22[†]	37[†]	63[†]	63[†]	63[†]	63[†]	63[†]
R.	PERU	14	3[†]	24	24	28	35	38	20	20[†]	20[†]
	WORLD	3,049	3,967	4,099	4,141	4,263	4,382	4,542	4,442	4,673	4,673

1. Thin sheets of wood of uniform thickness, rotary cut, sliced or sawn, for use in plywood, laminated construction, furniture, veneer containers, etc. In production the quantity given excludes veneer sheets used for plywood production within the country.

SOURCE: FAO-YFP, 1981–83, p. 216; 1984, p. 208.

Table 2312

TOTAL WOOD PULP PRODUCTION,[1] 9 LC, 1970-84[a]
(T MET)

	Country	1970	1975	1977	1978	1979	1980	1981	1982	1983	1984
A.	ARGENTINA	166	259	265	287	387	309	252	333	545	561
C.	BRAZIL	811	1,208	1,649	1,976	1,992	3,047	2,952	3,279	3,428	3,433
D.	CHILE	356	452	599	665	700	763	743	667	796	839
E.	COLOMBIA	42	82	110	105	119	123	126	115	114	114[†]
F.	COSTA RICA	#	4	#	#	5	5	3	3	2	2
N.	MEXICO	319	366	437	476	461	447	462	482	455	482
R.	PERU	#	#[‡]	5[‡]	5[‡]	5[‡]	7[‡]	4[‡]	1[‡]	1[†]	1[†]
S.	URUGUAY	6	15	14	19	23	24	22	21	23	23[†]
T.	VENEZUELA	#	29	46[‡]	44[‡]	56	63	46	46	60	67[‡]
	UNITED STATES	37,318	36,808	44,618	43,145	45,318	46,187	47,200	44,786	47,660	50,423
	WORLD	102,118	102,132	112,863	118,584	123,288	125,729	124,952	119,392	128,198	135,350

1. Wood pulp obtained by grinding or milling into their fibers, coniferous or non-coniferous rounds, quarters, billets, etc. of through refining coniferous or non-coniferous chips. Also called groundwood pulp and refiner pulp. It can be bleached or unbleached. It excludes exploded and defibrated pulp.

a. For 1962-69 data, see SALA, 21-1705.

SOURCE: FAO-YFP, 1981–83, p. 261; 1984, p. 253.

Table 2313

TOTAL PAPER AND PAPERBOARD PRODUCTION,[1] 17 LC, 1970-84
(T MET)

	Country	1970	1975	1977	1978	1979	1980	1981	1982	1983	1984
A.	ARGENTINA	644	650	539	645	789	713	669	730	899	946
B.	BOLIVIA	1[‡]	1	1[†]	1[†]	1[†]	1[†]	1[†]	1[†]	1[†]	1[†]
C.	BRAZIL	1,219	1,688	2,236	2,534	2,979	3,361	3,102	3,329	3,426	3,768
D.	CHILE	234	266	296	294	276	356	318	306	325	375
E.	COLOMBIA	220	258	281	307	325	351	407	366	366	366[†]
F.	COSTA RICA	5[†]	7	8	8[†]	11	12	15	18	13	14
G.	CUBA	80	123	70	73	73[†]	73[†]	73[†]	112	109	109[†]
H.	DOMINICAN REP.	8	9[†]	9[†]	9[†]	9[†]	9[†]	9[†]	9[†]	9[†]	9[†]
I.	ECUADOR	8	34	34	36	21	26	31	34	34[†]	34[†]
J.	EL SALVADOR	1[†]	5	5[†]	5	16	16	16	16[†]	16	16[†]
K.	GUATEMALA	14	19	23	27	29	32	29	12	16	17
N.	MEXICO	897	1,184	1,463	1,596	1,684	1,979	1,893	1,924	2,019	2,191
P.	PANAMA	15	9	20[†]	20[†]	20[†]	20[†]	43	43[†]	43[†]	43[†]
Q.	PARAGUAY	#	1	1	8	12	13	13	13[†]	13[†]	13[†]
R.	PERU	124	142	149	159	207	205	272	272[†]	146	146[†]
S.	URUGUAY	40[‡]	29	35[†]	41	52	52	48	39	43	47
T.	VENEZUELA	250	395[‡]	464[‡]	477	492	501	503	482	487	557
	UNITED STATES	46,117	45,248	53,347	55,154	57,410	56,839	57,667	54,899	58,804	62,366

1. Includes printing and writing paper, newsprint, other paper and paperboard products, household and sanitary paper, wrapping and packaging paper, and paperboard.

SOURCE: FAO-YFP, 1981–83, p. 306; 1984, p. 298.

Table 2314

PRINTING AND WRITING PAPER PRODUCTION, 12 LC, 1970-84[a]

(T MET)

	Country	1970	1975	1977	1978	1979	1980	1981	1982	1983	1984
A.	ARGENTINA	123	94	142	142	236	152	139	156	174	185
C.	BRAZIL	254	416	577	638	764	876	876	913	952	1,075
D.	CHILE	#	41	44	56	34	48	52	37	53	61
E.	COLOMBIA	44	44	61	65	66	71	84	70	67	67[†]
G.	CUBA	20	30	31	31[†]	31[†]	31[†]	31[†]	37	34	34[†]
I.	ECUADOR	#	3	3	4	4	4	5	5	5[†]	5[†]
K.	GUATEMALA	7	9	12	13	15	15	15	7	10	11
N.	MEXICO	122	256	304	350	360	526	427	390	404	461
P.	PANAMA	#	#	3[†]	3[†]	3[†]	3[†]	5	5[†]	5[†]	5[†]
R.	PERU	22	38[‡]	41[‡]	36	41	42[†]	68[†]	68[†]	37	37[†]
S.	URUGUAY	15[‡]	11	11[†]	18	25	25	23	19	18	18[†]
T.	VENEZUELA	26	56[‡]	69[‡]	81[‡]	84[‡]	84[†]	84[†]	84	82	113[†]
	UNITED STATES	10,046	9,708	12,299	12,933	13,592	13,829	13,958	13,898[‡]	15,405	16,348
	WORLD	27,290	28,192	34,825	37,944	40,367	41,401	41,239	41,542	45,009	48,835

a. For 1962-69 data, see SALA, 21-1707.

SOURCE: FAO-YFP, 1981–83, p. 323; 1984, p. 315.

Table 2315

NEWSPRINT PRODUCTION, 6 LC, 1970-84[a]

(T MET)

	Country	1970	1975	1977	1978	1979	1980	1981	1982	1983	1984
A.	ARGENTINA	3	#	16	38	94	97	110	94	158	204
C.	BRAZIL	103	125	107	116	109	105	105	107	106	109
D.	CHILE	124	120	132	132	134	131	131	124	155	170
K.	GUATEMALA	#	1	#	#	#	#	#	#	#	#
N.	MEXICO	40	29	90	84	95	116	129	125	157	199
S.	URUGUAY	#	1	#	#	#	#	#	#	~	~
	UNITED STATES	3,035	3,348[‡]	3,512[‡]	3,418[‡]	3,685[‡]	4,238	4,753[‡]	4,574[‡]	4,687[‡]	5,029
	WORLD	21,563	20,807	22,743	23,951	25,234	26,237	27,420	25,809	26,920	28,916

a. For 1962-69 data see SALA, 21-1707.

SOURCE: FAO-YFP, 1981–83, p. 316; 1984, p. 308.

Part VIII: Foreign Trade

CHAPTER 24

SELECTED COMMODITIES IN FOREIGN TRADE

Chapter Outline

NOTE: This volume contains statistics from numerous sources. Alternative data on many topics are presented. Variations in statistics can be attributed to differences in definition, parameters, coverage, methodology, as well as date gathered, prepared, or adjusted. See also Editor's Note on Methodology.

Table 2400

PRINCIPAL EXPORT COMMODITIES,[1] 19 LC, 1975

Country and Commodity	Value (M US)	% of Total Exports	Country and Commodity	Value (M US)	% of Total Exports
A. ARGENTINA			M. HONDURAS		
Total Exports	2,961.3	100.0	Total Exports	283.3	100.0
Wheat	300.7	10.2	Bananas	45.3	15.9
Corn	517.8	17.5	Coffee	57.1	20.1
Meat	281.5	9.5	Silver	13.7	4.8
Wool	104.2	3.5	Wood	39.1	13.8
Hides and Skin	71.1	2.4	N. MEXICO		
B. BOLIVIA			Total Exports	2,908.6	100.0
Total Exports	443.2	100.0	Cotton	174.0	5.9
Tin	182.3	41.1	Coffee	184.1	6.3
Tungsten	22.3	5.0	Lead	~	~
Lead	7.4	1.7	Zinc	85.9	2.9
Zinc	39.6	8.9	Sugar	162.1	5.5
Silver	28.5	6.4	Shrimp	118.5	4.0
Antimony	17.1	3.8	Copper	~	~
Crude Petroleum	114.5	25.8	O. NICARAGUA		
C. BRAZIL			Total Exports	376.5	100.0
Total Exports	8,670.0	100.0	Cotton	95.9	25.4
Coffee	855	9.8	Coffee	48.2	12.8
Cotton	98	1.1	Sugar	42.7	11.3
Cacao	220	2.5	Meat	27.0	7.1
Iron Ore	921	10.6	Cotton Seed	~	~
Sugar	974	11.2	P. PANAMA		
D. CHILE[2]			Total Exports	282.5	100.0
Total Exports	2,480.5	100.0	Bananas	59.5	21.0
Copper	1,653.6	66.6	Refined Petroleum	128.6	45.5
Nitrates	496.6	20.0	Shrimp	19.0	6.7
Iron Ore	72.7	2.9	Q. PARAGUAY		
E. COLOMBIA[2]			Total Exports	173.0	100.0
Total Exports	1,508.8	100.0	Timber	27.7	16.0
Coffee	624.8	41.4	Cotton	19.7	11.3
Petroleum	4.5	.2	Quebracho Extract	2.5	1.4
F. COSTA RICA			Hides	1.9	1.0
Total Exports	488.5	100.0	Oilseeds (Vegetable Oils)	10.4	6.0
Bananas	132.8	27.1	Meat	31.6	18.2
Coffee	97.0	19.8	Tobacco	11.8	6.8
H. DOMINICAN REP.			R. PERU[2]		
Total Exports	893.8	100.0	Total Exports	1,499.2	100.0
Sugar	577.2	64.5	Fishmeal	195.8	13.0
Coffee	43.2	4.8	Cotton	93.8	6.2
Cacao	29.0	3.2	Sugar	155.9	10.3
Tobacco	34.5	3.8	Copper	347.9	23.2
Bauxite	16.7	1.8	Silver	165.0	11.0
I. ECUADOR			Iron Ore	60.1	4.0
Total Exports	910.3	100.0	Zinc	160.0	10.6
Bananas	155.6	17.0	Lead	25.8	1.7
Coffee	64.3	7.0	Coffee	34.8	2.3
Cacao	42.3	4.6	S. URUGUAY		
Crude Petroleum	515.9	56.6	Total Exports	383.8	100.0
J. EL SALVADOR			Wool	86.6	22.5
Total Exports	514.7	100.0	Meat	73.4	19.1
Coffee	168.7	32.7	Hides	16.6	4.3
Cotton	76.3	14.8	T. VENEZUELA		
K. GUATEMALA			Total Exports	10,134.4	100.0
Total Exports	646.8	100.0	Petroleum	9,653.9	95.2
Coffee	161.7	25.0	Iron Ore	~	~
Bananas	26.9	4.1	UNITED STATES[2]		
Cotton	74.0	11.4	Total Exports	97,143	100.0
Sugar	115.6	17.8	Food and Live Animals	13,983	14.4
L. HAITI[2]			Crude Metals, Inedibles Except Fuels	10,934	11.3
Total Exports	71.6	100.0	Minerals, Fuel and Related Materials	3,442	3.5
Coffee	23.8	33.2	Chemicals	8,822	9.1
Sisal	3.2	4.4	Machinery and Transport Equipment	38,189	39.3
Sugar	6.4	8.9	Other Manufactured Goods	16,516	17.0
Bauxite	5.9	8.2			

1. Principal exports do not add to 100.0%.
2. 1974.

SOURCE: IMF-IFS, Jan. 1975, Sept. 1976; and U.S. Bureau of the Census, *Statistical Abstract of the United States*, 1974, table 1328. Cf. SALA, 18–2709.

Table 2401

PRINCIPAL EXPORT COMMODITIES,[1] 19 LC, 1980

Country and Commodity	Value (M US)	% of Total Exports		Country and Commodity	Value (M US)	% of Total Exports
A. ARGENTINA				L. HAITI (M Gourdes)		
Total Exports	8,021.4	100.0		Total Exports	972.5	100.0
Wheat	816.1	10.2		Coffee	334.2	34.4
Wool	269.8	3.4		Bauxite	80.5	8.3
Hides and Skin	354.6	4.4		Sugar	24.6	2.5
Meat	935.8	11.7				
Corn	513.3	6.4		H. HONDURAS (M Lempiras)		
				Total Exports	1700.5	100.0
B. BOLIVIA				Bananas	456	26.8
Total Exports	942.2	100.0		Coffee	408.2	24.0
Tin	378.2	40.1		Wood	72.4	4.3
Silver	118.3	12.6		Frozen Beef	121.5	7.1
Antimony	26.4	2.8		Sugar	58.7	3.5
Natural Gas	220.9	23.4				
Zinc	36.7	3.9		N. MEXICO (B Pesos)		
Wolfram	47.4	5.0		Total Exports	357.5	100.0
				Cotton	7.2	2.0
C. BRAZIL				Shrimp	8.0	2.2
Total Exports	20,132	100.0		Petroleum	225.7	63.1
Coffee	2,486	12.3		Coffee	10.2	2.9
Soybeans and Products	2,277	11.3				
Iron Ore	1,564	7.8		O. NICARAGUA (M Córdobas)		
Sugar	942	4.7		Total Exports	4,528.8	100.0
				Cotton	305.6	6.7
D. CHILE				Meat	588.4	13.0
Total Exports	4,671	100.0		Coffee	1,665	36.8
Copper	2,153	46.1				
Iron Ore	158	3.4		P. PANAMA (M Balboas)		
				Total Exports	360.5	100.0
E. COLOMBIA				Bananas	61.6	17.1
Total Exports	3,945	100.0		Refined Petroleum	81.8	22.7
Coffee	2,375.2	60.2		Shrimp	43.7	12.1
Fuel Oil	238.9	6.1		Sugar	65.8	18.3
Cotton	86.1	2.2				
Sugar	160.9	4.1		Q. PARAGUAY (M Guaraníes)		
				Total Exports	39,089	100.0
F. COSTA RICA (M Colones)				Sawn Timber	8,357	21.4
Total Exports	8,585	100.0		Cotton	13,335	34.1
Coffee	2,113	24.6		Soybeans	5,304	13.6
Sugar	348	4.1		Vegetable Oils	2,157	5.5
Beef	606	7.1				
				R. PERU		
H. DOMINICAN REP.				Total Exports	3,898.3	100
Total Exports	961.9	100.0		Copper	751.6	19.3
Sugar	309.9	32.2		Crude Petroleum	628.9	16.1
Coffee	76.8	8.0		Petroleum Products	147.9	3.8
Cocoa Beans and Products	55.8	5.8		Fishmeal	191.8	4.9
Bauxite	18.5	1.9		Iron Ore	94.7	2.4
Dore	259.5	27.0		Silver	312.2	8.0
Ferronickel	101.3	10.5		Zinc	210.3	5.4
				Lead	383.2	9.8
I. ECUADOR						
Total Exports	2,480.8	100.0		S. URUGUAY		
Bananas	237.1	9.6		Total Exports	1,058.6	100.0
Coffee	130.4	5.3		Wool	212.3	20.1
Cocoa Paste	143.2	5.8		Meat	181.8	17.2
Cocoa Butter	34.1	1.4		Hides	40.2	3.8
Crude Petroleum	1,393.9	56.2				
				T. VENEZUELA (M Bolívares)		
J. EL SALVADOR (M Colones)				Total Exports	82,507	100
Total Exports	2,684	100.0		Petroleum	78,328	94.9
Coffee	1,538	57.3				
Cotton	217.9	8.1		UNITED STATES		
				Total Exports (B US)	220.79	100
K. GUATEMALA (M Quetzales)						
Total Exports	1,557.1	100.0				
Coffee	464.9	29.9				
Bananas	82.7	5.3				
Cotton	166.1	10.7				
Sugar	69.3	4.5				
Fresh Meat	29.1	1.9				

1. Principal exports do not add up to 100%

SOURCE: Percentages calculated from IMF-IFS, March 1987.

Table 2402

PRINCIPAL EXPORT COMMODITIES,[1] 19 LC, 1985

Country and Commodity	Value (M US)	% of Total Exports	Country and Commodity	Value (M US)	% of Total Exports
A. ARGENTINA			L. HAITI (M Gourdes)		
Total Exports	8,396.1	100.0	Total Exports	871	100.0
Wheat	1,133.2	13.5	Bauxite (1982)	74.6	8.6
Wool	269.8	3.2	Coffee	226.4	26.0
Hides and Skin	286.1	3.4	Sugar (1984)	1.9	.2
Meat	370.1	4.4			
Corn	766.1	9.1	M. HONDURAS (M Lempiras)		
			Total Exports	1,491.3	100.0
B. BOLIVIA			Bananas (1984)	464.5	31.1
Total Exports	623.4	100.0	Coffee (1984)	338.2	22.7
Tin	186.7	29.9	Wood (1984)	69.8	4.7
Silver	10.2	1.6	Frozen Beef (1984)	42.4	2.8
Antimony	15.9	2.6	Sugar (1984)	51.3	3.4
Natural Gas	372.6	59.8			
Zinc	29.5	4.7	N. MEXICO (B Pesos)		
Wolfram	10.3	1.7	Total Exports	5,705.1	100.0
			Cotton	23.5	.4
C. BRAZIL			Shrimp	92	1.6
Total Exports	25,639	100.0	Petroleum	3,799	66.6
Coffee	2,369	9.2	Coffee	139.6	2.4
Soybeans and Products	2,540	9.9			
Iron Ore	1,658	6.5	O. NICARAGUA (M Córdobas)		
Sugar	199	0.8	Total Exports	3,945.4	100.0
			Cotton	1,344.8	34.1
D. CHILE			Coffee	1,198.4	30.4
Total Exports	3,823	100.0	Meat	176.9	4.5
Copper	1,761	46.1			
Iron Ore	91	2.4	P. PANAMA (M Balboas)		
			Total Exports	335.35	100.0
E. COLOMBIA			Bananas	78.08	23.3
Total Exports	3,551.6	100.0	Refined Petroleum	19.96	6.0
Coffee	1,784	50.2	Shrimp	59.77	17.8
Fuel Oil	408.8	11.5	Sugar	27.33	8.1
Cotton	58.4	1.6			
Sugar	37	1.0	Q. PARAGUAY (M Guaraníes)		
			Total Exports	96,708	100.0
F. COSTA RICA (M Colones)			Sawn Timber	3,072	3.2
Total Exports	48,526	100.0	Cotton	47,281	48.9
Bananas	10,706	22.1	Soybeans	32,134	33.2
Coffee	15,644	32.2	Vegetable Oils	4,278	4.4
Sugar	478	1.0			
Beef	2,811	5.8	R. PERU		
			Total Exports	2,966.4	100.0
H. DOMINICAN REP.			Fishmeal	116.6	3.9
Total Exports	735.2	100.0	Crude Petroleum	227.3	7.7
Sugar	190.1	25.9	Petroleum Products	418.1	14.1
Coffee	57.6	7.8	Copper	464.2	15.6
Cocoa Beans and Products	64.8	8.8	Silver	139.3	4.7
Tobacco	17.6	2.4	Iron Ore	72.8	2.5
Bauxite	0	0.0	Zinc	268.9	9.1
Dore	113.6	15.5	Lead	200.5	6.8
Ferronickel	120.7	16.4			
			S. URUGUAY		
I. ECUADOR			Total Exports	854.5	100.0
Total Exports	2,904	100.0	Wool	163.8	19.2
Bananas	220	7.6	Meat	117.9	13.8
Coffee	190.8	6.6	Hides	61.3	7.2
Cocoa Paste	2.5	.1			
Cocoa Butter	13.2	.5	T. VENEZUELA (M Bolívares)		
Crude Petroleum	1,824.7	62.8	Total Exports	92,042	100.0
			Petroleum	77,599	84.3
J. EL SALVADOR (M Colones)					
Total Exports	1,690.3	100.0	UNITED STATES		
Coffee	1,131.4	66.9	Total Exports (B US)	213.14	100.0
Cotton	76.9	4.5			
K. GUATEMALA (M Quetzales)					
Total Exports	1,060.1	100.0			
Coffee	450.8	42.5			
Bananas (1984)	56.3	5.0			
Cotton	71.6	6.8			
Sugar	43.8	4.1			
Fresh Meat	9.9	.9			

1. Principal exports do not add up to 100%.

SOURCE: Percentages calculated from IMF-IFS, March 1987.

Table 2403

TWO LEADING EXPORTS AS SHARE OF TOTAL EXPORT VALUE, 20 LC, 1955–85

Country	1955 Exports	1955 % of Total	1960 Exports	1960 % of Total	1965 Exports	1965 % of Total	1970 Exports	1970 % of Total	1975 Exports	1975 % of Total	1980 Exports	1980 % of Total	1985 Exports	1985 % of Total
A. ARGENTINA	Cereals	27.4	Meats	30.5	Wheat	24.9	Meat	24.7	Wheat	10.2	Meat	11.7	Wheat	13.5
	Meats	26.3	Cereals	29.4	Meat	22.0	Corn	14.9	Corn	17.5	Wheat	10.2	Corn	9.1
B. BOLIVIA	Tin	54.9	Tin	64.8	Tin	67.0	Tin	56.8	Tin	41.1	Tin	40.1	Natural Gas	59.8
	Wolframite	13.4	Lead	7.3	Silver	4.7	Antimony	16.3	Tungsten	5.0	Natural Gas	23.4	Zinc	29.9
C. BRAZIL	Coffee	60.8	Coffee	56.2	Coffee	43.9	Coffee	34.3	Coffee	9.8	Coffee	12.3	Soybeans and Products	9.9
	Cacao	5.0	Cacao	7.4	Cotton	6.4	Iron Ore	12.0	Cotton	1.1	Soybeans and Products	11.3	Coffee	9.2
D. CHILE	Metal and Ores	85.6	Copper	70.1	Copper	70.1	Copper	75.8	Copper	66.6	Copper	46.1	Copper	46.1
	Iron	3.8	Iron Ore	6.4	Iron Ore	11.4	Iron Ore	6.6	Nitrates	20.0	Iron Ore	3.4	Iron Ore	2.4
E. COLOMBIA	Coffee	76.7	Coffee	71.7	Coffee	64.8	Coffee	56.6	Coffee	41.4	Coffee	60.2	Coffee	50.2
	Petroleum	14.9	Petroleum	17.2	Petroleum	13.9	Petroleum	9.3	Petroleum	.2	Fuel Oil	6.1	Fuel Oil	11.5
F. COSTA RICA	Coffee	48.6	Coffee	49.3	Coffee	37.9	Coffee	31.8	Bananas	27.1	Coffee	24.6	Coffee	32.2
	Bananas	38.7	Bananas	28.0	Bananas	24.0	Bananas	29.0	Coffee	19.8	Bananas	20.1	Bananas	22.1
G. CUBA	Sugar	81.2	Sugar	75.7	Sugar	74.4	Sugar	76.9	Sugar	89.0	Sugar	83.0	Sugar	~
	Tobacco	5.9	Tobacco	10.2	Nickel, Cobalt	.4	Nickel, Cobalt	16.5	~	~	~	~	~	~
H. DOMINICAN REP.	Sugar	58.6	Sugar	49.6	Sugar	55.8	Sugar	51.8	Sugar	64.5	Sugar	32.2	Sugar	25.9
	Coffee	15.6	Coffee	12.6	Coffee	15.3	Coffee	13.5	Coffee	4.8	Dore	27	Ferronickel	16.4
I. ECUADOR	Bananas	35.6	Bananas	61.5	Bananas	57.0	Bananas	50.9	Bananas	17.0	Crude Petroleum	56.2	Crude Petroleum	62.8
	Coffee	30.4	Coffee	15.0	Coffee	14.7	Coffee	23.1	Coffee	7.0	Bananas	9.6	Bananas	7.6
J. EL SALVADOR	Coffee	78.2	Coffee	69.3	Coffee	46.3	Coffee	49.6	Coffee	32.7	Coffee	57.3	Coffee	66.9
	Cotton	15.6	Cotton	13.5	Cotton	14.2	Cotton	10.1	Cotton	14.8	Cotton	8.1	Cotton	4.5
K. GUATEMALA	Coffee	79.0	Coffee	65.8	Coffee	49.1	Coffee	34.4	Coffee	25.0	Coffee	29.9	Coffee	42.2
	Bananas	8.0	Bananas	16.7	Cotton	18.4	Cotton	9.1	Bananas	4.1	Cotton	10.7	Sugar	6.8
L. HAITI	Coffee	71.9	Coffee	55.6	Coffee	54.8	Coffee	38.1	Coffee	33.2	Coffee	34.4	Coffee	26.0
	Sisal	13.6	Sisal	12.2	Sisal	7.2	Bauxite	16.4	Sisal	4.4	Bauxite	8.3	~	~
M. HONDURAS	Bananas	61.1	Bananas	46.1	Bananas	49.8	Bananas	40.6	Bananas	15.9	Bananas	26.8	Bananas	35.1
	Coffee	19.0	Coffee	18.9	Coffee	13.6	Coffee	14.7	Coffee	20.1	Coffee	24.0	Coffee	23.7
N. MEXICO	Cotton	14.5	Cotton	20.7	Cotton	19.7	Cotton	8.8	Cotton	5.9	Petroleum	63.1	Petroleum	66.6
	Coffee	13.2	Coffee	9.4	Coffee	7.4	Sugar	7.0	Coffee	6.3	Coffee	2.9	Coffee	2.4
O. NICARAGUA	Coffee	40.0	Coffee	34.4	Cotton	41.3	Cotton	29.4	Cotton	25.4	Coffee	36.8	Cotton	34.1
	Cotton	30.6	Cotton	26.3	Coffee	15.8	Meat	13.5	Coffee	12.8	Meat	12.9	Coffee	30.4
P. PANAMA	Bananas	64.0	Bananas	72.9	Bananas	49.8	Bananas	57.4	Bananas	21.0	Refined Petroleum	22.7	Bananas	23.3
	Shrimp	25.8	Coffee	3.8	Refined Petroleum	29.0	Refined Petroleum	18.8	Refined Petroleum	45.5	Sugar	18.3	Shrimp	17.8
Q. PARAGUAY	Meat	37.2	Meat	26.5	Meat	28.6	Meat	23.9	Timber	16.0	Cotton	34.1	Cotton	48.9
	Quebracho Extract	20.4	Wood	18.6	Timber	21.7	Timber	19.7	Cotton	11.3	Sawn Timber	21.4	Soybeans	33.2
R. PERU	Cotton	25.1	Cotton	16.9	Fishmeal	24.4	Fishmeal	27.6	Fishmeal	13.0	Copper	19.3	Copper	15.6
	Lead	11.9	Sugar	11.0	Copper	23.8	Copper	25.0	Cotton	6.2	Crude Petroleum	16.1	Petroleum Products	14.1
S. URUGUAY	Wool	51.0	Wool	34.8	Wool	45.4	Wool	37.7	Wool	22.5	Wool	20.1	Wool	19.2
	Meat	19.7	Meat	23.8	Meat	24.3	Meat	31.5	Meat	19.1	Meat	17.2	Meat	13.8
T. VENEZUELA	Petroleum	91.9	Petroleum	90.6	Petroleum	93.6	Petroleum	90.2	Petroleum	95.2	Petroleum	94.9	Petroleum	84.3
	Iron Ore	4.8	Iron Ore	6.8	Iron Ore	5.0	Iron Ore	5.7	Iron Ore	~	Crude Petroleum	64.4	Crude Petroleum	48.5
UNITED STATES	Manufacturing Goods	54.8	Machinery	34.3	Machinery	20.4	Machinery	43.7	Food and Live Animals	14.4	~	~	~	~
	Semi-Manufactured Goods	15.6	Vegetable Food Products	8.6	Motor Vehicles	7.2	Other Manufactured Goods	18.7	Crude Metals, Inedible except Fuels	11.3	~	~	~	~

SOURCE: IMF-IFS, Jan. 1975, Dec. 1969, Aug. 1967, Aug. 1961, Sept. 1958, Mar. 1976, and Jan. 1971. Cuban data beginning 1960 are from UCLA, 6 (1962) and 10 (1966), UCLA-Cuba, and Cuba, DGE, AE, 1973, Cf. SALA, 18–2801; SALA, 24–2401.

Figure 24:1

SHARE OF FOURTEEN MAJOR COMMODITY EXPORTS IN LATIN AMERICA'S TOTAL EXPORT EARNINGS,[1] 1960–81

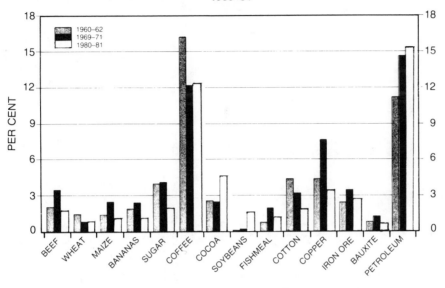

1. Includes Bahamas, Barbados, Guyana, Jamaica, and Trinidad and Tobago.

SOURCE: IDB-SPTF, 1983, p. 13.

Table 2404

CONTRIBUTION OF THE TEN MAIN LATIN AMERICAN PRIMARY EXPORT PRODUCTS TO EACH COUNTRY'S TOTAL VALUE OF MERCHANDISE EXPORTS, 19 LR, 1972–86a

(%)

	Beef			Maize			Bananas			Sugar			Coffee			Cocoa		
Country	1972–76	1981–85	1986‡	1972–76	1981–85	1986‡	1972–76	1981–85	1986‡	1972–76	1981–85	1986‡	1972–76	1981–85	1986‡	1972–76	1981–85	1986‡
A. ARGENTINA	9.4	4.3	3.2	13.0	10.1	11.2	#	#	#	#	#	#	#	#	#	#	#	#
B. BOLIVIA	#	#	#	#	#	#	#	#	#	#	#	#	#	#	#	#	#	#
C. BRAZIL	#	#	#	#	#	#	#	#	#	9.1	1.9	1.0	16.6	9.0	10.2	#	#	#
D. CHILE	#	#	#	#	#	#	#	#	#	#	#	#	#	#	#	#	#	#
E. COLOMBIA	#	#	#	#	#	#	#	#	#	5.8	2.4	1.1	49.4	50.1	45.5	#	#	#
F. COSTA RICA	7.7	5.6	5.5	#	#	#	24.8	24.2	17.1	#	#	#	25.5	27.6	31.2	#	#	#
H. DOMINICAN REP.	#	#	#	#	#	#	#	#	#	48.3	34.1	26.5	7.3	10.0	23.4	5.6	6.5	9.7
I. ECUADOR	#	#	#	#	#	#	14.3	6.9	8.5	#	#	#	10.5	6.0	10.8	#	#	#
J. EL SALVADOR	#	#	#	#	#	#	#	#	#	8.3	3.5	5.0	41.9	58.2	81.3	#	#	#
K. GUATEMALA	#	#	#	#	#	#	#	#	#	11.1	5.4	4.5	29.8	30.8	40.4	#	#	#
L. HAITI	#	#	#	#	#	#	#	#	#	5.0	.8	.3	32.1	25.4	40.6	#	#	#
M. HONDURAS	6.7	4.4	3.0	#	#	#	26.1	30.2	39.0	#	#	#	18.5	22.4	28.2	#	#	#
N. MEXICO	#	#	#	#	#	#	#	#	#	#	#	#	#	#	#	#	#	#
O. NICARAGUA	9.3	6.1	10.0	#	#	#	#	#	#	7.5	5.3	3.6	7.7	2.1	4.4	#	#	#
P. PANAMA	7.2	1.2	1.5	#	#	#	30.1	25.4	44.9	11.7	11.3	10.1	15.9	31.1	46.6	#	#	#
Q. PARAGUAY	#	#	#	#	#	#	#	#	#	#	#	#	#	#	#	#	#	#
R. PERU	–	–	–	#	#	#	#	#	#	11.4	.6	1.1	#	#	#	#	#	#
S. URUGUAY	29.1	16.3	8.6	#	#	#	#	#	#	#	#	#	#	#	#	#	#	#
T. VENEZUELA	#	#	#	#	#	#	#	#	#	#	#	#	#	#	#	#	#	#
LATIN AMERICA	2.0	1.1a	n.a.	1.5	1.0	1.1	1.3	.8	1.0	5.4	1.2	1.0	8.7	6.4	10.0	1.1	.4	.7

	Soybeans			Cotton			Iron Ore			Copper			Total 10 Products			Total Merchandise Exports
Country	1972–76	1981–85	1986‡	1972–76	1981–85	1986‡	1972–76	1981–85	1986‡	1972–76	1981–85	1986‡	1972–76	1981–85	1986‡	
A. ARGENTINA	**	6.7	10.4	#	#	#	#	#	#	#	#	#	22.4	21.0	24.7	100.0
B. BOLIVIA	#	#	#	#	#	#	#	#	#	#	#	#	#	#	#	100.0
C. BRAZIL	13.1	6.6	4.0	#	#	#	8.3	7.1	7.4	#	#	#	47.1	24.6	22.6	100.0
D. CHILE	#	#	#	#	#	#	5.4	3.6	3.0	66.0	45.1	36.6	71.4	48.7	39.6	100.0
E. COLOMBIA	#	#	#	#	#	#	#	#	#	#	#	#	49.4	50.1	45.5	100.0
F. COSTA RICA	#	#	#	#	#	#	#	#	#	#	#	#	63.8	59.8	54.8	100.0
H. DOMINICAN REP.	#	#	#	#	#	#	#	#	#	#	#	#	61.2	50.5	59.5	100.0
I. ECUADOR	#	#	#	#	#	#	#	#	#	#	#	#	35.3	12.9	19.2	100.0
J. EL SALVADOR	#	#	#	10.7	5.6	5.4	#	#	#	#	#	#	60.9	67.3	91.7	100.0
K. GUATEMALA	#	#	#	11.3	7.6	6.9	#	#	#	#	#	#	52.2	43.9	50.8	100.0
L. HAITI	#	#	#	#	#	#	#	#	#	#	#	#	37.1	26.2	40.9	100.0
M. HONDURAS	#	#	#	#	#	#	#	#	#	#	#	#	51.3	34.7	42.0	100.0
N. MEXICO	#	#	#	5.6	.9	1.3	#	#	#	#	#	#	13.3	3.0	5.7	100.0
O. NICARAGUA	#	#	#	26.8	26.3	31.1	#	#	#	#	#	#	59.5	68.8	91.3	100.0
P. PANAMA	#	#	#	#	#	#	#	#	#	#	#	#	41.8	36.6	55.0	100.0
Q. PARAGUAY	9.8	24.3	35.2	8.7	46.3	23.7	#	#	#	#	#	#	25.7	71.8	60.4	100.0
R. PERU	–	–	–	5.5	1.6	1.7	6.3	2.1	1.7	15.6	12.9	16.5	27.4	17.1	21.0	100.0
S. URUGUAY	#	#	#	#	#	#	#	#	#	#	#	#	29.1	16.3	8.6	100.0
T. VENEZUELA	#	#	#	#	#	#	#	#	#	#	#	#	#	#	#	100.0
LATIN AMERICA	2.9	1.9	2.2	2.0	.9a	**	3.0	2.3	3.0	3.0	1.9	2.2	49.7	18.0	**	100.0

a. For previous years after 1971, see SALA, 24-2403.

SOURCE: IDB-SPTF, 1986, table 64; 1987, table 67.

Table 2405

LATIN AMERICA PARTICIPATION IN TOTAL COMMERCE OF DEVELOPING COUNTRIES, BY GROUPS OF PRIMARY COUNTRIES, 1966 and 1983

(%)

Groups of Basic Products	Exports		Imports	
	1966	1983	1966	1983
All Food Types	46.1	51.6	23.8	20.6
Agricultural Value	25.1	16.6	27.3	14.5
Minerals and Metals	40.9	46.6	40.8	17.4
Total Primary Products	40.4	45.1	26.0	19.4
Fuel	30.1	19.6	45.4	34.4
Total of Primary Products Including Fuel	36.8	27.0	31.2	27.4

SOURCE: SELA, chapter 15, January–March 1987, p. 37.

Table 2406

LATIN AMERICA PARTICIPATION IN WORLD EXPORTS OF SELECTED BASIC PRODUCTS, 1983

(%)

Product	%
Bananas	79.92
Coffee	61.03
Sugar	58.48
Bauxite	39.15
Soya Oil	33.60
Copper	31.48
Iron Ore	31.48
Cocoa Beans	22.14
Albumine	21.28
Tobacco Leaves	15.92
Hides and Tallow	13.90
Fishery Products	13.03
Cotton	9.71
Wheat and Wheat Powder	8.47
Corn	7.19
Animal Skin	.82

SOURCE: SELA, chapter 15, January–March 1987, p. 37.

Table 2407

FOOD TRADE BY CATEGORY, 20 LR, AVERAGE 1981–85
(M US)[1]

| | Cereals and Preparations | | Meat and Preparations | | Dairy Products and Eggs | | Fruits and Vegetables | | Sugar and Honey | | Animal and Vegetable Oils | | Subtotal | | Coffee, Tea, and Cocoa | | Total | | Trade Balance |
Country	Exports	Imports	Exports	Imports	Exports	Imports	Exports	Imports	Exports	Imports	Exports	Imports	Exports	Imports	Exports	Imports	Exports	Imports	
A. ARGENTINA	2,420	3	836	10	35	11	353	58	160	4	1,211	7	5,015	92	43	99	5,059	192	4,867
B. BOLIVIA	1	65	0	1	0	10	0	2	8	1	3	15	12	94	14	1	26	95	–70
C. BRAZIL	62	1,040	1,155	41	8	25	899	147	674	2	1,142	206	3,939	1,461	2,972	0	6,911	1,461	5,450
D. CHILE	12	203	4	15	0	28	334	25	14	57	0	61	392	389	0	44	392	433	–41
E. COLOMBIA	12	170	30	4	5	19	171	74	68	4	0	117	286	388	1,654	5	1,940	393	1,547
F. COSTA RICA	16	41	57	6	1	5	247	18	22	3	0	4	347	77	261	2	608	79	530
H. DOMINICAN REP.	1	72	8	8	2	13	29	7	318	3	4	55	362	157	150	0	513	157	355
I. ECUADOR	1	81	0	0	0	7	185	6	10	21	2	46	198	162	294	0	492	162	330
J. EL SALVADOR	3	42	2	9	0	17	3	34	29	4	0	22	37	127	430	1	468	129	339
K. GUATEMALA	7	38	45	3	2	12	98	9	81	3	0	23	233	88	350	2	583	89	494
L. HAITI	0	47	2	3	0	13	3	3	2	7	0	27	6	101	50	0	57	101	–44
M. HONDURAS	1	23	33	9	0	14	253	7	35	1	6	7	328	61	167	1	496	62	434
N. MEXICO	14	842	17	80	0	178	513	247	49	154	0	430	594	1,931	476	1	1,070	1,932	–862
O. NICARAGUA	5	41	23	7	1	13	23	20	32	3	0	30	84	114	115	0	199	115	85
P. PANAMA	1	25	4	19	4	13	78	26	37	2	0	16	124	101	17	5	141	106	34
Q. PARAGUAY	0	4	1	11	0	5	0	5	0	1	0	2	1	28	1	2	2	30	–29
R. PERU	1	248	3	30	0	62	15	16	14	35	1	36	34	426	139	6	173	433	–260
S. URUGUAY	130	18	206	1	27	1	13	13	5	3	10	6	390	41	1	19	390	60	331
T. VENEZUELA	2	501	3	53	2	215	74	157	0	178	0	196	81	1,301	34	3	115	1,304	–1,189
LATIN AMERICA	2,753	3,731	2,431	472	91	789	3,328	1,032	1,750	533	2,384	1,374	12,768	7,932	7,193	210	19,961	8,142	11,820

1. Exports are valued fob and imports cif.

SOURCE: IDB-SPTF, 1986, p. 45; 1987, p. 94.

Table 2408

FOOD TRADE BALANCES, 20 L, 1961–75

(M US)

Division	Exports (FOB)			Imports (CIF)			Balance		
	1961	1971	1975	1961	1971	1975	1961	1971	1975
LAFTA	**3,284**	**5,290**	**10,496**	**871**	**1,454**	**3,835**	**2,413**	**3,836**	**6,661**
Andean Pact	650	974	2,102	472	741	1,610	178	233	492
B. BOLIVIA	3	13	73	22	38	57	–19	–25	16
D. CHILE	36	43	120	123	232	455	–32	–189	–335

Continued in SALA, 24–2405.

Table 2409

CEREAL IMPORTS, 20 LC, 1974 AND 1985

(T MET)

	Country	1974	1985
A.	ARGENTINA	#	1
B.	BOLIVIA	209	459
C.	BRAZIL	2,485	4,857
D.	CHILE	1,737	486
E.	COLOMBIA	503	1,021
F.	COSTA RICA	110	146
G.	CUBA	~	~
H.	DOMINICAN REP.	252	492
I.	ECUADOR	152	293
J.	EL SALVADOR	75	224
K.	GUATEMALA	138	164
L.	HAITI	83	227
M.	HONDURAS	52	99
N.	MEXICO	2,881	4,507
O.	NICARAGUA	44	114
P.	PANAMA	63	115
Q.	PARAGUAY	71	83
R.	PERU	637	1,187
S.	URUGUAY	70	31
T.	VENEZUELA	1,270	2,793
	UNITED STATES	460	992

SOURCE: WB-WOR, 1987, table 6.

Table 2410

FISH EXPORTS,[1] 10 LC, 1978–84

		Value of Exports (T US)						Value as % of World Exports					
	Country	1978	1980	1981	1982	1983	1984	1978	1980	1981	1982	1983	1984
A.	ARGENTINA	106,014	126,908	117,104	130,366	85,542	78,333[†]	2.8	2.7	3.8	3.2	~	~
C.	BRAZIL	25,434	36,605	43,089	34,452	32,213	22,052	#	#	#	#	~	~
D.	CHILE	6,865	37,909	46,831	46,900	31,900	36,800	#	#	#	#	~	~
E.	COLOMBIA	7,128	13,591	15,451	9,175	4,009	3,036	#	#	#	#	~	~
G.	CUBA	18,099	30,984	18,405	14,163	17,611	94,322[†]	#	#	#	#	~	~
I.	ECUADOR	10,707	19,160	11,085	5,971	6,299[†]	10,966	#	#	#	#	~	~
N.	MEXICO	26,120	7,970[†]	10,795[†]	22,256[†]	5,581	11,052[†]	#	#	#	#	~	~
R.	PERU	29,725	36,013	15,961	10,438	5,965[†]	4,723	#	#	#	#	~	~
S.	URUGUAY	21,277	47,399	55,734	43,872	36,867	39,596	#	#	#	#	~	~
T.	VENEZUELA	~	100	63	18,457[†]	32,966[†]	33,855	#	#	#	#	~	~
	LAIA	233,521	326,625	316,736	321,979	241,413	240,037	6.2	6.9	6.2	6.4	4.9[†]	4.7[†]
	CACM	3,726	2,645	2,767	3,316	5,248	10,956	.1	.1	.1	.1	.1[†]	.2[†]
	UNITED STATES	366,435	348,097	545,055	588,078	524,496	519,691	9.7	7.3	10.7	11.6	10.6	10.1

1. Fresh, chilled, and frozen.

SOURCE: UN-YITS, 1982, vol. 2, p. 21; 1983, vol. 2, p. 9; 1985, vol. 2, p. 43.

Table 2411

FISHERY EXPORTS, 11 OASL, 1970–80

(% and M US)

Category	1970		%[a]	1975		%[a]	1980		%[a]
Total fishery commodities	R.	PERU	65	R.	PERU	33	N.	MEXICO	30
	N.	MEXICO	14	N.	MEXICO	25	D.	CHILE	19
	D.	CHILE	5	C.	BRAZIL	7	R.	PERU	16
				D.	CHILE	6	I.	ECUADOR	9
				I.	ECUADOR	6	A.	ARGENTINA	7
							B.	BRAZIL	7
								Rest of OASL	12
								$1,942.7	100

Continued in SALA, 24–2407.

Table 2412

MEAT IMPORT VOLUME,[1] 16 L, 1975–85[a]

(T MET)

Country	1975	1977	1978	1979	1980	1981	1982	1983	1984	1985
A. ARGENTINA	~	#	#	9	20	11	2	2	2	~
B. BOLIVIA	~	#	~	~	~	~	~	~	~	~
C. BRAZIL	244	27	122	122	70	66	22	23	36	56
D. CHILE	11	4	14	6	11	17	9	3	6	7
E. COLOMBIA	~	#	#	#	#	.5	1	1	1	2
F. COSTA RICA	9	1	3	2	2	#	#	#	#	#
G. CUBA	~	6	11	16	20	22	23	21	18	25
H. DOMINICAN REP.[3]	14	#	#	2	12	11	10	9	3	11
J. EL SALVADOR	3	#	#	#	.5	#	#	#	#	#
K. GUATEMALA	~	#	1	.5	#	.6	#	~	#	#
M. HONDURAS	~	#	#	#	#	#	#	#	.3	.3
N. MEXICO[4,3]	147	19	11	45	47	94	78	49	82	135
O. NICARAGUA[3]	3	#	#	#	3	3	3	1	#	#
P. PANAMA[2]	1	#	#	#	#	1	2	#	#	.5
R. PERU	157	8	4	1	7	25	31	19	25	22
T. VENEZUELA[3]	102	40	75	56	27	47	40	21	8	6

1. Includes meat fresh, chilled, and frozen. Figures refer to "special trade" except where otherwise noted. "Special" imports include goods for domestic consumption and withdrawals from bonded warehouses or free zones for purposes of domestic consumption.
2. Data exclude the free zone of Colón and the Canal Zone.
3. Figures refer to "general trade," i.e., total imports.
4. Imports through free zones are included.

a. For 1934–74, see SALA, 20-2927.

SOURCE: FAO-TY, 1978; 1980, table 10; 1981, table 10; 1982, table 10; 1984, table 10; 1985, table 11.

Table 2413

MEAT EXPORT VOLUME,[1] 17 LC, 1975–85[a]

(T MET)

Country	1975	1977	1978	1979	1980	1981	1982	1983	1984	1985
A. ARGENTINA	79	389	481	489	313	342	363	282	180	170
B. BOLIVIA	2	.1	~	~	~	~	#	#	#	~
C. BRAZIL	5	116	110	120	213	383	428	444	436	458
D. CHILE	- -	3	2	4	5	4	4	2	2	2
E. COLOMBIA	18	14	30	16	12	22	21	14	5	4
F. COSTA RICA	29	32	35	32	26	33	25	14	21	25
H. DOMINICAN REP.[2]	4	1	1	1	1	4	4	3	#	8
J. EL SALVADOR	2	3	5	5	2	.6	1	2	1	1
K. GUATEMALA	15	19	15	16	11	15	14	12	7	14
L. HAITI[2]	~	1	1	2	.7	2[‡]	2	1	1	1[†]
M. HONDURAS	23	18	23	30	29	23	16	16	14	10
N. MEXICO[2]	5	36	55	26	19	14	11	9	9	4
O. NICARAGUA[2]	22	28	37	38	21	15	15	14	11	7
P. PANAMA[4]	1	1	.3	.6	1	2	4	2	1	#
Q. PARAGUAY	8	4	4	4	1	1	1	7	7	#
R. PERU	2[†]	2[†]	2[‡]	2	1	1	1	2	#	#
S. URUGUAY[2]	79	120	103	69	113	167	140	177	108	101
UNITED STATES[2,3]	370	574	578	597	731	800	674	629	617	638
WORLD	2,394	6,744	7,070	7,838	8,115	8,889	8,579	8,944	8,793	8,965

1. Includes meat fresh, chilled or frozen. Figures refer to "special trade" except where otherwise indicated. "Special" exports comprise exports of goods wholly or partly produced or manufactured in the country, together with exports of "nationalized" goods, but not of goods held in bonded warehouses or free zones.
2. Figures refer to "general trade," i.e., total exports including re-exports.
3. The customs area includes the Commonwealth of Puerto Rico.
4. Data exclude the free zone of Colón and the Canal Zone.

a. For 1934–74, see SALA, 20-2925. See SALA, 20-2926 for comparison of Argentina and Australia beef cattle exports.

SOURCE: FAO-TY, 1978; 1980, table 10; 1981, table 10; 1984, table 10; 1985, table 11.

Table 2414

MEAT EXPORTS,[1] 15 LC, 1980–84

	Country	Value of Exports (T US)					Value as % of World Exports				
		1980	1981	1982	1983	1984	1980	1981	1982	1983	1984
A.	ARGENTINA	519,738	522,209	455,819	322,801	415,836[†]	6.4	6.9	6.0	4.5	6.3
C.	BRAZIL	18,399	123,568	188,288	210,318	214,528	#	#	#	#	~
D.	CHILE	36	24	1,684[†]	1,666[†]	1,784[†]	#	#	#	#	~
E.	COLOMBIA	26,917	53,217	45,386	30,529	10,521	#	#	#	#	~
F.	COSTA RICA	70,722	73,948	53,058	32,253[†]	43,525[†]	#	#	~	~	~
H.	DOMINICAN REP.	2,883	8,435	8,829	6,711	1,600[†]	#	#	#	~	~
J.	EL SALVADOR	4,146	961	2,600	3,680[†]	3,679[†]	#	#	#	~	~
K.	GUATEMALA	34,735	30,572	7,709[†]	18,285[†]	15,941[†]	#	#	#	~	~
L.	HAITI	1,463[†]	3,233[†]	1,330[†]	243[†]	29[†]	#	#	#	~	~
M.	HONDURAS	60,739	46,471	33,922	31,339	23,700[†]	#	#	#[†]	~	~
N.	MEXICO	3,006[†]	4,137[†]	2,911[†]	3,130[†]	7,770[†]	#[†]	#[†]	#[†]	~	~
O.	NICARAGUA	58,551	21,232	33,818	31,952[†]	22,475[†]	#	#	#	~	~
P.	PANAMA	3,148	5,066	9,353	4,109	210[†]	#	#	#	~	~
Q.	PARAGUAY	32	583[†]	2,426[†]	2,529[†]	4,097[†]	#	#[†]	#[†]	~	~
S.	URUGUAY	155,777	214,476	171,174	218,498	97,102[†]	#	#	#	~	~
	LAIA	723,905	918,214	868,279	800,338	752,284[†]	9.0	12.1	11.5	11.1	11.3[†]
	CACM	228,893	173,186	131,108	117,508[†]	109,319[†]	2.8	2.3	1.7	1.6[†]	1.6
	UNITED STATES	235,436	280,732	352,286	371,255	451,119	2.9	3.7	4.7	5.1	6.8

1. Bovine, fresh and frozen.

SOURCE: UN-YITS, 1982, vol. 2, p. 256; 1983, vol. 2, p. 244; 1984, vol. 2, p. 278.

Table 2415

MEAT (FRESH) EXPORT VOLUME,
15 LRC, 1960-75

(T MET)

	Country	1960	1965	1970	1975
A.	ARGENTINA	280	349	352	79
B.	BOLIVIA	~	~	~	2

Continued in SALA, 24-2411, with yearly data.

Table 2416

COMPARISON OF ARGENTINA AND AUSTRALIA
BEEF CATTLE EXPORTS, 1938–77
(T MET)

Year	(1) Argentina Exports	(2) Australia Exports	(2/1) Australia % Argentina
1938–43	472.2	110.7	23.4
1955	411.4	224.5	54.6

Continued in SALA, 24–2412.

Table 2417

BANANA EXPORT VOLUME,[1] 14 LC, 1975–85[a]
(T MET)

	Country	1975	1977	1978	1979	1980	1981	1982	1983	1984	1985
B.	BOLIVIA	~	20	~	#	#	#	#	~	#	~
C.	BRAZIL	147	112	132	128	67	67	59	89	103	100[‡]
E.	COLOMBIA	486	455	592	626	692	795[‡]	804	787	1,030	786
F.	COSTA RICA	1,077	1,013	1,007	1,007	1,027	950	1,011	1,033	1,030	882
H.	DOMINICAN REP.[2]	26	18	11	6	11	28	18	6	6	6[†]
I.	ECUADOR[2]	1,450	1,318	1,425	1,386	1,437	1,230	1,261	910	906[‡]	1,074
K.	GUATEMALA	260	320	316	299	336	370	404	316	324[‡]	380[‡]
L.	HAITI[2]	~	#	#	#	#	#	#	#	#	#[†]
M.	HONDURAS	420	777	760	897	987	820	914	714	830	920[‡]
N.	MEXICO[2]	3	16	18	17	16	6[‡]	7	31	32	38
O.	NICARAGUA[2]	135	112	123	119	121	100	147	69	83	89
P.	PANAMA[3]	558	547	628	565	505	573	566	652	655	686
R.	PERU	~	~	~	#	#	#	#[†]	#	~	~
T.	VENEZUELA[2]	7	5	6	5	6	7[‡]	7[†]	14	26	27
	WORLD	6,641	6,668	7,149	7,097	6,956	6,929	7,147	6,335	6,999	6,946

1. Figures refer to "special trade" except where otherwise indicated. For explanation of "Special" exports, see table 2413, n. 1.
2. Figures refer to "general trade," i.e., total exports including re-exports.
3. Data exclude the free zone of Colón and the Canal Zone.

a. For 1934–74, see SALA, 20-2916.

SOURCE: FAO-TY, 1978; 1980; 1981, table 55; 1982, table 55; 1984, table 55; 1985, table 56.

Table 2418

BANANA EXPORTS,[1] 12 LC, 1980–84

	Country	Value of Exports (T US)					Value as % of World Exports				
		1980	1981	1982	1983	1984	1980	1981	1982	1983	1984
C.	BRAZIL	11,164	12,741	10,520	10,676	14,656	#	#	#	~	~
D.	CHILE	330	215[†]	552[‡]	581[†]	~	#	#[†]	#[†]	~	~
E.	COLOMBIA	94,141	122,430	151,119	147,696	197,915	7.3	8.8	10.2	9.3	10.4
F.	COSTA RICA	214,501	229,128	218,188	295,202[†]	323,377[†]	16.6	16.4	14.7	18.6[†]	17.0[†]
H.	DOMINICAN REP.	1,605	4,572	2,836	887	1,530[†]	#	#	#	~	~
I.	ECUADOR	195,591	212,766	214,312	269,513[†]	313,261[†]	15.1	15.2	14.5	17.0	16.4
K.	GUATEMALA	52,418	58,476	101,263[†]	76,659[†]	64,334[†]	4.1	4.2	6.8[†]	4.8[†]	3.4[†]
M.	HONDURAS	233,143	201,457	221,320	199,573	282,524[†]	18.0	14.4	15.0	12.6	14.8[†]
N.	MEXICO	~	~	~	3,663	5,603	~	~	~	~	~
O.	NICARAGUA	8,386	20,904	9,802	30,789[†]	33,235[†]	#	#	#	~	~
P.	PANAMA	61,714	69,683	66,546	75,492	40,801[†]	4.8	5.0	4.5	4.7	2.1[†]
T.	VENEZUELA	1,649	2,633	685[†]	3,567[†]	5,258[†]	4.7	4.9	4.5	3.9	~
	LAIA	302,893	352,541	377,834	436,582[†]	538,314[†]	23.4	25.3	25.5	27.5[†]	28.2[†]
	CACM	508,448	510,078	550,730[†]	602,237[†]	703,487[†]	39.3	36.5	37.2[†]	37.9[†]	36.9[†]
	UNITED STATES	71,505	75,896	72,988	72,148	70,640	5.5	5.4	4.9	4.5	3.7

1. Including fresh and dry plantain.

SOURCE: UN-YITS, 1982, vol 2, p. 292; UN-YITS, 1983, vol. 2, p. 280; UN-YITS, 1984,
vol. 2, p. 314.

Table 2419

BARLEY IMPORT VOLUME,[1] 17 LC, 1975–85[a]
(T MET)

	Country	1975	1977	1978	1979	1980	1981	1982	1983	1984	1985
A.	ARGENTINA	~	~	~	#	#	#	#	~	~	~
C.	BRAZIL	22	11	32	41	93	119	102	169	146	178
D.	CHILE	~	~	~	70	38	6	#	~	120	55
E.	COLOMBIA	12	88	108	49	39	80	98	118	116	130[†]
F.	COSTA RICA	#	#	#	32	17	#	#	#	#	~
G.	CUBA	31	42	44	23	57	60[‡]	43	41	43	42
H.	DOMINICAN REP.	~	~	~	#	#	#	#	~	~	~
I.	ECUADOR[3]	10[‡]	12	28	22	23	36	26	27	36[‡]	18
J.	EL SALVADOR	#	~	~	#	#	#	#	#	#	#
K.	GUATEMALA	~	~	~	#	#	#	#	~	~	~
M.	HONDURAS	~	~	~	#	#	#	#	~	~	~
N.	MEXICO[2,3]	150	.1	88	44	176	91	20	67	88	38
O.	NICARAGUA	~	~	~	#	#	#	#	#	~	#
P.	PANAMA	#	#	#	#	#	#	#	#	#	#
R.	PERU	33[‡]	20	21[‡]	34	36	36	37	19	33	89[†]
S.	URUGUAY[3]	4	#	#	19	7	22	23	31	30	15[†]
T.	VENEZUELA[3]	#	#	#	#	#	#	#	#	#	#
	UNITED STATES	~	~	~	157	140	127	198	141	146	105
	WORLD	~	~	~	14,824	14,997	18,599	18,670	17,691	22,726	20,102

1. Figures refer to "special trade" except where otherwise indicated. For explanation of
"Special" imports, see table 2412, n. 1.
2. Imports through free zones included.
3. Figures refer to "general trade," i.e., total imports.

a. For 1934–74, see SALA, 20-2918.

SOURCE: FAO-TY, 1978; 1980; 1981; 1982, table 40;1984, table 40; 1985, table 41.

Table 2420

BARLEY EXPORT VOLUME,[1] 4 LC, 1975–85[a]
(T MET)

	Country	1975	1977	1978	1979	1980	1981	1982	1983	1984	1985
A.	ARGENTINA	18	75	15	58	43	6	1	31	18	34
D.	CHILE	7	4	#	#	9	#	8	5	14	#
N.	MEXICO[3]	1	50	- -	#	#	#	#	#	#	#
S.	URUGUAY[3]	3	1	3	#	22	26	15	23	63	48[†]
	UNITED STATES[2,3]	651	1,553	649	721	1,463	2,067	1,375	1,521	1,971	706
	WORLD	12,412	13,109	14,596	14,111	16,215	19,299	18,472	17,754	23,008	21,808

1. Figures refer to "special trade" except where otherwise indicated. See table 2413 n. 1,
   for explanation of "special" exports.
2. The customs area includes the Commonwealth of Puerto Rico.
3. Figures refer to "general trade," i.e., total exports including re-exports.

a. For 1934–74, see SALA, 20-2917.

SOURCE: FAO-TY, 1978; 1980; 1981, table 40; 1982, table 40; 1984, table 40; 1985,
   table 41.

Table 2421

BUTTER IMPORT VOLUME,[1] 18 LC, 1975–85[a]
(T MET)

	Country	1975	1977	1978	1979	1980	1981	1982	1983	1984	1985
A.	ARGENTINA	4	.3	2	3	1	2[‡]	.5[‡]	#	#	1[†]
B.	BOLIVIA	~	~	~	#	#	#	#	#	#	#
C.	BRAZIL	4	2	#	1	6	#	#	#	#	~
D.	CHILE	50	4	6	9	7	4	5	2	2	#
E.	COLOMBIA	~	~	~	3	3	#	#	1	#	#
F.	COSTA RICA	2	.4	.5	1	1	#	#	~	~	~
G.	CUBA	~	18	17	17	21	20[‡]	15	16	17	17
H.	DOMINICAN REP.[3]	#	#	#	#	#	#	#	#	2	2[‡]
J.	EL SALVADOR	1	#	#	#	#	#[†]	#	#	#[‡]	#[‡]
K.	GUATEMALA	~	#	.1[‡]	#	#[‡]	#[‡]	#[‡]	#[‡]	#[‡]	#[‡]
L.	HAITI[3]	#	#	.4[‡]	#	#[‡]	#[‡]	#[‡]	#[‡]	#[‡]	#[‡]
M.	HONDURAS	1	.1	1[‡]	#	#	1[‡]	.8[‡]	#	#[‡]	#[†]
N.	MEXICO[2,3]	31	14	23[‡]	19[‡]	25	24	18	17	18	25
O.	NICARAGUA	~	~	~	#	#	1[‡]	.8[‡]	1	1	1[‡]
P.	PANAMA[4]	1	2	2	2	2	1	1[‡]	1	1	1[‡]
R.	PERU	110	12	12	13	8	7	9	14	13	13[‡]
S.	URUGUAY	~	~	~	#	#	#	#	~	~	~
T.	VENEZUELA[3]	1	4	4	2	2	3[‡]	1	#	#	15[‡]
	UNITED STATES		~	~	#	#	1	1	1	1	1
	WORLD	1,014	~	~	1,221	1,380	1,478	1,310	1,283	1,233	1,370

1. Figures refer to "special trade" except where otherwise indicated. See table 2412, n.1,
   for explanation of "special" imports.
2. Imports through free zones are included.
3. Figures refer to "general trade," i.e., total imports.
4. Data exclude the free zone of Colón and the Canal Zone.

a. For 1934-76, see SALA, 20-2919.

SOURCE: FAO-TY, 1976; 1978; 1980; 1981, table 30; 1982, table 30; 1984, table 30; 1985,
   table 31.

Table 2422

CACAO BEAN EXPORT VOLUME,[1] 9 LC, 1975–85[a]
(T MET)

	Country	1975	1977	1978	1979	1980	1981	1982	1983	1984	1985
C.	BRAZIL	177	108	134	157	124	125	143	153	107	172
F.	COSTA RICA	5	6	6	4	2	2‡	2	1	1	1
H.	DOMINICAN REP.[2]	22	26	28	26	23	27	39	34	32	31
I.	ECUADOR[2]	38	19	16	15	14	24	42	6	47	69
K.	GUATEMALA	1	4	3	2†	1	#	#	1	1‡	1‡
L.	HAITI[2]	1	2	2‡	3	2	3	2	4	2	3‡
N.	MEXICO[2]	4	5	4	2	1	#	3	2	2	2
P.	PANAMA[3]	~	1	1	1	1	#	1	#	#	#
T.	VENEZUELA[2]	16	9	7	7	8	8‡	7	9	6	6
	WORLD	1,169	962	108	1,017	1,090	1,171	1,251	1,206	1,349	1,444

1. Figures refer to "special trade" except where otherwise indicated. See table 2413, n.1, for explanation of "special" imports.
2. Figures refer to "general trade," i.e., total exports including re-exports.
3. Data excluded the free zone of Colón and the Canal Zone.

a. For 1934-74, see SALA, 20-2920.

SOURCE: FAO-TY, 1978; 1980; 1981; table 71; 1982, table 71; 1984, table 71; 1985, table 72.

Table 2423

COCOA EXPORTS, 13 LC, 1980–84

	Country	Value of Exports (T US)					Value as % of World Exports				
		1980	1981	1982	1983	1984	1980	1981	1982	1983	1984
B.	BOLIVIA	1,663†	1,597†	1,335†	~	~	#†	#†	#†	~	~
C.	BRAZIL	696,586	596,757	428,991	556,587	657,994	15.0	15.5	13.4	17.4	16.4
E.	COLOMBIA	4,757	5,697	3,723	5,825	17,921	#	#	#	~	~
F.	COSTA RICA	13,979	8,058	5,616	3,304†	6,673†	#	#	~	~	~
G.	CUBA	2,677	645†	1,839†	9,041†	24,648†	#†	#†	#†	~	~
H.	DOMINICAN REP.	53,790	48,203	57,480	58,223	60,894†	#	#	#	~	~
I.	ECUADOR	210,188	135,093	87,941	64,253†	132,986†	4.5	3.5	2.7	2.0†	3.3†
K.	GUATEMALA	3,394	758	467†	1,836†	~	#	#	#†	~	~
L.	HAITI	6,688†	3,682†	3,558†	7,025†	~	#†	#†	#†	~	~
N.	MEXICO	29,794	8,142	3,971†	~	25,891†	#	#	#†	~	~
P.	PANAMA	2,118	1,192	2,309	2,416	627†	#	#	#	~	~
R.	PERU	16,742	15,936	17,731	12,792†	8,110†	#	#	#	~	~
T.	VENEZUELA	28,626	20,634	16,780†	24,476†	25,509†	#	#	#†	~	~
	LAIA	988,037	788,730	559,911	670,657†	870,348†	21.2	20.4	17.5	20.9†	21.7†
	CACM	18,349	9,620	7,888	6,963†	12,410†	.4	.2	.2	.2†	.3†
	UNITED STATES	6,547	46,068	42,192	43,834	53,420	#	#	#	~	~

SOURCE: UN-YITS, 1982, vol. 2, p. 40; 1983, vol. 2, p. 28; 1984, vol. 2, p. 62.

Table 2424

COFFEE BEAN EXPORT VOLUME,[1] 17 LC, 1975–85

(T MET)

	Country	1975	1978	1979	1980	1981	1982	1983	1984	1985
B.	BOLIVIA	5	6	7.5	5	5	7	7	3	8[‡]
C.	BRAZIL	774	621	562	785	825	888	940	1,032	1,014
E.	COLOMBIA	489	509	657	660	544	525	539	599	585
F.	COSTA RICA	75	87	97	72	106	96	108	113	122
G.	CUBA	8	9[‡]	7	9	6	9[†]	17	10	12
H.	DOMINICAN REP.[2]	32	27	43	26	32	36	30	35	34
I.	ECUADOR[2]	64	103	82	54	56	74	75	72	79
J.	EL SALVADOR	141	121	185	147	212[‡]	141	159	161	148
K.	GUATEMALA	125	132	147	125	132[‡]	141	143	127	159
L.	HAITI	18	15[‡]	14	25	14	15	24	19	24[‡]
M.	HONDURAS	49	58	66	60	70[‡]	58	75	69	72[‡]
N.	MEXICO	142	115	175	130	122	126	185	174	193
O.	NICARAGUA[2]	41	55	55	46	49[‡]	57	56	42	41
P.	PANAMA[4]	2	3	3	3	5	4	6	5	5
Q.	PARAGUAY	6	#	1	.6	#	#	~	~	~
R.	PERU	43	55	70	43	40	40	56	54	61
T.	VENEZUELA[2]	14	14	8	2	2	1	2	5	9
	UNITED STATES[2,3]	55	58	79	79	70	60	43	63	52
	WORLD	3,550	3,391	3,800	3,717	3,763	3,939	4,039	4,210	4,404

1. Figures refer to "special trade" except where otherwise indicated. See table 2413, n.1,
   for explanation of "special" imports.
2. Figures refer to "general trade," i.e., total exports including re-exports.
3. The customs area includes the Commonwealth of Puerto Rico.
4. Data exclude the free zone of Colón and the Canal Zone.

a. For 1934–75, see SALA, 20-2921.

SOURCE: FAO-TY, 1978; 1980; 1981; table 70; 1982, table 70; 1984, table 70; 1985,
   table 70.

Table 2425

COFFEE EXPORTS,[1] 16 LC, 1980–84

	Country	Value of Exports (T US)					Value as % of World Exports				
		1980	1981	1982	1983	1984	1980	1981	1982	1983	1984
B.	BOLIVIA	17,178[†]	14,423[†]	24,529[†]	13,066	11,370[†]	#[†]	#[†]	#[†]	~	~
C.	BRAZIL	2,486,055	1,516,640	1,854,358	2,935,547	2,347,119	20.3	18.3	20.6	28.9	21.2
E.	COLOMBIA	2,360,804	1,423,621	1,561,494	1,506,187	1,764,504	19.2	17.2	17.4	14.8	15.9
F.	COSTA RICA	247,827	240,059	241,545	177,528[†]	205,385[†]	#	#	~	~	~
G.	CUBA	31,388[†]	42,566[†]	19,767[†]	327,924[†]	376,498[†]	#[†]	#[†]	#[†]	~	~
H.	DOMINICAN REP.	77,214	75,510	96,877	76,200	68,115[†]	#	#	#	~	~
I.	ECUADOR	132,181	104,621	156,630	145,009	176,172	#[†]	#[†]	#[†]	~	~
J.	EL SALVADOR	262,039	146,584	112,117	392,579[†]	418,794[†]	2.0	1.6	4.2[†]	~	~
K.	GUATEMALA	469,305	268,431	368,043[†]	342,597[†]	346,024[†]	3.8	3.2	4.1[†]	3.4[†]	3.1[†]
L.	HAITI	98,592	33,131[†]	35,876[†]	28,529[†]	60,848[†]	#[†]	#[†]	#[†]	~	~
M.	HONDURAS	207,458	170,623	153,407	150,377	163,641[†]	#	#	#[†]	~	~
N.	MEXICO	437,109	343,403	371,113	424,273	475,419	3.6	4.2	4.1	4.2	4.3
O.	NICARAGUA	165,670	136,530	124,002	129,821[†]	131,145[†]	#	#	#	~	~
P.	PANAMA	10,441	13,633	12,394	16,019	2,141[†]	#	#	#	~	~
R.	PERU	139,760	99,272	104,246	121,901[†]	107,831[†]	#	#	#	~	~
T.	VENEZUELA	7,931	3,330	10,029[†]	~	~	#	#	#	~	~
	LAIA	5,583,342	3,507,509	4,115,470	5,172,357	4,938,451	45.5	42.4	45.8	50.9	44.5
	CACM	1,352,299	962,228	999,115[†]	1,192,902	1,264,989	11.0	11.6	11.1[†]	11.7[†]	11.4[†]
	UNITED STATES	319,098	249,444	217,710	161,604	214,851	3.0	3.4	2.9	1.9	~

1. Including green, roasted, and substitutes.

SOURCE: UN-YITS, 1982, vol. 2, p. 39; 1983, vol. 2, table 071; 1984, vol. 2, p. 324.

Table 2426

BRAZIL SHARE OF WORLD COFFEE
EXPORTS, 1953–85

(T 60-kg Bags)

Year	Total	Brazil	% Brazil
1953	34,647	15,562	44.9
1954	29,918	10,918	37.8
1955	33,698	13,696	40.7
1956	38,394	16,804	43.8
1957	36,057	14,319	39.7
1958	36,505	12,894	35.3
1959	42,587	17,723	41.6
1960	42,491	16,819	39.6
1961	43,725	16,971	38.8
1962	46,256	16,377	35.4
1963	48,906	19,514	39.9
1964	46,721	14,948	32.0
1965	44,969	13,497	30.0
1966	49,028	17,031	34.7
1967	50,219	17,331	34.5
1968	53,608	19,035	35.5
1969	54,196	19,613	36.2
1970	52,722	17,085	32.4
1971	53,489	18,399	34.4
1972	57,866	19,215	33.2
1973	62,584	19,817	31.7
1974	54,787	13,280	24.2
1975	57,913	14,604	25.3
1976	58,806	15,602	26.5
1977	47,168	10,083	21.4
1978	56,208	12,551	22.3
1979	62,865	12,010	19.1
1980	59,861	15,269	25.5
1981	60,612	15,697	25.9
1982	64,553	17,208	26.7
1983	66,254	17,846	26.9
1984	68,582	19,505	28.6
1985	70,980	19,153	27.0

SOURCE: *Anuário Estatístico*, 1986, p. 69.

Figure 24:2

BRAZIL SHARE OF WORLD COFFEE EXPORTS, 1953–85

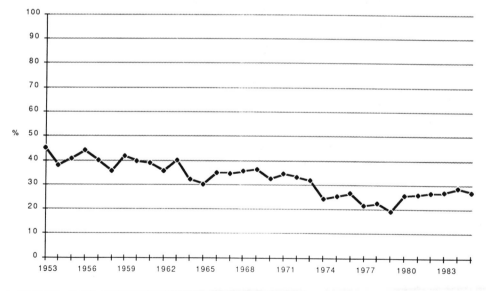

YEAR

SOURCE: Table 2426, above.

Table 2427

BRAZIL COFFEE EXPORTS TO UNITED STATES AND EUROPEAN COUNTRIES, 1979–85[a]

(T 60 kg Bags)

Importer	1979/80	1980/81	1981/82	1982/83	1983/84	1984/85
Total	26,083	26,979	26,585	27,054	25,408	25,388
United States	10,361	10,441	9,721	10,035	9,131	8,975
European Economic Community (ECC)	13,150	13,826	14,169	14,347	13,749	13,904
Belguim and Luxembourg	805	878	839	902	856	814
France	3,479	3,489	3,574	3,524	3,473	3,499
West Germany	5,043	5,349	5,499	5,610	5,344	5,422
Low Countries	1,291[‡]	1,376[‡]	1,350	1,407	1,414	1,443
Spain	989	1,058	1,164	1,122	1,082	1,145
United Kingdom	1,543[‡]	1,676	1,743	1,782	1,580	1,581
Other Importers	2,572	2,712	2,695	2,672	2,528	2,509
Austria	396	429	443	479	495	494
Norway	509	534	548	537	514	520
Sweden	1,198	1,262	1,216	1,180	1,046	1,027
Switzerland	469	487	488	476	473	468

a. October–September.

SOURCE: *Anuário Estatístico*, 1986, p. 39.

Table 2428

COLOMBIAN SHARE OF COFFEE IMPORTS, SELECTED MARKETS

(1986)

Market	Volume of Coffee Imports (T 60 kg Bags)	Colombian Share (%)
West Germany	2,770	36.7
United States	2,629	13.5
Netherlands	720	30.6
Japan	668	16.5
Sweden	574	36.9
France	369	7.9
Finland	337	35.0
United Kingdom	306	19.5
Denmark	206	24.8
Belgium	185	13.6

SOURCE: *Colombia Today*, vol. 22, no. 2, 1987.

Figure 24:3

COLOMBIA MAJOR MARKETS FOR COFFEE
(1986)

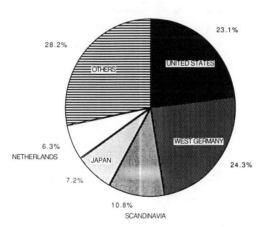

SOURCE: *Colombia Today*, vol. 22, no. 2, 1987.

Table 2429

UNITED STATES LEADING SUPPLIERS OF COFFEE
(1986)

Source		Volume (T 60-kg Bags)	%	Value (M US)
E.	COLOMBIA	2,629	13.5	656.8
C.	BRAZIL	2,200	11.3	501.9
N.	MEXICO	2,125	10.9	500.4
K.	GUATEMALA	1,658	8.5	363.0
I.	ECUADOR	1,371	7.0	257.2
	Indonesia	1,346	6.9	217.0
J.	EL SALVADOR	1,108	5.7	263.0
	Uganda	737	3.8	132.3
	Ivory Coast	694	3.6	125.2
R.	PERU	675	3.4	148.9
	Others	4,940	25.4	1,061.8
	Total	19,483	100.0	4,287.5

SOURCE: *Colombia Today*, vol. 22, no. 2, 1987.

Table 2430

MAIZE IMPORT VOLUME,[1] 17 L, 1975–85[a]
(T MET)

Country		1975	1978	1979	1980	1981	1982	1983	1984	1985
B.	BOLIVIA	~	~	#	#	#	#	1	5	1[‡]
C.	BRAZIL	2	1,262	1,526	1,594	902	#	213	254	262
D.	CHILE	86	253	200	357	309	397	144	36	#
E.	COLOMBIA	18	83[‡]	60	193	80	89	69	10	59[‡]
F.	COSTA RICA	13	6	4	61	25	72	51	33	25[‡]
G.	CUBA	~	481	350	610	580[‡]	367	402	423	386
H.	DOMINICAN REP.[3]	54	87	102	171	162	172	196	174	185[‡]
J.	EL SALVADOR	27	76	12	14	11	27	102	87	55[‡]
K.	GUATEMALA	68	84	55	81	52	6	1	#	2[‡]
L.	HAITI[3]	~	5[‡]	25[‡]	5[‡]	10[‡]	8[‡]	8	8[‡]	30[‡]
M.	HONDURAS	44	40	7	64	23[‡]	6	14	15	~
N.	MEXICO[4,3]	2,636	1,418	744	3,777	3,065	233	4,687	2,498	1,726
O.	NICARAGUA[3]	21	17	2	48	40	25	137	12	34
P.	PANAMA[2]	6	.1	25	39	26	33	30	14	41[‡]
R.	PERU	236	150[‡]	101	261	336	498	362	158	248[‡]
S.	URUGUAY[3]	#	.6	44	10[‡]	14[‡]	6	2	5	8[‡]
T.	VENEZUELA[3]	508	339	448	1,227	1,008	1,033	1,393	1,323	668

1. Figures refer to "special trade" except where otherwise noted. See table 2412, n.1, for explanation of "special" imports.
2. Data exclude the free zone of Colón and the Canal Zone.
3. Figures refer to "generate trade," i.e., total imports.
4. Imports through free zones are included.

a. For 1934–74, see SALA, 20-2924.

SOURCE: FAO-TY, 1978; 1980; 1981, table 47; 1982, table 44; 1984, table 41; 1985, table 42.

Table 2431

MAIZE EXPORT VOLUME,[1] 15 LC, 1975-85[a]
(T MET)

	Country	1975	1978	1979	1980	1981	1982	1983	1984	1985
A.	ARGENTINA	4,001	5,895	5,960	3,481	9,163	5,226	6,525	5,518	7,041
C.	BRAZIL	1,200	14	10	6	7	544	766	178	#
D.	CHILE	~	~	#	#	#	#	~	~	~
E.	COLOMBIA	~	~	#	#	#	#	~	~	~
F.	COSTA RICA	~	~	#	#	#	#	#	#	#
H.	DOMINICAN REP.[2]	~	~	#	#	#	#	#	#	#
I.	ECUADOR[2]	~	~	#	#	1	15	#	#	#
J.	EL SALVADOR	~	~	2	20	10	#	#	#	#
K.	GUATEMALA	~	.1[‡]	#	#	#	#	3	#	#
M.	HONDURAS	~	#	#	#	#	6	3	~	#
N.	MEXICO[2]	4	~	#	1	#	1	21	5	4
O.	NICARAGUA[2]	~	.1	3	#	#	#	#	#	#
Q.	PARAGUAY	6	~	#	25	2	7	~	12	#
R.	PERU	7	4[†]	2	3	2[‡]	1	1	1[‡]	2[‡]
S.	URUGUAY[2]	~	10	4	2	6	#	~	~	6
	WORLD	49,638	68,626	76,087	80,280	78,930	69,984	69,046	68,961	69,593

1. Figures refer to "special trade" except where otherwise indicated. See table 2413, n. 1,
   for explanation of "special" imports.
2. Figures refer to "general trade," i.e., total exports including re-exports.

a. For 1934-74, see SALA, 20-2923.

SOURCE: FAO-TY, 1978; 1980; 1981, table 41; 1982, table 41; 1984, table 41; 1985,
   table 42.

Table 2432

MILK (DRY) IMPORT VOLUME,[1] 19 L, 1975-85[a]
(T MET)

	Country	1975	1977[b]	1978[b]	1979[b]	1980	1981	1982	1983	1984	1985
A.	ARGENTINA	~	9	13	18	18	4	#	~	#[‡]	#[‡]
B.	BOLIVIA	5	2	8[‡]	7	8[‡]	7[‡]	4	1	11	7[‡]
C.	BRAZIL	14	46	12	10	62	8	8	19	30	31[‡]
D.	CHILE	9	14[‡]	14	18	16	14	11	15	17	3
E.	COLOMBIA[6]	4	15	19[‡]	7	19	36	7	6	3	4[‡]
F.	COSTA RICA	3	5	3	2	2	2	2	2	#	~
G.	CUBA	~	38	35[‡]	40	39	43	24	33	35	39
H.	DOMINICAN REP.[2,5]	2	5	6	7	9	7	3	10	13	8[‡]
I.	ECUADOR[5]	3	5	4	7	7	3	4	4	4[‡]	11
J.	EL SALVADOR[2]	8	9	11	11	12	12	8	11	4	5
K.	GUATEMALA	3	5	5[‡]	6	8	7	7	9[‡]	18[‡]	10
L.	HAITI[6,5]	5	1	5[‡]	2[‡]	4[‡]	2[‡]	5	5[‡]	5[‡]	7[‡]
M.	HONDURAS	5	3	4	5	6	6	4	6	8[‡]	7[‡]
N.	MEXICO[3,5]	38	58	60	85	185	91	71	108	111	161
O.	NICARAGUA[5]	1	1	1	4	2	5[‡]	11	8	12	8
P.	PANAMA[4]	3	3	2	2	2	3	3	4	4	4[‡]
Q.	PARAGUAY[6]	#	#	#	#	.6	1	1[‡]	2	2	1
R.	PERU	18	26	18[‡]	16	27	18	27	23	21	21[‡]
T.	VENEZUELA[5]	28	130	103	73	89	103	103	73	106	79[‡]

1. Figures refer to "special trade" except where otherwise indicated. See table 2412, n. 1,
   for explanation of "special" imports.
2. Includes condensed and powdered milk.
3. Imports through free zones included.
4. Data exclude the free zone of Colón and the Canal Zone.
5. Figures refer to "general trade," i.e., total imports.
6. Includes fresh, condensed, and powdered milk.

a. For 1934-74, see SALA, 20-2928.
b. Powdered milk only.

SOURCE: FAO-TY, 1978; 1980; 1982, table 28; 1984, table 28; 1984, table 29.

Table 2433

OAT IMPORT VOLUME,[1] 13 L, 1975–85[a]

(T MET)

	Country	1975	1977	1978	1979	1980	1981	1982	1983	1984	1985
B.	BOLIVIA	~	~	~	~	~	~	.5‡	#‡	66	#‡
C.	BRAZIL	254	23	33	40	24	18	4	18	11	5
E.	COLOMBIA	75	9	9‡	13	10	10	11	6	7	7‡
F.	COSTA RICA	1	#	#	#	#	#	#	.5	.9	~
G.	CUBA	~	22	27	26	13	10	15	13	10	16
H.	DOMINICAN REP.[3]	65	2	1	2	2	2	1	2	2	2†
I.	ECUADOR[3]	191	18	18	22	11	12	25	15	18‡	15
N.	MEXICO[4,3]	1	#	#	#	.7	21	1	1‡	#	1‡
O.	NICARAGUA[3]	22	4	2	3	6	6†	2	2	2	1
P.	PANAMA[2]	4	.6	.9	#	#‡	#‡	#	#	#	#‡
R.	PERU	5	9‡	4‡	4	#	5	8	6	6	7‡
S.	URUGUAY[3]	1	2	1	19	2	3	7	12	12	8‡
T.	VENEZUELA[3]	60	8	6	4	3	7	4	4	4	6

1. Figures refer to "special trade" except where otherwise indicated. See table 2412, n. 1,
   for explanation of "special" imports.
2. Data exclude the free zone of Colón and the Canal Zone.
3. Figures refer to "general trade," i.e., total imports.
4. Imports through free zones included.

a. For 1934–74, see SALA, 20-2930.

SOURCE: FAO-TY, 1978; 1980; 1982, table 43; 1984, table 43; 1985, table 44.

Table 2434

OAT EXPORT VOLUME,[1] 4 L, 1975–85[a]

(T MET)

	Country	1975	1978	1979	1980	1981	1982	1983	1984	1985
A.	ARGENTINA	204	337	83	62	123	54	83	46	104
D.	CHILE	6	1	#	2‡	1‡	1‡	1‡	1‡	2‡
N.	MEXICO[2]	1	~	#	#	#	#	~	~	~
S.	URUGUAY	2	1	#	2	1	2‡	~	~	~

1. Figures refer to "special trade" except where otherwise noted. See table 2413, n. 1,
   for explanation of "special" imports.
2. Figures refer to "general trade," i.e., total exports including re-exports.

a. For 1934–74, see SALA, 20-2929.

SOURCE: FAO-TY, 1978; 1980; 1982, table 43; 1984, table 43; 1985, table 44.

Table 2435

RICE IMPORT VOLUME,[1] 20 L, 1975-85[a]

(T MET)

	Country	1975	1978	1979	1980	1981	1982	1983	1984	1985
A.	ARGENTINA	~	2	10	3	5‡	#	~	#	~
B.	BOLIVIA	2	~	~	~	~	3	35	8	19
C.	BRAZIL	44	30	711	239	143	137	315	#	340
D.	CHILE	21	11	9	48	16	21	31	8	3
E.	COLOMBIA	~	~	14	4	#	#	#	#	~
F.	COSTA RICA	1	#	#	#	#	1	39	#	#†
G.	CUBA	~	171	161	224	200‡	201	207	184	242
H.	DOMINICAN REP.[3]	50	18	#	33	65	#	~	~	49‡
I.	ECUADOR[3]	20	#	25	22	10	9‡	35	4	14
J.	EL SALVADOR	8	1	5	5	5	3‡	7	12	18‡
K.	GUATEMALA	6	12	10	4	4	#	4	2‡	7‡
L.	HAITI[3]	2	15‡	17‡	23‡	24‡	25‡	15‡	5‡	7‡
M.	HONDURAS	11	10	5	4	4	3	2	2‡	2‡
N.	MEXICO[4,3]	~	#	36	93	74	22	#	170	166
O.	NICARAGUA[3]	~	1	10	37	22	#	5	18	33
P.	PANAMA[2]	#	#	#	#	#	#	#	#	~
Q.	PARAGUAY	~	~	#	#	#	#	~	~	~
R.	PERU	78	80	202	211	111	59	103‡	59	5
S.	URUGUAY[3]	~	~	#	#	#	#	#	#	~
T.	VENEZUELA[3]	~	~	1	#	#	1	#	~	~

1. Figures refer to "special trade" except where otherwise noted. See table 2412, n. 1, for explanation of "special" imports.
2. Data exclude the free zone of Colón and the Canal Zone.
3. Figures refer to "general trade," i.e., total imports.
4. Imports through free zones included.

a. For 1934-74, see SALA, 20-2931.

SOURCE: FAO-TY, 1978; 1980; 1982, table 39; 1984, table 39; 1985, table 40.

Table 2436

SOYBEAN EXPORTS, 11 LC, 1979-83

	Country	Value of Exports (T US)					Value as % of World Exports				
		1979	1980	1981	1982	1983	1979	1980	1981	1982	1983
A.	ARGENTINA	702,937	548,418†	331,302†	255,400†	309,324†	10.3	8.6	7.9	6.1	4.5
B.	BOLIVIA	172	~	~	~	~	#	~	~	~	~
C.	BRAZIL	179,506	393,930	403,672	123,457	308,571	2.6	5.6	3.3	1.8	4.5
E.	COLOMBIA	~	98	62†	~	~	~	#	#†	~	~
F.	COSTA RICA	~	32	8†	~	~	~	#	#†	~	~
K.	GUATEMALA	29	#	1	85†	60†	#	#	#	#†	~
M.	HONDURAS	7†	7†	3†	6†	45†	#†	#†	#†	#†	~
N.	MEXICO	#	3†	3†	2†	4†	#	#†	#†	#†	~
O.	NICARAGUA	46†	3	111†	6†	1†	#†	#	#†	#†	~
Q.	PARAGUAY	78,617	42,098	47,533	177,101†	301,773†	1.2	.6	.6	.9†	4.4†
S.	URUGUAY	1,815	1,895	6,066	4,911	2,137	#	#	.1	.1	#†
	LAIA	963,594	986,444†	788,588†	561,579†	922,326†	14.2	14.8	14.1	8.9	13.3
	CACM	76†	42†	120†	91†	119†	#†	#†	#†	#†	#†
	UNITED STATES	5,708,063	5,882,911	6,199,640	6,239,881	5,925,421	84.0	83.4	84.5	89.7	85.7

Source: UN-YITS, 1982, vol. 2, p. 329; 1983, vol. 2, table 2222.

Table 2437

SOYBEAN OIL IMPORT VOLUME,[1] 19 L, 1975-85[a]

(T MET)

	Country	1975	1978	1979	1980	1981	1982	1983	1984	1985
A.	ARGENTINA	~	~	#	#	#	#	~	~	~
B.	BOLIVIA	3	8[‡]	4	13[‡]	15[‡]	7	8	1	5[‡]
C.	BRAZIL	2	~	77	50	#	22	32	123	114
D.	CHILE	74	54	53	59	65	75[‡]	90[‡]	83	59
E.	COLOMBIA	60	48	76	79	109	125	104	109	66[‡]
F.	COSTA RICA	3	1	2	7	4[‡]	2[‡]	#	1	2[‡]
H.	DOMINICAN REP.[3]	170	13	19	22	20	39	36	27	35[‡]
I.	ECUADOR[3]	156	24	20	30	26	36	65	44[‡]	35
J.	EL SALVADOR	1	#	2	.6	3	1	2	1	1
K.	GUATEMALA	#	1[‡]	1	#	#	2	3[‡]	5[‡]	8[‡]
L.	HAITI[3]	53	15[‡]	17	25[‡]	19[‡]	16[‡]	14[‡]	13[‡]	22[‡]
M.	HONDURAS	1	#	1	#	.9[‡]	#	1	1[‡]	1[‡]
N.	MEXICO[4,3]	18	34	#	42	5[‡]	104	#	86	45
O.	NICARAGUA[3]	1	~	1	1	.6[‡]	#	~	3	~
P.	PANAMA[2]	108	14	20	32	18	19	21	18	25[‡]
Q.	PARAGUAY	~	~	#	#	#	#	~	~	~
R.	PERU	548	82	14	35	70	64	75	56	34[‡]
S.	URUGUAY[3]	#	2[‡]	.9	#[‡]	#	2	2	#	2[†]
T.	VENEZUELA[3]	~	15	36	20	56[‡]	45	57	111	79

1. Figures refer to "special trade" except where otherwise indicated. See table 2412, n. 1, for explanation of "special" imports.
2. Data exclude the free zone of Colón and the Canal Zone.
3. Figures refer to "general trade," i.e., total imports.
4. Imports through free zones included.

a. For 1934-74, see SALA, 20-2932.

SOURCE: FAO-TY, 1978; 1980; 1982, table 116; 1984, table 116; 1985, table 116.

Table 2438

SOYBEAN OILCAKE EXPORTS, 8 LC, 1980-84

	Country	Value of Exports (T US)					Value as % of World Exports				
		1980	1981	1982	1983	1984	1980	1981	1982	1983	1984
A.	ARGENTINA	60,463[†]	111,848[†]	163,125[†]	243,578[†]	511,988[†]	~	2.3	3.8	4.2	12.7
B.	BOLIVIA	6,888[†]	2,532[†]	2,561[†]	1,979[†]	1,980[†]	#	#	#	~	~
C.	BRAZIL	1,361,920[†]	2,096,246[†]	1,595,366[†]	2,661,069[†]	1,394,397[†]	33.3	42.2	36.9	46.2	34.6
I.	ECUADOR	467[†]	478[†]	430[†]	~	~	#	#	#	~	~
P.	PANAMA	118[†]	30[†]	9[†]	~	~	#	#	#	~	~
Q.	PARAGUAY	7,062[†]	129[†]	1,832[†]	3,506		#	#	#	~	~
R.	PERU	~	11[†]	11[†]	~	~	~	#	#	~	~
S.	URUGUAY	3,538[†]	539[†]	324[†]	651[†]	~	#	#	~	~	~
	LAIA	1,439,872	2,211,294	1,763,207	2,918,694	1,909,382	35.2	44.6	40.8	50.6	47.4
	UNITED STATES	1,654,233	1,588,551	1,411,441	1,527,074	1,019,337	40.9	32.0	32.7	26.5	25.3

SOURCE: UN-YITS, 1982, vol. 2, p. 311; 1984, vol. 2, table 08131.

Table 2439

SUGAR EXPORT VOLUME,[1] 19 L, 1975-85[a]

(T MET)

	Country	1975	1978	1979	1980	1981	1982	1983	1984	1985
A.	ARGENTINA	197	362	361	487	726	255	892	416	157[‡]
B.	BOLIVIA	62	78	125	107	20	44	53	17	17
C.	BRAZIL	1,750	2,015	1,867	2,626	2,781	2,805	2,572	3,165	2,611
D.	CHILE	56	17	18	39	13	#	2	#	~
E.	COLOMBIA	198	132	241	278	177	314	301	183	295
F.	COSTA RICA	102	70	69	72	83	55	54	103	56[†]
G.	CUBA	~	7,231[‡]	7,199[‡]	6,170[‡]	7,071[‡]	7,436	6,747	6,746	6,940
H.	DOMINICAN REP.[2]	950	901	986	794	855	827	918	861	722
I.	ECUADOR[2]	21	39	69	67	47	#	~	35	19
J.	EL SALVADOR	128	133	138	37	34	54	92	75	116
K.	GUATEMALA	204	153	157	199	228	127	267	204	180
L.	HAITI[2]	25	5[‡]	#	19	#	6	13	5	5[‡]
M.	HONDURAS	10	23	55	78	95	96	106	102	102
N.	MEXICO[2]	178	71	101	#	#	#	15	#	93
O.	NICARAGUA[2]	89	98	91	62	89	79	112	91	58
P.	PANAMA[3]	82	119	135	130	94	107	120	82	84
Q.	PARAGUAY	14	~	#	6	#	15	15	11	10
R.	PERU	422	266	181	54	#	140	10	40	60
T.	VENEZUELA[2]	~	#	#	#	#	#	#	~	~

1. Figures refer to "special trade" except where otherwise indicated. See table 2413, n. 1, for explanation of "special" imports.
2. Figures refer to "general" trade.
3. Data exclude the free zone of Colón and the Canal Zone.

a. For 1934-74, see SALA, 20-2933.

SOURCE: FAO-TY, 1978; 1980; 1982, table 66; 1984, table 66; 1985.

Table 2440

U.S. SUGAR IMPORT QUOTAS, 16 L

(1986-87)

	Country	Annual Quota %	Short Tons Raw Value[1]	Imported as of June 13	% of Quota
A.	ARGENTINA	4.3	39,130	10,348	41.8
B.	BOLIVIA	.8	7,500	7,462	99.5
C.	BRAZIL	14.5	131,950	62,535	47.4
E.	COLOMBIA	2.4	21,840	11,464	52.5
F.	COSTA RICA[2]	1.5	17,583	Quota Filled	100
H.	DOMINICAN REP.	17.6	160,160	68,081	42.5
I.	ECUADOR	1.1	10,010	Quota Filled	100
J.	EL SALVADOR[2]	2.6	26,020	~	~
K.	GUATEMALA	4.8	43,680	20,429	46.8
L.	HAITI	mQ[3]	7,500	Quota Filled	100
M.	HONDURAS[2]	1.0	15,917	12,752	80.1
N.	MEXICO	mQ	7,500	Quota Filled	100
P.	PANAMA	2.9	26,390	9,907	37.5
Q.	PARAGUAY	mQ	7,500	~	~
R.	PERU	4.1	37,310	9,318	25.0
S.	URUGUAY	mQ	7,500	7,376	98.3

1. Value of sugar ranging from 94°-98° polarization.
2. Costa Rica, El Salvador, and Honduras each received a portion of Nicaragua's quota.
3. Minimum quota.

SOURCE: Amerop Sugar Corporation/Westway Trading Company (New Jersey), Newsletter, July, 1987.

Table 2441

SUGAR EXPORTS,[1] 16 LC, 1978–84

	Country	Value of Exports (T US)						Value of % of World Exports						
		1978	1980	1981	1982	1983	1984	1978	1979	1980	1981	1982	1983	1984
A.	ARGENTINA	30,639	260,053	260,478[†]	41,506	129,708	7,266[†]	.5	.5	2.6	2.8	.5	1.7	.1[†]
B.	BOLIVIA	~	674[†]	11,666[†]	11,666[†]	11,666[†]	~	~	#[†]	#[†]	#[†]	#[†]	~	~
C.	BRAZIL	228,693	941,936	665,806	327,075	358,960	361,652	3.6	3.9	9.3	7.1	4.2	4.6	6.6
E.	COLOMBIA	19,536	164,685	76,881	54,720	68,922	37,071	.8	.6	1.7	.8	.7	.9	~
F.	COSTA RICA	15,909	40,746	42,007	13,230	~	9[†]	#	#	#	#	~	~	~
G.	CUBA	3,854,825	4,581,429	4,159,026	4,506,954	4,859,667	3,292,432	60.0	59.3	45.2	44.5	57.2	62.6	60.5[†]
H.	DOMINICAN REP.	171,540	286,904	516,650	261,487	262,129	10,419[†]	2.7	2.8	2.8	5.5	3.3	3.4	.2[†]
I.	ECUADOR	5,453	36,678	20,199	~	~	~	#	#	#[†]	#[†]	#[†]	~	~
J.	EL SALVADOR	18,915	13,367	14,832	15,081	~	~	#	#	#	#	~	~	~
K.	GUATEMALA	45,753	80,379	84,094	1,012[†]	3,630[†]	1,901[†]	#	#	#	#	~	~	~
M.	HONDURAS	5,501	27,975	37,890	24,506	27,840	~	#	#	#	#	~	~	~
N.	MEXICO	~	~	~	~	~	~	~	#	~	~	~	~	~
O.	NICARAGUA	25,549	20,458	39,708	22,346	2,848[†]	2,602[†]	#	#	#	#	#	~	~
P.	PANAMA	19,957	65,809	52,608	23,676	41,308	~	#	#	#	#	#	~	~
Q.	PARAGUAY	~	97[†]	3[†]	2,169[†]	2,486[†]	~	~	~	~	~	~	~	~
R.	PERU	43,641	13,440	144[†]	16,870	21[†]	~	#	#	#	#[†]	#	~	~
	LAIA	327,973	1,416,900	1,035,034	451,837	557,771	406,185	5.1	6.4	14.0	11.1	5.7	7.2	7.5
	CACM	111,627	182,925	218,531	76,175	34,319	4,513	1.7	1.9	1.8	2.3	1.0	.4[†]	.1[†]

1. Raw beet and cane sugar.

SOURCE: UN-YITS, 1982, vol. 2, p. 300; 1983, 1984, vol. 2, table 0611.

Table 2442

CUBA SUGAR EXPORTS AS SHARE OF CUBA'S TOTAL EXPORT VALUE,[1] 1900–84

Year	%	Year	%	Year	%
1900	37	1928	81	1956	79
1901	51	1929	80	1957	81
1902	48	1930	71	1958	81
1903	54	1931	70	1959	77
1904	62	1932	77	1960	79
1905	66	1933	73	1961	85
1906	57	1934	74	1962	83
1907	63	1935	80	1963	87
1908	56	1936	82	1964	88
1909	65	1937	80	1965	86
1910	73	1938	79	1966	85
1911	65	1939	79	1967	82
1912	72	1940	75	1968	77
1913	72	1941	79	1969	77
1914	77	1942	79	1970	77
1915	84	1943	80	1971	77
1916	85	1944	75	1972	75
1917	86	1945	72	1973	79
1918	85	1946	74	1974	89
1919	89	1947	89	1975	89
1920	92	1948	90	1976	86
1921	85	1949	88	1977	83
1922	86	1950	89	1978	86
1923	89	1951	88	1979	86
1924	88	1952	86	1980	84
1925	84	1953	83	1981	79
1926	83	1954	80	1982	77
1927	85	1955	80	1983	74
				1984	77

1. Raw Sugar, 96° base.

SOURCE: For most years data are from Cuban Economic Research Project, *A Study on Cuba: The Colonial and Republic Periods; the Socialist Experiment* (Coral Gables: University of Miami Press, 1965), pp. 280, 403, 616; and Cuba, JUCEPLAN, AE, 1973, pp. 193-194. Data for scattered years are from SALA-Cuba, pp. 169 and 174; IBRD (WB), *Report on Cuba* (Baltimore: Johns Hopkins, 1951), p. 801; FAO-TY, 1971, p. 225; K. S. Karol, *Guerrillas in Power: The Course of the Cuban Revolution* (New York: Hill and Wang, 1970), p. 587. Data for 1973-74 are from U.S. Central Intelligence Agency, *Cuba: Foreign Trade*, Intelligence Handbook A(ER) 75-69 (July 1975), tables 1, 4, and 9; and CIA, *Cuban Economy . . . 1968-76*, p. 9. Data for 1975-80 are from Cuba–CEE, AE, 1981, pp. 189, 195; since 1981, FAO-TY, 1985.

Table 2443

WHEAT IMPORT VOLUME,[1] 20 L, 1975–85[a]

(T MET)

	Country	1975	1977	1978	1979	1980	1981	1982	1983	1984	1985
A.	ARGENTINA	~	#	#	#	#	#	#	~	~	~
B.	BOLIVIA	194	238	281	371	282	252	300	336	230	436
C.	BRAZIL	2,106	2,626	4,335	3,658	4,759	4,363	4,225	4,182	4,869	4,048
D.	CHILE	6,844	474	926	739	1,069	1,054	1,006	1,177	964	476
E.	COLOMBIA	302	216	295	338	641	507[‡]	535	697	661	688[‡]
F.	COSTA RICA	83	76	85	88	104	96	101	104	124	120
G.	CUBA	~	1,208	1,124	1,294	1,228	1,244[‡]	1,268	1,442	1,482	1,387
H.	DOMINICAN REP.	125	111	159	144	158	198	128	188	126	256[‡]
I.	ECUADOR	210	241	222	168	200	249	326	281	245	225[‡]
J.	EL SALVADOR	34	105	68	105	116	106	135	123	148	151
K.	GUATEMALA	72	111	65	96	108	108[‡]	93[†]	114	129	160[‡]
L.	HAITI	82	122	126[‡]	149[‡]	149[‡]	199[‡]	167[‡]	185[‡]	177[‡]	190[‡]
M.	HONDURAS	52	60	63	69	71	78	80	68	90	97
N.	MEXICO[2]	864	477	506	1,148	823	1,028	398	423	344	320
O.	NICARAGUA	50	51	56	27	52	37[‡]	40	69	136	45
P.	PANAMA[3]	55	68	57	47	47	62	57	55	63	73
Q.	PARAGUAY	27	44	49	65	75	68	38	93	72	83
R.	PERU	833	833	732[‡]	781	800	756	861	805	763	837[‡]
S.	URUGUAY[4]	~	#	112[‡]	92	55	4	#	65	48	~
T.	VENEZUELA	620	705	506	719	785	890	773	875	968	1,105

1. Wheat and wheat flour in wheat equivalent. Figures refer to "special trade" unless otherwise indicated. See table 2412, n. 1, for explanation of "special" imports.
2. Imports through free zones included.
3. Data exclude the free zone of Colón and the Canal Zone.
4. Figures refer to "general trade," i.e., total exports.

a. For 1934–74, see SALA, 20-2936.

SOURCE: FAO-TY, 1978; 1980; 1982, table 37; 1984, table 37; 1985, table 38.

Table 2444

WHEAT EXPORT VOLUME,[1] 5 L, 1975–85[a]

(T MET)

	Country	1975	1978	1979	1980	1981	1982	1983	1984	1985
A.	ARGENTINA	1,920	1,776	4,364	4,538	3,788	3,837	1,023	7,370	9,716
D.	CHILE	~	- -	#	#	#	#	~	~	~
M.	HONDURAS	~	#	2	1	1	1	~	~	~
N.	MEXICO[2]	31	17	14	23	23	#	#	#	~
S.	URUGUAY[2]	68	~	#	#	112	147	128	74	~

1. Includes wheat and wheat flour in wheat equivalent. Figures refer to "special trade" except where otherwise indicated. See table 2413, n. 1, for explanation of "special" exports.
2. Figures refer to "general trade," i.e., total exports including re-exports.

a. For 1934–74, see SALA, 20-2934.

SOURCE: FAO-TY, 1978; 1980, table 347; 1984, table 37; 1985, table 38.

Table 2445

WHEAT EXPORTS,[1] 9 LC, 1980–84

	Country	Value of Exports (T US)					Value as % of World Exports				
		1980	1981	1982	1983	1984	1980	1981	1982	1983	1984
A.	ARGENTINA	816,137	763,639	676,552	1,474,040	93,265[†]	5.2	4.5	4.3	9.3	.6[†]
C.	BRAZIL	39	36	247	602	~	#	#	#	~	~
D.	CHILE	#	3,466[†]	~	~	~	#	#[†]	#[†]	~	~
G.	CUBA	~	~	7,296[†]	54,040[†]	72,139	~	~	~	~	~
K.	GUATEMALA	~	240[†]	240[†]	233[†]	~	~	#	#	#	~
N.	MEXICO	1,042[†]	717[†]	3,695[†]	210[†]	~	#[†]	#[†]	#[†]	~	~
O.	NICARAGUA	#	1,065	1,192	12	11[†]	#	#	#	~	~
P.	PANAMA	827[†]	60[†]	~	4,443[†]	~	~	~	~	~	~
S.	URUGUAY	~	16,094	21,887	19,058	~	~	#	#	~	~
	LAIA	817,289	783,235	698,685	1,493,879	93,266[†]	5.2	4.7	4.4	9.4	.6[†]
	CACM	#	1,407[†]	1,432[†]	245	11[†]	~	#	#	#	#[†]
	UNITED STATES	6,374,561	7,843,960	6,675,575	6,239,284	6,476,910	40.3	46.6	42.3	39.4	40.4

1. Unmilled.

SOURCE: UN-YITS, 1982, vol. 2, p. 25; 1983, vol. 2, table 041; 1984, table 041.

Table 2446

WOOL (CLEAN) EXPORT VOLUME,[1] 5 LC, 1975–85[a]
(T MET)

	Country	1975	1978	1979	1980	1981	1982	1983	1984	1985
A.	ARGENTINA	27	29	22	27	34[‡]	24	28	27	26[‡]
C.	BRAZIL	1	#	#	.4	.6	.4	.7	.4[‡]	.4[‡]
D.	CHILE	1	1	#	.2	.06	.7	#	#	#
R.	PERU	1	2[b]	#	.2[‡]	.5[‡]	#	.6	.9[‡]	~
S.	URUGUAY[2]	6	6	5	6	7	5	9	6	6[‡]
	UNITED STATES	~	.4	.4	.4	.3	.9	.4	.5	.9
	WORLD	~	278	299	323	346	323	344	360	395

1. Figures refer to "special trade" unless othewise indicated. See table 2413, n. 1, for explanation of "special" exports.
2. Figures refer to "general trade," i.e., total exports including re-exports.

a. For 1934–74, see SALA, 20-2937.
b. Greasy wool.

SOURCE: FAO-TY, 1978; 1980; 1982, table 114; 1984, table 114; 1985, table 114.

Table 2447

WOOL EXPORTS, 7 LC, 1980–84

	Country	Value of Exports (T US)					Value as % of World Exports				
		1980	1981	1982	1983	1984	1980	1981	1982	1983	1984
A.	ARGENTINA	247,618	297,721	191,546	185,572	199,441[†]	5.6	6.5	4.9	4.5	4.6[†]
B.	BOLIVIA	609[†]	643[†]	537[†]	~	~	#[†]	#[†]	#[†]	~	~
C.	BRAZIL	69,714	82,502	52,864	65,060	12,698[†]	1.6	1.8	1.4	1.6	.3
D.	CHILE	22,811	19,879	29,473[†]	20,778[†]	24,321[†]	#	#[†]	#[†]	~	~
Q.	PARAGUAY	23,158[†]	16,185[†]	548[†]	~	382[†]	#[†]	#[†]	#[†]	~	~
R.	PERU	30,169	9,465	7,086	47,040[†]	41,911[†]	#	#	#	~	~
S.	URUGUAY	134,031	144,216	132,398	105,977	55,112[†]	3.1	3.2	3.4	2.6	1.3[†]
	LAIA	528,187	570,285	414,082	425,134[†]	330,243[†]	12.0	12.5	10.6	10.2[†]	7.8[†]
	CACM	90	100[†]	156[†]	110[†]	68[†]	#	#[†]	#[†]	#[†]	#[†]
	UNITED STATES	36,976	48,155	43,900	64,092	55,400	.8	1.1	1.1	1.5	1.3

SOURCE: UN-YITS, 1982, vol. 2, p. 69; 1983, 1984, vol. 2, table 268.

Table 2448

FOREST PRODUCT EXPORTS, 10 OASL, 1970–80

(% and M US)

Category	1970		%[a]	1975		%[a]	1980		%[a]
All Forest Products	C.	BRAZIL	51	C.	BRAZIL	39	C.	BRAZIL	53
	D.	CHILE	18	D.	CHILE	26	D.	CHILE	30
	M.	HONDURAS	6	M.	HONDURAS	10			
	Q.	PARAGUAY	6	Q.	PARAGUAY	5			
				B.	BOLIVIA	5			

Continued in SALA, 24-2440.

Table 2449

ROUNDWOOD[1] TRADE, 17 LC, 1977–85

(T US)

PART I. VALUE OF IMPORTS

	Country	1977	1979	1980	1981	1982	1983	1984	1985
A.	ARGENTINA	495	2,457	4,613	2,659	2,216	2,718	2,281	2,281[†]
C.	BRAZIL	3,911	6,239	6,912	6,485	6,616	6,556	8,125	8,001
D.	CHILE	#	#	#	#	#	~	~	~
E.	COLOMBIA	#	#	#	#	#	~	~	~
F.	COSTA RICA	726	602	891	577	374	261	261	261
G.	CUBA	200[†]	#	#	#	#	~	3,364	3,228
H.	DOMINICAN REP.	#	#	9,659	8,478	5,046	6,517	4,630	3,661
J.	EL SALVADOR	49	60	102	102	102	~	~	~
K.	GUATEMALA	#	149	149	143	320	320	14	22
L.	HAITI	234	234[†]	#	#	#	~	~	~
M.	HONDURAS	#	#	#	#	#	~	~	~
N.	MEXICO	1,021	8,895	16,310	9,201	4,075	4,075	2,473	2,919
O.	NICARAGUA	720[†]	1,171	1,171[†]	1,171[†]	65	65[†]	65[†]	65[†]
P.	PANAMA	581	1,055	900	2,269	1,495	359	445	445
R.	PERU	288	24	411	54	252	252	180	32
S.	URUGUAY	790	1,034	1,070	372	133	62	62	62
T.	VENEZUELA	2,489	2,421	2,329	11,500	15,530	15,507	15,507	15,507
	UNITED STATES	74,805	83,562	93,867	96,907	90,685	113,959	95,711	79,702

PART II. VALUE OF EXPORTS

	Country	1977	1979	1980	1981	1982	1983	1984	1985
A.	ARGENTINA	43	346	410	302	234	440	625	625[†]
B.	BOLIVIA	925	~	~	~	~	~	~	~
C.	BRAZIL	1,465	3,951	3,072	2,370	1,652	1,892	2,039	2,231
D.	CHILE	4,302	31,235	56,835	17,672	36,891	34,587	29,880	40,371
E.	COLOMBIA	234[†]	~	~	~	~	~	~	~
F.	COSTA RICA	900	942	17	17	46	46	146	146
H.	DOMINICAN REP.	~	~	~	17	17[†]	~	~	~
K.	GUATEMALA	~	11	11	78	16	32	53	105
L.	HAITI	~	~	~	~	~	~	~	~
M.	HONDURAS	2,678	2,353	4,414	2,774	2,454	632	710	710
N.	MEXICO	145	769	613	746	293	485	196	180
O.	NICARAGUA	322[†]	1,008	1,511	1,511[†]	~	~	~	~
P.	PANAMA	3	~	~	~	~	250	222	222[†]
Q.	PARAGUAY	148	15	23	23	~	~	~	~
R.	PERU	23	~	~	~	~	~	~	~
T.	VENEZUELA	~	~	~	~	~	~	~	~
	UNITED STATES	1,167,383	1,998,552	2,006,672	1,584,554	1,528,020	1,371,513	1,374,395	1,451,220

1. For definitions of roundwood, fuelwood, etc., see SALA, 25-2301.

SOURCE: FAO-YFP, 1982, pp. 68, 72; 1984, pp. 68, 72; 1985, pp. 5, 8.

Table 2450

SAWNWOOD AND SLEEPERS TRADE,[1] 18 LC, 1976-85

(T US)

PART I. VALUE OF IMPORTS

	Country	1976	1978	1979	1980	1981	1982	1983	1984	1985
A.	ARGENTINA	24,836	44,829	103,028	139,409	90,217	51,714	48,850	51,475	42,899
C.	BRAZIL	8,782	19,646	16,084	24,297	17,663	12,871	8,582	10,299	12,840
D.	CHILE	#	#	#	#	#	#	~	~	~
E.	COLOMBIA	31[†]	31[†]	31[†]	1,365	1,008	390	277	277[†]	277[†]
F.	COSTA RICA	254	425	220	142	227	226	~	~	~
G.	CUBA	36,100	66,758	39,390	88,470	84,475[†]	84,949	70,630	101,759	118,748
H.	DOMINICAN REP.	21,500[‡]	49,600[‡]	9,961	21,361	16,388	13,289	10,092	8,932	5,831
J.	EL SALVADOR	2,780	5,058	2,783	680	3,600	800	1,055	1,163	2,538
K.	GUATEMALA	487	421	240	74	166	25	4	~	~
L.	HAITI	1,700	1,906	1,906	1,906	1,906	1,906	1,906	1,906	1,906
M.	HONDURAS	#	521	#	#	#	#	~	~	~
N.	MEXICO	20,353	4,872[†]	24,000	66,547	74,335	38,052	49,936	36,900	39,632
O.	NICARAGUA	#	#	#	#	#	#	~	~	~
P.	PANAMA	1,091[†]	1,163	1,414	1,707	1,204	536	1,079	193	193
Q.	PARAGUAY	#	#	#	#	#	#	~	~	~
R.	PERU	1,838	906	1,567	2,827	3,182	2,940	2,940[†]	3,251	2,179
S.	URUGUAY	3,358	5,110	10,682	11,070	9,806	6,212	3,083	3,083	3,083
T.	VENEZUELA	32,491	25,775	35,623	30,656	23,729	24,343	28,480[†]	28,480[†]	28,480[†]
	UNITED STATES	1,299,567	2,857,217	2,644,010	1,915,294	1,850,925	1,670,556	2,799,948	2,722,957	2,941,629

PART II. VALUE OF EXPORTS

	Country	1976	1978	1979	1980	1981	1982	1983	1984	1985
A.	ARGENTINA	16	185	112	198	471	383	383[†]	429	429
B.	BOLIVIA	22,000[†]	9,667	18,000[†]	19,000[†]	9,800[†]	12,150[†]	5,500[†]	5,500[†]	5.500[†]
C.	BRAZIL	70,546	104,440	207,987	211,471	210,404	139,855	178,815	142,981	121,773
D.	CHILE	22,580	51,223	92,683	149,027	95,879	63,524	65,764	74,142	57,508
E.	COLOMBIA	3,002	3,002	4,273	2,597	4,807	536	297	297[†]	297[†]
F.	COSTA RICA	425	76	17	20	505	805	1,113	1,462	1,457
I.	ECUADOR	8,997	2,000	2,000	4,078	6,300[†]	5,444	12,044[†]	15,900	16,588
J.	EL SALVADOR	#	#	#	#	#	#	~	~	~
K.	GUATEMALA	3,112	3,718	3,854	3,971	4,448	2,950	1,082	1,374	2,908
L.	HAITI	#	#	#	#	#	#	~	~	~
M.	HONDURAS	40,005	39,314	39,522	20,208[†]	25,106	43,162	34,748	30,370	30,370
N.	MEXICO	71	30	563	246	359	225	3,725	3,725	982
O.	NICARAGUA	5,866[†]	7,129	3,257	539	777	590	1,165	1,165	1,165
P.	PANAMA	29[†]	#	#	#	#	#	~	~	~
Q.	PARAGUAY	9,989	16,719	32,152	52,195	48,836[†]	62,636[†]	49,936[†]	62,400	65,100
R.	PERU	1,107	2,606	3,293	3,032	2,741	2,741	2,741	936	745
S.	URUGUAY	33	44[†]	#	#	#	#	~	~	~
	UNITED STATES	566,114	568,430	1,009,775	1,053,683	925,864	805,025	897,979	834,899	753,780

1. Cf. SALA, 23-2904 and 2905 for coniferous and nonconiferous sawnwood trade.

SOURCE: FAO-YFP, 1982, pp. 176, 180; 1984, pp. 172, 176; 1985, pp. 114, 118.

Table 2451

WOOD PULP TRADE, 15 LC, 1975–85
(T US)

PART I. VALUE OF IMPORTS

	Country	1975	1979	1980	1981	1982	1983	1984	1985
A.	ARGENTINA	57,713	65,291	68,391	73,314	73,350	30,886	25,640	17,392
C.	BRAZIL	44,397	35,300	37,755	21,483	9,349	5,840	11,236	12,180
D.	CHILE	1,050	#	#	#	#	~	~	~
E.	COLOMBIA	9,921	22,548	29,661	38,547	26,240	25,410	25,410[†]	30,953[†]
F.	COSTA RICA	1,401	1,772	4,542	2,995	2,778	1,203[†]	2,567	1,056[†]
G.	CUBA	6,800	15,456	22,687	14,761	15,037	18,190	16,352	17,627
H.	DOMINICAN REP.	1,000[†]	1,362	969[†]	969[†]	969[†]	969[†]	37	53
I.	ECUADOR	886	3,426	5,248	32,857	30,745	29,984	10,500	3,563
J.	EL SALVADOR	375	463	284	284[†]	284[†]	3,653	3,653[†]	3,653[†]
K.	GUATEMALA	2,112	6,038	17,038	7,112	868	5,640	4,430	4,286
N.	MEXICO	56,638	62,815	107,000	136,000	121,196	80,600	98,100	116,000
P.	PANAMA	24	828	642	683	344	805	636	636[†]
R.	PERU	14,524	16,451	14,469	13,770	20,253	13,553	17,312	6,315
S.	URUGUAY	3,947	5,260	5,174	3,396	2,787	4,175	4,175	4,175
T.	VENEZUELA	27,507[†]	42,700[†]	54,870[†]	63,135[†]	74,698[†]	49,278[†]	75,872[†]	81,822[†]
	UNITED STATES	1,037,051	1,452,468	1,673,405	1,753,467	1,484,974	1,485,257	1,844,779	1,517,089

PART II. VALUE OF EXPORTS

	Country	1975	1979	1980	1981	1982	1983	1984	1985
C.	BRAZIL	30,503	181,266	364,211	365,531	278,504	310,744	396,412	278,043
D.	CHILE	59,593	166,615	197,276	203,856	171,800	156,400	200,042	180,811
R.	PERU	#	#	#	#	#	~	~	~
	LATIN AMERICA	90,096	347,881	561,487	569,387	450,304	467,144	596,454	458,854
	UNITED STATES	896,516	1,092,702	1,628,666	1,655,709	1,407,655	1,350,732	1,483,491	1,343,466

SOURCE: FAO-YFP, 1982, pp. 264, 267; 1984, pp. 256, 258; 1985.

Table 2452

PAPER AND PAPERBOARD TRADE, 20 LC, 1975–85[a]

(T US)

PART I. VALUE OF IMPORTS

	Country	1975	1977	1978	1979	1980	1981	1982	1983	1984	1985
A.	ARGENTINA	104,627	100,544	110,585	111,167	183,304	162,262	83,392	87,563	50,129	29,100[†]
B.	BOLIVIA	3,460[†]	8,731	8,937	10,200[†]	11,700	12,500[†]	12,400[†]	12,400[†]	11,400[†]	10,900[†]
C.	BRAZIL	109,352	137,450	131,747	157,285	191,085	223,890	259,216	133,181	138,499	109,251
D.	CHILE	3,920	23,800	24,350	43,300	45,100	43,300	24,900	49,300	47,413	41,600
E.	COLOMBIA	41,458	35,900[‡]	40,950[‡]	66,977	82,441	118,273	123,952	82,359	81,154[†]	78,756[†]
F.	COSTA RICA	32,063	35,298	22,321	52,164	52,810	75,171	67,763	63,145	65,908	65,402[†]
G.	CUBA	18,900[†]	22,200[†]	30,790	38,608	75,654	64,322[†]	71,013	77,132	97,957	86,103
H.	DOMINICAN REP.	7,873	20,551[‡]	21,634	25,366	38,484	46,489	42,101	40,371	44,312	35,993
I.	ECUADOR	40,062	55,792	48,330	53,554	88,708	89,685	106,934	93,113	109,262	117,884[†]
J.	EL SALVADOR	21,768	25,288	25,655[†]	25,241[†]	26,287	27,450	32,000	27,460	27,460[†]	27,460[†]
K.	GUATEMALA	10,411	15,262	30,740	30,065	74,055	55,309	54,599	54,543	55,302	39,586
L.	HAITI	945[†]	3,076	3,077	3,033	2,906	3,141	3,054[†]	3,049[†]	3,049[†]	3,049[†]
M.	HONDURAS	13,787	33,116	37,567	26,749	27,470	31,375	28,412	20,719	20,843[†]	20,843[†]
N.	MEXICO	90,673	297,909[†]	113,200[†]	138,350[†]	398,700	394,000	473,598	227,841	73,100[†]	139,400[†]
O.	NICARAGUA	10,008	12,927[†]	10,800	8,428	12,014	13,014	12,268	12,268	12,268[†]	12,268[†]
P.	PANAMA	15,018	19,303	26,740	24,772	29,911	30,522	29,559	24,090	34,645	34,645[†]
Q.	PARAGUAY	4,747[†]	5,692	6,534	8,611	11,524	8,902	11,971	6,077	7,450	8,566
R.	PERU	34,249	28,513	15,064	8,572	20,120	40,026	50,800[†]	31,400[†]	29,152[†]	28,923[†]
S.	URUGUAY	6,527	7,044	7,193	8,814	14,489	18,753	11,301	6,130	6,130[†]	6,130[†]
T.	VENEZUELA	48,322[†]	65,393[†]	113,451	118,094[†]	116,740[†]	126,416[†]	167,214	148,821	132,800[†]	129,375[†]
	UNITED STATES	1,613,910	2,279,547	2,773,293	3,153,597	3,313,973	3,346,918	4,338,482	3,734,478	5,066,782	5,221,707

PART II. VALUE OF EXPORTS

	Country	1975	1977	1978	1979	1980	1981	1982	1983	1984	1985
A.	ARGENTINA	4,284	11,399	11,343	17,636	11,649	7,690	5,577	4,643	7,498	5,242
C.	BRAZIL	4,540	20,571	54,044	94,048	160,862	224,833	170,431	208,434	345,560	262,587
D.	CHILE	44,124	38,900	38,106	46,028	48,704	45,295	39,323	47,616	58,313	62,298[†]
E.	COLOMBIA	541	541[†]	541[†]	9,201	10,786	9,904	5,039	8,304	14,300[†]	12,500[†]
F.	COSTA RICA	594	552	239	3,412	13,217	11,625	12,275	15,145	9,559	9,559
J.	EL SALVADOR	1,171	771	807	871	921	957	971	6,587	6,587	6,587
K.	GUATEMALA	6,163	8,839	5,823	12,695	17,992	18,840	11,991	12,717	8,781	8,199
M.	HONDURAS	754[†]	599	2,494	2,375	4,999	4,999	~	~	~	~
N.	MEXICO	919[†]	1,033	1,033[†]	1,100[†]	2,700[†]	4,000[†]	5,000	5,000[†]	5,000[†]	5,000[†]
P.	PANAMA	122	270	124	191	635	670	947	538	223	223[†]
R.	PERU	1,285	3,489	3,489	3,489	1,427	1,165	509	1,970	1,970	1,970
S.	URUGUAY	793	2,711	4,165	6,535	10,381	7,663	4,579	6,646	6,646[†]	6,646[†]
T.	VENEZUELA	2,545	~	~	~	~	~	~	~	~	~
	UNITED STATES	1,100,742	1,121,609	1,104,708	1,340,141	2,016,959	2,013,112	1,714,085	1,719,220	1,813,021	1,559,267

a. For 1962-74 data see SALA, 21-2805.

SOURCE: FAO-YFP, 1982, pp. 314 and 310; 1984, pp. 302, 306; 1985, pp. 249, 253.

Table 2453

WOOD-BASED PANEL TRADE,[1] 18 LC, 1975-85[a]

(T US)

PART I. VALUE OF IMPORTS

	Country	1975	1979	1980	1981	1982	1983	1984	1985
A.	ARGENTINA	3,075	8,102	15,906	8,465	3,612	4,727	3,050	3,050
B.	BOLIVIA	#	105	105	105	105	~	~	~
C.	BRAZIL	1,248	7,727	19,107	12,566	10,696	7,087	6,499	6,113
D.	CHILE	#	#	#	#	#	~	~	~
E.	COLOMBIA	#	4,274	5,633	11,790	7,598	6,598	6,598[†]	6,598[†]
F.	COSTA RICA	924	628	1,160	245	245	245	282	129
G.	CUBA	2,086	9,620	17,215	17,215[†]	26,271	41,783	34,117	27,041
H.	DOMINICAN REP.	713[†]	10,143	919	821	885	885[†]	3,426	3,458
I.	ECUADOR	46	#	#	#	#	~	~	~
J.	EL SALVADOR	1,790	1,721	2,498	3,241	2,441	3,090	3,090	3,090
K.	GUATEMALA	#	2,712	2,616	1,912	2,279	2,563	1,517	784
M.	HONDURAS	222	842	842	420	420	~	~	~
N.	MEXICO	4,304	11,261	20,825	18,919	4,936	4,936	8,554	9,054
O.	NICARAGUA	467	117	136	136	35	35	35	35
P.	PANAMA	740	1,086	1,104	878	1,439	1,119	962	962
R.	PERU	448	2	2	2	69	69	69	69
S.	URUGUAY	1,062	723	1,423	765	362	206	206	206
T.	VENEZUELA	1,972	18,628	22,401	22,401	36,344	31,618	31,618	31,618
	UNITED STATES	333,518	792,641	585,526	660,463	504,468	852,923	766,153	790,805

PART II. VALUE OF EXPORTS

	Country	1979	1979	1980	1981	1982	1983	1984	1985
A.	ARGENTINA	932	1,563	4,144	3,993	4,898	3,335	2,966	2,966
B.	BOLIVIA	#	1,150[†]	1,450[†]	1,510[†]	1,590[†]	423[†]	423[†]	423[†]
C.	BRAZIL	50,568	104,035	124,976	141,179	104,942	122,147	140,088	135,981
D.	CHILE	54	4,759	6,919	5,895	9,362	7,741	8,852	8,948
E.	COLOMBIA	416	471	541	1,073	2,059	738	738[†]	738[†]
F.	COSTA RICA	1,697	4,177	7,647	8,229	6,383	6,007	5,392	5,780
I.	ECUADOR	450	7,278	23,256	22,187	23,228	4,125	2,757	3,127
K.	GUATEMALA	822	1,530	480	251	161	310	116	~
M.	HONDURAS	922	2,243	1,718	1,580	769	~	~	~
N.	MEXICO	473	2,081	7,375	1,975	503	9,024	9,024	9,822
O.	NICARAGUA	1,412	3,125	2,220	1,413	1,360	1,404	1,404[†]	1,404[†]
Q.	PARAGUAY	1,869[†]	7,310	14,233	10,430	29,223[†]	20,699	24,836	25,930
R.	PERU	373	3,842	2,371	3,227	3,206[†]	3,206[†]	509	899
	UNITED STATES	222,018	246,832	283,990	349,142	251,198	311,246	236,077	227,618

1. Includes veneer sheets, plywood, particle board, and fiberboard.

a. For 1962-74 data see SALA, 21-2802.

SOURCE: FAO-YFP, 1982, pp. 214 and 210; 1984, pp. 202, 206; 1985, pp. 144, 148.

Table 2454

FUEL[1] AS SHARE OF TOTAL COUNTRY IMPORTS,
20 LC, 1970-80

(% Value)

Year	A. ARGENTINA	B. BOLIVIA	C. BRAZIL
1970	4.7	1.2	12.3
1975	13.2	2.2	26.2
1980	10.3	1.0	50.5[a]

1. Includes coal, petroleum, and natural gas.

a. 1981.

SOURCE: UN-YITS, vol. 1, special table M, 1981.

Table 2455

FUELWOOD AND CHARCOAL TRADE, 7 LC, 1975-85

(T US)

PART I. VALUE OF IMPORTS

Country	1975	1978	1979	1980	1981	1982	1983	1984	1985
C. BRAZIL	14	#	#	#	#	#	~	~	~
D. CHILE	#	#	#	#	#	#	~	~	~
F. COSTA RICA	184	82	#	#	#	#	~	~	~
J. EL SALVADOR	#	#	#	#	#	#	~	~	~
N. MEXICO	118	102	146	194	768	236	236[†]	88	136
S. URUGUAY	#	#	#	#	#	#	~	~	~
T. VENEZUELA	26[†]	26[†]	26[†]	26[†]	26[†]	26[†]	~	~	~
UNITED STATES	1,030	4,844	3,837	5,967	3,093	1,561	2,089	3,582	3,668

PART II. VALUE OF EXPORTS

Country	1975	1978	1979	1980	1981	1982	1983	1984	1985
C. BRAZIL	#	808	2,000	1,582	1,010	282	984	~	~
F. COSTA RICA	1,088	905	905[†]	#	#	#	20	~	~
N. MEXICO	158	119[†]	769	613	746	293	485	196	180
UNITED STATES	4,881	5,672	7,003	4,566	9,225	5,609	5,609[†]	2,882	2,742

SOURCE: FAO-YFP, 1982, pp. 81, 83; 1984, pp. 81, 83; 1985, pp. 19, 21.

Table 2456

CRUDE OIL TRADE, 20 L, 1982–86

(T Barrels)

	Country	PART I. VOLUME OF IMPORTS					PART II. VOLUME OF EXPORTS				
		1982	1983	1984	1985	1986[‡]	1982	1983	1984	1985	1986[‡]
A.	ARGENTINA	5,177	#	#	#	#	#	#	#	3,287	#
B.	BOLIVIA	#	#	#	#	#	#	1,039	310	#	#
C.	BRAZIL	268,795	266,450	235,060	198,925	219,343	8,057	3,711	#	#	#
D.	CHILE	8,950	13,839	14,479	15,135	19,093	#	#	#	#	#
E.	COLOMBIA	7,327	13,834	9,801	6,748	#	#	#	#	#	31,310
F.	COSTA RICA	3,334	3,352[†]	3,250[†]	3,065	3,000[†]	#	#	#	#	#
G.	CUBA	~	~	~	~	~	#	#	#	#	~
H.	DOMINICAN REP.	9,944	11,450	13,001	12,485	13,171	#	#	#	#	#
I.	ECUADOR	#	#	#	#	#	42,669	59,305	61,344	70,694	63,300
J.	EL SALVADOR	3,909	4,436	4,419	4,489[†]	4,100[†]	#	#	#	#	#
K.	GUATEMALA	4,341	4,376	5,331	4,909	3,753	1,546	2,206	1,128	458	1,783
L.	HAITI	#	#	#	#	#	#	#	#	#	#
M.	HONDURAS	705	2,369	3,303	2,389	1,231	#	#	#	#	#
N.	MEXICO	#	#	#	#	#	544,614	561,005	558,004	524,943	470,704
O.	NICARAGUA	4,269	3,769	3,162	3,576	3,963	#	#	#	#	#
P.	PANAMA	11,752	10,370	10,557	7,965	10,100[†]	#	#	#	#	#
Q.	PARAGUAY	1,666	1,411	1,407	1,463[†]	1,300[†]	#	#	#	#	#
R.	PERU	#	#	#	#	#	~	8,190	7,240	9,175	4,851
S.	URUGUAY	12,481	8,930	9,074	7,878	9,896	#	#	#	#	#
T.	VENEZUELA	#	#	#	#	#	386,134	359,890	367,555	302,585	346,385

SOURCE: IDB, 1986, table 67; 1987, table 70 and 71.

Table 2457

REFINED OIL TRADE, 20 L, 1982–86

(T Barrels)

	Country	PART I. VOLUME OF IMPORTS					PART II. VOLUME OF EXPORTS				
		1982	1983	1984	1985	1986	1982	1983	1984	1985	1986
A.	ARGENTINA	736	656	985	423	0	13,831	14,549	12,228	25,638	6,646
B.	BOLIVIA	134	56	50[†]	50	40[†]	164	155	6	#	#
C.	BRAZIL	25,216	11,171	4,015	13,140	15,920	39,412	43,620	55,115	49,275	#
D.	CHILE	7,790	3,675	3,965	2,444	4,197	462	240	215	#	#
E.	COLOMBIA	11,033	7,435	5,749	9,414	7,741	12,019	15,732	16,862	18,975	20,511
F.	COSTA RICA	3,184[†]	2,883[†]	2,581[†]	2,279	2,100[†]	#	#	#	305	#
G.	CUBA	~	~	~	~	~	~	~	~	~	~
H.	DOMINICAN REP.	4,333	4,806	4,693	3,597	5,031	#	#	#	#	#
I.	ECUADOR	5,571	6,896	4,209	4,884	4,100[†]	5,868	4,405	6,764	5,380	4,500[†]
J.	EL SALVADOR	256	184	99	101	100[†]	#	461	575	#	#
K.	GUATEMALA	3,932	3,571	3,527	3,993	3,851	#	#	#	#	#
L.	HAITI	1,528[†]	1,614[†]	1,600[†]	1,600	1,500[†]	#	#	#	#	#
M.	HONDURAS	3,327	2,437	2,124	2,390	3,300[†]	35	#	#	#	#
N.	MEXICO	3,016	6,347	12,111	19,377	21,899	15,358	30,710	40,944	49,413	42,215
O.	NICARAGUA	418	477	1,206	1,284	1,207	46	5	#	#	#
P.	PANAMA	607	925	1,052	1,057	950[†]	29,755	13,560	200	864	#
Q.	PARAGUAY	1,591	1,667	2,268	2,313	2,200[†]	#	#	#	#	#
R.	PERU	559	2,174	696	223	1,588	8,612	12,885	17,081	18,449	17,240
S.	URUGUAY	111	321	332	288	1,098	126	223	#	#	230
T.	VENEZUELA	#	#	#	#	#	180,049	187,245	186,150	197,830	213,525

SOURCE: IDB-SPTF, 1986, table 67; 1987, table 70, 71.

Table 2458

PETROLEUM AND DERIVATIVES TRADE, 19 L, 1977–86

(M US)

PART I. VALUE OF NET IMPORTS

	Country	1977	1979	1981	1982	1983	1984	1985	1986[‡]
A.	ARGENTINA	413.4	941.7	281.4	~	~	~	~	#
C.	BRAZIL	4,010.8	6,410.3	9,672.0	8,612.3	6,791.2	5,074.0	4,306.0	2,410.0
D.	CHILE	418.0	846.9	983.2	892.0	482.7	495.0	452.1	322.6
E.	COLOMBIA	82.4	420.5	412.2	371.6	239.0	~	#	#
F.	COSTA RICA	102.2	168.4	180.5	168.0	157.0	151.3	158.9	120.0[†]
H.	DOMINICAN REP.	187.8	314.9	472.3	451.6	461.3	504.7	426.8	264.5
I.	ECUADOR	**	**	**	**	**	**	**	**
J.	EL SALVADOR	73.0	113.3	167.9	134.2	126.6	130.3	133.0	100.0[†]
K.	GUATEMALA	28.0	254.9	344.3	241.5	195.7	240.6	254.5	136.0
L.	HAITI	28.0	45.0	62.0	62.0	60.0[†]	60.0[†]	60.0[†]	32.0[†]
M.	HONDURAS	72.0	112.8	161.1	167.0	163.6	179.4	161.2	102.8
N.	MEXICO	**	**	**	**	**	**	**	#
O.	NICARAGUA	105.1	76.6	187.7	169.3	159.6	141.0	158.7	123.8
P.	PANAMA	268.2	319.4	415.4	399.2	263.3	288.6	294.0	200.0[†]
Q.	PARAGUAY	60.9	123.9	169.3	180.6	145.7	93.5	114.6	84.0[†]
R.	PERU	234.0	**	**	**	**	**	**	#
S.	URUGUAY	240.2	303.2	493.5	416.0	240.6	260.1	237.0	133.0
T.	VENEZUELA	**	**	**	**	**	**	**	**

PART II. VALUE OF NET EXPORTS

	Country	1977	1979	1981	1982	1983	1984	1985	1986[‡]
A.	ARGENTINA	**	**	**	135.5	243.0	275.3	652.2	400.0[†]
B.	BOLIVIA	67.4	44.0	3.3	4.5	34.2	8.5	5.0	3.0[†]
C.	BRAZIL	**	**	**	**	**	**	**	**
D.	CHILE	**	**	**	**	**	**	**	**
E.	COLOMBIA	**	**	**	**	**	2.1	0.1	526.0
F.	COSTA RICA	**	**	**	**	**	**	**	**
H.	DOMINICAN REP.	**	**	**	**	**	**	**	**
I.	ECAUDOR	484.1	989.1	1,710.0	1,508.0	1,733.0	1,835.0	1,728.4	803.0
J.	EL SALVADOR	**	**	**	**	**	**	**	**
K.	GUATEMALA	**	**	**	**	**	**	**	**
L.	HAITI	**	**	**	**	**	**	**	**
M.	HONDURAS	**	**	**	**	**	**	**	**
N.	MEXICO	810.6	3,446.3	13,902.5	16,044.5	15,565.0	15,669.0	14,050.4	5,752.7
O.	NICARAGUA	**	**	**	**	**	**	**	**
P.	PANAMA	**	**	**	**	**	**	**	**
Q.	PARAGUAY	**	**	**	**	**	**	**	**
R.	PERU	**	645.7	672.2	732.9	477.3	614.2	650.0	217.0
S.	URUGUAY	**	**	**	**	**	**	**	**
T.	VENEZUELA	9,088.8	13,557.2	19,351.5	15,564.0	13,933.0	14,993.0	13,063.0	7,218.0

SOURCE: IDB-SPTF, 1983, p. 126; 1986, table 69; 1987, table 72.

Table 2459

CRUDE OIL PRODUCTION IN OPEC[1]
MEMBER COUNTRIES, 1965–85

(T Barrels per Day)

Year	Production
1965	14,338
1966	15,770
1967	16,850
1968	18,786
1969	20,906
1970	23,413
1971	25,326
1972	27,094
1973	30,989
1974	30,729
1975	27,155
1976	30,738
1977	31,253
1978	29,805
1979	30,929
1980	26,879
1981	22,599
1982	18,992
1983	16,992
1984	16,347
1985	15,554

1. The 13 OPEC countries include Ecuador and Venezuela.

SOURCE: *OPEC Annual Statistical Bulletin*, 1985, table 13.

Figure 24:4

OPEC OIL PRODUCTION, 1965–85

(T Barrels per Day)

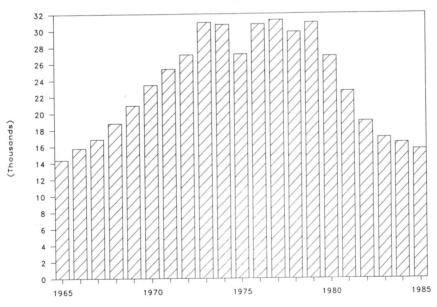

SOURCE: Table 2459, above.

Table 2460

OPEC[1] CRUDE OIL EXPORTS TO U.S., 1965–85
(T Barrels per Day)

Year	Exports
1965	992
1966	981
1967	740
1968	926
1969	940
1970	935
1971	1,427
1972	1,879
1973	2,406
1974	2,579
1975	2,726
1976	3,635
1977	5,069
1978	5,113
1979	5,102
1980	3,795
1981	2,735
1982	1,441
1983	1,259
1984	1,279
1985	887

1. The 13 OPEC countries include Ecuador and Venezuela.

SOURCE: *OPEC Annual Statistical Bulletin*, 1985, table 24.

Figure 24:5

OPEC CRUDE OIL EXPORTS TO U.S., 1965–85
(T Barrels per Day)

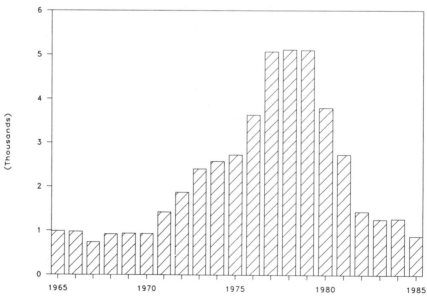

SOURCE: Table 2460, above.

Table 2461

U.S. OIL AND OIL PRODUCTS IMPORTED
(1987)[a]

Country	Barrels Per Day
Canada	785,500
VENEZUELA	764,400
MEXICO	658,600
Saudi Arabia	607,000
Nigeria	482,500
United Kingdom	373,600
Virgin Islands	268,000
Algeria	253,600
Angola	140,400
Iran	45,000

a. Imported between January and May, 1987.

SOURCE: *Los Angeles Times*, August 13, 1987.

Table 2462

LEAD EXPORTS, 8 LC, 1979–84

	Country	Value of Exports (T US)						Value as % of World Exports					
		1979	1980	1981	1982	1983	1984	1979	1980	1981	1982	1983	1984
A.	ARGENTINA	673	3	244	356	#	~	#	#	#[t]	#[t]	~	~
B.	BOLIVIA	1,949	57[t]	296[t]	309[t]	90[t]	104[t]	#	#[t]	#[t]	#[t]	~	~
C.	BRAZIL	400	898	186	29	120	~	#	#	#	#	~	~
E.	COLOMBIA	94	131	107	30	4	~	#	#	#	#	~	~
N.	MEXICO	79,671	55,462	29,620	22,047	31,370[t]	49,084	4.8	3.1	2.8	2.3	3.6[t]	5.8[t]
P.	PANAMA	502	632	690	581	148	~	#	#	#	#	~	~
R.	PERU	85,038	58,510	46,934	36,786	35,666	19,686	5.1	3.3	4.4	3.8	4.1[t]	2.3[t]
T.	VENEZUELA	13	2	433	~	~	~	#	#	#	~	~	~
	LAIA	167,838	115,064	77,822	65,783	68,848	68,877	10.1	6.5	7.3	6.7	7.9[t]	8.2[t]
	CACM	75	41	170	108[t]	642[t]	663[t]	#	#	#	#[t]	.1[t]	.1[t]
	UNITED STATES	13,947	164,836	26,050	49,102	19,124	15,240	.8	9.4	2.4	5.0	2.2	1.8

SOURCE: UN-YITS, 1982, vol. 2, p. 159; 1983, vol. 2, p. 147; 1984, vol. 2, p. 178.

Table 2463

COPPER EXPORTS,[1] 9 LC, 1979-84

	Country	Value of Exports (T US)						Value as % of World Exports					
		1979	1980	1981	1982	1983	1984	1979	1980	1981	1982	1983	1984
A.	ARGENTINA	504	411	2,217	2,572	1,123	2,954	#	#	#[t]	#[t]	~	~
B.	BOLIVIA	1,191[t]	615[t]	1,004[t]	16[t]	56[t]	~	#[t]	#[t]	#[t]	#[t]	~	~
C.	BRAZIL	11,856	10,606	23,932	21,867	30,213	74,865[t]	#	#	#	#	~	~
D.	CHILE	1,799,600	2,009,061	1,578,285	1,759,000	1,859,100	1,613,900	16.3	15.0	14.9	18.0	17.6	16.6
E.	COLOMBIA	222	145	105	209	~	~	#	#	#	#	~	~
K.	GUATEMALA	228	335	91	8[t]	~	~	#	#	#	#[t]	~	~
N.	MEXICO	14,109	32,831[t]	69,201[t]	51,103[t]	56,755[t]	69,493[t]	#	#[t]	#[t]	#[t]	~	~
R.	PERU	667,147	609,927	317,932	382,923	350,525[t]	324,509[t]	6.1	4.7	3.2	4.2	3.7[t]	~
T.	VENEZUELA	1[t]	53	484	484[t]	1,341[t]	1,194[t]	~	#	#	#[t]	~	~
	LAIA	2,493,636	3,962,032	3,030,108	2,993,251	3,277,683	3,108,519	22.6	19.9	18.8	22.7	21.7[t]	21.4[t]
	CACM	367	344	131	132[t]	477[t]	450	#	#	#	#[t]	#[t]	#[t]
	UNITED STATES	437,119	443,693	452,943	330,584	392,441	402,969	4.0	3.3	4.3	3.4	3.7	4.1

1. Except cement copper.

SOURCE: UN-YITS, 1982, vol. 2, p. 156; 1983, vol. 2, p. 144; 1984, vol. 2, p. 178.

Table 2464

TIN EXPORTS, 9 LC, 1980–84

Country	Value of Exports (T US)					Value as % of World Exports				
	1980	1981	1982	1983	1984	1980	1981	1982	1983	1984
A. ARGENTINA	11	12	3	45	3[†]	~	~	~	~	~
B. BOLIVIA	177,430[†]	179,947[†]	151,228[†]	164,583[†]	153,911[†]	5.7[†]	6.5[†]	6.7[†]	8.8[†]	7.5[†]
C. BRAZIL	63,534	67,143	56,893	112,141	216,338[†]	2.1	2.4	2.5	6.0	10.5[†]
D. CHILE	5,154[†]	4,778[†]	6,631[†]	8,264[†]	~	#	#	#	~	~
F. COSTA RICA	~	9	~	~	~	~	#	~	~	~
J. EL SALVADOR	1	~	~	~	~	#	~	~	~	~
K. GUATEMALA	~	16	~	~	~	~	#	~	~	~
N. MEXICO	62[†]	717[†]	201[†]	15[†]	283[†]	#	#	#	~	~
R. PERU	269	266	179	808[†]	626[†]	#	#	#	~	~
LAIA	241,306[†]	248,097[†]	205,503[†]	277,630[†]	371,219[†]	7.8[†]	9.0[†]	9.2[†]	14.8[†]	18.1[†]
CACM	103	52	35[†]	25[†]	26[†]	#	#	#[†]	#[†]	#[†]
UNITED STATES	31,120	108,225	148,869	57,165	48,945	1.0	3.9	6.6	3.1	2.4

SOURCE: UN-YITS, 1982, vol. 2, p. 584; 1983, vol. 2, p. 149; 1984, vol. 2, p. 183.

Table 2465

ZINC EXPORTS, 7 LC, 1980–84

Country	Value of Exports (T US)					Value as % of World Exports				
	1980	1981	1982	1983	1984	1980	1981	1982	1983	1984
A. ARGENTINA	185	1,562	3,236	4	~	#	#[†]	#[†]	~	~
C. BRAZIL	106	2,508	2,043	24	6,065	#	#	#	~	~
D. CHILE	#	1,293[†]	6,601[†]	~	~	#	#[†]	#[†]	~	~
H. DOMINICAN REP.	~	104	~	~	~	~	#	~	~	~
K. GUATEMALA	120	68	19[†]	121[†]	107[†]	#	#	~	~	~
N. MEXICO	46,588	18,588	10,853	51,012[†]	69,124[†]	#	#	#	~	~
R. PERU	32,759	90,207	113,959	73,417[†]	64,717[†]	2.2	5.2	6.8	4.2[†]	3.0[†]
LAIA	79,686	114,350	136,747	124,514[†]	139,948[†]	5.3	6.5	8.2	7.1[†]	6.5[†]
CACM	131	149	36[†]	173[†]	158[†]	#	#	#[†]	#[†]	#[†]
UNITED STATES	14,081	15,000	9,530	9,212	9,331	#	#	#	~	~

SOURCE: UN-YITS, 1982, vol. 2, p. 160; 1983, vol. 2, p. 148; 1984, vol. 2, p. 182.

Table 2466

MERCHANDISE TRADE,[1] 25 ECLA: LR, 1980–86

(M US)

Country	1980 Exports	1980 Imports	1981 Exports	1981 Imports	1982 Exports	1982 Imports	1983 Exports	1983 Imports	1984[‡] Exports	1984[‡] Imports	1985[‡] Exports	1985[‡] Imports	1986[‡] Exports	1986[‡] Imports
A. ARGENTINA	8,020.0	9,398.3	9,169.1	8.414.5	7.156.9	4,573.3	7,833.6	4,123.1	8,072.0	4,131.8	8,396.0	3,766.0	6,987.0	4,392.0
Bahamas	200.4	801.5	176.9	789.8	200.5	698.9	224.9	802.5	262.5	856.4	295.8	891.2	283.0	864.0
Barbados	180.8	479.0	162.7	521.4	196.2	472.1	272.2	564.8	339.6	600.8	302.2	568.0	238.5	614.0
B. BOLIVIA	941.8	680.6	913.3	681.8	779.8	402.6	755.1	473.1	724.4	412.5	623.4	462.8	504.3	478.2
C. BRAZIL	20,139.9	22,951.2	23,341.5	22,099.8	19,020.3	18,276.6	21,923.1	15,437.4	27,050.0	13,936.0	25,538.8	13,127.3	22,393.0	12,866.0
D. CHILE	4,705.0	5,469.0	3,835.8	6,512.5	3,491.6	3,432.3	3,827.0	2,818.0	3,650.1	3,356.9	3,804.0	2,955.0	4,050.0	3,074.0
E. COLOMBIA	3,986.6	4,283.3	3,157.8	4.729.6	2,933.1	5,047.6	2,969.7	4,464.0	3,424.0	3,980.0	3,518.0	3,734.0	5,008.0	3,464.0
F. COSTA RICA	1,001.5	1,374.9	1,002.4	1,089.1	817.7	758.6	853.2	898.9	955.3	995.2	930.4	1,005.1	1,076.6	1,046.5
H. DOMINICAN REP.	962.0	1,519.7	1,188.0	1,451.7	723.3	1,184.5	785.2	1,282.2	868.1	1,257.1	738.5	1,285.9	724.5	1,251.4
I. ECUADOR	2,544.2	2,241.8	2,544.2	2,361.5	2,207.4	2,054.7	2,365.0	1,408.0	2,622.0	1,567.0	2,905.0	1,611.0	2,181.0	1,677.0
J. EL SALVADOR	1,075.3	897.0	798.1	898.4	663.4	778.1	735.4	830.9	725.8	914.4	678.9	899.5	727.1	933.9
K. GUATEMALA	1,518.9	1,471.9	1,282.3	1,544.2	1,100.8	1,211.1	1,090.8	1,056.6	1,130.9	1,183.0	1,059.7	1,076.7	1,058.3	919.6
Guyana	388.9	386.4	346.4	399.6	227.5	239.4	193.4	225.8	205.0	199.7	214.2	209.3	209.6	239.5
L. HAITI	215.1	318.1	147.2	350.7	163.7	279.1	185.5	323.9	203.7	333.0	223.0	344.7	190.8	303.3
M. HONDURAS	850.3	954.0	783.8	898.6	637.4	641.3	694.2	760.7	745.7	879.6	805.0	879.0	900.9	902.1
Jamaica	962.7	1,038.2	974.0	1,296.7	723.0	1,138.9	685.7	1,124.2	738.7	1,034.4	568.6	1,004.2	580.0	860.0
N. MEXICO	16,070.0	18,902.1	19,891.3	24,050.1	20,054.2	13,515.1	22,329.3	8,564.8	24,041.6	11,287.4	21,663.8	13,312.2	16,031.0	11,432.4
O. NICARAGUA	450.4	802.9	508.2	922.5	382.5	681.6	428.3	778.1	385.4	799.6	301.5	878.2	239.2	714.4
P. PANAMA	2,267.1	2,994.6	2,540.1	3,315.4	2,271.5	2,868.3	1,673.5	2,321.7	1,685.8	2,509.4	1,958.9	2,712.3	2,412.0	2,955.0
Q. PARAGUAY	400.4	675.4	398.6	772.3	373.3	670.1	326.0	551.4	361.3	649.1	341.2	515.9	289.6	580.0
R. PERU	3,899.4	3,065.1	3,248.6	3,804.0	3,105.7	3,508.3	3,018.9	2,723.8	3,148.8	2,141.2	2,965.8	1,871.3	2,491.0	2,486.0
Suriname	514.5	454.1	473.8	507.0	402.8	433.8	367.3	402.1	356.4	344.8	314.2	298.5	287.6	250.6
Trin. & Tobago	2,541.0	1,764.1	2,607.8	1,733.1	2,096.0	2,302.3	2,272.9	2,315.7	2,106.3	1,718.4	2,089.4	1,394.2	1,399.9	1,318.0
S. URUGUAY	1,058.5	1,668.2	1,229.7	1,592.1	1,183.6	978.3	1,156.4	739.7	924.6	733.2	853.6	675.4	1,087.8	791.0
T. VENEZUELA	19,050.5	10,876.9	19,963.2	12,122.9	15,386.2	12,797.4	14,570.5	6,408.7	15,850.8	7,877.2	14,178.0	7,388.0	8,704.0	7,601.0
LATIN AMERICA[2]	93,946.0	95,468.3	100,684.7	102,859.5	86,298.3	78,944.4	91,537.1	61,400.0	100,578.6	63,698.3	95,267.7	62,865.5	80,054.7	62,013.9

1. Exports and imports f.o.b. values.
2. Totals may not add because of rounding.

SOURCE: IDB-SPTF, 1986, p. 419; 1987, p. 451.

Table 2467

GROWTH RATE OF MERCHANDISE IMPORTS, 7 L, 1974–84

(AA–GR of Dollar Value)

Country	1974–78	1979–80	1981	1982	1983	1984
A. ARGENTINA	2.0	64.0	–10.5	–45.7	–9.8	1.8
C. BRAZIL	2.0	29.0	–3.8	–12.2	–20.4	–9.7
D. CHILE	11.0	38.0	19.9	–47.8	–17.8	19.0
E. COLOMBIA	14.1	29.0	10.8	13.5	–17.4	–10.8
N. MEXICO	8.3	54.0	27.2	–40.0	–46.5	33.1
R. PERU	–4.5	36.0	23.0	–2.1	–26.9	–19.8
T. VENEZUELA	30.5	–1.6	11.5	12.1	–52.8	12.3

SOURCE: IDB-SPTF, 1985, table I-4.

Table 2468

GROWTH RATE OF MERCHANDISE EXPORTS, 7 L, 1974–84
(AA–GR of Dollar Value)

	Country	1974–78	1979–80	1981	1982	1983	1984
A.	ARGENTINA	13.0	11.9	14.3	−21.9	9.5	11.1
C.	BRAZIL	12.3	26.0	15.7	−13.4	8.5	23.2
D.	CHILE	3.4	38.4	−15.8	−11.8	9.6	−5.0
E.	COLOMBIA	21.0	12.6	−20.8	−.1	−7.6	15.0
N.	MEXICO	20.1	61.0	23.8	6.7	.8	9.7
R.	PERU	6.4	42.2	−17.2	−4.4	−2.8	2.6
T.	VENEZUELA	−5.1	45.0	4.8	−17.3	−10.6	7.7

SOURCE: IDB-SPTF, 1985, table I–7.

Table 2469

STRUCTURE OF TOTAL MERCHANDISE
IMPORTS, 20 LC, 1960–73[a]

		Food and Raw Materials (%)			
	Country	1960	1965	1970	1973
A.	ARGENTINA	26.7	42.2	36.5	~

a. Other categories are fuels and lubricants, machinery and equipment, other manufactured products, and total merchandise imports.

Continued in SALA, 24–2455.

Table 2470

MANUFACTURED GOODS[1] AS SHARE OF
TOTAL VALUE OF COUNTRY TRADE,
20 LC, 1970–80

	Country	Year	Imports CIF	Exports FOB
A.	ARGENTINA	1970	78.2	14.0
		1975	71.6	24.4
		1980	78.9	24.9

Continued in SALA, 24–2456.

Table 2471

CAPITAL GOODS EXPORTS,[1] 16 LR, 1970–82

(M US)

Exporting Country	1970	1971	1972	1973	1974	1975	1976	1977	1978	1979	1980	1981	1982
A. ARGENTINA	55	71	97	205	289	320	311	366	386	393	413	366	469
B. BOLIVIA	0	0	0	0	0	1	0	0	2	5	9	7	5

Continued in SALA, 25-2461.

Table 2472

CAPITAL GOODS IMPORTS AS SHARE OF TOTAL GOODS IMPORTED, 16 LR, 1970–82

(%)

Importing Country	1970	1971	1972	1973	1974	1975	1976	1977	1978	1979	1980	1981	1982
A. ARGENTINA	30.0	31.6	33.2	25.2	17.6	19.1	22.6	33.7	37.5	30.6	33.6	35.0	30.0
B. BOLIVIA	38.5	34.7	34.6	- -	35.8	42.1	45.1	38.7	44.2	38.9	31.0	43.5	37.9

Continued in SALA, 25-2462

Table 2473

TOTAL MERCHANDISE EXPORTS AS SHARE
OF COUNTRY GDP, 1970–82

(%)

Country	1970	1975	1978	1979	1980	1981	1982
LAIA							
A. ARGENTINA	4.2	6.1	12.9	14.7	15.0	18.1	16.0
C. BRAZIL	3.2	6.0	7.4	8.4	10.3	12.1	10.5

Continued in SALA, 24-2457.

Table 2474

COTTON EXPORTS, 11 LC, 1980–84

	Country	Value of Exports (T US)					Value as % of World Exports				
		1980	1981	1982	1983	1984	1980	1981	1982	1983	1984
A.	ARGENTINA	126,791	31,087	69,432	10,293	89,140[†]	1.9	3.2[†]	3.0[†]	~	~
B.	BOLIVIA	3,395[†]	3,261[†]	2,726[†]	~	~	#[†]	#[†]	#[†]	~	~
C.	BRAZIL	17,452	45,050	64,593	196,387	61,209	#	#	#	~	~
E.	COLOMBIA	82,359	93,812	26,707	23,195	49,076	#	#	#	~	~
J.	EL SALVADOR	87,142	55,213	45,394	53,617	13,773	#	#	#[†]	~	~
K.	GUATEMALA	172,330	111,434	95,686[†]	57,174[†]	67,313	2.5	1.8	2.0	1.3[†]	~
M.	HONDURAS	13,649	12,577	6,629	4,228	5,356	#	#	#[†]	~	~
N.	MEXICO	324,173	306,490	183,825	115,698	208,166	4.8	5.2	3.7	2.3	3.6
O.	NICARAGUA	30,922	123,639	89,095	99,109[†]	119,453[†]	#	#	#	~	~
Q.	PARAGUAY	105,833	129,288	122,415	79,000	91,883[†]	1.6	2.2	2.4	1.6	1.6[†]
R.	PERU	62,565	59,657	74,691	52,566[†]	15,788[†]	#	#	#	~	~
	LAIA	722,152	671,240	541,687	477,502	516,589[†]	10.7	11.4	10.8	9.6	8.9[†]
	LACM	305,503	302,875	236,805[†]	214,134[†]	205,900[†]	4.5	5.2	4.7[†]	4.3[†]	3.5[†]
	UNITED STATES	2,906,646	2,299,164	2,004,918	1,859,514	2,476,094	43.1	39.2	40.0	37.3	42.5

a. Datum for 1978: 2.1.

SOURCE: UN-YITS, 1982, vol. 2, p. 64; 1983, vol. 2, p. 52; 1984, vol. 2, p. 86.

Table 2475

U.S. COTTON IMPORT QUOTAS, 3 LR,[1] 1986

(% of World Quota)

	Country	%
C.	BRAZIL	4.3
N.	MEXICO	61.2
R.	PERU	1.7
	LATIN AMERICA	67.2

1. Other Latin American producers are Argentina, Colombia, Ecuador, Haiti, Honduras, and Paraguay. These countries were assigned smaller quotas.

SOURCE: NAFINSA-MV, no. 40, p. 944.

Table 2476

COTTON LINT EXPORT VOLUME,[1] 13 LC, 1975–85

(T MET)

	Country	1975	1978	1979	1980	1981	1982	1983	1984	1985
A.	ARGENTINA	6	147	62	86	24[‡]	69	8	56	80[‡]
B.	BOLIVIA	15	8	10	.6	#	#	#	~	~
C.	BRAZIL	83	45	#	9	30	56	180	32	102
E.	COLOMBIA	86	54	26	48	52[‡]	18	14	27	56[‡]
F.	COSTA RICA	~	9	#	1	#	#	~	~	~
H.	DOMINICAN REP.[3]	~	~	#	#	#	#	#	#	#
J.	EL SALVADOR	53	58	56	53	30	32	37	5	24
K.	GUATEMALA	107	130	147	137	110[‡]	66	39	52	57
M.	HONDURAS	4	13	9	9	7[‡]	6	3	5	5[†]
N.	MEXICO[3]	166	200	212	172	183	126	69	123	77
O.	NICARAGUA[3]	132	129	114	20	73[‡]	60	79	82	67
Q.	PARAGUAY	17	84	77	75	91	112	79	89	159
R.	PERU	46	21[‡]	20	30	32[‡]	53	31	8	39[‡]
	UNITED STATES[2,3]	871	1,279	1,527	1,823	1,269	1,392	1,205	1,497	1,097
	WORLD	3,879	4,387	4,374	4,815	4,296	4,416	4,307	4,316	4,203

1. Figures refer to "special trade" except where otherwise indicated. See table 2413, n. 1, for explanation of "special" exports.
2. The customs area includes the Commonwealth of Puerto Rico.
3. Figures refer to "general trade," i.e., total exports including re-exports.

a. For 1934–75 see SALA, 20-2922.

SOURCE: FAO-TY, 1958; 1980; 1981, table 109; 1982, table 109; 1984, table 109; 1985, table 110.

Table 2477

FERTILIZER IMPORTS,[1] 20 LRC, 1974–85[a]

(T MET)

	Country	1974/75	1975/76	1976/77	1977/78	1978/79	1979/80	1980/81	1981/82	1982/83	1983/84	1984/85
A.	ARGENTINA	52[‡]	36[‡]	48	43	80	119	93	74	91	99[‡]	122[‡]
B.	BOLIVIA	6[‡]	3[‡]	3[‡]	4	5	3	3	7	3[‡]	8	5
C.	BRAZIL	1,197	1,223	1,402	1,855	1,825	2,035	2,238	1,221	1,221	832	1,301
D.	CHILE	125	86	35	82	93	112	123	122	49	115	157
E.	COLOMBIA	172	31	112	200[‡]	225	206	221[‡]	199[‡]	264	255	294[‡]
F.	COSTA RICA	80	53	61	65	85	64[‡]	60[‡]	47[‡]	40[‡]	59[‡]	67
G.	CUBA	282	352	315	359	413	324	411	459	454	471	478
H.	DOMINICAN REP.	98	84[‡]	66[‡]	52	61	79[‡]	65[‡]	68[‡]	66[‡]	71[‡]	72[‡]
I.	ECUADOR	35	26	74	86	70	75	73	60[‡]	60	74[‡]	83[‡]
J.	EL SALVADOR	103[‡]	95	111	106	104	67	64	88	60	82	55
K.	GUATEMALA	65	52[‡]	84	107	70	102[‡]	86[‡]	89	87	74	96
L.	HAITI	2	2[‡]	~	3[‡]	4[‡]	4[‡]	~	6[‡]	5[‡]	3[‡]	4[‡]
M.	HONDURAS	18[‡]	20[‡]	25[‡]	28[‡]	23[‡]	20[‡]	31[‡]	26	24	28	35[‡]
N.	MEXICO	81	210	308	229	313	331	327	461	515	233	290
O.	NICARAGUA	45[‡]	10[‡]	48	58	39	23[‡]	65[‡]	55[‡]	23[‡]	72	49
P.	PANAMA	28	25	23[‡]	23[‡]	23[‡]	30[‡]	31[‡]	30[‡]	27[‡]	23[‡]	28[‡]
Q.	PARAGUAY	2	1	1[‡]	1[‡]	3[‡]	6	6	9	8	9[‡]	9[‡]
R.	PERU	134	84	30	63	61	54	44	46	47	68	59
S.	URUGUAY	24	37	58	49	45	67	60	47[‡]	42[‡]	34[‡]	44[‡]
T.	VENEZUELA	92	63	176[‡]	165	136[‡]	155	175	173	64[‡]	21[‡]	94[‡]
	LATIN AMERICA	2,641	2,493	2,980	3,578	3,620	3,809	4,163	3,280	3,150	2,629	3,342
	UNITED STATES	4,827	4,852	6,389	6,408	6,808	7,491	7,430	6,823	6,542	8,370	8,299
	WORLD	24,983	24,282	26,344	29,526	32,819	33,966	35,888	33,252	34,251	38,087	42,390

1. Includes nitrogenous, phosphate, and potash fertilizers.

a. For 1961–70 data see SALA, 23-1522.

SOURCE: FAO-FY, 1979 and 1981, table 32; 1984, table 31; 1985, table 30.

Table 2478

FERTILIZER EXPORTS,[1] 9 LC, 1970–85[a]

(T MET)

	Country	1970/71	1975/76	1976/77	1977/78	1978/79	1979/80	1980/81	1981/82	1982/83	1983/84	1984/85
A.	ARGENTINA	#	#	#	#	1	2[‡]	1	~[‡]	~[‡]	~	~
C.	BRAZIL	#	#	#	#	5[‡]	8[‡]	4[‡]	5[‡]	4[‡]	128	24
D.	CHILE	82	66	73	77	82	89	96	83	58	67	59
E.	COLOMBIA	2	23[‡]	9[‡]	2	5[‡]	5[‡]	8[‡]	3[‡]	~[‡]	2	1
F.	COSTA RICA	9	13[‡]	17	19	18	13[‡]	11[‡]	9[‡]	11[‡]	2[‡]	8
J.	EL SALVADOR	5	8	16	20	15	12[‡]	~	~	~	~	~
N.	MEXICO	78	1	30	75	51	48	28	9	6	87	58
S.	URUGUAY	#	#	#	#	4	9	7[‡]	4[‡]	4[‡]	1[‡]	1[‡]
T.	VENEZUELA	#	3[‡]	54[‡]	33[‡]	9	75	71[‡]	114	106[‡]	151[‡]	138[‡]
	UNITED STATES	2,355	3,924	4,305	5,511	6,641	6,908	7,569	6,226	6,005	6,316	8,512
	WORLD	19,142	22,834	26,646	30,778	34,177	34,356	37,377	32,913	33,491	38,489	42,610

1. Includes nitrogenous, phosphate, and potash fertilizers.

a. For 1961–70 data see SALA, 23-1523.

SOURCE: FAO-FY, 1979 and 1981, table 32; 1984, table 31; 1985, table 31.

CHAPTER 25

STRUCTURE AND TERMS OF TRADE

Table 2500

ARGENTINA PERCENTAGE VALUE OF TRADE, 1970–84

	Imports by Broad Economic Category*						
Category	1970	1975	1980	1981	1982	1983	1984
Total Imports	100.0	100.0	100.0	100.0	100.0	100.0	100.0
1. Food and Beverages	5.5	4.4	5.4	4.8	4.3	3.7	4.3
Primary	4.2	3.6	3.1	2.6	3.0	2.7	2.9
For Industry	2.6	2.1	1.1	1.0	1.7	1.8	1.5
For Hshold Consm	1.6	1.5	2.0	1.6	1.3	.9	1.3
Processed	1.3	.8	2.3	2.2	1.3	1.0	1.5
For Industry	.3	.3	.5	.4	.6	.6	.9
For Hshold Consm	1.0	.5	1.8	1.8	.7	.4	.5
2. Ind. Supplies Nes	53.2	58.3	32.7	30.7	41.5	48.1	48.3
Primary	5.0	6.4	2.6	2.7	3.7	4.6	4.9
Processed	48.1	51.9	30.1	28.0	37.8	43.4	43.4
3. Fuels	4.6	13.1	10.1	10.6	12.4	10.0	10.3
Primary	2.8	11.2	8.9	8.4	11.4	9.3	9.2
Processed	1.8	1.9	1.2	2.2	1.0	.7	1.1
4. Motor Spirit	0	.2	.7	1.5	.3	0	0
Other	1.8	1.7	.5	.8	.7	.7	1.0
5. Machinery	25.8	16.7	27.3	29.4	28.9	25.7	23.1
Machines Capt. Eqp	21.0	13.3	23.5	25.4	24.2	20.1	17.2
Parts Accessories	4.8	3.4	3.8	4.0	4.7	5.7	5.9
6. Transport	6.1	4.4	10.6	11.5	6.8	8.4	9.7
Passenger Cars	.1	0	2.3	2.6	.5	.1	0
Other	.7	1.3	4.3	4.4	1.6	2.2	2.4
Parts Accessories	5.3	3.1	4.0	4.5	4.6	6.1	7.3
7. Consumer Goods	4.7	3.0	13.8	13.0	6.1	4.0	4.3
Durable	1.6	1.3	6.1	5.6	2.2	1.3	1.5
Semi-Durable	1.3	.5	5.4	5.2	2.1	1.3	1.2
Non-Durable	1.8	1.2	2.3	2.2	1.8	1.5	1.5
8. Other	.1	.1	0	.1	.1	0	0

	Exports by Industrial Origin						
Origin	1970	1975	1980	1981	1982	1983	1984
Total Exports (1 + 2 + 3)	100.0	100.0	100.0	100.0	100.0	100.0	100.0
1. Agriculture	39.4	47.1	38.7	45.7	40.1	49.0	47.0
2. Mining Quarrying	.3	.4	.4	.3	.3	.3	.3
3. Manufacturing	60.2	52.6	60.9	54.0	59.6	50.6	52.7
31. Food, Bev., Tobac.	43.3	25.8	30.6	24.2	25.3	27.4	28.7
32. Textiles	5.5	4.9	8.9	6.9	6.6	5.5	5.7
33. Wood, Wood Prod.	#	0	0	0	0	0	0
34. Paper and Prod.	.9	.9	.9	.6	.6	.5	.6
35. Chemicals	4.0	4.7	8.8	11.6	12.8	9.4	8.8
36. Non-Metal Minrl	.1	.2	.4	.3	.5	.2	.2
37. Basic Metal Ind.	1.7	.8	3.5	4.4	5.7	3.5	3.4
38. Metal Manufact.	4.5	15.1	7.6	5.5	7.9	4.1	5.3
39. Oth. Manf. Ind.	.1	.1	.2	.3	.1	0	0

SOURCE: UN-YITS, 1976; 1981; 1983; 1984; 1985.

Table 2501

BOLIVIA PERCENTAGE VALUE OF TRADE, 1971–82

Category	Imports by Broad Economic Category*						
	1971	1975	1978	1979	1980	1981	1982
Total Imports	100.0	100.0	100.0	100.0	100.0	100.0	100.0
1. Food and Beverages	20.2	16.7	13.1	13.0	18.0	13.7	18.1
Primary	3.3	3.2	5.1	5.1	6.7	5.2	9.2
For Industry	2.4	2.5	4.2	4.5	5.7	4.3	9.0
For Hshold Consm	.9	.6	.9	.6	.9	.9	.2
Processed	17.0	13.5	8.0	7.9	11.3	8.5	8.8
For Industry	10.5	8.8	2.9	3.5	3.2	2.6	4.3
For Hshold Consm	6.4	4.8	5.2	4.4	8.1	5.9	4.6
2. Ind. Supplies Nes.	32.0	28.8	23.4	22.9	27.1	27.7	30.0
Primary	.8	.7	.5	.4	.5	.5	.7
Processed	31.2	28.1	22.9	22.4	26.6	27.1	29.3
3. Fuels	.7	1.7	.9	.7	.3	1.6	1.8
Primary	0	0	0	0	0	0	0
Processed	.7	1.6	.9	.7	.3	1.6	1.7
Motor Spirit	.5	.6	.5	.3	0	0	0
Other	.2	1.0	.4	.3	.3	1.6	1.7
4. Machinery	21.7	19.8	31.3	26.7	24.6	25.1	25.6
Machines Capt. Eqp	18.5	18.1	29.0	24.2	21.5	22.9	22.8
Parts Accessories	3.2	1.7	2.3	2.6	3.1	2.3	2.8
5. Transport	13.0	21.7	17.4	19.8	18.5	21.2	14.6
Passenger Cars	.6	4.3	3.0	3.7	6.1	7.5	3.1
Other	6.4	11.9	9.1	10.6	5.4	6.9	4.8
Industrial	6.1	11.3	8.5	10.0	5.2	6.4	4.2
Non-Industrial	.2	.6	.7	.5	.3	.5	.6
Parts Accessories	6.0	5.5	5.3	5.5	6.9	6.8	6.7
6. Consumer Goods	12.2	11.2	12.7	11.5	11.5	10.1	7.9
Durable	3.2	4.4	4.4	4.3	3.1	2.5	2.3
Semi-Durable	3.0	2.4	3.0	2.3	2.8	3.1	2.1
Non-Durable	6.0	4.4	5.3	5.0	5.6	4.4	3.5
7. Other	.2	.1	1.2	5.4	.2	.6	2.0

Origin	Exports by Industrial Origin							
	1971	1974	1975	1978	1979	1980	1981	1982
Total Exports (1 + 2 + 3)	100.0	100.0	100.0	100.0	100.0	100.0	100.0	100.0
1. Agriculture	5.4	4.5	5.7	6.5	5.2	3.3	2.7	2.9
2. Mining Quarrying	39.3	49.8	48.9	57.4	52.9	58.2	61.2	63.1
3. Manufacturing	55.3	45.7	45.3	36.1	41.9	38.5	36.1	33.9
31. Food, Bev., Tobac.	1.5	3.6	3.5	2.6	4.7	5.6	1.5	2.3
32. Textiles	.3	.1	.2	.3	.6	.4	.6	.7
33. Wood, Wood Prod.	1.4	1.8	1.6	1.7	2.7	3.1	2.1	1.7
34. Paper and Prod.	0	~	0	0	0	0	0	0
35. Chemicals	2.3	2.1	3.2	.3	1.0	2.3	1.2	.7
36. Non-Metal Minrl	0	.1	0	0	0	0	0	0
37. Basic Metal Ind.	49.5	37.9	36.5	30.4	29.7	25.3	29.0	27.3
38. Metal Manufact.	.3	.1	.1	.6	.9	1.6	1.6	1.1
39. Oth. Manf. Ind.	0	.1	.2	.1	2.3	0	.1	.1

SOURCE: UN-YITS, 1976; 1977; 1978; 1983; 1985.

Table 2502

BRAZIL PERCENTAGE VALUE OF TRADE, 1970–84

Category	Imports by Broad Economic Category						
	1970	1975	1978	1980	1982	1983	1984
Total Imports	100.0	100.0	100.0	100.0	100.0	100.0	100.0
1. Food and Beverages	10.4	5.9	8.7	8.2	8.3	8.0	8.8
Primary	8.3	4.7	7.4	6.7	7.5	6.5	7.4
For Industry	5.2	3.2	4.8	5.1	6.2	5.5	6.2
For Hshold Consm	3.1	1.5	2.6	1.6	1.3	1.0	1.2
Processed	2.1	1.1	1.3	1.5	.8	1.6	1.3
For Industry	.8	.6	.7	.5	.5	.6	1.0
For Hshold Consm	1.3	.5	.6	1.0	.3	1.0	.3
2. Ind. Supplies Nes.	36.5	33.9	29.4	27.0	18.6	17.2	20.8
Primary	2.0	2.0	3.5	3.4	1.6	2.2	3.0
Processed	34.5	31.9	25.9	23.6	17.0	15.0	17.8
3. Fuels	12.2	25.3	32.5	43.0	53.4	55.8	52.7
Primary	10.6	24.3	31.4	40.7	51.4	54.3	52.1
Processed	1.6	.9	1.1	2.2	2.1	1.5	.6
Motor Spirit	.1	.1	.1	.2	.3	.3	.3
Other	1.5	.8	.9	2.0	1.8	1.2	.3
4. Machinery	27.5	27.8	23.3	15.7	14.6	12.0	11.5
Machines Capt. Eqp	23.6	24.0	18.9	11.9	10.7	8.4	7.8
Parts Accessories	3.9	3.8	4.5	3.7	3.9	3.6	3.7
5. Transport	9.0	4.8	3.6	4.5	3.3	5.0	4.7
Passenger Cars	.1	.1	0	0	~	~	~
Other	5.5	1.9	.9	2.0	1.0	2.5	1.8
Industrial	5.4	1.8	.9	1.9	1.0	2.5	1.8
Non-Industrial	#	0	0	0	0	0	0
Parts Accessories	3.5	2.8	2.7	2.6	2.3	2.4	2.8
6. Consumer Goods	3.7	2.3	2.3	1.6	1.7	1.8	1.4
Durable	1.6	1.1	1.0	.6	.5	.4	.4
Semi-Durable	.9	.5	.4	.3	.3	.4	.3
Non-Durable	1.2	.7	.9	.7	.8	.9	.7
7. Other	.6	.1	.2	.1	.1	.2	.2

Origin	Exports by Industrial Origin							
	1970	1975	1978	1979	1980	1981	1982	1983
Total Exports (1 + 2 + 3)	100.0	100.0	100.0	100.0	100.0	100.0	100.0	100.0
1. Agriculture	53.6	28.4	25.8	22.1	19.9	13.5	16.1	17.6
2. Mining Quarrying	10.2	13.5	9.5	9.7	9.2	10.0	11.6	8.2
3. Manufacturing	36.2	58.1	64.7	68.2	70.9	76.6	72.3	74.1
31. Food, Bev., Tobac.	18.1	27.6	27.3	25.2	26.9	28.5	24.1	24.0
32. Textiles	2.6	7.6	8.1	8.9	7.1	7.0	6.8	8.0
33. Wood, Wood Prod.	3.9	1.6	1.5	1.8	1.9	1.7	1.4	1.4
34. Paper and Prod.	.3	.9	1.2	2.1	2.7	2.6	2.4	2.4
35. Chemicals	2.1	3.7	3.9	5.1	6.4	9.4	11.3	11.9
36. Non-Metal Minrl	.4	.5	.6	.7	.8	.8	.6	.5
37. Basic Metal Ind.	3.8	2.3	4.0	5.6	4.9	4.9	5.5	9.1
38. Metal Manufact.	4.0	11.5	16.8	17.6	18.6	19.9	18.8	15.3
39. Oth. Manf. Ind.	1.0	2.4	1.2	1.2	1.6	1.8	1.4	1.4

SOURCE: UN-YITS, 1977; 1978; 1979; 1980; 1983; 1985.

Table 2503

CHILE PERCENTAGE VALUE OF TRADE, 1970–81

Category	1970	1975	1976	1977	1978	1979	1980	1981
Imports by Broad Economic Category								
Total Imports	100.0	100.0	100.0	100.0	100.0	100.0	100.0	100.0
1. Food and Beverages	12.5	16.3	24.3	10.8	14.6	11.2	13.1	10.4
Primary	8.4	9.8	18.0	5.9	8.1	6.1	5.5	5.1
For Industry	5.2	8.2	16.5	4.1	6.1	4.5	4.0	3.7
For Hshold Consm	3.2	1.6	1.5	1.9	2.0	1.6	1.5	1.4
Processed	4.0	6.5	6.4	4.8	6.4	5.1	7.5	5.3
For Industry	1.9	5.7	5.2	2.3	3.2	2.9	2.9	1.1
For Hshold Consm	2.2	.8	1.2	2.6	3.3	3.0	4.6	4.2
2. Ind. Supplies Nes.	31.1	25.7	22.4	24.2	24.6	21.9	22.5	22.6
Primary	5.6	4.4	5.5	4.2	4.3	3.0	3.2	2.8
Processed	25.5	21.3	16.9	20.0	20.3	18.9	19.3	19.8
3. Fuels	6.0	19.6	11.6	19.8	16.6	21.0	18.3	19.4
Primary	4.1	19.1	10.7	18.7	15.6	20.0	17.0	12.0
Processed	1.9	.6	.9	1.1	1.0	1.1	1.3	2.4
Motor Spirit	.3	0	.2	0	0	0	.2	1.0
Other	1.7	.6	.8	1.1	1.0	1.1	1.0	1.4
4. Machinery	27.7	22.6	21.9	23.1	19.9	15.6	15.7	16.1
Machines Capt. Eqp	23.7	18.7	17.6	19.9	16.9	14.1	13.6	14.0
Parts Accessories	4.0	3.9	4.3	3.2	2.9	1.5	2.1	2.1
5. Transport	16.6	11.5	13.2	12.2	11.4	12.9	14.9	18.2
Passenger Cars	2.5	.8	.8	3.5	2.6	4.5	5.0	7.6
Other	9.0	7.3	7.5	5.6	5.2	6.8	7.3	7.8
Industrial	8.9	7.2	7.3	5.0	4.6	6.5	7.1	7.5
Non-Industrial	#	.1	.1	.6	.6	.3	.2	.2
Parts Accessories	5.1	3.5	4.9	3.1	3.5	1.5	2.6	2.8
6. Consumer Goods	5.8	3.7	5.7	8.1	10.5	10.6	11.9	15.6
Durable	1.5	.9	.9	3.5	5.0	4.6	5.3	6.1
Semi-Durable	1.7	1.0	1.1	2.9	3.4	4.1	4.7	7.1
Non-Durable	2.7	1.7	3.7	1.8	2.0	1.9	2.0	2.4
7. Other	.3	.5	.9	1.8	2.5	6.7	3.6	2.7
Exports by Industrial Origin								
Total Exports (1 + 2 + 3)	100.0	100.0	100.0	100.0	100.0	100.0	100.0	100.0
1. Agriculture	3.2	5.7	5.5	8.4	9.9	8.4	8.7	10.6
2. Mining Quarrying	10.0	9.9	10.7	8.7	11.4	12.9	11.1	17.0
3. Manufacturing	86.8	84.5	83.8	82.9	78.6	78.6	80.2	72.4
31. Food, Bev., Tobac.	2.2	6.1	5.9	7.7	8.2	7.0	8.9	9.3
32. Textiles	#	.4	1.0	.4	.4	.2	.2	.2
33. Wood, Wood Prod.	.7	1.5	1.6	2.6	2.7	2.8	3.0	2.5
34. Paper and Prod.	2.7	6.0	6.0	6.0	7.0	5.7	5.6	6.3
35. Chemicals	1.3	4.3	3.6	8.7	4.7	3.7	5.4	4.3
36. Non-Metal Minrl	#	.3	.2	.3	.2	.2	.2	.1
37. Basic Metal Ind.	78.3	64.2	63.2	54.3	52.5	56.9	53.2	46.1
38. Metal Manufact.	1.3	1.6	2.3	2.5	2.2	2.2	2.8	3.3
39. Oth. Manf. Ind.	.1	0	0	.4	.7	0	.8	.3

SOURCE: UN-YITS, 1976; 1980; 1983; 1984; 1985.

Table 2504

COLOMBIA PERCENTAGE VALUE OF TRADE, 1970–84

| | | Imports by Broad Economic Category | | | | | | |
Category	1970	1975	1976	1980	1982	1983	1984
Total Imports	100.0	100.0	100.0	100.0	100.0	100.0	100.0
1. Food and Beverages	5.6	8.2	10.8	9.2	8.5	8.9	8.1
Primary	3.6	5.2	5.7	5.1	4.4	5.7	5.0
For Industry	3.2	4.3	4.6	3.9	3.2	4.4	4.2
For Hshold Consm	.5	.9	1.1	1.1	1.2	1.4	.7
Processed	1.9	3.1	5.2	4.2	4.1	3.1	3.1
For Industry	.9	1.4	3.0	1.9	2.4	1.7	1.8
For Hshold Consm	1.0	1.6	2.2	2.3	1.8	1.4	1.3
2. Ind. Supplies Nes.	39.8	45.2	39.2	35.1	34.4	32.7	39.5
Primary	3.3	3.1	3.2	2.9	2.5	2.2	2.4
Processed	36.5	42.1	36.0	32.2	31.9	30.5	37.1
3. Fuels	.4	1.0	2.3	12.1	12.1	12.9	10.4
Primary	#	0	1.9	3.2	4.3	7.7	6.3
Processed	.4	1.0	.4	8.9	7.8	5.2	4.1
Motor Spirit	#	.7	.1	6.6	4.5	4.3	3.7
Other	.4	.2	.3	2.4	3.3	.9	.3
4. Machinery	27.6	23.1	23.6	23.4	24.5	26.2	24.6
Machines Capt. Eqp	23.8	19.1	19.9	20.6	21.3	23.0	21.4
Parts Accessories	3.8	3.9	3.7	2.8	3.2	3.1	3.2
5. Transport	20.0	17.1	16.6	15.0	15.6	14.0	11.7
Passenger Cars	3.5	1.4	1.6	3.9	5.1	4.0	3.2
Other	8.0	9.5	8.4	5.1	5.1	5.1	3.3
Industrial	7.9	9.5	8.3	4.4	4.8	4.9	3.1
Non-Industrial	#	.1	.2	.7	.3	.2	.2
Parts Accessories	8.5	6.2	6.6	5.9	5.4	4.9	5.2
6. Consumer Goods	6.1	4.8	4.3	4.4	4.2	4.2	3.7
Durable	1.2	.8	.9	1.0	.9	.8	.7
Semi-Durable	.8	1.3	1.2	1.1	1.1	1.2	1.2
Non-Durable	4.1	2.7	2.2	2.3	2.1	2.2	1.8
7. Other	.6	.6	3.2	.8	.7	1.2	2.0

| | | Exports by Industrial Origin | | | | | | |
Origin	1970	1975	1976	1980	1982	1983	1984
Total Exports (1 + 2 + 3)	100.0	100.0	100.0	100.0	100.0	100.0	100.0
1. Agriculture	76.6	60.1	67.6	69.1	62.7	60.3	63.5
2. Mining Quarrying	8.6	1.1	.9	2.0	1.9	1.7	1.9
3. Manufacturing	14.8	38.8	31.6	28.9	35.4	37.9	34.7
31. Food, Bev., Tobac.	3.8	11.2	5.6	7.4	5.2	5.5	3.7
32. Textiles	2.8	8.1	9.1	7.4	8.9	5.3	4.2
33. Wood, Wood Prod.	.6	.4	.7	.3	.4	.3	.2
34. Paper and Prod.	.5	1.1	2.0	1.8	2.4	1.8	2.0
35. Chemicals	3.9	11.7	7.5	5.3	10.4	18.0	17.2
36. Non-Metal Minrl	1.2	1.8	2.3	1.8	2.0	1.1	1.0
37. Basic Metal Ind.	.7	.4	.4	.1	.1	1.6	2.2
38. Metal Manufact.	1.3	3.6	3.6	3.7	5.1	2.5	1.7
39. Oth. Manf. Ind.	.1	.6	.4	1.1	.8	1.8	2.4

SOURCE: UN-YITS, 1976; 1981; 1983; 1985.

Table 2505

COSTA RICA PERCENTAGE VALUE OF TRADE, 1970–82

Category	1970	1975	1978	1979	1980	1981	1982
	Imports by Broad Economic Category						
Total Imports	100.0	100.0	100.0	100.0	100.0	100.0	100.0
1. Food and Beverages	8.8	8.5	6.2	6.2	7.1	6.7	6.6
Primary	4.8	4.9	2.4	2.5	3.3	3.8	3.7
For Industry	2.6	4.0	1.8	1.8	2.0	2.7	2.2
For Hshold Consm	2.3	.9	.6	.8	1.3	1.1	1.4
Processed	4.0	3.6	3.8	3.7	3.8	2.8	2.9
For Industry	1.3	1.2	.9	.8	1.0	.9	1.1
For Hshold Consm	2.7	2.4	2.9	2.9	2.8	2.0	1.8
2. Ind. Supplies Nes.	44.1	43.0	37.0	35.3	38.4	39.6	41.3
Primary	2.6	1.7	1.3	1.5	2.3	1.8	2.9
Processed	41.5	41.3	35.7	33.8	36.1	37.8	38.4
3. Fuels	3.6	10.3	9.3	12.7	14.7	15.9	19.8
Primary	1.8	3.8	3.9	4.5	8.0	10.4	11.2
Processed	1.8	6.5	5.4	8.2	6.7	5.5	8.6
Motor Spirit	.4	1.5	1.2	1.5	1.7	1.1	1.7
Other	.4	5.0	4.2	6.6	4.9	4.4	6.9
4. Machinery	16.8	16.8	17.3	19.2	15.2	16.1	10.7
Machines Capt. Eqp	15.9	15.7	16.3	18.2	14.2	15.2	9.7
Parts Accessories	.9	1.1	1.0	1.0	1.0	.9	1.0
5. Transport	10.9	10.4	12.5	11.2	8.7	6.5	4.4
Passenger Cars	2.2	1.9	2.5	2.4	2.1	1.0	.2
Other	3.8	4.0	4.9	4.3	2.1	1.7	1.8
Industrial	3.0	3.8	4.6	4.0	1.7	1.5	1.7
Non-Industrial	.3	.2	.3	.3	.4	.2	.1
Parts Accessories	5.4	4.5	5.0	4.5	4.4	3.8	2.4
6. Consumer Goods	15.6	10.4	12.7	11.8	11.7	8.9	7.9
Durable	2.6	1.1	2.4	2.1	1.8	1.4	.8
Semi-Durable	7.0	4.3	5.1	4.6	4.7	3.1	2.5
Non-Durable	6.0	5.0	5.2	5.2	5.2	4.5	4.6
7. Other	.2	.7	5.0	3.6	4.2	6.2	9.3

Origin	1970	1975	1978	1979	1980	1981	1982
	Exports by Industrial Origin						
Total Exports (1 + 2 + 3)	100.0	100.0	100.0	100.0	100.0	100.0	100.0
1. Agriculture	63.4	53.3	58.1	58.6	48.1	49.1	58.7
2. Mining Quarrying	0	0	0	0	.1	0	0
3. Manufacturing	36.6	46.7	41.9	41.4	51.8	50.8	41.3
31. Food, Bev., Tobac.	16.4	20.2	13.1	16.7	16.8	17.6	11.8
32. Textiles	4.4	4.6	3.8	4.5	6.8	5.4	4.6
33. Wood, Wood Prod.	.6	.6	.7	.6	.9	1.0	1.0
34. Paper and Prod.	1.1	1.3	.7	1.0	1.9	1.5	1.7
35. Chemicals	6.9	11.2	8.2	8.3	10.2	12.0	10.4
36. Non-Metal Minrl	.1	.1	.3	.9	.9	2.3	1.3
37. Basic Metal Ind.	.7	.9	1.2	1.2	1.7	1.3	.9
38. Metal Manufact.	4.7	5.1	5.2	5.4	6.3	6.2	5.9
39. Oth. Manf. Ind.	1.6	2.8	8.7	2.7	6.4	3.4	3.8

SOURCE: UN-YITS, 1976; 1981; 1983; 1984; 1985.

Table 2506

CUBA TOTAL TRADE VALUE, 1950–85, AND PERCENTAGES ACCORDING TO ORIGIN, 1970–83

Historical Series, 1950-80, Special Trade, Imports CIF, Exports FOB.
(M Pesos)

Year	Imports	Exports
1950	515.4	642.0
1951	640.2	766.1
1952	618.2	675.3
1953	489.7	640.3
1954	487.9	539.0
1955	575.1	594.2
1956	649.0	666.2
1957	772.8	807.7
1958	777.0	733.5
1959	673.5	637.4
1960	579.9	618.2
1961	638.7	624.7
1962	759.3	520.7
1963	867.3	543.8
1964	1,018.8	713.8
1965	866.2	690.6
1966	925.5	597.8
1967	999.1	705.0
1968	1,102.3	651.4
1969	1,221.6	666.7
1970	1,311.0	1,049.5
1971	1,386.6	861.2
1972	1,189.8	770.9
1973	1,467.0	1,153.0
1974	2,225.9	2,236.5
1975	3,113.0	2,952.2
1976	3,179.7	2,692.3
1977	3,461.6	2,918.4
1978	3,573.8	3,440.1
1979	3,687.0	3,500.4
1980	4,627.0	3,967.0
1981	5,114.0	4,224.0
1982	5,531.0	4,933.0
1983	6,218.0	5,523.0
1984	7,207.2	5,462.1
1985	5,982.8	7,904.5

Exports by Industrial Origin
(Percentage of Total Value)[1]

Origin	1970	1975	1976	1977	1978	1979	1980	1981	1982	1983
Total Exports (1 + 2 + 3)	100.0	100.0	100.0	100.0	100.0	100.0	100.0	100.0	100.0	100.0
1. Agriculture	5.2	3.5	4.3	4.4	4.4	5.4	4.3	4.7	5.0	4.8
2. Mining Quarrying	16.4	4.6	5.9	6.3	4.5	4.4	4.6	7.9	5.9	5.4
3. Manufacturing	78.4	91.9	89.8	89.3	91.1	90.2	91.1	87.4	89.1	89.8
31. Food, Bev., Tobac.	78.4	91.9	89.2	86.1	88.9	87.7	85.6	81.9	81.6	78.6
32. Textiles	~	0	0	~	~	~	~	~	~	~
33. Wood, Wood Prod.	~	~	~	~	~	~	~	~	~	~
34. Paper and Prod.	~	~	~	~	~	~	~	~	~	~
35. Chemicals	~	4.6	5.9	~	0	0	0	4.4	7.1	10.9
36. Non-Metal Minrl	~	~	~	~	~	~	~	.3	.2	~
37. Basic Metal Ind.	~	~	~	~	~	~	~	.1	.4	.3
38. Metal Manufact.	~	~	~	~	~	~	~	~	~	~
39. Oth. Manf. Ind.	~	~	.6	3.1	2.1	2.5	5.4	1.1	1.2	~

1. No percentages on imports available in source.

SOURCE: UN-YITS, 1976; 1981, 1983; 1984; 1985.

Table 2507

DOMINICAN REPUBLIC PERCENTAGE VALUE OF TRADE, 1970–83

Category	Imports by Broad Economic Category						
	1970	1978	1979	1980	1981	1982	1983
Total Imports	100.0	100.0	100.0	100.0	100.0	100.0	100.0
1. Food and Beverages	12.7	13.1	13.7	13.5	14.2	12.5	11.7
Primary	3.9	6.1	4.8	6.7	7.5	4.5	4.8
For Industry	1.4	4.3	2.2	4.0	5.3	2.5	3.1
For Hshold Consm	2.5	1.8	2.5	2.7	2.2	2.1	1.7
Processed	8.8	7.0	8.9	6.8	6.7	7.9	6.9
For Industry	.9	3.4	5.2	3.3	3.3	5.6	3.8
For Hshold Consm	7.9	3.6	3.7	3.5	3.4	2.4	3.0
2. Ind. Supplies Nes.	28.7	32.4	32.2	31.4	26.3	28.4	28.1
Primary	2.0	3.8	3.7	3.8	3.5	2.9	3.4
Processed	26.7	28.6	28.5	27.6	22.7	25.5	24.6
3. Fuels	6.9	22.0	25.9	24.9	32.5	33.7	35.9
Primary	2.4	20.8	23.7	23.7	27.5	26.3	26.7
Processed	4.5	1.2	2.2	1.2	5.0	7.5	9.1
Motor Spirit	2.5	.1	.5	.2	.2	.1	.4
Other	1.9	1.1	1.7	1.0	4.8	7.3	8.7
4. Machinery	22.7	14.6	12.9	14.9	13.7	13.1	12.3
Machines Capt. Eqp	~	13.2	11.3	13.4	12.5	11.9	10.0
Parts Accessories	~	1.3	1.6	1.5	1.2	1.2	1.7
5. Transport	13.3	9.5	8.1	8.6	7.6	6.2	5.5
Passenger Cars	~	1.9	1.6	1.4	.6	1.0	.4
Other	~	3.6	3.1	3.8	3.6	2.0	1.7
Industrial	~	3.3	2.7	2.8	2.7	1.3	1.0
Non-Industrial	~	.2	.4	1.0	.9	.7	.7
Parts Accessories	~	4.1	3.4	3.4	3.4	3.2	3.5
6. Consumer Goods	12.5	8.2	7.0	6.5	5.7	6.1	6.6
Durable	.4	1.4	1.2	1.2	.9	.9	1.0
Semi-Durable	4.3	2.3	1.9	1.7	1.4	1.3	1.5
Non-Durable	7.9	4.6	3.9	3.6	3.4	3.9	4.1
7. Other	3.0	.1	.1	.1	0	0	0

Origin	Exports by Industrial Origin						
	1970	1978	1979	1980	1981	1982	1983
Total Exports (1 + 2 + 3)	100.0	100.0	100.0	100.0	100.0	100.0	100.0
1. Agriculture	32.0	41.3	40.2	26.2	21.7	31.9	28.1
2. Mining Quarrying	7.3	4.2	3.1	3.0	1.8	1.2	.3
3. Manufacturing	60.7	54.5	56.7	70.8	76.4	66.9	71.7
31. Food, Bev., Tobac.	55.6	33.3	30.8	47.1	57.6	50.5	47.0
32. Textiles	.1	1.4	1.3	1.1	.7	1.2	1.1
33. Wood, Wood Prod.	0	0	0	0	0	0	0
34. Paper and Prod.	.1	.1	.1	.1	.1	.1	.1
35. Chemicals	3.2	5.9	5.4	6.0	4.5	5.7	4.2
36. Non-Metal Minrl	.1	.1	.3	.7	1.0	1.2	.5
37. Basic Metal Ind.	.1	12.3	16.5	14.5	11.2	3.9	13.1
38. Metal Manufact.	.2	1.3	2.4	1.2	1.3	4.3	5.1
39. Oth. Manf. Ind.	1.4	0	0	.1	0	0	0

SOURCE: UN-YITS, 1976; 1981; 1983; 1985.

Table 2508

ECUADOR PERCENTAGE VALUE OF TRADE, 1972–82

Category	Imports by Broad Economic Category							
	1972	1975	1976	1977	1978	1980	1981	1982
Total Imports	100.0	100.0	100.0	100.0	100.0	100.0	100.0	100.0
1. Food and Beverages	7.8	7.1	6.8	5.4	6.3	7.6	5.6	4.3
Primary	3.5	4.2	3.2	2.3	2.5	3.8	3.1	1.6
For Industry	3.4	4.0	2.9	2.1	2.1	3.5	2.9	1.4
For Hshold Consm	.2	.2	.3	.2	.4	.3	.2	.2
Processed	4.3	2.9	3.6	3.1	3.8	3.8	2.5	2.6
For Industry	2.6	1.0	1.7	1.2	1.2	1.1	.7	1.5
For Hshold Consm	1.7	1.9	1.9	1.9	2.6	2.6	1.8	1.1
2. Ind. Supplies Nes.	33.5	34.7	36.0	35.5	31.9	34.6	27.9	40.2
Primary	2.0	1.5	2.0	2.3	1.9	1.2	1.1	1.5
Processed	31.5	33.2	34.0	33.2	30.0	33.4	26.7	38.7
3. Fuels	6.3	1.9	1.0	.6	.7	1.0	12.9	1.3
Primary	1.7	.2	.1	0	0	0	1.3	0
Processed	4.6	1.6	.9	.6	.7	1.0	11.6	1.3
Motor Spirit	.2	0	~	0	0	0	6.4	0
Other	4.4	1.6	.9	.6	.7	1.0	5.2	1.3
4. Machinery	25.3	29.9	30.4	28.9	30.4	28.3	29.4	29.4
Machines Capt. Eqp	22.8	27.9	27.9	26.7	28.0	25.9	27.1	26.2
Parts Accessories	2.5	2.0	2.4	2.2	2.3	2.4	2.3	3.3
5. Transport	15.2	17.1	15.6	20.8	20.0	21.2	17.6	15.8
Passenger Cars	1.9	.6	.4	.5	2.9	2.6	1.7	2.2
Other	7.3	11.5	10.1	14.6	11.2	11.9	8.5	6.2
Industrial	7.3	11.3	9.9	14.5	11.1	11.8	8.5	6.1
Non-Industrial	0	.2	.1	.1	.1	0	.1	.1
Parts Accessories	5.9	5.1	5.2	5.7	5.9	6.8	7.4	7.3
6. Consumer Goods	11.5	8.6	8.5	7.9	8.7	6.4	6.2	8.8
Durable	2.9	2.2	2.3	2.2	3.0	1.9	1.4	1.7
Semi-Durable	1.5	1.8	1.8	1.8	1.8	1.9	1.4	2.2
Non-Durable	7.1	4.5	4.4	3.8	3.8	2.5	3.4	4.9
7. Other	.3	.7	1.7	1.0	2.1	.8	.3	.1

Origin	Exports by Industrial Origin							
	1972	1975	1976	1977	1978	1980	1981	1982
Total Exports (1 + 2 + 3)	100.0	100.0	100.0	100.0	100.0	100.0	100.0	100.0
1. Agriculture	70.8	29.1	29.6	30.4	33.0	18.8	22.2	25.4
2. Mining Quarrying	18.6	60.3	58.9	49.0	40.0	55.5	54.2	64.3
3. Manufacturing	10.7	10.6	11.5	20.6	26.9	25.7	23.5	10.4
31. Food, Bev., Tobac.	8.0	7.3	8.3	17.1	17.7	14.4	11.8	6.8
32. Textiles	.8	1.0	1.1	.6	.6	.6	.6	.4
33. Wood, Wood Prod.	.4	1.0	.9	.9	1.0	1.2	1.6	1.5
34. Paper and Prod.	.2	.1	.1	.1	.1	.1	.1	.1
35. Chemicals	.8	.4	.4	1.0	6.4	7.9	8.2	.3
36. Non-Metal Minrl	0	0	0	0	0	.1	.2	.1
37. Basic Metal Ind.	0	0	0	0	0	.1	.1	.1
38. Metal Manufact.	.4	.5	.5	.7	1.0	1.2	1.0	1.0
39. Oth. Manf. Ind.	.1	.2	.1	.1	.1	.1	.1	.1

SOURCE: UN-YITS, 1977; 1981; 1983; 1984; 1985.

Table 2509

EL SALVADOR PERCENTAGE VALUE OF TRADE, 1970–82

	Imports by Broad Economic Category						
Category	1970	1975	1976	1979	1980	1981	1982
Total Imports	100.0	100.0	100.0	100.0	100.0	100.0	100.0
1. Food and Beverages	11.4	9.9	9.6	10.1	15.3	13.7	14.8
Primary	4.9	4.8	4.4	4.2	7.9	6.3	8.3
For Industry	2.4	2.9	2.8	2.1	2.9	1.1	3.6
For Hshold Consm	2.5	1.9	1.6	2.1	5.0	5.1	4.7
Processed	6.5	5.1	5.2	5.9	7.3	7.5	6.5
For Industry	1.2	.6	1.1	.8	1.2	1.6	1.7
For Hshold Consm	5.3	4.5	4.1	5.1	6.1	5.8	4.8
2. Ind. Supplies Nes.	45.0	41.6	40.6	41.1	37.4	38.4	35.0
Primary	1.5	2.2	1.4	2.2	1.7	1.7	1.6
Processed	43.6	39.4	39.2	38.9	35.7	36.6	33.4
3. Fuels	2.2	8.3	7.2	9.3	17.6	20.7	24.4
Primary	1.4	7.7	6.7	8.7	17.0	20.0	23.5
Processed	.8	.6	.5	.6	.6	.7	.9
Motor Spirit	.1	.1	.1	.1	.1	.1	.3
Other	.6	.5	.5	.5	.5	.6	.6
4. Machinery	14.1	19.1	20.1	14.7	9.3	8.2	8.6
Machines Capt. Eqp	13.2	18.2	19.2	13.5	8.5	7.4	7.9
Parts Accessories	.9	.9	.9	1.1	.8	.8	.8
5. Transport	9.8	8.0	9.2	9.7	4.5	4.8	3.9
Passenger Cars	3.0	1.2	1.7	1.3	.6	.2	.2
Other	3.0	3.9	4.6	5.1	1.6	2.2	1.0
Industrial	3.0	3.7	4.4	4.8	1.4	2.1	.9
Non-Industrial	.1	.1	.2	.3	.2	.1	.1
Parts Accessories	3.8	2.9	2.9	3.3	2.4	2.4	2.6
6. Consumer Goods	17.3	13.1	13.1	14.9	15.8	14.2	13.2
Durable	2.4	1.7	1.8	2.3	1.3	1.0	.8
Semi-Durable	5.3	4.6	4.7	5.0	5.9	4.7	4.1
Non-Durable	9.6	6.8	6.7	7.7	8.7	8.5	8.2
7. Other	.2	.1	.2	.2	.1	.1	.2

	Exports by Industrial Origin						
Origin	1970	1975	1976	1979	1980	1981	1982
Total Exports (1 + 2 + 3)	100.0	100.0	100.0	100.0	100.0	100.0	100.0
1. Agriculture	62.8	50.5	64.5	66.8	53.5	49.4	46.1
2. Mining Quarrying	.2	.3	.3	.1	.4	.3	.5
3. Manufacturing	37.0	49.2	35.2	33.1	46.1	50.3	53.3
31. Food, Bev., Tobac.	6.7	19.9	9.3	6.6	5.4	6.6	8.5
32. Textiles	13.8	10.9	10.3	10.4	16.1	16.4	17.5
33. Wood, Wod Prod.	0	0	0	.1	.1	.1	0
34. Paper and Prod.	1.9	2.9	2.8	3.0	4.8	5.7	6.8
35. Chemicals	7.1	8.4	7.1	6.2	10.1	11.8	10.9
36. Non-Metal Minrl	.2	.2	.2	.8	.9	1.0	1.2
37. Basic Metal Ind.	2.0	1.6	1.3	2.0	2.5	2.3	1.7
38. Metal Manufact.	4.6	4.5	3.5	3.4	5.2	5.4	5.6
39. Oth. Manf. Ind.	.5	.8	.7	.6	.9	1.0	1.1

SOURCE: UN-YITS, 1976; 1981; 1983; 1984; 1985.

Table 2510

GUATEMALA PERCENTAGE VALUE OF TRADE, 1970–81

Category	Imports by Broad Economic Category					
	1970	1975	1978	1979	1980	1981
Total Imports	100.0	100.0	100.0	100.0	100.0	100.0
1. Food and Beverages	8.7	7.1	5.1	5.4	5.6	4.5
Primary	3.5	3.7	1.7	2.0	2.3	1.9
For Industry	2.9	2.6	1.2	1.6	1.8	1.4
For Hshold Consm	.6	1.0	.5	.4	.5	.5
Processed	5.1	3.4	3.5	3.4	3.3	2.7
For Industry	1.0	.6	.9	.8	.8	.8
For Hshold Consm	4.2	2.8	2.6	2.6	2.5	1.9
2. Ind. Supplies Nes.	46.7	40.9	40.0	40.3	38.5	32.2
Primary	1.7	2.4	2.0	1.9	2.6	1.7
Processed	45.0	38.6	38.0	38.5	35.9	30.4
3. Fuels	1.4	13.7	12.4	10.2	23.8	37.4
Primary	.4	10.1	7.0	1.3	11.4	5.6
Processed	1.1	3.6	5.4	8.9	12.4	31.8
Motor Spirit	.2	1.9	1.8	3.2	5.1	2.3
Other	.9	1.7	3.5	5.7	7.4	29.5
4. Machinery	16.9	16.2	18.1	18.6	12.9	11.4
Machines Cap. Eqp	15.8	15.2	16.8	17.4	11.8	10.5
Parts Accessories	1.1	1.1	1.3	1.2	1.1	.8
5. Transport	9.9	10.9	11.8	12.4	9.0	5.5
Passenger Cars	2.3	1.6	2.6	3.2	2.1	1.2
Other	3.6	5.5	5.3	5.5	3.9	2.0
Industrial	3.5	5.4	5.3	5.4	3.8	1.9
Non-Industrial	.1	0	.1	0	0	.1
Parts Accessories	4.0	3.9	3.9	3.7	3.1	2.3
6. Consumer Goods	16.2	11.0	12.3	12.7	10.0	8.8
Durable	2.6	2.0	2.9	2.8	2.2	1.7
Semi-Durable	6.8	4.6	5.0	4.8	3.9	3.8
Non-Durable	6.8	4.5	4.4	5.0	4.0	3.3
7. Other	.2	.1	.3	.3	.1	.2

Origin	Exports by Industrial Origin					
	1970	1975	1978	1979	1980	1981
Total Exports (1 + 2 + 3)	100.0	100.0	100.0	100.0	100.0	100.0
1. Agriculture	55.4	47.6	66.4	65.8	57.6	51.3
2. Mining Quarrying	.3	.7	.3	.4	1.4	2.2
3. Manufacturing	44.3	51.7	33.3	33.8	41.0	46.5
31. Food, Bev., Tobac.	15.2	26.0	11.4	9.4	11.9	16.6
32. Textiles	10.6	7.7	5.6	6.7	7.0	7.0
33. Wood, Wood Prod.	.8	.6	.5	.3	.2	.3
34. Paper and Prod.	1.7	1.6	1.2	1.4	1.5	2.0
35. Chemicals	8.7	8.7	8.4	8.9	10.6	13.6
36. Non-Metal Minrl	2.1	2.7	2.2	1.8	1.6	2.1
37. Basic Metal Ind.	1.3	.8	1.1	2.4	5.3	1.4
38. Metal Manufact.	3.5	3.1	2.5	2.6	2.6	3.1
39. Oth. Manf. Ind.	.3	.5	.3	.3	.4	.4

SOURCE: UN-YITS, 1976; 1981; 1983; 1984; 1985.

Table 2511

HAITI PERCENTAGE VALUE OF TRADE, 1970–79

	Imports by Broad Economic Category							
Category	1970	1972	1974	1975	1976	1977	1978	1979
Total Imports	100.0	100.0	100.0	100.0	100.0	100.0	100.0	100.0
1. Food and Beverages	16.5	22.2	19.7	25.1	27.0	23.7	21.9	19.9
Primary	3.0	7.0	6.3	13.1	11.1	9.3	7.8	5.7
For Industry	1.9	5.8	5.2	12.0	10.0	8.0	6.3	4.1
For Hshold Consm	1.2	1.2	1.1	1.1	1.2	1.3	1.5	1.6
Processed	13.4	15.2	13.4	11.9	15.9	14.4	14.1	14.1
For Industry	6.2	6.8	5.2	4.7	6.4	7.8	4.3	5.5
For Hshold Consm	7.2	8.4	8.2	7.3	9.4	6.6	9.8	8.6
2. Ind. Supplies Nes.	32.1	32.0	33.1	29.0	29.5	29.2	30.3	32.3
Primary	2.0	2.2	3.5	4.0	3.3	3.1	3.5	2.4
Processed	30.1	29.9	29.6	25.0	26.3	26.1	26.8	29.9
3. Fuels	5.5	6.0	11.2	9.1	8.2	11.0	11.0	12.9
Primary	~	.2	.3	.3	.2	.2	.2	.2
Processed	~	5.8	10.8	8.8	8.0	10.7	10.7	12.7
Motor Spirit	~	1.5	3.8	2.6	2.2	3.0	3.2	3.8
Other	~	4.3	7.1	6.2	5.8	7.7	7.6	8.9
4. Machinery	12.7	10.0	7.6	10.7	10.1	11.3	7.5	7.6
Machines Capt. Eqp	~	~	7.1	10.2	9.8	10.9	7.2	6.8
Parts Accessories	~	~	.5	.5	.3	.4	.3	.9
5. Transport	10.3	9.2	8.6	9.3	8.0	8.9	12.8	11.9
Passenger Cars	~	2.7	1.6	1.7	1.9	2.1	2.7	5.0
Other	~	.4	3.9	4.3	3.2	3.7	6.6	3.5
Industrial	~	.4	3.9	4.2	3.2	3.6	6.4	3.3
Non-Industrial	~	~	0	.1	.1	.1	.2	.1
Parts Accessories	~	6.1	3.1	3.4	2.8	3.2	3.4	3.4
6. Consumer Goods	20.2	17.0	15.9	12.9	13.6	15.4	16.0	14.8
Durable	2.1	2.0	4.2	3.1	2.7	2.6	2.9	2.5
Semi-Durable	9.7	8.1	5.4	4.6	6.2	8.2	7.9	6.7
Non-Durable	8.4	6.8	6.3	5.2	4.7	4.6	5.2	5.6
7. Other	2.7	3.7	3.9	3.9	3.6	.6	.5	.6

	Export by Industrial Origin							
Origin	1970	1972	1974	1975	1976	1977	1978	1979
Total Exports (1 + 2 + 3)	100.0	100.0	100.0	100.0	100.0	100.0	100.0	100.0
1. Agriculture	47.0	40.7	43.0	28.2	41.4	49.8	45.2	35.2
2. Mining Quarrying	16.9	16.6	9.6	12.9	15.6	12.1	10.8	12.1
3. Manufacturing	36.1	42.7	47.4	58.9	43.0	38.1	44.0	52.6
31. Food, Bev., Tobac.	10.4	13.7	10.0	19.0	5.3	2.5	4.9	1.5
32. Textiles	8.9	8.3	13.5	14.5	9.2	9.3	6.8	10.6
33. Wood, Wood Prod.	1.7	1.8	1.3	.9	.7	.5	~	~
34. Paper and Prod.	~	~	0	0	0	0	0	.8
35. Chemicals	9.2	9.6	9.2	6.1	7.2	4.7	6.4	5.0
36. Non-Metal Minrl	~	0	0	.1	2.1	2.2	1.8	.5
37. Basic Metal Ind.	~	~	0	~	~	~	~	~
38. Metal Manufact.	2.3	5.9	9.5	14.8	14.2	13.3	15.5	9.2
39. Oth. Manf. Ind.	3.5	3.4	3.8	3.5	4.2	5.6	8.5	25.0

SOURCE: UN-YITS, 1976; 1981; 1983; 1984; 1985.

Table 2512

HONDURAS PERCENTAGE VALUE OF TRADE, 1970–83

Category	Imports by Broad Economic Category							
	1970	1975	1976	1979	1980	1981	1982	1983
Total Imports	100.0	100.0	100.0	100.0	100.0	100.0	100.0	100.0
1. Food and Beverages	10.0	10.1	8.8	7.1	7.7	8.7	8.5	8.1
Primary	2.4	3.4	2.5	2.1	2.2	2.3	2.7	2.0
For Industry	1.7	3.1	2.1	1.7	1.7	1.7	2.3	1.7
For Hshold Consm	.7	.3	.4	.4	.6	.7	.4	.3
Processed	7.5	6.6	6.3	5.0	5.4	6.3	5.8	6.1
For Industry	1.6	1.4	1.8	.7	1.1	1.5	1.0	1.0
For Hshold Consm	5.9	5.2	4.5	4.3	4.3	4.9	4.8	5.2
2. Ind. Supplies Nes.	36.1	34.0	37.3	36.1	33.7	34.7	35.0	38.1
Primary	.8	3.1	1.7	1.2	2.4	1.5	1.1	1.6
Processed	35.4	31.0	35.7	34.9	31.3	33.2	33.9	36.5
3. Fuels	6.3	16.7	10.2	12.6	15.6	15.5	21.4	22.0
Primary	4.9	15.0	8.8	9.7	11.8	7.3	2.5	12.4
Processed	1.4	1.7	1.4	2.9	3.8	8.2	18.9	9.6
Motor Spirit	.3	.2	.2	.7	.7	2.1	4.4	2.4
Other	1.1	1.5	1.2	2.2	3.0	6.2	14.5	7.2
4. Machinery	16.8	17.0	16.5	19.3	18.6	17.1	12.1	12.9
Machines Capt. Eqp	16.2	16.3	15.8	18.8	18.0	16.5	11.6	12.3
Parts Accessories	.6	.7	.7	.5	.6	.6	.5	.6
5. Transport	12.8	10.6	13.1	12.2	11.1	9.2	8.1	6.4
Passenger Cars	2.1	1.0	1.1	1.4	1.3	1.3	1.3	.5
Other	6.3	5.7	7.3	.8	5.9	4.3	3.3	1.8
Industrial	6.1	5.5	7.1	.8	5.8	4.1	3.1	1.8
Non-Industrial	.2	.1	.2	.1	.2	.2	.2	.1
Parts Accessories	4.4	3.9	4.7	9.9	3.9	3.7	3.5	4.1
6. Consumer Goods	17.7	11.3	13.8	12.5	13.2	14.4	14.1	12.1
Durable	2.6	2.2	2.7	2.1	2.6	2.7	2.1	1.5
Semi-Durable	7.8	3.5	4.4	4.7	4.7	5.1	4.8	3.1
Non-Durable	7.3	5.7	6.7	5.8	5.9	6.5	7.2	7.4
7. Other	.3	.4	.3	.3	.2	.3	.7	.4

Origin	Exports by Industrial Origin							
	1970	1975	1976	1979	1980	1981	1982	1983
Total Exports (1 + 2 + 3)	100.0	100.0	100.0	100.0	100.0	100.0	100.0	100.0
1. Agriculture	64.0	49.9	62.1	63.5	63.7	63.3	67.8	65.1
2. Mining Quarrying	5.2	10.8	8.2	6.2	6.5	5.2	3.9	6.5
3. Manufacturing	30.8	39.3	29.7	30.3	29.8	31.5	28.2	28.4
31. Food, Bev., Tobac.	9.3	11.5	9.9	13.6	14.3	16.2	13.0	14.0
32. Textiles	2.8	2.3	2.5	2.2	2.8	2.7	1.8	1.5
33. Wood, Wood Prod.	9.6	13.7	10.6	8.4	4.9	5.5	8.3	7.1
34. Paper and Prod.	.7	.4	.3	.5	.6	.7	.6	.6
35. Chemicals	7.6	8.4	4.1	3.9	5.1	4.6	3.4	4.0
36. Non-Metal Minrl	.1	1.1	.3	0	.1	.4	.1	0
37. Basic Metal Ind.	.5	.4	.3	.2	.2	.1	.1	0
38. Metal Manufact.	.2	1.4	1.5	1.4	1.5	1.4	1.0	1.1
39. Oth. Manf. Ind.	0	.1	.1	1.1	.1	.1	.1	.1

SOURCE: UN-YITS, 1976; 1981; 1983; 1985.

Table 2513

MEXICO PERCENTAGE VALUE OF TRADE, 1970–82

Category	Imports by Broad Economic Category								
	1970	1974	1975	1976	1977	1978	1979	1981	1982
Total Imports	100.0	100.0	100.0	100.0	100.0	100.0	100.0	100.0	100.0
1. Food and Beverages	3.8	12.0	5.9	5.2	8.9	8.2	7.5	8.6	8.3
Primary	1.9	8.0	4.5	3.3	6.6	6.3	5.7	6.1	5.9
For Industry	1.3	7.1	3.2	2.9	5.9	5.7	5.0	4.8	4.7
For Hshold Consm	.6	1.0	1.4	.4	.7	.6	.7	1.4	1.2
Processed	2.0	4.0	1.4	1.9	2.4	1.9	1.8	2.4	2.4
For Industry	.5	1.2	.2	.3	.7	.6	.1	1.5	1.0
For Hshold Consm	1.4	2.8	1.2	1.6	1.7	1.4	1.7	.9	1.5
2. Ind. Supplies Nes.	35.5	38.8	38.8	34.0	37.9	40.0	35.4	26.3	28.5
Primary	8.6	9.0	11.4	6.2	8.2	7.3	6.3	3.9	3.0
Processed	26.8	29.8	27.4	27.8	29.7	32.8	29.1	22.4	25.5
3. Fuels	2.8	6.7	5.0	5.3	2.3	2.7	2.1	1.4	2.8
Primary	1.3	3.5	2.1	1.8	1.5	1.3	.8	.6	1.2
Processed	1.5	3.2	2.9	3.4	.8	1.4	1.3	.8	1.6
Motor Spirit	.4	2.0	1.0	1.1	.2	0	0	0	.4
Other	1.1	1.2	1.9	2.3	.6	1.4	1.3	.8	1.2
4. Machinery	33.4	23.4	27.0	33.2	29.1	27.1	28.8	23.6	27.7
Machines Capt. Eqp	28.1	20.4	23.6	28.9	24.6	22.7	24.7	23.6	27.7
Parts Accessories	5.3	3.0	3.4	4.3	4.5	4.5	4.1	~	~
5. Transport	17.6	14.9	19.4	18.1	17.4	17.7	18.6	16.4	15.2
Passenger Cars	4.6	4.2	.1	.1	.1	.1	.1	~	~
Other	6.7	6.3	6.6	4.1	5.0	5.0	7.3	4.2	4.3
Industrial	6.7	6.3	6.5	4.1	5.0	5.0	7.3	4.2	4.3
Non-Industrial	0	0	0	0	0	0	0	~	~
Parts Accessories	6.2	4.3	12.7	13.8	12.4	12.6	11.2	12.3	10.8
6. Consumer Goods	6.8	4.1	3.8	4.3	4.2	4.1	4.6	4.4	4.6
Durable	1.5	1.2	1.2	1.2	1.2	1.2	1.4	1.3	1.2
Semi-Durable	3.1	1.3	1.3	1.5	1.4	1.4	1.5	1.4	1.4
Non-Durable	2.2	1.6	1.4	1.7	1.6	1.5	1.6	1.7	1.9
7. Other	.1	.2	0	0	0	.1	3.2	19.2	12.9

Origin	Exports by Industrial Origin								
	1970	1974	1975	1976	1977	1978	1979	1981	1982
Total Exports (1 + 2 + 3)	100.0	100.0	100.0	100.0	100.0	100.0	100.0	100.0	100.0
1. Agriculture	34.1	27.3	28.9	36.2	33.0	30.1	24.8	9.3	7.9
2. Mining Quarrying	8.7	7.5	20.3	20.7	25.6	31.9	46.8	75.8	80.5
3. Manufacturing	57.2	65.2	50.8	43.1	41.4	38.0	28.4	14.9	11.6
31. Food, Bev., Tobac.	14.2	13.3	9.1	5.7	5.9	6.0	4.3	.8	.6
32. Textiles	3.8	8.9	5.5	5.1	4.1	2.8	2.4	.8	.6
33. Wood, Wood Prod.	.6	.7	.6	.8	.9	.8	.6	.2	.1
34. Paper and Prod.	2.1	1.2	1.3	1.3	1.3	1.1	.9	.4	.4
35. Chemicals	11.1	13.9	9.0	8.8	8.0	6.7	6.1	5.7	4.0
36. Non-Metal Minrl	1.4	1.9	2.0	2.3	3.3	2.4	1.5	.5	.4
37. Basic Metal Ind.	10.1	12.2	11.2	9.3	8.5	5.9	3.2	.6	.9
38. Metal Manufact.	12.7	12.0	11.2	9.1	8.5	11.7	8.8	3.0	4.0
39. Oth. Manf. Ind.	1.3	1.2	.9	.8	.9	.6	.6	2.9	.5

SOURCE: UN-YITS, 1976; 1981; 1983; 1984; 1985.

Table 2514

NICARAGUA PERCENTAGE VALUE OF TRADE, 1970–82

Imports by Broad Economic Category

Category	1970	1974	1975	1976	1977	1978	1979	1980	1981	1982
Total Imports	100.0	100.0	100.0	100.0	100.0	100.0	100.0	100.0	100.0	100.0
1. Food and Beverages	8.2	6.6	7.3	7.3	6.5	8.3	11.9	13.0	15.3	10.3
Primary	3.4	2.9	3.6	3.1	2.6	3.6	3.5	6.0	9.8	4.4
For Industry	2.0	2.0	2.6	2.1	1.5	2.2	1.4	2.1	5.6	3.4
For Hshold Consm	1.4	1.0	1.0	1.0	1.1	1.4	2.1	3.9	4.2	1.0
Processed	4.8	3.7	3.7	4.2	3.9	4.7	8.4	6.9	5.5	5.9
For Industry	.7	.7	.6	.5	.7	.9	1.9	1.9	1.9	1.8
For Hshold Consm	4.1	3.0	3.1	3.7	3.2	3.8	6.6	5.0	3.5	4.2
2. Ind. Supplies Nes.	40.3	44.7	36.7	37.2	35.4	38.7	35.1	37.2	30.6	31.3
Primary	2.2	1.6	1.2	1.8	1.2	1.9	1.5	2.5	1.6	1.4
Processed	38.1	43.2	35.5	35.4	34.1	36.8	33.6	34.7	29.0	29.8
3. Fuels	5.8	10.7	14.2	12.9	13.6	15.1	21.1	19.8	19.9	23.1
Primary	4.0	9.1	12.3	10.7	10.2	9.7	18.2	16.8	17.5	19.5
Processed	1.8	1.5	1.9	2.3	3.4	5.3	2.9	3.0	2.4	3.6
Motor Spirit	.3	.3	.4	.7	.7	1.4	.8	.6	.6	1.0
Other	1.5	1.2	1.5	1.6	2.7	4.0	2.1	2.4	1.9	2.7
4. Machinery	16.3	13.8	17.4	15.4	17.3	13.7	8.8	7.9	13.3	15.2
Machines Capt. Eqp	15.3	13.0	16.5	14.6	16.4	12.8	8.2	7.2	12.5	14.2
Parts Accessories	1.0	.9	.9	.8	.9	.9	.6	.7	.8	1.0
5. Transport	11.4	10.8	10.4	11.4	14.1	11.0	7.2	7.0	9.4	10.2
Passenger Cars	2.4	2.2	2.6	3.4	3.3	2.2	.9	.9	1.1	1.1
Other	4.3	5.0	3.9	4.0	6.5	4.1	2.6	2.8	4.7	4.1
Industrial	4.2	4.8	3.7	3.8	6.3	3.9	2.5	2.7	4.6	4.0
Non-Industrial	.1	.2	.2	.2	.2	.1	.1	.1	.1	0
Parts Accessories	4.7	3.7	3.9	4.0	4.3	4.7	3.6	3.3	3.6	5.1
6. Consumer Goods	17.8	13.1	13.5	15.6	12.9	13.0	15.6	15.1	11.3	9.8
Durable	2.1	1.9	1.6	1.7	1.6	1.3	.7	.9	.7	.4
Semi-Durable	6.5	5.3	4.9	5.9	4.8	4.4	5.9	6.6	3.1	2.8
Non-Durable	9.2	6.0	7.1	8.0	6.5	7.3	9.0	7.6	7.5	6.6
7. Other	.2	.2	.4	.2	.2	.2	.3	.1	.2	.1

Exports by Industrial Origin

Origin	1970	1974	1975	1976	1977	1978	1979	1980	1981	1982
Total Exports (1 + 2 + 3)	100.0	100.0	100.0	100.0	100.0	100.0	100.0	100.0	100.0	100.0
1. Agriculture	48.2	57.3	49.6	55.0	62.7	58.9	59.6	58.7	67.1	66.2
2. Mining Quarrying	3.0	2.7	1.5	.9	.8	.4	.1	.1	.1	.1
3. Manufacturing	48.7	40.0	48.8	44.0	36.5	40.7	40.3	41.3	32.8	33.7
31. Food, Bev., Tobac.	29.7	16.9	28.3	24.2	16.6	21.3	26.5	23.8	20.1	24.0
32. Textiles	6.3	4.8	5.3	4.9	4.9	3.6	2.7	2.5	1.7	1.2
33. Wood, Wood Prod.	2.2	2.1	2.0	2.5	1.8	1.6	1.2	.7	.5	.5
34. Paper and Prod.	.3	.4	.1	.2	.2	.2	.1	.1	0	0
35. Chemicals	6.0	10.3	8.9	8.4	8.7	9.0	6.9	10.6	8.3	6.3
36. Non-Metal Minrl	1.0	1.0	.8	.9	.9	1.0	.7	.7	.2	.1
37. Basic Metal Ind.	.9	.6	1.0	.7	.8	1.3	.6	1.4	.6	.3
38. Metal Manufact.	2.3	3.1	2.2	2.2	2.4	2.6	1.7	1.5	1.3	1.2
39. Oth. Manf. Ind.	.1	.1	.2	.1	.1	0	0	0	0	0

SOURCE: UN-YITS, 1976; 1981; 1983; 1984; 1985.

Table 2515

PANAMA PERCENTAGE VALUE OF TRADE, 1970–83

	Imports by Broad Economic Category						
Category	1970	1975	1979	1980	1981	1982	1983
Total Imports	100.0	100.0	100.0	100.0	100.0	100.0	100.0
1. Food and Beverages	7.9	7.9	8.5	8.6	7.8	8.1	9.2
Primary	2.4	2.2	2.2	2.0	2.5	2.3	2.4
For Industry	1.0	1.3	.9	.9	1.2	.9	.9
For Hshold Consm	1.4	.9	1.3	1.2	1.3	1.4	1.4
Processed	5.5	5.7	6.3	6.6	5.4	5.9	6.8
For Industry	.7	2.0	2.0	2.0	1.5	1.6	1.9
For Hshold Consm	4.8	3.7	4.3	4.6	3.9	4.2	4.9
2. Ind. Supplies Nes.	27.8	21.4	26.9	25.4	25.9	24.0	23.8
Primary	.7	.7	1.0	1.2	1.0	1.1	.9
Processed	27.1	20.7	25.9	24.2	24.9	22.9	22.8
3. Fuels	18.7	40.3	28.4	30.2	28.0	26.5	27.7
Primary	18.0	39.0	27.2	28.6	24.4	25.2	24.8
Processed	.7	1.4	1.2	1.5	3.6	1.3	2.8
Motor Spirit	0	0	.5	.5	3.0	.9	2.6
Other	.7	1.4	.7	1.0	.6	.4	.3
4. Machinery	15.4	12.2	11.3	11.3	13.8	15.9	12.5
Machines Capt. Eqp	14.8	11.2	10.1	10.5	12.8	14.6	11.6
Parts Accessories	.5	1.1	1.2	.9	1.0	1.3	.9
5. Transport	12.1	7.2	9.1	9.7	10.4	11.2	10.7
Passenger Cars	3.5	1.4	3.2	3.4	3.4	4.4	4.5
Other	4.0	2.7	2.2	2.9	3.3	2.8	2.7
Industrial	3.8	2.6	2.0	2.5	3.1	2.7	2.5
Non-Industrial	.2	.1	.2	.4	.2	.1	.2
Parts Accessories	4.6	3.1	3.7	3.3	3.7	4.0	3.5
6. Consumer Goods	17.8	10.9	15.7	14.7	13.9	14.1	16.0
Durable	4.0	2.4	4.2	3.6	3.4	3.6	3.8
Semi-Durable	8.7	4.3	6.5	6.3	5.8	5.5	6.2
Non-Durable	5.1	4.1	5.1	4.8	4.8	5.0	5.9
7. Other	.3	.1	.1	.2	.1	.2	.2

	Exports by Industrial Origin						
Origin	1970	1975	1979	1980	1981	1982	1983
Total Exports (1 + 2 + 3)	100.0	100.0	100.0	100.0	100.0	100.0	100.0
1. Agriculture	68.6	29.4	44.2	36.4	42.7	45.6	50.8
2. Mining Quarrying	0	~	~	0	~	~	~
3. Manufacturing	31.3	70.6	55.8	63.6	57.3	54.4	49.2
31. Food, Bev., Tobac.	8.2	21.0	19.6	31.0	28.2	18.7	26.3
32. Textiles	.2	1.9	5.6	4.2	5.6	7.9	4.6
33. Wood, Wood Prod.	0	0	.1	.1	.2	.1	.2
34. Paper and Prod.	.5	.4	1.2	1.6	1.1	1.3	1.1
35. Chemicals	20.4	45.6	26.4	24.7	19.8	24.5	14.8
36. Non-Metal Minrl	0	.1	1.1	0	.5	.3	.4
37. Basic Metal Ind.	.5	.4	.8	.6	.4	.4	.7
38. Metal Manufact.	1.4	1.1	.8	1.0	1.0	.7	1.0
39. Oth. Manf. Ind.	~	.1	.3	.5	.4	.5	.1

SOURCE: UN-YITS, 1976; 1981; 1983; 1984; 1985.

Table 2516

PARAGUAY PERCENTAGE VALUE OF TRADE, 1970–81

Category	Imports by Broad Economic Category					
	1970	1975	1976	1977	1978	1979
Total Imports	~	100.0	100.0	100.0	100.0	100.0
1. Food and Beverages	~	11.9	12.9	9.1	9.7	9.4
Primary	~	1.8	3.1	2.5	2.4	2.2
For Industry	~	1.6	2.8	2.1	2.1	1.9
For Hshold Consm	~	.2	.3	.4	.3	.3
Processed	~	10.1	9.8	6.7	7.3	7.2
For Industry	~	1.3	2.4	.7	.4	.4
For Hshold Consm	~	8.8	7.5	6.0	6.9	6.8
2. Ind. Supplies Nes.	~	22.2	21.2	19.5	18.4	20.6
Primary	~	.9	1.1	1.1	.9	.8
Processed	~	21.3	20.1	18.5	17.5	19.8
3. Fuels	~	20.3	23.8	19.6	22.4	24.0
Primary	~	16.8	16.7	12.0	14.3	14.2
Processed	~	3.5	7.0	7.6	8.2	9.9
Motor Spirit	~	1.4	3.2	2.2	2.7	2.6
Other	~	2.1	3.8	5.3	5.5	7.2
4. Machinery	~	20.1	18.4	24.3	18.5	19.1
Machines Capt. Eqp	~	18.6	17.3	23.1	17.4	18.0
Parts Accessories	~	1.4	1.1	1.1	1.2	1.1
5. Transport	~	15.9	15.1	17.5	20.1	16.5
Passenger Cars	~	2.8	3.2	3.5	3.4	4.0
Other	~	9.3	8.8	9.8	12.2	9.3
Industrial	~	8.9	8.3	8.9	11.0	8.5
Non-Industrial	~	.4	.5	.8	1.1	.8
Parts Accessories	~	3.8	3.1	4.2	4.5	3.2
6. Consumer Goods	~	9.1	8.2	9.7	10.8	10.3
Durable	~	1.7	1.8	2.2	2.0	1.7
Semi-Durable	~	2.0	1.5	2.0	2.3	1.8
Non-Durable	~	5.5	4.9	5.5	6.5	6.8
7. Other	~	.5	.3	.3	.1	.1

Origin	Exports by Industrial Origin							
	1970	1975	1976	1977	1978	1979	1980	1981
Total Exports (1 + 2 + 3)	100.0	100.0	100.0	100.0	100.0	100.0	100.0	100.0
1. Agriculture	32.7	39.6	53.1	59.9	60.8	64.9	65.5	62.1
2. Mining Quarrying	0	0	~	~	~	0	~	~
3. Manufacturing	67.2	60.4	46.9	40.1	39.2	35.1	34.5	37.9
31. Food, Bev., Tobac.	50.6	35.6	28.4	24.0	21.5	13.7	14.9	14.5
32. Textiles	.5	1.2	2.0	2.0	3.7	2.6	1.2	2.2
33. Wood, Wood Prod.	9.0	15.9	6.7	7.1	7.9	13.8	13.5	14.1
34. Paper and Prod.	0	0	0	0	0	0	~	~
35. Chemicals	6.4	6.1	8.5	6.4	5.7	4.5	4.5	4.1
36. Non-Metal Minrl	.5	.4	0	0	0	0	~	~
37. Basic Metal Ind.	~	~	~	~	~	0	~	~
38. Metal Manufact.	.1	0	~	~	0	0	~	~
39. Oth. Manf. Ind.	.1	1.2	1.2	.5	.5	.4	.4	2.9

SOURCE: UN-YITS, 1976; 1981; 1983; 1984; 1985.

Table 2517

PERU PERCENTAGE VALUE OF TRADE, 1970–82

Category	Imports by Broad Economic Category						
	1970	1975	1978	1979	1980	1981	1982
Total Imports	100.0	100.0	100.0	100.0	100.0	100.0	100.0
1. Food and Beverages	19.5	13.7	15.9	18.9	17.5	16.3	14.8
Primary	14.1	7.5	8.2	10.8	9.0	8.1	8.7
For Industry	11.1	7.1	8.0	10.7	7.9	6.8	6.4
For Hshold Consm	3.0	.4	.2	.1	1.1	1.2	2.3
Processed	5.4	6.2	7.7	8.1	8.5	8.3	6.1
For Industry	1.5	2.4	4.9	1.5	1.9	2.4	2.2
For Hshold Consm	3.9	3.8	2.8	6.6	6.5	5.8	3.9
2. Ind. Supplies Nes.	35.5	37.0	36.8	35.3	34.8	27.3	31.7
Primary	1.7	3.6	3.0	3.0	3.2	3.9	3.6
Processed	33.8	33.4	33.8	32.4	31.6	23.4	28.0
3. Fuels	1.7	11.8	5.3	2.9	2.0	1.1	1.5
Primary	.3	8.3	.7	.2	.2	.1	.1
Processed	1.5	3.5	4.6	2.8	1.8	1.0	1.4
Motor Spirit	.1	.4	.3	.2	0	.2	0
Other	1.3	3.0	4.3	2.5	1.8	.8	1.4
4. Machinery	23.6	24.5	27.8	29.0	27.2	27.7	27.6
Machines Capt. Eqp	19.4	21.9	23.4	24.7	23.7	24.5	24.2
Parts Accessories	4.2	2.6	4.4	4.4	3.5	3.2	3.3
5. Transport	12.5	9.1	9.1	10.1	13.3	20.1	16.4
Passenger Cars	3.9	1.3	1.3	1.1	2.2	13.2	9.9
Other	1.1	4.1	3.2	4.1	6.0	2.7	2.3
Industrial	1.1	3.9	3.0	4.0	5.8	2.4	2.0
Non-Industrial	0	.2	.2	.1	.2	.3	.3
Parts Accessories	7.5	3.7	4.6	4.9	5.1	4.2	4.2
6. Consumer Goods	7.0	3.8	4.6	3.6	4.8	7.4	8.0
Durable	1.4	1.2	2.0	1.5	2.1	4.1	3.4
Semi-Durable	1.5	.9	.7	.7	1.2	1.7	1.9
Non-Durable	4.1	1.7	1.9	1.4	1.4	1.6	2.6
7. Other	.1	.1	.6	.2	.5	0	.1

Origin	Exports by Industrial Origin						
	1970	1975	1978	1979	1980	1981	1982
Total Exports (1 + 2 + 3)	100.0	100.0	100.0	100.0	100.0	100.0	100.0
1. Agriculture	10.5	10.3	15.2	11.1	8.5	8.7	8.2
2. Mining Quarrying	19.6	19.8	22.0	28.1	35.9	35.4	32.8
3. Manufacturing	69.9	69.9	62.9	60.8	55.6	56.0	59.0
31. Food, Bev., Tobac.	38.8	39.2	15.5	10.6	9.5	8.3	7.2
32. Textiles	.3	1.1	5.3	7.6	7.5	9.5	8.7
33. Wood, Wood Prod.	.1	0	.3	.4	.4	.4	.2
34. Paper and Prod.	.3	.1	.3	.4	.2	.1	.1
35. Chemicals	.4	4.0	8.1	6.0	9.1	12.1	12.2
36. Non-Metal Minrl	.1	.1	.9	1.3	1.2	.8	.6
37. Basic Metal Ind.	29.6	23.8	29.6	30.5	24.6	20.8	26.7
38. Metal Manufact.	.1	1.4	2.4	2.5	2.3	2.5	2.3
39. Oth. Manf. Ind.	.1	.2	.4	1.5	.8	1.5	1.0

SOURCE: UN-YITS, 1976; 1981; 1983; 1984; 1985.

Table 2518

URUGUAY PERCENTAGE VALUE OF TRADE, 1970–84

Category	Imports by Broad Economic Category					
	1970	1975	1980	1982	1983	1984
Total Imports	100.0	100.0	100.0	100.0	100.0	100.0
1. Food and Beverages	9.0	6.6	6.6	4.7	6.1	7.0
Primary	3.8	3.9	4.2	3.2	4.8	5.1
For Industry	1.5	1.1	1.4	.9	2.5	2.4
For Hshold Consm	2.3	2.8	2.9	2.3	2.3	2.8
Processed	5.2	2.7	2.4	1.5	1.3	1.9
For Industry	3.7	2.3	.6	.3	.3	.4
For Hshold Consm	1.5	.3	1.8	1.2	1.0	1.5
2. Ind. Supplies Nes.	40.8	41.4	29.6	25.4	29.4	35.8
Primary	8.3	7.1	3.9	3.1	4.1	4.8
Processed	32.5	34.3	25.6	22.3	25.3	31.0
3. Fuels	14.1	31.0	28.4	38.9	35.9	36.0
Primary	~	28.6	25.6	37.8	33.6	33.6
Processed	~	2.5	2.8	1.1	2.2	2.4
Motor Spirit	~	.2	.2	~	.1	~
Other	~	2.3	2.6	1.1	2.1	2.4
4. Machinery	12.4	12.0	15.8	13.3	20.4	12.1
Machines Capt. Eqp	~	10.4	14.2	12.0	19.0	10.7
Parts Accessories	~	1.6	1.6	1.3	1.5	1.4
5. Transport	16.4	6.7	14.0	10.9	3.7	4.2
Passenger Cars	~	1.7	6.2	3.2	1.3	2.0
Other	~	3.2	5.6	6.0	1.2	1.0
Industrial	~	2.9	4.6	5.6	1.1	1.0
Non-Industrial	~	.3	1.0	.4	.1	0
Parts Accessories	~	1.9	2.2	1.7	1.2	1.1
6. Consumer Goods	6.5	2.3	5.5	6.8	4.4	4.9
Durable	.3	.8	2.5	3.0	1.5	1.5
Semi-Durable	2.0	.4	1.6	1.9	1.1	1.4
Non-Durable	4.2	1.1	1.4	1.9	1.9	2.1
7. Other	.7	0	.2	0	0	0

Origin	Exports by Industrial Origin							
	1970	1975	1979	1980	1981	1982	1983	1984
Total Exports (1 + 2 + 3)	100.0	100.0	100.0	100.0	100.0	100.0	100.0	100.0
1. Agriculture	22.8	30.6	16.1	21.5	24.6	27.8	22.7	21.2
2. Mining Quarrying	1.9	.3	.8	.7	.5	.2	.1	.2
3. Manufacturing	75.3	69.1	83.1	77.8	74.9	72.0	77.2	78.6
31. Food, Bev., Tobac.	51.4	29.7	26.9	30.7	35.4	31.0	40.0	29.7
32. Textiles	21.1	28.3	39.2	32.3	28.0	29.7	28.7	38.4
33. Wood, Wood Prod.	0	0	0	0	0	0	0	0
34. Paper and Prod.	.1	.6	1.2	1.3	.9	.7	1.1	1.2
35. Chemicals	.4	3.4	5.8	4.9	5.9	6.6	3.9	5.2
36. Non-Metal Minrl	.5	3.8	3.1	2.6	1.5	1.2	.8	.9
37. Basic Metal Ind.	.1	.5	.8	.7	.4	.4	.4	.7
38. Metal Manufact.	1.3	2.8	5.6	5.0	2.5	1.7	1.6	1.7
39. Oth. Manf. Ind.	.3	.1	.4	.4	.2	.6	.6	.8

SOURCE: UN-YITS, 1976; 1981; 1983; 1985.

Table 2519

VENEZUELA PERCENTAGE VALUE OF TRADE, 1970–81

Imports by Broad Economic Category

Category	1970	1975	1977	1978	1979	1980	1981
Total Imports	100.0	100.0	100.0	100.0	100.0	100.0	100.0
1. Food and Beverages	9.2	11.4	10.3	10.5	10.7	11.2	14.1
Primary	5.3	6.3	4.3	4.0	4.6	3.9	5.3
For Industry	3.8	5.2	2.7	2.3	2.9	2.5	3.4
For Hshold Consm	1.5	1.0	1.6	1.7	1.8	1.4	1.9
Processed	3.9	5.2	5.9	6.4	6.0	7.3	8.9
For Industry	1.3	2.3	1.8	2.4	1.7	2.5	3.3
For Hshold Consm	2.7	2.9	4.1	4.1	4.3	4.8	5.6
2. Ind. Supplies	34.3	31.4	32.8	28.1	32.1	33.7	31.5
Primary	2.7	1.4	2.7	1.7	2.9	4.0	3.0
Processed	31.6	30.0	30.1	26.4	29.2	29.7	28.5
3. Fuels	1.3	.5	.4	.2	.7	1.0	.1
Primary	.1	0	.1	0	.2	.5	0
Processed	1.2	.5	.3	.2	.5	.4	.1
Motor Spirit	.3	0	0	0	.2	.1	0
Other	.9	.5	.3	.1	.3	.4	.1
4. Machinery	28.6	31.8	35.1	32.2	30.0	28.0	26.3
Machines Capt. Eqp	25.4	28.7	32.8	29.3	26.7	24.5	22.7
Parts Accessories	3.2	3.1	2.3	2.9	3.3	3.5	3.6
5. Transport	15.6	16.8	14.3	20.0	16.6	14.3	16.7
Passenger Cars	5.6	6.5	4.4	5.5	5.7	5.4	6.1
Other	4.0	5.6	6.0	9.8	6.8	4.2	5.6
Industrial	3.8	5.4	5.8	9.5	6.4	3.8	5.2
Non-Industrial	.2	.3	.2	.3	.3	.3	.4
Parts Accessories	5.9	4.7	3.9	4.7	4.1	4.7	5.0
6. Consumer Goods	10.1	7.7	7.0	8.9	9.8	11.6	11.1
Durable	3.8	3.3	2.9	3.3	3.3	4.7	4.4
Semi-Durable	3.7	3.0	2.9	4.2	4.7	5.0	4.9
Non-Durable	2.6	1.4	1.2	1.5	1.8	1.9	1.8
7. Other	.9	.3	.1	.1	.1	.2	.1

Exports by Industrial Origin

Origin	1970	1975	1977	1978	1979	1980	1981
Total Exports (1 + 2 + 3)	100.0	100.0	100.0	100.0	100.0	100.0	100.0
1. Agriculture	1.4	.7	.9	.9	.5	.3	.4
2. Mining Quarrying	68.4	71.0	67.3	64.2	64.2	66.3	80.7
3. Manufacturing	30.2	28.3	31.8	34.9	35.3	33.5	18.9
31. Food, Bev., Tobac.	.2	.3	.1	.2	.1	.1	.1
32. Textiles	0	0	0	0	0	0	0
33. Wood, Wood Prod.	0	0	0	0	0	0	0
34. Paper and Prod.	0	.1	.1	.1	.1	.1	.1
35. Chemicals	28.5	27.5	31.1	33.7	33.2	30.1	14.8
36. Non-Metal Minrl	.1	0	0	0	0	0	0
37. Basic Metal Ind.	.7	.1	.2	.5	1.6	2.7	3.2
38. Metal Manufact.	.5	.2	.2	.4	.2	.5	.6
39. Oth. Manf. Ind.	.1	0	0	0	0	0	0

SOURCE: UN-YITS, 1976; 1981; 1983; 1984; 1985.

Table 2520

UNITED STATES PERCENTAGE VALUE OF TRADE,[1] 1970–85

Category	Imports by Broad Economic Category								
	1970	1975	1979	1980	1981	1982	1983	1984	1985
Total Imports	100.0	100.0	100.0	100.0	100.0	100.0	100.0	100.0	100.0
1. Food and Beverages	15.5	10.2	8.8	7.9	7.3	7.4	7.4	6.8	6.7
Primary	8.8	4.9	5.2	4.4	3.9	4.2	4.1	3.5	3.6
For Industry	4.0	2.2	2.3	2.0	1.5	1.5	1.4	1.3	1.3
For Hshold Consm	4.8	2.7	2.9	2.5	2.4	2.7	2.7	2.3	2.3
Processed	6.7	5.3	3.6	3.4	3.4	3.2	3.3	3.2	3.1
For Industry	1.3	.9	.6	.4	.4	.3	.4	.4	.4
For Hshold Consm	5.4	4.4	3.0	3.0	3.1	2.9	3.0	2.9	2.7
2. Ind. Supplies Nes.	32.5	24.6	22.8	21.0	21.7	20.5	20.8	21.3	20.1
Primary	7.0	4.8	3.9	3.7	3.6	3.0	3.0	2.9	2.6
Processed	25.5	19.8	18.9	17.2	18.1	17.4	17.8	18.4	17.6
3. Fuels	7.6	27.0	29.1	32.7	30.9	26.5	22.2	18.5	15.3
Primary	3.9	20.4	24.3	27.9	25.8	21.1	16.4	12.7	10.7
Processed	3.6	6.6	4.9	4.8	5.1	5.4	5.8	5.8	4.7
Motor Spirit	0	.3	1.0	.9	1.0	1.4	1.6	1.7	1.6
Other	3.6	6.2	3.8	3.9	4.1	4.0	4.2	4.2	3.0
4. Machinery	8.7	9.2	10.3	10.5	11.2	12.6	14.0	16.2	16.2
Machines Capt. Eqp	7.0	7.2	7.8	7.8	8.4	9.1	10.0	11.3	12.1
Parts Accessories	1.6	2.0	2.5	2.7	2.8	3.5	4.0	4.8	4.1
5. Transport	17.2	14.9	14.6	14.1	14.2	16.1	17.4	18.1	20.6
Passenger Cars	9.8	7.8	7.4	7.2	7.0	8.5	9.3	9.2	10.9
Other	2.0	1.8	1.9	2.2	2.9	3.0	2.7	2.9	3.3
Industrial	1.1	.9	1.4	1.6	2.3	2.5	2.4	2.7	2.9
Non-Industrial	.9	.8	.5	.5	.6	.5	.3	.2	.3
Parts Accessories	5.4	5.4	5.3	4.7	4.3	4.6	5.4	6.0	6.5
6. Consumer Goods	15.4	11.4	12.7	12.1	12.8	14.7	15.9	17.1	18.5
Durable	5.6	4.2	4.7	4.6	4.8	5.3	5.8	6.2	7.0
Semi-Durable	8.8	6.5	7.3	6.8	7.1	8.4	9.2	9.8	10.5
Non-Durable	.9	.6	.7	.7	.8	1.0	1.0	1.1	1.1
7. Other	3.3	2.6	1.6	1.7	1.9	2.3	2.2	2.1	2.4

Origin	Exports by Industrial Origin								
	1970	1975	1979	1980	1981	1982	1983	1984	1985
Total Exports (1 + 2 + 3)	100.0	100.0	100.0	100.0	100.0	100.0	100.0	100.0	100.0
1. Agriculture	12.6	17.1	16.3	15.4	15.2	14.1	14.5	14.0	10.8
2. Mining Quarrying	4.3	4.7	4.2	4.6	4.5	4.7	3.8	3.5	3.7
3. Manufacturing	83.1	78.2	79.6	80.0	80.3	81.3	81.7	82.5	85.5
31. Food, Bev., Tobac.	5.9	4.9	5.9	5.5	5.4	5.2	5.5	5.2	4.8
32. Textiles	2.3	2.3	2.8	2.7	2.5	2.2	2.0	1.9	1.9
33. Wood, Wood Prod.	.8	.8	.9	.9	.8	.7	.8	.7	.6
34. Paper and Prod.	3.4	2.8	2.5	2.8	2.7	2.7	2.8	2.8	2.6
35. Chemicals	12.0	10.8	12.9	12.9	12.8	14.2	14.4	14.7	14.5
36. Non-Metal Minrl	.9	.7	.8	.8	.8	.8	.8	.8	.7
37. Basic Metal Ind.	5.3	3.6	2.9	4.0	2.7	2.3	2.0	1.8	1.7
38. Metal Manufact.	49.7	49.6	48.0	47.1	49.7	50.5	50.8	51.0	54.3
39. Oth. Manf. Ind.	2.9	2.6	2.8	3.3	2.7	2.6	2.6	3.6	4.3

1. Includes Puerto Rico

SOURCE: UN-YITS, 1977; 1978; 1979; 1980; 1981; 1983; 1985.

Table 2521

ARGENTINA ABSOLUTE VALUE OF TRADE, 1970-84

(T US)

Imports

Category	1970	1975	1979	1980	1981	1982	1983	1984
Total Merchandise Trade	1,684,639	3,946,501	6,700,060	10,540,600	9,430,230	5,336,910	4,504,160	4,584,670
Agricultural Products, Total	120,070	238,534	531,910	682,120	544,520	282,550	247,190	288,360
Food and Animals	84,502	155,765	388,080	506,040	384,590	200,400	149,150	183,380
Live Animals	1,409	7,762	750	7,440	5,920	7,690	16,580	2,430
Meat and Meat Prep	3	255	14,660	49,550	28,240	4,090	2,140	2,040
Dairy Products Eggs	6,207	1,652	35,970	46,210	30,900	4,200	3,510	6,270
Cereals and Prep	651	84	8,440	18,080	12,130	2,180	1,010	2,550
Fruits and Vegetables	24,885	53,263	151,040	185,690	133,210	52,630	28,510	50,130
Sugar and Honey	419	795	7,000	14,790	10,140	2,220	1,650	1,280
Coffee, Tea, Cocoa Sp	47,038	89,267	165,220	164,440	135,000	115,970	89,720	109,060
Feeding Stuff	1,040	362	1,010	4,000	3,160	1,620	1,560	2,260
Miscellaneous Food	2,850	2,323	3,970	15,860	25,900	9,810	4,480	7,360
Beverages Tobacco	7,113	10,875	45,044	56,368	46,280	12,405	8,470	5,180
Beverages	6,118	10,308	41,274	44,821	34,260	10,407	6,530	3,970
Tobacco	995	567	3,770	11,547	12,030	1,998	1,940	1,210
Crude Materials	26,719	64,323	91,675	109,330	104,490	60,790	83,010	91,500
Hides and Skins	666	515	524	3,810	1,640	150	620	1,080
Oilseeds	204	292	4,080	2,370	6,106	950	1,900	2,380
Natural Rubber	12,406	20,489	40,577	38,540	25,691	25,110	38,320	41,130
Textile Fibers	11,304	27,057	25,803	23,980	45,720	13,913	18,880	21,540
Crude Mat Nes	2,139	15,970	20,691	40,630	25,330	20,672	23,300	25,380
Animal Vegetable Oil	1,736	7,571	7,117	10,380	9,160	8,950	6,560	8,300
Animal Fats	75	126	569	500	350	500	530	360
Fixed Vegetable Oils	1,298	4,703	3,997	4,350	4,300	5,420	4,280	6,260
Processed Oils	363	2,742	2,551	5,530	4,510	3,030	1,760	1,680
Fish and Fishery Products	~	~	21,360	23,910	25,900	13,910	7,670	8,360
Forest Products	~	~	290,050	411,620	337,920	214,340	175,270	176,740
Agricultural Requisites	24,289	52,619	139,092	196,157	129,160	98,170	111,710	140,330
Crude Fertilizers	858	1,934	826	584	807	653	300	600
Manuf Fertilizers	5,259	16,104	31,326	38,539	26,866	29,656	25,990	47,470
Pesticides	5,713	15,364	36,171	43,643	39,500	49,092	67,930	81,600
Agriculture Machines	12,459	19,217	70,769	113,391	61,980	18,770	17,500	10,660

Exports

Category	1970	1975	1979	1980	1981	1982	1983	1984
Total Merchandise Trade	1,773,167	2,961,264	7,809,924	8,021,418	9,143,044	7,624,940	7,836,060	8,107,410
Agricultural Products, Total	1,490,606	2,180,259	5,552,530	5,522,120	6,377,530	4,863,580	5,902,190	6,063,740
Food and Animals	1,207,026	1,891,051	3,883,880	3,855,220	4,909,190	3,623,200	4,763,020	3,872,740
Live Animals	22,673	2,942	11,075	5,697	5,880	6,110	3,370	2,870
Meat and Meat Prep	441,313	287,548	1,226,421	965,700	930,420	804,910	613,030	413,050
Dairy Products Eggs	1,908	22,080	17,922	21,110	27,070	52,327	48,650	16,410
Cereals and Prep	518,523	1,106,315	1,649,257	1,656,781	2,841,610	1,836,380	2,918,590	2,268,020
Fruits and Vegetables	75,683	175,934	425,884	389,925	341,220	352,570	274,630	253,940
Sugar and Honey	17,608	132,587	98,832	339,357	315,470	91,270	211,620	127,730
Coffee, Tea, Cocoa Sp	10,344	16,919	27,288	38,950	33,400	35,770	43,690	62,980
Feeding Stuff	114,016	141,660	407,749	412,558	396,610	438,080	642,310	723,450
Miscellaneous Food	4,958	5,066	19,452	25,159	17,510	5,780	7,150	4,290
Beverages Tobacco	7,128	36,844	48,726	42,070	42,570	71,073	58,330	54,580
Beverages	793	4,738	17,237	15,210	14,090	12,215	8,380	8,270
Tobacco	6,335	32,106	31,489	26,864	28,480	58,858	49,950	46,310
Crude Materials	177,042	163,468	1,091,890	1,118,700	1,045,040	742,960	546,140	1,208,700
Hides and Skins	62,681	10,047	37,915	54,060	54,220	13,560	10,490	11,770
Oilseeds	282	1,877	751,778	662,194	639,330	454,250	361,020	948,210
Natural Rubber	- -	#	#	2	#	#	#	#
Textile Fibers	113,689	139,234	276,124	374,880	328,818	260,980	163,720	240,420
Crude Mat Nes	390	12,310	26,071	27,543	22,665	14,170	10,910	8,300
Animal Vegetable Oils	99,410	88,896	528,034	506,123	380,730	426,360	534,710	927,730
Animal Fats	21,192	41	49,830	28,894	35,380	14,250	13,240	12,900
Fixed Vegetable Oils	73,800	87,938	472,534	471,885	339,960	408,820	517,690	908,860
Processed Oils	4,418	917	5,670	5,344	5,390	3,284	3,770	5,970
Fish and Fishery Products	~	~	205,350	143,260	139,350	190,590	181,180	149,620
Forest Products	~	~	19,660	16,400	12,460	11,090	8,460	8,220
Agricultural Requisites	5,717	43,040	47,213	20,862	17,428	37,972	3,350	7,980
Crude Fertilizers	4	579	2	#	129	100	#	#
Manuf Fertilizers	239	94	246	#	623	#	140	160
Pesticides	214	1,118	3,147	2,457	2,310	1,171	910	2,500
Agricultural Machines	5,260	41,249	43,805	18,405	14,366	36,701	2,300	5,310

SOURCE: FAO-TY, 1975, Section IV; 1980, Section IV; 1981, Section IV; 1983, Section IV; 1985, Section IV.

Table 2522

BOLIVIA ABSOLUTE VALUE OF TRADE, 1975–84

(T US)

Imports

Category	1975	1979	1980	1981	1982	1983	1984
Total Merchandise Trade	557,900	894,720	665,393	917,081	554,135	532,352	631,000
Agricultural Products, Total	88,687	114,184	121,846	118,602	102,774	147,312	73,153
Food and Animals	85,590	101,054	105,565	100,197	90,561	105,614	64,422
Live Animals	1,900	447	114	#	80	221	465
Meat and Meat Prep	75	81	305	900	317	421	69
Dairy Products Eggs	9,702	11,954	18,343	13,175	11,154	4,555	8,293
Cereals and Prep	60,020	62,448	55,923	53,548	66,545	84,509	45,876
Fruits and Vegetables	1,876	4,139	4,677	4,531	1,545	2,706	1,115
Sugar and Honey	#	2,175	807	1,700	364	290	320
Coffee, Tea, Cocoa Sp	1,555	2,611	2,671	4,561	580	2,626	660
Feeding Stuff	#	1,059	575	1,639	818	#	1,180
Miscellaneous Food	10,862	16,140	22,142	20,143	9,091	10,286	6,444
Beverages Tobacco	2,897	4,729	4,632	4,131	3,800	22,865	1,326
Beverages	#	917	515	504	244	636	592
Tobacco	2,897	3,812	4,117	3,627	3,556	22,229	734
Crude Materials	#	2,071	2,088	2,712	2,358	4,634	6,085
Hides and Skins	#	#	#	#	#	#	#
Oilseeds	#	177	14	1,378	695	3,210	1,297
Natural Rubber	#	40	296	32	110	#	77
Textile Fibers	#	705	778	302	553	424	3,711
Crude Mat Nes	#	1,149	1,000[†]	1,000[†]	1,000[†]	1,000[†]	1,000[†]
Animal Vegetable Oil	200	6,330	9,561	11,562	6,055	14,199	1,320
Animal Fats	#	117	107	114	148	6,578	45
Fixed Vegetable Oils	200	3,091	6,838	10,000	4,651	5,173	1,149
Processed Oils	#	3,122	2,616	1,448	1,256	2,448	126
Fish and Fishery Products	~	4,143	4,724	6,321	6,000[†]	1,133	1,160[†]
Forest Products	~	10,305	11,805	12,605	12,400	12,400	12,400
Agricultural Requisites	16,107	23,793	18,376	36,262	24,353	11,939	26,368
Crude Fertilizers	#	27	28	1	776	#	4
Manuf Fertilizers	3,203	2,973	824	5,029	1,355	2,084	7,424
Pesticides	1,200[†]	4,670	5,334	7,231	6,000[†]	3,156	6,959
Agriculture Machines	11,704	16,123	12,190	24,001	16,222	6,699	11,981

Exports

Category	1975	1979	1980	1981	1982	1983	1984
Total Merchandise Trade	444,700	857,207	1,037,185	938,968	898,531	818,000	781,508
Agricultural Products, Total	67,998	92,355	103,797	46,449	52,649	41,653	22,451
Food and Animals	49,273	73,608	96,514	39,906	43,574	38,172	20,699
Live Animals	17,000	16,000	11,420	9,975	11,935	5,892	1,696
Meat and Meat Prep	#	#	#	#	587	122	343
Dairy Products Eggs	#	#	#	#	#	#	#
Cereals and Prep	30	855	505	20	957	1,475	1,221
Fruits and Vegetables	1,611	3,076	3,095	3,539	1,749	1,499	2,510
Sugar and Honey	23,553	29,676	52,506	5,851	8,860	12,426	6,277
Coffee, Tea, Cocoa Sp	7,070	21,571	22,503	16,920	15,995	13,480	6,796
Feeding Stuff	9	2,430	6,485	3,601	3,491	3.278	1,856
Miscellaneous Food	#	#	#	#	#	#	#
Beverages Tobacco	774	958	1,072	838	1,492	576	95
Beverages	724	945	1,072	838	1,492	576	95
Tobacco	50	13	#	#	#	#	#
Crude Materials	17,951	17,789	6,181	5,705	7,078	2,846	1,657
Hides and Skins	600	4,834	433	2,200	2,638	54	645
Oilseeds	#	172	#	#	#	#	#
Natural Rubber	2,012	1,904	4,574	3,405	4,146	2,760	750
Textile Fibers	15,339	10,759	1,174	100	294	32	262
Crude Mat Nes	#	120	#	#	#	#	#
Animal Vegetable Oils	#	#	30	#	505	59	#
Animal Fats	#	#	#	#	#	#	#
Fixed Vegetable Oils	#	#	30	#	505	59	#
Processed Oils	#	#	#	#	#	#	#
Fish and Fishery Products	~	#	#	#	#	12	#
Forest Products	~	19,150	20,450	11,310	13,740	5,923	5,923
Agricultural Requisites	#	#	#	#	#	#	#
Crude Fertilizers	#	#	#	#	#	#	#
Manuf Fertilizers	#	#	#	#	#	#	#
Pesticides	#	#	#	#	#	#	#
Agricultural Machines	#	#	#	#	#	#	#

SOURCE: FAO-TY, 1980, Section IV; 1981, Section IV; 1983, Section IV; 1985, Section IV.

Table 2523

BRAZIL ABSOLUTE VALUE OF TRADE, 1970–84
(T US)

Imports

Category	1970	1975	1979	1980	1981	1982	1983	1984
Total Merchandise Trade	2,849,243	13,592,463	19,804,320	24,960,544	24,079,000	21,069,310	16,800,570	15,208,700
Agricultural Products, Total	300,618	867,719	2,361,048	2,470,568	2,186,003	1,797,950	1,458,970	1,503,700
Food and Animals	253,999	728,968	1,974,465	2,050,629	1,707,793	1,330,280	1,293,170	1,199,820
Live Animals	11,188	34,033	73,939	33,616	22,060	19,740	16,510	10,230
Meat and Meat Prep	895	16,804	166,724	95,715	76,594	1,016,310	20,880	31,300
Dairy Products Eggs	14,351	16,777	15,614	90,784	22,100	236,750	28,180	21,600
Cereals and Prep	155,130	479,168	1,212,704	1,537,363	1,355,944	2,670	1,064,690	986,330
Fruits and Vegetables	68,974	169,977	287,077	274,764	212,475	6,260	154,440	143,000
Sugar and Honey	168	1,868	3,235	4,147	4,445	2,930	1,680	920
Coffee, Tea, Cocoa Sp	1,675	4,344	205,177	6,184	6,359	6,262	4,110	4,470
Feeding Stuff	1,411	4,425	9,083	7,213	6,282	2,934	1,890	1,320
Miscellaneous Food	207	1,572	912	843	1,527	905	800	660
Beverages Tobacco	6,859	21,906	25,667	19,500	15,179	13,381	13,300	9,900
Beverages	6,782	21,025	24,015	17,801	14,510	12,459	12,330	9,770
Tobacco	77	881	1,652	1,699	669	922	970	140
Crude Materials	18,080	77,988	219,610	295,474	419,927	411,150	98,920	168,960
Hides and Skins	1,174	5,466	6,181	6,511	8,089	4,060	1,740	3,590
Oilseeds	65	466	91,580	131,002	278,964	316,634	12,710	43,320
Natural Rubber	6,519	30,361	81,917	97,306	80,122	46,265	43,730	68,890
Textile Fibers	4,378	18,352	3,281	24,487	21,687	15,468	12,110	31,360
Crude Mat Nes	5,944	23,343	36,651	36,168	31,065	28,730	28,640	21,810
Animal Vegetable Oil	21,680	38,857	141,306	104,965	43,104	43,140	53,580	125,010
Animal Fats	8,220	18,304	50,485	42,567	18,234	10,240	13,960	24,560
Fixed Vegetable Oils	13,327	20,194	90,424	61,880	24,649	32,508	39,490	100,340
Processed Oils	133	359	397	518	221	393	140	110
Fish and Fishery Products	~	~	106,450	89,650	68,080	77,310	43,160	33,580†
Forest Products	~	~	222,720	274,220	282,150	298,920	161,440	174,670
Agricultural Requisites	185,272	775,237	658,622	909,995	511,649	345,325	189,000	307,250
Crude Fertilizers	8,149	65,355	43,719	57,830	37,650	16,637	1,980	2,390
Manuf Fertilizers	70,637	349,672	522,511	777,850	436,403	297,256	169,770	297,230
Pesticides	18,771	100,653	52,999	30,991	7,855	7,538	4,950	3,060
Agriculture Machines	87,715	259,557	39,393	43,324	29,741	23,894	12,290	4,570

Exports

Category	1970	1975	1979	1980	1981	1982	1983	1984
Total Merchandise Trade	2,738,922	8,669,944	15,244,370	20,132,400	23,293,040	20,175,072	21,899,320	27,005,340
Agricultural Products, Total	1,972,459	4,896,894	7,052,910	9,377,840	9,687,830	8,077,750	9,037,700	10,462,670
Food and Animals	1,589,558	3,545,149	5,850,230	7,769,390	7,778,820	6,720,930	7,293,850	8,469,360
Live Animals	20,320	39,130	1,400	3,100	2,820	1,700	2,260	2,690
Meat and Meat Prep	101,208	147,424	292,260	540,170	869,730	810,290	826,770	867,210
Dairy Products Eggs	435	230	2,676	12,769	23,440	6,342	5,520	2,750
Cereals and Prep	88,034	162,452	12,896	20,243	48,191	75,102	83,440	59,570
Fruits and Vegetables	59,868	214,805	455,864	543,510	871,738	780,810	797,820	1,622,140
Sugar and Honey	134,492	1,157,461	434,342	1,398,202	1,161,426	599,920	571,050	635,530
Coffee, Tea, Cocoa Sp	1,107,567	1,305,103	3,354,741	3,592,827	2,486,050	2,637,140	2,996,660	3,650,150
Feeding Stuff	77,541	507,056	1,269,710	1,609,672	2,272,490	1,780,740	1,971,480	1,595,620
Miscellaneous Food	93	11,488	26,349	48,899	42,936	28,908	38,870	33,710
Beverages Tobacco	34,440	152,814	305,211	308,328	385,731	486,440	477,110	475,230
Beverages	1,471	3,825	10,794	13,067	17,067	9,520	5,160	6,660
Tobacco	32,969	148,989	294,417	295,261	368,664	476,926	471,950	468,570
Crude Materials	280,597	931,727	306,674	609,265	643,584	319,110	668,210	657,300
Hides and Skins	25,539	8,684	1,496	470	1,369	8,690	11,420	2,650
Oilseeds	40,758	717,815	195,464	415,681	436,262	138,131	316,940	464,770
Natural Rubber	4,424	1,749	497	91	104	76	10	140
Textile Fibers	203,009	180,029	66,707	154,027	169,572	141,199	308,300	152,280
Crude Mat Nes	6,867	23,450	42,510	38,996	36,277	29,900	31,540	37,460
Animal Vegetable Oils	67,864	267,204	590,790	690,852	879,699	550,431	598,530	860,780
Animal Fats	22	111	#	56	89	64	#	90
Fixed Vegetable Oils	57,769	250,873	569,154	670,790	858,680	142,310	581,590	845,140
Processed Oils	10,073	16,220	21,629	20,006	20,930	29,900	16,940	15,550
Fish and Fishery Products	~	~	145,450	132,760	155,860	551,270	137,290	177,690
Forest Products	~	~	591,290	864,590	944,320	695,380	822,030	1,028,590
Agricultural Requisites	2,214	42,348	164,850	231,863	269,021	203,963	167,360	199,670
Crude Fertilizers	108	114	#	412	294	194	10	20
Manuf Fertilizers	11	3,006	3,737	2,760	4,197	8,581	36,920	13,660
Pesticides	376	6,064	22,406	27,320	31,794	42,706	45,420	59,370
Agricultural Machines	1,719	33,164	138,707	201,371	232,736	152,482	85,000	126,620

SOURCE: FAO-TY, 1975, Section IV; 1980, Section IV; 1981, Section IV; 1983, Section IV; 1985, Section IV.

Table 2524

CHILE ABSOLUTE VALUE OF TRADE, 1970-84

(T US)

				Imports				
Category	1970	1975	1979	1980	1981	1982	1983	1984
Total Merchandise Trade	960,820	1,876,200	4,229,316	5,123,135	6,277,185	3,830,900	2,968,800	3,480,500
Agricultural Products, Total	175,477	323,487	587,471	812,276	793,258	551,821	511,313	464,987
Food and Animals	121,104	248,047	446,535	668,988	632,872	447,648	397,105	332,658
Live Animals	24,747	1,732	2,400	3,958	6,627	1,500	1,200	1,250
Meat and Meat Prep	8,765	396	11,569	18,554	28,925	17,570	4,965	10,080
Dairy Products Eggs	6,548	1,233	37,566	43,087	48,171	33,000	28,100	23,730
Cereals and Prep	37,508	142,413	187,269	261,580	280,553	243,900	239,800	173,278
Fruits and Vegetables	13,435	14,947	37,751	34,583	43,029	27,078	17,660	18,115
Sugar and Honey	4,598	62,431	75,951	214,691	125,223	61,000	51,150	44,320
Coffee, Tea, Cocoa Sp	19,224	19,323	74,005	63,590	60,011	43,800	38,030	47,085
Feeding Stuff	1,695	4,000	11,282	13,794	17,083	10,300	9,800	8,000
Miscellaneous Food	4,584	1,572	8,742	15,151	23,250	9,500	6,400	6,800
Beverages Tobacco	4,197	1,604	31,505	45,342	54,618	34,600	12,200	6,600
Beverages	308	315	18,856	23,374	28,223	13,100	8,200	5,800
Tobacco	3,889	1,289	12,649	21,968	26,395	21,500	4,000	800
Crude Materials	34,798	30,773	62,552	49,154	49,903	23,373	38,970	50,800
Hides and Skins	3,663	4,812	3,600	4,077	3,265	#	#	#
Oilseeds	214	94	950	1,420	1,177	1,000	800	900
Natural Rubber	3,441	2,954	7,500	8,253	7,517	1,500	6,300	8,000
Textile Fibers	25,388	17,913	44,034	26,881	29,083	13,873	22,870	32,900
Crude Mat Nes	2,092	5,000[†]	6,468	8,523	8,861	7,000[†]	9,000[†]	9,000[†]
Animal Vegetable Oil	15,378	43,063	46,879	48,792	55,865	46,200	63,038	74,929
Animal Fats	1,512	1,105	3,620	3,694	3,109	3,000	3,500	4,300
Fixed Vegetable Oils	13,428	40,976	43,099	40,781	48,941	43,200	59,538	70,629
Processed Oils	438	982	160	4,317	3,815	#	#	#
Fish and Fishery Products	~	~	1,583	4,914	5,884	3,894	#	#
Forest Products	~	~	43,300	45,100	43,300	24,900	49,300	49,300
Agricultural Requisites	40,797	70,837	86,339	119,504	117,801	39,173	58,218	81,855
Crude Fertilizers	1,200[†]	1,969	1,697	6	2,803	#	#	400
Manuf Fertilizers	20,526	32,170	40,765	65,778	61,540	19,073	37,803	51,850
Pesticides	4,751	5,151	14,985	20,218	21,193	12,500	14,000[†]	16,000[†]
Agriculture Machines	14,320	31,547	28,892	33,502	32,265	7,600	6,415	13,605

				Exports				
Category	1970	1975	1979	1980	1981	1982	1983	1984
Total Merchandise Trade	1,253,390	1,661,329	4,229,390	4,583,915	3,744,828	3,709,500	3,835,500	3,657,200
Agricultural Products, Total	40,221	154,282	303,884	391,611	394,149	385,737	365,708	431,568
Food and Animals	26,331	123,245	229,362	316,356	325,247	312,455	298,350	362,298
Live Animals	110	763	1,900	2,452	2,434	2,900	2,300	2,100
Meat and Meat Prep	- -	1,210	6,400	7,490	6,752	5,100	3,000	2,319
Dairy Products Eggs	- -	1,705	192	2,360	218	#	#	#
Cereals and Prep	1,686	10,435	20,525	21,993	17,493	14,655	9,560	12,515
Fruits and Vegetables	24,230	64,140	183,025	236,590	275,539	280,400	258,670	339,800
Sugar and Honey	45	40,395	7,590	29,362	13,011	1,000	17,770	1,004
Coffee, Tea, Cocoa Sp	28	119	#	439	247	#	#	#
Feeding Stuff	330	4,471	9,630	15,539	9,310	8,000	6,600	4,100
Miscellaneous Food	- -	7	100[†]	131	243	400	450[†]	460[†]
Beverages Tobacco	1,840	3,971	21,813	20,445	17,125	14,482	12,717	13,270
Beverages	1,840	3,971	21,813	20,414	16,631	11,182	9,417	9,070
Tobacco	- -	#	#	31	494	3,300	3,300	4,200
Crude Materials	11,654	26,341	50,755	53,287	50,346	52,700	53,541	55,200
Hides and Skins	1,026	1,696	6,400	4,777	3,099	6,000	3,200	3,800
Oilseeds	788	791	570	159	368	#	#	#
Natural Rubber	- -	#	#	#	#	#	#	#
Textile Fibers	6,477	11,748	23,115	22,797	19,799	21,300	15,441	16,200
Crude Mat Nes	3,363	12,106	20,670	25,554	27,080	30,400	34,900[‡]	35,200[‡]
Animal Vegetable Oils	396	725	1,954	1,523	1,431	1,100	1,100	800
Animal Fats	- -	6	43	28	13	#	#	#
Fixed Vegetable Oils	- -	#	268[‡]	#	#	#	#	#
Processed Oils	396	719	1,643	1,495	1,418	1,100	1,100	800
Fish and Fishery Products	~	~	225,196	322,983	326,554	386,340	419,148	419,373
Forest Products	~	~	341,320	458,761	368,597	320,900	312,108	371,229
Agricultural Requisites	17,644	45,360	88,495	57,056	51,106	62,100	64,550	66,800
Crude Fertilizers	17,519	43,707	42,300	37,377	34,380	28,200	30,000	32,000
Manuf Fertilizers	- -	773	44,386	17,640	16,256	32,200	32,800[†]	33,000[†]
Pesticides	125	499	1,721	1,722	351	1,500	1,550[†]	1,600[†]
Agricultural Machines	- -	381	88	317	119	200	200	200

SOURCE: FAO-TY, 1975, Section IV; 1980, Section IV; 1981, Section IV; 1983, Section IV; 1985, Section IV.

Table 2525

COLOMBIA ABSOLUTE VALUE OF TRADE, 1970-84

(T US)

Imports

Category	1970	1975	1979	1980	1981	1982	1983	1984
Total Merchandise Trade	754,600	1,494,794	3,233,194	4,662,604	5,199,149	5,463,080	4,966,900	4,492,390
Agricultural Products, Total	81,137	151,756	323,657	534,818	494,054	556,281	541,171	440,072
Food and Animals	40,566	106,586	165,717	334,314	267,991	319,376	344,240	250,759
Live Animals	616	1,213	5,797	6,742	4,229	7,078	8,049	6,412
Meat and Meat Prep	230	104	353	1,049	2,115	2,847	2,918	2,833
Dairy Products Eggs	4,565	5,141	11,969	36,581	53,991	14,450	15,027	6,940
Cereals and Prep	21,055	60,034	82,078	202,551	121,966	177,865	211,277	164,749
Fruits and Vegetables	3,651	12,337	32,610	55,932	48,851	67,638	68,219	32,105
Sugar and Honey	587	1,552	3,933	5,399	5,594	5,087	3,386	2,982
Coffee, Tea, Cocoa Sp	9,366	15,631	15,654	10,019	10,044	13,418	6,689	7,742
Feeding Stuff	255	1,736	6,059	5,244	6,997	15,842	17,361	17,603
Miscellaneous Food	241	8,838	7,264	10,797	14,204	15,151	11,314	9,393
Beverages Tobacco	13,009	8,308	28,191	49,199	46,335	49,474	42,613	23,541
Beverages	4,007	6,889	13,866	23,456	23,351	24,156	18,651	13,850
Tobacco	9,002	1,419	14,325	25,743	22,984	25,318	23,962	9,691
Crude Materials	17,926	21,149	48,828	62,253	49,044	74,595	74,348	80,414
Hides and Skins	43	1,173	586	15	86	295	50	#
Oilseeds	613	166	2,735	10,360	1,149	20,494	27,386	24,902
Natural Rubber	4,256	7,660	17,105	19,316	19,685	17,664	17,245	20,809
Textile Fibers	9,675	6,696	17,893	20,156	17,616	21,229	13,884	13,820
Crude Mat Nes	3,339	5,454	10,509	12,406	10,508	14,913	15,783	20,883
Animal Vegetable Oil	14,636	15,713	80,921	89,052	130,684	112,836	79,970	85,358
Animal Fats	5,369	9,430	19,405	23,161	21,141	25,720	24,398	27,245
Fixed Vegetable Oils	8,650	5,050	54,542	60,114	107,124	84,566	52,294	53,856
Processed Oils	617	1,233	6,974	5,777	2,419	2,550	2,978	4,257
Fish and Fishery Products	~	~	63,385	62,983	84,249	84,183	46,549	47,220[†]
Forest Products	~	~	93,830	119,100	169,618	158,180	114,644	114,644
Agricultural Requisites	35,573	77,093	95,359	151,198	153,487	184,346	160,378	158,136
Crude Fertilizers	138	3,014	2,483	2,535	2,752	4,399	2,976	1,967
Manuf Fertilizers	20,418	38,111	39,385	74,798	66,575	88,075	67,738	83,721
Pesticides	1,355	6,903	16,244	19,403	21,406	28,857	30,021	33,249
Agriculture Machines	13,662	29,065	37,247	54,462	62,754	63,015	59,643	39,199

Exports

Category	1970	1975	1979	1980	1981	1982	1983	1984
Total Merchandise Trade	735,657	1,465,187	3,300,443	3,945,048	2,956,400	3,073,860	3,080,893	3,483,140
Agricultural Products, Total	597,394	1,089,814	2,489,924	3,045,363	2,102,763	2,154,057	2,088,123	2,364,240
Food and Animals	551,115	980,917	2,345,012	2,822,806	1,867,532	1,982,215	1,916,797	2,159,144
Live Animals	36,253	93,550	78,322	63,247	71,152	98,180	86,212	54,278
Meat and Meat Prep	4,734	23,216	28,587	27,289	53,637	45,662	30,597	10,523
Dairy Products Eggs	417	1,188	17,088	20,448	16,745	10,089	273	#
Cereals and Prep	1,546	26,267	17,900	22,836	14,374	5,911	10,472	16,290
Fruits and Vegetables	19,927	46,592	104,943	107,471	142,398	169,355	158,432	205,735
Sugar and Honey	15,119	101,493	60,861	195,990	93,046	64,482	78,877	42,763
Coffee, Tea, Cocoa Sp	466,765	678,454	2,030,069	2,380,803	1,470,213	1,584,532	1,548,729	1,826,853
Feeding Stuff	6,252	9,396	861	1,546	1,541	906	552	795
Miscellaneous Food	102	761	6,381	3,176	4,426	3,098	2,653	1,907
Beverages Tobacco	7,217	13,015	22,330	26,862	21,901	24,656	24,988	24,382
Beverages	32	108	333	550	960	1,078	1,493	2,139
Tobacco	7,185	12,907	21,997	26,312	20,941	23,578	23,495	22,243
Crude Materials	39,038	95,878	122,494	195,611	213,283	147,147	146,283	180,698
Hides and Skins	1,671	#	#	#	#	#	#	#
Oilseeds	1,182	434	10,137	11,317	6,750	5,249	158	238
Natural Rubber	226	74	65	160	5	61	#	#
Textile Fibers	34,640	75,072	38,072	82,603	93,857	26,829	23,499	49,224
Crude Mat Nes	1,319	20,298	74,220	101,531	112,671	115,008	122,826	131,236
Animal Vegetable Oils	24	4	88	84	47	39	55	16
Animal Fats	- -	#	#	#	#	#	#	#
Fixed Vegetable Oils	- -	#	82	26	3	10	#	#
Processed Oils	24	4	6	58	44	29	55	16
Fish and Fishery Products	~	~	27,231	35,036	33,170	32,712	27,365	30,286[†]
Forest Products	~	~	41,342	26,726	60,958	48,104	49,824	49,824
Agricultural Requisites	719	21,724	18,496	32,415	28,038	25,589	28,809	26,717
Crude Fertilizers	- -	#	#	6	2	53	70	100
Manuf Fertilizers	6	8,342	440	7,893	2,357	25	2,503	35
Pesticides	424	11,879	13,567	21,042	21,274	20,948	25,124	25,271
Agricultural Machines	289	1,503	4,489	3,474	4,405	4,563	1,112	1,311

SOURCE: FAO-TY, 1975, Section IV; 1980, Section IV; 1981, Section IV; 1983, Section IV; 1985, Section IV.

Table 2526

COSTA RICA ABSOLUTE VALUE OF TRADE, 1970–84

(T US)

Country	Imports							
	1970	1975	1979	1980	1981	1982	1983	1984
Total Merchandise Trade	316.687	693,969	1,396,800	1,523,800	1,208,500	893,200	988,500	1,093,739
Agricultural Products, Total	35,079	71,031	110,118	143,097	114,736	90,034	106,661	103,463
Food and Animals	28,037	57,653	84,949	108,324	92,075	74,596	90,607	82,347
Live Animals	1,885	4,930	3,067	1,198	476	868	3,811	2,449
Meat and Meat Prep	1,011	2,885	6,721	7,858	3,259	2,237	3,616	3,784
Dairy Products Eggs	1,696	3,095	9,513	9,672	7,139	4,608	4,984	5,061
Cereals and Prep	10,775	30,942	29,140	45,407	43,133	36,723	50,158	35,675
Fruits and Vegetables	6,665	6,100	13,978	20,316	15,377	15,140	9,266	12,481
Sugar and Honey	1,053	1,784	2,865	3,067	1,770	5,323	1,373	2,345
Coffee, Tea, Cocoa Sp	562	922	1,735	3,538	2,608	1,533	2,392	3,365
Feeding Stuff	2,612	5,103	13,350	11,374	15,616	5,756	12,038	12,320
Miscellaneous Food	1,677	1,892	4,580	5,894	2,697	2,408	2,969	4,867
Beverages Tobacco	1,644	2,487	8,384	10,157	7,560	4,745	5,630	6,682
Beverages	1,113	2,079	7,537	9,611	7,371	4,571	5,121	6,370
Tobacco	531	408	847	546	189	174	509	312
Crude Materials	2,075	4,897	8,349	13,096	7,871	6,218	8,172	9,952
Hides and Skins	32	4	8	1,780	134	710	681	889
Oilseeds	630	1,034	707	3,244	479	407	433	671
Natural Rubber	490	1,140	3,110	2,171	4,319	2,615	2,860	3,060
Textile Fibers	419	1,483	509	1,485	860	482	1,198	459
Crude Mat Nes	504	1,236	4,015	4,416	2,079	2,004	3,000	4,873
Animal Vegetable Oil	3,323	5,994	8,436	11,520	7,230	4,475	2,252	4,482
Animal Fats	63	384	817	871	579	415	420	518
Fixed Vegetable Oils	3,126	5,423	7,105	10,073	5,619	3,694	1,520	3,549
Processed Oils	134	187	514	576	1,032	366	312	415
Fish and Fishery Products	~	~	2,660	4,754	1,829	907	2,931	2,205[†]
Forest Products	~	~	55,386	59,545	79,215	71,386	64,854	69,018
Agricultural Requisites	17,236	69,392	72,879	82,679	58,596	55,117	70,126	75,437
Crude Fertilizers	9	#	285	141	407	139	1,104	2,675
Manuf Fertilizers	7,497	37,905	17,191	29,724	15,841	15,977	18,249	21,828
Pesticides	5,432	14,644	31,734	35,287	34,954	35,268	42,713	36,508
Agricultural Machines	4,298	16,843	23,669	17,527	7,394	3,733	8,060	14,426

Category	Exports							
	1970	1975	1979	1980	1981	1982	1983	1984
Total Merchandise Trade	231,163	493,305	934,391	1,001,700	1,008,100	871,582	874,626	985,914
Agricultural Products, Total	182,315	361,164	690,583	659,967	667,286	607,758	542,912	669,931
Food and Animals	179,984	357,176	675,010	645,613	656,540	594,995	526,715	647,103
Live Animals	101	5,952	852	1,155	2,680	1,665	3,000	235
Meat and Meat Prep	18,467	33,069	84,164	75,547	79,665	56,257	33,488	46,694
Dairy Products Eggs	538	1,994	526	363	233	450	1,257	1,633
Cereals and Prep	1,174	5,024	17,243	18,910	27,756	8,580	17,089	17,797
Fruits and Vegetables	68,943	149,891	205,558	229,885	241,723	255,411	234,632	271,290
Sugar and Honey	10,868	49,308	18,896	42,701	43,800	14,569	18,803	22,832
Coffee, Tea, Cocoa Sp	75,773	106,354	338,650	265,601	251,572	249,730	214,066	276,458
Feeding Stuff	308	957	1,385	1,337	1,611	1,201	951	838
Miscellaneous Food	3,852	4,627	7,736	10,114	7,500	7,132	3,429	9,326
Beverages Tobacco	228	859	3,503	1,058	1,068	1,502	548	659
Beverages	65	166	2,442	249	402	235	96	138
Tobacco	163	693	1,061	809	666	1,267	452	521
Crude Materials	1,874	2,976	12,052	13,206	9,479	11,080	15,490	22,029
Hides and Skins	269	#	4	12	#	#	#	2
Oilseeds	292	696	2,410	1,032	168	581	496	535
Natural Rubber	- -	#	#	#	#	#	#	
Textile Fibers	403	205	523	1,460	14	4	5	18
Crude Mat Nes	910	2,075	9,115	10,702	9,297	10,495	14,989[‡]	21,474[‡]
Animal Vegetable Oil	229	153	18	90	199	181	159	140
Animal Fats	124	#	#	#	#	#		
Fixed Vegetable Oils	92	153	10	9	27	181	159	#
Processed Oils	13	#	8	81	172	#	#	140
Fish and Fishery Products	~	~	11,352	9,247	7,469	6,754	12,276	17,400
Forest Products	~	~	8,548	20,901	20,376	19,509	22,311	16,559
Agricultural Requisites	3,092	23,741	21,297	20,931	25,834	21,817	15,667	12,637
Crude Fertilizers	- -	#	#	#	#	#	#	#
Manuf Fertilizers	2,410	18,305	9,331	10,057	15,631	7,864	5,441	5,852
Pesticides	581	5,399	11,861	10,709	10,006	13,749	10,000[†]	6,540
Agricultural Machines	101	37	105	165	197	204	226	245

SOURCE: FAO-TY, 1975, Section IV; 1980, Section IV; 1981, Section IV; 1983, Section IV; 1985, Section IV.

Table 2527

CUBA ABSOLUTE VALUE OF TRADE, 1975–84

(T US)

Category	Imports						
	1975	1979	1980	1981	1982	1983	1984
Total Merchandise Trade	3,883,000	5,084,373	6,349,800	6,498,800	6,616,886	7,435,406	8,310,000
Agricultural Products, Total	748,869	858,515	1,140,148	1,158,179	1,055,647	1,076,008	1,144,193
Food and Animals	658,876	701,540	931,942	963,371	878,895	873,529	917,449
Live Animals	2,600	#	#	#	#	#	#
Meat and Meat Prep	53,745	75,509	84,585	96,933	121,343	118,084	122,151
Dairy Products Eggs	79,445	80,775	94,417	82,942	73,702	93,197	92,331
Cereals and Prep	364,428	359,484	501,760	532,899	477,445	425,997	453,300
Fruits and Vegetables	56,605	70,903	93,848	108,799	79,555	68,484	81,597
Sugar and Honey	#	#	#	#	#	#	#
Coffee, Tea, Cocoa Sp	33,504	24,457	28,584	25,531	9,425	30,466	24,226
Feeding Stuff	20,509	44,418	56,397	58,045	61,687	69,728	90,921
Miscellaneous Food	48,040	46,003	72,351	58,222	55,738	67,573	52,923
Beverages Tobacco	110	3,410	22,844	14,253	11,901	18,279	8,588
Beverages	110	3,410	5,882	9,535	7,286	15,971	8,213
Tobacco	#	#	16,962	4,718	4,615	2,308	375
Crude Materials	37,561	78,259	108,699	112,688	107,374	103,573	135,887
Hides and Skins	#	~	~	~	~	~	~
Oilseeds	4,600	#	165	459	#	7,054	9,468
Natural Rubber	#	3,156	4,871	3,453	1,623	3,761	5,039
Textile Fibers	32,961	45,103	62,932	64,963	62,584	61,028	78,876
Crude Mat Nes	~	30,000[‡]	40,731	43,813	43,167	31,730	42,504
Animal Vegetable Oil	52,322	75,297	76,663	67,867	57,477	80,627	82,269
Animal Fats	10,555	18,000[†]	16,028	15,869	15,340	18,029	16,473
Fixed Vegetable Oils	41,767	57,297	60,635	51,998	42,137	61,849	65,433
Processed Oils	#	#	#	#	#	749	363
Fish and Fishery Products	~	52,720	81,357	85,250	35,144	36,372	32,200[†]
Forest Products	~	97,108	200,881	178,120	187,429	188,943	188,943
Agricultural Requisites	221,797	244,600[†]	233,974	250,270	271,508	271,321	312,027
Crude Fertilizers	1,700[†]	300[†]	1,075	1,032	707	267	1,298
Manuf Fertilizers	101,121	98,300[†]	112,690	99,351	134,791	141,323	144,990
Pesticides	65,758	40,000[†]	30,463	38,544	23,432	27,848	33,192
Agriculture Machines	53,218	106,000[†]	89,746	111,343	112,578	101,883	132,547

Category	Exports						
	1975	1979	1980	1981	1982	1983	1984
Total Merchandise Trade	3,684,000	4,827,052	5,541,500	5,304,700	5,902,800	6,614,213	6,197,000[‡]
Agricultural Products, Total	3,432,455	4,345,093	4,843,859	4,465,565	4,895,039	5,292,591	5,074,585
Food and Animals	3,347,144	4,239,072	4,753,591	4,369,806	4,736,655	5,116,566	4,948,337
Live Animals	#	#	343	195	795	499	2,644
Meat and Meat Prep	#	#	334	12	#	704	549
Dairy Products Eggs	#	164	116	392	181	966	1,841
Cereals and Prep	#	#	#	#	#	#	#
Fruits and Vegetables	17,958	59,147	71,732	114,770	133,199	156,127	153,905
Sugar and Honey	3,312,904	4,145,980	4,648,556	4,216,176	4,556,593	4,901,925	4,764,802
Coffee, Tea, Cocoa Sp	16,282	33,781	32,510	38,261	45,887	56,345	24,596
Feeding Stuff	#	#	#	#	#	#	#
Miscellaneous Food	#	#	#	#	#	#	#
Beverages Tobacco	85,311	106,021	86,268	91,889	155,110	158,025	105,248
Beverages	19,474	26,674	35,136	20,675	31,495	34,944	40,382
Tobacco	65,837	79,347	51,132	71,214	123,615	123,081	64,866
Crude Materials	#	#	4,000	3,870	3,274	18,000	21,000
Hides and Skins	#	~	~	~	~	~	~
Oilseeds	#	#	#	#	#	#	#
Natural Rubber	#	#	#	#	#	#	#
Textile Fibers	#	#	#	1,870	774	#	#
Crude Mat Nes	#	#	4,000[‡]	2,000[‡]	2,500[‡]	18,000[‡]	21,000[‡]
Animal Vegetable Oils	#	#	#	#	#	#	#
Animal Fats	#	#	#	#	#	#	#
Fixed Vegetable Oils	#	#	#	#	#	#	#
Processed Oils	#	#	#	#	#	#	#
Fish and Fishery Products	~	132,062	123,813	120,178	146,259	157,523	157,900[†]
Forest Products	~	#	#	#	#	#	#
Agricultural Requisites	#	#	#	#	#	79	83
Crude Fertilizers	#	#	#	#	#	#	#
Manuf Fertilizers	#	#	#	#	#	79	83
Pesticides	#	#	#	#	#	#	#
Agricultural Machines	#	#	#	#	#	#	#

SOURCE: FAO-TY, 1980, Section IV; 1981, Section IV; 1983, Section IV; 1985, Section IV.

Table 2528

DOMINICAN REPUBLIC ABSOLUTE VALUE OF TRADE, 1970–84

(T US)

				Imports				
Country	1970	1975	1979	1980	1981	1982	1983	1984
Total Merchandise Trade	278,034	717,752	1,080,433	1,498,397	1,450,169	1,255,817	1,278,125	1,253,800
Agricultural Products, Total	35,978	136,362	164,666	217,082	240,024	183,297	175,208	165,663
Food and Animals	25,146	99,040	92,830	148,909	174,667	104,989	122,102	104,655
Live Animals	1,197	1,273	1,531	2,049	1,518	2,972	3,702	859
Meat and Meat Prep	835	1,135	4,129	17,781	15,038	11,823	7,364	2,280
Dairy Products Eggs	6,926	3,204	10,436	15,370	13,740	8,618	15,239	16,755
Cereals and Prep	6,148	75,001	44,625	75,157	104,551	52,623	66,000	58,801
Fruits and Vegetables	4,579	8,634	10,208	9,836	5,725	4,839	4,350	4,176
Sugar and Honey	343	1,220	2,228	2,895	3,042	2,401	3,396	1,769
Coffee, Tea, Cocoa Sp	526	793	952	591	410	645	867	727
Feeding Stuff	2,168	4,150	8,208	10,714	14,147	12,908	16,585	14,778
Miscellaneous Food	2,424	3,630	10,513	14,516	16,496	8,194	4,599	4,510
Beverages Tobacco	2,670	6,366	11,054	6,366	7,539	5,816	3,591	3,357
Beverages	854	2,766[†]	3,692	2,298	2,428	2,178	1,031	1,670
Tobacco	1,816	3,600	7,362	4,068	5,111	3,638	2,560	1,687
Crude Materials	803	4,058	6,551	16,283	14,430	4,805	7,894	9,810
Hides and Skins	- -	#	1,747	1,331	454	#	#	#
Oilseeds	- -	3,528	401	10,327	9,890	5,959	4,544	6,060
Natural Rubber	- -	#	207	129	266	254	317	477
Textile Fibers	613	530	1,430	1,287	943	678	299	273
Crude Mat Nes	190[‡]	#	2,766	3,215	2,877	2,569	2,734	3,000[†]
Animal Vegetable Oil	7,359	26,898	54,231	45,518	43,388	63,032	41,621	47,841
Animal Fats	1,105	5,000	10,470	9,988	10,963	14,172	8,068	13,706
Fixed Vegetable Oils	6,248	21,898	40,549	30,290	26,032	46,994	28,218	33,109
Processed Oils	6	#	3,212	5,240	6,393	1,866	5,335	1,026
Fish and Fishery Products	~	~	19,958	24,205	19,027	16,847	15,984	8,360[†]
Forest Products	~	~	46,832	71,392	73,145	62,290	58,834	58,834[†]
Agricultural Requisites	8,248	19,936	38,015	71,495	56,621	37,654	34,290	33,775
Crude Fertilizers	- -	#	2	12	1,113	3	43	112
Manuf Fertilizers	2,300	7,600[†]	21,111	37,401	25,865	18,780	14,595	14,430
Pesticides	1,750[‡]	4,718	9,076	13,693	16,265	11,042	13,345	11,476
Agriculture Machines	4,198	7,618	7,826	20,389	13,378	7,829	6,307	7,757

				Exports				
Category	1970	1975	1979	1980	1981	1982	1983	1984
Total Merchandise Trade	213,957	890,007	876,797	963,309	1,198,738	791,365	787,710	872,373
Agricultural Products, Total	186,876	711,800	530,556	515,137	786,223	517,757	490,681	567,211
Food and Animals	171,598	675,182	472,231	478,827	714,213	489,266	461,566	518,376
Live Animals	- -	6	32	35	40	43	24	64
Meat and Meat Prep	3,390	4,733	3,502	2,886	8,564	8,838	6,718	897
Dairy Products Eggs	2	20	178	20	#	82	64	#
Cereals and Prep	214	833	710	889	1,510	1,026	675	777
Fruits and Vegetables	6,243	17,831	20,758	26,648	30,016	29,979	32,240	39,634
Sugar and Honey	111,248	576,771	206,603	307,540	538,028	283,587	275,722	302,162
Coffee, Tea, Cocoa Sp	48,955	72,620	234,753	133,485	126,061	156,128	136,818	172,165
Feeding Stuff	1,380	333	1,035	1,642	1,876	1,063	1,822	1,402
Miscellaneous Food	166	2,035	4,660	5,682	8,118	8,520	7,483	1,275
Beverages Tobacco	14,648	35,624	53,973	34,374	67,675	24,571	24,524	33,820
Beverages	- -	83	100	275	366	193	384	2,948
Tobacco	14,648	35,541	53,873	34,099	67,309	24,378	24,140	30,872
Crude Materials	324	556	1,007	1,243	1,655	1,702	2,301	1,854
Hides and Skins	35	26	81	74	89	89	24	#
Oilseeds	252	1	4	23	45		23	2
Natural Rubber	- -	#	#	#	#	#	#	#
Textile Fibers	37	6	#	#	#	#	617	352
Crude Mat Nes	- -	523	922	1,146	1,521	1,609	1,637	1,500[†]
Animal Vegetable Oils	306	438	3,345	693	2,680	2,218	2,290	13,161
Animal Fats	- -	#	#	#	#	#	#	#
Fixed Vegetable Oils	- -	#	2,559	#	1,800	1,517	1,600	12,500
Processed Oils	306	438	786	693	880	701	690	661
Fish and Fishery Products	~	~	913	1,098	1,271	1,287	1,442	3,720[†]
Forest Products	~	~	~	17	17	#	#	#
Agricultural Requisites	- -	18	10,973	19,701	15,750	7,597	1,812	6,147
Crude Fertilizers	- -	#	#	7	#	#	1	#
Manuf Fertilizers	- -	#	10,891	19,638	15,705	7,569	1,790	6,129
Pesticides	- -	18	65	55	36	7	12	10[†]
Agricultural Machines	- -	#	17	1	9	21	9	8

SOURCE: FAO-TY, 1975, Section IV; 1980, Section IV; 1981, Section IV; 1983, Section IV;
1985, Section IV.

Table 2529

ECUADOR ABSOLUTE VALUE OF TRADE, 1970–84

(T US)

Imports

Category	1970	1975	1979	1980	1981	1982	1983	1984
Total Merchandise Trade	238,317	863,778	1,599,714	2,253,305	2,246,100	1,988,374	1,464,954	1,715,777
Agricultural Products, Total	19,376	83,548	137,157	181,864	180,704	178,868	212,929	248,000
Food and Animals	9,839	51,486	75,978	117,178	113,994	119,522	139,792	160,400
Live Animals	317	3,380	1,452	1,859	4,711	6,219	5,155	5,930
Meat and Meat Prep	40	#	62	81	47	66	180	180
Dairy Products Eggs	934	1,449	9,597	8,332	6,131	6,916	5,757	5,550
Cereals and Prep	6,503	41,810	51,356	86,270	87,596	83,522	90,169	68,400
Fruits and Vegetables	533	1,534	4,039	5,220	5,334	4,312	1,851	8,450
Sugar and Honey	116	227	1,461	1,713	1,215	8,600	28,675	65,639
Coffee, Tea, Cocoa Sp	340	827	1,032	1,247	983	805	20	#
Feeding Stuff	16	103	1,547	3,232	1,810	3,349	2,972	1,100
Miscellaneous Food	1,040	2,156	5,432	9,224	6,167	5,733	5,012	5,151
Beverages Tobacco	1,923	14,512	23,343	21,396	13,438	13,945	2,639	2,400
Beverages	364	7,161	10,741	11,457	7,738	7,430	642	500
Tobacco	1,559	7,351	12,602	9,939	5,700	6,515	1,997	1,900
Crude Materials	939	2,595	5,382	7,621	15,641	13,301	30,884	40,100
Hides and Skins	- -	8	#	#	#	#	#	#
Oilseeds	- -	80	1,091	143	6,136	4,439	11,143	13,650
Natural Rubber	310	1,426	1,606	4,063	6,714	2,262	2,159	2,200[†]
Textile Fibers	461	524	757	772	715	949	11,582	18,250
Crude Mat Nes	168	557	1,928	2,643	2,076	5,651	6,000[†]	6,000[†]
Animal Vegetable Oil	6,675	14,955	32,454	35,669	37,631	32,100	39,614	45,100
Animal Fats	3,520	7,314	16,386	10,518	7,604	5,828	7,019	7,200
Fixed Vegetable Oils	2,924	7,501	15,794	24,892	29,937	26,103	32,433	37,900
Processed Oils	231	140	274	259	90	169	162	#
Fish and Fishery Products	~	~	104,398	199,968	188,568	219,311	218,268	219,348
Forest Products	~	~	9,278	27,334	28,487	28,672	16,169	18,657
Agricultural Requisites	10,430	86,696	53,632	84,126	70,469	93,198	87,200	96,900
Crude Fertilizers	- -	497	296	865	901	300	#	#[†]
Manuf Fertilizers	4,092	29,438	9,714	27,723	16,668	25,603	20,100[†]	25,900[†]
Pesticides	2,605	13,379	14,884	17,966	19,635	25,209	26,000[†]	30,000[†]
Agriculture Machines	3,733	43,382	28,738	35,572	33,265	42,086	41,100[†]	41,000[†]

Exports

Category	1970	1975	1979	1980	1981	1982	1983	1984
Total Merchandise Trade	210,300	973,882	2,104,232	2,480,804	530,822	2,140,033	2,224,145	2,581,025
Agricultural Products, Total	175,760	322,732	749,819	623,348	504,302	515,892	378,634	520,124
Food and Animals	170,998	310,050	728,493	604,858	497,450	497,583	362,693	501,321
Live Animals	2,579	#	#	#	#	23	4	28
Meat and Meat Prep	- -	79	138	57	47	657	368	75
Dairy Products Eggs	- -	32	4	#	#	#	#	#
Cereals and Prep	- -	5,479	12	68	235	3,021	188	271
Fruits and Vegetables	84,481	141,890	160,211	199,204	212,829	219,835	157,574	139,475
Sugar and Honey	8,739	25,165	11,741	44,257	21,747	2,072	97	16,834
Coffee, Tea, Cocoa Sp	75,112	137,007	552,387	358,533	268,175	271,758	203,874	344,638
Feeding Stuff	87	398	3,579	2,239	791	51	588	#
Miscellaneous Food	- -	#	421	500	478	166	#	#
Beverages Tobacco	525	411	2,114	1,964	2,065	2,506	1,451	1,154
Beverages	5	10	603	733	931	955	181	161
Tobacco	520	401	1,511	1,231	1,134	1,551	1,270	993
Crude Materials	4,237	12,270	15,676	12,865	19,842	2,739	13,175	16,049
Hides and Skins	155	#	861	428	331	8	#	#
Oilseeds	1,659	3,462	98	545	#	#	148	201
Natural Rubber	- -	#	#	#	#	#	#	#
Textile Fibers	421	5,774	11,116	8,442	16,079	9,152	9,027	11,848
Crude Mat Nes	2,002	3,034	3,601	3,450	3,432	3,579	4,000[†]	4,000[†]
Animal Vegetable Oils	- -	1	3,536	3,661	4,613	3,064	1,315	1,600[†]
Animal Fats	- -	#	#	#	#	#	#	#
Fixed Vegetable Oils	- -	1	3,536	3,661	4,613	3,064	1,315	1,600[†]
Processed Oils	- -	#	#	#	#	#	#	#
Fish and Fishery Products	~	~	57	69	#	#	#	#
Forest Products	~	~	56,980	93,956	122,542	137,679	123,097	119,762
Agricultural Requisites	13	56	451	350	252	687	500	600
Crude Fertilizers	- -	#	#	#	#	#	#	#
Manuf Fertilizers	- -	#	#	#	#	#	#	#
Pesticides	13	56	420	209	250[†]	687	500[†]	600[†]
Agriculture Machines	- -	#	31	141	2	#	#	#

SOURCE: FAO-TY, 1975, Section IV; 1980, Section IV; 1981, Section IV; 1983, Section IV;
1985, Section IV.

Table 2530

EL SALVADOR ABSOLUTE VALUE OF TRADE, 1970–84

(T US)

				Imports				
Category	1970	1975	1979	1980	1981	1982	1983	1984
Total Merchandise Trade	213,600	598,037	1,011,972	1,106,880	985,800	944,839	891,495	977,430
Agricultural Products, Total	30,837	74,646	137,932	173,573	184,180	164,598	157,395	131,118
Food and Animals	23,833	62,924	106,152	144,762	148,907	138,786	134,900	106,413
Live Animals	1,015	1,440	944	885	681	788	6,916	9,609
Meat and Meat Prep	812	2,823	4,584	7,046	5,239	4,730	4,602	5,503
Dairy Products Eggs	4,458	9,194	17,739	21,938	32,350	17,881	19,821	5,934
Cereals and Prep	5,808	27,680	31,399	43,840	37,529	43,980	45,823	51,081
Fruits and Vegetables	6,421	12,507	28,270	46,473	48,905	43,050	32,902	17,562
Sugar and Honey	1,650	2,301	5,521	4,650	3,733	4,811	3,525	4,420
Coffee, Tea, Cocoa Sp	757	1,073	3,155	4,140	1,952	2,519	1,989	2,043
Feeding Stuff	1,605	2,949	7,251	7,198	10,088	11,409	10,435	9,750
Miscellaneous Food	1,307	2,957	7,289	8,592	8,430	9,618	8,887	511
Beverages Tobacco	1,810	2,120	3,897	4,538	3,643	2,985	2,441	1,978
Beverages	474	927	2,514	2,075	1,082	1,022	1,132	937
Tobacco	1,336	1,193	1,383	2,463	2,561	1,963	1,309	1,041
Crude Materials	2,049	4,251	8,574	7,107	9,077	3,607	3,164	3,103
Hides and Skins	417	881	713	795	1,971	547	1,560	1,198
Oilseeds	255	79	259	295	270	282	46	185
Natural Rubber	384	729	1,781	1,868	2,338	1,553	98	28
Textile Fibers	696	2,023	4,466	1,542	2,932	90	69	585
Crude Mat Nes	297	539	1,355	2,607	1,566	1,135	1,391	1,107
Animal Vegetable Oil	3,145	5,351	19,309	17,166	22,540	19,220	16,890	19,624
Animal Fats	2,269	5,092	16,260	12,022	12,891	11,776	11,732	17,100[†]
Fixed Vegetable Oils	850	184	2,180	5,034	8,915	5,460	3,956	2,306
Processed Oils	26	75	869	110	734	1,984	1,202	218
Fish and Fishery Products	~	~	2,506	3,738	2,417	948	570	1,541
Forest Products	~	~	30,268	29,851	34,677	35,525	35,240	35,240
Agricultural Requisites	33,485	62,319	55,625	42,846	66,717	36,757	41,715	40,850
Crude Fertilizers	109	300	386	#	#	#	8	#
Manuf Fertilizers	10,287	45,256	28,305	27,634	48,089	18,360	26,149	19,800[†]
Pesticides	21,248	7,103	17,460	10,835	15,599	15,811	11,387	17,000[†]
Agriculture Machines	1,841	9,660	9,474	4,377	3,029	2,586	4,171	4,050[†]

				Exports				
Category	1970	1975	1979	1980	1981	1982	1983	1984
Total Merchandise Trade	228,320	513,378	1,031,720	1,080,100	791,920	704,040	735,300	717,373
Agricultural Products, Total	161,881	352,884	746,959	832,714	565,751	494,817	528,940	463,180
Food and Animals	136,536	272,107	650,622	734,721	501,473	444,041	465,119	444,473
Live Animals	914	246	1,328	1,472	1,545	854	984	749
Meat and Meat Prep	68	2,896	14,549	5,063	1,320	2,819	3,571	2,038
Dairy Products Eggs	824	312	1,090	530	212	396	743	87
Cereals and Prep	2,025	2,834	5,064	7,667	6,840	2,702	1,967	1,332
Fruits and Vegetables	130	1,265	7,311	6,056	5,003	7,135	2,830	2,686
Sugar and Honey	8,008	87,457	32,935	17,154	19,152	20,963	43,993	28,934
Coffee, Tea, Cocoa Sp	120,971	173,425	586,392	694,709	464,487	406,819	409,692	408,647
Feeding Stuff	1,931	1,703	532	804	1,373	1,341	290	#
Miscellaneous Food	1,665	1,969	1,421	1,266	1,541	1,012	1,049	#
Beverages Tobacco	204	844	2,202	3,430	2,656	2,233	1,878	1,140
Beverages	164	317	886	1,003	640	498	644	630
Tobacco	40	527	1,316	2,427	2,016	1,735	1,234	510
Crude Materials	24,360	79,355	93,349	93,783	61,337	48,415	61,688	17,186
Hides and Skins	- -	3	11	#	5	#	225	10
Oilseeds	338	1,697	3,930	4,063	3,690	992	1,420	4,826
Natural Rubber	- -	3	19	28	8	#	#	#
Textile Fibers	23,455	76,537	87,064	87,143	55,275	45,396	58,390	10,350
Crude Mat Nes	567	1,115	2,325	2,549	2,359	2,027	1,653	2,000[†]
Animal Vegetable Oils	781	578	786	780	285	128	255	381
Animal Fats	- -	#	#	#	#	#	#	#
Fixed Vegetable Oils	759	566	693	714	252	110	207	300
Processed Oils	22	12	93	66	33	18	48	81
Fish and Fishery Products	~	~	13,484	17,319	23,344	22,010	14,484	17,601
Forest Products	~	~	871	921	957	971	6,587	6,587
Agricultural Requisites	5,188	9,367	14,587	8,458	4,632	3,446	5,298	4,225
Crude Fertilizers	2	#	2	#	1	#	#	#
Manuf Fertilizers	3,211	4,500	9,662	#	17	100	2	#
Pesticides	1,920	4,832	4,291	6,077	4,015	2,924	5,111	4,000[†]
Agricultural Machines	55	35	632	2,381	599	422	185	225

SOURCE: FAO-TY, 1975, Section IV; 1980, Section IV; 1981; Section IV; 1983, Section IV;
1985, Section IV.

Table 2531

GUATEMALA ABSOLUTE VALUE OF TRADE, 1970–84

(T US)

Category	Imports							
	1970	1975	1979	1980	1981	1982	1983	1984
Total Merchandise Trade	284,274	732,368	1,449,396	1,559,085	1,623,612	1,420,370	1,154,340	1,278,496
Agricultural Products, Total	32,129	69,668	140,969	146,455	155,520	124,115	106,874	118,210
Food and Animals	23,911	60,270	120,227	119,543	126,980	91,670	79,437	84,790
Live Animals	1,769	1,426	45,450	23,828	28,331	1,293	800	918
Meat and Meat Prep	724	976	1,603	1,980	2,967	2,459	1,160	1,105
Dairy Products Eggs	2,849	2,866	5,638	13,033	10,023	13,409	9,515	18,390
Cereals and Prep	10,123	37,525	46,031	55,146	154,008	36,376	39,408	37,826
Fruits and Vegetables	1,813	8,915	10,241	11,146	13,322	14,731	9,331	9,763
Sugar and Honey	659	1,362	2,566	2,132	2,958	3,478	2,688	2,784
Coffee, Tea, Cocoa Sp	746	1,054	2,211	3,149	2,947	2,652	1,780	1,834
Feeding Stuff	2,355	4,288	4,648	7,287	10,146	14,987	13,145	10,480
Miscellaneous Food	2,873	1,858	1,839	1,842	2,278	2,285	1,610	1,691
Beverages Tobacco	1,817	3,249	5,882	5,711	4,583	2,808	6,091	4,712
Beverages	1,258	2,556	3,800	3,128	3,136	2,208	5,091	3,712
Tobacco	559	693	2,082	2,583	1,447	600	1,000	1,000
Crude Materials	2,322	2,420	7,005	10,662	7,450	5,408	6,033	5,673
Hides and Skins	138	189	346	668	487	98	#	#
Oilseeds	295	274	1,821	2,278	1,789	1,487	2,130	1,620
Natural Rubber	567	168	285	88	28	14	#	#
Textile Fibers	727	999	1,469	4,801	2,498	1,934	903	1,053
Crude Mat Nes	595	790	3,084	2,527	2,648	1,875	3,000[†]	3,000
Animal Vegetable Oil	4,079	3,729	7,855	10,539	16,507	24,229	15,313	23,034
Animal Fats	2,672	2,907	5,555	6,919	9,722	11,472	7,800	12,000
Fixed Vegetable Oils	1,328	672	1,881	3,241	5,791	11,392	7,030[‡]	10,530[†]
Processed Oils	79	150	419	379	994	1,365	483	504
Fish and Fishery Products	~	~	2,643	2,446	2,301	2,213	1,815[†]	1,820[†]
Forest Products	~	~	39,204	93,932	64,642	58,091	63,070	56,263
Agricultural Requisites	13,717	72,748	80,245	76,253	83,139	55,449	58,490	68,090
Crude Fertilizers	- -	53	77	47	40	94	110	110
Manuf Fertilizers	5,000	44,944	33,782	43,124	50,724	30,906	25,800[†]	32,200[†]
Pesticides	3,714	9,342	27,263	16,506	17,092	16,942	20,000[†]	21,000[†]
Agriculture Machines	5,003	18,409	19,123	16,576	15,283	7,507	12,580[†]	14,780[†]

Category	Exports							
	1970	1975	1979	1980	1981	1982	1983	1984
Total Merchandise Trade	290,182	623,621	1,217,076	1,472,796	1,109,241	1,083,800	1,118,353	1,122,286
Agricultural Products, Total	203,978	451,127	921,045	1,032,634	769,122	725,801	712,939	690,550
Food and Animals	163,843	346,913	638,047	769,573	588,287	573,514	619,512	568,693
Live Animals	523	369	9,759	17,441	13,728	11,919	5,069	8,859
Meat and Meat Prep	14,599	20,983	49,643	47,693	51,060	41,228	27,607	21,159
Dairy Products Eggs	1,162	1,028	2,251	3,025	3,135	2,122	1,330	1,280
Cereals and Prep	3,064	3,212	6,911	11,736	7,362	10,439	7,180	7,541
Fruits and Vegetables	22,025	24,868	50,168	100,683	93,991	108,104	97,784	80,558
Sugar and Honey	13,146	122,362	65,432	90,765	107,029	35,991	113,216	84,360
Coffee, Tea, Cocoa Sp	103,927	167,604	441,810	484,265	300,916	355,488	359,912	356,769
Feeding Stuff	2,212	3,158	4,199	4,779	3,257	2,513	#	#
Miscellaneous Food	3,185	3,329	7,874	9,186	8,209	5,710	7,413	8,167
Beverages Tobacco	3,084	7,492	14,994	17,887	17,257	20,056	13,810	16,199
Beverages	565	384	520	504	387	276	100	100
Tobacco	2,519	7,108	14,474	17,383	16,870	19,780	13,710	16,099
Crude Materials	36,345	96,701	267,863	244,860	163,484	132,054	79,453	105,504
Hides and Skins	107	14	133	83	27	30	#	#
Oilseeds	1,074	3,895	12,977	11,170	15,431	11,454	9,086	11,584
Natural Rubber	- -	#	#	#	#	#	#	#
Textile Fibers	27,215	75,925	187,096	172,336	111,433	82,107	50,367	73,920
Crude Mat Nes	7,949	16,867	67,657	61,271	36,593	38,463	20,000[‡]	20,000[‡]
Animal Vegetable Oils	706	21	141	314	94	177	164	154
Animal Fats	17	1	#	#	#	28	#	#
Fixed Vegetable Oils	633	8	104	222	79	56	150	140
Processed Oils	56	12	37	92	15	93	14	14
Fish and Fishery Products	~	~	6,176	8,854	7,294	12,843	8,934	11,900
Forest Products	~	~	18,090	22,454	23,617	15,118	14,141	10,324
Agricultural Requisites	587	7,369	13,946	28,135	33,417	29,898	33,832	36,782
Crude Fertilizers	- -	1	17	#	1	2	#	#
Manuf Fertilizers	- -	240	157	4,873	5,175	5,572	5,550	6,500
Pesticides	587	7,128	13,566	23,052	27,992	23,942	28,000[†]	30,000[†]
Agricultural Machines	- -	#	206	210	249	382	282	282

SOURCE: FAO-TY, 1975, Section IV; 1980, Section IV; 1981, Section IV; 1983, Section IV;
1985, Section IV.

Table 2532

HAITI ABSOLUTE VALUE OF TRADE, 1975–84

(T US)

	Imports						
Category	1975	1979	1980	1981	1982	1983	1984
Total Merchandise Trade	142,516	266,163	354,158	447,960	387,280	440,300	474,080
Agricultural Products, Total	41,335	92,068	120,663	127,927	114,527	113,783	110,783
Food and Animals	29,631	68,069	87,474	91,535	87,427	88,368	79,683
Live Animals	112	144	189	81	#	220	100
Meat and Meat Prep	570	852	1,430	1,304	1,175	1,383	3,725
Dairy Products Eggs	4,006	8,333	12,847	13,933	14,570	11,690	10,950
Cereals and Prep	20,918	46,312	53,120	54,689	53,445	49,775	42,698
Fruits and Vegetables	1,381	2,409	2,408	2,867	3,222	3,130	3,295
Sugar and Honey	505	3,233	11,769	7,703	4,615	11,920	6,620
Coffee, Tea, Cocoa Sp	209	1,023	1,052	1,386	1,120	1,240	2,100
Feeding Stuff	366	1,022	1,159	1,613	80	110	145
Miscellaneous Food	1,483	4,741	3,500	7,959	9,200	8,900	10,050[†]
Beverages Tobacco	2,635	3,895	7,066	6,912	5,490	4,630	6,470
Beverages	956	1,425	1,382	2,159	1,990[†]	1,630[†]	2,370[†]
Tobacco	1,679	2,470	5,684	4,753	3,500	3,000	4,100
Crude Materials	1,145	1,144	1,521	1,996	1,420	1,420	1,450
Hides and Skins	#	13	20	#	#	#	#
Oilseeds	#	#	#	#	#	#	#
Natural Rubber	171	#	10	12	#	#	#
Textile Fibers	719	132	491	790	220	220	250
Crude Mat Nes	255	999	1,000[†]	1,194	1,200[†]	1,200[†]	1,200[†]
Animal Vegetable Oil	7,924	18,960	24,602	27,484	20,190	19,365	23,180
Animal Fats	2,217	5,900	8,125	9,871	9,000[†]	9,500[†]	11,600[†]
Fixed Vegetable Oils	5,534	12,674	16,477	16,844	11,190	9,865	11,580
Processed Oils	173	386	#	769	#	#	#
Fish and Fishery Products	~	3,118	4,784	2,050	3,560[†]	3,650[†]	6,580[†]
Forest Products	~	5,173	4,812	5,047	4,960	4,955	4,955
Agricultural Requisites	2,372	5,380	3,719	6,842	6,212	5,513	6,130
Crude Fertilizers	19	26	#	#	#	#	#
Manuf Fertilizers	108	2,174	1,020	3,292	1,900[†]	900[†]	1,250[†]
Pesticides	430	913	1,283	1,755	2,000[†]	2,200[†]	2,300[†]
Agriculture Machines	1,815	2,267	1,416	1,795[†]	2,312	2,413[†]	2,580[†]

	Exports						
Category	1975	1979	1980	1981	1982	1983	1984
Total Merchandise Trade	102,000	148,386	225,700	155,100	181,320	188,700	219,380
Agricultural Products, Total	37,752	54,061	112,303	46,450	50,345	71,958	64,903
Food and Animals	33,633	52,203	108,829	44,703	46,994	68,415	61,575
Live Animals	#	#	#	#	#	#	#
Meat and Meat Prep	771	3,178	1,802	3,877	2,138	1,708	1,305
Dairy Products Eggs	#	#	#	#	#	#	#
Cereals and Prep	167	4	#	#	#	#	#
Fruits and Vegetables	499	1,892	2,108	2,304	2,509	2,408	2,642
Sugar and Honey	11,083	661	7,019	615	2,130	4,072	971
Coffee, Tea, Cocoa Sp	20,323	46,098	95,400	36,107	38,137	58,600	50,884
Feeding Stuff	790	380	2,500	1,800	2,080	1,627	5,773
Miscellaneous Food	#	#	#	#	#	#	#
Beverages Tobacco	138	226	267	#	187	298	371
Beverages	138	226	267	#	187	298	371
Tobacco	#	#	#	#	#	#	#
Crude Materials	3,920	1,539	3,078	1,323	3,164	3,245	2,957
Hides and Skins	469	497	1,449	771	1,332	2,955	2,671
Oilseeds	47	126	41	1	10	#	#
Natural Rubber	#	#	#	#	#	#	#
Textile Fibers	3,221	745	1,508	461	1,722	190	186
Crude Mat Nes	183	171	80[†]	90[†]	100[†]	100[†]	100[†]
Animal Vegetable Oils	61	93	129	118	#	#	#
Animal Fats	#	#	#	#	#	#	#
Fixed Vegetable Oils	#	#	#	#	#	#	#
Processed Oils	61	93	129	118	#	#	#
Fish and Fishery Products	~	517	612	226	#	#	#
Forest Products	~	#	#	#	#	#	#
Agricultural Requisites	#	517	612	226	#	#	#
Crude Fertilizers	#	#	#	#	#	#	#
Manuf Fertilizers	#	#	#	#	#	#	#
Pesticides	#	#	#	#	#	#	#
Agricultural Machines	#	#	#	#	#	#	#

SOURCE: FAO-TY, 1980, Section IV; 1981, Section IV; 1983, Section IV; 1985, Section IV.

Table 2533

HONDURAS ABSOLUTE VALUE OF TRADE, 1970–84

(T US)

Imports

Category	1970	1975	1979	1980	1981	1982	1983	1984
Total Merchandise Trade	220,668	404,284	825,778	1,008,689	945,105	692,118	822,950	956,400
Agricultural Products, Total	25,740	53,691	178,632	138,483	120,478	68,667	82,726	90,875
Food and Animals	20,728	43,396	162,888	117,941	97,303	55,884	71,445	74,761
Live Animals	485	613	108,517	35,164	22,609	740	600	200
Meat and Meat Prep	653	1,079	2,728	3,430	4,480	1,935	5,851	5,860
Dairy Products Eggs	3,315	5,196	7,724	11,887	13,151	8,540	14,703	16,460
Cereals and Prep	8,123	27,707	23,495	42,631	30,490	22,683	25,522	25,996
Fruits and Vegetables	2,652	2,968	6,348	7,970	8,541	5,616	5,607	6,837
Sugar and Honey	744	383	1,142	1,147	1,348	683	476	1,292
Coffee, Tea, Cocoa Sp	510	758	1,946	1,863	2,132	1,309	1,578	1,698
Feeding Stuff	824	1,364	3,688	4,909	4,305	5,255	6,326	6,200
Miscellaneous Food	3,389	3,328	7,300	8,940	10,247	9,123	10,782	10,219
Beverages Tobacco	1,684	1,396	5,159	4,406	7,069	4,457	2,509	6,629
Beverages	432	1,124	4,168	3,410	4,636	3,130	1,900	3,459
Tobacco	1,252	272	991	996	2,433	1,327	609	3,170
Crude Materials	469	4,456	3,678	4,502	4,774	2,956	3,830	2,955
Hides and Skins	105	18	#	7	#	#	#	#
Oilseeds	36	1,102	268	108	52	234	260	305
Natural Rubber	- -	115	198	105	1,022	174	398	#
Textile Fibers	74	2,442	1,294	1,943	2,385	1,633	1,837	1,650
Crude Mat Nes	254	779	1,918	2,339	1,315	915	1,335	1,000[†]
Animal Vegetable Oil	2,870	4,443	6,907	11,634	11,332	5,370	4,942	6,530
Animal Fats	1,615	2.411	4,290	5,001	2,669	2,111	2,236	1,800[‡]
Fixed Vegetable Oils	1,224	1,949	2,561	6,245	8,428	3,072	2,563	4,440
Processed Oils	31	83	56	388	235	187	143	290
Fish and Fishery Products	~	~	1,437	2,042	1,955	1,285	1,560	2,240
Forest Products	~	~	27,591	28,312	31,795	28,832	20,719	20,843
Agricultural Requisites	13,206	28,752	61,582	57,681	66,761	45,657	50,685	52,160
Crude Fertilizers	12	#	9	148	215	77	7	#
Manuf Fertilizers	3,329	8,656	9,686	16,507	21,997	12,602	15,654	16,400[†]
Pesticides	3,086	7,360	24,579	21,321	30,065	26,335	27,088	27,000[†]
Agriculture Machines	6,779	12,736	27,308	19,705	14,484	6,643	7,936	8,760[†]

Exports

Country	1970	1975	1979	1980	1981	1982	1983	1984
Total Merchandise Trade	169,738	293,263	733,616	829,414	728,276	667,772	670,367	738,100
Agricultural Products, Total	123,766	166,670	566,110	625,798	572,332	498,111	480,812	526,466
Food and Animals	119,115	152,136	528,574	584,800	532,650	467,526	446,820	487,741
Live Animals	565	325	40,049	21,049	24,000	57	562	600
Meat and Meat Prep	9,719	18,571	61,146	60,923	47,340	34,560	31,520	29,585
Dairy Products Eggs	1	45	472	375	531	21	#	#
Cereals and Prep	1,038	338	1,378	2,318	2,302	2,533	1,684	#
Fruits and Vegetables	78,733	66,735	209,094	255,349	226,001	245,524	227,490	256,877
Sugar and Honey	1,675	7,826	17,794	34,081	56,753	28,261	30,853	32,100
Coffee, Tea, Cocoa Sp	26,061	57,340	196,674	208,678	174,143	155,380	152,745	167,375
Feeding Stuff	208	617	1,082	848	499	271	376	#
Miscellaneous Food	1,115	339	885	1,179	1,081	919	1,590	1,205
Beverages Tobacco	2,599	7,601	14,833	18,821	20,704	17,701	19,477	15,562
Beverages	6	68	3	12	52	#	9	#
Tobacco	2,593	7,533	14,830	18,809	20,652	17,701	19,468	15,562
Crude Materials	1,979	6,877	22,192	21,768	18,818	12,304	10,134	15,063
Hides and Skins	324	189	3,256	1,682	1,420	1,827	2,274	4,020
Oilseeds	276	338	3,102	2,814	1,360	788	1,152	320
Natural Rubber	57	121	265	82	35	9	#	#
Textile Fibers	1,232	4,572	11,512	13,648	12,578	6,630	4,229	7,723
Crude Mat Nes	90	1,657	4,057	3,542	3,425	3,050	2,479	3,000[†]
Animal Vegetable Oils	73	56	511	409	160	580	4,381	8,100
Animal Fats	23	9	8	93	#	#	#	#
Fixed Vegetable Oils	49	43	499	309	114	576	4,367	8,100
Processed Oils	1	4	4	7	46	4	14	#
Fish and Fishery Products	~	~	24,985	18,700	26,441	28,228	36,143	33,455
Forest Products	~	~	46,493	31,339	34,459	46,385	35,380	31,080
Agricultural Requisites	52	74	1,038	369	275	89	22	30
Crude Fertilizers	2	#	13	8	4	3	4	#
Manuf Fertilizers	- -	13	842	129	6	#	#	#
Pesticides	50	61	183	232	265	86	18	30[†]
Agricultural Machines	- -	#	#	#	#	#	#	#

SOURCE: FAO-TY, 1975, Section IV; 1980, Section IV; 1981, Section IV; 1983, Section IV
1985, Section IV.

Table 2534

MEXICO ABSOLUTE VALUE OF TRADE, 1970–84

(T US)

Imports

Category	1970	1975	1979	1980	1981	1982	1983	1984
Total Merchandise Trade	2,319,520	6,570,490	12,586,430	19,516,960	25,053,610	15,067,730	9,005,760	11,788,190
Agricultural Products, Total	216,277	935,594	1,342,150	3,140,600	3,381,250	1,900,810	2,352,710	2,332,370
Food and Animals	123,497	782,525	806,850	2,411,600	2,434,700	1,173,490	1,663,370	1,290,350
Live Animals	9,144	24,817	37,439	32,727	68,420	58,520	10,020	59,000
Meat and Meat Prep	5,192	10,180	29,469	45,604	84,683	61,300	43,280	67,210
Dairy Products Eggs	18,166	35,268	101,910	239,057	236,273	220,420	150,480	132,510
Cereals and Prep	65,517	581,111	510,920	1,142,671	1,166,280	464,060	1,145,520	835,420
Fruits and Vegetables	10,685	81,215	36,180	276,760	395,120	134,110	20,140	60,430
Sugar and Honey	2,281	2,616	5,770	568,010	366,700	141,700	188,000	75,430
Coffee, Tea, Cocoa Sp	3,030	5,078	13,550	8,278	22,050	12,400	4,600	7,050
Feeding Stuff	1,945	29,729	40,170	92,400	83,820	52,400	89,050	31,520
Miscellaneous Food	7,537	12,151	31,445	6,083	11,356	28,580	12,280	21,770
Beverages Tobacco	4,926	24,812	44,931	73,388	98,580	21,480	1,180	6,300
Beverages	4,100	24,531	44,798	72,244	98,520	21,840	1,180	6,290
Tobacco	826	281	133	1,144	59	#	#	#
Crude Materials	76,323	93,460	440,330	513,094	788,970	577,060	581,770	863,380
Hides and Skins	18,248	26,016	89,140	68,100	75,182	67,700	59,530	62,820
Oilseeds	18,524	9,746	218,420	308,514	539,481	388,880	392,090	689,890
Natural Rubber	12,847	24,327	58,340	73,659	68,360	53,280	53,720	56,200
Textile Fibers	16,068	12,521	31,250	37,590	42,060	27,570	16,980	23,170
Crude Mat Nes	10,636	20,850	43,179	50,400‡	63,880‡	39,630‡	59,440	31,300‡
Animal Vegetable Oil	11,531	34,797	52,207	117,357	59,010	128,420	106,390	172,340
Animal Fats	3,290	10,746	35,950	49,938	38,880	39,400	36,030	58,640
Fixed Vegetable Oils	5,293	18,960	4,297	55,448	5,450	74,320	55,640	111,260
Processed Oils	2,948	5,091	11,960	11,971	14,677	14,704†	14,720	2,450
Fish and Fishery Products	~	~	29,680	35,210	33,870	27,570	4,680	8,000†
Forest Products	~	~	245,320	609,380	632,460	641,860	367,390	356,370
Agricultural Requisites	76,879	306,824	417,780	390,355	506,764	550,110	479,000	520,610
Crude Fertilizers	7,077	42,844	41,666	73,276	67,294	51,400	48,000	43,030
Manuf Fertilizers	5,758	75,565	74,776	68,147	98,860	129,010	61,200†	88,170
Pesticides	3,645	11,390	13,308	19,741	17,933	19,000†	20,000†	22,000†
Agriculture Machines	60,399	177,025	288,030	229,191	322,680	350,700†	349,800†	367,420

Exports

Category	1970	1975	1979	1980	1981	1982	1983	1984
Total Merchandise Trade	1,282,000	2,861,031	8,816,978	15,307,480	19,419,610	21,229,664	22,312,040	24,053,560
Agricultural Products, Total	694,505	972,500	2,043,900	1,720,210	1,564,370	1,396,330	1,622,400	1,709,480
Food and Animals	521,228	697,796	1,444,920	1,146,704	1,014,970	988,330	1,309,390	1,263,020
Live Animals	79,184	29,052	120,594	98,350	71,233	107,676	168,480	114,320
Meat and Meat Prep	46,109	9,470	39,460	27,356	28,249	21,339	11,800	15,900
Dairy Products Eggs	27	176	81	35	11	#	30	130
Cereals and Prep	5,993	16,110	11,757	13,640	6,120	17,880	39,900	3,360
Fruits and Vegetables	187,148	257,411	500,510	439,444	499,440	412,450	456,630	562,350
Sugar and Honey	103,020	171,052	117,110	73,793	43,466	34,260	66,400	52,250
Coffee, Tea, Cocoa Sp	98,486	211,718	648,567	491,213	364,073	392,650	564,080	512,740
Feeding Stuff	505	175	810	1,838	973	270	270	80
Miscellaneous Food	756	2,632	6,026	1,035	1,400	1,800	1,800	1,890
Beverages Tobacco	15,838	53,394	101,682	126,254	120,920	114,920	101,520	124,780
Beverages	4,272	27,824	62,187	77,444	72,110	67,350	79,180	94,360
Tobacco	11,566	25,570	39,500	48,810	48,810	47,564	22,340	30,420
Crude Materials	155,619	219,034	493,940	442,240	425,870	290,940	209,150	319,580
Hides and Skins	16	31	65	1,256	1,611	#	370	1,050
Oilseeds	2,382	12,212	92,451	57,995	45,567	29,162	26,430	48,970
Natural Rubber	3,722	2,822	3,094	3,251	2,846	3,300	860	740
Textile Fibers	135,194	174,691	363,589	329,738	320,848	195,480	26,490	218,820
Crude Mat Nes	14,305	29,278	34,741	50,000‡	55,000‡	63,000‡	55,000‡	50,000‡
Animal Vegetable Oils	1,820	2,276	3,365	5,014	2,613	2,150	2,340	2,110
Animal Fats	- -	#	522	468	207	#	40	
Fixed Vegetable Oils	- -	#	128	442	450	#	90	180
Processed Oils	1,820	2,276	2,715	4,104	1,956	2,150	2,210	1,930
Fish and Fishery Products	~	~	455,340	580,040	494,480	396,180	436,750	468,230
Forest Products	~	~	4,510	10,930	7,080	6,020	18,230	17,950
Agricultural Requisites	9,724	7,700	26,083	27,688	17,612	15,750	35,900	30,710
Crude Fertilizers	344	4	#	#	1,127	1,400	#	#
Manuf Fertilizers	8,051	1,548	12,647	12,440	5,108	2,210†	23,150†	18,590
Pesticides	938	1,744	4,870	5,838	2,223	2,500†	2,800†	2,540
Agricultural Machines	391	4,404	8,566	9,410	9,154	9,640	9,950	9,580

SOURCE: FAO-TY, 1975, Section IV; 1980, Section IV; 1981, Section IV; 1983, Section IV;
1985, Section IV.

Table 2535

NICARAGUA ABSOLUTE VALUE OF TRADE, 1970–84

(T US)

Imports

Category	1970	1975	1979	1980	1981	1982	1983	1984
Total Merchandise Trade	198,748	516,864	360,196	887,211	999,441	775,548	847,470	792,200
Agricultural Products, Total	19,996	44,139	50,867	138,393	136,420	94,602	109,682	140,158
Food and Animals	15,870	37,805	41,447	109,412	109,979	71,177	79,934	95,645
Live Animals	737	1,271	651	2,708	4,561	1,464	1,598	2,179
Meat and Meat Prep	385	1,208	2,444	7,630	7,607	910	2,431	4,657
Dairy Products Eggs	1,055	1,719	4,148	6,810	11,628	17,756	11,692	15,554
Cereals and Prep	4,817	18,630	16,962	48,176	38,558	32,315	52,364	47,916
Fruits and Vegetables	3,494	6,850	9,619	32,442	35,256	7,403	5,758	11,068
Sugar and Honey	1,009	1,777	2,158	2,580	5,316	5,234	3,636	47
Coffee, Tea, Cocoa Sp	379	1,114	866	2,234	1,338	446	408	187
Feeding Stuff	429	1,033	724	453	458	93	326	3,637
Miscellaneous Food	3,565	4,203	3,875	6,379	5,257	5,556	1,721	10,400
Beverages Tobacco	1,304	1,524	1,629	1,080	559	197	552	259
Beverages	746	1,118	1,224	550	410	184	389	122
Tobacco	558	406	435	530	149	13	133	137
Crude Materials	1,185	1,405	2,514	9,470	6,814	7,185	9,859	9,863
Hides and Skins	39	188	#	#	#	#		
Oilseeds	391	537	500	5,458	2,984	5,756	7,827	8,310
Natural Rubber	140	12	84	230	698	220	853	553
Textile Fibers	428	50	1,538	3,023	15	93	179	
Crude Mat Nes	187	618	392	759	3,117	1,116	1,000[†]	1,000[†]
Animal Vegetable Oil	1,637	3,405	5,247	18,431	19,068	16,043	19,367	34,391
Animal Fats	1,160	2,707	3,698	6,127	9,220	6,814	7,555	8,533
Fixed Vegetable Oils	381	603	1,490	12,149	9,747	8,999	11,591	25,732
Processed Oils	96	95	59	155	101	230	221	126
Fish and Fishery Products	~	~	713	1,428	220	1,157	1,896	1,150[†]
Forest Products	~	~	9,716	13,321	14,321	12,368	12,368	12,368
Agricultural Requisites	9,139	39,549	19,996	75,592	72,742	50,622	64,151	71,029
Crude Fertilizers	~	#	#	1	#	#	#	#
Manuf Fertilizers	4,112	22,002	6,768	35,455	24,243	12,003	21,352	22,498
Pesticides	2,744	7,733	6,274	21,458	24,816	15,649	24,766	24,706
Agriculture Machines	2,283	9,814	6,954	18,678	23,683	22,970	18,033	23,825

Exports

Category	1970	1975	1979	1980	1981	1982	1983	1984
Total Merchandise Trade	178,623	375,172	566,555	450,442	499,833	405,793	428,336	392,575
Agricultural Products, Total	131,901	277,198	582,169	343,807	418,493	341,359	339,565	314,645
Food and Animals	82,914	154,921	427,752	301,602	278,643	237,278	212,775	162,249
Live Animals	581	2,444	100,135	30,041	20,031	#	65	61
Meat and Meat Prep	26,901	28,608	95,384	58,800	21,273	31,404	29,594	19,283
Dairy Products Eggs	2,356	6,794	2,554	2	1,877	4,234	#	#
Cereals and Prep	5,218	7,151	3,580	4,615	8,283	4,850	2,532	1,963
Fruits and Vegetables	1,633	5,785	8,325	9,825	24,409	31,254	20,205	17,722
Sugar and Honey	10,367	45,148	22,841	25,998	54,330	31,254	32,898	22,912
Coffee, Tea, Cocoa Sp	32,845	49,272	180,183	169,716	141,896	128,579	120,191	92,857
Feeding Stuff	2,983	9,691	14,576	2,477	6,488	5,014	7,290	7,451
Miscellaneous Food	30	28	174	128	56	#	#	#
Beverages Tobacco	2,442	5,825	4,374	2,660	5,663	7,034	5,585	4,485
Beverages	32	186	237	98	139	882	508	263
Tobacco	2,410	5,639	4,137	2,562	5,524	6,152	5,077	4,222
Crude Materials	42,505	107,930	145,867	39,537	133,660	96,573	121,146	147,880
Hides and Skins	265	482	2,282	586	641	164	94	190
Oilseeds	3,577	4,657	3,493	6,957	9,080	6,552	6,528	6,751
Natural Rubber	- -	#	#	#	#	#	#	#
Textile Fibers	35,262	98,524	139,166	30,922	123,656	85,817	113,524	139,939
Crude Mat Nes	3,401	4,267	926	1,072	303	762	1,000[†]	1,000[†]
Animal Vegetable Oils	4,040	8,522	4,176	8	507	474	59	31
Animal Fats	- -	#	129	#	#	#	#	#
Fixed Vegetable Oils	4,035	8,515	4,039	8	507	474	59	31
Processed Oils	5	7	8	#	#	#	#	#
Fish and Fishery Products	~	~	23,234	31,335	16,839	18,179	12,435	12,604
Forest Products	~	~	7,390	4,270	3,701	1,950	2,569	2,569
Agricultural Requisites	570	4,122	2,598	1,907	736	440	540	500
Crude Fertilizers	~	#	#	#	#	#	#	#
Manuf Fertilizers	30	201	91	#	6	#	#	#
Pesticides	540	3,827	2,507	1,907	730	440	540	500[†]
Agricultural Machines	- -	94	#	#	#	#	#	#

SOURCE: FAO-TY, 1975, Section IV; 1980, Section IV; 1981, Section IV; 1983, Section IV;
1985, Section IV.

Table 2536

PANAMA ABSOLUTE VALUE OF TRADE, 1970–84

(T US)

				Imports				
Category	1970	1975	1979	1980	1981	1982	1983	1984
Total Merchandise Trade	326,352	815,568	1,062,913	1,288,884	1,391,819	1,407,407	1,266,174	1,269,820
Agricultural Products, Total	28,227	65,890	95,605	120,104	130,383	122,375	124,158	122,909
Food and Animals	22,128	50,272	71,944	91,204	107,150	97,078	98,931	96,604
Live Animals	318	301	314	146	282	383	307	249
Meat and Meat Prep	4,106	6,633	10,170	12,427	13,919	12,236	14,631	8,928
Dairy Products Eggs	3,250	8,327	9,705	16,920	9,786	13,504	15,247	16,007
Cereals and Prep	4,863	17,037	18,941	23,760	32,876	26,156	24,170	24,918
Fruits and Vegetables	5,954	8,509	19,066	21,254	24,915	23,606	22,622	22,914
Sugar and Honey	423	3,516	1,641	2,011	2,240	2,388	2,340	2,470
Coffee, Tea, Cocoa Sp	1,109	1,959	3,770	4,560	4,912	5,028	6,718	7,714
Feeding Stuff	1,192	2,411	5,587	6,683	11,828	9,819	9,425	9,882
Miscellaneous Food	809	1,579	2,750	3,413	3,842	3,958	3,471	3,522
Beverages Tobacco	3,116	4,535	6,933	7,829	9,814	8,729	7,882	8,062
Beverages	1,883	2,704	4,439	5,359	7,274	6,331	6,000	6,604
Tobacco	1,233	1,831	2,494	2,470	2,540	2,398	1,882	1,458
Crude Materials	481	1,338	2,062	2,540	2,455	2,594	2,343	3,119
Hides and Skins	- -	#	102	22	37	32	22	#
Oilseeds	111	184	582	348	204	273	288	375
Natural Rubber	- -	3	235	595	560	841	797	950[†]
Textile Fibers	121	163	99	332	188	279	138	207
Crude Mat Nes	249	988	1,044	1,243	1,466	1,169	1,098	1,587
Animal Vegetable Oil	2,606	9,745	14,666	18,531	13,514	13,974	15,002	15,124
Animal Fats	5	492	821	1,273	1,231	990	1,255	1,219
Fixed Vegetable Oils	2,594	9,191	13,741	17,016	12,104	12,847	13,559	13,748
Processed Oils	7	62	104	242	179	137	188	157
Fish and Fishery Products	~	~	5,466	6,313	6,526	6,674	7,984	4,950[†]
Forest Products	~	~	29,155	34,264	35,556	33,373	27,452	36,881
Agricultural Requisites	12,640	41,904	35,532	41,004	45,125	41,289	32,717	36,424
Crude Fertilizers	1	#	#	#	5	1	4	4
Manuf Fertilizers	2,948	13,314	14,959	17,715	18,431	10,068	8,163	8,526
Pesticides	2,617	10,037	12,052	14,706	17,534	20,539	18,747	22,532
Agriculture Machines	7,074	18,553	8,521	8,583	9,155	10,681	5,803	5,362

				Exports				
Category	1970	1975	1979	1980	1981	1982	1983	1984
Total Merchandise Trade	109,497	286,445	294,739	353,377	319,420	390,313	303,545	256,307
Agricultural Products, Total	71,592	120,439	132,549	170,938	165,970	136,181	165,582	150,830
Food and Animals	70,844	118,714	127,168	164,803	159,904	129,792	158,962	144,220
Live Animals	7	795	351	1,382	1,715	2,965	4,109	2,251
Meat and Meat Prep	2,448	1,569	1,564	3,125	5,094	9,352	4,110	1,462
Dairy Products Eggs	8	345	4,035	7,832	7,548	3,888	3,586	3,502
Cereals and Prep	5	40	3,461	115	200	1,335	1,735	146
Fruits and Vegetables	60,922	61,479	70,792	65,763	75,321	70,652	81,458	80,664
Sugar and Honey	5,689	50,885	26,982	69,702	52,650	24,516	42,607	35,043
Coffee, Tea, Cocoa Sp	1,717	3,101	13,928	13,024	15,356	15,104	18,963	18,574
Feeding Stuff	- -	9	189	584	115	207	54	178
Miscellaneous Food	48	491	2,695	3,276	1,905	1,773	2,340	2,400
Beverages Tobacco	20	1,103	4,335	5,289	5,448	5,027	5,330	4,464
Beverages	18	303	2,661	3,886	3,264	2,753	3,214	2,591
Tobacco	2	800	1,674	1,403	2,184	2,274	2,116	1,873
Crude Materials	728	622	1,013	846	617	1,362	1,290	2,146
Hides and Skins	537	325	440	396	432	913	916	257
Oilseeds	- -	#	#	#	#	#	#	#
Natural Rubber	34	#	#	#	#	#	#	#
Textile Fibers	- -	#	#	#	#	#	#	#
Crude Mat Nes	157	297	573	450	185	449	374	1,889
Animal Vegetable Oils	- -	#	33	#	1	#	#	#
Animal Fats	- -	#	#	#	#	#	#	#
Fixed Vegetable Oils	- -	#	33	#	1	#	#	#
Processed Oils	- -	#	#	#	#	#	#	#
Fish and Fishery Products	~	~	56,904	66,040	57,816	69,000	72,569	85,890[†]
Forest Products	~	~	405	1,038	1,156	1,234	1,237	1,029
Agricultural Requisites	- -	700	906	1,812	169	149	536	1,384
Crude Fertilizers	- -	#	#	#	#	#	#	#
Manuf Fertilizers	- -	#	#	#	17	7	#	#
Pesticides	- -	700[†]	906	588	152	142	536	1,384
Agricultural Machines	- -	#	#	1,224	#	#	#	#

SOURCE: FAO-TY, 1975, Section IV; 1980, Section IV; 1981, Section IV; 1983, Section IV;
1985, Section IV.

Table 2537

PARAGUAY ABSOLUTE VALUE OF TRADE, 1975-84

(T US)

Imports

Category	1975	1979	1980	1981	1982	1983	1984
Total Merchandise Trade	178,361	437,722	517,141	506,111	581,474	478,264	513,054
Agricultural Products, Total	70,657	64,135	64,648	66,510	57,677	42,675	33,590
Food and Animals	52,484	17,599	18,983	23,987	15,193	24,406	9,176
Live Animals	45,000	1,029	727	870	557	451	623
Meat and Meat Prep	#	#	850	600	150	135	120
Dairy Products Eggs	409	230	1,294	2,648	1,364	2,202	1,769
Cereals and Prep	5,526	10,362	14,406	17,148	9,395	18,809	4,518
Fruits and Vegetables	298	1,417	1,057	1,946	2,438	1,499	811
Sugar and Honey	65	325	304	423	957	986	1,000
Coffee, Tea, Cocoa Sp	#	6	#	#	30	50	35
Feeding Stuff	#	#	#	#	#	#	#
Miscellaneous Food	1,186	4,230	345‡	352	302	274	300†
Beverages Tobacco	18,173	45,766	45,665	41,223	39,684	16,569	22,764
Beverages	13,324	28,438	31,392	31,194	28,006	11,458	13,800
Tobacco	4,849	17,328	14,273	10,029	11,678	5,111	8,964
Crude Materials	#	770	#	1,300	2,800	1,700	1,650
Hides and Skins	#	#	#	#	#	#	#
Oilseeds	#	282	#	1,300	2,800	1,700	1,650
Natural Rubber	#	#	#	#	#	~	~
Textile Fibers	#	#	#	#	#	#	#
Crude Mat Nes	#	488	#	#	#	#	#
Animal Vegetable Oil	#	#	#	#	#	#	#
Animal Fats	#	#	#	#	#	~	~
Fixed Vegetable Oils	#	#	#	#	#	#	#
Processed Oils	#	#	#	#	#	~	~
Fish and Fishery Products	~	~	~	~	~	~	~
Forest Products	~	8,611	11,524	8,902	11,971	6,077	7,450
Agricultural Requisites	10,590	21,520	25,200	25,155	25,855	26,820	28,130
Crude Fertilizers	131	#	#	#	#	~	#
Manuf Fertilizers	560	1,020†	2,500†	3,400†	2,240†	2,500†	2,710†
Pesticides	1,167	2,800†	3,000†	2,900†	3,100†	3,150†	3,200†
Agriculture Machines	8,732	17,700†	19,700†	18,855†	20,515†	21,170†	22,220†

Exports

Category	1975	1979	1980	1981	1982	1983	1984
Total Merchandise Trade	176,711	305,176	310,230	295,541	329,784	269,176	334,502
Agricultural Products, Total	146,823	249,379	229,605	245,136	278,096	243,705	302,965
Food and Animals	80,849	40,726	46,033	24,602	31,272	31,808	26,066
Live Animals	12,000†	#	#	#	#	#	#
Meat and Meat Prep	32,050	5,400	1,054	3	2,187	6,121	4,785
Dairy Products Eggs	#	#	#	#	#	#	#
Cereals and Prep	635	24	2,493	295	580	#	695
Fruits and Vegetables	10,508	6,023	11,247	6,650	9,812	3,779	3,405
Sugar and Honey	7,523	27	3,112	101	3,924	5,438	4,183
Coffee, Tea, Cocoa Sp	8,987	5,325	4,233	1,609	475	42	178
Feeding Stuff	5,148	14,155	22,394	14,344	12,706	14,528	10,820
Miscellaneous Food	3,998	1,772	1,500†	1,600†	1,700†	1,900†	2,000†
Beverages Tobacco	12,017	8,564	10,197	6,489	5,979	10,171	14,653
Beverages	#	1	55	31	#	#	#
Tobacco	12,017	8,563	10,142	6,458	5,979	10,171	14,653
Crude Materials	43,345	188,978	156,394	191,624	222,062	182,239	243,156
Hides and Skins	2,776	7,034	3,903	6,960	7,203	7,421	7,262
Oilseeds	19,092	81,349	45,272	52,541	90,964	88,487	104,638
Natural Rubber	#	#	#	#	#	~	~
Textile Fibers	21,189	100,296	106,967	131,889	123,752	86,262	131,156
Crude Mat Nes	288	299	252	234	143	69	100†
Animal Vegetable Oils	10,612	19,111	16,981	22,421	18,783	19,487	19,090
Animal Fats	#	#	#	#	#	~	~
Fixed Vegetable Oils	10,612	19,111	16,981	22,421	18,783	19,487	19,090
Processed Oils	#	#	#	#	#	~	~
Fish and Fishery Products	~	~	~	~	~	~	~
Forest Products	~	39,477	66,451	59,289	91,859	70,635	87,236
Agricultural Requisites	#	#	#	#	#	#	#
Crude Fertilizers	#	#	#	#	#	~	~
Manuf Fertilizers	#	#	#	#	#	#	#
Pesticides	#	#	#	#	#	#	#
Agricultural Machines	#	#	#	#	#	#	#

SOURCE: FAO-TY, 1980, Section IV; 1981, Section IV; 1983, Section IV; 1985, Section IV.

Table 2538

PERU ABSOLUTE VALUE OF TRADE, 1970–84

(T US)

Imports

Category	1970	1975	1979	1980	1981	1982	1983	1984
Total Merchandise Trade	621,763	2,379,578	1,475,510	2,573,365	3,159,530	2,940,255	2,722,000	2,140,000[‡]
Agricultural Products, Total	125,526	389,991	313,752	524,117	643,967	532,853	484,319	356,220
Food and Animals	106,421	322,710	270,235	466,220	566,880	467,764	413,983	290,387
Live Animals	24,201	4,389	2,929	1,815	2,402	3,812	2,189	2,109
Meat and Meat Prep	13,007	8,794	1,476	12,416	23,566	52,147	24,152	22,378
Dairy Products Eggs	11,985	41,742	24,627	42,089	38,685	62,631	52,090	35,639
Cereals and Prep	43,668	252,337	234,300	325,356	359,673	289,994	251,946	179,217
Fruits and Vegetables	7,256	2,624	1,713	23,596	24,209	24,078	13,080	10,248
Sugar and Honey	71	660	218	34,894	85,166	2,417	59,103	28,093
Coffee, Tea, Cocoa Sp	2,376	5,607	2,966	6,419	15,035	17,520	3,180	3,758
Feeding Stuff	1,617	160	163	15,587	13,917	10,349	4,213	4,595
Miscellaneous Food	2,240	6,397	1,843	4,048	4,227	4,816	4,030	4,350
Beverages Tobacco	2,410	5,054	3,614	9,018	8,875	14,716	10,276	7,259
Beverages	1,948	1,832	1,334	5,559	4,975	10,107	7,852	4,086
Tobacco	462	3,222	2,280	3,459	3,900	4,609	2,424	3,173
Crude Materials	6,886	20,708	22,205	19,670	31,569	18,458	17,359	18,246
Hides and Skins	1,697	4,694	543	3,008	8,962	1,685	119	309
Oilseeds	788	4,359	8,520	239	2,881	452	3,026	1,590
Natural Rubber	2,001	5,004	9,828	10,196	8,700	5,298	5,196	6,847
Textile Fibers	627	1,771	290	214	87	911	18	#
Crude Mat Nes	1,773	4,880	3,024	6,013	10,939	10,112	9,000[†]	9,500[†]
Animal Vegetable Oil	9,809	41,519	17,698	29,209	36,643	31,915	42,701	40,328
Animal Fats	720	2,549	2,028	1,730	1,661	1,117	2,731	1,197
Fixed Vegetable Oils	8,804	37,311	15,052	26,694	31,333	28,109	37,140	38,390
Processed Oils	285	1,659	618	785	3,649	2,689	2,830	741
Fish and Fishery Products	~	~	464	3,742	2,721	655	20,251	600[†]
Forest Products	~	~	26,616	37,829	57,034	74,314	48,214	48,214
Agricultural Requisites	16,386	99,837	51,079	77,020	71,646	70,462	70,417	72,298
Crude Fertilizers	111	400	#	735	62	14	#	1,216
Manuf Fertilizers	5,465	58,329	18,993	26,631	12,722	11,103	7,827	7,624
Pesticides	4,258	17,303	12,691	14,335	16,021	12,344	14,090	12,748
Agriculture Machines	6,552	23,805	19,395	35,319	42,841	47,001	48,500[†]	50,710[†]

Exports

Category	1970	1975	1979	1980	1981	1982	1983	1984
Total Merchandise Trade	1,047,858	1,314,599	3,389,905	3,308.990	2,407,711	2,812,830	3,257,558	3,362,110
Agricultural Products, Total	177,463	434,526	463,715	320,861	223,502	263,547	223,193	252,334
Food and Animals	114,797	353,681	359,489	214,256	142,099	170,691	154,118	196,129
Live Animals	247	249	2,784	1,136	1,277	1,007	522	588
Meat and Meat Prep	- -	621	1,951	2,450	946	1,631	1,950	389
Dairy Products Eggs	- -	40	3,841	1,435	180	50	#	#
Cereals and Prep	140	1,502	3,560	5,021	2,586	2,054	1,329	733
Fruits and Vegetables	2,900	4,582	22,258	23,635	16,708	22,309	13,002	16,589
Sugar and Honey	66,245	296,435	63,837	15,426	928	18,081	4,006	19,071
Coffee, Tea, Cocoa Sp	44,996	49,658	254,804	162,770	116,501	123,016	131,789	156,115
Feeding Stuff	243	16	1,816	1,680	1,503	1,492	220	1,223
Miscellaneous Food	26	578	4,638	703	1,470	1,051	1,300	1,421
Beverages Tobacco	285	1,365	2,427	1,145	1,165	929	336	581
Beverages	91	199	674	849	915	731	141	289
Tobacco	194	1,166	1,753	296	250	198	195	292
Crude Materials	61,387	77,929	92,802	100,404	78,391	90,207	68,239	55,314
Hides and Skins	2,274	610	1,158	201	25	41	36	#
Oilseeds	- -	#	40	52	34	12	5	41
Natural Rubber	- -	#	#	10	19	#	#	#
Textile Fibers	55,803	71,204	82,210	93,896	68,775	81,764	53,098	41,173
Crude Mat Nes	3,310	6,115	9,394	6,245	9,538	8,390	15,100[‡]	14,100[‡]
Animal Vegetable Oils	994	1,551	8,997	5,056	1,817	1,720	500	310
Animal Fats	- -	#	#	#	#	#	#	#
Fixed Vegetable Oils	- -	#	#	#	#	#	#	#
Processed Oils	994	1,551	8,997	5,056	1,847	1,720	500	310
Fish and Fishery Products	~	~	278,075	321,821	271,461	288,758	143,929	213,468
Forest Products	~	~	10,624	6,830	7,133	6,456	7,917	7,917
Agricultural Requisites	454	1,432	1,441	3,980	1,654	1,928	1,537	1,638
Crude Fertilizers	410	1,016	200	33	388	562	131	354
Manuf Fertilizers	19	15	28	2,720	25	6	#	4
Pesticides	22	120	803	1,043	986	387	636	450[†]
Agricultural Machines	3	281	410	184	255	973	770	830

SOURCE: FAO-TY, 1975, Section IV; 1980, Section IV; 1981, Section IV; 1982, Section IV; 1985, Section IV.

Table 2539

URUGUAY ABSOLUTE VALUE OF TRADE, 1975–84

(T US)

				Imports			
Category	1975	1979	1980	1981	1982	1983	1984
Total Merchandise Trade	516,198	1,206,290	1,680,350	1,641,120	1,109,976	787,508	785,831
Agricultural Products, Total	60,507	170,155	153,742	134,722	82,442	81,426	94,765
Food and Animals	22,627	101,954	87,495	91,423	47,047	45,378	51,614
Live Animals	302	738	1,637	1,727	216	174	241
Meats and Meat Prep	60	219	1,171	1,778	528	26	128
Dairy Products Eggs	761	969	1,141	1,494	772	190	258
Cereals and Prep	652	52,526	9,912	14,538	8,307	18,979	19,068
Fruits and Vegetables	5,926	16,372	22,526	24,159	14,977	7,770	10,930
Sugar and Honey	64	4,206	8,357	14,190	1,198	363	542
Coffee, Tea, Cocoa Sp	13,686	23,425	36,783	28,206	16,843	15,787	18,268
Feeding Stuff	1,094	2,901	4,858	3,359	2,276	1,201	1,384
Miscellaneous Food	82	598	1,110	1,972	1,930	888	795
Beverages Tobacco	6,206	14,809	19,368	17,573	15,023	7,188	9,626
Beverages	912	7,235	9,323	8,759	6,655	3,540	4,784
Tobacco	5,294	7,574	10,045	8,814	8,368	3,648	4,842
Crude Materials	17,890	35,891	35,613	22,919	17,054	22,619	24,929
Hides and Skins	3,885	9,418	7,601	4,175	3,085	3,380	8,684
Oilseeds	23	1,019	489	159	94	286	177
Natural Rubber	2,284	5,465	7,345	4,505	1,204	2,174	2,357
Textile Fibers	8,301	15,277	13,336	9,365	9,326	13,627	11,750
Crude Mat Nes	3,397	4,712	6,842	4,715	3,345	3,152	1,961
Animal Vegetable Oil	13,784	17,501	11,266	2,807	3,318	6,241	8,596
Animal Fats	224	6,763	4,026	148	174	70	840
Fixed Vegetable Oils	13,390	10,492	6,951	2,435	2,971	6,061	7,542
Processed Oils	170	246	289	224	173	110	214
Fish and Fishery Products	~	2,796	4,842	1,470	1,328	412	#
Forest Products	~	26,513	33,226	33,092	20,795	13,656	13,656
Agricultural Requisites	40,148	75,986	84,000	54,315	33,042	25,243	36,748
Crude Fertilizers	6,743	7,100	6,800	3,057	1,793	1,077	1,722
Manuf Fertilizers	17,397	22,904	27,661	22,313	18,704	13,998	18,269
Pesticides	2,748	7,323	8,088	7,366	7,101	6,508	7,393
Agriculture Machines	13,260	38,659	41,451	21,579	26,800	3,660	9,364

				Exports			
Category	1975	1979	1980	1981	1982	1983	1984
Total Merchandise Trade	381,198	788,134	1,058,550	1,215,380	1,022,884	1,045,147	928,906
Agricultural Products, Total	260,116	367,292	595,123	771,154	635,198	678,284	521,489
Food and Animals	156,656	235,965	337,380	500,011	397,942	476,403	326,350
Live Animals	5,024	10,907	7,905	13,493	14,971	31,028	8,785
Meats and Meat Prep	85,692	111,467	187,477	263,714	208,372	255,504	157,997
Dairy Products Eggs	2,174	11,030	16,701	23,597	15,962	33,228	17,893
Cereals and Prep	50,184	74,315	88,070	166,622	138,875	124,742	113,354
Fruits and Vegetables	5,542	12,440	12,914	11.762	7,089	11,603	13,088
Sugar and Honey	708	1,245	2,382	3,097	2,300	8,041	6,007
Coffee, Tea, Cocoa Sp	109	1,113	1,972	1,573	395	350	716
Feeding Stuff	6,371	10,545	15,345	10,796	8,428	11,675	8,486
Miscellaneous Food	852	2,903	4,614	5,357	1,550	232	24
Beverages Tobacco	288	1,570	1,053	319	443	13	1,157
Beverages	279	1,490	952	282	366	#	21
Tobacco	9	80	101	37	77	13	1,136
Crude Materials	95,724	119,322	238,264	262,992	231,488	193,813	187,515
Hides and Skins	2,411	2,534	3,448	4,245	7,038	6,902	4,541
Oilseeds	#	2,440	6,316	6,402	6,072	2,184	2,135
Natural Rubber	#	60	125	3	262	26	6
Textile Fibers	90,524	110,318	221,220	241,678	209,575	175,888	172,331
Crude Mat Nes	2,789	3,970	7,155	10,664	8,541	8,813	8,502
Animal Vegetable Oil	7,488	10,435	18,426	7,832	5,325	8,055	6,467
Animal Fats	261	4,810	7,170	2,633	2,253	6,241	3,775
Fixed Vegetable Oils	7,089	5,283	10,722	4,187	2,017	686	1,480
Processed Oils	98	342	534	1,012	1,055	1,128	1,212
Fish and Fishery Products	~	36,353	50,898	61,300	47,500	45,694	48,860
Forest Products	~	6,535	10,381	7,663	4,579	6,646	6,646
Agricultural Requisites	187	5,322	6,483	3,953	4,221	1,105	1,648
Crude Fertilizers	#	#	#	#	#	#	50
Manuf Fertilizers	187	4,338	6,122	3,680	3,338	593	1,118
Pesticides	#	32	41	63	226	263	230
Agriculture Machines	#	952	320	210	657	249	250

SOURCE: FAO-TY, 1980, Section IV; 1981, Section IV; 1982, Section IV; 1985, Section IV.

Table 2540

VENEZUELA ABSOLUTE VALUE OF TRADE, 1970–84

(T US)

Imports

Category	1970	1975	1979	1980	1981	1982	1983	1984
Total Merchandise Trade	1,665,031	5,807,319	9,598,400	10,669,150	11,810,900	11,665,000	7,851,000‡	6,676,000‡
Agricultural Products, Total	200,829	698,674	1,298,090	1,714,550	2,002,940	1,764,990	1,403,920	1,774,990
Food and Animals	151,369	482,918	952,340	1,331,100	1,629,720	1,456,160	1,105,260	1,222,710
Live Animals	23,510	60,449	85,686	67,439	74,114	99,710	84,670	58,180
Meat and Meat Prep	3,934	8,952	84,110	52,040	88,433	74,590	56,180	21,200
Dairy Products Eggs	13,079	55,566	88,316	132,261	212,226	217,130	133,940	166,460
Cereals and Prep	70,005	261,143	338,482	586,025	585,451	445,730	456,900	540,530
Fruits and Vegetables	28,303	60,496	128,010	125,240	178,420	138,800	86,300	91,020
Sugar and Honey	418	2,756	83,503	221,058	301,323	254,270	129,980	134,280
Coffee, Tea, Cocoa Sp	1,931	3,595	7,656	7,705	9,501	9,780	5,480	12,750
Feeding Stuff	3,198	19,816	91,924	103,977	119,053	144,640	135,700	161,190
Miscellaneous Food	6,469	10,145	44,650	35,351	61,201	71,520	16,110	37,100
Beverages Tobacco	16,550	61,238	113,378	152,668	127,729	120,570	108,770	144,630
Beverages	16,355	59,823	112,305	150,713	126,057	117,920	107,620	143,490
Tobacco	195	1,415	1,073	1,955	1,672	2,651	1,150	1,140
Crude Materials	22,233	71,549	63,951	77,899	85,499	86,180	61,830	129,960
Hides and Skins	473	1,690	617	3,013	2,848	3,500	4,040	8,110
Oilseeds	8,170	50,283	15,856	19,735	21,529	18,320	19,610	35,420
Natural Rubber	4,869	5,017	15,182	20,449	19,501	14,280	21,150	24,280
Textile Fibers	5,504	5,537	17,673	3,536	11,931	30,380	7,040	42,160
Crude Mat Nes	3,217	9,022	14,623	31,166	29,690	19,710	10,000‡	20,000†
Animal Vegetable Oil	10,677	82,969	168,424	152,888	159,990	102,080	128,070	277,700
Animal Fats	1,570	4,256	10,960	15,716	11,422	11,220	13,500	22,510
Fixed Vegetable Oils	8,501	76,669	153,448	132,469	145,202	87,330	112,270	251,460
Processed Oils	606	2,044	4,016	4,703	3,366	3,530	2,290	3,720
Fish and Fishery Products	~	~	21,450	25,600	29,320	31,060	9,970	5,860
Forest Products	~	~	217,470	227,000	247,180	318,130	265,700	284,280
Agricultural Requisites	36,833	178,606	150,688	223,753	230,632	177,070	64,460	86,780
Crude Fertilizers	- -	4	4,937	4,741	2,907	5,100	1,600	2,540
Manuf Fertilizers	12,052	29,876	56,177	117,390	86,095	19,900	2,910	25,410
Pesticides	2,236	3,206	5,977	10,564	13,468	11,464	5,350	9,910
Agriculture Machines	22,545	145,520	83,597	91,058	128,162	140,601	54,600	48,930

Exports

Category	1970	1975	1979	1980	1981	1982	1983	1984
Total Merchandise Trade	3,147,702	9,009,643	14,267,110	19,292,832	17,517,960	16,498,000	14,759,000‡	15,847,000‡
Agricultural Products, Total	43,337	64,904	90,700	77,460	77,014	94,580	123,870	171,980
Food and Animals	36,531	61,074	87,623	69,030	60,327	80,230	107,390	151,620
Live Animals	19	#	#	#	4	690	1,340	2,320
Meat and Meat Prep	213	533	666	747	642	530	1,000	2,260
Dairy Products Eggs	186	661	409	51	119	260	250	1,800
Cereals and Prep	7,600	12,606	3,492	6,756	264	4,460	2,100	690
Fruits and Vegetables	2,893	8,388	23,082	21,940	33,919	55,580	70,310	94,010
Sugar and Honey	5,690	298	50	15	#	#	30	80
Coffee, Tea, Cocoa Sp	19,607	36,503	57,545	36,688	23,998	18,180	31,110	49,260
Feeding Stuff	238	1	#	#	2	#	170	260
Miscellaneous Food	85	2,084	2,379	2,834	1,373	540	1,080	930
Beverages Tobacco	397	2,045	1,514	6,220	14,691	13,256	14,770	14,990
Beverages	50	1,041	703	499	537	334	400	610
Tobacco	347	1,004	811	5,721	14,154	12,922	14,370	14,380
Crude Materials	6,409	1,744	1,460	2,198	1,995	1,080	1,460	4,650
Hides and Skins	50	41	#	#	#	#		
Oilseeds	5,850	#	#	#	#	#	#	#
Natural Rubber	69	18	2	#	10	#	260	1,940
Textile Fibers	- -	693	31	187	106	#	#	#
Crude Mat Nes	440	992	1,427	2,005	1,879	1,080	150	710
Animal Vegetable Oils	- -	41	103	#	1	11	1,050	2,000†
Animal Fats	- -	#	3	#	1	11	250	710
Fixed Vegetable Oils	- -	39	100	#	#	#	70	#
Processed Oils	- -	2	#	#	#	#	180	710
Fish and Fishery Products	~	~	9,450	4,890	12,430	24,100	55,450	76,830
Forest Products	~	~	#	#	#	#	#	#
Agricultural Requisites	- -	2,647	22,287	30,733	44,793	32,756	39,390	45,300
Crude Fertilizers	- -	#	#	#	#	#	#	#
Manuf Fertilizers	- -	2,124	18,526	26,657	43,351	31,404	37,620	43,580
Pesticides	- -	523	393	646	700	203	520	420
Agricultural Machines	- -	#	3,368	3,430	742	1,141	1,250	1,290

SOURCE: FAO-TY, 1975, Section IV; 1980, Section IV; 1981, Section IV; 1982, Section IV; 1985, Section IV.

Table 2541

UNITED STATES ABSOLUTE VALUE OF TRADE, 1970-84

(T US)

Imports

Category	1970	1975	1979	1980	1981	1982	1983	1984
Total Merchandise Trade	39,963,200	9,694,034	20,713,101	24,119,480	26,098,184	24,395,200	25,804,780	32,572,560
Agricultural Products, Total	6,306,490	1,016,017	1,784,520	1,818,910	1,834,120	1,688,170	1,767,860	2,105,170
Food and Animals	4,537,822	714,909	1,248,760	1,289,320	1,262,190	1,140,590	1,190,700	1,445,960
Live Animals	156,674	14,198	37,697	40,276	33,223	47,292	53,360	62,540
Meat and Meat Prep	1,015,480	114,039	253,483	234,220	199,427	207,541	203,440	203,400
Dairy Products Eggs	99,814	17,646	30,639	31,990	35,743	37,162	40,190	42,260
Cereals and Prep	69,612	17,970	17,931	21,663	24,170	29,686	31,550	42,020
Fruits and Vegetables	734,982	100,669	205,110	203,410	296,300	294,110	303,890	409,040
Sugar and Honey	806,463	207,622	123,190	221,380	240,460	107,894	133,830	161,400
Coffee, Tea, Cocoa Sp	1,602,590	232,794	562,940	516,020	407,500	390,656	389,460	481,030
Feeding Stuff	29,093	5,236	8,281	9,190	11,226	10,993	13,890	15,570
Miscellaneous Food	22,673	4,735	9,492	11,150	14,134	15,259	21,080	28,710
Beverages Tobacco	854,992	141,864	256,349	277,003	313,881	336,399	340,760	365,340
Beverages	726,519	103,597	206,897	224,789	243,254	255,333	268,810	293,860
Tobacco	128,473	38,267	49,452	52,214	70,627	81,066	71,950	71,480
Crude Materials	761,759	104,197	206,051	200,016	210,806	171,320	187,430	224,600
Hides and Skins	110,186	15,831	32,134	23,008	26,887	19,749	18,950	22,960
Oilseeds	52,163	3,786	5,763	5,972	9,885	7,250	9,190	8,780
Natural Rubber	240,818	36,789	90,324	82,099	78,059	53,550	65,530	82,460
Textile Fibers	154,504	12,315	18,210	19,600	25,710	20,210	21,690	26,790
Crude Mat Nes	204,088	35,476	59,616	69,337	70,263	70,562	72,080	83,620
Animal Vegetable Oil	152,358	55,048	73,362	52,570	47,240	39,858	48,960	69,280
Animal Fats	4,198	933	414	600	466	428	470	790
Fixed Vegetable Oils	140,510	52,952	71,108	49,918	44,683	37,694	46,680	66,260
Processed Oils	7,650	1,162	1,841	2,057	2,091	1,736	1,810	2,230
Fish and Fishery Products	~	138,127	267,417	263,316	298,820	317,463	362,140	370,250
Forest Products	~	395,664	812,628	758,210	770,868	808,920	898,660	1,061,840
Agricultural Requisites	466,106	155,797	253,872	272,656	269,440	229,200	246,360	291,400
Crude Fertilizers	8,744	2,772	3,630	3,669	2,848	2,286	1,960	2,190
Manuf Fertilizers	192,202	55,689	81,828	97,862	110,207	96,300	99,710	114,200
Pesticides	10,870	10,130	19,420	26,624	28,373	26,454	25,120	30,790
Agriculture Machines	254,290	87,205	148,989	144,500	128,012	104,161	119,560	144,220

Exports

Category	1970	1975	1979	1980	1981	1982	1983	1984
Total Merchandise Trade	42,593,300	10,765,183	17,857,800	21,659,222	22,888,782	20,715,800	19,596,930	21,205,700
Agricultural Products, Total	7,381,756	2,241,988	3,621,540	4,289,110	4,505,290	3,824,260	3,754,320	3,932,290
Food and Animals	4,226,991	1,530,650	2,161,450	2,722,320	2,958,110	2,323,610	2,347,690	2,392,520
Live Animals	60,115	13,978	20,073	21,596	27,101	30,794	34,520	30,120
Meat and Meat Prep	103,615	53,150	113,081	129,756	148,502	128,900	119,530	121,280
Dairy Products Eggs	137,348	13,428	16,155	25,559	42,400	41,110	37,500	37,030
Cereals and Prep	2,588,402	1,164,390	1,445,180	1,808,333	1,946,262	1,475,357	1,516,740	1,607,730
Fruits and Vegetables	581,117	133,788	221,322	302,266	342,072	281,642	252,170	252,010
Sugar and Honey	22,677	15,567	14,748	48,719	69,406	12,441	14,550	15,800
Coffee, Tea, Cocoa Sp	31,186	16,566	52,966	49,903	45,296	41,391	35,080	41,970
Feeding Stuff	496,171	95,549	231,273	284,950	272,195	242,395	278,150	222,380
Miscellaneous Food	143,437	24,234	46,653	51,242	64,882	69,581	59,440	64,190
Beverages Tobacco	701,657	133,981	236,081	269,106	294,031	303,566	283,210	285,760
Beverages	22,637	6,213	19,998	24,619	20,306	19,052	17,400	16,250
Tobacco	679,020	127,768	216,083	244,487	273,726	284,514	265,810	269,510
Crude Materials	1,967,353	483,214	1,042,030	1,105,810	1,080,730	1,045,060	982,240	1,067,910
Hides and Skins	193,660	41,521	133,380	105,090	103,060	102,740	100,580	137,170
Oilseeds	1,263,167	313,653	638,990	656,060	687,760	683,780	634,400	619,630
Natural Rubber	8,903	2,896	2,661	4,050	3,294	2,623	2,990	4,900
Textile Fibers	396,678	104,317	228,229	294,911	234,465	205,110	192,250	253,340
Crude Mat Nes	104,945	20,827	38,766	45,700	52,150	50,809	52,020	52,860
Animal Vegetable Oils	488,678	94,144	181,977	191,872	172,416	152,023	141,190	186,110
Animal Fats	198,731	33,181	69,892	72,871	70,231	61,290	56,770	64,820
Fixed Vegetable Oils	263,274	57,602	106,238	110,501	95,540	82,224	80,360	115,580
Processed Oils	26,673	3,361	5,847	8,500	6,644	8,509	4,060	5,710
Fish and Fishery Products	~	29,803	107,080	99,335	114,203	103,220	99,670	92,390
Forest Products	~	350,375	568,800	698,997	652,838	570,598	565,070	574,190
Agricultural Requisites	999,095	401,058	501,378	652,231	626,384	480,886	397,050	470,550
Crude Fertilizers	91,121	46,572	43,199	50,853	42,000	38,355	42,340	39,200
Manuf Fertilizers	177,659	108,386	140,550	226,810	173,633	138,838	127,760	181,540
Pesticides	102,142	35,491	51,885	55,454	54,712	60,860	63,130	70,810
Agricultural Machines	628,123	210,609	265,740	319,110	356,039	242,832	163,830	178,990

SOURCE: FAO-TY, 1975, Section IV; 1980, Section IV; 1981, Section IV; 1982, Section IV; 1985, Section IV.

Table 2542

IMF IMPORT UNIT VALUE INDEX, 4 LC, 1953–86

(YA, 1980 = 100)

Country	1953	1954	1955	1956	1957	1958	1959	1960	1961	1962	1963	1964	1965	1966	1967	1968
C. BRAZIL	~	~	~	~	~	~	~	~	23.7	23.9	24.5	23.7	24.1	24.6	25.1	25.9
E. COLOMBIA	40.3	40.3	41.1	42.0	45.1	41.0	41.3	40.8	41.3	40.1	39.2	38.8	35.5	36.3	37.4	37.0
J. EL SALVADOR	39.0	28.0	28.0	29.0	29.0	29.0	27.0	28.0	29.0	29.0	31.0	32.0	32.0	40.0	35.0	32.0
O. NICARAGUA	~	~	~	~	~	28.9	28.5	28.9	27.2	27.4	28.2	27.3	28.3	30.9	29.3	31.6
UNITED STATES	22.2	22.6	22.6	22.9	23.3	22.2	21.8	22.1	21.8	21.3	21.4	22.0	22.2	22.8	23.0	23.3

Country	1969	1970	1971	1972	1973	1974	1975	1976	1977	1978	1979	1980	1981	1982	1983	1984	1985
C. BRAZIL	25.4	25.9	26.9	26.5	35.9	52.5	57.1	58.7	61.0	65.2	78.1	100.0	111.0	107.1	102	97	91
E. COLOMBIA	37.6*	38.0	38.6	41.1	48.7	62.6	66.8	69.7	73.8	82.7	91.2	100.0	106.1	108.4	106.1	~	~
J. EL SALVADOR	32.0	33.0	33.0	35.0	41.0	59.0	65.0	63.0	63.0	70.0	79.0	100.0	111.0	119.0	111.0	~	~
O. NICARAGUA	33.0	34.5	36.1	38.0	42.6	56.1	68.5	67.4	70.9	74.8	80.3	100.0	~	~	~	~	~
UNITED STATES	24.0	25.7	27.0	28.9	34.4	50.9	55.5	57.2	62.0	66.9	80.4	100.0	105.5	103.8	99.5	101.3	98.8

Country	1986
C. BRAZIL	71.76
E. COLOMBIA	~
J. EL SALVADOR	~
O. NICARAGUA	~
UNITED STATES	95.4

SOURCE: IMF-IFS-Y, 1984, line 75d; 1986, line 75d; September 1987, line 75d.

Table 2543

IMF EXPORT UNIT VALUE INDEX, 11 LC, 1953–86
(YA, 1980 = 100)

Country	1953	1954	1955	1956	1957	1958	1959	1960	1961	1962	1963	1964	1965	1966	1967	1968
B. BOLIVIA	10.8	10.8	10.8	11.3	10.0	9.6	10.0	10.0	10.8	10.8	11.3	14.6	16.7	15.9	15.0	15.0
C. BRAZIL	41.6	48.7	38.7	37.1	37.8	34.9	29.5	29.0	30.5	26.6	26.5	31.7	32.0	30.7	30.6	30.2
E. COLOMBIA	~	~	~	36.8	38.3	29.6	25.2	25.7	25.5	23.2	20.5	24.5	22.9	18.5	22.5	23.0
H. DOMINICAN REP.	27.1	32.9	27.8	26.7	34.0	29.4	25.4	25.6	26.3	29.7	32.6	34.5	30.6	33.3	33.2	36.0
I. ECUADOR	12.9	15.6	13.3	13.3	13.3	13.3	12.2	12.9	12.2	15.6	13.3	16.0	16.7	16.7	16.7	17.1
J. EL SALVADOR	35.0	44.0	39.0	39.0	39.0	32.0	26.0	26.0	25.0	23.0	26.0	29.0	31.0	30.0	28.0	27.0
M. HONDURAS	27.4	28.5	29.9	30.3	28.1	26.2	23.7	27.8	30.0	31.8	30.4	32.3	31.1	30.9	31.0	30.1
O. NICARAGUA	44.2	55.7	47.7	50.4	47.3	40.7	34.9	37.5	38.4	39.5	37.6	36.9	38.7	38.9	37.3	37.5
P. PANAMA	28.0	32.0	31.0	31.0	29.0	27.0	26.0	24.0	23.0	27.0	25.0	26.0	27.0	27.0	28.0	29.0
Q. PARAGUAY	29.9	39.7	38.8	35.0	34.9	34.0	32.9	26.2	25.9	26.4	30.9	35.8	36.3	37.1	33.7	36.3
R. PERU	~	~	~	~	~	~	~	20.0	19.0	19.0	20.0	23.0	24.0	28.0	25.0	27.0
UNITED STATES	29.4	28.9	29.3	30.4	31.4	31.1	31.1	31.3	31.9	31.7	31.7	32.0	33.0	34.0	34.7	35.2

Country	1969	1970	1971	1972	1973	1974	1975	1976	1977	1978	1979	1980	1981	1982	1983	1984	1985
B. BOLIVIA	16.3	21.1	17.1	17.8	23.3	40.6	38.8	43.8	54.4	61.5	74.0	100.0	97.1	92.3	94.5	93.0	88.6
C. BRAZIL	31.1	35.1	33.9	38.3	52.7	66.4	66.4	76.6	93.5	86.0	94.4	100.0	94.1	88.0	84.0	85.0	80.0
E. COLOMBIA	23.1*	28.5	27.1	30.3	38.2	51.2	50.6	74.1	108.9	91.0	89.7	100.0	89.5	88.8	89.0	~	~
H. DOMINICAN REP.	39.3	37.6	35.4	39.3	48.0	72.7	114.3	76.5	84.5	76.9	81.1	100.0	132.0	88.0	~	~	~
I. ECUADOR	15.2	17.1	18.2	15.2	20.9	43.2	39.8	44.8	57.4	52.2	72.9	100.0	91.9	99.2	83.7	80.2	83.3
J. EL SALVADOR	27.0	32.0	31.0	33.0	41.0	51.0	53.0	77.0	102.0	85.0	97.0	100.0	93.0	88.0	71.0	~	~
M. HONDURAS	30.0	33.6	32.6	34.2	40.3	47.0	56.2	66.4	91.2	90.7	85.6	100.0	94.0	90.0	92.0	96.0	97.0
O. NICARAGUA	38.2	39.0	39.4	42.8	47.4	60.7	57.0	74.8	92.6	87.2	71.0	100.0	107.0	91.0	93.0	104.0	~
P. PANAMA	28.0	28.0	28.0	29.0	49.0	69.0	80.0	73.0	66.0	64.0	78.0	100.0	105.0	84.0	92.0	91.0	86.0
Q. PARAGUAY	37.2	39.9	40.6	44.9	56.3	67.1	71.7	72.7	98.4	90.1	94.0	100.0	112.7	121.6	104.9	182.8	187.0
R. PERU	30.0	31.0	28.0	30.0	49.0	60.0	41.0	47.0	51.0	50.0	76.0	100.0	83.0	72.0	76.0	68.0	62.0
UNITED STATES	36.2	38.2	39.4	40.7	47.4	60.5	67.6	69.9	72.4	77.4	88.1	100.0	109.2	110.4	111.6	113.1	112.2

Country	1986
B. BOLIVIA	~
C. BRAZIL	~
E. COLOMBIA	~
H. DOMINICAN REP.	~
I. ECUADOR	~
J. EL SALVADOR	~
M. HONDURAS	~
O. NICARAGUA	~
P. PANAMA	~
Q. PARAGUAY	~
R. PERU	51.0
UNITED STATES	112.5

SOURCE: IMF-IFS-Y, 1984, line 74d; 1986, line 74d; September 1987, line 75d.

Table 2544

IMF TERMS OF TRADE INDEX,[1] 7 LC, 1960–81

(YA, 1975 = 100)

Year	B. BOLIVIA	H. DOMINICAN REP.	I. ECUADOR	M. HONDURAS	Q. PARAGUAY	R. PERU	T. VENEZUELA	UNITED STATES
1960	52.9	54.9	76.6	145.4	86.2	69.4	33.6	116.3
1961	57.5	56.3	72.0	156.9	85.6	68.5	38.7	120.4
1962	58.0	63.9	92.8	167.0	88.2	71.0	38.8	122.5
1963	59.4	69.2	77.9	157.7	101.8	74.8	37.7	121.2

Continued in SALA, 24-2544.

Table 2545

IMF TERMS OF TRADE INDEX,[1] 4 L, 1955–85

(YA, 1980 = 100)

Year	C. BRAZIL	E. COLOMBIA	J. EL SALVADOR	O. NICARAGUA
1955	~	~	126.2	~
1956	~	87.6	132.4	~
1957	~	84.9	131.4	~
1958	~	72.2	110.7	97.2
1959	~	61.0	95.6	103.5
1960	~	63.0	91.6	85.5
1961	128.7	61.7	86.6	95.2
1962	111.3	58.9	79.0	96.4
1963	108.2	52.3	85.9	109.6
1964	133.8	63.1	92.1	131.1
1965	132.9	64.5	94.7	128.3
1966	124.8	51.0	75.0	120.1
1967	121.9	60.2	81.4	115.0
1968	116.6	62.2	85.3	114.9
1969	122.4	61.4	82.4	115.8[†]
1970	135.5	75.0*	97.6	113.0
1971	126.0	70.2	93.1	109.1
1972	144.5	73.7	93.8	112.6
1973	146.8	78.4	100.0	111.3
1974	126.5	81.8	87.6	108.2
1975	116.3	75.7	81.6	83.2
1976	130.5	106.3	122.6	111.0
1977	153.3	147.6	160.6	130.6
1978	131.9	110.0	120.9	116.6
1979	120.9	98.4	123.1	112.0
1980	100.0	100.0	100.0	100.0
1981	84.7	84.4	83.8	~
1982	82.3	81.9	74.2	~
1983	82.2	83.9	64.4	~
1984	88.3	86.8	~	~
1985	88.4	86.0	~	~

1. Export unit value divided by import unit value; 100.0 = base; numbers above
   100.0 are favorable and those below 100.0 are unfavorable, relative to 1980.

SOURCE: IMF-IFS-Y, 1984; IMF-IFS-S, 1986.

Table 2546

TERMS OF TRADE,[1] 6 L, 1929–38

Export unit value index divided by import unit value index (1929 = 100)

Year	A. ARGENTINA	C. BRAZIL	D. CHILE	E. COLOMBIA	G. CUBA	N. MEXICO
1929	100.0	100.0	100.0	100.0	100.0	100.0
1930	95.9	61.6	95.7	73.6	82.1	77.5
1931	71.4	53.6	67.0	83.6	96.1	59.5
1932	74.5	67.5	55.1	72.9	83.6	59.8
1933	70.4	60.3	60.0	63.6	105.2	61.8
1934	85.7	62.9	57.3	81.4	110.0	66.7
1935	85.7	55.0	61.6	64.3	117.5	77.5
1936	105.1	54.3	70.3	64.3	128.4	64.7
1937	120.4	58.3	76.8	67.1	128.4	61.8
1938	110.2	43.0	54.1	60.0	~	132.4

SOURCE: Angus Maddison, *Two Crises: Latin America and Asia, 1929–38 and 1973–83*
(Paris: Development Centre of the Organisation for Economic Co-operation and
Development, 1985).

Table 2547

ECLA IMPORT UNIT VALUES (FOB), 19 L, 1960-84

(1970 = 100)

	Country	1960	1965	1971	1972	1973	1974	1975	1976	1977	1978	1979	1980	1981	1982	1983	1984
A.	ARGENTINA	89.5	86.2	109.6	106.3	127.8	188.9	216.1	225.4	238.2	266.8	327.3	328.8	318.0	311.9	289.7	280.6
B.	BOLIVIA	86.1	93.5	101.8	107.0	125.9	154.6	175.9	183.0	204.0	226.1	273.5	309.7	315.5	307.5	296.8	305.1
C.	BRAZIL	87.5	98.0	110.6	119.3	141.7	218.3	232.6	246.6	253.1	270.9	324.9	418.4	464.2	447.5	420.0	402.8
D.	CHILE	90.5	93.3	102.4	108.2	134.5	178.1	216.0	219.3	243.7	263.4	323.6	403.3	433.2	399.8	368.1	374.2
E.	COLOMBIA	90.9	94.0	101.7	105.2	128.6	164.7	175.6	183.4	194.0	217.9	240.4	263.8	282.8	270.4	253.5	259.5
F.	COSTA RICA	95.4	92.8	102.8	109.6	131.3	190.0	201.8	189.9	208.0	221.2	269.3	318.4	322.3	289.5	297.3	304.1
H.	DOMINICAN REP.	92.7	96.9	104.0	108.2	129.9	165.2	187.7	196.8	208.3	225.8	249.3	306.3	317.4	324.4	319.0	324.5
I.	ECUADOR	103.6	104.0	102.5	110.0	127.2	137.0	151.0	152.9	168.3	177.2	205.9	231.3	246.8	246.7	243.9	247.4
J.	EL SALVADOR	81.9	87.6	101.9	104.5	122.5	185.5	187.6	190.9	196.8	204.1	240.2	313.0	310.3	327.9	333.7	341.0
K.	GUATEMALA	73.6	83.6	103.6	114.4	131.3	188.8	219.0	197.0	200.1	213.7	253.5	302.3	316.2	336.3	346.8	354.0
L.	HAITI	91.8	96.2	103.0	106.9	127.2	164.7	185.0	198.8	214.9	230.8	257.3	293.2	302.7	330.9	337.0	337.0
M.	HONDURAS	73.0	77.1	102.1	109.6	127.6	163.0	184.5	200.0	222.6	233.4	249.9	295.0	311.9	315.1	311.9	323.2
N.	MEXICO	75.6	95.3	103.1	105.8	124.1	161.2	175.7	182.6	187.8	203.0	230.5	260.5	280.0	288.4	272.1	281.3
O.	NICARAGUA	80.1	82.5	101.2	103.2	123.1	162.3	187.1	193.2	205.2	226.4	259.4	312.9	324.6	341.9	354.5	355.2
P.	PANAMA	96.8	95.7	101.9	106.4	123.0	190.6	220.4	233.6	245.8	261.3	319.5	399.3	409.8	429.7	436.2	445.3
Q.	PARAGUAY	85.3	89.3	102.9	110.9	125.0	186.9	211.4	199.3	212.7	218.6	262.6	311.2	321.1	333.2	318.9	287.3
R.	PERU	83.7	99.5	102.7	109.5	137.9	141.8	167.1	170.8	188.6	217.1	241.4	270.6	291.8	297.7	307.5	313.1
S.	URUGUAY	82.7	96.2	101.3	112.4	120.6	173.4	210.9	214.7	215.1	219.5	270.5	344.3	381.7	354.6	324.6	316.2
T.	VENEZUELA	72.1	91.5	104.3	109.9	120.6	139.1	156.6	168.4	181.1	194.1	208.2	242.8	271.7	256.3	241.9	238.2
	LATIN AMERICA[1]	83.0	92.8	105.1	110.2	130.5	177.6	193.7	200.5	209.4	225.0	262.1	310.0	327.2	~	~	~

1. Includes Barbados, Guyana, Jamaica, Suriname, and Trinidad and Tobago.

SOURCE: ECLA-AE, 1981, pp. 508-509; except data for 1972 from ECLA-AE, 1980,
and data for 1971 from ECLA-AE, 1978; ECLA-AE, 1984, p. 527. ECLA-AE, 1985.

Table 2548

ECLA EXPORT UNIT VALUES, 19 L, 1960–84

(1970 = 100)

Country	1960	1965	1971	1972	1973	1974	1975	1976	1977	1978	1979	1980	1981	1982	1983	1984
A. ARGENTINA	91.9	94.2	114.0	131.7	186.3	238.8	214.8	198.7	203.9	211.0	260.7	306.2	307.4	254.8	229.6	244.9
B. BOLIVIA	50.0	92.4	83.6	86.6	109.9	218.0	195.6	208.0	244.1	271.6	322.7	430.3	416.2	401.6	413.9	426.4
C. BRAZIL	90.2	91.1	96.6	116.4	150.6	195.8	196.4	226.7	252.9	235.3	256.8	277.3	259.3	239.1	228.8	238.5
D. CHILE	56.0	63.1	80.1	78.5	111.3	155.9	113.2	124.0	123.4	129.5	169.5	190.5	165.0	137.4	134.1	128.2
E. COLOMBIA	88.0	90.0	92.2	103.7	132.7	159.1	143.3	220.7	368.7	311.2	286.6	335.2	288.3	297.8	285.7	303.4
F. COSTA RICA	94.0	99.3	92.3	96.3	115.8	133.3	164.3	176.9	252.5	246.5	260.1	302.1	269.8	259.8	247.6	260.0
H. DOMINICAN REP.	67.0	79.0	96.9	106.3	121.4	175.8	278.6	196.2	185.8	191.7	214.4	309.2	332.1	232.5	248.5	271.5
I. ECUADOR	98.0	85.0	95.9	93.2	117.2	267.6	244.5	280.3	335.0	303.9	439.9	553.0	530.9	490.0	451.7	450.1
J. EL SALVADOR	94.3	93.7	97.0	104.8	129.9	161.5	163.4	232.8	354.5	246.0	266.5	288.0	262.4	268.1	237.9	265.8
K. GUATEMALA	91.8	93.0	93.2	94.9	114.2	135.7	152.1	177.1	241.1	242.6	243.4	280.1	259.1	238.9	235.1	247.0
L. HAITI	83.9	89.6	94.0	96.6	112.7	144.4	171.2	191.9	265.3	260.4	249.5	288.1	270.0	272.4	260.9	280.3
M. HONDURAS	78.2	97.6	101.4	105.7	122.4	157.4	168.3	196.9	252.0	263.4	257.0	309.3	284.6	273.1	255.3	265.5
N. MEXICO	76.0	85.1	101.5	105.1	126.5	180.0	186.0	210.2	231.6	241.3	305.7	427.3	446.5	388.0	347.8	362.0
O. NICARAGUA	87.6	93.2	98.6	111.9	126.4	159.5	148.1	186.7	230.6	218.7	210.6	243.0	223.6	210.2	190.3	204.4
P. PANAMA	82.3	100.3	104.2	114.4	133.9	212.6	239.3	199.6	197.6	191.8	232.0	283.2	290.8	247.8	256.6	269.3
Q. PARAGUAY	85.2	100.0	105.0	117.1	168.6	219.5	220.1	219.5	295.8	269.6	287.8	299.0	322.5	281.6	257.9	312.3
R. PERU	58.5	71.3	93.0	92.2	131.8	193.4	174.5	186.0	192.3	188.1	282.4	367.3	313.5	280.8	290.9	292.6
S. URUGUAY	93.6	95.3	100.9	131.4	185.1	181.0	156.4	158.3	172.9	185.4	241.4	271.0	268.6	251.1	232.7	236.5
T. VENEZUELA	119.0	101.0	122.4	131.0	186.9	489.5	532.4	553.6	629.9	605.8	844.8	1,241.0	1,375.2	1,287.5	1,247.3	1,223.7
LATIN AMERICA[1]	88.1	89.1	102.3	112.2	147.1	234.3	224.5	240.8	266.8	256.5	309.5	377.6	367.6	≈	≈	≈

1. Includes Barbados, Guyana, Jamaica, Suriname, and Trinidad and Tobago.

SOURCE: ECLA-AE, 1981, pp. 502-503; except data for 1972 from ECLA-AE, 1980,
and data for 1971 from ECLA-AE, 1978; ECLA-AE, 1984, p. 501; ECLA-AE, 1985.

Table 2549

ECLA TOTAL IMPORT, EXPORT, AND TERMS OF
TRADE INDEXES FOR LATIN AMERICA,[1]
1930–60[a]

(1970 = 100)

Year	Import Unit Value[2]	Export Unit Value[2]	Terms of Trade[3]
1930	53.6	54.9	102.4
1931	45.1	37.3	82.7

Continued in SALA, 24-2548.

Table 2550

VOLUME OF LATIN AMERICAN EXPORTS, 6 L, 1929–38

	A. ARGENTINA	C. BRAZIL	D. CHILE	E. COLOMBIA	G. CUBA	N. MEXICO
1929 Values ($ M US)	907.6	461.5	282.8	123.5	272.4	284.6
Index (1929 = 100)						
1929	100.0	100.0	100.0	100.0	100.0	100.0
1930	69.3	109.6	65.0	109.8	76.5	81.1
1931	95.3	117.3	60.0	96.1	63.0	82.1
1932	87.4	80.8	28.8	98.0	61.2	58.5
1933	81.9	100.0	41.3	98.0	53.2	62.3
1934	85.8	111.5	66.3	103.9	52.1	84.9
1935	90.6	128.9	67.5	113.7	54.5	86.8
1936	81.9	142.3	67.5	127.5	57.3	95.3
1937	95.6	128.8	95.0	125.5	61.8	112.3
1938	61.4	155.8	88.8	131.4	~	50.0

SOURCE: Angus Maddison, *Two Crises: Latin America and Asia, 1929–38 and 1973–83*
(Paris: Development Centre of the Organisation for Economic Co-Operation and
Development, 1985).

Table 2551

VOLUME OF LATIN AMERICAN IMPORTS, 6 L, 1929–38

	A. ARGENTINA	C. BRAZIL	D. CHILE	E. COLOMBIA	G. CUBA	N. MEXICO
1929 Values ($ M US)	819.5	421.7	196.8	123.0	216.2	184.2
Index (1929 = 100)						
1929	100.0	100.0	100.0	100.0	100.0	100.0
1930	87.8	59.4	92.0	52.3	76.8	74.1
1931	61.5	39.1	48.0	44.6	51.4	48.1
1932	46.8	36.2	17.0	36.9	40.7	38.9
1933	51.3	50.7	19.0	50.8	35.4	44.4
1934	56.4	55.1	25.0	63.1	49.3	55.6
1935	58.3	62.3	38.0	69.2	60.1	57.4
1936	61.5	63.8	43.0	78.5	61.8	66.7
1937	80.8	78.3	48.0	90.8	69.6	85.2
1938	76.3	72.5	44.0	84.6	~	70.4

SOURCE: Angus Maddison, *Two Crises: Latin America and Asia, 1929–38 and 1973–83*
(Paris: Development Centre of the Organisation for Economic Co-Operation and
Development, 1985).

Table 2552

VALUE, INDEXES, AND PURCHASING POWER OF FOREIGN TRADE, 19 LR, 1928–76

(Value in Current and 1970 M US; Indexes 1970 = 100)

A. ARGENTINA

Year	Exports Value Current	1970	Unit Value[1]	Quantum[2]	Imports Value Current	1970	Value[1]	Quantum[3]	Terms of Trade	Exports Purchasing Power
	A	B	C(A/B)	D	E	F	G	H	I(C/G)	J(D x I)
1928	1,719.0	1,856.4	92.6	104.7	1,364.0	1,833.3	74.4	108.2	124.5	130.4

Continued in SALA, 24-2550.

Table 2553

PURCHASING POWER OF LATIN AMERICAN EXPORTS, 1929–38

	A. ARGENTINA	C. BRAZIL	D. CHILE	E. COLOMBIA	G. CUBA	N. MEXICO
1929 Values ($ M US)	907.6	461.5	282.8	123.5	272.4	284.6
Index (1929 = 100)						
1929	100.0	100.0	100.0	100.0	100.0	100.0
1930	66.9	67.1	62.2	81.7	62.8	63.0
1931	68.5	62.0	40.5	80.3	60.5	49.1
1932	65.3	54.4	15.5	71.8	51.2	35.2
1933	58.1	59.5	25.0	63.4	56.0	38.9
1934	74.2	69.6	37.8	84.5	57.3	56.5
1935	78.2	70.9	41.9	73.2	64.0	67.6
1936	86.3	77.2	47.3	83.1	73.6	62.0
1937	115.3	74.7	73.0	84.5	79.4	69.4
1938	67.7	67.1	48.0	78.9	n.a.	66.7

SOURCE: Angus Maddison, *Two Crises: Latin America and Asia, 1929–38 and 1973–83* (Paris: Development Centre of the Organisation for Economic Co-Operation and Development, 1985).

Table 2554

ECLA MERCHANDISE TERMS OF TRADE INDEX[1] (FOB/CIF),[2] 19 L, 1960–84;

(1970 = 100)

Country	1960	1965	1971	1972	1973	1974	1975	1976	1977	1978	1979	1980	1981	1982	1983	1984
A. ARGENTINA	104.9	109.2	109.0	123.2	146.2	127.6	100.7	88.9	86.3	79.9	81.1	94.2	97.2	82.0	79.5	86.4
B. BOLIVIA	59.2	99.8	82.1	80.2	87.6	139.7	111.0	113.4	119.8	121.2	120.6	143.6	134.8	132.1	140.4	138.1
C. BRAZIL	104.4	93.9	87.3	97.7	106.9	90.9	85.4	92.8	100.8	87.6	79.9	67.4	56.7	54.2	55.1	59.5
D. CHILE	63.9	68.4	78.2	72.0	83.3	88.1	53.2	57.1	51.3	49.8	53.4	49.0	39.5	35.4	37.2	34.5
E. COLOMBIA	97.7	96.3	90.7	97.9	103.6	96.6	81.5	120.2	189.8	150.1	129.6	126.3	102.1	109.9	112.2	115.4
F. COSTA RICA	101.1	107.6	90.3	87.5	88.7	71.2	85.5	93.3	121.7	111.9	97.9	97.3	84.9	90.0	83.8†	84.7
H. DOMINICAN REP.	73.6	82.3	93.2	97.5	94.1	106.5	149.4	100.2	89.5	85.5	86.6	103.2	106.0	72.7	78.9	83.4
I. ECUADOR	99.1	83.7	93.6	84.3	92.4	192.0	159.0	179.2	194.8	171.7	211.7	237.6	213.2	196.9	183.5	177.7
J. EL SALVADOR	116.1	107.0	95.2	99.3	106.0	87.9	87.4	122.1	179.9	120.2	111.2	93.6	85.5	82.6	72.3	78.0
K. GUATEMALA	124.6	110.8	90.0	82.9	87.6	73.0	70.2	90.3	120.4	113.6	96.6	94.2	82.9	72.1	69.0	70.1
L. HAITI	93.2	94.2	91.3	89.4	89.2	87.8	92.8	97.4	124.8	114.4	98.2	100.7	90.4	85.9	80.9	83.2
M. HONDURAS	106.8	125.3	99.3	96.0	96.2	96.6	91.4	98.9	114.2	113.8	103.4	106.4	92.2	87.5	82.6	81.9
N. MEXICO	100.5	89.7	98.4	99.0	102.0	111.6	105.7	114.9	122.9	118.6	132.5	164.3	159.6	134.7	129.4	127.7
O. NICARAGUA	110.2	112.3	97.4	107.6	102.7	98.2	79.4	96.8	112.5	97.0	81.5	78.7	69.5	62.3	54.5	57.7
P. PANAMA	87.7	105.8	102.3	106.8	108.9	113.1	110.7	87.1	82.1	75.2	75.3	75.2	75.2	61.3	62.8	62.8
Q. PARAGUAY	101.4	112.4	102.0	105.2	135.1	119.2	106.1	110.7	139.8	123.8	111.3	98.7	102.3	86.2	81.9	106.9
R. PERU	70.9	72.9	90.6	83.8	96.6	135.3	104.0	108.3	101.6	86.8	117.2	131.1	105.6	93.8	92.6	93.0
S. URUGUAY	114.6	100.3	99.6	116.5	153.1	105.1	75.4	74.5	80.8	84.7	90.1	81.4	72.0	71.6	72.2	74.7
T. VENEZUELA	164.4	111.0	117.4	118.7	154.7	353.3	335.3	325.1	344.6	309.6	401.1	509.9	501.4	492.1	476.1	500.5
LATIN AMERICA[3]	107.3	96.5	97.3	101.5	113.2	132.6	116.6	120.7	127.7	114.5	119.0	123.5	113.6	~	~	~

1. Export unit value divided by import unit value; 100.0 = base; numbers above 100.0 are favorable and those below 100.0 are unfavorable, relative to 1970.

2. ECLA uses the following procedures to calculate external trade indexes. Sample selection is made bearing in mind: (a) that the products considered were the most important in terms of their value; (b) that the products were homogeneous; (c) that the sample covered a large universe. Laspeyres indexes are used for quantities, Paasche for prices. For imports, indexes are calculated first for nine groupings of the "Foreign Trade Classification by Economic Use or Destination." For the period 1960–69 the year 1963 is used as the base; the data are then linked to the following period using 1970 as the base year; for imports this is done for each group of the "Foreign Trade Classification by Economic Use or Destination"; for exports, the total unit value indexes were linked together since similar groupings are not available.

Global values of exports and imports are FOB values according to the balance of payments. The values of imports by groupings under the "Foreign Trade Classification" are CIF values and are based on customs declarations.

3. Includes Barbados, Guyana, Jamaica, Suriname and, Trinidad and Tobago.

SOURCE: ECLA-AE, 1981, pp. 504-506; except data for 1972 from ECLA-AE, 1980, and data for 1971 from ECLA-AE, 1978; ECLA-AE, 1984, p. 523; ECLA-AE, 1985.

Table 2555

MERCHANDISE IMPORTS, 20 LC, 1965 AND 1985

(AA)

	Country	Food		Fuels		Machinery and Transport Equipment	
		1965	1985	1965	1985	1965	1985
A.	ARGENTINA	6	4[a]	10	10[a]	25	32[a]
B.	BOLIVIA	19	23[a]	1	2[a]	34	25[a]
C.	BRAZIL	20	9[a]	21	53[a]	22	15[a]
D.	CHILE	20	18[a]	6	21[a]	35	22[a]
E.	COLOMBIA	8	10[a]	1	11[a]	45	35[a]
F.	COSTA RICA	9	10[a]	5	17[a]	29	18[a]
G.	CUBA	~	~	~	~	~	~
H.	DOMINICAN REP.	24	14[a]	10	36[a]	23	17[a]
I.	ECUADOR	10	10[a]	9	2[a]	33	36[a]
J.	EL SALVADOR	15	20[a]	5	9[a]	28	21[a]
K.	GUATEMALA	11	9[a]	7	17[a]	29	18[a]
L.	HAITI	~	~	~	~	~	~
M.	HONDURAS	11	10[a]	6	22[a]	26	18[a]
N.	MEXICO	5	17[a]	2	3[a]	50	45[a]
O.	NICARAGUA	12	13[a]	5	19[a]	30	21[a]
P.	PANAMA	11	10[a]	21	26[a]	21	22[a]
Q.	PARAGUAY	14	8[a]	14	27[a]	37	33[a]
R.	PERU	17	25[a]	3	3[a]	41	38[a]
S.	URUGUAY	7	8[a]	17	36[a]	24	19[a]
T.	VENEZUELA	12	19[a]	1	1[a]	44	43[a]
	UNITED STATES	19	17	10	16	14	38

a. Figures are for years other than those specified.

SOURCE: *World Development Report 1987*, table 12.

Table 2556

GROWTH OF MERCHANDISE TRADE, 20 LC, 1965–85

(AA)

	Country	Exports		Imports	
		1965–80	1980–85	1965–80	1980–85
A.	ARGENTINA	4.7	3.2	1.8	−17.2
B.	BOLIVIA	2.5	−2.4	5.0	−4.3
C.	BRAZIL	9.4	6.6	8.3	−9.1
D.	CHILE	7.9	2.3	1.5	−12.5
E.	COLOMBIA	1.5	1.6	5.3	−1.4
F.	COSTA RICA	7.1	.4	5.8	−4.4
G.	CUBA	~	~	~	~
H.	DOMINICAN REP.	3.7	−1.5	5.0	−.3
I.	ECUADOR	15.2	6.3	6.9	−4.3
J.	EL SALVADOR	2.4	−5.3	2.7	1.8
K.	GUATEMALA	4.9	−1.3	4.6	−6.1
L.	HAITI	2.5	1.3[a]	5.5	1.9[a]
M.	HONDURAS	3.1	−7.2	2.6	−5.2
N.	MEXICO	7.7	10.1	5.7	−11.3
O.	NICARAGUA	2.4	−2.9	1.3	−.1
P.	PANAMA	~	−3.6	~	−1.5
Q.	PARAGUAY	6.5	4.0	3.6	−1.7
R.	PERU	2.3	1.4	−.2	−10.3
S.	URUGUAY	4.6	#	1.2	−16.5
T.	VENEZUELA	−9.4	−5.8	8.7	−9.1
	UNITED STATES	6.7	−2.8	6.6	8.4

a. Figures are for years other than those specified.

SOURCE: *World Development Report 1987*, table 10.

CHAPTER 26

DIRECTION OF TRADE AND
MAJOR TRADING PARTNERS

Table 2600

SHARE IN VALUE OF WORLD EXPORTS,[1] 20 LRC AND REGIONAL GROUPINGS, 1950–80

(%)

	Area	1950	1960	1970	1980
	World	100.00	100.00	100.00	100.00
A.	ARGENTINA	1.92	.84	.56	.40
B.	BOLIVIA	.12	.04	.06	.05
C.	BRAZIL	2.22	.99	.87	1.01
D.	CHILE	.47	.38	.39	.24
E.	COLOMBIA	.65	.36	.23	.21
F.	COSTA RICA	.09	.07	.07	.05
G.	CUBA	1.10	.48	.33	.20[a]
H.	DOMINICAN REP.	.14	.14	.07	.05
I.	ECUADOR	.12	.11	.06	.13
J.	EL SALVADOR	.11	.09	.07	.05
K.	GUATEMALA	.13	.09	.09	.08
L.	HAITI	.06	.02	.01	.01
M.	HONDURAS	.09	.05	.06	.04
N.	MEXICO	.86	59	.40	.81
O.	NICARAGUA	.04	.04	.06	.03
P.	PANAMA	.03	.02	.03	.02
Q.	PARAGUAY	.05	.02	.02	.02
R.	PERU	31	.34	.33	.19
S.	URUGUAY	.42	.10	.07	.05
T.	VENEZUELA	1.91	1.90	1.00	.96
	LATIN AMERICA	10.91	6.70	4.85	4.60
	ALADI	9.06	5.67	4.02	4.07
	Andean Group	3.13	2.74	1.70	1.54
	CACM	.48	.34	.36	.24
	UNITED STATES	16.91	15.91	13.60	10.87
	JAPAN	1.37	3.16	6.17	6.48
	WEST GERMANY	3.29	8.90	10.91	9.70

1. Excluding, through 1970, China and Mongolia and through 1980 North Korea and Vietnam. In 1980 the share for China and Mongolia combined was .93%.

a. Calculated from data in SALA, 23-2800 and Part II of 23-2829.

SOURCE: *CEPAL Review*, Aug. 1982, p. 53; UN-YITS, 1978, I, pp. 21, 23, 27; UN-MB, Oct. 1983, pp. 106, 112, 120.

Figure 26:1
WESTERN HEMISPHERE DECLINING SHARE IN
WORLD EXPORTS, 1950–80[a]
(%)

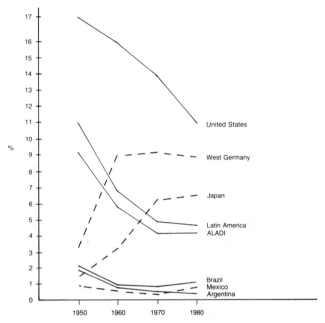

a. Trend line has been smoothed between the 5-year points sampled here.

SOURCE: SALA, 24-2600.

Table 2601

IMPORTS AS A PERCENTAGE OF WORLD IMPORTS,
20 LRC, 1950–75[a]
(Value, CIF)

	Country	1950	1955	1960	1965	1970	1975
A.	ARGENTINA	1.66	1.32	1.05	.68	.58	.48
B.	BOLIVIA	.10	.09	.06	.07	.05	.07
C.	BRAZIL	1.87	1.48	1.22	62	.97	1.66
D.	CHILE	.42	.42	.44	.34	.32	.19
E.	COLOMBIA	.63	.76	.42	.26	.29	.18
F.	COSTA RICA	.08	.10	.09	.10	.11	.09
G.	CUBA	.88	.65	.48	.49	.44	.38
H.	DOMINICAN REP.	.09	.13	.08	.06	.10	.11
I.	ECUADOR	.09	.13	.10	.10	.09	.12
J.	EL SALVADOR	.08	.10	.10	.11	.07	.07
K.	GUATEMALA	.12	.12	.10	.13	.10	.09
L.	HAITI	.06	.05	.03	.02	.02	.02
M.	HONDURAS	.08	.08	.06	.07	.07	.05
N.	MEXICO	.95	1.00	.99	.89	.84	.81
O.	NICARAGUA	.04	.08	.06	.09	.07	.06
P.	PANAMA	.12	.09	.10	.12	.12	.11
Q.	PARAGUAY	.04	.04	.03	.03	.03	.03
R.	PERU	.31	.34	.32	.42	.20	.31
S.	URUGUAY	.34	.26	.18	.09	.08	.07
T.	VENEZUELA	1.02	1.24	1.08	.86	.68	.74
	LATIN AMERICA	8.10	7.83	6.53	5.07	4.77	5.81
	UNITED STATES	16.53	14.10	13.70	13.21	14.44	12.68

a. For yearly data 1948–71, see SALA-SNP, pp. 295–296.

SOURCE: SALA-SNP, pp. 295–296; and IFS, March 1978, except Cuban data (problematic
    since the 1960s because of dollar exchange rate) calculated from Cuba, DGE, AE, 1957, and
    Cuba, JUCEPLAN, AE, 1972 and 1975.

Table 2602

MAJOR TRADING PARTNERS, 20 L, 1976-86[a]

(%)

Trade with Major Individual Countries

Country	Category	United States							United Kingdom						
		1976	1980	1982	1983	1984	1985	1986	1976	1980	1982	1983	1984	1985	1986
A. ARGENTINA	Export	7.3	8.9	13.4	9.9	10.8	12.2	9.27	3.1	2.5	1.0	~	~	#	.4
	Import	17.9	22.6	22.0	21.9	18.5	18.2	18.5	4.2	3.3	1.3	.1	#	#	.2
B. BOLIVIA	Export	34.4	17.3	26.1	20.5	20.9	14.1	17.5	9.0	7.1	3.5	2.6	3.5	9.3	2.1
	Import	25.7	18.3	29.0	28.2	16.9	21.6	17.9	2.6	2.1	4.0	3.9	3.6	2.3	.9
C. BRAZIL	Export	18.3	17.4	20.5	23.2	28.5	26.9	26.7	3.8	2.7	3.3	3.3	2.6	2.6	2.7
	Import	22.6	18.6	15.0	15.6	16.6	19.7	24.6	2.5	1.9	1.3	1.5	2.0	1.9	2.7
D. CHILE	Export	10.1	12.1	21.6	28.1	26.0	22.7	21.7	6.7	6.1	5.0	5.4	5.4	6.6	5.2
	Import	23.8	27.2	25.9	19.9	21.5	21.3	20.5	3.1	2.1	2.2	2.0	2.3	2.7	2.8
E. COLOMBIA	Export	31.2	30.1	23.4	28.3	31.5	32.8	35.8	2.0	1.8	1.5	1.7	2.5	3.0	2.4
	Import	42.5	38.5	34.6	35.6	34.2	35.3	35.6	3.6	2.2	2.1	2.2	2.1	2.4	2.3
F. COSTA RICA	Export	39.7	33.8	33.5	31.8	37.8	39.5	44.6	.2	.3	2.3	2.6	3.7	2.9	3.5
	Import	34.6	34.3	35.6	37.8	36.3	34.7	42.7	2.8	1.8	2.7	1.3	1.3	1.9	1.8
G. CUBA[1]	Export	~	#	.1	~	~	#	#	6.1†	5.0†	2.4	1.9	1.8	1.0	1.3
	Import	#	#	.1	#	.1	#	.1	5.4†	4.6†	7.7	4.8	4.5	3.0	3.7
H. DOMINICAN REP.	Export	69.6	46.3	54.0	67.4	76.7	75.9	16.6	1.0	.2	.2	.5	.1	.1	4.5
	Import	47.8	44.8	38.9	35.9	34.2	34.7	1.6	1.8	1.3	1.1	.9	.9	1.1	2.8
I. ECUADOR	Export	37.7	28.9	47.9	56.6	64.2	53.5	49.6	.1	.3	.1	.1	.3	.3	.5
	Import	39.1	38.3	37.3	34.0	29.9	33.1	31.9	3.7	2.6	3.0	3.1	1.8	3.4	3.7
J. EL SALVADOR	Export	32.7	39.7	35.4	38.6	37.6	48.2	46.2	.2	.6	.1	#	.2	.2	.2
	Import	28.6	32.4	27.2	32.5	33.3	33.9	48.1	2.5	1.3	.6	1.0	1.2	1.2	.9
K. GUATEMALA	Export	35.1	27.7	27.3	34.9	33.5	34.0	40.0	.4	.6	1.7	1.1	.9	.5	.7
	Import	36.4	34.5	31.1	32.2	32.5	37.4	39.8	3.1	2.3	1.2	1.1	1.2	1.6	1.3
L. HAITI	Export	66.8	69.5	78.6	76.1	79.7	87.2	77.0	.4	.6	1.1	.5	.4	.4	.3
	Import	56.4	57.2	61.0	63.3	67.2	67.3	65.2	2.3	1.2	1.3	1.1	.8	1.0	1.3
M. HONDURAS	Export	56.3	49.1	52.6	63.4	52.9	48.4	47.9	.1	.9	1.1	1.3	1.9	1.6	.8
	Import	43.7	40.4	41.0	45.1	40.6	39.0	44.9	2.1	2.9	2.1	2.2	1.2	1.5	1.7
N. MEXICO	Export	60.9	63.2	52.0	58.4	58.4	60.4	67.3	.8	.5	4.2	4.1	4.1	3.1	1.0
	Import	62.5	65.6	59.9	60.5	62.3	66.6	67.1	3.1	2.2	1.8	1.9	1.8	2.1	1.8
O. NICARAGUA	Export	31.1	37.6	24.4	22.5	14.1	14.2	.3	.3	.6	1.4	.5	.6	.5	.6
	Import	31.5	32.7	18.9	18.6	17.1	7.9	.6	2.5	.8	1.4	.5	1.0	1.6	2.2
P. PANAMA	Export	48.3	49.3	41.5	53.7	60.8	64.1	53.8	.1	.1	.2	.3	.1	.7	.7
	Import	32.1	33.8	35.0	32.3	31.7	31.5	16.7	1.6	1.1	1.2	.8	.9	1.0	1.5
Q. PARAGUAY	Export	11.9	5.5	2.8	8.6	6.3	1.2	4.3	6.0	.6	1.2	.7	.2	.5	.4
	Import	10.3	9.9	9.0	7.3	8.8	7.9	13.7	7.6	5.6	5.8	5.2	4.2	4.2	6.4
R. PERU	Export	24.9	33.0	31.0	35.6	39.6	33.9	30.1	5.9	4.1	4.4	5.3	4.5	4.5	4.7
	Import	30.5	38.1	30.6	32.8	29.4	28.2	27.2	3.4	3.5	1.9	1.8	1.8	2.7	2.9
S. URUGUAY	Export	10.9	7.8	7.4	9.7	14.9	15.2	32.6	3.8	3.5	3.6	3.9	3.9	4.2	4.1
	Import	8.7	9.8	12.2	8.3	8.5	8.6	10.3	3.7	4.2	2.4	2.2	2.1	2.7	3.7
T. VENEZUELA	Export	38.4	27.8	26.3	31.4	39.9	46.0	44.7	2.1	1.2	1.3	1.7	1.9	1.7	2.4
	Import	44.8	48.2	43.6	47.9	50.1	47.5	45.9	3.2	2.9	2.2	2.2	2.0	3.0	4.1

Table 2602 (Continued)

MAJOR TRADING PARTNERS, 20 L, 1976–86[a]

(%)

Trade with Major Individual Countries

Country	Category	Germany 1976	1980	1982	1983	1984	1985	1986	Japan 1976	1980	1982	1983	1984	1985	1986	Trade with EEC 1976	1980	1982	1983	1984	1985	1986
A. ARGENTINA	Export	5.2	5.1	4.4	3.2	3.7	3.4	6.8	5.3	2.6	3.7	4.8	3.3	4.3	6.7	33.2	27.6	21.3	23.9	27.7	24.5	30.8
	Import	11.2	9.4	9.0	10.5	9.7	10.6	12.0	8.2	9.3	8.0	6.8	8.2	7.0	7.0	27.4	25.9	22.1	27.2	24.6	28.0	30.8
B. BOLIVIA	Export	3.4	2.6	3.7	2.9	5.6	4.6	1.8	3.3	2.7	1.8	1.9	1.2	.4	1.2	18.8	21.4	15.0	18.1	15.4	20.9	12.1
	Import	7.7	4.3	7.3	5.5	4.6	5.3	4.2	11.1	7.0	11.0	7.3	3.3	8.5	4.7	15.4	12.4	16.3	16.9	14.9	14.2	12.8
C. BRAZIL	Export	8.9	6.6	5.9	5.2	4.7	5.0	5.1	6.3	6.1	6.5	6.5	5.6	5.5	6.4	30.7	27.2	26.9	28.9	25.2	26.8	25.0
	Import	8.7	7.0	4.4	4.5	4.5	6.5	8.5	7.3	4.8	4.6	3.7	4.0	4.3	6.5	20.0	15.4	12.6	12.5	12.6	14.6	22.3
D. CHILE	Export	14.8	12.2	11.5	12.6	9.9	9.5	10.4	10.7	10.3	11.9	9.0	11.1	9.9	10.4	35.7	36.8	31.4	34.5	31.1	33.7	34.1
	Import	5.7	5.4	6.1	6.2	6.2	6.8	8.0	11.1	10.4	6.5	5.4	8.9	6.1	9.5	13.8	15.2	16.8	17.2	18.0	19.6	21.5
E. COLOMBIA	Export	16.2	15.7	18.1	18.4	16.6	16.2	17.5	3.4	4.0	4.1	4.4	4.4	4.2	4.8	29.9	33.1	35.3	39.5	37.5	34.8	34.9
	Import	10.2	6.4	5.8	4.9	5.5	6.4	7.5	7.7	11.1	11.1	11.1	9.6	10.4	10.5	23.0	17.3	14.9	16.5	18.2	19.6	22.9
F. COSTA RICA	Export	10.5	11.3	14.3	12.8	13.3	12.8	11.8	1.2	.8	.7	.6	.5	.6	.9	19.0	23.2	25.9	24.1	25.9	23.5	25.0
	Import	5.2	4.8	3.9	4.7	5.2	5.3	5.3	11.4	11.6	4.2	5.3	7.6	9.6	10.3	12.2	11.1	10.9	12.3	14.2	15.1	14.7
G. CUBA[1]	Export	2.5†	3.9	2.3	2.6	1.3	2.1	2.0	6.8†	12.8	8.2	8.3	8.4	9.7	13.7	19.1	31.5	27.0	31.3	29.9	31.7	29.6
	Import	6.2†	5.5	4.3	4.5	4.2	4.1	4.6	13.5†	12.1	8.4	7.2	13.1	11.8	12.8	28.3	40.8	33.2	30.7	31.9	27.8	29.1
H. DOMINICAN REP.	Export	.4	.2	.2	.2	.3	.2	5.6	.6	.9	.8	1.9	1.7	2.3	4.7	12.0	8.4	6.6	11.2	11.1	13.2	38.7
	Import	3.5	2.6	2.2	3.2	2.7	3.9	6.3	6.3	8.0	5.1	4.3	4.7	6.3	17.1	10.3	8.8	4.1	11.3	9.2	10.3	20.6
I. ECUADOR	Export	2.9	1.6	1.1	.8	1.2	1.9	3.7	1.1	12.2	.8	1.8	.7	2.0	2.4	8.2	7.6	4.1	2.6	3.5	4.6	7.7
	Import	8.6	7.3	8.0	8.7	7.2	9.6	9.0	16.5	13.7	12.4	9.3	13.7	11.9	14.5	18.2	18.2	18.9	23.9	18.0	28.1	23.4
J. EL SALVADOR	Export	14.3	19.4	29.3	18.9	22.5	21.0	16.4	7.9	3.3	3.3	4.9	5.5	5.1	3.9	25.2	28.8	19.8	23.3	25.8	25.7	23.5
	Import	5.9	2.8	4.6	4.1	4.4	4.4	3.2	9.7	3.7	3.1	3.5	4.3	5.2	3.1	16.2	10.0	8.1	11.8	10.2	10.5	9.0
K. GUATEMALA	Export	10.7	8.3	7.0	5.4	2.7	3.5	4.3	8.3	2.8	5.0	3.4	4.7	3.0	3.6	18.3	24.1	17.5	16.9	10.8	13.2	12.5
	Import	7.0	5.4	5.6	5.0	5.1	5.5	5.4	11.1	8.0	5.2	4.9	5.1	4.7	4.6	15.5	12.5	11.8	11.5	11.8	13.6	14.4
L. HAITI	Export	.7	2.6	3.2	3.9	3.4	2.7	2.9	.6	.2	.7	.4	.3	.5	.5	26.8	23.3	15.4	16.9	12.7	13.1	17.2
	Import	3.3	1.8	2.3	2.4	1.9	1.9	2.2	5.8	5.4	5.2	4.3	4.8	6.0	4.6	14.3	9.5	10.7	11.1	8.7	12.1	11.6
M. HONDURAS	Export	11.7	11.5	8.8	5.5	5.8	8.5	6.1	3.1	3.7	5.8	5.5	7.2	5.5	9.9	19.9	18.0	21.0	15.6	17.6	25.0	22.3
	Import	4.7	2.1	3.4	2.7	3.6	3.0	2.8	8.8	8.9	6.8	5.9	4.6	5.9	8.8	12.0	10.5	11.1	14.3	14.4	13.9	11.7
N. MEXICO	Export	2.6	1.7	4.3	1.2	.9	1.3	2.4	5.1	3.7	6.7	6.8	7.5	7.7	6.4	8.6	6.6	12.0	17.9	17.8	18.2	12.4
	Import	7.0	5.2	6.1	4.0	4.1	4.0	5.9	5.1	5.3	5.7	3.9	4.2	5.4	6.3	16.3	13.8	14.8	15.0	13.1	13.0	14.3
O. NICARAGUA	Export	9.7	8.6	9.3	8.0	6.8	9.7	10.9	13.0	2.6	12.0	15.1	21.5	17.2	12.3	19.7	19.7	23.4	23.9	25.7	31.0	40.9
	Import	6.3	2.0	2.2	1.8	2.8	2.9	3.8	7.9	2.7	1.4	1.2	2.0	4.4	1.9	13.0	6.6	12.2	12.4	17.6	23.1	30.5
P. PANAMA	Export	8.5	5.1	5.9	5.7	5.9	5.8	7.1	.3	.4	.1	.4	.4	#	3.1	20.4	12.9	13.7	14.4	17.0	16.2	17.5
	Import	1.8	1.8	1.8	2.3	2.0	2.3	1.9	5.6	6.1	7.6	7.8	8.3	8.9	11.7	7.7	6.4	7.1	8.7	8.0	8.3	14.2
Q. PARAGUAY	Export	11.2	12.4	12.4	11.8	11.8	13.5	3.3	3.5	3.6	7.7	1.9	2.4	1.0	.8	40.0	25.3	24.4	36.6	40.1	44.9	19.2
	Import	8.5	6.5	6.4	6.8	3.1	5.0	6.5	4.7	8.1	5.5	4.2	11.8	4.6	5.7	20.0	16.1	17.5	20.7	15.0	15.9	18.2
R. PERU	Export	7.2	3.9	3.6	3.1	4.1	4.5	5.6	13.7	10.9	14.6	14.4	11.5	8.6	9.1	26.7	16.6	18.4	18.5	19.4	22.5	24.9
	Import	7.2	6.3	6.6	6.7	5.2	8.6	9.1	7.7	10.0	8.8	6.6	6.3	10.0	9.5	20.6	21.7	17.3	18.5	18.7	23.4	21.1
S. URUGUAY	Export	12.3	12.9	8.9	7.6	8.2	7.7	5.9	1.7	.9	1.8	1.9	2.2	2.2	1.3	37.5	30.1	23.5	20.5	20.7	22.8	20.6
	Import	7.6	6.7	6.9	6.0	5.9	7.3	7.4	1.8	4.1	2.7	2.4	1.8	2.3	3.2	18.3	17.9	15.3	15.1	17.4	19.3	22.1
T. VENEZUELA	Export	1.3	1.1	2.6	7.4	5.8	4.3	5.8	.4	3.5	3.8	3.4	2.7	2.9	3.3	8.7	12.6	12.7	19.4	16.0	20.2	15.7
	Import	9.7	6.8	4.7	4.3	4.6	5.7	7.4	8.7	8.1	9.8	6.0	5.2	5.7	6.9	24.8	20.6	20.9	22.2	23.0	23.1	26.9

1. Cuban % trade total here excludes Cuba's trade with socialist countries.

a. For prior years from 1915, see SALA, SNP, table XV-3.

SOURCE: Calculated from IMF-DOT-Y, 1982, 1986, and 1987.

Table 2603

LAFTA, CACM, AND ECLA:L INTRAZONAL IMPORTS AS SHARE OF EACH
COUNTRY'S TOTAL IMPORTS, 25 ECLA:L, 1960–85

(%)

	Country	1960	1970	1975	1980	1981	1982	1983	1984	1985
A.	ARGENTINA	13.6	21.1	25.8	19.3	19.5	29.2	26.9	32.5	31.0
B.	BOLIVIA	12.5	20.4	36.1	50.3	44.0	48.0	49.8	41.6	49.3
C.	BRAZIL	13.7	10.8	5.6	11.6	14.0	15.4	14.1	14.1	12.0
D.	CHILE	17.1	19.4	29.3	26.9	24.5	26.8	27.7	25.6	27.7
E.	COLOMBIA	1.9	8.6	11.0	15.7	19.5	20.9	20.6	20.7	21.8
I.	ECUADOR	6.2	9.8	13.9	14.3	12.8	14.5	16.7	19.2	19.8
N.	MEXICO	.2	2.8	5.6	3.8	4.6	3.3	2.1	3.3	3.2
Q.	PARAGUAY	28.9	37.7	61.0	59.7	62.3	64.6	61.4	58.8	55.3
R.	PERU	7.9	15.0	16.7	15.2	15.1	16.7	14.4	19.0	24.7
S.	URUGUAY	26.9	35.2	36.1	37.6	46.6	45.4	41.3	35.9	39.3
T.	VENEZUELA	1.9	3.7	6.9	9.0	11.5	10.8	10.2	11.2	9.7
	Total LAFTA	8.9	11.0	11.4	13.1	13.9	14.7	14.4	14.9	13.4
F.	COSTA RICA	6.3	30.5	35.2	33.1	36.8	38.9	30.8	30.4	26.6
J.	EL SALVADOR	15.1	32.0	37.5	45.4	48.0	47.1	40.6	39.3	36.9
K.	GUATEMALA	10.3	33.1	35.0	34.7	32.4	35.3	42.3	37.9	35.8
M.	HONDURAS	8.8	32.4	34.6	29.4	28.8	34.8	25.6	27.1	26.5
Q.	NICARAGUA	9.0	32.9	40.8	56.4	57.9	46.8	47.0	34.4	38.2
	Total CACM	10.3	32.1	36.4	38.4	39.3	40.1	37.6	34.1	32.7
	Barbados	6.7	28.0	31.7	21.1	23.2	23.6	22.8	18.1	25.3
	Guyana	12.5	17.0	23.1	31.5	35.5	49.2	48.3	51.9	53.9
	Jamaica	3.2	9.3	25.1	10.4	27.9	25.7	19.8	13.1	22.4
	Trinidad and Tobago	32.4	28.8	3.4	5.5	6.8	8.1	8.2	7.2	9.0
	Bahamas	5.4	6.7	7.2	4.9	3.0	3.4	4.3	2.4	3.7
L.	HAITI	~	2.4	3.8	8.5	10.4	7.6	8.4	6.7	4.0
P.	PANAMA	8.1	13.2	13.5	8.2	10.0	8.6	12.0	8.5	6.7
H.	DOMINICAN REP.	~	5.4	18.8	6.0	28.2	29.8	32.7	37.8	34.2
	Suriname	.7	3.1	17.4	36.2	36.2	30.3	27.6	27.5	27.1
	Total Region	9.4	12.9	13.0	13.7	14.9	15.6	15.9	15.5	14.4

SOURCE: ECLA-AE, 1986, p. 190.

Table 2604

CACM INTRAREGIONAL TRADE, 5 LR, 1985 AND 1986[†]

(T US)

			Exporting Countries				
	Importing Countries	Total CACM	K. GUATEMALA	J. EL SALVADOR	M. HONDURAS	O. NICARAGUA	F. COSTA RICA
K.	GUATEMALA						
	1985	99,457	**	49,444	5,146	7,665	37,202
	1986	98,416	**	51,728	4,758	2,232	39,878
J.	EL SALVADOR						
	1985	216,771	148,646	**	10,594	2,396	54,135
	1986	145,367	101,653	**	8,289	1,735	33,690
M.	HONDURAS						
	1985	74,846	32,755	7,072	**	1,936	33,083
	1986	53,687	23,688	6,683	**	1,379	21,937
O.	NICARAGUA						
	1985	56,742	25,522	9,073	7,002	**	15,145
	1986	28,482	8,355	5,850	2,525	**	11,752
F.	COSTA RICA						
	1985	99,838	49,366	33,069	7,802	9,601	**
	1986	95,031	50,682	33,403	5,622	5,324	**
	CACM						
	1985	547,654	257,289	98,658	30,544	21,598	139,565
	1986	420,983	184,378	97,664	27,014	10,670	107,257

SOURCE: IDB-SPTF, 1987, table V-3.

Table 2605

CACM TRADE WITH 18 ECR COUNTRIES,[1] 1970-80

(%)

Country	1970	1971	1972	1973	1974	1975	1976	1977	1978	1979	1980	Average 1970-1980
Exports	1.2	1.4	1.6	1.8	2.2	1.7	1.1	1.0	1.1	1.0	1.0[a]	1.2[b]
F. COSTA RICA	.2	.3	.2	.2	.4	.3	.3	1.0	1.8	1.8	1.5	1.0
J. EL SALVADOR	.1	.1	.1	.1	.1	.2	.3	.2	.3	.2	~	.2[c]
Imports	.8	1.1	.6	1.0	1.0	1.0	2.9	3.5	2.8	5.2	4.5[a]	2.9[b]
F. COSTA RICA	.7	.8	.7	.9	1.1	1.3	2.5	6.1	2.2	8.8	2.0	3.3
J. EL SALVADOR	.5	.3	.4	.1	.2	.3	.3	.2	.2	.2	~	.2[c]

Continued in SALA, 24-2611.

Table 2606

LAIA INTRAREGIONAL TRADE, 11 LR, 1985 AND 1986[†]

(M US)

Importing Countries	Total LAIA	A. ARGENTINA	B. BOLIVIA	C. BRAZIL	D. CHILE	E. COLOMBIA	I. ECUADOR	N. MEXICO	Q. PARAGUAY	R. PERU	S. URUGUAY	T. VENEZUELA
A. ARGENTINA												
1985	1,191.2	**	375.5	547.8	84.5	31.4	7.8	36.7	15.7	28.8	63.1	.6
1986	1,600.2	**	416.8	632.5	160.6	65.7	25.0	112.0	35.2	59.2	88.7	4.5
B. BOLIVIA												
1985	265.6	69.3	**	171.4	14.3	.8	#	.2	.3	8.1	1.0	.3
1986	292.2	56.4	**	198.2	30.5	1.5	.1	.8	#	3.3	.9	.4
C. BRAZIL												
1985	1,521.7	496.3	4.5	**	210.0	5.1	2.2	297.8	60.1	50.6	143.3	251.8
1986	1,674.3	684.9	15.2	**	292.9	10.3	20.3	154.0	91.8	49.0	296.0	59.9
D. CHILE												
1985	733.1	111.1	10.7	238.8	**	22.8	44.3	16.4	13.1	39.3	4.0	232.8
1986	699.8	121.7	9.7	235.7	**	35.0	64.9	26.0	13.6	59.5	6.6	127.1
E. COLOMBIA												
1985	739.4	132.7	3.9	102.4	44.8	**	62.8	121.2	.9	70.1	6.7	193.8
1986	546.3	62.5	4.2	107.0	40.5	**	44.0	111.4	.2	51.1	4.4	121.0
I. ECUADOR												
1985	346.4	14.6	.1	119.5	34.5	63.9	**	48.3	#	62.0	1.4	2.1
1986	330.5	11.4	.1	135.8	28.1	67.9	**	53.1	0	23.6	1.0	9.5
N. MEXICO												
1985	562.0	255.6	.2	220.2	51.0	6.5	1.6	**	.2	7.6	6.8	12.5
1986	337.3	131.5	.1	164.2	9.7	11.5	5.4	**	.3	2.3	7.1	5.1
Q. PARAGUAY												
1985	383.8	72.2	.1	298.8	5.8	#	.3	.3	**	#	6.1	#
1986	362.7	68.7	#	283.0	5.4	.1	#	.6	**	.1	4.6	.1
R. PERU												
1985	382.7	162.0	12.7	92.1	45.7	32.7	6.0	13.0	.6	**	1.8	16.0
1986	591.8	170.9	14.4	150.2	65.9	91.0	8.9	32.9	3.8	**	10.1	43.7
S. URUGUAY												
1985	286.5	99.0	.2	140.3	12.3	.3	.1	24.3	6.4	2.4	**	1.1
1986	391.8	111.2	.2	187.5	11.0	.6	4.1	62.4	6.4	2.2	**	6.2
T. VENEZUELA												
1985	637.1	72.8	#	302.8	33.7	142.8	2.0	39.1	.2	40.0	3.7	**
1986	729.4	42.6	#	345.0	40.6	182.6	1.8	55.2	.1	59.0	2.5	**
LAIA												
1985	7,050.0	1,485.5	407.8	2,233.9	536.6	306.4	127.2	597.4	97.5	308.9	237.8	711.1
1986	7,556.4	1,461.8	460.8	2,439.1	685.2	466.3	174.6	608.4	151.6	309.3	421.9	377.5

SOURCE: IDB-SPTF, 1987, table V-1.

Table 2607

ANDEAN GROUP INTRAREGIONAL TRADE, 6 LR, 1985 AND 1986[†]

(M US)

Importing Countries	Andean Group	Exporting Countries				
		B. BOLIVIA	E. COLOMBIA	I. ECUADOR	R. PERU	T. VENEZUELA
B. BOLIVIA						
1985	9.3	**	.1	#	8.1	.3
1986	5.3	**	1.5	.1	3.3	.4
E. COLOMBIA						
1985	330.7	3.9	**	62.8	70.1	193.8
1986	220.3	4.2	**	44.0	51.1	121.0
I. ECUADOR						
1985	128.2	.1	63.9	**	62.0	2.1
1986	101.1	.1	67.9	**	23.6	9.5
R. PERU						
1985	67.5	12.7	32.7	6.0	**	16.0
1986	158.0	14.4	97.0	8.9	**	43.7
T. VENEZUELA						
1985	184.8	#	142.8	2.0	40.0	**
1986	243.4	#	182.6	1.8	59.0	**
Andean Group						
1985	720.4	16.7	240.3	70.9	180.3	212.3
1986	728.1	18.7	343.0	54.8	137.0	174.6

SOURCE: IDB-SPTF, 1987, table V-3.

Table 2608

ORIGIN OF ANDEAN GROUP IMPORTS, 1961–77

(%)

Origin	1961-63	1975-77
United States	49.0	39.0
European Economic Community	29.0	25.5
Canada	3.0	3.5
Japan	4.0	9.5
Latin America		
(including Andean Group)	6.5	12.5
Rest of World	8.5	10.0
Total	100.0	100.0

SOURCE: *Colombia Today* 15:9 (1980)

Table 2609

INTRAREGIONAL EXPORTS AS A PERCENTAGE OF TOTAL EXPORTS, 25 LR, 1960–85

(%)

	Country	1960	1970	1975	1980	1981	1982	1983	1984	1985[‡]
A.	ARGENTINA	15.8	21.0	25.9	23.6	19.3	20.3	14.0	18.2	18.7
B.	BOLIVIA	12.3	8.9	35.9	36.7	42.5	51.8	55.0	57.0	63.5
C.	BRAZIL	7.1	11.6	15.5	18.1	19.1	15.0	10.3	11.3	9.6
D.	CHILE	7.7	12.2	23.7	23.5	21.6	19.3	11.9	15.0	14.3
E.	COLOMBIA	3.2	9.6	20.7	16.6	22.7	20.8	11.1	10.3	11.1
I.	ECUADOR	7.8	10.0	33.6	20.2	17.9	22.2	18.3	9.9	8.4
N.	MEXICO	2.9	9.5	13.0	5.8	9.7	8.4	7.6	6.1	5.1
Q.	PARAGUAY	33.0	38.2	35.6	45.3	50.2	50.8	40.2	37.9	27.6
R.	PERU	9.8	6.5	16.9	21.2	12.7	11.2	8.8	9.8	10.6
S.	URUGUAY	2.5	12.6	29.3	37.3	26.7	30.8	23.3	26.4	28.0
T.	VENEZUELA	11.2	12.5	12.3	9.8	14.5	15.2	14.0	12.6	11.4
	Total LAFTA	9.3	12.5	17.4	15.4	16.4	15.0	11.6	11.3	10.4
F.	COSTA RICA	5.2	23.8	29.0	34.3	33.2	28.0	29.0	26.0	22.9
J.	EL SALVADOR	10.8	31.7	30.0	28.5	27.2	26.3	25.3	23.1	19.7
K.	GUATEMALA	5.2	36.7	29.9	32.6	41.3	37.6	34.4	30.6	30.3
M.	HONDURAS	18.0	17.0	22.0	13.5	17.2	13.6	12.5	10.2	10.8
O.	NICARAGUA	4.5	27.4	25.7	10.3	16.1	17.4	10.1	11.5	10.4
	Total CACM	8.4	28.4	28.0	26.4	29.4	26.9	25.0	22.4	21.1
	Barbados	5.4	6.6	12.5	17.3	22.8	22.6	18.5	17.2	18.1
	Guyana	14.1	1.7	15.3	14.1	27.7	21.8	23.4	13.8	13.0
	Jamaica	2.0	4.1	5.6	7.6	9.9	14.6	14.4	9.1	9.1
	Trinidad and Tobago	5.9	9.9	11.1	15.0	16.8	18.9	14.3	13.0	11.7
	Bahamas	1.8	3.9	4.1	2.0	2.3	2.1	2.6	2.6	2.0
L.	HAITI	~	1.5	1.2	1.8	1.1	1.2	3.3	3.1	2.3
P.	PANAMA	.5	4.2	6.6	19.2	16.0	16.0	13.1	13.3	5.5
H.	DOMINICAN REP.	.2	.9	1.0	10.4	8.4	5.8	3.2	5.3	2.5
	Suriname	1.6	.7	#	2.9	2.6	14.1	14.0	6.5	7.0
	Total Region	8.8	12.8	16.0	15.4	16.5	15.3	12.0	11.6	10.7

SOURCE: ECLA-AE, 1986, p. 187.

Table 2610

VALUE OF IMPORTS FROM COUNTRIES WITH CENTRALLY PLANNED ECONOMIES, 9 L, 1965–83[a]

(M US)

	Country	Year	Total[1]	Asia[2]	Europe,[3] USSR	China[2]	Bulgaria	Czechoslovakia	German Dem. Rep.[4]	Hungary[5]	Poland	Romania	USSR
A.	ARGENTINA	1965	192	84	108	84	#	10	2	10	13	1	72
		1970	85	4	81	3	1	9	#	13	18	9	31
		1975	485	21	464	21	9	16	2	10	20	1	407
		1979	844	193	651	193	11	48	45	10	62	33	440
		1980	2,167	197	1,970	189	7	44	35	7	80	7	1,791
		1981	3,574	116	3,458	116	7	44	31	8	40	40	3,289
		1982	1,989	150	1,839	150	7	30	19	14	24	#	1,745
		1983	2,586	651	1,936	651	~	30	#	11	26	~	1,751

Continued in SALA, 25-2616.

Table 2611

VALUE OF EXPORTS TO COUNTRIES WITH CENTRALLY PLANNED ECONOMIES, 9 L, 1965–83[a]

(M US)

	Country	Year	Total[1]	Asia[2]	Europe,[3] USSR	China[2]	Bulgaria	Czechoslovakia	German Dem. Rep.[4]	Hungary[5]	Poland	Romania	USSR
A.	ARGENTINA	1965	30	#	30	#	#	4	1	1	3	1	20
		1970	19	1	18	1	#	5	#	1	10	#	2
		1975	95	1	94	1	#	9	#	2	33	34	15
		1979	129	11	118	11	4	20	#	7	20	24	38
		1980	151	32	119	32	6	19	15	10	14	8	47
		1981	153	24	128	24	4	40	12	12	11	7	42
		1982	74	5	69	5	2	9	4	3	12	#	38
			170	4	~		11		#	3			38

Continued in SALA, 25-2617.

Table 2612

ARGENTINA ABSOLUTE VALUE OF GOODS TRADED WITH SELECTED REGIONS AND COUNTRIES,[1] 1980–86
(M US)[2]

Category	Exports FOB							Imports CIF						
	1980	1981	1982	1983	1984	1985	1986	1980	1981	1982	1983	1984	1985	1986
I. World	8,024.8	9,142.9	7,622.6	7,835.7	8,107.3	8,396.1	7,476.6	10,540.9	9,432.2	5,341.0	4,504.0	4,584.6	3,814.2	5,067.3
II. Industrial Countries	3,455.2	3,389.5	3,263.3	3,097.5	3,466.9	3,525.1	3,551.5	7,186.4	6,516.3	3,356.1	2,833.3	2,664.8	2,304.3	3,196.2
United States	717.6	863.5	1,022.1	773.2	876.9	1,027.9	693.1	2,380.4	2,093.7	1,177.1	986.6	847.4	694.4	935.4
Canada	42.5	73.3	40.1	32.1	49.0	58.8	59.5	109.8	144.7	55.5	54.1	66.9	35.2	50.4
Australia	6.2	9.9	3.7	8.8	10.5	28.9	27.9	83.7	123.2	53.9	48.2	62.2	51.1	56.4
Japan	210.9	166.5	283.1	376.6	271.2	360.9	501.6	978.3	967.6	429.6	307.3	375.9	265.5	376.1
New Zealand	1.0	.6	.5	1.7	1.9	3.4	10.5	9.9	1.3	1.0	2.0	.7	.6	.9
Austria	7.0	4.1	8.1	4.6	2.7	4.0	6.0	45.9	44.2	29.6	33.5	26.8	29.6[a]	25.6
Belgium	59.4	86.9	68.6	123.3	207.2	148.8	224.5	159.0	105.7	75.1	75.7	100.0	72.4	101.3
Denmark	77.5	72.6	86.2	66.0	35.2	20.7	60.9	42.8	31.7	27.3	22.3	22.1	10.8	15.7
Finland	19.9	8.1	10.0	6.1	5.9	4.8	10.8	75.4	61.7	24.3	15.5	14.1	14.9	17.8
France	186.2	145.2	141.5	133.5	132.1	122.3	135.9	374.2	353.2	196.8	197.3	204.1	207.9	284.0
Germany	407.5	354.7	335.9	248.7	297.6	289.2	511.6	984.8	904.8	478.7	474.5	442.5	404.0	610.6
Iceland	~	~	.1	.1	~	.1	.1	~	~	~	~	~	~	~
Ireland	2.0	4.5	4.0	1.2	1.3	1.5	5.5	10.7	15.7	7.7	4.2	5.6	3.8	7.5
Italy	520.3	376.4	288.9	340.3	377.2	300.7	354.6	576.9	488.0	230.7	230.4	190.5	233.9	296.3
Netherlands	716.3	696.8	604.0	734.9	892.5	856.4	624.7	232.6	211.6	97.1	63.5	65.8	63.1	97.7
Norway	13.3	8.6	9.2	6.4	34.0	28.3	39.9	23.6	20.4	11.9	6.0	3.1	8.1	5.7
Spain	187.6	209.8	224.2	198.3	232.7	230.9	201.0	399.1	322.3	181.9	153.0	89.8	67.9	132.1
Sweden	21.2	44.3	23.3	15.7	21.1	17.3	20.9	139.9	131.5	76.8	49.2	54.4	36.0	54.9
Switzerland	55.6	46.1	36.3	26.0	18.0	20.3	30.5	216.2	173.0	132.7	106.7	92.6	103.4	115.8
United Kingdom	203.4	217.8	73.7	~	~	.2	32.3	343.4	322.2	68.5	3.4	.4	1.8	12.0
III. Developing Countries														
Oil Exporting Countries	267.1	296.7	544.9	596.7	667.7	493.6	454.5	593.0	429.0	174.0	6.1	5.6	6.1	1.0
Algeria	56.3	41.0	136.6	55.3	75.2	28.0	73.8	6.0	7.3	~	~	~	~	~
Indonesia	5.6	1.5	12.5	15.5	9.6	27.0	11.9	.2	.7	~	.1	~	~	~
Iran, I.R. of	86.3	30.8	134.4	396.4	430.2	313.9	293.6	~	9.7	~	~	~	~	~
Iraq	11.5	36.7	115.5	9.5	2.8	.4	1.2	127.5	~	~	~	~	~	~
Kuwait	2.2	20.8	2.0	1.7	1.4	1.3	1.2	5.7	~	~	~	~	~	~
Libya	1.1	.3	.6	.3	7.8	.3	14.0	5.9	~	~	~	~	~	~
Nigeria	17.5	21.9	22.5	20.7	6.4	33.7	16.7	37.4	66.7	~	~	~	~	~
Oman	~	1.4	~	2.8	2.5	~	~	~	~	~	~	~	~	~
Qatar	~	~	.3	.2	.1	~	.1	~	~	~	~	~	~	~
Saudi Arabia	21.5	39.3	23.0	33.9	15.8	12.7	15.7	338.7	280.8	153.5	~	~	4.6[b]	~
United Arab Emirates	.1	1.2	.1	2.0	1.9	3.3	.9	~	~	~	~	.7	~	~
T. VENEZUELA	65.1	101.7	97.4	58.4	114.0	72.8	25.5	71.5	63.6	20.5	6.0	4.9	1.6	1.0
Non-Oil Developing Countries	2,448.4	2,299.0	2,086.9	2,246.8	2,267.1	2,730.5	2,708.7	2,588.4	2,297.2	1,722.0	1,581.8	1,820.7	1,430.0	1,783.3
Africa	99.9	107.7	113.6	245.7	214.9	260.4	278.9	97.2	48.1	32.4	29.1	18.1	14.9	27.1
Angola	26.9	31.5	16.0	17.3	20.6	36.2	28.7	21.3	~	~	~	~	~	~
Benin	1.1	~	.9	~	~	5.2	6.4	~	~	~	~	~	~	~
Cameroon	~	.5	7.9	3.3	.2	.8	2.0	.5	~	~	~	~	~	~
Cape Verde	.7	~	~	2.6	2.5	2.2	1.5	~	~	~	~	~	~	~
Central African Rep.	~	~	~	~	~	~	6.9	~	~	~	~	~	~	~
Congo	.3	1.9	3.8	3.3	.7	.5	.7	20.0	1.6	.7	.8	1.4	.3	.2
Ethiopia	~	~	.1	~	.1	.8	.4	~	~	~	~	~	~	~
Gabon	2.5	3.5	4.5	3.7	2.4	3.1	3.0	~	~	~	~	~	~	~
Gambia, The	~	~	~	~	~	~	~	~	~	~	~	~	~	~
Ghana	1.1	2.7	~	1.7	.8	~	~	~	~	~	~	~	~	~
Guinea	~	~	~	~	~	~	3.9	~	~	~	~	~	~	~
Ivory Coast	3.6	3.4	2.8	.7	.1	8.7	6.9	~	~	~	~	~	~	~
Kenya	.1	~	~	2.9	1.1	6.5	.1	~	~	~	.2	~	~	~
Liberia	11.6	16.9	2.2	.2	~	.1	.1	~	~	~	~	~	~	1.1
Madagascar	~	~	~	~	~	~	~	~	~	~	4.6	~	~	~
Mali	.1	~	~	~	.4	~	~	~	~	~	~	~	.2	~
Mauritania	.1	~	3.7	~	.7	~	1.0	~	~	.1	~	~	~	.3
Mauritius	.1	~	~	~	~	~	~	~	~	~	~	~	~	~

Table 2612 (Continued)

ARGENTINA ABSOLUTE VALUE OF GOODS TRADED WITH SELECTED REGIONS AND COUNTRIES,[1] 1980–86
(M US$)[2]

Category	Exports FOB 1980	1981	1982	1983	1984	1985	1986	Imports CIF 1980	1981	1982	1983	1984	1985	1986
III. Developing Countries (Continued)														
Non-Oil Developing Countries														
Morocco	2.9	11.4	14.5	10.6	13.1	22.7	9.8	?	.1	?	?	?	?	?
Mozambique	?	?	.1	1.3	4.9	.9	.9	?	?	?	?	?	?	?
Niger	?	?	?	?	?	?	?	?	?	?	?	?	?	?
Reunion	?	3.4	?	?	?	?	?	?	?	?	?	?	?	?
Senegal	7.5	6.2	8.2	6.4	2.6	1.0	1.4	?	?	?	?	?	?	?
Sierra Leone	1.0	?	.1	.1	.7	?	?	?	?	?	?	?	?	?
Somalia	?	?	?	?	?	?	?	?	?	?	?	?	?	?
South Africa	15.6	18.1	19.2	172.0	122.7	77.4	83.1	53.4	44.2	31.1	23.5	16.5	14.4	25.0
Sudan	3.7	.1	.1	.1	.4	?	.6	?	1.7	?	?	?	?	?
Swaziland	?	?	?	?	?	?	?	?	?	?	?	?	?	?
Tanzania	?	?	1.9	?	.7	5.4	1.1	?	?	?	?	?	?	?
Togo	?	?	.3	?	.1	.1[b]	5.7	?	?	?	?	?	?	?
Tunisia	17.7	3.1	4.5	6.8	27.9	20.1	17.0	1.4	?	?	?	?	?	?
Upper Volta	.1	?	?	?	?	?	?	?	?	?	?	?	?	?
Zaire	3.4	5.2	22.9	8.2	4.1	5.5	5.1	.2	?	?	?	?	.1	?
Zimbabwe	?	?	?	?	8.3	?	.1	?	?	.3	.2	.1	.1	.6
Asia	267.5	242.9	269.8	742.3	372.0	517.9	488.3	259.3	249.1	74.4	61.7	80.5	42.6	96.1
Bangladesh	.1	2.6	2.1	.1	2.4	8.0	5.5	.8	1.8	.1	.2	.2	?	?
Brunei	?	.1	.1	.5	.1	?	?	.1	?	?	?	?	?	?
China, People's Rep.	188.8	92.1	136.6	498.6	74.9	311.0	269.2	32.7	21.4	10.3	4.7	6.1	4.3	8.9
Guam	?	.1	?	.1	.1	?	?	?	?	?	?	?	?	?
Hong Kong	21.9	19.4	3.3	.3	.4	8.2	8.5	110.9	95.8	17.7	1.9	1.7	.2	7.3
India	22.2	60.9	11.5	37.9	163.7	55.4	29.8	6.5	5.4	1.4	2.1	1.3	1.2	1.3
Korea	7.3	17.3	15.1	49.1	26.6	19.5	80.1	50.5	79.9	14.6	8.9	20.7	11.1	31.8
Malaysia	5.0	10.7	15.2	69.9	14.7	28.1	30.6	2.8	1.1	1.5	.3	.1	.1	7.3
Nepal	?	?	?	?	?	?	?	?	?	?	?	?	?	?
Pakistan	8.4	4.9	6.3	10.2	9.0	17.1	18.4	.8	.5	.7	.7	.4	.1	1.2
Philippines	.8	1.6	.7	9.1	38.6	.9	1.1	1.8	.7	.5	.2	.1	.7	.6
Singapore	5.3	36.1	76.4	36.1	16.3	9.0	9.3	50.7	40.6	26.6	41.9	49.5	23.4	35.6
Sri Lanka	.2	2.9	.1	19.7	4.3	25.2	5.5	1.6	1.7	1.0	.5	.3	.7	1.3
Thailand	4.7	4.3	2.3	10.9	21.0	8.7	17.4	.1	.1	?	.5	?	?	.1
Viet Nam	2.7	?	?	?	?	?	?	?	?	?	?	?	?	?
Oceania not specified	.1	?	?	?	.1	?	?	?	?	?	?	?	?	?
Europe	134.6	106.2	77.5	59.5	129.4	311.4	400.7	31.3	61.5	22.3	16.7	44.0	42.3	47.9
Cyprus	3.6	1.7	4.9	8.7	4.9	1.1	10.4	?	?	?	?	?	?	?
Gibraltar	?	.2	?	?	?	?	?	?	?	?	?	?	?	?
Greece	39.4	20.2	22.6	8.2	11.3	14.4	18.5	1.9	31.8	.4	.1	2.9	.1	?
Hungary	5.8	6.9	11.1	6.6	3.7	11.1	20.6	6.0	11.6	7.1	2.6	4.5	5.7	15.3
Malta	1.0	4.1	7.3	5.7	3.1	3.6	7.5	?	?	?	1.0	?	?	?
Portugal	42.3	34.5	28.6	23.6	59.2	73.9	35.8	6.7	5.7	3.3	2.8	2.2	2.9	3.5
Romania	23.3	27.8	.4	4.3	24.5	16.7	49.2	13.6	7.8	10.0	7.6	29.4	9.6	5.8
Turkey	1.2	.1	.5	1.6	3.2	76.7	57.5	.3	1.1	.1	?	?	?	.2
Yugoslavia	18.0	10.7	2.0	.7	19.7	15.9	30.2	2.7	3.5	1.5	1.8	1.4	1.3	3.4
Europe not specified	?	?	?	?	.1	?	.1	?	?	?	?	?	?	?
Middle East	98.8	134.1	166.5	154.5	164.1	564.0	542.0	17.7	14./	10.8	10.8	9.7	14.8	18.1
Bahrain	?	1.7	.1	.1	.1	.4	.5	?	.3	?	?	?	?	?
Egypt	29.4	68.6	108.6	88.6	67.2	143.7	115.3	?	?	?	?	?	?	.2
Israel	39.9	51.7	40.8	51.1	38.4	31.1	26.4	17.6	14.4	10.7	10.5	9.7	10.1	17.9
Jordan	10.6	2.0	8.7	3.9	6.4	12.7	4.0	?	?	?	?	?	?	?
Lebanon	10.1	3.3	4.3	5.9	35.3	39.9	34.5	.1	?	?	.1	.1	?	?
Syrian Arab Rep.	8.4	8.2	4.0	4.8	16.7	4.3	34.8	?	?	.1	.2	.2	?	?
Yemen Arab Rep.	.3	.3	?	?	.1	?	?	?	?	?	?	?	?	?
Yemen P.D. Rep.	?	?	?	?	?	?	?	?	?	?	?	?	?	?
Middle East not specified	?	?	?	?	?	?	?	?	?	?	?	?	?	?

Table 2612 (Continued)

ARGENTINA ABSOLUTE VALUE OF GOODS TRADED WITH SELECTED REGIONS AND COUNTRIES,[1] 1980-86
(M US)[2]

Category	Exports FOB							Imports CIF						
	1980	1981	1982	1983	1984	1985	1986	1980	1981	1982	1983	1984	1985	1986
IV. Latin America[3]	1,912.8	1,799.8	1,556.8	1,103.3	1,500.7	1,570.3	1,453.3	2,254.5	1,987.6	1,602.9	1,469.7	1,672.5	1,321.6	1,595.2
Antigua and Barbuda	~	~	.1	.1	~	.1c	~	~	~	~	~	~	~	~
Bahamas	1.1	.3	.8	.7	.3	~	.6	1.2	.3	.4	.3	1.0	.9	~
Barbados	2.0	1.3	.9	1.9	.8	1.7	1.3	~	.3	~	~	~	~	1.1
Belize	.1	.1	.1	.1	.1	~	~	~	~	~	~	~	~	~
Bermuda	1.1	.3	.2	~	.1	~	~	.9	.2	~	~	~	~	~
B. BOLIVIA	133.4	125.9	113.9b	56.4	88.2	69.3	69.7	252.4	343.8	395.7	394.5	391.7	382.9	378.3
C. BRAZIL	765.1	595.1	567.5	358.4	478.2	496.3	575.1	1,072.4	893.2	687.9	666.4	831.2	611.6	701.2
D. CHILE	217.6	189.0	164.2	188.9	149.9	111.1	126.5	254.7	189.5	146.6	116.1	118.5	85.4	158.6
E. COLOMBIA	39.0	51.2	69.9	59.5	66.6	132.7	115.9	52.1	41.0	25.9	24.3	24.5	23.2	65.4
F. COSTA RICA	5.5	5.2	1.6	1.9	7.8	3.5	2.9	2.1	1.3	.3	.2	.1	2.4	6.0
Dominica	.1	~	~	~	~	~	~	~	~	~	.2	~	~	~
H. DOMINICAN REP.	1.4	.8	1.0	10.9	31.9	9.9	14.6	.2	~	~	~	~	~	~
I. ECUADOR	17.5	16.9	19.8	13.4	15.6	14.6	11.6	61.1	50.1	35.7	12.1	8.8	11.5	18.4
J. EL SALVADOR	1.9	.3	9.4	2.6	1.7	3.6	3.7	.1	.1	~	.4	1.7	.3	~
Grenada	.2	~	.1	.1	.5	.1	.1	.1	.1	~	.3	.1	.1	.2
Guadeloupe	~	~	~	~	~	~	~	~	~	~	~	~	~	~
K. GUATEMALA	3.2	3.7	1.8	1.8	2.0	2.6	1.7	.2	.1	1.2	~	~	~	~
Guyana	.4	~	~	~	~	~	1.1	1.7	~	~	~	~	~	~
L. HAITI	.3	.3	.3	20.9	11.5	6.4	5.2	~	~	~	~	~	~	~
M. HONDURAS	4.2	3.0	4.3	.3	1.4	6.9	9.5	.5	~	.1	~	~	~	~
Jamaica	1.8	1.7	.2	.6	.7	.3	.4	~	~	21.7	~	~	~	~
Leeward Islands	~	~	~	~	~	~	~	~	~	~	~	~	~	~
Martinique	~	.1	~	~	~	~	~	~	~	~	~	~	~	~
N. MEXICO	121.3	275.3	111.8	33.4	171.6	255.5	115.5	71.7	66.6	61.9	69.3	78.5	59.8	89.6
Netherlands Antilles	6.7	31.3	3.7	6.8	21.8	8.8	8.5	11.9	41.1	10.4	.9	3.2	2.0	1.3
O. NICARAGUA	4.5	5.1	2.2	17.3	21.1	26.4	26.0	.1	~	~	~	~	~	~
P. PANAMA	14.0	2.8	5.4	7.1	10.3	8.8	21.6	90.9	56.7	25.6	18.8	24.8	17.2	19.6
Q. PARAGUAY	189.4	169.3	145.9	87.3	94.4	72.9	68.4	84.6	92.0	49.3	38.6	50.4	20.1	43.2
R. PERU	116.8	89.1	109.8	94.6	127.9	162.0	119.9	69.6	27.2	21.3	31.4	35.0	36.5	35.5
St. Christopher-Nevis	.1	~	.1	.1	.1	.3	.3	~	~	~	~	~	~	~
St. Lucia	.2	~	.1	.1	.1	.2	.2	~	~	~	~	~	~	~
St. Vincent	.1	.1	.1	.2	.1	.2	.1	~	~	~	~	~	~	~
Suriname	.1	~	.1	.1	.1	.1	.1	~	~	~	~	~	~	~
Trinidad and Tobago	2.0	1.6	9.3	2.8	4.9	4.2	5.9	4.9	~	~	~	~	~	~
S. URUGUAY	185.3	128.1	115.5	76.8	82.9	99.0	121.3	148.1	120.5	89.9	89.0	98.1	65.9	75.9
Windward Islands	~	~	~	~	~	~	~	~	~	~	~	~	~	~
British West Indies	11.4	.4	~	~	~	~	~	1.4	~	~	~	~	~	~
V. USSR, Eastern Europe, etc.	1,835.2	3,144.9	1,709.1	1,850.9	1,678.8	1,622.3	730.3	75.3	105.6	69.8	68.9	78.2	41.9	69.1
Albania	~	~	.4	~	~	1.5	1.5	~	~	~	~	~	~	~
Bulgaria	7.6	6.3	3.6	31.2	24.6	51.7	61.3	7.0	3.9	5.4	6.9	7.6	5.0	1.4
G. CUBA	66.3	76.8	47.9	128.4	233.7	283.4	234.1	.3	~	~	.1	.6	.3	.6
Czechoslovakia	25.1	24.8	30.1	31.0	93.7	58.0	75.7	16.6	33.1	14.9	8.5	4.4	5.2	3.5
Eastern Germany	35.4	31.0	19.0	6.6	17.5	16.4	9.7	14.6	11.8	3.8	2.7	4.5	8.8	2.5
Mongolia	~	~	~	~	~	~	~	~	~	~	~	~	~	~
North Korea	4.7	~	~	.2	~	.1	2.2	~	~	~	~	~	~	~
Poland	81.9	42.9	21.8	17.5	121.5	98.2	70.9	22.2	24.5	12.4	19.3	25.5	22.6	19.6
USSR	1,614.2	2,963.2	1,586.4	1,635.9	1,187.8	1,212.7	345.7	14.6	32.4	33.3	31.5	35.6	41.9	61.1
EEC	2,441.8	2,219.3	1,876.2	1,878.1	2,246.1	2,058.8	2,305.1	3,132.0	2,792.6	1,367.5	1,227.1	1,126.1	1,068.6	1,560.8

Table 2612 (Continued)

ARGENTINA ABSOLUTE VALUE OF GOODS TRADED WITH SELECTED REGIONS AND COUNTRIES,[1] 1980-86
(M US)[2]

Category	Exports FOB							Imports CIF						
	1980	1981	1982	1983	1984	1985	1986	1980	1981	1982	1983	1984	1985	1986
VI. Percent Distribution														
Industrial Countries	43.1	37.1	42.8	39.5	42.8	42.0	47.5	68.2	69.1	63.8	62.9	58.1	60.4	63.1
Oil Exporting Countries	3.3	3.2	7.1	7.6	8.2	5.9	6.1	5.6	4.5	3.3	.1	.1	.2	#
Non-Oil Developing Countries	30.5	25.1	27.4	28.7	28.0	32.5	36.2	24.6	24.4	32.2	35.1	39.7	37.5	35.2
Africa	1.2	1.2	1.5	3.1	2.7	3.1	3.7	.9	.5	1.4	.6	.4	.4	.5
Asia	3.3	2.8	3.5	9.5	4.6	6.2	6.5	2.5	2.6	1.4	1.4	1.8	1.1	1.9
Europe	1.7	1.2	1.0	.8	1.6	3.7	5.4	.3	.7	.4	.4	1.0	1.1	.9
Middle East	1.2	1.5	2.2	2.0	2.0	6.7	7.2	.2	.2	.2	.2	.2	.4	.9
Non-industrial Western Hemisphere[3]	23.0	18.6	19.1	13.3	17.1	18.7	19.4	20.7	20.4	29.6	32.5	36.4	34.6	31.5
USSR, Eastern Europe, etc.	22.9	34.4	22.4	23.6	20.7	19.3	9.8	.7	1.1	1.3	1.5	1.7	1.6	1.4
VII. Annual Percent Change														
World	2.8	13.9	-16.6	2.8	3.5	3.6	-11.0	57.1	-10.5	-43.4	-15.7	1.8	-16.8	32.9
Industrial Countries	-16.5	-1.9	-3.7	-5.1	11.9	1.7	.7	64.8	-9.3	-48.5	-15.6	-5.9	-13.5	38.7
Oil Exporting Countries	-22.2	11.1	83.7	9.5	11.9	-26.1	-7.9	195.3	-27.7	-59.4	-96.5	-8.2	8.9	-83.6
Non-Oil Developing Countries	-8.2	-6.1	-9.2	7.7	.9	14.3	-.8	27.7	-11.3	-25.0	-8.1	15.1	-22.5	24.7
Africa	3.8	7.9	5.5	116.3	-12.5	-12.2	7.1	-65.1	-50.6	-32.6	-10.2	-37.8	-18.3	82.1
Asia	-9.8	-5.4	6.7	175.1	-49.9	35.7	-5.7	163.2	-4.0	-70.1	-17.1	30.5	-47.6	125.6
Europe	-26.0	-21.1	-27.0	-23.2	117.5	24.1	28.7	-31.5	96.6	-63.7	-25.1	163.5	-39.1	13.2
Middle East	-50.4	35.7	24.2	-7.2	6.2	-10.0	-3.9	-2.5	-17.2	-26.5	#	-10.2	41.9	22.3
Non-industrial Western Hemisphere[3]	-2.4	-8.1	-14.1	-28.4	32.7	4.6	-7.5	37.6	-11.9	-17.8	-7.5	14.0	-21.0	20.7
USSR, Eastern Europe, etc.	195.7	71.4	-45.7	8.3	-9.3	4.2	-55.0	-18.6	40.1	-33.9	-1.3	13.5	16.1	13.0

1. DOT data may differ between countries and from IFS data because of the time it takes for an export to become an import, etc.
2. Data may be calculated from partner's reported data or estimated on basis of less than 12 months.
3. Cuba is included in category V; Venezuela is included in category III.

a. Nine months of reported data, 3 months derived from partner.
b. Nine months or reported data, 3 months extrapolated.
c. Nine months of reported data, 3 months derived or extrapolated.

SOURCE: Adapted from IMF-DOT-Y, 1982, 1986, and 1987.

Table 2613

BOLIVIA ABSOLUTE VALUE OF GOODS TRADED WITH SELECTED REGIONS AND COUNTRIES,[1] 1980–86
(M US)[2]

Category	Exports FOB							Imports CIF						
	1980	1981	1982	1983	1984	1985	1986	1980	1981	1982	1983	1984	1985	1986
I. World	1,036.2	995.3	898.5	786.7	781.5	672.5	657.0	813.8	918.2	496.3	530.7	409.0	608.2	685.2
II. Industrial Countries	587.4	519.5	425.9	335.7	350.7	248.8	219.3	497.2	532.0	296.8	295.6	186.9	283.8	263.9
United States	266.6	266.2	260.5	160.9	145.7	94.8	115.2[a]	231.7	210.3	143.8	149.5	116.1[a]	131.6[a]	122.8[a]
Canada	8.9	.4	.1	~	.1[a]	.1	6.7[a]	5.8	8.7	5.8	4.0	3.2	2.4[a]	1.1[a]
Australia	~	~	~	~	~	~	~	~	~	~	~	~	~	~
Japan	9.2	9.4	16.5	15.1	8.4	2.9	8.1[a]	7.8	109.0	54.4	39.0	24.1	51.7[a]	31.9[a]
Austria	~	~	~	.2	~	~	5.8[a]	~	~	~	1.3	.7	1.3[a]	.8[a]
Belgium–Luxembourg	36.2	28.1	18.4	31.6	31.5	13.9	7.5[a]	29.6	11.1	3.7	2.8	7.9[a]	6.5	11.2[a]
Denmark	~	~	~	~	~	.1	1.4[a]	~	~	~	3.4	.9	1.1	6.9[a]
Finland	~	~	~	~	~	~	2.3[a]	~	~	~	.6	.1[a]	.8[a]	.6[a]
France	44.4	24.7	14.8	14.5	5.6	7.6	28.0[a]	4.4	16.9	6.4	21.1	7.4	13.7[a]	6.1[a]
Germany	54.8	34.6	24.1	22.5	25.7	31.2	11.5[a]	78.1	74.0	36.3	29.2	28.3	32.2[a]	28.5
Ireland	~	~	~	~	~	~	~	~	~	~	.2	.4	.5[a]	1.2[a]
Italy	1.3	1.9	.9	.6	.5	.7	6.9[a]	11.6	9.4	8.5	3.9	3.6	4.7[a]	18.0[a]
Netherlands	45.4	72.3	36.3	46.7	74.1	21.6	1.0[a]	9.5	15.5	6.3	5.7	6.3	9.7[a]	5.6[a]
Norway	~	~	4.7	6.1	2.9	2.6	9.5[a]	~	~	~	.1	.1	.3[a]	.3[a]
Spain	.1	.9	.6	.1	.1[a]	~	.1[a]	15.7	24.5	5.9	2.2	4.0	4.0[a]	4.1[a]
Sweden	42.5	18.6	16.6	1.8	14.5	10.6	1.5[a]	7.9	8.5	5.9	7.2	3.2	5.2[a]	5.9[a]
Switzerland	42.5	18.6	16.6	1.8	14.5	10.6	1.5[a]	5.9	8.5	5.9	4.5	3.8	4.3[a]	6.9[a]
United Kingdom	71.3	38.5	30.4	20.6	41.5	62.7	13.7[a]	24.1	44.1	19.8	20.8	10.7	14.0[a]	5.9[a]
III. Developing Countries														
Oil Exporting Countries	4.8	3.8	4.3	.2	1.4	~	~	.5	.5	.1	.7	.5	~	~
T. VENEZUELA	4.8	3.8	4.3	.2	1.4	~	~	.5	.5	.1	.5	.4	~	~
Non-Oil Developing Countries	376.9	438.1	464.9	435.5	413.8	405.8	419.0	265.5	354.2	179.3	226.3	206.6	309.8	405.3
Africa	~	~	~	~	~	~	~	~	~	~	3.5	.5	1.1	.8
South Africa	~	~	~	~	~	~	~	~	~	~	3.3	.5	1.1	.8
Asia	.2	12.3	.4	~	5.0	~	2.3	16.8	28.8	8.1	2.4	4.9	5.6	7.5
China, People's Rep.	~	~	~	~	~	~	.7[a]	~	~	~	.7	.4	1.0[a]	1.6[a]
Hong Kong	~	~	~	~	~	~	~	~	~	~	.2	.2	.3[a]	.5[a]
Korea	~	~	~	~	5.0[a]	~	1.5[a]	~	~	~	1.2	.9	4.1[a]	4.0[b]
Malaysia	~	~	~	~	~	~	~	~	~	~	~	3.1	~	-.1[a]
Sri Lanka	~	~	~	~	~	~	~	~	~	~	.1	.2	~	~
Thailand	~	~	.4[a]	~	~	~	~	~	~	~	~	~	~	~
Asia not specified	.2	12.3	~	~	~	~	~	16.8	28.8	8.1	~	~	~	~
Europe	1.0	5.9	5.4	3.0	2.7	1.1	1.2	19.5	24.9	8.4	1.0	5.0	4.1	4.5
Greece	~	~	~	~	.8[a]	~	~	~	~	~	~	~	~	~
Portugal	~	~	~	~	.3[a]	~	~	~	~	~	.2	.1	.2[a]	.4[b]
Yugoslavia	~	~	~	~	~	~	~	~	~	~	~	~	~	~
Europe not specified	1.0	5.9	~	~	.1	~	~	19.5	24.9	8.4	~	~	~	~
Middle East	~	~	~	~	~	~	~	~	~	~	.2	.9	2.0	1.7
Israel	~	~	~	~	.1	~	~	~	~	~	.1	.9	2.0[a]	1.7[a]
IV. Latin America[3]	380.5	423.7	463.8	432.7	412.4	404.7	415.5	229.7	301.1	162.9	220.0	195.7	297.0	390.7
A. ARGENTINA	245.2	359.7	399.7	362.6	382.3	375.9	394.7[c]	89.6	90.8	72.4	75.6	63.4	76.2[a]	76.7[b]
C. BRAZIL	36.3	12.7	18.2	39.4	8.1	4.5	4.7[c]	53.5	129.4	50.5	73.9	89.3	188.5[a]	266.6[b]
D. CHILE	46.9	8.5	11.1	6.8	5.0	5.6	4.5[a]	30.9	36.4	14.8	16.2	14.1	15.7[a]	33.6[a]
E. COLOMBIA	9.8	5.9	5.8	3.8	4.6	4.1	4.3[c]	3.3	3.6	1.8	1.6	1.5[b]	.8[a]	.8[b]
F. COSTA RICA	~	~	~	~	~	~	~	~	~	~	.8	1.0	~	~
I. ECUADOR	1.6	.8	1.0	5.0	.1	.1	.1[c]	1.0	.9	.6	.3	.1	.1[b]	.1[b]
N. MEXICO	2.9	.9	.2	.1	.1	.2	.1[c]	2.6	5.5	1.8	32.5	~	2.0[b]	.7[b]
P. PANAMA	~	~	~	.1	1.2	1.5	1.6[c]	~	~	5.0	2.7	2.8	~	.1[b]
Q. PARAGUAY	.5	~	~	~	~	~	~	.5	~	5.0	~	.7	~	~
R. PERU	32.3	31.2	23.1	14.8	9.6	12.6	5.3[a]	44.4	28.8	13.6	13.5	21.8	14.4[a]	11.6[a]
S. URUGUAY	.6	.3	.3	~	~	~	~	1.1	1.8	1.0	2.4	1.3	1.1[a]	1.2[b]
Other Latin America not specified	~	.3	~	~	~	~	~	2.4	2.4	1.3	~	~	~	~

Table 2613 (Continued)

BOLIVIA ABSOLUTE VALUE OF GOODS TRADED WITH SELECTED REGIONS AND COUNTRIES,[1] 1980–86 (M US)[2]

Category	Exports FOB							Imports CIF						
	1980	1981	1982	1983	1984	1985	1986	1980	1981	1982	1983	1984	1985	1986
V. USSR, Eastern Europe, etc.	45.5	31.6	2.6	14.2	15.7	17.9	18.8	11.7	13.0	7.5	6.9	13.8	13.8	14.5
G. CUBA	~	~	~	~	~	~	~	~	~	~	.1	.1[c]	.1	.1
Czechoslovakia	~	~	~	~	~	15.0	15.7	~	~	~	~	~	~	2.0
Poland	~	~	~	~	13.8	1.1	1.2	~	~	~	2.9	1.9	1.9	4.1
USSR	~	~	2.3	8.9	1.9	2.9	3.1	~	~	~	.7[c]	3.9	3.9	12.4
USSR, etc. not specified	45.5	31.6	~	~	~	~	~	11.7	13.0	7.5	3.9	11.8	11.8	~
Country or area not specified	21.6	2.3	~	1.1	0	~	~	38.9	18.5	12.6	~	~	~	~
EEC	253.3	200.2	129.6	142.7	181.7	140.5	79.6	157.4	170.9	81.0	89.5	65.5	86.5	88.0
VI. Percent Distribution														
Industrial Countries	56.7	52.2	47.4	42.7	44.9	37.0	33.4	61.1	57.9	59.8	55.7	45.7	46.7	38.5
Oil Exporting Countries	.5	.5	.5	#	.2	~	~	.1	.1	#	#	.1	#	~
Non-Oil Developing Countries	42.3	44.0	51.7	55.4	53.8	46.1	63.8	32.6	38.6	36.1	42.5	50.5	50.9	59.2
Africa	#	~	~	~	~	~	.3	~	~	#	.6	.1	.2	.1
Asia	.1	1.2	#	~	~	.2	.2	2.1	3.1	1.6	.4	1.2	.9	1.1
Europe	~	.6	1.8	~	.3	.2	~	2.4	2.4	2.9	~	1.2	.7	.7
Middle East	~	~	~	~	~	~	~	~	~	~	~	.2	.3	.2
Non-industrial Western Hemisphere[3]	36.3	42.2	51.1	54.9	52.8	60.2	63.2	28.2	32.8	32.8	41.4	47.8	48.8	57.0
USSR, Eastern Europe, etc.	4.4	3.2	.3	1.8	2.0	2.7	2.9	1.4	1.4	1.5	1.4	3.4	2.3	2.1
VII. Annual Percent Change														
World	20.9	-3.9	-9.7	-12.4	-.7	-13.9	-2.3	-5.5	12.8	-45.9	6.9	-22.9	48.7	12.7
Industrial Countries	10.5	-11.6	-18.0	-21.2	4.5	-29.0	11.9	-5.4	7.0	-44.2	-.4	-36.8	51.8	-7.0
Oil Exporting Countries	38.3	-22.0	6.1	-6.3	60.0	-100.0	~	-19.1	33.4	-49.4	25.9	-28.6	-100.0	~
Non-Oil Developing Countries	-99.5	1,416.7	-97.8	~	-5.0	-1.9	3.3	-87.3	47.9	-68.5	-65.7	-8.7	50.0	30.8
Asia	-90.4	~	-97.7	~	-15.4	-81.8	8.4	-24.2	71.4	-71.9	-72.8	104.9	14.9	34.0
Europe	38.7	506.6	~	~	-10.5	-59.1	~	-8.2	27.8	-66.1	-95.7	382.5	-17.1	10.3
Middle East	~	~	~	~	33.3	~	~	~	~	~	~	494.9	114.7	-16.6
Non-industrial Western Hemisphere[3]	52.1	11.8	9.4	-5.9	-4.7	-1.9	2.7	-5.5	31.2	45.9	34.8	-11.0	51.8	31.6
USSR, Eastern Europe, etc.	1.5	-30.5	-91.7	442.8	10.5	14.1	5.0	-5.5	11.1	-42.1	.3	100.9	~	5.0

1. DOT data may differ between countries and from IFS data because of the time it takes for an export to become an import, etc.

2. Data may be calculated from partner's reported data or estimated on basis of less than 12 months.

3. Cuba is included in category V; Venezuela is included in category III.

a. Data derived from partner country for the entire year.

b. Five or fewer months of reported data; seven or more months derived or extrapolated.

c. Data extrapolated for the entire year.

SOURCE: Adapted from the IMF-DOT-Y, 1982, 1986, and 1987.

Table 2614

BRAZIL ABSOLUTE VALUE OF GOODS TRADED WITH SELECTED REGIONS AND COUNTRIES,[1] 1980–86
(M US)[2]

PART I

Category	Exports FOB							Imports CIF						
	1980	1981	1982	1983	1984	1985	1986	1980	1981	1982	1983	1984	1985	1986
I. World	20,132	23,329	20,168	21,853	27,007	25,256	24,551	24,961	24,074	21,069	16,803	15,210	14,335	16,390
II. Industrial Countries	11,539	12,513	12,048	13,639	17,107	15,987	15,408	11,626	10,058	8,122	6,440	6,038	6,471	10,044
United States	3,510	4,111	4,131	5,061	7,710	6,801	6,543	4,634	3,933	3,164	2,627	2,526	2,825	4,029
Canada	243	290	231	311	408	414	483	985	637	516	556	582	448	585
Australia	98	135	137	136	201	162	155	40	54	20	52	64	75	77
Japan	1,232	1,220	1,313	1,428	1,515	1,394	1,568	1,192	1,380	973	618	609	613	1,063
New Zealand	13	16	17	24	26	22	14	2	1	~	1	~	~	42
Austria	68	57	58	96	92	114	118	24	21	20	21	8	12	41
Belgium–Luxembourg	356	413	401	504	638	570	466	175	146	155	81	85	82	106
Denmark	131	93	91	104	123	85	110	32	26	21	20	17	18	55
Finland	70	62	64	75	87	54	65	79	55	46	49	28	31	43
France	822	851	863	884	836	780	784	719	649	597	489	397	326	720
Germany	1,337	1,317	1,182	1,130	1,256	1,274	1,247	1,741	1,180	934	758	682	933	1,394
Iceland	5	3	2	1	3	20	5	2	1	1	3	2	~	~
Ireland	21	30	40	30	34	20	20	13	9	8	8	10	11	56
Italy	979	961	984	978	1,115	1,125	953	415	661	518	229	216	201	405
Netherlands	1,150	1,470	1,132	1,259	1,361	1,552	1,262	263	228	149	172	156	178	257
Norway	117	111	92	88	104	85	102	93	72	64	34	47	46	97
Spain	521	372	368	526	495	523	465	218	107	102	76	45	61	99
Sweden	197	157	171	176	233	181	207	166	237	286	156	72	102	175
Switzerland	120	109	97	108	161	165	169	349	295	278	237	190	235	352
United Kingdom	550	735	672	721	708	663	671	483	367	270	253	304	273	447
III. Developing Countries														
Oil Exporting Countries	1,461	2,350	1,795	1,896	2,334	2,467	1,930	9,087	9,962	8,825	6,891	5,995	5,017	3,285
Algeria	167	267	125	150	239	136	150	83	303	185	163	130	207	197
Indonesia	41	122	87	59	56	62	60	76	300	14	~	1	4	7
Iran, I.R. of	239	195	210	347	298	212	218	766	~	52	421	185	108	134
Iraq	289	298	318	412	350	635	480	3,948	2,031	2,765	2,249	2,203	1,973	1,329
Kuwait	42	79	24	28	39	34	40	797	607	229	295	246	~	~
Libya	35	11	11	17	9	13	20	140	369	350	84	~	~	2
Nigeria	272	770	244	194	654	842	350	90	756	237	87	1,019	1,422	768
Oman	8	3	2	5	8	11	12	~	~	~	~	~	~	~
Qatar	14	15	19	13	14	16	21	201	231	339	272	145	~	~
Saudi Arabia	96	161	267	377	261	168	244	2,177	4,038	3,196	2,396	1,478	1,025	810
United Arab Emirates	29	21	16	25	41	35	29	212	278	411	206	~	~	~
T. VENEZUELA	230	408	470	270	365	303	305	598	1,048	1,048	719	587	278	37
Non-Oil Developing Countries	5,749	6,624	5,001	4,748	6,106	5,535	5,817	3,984	3,815	3,621	2,930	2,865	2,644	2,841
Africa	680	688	850	723	821	1,662	1,046	860	652	459	346	1,374	1,835	1,164
Angola	119	107	85	47	90	129	122	113	162	105	228	135	155	153
Benin	2	7	17	13	25	18	20	~	~	~	~	~	~	~
Burkina Faso	~	1	~	~	~	1	5	~	~	~	~	~	~	~
Cameroon	2	17	4	4	6	6	9	~	~	~	~	~	~	~
Cape Verde	2	~	~	3	3	7	4	~	~	~	~	~	~	~
Comoros	~	~	~	~	~	~	2	~	~	~	~	~	~	~
Congo	36	73	65	10	8	9	4	85	116	~	~	~	~	1
Djibouti	~	~	~	~	~	~	~	~	~	~	~	~	~	~
Ethiopia	2	6	2	7	1	1	~	~	~	~	~	~	~	~
Gabon	10	23	5	2	8	1	1	311	217	226	42	21	21	~
Gambia, The	~	~	~	2	~	~	1	~	~	~	~	~	~	~
Ghana	1	6	16	19	11	6	4	~	~	~	~	~	~	~
Guinea	1	9	31	20	35	32	24	~	~	~	~	~	~	~
Guinea-Bissau	~	~	~	1	~	~	~	~	~	~	~	~	~	~
Ivory Coast	30	78	60	6	13	13	23	~	~	~	~	~	2	2
Kenya	3	6	3	4	6	5	12	~	~	~	~	~	~	~
Liberia	44	28	62	80	37	124	49	~	~	~	~	~	~	~
Madagascar	1	2	3	2	2	1	1	~	~	~	~	~	~	~
Mauritania	1	1	4	2	1	~	1	~	~	~	~	~	~	~
Mauritius	1	2	2	3	1	~	3	~	~	~	~	~	~	~

Table 2614 (Continued)

BRAZIL ABSOLUTE VALUE OF GOODS TRADED WITH SELECTED REGIONS AND COUNTRIES,[1] 1980–86
(M US)[2]

Category	Exports FOB							Imports CIF						
	1980	1981	1982	1983	1984	1985	1986	1980	1981	1982	1983	1984	1985	1986
III. Developing Countries (Continued)														
Non-Oil Developing Countries														
Morocco	86	36	56	52	53	31	30	55	14	2	3	12	1	9
Mozambique	72	37	99	87	20	4	5	…	1	14	11	…	…	…
Niger	…	2	1	…	…	2	1	…	…	…	…	…	…	…
Reunion	4	3	7	2	…	…	…	…	…	…	…	…	…	…
Senegal	…	…	7	2	85	44	27	…	…	…	…	…	…	…
Seychelles	…	…	…	…	…	…	…	…	…	…	…	…	…	…
Sierra Leone	2	1	1	1	1	1	1	…	…	…	…	…	…	…
Somalia	…	…	…	…	3	1	4	…	…	…	…	…	…	…
South Africa	103	132	103	138	131	53	57	227	104	85	25	51	22[c]	24
Sudan	7	4	8	3	4	8	6	…	…	…	…	…	…	…
Tanzania	15	10	7	13	3	2	2	…	…	…	…	…	…	…
Togo	8	…	7	5	3	1	3	3	…	31	…	…	1[a]	…
Tunisia	25	17	35	28	28	21	12	…	…	…	…	…	…	…
Uganda	…	…	1	1	1	…	…	…	…	…	…	…	…	…
Upper Volta	106	78	147	148	126	135	104	58	25	15	3	3	2[b]	2
Zaire	…	1	13	15	1	2	2	5	12	10	3	2	…	2
Zambia	…	3	7	2	106	24	8	…	…	…	…	…	…	…
Zimbabwe	5	5	…	…	…	…	…	…	…	…	…	…	…	…
Asia	687	859	749	1,126	1,473	1,687	494	459	560	441	743	596	673	653
Bangladesh	6	5	1	5	9	6	12	10	6	2	4	4	1[a]	12
Burma	…	…	2	2	…	…	4	26	20	…	4	…	…	4
China, People's Rep.	72	104	86	272	453	818	586	263	396	366	596	434	502	353
Fiji	3	…	…	…	…	…	…	…	…	…	…	…	…	…
Guam	…	…	…	…	…	…	…	…	…	…	…	…	…	…
Hong Kong	33	88	83	106	137	123	95	16	13	19	19	9	16	31
India	247	310	180	281	404	333	251	3	4	2	1	1	2[b]	4
Korea	37	82	110	163	159	125	176	3	2	4	4	2	9	27
Malaysia	12	17	19	26	43	35	49	7	7	5	34	97	40	40
Pakistan	90	41	35	48	84	29	50	10	…	5	27	…	19	45
Papua New Guinea	3	2	5	1	1	…	…	…	…	5	5	3	2	1
Philippines	86	86	100	91	37	34	79	16	16	…	5	3	2	…
Singapore	50	69	72	63	72	55	57	92	60	39	26	44	45	63
Sri Lanka	26	…	1	2	8	7	13	…	…	…	…	2	1[a]	…
Thailand	21	55	52	64	64	57	64	11	36	…	26	…	33	66
Europe	648	527	430	617	641	703	836	102	118	84	73	206	222	394
Cyprus	9	15	35	40	10	8	10	2	…	…	…	…	…	…
Greece	120	63	61	79	85	56	79	10	11	11	14	10	19	32
Hungary	114	160	138	215	222	121	104	…	…	…	…	…	…	…
Malta	9	6	11	5	8	9	8	…	…	…	…	…	…	…
Portugal	154	104	68	106	162	131	90	48	49	25	17	13	17	108
Romania	104	131	57	85	56	75	68	40	48	44	41	18	27	41
Turkey	24	…	23	46	57	90	138	1	6	2	1	…	…	…
Yugoslavia	115	48	38	40	41	53	90	2	2	1	8	3	2	1
Middle East	314	463	303	286	433	1,473	1,375	43	28	26	8	4,281	3,145	2,324
Bahrain	2	2	3	3	6	8	9	2	1	…	…	…	…	…
Egypt	159	258	154	157	258	241	203	1	27	26	8	21	29	38
Israel	13	24	28	35	67	36	34	40	…	…	…	3	10	11
Jordan	64	51	44	32	35	25	15	…	…	…	…	…	…	…
Lebanon	12	36	25	31	21	12	26	…	…	…	…	…	…	…
Syrian Arab Rep.	9	57	20	22	40	24	20	…	…	…	…	…	…	…
Yemen Arab Rep.	40	…	3	6	6	3	3	…	…	…	…	…	…	…
Middle East not specified	40	…	…	6	…	…	…	…	…	…	…	…	…	…

Table 2614 (Continued)

BRAZIL ABSOLUTE VALUE OF GOODS TRADED WITH SELECTED REGIONS AND COUNTRIES,[1] 1980–86

(M US)[2]

Category	Exports FOB							Imports CIF						
	1980	1981	1982	1983	1984	1985	1986	1980	1981	1982	1983	1984	1985	1986
IV. Latin America[3]	3,650	3,496	3,140	2,271	3,110	2,477	2,997	3,119	3,507	3,660	2,479	2,403	1,786	1,590
A. ARGENTINA	1,092	880	650	661	853	548	797	841	634	594	374	539	493	589
Bahamas	7	43	30	30	3	8	10	34	24	28	35	37	9	9
Barbados	7	7	5	6	5	5	6	~	2	3	1	8	2[b]	3
Bermuda	~	~	~	~	2	3	2	2	2	3	20	16	10[b]	11
B. BOLIVIA	180	255	80	108	141	171	242	47	27	30	20	16	10[b]	11
D. CHILE	451	641	289	208	281	239	258	462	326	330	177	240	228[b]	310
E. COLOMBIA	136	204	272	146	171	102	134	10	6	4	2	6	5[b]	4
F. COSTA RICA	20	13	10	13	19	18	28	2	~	~	~	~	~	~
H. DOMINICAN REP.	17	23	17	22	21	27	37	~	11	~	~	~	~	~
I. ECUADOR	50	69	65	69	141	119	147	36	26	254	72	2	6[b]	8
J. EL SALVADOR	3	2	2	4	4	5	6	7	~	~	~	~	~	~
Greenland														
Grenada	1	2	1	1	~	~	1	~	~	~	~	~	~	~
Guadeloupe	12	15	10	6	14	12	16	~	~	~	1	~	1[b]	1
K. GUATEMALA	1	1	1	1	1	1	16	~	~	~	~	2	1[b]	1
Guiana, French	1	1	5	2	6	7	3	3	4	5	1	~	~	~
Guyana	7	8	5	2	6	7	3	~	~	~	1	~	~	1
L. HAITI	7	4	4	4	6	7	5	1	1	~	~	~	~	~
M. HONDURAS	16	13	5	11	30	12	27	~	6	2	9	16	3	~
Jamaica	2	16	18	12	8	6	12	~	~	~	~	~	~	~
Martinique	1	1	~	~	~	1	1	~	~	~	~	~	~	~
N. MEXICO	470	643	324	168	285	220	197	468	835	845	761	681	414	191
Netherlands Antilles	8	21	14	13	40	4	11	91	51	77	56	23	10	10
O. NICARAGUA	18	20	5	11	14	7	10	~	~	~	~	~	~	~
P. PANAMA	26	40	36	40	44	60	54	48	29	36	23	19	32	35
Panama Canal Zone														
Q. PARAGUAY	409	450	324	234	333	299	277	99	213	170	33	41	76	123
R. PERU	130	285	222	75	124	92	133	130	63	75	60	51	59	23
Suriname	12	16	15	15	26	15	13	15	4	6	2	10	4	12
Trinidad and Tobago	24	39	30	31	29	32	30	22	10	6	2	10	6[a]	2
S. URUGUAY	311	373	138	104	136	140	217	203	185	156	134	125	142	206
British West Indies	1	1	94	~	~	5	~	~	~	~	~	~	3[b]	~
V. USSR, Eastern Europe, etc.	1,091	1,408	969	1,146	870	635	800	250	229	486	524	465	337	392
Albania	~	~	1	~	1	1	1	~	~	~	~	~	~	~
Bulgaria	15	7	21	56	179	48	37	6	~	10	4	3	3	3
Czechoslovakia	95	132	83	127	82	53	51	26	36	19	16	12	5[b]	7
Eastern Germany	85	140	187	164	206	83	133	97	82	116	98	121	102	103
North Korea	2	~	~	3	~	~	1	~	~	~	~	~	~	1
Poland	523	507	168	125	211	162	248	84	89	127	216	161	131[b]	207
USSR	370	621	509	671	402	450	330	37	22	213	190	168	75	72
USSR, etc., not specified														
Country or area not specified	1	~	~	~	~	293	468	~	~	~	~	~	~	~
Special categories	259	355	261	273	283	245	197	~	~	~	~	~	~	~
EEC	6,141	6,409	5,862	6,320	6,815	6,778	6,147	4,110	3,422	2,779	2,104	1,924	7,100	3,648
VI. Percent Distribution														
Industrial Countries	57.3	53.6	59.7	62.4	63.3	63.3	62.8	46.6	41.8	38.6	38.3	39.7	45.1	61.3
Oil Exporting Countries	7.3	10.1	8.9	8.7	8.6	9.8	7.9	36.4	41.4	41.9	41.0	39.4	33.2	20.0
Non-Oil Developing Countries	28.6	28.4	24.8	21.7	22.6	21.9	23.7	16.0	15.8	17.2	17.4	17.7	17.6	17.3
Africa	5.6	7.4	6.0	4.9	6.3	6.6	4.3	4.1	7.1	4.2	3.6	9.0	12.8	7.1
Asia	3.6	4.2	4.1	5.4	5.7	6.7	6.1	2.1	3.6	2.2	4.4	3.9	4.7	4.0
Europe	5.8	4.4	3.0	3.4	3.2	2.8	3.4	.7	.9	1.0	1.7	1.4	1.6	2.4
Middle East	5.3	5.3	5.8	6.9	5.4	5.8	5.6	3.2	31.5	35.0	35.3	28.1	31.9	14.2
Non-industrial Western Hemisphere[3]	18.1	19.3	15.6	10.4	11.5	9.8	12.2	12.5	14.6	17.4	14.8	15.8	12.5	9.7
USSR, Eastern Europe, etc.	2.8	3.9	4.0	4.7	3.2	2.5	2.2	.7	.6	1.7	1.8	2.0	1.3	1.1

Table 2614 (Continued)

BRAZIL ABSOLUTE VALUE OF GOODS TRADED WITH SELECTED REGIONS AND COUNTRIES,[1] 1980-86
(M US)[2]

Category	Exports FOB							Imports CIF						
	1980	1981	1982	1983	1984	1985	1986	1980	1981	1982	1983	1984	1985	1986
VII. Annual Percent Change														
World	32.0	15.9	-13.5	8.4	23.6	-6.5	-2.8	26.0	-3.5	-12.5	-20.2	-9.5	-5.8	-14.3
Industrial Countries	22.3	8.4	-3.7	13.2	25.4	-6.5	-3.6	20.0	-13.5	-19.2	-20.7	-6.2	7.2	55.2
Oil Exporting Countries	82.6	60.9	-23.6	5.6	23.1	5.7	-21.8	38.7	9.6	-11.4	-21.9	-13.0	-18.7	-34.5
Non-Oil Developing Countries	44.3	15.2	-24.5	-5.1	28.6	-12.0	5.1	19.2	-4.3	-5.1	-19.1	-7.7	-4.4	7.5
Africa	75.9	54.3	-29.4	-12.9	60.8	-2.6	-37.1	115.9	65.6	-48.5	-32.3	130.2	33.6	-36.6
Asia	22.9	34.7	-14.8	41.9	28.9	10.4	-11.4	21.9	60.7	-47.1	63.4	-19.7	12.9	-2.9
Europe	42.2	-11.7	-42.2	24.2	14.8	-17.5	18.9	-17.6	11.2	2.1	37.1	-29.0	8.2	77.1
Middle East	103.3	16.8	-5.8	28.7	-3.7	1.4	-6.6	32.2	-8.5	-2.8	-19.5	-27.8	-26.5	-26.1
Non-industrial Western Hemisphere[3]	38.2	23.2	-30.1	-27.7	37.0	-20.4	21.0	20.7	12.4	4.4	-32.3	-3.0	-25.7	-10.9
USSR, Eastern Europe, etc.	36.4	58.7	-11.1	27.5	-14.7	-27.1	-13.0	50.1	-15.3	156.0	-14.3	-1.2	-39.6	1.8

1. DOT data may differ between countries and from IFS data because of the time it takes for an export to become an import, etc.

2. Data may be calculated from partner's reported data or estimated on basis of less than 12 months.

3. No trade with Cuba; Venezuela is included in category III.

a. Nine months of reported data, 3 months derived from partner.

b. Nine months of reported data, 3 months extrapolated.

c. Nine months of reported data, 3 months derived or extrapolated.

SOURCE: Adapted from IMF-DOT-Y, 1982, 1986, and 1987.

Table 2614 (Continued)

BRAZIL ABSOLUTE VALUE OF GOODS TRADED WITH SELECTED REGIONS AND COUNTRIES,[1] 1980–86

(M US)[2]

PART II

(Brazil Indicators of Trade with the United States, 1964–84)

Year	% of Total Foreign Trade			AA-GR		Bilateral Trade Balance
	Exports	Imports		Exports	Imports	
		Total	Excluded Crude Oil			
1964	33.2	26.2	39.4	−10.7	−6.7	99.4
1965	32.6	17.7	34.3	9.7	−24.9	238.6
1966	33.4	30.0	44.5	11.8	85.7	58.5
1967	33.1	−30.9	38.4	−5.8	−2.4	37.2
1968	33.3	32.6	35.7	14.5	20.0	14.3
1969	26.4	26.5	33.2	−2.7	.1	−3.5
1970	24.7	30.1	35.3	10.9	34.3	−147.7
1971	26.2	32.9	31.9	12.4	15.9	−194.9
1972	23.3	30.4	42.0	22.5	26.9	−280.6
1973	18.1	29.3	32.6	20.5	50.1	−696.0
1974	21.9	38.7	30.5	54.8	69.3	−1,341.5
1975	15.4	35.2	32.5	−23.0	.2	−1,748.9
1976	18.2	28.0	31.8	37.8	−8.0	−996.3
1977	17.7	19.8	28.5	16.6	−15.4	−252.7
1978	22.7	22.8	30.0	33.5	20.3	−19.6
1979	19.3	21.3	27.4	2.5	12.1	−298.7
1980	17.4	20.4	30.2	19.3	26.6	−591.4
1981	17.7	15.0	30.5	17.1	−14.6	607.8
1982	20.0	14.2	28.9	−1.9	−18.3	1,173.0
1983	23.1	15.6	31.7	25.5	−15.8	2,654.3
1984 first quarter	30.4	14.3	29.5	64.1[a]	−18.0[a]	1,253.3

a. As compared to first quarter of 1983.

SOURCE: ECLA-EIC, 1985, p. 80.

Table 2615

CHILE ABSOLUTE VALUE OF GOODS TRADED WITH SELECTED REGIONS AND COUNTRIES,[1] 1980–86 (M US)[2]

Category	Exports FOB							Imports CIF						
	1980	1981	1982	1983	1984	1985	1986	1980	1981	1982	1983	1984	1985	1986
I. World	4,687.5	3,949.3	3,709.5	3,850.0	3,658.0	3,872.5	4,225.5	5,123.7	6,363.8	3,536.1	2,967.7	3,480.5	3,079.3	3,131.6
II. Industrial Countries	2,959.4	2,530.0	2,590.1	2,868.7	2,545.4	2,665.6	2,853.0	3,079.8	3,860.0	2,015.5	1,486.5	1,817.6	1,575.7	1,764.2
United States	588.9	591.9	800.7	1,083.3	951.2	877.3	915.2	1,464.3	1,631.9	916.1	703.5	747.8	654.6	641.5
Canada	78.8	140.7	33.6	60.4	31.1	75.9	58.4	76.6	94.3	55.5	60.9	66.5	59.2	54.3
Australia	~	~	~	~	~	.6[a]	~	~	~	~	~	~	2.0[b]	~
Japan	506.6	426.7	440.0	348.1	407.7	384.9	420.1	370.3	673.0	229.6	161.2	312.7	188.5	296.4
New Zealand	~	~	~	~	~	.3[a]	~	~	~	~	~	~	.4[b]	~
Belgium–Luxembourg	147.3	85.4	100.0	95.3	67.1	89.1	77.9	35.2	47.6	36.7	24.8	44.6	32.0	45.7
Denmark	3.1	.5	.5	.5	1.0	1.2	1.2	16.0	32.7	27.3	11.3	10.9	12.2	12.6
Finland	~	~	~	~	~	.1[a]	~	~	~	~	~	~	2.2[b]	~
France	215.2	191.5	151.7	176.7	163.4	142.4	153.1	195.6	219.4	124.6	82.9	97.6	78.6	94.1
Germany	612.9	453.5	426.3	484.8	365.5	370.6	441.2	308.7	354.5	214.3	185.2	215.7	209.0	250.1
Ireland	~	.7	2.5	.8	.4	.9	13.6	5.1	10.6	6.6	2.8	2.8	2.6	3.4
Italy	249.9	212.7	174.8	169.8	160.9	196.0	215.8	103.8	146.6	73.1	51.3	66.1	50.3	64.0
Netherlands	142.4	120.8	106.0	106.2	92.2	141.3	153.6	72.2	84.3	36.0	26.9	28.2	24.8	30.1
Norway	~	~	~	~	~	.2[a]	~	~	~	~	~	~	3.1[b]	~
Spain	92.4	83.4	85.5	72.2	75.8	73.5	122.2	143.6	213.2	149.8	64.3	81.1	105.5	82.2
Sweden	50.3	50.9	40.3	46.6	24.6	51.1	53.5	28.6	36.3	26.1	24.0	33.1	41.1	47.6
Switzerland	23.5	5.8	41.4	14.7	8.4	5.2	7.4	118.1	144.6	43.7	26.9	30.9	33.0	53.7
United Kingdom	248.1	165.5	186.8	209.3	196.1	256.2	219.8	141.7	171.0	76.1	60.7	79.6	84.3	88.5
III. Developing Countries														
Oil Exporting Countries														
Iran, I.R. of	186.1	182.9	97.3	107.4	108.8	101.2	108.4	268.2	484.1	272.0	310.7	277.9	256.0	197.7
Iraq	10.3	31.7	12.5	12.5	~	~	~	11.1	~	5.5	~	~	~	~
Kuwait	7.9	5.1	6.6	7.7	15.1	14.7	9.2	~	~	~	~	~	~	~
Libya	~	~	~	~	~	~	~	~	~	~	~	~	~	~
Qatar	~	~	~	~	~	~	~	~	~	~	~	~	~	~
Saudi Arabia	30.2	23.5	28.4	30.5	30.5	39.9	44.6	~	124.6	6.1	30.7	26.1	.1	~
United Arab Emirates	59.3	50.6	18.9	27.0	23.0	16.6	14.0	~	~	~	40.1	~	~	~
T. VENEZUELA	78.4	72.0	43.4	29.7	40.2	33.7	40.6	257.1	359.5	260.4	224.8	251.8	267.1	148.2
Non-Oil Developing Countries	1,402.8	1,080.8	926.7	730.8	876.4	940.9	1,133.0	1,584.8	1,653.7	772.3	876.5	1,045.4	917.9	898.4
Africa	21.5	55.4	20.7	31.3	40.4	39.3	32.5	305.6	176.7	20.4	102.1	164.7	126.6	86.8
Gabon	6.6	6.8	~	~	~	26.1[c]	29.3	276.6	105.1	~	~	113.3	27.1	~
South Africa	~	~	~	~	~	.1[a]	~	290.0	14.6	~	~	~	20.5[e]	34.6
Tunisia	~	~	~	~	~	13.1[c]	3.2	~	~	~	~	~	~	~
Africa not specified	14.9	48.6	20.7	31.3	40.4	~	~	9.2	57.0	20.4	102.1	164.7	106.1[d]	2.7
Asia	208.5	143.5	159.0	177.0	225.8	264.3	262.9	120.5	158.4	144.1	78.5	113.4	98.6	130.0
China, People's Rep.	105.3	60.7	61.9	93.7	125.3	124.9	100.2	21.2	35.0	21.7	9.9	12.4	24.0	21.0
Hong Kong	15.4	2.1	7.5	3.4	8.5	9.6	13.3	29.8	4.7	27.3	13.7	19.8	11.3	15.7
Korea	69.5	60.5	52.1	56.6	64.9	88.4	91.8	30.0	40.5	51.2	23.3	40.7	24.2	48.0
Malaysia	4.4	~	~	~	~	.1[a]	~	~	~	~	~	~	.7[b]	~
Philippines	~	~	~	~	~	~	~	~	~	~	~	~	.1[b]	~
Singapore	~	~	~	~	~	~	~	~	~	~	~	~	1.5[b]	~
Sri Lanka	~	~	~	~	~	1.9[a]	~	~	~	~	~	~	.7[b]	~
Thailand	~	~	~	~	~	.2[a]	~	~	~	~	~	~	1.0[b]	~
Asia not specified	13.9	20.2	37.5	23.1	27.1	85.2	57.6	30.4	78.2	43.9	31.6	40.5	29.5	45.3
Oceania not specified	.9	2.7	7.7	1.8	2.9	5.2[c]	~	14.4	14.5	7.2	14.1	21.6	15.4[d]	~
Europe	112.5	80.2	52.3	74.4	70.5	87.7	136.2	28.9	48.0	38.8	30.1	37.9	43.9	61.7
Cyprus	~	~	~	~	~	~	~	~	~	~	~	~	~	~
Greece	20.2	20.8	15.1	12.9	14.8	22.0	29.0	~	~	~	~	.1	.1	.2
Portugal	5.8	~	~	~	12.9	11.9	13.9	~	~	~	~	2.5	2.8	3.2
Romania	31.2	17.4	6.3	8.6	7.5	6.8	10.9	~	~	~	~	~	~	~
Yugoslavia	39.4	27.6	15.1	19.3	15.3	12.9	33.2	28.9	48.0	38.8	30.1	35.3	42.3	58.3
Europe not specified	15.9	14.4	15.8	33.6	20.6	26.6	49.2	~	~	~	~	~	~	~

Table 2615 (Continued)

CHILE ABSOLUTE VALUE OF GOODS TRADED WITH SELECTED REGIONS AND COUNTRIES,[1] 1980–86 (M US)[2]

Category	Exports FOB							Imports CIF						
	1980	1981	1982	1983	1984	1985	1986	1980	1981	1982	1983	1984	1985	1986
Non-Oil Developing Countries (Continued)														
Middle East														
Egypt	~	8.9	18.2	12.8	29.9	22.7	89.4	~	~	~	2.0	3.2	56.6	38.1
Israel	~	8.9	7.8	2.9	13.3	9.1c	.2c	~	~	~	~	.7b	76.8	34.1
Middle East not specified	~	~	10.4	9.9	16.6	13.8	10.8	~	~	~	2.0	3.2	3.1	4.0
IV. Latin America[3]	1,138.7	864.8	719.9	465.0	550.0	565.9	720.4	1,386.9	1,630.1	829.4	888.6	978.0	817.2	779.5
A. ARGENTINA	280.6	191.3	151.3	119.4	116.7	84.5	160.6	157.4	141.7	151.9	200.6	160.9	105.9	122.5
Barbados	~	~	~	~	~	~	~	~	~	~	~	~	~	~
B. BOLIVIA	26.4	23.8	11.2	11.0	14.7	14.3	30.5	26.3	9.0	9.0	8.7	6.6	4.5	5.0
C. BRAZIL	448.6	288.2	308.2	164.3	227.5	211.3	292.9	394.8	570.5	258.4	190.2	296.4	248.9	247.6
E. COLOMBIA	76.8	70.9	46.3	42.3	43.0	54.8	40.5	17.8	25.6	11.2	12.8	21.5	21.9	38.3
F. COSTA RICA	~	~	~	~	~	~	~	~	~	~	~	~	~	~
H. DOMINICAN REP.	12.8	3.1	4.7	5.1	4.8	5.7	7.3	~	~	~	~	~	~	~
I. ECUADOR	21.6	14.2	51.3	33.8	27.8	33.6	28.1	210.2	99.5	32.8	40.4	46.0	48.1	58.8
J. EL SALVADOR	~	~	~	~	~	~	~	~	~	~	~	~	~	~
N. MEXICO	67.9	86.8	22.3	1.0	8.9	51.0	9.7	28.2	42.6	11.0	16.9	21.8	14.7	20.1
Netherlands Antilles	~	~	~	~	~	~	~	81.0	152.0	~	120.2	74.8	29.1	41.9
P. PANAMA	10.8	11.1	6.8	3.8	5.3	5.5	6.5	91.7	108.8	21.1	3.2	1.0	2.4	4.3
Q. PARAGUAY	7.7	7.2	7.5	2.4	4.5	5.8	5.4	7.3	11.9	14.0	22.4	36.5	27.0	29.4
R. PERU	70.7	70.3	49.0	39.4	44.9	45.6c	65.9	40.6	66.9	33.4	37.2	49.2	41.1	56.3
S. URUGUAY	29.6	16.1	13.1	6.2	8.7	12.3	11.0	21.6	33.0	21.2	8.0	9.3	4.1	6.2
America not specified	6.8	9.8	4.8	5.3	3.0	6.0c	21.4	52.9	9.1	5.0	3.2	2.2	1.6d	.9
Other Latin America not specified	~	~	~	1.3	~	~	~	~	~	~	~	~	~	~
V. USSR, Eastern Europe, etc.	20.8	23.3	20.1	53.9	32.6	43.6	30.8	2.3	7.5	7.2	4.2	6.6	5.6	8.3
Bulgaria	4.1	4.7	~	~	~	~	~	~	~	~	~	~	~	~
Eastern Germany	14.7	18.6	19.5	48.7	32.5	39.9	24.4	~	~	~	~	~	~	~
North Korea	~	~	~	~	~	~	~	~	~	~	~	~	~	~
USSR, etc., not specified	2.0	~	.6	5.2	.1	3.7	6.4	2.3	7.5	7.2	4.2	6.6	5.6	8.3
Country or area not specified	90.1	72.8	56.3	58.3	50.1	38.3c	38.9	144.3	273.7	421.7	263.1	295.7	276.2d	225.1
EEC	1,737.3	1,334.8	1,249.2	1,328.5	1,137.2	1,285.3	1,441.3	1,737.3	1,334.8	1,249.2	1,328.5	1,137.2	1,285.3	674.1
VI. Percent Distribution														
Industrial Countries	63.1	64.1	69.8	74.5	69.6	68.8	67.5	60.1	60.7	57.0	50.1	52.2	51.2	56.3
Oil Exporting Countries	4.0	4.6	2.5	2.9	2.9	2.7	2.6	5.2	7.6	7.7	10.5	7.9	8.3	6.3
Non-Oil Developing Countries	29.9	27.4	24.7	18.9	23.9	24.8	26.8	30.9	26.0	21.8	29.5	30.0	29.7	28.7
Africa	.5	1.4	.7	.8	1.1	.9	.8	5.0	2.8	.8	3.4	4.7	3.3	2.8
Asia	4.4	3.6	4.4	4.6	6.2	8.0	6.2	2.4	2.5	4.1	2.6	3.3	2.9	4.2
Europe	2.4	2.0	1.4	1.9	1.9	2.1	3.2	.6	.8	1.1	1.0	1.1	1.5	2.0
Middle East	2.3	3.0	1.9	2.4	2.7	2.4	2.1	.2	2.0	.3	3.0	.8	2.6	1.2
Non-Industrial Western Hemisphere[3]	24.3	21.9	19.4	12.1	15.0	14.6	17.0	27.1	25.6	23.5	29.9	28.1	26.5	24.9
USSR, Eastern Europe, etc.	.4	.6	.5	1.4	.9	1.1	.7	~	.1	.2	.1	.2	.2	.3

Table 2615 (Continued)

CHILE ABSOLUTE VALUE OF GOODS TRADED WITH SELECTED REGIONS AND COUNTRIES,[1] 1980-86 (M US)[2]

Category	Exports FOB							Imports CIF						
	1980	1981	1982	1983	1984	1985	1986	1980	1981	1982	1983	1984	1985	1986
VII. Annual Percentage Change														
World	20.6	-15.7	-6.1	3.8	-5.0	5.9	9.1	21.5	24.2	-44.4	-16.1	17.3	-11.5	1.7
Industrial Countries	23.7	-14.5	2.4	10.8	-11.3	4.7	7.0	34.7	25.3	-47.8	-26.2	22.3	-13.3	12.0
Oil Exporting Countries	49.2	-1.7	-46.8	10.3	1.3	-6.9	3.3	-49.9	80.5	-43.8	14.2	-10.6	-7.9	-37.9
Non-Oil Developing Countries	25.2	-23.0	-14.3	-21.1	19.9	7.4	15.8	30.1	4.3	-53.3	13.5	19.3	-12.2	10.3
Africa	147.1	157.7	-62.6	51.2	29.1	-13.9	-6.6	64.4	-42.2	-88.5	400.5	61.3	-38.6	-14.1
Asia	14.7	-31.2	10.8	11.3	27.6	36.4	-14.7	23.1	31.5	-9.0	-45.5	44.5	-21.5	46.1
Europe	129.1	-28.7	-34.8	42.3	-5.2	13.8	69.8	~	66.1	-19.2	-22.4	25.9	19.3	36.5
Middle East	101.3	11.2	-39.8	25.5	8.8	-4.5	-5.0	-97.1	~	-90.7	651.8	-66.7	173.0	-52.4
Non-Industrial Western Hemisphere[3]	19.6	-24.1	-16.8	-35.4	18.3	2.9	27.3	27.5	17.5	-49.1	7.1	10.1	-26.6	-4.6
USSR, Eastern Europe, etc.	18.9	12.0	-13.7	168.2	-39.5	33.7	-29.4	~	226.1	-4.0	-41.7	57.1	-15.2	48.2

1. DOT data may differ between countries and from IFS data because of the time it takes for an export to become an import. etc.

2. Data may be calculated from partner's reported data or estimated on basis of less than 12 months.

3. No trade with Cuba; Venezuela is included in category III.

a. Eleven months of reported data, 1 month derived from partner.

b. Ten months of reported data, 2 months derived from partner.

c. Eleven months of reported data, 2 months derived from partner.

d. Ten months of reported data, 2 months extrapolated.

e. Ten months of reported data, 1 month derived and 1 month extrapolated.

SOURCE: Adapted from IMF-DOT-Y, 1982, 1986, and 1987.

Table 2616

ASSOLUTE VALUE OF GOODS TRADED WITH SELECTED REGIONS AND COUNTRIES,[1] 1980–86

(M US)[2]

Category	Exports FOB							Imports CIF						
	1980	1981	1982	1983	1984	1985	1986	1980	1981	1982	1983	1984	1985	1986
I. World	3,945.0	2,956.4	3,095.0	3,080.8	3,482.8	3,551.8	5,174.3	4,662.6	5,199.1	5,477.7	4,968.1	4,492.4	4,130.7	4,076.7
II. Industrial Countries	2,978.0	2,073.8	2,244.7	2,411.4	2,821.5	2,801.9	4,449.1	3,511.5	3,676.4	3,855.7	3,514.5	3,217.2	3,007.6	3,159.2
United States	1,069.3	692.8	722.7	872.1	1,097.5	1,165.9	1,853.7	1,839.8	1,787.4	1,895.6	1,768.6	1,535.5	1,456.6	1,450.5
Canada	58.3	30.7	34.0	26.8	56.9	40.0	89.3	109.5	179.8	190.2	176.2	232.3	159.0	147.8
Australia	1.1	1.1	1.2	3.9	1.6	1.9	3.4	1.6	1.7	1.2	.7	.9	.3	17.2
Japan	147.6	126.5	127.6	136.8	153.5	149.9	246.3	434.1	497.7	608.0	551.6	431.2	428.6	428.3
New Zealand	.1	.1	.1	.2	.2	.1	.2	.1	.2	.2	.5	.4	1.5	1.4
Austria	3.2	2.3	3.8	6.3	5.0	9.8	60.0	10.9	15.5	12.0	16.1	11.9	10.9	16.0
Belgium-Luxembourg	39.3	26.4	42.4	67.1	103.8	63.4	62.4	26.2	40.3	43.0	29.8	34.6	29.0	27.8
Denmark	35.4	26.6	27.7	19.3	20.1	33.9	97.8	51.5	20.5	28.2	16.4	26.6	15.1	8.7
Finland	79.9	57.8	59.6	49.1	62.9	67.8	113.3	18.4	18.8	27.1	24.0	21.5	24.0	19.5
France	91.5	54.9	56.0	71.4	73.2	75.1	149.5	131.3	162.9	145.7	161.1	188.3	136.3	170.4
Germany	741.0	582.5	560.8	566.6	577.7	574.4	905.1	131.3	334.0	317.6	241.0	245.3	265.9	307.1
Iceland	1.6	.7	.2	.3	.4	.5	1.3	.5	.2	.2	.3	.3	.4	.6
Ireland	.6	4.4	3.8	6.9	19.2	9.0	5.2	1.5	2.4	2.4	4.6	5.3	6.9	4.1
Italy	63.6	64.0	181.8	169.2	135.9	98.2	93.0	120.9	129.5	129.4	98.7	91.3	68.6	110.2
Netherlands	271.9	146.5	174.4	168.2	204.8	190.1	213.7	29.4	29.2	39.7	32.8	40.9	62.3	45.1
Norway	40.4	27.5	24.9	25.1	37.6	33.7	60.9	13.1	24.9	3.0	3.1	2.2	2.2	4.2
Spain	150.6	84.4	76.3	82.1	82.5	78.4	137.5	143.9	136.4	141.4	129.1	90.6	127.6	165.8
Sweden	118.2	85.7	88.1	75.2	90.9	85.5	156.8	54.2	61.9	75.9	72.3	83.7	41.1	63.5
Switzerland	23.1	9.8	13.3	11.2	12.2	18.3	73.8	78.8	93.2	83.5	80.6	81.9	72.3	77.7
United Kingdom	42.1	49.3	46.2	53.7	85.7	106.2	126.0	111.9	145.8	116.2	107.3	92.5	98.9	93.5
III. Developing Countries														
Oil Exporting Countries														
Algeria	332.1	370.8	388.1	141.5	146.4	117.1	126.5	1,972.2	409.7	355.0	393.6	387.4	348.7	115.5
Indonesia	52.1	27.6	19.3	20.4	49.3	60.5	45.4	~	~	~	~	~	~	~
Iran, I.R. of	.5	~	~	~	~	.3	~	~	~	~	~	~	~	~
Iraq	~	~	~	~	~	~	~	~	~	~	~	~	~	~
Kuwait	~	.1	.1	.5	.2	.4	.3	~	~	~	~	~	~	~
Libya	~	1.5	.3	~	~	.5	.3	~	~	~	~	~	~	~
Nigeria	.1	.3	1.9	~	~	~	~	~	.1	.3	~	~	~	~
Qatar	~	~	~	~	~	~	~	~	~	~	~	~	~	~
Saudi Arabia	.1	~	.4	2.6	.1	.1	.3	.1	~	~	~	.1	~	~
United Arab Emirates	~	~	~	.1	.2	.1c	.1	~	~	~	~	~	~	~
T. VENEZUELA	279.2	341.2	366.1	117.9	96.6	129.0	80.0	197.0	409.6	354.6	393.6	387.4	238.5	115.5
Non-Oil Developing Countries	509.1	433.4	362.4	388.9	443.6	223.0	495.6	858.4	1,022.1	1,188.3	932.2	813.9	454.3	745.5
Africa	58.2	30.4	25.2	28.6	53.4	65.5	50.6	15.6	9.9	10.5	9.1	5.0	.1a	2.7
Burundi	~	~	~	~	~	~	~	.1	~	~	~	~	~	~
Cameroon	.1	~	~	~	~	~	~	~	~	.1	.1	.1	.1	.1
Ethiopia	.1	~	~	~	~	~	~	~	~	~	~	~	~	~
Gambia, The	.1	~	~	~	.2	.2c	~	~	~	~	~	~	~	~
Ghana	~	~	~	~	~	~	~	~	~	~	~	~	~	~
Guinea	~	~	~	.1	~	~	~	~	~	~	~	~	~	~
Kenya	.1	~	~	.1	.1	.1c	~	~	.1	~	~	~	~	~
Ivory Coast	~	.5	.5	.5	~	~	.1	~	~	~	~	~	~	~
Liberia	~	~	~	~	.1	.1c	~	~	~	~	~	~	.1c	~
Madagascar	~	~	~	~	~	.1c	.1	~	~	~	~	.1	~	~
Mauritius	3.8	1.8	2.4	4.9	2.8	4.5	4.7	.1	.5	~	~	~	~	~
Morocco	.7	~	~	.3	~	~	~	~	~	~	.1	~	~	~
Mozambique	.1	~	~	~	~	~	~	~	~	~	~	~	~	~
Senegal	.5	.5	.5	.4	.5	.2	.2	15.4	9.3	10.2	9.0	4.9	2.3	2.4
Seychelles	.1	.1	.1	.1	.1	.1	.1	~	~	~	~	~	~	~
South Africa	.3	.1	.9	1.7	.3	.5a	~	~	~	~	~	~	~	~
Sudan														
Tunisia														

Table 2616 (Continued)

COLOMBIA ABSOLUTE VALUE OF GOODS TRADED WITH SELECTED REGIONS AND COUNTRIES,[1] 1980–86
(M US)[2]

Category	Exports FOB 1980	1981	1982	1983	1984	1985	1986	Imports CIF 1980	1981	1982	1983	1984	1985	1986
Non-Oil Developing Countries (Continued)														
Africa (Continued)														
Uganda	?	?	?	?	?	?	?	?	?	?	?	?	?	?
Zaire	?	.1	.2	?	?	?	?	?	?	?	?	?	?	?
Zambia	?	?	?	?	?	?	?	?	?	.3[b]	?	?	?	?
Zimbabwe	?	?	?	?	?	?	?	?	?	?	?	?	?	?
Spanish Africa	?	?	?	?	?	?	?	.1	?	?	?	?	?	?
III. Developing Countries														
Non-Oil Developing Countries														
Asia														
Bangladesh	12.6	7.4	14.2	20.2	19.8	31.6	41.0	27.9	33.1	32.2	23.1	27.8	23.1	29.1
China, People's Rep.	.9	.1	6.7	?	1.1	?	1.9	.3	.6	.9	1.7	2.1	.9	2.9
French Polynesia	?	?	?	?	?	?	?	?	?	?	.1	?	?	?
Hong Kong	5.2	1.9	1.1	.2	.4	2.2	4.9	3.7	4.9	4.8	2.8	2.1	1.2	2.0
India	.7	?	?	2.2	?	15.1	15.9	.4	.1	.4	.5	.9	1.2	1.3
Korea	3.6	1.6	4.8	14.8	14.3	13.6	14.2	7.1	9.6	10.6	5.0	6.8	2.8	2.9
Malaysia	?	?	.3	?	?	.1	.1	2.6	1.5	1.6	.8	.6	.4	4.0
Pakistan	?	?	?	?	?	?	.2	.2	.1	.2	.2	.2	.2	.1
Papua New Guinea	?	.7	.3	2.7	?	?	?	.2	.3	.1	.1	.4	.2	.2
Philippines	.6	.2	.1	.1	.1	.1	?	.3	1.0	.9	?	?	.1	.1
Singapore	1.1	?	?	?	?	?	3.6	13.2	14.7	12.2	11.9	14.3	16.0	14.3
Sri Lanka	.1	.2	1.1	.1	.2	.2	.2	?	.2	.4	.1	.3	?	1.0
Thailand	?	2.8	?	.1	.2	?	.2	.1	?	?	?	?	?	.2
Viet Nam	?	?	?	?	3.7	?	?	?	.1	?	?	?	?	?
Oceania not specified	.3	.1	?	?	?	?	?	.3	?	?	?	?	?	?
Europe	66.9	56.9	37.6	44.0	43.9	?	38.8	53.4	21.4	24.0	27.1	22.3	25.8	28.7
Gibraltar	9.1	?	?	?	?	?	?	.1	.1	.1	.1	?	?	?
Greece	.5	1.9	.9	1.9	.3	?	11.2	1.0	.1	.1	.1	?	?	?
Hungary	9.6	26.3	7.5	17.7	37.8	?	?	.7	.8	1.2	1.1	3.2	?	.1
Malta	.2	?	?	?	?	6.4[a]	2.7	?	?	?	?	?	.1[a]	.3
Portugal	13.9	9.2	1.3	3.2	2.1	2.8[c]	6.2	1.2	.9	.9	.4	.6	.5[a]	.3
Romania	13.5	8.0	27.5	20.9	3.0	.6[c]	.3	39.9	9.9	13.6	14.8	11.8	11.2[c]	9.1
Turkey	?	1.2	.4	.3	.6	?	?	?	1.4	1.6	1.6	1.1	1.0[c]	.2
Yugoslavia	19.8	10.3	?	?	?	2.8[a]	16.6	10.5	8.2	8.2	9.1	5.6	12.8[a]	12.5
Europe not specified	?	?	?	.1	?	.1[c]	?	?	?	.1	.1	.1	.1[c]	.1
Middle East	10.8	7.4	2.4	4.8	3.1	11.9	2.6	5.1	8.0	6.5	5.4	10.5	12.6	18.5
Bahrain	?	?	?	?	.1	.2	.2	?	?	?	?	?	?	?
Egypt	?	.7	.2	?	?	?	?	.1	?	?	?	?	?	?
Israel	6.8	3.4	1.2	.8	2.6	10.0	1.0	4.9	8.0	6.5	5.3	10.4	12.5	18.5
Jordan	?	.1	.2	?	?	.3	?	?	?	?	?	?	?	?
Lebanon	.7	.2	.2	.8	?	?	.3	?	?	?	?	?	?	?
Syrian Arab Rep.	2.5	1.3	?	?	?	?	?	?	?	?	?	?	?	?
IV. Latin America[3]	692.7	702.1	671.2	432.8	469.8	498.8	489.1	953.6	1,359.3	1,470.1	1,261.1	1,135.8	1,002.7	782.1
A. ARGENTINA	68.7	51.4	36.4	43.0	58.7	36.7	38.5	42.8	47.8	73.3	49.9	45.6	106.2	111.5
Antigua and Barbuda	.4	.5	?	.4	?	?	?	3.2	8.9	1.0	9.9	1.2	.1	.1
Bahamas	.6	.4	7.6	.8	9.2	36.0	37.8	?	?	?	?	?	?	?
Barbados	.3	.5	1.2	.8	.4	.6	.7	.2	?	?	.2	?	?	?
Belize	?	?	.4	?	?	.7	.8	?	?	?	?	?	?	?
Bermuda	?	?	?	?	1.3	?	?	48.8	29.1	10.1	3.4	7.5	1.7	1.7
B. BOLIVIA	2.2	3.8	.9	1.6	14.3	6.0	6.3	7.4	12.0	6.8	4.1	5.5	5.1	5.3
C. BRAZIL	9.0	4.5	3.7	5.4	16.0	20.9	34.8	127.1	176.1	286.3	166.7	178.8	129.2	135.7
D. CHILE	64.3	28.3	11.7	11.1	7.3	8.2	8.6	82.5	84.9	68.0	56.7	48.8	52.7	44.6
F. COSTA RICA	5.5	4.6	3.9	5.0	?	?	?	1.0	2.2	2.8	1.6	1.3	.9	.9
Dominica	.1	.1	?	?	?	?	?	.1	?	.5	?	?	?	?

Table 2616 (Continued)

COLOMBIA ABSOLUTE VALUE OF GOODS TRADED WITH SELECTED REGIONS AND COUNTRIES,[1] 1980-86
(M US)[2]

Category	Exports FOB 1980	1981	1982	1983	1984	1985	1986	Imports CIF 1980	1981	1982	1983	1984	1985	1986
IV. Latin America[3] (Continued)														
H. DOMINICAN REP.	6.0	5.8	4.5	5.1	5.6	19.8	20.8	1.2	2.1	3.9	1.3	.4	.9	1.0
I. ECUADOR	77.3	66.3	51.9	42.7	47.3	56.3	42.3	77.5	83.4	90.2	160.1	68.9	81.4	57.0
J. EL SALVADOR	1.2	1.7	1.1	7.6	5.8	10.4	10.9	.2	.4	.5	.1	.3	1.9	2.0
Grenada	1.7	.7	~	~	.2	.4	.4	~	~	~	~	~	~	~
K. GUATEMALA	5.9	4.5	3.3	3.7	4.7	5.2	5.4	.9	.7	.3	.1	.5	1.3	1.4
Guiana, French	.2	.1	.1	.1	~	~	~	~	~	~	~	~	~	~
Guyana	~	~	.6	.4	.2	~	~	~	~	.1	~	~	~	~
L. HAITI	1.4	1.1	.5	.8	.8	1.9	1.9	~	~	~	~	~	~	~
M. HONDURAS	5.8	5.2	3.2	4.5	4.8	5.3	5.6	1.4	1.2	1.1	1.4	.7	1.2	1.3
Jamaica	1.3	.4	.6	1.3	.4	.5	4.4	.1	1.0	1.3	.1	.3	1.2	.1
Leeward Islands	.3	.1	.1	.1	.1	.1	.1	~	~	~	~	~	.1	.1
Martinique	.6	.3	.1	~	~	~	~	~	~	~	~	~	~	~
N. MEXICO	19.9	21.0	17.2	20.8	9.7	6.4	4.8	61.7	67.9	80.9	99.2	111.8	149.3	104.5
Montserrat	~	~	~	~	~	.1	~	~	~	~	~	~	~	~
Netherlands Antilles	33.5	28.0	24.8	65.4	107.1	73.2	76.9	132.1	143.3	146.8	161.2	89.1	34.1	35.8
O. NICARAGUA	3.8	2.3	2.7	4.9	13.7	3.6	3.8	.2	.1	.3	.1	~	~	~
P. PANAMA	59.2	61.3	67.9	52.1	31.7	36.8	38.7	65.4	169.5	175.1	80.3	84.0	71.8	75.4
Panama Canal Zone	~	~	~	.2	~	~	~	~	~	~	~	~	~	~
Q. PARAGUAY	.6	.7	.4	~	.1	.1	~	.4	10.6	1.8	1.1	1.5	1.7	~
R. PERU	13.7	29.2	34.0	19.6	23.3	31.9	51.9	97.0	102.6	151.5	62.6	92.9	108.4	72.6
St. Lucia	.8	.9	.9	.4	.7	.5	.6	~	~	~	~	~	~	~
St. Pierre-Miquelon	~	~	~	~	~	~	~	~	~	~	~	~	~	~
St. Vincent	.4	.2	.8	.4	.4	.4	.5	~	~	~	~	~	~	~
Suriname	1.6	1.5	2.1	2.9	2.8	3.1	3.2	.4	.1	.1	2.5	~	~	.5
Trinidad and Tobago	10.1	16.7	20.4	13.1	5.4	3.1	1.9	~	.5	~	.5	.6	.2	~
S. URUGUAY	.9	2.1	.8	.4	.1	.3	.4	4.0	4.0	10.3	4.4	8.7	9.7	10.2
Windward Islands	~	.2	.5	.3	~	~	~	~	~	2.6	~	~	~	~
British West Indies	.5	~	~	~	.2	~	~	~	.2	.1	~	.4	~	~
V. USSR, Eastern Europe, etc.	74.2	34.8	62.4	71.4	33.7	53.7	56.3	60.1	54.3	45.0	39.5	28.4	26.3	27.6
Bulgaria	4.6	.7	~	4.5	.1	2.5	2.6	2.0	2.9	.2	.6	.3	.1	.1
G. CUBA	5.6	3.5	4.5	1.6	1.9	4.6	4.9	.8	.7	.6	5.8	.2	3.8	4.0
Czechoslovakia	3.3	9.2	6.9	12.8	10.5	13.3	14.0	7.9	8.3	9.3	7.2	6.2	4.7	5.0
Eastern Germany	40.6	26.1	33.9	31.0	1.2	12.0	12.6	33.7	32.7	27.2	18.2	16.2	13.4	14.1
North Korea	~	~	~	~	~	~	~	.7	.3	.5	1.5	.4	.4	.1
Poland	51.3	22.0	35.7	1.7	1.5	1.4[c]	1.7	17.9	18.1	14.0	74.8	29.8	28.3[c]	6.4
USSR	20.2	15.2	17.1	21.6	20.0	21.2	22.3	15.0	9.4	7.4	6.2	5.1	4.1	4.3
Country or area not specified	~	.8	.7	66.0	36.1	44.6	46.8	1.0	.7	.7	.6	2.3	6.0	6.3
Special categories	~	.7	~	~	~	~	~	.4	.5	5.2	4.3	9.1	19.1	20.1
EEC	1,951.3	1,050.3	1,171.6	1,209.7	1,305.2	1,235.8	1,803.9	952.8	996.1	959.6	821.0	816.0	810.9	932.9
VI. Percent Distribution														
Industrial Countries	75.5	70.1	72.5	78.3	81.0	78.9	86.0	75.3	70.7	70.9	70.7	71.6	72.8	77.5
Oil Exporting Countries	8.4	12.5	12.5	4.6	4.2	3.5	2.4	4.2	7.9	6.5	7.9	8.6	8.5	2.8
Non-Oil Developing Countries	12.9	14.7	11.7	12.6	12.7	6.7	9.6	18.4	19.7	21.7	18.8	18.1	11.0	18.3
Africa	1.5	1.0	.8	.9	1.5	1.8	1.6	.3	.2	.2	.2	.1	.1	.1
Asia	.2	.2	.5	.7	.6	.9	.8	.6	.6	.6	.5	.6	.6	.7
Europe	1.7	1.9	1.2	1.4	1.3	.5	1.2	1.5	.8	.7	2.1	1.2	.7	.7
Middle East	.3	.2	.1	.1	.1	#	.3	.1	.2	.7	.1	.2	.3	.5
Latin America[3]	17.6	23.7	21.7	14.0	13.5	14.0	9.5	20.5	26.1	26.8	25.4	25.3	24.3	19.2
USSR, Eastern Europe, etc	3.2	2.6	3.2	2.4	1.0	1.5	1.1	1.3	1.0	.8	.8	.6	.6	.7

Table 2616 (Continued)

COLOMBIA ABSOLUTE VALUE OF GOODS TRADED WITH SELECTED REGIONS AND COUNTRIES,[1] 1980-86
(M US)[2]

Category	Exports FOB							Imports CIF						
	1980	1981	1982	1983	1984	1985	1986	1980	1981	1982	1983	1984	1985	1986
VII. Annual Percent Change														
World	18.6	-25.1	4.7	-.5	13.0	2.0	45.7	44.2	11.5	5.4	-9.3	-9.6	-8.1	-1.3
Industrial Countries	18.1	-30.4	8.2	7.4	17.0	-.7	58.8	44.0	4.7	4.9	-8.8	-8.5	-6.5	5.0
Oil Exporting Countries	-13.5	11.7	4.7	-63.5	3.5	-20.0	-33.8	83.5	107.7	-13.4	10.9	-1.6	-9.9	51.6
Non-Oil Developing Countries	49.0	-14.9	-16.4	7.3	14.1	-49.7	7.6	35.8	19.1	16.3	-21.6	-12.7	-44.2	-10.3
Africa	30.6	-47.7	-17.2	13.5	86.6	22.8	-22.7	42.9	-36.4	5.3	-11.8	-45.8	-49.4	5.1
Asia	34.1	-41.7	93.2	42.3	-2.1	59.8	29.6	4.0	18.5	-2.8	-28.2	20.2	-16.9	26.3
Europe	37.4	-33.2	-7.1	-37.6	-.7	-3.3	-11.5	142.6	-44.7	-3.8	168.5	-48.9	-45.4	.8
Middle East	37.3	-31.1	-68.2	102.1	-34.2	279.3	-78.5	361.8	57.7	-18.7	-17.8	95.3	20.1	47.4
Latin America[3]	12.0	1.4	-4.4	-35.5	8.6	6.2	-1.9	39.7	62.5	8.1	-14.2	-9.9	-11.7	-22.0
USSR, Eastern Europe, etc.	101.7	-26.1	13.8	14.5	-52.9	59.4	5.0	98.1	-9.6	-17.0	-12.4	-28.1	-7.5	5.0

1. DOT data may differ between countries and from IFS data because of the time it takes for an export to become an import, etc.
2. Data may be calculated from partner's reported data or estimated on basis of less than 12 months.
3. Cuba is included in category V; Venezuela is included in category III.
a. Data acquired from partner country for the entire year.
b. Five or fewer months of reported data; seven or more months derived or extrapolated.
c. Data extrapolated for the entire year.

SOURCE: Adapted from IMF-DOT-Y, 1982, 1986, and 1987.

Table 2617

COSTA RICA ABSOLUTE VALUE OF GOODS TRADED WITH SELECTED REGIONS AND COUNTRIES,[1] 1980–86 (M US)[2]

Category	Exports FOB							Imports CIF						
	1980	1981	1982	1983	1984	1985	1986	1980	1981	1982	1983	1984	1985	1986
I. World	980.9	1,008.2	871.4	860.9	985.6	923.7	1,212.9	1,470.8	1,208.9	893.3	989.7	1,091.2	1,096.7	1,136.6
II. Industrial Countries	616.9	602.2	570.4	525.5	675.8	643.9	976.2	936.2	735.9	502.7	581.5	673.5	692.2	810.5
United States	331.4	327.3	291.8	273.8	372.1	364.8	540.6	503.8	402.7	318.2	374.3	395.8	380.2	484.9
Canada	3.7	5.2	7.0	6.5	5.5	10.9	30.6	34.5	26.4	14.2	18.6	21.8	18.5	17.9
Australia	.7	.9	.9	.8	.5	3.4	.9	1.3	.3	.4	.1	.2	.3	.5
Japan	8.0	5.4	6.1	4.9	4.8	5.2	11.3	171.3	118.3	37.2	52.8	82.4	105.2	116.9
New Zealand	.8	?	.1	.2	.2	.3	.1	.3	.2	?	.1	?	?	?
Austria	.8	?	.1	.8	.1	?	10.9	2.1	2.9	1.3	2.7	2.9	4.4	2.8
Belgium-Luxembourg	26.0	23.8	11.0	9.6	10.5	11.1	9.1	7.0	7.7	4.8	4.7	5.8	9.5	7.8
Denmark	.8	.3	.4	.2	.6	?	3.1	4.3	3.9	1.8	1.4	1.8	2.3	3.1
Finland	25.6	17.5	19.3	19.7	19.4	21.8	28.1	.4	.5	1.3	1.3	7.2	2.2	1.7
France	18.9	9.7	11.5	11.1	11.5	11.6	17.8	17.6	20.9	11.6	9.8	21.2	16.0	17.1
Germany	110.5	123.3	124.5	110.6	131.5	117.9	142.6	70.9	55.4	35.1	46.7	56.7	58.3	60.8
Iceland	.1	.1	.3	.3	.7	.4	.8	?	?	.1	?	?	?	?
Ireland	.4	.3	.6	.8	.7	.3	.7	2.7	4.1	3.3	6.8	3.3	3.8	3.2
Italy	39.0	29.1	32.9	27.3	33.9	19.8	48.9	23.4	24.9	13.3	17.1	20.3	20.2	22.7
Netherlands	28.8	25.5	24.9	21.0	22.2	19.3	24.7	11.1	7.0	4.1	6.1	10.5	9.7	12.5
Norway	2.9	2.2	3.6	4.0	5.1	4.6	9.7	.8	.4	.4	.3	.9	.7	.4
Spain	4.9	5.1	5.4	4.4	8.6	9.4	12.7	33.2	24.5	17.1	16.0	21.2	25.7	19.1
Sweden	9.2	12.3	8.8	6.8	10.0	12.0	24.4	12.2	8.8	9.6	2.8	3.8	5.4	8.1
Switzerland	2.4	3.9	1.8	1.6	1.3	4.0	17.5	10.5	8.8	5.3	7.4	9.6	9.4	10.7
United Kingdom	2.7	10.5	19.8	22.0	36.7	27.1	41.9	25.8	18.3	23.8	12.6	14.2	20.4	20.3
III. Developing Countries														
Oil Exporting Countries														
Algeria	4.2	8.3	11.4	11.9	6.5	10.2	3.4	85.1	92.0	107.7	72.7	93.6	123.9	15.7
Indonesia	.1	.3	.1	?	?	?	?	.2	?	.4	.3	?	?	.1
Iran, I.R. of	?	.1	.1	?	?	?	.7	?	?	?	?	?	.2	.2
Iraq	?	?	?	?	?	?	?	?	?	?	?	?	?	?
Kuwait	?	.2	.7	2.8	1.4	1.6	.7	?	?	?	?	?	?	?
Libya	?	1.1	?	?	?	?	?	?	?	?	?	?	?	?
Oman	?	.2	.7	1.9	2.3	1.7	1.1	?	?	?	?	?	?	?
Qatar	?	.3	.1	.1	.1	1.0	.1	?	?	?	?	?	?	?
Saudi Arabia	1.6	3.0	4.3	4.1	1.0	1.0	?	.2	.1	?	?	?	?	.1
T. VENEZUELA	2.4	3.1	5.6	3.0	1.8	5.7	1.4	84.9	92.0	107.3	72.4	93.6	123.7	15.3
Non-Oil Developing Countries	354.9	373.9	265.1	282.8	282.8	245.6	213.3	432.0	369.7	275.5	322.7	301.2	256.3	281.2
Africa	.3	1.2	2.1	3.6	1.7	.8	1.3	.7	.3	.1	.1	.1	?	.1
Botswana	?	?	?	.4	.1	?	?	?	?	?	?	?	?	?
Djibouti	?	?	?	.1	?	?	?	?	?	?	?	?	?	?
Guinea	?	?	?	?	?	?	?	?	.1	?	?	?	?	?
Ivory Coast	.2	.2	.7	2.8	1.4	1.6	.6	?	?	?	?	?	?	?
Lesotho	?	1.1	1.6	.7	.3	.6	.6	?	?	?	?	?	?	?
Liberia	.1	.1	?	.1	?	?	?	?	.2	.1	.7	.3	.6	.6
Morocco	?	.5	.4	.6	.2	.3	.3	.2	.1	?	?	.2	?	?
South Africa	.3	.2	.1	1.8	1.1	.4	.1	.4	.1	?	?	?	?	?
Africa not specified	?	?	?	?	?	?	?	.1	?	?	?	?	?	?
Asia	1.4	3.1	2.7	3.3	2.3	2.2	1.8	8.2	14.3	19.7	8.9	11.8	14.5	25.4
China, People's Rep.	.3	.1	.1	.4	.1	.3	.2	.1	.1	.2	.2	.3	.3	.6
Hong Kong	?	.2	.1	.1	.3	.7	.1	?	?	.1	.2	.3	.3	.3
India	.4	.6	1.0	.4	.3	.7	.1	3.7	2.0	1.2	2.5	3.7	5.4	7.3
Kampuchea, Dem.	?	?	?	.1	.1	.1	?	?	?	?	.1	.1	.1	.1
Kiribati, Rep. of	?	?	?	?	?	?	?	?	?	?	?	?	?	?
Korea	.1	.3	.1	1.4	.4	.3	.3	2.3	11.5	5.3	5.6	7.3	7.1	16.0
Malaysia	?	.1	.1	.1	.1	?	.2	.1	.1	?	.1	?	.1	.9
Pakistan	?	?	.2	.1	.2	?	.2	?	?	?	?	?	?	?
Philippines	.2	.3	.2	.3	.4	.1	.1	?	?	?	?	?	?	?

Table 2617 (Continued)
COSTA RICA ABSOLUTE VALUE OF GOODS TRADED WITH SELECTED REGIONS AND COUNTRIES,[1] 1980–86
(M US)[2]

Category	Exports FOB							Imports CIF						
	1980	1981	1982	1983	1984	1985	1986	1980	1981	1982	1983	1984	1985	1986
Non-Oil Developing Countries (Continued)														
Asia (Continued)														
Singapore	.3	1.0	.3	.3	.1	.1	.1	—	.4	12.8	.3	.3	.9	.1
Sri Lanka	.5	—	.7	.6	—	—	—	—	.1	—	—	.1	.1	—
Thailand	—	.9	—	—	1.0	.9	.8	.8	—	—	—	—	—	—
Tuvalu	—	—	—	—	—	—	—	—	—	—	—	—	—	—
Oceania not specified	—	—	—	—	—	—	—	—	—	—	—	—	—	—
Non-Oil Exporting Countries														
Europe	6.6	8.9	3.3	5.8	11.8	23.9	15.3	4.6	1.4	.8	.8	1.6	1.3	1.3
Cyprus	.2	—	—	.1	.1	—	—	—	—	—	—	—	—	—
Gibraltar	—	—	—	.6	—	—	—	—	—	—	—	—	—	—
Greece	—	4.0	—	.3	4.1	4.9[a]	.1	2.9	—	.1	.2	.2	—	.2
Hungary	—	—	—	.3	4.1	8.5	—	—	.1	—	—	.2	.1	—
Malta	—	.2	—	—	—	—	—	—	.4	.3	.3	.4	.4	.5
Portugal	—	.2	—	1.7	.9	.6	1.4	.6	.1	—	—	.3	.1	.1
Romainia	—	3.0	2.5	.1	.1	.9[a]	—	.2	—	—	—	—	—	—
Turkey	—	.1	.2	.1	.1	.2	—	.5	.2	.3	.3	.3	.3	.2
Yugoslavia	6.3	.7	.1	.1	—	—	—	—	—	.3	.3	.3	.1[a]	—
Europe not specified	—	—	.1	.1	.4	.1[a]	—	—	—	—	—	—	—	—
Middle East	7.0	9.0	11.9	16.6	10.5	12.6	5.0	.8	1.1	.6	2.6	1.5	2.5	3.6
Bahrain	—	.2	—	.1	—	.1	.1	—	—	—	—	—	—	.1
Egypt	2.9	.4	1.0	.1	.2	.1[a]	1.4	—	—	—	—	—	—	—
Israel	.7	.1	1.1	4.1	2.6	5.2	.6	.8	1.1	.6	2.6	1.5	2.2	3.2
Jordan	.5	1.5	.6	2.5	2.5	1.8	.2	—	—	—	—	—	—	—
Lebanon	1.2	1.7	3.0	.8	.1	.4	.6	—	—	—	—	—	—	—
Syrian Arab Rep.	—	.3	.4	—	—	.5	—	—	—	—	—	—	—	—
Yemen Arab Rep.	—	—	—	—	—	—	—	—	—	—	—	—	—	—
Yemen, P.D. Rep.	—	—	—	.4	.4	.4[a]	.6	—	—	—	—	—	—	—
IV. **Latin America[3]**	343.6	359.7	355.0	263.6	262.6	214.5	193.3	503.1	445.1	361.7	382.7	380.3	361.9	266.7
A. ARGENTINA	2.2	1.7	.1	.2	.1	2.1	6.9	6.6	4.4	1.9	2.5	2.5	6.9	3.4
Antigua and Barbuda	—	.1	.1	.2	.1	.1	.1	—	—	—	.1	.2	—	.1
Bahamas	.2	.3	.3	.2	.1	.1	.1	—	—	—	—	—	—	—
Barbados	.2	.4	.5	.4	.3	.2	.5	—	—	—	—	—	—	—
Belize	.2	.6	.8	.4	.4	.3	.4	—	—	—	—	—	—	—
Bermuda	—	.6	.2	.2	.2	—	—	.1	.1	—	—	—	.1	.1
B. BOLIVIA	1.7	.6	.2	.2	.9	.7	.2	—	—	—	—	—	—	—
C. BRAZIL	2.9	4.0	2.4	.6	.2	.7	.7	21.7	18.7	1.2	14.1	20.2	23.9	31.3
D. CHILE	1.7	—	—	—	.2	.1	—	7.5	5.0	1.3	3.1	1.0	3.6	2.5
E. COLOMBIA	3.6	5.4	3.4	1.9	1.7	1.8	2.0	5.7	4.3	4.2	5.5	8.6	7.2	7.3
Dominica	.1	.1	—	.2	—	—	—	—	—	—	—	—	—	—
H. DOMINICAN REP.	3.1	3.3	2.3	2.7	2.3	2.6	5.2	.7	.9	1.4	3.9	.9	.1	.2
I. ECUADOR	1.4	18.3	1.6	.4	1.4	2.6	2.0	2.1	1.2	.8	.4	1.5	15.6	22.6
J. EL SALVADOR	52.5	43.5	33.1	41.6	44.6	46.3	37.0	67.6	37.2	22.7	29.7	30.8	30.1	31.0
Grenada	.1	.1	.1	.2	.5	.1	.3	—	—	—	—	—	—	—
Guadeloupe	.1	.1	.1	—	—	—	—	—	—	—	—	—	—	—
K. GUATEMALA	65.5	75.8	64.3	88.5	75.9	39.2	33.7	100.6	64.9	56.2	59.4	59.4	46.4	45.5
Guiana, French	.4	.5	.1	.3	.4	—	.8	—	—	—	—	—	—	—
Guyana	.1	.7	—	—	—	.6	—	—	—	—	—	—	—	—
L. HAITI	.7	.7	1.2	27.2	44.8	30.8	25.9	18.8	16.4	11.9	11.0	8.3	7.2	6.2
M. HONDURAS	28.3	34.8	23.2	.9	.5	1.2	1.0	.1	—	—	—	—	—	.1
Jamaica	.4	1.1	—	.3	.3	.8	—	.1	—	—	—	—	.6	—
Leeward Islands	—	—	—	—	—	—	1.1	—	—	—	—	—	—	—
Martinique	—	—	—	.3	.3	—	—	—	—	—	—	—	—	—

Table 2617 (Continued)

COSTA RICA ABSOLUTE VALUE OF GOODS TRADED WITH SELECTED REGIONS AND COUNTRIES,[1] 1980–86 (M US)[2]

Category	Exports FOB							Imports CIF						
	1980	1981	1982	1983	1984	1985	1986	1980	1981	1982	1983	1984	1985	1986
IV. Latin America[3] (Continued)														
N. MEXICO	1.1	19.1	13.5	.1	13.5	7.7	.5	75.5	110.7	80.3	81.6	76.4	32.0	52.5
Netherlands Antilles	5.7	12.8	7.2	11.0	4.7	2.1	1.5	38.5	25.9	20.7	46.6	24.1	16.7	10.2
O. NICARAGUA	124.1	83.8	46.6	40.9	27.9	27.2	23.8	32.8	33.8	21.6	20.2	16.3	8.9	8.1
P. PANAMA	41.8	46.3	41.4	37.1	37.2	39.7	43.8	31.6	21.2	13.8	20.7	25.6	20.5	22.9
Panama Canal Zone	~	~	~	~	~	~	~	~	~	~	~	~	~	~
R. PERU	.9	1.4	1.4	1.0	.4	.2	2.6	5.9	5.0	3.0	3.7	8.0	14.0	2.3
St. Lucia	.1	.1	.3	.2	.1	.3	.4	.2	~	~	~	~	~	~
St. Pierre-Miquelon	~	~	~	~	~	~	~	~	~	~	~	~	~	~
St. Vincent	.1	.1	.3	.3	~	~	~	~	~	~	~	~	~	~
Suriname	.3	.6	.4	.3	.2	.9	1.2	~	~	~	~	~	~	~
Trinidad and Tobago	1.5	.6	1.6	.9	1.5	1.3	.6	1.7	3.4	2.2	3.0	1.2	1.5	2.7
S. URUGUAY	.3	.1	~	~	~	~	~	~	~	~	~	.1	.1	~
Windward Islands	.2	.2	1.3	.9	.6	.5[a]	~	.7	~	.2	.2	~	~	.2
British West Indies	~	~	~	~	~	~	.6	~	~	~	~	~	~	~
Other Latin America not specified	.1	~	~	~	~	.5	.6	.7	~	~	~	~	1.8	2.3
V. USSR, Eastern Europe, etc.	4.4	23.3	23.6	39.5	20.0	22.6	9.4	4.9	3.0	1.7	1.9	3.0	2.3	2.4
Albania	~	.3	7.3	3.5	.4	.4[a]	~	~	~	~	~	~	~	~
Bulgaria	4.4	~	1.6	1.5	.2	.3	~	~	~	~	~	~	~	~
G. CUBA	4.4	~	~	~	~	~	~	.1	.1	~	~	~	~	~
Czechoslovakia	~	7.9	7.4	8.9	12.1	18.5	7.9	2.0	1.2	1.1	1.3	1.5	1.4	1.4
Eastern Germany	2.0	10.7	5.7	.4	.4	3.8	1.5	~	~	.1	.2	.2	.2	.2
North Korea	1.1	.2	~	.3	.1	.1[a]	~	1.1	.3	~	~	1.2	.1[a]	.1
Poland	.4	.9	.4	2.9	6.4	12.3[a]	13.7	.4	.5	.1	.1	.5	.4[a]	.3
USSR	1.8	1.3	1.3	24.7	6.9	6.5[a]	~	1.8	1.4	.5	.4	.2	.6	.6
Country or area not specified	~	~	~	~	~	.8[a]	~	~	~	~	~	1.4	.7	~
Special categories	.5	~	~	~	~	.8[a]	9.1	~	~	.7	~	~	.6	3.0
EEC	232.0	231.5	231.1	207.1	256.1	217.1	302.9	196.7	167.0	115.1	121.4	155.3	167.1	167.1
VI. Percent Distribution														
Industrial Countries	62.9	59.7	65.5	61.0	68.6	69.7	80.5	63.7	60.9	56.3	58.8	61.7	63.1	71.3
Oil Exporting Countries	.4	.8	1.3	1.4	.7	.7	.3	5.8	7.6	12.1	7.3	8.6	9.8	1.4
Non-Oil Developing Countries	36.2	37.0	30.3	32.5	28.1	24.9	17.6	29.4	30.6	30.8	32.6	27.6	22.9	24.7
Africa	~	.1	.2	.4	.2	.3	.1	.6	#	#	.9	#	.3	.2
Asia	.1	.3	.3	.4	.2	.2	.2	.3	.9	2.2	1.1	.2	.2	.2
Europe	.7	.9	.4	.7	1.2	2.6	1.3	.6	1.2	.1	.2	.1	.1	.3
Middle East	.7	.9	1.4	1.9	1.1	1.4	.4	.3	.1	.1	.3	.2	.1	.1
Non-industrial Western Hemisphere[3]	35.0	35.7	29.3	30.6	26.6	23.2	15.9	34.2	36.8	40.5	38.7	34.8	33.0	23.5
USSR, Eastern Europe, etc.	.4	2.3	2.7	4.6	2.0	2.5	.8	.3	.2	.2	.3	.3	.2	.2
VII. Annual Percent Change														
World	5.0	2.8	-13.6	-1.2	14.5	-6.3	31.3	5.2	-17.8	-26.1	10.8	10.3	.5	3.6
Industrial Countries	-7.7	-2.4	-5.3	-7.9	28.6	-4.7	51.6	7.4	-21.4	-31.7	15.7	15.8	2.8	17.1
Oil Exporting Countries	-21.2	97.6	37.3	4.4	-45.4	15.4	-66.7	58.7	8.1	17.1	-32.5	28.7	18.8	-87.3
Non-Oil Developing Countries	41.2	5.1	-29.1	5.8	-1.3	-3.7	-13.2	-6.1	-14.4	-25.5	17.1	-6.7	-13.9	9.7
Africa	-65.2	361.1	139.3	57.5	-60.4	22.4	-50.2	253.4	-60.7	-48.9	-60.6	-13.0	-19.1	47.4
Asia	18.3	118.3	-12.4	17.0	-31.4	-2.5	-17.1	-31.0	70.4	40.8	-54.4	28.5	22.7	75.4
Europe	-15.1	34.4	-62.9	76.4	103.6	102.5	-35.9	5.8	-69.4	-40.3	-8.5	113.9	-24.0	1.7
Middle East	-4.3	27.3	32.7	39.3	-36.6	19.8	-60.5	11.0	39.3	-48.9	365.7	-42.8	69.8	41.9
Non-industrial Western Hemisphere[3]	43.5	4.7	-29.1	3.4	-.4	-18.3	-9.9	1.2	-11.5	-18.8	5.9	-.7	-4.8	-26.3
USSR, Eastern Europe, etc.	-50.2	428.7	1.5	67.0	-49.3	13.1	-58.3	67.2	-39.2	-41.9	9.7	59.3	-22.8	3.5

1. DOT may differ between countries and from IFS data because of the time it takes for an export to become an import, etc.
2. Data may be calculated from partner's reported data or estimated on basis of less than 12 months.
3. Cuba is included in category V; Venezuela is included in category III.

a. Five or fewer months of reported data, 7 or more months derived or extrapolated.

SOURCE: Adapted from IMF-DOT-Y, 1982, 1986, and 1987.

Table 2618

CUBA ABSOLUTE VALUE OF GOODS TRADED WITH SELECTED REGIONS AND COUNTRIES,[1] 1980-86
(M US)[2]

PART I. NON-COMMUNIST TRADE

Category	Exports FOB							Imports CIF						
	1980	1981	1982	1983	1984	1985	1986	1980	1981	1982	1983	1984	1985	1986
I. World	1,381.3	1,488.6	1,292.6	1,046.4	843.7	868.8	874.6	2,272.3	2,140.4	1,640.3	1,667.0	2,291.8	2,821.6	2,543.1
II. Industrial Countries[4]	766.3	604.7	521.5	462.1	390.7	417.7	446.3	1,637.3	530.6	1,022.2	985.5	1,327.3	1,494.3	1,456.6
United States	~	~	1.5	~	~	~	~	~	.6	1.0	.7	1.1	1.1	1.5
Canada	134.2	163.3	77.1	45.3	49.5	31.9	50.2	374.4	414.1	289.8	323.9	287.1	270.6	287.9
Australia	.5	.4	.5	.6	1.2	1.5	.3	1.7	2.0	.5	1.6	9.3	5.3	5.7
Japan	170.7	139.8	103.5	83.8	71.0	84.7	120.2	264.7	293.1	138.6	115.2	274.7	333.6	326.0
New Zealand	~	~	~	~	~	~	~	~	~	5.2	~	5.2	~	19.0
Austria	5.1	2.8	4.2	1.9	2.2	2.0	1.9	9.6	9.1	7.1	9.3	13.7	18.1	23.8
Belgium	36.0	6.9	3.5	12.0	6.1	1.8	3.0	30.4	36.9	17.0	15.4	13.5	29.7	25.2
Denmark	2.7	2.4	.5	1.2	3.4	1.9	1.1	8.1	8.4	6.7	6.2	8.2	10.0	9.8
Finland	48.7	43.9	24.0	13.3	4.4	13.7	9.4	7.2	8.3	3.0	2.6	4.0	3.0	4.3
France	59.7	50.7	50.5	51.6	30.7	36.2	50.3	291.6	172.5	62.1	111.3	113.6	115.6	59.2
Germany	51.9	25.2	29.0	26.9	10.8	18.4	17.3	120.4	102.1	71.0	70.8	87.0	115.7	116.6
Iceland	~	.8	.3	.2	.1	.7	.6	8.9	16.2	27.9	28.5	27.2	~	~
Ireland	2.7	34.3	39.5	33.6	42.2	34.7	49.8	22.9	47.8	42.3	32.6	79.7	69.3	74.0
Italy	42.8	25.2	43.0	81.9	56.0	57.0	37.9	59.7	43.2	65.6	43.5	43.7	32.6	32.9
Netherland	64.6	.1	.1	.2	.1	.7	3.7	49.9	43.5	65.6	43.5	79.7	1.4	.9
Norway	.5	.1	.1	.2	.1	.7	.6	2.4	2.1	1.4	1.1	1.1	1.4	.9
Spain	83.1	55.3	100.0	85.0	79.6	112.5	79.4	207.6	192.9	120.7	98.1	196.3	320.0	320.8
Sweden	1.2	17.1	6.4	5.1	5.4	5.8	7.3	57.3	63.2	22.4	18.6	43.1	32.9	29.7
Switzerland	6.6	5.8	6.4	5.1	2.0	5.5	2.6	30.5	36.1	19.4	29.6	24.4	30.9	24.1
United Kingdom	55.4	30.5	28.5	19.6	15.4	8.5	11.4	90.2	81.7	125.7	76.6	94.7	83.5	95.3
III. Developing Countries														
Oil Exporting Countries	184.0	159.1	130.6	105.6	62.7	67.6	42.7	108.9	86.1	22.3	93.4	224.4	467.5	396.0
Algeria	106.7	115.0	82.5	67.6	32.9	28.0	21.0	.5[a]	.5[a]	.2[a]	1.0[a]	.9[b]	.8[b]	~
Indonesia	36.3[a]	5.3[a]	9.2[a]	~	~	~	~	~	4.5[a]	~	~	~	~	~
Iran, I.R. of	~	~	~	~	~	~	~	~	~	~	~	~	~	~
Iraq	~	~	~	~	~	~	16.0	~	~	~	~	~	~	~
Libya	31.9[a]	31.1[a]	31.1	27.9	25.2	21.4	16.0	.1[a]	.1[a]	.1[a]	~	~	~	~
Saudi Arabia	2.6	3.9	3.8	9.0	2.5	2.1	1.6	~	~	~	~	~	~	~
United Arab Emirates	.1[a]	.3[a]	.1[a]	.2[a]	.2[a]	.1[a]	.1	~	~	~	~	~	~	~
T. VENEZUELA	7.0[a]	3.5[a]	4.0	1.0	2.0	16.0	4.0	108.4[a]	81.2[a]	22.0	92.4	224.4	467.5	396.0
Non-Oil Developing Countries	381.1	684.2	602.7	442.7	360.5	302.8	385.6	434.6	458.1	555.6	544.4	711.7	853.3	690.4
Africa	115.1	146.1	87.1	72.0	37.9	34.3	30.2	10.0	2.7	6.2	9.3	5.2	4.0	8.4
Angola	.1[b]	.1[b]	.1[b]	.1[b]	.1[b]	.1[b]	.1	~	~	~	~	~	~	~
Burundi	~	.1[a]	.1[a]	~	~	~	~	~	~	~	~	~	~	~
Comoros	~	.1[b]	.1[b]	.1[b]	.1[b]	.1[b]	.1[b]	~	~	~	~	~	~	~
Congo	~	~	~	~	~	~	~	~	~	~	~	~	~	~
Ethiopia	~	.2[b]	.2[b]	~	.1[a]	.1[b]	.1	~	~	~	~	~	~	~
Gabon	.2[b]	.2[b]	.2[b]	~	.2[a]	~	~	~	~	~	~	~	~	~
Ghana	~	.6[a]	.6[c]	.6[b]	.7[b]	.7	.7	~	~	~	~	~	~	~
Guinea-Bissau	~	~	~	~	~	~	~	~	~	~	~	~	~	~
Mali	~	~	~	~	~	~	~	~	~	~	~	~	~	~
Morocco	~	21.2[a]	.9[a]	1.0[b]	1.1[b]	1.0[b]	~	4.7[a]	2.3[a]	4.1[a]	1.6[a]	~	~	~
Senegal	~	8.3[a]	.9[a]	1.0[b]	~	~	~	~	~	~	~	~	~	~
Somalia	~	~	~	~	~	~	~	~	~	~	~	~	~	~
Sudan	~	~	~	3.2[a]	4.0[a]	5.1[a]	8.1	~	~	~	6.7[a]	~	~	~
Tunisia	8.6[a]	~	~	~	~	~	~	4.9[a]	~	~	~	5.2[a]	4.0[a]	8.4

Table 2618 (Continued)

CUBA ABSOLUTE VALUE OF GOODS TRADED WITH SELECTED REGIONS AND COUNTRIES,[1] 1980–86 (M US)[2]

PART I. NON-COMMUNIST TRADE (Continued)

Category	Exports FOB							Imports CIF						
	1980	1981	1982	1983	1984	1985	1986	1980	1981	1982	1983	1984	1985	1986
III. Developing Countries (Continued)														
Non-Oil Developing Countries														
Asia	162.2	214.4	270.0	198.0	136.7	108.3	88.6	133.1	95.4	139.9	120.6	118.3	147.1	107.0
Bangladesh	~	~	~	~	~	~	~	~	~	~	~	.9	~	~
China, People's Rep.	115.7[a]	171.7[a]	243.7[a]	182.7[a]	121.1[a]	97.8[a]	76.5	102.1[a]	84.4[a]	128.7[a]	106.8[a]	104.2[a]	128.5[a]	105.4
Hong Kong	.4[a]	.3[a]	.3[a]	.4[a]	.1[a]	.2[a]	.2	4.1[a]	2.2[a]	1.0[a]	.1[a]	.2[a]	.2[a]	.1
India	~	.3[a]	3.7	3.1	3.4	3.4	3.5	7.1[a]	.6[a]	~	.5	.6[b]	.6[b]	.6
Malaysia	7.6[a]	36.7[a]	13.5[a]	7.2[a]	10.8[a]	4.3[a]	8.2	1.9[a]	2.6[a]	.2[a]	.6[a]	.6[a]	.7[a]	.1
Papua New Guinea	.1[a]	~	~	~	~	~	~	~	~	~	~	~	~	~
Philippines	~	~	~	~	~	~	~	.1[a]	~	~	.1[a]	~	~	~
Singapore	2.2[a]	.1[a]	.2[a]	.2[a]	1.3[a]	.8[a]	.2	5.3[a]	5.7[a]	2.6[a]	3.0[a]	1.8[a]	1.8[a]	.8
Sri Lanka	~	~	~	4.4[a]	~	1.9[a]	.2	~	~	~	~	~	1.2[a]	~
Thailand	~	~	~	~	~	~	~	12.5[a]	~	7.0[c]	9.4[a]	10.0[a]	14.2[a]	~
Europe	131.7	226.3	164.9	111.9	144.5	180.3	187.8	244.4	273.5	316.7	266.4	255.1	302.3	247.5
Cyprus	.1[a]	.3[a]	.1[a]	.7[a]	.5[a]	.6[a]	.1	~	~	~	~	~	~	~
Greece	.4[a]	.4[a]	.1[a]	.1[a]	.1[a]	.3[a]	5.0	~	~	4.3[a]	~	~	~	~
Hungary	23.3[a]	67.1[a]	54.1[a]	11.2[a]	16.4[a]	20.4[a]	15.9	50.6[a]	56.0[a]	77.9[a]	69.8[a]	83.7[a]	83.7[a]	57.5
Malta	.1[a]	.1[a]	.5[a]	~	~	~	~	~	~	~	~	~	~	~
Portugal	20.5[a]	51.7[a]	39.9[a]	5.8[a]	8.5[a]	3.7[a]	3.4	9.8[a]	10.2[a]	4.2[a]	4.3[a]	5.4[a]	7.7[a]	7.5
Romania	31.1[a]	59.7[a]	37.5[a]	62.5[a]	89.1[a]	125.6	131.9	83.0[a]	134.8[a]	165.1[a]	133.4[a]	124.3[a]	92.5	97.1
Turkey	~	~	~	~	~	1.5	1.6	.6[a]	.5[a]	.6[a]	.2[a]	.2[a]	.3	~
Yugoslavia	6.0[a]	6.7[a]	.1[c]	~	3.2[a]	1.5[a]	2.1	9.1[a]	6.6[a]	7.1[a]	5.5	~	76.8[a]	41.6
Middle East	70.6	147.7	141.5	126.9	65.9	63.4	59.5	5.9	5.8	5.5	5.5	6.1	6.4	6.7
Bahrain	~	~	~	~	~	~	~	~	~	~	~	~	~	~
Egypt	25.9[a]	85.3[a]	51.1[a]	31.5[a]	12.6[a]	26.3	27.6	~	~	~	~	~	.4	.4
Jordan	.1[a]	~	~	~	~	.1	.1	~	~	~	~	~	~	~
Lebanon	~	~	~	~	~	~	~	~	~	~	~	~	~	~
Syrian Arab Rep.	7.5[a]	24.9[a]	55.4[a]	57.1[a]	24.0	11.9	12.4	5.8[b]	5.8[b]	5.5	5.5	6.0	6.0	6.3
Yemen Arab Rep.	2.5[a]	2.3[a]	.2[a]	1.4[a]	1.5[b]	1.5	1.6	~	~	~	~	~	~	~
IV. Latin America[3]	135.5	149.3	107.5	75.5	68.0	64.8	62.2	241.6	227.9	149.8	279.7	579.8	867.4	716.8
A. ARGENTINA	.3[a]	.1[a]	.1[a]	.1[a]	.6[a]	.3	.5	73.0[a]	84.5[a]	52.7[a]	141.2[a]	257.1[a]	311.7	257.5
Bahamas	.2[b]	.2[b]	.1[b]	.2[b]	.2[b]	.3	.2	~	~	~	~	~	~	~
Barbados	3.0[a]	4.0[a]	2.6[a]	1.4[a]	.4[a]	.1[a]	.2	~	~	~	~	~	~	~
Bermuda	.1[a]	~	.1[a]	.2[a]	.1[b]	.1[b]	.1	~	~	.1[a]	~	~	~	~
B. BOLIVIA	~	~	~	.1[a]	.2[a]	.1[b]	~	~	~	~	~	~	~	~
E. COLOMBIA	.7[a]	.6[a]	.5[a]	5.3[a]	~	3.5	3.6	6.1[a]	3.8[a]	4.9[a]	1.8[a]	2.1[a]	5.1	5.3
F. COSTA RICA	.1[a]	.1[a]	~	.1[a]	.2[a]	~	~	4.8[a]	~	~	~	~	~	~
H. DOMINICAN REP.	~	~	~	~	~	~	~	~	~	34.4[a]	~	~	~	~
Grenada	.9[a]	.9[a]	2.3[a]	2.3	2.5	2.5[b]	2.6	.1[a]	.1[a]	.1[a]	.1[b]	.1[b]	.1[b]	.1
Guadeloupe	~	~	.3[a]	.3[a]	.4[b]	.4	.4	~	~	~	~	~	~	~
Guiana, French	.8[a]	.7[a]	.4[a]	~	.3	.3	~	~	.1[a]	1.5[a]	.1[b]	~	~	~
Guyana	.3[a]	1.2[a]	1.1[a]	~	~	~	~	~	~	~	~	~	~	~
Jamaica	.8[a]	.9[a]	2.4[a]	~	~	~	~	.8[a]	~	~	~	~	~	~
N. MEXICO	14.7[a]	23.1[a]	58.7[a]	23.2[a]	12.3[a]	2.3	2.0	29.4[a]	21.0[a]	28.8[a]	38.9[a]	89.2[a]	76.7	49.0
Netherlands Antilles	5.7[b]	5.7[b]	5.4	5.4	6.0	6.0	6.3	3.1[b]	3.1[b]	3.0	3.0	3.3	3.3	3.4
O. NICARAGUA	~	7.5[a]	27.8[a]	27.8	30.6	30.6	32.1	~	~	1.4[a]	1.4	1.5	1.5[b]	1.6
P. PANAMA	.1[a]	.5[a]	.1[a]	.3[a]	.1[a]	.2[c]	.2	.5[a]	12.4[a]	1.4[a]	1.4	1.5	1.5[b]	1.6
R. PERU	~	.3[b]	.1[a]	5.7	10.0	.1	7.5	14.5[a]	20.3[a]	18.3[b]	14.6[b]	13.2[b]	11.8[b]	1.4
St. Vincent	.3[b]	.3[b]	.3[b]	.3[b]	.3[b]	.3[b]	.3	~	~	~	~	~	~	~
Suriname	.2[a]	.1[a]	1.4[a]	1.9[a]	2.1	2.1	2.2	.9[a]	.4[a]	.3[a]	.2[a]	.2[a]	~	2.2
Trinidad and Tobago	.2[a]	.1[c]	.2[c]	.2[a]	.1[a]	~	~	~	~	.3[a]	.2[a]	.2[a]	~	~
EEC	419.8	282.9	340.2	317.8	252.8	275.7	259.1	890.6	711.7	547.4	487.2	669.2	784.3	741.2

Table 2618 (Continued)

CUBA ABSOLUTE VALUE OF GOODS TRADED WITH SELECTED REGIONS AND COUNTRIES,[1] 1980–86
(M US)[2]

PART I. NON-COMMUNIST TRADE (Continued)

Category	Exports FOB							Imports CIF						
	1980	1981	1982	1983	1984	1985	1986	1980	1981	1982	1983	1984	1985	1986
V. Annual Percentage Change														
Industrial Countries	39.6	-21.1	-13.8	-11.4	-15.5	6.9	6.9	54.2	-6.5	-33.3	-3.6	34.7	12.6	-2.5
Oil Exporting Countries	179.2	-13.5	-16.0	-16.9	-14.9	-19.9	-36.8	89.1	-20.9	-14.9	-18.8	-10.1	-9.9	-15.3
Non-Oil Developing Countries	41.0	79.5	-11.9	-26.5	-18.6	-16.0	.5	35.5	5.4	21.3	-2.0	30.7	19.9	-19.7
Africa	151.9	27.0	-40.4	-17.4	-47.3	-9.5	-12.1	-13.5	-72.8	128.3	49.6	-43.8	-24.3	111.4
Asia	28.0	32.2	25.9	-26.7	-30.9	-20.8	-18.2	21.3	-24.9	40.1	-13.9	-1.9	24.4	-27.3
Europe	6.1	71.9	-27.1	-32.2	29.2	24.7	4.2	68.5	11.9	15.8	-15.9	-4.2	-18.5	-18.1
Middle East	25.3	109.2	-4.2	-10.3	-48.1	-3.7	-6.2	10.3	-1.7	-4.2	-.2	10.0	5.9	4.8
Non-Industrial Western Hemisphere[3]	516.2	10.2	-28.0	-29.7	-10.0	-4.7	-4.0	62.3	-5.7	-34.3	86.8	107.3	49.6	-17.4

1. DOT data may differ between countries and from IFS data because of the time it takes for an export to become an import, etc.
2. Data may be calculated from partner's reported data or estimated on basis of less than 12 months.
3. Venezuela is included in category III.
4. Data derived from partner country for the entire year.
a. Data derived from partner country for the entire year.
b. Data extrapolated for the entire year.
c. Five of fewer months of reported data; seven or more months derived or extrapolated.

SOURCE: Adapted from IMF-DOT-Y, 1982, 1986, and 1987.

PART II. ALL TRADE
(M Pesos)

Category	1970	1973	1974	1975	1976	1977	1978	1979[‡]	1980	1981[‡]	1982	1983	1984	1985[‡]
Exports	1,050	1,153	2,237	2,952	2,962	2,312	3,440	3,500	3,967	4,259	4,940	5,535	5,462	5,983
USSR	529	477	811	1,662	1,638	2,066	2,496	2,370	2,253	2,455	3,297	3,882	3,938	4,468
Rest of Socialist Countries	248	268	472	341	452	378	420	514	534	823	882	883	953	842
Rest of World	273	408	954	949	602	468	524	616	1,180	981	761	770	571	673
Imports	1,311	1,463	2,226	3,113	3,180	3,433	3,574	3,687	4,627	5,081	5,537	6,222	7,207	7,905
USSR	691	811	1,025	1,250	1,490	1,858	2,328	2,524	2,904	3,223	3,756	4,245	4,776	5,310
Rest of Socialist Countries	226	224	328	437	374	467	521	534	709	877	1,153	1,169	1,282	1,330
Rest of World	394	428	873	1,456	1,316	1,108	725	629	1,014	981	628	808	1,149	1,265
Balance	-261	-310	11	-161	-488	-521	-134	-187	-660	-822	-597	-687	-1,745	-1,922
USSR	-162	-334	-214	412	148	208	168	-154	-651	-768	-459	-363	-838	-841
Rest of Socialist Countries	22	44	144	-66	78	-89	-101	-20	-175	-54	-271	-286	-329	-488
Rest of World	-121	-20	81	-507	-714	-640	-201	-13	166	~	133	-38	-578	-593

SOURCE: ECLA-S, 19881, p. 691; 1983, p. 255; 1985, p. 236.

Table 2618 (Continued)

CUBA ABSOLUTE VALUE OF GOODS TRADED WITH SELECTED REGIONS AND COUNTRIES,[1] 1980-86 (M US)[2]

PART III. TRADE WITH WORLD REGIONS, 1959-73

	1959-68[a]		1969		1970		1971		1972[‡]		1973[‡]	
	Export	Import	Export	Import	Export	Import	Export	Import	Export	Import	Export	Import
Absolute Total (M pesos)	630	843	667	1,222	1,049	1,312	861	1,388	771	1,190	1,151	1,391
Percentage Total	100	100	100	100	100	100	100	100	100	100	100	100
Socialist Eastern Europe	50	57	54	66	65	63	54	63	45	70	56	65
Other Eastern Europe	5	4	7	4	4	3	5	2	6	2	4	3
European Common Market	4	7	6	10	3	13	3	11	4	6	6	13
European Free Trade Area	4	4	4	8	3	7	3	7	4	6	2	1
Asia	16	12	24	9	22	10	25	12	28	11	24	13
Middle East	3	1	2	1	1	--	3	1	5	--	2	--
Africa	3	1	2	1	1	1	3	--	2	--	2	--
Americas	15	14	1	1	1	2	4	3	5	4	3	5

a. Yearly average.

SOURCE: Cuba: JUCEPLAN, AE, 1973, pp. 188-191.

PART IV. TRADE WITH LATIN AMERICAN COUNTRIES, 1959-73 (%)

	D. CHILE		N. MEXICO		R. PERU		OTHER	
Year	Exports	Imports	Exports	Imports	Exports	Imports	Exports	Imports
1959-68[a]	#	#	#	#	#	#	.1	.2
1969	#	#	#	#	#	#	#	#
1970	#	#	#	#	#	#	#	#
1971	.2	.1	#	#	#	#	#	#
1972	.4	.1		.1	#	.1	#	#
1973	.2	.1		.1	#	#	#	#

a. Yearly average.

SOURCE: Cuba, JUCEPLAN, AE, 1973, pp. 1980-191.

Table 2619

CUBA'S MOST IMPORTANT TRADING
PARTNERS, 1900–80

(% Value)

PART I. UNITED STATES, 1900-62				PART II. SOVIET UNION, 1960-80		
Year	Exports from Cuba	Imports to Cuba		Year	Exports from Cuba	Imports to Cuba
1900	71	43		1960	17	14
1905	87	45		1961	48	45
1910	86	53		1962	42	54
1915	83	64		1963	30	53
1919	77	76		1964	39	40
1925	75	63		1965	47	50
1929	77	59		1966	46	56
1937	81	69		1967	52	58
1942	90[a]	84[b]		1968	45	61
1945	79	79		1969	35	55
1950	59	79		1970	50	53
1955	67	74		1971	35	53
1959	73	73		1972	29	60
1960	59	39		1973	41	56
1961	6	2		1974	36	46
1962	1	2		1975	56	40
				1976	61	47
				1977	71	54
				1978	73[c]	65
				1979	68	68[c]
				1980	57	62

a. Highest U.S. figure.
b. Second highest U.S. figure; highest import figure, 87%, came in 1942.
c. Highest Soviet figure.

SOURCE: For U. S. trade, SALA-SNP, p. 284, revised with data in Schroeder, pp. 432-433, and William M. Leogrande, *Cuban Dependency* (Buffalo, N. Y.: Special Studies Series, Council on International Studies, 1978), p. 17. For Soviet data, Leogrande, *Cuban Dependency*, p. 18; SALA-Cuba, p. 168; ECLS-S, 1980, p. 201.

Table 2620

CROSS REFERENCES TO CUBA DATA IN SALA 20

Table 2621

DOMINICAN REPUBLIC ABSOLUTE VALUE OF GOODS TRADED WITH SELECTED REGIONS AND COUNTRIES,[1] 1980–86
(M US)[2]

Category	Exports FOB							Imports CIF						
	1980	1981	1982	1983	1984	1985	1986	1980	1981	1982	1983	1984	1985	1986
I. World	963.4	1,187.1	809.0	803.6	874.8	746.8	211.9	1,425.7	1,414.5	1,250.0	1,277.5	1,256.9	1,248.3	748.3
II. Industrial Countries	812.0	1,045.1	623.4	711.1	799.8	696.9	162.3	958.8	870.7	728.3	704.6	638.9	678.3	360.1
United States	502.6	795.4	437.2	541.4	670.9	566.6	35.1	539.1	608.3	486.1	458.6	429.5	433.6	11.6
Canada	2.9	15.0	10.0	16.9	15.4	10.7	25.9	34.9	37.0	32.5	29.7	19.2	18.2	37.6
Australia	~	.1	~	~	~	~	.1	.4	.8	.1	.1	.1	.1	.1
Japan	8.7	15.1	6.1	15.0	15.2	17.3	9.9	113.7	82.3	64.3	55.0	58.6	78.4	128.1
New Zealand	~	~	~	~	~	~	.4	2.6	5.0	.6	5.7	7.1	9.2	9.4
Austria	~	~	~	~	~	~	~	2.4	1.5	.6	.4	.4	.4	1.4
Belgium – Luxembourg	21.1	25.2	24.2	19.5	11.7	10.3	27.0	10.9	9.7	9.8	10.7	7.5	9.3	8.8
Denmark	2.0	.2	.2	2.7	.6	.1	.7	1.6	1.0	2.8	1.0	.9	.9	2.8
Finland	~	~	~	~	~	~	4.0	1.1	.6	.8	.9	.5	.5	1.4
France	3.2	4.7	3.5	1.5	.5	2.1	6.0	16.3	10.4	13.8	13.8	9.4	8.6	27.6
Germany	1.6	1.5	1.3	1.3	2.9	1.2	11.9	37.6	33.5	28.1	40.4	33.4	48.7	46.8
Iceland	~	~	~	~	~	~	~	~	~	~	~	~	~	~
Ireland	~	~	~	~	~	~	~	.9	.7	.2	.1	.7	.3	2.0
Italy	2.0	2.4	2.4	2.1	2.4	1.9	~	24.9	15.3	10.5	11.3	9.8	13.1	13.1
Netherlands	48.1	26.9	20.6	36.6	62.1	68.4	1.5	14.8	12.9	8.7	10.3	14.8	11.9	13.1
Norway	.1	~	1.9	~	~	~	~	5.4	4.8	2.4	3.3	2.8	5.5	5.1
Spain	14.0	47.4	13.1	21.9	15.2	13.3	24.7	22.7	21.2	46.5	43.9	27.9	21.4	31.9
Sweden	~	3.4	1.0	~	2.0	3.2	3.9	2.2	1.0	1.8	2.4	1.7	1.5	2.4
Switzerland	204.5	102.9	100.5	48.1	3.0	.6	1.6	8.3	6.7	4.3	4.4	3.0	3.2	9.3
United Kingdom	1.2	4.8	1.3	4.1	.7	1.0	9.5	19.2	17.9	14.3	12.7	11.7	13.5	20.8
III. Developing Countries														
Oil Exporting Countries	91.3	82.1	31.2	3.8	17.7	1.8	2.0	301.5	275.6	221.1	268.9	334.5	332.7	135.2
Algeria	7.0	10.7	3.0	~	~	~	~	~	~	.1	~	~	.1[a]	~
Iraq	~	~	~	~	~	~	~	~	.1	~	~	~	~	~
Nigeria	~	~	~	~	~	~	~	~	~	~	~	~	~	~
T. VENEZUELA	84.3	71.4	28.2	3.8	17.7	1.8	2.0	301.5	275.6	221.0	268.9	332.7	332.3	135.0
Non-Oil Developing Countries	55.1	45.8	54.6	45.7	42.8	26.1	24.5	142.5	249.6	285.9	286.0	267.2	221.4	218.2
Africa	18.6	7.1	14.4	13.0	7.1	1.4	3.2	4.9	1.7	2.6	.3	.5	3.1	1.2
Benin	.9	~	~	~	~	~	~	~	~	~	~	~	~	~
Ivory Coast	1.4	~	~	~	~	~	~	~	~	~	~	~	~	~
Kenya	~	~	~	~	~	~	~	~	~	~	~	~	~	~
Liberia	~	~	~	~	~	~	~	.2	~	~	~	~	~	~
Morocco	1.7	2.5	9.8	7.1	7.1	1.1	1.2	~	~	~	~	~	~	~
Senegal	12.9	4.3	4.2	4.7	~	.3	~	~	~	~	~	~	~	~
South Africa	~	~	~	~	~	~	~	4.6	1.2	2.5	.2	.5	2.8	.9
Togo	1.6	.3	.3	1.1	~	~	~	~	~	~	~	~	~	~
Tunisia	~	~	~	~	~	~	2.0	~	~	~	~	~	~	~
Africa not specified	~	~	~	~	~	~	~	.1	.5	.1	~	~	.2	.2
Asia	~	.1	~	6.0	~	.7	.9	10.7	7.3	7.4	8.2	8.2	13.9	24.7
Brunei	~	~	~	~	~	~	~	~	~	~	.1	.1	.1	~
China, People's Rep.	~	~	~	~	~	.1[a]	.1	~	~	~	.1	.1	.1	~
Hong Kong	~	~	~	~	~	~	~	3.3	2.7	2.1	3.0	2.2	2.1	14.6
India	~	.1	~	~	~	~	.3	.3	.1	.1	.1	.2	.7	.7
Korea	~	~	~	~	~	.3	.3	6.6	4.0	4.6	4.0	5.0	8.7	6.4
Macao	~	~	~	~	~	~	~	~	~	~	.2	.1	.1[a]	~
Pakistan	~	~	~	~	~	~	~	~	~	~	~	~	.1[a]	~
Philippines	~	~	~	6.0	.1	.1[a]	.1	.2	.1	.1	.3	.1	1.7	.1
Singapore	~	~	~	~	~	~	~	.2	.2	.3	.4	.3	.4	1.0
Thailand	~	~	~	~	~	~	~	~	.1	.1	~	~	.1[a]	1.7
Oceania not specified	~	~	~	~	~	~	~	~	~	.1	~	~	~	~

Table 2621 (Continued)

DOMINICAN REPUBLIC ABSOLUTE VALUE OF GOODS TRADED WITH SELECTED REGIONS AND COUNTRIES,[1] 1980–86

(M US)[2]

Exports FOB

Category	1980	1981	1982	1983	1984	1985	1986
III. Developing Countries (Continued)							
Non-Oil Developing Countries							
Europe							
Gibraltar	8.5	.2	13.3	.2	1.2	.1	.7
Greece	3.6	?	?	?	?	.1	.1
Hungary	?	?	?	?	?	?	?
Portugal	4.8	.2	13.3	.2	.7	.1	.6
Romania	?	?	?	?	?	.5[a]	?
Turkey	?	?	?	?	?	?	?
Yugoslavia	?	?	?	?	?	?	?
Europe not specified	.2	?	?	?	?	?	?
Middle East							
Israel	?	?	?	?	?	?	?
IV. Latin America[3]	112.3	109.8	53.1	30.3	52.1	26.1	21.7
A. ARGENTINA	.3	.1	?	.1	.2	.1	.2
Antigua and Barbuda	?	?	.3	?	.2	.1	.8
Bahamas	.4	.1	1.2	.1	.2	.8	.4
Barbados	.1	.1	?	?	.1	.2[a]	.1
Belize	?	.1	?	?	?	.2[a]	?
Bermuda	.7	6.2	?	?	.5	.2[a]	.4
C. BRAZIL	.7	.7	?	?	.3	.4	.4
D. CHILE	.9	3.7	2.3	2.8	.5	.2[a]	.4
E. COLOMBIA	.9	.5	3.0	4.2	.3	.3[a]	.3
F. COSTA RICA	.4	1.6	.7	.2	.4	.1	.1
Dominica	?	?	.1	.1	4.1	?	?
I. ECUADOR	.7	.4	.1	?	.3	.6	.7
J. EL SALVADOR	?	1.7	.2	.6	.6	1.3	1.4
Grenada	2.8	.4	.9	.1	1.0	.3	.3
Guadeloupe	.1	?	.1	?	.1	?	?
K. GUATEMALA	.2	.4	?	?	.1	.4	.4
Guiana, French	?	?	?	?	?	?	?
Guyana	.3	?	?	?	?	?	?
L. HAITI	9.2	7.1	5.1	5.6	6.4	6.1	6.4
M. HONDURAS	.3	.6	.5	1.8	1.1	.7	.8
Jamaica	.7	4.9	1.3	2.1	4.2	.6	.6
Leeward Islands	?	?	?	?	.2	.3	.3
Martinique	3.3	.1	.1	.1	.1	.1	.1
N. MEXICO	.1	.6	?	1.7	.1	.6	?
Montserrat	?	?	?	?	?	?	?
Netherlands Antilles	1.5	2.3	2.7	1.8	2.5	1.7	1.8
O. NICARAGUA	.7	.1	?	.5	.1	.8	.8
P. PANAMA	?	.5	.8	.5	?	?	?
Panama Canal Zone	?	?	?	?	?	?	?
Q. PARAGUAY	?	?	?	?	.3	.2	.2
R. PERU	.1	?	.5	?	.4	.2	.3
St. Kitts-Nevis	?	?	?	?	?	?	?
St. Lucia	1.5	1.5	1.8	.6	.3	.2	.2
St. Vincent	1.1	1.2	1.4	.6	.3	.3	.3
Suriname	1.2	2.5	.8	.6	.7	1.2	1.3
Trinidad and Tobago	.2	1.2	2.4	2.0	10.0	6.5	1.4
S. URUGUAY	.2	.1	.1	.1	.1	?	?
Windward Islands	?	?	?	?	?	?	?
America not specified	.2	.4	.5	.2	?	?	?
British West Indies	?	?	?	.7	?	?	?
French West Indies not specified	?	?	?	.3	?	?	?

Imports CIF

Category	1980	1981	1982	1983	1984	1985	1986
III. Developing Countries (Continued)							
Non-Oil Developing Countries							
Europe							
Gibraltar	1.1	.6	.5	.4	1.0	1.6	.4
Greece	?	?	?	?	.4	.4	.1
Hungary	.1	.1	.1	?	?	.6	.3
Portugal	.8	.5	.3	.3	.5	.6[a]	?
Romania	?	?	?	?	.5	.1	?
Turkey	.2	?	.2	?	.1	.1	?
Yugoslavia	?	?	?	?	?	?	?
Europe not specified	.3	.3	.3	.7	2.4	1.3	3.4
Middle East							
Israel	.3	.3	.2	.7	.7	.9	3.2
IV. Latin America[3]	427.0	515.3	496.3	545.3	589.8	534.3	323.7
A. ARGENTINA	1.2	.7	1.0	6.2	20.3	16.4	10.5
Antigua and Barbuda	?	?	?	?	.1	?	?
Bahamas	.1	.1	.8	.2	.6	.8	.9
Barbados	?	?	?	?	.2	.1[a]	.1[a]
Belize	.1	.1	.2	.1	.2	?	?
Bermuda	?	?	?	?	?	?	?
C. BRAZIL	11.7	21.6	15.0	20.1	21.5	22.6	27.6
D. CHILE	10.7	2.8	4.5	5.2	4.3	5.3[a]	7.3
E. COLOMBIA	5.4	6.1	3.8	5.1	4.4	15.0	15.8
F. COSTA RICA	2.4	2.9	1.9	2.6	2.1	2.2[a]	4.0
Dominica	?	?	?	?	?	?	.3
I. ECUADOR	1.3	1.5	1.6	1.9	1.0	1.4	1.5
J. EL SALVADOR	.7	?	?	?	?	.1	.7
Grenada	.4	?	.9	.6	1.0	.6	1.4
Guadeloupe	.1	?	.1	.1	.1	.1	.3
K. GUATEMALA	2.8	7.6	7.3	5.7	3.7	5.2	5.5
Guiana, French	.2	.4	?	?	.1	?	?
Guyana	.3	?	?	?	?	?	.1
L. HAITI	3.2	.5	2.4	10.8	10.6	5.9	6.2
M. HONDURAS	2.2	2.0	2.5	1.7	.5	.4	.4
Jamaica	1.4	2.1	1.7	3.1	2.8	1.5	1.3
Leeward Islands	?	?	.4	?	.4	?	?
Martinique	?	?	?	?	?	?	?
N. MEXICO	9.1	81.0	170.7	151.8	147.7	101.8	93.9
Montserrat	?	?	?	?	?	?	?
Netherlands Antilles	58.1	97.5	48.3	45.6	23.2	6.7	7.1
O. NICARAGUA	?	?	?	.3	.3	?	.1
P. PANAMA	9.6	9.7	11.4	13.4	11.7	3.7	.1
Panama Canal Zone	?	?	?	?	?	?	?
Q. PARAGUAY	.5	.1	.2	.2	.3	.1	?
R. PERU	.1	.1	?	?	?	.8	?
St. Kitts-Nevis	?	.2	?	?	?	?	?
St. Lucia	?	?	?	?	?	?	?
St. Vincent	?	?	.3	?	?	?	?
Suriname	.1	.2	.6	.6	1.5	.5	.5
Trinidad and Tobago	2.6	2.5	1.0	1.6	.6	1.3	5.8
S. URUGUAY	?	.1	.1	?	?	?	?
Windward Islands	?	?	?	?	?	?	?
America not specified	?	?	?	?	?	?	?
British West Indies	?	?	?	?	?	?	?
French West Indies not specified	?	?	?	?	?	?	?

Table 2621 (Continued)
DOMINICAN REPUBLIC ABSOLUTE VALUE OF GOODS TRADED WITH SELECTED REGIONS AND COUNTRIES,[1] 1980-86
(M US)[2]

Category	Exports FOB							Imports CIF						
	1980	1981	1982	1983	1984	1985	1986	1980	1981	1982	1983	1984	1985	1986
V. USSR, Eastern Europe, etc.														
G. CUBA	5.0	14.1	99.8	41.6	13.7	22.1	23.0	1.3	1.4	.2	.2	.2	.5	.6
Czechoslovakia	?	?	31.2	?	?	?	?	?	?	?	?	?	?	?
Eastern Germany	1.7	?	?	?	2.5	2.4[a]	?	.3	.4	.1	.1	.1	.1[a]	.1
North Korea	?	?	?	?	.1	?	?	?	.9	.1	.1	.1	.3	.3
Poland	?	?	?	?	?	?	?	?	?	?	?	?	?	?
USSR	3.4	14.1	68.5	41.6	11.2	21.9	23.0	.1	.2	?	?	?	?	?
EEC	98.0	113.2	79.9	89.8	96.7	98.5	82.1	149.5	123.1	135.1	144.4	116.1	128.7	154.2
VI. Percent Distribution														
Industrial Countries	84.3	88.0	77.1	88.5	91.4	93.3	76.6	67.3	61.6	58.3	55.2	50.8	54.3	48.1
Oil Exporting Countries	9.5	6.9	3.9	.5	.4	1.4	.9	21.1	19.5	17.7	21.0	26.6	22.2	18.1
Non-Oil Developing Countries	5.7	3.9	6.7	5.7	4.9	2.6	11.6	10.0	17.6	22.9	22.4	21.3	14.4	29.2
Africa	2.7	1.5	2.2	1.6	.8	.1	1.5	.3	.1	.2	#	#	.2	.2
Asia	?	?	?	.7	#	#	.4	.8	.5	.6	.6	.7	1.1	3.3
Europe	.9	?	1.6	#	.1	#	.3	.1	?	?	#	.1	.1	.1
Middle East	?	?	?	.1	.2	?	?	?	?	?	.1	.2	.1	.5
Non-industrial Western Hemisphere[3]	11.7	9.3	6.8	3.8	6.0	3.5	10.2	30.0	36.4	39.7	42.7	46.9	42.8	43.3
USSR, Eastern Europe, etc.	.5	1.2	12.3	5.2	1.6	3.0	10.9	.1	.1	?	#	#	#	.1
VII. Annual Percentage Change														
World	10.1	23.2	-31.9	-.7	8.9	-14.6	-71.6	35.0	-.8	-11.6	2.2	-1.6	-.7	-40.1
Industrial Countries	1.4	28.7	-40.3	14.1	12.5	-12.9	-76.7	37.8	-9.2	-16.4	3.3	-9.3	6.2	-46.9
Oil Exporting Countries	75.3	-10.1	-62.0	-87.8	365.8	-17.5	11.1	58.6	-8.6	-19.8	21.6	24.4	3.6	59.4
Non-Oil Developing Countries	152.0	-16.7	19.1	-16.3	-6.3	-38.6	-6.1	-7.6	75.2	14.5	#	-6.6	-15.7	-1.4
Africa	371.1	-30.2	-7.7	-25.6	-45.2	-84.5	190.4	218.7	-64.6	50.5	-90.0	78.7	559.3	-61.4
Asia	-96.2	?	-45.5	?	-98.5	619.4	35.4	65.1	-31.6	.6	11.2	-.2	69.6	77.7
Europe	806.3	-97.8	?	-98.5	500.0	-58.3	?	48.1	-42.8	-18.9	-20.0	125.0	11.1	-72.1
Middle East	?	?	?	?	?	?	?	118.7	.4	2.1	179.1	226.1	-46.0	168.5
Non-industrial Western Hemisphere[3]	66.5	-2.2	-49.8	-45.0	72.0	-50.0	-16.7	27.4	20.7	-3.7	9.9	8.2	-9.4	-39.4
USSR, Eastern Europe, etc.	?	180.2	608.5	-58.3	-67.0	60.6	4.4	81.0	11.8	-86.3	-13.2	3.3	210.5	5.1

1. DOT data may differ between countries and from IFS data because of the time it takes for an export to become an import, etc.
2. Data may be calculated from partner's reported data or estimated on basis of less than 12 months.
3. Venezuela is included in category III and Cuba in category V.
a. Five or fewer months of reported data, 7 or more months derived or extrapolated.

SOURCE: Adapted from IMF-DOT-Y, 1982, 1986, and 1987.

Table 2622

ECUADOR ABSOLUTE VALUE OF GOODS TRADED WITH SELECTED REGIONS AND COUNTRIES,[1] 1980-86
(M US)[2]

Category	Exports FOB 1980	1981	1982	1983	1984	1985	1986	Imports CIF 1980	1981	1982	1983	1984	1985	1986
I. World	2,475.8	2,540.3	2,139.9	2,227.5	2,580.1	3,056.7	2,940.4	2,253.7	2,246.3	1,988.2	1,465.2	1,767.3	1,737.5	2,073.5
II. Industrial Countries	1,317.5	1,413.0	1,149.1	1,379.1	1,775.1	1,866.8	1,858.3	1,663.4	1,650.1	1,564.6	1,088.6	1,235.1	1,324.1	1,597.8
United States	805.9	983.9	1,025.3	1,259.9	1,657.2	1,636.5	1,457.3	801.3	757.3	741.2	498.2	528.0	574.6	660.8
Canada	1.5	1.3	4.0	2.1	3.3	20.3	66.5	57.0	82.2	53.1	39.9	29.0	52.1	66.9
Australia	1.6	1.6	2.4	2.1	1.8	2.2	4.2	7.9	16.3	10.2	2.5	11.9	6.6	2.3
Japan	304.1	310.7	16.9	39.9	16.9	61.7	70.9	267.0	263.3	245.3	136.4	242.3	206.5	301.0
New Zealand	2.4	5.1	6.6	4.5	3.9	2.0	8.0	.3	.4	.1	5.1	13.8	5.4	4.8
Austria	5.2	.8	~	.3	~	1.8	7.3	6.3	9.6	5.5	9.2	7.4	6.2	12.3
Belgium–Luxembourg	23.3	22.7	21.0	15.1	7.5	7.2	9.6	12.2	14.3	10.3	8.0	20.0	13.8	13.8
Denmark	~	~	~	.1	.1	.4	2.3	6.0	9.0	19.0	2.7	9.8	4.6	6.8
Finland	1.3	2.9	2.5	1.6	2.0	2.7	9.2	3.8	1.8	1.6	4.9	3.2	1.5	2.3
France	16.3	4.2	6.4	2.5	2.8	10.9	18.9	28.1	29.8	28.5	31.8	29.2	24.6	32.4
Germany	30.8	29.3	24.0	17.3	31.2	58.6	108.3	145.9	166.4	158.8	127.4	127.4	166.9	185.8
Ireland	3.4	4.7	4.4	3.2	3.2	5.7	9.2	1.0	1.0	2.2	2.5	1.8	4.3	3.1
Italy	80.8	14.3	13.7	6.4	9.0	23.5	30.3	79.8	83.4	70.7	73.5	39.3	50.2	68.5
Netherlands	19.2	22.5	15.4	6.4	18.6	18.2	11.5	19.9	24.3	22.9	13.9	17.4	34.9	34.8
Norway	~	.1	.1	~	~	.1	.5	42.7	18.6	8.8	1.3	14.4	2.4	1.6
Spain	14.5	3.7	3.7	3.1	8.7	4.3	16.2	42.0	35.5	49.9	41.4	36.6	50.3	61.1
Sweden	.4	.4	.1	~	.1	.3	3.3	28.1	10.9	24.5	11.7	37.7	22.6	21.8
Switzerland	1.0	.4	.1	~	.4	1.0	9.2	46.5	60.2	52.1	32.2	34.2	37.5	41.2
United Kingdom	5.5	3.1	2.4	3.0	8.1	9.4	15.7	67.5	65.8	60.1	45.9	31.7	59.5	76.8
III. Developing Countries														
Oil Exporting Countries	40.9	53.0	54.3	2.2	3.2	2.1	2.3	23.7	23.6	19.8	11.0	14.1	6.1	9.3
Indonesia	~	~	~	~	~	~	~	.4	1.1	2.1	2.3	.3	2.0	.3
Iran, I.R. of	~	~	~	~	~	~	~	~	~	~	~	~	~	~
Libya	~	~	~	.2	~	~	~	~	~	~	~	~	~	~
Saudi Arab	~	~	~	~	~	~	~	~	~	2.4	2.2	11.0	~	3.5
T. VENEZUELA	40.9	53.0	54.3	2.0	3.1	1.4	2.0	23.4	22.6	15.3	6.5	2.7	1.1	5.5
Non-Oil Developing Countries	1,106.6	1,045.9	908.3	743.6	724.3	1,045.5	988.0	525.4	503.5	346.2	320.6	484.6	369.6	439.4
Africa	1.6	1.1	21.8	4.1	1.3	5.1	4.3	30.6	27.4	16.0	8.6	6.5	7.6	6.4
Morocco	~	~	~	~	~	.3[a]	.8	~	~	~	~	~	~	~
South Africa	.8	.7	.9	1.9	.6	.4[a]	.3	29.8	26.5	15.6	6.9	6.3	6.9	6.1
Tunisia	~	~	~	~	~	.4[a]	.4	~	~	~	~	~	~	~
Africa not specified	.8	.4	20.9	2.2	.7	4.0[a]	2.8	.3	.7	.5	1.6	.1	~	~
Asia	17.3	493.7	400.7	250.5	384.6	706.6	659.8	56.1	175.7	28.6	22.0	30.0	36.8	45.7
China, People's Rep.	~	~	~	~	~	2.8[a]	2.1	19.9	~	.7	.1	~	1.2[a]	5.0
Hong Kong	~	~	~	~	~	.3[a]	1.1	~	~	~	~	~	1.0[a]	1.9
India	~	~	~	~	~	~	~	~	~	~	~	~	~	~
Korea	~	~	~	~	~	178.1	287.7	~	~	~	~	~	7.8	17.1
Malaysia	.6	.2	.3	~	~	.9[a]	1.1	6.3	1.3	1.8	2.2	3.4	.7[a]	2.6
Pakistan	~	~	~	~	~	~	~	~	~	~	~	~	~	.3
Philippines	~	~	~	~	~	~	~	~	~	~	~	~	~	.1
Singapore	~	~	~	~	~	.3[a]	~	~	~	~	~	~	7.5	~
Sri Lanka	~	~	~	~	~	.3[a]	1.1	~	~	~	~	~	7.5[a]	4.2
Western Samoa	~	~	~	~	~	~	~	~	~	~	~	~	~	~
Asia not specified	16.8	493.5	400.4	250.5	384.5	523.6	366.5	29.6	173.3	24.1	17.4	26.2	17.5	13.1
Oceania not specified	~	~	~	~	~	~	~	1.0	~	~	~	~	~	~

Table 2622 (Continued)

ECUADOR ABSOLUTE VALUE OF GOODS TRADED WITH SELECTED REGIONS AND COUNTRIES,[1] 1980–86
(M US)[2]

Category	Exports FOB							Imports CIF						
	1980	1981	1982	1983	1984	1985	1986	1980	1981	1982	1983	1984	1985	1986
III. Developing Countries (Continued)														
Non-Oil Developing Countries														
Europe														
Cyprus	48.6	26.8	15.2	13.2	14.4	44.3	41.0	37.1	22.2	11.4	12.4	20.4	18.6	25.8
Greece	1.2	~	.1	~	~	.9[a]	1.1	~	~	2.9	~	~	~	.2
Hungary	19.0	11.8	7.7	2.9	8.8	29.7[a]	16.9	.3	12.2	.9	4.0	6.9	5.5[a]	7.3
Malta														
Portugal	1.8	1.6	.9	.8	.6	.6[a]	3.8	1.4	2.4	1.9	2.4	4.3	3.2[a]	2.6
Romania	1.6		1.2	.1	.8	2.8	1.9	1.3	.1		3.6	2.6	.1	
Turkey														
Yugoslavia	24.2	12.8	5.2	3.7	2.7	6.5[a]	15.2	8.3	5.7	3.1	1.6	3.1	7.0[a]	13.6
Europe not specified		.6	.1	.2	.2	2.0[a]	1.4		.2	.1		1.8	1.4[a]	1.0
Middle East														
Israel	~	~	~	.2	~	.2	~	~	~	~	~	~	18.2	18.5
Jordan	~	~	~	~	~	.2[a]	~	~	~	~	~	~	18.2[a]	15.0
Syrian Arab Rep.	~	~	~	~	~	~	~	~	~	~	~	~	~	~
IV. Latin America[3]	1,072.6	577.3	524.9	477.9	327.2	291.5	285.2	625.3	301.9	307.7	286.5	430.8	291.1	352.3
A. ARGENTINA	31.1	31.8	25.3	8.6	5.0	9.1	17.0	13.5	19.0	24.4	15.9	20.3	14.9	12.7
B. BOLIVIA	.6	.7	.2	.1		.1	.1	11.6	1.3	1.3			.1	
C. BRAZIL	34.7	65.5	155.8	2.7	1.6	2.3	7.1	49.8	83.1	77.9	73.9	224.9	123.2	161.7
D. CHILE	220.4	73.7	29.2	37.0	27.1	44.2	53.5	24.4	16.7	34.8	42.7	33.9	30.8	30.9
E. COLOMBIA	93.3	82.7	91.9	133.6	44.5	46.5	32.5	52.4	47.9	47.4	49.6	42.0	30.1	22.6
F. COSTA RICA	2.2	1.2	.4	.5	1.1	14.2	20.5	1.4	14.6	4.3	1.9	1.9	5.6	2.2
H. DOMINICAN REP.	.2	.4	.6		.3	.2	.1	1.9	.1		.1		.1	
J. EL SALVADOR	.3	.7	.3		.4	.2	.2	1.4	1.9	9.5	25.8	8.5	2.3	1.7
K. GUATEMALA	~	~	~	~	~	~	~	~	~	~	~	11.3	~	~
L. HAITI	.1				.1	.6	.4			1.3	1.3			
M. HONDURAS	~	~	~	~	~	~	24.5	~	~	~	~	~	~	~
Jamaica	13.2	16.3	2.4	.3	1.2	1.8	4.8	37.8	23.7	21.4	16.9	27.0	29.1	56.0
N. MEXICO														
Netherlands Antilles	~	~	~	~	~	.4	.3	~	~	~	~	~	~	~
O. NICARAGUA	25.2	17.3	70.1	216.9	165.5	119.7	83.8	3.9	17.2	16.5	1.1	3.7	6.3	3.4
P. PANAMA	.3	.3	.1	.1	.1	.1	.8		.1		.1	.4	.4	
Panama Canal Zone														
Q. PARAGUAY	12.9	9.6	11.3	4.5	6.3	3.9	5.1	56.8	38.0	36.0	29.1	30.1	17.9	31.6
R. PERU	1.6	100.8	32.4	.3	.1	.2	.5	.9	.8	.6	1.0	1.6	.6	2.5
Trinidad and Tobago													.7	
S. URUGUAY	595.7	123.4	50.7	71.4	70.7		32.8	146.0	15.0	18.3	15.8	21.1		21.1
America not specified	~	~	~	~	~	~	~	~	~	~	~	~	~	~
Other Latin America not specified	~	~	~	~	~	~	~	~	~	~	~	~	~	~
V. USSR Eastern Europe, etc.	17.4	13.9	16.3	9.7	8.4	11.5	8.0	16.2	36.6	13.8	19.0	8.1	8.4	6.3
Bulgaria		1.3	2.1	.4	.8	.4	.3	.8	1.6	1.1	.3	.5	.1[a]	.1
Czechoslovakia	4.8	4.8	6.3	3.4	3.3	3.0	2.1	7.3	5.7	6.4	5.8	6.5	5.6	5.6
Eastern Germany	8.7	3.2	.9	.1	.1	1.0[a]	.7	2.2	23.1	.3	9.9	.7	.1[a]	.1[a]
Poland	.8			5.4	1.3	1.1[a]	.8	25.8	1.8	2.5	.7	1.8	1.4[a]	1.1
USSR	3.9	4.6	7.0	5.9	4.3	7.1	5.0	5.8	6.1	6.1	3.0	.4	.8[a]	.6
USSR, etc., not specified	~	~	~	~	~	~	~	~	~	~	~	~	~	~
Country or area not specified		.2	.3	.1				.1	.3					
Special categories	~	~	~	~	~	~	~	~	~	~	~	1.7	~	~
EEC	196.9	106.1	92.0	57.9	89.9	139.8	226.7	403.9	431.8	427.1	349.5	317.4	412.2	485.7

Table 2622 (Continued)

ECUADOR ABSOLUTE VALUE OF GOODS TRADED WITH SELECTED REGIONS AND COUNTRIES,[1] 1980-86
(M US)[2]

Category	Exports FOB							Imports CIF						
	1980	1981	1982	1983	1984	1985	1986	1980	1981	1982	1983	1984	1985	1986
VI. Percent Distribution														
Industrial Countries	53.2	55.6	53.7	61.9	68.8	61.1	63.2	73.8	73.5	78.7	74.3	69.9	76.2	77.1
Oil Exporting Countries	1.7	2.1	2.5	2.6	3.5	4.6	#	1.1	1.7	.9	.8	.8	.5	.4
Non-Oil Developing Countries	44.4	41.2	42.4	33.1	28.0	33.9	33.6	22.2	22.3	17.3	21.8	27.3	20.9	21.2
Africa	.1	~	1.0	.2	.1	.2	.1	1.4	1.2	.8	.6	.4	.4	.3
Asia	.7	19.4	18.7	11.2	14.9	23.1	22.4	2.5	7.8	1.4	1.5	1.7	2.1	2.2
Europe	2.0	1.1	.7	.6	.6	1.4	1.4	1.6	1.0	.6	.8	1.2	1.1	1.2
Middle East	~	~	~	~	~	~	~	~	~	.1	.2	.6	1.3	.9
Non-industrial Western Hemisphere[3]	43.3	22.7	24.5	21.5	12.7	9.5	9.7	18.9	13.4	15.5	19.6	24.4	16.8	17.0
USSR, Eastern Europe, etc.	.7	.5	.8	.4	.3	.4	.3	.7	1.6	.7	1.3	.5	.5	.3
VII. Annual Percent Change														
World	17.5	2.6	-15.8	4.1	15.8	18.5	-3.8	40.9	-.3	-11.5	-26.3	20.6	-1.7	19.3
Industrial Countries	35.5	7.3	-18.7	20.0	28.7	5.2	-.5	31.5	-.8	-5.2	-30.4	13.5	7.2	20.7
Oil Exporting Countries	25.8	29.6	2.5	-946.1	40.9	-25.9	9.5	152.1	-.4	-16.1	-44.4	28.2	-37.6	52.5
Non-Oil Developing Countries	2.8	-4.8	-13.2	-18.7	-2.1	41.5	-5.5	87.9		-31.5	-6.9	50.9	-24.9	18.9
Africa	18.2	-35.8	~	-81.5	-67.5	282.4	-14.6	12.2	-10.5	-41.5	-46.7	-24.4	8.0	-9.0
Asia	27.2	~	-18.8	-37.5	53.5	83.7	-6.6	229.3	213.0	-83.7	-23.0	36.2	22.8	24.2
Europe	-46.0	-44.8	-43.3	-13.5	9.1	208.6	-7.5	-7.8	-40.1	-48.6	8.2	65.0	-8.8	38.7
Middle East	~	~	~	~	-80.0	350.0	~	~	~	~	-7.1	394.6	101.1	-16.2
Non-industrial Western Hemisphere[3]	7.1	-46.2	-9.1	-9.0	-31.5	-10.9	-2.1	89.2	-29.0	1.9	-6.9	50.4	-32.1	21.0
USSR, Eastern Europe, etc.	-40.2	-20.1	17.6	-40.4	-13.7	36.9	-30.1	74.2	126.0	-62.2	37.9	-57.4	3.9	-24.9

1. DOT data may differ between countries and from IFS data because of the time it takes for an export to become an import, etc.
2. Data may be calculated from partner's reported data or estimated on basis of less than 12 months.
3. No trade with Cuba; Venezuela is included in category III.
a. Eight, seven, or six months of reported data; four, five, or six months derived or extrapolated.

SOURCE: Adapted from IMF-DOT-Y, 1982, 1986, and 1987.

Table 2623

EL SALVADOR ABSOLUTE VALUE OF GOODS TRADED WITH SELECTED REGIONS AND COUNTRIES,[1] 1980-86
(M US)[2]

Category	Exports FOB							Imports CIF						
	1980	1981	1982	1983	1984	1985	1986	1980	1981	1982	1983	1984	1985	1986
I. World	1,070.3	796.5	699.5	741.3	717.6	679.0	788.8	971.4	981.4	856.7	891.5	977.4	961.4	1,185.6
II. Industrial Countries	710.1	376.6	505.9	506.8	506.5	552.2	654.6	348.3	460.3	398.2	452.7	488.6	499.3	747.2
United States	439.3	136.5	248.1	286.1	269.7	327.4	364.7	194.2	249.8	233.1	289.6	325.2	325.8	569.8
Canada	8.8	9.1	10.8	13.1	11.6	14.9	46.2	11.5	17.2	13.5	13.5	11.4	9.3	8.9
Australia	~	.1	.1	~	~	~	~	1.2	1.9	.7	.1	.1	~	.1
Japan	43.2	36.1	23.4	36.6	39.7	34.4	31.0	37.5	33.5	26.8	31.3	41.9	49.6	36.6
New Zealand	~	~	~	~	.6	~	~	.2	3.5	~	.4	.9	1.0	8.6
Austria	~	~	~	~	~	~	17.7	.2	.9	1.2	1.0	.9	1.0	2.2
Belgium	6.2	.5	.9	2.1	4.6	11.4	3.5	6.6	9.4	9.1	16.4	7.6	5.9	7.7
Denmark	~	~	.4	~	~	~	.5	3.3	2.6	1.8	1.2	1.7	1.2	2.0
Finland	~	~	~	~	~	~	1.5	4.7	.2	.2	2.1	.8	3.5	1.0
France	9.8	8.2	.5	6.6	.6	1.5	18.2	8.1	30.8	19.5	9.1	3.7	4.9	9.5
Germany	149.0	173.8	204.9	139.9	161.2	142.4	129.7	24.4	36.8	39.8	36.3	43.1	42.0	37.4
Iceland	~	~	~	~	~	~	.1	.8	5.2	.7	1.2	.1	.1	4.3
Ireland	~	~	~	~	~	~	~	~	~	~	~	~	~	~
Italy	12.2	2.6	7.7	2.9	.5	1.3	4.8	13.0	15.4	6.9	4.8	6.9	6.3	14.3
Netherlands	28.8	5.2	2.3	2.3	.6	.9	6.9	14.8	24.8	19.4	17.8	15.1	15.4	11.2
Norway	~	~	~	~	~	~	1.3	.1	.1	.1	.2	.1	1.9	3.3
Spain	5.4	~	5.2	16.7	15.2	15.1	20.1	9.8	12.0	6.6	8.7	9.4	12.5	7.7
Sweden	.4	~	~	.1	.6	1.0	2.5	3.3	3.5	10.7	3.9	5.5	4.2	3.5
Switzerland	3.3	1.5	.7	.3	~	.1	4.1	3.6	3.4	2.8	6.1	3.8	4.1	8.0
United Kingdom	3.8	3.0	.9	.3	1.6	1.6	1.8	11.1	9.2	5.3	9.2	11.4	11.4	11.1
III. Developing Countries	.4	.9	~	~	.1	.1	~	244.5	40.4	76.1	69.6	66.0	72.7	61.6
Oil Exporting Countries	.4	.8	~	~	.1	.1	~	244.5	40.4	76.1	69.6	66.0	72.7	61.6
Indonesia	~	~	~	~	~	~	~	~	~	~	~	~	~	~
Iran, I.R. of	~	.8	~	~	~	~	~	~	~	~	~	~	~	~
T. VENEZUELA	.4	.8	~	~	.1	.1[b]	~	244.5	40.4	76.1	69.6	66.0	72.7	61.6
Non-Oil Developing Countries	307.5	229.3	187.4	206.1	182.5	116.6	123.6	366.9	396.7	370.9	358.4	403.3	366.2	352.5
Africa	~	.1	~	.1	1.4	1.3	~	.3	.3	.2	.4	.3	.3	.2
Morocco	~	.1	~	.1	~	~	~	.1	.3	.1	.1	~	~	~
South Africa	.1	.1	~	.1	1.4	1.3[c]	~	.2	.2	.1	.3	.3	.2	.2
Asia	.1	2.3	1.5	7.6	.3	.3	.8	2.2	3.2	1.6	5.4	3.6	6.1	4.1
Bangladesh	~	~	~	~	~	~	~	~	~	~	~	~	~	~
China, People's Rep.	~	~	~	~	.2	2.2	.2	~	~	~	~	~	6.3[a]	1.8
Hong Kong	.1	.3	1.5	2.1	.2	.1	.3	1.6	1.1	1.2	.9	1.7	2.3[a]	1.7
India	~	~	~	~	~	~	~	.3	1.4	.4	.9	~	2.6	~
Korea	1.1	1.1	~	5.3	~	~	~	~	~	~	3.1	~	~	~
Malaysia	~	.1	~	~	~	~	~	~	~	~	~	~	~	~
Pakistan	~	~	~	~	~	~	~	~	~	~	~	~	~	~
Philippines	~	~	~	~	~	~	.3	~	.6	.4	~	~	~	~
Singapore	~	.6	~	.2	.2	.2	~	1.1	~	~	1.1	1.9	3.3	~
Sri Lanka	~	.1	~	.2	.2	~	.2	.2	.1	~	.2	~	.2[a]	.5
Thailand	~	~	~	~	~	~	~	~	~	~	~	~	~	.1
Europe	1.6	5.5	1.1	8.9	2.2	.4	.3	1.6	1.0	.3	.8	.9	1.3	1.3
Hungary	~	.1	~	~	~	~	~	.4	.1	.2	.8	.9	.2[a]	~
Portugal	1.6	3.1	1.1	1.8	.9	.3[a]	~	1.6	.3	.3	.8	.9	3.3	1.3
Romania	~	2.4	~	~	~	~	~	.2	.3	.3	~	~	.2[a]	~
Yugoslavia	~	~	~	~	~	~	.2	~	~	~	~	~	~	~
Middle East	~	.2	~	~	~	.1	.2	~	.2	~	~	~	.7	.7
Israel	~	.2	~	~	~	.1[a]	~	~	.2	~	~	~	.7[a]	.7

Table 2623 (Continued)

EL SALVADOR ABSOLUTE VALUE OF GOODS TRADED WITH SELECTED REGIONS AND COUNTRIES,[1] 1980–86 (M US)[2]

Category	Exports FOB							Imports CIF						
	1980	1981	1982	1983	1984	1985	1986	1980	1981	1982	1983	1984	1985	1986
IV. Latin America[3]	306.2	222.4	184.9	189.6	178.6	116.4	122.5	608.5	432.3	444.8	421.5	464.4	431.4	407.7
A. ARGENTINA	.1	.1	~	.7	1.5	.6	.6	2.2	.4	6.0	1.5	2.9	2.3	2.4
Bahamas	~	~	~	~	~	~	~	~	.2	~	~	~	~	~
Barbados	~	~	~	~	~	1.7a	~	~	~	.1	~	.1	.1b	~
Belize	.6	.7	.6	.6	.7	.4	.5	~	~	~	~	~	~	.1
C. BRAZIL	~	~	~	~	~	~	~	3.2	3.5	2.4	3.2	3.9	5.9	6.2
D. CHILE	.2	.1	.1	~	.1	~	~	1.5	.5	.1	.5	.3	.3	~
E. COLOMBIA	.1	~	~	~	.1	3.4	3.6	1.5	2.0	1.6	4.5	4.5	8.1	8.5
F. COSTA RICA	67.5	34.4	21.5	22.1	27.0	24.7	25.9	55.4	46.7	35.9	42.6	46.7	54.1	56.8
H. DOMINICAN REP.	.5	.8	1.3	1.8	1.5	1.3	1.4	~	~	~	.1	.1	~	~
I. ECUADOR	.4	.1	~	~	~	~	.1	.3	.2	.3	~	~	.1	.1
K. GUATEMALA	173.6	140.8	131.6	123.1	117.3	61.4	64.5	253.6	247.5	209.9	172.3	187.5	149.6	157.1
L. HAITI	~	~	.1	.1	.1	~	~	~	.3	.3	~	~	.3	.3
M. HONDURAS	~	1.4	3.8	7.9	7.9	6.4	6.7	~	~	8.2	15.2	16.7	10.6	11.1
Jamaica	~	~	~	~	~	~	~	~	~	~	~	~	~	1.6
N. MEXICO	.5	1.1	.1	1.9	12.1	.1	.1	11.8	50.6	70.6	82.3	97.4	89.5	62.7
Netherlands Antilles	1.6	4.7	.2	~	~	.1	~	1.6	1.4	1.0	1.0	1.6	1.7	1.8
O. NICARAGUA	54.7	30.0	17.3	15.0	5.1	3.2	3.4	11.4	10.2	6.8	3.5	3.2	2.4	2.5
P. PANAMA	7.3	8.1	8.2	15.9	5.3	14.8	15.5	20.6	25.7	23.9	23.7	31.4	30.6	32.1
Panama Canal Zone	~	~	~	~	~	~	~	~	~	~	~	~	~	~
Q. PARAGUAY	~	~	~	~	~	~	~	~	~	~	~	~	~	~
R. PERU	1.8	2.6	1.4	1.2	2.1	2.9	2.4	1.8	2.6	1.4	1.2	2.1	2.9	2.4
Suriname	~	~	~	~	~	~	.3	~	~	~	~	~	~	~
Trinidad and Tobago	~	~	~	.6	~	~	~	.3	.2	.2	.2	~	~	.1
S. URUGUAY	.3	.2	~	~	~	~	~	.3	.2	.2	~	.1	~	~
Other Latin America not specified	~	~	~	~	~	~	~	~	~	~	~	~	~	~
V. USSR, Eastern Europe, etc.	.4	.4	~	.7	1.4	~	~	.4	.4	.5	.2	.7	.3	.4
Czechoslovakia	.4	.4	~	.7	~	~	~	.4	.4	.5	.2	.6	.3	.4
Poland	~	~	~	7.0	1.4	1.3b	~	~	~	~	~	~	~	~
USSR	~	~	~	~	~	~	~	~	~	~	~	~	~	~
Country or area not specified	19.8	179.1	5.0	15.2	28.3	26.9b	8.6	6.3	77.0	5.3	3.9	10.8	10.3b	13.9
EEC	209.7	193.4	223.9	172.4	185.2	174.2	185.6	92.2	146.5	109.6	105.5	99.8	101.0	106.5
VI. Percent Distribution														
Industrial Countries	66.3	47.3	72.3	68.4	70.6	81.3	83.0	35.9	46.9	46.5	50.8	50.0	51.9	63.0
Oil Exporting Countries	~	.1	~	~	#	#	#	25.2	4.1	8.9	7.8	6.8	5.2	5.2
Non-Oil Developing Countries	28.7	28.8	26.8	26.9	25.2	21.7	15.7	37.8	40.4	43.3	40.2	41.3	34.2	29.7
Africa	~	.3	.2	1.0	.2	.2	.1	.2	.3	#	#	#	#	.3
Asia	.2	.7	.2	1.2	#	.3	~	.2	.3	#	.6	.4	.6	.1
Europe	~	~	~	~	#	#	~	.2	.1	#	.1	#	~	.1
Middle East	~	~	~	~	~	~	~	.1	.1	#	.1	.1	.1	.1
Non-industrial Western Hemisphere[3]	28.6	27.9	26.4	25.6	24.9	17.1	15.5	62.6	44.1	51.9	47.3	47.5	44.9	34.4
USSR, Eastern Europe, etc.	~	~	~	.7	.2	.2	~	~	~	.1	~	.1	.1	~

Table 2623 (Continued)

EL SALVADOR ABSOLUTE VALUE OF GOODS TRADED WITH SELECTED REGIONS AND COUNTRIES,[1] 1980–86
(M US)[2]

Category	Exports FOB							Imports CIF						
	1980	1981	1982	1983	1984	1985	1986	1980	1981	1982	1983	1984	1985	1986
VII. Annual Percent Change														
World	-12.5	-25.6	-12.2	6.0	-3.2	-5.4	16.2	-6.6	1.0	-12.7	4.1	9.6	-1.6	23.3
Industrial Countries	-22.0	-47.0	34.3	.2	-.1	9.0	18.5	-38.9	32.1	-13.5	13.7	7.9	2.2	49.7
Oil Exporting Countries	-17.9	103.1	~	~	~	#	#	112.0	-83.5	88.4	-8.5	-5.2	-10.0	-15.3
Non-Oil Developing Countries	8.8	-25.4	-18.3	6.2	-9.0	-3.4	6.0	7.2	8.1	-6.5	-3.4	12.5	-3.0	-3.7
Africa	~	~	~	~	~	.45	~	-49.3	-1.8	-43.2	72.9	.3	-33.7	5.1
Asia	-96.5	#	-35.1	413.7	-95.6	-16.2	182.0	-70.0	46.7	-49.6	229.3	-32.1	66.5	-32.2
Europe	33.3	235.6	-79.6	695.0	-74.9	-59.3	~	-37.1	155.6	-68.9	147.8	14.5	40.0	4.4
Middle East	~	~	~	~	~	~	~	~	~	~	~	~	~	~
Non-industrial Western Hemisphere[3]	10.3	-27.4	-16.9	2.5	-5.8	-34.8	5.2	35.8	-28.9	2.9	-5.2	10.2	-7.1	-5.5
USSR, Eastern Europe, etc.	~	~	~	~	-82.2	-5.0	~	-50.3	4.5	19.3	-48.7	183.2	-50.8	5.0

1. DOT data may differ between countries and from IFS data because of the time it takes for an export to become an import, etc.
2. Data may be calculated from partner's reported data or estimated on basis of less than 12 months.
3. No trade with Cuba; Venezuela is included in category III.
a. Data derived from partner country for the entire year.
b. Data extrapolated for the entire year.
c. Five or fewer months of reported data; seven or more months derived or extrapolated.

SOURCE: Adapted from IMF-DOT-Y, 1982, 1986, and 1987.

Table 2624

GUATEMALA ABSOLUTE VALUE OF GOODS TRADED WITH SELECTED REGIONS AND COUNTRIES,[1] 1980-86
(M US)[2]

Category	Exports FOB							Imports CIF						
	1980	1981	1982	1983	1984	1985	1986	1980	1981	1982	1983	1984	1985	1986
I. World	1,517.5	1,226.1	1,119.8	1,158.9	1,306.1	1,196.4	1,471.2	1,597.7	1,673.5	1,388.0	1,135.0	1,290.1	1,191.5	1,106.1
II. Industrial Countries	882.8	566.7	588.5	668.5	710.4	667.6	940.1	949.2	1,013.8	799.1	594.9	672.6	698.8	678.6
United States	419.9	223.3	306.0	405.1	435.5[a]	407.0[a]	588.0	551.8	565.9	432.3	365.3	414.2[a]	445.1[a]	439.7
Canada	6.0	4.2	4.8	5.2	28.2[a]	19.1[a]	29.0	20.2	17.2	18.8	18.5	18.6[a]	13.7[a]	11.8
Australia	.1	~	~	~	.5[a]	2.2[a]	.4	1.2	4.0	.2	1.2	.1[a]	.1[a]	.1
Japan	42.0	59.6	55.5	39.4	60.5[a]	36.3[a]	52.9	128.5	129.2	72.7	55.7	64.5[a]	56.5[a]	50.4
New Zealand	.1	~	.1	.1	.1[a]	~	~	.9	1.1	.3	.3	.7[a]	.8[a]	1.0
Austria	.3	.2	.6	1.6	8.0[a]	9.2[a]	12.8	1.9	2.2	2.6	2.1	4.2[a]	3.2[a]	3.5
Belgium-Luxembourg	21.6	12.1	10.1	10.2	5.8[a]	4.0[a]	7.5	7.9	13.9	8.8	5.7	5.1[a]	5.7[a]	10.8
Denmark	1.7	47.9	.9	.6	1.2[a]	1.9[a]	5.2	4.3	4.2	3.3	3.2	2.6[a]	2.7[a]	3.3
Finland	29.5	14.2	15.2	14.5	15.8[a]	13.6[a]	20.2	~	~	2.6	.2	.4[a]	1.8[a]	.5
France	13.5	15.1	8.4	37.9	8.5[a]	10.8[a]	12.3	27.3	30.4	19.2	16.8	16.1[a]	17.4[a]	15.4
Germany	126.0	100.0	78.2	62.4	35.6[a]	41.7[a]	62.6	86.7	107.8	77.1	56.6	64.8[a]	65.1[a]	59.2
Iceland	.1	~	~	~	.1[a]	.7[a]	.1	~	~	~	~	~	~	~
Ireland	~	~	~	~	~	~	~	1.9	1.5	6.5	4.6	3.2[a]	3.1[a]	5.1
Italy	73.3	31.8	41.1	34.6	48.7[a]	71.1[a]	54.8	21.5	24.1	18.0	11.6	8.9[a]	10.7[a]	17.2
Netherlands	63.1	33.5	38.5	31.3	17.6[a]	13.8[a]	17.9	13.8	13.4	13.9	5.7	19.7[a]	12.8[a]	11.8
Norway	2.5	3.9	3.3	1.1	4.8[a]	4.5[a]	3.6	.6	2.3	3.8	2.0	2.4[a]	3.2[a]	2.9
Spain	7.2	2.1	4.3	4.0	5.8[a]	2.2[a]	6.0	20.7	32.8	75.9	13.1	13.6[a]	21.5[a]	17.0
Sweden	2.6	3.2	1.5	4.4	5.8[a]	6.0[a]	27.2	4.5	5.6	5.0	3.1	3.7[a]	3.4[a]	3.5
Switzerland	6.7	1.1	1.4	3.0	16.0[a]	17.4[a]	28.0	18.4	27.1	20.6	16.5	14.3[a]	12.8[a]	10.5
United Kingdom	66.7	14.2	18.6	12.9	11.9[a]	5.9[a]	10.8	36.9	30.5	17.0	12.7	15.6[a]	19.3[a]	14.9
III. Developing Countries														
Oil Exporting Countries	11.6	14.6	23.0	15.0	99.6	81.3	61.6	159.0	113.4	82.5	102.2	102.3	81.4	45.2
Algeria	.9	2.0	.8	.2	1.9[a]	~	.4	~	~	~	~	~	~	~
Indonesia	~	~	~	~	.1[a]	1.6	1.2	~	~	~	~	~	~	~
Kuwait	~	~	~	~	~	~	~	~	.3	.9	.1	.2[a]	.5	.6
Oman	~	~	~	~	.1[a]	.7[a]	.4	~	~	~	~	~	~	~
Saudi Arabia	9.3	10.2	15.9	14.7	85.4[a]	72.6	54.4	~	~	~	~	~	~	~
T. VENEZUELA	1.3	2.4	6.3	.1	5.0	1.0	1.0	159.0	113.4	82.4	102.2	102.3	81.4	45.1
Non-Oil Developing Countries	613.7	613.1	481.4	452.1	458.5	416.2	136.5	462.8	508.1	481.3	423.3	496.7	391.8	362.0
Africa	.3	5.3	3.3	4.1	3.0	4.6	2.9	.2	.3	.9	.2	.2	.6	.6
Ethiopia	~	5.1	~	~	~	~	~	~	~	~	~	~	~	~
Morocco	~	~	.5	2.1	.5[a]	.6	.7	~	~	~	~	~	~	~
South Africa	~	.2	1.4	.4	.7[a]	.7	~	~	.3	.9	.1	.2[a]	.5	.6
Tunisia	~	~	~	.4	.4[b]	1.6[a]	.4	~	~	~	~	~	~	~
Africa not specified	.2	~	1.4	1.6	1.7	1.7	1.8	~	~	~	~	~	~	~
Asia	83.8	63.3	28.5	11.9	21.9	17.4	24.2	17.1	16.7	10.8	10.4	14.6	13.6	13.1
China, People's Rep.	62.5	44.5	15.1	.6	3.2[a]	.2[a]	~	2.0	1.3	.7	1.6	2.3[a]	1.5[a]	1.3
Hong Kong	1.0	1.1	.5	.2	.2[a]	.4[a]	.2	4.5	5.2	3.3	2.5	3.4[a]	4.3[a]	3.6
India	.1	.1	.2	.3	.4[b]	.4	.4	.2	.1	.1	.1	.1[b]	.1[b]	.1
Korea	~	2.5	1.2	.6	4.8[a]	1.0	1.1	7.6	7.8	3.3	3.6	7.1[a]	6.1	6.4
Malaysia	.1	~	~	~	~	~	.2	~	~	~	~	~	~	~
Pakistan	.1	.4	.1	.2	.2[a]	.1	.1	~	~	~	~	~	~	~
Philippines	.2	.6	.6	.2	~	~	.1	.1	.1	~	.1	~	.9	.1
Singapore	1.2	~	~	.1	.3[a]	.1	~	.9	1.1	.9	.7	.3[a]	.2	.2
Sri Lanka	~	~	~	~	~	~	~	.2	.5	.2	.4	.3[a]	.1[a]	.2
Thailand	.6	1.4	.3	~	.5[a]	4.9[a]	8.5	~	~	~	~	~	~	~
Asia not specified	17.2	10.9	9.8	9.4	10.3	10.3	10.8	1.5	.6	2.2	1.3	1.5	1.5	1.5

Table 2624 (Continued)

GUATEMALA ABSOLUTE VALUE OF GOODS TRADED WITH SELECTED REGIONS AND COUNTRIES,[1] 1980–86
(M US)[2]

Category	Exports FOB							Imports CIF						
	1980	1981	1982	1983	1984	1985	1986	1980	1981	1982	1983	1984	1985	1986
III. Developing Countries (Continued)														
Non-Oil Developing Countries														
Europe														
Greece	6.4	16.9	3.9	2.9	4.8	6.7	8.6	6.7	4.3	3.0	.8	1.2	6.0	4.5
Hungary	~	15.0	~	.9	~	~	~	~	.1	~	~	.1[a]	.1[a]	.1
Malta	~	~	~	~	~	.4[a]	.4	~	~	~	~	~	~	~
Portugal	6.0	1.0	2.8	1.8	4.7[a]	6.2[a]	6.5	1.4	4.1	2.8	.7	1.0[a]	3.8[a]	4.0
Romania	~	.3	.6	.1	~	~	~	~	~	~	~	~	~	~
Turkey	.4	~	~	.1	~	~	1.3	5.1	.1	.1	.1	.1[b]	2.0	.3
Yugoslavia	~	.6	.5	.1	.1[b]	.1[b]	.1	.1	.1	.1	.1	.1[b]	.1[b]	.1
Europe not specified	~	~	~	~	~	~	~	~	~	~	~	~	~	~
Middle East														
Bahrain	39.2	33.1	46.3	34.8	116.6	105.5	86.7	~	~	~	~	~	~	~
Egypt	3.6	.2	1.2	.1	1.4[a]	1.4[b]	1.5	~	~	~	~	~	~	~
Israel	.4	.5	.1	.1	.2[a]	1.2	1.3	1.5	.5	.6	.4	4.0[a]	1.0[a]	2.6
Jordan	~	~	~	~	.4[a]	.4[a]	.5	~	~	~	~	~	~	~
Lebanon	~	~	~	~	~	~	.3	~	~	~	~	~	~	~
Syrian Arab Rep.	~	~	~	~	~	~	~	~	~	~	~	~	~	~
Middle East not specified	25.8	22.2	29.1	19.9	21.9	21.9	23.0	~	~	~	~	~	~	~
IV. Latin America[3]	495.6	509.1	422.5	413.6	411.9	363.3	375.6	596.3	599.7	548.5	513.7	579.0	452.1	386.1
A. ARGENTINA	.4	.2	1.1	.5	.4[a]	.2[b]	.2	3.0	2.3	3.9	2.6	2.2[a]	3.1[c]	3.0
Bahamas	~	~	~	~	~	~	~	~	~	~	~	~	~	~
Barbados	~	~	~	~	~	~	~	~	~	~	~	~	~	~
B. BOLIVIA	.6	3.0	1.4	1.3	~	.6[a]	.6	~	.1	~	~	~	~	~
Belize	.6	.5	.1	~	1.4	1.4	1.4	~	~	~	1.3	.8[a]	.8[b]	.8
C. BRAZIL	2.1	.2	.2	6.8	~	~	~	13.9	17.1	14.6	6.6	15.8[a]	13.6[a]	14.3
D. CHILE	.3	~	.4	~	~	~	~	.6	3.9	2.1	2.2	5.1[a]	5.7	6.0
E. COLOMBIA	1.2	.8	4.8	.2	.5[a]	1.2	1.2	4.3	4.7	4.0	4.6	~	~	~
F. COSTA RICA	89.8	57.5	51.6	52.4	54.0[a]	42.2	44.3	65.3	57.3	58.0	82.0	83.5[a]	43.1	37.1
H. DOMINICAN REP.	6.0	7.7	7.2	5.6	3.7[a]	3.3[c]	5.5	.2	.2	.2	.1	.2	.1[c]	.4
I. ECUADOR	1.2	1.6	5.0	16.9	10.3[a]	8.8	6.6	.3	.4	1.3	.2	.4[a]	.4[c]	.2
J. EL SALVADOR	194.0	230.9	190.3	163.4	170.5[a]	136.0	142.8	99.3	102.8	117.5	103.8	129.0[a]	67.5	70.9
Guadeloupe	~	~	~	~	~	~	~	~	~	~	~	~	~	~
L. HAITI	.4	.6	.3	.2	.2[b]	.2[b]	.2	.2	.1	.1	.1	.1[b]	.1[b]	.1
M. HONDURAS	60.6	49.7	50.6	54.3	59.7	59.7	62.7	36.9	18.8	25.3	26.9	29.6	29.6	31.1
Jamaica	.9	.7	.5	2.8	4.1[a]	2.3[a]	3.2	.2	.1	.9	3.2	2.2[a]	1.3[a]	1.4
Martinique	~	~	~	~	~	~	~	~	~	~	~	~	~	~
N. MEXICO	23.3	65.1	35.1	14.8	9.1[a]	16.0	12.0	58.9	128.3	102.2	89.0	112.9[a]	111.3	77.9
Netherlands Antilles	.2	.1	.4	13.4	14.7	14.7	15.5	121.1	99.3	98.2	68.6	75.4	75.4	79.2
O. NICARAGUA	96.4	69.1	44.9	50.8	55.9	55.9	58.7	16.4	15.1	14.3	12.4	13.6	13.6	14.3
P. PANAMA	15.9	16.9	21.9	16.2	15.8[a]	15.5	16.2	6.6	5.7	4.4	5.5	3.3[a]	3.6	3.4
Panama Canal Zone	~	~	~	~	~	~	~	~	~	~	~	~	~	~
Q. PARAGUAY	~	~	~	~	~	~	~	.6	.7	.5	~	1.2[b]	1.0[b]	.2
R. PERU	.2	.3	.1	13.7	4.7	9.9[b]	.3	.2	.3	~	1.3	~	~	~
Suriname	~	~	~	~	~	~	~	~	~	~	~	~	~	~
Trinidad and Tobago	.2	1.2	.2	.1	1.5[a]	2.2[a]	3.0	9.4	29.3	18.3	2.4	2.7[a]	1.5[a]	.8
S. URUGUAY	~	~	~	~	~	~	~	.1	~	.1	~	~	~	~

Table 2624 (Continued)

GUATEMALA ABSOLUTE VALUE OF GOODS TRADED WITH SELECTED REGIONS AND COUNTRIES,[1] 1980–86
(M US)[2]

Category	Exports FOB							Imports CIF						
	1980	1981	1982	1983	1984	1985	1986	1980	1981	1982	1983	1984	1985	1986
V. USSR, Eastern Europe, etc.	.9	5.1	19.1	19.9	21.9	21.9	23.0	4.1	4.2	8.4	3.5	3.9	3.9	4.1
Bulgaria	~	~	~	~	~	~	~	~	~	~	~	~	~	~
Czechoslovakia	.8	3.7	8.4	1.0	1.1b	1.1	1.2	1.5	1.9	1.3	.7	.8b	.8	.9
Eastern Germany	~	~	~	~	~	~	~	~	~	~	~	~	~	~
Poland	~	~	~	~	~	~	~	~	~	~	~	~	~	~
USSR	~	~	~	~	~	~	~	~	~	~	~	~	~	~
USSR, etc., not specified	.1	1.4	10.7	18.9	20.8	20.8	21.8	2.6	2.3	7.0	2.8	3.0	3.0	3.2
Country or area not specified	1.8	2.4	1.3	3.0	3.3	3.3	3.5	13.1	20.3	5.6	.6	.7b	.7	.7
EEC	379.1	272.8	203.0	196.7	139.8	157.8	183.8	222.4	262.8	242.7	130.7	150.6	162.0	158.9
VI. Percent Distribution														
Industrial Countries	58.2	46.2	52.6	57.7	54.4	55.8	63.9	59.4	60.6	57.6	52.4	52.1	58.6	61.3
Oil Exporting Countries	.8	1.2	2.1	1.3	7.3	6.1	4.2	9.9	6.8	5.9	9.0	7.2	6.7	4.1
Non-Oil Developing Countries	40.4	50.0	42.9	39.0	35.3	35.9	29.7	29.0	30.4	34.7	37.3	38.6	36.6	32.7
Africa	~	.4	.3	.4	.2	.4	.2	~	~	.1	~	~	~	.1
Asia	5.5	5.0	2.5	1.0	1.7	1.5	1.6	1.1	1.0	.8	.9	1.1	1.1	1.2
Europe	.4	1.4	.4	.2	.4	.6	.6	.4	.3	.2	.1	.1	.5	.4
Middle East	2.6	2.7	4.1	3.0	8.9	8.8	5.9	.1	~	~	~	.3	.1	.2
Non-industrial Western Hemisphere[3]	32.7	41.5	37.7	35.7	31.5	30.4	25.5	37.3	35.8	39.5	45.3	44.9	37.9	34.9
USSR, Eastern Europe, etc.	.1	.4	1.7	1.7	1.7	1.8	1.6	.3	.2	.6	.3	.3	.3	.4
VII. Annual Percent Change														
World	22.0	-19.2	-8.7	3.5	12.7	-8.4	23.0	6.2	4.7	-17.1	-18.2	13.7	-7.6	-7.2
Industrial Countries	14.1	-35.8	3.8	13.6	6.3	-6.0	40.8	4.6	6.8	-21.2	-25.6	13.1	3.9	-2.9
Oil Exporting Countries	2.7	25.8	57.5	-34.8	531.3	-21.6	-24.2	44.1	-28.6	-27.2	23.9	-9.9	-10.0	-44.5
Non-Oil Developing Countries	36.2	-.1	-21.5	-6.1	1.4	-5.2	4.9	5.7	9.8	-5.3	-12.1	16.3	-6.2	-7.6
Africa	744.1	~	-38.6	25.5	-26.5	54.5	-37.1	-77.0	45.3	179.2	-78.8	12.1	185.8	5.0
Asia	17.0	-24.4	-55.0	-58.3	84.1	-20.6	39.6	25.6	-2.3	-35.5	-4.0	41.0	-7.0	-3.2
Europe	-3.1	162.9	-76.6	-26.8	66.2	40.0	28.2	267.6	-35.7	-29.6	-72.7	42.8	405.8	-24.0
Middle East	-7.2	-15.5	39.9	-24.9	235.1	-9.5	-17.8	101.9	-61.3	1.2	-12.1	670.4	-73.7	154.7
Non-industrial Western Hemisphere[3]	45.1	2.7	-17.0	-2.1	-.4	-11.8	3.4	12.3	.6	-8.5	-6.3	12.7	-21.9	-14.6
USSR, Eastern Europe, etc.	-58.1	458.8	278.6	4.1	10.0	-5.0	5.0	-7.3	1.0	100.7	-58.0	10.0	-5.0	5.0

1. DOT data may differ between countries and from IFS data because of the time it takes for an export to become an import, etc.
2. Data may be calculated from partner's reported data or estimated on basis of less than 12 months.
3. No trade with Cuba; Venezuela is included in category III.
a. Data derived from partner country for the entire year.
b. Data extrapolated for the entire year.
c. Five or fewer months of reported data; seven or more months derived or extrapolated.

SOURCE: Adapted from IMF-DOT-Y, 1982, 1986, and 1987.

Table 2625

HAITI ABSOLUTE VALUE OF GOODS TRADED WITH SELECTED REGIONS AND COUNTRIES,[1] 1980–86

(M US)[2]

Category	Exports FOB							Imports CIF						
	1980	1981	1982	1983	1984	1985	1986	1980	1981	1982	1983	1984	1985	1986
I. World	225.74	153.10	376.48	420.36	448.26	448.83	461.21	354.18	375.70	536.89	630.89	685.49	698.95	653.60
II. Industrial Countries[4]	220.01	149.14	367.94	403.95	433.79	440.07	448.32	270.94	292.21	445.27	521.62	577.17	588.82	555.00
United States	127.75	112.53	296.00	319.73	358.64	369.00	355.09	188.95	195.75	328.46	402.49	461.23	435.49	426.03
Canada	3.49	1.58	6.97	8.72	12.95	7.01	8.83	17.58	24.80	20.96	13.61	16.15	20.83	16.57
Australia	.08	.49	.49	.42	.59	.46	.31	.04	.13	.01	.01	.71	.27	.06
Japan	.41	~	2.77	1.89	1.54	2.41	2.36	19.32	23.81	28.04	27.49	32.73	41.26	30.14
New Zealand	~	.01	.01	.02	.02	~	.01	.22	.65	.88	.87	.41	1.22	.39
Austria	.11	.01	.14	.14	.56	.32	~	.16	.06	.96	.64	1.46	1.00	~
Belgium–Luxembourg	14.99	6.01	8.98	8.56	8.60	9.79	10.44	2.48	1.19	3.88	3.64	3.27	3.38	3.52
Denmark	.95	.58	.81	1.48	.77	.67	1.82	1.29	1.24	.77	.87	1.21	.86	1.58
Finland	~	.04	.97	1.13	.80	.70	.25	.13	.28	.25	.25	.27	.27	.33
France	29.88	13.42	18.15	20.47	14.84	14.96	24.24	12.26	10.07	15.34	25.79	18.60	27.06	26.97
Germany	6.74	4.11	12.02	16.41	15.38	12.10	13.45	8.28	7.75	12.52	15.09	12.77	13.14	14.19
Iceland	.01	~	~	~	~	.07	~	.03	.01	~	~	~	~	~
Ireland	~	1.41	.58	.02	.09	~	.03	~	~	.25	.67	.42	.48	.27
Italy	28.67	7.69	11.33	17.63	12.62	16.47	20.83	2.57	1.39	7.53	8.26	6.58	15.20	5.09
Netherlands	3.96	1.96	1.49	3.61	1.91	2.86	3.91	5.87	13.28	10.00	8.39	9.99	12.88	12.79
Norway	.41	.18	.04	.08	.09	.06	.17	1.49	1.79	2.38	1.50	1.54	2.14	2.04
Spain	.12	.04	.99	.73	1.24	.48	3.49	2.02	1.45	1.08	1.02	1.28	2.21	3.04
Sweden	1.06	.12	.11	.13	.05	.08	.26	.76	.64	1.63	1.42	.52	.79	.66
Switzerland	.19	.06	1.96	.49	1.43	.85	1.63	1.93	4.05	3.14	2.66	2.37	3.06	3.03
United Kingdom	1.20	.84	4.14	2.28	1.67	1.80	1.21	5.56	4.02	7.22	6.97	5.65	7.29	8.31
III. Developing Countries														
Oil Exporting Countries														
Nigeria	.53	.66	1.0	2.0	.62	.50	4.0	.29	~	~	~	3.3	14.3	4.0
Saudi Arabia	~	.54a	~	~	~	~	~	~	~	~	~	~	~	~
T. VENEZUELA	.43	.47	1.0	2.0	.62b	.50b	4.0	.21	~	~	~	3.3	14.3	4.0
Non-Oil Developing Countries	5.21	3.0	6.69	14.12	13.93	8.42	8.35	82.13	82.63	83.31	101.5	92.7	79.95	78.96
Africa	.03	.08	~	.02	.02	.02	.02	1.66	.71	.22	.96	.05	.05	.67
Madagascar	~	~	~	~	~	~	~	.11	~	~	~	~	~	~
Mauritius	~	~	~	~	~	~	~	~	~	.01a	~	~	~	~
Morocco	~	.08a	~	~	~	~	~	~	~	~	~	~	~	~
Mozambique	~	~	~	~	~	~	~	~	~	~	~	~	~	~
Senegal	~	~	~	~	~	~	~	~	~	~	~	~	~	~
South Africa	~	~	~	~	~	~	~	.01	~	~	.95a	.05	.05	.05
Tanzania	.01	~	~	.02a	~	~	~	~	.04a	~	.01a	~	~	~
Tunisia	~	~	~	~	~	~	~	~	.11a	~	~	~	~	~
Zambia	~	~	~	~	~	~	~	1.54	.45	~	~	~	~	~
Zimbabwe	~	.06	~	~	~	~	~	.64	.24	.21a	~	~	~	.62
Asia	.13	.32	.18	.24	.12	.11	.14	15.87	10.37	8.30	10.97	9.7	13.98	13.36
China, People's Rep.	.04	.02a	.09a	.17a	.06a	.05a	.07	7.87	4.27	.05a	.14a	.26a	.33a	.15
Hong Kong	.09	~	~	.01	~	.05a	~	2.38	2.52	3.90a	4.24a	3.77a	4.46a	4.90
India	~	~	~	~	~	~	~	.09	.09	.09	.09	.1	.1	.10
Korea	~	~	~	.01	~	~	~	4.30	2.08	4.24a	4.93a	5.41a	9.08	7.94
Pakistan	~	~	.03a	~	~	~	~	.11	.04a	.03a	.01a	.01a	~	.05
Philippines	~	~	~	~	~	~	~	~	.11a	~	~	~	~	~
Singapore	.01	.06	~	~	~	~	~	.49	.45	~	~	~	~	~
Thailand	~	~	~	~	~	~	~	.64	.24	~	1.56	.15a	.03a	.20

Table 2625 (Continued)

HAITI ABSOLUTE VALUE OF GOODS TRADED WITH SELECTED REGIONS AND COUNTRIES,[1] 1980-86 (M US)[2]

Category	Exports FOB							Imports CIF						
	1980	1981	1982	1983	1984	1985	1986	1980	1981	1982	1983	1984	1985	1986
III. Developing Countries (Continued)														
Non-Oil Developing Countries														
Europe														
Gibraltor	.1	.01	1.83	.04	.07	.06	.03	1.03	.78	.31	.19	.16	.19	.14
Greece	—	.01[a]	.66[a]	.01[a]	.04[a]	.05[a]	.02	.08	.04[a]	.02[a]	—	.01[a]	.10[a]	.06
Hungary	—	—	—	—	—	—	—	.11	.09	—	—	—	—	—
Malta	—	—	1.15[a]	—	—	—	—	—	—	—	—	—	—	—
Portugal	—	—	—	.03[a]	—	.01[a]	.01	.04	.01[a]	.12[a]	.19[a]	.15[a]	.08[a]	.08
Romania	—	—	—	—	—	—	—	.23	.27	—	—	—	—	—
Turkey	—	—	.02[a]	—	.03[a]	.03[b]	—	.07	.28	—	—	—	—	—
Yugoslavia	—	—	—	—	—	—	—	—	—	.18[a]	—	—	—	—
Middle East														
Israel	.11	.75	—	.27	—	—	—	.02	.11	.11	.33	.99	.11	—
Jordan	.01	.75	—	.27	—	—	—	.01	.11[a]	.11[a]	.33[a]	.99[a]	.11[a]	—
Lebanon	—	—	—	—	—	—	—	—	—	—	—	—	—	—
Yemen Arab Rep.	—	—	—	—	—	—	—	—	—	—	—	—	—	—
IV. Latin America[3]	5.36	2.59	5.68	15.55	13.71	8.24	12.16	63.84	70.77	74.37	89.06	85.10	79.89	64.69
A. ARGENTINA	—	—	—	—	—	.01[c]	—	.67	.28[a]	.31[a]	22.98[a]	12.65[a]	7.03	5.68
Bahamas	.33	.23	.22	.22	.24	.24	.25	.08	.22	.35	.42	.47	.47	.49
Barbados	.06	.02	.14[a]	.56[a]	.10[a]	.22[a]	.10	.22	.20	.40[a]	.42[a]	.25[a]	.32[a]	.46
Belize	.01	—	—	—	—	—	—	—	—	—	—	—	—	—
B. BOLIVIA	—	.01[a]	—	.01[a]	.01[a]	.01[a]	—	—	—	—	—	—	—	—
C. BRAZIL	.03	.04	.01[a]	.01[a]	—	.01[c]	.01	5.65	3.9	4.68[a]	4.26[a]	6.18[a]	7.44[a]	5.02
D. CHILE	—	—	—	—	—	—	—	.05	.04	—	—	—	—	—
E. COLOMBIA	.03	.01[a]	.01[a]	—	.02[a]	.02[b]	—	.83	.51	.59[a]	.83[a]	.84[a]	2.04	2.14
F. COSTA RICA	.02	—	—	.83[a]	.78[a]	.58	.19	.13	.77[a]	1.37[a]	1.49[a]	.44[a]	.61	.91
H. DOMINICAN REP.	.96	.45	2.42[a]	10.84[a]	10.59[a]	5.94	6.23	4.99	6.35	5.62[a]	6.18[a]	7.08[a]	6.75	7.09
I. ECUADOR	.01	—	—	—	—	—	—	.05	.02[a]	.06[a]	.07[a]	.15[a]	.05	.05
J. EL SALVADOR	.90	.24	.24[a]	.32[a]	.35	.28	.29	.09	.26	.35[a]	.17[a]	.19	.19	.29
Guadeloupe	.21	.2	.45[a]	.07[a]	.35	.35	.37	.48	.72	.08[a]	.12[a]	.09	.09	.37
K. GUATEMALA	.03	.23	.10[a]	.07[b]	—	—	.08	—	—	—	—	—	—	—
Guiana, French	—	—	—	—	—	—	—	—	—	—	—	—	—	—
Guyana	—	.05	.02[a]	—	.01	.01	—	—	.08[a]	—	.01[a]	.01[b]	.01[b]	—
M. HONDURAS	.04	.12	.06[a]	.05[a]	.31[a]	.03[a]	.12	.14	—	—	—	—	—	—
Jamaica	.20	.24[b]	.22[b]	.24[b]	.25[b]	.24[b]	—	1.19	.92	.96[a]	.94[a]	.97[a]	1.29[a]	1.17
Leeward Islands	.24	.13	.19[a]	.22	.21	.21[b]	.22	—	—	—	—	—	—	—
Martinique	.51	.01[a]	.03[a]	.10[a]	.09	.09	.10	.06	.09	.1	1.01	.23	.23	.24
N. MEXICO	.55	.09	.09	.09	.09	.09	.10	1.16	1.11	.21[a]	.58[a]	.76[a]	1.24	.43
Netherlands Antilles	.01	.30	.09[a]	.01[a]	—	.03	.03	38.30	33.62	31.93	31.93	35.13	35.13	36.88
O. NICARAGUA	.18	—	—	—	—	—	—	—	—	—	—	—	—	—
P. PANAMA	.06	.05[a]	.06[b]	.05[b]	.01	.04[b]	.03	1.62	2.17	.03[a]	.02[a]	.13[a]	.04	.03
Panama Canal Zone	—	—	—	—	—	—	—	—	—	—	—	—	—	—
R. PERU	—	—	—	—	—	.04[b]	—	.06	.03[a]	.37	.12	.15	.19	.10
St. Vincent	—	—	.01[a]	.05[b]	—	.05[a]	—	—	—	—	—	—	—	—
Suriname	—	—	—	—	—	—	—	—	—	—	—	—	—	—
Trinidad and Tobago	.02	.14	.52[a]	.15[a]	.80[a]	.05[a]	.04	7.67	18.47	26.63[a]	17.43[a]	160.01[a]	2.39[a]	3.70
Windward Islands	—	—	—	—	—	—	—	—	—	—	—	—	—	—
British West Indies	.42	.42[b]	.38[b]	.42[b]	.44[b]	.42[b]	—	.51	.51[b]	.46[b]	.51[b]	.53[b]	.51[b]	—
V. USSR, Eastern Europe, etc.	—	—	—	—	—	—	—	—	—	—	—	—	—	—
Bulgaria	—	.6	—	—	—	—	—	.82	.85	.81	.81	.89	.89	.94
Czechoslovakia	—	.16	.15	.15	.17	.17	.18	.04	.04[b]	.03[b]	.04[b]	.04[b]	.04[b]	—
Poland	.10	.10[b]	.09[b]	.10[b]	.10[b]	.10[b]	—	.78	.78[b]	.70[b]	.77[b]	.81[b]	.79[b]	.94
EEC	86.51	34.64	59.15	71.23	57.16	59.25	79.44	40.49	40.42	58.71	70.88	59.93	82.68	75.89

Table 2625 (Continued)

HAITI ABSOLUTE VALUE OF GOODS TRADED WITH SELECTED REGIONS AND COUNTRIES,[1] 1980–86
(M US)[2]

Category	Exports FOB							Imports CIF						
	1980	1981	1982	1983	1984	1985	1986	1980	1981	1982	1983	1984	1985	1986
VI. Percent Distribution														
Industrial Countries	97.50	97.4	97.8	96.10	96.8	98.0	97.2	76.50	77.8	82.9	82.7	84.2	84.2	84.9
Oil Exporting Countries	.23	.38	.20	.16	.14	.11	.86	.08	~	~	~	~	~	~
Non-Oil Developing Countries	2.26	1.15	2.08	3.67	3.38	2.71	1.81	23.04	18.20	15.80	16.70	14.10	11.80	12.1
Africa	#	#	~	#	#	#	~	.50	.2	#	.20	~	~	.1
Asia	.10	.2	#	.1	#	#	~	4.50	2.8	1.50	1.70	1.40	2.00	2.0
Europe	~	#	.50	#	#	#	~	.3	.2	.10	#	#	#	~
Middle East	#	.5	~	.10	~	~	~	#	#	~	.10	.10	#	~
Non-Industrial														
Western Hemisphere[3]	2.4	1.7	1.5	3.7	3.1	1.8	2.6	18.0	18.8	13.9	14.1	12.4	11.4	9.9
USSR, Eastern Europe, etc.	#	.1	#	#	#	#	~	.2	.20	.20	.1	.1	.1	.1
VII. Annual Percent Change														
World	52.80	-32.2	145.7	11.7	6.6	.1	2.8	33.1	6.1	42.9	17.5	8.7	2.0	-6.5
Industrial Countries	54.10	-32.2	146.7	9.80	7.40	1.40	1.9	34.30	7.9	52.4	17.10	10.60	2.0	-5.7
Oil Exporting Countries	15.22	133.96	-37.90	-10.39	-10.14	-19.35	100.0	190.00	~	~	~	~	~	-100.0
Non-Oil Developing Countries	14.32	-26.03	107.94	96.18	-1.36	-19.32	-.8	30.13	30.83	-20.36	24.81	8.87	-16.61	-1.2
Africa	180.00	200.00	-98.80	~	4.3	-4.5	-4.8	56.90	-57.0	-69.7	342.1	-95.0	2.1	~
Asia	#	-85.30	536.80	47.90	-67.60	-20.70	24.1	61.90	-45.10	-4.10	32.30	-11.60	43.60	-4.4
Europe	50.00	300.00	#	-97.90	84.20	-21.4	-47.3	-36.5	-24.0	-60.8	-38.80	-15.40	18.20	-26.1
Middle East	404.5	579.3	~	~	~	~	~	-15.0	547.10	#	200.0	200.0	-88.90	~
Non-Industrial														
Western Hemisphere[3]	9.7	-51.8	119.8	173.7	-11.8	-39.9	47.7	24.80	10.9	5.1	19.8	-4.4	-6.1	-19.0
USSR, Eastern Europe, etc.	10.8	~	-4.9	10.20	9.7	-4.90	4.7	10.8	4.0	-5.0	9.90	10.0	-5.00	5.1

1. DOT data may differ between countries and from IFS data because of the time it takes for an export to become an import, etc.

2. Data may be calculated from partner's reported data or estimated on basis of less than 12 months.

3. No trade with Cuba, Venezuela is included in category III.

4. For 1981–85 figures, data derived from partner country for the entire year.

a. Data derived from partner country for the entire year.

b. Data extrapolated for the entire year.

c. Five of fewer months of reported data; seven or more derived or extrapolated.

SOURCE: Adapted from IMF-DOT-Y, 1982, 1986, and 1987.

Table 2626

HONDURAS ABSOLUTE VALUE OF GOODS TRADED WITH SELECTED REGIONS AND COUNTRIES,[1] 1980-86

(M US)[2]

Category	Exports FOB 1980	1981	1982	1983	1984	1985	1986	Imports CIF 1980	1981	1982	1983	1984	1985	1986
I. World	829.41	728.20	667.76	660.06	785.43	812.97	925.28	1,005.08	945.10	692.11	819.99	974.32	867.39	890.27
II. Industrial Countries[4]	691.64	612.27	560.89	535.51	662.96	700.96	802.35	673.57	612.73	416.87	475.38	566.39	534.77	607.17
United States	437.85	398.89	351.32	363.67	409.09	393.18	443.09	426.04	391.95	273.50	295.95	354.09	338.69	399.63
Canada	.88	3.82	1.34	2.74	23.58	15.31	14.89	17.87	18.60	8.93	9.90	26.39	11.52	10.65
Australia	8.48	.05	~	.24	.46	.12	.13	1.90	.38	.03	.01	.03	.02	.02
Japan	34.00	45.41	38.49	39.67	55.57	45.09	91.34	99.37	63.00	45.20	36.7	40.33	51.54	77.91
New Zealand	~	~	~	~	.05	.11	~	~	~	~	~	.45	.37	.42
Austria	~	~	~	8.68	6.28	8.47	12.23	1.46	1.98	1.13	1.89	1.98	3.38	1.85
Belgium–Luxembourg	15.39	28.78	38.73	26.07	10.80	17.33	11.86	9.57	10.41	5.73	7.35	7.18	4.47	5.14
Denmark	.01	.12	.13	2.72	1.70	1.97	1.93	7.31	9.42	1.61	2.88	2.12	2.80	2.97
Finland	.20	.77	.66	.32	4.23	3.89	3.42	.18	.32	.27	.12	1.01	.31	.55
France	3.93	4.76	5.64	3.3	9.04	9.59	15.81	15.88	14.57	6.61	22.6	14.63	19.19	22.27
Germany	102.28	56.96	58.51	35.11	44.71	69.17	56.24	28.71	34.35	22.63	27.92	31.71	25.75	24.59
Iceland	~	~	~	.38	.13	1.29	.46	.01	.01	.01	~	~	.19	~
Ireland	~	~	.02	.02	.05	.23	1.48	.30	.56	.58	2.34	3.49	3.37	4.86
Italy	12.84	13.75	14.67	14.45	20.54	55.88	66.71	10.00	17.71	13.51	14.60	16.67	13.54	8.18
Netherlands	37.86	25.24	17.34	14.76	11.87	15.35	15.88	15.96	13.01	9.33	17.69	13.35	17.98	11.11
Norway	4.04	4.69	2.58	2.84	3.67	2.68	2.89	.12	.16	.08	.25	.59	.37	.51
Spain	8.65	15.52	21.63	17.80	20.29	19.73	28.05	8.49	9.11	4.85	5.45	25.25	16.76	9.45
Sweden	2.54	6.24	3.48	4.73	11.00	10.18	6.83	3.24	3.69	4.11	2.31	2.27	2.36	2.73
Switzerland	.58	.79	.94	.95	15.09	18.46	21.97	5.90	5.90	4.76	12.24	13.97	9.10	9.42
United Kingdom	22.09	6.48	5.43	9.08	14.79	12.92	7.13	21.27	17.59	14.03	15.19	10.86	13.07	14.90
III. Developing Countries														
Oil Exporting Countries	2.18	4.53	6.25	9.73	2.91	1.61	1.28	104.87	41.48	13.46	83.56	108.9	106.70	49.50
Indonesia	~	~	~	~	~	~	.07	.04	.07	.03	.01[a]	~	~	~
Iran, I.R. of	~	~	~	~	~	~	~	.02	~	~	~	~	~	~
Libya	~	~	~	~	~	~	~	~	~	~	~	~	~	~
Nigeria	~	~	~	~	~	~	.09	~	.05	~	~	~	~	~
Oman	~	.33	.16	.20[a]	1.16[a]	.12	~	~	.05	~	~	~	~	~
Saudi Arabia	~	3.69	6.02	8.08	1.75[a]	1.49	1.11	~	~	~	~	~	~	~
T. VENEZUELA	2.18	4.53	6.02	8.08	1.75[a]	1.49	1.11	104.82	41.41	13.43	83.56	108.9	106.7	49.50
Non-Oil Developing Countries	127.22	107.04	96.35	105.98	109.64	100.43	108.29	214.66	280.98	253.81	252.20	278.24	206.33	212.87
Africa	.03	.28	.03	3.08	5.40	4.12	3.73	1.20	.14	.53	.58	.96	2.48	.12
Cameroon	~	3.56	1.74	1.46	.45	.37	5.23	~	~	~	~	~	~	~
Madagascar	~	.80	1.65	~	~	~	~	~	~	~	~	~	~	~
Morocco	.01	.06	.03	.12[a]	.13[a]	.12[a]	.14	.05	.05	.03	~	~	~	~
South Africa	~	.22	.03	.26[a]	.51[a]	.22	.01	1.15	.05	.49	.58	.94[a]	2.39[c]	.08
Sudan	~	~	~	~	~	~	~	~	~	~	~	~	~	~
Zambia	~	~	~	.01[a]	.28[a]	.02[a]	.03	~	~	~	.02[a]	.02[a]	.02[b]	.02
Africa not specified	.03	~	~	3.08	3.39	3.39	3.55	~	~	~	~	~	~	~
Asia	12.75	10.49	9.71	8.08	11.99	14.63	16.03	12.75	10.49	9.71	8.08	11.99	14.63	16.03
China, People's Rep.	4.58	3.67	2.83	1.64	2.50[a]	2.28[a]	2.68	4.58	3.67	2.83	1.64	2.50[a]	2.28[a]	2.68
Hong Kong	2.77	2.69	1.78	1.55	3.77[a]	4.03[a]	3.53	2.77	2.69	1.78	1.55	3.77[a]	4.03[a]	3.53
India	.21	.23	.35	.18	.19	.19	.20	.21	.23	.35	.18	.19	.19	.20
Korea	4.38	3.25	3.21	4.39	5.03[a]	8.72	9.07	4.38	3.25	3.21	4.39	5.03[a]	8.72	9.07
Malaysia	.08	.11	1.19	.08	.04[a]	.05[a]	.21	.08	.11	1.19	.08	.04[a]	.05[a]	.21
Pakistan	.04	.05	.08	.02[a]	.05[a]	.03[a]	.09	.04	.05	.08	.02[a]	.05[a]	.03[a]	.09
Philippines	.22	.02	~	.10[b]	.05[a]	.02[b]	~	.22	.02	~	.10[b]	.05[a]	.02[b]	~
Singapore	.23	.15	.14	.03[a]	.17[a]	.16[a]	.06	.23	.15	.14	.03[a]	.17[a]	.16[a]	.06
Sri Lanka	.22	.24	.10	.03[a]	.04[a]	.02[a]	.16	.22	.24	.10	.03[a]	.04[a]	.02[a]	.16
Thailand	.02	2.37	~	.12[a]	.01[a]	~	.34	.03	~	~	.03[a]	.04[a]	.02[a]	.16

Table 2626 (Continued)

HONDURAS ABSOLUTE VALUE OF GOODS TRADED WITH SELECTED REGIONS AND COUNTRIES,[1] 1980–86 (M US)[2]

Category	Exports FOB							Imports CIF						
	1980	1981	1982	1983	1984	1985	1986	1980	1981	1982	1983	1984	1985	1986
III. Developing Countries (Continued)														
Non-Oil Developing Countries														
Europe														
Gibraltar	10.55	2.94	.72	7.39	2.05	1.03	12.26	2.01	1.83	.54	1.47	.61	3.78	.89
Greece	~	.85	~	.09[a]	.06[a]	.23[a]	.17	.07	.02	.01	.01[b]	.01[b]	.01[b]	~
Hungary	~	~	.22	1.95	~	~	.16	.01	.01	~	.05[a]	.20[a]	.01[a]	.13
Malta	~	.20	~	.02[a]	~	~	~	.41	.23	.18	.15	~	~	~
Portugal	.57	.54	.15	.05	1.98[a]	.59[a]	.91	.48	.87	.22	.94	.41[a]	3.74[a]	.71
Romania	~	.18	~	~	~	~	~	.11	.13	.02	.36	~	~	~
Turkey	~	~	~	~	~	~	~	.43	.05	.04	~	~	~	~
Yugoslavia	9.98	1.08	~	1.09	.02[a]	.11	.12	.17	.44	.02	.02	.01[b]	.02[a]	.06
Europe not specified	~	~	~	~	~	.05[a]	10.84	~	.02	.01	.01[b]	.01[b]	.01[b]	~
Middle East														
Egypt	.53	2.83	1.43	17.63	5.24	3.11	2.59	.39	.41	.26	.59	.33	.55	2.31
Israel	~	.15	.65	1.24	.64[b]	.61[b]	~	~	~	~	~	~	~	~
Syrian Arab Rep.	.53	.31	~	.53	.36[a]	.18[a]	~	.30	.40	.26	.59	.33[a]	.55[a]	2.31
Yemen, P.D. Rep.	~	~	~	~	~	~	~	.08	.01	~	~	~	~	~
IV. Latin America[3]	118.29	101.96	98.69	87.55	99.35	93.20	85.76	303.13	309.60	256.24	325.28	373.46	290.72	243.01
A. ARGENTINA	.29	.06	.04	.02[a]	~	~	.18	2.89	2.58	1.04	1.25	1.55[a]	7.6	10.39
Antigua and Barbuda	.23	.44	.71	.53	.58	.58	.61	.01	.03	.03	.03[b]	.03[b]	.03[b]	~
Bahamas	~	~	~	~	3.13[a]	3.10[a]	4.22	.01	.03	.03	.03[b]	.08[a]	.45[a]	.03
Barbados	.27	.28	.98	1.86	.65	.65	.68	.07	~	.06	.25[a]	.15[a]	.15	.16
Belize	2.80	2.49	2.37	.59	~	~	~	.02	.63	.48	.69	.09[a]	.81	.85
Bermuda	~	~	~	~	~	~	~	~	~	~	~	~	~	~
C. BRAZIL	.85	.53	.04	.09	.02[a]	.07[c]	.05	17.83	16.29	8.44	10.62	32.94[a]	12.89[a]	30.01
D. CHILE	~	~	.01	~	~	~	~	.43	.14	.05	.09	~	~	~
E. COLOMBIA	1.06	2.64	1.33	1.22	.61	1.08	1.13	4.99	3.91	2.90	5.37	5.24[a]	5.83	6.12
F. COSTA RICA	17.57	15.56	10.65	9.61	7.56[a]	6.55	5.59	31.35	42.55	26.09	34.23	49.23[a]	33.90	28.45
Dominica	.09	.06	.10	.11[b]	.12[b]	.11[b]	~	~	.03	.01	.01[b]	.01[b]	.01[b]	.01[b]
H. DOMINICAN REP.	2.10	1.52	2.27	.34	.46[a]	.42	.44	.34	.69	.48	.69	1.20[a]	.81	.85
I. ECUADOR	~	.51	.13	1.21[a]	~	~	~	.03	.63	.06	.81	.09[a]	.64	.45
J. EL SALVADOR	~	2.49	10.47	13.84	15.17[a]	9.63	10.11	~	1.52	3.84	8.25	8.65[a]	7.06	7.41
Grenada	.02	.13	~	~	~	~	~	~	~	~	~	~	~	~
Guadeloupe	1.88	1.48	2.68	2.45	2.70	2.70	2.83	~	~	~	~	~	~	~
K. GUATEMALA	41.20	31.95	26.38	28.23	31.05	31.05	32.61	57.73	61.05	48.04	58.72	64.59	64.59	67.82
Guyana	.09	.08	~	.04	~	~	~	.03	~	.01	.01[b]	.01[b]	.01[b]	~
L. HAITI	.19	1.83	1.45	.04	.18[a]	.76[a]	1.45	1.41	.75	.45	.62	3.25[a]	1.86[a]	.07
Jamaica	~	.55	~	.73	~	~	~	~	~	~	~	~	~	~
Leeward Islands	~	.36	~	.07	~	~	~	~	~	~	~	~	~	~
Martinique	~	.07	~	~	~	~	~	~	~	~	~	~	~	~
N. MEXICO	.37	.14	.33	.36[b]	1.18	5.77	3.01	22.59	17.16	15.18	35.05	51.01[a]	31.09	24.53
Montserrat	.62	~	.19	.21[b]	.22[b]	.21[b]	~	~	~	~	~	~	~	~
Netherlands Antilles	~	20.83	4.77	.07	.16[a]	~	~	3.02	7.71	6.81	8.46	9.30	9.30	9.77
O. NICARAGUA	32.62	2.32	8.26	9.96	10.63	10.63	11.16	14.46	13.26	8.88	3.55	3.91	3.91	4.10
P. PANAMA	5.73	~	1.79	1.49	1.17[a]	1.94	2.04	8.03	12.47	18.38	37.80	2.19	2.28	2.66
Panama Canal Zone	~	~	~	~	~	~	~	~	~	~	~	~	~	~
R. PERU	~	.14	.03	.27	.30	.31	.31	.73	.16	.12	.58	~	.79	.40
St. Lucia	.49	.71	.35	.43	.48	.48	.40	~	~	.01	.01[b]	.01[b]	.01[b]	~
St. Pierre-Miquelon	.09	~	~	~	~	~	~	~	.02	.01	.01[b]	.01[b]	.01[b]	~
St. Vincent	.12	.22	~	.43	~	~	.50	.03	~	~	~	~	~	~
Surname	1.13	2.05	1.69	1.63	1.79	1.79	1.88	1.13	~	~	~	~	~	~
Trinidad and Tobago	5.77	7.89	13.98	14.28	21.47[a]	14.45[a]	5.63	32.13	87.44	101.74	36.15	31.16[a]	.87[a]	.28

Table 2626 (Continued)

HONDURAS ABSOLUTE VALUE OF GOODS TRADED WITH SELECTED REGIONS AND COUNTRIES,[1] 1980–86
(M US)[2]

Category	Exports FOB							Imports CIF						
	1980	1981	1982	1983	1984	1985	1986	1980	1981	1982	1983	1984	1985	1986
IV. Latin America[3] (Continued)														
S. URUGUAY	.01	~	.06	~	~	~	~	.09	.31	.04	.03[a]	.03[c]	.01	.01
Windward Islands	~	~	~	~	~	~	~	~	~	~	~	~	~	~
America not specified	~	~	~	~	~	~	~	~	~	~	~	~	~	~
British West Indies	~	~	~	~	~	~	~	~	~	.01	.01[b]	.01[b]	.01[b]	~
Other Latin America not specified	.53	.96	.13	.07	.08[b]	.08[b]	.08[b]	.13	.09	.22	.24[b]	.26[b]	.24[b]	~
V. USSR, Eastern Eruope, etc.	~	~	.41	4.54	4.99	4.99	5.24	3.65	2.73	2.08	1.15	1.27	1.27	1.33
Albania	~	~	~	1.87	1.83	1.83	1.92	.01	.01	~	~	~	~	~
Bulgaria	~	~	~	~	~	~	~	.17	~	~	~	~	~	~
Czechoslovakia	~	~	.04	2.87	3.16	3.16	3.32	1.87	1.38	.88	.51	.56	.56	.58
East Germany	~	~	.37	.40[b]	.42[b]	.40[b]	~	.42	.21	.27	.36	.39	.39	.41
North Korea	~	~	~	~	~	~	~	.07	.06	.09	.10[b]	.10[b]	.10[b]	~
Poland	~	~	~	.38[b]	.40[b]	.38[b]	.40	.33	.07	.02	.03[b]	.03[b]	.03[b]	~
USSR	~	~	~	~	~	~	~	1.10	1.06	.84	.29	.32	.32	.34
Country or area not specified	.17	.01	.07	4.3	4.73	4.73	4.97	.15	.03	.34	7.70	8.47	8.47	8.89
EEC	203.63	153.0	162.25	120.64	135.84	202.99	206.17	117.97	127.62	79.08	116.96	125.88	120.68	104.32
VI. Percent Distribution														
Industrial Countries	83.4	84.10	84.00	81.1	84.4	86.2	86.7	67.0	64.80	60.20	58.0	58.1	61.7	68.20
Oil Exporting Countries	.3	.62	.94	1.51	1.01	.78	.14	10.4	4.39	1.94	1.48	1.11	1.11	5.56
Non-Oil Developing Countries	15.3	14.70	14.37	14.40	13.09	11.71	11.70	21.3	29.72	36.67	27.97	32.33	28.97	23.91
Africa	~	#	#	.5	.7	.5	.40	.1	#	.10	.10	.10	.30	~
Asia	1.3	.50	.30	.20	.10	.1	.6	1.3	1.10	1.40	1.10	1.2	1.8	1.8
Europe	~	.40	.10	1.1	.30	.10	1.3	.2	.20	.10	.2	.10	.4	.1
Middle East	.1	.4	.2	2.7	.7	.4	.3	~	#	#	.1	#	.10	.3
Non-Industrial														
Western Hemisphere[3]	14.3	14.0	14.8	13.3	12.6	11.5	9.3	30.2	32.8	37.0	39.7	38.3	33.5	27.3
USSR, Eastern Europe, etc.	~	~	.10	.7	.6	.6	.6	.4	.30	.30	.1	.1	.1	.1
VII. Annual Percentage Change														
World	13.1	-12.20	-8.30	-1.2	19.0	2.5	13.8	21.7	-6.00	-26.80	18.5	18.8	-11.0	2.6
Industrial Countries	9.7	-11.50	-8.40	-4.5	23.8	5.70	14.5	23.6	-9.0	-32.0	14.0	19.1	-5.6	13.5
Oil Exporting Countries	-67.4	107.80	37.97	79.20	-30.54	-19.92	-20.5	51.5	-60.45	-67.55	-20.13	-10.05	-10.03	-53.6
Non-Oil Developing Countries	32.3	-15.86	-10.30	10.99	-5.02	-7.72	7.8	6.7	31.06	-9.65	-19.82	38.53	-19.52	3.2
Africa	~	#	-90.30	851.90	75.5	-73.6	-9.6	349.3	-88.80	290.40	10.4	64.3	158.20	-95.2
Asia	-85.3	#	-51.10	-96.5	755.0	12.9	803.1	10.9	-18.00	-7.40	-19.2	50.3	31.7	3.3
Europe	300.8	-72.1	-75.5	925.4	-72.3	-49.7	~	-23.7	-9.0	-70.6	173.8	-58.6	519.0	-76.3
Middle East	-83.5	430.1	-49.5	-37.01	-70.3	-40.6	-16.6	30.1	.5	-35.3	122.0	-43.7	66.67	320.0
Non-Industrial														
Western Hemisphere[3]	22.1	13.8	-3.2	-11.3	13.5	-6.2	-8.0	18.6	2.1	-17.2	26.9	14.8	-22.2	-16.4
USSR, Eastern Europe, etc.	~	#	#	10.00	10.0	-4.90	5.0	56.4	-25.2	-23.7	-44.7	10.0	-5.00	5.1

1. DOT data may differ between countries and from IFS data because of the time it takes for an export to become an import, etc.
2. Data may be calculated from partner's reported data or estimated on basis of less than 12 months.
3. No trade with Cuba; Venezuela is included in category III.
4. For 1983–85 figures, data derived from partner country for entire year.
a. Data derived from partner country for the entire year.
b. Data extrapolated for the entire year.
c. Five or fewer months of reported data: seven or more months derived or extrapolated.

SOURCE: Adapted from IMF-DOT-Y, 1982, 1986, and 1987.

Table 2627

MEXICO ABSOLUTE VALUE OF GOODS TRADED WITH SELECTED REGIONS AND COUNTRIES,[1] 1980–86 (M US)[2]

Category	Exports FOB 1980	1981	1982	1983	1984	1985	1986	Imports CIF 1980	1981	1982	1983	1984	1985	1986
I. World	15,557	19,381	21,209	22,313	24,382	22,105	16,579	17,687	21,933	13,687	8,200	10,327	13,441	12,320
II. Industrial Countries	13,279	16,171	17,682	19,080	20,950	19,484	14,654	15,171	19,223	12,058	6,897	8,871	12,099	11,455
United States	10,072	10,716	11,129	13,034	14,130	13,341	11,163	10,890	13,998	8,188	4,958	6,440	8,954	8,272
Canada	117	661	584	467	495	393	302	321	405	291	206	207	235	227
Australia	9	14	13	7	10	15	18	30	38	19	6	39	75	25
Japan	671	1,157	1,450	1,512	1,868	1,709	1,065	899	1,095	777	320	457	723	771
New Zealand	1	2	2	2	4	6	9	21	27	32	15	33	11	25
Austria	1	3	54	102	85	38	38	18	23	31	6	9	38	22
Belgium-Luxembourg	77	66	67	58	82	62	85	141	109	74	42	75	88	92
Denmark	2	5	2	8	5	6	9	26	31	40	15	11	16	15
Finland	4	12	11	6	2	6	2	31	57	22	16	10	19	13
France	567	900	931	832	928	816	382	473	534	318	327	230	275	240
Germany	256	212	240	270	231	293	390	884	1,081	831	331	440	536	723
Ireland	2	~	~	~	1	~	1	59	77	19	5	22	41	25
Italy	101	112	418	149	305	301	101	277	393	393	152	204	210	186
Netherlands	76	89	18	40	35	89	54	90	120	94	55	54	77	75
Norway	1	3	~	3	7	3	8	19	19	8	13	30	18	16
Spain	1,238	1,921	1,815	1,617	1,703	1,700	791	316	429	336	152	179	214	190
Sweden	19	46	14	10	8	8	8	139	194	161	50	96	137	165
Switzerland	23	13	22	48	33	25	56	170	201	173	74	144	148	157
United Kingdom	43	242	913	916	1,020	678	174	368	390	253	155	191	284	217
III. Developing Countries														
Oil Exporting Countries														
Algeria	81	91	112	65	82	69	58	37	34	36	18	18	24	24
Indonesia	9	12	2	15	32	17	9	~	~	18	17	10	10	13
Iran, I.R. of	6	7	3	1	1	2	1	11	14	18	~	1	1	1
Iraq	~	~	10	4	6	2	~	1	2	~	~	1	~	~
Kuwait	~	2	2	~	1	~	1	~	~	~	~	~	~	~
Libya	~	~	~	3	~	~	1	1	~	.1	~	~	~	1
Nigeria	1	1	1	10	4	7	1	~	1	1	~	~	~	~
Saudi Arabia	4	~	6	~	2	3	2	13	9	8	1	6	6	3
T. VENEZUELA	62	69	88	32	35	39	44	26	18	9	1	1	13	7
Non-Oil Developing Countries	1,886	3,082	3,108	2,679	2,511	2,067	1,536	1,001	1,462	925	377	601	879	643
Africa	19	40	16	57	51	81	34	26	60	40	20	42	78	66
Ivory Coast	~	~	~	~	~	~	1	~	~	~	~	~	~	1
Kenya	4	16	7	4	3	48	3	7	11	6	7	18	13	10
Liberia	~	~	3	15	4	5	6	1	21	26	9	18	21	16
Morocco	~	~	~	~	~	~	1	~	~	1	~	~	1	19
Mozambique	~	~	~	~	~	~	~	~	~	~	~	~	~	~
Namibia	~	~	~	~	~	~	~	~	~	~	~	~	~	~
South Africa	3	1	~	1	1	1	1	13	6	4	18	2	1	~
Zaire	~	2	6	~	3	1	3	5	9	1	9	17	21	8
Africa not specified	2	9	2	11	7	3	15	5	14	3	2	5	35	14
Asia	160	448	418	327	314	289	265	226	296	240	102	100	154	149
China, People's Rep.	94	170	87	54	92	83	109	60	105	59	10	22	62	42
Hong Kong	4	8	5	18	21	14	12	40	76	66	4	5	12	14
India	6	57	3	7	10	17	18	9	14	21	4	5	7	5
Korea	13	68	207	136	156	102	69	35	22	23	19	14	11	19
Malaysia	2	1	3	4	2	~	1	10	15	5	3	3	5	12
Pakistan	~	~	1	1	~	1	1	10	3	1	~	~	~	17
Philippines	6	90	81	74	3	4	3	7	2	4	18	2	~	8
Singapore	1	2	1	2	~	5	4	2	19	13	9	17	21	6
Sri Lanka	~	~	~	1	3	18	26	32	17	8	2	4	9	6
Thailand	1	9	4	1	3	17	21	10	17	~	~	13	9	1
Asia not specified	2	36	22	29	25	25	~	2	1	22	~	5	7	10
Oceania not specified	5	~	~	~	1	1	~	14	~	14	~	1	2	~

Table 2627 (Continued)

MEXICO ABSOLUTE VALUE OF GOODS TRADED WITH SELECTED REGIONS AND COUNTRIES,[1] 1980–86
(M US)[2]

Category	Exports FOB							Imports CIF						
	1980	1981	1982	1983	1984	1985	1986	1980	1981	1982	1983	1984	1985	1986
III. Developing Countries (Continued)														
Non-Oil Developing Countries														
Europe														
Greece	73	102	167	153	171	129	122	29	49	22	10	18	31	56
Hungary	10	18	1	1	4	2	2	6	18	4	3	4	3	1
Portugal	1	3	10	40	7	10	1	5	5	3	~	~	4	3
Romania	6	19	109	101	129	83	70	3	2	4	3	5	2	2
Turkey	4	11	28	2	6	5	10	3	9	4	1	1	6	14
Yugoslavia	1	16	12	~	1	8	15	1	1	~	2	3	1	1
Europe not specified	43	26	4	~	3	3	15	3	4	4	3	9	6	35
Middle East	647	678	762	543	505	439	133	8	16	23	3	9	18	18
Egypt	~	~	2	1	1	1	2	2	~	~	~	~	~	~
Israel	641	672	738	531	486	432	125	5	10	11	2	6	8	13
Lebanon	~	~	~	4	3	3	3	~	~	~	~	~	~	~
Middle East not specified	2	1	4	4	4	2	3	1	3	3	2	~	1	2
IV. Latin America[3]	1,068	1,905	1,858	1,665	1,552	1,199	1,041	749	1,057	635	261	446	630	378
A. ARGENTINA	44	35	50	37	45	32	99	100	235	122	32	155	269	118
Bahamas	1	59	14	9	24	3	37	4	5	3	1	2	4	3
Belize	7	6	5	6	6	5	8	2	~	~	~	~	~	~
Bermuda	84	14	1	1	1	~	1	2	~	~	~	3	4	1
B. BOLIVIA	3	3	1	1	1	2	1	~	1	1	~	~	4	1
C. BRAZIL	406	748	715	640	562	298	161	421	554	315	125	209	204	170
D. CHILE	27	40	11	17	16	16	26	60	49	25	4	13	52	10
E. COLOMBIA	48	48	48	69	69	121	103	15	16	12	8	8	6	11
F. COSTA RICA	97	103	72	68	60	21	47	1	16	13	8	13	8	1
H. DOMINICAN REP.	10	124	166	150	163	132	111	~	~	~	3	~	~	~
I. ECUADOR	39	77	22	25	39	48	51	13	16	3	~	1	2	5
J. EL SALVADOR	19	77	69	89	77	89	54	1	1	5	~	~	~	15
K. GUATEMALA	59	129	107	69	103	101	67	23	66	35	12	9	16	15
Guyana	~	~	~	~	3	1	~	5	3	1	1	2	2	1
L. HAITI	1	12	10	22	1	28	22	~	1	~	~	~	~	~
M. HONDURAS	19	20	77	51	46	47	10	3	2	6	3	6	6	7
Jamaica	4	88	2	15	13	15	5	~	~	~	~	~	~	~
Netherlands Antilles	29	2	141	154	11	30	9	11	7	56	54	8	11	19
O. NICARAGUA	54	86	150	134	69	119	98	~	~	3	1	6	~	2
P. PANAMA	22	127	26	17	151	13	1	~	~	~	~	1	~	~
Q. PARAGUAY	~	31	26	6	14	13	26	6	15	3	2	6	11	26
R. PERU	26	31	26	17	14	13	26	23	17	5	2	6	11	26
Trinidad and Tobago	1	6	~	6	14	13	1	~	10	3	2	6	6	1
S. URUGUAY	8	6	80	49	43	24	58	6	~	5	3	5	6	~
Windward Islands	~	1	2	3	2	1	~	8	6	3	3	3	5	~
America not specified	1	1	1	1	2	1	~	~	~	~	2	3	~	2
British West Indies	1	~	2	4	3	9	2	8	7	3	3	3	5	~
Other Latin America not specified	2	1	~	~	~	~	~	8	7	3	3	3	5	2
V. USSR, Eastern Europe, etc.	52	37	51	109	126	92	66	290	169	90	33	29	26	20
G. CUBA	27	19	26	35	81	70	45	238	123	59	23	12	2	2
Czechoslovakia	21	5	15	30	19	11	14	18	17	14	6	10	14	10
Eastern Germany	~	10	2	38	12	3	~	23	13	6	1	3	3	2
Poland	9	2	3	9	22	28	9	6	9	6	3	1	9	1
USSR	4	4	8	6	14	8	7	11	15	11	3	4	7	5
USSR, etc., not specified	~	~	~	~	~	8	~	~	17	~	~	~	~	~
Country or area not specified	~	~	4	380	376	131	12	324	56	15	462	323	413	179
Special categories	259	252	252	~	338	263	251	862	990	563	414	485	184	~
EEC	2,378	3,584	4,515	3,992	4,442	4,030	2,057	2,643	3,185	2,361	1,234	1,411	1,744	1,766

Table 2627 (Continued)

MEXICO ABSOLUTE VALUE OF GOODS TRADED WITH SELECTED REGIONS AND COUNTRIES,[1] 1980–86 (M US)[2]

Category	Exports FOB							Imports CIF						
	1980	1981	1982	1983	1984	1985	1986	1980	1981	1982	1983	1984	1985	1986
VI. Percent Distribution														
Industrial Countries	85.4	83.4	83.4	85.5	85.9	88.1	88.4	85.8	87.6	88.1	84.1	85.9	90.0	93.0
Oil Exporting Countries	.5	.5	.5	.3	.3	.3	.3	.5	.2	.3	.2	.2	.1	.2
Non-Oil Developing Countries	12.1	15.9	14.6	11.9	9.9	7.8	9.3	12.1	6.6	6.7	4.6	5.6	4.9	5.2
Africa	.1	.2	.1	.3	.2	.4	.2	.1	.3	.3	.2	.4	.6	.5
Asia	1.0	2.3	2.0	1.5	1.3	1.3	1.6	1.3	1.4	1.8	1.2	1.0	1.1	1.2
Europe	.5	.5	.8	.7	.7	.6	.7	.2	.2	.2	.1	.2	.2	.5
Middle East	4.2	3.5	3.6	2.4	2.1	2.0	.8	#	.1	.2	#	.1	.2	.1
Non-industrial Western Hemisphere[3]	6.9	9.8	8.8	7.5	6.4	5.4	6.3	4.2	4.9	4.6	3.2	4.3	4.7	3.1
USSR, Eastern Europe, etc.	.3	.2	.2	.5	.5	.4	.4	1.6	.8	.7	.4	.3	.2	.2
VII. Annual Percent Change														
World	73.2	24.6	9.4	5.2	9.3	-9.3	-25.0	61.0	24.0	-37.6	-40.1	25.9	30.2	-8.3
Industrial Countries	74.8	21.8	9.3	7.9	9.8	-7.0	-24.8	50.2	26.7	-37.3	-42.8	28.6	36.4	-5.3
Oil Exporting Countries	-39.0	11.8	23.1	-41.9	26.2	-20.7	-15.9	-13.9	-8.1	5.9	-50.0	#	27.7	#
Non-Oil Developing Countries	84.0	64.1	.8	-14.0	-6.8	-24.3	-25.7	31.4	46.1	-36.8	-58.9	59.2	32.7	-26.8
Africa	10.6	111.7	-60.3	258.2	-10.2	58.5	-57.8	-44.1	133.5	-33.3	-51.4	113.5	86.3	-15.4
Asia	.2	180.6	-6.7	-71.7	-4.0	-8.0	-8.3	83.5	31.0	-19.0	-57.6	-1.7	54.2	-3.8
Europe	-5.6	39.4	64.0	-8.0	11.7	-24.4	-6.1	17.3	67.9	-54.0	-56.6	92.4	70.3	79.9
Middle East	105.9	4.8	12.3	-28.8	-7.0	-13.1	-69.7	69.1	83.9	48.0	-87.7	338.7	-23.5	95.2
Non-industrial Western Hemisphere[3]	73.7	78.3	-2.5	-10.4	-6.8	-22.8	-13.1	23.3	43.6	-40.9	-58.9	71.0	41.2	-40.1
USSR, Eastern Europe, etc.	-28.1	37.4	111.3	15.8	-27.3	-27.3	-27.8	850.9	-41.9	-46.6	-63.4	-13.2	-7.9	-25.5

1. DOT data may differ between countries and from IFS data because of the time it takes for an export to become an import, etc.
2. Data may be calculated from partner's reported data or estimated on basis of less than 12 months.
3. Cuba is included in category V; Venezuela is included in catetory III.

SOURCE: Adapted from IMF-DOT-Y, 1982, 1986, and 1987.

Table 2628

NICARAGUA ABSOLUTE VALUE OF GOODS TRADED WITH SELECTED REGIONS AND COUNTRIES,[1] 1980-86
(M US)[2]

Category	Exports FOB							Imports CIF						
	1980	1981	1982	1983	1984	1985	1986	1980	1981	1982	1983	1984	1985	1986
I. World	413.84	475.91	370.19	429.19	424.36	317.03	315.05	881.88	984.22	774.88	741.5	698.7	586.98	543.89
II. Industrial Countries[4]	318.83	306.68	249.65	304.51	323.17	227.52	228.60	370.15	456.40	320.72	288.45	318.58	265.94	236.07
United States	160.25	136.34	82.34	98.64	62.55	45.09	.82	242.11	261.36	147.56	145.09	122.65	46.20	3.19
Canada	1.51	2.54	1.57	22.84	35.41	18.88	24.59	10.83	23.88	12.59	14.19	19.82	14.91	17.83
Australia	.18	.20	.16	.39	.51	.18	.18	.50	.30	.32	.03	~	.10	.05
Japan	12.76	55.72	42.60	66.01	95.33	54.38	38.75	28.61	28.26	18.51	9.62	14.28	25.92	10.49
New Zealand	~	~	~	.07	.05	~	~	~	.59	~	.89	2.32	~	.02
Austria	~	~	~	5.31	6.19	3.48	16.75	.37	.49	1.05	6.79	7.49	4.05	3.70
Belgium and Luxembourg	15.50	8.53	6.71	2.67	3.83	4.49	12.96	3.41	3.04	3.03	2.25	2.82	1.57	6.86
Denmark	.14	2.76	1.53	.13	.72	1.56	2.78	2.00	.79	1.56	.70	1.49	2.19	9.14
Finland	.88	2.09	1.90	.45	3.30	1.04	2.39	.35	.25	.05	1.34	3.07	3.98	5.29
France	22.87	18.29	19.25	25.80	36.20	20.15	25.07	10.32	9.21	32.43	30.69	34.08	39.35	48.45
Germany	55.74	50.35	52.46	34.90	30.18	30.87	34.45	28.23	60.02	28.85	13.70	19.91	17.18	20.65
Ireland	~	~	.15	.15	.41	.39	.24	.12	3.95	8.25	1.45	2.36	2.92	1.23
Italy	14.08	13.72	8.42	14.00	10.53	7.69	11.39	4.64	9.93	20.86	13.25	15.07	17.02	23.17
Netherlands	19.39	7.22	16.27	9.08	8.29	9.40	18.53	13.62	13.75	10.26	8.77	8.95	9.10	12.86
Norway	~	.75	.03	.24	.02	.16	.38	.03	.04	.03	.21	1.78	2.61	2.95
Spain	13.63	7.00	13.79	15.15	20.52	21.49	21.51	8.33	11.59	21.99	21.08	33.80	36.72	30.75
Sweden	.15	.02	.03	.23	.32	.17	.43	.39	8.18	1.57	5.64	9.27	11.37	8.02
Switzerland	~	~	~	6.18	6.22	6.55	15.64	8.99	9.63	7.51	8.81	12.41	21.47	19.55
United Kingdom	1.75	2.16	2.61	2.26	2.58	1.55	1.74	7.30	11.13	4.31	3.96	7.02	9.26	11.89
III. Developing Countries														
Oil Exporting Countries	.22	1.24	.62	30.59	16.16	13.04	10.08	149.14	87.10	40.46	2.2	5.5	5.50	7.70
Algeria	.22	.62	~	30.41[a]	15.41	13.12	9.84	~	~	~	~	~	~	~
Indonesia	~	~	.12	.09[a]	.73[a]	.53	.24	~	~	~	~	~	~	~
Iran, I.R. of	~	~	~	~	~	~	~	~	~	~	~	~	~	~
Nigeria	~	~	.40	~	.02	~	~	~	~	~	~	~	~	~
Saudi Arabia	~	.62	.10	.09	.08	.07[b]	~	~	~	~	~	~	~	~
T. VENEZUELA	~	~	~	~	~	~	~	149.14	87.10	40.46	2.2	5.5	5.5	7.70
Non-Oil Developing Countries	85.91	121.67	88.03	56.17	41.79	31.40	36.26	358.58	412.30	317.06	350.22	266.67	201.69	184.04
Africa	~	~	~	30.43	15.43	13.15	9.86	.06	.04	1.82	.02	~	~	.09
Cape Verde	~	~	~	~	~	~	~	~	~	~	~	~	~	~
Ethiopia	~	~	~	~	~	~	~	~	~	~	~	~	~	~
Morocco	~	~	~	~	~	~	~	~	~	~	~	~	~	~
Senegal	~	~	~	~	~	~	~	~	~	~	~	~	~	~
South Africa	~	~	~	~	~	~	~	.06	.04	1.82	~	~	~	.09
Tunisia	~	~	~	~	~	~	.02	~	~	~	.02[a]	~	~	~
Asia	2.79	34.06	19.81	9.38	1.22	3.24	5.33	4.89	4.62	4.43	2.33	7.12	4.22	2.81
Bangladesh	~	~	~	~	~	~	~	~	~	~	~	~	~	~
China, People's Rep.	1.94	20.75	19.52	8.43[a]	~	~	~	~	~	.20	.06[a]	.04[a]	1.30[a]	1.27
Hong Kong	~	5.97	.04	~	~	~	~	.70	.77	.53	.07[a]	.33	.33[b]	.35
India	~	3.86	~	~	.47[a]	.12[c]	1.02	.36	.61	.30	.30	4.42[a]	2.52	1.12
Korea	~	.37	~	~	.01[a]	.08[a]	~	2.79	2.82	3.24	1.83[a]	~	~	~
Malaysia	~	~	~	~	~	~	~	.63	.22	~	~	~	~	~
Pakistan	~	.08	~	~	~	~	2.00	~	~	~	~	~	~	~
Philippines	~	.36	~	.84[a]	~	~	.07	.29	~	~	~	~	.02[a]	~
Singapore	~	~	~	~	~	~	~	~	~	~	~	~	~	~
Sri Lanka	~	2.04	~	.01[a]	~	2.34[a]	1.99	.12	.20	.15	.07[a]	.07[a]	.04[a]	~
Thailand	.38	~	.04	~	~	.04[a]	~	~	~	~	~	2.26[a]	~	~

Table 2628 (Continued)

NICARAGUA ABSOLUTE VALUE OF GOODS TRADED WITH SELECTED REGIONS AND COUNTRIES,[1] 1980-86

(M US)[2]

Category	Exports FOB							Imports CIF						
	1980	1981	1982	1983	1984	1985	1986	1980	1981	1982	1983	1984	1985	1986
III. Developing Countries (Continued)														
Non-Oil Developing Countries														
Europe														
Gibraltar	1.57	1.08	.45	.64	.77	1.51	.86	.64	.58	.41	.49	.82	3.26	4.28
Cyprus	~	~	.41	.41	.45	.45[b]	.48	~	~	~	~	~	~	~
Greece	~	~	~	.03[a]	.01[a]	.34[a]	.19	~	~	~	.20[a]	.81[a]	~	.05
Hungary	~	1.03	~	~	.02[a]	~	~	.09	.15	.16	.29[a]	.01[a]	.01[a]	~
Portugal	.12	.05	.04	.19[a]	.28[a]	.37[a]	.13	.13	.27	.15	~	~	~	.67
Romania	~	~	~	~	~	~	~	.23	.10	.02	~	~	~	~
Yugoslavia	1.46	~	.09	~	~	.35[a]	~	.02	.07	.09	~	~	3.25[a]	3.56
Middle East														
Israel	~	.96	.09	.09[a]	~	.01	.01	.08	.03	1.18	1.43	1.10	.11	.22
Lebanon	~	~	~	~	~	~	~	.08	.03	1.18	1.43[a]	1.10[a]	.11[a]	.22
IV. Latin America[3]														
A. ARGENTINA	81.77	86.82	67.99	46.15	40.53	27.18	30.29	502.22	494.33	349.68	348.16	263.13	199.6	184.34
Barbados	~	~	~	~	~	~	~	3.15	8.89	3.42	18.97[a]	23.22[a]	29.07[a]	28.57
Belize	~	~	~	~	~	~	~	~	~	~	.01[a]	~	~	~
B. BOLIVIA	~	~	~	~	~	~	.01	~	~	~	~	~	~	~
C. BRAZIL	~	~	~	~	~	~	~	4.65	36.91	7.81	11.62[a]	15.95[a]	7.29[a]	10.47
D. CHILE	~	~	~	~	~	~	~	~	.03	1.33	~	~	~	~
E. COLOMBIA	~	.06	.19	.12[a]	.01[a]	.02	.02	2.39	6.06	1.58	5.40[a]	15.08[a]	3.97	4.17
F. COSTA RICA	36.66	34.10	24.85	18.32[a]	14.85	~	7.40	116.27	79.86	46.06	44.94[a]	30.66[a]	29.95	26.14
H. DOMINICAN REP.	~	~	~	.32[a]	.01[a]	~	~	~	~	~	~	~	~	~
I. ECUADOR	~	~	~	.07[a]	~	~	~	~	~	~	~	.01[a]	.40[c]	.28
J. EL SALVADOR	9.97	9.35	5.49	3.20[a]	2.93[a]	2.18	2.29	50.44	34.12	18.02	16.45[a]	5.65[a]	3.57	3.75
K. GUATEMALA	16.24	15.95	14.29	11.25[a]	12.37	12.37	12.99	102.00	76.98	44.30	55.87[a]	61.46	61.46	64.53
L. HAITI	.41	.09	~	~	~	~	~	~	~	~	~	~	~	~
M. HONDURAS	12.54	11.33	7.45	3.32	3.55	3.55	3.73	30.37	19.56	8.37	10.63	11.69	11.69	12.28
Jamaica	.10	~	~	~	~	~	.03	.10	.04	~	~	.01[a]	~	~
N. MEXICO	.11	9.25	14.18	8.40[a]	6.11[a]	.08[c]	2.92	17.84	119.40	154.93	169.40[a]	75.48[a]	33.36	9.93
Netherlands Antilles	~	~	~	~	~	~	~	11.80	6.64	9.38	9.38	10.32	10.32	10.84
P. PANAMA	5.53	5.28	1.44	1.25[a]	.70[a]	.77[c]	.90	13.48	17.92	12.26	.95[a]	1.27[a]	1.67[c]	2.28
R. PERU	.21	.80	~	~	~	~	~	.31	.65	1.57	2.32	6.83	1.73	3.42
Trinidad and Tobago	~	~	~	~	~	~	~	.27	~	~	~	~	~	~
S. URUGUAY	~	~	~	~	.01[a]	~	~	~	~	~	.02[a]	~	.03[a]	~
British West Indies	~	~	~	~	~	~	~	~	~	~	~	~	~	~
V. USSR, Eastern Europe, etc.	8.32	28.67	24.01	24.01	26.41	26.41	27.73	.99	33.41	88.86	88.86	97.74	97.74	102.63
Bulgaria	~	2.58	4.38	4.38	4.82	4.82	5.06	~	.63	6.27	6.27	6.89	6.89	7.24
Cuba	~	11.25	1.27	1.27	1.40	1.40[b]	1.47	.09	8.23	30.58	30.58	33.64	33.64	35.32
Czechoslovakia	~	.39	5.42	5.42	5.96	5.96	6.25	~	.23	1.47	1.47	1.62[b]	1.62	1.70
Eastern Germany	~	3.64	4.77	4.77	5.25	5.25	5.51	~	17.86	11.63	11.63	12.79	12.79	13.43
North Korea	~	1.39	~	~	~	~	~	~	.98	.12	.13	.13	.13[b]	.14
Poland	~	~	~	~	~	~	~	~	~	~	.02[a]	~	~	~
USSR	8.32	9.41	8.17	8.17	8.99	8.99	9.44	.90	5.47	38.79	42.67	42.67	42.67	44.80
ECC	143.21	110.07	121.07	104.35	113.57	98.31	128.98	78.10	123.67	131.68	96.33	126.32	135.32	165.71

Table 2628 (Continued)

NICARAGUA ABSOLUTE VALUE OF GOODS TRADED WITH SELECTED REGIONS AND COUNTRIES,[1] 1980–86
(M US)[2]

Category	Exports FOB							Imports CIF						
	1980	1981	1982	1983	1984	1985	1986	1980	1981	1982	1983	1984	1985	1986
VI. Percent Distribution														
Industrial Countries	77.00	64.40	67.40	70.9	76.2	71.8	72.6	42.00	45.90	41.40	38.9	45.6	45.3	43.4
Oil Exporting Countries	#	.26	.16	6.99	6.37	6.75	3.2	16.91	8.85	5.22	4.15	4.06	4.16	1.4
Non-Oil Developing Countries	20.76	25.57	23.78	10.59	10.46	11.64	11.5	40.66	41.89	40.92	44.72	35.77	35.56	33.8
Africa	~	~	~	7.1	3.6	4.1	3.1	#	#	.20	.30	#	#	~
Asia	.70	7.20	5.40	2.2	.30	1.0	1.7	.60	.50	.60	.30	1.00	.7	.5
Europe	.40	.20	.10	.1	.20	.5	.3	.10	.10	.10	.10	.10	.6	.8
Middle East	~	.2	.1	#	~	~	~	~	~	.20	.20	.20	~	~
Non-industrial Western Hemisphere[3]	19.8	18.2	18.4	10.8	9.6	8.6	9.6	56.9	49.7	45.1	47.0	37.7	34.0	33.9
USSR, Eastern Europe, etc.	2.00	6.00	6.50	5.6	6.2	8.3	8.8	.10	3.40	11.50	12.0	14.0	16.7	18.9
VII. Annual Percent Change														
World	-27.00	15.00	-22.20	15.9	-1.1	-25.3	-.6	145.00	12.70	-22.10	-4.3	-5.8	-16.0	-7.3
Industrial Countries	-17.00	-3.80	-18.60	22.00	6.10	-29.60	.5	135.10	23.30	-29.70	-10.10	10.40	-16.50	-11.2
Oil Exporting Countries	-86.90	463.64	-50.00	4,833.87	-7.85	-20.22	-26.1	124.41	-41.60	-53.55	-19.99	-10.00	-9.99	40.0
Non-Oil Developing Countries	-47.87	41.62	-27.65	-30.51	-24.29	-16.28	15.5	165.50	14.98	-23.10	9.98	-26.39	-12.84	-8.8
Africa	~	~	~	~	-49.3	-15.0	-24.8	5.30	-36.70	~	-98.80	~	~	~
Asia	-96.00	~	-41.80	-52.70	-87.00	166.1	64.6	85.80	-5.60	-4.20	-47.4	206.1	-40.8	-33.4
Europe	396.20	-31.50	-58.30	41.6	20.9	96.2	-43.1	-14.2	-8.3	-29.9	19.1	68.7	297.6	31.3
Middle East	~	~	-58.60	-77.10	-96.70	133.3	~	69.40	-61.40	~	21.10	-23.10	-90.00	100.0
Non-industrial Western Hemisphere[3]	-14.6	6.2	-21.7	-32.1	-12.2	-32.9	11.4	153.6	-1.6	-29.2	-.4	-24.4	-24.1	-7.6
USSR, Eastern Europe, etc.	~	244.60	-16.30	10.00	10.0	-5.00	5.0	798.2	~	166.00	10.00	10.0	-5.00	5.0

1. DOT data may differ between countries and from IFS data because of the time it takes for an export to become an import, etc.
2. Data may be calculated from partner's reported data or estimated on basis of less than 12 months.
3. Cuba is included in category V; Venezuela is included in category III.
4. For 1983–85 figures, data derived from partner country for entire year.

a. Data derived from partner country for entire year.
b. Data extrapolated for entire year.
c. Five or fewer months of reported data; seven or more months derived or extrapolated.

SOURCE: Adapted from IMF-DOT-Y, 1982, 1986, and 1987.

Table 2629

PANAMA ABSOLUTE VALUE OF GOODS TRADED WITH SELECTED REGIONS AND COUNTRIES,[1] 1980–86
(M US)[2]

Category	Exports FOB							Imports CIF						
	1980	1981	1982	1983	1984	1985	1986	1980	1981	1982	1983	1984	1985	1986
I. World	350.2	316.6	308.1	299.3	251.5	300.6	575.8	1,448.4	1,539.9	1,569.3	1,411.9	1,423.0	1,391.4	4,685.2
II. Industrial Countries														
United States	224.1	228.0	189.3	214.0	201.9	248.1	472.4	718.4	786.3	841.7	724.4	739.5	744.6	2,551.7
Canada	172.6	167.0	127.9	160.8	152.9	192.6	309.8	489.1	535.6	549.0	456.4	450.5	438.0	782.7
Australia	1.0	1.2	13.2	2.7	.6	6.7	5.0	12.6	17.0	13.6	13.7	15.1	28.5	38.6
Japan	1.3	.3	.3	.9	1.0	.2	17.8	89.0	94.6	119.5	110.2	117.9	123.5	546.5
New Zealand	~	~	~	~	~	~	~	7.9	5.4	2.2	2.7	5.5	6.7	5.0
Austria	~	~	~	~	~	4.6	3.2	1.3	.9	1.8	1.4	1.2	1.8	2.6
Belgium–Luxembourg	~	9.4	13.4	15.4	13.4	17.1	16.7	5.6	7.6	5.7	8.6	10.8	5.3	12.7
Denmark	~	~	~	~	~	1.4	1.5	4.1	3.7	4.2	5.9	3.9	3.1	74.0
Finland	~	~	~	~	~	2.4	2.0	1.0	1.1	.9	1.1	1.1	.4	4.1
France	.3	1.0	.6	.6	.3	.5	3.7	10.5	15.3	24.5	16.6	15.6	14.5	85.5
Germany	17.7	24.2	18.2	17.1	14.8	17.5	40.6	25.8	27.8	28.7	32.0	29.2	31.4	87.8
Iceland	~	~	~	~	~	.1	.4	.4	.3	.5	.2	.1	.2	.1
Ireland	~	~	~	~	~	.1	5.3	2.7	1.5	1.3	2.2	2.5	2.9	5.3
Italy	5.4	17.0	8.2	8.1	10.8	6.7	20.0	14.5	17.3	17.1	23.7	14.7	15.2	195.7
Netherlands	21.2	3.9	1.2	.8	1.2	4.1	8.7	14.3	11.9	10.9	7.1	8.4	9.2	46.7
Norway	3.6	2.8	3.0	1.1	1.2	1.5	4.6	1.2	1.6	5.5	2.0	1.4	1.3	378.2
Spain	.4	.4	.1	.2	3.0	3.6	5.0	10.0	12.6	13.3	13.6	14.7	18.4	79.1
Sweden	.6	.3	2.6	5.1	3.5	4.1	12.6	7.2	9.1	17.3	9.2	8.8	8.4	24.6
Switzerland	.1	.1	.1	.3	~	26.7	16.6	4.8	5.4	6.3	5.5	24.7	33.8	108.8
United Kingdom	.4	.3	.5	.9	.3	5.7	3.9	15.6	16.2	18.3	12.0	12.6	13.6	72.6
III. Developing Countries														
Oil Exporting Countries	6.0	10.5	14.9	4.5	10.5	6.2	6.1	376.5	245.5	159.9	212.9	103.7	88.8	81.6
Indonesia	~	~	~	~	~	~	~	~	.2	.1	~	~	.1	34.0
Iran, I.R. of	~	~	~	~	~	~	~	~	~	~	~	~	~	~
Iraq	~	~	~	~	~	~	~	~	~	~	~	~	~	~
Kuwait	~	~	~	~	~	~	~	~	.1	~	~	~	~	~
Libya	~	~	~	~	~	~	~	~	~	~	~	~	~	~
Nigeria	~	~	~	~	~	~	~	~	.1	2.1	.4	~	~	~
Saudi Arabia	.8	2.0	2.3	3.4	3.7	3.7	2.3	266.6	118.5	~	~	~	~	2.3
United Arab Emirates	~	~	~	~	5.7	~	.6	~	~	~	~	3.7	.1	.6
T. VENEZUELA	5.1	8.2	12.5	1.1	1.1	2.5	3.2	109.9	126.7	157.7	121.9	103.7	88.3	47.3
Non-Oil Developing Countries	67.2	59.7	45.8	43.9	37.5	45.0	95.7	200.0	346.5	395.2	384.5	534.7	521.4	1,730.4
Africa	~	.1	2.0	~	.2	.5	~	.2	.2	.3	.6	.2	.3	1.2
South Africa	~	.1	2.0	~	.2	.5	~	.2	.1	.3	.6	.2	.2	.4
Africa not specified	~	~	2.0	~	.2	~	~	~	.1	~	~	~	.1	.1
Asia	.4	.4	.2	.2	.3	.1	31.4	27.7	30.5	28.1	22.9	24.0	25.7	1,168.0
China, People's Rep.	.4	.4	.2	.2	.3	1.5	1.1	2.6	4.2	2.2	2.1	1.3	1.2	17.8
Hong Kong	~	.2	.2	.2	.3	.1	1.7	11.2	10.9	10.7	9.6	10.5	11.2	218.1
India	.1	~	.1	.1	.1	.4	.4	.6	.5	.5	.4	.1	.4	~
Korea	~	~	~	~	~	170.4	27.5	11.5	13.2	12.5	9.4	10.9	595.6	595.6
Malaysia	~	~	~	~	~	.1	~	.2	.1	.4	.4	.1	.1	7.8
Pakistan	~	~	~	~	~	.2	~	.3	.2	.3	.3	.1	.2	1.1
Philippines	~	~	~	~	~	.3	~	.6	.4	.7	.6	.8	.3	27.9
Singapore	~	.1	~	.1	~	3.6	1.1	.2	.3	.7	.6	.2	.4	244.0
Sri Lanka	~	~	~	~	~	~	~	.1	.1	.4	.1	.1	.1	.2
Thailand	.3	~	~	~	~	3.2	~	.2	.2	~	~	~	~	20.6
Asia not specified	~	~	~	~	~	~	~	~	.1	~	~	~	~	~

Table 2629 (Continued)

PANAMA ABSOLUTE VALUE OF GOODS TRADED WITH SELECTED REGIONS AND COUNTRIES,[1] 1980-86
(M US)[2]

Category	Exports FOB 1980	1981	1982	1983	1984	1985	1986	Imports CIF 1980	1981	1982	1983	1984	1985	1986
III. Developing Countries (Continued)														
Non-Oil Developing Countries														
Europe														
Greece	2.5	11.6	?	?	?	.5	3.7	2.7	2.0	1.7	3.5	1.9	2.4	57.7
Hungary	?	?	?	?	?	?	.2	?	.1	.1	.1	.1	.1	4.4
Malta	?	?	?	?	?	?	?	.2	?	?	.9	.5	.4	?
Portugal	?	?	?	?	?	.8	.4	.5	.4	1.1	1.5	1.0	1.2	1.6
Romania	?	?	?	?	?	.1	?	.3	.2	.1	.1	?	.1	.1
Turkey	?	8.1	?	?	?	?	?	.2	?	.1	?	?	.1	.1
Yugoslavia	2.4	3.5	?	?	?	.3	2.3	?	.3	.1	?	?	.3	51.4
Middle East														
Egypt	.9	2.8	3.0	3.6	9.5	4.1	4.8	266.8	118.8	.9	.5	.5	1.9	7.7
Israel	?	.2	.3	.2	?	.4	1.8	?	.2	.9	.4	.5	1.4	7.4
Syrian Arab Rep.	?	.2	.2	.2	.1	?	?	?	?	?	?	?	?	?
Yemen Arab Rep.	?	.4	.2	?	?	?	?	?	?	?	?	?	?	?
V. Latin America[3]	69.3	55.3	55.4	44.6	38.0	46.5	62.0	279.1	440.6	522.0	478.6	611.9	579.9	577.3
A. ARGENTINA	3.2	.3	.1	?	?	2.5	6.8	2.3	1.5	1.7	2.3	5.2	3.8	19.6
Bahamas	.5	.5	?	?	?	.1	?	?	?	?	?	?	.1	?
Barbados	?	?	?	?	?	?	?	?	?	?	?	?	.1	?
Belize	.1	.5	?	.2	?	?	.1	.1	.1	.1	?	.1	.1	.1
B. BOLIVIA	.7	.5	?	.2	?	4.7	.5	12.7	20.3	20.7	20.1	22.2	28.7	46.7
C. BRAZIL	.1	.6	.3	?	.2	.1	.4	3.2	2.9	5.5	3.7	3.6	4.7	7.2
D. CHILE	.6	2.0	3.7	4.1	1.0	1.1	2.2	10.1	11.3	9.7	8.4	12.4	12.6	13.2
E. COLOMBIA	3.7	11.9	10.1	15.2	20.6	17.6	22.3	36.8	42.8	39.5	36.1	35.0	34.6	42.8
F. COSTA RICA	22.6	1.6	.7	.9	.2	.9	.2	.7	.3	.7	.3	.2	.2	.2
H. DOMINICAN REP.	1.4	1.1	2.3	.5	.7	1.6	3.1	34.9	18.7	86.7	110.5	83.1	81.4	57.0
I. ECUADOR	1.8	1.1	.7	.9	.2	.9	.2	6.3	5.5	5.7	5.8	5.3	5.7	5.9
J. EL SALVADOR	4.6	4.3	3.4	4.8	2.4	2.9	4.0	?	?	?	?	.1	?	?
Guadeloupe	?	?	?	?	?	?	?	?	?	?	?	.1	?	?
K. GUATEMALA	7.0	2.8	2.5	2.2	3.0	3.3	3.1	15.9	18.0	17.9	15.9	17.4	17.0	17.9
Guiana, French	.3	.3	.4	.6	.2	?	.2	?	.3	?	?	.1	.1	?
Guyana	.5	1.6	?	?	.2	.1	?	.4	.2	.1	?	?	?	?
L. HAITI	.4	.2	?	.1	.1	.1	.1	2.1	2.2	2.3	1.8	1.3	2.1	2.4
M. HONDURAS	1.5	6.7	9.1	1.8	2.0	2.1	2.4	.7	.2	.2	1.1	.7	.1	.1
Jamaica	.2	.3	.5	.1	.1	.3	.1	?	.3	?	?	?	?	?
Leeward Islands	?	.3	.9	?	?	.1	1.0	?	?	?	?	?	?	?
N. MEXICO	.2	.3	.9	?	?	.1	1.0	14.4	118.5	146.1	127.1	129.0	110.2	110.2
Netherlands Antilles	3.1	3.7	4.9	4.3	2.7	2.6	3.7	4.1	6.2	9.7	13.1	31.1	10.2	10.7
O. NICARAGUA	10.7	7.1	2.5	.9	1.2	1.2	2.1	3.6	3.6	2.1	1.4	.8	1.0	1.0
Panama Canal Zone	?	?	?	?	?	?	?	.1	?	?	.1	.1	?	?
Q. PARAGUAY	.1	.1	?	.1	.1	?	.7	3.4	3.6	4.5	5.3	7.0	7.0	16.0
R. PERU	.2	.3	.9	4.5	.4	1.2	.7	.1	.2	.4	.4	.2	.2	.2
St. Pierre-Miquelon	?	?	?	?	?	?	?	?	?	?	?	?	?	?
Suriname	.3	.2	.2	.2	?	.2	.1	.3	.2	.2	?	?	?	?
Trinidad and Tobago	.1	.4	.1	2.8	?	.5	.3	17.1	57.5	9.0	3.5	8.2	6.4	4.2
S. URUGUAY	.5	.1	?	.1	.1	?	?	.1	.1	1.6	.2	.1	.1	.1
Windward Islands	?	?	?	?	?	?	?	?	?	?	?	?	?	?
French West Indies not specified	?	?	?	?	1.8	?	?	?	?	?	?	?	?	?
Other Latin America not specified	?	?	?	1.8	?	1.8	5.4	?	?	?	.1	145.1	165.7	173.9

Table 2629 (Continued)

PANAMA ABSOLUTE VALUE OF GOODS TRADED WITH SELECTED REGIONS AND COUNTRIES,[1] 1980–86 (M US)[2]

Category	Exports FOB							Imports CIF						
	1980	1981	1982	1983	1984	1985	1986	1980	1981	1982	1983	1984	1985	1986
V. Developing Countries (Continued)														
Non-Oil Developing Countries														
USSR, Eastern Europe, etc.														
G. CUBA	.5	.8	.5	1.3	1.7	1.3	1.6	3.2	3.3	1.3	1.3	1.0	2.1	2.2
Czechoslovakia	.5	.8	.5	.8	1.7	~	1.2	.1	.5	.1	.3	.1	.2	.2
Eastern Germany	~	~	~	.3	~	~	.3	1.3	1.3	.7	.9	.7	1.6	1.7
Poland	.1	~	~	~	.1	~	~	~	.1	.2	~	~	~	~
USSR	~	~	~	.3	~	.2	.7	1.4	.9	.2	.8	.2	.3	.2
Country or area not specified	~	~	~	~	~	~	~	1.7	1.3	.4	~	.1	.3	.4
Special categories	52.4	17.6	57.7	35.6	42.7	48.6		134.4	140.8	152.9	161.7	21.1	9.7	10.7
EEC	45.1	56.1	42.3	43.1			100.7	376.5	245.5	125.1	123.4	103.7	88.8	665.4
VI. Percent Distribution														
Industrial Countries	64.0	72.0	61.4	71.5	80.3	82.5	82.0	49.6	51.1	53.6	51.3	52.0	53.5	54.5
Oil Exporting Countries	1.7	3.3	4.8	1.5	4.2	1.1	1.1	26.0	15.9	10.2	8.6	7.3	2.2	1.7
Non-Oil Developing Countries	19.2	18.9	14.9	14.7	14.9	29.2	16.6	13.7	22.4	25.2	27.2	37.5	32.6	36.9
Africa	~	.1	.7	.1	.1	.1	.1	.2	~	.2	.1	#	#	~
Asia	.1	.1	.7	.1	.1	23.0	5.5	1.9	2.0	1.8	1.6	1.7	1.8	24.9
Europe	.7	3.7	~	.1	~	.2	.6	.2	.1	.1	.2	.1	.2	1.2
Middle East	.3	.9	1.0	1.2	3.8	1.4	.8	18.4	7.7	.1	~	~	.1	.2
Non-Industrial														
Western Hemisphere[3]	19.8	17.5	18.0	14.9	15.1	15.5	10.8	19.3	28.6	33.3	33.9	43.0	41.7	12.3
USSR, Eastern Europe, etc	.1	.2	.1	.4	.7	.4	.3	.2	.2	.1	.2	.1	.2	~
VII. Annual Percent Change														
World	15.6	-9.6	-2.7	-2.8	-16.0	19.5	91.5	22.3	6.3	1.9	-10.0	.8	-2.2	236.7
Industrial Countries	17.5	1.7	-17.0	13.1	-5.7	22.9	90.4	22.6	9.5	7.0	-13.9	2.1	.7	242.7
Oil Exporting Countries	15.3	75.4	41.4	-69.8	133.3	-19.0	-1.6	142.2	-34.8	-34.9	-23.8	-14.9	-32.6	-8.1
Non-Oil Developing Countries	-32.3	-11.1	-23.2	-4.1	-14.6	515.2	112.7	-53.1	74.0	14.3	-2.8	39.2	91.7	231.9
Africa	-99.6	905.3	960.7	-99.7	~	-99.5	~	-21.3	-35.6	50.0	-55.3	-83.2	57.9	324.2
Asia	~	-20.1	-38.3	-16.7	68.9	-71.7	~	19.6	10.2	-7.8	-18.6	4.6	7.2	~
Europe	93.6	356.9	~	~	~	~	582.1	-.6	-25.9	-16.5	110.4	-46.4	27.0	310.4
Middle East	-49.6	212.0	7.8	18.4	164.3	-57.0	16.8	193.1	-55.5	-99.2	-48.5	9.9	760.3	
Non-Industrial														
Western Hemisphere[3]	-30.8	-70.3	.3	-19.5	-14.8	22.5	33.2	-21.0	57.9	18.5	-8.3	27.8	-5.2	-.5
USSR, Eastern Europe, etc.	189.2	62.7	-41.5	193.2	24.0	-22.1	25.7	28.0	3.1	-61.5	5.6	-26.7	118.3	5.0

1. DOT data may differ between countries and from IFS data because of the time it takes for an export to become an import, etc.
2. Data may be calculated from partner's reported data or estimated on basis of less then 12 months.
3. Cuba is included in category V; Venezuela is included in category III.
a. Eight, seven, or six months of reported data; four, five, or six months derived or extrapolated.

SOURCE: Adapted from IMF-DOT-Y, 1982, 1986, and 1987.

Table 2630

PARAGUAY ABSOLUTE VALUE OF GOODS TRADED WITH SELECTED REGIONS AND COUNTRIES,[1] 1980–86
(M US)[2]

Category	Exports FOB							Imports CIF						
	1980	1981	1982	1983	1984	1985	1986	1980	1981	1982	1983	1984	1985	1986
I. World	310.23	297.16	329.80	269.18	334.47	303.92	233.74	521.65	506.28	581.51	478.27	514.35	442.27	508.81
II. Industrial Countries	143.78	120.82	136.20	138.15	156.07	163.37	70.57	191.94	196.96	200.70	162.72	199.48	134.27	199.97
United States	17.10	16.60	9.10	23.27	17.73	3.61	10.09	51.37	50.32	52.30	54.81	45.16	35.00	69.76
Canada	.04	.01	~	.47	.20	~	~	.26	.62	.40	.42	9.87	~	~
Australia	~	~	~	~	~	~	~	~	.01	~	~	~	~	~
Japan	11.30	24.90	25.50	5.24	7.90	3.17	1.90	42.03	42.05	32.00	20.17	60.74	20.20	29.13
Austria	~	~	~	.05	.03	~	~	2.13	2.25	1.10	1.00	.44	~	~
Belgium-Luxembourg	5.74	3.74	6.10	6.61	9.75	18.59	5.79	1.64	2.37	2.10	1.78	1.15	1.27	1.23
Denmark	1.81	~	.30	.14	~	~	~	.36	.80	1.00	.50	.26	~	~
Finland	~	~	~	~	~	~	~	.63	.10	.10	.04	.02	~	~
France	5.03	4.60	7.20	4.91	8.07	23.79	1.92	12.03	9.10	10.60	16.95	25.97	6.97	12.73
Germany	38.45	32.83	40.90	31.86	39.56	41.00	7.77	33.53	41.00	37.30	32.32	16.06	21.97	32.97
Ireland	.01	~	.40	.01	.02	~	~	.01	~	~	.02	.02	~	~
Italy	6.05	3.38	5.70	3.11	6.01	3.60	4.29	4.71	6.08	6.60	4.89	3.17	3.54	6.68
Netherlands	19.75	13.30	16.00	38.59	41.26	38.39	22.52	2.15	3.34	9.90	1.71	6.67	2.31	2.12
Norway	.03	~	~	~	.03	~	~	.27	.10	.10	.10	.02	~	~
Spain	4.80	3.80	6.90	2.81	12.11	9.64	1.77	5.50	6.51	6.10	16.08	2.50	16.00	4.63
Sweden	.27	.01	~	~	~	~	~	3.56	4.39	2.20	2.26	.88	1.73	2.25
Switzerland	31.61	14.70	14.20	19.18	12.76	20.02	13.61	2.90	3.03	4.90	4.94	5.10	6.79	6.03
United Kingdom	1.80	2.95	3.90	1.91	.65	1.57	.93	28.84	24.90	23.00	24.73	21.46	18.48	32.42
III. Developing Countries														
Oil Exporting Countries	1.27	4.60	12.80	3.64	7.76	~	~	38.35	37.37	75.70	65.65	48.63	41.33	33.56
Algeria	1.26	.10	.90	.74	~	~	~	37.08	27.50	75.60	65.56	48.45	41.33	33.56
Indonesia	~	.15	1.70	~	~	~	~	~	~	~	~	~	~	~
Iraq	~	~	.10	~	~	~	~	~	~	~	~	~	~	~
Nigeria	~	.380	.80	~	~	~	~	~	9.80	.10	.09	.18	~	~
Saudi Arabia	.01	.55	9.30	2.91	7.75	~	~	.01	.07	.10	~	~	~	~
T. VENEZUELA	161.25	169.14	180.00	126.94	169.03	83.40	133.70	283.37	265.85	298.9	246.31	264.78	241.33	234.76
Non-Oil Developing Countries	1.17	1.65	7.60	5.43	12.26	~	~	1.93	.58	.90	2.09	1.20	~	33.56
Africa	~	~	~	~	~	~	~	~	~	~	~	~	~	~
Cameroon	.02	.04	.20	~	~	~	~	~	~	~	~	~	~	~
Congo	~	~	.20	~	~	~	~							
Ivory Coast	~	.29	.20	.96	.30	~	~	~	~	~	~	~	~	~
Madagascar	~	.03	.10	~	.02	~	~							
Mali	~	~	.40	~	~	~	~							
Morocco	~	.16	.30	~	~	~	~							
Senegal	.49	.58	~	~	~	~	~							
South Africa	.65	.14	6.20	4.40	11.04	~	~	.65	.38	.90	2.09	1.20	~	~
Tunisia	~	.40	.20	~	~	~	~		.20					
Upper Volta	~	~	~	~	~	~	~							
Africa not specified	1.28	~	~	1.03	1.21	~	~							
Asia	4.85	4.52	6.00	1.73	6.23	~	~	8.42	3.01	2.80	2.04	1.00	~	~
Burma	~	.20	.20	~	~	~	~	5.86	.03	~	~	~	~	~
China, People's Rep.	~	~	.80	.96	.30	~	~	.91	.66	.80	~	.22	~	~
Hong Kong	~	.20	~	~	.02	~	~	.42	.47	.40	1.25	.05	~	~
India	~	1.40	~	.37	.61	~	~	1.12	1.70	1.60	.21	.68	~	~
Korea	~	.30	1.50	~	~	~	~	~	.01	~	.39	~	~	~
Malaysia	~	~	.50	~	~	~	~	~	.03	~	~	~	~	~
Pakistan	~	~	.10	~	~	~	~	~	~	~	~	~	~	~
Philippines	.19	1.00	1.20	~	~	~	~	.01	.11	~	~	~	~	~
Singapore	~	1.20	1.20	~	~	~	~	~	.03	~	~	~	~	~
Sri Lanka	4.66	.07	~	.40	5.31	~	~	.10	~	~	.19	.05	~	~
Asia not specified	~	.07	~	~	~	~	~	~	~	~	~	~	~	~
Oceania not specified	~	~	~	.02	~	~	~	~	~	~	.04	.01	~	~

Table 2630 (Continued)

PARAGUAY ABSOLUTE VALUE OF GOODS TRADED WITH SELECTED REGIONS AND COUNTRIES,[1] 1980-86
(M US)[2]

Category	Exports FOB							Imports CIF						
	1980	1981	1982	1983	1984	1985	1986	1980	1981	1982	1983	1984	1985	1986
III. Developing Countries (Continued)														
Non-Oil Developing Countries														
Europe														
Greece	13.25	14.52	9.40	8.69	16.60	~	~	.13	2.2	1.3	.12	.17	~	~
Hungary	~	~	~	.67	4.79	~	~	.01	.02	~	.04	.01	~	~
Portugal	12.17	12.87	8.90	8.02	11.82	~	~	.11	.09	.20	.06	.15	~	~
Romania	~	~	~	~	~	~	~	.11	.11	.40	.06	.15	~	~
Turkey	~	~	~	~	~	~	~	.01	.07	.10	.02	.02	~	~
Yugoslavia	1.07	1.65	.50	~	.04	~	~	.01	.01	~	~	~	~	~
Middle East														
Israel	.02	~	.50	1.00	1.14	~	~	1.80	.27	.40	.33	.15	~	~
Syrian Arab Rep.	.02	~	.50	~	~	~	~	~	~	.40	~	~	~	~
Middle East not specified	~	~	~	1.00	1.14	~	~	1.80	~	~	.33	.15	~	~
IV. Latin America[3]	141.99	149.14	167.5	113.0	140.51	83.4	133.70	271.11	259.57	293.6	241.82	262.33	241.33	234.76
A. ARGENTINA	74.18	68.59	59.20	32.14	40.53	16.90	35.17	106.44	100.10	113.20	90.36	80.96	74.88	69.54
B. BOLIVIA	.58	1.18	.40	.36	.01	~	~	.07	.28	.20	.11	.07	~	~
C. BRAZIL	40.24	54.34	83.40	56.62	53.22	60.08	92.13	140.50	131.30	154.30	136.21	167.89	159.87	160.81
D. CHILE	11.31	11.10	6.90	8.87	16.75	~	~	4.30	3.92	7.30	2.72	3.61	~	~
E. COLOMBIA	.14	.07	.20	.01	~	~	~	.20	.34	.40	.06	.04	~	~
F. COSTA RICA	~	~	~	~	~	~	~	~	.04	~	~	~	~	~
H. DOMINICAN REP.	~	~	~	~	~	~	~	~	.01	~	~	~	~	~
I. ECUADOR	~	~	~	.02	.17	~	~	.34	.42	.10	.06	.01	~	~
J. EL SALVADOR	~	~	~	~	~	~	~	~	.08	~	~	~	~	~
K. GUATEMALA	~	~	~	~	~	~	~	~	.02	~	~	~	~	~
Jamaica	~	~	~	~	~	~	~	~	~	~	~	~	~	~
N. MEXICO	4.02	2.49	.90	.14	.06	~	~	.50	.64	2.80	.29	.17	~	~
Netherlands Antilles	~	~	~	~	~	~	~	~	~	~	~	~	~	~
P. PANAMA	~	1.20	2.60	~	~	~	~	2.89	2.61	3.30	2.49	1.29	~	~
R. PERU	.02	.49	.20	2.32	1.34	~	~	.13	3.53	2.40	.11	.11	~	~
Trinidad and Tobago	~	~	~	~	~	~	~	~	.30	.20	.11	.11	~	~
S. URUGUAY	10.16	9.13	4.40	4.70	6.80	6.43	6.40	14.95	15.50	8.20	7.67	4.77	5.79	4.41
America not specified	1.32	~	~	4.92	13.88	~	~	1.65	~	~	1.60	3.30	~	~
Other Latin America not specified	~	~	~	4.92	13.88	~	~	.76	.24	~	1.65	3.33	~	~
V. USSR, Eastern Europe, etc.	.08	.90	~	~	.44	~	~	2.13	.78	1.00	1.01	.40	~	~
Bulgaria	~	.90	~	~	~	~	~	~	.10	.10	~	~	~	~
Czechoslovakia	~	~	~	~	~	~	~	~	.60	.90	~	~	~	~
North Korea	~	~	~	~	~	~	~	~	.01	~	~	~	~	~
Poland	~	~	~	~	~	~	~	~	1.89	.60	~	~	~	~
USSR	~	~	~	~	~	~	~	~	.07	~	~	~	~	~
USSR, etc., not specified	.08	~	~	~	.44	~	~	2.13	~	~	~	~	~	~
Country or area not specified	3.84	~	~	~	.44	57.14	29.46	1.49	.15	.01	1.01	.40	.79	~
ECC	95.60	77.46	96.30	98.63	134.04	136.57	44.98	88.90	94.23	108.00	99.08	77.40	70.53	92.79
VI. Percent Distribution														
Industrial Countries	46.3	40.7	41.3	51.3	46.7	53.8	30.2	36.8	38.9	34.5	34.0	38.8	30.4	39.3
Oil Exporting Countries	.4	1.5	3.9	1.4	2.3	~	~	7.2	7.4	13.0	13.7	9.5	9.3	6.6
Non-Oil Developing Countries	52.0	56.9	54.6	47.2	50.5	27.4	57.2	55.0	52.0	51.3	51.5	51.5	54.6	46.1
Africa	.8	1.9	2.8	2.3	3.7	~	~	7.7	5.5	13.2	14.1	9.7	9.3	6.6
Asia	1.6	1.5	1.8	.6	1.9	~	~	1.6	.6	.5	.4	.2	~	~
Europe	4.3	4.9	2.9	3.2	5.0	~	~	.3	.1	.1	#	#	~	~
Middle East	~	~	.2	.4	.3	~	~	~	2.0	.1	.1	#	~	~
Non-industrial Western Hemisphere[3]	45.8	50.2	50.8	42.0	42.0	27.4	57.2	52.6	51.2	50.5	50.6	51.0	54.6	46.1
USSR, Eastern Europe, etc.	~	.3	~	.4	.1	~	~	.4	.2	.2	.2	.1	~	~

Table 2630 (Continued)

PARAGUAY ABSOLUTE VALUE OF GOODS TRADED WITH SELECTED REGIONS AND COUNTRIES,[1] 1980–86 (M US)[2]

Category	Exports FOB							Imports CIF						
	1980	1981	1982	1983	1984	1985	1986	1980	1981	1982	1983	1984	1985	1986
VII. Annual Percent Change														
World	2.0	-4.2	11.0	-18.4	24.3	-9.1	-23.1	19.1	-2.9	14.8	-17.8	7.5	-14.0	15.0
Industrial Countries	-21.3	-16.0	12.7	1.4	13.0	4.7	-56.8	8.8	2.6	1.9	-18.9	22.6	-32.7	48.9
Oil Exporting Countries	887.6	261.1	178.3	-71.6	113.2	~	~	-26.0	.7	102.6	-13.3	-25.9	-15.0	-13.9
Non-Oil Developing Countries	38.4	4.9	6.4	-29.5	33.2	-50.7	60.3	42.6	-7.4	13.2	-17.4	7.5	-8.9	-2.7
Africa	202.7	128.9	-67.5	-33.7	98.7	~	~	-24.2	-30.3	172.4	-11.6	-26.6	-16.8	-18.8
Asia	219.2	-6.7	32.7	-71.2	261.0	~	~	423.1	-64.3	-6.9	-27.0	-51.0	~	~
Europe	41.9	9.6	-35.3	-7.6	91.7	~	~	-19.3	127.4	-40.8	-90.9	46.9	~	~
Middle East	171.4	~	~	66.3	13.8	~	~	35.6	458.1	-96.0	-17.7	-54.1	~	~
Non-industrial Western Hemisphere[3]	35.3	5.0	12.3	24.3	-40.6	60.3	60.3	~	-4.3	13.1	-17.6	8.5	-8.0	-2.7
USSR, Eastern Europe, etc.	-97.8	~	~	~	~	~	~	-12.7	-63.2	27.6	-1.0	-60.5	~	~

1. DOT data may differ between countries and from IFS data because of the time it takes for an export to become an import, etc.
2. Data may be calculated from partner's reported data or estimated on basis of less than 12 months.
3. No trade with Cuba; Venezuela is included in category III.

SOURCE: Adapted from IMF-DOT-Y, 1982, 1986, and 1987.

Table 2631

PERU ABSOLUTE VALUE OF GOODS TRADED WITH SELECTED REGIONS AND COUNTRIES,[1] 1980–86 (M US)[2]

Category	Exports FOB							Imports CIF						
	1980	1981	1982	1983	1984	1985	1986	1980	1981	1982	1983	1984	1985	1986
I. World	3,914.7	3,246.9	2,919.1	2,577.4	3,086.4	2,980.6	2,504.5	2,610.5	3,433.7	3,001.3	2,034.9	1,492.3	1,423.8	1,740.9
II. Industrial Countries[4]	2,489.8	2,163.3	2,099.4	2,044.8	2,225.4	2,093.4	1,707.5	1,618.5	2,290.4	2,313.9	1,597.1	1,070.3	991.7	1,207.0
United States	1,257.7	1,089.8	1,045.6	972.3	1,141.8	1,009.3	754.2	776.0	1,136.6	1,118.7	773.0	468.8	401.3	473.2
Canada	20.9	24.0	24.4	57.4	54.5	2.9	18.2	26.0	48.1	65.0	64.7	53.9	28.3	51.2
Australia	4.9	1.3	1.8	1.8	6.0	2.9	2.1	6.9	8.9	5.1	5.1	7.7	7.7	9.3
Japan	371.2	484.1	432.7	410.7	319.8	303.5	266.1	209.1	295.7	367.4	207.8	136.5	142.7	165.5
New Zealand	.6	1.1	.3	.2	.1	.1	.1	14.8	19.7	50.1	23.0	13.5	12.2	33.1
Austria	20.3	2.0	1.2	.4	~	44.8	5.6	5.8	14.0	18.5	5.9	3.5	6.8	8.1
Belgium–Luxembourg	99.3	68.5	95.1	89.5	130.1	136.3	108.5	62.6	36.6	25.0	20.2	25.6	26.4	22.8
Denmark	4.5	5.3	4.8	4.9	5.9	3.8	5.1	5.1	9.0	7.9	3.3	2.3	~	5.5
Finland	6.9	3.2	3.4	10.2	2.5	6.6	1.4	4.3	10.3	6.5	5.7	3.7	5.7	6.0
France	43.8	41.1	52.7	35.5	58.6	41.7	26.6	38.0	69.8	60.7	98.8	33.3	48.0	39.7
Germany	185.7	100.1	84.7	79.6	118.4	134.8	140.8	178.1	228.2	198.2	138.9	111.4	122.4	159.2
Iceland	~	.5	.1	.1	.3	1.5	.8	.4	~	~	~	~	~	~
Ireland	~	~	~	~	~	~	~	3.0	2.9	3.1	1.5	2.5	5.2	9.8
Italy	167.6	80.1	91.9	82.6	96.5	79.5	81.1	59.2	83.3	77.6	45.4	33.3	28.1	50.2
Netherlands	90.1	87.3	89.6	106.6	75.3	107.1	99.9	22.3	39.4	34.8	29.3	16.2	23.4	27.6
Norway	.7	1.0	2.0	1.0	3.0	.9	3.6	3.2	2.5	3.3	8.1	2.1	1.1	2.1
Spain	23.9	13.4	14.2	18.0	20.8	11.4	23.3	4.0	57.9	121.4	64.4	63.1	39.6	23.9
Sweden	21.7	9.8	13.2	15.6	77.1	20.5	19.1	79.0	79.2	40.2	33.4	34.7	28.4	23.9
Switzerland	15.5	18.0	5.3	6.1	12.0	36.3	33.6	33.8	56.3	41.7	26.4	25.2	25.7	68.5
United Kingdom	154.4	132.9	136.4	152.2	152.4	133.4	117.2	86.7	92.1	64.0	42.4	33.1	39.0	51.0
III. Developing Countries														
Oil Exporting Countries														
Algeria	75.7	69.2	60.4	32.7	50.5	48.7	84.0	28.7	38.3	19.1	20.7	25.9	26.1	39.2
Indonesia	4.0	~	.4	.7[a]	.7[b]	.7[b]	9.0	.2	.3	~	~	~	.1	~
Iran, I.R. of	.1	1.7	3.6	3.3	12.4[a]	1.5[c]	4.4	~	~	.1[a]	~	~	~	~
Nigeria	18.4	22.5	5.9	16.2[b]	17.0[b]	4.9	24.6	.1	.4	~	~	~	~	~
Saudi Arabia	1.2	~	.2	1.7	1.7	.9	.3	~	~	.4[a]	~	~	~	~
T. VENEZUELA	52.0	45.0	50.0	27.1	50.5	41.6	45.7	28.4	37.6	19.0	20.7	25.1	26.0	39.0
Non-Oil Developing Countries	1,092.3	607.8	628.0	346.1	366.7	620.4	534.9	358.5	524.0	620.4	393.3	357.9	366.3	465.3
Africa	14.6	26.7	12.0	15.7	3.5	1.7	18.5	11.9	20.2	~	~	~	~	.2
Angola	~	~	~	~	~	~	~	~	~	~	~	~	~	~
Madagascar	~	~	~	~	~	~	~	~	.1	~	~	~	~	~
Mauritius	~	~	.5[a]	~	~	~	~	~	~	~	~	~	~	~
Mozambique	~	~	~	.3[a]	~	~	~	~	~	~	~	~	~	~
South Africa	14.2	26.2	11.7[a]	15.0[a]	2.9[a]	1.4[c]	1.2	11.3	19.6	12.0[a]	12.2[a]	8.9[a]	8.4[c]	~
Zimbabwe	.3	.5	.4[b]	.3[b]	.3[b]	.2[b]	.3	.6	.5	.5[b]	.4[b]	.4[b]	.3[b]	~
Africa not specified	~	~	~	~	~	~	~	~	~	~	~	~	~	~
Asia	142.0	137.3	89.6	60.6	15.7	142.5	142.4	29.1	34.9	32.4	18.7	22.4	15.1	34.5
China, People's Rep.	88.2	70.7	93.6[a]	19.4	.3	55.5	63.4	.2	.8	1.4	1.1	4.3	1.1	6.7
Fiji	~	~	.2[a]	.2[a]	~	1.7	~	~	~	~	~	~	~	~
Hong Kong	2.9	3.6	4.3	2.5	12.5	7.2	9.0	3.0	12.0	12.7	4.6	3.0	2.3	3.1
India	2.6	.6	12.4	3.2	.7	7.9	12.3	4.8	1.3	2.4	.7	.5	.4	.7
Korea	42.1	54.5	55.2	29.2	2.2	63.9	43.0	1.7	7.5	8.6	11.0	2.8	4.7	9.3
Malaysia	1.3	.2	2.6	.4	~	.2	.9	.2	.1	.1	.2	.2	.9[a]	.4
Pakistan	1.2	1.4	.9	.5	.6[a]	.7	~	5.6	.2	.1[a]	.1	.7	.1	.2
Papua New Guinea	1.0	.4	.8	.1	.5[b]	.4[b]	~	~	~	~	~	1.5	~	~
Philippines	1.6	2.3	4.4	.7	~	4.1	7.5	~	~	1.5	~	~	.1	~
Singapore	.7	1.5	2.8	1.1	3.5[a]	.4	.2	8.5	8.0	4.6	4.3[a]	8.5[a]	5.3	5.5
Sri Lanka	~	~	.1[a]	.1[a]	.5[a]	.4	.2	~	~	.5	.9	1.1[a]	.7	~
Thailand	~	~	.4[a]	.4[a]	.8[a]	.1	~	~	~	.1[a]	~	~	~	~
Asia not specified	.4	.4	.3[b]	.3[b]	.3[b]	.3[b]	~	4.9	4.7	.1[a]	4.3[b]	3.9[b]	3.1[b]	~
Oceania not specified	~	~	~	~	~	~	~	.1	.3	.3[b]	.3[b]	.3[b]	.2[b]	~

Table 2631 (Continued)

PERU ABSOLUTE VALUE OF GOODS TRADED WITH SELECTED REGIONS AND COUNTRIES,[1] 1980–86
(M US)[2]

Category	Exports FOB							Imports CIF						
	1980	1981	1982	1983	1984	1985	1986	1980	1981	1982	1983	1984	1985	1986
III. Developing Countries (Continued)														
Non-Oil Developing Countries														
Europe	152.2	73.3	76.2	35.4	33.7	79.3	66.2	37.7	13.9	14.5	7.5	5.1	3.2	7.4
Greece	1.8	.3	5.9	3.0	.5	10.0	8.5	6.0	1.7	2.6	2.6	.1	.2	.8
Hungary	4.1	3.2	4.4	2.5	3.5	11.0	8.3	3.5	2.2	1.2	.9	2.5	1.3[a]	1.8
Malta	.1	~	.1[a]	.1[a]	.1[a]	.2[a]	~	~	.1	~	~	.1[a]	1.2	.7
Portugal	9.8	6.1	8.8	8.3	9.7	11.3	11.7	1.0	2.1	2.1	1.5	1.2	1.2	1.6
Romania	14.2	~	15.8	~	1.3	7.8	2.3	.5	3.2	7.0	.4[a]	.1[a]	.1[b]	1.1
Turkey	85.7	51.3	37.3	14.2	16.6	26.7	31.4	.6	1.7	.4	.3	.4	.2	.8
Yugoslavia	~	~	~	~	~	4.4	~	.4	.8	.9[b]	.8[b]	.7[a]	.3	.3
Europe not specified	~	.5	.5[b]	.4[b]	.3[b]	.3[b]	~	~	.8	.1[b]	.1[b]	.7[b]	.6	~
Middle East	24.2	23.9	7.9	1.6	2.1	10.1	29.5	1.8	.5	1.0	.9	2.3	1.3	1.1
Egypt	2.5	~	.6	.6	.4[a]	.4[b]	~	1.6	.4	.8	.8	1.5	1.3	.9
Israel	1.1	.6	.3	.1	.8[a]	4.4	4.2	~	~	~	~	~	~	~
Jordan	~	.1	.2	.1	~	~	~	~	~	~	~	~	~	~
Lebanon	~	.6	.2[b]	.1[b]	.1[b]	.1[b]	.4	~	~	~	~	~	~	~
Syrian Arab Rep.	~	.2	.5	.2	.1	.5	~	~	~	~	~	~	~	~
Middle East not specified	2.1	.5	.5[b]	.4[b]	.3[b]	.3[b]	~	~	.1	.1[b]	.1[b]	~	~	~
IV. Latin America[3]	829.6	415.9	448.3	267.4	367.7	420.9	362.4	306.7	492.6	573.0	373.2	352.8	364.1	461.4
A. ARGENTINA	59.4	19.7	22.2	29.9	34.1	35.9	57.2	71.6	60.2	110.3	105.4	128.8	144.6	133.1
Bahamas	126.6	14.1	10.1[b]	10.1[b]	7.0	6.0	~	~	.1	.1[b]	.1[b]	.4	.1	.4
Bermuda	~	.1[a]	.1[a]	~	~	~	~	~	~	~	~	~	~	~
B. BOLIVIA	69.2	24.5	22.5	13.5	30.0	13.1	10.6	11.4	7.3	21.2	16.1	3.1	10.0	5.3
C. BRAZIL	124.2	47.9	63.7	51.8	45.5	53.5	73.8	81.3	194.0	240.0	90.6	91.8	84.8	116.6
D. CHILE	45.0	58.9	39.4	50.8	59.8	49.9	49.0	34.0	40.8	43.8	35.8	27.0	47.0	46.7
E. COLOMBIA	55.9	91.9	123.9	40.0	75.4	75.4	66.0	22.6	37.0	29.7	20.2	20.2	24.2	57.9
F. COSTA RICA	5.1	4.3	1.8	3.1	7.3[a]	15.5	5.2	.3	1.6	1.1	1.5	.5	.4[c]	3.3
H. DOMINICAN REP.	~	.1	.1	.2	.3[a]	.5	.5	~	~	.5[a]	~	.3[a]	.2[c]	~
I. ECUADOR	83.8	11.5	42.7	28.4	29.9	74.9	28.7	5.5	6.4	29.5	5.6	2.7	6.8	5.1
J. EL SALVADOR	2.8	1.9	1.4	1.0	1.9[a]	3.1	2.2	~	~	.1[a]	~	~	.9[b]	.3
K. GUATEMALA	.3	.4	.1	.5	1.1[b]	.9[b]	.2	.3	.1	~	17.7	4.7	~	~
Guiana, French	.3	~	.3	.1[a]	.1[b]	~	~	~	~	.1	.5	.2[a]	.2[b]	~
Guyana	~	~	.1[a]	~	.1	.2	.1	.1	.4	.1[b]	.1	.6	~	~
L. HAITI	~	~	.1[a]	.5	.1	.2	.4	~	.1	.3	.1	~	~	~
M. HONDURAS	.1	.2	.1[a]	~	.1[b]	.7	~	.1	.1	.1[a]	~	~	~	~
Jamaica	.1	.2	.1[a]	~	.1[a]	.2	~	.1	.2	.1[a]	~	~	~	~
Martinique	~	10.5	~	~	~	~	~	~	10.5	~	~	~	~	~
N. MEXICO	90.7	43.0	13.3	14.0	19.1	11.0	3.4	17.2	33.8	26.6	22.9	18.4	4.2	23.7
Netherlands Antilles	.2	.3	5.6	.1	.2[b]	.2[b]	6.0	13.1	25.2	10.2	14.8	9.4	1.4	.1
O. NICARAGUA	.5	.6	1.2	2.1	6.2	1.6	3.1	.2	.3	~	~	~	~	~
P. PANAMA	102.3	48.7	63.1	9.5	16.5	35.3	14.5	13.0	28.7	20.7	11.3	10.2	9.9	10.8
Q. PARAGUAY	.5	.4	.1	.1[a]	.1[a]	.1[b]	.1	.2	.8	1.4	3.6	2.3	2.2	9.6
Trinidad and Tobago	.4	.1	.1	.6[a]	.6[a]	.4[a]	3.8	~	~	~	~	.7[a]	.6[a]	.1
S. URUGUAY	10.2	2.1	1.3	2.0	2.6	2.4	2.1	7.5	7.5	18.0	6.4	7.5	1.8	9.2
America not specified	~	~	~	~	~	~	~	~	~	~	~	~	~	~
Other Latin America not specified	~	~	~	~	~	~	~	~	~	~	~	~	~	~
V. USSR, Eastern Europe, etc.	67.4	73.9	23.8	30.1	8.5	161.5	125.9	6.7	8.7	9.2	9.1	24.1	2.2	15.4
Bulgaria	7.3	10.8	14.7	6.4	8.5	15.2	6.0	1.3	.3	.3	.3[b]	.3[b]	.2[b]	.1
G. CUBA	13.2	18.5	16.6[b]	13.3[b]	12.0[b]	10.8[b]	2.0	~	~	~	5.7	10.0	.1	7.5
Czechoslovakia	6.8	4.1	3.6[b]	4.1	2.6[b]	3.2	14.3	4.3	4.9	5.8	2.6	3.5	1.3	2.5
Eastern Germany	24.2	28.6	25.7[b]	1.6	18.5[b]	.1	.1	~	~	~	.2	9.7	.5	2.6
North Korea	~	.4	.8	.9	.1[a]	4.6	3.8	.2	.8	.9[b]	.7[a]	.8[b]	.1	.1
Poland	36.8	12.4	11.2[b]	8.9[b]	8.1[b]	7.2[b]	3.6	26.1	2.1	2.4[b]	.4	1.9[b]	1.5[b]	.3
USSR	16.0	12.1	8.2	17.1	7.8[b]	137.3	99.6	~	2.5	3.0	.4	.8	.2	.8
Country or area not specified	178.6	312.2	281.0[b]	224.8[b]	202.3[b]	182.1[b]	16.1	563.5	536.1	589.9[b]	530.7[b]	477.6[b]	382.1[b]	1.0
EEC	781.0	535.5	584.3	580.3	668.7	670.7	623.5	466.1	623.0	597.1	448.2	322.1	333.1	368.2

Table 2631 (Continued)

PERU ABSOLUTE VALUE OF GOODS TRADED WITH SELECTED REGIONS AND COUNTRIES,[1] 1980–86 (M US)[2]

Category	Exports FOB							Imports CIF						
	1980	1981	1982	1983	1984	1985	1986	1980	1981	1982	1983	1984	1985	1986
VI. Percent Distribution														
Industrial Countries	63.6	66.6	71.9	79.3	72.1	70.2	68.2	62.0	66.7	77.1	78.5	71.7	69.7	69.3
Oil Exporting Countries	1.9	2.1	2.2	1.9	2.0	1.8	3.4	1.1	1.1	.9	.9	1.1	1.4	2.3
Non-Oil Developing Countries	27.0	18.3	19.7	15.2	14.4	17.8	21.4	12.7	15.2	16.7	14.1	17.9	21.5	26.7
Africa	.5	.8	2.3	.5	.1	.5	.7	.5	.6	.6	.6	.1	.6	~
Asia	3.6	4.2	3.1	2.4	.5	4.8	5.7	1.1	1.0	1.1	.9	1.5	1.1	2.0
Europe	3.9	2.3	2.6	1.4	1.1	2.7	2.6	1.4	.4	.5	.5	.3	.2	.4
Middle East	.6	.7	.3	.1	~	.3	1.2	.1	~	.2	.1	.2	.1	.1
Non-Industrial														
Western Hemisphere[3]	21.2	12.8	15.4	10.4	11.9	14.1	14.5	11.8	14.3	19.1	18.3	23.6	25.6	26.5
USSR, Eastern Europe, etc	1.7	2.3	.8	1.2	.3	5.4	5.0	.3	.3	.3	.4	1.6	.2	.9
VII. Annual Percent Change														
World	6.5	-17.1	-10.7	-11.7	19.7	-3.4	-16.0	55.0	31.5	-12.6	-32.2	-26.7	-4.6	22.3
Industrial Countries	9.6	-13.1	-3.0	-7.6	8.8	-5.9	-18.4	50.9	41.5	1.0	-31.0	-33.0	-7.3	21.7
Oil Exporting Countries	5.9	-8.6	6.1	-20.4	10.8	-16.8	72.5	22.9	33.4	-11.2	-20.3	5.2	#	50.2
Non-Oil Developing Countries	31.6	-43.6	11.8	-30.0	-.5	12.8	-13.8	57.3	57.0	20.3	-38.4	18.3	-5.3	27.0
Africa	35.0	148.9	-79.1	-99.9	~	-51.4	13.3	29.6	71.8	-9.1	-37.1	-89.7	672.6	-97.9
Asia	635.1	-3.3	-34.8	-32.3	-74.0	805.6	-.1	83.1	19.8	-7.1	-42.3	20.0	-32.7	128.5
Europe	22.3	-51.9	3.8	-53.6	-4.7	135.4	-16.5	31.2	-63.2	4.5	-34.3	-46.3	-37.7	131.4
Middle East	~	-1.2	-66.8	-79.9	-87.9	-38.1	193.2	54.8	-73.8	109.8	-6.5	151.0	-43.8	-13.5
Non-Industrial														
Western Hemisphere[3]	8.6	-49.9	7.8	-40.4	37.5	14.5	-13.9	50.3	60.6	16.3	-34.9	-5.5	3.2	26.7
USSR, Eastern Europe, etc.	-45.8	9.7	-67.9	26.5	-71.7	-10.0	-22.1	173.3	29.3	6.3	-1.2	164.7	-91.0	606.7

1. DOT data may differ between countries and from IFS data because of the time it takes for an export to become an import, etc.
2. Data may be calculated from partner's reported data or estimated on basis of less than 12 months.
3. Cuba is included in category V; Venezuela is included in category III.
4. For the 1982–85 figures, data derived from partner country for the entire year.
a. Data derived from partner country for the entire year.
b. Data extrapolated for entire year.
c. Five or fewer months of reported data; seven or more months derived or extrapolated.

SOURCE: Adapted from IMF-DOT-Y, 1982, 1986, and 1987.

Table 2632

URUGUAY ABSOLUTE VALUE OF GOODS TRADED WITH SELECTED REGIONS AND COUNTRIES,[1] 1980–86
(M US)[2]

Category	Exports FOB							Imports CIF						
	1980	1981	1982	1983	1984	1985	1986	1980	1981	1982	1983	1984	1985	1986
I. World	1,057.5	1,174.7	1,032.3	1,063.2	920.9	850.5	1,354.7	1,649.3	1,626.5	1,110.0	624.2	774.3	819.9	1,066.2
II. Industrial Countries	425.7	487.8	375.6	378.4	369.3	335.9	775.3	592.7	581.7	385.3	185.9	246.0	281.6	425.1
United States	82.6	94.9	76.7	103.5	137.7[a]	128.9	442.0	161.1	158.2	135.0	52.1	66.0	70.7[a]	109.8
Canada	7.1	8.4	7.3	25.9	9.0[a]	6.8	10.7	13.6	19.4	10.2	2.6	6.3	4.4[b]	9.5
Australia	.4	.7	.6	.9	2.6[a]	2.8	2.4	2.4	8.0	5.3	4.4	3.2	1.8[b]	2.8
Japan	9.3	13.1	18.1	20.0	20.1[a]	19.0	17.4	67.9	79.7	30.5	14.9	14.3	18.6[b]	33.6
New Zealand	—	—	—	.2	.10	.1[a]	~	.5	.3	.1	.1	3.0	.2[b]	.8
Austria	3.3	3.6	6.8	3.2	3.3[a]	.6	9.8	4.9	4.8	3.8	2.5	2.3	4.8[b]	4.6
Belguim-Luxembourg	18.2	23.6	15.5	11.6	6.6[a]	5.1	6.0	7.5	8.2	4.1	3.1	4.1	4.6[b]	5.6
Denmark	2.6	.7	.7	.5	.4[a]	.3	2.0	15.2	4.0	2.8	1.4	1.5	4.2[b]	4.4
Finland	.6	5.0	4.5	4.5	5.5[a]	4.2	6.6	1.3	1.7	.4	.1	.4	.7[b]	1.9
France	14.3	21.9	23.4	17.8	13.5[a]	14.2	35.8	29.7	41.9	26.6	15.0	14.8	23.4[b]	35.6
Germany	136.9	123.1	91.8	80.4	75.7[a]	66.1	79.4	111.4	99.7	77.0	37.4	45.9	59.8[b]	78.7
Ireland	.1	.1	~	~	~	1.1[b]	1.0	.7	.8	.6	.7	.6	.6[b]	.8
Italy	46.2	55.9	38.3	20.7	18.9[a]	22.2	40.0	46.7	38.2	21.8	9.6	30.4	20.0[b]	36.4
Netherlands	45.3	57.5	29.6	30.4	22.3[a]	27.4	26.2	15.1	14.0	9.0	7.3	8.4	8.2[b]	14.6
Norway	.3	.5	.2	.3	1.0[a]	.2	1.3	2.1	7.5	.6	.5	.1	1.0[b]	.6
Spain	10.3	16.2	11.0	6.9	8.6[a]	13.1	17.5	19.1	23.3	13.2	5.7	12.6	15.1[b]	19.7
Sweden	5.3	1.5	2.3	1.5	1.2[a]	1.0	4.5	7.5	6.7	4.2	3.8	1.8	8.2[b]	9.8
Switzerland	5.6	8.0	12.1	8.2	6.6[a]	6.3	17.2	17.0	17.4	12.8	10.9	14.1	13.2[b]	16.9
United Kingdom	37.4	53.0	36.7	41.9	36.1[a]	35.6	55.4	69.1	47.8	27.1	13.8	16.1	22.0[b]	39.3
III. Developing Countries	71.3	131.8	92.1	174.0	88.5	82.7	62.3	418.3	347.7	308.1	185.7	194.4	164.9	114.7
Oil Exporting Countries	1.0	7.1	.3	.3	.6	.3	.2	~	.1	~	.3	~	~	~
Algeria	—	—	—	1.3	—	—	—							
Indonesia	37.5	47.3	55.0	119.8	48.5[c]	61.6	46.2	~	~	89.2	29.2	78.8	66.9	46.9
Iran, I.R. of	—	2.6	.2	8.1	.2[c]	.2[c]	1.6	~	~	~	~	~	~	~
Iraq	211.1	~	~	~	~	~	~	~	~	~	~	~	~	~
Kuwait	4.3	3.2	8.4	2.4	3.1[c]	2.2		~	~	~	~	~	~	~
Libya	—	7.4	—	.2	1.9[c]	1.5[d]	.1	134.4	210.1	127.8	103.1	114.0	96.9	67.8
Nigeria	15.1	47.7	14.7	10.8	2.5[c]	.2	.1	~	~	~	~	~	~	~
Oman	—	.2	—	—	~	~	.8	~	17.0	~	~	~	~	~
Saudi Arabia	10.2	12.6	11.2	26.4	20.8[a]	14.3	10.7	72.8	120.5	91.1	53.1	~	1.1	3.0
United Arab Emirates	—	1.9	.1	—	6.7[a]	.6	.4	~	.1	~	~	1.7	~	~
T. VENEZUELA	3.0	1.8	2.1	2.4	4.3	3.7	3.0	.8	~	~	~	~	1.1	~
Non-Oil Developing Countries	483.1	472.4	455.8	412.9	352.1	341.7	439.3	609.0	677.3	405.8	238.7	301.7	340.2	488.6
Africa	30.1	77.2	30.8	23.0	20.7	9.2	10.0	148.4	222.6	136.3	108.5	117.4	100.6	72.3
Angola	.7	1.1	~	.5	1.2[d]	3.2[d]	~							
Benin	.1	—	—	1.0	1.2[c]	1.2[d]	2.1							
Cameroon	—	—	.6	—	.5	2.0								
Cape Verde	—	—	—	.4	.8[c]	.6[d]								
Congo	.2	.2	—	.1	.2[a]	.2[d]	.1							
Gabon	.1	.1	.3	2.2	~	.7	.8							
Ghana	1.1	6.3	1.0	.5	.4[c]	.3[d]	~							
Ivory Coast	.5	.3	—	—	.4[c]	.3[d]	.3							
Liberia	~	~	~	~	~	~	~							
Madagascar	~	~	~	~	~	.1	~							
Mauritius	~	~	~	~	~	~	~							
Morocco	.1	.2	2.0	.6	.8[a]	.1	.1		.4	.2				
Niger	.2	~	~	~	~	~	~	4.1	4.1			1.1[d]	1.1[d]	1.2
Senegal	~	~	~	~	~	~	~	8.4	4.8	2.9	4.1	1.6	1.9[e]	
South Africa	11.3	10.9	7.8	5.3	9.9[a]	5.5	6.1	2.0	1.9					2.6
Togo	~	2.9	4.2	~	~	~	~	1.8	1.1	.5				
Tunisia	~	~	~	1.1	~	.1[b]	.1			3.9	.2	.2	.1[d]	.2
Zaire	~	~	~	1.1	.4[c]	.3	.3						.3[b]	.3

Table 2632 (Continued)

URUGUAY ABSOLUTE VALUE OF GOODS TRADED WITH SELECTED REGIONS AND COUNTRIES,[1] 1980–86
(M US)[2]

Category	Exports FOB							Imports CIF						
	1980	1981	1982	1983	1984	1985	1986	1980	1981	1982	1983	1984	1985	1986
III. Developing Countries (Continued)														
Non-Oil Developing Countries														
Africa (Continued)														
Zimbabwe	?	?	?	?	?	?	?	?	.2	.3	.3	.3	.1	.1
British Africa not specified	?	?	?	?	?	?	?	?	?	?	?	?	?	?
Spanish Africa	?	?	?	?	?	?	?	?	?	?	?	?	?	.1
Asia														
Bangladesh	8.1	12.6	17.0	25.0	53.7	61.6	83.5	32.9	30.1	16.6	8.2	9.5	10.4	18.6
China, People's Rep.	.6	.4	9.0	12.2	38.2a	43.1	58.4	1.1	1.1	1.6	1.7	2.3	.9b	.5
Hong Kong	6.6	8.4	5.8	5.6	6.5a	9.4	14.5	3.2	4.0	2.4	.6	.5	.6b	1.2
India	.2	.8	.4	.1	.2c	.2d	?	5.8	6.3	4.0	.9	1.3	2.5b	6.5
Korea	.2	2.3	1.0	5.0	6.4a	3.6	2.4	6.4	3.5	1.8	1.4	1.3	.3	.3
Malaysia	.1	.5	.2	.2	.2a	.6	.9	5.7	7.2	2.1	.5	.8	2.2	3.5
Pakistan	?	?	?	?	?	?	?	6.5	4.8	1.6	1.6	2.5	.9b	1.8
Philippines	.2	.1	.3	.4	.1a	.8	1.5	.1	.1	.1	?	?	.1b	?
Singapore	.3	.1	.2	.3	.2a	2.2	3.9	.2	2.0	2.2	.7	1.2	2.5b	4.2
Sri Lanka	?	?	?	?	?	?	?	.6	.8	.7	.3	.5	.4b	.5
Thailand	?	?	?	?	?	1.1	1.1	.2	.1	?	?	?	?	?
Asia not specified	1.5	8.0	?	?	?	?	?	?	?	?	?	?	?	?
Europe														
Cyprus	36.8	37.6	32.6	20.9	17.9	20.6	19.8	12.2	9.6	6.1	2.0	1.2	8.0	1.1
Greece	.5	.4	.5	.3	.1a	.1b	.1	.2	.7	.1	.2	.1	.9b	?
Hungary	17.0	7.6	6.3	2.4	4.1a	3.1	5.6	.2	.7	.1	.2	.1	.2b	.3
Malta	3.0	5.0	6.7	3.9	4.1a	7.5	?	1.2	1.1	1.1	.4	.4	?	?
Portugal	4.2	.4	.4	.5	.5a	.7	.4	?	?	?	?	?	?	?
Romania	?	7.5	7.3	5.2	5.0a	6.8	10.6	.3	1.1	.4	.2	.2	.4b	.4
Turkey	.3	1.4	1.5	.1	.5a	.5d	?	1.2	1.7	1.1	.1	.2	.2d	?
Yugoslavia	5.2	9.5	8.1	3.4	2.9a	.5b	.9	.1	.1	.1	.1	.1	.1d	.1
Europe not specified	?	?	?	?	?	?	?	.1	.6	2.5	.8	?	7.0b	?
Middle East														
Egypt	82.9	153.7	149.2	266.4	113.5	93.5	73.9	213.4	19.9	90.8	29.4	79.7	69.0	50.6
Israel	27.2	55.7	46.6	83.5	12.6a	12.0d	?	2.4	2.9	1.7	.3	.9	2.1b	3.7
Jordan	3.5	16.0	12.7	21.0	19.5a	14.2	14.9	?	?	?	?	?	?	?
Lebanon	?	3.2	11.3	2.4	.2c	.2d	?	?	?	?	?	?	?	?
Syrian Arab Rep.	?	.5	3.6	.3	?	?	?	?	?	?	?	?	?	?
IV. Latin America[3]	395.0	315.1	318.2	251.7	234.9	238.5	313.3	620.4	742.8	464.1	276.3	288.3	317.0	460.8
A. ARGENTINA	142.3	101.8	109.1	91.1	83.7a	62.8	71.3	174.1	128.8	86.0	62.3	87.4	108.2	133.5
Bahamas	.2	.6	.2	.1	.2c	.1	.1	.1	?	?	.1	.1	.1d	.1
Barbados	.3	.2	.2	.2	.3a	.1	.4	?	?	?	?	?	?	?
B. BOLIVIA	1.7	2.0	1.0	1.8	1.2	1.0	1.1	1.9	.2	?	.1	.1	.1d	?
C. BRAZIL	191.0	152.7	145.8	121.3	109.9a	143.4	201.6	284.0	322.0	140.6	69.9	127.1	154.3b	239.0
D. CHILE	23.3	24.8	21.8	9.3	10.3a	4.0e	5.6	19.6	13.6	9.0	5.7	6.1	13.5	12.1
E. COLOMBIA	3.6	2.9	3.0	3.6	3.8a	6.8	7.2	1.5	3.0	.5	.3	.1	.4	.4
F. COSTA RICA	?	?	?	?	?	.1	.1	.1	.2	.4	.4	.1	?	?
H. DOMINICAN REP.	.8	.7	1.2	.9	.2a	1.4	1.0	.4	.2	.4	.2	.2	.2	?
I. ECUADOR	.1	?	?	?	1.1a	?	?	6.3	105.0	34.4	.4	.2	.1e	.1
K. GUATEMALA	?	?	?	?	?	?	?	?	?	?	?	?	?	?
L. HAITI	.7	.7	.9	?	?	?	?	.2	.7	.9	?	?	?	?
M. HONDURAS	.7	.7	?	?	?	.1	.1	?	?	?	?	?	?	?
Jamaica	?	?	?	?	?	?	?	.2	?	?	?	?	?	?
Leeward Islands	.1	.1	?	?	?	?	?	?	?	?	?	?	?	?
N. MEXICO	5.1	6.2	3.9	3.3	4.7a	6.8	7.7	11.6	11.0	83.3	66.1	47.3	26.8	64.0
Netherlands Antilles	?	.2	?	?	?	?	?	6.1	.45	6.0	4.7	2.1	2.0d	2.2
O. NICARAGUA	?	.1	?	?	?	?	?	?	?	?	?	?	?	?

Table 2632 (Continued)

URUGUAY ABSOLUTE VALUE OF GOODS TRADED WITH SELECTED REGIONS AND COUNTRIES,[1] 1980–86
(M US)[2]

Category	Exports FOB							Imports CIF						
	1980	1981	1982	1983	1984	1985	1986	1980	1981	1982	1983	1984	1985	1986
IV. Latin America[3] (Continued)														
P. PANAMA	.3	.2	3.2	.5	.3[a]	.3	.3	7.1	8.7	2.3	3.4	1.6	~	~
Panama Canal Zone	~	~	~	~	~	~	~	~	~	~	~	~	~	~
Q. PARAGUAY	14.6	12.9	9.9	8.2	6.7[a]	6.1	4.4	19.5	19.4	5.7	7.0	11.4	7.1[b]	7.0
R. PERU	8.0	7.5	16.6	5.0	5.6	1.8	9.2	10.8	2.6	1.0	2.0	2.7	2.6	2.3
Trinidad and Tobago	~	~	~	.2	.4[a]	.4[b]	~	2.7	2.4	2.6	1.1	.5	~	~
Windward Islands	~	~	~	~	~	~	~	~	~	.1	~	~	~	~
America not specified	~	~	~	3.7	2.2	.1	.1	~	~	.1	~	~	~	.1
V. USSR, Eastern Europe, etc.	70.5	82.7	92.5	73.6	82.4	56.3	59.1	8.0	9.3	4.7	12.3	29.7	29.7	31.2
Bulgaria	~	.1	.1	.4	.5[c]	.4	.4	2.7	1.1	1.2	.3	.6	.6	.4
Czechoslovakia	14.3	9.6	6.4	8.2	15.3	11.7	12.3	10.6	4.4	1.2	9.3	.6	.7[d]	.6
Eastern Germany	8.0	6.2	7.4	3.1	4.2[c]	4.5	4.7	1.5	.6	.6	.3	.7	.7[d]	.7
Poland	6.5	3.9	1.8	3.9	1.0[c]	1.0[d]	1.9	9.2	4.2	.8	.3	.3	.3	.3
USSR	48.3	66.9	78.6	61.9	62.3	39.7	41.7	3.3	3.2	1.7	2.4	28.4	28.4	29.9
USSR, etc., not specified	.3	~	.7	11.7	8.6[c]	1.5	1.6	.1	~	.2	~	.1	.1	.1
Country or area not specified	~	~	~	~	~	~	~	~	~	~	~	~	~	~
Special categories	~	~	3.2	~	~	~	~	~	~	~	~	~	~	~
EEC	332.5	367.2	260.5	217.8	191.3	193.9	279.5	315.0	279.8	182.9	94.4	134.6	158.6	235.7
VI. Percent Distribution														
Industrial Countries	40.2	41.3	36.4	35.6	40.1	41.6	57.2	35.9	35.8	34.7	29.8	31.8	34.3	39.9
Oil Exporting Countries	6.7	11.1	8.9	16.4	9.7	5.7	4.6	25.4	21.4	27.8	29.8	25.1	22.9	10.8
Non-Oil Developing Countries	45.0	39.6	43.9	38.5	38.3	25.2	32.4	36.4	41.4	36.5	38.2	38.9	36.2	45.8
Africa	2.8	6.6	3.0	2.2	2.2	1.1	.7	9.0	13.7	12.3	17.4	15.2	12.3	6.8
Asia	.8	1.1	1.6	2.3	5.8	7.2	6.2	2.0	1.8	1.5	1.3	1.2	1.3	1.7
Europe	3.5	3.2	3.2	2.0	1.9	2.4	1.5	.7	.6	.5	.3	.3	1.0	.1
Middle East	7.8	13.1	14.5	25.1	12.3	11.0	5.5	12.9	1.2	8.2	4.7	10.3	8.4	4.7
Non-industrial Western Hemisphere[3]	37.4	26.8	30.8	23.7	25.5	28.0	23.1	37.6	45.7	41.8	44.3	37.2	38.7	43.2
USSR, Eastern Europe, etc.	6.7	7.0	9.0	6.9	8.9	6.0	4.4	1.1	.6	.4	2.0	3.8	3.6	2.9
VII. Annual Percent Change														
World	34.0	11.1	-12.1	3.0	-13.4	-7.6	59.3	38.1	-1.4	-31.8	-43.8	24.0	5.9	30.0
Industrial Countries	8.1	14.6	-23.0	.7	-2.4	-4.2	119.1	42.4	-1.8	-33.8	-51.7	32.3	14.5	51.0
Oil Exporting Countries	432.9	85.0	-30.1	88.9	-48.9	-20.0	-24.7	59.2	-16.9	-11.4	-39.7	4.7	-9.9	-30.4
Non-Oil Developing Countries	35.2	-1.7	-3.1	-9.9	-13.7	-10.8	28.6	21.0	12.2	-39.8	-41.1	26.4	-8.1	43.6
Africa	193.9	156.6	-60.1	-25.2	-10.3	-55.2	7.9	128.9	50.0	-38.8	-20.4	8.2	-14.3	-28.2
Asia	205.3	55.6	34.7	46.7	115.1	14.7	35.6	88.6	-8.5	-44.8	-50.4	15.0	10.0	78.1
Europe	85.4	2.4	-13.3	-36.1	-14.0	14.6	-3.8	8.7	-21.4	-36.9	-67.8	-36.8	550.2	-86.2
Middle East	292.8	85.5	-2.9	78.6	-57.4	-17.6	-20.9	49.3	-90.7	356.3	-67.6	170.6	-13.4	-26.7
Non-industrial Western Hemisphere[3]	24.9	-20.2	1.0	-20.9	-6.7	1.6	31.3	17.0	19.7	-37.5	-40.5	4.4	10.0	45.4
USSR, Eastern Europe, etc.	192.5	17.3	11.9	-20.5	11.9	-31.7	5.0	156.6	-48.5	-49.6	161.9	142.4	-5.0	5.0

1. DOT data may differ between countries and from IFS data because of the time it takes for an export to become an import, etc.
2. Data may be calculated from partner's reported data or estimated on basis of less than 12 months.
3. No trade with Cuba; Venezuela is included in category III.

a. Eleven months of reported, one month derived from partner.
b. Data derived from partner country for the entire year.
c. Eleven months of reported, one month extrapolated.
d. Data extrapolated for the entire year.
e. Eight, seven, or six months of reported data; four, five, or six months derived or extrapolated.

SOURCE: Adapted from IMF-DOT-Y, 1982, 1986, and 1987.

Table 2633

VENEZUELA ABSOLUTE VALUE OF GOODS TRADED WITH SELECTED REGIONS AND COUNTRIES,[1] 1980–86
(M US)[2]

Category	Exports FOB							Imports CIF						
	1980	1981	1982	1983	1984	1985	1986	1980	1981	1982	1983	1984	1985	1986
I. World	19,261	20,002	16,957	14,755	16,094	14,189	8,412	11,183	12,098	11,650	5,786	7,007	7,304	7,635
II. Industrial Countries[4]	11,220	11,642	10,523	10,470	10,696	10,871	5,739	9,650	10,416	9,789	4,777	5,757	6,076	6,513
United States	5,344	5,114	4,712	4,588	6,772	6,526	3,764	5,350	5,844	5,332	2,673	3,395	3,469	3,503
Canada	1,772	1,910	1,440	557	730	716	272	533	564	458	291	267	281	194
Australia	~	~	759	1,696	236	153	1	14	14	33	3	9	5	8
Japan	682	781	563	394	376	415	279	896	969	1,190	328	337	416	529
New Zealand	~	~	~	9	4	6	~	14	19	48	34	28	33	15
Austria	4	~	~	5	4	20	19	8	11	17	12	12	27	41
Belgium—Luxembourg	208	215	148	218	118	98	69	145	161	146	64	92	88	117
Denmark	23	7	6	21	10	40	~	48	49	34	38	50	46	34
Finland	~	~	3	5	6	1	~	37	39	14	34	25	28	26
France	343	461	256	196	182	166	134	334	364	392	240	238	256	331
Germany	203	190	391	595	573	606	487	758	766	600	313	373	414	562
Iceland	~	4	~	1	~	~	~	~	~	~	~	~	~	~
Ireland	~	~	~	~	16	7	8	10	20	23	11	16	7	8
Italy	1,123	1,401	980	843	669	742	147	471	487	549	211	300	312	356
Netherlands	301	523	417	801	442	720	237	196	208	211	129	165	155	132
Norway	13	~	6	2	20	43	30	20	23	14	5	10	21	16
Spain	699	632	383	173	138	224	41	340	358	307	150	152	183	193
Sweden	281	215	221	140	114	154	55	62	78	63	46	44	40	39
Switzerland	~	~	2	1	4	6	1	96	101	98	58	73	75	97
United Kingdom	225	190	236	240	316	242	203	320	341	260	127	171	220	312
III. Developing Countries														
Oil Exporting Countries														
Algeria	26	21	4	71	31	28	9	40	9	11	8	16	6	6
Indonesia	~	~	~	5	20	10	7	~	~	~	~	~	~	1
Iran, I.R. of	7	21	1[a]	2[a]	7	~	~	10	8	11	7	10	6	5
Iraq	~	~	~	66	3	~	2	~	1	~	~	~	~	2
Nigeria	3	~	~	~	~	~	2	~	~	~	~	~	~	~
Saudi Arabia	16	~	3[a]	~	~	18	~	29	~	~	1	6	~	~
Non-Oil Developing Countries	7,738	7,974	3,926	3,348	3,736	2,812	1,804	1,418	1,591	1,678	896	1,144	1,099	1,008
Africa	186	175	5	156	26	10	7	109	111	5	3	2	50	34
Congo	17	~	~	~	~	~	~	~	~	~	~	~	~	~
Ivory Coast	149	171	60[a]	21[a]	23[a]	20[b]	~	~	~	~	~	~	~	~
Liberia	~	~	~	~	~	~	~	13	~	~	~	~	~	~
Malawi	~	~	~	~	~	~	~	~	~	~	~	~	~	~
Mauritius	~	~	~	~	~	~	~	~	~	~	~	~	~	~
Morocco	2	2	1[a]	~	1[a]	1[c]	~	1	1	6[a]	3[a]	2[a]	2[c]	2
Mozambique	~	~	~	~	~	~	~	~	~	~	~	~	~	~
Namibia	~	~	~	~	~	~	~	~	~	~	~	~	~	~
Senegal	~	~	~	~	1[a]	~	~	~	~	~	~	~	~	~
South Africa	2	1	~	~	~	~	~	~	111	68[a]	36[a]	14[a]	30	26
Tunisia	~	1	~	~	~	~	~	~	~	~	3[a]	4[a]	2[a]	5
Africa not specified	~	~	5	151	6	~	~	66	~	4	3	2	18	5
Asia	141	261	137	21	30	177	95	165	184	184	52	83	80	81
China, People's Rep.	~	~	~	4[a]	8[a]	115[a]	45	45	55	49	11	13	14	3
Hong Kong	19	14	1[a]	3	3	11	5	62	60	52	15	13	28	25
India	54	134	57	~	9	14	6	3	5	1	5	1	1	1
Korea	24	89	50	4	1	20	2	32	37	45	14	37	27	33
Malaysia	~	~	3[a]	~	~	~	~	8	5	1[a]	2[a]	1[a]	2[a]	~
Papua New Guinea	~	~	~	2[a]	~	~	~	~	4	~	~	1[a]	~	~
Philippines	~	~	~	~	~	~	~	1	2	2	1	1[a]	1[a]	5

Table 2633 (Continued)

VENEZUELA ABSOLUTE VALUE OF GOODS TRADED WITH SELECTED REGIONS AND COUNTRIES,[1] 1980–86

(M US)[2]

Category	Exports FOB							Imports CIF						
	1980	1981	1982	1983	1984	1985	1986	1980	1981	1982	1983	1984	1985	1986
III. Developing Countries (Continued)														
Non-Oil Developing Countries														
Africa (Continued)														
Singapore	21	~	25[a]	8[a]	6	~	~	4	8	7	3	5	4	~
Thailand	16	3	2	12	10	18	12	~	~	13	~	4	~	6
Asia not specified	~	~	1	~	~	~	25	~	~	~	~	~	~	2
Oceania not specified	~	~	~	~	~	~	~	~	~	~	~	~	~	~
Europe	233	232	141	70	108	32	23	30	49	39	6	16	36	41
Gibraltar	8	~	~	~	~	5[a]	1	~	~	~	~	~	~	~
Greece	76	34	33	~	~	~	~	~	~	6	~	1[a]	1[a]	1
Hungary	~	~	~	~	~	~	1	1	2	2	2[a]	1	1	~
Malta	3	~	1[a]	~	~	~	~	~	~	~	~	~	~	~
Portugal	142	150	103	67	99	18	3	17	18	20	5[a]	7	7	7
Romania	3	17	7[a]	9[a]	3[a]	3[b]	12	1	11	3	~	1	16	24
Turkey	~	3	7	~	5[a]	4[b]	2	1	1	2	1[a]	2	7	6
Yugoslavia	~	~	~	~	4[a]	4[a]	1	4	11	3	~	1	5	2
Europe not specified	~	28	25[b]	20[b]	18[b]	16[b]	~	~	~	~	~	~	~	2
Middle East	3	~	15	81	12	18	2	7	6	5	7	6	3	~
Egypt	~	~	14	2	~	~	~	~	~	2	~	~	~	~
Israel	~	~	1[a]	~	~	~	~	7	6	3	6	10	12	~
IV. Latin America[3]	7,201	7,327	3,628	3,091	3,091	2,603	1,686	1,146	1,249	1,456	836	1,053	936	858
A. ARGENTINA	56	37	14	4	3	1[c]	8	85	97	133	60	126	84	42
Antigua and Barbuda	~	~	~	~	~	~	~	~	~	~	~	~	~	~
Bahamas	44	1	~	~	~	~	21	2	2	1[b]	1[b]	1[b]	1[b]	~
Barbados	29	31	26	20	20	31	~	2	1	~	~	~	~	~
Bermuda	~	~	1[a]	~	~	~	~	1	3	4[a]	~	~	~	~
B. BOLIVIA	~	~	~	~	~	~	~	3	3	~	~	~	~	~
C. BRAZIL	678	933	900	553	510	252	69	186	254	469	345	366	310	344
D. CHILE	242	336	241	209	226	240	116	81	71	51	36	41	34	40
E. COLOMBIA	273	330	301	323	321	225	105	183	195	239	91	113	111	80
F. COSTA RICA	82	88	104	63	92	122	51	1	2	3	3	2	5	6
Dominica	~	~	~	1[a]	~	~	~	~	~	~	~	~	~	1
H. DOMINICAN REP.	237	267	239	287	324	277	135	136	67	46	4[a]	29	4	2
I. ECUADOR	17	20	36	6	2	2[c]	5	38	43	56	4	3[a]	2[c]	1
J. EL SALVADOR	106	85	78	70	73	79	56	~	1	1	~	5	1	~
K. GUATEMALA	132	103	78	97	93	74	41	1	1	10	~	~	~	~
Guiana, French	~	~	1[a]	1[a]	~	~	~	1	1	1[a]	1[b]	1[b]	1[b]	4
Guyana	~	3	~	~	3	~	~	34	59	7[a]	9[a]	8[b]	7[b]	~
L. HAITI	~	~	~	~	3	13	~	3	6	~	~	~	~	~
M. HONDURAS	86	37	26	67	99	97	45	3	6	6[a]	9[a]	8[b]	7[b]	60
Jamaica	158	171	206	144	93	146	63	14	~	~	~	~	~	~
N. MEXICO	24	26	22	1	2	13	6	84	86	79	56	57	55	91
Netherlands	4,590	4,308	3,877[b]	3,101[b]	2,791[b]	2,512[b]	7	94	91	95[b]	86[b]	77[b]	62[b]	~
O. NICARAGUA	85	83	39	2	5	5	7	~	~	~	~	~	~	~
P. PANAMA	168	194	179	121	120	118	43	121	160	191	43	84	106	91
Panama Canal Zone	~	3	1[a]	1[a]	~	~	~	~	~	~	1[b]	~	~	~
Q. PARAGUAY	1	2	2[b]	1[b]	1[b]	2[c]	1	~	~	12	1	23	7	21
R. PERU	26	28	20	21	20	27	31	57	60	50	29	45	47	54
St. Lucia	1	2	2[b]	1[b]	1[b]	1[b]	~	~	~	~	~	~	~	~
St. Vincent	~	~	1[a]	1[a]	~	~	~	~	~	~	~	~	~	~
Suriname	7	10	8	82	87	52	2	~	5	12[a]	2[a]	9	8	14
Trinidad and Tobago	~	~	~	11	2[a]	1[b]	34	11	8	33	21	22	27	21
S. URUGUAY	80	125	99[b]	79[b]	71[b]	64[b]	~	4	4	4	3	8	8[b]	3
French West Indies not specified	78	110	~	~	~	~	~	3	~	~	~	~	~	~

Table 2633 (Continued)

VENEZUELA ABSOLUTE VALUE OF GOODS TRADED WITH SELECTED REGIONS AND COUNTRIES,[1] 1980-86
(M US)[2]

Category	Exports FOB							Imports CIF						
	1980	1981	1982	1983	1984	1985	1986	1980	1981	1982	1983	1984	1985	1986
V. USSR, Eastern Europe, etc.	128	96	27	98	205	442	363	26	22	19	9	13	24	15
Bulgaria	~	~	~	~	~	~	~	~	~	1	1	1	~	~
G. CUBA	99	74	20	84	204	425	360	1	4	4b	8	2	16	4
Czechoslovakia	3	1	1	1b	1b	1b	~	7	4	13	~	10	7	10
Eastern Germany	19	21	6	8	14b	14	3	17	18	~	~	~	~	~
North Korea	~	~	~	~	~	~	~	~	~	~	~	~	~	~
Poland	1	~	~	~	~	~	4	7	6	7b	6b	6b	4b	~
USSR	8	~	1	6	~	3	~	~	1	1b	1b	1b	1b	1
Country or area not specified	137	261	2,463	755	1,922	21	494	~	~	86	73	50	25	24
EEC	3,343	3,802	2,953	3,154	2,537	2,861	1,322	2,638	2,772	2,548	1,298	1,565	1,688	2,053
VI. Percent Distribution														
Industrial Countries	58.3	58.2	62.1	71.0	66.5	76.6	68.2	86.3	86.1	84.0	82.6	82.2	83.2	85.3
Oil Exporting Countries	.1	.1	#	.1	.1	.1	.1	.4	.1	#	#	#	~	#
Non-Oil Developing Countries	40.2	39.9	41.8	37.7	33.1	30.8	21.4	12.6	13.1	14.1	13.8	14.3	12.1	13.2
Africa	1.0	.9	.4	1.1	.2	.1	.1	1.0	.9	.6	.1	.4	.7	.4
Asia	.7	1.3	.8	.2	.2	1.2	1.1	1.5	1.5	1.6	.9	1.2	1.1	1.1
Europe	1.2	1.2	.8	.5	.7	.2	.3	.3	.4	.3	.1	.2	.5	.5
Middle East	~	~	.1	.5	.1	.1	~	.1	.1	.2	.1	.1	.2	~
Non-Industrial														
Western Hemisphere[3]	37.4	36.6	21.4	20.9	19.2	18.3	20.0	10.2	10.3	12.5	14.4	15.0	12.8	11.2
USSR, Eastern Europe, etc.	.7	.5	.2	.7	1.3	3.1	4.3	.2	.2	.2	.2	.2	.3	.2
VII. Annual Percentage Change														
World	34.6	3.8	-15.2	-13.0	9.1	-11.8	-40.7	16.3	8.2	-3.7	-50.3	21.1	4.2	4.5
Industrial Countires	24.4	3.8	-9.6	-1.5	2.2	1.6	-47.2	17.7	7.9	-6.0	-51.2	20.5	5.5	7.2
Oil Exporting Countries	220.0	-16.4	-80.9	150.0	#	-10.0	-67.9	~	-78.0	-77.7	#	-50.0	~	#
Non-Oil Developing Countries	56.9	3.1	-12.3	-19.4	-8.7	-9.5	-35.8	6.9	12.3	6.4	-51.9	19.3	-14.1	-8.3
Africa	33.8	-6.0	-97.1	-56.2	-83.3	-61.5	-30.0	124.3	2.2	-95.5	-40.0	-33.3	-15.4	-32.0
Asia	857.8	85.3	-47.5	-84.7	42.9	490.3	-46.3	26.7	11.0	.2	-71.7	59.6	-3.6	1.2
Europe	368.3	-.5	~	-50.4	54.3	-70.4	-28.1	9.3	64.5	-21.0	-84.6	166.7	125.0	13.9
Middle East	-40.4	~	-39.2	440.0	-85.2	50.0	-88.9	46.3	-11.4	-21.4	40.0	-14.3	-50.0	~
Non-Industrial														
Western Hemisphere[3]	52.2	1.8	-50.5	-14.8	-8.7	-15.8	-35.2	2.5	9.1	16.5	-42.6	26.0	-11.1	-8.3
USSR, Eastern Europe, etc.	98.6	-25.1	-71.9	263.0	109.2	115.6	-17.9	57.2	-13.8	-14.3	-52.6	44.4	84.6	-37.5

1. DOT data may differ between countries and from IFS data because of the time it takes for an export to become an import, etc.
2. Data may be calculated from partner's reported data or estimated on basis of less than 12 months.
3. No trade with Cuba.
4. For the 1982-85 figures, data derived from partner country for the entire year.
a. Data derived from partner country for the entire year.
b. Data extrapolated for the entire year.
c. Five or fewer months of reported data; seven or more months derived or extrapolated.

SOURCE: Adapted from IMF-DOT-Y, 1982, 1986, and 1987.

Table 2634

UNITED STATES VALUE OF GOODS TRADED WITH EACH LATIN AMERICAN COUNTRY, 19 LC, 1980–86
(M US)

	Country	Exports							Imports, FOB						
		1980	1981	1982	1983	1984	1985	1986	1980	1981	1982	1983	1984	1985	1986
A.	ARGENTINA	2,630	2,192	1,294	965	900	721	943	792	1,214	1,222	939	1,024	1,167	939
B.	BOLIVIA	172	189	99	102	106	120	112	189	184	113	172	160	101	127
C.	BRAZIL	4,352	3,798	3,423	2,557	2,640	3,140	3,885	4,000	4,852	4,643	5,381	8,273	8,147	7,340
D.	CHILE	1,354	1,465	925	729	805	682	824	559	661	729	1,053	871	858	935
E.	COLOMBIA	1,736	1,771	1,903	1,514	1,450	1,468	1,319	1,327	900	883	1,058	1,253	1,456	2,039
F.	COSTA RICA	498	373	330	382	423	422	483	405	426	421	453	544	570	720
H.	DOMINICAN REP.	795	779	664	632	646	742	921	828	977	669	855	1,068	1,031	1,139
I.	ECUADOR	864	854	828	597	655	591	601	953	1,103	1,227	1,520	1,804	1,975	1,603
J.	EL SALVADOR	273	308	292	365	426	446	518	444	270	333	362	406	413	401
K.	GUATEMALA	553	559	390	316	377	405	400	465	384	365	404	479	448	647
L.	HAITI	311	301	299	366	419	396	387	264	287	326	352	395	406	391
M.	HONDURAS	379	349	275	299	322	308	363	475	493	426	435	450	433	487
N.	MEXICO	15,146	17,789	11,817	9,082	11,992	13,635	12,392	12,835	14,013	15,770	17,019	18,267	19,392	17,558
O.	NICARGUA	250	184	119	132	112	42	3	227	152	98	109	69	50	1
P.	PANAMA	699	884	845	748	757	675	712	353	329	289	378	365	467	412
Q.	PARAGUAY	109	108	78	37	64	99	171	85	52	41	34	44	25	31
R.	PERU	1,172	1,486	1,117	900	751	496	693	1,443	1,277	1,150	1,204	1,402	1,152	858
S.	URUGUAY	183	163	190	86	80	64	100	103	165	265	390	576	571	486
T.	VENEZUELA	4,577	5,445	5,206	2,811	3,377	3,399	3,141	5,571	5,800	4,957	5,173	6,820	6,830	5,446
	WORLD	220,781	233,738	212,274	200,528	217,889	213,146	217,291	256,959	272,351	254,882	269,880	341,170	361,620	387,075

SOURCE: Adapted from IMF-DOT-Y, 1982, 1986, and 1987.

Table 2635

SHARE OF THE TRANSNATIONAL CORPORATIONS IN INDUSTRIAL EXPORTS, 6 L, 1976–80

(%)

	Country	1976	1977	1978	1979	1980
C.	BRAZIL	~	~	49.8	52.4	~
D.	CHILE	~	~	~	21.7	~
E.	COLOMBIA	22.7	24.0	19.6	14.0	16.9
F.	COSTA RICA	~	~	~	~	26.0
N.	MEXICO	37.2	42.4	~	~	~
S.	URUGUAY	~	10.1	12.6	~	~

SOURCE: *CEPAL Review*, April 1985, no. 25, p. 53.

Table 2636

SOVIET TRADE WITH THE WESTERN HEMISPHERE, 20 LC, 1984

(M US)[1]

	Country	Exports to	Imports from	Soviet Deficit
A.	ARGENTINA	1,361.3	30.8	1,330.5
B.	BOLIVIA	4.3	1.2	3.1
C.	BRAZIL	563.6	114.8	448.8
D.	CHILE	- -	- -	- -
E.	COLOMBIA	21.9	4.46	17.4
F.	COSTA RICA	- -	- -	- -
G.	CUBA	8,694.1	4,520.7	4,173.4
H.	DOMINICAN REP.	- -	- -	- -
I.	ECUADOR	4.2	.1	4.1
J.	EL SALVADOR	- -	- -	- -
K.	GUATEMALA	- -	- -	- -
L.	HAITI	- -	- -	- -
M.	HONDURAS	- -	- -	- -
N.	MEXICO	19.4	2.1	17.3
O.	NICARAGUA	166.9	166.3	.6
P.	PANAMA	11.3	11.2	.1
Q.	PARAGUAY	- -	- -	- -
R.	PERU	81.4	30.1	51.3
S.	URUGUAY	83.7	27.3	56.4
T.	VENEZUELA	- -	- -	- -
	LATIN AMERICA	11,012.3	4,909.2	6,103.1
	UNITED STATES	3,776.9	368.5	3,408.4

1. Converted from rubles at the rate of 83 to 1.

SOURCE: Soviet Ministry of Trade.

Part IX: Financial Flows

CHAPTER 27

BALANCE OF PAYMENTS

AND

INTERNATIONAL LIQUIDITY

Note: This volume contains statistics from numerous sources. Alternative data on many topics are presented. Variations in statistics can be attributed to differences in definition, parameters, coverage, methodology, as well as date gathered, prepared, or adjusted. See also Editor's Note on Methodology.

Table 2700

GUIDE TO BALANCE OF PAYMENTS ANALYSIS

(IMF Focuses on Reserves; ECLA Focuses on the Balance of Current and Capital Accounts)

A. Current Account[1,7]
Merchandise: exports f.o.b.
Merchandise: imports f.o.b.
   Trade Balance
Other goods, services, and income:
   credit

Other goods, services, and income:
   debit

     Total goods, services and income
Private unrequited transfers[2,a]
     Total, excl. official unrequited transfers
Official unrequited transfers[2,b]

B. Direct Investment and Other Long-Term[3] Capital
Direct investment

Portfolio investment
Other long-term capital
   Resident official sector

   Deposit money banks

   Other sectors

     Total, Groups A plus B

C. Other Short-Term Capital[3]

Resident official sector

Deposit money banks

Other sectors

D. Net Errors and Omissions

   Total, Groups A through D

E. Counterpart Items
Monetization/demonetization of gold
Allocation/cancellation of SDRs
Valuation changes in reserves

   Total, Groups A through E

F. Exceptional Financing

   Total, Groups A through F

G. Liabilities Constituting Foreign[5] Authorities' Reserves

   Total, Groups A through G

H. Total Change in Reserves[4,6]
Monetary gold
SDRs
Reserve position in the Fund
Foreign exchange assets
Other claims
Use of Fund credit

1. ECLA inclusions are as follows (cf. table 2725):
   A. Goods, Services and Income
      Merchandise
      Shipment
      Other Transportation
         Passenger Services
         Port Services, etc.
      Travel
      Investment Income
         Direct Investment Income
            Reinvested Earnings
            Distributed Earnings
         Other
            Resident Official, Including Interofficial
            Foreign Official, Excluding Interofficial
            Private
      Other Goods, Services, and Income
         Official
            Interofficial
            Other, Resident Official
            Other, Foreign Official
         Private
            Labor Income, nie
            Property Income, nie
            Other
   B. Private Unrequited Transfers
      Migrants' Transfers
      Workers' Remittances
      Other
2. Required = payment for goods or services.
3. ECLA inclusions are as follows:
   A. Official Unrequited Transfers
      Interofficial
      Other, Resident Official
      Other, Foreign Official
   B. Capital Other Than Reserves
      Long-Term Capital
      Direct Investment
      Other Private Loans
      General Government Securities and Assets
      Short-Term Capital
      Deposit Money Banks
      Other Private
      Reserve Banks
   C. Net Errors and Omissions

   D. Exceptional Financing
   E. Counterpart Items
      Monetization/Demonetization of Gold
      Allocation of SDRs
4. Reserves (and related items) bring categories I and II into zero balance and include:
   A. Use of IMF Credit
   B. Other Liabilities
   C. Monetary Gold
   D. SDRs
   E. Reserve Position in IMF
   F. Foreign Exchange and Other Claims

According to Høst (cited in Source, below, pp. 50-51), "reserves and related items, as now defined, have always been considered to be the hard core of financing below the line of the balance of payments surpluses and deficits, as representing the response of monetary authorities at home or abroad to surplus or deficit situations. It was invariably so considered when the concept of compensatory official financing was used in the early days of the Fund's activities. For many years, a similar concept was used in the United States in its publication of balance of payments statistics as one measure of surplus or deficit, the so-called official settlements balance. Such a balance ceased to be published in the United States in 1976. For several reasons, reserves and related items have become less adequate for the assessment of the balance of payments. First, a build-up of reserves by the monetary authorities of a number of countries in a reserve center or other financial centers may not, in an environment of general floating of exchange rates, reflect surpluses or deficits in the countries holding the reserves. It may be the response to interest differentials between financial markets or confidence factors, inducing countries to adjust the currency composition of their foreign exchange portfolios. Moreover, after the sharp rise in the price of oil which began in 1973, part of the foreign assets held by the monetary authorities of some of the major oil exporting countries must be regarded to be in the nature of investments rather than balances held for the financing of balance of payments deficits. For all these reasons, it has become increasingly difficult to assess the surplus or deficit in the balance of payments calling for adjustment. But these difficulties do not apply to the great majority of developing countries."

5. Liabilities Constituting Foreign Authorities' Reserves.
6. Cf. ECLA's concept of compensatory financing in table 2725ff., the last three items of which equal change in reserves.
7. Because the Basic Balance (current account + official unrequited transfers) is not separately available prior to 1967 for most countries, IFS-Y standard format for all years precludes presentation for Basic Balance for any years.

a. One definition considers this item to belong to capital account.
b. ECLA's definition considers this item to belong to capital account.

SOURCE: Data are from IMF-IFS-Y, 1979. Analysis is also adapted from Poul Høst-Madsen, *Macroeconomic Accounts: An Overview*, Pamphlet Series No. 29 (Washington, D.C.: IMF, 1979), pp. 39, 49-51. Cf. table 2725ff.

Table 2701

IMF BALANCE OF PAYMENTS, 19 LC, 1981–85[a]

(M SDR)

A. ARGENTINA

Category	1983	1984	1985
A. Current Account	-2,282	-2,480	-948
Merchandise: exports f.o.b.	7,328	7,875	8,292
Meat	552	380	365
Other	6,776	7,495	7,927
Merchandise: imports f.o.b.	-3,857	-4,031	-3,470
Trade balance	3,471	3,845	4,822
Other goods, services, and income: credit	1,805	1,762	1,905
Other goods, services, and income: debit	-7,573	-8,089	-7,675
Total: goods, services, and income	-2.297	-2,482	-948
Private unrequited transfers	15	2	#
Total, excl. official unrequited transfers	-2.282	-2,480	-948
Official unrequited transfers	#	#	#
B. Direct Investment and Other Long-Term Capital	-579	-1,210	-1,012
Direct investment	170	262	953
Portfolio investment	612	361	-603
Other long-term capital			
Resident official sector	-1.350	880	117
Loans received by general government	-805	1,744	1,177
Loans received by Central Bank	-534	-520	-906
Other liabilities	#	#	#
Assets	-11	-343	-154
Deposit money banks	36	-31	#
Other sectors	-46	-2,681	-1,478
Loans received	119	-2,511	-1,490
Other	-165	-171	12
Total, Groups A plus B	-2,861	-3,690	-1,960
C. Other Short-Term Capital	-1,335	1,290	1,104
Resident official sector	-219	154	446
Deposit money banks	298	-510	641
Other sectors	-1,415	1,646	16
D. Net Errors and Omissions	-414	-51	-308
Total, Groups A through D	-4,610	-2,452	-1,163
E. Counterpart Items	119	-115	#
Monetization/demonetization of gold	#	#	#
Allocation/cancellation of SDRs	#	#	#
Valuation changes in reserves	119	-115	#
Total, Groups A through E	-4,492	-2,567	-1,163
F. Exceptional Financing	2,438	2,395	2,344
Bonds issued to cancel external obligations	459	375	108
Loans received by Central Bank	1,676	609	-604
Payments arrears	304	910	-2,393
Total, Groups A through F	-2,054	-172	1,181
G. Liabilities Constituting Foreign Authorities' Reserves	-141	196	-217
Total, Groups A through G	-2,194	25	964
H. Total Change in Reserves	2,194	-25	-964
Monetary gold	#	#	#
SDRs	#	#	1
Reserve position in the Fund	91	#	#
Foreign exchange assets	983	-24	-1,949
Other claims	#	#	#
Use of Fund credit	1,121	#	985
Conversion rates: Austral per SDR	.01126	.06934	.61104
Conversion rates: U.S. dollars per SDR	1.0690	1.0250	1.0153

B. BOLIVIA

Category	1983	1984	1985
A. Current Account	-140.9	-170,6	-278,1
Merchandise: exports f.o.b.	706.4	706.8	614.0
Crude petroleum and gas			
Metals	269.4	306.1	207.4
Other	55.8	26.0	39.6
Merchandise: imports f.o.b.	-442.6	-402.2	-455.8
Trade balance	263.8	304.6	158.2
Other goods, services, and income: credit	118.6	120.5	112.3
Other goods, services, and income: debit	-621.9	-681.4	-626.9
Total: goods, services, and income	-239.5	-256.3	-356.4
Private unrequited transfers	37.6	21.3	19.4
Total, excl. official unrequited transfers	-201.9	-235.0	-337.0
Official unrequited transfers	61.0	64.4	58.9
B. Direct Investment and Other Long-Term Capital	-392.0	-143.8	-231.3
Direct investment	6.5	6.8	9.8
Portfolio investment	#	-.9	-.9
Other long-term capital			
Resident official sector	-238.0	-108.3	-196.5
Loans received by general government	-224.6	~	~
Loans received by Central Bank	-9.5	~	~
Other	-3.8	~	~
Deposit money banks	-32.7	-11.6	-8.5
Other sectors	-127.7	-29.9	-35.3
Total, Groups A plus B	-532.8	-314.4	-509.4
C. Other Short-Term Capital	-109.2	199.9	-2.2
Resident official sector	12.7	2.7	1.3
Deposit money banks	-29.9	13.3	-26.3
Other sectors	-92.0	183.9	22.8
D. Net Errors and Omissions	75.7	-11.7	183.2
Total, Groups A through D	-566.3	-126.2	-328.4
E. Counterpart Items	8.8	18.7	-19.7
Monetization/demonetization of gold	.8	.9	-.1
Allocation/cancellation of SDRs	#	#	#
Valuation changes in reserves	7.9	17.8	-19.6
Total, Groups A through E	-557.5	-107.6	-348.1
F. Exceptional Financing	834.4	276.0	347.3
Grants from Subsidy Account	.8	.7	.5
IBRD structural adjustment loan	#	#	#
Loans from Argentine banks	#	#	#
Loans from U.S. commercial banks	#	#	#
Trust Fund loans	#	#	#
Rescheduled debt			
Resident official sector	298.1	#	#
Deposit money banks	32.4	-157.8	#
Other sectors	124.2	-26.5	#
Payments arrears	378.9	-94.9	#
Total, Groups A through F	276.9	168.4	-.8
G. Liabilities Constituting Foreign Authorities' Reserves	-252.7	-36.8	-61.8
Total, Groups A through G	24.2	131.7	-62.6
H. Total Change in Reserves	-24.2	-131.7	62.6
Monetary gold	-.8	-.9	.1
SDRs	-.1	.1	#
Reserve position in the Fund	#	#	#
Foreign exchange assets	-11.4	-104.3	71.7
Other claims	-19.0	-6.2	8.9
Use of Fund credit	7.2	-20.3	-18.2
Conversion rates: Bolivian pesos per SDR	246	2,372	~
Conversion rates: U.S. dollars per SDR	1.0690	1.0250	1.0153

Table 2701 (Continued)

IMF BALANCE OF PAYMENTS, 19 LC, 1981–85[a]

(M SDR)

C. BRAZIL

Category	1983	1984	1985
A. Current Account	-6,360	52	-333
Merchandise: exports f.o.b.	20,508	26,390	25,153
Coffee	1,962	2,500	2,340
Iron ore	1,415	1,567	1,627
Other	17,131	22,322	21,186
Merchandise: imports f.o.b.	-14,441	-13,596	-12,929
Trade balance	6,068	12,794	12,224
Other goods, services, and income: credit	2,288	3,131	3,633
Other goods, services, and income: debit	-14,816	-16,039	-16,342
Investment income	-10,954	-12,426	-12,611
Other	-3,862	-3,614	-3,731
Total: goods, services, and income	-6,461	-115	-485
Private unrequited transfers	99	157	138
Total, excl. official unrequited transfers	-6,362	42	-348
Official unrequited transfers	2	10	15
B. Direct Investment and Other Long-Term Capital	124	-2,759	-6,496
Direct investment	1,285	1,517	1,262
Portfolio investment	-270	-265	-231
Other long-term capital			
Resident official sector	1,894	-1,256	-2,562
Loans received by general government	1,802	6,425	3,527
Loans received by Central Bank	-6	-7,827	-5,911
Other	98	145	-178
Deposit money banks	-1,786	-1,378	-2,590
Other sectors	-1,000	-1,377	-2,375
Loans received	-778	~	~
Other	-13	~	~
Total, Groups A plus B	-6,236	-2,707	-6,828
C. Other Short-Term Capital	-1,076	-3,110	-1,526
Resident official sector	-78	-280	-18
Deposit money banks	-663	958	-547
Other sectors	-335	-3,788	-960
D. Net Errors and Omissions	-57	396	-488
Total, Groups A through D	-7,889	-5,421	-8,842
E. Counterpart Items	751	815	-987
Monetization/demonetization of gold	521	328	257
Allocation/cancellation of SDRs	#	#	#
Valuation changes in reserves	230	487	-1,244
Total, Groups A through E	-7,138	-4,606	-9,829
F. Exceptional Financing	7,350	10,208	8,763
Rescheduled debt			
Resident official sector	1,060	~	~
Deposit money banks	366	~	~
Other sectors	209	~	~
Short-term loans	314	201	#
Deferred payments	3,210	~	~
Payments arrears	2,192	-2,231	#
Total, Groups A through F	212	5,601	-1,066
G. Liabilities Constituting Foreign Authorities' Reserves	-1,213	491	-436
Total, Groups A through G	-1,001	6,093	-1,502
H. Total Change in Reserves	1,001	-6,093	1,502
Monetary gold	-147	-328	-551
SDRs	#	-1	#
Reserve position in the Fund	260	#	#
Foreign exchange assets	-859	-7,368	1,993
Other claims	-279	-140	124
Use of Fund credit	2,027	1,744	-64
Conversion rates: cruzeiros per SDR	616.9	1,894.2	6,296
Conversion rates: U.S. dollars per SDR	1.0690	1.0250	1.0153

D. CHILE

Category	1983	1984	1985
A. Current Account	-1,004	-2,010	-1,287
Merchandise: exports f.o.b.	3,580	3,561	3,686
Copper	1,750	1,565	1,743
Other	1,830	1,996	1,943
Merchandise: imports f.o.b.	-2,636	-3,275	-2,909
Trade balance	944	286	777
Other goods, services, and income: credit	912	1,136	940
Other goods, services, and income: debit	-2,946	-3,528	-3,064
Investment income	-1,781	-2,281	-2,069
Other	-1,165	-1,247	-995
Total: goods, services, and income	-1,090	-2,106	-1,347
Private unrequited transfers	46	40	46
Total, excl. official unrequited transfers	-1,044	-2,066	-1,301
Official unrequited transfers	40	57	14
B. Direct Investment and Other Long-Term Capital	1,132	-576	-1,627
Direct investment	138	65	110
Portfolio investment	#	#	#
Other long-term capital			
Resident official sector	1,075	128	73
Loans received by general government	-108	151	174
Loans received by Central Bank	1,182	-23	-101
Other	#	#	#
Deposit money banks	-8	-479	-1,060
Other sectors	-73	-290	-750
Drawings on loans received	478	~	~
Repayments on loans received	-551	~	~
Total, Groups A plus B	128	-2,585	-2,914
C. Other Short-Term Capital	-675	575	359
Resident official sector	94	#	#
Deposit money banks	-395	244	27
Other sectors	-374	331	333
D. Net Errors and Omissions	53	97	-10
Total, Groups A through D	-495	-1,914	-2,565
E. Counterpart Items	107	212	-253
Monetization/demonetization of gold	22	60	2
Allocation/cancellation of SDRs	#	#	#
Valuation changes in reserves	85	151	-255
Total, Groups A through E	-387	-1,702	-2,818
F. Exceptional Financing	~	1,931	2,474
Total, Groups A through F	-387	230	-344
G. Liabilities Constituting Foreign Authorities' Reserves	11	72	-4
Total, Groups A through G	-376	301	-347
H. Total Change in Reserves	376	-301	347
Monetary gold	43	-60	-2
SDRs	12	-7	11
Reserve position in the Fund	71	#	#
Foreign exchange assets	-324	-450	142
Other claims	#	#	#
Use of Fund credit	573	216	196
Conversion rates: Chilean pesos per SDR	84.28	101.12	163.55
Conversion rates: U.S. dollars per SDR	1.0690	1.0250	1.0153

Table 2701 (Continued)

IMF BALANCE OF PAYMENTS, 19 LC, 1981–85[a]

(M SDR)

E. COLOMBIA

Category	1983	1984	1985
A. Current Account	−2,567	−1,367	−1,369
Merchandise: exports f.o.b.	2,778	4,169	3,657
Coffee	1,350	1,692	1,686
Petroleum products	415	434	404
Other	1,013	2,043	1,567
Merchandise: imports f.o.b.	−4,176	−3,929	−3,678
Trade balance	−1,397	240	−21
Other goods, services, and income: credit	1,060	1,029	1,094
Transportation	332	385	422
Other	695	644	673
Other goods, services, and income: debit	−2,384	−2,928	−2,900
Transportation	−598	−581	−564
Investment income	−1,121	−1,591	−1,599
Other	−665	−755	−736
Total: goods, services, and income	−2,720	−1,659	−1,826
Private unrequited transfers	136	282	435
Total, excl. official unrequited transfers	−2,585	−1,377	−1,391
Official unrequited transfers	18	10	22
B. Direct Investment and Other Long-Term Capital	1,429	1,778	2,027
Direct investment	480	547	718
Portfolio investment	−2	−3	−1
Other long-term capital			
Resident official sector	95	346	299
Loans received by general government	98	359	279
Loans received by Bank of the Republic	−3	−13	21
Other	#	#	#
Deposit money banks	#	#	#
Other sectors	855	887	1,010
Government-owned enterprises	787	841	832
Private enterprises	68	46	178
Total, Groups A plus B	−1,138	411	658
C. Other Short-Term Capital	−364	−860	−204
Resident official sector	79	18	14
Deposit money banks	54	183	−249
Other sectors	−497	−695	32
D. Net Errors and Omissions	−226	−66	−527
Total, Groups A through D	−1,728	−516	−73
E. Counterpart Items	236	−518	105
Monetization/demonetization of gold	166	−635	167
Allocation/cancellation of SDRs	#	#	#
Valuation changes in reserves	70	117	−62
Total, Groups A through E	−1,492	−1,035	32
F. Exceptional Financing	#	#	#
Total, Groups A through F	−1,492	−1,035	32
G. Liabilities Constituting Foreign Authorities' Reserves	5	4	−1
Total, Groups A through G	1,487	−1,031	31
H. Total Change in Reserves	1,487	1,031	−31
Monetary gold	−166	635	−167
SDRs	−26	189	#
Reserve position in the Fund	−87	262	#
Foreign exchange assets	1,766	−55	136
Other claims	#	#	#
Use of Fund credit	#	#	#
Conversion rates: Colombian pesos per SDR	84,30	103.34	144.49
Conversion rates: U.S. dollars per SDR	1.0690	1.0250	1.0153

F. COSTA RICA

Category	1983	1984	1985
A. Current Account	−286.7	−250.0	−320.4
Merchandise: exports f.o.b.	807.5	972.8	918.4
Bananas	225.1	244.1	209.6
Coffee	215.3	260.7	306.5
Other	367.2	467.9	402.4
Merchandise: imports f.o.b.	−840.9	−972.2	−990.2
Trade balance	−33.4	.5	−71.7
Other goods, services, and income: credit	299.4	308.2	331.8
Other goods, services, and income: debit	−586.7	−598.7	−626.7
Total: goods, services, and income	−320.7	−289.9	−366.7
Private unrequited transfers	21.4	31.1	33.8
Total, excl. official unrequited transfers	−299.3	−258.8	−332.9
Official unrequited transfers	12.5	8.8	12.5
B. Direct Investment and Other Long-Term Capital	−54.9	−179.8	−130.1
Direct investment	51.7	50.7	66.0
Portfolio investment	−2.5	−.2	−13.2
Other long-term capital			
Resident official sector	−55.5	−120.5	−127.1
Loans received by general government	17.9	27.5	6.3
Loans received by Central Bank	−72.3	−123.9	−96.3
Other	−1.1	−24.1	−37.1
Deposit money banks	−14.2	−26.2	−25.0
Other sectors	−34.5	−83.6	−30.9
Loans received by government enterprises	−3.6	−52.7	−16.0
Loans recieved by private enterprises	−30.9	−30.8	−15.0
Total, Groups A plus B	−341.7	−429.8	−450.6
C. Other Short-Term Capital	−56.2	−96.2	−53.9
Resident official sector	.5	.6	−1.3
Deposit money banks	−32.1	10.5	−25.5
Other sectors	−24.6	−107.3	−27.2
D. Net Errors and Omissions	52.1	107.9	109.4
Total, Groups A through D	−345.7	−418.1	−395.1
E. Counterpart Items	29.6	−15.8	−15.6
Monetization/demonetization of gold	7.0	−12.9	11.4
Allocation/cancellation of SDRs	#	#	#
Valuation changes in reserves	22.6	−2.9	−27.0
Total, Groups A through E	−316.2	−433.9	−410.7
F. Exceptional Financing	410.6	417.6	516.6
Grants from AID	30.6	99.9	160.4
Long-term borrowing by Central Bank	1,174.6	243.2	478.1
Short-term borrowing by Central Bank	−14.3	84.1	−4.5
Payment arrears			
Resident official sector	−465.2	128.8	−119.0
Deposit money banks	−58.4	1.6	−2.0
Other sectors	−256.8	28.1	−33.5
Rescheduling of government enterprises' arrears	#	#	#
Total, Groups A through F	94.4	−16.3	106.0
G. Liabilities Constituting Foreign Authorities' Reserves	−21.6	−48.5	−53.3
Total, Groups A through G	72.8	−64.8	52.6
H. Total Change in Reserves	−72.8	64.8	−52.6
Monetary gold	−1.2	12.9	−9.8
SDRs	−2.8	2.7	.1
Reserve position in the Fund	#	#	#
Foreign exchange assets	−178.0	52.7	−47.9
Other claims	10.1	20.8	−7.7
Use of Fund credit	99.1	−24.3	12.7
Conversion rates: Costa Rican colones per SDR	43.930	45.646	51.227
Conversion rates: U.S. dollars per SDR	1.0690	1.0250	1.0153

Table 2701 (Continued)

IMF BALANCE OF PAYMENTS, 19 LC, 1981–85[a]

(M SDR)

H. DOMINICAN REP.

Category	1982	1983	1984
A. Current Account	−400.3	−390.9	−159.4
Merchandise: exports f.o.b.	695.4	734.5	846.9
Sugar	279.5	279.6	312.2
Other	415.8	454.9	534.7
Merchandise: imports f.o.b.	−1,138.8	−1,196.4	−1,226.4
Trade balance	−443.5	−461.9	−379.5
Other goods, services, and income: credit	342.8	433.6	494.9
Other goods, services, and income: debit	−485.3	−563.7	−533.4
Investment income	−234.1	−284.4	−241.2
Other	−251.2	−279.3	−292.2
Total: goods, services and income	−586.0	−592.0	−417.9
Private unrequited transfers	172.1	182.4	200.0
Total, excl. official unrequited transfers	−413.9	−409.6	−217.9
Official unrequited transfers	13.6	18.7	58.5
B. Direct Investment and Other Long-Term Capital	177.2	58.6	286.9
Direct investment	−1.3	45.1	66.8
Portfolio investment	#	#	#
Other long-term capital			
Resident official sector	202.3	75.4	231.5
Loans received by general government	~	~	~
Loans received by Central Bank	~	~	~
Other	~	~	~
Deposit money banks	−.8	8.5	−2.3
Other sectors	−23.0	−70.4	−9.1
Total, Groups A plus B	−223.1	−332.4	127.5
C. Other Short-Term Capital	−147.6	−125.7	−68.3
Resident official sector	−31.6	−9.4	−118.2
Deposit money banks	−41.1	−219.4	−21.1
Other sectors	−74.8	103.1	71.0
D. Net Errors and Omissions	−.6	12.2	28.9
Total, Groups A through D	−371.3	−445.8	88.1
E. Counterpart Items	−3.6	−8.5	−14.1
Monetization/demonetization of gold	−14.9	−13.7	−21.6
Allocation/cancellation of SDRs	#	#	#
Valuation changes in reserves	11.2	5.2	7.5
Total, Groups A through E	−374.9	−454.3	74.0
F. Exceptional Financing	147.2	337.8	−1.1
Long-term borrowing by Central Bank	60.5	38.4	~
Short-term borrowing by Central Bank	−21.6	−28.3	−29.3
Commercial arrears	108.2	−97.3	28.2
Deposits received for balance of payments support	#	#	#
Total, Groups A through F	−227.7	−116.6	73.0
G. Liabilities Constituting Foreign Authorities' Reserves	91.9	−19.6	7.6
Total, Groups A through G	−135.8	−136.1	80.6
H. Total Change in Reserves	135.8	136.1	−80.6
Monetary gold	14.9	11.7	21.6
SDRs	1.1	.3	−.2
Reserve position in the Fund	#	−7.4	7.4
Foreign exchange assets	75.4	−39.6	−102.2
Other claims	.1	#	2.3
Use of Fund credit	44.3	171.1	−9.5
Conversion rates: Dominican pesos per SDR	1.1040	1.0690	1.0250
Conversion rates: U.S. dollars per SDR	1.0690	1.0250	1.0153

I. ECUADOR

Category	1983	1984	1985
A. Current Account	−97.3	−241.9	−83.7
Merchandise: exports f.o.b.	2,212.3	2.558.0	2,826.6
Bananas	143.1	132.7	187.1
Coffee	139.4	170.7	181.2
Crude petroleum	1,537.9	1,638.0	1,797.4
Other	392.0	616.6	660.9
Merchandise: imports f.o.b.	−1,317.1	−1,528.8	−1,697.0
Trade balance	895.2	1,029.3	1,129.7
Other goods, services, and income: credit	302.2	341.5	384.1
Other goods, services, and income: debit	−1,317.1	−1,632.2	−1,622.1
Shipment	−104.8	−147.3	−118.2
Investment income	−732.5	−935.6	−977.0
Other	−479.9	−549.3	−526.9
Total: goods, services, and income	−119.7	−261.5	−108.3
Private unrequited transfers	#	~	~
Total, excl. official unrequited transfers	−119.7	−261.5	−108.3
Official unrequited transfers	22.5	19.5	24.6
B. Direct Investment and Other Long-Term Capital	−1,075.8	−827.3	−674.7
Direct investment	46.8	48.8	59.1
Portfolio investment	#	#	#
Other long-term capital			
Resident official sector	−240.4	−319.0	−636.2
Loans received by general government	−228.3	−310.2	−636.2
Other	−12.2	−8.8	#
Deposit money banks	−6.5	−8.8	#
Other sectors	−875.6	−548.3	−97.5
Total, Groups A plus B	−1,173.1	−1,069.3	−758.4
C. Other Short-Term Capital	−1,027.1	−242.9	~
Resident official sector	−555.7	−22.4	~
Deposit money banks	6.5	33.2	~
Other sectors	−478.0	−253.7	~
D. Net Errors and Omissions	−79.7	9.1	−83.3
Total, Groups A through D	−2,279.9	−1,303.1	−841.7
E. Counterpart Items	33.6	47.3	−80.1
Monetization/demonetization of gold	#	#	#
Allocation/cancellation of SDRs	#	#	#
Valuation changes in reserves	33.6	47.3	−80.1
Total, Groups A through E	−2,246.3	−1,255.8	−921.8
F. Exceptional Financing	2,313.4	1,294.6	867.7
Debt rescheduling			
Residential official sector	1,956.0	1,176.6	1,127.7
Other sectors	#	#	18.7
Long-term loans received from commercial banks	403.2	#	~
Payments arrears	−45.8	118.0	−278.7
Total, Groups A through F	67.1	38.8	−54.1
G. Liabilities Constituting Foreign Authorities' Reserves	69.2	−70.2	~
Total, Groups A through G	136.3	−31.4	−54.1
H. Total Change in Reserves	−136.3	31.4	54.1
Monetary gold	#	#	#
SDRs	−.1	−.4	−25.7
Reserve position in the Fund	−11.4	11.4	#
Foreign exchange assets	−328.3	−19.0	−4.6
Other claims	#	#	#
Use of Fund credit	203.5	39.4	84.4
Conversion rates: sucres per SDR	47.159	64.100	70.623
Conversion rates: U.S. dollars per SDR	1.0690	1.0250	1.0153

Table 2701 (Continued)

IMF BALANCE OF PAYMENTS, 19 LC, 1981–85[a]

(M SDR)

J. EL SALVADOR

Category	1982	1983	1984
A. Current Account	−138.0	−60.8	−52.2
Merchandise: exports f.o.b.	637.8	688.0	708.2
Coffee	364.7	376.3	438.8
Cotton	42.6	51.9	8.9
Other	230.5	259.8	260.5
Merchandise: imports f.o.b.	−748.1	−777.3	−892.2
Trade balance	−110.3	−89.3	−184.0
Other goods, services, and income: credit	152.4	161.7	222.7
Other goods, services, and income: debit	−334.8	−360.9	−391.1
Total: goods, services, and income	−292.7	−288.5	−352.3
Private unrequited transfers	46.8	49.2	115.1
Total, excl. official unrequited transfers	−245.8	−239.3	−237.2
Official unrequited transfers	107.8	178.5	185.0
B. Direct Investment and Other Long-Term Capital	135.8	307.5	23.8
Direct investment	−.9	26.3	12.1
Portfolio investment	−.9	.1	#
Other long-term capital			
Resident official sector	132.3	276.2	21.5
Loans received by general government	129.3	151.0	91.5
Loans received by Central Reserve Bank	158.0	126.7	−67.9
Other	−155.1	−1.5	−2.1
Deposit money banks	−.1	−.8	−.5
Other sectors	5.5	5.8	−9.3
Loans received	5.5	5.8	−9.3
Other	#	#	#
Total, Groups A plus B	−2.2	246.8	−28.4
C. Other Short-Term Capital	20.6	−111.0	−14.5
Resident official sector	−5.5	−23.5	−32.4
Deposit money banks	26.2	−30.5	−7.0
Other sectors	#	−57.0	24.9
D. Net Errors and Omissions	−86.5	−23.8	−41.3
Total, Groups A through D	−68.2	111.9	−84.3
E. Counterpart Items	3.5	15.1	14.8
Monetization/demonetization of gold	#	#	#
Allocation/cancellation of SDRs	#	#	#
Valuation changes in reserves	3.5	15.1	14.8
Total, Groups A through E	−64.7	127.1	−69.5
F. Exceptional Financing	74.1	−84.6	77.7
Long-term loans received by the Central Reserve Bank	95.1	~	48.7
Short-term borrowing by the Central Reserve Bank	−21.0	−84.6	29.0
Total, Groups A through F	9.4	42.5	8.2
G. Liabilities Constituting Foreign Authorities' Reserves	−32.6	−5.2	13.3
Total, Groups A through G	−23.1	37.3	21.5
H. Total Change in Reserves	23.1	−37.3	−21.5
Monetary gold	#	1.9	#
SDRs	−1.6	1.6	.1
Reserve position in the Fund	#	#	#
Foreign exchange assets	−35.0	−56.2	−16.2
Other claims	#	#	#
Use of Fund credit	59.7	15.5	−5.4
Conversion rates: Salvadoran colones per SDR	2.7600	2.6725	2.5625
Conversion rates: U.S. dollars per SDR	1.0690	1.0250	1.0153

K. GUATEMALA

Category	1983	1984	1985
A. Current Account	−211.7	−372.4	−236.8
Merchandise: exports f.o.b.	1,020.4	1,103.6	1,049.3
Coffee	289.0	352.5	444.8
Other	731.4	751.1	604.5
Merchandise: imports f.o.b.	−988.4	−1,154.1	−1,061.4
Trade balance	32.1	−50.5	−12.2
Other goods, services, and income: credit	105.8	126.7	127.9
Other goods, services, and income: debit	−378.1	−476.6	−372.1
Shipment and other transportation	−92.5	−109.4	−105.8
Investment income	−133.6	−229.3	−189.0
Other	−152.0	−137.9	−77.2
Total: goods, services, and income	−240.2	−400.5	−256.3
Private unrequited transfers	27.8	27.4	18.7
Total, excl. official unrequited transfers	−212.4	−373.1	−237.6
Official unrequited transfers	.8	.7	.8
B. Direct Investment and Other Long-Term Capital	25.3	−47.5	−65.5
Direct investment	42.0	37.1	59.9
Portfolio investment	−.1	−9.2	−25.7
Other long-term capital			
Resident official sector	−11.2	−29.0	−100.1
Loans received by general government	86.8	41.3	66.1
Loans received by Bank of Guatemala	−98.0	−73.4	−144.6
Other	#	3.1	−21.6
Deposit money banks	#	#	#
Other sectors	−5.4	−46.5	.3
Loans received	−6.7	−46.8	1.1
Other	1.2	.3	−.7
Total, Groups A plus B	186.4	−419.9	−302.4
C. Other Short-Term Capital	113.7	−61.2	−73.3
Resident official sector	34.3	−88.5	−179.0
Deposit money banks	66.9	9.2	−63.8
Other sectors	12.5	18.1	169.6
D. Net Errors and Omissions	−34.9	14.1	43.4
Total, Groups A through D	−107.6	−467.0	−332.2
E. Counterpart Items	13.3	21.6	−38.7
Monetization/demonetization of gold	#	#	#
Allocation/cancellation of SDRs	#	#	#
Valuation changes in reserves	13.3	21.6	−38.7
Total, Groups A through E	−94.2	−445.4	−370.9
F. Exceptional Financing	116.7	487.0	428.9
Bonds issued to cancel external obligations	73.5	66.3	166.9
Long-term borrowing by Bank of Guatemala	167.4	179.1	139.2
Short-term borrowing by Bank of Guatemala	−50.7	4.0	56.3
Payments arrears	−73.5	237.6	67.5
Total, Groups A through F	22.5	41.6	58.0
G. Liabilities Constituting Foreign Authorities' Reserves	39.3	−5.9	3.8
Total, Groups A through G	61.8	35.6	61.8
H. Total Change in Reserves	−61.8	−35.6	−61.8
Monetary gold	#	#	#
SDRs	−.5	−1.5	2.0
Reserve position in the Fund	−7.9	7.9	#
Foreign exchange assets	−90.6	−85.5	3.8
Other claims	−1.1	24.3	−19.8
Use of Fund credit	38.3	19.1	−47.8
Conversion rates: quetzales per SDR	1.0690	1.0250	1.0153
Conversion rates: U.S. dollars per SDR	1.0690	1.0250	1.0153

Table 2701 (Continued)

IMF BALANCE OF PAYMENTS, 19 LC, 1981–85[a]

(M SDR)

L. HAITI

Category	1983	1984
A. Current Account	−106.0	−107.5
Merchandise: exports f.o.b.	173.5	198.7
Bauxite	#	#
Coffee	47.6	44.0
Other	125.9	154.7
Merchandise: imports f.o.b.	−303.0	−324.9
Trade balance	−129.6	−126.3
Other goods, services, and income: credit	100.4	104.1
Other goods, services, and income: debit	−179.5	−203.6
Shipment and other transportation	−82.5	−94.1
Distributed earnings on direct investment	−11.1	−5.8
Other	−86.0	−103.8
Total: goods, services, and income	−208.7	−225.8
Private unrequited transfers	43.1	43.3
Total, excl. official unrequited transfers	−165.5	−182.5
Official unrequited transfers	59.5	75.0
B. Direct Investment and Other Long-Term Capital	42.7	60.8
Direct investment	7.8	4.3
Portfolio investment	#	#
Other long-term capital		
Resident official sector	29.4	53.8
Deposit money banks	#	#
Other sectors	5.5	2.7
Total, Groups A plus B	−63.3	−46.6
C. Other Short-Term Capital	−5.3	−7.8
Resident official sector	−.1	#
Deposit money banks	−5.2	−7.8
Other sectors	#	#
D. Net Errors and Omissions	37.7	25.5
Total, Groups A through D	−30.9	−28.9
E. Counterpart Items	#	#
Monetization/demonetization of gold	#	#
Counterpart to allocation/cancellation	#	#
Valuation changes in reserves	#	#
Total, Groups A through E	−30.9	−28.9
F. Exceptional Financing	.1	.8
Subsidy Account grants	#	#
Trust Fund loans	#	#
Total, Groups A through F	−30.7	−28.1
G. Liabilities Constituting Foreign Authorities' Reserves	#	#
Total, Groups A through G	−30.7	−28.1
H. Total Change in Reserves	30.7	28.1
Monetary gold	#	#
SDRs	−3.0	3.1
Reserve position in the Fund	#	#
Foreign exchange assets	9.7	4.0
Other claims	#	#
Use of Fund credit	24.0	21.0
Conversion rates: gourdes per SDR	5.1988	5.1988
Conversion rates: U.S. dollars per SDR	1.0250	1.0153

M. HONDURAS

Category	1983	1984	1985
A. Current Account	−210.6	−294.5	−258.8
Merchandise: exports f.o.b.	649.4	727.5	822.5
Bananas	190.0	226.6	283.7
Coffee	141.4	165.0	182.4
Wood	37.8	34.0	32.1
Other	280.1	301.9	324.3
Merchandise: imports f.o.b.	−711.6	−858.1	−939.9
Trade balance	−62.2	−130.6	−117.4
Other goods, services, and income: credit	108.8	123.2	129.4
Other goods, services, and income: debit	−298.8	−365.1	−392.4
Total: goods, services, and income	−252.2	−372.5	−380.5
Private unrequited transfers	9.1	10.0	12.2
Total, excl. official unrequited transfers	−243.2	−362.5	−368.3
Official unrequited transfers	32.6	68.0	109.4
B. Direct Investment and Other Long-Term Capital	151.8	248.9	218.7
Direct investment	19.6	20.0	27.1
Portfolio investment	.1	−1.8	1.2
Other long-term capital			
Resident official sector	32.1	75.5	99.1
Loans received by general government	44.7	57.5	47.8
Loans received by Central Bank	−4.4	20.4	63.7
Other	−8.1	−2.4	−12.3
Deposit money banks	−2.3	−3.8	4.0
Other sectors	102.2	159.1	87.3
Total, Groups A plus B	−58.8	−45.6	−40.2
C. Other Short-Term Capital	−19.4	16.4	−3.5
Resident official sector	−31.6	7.1	13.1
Deposit money banks	7.2	−6.1	5.3
Other sectors	5.0	15.4	−21.9
D. Net Errors and Omissions	20.9	−29.4	10.3
Total, Groups A through D	−57.3	−58.6	−33.3
E. Counterpart Items	7.0	14.8	−26.9
Monetization/demonetization of gold	#	#	#
Allocation/cancellation of SDRs	#	#	#
Valuation changes in reserves	7.0	14.8	−26.9
Total, Groups A through E	−50.3	−43.7	−60.2
F. Exceptional Financing	17.0	44.1	44.3
Loans from CAMSF	#	#	#
Loans from VIF	17.0	13.2	12.1
Trust Fund loans	#	#	#
Total, Groups A through F	−33.4	.3	−16.0
G. Liabilities Constituting Foreign Authorities' Reserves	−3.9	24.8	#
Total, Groups A through G	−37.2	25.2	−16.0
H. Total Change in Reserves	37.2	−25.2	16.0
Monetary gold	#	#	#
SDRs	−.5	2.0	.2
Reserve position in the Fund	−4.2	4.2	#
Foreign exchange assets	−2.1	−28.4	34.3
Other claims	−1.9	−1.4	−1.7
Use of Fund credit	45.9	−1.6	−16.7
Conversion rates: lempiras per SDR	2.1380	2.0500	2.0307
Conversion rates: U.S. dollars per SDR	1.0690	1.0250	1.0153

Table 2701 (Continued)

IMF BALANCE OF PAYMENTS, 19 LC, 1981–85ᵃ

(M SDR)

N. MEXICO			
Category	1983	1984	1985
A. **Current Account**	4,979	4,078	517
Merchandise: exports f.o.b.	20,888	23,595	21,541
Merchandise: imports f.o.b.	–8,012	–11,013	–13,261
Trade balance	12,876	12,581	8,280
Other goods, services, and income: credit	5,893	8,073	7,745
Travel	2,551	3,200	2,882
Other	3,343	4,873	4,863
Other goods, services, and income: debit	–14,075	–16,978	–15,950
Travel	–1,483	–2,123	–2,233
Investment income	–9,980	–11,938	–10,460
Other	–2,612	–2,917	–3,258
Total: goods, services, and income	4,695	3,677	76
Private unrequited transfers	116	224	284
Total, excl. official unrequited transfers	4,811	3,901	359
Official unrequited transfers	167	177	158
B. **Direct Investment and Other Long-Term Capital**	4,448	2,449	–305
Direct investment	425	381	495
Portfolio investment	–583	–739	–901
Other long-term capital			
Resident official sector	3,978	2,779	752
Deposit money banks and other institutions	1,343	451	–18
Other sectors	–715	–422	–632
Total, Groups A plus B	9,426	6,528	212
C. **Other Short-Term Capital**	–5,510	–3,473	–1,523
Resident official sector	#	#	#
Deposit money banks	318	328	–47
Other sectors	–5,829	–3,801	–1,477
D. **Net Errors and Omissions**	–885	–974	–1,410
Total, Groups A through D	3,032	2,082	–2,721
E. **Counterpart Items**	91	273	–504
Monetization/demonetization of gold	112	63	71
Allocation/cancellation of SDRs	#	#	#
Valuation changes in reserves	–21	210	–574
Total, Groups A through E	3,123	2,355	–3,225
F. **Exceptional Financing**	~	~	~
Total, Groups A through F	3,123	2,355	–3,225
G. **Liabilities Constituting Foreign Authorities' Reserves**	–1,141	#	#
Total, Groups A through G	1,982	2,355	–3,225
H. **Total Change in Reserves**	–1,982	–2,355	3,225
Monetary gold	–3	123	–23
SDRs	–17	19	3
Reserve position in the Fund	–91	91	#
Foreign exchange assets	–2,874	–3,791	2,949
Other claims	#	#	#
Use of Fund credit	1,003	1,204	296
Conversion rates: Mexican pesos per SDR	128.38	172.02	260.81
Conversion rates: U.S. dollars per SDR	1.0690	1.0250	1.0153

O. NICARAGUA			
Category	1981	1982	1983
A. **Current Account**	–429.0	–426.4	–415.2
Merchandise: exports f.o.b.	431.0	367.8	400.7
Coffee	116.0	112.3	143.8
Cotton	104.7	79.0	102.4
Other	210.3	176.4	154.5
Merchandise: imports f.o.b.	–782.3	–655.3	–727.9
Trade balance	–251.3	–287.6	–327.1
Other goods, services, and income: credit	62.2	44.8	38.4
Other goods, services, and income: debit	–199.6	–230.3	–200.7
Total: goods, services, and income	–488.7	–473.0	–489.4
Private unrequited transfers	11.2	7.2	3.4
Total, excl. official unrequited transfers	–477.5	–465.8	–486.0
Official unrequited transfers	48.4	39.4	70.8
B. **Direct Investment and Other Long-Term Capital**	505.8	397.9	509.7
Direct investment	#	#	7.2
Portfolio investment	#	#	#
Other long-term capital			
Resident official sector	436.3	383.1	504.9
Deposit money banks	69.5	18.5	31.3
Other sectors	#	–3.7	–33.8
Total, Groups A plus B	76.7	–28.5	94.5
C. **Other Short-Term Capital**	–31.6	–44.4	–18.7
Resident official sector	#	#	#
Deposit money banks	#	#	#
Other sectors	–31.6	–44.4	–18.7
D. **Net Errors and Omissions**	–.3	–18.1	–24.5
Total, Groups A through D	44.8	–91.0	51.3
E. **Counterpart Items**	9.4	5.4	8.4
Monetization/demonetization of gold	#	#	#
Allocation/cancellation of SDRs	3.5	#	#
Valuation changes in reserves	5.9	5.4	8.4
Total, Groups A through E	54.1	–85.6	59.7
F. **Exceptional Financing**	~	2.1	11.8
Loans from CAMSF	~	~	~
Loans from VIF	~	~	~
Total, Groups A through F	54.1	–83.5	71.5
G. **Liabilities Constituting Foreign Authorities' Reserves**	#	#	#
Total, Groups A through G	54.1	–83.5	71.5
H. **Total Change in Reserves**	–54.1	83.5	–71.5
Monetary gold	#	#	#
SDRs	–.1	–.8	.9
Reserve position in the Fund	#	#	#
Foreign exchange assets	–45.1	–58.6	–12.6
Other claims	8.5	146.6	–55.5
Use of Fund credit	–17.5	–3.7	–4.3
Conversion rates: córdobas per SDR	11.851	11.095	10.743
Conversion rates: U.S. dollars per SDR	1.1792	1.1040	1.0690

Table 2701 (Continued)

IMF BALANCE OF PAYMENTS, 19 LC, 1981–85[a]

(M SDR)

P. PANAMA

Category	1983	1984	1985
A. Current Account	181.9	–68.4	20.9
Merchandise: exports f.o.b.	1,537.6	1,644.7	1,919.7
To Canal Zone	#	#	#
To rest of world			
By enterprises in colón Free Zone	1,252.5	1,364.7	1,594.8
By others			
Bananas	70.2	72.8	76.9
Petroleum	34.0	5.1	19.7
Other	181.0	202.1	228.3
Merchandise: imports f.o.b.	–2,174.7	–2,448.2	–2,563.4
By enterprises in Colón Free Zone	–1,074.6	–1,305.3	–1,485.4
By others	–1,100.1	–1,142.9	–1,078.0
Trade balance	–637.1	–803.5	–643.7
Other goods, services, and income: credit	4,994.9	4,740.5	4,361.3
Other goods, services, and income: debit	–4,214.2	–4,053.5	–3,778.7
Total: goods, services, and income	143.5	–116.5	–61.2
Private unrequited transfers	–54.8	–61.1	–52.5
Total, excl. official unrequited transfers	88.7	–177.6	–113.7
Official unrequited transfers	93.2	109.2	134.5
B. Direct Investment and Other Long-Term Capital	162.3	239.4	~
Direct investment	46.0	35.8	~
Portfolio investment	59.6	60.5	~
Other long-term capital			
Resident official sector	150.8	79.4	~
Deposit money banks	–12.4	100.9	~
Other sectors	–81.7	–37.2	~
Loans received by public enterprises	59.8	51.5	~
Loans received by private enterprises	–146.7	–90.0	~
Other	5.2	1.4	~
Total, Groups A plus B	344.2	171.0	20.9
C. Other Short-Term Capital	–36.8	–174.8	~
Resident official sector	.8	1.9	~
Deposit money banks	63.0	–74.8	~
Other sectors	–100.7	–101.9	~
D. Net Errors and Omissions	–319.4	–102.0	–144.5
Total, Groups A through D	–12.1	–105.8	–123.6
E. Counterpart Items	10.0	16.4	–14.0
Monetization/demonetization of gold	#	#	#
Allocation/cancellation of SDRs	#	#	#
Valuation changes in reserves	10.0	16.4	–14.0
Total, Groups A through E	–2.1	–89.4	–137.6
F. Exceptional Financing	#	19.5	#
Total, Groups A through F	–2.1	–69.9	–137.6
G. Liabilities Constituting Foreign Authorities' Reserves	#	#	#
Total, Groups A through G	–2.1	–69.9	–137.6
H. Total Change in Reserves	2.1	69.9	137.6
Monetary gold	#	#	#
SDRs	3.4	.4	–11.7
Reserve position in the Fund	–8.7	8.7	#
Foreign exchange assets	–100.6	–31.6	142.5
Other claims	#	#	#
Use of Fund credit	108.0	92.5	6.8
Conversion rates: balboas per SDR	1.0690	1.0250	1.0153
Conversion rates: U.S. dollars per SDR	1.0690	1.0250	1.0153

Q. PARAGUAY

Category	1983	1984	1985
A. Current Account	–231.4	–309.7	–222.1
Merchandise: exports f.o.b.	305.0	352.5	319.5
Cotton	73.8	128.0	139.7
Soybeans	70.8	96.9	99.0
Other	160.3	127.6	80.9
Merchandise: imports f.o.b.	–515.8	633.3	–508.1
Trade balance	–210.9	–280.8	–188.6
Other goods, services, and income: credit	229.8	492.4	841.3
Other goods, services, and income: debit	–256.2	–530.3	–882.2
Total: goods, services, and income	–237.2	–318.7	–229.5
Private unrequited transfers	1.3	2.0	1.8
Total, excl. official unrequited transfers	–235.9	–316.7	–227.7
Official unrequited transfers	4.5	7.0	5.6
B. Direct Investment and Other Long-Term Capital	270.5	214.0	119.5
Direct investment	4.6	5.1	.7
Portfolio investment	3.1	#	8.2
Other long-term capital			
Resident official sector	129.7	123.8	107.2
Deposit money banks	6.7	31.0	14.7
Other sectors	126.4	54.1	–11.2
Trade credits received	–2.1	–18.4	–7.0
Other loans received	128.4	72.6	–4.2
Other	#	#	#
Total, Groups A plus B	39.1	–95.6	–102.6
C. Other Short-Term Capital	–44.1	63.2	–66.6
Resident official sector	23.2	93.2	–60.8
Deposit money banks	.7	–5.2	13.6
Other sectors	–68.0	–24.9	–19.4
D. Net Errors and Omissions	10.5	17.2	36.8
Total, Groups A through D	5.5	–15.2	–132.4
E. Counterpart Items	–20.8	39.4	–56.2
Monetization/demonetization of gold	#	#	#
Allocation/cancellation of SDRs	#	#	#
Valuation changes in reserves	–20.8	39.4	–56.2
Total, Groups A through E	–15.3	24.2	–188.6
F. Exceptional Financing	#	#	#
Total, Groups A through F	–15.3	24.2	–188.6
G. Liabilities Constituting Foreign Authorities' Reserves	–2.5	1.8	6.0
Total, Groups A through G	–17.8	26.0	–182.6
H. Total Change in Reserves	17.8	–26.0	182.6
Monetary gold	.2	#	#
SDRs	–6.7	–4.6	–3.8
Reserve position in the Fund	–4.7	#	.7
Foreign exchange assets	31.6	–25.4	184.7
Other claims	–2.5	4.0	1.0
Use of Fund credit	#	#	#
Conversion rates: guaraníes per SDR	134.69	206.03	243.68
Conversion rates: U.S. dollars per SDR	1.0690	1.0250	1.0153

Table 2701 (Continued)

IMF BALANCE OF PAYMENTS, 19 LC, 1981–85[a]

(M SDR)

R. PERU

Category	1983	1984	1985
A. **Current Account**	–820	–220	47
Merchandise: exports f.o.b.	2,824	3,072	2,921
Copper	415	430	457
Petroleum and petroleum products	509	604	636
Other	1,900	2,038	1,828
Merchandise: imports f.o.b.	–2,548	–2,089	–1,843
Trade balance	275	983	1,078
Other goods, services, and income: credit	775	809	811
Other goods, services, and income: debit	–2,072	–2,163	–1,966
Total: goods, services, and income	–1,022	–372	–77
Private unrequited transfers	#	#	#
Total, excl. official unrequited transfers	1,022	–372	–77
Official unrequited transfers	202	152	123
B. **Direct Investment and Other Long-Term Capital**	182	–605	–906
Direct investment	35	–86	–58
Portfolio investment	#	#	#
Other long-term capital			
Resident official sector	227	–408	–726
Deposit money banks	#	#	#
Other sectors	–80	–111	–122
Total, Groups A plus B	–636	–824	–860
C. **Other Short-Term Capital**	–7	–281	–402
Resident official sector	57	–100	–191
Deposit money banks	–1	39	30
Other sectors	–62	–219	–242
D. **Net Errors and Omissions**	–402	–412	73
Total, Groups A through D	–1,047	–1,517	–1,188
E. **Counterpart Items**	66	116	–191
Monetization/demonetization of gold	#	#	#
Allocation/cancellation of SDRs	#	#	#
Valuation changes in reserves	68	116	–191
Total, Groups A through E	–980	–1,402	–1,380
F. **Exceptional Financing**	983	1,765	1,500
Grants from Subsidy Account	3	2	2
Long-term financing received by			
Monetary authorities	#	#	#
Government (debt rescheduling)	980	478	206
Short-term financing received by			
Monetary authorities	#	#	#
Deposit money banks	#	#	#
Total, Groups A through F	3	363	121
G. **Liabilities Constituting Foreign Authorities' Reserves**	#	#	#
Total, Groups A through G	3	363	121
H. **Total Change in Reserves**	–3	–363	–121
Monetary gold	#	#	–147
SDRs	29	–22	23
Reserve position in the Fund	#	#	#
Foreign exchange assets	–110	–336	–23
Other claims	~	–27	76
Use of Fund credit	78	22	–49
Conversion rates: soles per SDR	1,741.0	3,553.6	11.143
Conversion rates: U.S. dollars per SDR	1.0690	1.0250	1.0153

S. URUGUAY

Category	1983	1984	1985
A. **Current Account**	–55.9	–125.9	–106.5
Merchandise: exports f.o.b.	1,081.8	902.0	840.7
Hides	70.5	89.4	60.4
Meat	231.4	142.3	116.1
Wool	157.7	160.5	161.3
Manufactures: leather	59.6	53.6	51.8
Manufactures: wool	91.7	114.3	96.2
Other	470.8	341.9	354.9
Merchandise: imports f.o.b.	–692.0	–714.3	–665.2
Trade balance	389.8	187.7	175.5
Other goods, services, and income: credit	297.0	441.0	446.2
Other goods, services, and income: debit	–753.0	–764.4	–758.9
Total: goods, services, and income	–66.2	–135.7	–117.1
Private unrequited transfers	10.3	#	#
Total, excl. official unrequited transfers	–55.9	–135.7	–117.1
Official unrequited transfers	#	9.8	10.6
B. **Direct Investment and Other Long-Term Capital**	602.0	29.5	58.3
Direct investment	5.2	3.3	–7.8
Portfolio investment	–14.6	6.6	94.5
Other long-term capital			
Resident official sector	308.0	45.0	–22.5
Deposit money banks	34.4	–1.1	–4.9
Other sectors	268.8	–24.4	–1.1
Total, Groups A plus B	546.0	–96.5	–48.2
C. **Other Short-Term Capital**	–336.0	155.1	–134.0
Resident official sector	37.9	47.0	123.0
Deposit money banks	–62.3	65.8	–145.9
Other sectors	–311.6	42.3	–111.2
D. **Net Errors and Omissions**	–276.1	–140.6	245.9
Total, Groups A through D	–66.1	–81.9	63.7
E. **Counterpart Items**	–41.5	17.2	–5.6
Monetization/demonetization of gold	48.6	7.4	5.6
Allocation/cancellation of SDRs	#	#	#
Valuation changes in reserves	7.2	9.8	–11.2
Total, Groups A through E	–107.6	–64.8	58.1
F. **Exceptional Financing**	#	#	#
Commercial arrears	#	#	#
Total, Groups A through F	–107.6	–64.8	58.1
G. **Liabilities Constituting Foreign Authorities' Reserves**	.3	–1.2	–.3
Total, Groups A through G	–107.3	–65.9	57.8
H. **Total Change in Reserves**	107.3	65.9	–57.8
Monetary gold	48.6	–7.4	–5.6
SDRs	–1.9	–1.5	–8.2
Reserve position in the Fund	–9.5	9.5	#
Foreign exchange assets	–80.7	53.7	–13.2
Other claims	10.8	11.7	–122.5
Use of Fund credit	140.0	#	91.8
Conversion rates: new pesos per SDR	36.923	57.525	102.99
Conversion rates: U.S. dollars per SDR	1.0690	1.0250	1.0153

Table 2701 (Continued)

IMF BALANCE OF PAYMENTS, 19 LC, 1981–85[a]

(M SDR)

T. VENEZUELA

Category	1983	1984	1985
A. **Current Account**	4,141	5,286	2,879
Merchandise: exports f.o.b.	13,630	15,577	13,964
Oil	12,609	14,433	12,668
Other	1,022	1,144	1,296
Merchandise: imports f.o.b.	–5,995	–7,085	–7,276
Trade balance	7,635	8,493	6,687
Other goods, services, and income: credit	2,591	2,946	2,510
Other goods, services, and income: debit	5,888	–6,019	–6,193
Total: goods, services, and income	4,339	5,419	3,005
Private unrequited transfers	–175	–105	–100
Total, excl. official unrequited transfers	4,164	5,314	2,904
Official unrequited transfers	–22	–28	–26
B. **Direct Investment and Other Long-Term Capital**	224	–997	–690
Direct investment	80	41	104
Portfolio investment	188	–125	~
Other long-term capital			
Resident official sector	311	–904	–802
Deposit money banks	#	#	#
Other sectors	–355	–9	7
Assets of Venezuelan Investment Fund	–90	231	–45
Other	–266	–240	52
Total, Groups A plus B	4,365	4,289	2,188
C. **Other Short-Term Capital**	–4,058	–3,790	–739
Resident official sector	–16	23	23
Deposit money banks	–774	–398	79
Other sectors	–3,268	–3,416	–840
D. **Net Errors and Omissions**	–2,747	1,051	–1,080
Total, Groups A through D	314	1,549	370
E. **Counterpart Items**	320	731	–1,307
Monetization/demonetization of gold	#	#	#
Allocation/cancellation of SDRs	#	#	#
Valuation changes in reserves	320	731	–1,307
Total, Groups A through E	634	2,281	–937
F. **Exceptional Financing**	~	~	~
Total, Groups A through F	634	2,281	–937
G. **Liabilities Constituting Foreign Authorities' Reserves**	#	#	#
Total, Groups A through G	634	2,281	–937
H. **Total Change in Reserves**	–634	–2,281	937
Monetary gold	#	#	#
SDRs	62	–45	–69
Reserve position in the Fund	–195	50	82
Foreign exchange assets	–1,209	–1,788	–256
Other claims	707	–497	1,180
Use of Fund credit	#	#	#
Conversion rates: bolívares per SDR	4.5940	7.1930	7,6151
Conversion rates: U.S. dollars per SDR	1.0690	1.0250	1.0153

UNITED STATES

Category	1983	1984	1985
A. **Current Account**	–38.51	–104.18	–115.66
Merchandise: exports f.o.b.	187.84	214.64	211.53
Merchandise: imports f.o.b.	–246.09	–324.54	–333.44
Trade balance	–58.24	–109.90	–121.90
Other goods, services, and income: credit	124.31	136.84	141.66
Reinvested earnings	8.98	8.76	20.12
Other investment income	64.07	75.40	68.18
Other	51.26	52.68	53.36
Other goods, services, and income: debit	–96.67	–119.18	–120.74
Reinvested earnings	–.09	–2.82	–1.16
Other investment income	–49.20	–63.06	–62.80
Other	–46.38	–53.29	–56.77
Total: goods, services, and income	–29.61	–92.23	–100.98
Private unrequited transfers	–.94	–1.40	–1.59
Total, excl. official unrequited transfers	–30.54	–93.63	–102.57
Official unrequited transfers	–7.97	–10.55	-13.08
Grants (excluding military)	–5.90	–8.40	–10.95
Other	–2.06	–2.16	–2.13
B. **Direct Investment and Other Long-Term Capital**	–6.25	36.74	69.28
Direct investment	6.11	20.87	–.31
In United States	11.20	24.73	17.69
Abroad	–5.09	–3.86	–18.00
Portfolio investment	4.60	28.45	62.22
Other long-term capital			
Resident official sector	–4.41	–4.48	–1.42
Disbursements on loans extended	–7.64	–7.60	–5.75
Repayments on loans extended	4.29	3.97	4.14
Other	–1.05	–.86	.20
Deposit money banks	–12.54	–8.11	8.79
Other sectors	~	~	~
Total, Groups A plus B	–44.75	–67.44	–46.38
C. **Other Short-Term Capital**	30.28	40.84	28.74
Resident official sector	5.24	1.39	–1.75
Deposit money banks	26.73	26.47	23.72
Other sectors	–1.69	12.98	6.78
D. **Net Errors and Omissions**	10.64	26.83	23.29
Total, Groups A through D	–3.84	.23	5.66
E. **Counterpart Items**	–.43	–.59	1.23
Monetization/demonetization of gold	–.26	–.23	–.04
Allocation/cancellation of SDRs	#	#	#
Valuation changes in reserves	–.17	–.36	1.27
Total, Groups A through E	–4.27	–.36	6.88
F. **Exceptional Financing**	#	#	#
Security issues in foreign currencies	#	#	#
Total, Groups A through F	–4.27	–.36	6.88
G. **Liabilities Constituting Foreign Authorities' Reserves**	4.86	2.83	–2.04
Total, Groups A through G	.68	2.48	4.85
H. **Total Change in Reserves**	–.68	–2.48	–4.85
Monetary gold	.25	.23	.05
SDRs	–.04	–.95	–.88
Reserve position in the Fund	–4.14	–.97	.90
Foreign exchange assets	3.25	–.78	–4.91
Other claims	#	#	#
Use of Fund credit	#	#	#
Conversion rates: U.S. dollars per SDR	1.0690	1.0250	1.0153

a. For an alternative series, 1953–81 data, see SALA, 23-2720; for data for previous years, see SALA, 24-2701 through 2720.

SOURCE: IMF-BPS-Y, vol. 36, no. 1, 1985, and vol. 37, no. 1, 1986.

Table 2702

VALUE OF MERCHANDISE IMPORTS,[1] 19 LC, 1951–85
(M US)

Year	A. ARGENTINA	B. BOLIVIA	C. BRAZIL	D. CHILE	E. COLOMBIA	F. COSTA RICA	H. DOMINICAN REP.	I. ECUADOR	J. EL SALVADOR	K. GUATEMALA
1951	~	90.3	1,703	-308	~	47.7	76.9	52.0	67.0	78.9
1952	~	97.3	-1,702	-331	~	59.2	97.0	57.8	68.8	73.4
1953	-704	-71.4	-1,116	-304	~	-64.8	-86.0	-61.8	-74.4	-78.5
1954	-866	-71.6	-1,408	-298	~	-70.9	-83.4	-100.0	-86.7	-85.8
1955	-1,038	-77.6	-1,099	-327	~	-77.7	-100.2	-94.7	-91.9	-98.1
1956	-988	-79.1	-1,046	-332	-614	-81.6	-110.0	-95.9	-105.0	-126.9
1957	-1,160	-85.9	-1,285	-383	-451	-92.0	-117.5	-98.5	-115.2	-136.1
1958	-1,091	-74.1	-1,179	-363	-384	-88.9	-134.4	-102.2	-108.3	-138.1
1959	-879	-62.4	-1,210	-361	-402	-93.5	-111.5	-96.1	-99.7	124.3
1960	-1,106	-68.2	-1,293	-474	-496	-98.9	-90.3	-109.8	-122.6	-124.8
1961	-1,200	-74.7	-1,292	-532	-531	-96.0	-72.1	-108.7	-109.0	-120.6
1962	-1,200	-92.5	-1,304	-512	-537	-102.4	-132.3	-112.1	-124.9	-122.9
1963	-868	-98.1	-1,294	-490	-497	-112.7	-164.6	-118.7	-152.2	-150.4
1964	-953	-106.7	-1,086	-529	-582	-125.8	-202.4	-140.0	-191.8	-180.5
1965	-1,062	-126.6	-941	-530	-430	-160.9	-120.7	-151.8	-185.7	-206.1
1966	-995	-138.8	-1,303	-661	-639	-162.1	-166.9	-160.3	-201.0	-201.8
1967	-970	-151.8	-1,441	-651	-464	-173.7	-174.7	-195.7	-204.9	-226.5
1968	-1,035	-161.5	-1,855	-726	-615	-193.7	-196.8	-231.6	-198.2	-237.6
1969	-1,395	-173.4	-1,993	-786	-648	-221.5	-217.2	-218.7	-193.0	-240.9
1970	-1,499	-132.2	-2,507	-867	-802	-286.8	-278.0	-249.6	-194.7	-266.6
1971	-1,653	-144.3	-3,256	-927	-903	-317.2	-390.7	-306.8	-226.0	-290.0
1972	-1,685	-153.2	-4,193	-1,012	-850	-337.1	-337.7	-284.1	-249.7	-294.8
1973	-1,978	-193.2	-6,154	-1,329	-983	-412.1	-421.9	-397.5	-339.8	-391.4
1974	-3,216	-324.1	-12,562	-1,901	-1,511	-648.9	-673.0	-875.2	-522.2	-631.5
1975	-3,510	-469.9	-12,042	-1,520	-1,415	-627.2	-772.7	-1,006.3	-550.7	-672.4
1976	-2,765	-512.3	-12,347	-1,473	-1,654	-695.4	-763.6	-1,047.9	-681.0	-950.7
1977	-3,799	-579.0	-12,023	-2,151	-1,970	-925.1	-849.3	-1,360.5	-861.0	-1,087.0
1978	-3,488	-723.9	-13,631	-2,886	-2,552	-1,049.4	-862.4	-1,704.0	-951.1	-1,283.8
1979	-6,028	-815.0	-17,961	-4,190	-2,978	-1,257.2	-1,137.5	-2,096.8	-954.7	-1,401.7
1980	-9,394	-680.1	-22,955	-5,469	-4,283	-1,375.2	-1,519.7	-2,241.8	-897.0	-1,472.6
1981	-8,431	-680.1	-22,091	-6,513	-4,730	-1,090.6	-1,451.7	-2,361.5	-898.4	-1,540.0
1982	-4,859	-428.7	-19,395	-3,643	-5,358	-804.9	-1,257.3	-2,181.0	-825.9	-1,284.3
1983	-4,119	-481.8	-15,429	-2,818	-4,464	-897.8	-1,279.0	-1,408.0	-830.9	-1,056.0
1984	-4,118	-412.3	-13,916	-3,357	-4,027	-996.7	-1,257.1	-1,567.0	-914.5	-1,182.2
1985	-3,519	-462.8	-13,168	-2,954	-3,734	-1,005.1	~	-1,723.0	~	-1,076.7

Table 2702 (Continued)

VALUE OF MERCHANDISE IMPORTS,[1] 19 LC, 1951–85
(M US)

Year	L. HAITI	M. HONDURAS	N. MEXICO	O. NICARAGUA	P. PANAMA	Q. PARAGUAY	R. PERU	S. URUGUAY	T. VENEZUELA	UNITED STATES[2]
1951	~	47.6	~	~	~	26.9	~	~	~	~
1952	~	58.4		~	~	32.7	~	~	~	~
1953	~	-54.6	-768	~	~	-30.9	~	~	~	-10.96
1954	~	-52.3	-760	~	~	-34.4	~	~	~	-10.35
1955	~	-55.3	-840	~	-98	-33.9	~	~	~	-11.52
1956	~	-57.7	-1,108	-57.6	-107	-37.1	-341		-1,170	-12.78
1957	~	-68.6	-1,102	-68.4	-122	-39.2	-397	~	-1,775	-13.29
1958	~	-65.7	-1,090	-65.3	-94	-44.3	-331	~	-1,512	-12.95
1959	~	-61.6	-964	-52.7	-97	-36.5	-273	-151.7	-1,520	-15.31
1960	~	-64.1	-1,132	-56.4	-109	-43.9	-327	-187.9	-1,145	-14.76
1961	~	-65.2	-1,086	-58.7	-124	-47.9	-408	-182.8	-1,055	-14.54
1962	~	-72.8	-1,097	-78.7	-145	-41.1	-468	-207.6	-1,161	-16.26
1963	-39.1	-88.3	-1,186	-91.0	-164	-41.4	-509	-151.6	-1,037	-17.05
1964	-37.1	-94.7	-1,424	-109.8	-168	-45.1	-511	-168.6	-1,192	-18.70
1965	-42.6	-113.2	-1,498	-133.9	-192	-56.7	-653	-123.1	-1,354	-21.51
1966	-43.7	-138.0	-1,581	-151.8	-218	-63.3	-803	-132.2	-1,316	-25.49
1967	-40.3	-152.0	-1,760	-172.2	-232	-65.7	-810	-146.4	-1,366	-26.87
1968	-38.7	-169.4	-1,892	-166.5	-246	-73.5	-673	-135.9	-1,510	-32.99
1969	-42.1	-169.7	-1,983	-159.3	-285	-81.2	-659	-170.0	-1,554	-35.81
1970	-47.8	-203.4	-2,236	-178.6	-331	-76.6	-699	-203.1	-1,713	-39.86
1971	-53.2	-178.0	-2,158	-190.2	-364	-82.9	-730	-203.0	-1,896	-45.58
1972	-57.3	-176.5	-2,610	-205.5	-409	-78.7	-812	-178.7	-2,222	-55.80
1973	-66.5	-243.4	-3,656	-327.5	-458	-127.3	-1,097	-248.6	-2,626	-70.50
1974	-96.5	-387.5	-5,791	-541.8	-761	-198.3	-1,909	-433.6	-3,876	-103.82
1975	-122.1	-372.4	-6,278	-482.1	-823	-227.3	-2,389	-494.0	-5,462	-98.18
1976	-164.2	-432.5	-5,771	-485.0	-783	-236.4	-2,099	-536.6	-7,337	-124.23
1977	-199.9	-550.1	-5,625	-704.2	-790	-360.1	-2,164	-686.7	-10,194	-151.91
1978	-207.4	-654.5	-7,992	-553.3	-862	-432.0	-1,601	-709.8	-11,234	-176.03
1979	-220.1	-783.5	-12,131	-388.9	-1,086	-577.1	-1,951	-1,166.2	-10,004	-212.03
1980	-319.0	-954.1	-18,896	-802.9	-2,995	-675.3	-3,062	-1,668.2	-10,877	-249.77
1981	-360.1	-898.6	-24,007	-922.4	-3,316	-772.4	-3,802	-1,592.1	-12,123	-265.08
1982	-301.9	-680.7	-14,435	-723.5	-3,045	-711.3	-3,721	-1,038.4	-13,584	-247.67
1983	-325.9	-760.7	-7,721	-778.1	-2,325	-551.4	-2,722	-739.7	-6,409	-266.77
1984	-360.1	-879.6	-11,255	~	-2,478	-649.1	-2,140	-733.2	-7,877	-328.59
1985	~	-954.4	-13,460	~	-2,712	-515.9	-1,868	-675.4	-7,388	-338.86

1. FOB.
2. Data in billions.

SOURCE: IMF-IFS-Y, 1981 and 1985; IMF-IFS, June 1987.

Table 2703

VALUE OF MERCHANDISE EXPORTS,[1] 19 LC, 1951-85

(M US)

Year	A. ARGENTINA	B. BOLIVIA	C. BRAZIL	D. CHILE	E. COLOMBIA	F. COSTA RICA	H. DOMINICAN REP.	I. ECUADOR	J. EL SALVADOR	K. GUATEMALA
1951	1,169	124.5	1,770	378	~	60.9	119.5	70.5	83.6	82.5
1952	678	95.1	1,416	462	~	71.9	116.6	101.7	87.0	88.8
1953	1,102	64.0	1,539	339	~	79.3	104.3	92.3	93.6	99.5
1954	1,027	72.3	1,558	406	~	85.7	121.0	125.1	104.6	104.8
1955	929	81.0	1,419	487	~	80.7	115.0	114.9	106.5	106.3
1956	944	84.6	1,483	489	654	64.7	121.8	117.8	123.0	122.5
1957	974	76.9	1,392	402	590	82.7	161.5	137.1	127.1	115.9
1958	994	51.3	1,244	364	527	93.1	126.4	136.9	118.0	107.9
1959	1,009	61.6	1,282	451	514	76.0	131.8	144.2	111.8	103.7
1960	1,079	54.4	1,270	480	480	87.0	157.4	146.3	102.6	115.9
1961	964	63.8	1,405	444	462	83.3	138.9	132.0	118.8	114.0
1962	1,216	63.6	1,215	484	462	92.7	169.6	149.1	138.9	119.0
1963	1,365	71.9	1,406	493	474	94.9	174.3	150.9	150.2	153.4
1964	1,410	100.1	1,430	592	623	114.4	179.4	161.9	175.5	174.3
1965	1,493	115.1	1,596	692	581	111.7	125.5	181.0	190.0	192.1
1966	1,593	130.9	1,741	860	526	135.7	136.7	187.3	189.5	231.9
1967	1,464	153.2	1,654	883	552	143.3	156.2	198.9	207.9	203.9
1968	1,368	155.5	1,881	908	605	170.0	163.5	210.7	211.7	233.5
1969	1,612	177.8	2,311	1,172	672	189.6	183.4	193.4	202.1	262.5
1970	1,773	190.4	2,739	1,113	788	231.0	214.0	234.9	236.1	297.1
1971	1,740	181.6	2,891	1,000	754	225.3	240.7	238.0	243.9	286.9
1972	1,941	201.3	3,941	851	979	278.8	347.6	323.2	301.7	335.9
1973	3,266	260.8	6,093	1,316	1,263	344.8	442.1	584.7	358.4	442.0
1974	3,930	556.5	7,814	2,152	1,495	440.2	636.8	1,225.4	464.5	582.3
1975	2,961	444.7	8,492	1,590	1,683	493.1	893.8	1,012.8	533.0	640.9
1976	3,918	563.0	9,961	2,116	2,202	592.4	716.4	1,307.2	744.6	760.4
1977	5,651	634.3	11,923	2,186	2,660	827.8	780.5	1,400.8	973.5	1,160.2
1978	6,401	627.3	12,473	2,460	3,155	863.9	675.5	1,529.2	801.6	1,092.4
1979	7,810	761.8	15,244	3,835	3,441	942.1	868.6	2,150.5	1,132.3	1,221.4
1980	8,021	941.9	20,132	4,705	3,986	1,000.9	961.9	2,544.2	1,075.3	1,519.8
1981	9,143	909.1	23,276	3,836	3,158	1,002.6	1,188.0	2,544.2	798.0	1,291.3
1982	7,623	827.7	20,173	3,706	3,114	869.0	767.7	2,343.0	704.1	1,170.4
1983	7,835	756.8	21,898	3,827	2,970	862.4	785.2	2,365.0	735.4	1,091.7
1984	8,100	724.5	27,002	3,650	4,310	932.9	868.1	2,622.0	725.9	1,132.2
1985	8,396	623.4	25,634	3,743	3,713	930.3	~	2,870.0	~	1,059.7

Table 2703 (Continued)

VALUE OF MERCHANDISE EXPORTS,[1] 19 LC, 1951–85

(M US)

Year	L. HAITI	M. HONDURAS	N. MEXICO	O. NICARAGUA	P. PANAMA	Q. PARAGUAY	R. PERU	S. URUGUAY	T. VENEZUELA	UNITED STATES[2]
1951	~	67.7	~	~	~	38.3	~	~	~	~
1952	~	64.9	~	~	~	31.8	~	~	~	12.25
1953	~	69.9	-169	~	~	25.4	~	~	~	12.81
1954	~	56.4	668	~	~	34.8	~	~	~	~
1955	~	53.7	861	~	76	38.7	~	~	~	14.26
1956	~	72.9	844	65.5	73	36.8	-321	~	2,221	17.35
1957	~	64.8	740	70.6	70	36.9	332	~	2,764	19.39
1958	~	69.5	752	70.4	40	33.4	292	~	2,508	16.26
1959	~	68.5	744	75.0	43	35.4	323	108.3	2,326	16.30
1960	~	63.1	778	63.9	39	36.5	445	129.4	2,384	19.65
1961	~	73.0	826	69.9	41	43.1	510	174.7	2,453	20.11
1962	~	81.5	930	90.4	60	40.4	556	153.5	2,544	20.78
1963	43.2	84.4	985	106.6	73	39.5	555	166.2	2,464	22.27
1964	37.9	95.1	1,054	125.5	82	46.2	685	183.6	2,480	25.50
1965	37.8	128.2	1,146	149.2	93	60.8	685	196.3	2,482	26.46
1966	34.8	144.4	1,244	142.5	103	53.6	789	190.3	2,404	29.31
1967	32.3	155.9	1,152	147.9	109	50.4	742	159.8	2,495	30.67
1968	36.3	181.0	1,258	162.3	118	50.0	850	179.3	2,468	33.63
1969	36.7	170.9	1,454	158.7	133	55.2	881	199.2	2,409	36.41
1970	39.1	178.2	1,348	178.6	130	65.3	1,034	224.1	2,602	42.45
1971	45.3	194.6	1,409	187.3	138	66.5	890	196.8	3,103	43.31
1972	39.2	212.1	1,717	249.4	146	85.6	945	281.6	3,152	49.38
1973	49.6	266.6	2,141	278.4	162	128.0	1,112	327.6	4,721	71.41
1974	62.8	300.3	2,999	381.0	251	173.2	1,506	281.4	11,085	98.31
1975	71.2	309.7	3,007	374.9	331	188.0	1,291	384.9	8,853	107.09
1976	99.7	411.7	3,475	541.8	269	202.1	1,360	565.0	9,253	114.74
1977	137.6	529.9	4,604	636.2	289	327.1	1,726	611.5	9,556	120.81
1978	149.9	626.2	6,246	646.0	304	356.1	1,941	686.1	9,084	142.05
1979	138.0	756.5	9,301	615.9	356	384.5	3,491	788.1	14,159	184.47
1980	215.8	850.3	16,066	450.4	2,267	400.3	3,898	1,058.5	19,051	224.27
1981	151.1	783.8	19,838	508.2	2,540	398.5	3,249	1,229.7	19,963	237.01
1982	177.1	676.5	22,081	406.0	2,355	396.2	3,293	1,256.4	16,332	211.21
1983	186.6	694.2	22,228	428.4	1,644	326.0	3,015	1,156.4	14,571	200.75
1984	206.6	745.7	24,196	~	1,686	361.3	3,147	924.6	15,851	220.32
1985	214.6	835.1	21,867	~	1,959	324.4	2,967	853.6	14,178	214.42

1. FOB.
2. Data in billions.

SOURCE: IMF-IFS-Y, 1981 and 1985; and IMF-IFS, June 1987.

Table 2704

TRADE BALANCES, 19 LC, 1951–85
(M US)

Year	A. ARGENTINA	B. BOLIVIA	C. BRAZIL	D. CHILE	E. COLOMBIA	F. COSTA RICA	H. DOMINICAN REP.	I. ECUADOR	J. EL SALVADOR	K. GUATEMALA
1951	~	34.2	67	70	~	13.2	42.6	18.5	16.6	3.6
1952	~	-2.2	-286	131	~	131.1	213.6	159.5	155.8	162.2
1953	398	-7.4	423	35	~	14.5	18.3	30.5	19.2	21.0
1954	161	.7	150	108	~	14.8	37.6	25.1	17.9	19.0
1955	-109	3.4	320	160	~	3.0	14.8	20.2	14.6	8.2
1956	-54	5.5	437	157	40	-16.9	11.8	21.9	18.0	-4.4
1957	-186	-9.0	107	19	139	-9.3	44.0	38.6	11.9	-20.2
1958	-97	-22.8	65	1	143	4.2	-8.0	34.7	9.7	-30.2
1959	130	-.8	72	90	112	-17.5	20.3	48.1	12.1	-20.6
1960	-27	-13.8	-23	6	-16	-11.9	67.1	36.5	-20.0	-8.9
1961	-328	-10.9	113	-88	-69	-12.7	66.8	23.3	9.8	-6.6
1962	16	-28.9	-89	-28	-75	-9.7	37.3	37.0	14.0	-3.9
1963	497	-26.2	112	3	-23	-17.8	9.7	32.2	-2.0	3.0
1964	457	-6.6	344	63	41	-11.4	-23.0	21.9	-16.3	-6.2
1965	431	-11.5	655	162	151	-49.2	4.8	29.2	4.3	-14.0
1966	598	-7.9	438	199	-113	-26.4	-30.2	27.0	-11.5	30.1
1967	494	1.4	213	232	88	-30.4	-18.5	3.2	3.0	-22.6
1968	333	-6.0	26	182	-10	-23.7	-33.3	-20.9	13.5	-4.1
1969	217	4.4	318	386	24	-31.9	-33.8	-25.3	9.1	21.6
1970	274	55.2	232	246	-14	-55.8	-64.0	-14.7	41.4	30.5
1971	87	37.3	-365	73	-148	-92.0	-69.0	-68.8	18.0	-3.1
1972	256	48.1	-252	-161	129	-58.3	9.9	39.1	52.0	41.1
1973	1,289	67.6	-61	-13	280	-67.4	20.2	187.3	18.6	50.7
1974	714	232.4	-4,748	250	-17	-208.8	-36.2	350.2	-57.7	49.2
1975	-549	-25.1	-3,550	70	268	-134.2	121.1	6.6	-17.7	-31.4
1976	1,153	50.7	-2,386	643	548	-103.0	-47.2	259.3	63.7	-190.3
1977	1,852	55.3	-100	35	690	-97.3	-68.8	40.3	112.5	73.2
1978	2,913	-96.6	-1,158	-426	603	-185.5	-186.9	-174.8	-149.4	-191.4
1979	1,782	-53.2	-2,717	-355	464	-315.1	-268.9	53.7	177.6	-180.3
1980	-1,373	261.8	2,833	-764	-297	-374.3	-557.8	302.4	178.4	47.2
1981	712	229.0	1,185	-2,677	-1,572	-88.0	-263.7	182.7	-100.3	-248.7
1982	2,764	399.0	778	63	2,244	64.1	-489.6	162.0	-121.8	-113.9
1983	3,716	259.1	6,469	1,009	-1,494	-35.4	-493.8	957.0	-95.5	35.7
1984	3,982	312.2	13,086	293	246	-56.0	-398.0	1,055.0	-188.6	-50.0
1985	4,877	160.6	12,466	789	-21	-74.8	~	1,147.0	~	-17.0

Table 2704 (Continued)

TRADE BALANCES, 19 LC, 1951–85

(M US)

Year	L. HAITI	M. HONDURAS	N. MEXICO	O. NICARAGUA	P. PANAMA	Q. PARAGUAY	R. PERU	S. URUGUAY	T. VENEZUELA	UNITED STATES[1]
1951	5.7	20.1	?	?	?	11.4	?	?	?	?
1952	2.6	123.3	?	?	?	64.5	?	?	?	?
1953	-6.7	15.3	-16.9	?	?	-5.5	?	?	?	1.29
1954	8.0	4.1	-9.2	?	?	.4	?	?	?	2.46
1955	-17.1	-1.6	21	?	-21	4.8	?	?	?	2.75
1956	-6.1	15.2	-174	7.9	-34	-.3	-20	?	1,051	4.57
1957	-13.3	-3.8	-362	2.2	-52	-2.3	-65	?	989	6.10
1958	-5.4	3.8	-338	5.1	-54	-10.9	-39	?	996	3.31
1959	-9.5	6.9	-220	22.3	-54	-1.1	50	-43.4	806	.99
1960	-5.3	-1.0	-354	7.5	-70	-7.4	118	-58.5	1,239	4.89
1961	-21.4	7.8	-260	11.2	-82	-4.8	102	-8.1	1,398	5.57
1962	-7.1	8.7	-167	11.7	-85	-.7	88	-54.1	1,383	4.52
1963	4.1	-3.9	-201	15.6	-91	-1.9	46	14.6	1,427	5.22
1964	.8	.4	-370	15.7	-86	1.1	174	15.0	1,288	6.80
1965	-4.8	15.0	-325	15.3	-100	4.1	32	73.2	1,128	4.95
1966	-8.9	6.4	-337	-9.3	-114	-9.7	-14	58.1	1,088	3.82
1967	-8.0	3.9	-608	-24.3	-123	-15.3	-68	13.4	1,129	3.80
1968	-2.4	11.6	-634	-4.2	-129	-23.5	177	43.4	958	.64
1969	-5.4	1.2	-529	-.6	-153	-26.0	222	29.2	855	.60
1970	-8.7	-25.2	-888	#	-201	-11.3	335	21.0	889	2.59
1971	-9.7	16.5	-749	-2.9	-226	-16.4	159	-6.2	1,207	-2.27
1972	-18.0	35.6	-894	43.9	-263	6.8	133	102.9	930	-6.42
1973	-16.9	23.1	-1,515	-49.1	-296	.7	15	79.0	2,095	.91
1974	-33.7	-87.2	-2,791	-160.8	-510	-25.1	-403	-52.2	7,209	-5.51
1975	-50.9	-62.7	-3,272	-107.2	-492	-39.3	-1,099	-109.2	3,391	8.91
1976	-64.5	-20.8	-2,295	56.8	-514	-34.3	-740	28.4	1,916	-9.49
1977	-62.3	-20.3	-1,021	-68.0	-502	-33.0	-438	-75.2	-638	-31.10
1978	-57.5	-28.4	-1,745	92.7	-558	-75.9	340	-23.7	-2,150	-33.98
1979	-82.1	-26.9	-2,830	227.0	-730	-192.6	1,540	-378.1	4,155	-27.56
1980	-103.2	-103.8	-2,830	-352.5	-727	-275.0	837	-609.7	8,174	-25.50
1981	-209.0	-114.8	-4,099	414.2	-775	-373.9	-553	-362.4	7,840	-27.98
1982	-124.8	-4.2	7,646	-317.5	-689	-315.1	-428	218.0	2,748	-36.47
1983	-139.3	-66.5	14,507	-349.5	-681	-225.4	293	416.7	8,162	-62.02
1984	-131.3	-133.9	12,941	?	-817	-287.8	1,007	191.4	7,974	-108.27
1985	-145.5	-119.3	8,407	?	-754	-191.5	1,098	178.2	6,790	-124.44

1. Data in billions.

SOURCE: IMF-IFS-Y, 1982 and 1985; and IMF-IFS, June 1987.

Table 2705

REAL TRADE BALANCES, 19 L, 1951–85

(M US of 1980)

Country	1951	1952	1953	1954	1955	1956	1957	1958	1959	1960	1961	1962
A. ARGENTINA[1]	~	~	1,353.7	557.1	–372.0	–176.5	–592.4	–311.9	418.0	–86.3	–1,028.2	50.5
B. BOLIVIA	115.2	–7.5	–25.2	2.4	11.6	18.0	–28.7	–73.3	–2.6	–44.1	–34.2	–91.2
C. BRAZIL	225.6	–969.5	1,438.8	519.0	1,092.2	1,428.1	340.8	209.0	231.5	–73.5	354.2	–280.8
D. CHILE	235.7	444.1	119.1	373.7	546.1	513.1	60.5	3.22	289.4	19.2	–275.9	–88.3
E. COLOMBIA	~	~	~	~	~	130.7	442.7	459.8	360.1	–51.1	–216.3	–236.6
F. COSTA RICA	44.4	444.4	49.3	51.2	10.2	–55.2	–29.6	13.5	–56.3	–38.0	–39.8	–30.6
H. DOMINICAN REP.	143.4	724.1	62.2	130.1	50.6	38.6	140.1	–25.7	65.3	214.4	209.4	117.7
I. ECUADOR	62.3	540.7	103.7	86.9	68.9	71.6	122.9	111.6	154.7	116.6	73.0	116.7
J. EL SALVADOR	55.9	528.1	65.3	61.9	49.8	58.8	37.9	31.2	38.9	–63.9	30.7	44.2
K. GUATEMALA	12.1	549.8	71.4	65.7	28.0	–14.4	–64.3	–97.1	–66.2	–28.4	–20.7	–12.3
L. HAITI	19.2	8.8	–22.8	27.7	–58.4	–19.9	–42.4	–17.4	–30.6	–16.9	–67.1	–22.4
M. HONDURAS	67.7	418.0	52.0	14.2	–5.4	49.7	–12.1	12.2	22.2	–3.2	24.5	27.4
N. MEXICO	~	~	–57.5	–31.8	71.7	–568.6	–1,152.9	–1,086.8	–707.4	–1,131.0	–815.1	–526.8
O. NICARAGUA	~	~	~	~	~	25.8	7.0	16.4	71.7	24.0	35.1	36.9
P. PANAMA	~	~	~	~	–71.7	–111.1	–165.6	–173.6	–173.6	–223.6	–257.1	–268.1
Q. PARAGUAY	38.4	218.6	–18.7	1.4	16.4	–1.0	–7.3	–35.1	–3.5	–23.6	–15.1	–2.2
R. PERU	~	~	~	~	~	–65.4	–207.0	–125.4	160.8	377.0	319.8	277.6
S. URUGUAY	~	~	~	~	~	~	~	~	–139.6	–186.9	–25.4	–170.7
T. VENEZUELA	~	~	~	~	~	3,434.6	3,149.7	3,202.6	2,591.6	3,958.4	4,382.5	4,362.8
UNITED STATES[2]	~	~	4.4	8.5	9.4	14.9	19.4	10.6	3.2	15.6	17.4	14.3

Country	1963	1964	1965	1966	1967	1968	1969	1970	1971	1972	1973	1974
A. ARGENTINA[1]	1,567.8	1,428.3	1,306.1	1,758.8	1,423.6	946.0	599.5	717.3	220.8	629.0	2,719.4	1,180.2
B. BOLIVIA	–82.3	–20.6	–34.9	–23.2	4.0	–17.1	12.2	144.5	94.7	118.2	142.6	384.1
C. BRAZIL	353.3	1,075.0	1,984.9	1,288.2	613.8	73.9	878.5	607.3	–926.4	–619.2	–128.7	–7,847.9
D. CHILE	9.46	196.9	490.9	585.3	668.6	517.1	1,066.3	644.0	185.3	–395.6	–27.4	413.2
E. COLOMBIA	–72.6	128.1	457.6	–332.4	253.6	–28.4	66.3	–36.7	–375.6	317.0	590.7	–28.1
F. COSTA RICA	–56.2	–35.6	–149.1	–77.7	–87.6	–67.3	–88.1	–146.1	–233.5	–143.2	–142.2	–345.1
H. DOMINICAN REP.	30.6	–71.9	14.6	–88.8	–53.3	–94.6	–93.4	–167.5	–175.1	24.3	42.6	–59.8
I. ECUADOR	101.6	68.4	88.4	79.4	9.22	–59.4	–69.9	–38.4	–174.6	96.1	395.1	578.8
J. EL SALVADOR	–6.3	–50.9	13.0	–33.8	8.65	38.4	25.1	108.4	45.7	127.8	39.2	–95.4
K. GUATEMALA	9.5	–19.4	–42.4	88.5	–65.1	–11.7	59.7	79.8	–7.9	101.0	107.0	81.3
L. HAITI	12.9	2.5	–14.6	–26.2	–23.1	–6.8	–14.9	–22.8	–24.6	–44.2	–35.7	–55.7
M. HONDURAS	–12.3	1.3	45.5	18.8	11.2	33.0	3.3	–66.0	41.9	87.4	48.7	–144.1
N. MEXICO	–634.1	–1,156.3	–984.9	–991.2	–1,752.2	–1,801.1	–1,461.3	–2,324.6	–1,901.0	–2,196.6	–3,196.2	–4,613.2
O. NICARAGUA	49.2	49.1	46.4	–27.4	–70.0	–11.9	–1.7	0	–7.36	107.9	–103.6	–265.8
P. PANAMA	–287.1	–268.8	–303.0	–335.3	–354.5	–366.4	–422.7	–526.2	–573.6	–646.2	–624.5	–843.0
Q. PARAGUAY	–6.0	3.4	12.4	–28.5	–44.1	–66.8	–71.8	–29.6	–41.6	16.7	1.5	–41.4
R. PERU	145.1	543.8	97.0	–41.2	–196.0	502.8	613.3	877.0	404.0	326.8	31.6	–666.1
S. URUGUAY	46.1	46.9	221.8	170.9	38.6	123.3	80.7	55.0	–15.7	252.8	166.7	–86.3
T. VENEZUELA	4,501.6	4,025.0	3,418.2	3,200.0	3,253.6	2,721.6	2,361.9	2,327.2	3,063.5	2,285.0	4,420.0	11,915.7
UNITED STATES[2]	16.4	21.3	15.0	11.2	11.0	1.8	1.7	6.8	–5.8	–15.8	1.9	–9.1

Table 2705 (Continued)

REAL TRADE BALANCES, 19 L, 1951–85

(M US of 1980)

	Country	1975	1976	1977	1978	1979	1980	1981	1982	1983	1984	1985
A.	ARGENTINA[1]	–812.1	1,649.5	2,558.0	3,763.6	2,022.7	–1,373.0	652.0	2,503.6	3,329.8	3,520.8	4,346.7
B.	BOLIVIA	–37.1	72.5	76.4	–124.8	–60.4	261.8	209.7	361.4	232.2	276.0	143.1
C.	BRAZIL	–5,251.5	–3,413.5	–138.1	1,496.1	3,084.0	2,833.0	1,085.2	704.7	5,796.6	11,570.3	11,110.5
D.	CHILE	103.6	919.9	48.3	–550.4	–403.0	–764.0	–2,451.5	57.1	904.1	259.1	703.2
E.	COLOMBIA	396.5	784.0	953.0	779.1	526.7	–297.0	–1,439.6	2,032.6	–1,338.7	217.5	–18.7
F.	COSTA RICA	–199.0	–147.4	–134.4	–239.7	–357.7	–374.3	–80.6	58.1	–31.7	–49.5	–66.7
H.	DOMINICAN REP.	179.1	–67.5	–95.0	–241.4	–305.2	–557.8	–241.4	–443.4	442.4	–351.9	–66.7
I.	ECUADOR	9.8	371.0	55.7	–225.8	60.9	302.4	167.3	146.7	857.5	932.8	1,022.3
J.	EL SALVADOR	–26.2	91.1	155.4	–193.0	201.6	178.4	–91.9	–110.3	–85.6	–166.8	~
K.	GUATEMALA	–46.5	–272.3	101.1	–247.3	–204.7	47.2	–227.8	–103.2	32.0	–44.2	–15.2
L.	HAITI	–75.3	–92.3	–86.1	–74.3	–93.2	–103.2	–191.4	–113.0	–124.8	–116.1	–129.7
M.	HONDURAS	–92.8	–29.8	–28.0	–36.7	–30.5	–103.8	–105.1	–3.8	–59.6	–118.4	–106.3
N.	MEXICO	–4,840.2	–3,283.3	–1,410.2	–2,254.5	–3,212.3	–2,830.0	–3,753.7	6,925.7	12,999.1	11,442.1	7,492.9
O.	NICARAGUA	–158.6	81.3	–93.9	119.8	257.7	–352.5	379.3	–287.6	–313.2	~	~
P.	PANAMA	–727.8	–735.3	–693.4	–720.9	–828.6	–727.0	–709.7	–624.1	–610.2	–722.4	–672.0
Q.	PARAGUAY	–58.1	–49.1	–45.6	–98.1	218.6	–275.0	–342.4	285.4	–202.0	–254.4	–170.7
R.	PERU	–1,625.7	–1,058.7	–605.0	–439.3	1,748.0	837.0	–506.4	–387.7	262.5	890.4	978.6
S.	URUGUAY	–161.5	40.6	–103.9	–30.6	–429.2	–609.7	–331.9	197.4	373.3	169.2	158.8
T.	VENEZUELA	5,016.3	2,741.1	–881.2	–2,777.8	4,716.2	8,174.0	7,179.4	2,489.1	7,313.6	7,050.4	6,212.1
	UNITED STATES[2]	13.2	–13.6	–43.0	–43.9	–31.3	–25.5	–25.6	–33.0	–55.6	–95.7	–110.9

1. Nominal data in source deflated here using U.S. export price index (table 3231).
2. B US of 1980.

SOURCE: IMF-IFS-Y, 1987.

Figure 27:1

ARGENTINA REAL TRADE BALANCE, 1953–85

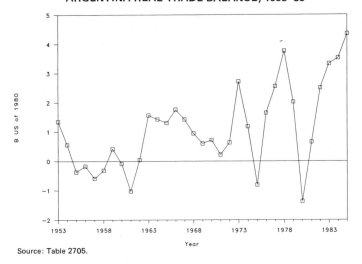

Source: Table 2705.

Figure 27:2

BOLIVIA REAL TRADE BALANCE, 1951–85

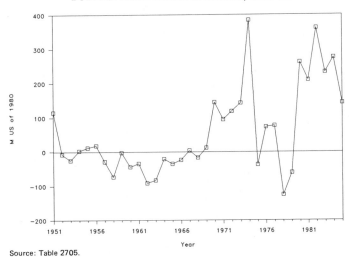

Source: Table 2705.

Figure 27:3

BRAZIL REAL TRADE BALANCE, 1951–85

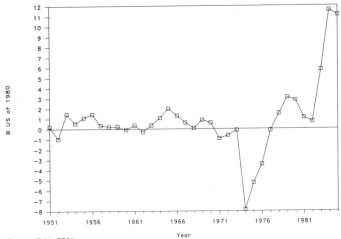

Source: Table 2705.

Figure 27:4

CHILE REAL TRADE BALANCE, 1951-85

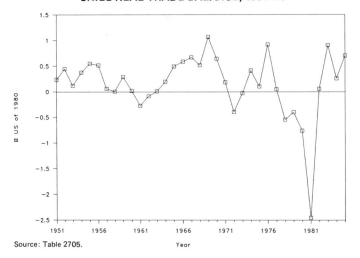

Source: Table 2705.

Figure 27:5

COLOMBIA REAL TRADE BALANCE, 1956-85

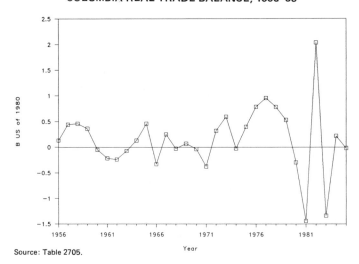

Source: Table 2705.

Figure 27:6

COSTA RICA REAL TRADE BALANCE, 1956-85

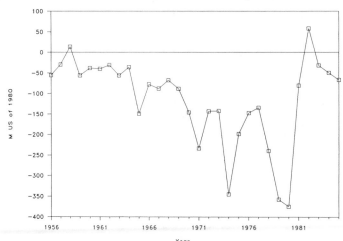

Source: Table 2705.

Figure 27:7

DOMINICAN REPUBLIC REAL TRADE BALANCE, 1956–85

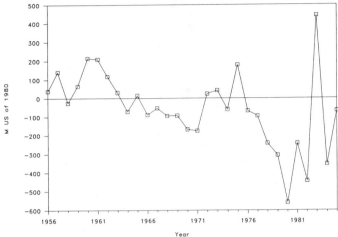

Source: Table 2705.

Figure 27:8

ECUADOR REAL TRADE BALANCE, 1956–85

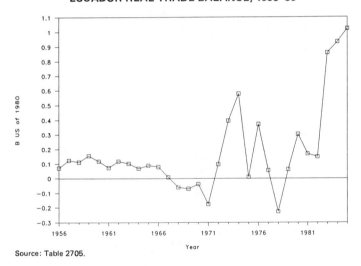

Source: Table 2705.

Figure 27:9

EL SALVADOR REAL TRADE BALANCE, 1956–84

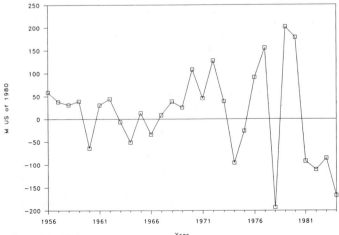

Source: Table 2705.

Figure 27:10

GUATEMALA REAL TRADE BALANCE, 1956–85

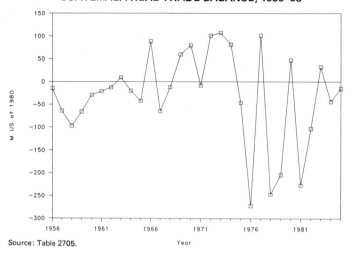

Source: Table 2705.

Figure 27:11

HAITI REAL TRADE BALANCE, 1956–85

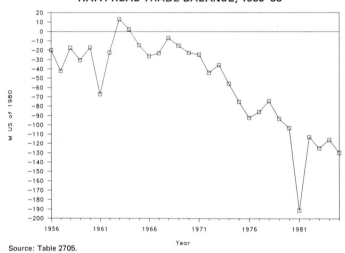

Source: Table 2705.

Figure 27:12

HONDURAS REAL TRADE BALANCE, 1956–85

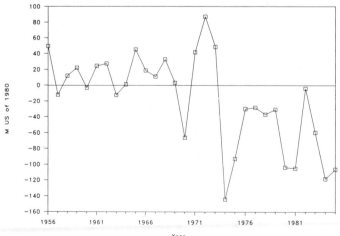

Source: Table 2705.

Figure 27:13

MEXICO REAL TRADE BALANCE, 1953–85

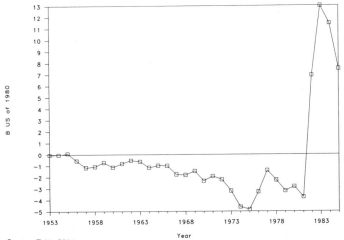

Source: Table 2705.

Figure 27:14

NICARAGUA REAL TRADE BALANCE, 1956–83

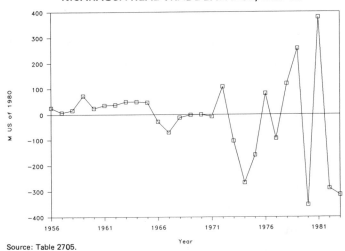

Source: Table 2705.

Figure 27:15

PANAMA REAL TRADE BALANCE, 1955–85

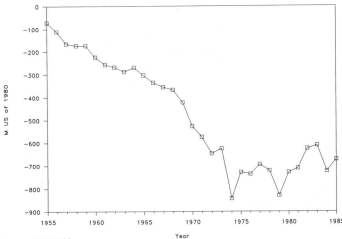

Source: Table 2705.

Figure 27:16

PARAGUAY REAL TRADE BALANCE, 1951–85

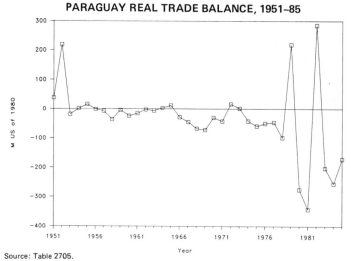

Source: Table 2705.

Figure 27:17

PERU REAL TRADE BALANCE, 1956–85

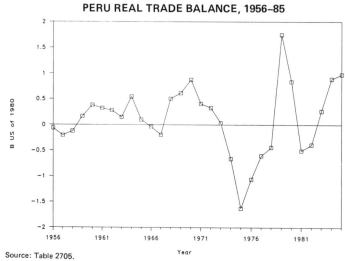

Source: Table 2705.

Figure 27:18

URUGUAY REAL TRADE BALANCE, 1959–85

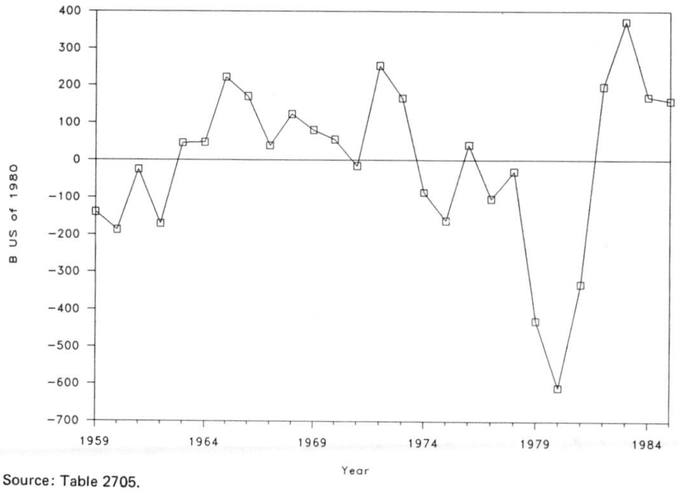

Source: Table 2705.

Figure 27:19

VENEZUELA REAL TRADE BALANCE, 1956–85

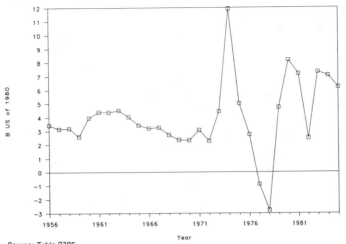

Source: Table 2705.

Figure 27:20

UNITED STATES REAL TRADE BALANCE, 1956–85

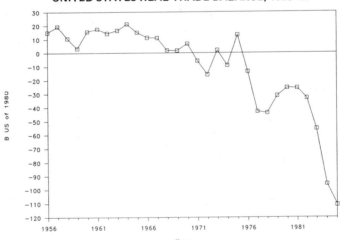

Source: Table 2705.

Table 2706

PHYSICAL HOLDINGS OF GOLD, 18 LC, 1950-85[a]

(M Ounces, YE)

	Country	1950	1951	1952	1953	1954	1955	1956	1957	1958	1959	1960	1961	1962	1963	1964	1965	1966	1967	1968	1969	1970
A.	ARGENTINA	2.36	5.57	8.19	10.61	10.61	10.61	6.40	3.59	1.70	1.60	2.96	5.42	1.73	2.22	2.03	1.88	2.39	2.39	3.11	3.85	3.99
B.	BOLIVIA	.65	.65	.59	.63	.14	.63	.03	.02	.03	.03	.03	.03	.09	.06	.13	.19	.21	.27	.31	.33	.36
C.	BRAZIL	9.09	9.11	9.14	9.17	9.20	9.23	9.26	9.26	9.29	9.33	8.20	8.14	7.87	8.15	2.61	1.80	1.30	1.30	1.29	1.29	1.29
D.	CHILE	1.15	1.29	1.19	1.20	1.21	1.27	1.31	1.15	1.15	1.19	1.29	1.37	1.22	1.23	1.23	1.25	1.29	1.29	1.32	1.35	1.33
E.	COLOMBIA	2.11	1.37	2.14	2.46	2.43	2.46	1.63	1.77	2.06	2.03	2.23	2.51	1.63	1.77	1.66	1.00	.71	.89	.89	.74	.49
F.	COSTA RICA	.06	.06	.06	.06	.06	.06	.06	.06	.06	.06	.06	.06	.06	.06	.06	.06	.06	.06	.06	.06	.06
H.	DOMINICAN REP.	.11	.35	.35	.35	.35	.35	.33	.33	.33	.30	.30	.09	.09	.09	.09	.09	.09	.09	.09	.09	.09
I.	ECUADOR	.54	.64	.65	.65	.65	.65	.62	.62	.62	.58	.57	.55	.55	.53	.32	.32	.31	.49	.75	.63	.55
J.	EL SALVADOR	.66	.73	.84	.83	.82	.81	.80	.90	.90	.87	.86	.51	.51	.51	.51	.52	.51	.51	.51	.49	.49
K.	GUATEMALA	.78	.78	.78	.78	.78	.78	.78	.78	.78	.67	.67	.67	.67	.66	.66	.62	.57	.57	.57	.57	.50
L.	HAITI	.07	.07	.07	.06	.06	.06	.06	.02	.02	.02	.02	.02	.02	.02	.02	.02	#	#	#	#	#
M.	HONDURAS	#	#	#	#	#	#	#	#	#	#	#	#	#	#	#	#	#	#	#	#	#
N.	MEXICO	5.94	5.94	4.11	4.51	1.77	4.06	4.77	5.14	4.09	4.06	3.89	3.20	2.69	3.97	4.83	4.51	3.11	4.74	4.71	4.83	5.03
O.	NICARAGUA	.08	.08	.08	.08	.08	.08	.04	.04	.04	.01	.01	.01	.01	.01	.01	.01	.03	.02	.02	.01	.02
Q.	PARAGUAY	.01	.01	.01	.01	.01	.01	.01	#	#	#	#	#	#	#	#	#	#	#	#	#	#
R.	PERU	.89	1.31	1.31	1.04	1.00	1.00	1.00	.79	.55	.80	1.21	1.35	1.35	1.64	1.93	1.92	1.85	.58	.57	.71	1.13
S.	URUGUAY	6.74	6.31	5.91	6.49	6.49	6.16	5.33	5.13	5.13	5.13	5.13	5.13	5.13	4.90	4.90	4.43	4.19	3.99	3.81	4.71	4.61
T.	VENEZUELA	10.66	10.66	10.66	10.66	11.51	11.54	17.29	20.57	20.57	18.71	11.46	11.46	11.46	11.46	11.46	11.46	11.46	11.46	11.51	11.51	10.97
	UNITED STATES	652.00	653.51	664.34	631.17	622.66	621.51	630.23	653.06	588.06	557.34	508.69	484.20	458.77	445.60	442.03	401.86	378.14	344.71	311.20	338.83	316.34

	Country	1971	1972	1973	1974	1975	1976	1977	1978	1979	1980	1981	1982	1983	1984	1985
A.	ARGENTINA	2.56	3.99	4.00	4.00	4.00	4.00	4.18	4.28	4.37	4.37	4.37	4.37	4.37	4.37	4.37
B.	BOLIVIA	.38	.41	.41	.41	.41	.41	.60	.64	.68	.76	.83	.89	.91	.91	.89
C.	BRAZIL	1.32	1.33	1.33	1.33	1.33	1.33	1.52	1.61	1.70	1.88	2.20	.15	.54	1.47	3.10
D.	CHILE	1.35	1.36	1.38	1.44	1.30	1.34	1.36	1.39	1.52	1.70	1.70	1.71	1.53	1.53	1.53
E.	COLOMBIA	.40	.43	.43	.43	1.13	1.41	1.73	1.96	2.32	2.79	3.37	3.82	4.22	1.37	1.84
F.	COSTA RICA	.06	.06	.06	.06	.06	.06	.07	.08	.09	.13	.14	.05	.08	.02	.06
H.	DOMINICAN REP.	.09	.09	.09	.09	.09	.09	.10	.10	.11	.13	.14	.09	.08	.02	.02
I.	ECUADOR	.53	.36	.39	.39	.39	.39	.40	.41	.41	.41	.41	.41	.41	.41	.41
J.	EL SALVADOR	.49	.49	.49	.49	.49	.49	.50	.50	.51	.52	.52	.52	.47	.47	.47
K.	GUATEMALA	.50	.49	.49	.49	.49	.49	.51	.51	.52	.52	.52	.52	.52	.52	.52
L.	HAITI	~	~	~	#	#	#	.01	.01	.02	.02	.02	.02	.02	.02	.02
M.	HONDURAS	#	#	#	#	#	#	.01	.01	.01	.02	.02	.02	.02	.02	.02
N.	MEXICO	5.26	4.94	4.63	3.66	3.66	1.60	1.76	1.89	1.98	2.06	2.26	2.07	2.31	2.42	2.36
O.	NICARAGUA	.02	.01	.02	.02	.02	.02	.03	.03	.02	.04	.04	.02	.12	~	~
Q.	PARAGUAY	#	#	#	#	#	#	.01	.01	.04	.04	.04	.04	.04	.04	.04
R.	PERU	1.13	1.09	1.00	1.00	1.00	1.00	1.00	1.00	1.16	1.40	1.40	1.40	1.40	1.40	1.95
S.	URUGUAY	4.23	3.54	3.54	3.54	3.54	3.54	3.58	3.64	3.31*	3.42	3.39	2.86	2.60	2.62	2.62
T.	VENEZUELA	11.17	11.17	11.17	11.18	11.18	11.18	11.32	11.39	11.46	11.46	11.46	11.46	11.46	11.46	11.46
	UNITED STATES	291.60	275.97	275.97	275.97	274.71	274.68	277.55	276.41	264.60	264.32	264.11	264.03	263.39	262.79	262.65

a. Cf. table 2725.

SOURCE: IMF-IFS-Y, 1980, pp. 40-43, and 1986, pp. 60-63.

Table 2707

WEEKS OF IMPORTS AVAILABLE IN TERMS OF TOTAL RESERVES (EXCLUDING GOLD), 19 L, 1950–86

Country	1950	1955	1959	1960	1961	1962	1963	1964	1965	1966	1967	1968	1969	1970	1971
A. ARGENTINA	24.0	3.8	11.5	17.6	7.0	2.1	10.2	4.0	7.4	6.1	30.5	28.9	13.3	16.3	5.4
B. BOLIVIA	5.6	4.0	4.9	4.2	4.3	.5	4.2	9.0	11.6	12.7	9.8	9.7	9.5	10.7	12.2
C. BRAZIL	16.6	6.7	1.5	2.1	6.6	2.1	2.4	6.3	20.0	13.2	4.8	5.2	14.0	20.8	23.8
D. CHILE	3.1	5.7	10.9	6.5	2.3	3.3	3.2	3.9	8.1	8.8	5.9	11.3	17.0	18.9	9.0
E. COLOMBIA	5.6	3.9	18.1	9.2	4.9	2.7	2.6	4.1	7.0	4.0	5.4	11.5	14.8	11.7	10.5
F. COSTA RICA	3.3	11.1	6.3	5.3	2.0	4.8	5.7	6.2	5.2	4.4	4.4	4.5	5.7	2.3	4.0
H. DOMINICAN REP.	17.3	11.6	11.9	8.0	3.9	5.8	11.0	9.0	25.6	11.6	7.8	7.6	7.8	5.0	7.7
I. ECUADOR	20.8	5.5	12.2	9.4	9.3	13.0	13.3	13.9	10.9	15.0	12.6	6.3	9.2	10.5	5.7
J. EL SALVADOR	19.8	6.2	3.8	1.3	3.2	3.5	9.1	9.7	10.0	9.2	8.6	10.7	11.6	11.1	9.7
K. GUATEMALA	8.3	14.1	9.0	13.1	13.4	9.7	10.2	9.4	10.5	10.2	9.5	9.5	11.2	11.1	12.8
L. HAITI	7.6	9.6	4.5	5.5	4.7	3.1	3.5	2.6	2.2	3.0	2.7	3.5	4.7	4.1	8.9
M. HONDURAS	12.4	14.6	9.2	9.6	8.8	8.6	6.7	10.0	9.9	9.5	7.9	8.8	8.7	4.7	5.9
N. MEXICO	8.3	17.6	16.3	13.4	13.7	15.1	17.2	14.6	12.7	14.7	12.5	13.1	12.3	12.0	17.4
O. NICARAGUA	1.7	8.7	9.0	8.3	9.6	9.3	14.8	14.7	18.5	16.4	8.0	13.4	12.8	12.7	14.4
P. PANAMA	3.2	4.0	2.0	3.2	1.9	1.6	2.1	1.5	1.4	1.3	1.4	2.2	2.5	2.3	2.8
Q. PARAGUAY	4.6	7.7	6.1	1.2	3.1	2.7	4.2	7.0	9.6	10.1	8.9	8.7	6.5	12.8	13.1
R. PERU	7.0	4.0	5.5	4.6	7.0	6.7	7.3	8.3	7.7	5.7	6.8	7.5	12.3	24.8	26.3
S. URUGUAY	18.6	.5	2.0	2.1	2.8	5.2	4.2	3.9	8.2	9.5	6.8	11.1	5.1	3.1	4.6
T. VENEZUELA	.4	6.1	2.3	9.1	7.8	7.3	14.6	18.2	15.6	14.4	16.9	16.2	16.0	17.7	27.4

Country	1972	1973	1974	1975	1976	1977	1978	1979	1980	1981	1982	1983	1984	1985	1986
A. ARGENTINA	8.6	26.8	16.4	3.8	24.8	39.4	67.4	72.9	33.1	18.0	24.4	13.5	14.1	42.6	~
B. BOLIVIA	12.4	12.4	25.0	12.6	13.2	18.6	11.5	9.5	8.1	5.3	14.0	14.1	26.6	18.8	~
C. BRAZIL	44.9	47.3	19.1	15.2	24.6	28.2	40.9	23.5	12.0	14.3	9.7	13.5	39.3	38.5	~
D. CHILE	5.3	5.8	1.1	2.2	12.8	9.8	18.9	23.9	31.7	26.3	26.7	38.4	37.5	46.5	42.0
E. COLOMBIA	18.7	25.3	14.0	16.5	33.5	44.8	43.4	61.8	53.9	47.4	36.7	19.9	15.8	20.0	36.3
F. COSTA RICA	5.7	5.5	3.0	3.7	6.4	9.7	8.6	4.4	4.9	5.7	13.2	16.4	19.3	24.0	23.6
H. DOMINICAN REP.	7.4	9.0	5.6	6.6	7.3	9.6	8.1	10.2	6.4	7.0	4.6	6.1	9.1	11.9	~
I. ECUADOR	19.8	27.5	24.4	13.3	25.9	27.3	22.0	23.5	23.4	14.6	8.0	22.9	18.5	23.2	18.5
J. EL SALVADOR	11.9	5.7	7.2	9.3	13.1	11.8	13.6	7.1	4.2	3.8	6.6	9.3	8.8	9.7	~
K. GUATEMALA	18.7	23.1	13.5	20.1	30.4	33.0	30.0	24.1	14.5	4.7	4.2	9.6	11.2	13.3	30.4
L. HAITI	13.5	10.7	8.2	4.3	7.0	8.3	8.6	10.5	2.2	2.7	~	~	.8	.4	~
M. HONDURAS	9.5	8.3	6.1	12.5	15.0	16.1	13.7	13.2	7.5	5.4	7.9	7.2	7.0	6.2	~
N. MEXICO	18.7	15.8	10.6	10.9	10.2	14.6	12.7	8.9	7.9	8.8	2.9	25.4	32.1	18.2	~
O. NICARAGUA	19.1	18.5	9.7	12.2	14.3	10.1	4.4	21.2	3.8	5.8	11.5	11.8	~	~	~
P. PANAMA	5.1	4.3	2.5	2.0	4.8	4.3	8.3	5.2	4.2	4.0	3.3	7.6	7.9	3.7	~
Q. PARAGUAY	19.8	24.2	22.8	29.1	37.2	45.2	60.9	60.8	64.4	69.9	57.2	64.8	59.1	56.7	40.3
R. PERU	28.9	26.9	31.4	8.7	7.4	9.7	10.3	43.4	41.2	14.6	16.8	23.3	38.3	47.0	26.3
S. URUGUAY	17.0	18.4	8.6	5.5	15.6	23.0	24.2	13.9	11.9	13.6	5.4	13.7	9.0	12.8	30.5
T. VENEZUELA	28.0	35.9	75.0	72.8	55.1	36.8	26.7	35.7	29.0	32.4	26.4	45.6	60.9	64.7	35.1

SOURCE: IMF-IFS-Y, 1987, pp. 48–49.

Table 2708

SDR DEFINED

SDRs were initially expressed in terms of a fixed amount of gold that was equivalent to the gold content of the U.S. dollar. After the value of the dollar was severed from gold and allowed to float in exchange markets, the value of the SDR had to be redefined. Thus, since June 1974 the value of the SDR in terms of the U.S. dollar is determined by the sum of the dollar value of sixteen currencies, based on market exchange rates. The weight given to each of these currencies is based on the country's participation in world trade, subject to some modifications.[1] The new approach to the valuation of SDRs created a relatively stable measure of value in a time when the values of independent currencies were fluctuating widely in the foreign exchange market. As a result, many participants in the international financial markets who were looking for some stability in the value of international financial transactions began to use the SDR as a unit of account.

1. Effective July 1, 1978, the value of the SDR is the sum of the dollar value of the following number of units in each of the sixteen currencies:

U.S. dollar	.40	Belgian franc	1.60
German mark	.32	Saudi Arabian riyal	.13
Japanese yen	21.00	Swedish krona	.11
French franc	.42	Iranian rial	1.70
Pound sterling	.05	Australian dollar	.017
Italian lira	52.00	Spanish peseta	1.50
Netherlands guilder	.14	Norwegian krone	.10
Canadian dollar	.07	Austrian schilling	.28

SOURCE: Rita Rodríguez and Eugene Carter, *International Financial Management* (Englewood Cliffs, N.J.: Prentice-Hall, 1978), p. 85.

Table 2709

ARGENTINA TOTAL REAL SDR RESERVES, MINUS GOLD,[1] 1950–86

(M US of 1980)

Year	Nominal Value	Real Value	Year	Nominal Value	Real Value
1950	445	1,718.146	1969	403	1,113.26
1951	253	851.85	1970	533	1,395.29
1952	133	450.85	1971	177	449.24
1953	160	544.22	1972	289	710.07
1954	152	525.95	1973	952	2,008.44
1955	85	290.10	1974	935	1,545.45
1956	158	516.34	1975	246	363.91
1957	160	509.55	1976	1,244	1,779.69
1958	38	122.19	1977	2,596	3,595.57
1959	220	707.40	1978	3,812	4,925.06
1960	422	1,348.24	1979	7,127	8,089.67
1961	196	614.42	1980	5,268	5,268.00
1962	54	170.35	1981	2,808	2,571.43
1963	192	605.68	1982	2,272	2,057.97
1964	82	256.25	1983	1,120	1,003.58
1965	170	515.15	1984	1,268	1,121.13
1966	132	388.24	1985	2,844	2,534.76
1967	643	1,853.03	1986	1,887	1,677.33
1968	651	1,849.43			

1. Nominal data in source deflated here using U.S. export price index (table 3231).

SOURCE: IMF-IFS-Y, 1987.

Figure 27:21

ARGENTINA TOTAL REAL SDR RESERVES, MINUS GOLD, 1950–86

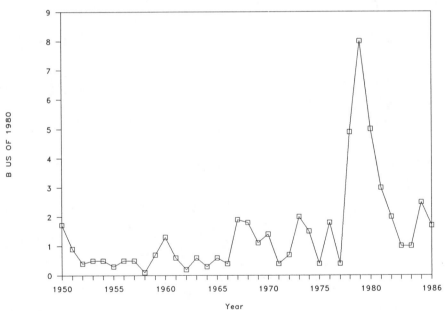

Source: Table 2709.

Table 2710

BOLIVIA TOTAL REAL SDR RESERVES, MINUS GOLD,[1] 1950–85

(M US of 1980)

Year	Nominal Value	Real Value	Year	Nominal Value	Real Value
1950	6	23.17	1968	29	82.39
1951	12	40.40	1969	30	82.87
1952	8	27.12	1970	33	86.39
1953	3	10.20	1971	37	93.91
1954	6	20.76	1972	41	100.74
1955	6	20.48	1973	46	97.05
1956	3	9.80	1974	144	238.02
1957	6	19.11	1975	119	176.04
1958	2	6.43	1976	130	185.98
1959	6	19.29	1977	174	241.00
1960	6	19.17	1978	130	167.96
1961	6	18.81	1979	135	153.23
1962	1	3.15	1980	83	83.00
1963	8	25.24	1981	86	78.75
1964	18	56.25	1982	141	127.72
1965	30	90.91	1983	153	137.10
1966	34	100.00	1984	257	227.23
1967	29	83.57	1985	182	162.21

1. Nominal data in source deflated here using U.S. export price index (table 3231).

SOURCE: IMF-IFS-Y, 1987.

Figure 27:22

BOLIVIA TOTAL REAL SDR RESERVES, MINUS GOLD, 1950–85

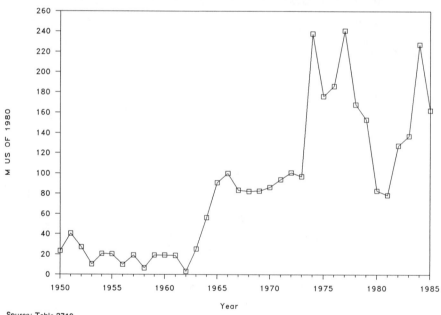

Source: Table 2710.

Table 2711

BRAZIL TOTAL REAL SDR RESERVES, MINUS GOLD,[1] 1950–86

(M US of 1980)

Year	Nominal Value	Real Value	Year	Nominal Value	Real Value
1950	348	1,343.629	1969	611	1,687.85
1951	198	666.67	1970	1,142	2,989.53
1952	209	708.47	1971	1,563	3,967.01
1953	284	965.99	1972	3,806	9,351.35
1954	161	557.09	1973	5,272	11,122.36
1955	168	573.38	1974	4,260	7,041.32
1956	287	937.91	1975	3,400	5,029.59
1957	152	484.08	1976	5,584	7,988.56
1958	140	450.16	1977	5,921	8,200.83
1959	40	128.62	1978	9,078	11,728.68
1960	58	185.30	1979	6,806	7,725.31
1961	185	579.94	1980	4,524	4,524.00
1962	60	189.27	1981	5,673	5,195.05
1963	69	217.67	1982	3,561	3,225.54
1964	154	481.25	1983	4,160	3,727.60
1965	421	1,275.76	1984	11,740	10,380.19
1966	380	1,117.65	1985	9,654	8,604.28
1967	154	443.80	1986	4,744	4,216.89
1968	212	602.27			

1. Nominal data in source deflated here using U.S. export price index (table 3231).

SOURCE: IMF-IFS-Y, 1987.

Figure 27:23

BRAZIL TOTAL REAL SDR RESERVES, MINUS GOLD, 1950–86

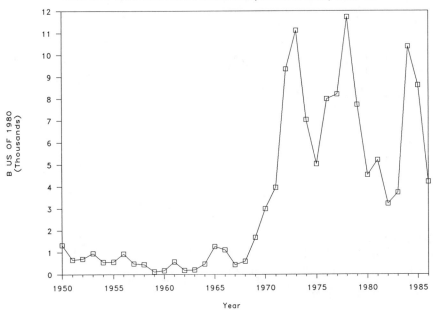

Source: Table 2711.

Table 2712

CHILE TOTAL REAL SDR RESERVES, MINUS GOLD,[1] 1950–86

(M US of 1980)

Year	Nominal Value	Real Value	Year	Nominal Value	Real Value
1950	15	57.92	1969	296	817.68
1951	15	50.51	1970	342	895.29
1952	33	111.86	1971	157	398.48
1953	26	88.44	1972	89	218.67
1954	13	44.98	1973	101	213.08
1955	42	143.34	1974	34	56.20
1956	38	124.18	1975	48	71.01
1957	11	35.03	1976	349	499.28
1958	23	73.95	1977	351	486.15
1959	86	276.53	1978	837	1,081.40
1960	66	210.86	1979	1,471	1,669.69
1961	26	81.50	1980	2,449	2,449.00
1962	36	113.56	1981	2,761	2,528.39
1963	34	107.26	1982	1,645	1,490.04
1964	46	143.75	1983	1,945	1,742.83
1965	94	284.85	1984	2,349	2,076.92
1966	127	373.53	1985	2,230	1,987.52
1967	81	233.43	1986	1,922	1,708.44
1968	162	460.23			

1. Nominal data in source deflated here using U.S. export price index (table 3231).

SOURCE: IMF-IFS-Y, 1987.

Figure 27:24

CHILE TOTAL REAL SDR RESERVES, MINUS GOLD, 1950–86

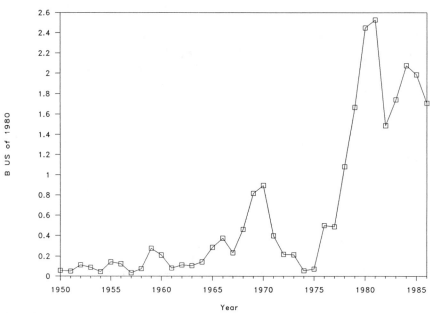

Source: Table 2712.

Table 2713

COLOMBIA TOTAL REAL SDR RESERVES, MINUS GOLD,[1] 1950–86

(M US of 1980)

Year	Nominal Value	Real Value	Year	Nominal Value	Real Value
1950	40	154.44	1969	195	538.67
1951	90	303.03	1970	189	494.76
1952	92	311.86	1971	173	439.09
1953	117	397.96	1972	285	700.25
1954	172	595.16	1973	428	902.95
1955	50	170.65	1974	352	581.82
1956	74	241.83	1975	405	599.11
1957	83	264.33	1976	947	1,354.79
1958	89	286.17	1977	1,438	1,991.69
1959	145	466.24	1978	1,816	2,346.25
1960	92	293.93	1979	2,918	3,312.15
1961	52	163.01	1980	3,788	3,788.00
1962	28	88.33	1981	4,124	3,776.56
1963	25	78.86	1982	3,500	3,170.29
1964	46	143.75	1983	1,816	1,627.24
1965	61	184.85	1984	1,392	1,230.77
1966	52	152.94	1985	1,452	1,294.12
1967	52	149.86	1986	2,204	1,959.11
1968	142	403.41			

1. Nominal data in source deflated here using U.S. export price index (table 3231).

SOURCE: IMF-IFS-Y, 1987.

Figure 27:25

COLOMBIA TOTAL REAL SDR RESERVES, MINUS GOLD, 1950–86

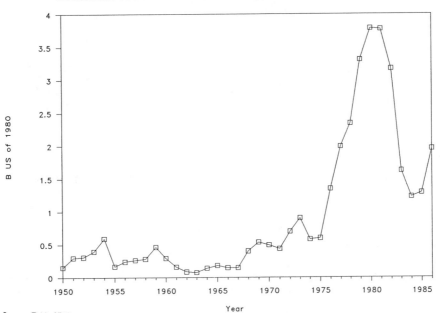

Source: Table 2713.

Table 2714

COSTA RICA TOTAL REAL SDR RESERVES, MINUS GOLD,[1] 1950–86

(M US of 1980)

Year	Nominal Value	Real Value	Year	Nominal Value	Real Value
1950	3	11.58	1969	27	74.59
1951	7	23.57	1970	14	36.65
1952	14	47.46	1971	25	63.45
1953	17	57.82	1972	37	90.91
1954	15	51.90	1973	40	84.39
1955	19	64.85	1974	34	56.20
1956	11	35.95	1975	42	62.13
1957	11	35.03	1976	82	117.31
1958	19	61.09	1977	157	216.85
1959	12	38.59	1978	149	192.51
1960	11	35.14	1979	90	102.16
1961	4	12.54	1980	114	114.00
1962	11	34.70	1981	113	103.48
1963	14	44.16	1982	205	185.69
1964	17	53.13	1983	297	266.13
1965	18	54.55	1984	413	365.16
1966	15	44.12	1985	461	410.87
1967	16	46.11	1986	428	380.44
1968	18	51.14			

1. Nominal data in source deflated here using U.S. export price index (table 3231).

SOURCE: IMF-IFS-Y, 1987.

Figure 27:26

COSTA RICA TOTAL REAL SDR RESERVES, MINUS GOLD, 1950–86

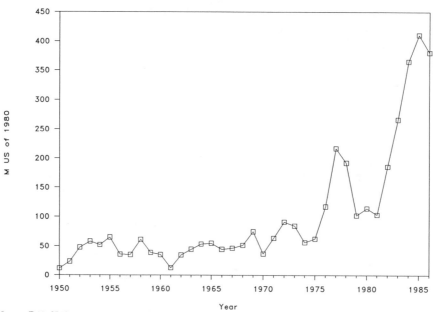

Source: Table 2714.

Table 2715

DOMINICAN REPUBLIC TOTAL REAL SDR RESERVES, MINUS GOLD,[1] 1950–86

(M US of 1980)

Year	Nominal Value	Real Value	Year	Nominal Value	Real Value
1950	17	65.64	1969	37	102.21
1951	19	63.97	1970	29	75.92
1952	21	71.19	1971	49	124.37
1953	17	57.82	1972	51	125.31
1954	25	86.51	1973	70	147.68
1955	25	85.32	1974	71	117.36
1956	28	91.50	1975	96	142.01
1957	37	117.83	1976	106	151.65
1958	36	115.76	1977	148	204.42
1959	31	99.68	1978	118	152.45
1960	15	47.92	1979	181	205.45
1961	6	18.81	1980	158	158.00
1962	17	53.63	1981	193	176.74
1963	39	123.03	1982	117	105.98
1964	38	118.75	1983	164	146.95
1965	48	145.45	1984	259	229.00
1966	41	120.59	1985	310	276.29
1967	29	83.57	1986	308	273.78
1968	33	93.75			

1. Nominal data in source deflated here using U.S. export price index (table 3231).

SOURCE: IMF-IFS-Y, 1987.

Figure 27:27

DOMINICAN REPUBLIC TOTAL REAL SDR RESERVES, MINUS GOLD, 1950–86

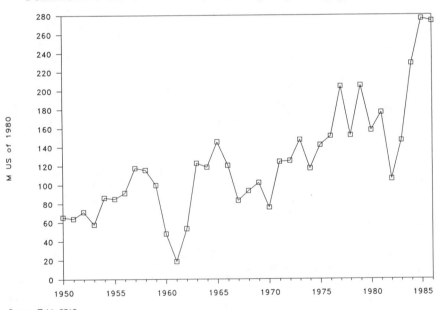

Source: Table 2715.

Table 2716

ECUADOR TOTAL REAL SDR RESERVES, MINUS GOLD,[1] 1950–86

(M US of 1980)

Year	Nominal Value	Real Value	Year	Nominal Value	Real Value
1950	20	77.22	1969	43	118.78
1951	10	33.67	1970	55	143.98
1952	22	74.58	1971	34	86.29
1953	17	57.82	1972	112	275.18
1954	17	58.82	1973	174	367.09
1955	12	40.96	1974	260	429.75
1956	13	42.48	1975	216	319.53
1957	17	54.14	1976	411	587.98
1958	16	51.45	1977	513	708.56
1959	23	73.95	1978	488	630.49
1960	21	67.09	1979	548	622.02
1961	19	59.56	1980	794	794.00
1962	24	75.71	1981	543	497.25
1963	33	104.10	1982	276	250.00
1964	40	125.00	1983	616	551.97
1965	35	106.06	1984	624	551.72
1966	50	147.06	1985	654	582.89
1967	52	149.86	1986	527	468.44
1968	31	88.07			

1. Nominal data in source deflated here using U.S. export price index (table 3231).

SOURCE: IMF-IFS-Y, 1987.

Figure 27:28

ECUADOR TOTAL REAL SDR RESERVES, MINUS GOLD, 1950–86

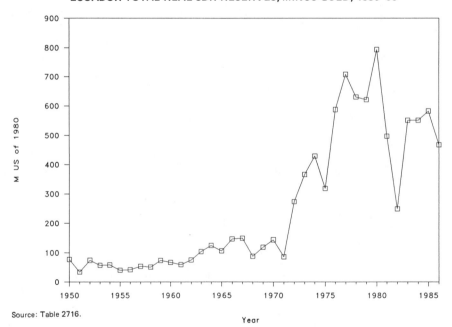

Source: Table 2716.

Table 2717

EL SALVADOR TOTAL REAL SDR RESERVES, MINUS GOLD,[1] 1950–86
(M US of 1980)

Year	Nominal Value	Real Value	Year	Nominal Value	Real Value
1950	19	73.36	1969	47	129.83
1951	17	57.24	1970	45	117.80
1952	15	50.85	1971	43	109.14
1953	15	51.02	1972	59	144.96
1954	16	55.36	1973	34	71.73
1955	11	37.54	1974	63	104.13
1956	11	35.95	1975	91	134.62
1957	10	31.85	1976	160	228.90
1958	8	25.72	1977	174	240.33
1959	7	22.51	1978	206	266.15
1960	3	9.58	1979	108	122.59
1961	7	21.94	1980	61	61.00
1962	9	28.39	1981	62	56.78
1963	27	85.17	1982	98	88.77
1964	36	112.50	1983	153	137.10
1965	38	115.15	1984	169	149.43
1966	39	114.71	1985	164	146.17
1967	37	106.63	1986	139	123.56
1968	44	125.00			

1. Nominal data in source deflated here using U.S. export price index (table 3231).

SOURCE: IMF-IFS-Y, 1987.

Figure 27:29

EL SALVADOR TOTAL REAL SDR RESERVES, MINUS GOLD, 1950–86

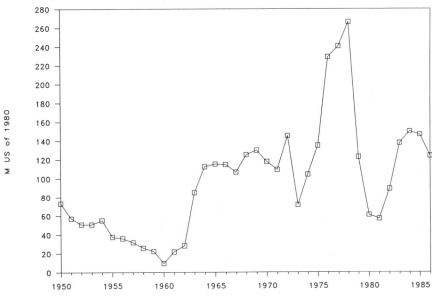

Source: Table 2717.

Table 2718

GUATEMALA TOTAL REAL SDR RESERVES, MINUS GOLD, [1] 1950–86
(M US of 1980)

Year	Nominal Value	Real Value	Year	Nominal Value	Real Value
1950	11	42.47	1969	47	129.83
1951	14	47.14	1970	45	117.80
1952	17	57.63	1971	69	175.13
1953	15	51.02	1972	107	262.90
1954	16	55.36	1973	159	335.44
1955	11	37.54	1974	148	244.63
1956	11	35.95	1975	242	357.99
1957	10	31.85	1976	423	605.15
1958	8	25.72	1977	551	761.05
1959	7	22.51	1978	569	735.14
1960	3	9.58	1979	529	600.45
1961	7	21.94	1980	349	349.00
1962	9	28.39	1981	129	118.13
1963	27	85.17	1982	102	92.39
1964	36	112.50	1983	201	180.11
1965	38	115.15	1984	280	247.57
1966	39	114.71	1985	274	244.21
1967	37	106.63	1986	296	263.11
1968	44	125.00			

1. Nominal data in source deflated here using U.S. export price index (table 3231).

SOURCE: IMF-IFS-Y, 1987.

Figure 27:30

GUATEMALA TOTAL REAL SDR RESERVES, MINUS GOLD, 1950–86

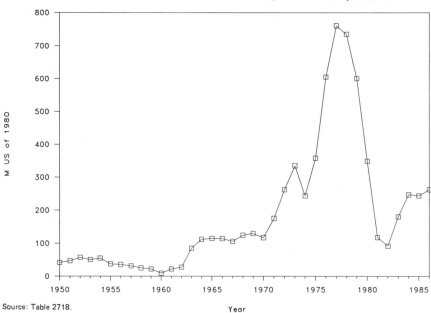

Source: Table 2718.

Table 2719

HAITI TOTAL REAL SDR RESERVES, MINUS GOLD, [1] 1950–86
(M US of 1980)

Year	Nominal Value	Real Value	Year	Nominal Value	Real Value
1950	5	19.31	1969	4	11.05
1951	9	30.30	1970	4	10.47
1952	10	33.90	1971	10	25.38
1953	5	17.01	1972	16	39.31
1954	10	34.60	1973	14	29.54
1955	7	23.89	1974	16	26.45
1956	6	19.61	1975	11	16.27
1957	6	19.11	1976	24	34.33
1958	0	0	1977	28	38.67
1959	3	9.65	1978	30	38.76
1960	4	12.78	1979	42	47.67
1961	3	9.40	1980	13	13.00
1962	2	6.31	1981	21	19.23
1963	3	9.46	1982	4	3.62
1964	2	6.25	1983	9	8.06
1965	1	3.03	1984	13	11.49
1966	2	5.88	1985	6	5.35
1967	2	5.76	1986	13	11.56
1968	3	8.52			

1. Nominal data in source deflated here using U.S. export price index (table 3231).

SOURCE: IMF-IFS-Y, 1987.

Figure 27:31

HAITI TOTAL REAL SDR RESERVES, MINUS GOLD, 1950–86

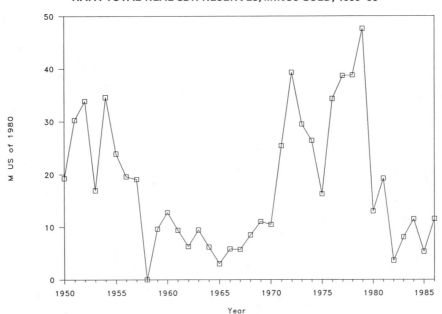

Source: Table 2719.

Table 2720

HONDURAS TOTAL REAL SDR RESERVES, MINUS GOLD, [1] 1950–86

(M US of 1980)

Year	Nominal Value	Real Value	Year	Nominal Value	Real Value
1950	11	42.47	1969	31	85.64
1951	20	67.34	1970	20	52.36
1952	23	74.58	1971	20	50.76
1953	22	78.23	1972	32	78.62
1954	24	83.04	1973	35	73.84
1955	20	68.26	1974	36	59.50
1956	18	58.82	1975	83	122.78
1957	16	50.96	1976	113	161.66
1958	30	32.15	1977	148	204.42
1959	12	38.59	1978	142	183.46
1960	13	41.53	1979	159	180.48
1961	12	37.62	1980	117	117.00
1962	13	41.01	1981	87	79.67
1963	12	37.85	1982	102	92.39
1964	20	62.50	1983	109	97.67
1965	23	69.70	1984	131	115.83
1966	27	79.41	1985	96	85.56
1967	25	72.05	1986	91	80.89
1968	31	88.07			

1. Nominal data in source deflated here using U.S. export price index (table 3231).

SOURCE: IMF-IFS-Y, 1987.

Figure 27:32

HONDURAS TOTAL REAL SDR RESERVES, MINUS GOLD, 1950–86

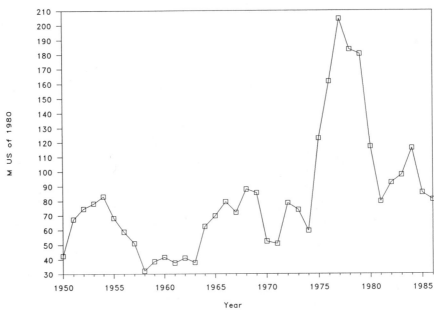

Source: Table 2720.

Table 2721

MEXICO TOTAL REAL SDR RESERVES, MINUS GOLD, [1] 1950–86
(B US of 1980)

Year	Nominal Value	Real Value	Year	Nominal Value	Real Value
1950	89	343.63	1969	493	1,361.88
1951	89	299.66	1970	568	1,486.91
1952	138	467.80	1971	693	1,758.88
1953	92	312.93	1972	899	2,208.85
1954	147	508.65	1973	962	2,029.54
1955	299	1,020.48	1974	1,011	1,671.07
1956	345	1,127.45	1975	1,182	1,748.52
1957	296	942.68	1976	1,023	1,463.52
1958	248	797.43	1977	1,357	1,874.31
1959	316	1,016.08	1978	1,414	1,826.87
1960	306	977.64	1979	1,573	1,785.47
1961	301	943.57	1980	2,321	2,321.00
1962	333	1,050.47	1981	3,500	3,205.13
1963	409	1,290.22	1982	756	684.78
1964	418	1,306.25	1983	3,737	3,348.57
1965	380	1,151.52	1984	7,419	6,559.68
1966	455	1,338.24	1985	4,467	3,981.28
1967	420	1,210.37	1986	4,635	4,120.00
1968	492	1,397.73			

1. Nominal data in source deflated here using U.S. export price index (table 3231).

SOURCE: IMF-IFS-Y, 1987.

Figure 27:33

MEXICO TOTAL REAL SDR RESERVES, MINUS GOLD, 1950–86

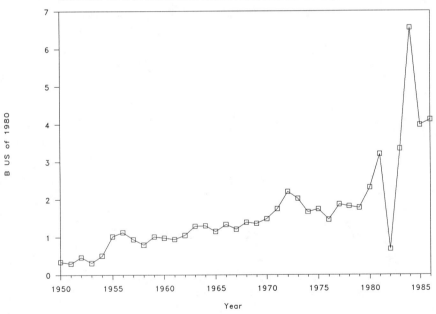

Source: Table 2721.

Table 2722

NICARAGUA TOTAL REAL SDR RESERVES, MINUS GOLD, [1] 1950–86
(M US of 1980)

Year	Nominal Value	Real Value	Year	Nominal Value	Real Value
1950	1	3.86	1969	44	121.55
1951	6	20.20	1970	49	128.27
1952	13	44.07	1971	54	137.06
1953	14	47.62	1972	74	181.82
1954	11	38.06	1973	96	202.53
1955	12	40.96	1974	85	140.50
1956	6	19.61	1975	104	153.85
1957	10	31.85	1976	126	180.26
1958	6	19.29	1977	122	168.51
1959	12	38.59	1978	39	50.39
1960	11	35.14	1979	111	125.99
1961	13	40.75	1980	51	51.00
1962	17	53.63	1981	96	87.91
1963	32	100.95	1982	155	140.40
1964	39	121.88	1983	176	157.71
1965	57	172.73	1984	~	~
1966	57	167.65	1985	~	~
1967	31	89.34	1986	~	~
1968	48	136.36			

1. Nominal data in source deflated here using U.S. export price index (table 3231).

SOURCE: IMF-IFS-Y, 1987.

Figure 27:34

NICARAGUA TOTAL REAL SDR RESERVES, MINUS GOLD, 1950–83

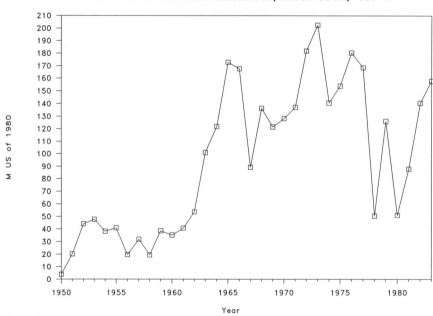

Source: Table 2722.

Table 2723

PANAMA TOTAL REAL SDR RESERVES, MINUS GOLD, [1] 1950–86

(M US of 1980)

Year	Nominal Value	Real Value	Year	Nominal Value	Real Value
1950	4	15.44	1969	14	38.67
1951	2	6.73	1970	16	41.88
1952	3	10.17	1971	19	48.22
1953	5	17.01	1972	40	98.28
1954	7	24.22	1973	35	73.84
1955	6	20.48	1974	32	52.89
1956	8	26.14	1975	30	44.38
1957	4	12.74	1976	68	97.28
1958	9	28.94	1977	58	80.11
1959	4	12.86	1978	116	149.87
1960	7	22.36	1979	90	102.16
1961	5	15.67	1980	92	92.00
1962	5	15.77	1981	103	94.32
1963	7	22.08	1982	92	83.33
1964	5	15.63	1983	197	176.52
1965	6	18.18	1984	220	194.52
1966	6	17.65	1985	89	79.32
1967	7	20.17	1986	139	123.56
1968	11	31.25			

1. Nominal data in source deflated here using U.S. export price index (table 3231).

SOURCE: IMF-IFS-Y, 1987.

Figure 27:35

PANAMA TOTAL REAL SDR RESERVES, MINUS GOLD, 1950–86

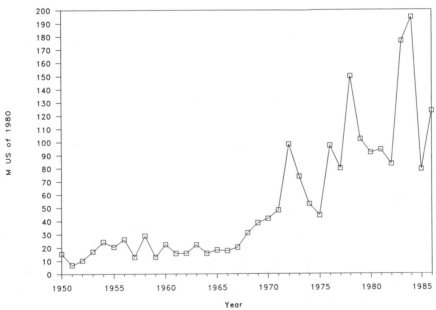

Source: Table 2723.

Table 2724

PARAGUAY TOTAL REAL SDR RESERVES, MINUS GOLD, [1] 1950–86
(M US of 1980)

Year	Nominal Value	Real Value	Year	Nominal Value	Real Value
1950	2	7.72	1969	10	27.62
1951	13	43.77	1970	18	47.12
1952	7	23.73	1971	19	48.22
1953	6	20.41	1972	29	71.25
1954	5	17.30	1973	47	99.16
1955	6	20.48	1974	71	117.36
1956	8	26.14	1975	98	144.97
1957	5	15.92	1976	136	194.56
1958	7	22.51	1977	221	305.25
1959	4	12.86	1978	344	444.44
1960	1	3.19	1979	462	524.40
1961	2	6.27	1980	597	597.00
1962	2	6.31	1981	692	633.70
1963	3	9.46	1982	670	606.88
1964	5	15.63	1983	650	582.44
1965	10	30.30	1984	680	601.24
1966	11	32.35	1985	498	443.85
1967	12	34.58	1986	366	325.33
1968	12	34.09			

1. Nominal data in source deflated here using U.S. export price index (table 3231).

SOURCE: IMF-IFS-Y, 1987.

Figure 27:36

PARAGUAY TOTAL REAL SDR RESERVES, MINUS GOLD, 1950–86

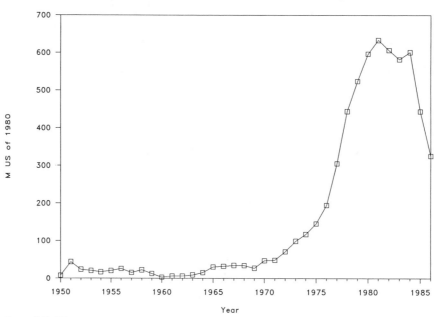

Source: Table 2724.

Table 2725

PERU TOTAL REAL SDR RESERVES, MINUS GOLD, [1] 1950–86

(M US of 1980)

Year	Nominal Value	Real Value	Year	Nominal Value	Real Value
1950	26	100.39	1969	142	392.27
1951	18	60.61	1970	296	774.87
1952	16	54.24	1971	351	890.86
1953	19	64.63	1972	408	1,002.46
1954	27	93.43	1973	436	919.83
1955	23	78.50	1974	756	1,249.59
1956	38	124.18	1975	363	536.98
1957	12	38.22	1976	249	356.22
1958	12	38.59	1977	294	406.08
1959	31	99.68	1978	299	386.30
1960	34	108.63	1979	1,154	1,309.88
1961	63	197.49	1980	1,552	1,552.00
1962	69	217.67	1981	1,031	944.14
1963	78	246.06	1982	1,223	1,107.79
1964	93	290.63	1983	1,304	1,168.46
1965	107	324.24	1984	1,663	1,470.38
1966	90	264.71	1985	1,663	1,482.17
1967	106	305.48	1986	1,169	1,039.11
1968	91	258.52			

1. Nominal data in source deflated here using U.S. export price index (table 3231).

SOURCE: IMF-IFS-Y, 1987.

Figure 27:37

PERU TOTAL REAL SDR RESERVES, MINUS GOLD, 1950–86

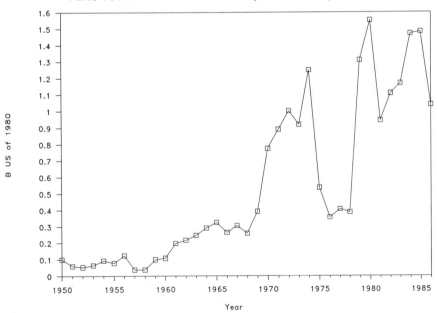

Source: Table 2725.

Table 2726

URUGUAY TOTAL REAL SDR RESERVES, MINUS GOLD, [1] 1950–86

(M US of 1980)

Year	Nominal Value	Real Value	Year	Nominal Value	Real Value
1950	76	293.44	1969	19	52.49
1951	46	154.88	1970	14	36.65
1952	113	383.05	1971	19	48.22
1953	141	479.59	1972	64	157.25
1954	106	366.78	1973	83	175.11
1955	2	6.83	1974	66	109.09
1956	9	29.41	1975	50	73.96
1957	2	6.37	1976	152	217.45
1958	8	25.72	1977	265	366.02
1959	7	22.51	1978	271	350.13
1960	9	28.75	1979	245	278.09
1961	11	34.48	1980	301	301.00
1962	23	72.56	1981	369	337.91
1963	14	44.16	1982	105	95.11
1964	15	46.88	1983	198	177.42
1965	24	72.73	1984	137	121.13
1966	30	88.24	1985	159	141.71
1967	22	63.40	1986	394	350.22
1968	34	96.59			

1. Nominal data in source deflated here using U.S. export price index (table 3231).

SOURCE: IMF-IFS-Y, 1987.

Figure 27:38

URUGUAY TOTAL REAL SDR RESERVES, MINUS GOLD, 1950–86

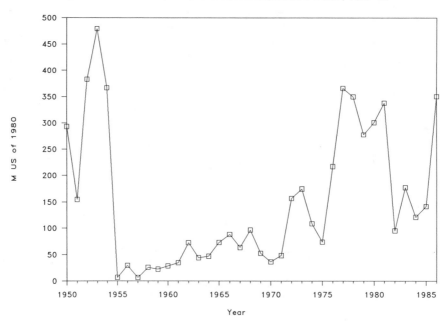

Source: Table 2726.

Table 2727

VENEZUELA TOTAL REAL SDR RESERVES, MINUS GOLD, [1] 1950–86

(M US of 1980)

Year	Nominal Value	Real Value	Year	Nominal Value	Real Value
1950	5	19.31	1969	530	1,464.09
1951	4	13.47	1970	637	1,667.54
1952	70	237.29	1971	1,010	2,563.45
1953	111	377.55	1972	1,204	2,958.23
1954	79	273.36	1973	1,609	3,394.51
1955	130	443.69	1974	4,928	8,145.45
1956	347	1,133.99	1975	7,178	10,618.34
1957	739	2,353.50	1976	6,992	10,002.86
1958	342	1,099.68	1977	6,368	8,795.58
1959	69	221.86	1978	4,632	5,984.50
1960	208	664.54	1979	5,557	6,307.60
1961	179	561.13	1980	5,178	5,178.00
1962	182	574.13	1981	7,014	6,423.08
1963	344	1,085.17	1982	5,964	5,402.17
1964	431	1,346.88	1983	7,300	6,541.22
1965	418	1,266.67	1984	9,081	8,029.18
1966	376	1,105.88	1985	9,332	8,317.29
1967	471	1,357.35	1986	5,623	4,998.22
1968	519	1,474.43			

1. Nominal data in source deflated here using U.S. export price index (table 3231).

SOURCE: IMF-IFS-Y, 1987.

Figure 27:39

VENEZUELA TOTAL REAL SDR RESERVES, MINUS GOLD, 1950–86

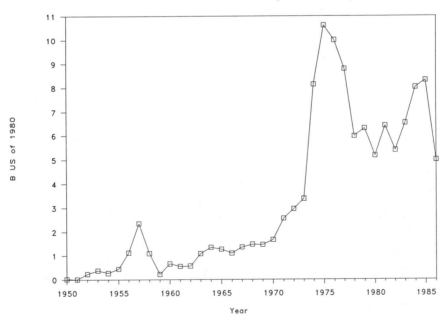

Source: Table 2727.

Table 2728

UNITED STATES TOTAL REAL SDR RESERVES, MINUS GOLD, [1] 1950–86

(M US of 1980)

Year	Nominal Value	Real Value	Year	Nominal Value	Real Value
1950	1,446	5,583.01	1969	5,105	14,102.21
1951	1,426	4,801.35	1970	3,415	8,939.79
1952	1,462	4,955.93	1971	1,942	4,928.93
1953	1,367	4,649.66	1972	2,453	6,027.03
1954	1,185	4,100.35	1973	2,260	4,767.93
1955	1,044	3,563.14	1974	3,456	5,712.40
1956	1,608	5,254.90	1975	3,952	5,846.15
1957	1,975	6,289.81	1976	6,153	8,802.58
1958	1,958	6,295.82	1977	6,250	8,632.60
1959	1,998	6,424.44	1978	5,357	6,921.19
1960	1,555	4,968.05	1979	5,909	6,707.15
1961	1,806	5,661.44	1980	12,228	12,228.00
1962	1,163	3,668.77	1981	16,258	14,888.28
1963	1,247	3,933.75	1982	20,677	18,729.17
1964	1,201	3,753.13	1983	21,612	19,365.59
1965	1,385	4,196.97	1984	24,319	21,502.21
1966	1,647	4,844.12	1985	29,220	26,042.78
1967	2,765	7,968.30	1986	30,619	27,216.89
1968	4,848	13,687.50			

1. Nominal data in source deflated here using U.S. export price index (table 3231).

SOURCE: IMF-IFS-Y, 1987.

Figure 27:40

UNITED STATES TOTAL REAL SDR RESERVES, MINUS GOLD, 1950–86

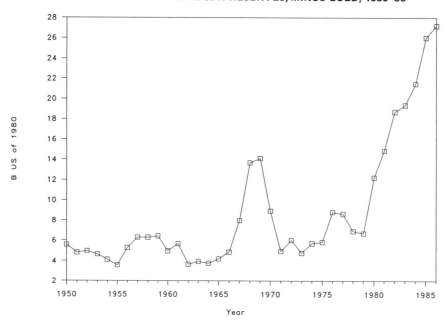

Source: Table 2728.

Table 2729

TOTAL CHANGE IN DOLLAR RESERVES, 19 LC, 1951–85
(M US)

Year	A. ARGENTINA	B. BOLIVIA	C. BRAZIL	D. CHILE	E. COLOMBIA	F. COSTA RICA	H. DOMINICAN REP.	I. ECUADOR	J. EL SALVADOR	K. GUATEMALA
1951	25	-5.5	137	-2	~	-4.7	-10.3	5.0	-1.6	-2.3
1952	49	4.0	-32	-19	~	-6.2	-2.5	-11.5	-1.0	-3.2
1953	-86	6.9	63	10	~	.2	4.0	2.9	.2	.1
1954	-30	12.1	38	15	~	-7.3	-7.6	2.3	-.8	2.5
1955	68	3.3	-15	-21	~	-3.9	-1.4	5.8	5.5	-15.5
1956	38	9.9	-148	3	8	7.8	-2.3	.2	2.6	-15.7
1957	175	-3.8	173	51	-7	#	-8.2	-2.4	-5.0	-3.9
1958	154	1.5	49	-1	-9	-7.8	.7	-1.2	2.0	26.0
1959	-178	-6.7	8	-73	-70	6.2	5.7	-5.9	4.7	5.1
1960	-258	3.9	24	4	41	1.2	21.1	2.8	10.4	-10.0
1961	232	-1.9	-101	92	69	10.9	16.8	12.7	5.0	-1.1
1962	297	4.7	114	-18	61	-10.0	-11.7	-7.1	-7.0	9.9
1963	-141	-5.1	39	42	47	6.4	-26.6	-11.7	-15.9	-12.0
1964	74	-16.5	-33	-2	-30	-4.0	9.3	-4.8	-10.9	-4.5
1965	-127	-14.0	-219	-50	-16	4.4	6.8	11.7	-5.2	-8.8
1966	-26	-4.6	14	-49	17	3.2	13.5	-10.1	14.5	12.8
1967	-541	3.3	193	30	28	-4.8	7.9	-8.8	2.1	4.8
1968	-33	3.5	-70	-73	-69	-10.4	-10.6	1.6	-4.2	-2.8
1969	222	.5	-399	-157	-55	-17.4	1.1	4.5	-4.6	-12.3
1970	-135	-5.5	-530	-99	-36	11.6	-.4	-7.7	-6.4	14.6
1971	390	-6.5	-55.6	213	7	-13.0	-18.9	10.7	3.9	-13.4
1972	14	-4.1	-2,437	116	-180	-19.9	-10.1	-74.3	-19.0	-42.9
1973	-814	2.5	-2,227	-16	-207	-16.5	-33.4	-99.5	13.1	-77.3
1974	-127	-127.2	1,144	16	85	33.0	-2.8	-108.2	-14.4	-6.3
1975	1,071	33.5	1,235	271	-97	16.6	-25.3	65.3	-30.4	-102.5
1976	-921	-47.1	-2,508	-333	-633	-64.1	14.4	-224.0	-84.5	-219.4
1977	-1,828	-75.8	-712	-156	-668	-109.5	-50.3	-146.3	-41.0	-182.9
1978	-2,297	81.8	-4,638	-724	-669	-25.6	41.3	-13.0	-56.9	-10.4
1979	-4,381	-25.4	2,860	-1,128	-1,615	113.6	-7.8	-86.5	125.2	18.3
1980	2,749	137.0	3,321	-1,402	-1,231	-98.9	-44.4	-291.0	71.4	252.5
1981	3,437	-21.7	-750	-77	-218	66.6	-54.1	380.6	42.7	300.8
1982	758	-37.2	4,160	1,372	722	-137.1	160.4	328.2	27.0	33.0
1983	2,427	-9.7	1,215	499	1,753	-61.0	149.2	-127.2	-38.9	-56.4
1984	-16	~	~	-197	1,166	57.6	~	58.3	-18.4	-20.9
1985	~	~	~	173	-199	~	~	~	~	-97.0

Table 2729 (Continued)
TOTAL CHANGE IN DOLLAR RESERVES, 19 LC, 1951–85
(M US)

Year	L. HAITI	M. HONDURAS	N. MEXICO	O. NICARAGUA	P. PANAMA	Q. PARAGUAY	R. PERU	S. URUGUAY	T. VENEZUELA	UNITED STATES[1,2]
1951	-1.6	-9.7	~	~	~	-6.2	~	~	~	~
1952	-2.8	-2.1	~	~	~	1.9	~	~	~	~
1953	5.8	-.6	32	~	~	1.5	~	~	~	1.26
1954	-4.5	-1.2	40	~	~	5.8	~	~	~	.48
1955	2.7	4.1	-231	~	#	2.3	~	~	~	.18
1956	1.2	2.0	-72	7.3	-2	-21	-15	~	-417	-.87
1957	3.2	4.1	36	-2.4	4	4.0	33	~	-505	-1.16
1958	2.9	4.3	80	1.9	-4	-.3	3	~	395	2.29
1959	1.6	-.8	-62	-4.6	5	1.6	-32	2.6	338	1.04
1960	-2.2	-.4	16	.1	-3	2.7	-17	-5.9	115	2.14
1961	-2.8	1.8	29	.1	3	-3.4	-34	-5.9	29	.61
1962	4.1	.2	-14	-3.9	#	-.1	-6	6.4	-2	1.53
1963	2.5	-.1	-120	-8.5	-3	-1.5	-19	17.0	-163	.38
1964	.3	-4.7	-42	-6.2	2	-2.3	-25	-.6	-86	.17
1965	.9	-6.2	61	-18.2	-1	-5.5	-15	8.0	-11	1.22
1966	1.2	5.0	-2	-2.6	#	-.4	17	1.2	67	.57
1967	2.0	-.4	-27	19.4	-1	-.7	30	8.2	-95	.05
1968	-3.1	-6.5	-94	-4.0	-2	.1	18	15.7	-50	-.88
1969	-1.2	.6	53	4.7	-3	2.0	-31	-28.4	-11	-1.26
1970	-3.8	9.7	-75	-11.3	-4	-7.3	-187	16.7	-87	2.48
1971	-10.7	-2.6	-197	-8.1	-3	-3.4	-90	-.4	-469	2.18
1972	-9.8	-13.3	-223	-27.5	-22	-10.4	-30	-3.1	-208	#
1973	3.5	-6.9	-168	-67.8	2	-25.7	-94	-23.8	-637	-.06
1974	11.4	17.4	-43	35.2	11	-30.1	-413	40.9	-4,480	-1.46
1975	8.5	-54.1	-112	-41.3	16	-27.9	499	57.0	-2,669	-.20
1976	-11.1	-38.0	682	-2.9	-15	-42.4	312	-73.8	-2,377	-2.52
1977	-12.1	-66.2	-384	-9.3	10	-112.4	-59	-174.3	-847	-.56
1978	-14.3	-9.9	-455	82.8	-78	-179.5	-5	-152.0	977	1.06
1979	-11.4	-25.0	-396	-35.0	21	-165.1	-1,066	-123.1	-4,234	2.76
1980	26.3	73.0	-1,027	196.6	-17	-152.9	-609	-113.6	-3,823	-7.64
1981	56.7	69.0	-1,122	-62.4	68	-43.1	575	-20.1	12	-3.21
1982	46.3	52.8	3,470	96.7	9	65.0	112	505.1	8,215	-3.86
1983	33.1	39.4	-2,050	33.2	3	56.3	33	114.8	-95	45
1984	29.2	-26.8	-2,138	~	69	19.0	-296	63.0	-1,517	-.97
1985		18.6	~	~	158	~	-277	~	~	-8.21

1. Cf. SALA, 25-2701 to 2720.
2. Data in billions.

SOURCE: IMF-IFS-Y, 1981, line 79 kd, and 1986, line 79 cd.

Table 2730

ECLA BALANCE OF PAYMENTS, 19 L, 1982–85

(M US)

Category	A. ARGENTINA				B. BOLIVIA				C. BRAZIL				D. CHILE			
	1982	1983	1984	1985‡	1982	1983	1984	1985‡	1982	1983	1984	1985‡	1982	1983	1984	1985‡
Balance on current account	-2,477	-2,436	-2,542	-950	-121	-216	-238	-325	-16,314	-6,842	43	-650	-2,378	-1,116	-2,118	-1,342
Trade balance	2,600	3,469	3,591	4,800	280	165	170	12	-2,795	4,079	11,367	10,740	-385	635	-108	542
Exports of goods and services	9,022	9,291	9,578	9,950	912	858	818	722	21,967	23,619	28,986	27,579	4,641	4,601	4,495	4,470
Goods FOB	7,598	7,838	8,072	8,400	828	755	724	624	20,172	21,906	27,050	25,639	3,706	3,827	3,650	3,804
Real services[1]	1,422	1,454	1,505	1,550	85	103	93	98	1,791	1,712	1,936	1,940	936	774	845	666
Transport and insurance	682	755	830	860	26	35	35	38	1,013	1,119	1,309	1,370	318	269	308	302
Travel	516	453	440	450	30	42	32	30		40	66	60	125	95	129	116
Imports of goods and services	6,422	5,822	5,987	5,150	633	693	648	710	24,762	19,540	17,619	16,839	5,027	3,966	4,602	3,928
Goods FOB	4,873	4,120	4,132	3,400	429	473	412	463	19,395	15,434	13,936	13,189	3,643	2,818	3,357	2,955
Real services[1]	1,550	1,700	1,855	1,750	204	220	235	247	5,365	4,106	3,683	3,650	1,383	1,148	1,245	973
Transport and insurance	649	737	900	760	101	128	121	149	2,460	2,025	2,071	2,000	630	511	615	514
Travel	566	507	600	600	40	20	30	30	913	431	218	450	195	214	327	269
Factor services	-5,107	-5,922	-6,135	-5,750	-418	-421	-436	-363	-13,509	-11,025	-11,484	-11,540	-2,035	-1,800	-2,051	-1,931
Profits	-351	-424	-437	-400	-24	-59	-36	-35	-2,144	-1,453	-1,270	-1,140	-128	-77	-113	-155
Interest received	525	440	264	~	7	22	18	26	1,198	707	1,252	1,300	506	187	316	197
Interest paid	-4,930	-5,425	-5,542	~	-397	-381	-415	-353	-12,550	-10,267	-11,463	-11,700	-2,299	-1,813	-2,158	-1,943
Others	-351	-514	-420	-450	-3	-2	-2	-14	-14	-13	-2	#	114	-97	-96	-30
Unrequited private transfer payments	32	16	2	--	17	40	28	26	-11	106	161	150	41	49	41	47
Balance on capital account	1,809		2,686	3,600	153	232	465	343	11,119	4,943	5,367	664	1,038	600	2,210	1,240
Unrequited official transfer payments	#	#	#	#	29	66	60	54	2	2	10	#	68	43	58	14
Long-term capital	3,788	1,715	277	3,600	164	67	161	-237	8,011	1,850	6,381	3,048	1,680	1,210	1,208	1,015
Direct investment	270	183	269		37	7	7	10	2,534	1,372	1,555	800	384	148	67	112
Portfolio investment	3,028	1,140	754		#	#	#	#	-1	-286	-272	#	#	#	#	#
Other long-term capital	491	393	-746		128	60	154	-247	5,478	764	5,097	7,248	1,296	1,063	1,142	903
Official sector[2]	-29	376	393		116	64	351	-203	1,744	3,132	7,921	~	134	1,149	957	1,210
Loans disbursed	227	2,497	2,034		132	393	737	97	3,368	4,679	9,305	~	296	1,300	1,047	1,431
Amortization payments	-208	-2,110	-548		-67	-324	-379	-300	-1,286	-1,520	-1,412	~	-162	-151	-90	-221
Commercial banks[2]	268	38	-32		-13	#	-38	-9	1,681	1,136	1,230	~	327	-9	23	-69
Loans disbursed	812	264	8		6	39	11	1	4,239	-848	-2,639	~	701	135	90	1,131
Amortization payments	-542	-227	-40		-19	-39	-49	-9	-2,559	2,527	-1,411	~	-309	-161	-75	-1,200
Other sectors[2]	251	-22	-2,748		24	-4	-159	-35	-2,053	-3,358	2,076	~	836	-78	162	-238
Loans disbursed	2,761	2,447	281		55	154	43	8	6,675		-4,149	~	1,613	511	484	795
Amortization payments	-2,097	-1,289	-2,854		-35	-157	-202	-43	-4,264		-1,430	~	-788	-589	-322	-1,033
Short-term capital (net)	-1,708	-91	2,462	2,650	-7	18	250	376	3,879	3,682	1,471	-1,648	-647	-710	844	-159
Official sector	2,682	311	1,298		118	148	66	365	-136	4,756	982	~	15	112	254	214
Commercial banks	304	-1,509	-523		20	-32	-4	-12	-267	-710	-3,883	~	68	-422	250	36
Other sectors	-4,693	-440	1,687		-145	-98	188	23	-369	-364	406	~	-731	-400	339	337
Errors and omissions	-273	-2,450	-52	~	-34	81	-7	150	-3,516	-592	406	-736	-64	57	100	-3
Global balance[3]	-668		144	-2,500	32	16	226	18		-1,899	5,410	14	-1,340	-516	92	-102
Total variation in reserves (minus sign indicates an increase)	762	2,379	~	~	-38	1	-256	-28	4,157	1,214	-6,105	~	1,112	652	-352	190
Monetary gold	#	#	~	~	-2	-1	-1	#	824	-156	-336	~	-2	46	-62	22
Special Drawing Rights	404	100	~	~	#	#	#	-1	452	287	#	~	-1	14	-6	11
IMF reserve position	178	1,105	~	~	#	#	#	#	-23	-714	#	~	-3	78	#	#
Foreign exchange assets	180	#	~	~	-56	19	-116	31	2,245	-297	-7,173	~	1,160	-87	-458	-145
Other assets	#	1,174	~	~	5	-20	-114	-46	109	2,094	-144	~	#	#	#	#
Use made of IMF credit	#	#	~	~	15	3	-25	-12	550		1,549	~	-42	600	175	302

Table 2730 (Continued)

ECLA BALANCE OF PAYMENTS, 19 L, 1982–85

(M US)

Category	E. COLOMBIA 1982	1983	1984	1985‡	F. COSTA RICA 1982	1983	1984	1985‡	H. DOMINICAN REPUBLIC 1982	1983	1984	1985‡	I. ECUADOR 1982	1983	1984	1985‡
Balance on current account	-3,196	-3,022	-2,020	-1,364	-206	-330	-342	-371	-457	-441	-223	-317	-1,215	-128	-268	-110
Trade balance	-2,503	-1,970	-888	-417	113	-16	-37	-60	-393	-339	-187	-273	-368	735	855	966
Exports of goods and services	4,897	3,784	4,482	5,000	1,070	1,133	1,210	1,202	1,142	1,242	1,369	1,318	2,690	2,643	2,895	3,234
Goods FOB	3,549	2,970	3,668	4,036	871	853	933	928	768	785	868	739	2,343	2,365	2,622	2,870
Real services[1]	1,348	815	814	964	201	280	277	274	374	457	501	579	347	278	273	364
Transport and insurance	481	390	340	369	31	59	58	57	21	27	29	36	139	95	95	146
Travel	422	235	270	297	133	133	116	113	266	320	371	439	131	120	120	143
Imports of goods and services	7,400	5,754	5,370	5,416	957	1,149	1,247	1,261	1,535	1,581	1,556	1,591	3,058	1,908	2,040	2,268
Goods FOB	5,967	4,464	3,980	4,027	780	898	989	997	1,257	1,282	1,257	1,286	2,181	1,408	1,567	1,723
Real services[1]	1,433	1,290	1,390	1,389	177	250	258	264	277	299	299	305	877	500	473	545
Transport and insurance	875	639	553	531	92	133	142	145	138	150	127	145	164	238	296	269
Travel	235	315	260	240	47	52	55	58	87	88	89	83	250	152	155	167
Factor services	-878	-1,197	-1,311	-1,352	-348	-337	-330	-338	-254	-297	-241	-286	-847	-863	-1,123	-1,076
Profits	-152	-437	-183	-211	-8	7	-18	-17	4	#	#	~	-80	-60	-70	-120
Interest received	550	272	110	91	20	34	33	35	#	7	6	~	44	45	77	26
Interest paid	-1,266	-1,011	-1,196	-1,203	-357	-374	-338	-349	-258	-304	-247	~	-811	-723	-936	-872
Others	-9	-21	-42	-29	-4	-4	-6	-7	#	#	#	~	#	-125	-194	-110
Unrequited private transfer payments	184	145	179	405	29	23	24	27	190	195	205	242	#	#	#	#
Balance on capital account	2,222	1,180	741	1,687	331	377	271	463	311	303	321	342	875	238	187	135
Unrequited official transfer payments	2	19	26	59	6	46	109	175	15	20	60	114	20	24	20	25
Long-term capital	1,774	1,528	1,672	2,200	38	1,197	91	245	262	506	294	281	162	1,372	358	~
Direct investment	372	514	411	729	33	55	54	60	-1	48	69	27	40	50	50	60
Portfolio investment	-8	-2	-3	-5	#	-3	-3	#	#	#	#	#	#	#	#	#
Other long-term capital	1,410	1,016	1,264	1,476	5	1,144	39	185	264	458	225	254	122	1,322	308	254
Official sector[2]	355	102	~	~	27	1,196	122	190	290	542	237	~	-261	2,265	879	~
Loans received	558	290	~	~	122	1,362	382	596	393	734	273	~	192	2,641	1,531	~
Amortization payments	-198	-188	~	~	-95	-180	-246	-406	-103	-192	-36	~	-437	-363	-643	~
Commercial banks[2]	#	#	~	~	-21	-15	-19	-5	-1	11	-2	~	8	-7	-9	~
Loans received			~	~	7			~				~				~
Amortization payments			~	~	-28			~				~				~
Other sectors[2]	1,054	914	~	~	-1	-37	-64	#	-25	-95	-10	~	383	-936	-562	~
Loans received	1,334	1,360	~	~	170	64	41	~	26	17	20	~	1,112	150	78	~
Amortization payments	-279	-446	~	~	-171	-101	-105	~	-51	-111	-30	~	-728	-1,085	-639	~
Short-term capital (net)	384	-391	-835	-210	186	-933	-16	-30	34	-241	-64	~	921	-1,073	-200	~
Official sector	42	90	-186	~	181	-535	12	43	162	-131	-115	~	585	-520	-95	~
Commercial banks	146	58	-414	-445	40	-97	-15	-30	-45	-235	-22	~	50	7	34	~
Other sectors	197	-539	-235	~	-35	-301	-13	~	-83	124	73	~	286	-560	-139	~
Errors and omissions	63	25	-122	-362	101	66	88	73	-1	18	31	-53	-286	-85	9	~
Global balance[3]	-974	-1,842	-1,279	323	125	47	-71	92	-146	-139	98	25	-340	110	-81	25
Total variation in reserves (minus sign indicates an increase)	694	1,782	1,261	-284	-95	-170	84	-67	160	150	-84	-13	328	-127	58	-25
Monetary gold	-187	-177	~	~	#	11	13	-10	16	16	23	-2	#	#	#	~
Special Drawing Rights	-40	-19	~	~	#	#	3	#	1	#	#	-31	34	#	#	~
IMF reserve position	-16	-81	~	~	#	#	#	#	#	#	#	#	29	-12	12	~
Foreign exchange assets	936	2,060	~	~	-85	99	82	~	95	-8	8	-56	266	-328	21	~
Other assets	#	#	~	~	#	#	22	~	#	#	-90	#	#	#	#	~
Use made of IMF credit	#	#	~	~	-10	~	-36	32	48	176	-25	76	#	213	25	~

Table 2730 (Continued)
ECLA BALANCE OF PAYMENTS, 19 L, 1982–85
(M US)

Category	J. EL SALVADOR				K. GUATEMALA				L. HAITI				M. HONDURAS			
	1982	1983	1984	1985‡	1982	1983	1984	1985‡	1982	1983	1984	1985‡	1982	1983	1984	1985‡
Balance on current account	-271	-256	-313	-341	-376	-225	-383	-247	-160	-177	-182	-191	-249	-260	-311	-378
Trade balance	-218	-187	-328	-367	-323	-142	-201	-86	-195	-209	-208	-220	-56	-120	-139	-203
Exports of goods and services	822	873	862	866	1,307	1,172	1,228	1,183	270	288	299	342	767	797	875	937
Goods FOB	704	735	726	723	1,200	1,092	1,131	1,062	174	186	199	223	677	694	766	821
Real services[1]	118	138	136	143	107	80	97	121	96	103	101	119	90	102	109	116
Transport and insurance	23	30	30	31					7	7	7	8	37	44	45	50
Travel	20	24	26	28					80	85	81	93	25	22	24	25
Imports of goods and services	1,041	1,061	1,190	1,233	1,630	1,314	1,429	1,269	465	497	507	562	823	917	1,014	1,140
Goods FOB	826	831	905	954	1,284	1,056	1,183	1,081	296	324	325	345	681	761	844	945
Real services[1]	215	230	285	279	346	257	246	188	169	173	182	217	142	156	170	195
Transport and insurance	72	81	94	95	141	99	112	107	77	88	94	114	69	78	74	94
Travel	60	74	74	73	100	89	61	24	41	39	39	43	23	21	22	27
Factor services	-105	-121	-116	-120	-115	-113	-209	-180	-14	-14	-18	-20	-202	-149	-184	-188
Profits	-45	-36	-78	-59	-41	-39	-83	-70	-8	-8	-2	-2	-45	-30	-46	-58
Interest received	14	13	20	18	20	27	30	30	#	1	#	#	15	12	12	15
Interest paid	-98	-107	-105	-109	-101	-102	-152	-139	-6	-7	-16	-18	-172	-131	-150	-145
Labour and property	24	10	47	30	7	#	-4	-1								
Unrequited private transfer payments	52	53	131	146	62	30	28	19	49	46	43	49	9	10	12	13
Balance on capital account	242	280	320	388	338	276	397	316	115	144	154	168	203	213	301	389
Unrequited official transfer payments	119	191	196	222	1	1	1	#	61	64	75	97	21	35	68	111
Long-term capital	255	329	69	92	341	283	205	139	43	46	62	∼	168	180	245	236
Direct investment	-1	28	#	#	77	45	38	60	7	8	4	5	14	21	7	28
Portfolio investment	-1	#	#	#	#	77	59	-2	#	#	#	∼	#	#	#	#
Other long-term capital	257	301	69	92	263	161	109	81	36	37	57	∼	155	159	238	208
Official sector[2]	251	296	69	92	142	167	157	82	33	32	55	∼	79	52	305	172
Disbursements	358	438	265	300	197	310	283	177	38	35	61	∼	125	104	291	248
Amortization payments[2]	-87	-141	-196	-208	-55	-143	-126	-95	-4	-3	-6	∼	-38	-43	-54	-58
Commercial banks[2]	#	-1	#	#	#	#	#	#	#	#	#	∼	-2	-2	-2	5
Disbursements	1	-1	#	#	#	#	#	#	#	#	#	∼	3	2	1	7
Amortization payments	-1	-1	}	}	#	#	#	#	#	#	#	∼	-5	-5	-2	-2
Other sectors[2]	6	6	}	}	121	-6	-48	-1	4	6	3	∼	80	109	-65	31
Disbursements	36	28	}	}	121	11	6	89	8	12	20	∼	142	173	54	113
Amortization payments	-31	-22	}	}	-15	-18	-54	-90	-5	-7	-17	∼	-62	-64	-118	-40
Short-term capital (net)	-66	215	55	74	-29	29	179	186	-8	-6	-8	∼	19	-75	16	10
Official sector	-65	121			-15	24	-93	∼	-8	-6	-8	∼	39	-38	16	32
Commercial banks	29	-33			14	71	9	∼	#	#	#	∼	18	8	#	#
Other sectors	#	-61			-1	-67	262	∼	#	#	#	∼	-37	5	16	-22
Errors and omissions	-95	-26	7	47	-33	-37	12	-10	19	40	26	23	-5	22	-28	32
Global balance[3]	-29	24			-38	51	14	69	-45	-33	-28	∼	-46	-47	-10	11
Total variation in reserves (minus sign indicates an increase)	27	-39	-19	-30	16	-64	-30	-69	3	32	6	∼	53	39	7	-11
Monetary gold	#	2	#	#	#	-1	-1	1	1	#	#	∼	#	#	∼	#
Special Drawing Rights	-2	2	#	#	3	#	8	2	#	-1	1	∼	#	∼	2	#
IMF reserve position	#	#	#	#	10	-8	#	#	#	#	#	∼	#	-4	4	#
Foreign exchange assets	-35	-53	-6	-14	25	-89	-72	-29	-16	10	-5	∼	-11	3	∼	-9
Other assets	#	#	#	#	-15	25	25	-8	#	#	#	∼	-2	-2	∼	-2
Use made of IMF credit	64	11	-13	-17	-6	35	10	-34	18	22	11	∼	66	43	-11	#

Note: In the J. EL SALVADOR columns for 1984 and 1985, the commercial-bank and other-sector long-term capital detail rows are joined by a brace (}) in the original. The symbol ∼ represents a "not available" (squiggle) mark in the source.

Table 2730 (Continued)
ECLA BALANCE OF PAYMENTS, 19 L, 1982–85
(M US)

Category	N. MEXICO				O. NICARAGUA				P. PANAMA				Q. PARAGUAY			
	1982	1983	1984	1985‡	1982	1983	1984	1985‡	1982	1983	1984	1985‡	1982	1983	1984	1985‡
Balance on current account	-5,316	5,151	3,704	298	-512	-519	-508	-569	-538	143	-227	91	-391	-252	-329	-192
Trade balance	5,436	14,494	13,869	8,852	-381	-462	-464	-527	-253	103	-69	139	-446	-233	-276	-142
Exports of goods and services	27,257	27,183	30,025	27,658	448	463	422	353	1,603	2,969	2,981	3,286	617	476	543	518
Goods FOB	21,230	22,380	24,042	21,866	408	428	385	293	345	1,674	1,683	1,949	396	326	361	341
Real services [1]	6,027	4,863	5,983	5,792	41	35	37	60	1,258	1,296	1,298	1,336	221	150	182	177
Transport and insurance	426	467	530	548	12	10	5	3	574	730	723	750	2	~	~	~
Travel	4,751	2,727	3,278	2,900	20	5	5	3	172	172	186	200	59	49	~	~
Imports of goods and services	21,821	12,689	16,155	18,806	829	925	886	880	1,856	2,866	3,050	3,147	1,063	709	819	660
Goods FOB	14,437	8,553	11,287	13,460	723	778	761	763	1,441	2,322	2,478	2,603	711	551	649	516
Real services [1]	7,384	4,136	4,868	5,346	106	147	125	117	415	545	572	544	352	157	170	144
Transport and insurance	1,729	1,275	1,354	1,380	49	50	49	51	243	373	403	366	106	75	98	72
Travel	4,365	1,581	2,174	2,262	20	7	6	3	78	71	67	65	42	44	44	47
Factor services	-10,855	-9,466	-10,339	-8,762	-140	-61	-46	-44	-231	100	-95	-67	53	-21	-55	-58
Profits	-797	-380	-454	-618	#	-1	#	#	-35	-92	-73	-67	-16	-39	-49	-50
Interest received	1,248	1,280	2,054	1,728	#	7	5	2	2,816	4,323	3,899	3,085	122	63	70	79
Interest paid	-10,878	-10,286	-11,912	-9,917	-149	-66	-51	-46	-3,017	-4,122	-3,911	-3,285	-92	-78	-95	-108
Work and ownership	-428	-80	-27	45	#	4	#	#	6	-10	-10	273	39	33	19	21
Unrequited private transfer payments	103	123	175	208	8	8	2	2	-55	-60	-63	-53	2	1	8	8
Balance on capital account	2,431	-3,118	-1,570	-2,722	578	586	518	592	524	-156	141	200	329	255	305	84
Unrequited official transfer payments	179	179	201	243	43	76	88	93	85	104	111	137	4	5	7	6
Long-term capital	8,466	4,730	2,636	295	445	557	517	487	1,385	179	~	~	265	289	215	163
Direct investment	874	460	392	491	#	8	2	#	277	56	~	~	44	5	5	11
Portfolio investment	630	-625	-625	-667	#	#	#	#	262	63	~	~	#	3	#	8
Other long-term capital	6,962	4,895	2,870	471	445	549	515	487	846	60	~	~	221	281	210	144
Official sector [2]	2,645	4,256	2,849	-9	368	552	538	~	368	161	~	~	60	139	127	109
Loans received	3,094	5,195	2,849	1,997	407	580	554	~	553	232	~	~	83	162	150	137
Amortization payments	-449	-938	#	-2,006	-39	-28	-16	-12	-183	-70	~	~	-22	-23	-23	-28
Commercial banks [2]	2,346	1,422	474	480	24	33	8	~	256	-13	~	~	11	7	32	}35
Loans received	3,355	2,373	1,464	1,570	30	38	20	~	256	4	~	~	16	10	40	
Amortization payments	-1,008	-951	-991	-1,090	-7	-4	-12	-13	#	-17	~	~	-6	-3	-9	
Other sectors [2]	1,971	-783	-452	~	54	-36	-31	-59	222	-87	~	~	150	135	51	
Loans received	4,160	1,417	907	~	61	14	#	-59	334	145	~	~	217	168	109	
Amortization payments	-1,837	-2,080	-1,366	~	-11	-50	-33	44	-113	-235	~	~	-52	-33	-58	-65
Short-term capital	-2,256	-7,050	-4,170	-1,571	-44	-20	#	#	-1,309	-63	~	~	74	-50	67	~
Official sector	-137	-1,216	#	#	#	#	#	#	5	1	~	~	10	22	93	~
Commercial banks	-8	340	336	-800	4	-20	-33	44	-630	67	~	~	1	1	-5	~
Other sectors	-2,111	-6,174	-4,506	-771	-48	-26	-54	-31	-684	-131	~	~	62	-73	-21	~
Net errors and omissions	-3,958	-972	-238	-1,689	134	67	10	23	364	-376	30	88	-14	11	16	~
Global balance [3]	-2,885	2,033	2,134	-2,424	66	-48	-10	-23	-14	-13	-86	291	-63	3	-24	-108
Total variation in reserves (minus sign indicates an increase)	3,185	-2,045	-2,143	2,328	~	1	1	#	9	3	70	~	121	49	3	132
Monetary gold	7	-5	125	~	~	1	1	#	#	4	#	#	#	#	~	~
Special Drawing Rights	~	-17	20	~	~	~	#	#	-1	-9	4	#	-9	-6	~	~
IMF reserve position	~	-95	95	~	~	~	-33	#	20	-9	9	~	-1	-3	~	~
Foreign exchange assets	~	#	#	~	~	-86	#	~	#	-100	-19	~	133	60	~	~
Other assets	~	-2,967	-3,488	~	-11	42	-33	~	-10	#	79	~	-2	-3	~	~
Use made of IMF credit	~	1,039	1,104	~	-5	-5	-5	~		109			#	#	132	-108

Table 2730 (Continued)

ECLA BALANCE OF PAYMENTS, 19 L, 1982-85
(M US)

Category	R. PERU 1982	1983	1984	1985‡	S. URUGUAY 1982	1983	1984	1985‡	T. VENEZUELA 1982	1983	1984	1985‡
Balance on current account	-1,823	-1,091	-412	-61	-235	-60	-124	-125	-4,222	4,451	5,001	3,950
Trade balance	-769	39	787	949	-48	217	227	220	-2,077	6,745	6,223	6,019
Exports of goods and services	4,061	3,728	3,820	3,616	1,537	1,411	1,289	1,251	17,557	15,825	16,696	15,089
Goods FOB	3,230	3,017	3,149	2,966	1,256	1,156	925	854	16,332	14,570	15,851	14,197
Real services[1]	830	711	671	650	281	255	365	397	1,225	1,254	845	887
Transport and insurance	291	262	206	195	81	71	69	68	664	673	440	488
Travel	322	209	209	200	106	90	210	235	309	310	358	245
Imports of goods and services	4,830	3,689	3,033	2,667	1,585	1,194	1,062	1,031	19,634	9,080	10,474	9,065
Goods FOB	3,787	2,723	2,141	1,869	1,038	740	733	697	13,584	6,409	7,877	6,593
Real services[1]	1,043	966	892	798	547	455	329	334	6,050	2,671	2,597	2,472
Transport and insurance	523	447	379	330	116	85	74	68	1,524	930	1,116	970
Travel	153	191	181	160	304	259	154	162	2,925	1,073	1,075	830
Factor services	-1,053	-1,132	-1,199	-1,010	-197	-288	-362	-356	-1,530	-2,107	-1,072	-1,950
Profits	-160	-137	-53	#	#	#	#	#	-401	-188	-152	-155
Interest received	109	115	158	?	147	63	87	72	2,565	1,500	2,169	1,720
Interest paid	-1,004	-1,110	-1,303	?	-344	-350	-449	-428	-3,694	-3,425	-3,029	-3,515
Others	#	#	#	?	#	#	#	#	-615	-187	-149	-119
Unrequited private transfer payments	#	#	#	#	10	11	10	11	-3,930	-4,116	-3,433	-2,279
Balance on capital account	1,753	1,006	662	379	-182	-11	39	96	-24	-24	-29	-23
Unrequited official transfer payments	179	220	159	127	#	#	#		3,155	239	-318	
Long-term capital	1,263	1,237	1,231	?	468	643	30		253	86	58	
Direct investment	59	38	-88	?	-14	6	3		1,582	201	-130	
Other long-term capital	1,204	1,199	1,319	?	488	653	20		1,320	-47	-246	
Official sector[2]	1,048	1,284	1,433	?	419	329	46		1,317	332	-308	
Loans disbursed	2,028	2,577	2,681	?	462	531	90		2,741	1,259	434	
Amortization payments	-980	-1,292	-1,624	?	-39	-198	-43	96	-1,492	-827	-752	
Commercial banks[2]	157	#	#	?	-5	-37	-1		#	#	#	
Loans disbursed	378	-85	-114	?	1	43	#		#	#	#	
Amortization payments	-221	131	100	?	-2	-9	-1		#	#	#	
Other sectors[2]	457	-217	-214	252	75	287	-25		3	-379	62	-1,353
Loans disbursed	-291	-26	-170	?	107	346	62		1,284	505	28	
Amortization payments	#	#	#	?	-31	-58	-87		-1,068	-702	-269	
Short-term capital (net)	749	61	#	?	511	-359	158		-4,914	-4,338	-3,189	
Official sector	#	#	#	?	83	41	47		-57	-17	24	
Commercial banks	-148	-22	61	?	239	-67	67		916	-827	-197	
Other sectors	-70	#	#	?	189	-333	43		-5,773	-3,493	-3,016	
Errors and omissions	#	-66	-170	?	-1,161	-295	-149		-2,146	7	104	
Global balance[3]	#	-425	-557	?	-417	-70	-85	-29	-8,152	336	1,568	
Total variation in reserves (minus sign indicates an increase)	57	53	-290	?	497	71	70	22	7,635	-283	-1,797	-1,671
Monetary gold	#	#	#	?	85	52	-8	#	#	#	#	#
Special Drawing Rights	-22	32	-22	?	41	-2	-1	-10	5	87	-22	-121
IMF reserve position	#	#	#	?	33	-10	10	#	-113	-166	106	-7
Foreign exchange assets	-119	-48	-246	?	240	-122	65	-30	1,695	-960	-1,392	-1,153
Other assets	-65	21	#	?	3	12	12	#	6,048	756	-489	-390
Use made of IMF credit	262	48	-22	?	96	142	-8	128	#	#	#	#

1. Real services also include other official and private transactions, but exclude factor services.
2. In addition to loans received and amortization payments on these, this entry includes net loans granted and other assets and liabilities.
3. The global balance is the sum of the balance on the capital and current accounts. The difference between the total variation in reserves with the opposite sign and the global balance represents the value of counterpart items: monetization of gold, allocation of Special Drawing Rights and variations due to revaluation.
a. Cf. SALA, 21-2637; for 1977-81, see SALA, 25, 2728-2746.

SOURCE: ECLA-S, 1982, vol. 1, p. 444; 1983, vol. 1, p. 454; 1985, vol. 1.

Table 2731

LATIN AMERICA: ECLA BALANCE OF PAYMENTS, 1950–77[a]
(M US)

Item	1950
Current Account	
Exports of Goods and Services	6,608.3
Goods FOB	6,037.2
Services	571.1
Transport	99.8
Travel	338.2

a. For data on LAFTA, AG, and CACM, see SALA, 24-2748, 24-2749, 24-2450. For
    Current account data for 1950–77, see SALA, 24-2751.

CHAPTER 28

DEBT AND ASSISTANCE

Table 2800

DISBURSED FOREIGN DEBT,[1] 19 LR, 1978–86

(B US YE)

Grouping and Country	1978	1980	1981	1982	1983	1984	1985	1986[†]
Oil Exporters	64,390	93,675	126,489	142,690	152,185	155,154	156,289	161,060
B. BOLIVIA[a]	1,762	2,220	2,622	2,502	3,156	3,281	3,355	3,340
I. ECUADOR	2,975	4,652	5,868	6,187	6,712	6,949	7,440	7,540
N. MEXICO[d]	33,946	50,700	74,900	88,300[d]	92,100	96,700	97,800	100,000
R. PERU	9,324	9,594	9,638	11,097	12,442	13,389	13,794	14,300
T. VENEZUELA[f]	16,383	26,509	33,411	35,061	35,997	34,835	33,900	35,880
Non-Oil Exporters	86,503	128,882	161,269	188,018	198,621	211,738	216,911	221,020
A. ARGENTINA	12,496	27,162	35,671	43,634	45,087	46,903	48,312	50,300
C. BRAZIL[b]	52,285	68,354	78,580	87,580	96,500	102,039	101,920	101,750
D. CHILE[c]	6,664	11,084	15,591	17,159	18,037	19,669	20,413	20,690
E. COLOMBIA	4,247	6,300	7,885	9,410	10,405	11,551	12,831	13,430
F. COSTA RICA	1,870	3,183	3,360	3,497	3,848	3,955	4,084	4,000
H. DOMINICAN REP.	1,309	1,839	2,286	3,076	3,237	3,447	3,701	4,050
J. EL SALVADOR	986	1,176	1,471	1,710	1,891	1,949	2,003	2,120
K. GUATEMALA	821	1,053	1,305	1,560	2,130	2,463	2,644	2,530
L. HAITI[a]	210	290	372	410	551	607	599	680
M. HONDURAS	971	1,510	1,708	1,986	2,162	2,392	2,615	2,880
O. NICARAGUA[a]	961	1,588	2,566	3,139	3,788	3,901	4,616	5,260
P. PANAMA[e]	1,774[a]	2,266[a]	5,047	5,960	5,924	6,537	6,500	6,450
Q. PARAGUAY	669	861	949	1,204	1,469	1,654	1,773	1,890
S. URUGUAY	1,240	2,156	3,112	4,238	4,572	4,671	4,900	4,990
LATIN AMERICA	150,893	222,497	287,758	330,708	350,806	366,892	373,200	382,080

1. Comparability varies between countries and over time. Data for any country may or may not include short-term debts (less than 90 days or one year) and/or debts non-guaranteed by government. Debt of the private commercial banks is generally excluded, except for Mexico after the 1982 nationalization of the private banking system.

a. Public debt.

b. Including the total medium-term and long-term debt plus the short-term debt with financial institutions reporting to the Bank for International Settlements.

c. Short-term, medium-term, and long-term debt, excluding debt with the IMF and short-term credits for foreign trade operations.

d. Beginning in 1982, includes nationalized private-commercial bank debts.

e. Excludes financial institutions serving Panama's role as an "international financial center."

f. Including the public debt plus the non-guaranteed long-term and short-term debt with financial institutions reporting to the Bank for International Settlements.

SOURCE: ECLA-SP, 1985, p. 32; 1986, p. 21.

Table 2801

RELATIONSHIP BETWEEN TOTAL PUBLIC AND PRIVATE INTEREST PAYMENTS AND THE EXPORTATION OF GOODS AND SERVICES,[1] 20 LC, 1977–85

(%)

Country	1977	1978	1979	1980	1981	1982	1983	1984	1985[‡]
Non-Petroleum Exporters									
A. ARGENTINA	7.6	9.6	12.8	22.0	35.5	53.6	58.4	58.7	54.5
C. BRAZIL	18.9	24.5	31.5	34.1	40.4	57.1	43.5	38.7	43.5
D. CHILE	13.7	17.0	16.5	19.3	38.8	49.5	39.4	50.0	46.5
E. COLOMBIA	7.4	7.7	10.1	11.8	21.8	25.8	26.5	23.6	23.0
F. COSTA RICA	7.1	9.9	12.8	18.0	28.0	36.1	32.8	30.7	28.0
G. CUBA	~	~	~	~	~	~	~	~	~
H. DOMINICAN REP.	8.8	14.0	14.4	14.7	20.2	22.6	24.5	19.7	18.5
J. EL SALVADOR	2.9	5.1	5.3	5.9	7.9	11.9	12.3	13.2	14.0
K. GUATEMALA	2.4	3.6	3.1	5.3	7.5	7.8	8.7	8.9	11.5
L. HAITI	2.3	2.8	3.3	2.0	2.5	2.2	2.4	5.3	5.0
M. HONDURAS	7.2	8.2	8.6	10.6	14.5	22.4	16.4	17.1	17.0
O. NICARAGUA	7.0	9.3	9.7	17.8	22.2	32.2	14.3	11.7	17.0
P. PANAMA	~	~	~	~	~	~	~	~	~
Q. PARAGUAY	6.7	8.5	10.7	14.3	16.4	15.6	16.4	14.3	13.0
S. URUGUAY	9.8	10.4	9.0	11.0	12.9	22.4	24.8	33.8	35.5
TOTAL	11.9	15.1	18.8	23.1	32.7	45.2	39.4	38.7	40.0
Petroleum Exporters									
B. BOLIVIA	9.9	13.7	18.1	24.5	32.1	43.5	44.4	63.1	60.0
I. ECUADOR	4.8	10.3	13.6	18.2	24.3	30.1	27.4	27.8	24.5
N. MEXICO	25.4	24.0	24.8	23.3	29.0	46.0	39.3	40.2	37.0
R. PERU	17.9	21.2	14.7	16.0	24.1	25.1	29.8	34.0	34.5
T. VENEZUELA	4.0	7.2	6.9	8.1	12.7	21.0	21.6	17.5	22.5
TOTAL	13.0	16.0	15.7	16.6	22.6	35.1	32.4	32.2	32.0
LATIN AMERICA	12.4	15.5	17.4	19.9	27.6	40.5	35.9	35.7	36.0

1. Interest payments include short-term debt interest.

SOURCE: Mexico, NAFINSA-MV, January 1984, No. 4, p. 89; and February 1985, No. 5, pp. 134–135.

Table 2802

EXTERNAL PUBLIC SECTOR DEBT OUTSTANDING,[1] 19 L, 1960–84

(M US YE)[2]

	Country	1960	1970	1975	1976	1977	1978	1979	1980	1981	1982	1983	1984
A.	ARGENTINA	1,275	2,455	5,249	6,519.5	7,530.1	8,944.1	10,763.4	12,335.2	14,414.1	18,323	26,503.6	30,620.7
B.	BOLIVIA	179	553.3	1,288.7	1,666.9	2,074.8	2,454.9	2,870.4	3,075.4	3,352.2	3,380.5	4,044.6	4,156.0
C.	BRAZIL	2,407	4,706	17,897	23,430	29,018	38,903	46,127	50,922	57,476	64,233.6	67,433.4	75,711.4
D.	CHILE	562	2,536.5	4,390.3	4,289.9	4,643.7	5,614.4	5,539.2	5,178.3	5,047.1	6,001.8	7,906.6	11,718.3
E.	COLOMBIA	377	1,878.8	3,037.0	3,381.2	3,716.2	4,350.2	5,320.4	6,538.1	7,803.5	9,734.9	10,592.2	12,630.3
F.	COSTA RICA	55	229.1	731.6	1,008.1	1,292.0	1,618.4	1,934.8	2,530.5	3,103.9	3,371.9	4,153.1	4,106.1
H.	DOMINICAN REP.	6	307.1	707.7	831.5	924.3	1,017.2	1,440.4	1,889.7	2,072.1	2,350.5	2,959.6	3,031.6
I.	ECUADOR	95	332.6	744.8	1,039.1	1,757.2	2,890.3	3,474.2	4,339.7	5,072.1	4,897.9	7,673.2	7,684.7
J.	EL SALVADOR	33	126.1	382.7	450.5	450.6	645.4	722.3	933.1	1,102.7	1,405.9	1,645.5	1,737.0
K.	GUATEMALA	51	175.7	267.8	542.0	634.3	743.7	819.5	1,050.3	1,378.4	1,540.9	1,838.4	1,987.3
L.	HAITI	38	45.2	106.4	192.6	222.0	278.0	367.4	411.3	497.4	546.9	630.2	676.6
M.	HONDURAS	23	149.1	452.3	593.2	812.8	971.2	1,261.0	1,725.2	1,987.9	2,091.1	2,440.9	2,502.0
N.	MEXICO	1,151	3,751.0	13,682.2	18,150.6	24,995.6	30,719.2	35,727.5	38,382.6	47,396.3	56,573.1	73,370.4	74,191.0
O.	NICARAGUA	41	208.7	801.6	956.9	1,102.9	1,168.0	1,425.6	2,135.7	2,009.9	3,159.1	4,100.7	4,177.6
P.	PANAMA	59	290.5	1,124.1	1,435.5	1,832.9	2,380.0	2,581.4	2,860.5	3,155.2	3,414.7	3,928.3	3,566.7
Q.	PARAGUAY	22	158.8	429.5	462.8	545.1	747.2	1,154.3	1,198.4	1,527.6	1,904.4	1,992.6	2,011.8
R.	PERU	265	1,092.5	4,002.2	5,559.3	6.458.7	6,771.8	8,033.4	8,457.0	8,523.4	10,008.5	11,895.8	12,684.5
S.	URUGUAY	132	355.8	1,034.3	1,152.6	1,204.7	1,249.2	1,415.5	1,645.5	1,930.8	2,255.3	3,063.6	3,250.9
T.	VENEZUELA	363	924.1	1,393.3	3,204.0	4,780.7	7,384.4	10,238.8	11,150.5	11,534.9	12,957.6	13,515.7	17,564.9

1. Includes the undisbursed portion. Does not necessarily include external debt of decentralized agencies. For total public and private sector loans, see table 2808, below.
2. Excludes loans under one year. Debts under 90 days normally have been considered to involve only "cash flow" management, but in recent years such loans have been simply "rolled over" to disguise what are in effect loans for an unspecified term. Excludes private sector debt and "purchase" and "repurchase" transactions with IMF.

SOURCE: IDB-SPTF, 1985, p. 424; 1986, p. 430.

Table 2803

DISBURSED PORTION OF THE EXTERNAL PUBLIC SECTOR DEBT OUTSTANDING,[1]
19 L, 1960–84
(M US)[2]

	Country	1960	1970	1975	1976	1977	1978	1979	1980	1981	1982	1983	1984
A.	ARGENTINA	987	1,878.4	3,120.7	4,428.6	5,032.9	6,743.4	8,597.2	10,185.7	10.584.6	15,886.2	24,583.3	28,670.6
B.	BOLIVIA	168	4,81.4	824.3	1,065.6	1,429.4	1,719.2	1,908.4	2,226.9	2,677.5	2,767.8	3,105.1	3,203.4
C.	BRAZIL	2,202	3,233.4	13,923.1	17,637.9	22,082.8	30.195.3	35,615.3	39.894.1	44,833.5	49,910.8	57,159.4	60,502.1
D.	CHILE	456	2,067.3	3,733.4	3,593.0	3,665.0	4,355.9	4,813.1	4,739.7	4,528.0	5,277.9	6,871.6	10,838.8
E.	COLOMBIA	312	1,298.5	2,377.3	2,476.4	2,696.4	2,806.9	3,378.7	4,083.6	5,072.8	5,986.4	6,885.2	7,980.4
F.	COSTA RICA	44	134.2	420.9	541.9	736.7	950.8	1,304.7	1,701.0	2,252.0	2,469.5	3,314.6	3,380.3
H.	DOMINICAN REP.	6	226.4	449.0	574.9	652	777.0	907.9	1,229.2	1,408.0	1,660.4	2,213.6	2,338.2
I.	ECUADOR	71	193.1	434.0	590.0	1,110.5	2,216.8	2,602.3	3,300.4	4,192.1	3,885.1	6,268.8	6,630.4
J.	EL SALVADOR	23	126.1	382.7	450.5	450.6	645.4	722.3	933.1	1,102.7	1,405.9	1,654.5	1,737.0
K.	GUATEMALA	26	175.7	267.8	542.0	634.3	743.7	819.5	1,050.3	1,378.4	1,540.9	1,838.4	1,987.0
L.	HAITI	37	45.2	100.4	182.6	222.0	278.0	367.4	411.3	497.4	546.9	630.2	676.6
M.	HONDURAS	11	149.1	452.3	593.2	812.8	971.2	1,261.0	1,725.2	1,987.9	2,091.1	2,440.9	2,502.0
N.	MEXICO	827	3,751.0	13,682.2	18,150.6	24,995.6	30.719.2	35,727.5	38.382.6	47.396.3	56,573.1	75,370.4	74,191.4
O.	NICARAGUA	22	208.7	801.6	956.9	1,102.9	1,168.0	1,425.6	2,135.7	2,609.9	3,159.1	4,100.7	4,177.6
P.	PANAMA	32	290.5	1,124.1	1,435.5	1,832.9	2,380.0	2,581.4	2,860.5	3,155.2	3,414.7	3,928.3	3,566.7
Q.	PARAGUAY	20	158.8	429.5	462.8	545.1	747.2	1,154.3	1,198.4	1,527.6	1,904.4	1,992.6	2,011.8
R.	PERU	162	1,092.5	4,002.2	5,559.3	6,458.7	6,771.8	8,033.4	8,457.0	8,523.4	10,008.5	11,895.8	12,684.5
S.	URUGUAY	115	355.8	1,034.3	1,152.6	1,204.7	1,249.2	1,415.5	1,645.5	1,930.8	2,255.3	3,063.6	3,250.9
T.	VENEZUELA	252	924.1	1,393.3	3,204.0	4,780.7	7,384.4	10,238.8	11,150.5	11,534.9	12,957.6	13,515.7	17,564.9

1. Included in table 2802, above.
2. Excludes loans under one year. Debts under 90 days normally have been considered
   to involve only "cash flow" management, but in recent years such loans have been
   simply "rolled over" to disguise what are in effect loans for an unspecified term.
   Excludes private sector debt and "purchase" and "repurchase" transactions with
   IMF.

SOURCE: IDB-SPTF, 1985, p. 425; 1986, p. 431.

Table 2804

STRUCTURE OF THE LATIN AMERICAN EXTERNAL PUBLIC SECTOR DEBT,[1]
BY TYPE OF CREDITOR, 1961–84
(%)[2]

	Private					Official				
Year	Suppliers	Banks[3]	Bond Issues	Nationa- lization	Total Private	Multi- lateral	Bilateral	Total Debt	Disbursed Portion	Undisbursed Portion
1961	25.0	14.2	8.1	.9	48.2	15.3	36.5	51.8	74.6	25.4
1962	31.6	11.5	8.0	.7	51.8	15.8	32.4	48.2	79.1	20.9
1963	29.0	11.2	7.7	.5	48.4	18.5	33.1	51.6	75.2	24.8
1964	25.6	13.1	7.2	.8	46.7	19.8	33.5	53.3	76.3	23.7
1965	20.2	12.0	7.5	1.0	40.7	22.5	36.8	59.3	76.8	23.2
1966	19.5	10.5	7.7	1.6	39.3	23.4	37.3	60.7	75.5	24.5
1967	17.2	11.1	6.1	4.4	38.8	22.1	39.1	61.2	74.2	25.8
1968	17.4	12.0	6.7	3.4	39.5	22.8	37.7	60.5	73.2	26.8
1969	16.7	18.3	6.6	2.1	43.7	24.0	32.3	56.3	75.0	25.0
1970	17.0	19.2	5.9	2.3	44.4	24.3	31.3	55.6	75.7	24.3
1971	16.4	22.2	5.6	2.3	46.5	24.6	28.9	53.5	73.7	26.3
1972	14.6	26.0	5.4	1.9	47.9	24.4	27.7	52.1	74.1	25.9
1973	12.8	32.7	4.6	1.4	51.5	22.6	25.9	48.5	73.9	26.1
1974	11.9	37.7	4.0	2.0	55.6	19.9	24.5	44.4	75.1	24.9
1975	10.7	42.6	3.7	1.4	58.4	20.0	21.6	41.6	75.9	24.1
1976	9.0	46.1	3.6	2.2	60.9	18.8	20.3	39.1	76.0	24.0
1977	8.0	50.0	5.8	1.3	65.1	17.3	17.6	34.9	76.2	23.8
1978	7.1	52.5	7.2	.9	67.7	16.4	15.9	32.3	78.1	21.9
1979	6.8	55.9	6.5	.6	69.8	16.6	13.6	30.2	77.9	22.1
1980	6.1	56.3	6.2	.3	68.9	17.2	13.9	31.1	80.4	19.6
1981	5.6	57.6	6.0	.2	69.4	17.5	13.1	30.6	80.6	19.4
1982	4.8	58.3	6.6	.2	69.9	17.7	12.4	30.1	81.7	18.3
1983	4.0	62.9	5.0	.1	72.0	16.3	11.7	28.0	85.8	14.2
1984	3.4	64.7	4.1	.1	72.3	15.9	11.8	27.7	88.0	12.0

1. Including the undisbursed portion at year end. Does not necessarily include external
   debts of decentralized agencies.
2. Excludes debts under one year. Debts under 90 days normally have been considered
   to involve only "cash flow" management, but in recent years such loans have been
   simply "rolled over" to disguise what are in effect loans for an unspecified term.
3. Includes also financial institutions other than banks.

SOURCE: IDB-SPTF, 1985, p. 426; 1986, p. 432.

Table 2805

INTEREST PAYMENTS ON THE EXTERNAL PUBLIC SECTOR DEBT,[1]
19 L, 1960–84
(M US)[2]

	Country	1960	1970	1975	1976	1977	1978	1979	1980	1981	1982	1983	1984
A.	ARGENTINA	50	121	264	265	318	503	568	841	1,060	1,280	1,328	2,392
B.	BOLIVIA	3	7	24	38	59	86	122	164	171	181	173	201
C.	BRAZIL	134	133	856	961	1,193	1,845	2,919	4,189	5,147	5,941	5,004	6,433
D.	CHILE	14	78	157	209	201	290	355	484	488	551	557	939
E.	COLOMBIA	14	44	115	125	140	169	230	279	409	571	521	547
F.	COSTA RICA	1	7	23	27	36	65	84	130	115	81	503	207
H.	DOMINICAN REP.	~	5	19	20	25	41	57	93	121	110	109	108
I.	ECUADOR	2	7	17	25	45	97	208	288	441	562	373	790
J.	EL SALVADOR	1	4	7	14	15	18	21	24	30	36	63	72
K.	GUATEMALA	1	6	7	8	9	16	22	30	38	59	76	821
L.	HAITI	#	#	1	1	4	4	4	5	6	7	6	6
M.	HONDURAS	1	3	10	16	22	31	46	59	79	97	83	80
N.	MEXICO	29	216	829	1,082	1,310	1,859	2,851	3,847	4,784	6,124	6,422	7,428
O.	NICARAGUA	1	7	36	41	52	50	37	38	91	109	36	34
P.	PANAMA	1	7	41	56	73	122	196	252	279	332	283	288
Q.	PARAGUAY	1	4	8	8	11	16	22	35	32	41	45	58
R.	PERU	7	44	187	199	248	317	437	544	528	548	397	286
S.	URUGUAY	4	16	46	57	58	61	71	104	124	156	210	284
T.	VENEZUELA	18	40	103	122	223	393	659	1,229	1,237	1,629	1,720	1,437

1. Included in table 2806, below.
2. Does not necessarily include external debts of decentralized agencies. Includes also
   financial institutions other than banks. Excludes debts under one year. Debts under
   90 days normally have been considered to involve only "cash flow" management,
   but in recent years such loans have been simply "rolled over" to disguise what are in
   effect loans for an unspecified term.

SOURCE: IDB-SPTF, 1985, p. 427; 1986, p. 433.

Table 2806

AMORTIZATION PAYMENTS ON THE EXTERNAL PUBLIC SECTOR DEBT, 19 L,[1] 1970–84
(M US)[2]

	Country	1970	1975	1976	1977	1978	1979	1980	1981	1982	1983	1984
A.	ARGENTINA	341.5	522.5	604.1	721.9	1,613.4	895.3	1,145.9	1,092.8	1,015.2	963.9	486.4
B.	BOLIVIA	17.0	51.4	70.7	100.1	274.9	149.9	126.4	110.3	105.9	109.4	119.3
C.	BRAZIL	255.2	925.2	1,086.3	1,680.0	2,637.9	3,601.3	3,850.3	3,923.4	4,157.8	1,788.5	1,603.4
D.	CHILE	163.5	345.1	546.4	684.8	925.1	903	891.2	1,175.8	480.4	329.3	320.8
E.	COLOMBIA	78	123.9	144.6	175.9	219.2	407.8	250.1	263.0	308.8	398.8	548.0
F.	COSTA RICA	20.6	40.9	40.3	51.2	173.4	172	75.3	81.8	56.4	91.8	114.1
G.	CUBA	~	~	~	~	~	~	~	~	~	~	~
H.	DOMINICAN REP.	7.3	32.1	38.7	47.3	49.4	192.5	63.5	111.1	149.5	116.1	38.3
I.	ECUADOR	15.5	32.0	55.5	71.3	109.2	739.6	271.5	481.2	544.8	157.2	201.8
J.	EL SALVADOR	5.9	47.2	22.2	54.0	12.3	12.7	17.2	17.7	32.3	92.8	122.3
K.	GUATEMALA	19.9	7.5	9.2	8.0	10.4	14.8	15.2	22.6	43.8	65.0	111.6
L.	HAITI	3.6	6.4	8.7	15.0	14.1	8.6	15.3	15.1	8.6	7.8	11.3
M.	HONDURAS	3.4	6.7	13.8	20.1	28.4	63.0	39.5	38.4	51.8	38.3	54.7
N.	MEXICO	475	753.4	1,144.3	2,230.6	4,399.3	7,101.4	4,009.3	3,702	3,276.2	4,555.7	3,663
O.	NICARAGUA	16.2	19.4	34.0	46.6	47.3	15.5	44.4	70.1	53.2	45.6	25.2
P.	PANAMA	23.7	31.1	44.7	88.2	444	190.1	213.7	213.9	282.3	188.9	231.2
Q.	PARAGUAY	7.1	14.2	11.8	16.1	19.9	30.8	44.8	38.8	38.8	39.5	39.0
R.	PERU	100.7	253.8	256.1	404.9	432.3	487.6	956.7	1,367	978.4	362.3	320.6
S.	URUGUAY	47.1	182.2	148.5	187.2	366.0	54.8	92.9	60.7	70.6	94.0	127.1
T.	VENEZUELA	41.8	435.9	285.1	604.6	356.2	889.7	1,735	1,351.5	1,592	936.2	1,099,1

1. Included in table 2807, below.
2. Excludes loans under one year. Debts under 90 days normally have been considered to
   involve only "cash flow" management, but in recent years such loans have been simply
   "rolled over" to disguise what are in effect loans for an unspecified term.

SOURCE: IDB-SPTF, 1986, p. 434.

Table 2807

SERVICE PAYMENTS ON THE EXTERNAL PUBLIC SECTOR DEBT,[1] 19 L, 1960–84
(M US)[2]

	Country	1960	1966	1970	1975	1977	1978	1979	1980	1981	1982	1983	1984
A.	ARGENTINA	254	455	462.5	788.9	1,039.9	2,116.0	1,463.7	1,987.1	2,152.5	2,294.9	2,291.5	2,878.8
B.	BOLIVIA	16	7	23.6	75.9	159.1	361.2	272.1	290.3	281.3	286.8	282.3	320.7
C.	BRAZIL	554	573	388.6	1,781.3	2,872.7	4,483.2	6,520.6	8,039.2	9,070.8	10,098.9	6,792.7	8,036.5
D.	CHILE	78	103	241.5	501.8	886.2	1,215.0	1,258.5	1,374.9	1,663.6	1,031.6	886.0	1,259.5
E.	COLOMBIA	82	109	122.1	238.7	315.6	388.2	637.5	529.1	672.4	880.1	919.6	1,095.1
F.	COSTA RICA	5	20	27.7	64.2	87.0	238.4	255.5	205.0	196.6	137.6	595.2	321.5
H.	DOMINICAN REP.	~	20	12.0	51.2	72.1	90.7	249.1	156.7	232.0	259.7	225.2	146.4
I.	ECUADOR	11	13	22.2	49.1	115.9	206.6	947.6	559.3	922.6	1,107.1	529.8	991.6
J.	EL SALVADOR	3	6	9.5	54.1	69.4	29.9	33.4	41.7	47.6	68.1	156.0	194.2
K.	GUATEMALA	2	10	26.1	14.1	17.2	26.1	37.3	44.9	60.4	102.7	140.7	196.0
L.	HAITI	2	~	4.0	7.6	18.8	18.5	12.3	20.5	20.9	15.4	14.3	17.4
M.	HONDURAS	2	3	6.1	16.9	42.0	59.6	109.0	98.4	117.3	149.0	121.7	134.8
N.	MEXICO	210	456	691.2	1,582.0	3,540.8	6,258.7	9,952.9	7,856.0	8,486.0	9,400.0	10,977.5	11,090.7
O.	NICARAGUA	3	9	22.9	54.9	98.2	97.7	52.4	82.2	160.6	162.4	82.0	59.2
P.	PANAMA	2	7	30.5	72.3	161.4	565.9	386.3	465.2	493.3	614.0	472.2	519.2
Q.	PARAGUAY	3	5	10.6	21.8	26.6	35.5	52.8	80.1	70.7	80.8	84.5	117.4
R.	PERU	52	89	144.4	440.3	653.4	749.8	924.5	1,500.8	1,895.2	1,526.1	758.8	606.7
S.	URUGUAY	10	31	62.9	228.4	245.0	427.2	125.5	197.4	184.3	226.4	304.1	410.7
T.	VENEZUELA	111	67	82.1	539.4	827.2	749.5	1,548.4	2,964.2	2,588.4	3,220.7	2,655.8	2,536.4

1. Service = amortization plus interest on the debt. Does not necessarily include service
    payments on external debt by decentralized agencies.
2. Excludes loans under one year. Debts under 90 days normally have been considered to
    involve only "cash flow" management, but in recent years such loans have been simply
    "rolled over" to disguise what are in effect loans for an unspecified term.

SOURCE: IDB-SPTF, 1985, p. 429; 1986, p. 435.

Table 2808

EXTERNAL PUBLIC SECTOR DEBT SERVICE AS SHARE OF EXPORTS OF GOODS[1]
AND SERVICES, 19 L, 1960–85
(%)[2]

	Country	1960	1966	1970	1973	1975	1976	1977	1978	1979	1980	1981	1982	1983	1985
A.	ARGENTINA	20.5	25.5	21.8	17.9	22.4	18.8	15.7	28.2	16.1	19.9	18.2	24.5	24.0	41.8
B.	BOLIVIA	27.6	4.9	11.0	15.5	14.6	16.2	21.5	49.8	30.3	26.2	27.0	28.2	30.5	29.1
C.	BRAZIL	38.7	30.6	12.6	13.9	17.5	19.3	21.5	31.9	38.5	36.1	31.9	42.1	28.7	26.5
D.	CHILE	14.2	10.5	19.2	10.9	28.7	31.5	33.4	40.9	27.1	23.5	27.2	18.8	18.3	26.2
E.	COLOMBIA	13.9	16.4	11.9	13.4	11.5	9.9	9.1	10.0	14.5	11.2	13.4	17.5	21.3	29.2
F.	COSTA RICA	4.8	12.3	10.0	10.3	10.6	9.5	9.0	23.4	23.0	16.7	15.3	12.5	50.6	36.6
H.	DOMINICAN REP.	~	12.5	4.7	5.6	5.0	6.5	7.5	10.8	21.6	12.8	10.6	18.7	22.7	16.1
I.	ECUADOR	7.1	6.4	9.3	7.5	4.5	5.8	7.3	12.1	30.0	14.4	17.8	30.8	32.5	28.8
J.	EL SALVADOR	2.6	2.9	3.5	5.3	9.1	4.4	6.3	3.0	2.4	3.5	3.5	4.6	6.4	16.3
K.	GUATEMALA	1.5	5.7	7.4	3.6	1.7	1.5	1.3	2.2	2.7	3.7	3.3	6.6	11.7	21.3
L.	HAITI	3.6	~	7.5	7.7	7.5	7.1	6.9	5.6	3.6	4.5	6.6	5.1	5.0	5.8
M.	HONDURAS	2.8	1.9	3.0	3.7	4.9	6.4	7.2	8.7	12.9	10.2	12.7	18.8	14.9	17.6
N.	MEXICO	15.5	20.9	24.2	24.3	25.5	31.6	44.3	56.7	65.6	33.2	28.2	29.5	35.9	37.0
O.	NICARAGUA	3.8	5.2	11.2	22.0	12.5	12.3	14.1	13.7	8.1	14.6	~	~	18.3	~
P.	PANAMA	1.6	2.8	7.6	16.9	8.5	12.3	17.9	60.1	34.6	33.5	11.5	13.8	6.8	6.9
Q.	PARAGUAY	6.8	7.8	11.2	10.7	10.5	8.1	6.7	7.6	9.7	12.8	9.8	10.3	14.9	12.9
R.	PERU	10.5	9.8	11.7	29.7	26.1	26.1	30.7	31.5	22.7	32.7	44.9	36.7	19.6	7.9
S.	URUGUAY	5.8	12.5	21.7	22.9	41.4	29.6	30.3	46.8	10.4	12.3	9.5	13.4	19.8	30.6
T.	VENEZUELA	4.4	2.7	3.0	6.1	5.8	4.2	8.1	7.7	10.3	14.8	12.4	15.6	15.0	12.8

1. Service = amortization plus interest. Exports of merchandise (f.o.b.). Does not
    necessarily include external debt service of decentralized agencies.
2. Excludes loans under one year. Debts under 90 days normally have been considered to
    involve only "cash flow" management, but in recent years such loans have been simply
    "rolled over" to disguise what are in effect loans for an unspecified term.

SOURCE: IDB-SPTF, 1982, p. 393; and for 1981–83 data, WB-WDR, 1983–85, table 16; 1987, table 19.

Table 2809

LATIN AMERICAN LOAN VALUES ON THE SECONDARY MARKET, 11 L, 1984–87

(Real % of Nominal Value)

Country	12/84	12/85	1/86	2/86	3/86	4/86	5/86	6/86	7/86	8/86	9/86	10/86	11/86	12/86	1/87	2/87	3/87	4/87	5/87	6/87	7/87	8/87
A. ARGENTINA	66.00	66.00	66.00	66.00	66.00	65.75	65.75	65.75	66.50	66.00	66.00	65.00	64.00	64.00	63.50	63.50	62.50	59.00	59.00	52.00	46.50	46.00
B. BOLIVIA	25.00	8.50	7.75	7.75	7.75	7.75	7.75	7.75	8.00	8.00	8.00	8.00	9.00	9.00	9.00	10.00	10.00	12.00	12.00	12.00	12.00	12.00
C. BRAZIL	85.00	78.00	75.50	76.50	76.50	77.00	75.00	75.00	75.00	75.00	75.00	75.00	74.50	74.00	72.50	71.00	63.00	63.00	64.00	60.00	53.00	47.00
D. CHILE	65.00	68.00	69.00	69.00	69.00	67.50	68.00	68.50	68.50	68.50	68.50	68.50	68.50	68.50	68.50	68.50	68.50	69.00	69.50	68.50	67.00	62.00
E. COLOMBIA	85.00	85.00	83.00	83.00	83.00	83.00	83.00	83.00	83.00	83.00	84.00	84.00	84.00	84.00	84.00	84.00	84.00	84.00	84.00	83.00	83.00	80.00
F. COSTA RICA[1]	0	0	36.00	36.00	36.00	36.00	36.00	36.00	36.00	36.00	36.00	36.00	36.00	36.00	36.00	36.00	36.00	36.00	36.00	35.00	35.00	32.00
I. ECUADOR	72.00	72.00	69.50	69.00	68.50	64.00	64.00	64.00	65.00	65.00	65.00	65.00	66.00	65.00	64.00	63.50	60.00	55.00	52.00	49.00	45.00	38.00
N. MEXICO	83.00	70.00	70.00	64.00	58.00	58.00	58.00	58.00	58.00	58.00	58.00	57.00	56.00	56.00	57.00	58.00	58.00	58.00	59.00	56.00	53.00	50.00
P. PANAMA	80.00	78.00	73.00	73.00	70.00	70.00	70.00	70.00	67.00	67.00	67.00	67.00	67.00	67.00	67.00	67.00	67.00	67.00	67.00	65.00	60.00	55.00
R. PERU[1]	0	0	0	0	0	22.00	22.00	22.00	22.00	22.00	22.00	22.00	22.00	21.00	20.00	18.00	17.00	15.00	15.00	13.00	13.00	8.00
T. VENEZUELA	83.00	82.00	80.00	78.00	76.00	77.50	76.00	76.00	75.00	75.00	75.00	74.50	74.00	73.50	73.50	73.50	73.50	73.50	73.50	71.00	66.00	64.00

Month and Year

1. Price "0" is used so calculation will not be distorted.

SOURCE: Supplied by Merrill Lynch International, August 12, 1987.

Table 2810

WORLD BANK (INTERNATIONAL BANK FOR RECONSTRUCTION AND DEVELOPMENT) ACTUAL LOANS, 20 LR, FY 1949–46
(M US)[1]

A. ARGENTINA

1949	1950	1951	1952	1953	1954	1955	1956	1957	1958	1959	1960	1961
#	#	#	#	#	#	#	#	#	#	#	#	#

1962	1963	1964	1965	1966	1967	1968	1969	1970	1971	1972	1973	1974	1975	1976
5.9	47.5	36.0	17.1	5.2	4.2	7.0	28.5	44.0	31.6	44.9	54.2	50.2	41.4	13.3

Continued in SALA, 22-3108.

Table 2811

IMF FINANCIAL TARGETS ESTABLISHED IN AGREEMENTS WITH 13 LC
(AA–GR)

Country	Date of Agreement	Ultimate Targets — Net External Assets	Inflation 1	Inflation 2	Ex-post Real Exchange Rate (1980 + 100) 1981	1982	1983[‡]	Money[4] M_1	M_2	Operational Targets — Monetary Base	Public External Indebtedness[5]	Public-Sector Deficit (as Percentage of GDP[6]) 1982	1983	1984	Net Domestic Credit to Public Sector Nominal	Real[7]
					Stand-by Arrangements											
A. ARGENTINA	24 Jan. 1983	−29	−23	−16	143	189	191	170	44	119	8.3	14.0	8.0	5.0	209	−4
Barbadoes	1 Oct. 1982	~	~	~	95	88	85	~	~	~	~	6.6	~	1.8	~	~
D. CHILE	10 Jan. 1983	−23	100	−29	99	125	138	−14	−18	−18	9.4	4.0	2.3	~	10	−10
F. COSTA RICA	20 Dec. 1982	−2	−95	−45	168	141	124	5	#	#	3.3	9.5	4.5	~	15	−40
I. ECUADOR	25 July 1983	~	−27	−10	97	107	114	41	43	44	10.0	7.5	4.0	~	29	−18
K. GUATEMALA	31 Aug. 1983	~	~	~	98	100	100	~	~	~	~	5.0	~	3.0	~	~
L. HAITI	7 Nov. 1983	~	~	~	103	98	~	~	~	~	~	4.8	~	~	~	~
M. HONDURAS	5 Nov. 1982	~	~	~	99	92	86	~	~	~	~	~	~	~	~	~
P. PANAMA	21 June 1983	~	~	~	102	100	99	~	~	~	~	~	~	~	~	~
S. URUGUAY	22 April 1983	~	~	~	105	129	176	~	~	~	~	8.0	3.0	1.0	~	~
					Extended Fund Facility Agreements											
C. BRAZIL																
First letter	6 Jan. 1983	−67	−43	−22	~	~	~	60	60	63	7.4	16.9	7.9	~	98	−1
Second letter	24 Feb. 1983	−67	−44	−23	93	95	118	58	58	61	7.4	16.9	8.8	~	123	9
Third letter	15 Sep. 1983	~	~	~	~	~	~	~	~	61	11.0	16.9	15.2	~	118	19
Dominica	6 Feb. 1981	~	~	~	96	94	91	~	~	~	~	~	~	~	~	~
Grenada	24 Aug. 1983	~	~	~	~	~	~	~	~	~	~	~	17.0	8.5	~	~
Jamaica	13 April 1981	17	−33	−5	97	92	87	13	15	13	11.0	~	~	~	31	18
		14	92	9				14	16	8	~	~	~		10	13
N. MEXICO	1 Jan. 1983	~	~	~	94	137	152	~	~	~	~	16.5	8.5	5.5	~	~
R. PERU	7 June 1982	−12	−22	−9	91	94	132	57	52	51	8.8	4.0		2.0	9	−37
H. DOMINICAN REP.	21 Jan. 1983	~	~	~	101	96	94	~	~	~	~	4.0	~	3.0	~	~

1. Implicit target for reduction of inflation, i.e., the implicit target for the growth of M_1 divided by the prevailing rate of inflation (variation in consumer price index during the 12 preceding months) at the time of entry into force of the agreement with the IMF.
2. Implicit degree of monetary deflation, i.e., the implicit target for the stock of M_1 deflated by the prevailing inflation rate.
3. The data for 1983 represent the average from January to September.
4. The targets for the growth of M_1 and M_2 are implicit. Calculations were made by using the monetary multiplier observed in the years preceding the entry into force of the IMF agreement, according to the formula mentioned in the text.
5. In the case of Brazil, includes State-guaranteed private indebtedness.
6. The figures for the first year reflect the situation prior to the agreement and the following ones refer to targets, except in the case of Peru, where only targets are shown. In 1981, its deficit was 8.0% of GDP.
7. Deflated by the prevailing rate of inflation at the time of entry into force of the agreement.

SOURCE: Richard Lynn Ground, "Orthodox Adjustment Programmes in Latin America: A Critical Look at the Policies of the International Monetary Fund," *Cepal Review* (Santiago, 1984).

Table 2812

IMF FINANCING AGREEMENTS, 13 LC

(In Force at End of 1983)

		Date of Agreement	Duration (Months)	Conditioned Financing — Millions of SDRs	Conditioned Financing — In Relation to IMF Quota[2]	Non-Conditioned Financing[1] — Millions of SDRs	Non-Conditioned Financing[1] — In Relation to IMF Quota[2]	Total Financing — In Relation to Deficit on Current Account[3] 1981	1982	1983	Amount Drawn — On Date of Agreement Conditioned	Total	To Date Total
	Stand-by Arrangements												
A.	ARGENTINA	24 Jan. 1983	15	500	187	520	65	40	72	91	20	41	55
	Barbados	1 Oct. 1982	20	32	125	13	51	12	31	~	30	64	91
F.	COSTA RICA	20 Dec. 1982	12	92	150	16	26	31	58	29	#	#	77
D.	CHILE	10 Jan. 1983	24	500	154	295	91	10	19	39	24	53	65
I.	ECUADOR	25 July 1983	12	158	157	#	#	18	16	29	50	50	50
K.	GUATEMALA	31 Aug. 1983	16	115	150	#	#	20	28	34	~	11	11
L.	HAITI	7 Nov. 1983	24	60	174	#	#	16	23	19	~	~	~
M.	HONDURAS	5 Nov. 1982	12	77	150	23	45	36	44	48	20	39	46
P.	PANAMA	24 June 1983	18	150	222	59	87	33	29	40	7	33	43
S.	URUGUAY	22 April 1983	24	378	300	#	#	47	89	224	13	13	25
	Extended Fund Facility Agreements												
C.	BRAZIL	6 Jan. 1983[4]	36	239	425	965	97	17	12	24	9	26	26
	Dominica	6 Feb. 1981	36	9	295	2	67	21	21	~	9	26	87
	Grenada	24 Aug. 1983	36	14	300	#	#	22	14	~	8	8	8
	Jamaica	13 April 1981	36	478	450	42	38	55	33	~	14	17	71
N.	MEXICO	1 Jan. 1983	36	411	425	#	#	8	40	35[5]	6	6	26
R.	PERU	7 June 1982	36	650	265	192	78	18	17	22	#	23	88
H.	DOMINICAN REP.	21 Jan. 1983	36	371	450	55	66	40	34	39	12	21	35

1. Includes financing from Compensatory Financing Facility as of dates of agreements (Stand-by and Extended Fund Facility) mentioned. However, also included is SDR 499 million obtained by Brazil from that Facility in December 1982 and SDR 12.6 million obtained by the Dominican Republic from the Buffer Stock Financing Facility (August 1983).
2. Percentage.
3. Average annual flow (without adjustments for suspension of drawings) to average value of SDR each year for all countries, except Dominica and Jamaica, for which actual figures are given.
4. This agreement was replaced by the agreement of 24 February 1983, which in turn was replaced by the agreement of 15 September 1983.
5. Surplus.

SOURCE: Richard Lynn Ground, "Orthodox Adjustment Programmes in Latin America: A Critical Look at the Policies of the International Monetary Fund," *Cepal Review* (Santiago, 1984).

Table 2813

IMF DEFINITIONS FOR FUND ACCOUNT DATA

Members of the Fund may draw on its financial resources to meet their balance of payments needs through a **reserve tranche** and four additional **credit tranches**. When a member borrows from ("draws on") the Fund, it uses its own currency to *purchase* the currencies of other members or SDRs held by the Fund's General Account. Thus, a drawing results in an increase in the Fund's holdings of a member's currency and in a corresponding decrease in the General Account's holdings of the currencies of other members or of SDRs. As a result, the composition of the Fund's resources changes without affecting the total. Drawings under reserve tranche policies do not cause Fund holdings of a member's currency to exceed its quota; they are unconditional and are referred to as reserve tranche drawings. Drawings in each of four credit tranches are available in amounts equal to 25 percent of a member's quota. The conditionality imposed by the Fund for these drawings is progressively more rigorous after the first tranche. Most credit tranche drawings are made under **stand-by** arrangements, which assure a member that it will be able to draw on the Fund's resources up to a specified amount without a further review of its position and policies. A member is required to repurchase drawings under regular tranche policies in three to five years, or earlier, if its balance of payments position improves.

The Fund's special facilities permit additional use of Fund resources under particular circumstances. The **compensatory financing facility** enables members to draw on the Fund up to 100 percent of quota when they experience pay-

ments difficulties as a result of temporary shortfalls in export receipts—or up to 100 percent of quota when they experience payments difficulties as a result of excess cereal import costs—and their payments difficulties are largely beyond their control, as long as total drawings under the facility do not exceed 125 percent of quota. The **buffer stock financing facility** may be used by members in balance of payments difficulty to draw up to 50 percent of quota to finance contributions to international buffer stock arrangements. The **extended facility** assists members suffering from serious balance of payments difficulties resulting from structural imbalances in production, trade, and prices, or having economies characterized by slow growth and inherently weak payments positions, when the Fund is satisfied that its resources are required for longer periods and in larger amounts relative to quota than are available under the regular tranche policies.

Under the Fund's **enlarged access policy**, which replaced the **supplementary financing facility**, the Fund provides supplementary financing in conjunction with the use of the Fund's ordinary resources to all members facing serious payments imbalances that are large in relation to their quotas. It is used only in support of economic programs under stand-by arrangements reaching into the upper credit tranches or under extended arrangements. Such drawings are subject to Fund conditionality, phasing, and performance criteria. The period of such arrangements normally exceeds one year and may extend up to three years in certain cases.

IMF Fund Account Data Abbreviations

Amt. Appr.	Amount Approved	Imp.	Import
Comp. Financ. Pur	Compensatory Financing Facility Purchases	Oil Fac.	Oil Facility
		Ord.	Ordinary
Dist.	Distribution	Outstand. Sh-Term Fund Borrow	Outstanding Short-Term Fund Borrowing
EAR	Enlarged Access to the Fund's Resources	Pur.	Purchases
Exp.	Expected	Repurch.	Repurchases
Extend.	Extended	SFF	Supplement Financing Facility
GAB	Guaranteed Arrangements to Borrow	St-By	Stand-by

Table 2814

IMF FUND ACCOUNTS, 19 L, 1985–86

Category[1]	A. ARGENTINA 1985	A. ARGENTINA 1986	B. BOLIVIA 1985	B. BOLIVIA 1986	C. BRAZIL 1985	C. BRAZIL 1986	D. CHILE 1985	D. CHILE 1986	E. COLOMBIA 1985	E. COLOMBIA 1986	F. COSTA RICA 1985	F. COSTA RICA 1986
General Department						Millions of SDRs End of Period						
Quota	1,113.0	1,113.0	90.7	90.7	1,461.0	1,461.0	440.5	440.5	394	394	84.1	84.1
St-By Arrangements Amount Drawn	710	#	#	32.7	#	#	#	#	#	#	34.0	#
St-By Arrangements Undrawn Balance	710	#	#	17.3	#	#	#	#	#	#	20.0	#
Reserve Position in the Fund	#	#	#	#	#	#	#	#	#	#	26.1	16.3
Use of Fund Credit	2,105	2,241	46.7	136.3	4,205	3,680	990.6	1,088.3	#	#	#	#
Comp. Financ. Purch. Exp. Shortfalls	795	600	17.9	75.3	1,213	789	365.6	255.0	#	#	~	~
Fund Holdings of Currency: Amount	3,218	3,354	137.4	208.9	5,667	5,141	1,431.1	1,528.8	394	394	255.8	225.1
Percent of Quota	289	301	151.5	230.3	388	352	324.9	347	100	100	304.1	267.6
						Millions of SDRs During Period						
Total Purchases[2]	984.5	473	#	96.8	#	#	195.6	250	#	#	34	#
Reserve Tranche	~	~	~	~	~	~	~	~	~	~	~	~
Gold Distributionns	~	~	~	~	~	~	~	~	#	#	~	~
Total Repurchases	#	337.3	18.2	25.3	64.5	525.5	#	152.4	#	#	21.4	30.7
Repurchases of Purchases	#	337.3	18.2	25.3	64.5	525.5	#	152.4	#	#	21.4	30.7
SDR Department						Millions of SDRs End of Period						
Net Cumulative Allocations	~	#	#	#	1	#	0.3	0.2	#	114	.02	.01
SDR Holdings: Amount	~	#	#	7.6	#	#	0.2	0.1	#	100	~	~
Percent of Allocations	~	#	#	#	#	#	#	#	#	#	.08	.04

Category[1]	H. DOMINICAN REP. 1985	H. DOMINICAN REP. 1986	I. ECUADOR 1985	I. ECUADOR 1986	J. EL SALVADOR 1985	J. EL SALVADOR 1986	K. GUATEMALA 1985	K. GUATEMALA 1986	L. HAITI 1985	L. HAITI 1986	M. HONDURAS 1985	M. HONDURAS 1986
General Department						Millions of SDRs End of Period						
Quota	112.1	112.1	150.7	150.7	89	89	108	108	44.1	44.1	67.8	67.8
St-By Arrangements: Amount Drawn	61.4	#	84.4	15.1	#	#	#	#	#	#	#	#
St-By Arrangements: Undrawn Balance	17.1	#	21.1	60.3	#	#	#	#	#	#	#	#
Reserve Position in the Fund	#	#	#	#	#	#	#	#	.1	.1	#	#
Use of Fund Credit	270.4	248.8	327.3	397.7	80.9	35.1	~	~	74.4	63.5	121.7	80.3
Comp. Financ. Purch. Exp. Shortfalls	85.2	51.2	85.4	125.1	40.3	12.1	105.2	57.2	10.6	#	#	#
Fund Holdings of Currency: Amount	382.5	360.9	478	548.4	169.9	124.1	213.2	165.2	118.4	98.7	189.5	148.1
Percent of Quota	341.2	322	317.2	363.9	190.9	139.4	197.4	153.0	268.6	223.8	279.5	218.4
						Millions of SDRs During Period						
Total Purchases[2]	76.9	17.1	84.4	75.9	#	#	#	#	#	#	#	#
Reserve Tranche	~	~	~	~	~	~	~	~	~	~	~	~
Gold Distributions	~	~	~	~	~	~	~	~	~	~	~	~
Total Repurchases	32.2	38.7	#	5.5	26.6	45.8	47.8	48	11.8	19.7	16.7	41.4
Repurchases of Purchases	32.2	38.7	#	5.5	26.6	45.8	47.8	48	11.8	19.7	16.7	41.4
SDR Department						Millions of SDRs End of Period						
Net Cumulative Allocations	#	#	#	#	#	#	#	#	#	#	#	#
SDR Holdings: Amount	28.8	#	26.2	45.7	#	#	#	#	#	5.4	#	#
Percent of Allocations	91.9	#	79.5	138.9	.2	#	#	#	.1	39.3	.01	#

Table 2814 (Continued)

IMF FUND ACCOUNTS, 19 L, 1985–86

Category[1]	N. MEXICO 1985	N. MEXICO 1986	O. NICARAGUA 1985	O. NICARAGUA 1986	P. PANAMA 1985	P. PANAMA 1986	Q. PARAGUAY 1985	Q. PARAGUAY 1986	R. PERU 1986	S. URUGUAY 1985	S. URUGUAY 1986	T. VENEZUELA 1985	T. VENEZUELA 1986
General Department					Millions of SDRs: End of Period								
Quota	1,166	1,166	68.2	68.2	102.2	102.2	48.4	48.4	330.9	164	164	1,372	1,372
St-By Arrangements: Amount Drawn	#	450	#	#	35	79	#	#	#	35	88	~	~
St-By Arrangements: Undrawn Balance	#	950	#	#	55	11	31.6	24.9	#	88	35	~	~
Reserve Position in the Fund	#	#	.01	#	#	#	#	#	#	#	#	~	~
Use of Fund Credit	2,703	3,319	#	#	283.4	288.6	~	~	595.5	319	323	~	~
Comp. Financ. Purch. Exp. Shortfalls	#	#	#	#	55.9	44.2	~	~	238.6	105	83	~	~
Fund Holdings of Currency: Amount	3,869	4,485	68.2	68.2	385.6	390.8	~	~	926.4	482	487	892	891
Percent of Quota	332	385	100	100	377.3	382.4	34.8	48.7	280	294	297	65	65
					Millions of SDRs During Period								
Total Purchases[2]	295.8	741.4	#	#	35	44	#	#	#	101.2	52.7	~	~
Reserve Tranche	~	~	~	~	~	~	~	~	~	~	~	~	~
Gold Distributions	~	~	~	~	~	~	~	~	~	~	~	~	~
Total Repurchases	#	125.4	9	#	28.3	38.7	#	#	43.5	9.5	48.2	~	~
Repurchases of Purchases	#	125.4	9	#	28.3	38.7	#	#	43.5	9.5	48.2	~	~
SDR Department					Millions of SDRs End of Period								
Net Cumulative Allocations	#	7	#	#	11.7	1.4	38.8	42.1	#	13	10	451	495
SDR Holdings: Amount	#	2	#	#	44.5	5.5	283.2	307.2	#	27	19	142	157
Percent of Allocations			#	#	~	~	~	~	#	~	~	~	~

1. For definitions of terms, see table 2811. For SDR exchange rate, see tables 3102 and 3103.
2. Equals "all drawing."

a. For data from years 1947–74, see SALA, 23-3100 through 3118.

SOURCE: IMF-IFS-Y, 1985, 1986, 1987.

Table 2815

INTER-AMERICAN DEVELOPMENT BANK LOANS, YEARLY LENDING, 19 L, 1974–86
(M US)

	Country	1974	1975	1977	1978	1979	1980	1981	1982	1983	1984	1985	1986
A.	ARGENTINA	89.1	201.0	317.8	57.1	280.5	359.2	292.4	402.4	80.1	458.8	108.9	516.3
B.	BOLIVIA	46.2	54.1	83.3	180.7	12.2	42.6	97.0	201.0	58.9	78.0	~	20.9
C.	BRAZIL	187.0	269.5	361.5	283.2	365.5	424.4	383.1	372.2	441.0	393.7	395.3	428.8
D.	CHILE	97.3	70.7	24.5	54.0	~	19.9	161.0	302.5	548.0	293.3	522.5	359.8
E.	COLOMBIA	#	75.8	112.7	199.0	151.0	194.6	180.6	191.2	405.9	405.0	413.3	87.0
F.	COSTA RICA	53.8	41.6	79.6	90.0	35.9	132.9	35.2	67.4	41.8	92.6	6.0	179.9
H.	DOMINICAN REP.	36.7	35.5	#	66.3	195.5	80.5	71.8	155.4	96.2	205.5	146.2	140.0
I.	ECUADOR	55.5	43.7	73.1	94.3	210.0	84.5	168.5	101.4	83.3	306.4	274.4	272.7
J.	EL SALVADOR	33.4	43.0	109.4	13.2	47.8	63.4	52.4	128.4	25.0	110.2	26.2	25.2
K.	GUATEMALA	19.4	120.6	60.5	#	15.0	76.5	112.5	46.0	167.9	13.9	192.0	65.8
L.	HAITI	#	41.1	15.7	43.5	4.1	10.1	8.7	33.4	18.8	.4	27.4	56.5
M.	HONDURAS	35.6	28.7	32.0	114.0	15.8	67.6	7.5	49.0	130.2	42.0	69.8	122.9
N.	MEXICO	186.4	167.3	256.9	238.2	266.4	284.0	279.0	323.2	286.2	229.8	401.5	327.9
O.	NICARAGUA	10.5	16.5	20.0	32.0	81.5	70.6	8.0	35.1	30.5	~	~	~
P.	PANAMA	14.5	42.2	122.0	19.0	27.6	77.7	90.2	37.3	112.0	8.4	52.8	98.4
Q.	PARAGUAY	49.0	3.2	13.8	60.5	32.4	27.4	32.5	98.3	48.6	37.5	~	~
R.	PERU	65.5	16.0	21.0	29.5	148.6	177.6	226.7	180.1	264.9	195.8	14.5	19.2
S.	URUGUAY	21.4	35.4	29.7	#	35.5	57.5	78.0	10.0	50.0	119.8	21.6	73.2
T.	VENEZUELA	#	#	#	#	#	#	#	#	#	30.0	448.3	238.0	~

SOURCE: *IMF Survey*, April 17, 1978, p. 115; IDB-AR, 1980; 1982, p. 41; and 1985, p. 47, 1986, p. 47.

Table 2816

INTER-AMERICAN DEVELOPMENT BANK LOANS, 19 L, 1983–86

(M US)

	Country	1983	1984	1985	1986
A.	ARGENTINA	80.1	458.8	108.9	516.3
B.	BOLIVIA	58.9	78.0	~	140.4
C.	BRAZIL	441.0	393.7	395.3	428.8
D.	CHILE	548.0	293.3	522.5	359.8
E.	COLOMBIA	405.9	405.0	413.3	87.0
F.	COSTA RICA	41.8	92.6	6.0	179.9
H.	DOMINICAN REP.	96.2	205.5	146.2	140.0
I.	ECUADOR	83.3	306.4	274.4	272.7
J.	EL SALVADOR	25.0	110.2	26.2	25.2
K.	GUATEMALA	167.9	13.9	192.0	65.8
L.	HAITI	18.8	.4	24.7	~
M.	HONDURAS	130.2	42.0	69.8	122.9
N.	MEXICO	286.4	229.8	401.5	327.9
O.	NICARAGUA	30.8	~	~	~
P.	PANAMA	112.0	8.4	52.8	98.4
Q.	PARAGUAY	48.6	37.5	~	~
R.	PERU	264.9	195.8	14.5	19.2
S.	URUGUAY	50.0	119.8	21.6	73.2
T.	VENEZUELA	30.0	448.3	238.8	~
	TOTAL	2,919.8	3,439.0	2,908.5	2,857.5

SOURCE: Mexico-BNCE-CE, June 1987, p. 465.

Table 2817

INTER-AMERICAN DEVELOPMENT BANK LOAN DISTRIBUTION BY SECTOR, 1961–86

(M US)

Sector	1986	%	1961–86	%
Productive Sectors				
Agriculture and Fishing	636.0	20.9	7,483.1	21.1
Mining and Industry	102.0	3.4	5,639.4	15.9
Tourism	156.0	5.2	511.0	1.4
Physical Infrastructure				
Energy	750.7	24.7	9,777.2	27.6
Transportation, Communication	362.9	11.9	4,544.7	12.8
Social Infrastructure				
Public Health and Welfare	468.6	15.5	3,175.9	9.0
Education, Science, Technology	179.2	5.9	1,584.0	4.5
Urban Development	288.8	9.5	1,443.1	4.1
Other				
Export Financing	68.4	2.2	713.1	2.0
Preinvestment	7.2	.2	407.8	1.2
Other	17.2	.6	158.5	.4
Total	3,037.0	100	35,437.7	100

SOURCE: Mexico-BNCE-CE, June 1987, p. 465.

Table 2818

A.I.D. ACTUAL DISBURSEMENT FOR LOANS AND GRANTS, 19 L, 1979–85

(T US)

	Country	1979	1980	1981	1982	1983	1984	1985
A.	ARGENTINA	2	~	~	~	~	~	~
B.	BOLIVIA	26,524	21,162	16,397	11,289	8,851	9,926	24,604
C.	BRAZIL	6,762	92	327	95	563	87	132
D.	CHILE	9,144	3,098	588	4	~	~	~
E.	COLOMBIA	11,425	8,061	1,063	220	95	297	242
F.	COSTA RICA	7,067	4,873	4,026	24,729	109,948	146,337	224,234
H.	DOMINICAN REP.	11,992	17,621	19,517	23,113	54,754	50,139	110,038
I.	ECUADOR	705	1,752	2,492	3,306	6,953	14,871	22,205
J.	EL SALVADOR	3,787	12,692	89,869	134,987	148,728	151,412	247,645
K.	GUATEMALA	5,756	7,442	11,922	13,544	26,631	13,735	17,829
L.	HAITI	10,277	11,397	15,423	16,298	17,296	19,608	25,097
M.	HONDURAS	15,599	16,445	22,093	62,153	45,075	102,625	132,353
N.	MEXICO	85	107	131	117	192	300	405
O.	NICARAGUA	11,228	31,882	53,873	6,945	4,315	1,145	336
P.	PANAMA	12,503	14,399	13,441	19,039	14,902	15,982	67,775
Q.	PARAGUAY	4,920	1,711	2,656	2,094	2,301	1,447	2,250
R.	PERU	14,843	20,782	22,860	20,440	21,581	63,904	82,952
S.	URUGUAY	2,281	4,042	2,835	91	~	~	~
T.	VENEZUELA	72	66	34	30	~	~	~
	TOTAL	154,973	177,626	279,547	338,495	462,184	591,815	958,098

SOURCE: Unpublished data provided by A.I.D. W-211.

Table 2819

A.I.D. STATUS OF LOAN AGREEMENTS, 20 L, 1958–86

(T US)

	Country	Agreement Amount	Amount Utilized	Principal Repayments	Balance Outstanding	Interest Collection
A.	ARGENTINA	130,467.61	130,467.61	81,320.92	35,185.25	27,982.68
B.	BOLIVIA	391,793.92	337,648.67	57,221.66	261,787.11	64,614.38
C.	BRAZIL	1,428,366.86	1,428,344.18	225,810.83	1,005,671.77	309,862.05
D.	CHILE	633,837.29	633,837.29	260,963.06	354,549.60	167,898.44
E.	COLOMBIA	880,492.49	880,492.49	252,130.15	600,662.37	254,489.39
F.	COSTA RICA	365,158.14	321,381.83	17,276.26	303,808.69	26,654.91
G.	CUBA	~	~	~	~	~
H.	DOMINICAN REP.	412,044.34	357,035.17	68,116.93	288,918.24	56,954.82
I.	ECUADOR	176,478.51	142,928.25	54,335.72	88,166.82	30,392.39
J.	EL SALVADOR	306,642.91	272,632.98	20,161.86	252,471.11	27,863.03
K.	GUATEMALA	233,661.91	176,182.59	28,006.27	148,176.32	27,391.87
L.	HAITI	21,475.20	21,217.25	2,781.44	18,199.00	5,900.50
M.	HONDURAS	344,388.13	272,869.14	22,132.71	250,736.43	32,312.88
N.	MEXICO	83,996.55	83,996.55	59,108.91	24,887.63	29,649.34
O.	NICARAGUA	218,072.95	218,072.95	12,520.20	205,552.75	21,470.36
P.	PANAMA	252,688.73	223,193.55	46,112.01	177,081.54	46,094.42
Q.	PARAGUAY	70,370.35	69,766.82	30,341.77	36,920.35	20,292.99
R.	PERU	442,925.84	392,931.77	77,916.32	308,339.96	53,398.64
S.	URUGUAY	76,202.98	76,202.98	19,448.06	42,405.55	18,466.21
T.	VENEZUELA	55,000.00	55,000.00	55,000.00	#	11,087.56

SOURCE: *Status of Loan Agreements* (Office of Financial Management, Agency for International Development, September 1986).

Table 2820

EX-IM BANK ACTUAL LOANS, 20 L, 1973–81[a]

(T US)

						FY				
	Country	1973	1974	1975	1976	1977	1978	1979	1980	1981
A.	ARGENTINA	32,212	5,945	29,142	36,098	19,636	21,000	19,893	11,767	33,552
B.	BOLIVIA	#	#	#	4,261	107	6,215	8,188	#	96

Continued in SALA, 24-2844.

Table 2821

EX-IM BANK AUTHORIZATIONS BY COUNTRY
(October 1, 1980 – September 30, 1986)
(T US)

Country	1980-81	1981-82	1982-83	1983-84	1984-85	1985-86
A. ARGENTINA						
Direct Loans	81,460	500,000	#	#	#	#
Off Loans	1,154	#	#	#	#	#
Financial and Other Guar	#	16,150	#	#	#	#
Bank, Preship, and CNG Guar	13,532	7,820	135	#	#	#
M/T Insurance Policies	25,590	13,328	#	#	#	#
Total Authorizations	121,736	587,298	135	#	#	#
S/T Insurance Shipments	168,850	72,214	7,553	1,473	328	161
Total Auth and Shipments	290,585	659,512	7,688	#	328	161
B. BOLIVIA						
M/T Insurance Policies	231	#	#	#	#	#
Total Authorizations	231	#	#	#	#	#
S/T Insurance Shipments	9,278	1,535	–29	–50	#	#
Total Auth and Shipments	9,509	1,535	–29	–50	#	#
C. BRAZIL						
Direct Loans	141,445	109,083	29,275	28,538	37,400	124,355
Off Loans	7,255					
Financial and Other Guar	110,702	16,698	9,008	18,556	135,260	14,821
Off Guars and Colps	6,380	#	#	#	#	#
Bank, Preship, and CNG Guar	19,184	21,796	27,990	25,196	134,865	67,322
M/T Insurance Policies	10,693	35,115	28,477	30,778	35,965	40,933
Total Authorizations	295,659	182,692	94,749	103,067	343,490	247,431
S/T Insurance Shipments	148,275	164,240	127,218	385,388	292,084	196,840
Total Auth and Shipments	443,934	346,932	221,967	488,455	635,574	444,271
D. CHILE						
Direct Loans	#	#	#	#	1,275	#
Financial and Other Guar	#	#	#	11,454	14,988	40,000
Bank, Preship, and CNG Guar	19,804	10,099	60,425	6,255	8,330	8,907
M/T Insurance Policies	9,712	7,285	490	6,557	7,859	11,599
Total Authorizations	29,156	17,584	60,915	24,465	32,453	60,506
S/T Insurance Shipments	13,744	60,383	39,186	28,593	67,271	54,474
Total Auth and Shipments	43,260	77,967	100,101	52,859	99,724	114,980
E. COLOMBIA						
Direct Loans	45,116	540,264	3,778	4,015	130,000	#
Financial and Other Guar	8,164	67,500	2,642	535	182,360	#
Bank, Preship, and CNG Guar	7,733	4,731	22,883	55,559	55,225	48,186
M/T Insurance Policies	19,305	19,106	6,298	33,131	3,453	13,183
Total Authorizations	80,318	631,601	35,601	93,240	371,038	61,369
S/T Insurance Shipments	60,548	77,166	707,027	45,734	58,445	61,840
Total Auth and Shipments	140,866	708,767	106,328	138,974	429,483	123,209
F. COSTA RICA						
Off Loans	942	#	#	#	#	#
Financial and Other Guar	1,277	#	#	#	#	#
Off Guars and Colps	942	#	#	#	#	#
Bank, Preship, and CNG Guar	897	#	#	#	#	#
M/T Insurance Policies	4,623	442	#	#	#	#
Total Authorizations	12,833	442	#	#	#	#
S/T Insurance Shipments	51,968	13,437	20,859	10,338	19,451	44,862
Total Auth and Shipments	64,801	13,879	20,859	10,338	19,451	44,862
H. DOMINICAN REP.						
Off Loans	1,155	#	#	#	#	#
Financial and Other Guar	8,955	#	19,975	#	#	#
Bank, Preship, and CNG Guar	6,336	#	4,677	#	#	#
M/T Insurance Policies	3,557	319	861	#	145	#
Total Authorizations	20,003	319	25,513	#	145	#
S/T Insurance Shipments	20,949	26,428	20,985	7,016	7,909	159
Total Auth and Shipments	40,952	26,747	46,498	7,016	8,054	159
I. ECUADOR						
Financial and Other Guar	7,225	#	#	14,100	#	#
Bank, Preship, and CNG Guar	24,718	11,540	1,126	2,180	5,625	18,103
M/T Insurance Policies	39,882	17,404	8,932	1,297	#	23,376
Total Authorizations	71,825	28,943	10,058	17,577	5,625	41,480
S/T Insurance Shipments	78,897	77,831	45,071	25,164	31,419	47,315
Total Auth and Shipments	150,722	106,775	55,129	42,741	37,044	88,795

Table 2821 (Continued)

EX-IM BANK AUTHORIZATIONS BY COUNTRY
(October 1, 1980 – September 30, 1986)
(T US)

Country	1980-81	1981-82	1982-83	1983-84	1984-85	1985-86
J. EL SALVADOR						
Bank, Preship, and CNG Guar	#	#	#	102	5,683	6,706
M/T Insurance Policies	12	–230	#	7,650	#	452
Total Authorizations	12	–230	#	7,752	5,683	7,158
S/T Insurance Shipments	11,617	6,223	4,823	6,309	12,621	62,007
Total Auth and Shipments	11,628	5,993	4,823	14,061	18,304	69,165
K. GUATEMALA						
Financial and Other Guar	540	#	#	#	#	#
Bank, Preship, and CNG Guar	1,778	1,775	4,688	1,523	3,877	826
M/T Insurance Policies	4,463	3,158	622	#	11,422	#
Total Authorizations	6,781	4,913	5,130	1,523	15,300	826
S/T Insurance Shipments	66,143	44,254	25,377	7,055	3,464	34,584
Total Auth and Shipments	72,925	49,167	30,687	8,578	18,764	35,410
L. HAITI						
S/T Insurance Shipments	271	1,031	960	525	836	168
Total Auth and Shipments	271	1,031	960	525	836	168
M. HONDURAS						
Off Loans	888					
Off Guars and Colps	891	#	#	#	#	#
Bank, Preship, and CNG Guar	7,011	18,320	3,105	327	#	#
M/T Insurance Policies	5,171	1,797	250		#	#
Total Authorizations	13,962	20,117	3,355	327	#	#
S/T Insurance Shipments	38,848	26,337	14,542	11,806	20,192	19,253
Total Auth and Shipments	52,810	46,454	17,897	12,132	20,192	19,253
N. MEXICO						
Direct Loans	654,519	293,448	37,189	66,517	10,141	#
Financial and Other Guar	3,520		205,717	54,867	89,031	39,525
Bank, Preship, and CNG Guar	145,728	95,631	20,152	11,021	23,748	92,527
M/T Insurance Policies	144,764	80,503	24,467	100,203	82,999	17,482
Total Authorizations	948,530	469,581	287,525	232,609	205,919	149,534
S/T Insurance Shipments	858,140	906,192	226,229	302,277	478,512	587,868
Total Auth and Shipments	1,780,670	1,375,773	513,754	534,885	684,431	737,402
O. NICARAGUA						
M/T Insurance Policies	12	#	#	#	#	#
Total Authorizations	12	#	#	#	#	#
S/T Insurance Shipments	–58	4,669	#	#	#	#
Total Auth and Shipments	–46	4,669	#	#	#	#
P. PANAMA						
Financial and Other Guar	32,461	#	#	#	#	#
Bank, Preship, and CNG Guar	2,466	7,054	510	1,018	383	425
M/T Insurance Policies	2,775	4,096	873	9,791	395	541
Total Authorizations	37,702	11,149	1,383	10,809	778	966
S/T Insurance Shipments	64,753	56,238	41,890	21,335	15,849	13,305
Total Auth and Shipments	102,455	67,338	43,273	32,144	16,626	14,271
Q. PARAGUAY						
Bank, Preship, and CNG Guar	1,048	2,591	1,286	36	1,466	#
M/T Insurance Policies	2,302	1,666	878	1,443	2,550	#
Total Authorizations	3,350	4,258	2,165	1,479	4,016	#
S/T Insurance Shipments	17,886	9,393	4,694	483	509	237
Total Auth and Shipments	21,236	13,650	6,858	1,962	4,525	237
R. PERU						
Direct Loans	8,503	63,890	26,250	#	#	#
Off Loans	4,613					
Financial and Other Guar	720	7,568	23,475	#	#	#
Off Guars and Colps	3,620	#	#	#	#	#
Bank, Preship, and CNG Guar	44,543	63,156	29,232	16,676	#	#
M/T Insurance Policies	10,344	11,237	8,044	1,452	#	#
Total Authorizations	72,343	145,850	87,001	18,127	#	#
S/T Insurance Shipments	60,182	51,866	36,730	16,034	27,823	2,623
Total Auth and Shipments	132,525	197,715	123,731	34,161	27,823	2,623

Table 2821 (Continued)

EX-IM BANK AUTHORIZATIONS BY COUNTRY
(October 1, 1980 – September 30, 1986)
(T US)

Country	1980-81	1981-82	1982-83	1983-84	1984-85	1985-86
S. URUGUAY						
Direct Loans	14,850	#	#	#	#	#
Bank, Preship, and CNG Guar	4,244	1,383	643	4,526	638	#
M/T Insurance Policies	3,078	1,458	3,725	850	#	85
Total Authorizations	22,171	2,841	4,368	5,376	638	85
S/T Insurance Shipments	23,967	20,525	5,989	6,629	5,093	2,771
Total Auth and Shipments	46,138	23,366	10,356	12,005	5,730	2,856
V. Venezuela						
Direct Loans	59,516	26,000	12,000	#	#	#
Off Loans	637	#	#	#	#	#
Financial and Other Guar	#	#	#	177,497	#	#
Bank, Preship, and CNG Guar	51,741	43,102	1,600	2,261	#	#
M/T Insurance Policies	69,714	82,974	15,465	14,373	272	53
Total Authorizations	181,607	152,076	105,587	194,131	272	53
S/T Insurance Shipments	460,078	392,378	218,814	34,378	16,467	7,407
Total Auth and Shipments	641,685	594,454	324,401	228,509	16,739	7,460
LATIN AMERICAN						
Direct Loans	1,052,875	1,637,244	112,971	142,372	195,066	126,305
Off Loans	16,644	#	#	#	#	#
Financial and Other Guar	185,738	119,057	280,338	277,062	421,640	113,801
Off Guars and Colps	11,833	#	#	#	#	#
Bank, Preship, and CNG Guar	366,207	313,475	225,321	145,388	247,232	256,776
M/T Insurance Policies	359,770	286,892	168,626	212,450	154,853	108,550
Total Authorizations	1,993,067	2,356,668	787,256	777,274	1,018,791	605,432
S/T Insurance Shipments	2,280,860	2,188,518	1,086,147	1,029,127	1,143,839	1,206,861
Total Auth and Shipments	4,273,927	4,545,186	1,873,403	1,806,400	2,162,630	1,812,293

SOURCE: Data provided by Joe Sorbera, Reports Division, Export-Import Bank.

Table 2822

AVERAGE FINANCING TERMS OF LOANS TO LATIN AMERICA AUTHORIZED BY THE U.S. GOVERNMENT AND MULTILATERAL INSTITUTIONS, 1961–86

(%)

Agency	1961-65	1966-70	1971	1972	1973	1974	1975	1976	1977	1978	1979	1980	1981	1982	1983	1984	1985	1986
Average interest rate																		
AID	3.63	4.73	5.53	5.84	5.71	5.90	6.75	6.90	7.09	6.41	6.71	~	~	~	~	~	~	~
IDB	1.55	2.43	2.78	2.80	2.76	2.75	2.80	2.75	2.70	2.58	2.64	~	~	~	~	~	~	~
IBRD	3.68	4.38	4.57	5.10	5.17	5.54	5.20	5.29	5.97	5.36	5.80	5.82	7.35	7.73	9.71	8.88	8.84	~
Ex-Im Bank	5.60	5.96	6.00	6.01[a]	6.00	6.26	8.09	8.33	8.50	8.19	7.17	8.45	9.87	11.56	10.47	9.89	8.82	~
Grace period (years)																		
AID	5.63	5.66	5.43	5.92	6.27	6.41	6.02	5.32	4.95	5.33	5.11	~	~	~	~	~	~	~
IDA	10.00	9.80	9.08	9.78	9.84	9.79	9.67	10.00	8.56	9.70	10.00	~	~	~	~	~	~	~
IDB	10.00	10.00	10.00	10.00	10.00	10.00	10.00	10.00	10.00	10.00	10.00	~	~	~	~	~	~	~
IBRD	2.83	4.25	4.40	6.34	6.35	6.58	6.49	6.45	6.12	6.86	6.24	~	~	~	~	~	~	~
Ex-Im Bank	4.05	5.08	4.68	4.81	4.93	5.30	4.96	4.04	4.00	3.62	3.84	~	~	~	~	~	~	~
Amortization period (years)																		
AID	19.16	19.01	17.86	16.90	17.86	16.98	17.40	16.85	14.86	14.80	14.05	~	~	~	~	~	~	~
IDA	26.10	29.46	28.26	29.33	29.70	29.79	28.76	30.00	20.44	13.88	18.46	~	~	~	~	~	~	~
IDB	40.00	40.00	40.00	40.00	40.00	40.00	40.00	40.00	40.00	40.00	40.00	~	~	~	~	~	~	~
IBRD	15.94	17.98	18.34	19.29	20.48	20.36	20.63	19.93	19.94	18.86	18.46	~	~	~	~	~	~	~
Ex-Im Bank	9.19	8.91	7.01	5.94	5.08	4.81	4.64	4.25	6.25	5.20	5.18	~	~	~	~	~	~	~

a. Includes three loans to Brazil totaling more than $6.3 million, at an interest rate of 6.5 percent.

SOURCE: IDB-SPTF, 1979, p. 90; 1980, p. 92; 1987, p. 34.

Table 2823

LATIN AMERICAN EXPOSURE OF U.S. BANKS BY PERCENT OF EQUITY AND OUTSTANDING LOANS
(1986)

| | Equity | | Outstanding Loans | |
Bank	Rank	Percent	Rank	Amount (M US)
Mfrs. Hanover	1	199	3	7,505
BankAmerica	2	188	2	7,623
Irving Bank	3	146	11	1,541
Chase Manhattan	4	143	4	7,020
Chemical New York	5	142	6	4,445
Bankers Trust N.Y.	6	118	7	3,222
Citicorp	7	114	1	10,400
Marine Midland Bks	8	107	12	1,474
First Chicago	9	102	8	2,410
J. P. Morgan & Co.	10	89	5	4,614
Continental Illinois	11	88	9	1,816
Wells Fargo	12	69	10	1,638
Republicbank	13	64	17	786
Republic New York	14	61	18	699
Bank of Boston	15	60	15	1,065
Mellon Bank	16	54	16	998
First Interstate	17	51	14	1,414
Security Pacific	18	49	13	1,424
Bank of New York	19	47	19	504
First Bank System	20	30	20	426
PNC Financial	21	29	21	410
Bank of New England	22	23	22	274
NBD Bancorp	23	20	23	232
MCORP	24	16	25	194
NCNB Corp	25	15	24	204
Sun Trust Banks	26	8	26	129
First Union	27	4	27	72

SOURCE: *Barrons*, May 25, 1987, p. 11.

Table 2824

EXPOSURE OF U.S. BANK HOLDING COMPANIES, 4 L
(B US, Sept. 30, 1983)[a]

Country	Citicorp	Bank America	Chase Manhattan	Manufacturers Hanover	J. P. Morgan	Chemical N.Y.	First Interstate	Continental Illinois	Security Pacific	Bankers Trust
A. ARGENTINA	1.1	.3	.8	1.3	.7	.4	.8	.4[a]	.2[†]	.2[†]
C. BRAZIL	4.7	2.5	2.6	2.1	1.8	1.3	.5	.5[a]	.5	.7

Continued in SALA, 24-2845.

Table 2825

U.S. CLAIMS ON FOREIGN COUNTRIES HELD BY U.S. OFFICES AND FOREIGN BRANCHES OF U.S. – CHARTERED BANKS,[1] 9 L, 1979–87

(B US)

	Country	1979	1980	1981	1982	1983	1984	1985[a]	1986[a]	1987[‡,b]
A.	ARGENTINA	5.0	7.9	9.4	8.9	9.5	8.7	8.9	9.5	9.5
C.	BRAZIL	15.2	16.2	19.1	22.9	23.1	26.3	25.6	25.2	25.6
D.	CHILE	2.5	3.7	5.8	6.3	6.4	7.0	7.0	7.1	7.2
E.	COLOMBIA	2.2	2.6	2.6	3.1	3.2	2.9	2.7	2.1	2.0
I.	ECUADOR	1.7	2.1	2.2	2.2	2.2	2.2	2.1	2.2	2.1
M.	MEXICO	12.0	15.9	21.6	24.5	26.1	25.7	24.2	23.8	23.8
P.	PANAMA[2]	4.3	5.4	7.7	7.5	5.8	6.7	6.0	5.1	5.5
R.	PERU	1.5	1.8	2.0	2.6	2.4	2.2	1.8	1.4	1.4
T.	VENEZUELA	8.7	9.1	9.9	10.5	9.9	9.3	8.9	8.6	8.7

1. The banking offices covered by these data are the U.S. offices and foreign branches of U.S.-owned banks and of U.S. subsidiaries of foreign-owned banks. Offices *not* covered include (1) U.S. agencies and branches of foreign banks, and (2) foreign subsidiaries of U.S. banks. To minimize duplication, the data are adjusted to exclude the claims on foreign branches held by a U.S. office or another foreign branch of the same banking institution.
2. Includes Canal Zone, beginning Dec. 1979.

a. Preliminary data as of Dec. of corresponding year.
b. Projected data for March 1987.

SOURCE: USBG-FRB, Sept. 1984, Sept. 1986, August 1987, table 321.

Table 2826

U.S. CLAIMS ON UNAFFILIATED FOREIGNERS[1] AS REPORTED BY NONBANKING BUSINESS ENTERPRISES TO THE FEDERAL RESERVE, 3 L, 1980–86

(M US)

	Country	Financial Claims							Commercial Claims						
		1980	1981	1982	1983	1984	1985[a]	1986[a]	1980	1981	1982	1983	1984	1985[a]	1986[a]
C.	BRAZIL	96	30	62	53	100	78	67	861	668	258	493	214	206	229
N.	MEXICO	208	313	274	293	215	180	173	1,102	1,022	775	884	583	510	385
T.	VENEZUELA	137	148	139	134	125	48	24	410	424	351	272	206	157	216

1. The term "foreigners" covers all institutions and individuals domiciled outside the United States (including U.S. citizens domiciled abroad), and the foreign branches, subsidiaries, and offices of U.S. banks and business concerns; the central governments, central banks, and other official institutions of foreign countries, wherever located; and international and regional organizations, wherever located. The term "foreigners" also includes persons in the United States when it is known by reporting institutions that they are acting on behalf of foreigners. (See the *Annual Statistical Digest*, 1970–1979, of the Board of Governors of the Federal Reserve System, pp. 580–582, for an outline of revisions in international statistics.)

a. As of Dec. of corresponding year.

SOURCE: USBG-FRB, June 1985, Sept. 1986, August 1987, table 3.23.

Table 2827

U.S. BANKS' OWN CLAIMS ON FOREIGNERS AS REPORTED
TO THE FEDERAL RESERVE, 12 L, 1981–87

(M US, YE)

	Country	1981[a]	1982	1983	1984	1985[b]	1986[b]	1987[‡,c]
A.	ARGENTINA	7,527	10,974	11,749	11,050	11,462	12,079	12,154
C.	BRAZIL	16,926	23,271	24,667	26,315	25,283	25,586	26,221
D.	CHILE	3,690	5,513	6,072	6,839	6,603	6,533	6,399
E.	COLOMBIA	2,018	3,211	3,745	3,499	3,249	2,819	2,679
G.	CUBA	3	3	0	0	0	0	9
I.	ECUADOR	1,531	2,062	2,307	2,420	2,390	2,430	2,388
K.	GUATEMALA	124	124	129	158	194	140	120
N.	MEXICO	22,439	29,552	34,802	34,885	31,799	30,490	30,084
P.	PANAMA	6,794	10,210	7,848	7,707	6,645	5,423	5,849
R.	PERU	1,218	2,357	2,536	2,384	1,947	1,637	1,584
S.	URUGUAY	157	686	977	1,088	960	940	957
T.	VENEZUELA	7,069	10,643	11,287	11,017	10,871	11,052	11,063

a. Liabilities and claims of banks in the United States were increased, beginning in December 1981, by the shift from foreign branches to international banking facilities in the United States of liabilities to, and claims on, foreign residents.
b. Preliminary data as of Dec. of corresponding year.
c. Projected data for April, 1987.

SOURCE: USBG-FRB, June 1985, Sept. 1986, August 1987, table 3.18.

Table 2828

U.S. LIABILITIES DUE TO FOREIGNERS AS REPORTED
TO THE FEDERAL RESERVE, 12 L, 1981–87

(M US)

	Country	1981[a]	1982	1983	1984	1985	1986[b]	1987[‡,c]
A.	ARGENTINA	2,445	3,578	4,038	4,394	6,032	4,754	9,461
C.	BRAZIL	1,568	2,014	3,168	5,275	5,373	4,321	3,713
D.	CHILE	664	1,626	1,842	2,001	2,049	2,053	2,252
E.	COLOMBIA	2,993	2,594	1,689	2,514	3,104	4,281	4,373
G.	CUBA	9	9	8	10	11	7	6
I.	ECUADOR	434	455	1,047	1,092	1,239	1,235	1,044
K.	GUATEMALA	479	670	788	896	1,071	1,122	1,164
N.	MEXICO	7,235	8,377	10,392	12,303	14,060	13,631	14,963
P.	PANAMA	4,857	4,805	5,924	6,951	7,514	6,865	7,125
R.	PERU	694	1,147	1,166	1,266	1,167	1,163	1,086
S.	URUGUAY	367	759	1,244	1,394	1,552	1,537	1,540
T.	VENEZUELA	4,245	8,417	8,632	10,545	11,922	10,452	10,562

a. Liabilities and claims of banks in the United States were increased, beginning in December 1981, by the shift from foreign branches to international banking facilities in the United States of liabilities to, and claims on, foreign residents.
b. Preliminary data as of Dec. of corresponding year.
c. Projected data for April 1987.

SOURCE: USBG-FRB, June 1985, Sept. 1986, August 1987, table 3.17.

Table 2829

CHILE REAL DEBT, 1960–85
(M US of 1983)

	(A)	(B)	(C)	(D)
			Net Position	
	Debt	Reserves	(as of Dec. 31)	Interest
Year	(as of Dec. 31)	(as of Dec. 31)	(A – B)	Payments
1960	746	73	673	19
1961	1,010	−5	1,015	28
1962	1,255	15	1,240	36
1963	1,469	−24	1,493	42

Continued in SALA, 25-2837.

Table 2830

THREE VIEWS OF THE CUMULATIVE FOREIGN LOANS DISBURSED TO MEXICO'S PUBLIC SECTOR,[1] 1970-82

(YE)

| | M US[3] | | 1981 = 100.0 | M US of 1981 |
| | (A) Nominal Debt | (B) Nominal Debt | (C) U.S. Export | (D) Real Debt |
Year	One Year or Longer	90 Days or Longer[2]	Price Index	90 Days or Longer[2] (B/C)
1970	3,245	4,262	35.2	12,108
1971	3,523	4,546	36.3	12,523
1972	3,962	5,064	37.3	13,576

Continued in SALA, 25-2838.

Table 2831

MEXICO PUBLIC DEBT, 1982-86

(M US)

Category	1982	1983	1984	1985	1986
Balance on Public External Debt (Credits Users)	58,874.2	62.556.2	69,377.9	72,080.1	73,350.9
Long Run	49,548.7	52,778.7	68,994.4	71,626.0	73,956.8
Short Run	9,325.5	9,777.5	383.5	454.1	1,394.1
Structure by User					
Federal Government	12,476.1	16,962.9	24,652.8	25,634.3	31,678.6
Organizations and Companies	27,239.0	26,582.3	27,247.5	29,187.8	22,646.3
Financing Institutions	15,348.5	14,957.9	14,528.5	14,221.0	17,999.0
Non-Financing Institutions	3,810.6	4,053.1	2,949.1	3,037.0	3,027.0
Balance on Foreign Debt by Financing Sources	58,874.2	62,556.2	69,377.9	72,080.1	75,350.9
Private Banks	14,984.5	15,177.1	3,043.7	591.1	1,753.6
Unionized	30,414.2	34,909.8	30,678.6	8,575.9	8,269.1
OFIS	5,041.4	4,432.3	4,879.4	5,945.5	7,410.9
Bilaterals	2,717.9	3,068.6	3,381.2	4,414.7	5,618.7
Public Bonds	4,083.3	3,766.3	3,295.3	3,085.2	2,720.6
Private Bonds	1,372.6	864.7	709.8	655.3	680.9
Supplier	128.7	337.4	247.0	167.2	132.2
Other	131.6	#	#	#	#
Restructured	#	#	23,142.9	48,645.2	48,764.9
Flow of Resources	6,260.5	4,352.4	2,612.8	762.9	1,386.7
Federal Government	4,180.7	4,299.5	2,726.7	580.2	897.2
Organizations and Companies	1,016.3	−27.4	−1,118.3	−534.8	−431.2
Financing Institutions	595.6	84.8	976.0	602.0	942.7
Non-Financing Institutions	467.9	−4.5	28.4	115.5	−22.0
Interest Payments on External Debt	7,791.3	6,468.8	7,611.1	7,601.0	6,130.8
Balance of the National Societies of Credit	7,957.9	10,321.4	6,183.0	4,823.7	5,551.4
Balance of the Internal Debt of the Federal Government (MMP)	2,627.8	4,086.2	5,335.1	9,772.8	23,755.7
Balance Structure					
Banxico	2,137.7	3,084.4	4,122.1	5,930.5	8,454.9
Values	305.1	573.3	739.7	2,334.6	8,107.6
Banking System	185.0	428.5	473.3	1,507.7	7,139.2
Net Internal Debt	1,269.1	1,204.3	1,329.7	4,006.4	9,903.8
Interest Payments on Internal Debt	363.7	1,388.0	1,673.4	3,395.8	7,471.0

SOURCE: NAFINSA-MV, April 27, 1987.

Table 2832

MEXICO AMORTIZATION CALENDAR WITH COMMERCIAL BANKS AFTER DEBT RESTRUCTURING
(M US)

Year	Before	After
1986	1,208	258
1987	513	0
1988	1,016	0
1989	3,000	572
1990	3,499	1,897
1991	4,291	1,897
1992	4,803	1,897
1993	5,293	1,897
1994	5,492	1,606
1995	5,582	1,026
1996	5,811	2,623
1997	6,091	1,872
1998	6,118	2,666
1999	~	3,182
2000	~	3,672
2001	~	4,652
2002	~	5,609
2003	~	5,839
2004	~	6,120
2005	~	3,072
2006	~	3,072

SOURCE: *Mexico Today*, April 1987.

Table 2833

MEXICO RESULTS OF NEGOTIATIONS WITH PRIVATE BANKS
(M US)

1. Restructured Debt, 1985–90	43,700
2. Previous Credits, 1983–84	8,500
3. New Credits	6,000
4. Credit to Ensure Growth[1]	500
5. Credit to Ensure Investment[1]	1,200
6. Private Debt (FIORCA)	9,700
7. Inter-Banking Lines of Credit	6,000
Total	75,650

1. Contingencies.

SOURCE: *Mexico Today*, April 1987.

Table 2834

MEXICO NEW FINANCING, 1987
(M US)

New Credit	12,000
Official Sources	6,000
IMF	1,700
Multilateral	2,500
Bilateral	1,800
Commercial Banks	6,000
Facility 1	5,000
Facility	1,000
Credit Contingencies	2,420
Oil	720
Facility 3	500
Facility 4	1,200
Total	14,420

SOURCE: *Mexico Today*, April 1987.

Table 2835

ASSISTANCE FROM INTERNATIONAL ORGANIZATIONS,[1] 20 LRC, 1946–86

(M US)

Country/Organization	1946–48	1949–52	1953–61	1962–78	1979	1980	1981	1982	1983	1984	1985	1986	Total
A. ARGENTINA													
Total	0	0	42.1	2,739.7	388.7	485.9	479.4	533.4	593.9	210.8	563.5	826.5	6,332.7
IBRD	0	0	31.0	963.2	96.0	237.0	68.0	400.0	100.0	0	180.0	544.5	2,592.1
IFC	0	0	5.2	83.5	6.0	15.0	65.0	10.0	.5	42.7	63.4	156.4	446.0
IDB	0	0	0	1,653.7	280.7	232.2	346.4	119.2	490.5	167.6	319.1	125.6	323.8
UNDP	0	0	5.0	36.8	6.0	1.7	#	4.2	2.9	.5	1.0	0	58.2
Other U.N.	0	0	.9	2.5	0	0	0	0	0	0	0	0	3.6
B. BOLIVIA													
Total	0	0	15.4	788.0	149.7	99.3	8.2	99.9	211.3	130.6	2.6	70.0	1,487.2
IBRD	0	#	0	249.3	0	50.0	0	0	0	0	0	0	296
IFC	0	0	0	3.6	0	0	5.7	0	0	0	0	0	9.3
IDA	0	0	0	69.3	10.5	25.0	0	0	0	0	0	70.0	174.8
IDB	0	0	10.0	431.5	136.6	22.6	0	97.0	211.1	126.8	0	0	951.2
UNDP	0	#	4.7	27.9	2.6	1.5	1.0	2.9	.2	.8	2.6	0	44.1
Other U.N.	0	0	.7	6.4	0	.2	1.5	0	0	3.0	0	0	11.8
C. BRAZIL													
Total	0	117.6	178.8	6,903	963.3	1,102.8	1,551.1	1,222.8	1,807.0	2,192.8	2,010.3	1,834.9	19,689
IBRD	0	117.5	149.5	3,666.7	674.0	695.0	844.0	722.1	1,457.5	1,604.3	1,523.0	1,620.0	13,044.4
IFC	0	0	9.9	389.1	65.1	74.0	229.2	206.6	77.5	61.2	44.6	107.1	1,228.9
IDB	0	0	11.2	2,767.8	221.3	329.9	477.3	284.6	269.5	524.6	442.5	107.3	5,306.2
UNDP	0	.1	7.2	64.5	2.5	2.6	.6	8.2	2.0	0	.2	0	87.8
Other U.N.	0	0	1.0	14.7	.4	1.3	0	1.3	.5	2.7	0	0	21.7
D. CHILE													
Total	16.0	1.0	135.3	881.4	35.0	43.8	260.1	192.4	573.7	355.8	545.2	712.8	3,968.1
IBRD	16.0	.9	95.1	247.5	0	38.0	78.0	0	128.0	0	287.0	456.0	1,343.8
IFC	0	0	5.8	15.4	0	0	0	10.2	44.5	0	73.7	0	142.7
IDA	0	0	19.0	~	0	0	0	0	0	0	0	0	19.0
IDB	0	0	5.7	568.0	35.0	0	180.9	182.0	400.5	352.2	182.8	256.8	2,389.6
UNDP	0	.1	9.0	43.7	#	5.8	.9	.2	.7	3.6	1.5	0	65.1
Other U.N.	0	0	.7	6.8	0	0	.3	0	0	0	.2	0	7.9
E. COLOMBIA													
Total	0	30.1	191.5	2,708.6	523.8	727.4	830.7	512.3	222.4	1,043.8	1,210.1	825.0	7,247.9
IBRD	0	30.0	170.6	1,710.1	311.5	518.0	550.0	291.3	78.4	464.1	707.5	700.3	5,524.3
IFC	0	0	2.2	49.2	0	.3	34.8	14.6	28.8	6.8	23.0	8.9	162.0
IDA	0	0	0	19.5	0	0	0	0	0	0	0	0	19.5
IDB	0	0	10.8	876.1	206.0	201.0	244.6	206.1	106.2	570.4	478.1	115.8	1,451.4
UNDP	0	.1	6.9	41.1	4.9	1.0	1.3	.3	3.2	2.5	1.5	0	62.7
Other U.N.	0	0	1.0	12.6	1.4	7.1	0	0	5.8	0	0	0	28.0
F. COSTA RICA													
Total	0	#	18.8	642.5	36.4	105.6	120.4	29.8	124.4	35.8	155.4	105.0	818.5
IBRD	0	0	17.3	271.8	34.0	30.0	29.0	0	25.2	0	83.5	0	489.9
IFC	0	0	0	3.1	2.1	0	0	0	1.5	0	0	0	6.7
IDA	0	0	0	4.6	0	0	0	0	0	0	0	0	4.6
IDB	0	0	0	351.6	.1	74.5	91.3	29.2	97.2	35.8	71.6	105.0	301.6
UNDP	0	#	1.1	8.8	.2	1.0	.1	.6	.4	#	.1	0	12.2
Other U.N.	0	0	.4	2.6	0	.1	0	0	.1	0	.2	0	3.5

U.S. Fiscal Year

Table 2835 (Continued)

ASSISTANCE FROM INTERNATIONAL ORGANIZATIONS,[1] 20 LRC, 1946-86

(M US)

U.S. Fiscal Year

Country/Organization	1946-48	1949-52	1953-61	1962-78	1979	1980	1981	1982	1983	1984	1985	1986	Total
G. CUBA													
Total	0	#	1.7	26.5	3.0	1.6	#	7.7	1.3	1.0	.3	0	43.2
UNDP	0	#	1.5	22.9	3.0	1.3	#	7.7	1.1	1.0	.3	0	39.0
Other U.N.	0	0	.2	3.6	0	.3	0	0	.2	0	0	0	4.2
H. DOMINICAN REP.													
Total	0	0	.6	352.6	176.1	210.5	119.9	91.2	168.4	119.2	193.3	188.9	727.4
IBRD	0	0	0	64.0	52.0	120.0	24.0	25.4	7.1	3.8	5.8	35.8	337.9
IFC	0	0	0	13.4	0	2.0	.4	0	10.5	0	0	7.6	33.7
IDA	0	0	0	22.0	0	0	0	0	0	0	0	0	22.0
IDB	0	0	0	232.4	120.5	87.5	95.0	61.9	150.0	113.7	187.0	145.5	300.3
UNDP	0	0	.4	17.0	1.8	1.0	.5	3.9	.8	.3	.5	0	26.4
Other U.N.	0	0	.2	3.8	1.8	0	0	0	0	1.4	0	0	7.1
I. ECUADOR													
Total	0	.1	52.5	718.8	182.1	270.7	94.6	444.0	209.1	117.8	287.8	408.4	2,778.2
IBRD	0	0	45.0	205.5	58.0	106.0	20.0	228.7	40.6	0	8.0	253.5	964.1
IFC	0	0	0	22.4	4.3	1.3	10.8	9.3	.1	.1	0	0	48.2
IDA	0	0	0	36.9	0	0	0	0	0	0	0	0	36.5
IDB	0	0	0	419.6	113.2	161.0	63.5	202.5	167.3	117.7	279.0	153.1	1,670.7
UNDP	0	.1	6.3	28.3	6.1	.6	.3	3.5	.2	#	8	0	46.5
Other U.N.	0	0	1.2	6.1	.5	1.8	0	0	.9	0	1.8	1.8	12.2
J. EL SALVADOR													
Total	0	12.6	24.7	443.4	60.0	48.9	40.5	112.8	53.3	115.2	23.1	0	906.9
IBRD	0	12.5	22.2	157.2	23.5	0	0	0	0	0	0	0	215.1
IFC	0	0	.1	.8	.8	0	0	0	0	0	0	0	1.0
IDA	0	0	0	25.6	0	0	0	0	0	0	0	0	25.6
IDB	0	0	.2	242.7	29.5	48.5	40.4	112.4	52.9	114.0	21.0	0	634.2
UNDP	0	.1	1.8	12.9	5.6	.4	.1	.4	.4	.9	1.2	0	23.8
Other U.N.	0	0	.4	4.2	1.4	0	0	0	0	.3	.9	0	7.2
K. GUATEMALA													
Total	0	#	21.6	595.6	2.2	86.9	26.5	45.9	102.4	135.8	237.4	81.0	1,451.5
IBRD	0	0	18.2	242.3	0	17.0	0	0	18.5	50.0	44.6	81.0	471.6
IFC	0	0	.2	18.0	0	0	0	0	0	0	0	0	18.2
IDB	0	0	.1	315.7	.3	66.0	25.5	42.5	83.3	84.5	191.0	0	925.1
UNDP	0	#	2.3	12.8	1.9	2.8	1.0	.9	.6	1.3	0	0	25.3
Other U.N.	0	0	.8	6.8	0	1.1	0	2.5	0	0	0	0	11.3
L. HAITI													
Total	0	.1	8.4	225.7	61.1	9.8	33.9	47.2	89.5	38.1	45.7	9.7	600.7
IBRD	0	0	2.6	0	0	0	0	0	0	0	0	0	2.6
IFC	0	0	0	0	0	0	3.2	0	0	0	0	0	3.2
IDA	0	0	0	93.5	16.5	0	21.2	18.0	56.0	19.1	32.1	0	256.4
IDB	0	0	2.9	109.7	38.3	4.1	9.1	17.6	32.6	17.4	11.9	9.7	284.8
UNDP	0	.1	2.4	16.3	6.3	3.7	.4	6.5	.9	1.6	1.7	0	40.0
Other U.N.	0	0	.5	6.2	0	2.0	0	5.1	0	0	0	0	13.7

Table 2835 (Continued)

ASSISTANCE FROM INTERNATIONAL ORGANIZATIONS,[1] 20 LRC, 1946–86

(M US)

Country/Organization	1946–48	1949–52	1953–61	1962–78	1979	1980	1981	1982	1983	1984	1985	1986	Total
M. HONDURAS													
Total	0	#	32.5	504.5	177.0	224.0	35.5	37.0	89.6	154.3	16.5	108.0	1,390.8
IBRD	0	0	19.9	167.9	65.0	128.0	28.0	30.0	45.0	19.6	6.9	37.4	547.6
IFC	0	0	0	10.4	0	0	0	0	0	0	0	.6	11.0
IDA	0	0	8.4	49.2	0	25.0	0	0	0	0	0	0	82.6
IDB	0	0	2.2	259.9	106.3	71.0	7.5	0	42.2	134.1	8.4	70.0	713.6
UNDP	0	#	1.7	13.2	4.2	#	0	7.0	2.4	0	1.2	0	29.7
Other U.N.	0	0	.3	3.9	1.5	0	0	0	0	.6	0	0	6.3
N. MEXICO													
Total	0	80.4	153.7	4,945.4	963.4	971.7	1,439.4	804.5	1,373.2	883.3	674.9	1,187.3	12,260.5
IBRD	0	80.3	145.8	3,013.8	552.0	300.0	1,081.0	657.3	887.9	598.0	598.0	904.0	8,700.4
IFC	0	0	1.4	99.0	125.6	275.3	61.2	10.5	179.2	25.2	74.3	39.0	815.6
IDB	0	0	0	1,777.7	280.2	396.2	295.5	134.1	306.0	281.0	0	244.3	2,664.5
UNDP	0	.1	4.3	40.4	5.0	.2	.2	.9	.1	.8	.1	0	53.8
Other U.N.	0	0	2.2	14.5	.6	0	1.5	2.6	0	0	2.5	0	21.2
O. NICARAGUA													
Total	0	5.2	33.7	410.7	39.0	55.3	117.9	51.3	31.3	.8	.3	1.1	736.6
IBRD	0	5.2	30.2	126.0	0	20.0	33.7	16.0	0	0	0	0	231.1
IFC	0	0	0	9.5	0	0	0	0	0	0	0	0	9.5
IDA	0	0	0	23.0	0	32.0	5.0	0	0	0	0	0	60.0
IDB	0	0	2.0	236.0	36.8	0	75.0	34.4	30.7	0	0	0	405.4
UNDP	0	0	1.0	11.9	1.7	3.3	3.5	.9	.6	.5	.3	0	23.8
Other U.N.	0	0	.5	3.7	.5	0	.7	0	0	.3	0	1.1	6.8
P. PANAMA													
Total	0	#	15.4	505.1	68.2	149.9	74.5	126.9	137.7	82.6	137.4	39.4	1,268.3
IBRD	0	0	14.0	209.7	34.0	58.0	45.5	24.4	85.0	74.2	51.0	0	595.8
IFC	0	0	0	5.3	3.0	0	0	0	0	0	37.5	23.2	69.0
IDB	0	0	0	267.8	29.0	91.4	28.5	99.0	52.0	8.4	48.7	16.2	572.2
UNDP	0	#	1.0	18.9	1.7	.5	.5	3.5	.6	0	.1	0	26.8
Other U.N.	0	0	.4	3.4	.5	0	0	0	.1	0	.1	0	4.5
Q. PARAGUAY													
Total	0	4.6	6.7	450.2	97.2	76.6	88.8	176.4	114.7	45.4	40.3	0	1,090.4
IBRD	0	4.5	0	124.9	64.0	36.0	58.8	99.4	40.0	30.0	.8	0	457.6
IFC	0	0	0	5.4	0	0	1.2	10.4	0	.3	0	0	18.0
IDA	0	0	0	45.5	0	0	0	0	0	0	0	0	45.5
IDB	0	0	3.2	253.5	31.2	39.4	27.5	64.9	72.9	14.1	37.5	0	533.8
UNDP	0	.1	2.8	16.3	1.4	1.2	1.3	1.0	1.8	1.0	1.0	0	28.0
Other U.N.	0	0	.7	4.6	.6	0	0	.7	0	0	1.0	0	7.5
R. PERU													
Total	0	2.5	93.9	997.1	191.2	247.5	461.6	443.3	454.1	317.6	73.3	24.6	3,327.9
IBRD	0	2.4	79.6	470.5	123.8	111.0	148.0	286.7	302.2	122.5	31.0	13.5	1,690.9
IFC	0	0	4.4	19.3	2.5	3.2	8.5	18.2	8.0	9.2	16.8	10.0	100.1
IDB	0	0	3.9	461.9	60.2	132.5	305.0	130.0	142.3	184.8	24.3	0	1,466.7
UNDP	0	.1	5.2	36.6	2.7	.8	.1	5.4	1.6	1.1	1.2	0	54.5
Other U.N.	0	0	.8	8.8	2.0	0	0	3.0	0	0	0	1.1	15.7

Table 2835 (Continued)

ASSISTANCE FROM INTERNATIONAL ORGANIZATIONS,[1] 20 LRC, 1946-86
(M US)

U.S. Fiscal Year

Country/Organization	1946-48	1949-52	1953-61	1962-78	1979	1980	1981	1982	1983	1984	1985	1986	Total
S. URUGUAY													
Total	0	33.0	39.4	375.6	70.3	168.5	108.1	51.3	49.1	167.8	74.5	56.6	851.9
IBRD	0	33.0	38.0	145.9	26.5	98.0	30.0	40.0	45.0	0	64.0	45.2	551.4
IFC	0	0	0	3.8	6.4	10.7	0	0	2.8	0	8.9	3.0	35.5
IDB	0	0	0	209.1	35.7	57.5	78.0	10.0	0	167.8	1.6	8.4	238.4
UNDP	0	0	1.2	16.2	1.7	2.3	.1	1.3	1.3	0	0	0	25.7
Other U.N.	0	0	.2	.6	0	0	0	0	0	0	0	0	.9
T. VENEZUELA													
Total	0	#	15.2	710.3	6.2	1.8	.1	2.0	.4	64.8	514.3	138.0	1,277.9
IBRD	0	0	0	378.0	0	0	0	0	0	0	0	0	348.0
IFC	0	0	3.2	22.2	0	0	0	0	0	0	0	0	25.4
IDB	0	0	9.2	283.5	2.3	0	0	0	0	64.3	514.0	138.0	866.2
UNDP	0	#	2.6	24.6	3.9	1.8	.1	2.0	.4	.5	0	0	36.2
Other U.N.	0	0	.2	2.0	0	0	0	0	0	0	0	0	2.1
LATIN AMERICA REGIONAL[3]													
Total	0	.1	32.8	350.7	225.7	1.3	56.3	30.0	4.1	1.0	31.5	.8	814.9
IFC	0	0	0	10.0	0	0	0	0	0	0	0	0	10.0
IDB	0	0	0	130.4	210.2	0	50.3	24.0	0	0	29.6	0	526.2
UNDP	0	.1	18.2	99.9[a]	14.6	.6	4.7	6.0	2.6	1.0	1.9	0	149.8
Other U.N.	0	0	11.1	29.8	.9	.7	1.3	0	1.5	0	0	.8	44.4
EEC	0	0	3.5	80.6	0	0	0	0	0	0	0	0	84.5
LATIN AMERICA (TOTAL)													
Total	16.0	287.5	1,119.7	27,194.0	4,617.6	5,214.9	6,123.1	5,326.3	6,605.5	6,445.1	7,285.9	6,757.5	71,416.7
IBRD	16.0	286.3	880.1	12,808.0	2,232.8	2,595.0	3,119.0	2,962.9	3,396.6	3,003.4	3,654.3	4,701.2	39,438.6
IFC	0	0	32.6	787.2	218.2	389.0	422.2	301.1	353.3	146.3	546.3	366.5	3,504.1
IDA	0	0	27.4	412.6	32.0	89.1	34.2	25.0	63.0	24.1	45.9	70.0	822.8
IDB	0	0	61.3	12,229.3	2,030.0	2,090.6	2,507.9	1,946.6	2,735.6	3,238.1	3,005.0	1,577.2	26,115.4
UNDP	0	1.2	89.7	672.3	84.0	40.9	24.0	78.0	32.7	21.2	25.5	0	1,070.0
Other U.N.	0	0	25.1	156.2	12.6	15.2	5.8	12.7	9.3	10.0	4.9	5.0	254.4
EEC	0	0	3.5	128.4	8.0	2.5	10.0	0	15.0	2.0	4.0	37.6	211.4
WORLD REGIONAL[4]													
Total	512.8	835.4	5,071.1	80,526.5	14,401.0	16,856.8	18,468.3	18,873.5	20,804.3	23,317.8	22,633.5	23,061.2	238,768.0
IBRD	512.8	830.8	4,252.8	39,101.8	6,989.0	7,644.2	8,808.9	10,329.6	11,136.3	11,949.2	11,358.3	13,328.8	125,248.3
IFC	0	0	41.8	1,959.5	425.4	680.6	810.7	611.8	844.5	695.6	937.2	1,156.2	8,091.5
IDA	0	0	99.3	13,983.9	2,961.5	3,829.5	3,482.1	2,686.5	3,340.7	3,575.0	3,028.1	3,114.6	39,925.8
IDB	0	0	61.3	12,229.3	2,030.0	2,090.6	2,507.9	1,946.6	2,735.6	3,238.1	3,005.0	1,577.2	26,115.4
ADB	0	0	0	4,749.4	985.8	1,433.4	1,453.0	1,661.2	1,656.1	2,116.5	2,009.3	1,942.2	18,015.2
AFDB[5]	0	0	0	923.3	170.9	247.7	250.0	428.3	238.5	910.3	1,110.0	1,273.4	5,542.2
UNDP	0	4.6	329.4	3,185.4	471.9	335.4	337.5	567.7	333.0	300.9	261.8	~	6,058.2
Other U.N.	0	0	98.2	1,470.6	186.3	164.5	355.8	206.4	109.4	105.0	303.1	84.5	3,109.2
ECC	0	0	188.3	2,923.6	180.2	430.9	462.4	435.4	410.2	427.2	620.7	584.3	6,662.2

Table 2835 (Continued)

ASSISTANCE FROM INTERNATIONAL ORGANIZATIONS,[1] 20 LRC, 1946–86

(M US)

1. The data represent assistance from all sources available to the various organizations, including contributions, subscriptions, bond issues, etc. The data do not represent the United States contributions to these organizations. Data are based on United States fiscal years except for "UNDP" and "Other U.N." programs. These are calendar year figures, shown in the fiscal year in which the calendar year ends. As of FY 1982 UNDP data are based on United States fiscal years. Recipient countries have been grouped by region.

WORLD BANK GROUP

International Bank for Reconstruction and Development (IBRD): Data cover loan authorizations of the IBRD made either to governments, government enterprises, or to private firms with government guarantee. No adjustments are made for subsequent sales of loans. Cancellations are deducted from loans authorized in the year originally authorized. Fiscal year activity from FY 1978 onward contains only new loan authorizations.

International Development Association (IDA): Data cover value of agreements with governments for development credits. Cancellations are deducted from credits authorized in the year originally authorized. Fiscal year activity from FY 1978 onward contains only new loan authorizations.

International Finance Corporation (IFC): Data cover the commitments made by the IFC to invest in private enterprises in the various countries. Cancellations are deducted from commitments in the year originally committed.

Starting in FY 1974 reductions are reflected in the cumulative total with no adjustments in annual amounts. Fiscal year activity for FY 1980 onward contains only new loan authorizations; increases in loans authorized in prior years appear only in cumulative data.

OTHER INTERNATIONAL ORGANIZATIONS

Asian Development Bank (ADB): Data cover loan authorizations of the Asian Development Bank which made its first loan in 1968.

African Development Bank (AFDB): Data cover loan authorizations of the African Development Bank which made its first loans in U.S. FY 1968; and the African Development Fund with its first loans in U.S. FY 1974.

Inter-American Development Bank (IDB): Data cover loan authorizations of the IDB made either to governments, government enterprises or to private firms from Ordinary Capital and from the Fund for Special Operations. Cancellations are deducted from authorizations in the year originally authorized. Data exclude original loans from the Social Progress Trust Fund administered by the Bank for the United States; they include, however, any loans purchased from the Bank with SPTF reflows.

United Nations Development Program: Data are shown combining the Special Fund (UNDP-SF) and Technical Assistance (UNDP-TA). Each was previously a separate program—the Special Fund and the Expanded Program of Technical Assistance (EPTA), respectively. These were combined to form the United Nations Development Programme (UNDP). The Special Fund data cover allocations primarily for costs of preinvestment surveys. In FY 1973 the data represent the value of large-scale and small-scale projects approved and budgeted in the previous calendar year. Starting in FY 1974 the data are project approvals from the UNDP Compendium of Approved Projects.

Other United Nations Programs: Data cover allocations for approved projects and for administrative and operational services financed from government contributions and other sources by the United Nations Childrens' Fund (UNICEF). The data also include the Regular and other programs of technical assistance by U.N. specialized agencies (UNTA). Data for the specialized agencies are not available from FY 1969 onward.

European Economic Community (EEC): Data include obligations from the European Development Funds and from the European Investment Bank (EIB) for developing countries.

2. Transitional quarter.
3. Latin America Regional

AID and Predecessor Agencies. — Excludes Alliance for Progress funds obligated for nonregional programs in FY 1963–71.

Food for Peace (PL 480), Title II—Total Grants, Voluntary Relief Agencies. — Includes programs for French Guiana, Guadeloupe, and Martinique.

Other Economic Assistance, Other. — Represents primarily technical assistance grants for various countries and administrative funds under the Social Progress Trust Fund; Inter-American Foundation, $38.3 million.

Other U.S. Loans, All Other. — Represents OPIC direct loan.
4. World Regional

A.I.D. and Predecessor Agencies, Grants. — Excludes reimbursements by the Department of Defense for grants to Vietnam.

Other Economic Assistance, Contributions to International Financial Institutions (IFI). — Data excludes callable capital.

Other U.S. Loans, All Other. — Represents short-term credits by the Department of Agriculture under the Commodity Credit Corporation Charter Act unless otherwise identified on individual country pages.
5. Data exclude African Development Bank from FY 1979 onward.

a. Includes $825,000 approved in FY 1965 for Paraguay, transferred to Latin America Regional in FY 1971.

SOURCE: USAID-OLG, July 1, 1945–September 30, 1986, pp. 195, 203–212.

Table 2836

GROSS PROJECTED U.S. ASSISTANCE FOR GRANTS AND LOANS,[1] 19 L, 1970-86[a]

(M US)

Country	Fiscal Year	Total[2] Loans and Grants[3] (A+C)	"Other" Loans		Economic and Military Loans and Grants			Some Economic and Military Subtotals			I. Total Loans[12] (A+H)
			A. Total[4]	B. IMF Subtotal[5]	C. Total[6] (D+E)	D. Military[7]	E. Economics[8]	F. AID[9]	G. Food[10]	H. Loans[11]	
A. ARGENTINA	1970	23.9	22.3	22.3	1.6	.6	1.0	1.0	#	#	22.3
	1975	94.9	64.7	64.7	30.2	30.1	.1	#	#	30.0	94.7
	1978	27.4	27.4	27.4	#	#	#	#	#	#	27.4
	1979	32.8	32.7	32.7	.1	#	.1	#	#	.1	32.8
	1980	81.0	81.0	81.0	#	#	#	#	#	#	81.0
	1981	82.6	82.6	82.6	#	#	#	#	#	#	82.6
	1982	551.1	551.0	551.0	.1	#	.1	#	#	#	551.0
	1983	#	#	#	#	#	#	#	#	#	#
	1984	.1	#	#	.1	#	.1	#	#	#	#
	1985	~	~	~	~	~	~	~	~	~	~
	1986	~	~	~	~	~	~	~	~	~	~
B. BOLIVIA	1970	9.5	#	#	9.5	1.5	8.0	3.0	3.6	#	#
	1975	33.2	#	#	33.2	7.4	25.8	20.1	5.1	21.2	21.2
	1978	71.5	17.5	5.5	54.0	.8	53.2	34.3	16.5	39.1	56.6
	1979	57.9	#	#	57.9	6.7	51.2	28.9	19.0	38.0	38.0
	1980	30.4	#	#	30.4	.3	30.1	4.5	24.8	17.3	17.3
	1981	12.8	#	#	12.8	#	12.8	2.3	9.5	.2	.2
	1982	19.7	#	#	19.7	#	19.7	2.1	16.4	10.0	10.0
	1983	63.0	#	#	63.0	#	63.0	11.4	49.2	40.4	40.4
	1984	78.1	#	#	78.1	.1	78.0	52.3	22.1	49.5	49.5
	1985	54.0	#	#	54.0	3.4	50.6	18.4	29.5	24.0	24.0
	1986	76.1	#	#	76.1	1.5	74.6	38.4	32.2	28.3	28.3
C. BRAZIL	1970	218.0	63.2	63.2	154.8	.8	154.0	88.0	62.4	95.0	158.2
	1975	337.2	257.1	256.5	80.1	65.4	14.7	3.1	8.4	60.0	317.1
	1978	106.8	104.7	104.7	2.1	#	2.1	#	.1	#	104.7
	1979	262.0	259.9	212.6	2.1	#	2.1	#	.6	#	259.9
	1980	101.7	99.3	68.8	2.4	#	2.4	#	1.4	#	99.3
	1981	117.0	115.9	115.9	1.1	#	1.1	#	.6	#	115.9
	1982	91.7	91.0	91.0	.7	#	.7	#	.3	.1	91.1
	1983	30.7	30.3	29.3	.4	#	.4	#	.1	#	30.3
	1984	28.5	28.5	28.5	#	#	#	#	#	#	28.5
	1985	.8	37.4	37.4	.8	#	.8	#	#	#	37.4
	1986	.7	124.4	124.4	.7	#	.7	#	#	#	124.4
D. CHILE	1970	27.1	#	#	27.1	.8	26.3	18.0	7.2	15.0	15.0
	1975	128.6	32.4	23.0	96.2	.7	95.5	31.3	62.4	88.2	120.6
	1978	53.1	46.0	#	7.1	#	7.1	.2	5.6	#	46.0
	1979	13.6	#	#	13.6	#	13.6	.3	9.0	#	#
	1980	10.2	#	#	10.2	#	10.2	.1	5.0	#	#
	1981	12.1	#	#	12.1	#	12.1	#	7.7	.1	.1
	1982	6.7	#	#	6.7	#	6.7	#	2.3	#	#
	1983	2.8	#	#	2.8	#	2.8	#	1.0	#	#
	1984	1.7	#	#	1.7	#	1.7	#	#	#	#
	1985	1.3	1.3	#	1.3	#	1.3	#	#	#	1.3
	1986	1.1	1.1	#	1.1	#	1.1	#	#	#	1.1
E. COLOMBIA	1970	151.8	13.3	13.3	138.5	7.4	131.1	75.8	53.5	84.1	97.4
	1975	32.7	3.5	3.5	29.2	.7	28.5	14.0	11.5	12.2	15.7
	1978	89.5	30.0	30.0	59.5	52.2	7.3	#	2.6	51.0	81.0
	1979	64.5	42.5	42.5	22.0	13.0	9.0	.3	1.6	12.5	55.0
	1980	47.5	24.1	24.1	23.4	.3	23.1	.3	4.6	#	24.1
	1981	51.1	45.1	45.1	6.0	.3	5.7	#	#	#	45.1
	1982	553.5	540.3	540.3	13.5	10.5	3.0	#	#	10.0	550.3
	1983	4.6	3.8	3.8	4.6	.7	3.9	#	#	#	#
	1984	33.5	4.0	4.0	33.5	25.3	8.2	#	#	24.5	28.5
	1985	12.1	130.0	130.0	12.1	.8	11.3	#	#	#	130.0
	1986	15.8	#	#	15.8	4.3	11.5	#	#	#	#
F. COSTA RICA	1970	20.9	.2	.2	20.7	#	20.7	19.5	.5	17.5	17.7
	1975	9.0	5.3	3.8	3.7	#	3.7	.7	1.0	#	5.3
	1978	13.2	4.1	4.0	9.1	#	9.1	6.9	.8	5.5	9.6
	1979	22.7	4.8	2.7	17.9	#	17.9	16.4	#	15.1	19.9
	1980	22.4	6.4	6.0	16.0	#	16.0	13.6	.4	12.0	18.4
	1981	20.4	5.1	5.1	15.3	#	15.3	11.5	1.8	10.0	15.1
	1982	56.8	3.0	#	53.8	#	51.7	31.5	19.1	42.7	45.7
	1983	218.7	#	#	218.7	4.6	214.1	184.2	28.2	166.2	166.2
	1984	179.0	2.1	2.1	179.0	9.1	169.9	145.5	22.5	69.9	72.0
	1985	231.2	.9	.9	231.2	11.2	220.0	195.5	21.6	32.1	33.0
	1986	165.4	1.6	1.6	165.4	2.6	162.8	139.2	20.3	26.3	27.9

Table 2836 (Continued)

GROSS PROJECTED U.S. ASSISTANCE FOR GRANTS AND LOANS,[1] 19 L, 1970-86[a]
(M US)

Country	Fiscal Year	Total[2] Loans and Grants[3] (A+C)	"Other" Loans A. Total[4]	B. IMF Subtotal[5]	Economic and Military Loans and Grants C. Total[6] (D+E)	D. Military[7]	E. Economics[8]	Some Economic and Military Subtotals F. AID[9]	G. Food[10]	H. Loans[11]	I. Total Loans[12] (A+H)
H. DOMINICAN REP.	1970	21.9	#	#	21.9	2.1	19.8	5.2	14.0	9.6	9.6
	1975	20.6	7.3	7.3	13.3	1.6	11.7	5.6	5.5	5.3	12.6
	1978	7.0	.2	.2	6.8	.7	6.1	1.3	3.9	#	.2
	1979	75.4	26.0	.7	49.4	1.0	48.4	26.4	20.7	39.2	65.2
	1980	70.1	10.8	3.7	59.3	3.5	55.8	34.6	19.7	36.9	47.7
	1981	43.1	1.2	1.2	41.9	3.4	38.5	17.4	18.6	32.0	33.2
	1982	87.9	#	#	87.9	5.5	82.4	60.0	19.3	76.5	76.5
	1983	69.7	#	#	69.7	6.6	63.1	34.6	25.3	57.4	57.4
	1984	104.6	#	#	104.6	6.4	98.1	64.4	31.3	87.8	87.8
	1985	179.3	.5	.5	179.3	8.7	170.6	125.5	42.4	57.4	57.9
	1986	106.3	1.5	1.5	106.3	4.5	101.8	67.1	31.8	41.2	42.7
I. ECUADOR	1970	31.2	3.0	3.0	28.2	2.4	25.8	23.2	1.6	19.4	22.4
	1975	14.4	6.0	6.0	8.4	.4	8.0	2.1	3.4	#	6.0
	1978	19.9	3.7	.5	16.2	10.7	5.5	.8	2.4	10.0	13.7
	1979	33.1	26.4	26.4	6.7	.4	6.3	.5	2.7	#	26.4
	1980	16.3	1.2	#	15.1	3.3	11.8	8.3	.9	9.0	10.2
	1981	25.5	2.7	#	22.8	4.3	18.5	12.5	2.3	13.6	6.7
	1982	27.9	#	#	27.9	5.0	22.9	17.3	2.4	16.6	16.6
	1983	31.2	#	#	31.2	4.6	26.6	21.5	1.8	6.7	6.7
	1984	35.6	1.5	1.5	6	6.7	28.9	22.6	2.7	6.0	6.5
	1985	58.6	#	#	#	6.0	51.9	33.2	14.9	4.0	4.0
	1986	64.9	#	#	#	.7	60.4	49.8	6.5	3.8	3.8
J. EL SALVADOR	1970	13.2	#	#	13.2	.6	12.6	10.3	1.8	7.8	7.8
	1975	10.0	.6	.6	9.4	5.5	3.9	1.3	1.6	3.0	3.6
	1978	10.9	#	#	10.9	#	10.9	8.0	1.7	5.7	57
	1979	11.5	.1	.1	11.4	#	11.4	6.9	2.9	4.2	4.3
	1980	64.3	.1	.1	64.2	5.9	58.3	52.3	5.5	46.1	47.2
	1981	149.5	#	#	149.5	35.5	114.0	78.3	35.3	90.0	90.0
	1982	264.2	#	#	264.2	82.0	182.2	154.6	27.6	80.3	80.3
	1983	326.9	#	#	326.9	81.3	245.6	198.8	46.8	133.1	133.1
	1984	412.5	#	#	412.5	196.6	215.9	161.4	54.5	99.7	99.7
	1985	570.2	#	#	570.2	136.3	433.9	376.1	57.8	80.0	80.0
	1986	444.4	#	#	444.4	121.8	322.6	268.2	54.4	52.0	52.0
K: GUATEMALA	1970	33.6	#	#	33.6	1.4	32.2	29.1	2.5	25.1	25.1
	1975	17.8	.8	.8	17.0	2.9	14.1	9.4	3.4	9.3	10.1
	1978	10.6	#	#	10.6	#	10.6	4.5	4.6	#	#
	1979	24.7	#	#	24.7	#	24.7	17.4	5.3	14.6	14.6
	1980	13.8	.8	#	13.0	#	13.0	7.8	3.3	5.0	5.8
	1981	19.0	#	#	19.0	#	19.0	9.1	7.5	5.6	5.6
	1982	15.5	#	#	15.5	#	15.5	8.2	5.6	3.0	3.0
	1983	29.7	#	#	19.7	#	29.7	22.3	5.4	17.5	17.5
	1984	20.3	#	#	20.3	#	20.3	4.5	13.2	6.7	6.7
	1985	107.4	.2	#	106.9	#	106.9	75.7	28.2	59.7	59.9
	1986	122.1	#	#	116.7	#	116.7	89.8	24.0	47.9	47.9
L. HAITI	1970	3.8	.1	.1	3.7	#	3.7	1.6	2.1	#	.1
	1975	9.3	#	#	9.3	#	9.3	3.6	5.6	2.3	2.3
	1978	29.4	1.2	#	28.2	.7	27.5	8.9	18.5	11.0	12.2
	1979	25.5	.3	#	25.2	.4	24.8	9.1	15.4	8.8	9.1
	1980	27.2	#	#	27.2	.1	27.1	11.1	15.8	8.6	8.6
	1981	35.8	.8	#	35.0	.4	34.6	9.2	24.5	8.9	9.7
	1982	35.6	.8	#	34.8	.5	34.3	12.0	22.2	13.3	14.1
	1983	48.2	1.3	#	46.9	.7	46.2	27.3	18.5	11.3	12.6
	1984	47.5	#	#	47.5	1.0	46.5	25.7	19.8	11.0	11.0
	1985	56.3	.4	#	56.3	.7	55.6	30.7	23.2	15.0	15.4
	1986	79.6	.5	#	79.6	1.9	77.7	46.9	29.2	15.0	15.5
M. HONDURAS	1970	8.6	1.0	1.0	7.6	.4	7.2	5.5	.9	2.7	3.7
	1975	41.1	1.3	1.3	39.8	4.2	35.6	25.4	9.0	27.3	28.6
	1978	20.8	.5	.5	20.3	3.2	17.1	13.0	2.4	12.5	13.0
	1979	32.3	.8	.8	31.5	2.3	29.1	22.0	4.8	20.0	20.8
	1980	66.8	13.7	12.5	57.0	3.9	53.1	45.8	5.2	44.1	156.1
	1981	37.3	.9	.9	45.3	8.9	36.4	25.7	8.2	32.2	33.1
	1982	112.6	.6	.3	112.0	31.3	80.7	67.9	10.1	80.5	81.1
	1983	154.3	#	#	154.3	48.3	106.0	87.3	15.5	54.0	54.0
	1984	172.6	.2	#	172.4	77.4	95.0	71.0	20.2	38.3	38.5
	1985	296.4	2.0	#	296.4	67.4	229.0	204.6	19.4	34.8	36.8
	1986	197.7	.4	#	197.7	61.1	136.6	111.8	19.6	30.6	31.0

Table 2836 (Continued)

GROSS PROJECTED U.S. ASSISTANCE FOR GRANTS AND LOANS,[1] 19 L, 1970-86[a]

(M US)

Country	Fiscal Year	Total[2] Loans and Grants[3] (A+C)	"Other" Loans A. Total[4]	B. IMF Subtotal[5]	Economic and Military Loans and Grants C. Total[6] (D+E)	D. Military[7]	E. Economics[8]	Some Economic and Military Subtotals F. AID[9]	G. Food[10]	H. Loans[11]	I. Total Loans[12] (A+H)
N. MEXICO	1970	36.6	35.5	35.5	1.1	.1	1.0	1.0	#	#	35.5
	1975	196.0	195.7	195.7	.3	.1	.2	#	#	#	195.7
	1978	629.1	608.5	608.5	20.6	.1	20.5	#	#	#	608.5
	1979	170.9	157.2	157.2	13.7	.2	13.5	#	#	#	157.2
	1980	188.3	180.8	180.8	7.5	.1	7.4	#	#	#	180.8
	1981	662.5	652.6	652.6	9.9	.1	9.8	#	#	#	652.6
	1982	302.2	293.4	293.4	8.8	.1	8.7	#	#	#	293.4
	1983	96.5	88.2	37.2	8.3	.1	8.2	#	#	#	88.2
	1984	88.0	79.4	66.5	8.6	.2	8.4	#	#	#	79.4
	1985	21.4	10.1	10.1	11.3	.2	11.1	#	1.2	#	79.4
	1986	12.1	#	#	12.1	.2	11.9	#	.3	#	10.1
O. NICARAGUA	1970	4.4	.1	#	4.3	1.2	3.1	2.3	.4	#	4.4
	1975	46.8	.3	#	46.5	4.3	42.2	40.1	1.4	42.0	42.3
	1978	14.6	.2	.2	14.4	.4	14.0	12.5	.1	10.5	10.7
	1979	18.5	#	#	18.5	#	18.5	9.7	7.0	2.6	2.6
	1980	38.7	#	#	38.7	#	38.7	19.4	18.0	30.0	30.0
	1981	59.9	#	#	59.9	#	59.9	58.4	1.2	48.0	48.0
	1982	6.3	#	#	6.3	#	6.3	5.8	.4	#	#
	1983	#	#	#	#	#	#	#	#	#	#
	1984	.1	#	#	.1	#	.1	#	#	#	#
	1985	#	#	#	#	#	#	#	#	#	#
	1986	#	#	#	#	#	#	#	#	#	#
P. PANAMA	1970	17.0	2.5	2.5	14.5	1.0	13.5	11.8	1.0	8.5	11.0
	1975	51.9	30.1	30.1	21.8	.6	21.2	8.3	.9	6.7	36.8
	1978	23.6	#	#	23.6	.5	23.1	21.3	1.3	20.0	20.0
	1979	26.3	3.7	3.6	22.6	1.4	21.2	19.9	1.1	17.0	20.7
	1980	2.3	#	#	2.3	.3	2.0	1.0	1.0	#	#
	1981	11.0	#	#	11.0	.4	10.6	8.7	1.9	6.4	6.4
	1982	18.4	#	#	18.4	5.4	13.0	11.7	1.3	13.1	13.1
	1983	12.9	#	#	12.9	5.5	7.4	6.3	1.1	8.8	8.8
	1984	25.7	.2	#	25.5	13.5	12.0	10.7	1.3	10.0	10.2
	1985	85.1	#	#	85.1	10.6	74.5	74.3	.1	7.9	7.9
	1986	41.6	.3	.3	41.6	8.2	33.4	33.3	.1	11.3	11.6
Q. PARAGUAY	1970	9.3	#	#	9.3	1.2	8.1	7.1	.5	4.6	4.6
	1975	9.6	#	#	9.6	1.6	8.0	6.7	.4	5.2	5.2
	1978	4.1	#	#	4.1	.6	3.5	1.8	.3	#	#
	1979	10.3	#	#	10.3	#	10.3	7.1	.3	5.0	5.0
	1980	3.6	#	#	3.6	#	3.6	1.3	.4	#	#
	1981	6.2	#	#	6.2	#	6.2	2.0	.7	#	#
	1982	67.7	63.9	63.9	3.8	#	3.8	#	.1	#	63.9
	1983	4.4	1.1	#	3.3	.1	3.2	#	#	#	1.1
	1984	2.8	#	#	2.8	.1	2.7	.2	#	#	#
	1985	3.6	#	#	3.7	.1	3.6	1.0	#	#	#
	1986	3.4	#	#	3.4	.1	3.4	1.1	#	#	#
R. PERU	1970	17.5	#	#	17.5	.6	16.9	11.3	4.2	#	#
	1975	68.8	31.3	16.3	37.5	21.4	16.1	8.9	6.4	27.5	58.8
	1978	138.5	74.9	.7	63.6	8.9	54.7	22.0	31.9	52.0	126.9
	1979	139.0	62.8	#	76.2	5.5	70.7	34.1	35.3	53.8	116.6
	1980	102.9	46.3	6.2	56.6	3.3	53.3	18.7	33.0	36.0	82.3
	1981	100.5	16.0	13.1	84.5	4.3	80.2	34.5	42.5	51.0	67.0
	1982	59.6	#	#	59.6	5.0	54.6	35.8	16.2	48.7	48.7
	1983	124.4	26.3	26.3	98.1	4.6	93.5	35.5	55.9	52.5	78.8
	1984	175.6	.3	#	175.3	10.7	164.6	118.9	42.9	129.0	129.3
	1985	87.8	1.3	#	87.8	8.7	79.1	37.9	38.8	33.5	34.8
	1986	59.0	#	#	59.0	.6	58.4	25.9	28.8	20.0	20.0
S. URUGUAY	1970	22.9	#	#	22.9	3.5	19.4	16.9	2.4	17.4	17.4
	1975	22.2	#	#	22.2	9.2	12.9	12.8	#	19.3	19.3
	1978	.2	#	#	2	#	.2	#	#	#	#
	1979	.2	#	#	.2	#	.2	#	#	#	#
	1980	#	#	#	#	#	#	#	#	#	#
	1981	15.0	14.9	14.9	.1	#	.1	#	#	#	14.9
	1982	.8	#	#	.8	#	.8	#	#	#	#
	1983	1.1	#	#	1.1	.1	1.0	#	#	#	#
	1984	.7	#	#	.7	.1	.6	#	#	#	#
	1985	.1	#	#	.1	.1	#	#	#	#	#
	1986	14.5	#	#	14.5	.1	14.4	#	#	#	#

Table 2836 (Continued)

GROSS PROJECTED U.S. ASSISTANCE FOR GRANTS AND LOANS,[1] 19 L, 1970–86[a]

(M US)

Country	Fiscal Year	Total[2] Loans and Grants[3] (A+C)	"Other" Loans		Economic and Military Loans and Grants			Some Economic and Military Subtotals			I. Total Loans[12] (A+H)
			A. Total[4]	B. IMF Subtotal[5]	C. Total[6] (D+E)	D. Military[7]	E. Economics[8]	F. AID[9]	G. Food[10]	H. Loans[11]	
T. VENEZUELA	1970	17.0	13.5	13.5	3.5	.8	2.7	1.1	#	#	13.5
	1975	16.4	14.1	14.1	2.3	.7	1.6	#	#	#	14.1
	1978	22.4	22.3	22.3	.1	.1	#	#	#	#	22.3
	1979	18.5	18.5	18.5	#	#	#	#	#	#	18.5
	1980	160.2	160.2	160.2	#	#	#	#	#	#	160.2
	1981	59.6	59.5	59.5	.1	#	.1	#	#	#	59.5
	1982	26.2	26.0	26.0	.2	#	.2	#	#	#	26.0
	1983	12.2	12.0	12.0	.2	.1	.1	#	#	#	12.0
	1984	.4	#	#	.4	#	.4	#	#	#	.4
	1985	.9	#	#	#	.1	.8	#	#	#	#
	1986	.2	#	#	#	.1	.1	#	#	#	#

1. The definition of "assistance" is highly debatable and often full of irony as in the case of funding by the Export-Import (Ex-Im) Bank: The U.S. government formerly classified Ex-Im Bank loans as offering "assistance" when interest rates were relatively high in relation to other U.S. aid; since the 1970s when the government accepted criticism of its classification of Ex-Im Bank and took its funding out of figures on "assistance," however, other aid (including U.S. AID) rates and private rates have not compared so favorably and Ex-Im loans perhaps should be classified as offering assistance — indeed, U.S. business firms have complained that Ex-Im Bank loans offer more favorable terms to foreigners than to U.S. companies. Although it can be argued that Ex-Im Bank loans are tied to purchase of U.S. goods and services, it should be remembered that in the end Ex-Im Bank loans must compete in the international finance market or lose borrowers. (Cf. SALA-SNP, part III, for a discussion of supranational policy problems.) Ex-Im loans here are classified as part of U.S. assistance.
2. Total incluses all U.S. obligations (i.e., authorizations to expend in contrast to actual expenditures) for assistance administered by (a) the U.S. Agency for International Development (AID or USAID); (b) Peace Corps; (c) other U.S. agencies; and assistance administered through (d) Food for Peace Programs; (e) Social Progress Trust Funds of the Inter-American Development Bank; other selected U.S. programs (e.g., Inter-American Highway) — may include some disbursements; (f) military programs; as well as actual loans held by (h) the U.S. Ex-Im Bank. Does not include AID administrative overhead costs in the host country. Excludes regional obligations to more than one country. Excludes payments made through international agencies (e.g., IDB, IBRD) over which the U.S. has no direct control.
3. Grant and loan data are presented here in gross terms which revise previous methodology of reporting obligations in net terms; however, Ex-Im Bank data are still reported in net figures, as are AID data prior to FY 1955. Military sums are for deliveries prior to FY 1962, except exclude excess stocks deliveries include in SALA-SNP, XVII-5. Thus, although all data are subject to revisions (as in the case of shortfalls in Food for Peace deliveries), this new historical series will not fluctuate as much as previously.
4. Includes short-term credits by U.S. Department of Agriculture.
5. Before 1973 Ex-Im Bank deobligated sums (except for repayments) for years when originally authorized as it canceled, decreased, terminated, or sold loans to non-U.S. government purchasers. Includes (since 1969 only) loans of less than 5 years maturity. Excludes loans for military assistance (which are included under the military category.)

6. In source, this total is labeled "Total Economic and Military Grants and Loans," but actually economic obligations include funds for social purposes (such as education) as well as administrative functions (such as "Supporting Assistance" to maintain political stability for security objectives).
7. Military data included Ex-Im Bank military loans (but not guarantees) and also represent grant and loan actual assistance prior to FY 1962. Exclude AID obligations for Supporting Assistance (see notes 3 and 9). Excludes excess stock deliveries included in SALA-SNP, XVII-5.
8. Includes AID programs and Food for Peace.
9. AID was established November 4, 1961. Its predecessor agencies were, successively: Economic Cooperation Administration (April 3, 1948 — October 31, 1951); Mutual Security Agency (November 1, 1951 — July 31, 1953); Foreign Operations Administration (August 1, 1953 — June 30, 1955); International Cooperation Administration (July 1, 1955 — November 3, 1961); and the Development Loan Fund (August 14, 1957 — November 3, 1961); see AID/Washington, U.S. Economic Assistance Programs Administered by the Agency for International Development and Predecessor Agencies, April 3, 1948 — June 30, 1967. AID data include grant and loan Supporting Assistance for military infrastructure; and includes "402" Mutual Security Aid Program obligations for U.S. agricultural exports.
10. Food for Peace involves (a) sales on credit terms (for dollars and/or local currency) and (b) donations (for emergency relief or for volunteer relief agencies such as CARE) of surplus U.S. agricultural commodities. Former are valued at export market price; latter are valued at cost through FY 1969, subsequently at market value, plus ocean freight. (Donations to volunteer relief agencies do not, however, include ocean freight.) This subtotal does not include any funds generated by such activity as interest on local currency deposits.
11. Included in col. C.
12. Loans include "capitalized interest" (interest for prior years which is due but not paid) added during the year it becomes an accrued liability. Data exclude the export guarantees and insurance which are included in SALA-SNP, XVII-9. Refunding of loans generally is excluded.

a. For prior years, see SALA-SNP, XVII-1.

SOURCE: Adapted from USAID-OLG, July 1, 1945–June 30, 1975; July 1, 1945–September 30, 1983; and July 1, 1945–September 30, 1986. See pp. 1–3 of these volumes for discussion of concepts and terms as well as coverage.

Table 2837

A.I.D. COMMITMENTS TO INDIVIDUAL LATIN AMERICAN COUNTRIES, 20 L, 1949–86

(M US, Descending Order)

	Country	Amount	%
1.	BRAZIL	1,457.6	13.4
2.	EL SALVADOR	1,410.8	13.0
3.	COLOMBIA	1,008.3	9.3
4.	COSTA RICA	873.7	8.0
5.	HONDURAS	824.9	7.6
6.	DOMINICAN REP.	804.1	7.4
7.	BOLIVIA	732.8	6.7
8.	CHILE	703.4	6.5
9.	PERU	629.2	5.8
10.	GUATEMALA	502.1	4.6
11.	PANAMA	444.4	4.1
12.	ECUADOR	350.4	3.2
13.	NICARAGUA	313.5	2.9
14.	HAITI	313.3	2.9
15.	ARGENTINA	135.9	1.3
16.	PARAGUAY	126.8	1.2
17.	URUGUAY	86.0	.8
18.	MEXICO	78.9	.7
19.	VENEZUELA	72.0	.7
20.	CUBA	3.3	#
	LATIN AMERICA	10,871.4	100.0

SOURCE: Calculated from table 2829, above, by Stephen Bosworth.

Table 2838

PER CAPITA A.I.D. COMMITMENTS TO INDIVIDUAL LATIN AMERICA COUNTRIES, 20 L, 1949–86

(US, Descending Order)

	Country	Amount
1.	COSTA RICA	624
2.	EL SALVADOR	427.5
3.	PANAMA	317.4
4.	HONDURAS	317.3
5.	DOMINICAN REP.	201
6.	NICARAGUA	165
7.	BOLIVIA	162.8
8.	GUATEMALA	98.5
9.	CHILE	78.2
10.	HAITI	74.6
11.	ECUADOR	60.4
12.	PARAGUAY	55.1
13.	COLOMBIA	51.4
14.	PERU	48.4
15.	URUGUAY	34.4
16.	BRAZIL	16.3
17.	VENEZUELA	7.1
18.	ARGENTINA	5.9
19.	MEXICO	1.6
20.	CUBA	.4

SOURCE: Calculated from table 2829, above, by Stephen Bosworth.

Table 2839

GROSS PROJECTED A.I.D. ASSISTANCE DURING FOUR PERIODS, 20 L, 1949–86

(M US, Descending Order)

Mutual Security Years, 1949–58		Peak Years of Alliance for Progress, 1959–66		Years of U.S. Congressional Disillusionment, 1967–74		Years of Latin America's Rising Foreign Debt, 1975–86	
1. BOLIVIA	92.4	1. BRAZIL	842.8	1. COLOMBIA	647.3	1. EL SALVADOR	1,310.4
2. GUATEMALA	54.5	2. CHILE	499.2	2. BRAZIL	586.9	2. COSTA RICA	758.3
3. CHILE	24.2	3. COLOMBIA	316.3	3. DOMINICAN REP.	146.3	3. HONDURAS	699.0
4. BRAZIL	23.4	4. BOLIVIA	222.8	4. BOLIVIA	145.4	4. DOMINICAN REP.	453.9
5. PERU	18.4	5. DOMINICAN REP.	202.2	5. PANAMA	127.6	5. PERU	403.2
6. HAITI	16.6	6. ARGENTINA	141.0	6. CHILE	126.3	6. GUATEMALA	295.7
7. HONDURAS	16.1	7. PERU	116.1	7. GUATEMALA	98.2	7. BOLIVIA	272.2
8. ECUADOR	14.7[a]	8. ECUADOR	107.5	8. PERU	92.2	8. PANAMA	235.9
9. PARAGUAY	14.7[a]	9. MEXICO	70.9	9. NICARAGUA	87.3	9. HAITI	225.9
10. PANAMA	10.1	10. PANAMA	70.8	10. HONDURAS	68.4	10. EDUCADOR	168.6
11. COSTA RICA	8.7	11. VENEZUELA	64.2	11. COSTA RICA	59.7	11. NICARAGUA	165.0
12. COLOMBIA	8.1	12. NICARAGUA	56.3	12. ECUADOR	59.6	12. CHILE	53.7
13. MEXICO	6.4	13. GUATEMALA	53.7	13. EL SALVADOR	47.9	13. COLOMBIA	36.6
14. EL SALVADOR	5.5	14. COSTA RICA	47.0[a]	14. PARAGUAY	43.0	14. PARAGUAY	28.4
15. NICARAGUA	4.9	15. EL SALVADOR	47.0[a]	15. URUGUAY	42.1	15. URUGUAY	14.1
16. CUBA	2.6	16. HAITI	42.5	16. HAITI	28.6	16. BRAZIL	4.5
17. URUGUAY	1.9	17. HONDURAS	41.4	17. VENEZUELA	6.8	17. ARGENTINA[a]	#
18. DOMINICAN REP.	1.7	18. PARAGUAY	40.7	18. ARGENTINA	5.3	18. CUBA[a]	#
19. VENEZUELA	1.0	19. URUGUAY	27.9	19. MEXICO	1.6	19. MEXICO[a]	#
20. ARGENTINA	.2	20. CUBA	.7	20. CUBA	0	20. VENEZUELA[a]	#

a. Tie ranking.

SOURCE: Phillip Paul Boucher, "U.S. Foreign Aid to Latin America: Hypotheses and Patterns in Historical Statistics, 1934-1974," Ph.D. dissertation, University of California, Los Angeles, 1979, p. 98; 1975–86, calculated by Stephen Bosworth from table 2829, above.

Table 2840

PER CAPITA GROSS PROJECTED A.I.D. ASSISTANCE DURING FOUR PERIODS, 20 L, 1949–86

(M US, Descending Order)

Mutual Security Years, 1949–58		Peak Years of Alliance for Progress, 1959–66		Years of U.S. Congressional Disillusionment, 1967–74		Years of Latin America's Rising Foreign Debt, 1975–86	
1. BOLIVIA	28.90	1. PANAMA	64.40	1. PANAMA	85.10	1. BRAZIL	121.6
2. GUATEMALA	17.60	2. CHILE	61.60	2. NICARAGUA	45.90	2. COLOMBIA	26.6
3. PANAMA	11.20	3. DOMINICAN REP.	61.30	3. DOMINICAN REP.	35.70	3. PERU	17.6
4. HONDURAS	10.10	4. BOLIVIA	54.30	4. COSTA RICA	33.20	4. CHILE	11.2
5. PARAGUAY	9.80	5. NICARAGUA	37.50	5. BOLIVIA	31.60	5. ECUADOR	8.3
6. COSTA RICA	8.70	6. COSTA RICA	33.60	6. COLOMBIA	31.00	6. GUATEMALA	7.2
7. HAITI	4.60	7. ECUADOR	22.90	7. HONDURAS	26.30	7. BOLIVIA	5.7
8. ECUADOR[a]	4.10	8. PARAGUAY	21.40	8. PARAGUAY	18.70	8. DOMINICAN REP.	5.5
9. NICARAGUA[a]	4.10	9. HONDURAS	20.70	9. GUATEMALA	18.50	9. HAITI	5.0
10. CHILE	3.70	10. COLOMBIA	18.90	10. URUGUAY	15.60	10. EL SALVADOR	4.6
11. EL SALVADOR	2.60	11. EL SALVADOR	17.40	11. EL SALVADOR	13.70	11. HONDURAS	3.8
12. PERU	2.10	12. GUATEMALA	13.10	12. CHILE	13.30	12. PARAGUAY	3.2
13. URUGUAY	.83	13. HAITI	11.90	13. ECUADOR	9.80	13. NICARAGUA	2.8
14. DOMINICAN REP.	.68	14. BRAZIL	11.20	14. PERU	6.80	14. URUGUAY	2.4
15. COLOMBIA	.65	15. PERU	10.80	15. HAITI	6.70	15. PANAMA	1.9
16. CUBA	.43	16. URUGUAY	10.70	16. BRAZIL	6.30	16. COSTA RICA	1.6
17. BRAZIL	.40	17. VENEZUELA	8.00	17. VENEZUELA	.65	17. ARGENTINA[a]	#
18. MEXICO	.23	18. ARGENTINA	6.70	18. ARGENTINA	.22	18. CUBA[a]	#
19. VENEZUELA	.17	19. MEXICO	1.80	19. MEXICO	.03	19. MEXICO[a]	#
20. ARGENTINA	.01	20. CUBA	.09	20. CUBA	#	20. VENEZUELA[a]	#

a. Tie ranking.

SOURCE: Calculated by Stephen Bosworth from table 2829, above. Population statistics are from SALA, 25-Ch. 6; IMF-IFS, June 1987, and UN-MB, August 1987.

Table 2841

YEARLY U.S. PROJECTED ASSISTANCE TO LATIN AMERICA, 1946–86

(M US)

Fiscal Year	Total Grants and Loans[1]	Loans' Share
1946	104.7	91.7
1947	108.3	86.8
1948	55.9	17.1
1949	70.7	44.5
1950	196.9	169.2
1951	219.1	201.7
1952	103.0	78.7
1953	439.9	388.8
1954	95.0	17.9
1955	357.1	246.2
1956	368.6	217.1
1957	672.4	485.9
1958	398.9	238.6
1959	623.5	488.5
1960	306.1	174.5
1961	923.2	681.3
1962	1,036.0	695.4
1963	984.1	649.9
1964	1,164.2	836.9
1965	961.6	669.6
1966	1,090.6	761.0
1967	1,102.5	886.7
1968	1,080.0	890.2
1969	644.2	493.0
1970	685.1	461.5
1971	647.5	490.0
1972	1,007.3	823.2
1973	896,0	751.8
1974	1,216.2	1,079.1
1975	1,160.3	1,010.0
1976	959.1	809.7
TQ[2]	181.1	136.8
1977	537.0	383.6
1978	1,292.6	1,158.5
1979	1,039.7	866.6
1980	1,051.6	875.8
1981	1,520.9	1,297.4
1982	2,304.4	1,955.4
1983	1,235.1	710.9
1984	1,414.9	663.0
1985	1,766.5	322.4
1986	1,454.9	416.3

1. Excludes amounts and sums allocated to more than one country (e.g., Regional Programs in Central America — ROCAP).
2. Transitional quarter to new fiscal-year basis.

SOURCE: SALA-SNP, p. 360, and calculated from table 2829, first and last columns, above.

Table 2842

U.S. FOOD AID IN CEREALS, 20 L

(T MET)

	Country	1974/75	1984/85
A.	ARGENTINA	~	~
B.	BOLIVIA	22	111
C.	BRAZIL	31	10
D.	CHILE	323	10
E.	COLOMBIA	28	4
F.	COSTA RICA	1	164
G.	CUBA	~	~
H.	DOMINICAN REP.	16	107
I.	ECUADOR	13	18
J.	EL SALVADOR	4	194
K.	GUATEMALA	9	23
L.	HAITI	25	101
M.	HONDURAS	31	118
N.	MEXICO	~	6
O.	NICARAGUA	3	43
P.	PANAMA	3	1
Q.	PARAGUAY	10	4
R.	PERU	37	216
S.	URUGUAY	6	~
T.	VENEZUELA	--	--

SOURCE: WB-WDR, 1987, table 6.

Table 2843

INTER-AMERICAN FOUNDATION GRANTS, 19 L, 1972–86

(T US)

	Country	1985	1986	1972–86
A.	ARGENTINA	922	1,391	10,389
B.	BOLIVIA	1,646	1,166	14,574
C.	BRAZIL	1,594	1,979	12,911
D.	CHILE	1,251	1,137	30,792
E.	COLOMBIA	2,169	1,666	21,981
F.	COSTA RICA	2,038	1,224	7,973
H.	DOMINICAN REP.	367	968	9,887
I.	ECUADOR	634	1,004	7,308
J.	EL SALVADOR	12	323	3,934
K.	GUATEMALA	1,009	560	6,222
L.	HAITI	838	850	5,301
M.	HONDURAS	545	657	7,459
N.	MEXICO	1,130	771	16,055
O.	NICARAGUA	730	6	6,721
P.	PANAMA	656	929	6,766
Q.	PARAGUAY	721	154	10,114
R.	PERU	2,126	1,613	20,292
S.	URUGUAY	435	815	10,328
T.	VENEZUELA	768	582	2,354
	TOTAL	19,591	18,817	230,553

SOURCE: Adapted from *The Times of the Americas* (Washington, D.C.), Oct. 15, 1986, Part B, p. 8; *Inter-American Foundation–AR*, p. 63, 1986.

Table 2844

INTER-AMERICAN FOUNDATION[1] FUND ACCOUNT FOR LATIN AMERICA AND THE CARIBBEAN, 1971–85

(T US)

Fiscal Year	Budget Sources					Expenditures					
	Appropriations	%	Social Progress Trust Fund	%	Total Allocated	Grants and Other Programs[2]	%	Administrative Costs	%	Total Budget
1971	~	~	~	~	~	~	~	376	100	376
1972	2,794	100	~	~	2,794	2,794	71	1,125	29	3,919
1973	2,998	100	~	~	2,998	2,998	67	1,482	33	4,480
1974	7,210	57	5,494	43	12,704	12,704	89	1,604	11	14,308
1975	4,524	33	9,126	67	13,650	13,650	88	1,889	12	15,539
1976	5,257	42	7,335	58	12,592	12,592	83	2,552	17	15,144
1977	4,240	28	11,004	72	15,244	15,244	88	2,181	12	17,425
1978	3,905	32	8,280	68	12,185	12,185	85	2,219	15	14,404
1979	10,543	61	6,815	39	17,358	17,358	88	2,488	12	19,846
1980	8,945	39	14,017	61	22,962	22,962	89	2,943	11	25,905
1981	11,691	52	10,896	48	22,587	22,587	87	3,330	13	25,917
1982	11,952	53	10,458	47	22,410	22,410	86	3,631	14	26.041
1983	9,657	51	9,256	49	18,913	18,913	83	3,894	17	22,807
1984	9,041	47	10,180	53	19,221	19,221	82	4,095	18	23,316
1985	8,974	36	15,735	64	24,709	24,709	85	4,465	15	29,174
Total	101,731	46	118,596	54	220,327	220,327	85	38,274	15	258,601

1. The Foundations's funds come from Congressional appropriations and from the Social Progress Trust Fund. The Fund, which is administered by the Inter-American Development Bank, holds repayments from loans made under the Alliance for Progress by the U.S. government to Latin American and Caribbean countries.
2. Other program activities have included such items as evaluations, fellowships, in-country technical assistance, and publications. Approximately 9 million dollars has been utilized for this purpose during fiscal years 1972–85.

SOURCE: *The Times of the Americas* (Washington, D.C.), Oct. 15, 1986, Parb B, p. 8.

Table 2845

CONGRESSIONAL APPROPRIATIONS TO INTER-AMERICAN FOUNDATION
(FY, M US)

Year	Amount
1970–1978	50.0
1979	10.0
1980	12.6
1981	15.8
1982	12.0
1983	14.0
1984	13.0
1985	12.0
1986	11.5
1987	11.8

SOURCE: *Inter-American Foundation–AR*, 1986, p. 61.

Table 2846

RESOURCES OF SOCIAL PROGRESS TRUST FUND
(M US)

Year	Amount
1974–1976	31.0
1977–1979	48.0
1980–1982	48.0
1983–1985	48.0
1986–1988	48.6

SOURCE: *Inter-American Foundation–AR*, 1986, p. 61.

Table 2847

U.S. VOTING POWER IN MULTILATERAL AGENCIES
(%)

	United States	Central America
IMF	20.0	.8
IBRD	20.8	.6
IDA	21.4	1.2
IFC	28.4	.6
IDB	34.6	3.1

SOURCE: Tom Berry et al., *Dollars and Dictators* (Albuquerque, N.M.: The Resource Center, 1982), p. 55.

Table 2848

U.S. PEACE CORPS BUDGET, 1961–87

Fiscal Year	Budget Request Dollars (T US)	Appropriated Dollars (T US)	Volunteers (N)
1961	~	~	124
1962	40,000	30,000	2,816
1963	63,750	59,000	6,646
1964	108,000	95,964	10,078
1965	115,000	104,100	13,248
1966	125,200	114,000	15,556
1967	110,500	110,000	14,968
1968	124,400	107,500	13,823
1969	112,800	102,000	12,131
1970	109,800	98,000	9,513
1971	98,800	90,000	7,066
1972	71,200	72,500	6,894
1973	88,027	81,000	7,341
1974	77,000	77,000	8,044
1975	82,256	77,687	7,015
1976	80,826	81,266	5,958
1977	67,155	80,000	5,752
1978	74,800	86,234	7,072
1979	95,135	99,179	6,328
1980	105,404	105,795	5,994
1981	118,800	118,531	5,445
1982	121,900	105,000	5,380
1983	97,500	105,000	5,483
1984	108,500	117,000	5,699
1985	115,000	128,600	6,264
1986	124,400	124,200	5,564
1987	126,200	~	~

SOURCE: *The Times of the Americas* (Washington, D.C.), July 9, 1986, p. 14.

Table 2849

U.S. PEACE CORPS BUDGET, 1962–86

Fiscal Year	Appropriated Dollars (T US)	Constant Dollars (T US)	Volunteers and Trainees[1] (N)
1962	30,000	42,523	2,816
1963	59,000	82,414	6,554
1964	95,964	132,896	10,078
1965	104,000	140,070	13,248
1966	114,000	148,645	15,556
1967	110,000	139,205	14,968
1968	107,500	130,193	13,823
1969	102,000	117,620	12,131
1970	98,450	107,760	9,513
1971	90,000	93,730	8,398
1972	72,500	72,500	6,894
1973	81,000	76,473	7,354
1974	77,000	66,276	8,044
1975	77,687	63,584	6,895
1976	81,266	60,755	5,958
1977	80,000	56,493	6,916
1978	86,234	56,714	7,072
1979	99,179	59,927	6,328
1980	99,924	55,268	5,994
1986	130,000[a]	~	5,000[‡]

1. Volunteers and trainees on-board at the end of the fiscal year (1962–76: June 30; 1977–80: September 30).

a. Authorized amount.

SOURCE: U.S. Action, *Annual Report*, 1980, p. 42; and for 1986 data, Select Committee on Hunger, U.S. House of Representatives, *The Peace Corps: 25 Years of Alleviating Hunger* (Washington D.C.: U.S. Government Printing Office, March 1986), Chart 2.

Table 2850

U.S. PEACE CORPS VOLUNTEERS IN FULL-TIME
EQUIVALENTS (FTEs), 12 L, 1975–81
(FTEs for Each FY)

	Country	1975	1976	1977	1978	1979	1980	1981
C.	BRAZIL	106	140	120	142	89	32	3.4[a]
D.	CHILE	42	65	88	108	110	94	95.8

Continued in SALA, 25–2852.

Table 2851

U.S. PEACE CORPS VOLUNTEER CHARACTERISTICS
(1980)

Peace Corps Volunteers by Human Need Areas	%
Health/Nutrition/Water Supply	25
Food Production	18
Knowledge/Skills	40
Economic Development/Income Generation	7
Energy/Conservation	4
Community Services/Housing	6

Peace Corps Volunteers and Trainees at End of FY 1980	N
Africa	2,464
North Africa, Near East, Asia, and Pacific	1,802
Latin America	1,728
Total	5,994

Sex Ratio of Peace Corps Volunteers	%
Female	44
Male	56

Age of Peace Corps Volunteers	%
22 years or younger	1
23–25 years	53
26–28 years	24
29–35 years	14
36 years or older	8

SOURCE: U.S. Action, *Annual Report*, 1980, p. 44.

Table 2852

U.S. PEACE CORPS VOLUNTEERS, BY SKILL CLASSIFICATION, 9 LC
(N, 1980)

Country	Health	Nutrition	Food	Water	Knowledge/ Skills	Economic Development	Housing	Energy Conservation	Community Services	Total
Belize	9	0	8	0	27	7	0	0	7	58
B. BRAZIL	5	0	0	0	17	0	0	2	0	24

Continued in SALA, 25–2854.

Table 2853

U.S. PEACE CORPS SERVICE IN LATIN AMERICA, 17 L
(1986)

	Country	Entered	Departed
B.	BOLIVIA	1962	1971
C.	BRAZIL	1962	1981
D.	CHILE	1961	1982
E.	COLOMBIA	1961	1981
F.	COSTA RICA	1963	**
H.	DOMINICAN REP.	1962	**
I.	ECUADOR	1962	**
J.	EL SALVADOR	1962	1980
K.	GUATEMALA	1963	**
L.	HAITI	1983	**
M.	HONDURAS	1963	**
O.	NICARAGUA	1968	1979
P.	PANAMA	1963	1971
Q.	PARAGUAY	1967	**
R.	PERU	1962	1975
S.	URUGUAY	1963	1974
T.	VENEZUELA	1962	1977

SOURCE: Select Committee on Hunger, U.S. House of Representatives, *The Peace Corps: 25 Years of Alleviating Hunger* (Washington, D.C.: U.S. Government Printing Office, March 1986), Chart 2.

CHAPTER 29

INVESTMENTS AND
CORPORATE BUSINESS ACTIVITY

Table 2900

U.S. DIRECT INVESTMENT IN LATIN AMERICA, 19 LRC, 1950–86
(Cumulative M US in Book Value)

Country	Year	Total[2]	Mining	Petroleum	Manufacturing[3]	Transport, Communications, and Public Utilities	Trade	Other Industries
A. ARGENTINA	1950	356	~[a]	~[b]	161	77	35	16
	1951	360	~[a]	~[a]	167	~[a]	41	~
	1952	382	~[a]	~[a]	192	~[a]	47	~
	1953	391	~[a]	~[a]	193	~[a]	49	~
	1954	405	~[a]	~[a]	208	~[a]	47	~
	1955	418	~[a]	~[a]	218	~[a]	42	~
	1956	429	~[a]	~[a]	233	~[a]	40	~
	1957	333	~[a]	~[a]	164	~[a]	22	~
	1958	330	~[a]	~[a]	154	~[a]	19	~
	1959	366	~[a]	~[a]	160	~[a]	16	~
	1960	473	~[a]	~[a]	214	~[a]	21	~
	1961	560	~[a]	~[a]	307	22	29	~
	1962	799	~[a]	~[a]	413	23	34	~
	1963	829	~[a]	~[a]	454	24	38	~
	1964	882	~[a]	~[a]	500	25	40	~
	1965	992	~[a]	187	618	25	47	327
	1966	758	~[a]	121	510	9	23	~
	1967	803	~[a]	125	536	9	31	~
	1968	870	~[a]	120	589	10	~	50
	1969	973	~[a]	115	659	8	~	60
	1970	1,022	28	137	669	6	~[a]	~
	1971	1,089	39	148	712	5	~[a]	~
	1972	1,128	~[a]	~[a]	749	~[a]	~[a]	~
	1973	1,144	44	141	768	~[a]	~[a]	~
	1974	1,138	50	147	737	11	70	68
	1975	1,154	~	142	764	8	87	60
	1976	1,366	53	174	898	~[a]	105	~[a]
	1977	1,490	55	223	921	~	132	~
	1978	1,658	53	259	983	~	157	~
	1979	1,850	~	305	1,184	289	136	~
	1980	2,494	~	395	1,584	409	216	~
	1981	2,735	69	483	1,570	308	202	107
	1982	2,979	71	629	1,718	~[e]	168	93
	1983	2,702	~	500	1,555	~[d]	167	105
	1984	2,746	~	443	1,568	~[d]	174	122
	1985	2,713	~	471	1,505	174	135	112
	1986	2,986	~	473	1,749	255	158	101
B. BOLIVIA	1950	11	6	~	~[b]	2	2	~[b]
C. BRAZIL	1950	644	2	112	285	138	73	35
	1951	784	2	131	387	142	88	34
	1952	977	1	167	507	151	112	37
	1953	970	3	197	477	149	106	39
	1954	992	4	165	527	150	114	33
	1955	1,052	4	179	560	156	121	32
	1956	1,143	9	188	612	171	129	35
	1957	835	10	130	378	182	116	19
	1958	795	6	93	398	186	91	20
	1959	828	5	84	432	192	93	21
	1960	953	10	76	515	200	130	23
	1961	1,006	14	92	548	198	129	25
	1962	1,084	26	79	616	191	136	35
	1963	1,132	30	60	664	193	148	38
	1964	997	40	53	668	41	153	41
	1965	1,074	51	57	723	37	162	45
	1966	882	28	70	574	~	92	~
	1967	961	28	76	627	22	88	31
	1968	1,122	27	79	757	17	92	43
	1969	1,290	26	95	899	15	86	52
	1970	1,526	30	114	1,075	15	119	54
	1971	1,745	26	141	1,225	14	150	70
	1972	2,180	45	164	1,561	15	175	80
	1973	2,885	31	198	2,046	16	212	103
	1974	3,760	94	244	2,578	18	363	183
	1975	4,579	130	288	3,106	22	406	269
	1976	5,416	140	336	3,673	26	496	31
	1977	5,930	~	364	3,937	26	495	~

Table 2900 (Continued)

U.S. DIRECT INVESTMENT IN LATIN AMERICA, 19 LRC, 1950–86
(Cumulative M US in Book Value)

Country	Year	Total[2]	Mining	Petroleum	Manufacturing[3]	Transport, Communications, and Public Utilities	Trade	Other Industries
C. BRAZIL (Continued)	1978	7,170	268	424	4,684	25	552	521
	1979	7,186	110	301	4,902	548	506	194
	1980	7,703	141	365	5,145	679	571	206
	1981	8,253	152	422	5,420	590	581	216
	1982	9,031	138	448	5,958	633	625	223
	1983	9,060	~	358	6,451	734	394	212
	1984	9,377	~	302	6,764	899	410	178
	1985	8,889	~	206	6,888	1,026	375	99
	1986	9,135	~	151	7,095	1,187	452	112
D. CHILE	1950	540	351	~b	29	~b	15	3
	1951	582	382	~a	33	~a	14	~
	1952	626	423	~a	33	~a	11	~
	1953	660	452	~a	34	~a	9	~
	1954	635	418	~a	35	~a	10	~
	1955	643	421	~a	37	~a	11	~
	1956	682	454	~a	39	~a	12	~
	1957	666	483	~a	22	~a	9	~
	1958	687	498	~a	21	~a	8	~
	1959	729	526	~a	21	~a	10	~
	1960	738	517	~a	22	~a	12	~
	1961	735	504	~a	27	171	14	~
	1962	755	504	~a	29	187	14	~
	1963	768	503	~a	27	201	15	~
	1964	769	~a	~a	30	214	20	~
	1965	829	509	~a	39	~a	24	257
	1966	765	439	~a	47	~a	19	~
	1967	820	~	~a	56	~a	21	
	1968	916	566	~a	57	~a	21	12
	1969	817	443	~a	57	~a	20	16
	1970	758	490	~a	57	135	24	20
	1971	739	486	~a	48	133	23	19
	1972	642	~	~a	50	131	25	17
	1973	643	~	~a	47	131	28	16
	1974	287	25	~	44	129	27	23
	1975	174	12	~	49	4	28	~
	1976	179	5	~	49	6	34	~
	1977	193	~	~	56	7	39	~
	1978	230	~	~	71	10	51	26
	1979	250	5	70	~	~	49	~
	1980	536	209	91	~	~	64	~
	1981	834	~	98	112	~	80	~
	1982	854	~d	79	60	~	71	~d
	1983	108	~	59	-289	~d	64	151
	1984	46	~	44	-276	~d	49	136
	1985	85	~	49	-281	~d	42	123
	1986	193	~	48	-277	~d	37	125
E. COLOMBIA	1950	193	~a	112	25	29	9	~
	1951	221	~	131	27	31	11	~
	1952	261	~a	152	37	31	19	~
	1953	271	~a	159	41	28	22	~
	1954	310	~a	166	51	31	36	~
	1955	336	~a	178	58	33	42	~
	1956	371	~a	193	68	39	44	~
	1957	396	~a	245	61	24	34	~
	1958	383	~a	225	68	26	35	~
	1959	401	~a	225	77	28	41	~
	1960	424	~a	233	92	28	46	~
	1961	425	~a	230	95	29	49	~
	1962	455	~a	257	100	27	52	~
	1963	465	~a	246	120	27	52	~
	1964	508	~a	255	148	30	53	~
	1965	526	~a	269	160	29	49	20
	1966	459	~a	86	193	~	27	15
	1967	482	~a	105	200	~	29	17
	1968	520	~a	130	212	~	25	~
	1969	574	~a	147	240	27	29	~

Table 2900 (Continued)
U.S. DIRECT INVESTMENT IN LATIN AMERICA, 19 LRC, 1950–86
(Cumulative M US in Book Value)

Country	Year	Total[2]	Mining	Petroleum	Manufacturing[3]	Transport, Communications, and Public Utilities	Trade	Other Industries
E. COLOMBIA (Continued)	1970	584	12	137	250	26	37	~
	1971	650	~a	146	302	25	35	~
	1972	635	~a	129	299	26	37	~
	1973	608	~a	76	326	~a	45	14
	1974	617	18	58	366	14	54	~
	1975	648	17	62	381	13	64	16
	1976	654	11	56	388	~	64	~
	1977	696	9	72	432	~	66	~
	1978	769	9	85	490	~	69	~
	1979	842	~	198	492	~	95	~
	1980	1,012	~	265	548	~	97	~
	1981	1,174	~	318	574	~	98	~
	1982	1,655	~d	569	651	~d	105	~d
	1983	2,123	~	1,010	637	~d	91	~d
	1984	2,267	~	1,075	694	~d	83	~d
	1985	2,142	~	1,005	661	~d	51	~d
	1986	2,049	~	965	677	~d	42	~d
F. COSTA RICA	1950	60	~	4	~	11	1	~b
	1955‡	61	~	6	~	11	~b	~b
G. CUBA	1950	642	~b	20	54	271	21	269c
	1955	736	~b	~b	55	312	30	298
	1960‡	956	~a	147	111	313	44	341
H. DOMINICAN REP.	1950	106	~	~b	9	11	1	81
	1955‡	134	6	~b	13	5	~b	103
	1960	105	~b	~b	~b	~b	~b	~
I. ECUADOR	1950	14	~	~b	1	5	2	4
	1955‡	25	~	~b	~b	6	2	8
	1982	405	#	225	133	5	37	-9
	1983	442	~	~d	117	9	27	~d
	1984	371	~	192	126	10	26	11
	1985	361	~	~d	140	12	~	~d
	1986	536	~	319	152	13	28	12
J. EL SALVADOR	1950	19	~b	2	~b	17	1	~b
K. GUATEMALA	1950	106	~b	4	~b	72	3	~b
	1955‡	103	~b	6	~b	73	~b	~b
	1960	131‡	~a	26‡	~a	66‡	5‡	34‡
L. HAITI	1950	13	~	~b	~b	2	~b	8
	1955‡	18	~	~b	~b	3	~b	9
M. HONDURAS	1950	62	~a	~a	~a	9	~b	~a
	1955‡	101	~a	~a	~a	12	~b	~a
	1960	100‡	~a	~a	~a	23‡	1‡	76‡
N. MEXICO	1950	414	121	13	133	107	30	11
	1951	468	126	9	194	87	41	11
	1952	481	128	10	205	89	38	11
	1953	497	138	11	207	89	39	11
	1954	503	135	13	208	88	44	16
	1955	577	143	15	262	87	54	16
	1956	667	158	22	309	88	72	19
	1957	739	139	31	335	134	68	32
	1958	745	139	32	326	120	84	34
	1959	758	137	30	353	118	84	36
	1960	795	130	32	391	119	85	39
	1961	830	129	54	418	29	97	104
	1962	867	121	73	442	26	97	107
	1963	907	116	65	502	25	93	105
	1964	1,034	128	56	606	27	111	106
	1965	1,182	104	48	756	27	138	110
	1966	1,329	95	29	927	20	136	39
	1967	1,426	~a	26	1,016	18	151	~a
	1968	1,566	97	25	1,147	19	165	59
	1969	1,756	117	15	1,277	20	179	94
	1970	1,912	127	10	1,380	23	207	122
	1971	1,980	103	7	1,492	26	224	82
	1972	2,161	98	10	1,631	26	263	82
	1973	2,379	85	10	1,800	31	305	88

Table 2900 (Continued)

U.S. DIRECT INVESTMENT IN LATIN AMERICA, 19 LRC, 1950–86
(Cumulative M US in Book Value)

Country	Year	Total[2]	Mining	Petroleum	Manufacturing[3]	Transport, Communications, and Public Utilities	Trade	Other Industries
N. MEXICO	1974	2,854	83	18	2,173	34	400	550
(Continued)	1975	3,200	80	22	2,443	35	476	87
	1976	2,984	88	17	2,223	47	453	105
	1977	3,230	98	26	2,391	~	502	~
	1978	3,712	97	41	2,752	~	563	~
	1979	4,490	76	145	3,451	508	537	~
	1980	5,989	95	150	4,489	750	727	~
	1981	6,962	77	189	5,140	846	878	~
	1982	5,584	~e	193	4,166	726	626	~e
	1983	4,381	~	75	3,446	430	352	327
	1984	4,568	~	76	3,632	461	410	261
	1985	5,070	~	52	4,073	774	522	257
	1986	4,826	~	42	3,926	841	456	~d
O. NICARAGUA	1950	9	~b	~b	~b	1	1	~
P. PANAMA	1950	58	- -	6	2	18	11	23
	1951	67	- -	6	2	17	14	28
	1952	69	- -	6	3	18	12	30
	1953	86	- -	7	4	18	14	43
	1954	100	- -	9	4	20	18	49
	1955	109	- -	10	5	21	15	57
	1956	157	1	1	8	24	30	94
	1957	201	5	13	3	19	70	91
	1958	268	8	25	6	20	94	115
	1959	327	16	29	8	21	118	135
	1960	405	17	56	9	22	145	156
	1961	486	17	62	10	25	195	177
	1962	537	19	81	5	25	224	183
	1963	616	19	94	12	26	273	193
	1964	663	19	107	23	29	281	205
	1965	724	19	130	24	36	293	221
	1966	847	- -	70	18	52	235	151
	1967	872	- -	~a	~a	54	240	155
	1968	971	- -	47	48	60	250	178
	1969	1,055	- -	27	49	62	259	184
	1970	1,190	- -	39	64	60	274	211
	1971	1,380	- -	33	77	63	301	225
	1972	1,352	- -	25	88	51	318	230
	1973	1,549	1	~a	89	42	375	~a
	1974	1,604	−1	55	115	43	456	324
	1975	1,907	1	125	122	39	542	359
	1976	1,957	1	94	139	45	572	381
	1977	2,249	1	106	158	24	654	386
	1978	2,385	1	68	180	26	707	406
	1979	2,874	5	289	214	#	542	242
	1980	3,171	- -	503	262	#	601	~
	1981	3,671	- -	601	302	#	672	377
	1982	4,404	~e	776	327	#	655	~d
	1983	4,837	~	1,101	189	#	704	90
	1984	4,467	~	548	~d	#	701	~d
	1985	4,004	~	514	245	0	639	33
	1986	4,352	~	498	253	0	784	48
R. PERU	1950	145	55	~b	16	~b	13	1
	1951	199	107	~a	21	~a	18	~
	1952	233	129	~a	17	~a	24	~
	1953	274	150	~a	16	~a	29	~
	1954	278	150	~a	18	~a	31	~
	1955	292	154	~a	23	~a	36	~
	1956	332	178	~a	25	~a	38	~
	1957	383	196	86	29	14	42	16
	1958	409	218	86	29	19	38	18
	1959	428	242	79	31	19	36	20
	1960	496	307	79	35	19	42	20
	1961	486	292	71	36	20	45	23
	1962	503	298	66	46	20	48	26
	1963	498	290	56	64	21	41	27
	1964	514	291	60	65	27	46	31
	1965	515	262	60	79	21	54	38

Table 2900 (Continued)

U.S. DIRECT INVESTMENT IN LATIN AMERICA, 19 LRC, 1950–86
(Cumulative M US in Book Value)

Country	Year	Total[2]	Mining	Petroleum	Manufacturing[3]	Transport, Communications, and Public Utilities	Trade	Other Industries
R. PERU	1966	651	360	~[a]	128	~[a]	52	24
(Continued)	1967	712	416	57	140	~[a]	45	24
	1968	749	440	62	146	~[a]	~[a]	26
	1969	771	~[a]	66	154	−2	37	26
	1970	744	~[a]	67	156	−1	35	24
	1971	729	~[a]	74	156	−1	33	29
	1972	769	442	97	155	−3	32	36
	1973	859	466	149	161	−2	42	32
	1974	900	412	239	155	−2	54	74
	1975	1,221	700	246	166	−1	62	37
	1976	1,367	~	~	168	−1	64	43
	1977	1,397	807	316	159	−1	62	46
	1978	1,429	~[a]	~[a]	158	−1	57	47
	1979	1,537	~[a]	~[a]	~[a]	~[a]	52	24
	1980	1,665	~[a]	~[a]	~[a]	~[a]	64	19
	1981	1,928	~	~	106	10	76	~
	1982	2,262	~[d]	~[d]	106	30	76	23
	1983	2,042	~	1,213	127	~[d]	61	~[d]
	1984	1,903	~	1,083	111	~[d]	68	~[d]
	1985	1,652	~	906	55	0	64	~[d]
	1986	1,118	~	422	47	0	64	~[d]
S. URUGUAY	1950	55	~	3	33	2	4	13
	1955[‡]	74	~	4	36	2	10	22
	1960	47	~[a]	~[a]	20	~[a]	4	23
T. VENEZUELA	1950	993	~[b]	857	24	10	24	20
	1951	968	~[a]	811	29	11	30	~
	1952	1,134	~[a]	907	36	12	34	~
	1953	1,237	~[a]	939	41	13	38	~
	1954	1,271	~[a]	939	51	14	45	~
	1955	1,311	~[a]	965	67	15	57	~
	1956	1,676	~[a]	1,278	86	23	83	~
	1957	2,465	~[a]	1,934	124	24	113	~
	1958	2,658	~[a]	2,071	151	27	129	~
	1959	2,690	~[a]	2,046	161	29	166	~
	1960	2,569	~[a]	1,995	180	32	165	~
	1961	3,007	~[a]	2,368	195	34	185	~
	1962	2,816	~[a]	2,197	193	35	175	~
	1963	2,808	~[a]	2,166	202	36	185	~
	1964	2,780	~[a]	2,133	220	18	199	~
	1965	2,705	~[a]	2,024	246	19	223	192
	1966	2,136	~[a]	1,544	281	18	115	~
	1967	2,081	~[a]	1,481	288	18	131	~
	1968	2,158	~[a]	1,480	347	~[a]	~[a]	23
	1969	2,196	79	1,474	378	~[a]	~[a]	22
	1970	2,241	78	1,440	416	~[a]	~[a]	33
	1971	2,199	~[a]	1,327	461	~[a]	~[a]	31
	1972	2,172	~[a]	1,225	487	28	~[a]	37
	1973	2,051	~[a]	~[a]	517	30	214	70
	1974	1,804	21	659	620	31	244	94
	1975	1,872	~	687	668	32	268	~
	1976	1,571	−21	230	747	~	289	~
	1977	1,896	~	325	932	25	325	~
	1978	2,015	~	290	1,059	26	321	~
	1979	1,797	- -	57	940	22	319	~
	1980	1,908	- -	40	1,032	~	361	~
	1981	2,175	- -	126	1,156	−50	406	~
	1982	2,371	~[e]	~[d]	1,278	−39	445	~[e]
	1983	1,711	~	245	949	−16	180	81
	1984	1,762	~	265	950	−46	163	55
	1985	1,588	~	75	814	−98	253	144
	1986	1,843	~	243	928	101	212	154
LATIN AMERICA	1977	18,882	1,197	1,873	8,409	~	2,411	~[b]
	1978	21,467	1,248	2,148	10,961	~	2,644	~[b]
	1979	22,553	979	2,657	12,048	~	2,385	2,193
	1980	25,964	1,097	3,033	14,044	~	2,806	2,897

Table 2900 (Continued)

U.S. DIRECT INVESTMENT IN LATIN AMERICA, 19 LRC, 1950–86
(Cumulative M US in Book Value)

Country	Year	Total[2]	Mining	Petroleum	Manufacturing[3]	Transport, Communications, and Public Utilities	Trade	Other Industries
LATIN AMERICA (Continued)	1981	38,883	1,916	4,499	15,762	~	3,933	3,978
	1982	33,039	2,295	6,465	15,625	~	3,799	2,113
	1983	24,133	~	7,359	13,995	1,558	2,774	2,523
	1984	25,229	~	6,320	14,566	1,631	2,841	2,595
	1985	27,901	~	5,035	14,760	1,909	2,836	2,323
	1986	34,970	~	5,227	15,193	2,464	2,923	2,162
WORLD	1977	149,848	~	~	~	~	~	149,848
	1978	167,804	~	~	~	~	~	167,804
	1979	186,760	~	~	~	~	~	186,760
	1980	215,578	~	~	~	~	~	215,578
	1981	227,342	~	~	~	~	~	227,342
	1982	221,343	~	~	~	~	~	221,343
	1983	207,203	~	57,574	82,907	10,512	21,278	13,312
	1984	212,994	~	59,089	85,253	10,701	21,790	13,165
	1985	229,748	~	58,030	95,104	11,780	22,710	13,061
	1986	259,890	~	61,151	107,241	14,258	25,246	12,795

1. The table is updated only insofar as U.S. Department of Commerce data permit. Since post-1950 data for several republics (e.g., El Salvador, Nicaragua) have been included only under the general category of "Other Countries" in Latin America, latest data available for some countries are for 1950.
2. Subtotals do not necessarily add to total; finance and insurance excluded here.
3. Includes food products, chemicals and allied products, primary and fabricated metals, machinery, transportation equipment and other manufacturing.

a. Included in "Other."
b. Included in "Total."
c. Includes $262.7 million in agriculture.
d. Suppressed to avoid disclosure of data of individual companies.
e. Less than $500,000 (±).

SOURCE: U.S. Department of Commerce, *Selected Data on U.S. Direct Investment Abroad, 1966–78*; USDC-SCB, 61:8 (Aug. 1981), pp. 31–32; 62:8 (Aug. 1982), pp. 21–22; Aug. 1985, table 10; Aug. 1987.

Table 2901

DIRECT INVESTMENT FLOW,[1] 19 L, 1975–83[a]
(M US; Minus = Debit)

Country	1975	1976	1977	1978	1979	1980	1981	1982	1983
A. ARGENTINA	#	#	83	273	265	788	944	257	183
B. BOLIVIA	53.4	–8.1	–1.2	11.5	18.0	41.5	59.9	36.9	42.1

Continued in SALA, 24-2900.

Table 2902

U.S. DIRECT INVESTMENT ABROAD, 1977–86

(M US)

PART I. LATIN AMERICA

Year	Direct Investment Position	Net Capital Outflows (Minus = Inflows)	Equity and Intercompany Account Outflows (Minus = Inflows)	Reinvested Earnings of Incorporated Affiliates	Income	Fees and Royalties
1977	27,514	3,949	2,526	1,423	3,712	299
1978	31,770	4,014	2,096	1,918	4,779	372
1979	35,220	3,362	438	2,924	6,520	422
1980	38,761	2,833	−533	3,366	6,968	581
1981	38,864	−37	−197	3,497	6,143	671
1982	28,161	−5,138	−6,500	2,137	3,494	590
1983	24,133	−3,692	−3,066	1,712	1,034	514
1984	25,229	324	−2,230	2,554	1,327	151
1985	27,901	3,838	−1,182	1,599	2,109	119
1986	34,970	7,450	~	1,446	2,920	180

PART II. WORLD

Year	Direct Investment Position	Net Capital Outflows (Minus = Inflows)	Equity and Intercompany Account Outflows (Minus = Inflows)	Reinvested Earnings of Incorporated Affiliates	Income	Fees and Royalties
1977	145,990	11,893	5,497	6,396	19,673	3,883
1978	162,727	16,056	4,713	11,343	25,458	4,705
1979	187,858	25,222	6,258	18,964	38,183	4,980
1980	215,375	19,222	2,205	17,017	37,146	5,780
1981	228,348	9,680	−3,803	13,483	32,446	5,813
1982	207,752	−2,369	−4,756	6,375	21,380	5,572
1983	207,203	373	−4,209	9,090	20,449	6,275
1984	212,994	3,858	−5,268	9,126	21,509	3,923
1985	229,748	17,267	−1,912	18,357	32,665	4,224
1986	259,890	28,047	~	18,894	36,697	4,715

SOURCE: USDC-SCB, 59:8 (Aug. 1979); 60:8 (Aug. 1980); 61:8 (Aug. 1981); 62:8
(Aug. 1982); 64:8 (Aug. 1984); 66:8 (Aug. 1986); 67:8 (Aug. 1987).

Table 2903

ACCUMULATED DIRECT INVESTMENT IN LATIN AMERICA BY ORIGIN, 5 L, 1969–76

(M US and %)

Country of Origin	A. ARGENTINA 1973	C. BRAZIL 1971	C. BRAZIL 1976	E. COLOMBIA[1] 1971	E. COLOMBIA[1] 1975	N. MEXICO 1971	N. MEXICO 1975	P. PANAMA 1969	P. PANAMA 1974
I. TOTAL (M US)	2,274	2,911	9,005	503	632	2,997	4,736	214	534
II. %									
United States	39.5	37.7	32.2	55.9	48.1	80.9	68.7	90.8	86.3
Canada	3.9	10.1	5.3	10.1	10.1	1.7	2.3	~	~
Western Europe									
France	8.5	4.5	3.6	3.4	4.3	1.7	1.0	~	~
Germany	4.5	11.4	12.4	2.4	2.5	2.8	2.3	~	~

Continued in SALA 24-2903.

Table 2904

ACCUMULATED FOREIGN DIRECT INVESTMENT BY MAJOR INDUSTRIAL SECTOR, 5 L, 1969–76

Host Country	Year	Total (M US)	Share of Distribution (%) Extraction Sector	Share of Distribution (%) Manufacturing	Share of Distribution (%) Service	Share of Distribution (%) Other
A. ARGENTINA	1973	2,275.2	5.6	65.0	24.5	4.5

Continued in SALA, 23-3211.

Table 2905

ACCUMULATED DIRECT INVESTMENT BY DAC/OECD COUNTRIES,[1] 8 LRC, 1967–78[a]

(M US)

| Country | 1967 | | 1975 | 1978 | |
	DAC/OECD[1]	Other DAC/OECD[2]	DAC/OECD[1]	Other DAC/OECD[2]	DAC/OECD
A. ARGENTINA	1,821	804	2,000	846	3,340
C. BRAZIL	3,728	2,400	9,100	4,521	13,520

Continued in SALA, 24–2905.

Table 2906

BRITISH DIRECT INVESTMENT FLOWS, 9 L, 1969–75

(M US)[1]

Country	1969	1970	1971	1972	1973	1974	1975
A. ARGENTINA	12.7	−.7	−5.1	19.5	6.4	14.3	19.3

Continued in SALA, 23-3209.

Table 2907

PORTFOLIO INVESTMENT FLOW,[1] 19 L, 1976–85

(M SDR)

Country	1976	1978	1979	1980	1981	1982	1983	1984	1985
A. ARGENTINA	−57	81	173	118	957	267	612	361	−603
B. BOLIVIA	#	#	#	−2	#	#	#	#	#
C. BRAZIL	#	#	510	272	−1	−3	−270	−265	−231
D. CHILE	−5	#	39	#	#	#	#	#	#
E. COLOMBIA	−1	−2	−9	−2	−1	−6	−2	−3	−1
F. COSTA RICA	#	16.7	#	94.2	−2.1	−1.8	−2.5	−2.6	−13.2
H. DOMINICAN REP.	#	#	#	#	#	#	#	#	#
I. ECUADOR	4.9	#	#	#	#	#	#	#	#
J. EL SALVADOR	15.4	3.2	−4.4	−.8	#	−.9	.1	~	~
K. GUATEMALA	.1	9.4	4.2	3.0	.3	.4	.1	−9.2	−25.7
L. HAITI	#	#	#	#	#	#	#	#	~
M. HONDURAS	#	−.4	−.1	#	−.2	−.2	.1	−1.8	1.2
N. MEXICO	373	603	−306	−57	845	844	−584	−739	−901
O. NICARAGUA	#	#	#	#	#	#	#	#	#
P. PANAMA	.1	56.2	157.8	−680.3	172.2	318.7	58.6	60.5	~
Q. PARAGUAY	#	#	#	#	6	7.2	3.1	#	8.2
R. PERU	#	#	#	#	#	#	#	#	#
S. URUGUAY	28.2	−6.9	−24.1	−5.2	2.6	−6.2	−14.6	6.6	94.5
T. VENEZUELA	626	99	−57	1,007	70	1,433	188	−125	~
U.S. Dollars per SDR	1.1545	1.2520	1.2920	1.3015	1.1792	1.1040	1.0690	1.0250	1.0153

1. Portfolio Investments are miscellaneous holdings of stocks and bonds issued by foreign governments or corporations which do not usually exceed 25 percent of voting stock. Holdings of more than 25 percent of voting stock are usually considered Direct Foreign Investment (see Direct Investment, tables 2900–2906, above). For definitions, see SALA-SNP, p. 252.

SOURCE: IMF-BPS-Y, 1984; IMF-BPS, Nov. 1984; IMF-BPS, Jan. 1985; IMF-BPS-Y, 1986.

Table 2908

CAPITAL EXPENDITURES BY U.S. MAJORITY-OWNED FOREIGN AFFILIATES,[1] 9 LR, 1981–87

(M US)

Country	Year	All Industries	Mining	Petroleum	Manufacturing Total	Food and Kindred Products	Chemicals and Allied Products	Primary and Fabricated Metals	Machinery, Except Electrical	Electric and Electronic Equipment	Transportation Equipment	Other Manufacturing	Trade	Finance[2]	Other Industries
A. ARGENTINA	1981[a]	635	5	130	434	57	80	~ᶜ	142	4	~ᶜ	~ᶜ	57	#	9
	1982[b]	412	4	124	246	35	60	4	54	3	~ᶜ	~ᶜ	30	#	7
	1983[b]	425	4	124	263	61	42	7	~ᶜ	8	66	~ᶜ	25	#	9
	1984[d]	458	2	132	287	46	63	5	77	7	49	40	20	#	17
	1985	333	2	73	216	42	51	5	75	1	13	29	37	#	6
	1986	263	5	61	149	39	51	3	21	1	10	24	37	#	10
	1987	247	~	56	130	29	40	~ᶜ	5	2	~ᶜ	32	21	18	19
C. BRAZIL	1981[a]	1,640	2	86	1,325	108	247	88	250	60	385	188	175	~ᶜ	~ᶜ
	1982[b]	1,747	1	100	1,434	100	244	251	258	48	335	199	157	25	30
	1983[b]	1,962	~ᶜ	~ᶜ	1,656	119	292	~ᶜ	262	78	308	~ᶜ	165	9	27
	1984[d]	1,506	~ᶜ	125	1,136	62	170	~ᶜ	246	50	159	~ᶜ	187	10	~ᶜ
	1985	1,387	14	96	1,030	60	171	174	197	44	218	167	212	10	24
	1986	1,527	4	103	1,182	66	221	101	226	54	314	200	202	11	24
	1987	1,637	~	110	1,354	84	226	90	258	65	378	254	123	5	31
D. CHILE	1981[a]	287	~ᶜ	34	12	1	5	2	#	#	#	4	43	~ᶜ	~ᶜ
	1982[b]	142	65	27	13	2	3	3	#	1	#	5	21	~ᶜ	~ᶜ
	1983[b]	107	49	16	13	3	4	1	#	1	#	4	15	#	14
	1984[d]	144	78	17	19	1	2	~ᶜ	#	1	#	~ᶜ	25	#	5
	1985	104	~ᶜ	13	11	2	2	3	#	1	#	3	31	2	~ᶜ
	1986	139	75	17	12	3	3	3	#	1	#ᶜ	3	31	#	3
	1987	90	~	8	36	2	2	~ᶜ	#	1	3	2	10	3	32
E. COLOMBIA	1981[a]	345	3	235	61	10	32	3	~ᶜ	1	5	~ᶜ	40	1	6
	1982[b]	529	2	430	64	13	31	~ᶜ	#	2	~ᶜ	9	28	1	5
	1983[b]	602	1	492	73	21	28	3	#	1	~ᶜ	~ᶜ	25	~ᶜ	~ᶜ
	1984[a]	376	1	254	90	24	43	3	#	4	~ᶜ	~ᶜ	25	1	5
	1985	795	~ᶜ	510	41	10	16	1	#	1	1	12	13	2	~ᶜ
	1986	694	~ᶜ	438	63	12	23	2	#	2	1	22	20	1	~ᶜ
	1987	372	~	183	62	16	19	3	#	1	3	20	11	#	115
I. ECUADOR	1981[a]	62	#	25	21	3	5	1	#	2	#	9	17	#	#
	1982[b]	46	#	22	14	3	5	1	#	2	#	3	10	#	#
	1983[b]	48	#	29	11	2	3	1	#	2	#	3	8	#	#
	1984[d]	57	#	36	14	2	8	1	#	1	#	3	4	2	1
	1985	44	#	22	13	2	5	1	#	1	#	4	8	1	#
	1986	65	#	46	9	2	3	#	#	2	#	2	9	1	#
	1987	30	~	38	6	#	3	#	#	1	#	1	4	1	1
N. MEXICO	1981[a]	1,198	3	12	913	123	100	50	24	103	379	135	212	3	55
	1982[b]	933	2	10	745	56	91	33	20	73	328	144	140	2	34
	1983[b]	775	1	4	619	78	92	21	14	67	243	104	112	1	39
	1984[d]	690	#	3	544	52	100	18	7	68	248	51	120	#	23
	1985	788	#	3	623	41	89	16	23	36	335	84	145	1	16
	1986	949	#	3	786	60	91	13	34	38	478	72	145	1	13
	1987	720	~	3	635	35	102	25	123	61	193	96	57	2	14
P. PANAMA	1981[a]	74	#	3	5	2	2	#	#	#	#	1	7	22	37
	1982[b]	43	#	2	4	2	2	#	#	#	#	#	4	18	15
	1983[b]	32	#	2	5	2	2	#	#	#	#	1	6	15	4
	1984[d]	36	#	6	3	1	1	#	#	#	#	1	10	3	14
	1985	20	#	3	2	1	1	#	#	#	#	1	7	2	5
	1986	23	#ᶜ	5	3	1	2	#	#	#	#	1	8	3	4
	1987	38	~	15	3	2	1	#	#	#	#	1	11	4	3

Table 2908 (Continued)

CAPITAL EXPENDITURES BY U.S. MAJORITY-OWNED FOREIGN AFFILIATES,[1] 9 LR, 1981-87

(M US)

Country	Year	All Industries	Mining	Petroleum	Manufacturing								Trade	Finance[2]	Other Industries
					Total	Food and Kindred Products	Chemicals and Allied Products	Primary and Fabricated Metals	Machinery, Except Electrical	Electric and Electronic Equipment	Transportation Equipment	Other Manufacturing			
R. PERU	1981a	455	~c	345	9	2	2	3	#	1	#	2	~c	~c	~c
	1982b	419	32	340	15	2	7	2	#	1	#	4	30	~c	~c
	1983b	361	11	#	11	4	3	1	#	1	#	2	~c	2	2
	1984d	260	~c	191	10	2	2	2	#	1	#	3	25	~c	~c
	1985	108	8	75	4	#	1	#	#	#	#	2	20	1	1
	1986	174	~c	128	6	1	1	#	#	#	#	3	19	2	~c
	1987	86	~	57	9	#	5	2	#	#	#	1	6	#	13
T. VENEZUELA	1981a	377	#	66	197	42	58	7	~c	9	~c	28	93	1	20
	1982b	420	#	60	225	41	55	4	7	4	~c	~c	118	#	17
	1983b	380	#	37	188	57	50	5	~c	5	~c	18	145	#	10
	1984d	247	#	24	170	58	37	4	6	2	~c	~c	42	#	12
	1985	176	#	27	114	38	25	1	2	1	8	39	39	#	5
	1986	159	#	17	101	27	14	1	1	4	12	41	33	1	~c
	1987	153	~	19	97	33	13	~c	#	3	~c	33	23	#	10
LATIN AMERICA	1981a	5,072	13	936	3,077	348	531	154	416	180	669	367	644	27	127
	1982b	4,691	106	1,115	1,760	154	498	298	339	134	663	364	538	46	108
	1983b	4,692	66	704	2,839	347	516	39	276	163	617	132	501	27	105
	1984d	4,176	171	956	2,359	269	445	289	337	149	498	372	477	38	176
	1985	4,125	308	995	2,117	218	371	215	298	92	575	349	519	21	164
	1986	4,463	287	1,052	2,380	231	432	133	282	106	816	379	524	23	197
	1987	3,763	~	640	2,408	211	440	164	387	139	598	468	283	49	313

1. Capital expenditure estimates are for majority-owned nonbank foreign affiliates of nonbank U.S. parents. (An affiliate is majority owned when the combined ownership of all U.S. parents exceeds 50%.) Capital expenditures are those that are made to acquire, add to, or improve property, plant, and equipment, and that are charged to capital accounts. They are on a gross basis; sales and other dispositions of fixed assets are not netted against them. Capital expenditures are in current dollars; they are not adjusted for price changes in host countries or for changes in the value of foreign currencies because the data needed for these adjustments are unavailable.

2. Excludes banking, insurance, and real estate.

a. Based on survey taken in June 1982.

b. Based on survey taken in December 1982.

c. Data suppressed (by source) to avoid disclosure of individual companies.

d. Based on survey taken in December 1983.

SOURCE: USDC-SCB, 63:3 (March 1983); 64:3 (March 1984); 65:3 (March 1985); 67:3 (March 1987).

Table 2909

GROSS PRODUCT OF U.S. MAJORITY-OWNED FOREIGN AFFILIATES,[1] 9 LR

(M US, 1977)

Country	All Industries	Mining	Petroleum	Manufacturing Total	Trade	Finance	Other Industries
A. ARGENTINA	1,449	~2	306	945	143	3	~2
B. BRAZIL	6,485	12	736	5,169	311	26	231

Continued in SALA, 24-2909.

Table 2910

GROSS PRODUCT OF U.S. MAJORITY-OWNED FOREIGN AFFILIATES IN LATIN AMERICA[1]

(M US)

Category	1977
All Industries	16,036
Mining	579
Metal Mining	569
Iron	3
Copper, Lead, Zinc, Gold, and Silver	250
Bauxite, Other Ores, and Services	317
Coal and Other Nonmetallic Minerals	10
Petroleum	3,072
Oil and Gas Extraction	1,194
Crude Petroleum (No Refining) and Gas	1,033
Oil and Gas Field Services	161

Continued in SALA, 24–2910.

Table 2911

CORPORATE BUSINESS ACTIVITY,[1] 18 L

(1982, except asterisk indicates 1983)

A. ARGENTINA

Sales Rank	Company	Type of Business	M US — Sales/Turnover 1982	1982 Profit or Loss	1982 Employees	M US — 1982 Net Assets	Transnational Parent
1	YPF — Yacimentos Petroliferos Fiscales	Petroleum	2,420.7*	7,577.1	31,353	5,357.0	**
2	ENTEL — Emip Nac de Telecomunicaciones	Communications	809.0	–507.3	45,441	10,108.0	**
3	Massalin-Particulares	Tobacco	787.0	29.6	1,800	357.7	Phil mon US

Continued in SALA, 24–2911.

Part X: National Accounts, Government Policy and Finance, and Prices

CHAPTER 30

GOVERNMENT PLANS, REVENUE AND EXPENDITURE, AND MONEY SUPPLY

General notes:

Expenditures may be in projected or disbursed terms; deficits may not
include amortization of the debt and may exclude "off-budget"
spending; for example, for United States in 1981 such spending
reached $21.0 billion more than the registered deficit of $72.6 billion
shown in SALA, 23-2421. (With regard to "off-budget" spending, see
U.S. News and World Report, Oct. 4, 1982, p. 77.)

Central government expenditures may include subsidies for decentralized
agencies.

Note: This volume contains statistics from numerous sources. Alternative
data on many topics are presented. Variations in statistics can be attributed to differences in definition, parameters, coverage, methodology, as
well as date gathered, prepared, or adjusted. See also Editor's Note on
Methodology.

Table 3000

CURRENT DEVELOPMENT PLANS, 17 L

PART I. GOALS

Country	Scope[1]	Duration[3]	AAGR		Yearly % Planned Growth Rate									Share of Public Investment in Total Investment	Yearly % Planned Investment[2]			
			Population	Domestic Demand for Food	GDP	Total Employment	Agricultural Production Total	Cereals	Fertilizer Consumption	Export Earnings Total	Agricultural	Of GDP		Share of Agriculture in Total Investment	Public Investment	Land and Water Development in Total Investment	External Resources in Total Plan Outlay
A. ARGENTINA	PS	1974-77	1.3	2.0	7.5	2.8	6.5	~	~	19.6	~	9.8a	42.0	~	~	~	~
B. BOLIVIA	C/AS	1976-80	2.5	5.0	7.7b	2.9	7.4	6.8	9.2	~	17.9	28.0c	70.0	9.6	10.1	~	31.0

PART II. ACHIEVEMENTS (AAGR)

Country	Year	Total GDP Goal	Result	GDP/C Goal	Result	Total Manufacturing[1] Goal	Result
A. ARGENTINA	1970-75	7.0	3.2	5.5	1.8	8.6	4.5
C. BRAZIL	1972-74	9.0	9.3	6.0	6.6	11.0	10.2

Continued in SALA, 24-3000.

Table 3001

CENTRAL GOVERNMENT CURRENT REVENUES, 19 L, 1970–86
(% of GDP)

	Country	1970	1980	1982	1983	1984	1985	1986[‡]
A.	ARGENTINA[1]	7.8	12.7	11.3	5.9	5.7	10.5	22.5
B.	BOLIVIA	8.7	10.2	7.3	2.6	2.6	7.1	9.7
C.	BRAZIL	9.1	9.3	9.1	25.4	23.2	~	~
D.	CHILE[2]	35.7	34.6	36.0	30.3	31.6	31.2	32.6
E.	COLOMBIA	9.0	8.4	7.6	7.8	7.9	9.2	12.4
F.	COSTA RICA	12.9	12.8	14.4	16.6	16.6	16.6	16.6
H.	DOMINICAN REP.	16.1	14.3	9.5	10.6	10.7	11.2	13.3
I.	ECUADOR	10.6	12.8	11.0	22.1	22.4	25.3	28.5
J.	EL SALVADOR	10.9	11.4	12.3	12.4	13.5	13.4	14.8
K.	GUATEMALA	8.7	9.5	8.4	8.2	7.0	7.8	9.0
L.	HAITI[2]	13.6	9.5	11.6	11.7	11.8	13.2	14.9
M.	HONDURAS	12.3	15.3	13.8	13.4	15.1	15.6	15.7
N.	MEXICO	9.1	16.0	16.3	18.6	17.3	17.3	~
O.	NICARAGUA	10.7	21.5	25.1	31.0	35.0	32.1	32.1
P.	PANAMA	15.7	19.9	20.2	20.4	19.5	20.4	20.3
Q.	PARAGUAY	11.7	9.2	9.3	8.0	8.0	7.9	7.8
R.	PERU	16.1	20.5	17.5	14.2	16.3	17.3	15.0
S.	URUGUAY	13.8	16.2	15.2	15.9	13.5	14.8	15.9
T.	VENEZUELA	18.3	24.7	26.9	24.7	28.8	29.2	24.7

1. National Administration.
2. General Government.

SOURCE: IDB-SPTF, 1985 and 1986, table 19.

Table 3002

CENTRAL GOVERNMENT TAX REVENUES, 19 L, 1970–86
(% of Current Revenue)[1]

	Country	1970	1980	1982	1983	1984	1985	1986[‡]
A.	ARGENTINA[2]	88.1	75.1	78.5	91.6	95.6	85.6	87.4
B.	BOLIVIA	92.9	85.7	67.4	90.5	91.8	~	~
C.	BRAZIL	90.6	72.0	73.9	73.2	67.4	~	~
D.	CHILE[3]	77.1	74.4	52.5	64.0	64.7	64.2	62.0
E.	COLOMBIA	96.4	97.7	97.4	97.0	96.4	95.1	88.4
F.	COSTA RICA	95.6	96.6	97.8	96.3	92.0	92.7	88.5
H.	DOMINICAN REP.	89.7	77.4	88.4	86.1	89.9	93.8	94.4
I.	ECUADOR[3]	94.0	94.9	95.3	84.3	86.1	88.5	95.4
J.	EL SALVADOR	93.8	97.5	86.2	86.0	87.4	86.8	90.5
K.	GUATEMALA	90.0	90.8	85.8	82.8	78.8	78.6	78.9
L.	HAITI[3]	60.1	92.8	88.9	88.8	85.0	87.9	79.6
M.	HONDURAS	89.7	91.7	92.6	88.7	90.2	90.3	84.7
N.	MEXICO	90.3	94.9	93.0	94.2	95.4	94.9	~
O.	NICARAGUA	85.3	89.0	83.2	87.6	89.3	87.0	87.5
P.	PANAMA	80.5	76.0	74.6	74.0	73.6	69.1	75.2
Q.	PARAGUAY	89.1	89.3	86.8	78.7	82.2	85.6	85.8
R.	PERU	86.2	92.3	90.5	89.9	83.3	88.0	89.5
S.	URUGUAY	91.6	92.0	86.6	85.7	90.1	93.2	~
T.	VENEZUELA	63.6	81.6	78.7	83.7	84.4	81.4	76.7

1. Current Revenue: Includes all non-repayable receipts raised by the central government
   in the form of tax and non-tax, revenue, both excludes social security contributions
   and the sale of fixed government capital assets. Current revenue excludes the proceeds
   from central government borrowings and from the issuance of government bonds and
   the sale of other financial assets. In Haiti donations are included under current revenue
   and classified as a form of non-tax revenue.
2. National Administration.
3. General Government.

SOURCE: IDB-SPTF, 1985 and 1986, table 25.

Table 3003

CENTRAL GOVERNMENT DIRECT TAXES, 19 L, 1970–86
(% of Current Revenue)[1]

	Country	1970	1980	1982	1983	1984	1985	1986[‡]
A.	ARGENTINA[2]	33.8	21.8	10.4	4.8	2.7	11.2	13.3
B.	BOLIVIA	17.1	11.5	27.1	22.0	7.9	~	~
C.	BRAZIL	24.1	25.2	29.3	43.8	45.1	~	~
D.	CHILE[3]	~	69.2	15.8	16.8	11.2	10.6	10.0
E.	COLOMBIA	48.3	35.8	34.5	41.3	39.0	35.4	~
F.	COSTA RICA	23.7	22.5	22.9	24.1	20.0	17.6	17.0
H.	DOMINICAN REP.	22.4	20.0	29.9	26.8	25.6	22.4	21.3
I.	ECUADOR[3]	15.8	47.4	56.1	45.1	48.2	40.7	37.4
J.	EL SALVADOR	22.2	30.8	26.6	24.4	22.1	20.4	20.7
K.	GUATEMALA	15.0	13.5	14.7	18.1	12.8	14.6	13.2
L.	HAITI[3]	10.5	15.9	22.0	16.3	16.1	14.9	~
M.	HONDURAS	25.0	31.1	26.7	24.6	24.8	22.9	22.0
N.	MEXICO	39.7	36.9	31.1	23.4	25.0	24.5	~
O.	NICARAGUA	20.9	26.4	20.5	20.0	20.2	19.7	22.3
P.	PANAMA	38.8	34.0	36.6	41.0	39.4	36.4	~
Q.	PARAGUAY	15.4	21.9	30.1	22.5	27.4	28.5	27.5
R.	PERU	33.8	35.5	26.5	24.1	23.4	19.0	26.7
S.	URUGUAY	13.8	19.8	14.7	18.7	14.3	17.0	~
T.	VENEZUELA	48.3	71.9	66.6	59.6	62.3	61.3	47.7

1. For definition of current revenue, see table 3002.
2. National Administration.
3. General Government.

SOURCE: IDB-SPTF, 1985 and 1986, table 26.

Table 3004

CENTRAL GOVERNMENT INCOME TAXES, 19 L, 1970–86
(% of Current Revenue)[1]

	Country	1970	1980	1982	1983	1984	1985	1986[‡]
A.	ARGENTINA[2]	17.7	18.6	7.7	3.6	2.0	6.9	8.7
B.	BOLIVIA	15.0	10.9	27.1	21.8	7.9	~	~
C.	BRAZIL	24.1	25.2	29.3	19.2	21.8	~	~
D.	CHILE[3]	19.4	18.4	23.6	16.8	11.2	~	~
E.	COLOMBIA	45.4	31.0	33.6	41.2	39.0	34.7	~
F.	COSTA RICA	18.2	19.0	22.8	22.0	17.5	15.7	15.0
H.	DOMINICAN REP.	19.1	19.2	24.2	22.0	21.2	20.7	19.7
I.	ECUADOR[3]	15.8	46.8	55.3	32.7	38.0	31.7	28.8
J.	EL SALVADOR	14.2	23.2	20.3	18.7	17.3	15.6	13.6
K.	GUATEMALA	11.3	12.7	13.9	17.3	11.8	12.5	12.1
L.	HAITI[3]	7.0	12.7	16.5	13.5	13.1	12.1	~
M.	HONDURAS	23.9	30.3	25.8	23.7	23.9	22.1	21.3
N.	MEXICO	38.2	36.2	28.9	22.8	24.4	23.9	~
O.	NICARAGUA	9.4	8.3	10.9	14.7	15.4	15.8	18.4
P.	PANAMA	34.0	29.0	31.3	33.9	31.8	31.8	33.6
Q.	PARAGUAY	9.0	17.3	19.3	14.8	12.0	14.3	14.5
R.	PERU	29.8	29.2	14.8	17.4	14.9	12.5	22.1
S.	URUGUAY	8.1	15.8	7.1	12.1	9.6	11.2	~
T.	VENEZUELA	47.9	71.7	66.4	59.3	62.0	61.0	47.3

1. For definition of current revenue see table 3002.
2. National Administration.
3. General Government.

SOURCE: IDB-SPTF, 1985 and 1986, table 27.

Table 3005

CENTRAL GOVERNMENT PROPERTY TAXES, 18 L, 1970–86
(% of Current Revenue)[1]

	Country	1970	1980	1982	1983	1984	1985	1986[‡]
A.	ARGENTINA[2]	15.5	3.2	2.7	1.3	.7	4.3	4.6
B.	BOLIVIA	2.1	.6	.5	.1	#	~	~
C.	BRAZIL	#	#	#	#	#	~	~
D.	CHILE[3]	4.1	.3	.8	#	#	~	~
E.	COLOMBIA	1.6	.1	.3	.1	#	#	~
F.	COSTA RICA	.6	1.3	.9	.7	.6	.4	.5
H.	DOMINICAN REP.	3.3	.7	3.2	2.7	2.3	1.8	1.6
I.	ECUADOR[3]	0	.4	.5	~	~	~	~
J.	EL SALVADOR	6.4	5.9	4.7	4.0	3.2	3.0	5.9
K.	GUATEMALA	3.1	.7	.8	.7	.9	2.0	1.1
L.	HAITI[3]	3.6	1.5	1.7	1.3	1.4	1.2	~
M.	HONDURAS	1.1	.8	1.0	.9	.8	.8	.7
N.	MEXICO	#	#	#	~	~	~	~
O.	NICARAGUA	9.4	7.4	4.6	2.8	3.1	2.2	2.1
P.	PANAMA	4.3	3.9	3.9	4.1	4.6	4.5	~
Q.	PARAGUAY	6.3	4.6	12.0	7.7	5.9	4.8	4.5
R.	PERU	4.0	3.2	3.9	3.6	2.9	2.4	4.6
S.	URUGUAY	5.7	5.6	5.8	6.6	4.7	5.7	~
T.	VENEZUELA	.4	.2	.2	.3	.3	.4	.4

1. For definition of current revenue see table 3002.
2. National Administration.
3. General Government.

SOURCE: IDB-SPTF, 1985 and 1986, table 28.

Table 3006

CENTRAL GOVERNMENT PRODUCTION AND SALES TAX, 19 L, 1970–86
(% of Current Revenue)[1]

	Country	1970	1980	1982	1983	1984	1985	1986[‡]
A.	ARGENTINA[2]	32.8	39.3	44.2	12.3	10.3	29.5	52.5
B.	BOLIVIA	34.5	27.1	16.2	33.2	51.9	~	~
C.	BRAZIL	59.0	28.8	32.7	25.3	18.0	~	~
D.	CHILE[3]	43.4	4.2	3.5	24.6	23.5	23.2	37.6
E.	COLOMBIA	8.6	20.1	40.4	24.7	26.1	27.5	~
F.	COSTA RICA	40.7	39.6	31.4	35.6	41.0	41.5	38.1
H.	DOMINICAN REP.	20.2	21.5	33.8	32.6	35.5	36.0	39.1
I.	ECUADOR[3]	16.5	19.4	20.3	26.5	24.3	35.0	45.7
J.	EL SALVADOR	25.6	28.5	33.2	38.3	40.3	38.2	28.6
K.	GUATEMALA	43.3	39.9	51.2	15.2	32.3	24.9	27.9
L.	HAITI[3]	10.9	10.1	20.2	26.7	27.2	34.0	~
M.	HONDURAS	36.0	24.0	30.8	29.2	29.9	29.9	28.3
N.	MEXICO	27.5	24.0	24.5	30.5	32.2	31.4	~
O.	NICARAGUA	36.3	45.9	44.8	45.8	50.6	56.9	54.4
P.	PANAMA	14.2	26.7	23.3	9.7	9.7	9.3	8.3
Q.	PARAGUAY	27.1	16.2	22.9	18.8	7.3	8.6	9.7
R.	PERU	31.2	37.2	47.1	51.7	47.3	56.1	46.4
S.	URUGUAY	40.3	51.6	53.0	52.5	59.6	57.8	~
T.	VENEZUELA	6.1	3.2	4.9	3.9	2.8	4.0	5.2

1. For definition of current revenue see table 3002.
2. National Administration.
3. General Government.

SOURCE: IDB-SPTF, 1985 and 1986, table 30.

Table 3007

CENTRAL GOVERNMENT INTERNATIONAL TRADE TAXES, 19 L, 1970–86
(% of Current Revenue)[1]

	Country	1970	1980	1982	1983	1984	1985	1986[‡]
A.	ARGENTINA[2]	20.9	11.2	16.0	37.6	32.5	26.2	13.9
B.	BOLIVIA	67.5	56.8	53.1	20.5	27.6	~	~
C.	BRAZIL	7.1	7.2	5.1	4.1	4.3	~	~
D.	CHILE[3]	27.0	.9	3.1	18.0	23.5	25.3	7.7
E.	COLOMBIA	27.3	36.1	21.8	17.6	17.2	19.8	~
F.	COSTA RICA	29.8	26.3	38.1	36.6	31.0	33.6	33.3
H.	DOMINICAN REP.	45.1	31.1	24.7	26.8	28.8	33.5	32.4
I.	ECUADOR[3]	56.6	26.3	19.0	12.7	13.6	12.9	12.3
J.	EL SALVADOR	40.5	37.0	25.2	22.2	24.1	27.8	40.9
K.	GUATEMALA	28.0	34.7	17.1	19.7	20.0	10.2	24.8
L.	HAITI[3]	36.3	58.4	38.7	36.6	29.1	23.9	19.4
M.	HONDURAS	28.6	36.7	35.3	34.8	35.4	37.5	34.4
N.	MEXICO	18.2	27.0	21.5	39.5	37.2	38.3	~
O.	NICARAGUA	28.1	22.7	17.2	7.2	6.7	5.1	8.1
P.	PANAMA	23.5	12.9	12.3	12.9	13.7	13.0	13.8
Q.	PARAGUAY	34.2	33.2	15.2	17.4	11.6	12.0	12.9
R.	PERU	21.3	19.8	21.4	21.7	19.5	20.6	19.3
S.	URUGUAY	20.3	18.4	13.1	13.7	15.4	17.3	16.2
T.	VENEZUELA	7.8	5.4	6.7	17.5	17.2	14.0	19.3

1. For definition of current revenue see table 3002.
2. National Administration.
3. General Government.

SOURCE: IDB-SPTF, 1985 and 1986, table 31.

Table 3008

CENTRAL GOVERNMENT TOTAL EXPENDITURE, 19 L, 1970–86
(% of GDP)

	Country	1970	1980	1982	1983	1984	1985	1986[‡]
A.	ARGENTINA[1]	9.2	15.4	15.0	20.0	12.8	18.7	29.8
B.	BOLIVIA	9.5	17.0	13.5	9.3	32.2	12.0	11.9
C.	BRAZIL	9.5	9.2	9.0	30.8	28.5	~	~
D.	CHILE[2]	40.8	29.1	39.7	34.2	34.6	33.4	33.4
E.	COLOMBIA	10.0	9.6	11.9	11.4	12.1	11.9	14.1
F.	COSTA RICA	12.8	20.9	16.0	20.1	19.6	18.7	20.2
H.	DOMINICAN REP.	17.7	17.5	12.5	13.2	11.4	12.7	14.0
I.	ECUADOR[2]	13.4	14.3	15.5	26.0	25.6	26.5	28.0
J.	EL SALVADOR	12.8	18.6	20.0	21.4	20.7	17.1	18.8
K.	GUATEMALA	9.9	14.2	13.1	11.5	10.9	9.6	10.8
L.	HAITI[2]	14.3	14.9	16.6	23.0	21.9	20.8	20.4
M.	HONDURAS	15.4	23.3	23.5	23.8	26.5	25.0	23.0
N.	MEXICO	10.8	18.8	26.2	27.0	25.0	25.3	~
O.	NICARAGUA	11.9	29.6	36.4	63.8	59.3	54.9	48.9
P.	PANAMA	20.5	26.3	26.8	27.0	25.9	24.1	22.4
Q.	PARAGUAY	11.8	9.5	10.8	10.6	10.9	9.5	7.3
R.	PERU	17.5	23.4	21.6	23.1	21.4	20.2	19.4
S.	URUGUAY	15.1	15.8	23.9	19.9	18.8	17.6	17.1
T.	VENEZUELA	19.4	24.9	28.1	27.0	25.2	27.0	25.9

1. National Administration.
2. General Government.

SOURCE: IDB-SPTF, 1985 and 1986, table 20.

Table 3009

TOTAL EXPENDITURE[1] AND DEFICIT OF CENTRAL GOVERNMENTS, 19 L, 1975–85

(M NC)

Country	Code[2]	1975	1978	1979	1980	1981	1982	1983	1984	1985[‡]
A. ARGENTINA[3]	I	212	4.5	11.9	25.0	59.7	18.3	122.5	594.0	7,578
	II	–155	1.0	2.3	7.9	25.9	–9.2	–82.3	–300.0	2,867
B. BOLIVIA[5]	I	6,395	11,542	15,035	21,521	24,347	3,276	1,862	5,725	~
	II	706	–3,002	–6,651	–9,728	–10,461	–1,378	–6,696	–4,970	~
C. BRAZIL[3]	I	95.4	#	671.4	1,798.9	3,310.1	~	~	~	~
	II	#	4.9	2.3	2.0	3.0	~	~	~	~
D. CHILE[3,4]	I	7.4	94.5	151.2	226.4	291.5	323.4	400.3	501.3	~
	II	.5	5.9	5.9	13.0	25.4	22.7	52.0	59.0	~
E. COLOMBIA[3]	I	39,351	78.2	108.6	163.2	214.9	291.2	344.7	464.6	572.1
	II	–909	5.9	6.0	–11.4	–58.3	–101.4	–106.0	–161.9	126.8
F. COSTA RICA	I	2,942	5,484	6,629	8,279	9,911	16,294	27,656	34,867	30,942.0
	II	–681	–1,458	–2,390	–3,297	–2,457	–3,346	–6,599	–7,586.0	–6,838
H. DOMINICAN REP.	I	653	675	1,005	1,053	1,068	988	1,142	1,248	1,856
	II	–17	–97	–331	–184	–160	–243	–236	–64	–207
I. ECUADOR	I	11,755	26,155	28,189	46,156	53,395	66,536	74,234	106,657.0	170,825.0
	II	609	–7,098	–5,109	8,589	–20,098	–21,647	–14,047	6,785.0	10,777.0
J. EL SALVADOR	I	600	1,158	1,306	1,514	~	~	~	2,514.0	2,874.0
	II	–22	–131	–91	–484	~	~	~	969	–970.0
K. GUATEMALA	I	395	799	922	1,256	1,740	1,820	2,731	1,132.0	1,215.0
	II	–43	–138	–254	–509	–633	–710	–1,469	466.0	–362.0
L. HAITI	I	495	911	1,048	1,202	1,325	1,303	1,318	1,990.0	2,013.0
	II	–270	–370	–442	–511	–664	–540	–472	1,076.0	–889.0
M. HONDURAS	I	438	842	912	1,243	1,906	2,365	2,524	2,842	2,098.0
	II	–155	–301	–280	–485	–672	–1,030	–1,069	–1,173	–1,005.0
N. MEXICO[3]	I	156	476	733	1,061	1,318	2,658	4,607	6,718	11,535.0
	II	–54	–174	–321	–381	–383	–1,126	–1,426	–1,775	3,639.0
O. NICARAGUA	I	2,106	3,287	2,982	6,364	8,412	11,109	20,083	25,235	6,900.0
	II	–783	–1,666	–1,090	–1,838	–3,030	–3,863	–9,870	–9,322	–25.7
P. PANAMA	I	420	648	933	1,065	1,217	1,625	1,370	1,314	1,269.0
	II	–123	–251	–433	–370	–427	–777	–464	–428	–194.0
Q. PARAGUAY[3]	I	18,609	30,776	40,628	52,976	69,977	~	~	~	~
	II	–714	3,557	3,024	–1,385	–8,215	~	~	~	~
R. PERU[3]	I	131.4	430.0	728	1,370	2,276	3,051	6,083	12,496	32,164.0
	II	–43.5	–166	–176	–351	–753	–558	–2,351	–957	–3,999.0
S. URUGUAY	I	1,349	4,751	7,260	13,081	18,817	27,503	33,159	50,560	91,425.0
	II	–363	–401	123	75	–117	–11,210	–7,411	–15,676	–14,638.0
T. VENEZUELA[3]	I	32.3	51.2	51.0	72.9	94.0	180.2	169.9	191.7	99.6
	II	8,553	11,107	–903	–10,172	1,307	–6.5	–20.4	3.0	8.3

1. Current plus capital expenditures.
2. I = Total expenditure;
   II = Deficit (positive number indicates surplus), i.e., current income less total
   expenditure.
3. BNC.
4. M US of 1976.
5. M US at 1970 prices.

a. Excluding treasury certificates issued and redeemed in the same year, since their introduction in 1978.

SOURCE: ECLA-S, 1978, 1979, 1980, 1981, 1984, 1985.

Table 3010

FUNCTIONAL ANALYSIS OF CENTRAL GOVERNMENT EXPENDITURE, 20 LC

(%)

Country	Year	Total Expenditure[1]	General Public Services	Defense	Education	Health	Social Security and Welfare	Housing and Community Amenities	Other Community and Social Services	Subtotal[2] Economic Services	Agriculture, Forestry, Fishing, and Hunting	Roads	Other Transportation and Communication	Other Purposes
A. ARGENTINA	1984	100.0	9.94	8.81	9.51	1.81	37.81	.50	.65	20.26	.88	3.92	5.34	8.55
B. BOLIVIA	1984	100.0	~	5.40	12.23	1.48	5.21	.20	.10	5.29	.53	1.60	2.29	~
C. BRAZIL	1984	100.0	11.21	3.98	3.23	7.64	32.40	.30	.18	14.49	4.63	1.15	1.88	30.30
D. CHILE	1985	100.0	11.26	11.54	13.18	6.07	38.96	4.80	.69	7.07	1.71	3.00	.97	6.42
E. COLOMBIA	1983	100.0	19.78	8.15	21.84	4.61	19.25	4.89	.66	26.08	1.90	11.35	2.19	5.50
F. COSTA RICA	1983	100.0	8.78	3.04	19.37	22.48	14.45	2.67	5.11	20.16	5.30	12.58	.41	10.28
G. CUBA	~	~	~	~	~	~	~	~	~	~	~	~	~	~
H. DOMINICAN REP.	1984	100.0	11.95	8.38	15.13	10.28	8.58	6.61	1.75	35.21	16.17	1.07	7.62	3.44
I. ECUADOR	~	~	~	~	~	~	~	~	~	~	~	~	~	~
J. EL SALVADOR	1985	100.0	13.16	20.34	14.48	5.87	2.86	.58	.32	12.61	3.31	5.21	.47	6.67
K. GUATEMALA	1983	100.0	~	~	~	~	~	~	~	~	~	~	~	~
L. HAITI	1982	100.0	14.49	9.86	7.33	7.39	5.39	.17	4.00	19.55	4.71	7.05	.51	31.82
M. HONDURAS	1976	100.0	27.72	10.49	20.69	14.69	4.73	2.57	.93	18.76	3.10	12.35	~	~
N. MEXICO	1984	100.0	8.48	2.69	12.36	1.52	9.52	2.38	.52	27.18	5.12	1.93	3.69	36.60
O. NICARAGUA	1983	~	~	~	~	~	~	~	~	~	~	~	~	~
P. PANAMA	1982	100.0	29.01	~	11.0	13.14	8.31	3.84	.70	13.48	3.41	~	.58	20.45
Q. PARAGUAY	1984	100.0	12.76	10.24	10.69	5.85	30.41	2.51	.16	22.24	1.65	3.86	.16	5.13
R. PERU	1981	100.0	10.44	13.81	11.34	5.30	.15	.92	1.25	~	4.07	13.32	~	~
S. URUGUAY	1985	100.0	11.02	10.84	6.42	4.05	48.53	.07	.91	8.14	1.01	3.94	1.99	12.03
T. VENEZUELA	1984	100.0	5.40	6.14	17.65	7.61	7.62	7.10	1.50	22.80	3.86	.62	5.44	25.30
UNITED STATES	1985	100.0	5.24	24.94	1.82	11.29	29.17	2.49	.28	8.26	2.64	1.34	1.10	16.70

1. Owing to adjustment items and unallocated transactions, components may not add to totals.

2. Includes other unspecified categories, as well as Agriculture, Roads, and Transportation.

SOURCE: IMF-GFSY, 1986, pp. 34–35.

Table 3011

DEFENSE AND SOCIAL EXPENDITURES,[1] 20 L, 1972–85

| | | Total Expenditure (% of GNP) | | | | Central Government Expenditure[2] Per Capita (1975 dollars) | | | | | | | | | | | | | |
| | | | | | | Defense[3] | | | | Education[4] | | | | Health[5] | | | |
	Country	1972	1981	1983	1985	1972	1981	1983	1985	1972	1981	1983	1985	1972	1981	1983	1985
A.	ARGENTINA	16.5	23.6	22.3	18.0	8.8	11.4	9.1	8.8	8.8	7.3	7.6	9.5	2.9	1.4	1.4	1.8
B.	BOLIVIA	9.2	12.7	11.3	39.9	16.2	22.7	10.8	5.4	30.6	24.4	26.9	12.2	8.6	7.2	3.1	1.5
C.	BRAZIL	16.6	19.5	21.4	21.1	8.3	3.4	4.1	4.0	6.8	3.8	3.7	3.2	6.4	7.4	7.3	7.6
D.	CHILE	42.3	31.0	34.8	35.5	6.1	12.0	12.0	11.5	14.3	14.4	13.7	13.2	8.2	6.4	6.0	6.1
E.	COLOMBIA	13.0	~	~	~	~	~	~	~	~	~	~	~	~	~	~	~
F.	COSTA RICA	18.9	23.7	26.4	24.5	2.8	2.6	3.0	3.0	28.3	23.7	19.4	19.4	3.8	29.7	22.5	22.5
G.	CUBA	~	~	~	~	~	~	~	~	~	~	~	~	~	~	~	~
H.	DOMINICAN REP.	18.5	44.9	15.6	14.2	~	8.9	8.7	8.4	~	13.9	15.3	15.1	~	9.7	10.5	10.3
I.	ECUADOR	~	17.1	14.3	14.5	~	11.8	10.6	11.3	~	30.1	26.0	27.7	~	7.9	7.5	8.3
J.	EL SALVADOR	12.8	18.5	17.4	19.8	6.6	16.8	15.8	20.3	21.4	17.9	16.6	14.5	10.9	8.4	8.4	5.9
K.	GUATEMALA	9.9	16.2	13.1	~	11.0	~	10.6	~	19.4	~	26.0	~	9.5	~	7.5	~
L.	HAITI	14.5	19.4	17.6	18.8	~	~	~	8.4	~	~	~	6.0	~	~	~	5.7
M.	HONDURAS	15.4	~	~	~	12.4	~	~	~	22.3	~	~	~	10.2	~	~	~
N.	MEXICO	12.1	20.8	27.9	24.9	4.2	2.5	2.0	27.7	16.6	18.2	11.0	12.4	5.1	1.9	1.2	1.5
O.	NICARAGUA	15.5	30.2	~	~	12.3	11.0	~	~	16.6	11.6	~	~	4.0	14.6	~	~
P.	PANAMA	~	36.1	40.4	~	~	~	~	~	~	12.8	11.0	~	~	13.2	13.1	~
Q.	PARAGUAY	13.1	10.7	11.7	10.8	13.8	13.2	12.5	10.2	12.0	11.0	120	10.7	3.5	4.5	3.7	5.8
R.	PERU	17.1	20.2	18.6	12.9	14.8	13.8	27.6	~	22.7	11.3	18.5	~	6.2	5.3	6.2	~
S.	URUGUAY	25.0	24.4	25.9	24.8	5.6	12.9	12.7	10.8	9.5	7.7	6.5	6.4	1.6	3.8	3.4	4.1
T.	VENEZUELA	21.3	28.9	27.4	25.6	10.3	3.9	5.2	6.1	18.3	18.3	19.1	17.7	11.7	7.3	8.6	7.6

1. Both current and capital (development) expenditures are included. The inadequate statistical coverage of state, provincial, and local governments and the nonavailability of data for these lower levels of government have dictated the use of only central government data. This may seriously understate or distort the statistical portrayal of the allocation of resources for various purposes, especially in large countries where lower levels of government have considerable autonomy and are responsible for many social services. Great caution should therefore be exercised in using the data for cross-economy comparisons.
2. Central Government Expenditure comprises the expenditure by all government offices, departments, establishments, and other bodies that are agencies or instruments of the central authority of a country. It does not necessarily comprise all public expenditure.
3. Defense Expenditure comprises all expenditure, whether by defense or other departments, for the maintenance of military forces, including the purchase of military supplies and equipment, construction, recruiting, and training. Also falling in this category is expenditure for strengthening the public services to meet wartime emergencies, for training civil defense personnel, and for foreign military aid and contributions to military organizations and alliances.
4. Education Expenditure comprises public expenditure for the provision, management, inspection, and support of preprimary, primary, and secondary schools; of universities and colleges; and of vocational, technical, and other training institutions by central governments. Also included is expenditure on the general administration and regulation of the education system; on research into its objectives, organization, administration, and methods; and on such subsidiary services as transportation and medical and dental services in schools.
5. Health Expenditure covers public expenditure on hospitals, medical and dental centers, and clinics with a major medical component; on national health and medical insurance schemes; and on family planning and preventive care. Also included is expenditure on the general administration and regulation of relevant government departments, hospitals and clinics, health and sanitation, and national health and medical insurance schemes.

SOURCE: WB-WDR, 1983, 1986, table 22; 1987, table 23.

Table 3012

CENTRAL GOVERNMENT EXPENDITURES, LENDING PAYMENTS, AND DEFICITS, 20 LC

(%)

	Country	Year	Code[1]	(1) Total Expenditure and Lending Repayment (2 + 5)	(2) Total Expenditure (3 + 4)	(3) Current Expenditure	(4) Capital Expenditure	(5) Lending Minus Repayment
A.	ARGENTINA	1984	~	100.0	84.38	76.66	7.72	15.62
B.	BOLIVIA	1984	E	100.0	99.77	97.88	1.88	.23
C.	BRAZIL	1984	D	100.0	71.36	70.12	3.91	28.64
D.	CHILE	1985	A	100.0	99.17	89.30	9.88	.83
E.	COLOMBIA	1983	C	100.0	100.14	83.94	22.21	-.14
F.	COSTA RICA	1983	A	100.0	99.30	87.95	17.65	.70
G.	CUBA	~	~	~	~	~	~	~
H.	DOMINICAN REP.	1984	A	100.0	99.21	75.36	19.58	.79
I.	ECUADOR	~	~	~	~	~	~	~
J.	EL SALVADOR	1985	~	100.0	105.01	72.00	8.68	-5.01
K.	GUATEMALA	1983	B	100.0	98.11	74.51	25.23	1.89
L.	HAITI	1982	~	100.0	100.0	89.32	10.68	~
M.	HONDURAS	1976	A	100.0	99.47	63.47	36.00	.53
N.	MEXICO	1984	C	100.0	98.23	79.36	18.87	1.77
O.	NICARAGUA	1983	B	100.0	~	69.47	~	~
P.	PANAMA	1982	A	100.0	95.59	83.08	12.51	4.41
Q.	PARAGUAY	1984	A	100.0	95.40	74.51	20.89	4.60
R.	PERU	1981	~	100.0	100.0	75.54	24.46	~
S.	URUGUAY	1985	~	100.0	97.88	91.77	6.11	2.12
T.	VENEZUELA	1984	~	100.0	92.48	77.95	15.55	7.52
	UNITED STATES	1985	E	100.0	97.36	92.90	4.66	2.64

1. Letters A–G indicate percent of General Government tax revenue accounted by Central
   Government, where data are available, as follows: A, 95 and over; B, 90–94.9;
   C, 80–89.9; D, 70–79.9; E, 60–69.9; F, 50–59.9; G, 20–49.9.

SOURCE: IMF-GFSY, 1986, pp. 36–37.

Table 3013

CENTRAL GOVERNMENT CURRENT SAVINGS, 19 L, 1970–86

(% of GDP)

	Country	1970	1980	1982	1983	1984	1985	1986‡
A.	ARGENTINA[1]	1.2	2.4	1.0	-6.0	-4.5	-4.4	-1.3
B.	BOLIVIA	-.5	-4.5	-4.9	-6.3	-29.1	3.5	.5
C.	BRAZIL	2.7	3.0	3.4	5.8	3.8	~	~
D.	CHILE[2]	6.1	8.4	-2.0	-.2	1.5	2.8	5.0
E.	COLOMBIA	3.0	6.6	.6	-.8	-1.6	.4	1.2
F.	COSTA RICA	2.0	-3.6	.5	.4	.3	1.0	.5
H.	DOMINICAN REP.	4.3	2.6	-.7	.4	1.2	1.6	3.2
I.	ECUADOR[2]	#	.9	-1.8	.2	1.4	5.5	7.2
J.	EL SALVADOR	.3	-.7	-2.7	-2.3	-2.2	.1	1.1
K.	GUATEMALA	.9	.9	.2	.2	-1.1	.2	.2
L.	HAITI[2]	.5	-.6	-.3	-8.5	-7.7	-5.4	-3.5
M.	HONDURAS	1.6	.5	-1.7	-3.1	-1.6	-2.1	-2.3
N.	MEXICO	2.2	1.5	-3.8	-4.5	-4.4	-4.1	~
O.	NICARAGUA	1.8	-1.2	-6.3	-7.4	-8.3	-15.8	-12.2
P.	PANAMA	.9	.7	-1.3	-2.7	-2.0	-1.5	-.2
Q.	PARAGUAY	1.9	2.4	.6	-.9	.4	.9	1.3
R.	PERU	2.8	2.4	.2	-5.0	-1.1	.3	-.5
S.	URUGUAY	#	2.0	-4.7	-2.0	-3.7	-1.0	.3
T.	VENEZUELA	4.5	8.5	8.2	6.1	9.3	9.0	6.1

1. National Administration.
2. General Government.

SOURCE: IDB-SPTF, 1985 and 1986, table 21.

Table 3014

CENTRAL GOVERNMENT OVERALL SURPLUS OR DEFICIT, 19 L, 1970–86
(% of GDP)

	Country	1970	1980	1982	1983	1984	1985	1986‡
A.	ARGENTINA[1]	−1.4	−2.7	−3.7	−14.1	−7.2	−8.3	−6.5
B.	BOLIVIA	−.8	−7.2	−6.4	−6.7	−29.6	−4.9	−2.2
C.	BRAZIL	−.4	.1	.1	−4.0	−4.7	~	~
D.	CHILE[2]	−2.0	5.5	−2.3	−3.6	−2.9	−1.9	−.6
E.	COLOMBIA	−1.0	0	−3.8	−3.5	−4.2	−2.6	−1.8
F.	COSTA RICA	.1	−8.2	−3.0	−3.6	−3.0	−2.0	−3.6
H.	DOMINICAN REP.	−1.6	−3.1	−3.0	−2.5	−.7	−1.2	.6
I.	ECUADOR[2]	−2.8	−1.5	−4.5	.7	1.2	1.6	2.8
J.	EL SALVADOR	−1.6	−6.7	−7.7	−8.9	−7.1	−2.7	−1.8
K.	GUATEMALA	−1.3	−4.7	−4.7	−3.3	−3.8	−1.8	−1.4
L.	HAITI[2]	−.7	−5.4	−6.5	−3.4	−6.3	−2.2	−3.1
M.	HONDURAS	−3.1	−8.0	−9.7	−9.9	−9.5	−7.7	−5.6
N.	MEXICO	−1.7	−2.9	−9.8	−8.5	−7.7	−8.0	~
O.	NICARAGUA	−1.2	−9.0	−12.0	−31.3	−23.3	−22.0	−15.8
P.	PANAMA	−4.8	−6.0	−6.6	−6.3	−5.7	−3.4	−2.0
Q.	PARAGUAY	−.1	−.2	−.6	−2.6	−2.9	−1.5	.6
R.	PERU	−1.4	−2.8	−3.9	−8.9	−5.0	−2.7	−4.4
S.	URUGUAY	−1.3	.1	−7.2	−4.0	−5.3	−2.8	−1.2
T.	VENEZUELA	−1.2	−.2	−1.3	−2.3	3.6	2.3	−1.2

1. National Administration
2. General Government.

SOURCE: IDB-SPTF, 1985 and 1986, table 22.

Table 3015

CENTRAL GOVERNMENT NET DOMESTIC BORROWING, 19 L, 1970–86
(% of GDP)

	Country	1970	1980	1982	1983	1984	1985	1986‡
A.	ARGENTINA[1]	1.1	1.9	6.2	16.4	7.8	1.3	3.9
B.	BOLIVIA	.9	3.4	5.8	17.5	30.7	4.8	−1.7
C.	BRAZIL	.4	−.1	−.1	3.9	3.5	~	~
D.	CHILE[2]	2.0	−4.7	2.6	3.6	2.2	−.6	−2.7
E.	COLOMBIA	−.1	−1.0	3.2	3.7	3.6	2.0	1.2
F.	COSTA RICA	−.7	7.1	2.0	1.8	1.2	.5	1.8
H.	DOMINICAN REP.	.7	1.4	2.3	1.8	.1	#	#
I.	ECUADOR[2]	2.8	1.0	2.1	3.2	1.6	−.5	.2
J.	EL SALVADOR	1.3	5.3	5.0	.6	1.9	.8	.6
K.	GUATEMALA	−.1	3.3	3.6	2.8	2.9	1.4	−.1
L.	HAITI[2]	.3	2.9	2.7	1.6	4.5	1.9	.9
M.	HONDURAS	.8	2.9	3.0	4.8	2.8	3.2	3.0
N.	MEXICO	1.4	2.3	7.8	5.6	6.0	7.8	~
O.	NICARAGUA	.1	4.7	9.2	24.9	19.2	13.7	8.9
P.	PANAMA	.7	−.7	−.6	3.3	4.2	1.8	~
Q.	PARAGUAY	−.1	−.2	.6	1.9	1.9	.8	−.7
R.	PERU	.8	2.5	.9	4.1	1.0	−.6	~
S.	URUGUAY	1.2	−.1	7.4	4.2	5.6	3.2	1.4
T.	VENEZUELA	.5	−2.9	.1	2.8	−2.4	−1.1	3.1

1. National Administration.
2. General Government.

SOURCE: IDB-SPTF, 1985 and 1986, table 23.

Table 3016

CENTRAL GOVERNMENT NET FOREIGN BORROWING, 19 L, 1970-86
(% of GDP)

	Country	1970	1980	1982	1983	1984	1985	1986‡
A.	ARGENTINA[1]	.3	.7	-2.5	-2.3	-.6	~	3.8
B.	BOLIVIA	#	3.9	-.6	-.1	-.1	.1	3.9
C.	BRAZIL	.0	.0	.0	-.4	.6	~	~
D.	CHILE[2]	.0	-.8	-.3	.0	.8	2.6	3.2
E.	COLOMBIA	1.1	1.0	.6	-.2	.6	.6	.5
F.	COSTA RICA	.6	1.1	1.0	1.8	1.9	2.5	1.8
H.	DOMINICAN REP.	1.0	1.6	.7	.4	.9	1.6	1.0
I.	ECUADOR[2]	#	.5	2.4	~	~	~	~
J.	EL SALVADOR	.3	1.4	2.7	8.4	5.2	1.9	1.2
K.	GUATEMALA	1.3	1.4	1.1	.9	.2	.7	.6
L.	HAITI[2]	.4	2.6	3.8	1.9	1.8	.3	2.1
M.	HONDURAS	2.4	5.1	6.7	5.0	6.7	4.5	2.6
N.	MEXICO	.3	.6	2.0	2.9	1.7	.2	~
O.	NICARAGUA	1.1	4.3	2.8	6.4	4.1	8.3	6.9
P.	PANAMA	3.6	6.8	7.2	3.0	1.6	2.0	~
Q.	PARAGUAY	.4	.5	~	.7	1.4	.8	.1
R.	PERU	.6	.3	3.1	4.8	3.9	3.0	~
S.	URUGUAY	.2	.1	-.2	-.2	-.3	-.4	-.2
T.	VENEZUELA	.6	3.1	1.2	-.6	-1.2	-1.2	-1.9

1. National Administration.
2. General Government.

SOURCE: IDB-SPTF, 1985 and 1986, table 24.

Table 3017

CENTRAL GOVERNMENT INTEREST PAYMENTS, 19 L, 1970-86
(% of Total Expenditures)

	Country	1970	1980	1982	1983	1984	1985	1986‡
A.	ARGENTINA[1]	3.2	.3	1.2	.4	5.9	15.4	9.4
B.	BOLIVIA	5.3	10.5	11.0	7.1	4.7	~	~
C.	BRAZIL	4.5	5.1	2.5	12.1	20.9	~	~
D.	CHILE[2]	2.5	2.9	1.4	3.5	3.9	5.8	4.9
E.	COLOMBIA	4.7	5.4	6.0	~	~	5.7	7.6
F.	COSTA RICA	10.9	13.6	11.8	14.4	13.1	12.9	12.9
H.	DOMINICAN REP.	.5	7.3	6.2	7.8	5.9	4.7	.9
I.	ECUADOR[2]	12.3	8.8	18.5	16.9	17.9	15.0	11.1
J.	EL SALVADOR	1.2	2.4	9.0	8.4	8.0	7.0	7.6
K.	GUATEMALA	4.2	4.0	6.5	7.6	8.0	7.2	12.3
L.	HAITI[2]	4.1	2.5	3.3	2.1	.6	.3	~
M.	HONDURAS	3.3	4.7	6.1	8.9	8.5	9.3	11.8
N.	MEXICO	9.4	9.6	20.9	35.3	35.8	36.7	~
O.	NICARAGUA	2.6	7.6	12.8	5.9	3.2	4.3	2.2
P.	PANAMA	5.3	21.4	26.9	25.3	23.9	27.4	27.9
Q.	PARAGUAY	2.8	3.3	3.2	3.1	4.2	5.1	7.3
R.	PERU	5.2	18.4	18.3	23.2	23.5	25.3	14.2
S.	URUGUAY	3.1	2.2	4.2	6.1	9.5	11.5	10.4
T.	VENEZUELA	1.6	6.8	7.5	8.7	8.7	10.9	12.7

1. National Administration.
2. General Government.

SOURCE: IDB-SPTF, 1985 and 1986, table 35.

Table 3018

ARGENTINA CENTRAL GOVERNMENT REVENUE, EXPENDITURE, AND FINANCING THE DEFICIT, 1975–85

(B NC)

Category	1975	1977	1978	1979	1980	1981	1982	1983	1984	1985[‡]
1. Current Income	57	1,388	3.5	9.5	17.1	33.9	9.1	40.2	294.2	4,711
Tax Revenue	47	1,196	2.8	6.8	15.3	29.3	8.2	35.8	276.3	4,134
Non-Tax Revenue	9	192	.8	2.7	1.9	4.5	.9	4.4	17.9	577
2. Current Expenditure	182	1,422	3.9	10.3	22.1	48.6	16.4	84.2	444.3	4,259
Wages and Salaries	47	490	1.5	3.9	9.2	17.7	3.9	17.5	113.9	~
Non-Personal Goods and Services	~	167	.5	1.1	2.4	5.5	1.3	5.5	19.0	211
Interest	11	97	.2	.4	.1	.4	5.7	13.2	107.6	984
Transfers	114	660	1.6	4.8	10.2	24.3	5.6	46.1	197.5	2,067
Other Current Expenditure	10	8	~	.1	.2	.7	.6	2.9	6.3	79
3. Current Savings[1]	-125	-34	-.4	-.8	-4.9	-14.7	-7.3	-44.0	-150.1	453
4. Capital Expenditure	189	463	.6	1.6	2.9	11.1	1.9	38.3	149.7	3,320
Real Investment	7	184	.4	1.0	1.6	4.8	.8	2.2	6.8	33
Loans (Net of Repayments)	23	279	.2	.6	1.3	6.3	1.2	36.1	142.8	3,287
5. Total Expenditure[2]	212	1,885	4.5	11.9	25.0	59.7	18.3	122.5	594.0	7,578
6. Fiscal Deficit[3]	-155	-497	1.0	2.3	7.8	25.9	-9.2	-82.3	-299.8	2,867
7. Financing Deficit										
Central Bank	119	312	~	~	9.8	27.8	7.1	104.0	268.1	1,034
Unified Official Account Fund	20	231	.4	1.0	1.6	1.6	.6	3.2	22.4	42
Issue of Securities[4]	27	471	1.7	4.3	2.7	16.1	5.4	5.5	67.0	842
Bond of Amortization Payments	-11	-561	-1.0	-2.9	-1.5	-2.4	-2.1	-2.0	-56.6	-749
Other	#	44	.1	-.1	-.5	-2.3	-.3	-28.2	-1.0	1,746

1. Current Income minus Current Expenditure.
2. Current Expenditure plus Capital Expenditure.
3. For 1975 and 1976 the National Treasury calculated the deficit by considering Amortization of the Public Debt as expenditure and Issues of Securities as income.
4. Less debt amortization payments (1975 and 1976).

SOURCE: ECLA-S, 1978–80, 1984 and 1985.

Table 3019

BOLIVIA CENTRAL GOVERNMENT REVENUE, EXPENDITURE, AND FINANCING THE DEFICIT, 1975–85

Category	M NC					B NC				
	1975	1977	1978	1979	1980	1981	1982	1983	1984	1985[‡]
1. Current Income	5,689	7,641	8,540	8,384	11,793	14.0	19.2	46.9	560	193,035
Inland Revenue	1,724	2,748	3,165	3,621	4,460	5.1	7.9	22.5	216	23,452
Custom Revenue	1,550	1,694	1,960	2,064	2,563	3.1	3.8	5.8	123	22,702
Additional Export Tax	622	535	470	807	127	~	~	~	83	5,885
Mining Royalties	478	1,258	1,545	1,333	1,771	.9	1.7	1.6	79	127,811
Petroleum and Gas Royalties	819	918	919	80	1,852	2.4	4.2	4.5	59	13,185
Other Income	496	488	481	480	1,020	2.5	1.6	12.5	8,234	2,028,751
2. Current Expenditure	6,395	10,954	11,542	15,035	21,521	24.2	130.2	356.1	1,730	124,332
Personal Services	2,686	3,795	4,704	5,948	9,706	11.9	23.5	77.8	101	14,542
Non-personal Services	~	~	513	587	946	1.1	2.6	4.7	175	14,816
Materials and Supplies	744	931	684	692	1,512	2.5	3.3	10.5	110	8,201
Fixed and Financial Assets	230	293	256	317	1,345	1.6	1.6	5.5	546	36,037
Public Debt	845	925	1,165	1,831	3,817	3.1	75.9	171.7	4,481	14,408
Transfers and Contributions	1,789	3,153	3,211	3,424	2,552	2.7	5.9	30.7	1,091	1,816,415
Other Expenditure	300	1,857	1,009	2,236	1,642	1.3	17.4	55.2	~	~
3. Deficit	-706	-3,113	-3,002	-6,651	-9,728	-10.2	-111.0	309.2	7,674	1,835,716

SOURCE: ECLA-S, 1978–81, 1984, 1985.

Table 3020

BRAZIL CENTRAL GOVERNMENT REVENUE, EXPENDITURE, AND FINANCING THE DEFICIT, 1975–81

(B NC)

Category	1975	1976	1977	1978	1979	1980	1981[‡]
1. Current income	76.8	116.2	242.9	349.2	509.8	1,219.4	2,262.0
Tax Income	~	~	211.0	309.6	445.1	958.2	1,837.2

Continued in SALA, 24–3020.

Table 3021

CHILE CENTRAL GOVERNMENT REVENUE; EXPENDITURE, AND FINANCING THE DEFICIT, 1975–84

Category	1975	1976	1977	1978	1979	1980	1981	1982	1983	1984[‡]
A. INCOME AND EXPENDITURE IN NATIONAL CURRENCY										
(Billions of current pesos of each year)										
1. Current Income	7.9	25.2	57.6	100.4	157.1	239.4	319.9	300.7	348.3	442.3
Direct Taxes	2.4	6.5	14.7	24.7	45.3	65.6	81.1	80.1	70.0	86.5
Indirect Taxes	5.1	18.0	41.7	69.6	104.3	154.1	203.7	190.7	260.3	339.6
Non-tax Revenue	.4	.7	1.8	6.1	7.5	19.7	35.1	29.9	18.6	16.2
2. Total Expenditure	7.4	24.1	57.0	94.5	151.2	226.4	291.5	323.4	400.3	501.3
Servicing of Public Debt	~	.3	1.0	1.2	7.8	15.8	2.9	4.2	13.0	34.6
Other Expenditure	7.4	23.8	56.0	93.3	143.4	210.6	288.7	319.2	387.3	466.7
3. Deficit (1–2)	.5	1.1	.6	5.9	5.9	13.0	28.4	22.7	52.0	59.0
4. Deficit/Total (Percentage)	6.1	4.6	1.0	6.2	3.9	5.8	9.7	–7.0	–13.0	–11.8
B. INCOME AND EXPENDITURE IN FOREIGN CURRENCY										
(Millions of dollars at current prices)										
1. Current Income	219	383	374	360	864	1,007	523	439	548	422
Copper	177	352	353	331	840	976	449	402	518	361
Other	42	31	21	29	24	31	74	37	30	61
2. Total Expenditure	556	695	624	675	679	1,178	1,550	564	648	667
Service of Public Debt	388	544	445	507	524	958[a]	1,270[b]	410	462	369
Other Expenditure	168	151	179	168	156	220	280	154	18	298
3. Deficit (1–2)	–337	–312	–250	–315	184	–171	–1,037	–125	–100	245
4. Deficit/Total Expenditure (Percentage)	–60.6	–44.9	–40.1	–46.7	27.1	–14.5	–66.9	–22.2	–15.4	–36.7
C. CONSOLIDATED INCOME AND EXPENDITURE										
(Millions of dollars at 1976 prices)										
1. Current Income	2,360	2,313	2,499	2,688	3,104	3,579	3,842	3,239	3,025	3,235
Copper	193	352	314	253	509	519	219	192	244	166
Direct Taxes	674	515	564	604	752	842	915	809	559	598
Indirect Taxes	1,388	1,384	1,553	1,681	1,717	1,963	2,291	1,926	2,070	2,337
Non-tax Revenue	105	62	68	150	126	255	417	312	152	134
2. Total Expenditure	2,607	2,540	2,699	2,788	2,896	3,504	4,025	3,528	3,485	3,753
Servicing of Public Debt	447	566	435	418	446	710[c]	652[d]	238	321	407
Other Expenditure	2,160	1,974	2,264	2,370	2,450	2,797	3,373	3,290	3,164	3,346
3. Deficit (1–2)	–247	–227	–200	–200	208	75	–183	–289	–460	–518

a. Includes advance payments of US $422 million.
b. Includes advance payments of US $867 million.
c. Includes advance payments of US $346 million at 1976 prices.
d. Includes advance payments of US $423 million at 1976 prices.

SOURCE: ECLA-S, 1984.

Table 3022

COLOMBIA CENTRAL GOVERNMENT REVENUE, EXPENDITURE, AND FINANCING THE DEFICIT, 1975–85

(B NC)

Category	1975	1977	1978	1979	1980	1981	1982	1983	1984	1985[‡]
1. Current Income	38.4	63.4	84.1	114.6	151.8	156.6	189.8	238.7	302.7	445.3
Tax Revenue	37.4	62.2	82.0	112.6	148.8	152.8	184.8	231.6	291.2	430.1
Income and Complementary Taxes	18.0	23.9	30.4	37.3	47.1	53.0	65.2	97.8	118.2	157.9
Sales Taxes	7.7	12.6	17.5	23.0	30.5	40.3	49.6	58.7	.4	3.3
Customs Duties and Surcharges	5.4	9.4	13.4	16.6	24.8	29.4	36.6	37.8	79.1	124.0
Profits on Exchange Operations	3.6	8.8	10.9	23.8	30.1	~	~	~	48.3	84.0
Gasoline Taxes	1.7	4.5	5.8	8.0	11.3	18.1	20.1	24.7	3.6	5.6
Other	.8	3.0	4.0	4.3	4.9	4.8	6.7	8.8	30.6	37.7
Non-tax Revenue	.9	1.2	2.1	2.0	3.0	3.8	5.0	7.1	12.2	20.9
2. Current Expenditure	26.1	41.4	57.1	82.6	121.3	153.8	211.0	262.9	10.7	15.2
3. Current Savings	12.2	22.0	26.9	31.9	30.6	2.8	−21.2	−24.2	362.4	421.8
4. Investment	13.1	16.2	21.0	26.0	42.0	61.1	80.2	81.8	102.4	150.3
5. Total Expenditure	39.3	57.6	78.2	108.6	163.3	214.9	291.2	344.7	464.6	572.1
6. Fiscal Deficit (or surplus)	−.9	5.8	5.9	6.0	−11.4	−58.3	−101.4	−126.0	161.9	126.8
7. Financing of Deficit										
External Credit	−.5	−1.6	−2.2	5.2	16.5	19.5	14.9	9.9	3.0	8.1
Domestic Credit	1.3	−4.2	−3.7	−11.2	−5.9	38.8	80.5	96.1	126.4	118.7

SOURCE: ECLA-S, 1978–81, 1984, 1985.

Table 3023

COSTA RICA CENTRAL GOVERNMENT REVENUE, EXPENDITURE, AND FINANCING THE DEFICIT,[1] 1975–85

(M NC)

Category	1975	1976	1977	1979	1980	1981	1982	1983	1984	1985[‡]
1. Current Income	2,261	2,693	3,487	4,239	4,982	7,454	12,948	21,057	27,281	24,104
Tax Revenue	2,090	2,520	3,281	4,126	4,692	6,933	12,281	19,870	24,426	22,549
Direct	447	612	781	1,066	1,080	1,555	3,014	4,860	4,895	4,010
Indirect	1,643	1,170	1,501	3,060	3,612	2,255	3,573	6,264	~	18,539
On Foreign Trade	678	738	999	~	~	3,123	5,694	6,746	19,531[a]	
Non-tax Revenue	171	173	206	103	290	521	667	1,187	−2,855	23,045
2. Current Expenditure	2,210	2,727	3,372	5,152	6,349	7,938	13,108	21,514	25,999	9,116
Wages and Salaries	1,384	1,667	2,006	~	~	3,483	5,131	7,524	8,850	13,929
Other Current Expenditures	326	1,060	1,366	~	~	4,455	7,977	13,990	17,149	1,059
3. Current Saving (1–2)	51	−34	−115	−913	−1,367	−484	−160	−457	1,282	7,897
4. Capital Expenditure	732	1,251	1,282	1,477	1,930	1,973	3,186	6,142	8,932	3,375
Real Investment	370	625	696	~	~	1,201	1,444	2,843	4,252	~
Debt Amortization Payments	210	262	299	~	~	420	−807	1,164	2,839	2,283
Other Capital Expenditures	152	364	287	~	~	352	935	2,135	1,841	2,239
5. Total Expenditures (2+4)	2,942	3,978	4,654	6,629	8,279	9,911	16,294	27,656	34,931	30,942
6. Fiscal Deficit (1–5)	−681	−1,285	−1,167	−2,390	−3,297	−2,457	−3,346	−6,599	−7,650	−6,838
7. Financing of Deficit										
Domestic Financing	452	1,034	857	1,725	2,838	1,551	1,967	4,731	5,165	~
Central Bank	24	120	81	~	~	4,696	−1,533	−836	~	~
Issue of Securities	161	436	548	~	~	1,532	1,935	4,032	~	~
Other	268	478	228	~	~	−4,677	1,565	1,535	~	~
External Financing	229	251	310	665	459	906	1,379	1,868	2,485	~

1. Includes extra budgetary operations.

a. Includes indirect tax revenue.

SOURCE: ECLA-S, 1978–80, 1984, and 1985.

Table 3024

DOMINICAN REPUBLIC CENTRAL GOVERNMENT REVENUE, EXPENDITURE,
AND FINANCING THE DEFICIT, 1975–85

(M NC)

Category	1975	1977	1978	1979	1980	1981	1982	1983	1984	1985[‡]
1. Current Income	636	620	578	674	869	908	745	906	1,184	1,649
Tax Revenue	592	589	552	623	696	735	661	782	1,085	1,549
Direct	142	126	129	151	220	225	223	243	289	371
Indirect	95	140	144	166	189	238	253	296	428	596
On Foreign Trade	332	296	251	276	287	272	185	243	343	551
Others	22	27	28	30	~	~	~	~	~	~
Non-tax Revenue	45	31	26	51	173	173	84	124	100	100
Extraordinary Income	21	~	~	~	~	~	~	~	~	~
2. Total Expenditure	653	631	675	1,005	1,053	1,068	988	1,142	1,248	~
Current Expenditure	353	368	443	644	729	776	792	878	1,004	1,415
Capital Expenditure	300	263	232	356	324	292	196	264	244	~
Real Investment	249	176	155	97	128	121	98	116	78	131
Amortization of the Debt	8	15	17	25	~	~	~	~	~	~
Capital Transfers	43	65	53	166	193	160	83	118	116	~
Other Expenditures	~	7	7	68	3	11	15	30	50	~
3. Fiscal Deficit (–) or Surplus	–17	–11	–97	–331	–184	–160	–243	–236	–64	–207

SOURCE: ECLA-S, 1978–80, 1984, and 1985.

Table 3025

ECUADOR CENTRAL GOVERNMENT REVENUE, EXPENDITURE,
AND FINANCING THE DEFICIT, 1975–85

(M NC)

Category	1975	1977	1978	1979	1980	1981	1982	1983	1984	1985[‡]
1. Total Income[1]	12,364	16,453	13,057	23,080	37,631	39,297	45,996	60,187	99,872	181,602
Current Income	12,364	17,282	19,660	23,722	38,512	40,510	47,787	60,850	99,924	182,903
Traditional	~	14,628	17,501	19,372	23,915	25,379	25,741	31,864	51,052	71,842
Tax Revenue	10,826	16,262	16,748	18,445	22,445	23,744	23,454	30,526	48,111	68,002
Direct	3,333	4,722	2,954	3,419	4,179	6,137	6,007	7,153	9,428	14,221
Indirect	2,376	3,923	5,541	6,527	8,616	8,098	9,037	12,740	21,262	30,457
On Foreign Trade	5,184	7,617	8,253	8,499	9,650	9,509	8,410	10,633	17,421	23,324
Other Income	1,815	1,019	753	927	1,470	1,635	2,287	1,338	2,942	3,841
From Petroleum	2,490	2,654	2,159	4,350	14,229	15,131	21,627	28,950	46,804	109,185
2. Total Expenditure	11,755	20,745	26,155	28,189	47,557	59,395	64,579	74,018	106,657	170,825
3. Deficit (1-2)	609	4,293	–7,098	–5,109	9,926	–20,098	18,583	–13,832	–6,785	10,777
4. Financing	~	3,799	6,394	3,890	5,733	16,838	18,583	13,832	6,785	–10,777
Indebtedness	–237	3,549	6,541	4,260	5,956	8,301	17,587	14,189	9,472	10,078
Foreign	–235	1,081	1,179	~	1,553	7,658	9,988	–2,250	–4,058	–4,446
Domestic	2	2,468	5,362	4,260	4,403	643	7,599	16,439	13,530	–5,632
Cash Balances[2]	–1,176	250	–147	–370	–284	–1,220	280	–358	–2,687	–699
Difference (3-4)[3]	~	494	704	1,219	4,193	3,260	~	~	~	~

1. Net total income taxes paid with savings certificates and agrarian reform bonds have
    been deducted.
2. Use or net accumulation of funds during the financial year, according to whether the
    balance is positive or negative.
3. Balance of payments deferred until the next year (positive sign) and of payments made
    to cover expenditure of the previous year (negative sign).

SOURCE: ECLA-S, 1978–80, 1984, and 1985.

Table 3026

EL SALVADOR CENTRAL GOVERNMENT REVENUE, EXPENDITURE, AND FINANCING THE DEFICIT, 1975–85

(M NC)

Category	1975	1977	1978	1979	1980	1981	1982	1983	1984	1985[‡]
1. Current Income	578	1,182	1,027	1,215	1,040	1,107	1,110	1,262	1,545	1,903
Tax Revenue (a + b)	541	1,131	972	1,162	989	990	952	1,080	1,351	1,653
a. Direct	154	237	286	277	312	297	294	306	341	406
b. Indirect	~	894	686	885	677	693	658	774	1,010	1,248
c. On Foreign Trade	205	624	401	571	375	322	279	279	373	483
d. Non-tax Revenue	37	51	55	53	51	117	158	182	194	250
2. Current Expenditure	445	680	783	862	1,077	1,233	1,347	1,493	1,797	2,003
Wages and Salaries	229	349	411	475	618	657	~	~	~	~
Other Current Expenditure	217	331	372	387	459	576	~	~	~	~
3. Current Savings (1–2)	133	502	244	353	–37	–126	–237	–231	–118	–99
4. Capital Expenditure	154	352	375	444	584	507	472	1,238	717	871
Real Investment	62	214	219	274	438	381	298	366	383	506
Debt Amortization Payments	20	29	33	29	21	60	77	607	267	224
Other Capital Expenditure	73	109	123	141	125	66	97	265	67	141
5. Total Expenditure (2+4)	600	1,032	1,158	1,306	1,514	1,740	1,820	2,731	2,514	2,874
6. Fiscal Deficit (–) or Surplus (1–5)	–22	150	–131	–91	–484	–633	–710	–1,469	–969	–970
7. Financing of Deficit										
Domestic Financing[1]	–62	–199	72	33	393	375	448	641	361	528
Central Bank	~	~	8	–8	143	176	~	25	–6	~
Issue of Securities	~	~	22	100	300	299	333	–94	421	200
Other	~	~	42	–59	–50	–100	115	710	–54	~
External Financing	83	49	59	58	91	258	262	828	608	442

1. Includes financing provided by the Central Reserve Bank of El Salvador, sale of securities, changes in treasury position, use of balances remaining from previous financial years, etc. (1975–76).

SOURCE: ECLA-S, 1978–80, 1984, and 1985.

Table 3027

GUATEMALA CENTRAL GOVERNMENT REVENUE, EXPENDITURE, AND FINANCING THE DEFICIT, 1975–85

(M NC)

Category	1975	1977	1978	1979	1980	1981	1982	1983	1984	1985[‡]
1. Current Income	330	591	661	668	747	741	730	741	666	853
Tax Revenue (a + b)	301	557	621	621	678	652	626	573	498	673
a. Direct	63	80	102	97	100	110	108	134	86	124
b. Indirect	135	477	519	524	578	542	518	439	412	549
c. On Foreign Trade	91	249	264	241	259	171	125	106	107	88
2. Current Expenditure	269	405	476	540	678	759	710	721	767	830
Wages and Salaries	~	181	~	~	~	~	~	~	~	~
Other Current Expenditure	~	224	~	~	~	~	~	20	–101	23
3. Saving on Current Account (1–2)	61	186	185	128	69	–18	20	20	–101	23
4. Capital Expenditure	126	284	323	382	578	724	548	376	365	385
Real Investment[2]	85	204	216	310	438	621	432	316	263	269
Debt Amortization Payments	31	57	64	72	140	103	116	60	102	116
Other Capital Expenditure	~	23	43	~	~	~	~	~	~	~
5. Total Expenditure (2+4)	395	689	799	922	1,256	1,483	1,258	1,097	1,132	1,215
6. Fiscal Deficit (1–5)	–43	–98	–138	–254	–509	–742	–528	–356	–466	–362
7. Financing of Deficit										
Domestic Financing[1]	52	57	37	122	391	634	416	256	413	281
External Financing	19	41	101	132	118	108	112	100	53	81

1. Includes the floating debt (1975, 1976).
2. Includes other capital expenditure.

SOURCE: ECLA-S, 1978–80, 1984, and 1985.

Table 3028

HAITI CENTRAL GOVERNMENT REVENUE, EXPENDITURE, AND FINANCING THE DEFICIT,[1] 1975–85

(M NC)

Category	1975	1977	1978	1979	1980	1981	1982	1983	1984	1985[‡]
1. Current Income	225	358	541	606	691	661	763	846	914	1,124
Tax Revenue	185	299	428	494	629	645	710	831	907	1,104
Direct and Indirect	73	108	210	250	268	366	457	536	594	798
On Foreign Trade	112	191	218	244	361	279	253	295	313	306
2. Current Expenditure	204	269	325	407	540	797	817	807	1,775	1,803
Wages and Salaries	123	147	180	208	293	355	402	418	~	~
Other Current Expenditure	~	122	145	199	247	319	337	327	~	~
3. Saving on Current Account (1–2)	21	89	216	199	151	–136	–54	39	–861	–679
4. Capital Expenditure	291	542	586	641	662	528	486	511	215	210
Real Investment	~	535	569	626	642	365	173	105	~	~
Debt Amortization Payments	~	7	17	15	20	163	313	406	~	~
5. Total Expenditure (2+4)	495	811	911	1,048	1,202	1,325	1,303	1,318	1,990	2,013
6. Fiscal Deficit (1–5)	–270	–453	–370	–442	–511	–664	–540	–472	–1,076	–889
7. Financing of Deficit										
External Financing	153	361	~	330	340	434	124	92	572	218
Grants[2]	95	156	~	209	183	325	346	347	~	~
Loans	58	205	~	121	157	106	172	151	~	~
Domestic Financing	117	92	~	112	171	290	70	33	345	637

1. For 1975 and 1976, fiscal years October to September.
2. Excludes food imports from the U.S. on concessional terms under that country's law on agricutural surpluses (P. L. 480, Title I), and donations by non-governmental organizations.

SOURCE: ECLA-S, 1978–81, 1984, and 1985.

Table 3029

HONDURAS CENTRAL GOVERNMENT REVENUE, EXPENDITURE, AND FINANCING THE DEFICIT, 1975–85

(M NC)

Category	1975	1977	1978	1979	1980	1981	1982	1983	1984	1985[‡]
1. Current Income	283	486	541	632	758	741	770	782	953	1,093
Tax Revenue	252	444	503	574	697	695	715	713	881	986
Direct	78	95	128	153	236	186	206	199	242	249
Indirect	174	349	375	421	461	509	509	514	639	737
2. Current Expenditure	254	444	471	527	727	791	865	980	1,063	1,225
Wages and Salaries	160	212	258	299	353	468	~	~	~	~
Other Current Expenditure	94	232	213	278	374	323	~	~	~	~
3. Current Saving (1–2)	29	42	70	105	31	–50	–95	–198	–110	–132
4. Capital Expenditure	184	250	371	385	516	473	729	613	937	873
Real Investment	76	186	172	152	193	133	178	162	170	174
Debt Amortization Payments	37	65	70	88	93	114	144	202	312	386
Other Capital Expenditure	71	79	129	145	231	226	407	249	455	313
5. Total Expenditure (2+4)	438	694	842	912	1,243	1,265	1,594	1,593	2,000	2,098
6. Fiscal Deficit (1–5)	–155	–208	–301	–280	–485	–525	–824	–811	–1,047	–1,005
7. Financing										
Domestic	60	109	117	123	219	248	422	484	456	588
External	95	99	184	157	266	276	402	327	591	417

SOURCE: ECLA-S, 1978–80, 1984, and 1985.

Table 3030

MEXICO CENTRAL GOVERNMENT REVENUE, EXPENDITURE, AND FINANCING THE DEFICIT, 1975–85

(B NC)

Category	1975	1977	1978	1979	1980	1981	1982	1983	1984	1985[‡]
1. Current Income	102	192	302	412	680	935	1,532	3,181	4,975	7,896
Tax Revenue (a + b + c)	95	181	289	395	651	647	967	1,828	3,036	4,750
a. Direct	49	95	134	173	247	339	464	727	1,204	1,890
b. Indirect	37	63	120	158	220	241	418	1,015	1,695	2,580
c. On Foreign Trade	9	23	35	64	184	67	85	86	137	280
Non-tax Revenue	7	11	13	17	29	54	107	183	231	405
2. Current Expenditure	92	177	286	382	579	937	2,182	3,916	6,226	9,776
Wages and Salaries	34	64	93	120	159	225	~	~	~	~
Other Current Expenditure	58	113	193	262	420	712	~	~	~	~
3. Saving on Current Account (1–2)	10	15	16	30	101	–2	–650	–735	–1,251	–1,880
4. Capital Expenditure[1]	63	90	190	351	482	381	476	680	951	1,759
Real Investment	37	49	57	86	169	90	145	139	263	429
Debt Amortization Payments[1]	10	16	108	232	258	244	253	441	540	1,077
Other Capital Expenditure	16	25	133	265	313	47	77	100	148	253
5. Total Expenditure[1] (2+4)	156	267	476	733	1,061	1,318	2,658	4,597	7,177	11,535
6. Fiscal Deficit[1] (1–5)	–54	–75	–174	–321	–381	383	1,126	1,415	2,202	3,639
7. Financing of Fiscal Deficit										
Domestic Financing[1]	37	55	148	296	332	376	~	~	~	~
External Financing	17	20	26	25	49	24	~	~	~	~

1. Excluding treasury certificates issued and redeemed in the same year, since their introduction in 1978.

SOURCE: ECLA-S, 1978–81, 1984, and 1985.

Table 3031

NICARAGUA CENTRAL GOVERNMENT REVENUE, EXPENDITURE, AND FINANCING THE DEFICIT, 1975–85

Category	M NC						B NC			
	1975	1977	1978	1979	1980	1981	1982	1983	1984	1985[‡]
1. Current Income	1,323	1,796	1,621	1,892	4,526	5,382	7.2	10.2	15.8	37.2
Tax Revenue	1,151	1,638	1,449	1,487	3,991	4,576	5.8	8.5	13.8	31.7
Direct	265	392	363	309	934	1,199	1.3	1.8	3.2	7.2
Indirect	535	752	702	763	1,840	3,377	4.5	6.7	10.6	24.5
From Taxes on External Trade	352	494	384	415	1,217	806	~	~	~	~
Non-tax Revenue	172	158	~	~	~	~	1.5	1.7	1.9	5.5
2. Current Expenditure	1,121	1,539	1,875	2,587	5,008	6,986	9.1	12.7	19.2	51.0
Wages and Salaries	444	588	702	903	1,562	1,904	~	~	~	~
Other Current Expenditure	677	951	1,173	1,684	3,446	4,082	~	~	~	~
3. Saving on Current Account (1–2)	202	257	–254	–695	–482	–1,604	–1.8	–2.5	–3.5	–13.7
4. Capital Expenditure	985	1,539	1,412	395	1,356	1,426	2.0	7.4	7.8	11.9
Real Investment	291	921	921	314	972	882	1.1	2.2	3.6	7.9
Amortization of Debt	144	238	384	81	170	274	.3	.4	.5	.6
Other Capital Expenditure	550	380	107	~	214	270	.6	4.8	3.6	3.4
5. Total Expenditure (2+4)	2,106	3,078	3,287	2,982	6,364	8,412	11.1	20.0	26.9	62.9
6. Fiscal Deficit (–) or Surplus (1–5)	–783	–1,282	–1,666	–1,090	–1,838	–3,030	–3.9	–9.9	–11.1	–25.7
7. Financing of Deficit										
Domestic	49	130	920	996	450	2,096	1.5	1.7	1.9	1.8
External	734	1,152	746	94	1,388	934	2.3	8.2	9.2	23.9

SOURCE: ECLA-S, 1978–80, 1984 and 1985.

Table 3032

PANAMA CENTRAL GOVERNMENT REVENUE, EXPENDITURE,
AND FINANCING THE DEFICIT, 1975–85

(M NC)

Category	1975	1977	1978	1979	1980	1981	1982	1983	1984	1985[‡]
1. Current Income	297	348	397	490	695	790	848	906	916	1,075
Tax Revenue	227	281	327	406	507	582	615	661	635	689
Direct	114	130	143	193	255	315	332	366	321	363
Indirect	113	96	184	213	252	267	238	295	314	326
On Foreign Trade	58	55	68	80	91	99	106	115	121	130
Non-tax Revenue	~	67	~	~	~	208	233	245	281	257
2. Current Expenditure	283	342	464	612	766	771	930	929	955	950
Wages and Salaries	170	186	225	264	297	298	319	356	~	~
Other Current Expenditure	113	156	239	348	469	473	611	573	~	~
3. Current Saving (1–2)	14	6	–67	–122	–71	–19	–82	–23	–39	13
4. Capital Expenditure	134	133	184	321	299	446	695	441	538	319
Fixed Investment, Financial Investment, and Transfers	111	97	35	53	52	66	112	102	~	~
Other Capital Expenditure	~	~	82	210	162	271	384	138	~	~
Amortization of the Debt	23	36	67	58	85	111	199	229	256	154
5. Total Expenditure (2+4)	420	475	648	933	1,065	109	199	201	1,493	1,269
6. Fiscal Deficit (1–5)	–123	–127	–251	–443	–370	1,217	1,625	1,370	–577	–194
7. Financing of Deficit	~	~	113	138	179	–427	–777	–464	158	191
Domestic	8	6	48	52	71	82	42	49	55	59
External	115	121	138	305	191	248	300	7 6	2.0	44

a. Wages and purchase of non-personal goods and services.

SOURCE: ECLA-S, 1978–81, 1984, and 1985.

Table 3033

PARAGUAY CENTRAL GOVERNMENT REVENUE, EXPENDITURE, AND FINANCING THE DEFICIT, 1975–85

(M NC)

Category	1975	1977	1978	1979	1980	1981	1982	1983	1984	1985[a]
1. Current Income	17,394	26,379	34,333	43,629	51,592	59,107	68,200	65,600	84,600	110,200
Tax Revenue	15,877	23,492	30,334	38,810	46,137	52,351	60,900	53,100	70,100	94,400
Direct Taxes	~	~	~	8,449	11,323	14,235	20,500	18,800	20,900	29,600
On Personal Income	~	~	~	~	~	~	~	~	~	~
On Corporative Earnings	~	~	~	6,846	9,395	11,735	13,200	10,700	10,900	15,800
On Real Estate	~	~	~	1,603	1,928	2,500	7,300	8,100	10,000	13,800
Indirect Taxes	~	~	~	30,367	34,814	38,116	31,700	25,700	37,200	64,800
On External Trade	~	~	~	15,786	17,213	17,325	12,500	9,800	11,000	14,000
Imports	~	~	~	14,645	15,945	16,623	8,900	7,400	7,900	11,000
Exports	~	~	~	1,141	1,268	1,202	400	300	600	~
On Domestic Trade	~	~	~	6,945	8,280	8,691	18,300	15,100	25,300	34,600
Others	~	~	~	7,636	9,321	11,600	8,800	8,900	1,200	16,200
Non-tax Income	2,017	2,887	3,999	4,819	5,455	6,756	7,300	12,500	14,400	15,900
2. Current Expenditure	14,412	18,553	21,616	27,193	38,064	52,998	65,100	75,100	78,800	97,600
Consumption	~	13,977	16,306	20,105	28,278	40,191	38,700	43,500	45,200	60,300
Wages and Salaries	6,126	~	~	12,205	15,938	22,474	28,300	32,900	33,900	40,800
Goods and Non-Personal Services	~	~	~	5,344	7,324	9,803	10,400	10,600	11,300	14,800
Others	8,286	~	~	2,556	5,016	7,914	4,200	5,600	5,600	~
Interest Payments	~	~	~	1,345	1,766	2,147	2,500	2,700	5,300	6,700
Transfers	~	4,576	5,310	5,743	7,792	10,653	19,700	23,200	22,800	30,500
Subsidies	~	~	~	63	83	92	~	~	~	~
Transfers to the Private Sector	~	~	~	3,289	4,725	3,941	15,400	18,300	18,000	23,700
Transfers to the Public Sector	~	~	~	2,151	2,915	3,941	4,300	4,900	4,600	6,800
Other	~	~	~	241	298	357	420	560	560	3,100
3. Saving	3,482	7,826	12,717	16,436	13,527	6,117	3,100	–9,500	5,800	12,700
4. Capital Expenditure	4,198	7,246	9,160	13,434	14,912	25,974	21,900	24,400	23,500	34,700
Capital Formation	~	~	~	11,379	10,694	14,743	14,500	17,800	17,800	29,700
Financial Investment	3,471	6,051	7,887	257	2,533	9,075	~	~	~	~
Transfers to the Public	~	~	~	1,799	1,672	2,153	6,900	5,400	~	800
Other Capital Expenditure	727	~	~	~	~	~	500	1,100	~	~
5. Total Expenditure	18,609	25,799	30,776	40,628	52,976	78,964	87,000	99,500	102,300	132,800
6. Global Balance	–714	579	3,557	3,024	–1,385	–19,857	–12,500	–35,800	–19,700	–21,400
7. Financing	~	~	~	–3,024	–1,385	19,857	12,500	35,800	19,700	21,400
Domestic (net)	–649	–517	–263	–4,980	–1,153	17,646	5,800	19,100	6,800	10,700
Indebtedness	~	~	~	1,052	–1,813	2,644	~	~	~	~
Direct Loans	~	~	~	1,350	–1,011	2,801	~	~	~	~
Central Bank	91	340	270	585	236	379	3,200	17,100	2,500	7,700
Suppliers	~	~	~	435	230	3,417	~	~	~	~
Other	–774	–667	–125	330	–1,477	–995	~	~	~	~
Bonds	–217	–190	–407	–298	–802	–157	~	~	~	~
Sale	~	~	~	~	~	~	~	~	~	~
Amortization	~	~	~	–298	–802	–157	~	~	~	~
Cash Variation (minus sign indicates increase)	~	~	~	6,032	660	15,002	~	~	~	~
External (net)	1,363	2,526	1,968	1,956	2,538	2,211	6,600	16,800	12,800	10,700
Loans	~	~	~	1,923	2,515	2,167	~	~	~	~
Disbursements	~	~	~	4,226	4,066	4,639	9,200	19,700	18,700	16,100
Amortization	~	~	~	–2,303	–1,551	–2,472	–2,600	–2,900	75,800	–5,400
Variations in Reserves	~	2,589	5,262	~	~	~	~	~	~	~
Donations	~	~	~	33	23	45	~	~	~	~

a. Amounts actually registered (preliminary figures).

SOURCE: ECLA-S, 1978–80, 1984, and 1985.

Table 3034

PERU CENTRAL GOVERNMENT REVENUE, EXPENDITURE,
AND FINANCING THE DEFICIT, 1982–85

(M NC)

Category	1982	1983	1984 Actual	1985 Actual[‡]
1. Current Income	2,485	3,732	9,554	27,893
Tax Revenue	2,249	3,361	7,957	24,618
Income Tax	480	649	1,422	3,410
Property Tax	96	135	281	665
Tax on External Trade	942	1,257	1,860	6,241
Production and Consumer Taxes	822	1,488	4,518	15,330
Other Tax Revenue	83	118	536	1,091
Less Credit Documents[1]	−174	−286	−660	−2,119
Non-tax Revenue[2]	192	330	1,597	3,275
Other Resources and Transfers	44	41	~	~
2. Capital Income	8	~	92	272
3. Total Expenditure	3,051	6,083	12,563	32,164
Current Expenditure	2,456	5,065	10,203	27,064
Remunerations	545	1,009	2,907	7,412
Goods and Services	69	153	569	1,726
Transfers	230	563	1,714	3,475
Interest	557	1,411	2,957	8,140
Domestic Debt	259	492	724	2,255
External Debt	298	919	2,233	5,885
Defense and Interior	1,055	1,929	2,056	6,311
Capital Expenditure	595	1,018	2,360	5,100
Gross Capital Formation	440	599	2,075	4,540
Transfers	144	407	279	530
Others	11	12	6	30
Deficit (1–3)	−558	−2,351	−2,917	−3,999

1. Mainly tax reimbursements for non-traditional exports, tax capitalization, and tax
    payment promissory notes.
2. Mainly property income, fines, and deductions from pensions.

SOURCE: ECLA-S, 1984 and 1985.

Table 3035

URUGUAY CENTRAL GOVERNMENT REVENUE, EXPENDITURE, AND FINANCING THE DEFICIT, 1975–85

(M NC)

Category	1975	1977	1978	1979	1980	1981	1982	1983	1984	1985[‡]
1. Current Income	989	2,938	4,350	8,424	14,955	21,260	19,552	29,486	39,797	76,787
Internal Taxes	929	2,092	3,256	5,704	10,695	14,804	13,487	18,214	28,187	58,402
On Production, Consumption and Transactions	~	2,046	3,067	5,221	9,287	13,514	12,758	16,753	27,259	54,179
Value Added	~	1,002	1,526	2,751	5,676	8,515	7,970	9,718	15,942	30.218
Fuels	~	431	582	973	1,661	2,117	1,997	3,609	5,908	12,125
Tobacco	~	204	297	459	912	1,251	1,535	2,046	2,672	4,897
Other	~	409	662	1,038	1,038	1,631	1,256	1,380	2,737	6,937
On Income	~	349	569	1,038	2,363	2,427	2,028	3,147	2,942	4,764
On Wealth	~	171	211	282	725	1,094	1,293	2,074	1,935	4,369
Other	57	56	59	81	116	116	134	113	169	538
Less: Documents Received	~	−377	−527	−717	−1,475	−2,235	2,414	−2,964	−4,021	−5,448
Adjustments[1]	~	−153	−122	−198	−320	−111	−311	−909	−97	~
Taxes on Foreign Trade	~	424	550	1,597	2,753	3,199	2,669	4,582	5,917	10,227
Other Income	~	422	544	1,123	1,507	3,257	3,396	6,690	5,693	8,158
2. Current Expenditure	1,204	2,796	4,042	7,260	1,381	18,817	27,503	33,159	50,560	83,612
Wages and Salaries	871[a]	1,836[a]	1,948	3,282	5,980	8,800	~	~	~	~
Contributions and Assistance to Social Security	871[a]	1,836[a]	665	1,117	3,464	4,866	21,573	24,522	31,420	53,837
Purchase of Goods and Services	~	457	765	1,397	2,466	3,766	3,526	4,112	6,944	11,185
Other Current Expenditure[2]	333	970	664	1,104	846	978	1,594	2,289	6,911	7,787
3. Saving on Current Account (1–2)	−218	142	308	1,163	1,874	2,443	−7,951	−3,673	−10,763	−6,825
4. Investments	145[‡]	382	708	1,040	1,799	2,559	3,258	3,738	4,913	7,813
5. Total Expenditure (2+4)	1,349	3,178	4,750	8,301	14,880	21,377	30,761	36,897	55,473	91,425
6. Fiscal Deficit or Surplus (1–5)	−363	−241	−401	124	75	−117	−11,210	7,411	−15,676	−14,638
7. Financing										
Net Credit Central Bank	95	287	159	206	−168	396	8,915	5,765	7,470	1,405
Issue of Securities (Net)	263	78	151	−287	−220	54	1,680	1,557	9,413	16,053
Other	4	−90	123	−9	374	−238	815	532	−271	−760

1. Discrepancy between treasury information and tax office information.
2. Including transfer payments, interest payments on the public debt and affected income (1978–80).

a. Wages and salaries and contributions and assistance to Social Security combined.

SOURCE: ECLA-S, 1978–80, 1984, and 1985.

Table 3036

VENEZUELA CENTRAL GOVERNMENT REVENUE, EXPENDITURE, AND FINANCING THE DEFICIT, 1982–85[a]

(B NC)

Category	1982	1983	1984	1985[‡]
1. Current Income	78.2	71.8	99.2	107.9
Petroleum Revenue	47.0	42.0	62.1	−30.6
Income Tax	39.1	34.0	51.5	53.3
Income Tax on Petroleum Products	1.1	1.5	1.5	~
Royalties	6.7	6.5	9.1	8.8
Other Tax Revenue	21.5	24.6	32.2	34.4
Direct	13.0	8.8	10.3	12.8
Customs	5.2	2.5	2.8	~
Indirect Domestic	3.1	3.2	21.9	21.6
Exchange Profits	~	10.1	14.3	11.1
2. Current Expenditure	54.4	54.0	63.8	75.2
Remunerations	19.2	19.2	20.4	20.2
Financial Subsidies	3.1	1.7	1.6	1.1
Interest Payments	8.4	12.6	10.8	12.0
On External Debt	7.0	8.4	7.5	7.9
On Domestic Debt	1.4	4.2	3.3	4.1
Other Current Expenditure	23.8	20.4	4.8	5.9
3. Current Savings (1–2)	23.8	18.0	30.4	32.7
4. Capital Expenditure	27.4	20.5	19.5	24.4
Real Investment	6.1	4.5	4.0	3.6
Other Capital Expenditure	21.3	16.1	15.4	20.8
5. Total Expenditure (2+4)	81.9	74.3	88.3	99.6
6. Fiscal Deficit (1–5)	−3.6	−2.5	11.0	8.3
7. Financing of the Deficit	3.6	2.5	−11.0	−8.3
Use of Domestic Surplus	5.5	6.1	−5.2	−3.3
Central Bank	~	7.0	~	6.0
Sale of Securities	.4	1.3	3.6	4.1
Amortization	−.9	−1.7	−5.7	−5.9
Other Forms of Financing	6.0	−.5	~	~
External Financing	−1.9	−3.6	−5.7	−5.0
Disbursements	3.4	.4	~	~
Amortization	−5.3	−4.0	−5.7	−5.0

a. For 1975–81, see SALA, 24-3036.

SOURCE: ECLA-S, 1985.

Table 3037

UNITED STATES CENTRAL GOVERNMENT REVENUE, EXPENDITURE, AND FINANCING THE DEFICIT, 1970–85

(B NC)

Category	1970	1975	1976	1977	1978	1979	1980	1981	1982	1983	1984	1985
Deficit (−) or Surplus	−11.38	−53.93	−74.86	−52.23*	−58.74	−35.95	−76.18	−78.74	−125.69	−202.52	−178.26	−212.11
Revenue	190.49	292.70	311.30	371.52*	416.73	488.76	546.08	63.86	659.92	653.44	718.53	791.68
Expenditure and Lending	201.87	346.63	386.17	423.75*	475.67	524.71	622.26	718.60	785.61	855.96	896.79	1,003.79
Expenditure	201.00	333.12	375.29	414.28*	457.73	506.26	596.64	687.61	764.89	842.60	881.92	977.29
Lending Minus Repayments	.87	13.51	11.08	9.47*	17.94	18.45	25.62	30.99	20.72	13.36	14.87	26.50
Financing												
Net Borrowing	11.86	53.09	82.79	55.83*	61.99	39.82	76.61	84.80	138.76	215.59	174.08	200.54
Use of Cash Balances	−1.52	.84	−7.93	−3.60*	−3.05	−3.87	−.43	−6.06	−13.07	−13.07	4.18	11.57

SOURCE: IMF-IFS-Y, 1986, lines 80–87; IMF-IFS-S, June, 1987, lines 80–87.

Table 3038

ARGENTINA MONEY SUPPLY, 1976–85[a]
(M NC[1] YE)

Year	A, Money[2] (M_1)	B, Quasi- Money[3]	C, Total[4] (M_2)
1976	.11	.05	.16
1977	.23	.29	.52
1978	.59	.87	1.46
1979	1.40	2.95	4.35
1980	2.75	5.47	8.22
1981	4.67	12.82	17.49
1982	16.23	29.70	45.93
1983	74.96	155.20	230.20
1984	451.20	1,186.80	1,637.50
1985	3,029.70	5,400.90	8,430.60

1. Australes.
2. Sum of currency outside banks and private sector demand deposits.
3. Time, savings, and foreign currency deposits by residents.
4. Calculated by totaling series A and B.

a. For previous years see SALA, 24-3038.

SOURCE: IMF-IFS-Y, 1987.

Table 3039

BOLIVIA MONEY SUPPLY, 1952–85
(NC YE)

Year	A. Money[1] (M_1)	B. Quasi- Money[2]	C. Total[3] (M_2)
1952	9	1	10
1953	16	1	17
1954	27	1	28
1955	56	3	59
1956	197	6	203
1957	291	10	301
1958	301	9	310
1959	386	15	401
1960	419	16	435
1961	496	17	513
1962	556	29	585
1963	665	37	702
1964	803	50	853
1965	943	52	995
1966	1,153	100	1,253
1967	1,192	151	1,343
1968	1,287	226	1,513
1969	1,361	306	1,667
1970	1,532	381	1,913
1971	1,766	493	2,259
1972	2,210	634	2,844
1973	2,969	807	3,776
1974	4,257	1,192	5,449
1975	4,759	1,956	6,715
1976	6,497	3,405	9,902
1977	7,855	4,960	12,815
1978	8,831	5,650	14,481
1979	10,304	6,328	16,632
1980	14,694	8,430	23,124
1981	17,587	11,831	29,418
1982	57,827	39,375	97,202
1983	177,500	87,600	265,100
1984[a]	3,370	684	4,053
1985[a]	207*	88*	296

1. Sum of currency outside of banks and private sector demand deposits, source line 34.
2. Time, savings, and foreign currency deposits by residents, source line 35.
3. Calculated by adding columns A and B.

a. Thousands of Bolivianos for 1984 and millions for 1985.

SOURCE: IMF-IFS-Y, 1982 and 1987.

Table 3040

BRAZIL MONEY SUPPLY,[1] 1948–85
(M NC YE)

PART I. 1948–59

Year	A. Money[2] (M_1)	B. Quasi- Money[3]	C. Total[4] (M_2)
1948	49	16	65
1949	58	18	76
1950	78	19	97
1951	91	20	111
1952	104	21	125
1953	124	22	146
1954	151	25	176
1955	178	24	202
1956	217	25	242
1957	211	29	240
1958	353	33	386
1959	501	39	540

SOURCE: IMF-IFS-S, 1965–66.

PART II. 1960–85

Year	A. Money[1] (M_1)	B. Quasi- Money[2]	C. Total[3] (M_2)
1960	.7	.1	.8
1961	1.0	.1	1.1
1962	1.7	.1	1.8
1963	2.8	.1	2.9
1964	5.1	.2	5.3
1965	9.1	.3	9.4
1966	10.0	.9	10.9
1967	15.0	1.7	16.7
1968	21.3	2.7	24.0
1969	27.4	4.4	31.8
1970	34.7	6.0	40.7
1971	42.0*	3.3*	45.3
1972	59.0	6.1	65.1
1973	87.0	7.1	94.1
1974	116.8	8.1	124.9
1975	168.5	12.0	180.5
1976	231.1	19.1	250.2
1977	318.5	44.2	362.7
1978	434.0*	94.2	529.0*
1979	759.0	154.6	913,0
1980	1,288.0	184.4	1,472.0
1981	2,353.0	509.0	2,862.0
1982	3,963.0	1,335.0	5,297.0
1983	7,735.0	4,769.0	12,504.0
1984	23,090.0	21,905.0	44,995.0
1985	100,363.0	97,013.0	197,376.0

1. Differences between Parts I and II reflect a change in unit of account and not a discontinuity in the series.
2. Sum of currency outside of banks and private sector demand deposits.
3. Time, savings, and foreign currency deposits by residents.
4. Calculated by adding columns A and B.

SOURCE: IMF-IFS-Y, 1986 and 1987.

Table 3041

CHILE MONEY SUPPLY, 1955–84
(M NC YE)

PART I. 1955–64
(M NC)

Year	A. Money[1] (M_1)	B. Quasi- Money[3]	C. Total[3] (M_2)
1955	93	16	109
1956	130	25	155
1957	165	38	203
1958	222	54	276
1959	294	162	456
1960	384	211	595
1961	432	266	698
1962	557	389	946
1963	747	459	1,206
1964	1,129	720	1,849

SOURCE: IMF-IFS-S, 1965–66.

PART II. 1965–84
(B NC)

Year	A. Money[1] (M_1)	B. Quasi- Money[2]	C. Total[3] (M_2)
1965	.002	.001	.003
1966	.003	.002	.005
1967	.003	.002	.005
1968	.005	.003	.008
1969	.006	.005	.011
1970	.010	.007	.017
1971	.021	.011	.032
1972	.1	.03	.13
1973	.22	.22	.44
1974	.84	1.19	2.03
1975	2.98	4.52	7.50
1976	8.80	11.17	19.97
1977	18.32	27.62	45.94
1978	30.58	57.092	87.67
1979	50.31	96.59	146.90
1980	78.87	152.15	231.02
1981	74.12	237.11	311.23
1982	81.12	311.33	392.40
1983	102.72	308.99	411.71
1984	116.2	441.0	557.20

1. Sum of currency outside banks and private sector demand deposits.
2. Time, savings, and foreign currency deposits by residents.
3. Calculated by adding columns A and B.

SOURCE: IMF-IFS-Y, 1985 and 1987.

Table 3042

COLOMBIA MONEY SUPPLY, 1952–85
(B NC YE)

Year	A. Money[1] (M_1)	B. Quasi-Money[2]	C. Total[3] (M_2)
1952	1.32	.20	1.52
1953	1.55	.21	1.76
1954	1.84	.38	2.22
1955	1.91	.50	2.41
1956	2.38	.84	3.22
1957	2.70	.65	3.35
1958	3.26	.64	3.90
1959	3.63	.77	4.40
1960	3.99	.76	4.75
1961	4.96	.92	5.88
1962	5.93	1.55	7.48
1963	6.69	1.51	8.20
1964	8.25	1.45	9.70
1965	9.64	2.19	11.83
1966	11.24	1.81	13.05
1967	13.68	2.10	15.78
1968	15.86	2.22	18.08
1969	19.40	2.70	22.10
1970	22.40	3.38	25.78
1971	25.06	4.13	29.19
1972	31.85	5.86	37.71
1973	41.65	9.25	50.90
1974	49.07	14.64	63.71
1975	58.92	19.58	78.50
1976	79.38	25.76	105.14
1977	103.50	37.19	140.69
1978	132.93*	47.08*	180.01*
1979	165.89	55.10	220.99
1980	212.40	108.08	321.20
1981	256.37	178.36	434.73
1982	321.40	204.25	525.65
1983	396.74	262.49	659.23
1984	492.39	324.45	816.84
1985	545.26	436.84	982.10

1. Sum of currency outside of banks and private sector demand deposits, source line 34.
2. Time, savings, and foreign currency deposits by residents, source line 35.
3. Calculated by adding columns A and B.

SOURCE: IMF-IFS-Y, 1982 and 1987.

Table 3043

COSTA RICA MONEY SUPPLY, 1952–86
(M NC YE)

Year	A. Money[1] (M_1)	B. Quasi-Money[2]	C. Total[3] (M_2)
1952	265	38	303
1953	291	45	336
1954	325	49	374
1955	340	61	401
1956	342	71	413
1957	370	83	453
1958	399	103	502
1959	427*	120*	547
1960	433	128	561
1961	422	124	546
1962	480	137	617
1963	535	148	683
1964	568	166	734
1965	598	185	783
1966	622	186	808
1967	832	248	1,080
1968	849*	219	1,068
1969	959	236	1,195
1970	1,006	270	1,276
1971	1,317	494	1,811
1972	1,501	665	2,166
1973	1,874	767	2,641
1974	2,146	1,300	3,446
1975	2,771	2,133	4,904
1976	3,408	3,182	6,590
1977	4,504	4,160	8,664
1978	5,625	5,442	11,067
1979	6,226	8,642	14,868
1980	7,271	9,965	17,236
1981	10,832	21,439	32,271
1982	18,448	22,545	40,993
1983	25,619	30,524	56,143
1984	30,132	35,632	65,764
1985	32,439	43,563	76,002
1986	42,487	49,671	92,158

1. Sum of currency outside of banks and private sector demand deposits, source line 34.
2. Time, savings, and foreign currency deposits by residents, source line 35.
3. Calculated by adding columns A and B.

SOURCE: IMF-IFS-Y, 1982 and 1987.

Table 3044

DOMINICAN REPUBLIC MONEY SUPPLY,
1952–86

(M NC YE)

Year	A. Money[1] (M_1)	B. Quasi-Money[2]	C. Total[3] (M_2)
1952	62.1	13.1	75.2
1953	60.2	12.2	72.4
1954	68.6	26.2	94.8
1955	76.5	32.7	109.2
1956	76.9	37.4	114.3
1957	87.4	43.1	130.5
1958	107.2	36.8	144.0
1959	91.9	36.7	128.6
1960	101.9	27.2	129.1
1961	104.4	22.0	126.4
1962	114.0	26.0	140.0
1963	130.2	27.3	157.5
1964	116.6	30.8	147.4
1965	135.0	60.8	195.8
1966	116.1	49.3	165.4
1967	120.2	53.2	173.4
1968	139.1	72.2	211.3
1969	149.3	93.7	243.0
1970	171.7	118.1	289.8
1971	188.1	144.9	333.0
1972	222.5	188.2	410.7
1973	260.1	244.8	504.9
1974	364.2	361.3	725.5
1975	379.7	467.5	847.2
1976	390.4	484.6	875.0
1977	460.0	545.4	1,005.4
1978	458.0	533.1	991.1
1979	598.4	556.3	1,154.7
1980	579.6	594.9	1,174.5
1981	660.5	677.0	1,337.5
1982	731.5	803.9	1,535.4
1983	781.4	895.1	1,676.5
1984	1,159.5	1,010.4	2,169.9
1985	1,355.2	1,235.3	2,590.5
1986	1,988.7	2,296.7	4,285.4

1. Sum of currency outside of banks and private sector demand
   deposits, source line 34.
2. Time, savings, and foreign currency deposits by residents, source
   line 35.
3. Calculated by adding columns A and B.

SOURCE: IMF-IFS-Y, 1982 and 1987.

Table 3045

ECUADOR MONEY SUPPLY, 1952–84

(M NC YE)

Year	A. Money[1] (M_1)	B. Quasi-Money[2]	C. Total[3] (M_2)
1952	1,051	182	1,233
1953	1,088	230	1,318
1954	1,273	270	1,543
1955	1,193	352	1,545
1956	1,358	388	1,746
1957	1,412	469	1,881
1958	1,400	391	1,791
1959	1,577	440	2,017
1960	1,732	469	2,201
1961	1,778	598	2,376
1962	2,000	678	2,678
1963	2,241	609	2,850
1964	2,626	569	3,195
1965	2,670	616	3,286
1966	3,016	831	3,847
1967	3,439	1,021	4,460
1968	4,172	1,391	5,563
1969	4,751	1,547	6,298
1970	5,989	1,746	7,735
1971	6,719	2,175	8,894
1972	8,376	2,595	10,971
1973	11,299	3,132	14,431
1974	16,866	4,167	21,033
1975	18,343	4,741	23,084
1976	22,809	6,006	28,815
1977	29,876	6,087	35,963
1978	32,920	6,820	39,740
1979	41,952	10,227	52,179
1980	53,584	12,590	66,174
1981	61,807	13,896	75,703
1982	73,130	20,499	93,629
1983	95,145	22,868	118,013
1984	129,058	40,223	169,281

1. Sum of currency outside of banks and private sector demand
   deposits, source line 34.
2. Time, savings, and foreign currency deposits by residents, source
   line 35.
3. Calculated by adding columns A and B.

SOURCE: IMF-IFS-Y, 1982 and 1987.

Table 3046

EL SALVADOR MONEY SUPPLY, 1952–86
(M NC YE)

Year	A. Money[1] (M_1)	B. Quasi- Money[2]	C. Total[3] (M_2)
1952	163.7	10.3	174.0
1953	171.8	10.9	182.7
1954	190.4	15.6	206.0
1955	187.4	19.8	207.2
1956	215.0	26.1	241.1
1957	215.2	37.2	252.4
1958	202.3	55.0	257.3
1959	205.7	75.6	281.3
1960	193.0	83.0	276.0
1961	184.2	100.3	284.5
1962	183.4	122.8	306.2
1963	220.9	154.0	374.9
1964	233.5	189.6	423.1
1965	234.2	204.3	438.5
1966	247.0	231.6	478.6
1967	252.7	236.2	488.9
1968	264.7	244.8	509.5
1969	288.1	273.8	561.9
1970	295.3	300.2	595.5
1971	315.4	342.8	658.2
1972	389.6	417.5	807.1
1973	466.0	491.6	957.6
1974	556.6	559.7	1,116.3
1975	648.1	704.6	1,352.7
1976	916.7	853.7	1,770.4
1977	988.3	1,015.3	2,003.6
1978	1,086.9	1,154.4	2,241.3
1979	1,320.9	1,124.8	2,445.7
1980	1,428.6	1,134.7	2,563.3
1981	1,437.2	1,397.0	2,834.2
1982	1,716.6*	1,599.5*	3,316.1*
1983	1,657.0	1,979.0	3,637.0
1984	1,961.0	2,405.0	4,366.0
1985	2,488.0	3,068.0	5,556.0
1986	3,047.0	4,147.0	7,194.0

1. Sum of currency outside of banks and private sector demand deposits, source line 34.
2. Time, savings, and foreign currency deposits by residents, source line 35.
3. Calculated by adding columns A and B.

SOURCE: IMF-IFS-Y, 1982 and 1987.

Table 3047

GUATEMALA MONEY SUPPLY, 1952–86
(M NC YE)

Year	A. Money[1] (M_1)	B. Quasi- Money[2]	C. Total[3] (M_2)
1952	63.6	7.0	70.6
1953	76.1	7.2	83.3
1954	77.6	6.7	84.3
1955	86.7	8.6	95.3
1956	103.9	14.6	118.5
1957	116.3	19.0	135.3
1958	106.8	22.7	129.5
1959	108.8	26.4	135.2
1960	105.5	31.3	136.8
1961	106.7	36.4	143.1
1962	108.7	42.5	151.2
1963	121.4	48.4	169.8
1964	129.3	64.8	194.1
1965	135.6	73.8	209.4
1966	143.0	91.5	234.5
1967	148.3	114.5	262.8
1968	151.1	126.2	277.3
1969	160.9	148.3	309.2
1970	172.8	170.9	343.7
1971	178.9	204.4	383.3
1972	214.4	262.5	476.9
1973	264.3	315.5	579.8
1974	305.4	362.9	668.3
1975	353.6	454.9	808.5
1976	493.8	558.0	1,051.8
1977	594.1	655.0	1,249.1
1978	664.0	759.6	1,423.6
1979	734.9	802.3	1,537.2
1980	752.8	939.6	1,692.4
1981	777.8	1,128.9	1,906.7
1982	786.6	1,404.1	2,190.7
1983	833.8	1,321.3	2,155.1
1984	869.4	1,529.7	2,399.1
1985	1,346.5	1,846.4	3,192.9
1986	1,608.4	2,266.7	3,875.1

1. Sum of currency outside of banks and private sector demand deposits, source line 34.
2. Time, savings, and foreign currency deposits by residents, source line 35.
3. Calculated by adding columns A and B.

SOURCE: IMF-IFS-Y, 1982 and 1987.

Table 3048

HAITI MONEY SUPPLY, 1952–84

(M NC YE)

Year	A. Money[1] (M_1)	B. Quasi-Money[2]	C. Total[3] (M_2)
1952	98.3	21.2	119.5
1953	94.4	21.3	115.7
1954	116.8	27.8	144.6
1955	117.8	29.4	147.2
1956	126.9	34.8	161.7
1957	121.4	34.3	155.7
1958	102.6	32.0	134.6
1959	104.4	32.1	136.5
1960	104.3	34.1	138.4
1961	118.0	37.6	155.6
1962	122.5	37.8	160.3
1963	130.7	38.8	169.5
1964	132.5	38.7	171.2
1965	133.4	37.9	171.2
1966	123.2	38.1	161.4
1967	142.2	36.5	178.7
1968	160.0	40.8	200.8
1969	175.6	48.8	224.4
1970	190.6	58.0	248.6
1971	214.6	75.4	290.0
1972	271.2	110.3	381.6
1973	332.8	154.5	487.3
1974	342.4	241.3	583.7
1975	402.6	332.2	734.8
1976	549.6	465.6	1,015.2
1977	629.1	587.8	1,216.8
1978	717.8	713.7	1,431.5
1979	1,107.8	764.9	1,872.7
1980	945.4	992.9	1,938.3
1981	1,174.6	1,022.9	2,197.5
1982	1,164.3	1,102.9	2,267.2
1983	1,174.7	1,172.9	2,347.6
1984	1,400.1	1,268.6	2,668.7

1. Sum of currency outside of banks and private sector demand deposits, source line 34.
2. Time, savings, and foreign currency deposits by residents, source line 34.
3. Calculated by adding columns A and B.

SOURCE: IMF-IFS-Y, 1982 and 1987.

Table 3049

HONDURAS MONEY SUPPLY, 1952–86

(M NC YE)

Year	A. Money[1] (M_1)	B. Quasi-Money[2]	C. Total[3] (M_2)
1952	52.5	7.4	59.9
1953	59.4	8.8	68.2
1954	68.6	10.3	78.9
1955	60.6	11.5	72.1
1956	67.2	15.8	83.0
1957	64.3	12.6	76.9
1958	63.0	11.7	74.7
1959	65.9	14.7	80.6
1960	64.3	20.7	85.0
1961	65.7	23.7	89.4
1962	72.7	29.5	102.2
1963	79.1	34.7	113.8
1964	89.8	39.4	129.2
1965	104.6	46.5	151.1
1966	106.9	58.6	165.5
1967	114.3	68.7	183.0
1968	127.4	85.8	213.2
1969	148.1	104.2	252.3
1970	158.9	129.5	288.4
1971	169.4	151.7	321.1
1972	192.9	172.8	365.7
1973	238.4	206.6	445.0
1974	242.4	217.8	460.2
1975	262.7	244.5	507.2
1976	361.0	311.0	672.0
1977	411.3	384.5	795.8
1978	480.4	482.0	962.4
1979	545.6	494.8	1,040.4
1980	610.3	517.4	1,127.7
1981	637.4	588.9	1,226.3
1982	716.9	761.2	1,478.1
1983	814.9	918.5	1,733.4
1984	846.0	1,065.4	1,911.4
1985	855.6	1,016.6	1,872.2
1986	953.2	1,096.8	2,050.0

1. Sum of currency outside of banks and private sector demand deposits, source line 34.
2. Time, savings, and foreign currency deposits by residents, source line 35.
3. Calculated by adding columns A and B.

SOURCE: IMF-IFS-Y, 1982 and 1987.

Table 3050

MEXICO MONEY SUPPLY, INFLATION, AND GDP, 1952–86

	(A)	(B)	(C)	(D)	(E)	(F)
						Real M_2
		B NC YE		M_2 Index	Price Index[4]	Index (D/E)
Year	Money[1] (M_1)	Quasi-Money[2]	Total[3] (M_2)		(1980 = 100.0)	
1952	7.3	1.9	9.2	.7	~	~
1953	8.0	2.1	10.1	.8	~	~
1954	9.0	3.0	12.0	.9	~	~
1955	10.8	3.4	14.2	1.1	13.3	8.2
1956	12.0	3.7	15.7	1.2	~	~
1957	12.8	4.7	17.5	1.4	~	~
1958	13.7	5.5	19.2	1.5	~	~
1959	15.9	5.3	21.2	1.6	15.3	10.5
1960	17.4	5.4	22.8	1.8	16.1	11.2
1961	18.0	6.0	24.0	1.9	16.2	11.7
1962	20.9	6.6	27.5	2.1	16.5	12.7
1963	24.3	8.1	32.4	2.5	16.6	15.1
1964	28.6	9.2	37.8	2.9	17.3	16.8
1965	30.2	10.4	40.6	3.1	17.6	17.6
1966	33.9	11.8	45.7	3.5	17.8	19.7
1967	37.0	13.1	50.1	3.7	18.4	20.1
1968	42.3	14.8	57.1	4.4	18.7	23.5
1969	48.6	16.9	65.5	5.1	19.2	26.6
1970	53.8	18.2	72.0	5.6	20.3	27.6
1971	57.9	19.6	77.5	6.0	21.1	28.4
1972	68.2	22.9	91.1	7.0	21.7	32.3
1973	83.5	31.6	115.1	8.9	25.1	35.5
1974	100.8	38.4	139.2	10.7	30.7	34.9
1975	122.4	41.7	164.1	12.7	34.0	37.4
1976	158.0	85.0	243.0	18.7	41.5	45.1
1977	208.2[a],*	317.0[a]	525.2	40.5	58.6	69.1
1978	270.2	429.0	699.2	53.9	67.9*	79.4
1979	360.9	588.0	948.9	73.2	80.3	91.2
1980	477.2	820.0	1,297.2	100.0	100.0	100.0
1981	635.0	1,298.0	1,933.0	149.0	124.4	119.8
1982	1,031.0*	2,024.0*	3,055.0*	235.5	194.2	121.3
1983	1,447.0	3,498.0	4,945.0	381.2	402.7	94.7
1984	2,315.0	6,017.0	8,332.0	642.3	686.0	93.6
1985	3,462.0	8,474.0	11,936.0	920.1	1,053.4	87.3
1986	5,794.0	15,496.0	21,290.0	1,641.2	1,932.4	84.9

1. Sum of currency outside of banks and private sector demand deposits, source line 34.
2. Time, savings, and foreign currency deposits in Mexico by residents, source line 35.
   According to data calculated from Banco de México, *Indicadores Económicos*, August
   1982, p. 6, foreign currency in checking accounts, liquid savings, and in time deposits
   made up the following % of M_4 (or IMF's M_2): 1968, 5.1%; 1969, 4.3%; 1970, 3.8%;
   1971, 2.9%; 1972, 2.2%; 1973, 3.2%; 1974, 2.5%; 1975, 3.1%; 1976, 10.6%; 1977,
   14.0%; 1978, 12.5%; 1979, 14.8%; 1980, 18.1%; Mar. 1982, 25.0%. Cf. Leroy O.
   Laney, "Currency Substitution: The Mexican Case." *Voice* (Federal Reserve Bank of
   Dallas), January 1981, pp. 1-10.
3. Calculated by adding columns A and B.
4. Bank of Mexico Wholesale Price Index (210 national and import goods), period
   average, source line 63.

a. Expanded coverage which approximates the Bank of Mexico's concept of M_4.

Method: A,B: 1952-74, IFS-Y, 1982; IMF-IFS-Y, 1987, lines 34 and 35.
          C: Calculated (A + B).
          D: Calculated from column C.
          E: See source A, B, line 63.
          F: Calculated (D/E).

SOURCE: SALA 22-2.

Figure 30:1

MEXICO MONEY SUPPLY (M_2) AND INFLATION INDEXES, 1952–82

(1975 = 100)

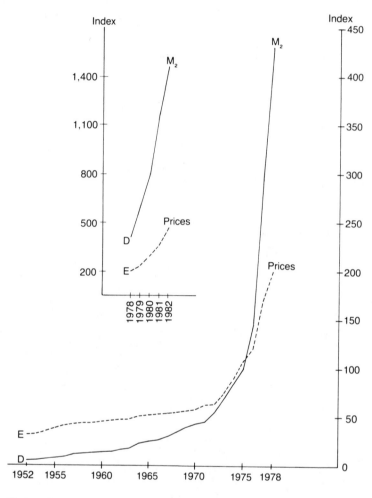

Trajectories D and E are keyed
to columns D and E in table 2

SOURCE: SALA, 22, p. xi.

	Table 3051
	NICARAGUA MONEY SUPPLY, 1952–83
	(M NC YE)

Year	A. Money[1] (M_1)	B. Quasi- Money[2]	C. Total[3] (M_2)
1952	180.2	2.0	182.2
1953	230.2	9.2	239.4
1954	264.4	7.5	271.9
1955	272.5	18.1	290.6
1956	267.0	18.1	285.1
1957	259.6	19.4	279.0
1958	251.6	22.9	274.5
1959	253.2	28.8	282.0
1960	264.0	33.1	297.1
1961	272.7	32.0	304.7
1962	352.9	31.5	384.4
1963	397.4	51.3	448.7
1964	460.3	84.9	545.2
1965	537.3	135.2	672.5
1966	565.1	185.8	750.9
1967	540.7	219.3	760.0
1968	484.8	197.2	682.0
1969	513.1	207.9	721.0
1970	578.2	250.5	828.7
1971	618.9	330.3	949.2
1972	748.7	477.3	1,226.0
1973	1,146.4	587.9	1,734.3
1974	1,313.3	703.0	2,016.3
1975	1,255.8	774.0	2,029.8
1976	1,615.5	1,083.7	2,699.2
1977	1,699.2	1,156.2	2,855.4
1978	1,579.3	1,072.9	2,652.2
1979	2,654.1	772.6	3,426.7
1980	4,102.4	1,644.2	5,746.6
1981	5,206.3	2,720.4	7,926.7
1982	6,545.8	3,349.3	9,895.1
1983	10,937.0	4,252.9	15,189.9

1. Sum of currency outside of banks and private sector demand deposits, source line 34.
2. Time, savings, and foreign currency deposits by residents, source line 35.
3. Calculated by adding columns A and B.

SOURCE: IMF-IFS-Y, 1982, 1986, and 1987.

	Table 3052
	PANAMA MONEY SUPPLY, 1952–85
	(M NC YE)

Year	A. Money[1] (M_1)	B. Quasi- Money[2]	C. Total[3] (M_2)
1952	26.6	17.7	44.3
1953	30.2	18.4	48.6
1954	32.6	18.5	41.1
1955	32.7	19.8	52.5
1956	34.2	22.1	56.3
1957	38.0	23.4	61.4
1958	39.9	25.3	65.2
1959	41.6	27.1	68.7
1960	42.1	28.2	70.3
1961	43.9	31.4	75.3
1962	48.8	38.1	86.9
1963	59.7	51.0	110.7
1964	50.8	54.1	104.9
1965	55.5	69.2	124.7
1966	61.9	87.0	148.9
1967	70.3	110.4	180.7
1968	80.9	125.6	206.5
1969	84.8	111.7*	196.5*
1970	100.5	155.8	256.3
1971	105.4	196.8	302.2
1972	153.6	239.3	392.9
1973	161.1	283.4	444.5
1974	196.3	333.9	530.2
1975	173.1	374.7	547.8
1976	190.0	388.0	578.0
1977	213.2	459.3	672.5
1978	246.0	586.7	832.7
1979	301.3	742.2	1,043.5
1980	335.3	980.4	1,315.7
1981	359.7	1,201.1	1,560.8
1982	379.3	1,369.8	1,749.1
1983	372.6	1,375.6	1,748.2
1984	381.0	1,481.9	1,862.9
1985	409.5	1,543.0	1,952.5

1. Sum of currency outside of banks and private sector demand deposits, source line 34.
2. Time, savings, and foreign currency deposits by residents, source line 35.
3. Calculated by adding columns A and B.

SOURCE: IMF-IFS-Y, 1982, 1986, and 1987.

Table 3053

PARAGUAY MONEY SUPPLY, 1952–86
(M NC YE)

Year	A. Money[1] (M_1)	B. Quasi- Money[2]	C. Total[3] (M_2)
1952	582	50	632
1953	861	82	943
1954	1,070	102	1,172
1955	2,384	376	2,545
1956	1,941	95	2,036
1957	1,997	180	2,177
1958	2,384	376	2,760
1959	2,609	265	2,874
1960	2,674	357	3,031
1961	3,391	542	3,933
1962	3,311	825	4,136
1963	3,685	1,244	4,929
1964	4,473	1,761	6,234
1965	4,913	2,365	7,279
1966	5,034	2,822	7,856
1967	6,691*	3,648*	10,339*
1968	5,786	4,324	10,111
1969	6,557	5,300	11,857
1970	7,308	6,200	13,508
1971	7,848	7,394	15,242
1972	9,421	9,420	18,840
1973	12,494	11,808	24,302
1974	15,120	14,260	29,380
1975	17,829	19,258	37,087
1976	21,590	24,159	45,749
1977	28,574	31,576	60,150
1978	39,812	38,682	78,494
1979	49,537	47,952	97,489
1980	62,364	68,893	131,257
1981	62,432	94,355	156,787
1982	60,200	105,487	165,687
1983	75,587	117,838	193,425
1984	97,807	128,131	225,938
1985	125,202	147,735	272,937
1986	158,674	188,977	347,651

1. Sum of currency outside of banks and private sector demand deposits, source line 34.
2. Time, savings, and foreign currency deposits by residents, source line 35.
3. Calculated by adding columns A and B.

SOURCE: IMF-IFS-Y, 1982, 1986, and 1987.

Table 3054

PERU MONEY SUPPLY, 1952–86
(M NC YE)

Year	A. Money[1] (M_1)	B. Quasi- Money[2]	C. Total[3] (M_2)
1952	2.7	1.6	4.3
1953	3.1	1.8	4.9
1954	3.4	2.0	5.4
1955	3.6	2.5	6.1
1956	4.2	3.0	7.2
1957	4.4	3.5	7.9
1958	4.7	3.8	8.5
1959	6.0	4.0	10.0
1960	7.1	4.7	11.8
1961	8.3	5.5	13.8
1962	8.9	6.6	15.5
1963	10.3	7.7	18.0
1964	13.0	9.6	22.6
1965	15.6	12.3	27.9
1966	17.8	13.7	31.5
1967	20.1	14.1	34.2
1968	22.2	14.4	36.6
1969	26.3	14.5	40.8
1970	40.8	14.1	54.9
1971	45.0	15.5	60.5
1972	57.9	16.8	74.7
1973	72.5	19.1	91.6
1974	102.6	21.2	123.8
1975	120.0	23.3	143.3
1976	151.0	26.9	177.9
1977	182.4	39.8	222.2
1978	265.3	91.9	357.2
1979	451.7	234.5	686.2
1980	712.6	546.1	1,258.7
1981	1,044.8	1,077.3	2,122.1
1982	1,408.4	2,191.2	3,599.6
1983	2,763.2	4,560.2	7,323.4
1984	5,967.0	11,038.0	17,006.0
1985	23,002.0	20,765.0	43,767.0
1986	42,713.0	24,117.0	66,830.0

1. Sum of currency outside of banks and private sector demand deposits, source line 34.
2. Time, savings, and foreign currency deposits by residents, source line 35.
3. Calculated by adding columns A and B.

SOURCE: IMF-IFS-Y, 1982, 1986, and 1987.

Table 3055

URUGUAY MONEY SUPPLY, 1952–86
(B NC YE)

Year	A. Money[1] (M_1)	B. Quasi-Money[2]	C. Total[3] (M_2)
1952	~	~	~
1953	~	~	~
1954	~	~	~
1955	~	~	~
1956	~	~	~
1957	~	~	~
1958	~	~	~
1959	~	~	~
1960	~	#	#
1961	#	#	#
1962	#	#	.01
1963	#	#	.01
1964	.01	.01	.02
1965	.01	.01	.02
1966	.01	.01*	.02*
1967	.03	.02	.05
1968	.05	.02	.07
1969	.08	.03	.11
1970	.09	.04	.13
1971	.14	.06	.20
1972	.20	.12	.32
1973	.36	.18	.54
1974	.59	.34	.92
1975	.83*	.78*	1.61*
1976	1.38	1.85	3.23
1977	1.94	3.9	5.83
1978	3.59	7.53	11.11
1979	6.16	14.44	20.60
1980	9.08	26.51	35.59
1981	9.84	43.45	53.29
1982	13.70*	58.77*	72.47*
1983	14.93	66.93	81.86
1984	22.16	110.76	132.88
1985	45.99	213.80	259.79
1986	85.79	397.16	482.91

1. Sum of currency outside of banks and private sector demand deposits, souce line 34.
2. Time savings, and foreign currency deposits by residents, source line 35.
3. Calculated by adding columns A and B.

SOURCE: IMF-IFS-Y, 1982, 1986, and 1987.

Table 3056

VENEZUELA MONEY SUPPLY, 1952–86
(M NC YE)

Year	A. Money[1] (M_1)	B. Quasi-Money[2]	C. Total[3] (M_2)
1952	1,909	273	2,182
1953	2,085	372	2,457
1954	2,169	494	2,663
1955	2,414	669	3,083
1956	2,756	922	3,678
1957	3,649	1,501	5,150
1958	4,017	1,860	5,877
1959	3,823	2,083	5,906
1960	3,574	1,691	5,265
1961	3,684	1,643	5,327
1962	3,604	1,806	5,410
1963	3,623	2,501	6,124
1964	4,399	3,022	7,421
1965	4,489	3,096	7,585
1966	4,620	2,928	7,548
1967	5,237	3,397	8,634
1968	5,699	3,771	9,470
1969	6,186	4,299	10,485
1970	6.732	4,718	11,450
1971	7,868	5,526	13,394
1972	9,467	6,981	16,448
1973	11,318	8,438	19,757
1974	16,006	9,980	25,987
1975	23,312	15,416	38,728
1976	27,105	21,567	48,671
1977	34,027	27,482	61,509
1978	38,987	31,848	70,835
1979	42,460	32,657	75,117
1980	50,209	38,432	88,642
1981	54,954	48,231	103,185
1982	58,015	57,979	115,994
1983	70,049	69,994	140,043
1984	86,693	76,787	163,481
1985	93,707‡	88,603‡	182,310
1986	98,479‡	119,418‡	217,897‡

1. Sum of currency outside of banks and private sector demand deposits, source line 34.
2. Time, savings, and foreign currency deposits by residents, source line 35.
3. Calculated by adding columns A and B.

SOURCE: IMF-IFS-Y, 1982, 1986, and 1987.

Table 3057

MONEY SUPPLY[1] CHANGES, 19 LC, 1958–86

(PC Calculated from Indexes)

	Country	1958	1959	1960	1961	1962	1963	1964	1965	1966	1967	1968	1969	1970	1971
A.	ARGENTINA	~	~	~	~	~	~	~	~	~	~	~	~	~	~
B.	BOLIVIA	~	22.2	13.4	18.1	14.6	15.6	23.1	22.7	19.9	5.2	7.3	9.6	9.0	10.9
C.	BRAZIL	~	27.1	38.5	44.3	53.3	58.2	86.1	83.7	38.6	34.6	42.0	32.3	29.2	31.1
D.	CHILE	~	~	~	~	~	~	~	~	~	~	~	~	52.9	99.3
E.	COLOMBIA	16.7	16.2	6.6	16.3	19.8	17.1	24.1	14.3	16.0	22.2	19.3	21.1	19.8	10.3
F.	COSTA RICA	7.0	7.2*	2.1	-6.3	13.0	12.3	11.0	4.5	2.6	19.6	16.9	.8	4.9	30.9
H.	DOMINICAN REP.	16.4	5.8	-7.7	12.9	-1.7	9.3	8.1	-2.5	-1.4	-2.3	9.1	8.8	14.4	7.4
I.	ECUADOR	3.7	8.3	10.6	6.0	5.9	12.0	26.3	-.9	8.4	15.5	17.5	11.7	22.6	20.5
J.	EL SALVADOR	-6.5	-5.7	1.7	-7.7	2.4	7.8	5.5	2.0	2.9	3.8	.4	5.7	7.6	3.6
K.	GUATEMALA	2.5	-4.7	-2.5	-1.7	.9	13.4	16.2	3.6	9.3	-3.5	6.9	1.1	6.4	-1.2
L.	HAITI	-3.1	-14.4	10.3	6.4	4.2	5.6	3.8	-3.0	3.8	3.8	11.3	10.7	10.3	18.0
M.	HONDURAS	-2.0	4.6	-2.4	2.2	10.7	8.7	14.5	13.9	6.9	-2.1	14.3	12.9	13.6	3.7
N.	MEXICO	6.6	13.1	12.1	6.0	8.3	14.0	19.8	9.0	8.4	10.1	12.3	12.6	11.3	8.1
O.	NICARAGUA	3.3	-6.4	1.9	4.8	21.3	21.2	11.3	17.4	6.8	-.7	-3.6	-1.7	6.6	4.6
P.	PANAMA	2.8	13.2	-.4	3.2	7.0	19.1	-9.7	9.3	11.5	8.9	11.2	7.7	13.7	9.5
Q.	PARAGUAY	12.3	14.7	3.0	18.6	12.6	2.9	17.8	16.0	-.9	5.6	4.1	-7.2	6.3	14.8
R.	PERU	3.6	6.9	19.3	13.0	7.4	8.6	36.5	25.3	14.6	8.5	16.9	12.0	42.5	27.2
S.	URUGUAY	~	~	~	~	~	~	~	~	68.6	49.0	87.0	69.4	31.4	32.1
T.	VENEZUELA	18.0	7.5	-16.5	7.0	-1.5	5.0	12.7	12.2	2.3	4.8	2.8	8.2	9.9	11.8
	UNITED STATES	1.6	2.1	5.0	2.2	2.4	3.2	3.8	4.2	4.6	4.0	7.0	5.9	3.8	6.8

	Country	1972	1973	1974	1975	1976	1977	1978	1979	1980	1981	1982	1983	1984	1985	1986
A.	ARGENTINA	~	72.7	83.5	90.5	310.8	144.2	145.6	131.4	115.9	53.9	195.7	287.8	522.6	650.2	~
B.	BOLIVIA	20.8	35.0	42.8	22.6	18.9	31.9	13.5	13.8	38.4	15.1	120.6	198.9	790.9	7,834.1	~
C.	BRAZIL	32.5	42.0	36.5	35.7	42.4	37.0	40.9	52.2	76.0	65.1	82.0	85.1	138.2	275.7	~
D.	CHILE	100.9	264.4	315.5	239.5	216.1	156.7	81.2	60.0	62.6	23.4	-5.5	28.3	18.9	~	~
E.	COLOMBIA	19.3	28.3	28.6	9.7	30.2	36.2	35.4	25.2	24.8	24.6	23.1	19.7	21.4	22.7	~
F.	COSTA RICA	19.5	23.0	42.7	68.0	83.7	31.4	21.9	10.4	9.6	38.8	70.4	45.3	26.2	8.6	~
H.	DOMINICAN REP.	15.5	17.0	26.1	26.9	-2.5	9.5	12.7	9.5	15.9	2.3	15.9	9.0	30.8	24.5	29.0
I.	ECUADOR	16.6	31.3	43.4	23.0	9.2	43.2	13.9	20.1	25.7	21.7	21.6	22.3	27.2	~	42.4
J.	EL SALVADOR	13.4	19.0	27.0	14.7	25.4	33.1	-1.2	12.0	25.2	-2.7	7.4	-1.0	5.1	26.0	23.5
K.	GUATEMALA	12.3	23.8	25.1	7.1	33.9	28.6	12.2	11.0	5.7	1.0	6.6	.1	5.0	24.8	37.8
L.	HAITI	17.3	22.9	15.1	-.5	37.2	21.3	17.5	12.8	13.2	24.9	2.1	4.3	13.5	.8	8.5
M.	HONDURAS	6.4	21.8	11.3	.3	27.5	26.7	11.4	17.6	7.3	8.5	3.0	13.4	13.6	~	8.5
N.	MEXICO	13.5	22.8	19.2	21.5	22.3	26.6	37.2	31.4	31.1	36.8	43.5	44.1	53.2	53.7	51.3
O.	NICARAGUA	17.8	51.4	25.6	-12.4	21.4	15.6	-2.2	18.5	105.3	21.7	19.9	73.0	~	~	~
P.	PANAMA	27.2	21.8	11.2	9.6	13.1	10.1	13.5	16.1	16.8	8.7	7.0	.7	3.7	3.0	~
Q.	PARAGUAY	14.1	33.0	21.4	16.6	20.6	36.6	34.1	32.2	20.4	13.7	-5.5	8.4	37.3	23.2	25.4
R.	PERU	19.6	26.9	31.3	28.8	21.6	21.6	34.3	59.5	71.1	43.4	33.7	75.4	97.3	204.2	175.6
S.	URUGUAY	49.3	63.5	80.0	50.1	64.2	46.5	56.5	99.5	34.9	33.9	-.8	27.7	24.0	71.8	95.4
T.	VENEZUELA	18.3	21.9	31.1	47.3	27.0	25.0	18.9	7.4	14.1	11.4	9.9	11.6	26.8	14.1	7.2
	UNITED STATES	7.2	7.2	5.0	4.6	5.7	7.6	8.2	8.0	6.3	7.1	6.6	11.1	7.0	9.2	13.4

1. "Money" equals M$_1$ (the sum of currency outside banks and private sector demand deposits).

SOURCE: IMF-IFS-Y, 1986 and 1987, pp. 88-91.

Table 3058

INCOME VELOCITY OF MONEY, 18 L, 1951-82

(1980 = 100)

Country	1951	1952	1953	1954	1955	1956	1957	1958	1959	1960	1961	1962
A. ARGENTINA	~	~	~	~	~	~	~	~	~	~	~	~
B. BOLIVIA	~	137.7	236.1	274.1	317.4	165.6	120.4	122.9	115.6	118.3	108.9	103.9

Country	1963	1964	1965	1966	1967	1968	1969	1970	1971	1972	1973	1974
A. ARGENTINA	44.4	43.6	46.6	45.1	42.8	37.7	37.6	36.6	50.7	61.2	55.6	40.2
B. BOLIVIA	96.8	88.6	80.3	74.1	79.6	84.2	83.2	85.5	84.4	89.0	99.5	115.9

Country	1975	1976	1977	1978	1979	1980	1981	1982
A. ARGENTINA	63.3	80.3	90.9	91.8	106.6	100.0	125.7	~
B. BOLIVIA	107.3	103.5	90.7	93.7	99.1	100.0	~	~

Continued in SALA, 24–3058.

Table 3059

INCOME VELOCITY OF MONEY PLUS QUASI-MONEY,[1] 19 LC, 1951-86

(1980 = 100)

Country	1951	1952	1953	1954	1955	1956	1957	1958	1959	1960	1961	1962
A. ARGENTINA	~	~	~	~	~	~	~	~	~	~	~	~
B. BOLIVIA	~	192.1	343.8	417.9	478.9	254.0	184.0	189.6	178.2	181.5	168.2	159.3
C. BRAZIL	~	~	~	~	~	~	~	~	41.0	46.1	46.2	47.2	50.4
D. CHILE	~	~	~	~	~	~	~	~	~	~	~	~
E. COLOMBIA					11.7	~	~	~	11.0	11.7	11.4	10.6
F. COSTA RICA	240.6	221.6	221.2	214.2	218.2	218.1	216.5	207.0	193.3*	199.9	213.6	208.0
H. DOMINICAN REP.	141.4	128.6	132.8	105.5	94.7	101.2	100.0	99.9	88.8	106.9	95.7	125.4
I. ECUADOR	165.3	153.5	152.1	145.2	154.0	138.9	137.7	137.2	134.1	133.1	130.8	127.7
J. EL SALVADOR	183.7	159.0	161.1	154.3	150.5	148.8	144.9	137.1	136.2	125.4	131.7	134.4
K. GUATEMALA	219.6	211.9	192.4	202.0	185.2	165.1	150.7*	148.6	160.4	160.0	159.6	162.0
L. HAITI	~	~	~	~	239.7	232.6	239.6	246.6	255.1	232.8	217.3	217.7
M. HONDURAS	189.6	178.4	169.9	139.0	159.8	144.4	156.7	182.4	171.7	166.7	168.5	160.7
N. MEXICO	123.3	122.7	110.4	106.5	110.9	116.0	115.2	113.6	110.8	117.7	117.5	117.2
O. NICARAGUA	~	~	~	~	~	~	~	~	~	184.1	189.4	174.6
P. PANAMA	~	~	~	~	231.1	224.5	227.0	219.4	208.2	211.0	225.3	221.1
Q. PARAGUAY	~	131.9	161.4	166.8	161.5	153.6	187.9	187.0	181.5	202.4	192.8	186.5
R. PERU	104.0	94.9	90.2	94.9	93.0	88.4	89.3	93.1	102.1	102.0	120.3	104.4
S. URUGUAY	~	~	~	~	~	~	~	~	~	~	~	~
T. VENEZUELA	257.9	235.0	221.2	226.0	214.5	205.8	172.1	144.5	132.5	158.0	162.9	178.2
UNITED STATES	74.3	74.1	76.3	73.5	92.4	77.2	79.1	89.8	94.4	94.5	91.6	91.4

Country	1963	1964	1965	1966	1967	1968	1969	1970	1971	1972	1973	1974
A. ARGENTINA	107.3	103.2	108.4	106.7	102.4	90.1	87.5	82.9	288.1	126.3	104.2	82.3
B. BOLIVIA	146.4	133.8	121.4	148.0	135.7	121.7	106.7	95.2	82.8	134.1	151.1	143.3
C. BRAZIL	67.8*	70.5	62.7	64.9	64.0	63.5	63.6	59.5	60.2	59.2	56.5	61.8*
D. CHILE	~	~	~	~	~	313.7	129.3	118.8	97.1	85.2	98.9	147.8
E. COLOMBIA	11.6	11.6	11.4	12.0	11.1	10.8	10.3	10.3	10.9	11.1	11.1	11.4
F. COSTA RICA	200.5	190.8	194.4	205.9	187.1	176.1	212.2	229.6	178.5	156.8	30.4	28.8
H. DOMINICAN REP.	131.1	131.4	110.3	118.2	119.5	106.5	107.1	98.5	98.1	98.2	91.9	85.3
I. ECUADOR	123.7	121.4	128.9*	125.1	119.9	107.4	104.8	101.4	95.8	95.7	98.1	104.3
J. EL SALVADOR	125.4	123.8	125.1	124.2	123.2	127.0	124.7	122.5	120.2	110.9	106.9	103.4
K. GUATEMALA	159.0	136.1	128.4	118.7	117.0	114.9	112.9	112.2	111.1	99.4	97.2	100.9
L. HAITI	219.8	235.0	263.5	273.2	265.0	241.7	229.7	215.1	196.1	163.9	173.4	124.6
M. HONDURAS	151.3	147.4	144.0	139.3	143.5	131.9	118.2	107.4	104.1	102.3	95.7	95.9
N. MEXICO	107.9	109.4	106.5	109.8	106.9	105.8	103.3	111.1	114.2	115.9	115.3	119.4
O. NICARAGUA	158.4	158.7	141.1	132.0	137.2	144.3	150.5	159.2	149.2	122.0	107.2	121.4
P. PANAMA	202.5	217.0	205.0	188.6	178.4	166.7	168.7	150.2	133.1	123.5	109.9	113.8
Q. PARAGUAY	181.2	158.3	141.9	140.6	131.9	126.9	132.0	127.8	120.1	118.1	115.8	127.6
R. PERU	99.2	93.9	89.1	91.1	97.2	104.0	108.3	98.9	91.2	86.7	85.2	84.1
S. URUGUAY	~	~	96.1*	130.2	142.6	166.7	140.2	127.7	114.6	125.3	160.4	160.2
T. VENEZUELA	176.3	169.4	161.8	161.1	161.4	161.2*	152.6	153.3	151.7	134.4	132.9	160.2
UNITED STATES	89.0	88.3	88.7	91.3	90.3	91.2	92.8	94.1	91.0	88.9	90.6	92.6

Table 3059 (Continued)

INCOME VELOCITY OF MONEY PLUS QUASI-MONEY,[1] 19 LC, 1951-86

(1980 = 100)

Country	1975	1976	1977	1978	1979	1980	1981	1982	1983	1984	1985	1986
A. ARGENTINA	147.4	189.7	146.7	117.3	114.5	100.0	101.1	112.7	134.3	~	~	~
B. BOLIVIA	137.1	123.5	102.8	99.2	99.9	100.0	102.9	119.6	158.5	317.9	501.9	~
C. BRAZIL	64.8	73.3	78.9	76.5	80.4	100.0	116.7	113.8	132.7	137.6	119.1	~
D. CHILE	143.1	163.6	147.6	125.3	112.4	100.0	75.4	57.7	70.3	67.9	~	~
E. COLOMBIA	12.9	13.0	12.8	91.6	97.2	100.0	86.9	83.2	86.0	86.9	87.5	~
F. COSTA RICA	21.7	12.4	42.1	115.2	101.9	100.0	90.7	108.1	96.1	103.9	103.4	107.4
H. DOMINICAN REP.	79.0	84.4	88.4	83.6	95.0	100.0	107.0	98.1	93.7	99.2	114.2	8.6
I. ECUADOR	99.7	110.0	100.5	103.4	103.5	100.0	100.4	96.8	108.5	117.1	~	~
J. EL SALVADOR	100.5	103.6	98.9	103.3	104.1	100.0	92.1	84.6	87.5	88.3	84.5	89.3
K. GUATEMALA	99.6	93.2	95.7	92.9	94.6	100.0	98.9	84.9	84.4	82.1	~	~
L. HAITI	131.9	120.8	106.4	90.5	83.8	100.0	85.7	83.3	85.7	85.9	~	~
M. HONDURAS	99.7	96.3	92.8	90.2	89.0	100.0	101.5	95.3	82.0	75.4	79.7	81.3
N. MEXICO	125.3	107.0	104.5	98.5	97.3	100.0	94.7	92.8	105.8	103.3	112.0	~
O. NICARAGUA	132.2	121.3	118.6	123.6	120.3	100.0	81.4	79.3	59.7	~	~	~
P. PANAMA	117.5	115.8	111.2	108.7	99.6	100.0	88.4	84.9	~	~	~	~
Q. PARAGUAY	118.5	106.5	98.0	92.4	97.2	100.0	101.6	93.3	93.2	102.3	112.2	125.3
R. PERU	82.1	95.6	107.4	118.6	122.9	100.0	104.7	101.3	99.4	104.0	103.0	~
S. URUGUAY	166.3	139.2	123.8	109.0	100.6	100.0	81.0	65.1	63.6	66.9	65.2	62.3
T. VENEZUELA	116.5	100.0	88.6	81.8	91.9	100.0	98.6	83.4	73.8	72.6	68.6	~
UNITED STATES	92.2	91.0	90.0	93.8	97.3	100.0	105.5	102.8	95.2	96.5	93.6	90.8

1. "Money" equals the sum of currency outside banks and private sector demand deposits. "Quasi-Money" is time, savings, and foreign currency deposits by residents. "Income Velocity" is here defined as "money" plus "quasi-money" divided by "GDP" and then converted to index format. Data "are designed to exhibit variability in the income velocity of money, and not international differences in the ratio of income to money. The ratio is therefore expressed in index number form, rather than in amounts of national currency income per unit of domestic currency" (IMF-IFS-S, no. 5, 1983, p. viii).

SOURCE: IMF-IFS-S, no. 5, 1983, pp. 54–57; IMF-IFS-Y, 1986 and 1987, pp. 100–103.

Table 3060

MONEY MULTIPLIERS, 12 LC, 1978–82

	Country	Monetary Multiplier (M$_1$)				Monetary Multiplier (M$_2$)			
		Average	Minimum	Maximum	Coefficient of Variation	Average	Minimum	Maximum	Coefficient of Variation
A.	ARGENTINA	1.26	.74	3.75	62.25	2.47	1.01	3.90	39.44
	Barbados	1.50	1.32	1.74	7.69	4.69	4.21	5.64	9.68
C.	BRAZIL	1.85	1.73	2.00	3.54	2.26	2.10	2.51	4.81
D.	CHILE	.85	.60	1.32	20.99	3.10	1.76	6.40	48.42
F.	COSTA RICA	1.42	1.01	1.85	15.51	3.28	3.01	3.65	6.06
H.	DOMINICAN REP.	1.00	.92	1.14	2.07	2.13	1.88	2.52	6.97
	Dominica	1.64	1.02	2.65	31.84	5.28	2.83	8.63	35.95
I.	ECUADOR	1.61	1.42	1.92	12.35	2.02	1.64	2.46	11.91
	Grenada	1.28	1.11	1.49	8.35	3.13	2.66	3.91	10.91
K.	GUATEMALA	1.06	.94	1.15	4.89	2.47	2.06	2.92	12.22
L.	HAITI	.97	.66	1.53	22.31	1.82	1.32	2.48	17.25
	Jamaica	1.68	1.30	2.02	11.81	4.33	3.35	6.40	19.93
M.	HONDURAS	1.52	1.45	1.83	9.54	3.19	2.73	4.03	10.30
N.	MEXICO	.64	.47	.72	13.88	1.75	1.60	1.90	4.42
R.	PERU	.92	.67	1.12	16.90	1.55	1.39	1.75	6.51
S.	URUGUAY	1.02	.77	1.32	12.64	4.56	2.30	6.76	29.76

SOURCE: Richard Lynn Ground, "Orthodox Adjustment Programmes in Latin America: A Critical Look at the Policies of the International Monetary Fund," *Cepal Review* (Santiago, 1984).

CHAPTER 31

EXCHANGE RATES

Table 3100

IMF SDR YEAR-END EXCHANGE RATES,[1] 19 LC, 1970–86

(NC per SDR)[2]

	Country	1970	1971	1972	1973	1974	1975	1976	1977	1978
A.	ARGENTINA	.004	.0005	.0005	.0006	.0006	.00001*	.00003	.00007	.00013
B.	BOLIVIA	11.88	12.90	21.71	24.13	24.49	23.41	23.24	24.29	26.06
C.	BRAZIL	4.95	.01*	.01	.01	.01	.01	.01	.02	.03
D.	CHILE	.01	.02	.03	.43	2.29	9.95	20.24	33.96	44.23
E.	COLOMBIA	19.09	22.70	24.74	29.91	35.05	38.59	42.20	46.11	53.41
F.	COSTA RICA	6.64	7.20	7.20	8.02	10.49	10.03	9.96	10.41	11.17
H.	DOMINICAN REP.	1.00	1.09	1.09	1.21	1.22	1.17	1.16	1.21	1.30
I.	ECUADOR	25.00	27.14	27.14	30.16	30.61	29.27	29.05	20.37	32.57
J.	EL SALVADOR	2.50	2.71	2.71	3.02	3.06	2.93	2.90	3.04	3.26
K.	GUATEMALA	1.00	1.09	1.09	1.21	1.22	1.17	1.16	1.21	1.30
L.	HAITI	5.00	5.43	5.43	6.03	6.12	5.85	5.81	6.07	6.51
M.	HONDURAS	2.00	2.17	2.17	2.41	2.45	2.34	2.32	2.43	2.61
N.	MEXICO	12.50	13.57	13.57	15.08	15.30	14.63	23.18	27.62	29.61
O.	NICARAGUA	7.03	7.63	7.63	8.48	8.60	8.23	8.16	8.54	9.15
P.	PANAMA	1.00	1.09	1.09	1.21	1.22	1.17	1.16	1.21	1.30
Q.	PARAGUAY	126.00	136.80	136.80	152.00	154.27	147.50	146.39	153.05	164.15
R.	PERU	.04*	.04	.04	.05	.05	.05	.08	.16	.26
S.	URUGUAY	.25	.40	.80	1.13	2.03	3.20	4.65	6.57	9.19
T.	VENEZUELA	4.45	4.72	4.72	5.17	5.25	5.02	4.99	5.21	5.59
	UNITED STATES	1.00	1.09	1.09	1.21	1.22	1.17	1.16	1.21	1.30

	Country	1979	1980	1981	1982	1983	1984	1985	1986
A.	ARGENTINA	.00021	.00025	.00084	.00536	.02435	.17520	.87929	1.53755
B.	BOLIVIA	32.29	31.26	28.53	216.21	523.48	8,821.89	1.8585	2.3522
C.	BRAZIL	.06	.08	.15	.28	1.03	3.12	11.52	18.27
D.	CHILE	51.38	49.74	45.39	81.00	91.64	125.71	201.96	250.42
E.	COLOMBIA	57.96	64.94	68.76	77.54	92.94	111.64	189.15	267.88
F.	COSTA RICA	11.290	10.930	42.007	44.400	45.438	46.805	58.985	72.015
H.	DOMINICAN REP.	1.3173	1.2754	1.1640	1.1031	1.0470	.9802	3.2294	3.7633
I.	ECUADOR	32.933	31.885	29.049	36.568	56.640	65.846	105.174	179.197
J.	EL SALVADOR	3.2933	3.1885	2.9099	2.7578	2.6174	2.4505	2.7461	6.1160
K.	GUATEMALA	1.3173	1.2754	1.1640	1.1031	1.0470	.9802	1.0984	3.0580
L.	HAITI	6.5867	6.3770	5.8198	5.5156	5.2347	4.9011	5.4921	6.1160
M.	HONDURAS	2.6347	2.5508	2.3279	2.2062	2.0939	1.9604	2.1968	2.4464
N.	MEXICO	30.04	29.66	30.53	106.43	150.55	188.75	408.28	1,129.62
O.	NICARAGUA	13.239	12.818	11.698	11.086	10.522	9.851	30.756	85.623
P.	PANAMA	1.3173	1.2754	1.1640	1.1031	1.0470	.9802	1.0984	1.2232
Q.	PARAGUAY	165.98	160.70	146.66	138.99	131.92	235.25	351.49‡	672.75‡
R.	PERU	.33	.44	.59	1.09	2.38	5.88	15.32	17.06
S.	URUGUAY	11.150	12.786	13.495	37.230	45.281	73.271	137.302	221.397
T.	VENEZUELA	5.6546	5.4747	4.9963	4.7351	4.5019	7.3516	8.2382	17.7363
	UNITED STATES	1.31733	1.27541	1.16396	1.10311	1.04695	.98021	1.09842	1.22319

1. Special Drawing Right (SDR) values are based on a market basket of currencies.
2. Line aa, Market Rate.

SOURCE: IMF-IFS-Y, 1986; IMF-1FS, June 1987.

Table 3101

IMF SDR AVERAGE EXCHANGE RATES,[1] 19 LC, 1970–86
(NC per SDR)[2]

	Country	1970	1971	1972	1973	1974	1975	1976	1977	1978
A.	ARGENTINA	.0004	.0005	.0009	.0011	.0011	.0044	.00002*	.00005	.00010
B.	BOLIVIA	11.88	11.92	14.43	23.84	24.05	24.28	23.09	23.35	25.04
C.	BRAZIL	~	.01*	.01	.01	.01	.01	.01	.02	.02
D.	CHILE	.01	.01	.02	.13	1.00	5.96	15.07	25.14	39.63
E.	COLOMBIA	18.44	19.99	23.74	28.18	31.35	37.55	40.06	42.94	48.95
F.	COSTA RICA	6.63	6.65	7.20	7.92	9.54	10.41	9.89	10.01	10.73
H.	DOMINICAN REP.	1.0000	1.0030	1.0857	1.1921	1.2026	1.2142	1.1545	1.1675	1.2520
I.	ECUADOR	20.917	25.074	27.143	29.803	30.066	30.354	28.863	29.188	31.300
J.	EL SALVADOR	2.5000	2.5075	2.7143	2.9803	3.0066	3.0354	2.8863	2.9188	3.1300
K.	GUATEMALA	1.0000	1.0030	1.0857	1.1921	1.2026	1.2142	1.1545	1.1675	1.2520
L.	HAITI	5.0000	5.0149	5.4286	5.9607	6.0132	6.0708	5.7726	5.8376	6.2600
M.	HONDURAS	2.0000	2.0060	2.1714	2.3843	2.4053	2.4283	2.3090	2.3350	2.5040
N.	MEXICO	12.500	12.537	13.571	14.902	15.033	15.177	17.809	26.354	28.505
O.	NICARAGUA	7.000	7.021	7.600	8.345	8.434	8.531	8.112	8.203	8.797
P.	PANAMA	1.0000	1.0030	1.0857	1.1921	1.2026	1.2142	1.1545	1.1675	1.2520
Q.	PARAGUAY	126.00	126.38	136.80	150.21	151.53	152.98	145.47	147.11	157.75
R.	PERU	.04*	.04	.04	.05	.05	.05	.06	.10	.20
S.	URUGUAY	.250	.256	.582	1.032	1.439	2.737	3.851	5.462	7.582
T.	VENEZUELA	4.5000	4.4600	4.7771	5.1315	5.1533	5.2026	4.9528	5.0116	5.3742
	UNITED STATES	1.00000	1.00298	1.08571	1.19213	1.20264	1.21415	1.15452	1.16752	1.25200

	Country	1979	1980	1981	1982	1983	1984	1985	1986
A.	ARGENTINA	.00017	.00024	.00052	.00286	.01126	.06934	.61104	1.10634
B.	BOLIVIA	26.81	31.90	28.90	70.79	245.63	2,232.24	.4487	2.2548
C.	BRAZIL	.03	.07	.11	.20	.62	1.89	6.30	16.02
D.	CHILE	48.12	50.76	45.99	56.20	84.28	101.123	163.55	226.440
E.	COLOMBIA	54.98	61.54	64.25	70.77	84.30	103.34	144.49	227.902
F.	COSTA RICA	11.07	11.15	25.66	41.30	43.93	45.646	51.227	65.681
H.	DOMINICAN REP.	1.2920	1.3015	1.1792	1.1040	1.0690	1.0250	3.1604	3.4073
I.	ECUADOR	32.300	32.538	29.479	33.149	47.159	64.100	70.623	144.041
J.	EL SALVADOR	3.2300	3.2538	2.9479	2.7600	2.6725	2.5625	2.5384	5.6924
K.	GUATEMALA	1.2920	1.3015	1.1792	1.1040	1.0690	1.0250	1.0153	2.1994
L.	HAITI	6.4600	6.5077	5.8958	5.5201	5.3450	3.1251	5.0767	5.8659
M.	HONDURAS	2.5840	2.6031	2.3583	2.2080	2.1380	2.0500	2.0307	2.3463
N.	MEXICO	29.464	29.871	28.907	62.268	128.380	172.025	260.812	717.713
O.	NICARAGUA	11.958	13.080	11.851	11.095	10.743	10.301	26.911	78.016
P.	PANAMA	1.2920	1.3015	1.1792	1.1040	1.0690	1.0250	1.0153	1.1732
Q.	PARAGUAY	162.79	163.99	148.57	139.11	134.69	206.03	311.37	397.90
R.	PERU	.29	.38	.50	.77	1.74	3.55	11.14	16.36
S.	URUGUAY	10.156	11.843	12.759	15.356	36.923	57.525	102.987	178.314
T.	VENEZUELA	5.5459	5.5868	5.0615	4.7390	4.5940	7.1930	7.6150	9.4831
	UNITED STATES	1.29200	1.30153	1.17916	1.10401	1.06900	1.02501	1.01534	1.17317

1. Special Drawing Right (SDR) values are based on a market basket of currencies.
2. Line rb, Market Rate.

SOURCE: IMF-IFS-Y, 1986; IMF-IFS-Y, 1987.

Table 3102

IMF DOLLAR VALUE OF SDR, 1969–86[a]
(YE and YA)

Year	US Dollar/SDR Rate (YE)	US Dollar/SDR Rate (YA)[1]	SDR/US Dollar Rate (YE)	SDR/US Dollar Rate (YA)[1]
1969	1.00000	1.00000	1.00000	1.00000
1970	1.00000	1.00000	1.00000	1.00000
1971	1.08571	1.00298	.92105	.99702
1972	1.08571	1.98571	.92105	.92105
1973	1.20635	1.19213	.82895	.83883
1974	1.22435	1.20264	.81676	.83150
1975	1.17066	1.21415	.85422	.82362
1976	1.16183	1.15452	.86071	.86616
1977	1.21471	1.16752	.82324	.85652
1978	1.30279	1.25200	.76758	.79872
1979	1.31733	1.29200	.75911	.77399
1980	1.27541	1.30153	.78406	.76833
1981	1.16396	1.17916	.85914	.84806
1982	1.10311	1.10401	.90653	.90579
1983	1.04695	1.06900	.95515	.93545
1984	.98021	1.02501	1.02019	.97560
1985	1.09842	1.01534	.91040	.98489
1986	1.22319	1.17317	.81753	.85239

1. Geometric average.
2. Prior to 1970 one dollar equals one SDR (Special Drawing Right).

SOURCE: IMF-IFS-Y, 1986; IMF-IFS, June 1987.

Table 3103

IMF DOLLAR YEAR-END EXCHANGE RATES,[1] 20 L, 1948-86[a]

(NC per US)

Year	A. ARGENTINA	B. BOLIVIA	C. BRAZIL	D. CHILE	E. COLOMBIA	F. COSTA RICA	G.[3] CUBA	H. DOMINICAN REP.	I. ECUADOR	J. EL SALVADOR	K. GUATEMALA
1948	.0481	.042	.019	.0066	1.960	6.200	1.00	1.00	13.500	2.500	1.00
1949	.0902	.042	.019	.0099	1.960	6.200	1.00	1.00	13.500	2.500	1.00
1950	.1402	.060	.019	.0073	1.960	5.920	1.00	1.00	15.000	2.500	1.00
1951	.1446	.060	.019	.0093	2.510	5.635	1.00	1.00	15.000	2.500	1.00
1952	.1398	.060	.019	.0013	2.510	5.635	1.00	1.00	15.000	2.500	1.00
1953	.1398	.190	.057	.0011	2.510	5.635	1.00	1.00	15.000	2.500	1.00
1954	.1398	.190	.074	.0011	2.510	5.635	1.00	1.00	15.000	2.500	1.00
1955	.3610	.190	.067	.0055	2.510	5.635	1.00	1.00	15.000	2.500	1.00
1956	.3745	7.760	.066	.0069	2.510	5.635	1.00	1.00	15.000	2.500	1.00
1957	.3745	8.565	.091	.0099	5.425	5.635	1.00	1.00	15.000	2.500	1.00
1958	.7000	11.935	.141	.0099	6.400	5.635	1.00	1.00	15.000	2.500	1.00
1959	.8325	11.880	.184	.0105	6.400	5.635	1.00	1.00	15.000	2.500	1.00
1960	.8270	11.880	.195	.0105	6.700	5.635	1.00	1.00	15.000	2.500	1.00
1961	.8302	11.880	.307	.0105	6.700	6.635	1.00	1.00	18.000	2.500	1.00
1962	1.341	11.880	.475	.0024	9.000	6.635	1.00	1.00	18.000	2.500	1.00
1963	1.325	11.880	.620	.0030	9.000	6.635	1.00	1.00	18.000	2.500	1.00
1964	1.509	11.880	1.850	.0033	9.000	6.635	1.00	1.00	18.000	2.500	1.00
1965	1.885	11.880	2.220	.004	3.500	6.635	1.00	1.00	18.000	2.500	1.00
1966	2.473	11.880	2.220	.044	13.500	6.635	1.00	1.00	18.000	2.500	1.00
1967	3.500	11.880	2.715	.0058	15.760	6.635	1.00	1.00	18.000	2.500	1.00
1968	3.500	11.880	3.830	.008	16.880	6.635	1.00	1.00	18.000	2.500	1.00
1969	4.00	11.880	4.350	.0010	17.880	6.635	1.00	1.00	18.000	2.500	1.00
1970	5.00	11.880	4.950	.0122	19.090	6.635	1.00	1.00	25.000	2.500	1.00
1971	5.00	11.880	5.635	.0158	20.910	6.635	.92	1.00	25.000	2.500	1.00
1972	5.00	20.000	6.215	.025	22.790	6.635	.92	1.00	25.000	2.500	1.00
1973	5.00	20.000	6.220	.360	24.790	6.650	.83	1.00	25.000	2.500	1.00
1974	5.00	20.000	7.435	1.870	28.630	8.570	.83	1.00	25.000	2.500	1.00
1975	60.9	20.000	9.070	8.500	32.960	8.500	.83	1.00	25.000	2.500	1.00
1976	274.5	20.000	12.345	17.420	36.320	8.570	.83	1.00	25.000	2.500	1.00
1977	597.5	20.000	16.050	27.960	37.960	8.570	.83	1.00	25.000	2.500	1.00
1978	.100	20.000	20.920	33.950	41.000	8.570	.740	1.00	25.000	2.500	1.00
1979	.162	24.510	42.530	39.000	44.000	8.570	.720	1.00	25.000	2.500	1.00
1980	.199	24.510	65.500	39.000	50.920	8.570	.710	1.00	25.000	2.500	1.00
1981	.725	24.510	127.80	39.000	59.070	36.090	.830	1.00	25.000	2.500	1.00
1982	4.855	196.000	252.67	73.430	70.290	40.250	.850	1.00	33.150	2.500	1.00
1983	23.261	500.000	.98*	87.530	88.770	43.400	.870	1.00	54.100	2.500	1.00
1984	178.735	9.000	3.18	128.240	113.890	47.750	.900	1.00	67.175	2.500	1.00
1985	.8005*	1.6920	10.49	183.860	172.200	53.700	.910[b]	2.9400	95.750	2.500	1.00
1986	1.2570	1.9230	14.94	204.730	219.000	58.875	.793[b]	3.0766	146.500	5.000	2.50[+]

Table 3103 (Continued)

IMF DOLLAR YEAR-END EXCHANGE RATES,[1] 20 L, 1948–86[a]

(NC per US)

Year	L. HAITI	M. HONDURAS	N. MEXICO	O. NICARAGUA	P. PANAMA	Q. PARAGUAY	R. PERU[2]	S. URUGUAY[2]	T. VENEZUELA[2]
1948	5.00	2.00	4.855	5.145	1.00	3.12	16.10	.0019	3.220
1949	5.00	2.00	8.650	5.145	1.00	3.12	14.81	.0019	3.220
1950	5.00	2.00	8.650	6.826	1.00	3.12	14.95	.0019	3.220
1951	5.00	2.00	8.650	6.826	1.00	6.00	15.28	.0019	3.220
1952	5.00	2.00	8.650	6.826	1.00	15.00	15.60	.0019	3.220
1953	5.00	2.00	8.650	6.826	1.00	15.00	19.89	.0019	3.220
1954	5.00	2.00	12.500	6.826	1.00	21.00	19.00	.0021	3.220
1955	5.00	2.00	12.500	6.826	1.00	21.00	19.00	.0021	3.220
1956	5.00	2.00	12.500	6.826	1.00	10.00	19.00	.0021	3.220
1957	5.00	2.00	12.500	6.826	1.00	111.30	19.00	.0021	3.220
1958	5.00	2.00	12.500	7.026	1.00	111.30	24.49	.0021	3.220
1959	5.00	2.00	12.500	7.026	1.00	122.00	27.70	.0110	3.220
1960	5.00	2.00	12.500	7.026	1.00	126.00	26.76	.0200	3.220
1961	5.00	2.00	12.500	7.026	1.00	126.00	26.81	.0110	3.220
1962	5.00	2.00	12.500	7.026	1.00	126.00	26.82	.0164	3.220
1963	5.00	2.00	12.500	7.026	1.00	126.00	26.82	.0187	3.220
1964	5.00	2.00	12.500	7.026	1.00	126.00	26.82	.0600	4.450
1965	5.00	2.00	12.500	7.026	1.00	126.00	26.82	.0762	4.450
1966	5.00	2.00	12.500	7.026	1.00	126.00	26.82	.2000	4.450
1967	5.00	2.00	12.500	7.026	1.00	126.00	38.70	.2500	4.450
1968	5.00	2.00	12.500	7.026	1.00	126.00	38.70	.2500	4.450
1969	5.00	2.00	12.500	7.026	1.00	126.00	38.70	.2500	4.450
1970	5.00	2.00	12.500	7.026	1.00	126.00	38.70	.2500	4.450
1971	5.00	2.00	12.500	7.026	1.00	126.00	38.70	.3700	4.350
1972	5.00	2.00	12.500	7.026	1.00	126.00	38.70	.7320	4.350
1973	5.00	2.00	12.500	7.026	1.00	126.00	38.70	.9370	4.285
1974	5.00	2.00	12.500	7.026	1.00	126.00	38.70	1.6560	4.285
1975	5.00	2.00	12.500	7.026	1.00	126.00	45.00	2.7300	4.293
1976	5.00	2.00	19.950	7.026	1.00	126.00	69.37	4.0000	4.293
1977	5.00	2.00	22.736	7.026	1.00	126.00	130.38	5.4100	4.293
1978	5.00	2.00	22.724	7.026	1.00	126.00	196.18	7.0540	4.293
1979	5.00	2.00	22.803	10.050	1.00	126.00	250.12	8.4640	4.293
1980	5.00	2.00	23.256	10.050	1.00	126.00	.342*	10.0250	4.293
1981	5.00	2.00	26.229	10.050	1.00	126.00	.507	11.5940	4.293
1982	5.00	2.00	96.480	10.050	1.00	126.00	.990	33.7500	4.293
1983	5.00	2.00	143.930	10.050	1.00	126.00	2.271	43.250	4.300
1984	5.00	2.00	192.560	10.050	1.00	240.00	5.696	43.250	4.300
1985	5.00	2.00	371.700	28.000	1.00	320.00‡	13.945	74.750	7.500
1986	5.00	2.00	923.500	70.000	1.00	550.00‡	13.950	125.000	7.500
								181.000	14.500

1. Line ae, Market Rate/Par Rate (or Central Rate).

2. For multiple exchange rates, see SALA, 17, ch. 24.

3. Beginning 1971, data reflect noncommercial rates applied to tourism and to remittances from outside the ruble area available at the U.N. Statistical Office.

a. For previous years after 1937, see SALA, 17, ch. 24.

b. Fourth quarter.

SOURCE: IMF-IFS-S, no. 1, 1981; IMF-IFS-Y, 1986, and IMF-AFS, June, 1987; Cuba data from UN-MB, various monthly, 1969–87.

Table 3104

IMF DOLLAR AVERAGE EXCHANGE RATES,[1] 19 L, 1965-86[a]
(NC per US)

Country	1965	1970	1971	1972	1973	1974	1975	1976	1977	1978	1979	1980	1981	1982	1983	1984	1985	1986
A. ARGENTINA	1.7	3.8	4.6	8.2	9.4	8.9	36.6	.00001*	.00004	.00008	.00013	.00018	.00044	.00259	.01053	.06765	.60181	.94303
B. BOLIVIA	11.88	11.88	11.88	13.29	20.00	20.00	20.00	20.00	20.00	20.00	20.39	24.51	24.51	64.12	229.78	2,177.78	.4419*	1.9220
C. BRAZIL	1.90	4.59	.01*	.01	.01	.01	.01	.01	.01	.02	.03	.05	.09	.18	.58	1.85	6.20	13.654
D. CHILE	.003	.012	.012	.020	.111	.832	4.911	13.054	21.529	31.656	37.246	39.000	39.000	50.909	78.842	98.656	161.081	193.020
E. COLOMBIA	10.475	18.443	19.932	21.886	23.637	26.064	30.929	34.694	36.775	39.095	42.550	47.280	54.491	64.085	78.854	100.817	142.311	194.260
F. COSTA RICA	6.625	6.625	6.626	6.635	6.647	7.930	8.570	8.570	8.570	8.570	8.570	8.570	21.763	37.580	41.094	44.533	50.453	55.986
H. DOMINICAN REP.	1.00	1.00	1.00	1.00	1.00	1.00	1.00	1.00	1.00	1.00	1.00	1.00	1.00	1.00	1.00	1.00	3.1126	2.9043
I. ECUADOR	18.000	20.917	25.000	25.000	25.000	25.000	25.000	25.000	25.000	25.000	25.000	25.000	25.000	30.026	44.115	62.536	69.556	122.779
J. EL SALVADOR	2.50	2.50	2.50	2.50	2.50	2.50	2.50	2.50	2.50	2.50	2.50	2.50	2.50	2.50	2.50	2.50	~	~
K. GUATEMALA	1.00	1.00	1.00	1.00	1.00	1.00	1.00	1.00	1.00	1.00	1.00	1.00	1.00	1.00	1.00	1.00	1.00	1.8750‡
L. HAITI	5.00	5.00	5.00	5.00	5.00	5.00	5.00	5.00	5.00	5.00	5.00	5.00	5.00	5.00	5.00	5.00	~	~
M. HONDURAS	2.00	2.00	2.00	2.00	2.00	2.00	2.00	2.00	2.00	2.00	2.00	2.00	2.00	2.00	2.00	2.00	~	~
N. MEXICO	12.500	12.500	12.500	12.500	12.500	12.500	12.500	15.426	22.573	22.767	22.805	22.951	24.515	56.402	120.094	167.828	256.872	611.770
O. NICARAGUA	7.000	7.000	7.000	7.000	7.000	7.013	7.026	7.026	7.026	7.026	9.255	10.050	10.050	10.050	10.050	10.050	26.504	66.500
P. PANAMA	1.00	1.00	1.00	1.00	1.00	1.00	1.00	1.00	1.00	1.00	1.00	1.00	1.00	1.00	1.00	1.00	1.00	~
Q. PARAGUAY	126.00	126.00	126.00	126.00	126.00	126.00	126.00	126.00	126.00	126.00	126.00	126.00	126.00	126.00	126.00	201.00	306.67	339.17
R. PERU	.03*	.04	.04	.04	.04	.04	.04	.06	.08	.16	.225	.29	.42	.70	1.63	3.47	10.97	13.95
S. URUGUAY	.0523	.2500	.2600	.5630	.8746	1.2155	2.2991	3.3950*	4.678	6.060	7.861	9.099	10.820	13.909	34.540	56.122	101.431	151.993
T. VENEZUELA	4.4997	4.4983	4.5007	4.4000	4.3045	4.2845	4.2850	4.2899	4.2925	4.2925	4.2925	4.2925	4.2925	4.2925	4.2975	7.0175	7.500	8.083

1. Line rf, Implicit Rate/Market Rate.

a. For previous years after 1937, see SALA, 17, ch. 24, and SALA, 22-2501. Rounding by source makes data for Argentina and Chile problematic for all but the last few years.

SOURCE: IMF-IFS-Y, 1986; IMF-IFS, June 1987.

Table 3105

EXCHANGE RATE HISTORY,[1] 13 L, 1937–74

(U per US; 1937–74 = A, 1948–74 = YE)

A. ARGENTINA

Year	Free	Official	Selling (P)	Selling (B)	Selling (A)	Selling (F)	Selling (C)	Buying (S)	Buying (P)	Buying (B)
1937[a]	3.41	*	3.23	3.23	*	3.33	*	*	3.03	3.03
1938	4.38	*	3.21	36.31	*	3.92	*	*	3.07	3.07
1939	4.40[g]	*	3.83[g]	3.83[g]	*	4.33	*	*	3.27	3.27
1940	*	*	3.73	4.23	*	4.37	*	*	3.36	3.26
1941	*	*	3.73	4.23	4.94	4.24	*	*	4.22	3.36
1942	*	*	3.73	4.23	4.94	4.23	*	*	4.22	3.36
1943	*	*	3.73	4.23	4.94	4.06	*	*	4.04	3.36
1944	*	*	3.73	4.23	4.94	4.02	*	*	3.98	3.36
1945	*	*	3.73	4.23	4.94	4.04	*	*	3.98	3.36
1946	*	*	3.73	4.23	4.94	4.09	*	*	3.98	3.36
1947	*	*	3.73	4.23	4.94	4.08	4.80	*	3.98	3.36
1948[b]	4.81	3.36	3.73	4.23	4.94	4.45	9.25	5.00[h]	3.98	3.36
1949[c]	9.02	3.36	5.37[i]	6.09	10.26	9.02	15.80	7.20[i]	5.73[i]	3.36
1950[d]	14.02	5.00	5.00[j]	5.00	*[k]	14.03	19.50	7.50[j]	7.50[j]	5.00[j]
1951	14.46	5.00	*	*	*	14.46	27.60	7.50	7.50	5.00
1952	13.98	5.00	*	*	*	13.98	23.20	7.50	7.50	5.00
1953	13.98	5.00	*	*	*	*	20.85	7.50	7.50	5.00
1954	13.98	5.00	*	*	*	*	*	*	*	*
1955	36.10	18.00	*	*	*	*	*	*	*	*
1956	37.45	18.00	*	*	*	*	*	*	*	*
1957	37.00	18.00	*	*	*	*	*	*	*	*
1958	70.00	18.00	*	*	*	*	*	*	*	*
1959[e]	*	83.25[l]	*	*	*	*	*	*	*	*
1960	*	82.70	*	*	*	*	*	*	*	*
1961	*	83.02	*	*	*	*	*	*	*	*
1962	*	134.10	*	*	*	*	*	*	*	*
1963	*	132.50	*	*	*	*	*	*	*	*
1964	*	150.90	*	*	*	*	*	*	*	*
1965	*	188.50	*	*	*	*	*	*	*	*
1966	*	247.30	*	*	*	*	*	*	*	*
1967	*	350.00	*	*	*	*	*	*	*	*
1968	*	350.00	*	*	*	*	*	*	*	*
1969	*	4.00[m]	*	*	*	*	*	*	*	*
1970	*	5.00	*	*	*	*	*	*	*	*
1971[f]	8.25[n]	5.00	*	*	*	*	*	*	*	*
1972	9.98	5.00	*	*	*	*	*	*	*	*
1973	9.98	5.00	*	*	*	*	*	*	*	*
1974	9.98[o]	5.00[o]	*	*	*	*	*	*	*	*

1. Code: A, auction; B, basic; C, curb; F, free; P, preferential; S, special

a. Selling rate: subdivided into preferential, basic auction free, and curb (1937–49); buying rate: special, preferential, basic.

b. 1948–72: two categories listed — free and official.

c. October 3, 1949: Argentina readjusted her multiple currency structure, the degree of adjustments varying widely depending upon the particular transactions and commodities to which applied.

d. On August 29, 1950, the number of effective rates was reduced from 9 to 3. The preferential import rates of 3.73 and 5.37 pesos per U.S. dollar and the basic export rate of 3.35 pesos were consolidated into a single rate of 5.00 per U.S. dollar. (Source: IFS, September 1950-country notes.)

e. A new exchange system was made effective January 12, 1959, when the previous official and free market were replaced by a single market for all transactions with a fluctuating exchange rate.

f. On September 20, 1971, a dual exchange rate system was introduced consisting of an official market with a fixed rate of 5.00 pesos per U.S. dollar and a financial market in which the rate is allowed to fluctuate.

g. January/August. Rates quoted for 1940 were established in August 1939. On August 1939 free market discontinued and a system of multiple official rates was established.

h. Beginning June 23.

i. Beginning October 3.

j. Beginning August 29.

k. Auction abolished August 28.

l. Beginning January 12, 1959.

m. A new peso equal to 100 old pesos was introduced on January 1, 1970.

n. On September 20, 1971, a dual exchange rate system was introduced, consisting of an official market with a fixed rate of 5.00 pesos per U.S. dollar and a financial market in which the rate is allowed to fluctuate.

o. August 1974.

Continued in SALA, 17-2401 through 2413.

Table 3106

LATIN AMERICA OFFICIAL, COMMERCIAL, FINANCIAL, PARALLEL, PREFERENTIAL, AND FREE MARKET EXCHANGE RATES, 20 L, 1986

(NC per US)

	Country	Currency	Rate	First Quarter 1986	Second Quarter 1986	Third Quarter 1986	Fourth Quarter 1986
A.	ARGENTINA	Austral[1]	Official	.8	.9	1.0	1.2
			Parallel	.9	.9	1.2	1.4
B.	BOLIVIA	Peso[2]	Official	1,900,000.0	1,900,000.0	1,900,000.0	1,000,000.0
			Parallel	2,200,000.0	1,900,000.0	1,900,000.0	2,000,000.0
C.	BRAZIL	Cruzeiro	Official	13.8	13.8	13.8	14.2
			Parallel	17.4	20.4	26.0	28.5
D.	CHILE	Peso	Official	186.0	190.4	194.6	200.0
			Parallel	200.0	198.0	204.0	209.0
E.	COLOMBIA	Peso	Official	179.9	196.4	202.9	216.0
			Parallel	181.0	197.0	203.0	217.0
F.	COSTA RICA	Colón	Official	54.3	55.9	56.3	58.3
			Parallel	57.5	58.0	58.0	59.0
G.	CUBA	Peso	Official	.9	.9	.9	.8
			Parallel	5.0	5.0	5.0	5.0
H.	DOMINICAN REP.	Peso	Official	2.8	2.8	2.8	3.0
I.	ECUADOR	Sucre	Official	110.0	110.0	~	146.5
			Free	144.7	171.0	166.5	145.1
J.	EL SALVADOR	Colón	Commercial	5.0	5.0	5.0	5.0
			Parallel	5.8	6.0	5.5	5.5
K.	GUATEMALA	Quetzal	Official	1.0	~	~	~
			Parallel	3.0	2.8	3.0	2.6
L.	HAITI	Gourde	Official	5.0	5.0	5.0	5.0
M.	HONDURAS	Lempiral	Official	2.0	2.0	2.0	2.0
			Parallel	2.7	2.7	2.2	2.1
N.	MEXICO	Peso	Free	483.0	630.0	742.0	852.3
			Preferential	~	~		
			Commercial	467.7	555.0	721.4	866.0
O.	NICARAGUA	Córdoba	Official	~	975.0	975.0	1,450.0
			Commercial	70.0	70.0	70.0	70.0
			Parallel	2,000.0	2,000.0	2,100.0	3,000.0
P.	PANAMA	Balboa	Official	1.0	1.0	1.0	1.0
Q.	PARAGUAY	Guaraní	Official	240.0	240.0	240.0	320.0
			Parallel	774.5	718.0	619.5	610.0
R.	PERU	Inti[3]	Commercial	14.0	14.0	14.0	14.0
			Parallel	17.7	17.4	17.4	18.4
S.	URUGUAY	Peso	Official	135.7	147.8	164.5	175.0
T.	VENEZUELA	Bolívar	Free	18.9	19.9	19.7	19.0
			Commercial	7.5	7.5	7.5	14.5

1. Change currency from peso to austral = 1,000 pesos on June 14, 1985.
2. Change currency from peso to potosí = 1,000,000 pesos.
3. Change currency from sol to inti = 1,000 soles on Feb. 1, 1985.

SOURCE: Adapted from *Latin America Weekly Report*, WR-86-13, March 28, 1986; WR-86-24, June 26, 1986; WR-86-37, Sept. 25, 1986; WR-86-50, Dec. 25, 1986.

Table 3107

PARALLEL OR BLACK MARKET EXCHANGE RATES OF U.S. DOLLARS, 12 L, 1968-83[a]

(NC per US, YE)

	Country	1968	1970	1972	1973	1974	1975	1976	1977	1978	1979	1980	1981	1982	1983
A.	ARGENTINA	350.0	4.4[b]	11.6	11.0	23.2	136.0	280.0	605.0	1,011.0	1,620.0	1,989.0	10,550.0	48,520.0	23.25*
B.	BOLIVIA	13.5	20.0	23.0	21.0	21.0	21.0	21.2	21.0	23.0	25.0	~	~	~	~
C.	BRAZIL	4.1	5.2	6.9	6.8	8.2	13.6	15.6	20.1	26.5	46.0	65.4	127.7	252.4	980.0
D.	CHILE	16.3	28.0	340.0	790.0	2,010.0	8.9[b]	19.0	28.3	34.8	41.0	~	38.9	72.6	87.3
E.	COLOMBIA	18.0	24.5	25.5	27.0	29.8	34.5	37.7	38.2	41.3	44.8	50.9	50.1	70.3	~
G.	CUBA	5.0	7.0	9.9	9.8	9.3	8.6	10.4	11.7	13.6	13.0	~	~	~[c]	~
H.	DOMINICAN REP.	1.2	1.2	1.2	1.2	1.3	1.3	1.3	1.4	1.4	1.3	~	~	~	179.0
I.	ECUADOR	22.4	28.5	27.7	25.0	25.2	26.2	27.8	26.0	26.4	27.1	28.0	33.1	64.5	86.5
J.	EL SALVADOR	2.9	2.9	2.9	2.9	2.9	3.0	3.2	3.3	3.0	3.9	~	~	3.75	3.95
O.	NICARAGUA	8.4	8.3	8.5	8.3	8.3	8.4	8.4	8.6	12.0	20.0	~	~[d]	~	28.0
R.	PERU	44.7	58.0	70.0	72.0	59.0	70.0	90.5	145.0	213.0	252.0	341.0	505.9	987.2	~
S.	URUGUAY	251.0	290.0	940.0	925.0	2,470.0	2.9[b]	4.1	5.3	7.0	8.4	9.9	11.6	33.5	43.0

a. For prior years, see SALA-SNP, p. 241.

b. "New peso."

c. Black market rate in Cuba in 1983 said to be 5 to 1, as told to James W. Wilkie during his visit in June 1983; dollars were accepted at 1 to 1 rate by Cuba's Intourist Agency and its hotels and restaurants.

d. Black market rate said to be 30 to 1, as told to James W. Wilkie during his visit in July 1981.

SOURCE: 1968-79: adapted from Pick's Currency Yearbook, 1976-77 and 1977-79; 1980-83: Statistische Beihefte Zu den Monatsberichten der Deutschen Bundesbank, Reihe 5 Die Währangen der Welt, Frankfurt.

Table 3108

CENTRAL AMERICA OFFICIAL, FINANCIAL, AND BLACK MARKET EXCHANGE RATES, 7 L, 1985–87

(NC per US)

PART I. FIRST QUARTER 1985

Country	Official	Financial or Tourist	Parallel, or Black Market
K. GUATEMALA (quetzal)	1.00	1.50-1.79	1.65
Belize (dollar)	2.00	~	~
J. EL SALVADOR (colón)	2.50	3.75	4.15-5.00
M. HONDURAS (lempira)	2.00	~	2.75
O. NICARAGUA (córdoba)	10.00	28.50	500-600
F. COSTA RICA (colón)	20.00	47.95	53
P. PANAMA (balboa)	1.00	~	~

PART II. SECOND QUARTER 1985

	Official	Parallel or Financial[1]	Free or Black Market[2]
K. GUATEMALA (quetzal)	1.00	2.00-2.85	2.90
Belize (dollar)	2.00	~	~
J. EL SALVADOR (colón)	2.50	3.75	4.65-4.90
M. HONDURAS (Lempira)	2.00	~	2.75
O. NICARAGUA (córdoba)	10.00	48.00-60.00	500-600
F. COSTA RICA (colón)	20.00	49.50	53
P. PANAMA (balboa)	1.00	~	~

PART III. THIRD QUARTER 1986

K. GUATEMALA (quetzal)	1.00-2.50	2.90-2.98	2.97
Belize (dollar)	2.00	~	~
J. EL SALVADOR (colón)	5.00	~	5.40-5.45
M. HONDURAS (Lempira)	2.00	~	2.30-2.35
O. NICARAGUA (córdoba)	28.00[a]	1,200	2,000
F. COSTA RICA (colón)	20.00[b]	56.30	57.50
P. PANAMA (balboa)	1.00	~	~

PART IV. SECOND QUARTER 1987

Belize (dollar)	2.00	~	~
F. COSTA RICA (colón)	20.00	60.50	63.50
J. EL SALVADOR (colón)	5.00	~	5.30
K. GUATEMALA (quetzal)	2.50	2.67	2.66
M. HONDURAS (lempira)	2.00	~	2.30
O. NICARAGUA (córdoba)	70.00	4,500	7,000
P. PANAMA (balboa)	1.00	~	~

1. An alternative, officially authorized, exchange rate for certain specified transactions. In some countries (such as Guatemala) it fluctuates; in others (such as Nicaragua) it is fixed.
2. Estimated, since in some countries (Honduras, Costa Rica) this market is clandestine, or (as in Nicaragua) the rate fluctuates widely.

a. For oil imports.
b. For students.

SOURCE: *Central America Report* (Guatemala City), first quarter 1985, second quarter 1985, third quarter 1986, and second quarter 1987.

Table 3109

ANNUAL VALUE OF THE U.S. DOLLAR IN BOLIVIAN PESOS, 1937–85

Year	Official Value		Parallel Market
	Average	End of Year if Varies from Average	End of Year
1937	17		
1938	30		
1939	32		
1940	39		
1941	46		
1942	46		
1943	42		
1944	42		
1945	42		
1946	42		
1947	42		
1948	42		91
1949	42		116
1950	60		130
1951	60		210
1952	60		275
1953	190		950
1954	190		1,820
1955	190		4,050
1956	7,760		8,000
1957	8,330	8,565	8,500
1958	9,698	11,935	11,940
1959	11,880		12,100
1960	11,880		11,990
1961	11,880		11,990
1962	11,880		11,990
1963	11.9[a]		13.0[a]
1964	11.9		13.0
1965	11.9		12.6
1966	11.9		14.0
1967	11.9		14.3
1968	11.9		13.6
1969	11.9		17.0
1970	11.9		20.0
1971	11.9		19.8
1972	13.3	20	23
1973	20.0		21
1974	20.0		21
1975	20.0		21
1976	20.0		21
1977	20.0		21
1978	20.0		23
1979	20.4	25	25
1980	24.5		
1981	24.5		
1982	64	196	290
1983	230	500	1,200[b]
1984	2,314	9,000	23,381[c]
1985	455,083	1,589,000	1,715,000[d]

a. Conversion: 1,000 to 1.
b. Average = 695.
c. Average = 8,191.
d. Average = 829,833.

SOURCE: James W. Wilkie, "Bolivia: Ironies in the National Revolutionary Process, 1952-1986," SALA, 25, ch. 35.

Table 3110

MONTHLY VALUE OF THE U.S. DOLLAR IN BOLIVIAN PESOS, 1984–86

Year	Month	A. Official Value	B. Parallel Market
1982	Nov.	200	250
	Dec.	200	290
1983	Jan.	200	390
	Feb.	200	500
	March	200	500
	April	200	420
	May	200	380
	June	200	390
	July	200	600
	Aug.	200	780
	Sept.	200	785
	Oct.	200	1,050
	Nov.	500	1,350
	Dec.	500	1,200
1984	Jan.	500	1,900
	Feb.	500	2,100
	March	500	2,780
	April	2,000	3,560
	May	2,000	3,480
	June	2,000	3,330
	July	2,000	3,500
	Aug.	5,000[a]	7,190
	Sept.	5,000[a]	13,515
	Oct.	5,000[a]	15,160
	Nov.	9,000	18,394
	Dec.	9,000	23,381
1985	Jan.	9,000	68,000
	Feb.	50,000	132,000
	March	50,000	126,000
	April	50,000	162,000
	May	75,000	250,000
	June	75,000	470,000
	July	75,000	847,000
	Aug.	75,000	1,149,000
	Sept.	1,081,000	1,065,000
	Oct.	1,107,000	1,118,000
	Nov.	1,225,000	1,333,000
	Dec.	1,589,000	1,715,000
1986	Jan.	2,040,000	2,279,000
	Feb.	1,840,000	1,890,000
	Oct.	1,921,000	1,935,000

a. Rate for essential imports = 2,000.

SOURCE: James W. Wilke, "Bolivia: Ironies in the National Revolutionary Process, 1952-1986," SALA, 25, ch. 35.

Table 3111

EXCHANGE RATE AGREEMENTS, 19 L

(As of March 31, 1987)

Currency Pegged to U.S. Dollar	Exchange Rate Adjusted According to a Set of Indicators[1]	Other Managed Floating	Independently Floating
J. EL SALVADOR	C. BRAZIL	A. ARGENTINA	B. BOLIVIA
K. GUATEMALA	D. CHILE	F. COSTA RICA	H. DOMINICAN REP.
L. HAITI	E. COLOMBIA	I. ECUADOR	S. URUGUAY
M. HONDURAS			UNITED STATES
O. NICARAGUA		N. MEXICO	
P. PANAMA		R. PERU	
Q. PARAGUAY			
T. VENEZUELA			

1. Includes exchange arrangements under which the exchange rate is adjusted at relatively frequent intervals, on the basis of indicators determined by the respective member countries.

SOURCE: IMF-IFS, June 1987.

Table 3112

IMF U.S. DOLLAR EFFECTIVE EXCHANGE RATE INDEX (MERM),[1] 1970–86

(1980 = 100, YA)

Year	Index	Year	Index
1970	128.6	1979	99.9
1971	125.4	1980	100.0
1972	116.4	1981	112.7
1973	106.8	1982	125.9
1974	109.5	1983	133.2
1975	106.7	1984	143.7
1976	112.2	1985	150.2
1977	111.7	1986	122.5
1978	102.1		

1. Combines the exchange rates here between U.S. currency and other major currencies with weights derived from IMF's Multilateral Exchange Rate Model (MERM).

SOURCE: IMF-IFS-Y, 1985, line amx; and IMF-IFS, June 1987, line amx.

Table 3113

INDEX NUMBERS OF EFFECTIVE EXCHANGE RATES, 7 L, 1975–84

(1980 = 100)

	Country	1975	1976	1977	1978	1979	1980	1981	1982	1983	1984
A.	ARGENTINA	269.9	195.1	225.6	181.6	129.7	100.0	119.7	260.0	226.1	235.7
C.	BRAZIL	71.2	70.2	71.2	74.8	82.4	100.0	86.3	81.4	108.5	116.6
D.	CHILE	111.5	100.6	94.7	115.2	115.0	100.0	83.8	95.1	113.9	119.4
E.	COLOMBIA	120.4	117.7	101.7	103.1	101.2	100.0	92.8	87.7	90.3	97.3
N.	MEXICO	91.4	102.6	125.3	118.9	112.2	100.0	89.1	133.8	143.4	125.0
R.	PERU	65.8	72.3	85.5	115.6	110.7	100.0	86.4	85.8	94.9	97.6
T.	VENEZUELA	108.9	106.7	106.1	109.1	108.0	100.0	91.4	85.9	92.0	122.9

SOURCE: IDB-SPTF, 1985, table III-1.

Table 3114

ARGENTINA EVOLUTION OF REAL EXCHANGE
RATES, 1970–85

(1980 = 100)

Year and Quarter	Nominal Exchange Rate (Australes per Dollar)	Indexes of Effective Real Exchange Rate[1]	
		Exports	Imports
1975	.000004	192.3	195.9
1976	.000014	126.4	129.3
1977	.00004	163.6	166.1
1978	.00008	148.3	149.3
1979	.00013	112.0	111.4
1980	.0002	100.0	100.0
1981	.0005[a]	131.0	136.0
1982	.0023[a]	156.9	160.4
1983	.0105	156.8	164.1
1984	.0677	144.8	155.4
1985	.6018	168.1	180.8
1982			
I	.0010	136.9	140.5
II	.0014	145.4	148.2
III	.0031	186.0	189.8
IV	.0039	159.3	163.0
1983			
I	.0058	164.4	168.8
II	.0078	164.2	170.7
III	.0107	148.9	157.8
IV	.0178	149.5	158.8
1984			
I	.0278	154.1	165.0
II	.0412	136.6	143.9
III	.0693	135.0	145.1
IV	.1322	153.6	167.6
1985			
I	.2495	159.3	174.2
II	.5567	162.2	179.3
III	.8005	174.3	186.8
IV	.8005	176.6	183.0

1. These indexes were obtained by multiplying the weightings of exports or imports by the real exchange rate indexes. The products are added together to give the effective real exchange rate indexes.

a. The second half of 1981 and 1982, for which the figure used is the 50/50 average of the commercial rate and the financial rate.

SOURCE: ECLA-S, 1985, vol. 1, p. 84.

Table 3115

BOLIVIA EVOLUTION OF REAL EXCHANGE RATES
AND PRICE INDEXES, 1970–85

PART I. EVOLUTION OF REAL EXCHANGE RATE INDEXES[1]

(1980 = 100)

	Bolivian Pesos per:				
Year	US Dollar	Japanese Yen	French Franc	Deutsch Mark	Dutch Guilder
1970	111.91	83.46	83.10	82.55	73.79
1971	111.08	81.97	84.47	87.69	79,17
1972	121.97	99.67	103.29	106.19	97.63
1973	157.84	147.51	143.75	155.27	138.15
1974	115.51	110.89	92.89	105.41	97.36
1975	116.75	103.99	107.68	108.80	105.37
1976	116.98	104.69	101.55	106.08	105.28
1977	114.77	108.85	99.97	110.34	111.53
1978	112.11	122.65	107.57	118.71	119.46
1979	107.46	107.64	107.56	115.52	113.90
1980	100.00	100.00	100.00	100.00	100.00
1981	82.51	79.15	66.81	64.55	64.29
Year	Swiss Franc	Pound Sterling	Argentine Peso	Brazilian Cruzeiro	Chilean Peso
1970	65.17	77.77	64.83	125.05	90.76
1971	69.95	83.45	69.57	127.86	174.66
1972	84.51	96.19	73.42	141.94	165.19
1973	126.81	117.88	111.19	181.50	202.53
1974	90.98	80.23	84.70	130.92	96.45
1975	103.68	87.17	55.59	129.09	71.93
1976	104.28	79.04	84.09	134.95	86.84
1977	101.89	82.20	66.53	133.72	104.02
1978	125.10	88.55	75.74	130.56	96.07
1979	118.62	94.65	97.42	115.99	94.97
1980	100.00	100.00	100.00	100.00	100.00
1981	68.76	73.88	66.17	88.00	90.61

Table 3115 (Continued)

BOLIVIA EVOLUTION OF REAL EXCHANGE RATES
AND PRICE INDEXES, 1970–85

PART II. EVOLUTION OF NOMINAL EXCHANGE RATES AND EFFECTIVE REAL
EXCHANGE RATE INDEXES FOR EXPORTS AND IMPORTS

| Year and Quarter | Nominal Exchange Rates in Pesos per Dollar | | 1980 = 100 | |
| | Official Exchange Rate[3] for Buyers | Parallel Marker Exchange Rate[4] for Buyers | Indexes of Effective Real Exchange Rate[2] | |
			Exports	Imports
1970	~	~	90.8	96.8
1971	~	~	95.1	99.2
1972	~	~	105.5	111.0
1973	~	~	141.9	150.8
1974	~	~	101.7	108.1
1975	20	~	96.6	102.7
1976	20	~	102.8	108.4
1977	20	~	99.1	106.4
1978	20	~	102.8	110.3
1979	20	~	104.8	107.5
1980	25	~	100.0	100.0
1981	25	~	71.4	79.3
1982	99[a]	153	110.5	127.2
1983	230	646	76.3	86.6
1984	2,314	8,278	56.7	63.7
1985	452,742	680,103	59.8	69.4
1984				
I	500	2,400	52.7	59.9
II	1,800	3,217	75.6	84.0
III	2,000	8,075	55.0	61.1
IV	4,956	19,418	43.3	49.6
1985				
I	31,452	101,418	44.5	51.6
II	62,634	277,962	35.1	40.0
III	409,944	975,331	51.2	59.4
IV	1,306,937	1,365,702	108.4	126.4

1. Corresponds to the quotient of the nominal exchange rate indexes divided by the relative price indexes. For Bolivia, the wholesale price index was used.
2. These indexes were obtained by multiplying the weightings of exports or imports by the real exchange rate indexes. The products are added together to give the effective real exchange rate indexes.
3. Exchange rates used in the banking system for converting foreign currency into domestic currency.
4. Quarterly average exchange rate.

a. During the period March–Oct. 1982, use was made of an exchange rate obtained from the average of the official rate weighted 40 percent and of the open market rate weighted 60 percent.

SOURCE: ECLA-S, 1981, Statistical Appendix, for Part I and 1970–74 of Part II; and for Part II, ECLA-S, 1985, vol. 1, p. 120.

Figure 31:1

BOLIVIA OFFICIAL AND FREE EXCHANGE RATES, 1982–84

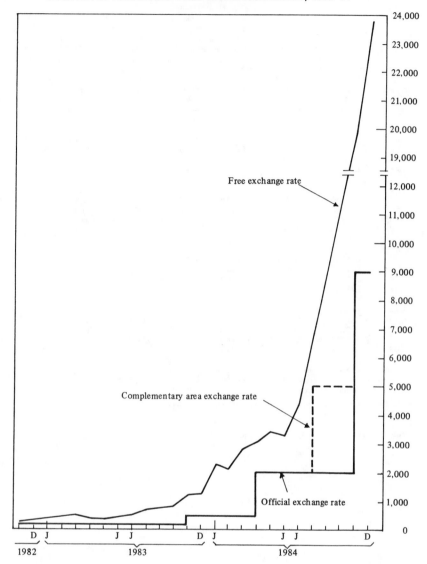

SOURCE: ECLA-S, 1984, vol. 1, p. 110.

Table 3116

BRAZIL EVOLUTION OF REAL EXCHANGE RATES AND PRICE INDEXES, 1980–85

	1980 = 100 Exchange Rate		1980 = 100 Indexes for Major Manufacturing Products		Real Exchange Rate	1980 = 100 Indexes of Effective Real Exchange Rate[1]		
Year and Quarter	Cruceiros per Dollar (1)	Index (2)	Brazil (3)	United States (4)	(2) × (4)/(3) (5)	Exports (6)	Imports (7)	(8)[a]
1980	52.71	100.0	100.0	100.0	100.0	100.0	100.0	100.0
1981	93.13	176.7	209.3	110.6	93.4	83.1	88.8	86.5
1982	179.51	340.6	422.8	113.7	91.6	80.1	85.9	83.7
1983	577.04	1,094.7	1,029.6	114.9	122.2	95.0	99.8	100.8
1984	1,848.03	3,506.0	3,334.5	117.4	123.4	88.9	92.6	93.8
1985	6,200.63	11,763.7	10,919.4	117.9	127.0	89.7	93.7	95.2
1983								
I	326.43	619.3	643.5	114.2	109.9	92.8	98.0	97.3
II	475.89	902.8	817.9	114.2	126.1	101.5	105.8	107.3
III	638.36	1,121.1	1,125.6	115.4	114.9	94.4	99.3	100.8
IV	867.50	1,645.8	1,531.8	115.9	124.5	91.3	96.1	97.7
1984								
I	1,140.67	2,164.0	2,017.2	116.7	125.2	91.0	94.8	96.2
II	1,514.42	2,873.1	2,623.9	117.6	128.8	91.5	94.1	95.5
III	2,004.75	3,803.4	3,629.7	117.6	123.2	88.4	92.2	93.3
IV	2,732.27	5,183.6	5,067.2	117.7	120.3	84.5	89.2	90.1
1985								
I	3,762.8	7,138.7	7,064.0	117.4	118.6	82.5	88.1	88.9
II	5,232.1	9,926.2	8,949.9	118.2	131.1	92.2	97.2	98.7
III	6,797.7	12,896.4	11,494.9	117.8	132.2	93.0	96.6	98.3
IV	9,009.9	17,093.3	16,168.8	118.2	125.0	91.2	92.8	95.0

1. These indexes were obtained by multiplying the weightings of exports or imports by the real exchange rate indexes. The products were added together to give the effective real exchange rate indexes.

a. Excludes the following petroleum-exporting countries: Saudia Arabia, Iraq, and Kuwait.

SOURCE: ECLA-S, 1985, vol. 1, pp. 145 and 146.

Table 3117

CHILE EVOLUTION OF REAL EXCHANGE RATES, 1975–85

| | Nominal Exchange Rates[1] | | | 1980 = 100 Indexes of Effective Real Exchange Rate | | | |
| | Official | | | Exports | | Imports | |
Year and Quarter	Principal	Preferential	Parallel	(1)[a]	(2)[b]	(1)[a]	(2)[b]
1975	4.91	~	~	135.7	142.6	131.1	137.8
1976	13.05	~	~	116.8	120.3	115.2	118.6
1977	21.53	~	~	113.8	100.2	110.9	97.6
1978	31.66	~	~	133.3	113.5	127.0	108.1
1979	37.25	~	~	118.6	114.5	114.2	110.2
1980	39.00	~	~	100.0	100.0	100.0	100.0
1981	39.00	~	~	89.1	82.0	93.3	85.8
1982	50.91	~	~	104.0	92.8	111.4	99.4
1983	78.84	64.87	92	112.1	110.9	121.3	120.1
1984	98.66	77.73	113	110.9	113.1	119.0	121.2
1985	161.08	~	180	128.3	140.6	138.6	152.0
1982							
I	39.00	~	~	92.6	78.1	98.2	82.8
II	40.34	~	~	95.8	80.2	102.2	85.5
III	55.01	50.49[c]	~	111.4	100.2	120.1	108.1
IV	69.28	55.43	77	116.0	112.5	125.0	121.2
1983							
I	74.96	59.95	99	123.1	117.1	131.8	125.3
II	75.34	62.55	91	112.0	108.8	120.6	117.3
III	79.75	66.19	86	104.9	108.2	114.3	117.8
IV	85.31	70.79	93	108.5	109.6	118.6	119.9
1984							
I	88.05	73.41	97	114.3	111.3	122.8	119.6
II	90.00	75.35	113	109.5	109.7	115.7	115.8
III	95.62	78.38	116	105.1	109.6	112.8	117.3
IV	120.95	83.77	124	114.6	121.6	124.5	132.1
1985							
I	135.82	91.53	139	116.2	124.4	128.0	137.0
II	152.14	98.29	172	121.6	132.2	132.6	144.2
III	175.50	~	200	133.5	149.0	143.8	160.5
IV	180.87	~	210	141.7	156.9	150.1	166.2

1. Pesos per dollar.

a. These indexes were obtained by multiplying the weightings of exports or imports by the real exchange rate indexes. The products are added together to give the effective real rate indexes. The wholesale price index for domestic products was used.

b. A procedure similar to that described in Note a was employed, except that the calculations were based on the following price indexes: 1975-78, corrected consumer price index of R. Cortázar and J. Marshall; 1979-85, consumer price index of the National Statistical Institute (INT).

c. Average for Aug. and Sept.

SOURCE: ECLA-S, 1985, vol. 1, p. 272.

Table 3118

COLOMBIA EVOLUTION OF REAL EXCHANGE
RATES, 1975–85

| | | 1980 = 100 | |
| | | Indexes of Effective Real Exchange Rate[1] | |
Year and Quarter	Nominal Exchange Rate (Pesos per Dollar)	Exports	Imports
1975	30.93	118.2	119.5
1976	34.70	112.0	113.1
1977	36.78	102.0	102.0
1978	39.10	103.1	103.4
1979	42.55	99.3	98.6
1980	47.28	100.0	100.0
1981	54.49	92.1	96.1
1982	64.08	86.5	90.0
1983	78.85	87.4	90.7
1984	100.82	88.7	95.3
1985	142.30	102.3	108.6
1982			
I	60.24	89.5	93.1
II	62.65	86.8	90.3
III	65.14	85.0	88.6
IV	68.31	84.5	88.1
1983			
I	72.13	87.1	90.0
II	76.35	85.0	87.7
III	80.87	87.0	90.6
IV	86.07	90.4	94.6
1984			
I	91.61	89.5	95.0
II	97.43	87.7	94.1
III	103.80	88.0	95.0
IV	110.44	89.5	96.9
1985			
I	118.88	89.1	96.3
II	135.38	96.2	102.6
III	150.28	105.6	111.5
IV	164.65	118.4	124.1

1. These indexes were obtained by multiplying the weightings of exports or imports by the real exchange rate indexes. The products were added together to give the effective real exchange rate indexes.

SOURCE: ECLA-S, 1985, vol. 1, p. 177.

Table 3119

COSTA RICA EVOLUTION OF REAL EXCHANGE RATES, 1975–85

Year and Quarter	Nominal Exchange Rates[1] (Colones per Dollar)			1980 = 100 Indexes of Effective Real Exchange Rate[2]	
	Exports	Imports		Exports	Imports
1975	8.75	8.57		106.9	104.0
1976	8.57	8.57		104.0	101.1
1977	8.57	8.57		105.4	102.3
1978	8.57	8.57		106.7	105.5
1979	8.57	8.57		102.6	100.1
1980	9.20	9.27		100.0	100.0
1981	21.15	20.01		147.4	143.2
1982	38.62	39.23		136.1	131.2
1983	42.24	42.16		122.6	114.5
1984	44.53	44.51		129.1	118.5
1985	50.62	50.62		141.5	126.7
1982					
I	36.24	35.04		158.3	156.9
II	36.45	39.77		138.7	133.5
III	40.14	40.30		125.0	117.9
IV	41.64	41.81		122.4	116.4
1983					
I	41.64	41.96		118.8	112.2
II	41.69	41.78		120.4	112.5
III	42.70	42.07		125.9	116.5
IV	42.93	42.84		125.2	116.7
1984					
I	43.40	43.40		125.2	117.1
II	43.53	43.53		127.0	117.8
III	44.23	44.13		129.3	117.4
IV	46.98	46.98		135.0	121.7
1985					
I	48.30	48.30		119.8	116.4
II	49.49	49.49		132.1	122.6
III	51.27	51.27		149.5	129.3
IV	53.42	53.42		164.5	138.5

1. These indexes were obtained by multiplying the weightings of exports or imports by the nominal exchange rate indexes. The products are added together to give the effective nominal exchange rate indexes.
2. These indexes were obtained by multiplying the weightings of exports or imports by the real exchange rate indexes. The products are added together to give the effective real exchange rate indexes. In calculating these indexes for Costa Rica, the wholesale price index was used.

SOURCE: ECLA-S, 1985, vol. 1, p. 204.

Table 3120

CUBA EVOLUTION OF REAL EXCHANGE
RATE INDEXES, 1980–85

		Cuban Pesos per:			
Year and Quarter	US Dollar	Pound Sterling	Swiss Franc	Deutsch Mark	Japanese[1] Yen
1980	.7113	1.6432	.4294	.3968	.3113
1981	.7814	1.6071	.4001	.3510	.3572
1982	.8333	1.4686	.4139	.3443	.3372
1983	.8598	1.3167	.4128	.3411	.3609
1984	.8861	1.1999	.3820	.3141	.3755
1985	.9138	1.1777	.3725	.3096	.3829
1985					
I	.9307	1.0499	.3474	.2907	.3674
II	.9246	1.1470	.3500	.2942	.3663
III	.9058	1.2286	.3780	.3126	.3749
IV	.8941	1.2854	.4145	.3410	.4232

1. 100 Yen.

SOURCE: ECLA-S, 1985, vol. 1, p. 240.

Table 3121

DOMINICAN REPUBLIC EVOLUTION OF REAL EXCHANGE
RATES AND PRICE INDEXES, 1970–85

			1970 = 100			Parity	1970 = 100
	Exchange Rate (Pesos per Dollar)	Exchange Rate Index	Price Index		Ratio (3) (4)	Exchange Rate (1.15 X column 5) (Pesos per Dollar) (6)	Index of Under- or Over- Valuation of the Exchange Rate (6) (1)
Year	(1)	(2)	Domestic (3)	Foreign (4)	(5)	(6)	(7)
1970	1.15	100.0	100.0	100.0	100.0	1.15	100.0
1971	1.14	99.1	104.3	104.3	100.0	1.15	100.9
1972	1.12	97.4	112.5	107.7	104.5	1.20	107.1
1973	1.13	98.3	129.5	114.4	113.2	1.30	115.0
1974	1.14	99.1	146.5	127.0	115.4	1.33	116.7
1975	1.18	102.6	167.7	138.6	121.0	1.39	117.8
1976	1.20	104.4	180.9	146.6	123.3	1.42	118.3
1977	1.22	106.1	204.1	156.2	130.7	1.50	123.0
1978	1.25	108.7	218.6	168.1	130.0	1.50	120.0
1979	1.23	107.0	238.6	187.0	127.6	1.47	119.5
1980	1.26	109.6	278.6	212.3	131.2	1.51	119.8
1981	1.28	111.3	299.6	234.4	127.8	1.47	114.8
1982	1.46	127.0	322.5	248.6	129.7	1.49	102.0
1983	1.60	139.1	344.8	256.7	134.3	1.55	96.9
1984	2.83	246.1	428.9	267.7	160.2	1.84	65.0
1985	3.12	271.3	589.8	277.3	212.7	2.45	78.5

SOURCE: ECLA-S, 1985, vol. 1, p. 596.

Table 3122

ECUADOR EVOLUTION OF REAL EXCHANGE RATES, 1975–85

1980 = 100

Year and Quarter	Nominal Exchange Rates (Sucres per Dollar)					Indexes of Effective Real Exchange Rates[1]	
	Official	Free[2]	Free	Exports	Imports	Exports	Imports
1975	25.00	~	25.40	~	~	111.5	109.0
1976	25.00	~	27.45	~	~	105.2	102.4
1977	25.00	~	27.47	~	~	99.0	98.0
1978	25.00	~	26.60	~	~	96.2	98.9
1979	25.00	~	27.61	~	~	99.2	100.2
1980	25.00	~	27.78	~	~	100.0	100.0
1981	25.00	~	30.76	~	~	95.6	92.6
1982	30.03	~	49.81	30.21	30.53	96.9	96.2
1983	44.12	83.22	83.47	45.38	48.30	102.0	104.4
1984	62.54	92.65	96.09	68.29	72.69	116.0	117.3
1985	69.56	96.50	116.29	89.62	93.51	116.7	117.0
1982							
I	25.00	~	36.97	25.77	26.50	92.1	91.3
II	28.80	~	47.64	27.50	29.50	94.4	97.6
III	33.15	~	58.65	31.94	32.36	103.4	101.0
IV	33.15	~	60.85	33.0	33.30	97.5	94.8
1983							
I	33.91	~	72.63	36.40	37.93	98.1	99.1
II	43.47	78.80	86.36	45.13	49.37	105.8	111.5
III	47.25	89.53	94.03	49.87	53.53	101.3	104.1
IV	51.83	85.47	86.14	53.80	56.07	102.9	102.8
1984							
I	56.44	89.23	90.48	59.91	60.29	110.3	106.6
II	60.94	90.00	90.29	65.67	71.51	115.0	120.0
III	65.58	95.00	97.00	71.63	77.85	119.6	123.2
IV	67.18	96.50	116.95	76.66	81.10	119.1	119.3
1985							
I	67.18	96.50	121.65	~	~	~	~
II	67.18	96.50	114.69	~	~	~	~
III	67.18	96.50	109.03	~	~	~	~
IV	76.70	96.50	123.57	~	~	~	~

1. These indexes were obtained by multiplying the weightings of exports or imports by the real exchange rate indexes. The products are added together to give the effective rate indexes.
2. Central Bank of Ecuador.

SOURCE: ECLA-S, 1985, vol. 1, p. 307.

Table 3123

GUATEMALA EVOLUTION OF REAL EXCHANGE RATES, 1980–1985

1970 = 100

Year	Nominal Exchange Rate		Wholesale Price Index		Indexes of Adjusted Effective Real Exchange Rate
	(Quetzales per Dollar)	Index	Internal	United States	
1980	1.00	100.0	264.3	243.6	92.2
1981	1.00	100.0	295.3	265.8	90.0
1982	1.00	100.0	278.2	271.2	97.5
1983	1.00	100.0	280.7	274.6	97.8
1984	1.00	100.0	296.5	281.1	94.8
1985	1.00	100.0	421.9	292.1	69.2

SOURCE: ECLA-S, 1985, vol. 1, p. 356.

Table 3124

HONDURAS EVOLUTION OF REAL EXCHANGE RATES, 1978–85

1978 = 100

Year	Nominal Exchange Rate (Lempiras per Dollar) (1)	Index (2)	Wholesale Price Indexes				Relation Between Wholesale Price Indexes			Indexes of Effective Real Exchange Rate		
			Trading Partners[1]				Exports (3/4) (7)	Imports (3/5) (8)	Foreign Trade[2] (3/6) (9)	Exports (2/7) (10)	Imports (2/8) (11)	Foreign Trade[2] (2/9) (12)
			Honduras (3)	Exports (4)	Imports (5)	Foreign Trade[2] (6)						
1978	2.00	100.0	100.0	100.0	100.0	100.0	100.0	100.0	100.0	100.0	100.0	100.0
1979	2.00	100.0	109.7	112.3	109.8	111.2	97.7	99.9	98.6	102.4	100.1	101.4
1980	2.00	100.0	125.6	127.1	125.7	126.4	98.8	99.9	99.4	101.2	100.1	100.6
1981	2.00	100.0	136.4	131.6	136.0	133.8	103.6	100.3	101.9	96.5	99.7	98.1
1982	2.00	100.0	150.3	133.0	137.8	136.2	113.0	109.1	110.4	88.5	91.7	90.6
1983	2.00	100.0	161.9	135.2	143.3	140.8	119.7	113.0	115.0	83.5	88.5	87.0
1984	2.00	100.0	164.1	138.5	146.4	143.4	118.5	112.1	114.4	84.4	89.2	87.4
1985[a]	2.00	100.0	164.9	148.7	165.2	158.6	110.9	99.8	104.0	90.2	100.2	96.2

1. Consists of 17 trading partners.
2. Includes exports and imports.

a. Includes the first three quarter averages.

SOURCE: ECLA-S, 1985, vol. 1, p. 414.

Table 3125

MEXICO EVOLUTION OF REAL EXCHANGE RATES, 1975–85

1980 = 100

Year and Quarter	Official Exchange Rates (Pesos per Dollar)		Indexes of Effective Real Exchange Rates[1]			
	Free	Controlled	Exports		Imports	
			(1)[a]	(2)[b]	(1)[a]	(2)[b]
1975	12.50	~	103.9	~	102.5	~
1976	15.43	~	109.4	~	107.6	~
1977	22.57	~	120.7	~	119.2	~
1978	22.77	~	114.1	~	114.8	~
1979	22.81	~	109.1	~	109.0	~
1980	22.95	~	100.0	~	100.0	~
1981	24.52	~	90.3	~	90.8	~
1982	57.18	~	131.8	~	133.2	~
1983	150.30	120.09	173.2	136.2	176.9	139.2
1984	185.19	167.83	124.7	112.9	127.3	115.3
1985	310.17	256.87	132.7	110.9	135.1	112.9
1982						
I	34.37	~	105.0	~	105.8	~
II	46.78	~	123.6	~	124.6	~
III	67.42	59.75	148.9	132.0	150.4	133.3
IV	80.13	55.91	149.8	103.3	151.8	104.8
1983						
I	148.72	102.02	214.3	147.0	218.4	149.8
II	148.63	114.20	175.3	134.7	179.1	137.6
III	148.41	126.12	155.3	132.0	159.0	135.1
IV	155.44	138.04	147.6	131.1	150.9	134.0
1984						
I	167.33	149.96	134.8	120.8	137.6	123.3
II	179.16	161.87	125.6	113.5	128.2	115.8
III	191.10	173.73	122.0	110.9	124.5	113.2
IV	203.17	185.74	116.5	106.5	118.9	108.7
1985						
I	217.86	200.57	109.6	100.9	112.0	103.1
II	235.97	218.57	107.2	99.3	109.4	101.3
III	336.20	274.75	142.2	116.2	144.6	118.2
IV	450.63	333.60	171.6	127.1	174.5	129.2

1. These indexes were obtained by multiplying the weightings of exports or imports by the real exchange rate indexes. The products are added together to give the effective real exchange rate indexes.

a. Based on the free rate.
b. Based on the controlled rate.

SOURCE: ECLA-S, 1985, vol. 1, p. 443.

Table 3126

OFFICIAL AND REAL MEXICAN PESO VALUES COMPARED TO MEXICO'S REAL TRADE DEFICITS, 1952–82

	(A)	(B)	(C)	(D)	(E)	(F)	(G)	(H)
						Mexico YE		
Year	Official Peso Exchange Rate for Dollars (YA)	Mexico's Wholesale Price Index	U.S. Wholesale Price Index	Peso 1963 Parity Exchange Rate[1] 12.5 in Col. A Times (B/C)	Peso's Value Index (D/A)[2]	Merchandise Trade Balance FOB	Trade Index 1963 Equals –100.0	Real Merchandise Balance Index[3] 1963 Equals –100
		YA; 1963=100.0			1963=100.0	M US		(G/C)
1952	8.650	65.6	93.9	8.7	100.6	~	~	~
1953	8.650	64.3	92.6	8.7	100.6	–169	–84.1	–90.8
1954	12.500	70.5	92.8	9.5	76.0	–92	–45.8	–49.4
1955	12.500	80.1	93.0	10.8	86.4	21	10.5	11.3
1956	12.500	83.8	96.1	10.9	87.2	–174	–86.6	–90.1
1957	12.500	87.5	98.7	11.1	88.8	–362	–180.1	–182.5
1958	12.500	91.4	100.2	11.4	91.2	–338	–168.2	–167.9
1959	12.500	92.4	100.4	11.5	92.0	–220	–109.5	–109.1
1960	12.500	96.9	100.6	12.0	96.0	–354	–176.1	–175.0
1961	12.500	97.7	100.2	12.2	97.6	–260	–129.4	–129.1
1962	12.500	99.6	100.4	12.4	99.2	–167	–83.1	–82.8
1963	12.500	100.0	100.0	12.5	100.0	–201	–100.0	–100.0
1964	12.500	104.3	100.2	13.0	104.0	–370	–184.1	–183.7
1965	12.500	106.4	102.2	13.0	104.0	–352	–175.1	–171.3
1966	12.500	107.6	105.7	12.7	101.6	–337	–167.7	–158.7
1967	12.500	110.7	105.9	13.1	104.8	–608	–302.5	–285.6
1968	12.500	112.9	108.5	13.0	104.0	–634	–315.4	–290.7
1969	12.500	115.8	112.8	12.8	102.4	–529	–263.2	–233.2
1970	12.500	122.5	116.9	13.1	104.8	–888	–441.8	–377.9
1971	12.500	127.3	120.8	13.2	105.6	–749	–372.6	–308.4
1972	12.500	130.7	126.1	13.0	104.0	–894	–444.8	–352.7
1973	12.500	151.4	142.6	13.3	106.4	–1,515	–753.7	–528.5
1974	12.500	185.5	169.4	13.7	109.6	–2,791	–1,388.6	–819.7
1975	12.500	204.9	185.2	13.8	138.0	–3,271	–1,627.4	–878.7
1976	15.426	250.6	193.7	16.2	105.0	–2,296	–1,142.3	–589.7
1977	22.573	353.7	205.6	21.5	95.2	–1,021	–508.0	–247.0
1978	22.767	409.4	221.7	23.1	101.5	–1,746	–868.7	–391.8
1979	22.805	484.4	249.4	24.3	106.6	–2,830	–1,408.0	–564.6
1980	22.951	603.1	284.4	26.5	115.5	–2,310	–1,149.3	–404.1
1981	24.515	752.0	310.2	30.3	123.6	–3,329	–1,656.2	–533.9
1982[a]	46.758	1,010.2	316.1[c]	39.9	85.3	116[b]	57.8[b]	33.9[b]

1. The year 1963 was selected for parity comparison because of the following characteristics: low increase of .4% in Mexican wholesale price index (column B); relatively low deficit of $201 million real dollars in merchandise trade balance (column F); and healthy real GDP gain of 8.0% (see SALA, 22-3).
2. More than 100.0 equals peso "overvaluation" which discourages exports from Mexico and foreign tourism to Mexico; it encourages imports to Mexico, Mexican tourism abroad, and a Mexican shift from pesos into "cheap" dollars. Also in terms of 1963 value, the greater the undervaluation of the peso the greater the chances to reduce Mexico's trade deficit, to increase Mexico's money balance from tourism, and to encourage investment in pesos rather than dollars. Undervalued pesos allow foreigners to buy more goods and services in Mexico than do overvalued pesos.
3. In no years did value of exports equal that of imports (theoretically zero on the index scale). The real merchandise trade deficit of $201 million equals –100.0 on the index scale.

a. May.
b. January–April.
c. January–April = 170.5 U.S. wholesale price index.

Method: A: 1952–74, IFS-Y, 1982; 1975–82, IFS, Aug. 1982, line *rf*.
B: Bank of Mexico 210-item wholesale price index calculated (base converted) from source A, line 63.
C: Calculated from source A, line 63.
D: Calculated (datum for 1963 in column A times B/C).
E: Calculated (A/D), according to ECLA methodology in ECLA-S2, 1980, p. 394.
F: 1952–74, IFS-Y, 1982, line 77*ad*; 1975–81, IFS, Aug. 1982, calculated from lines 77*aad* and 77*abd*; 1982 calculated from CE, Aug. 1982, p. 904.
G: Calculated from column F.
H: Calculated (G/C).

Source: SALA, 22-4.

Table 3127

PANAMA EVOLUTION OF REAL EXCHANGE RATES, 1970–85

| | Exchange Rate | | 1970 = 100 | | | |
| | | | Panama Wholesale Price Index (3) | US Wholesale Price Index (4) | Index of Adjusted Real Exchange Rate $(2)/\frac{(3)}{(4)}$ (5) | Parity Exchange Rate (3)/(4) (6) |
Year	(Balboa per Dollar) (1)	Index (2)				
1970	1,000	100.0	100.0	100.0	100.0	1.00
1980	1,000	100.0	300.7	243.6	81.0	1.23
1981	1,000	100.0	330.9	265.8	80.3	1.24
1982	1,000	100.0	358.2	271.2	75.7	1.32
1983	1,000	100.0	366.7	274.6	74.9	1.34
1984	1,000	100.0	370.4	281.1	75.9	1.32
1985	1,000	100.0	393.4	292.1[‡]	74.3	1.35

SOURCE: ECLA-S, 1985, vol. 1, p. 497.

Table 3128

PARAGUAY EVOLUTION OF REAL EXCHANGE RATES, 1975–85

| | Exchange Rates Guaraníes per Dollar) | | | 1980 = 100 Indexes of Effective Real Exchange Rates | | | |
| | Official | | | Official[1] | | Parallel[2] | |
Year and Quarter	Exports	Imports	Parallel	Exports	Imports	Exports	Imports
1975	126	126	143	92.6	87.6	110.1	108.7
1976	126	126	136	99.0	96.3	107.6	115.5
1977	126	126	133	97.5	93.6	105.0	109.2
1978	126	126	142	102.2	94.3	112.0	115.0
1979	126	126	138	95.0	89.3	97.6	98.9
1980	126	126	135	100.0	100.0	100.0	100.0
1981	126	126	153	84.6	88.5	99.7	107.7
1982	142	137	205	88.1	87.7	127.0	135.9
1983	158	146	321	74.7	69.7	153.1	152.7
1984	222	245	382	83.8	89.7	143.8	150.5
1985	312	387	613	91.4	112.8	182.5	185.7
1982							
I	134	126	161	78.1	75.8	92.0	98.1
II	144	136	169	91.8	88.4	104.9	113.6
III	147	145	227	93.2	95.9	147.1	157.8
IV	144	141	263	89.2	90.5	164.1	174.2
1983							
I	149	146	244	83.0	82.0	139.8	137.9
II	165	144	288	79.3	69.2	144.2	138.5
III	161	146	395	69.4	63.6	173.7	175.0
IV	156	147	355	67.1	64.0	154.6	159.2
1984							
I	180	146	339	78.2	64.6	150.4	154.2
II	227	198	373	93.8	82.8	155.0	160.2
III	240	306	421	88.0	111.6	150.9	160.0
IV	240	328	394	75.1	100.0	119.0	127.4
1985							
I	288	304	426	85.5	90.3	125.7	135.8
II	320	353	569	99.8	110.1	180.1	184.3
III	320	443	780	93.7	129.7	234.8	234.7
IV	320	447	675	86.6	121.0	189.3	188.0

1. These indexes were obtained by multiplying the weightings of exports or imports by the real exchange rate indexes. The products are added together to give the effective real exchange rate indexes.
2. These indexes correspond to a weighted average of the real exchange rate indexes for Paraguay with respect to Argentina, Brazil, the United States, Japan, Italy, France, and the Federal Republic of Germany, calculated on the basis of their relative shares in non-registered trade flows with this country. In calculating these indexes, the parallel exchange rate was used.

SOURCE: ECLA-S, 1985, vol. 1, p. 524.

Table 3129

PERU EVOLUTION OF REAL EXCHANGE RATES, 1975–85

1980 = 100

Year and Quarter	Nominal Exchange Rate (Intis per Dollar)	Indexes of Effective Real Exchange Rate[1]			
		Exports		Imports	
		(1)[a]	(2)[b]	(1)[a]	(2)[b]
1975	0.04	76.6	67.2	76.1	66.8
1976	0.06	80.7	73.7	81.5	74.5
1977	0.08	90.4	85.0	90.3	84.9
1978	0.16	113.1	113.0	112.8	112.7
1979	0.23	106.9	108.9	107.3	109.3
1980	0.29	100.0	100.0	100.0	100.0
1981	0.42	86.5	86.8	85.5	85.8
1982	0.70	88.8	85.3	88.1	84.6
1983	1.63	93.7	93.8	92.1	92.2
1984	3.47	88.9	94.7	87.6	93.4
1985	10.97	103.0‡	113.7	101.4‡	112.0
1983					
I	1.10	95.0	90.4	93.5	89.0
II	1.43	95.7	92.4	93.7	90.4
III	1.85	94.0	96.1	92.5	94.5
IV	2.12	90.2	96.2	88.7	94.6
1984					
I	2.45	85.9	90.7	84.5	89.2
II	3.02	89.0	93.8	87.7	92.4
III	3.71	87.6	95.0	86.5	93.8
IV	4.68	93.2	99.4	91.9	98.1
1985					
I	7.00	100.8	109.3	99.6	108.0
II	9.70	103.1	113.0	101.4	111.2
III	13.26	104.3	117.5	102.7	115.7
IV	13.94	103.8‡	115.0	102.0‡	113.2

1. These indexes were obtained by multiplying the weightings of exports or imports by the real exchange rate indexes. The products are added together to give the effective real exchange rate indexes.

a. Based on national price index.
b. Based on consumer index.

SOURCE: ECLA-S, 1985, vol. 1, p. 568.

Table 3130

VENEZUELA EVOLUTION OF REAL EXCHANGE RATES AND PRICE INDEXES, 1970–85

PART I. EVOLUTION OF REAL EXCHANGE RATE INDEXES[1]

(1980 = 100)

Year and Quarter	Venezuelan Bolivares per:				
	US Dollar	Canadian Dollar	Japanese Yen	Deutsch Mark	Spanish Peseta
1970	114.78	144.40	86.04	84.71	87.93
1971	116.06	150.27	85.47	91.36	91.68
1972	115.29	152.87	94.20	100.23	100.47
1973	119.00	148.54	110.96	116.72	111.52
1974	120.48	143.56	116.11	109.93	113.30
1975	115.23	133.79	102.49	107.19	111.97
1976	111.73	137.51	100.33	101.25	102.72
1977	105.54	122.57	100.37	101.30	94.38
1978	105.79	115.74	115.95	111.88	99.05
1979	107.83	111.43	108.25	115.54	113.47
1980	100.00	100.00	100.00	100.00	100.00
1981	94.82	95.35	91.28	74.06	77.29
I	98.18	96.95	102.05	82.98	85.81
II	95.94	94.97	91.79	73.89	77.77
III	92.57	92.61	84.56	67.01	71.51
IV	92.95	96.94	87.59	73.80	75.63

Year and Quarter	French Franc	Italian Lira	Pound Sterling	Netherlands Antilles Guilder	Brazilian Cruzeiro
1970	85.12	92.01	79.81	109.59	129.90
1971	88.14	94.21	87.15	110.20	132.44
1972	97.31	98.02	90.85	113.65	133.23
1973	108.01	105.75	88.77	112.12	137.71
1974	96.92	113.65	83.72	114.12	136.63
1975	106.34	107.86	86.14	115.46	127.10
1976	96.88	97.41	75.56	112.71	128.53
1977	91.78	95.18	75.65	105.75	122.99
1978	101.33	99.81	83.72	106.36	123.08
1979	107.76	106.49	94.97	107.24	116.56
1980	100.00	100.00	100.00	100.00	100.00
1981	76.64	77.06	84.88	97.50	102.51
I	86.06	86.42	97.25	100.42	110.07
II	76.05	76.58	87.64	97.74	106.20
III	70.59	69.91	75.33	95.16	98.62
IV	75.25	75.11	79.52	96.93	97.38

Table 3130 (Continued)

VENEZUELA EVOLUTION OF REAL EXCHANGE RATES AND PRICE INDEXES, 1970–85

PART II. EVOLUTION OF NOMINAL EXCHANGE RATE AND EFFECTIVE REAL EXCHANGE RATE INDEXES FOR EXPORTS AND IMPORTS

Year and Quarter	Nominal Exchange Rates (Bolívares per Dollar)			1980 = 100 Indexes of Effective Real Exchange Rates[2]	
	Commercial	Free	Average[3]	Exports	Imports
1975	4.29	#	4.29	117.1	112.0
1976	4.29	#	4.29	114.5	107.6
1977	4.29	#	4.29	107.0	103.0
1978	4.29	#	4.29	106.7	106.9
1979	4.29	#	4.29	107.8	108.8
1980	4.29	#	4.29	100.0	100.0
1981	4.29	#	4.29	91.4	43.1
1982	4.29	#	4.29	85.1	84.2
1983	~	10.59	5.01	91.9	91.5
1984	~	13.51	6.49	102.4	102.1
1985[‡]	7.50	13.97	7.05	92.1	91.9
1982					
I	4.29	#	4.29	86.7	86.1
II	4.29	#	4.29	85.6	84.9
III	4.29	#	4.29	84.1	83.1
IV	4.29	#	4.29	84.0	83.0
1983					
I	4.86	5.60	4.35	83.3	82.9
II	6.00	10.20	5.13	94.8	94.6
III	6.00	13.90	5.70	102.6	102.1
IV	6.00	12.75	4.87	86.9	86.4
1984					
I	7.00	13.65	5.45	94.5	94.1
II	7.50	15.30	6.94	114.7	114.5
III	7.50	12.57	6.77	103.8	103.5
IV	7.50	12.52	6.79	96.5	96.1
1985[‡]					
I	7.50	13.28	6.93	93.2	92.8
II	7.50	13.36	6.99	91.4	91.3
III	7.50	14.39	7.11	92.0	91.8
IV	7.50	14.85	7.17	91.8	91.7

1. Corresponds to the quotient of the nominal exchange rate indexes divided by the relative price indexes. For Venezuela, the wholesale price index for domestic products was used.
2. These indexes were obtained by multiplying the weightings of exports or imports by the real exchange rate indexes. The products are added together to give the effective real exchange rate indexes.
3. Central Bank of Venezuela.

SOURCE: ECLA-S, 1981, Statistical Appendix; for Part II, years 1975–84, ECLA-S, 1985, vol. 1, p. 658.

CHAPTER 32

PRICE CHANGES, COMMODITY PRICES, AND INTEREST RATES

Chapter Outline

Table 3200

GUIDE TO TABLES 3201–3223: CONSUMER PRICE CHANGES
(Calculations by Waldo W. Wilkie)

Alternative PC series are presented for each country to illustrate that there is no single measure of price change. The reader must look at the series to interpret trends.

Differences amounting to several percent between alternative series may be due only to rounding in the original data (e.g., between a figure ending in .4 that rounds downward and a figure ending in .5 that rounds upward).

Differences in series may also be due, however, to one or more of the following factors:

1. number of items included in the series
2. weights attached to each item
3. calculations based upon different base years
4. coverage geographically of capital city in contrast to major urban areas, all urban areas, or national scope
5. consumer prices keyed to varying definition of "consumer" as involving:
   a. all households
   b. wage earner households
   c. wage and salary earner households
   d. low income earners
   e. low and middle income earners
   f. middle income earners
   g. "average" working class family with a specified number of dependents
   h. government employees

According to IMF-IFS-S, No. 2, 1981, pp. ii-iii:

The increasing interdependence of national economies, and the increased transmission of inflation between them, has brought with it a need for global measures of price change in order to enable analysts to quantify the magnitude of global inflation and to examine its diffusion and dispersion around the world. The three most commonly used indicators of global price change are consumer prices, GDP deflators, and wholesale prices. GDP deflators have particular relevance in this context since they reflect, in concept, the aggregate price change of all goods and services produced in the domestic economy. As such they have been viewed as broader measures of price change than consumer price indexes, which cover only items of private consumption expenditure. The GDP deflator has several deficiencies, however, as a measure of global inflation. Although its sectoral coverage is wider than that of consumer or wholesale price indexes, the techniques used to obtain constant price data for components of the national accounts other than private consumption expenditure are less than satisfactory in most countries. . . .

[Therefore, the IMF emphasizes] consumer prices. There is a fair degree of similarity in concepts and methodologies between countries for these series. Country coverage is also more comprehensive than that for GDP deflators and wholesale prices.

[In summary,] it should be emphasized [that price] measures are only approximate indicators of overall price trends. In order to summarize into one aggregate measure the large number of transactions whose price movements they purport to reflect, a number of judgements must be made. Depending on the assumptions made concerning such aspects of methodology as the choice of base year, weights, formulae, sample selection, and specification of prices, different results, although perhaps equally appropriate depending on the context in which the measures are to be used, can ensue. In this sense, price index numbers cannot be rigorously defined independent of the methods used in their construction.

Table 3201

ARGENTINA COMPARATIVE PC OF PRICES,[1] 1980–86

(YA)

PART II.[a]

| Year | Consumer[2] | | | | | GDP Deflator | |
	A. Economía Argentina (1930–40)	B. Díaz Alejandro (1936–66)	C. Martin (1941–73)	D. IMF (1953–86)	E. UN-SY[3] (1973–86)	F. IMF (1961–86)	G. Díaz Alejandro (1936–65)
1980				100.8	100.8	95.3	
1981				104.5	104.5	107.9	
1982				164.8*	164.8	180.3	
1983				343.8	343.8	353.5	
1984				626.7*	626.7	~	
1985				672.1	672.1	~	
1986				90.1	~	~	

1. See table 3200.
2. Buenos Aires.
3. Greater Buenos Aires since 1981.

a. For 1914–1979, see SALA, 24-3201.

SOURCE: Calculations were made from the following:
  A. *Revista de Economía Argentina* 36 (1937), pp. 268-269, and 40 (1941), p. 105.
  B. Carlos F. Díaz Alejandro, *Essays on the Economic History of the Argentine Republic* (New Haven: Yale University Press, 1970), p. 528.
  C. J. L Martin, SALA, 18-1411.
  D. IMF-IFS-Y, 1983, pp. 70; IMF-IFS-Y, 1984, pp. 102-103; IMF-IFS-Y, 1986.
  E. UN-MB, Dec., 1984, p. 220; UN-SY, 1981, p.169, UN-MB, Nov. 1986, p. 212.
  F. IMF-IFS-S, No. 2, 1981, pp. 10-11; IMF-IFS-S, No. 8, 1984, pp. 76-77; IMF-IFS-Y, 1986; IMF-IFS-Y, 1987.
  G. See source B, above.

Table 3202

BOLIVIA COMPARATIVE PC OF PRICES,[1] 1980–86[a]

(YA)

| Year | Consumer[2] | | | | GDP Deflator |
	A. Wilkie (1932-66)	B. Martin (1941-75)	C. IMF (1953–86)	D. UN-SY (1973–86)	E. IMF (1957-86)
1980			47.2*	47.2	38.9
1981			28.6	32.2	27.8
1982			133.3	123.5	168.2
1983			269.0	275.6	270.7
1984			1,281.4	1,281.2	~
1985			11,749.6	11,749.6	~
1986			~	~	~

1. See table 3200.
2. La Paz.

a. For 1932–79, see SALA, 24-3202.

SOURCE: Calculations were made from the following:
  A. James W. Wilkie, *The Bolivian Revolution and U.S. Aid Since 1952* (Los Angeles: UCLA Latin American Center Publications, 1969), p. 4.
  B. J. L. Martin, SALA, 18-1412.
  C. IMF-IFS-Y, 1983, pp. 70; IMF-IFS-Y, 1984, pp. 102-103; IMF-IFS-Y, 1986.
  D. UN-MB, Dec. 1984, p. 220; UN-SY, 1981, p. 169, UN-MB, Nov. 1986, p. 212.
  E. IMF-IFS-S, No. 2, 1981, pp. 10-11; IMF-IFS, No. 8, 1984, pp. 76-77; IMF-IFS-Y, 1986; IMF-IFS-Y, 1987.

Table 3203

BRAZIL COMPARATIVE PC OF PRICES,[1] 1980–86

(YA)

PART II.[a]

Year	Consumer[2]					GDP Deflator
	A. Simonson (1930–39)	B. Martin (1941–75)	C. IMF (1958–86)	D. ILO (1930–45)	E. UN-SY (1937–86)	F. IMF (1964–86)
1980			82.8		78.0	91.6
1981			105.6		95.6	102.5
1982			97.8		89.3	92.8
1983			142.1		135.8	151.9
1984			197.0		172.5	210.6
1985			226.9		201.5	225.5
1986			145.2		~	-91.4

1. See table 3200.
2. Rio de Janeiro.

a. For 1913–79, see SALA, 24-3203.

SOURCE: Calculations were made from the following:
  A. Mario Henrique Simonson, "Brazilian Inflation: Postwar Experience and Outcome
     of the 1964 Reforms," *Economic Development Issues: Latin America* (New York:
     Committee for Economic Development, 1967), p. 269.
  B. J. L. Martin, SALA, 18-1413.
  C. IMF-IFS-Y, 1983, p. 70; IMF-IFS-Y, 1984, pp. 102-103; IMF-IFS-Y, 1986.
  D. ILO-YLS, 1945/1946, p. 194.
  E. UN-MB, Dec. 1984, p. 220; UN-SY, 1981, p. 169; UN-MB, Nov. 1986, p. 212.
  F. IMF-IFS-S, No. 8, 1984, pp. 76-77; IMF-IFS-Y, 1986; IMF-IFS-Y, 1987.

Table 3204

CHILE COMPARATIVE PC OF PRICES,[1] 1980–1986

(YA)

PART II.[a]

Year	Consumer[2]					GDP Deflator
	A. Latorre[3] (1929–57)	B. UN-SY (1931–86[b])	C. Martin (1941–75)	D. IMF (1964–86)	E. Chile (1930–40)	F. IMF (1962–86)
1980		35.1		82.8		29.2
1981		19.7		105.6*		12.2
1982		9.9		97.8		13.3
1983		27.3		142.1		26.6
1984		19.8		197.0		14.3
1985		30.4		226.9		32.8
1986		~		145.2		19.2

1. See table 3200.
2. Santiago.
3. Food only.

a. For 1899-1979, see SALA, 24-3204.
b. Selected periods only.

SOURCE: Calculations were made from the following:
  A. Adolfo Latorre Subercaseaux, "Relación Entre el Circulante y los Precios en Chile,"
     Memoria para Optar al Título de Ingeniero Comercial, Universidad Católica de Chile,
     1958.
  B. UN-SY, 1949-50, p. 401; UN-MB, Dec. 1984, p. 220; UN-SY, 1981, p. 170; UN-MB,
     Nov. 1986, p. 212.
  C. J. L. Martin, SALA, 18-1414.
  D. IMF-IFS-Y, 1984, pp. 102-103; IMF-IFS-Y, 1986.
  E. Chile, DGE, *Estadística Chilena*, Sept. 1933, Jan. 1936, Jan.-Feb., 1940,
     Aug. 1941.
  F. IMF-IFS-S, No. 8, 1984, pp. 76-77; IMF-IFS-Y, 1986, IMF-IFS-Y, 1987.

Table 3205

COLOMBIA COMPARATIVE PC OF PRICES,[1] 1980–86[a]

(YA)

Year	Consumer[2]					GDP Deflator
	A. Urrutia (1929-48)	B. IMF (1938-54)	C. Martin (1941-75)	D. IMF (1953-86)	E. UN-SY[3] (1973-86)	F. IMF (1951-86)
1980				26.5	28.0	27.6
1981				27.5	29.4	22.8
1982				24.5	24.0	24.8
1983				19.8	19.5	20.4
1984				16.1	16.2	22.2
1985				24.0	25.2	23.2
1986				18.9	~	25.3

1. See table 3200.
2. Bogotá.
3. Low income group.

a. For 1929–79, see SALA, 24-3205.

SOURCE: Calculations were made from the following:
- A. Miguel Urrutia Montoya and Mario Arrubla, eds., *Compendio de Estadísticas Históricas de Colombia* (Bogotá, D.E.: Universidad Nacional de Colombia, 1970), pp. 81-82.
- B. IMF-IFS, July 1950 and Jan. 1956.
- C. J. L. Martin, SALA, 18-1415.
- D. IMF-IFS-Y, 1983, p. 70; IMF-IFS-Y, 1984, pp. 102-103; IMF-IFS-Y, 1986.
- E. UN-MB, Dec. 1984, p. 220; UN-SY, 1981, p. 170; UN-MB, Nov. 1986, p. 212.
- F. IMF-IFS-S, No. 2, 1981, pp. 10-11; IMF-IFS-S, No. 8, 1984, pp. 76-77; IMF-IFS-Y, 1986; IMF-IFS-Y, 1987.

Table 3206

COSTA RICA COMPARATIVE PC OF PRICES,[1] 1980–86[a]

(YA)

Year	Consumer[2]				GDP Deflator
	A. Banco-Central (1937-68)	B. Martin (1941-75)	C. IMF (1953-86)	D. UN-SY[3] (1973-86)	E. IMF (1961-86)
1980			18.1	18.2	18.8
1981			37.1	37.0	41.1
1982			90.1	90.0	84.2
1983			32.6	32.7	26.0
1984			12.0	11.9	19.4
1985			15.1	14.5	16.9
1986			11.8	~	18.9

1. See table 3200.
2. San José.
3. Greater San José.

a. For 1937–79, see SALA, 24-3206.

SOURCE: Calculations were made from the following:
- A. Costa Rica, Banco Central, data provided to SALA.
- B. J. L. Martin, SALA, 18-1416.
- C. IMF-IFS-Y, 1983, p. 70; IMF-IFS-Y, 1984, pp. 102-103; IMF-IFS-Y, 1986.
- D. UN-MB, Dec. 1984, p. 220; UN-SY, 1981, p. 70; UN-MB, Nov. 1986, p. 212.
- E. IMF-IFS-S, No. 2, 1981, pp. 10-11; IMF-IFS-S, No. 8, 1984, pp. 76-77; IMF-IFS-Y, 1986; IMF-IFS-Y, 1987.

Table 3207

CUBA PRICES,[1] 1938–86

Year	A. DGE (1938-62)[a]	B. Havana Related to New York City[2]
1938	-.5	
1939	-5.8	
1940	-1.8	
1941	8.6	
1942	32.5	
1943	13.9	
1944	14.0	
1945	13.0	
1946	9.5	
1947	16.9	
1948	9.1	
1949	-13.2	
1950	-2.7	
1951	10.5	
1952	.3	
1953	-2.4	
1954	-5.5	
1955	-2.3	
1956	-.7	
1957	6.5	
1958	3.1	
1959	~	
1960	~	
1961	~	
1962	5.8[b]	
1963		~
1964		~
1965		~
1966		~
1967		~
1968		~
1969		-3.1[f]
1970		~
1971		~
1972		~
1973		~
1974		2.3[g]
1975		-5.6[h]
1976		0[i]
1977		0[j]
1978		-1.2[k]
1979		13.3
1980		~
1981		~
1982		10.3[d]
1983		-11.5[a]
1984		~
1985		~
1986		~

1. See table 3200.
2. Cost of living for U.N. officials converted to PC.

a. Havana food prices.
b. May 1961 to May 1962.
c. June 1978 to April 1979.
d. December 1981 to March 1982.
e. March 1982 to July 1983.
f. October 1968 to December 1969.
g. March 1973 to April 1974.
h. April 1974 to May 1975.
i. May 1975 to May 1976.
j. May 1976 to May 1977.
k. May 1977 to June 1978.

SOURCE: Calculations were made from the following:
    A. Cuba, DGE, AE, 1957, pp. 409-410, and for 1962, Dudley Seers, ed., *Cuba: The Economic and Social Revolution* (Chapel Hill: University of North Carolina Press, 1964), p. 33.
    B. SALA, 20-2520 and SALA, 24-3222; UN-MB, Nov. 1986, p. 212.

Table 3208

DOMINICAN REPUBLIC COMPARATIVE PC OF PRICES,[1] 1980–86[a]

(YA)

Year	Consumer[2]			GDP Deflator
	A. UN-SY[3] (1942-84)	B. Martin (1942-75)	C. IMF (1953-86)	D. IMF (1951-86)
1980	~		16.8	13.7
1981	7.5		7.5	5.3
1982	7.6		7.6	8.0
1983	7.0		4.8	3.4
1984	24.3		27.0	24.4
1985	~		37.5	38.3
1986	~		9.7	9.4

1. See table 3200.
2. Santo Domingo.
3. Including direct taxes, 1981–82.

a. For 1942–79, see SALA, 24-3208.

SOURCE: Calculations were made from the following:
- A. UN-SY, 1949-50, p. 41; for 1950–54 data, see UN-SY, 1955, p. 446; UN-MB, Dec. 1984, p. 220; UN-SY, 1981, p. 170. Selected periods only. UN-MB, Nov. 1986, p. 212.
- B. J.L. Martin, SALA, 18-1417.
- C. IMF-IFS-Y, 1983, p. 70; IMF-IFS-Y, 1984, pp. 102-103; IMF-IFS-Y, 1986.
- D. IMF-IFS-S, No. 2, 1981, pp. 10-11; IMF-IFS-S, No. 8, 1984, pp. 76-77; IMF-IFS-Y, 1986; IMF-IFS-Y, 1987.

Table 3209

ECUADOR COMPARATIVE PC OF PRICES,[1] 1980–85

(YA)

PART II.[a]

Year	Consumer[2]					GDP Deflator
	A. Rodríguez[2] (1930-42)	B. Banco Central[2] (1940-51)	C. Martin (1951-75)	D. IMF (1953-85)	E. UN-SY[3] (1973-85)	F. IMF (1951-84)
1980				13.0*	12.8	19.5
1981				13.0*	12.0	14.4
1982				16.3	16.3	17.8
1983				48.4	48.4	38.7
1984				31.1	31.2	38.3
1985				28.0	28.0	~

1. See table 3200.
2. Quito.
3. Quito.

a. For 1922–79, see SALA, 24-3209.

SOURCE: Calculations were made from the following:
- A. Linda A. Rodríguez, *The Search for Public Policy: Regional Politics and Government Finances in Ecuador*, 1830–1940 (Berkeley and Los Angeles: University of California Press, 1985).
- B. Ecuador, Banco Central, *Boletín*, July-Aug. 1952, p. 142.
- C. J. L. Martin, SALA, 18-1418.
- D. IMF-IFS-Y, 1983, p. 70; IMF-IFS-Y, 1984, pp. 102-103; IMF-IFS-Y, 1986.
- E. UN-MB, Dec. 1984, p. 220; UN-SY, 1981, p. 170; UN-MB, Nov. 1986, p. 212.
- F. IMF-IFS-S, No. 2, 1981, pp. 10-11; IMF-IFS-S, No. 8, 1984, pp. 76-77; IMF-IFS-Y, 1986; IMF-IFS-Y, 1987.

Table 3210

EL SALVADOR COMPARATIVE PC OF PRICES,[1] 1980–86[a]

(YA)

| Year | Consumer[2] | | | GDP Deflator |
	A. UN-SY[3] (1938-86)	B. Martin (1941-75)	C. IMF (1953-86)	D. IMF (1952-86)
1980	17.0		17.4	13.4
1981	14.7		14.8	5.7
1982	11.7		11.7	9.9
1983	13.2		13.3	12.3
1984	11.7		11.5	12.3
1985	22.2		22.3	20.6
1986	~		31.9	37.4

1. See table 3200.
2. San Salvador.
3. Urban areas since 1983. Selected periods.

a. For 1938–79, see SALA, 24-3210.

SOURCE: Calculations were made from the following:
  A. UN-SY, 1955, p. 446; UN-MB, Dec. 1984, p. 220; UN-SY, 1981, p. 170; UN-MB, Nov. 1986, p. 212.
  B. J. L. Martin, SALA, 18-1419.
  C. IMF-IFS-Y, 1983, p. 70; IMF-IFS-Y, 1984, pp. 102-103; IMF-IFS-Y, 1986.
  D. IMF-IFS-S, No. 2, 1981, pp. 10-11; IMF-IFS-S, No. 8, 1984, pp. 76-77; IMF-IFS-Y, 1986, IMF-IFS-Y, 1987.

Table 3211

GUATEMALA COMPARATIVE PC OF PRICES,[1] 1980–86[a]

(YA)

| Year | Consumer[2] | | | | GDP Deflator |
	A. Adler, et. al (1939-49)[b]	B. Martin (1941-75)	C. IMF (1953-86)	D. UN-SY[3] (1973-86)	E. IMF (1951-86)
1980			10.8	10.7	10.0
1981			11.4	11.4	8.5
1982			.3	#	5.0
1983			4.5	–12.0[c]	6.5
1984			3.4	1.8[d]	4.2
1985			18.7	18.6	18.7
1986			36.9	~	41.2

1. See table 3200.
2. Guatemala City.
3. Urban areas since 1975 (prior to 1975, Guatemala City only).

a. For 1939-79, see SALA, 24-3211.
b. Wholesale prices spliced to consumer price index beginning in 1946.
c. Marked break in series.
d. Base 1984 = 100 (beginning 1983).

SOURCE: Calculations were made from the following:
  A. John H. Adler et al., *Las Finanzas Públicas y el Desarrollo de Guatemala* (México, D.F.: Fondo de Cultura Económica, 1952), p. 256.
  B. J. L. Martin, SALA, 18-1420.
  C. IMF-IFS-Y, 1983, p. 70; IMF-IFS-Y, 1984, pp. 102-103; IMF-IFS-Y, 1986.
  D. UN-MB, Dec. 1984, p. 222; UN-SY, 1981, p. 171; UN-MB, Nov. 1986, p. 212.
  E. IMF-IFS-S, No. 2, 1981, pp. 10-11; IMF-IFS-S, No. 8, 1984, pp. 76-77; IMF-IFS-Y, 1986; IMF-IFS-Y, 1987.

Table 3212

HAITI COMPARATIVE PC OF PRICES,[1] 1980–86[a]

(YA)

Year	Consumer[2]		GDP Deflator
	A. IMF (1949-86)	B. UN-SY (1973-86)	C. IMF (1956-86)
1980	17.8*	17.9	19.5
1981	10.9*	11.0	6.0
1982	7.4	7.2	3.9
1983	10.2	10.3	8.9
1984	6.4	6.3	11.1
1985	10.6	10.7	10.4
1986	3.3	~	11.0

1. See table 3200.
2. Port-au-Prince.

a. For 1949–79, see SALA, 24-3212.

SOURCE: Calculations were made from the following.
A.   IMF-IFS-Y, 1972, p. 144; for 1954: IMF-IFS-Y, 1983, p. 70; since 1955: IMF-IFS-Y, 1984, pp. 102-103; IMF-IFS-Y, 1986.
B.   UN-MB, Dec. 1984, p. 222; UN-SY, 1981, p. 171; UN-MB, Nov. 1986, p. 214.
C.   IMF-IFS-S, No. 2, 1981, pp. 10-11; IMF-IFS-S, No. 8, 1984, pp. 76-77; IMF-IFS-Y, 1986; IMF-IFS-Y, 1987.

Table 3213

HONDURAS COMPARATIVE PC OF PRICES,[1] 1980–86

(YA)

PART II.[a]

Year	Consumer[2]				GDP Deflator
	A. Banco Central (1930–53)[b]	B. Martin (1949–75)	C. IMF (1953–86)	D. UN-SY[3] (1973–86)	E. IMF (1951–86)
1980			18.1	18.6	13.5
1981			9.4	9.4	7.5
1982			9.0	9.4	6.8
1983			8.3	8.9	5.0
1984			4.7	4.8	4.2
1985			3.4	1.8	4.6
1986			4.4	~	4.3

1. See table 3200.
2. Tegucigalpa.
3. Honduras.

a. For 1926–79, see SALA, 24-3213.
b. San Pedro Sula.
c. Marks break in the comparability of data. Data after "b" do not form a consistent series with those for earlier years.

SOURCE: Calculations were made from the following:
A.   Honduras, Banco Central, *Boletín*, 4: (1954), p. 38.
B.   J. L. Martin, SALA, 18-1421.
C.   IMF-IFS-Y, 1983, p. 70; IMF-IFS-Y, 1986.
D.   UN-MB, Dec. 1984, p. 222; UN-SY, 1981, p. 171; UN-MB, Nov. 1986, p. 214.
E.   IMF-IFS-S, No. 2, 1981, pp. 10-11; IMF-IFS-S, No. 8, 1984, pp. 76-77; IMF-IFS-Y, 1986; IMF-IFS-Y, 1987.

Table 3214

MEXICO COMPARATIVE PC OF PRICES,[1] 1980–86

(YA)

PART II.[a]

	Consumer[2]				GDP Deflator
Year	A. DGE (1930–75)	B. Martin (1935–75)	C. IMF (1953–86[b])	D. UN-SY (1973–86)	E. IMF (1949–86)
1980			26.4	26.3	28.7
1981			27.9	28.0	27.3
1982			58.9	58.9	61.2
1983			101.8	101.9	92.1
1984			65.5	65.5	61.8
1985			57.7	57.7	54.4
1986			86.2	~	~

1. See table 3200.
2. Mexico City.

a. For 1901–79, see SALA, 24-3214.
b. Bank of Mexico Series.

SOURCE: Calculations were made from the following:
- A. James W. Wilkie, *The Mexican Revolution: Federal Expenditure and Social Change Since 1910* (Berkeley: University of California Press, 1967), p. 23 (and sources cited there); and since 1964 Mexico, DGE, *Compendio Estadístico*, 1970, p. 296.
- B. J. L. Martin, SALA 18-1422.
- C. IMF-IFS-Y, 1983, p. 70; IMF-IFS-Y, 1984, pp. 102-103; IMF-IFS-Y, 1986.
- D. UN-MB, Dec. 1984, p. 222; UN-SY, 1981, p. 173; UN-MB, Nov. 1986, p. 216.
- E. IMF-IFS-S, No. 2, 1981, pp. 10-11; IMF-IFS-S, No. 8, 1984, pp. 76-77; IMF-IFS-Y, 1986; IMF-IFS-Y, 1987.

Table 3215

NICARAGUA COMPARATIVE PC OF PRICES,[1] 1980–86[a]

(YA)

	Consumer[2]					GDP Deflator
Year	A. UN-SY Food Prices (1938-49)	B. Martin (1941-71)	C. IMF (1956-86)	D. DeFranco and Chamorro (1969-77)	E. UN-SY[3] (1974-86)	F. IMF (1961-86)
1980			35.3*		35.1	37.1
1981			23.9		~	11.8
1982			24.8		~	16.6
1983			31.1		~	14.7
1984			35.4		~	~
1985			219.5		~	~
1986			~		~	~

1. See table 3200.
2. Managua.
3. Metropolitan area.

a. For 1938–79, see SALA, 24-3215.

SOURCE: Calculations were made from the following:
- A. UN-SY, 1949-50, p. 401.
- B. J. L. Martin, SALA, 18-1423.
- C. IMF-IFS-Y, 1972, pp. 156-157; IMF-IFS-Y, 1983, p. 71; IMF-IFS-Y, 1984, p. 103; IMF-IFS-Y, 1986.
- D. Mario A. De Franco and Carlos F. Chamorro, "Nicaragua: Crecimiento Industrial y Desempleo," in D. Camacho et al., *El Fracaso Social de la Integración Centroamericana* (San José, Costa Rica: Editorial Universitaria Centroamericano, 1979), cited in John A. Booth, *The End and the Beginning: The Nicaraguan Revolution* (Boulder, Colorado: Westview Press, 1982), p. 79.
- E. UN-SY, 1981, p. 173; UN-SY, 1982, p. 174.
- F. IMF-IFS-S, No. 2, 1981, p. 10; IMF-IFS-S, No. 8, 1984, pp. 76-77; IMF-IFS-Y, 1986; IMF-IFS-Y, 1987.

Table 3216

PANAMA COMPARATIVE PC OF PRICES,[1] 1980–86[a]

(YA)

Year	Consumer[2]			GDP Deflator
	A. Martin (1941-75)	B. IMF (1953-86)	C. UN-SY (1973-86)	D. IMF (1952-86)
1980		13.8	13.9	10.4
1981		7.3	7.3	4.6
1982		4.3	4.2	4.6
1983		2.1	2.1	1.8
1984		1.6	1.6	4.8
1985		1.0	1.0	2.7
1986		−.1	~	~

1. See table 3200.
2. Panama City.

a. For 1941–79, see SALA, 24-3216.

SOURCE: Calculations were made from the following:
    A. J. L. Martin, SALA, 18-1424.
    B. IMF-IFS-Y, 1983, p. 70; IMF-IFS-Y, 1984, pp. 102-103; IMF-IFS-Y, 1986.
    C. UN-MB, Dec. 1984, p. 224; UN-SY, 1981, p. 174; UN-MB, Nov. 1986, p. 216.
    D. IMF-IFS-S, No. 2, 1981, p. 10; IMF-IFS-S, No. 8, 1984, pp. 76-77; IMF-IFS-Y,
       1986; IMF-IFS-Y, 1987.

Table 3217

PARAGUAY COMPARATIVE PC OF PRICES,[1] 1980–86[a]

(YA)

Year	Consumer[2]			GDP Deflator
	A. UN-SY (1939-82)	B. Martin (1941-75)	C. IMF (1953-86)	D. IMF (1951-86)
1980	22.5		22.4	16.9
1981	13.0		14.0	16.6
1982	5.1		6.8	4.8
1983	~		13.4	14.4
1984	~		20.3	26.9
1985	~		25.2	25.2
1986			31.7	31.5

1. See table 3200.
2. Asunción.

a. For 1939–79, see SALA, 24-3217.

SOURCE: Calculations were made from the following:
    A. UN-SY, 1949-50, p. 402; UN-MB, Dec. 1984, p. 224; UN-SY, 1981, p. 174;
       UN-SY, 1986, p. 177.
    B. J. L. Martin, SALA, 18-1425.
    C. IMF-IFS-Y, 1983, p. 70; IMF-IFS-Y, 1984, pp. 102-103; IMF-IFS-Y, 1986.
    D. IMF-IFS-S, No. 2, 1981, p. 10; IMF-IFS-S, No. 8, 1984, pp. 76-77; IMF-IFS-Y,
       1986; IMF-IFS-Y, 1987.

Table 3218

PERU COMPARATIVE PC OF PRICES,[1] 1980–86

(YA)

PART II.[a]

	Consumer[2]					GDP Deflator
Year	A. Peru (1930–41)	B. UN-SY[3,4] (1931–86)	C. Martin (1941–75)	D. IMF (1938–86)	E. League (1929–38)	F. IMF (1961–86)
1980		~*		59.2		54.9
1981		75.4		75.4		66.3
1982		64.5		64.4		65.0
1983		111.2		111.2		110.8
1984		110.2		110.2		117.2
1985		163.3		163.4		159.7
1986		~		77.9		

1. See table 3200.
2. Lima.
3. Lima and Callao, 1973–80.
4. Metropolitan area, 1981–83.

a. For 1914–79, see SALA, 24-3218.

SOURCE: Calculations were made from the following:
    A. Peru, Dirección Nacional de Estadística, *Extracto Estadístico*, 1927, p. 103; English
       version, 1931-33, p. 53, 1941, p. 384.
    B. UN-SY, 1949-50, p. 402; UN-MB, Dec. 1984, p. 224; UN-SY, 1981, p. 174; UN-MB,
       Nov. 1986, p. 216.
    C. J. L. Martin, SALA, 18-1426.
    D. IMF-IFS-Y, 1983, p. 70; for 1938-52: IMF-IFS, June 1948 and Nov. 1950;
       IMF-IFS-Y, 1971; IMF-IFS-Y, 1984, pp. 102-103; IMF-IFS-Y, 1986.
    E. League of Nations, *Monthly Bulletin of Statistics*, Jan. 1939, p. 32.
    F. IMF-IFS-S, No. 2, 1981, p. 10; IMF-IFS-S, No. 8, 1984, pp. 76-77; IMF-IFS-Y, 1986;
       IMF-IFS-Y, 1987.

Table 3219

URUGUAY COMPARATIVE PC OF PRICES,[1] 1980–86[a]

(YA)

	Consumer[2]				GDP Deflator
Year	A. Instituto de Economía (1930-54)	B. UN-SY (1931-86)	C. Martin (1941-75)	D. IMF (1953-85)	E. IMF (1961-86)
1980		63.5		63.5	51.0
1981		34.0		34.0	30.3
1982		19.0		19.0	16.0
1983		49.2		49.2	52.7
1984		55.3		55.3	61.5
1985		72.2[b]		72.2	76.7
1986		76.4		~	70.9

1. See table 3200.
2. Montevideo.

a. For 1930–79, see SALA, 24-3219.
b. Marks a break in comparability of data. Hence data after "a" do not form
   a consistent series with those for earlier years.

SOURCE: Calculations were made from the following:
    A. Uruguay, Instituto de Economía, *Estadísticas Básicas* (Montevideo: Universidad
       de Uruguay, 1969), p. 93.
    B. UN-SY, 1949-50, p. 402; and since 1950: UN-SY, 1955, p. 448; UN-MB, Dec.
       1984, p. 226; UN-SY, 1981, p. 176; UN-MB, Nov. 1986, p. 216.
    C. J. L. Martin, SALA, 18-1427.
    D. IMF-IFS-Y, 1983, p. 70; IMF-IFS-Y, 1984, pp. 102-103; IMF-IFS-Y, 1986.
    E. IMF-IFS-S, No. 2, 1981, p. 10; IMF-IFS-S, No. 8, 1984, pp. 76-77; IMF-IFS-Y, 1986;
       IMF-IFS-Y, 1987.

Table 3220

VENEZUELA COMPARATIVE PC OF PRICES,[1] 1980–86[a]
(YA)

Year	Consumer[2]				GDP Deflator
	A. DGE (1929-48)	B. Martin (1941-75)	C. IMF (1953-86)	D. UN-SY[3] (1973-86)	E. IMF (1951-86)
1980			21.5	23.4	24.8
1981			16.2	16.0	12.5
1982			9.6	9.6	1.4
1983			6.3	6.4	5.7
1984			12.2[b]	12.2	21.6
1985			11.4	11.9	6.5
1986			11.5	~	~

1. See table 3200.
2. Caracas.
3. Metropolitan area.

a. For 1929–79, see SALA, 24-3220.
b. Marks a break in comparability of data. Hence data after "b" do not form a consistent series with those for earlier years.

SOURCE: Calculations were made from the following:
  A. Venezuela, DGE, *Boletín de Estadística*, July 1949, p. 18.
  B. J. L. Martin, SALA, 18-1428.
  C. IMF-IFS-Y, 1983, p. 68; IMF-IFS-Y, 1986.
  D. UN-MB, Dec. 1984, p. 226; UN-SY, 1981, p. 176; UN-MB, Nov. 1986, p. 216.
  E. IMF-IFS-S, No. 2, 1981, p. 8; IMF-IFS-S, No. 8, 1984, pp. 74-75; IMF-IFS-Y, 1986; IMF-IFS-Y, 1987.

Table 3221

UNITED STATES COMPARATIVE PC OF PRICES,[1] 1980–86
(YA)

PART II.[a]

Year	Consumer[2]				GDP Deflator
	A. USBC (1930-69)	B. Martin (1941-75)	C. IMF (1953-85)	D. UN-SY (1973-86)	E. IMF (1949-86)
1980			13.5	13.4	9.1
1981			10.4	10.4	9.6
1982			6.2	6.1	6.4
1983			3.2	3.2	3.9
1984			4.3	4.3	3.9
1985			3.6	3.5	3.4
1986			1.9	~	2.6

1. See table 3200.
2. National Index.

a. For 1901–79, see SALA, 24-3221.

SOURCE: Calculations were made from the following:
  A. USBC-HS, 1975, vol. I, series E135.
  B. J. L. Martin, SALA 18-1429.
  C. IMF-IFS-Y, 1983, p. 68; IMF-IFS-Y, 1984, pp. 100-101; IMF-IFS-Y, 1986, p. 111.
  D. UN-MB, Dec. 1984, p. 226; UN-SY, 1981, p. 176; UN-MB, Nov. 1986, p. 218.
  E. IMF-IFS-S, No. 2, 1981, p. 8; IMF-IFS-S, No. 8, 1984, pp. 74-75; IMF-IFS-Y, 1986, p. 165; IMF-IFS-Y, 1987.

Table 3222

SUMMARY OF IMF PC OF CONSUMER PRICE INDEX, 19 LC, 1970–86
(YA)

Country	1970	1971	1972	1973	1974	1975	1976	1977	1978	1979	1980	1981	1982	1983	1984	1985	1986
Antigua and Barbuda	~	~	~	~	~	~	~	~	~	~	~	~	~	~	~	~	~
A. ARGENTINA	13.6	34.8	58.4	61.2	23.5*	182.3	443.2	176.1	175.5	159.5	100.8	104.5	164.8*	343.8	626.7*	672.1	90.1
Bahamas, The	6.2	4.8	6.8	5.5	13.3	10.2	4.2	3.2	6.1	9.1	12.1	11.1	10.3	4.1	3.9	4.6	5.4
Barbados	7.8	12.4	7.0	16.9	38.9	20.3	5.0	8.3	9.5	13.2*	14.5	14.6	10.3	5.3	4.6	3.9	1.3
Belize	~	~	~	~	~	~	~	~	~	~	~	11.2	6.8	5.0	3.7	3.7	1.0
B. BOLIVIA	3.8	3.7	6.5	31.5	62.8	8.0	4.5	8.1	10.4	19.7	47.2*	28.6	133.3	269.0	1,281.4	11,749.6	~
C. BRAZIL	22.3	20.2	16.5	12.7	27.6	29.0*	42.0	43.7	38.7	52.7	82.8	105.6*	97.8	142.1	197.0	226.9	145.2
D. CHILE	33.0	19.2*	77.3	353.6	504.7	374.7*	211.8	91.9	40.1	33.4	35.1	19.7	9.9	27.3	19.9	30.7	19.5
E. COLOMBIA	6.8	9.0*	13.4	20.8	24.3	22.9	20.2	33.1	17.8	24.7	26.5	27.5	24.5	19.8	16.1	24.0	18.9
F. COSTA RICA	4.7	3.1	4.6	15.2	30.1	17.4*	3.5	4.2	6.0	9.2	18.1	37.1	90.1	32.6	12.0	15.1	11.8
Dominica	12.4	3.6	3.7	12.1	36.3	18.3	10.9	9.5	7.8	19.9	30.6	13.3	4.5	4.0	2.2	2.1	3.0
H. DOMINICAN REP.	3.8	4.3	7.8	15.1	13.2	14.5	7.8	12.8	3.5*	9.2	16.8	7.5	7.6	4.8	27.0	37.5	9.7
I. ECUADOR	5.1	8.4	7.9	13.0*	23.3	15.4	10.7	13.0	11.7	10.3	13.0*	16.4*	16.3	48.4	31.2	28.0	23.0
J. EL SALVADOR	2.8	.4	1.6	6.4	16.9	19.2	7.0	11.8	13.2	14.6	17.4	14.8	11.7	13.3	11.5	22.3	31.9
Grenada	~	~	~	~	~	~	~	18.5	18.1	21.5	21.2	18.8	7.8	6.1	5.6	2.5	.5
K. GUATEMALA	2.4	-.5	.5	13.8	16.5	13.2*	10.7*	12.3	8.3	11.3	10.8	11.4	.3	4.5	3.4	18.7	36.9
Guyana	3.4*	1.0	5.0	7.5	17.5	7.8	9.0	8.3	15.2	17.8	14.1	24.7	20.2	13.3	25.2	~	~
L. HAITI	1.3	9.5	3.2	22.7	15.0	16.8	7.0	6.5	-2.7	13.1	17.8*	10.9*	7.4	10.2	6.4	10.6	3.3
M. HONDURAS	2.9	2.2	3.6	5.2	12.8	8.4	4.9	8.4	5.7*	12.1	18.1	9.4	9.0	8.3	4.7	3.4	4.4
Jamaica	7.7*	5.3	5.4	17.7	27.2	17.4	9.8	11.2	34.9	29.1	27.3	12.7	6.5	11.6	27.8	25.7	15.1
N. MEXICO	5.2	5.3	5.0	12.0	23.8	15.2	15.8	29.0	17.5	18.2	26.4	27.9	58.9	101.8	65.5	57.7	86.2
Netherlands Antilles	3.6*	2.1	4.1	8.1	19.4	15.6	5.2	5.5	8.2	11.4	14.6	12.2	6.1	2.8	2.1	~	~
O. NICARAGUA	~	~	~	27.0	13.3	7.5	2.8	11.4	4.6	48.2	35.3*	23.9	24.8	31.1	35.4	219.5	~
P. PANAMA	3.1	2.0	5.3	6.9	16.8	5.5*	4.0	4.5	4.2	7.9	13.8	7.3	4.3	2.1	1.6	1.0	-.1
Q. PARAGUAY	-.7	4.8	9.5	12.5	25.2	6.8	4.6	9.3	10.6	28.3	22.4	14.0	6.8	13.4	20.3	25.2	31.7
R. PERU	5.0	6.8	7.2	9.5	16.9	23.6	33.5	38.1	57.8	66.7*	59.2	75.4	64.4	111.2	110.2	163.4	77.9
St. Lucia	13.4	8.4	7.9	13.4	34.2	17.8	9.7	8.9	10.9	9.4	19.5	15.1	4.6	1.5	1.2	1.3	2.3
St. Vincent	~	~	~	~	~	6.8	11.3	10.2	8.4	15.6	17.2*	12.7*	7.2	5.5	2.7	2.1	~
Suriname	2.6	.2	3.3	13.0	16.9	8.4	10.1	9.7	8.8*	14.9	14.1*	8.7	7.3	4.4	3.7	~	~
Trinidad and Tobago	2.5	3.5	9.3	14.8	22.0	17.0	10.6	11.8	10.2	14.7	17.5	14.3	11.5	16.7*	13.3	7.6	7.7
S. URUGUAY	17.0	24.0	76.5	97.0*	77.2	81.4	50.6	58.2	44.5	66.8	63.5	34.0	19.0	49.2	55.3	72.2*	76.4
T. VENEZUELA	2.5	3.2	2.8	4.1	8.3	10.3	7.6	7.8	7.1	12.4	21.5	16.2	9.6	6.3	12.2*	11.4	11.5
Western Hemisphere	12.3	14.8	20.0	28.5	28.0	37.3	51.0	44.0	37.8	50.5	54.8	59.8	73.4	118.5	146.1	161.5	82.0

SOURCE: IMF-IFS-Y, 1987.

Table 3223

RETAIL PRICE INDEX RELATING TO LIVING EXPENDITURES OF U.N. OFFICIALS IN LATIN AMERICAN CAPITALS, 20 L, 1966–86

(New York City = 100, December of Each Year)

Country	1966	1973	1974	1975	1976	1977	1978	1979	1980	1981	1982	1983	1984	1985	1986
A. ARGENTINA	~	78[a]	84[i]	46[h]	47[l]	78	143	143	216	110	81	80	73	73	87
B. BOLIVIA	81	73[b]	83[e]	82	85	95	93[e]	109	103	104	62[i]	83	89	43	83
C. BRAZIL	108	93	100[i]	101	102[a]	100	104[i]	78	94	84	84	64	61	46	60
D. CHILE	76	36[i]	68[i]	75	77	93	97	111	116	132	92	85	73	53	54
E. COLOMBIA	63	64[g]	67[i]	67	66[h]	79	84	96	96[i]	107	102[h]	90	66	56	53
F. COSTA RICA	84	79[a]	91	95[e]	95[j]	93	86	99	105	49	52	70[i]	70	69	70
G. CUBA	~	87[b]	89[c]	84[k]	84[k]	84[k]	83[da]	94[c]	~	87[a]	78[ba]	69	~	67[a]	83[a]
H. DOMINICAN REP.	~	94[g]	95[i]	100[g]	98	97	90[g]	88[g]	97	91[e]	95[d]	95[e]	102	57	57
I. ECUADOR	~	83[j]	82[i]	80	79	73	86	85	87[i]	80	60[j]	59	51	54	61
J. EL SALVADOR	~	83	89[e]	87[g]	87	86	96[f]	99	104[e]	98	87[f]	70[g]	70	61	70
K. GUATEMALA	91	77[d]	86[i]	88	88[j]	94	101	100[i]	100[i]	99	86[j]	86[b]	95	58	70
L. HAITI	~	86[g]	94[k]	92[d]	90[d]	94[g]	99[g]	98	92[d]	97[c]	104[c]	104	75	71	73
M. HONDURAS	~	88[k]	87[f]	90[e]	88	91	89[i]	94[g]	99	93	86[i]	87[i]	87	87	89
N. MEXICO	95	89[g]	90[i]	92	90[a]	71	79	86	95	100	71	61	54	39	43
O. NICARAGUA	~	88[k]	93[c]	91	95	98	91	87[c]	~	111[f]	1.0[h]	65	65	85	59
P. PANAMA	~	86[g]	88[g]	88[g]	88	88	90[g]	90[g]	95[h]	98	73[i]	90[i]	97	101	84
Q. PARAGUAY	~	71[g]	75[h]	80[h]	79	84	88[f]	104	110[f]	116[i]	101[h]	104[h]	46	41	49
R. PERU	94	82[e]	84[g]	90	93[g]	84	72	80	100	104	101	91	67	54	80
S. URUGUAY	66	70[d]	69[i]	72	73	83	81[i]	102[i]	115	123	100	70	55	56	63
T. VENEZUELA	103	91	88[g]	87[h]	87	92	123[h]	141[i]	142	141[g]	145[h]	71	68	47	35

a. Calculated on the basis of the cost of government or subsidized housing which is normally lower than prevailing rentals.
b. March.
c. April.
d. June.
e. July.
f. August.
g. September.
h. October.
i. November.
j. Prior to devaluation of the peso.
k. May.
l. November unless noted otherwise.

SOURCE: UN-MB, various monthly since 1966.

Table 3224

IMF WHOLESALE PRICE INDEX,[1] 13 LC, 1970-86

(YA, 1980 = 100)

Country	1970	1973	1974	1975	1976	1977	1978	1979	1981	1982	1983	1984	1985	1986
A. ARGENTINA[2]	.05	.18	.21	.62	3.73	9.30	22.87	57.00	209.58	746.60	3,440.5	23,175	176,798	289,708
C. 1. BRAZIL[3]	4.05	6.73	8.69	11.06	15.85	22.58	31.07	48.43	208.18	402	1,075	3,617	11,900	28,583
C. 2. BRAZIL[2]	4.11	6.79	8.78	11.23	15.75	22.15	30.76	47.80	213.04	412	1,088	3,625	11,718	28,092
D. 1. CHILE[2]	.007	.086	.965	5.616	18.032	33.549	47.963	71.654	109.085	116.927	107.2	211.5	303.3	363.3
D. 2. CHILE[4]	.008	.091*	.932	5.464	17.817	32.545	47.234	71.447	110.120	117.187	166.2	204.9	287.6	355.0
E. COLOMBIA[2]	11.95	20.16	27.42	34.39	42.27	53.56	62.99	80.52	124.06	155.92	189.8	224.5	280.5	342.3
F. COSTA RICA[5]	24.5	31.9	44.7	54.3	59.3	63.8	69.6	80.8	165.3	344.2	434.3	467.6	516.2	562.7
I. ECUADOR[6]	~	~	50.1	57.1	66.6	72.1	84.2	93.2	109.6	128.1	147.1	181.0	228.3	279.2
J. 1. EL SALVADOR[7]	32.6	39.6	49.6	50.5	68.0	100.2	80.3	86.4	110.0	119.4	127.5	134.9	153.6	~
J. 2. EL SALVADOR[8]	33.7	42.1	55.0	58.9	65.5	73.2	76.7	84.5	112.4	122.0	131.7	141.0	166.2	~
K. 1. GUATEMALA[9]	37.8	43.8	53.8	60.4	66.8	75.5	78.2	86.2	111.7	105.3	106.2	112.2	138.3	197.7
K. 2. GUATEMALA[10]	37.8	43.6	53.0	59.9	66.1	75.8	78.6	86.4	111.9	104.4	105.3	110.9	137.5	200.4
N. MEXICO[11]	20.32	25.11	30.75	33.97	41.55	58.64	67.89	80.31	124.44	194.20	402.7	686.0	1,053.4	1,932.4
P. PANAMA[12]	33.3	42.0	54.8	62.4	67.3	72.2	76.0	86.7	110.0	119.1	114.6	115.8	115.3	96.9
Q. PARAGUAY[13]	21.5	39.7	52.0	59.9	60.3	65.1	73.5	92.8	112.2	116.1	141.6	181.6	224.2	~
S. URUGUAY[14]	.77	3.78	6.74	11.63	17.51	26.32	39.10	70.54	123.44	139.36	241.77	428.85	757.24	1,265.9
T. 1. VENEZUELA[15]	39.6	45.3	52.8	60.1	64.4	71.0	76.3	83.3	113.84	123.03	131.62	154.6	182.8	211.5
T. 2. VENEZUELA[16]	37.5	42.2	49.4	56.4	61.0	68.5	73.7	81.3	115.1	124.9	134.3	157.5	188.9	225.5
UNITED STATES	41.1	50.1	59.6	65.0	68.1	72.2	77.9	87.6	109.1	111.3	112.7	115.4	114.9	111.52

1. For data covering period 1952-70 see SALA, 23-2623.
2. Home and import goods.
3. Wholesale prices.
4. Home goods.
5. Wholesale prices in San José. Home and import goods.
6. Index compiled by the Central University of Ecuador.
7. Index of wholesale prices based on a sample of 91 commodities, including coffee.
8. Index of wholesale prices based on a sample of 91 commodities, excluding coffee.
9. Wholesale prices in Guatemala City; compiled by the Dirección General de Estadística from a sample of 65 commodities.
10. Home and export goods series. Refers to national products in K.1. Guatemala.
11. Covers 210 home and import goods in Mexico City.
12. Index for the entire country, covering the agricultural, industrial and import sectors.
13. Data as reported directly by the Central Bank to the IMF; covers Asunción only.
14. Covers home and export goods in agriculture and manufacturing.
15. Covers home and import goods for domestic consumption.
16. Covers home goods for domestic consumption.

SOURCE: IMF-IFS-S, 1983; IMF-IFS, June 1984, line 63; IMF-IFS-Y, 1986; IMF-IFS-Y, 1986, line 63.

Table 3225

PC OF WHOLESALE PRICE INDEX, 13 LR, 1970-86
(YA)

	Country	1970	1971	1972	1973	1974	1975	1976	1977	1978	1979	1980	1981	1982	1983	1984	1985	1986
A.	ARGENTINA	14.0	39.0	76.7	50.4	19.9	192.5	499.1	149.5	146.0	149.3	75.4	109.6	256.2	360.9*	573.4	662.9	63.9
C.	BRAZIL	22.0*	20.0	18.6	16.8	29.2	27.2*	43.3	42.5	37.6	55.9	106.4	108.2*	93.2	167.4	236.3	229.0	140.2
D.	CHILE	36.8	17.7	70.3	510.7	1,021.3*	481.9	221.1	86.1	43.0	49.4	39.6	9.1	7.2	45.5	24.3	43.4	19.8
E.	COLOMBIA	7.6*	11.5	18.3	28.0	36.0	25.4	22.9	26.7	17.6	27.8	24.2	24.1	25.7	21.7	18.3	24.9	22.0
F.	COSTA RICA	6.5	6.4	5.5	16.3	39.8	21.6	9.3	7.5	7.8*	16.1	23.7	65.3	108.2	26.2	7.7	10.4	9.0
I.	ECUADOR	~	~	~	~	~	14.0	16.7	8.2	16.7	10.7	7.3	9.6	16.9	14.9	23.1	26.1	22.3
J.	EL SALVADOR	8.7	-5.4	5.9	21.1	25.3	1.8	34.7	47.3	-19.8*	7.6	15.8	10.0	8.5	6.8	5.9	13.8	~
K.	GUATEMALA	2.4	2.1	-.7	14.3	22.8	12.3	10.5	13.0	3.6	10.3	16.0	11.7	-5.8	.9	5.6	23.3	42.9
N.	MEXICO	6.0	3.7	2.8	15.7	22.5	10.5	22.3	41.2	15.8*	18.3	24.5	24.4	56.1	107.4	70.3	53.6	83.4
P.	PANAMA	3.1	5.4	8.5	10.5	30.2	14.0	7.8	7.2	5.4	14.0	15.3	10.0	8.3*	-3.8	1.1	-.4	-16.0
Q.	PARAGUAY	-4.0	12.9	18.5*	38.0	30.5	15.2	1.1	8.0	12.8	26.3	7.8	12.2	3.5	22.0	28.3	23.4	~
S.	URUGUAY	13.7	20.3	84.9	121.0	78.6	72.4	50.6	50.3	48.6	80.4	41.8	23.4	12.9	73.5	77.4	76.6	67.2
T.	VENEZUELA	1.6	3.5	3.4	6.7	16.7	13.7	7.2	10.3	7.4	9.3	20.0	13.8	8.1	7.0	17.5	18.2	15.7
	Western Hemisphere	13.5	15.9	24.2	34.6	32.1	38.8	60.1	47.7	35.7	52.2	56.9	61.0	84.6	134.9	160.8	161.6	76.2

SOURCE: IMF-IFS-Y, 1987.

Table 3226

U.N. WHOLESALE PRICE INDEX, 15 LC, 1971-81
(YA, 1970 = 100)

	Country	Index	1971	1972	1973	1974	1975	1976	1977	1978	1979	1980	1981
A.	ARGENTINA	General	140	247	370	455	1,301	7,770	19,412	47,729	119,082	209,098	437,826
		Finished goods[2]	136	280	354	441	1,379	8,117	19,860	49,190	122,360	220,324	465,074
		Domestic goods	140	247	369	440	1,270	7,408	18,678	47,086	120,457	213,880	~
		Imported goods	123	247	402	550	1,967	15,549	35,175	61,877	119,561	208,383	536,904
		Farm products	148	289	412	455	1,109	6,906	18,318	44,541	111,110	181,761	351,049
		Textiles	133	234	363	468	1,294	6,698	17,045	43,060	107,895	190,666	~

Continued in SALA, 23-2624.

Table 3227

ECLA IMPORT AND EXPORT PRICE CHANGES, 19 LR, 1976-80
(%)

Category	Imports					Exports				
	1976	1877	1978	1979	1880	1976	1977	1978	1979	1980
Oil-Exporting Countries	6.3	8.5	8.6	8.9	12.8	5.0	5.8	-6.3	35.3	35.6

Continued in SALA, 23-2630.

Table 3228

COMMODITY PRICES, 1970-86[a]

(YA)

Commodity	Code[1]	1970	1975	1978	1979	1980	1981	1982	1983	1984	1985	1986
Aluminum (US cents/pound)												
Canada (United Kingdom)	w	27.86	39.39	60.10	72.70	80.51	57.28	44.98	65.25	56.77	47.21	52.15
Bananas (US cents/pound)												
Latin America (US Ports)	w	7.53	11.15	13.00	14.78	17.01	18.20	16.99	19.46	16.76	17.25	17.93
Bauxite (US $/metric ton)												
Guyana (Baltimore)	w	42.39	105.31	138.42	152.60	212.45	216.34	203.35	179.54	164.95	164.28	~
Beef (US cents/pound)												
All Origins (US Ports)	w	59.16	60.20	96.99	130.82	125.19	112.12	108.39	110.67	103.11	97.67	94.98
Argentina (frozen)	u	33.14	38.87	52.54	86.91	93.12	76.87	64.07	66.59	57.78	~	~
Argentina (corned)	u	39.30	74.83	75.93	116.77	144.27	135.20	99.99	91.33	82.46	82.23	~
Butter (US cents/pound)												
New Zealand	w	28.61	50.46	68.08	69.34	73.80	78.79	79.05	110.06	75.55	57.15	56.89
Cacao (US cents/pound)												
Brazil	u	29.42	56.59	153.53	140.73	107.06	87.50	68.29	83.10	105.32	94.97	92.03
Coal (US $/short ton)												
US (Pennsylvania mines)	w	16.60	44.86	44.71	45.64	46.18	61.03	68.21	65.83	65.81	~	~
Coconut Oil (US cents/pound)												
Philippines	w	12.80	17.00	27.01	41.95	28.06	23.27	19.75	24.15	44.83	24.18	12.10
Coffee (US cents/pound)												
All Coffee (New York)	w	50.53	72.48	155.00	169.50	150.71	115.82	125.62	127.94	141.24	133.47	170.28
Brazil (New York)	w	55.80	82.58	165.29	178.47	208.79	186.44	143.68	142.75	149.65	148.93	231.19
Brazil	u	44.26	49.57	142.11	154.72	143.75	83.34	94.88	101.16	112.72	103.97	173.30
Colombia (New York)	w	56.66	81.71	185.20	183.40	178.83	128.09	139.71	131.69	144.25	145.56	192.74
Colombia	u	54.22	62.38	166.86	137.47	161.70	121.77	134.62	120.13	133.35	134.87	202.33
El Salvador	u	49.37	54.39	160.93	154.39	151.41	123.77	128.87	105.64	~	~	~
Uganda (New York)	w	41.44	61.05	147.47	165.47	147.15	102.91	111.04	124.12	138.18	121.24	148.24
Copper (US cents/pound)												
Canada	u	62.84	57.30	63.21	95.07	99.76	81.96	71.73	72.53	54.66	62.24	~
Copra (US $/metric ton)												
Philippines	u	179.91	226.41	356.00	615.27	390.45	310.53	276.66	275.78	~	~	140.60
Cotton (US cents/pound)												
United States (10 markets)	w	25.10	45.10	57.60	62.10	81.30	72.02	60.03	68.42	68.15	58.68	52.72
Mexico	u	26.26	51.14	69.91	74.24	83.36	74.82	64.57	77.90	~	~	~
Fishmeal (US $/metric ton)												
Peru	u	155.72	202.45	387.26	385.60	453.00	505.84	~	~	~	~	~
Gold (US $/fine ounce)												
United Kingdom (London)	w	35.94	159.25	193.24	306.67	607.87	459.75	375.80	422.47	360.36	317.18	367.68
Groundnuts (US $/metric ton)												
Nigeria (London)	w	228.17	432.97	630.92	562.75	485.57	622.72	383.20	349.44	349.76	349.85	~
Groundnut Cake (US $/metric ton)												
All Origins (Europe)	w	115.06	157.76	230.78	237.72	271.41	269.26	208.33	229.00	187.50	146.25	166.00
Groundnut Oil (US $/metric ton)												
West Africa (Europe)	w	378.54	778.17	1,079.17	888.67	858.75	1,042.75	585.17	710.92	1,016.67	905.25	569.42
Hides (US cents/pound)												
United States (Chicago)	w	12.90	23.28	47.54	73.13	45.92	41.72	38.56	45.13	58.87	51.18	63.76
Australia	u	24.79	43.92	73.87	90.57	84.65	60.76	57.72	48.73	51.94	47.08	58.09
Iron Ore (US $/metric ton)												
Brazil (North Sea Ports)	w	15.22	22.81	19.39	23.44	27.25	24.62	26.21	23.97	23.11	22.66	21.89
Jute (US $/metric ton)												
Bangladesh (Chita-Chaina)	w	269.60	370.98	397.88	385.01	313.65	278.38	283.22	298.39	569.80	698.57	326.03
Lamb (US cents/pound)												
New Zealand	u	24.33	39.80	55.62	63.94	72.28	74.90	64.97	62.37	56.75	53.86	51.84
Lead (US cents/pound)												
United States (New York)	w	15.70	21.60	33.80	53.00	43.50	37.46	26.69	22.53	27.00	19.63	20.30
Linseed Oil (US cents/pound)												
United States (Minneapolis)	w	11.00	41.00	21.80	29.10	30.80	37.17	33.13	31.95	36.36	37.62	~
Logs (US $/cubic meter)												
Philippines (Tokyo)	w	43.17	67.51	91.58	160.60	192.95	144.44	143.08	136.43	149.59	132.32	~
Maize (US $/bushel)												
United States (US Gulf Pts)	w	1.48	3.04	2.56	2.94	3.19	3.32	2.75	3.45	3.45	2.85	2.23
Manganese (US $/long ton)												
India (US Ports)	w	55.33	140.00	144.38	140.00	155.25	167.80	164.12	151.82	143.21	141.01	140.83
Newsprint (US $/short ton)												
United States (New York)	w	150.50	256.70	315.46	345.22	388.53	428.47	440.71	422.41	450.71	463.41	453.82
Nickel (US cents/pound)												
Canada (Canadian Ports)	w	127.63	207.33	209.17	271.00	295.68	270.03	219.43	211.95	215.56	222.22	176.39
Palm Kernels (US $/metric ton)												
Nigeria (Europe)	w	167.55	206.75	363.73	499.50	344.50	317.33	264.83	365.33	524.75	284.67	141.42
Palm Oil (US $/metric ton)												
Malaysia	u	214.82	473.33	532.02	594.21	529.53	490.91	416.81	437.54	650.55	493.83	269.97

Table 3228 (Continued)

COMMODITY PRICES, 1970–86[a]

(YA)

Commodity	Code[1]	1970	1975	1978	1979	1980	1981	1982	1983	1984	1985	1986
Pepper, Black (US cents/pound)												
Malaysia (New York)	w	57.30	90.95	106.43	96.12	90.43	71.84	70.43	76.63	103.34	173.20	219.16
Petroleum (US $/Barrel)												
Libya (Es Sidra)	w	2.58	11.59	13.71	21.06	35.87	39.83	35.49	30.89	30.15	29.66	~
Saudi Arabia (Ras Tanura)	w	1.30	10.72	12.70	17.26	28.67	32.50	33.47	29.31	28.47	~	~
Venezuela (Tia Juana)	w	1.73	10.89	12.42	16.77	27.60	32.03	32.03	28.05	27.03	26.44	~
Phosphate Rock (US $/metric ton)												
Morocco (Casablanca)	w	11.00	68.00	29.00	33.00	46.71	49.50	42.38	36.92	38.25	33.92	34.37
Potash (US $/metric ton)												
Canada (Vancouver)	w	31.50	81.33	56.38	76.04	115.71	113.67	83.25	75.50	83.71	83.96	68.79
Plywood (US cents/sheet)												
Philippines (Tokyo)	w	103.06	121.83	189.58	262.49	273.84	245.46	234.35	229.87	227.03	210.91	274.15
Pulp (US $/metric ton)												
Canada	u	154.16	373.04	292.63	380.18	470.23	481.36	435.46	368.08	440.34	354.24	~
Rice (US $/metric ton)												
United States (New Orleans)	w	189.60	418.87	399.03	381.40	496.04	565.48	366.70	378.46	379.74	382.50	342.83
Rubber (US cents/pound)												
All Origins (New York)	w	21.10	29.90	50.00	64.20	73.50	57.00	45.28	56.17	49.58	41.79	41.20
Sawnwood (US $/cubic meter)												
Malaysia (French Ports)	w	93.23	166.44	203.47	339.08	369.66	314.14	302.11	304.28	306.77	276.26	266.18
Shrimp (US $/pound)												
United States (N. York Gulf)	w	1.24	2.67	3.64	5.43	4.60	4.41	6.21	6.00	5.24	4.76	5.85
Silver (US cents/troy ounce)												
United States (New York)	w	177.10	441.90	540.10	1,109.00	2,057.80	1,052.1	794.9	1,144.1	814.1	614.2	546.9
Sisal (US $/metric ton)												
Tanzania	u	115.25	413.24	357.36	387.77	540.61	587.94	476.13	495.81	371.06	562.43	~
Sorghum (US $/metric ton)												
United States (U.S. Gulf Ports)	w	51.80	111.87	93.84	108.11	128.86	126.54	108.35	128.42	118.19	102.97	82.41
Soybeans (US $/metric ton)												
United States (Rotterdam)	w	116.92	221.67	265.33	297.75	296.25	288.42	244.50	281.67	282.08	224.42	208.42
Soybean Meal (US $/metric ton)												
United States (Rotterdam)	w	102.58	155.00	213.33	243.00	258.58	252.67	218.00	237.83	197.17	157.17	184.75
Soybean Oil (US $/metric ton)												
All Origins (Dutch Ports)	w	286.33	563.33	607.00	662.17	598.25	506.92	447.33	526.92	725.17	576.00	342.41
Sugar (US cents/pound)												
US Import Price (NY)	w	7.50	22.47	~	~	30.03	19.73	19.92	22.04	21.74	20.35	~
EEC Import Price	w	5.09	15.44	15.91	18.12	22.09	18.93	18.12	17.57	16.04	15.99	~
Caribbean (New York)	w	3.76	20.56	7.82	9.66	28.67	16.89	8.41	8.47	5.20	4.05	6.05
Brazil	u	5.10	29.18	7.70	8.79	21.79	16.92	9.42	9.46	9.17	6.66	7.09
Dominican Republic	u	6.15	26.77	8.63	8.73	16.41	27.47	14.45	13.02	~	~	~
Australia	u	4.97	19.95	12.07	13.30	21.07	19.16	9.99	10.32	7.82	5.84	7.97
Philippines	u	6.62	27.03	8.18	7.61	16.22	20.65	15.09	13.44	12.70	14.94	17.59
Superphosphate (US $/metric ton)												
United States (US Gulf Ports)	w	42.50	205.00	98.04	143.34	178.04	160.87	140.04	134.04	131.25	121.38	121.17
Tea (US cents/pound)												
Average Auction (London)	w	49.55	69.70	99.29	97.87	101.06	91.59	87.62	105.44	156.79	89.98	87.48
Tin (US cents/pound)												
All Origins (New York)	w	174.40	340.10	590.10	713.20	774.60	644.92	583.33	601.42	573.04	534.49	~
Bolivia	u	174.41	312.55	566.91	672.37	760.36	633.80	574.63	586.48	554.40	539.32	~
Tobacco (US cents/pound)												
United States (All Markets)	w	80.61	103.78	124.06	134.74	142.59	160.86	182.72	185.52	185.60	184.33	163.60
Urea (US $/metric ton)												
Any Origin (Europe)	w	48.25	197.67	144.83	146.46	221.88	217.33	159.54	124.46	171.29	136.33	107.00
Wheat (US $/bushel)												
Australia	u	1.42	4.57	3.09	3.94	4.91	5.07	4.41	4.67	3.89	3.50	3.14
United States (US Gulf Pts)	w	1.49	4.06	3.48	4.36	4.70	4.76	4.36	4.28	4.15	3.70	3.13
Argentina	u	1.48	4.65	3.21	3.85	4.94	5.51	4.54	3.90	3.63	3.13	~
Wool (US cents/kilogram)												
New Zealand (greasy wool)	u	66.14	131.82	217.83	264.98	275.58	243.55	212.98	197.79	208.83	201.29	214.33
Zinc (US cents/pound)												
United States (New York)	w	15.90	38.90	31.50	37.80	38.10	45.67	40.01	42.82	49.95	43.22	40.50
Canada	u	11.93	36.18	28.19	32.06	34.51	39.19	36.09	36.30	44.71	37.37	~
Peru	u	6.41	16.73	14.05	18.61	21.91	25.25	24.22	~	~	~	~

1. Code: w = wholesale price.
   u = unit price (reported value data divided by reported volume data).

a. For data 1949–70 see SALA, 21-2526.

SOURCE: IMF-IFS-Y, 1979; IMF-IFS-Y, 1980; IMF-IFS-Y, 1981; IMF-IFS-Y, 1982;
IMF-IFS, May 1985, pp. 74-77; IMF-IFS-Y, 1986, pp. 169–171; IMF-IFS-Y, 1986,
pp. 174–177.

Table 3229

REAL "MANUFACTURES PURCHASING POWER INDEX" OF PRIMARY COMMODITIES EXPORTED BY DEVELOPING COUNTRIES, 1948–85

(1977–79 = 100)

				Agriculture							Metals and Minerals (23.4)
					Food						
Year	Petroleum	33 Commodities[1] (Excluding Energy) (100.0)[a]	Total (71.8)	Total (58.1)	Beverages (26.4)	Cereals (7.5)	Fats and Oils (8.6)	Other (15.6)	Non-Food (13.6)	Timber (4.8)	
1948	47	109	116	110	58	162	162	145	139	54	100
1949	40	109	114	110	68	169	126	145	128	60	107
1950	41	146	158	142	99	183	153	190	227	72	125
1951	36	153	163	138	95	172	157	184	269	91	135
1952	34	130	128	115	86	164	125	135	179	65	150
1953	37	122	120	115	90	168	130	123	152	61	139
1954	40	132	134	132	131	160	124	125	143	86	136
1955	39	130	125	114	102	139	113	123	172	68	156
1956	38	128	122	115	104	136	112	126	152	63	159
1957	37	125	124	120	93	127	110	166	145	60	139
1958	34	109	107	101	83	126	102	120	131	56	127
1959	31	108	106	95	74	121	111	108	151	67	125
1960	29	107	104	92	71	114	104	111	155	72	125
1961	28	100	95	84	66	120	106	96	131	73	120
1962	26	98	94	85	62	130	98	97	128	79	115
1963	26	117	121	121	62	130	105	223	121	78	115
1964	24	115	111	109	70	129	106	167	120	65	138
1965	24	107	92	86	66	125	117	84	117	75	158
1966	23	106	89	83	62	136	110	76	114	76	164
1967	23	98	87	82	60	143	103	79	107	80	136
1968	23	100	88	82	60	140	100	80	112	83	140
1969	22	103	92	86	59	132	94	105	114	76	146
1970	20	102	91	89	64	113	104	109	100	76	143
1971	25	92	86	83	53	103	99	116	96	73	117
1972	26	94	92	92	54	101	89	155	91	67	107
1973	32	122	120	119	59	178	157	170	124	100	135
1974	108	157	164	175	56	212	150	374	114	99	149
1975	95	112	113	119	48	149	89	241	89	67	116
1976	100	109	110	110	90	119	94	149	111	89	111
1977	100	112	116	119	138	100	106	105	102	91	104
1978	87	93	94	93	89	104	97	93	97	80	92
1979	111	97	93	91	81	96	98	103	102	124	104
1980	166	113	113	115	66	105	82	219	106	137	106
1981	186	91	89	89	54	112	79	141	92	102	93
1982	186	77	73	70	58	84	66	86	83	106	85
1983	165	82	78	74	59	91	79	89	95	99	88
1984	164	81	78	75	70	88	96	65	90	113	85
1985	159	73	67	64	62	80	73	54	81	109	84

1. The commodities included in each group are: beverages—coffee, cocoa, tea; cereals—maize, rice, wheat, grain sorghum; fats and oils—palm oil, coconut oil, groundnut oil, soybeans, copra, groundnut meal, soybean meal; other foods—sugar, beef, bananas, oranges; non-foods—cotton, jute, rubber, tobacco; timber—logs; metals and minerals—copper, tin, nickel, bauxite, aluminum, iron ore, manganese ore, lead, zinc, phosphate rock.

a. Weighted by 1977–1979 developing countries export values.

SOURCE: WB, *Commodity Trade and Price Trends* (Baltimore: The Johns Hopkins University Press, 1986), p. 40.

Table 3230

WESTERN HEMISPHERE EXPORT PRICE INDEX, 12 LC, 1950–86

(1980 = 100)

	Country	1950	1955	1959	1960	1961	1962	1963	1964	1965	1966	1967	1968	1969	1970	1971
B.	BOLIVIA	9.6	10.8	10.0	10.0	10.8	10.8	11.3	14.6	16.7	15.8	15.0	15.0	16.3	21.1	17.1
C.	BRAZIL	36.2	38.7	29.6*	29.0	30.5*	26.6	26.5	31.7	32.0	30.7	30.6	30.2	31.1	35.1	33.9
E.	COLOMBIA	~	~	25.2	25.7	25.5	23.4	20.5	24.5	22.9	18.5	22.5	23.0	23.1	28.5*	27.1
H.	DOMINICAN REP.	27.2	27.8	25.4	25.6	26.3	29.7	32.6	34.5	30.6	33.3	33.2	36.0	39.3	37.6	35.4
I.	ECUADOR	~	13.3	12.2	12.9	12.2	15.6	13.3	16.0	16.7	16.7	16.7	17.1	15.2	17.1	18.2
J.	EL SALVADOR	35.2	38.5	26.1	26.1	25.1	22.9	26.3	29.1	30.6	30.0	28.1	27.2	26.6	32.1	30.9
	Grenada	~	~	~	~	~	~	~	~	~	~	~	28.9	31.8	29.7	26.9
	Guyana	~	~	~	~	19.0	19.3	23.8	22.5	20.2	20.7	20.4	20.5	21.7	24.7	26.5
M.	HONDURAS	24.7	29.9	23.7	27.8	30.0	31.8	30.4	32.3	31.1	30.9	31.0	30.1	30.0	33.6	32.6
O.	NICARAGUA	33.8	47.7	34.9	37.5	38.4	39.5	37.6	36.9	38.7	38.9	37.3	37.5	38.2	39.0	39.4
P.	PANAMA	26.7	30.9	26.3	23.5	23.1	27.3	24.8	26.3	27.0	27.5	27.7	29.5	27.6	27.6	27.6
Q.	PARAGUAY	31.8	38.8	29.5	24.7	25.9	26.4	30.9	35.8	36.3	37.1	33.7	36.3	37.2	39.9	40.6
R.	PERU	~	~	~	20.0	18.7	18.9	20.4	23.4	23.9	28.4	25.2	26.6	30.2	31.3	28.4
	Suriname	~	~	~	~	~	~	~	~	26.7	26.4	26.4	27.0	28.1	30.0	30.6
	Trinidad and Tobago	~	~	~	~	~	~	~	~	~	9.9	10.2	9.6	9.7	9.8	11.1
T.	VENEZUELA	~	5.3	5.4	5.6	6.5	6.5	6.5	6.7	6.7	6.7	6.7	6.7	6.6	6.7	8.4
	Western Hemisphere	~	17.5	15.5	15.9	17.0	16.4	16.4	18.1	18.0	17.9	17.9	18.0	18.4	19.8	20.8

	Country	1972	1973	1974	1975	1976	1977	1978	1979	1980	1981	1982	1983	1984	1985	1986
B.	BOLIVIA	17.8	23.3	40.6	38.8	43.8	54.4	61.5	74.9	100.0	97.1	92.3	94.5	93.0	88.6	~
C.	BRAZIL	38.3	52.7	66.4	66.4	76.6	93.5	86.0	94.4	100.0	94.1	88.4	83.6	85.3	80.5	~
E.	COLOMBIA	30.3	38.2	51.2	50.6	74.1	108.9	91.0	89.7	100.0	89.5	88.8	89.0	95.1	88.9	100.6
H.	DOMINICAN REP.	39.3	48.0	72.6	114.3	76.4	84.5	76.9	81.1	100.0	132.1	88.1	~	~	~	~
I.	ECUADOR	15.2	19.3	41.7	38.5	42.4	49.1	45.1	72.9	100.2	91.9	99.2	83.7	80.2	83.3	~
J.	EL SALVADOR	33.3	41.3	51.4	52.6	77.1	101.5	85.0	96.9	100.0	93.0	88.1	71.3	~	~	~
	Grenada	25.0	42.6	66.7	83.9	62.7	64.2	83.1	99.9	100.0	87.6	78.0	79.6	70.7	87.0	129.5
	Guyana	29.8	30.8	59.8	79.0	66.0	74.1	68.9	75.2	100.0	93.3	87.4	80.1	~	~	~
M.	HONDURAS	34.2	40.3	47.0	57.8	66.4	90.1	86.0	84.9	100.0	94.1	90.1	91.6	96.1	97.4	~
O.	NICARAGUA	42.8	47.4	60.7	57.0	74.8	92.6	87.2	89.9	100.0	~	~	~	~	~	~
P.	PANAMA	29.5	49.2	69.3	80.4	72.7	65.6	63.7	77.7	100.0	104.9	84.4	92.3	91.3	86.1	~
Q.	PARAGUAY	44.9	56.3	67.1	71.7	72.7	98.4	90.1	94.0	100.0	112.7	121.6	104.9	114.6	76.8	~
R.	PERU	29.9	49.4	59.6	41.2	46.8	50.9	50.2	76.5	100.0	83.0	71.7	75.9	68.3	62.2	51.2
	Suriname	31.3	31.2	42.3	57.0	61.9	68.8	74.5	81.9	100.0	109.0	105.7	95.4	89.2	68.8	67.1
	Trinidad and Tobago	11.6	14.9	38.0	41.6	42.8	47.4	47.3	62.6	100.0	110.3	105.6	104.8	104.1	96.5	~
T.	VENEZUELA	9.0	13.3	37.4	40.0	41.6	45.5	45.3	60.9	100.0	116.0	115.6	101.6	~	~	~
	Western Hemisphere	22.6	31.5	52.0	53.2	58.7	69.4	65.7	78.1	100.0	101.9	98.3	90.6	91.2	84.9	~

SOURCE: IMF-IFS-Y, 1987.

Table 3231

U.S. EXPORT PRICE INDEX,[1] 1880–1986

Year	1970 = 100	1980 = 100	Year	1970 = 100	1980 = 100
1880	37.5	14.3	1935	36.0	13.8
1881	38.3	14.6	1936	36.8	14.1
1882	39.5	15.1	1937	39.1	14.9
1883	37.4	14.3	1938	36.2	13.8
1884	36.0	13.8	1939	35.4	13.5
1885	33.6	12.8	1940	37.9	14.5
1886	31.6	12.1	1941	40.8	15.6
1887	31.5	12.0	1942	49.5	18.9
1888	33.1	12.6	1943	54.6	20.9
1889	31.7	12.1	1944	62.5	23.9
1890	31.4	12.0	1945	62.3	23.8
1891	32.4	12.4	1946	59.0	22.5
1892	30.2	11.5	1947	70.4	26.9
1893	29.6	11.3	1948	74.8	28.6
1894	26.0	9.9	1949	69.6	26.6
1895	26.5	10.1	1950	67.8	25.9
1896	26.2	10.0	1951	77.7	29.7
1897	25.5	9.7	1952	77.3	29.5
1898	25.2	9.6	1953	77.0	29.4
1899	26.7	10.2	1954	75.7	28.9
1900	30.0	11.5	1955	76.7	29.3
1901	29.3	11.2	1956	80.0	30.6
1902	30.0	11.5	1957	82.2	31.4
1903	32.0	12.2	1958	81.4	31.1
1904	32.1	12.3	1959	81.4	31.1
1905	31.0	11.8	1960	81.9	31.3
1906	36.5	13.9	1961	83.5	31.9
1907	35.1	13.4	1962	83.0	31.7
1908	33.2	12.7	1963	83.0	31.7
1909	34.8	13.3	1964	83.8	32.0
1910	37.7	14.4	1965	86.4	33.0
1911	34.5	13.2	1966	89.0	34.0
1912	35.2	13.4	1967	90.8	34.7
1913	36.9	14.1	1968	92.1	35.2
1914	36.1	13.8	1969	94.8	36.2
1915	38.8	14.8	1970	100.0	38.2
1916	50.0	19.1	1971	103.1	39.4
1917	65.3	24.9	1972	106.5	40.7
1918	76.1	29.1	1973	124.1	47.4
1919	80.0	30.6	1974	158.4	60.5
1920	86.6	33.1	1975	177.0	67.6
1921	56.5	21.6	1976	183.0	69.9
1922	52.4	20.0	1977	189.5	72.4
1923	59.8	22.8	1978	202.6	77.4
1924	55.1	21.0	1979	230.6	88.1
1925	51.8	19.8	1980	261.8	100.0
1926	55.1	21.0	1981	285.9	109.2
1927	48.1	18.4	1982	289.0	110.4
1928	48.9	18.7	1983	292.1	111.6
1929	48.5	18.5	1984	296.1	113.1
1930	43.3	16.5	1985	293.7	112.2
1931	33.3	12.7	1986	294.5	112.5
1932	28.8	11.0			
1933	30.0	11.5			
1934	35.3	13.5			

1. The U.S. export price index constructed here has been used to deflate the commodity prices in tables 3229 through 3241. Index prepared by David Lorey.

SOURCE: *Historical Statistics of the United States*, various years; IMF-IFS-4, 1987.

Figure 32:1

U.S. EXPORT PRICE INDEX, 1880–1986

PART I. 1880–1930

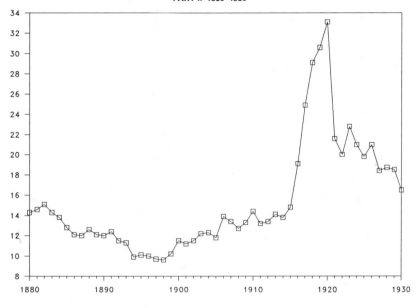

PART II. 1931–1986

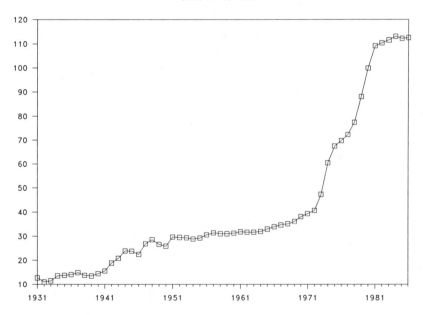

SOURCE: Table 3231.

Table 3232

BANANAS, REAL PRICE,[1] 1951–86
(US of 1970/lb)

Year	Real Price	Year	Real Price
1951	9.40	1971	6.17
1952	9.57	1972	6.88
1953	9.61	1973	6.02
1954	10.04	1974	5.27
1955	9.78	1975	6.30
1956	9.50	1976	6.41
1957	9.73	1977	6.53
1958	9.09	1978	6.42
1959	11.43	1979	6.41
1960	11.17	1980	6.50
1961	10.63	1981	6.37
1962	10.17	1982	5.88
1963	9.75	1983	6.66
1964	9.26	1984	5.66
1965	8.39	1985	5.87
1966	7.85	1986	6.09
1967	7.87		
1968	7.52		
1969	7.64		
1970	7.53		

1. Nominal data in source deflated here using U.S. export price index (table 3231).

SOURCE: IMF-IFS-Y, various years.

Figure 32:2

BANANAS, REAL PRICE, 1951–86
(US of 1970/lb)

SOURCE: Table 3232.

Table 3233

BAUXITE (GUYANIAN), REAL PRICE,[1] 1965–85
(US of 1970/MET)

Year	Real Price
1965	37.27
1966	40.73
1967	46.26
1968	46.74
1969	44.72
1970	42.39
1971	48.04
1972	50.05
1973	48.90
1974	45.40
1975	59.50
1976	64.09
1977	71.15
1978	68.32
1979	66.18
1980	81.15
1981	75.67
1982	72.09
1983	61.47
1984	55.71
1985	55.93

1. Nominal data in source deflated here using the U.S.
   export price index (table 3231).

SOURCE: IMF-IFS-Y, various years.

Figure 32:3

BAUXITE (GUYANIAN), REAL PRICE, 1965–85
(US of 1970/MET)

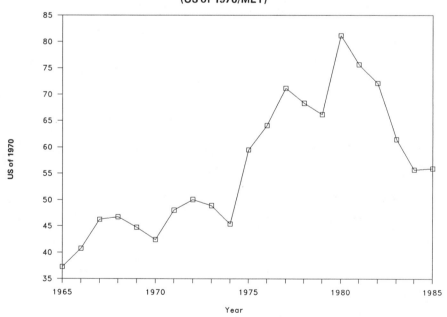

SOURCE: Table 3233.

Table 3234

BEEF (ARGENTINE FROZEN), REAL PRICE,[1] 1950–84

(US Cents of 1970/lb)

Year	Real Price	Year	Real Price
1950	14.07	1970	33.14
1951	18.21	1971	38.95
1952	16.56	1972	48.68
1953	20.70	1973	57.34
1954	20.67	1974	53.01
1955	25.24	1975	21.96
1956	19.15	1976	22.56
1957	18.14	1977	27.89
1958	21.56	1978	25.93
1959	23.81	1979	37.69
1960	24.76	1980	35.57
1961	21.74	1981	26.89
1962	19.65	1982	22.17
1963	20.81	1983	22.80
1964	27.92	1984	19.51
1965	32.84		
1966	28.94		
1967	23.63		
1968	30.42		
1969	26.91		

1. Nominal data in source deflated here using U.S. export price index (table 3231).

SOURCE: IMF-IFS-Y, various years.

Figure 32:4

BEEF (ARGENTINE FROZEN), REAL PRICE, 1950–84

(US Cents of 1970/lb)

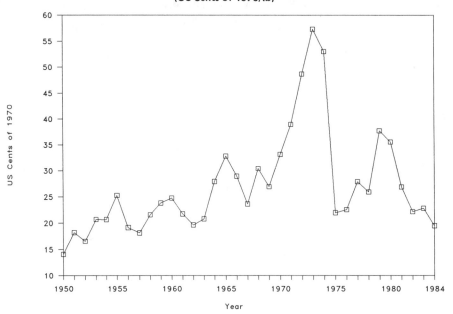

SOURCE: Table 3234.

Table 3235

CACAO, REAL PRICE,[1] 1913–86

(US Cents of 1970/lb)

Year	Real Price	Year	Real Price
1913	11.65	1953	40.77
1914	9.07	1954	67.17
1915	21.62	1955	44.09
1916	15.64	1956	30.29
1917	8.33	1957	35.06
1918	7.93	1958	48.17
1919	10.87	1959	41.63
1920	8.08	1960	30.54
1921	20.17	1961	23.95
1922	33.77	1962	23.93
1923	37.63	1963	27.87
1924	36.51	1964	25.23
1925	35.14	1965	15.81
1926	38.37	1966	22.98
1927	75.11	1967	25.85
1928	60.94	1968	29.95
1929	49.99	1969	42.22
1930	36.69	1970	29.42
1931	34.20	1971	22.79
1932	32.05	1972	24.64
1933	30.77	1973	39.09
1934	29.55	1974	46.31
1935	28.22	1975	31.97
1936	40.19	1976	42.09
1937	41.45	1977	96.85
1938	31.46	1978	75.78
1939	29.49	1979	61.03
1940	28.79	1980	40.89
1941	35.07	1981	30.61
1942	37.69	1982	23.63
1943	33.29	1983	28.45
1944	29.85	1984	35.57
1945	27.22	1985	32.34
1946	52.59	1986	31.25
1947	96.75		
1948	128.65		
1949	64.41		
1950	142.43		
1951	42.15		
1952	41.84		

1. Nominal data in source deflated here using U.S. export price index (table 3231).

SOURCE: IMF-IFS-Y, various years.

Figure 32:5

CACAO, REAL PRICE, 1913–86

(US Cents of 1970/lb)

PART I. 1913–50

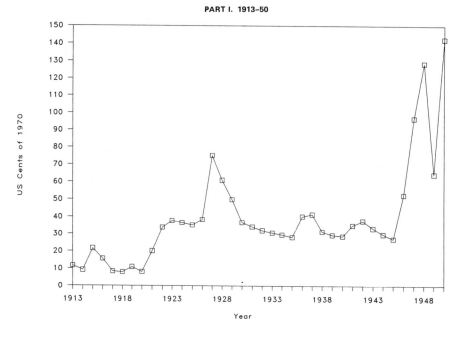

PART II. 1951–86

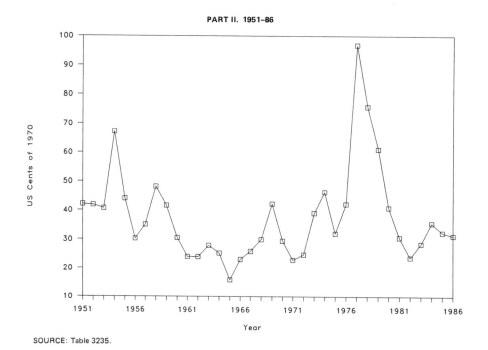

SOURCE: Table 3235.

Table 3236

COFFEE (BRAZILIAN), REAL PRICE,[1] 1950–86

(US Cents of 1980/lb)

Year	Real Price	Year	Real Price
1950	170.31	1970	141.94
1951	164.78	1971	116.75
1952	169.32	1972	122.46
1953	179.83	1973	140.95
1954	194.71	1974	113.06
1955	158.98	1975	92.28
1956	151.41	1976	168.08
1957	142.17	1977	299.30
1958	129.71	1978	215.58
1959	102.19	1979	156.04
1960	135.11	1980	161.70
1961	129.12	1981	111.51
1962	120.66	1982	121.94
1963	117.79	1983	113.02
1964	145.25	1984	117.90
1965	139.42	1985	120.20
1966	135.53	1986	179.85
1967	115.27		
1968	114.60		
1969	110.86		

1. Nominal data in source deflated here using U.S. export price index (table 3231).

SOURCE: IMF-IFS-Y, 1980, 1987.

Figure 32:6

COFFEE (BRAZILIAN), REAL PRICE,[1] 1950–86

(US Cents of 1980/lb)

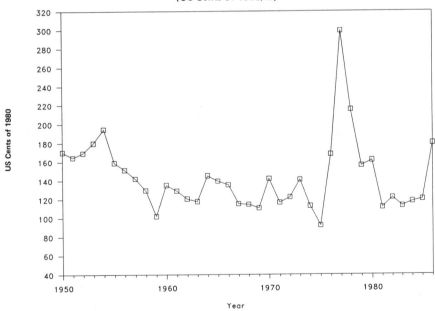

SOURCE: Table 3236.

Table 3237

COPPER, REAL PRICE,[1] 1950–85

(US Cents of 1980/lb)

Year	Real Price	Year	Real Price
1950	82.01	1970	150.97
1951	81.48	1971	130.53
1952	82.03	1972	124.37
1953	97.96	1973	124.20
1954	102.73	1974	126.69
1955	127.95	1975	93.99
1956	136.67	1976	98.47
1957	94.20	1977	90.90
1958	82.83	1978	84.64
1959	100.26	1979	104.73
1960	102.40	1980	101.40
1961	93.79	1981	76.94
1962	96.53	1982	66.04
1963	96.53	1983	69.77
1964	99.75	1984	59.13
1965	106.12	1985	58.71
1966	106.41		
1967	110.12		
1968	118.89		
1969	131.16		

1. Nominal data in source deflated here using U.S. export price index (table 3231).

SOURCE: IMF-IFS-Y, 1980, 1987.

Figure 32:7

COPPER, REAL PRICE, 1950–85

(US Cents of 1980/lb)

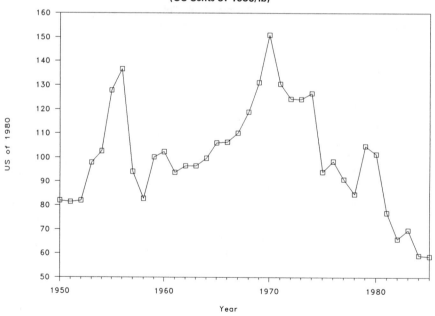

SOURCE: Table 3237.

Table 3238

COTTON (MEXICAN), REAL PRICE,[1] 1950–83

(US Cents of 1980/lb)

Year	Real Price	Year	Real Price
1950	14.94	1970	6.87
1951	13.01	1971	8.32
1952	12.46	1972	8.08
1953	10.00	1973	8.89
1954	11.61	1974	8.19
1955	10.10	1975	7.57
1956	9.24	1976	12.87
1957	8.67	1977	8.76
1958	8.14	1978	9.03
1959	7.16	1979	8.43
1960	7.24	1980	8.34
1961	7.45	1981	6.85
1962	7.35	1982	5.85
1963	7.56	1983	6.98
1964	7.54		
1965	7.13		
1966	6.89		
1967	6.94		
1968	6.95		
1969	6.63		

1. Nominal data in source deflated here using U.S. export price index (table 3231).

SOURCE: IMF-IFS-Y, various years.

Figure 32:8

COTTON (MEXICAN), REAL PRICE, 1950–83

(US Cents of 1980/lb)

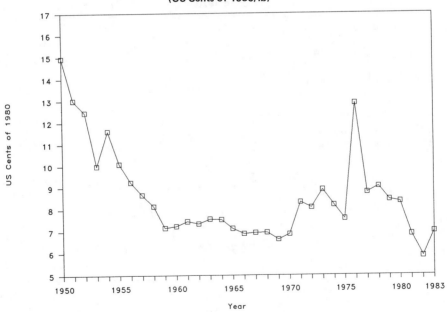

SOURCE: Table 3238.

Table 3239

IRON ORE (BRAZILIAN), REAL PRICE,[1] 1950–86
(T US of 1970/MET)

Year	Real Price	Year	Real Price
1950	18.29	1970	15.22
1951	26.55	1971	13.06
1952	28.85	1972	12.01
1953	26.04	1973	13.80
1954	22.59	1974	11.99
1955	23.73	1975	12.89
1956	26.70	1976	12.14
1957	27.31	1977	11.39
1958	26.39	1978	9.57
1959	20.98	1979	10.16
1960	20.85	1980	10.41
1961	21.31	1981	8.61
1962	20.18	1982	9.07
1963	18.90	1983	8.21
1964	18.72	1984	7.80
1965	18.16	1985	7.72
1966	17.13	1986	7.43
1967	14.87		
1968	13.71		
1969	12.32		

1. Nominal data in source deflated here using U.S. export price index (table 3231).

SOURCE: IMF-IFS-Y, various years.

Figure 32:9

IRON ORE (BRAZILIAN), REAL PRICE, 1950–86
(T US of 1970/MET)

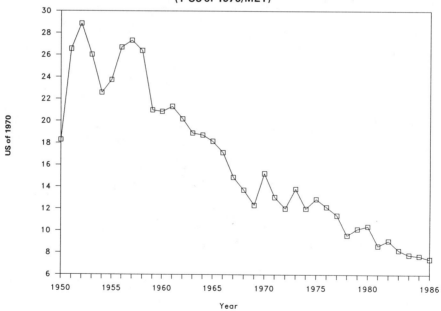

SOURCE: Table 3239.

Table 3240

PETROLEUM (VENEZUELAN), REAL PRICE,[1] 1950–85

(US of 1980/Barrel)

Year	Real Price	Year	Real Price
1950	5.48	1970	4.53
1951	4.78	1971	5.61
1952	4.44	1972	5.82
1953	4.32	1973	7.51
1954	4.33	1974	16.93
1955	4.23	1975	16.11
1956	3.99	1976	16.14
1957	3.50	1977	17.15
1958	3.70	1978	16.05
1959	4.18	1979	19.04
1960	4.35	1980	27.60
1961	5.42	1981	29.33
1962	5.46	1982	29.01
1963	5.46	1983	25.13
1964	5.41	1984	23.90
1965	5.24	1985	23.57
1966	5.09		
1967	4.99		
1968	4.91		
1969	4.78		

1. Nominal data in source deflated here using U.S. export price index (table 3231).

SOURCE: IMF-IFS-Y, various years.

Figure 32:10

PETROLEUM (VENEZUELAN), REAL PRICE, 1950–85

(US of 1980/Barrel)

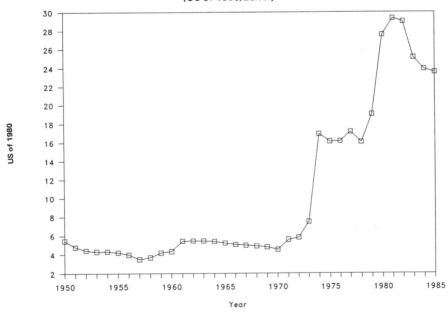

SOURCE: Table 3240.

Table 3241

SOYBEANS, REAL PRICE,[1] 1958–86

(US of 1970/MET)

Year	Real Price	Year	Real Price
1958	116.71	1974	174.82
1959	115.48	1975	125.24
1960	112.33	1976	126.32
1961	132.93	1977	147.85
1962	120.48	1978	132.44
1963	132.53	1979	129.12
1964	131.26	1980	113.16
1965	135.32	1981	100.88
1966	141.85	1982	84.60
1967	123.99	1983	96.43
1968	115.01	1984	95.27
1969	108.65	1985	76.41
1970	116.92	1986	70.77
1971	121.80		
1972	131.46		
1973	233.95		

1. Nominal data in source deflated here using U.S. export price index (table 3231).

SOURCE: IMF-IFS-Y, various years.

Figure 32:11

SOYBEANS, REAL PRICE, 1958–86

(US of 1970/MET)

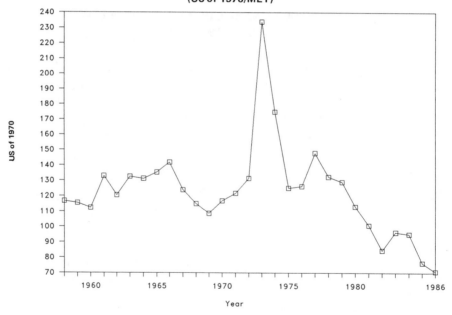

SOURCE: Table 3241.

Table 3242

SUGAR (BRAZILIAN), REAL PRICE,[1] 1951–86

(US Cents of 1980/lb)

Year	Real Price	Year	Real Price
1951	14.78	1971	13.96
1952	9.42	1972	17.74
1953	13.47	1973	18.90
1954	12.01	1974	41.95
1955	12.39	1975	43.17
1956	12.68	1976	16.48
1957	15.64	1977	11.38
1958	11.03	1978	9.95
1959	10.13	1979	9.98
1960	10.89	1980	21.79
1961	11.91	1981	15.49
1962	12.68	1982	8.53
1963	19.78	1983	8.48
1964	18.53	1984	8.11
1965	10.27	1985	5.94
1966	10.71	1986	6.30
1967	10.49		
1968	12.76		
1969	13.12		
1970	13.35		

1. Nominal data in source deflated here using U.S. export price index (table 3231).

SOURCE: IMF-IFS-Y, 1980, 1987.

Figure 32:12

SUGAR (BRAZILIAN), REAL PRICE, 1951–86

(US Cents of 1980/lb)

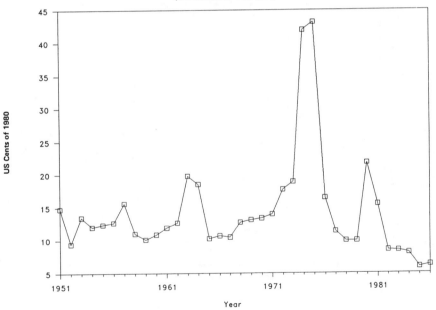

SOURCE: Table 3242.

Table 3243

TIN (BOLIVIAN), REAL PRICE,[1] 1950–85

(US of 1970/MET)

Year	Real Price	Year	Real Price
1950	133.24	1970	174.41
1951	161.90	1971	153.76
1952	153.04	1972	159.28
1953	120.78	1973	167.40
1954	122.85	1974	228.08
1955	119.43	1975	176.58
1956	123.41	1976	187.92
1957	112.17	1977	250.73
1958	112.53	1978	279.82
1959	121.25	1979	291.57
1960	120.40	1980	290.44
1961	131.84	1981	221.69
1962	135.22	1982	198.83
1963	135.53	1983	200.78
1964	179.45	1984	187.23
1965	201.63	1985	183.63
1966	181.18		
1967	165.63		
1968	154.97		
1969	163.66		

1. Nominal data in source deflated here using U.S. export price index (table 3231).

SOURCE: IMF-IFS-Y, various years.

Figure 32:13

TIN (BOLIVIAN), REAL PRICE, 1950–85

(US of 1970/lb)

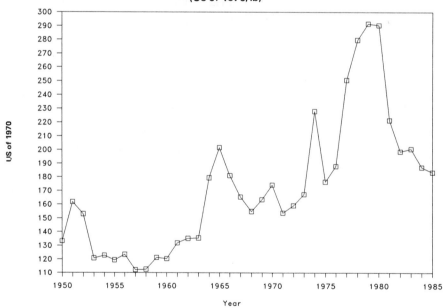

SOURCE: Table 3243.

Table 3244

WHEAT (ARGENTINE), REAL PRICE,[1] 1950–85

(US of 1980/Bushel)

Year	Real Price	Year	Real Price
1950	6.25	1970	3.87
1951	6.53	1971	4.11
1952	6.81	1972	4.45
1953	6.97	1973	5.59
1954	4.98	1974	8.69
1955	6.31	1975	6.88
1956	5.46	1976	5.32
1957	5.16	1977	3.60
1958	5.21	1978	4.15
1959	4.92	1979	4.37
1960	4.98	1980	4.94
1961	5.27	1981	5.05
1962	5.24	1982	4.11
1963	5.46	1983	3.49
1964	5.56	1984	3.21
1965	4.61	1985	2.79
1966	4.41		
1967	4.64		
1968	4.43		
1969	4.45		

1. Nominal data in source deflated here using U.S. export price index (table 3231).

SOURCE: IMF-IFS-Y, 1980, 1987.

Figure 32:14

WHEAT (ARGENTINE), REAL PRICE, 1950–85

(US of 1980/Bushel)

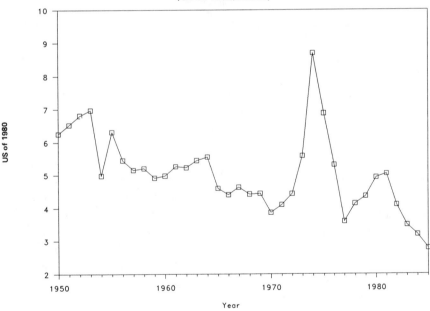

SOURCE: Table 3244.

Table 3245

WOOL (AUSTRALIAN), REAL PRICE,[1] 1958–86

(US Cents of 1970/kg)

Year	Real Price	Year	Real Price
1958	149.88	1974	159.10
1959	167.78	1975	103.06
1960	164.11	1976	108.19
1961	166.80	1977	119.79
1962	147.34	1978	115.96
1963	171.94	1979	110.36
1964	179.73	1980	115.48
1965	145.81	1981	114.81
1966	153.12	1982	105.91
1967	134.36	1983	92.26
1968	126.60	1984	95.18
1969	139.11	1985	88.01
1970	98.13	1986	80.74
1971	77.28		
1972	110.61		
1973	246.00		

1. Nominal data in source deflated here using U.S. export price index (table 3231).

SOURCE: IMF-IFS-Y, various years.

Figure 32:15

WOOL (AUSTRALIAN), REAL PRICE, 1958–86

(US Cents of 1970/kg)

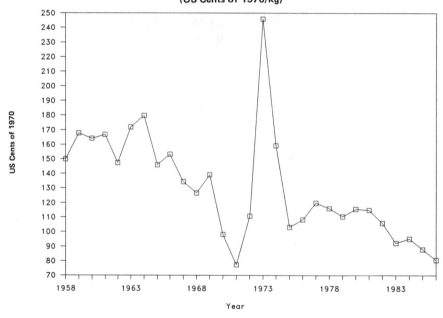

SOURCE: Table 3245.

Table 3246

MEXICAN BANK INTEREST PAID ON DEPOSITS, 1975–87
(AA)

Month	1975	1976	1977	1978	1979	1980	1981	1982	1983	1984	1985	1986	1987
January	#	11.86	12.05	14.33	15.98	17.90	25.46	32.34	50.29	55.95	47.17	68.55	95.89
February	#	11.83	12.00	14.47	15.97	18.39	25.98	33.43	54.24	55.16	47.33	70.30	96.20
March	#	11.78	11.99	14.62	15.98	19.20	26.59	33.67	56.16	53.11	49.36	71.79	96.26
April	#	11.79	12.03	14.87	15.99	19.83	26.91	34.39	57.21	51.10	51.93	73.48	95.79
May	#	11.78	11.93	15.02	16.02	20.39	27.22	36.26	58.14	50.12	53.76	75.02	94.79
June	#	11.76	12.59	15.16	16.04	20.47	27.66	39.59	58.63	50.38	54.92	76.97	93.76
July	#	11.74	13.25	15.26	16.08	20.53	28.42	43.23	58.73	50.69	57.00	81.36	92.91
August	11.91	11.74	13.52	15.29	16.10	20.82	29.50	46.42	58.23	50.93	59.06	84.40	92.15
September	11.91	11.74	13.57	15.38	16.51	21.51	30.45	47.88	57.78	50.60	60.98	87.72	91.02
October	11.91	11.96	13.64	15.49	16.69	22.42	31.22	45.99	57.14	49.34	62.29	91.48	90.30
November	11.92	12.03	13.93	15.81	17.37	22.77	31.77	45.51	56.82	48.31	63.39	94.19	~
December	11.97	12.12	14.04	15.88	17.52	24.25	31.81	46.12	56.44	47.54	65.66	95.33	~

SOURCE: NAFINSA-MV, April 20, 1987, and October 26, 1987.

Table 3247

PRIME RATE OF INTEREST CHARGED
BY U.S. BANKS, 1960–87

PART I. % PER YEAR

Year	%
1960	4.82
1965	4.54
1970	7.91
1971	5.72
1972	5.25
1973	8.03
1974	10.81
1975	7.86
1976	6.84
1977	6.83
1978	9.06
1979	12.67
1980	15.27
1981	18.87
1982	14.86
1983	10.79
1984	12.04
1985	9.93
1986	8.33

PART II. % PER MONTH

Month	1982	1983	1984	1985	1986	1987
January	15.75	11.16	11.00	10.61	9.50	7.50
February	16.66	10.98	11.00	10.50	9.50	7.50
March	16.50	10.50	11.21	10.50	9.10	7.50
April	16.50	10.50	11.93	10.31	8.83	7.75
May	16.50	10.50	12.39	9.78	8.50	8.14
June	16.50	10.50	12.60	9.50	8.50	8.25
July	16.26	10.50	13.00	9.50	8.16	~
August	14.39	10.89	13.00	9.50	7.90	~
September	13.50	11.00	12.97	9.50	7.50	~
October	12.52	11.00	12.58	9.50	7.50	~
November	11.85	11.00	11.77	9.50	7.50	~
December	11.50	11.00	11.06	9.50	7.50	~

SOURCE: 1960: USBC-SA, 1978, table 890; USBC-SA, 1981, table 873; USBC-SA, 1983, table 852; since 1982: USDC-SCB, May 1984, March 1985, USDC-SCB, September 1986, July 1987.

Table 3248

INTEREST ON U. S. COMMERCIAL PAPER, 1900–86
(4 to 6 month paper, YA)

Year	%	Year	%
1900	5.71	1944	.73
1901	5.40	1945	.75
1902	5.81	1946	.81
1903	6.16	1947	1.03
1904	5.14	1948	1.44
1905	5.18	1949	1.49
1906	6.25	1950	1.45
1907	6.66	1951	2.16
1908	5.00	1952	2.33
1909	4.67	1953	2.52
1910	5.72	1954	1.58
1911	4.75	1955	2.18
1912	5.41	1956	3.31
1913	6.20	1957	3.81
1914	5.47	1958	2.46
1915	4.01	1959	3.97
1916	3.84	1960	3.85
1917	5.07	1961	2.97
1918	6.02	1962	3.26
1919	5.37	1963	3.55
1920	7.50	1964	3.97
1921	6.62	1965	4.38
1922	4.52	1966	5.55
1923	5.07	1967	5.10
1924	3.98	1968	5.90
1925	4.02	1969	7.83
1926	4.34	1970	7.72
1927	4.11	1971	5.11
1928	4.85	1972	4.69
1929	5.85	1973	8.15
1930	3.59	1974	9.87
1931	2.64	1975	6.33
1932	2.73	1976	5.35
1933	1.73	1977	5.60
1934	1.02	1978	7.99
1935	.75	1979	10.91[a]
1936	.75	1980	12.29[a]
1937	.94	1981	14.76[a]
1938	.81	1982	11.89[a]
1939	.59	1983	8.89
1940	.56	1984	10.16
1941	.53	1985	8.01
1942	.66	1986	6.39
1943	.69		

a. Daily average.

SOURCE: 1900–54: USBC-HS, 1975, series X-445; 1954–78: USBG-FRB, Sept. 1984; since 1979, data are for 6 month paper: USDC-SCB, May 1979–85, USDC-SCB, May 1986, p. S-14, August 1987, p. S-14.

Table 3249

U.S. FEDERAL FUNDS[1] INTEREST RATE, 1955–87
(YA % Per Annum)

Year	%
1955	1.78
1956	2.73
1957	3.11
1958	1.58
1959	3.30
1960	3.22
1961	1.96
1962	2.68
1963	3.18
1964	3.50
1965	4.07
1966	5.12
1967	4.22
1968	5.67
1969	8.21
1970	7.18
1971	4.66
1972	4.43
1973	8.73
1974	10.50
1975	5.82
1976	5.05
1977	5.54
1978	7.93
1979	11.20
1980	13.36
1981	16.38
1982	12.26
1983	9.09
1984	10.23
1985	8.10
1986	6.81
1987[a]	6.38

1. Short-term borrowings between financial institutions.

a. Average Jan.–May.

SOURCE: IMF-IFS, July 1987, line 60 b.

CHAPTER 33

GROSS PRODUCT

DEFINITIONS OF TERMS
I. Market-Country System

National accounting results in a statistical statement of the gross value of goods and services produced by a country's economy in a given period of time, usually one year. Included are primary production (agriculture, forestry, fishing, and mining), whether or not it enters the exchange economy, and all other goods and services produced and exchanged. Nonprimary production performed by producers outside their own trade and consumed by themselves is omitted.

Gross value of output can be calculated either by factor cost or market price:

Gross value of output by *market price* (or purchasers' values) equals market value of output before depreciation provisions for fixed capital consumption.

Gross value of output by *factor cost* equals market value of output less indirect payments (such as excise and sales taxes, depreciation, government subsidies, transfer payments).

Gross domestic product (GDP) and **gross national product (GNP)** differ mainly in treatment of *factor income earned abroad*. Factor income earned abroad (or factor payment abroad) is foreign investment income (rent, interest, dividents, branch profits, undistributed earnings of subsidiaries) and income from working in other countries.

GDP (gross domestic product) equals total value of output accruing *within* a country. Thus, it includes factor income generated by foreign investors or suppliers in the country but excludes factor income invested or supplied abroad by normal residents of the country.

GNP (gross national product) equals total value of output accruing *to* a country. Thus, it excludes factor income earned by foreign investors or suppliers in the country but includes factor income earned in other countries by normal residents of the country.

II. Non-Market-Country System
(Cf. table 3307)

GSP   (Gross Social Product)

GMP   (Gross Material Product)

Figure 33:1

GDP SHARES OF IMPORTANT ACTIVITIES FOR TOTAL
LATIN AMERICA AND THE UNITED STATES,
TEN-YEAR INTERVALS, 1950-80

(%)

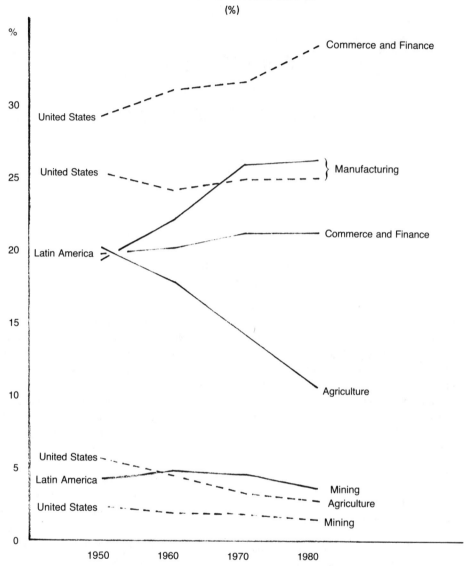

SOURCE: SALA, 23-2324; SALA, 23-2325; SALA, 23-2326; SALA, 23-2330.

Figure 33:2

LATIN AMERICA GDP ANNUAL RATES OF GROWTH, 1946–85

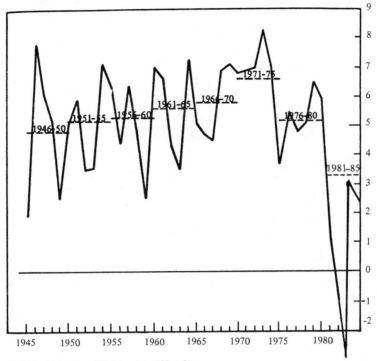

SOURCE: Adapted from ECLA-S, vol. 1, 1982, p. 21.

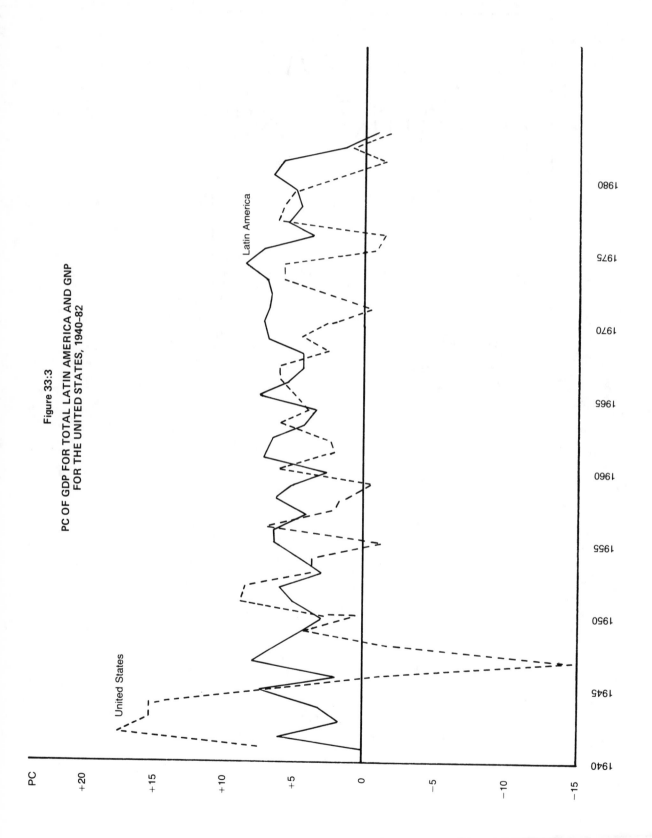

Figure 33:3

PC OF GDP FOR TOTAL LATIN AMERICA AND GNP
FOR THE UNITED STATES, 1940-82

SOURCE:
Latin America: SALA, 23-2331, "ECLA Factor" series through 1974, then "ECLA
Market" series; series overlap 1975-79 has an average difference in PC of .4%.

United States: SALA, 23-2322, USDC-SCB series.

Table 3300

GENERAL SOURCES AND METHODS FOR COMPARATIVE
PC OF REAL GDP SERIES PRESENTED IN
TABLES 3301 THROUGH 3322[a,b]

Series	Source[1]
ECLA Factor	At factor cost in 1970 prices: through 1976 from ECLA-SHCAL, pp. 74-195 and 25-88, then also from ECLA-S, 1981, 1980 (table 3 for each country), 1979, 1978, 1977. and for 1976–84 ECLA-SY, 1985, p. 231. Data for table 3301 are calculated from 1970 dollars at purchasing power exchange rate for each country. ECLA-SY, 1985. Cf "ECLA Market" series below.
IMF	In 1975 prices: through 1957 from IMF-IFS-Y, 1982; after 1957 from IMF-IFS-Y, 1986. IMF data are, in general, from UN sources at market prices. Revised with data in 1980 prices (calculated from indexes) in IMF-IFS-Y, 1986, IMF-IFS-Y, 1987.
OECD	Index 1968 = 100 for 1960–70, 1978 = 100 for 1971, and 1980 = 100 for 1972–83; data through 1959 from *National Accounts of Less Developed Areas, 1950-1966,* July 1968, p. 20; after 1960 data are from *Latest Information on National Accounts of Developing Countries, 1960-83,* Nov. 1983, p. 17 and Dec. 1985, No. 17, p. 19. Data are in market prices.
SALA	In 1970 dollars at official exchange rates, based upon USAID data synthesized in SALA-SNP, pp. 393-394 and also data and sources given in SALA, 18-2200. Data are, in general, at market prices. For comparison of USAID estimated at three different times, see SALA-SNP, pp. 395-396.
ECLA Market	At market prices in 1970 dollars (compared to factor cost terms in "ECLA Factor" given above). Data are from ECLA-S, 1980, ECLA-N, Jan. 1983, and Mexico-NAFINSA-MV, March 11, 1985; 1981–85 data from ECLA-SP, 1986, p. 24. ECLA-SP, 1986. Cf. "ECLA Factor" series above.
IDB	In 1984 dollars at market prices. Data from IDB-SPTF, 1986, table II-4; IDB-SPTF, 1987, table 11-6.

1. PC calculations by Waldo W. Wilkie.

a. For Cuba sources, see table 3307; for other Mexico sources, see table 3314; for U.S. sources, see table 3322.

b. For definition of GDP and GNP, see title page to this chapter and tables 3340 through 3360; on GSP and GMP, see table 3307. About GNP (and GDP), the World Bank's *World Development Report*, 1982, includes the following cautions (p. 20): "Gross national product (GNP) measures economic activity—not welfare. But as a measure of aggregate economic output and expenditure, GNP data are often ambiguous or deficient. Ambiguity exists, for example, because public services such as administration and defense are treated as final rather than as intermediate services, and purchases of consumer durables other than residences are regarded as consumption rather than investment. Moreover, GNP does not make allowance for the varying amounts of capital, including mineral and other natural resources, used up during production. These are notoriously difficult to estimate. Gaps exist in basic data, most notably for subsistence production in developing countries and for illegal activities in most countries. Measurement problems also arise because of lack of consistency among countries in calculating changes in real output over time; this is particularly true between the market economies and the centrally planned economies. Moreover, major problems arise in intercountry comparisons of levels of GNP converted to a common currency by using exchange rates.

Welfare could not be fully measured even if it were possible to collect perfect GNP data for each country, based on Standard National Accounting definitions, and make international comparisons. . . . GNP does not measure items that are important to welfare in most societies, such as the distribution of income and wealth, employment status, job security, and opportunities for advancement, availability of health and education services, unpaid services, the quality of the environment, and climatic differences. . . . [Thus economists settle] for partial measures such as GNP—which at least covers most of the goods and services available to meet important consumption needs. GNP data, however, need to be complemented by other indicators, particularly those which relate more directly to the 'quality of life'."

Table 3301

ARGENTINA COMPARATIVE PC OF REAL GDP, 1901–86

I. 1901-39		II. 1940–86						
Year	ECLA Factor (1901-39)	Year	ECLA Factor (1940-85)	IMF (1953-86)	OECD (1951-83)	SALA (1951-74)	ECLA Market (1975-86)	IDB (1981-86)
		1940	-2.0					
1901	8.5	1941	4.9					
1902	-2.1	1942	4.6					
1903	4.3	1943	.7					
1904	10.6	1944	9.7					
1905	13.2	1945	-4.8					
1906	5.0	1946	8.3					
1907	2.2	1947	13.7					
1908	9.8	1948	1.2					
1909	5.0	1949	-4.6					
1910	7.2	1950	1.6					
1911	1.8	1951	3.9		4.1	3.4		
1912	8.2	1952	-5.1		-6.4	-6.7		
1913	1.1	1953	5.4	6.9	7.1	6.8		
1914	-10.4	1954	4.1	5.0	3.8	3.2		
1915	.5	1955	7.1	12.5	6.9	7.4		
1916	-2.9	1956	2.8	-5.3	1.6	1.2		
1917	7.2	1957	5.1	-3.3	5.5	4.4		
1918	1.4	1958	6.1	8.0	7.2	6.7		
1919	3.7	1959	-6.4	-10.0	-5.8	-6.1		
1920	7.3	1960	7.8	11.1	7.9	8.5		
1921	2.6	1961	7.1	10.0	7.1	6.8		
1922	8.0	1962	-1.6	#	-1.6	-1.5		
1923	11.0	1963	-2.4	-3.7*	-2.4	-2.4		
1924	7.8	1964	10.3	-2.3	10.3	10.4		
1925	-.4	1965	9.1	11.6	9.2	9.3		
1926	4.8	1966	.6	10.1	.6	.4		
1927	7.1	1967	2.7	.8	2.6	2.5		
1928	6.2	1968	4.3	3.3	4.3	4.5		
1929	4.6	1969	8.6	4.9	8.5	7.9		
1930	-14.1	1970	5.4	2.6*	5.4	4.4		
1931	-6.9	1971	4.8	3.4	4.7	3.0		
1932	-3.3	1972	3.1	2.2	3.8	4.8		
1933	4.7	1973	6.1	3.2	3.4	5.6		
1934	7.9	1974	6.1	5.2	5.7	6.1		
1935	4.4	1975	-.9	#	-.4		-.9	
1936	1.2	1976	-1.7	#	-.5		-.2	
1937	8.1	1977	4.9	5.9	6.4		6.0	
1938	1.3	1978	-3.9	-2.8	-3.4		-3.9	
1939	3.6	1979	6.7	6.7	6.7		7.1	
		1980	.7	1.8	.7		3.7	
		1981	-6.7	-7.1	-6.2		-6.7	-6.8
		1982	-6.2	-3.8	-5.3		-6.3	-4.6
		1983	3.0	2.0	2.8		3.0	2.8
		1984	2.3	2.9			2.2	2.6
		1985	-4.4‡	-4.7			-4.4	-4.5
		1986		5.9			5.5‡	5.7‡

SOURCE AND METHODS: See table 3300.

Table 3302

BOLIVIA COMPARATIVE PC OF REAL GDP, 1946–86

Year	ECLA Factor (1946–85)	IMF (1953–86)	OECD (1951–83)	SALA (1951–74)	ECLA Market (1975–86)	IDB (1981-86)
1946	1.8					
1947	1.7					
1948	2.1					
1949	2.1					
1950	2.1					
1951	7.0		6.4	6.9		
1952	3.0		2.5	1.6		
1953	-9.5	-9.5	-11.4	-10.9		
1954	2.1	2.1	.7	0		
1955	5.3	5.3	7.0	7.1		
1956	-5.9	-5.9	-4.8	-5.0		
1957	-3.3	-3.3	-3.5	-3.4		
1958	2.4	2.4	2.9*	3.9		
1959	-.3	-.3	-.3	-1.3		
1960	4.3	8.6	4.3	6.3		
1961	2.1	1.3	2.1	2.1		
1962	5.6	2.4	5.6	5.8		
1963	6.4	6.8	6.4	6.0		
1964	4.8	4.0	4.8	4.5		
1965	4.9	4.9	6.9	6.9		
1966	7.2	7.2	7.0	6.9		
1967	6.3	6.3	6.3	4.1		
1968	8.5	8.5*	7.2	8.3		
1969	4.5	4.6	4.8	4.4		
1970	5.2	7.8	-.5	5.8		
1971	4.9	4.9	4.9	6.9		
1972	5.9	5.8	5.8	6.6		
1973	6.9	6.7	6.7	6.1		
1974	6.1	5.1	5.1	5.0		
1975	5.3	6.6	6.6		5.1	
1976	6.8	6.1	6.1		6.8	
1977	4.0	4.2	4.2		3.4	
1978	3.1	3.4	3.4		3.1	
1979	1.8	.2	1.8		1.8	
1980	.6	-1.4	.6		1.2	
1981	.4	.4	-1.1		.3	.3
1982	-2.8	-2.8	-9.1		-2.8	-2.8
1983	-6.5	-6.6	-7.6*		-6.6	-6.6
1984	-.8	-.9			-.9	-.9
1985	-1.7‡	-1.7			-1.7	-1.7
1986		~			-3.5‡	-2.9‡

SOURCE AND METHODS: See table 3300.

Table 3303

BRAZIL COMPARATIVE PC OF REAL GDP, 1921–86

I. 1921-39		II. 1940-86						
Year	ECLA Factor (1921–39)	Year	ECLA Factor (1940–85)	IMF (1966–86)	OECD (1951–83)	SALA (1952–74)	ECLA Market (1975–86)	IDB (1981-86)
		1940	1.0					
1921	.2	1941	4.9					
1922	5.0	1942	-2.8					
1923	5.8	1943	5.8					
1924	.2	1944	4.6					
1925	4.2	1945	.9					
1926	.2	1946	7.8					
1927	5.3	1947	2.4					
1928	8.2	1948	7.4					
1929	.7	1949	6.6					
1930	-3.4	1950	6.5					
1931	-.6	1951	5.9		5.1	5.9		
1932	1.1	1952	8.7		5.7	8.9		
1933	5.6	1953	2.5		3.2	2.4		
1934	6.8	1954	10.1		7.6	10.2		
1935	2.8	1955	6.9		6.8	6.8		
1936	9.1	1956	3.2		1.9	3.2		
1937	2.6	1957	8.1		6.9	8.1		
1938	4.1	1958	7.7		6.6	7.7		
1939	2.8	1959	3.0		7.3	5.6		
		1960	12.5		9.7	9.7		
		1961	10.3		10.3	10.3		
		1962	5.2		5.2	5.3		
		1963	1.6		1.5	1.6		
		1964	2.9	2.6	2.9	2.8		
		1965	2.7	23.1	2.7	2.9		
		1966	3.8	3.5	3.8	5.1		
		1967	4.9	5.4	4.9	4.8		
		1968	11.2	10.8	11.2	9.4		
		1969	9.9	9.8	9.9	9.0		
		1970	8.8	2.6	8.9	9.5		
		1971	13.3	12.2	12.0*	11.0		
		1972	11.7	10.9	11.1	11.7		
		1973	13.9	13.5	13.6	11.3		
		1974	9.8	9.7	9.7	10.9		
		1975	5.7	4.2	5.4		5.7	
		1976	9.0	9.8	9.7		9.0	
		1977	4.7	4.6	5.7		4.7	
		1978	6.0	4.8	5.0		6.0	
		1979	6.4	7.2	6.4		6.4	
		1980	7.2	9.1	7.2		6.8	
		1981	-1.9	-3.3	-1.6		-2.0	-3.3
		1982	1.5	.9	.9		1.4	.9
		1983	-2.6	-2.5	-3.2		-2.7	-2.5
		1984	4.9	5.7			4.8	5.7
		1985	8.3‡	8.3			8.2	8.3
		1986		~			8.0‡	8.2‡

SOURCE AND METHODS: See table 3300.

Table 3304

CHILE COMPARATIVE PC OF REAL GDP, 1946–86

Year	ECLA Factor (1940–86)	IMF (1953–86)	OECD (1951–83)	SALA (1951–74)	ECLA Market (1974–86)	IDB (1981-86)
1940	5.0					
1941	.1					
1942	5.5					
1943	4.2					
1944	1.4					
1945	9.1					
1946	6.2					
1947	–6.7					
1948	11.5					
1949	–.5					
1950	4.8					
1951	5.2		4.4	4.4		
1952	3.4		5.7	5.9		
1953	7.1	5.1	5.2	5.8		
1954	.7	.5	.3	.4		
1955	2.7	#	–.1	–1.0		
1956	.7	.5	.6	.2		
1957	2.7	10.5	10.5	11.8		
1958	4.8	3.9	2.7	3.9		
1959	6.9	–.6	–.5	–1.1		
1960	5.1	5.7	7.0	6.7		
1961	6.1	6.1	6.1*	6.2		
1962	4.6	4.5	4.6	4.7		
1963	5.1	4.9	5.1	4.9		
1964	4.3	4.7	4.3	4.0		
1965	5.1	5.0	5.1	4.6		
1966	7.0	6.9	7.0	6.1		
1967	2.4	2.5	2.4	1.9		
1968	3.0	2.9	3.0	3.0		
1969	3.5	3.3	3.5	3.2		
1970	3.6	1.4*	2.1	9.2[a]		
1971	7.7	9.0	9.0	9.0		
1972	–.1	–1.2	–1.2	1.8		
1973	–3.6	–5.6	–5.6	–3.6		
1974	5.7	1.0	1.0	3.7	5.7	
1975	–11.3	–12.9	–12.9		–12.9	
1976	4.1	3.5	3.5		3.5	
1977	8.6	9.9	9.9		9.9	
1978	7.8	8.2	8.2		8.2	
1979	8.3	8.3	8.3		8.3	
1980	7.8	7.8	7.8		8.0	
1981	5.2	5.5	5.7		5.2	5.5
1982	–13.0	–14.1	–14.3		–13.1	–14.1
1983	–.5	–.7	–.8		–.5	–.7
1984	6.2	6.3			6.0	6.3
1985	2.4[‡]	2.4			2.4	2.4
1986		5.7			5.0	5.5[‡]

a. USAID calculations in 1973 dollars show PC of 4.5%. Cf. SALA-SNP, p. 416.

SOURCE AND METHODS: See table 3300.

Table 3305

COLOMBIA COMPARATIVE PC OF REAL GDP, 1926–86

I. 1926–39		II. 1940–86						
Year	ECLA Factor (1926–39)	Year	ECLA Factor (1940–85)	IMF (1953–86)	OECD (1951–83)	SALA (1951–74)	ECLA Market (1975–86)	IDB (1981-86)
		1940	2.2					
1926	9.5	1941	1.7					
1927	9.0	1942	.2					
1928	7.3	1943	.4					
1929	3.6	1944	6.8					
1930	-.9	1945	4.7					
1931	-1.6	1946	9.1					
1932	6.6	1947	3.9					
1933	5.6	1948	3.1					
1934	-2.1	1949	5.5					
1935	11.2	1950	1.8					
1936	5.3	1951	3.1		3.1	3.4		
1937	1.6	1952	6.3		6.4	6.7		
1938	6.5	1953	5.8	6.1	6.0	6.0		
1939	6.1	1954	6.6	6.9	7.0	7.2		
		1955	4.0	3.9	3.9	4.0		
		1956	4.1	4.1	4.0	3.9		
		1957	2.4	2.2	2.2	1.5		
		1958	2.5	2.5	2.5	2.3		
		1959	7.1	7.2	6.9	7.8		
		1960	4.1	4.3	4.3	4.4		
		1961	5.0	5.1	5.1	4.8		
		1962	5.4	5.4	5.4	5.0		
		1963	3.2	3.3	3.3	3.5		
		1964	6.1	6.2	6.2	5.7		
		1965	3.5	3.6	3.6	3.6		
		1966	5.2	5.4	5.4	5.3		
		1967	4.2	4.2	4.2	4.1		
		1968	6.3	6.1	6.1	5.8		
		1969	6.3	6.3	6.4	6.0		
		1970	6.6	9.3	6.7	6.9		
		1971	5.8	6.0	6.0	6.0		
		1972	7.9	7.7	7.7	6.6		
		1973	7.6	6.7	6.7	8.0		
		1974	6.5	5.7	5.7	6.6		
		1975	4.3	2.3	2.3		3.8	
		1976	4.2	4.7	4.7		4.6	
		1977	4.7	4.2	4.1		4.9	
		1978	8.8	8.5	8.5		8.9	
		1979	4.3	5.4	5.4		5.1	
		1980	5.5	4.1	4.1		4.7	
		1981	2.3	2.3	2.3		2.3	2.3
		1982	1.1	.9	.9		1.0	.9
		1983	1.2	1.6	.8		1.9	1.6
		1984	3.7	3.4			3.6	3.4
		1985	2.5[‡]	2.4			2.6	2.4
		1986		5.1			5.0[‡]	5.1[‡]

SOURCE AND METHODS: See table 3300.

Table 3306

COSTA RICA COMPARATIVE PC OF REAL GDP, 1946–86

Year	ECLA Factor (1946–85)	IMF (1961–86)	OECD (1954–83)	SALA (1951–74)	ECLA Market (1975–86)	IDB (1981-86)
1946	7.9					
1947	19.0					
1948	5.7					
1949	4.0					
1950	4.1					
1951	2.7			3.6		
1952	12.1			12.6		
1953	15.2			11.5		
1954	.8		4.6	5.3		
1955	11.6		4.5	4.8		
1956	-2.8		1.4	2.3		
1957	8.5		9.2	6.9		
1958	12.4		6.7	6.4		
1959	3.7		3.1	3.9		
1960	8.7		6.1*	3.1		
1961	4.2	-.8	-1.0	2.0		
1962	6.1	8.1	8.1	6.2		
1963	8.6	4.8	4.8	6.4		
1964	4.9	4.1	4.1	-.9		
1965	9.1	9.8	9.8	9.6		
1966	7.8	7.9	7.9	6.6		
1967	6.1	5.7	5.7	8.6		
1968	7.7	8.5	8.5	9.2		
1969	6.7	5.5	5.5	9.5		
1970	6.6	7.5	7.5	5.4		
1971	6.6	6.8	6.8	4.0		
1972	8.2	8.2	8.2	6.7		
1973	7.7	7.7	7.7	7.2		
1974	5.5	5.5	5.5	4.2		
1975	2.1	2.1	2.1		2.1	
1976	5.5	5.5	5.5		5.5	
1977	8.9	8.9	8.9		8.9	
1978	6.3	6.3	6.3		6.3	
1979	4.9	4.9	4.9		4.9	
1980	.8	.8	.8		2.8	
1981	-2.3	-2.3	-2.3		-2.4	-2.3
1982	-7.2	-7.3	-9.1		-7.3	-7.3
1983	2.8	2.9	.8		2.7	2.9
1984	7.3	8.0			7.9	8.0
1985	1.7‡	1.0			.9	1.0
1986		4.2			3.0	3.0‡

SOURCE AND METHODS: See table 3300.

Table 3307

CUBA COMPARATIVE PC OF
REAL PRODUCT, 1947–85
(Cf. table 3300)

PART I. GMP AND GSP[1] DEFINED

(From SALA-Cuba, p. 204)

Category	Example[1] for 1962
(a) Personal Consumption	2,491.1
(b) Collective Consumption	417.1
(c) Gross Capital Formation	607.6
(d) Increase in Stock[2]	277.1
(e) Net Exports	–94.7
(I) Gross Material Product (a + b + c + d + e)	3,698.2
(f) Consumption of Fixed Capital	188.7
(II) Net Material Product (I) – (f)	3,509.5
(III) Expenditures on Non-material Services	2,384.2
(IV) Gross Social Product (I + III)	6,082.4

1. Data refer to the total expenditures (in millions of 1965 pesos) on Gross Social Product (GSP). GSP includes expenditures on Gross Material Product (GMP) which is defined as the total net value of goods and "productive" services (including agriculture, industry, construction, transportation, communication, commerce, and turn-over taxes) produced in the course of the year. In contrast, non-material services cover those economic activities classified as "non-productive" (including public administration, education, health, defense, personal and professional services, and similar activities). Readers should note that calculations of GSP and GMP do not correspond to standard GNP systems. Differences in national accounting practices prevent comparability without adjustment as in the SALA series given in Part II, below, where GNP was computed in source by adding to Cuba's GMP the value added in non-productive services. Cf. CEPAL, *Cuentas Nacionales y Producto Material en América Latina* (Santiago, 1982).
2. Data for "Increase in Stock" not available in original sources and have been approximated by subtracting the sum of available items from GMP.

Table 3307 (Continued)

CUBA COMPARATIVE PC OF REAL PRODUCT, 1947–85

PART II. SERIES, 1947–85

Year	CERP[1] GNP[2] (1947–58)	SALA[3] GNP (1951–75)[a]	Mesa-Lago[4] GMP (1963–80)	ECLA[5] GMP[6] (1971–84)	ECLA[7] GSP (1963–85)	Cuba-CEE[8] GSP (1977–81)
1947	12.1					
1948	-7.5					
1949	-.3					
1950	15.9					
1951	.5	0				
1952	4.3	5.9				
1953	-10.6	-12.0				
1954	1.7	-.1				
1955	2.1	1.0				
1956	9.5	5.1				
1957	6.0	10.7				
1958	-3.9	-3.5				
1959		~				
1960		~				
1961		~				
1962		~				
1963		0	1.0		-1.1	
1964		9.8	9.0		7.3	
1965		2.0	1.5		4.9	
1966		-3.9	-3.7		-.9	
1967		-2.0	2.4		7.5	
1968		6.2	6.7		1.7	
1969		-8.7	-4.0		-1.3	
1970		6.4	.6		15.5	
1971		-3.0	14.6	4.2	6.9	
1972		1.0	25.1	9.7	15.8	
1973		6.1	11.3	13.1	15.1	
1974		1.9	10.5	7.8	12.7	
1975		3.8	19.8	12.3	3.7	
1976			-.1	4.4	1.2	
1977			4.1	1.8	2.6	3.9
1978			9.4	7.7	11.8	4.2
1979			4.3	4.2	2.8	3.8
1980			3.0	2.2	-1.2	4.1
1981				16.2	16.0	14.8
1982				2.5	3.8	
1983				3.2	4.9	
1984				7.9[‡]	7.3	
1985					4.8[‡]	

1. CERP: *Cuban Economic Research Project: A Study on Cuba* (Coral Gables: University of Miami Press, 1965), p. 605, given in Schroeder, p. 570.
2. Deflated here with U.S. export price index given in SALA, 22-2625.
3. Calculated from index numbers in SALA, 19-200, 201. After 1969, Cuban data converted to GNP by CIA source wherein GMP adjusted to include "non-productive" services such as education and health (see Part I, above).
4. Carmelo Mesa-Lago, *The Economy of Socialist Cuba: A Two-Decade Appraisal* (Albuquerque: University of New Mexico Press, 1982), p. 34.
5. ECLA-S, 1978–81 and 1984, pp. 296 and 215 respectively. Cf. table 3346.
6. According to ECLA-S, e.g. 1979, p. 183, all data are in constant prices because for Cuba "current" and "constant" prices are equivalent in the case of material product (at producer prices). See also ECLA-S, 1981, p. 303, note 6, for discussion of frozen prices through 1980.
7. ECLA-AE, 1980, pp. 264–265; and for 1979–84 data at 1981 constant prices, ECLA-SY, 1985, pp. 312–313.
8. Cuba-CEE, AE, 1981, p. 67.

a. For 1950s, calculated from index based at 1950; for 1962–75, index based at 1970.

Table 3307 (Continued)

CUBA COMPARATIVE PC OF REAL PRODUCT, 1947–85

PART III. PEREZ–LOPEZ ESTIMATED OUTPUT INDICATORS, 1965–82

(1970 = 100)

Year	Industry	Agriculture	Material Product	GSP	GDP
1965	80	74	76	76	73
1966	83	70	78	80	77
1967	91	79	92	89	86
1968	90	79	85	81	81
1969	91	82	84	79	80
1970	82	96	80	76	77
1971	83	86	78	83	83
1972	88	85	87	88	87
1973	96	90	95	95	95
1974	100	100	100	100	100
1975	108	105	106	104	105
1976	107	111	105	106	108
1977	108	119	111	111	113
1978	115	124	112	114	120
1979	116	127	116	118	123
1980	113	129	111	116	120
1981	120	142	118	122	130
1982	120	141	119	124	133

PART IV. AA–GR FOR SELECTED INDICATORS OF ECONIMIC ACTIVITY[1]

(%)

Indicator	AA–GR			
	1966–70	1971–75	1976–80	1981–82
Industry				
Official	6.5	11.1	3.9	11.2
Brundenius	5.7	8.6	2.9	~
Estimated[2]	.5	5.7	.9	3.1
Agriculture				
Official	2.0	2.4	7.6	4.8
Brundenius	2.5	.2	4.4	~
Estimated	5.3	1.8	4.2	4.5
Material product				
Official	4.8	10.9	4.0	9.4
Brundenius	3.3	8.9	4.0	~
Estimated	1.0	5.8	.9	3.5
GSP				
Official	4.4	10.9	4.7	9.5
Estimated	0	6.5	2.2	3.4
GDP				
Official	~	12.3	7.0	~
Brundenius	.8	7.7	5.7	~
Estimated	1.1	6.4	2.7	5.3

1. Jorge F. Pérez–López, *Measuring Cuban Economic Performance* (Austin: University of Texas Press, 1987), pp. iii, 120.
2. Estimates are by Pérez–López; see note 1 above.

Table 3308

DOMINICAN REPUBLIC COMPARATIVE PC
OF REAL GDP, 1946–86

Year	ECLA Factor (1946–85)	IMF (1953–86)	OECD (1951–83)	SALA (1951–74)	ECLA Market (1975–86)	IDB (1981-86)
1946	-7.3					
1947	10.2					
1948	10.5					
1949	12.5					
1950	17.9					
1951	11.8		11.8	9.1		
1952	8.1		8.1	11.8		
1953	-1.3	-1.3	-1.3	.8		
1954	5.7	5.8	5.8	5.9		
1955	6.2	6.2	6.2	6.3		
1956	10.0	10.0	9.9	11.2		
1957	6.3	6.3	6.4	5.2		
1958	5.3	5.3	5.3	6.3		
1959	.6	.7	.6	.1		
1960	4.9	1.3	4.9	6.6		
1961	-2.3	-2.2	-2.2	-3.9		
1962	17.0	17.0	17.0	17.3		
1963	6.5	7.5	6.5	8.5		
1964	6.7	4.1	6.7	3.8		
1965	-12.4	-10.9	-12.4	-10.4		
1966	13.4	13.1	13.4	12.2		
1967	3.4	3.4	3.4	3.4		
1968	.2	.5	.2	1.0		
1969	10.9	12.2	11.0	12.0		
1970	10.6	8.5	10.6	11.1		
1971	10.6	10.9	10.9	11.0		
1972	10.4	10.4	10.4	11.7		
1973	12.9	12.9	12.9	8.9		
1974	5.5	6.0	6.0	8.2		
1975	2.1	5.2	5.2		5.2	
1976	5.5	6.7	6.7		6.7	
1977	8.9	5.0	5.0		5.0	
1978	5.7	2.1	2.1		2.2	
1979	4.5	4.5	4.5		4.8	
1980	6.1	6.1	6.1		5.3	
1981	4,0	4.1	4.1		4.0	4.1
1982	1.4	1.7	1.6		1.4	1.7
1983	4.4	3.9	3.9*		4.4	3.9
1984	.5	.4			.5	.4
1985	-2.1‡	-2.2			-2.0	-2.2
1986		2.0			.5‡	1.3‡

SOURCE AND METHODS: See table 3300.

Table 3309

ECUADOR COMPARATIVE PC OF REAL GDP, 1940–86

Year	ECLA Factor (1940–85)	IMF (1953–86)	OECD (1951–83)	SALA (1951–74)	ECLA Market (1974–86)	IDB (1981–86)
1940	6.6					
1941	.5					
1942	4.2					
1943	12.7					
1944	1.3					
1945	.4					
1946	11.9					
1947	11.1					
1948	13.7					
1949	1.8					
1950	8.7					
1951	1.1		2.7	3.4		
1952	12.3		10.4	8.6		
1953	2.1	8.6	3.3	3.6		
1954	8.1	8.1	8.1	8.7		
1955	2.6	2.6	2.6	2.5		
1956	3.7	3.7	3.6	3.0		
1957	4.5	5.1	5.3	5.4		
1958	2.9	2.3	2.3	3.0		
1959	5.4	5.2	5.1	4.6		
1960	6.5	6.6	4.5*	6.8		
1961	2.5	1.5	1.7	1.4		
1962	5.3	4.5	4.5	4.9		
1963	2.6	3.9	3.8	4.8		
1964	7.0	7.8	7.8	7.2		
1965	9.6	12.5	3.2	3.0		
1966	2.6	2.4	8.0	4.6		
1967	5.3	6.9	8.0	6.1		
1968	5.5	4.0	4.5	5.9		
1969	5.5	2.3	4.2	2.7		
1970	7.0	6.5	4.8	8.8		
1971	5.8	6.3	5.0	2.0		
1972	8.0	14.4	7.0*	8.4		
1973	17.9	25.3	25.4	13.0		
1974	4.0	6.4	6.4	4.8	9.0	
1975	7.5	5.6	5.6		6.8	
1976	8.1	9.2	9.3		9.3	
1977	6.4	6.5	6.5		7.5	
1978	6.6	6.6	6.5		5.4	
1979	5.3	5.3	5.1		5.1	
1980	4.9	4.9	4.8		5.1	
1981	3.8	3.9	4.3		3.8	3.9
1982	1.2	1.2	1.4		1.1	1.2
1983	-1.2	-2.8	-2.7		-1.2	-2.8
1984	4.5	4.2			4.5	4.0
1985	4.4‡	4.5			4.3	3.8
1986		2.9			1.5‡	1.7‡

SOURCE AND METHODS: See table 3300.

Table 3310

EL SALVADOR COMPARATIVE PC
OF REAL GDP, 1946–86

Year	ECLA Factor (1946–85)	IMF (1953–86)	OECD (1951–83)	SALA (1951–74)	ECLA Market (1975–86)	IDB (1981–86)
1946	1.6					
1947	25.8					
1948	27.4					
1949	–9.2					
1950	2.9					
1951	2.0		–3.6	5.0		
1952	7.5		8.0	7.3		
1953	3.1	2.6	11.5*	4.4		
1954	1.2	3.1	3.6*	2.1		
1955	5.1	4.3	3.6	4.1		
1956	7.9	6.0	4.6	4.0		
1957	5.3	5.6	5.0	5.7		
1958	2.2	1.0	1.0	0		
1959	4.5	4.5	1.9	1.8		
1960	4.1	4.0	4.1	3.0		
1961	3.5	3.5	3.5	3.4		
1962	12.0	12.0	12.0	11.6		
1963	4.3	4.3	4.3	4.3		
1964	9.3	9.3	9.3	9.4		
1965	5.4	5.4	5.4	5.1		
1966	7.2	7.2	7.2	7.3		
1967	5.4	5.4	5.4	5.4		
1968	3.2	3.2	3.2	3.3		
1969	3.5	3.5	3.5	3.4		
1970	3.0	3.0	3.0	3.6		
1971	4.6	4.8	4.8	4.0		
1972	5.7	5.5	5.5	5.8		
1973	5.1	5.1	5.1	5.4		
1974	6.4	6.4	6.4	5.2		
1975	5.6	5.6	5.6		5.6	
1976	4.0	4.0	4.0		4.0	
1977	5.0	6.1	6.1		5.9	
1978	4.4	6.4	6.4		4.4	
1979	–1.7	–1.7	–1.7		–1.5	
1980	–8.7	–8.7	–8.7		–5.3	
1981	–8.4	–8.3	–9.0		–8.4	–8.3
1982	–5.6	–5.6	–6.3		–5.7	–5.6
1983	.6	.8	#*		.6	.8
1984	1.5	2.3			1.4	2.3
1985	1.4‡	2.0			1.4	2.0
1986		1.0			–.5	1.0‡

SOURCE AND METHODS: See table 3300.

Table 3311

GUATEMALA COMPARATIVE PC
OF REAL GDP, 1946–86

Year	ECLA Factor (1946–85)	IMF (1953–86)	OECD (1951–83)	SALA (1951–74)	ECLA Market (1975–86)	IDB (1981–86)
1946	7.9					
1947	12.7					
1948	-.8					
1949	-7.9					
1950	.3					
1951	1.4		1.5	1.8		
1952	2.1		2.1	2.1		
1953	3.7	3.6	3.6	2.8		
1954	1.9	1.9	1.9	1.8		
1955	2.5	2.5	2.4	2.8		
1956	9.1	9.1	9.1	9.4		
1957	5.6	5.6	5.7	5.5		
1958	4.7	4.7	4.2	4.6		
1959	4.9	4.9	4.9	4.8		
1960	2.4	2.4	2.4	2.4		
1961	4.3	4.3	4.3	4.2		
1962	3.5	3.5	3.5	3.6		
1963	9.5	9.5	9.5	9.5		
1964	4.6	4.6	4.6	4.5		
1965	4.4	4.4	4.4	4.4		
1966	5.5	5.5	5.5	4.6		
1967	4.1	4.1	4.1	4.0		
1968	8.8	8.8	8.8	8.5		
1969	4.7	4.7	4.7	3.8		
1970	5.7	5.7	5.7	6.8		
1971	5.6	5.6	5.6	5.0		
1972	7.3	7.3	7.3*	8.1		
1973	6.8	6.8	7.3	8.1		
1974	6.4	6.4	6.1	6.6		
1975	1.9	1.9	1.9		1.9	
1976	7.4	7.4	7.4		7.4	
1977	7.8	7.8	7.8		7.8	
1978	5.5	5.0	5.0		5.0	
1979	4.7	4.7	4.7		4.7	
1980	3.8	3.7	3.7		4.2	
1981	1.0	.7	.9		1.0	.7
1982	3.3	-3.5	-3.4		-3.4	-3.5
1983	-2.7	-2.6	-2.0*		-2.7	-2.5
1984	.3	.5			#	.6
1985	-1.0	-.6			-.9	-1.0
1986		#			#	0‡

SOURCE AND METHODS: See table 3300.

Table 3312

HAITI COMPARATIVE PC OF REAL GDP, 1946–86

Year	ECLA Factor (1946–85)	IMF (1953–86)	OECD (1951–83)[a]	SALA (1951–74)[b]	ECLA Market (1975–86)	IDB (1981–86)
1945						
1946	.9					
1947	1.7					
1948	1.0					
1949	1.1					
1950	1.6					
1951	1.5		1.4	1.3		
1952	5.7		5.7	5.4		
1953	-3.2	-3.2	-3.3	-2.4		
1954	8.2	8.1	8.1	6.2		
1955	-4.0	-4.0	-4.0	-2.3		
1956	8.7	8.7	8.8	7.5		
1957	-5.9	-5.9	-6.1	-4.7		
1958	7.9	7.9	8.0	7.3		
1959	-4.7	-4.7	-4.8	-4.4		
1960	6.5	2.6	7.3	3.4*		
1961	-4.1	-2.4	-3.0	-2.5		
1962	9.6	8.3	7.9	8.2		
1963	-6.5	-2.9	-1.9	-2.1		
1964	-2.3	-1.6	-1.6	-1.1		
1965	1.1	2.1	2.1	1.1		
1966	-.6	.1	-.6	0		
1967	-2.0	-2.1	-2.1	-1.1		
1968	3.9	3.2	3.1	4.3		
1969	3.3	3.8	3.9	4.4		
1970	4.7	.7	.6	2.0		
1971	6.5	6.5	6.5	9.0		
1972	3.6	.9	-1.9	7.4		
1973	4.5	4.8	7.8	3.3		
1974	4.3	5.8	5.8	4.2		
1975	2.2	1.1	1.1		2.2	
1976	5.3	8.4	8.4		5.3	
1977	1.3	.5	.5		1.3	
1978	3.9	4.9	4.8		4.4	
1979	7.3	7.6	7.6		4.7	
1980	7.7	7.3	7.2		7.5	
1981	-2.7	-2.9	-2.7		-2.7	-2.7
1982	-3.4	-3.4	-4.0		-3.5	-3.5
1983	.7	.8	.9*		.6	.8
1984	.5	.3			.4	.3
1985	3.5[‡]	.2			3.5	1.1
1986		.6			-1.5	-.2

a. Data are at factor cost through 1959.
b. Through 1959 from UN-YNAS, 1970, III, p. 34.

SOURCE AND METHODS: See table 3300.

Table 3313

HONDURAS COMPARATIVE PC OF REAL GDP, 1926–86

I. 1926–39			II. 1940–86					
Year	ECLA Factor (1926–39)	Year	ECLA Factor (1940–85)	IMF (1953–86)	OECD (1951–83)	SALA (1951–74)	ECLA Market (1975–86)	IDB (1981–86)
		1940	6.9					
1926	.9	1941	–.3					
1927	9.8	1942	–8.6					
1928	12.5	1943	.2					
1929	–1.0	1944	15.2					
1930	6.5	1945	9.4					
1931	2.2	1946	7.6					
1932	–10.4	1947	6.4					
1933	–6.2	1948	2.1					
1934	–3.1	1949	1.4					
1935	–4.4	1950	3.2					
1936	1.8	1951	5.4		4.6	7.2		
1937	–4.4	1952	3.8		3.0	6.1		
1938	5.8	1953	7.8	6.1	6.0	6.4		
1939	2.8	1954	–5.7	–6.1	–5.1	.9		
		1955	2.6	5.9	2.7	3.0		
		1956	8.1	4.4	9.2	3.8		
		1957	4.6	4.2	6.4	11.1		
		1958	3.2	5.5	2.5	1.3		
		1959	2.5	2.3	4.5	5.2		
		1960	6.2	2.3	1.7	5.4		
		1961	2.6	2.0	2.8	.7		
		1962	5.8	5.2	5.1	3.5		
		1963	3.7	3.5	3.3	3.0		
		1964	5.2	5.7	6.0	1.2		
		1965	8.6	8.7	10.3	7.8		
		1966	5.8	5.4	5.9	8.3		
		1967	5.6	5.4	4.6	4.4		
		1968	5.9	6.3	7.3	8.9		
		1969	.8	.8	.3	2.9		
		1970	2.6	6.2	6.6*	5.3		
		1971	3.8	2.3	5.4*	4.0		
		1972	4.2	6.2	3.1*	3.8		
		1973	4.2	4.7	3.7*	5.5		
		1974	–.6	–.1	–.1	2.6		
		1975	–1.9	–2.6	–3.0		–1.7	
		1976	6.1	10.6	8.0		8.4	
		1977	5.8	1.0	11.5		8.7	
		1978	7.9	17.5	7.4		7.0	
		1979	6.1	6.3	6.8		6.6	
		1980	3.3	1.3	2.7		4.7	
		1981	.7	1.5	1.2		1.0	1.0
		1982	–.5	–2.0	–1.8		–1.6	–2.6
		1983	–1.2	–.2	–.7		–.6	–1.1
		1984	2.6	2.8			3.1	3.5
		1985	1.7	2.9			1.4	2.7
		1986		3.0			2.0	3.0

SOURCE AND METHODS: See table 3300.

Table 3314

MEXICO COMPARATIVE PC OF REAL GDP, 1896–1986[a]

PART I. 1896–1939

Year	ECLA Factor (1922–39)	Bank of Mexico[1] (1896–1939)
1896		3.1
1897		6.7
1898		5.8
1899		-4.8
1900		.8
1901		8.6
1902		-7.1
1903		11.2
1904		1.8
1905		10.4
1906		-1.1
1907		5.9
1908		-.2
1909		2.9
1910		.9
1911		≈
1912		≈
1913		≈
1914		≈
1915		≈
1916		≈
1917		≈
1918		≈
1919		≈
1920		≈
1921		7.7
1922	2.3	2.3
1923	3.4	3.4
1924	-1.6	-1.6
1925	6.2	6.2
1926	7.7	6.0
1927	-2.3	-4.4
1928	1.8	.6
1929	-3.3	-3.9
1930	-6.8	-6.3
1931	3.7	3.3
1932	-16.2	-14.9
1933	10.7	11.3
1934	6.6	6.8

PART II. 1940–86

Year	ECLA Factor (1940–85)	IMF (1953–86)	OECD (1951–83)	Bank of Mexico[2] (1940–80)	Bank of Mexico New System of National Accounts[3] (1971–84)	SALA (1951–74)	ECLA Market (1975–86)	IDB (1981–86)
1940	-.3			1.4				
1941	14.8			9.7				
1942	5.6			5.6				
1943	3.6			3.7				
1944	7.6			8.2				
1945	6.3			3.1				
1946	7.3			6.6				
1947	3.7			3.4				
1948	3.6			4.1				
1949	7.6			5.5				
1950	9.4	9.9		9.9				
1951	7.5	≈	7.8	7.7		9.1		
1952	3.0	≈	3.9	4.0		3.3		
1953	5.4	.3	.2	.3		4.6		
1954	5.4	10.0	10.5	10.0		5.4		
1955	7.9	8.6	8.8	8.5		7.5		
1956	5.3	6.8	6.6	6.9		5.3		
1957	7.5	7.5	7.7	7.6		7.5		
1958	4.6	5.4	5.4	5.4		4.2		
1959	4.3	3.0	2.9	3.0		3.9		
1960	7.5	8.1	8.1	8.1		7.6		
1961	4.9	4.9	4.9	4.9		4.9		
1962	4.7	4.7	4.7	4.7		4.5		
1963	8.0	8.0	8.0	8.0		8.0		
1964	11.7	11.7	11.7	11.7		11.6		
1965	6.5	6.5	6.5	6.5		6.3		
1966	6.9	6.9	6.9	6.9		6.8		
1967	6.3	6.3	6.3	6.3		6.1		
1968	8.1	8.1	8.1	8.1		8.0		
1969	6.3	6.3	6.3	6.3		6.4		
1970	6.9	6.9*	6.9*	6.9	6.9	6.8		
1971	3.4	4.2	3.4*	4.2	4.2	6.0		
1972	7.3	8.5	7.3*	8.5	8.5	4.7		
1973	7.6	8.4	7.6*	8.4	8.4	8.1		
1974	5.9	6.1	6.1	6.1	6.1	5.1		
1975	4.1	5.6	5.6	5.6	5.6		5.6	
1976	2.1	4.2	4.2	4.2	4.2		4.2	
1977	3.3	3.4	3.4	3.4	3.4		3.4	
1978	7.0	8.3	8.3	8.2	8.2		8.1	
1979	9.2	9.2	9.2	9.2	9.2		9.2	

Table 3314 (Continued)

MEXICO COMPARATIVE PC OF REAL GDP, 1896–1986[a]

PART I. 1896–1939

Year	ECLA Factor (1922–39)	Bank of Mexico[1] (1896–1939)
1935	5.1	7.4
1936	10.4	8.0
1937	3.4	3.3
1938	1.8	1.6
1939	5.3	5.4

PART II. 1940–86

Year	ECLA Factor (1940–85)	IMF (1953–86)	OECD (1951–83)	Bank of Mexico[2] (1940–80)	Bank of Mexico New System of National Accounts[3] (1971–84)	SALA (1951–74)	ECLA Market (1975–86)	IDB (1981–86)
1980	8.4	8.3	8.3	8.3	8.3		8.8	
1981	8.4	7.9	7.9	7.9	7.9		8.3	7.9
1982	-.5	-.6	-.6	-.5	-.5		#	-.5
1983	-5.1	-5.3	-4.6	-5.3	-5.3		-5.2	-5.3
1984	3.6	3.7		3.7	3.5		3.5	3.7
1985	2.5‡	2.7		2.8			2.7	2.8
1986		~		-3.8			-4.0‡	-3.8

1. Leopoldo Solís, *La Realidad Económica Mexicana: Retrovisión y Perspectivas*, rev. ed. (México, D.F.: Siglo XXI, 1981), p. 79.
2. SALA-SEM, "Introduction."
3. Data a are in 1970 prices from NAFINSA-EMC, 1981, p. 51; Banco Nacional de México, *Informe*, 1982, pp. 30 and 50; and Banco Nacional de México, *Review of the Economic Situation of Mexico*, Aug. 1985, vol. 61, p. 10.
a. SALA recommends that the Bank of Mexico series be used which is essentially the same as IMF.

SOURCE AND METHODS: See table 3300.

Table 3315

NICARAGUA COMPARATIVE PC
OF REAL GDP, 1946–86

Year	ECLA Factor (1946–85)	IMF (1953–86)	OECD (1951–83)	SALA (1951–74)[a]	ECLA Market (1975–86)	IDB (1981–86)
1946	8.6					
1947	.3					
1948	8.7					
1949	−1.8					
1950	16.6					
1951	6.8		6.8	6.8		
1952	16.9		16.9	14.5		
1953	2.4	2.4	2.4	1.5		
1954	9.3	9.3	9.4	12.5		
1955	6.7	6.8	6.7	3.5		
1956	−.1	−.1	−.1	1.8		
1957	8.4	8.5	8.5	9.5		
1958	.3	.3	.3	−.5		
1959	1.5	1.5	1.5	1.9		
1960	1.4	3.6	1.4	1.6		
1961	7.5	7.5	7.5*	7.3		
1962	10.9	10.9	10.9	10.2		
1963	10.9	10.9	10.9	6.7		
1964	11.7	11.7	11.7	11.2		
1965	9.5	9.5	9.5	9.9		
1966	3.3	3.3	3.3	3.0		
1967	7.0	7.0	7.0	6.7		
1968	1.3	1.4	1.3	.3		
1969	6.7	6.2	6.2	5.0		
1970	1.0	1.3	2.0	4.5		
1971	4.9	4.9	3.9	5.0		
1972	3.2	3.2*	4.2	4.8		
1973	5.1	6.4	4.3	1.8		
1974	12.7	14.2	13.0	9.4		
1975	2.2	−.2	1.4		2.2	
1976	5.0	5.2	5.8		5.0	
1977	6.3	8.4	6.6		6.3	
1978	−7.2	−7.8	−6.5		−7.2	
1979	−26.5	−26.4	−25.9		−25.5	
1980	10.0	10.0	10.0		−10.0	
1981	5.4	5.3	8.6		5.4	5.4
1982	−.8	−1.2	−1.3		−.8	−.8
1983	4.5	5.1	4.0		4.4	4.6
1984	−1.4	~			−1.4	−1.6
1985	−2.6‡	~			−2.6	−4.1
1986		~			#‡	−.4

a. Calculated from SALA, 19-2200.

SOURCE AND METHODS: See table 3300.

Table 3316

PANAMA COMPARATIVE PC
OF REAL GDP, 1946–86

Year	ECLA Factor (1946–85)	IMF (1953–86)	OECD (1951–83)	SALA (1951–74)	ECLA Market (1975–86)	IDB (1981–86)
1946	1.6					
1947	4.2					
1948	-5.9					
1949	2.3					
1950	.5					
1951	-.9		-.8	-.7		
1952	5.4		5.4	5.7		
1953	6.1	6.1	6.0	6.4		
1954	3.6	3.6	3.6	1.9		
1955	5.8	5.8	5.8	5.9		
1956	5.2	5.2	5.2	5.2		
1957	10.5	10.5	10.5	10.8		
1958	.8	.8	.8	1.8		
1959	6.4	6.4	6.3	7.6		
1960	6.0	6.0	6.0	7.3		
1961	10.8	10.8	10.8	11.7		
1962	8.4	8.2	8.2	8.8		
1963	9.4	8.5	8.5	8.8		
1964	4.3	4.4	4.4	5.2		
1965	8.8	9.2	9.2	7.4		
1966	7.4	7.6	7.6	7.7		
1967	8.4	8.6	8.6	7.7		
1968	7.3	7.0	7.0	6.9		
1969	7.8	8.4	8.4	8.9		
1970	6.0	4.1	6.9*	7.2		
1971	8.1	9.6	9.6	8.0		
1972	5.3	4.6	4.6	6.5		
1973	6.1	5.4	5.4*	6.1		
1974	.8	2.4	2.4	4.1		
1975	.6	1.7	1.7		.6	
1976	-1.1	1.7	1.6		-.3	
1977	3.3	1.1	1.1		4.6	
1978	3.8	9.8	9.8		6.5	
1979	4.5	4.5	4.5		7.0	
1980	15.1	15.1	15.2		9.7	
1981	4.0	4.2	4.2		4.0	4.2
1982	5.0	5.5	5.5		4.9	5.5
1983	~	.4	.4		-.1	.4
1984	-.3	-.4			-.4	-.4
1985	3.4‡	4.1			3.3	4.1
1986		~			3.0‡	2.8

SOURCE AND METHODS: See table 3300.

Table 3317

PARAGUAY COMPARATIVE PC
OF REAL GDP, 1939–86

Year	ECLA Factor (1939–85)	IMF (1953–86)	OECD (1951–83)	SALA (1951–74)	ECLA Market (1976–86)	IDB (1981–86)
1939	17.5					
1940	–15.1					
1941	13.3					
1942	5.9					
1943	2.1					
1944	2.1					
1945	–3.5					
1946	9.8					
1947	–13.0					
1948	1.1					
1949	16.8					
1950	–1.6					
1951	1.9		–.4	1.1		
1952	–1.7		3.1	–1.0		
1953	2.8	5.2	1.3	5.3		
1954	1.7	2.6	3.8	2.7		
1955	4.6	6.3	7.1	6.2		
1956	4.2	2.4	–1.2	2.5		
1957	4.6	6.0	7.0	10.8		
1958	5.6	6.6	5.3	1.9		
1959	.4	–1.1	–.3	–1.1		
1960	.2	–.4	–.5*	–.5		
1961	4.8	6.0	5.9	5.9		
1962	7.0	5.9	5.5	5.9		
1963	2.7	2.0	2.7	1.7		
1964	4.3	4.3	4.4	4.0		
1965	5.7	5.7	5.7	6.8		
1966	1.1	1.1	1.2	1.3		
1967	6.3	6.3	6.3	5.9		
1968	3.6	3.7	3.5	4.8		
1969	3.9	3.8	3.9	4.0		
1970	6.2	3.8	6.2*	5.7		
1971	4.4	5.4	5.4	5.0		
1972	5.1	6.5	6.5	4.8		
1973	7.8	7.2	7.2	7.2		
1974	8.3	8.2	8.2	8.5		
1975	5.0	6.3	6.3			
1976	7.5	7.0	7.0		7.0	
1977	11.8	12.8	12.8		12.8	
1978	10.3	10.8	10.8		10.9	
1979	11.4	10.7	10.7		10.7	
1980	11.4	11.4	11.4		11.4	
1981	8.7	8.5	8.4		8.7	8.7
1982	–.6	–.8	–2.0*		–.7	–1.0
1983	–2.9	–3.0	–3.7*		–3.0	–3.0
1984	3.3	3.1			3.3	3.1
1985	4.1‡	4.0			4.0	4.0
1986		#			1.0‡	0‡

SOURCE AND METHODS: See table 3300.

Table 3318

PERU COMPARATIVE PC
OF REAL GDP, 1946–86

Year	ECLA Factor (1946–85)	IMF (1953–86)[a]	OECD (1951–83)[b]	SALA (1951–74)	ECLA Market (1975–86)	IDB (1981–86)
1946	4.0					
1947	3.0					
1948	3.4					
1949	7.1					
1950	5.0					
1951	11.3		10.5	10.2		
1952	2.7		2.8	3.0		
1953	2.2	2.5	2.2	2.0		
1954	9.6	8.8	9.6	9.8		
1955	4.9	7.0	4.9	5.0		
1956	5.0	2.5	4.6	4.4		
1957	1.0	1.1	1.1	1.1		
1958	3.2	3.3	3.3	3.3		
1959	4.4	5.4	3.6	3.5		
1960	9.0	9.4	11.4	9.2		
1961	8.2	8.8	7.0	8.0[c]		
1962	8.8	10.3	8.2	9.3[c]		
1963	3.9	4.2	4.1	3.8		
1964	6.8	6.9	7.3	6.9		
1965	4.8	5.1	5.2	4.8		
1966	5.7	7.0	6.4	5.8		
1967	1.8	3.5	3.4	1.6		
1968	.6	#	-.3	.7		
1969	4.4	4.1	3.9	2.4		
1970	9.1	7.3	5.4	9.1		
1971	5.1	5.1	5.0	6.5[c]		
1972	5.8	5.8	1.7	6.1[c]		
1973	6.2	6.2	4.3	6.2		
1974	6.9	6.9	7.5	5.8		
1975	3.3	2.4	4.6		4.5	
1976	3.0	3.3	2.0		2.0	
1977	-1.2	-.3	-.1		-.1	
1978	-.5	-1.7	-.5		-.5	
1979	4.1	4.3	4.1		4.1	
1980	3.8	2.9	3.8		4.0	
1981	4.0	3.0	3.9		4.0	3.1
1982	.1	.9	.4		.1	.9
1983	-11.9	-12.0	-11.9*		-11.9	-12.0
1984	4.2	4.8			3.8	4./
1985	1.7	1.6			1.6	1.9
1986		~			8.5[‡]	8.5[‡]

a. 1970 prices through 1960.
b. GNP through 1959.
c. Corrects SALA, 18-2200; recalculated from USAID source, in 1973 dollars.

SOURCE AND METHODS: See table 3300.

Table 3319

URUGUAY COMPARATIVE PC OF REAL GDP, 1936–86

Year	ECLA Factor (1936–85)	IMF (1956–86)	OECD (1951–83)	SALA (1951–74)	ECLA Market (1975–86)	Kravis et al.[1] (1951–77)	IDB (1981–86)
1936	3.6						
1937	8.7						
1938	−4.9						
1939	−.8						
1940	−2.2						
1941	5.9						
1942	−9.1						
1943	1.5						
1944	12.9						
1945	2.3						
1946	11.1						
1947	6.7						
1948	2.6						
1949	3.7						
1950	3.1						
1951	−8.2		8.2	8.2		12.9	
1952	−.4		−.3	−.5		−3.5	
1953	6.5		6.4	6.5		4.6	
1954	5.7		5.8	5.7		5.5	
1955	1.6		1.5*	1.8		1.6	
1956	1.7	1.8	1.8	1.8		−.5	
1957	1.0	1.2	1.0	.9		13.5	
1958	−3.5	−3.5	−3.6	−3.6		−5.7	
1959	−2.8	−3.0	−2.8	−2.8		3.6	
1960	3.5	3.7	1.1	3.6		2.5	
1961	2.9	3.0	2.8	2.8		−.1	
1962	−2.3	−2.3	−2.3	−2.3		−2.9	
1963	.5	.6	.5	−1.1		−.5	
1964	2.0	1.8	2.0	2.8		1.6	
1965	1.2	1.2	1.2	1.0		−1.7	
1966	3.4	3.4	3.4	3.2		3.5	
1967	−4.1	−3.9	−4.1	−5.5		−5.8	
1968	1.6	1.1	1.6	1.3		.3	
1969	6.1	6.3	6.1	6.2		5.0	
1970	4.7	6.5	4.7*	5.9		4.1	
1971	−1.0	.1	.1	−1.0		−1.1	
1972	−3.3	−1.6	−1.6	−3.0		−2.1	
1973	.8	.4	.40			1.1	
1974	3.1	3.1	3.1	1.0		3.8	
1975	4.4	5.9	5.9		4.8	.2	
1976	2.6	4.0	4.0		4.2	3.0	
1977	3.4	1.2	1.2		1.8	1.9	
1978	3.9	5.3	5.3		6.2		
1979	6.2	6.2	6.2		9.6		
1980	6.1	6.0	6.0		6.0		
1981	1.5	1.9	1.9		1.5		1.9
1982	−10.0	−9.4	−9.7		−9.7		−9.4
1983	−6.0	−5.9	−4.7		−6.4		−5.9
1984	−2.1	−1.5			−2.4		−1.5
1985	.6‡	.7			.5		0
1986		6.3			5.0‡		6.3‡

1. Irving B. Kravis, Alan Heston, and Robert Summers, *World Product and Income: International Comparisons of Real Gross Product* (Baltimore: Published for the World Bank by the Johns Hopkins University Press, 1982), pp. 330–336. Kravis et al. give the results of the International Comparison Project (ICP), supervised by the UN Statistical Office with funding from a consortium organized by the World Bank, which developed international dollars comparable from country to country by applying a common set of prices (representative of the world price structure) to the quantities of the commodities and services entering into each country's final expenditure on GDP. The results theoretically overcome the problem of using nominal exchange rates, as does the "ECLA Factor approach." Data are calculated from 1975 dollars at market prices.

SOURCE AND METHODS: See table 3300.

Table 3320

VENEZUELA COMPARATIVE PC
OF REAL GDP, 1937–86

Year	ECLA Factor (1937–85)	IMF (1953–86)	OECD (1951–83)	SALA (1951–74)	ECLA Market (1975–86)	IDB (1981–86)
1937	7.3					
1938	3.2					
1939	4.3					
1940	2.8					
1941	7.9					
1942	-4.6					
1943	5.6					
1944	11.3					
1945	9.7					
1946	17.6					
1947	16.4					
1948	12.7					
1949	4.8					
1950	2.4					
1951	11.7		11.6	12.0		
1952	7.3		7.2	7.6		
1953	6.2	6.2	6.2	7.5		
1954	9.6	9.7	9.5	10.1		
1955	8.9	8.9	8.9	7.8		
1956	10.6	10.6	10.5	8.0		
1957	11.6	3.6	11.6	10.3		
1958	1.3	1.3	1.3	7.1		
1959	7.9	8.0	7.9	8.9		
1960	1.4	4.0	4.0*	3.3		
1961	5.0	4.9	5.0	4.5		
1962	9.1	9.1	9.1	8.3		
1963	6.9	7.0	6.9	7.1		
1964	9.7	9.6	9.7	12.9		
1965	5.9	6.0	5.9	5.7		
1966	2.3	2.5	2.3	2.7		
1967	4.0	3.8	4.0	4.6		
1968	5.3	4.9	5.3	5.2		
1969	4.5	4.5	4.5	3.9		
1970	7.1	8.8	8.8	6.2		
1971	3.3	3.0	3.0	0		
1972	3.0	2.7	2.7	5.0		
1973	6.7	6.3	6.3	4.8		
1974	5.8	6.1	6.1	7.3		
1975	5.2	6.1	6.1		5.9	
1976	7.8	8.8	8.8		8.4	
1977	7.6	6.7	6.7		6.8	
1978	4.8	2.1	2.1		3.2	
1979	1.3	1.3	1.3		.9	
1980	-2.0	-2.0	-2.0		-3.4	
1981	-.9	-.3	-.3		-1.0	-.3
1982	-1.2	.7	.7		-1.3	.7
1983	-5.5	-5.6	-4.8		-5.6	-5.6
1984	-1.0	-1.4			-1.1	-1.2
1985	-1.1‡	.3			-.6	.1
1986		~			1.5‡	3.1‡

SOURCE AND METHODS: See table 3300.

Table 3321

LATIN AMERICA COMPARATIVE PC
OF REAL GDP, 1940–86

Year	ECLA Factor[1] (1940–85)	IMF (1953–86)[2]	OECD[3] (1951–83)	SALA[4] (1951–74)	ECLA[5] Market (1975–86)	IDB (1981–86)
1940	.2					
1941	6.2					
1942	1.8					
1943	3.1					
1944	7.3					
1945	1.7					
1946	7.8					
1947	6.3					
1948	4.7					
1949	2.7					
1950	4.9					
1951	5.9		5.4	6.2		
1952	3.0		2.3	2.5		
1953	4.5	2.4	3.6	4.6		
1954	6.2	5.2	6.4	5.9		
1955	6.3	4.5	6.3	2.5		
1956	4.1	.7	3.8	3.3		
1957	6.1	2.6	6.4	6.3		
1958	4.9	5.7	4.9	4.5		
1959	2.6	1.7	2.2	1.9		
1960	7.0	6.3	7.4	6.0		
1961	6.6	5.6	6.6	6.6		
1962	4.2	3.6	4.3	4.0		
1963	3.4	3.2	3.2	3.2		
1964	7.5	4.4	6.9	7.6		
1965	5.4	12.0	5.1	5.4		
1966	4.4	6.2	4.4	4.5		
1967	4.3	4.0	4.4	4.1		
1968	6.9	6.9	6.9	6.3		
1969	7.1	6.8	7.1	6.7		
1970	6.9	4.5	6.6	7.0		
1971	6.7	6.5	5.9	7.0		
1972	6.9	6.8	6.1	6.5		
1973	8.5	7.7	8.0	7.9		
1974	7.1	7.0	6.1	7.3		
1975	3.2	4.1	3.3		3.7	
1976	4.6	6.1	5.6		5.5	
1977	4.6	5.0	5.1		4.8	
1978	4.7	4.4	4.4		5.0	
1979	6.4	6.4	6.1		6.5	
1980	5.7	5.0	5.2		6.1	
1981	.5	.5	1.5		.5	.5
1982	-1.4	-1.4	-1.1		-1.4	-.8
1983	-2.4	-2.4	-2.7		-2.4	-2.9
1984	3.4	3.3			3.2	3.8
1985	2.8‡	2.5			2.7	3.7
1986		~			3.4‡	3.8‡

1. Excludes Cuba and through 1944 excludes Bolivia, Costa Rica, Dominican Republic, El Salvador, Guatemala, Haiti, Nicaragua, Panama, and Peru, but the ten countries included generated 88.7% of GDP for the region in 1945.
2. Excludes Cuba and Venezuela. Includes Dominica since 1977, Guyana since 1978, Jamaica since 1961, St. Lucia since 1976, Suriname since 1974. (Reported as Western Hemisphere in Source.)
3. Includes Jamaica, Trinidad and Tobago and five other unspecified countries; includes Netherlands Antilles and Guyana for 1956–59; includes more than ten small republics of the Caribbean through 1959.
4. Excludes Cuba and Haiti.
5. Excludes Cuba, from 1981.

SOURCE AND METHODS: See table 3300.

Table 3322

UNITED STATES COMPARATIVE
PC OF REAL GNP, 1910–86[a]

PART I. 1910–39

Year	USBC[1] (1910–39)	USDC-SCB[2] (1930–39)
1910	2.8	
1911	2.6	
1912	5.7	
1913	.9	
1914	−4.3	
1915	−.8	
1916	7.9	
1917	.7	
1918	12.3	
1919	−3.5	
1920	−4.3	
1921	−8.6	
1922	15.8	
1923	12.1	
1924	−.2	
1925	8.4	
1926	5.9	
1927	.0	
1928	.6	
1929	6.7	
1930	−9.8	−9.5
1931	−7.6	−7.8
1932	−14.7	−13.8
1933	−1.8	−2.2
1934	9.1	7.6
1935	9.9	8.7
1936	13.9	13.7
1937	5.3	5.0
1938	−5.0	−4.4
1939	8.6	7.8

PART II. 1940–86

Year	USBC[1] (1940–70)	IMF[3] (1953–86)	SALA[4] (1951–74)	USDC-SCB[2] (1940–86)
1940	8.5			7.6
1941	16.1			16.3
1942	12.9			15.3
1943	13.2			15.6
1944	7.2			7.1
1945	−1.7			−1.5
1946	−11.9			−14.7
1947	−.9			−1.7
1948	4.5			4.1
1949	.1			.5
1950	9.6			8.7
1951	7.9		7.9	8.3
1952	3.1		3.1	3.7
1953	4.5	3.8	4.5	3.8
1954	−1.3	−1.2	−1.4	−1.2
1955	7.6	6.7	7.6	6.7
1956	1.9	2.1	1.9	2.1
1957	1.4	1.8	1.4	1.8
1958	−1.1	−.3	−1.1	−.4
1959	6.4	6.0	6.4	6.0
1960	2.5	2.1	2.5	2.2
1961	2.0	2.6	1.9	2.6
1962	6.6	5.7	6.5	5.8
1963	4.0	4.0	4.0	4.0
1964	5.5	5.2	5.5	5.3
1965	6.3	6.0	6.3	6.0
1966	6.5	6.1	6.5	6.0
1967	2.6	2.7	2.6	2.7
1968	4.7	4.6	4.7	4.6
1969	2.6	2.8	2.6	2.8
1970	−.6	−.5	−.7	−.2
1971		3.2	3.0	3.4
1972		5.3	6.8	5.7
1973		4.4	5.5	5.8
1974		−1.7	−1.7	−.6
1975		−1.9		−1.1
1976		6.0		6.1
1977		5.5		5.9
1978		4.9		5.0
1979		1.5		2.8
1980		−1.8		−.3
1981		2.2		2.0
1982		−1.9		−1.9
1983		5.0		3.7
1984		8.5		6.8
1985		2.8		3.0
1986		2.7		2.9

1. USBC-HS, Series F-31, in 1958 dollars.
2. USDC-SCB, *The National Income and Product Accounts of the United States, 1929–1976* (Washington, D.C., 1981), revised since 1976 with USDC-SCB, July 1982, April 1985 and Oct. 1986. All data calculated in 1972 dollars except for 1985 and 1986 in 1982 constant dollars.
3. IMF-IFS-Y, 1984 and 1986.
4. SALA, 18-2200.

a. At market prices.

SOURCE AND METHODS: See table 3300.

Table 3323

GDP LEVELS AND GROWTH, 6 L, 1929–83

	A. ARGENTINA	C. BRAZIL	D. CHILE	E. COLOMBIA	G. CUBA	N. MEXICO
1929 Levels, million 1929 $ at US Relative Prices	4,806	2,690	1,077	729	890	1,385
1929	100.0	100.0	100.0	100.0	100.0	100.0
1930	95.9	97.9	95.9	99.1	94.2	93.2
1931	89.2	94.7	76.9	97.6	79.1	96.6
1932	86.2	98.8	73.5	104.0	63.5	81.0
1933	90.3	107.6	83.5	109.9	68.7	89.7
1934	97.4	117.5	94.7	107.6	80.7	95.6
1935	101.7	120.9	98.4	119.6	94.4	100.5
1936	103.0	135.5	101.6	126.0	110.0	110.9
1937	111.3	141.7	109.4	127.9	126.4	114.7
1938	112.6	148.1	109.4	136.3	98.1	116.8
1950	159.6	268.3	172.5	212.1	193.0	239.1
1973	374.6	1,354.4	393.9	676.8	313.1	969.1
1973 Levels, million 1973 $ at US Relative Prices	62,074	124,564	14,750	16,949	9,685	46,858
1973	100.0	100.0	100.0	100.0	100.0	100.0
1974	105.7	109.7	101.0	105.7	88.7	106.1
1975	105.3	115.7	87.9	108.2	85.0	112.1
1976	104.8	126.9	91.0	113.3	86.1	116.8
1977	111.5	134.2	100.0	118.0	87.3	120.8
1978	107.7	140.9	108.2	128.0	88.4	130.8
1979	115.5	149.9	117.2	134.9	88.5	142.8
1980	115.8	160.7	126.3	140.4	88.6	154.7
1981	108.6	158.2	133.3	143.6	92.1	167.0
1982	102.8	159.7	114.5	145.0	94.4	166.0
1983	105.7	154.6	113.7	146.1	99.1	157.3

SOURCE: Angus Maddison, *Two Crises: Latin America and Asia, 1929–38 and 1973–83* (Paris: Development Centre of the Organisation for Economic Co-Operation and Development, 1985).

Table 3324

GDP IN CONSTANT DOLLARS OF 1970, 19 LR, 1940–85

(ECLA Factor Series)[1]

PART I. PURCHASING POWER EQUIVALENCES OF LATIN
AMERICAN CURRENCY IN RELATION
TO THE DOLLAR IN 1970

	Country	1 Dollar U.S. Currency Equals:
A.	ARGENTINA	2.95 pesos argentinos
B.	BOLIVIA	9.03 pesos bolivianos
C.	BRAZIL	4.14 novos cruzeiros
D.	CHILE	.01 pesos chilenos
E.	COLOMBIA	10.68 pesos colombianos
F.	COSTA RICA	5.09 colones costarricenses
H.	DOMINICAN REP.	.87 pesos dominicanos
I.	ECUADOR	14.00 sucres
J.	EL SALVADOR	1.70 colones salvadoreños
K.	GUATEMALA	.81 quetzales
L.	HAITI	3.99 gourdes
M.	HONDURAS	1.75 lempiras
N.	MEXICO	8.88 pesos mexicanos
O.	NICARAGUA	6.41 córdobas
P.	PANAMA	.76 balboas
Q.	PARAGUAY	85.41 guaraníes
R.	PERU	30.72 soles
S.	URUGUAY	.20 pesos uruguayos
T.	VENEZUELA	3.96 bolívares

1. Owing to timing of revisions, the implicit PC since 1970 here
   may not agree with explicit PC for ECLA factor series in tables
   3301 through 3321 above.

SOURCE: ECLA-SHCAL, p. 8.

Table 3324 (Continued)

PART II. SERIES, 1940-85 (M US)[1]

Year	A. ARGENTINA	B. BOLIVIA	C. BRAZIL	D. CHILE	E. COLOMBIA	F. COSTA RICA	H. DOMINICAN REPUBLIC	I. ECUADOR	J. EL SALVADOR	K. GUATEMALA
1940	10,048	~	8,024	2,495	3,013	~	~	424	~	~
1941	10,538	~	8,421	2,498	3,063	~	~	426	~	~
1942	11,028	~	8,183	2,636	3,070	~	~	444	~	~
1943	11,108	~	8,660	2,746	3,082	~	~	500	~	~
1944	12,189	~	9,057	2,785	3,090	~	~	507	~	~
1945	11,602	634	9,137	3,038	3,445	203[a]	356	509	336	795[a]
1946	12,567	645	9,851	3,225	3,757	218	330	570	342	857
1947	14,288	656	10,090	3,010	3,904	260	363	633	430	967
1948	14,464	670	10,841	3,357	4,025	274	402	719	548	883
1949	13,800	684	11,558	3,339	4,248	286	452	732	498	885
1950	14,018	698	12,309	3,499	4,325	298	533	796	512	885
1951	14,562	748	13,037	3,683	4,458	306	596	805	522	897
1952	13,821	770	14,169	3,810	4,739	343	644	904	561	916
1953	14,570	697	14,528	4,078	5,013	395	636	923	601	950
1954	15,164	712	15,996	4,108	5,344	398	673	997	608	967
1955	16,242	749	17,093	4,221	5,559	444	714	1,024	640	991
1956	16,693	705	17,636	4,251	5,788	431	786	1,062	690	1,081
1957	17,550	682	19,058	4,371	5,925	468	835	1,109	727	1,142
1958	18,623	698	20,526	4,582	6,072	526	880	1,142	742	1,196
1959	17,428	696	21,656	4,899	6,501	545	885	1,203	776	1,255
1960	18,789	726	23,774	5,147	6,768	593	929	1,281	807	1,286
1961	20,128	741	26,224	5,461	7,108	617	908	1,313	836	1,340
1962	19,802	782	27,599	5,714	7,490	655	1,062	1,383	935	1,388
1963	19,327	832	28,027	6,004	7,733	711	1,131	1.419	976	1,520
1964	21,327	872	28,848	6,262	8,202	746	1,207	1,518	1,067	1,591
1965	23,275	915	29,634	6,578	8,490	814*	1,057	1,665	1,124	1,660
1966	23,421	981	30,749	7,039	8,935	877	1,199	1,708	1,204	1,752
1967	24,053	1,043	32,250	7,211	9,309	931	1,239	1,799	1,270	1,824
1968	25,078	1,132	35,852	7,427	9,897	1,002	1,242	1,898	1,311	1,984
1969	27,228	1,182	39,412	7,684	10,523	1,069	1,377	2,002	1,357	2,077
1970	28,686	1,269	42,885	7,961	11,217	1,139	1,523	2,190	1,397	2,196
1971	30,065	1,332	48,590	8,574	11,865	1,217	1,689	2,278	1,462	2,319
1972	31,004	1,411	54,294	8,566	12,804	1,316	1,864	2,459	1,544	2,489
1973	32,020	1,485	61,842	8,256	13,781	1,139	2,105	2,855	1,622	2,658
1974	35,039	1,576	67,888	8,724	14,673	1,418	2,231	3,113	1,727	2,827
1975	34,735	1,680	71,748	7,472	15,300	1,496	2,347	3,324	1,823	2,882
1976	34,142	1,782	78,180	7,754	15,939	1,612	2,505	3,632	1,895	3,095
1977	35,828	1,857	81,825	8,506	16,697	1,755	2,630	3,905	2,010	3,337
1978	31,051	1,919	79,428	8,575	17,596	1,865	2,686	4,838	2,139	3,503
1979	33,134	1,954	84,492	9,285	18,345	1,958	2,808	5,094	2,102	3,669
1980	33,380	1,966	90,592	10,008	19,354	1,973	2,978	5,344	1,920	3,806
1981	31,299	1,980	89,157	10,561	19,906	1,928	3,097	5,555	1,761	3,832
1982	29,668	1,849	89,994	9,074	20,086	1,787	3,149	5,653	1,662	3,695
1983	30,580	1,690	87,163	9,009	20,286	1,829	3,272	5,464	1,651	3,596
1984	31,203	1,627	91,071	9,580	20,895	1,939	3,292	5,630	1,675	3,603
1985	29,830	1,599	98,630	9,810	21,417	1,972	3,223	5,877	1,698	3,567

Table 3324 (Continued)

PART II. SERIES, 1940–85 (M US)[1] (Continued)

Year	L. HAITI	M. HONDURAS	N. MEXICO	O. NICARAGUA	P. PANAMA	Q. PARAGUAY	R. PERU	S. URUGUAY	T. VENEZUELA	LATIN AMERICA
1940	~	229	6,632	~	~	342	~	1,273	1,528	38,341[b]
1941	~	229	7,614	~	~	347	~	1,348	1,649	40,736[b]
1942	~	209	8,041	~	~	367	~	1,226	1,572	41,461[b]
1943	~	209	8,333	~	~	375	~	1,244	1,661	42,749[b]
1944	~	241	8,967	~	~	383	~	1,404	1,849	45,854[b]
1945	377	264	9,563	176	363	370	~	1,436	2,029	46,653
1946	380	284	10,227	191	368	406	~	1,595	2,386	50,304
1947	386	302	10,605	192	384	353	~	1,703	2,778	53,470
1948	390	309	10,986	209	361	357	~	1,947	3,132	55,990
1949	394	313	11,819	205	369	417	~	1,811	3,282	57,488
1950	401	323	12,926	239	371	410	~	1,867	3,360	60,286
1951	407	340	13,897	255	368	418	~	2,021	3,752	63,871
1952	430	353	14,314	298	388	411	~	2,013	4,025	65,785
1953	416	381	15,087	305	411	423	~	2,143	4,274	68,772
1954	450	360	15,909	334	426	430	~	2,265	4,686	73,050
1955	432	369	17,167	356	450	450	~	2,301	5,102	77,686
1956	470	399	18,085	356	474	469	~	2,341	5,640	80,909
1957	442	417	19,443	386	524	490	~	2,363	6,296	85,814
1958	477	430	20,335	387	528	518	~	2,280	6,379	90,024
1959	454	441	21,219	393	561	520	~	2,216	6,881	92,393
1960	484	468	22,802	398	595	521	4,882	2,295	6,978	98,857
1961	464	480	23,926	428	659	546	~	2,360	7,329	105,433
1962	508	508	25,044	475	715	584	~	2,307	7,998	109,917
1963	475	527	27,045	526	782	600	~	2,319	8,550	113,663
1964	465	554	30,207	588	816	626	~	2,365	9,380	122,147
1965	470	602	32,166	644	887	662	6,641	2,392	9,935	128,743
1966	467	637	34,396	665	953	669	~	2,474	10,163	134,391
1967	457	673	36,552	712	1,033	712	~	2,371	10,573	140,219
1968	475	713	39,526	721	1,108	737	~	2,409	11,134	149,894
1969	491	719	42,026	769	1,194	766	~	2,556	11,630	160,585
1970	514	733	44,934	777	1,266	813	7,977	2,676	12,457	172,646
1971	547	780	46,480	815	1,369	848	~	2,650	12,873	184,167
1972	567	813	49,858	841	1,441	892	~	2,557	13,261	196,535
1973	592	848	53,495	883	1,529	978	8,882	2,577	14,101	212,649
1974	618	840	56,653	996	1,541	1,059	9,546	2,658	14,962	228,087
1975	632	823	58,964	1,018	1,550	1,126	9,979	2,776	15,848	235,497
1976	665	881	60,218	1,069	1,534	1,205	10,181	2,849	17,179	246,303
1977	674	932	62,182	1,136	1,558	1,358	10,175	2,945	18,352	257,664
1978	525	1,069	76,190	1,058	1,782	1,519	10,124	3,132	18,736	267,736
1979	563	1,134	83,199	778	1,862	1,691	10,542	3,326	18,987	289,923
1980	606	1,172	90,185	857	2,144	1,885	10,947	3,528	18,609	301,252
1981	590	1,180	97,353	902	2,234	2,049	11,373	3,595	18,553	306,902
1982	567	1,176	96,826	891	2,356	2,029	11,413	3,255	18,680	303,809
1983	568	1,164	91,719	933	2,366	1,968	10,173	3,093	17,630	294,154
1984	583	1,193	94,929	920	2,337	2,029	10,657	3,036	17,630	294,154
1985	603	1,213	97,302	896	2,416	2,112	10,838	3,054	17,155	312,044

1. Owing to timing of revisions, the implicit PC since 1970 here may not agree with
   explicit PC for ECLA factor series in tables 3301 through 3321 above.

a. ECLA estimate to arrive at total for Latin America in 1945.
b. Totals for years from 1940 to 1944 calculated by ECLA on basis of change in
   countries shown, countries which generated 88.7% of total GDP in 1945.

SOURCE: ECLA-SHCAL, pp. 14-19, except data since 1970 through 1979 from ECLA-AE,
   1979–81, pp. 128–129, 198–199, and 206–207, respectively; for 1980–84 data, ECLA-SY,
   1985, pp. 230–231; 1985 data calculated from tables 3301 through 3321, above.

Table 3325

STRUCTURE AND GROWTH OF GDP, BY SECTOR, 1960–86
(%)

| | Structure | | | | | | | | | Growth Rates | | | | | | | |
| | Average | | | Annual | | | | | | Average | | Annual | | | | | |
	1960–69	1970–79	1980–86	1981	1982	1983	1984	1985	1986‡	1961–70	1971–80	1981	1982	1983	1984	1985	1986‡
Primary	21.0	15.6	14.7	14.5	14.7	15.2	15.2	15.1	14.3	3.4	3.4	4.6	.1	.4	3.8	3.7	-2.0
Agriculture	16.5	12.5	11.7	11.6	11.7	12.1	12.0	12.1	11.3	3.3	3.6	4.7	-.2	.5	3.4	4.2	-2.4
Mining	4.5	3.2	3.0	2.9	3.0	3.1	3.1	3.1	2.9	3.8	2.8	4.1	1.3	-.0	5.2	1.7	-.4
Secondary	35.1	38.5	38.3	38.7	38.2	37.5	37.5	37.7	38.5	6.5	7.0	-2.1	-1.9	-4.9	4.0	4.3	5.9
Manufacturing	22.9	24.9	23.6	23.7	23.3	23.0	23.2	23.4	23.8	6.9	6.5	-4.5	-2.3	-4.3	5.0	4.4	5.8
Electricity	1.1	1.6	2.2	1.9	2.1	2.3	2.3	2.4	2.5	10.8	9.5	4.7	5.9	5.2	8.0	6.5	7.0
Construction	5.4	5.8	5.2	5.9	5.6	5.0	4.7	4.7	4.9	4.7	7.2	-.6	-5.2	-13.7	-2.1	4.6	6.9
Transport	5.7	6.3	7.2	7.2	7.2	7.3	7.2	7.2	7.3	5.9	8.0	3.4	0	-2.7	3.7	3.0	5.1
Tertiary	43.9	45.8	47.1	46.8	47.1	47.3	47.3	47.1	47.2	6.1	6.5	1.9	-.2	-2.3	3.7	3.3	3.8
Commerce	18.1	17.5	16.8	17.5	17.1	16.6	16.5	16.4	16.2	5.5	6.0	.5	-2.7	-6.3	3.6	2.8	2.9
Financial Services	11.7	13.5	12.1	11.7	11.9	12.3	12.4	12.5	12.5	6.8	5.2	3.2	.8	.4	4.4	4.7	4.1
Other Services	9.4	10.4	11.2	10.7	11.0	11.1	11.1	11.2	11.5	6.8	6.7	2.0	1.7	-1.6	3.8	4.5	6.5
Government	4.7	4.4	7.0	6.8	7.0	7.3	7.3	7.0	6.8	5.0	10.5	3.2	1.9	1.4	2.6	.5	1.0
G.D.P.	100.0	100.0	100.0	100.0	100.0	100.0	100.0	100.0	100.0	~	~	~	~	~	~	~	~

SOURCE: IDB-SPTF, 1987, table 11-7.

Table 3326

AGRICULTURAL SECTOR: VALUE ADDED, DISTRIBUTION, AND GROWTH, 19 LR, 1961-84

(%)

	Regional Distribution			Proportion of GDP			Average Annual Growth			Annual Variation		
Country	1961-70	1971-80	1981-84	1961-70	1971-80	1981-84	1961-70	1971-780	1981	1982	1983	1984[‡]
A. ARGENTINA	14.2	13.1	12.2	14.4	13.3	15.0	2.5	2.1	2.4	7.3	.7	2.6
B. BOLIVIA	.9	1.0	.8	20.5	17.5	18.1	3.0	3.9	7.0	-2.2	-22.0	3.5
C. BRAZIL	25.4	27.3	29.3	15.1	10.2	9.9	3.2	5.5	6.4	-2.5	2.2	4.3
D. CHILE	3.1	2.5	2.5	9.2	8.6	9.0	2.2	2.7	5.3	-2.3	-2.8	7.3
E. COLOMBIA	8.5	9.0	9.2	27.1	23.4	22.5	3.7	4.4	3.2	-1.9	1.8	2.0
F. COSTA RICA	1.0	1.1	1.0	24.4	20.6	20.0	5.2	2.6	5.1	-4.7	3.9	8.0
H. DOMINICAN REP.	1.7	1.7	1.7	26.0	18.5	17.2	1.7	3.5	5.5	4.3	3.4	-.2
I. ECUADOR	2.2	2.3	2.1	26.8	18.6	14.7	4.3	3.0	5.6	1.5	-14.3	11.6
J. EL SALVADOR	1.6	1.5	1.2	28.0	24.3	25.9	4.1	3.2	-6.4	-4.7	-3.2	1.2
K. GUATEMALA	3.1	3.6	3.4	28.7	27.0	25.1	4.5	4.7	1.2	-3.0	-2.7	.5
L. HAITI	1.1	.9	.7	44.6	38.2	32.3	.8	1.6	-1.5	-4.2	-.8	1.4
M. HONDURAS	1.2	1.2	1.2	35.9	31.3	30.4	5.6	3.2	2.2	-.8	3.3	2.4
N. MEXICO	20.8	20.4	21.0	14.3	10.4	9.2	3.9	3.5	6.1	-.6	2.9	2.4
O. NICARAGUA	1.2	1.2	.9	25.1	24.3	24.3	6.9	.6	10.1	2.9	6.3	-5.3
P. PANAMA	.7	.7	.6	16.7	12.5	10.0	5.5	1.7	8.3	-1.5	5.0	-1.2
Q. PARAGUAY	1.4[a]	1.8	2.1	30.3[b]	28.8	26.0	2.0[a]	6.8	10.1	.4	-2.4	5.7
R. PERU	5.1	4.3	3.9	17.8	14.1	14.0	4.3	0	9.9	3.0	-10.2	9.4
S. URUGUAY	1.6	1.2	1.1	13.9	12.2	12.1	3.8	.9	5.5	-11.4	2.6	-5.0
T. VENEZUELA	3.8	4.0	3.8	7.0	6.3	6.6	5.6	3.1	-1.9	3.6	.4	2.0
LATIN AMERICA[1]	100.0	100.0	100.0	15.5	12.1	11.6	3.6	3.6	4.9	-.3	.6	3.3

1. Includes Bahamas, Barbados, Guyana, Jamaica, Suriname, and Trinidad and Tobago.

a. 1963-70.

SOURCE: IDB-SPTF, 1986, Part Two, table 5.

Table 3327

MANUFACTURING SECTOR: VALUE ADDED, DISTRIBUTION, AND GROWTH, 19 LR, 1961-84

(%)

Country	Regional Distribution			Proportion of GDP			Average Annual Growth					
	1961-70	1971-80	1981-84	1961-70	1971-80	1981-84	1961-70	1971-80	1981	1982	1983	1984[‡]
A. ARGENTINA	17.4	13.0	9.3	26.1	27.1	23.5	5.5	1.8	-16.0	-4.7	10.9	4.3
B. BOLIVIA	.4	.4	.3	13.6	15.3	14.9	6.4	5.8	-3.8	-15.3	-7.5	-6.6
C. BRAZIL	31.2	38.5	40.3	27.2	29.4	27.9	7.0	9.2	-6.5	.2	-6.3	6.0
D. CHILE	5.6	3.5	2.8	24.3	23.4	20.2	5.4	1.8	2.6	-21.6	3.9	10.3
E. COLOMBIA	4.4	4.2	4.2	20.8	22.8	21.0	6.0	6.0	-2.6	-1.4	.5	6.3
F. COSTA RICA[1]	.5	.6	.6	16.4	21.0	21.7	9.0	7.5	-.5	-11.4	1.2	10.0
H. DOMINICAN REP.	.7	.8	.9	15.3	18.6	18.1	8.8	6.8	2.7	5.2	1.7	-3.0
I. ECUADOR	.8	1.0	1.4	14.9	17.4	20.2	9.4	9.5	7.5	6.2	-2.8	-1.5
J. EL SALVADOR	.7	.6	.4	17.1	18.7	17.0	8.2	3.1	-10.4	-8.4	-1.0	1.8
K. GUATEMALA	1.1	1.0	1.0	14.5	15.9	15.9	7.7	6.3	-3.1	-5.2	-1.9	.4
L. HAITI	.2	.2	.2	14.0	15.5	16.9	.7	8.6	-11.9	-3.6	5.6	3.0
M. HONDURAS	.3	.3	.3	12.7	14.9	15.2	7.1	5.9	.8	-7.2	-3.4	4.8
N. MEXICO	21.6	23.2	26.8	21.9	24.4	24.1	9.2	7.2	7.0	-2.9	-7.3	4.7
O. NICARAGUA	.6	.5	.5	19.1	22.2	24.5	10.2	3.5	2.8	-1.7	4.6	.2
P. PANAMA	.3	.3	.3	11.7	11.5	9.4	10.9	3.7	-3.3	2.2	-2.1	-.1
Q. PARAGUAY	.5[a]	.5	.7	15.6[a]	17.6	16.5	4.6[a]	8.4	4.3	-3.7	-4.2	4.1
R. PERU	4.4	3.7	3.0	22.7	24.9	22.3	6.2	3.9	-.1	-2.7	-17.2	1.7
S. URUGUAY[1]	1.9	1.2	.9	23.3	24.5	20.8	1.6	3.0	-4.6	-16.8	-7.0	4.0
T. VENEZUELA	5.8	5.2	5.3	15.7	16.9	18.7	7.6	5.2	-2.5	4.1	-1.7	2.8
LATIN AMERICA[2]	100.0	100.0	100.0	22.9	24.9	23.8	6.9	6.5	-2.8	-2.1	-4.3	4.8

1. Includes mining.
2. Includes Bahamas, Barbados, Guyana, Jamaica, Suriname, and Trinidad and Tobago.

SOURCE: IDB-SPTF, 1985, Part Two, table 7.

Table 3328

SHARES OF AGRICULTURAL GDP IN TOTAL GDP, 19 LR, 1950–75
(%)

Country	Agricultural GDP/Total GDP				Agricultural GDP PI/Nonagricultural GDP PI			
	1950-52	1959-61	1969-71	1973-75	1950-52	1959-61	1969-71	1973-75
A. ARGENTINA	16.5	15.5	12.8	12.0	60.4	73.6	75.1	76.9

Continued in SALA, 24-3328.

Table 3329

AGRICULTURE[1] SHARE IN GDP, 19 LR, 1920–85[a]
(%)[b]

Year	A. ARGENTINA	B. BOLIVIA	C. BRAZIL	D. CHILE	E. COLOMBIA	F. COSTA RICA	G. CUBA	H. DOMINICAN REPUBLIC	I. ECUADOR	J. EL SALVADOR	K. GUATEMALA	L. HAITI
1920	30.0	~	22.8	~	~	~	~	~	~	~	~	~
1930	22.6	~	23.5	~	52.4	~	~	~	~	~	~	~
1940	23.2	~	21.4	13.0	44.7	~	~	~	38.3	~	~	~
1950	16.2	25.4	16.8	11.6	37.7	38.4	~	34.5	42.1	40.9	35.5	52.2
1960	14.9	24.5	13.4	9.8	32.7	29.4	~	33.9	39.0	36.0	33.4	49.2
1970	12.9	19.7	10.0	7.9	28.6	25.0	~	25.8	29.7	30.6	30.1	50.8
1980	13.7	17.1	7.3	7.7	25.4	18.3	~	18.6	21.1	28.0	28.0	42.0
1981‡	15.2	18.4	8.1	6.9	25.6	19.8	~	18.3	15.3	29.9	27.7	42.0
1982‡	15.2	21.7	7.8	8.3	23.9	21.5	~	20.5	15.8	27.5	28.0	43.5
1983‡	15.4	17.4	8.4	8.2	24.0	21.5	~	19.2	13.8	29.5	27.8	34.2
1984‡	~	19.0	9.5	7.4	23.5	21.2	~	19.0	14.9	29.5	27.6	33.3
1985‡	10.9	19.6	14.3	8.3	18.5	19.8	~	20.4	11.5	26.6	25.1	33.2

Year	M. HONDURAS	N. MEXICO	O. NICARAGUA	P. PANAMA	Q. PARAGUAY	R. PERU	S. URUGUAY	T. VENEZUELA	LATIN AMERICA[2]	UNITED STATES
1920	~	~	~	~	~	~	~	~	~	~
1930	55.2	18.7	~	~	~	~	~	~	~	~
1940	50.5	19.7	~	~	49.2	~	16.3	19.2	~	~
1950	44.8	19.4	36.6	32.6	40.8	25.5	13.5	9.2	25.1	5.5
1960	32.8	16.2	29.5	26.1	39.2	24.4	11.0	7.9	19.7	4.4
1970	32.5	12.7	27.0	20.0	34.3	20.3	12.9	7.6	17.1	3.2
1980	27.0	9.4	26.8	17.0	30.0	13.3	9.8	7.0	13.8	2.7
1981‡	27.5	9.1	28.0	16.3	29.5	12.8	10.1	7.0	11.2[c]	~
1982‡	28.1	9.1	28.0	16.0	29.2	13.2	10.7	6.8	~	~
1983‡	28.6	10.0	28.2	10.4	28.7	13.2	11.1	6.6	~	~
1984‡	29.0	9.9	26.4	10.0	29.5	14.1	12.1	7.7	~	~
1985‡	27.5	8.7	24.6	9.1	31.4	10.1	12.3	6.9	~	~

1. Includes hunting, fishing, and forestry.
2. For coverage, see table 3321, note 1.

a. For yearly data since 1900, see SALA, 20-2205ff. and 22-2305ff.
b. Calculations based upon constant dollars, factor cost.
c. For 1979 from ECLA-AE, 1980, p. 119.

SOURCE: Latin American data calculated from ECLA-SHCAL, pp. 74ff.; and for 1960-85 from ECLA-S, 1980-85, table 3, by country. U.S. data calculated from USDC sources given in SALA, 25-3322, note 2.

Table 3330

MINING AND QUARRYING SHARE IN GDP, 19 LR, 1920-85[a]
(%)[b]

Year	A. ARGENTINA	B. BOLIVIA	C. BRAZIL	D. CHILE	E. COLOMBIA	F. COSTA RICA[1]	H. DOMINICAN REPUBLIC	I. ECUADOR	J. EL SALVADOR	K. GUATEMALA
1920	.3	~	.6	~	~	~	~	~	~	~
1930	.3	~	.4	~	3.0	~	~	~	~	~
1940	.9	~	.5	19.4	3.0	~	~	2.2	~	~
1950	.7	19.8	.4	12.4	2.4	~	.3	1.2	1.0	.2
1960	1.3	12.3	.5	11.1	2.7	~	1.9	1.4	.2	.2
1970	2.2	8.0	.8	11.7	2.1	~	1.7	1.2	.2	.1
1980	2.5	5.5	.9	12.2	1.1	~	4.9	4.7	.1	.4
1981‡	2.6	5.2	.9	10.7	1.2	~	5.0	5.0	.1	.4
1982‡	2.7	5.2	1.0	13.9	1.0	~	3.5	5.2	.2	.4
1983‡	2.8	5.8	.9	13.6	1.1	~	4.4	~	.2	.3
1984‡	2.7	5.1	1.0	13.4	1.3	~	4.7	.7	.2	.4
1985‡	2.7	12.6	1.1	10.3	4.1	~	5.3	8.3	.1	.3

Year	L. HAITI	M. HONDURAS	N. MEXICO	O. NICARAGUA	P. PANAMA	Q. PARAGUAY	R. PERU	S. URUGUAY[1]	T. VENEZUELA	LATIN AMERICA[2]	UNITED STATES
1920	~	~	~	~	~	~	~	~	~	~	~
1930	~	2.0	8.5	~	~	~	~	~	~	~	~
1940	~	3.1	6.0	~	~	~	~	~	20.3	4.3	2.1
1950	3.3	2.3	4.1	1.5	.2	~	7.2	~	27.3	4.0	1.8
1960	5.0	1.9	2.4	1.2	.3	~	11.2	~	27.5	4.6	1.8
1970	1.7	2.3	4.1	.7	.3	~	7.2	~	22.6	4.3	1.5
1980	.9	1.8	3.1	.2	.3	~	8.1	~	8.8	3.5[c]	~
1981‡	.5	1.8	3.4	.2	.3	~	7.3	~	8.8	~	~
1982‡	1.0	2.1	3.7	.1	.2	~	8.0	~	.7	~	~
1983‡	~	2.1	3.8	.2	.3	~	8.4	~	.6	~	~
1984‡	#	2.2	3.7	.1	.2	~	8.2	~	~	~	~
1985‡	.1	2.2	7.9	.4	.1	~	11.9	~	.4	~	~

1. Included in table 3331.
2. For coverage, see table 3321, note 1.

a. For yearly data since 1900, see SALA, 20-2205ff. and 22-2305ff.
b. Calculations based upon constant dollars, factor cost.
c. Includes petroleum refining.

SOURCE: See table 3329.

Table 3331

MANUFACTURING SHARE IN GDP, 19 LR, 1920-85[a]
(%)[b]

Year	A. ARGENTINA	B. BOLIVIA	C. BRAZIL	D. CHILE	E. COLOMBIA	F. COSTA RICA[1]	H. DOMINICAN REPUBLIC	I. ECUADOR	J. EL SALVADOR	K. GUATEMALA	UNITED STATES
1920	17.4	~	12.1	~	~	~	~	~	~	~	~
1930	20.5	~	12.0	~	5.5	~	~	~	~	~	~
1940	22.7	~	15.0	11.8	~	~	~	16.0	~	~	~
1950	23.7	12.2	21.2	23.1	14.5	11.5	8.3	16.0	12.9	11.1	24.7
1960	26.5	11.6	26.3	24.8	16.7	12.5	12.4	15.7	13.9	11.9	23.5
1970	28.0	14.5	28.4	27.2	17.5	15.1	14.6	16.8	17.6	14.6	24.2
1980	25.3	15.4	30.2	24.2	18.3	18.1	16.7	20.1	16.3	15.6	24.3
1981‡	22.1	15.4	29.0	21.8	17.6	18.4	16.6	23.0	15.2	15.3	~
1982‡	22.4	14.0	28.6	20.2	16.9	17.7	16.3	22.5	15.5	14.6	~
1983‡	24.1	14.2	26.1	20.8	15.8	16.5	16.8	~	16.1	14.5	~
1984‡	24.8	12.6	26.1	21.7	16.7	17.6	16.5		16.1	14.7	~
1985‡	23.5	9.8	26.4	20.1	22.5	18.7	14.2	26.7	14.9	16.7	~

Year	L. HAITI	M. HONDURAS	N. MEXICO	O. NICARAGUA	P. PANAMA	Q. PARAGUAY	R. PERU	S. URUGUAY[1]	T. VENEZUELA	LATIN AMERICA[2]
1920	~	~	~	~	~	~	~	~	~	~
1930	~	4.7	13.8	~	~	~	~	~	~	~
1940	~	6.8	16.9	~	~	16.0	~	17.3	13.6	16.6
1950	8.1	9.1	18.8	10.8	8.2	15.9	14.2	20.3	11.2	18.7
1960	8.9	15.3	19.3	13.0	11.8	15.1	17.1	24.3	14.0	21.3
1970	9.8	13.8	23.4	19.2	15.8	17.3	21.1	23.1	11.2	25.1[c]
1980	12.5	16.4	23.8	20.6	12.0	15.8	21.2	23.9	14.1	25.4[c]
1981‡	13.2	16.4	24.0	19.3	11.4	16.1	20.2	23.5	14.8	~
1982‡	12.1	14.4	23.5	18.5	9.7	15.7	19.6	21.5	14.5	~
1983‡	18.1	15.5	22.9	21.2	9.6	15.5	18.2	18.8	14.8	~
1984‡	17.4	13.9	23.4	21.7	9.3	15.1	17.8	20.8	18.7	~
1985‡	16.1	15.3	22.6	25.4	8.7	15.5	26.1	26.4	19.3	~

1. Includes mining and quarrying.
2. For coverage, see table 3321, note 1.

a. For yearly data since 1900, see SALA, 20-2205ff. and 22-2305ff.
b. Calculations based upon constant dollars, factor cost.
c. For 1979 from ECLA-S, 1980, p. 119.

SOURCE: See table 3329.

Table 3332
CONSTRUCTION SHARE IN GDP, 19 LR, 1920-85ᵃ
(%)ᵇ

Year	A. ARGENTINA	B. BOLIVIA	C. BRAZIL	D. CHILE	E. COLOMBIA	F. COSTA RICA	H. DOMINICAN REPUBLIC	I. ECUADOR	J. EL SALVADOR	K. GUATEMALA
1920	1.5	~	~	~	3.0	~	~	~	~	~
1930	5.5	~	~	~	4.5	~	~	~	~	~
1940	3.7	~	7.5	4.2	4.0	~	~	1.3	2.4	4.2
1950	5.3	1.6	9.2	4.4	4.7	4.7	3.8	1.3	3.3	2.7
1960	4.8	3.8	8.3	4.4	5.5	5.0	3.0	2.6	3.0	2.2
1970	6.4	4.4	5.8	4.2	3.5	4.7	5.5	4.4	4.6	4.0
1980	7.6	4.3	6.9	3.3	3.9	6.9	7.7	5.7	3.3	4.4
1981‡	7.8	3.9	6.7	4.5	4.4	5.4	7.4	3.4	3.3	4.2
1982‡	6.1	1.8	6.6	3.9	4.5	4.2	6.9	3.3	3.8	4.1
1983‡	4.7	1.8	5.1	3.9	4.5	4.0	7.6	2.8	~	~
1984‡	3.6	3.4	5.0	3.9	5.0	4.7	7.8	2.9	3.5	2.9
1985‡	4.1	3.3	4.0	5.6	~	4.2	6.4	6.2	3.4	2.7

Year	L. HAITI	M. HONDURAS	N. MEXICO	O. NICARAGUA	P. PANAMA	Q. PARAGUAY	R. PERU	S. URUGUAY	T. VENEZUELA	LATIN AMERICA[1]	UNITED STATES
1920	~	~	~	~	~	~	~	~	~	~	~
1930	~	3.5	3.2	~	~	~	~	~	~	~	~
1940	~	4.5	4.1	~	~	1.3	~	3.8	3.5	~	~
1950	~	5.4	4.8	1.2	4.2	1.3	6.7	5.0	6.5	4.4	5.5
1960	~	4.5	5.5	2.2	5.7	2.3	5.3	5.4	5.4	5.6	6.3
1970	2.3	4.8	5.7	3.5	6.3	3.0	3.2	3.9	4.2	5.5	5.0
1980	4.9	4.9	5.9	2.1	6.1	8.4	3.7	7.0	6.8	5.2	3.7
1981‡	5.5	4.6	5.7	2.6	5.5	8.7	3.8	6.5	6.1	5.7ᶜ	~
1982‡	4.5	4.9	5.1	2.5	9.3	8.4	4.0	5.8	5.8	~	~
1983‡	5.8	4.8	4.9	1.8	6.6	8.2	3.5	4.8	4.8	~	~
1984‡	5.8	5.6	5.5	2.0	5.4	7.5	3.3	3.3	4.1	~	~
1985‡	6.3	5.4	~	3.2	4.9	5.4	2.4	2.9	2.7	~	~

1. For coverage, see table 3321, note 1.
a. For yearly data since 1900, see SALA, 20-2205ff. and 22-2305ff.
b. Calculations based upon constant dollars, factor cost.
c. For 1977 from ECLA-ESDER, I, p. 22.

SOURCE: See table 3329.

Table 3333

UTILITIES[1] SHARE IN GDP, 19 LR, 1920-85ᵃ

(%)ᵇ

Year	A. ARGENTINA	B. BOLIVIA	C. BRAZIL	D. CHILE	E. COLOMBIA	F. COSTA RICA	H. DOMINICAN REPUBLIC	I. ECUADOR	J. EL SALVADOR	K. GUATEMALA
1920	.5	?	?	?	?	?	?	?	?	?
1930	.5	?	?	?	?	?	?	?	?	?
1940	.7	?	1.4	1.0	.7	1.3	?	.5	?	?
1950	.8	1.3	1.9	.9	.7	1.4	.3	.6	1.0	.3
1960	1.2	1.3	2.0	1.3	1.1	2.0	.9	1.3	1.6	.5
1970	2.3	1.4	2.4	1.4	1.5	2.4	1.3	1.3	2.7	.9
1980	3.5	1.6	3.3	2.2	1.8	2.7	1.9	1.8	2.8	1.3
1981‡	3.7	1.8	3.5	2.5	1.9	3.0	2.0	1.2	3.0	1.3
1982‡	4.1	2.1	3.6	2.9	1.6	3.6	1.8	1.2	3.0	1.3
1983‡	4.3	2.3	4.8	3.0	1.8	3.6	1.8	1.3	3.2	1.3
1984‡	4.4	2.4	3.6	3.0	1.7	3.4	2.0	1.3	3.2	1.3
1985‡	3.4	.9	2.1	2.5	1.5	2.8	.5	1.3	2.5	1.4

Year	L. HAITI	M. HONDURAS	N. MEXICO	O. NICARAGUA	P. PANAMA	Q. PARAGUAY[2]	R. PERU	S. URUGUAY	T. VENEZUELA	LATIN AMERICA[3]	UNITED STATES
1920	?	?	?	?	?	?	?	?	?	?	?
1930	?	?	?	?	?	?	?	?	?	?	?
1940	?	?	.5	?	?	.1	?	.5	.2	?	?
1950	.3	.2	.4	.4	.8	.3	?	.7	.3	.8	1.3
1960	.8	.7	.8	1.1	1.3	.7	.8	1.1	.9	.9	2.0
1970	1.3	1.4	1.0	1.7	2.0	1.2	.9	1.5	1.7	1.2	2.4
1980	1.7	1.6	1.3	3.1	3.6	2.5	1.5	1.7	2.8	1.8	2.4
1981‡	2.1	1.6	1.3	3.0	3.8	2.8	1.5	1.9	3.1	2.3ᶜ	?
1982‡	2.1	2.2	1.4	3.1	3.3	3.2	1.6	2.0	3.3	?	?
1983‡	.8	2.2	1.5	2.0	3.7	3.2	1.7	2.0	3.5	?	?
1984‡	.9	2.3	1.6	1.4	3.6	3.1	1.8	1.8	3.9	?	?
1985‡	.8	2.2	1.2	1.9	3.6	2.8	-.8	1.9	1.6	?	?

1. Includes electricity, gas, water, and sewerage.

2. Excludes gas before 1970.

3. For coverage, see table 3321, note. 1.

a. For yearly data since 1900, see SALA, 20-2205ff. and 22-2305ff.

b. Calculations based upon constant dollars, factor cost.

c. For 1977 from ECLA-ESDER, I., p. 22.

SOURCE: See table 3329.

Table 3334

TRANSPORT AND COMMUNICATION SHARE IN GDP, 19 LR, 1920-85[a]
(%)[b]

Year	A. ARGENTINA	B. BOLIVIA	C. BRAZIL	D. CHILE	E. COLOMBIA	F. COSTA RICA	H. DOMINICAN REPUBLIC	I. ECUADOR	J. EL SALVADOR	K. GUATEMALA
1920	7.4	~	2.7	~	~	~	~	~	~	~
1930	9.6	~	3.2	~	~	~	~	~	~	~
1940	9.2	~	3.7	~	~	~	~	4.1	3.7	2.3
1950	11.3	6.2	4.5	3.4	~	3.1	5.7	5.1	4.5	3.0
1960	10.7	9.6	5.3	3.8	6.5	4.5	6.1	4.7	5.3	3.5
1970	11.3	8.1	5.7	5.7	7.4	4.8	8.6	7.2	5.9	4.4
1980	10.9	11.6	6.6	6.3	9.7	7.5	9.2	7.1	5.4	4.5
1981‡	11.1	12.8	6.6	7.5	9.5	8.0	9.3	9.3	5.7	4.4
1982‡	11.4	12.5	6.8	7.6	12.0	8.4	9.1	9.6	5.7	4.3
1983‡	11.3	12.8	8.6	7.4	11.9	8.2	8.9	~	~	~
1984‡	11.6	12.2	7.5	7.4	12.1	7.6	8.9	9.3	6.0	4.4
1985‡	3.4	7.4	5.6	4.9	9.0	4.3	5.5	7.6	3.7	4.4

Year	L. HAITI	M. HONDURAS	N. MEXICO	O. NICARAGUA	P. PANAMA	Q. PARAGUAY	R. PERU	S. URUGUAY	T. VENEZUELA	LATIN AMERICA[1]	UNITED STATES
1920	~	~	~	~	~	~	~	~	~	~	~
1930	~	~	2.9	~	~	~	~	~	~	~	~
1940	~	~	2.7	~	~	~	~	11.1	~	~	~
1950	1.6	5.3	2.8	3.5	3.3	4.0	~	10.2	15.6	5.3	6.8
1960	2.1	8.2	2.7	6.0	4.0	4.5	5.8	9.6	10.8	6.4	5.8
1970	2.4	7.8	5.0	5.8	5.6	3.9	7.9	8.7	10.9	6.1	6.4
1980	3.2	9.6	7.3	5.7	11.4	4.2	7.6	8.7	12.9	6.1	7.3
1981‡	3.2	9.6	8.0	5.4	12.1	4.7	7.9	9.1	13.2	6.6[c]	~
1982‡	3.3	7.5	7.8	5.7	20.4	4.6	~	8.8	14.0	~	~
1983‡	2.1	7.1	7.8	6.0	26.9	4.6	7.6	8.5	~	~	~
1984‡	2.4	7.8	7.9	6.0	24.6	4.5	~	6.7	~	~	~
1985‡	1.8	7.1	6.6	5.0	23.6	4.3	5.9	5.7	9.7	~	~

1. For coverage, see table 3321, note 1.
a. For yearly data since 1900, see SALA, 20-2205ff. and 22-2305ff.
b. Calculations based upon constant dollars, factor cost.
c. For 1977 from ECLA-ESDER, I., p. 22.

SOURCE: See table 3329.

Table 3335

MANUFACTURING REAL RATES OF GROWTH, 18 LC, 1969–86ᵃ

(PC)

Country	1969	1970	1971	1972	1973	1974	1975	1976	1977	1978	1979	1980	1981	1982	1983	1984	1985	1986‡
A. ARGENTINA	25.0	#	4.8	4.5	4.3	8.3	-3.8	-4.0	8.3	-11.5	13.0	-3.8	-16.0	-4.7	10.9	4.3	-10.5	12.8
B. BOLIVIA	~	~	3.6	8.1	5.0	11.3	6.1	8.3	6.9	4.6	2.8	-1.0	-3.8	-15.3	-7.5	-6.6	-9.2	8.1
C. BRAZIL	~	~	60.7	11.1	14.0	17.5	7.5	18.1	2.4	6.9	7.5	7.0	-6.5	.2	-6.3	6.0	8.3	11.3
D. CHILE	~	~	12.9	2.5	-7.4	-2.7	-26.0	7.4	8.6	7.9	8.8	5.4	2.6	-21.6	3.9	10.3	1.2	8.0
E. COLOMBIA	~	~	7.6	11.3	8.9	8.1	1.1	4.3	2.0	10.0	5.5	1.7	-2.6	-1.4	.5	6.3	2.3	7.7
H. DOMINICAN REP.	19.9	18.8	13.1	8.0	13.4	4.7	7.3	6.8	5.7	-.2	4.8	5.0	2.7	5.2	1.7	-3.0	-5.0	3.0
I. ECUADOR	9.6	9.8	5.0	9.2	9.2	10.4	15.2	13.2	11.9	8.2	8.4	6.4	7.5	6.2	-2.8	-1.5	-1.8	.8
J. EL SALVADOR	.7	3.8	7.1	3.8	7.2	5.7	2.5	11.1	5.2	4.4	-3.9	-16.0	-10.4	-8.4	-1.0	1.8	3.8	2.3
K. GUATEMALA	7.1	3.7	7.1	5.6	8.1	4.6	-1.7	10.4	10.9	6.4	5.6	5.5	-3.1	-5.2	-1.9	.4	-.2	.3
L. HAITI	.4	-4.6	14.6	7.4	-.6	13.1	-8.3	19.4	11.1	5.4	8.9	12.8	-11.9	-3.6	5.6	3.0	-3.0	-2.8
M. HONDURAS	8.9	6.9	4.7	3.9	3.8	-1.0	2.6	10.3	9.8	9.7	8.1	7.9	.8	-7.2	-3.4	4.8	2.3	1.6
N. MEXICO	6.9	9.7	4.8	10.0	9.9	6.0	5.0	5.4	3.8	9.3	10.7	7.1	7.0	-2.9	7.3	4.7	5.8	-5.6
O. NICARAGUA	~	~	~	~	~	~	~	~	~	~	~	~	2.8	-1.7	4.6	.2	-4.7	1.6
P. PANAMA	9.1	6.9	6.3	5.2	5.6	1.3	-3.3	2.7	.7	2.0	11.0	4.1	-3.3	2.2	-2.1	-.1	1.9	2.0
Q. PARAGUAY	4.9	8.0	1.6	11.0	8.4	7.4	-1.8	5.5	20.1	9.8	7.7	12.6	4.3	-3.7	-4.2	4.1	5.0	-1.8
R. PERU	~	~	6.9	1.1	6.4	10.0	4.5	4.3	-5.0	-3.5	4.5	5.2	-.1	-2.7	-17.2	1.7	4.1	17.8
S. URUGUAY	#	#	.7	1.4	-.8	~	~	~	~	~	~	~	4.6ᵇ	-16.8ᵇ	-7.0ᵇ	4.0ᵇ	-1.6ᵇ	12.1ᵇ
T. VENEZUELA	~	~	1.7	~	~	~	~	~	~	~	~	~	2.5	4.1	-1.7	2.8	2.2	3.1
UNITED STATES	3.5	-5.3	1.7	9.3	11.4	-4.0	-7.5	9.2	6.5	5.4	3.1	-4.0	3.0	-7.2	~	~	~	~

a. For prior years, see SALA, 25-3335.
b. Includes mining.

SOURCE: IMF-IFS-S, No. 8, 1984; and for 1981–84 data, IDB-STPF, 1985, Part Two, table 7; IDB-SPTF, 1987, table 11.

Table 3336

AGRICULTURE, FORESTRY, AND FISHING REAL RATES OF GROWTH, 19 LC, 1969–86[a]

(PC)

Country	1969	1970	1971	1972	1973	1974	1975	1976	1977	1978	1979	1980	1981	1982	1983	1984	1985	1986[‡]
A. ARGENTINA	#	#	#	10.0	9.1	#	#	#	8.3	#	#	-7.7	8.3	7.0	2.1	3.6	-1.7	-.9
B. BOLIVIA	~	~	5.9	5.9	4.6	3.7	7.8	5.0	-.6	2.1	2.9	2.0	7.0	-2.2	-22.1	18.7	3.0	-1.9
C. BRAZIL	~	~	11.8	5.3	5.0	4.8	4.5	4.3	12.5	-3.7	7.7	3.6	6.8	-2.5	2.2	3.2	8.8	-7.3
D. CHILE	~	~	#	-8.3	-9.1	25.0	4.0	#	7.7	-3.6	7.4	3.4	5.3	-2.3	-.1	7.5	5.6	8.8
E. COLOMBIA	10.4	~	1.3	7.6	2.4	4.6	6.6	3.1	3.0	7.8	5.4	1.7	3.2	-1.3	2.0	1.8	.2	2.0
F. COSTA RICA	~	4.1	4.6	5.4	5.6	-1.7	3.1	.5	2.2	6.6	.5	-.5	1.2	-4.9	4.4	10.1	-2.8	#
H. DOMINICAN REP.	~	~	~	~	~	#	-2.4	7.3	1.9	4.6	1.1	4.8	5.6	3.8	3.5	-.2	-4.5	-2.7
I. ECUADOR	6.2	-9.1	5.0	4.0	1.0	9.0	2.3	2.9	2.4	-3.9	3.6	5.2	4.0	1.1	-14.9	8.9	4.8	4.4
J. EL SALVADOR	3.7	6.5	3.8	1.4	1.8	10.3	6.5	-8.1	3.6	14.1	3.5	-4.8	-10.1	-3.4	#	3.4	-1.1	-2.1
K. GUATEMALA	2.4	5.8	6.9	9.7	5.2	6.4	2.5	4.5	3.8	3.2	2.8	1.6	1.4	-2.0	-2.5	1.5	-.8	-.2
L. HAITI	1.8	.7	3.1	-.3	2.3	2.4	3.8	1.0	-6.0	1.8	4.4	-1.4	-2.2	-4.1	3.1	3.7	.5	2.6
M. HONDURAS	-2.8	-1.5	9.1	1.1	4.7	-8.7	-9.3	9.3	5.6	8.0	7.8	3.1	.9	.1	-.1	1.2	1.9	1.5
N. MEXICO	#	6.1	5.6	18	3.4	1.7	3.3	#	7.9	5.9	-1.4	7.0	5.3	-.1	3.4	2.5	3.8	-2.1
O. NICARAGUA	~	~	~	~	~	~	~	~	~	~	~	~	10.1	2.0	11.7	-5.4	-4.9	-5.4
P. PANAMA	5.2	-.6	8.1	-3.7	1.3	-5.7	7.4	5.0	4.8	8.0	-4.2	-1.7	2.8	#	3.1	1.5	4.9	-2.0
Q. PARAGUAY	2.6	2.1	6.5	6.2	6.4	9.8	8.2	3.7	11.1	5.9	6.7	9.2	6.7	-3.0	-4.8	5.9	4.6	-5.9
R. PERU	~	~	#	-6.8	-1.8	5.6	#	1.8	#	#	3.4	-5.0	10.5	2.8	-11.5	12.9	2.7	3.7
S. URUGUAY	50.0	#	-6.3	-10.5	2.6	3.3	5.6	1.9	3.2	-6.7	-.4	16.2	1.0	-6.8	-2.6	-6.8	4.6	3.2
T. VENEZUELA	~	~	~	~	~	~	~	~	~	~	~	~	-1.9	3.6	#	.8	5.7	6.8
UNITED STATES	2.4	4.9	4.6	-1.0	1.5	.5	2.6	-4.9	1.9	1.0	5.4	1.5	15.5	-4.4	~	~	~	~

a. For prior years, see SALA, 25-3336.

SOURCE: IMF-IFS-S, No. 8, 1984, pp. 38–41; IDB-STPF, 1984, table 9, p. 423; IDB-SPTF, 1987, table 9.

Table 3337

HOUSING, DEFENSE, GOVERNMENT, AND OTHER SERVICES SHARE IN GDP, 1920–79

A. ARGENTINA

Year	Housing	Defense and Government Services	Other Services
1920	2.7	9.8	9.0
1925	2.4	9.2	8.6

a. Included in "Other Services."

Continued in SALA 20, 2206-2224.

Table 3338

EXPENDITURE ON GDP,[1] 19 LC, 1960–73

(%)[2]

Country	Year	Government Final Consumption Expenditure	Private Final Consumption Expenditure	Increase in Stocks	Gross Fixed Capital Formation	Goods and Services	
						Exports	Less Imports
A. ARGENTINA	1960	9	71	1	21	10	11
	1963	9	72	1	18	11	9

Continued in SALA, 17-2206

Table 3339

GDP, NATIONAL CURRENCY, AND CURRENT PRICES,[1] 18 LC, 1935–66

(M)

Year	A. ARGENTINA[3]	B. BOLIVIA	C. BRAZIL[4]	D. CHILE[2]	E. COLOMBIA	F. COSTA RICA	H. DOMINICAN REP.	I. ECUADOR	J. EL SALVADOR
1935	9,300.0	~	~	~	~	~	~	~	~
1936	9,800.0	~	~	~	~	~	~	~	~

Continued in SALA, 17-2205.

Table 3340

ARGENTINA EXPENDITURE ON GDP AND GNP,[1] 1976–86

(M NC)

Category	1976	1977	1978	1979	1980	1981	1982	1983	1984	1985	1986
Exports[2]	.1	.3	.6	1.3	1.9	5.2	19.9	100.2	~	~	~
Government Consumption	.1	.2	.6	1.6	3.7	7.2	15.4	88.4	~	~	~
Gross Fixed Capital Formation	.2	.6	1.3	3.3	6.3	10.2	24.4	121.8	~	~	~
Increase in Stocks	#	#	#	#	.2	-.3	2.3	.6	~	~	~
Private Consumption	.4	1.3	3.2	9.4	18.8	37.8	100.8	438.6	~	~	~
Less: Imports[2]	-.1	-.2	-.4	-1.2	-2.6	-5.4	-15.1	-66.9	~	~	~
Gross Domestic Product	.8	2.1	5.2	14.3	28.3	54.8	147.6	682.7	~	~	~
Net Factor Income from Abroad	#	#	-.1	-.1	-.3	-2.4	-12.9	-64.4	~	~	~
Gross National Expenditure = GNP	.7	2.1	5.2	14.1	28.1	52.4	134.7	618.2	~	~	~

1. Cf. SALA, 18-2208; for historical series comparing GDP to GNP, see SALA, 19-2202.
2. Exports and imports include nonfactor services as well as goods.

SOURCE: IMF-IFS-Y, 1987.

Table 3341

BOLIVIA EXPENDITURE ON GDP AND GNP, 1976–86

(T NC through 1984; M NC since 1985)

Category	1976	1977	1978	1979	1980	1981	1982	1983	1984	1985	1986
Exports[1]	12.7	14.5	17.0	21.8	31.5	37.5	155.7	401.4	4,908.4	538	~
Government Consumption	6.7	8.6	9.5	13.6	15.9	19.6	40.1	134.1	1,737.2	224	~
Gross Fixed Capital Formation	10.7	12.4	16.4	17.4	17.5	21.6	59.6	204.6	2,805.4	323	~
Increase in Stocks	1.3	1.1	2.2	1.4	.5	3.9	.8	-54.4	-452.1	-85	~
Private Consumption	39.1	44.9	52.7	60.7	82.3	105.0	275.9	1,125.9	16,361.1	2,248	~
Less: Imports[1]	-14.0	-16.4	-22.6	-24.7	-24.8	-33.4	-112.2	-310.2	-3,853.1	499	~
Gross Domestic Product	56.4	65.2	75.2	90.2	122.9	154.2	419.9	1,501.4	21,506.9	2,769	~
Less: Net Factor Payments Abroad	.9	1.7	2.3	3.6	6.6	9.0	49.3	87.8	1,098.4	-171	~
Gross National Expenditure = GNP	55.6	63.5	72.9	86.6	116.3	145.2	370.6	1,413.6	20.408.5	2,599	~

1. Exports and imports include nonfactor services as well as goods.

SOURCE: IMF-IFS-Y, 1987.

Table 3342

BRAZIL EXPENDITURE ON GDP AND GNP, 1976–86

(M NC)

Category	1976	1977	1978	1979	1980	1981	1982	1983	1984	1985	1986
Exports[1]	115	180	242	431	1,121	2,311	3,846	13,393	52,306	169,331	~
Government Consumption	171	235	350	590	1,139	2,285	5,057	11,328	31,987	136,445	~
Gross Fixed Capital Formation	366	530	789	1,375	2,782	5,485	9,907	20,209	64,162	253,700	704,023
Increase in Stocks	10	17	28	-13	55	36	-172	-1,695	#	#	~
Private Consumption	1,118	1,722	2,497	4,214	8,942	17,024	33,692	85,523	270,108	944,683	~
Less: Imports[1]	-154	-197	-285	-556	-1,400	-2,404	-4,182	-10,563	-30,595	-98,094	~
Gross Domestic Product	1,626	2,487	3,621	6,041	12,639	24,737	48,148	118,195	387,968	1,406,065	3,586,291
Less: Net Factor Payments Abroad	-25	-40	-84	-163	-404	-1,015	-2,590	-6,840	-21,941	-73,661	-158,353
Gross National Expenditure = GNP	1,600	2,447	3,680	6,149	12,760	24,617	48,225	113,428	365,827	~	~

1. Exports and imports include nonfactor services as well as goods.

SOURCE: IMF-IFS-Y, 1987.

Table 3343

CHILE EXPENDITURE ON GDP AND GNP, 1976–86

(B NC)

Category	1976	1977	1978	1979	1980	1981	1982	1983	1984	1985	1986
Exports[1]	32.3	59.3	100.4	179.7	245.4	209.0	239.9	374.5	459.5	749.2	994.2
Government Consumption	18.0	41.9	70.4	110.4	133.9	167.4	190.1	220.7	273.8	367.1	410.7
Gross Fixed Capital Formation	17.1	38.4	71.6	115.0	178.9	236.8	181.5	186.5	233.8	366.4	472.7
Increase in Stocks	-.6	3.2	15.2	22.4	46.7	52.2	-41.6	-33.7	24.2	-13.2	13.9
Private Consumption	88.7	209.5	346.6	546.3	760.5	948.3	932.7	1,141.9	1,381.7	1,785.3	2,237.3
Less: Imports[1]	-26.8	-64.5	-116.7	-201.6	-290.1	-340.6	-263.4	-332.1	-479.6	-678.1	-870.2
Gross Domestic Product	128.7	287.8	487.5	772.2	1,075.3	1,273.1	1,239.1	1,557.7	1,893.4	2,576.6	3,246.1
Less: Net Factor Payments Abroad	-4.2	-7.6	-13.3	-24.7	-36.3	-57.1	-95.5	-134.2	~	~	~
Gross National Expenditure = GNP	124.5	280.2	474.2	747.5	1,039.0	1,216.0	1,143.6	1.423.5	~	~	~

1. Exports and imports include nonfactor services as well as goods.

SOURCE: IMF-IFS-Y, 1987.

Table 3344

COLOMBIA EXPENDITURE ON GDP AND GNP, 1976–86

(B NC)

Category	1976	1977	1978	1979	1980	1981	1982	1983	1984	1985	1986
Exports[1]	90.7	120.8	151.2	180.9	256.1	235.0	272.5	319.5	458.4	691.5	1,269.2
Government Consumption	43.7	55.2	77.8	110.7	159.4	206.9	272.8	334.6	425.6	521.3	663.2
Gross Fixed Capital Formation	84.6	104.0	139.9	183.3	264.9	350.1	436.1	524.9	654.5	805.9	1,039.0
Increase in Stocks	8.9	30.2	26.4	32.5	36.2	58.9	75.5	82.7	76.9	54.6	#
Private Consumption	378.3	500.3	639.7	841.3	1,108.8	1,437.7	1,819.7	2,196.9	2,721.9	3,416.8	4,275.9
Less: Imports[1]	-74.0	-94.5	-125.5	-159.8	-246.3	-305.7	-379.4	-404.4	-480.7	-625.0	-840.0
Gross Domestic Product	532.3	716.0	909.5	1,188.8	1,579.1	1,982.8	2,497.3	3,054.1	3,856.6	4,865.1	6,407.3
Less: Net Factor Payments Abroad	-9.1	-7.7	-7.9	-7.2	-5.7	-10.5	-37.5	-63.2	-99.1	-139.7	~
Gross National Expenditure = GNP	523.2	708.3	901.6	1,181.6	1,573.4	1,972.3	2,459.8	2,982.7	3,757.5	4,725.4	~

1. Exports and imports include nonfactor services as well as goods.

SOURCE: IMF-IFS-Y, 1987.

Table 3345

COSTA RICA EXPENDITURE ON GDP AND GNP, 1976–86

(M NC)

Category	1976	1977	1978	1979	1980	1981	1982	1983	1984	1985	1986
Exports[1]	6,082	8,198	8,589	9,311	10,963	24,707	43,959	45,601	56,046	60,618	75,926
Government Consumption	3,306	4,208	5,069	6,243	7,544	8,987	14,192	19,802	25,503	31,175	39,686
Gross Fixed Capital Formation	4,846	5,889	6,952	9,050	9,895	13,738	19,809	23,057	32,679	37,308	45,515
Increase in Stocks	46	502	132	-295	1,109	2,838	4,261	8,161	4,324	7,535	9,669
Private Consumption	13,690	17,143	20,388	23,139	27,140	34,344	56,397	76,925	99,837	119,337	141,653
Less: Imports[1]	-7,295	-9,608	-10,936	-12,863	-15,245	-27,510	-41,113	-47,208	-55,378	-63,548	-73,982
Gross Domestic Product	20,676	26,331	30,194	34,584	41,406	57,103	97,505	126,337	163,011	192,425	238,468
Less: Net Factor Payments Abroad	-627	-655	-903	-1,279	-1,987	-6,434	-16,087	-15,229	-13,804	-15,962	16,154
Gross National Expenditure = GNP	20,049	25,676	29,291	33,305	39,419	50,669	81,418	111,108	149,207	176,463	254,622

1. Exports and imports include nonfactor services as well as goods.

SOURCE: IMF-IFS-Y, 1987.

Table 3346

CUBA GROSS MATERIAL PRODUCT,[1] BY ECONOMIC SECTOR, 1970-84

	1970	1971	1972	1973	1974	1975	1976	1977	1978	1979	1980	1981[†,5]	1982[†]	1983[†]	1984[†]
M Constant Pesos[2]															
Total Material Product	5,666	5,904	6,478	7,328	7,900	8,142	8,431	10,181	10,962	11,428	11,684	13,051	15,260	15,747	16,984
Agriculture	1,230	1,153	1,216	1,271	1,328	1,607	1,665	1,735	1,842	1,942	2,001	2,183	3,698a	3,687a	3,889a
Industry[3]	4,000	4,177	4,458	4,988	5,393	5,285	5,446	6,996	7,563	7,917	8,115	9,085	9,707	10,075	10,795
Construction	436	574	804	1,069	1,179	1,250	1,320	1,450	1,557	1,569	1,568	1,818	1,802	1,988	2,310
Structure (%)[4]															
Total Material Product	100.0	100.0	100.0	100.0	100.0	100.0	100.0	100.0	100.0	100.0	100.0	100.0	65.9	66.2	66.6
Agriculture	21.7	19.5	18.8	17.3	16.8	19.7	19.7	~	~	~	17.1	16.7	15.9	15.6	15.3
Industry[3]	70.6	70.8	68.8	68.1	68.3	64.9	64.6	~	~	~	69.5	69.5	42.2	42.2	42.3
Construction	7.7	9.7	12.4	14.6	14.9	15.4	15.7	~	~	~	13.4	13.9	7.8	8.3	9.0
AAGR[4]															
Total Material Product	~	4.2	9.7	13.1	7.8	3.1	3.5	~	7.7	4.2	2.2	16.2	2.5	3.2	7.9
Agriculture	~	-6.3	5.5	4.5	4.5	21.0	3.6	~	6.2	5.4	3.0	13.0	-2.4	-.3	3.5
Industry[3]	~	4.4	6.7	11.9	8.1	-2.0	3.0	~	8.1	4.7	2.5	16.9	4.3	3.8	7.1
Construction	~	31.7	40.1	33.0	10.3	6.0	5.6	~	7.4	.8	#	19.3	.8	10.3	16.2

1. The material product consists of the value of the agricultural, fishery, mining, manufacturing, construction, and electrical energy sectors.
2. The *Anuario Estadístico de Cuba* describes all this information as valued at current prices, whereas according to the National Bank of Cuba, with the exception of trade and transport, the "other sectors"—the material product plus communications—are given at constant 1965 prices. In addition, sources in the State Statistical Committee explained that as of 1965 prices were frozen for inputs and final goods—agricultural, industrial and construction—and only new products were valued at different prices from those fixed then, but at prices frozen from the year in which they were incorporated in the Cuban economic system. Thus the terms current prices and constant prices in the case of the material product (at producer prices) are equivalent, and bearing in mind—according to the National Bank of Cuba— that the group of new products is very small, it is considered that the interpretation stemming from the resulting real growth rates is not affected.
3. Includes mining, manufacturing, and electrical energy; the fishing industry is included in manufacturing.
4. The percentage structure and growth rates correspond to the real and not the rounded figures.
5. Individual activities and total were extrapolated independently on the basis of the variations at constant 1981 prices estimated by the state statistical committee. The sum of the activities does not coincide with the total for 1981.

a. Includes fishing and forestry.

SOURCE: ADAPTED FROM ECLA-5, 1979–81, 1984, pp. 183, 192, 296, and 215 respectively.

Table 3347

DOMINICAN REPUBLIC EXPENDITURE ON GDP AND GNP, 1976–86

(M NC)

Category	1976	1977	1978	1979	1980	1981	1982	1983	1984	1985	1986
Exports[1]	36.6	40.5	49.1	32.4	35.1	61.8	80.2	88.8	86.4	~	~
Government Consumption	23.4	33.4	27.0	41.1	43.8	45.9	48.9	53.4	57.8	~	~
Gross Fixed Capital Formation	19.2	19.9	29.0	33.2	79.7	57.0	54.9	57.6	88.6	~	~
Increase in Stocks	#	#	#	10.0	#	#	#	#	.3	~	~
Private Consumption	43.2	62.7	94.6	104.9	148.2	154.5	144.9	147.3	163.5	~	~
Less: Imports[1]	−49.9	−59.9	−79.1	−108.8	−147.7	−140.7	−135.3	−136.1	−165.9	~	~
Gross Domestic Product	72.5	96.6	120.6	112.8	159.1	178.5	193.6	211.0	230.7	~	~
Less: Net Factor Payments Abroad	−123.8	−135.7	−187.7	−210.2	−293.1	−254.1	−297.1	~	~	~	~
Gross National Expenditure = GNP	3,827.7	4,592.7	5,302.5	6,415.0	6,933.4	7,663.4	8,277.7	~	~	~	~

1. Exports and imports include nonfactor services as well as goods.

SOURCE: IMF-IFS-Y, 1987.

Table 3348

ECUADOR EXPENDITURE ON GDP AND GNP, 1976–86

(B NC)

Category	1976	1977	1978	1979	1980	1981	1982	1983	1984	1985	1986
Exports[1]	34.17	41.32	40.83	60.62	73.80	75.91	87.56	133.06	209.86	305.02	321.54
Government Consumption	18.63	24.66	26.45	30.08	42.56	49.74	58.15	70.06	99.63	126.97	157.40
Gross Fixed Capital Formation	29.47	39.29	50.09	55.43	69.33	77.63	94.17	93.03	125.23	178.68	255.99
Increase in Stocks	2.11	4.85	4.35	3.86	7.30	3.16	10.65	5.41	14.73	20.01	20.73
Private Consumption	84.52	102.58	121.24	143.29	174.88	214.67	262.21	369.33	520.59	712.86	927.89
Less: Imports[1]	−35.98	−46.31	−51.61	−59.33	−74.53	−72.44	−97.03	−110.62	−157.41	−231.87	−317.25
Gross Domestic Product	132.91	166.38	191.35	233.96	293.34	348.66	415.72	560.27	812.63	1,111.67	1,366.30
Less: Net Factor Payments Abroad	−4.06	−4.48	−5.52	−9.95	−14.54	−18.31	−30.89	−41.79	−72.57	−81.76	−121.68
Gross National Expenditure = GNP	128.85	161.90	185.82	224.01	278.80	330.36	384.83	518.48	740.06	1,029.91	1,244.62

1. Exports and imports include nonfactor services as well as goods.

SOURCE: IMF-IFS-Y, 1987.

Table 3349

EL SALVADOR EXPENDITURE ON GDP AND GNP,[1] 1976–86

(M NC)

Category	1976	1977	1978	1979	1980	1981	1982	1983	1984	1985	1986
Exports[2]	2,028	2,735	2,328	3,182	3,046	2,307	2,042	2,486	2,536	3,040	4,625
Government Consumption	686	805	996	1,133	1,247	1,369	1,415	1,607	1,869	2,220	2,717
Gross Fixed Capital Formation	1,145	1,521	1,652	1,512	1,210	1,173	1,130	1,180	1,336	1,723	2,550
Increase in Stocks	−26	158	183	45	−27	58	56	44	59	−169	89
Private Consumption	4,015	4,607	5,514	5,933	6,405	6,644	6,877	7,871	9,184	11,568	15,778
Less: Imports[2]	−2,101	−2,686	−3,041	−3,197	−2,964	−2,904	−2,553	−3,036	−3,327	−4,051	−5,866
Gross Domestic Product	5,706	7,167	7,692	8,607	8,917	8,647	8,966	10,152	11,657	14,331	19,895
Less: Net Factor Payments Abroad	−17	−72	−130	−60	−128	−149	−229	−370	−343	−353	−453
Gross National Expenditure = GNP	5,689	7,095	7,562	8,547	8,789	8,498	8,737	9,782	11,314	13,978	19,442

1. Cf. Joseph P. Mooney, "Gross Domestic Product, Gross National Product, and Capital Formation in El Salvador, 1945–1965," *Estadística*, Sept. 1968, pp. 491–517.
2. Exports and imports include nonfactor services as well as goods.

SOURCE: IMF-IFS-Y, 1987.

Table 3350

GUATEMALA EXPENDITURE ON GDP AND GNP, 1976-86
(M NC)

Category	1976	1977	1978	1979	1980	1981	1982	1983	1984	1985	1986
Exports[1]	942	1,340	1,304	1,474	1,748	1,471	1,289	1,176	1,256	2,068	2,542
Government Consumption	297	354	435	488	627	680	676	688	726	777	1,107
Gross Fixed Capital Formation	900	1,039	1,218	1,286	1,295	1,443	1,310	950	912	1,225	1,543
Increase in Stocks	34	60	95	8	-44	23	76	52	184	61	57
Private Consumption	3,396	4,127	4,675	5,432	6,217	7,022	7,150	7,501	7,856	9,296	12,837
Less: Imports[1]	-1,204	-1,439	-1,655	-1,784	-1,963	-2,032	-1,629	-1,317	-1,464	-2,247	-2,300
Gross Domestic Product	4,365	5,481	6,071	6,903	7,879	8,608	8,717	9,050	9,470	11,180	15,785
Less: Net Factor Payments Abroad	-74	-33	-26	-12	-71	-103	-121	-113	-207	-331	-462
Gross National Expenditure = GNP	4,291	5,448	6,045	6,891	7,809	8,505	8,596	8,937	9,264	10,849	15,324

1. Exports and imports include nonfactor services as well as goods.

SOURCE: IMF-IFS-Y, 1987.

Table 3351

HAITI EXPENDITURE ON GDP AND GNP, 1976-86
(M NC)

Category	1976	1977	1978	1979	1980	1981	1982	1983	1984	1985	1986
Exports[1]	1,046	1,249	1,495	1,522	2,148	1,944	2,139	2,015	2,172	2,381	2,063
Gross Fixed Capital Formation	678	748*	857	938	1,238	1,252	1,230	1,331	1,442	1,673	1,614
Increase in Stocks	26	~	~	~	~	~	~	~	~	~	~
Private Consumption	4,101	4,592	4,690	5,245	6,835	7,535	7,188	7,866	8,678	9,471	10,513
Less: Imports[1]	-1,430	-1,692	-1,982	-2,068	-3,038	-3,334	-3,132	-3,064	-3,210	-3,682	-2,972
Gross Domestic Product	4,395	4,897	5,060	5,600	7,183	7,397	7,425	8,148	9,082	10,047	11,218
Less: Net Factor Payments Abroad	-36	-63	-76	-70	-72	-66	-72	-73	-92	-101	-78
Gross National Expenditure = GNP	4,359	4,834	4,984	5,530	7,111	7,331	7,353	8,075	8,990	9,946	11,119

1. Exports and imports include nonfactor services as well as goods.

SOURCE: IMF-IFS-Y, 1987.

Table 3352

HONDURAS EXPENDITURE ON GDP AND GNP, 1976-86
(M NC)[1]

Category	1976	1977	1978	1979	1980	1981	1982	1983	1984	1985	1986
Exports[2]	898	1,149	1,366	1,649	1,860	1,735	1,520	1,556	1,663	1,787	1,996
Government Consumption	348	417	442	520	678	758	800	877	952	1,046	1,144
Gross Fixed Capital Formation	550	711	941	1,004	1,235	1,051	966	1,073	1,246	1,215	1,094
Increase in Stocks	-32	59	93	170	13	100	-190	-176	-15	16	50
Private Consumption	1,985	2,335	2,511	2,945	3,563	4,035	4,295	4,504	4,742	5,015	5,376
Less: Imports[2]	-1,032	-1,311	-1,555	-1,863	-2,261	-2,126	-1,629	-1,799	-2,126	-2,120	-2,183
Gross Domestic Product	2,717	3,360	3,798	4,425	5,088	5,553	5,762	6,035	6,462	6,959	7,477
Less: Net Factor Payments Abroad	-102	-124	157	-210	275	269	385	-284	308	336	382
Gross National Expenditure = GNP	2,615	3,236	3,641	4,215	4,813	5,284	5,377	5,751	6,154	6,623	7,095

1. Year ending Sept. 30.
2. Exports and imports include nonfactor services as well as goods.

SOURCE: IMF-IFS-Y, 1987.

Table 3353

MEXICO EXPENDITURE ON GDP AND GNP, 1976–86

(B NC)

Category	1976	1977	1978	1979	1980	1981	1982	1983	1984	1985	1986
Exports[1]	116.4	190.8	244.7	343.3	537.2	701.6	1,636.5	3,340.6	5,101.9	~	~
Government Consumption	150.9	199.0	255.2	334.3	462.8	684.5	1,057.6	1,590.3	2,737.0	~	~
Gross Fixed Capital Formation	288.4	363.3	492.4	718.5	1,032.9	1,509.4	2,098.8	2,972.3	5,163.6	~	~
Increase in Stocks	17.2	59.1	59.2	77.6	169.8	193.2	-98.0	499.9	1,053.2	~	~
Private Consumption	933.4	1,226.1	1,543.8	1,975.9	2,651.5	3,583.8	5,776.1	10,356.0	17,468.6	~	~
Less: Imports[1]	-135.3	-189.0	-258.0	-382.0	-577.8	-798.1	-1,053.9	-1,617.4	-2,775.3	~	~
Gross Domestic Product	1,371.0	1,849.3	2,337.4	3,067.5	4,276.5	5,874.4	9,417.1	17,141.7	28,748.9	45,588.5	~
Less: Net Factor Payments Abroad	-29.0	-42.9	-52.5	-77.1	-117.2	-200.2	-519.3	-1,073.3	-1,719.3	~	~
Gross National Expenditure = GNP	1,342.0	1,806.3	2,284.9	2,990.4	4,159.3	5,674.2	8,897.8	16,068.4	27,029.6	~	~

1. Exports and imports include nonfactor services as well as goods.

SOURCE: IMF-IFS-Y, 1987.

Table 3354

NICARAGUA EXPENDITURE ON GDP AND GNP, 1976–86

(M NC)

Category	1976	1977	1978	1979	1980	1981	1982	1983	1984	1985	1986
Exports[1]	4,268	5,032	5,160	6,100	5,039	5,470	4,530	4,500	~	~	~
Government Consumption	1,208	1,396	1,762	2,591	4,107	5,376	6,649	9,782	~	~	~
Gross Fixed Capital Formation	2,613	3,620	2,180	967	2,882	5,055	4,497	5,384	~	~	~
Increase in Stocks	-252	326	-282	-1,800	482	567	653	787	~	~	~
Private Consumption	8,876	10,238	10,132	10,739	18,381	19,534	21,204	23,607	~	~	~
Less: Imports[1]	-4,119	-5,868	-4,686	-4,083	-8,999	-10,229	-7,837	-8,277	~	~	~
Gross Domestic Product	12,594	14,744	14,266	14,514	21,892	25,773	29,696	35,783	~	~	~
Less: Net Factor Payments Abroad	-491	-604	-602	-801	-922	-1,016	-1,380	-671	~	~	~
Gross National Expenditure = GNP	12,103	14,140	13,664	13,713	20,970	24,757	28,316	35,112	~	~	~

1. Exports and imports include nonfactor services as well as goods.

SOURCE: IMF-IFS-Y, 1987.

Table 3355

PANAMA EXPENDITURE ON GDP AND GNP, 1976–86

(M NC)

Category	1976	1977	1978	1979	1980	1981	1982	1983	1984	1985	1986
Exports[1]	837.8	921.1	986.4	1,124.8	1,567.1	1,632.0	1,689.6	1,709.5	1,622.1	1,740.4	~
Government Consumption	386.1	412.1	482.9	567.2	680.5	812.9	962.6	941.5	1,001.3	1,037.8	~
Gross Fixed Capital Formation	608.6	445.9	606.3	661.2	866.4	1,079.6	1,185.4	917.8	779.9	736.5	~
Increase in Stocks	10.2	45.0	45.4	124.5	120.5	87.6	-.8	16.3	-18.9	-26.3	~
Private Consumption	1,088.8	1,242.6	1,431.7	1,693.8	2,009.5	2,107.4	2,311.5	2,480.0	2,878.0	3,091.4	~
Less: Imports[1]	-975.2	-996.9	-1,100.2	-1,371.3	-1,685.2	-1,841.5	-1,869.4	-1,691.4	-1,696.9	-1,698.3	~
Gross Domestic Product	1,956.3	2,069.8	2,452.5	2,800.2	3,558.8	3,878.0	4,278.9	4,373.7	4,565.5	4,881.5	~
Less: Net Factor Payments Abroad	-55.5	-63.1	-57.4	-102.8	-110.0	-78.6	-138.9	2.2	-123.6	-47.0	~
Gross National Expenditure = GNP	1,900.8	2,006.7	2,395.1	2,697.4	3,448.8	3,799.4	4,140.0	4,375.9	4,441.9	4,834.5	~

1. Exports and imports include nonfactor services as well as goods.

SOURCE: IMF-IFS-Y, 1987.

Table 3356

PARAGUAY EXPENDITURE ON GDP AND GNP, 1976–86

(B NC)

Category	1976	1977	1978	1979	1980	1981	1982	1983	1984	1985	1986
Exports[1]	31.38	51.28	59.41	69.13	77.60	79.11	89.46	70.05	194.36	286.60	300.98
Government Consumption	13.41	16.35	21.50	24.71	34.73	48.63	52.27	58.02	69.28	90.21	121.40
Gross Fixed Capital Formation	48.75	62.92	81.26	116.14	152.65	194.22	176.87	164.51	226.79	259.24	350.50
Increase in Stocks	3.97	2.15	6.46	6.83	8.55	10.06	12.05	10.72	14.30	18.50	23.68
Private Consumption	155.17	190.06	225.24	306.50	399.40	504.07	552.02	642.20	835.15	1,066.04	1,410.92
Less: Imports[1]	–38.62	–59.16	–71.33	–92.80	–112.37	–127.40	–145.63	–127.39	–269.43	–326.70	–373.68
Gross Domestic Product	214.07	263.61	322.54	430.51	560.46	708.69	737.04	818.11	1,070.44	1,393.89	1,833.80
Less: Net Factor Payments Abroad	–1.09	.36	1.77	1.29	5.26	8.76	8.26	5.00	–2.32	6.54	10.76
Gross National Expenditure = GNP	212.98	263.97	324.31	431.81	565.72	717.45	745.30	823.10	1,068.12	1,386.99	1,823.04

1. Exports and imports include nonfactor services as well as goods.

SOURCE: IMF-IFS-Y, 1987.

Table 3357

PERU EXPENDITURE ON GDP AND GNP, 1976–86

(B NC)

Category	1976	1977	1978	1979	1980	1981	1982	1983	1984	1985	1986
Exports[1]	96	176	375	942	1,335	1,697	2,862	6,141	13,312	40,545	~
Government Consumption	101	157	209	301	628	1,096	1,939	3,559	6,720	17,841	~
Gross Fixed Capital Formation	128	154	235	441	847	1,734	3,083	4,781	9,630	22,668	~
Increase in Stocks	9	5	9	7	33	152	118	–308	–189	–362	~
Private Consumption	570	780	1,171	1,982	3,273	5,917	9,564	18,216	40,995	107,010	~
Less: Imports[1]	–139	–214	–320	–553	–1,145	–2,076	–3,382	–6,076	–10,602	–29,725	~
Gross Domestic Product	765	1,058	1,678	3,119	4,972	8,520	14,183	26,313	59,865	157,977	~
Less: Net Factor Payments Abroad	–12	–23	–69	–142	–142	–245	–406	–979	–1,751	–4,918	~
Gross National Expenditure = GNP	753	1,036	1,609	2,977	4,830	8,275	13,778	25,334	58,114	153,059	~

1. Exports and imports include nonfactor services as well as goods.

SOURCE: IMF-IFS-Y, 1987.

Table 3358

URUGUAY EXPENDITURE ON GDP AND GNP, 1976–86

(M NC)

Category	1976	1977	1978	1979	1980	1981	1982	1983	1984	1985	1986
Exports[1]	2,350	3,774	5,530	9,400	13,861	17,987	18,072	44,700	72,065	122,080	227,097
Government Consumption	1,755	2,451	3,821	6,789	11,482	17,336	20,100	25,653	36,851	69,084	129,582
Gross Fixed Capital Formation	1,952	3,030	4,943	9,312	15,422	19,205	19,382	20,329	27,331	38,304	69,279
Increase in Stocks	–81	–2	8	663	572	–403	–827	–1,902	1,784	1,467	2,885
Private Consumption	9,107	15,018	22,919	43,441	70,479	91,147	94,076	137,826	216,282	392,451	691,858
Less: Imports[1]	–2,445	–4,356	–6,291	–11,980	–19,612	–22,819	–22,107	–41,600	–59,954	–103,228	–175,664
Gross Domestic Product	12,638	19,915	30,930	57,625	92,204	122,453	128,696	185,006	294,359	520,158	945,037
Less: Net Factor Payments Abroad	–244	–317	–465	–454	–864	–797	–2,729	–9,895	–20,210	–35,592	–41,616
Gross National Expenditure = GNP	12,783	19,598	30,115	57,171	91,340	121,656	125,967	175,111	274,149	484,566	903,421

1. Exports and imports include nonfactor services as well as goods.

SOURCE: IMF-IFS-Y, 1987.

Table 3359

VENEZUELA EXPENDITURE ON GDP AND GNP, 1976–86

(B NC)

Category	1976	1977	1978	1979	1980	1981	1982	1983	1984	1985	1986
Exports[1]	41.06	43.51	41.96	64.03	85.46	89.62	75.20	74.07	105.15	101.60	~
Government Consumption	19.78	22.96	24.05	27.76	35.12	42.64	42.59	41.34	44.65	48.73	~
Gross Fixed Capital Formation	42.77	60.48	71.84	65.55	64.15	69.78	70.16	55.35	47.75	57.47	~
Increase in Stocks	3.73	4.18	.58	.10	−1.35	−4.37	5.17	−21.20	8.14	−2.89	~
Private Consumption	66.94	80.11	94.76	110.33	135.38	160.53	182.24	183.44	208.73	232.18	~
Less: Imports[1]	−39.18	−55.53	−64.13	−60.03	−64.55	−72.99	−84.09	−42.50	−65.96	−65.06	~
Gross Domestic Product	135.10	155.71	169.06	207.74	254.20	285.21	291.27	290.49	348.45	372.03	~
Less: Net Factor Payments Abroad	.18	−.36	−.63	−.76	1.20	2.26	−6.60	−9.86	−6.71	−14.77	~
Gross National Expenditure = GNP	135.29	155.34	168.43	206.98	255.40	287.47	284.67	280.63	339.01	357.26	~

1. Exports and imports include nonfactor services as well as goods.

SOURCE: IMF-IFS-Y, 1987.

Table 3360

UNITED STATES EXPENDITURE ON GDP AND GNP, 1976–86

(B US)

Category	1976	1977	1978	1979	1980	1981	1982	1983	1984	1985	1986
Exports[1]	146.2	155.5	181.8	223.1	272.6	292.3	270.3	263.8	282.1	278.6	284.0
Government Consumption and Investment	357.0	387.3	425.2	467.8	530.3	588.1	641.7	675.0	733.4	815.4	864.2
Of Which Gross Fixed Capital Formation	49.0	51.5	56.7	60.5	71.5	73.1	77.2	64.4	73.3	97.1	101.1
Private Gross Fixed Capital Formation	261.7	322.8	388.2	441.9	445.3	491.5	471.8	509.4	598.0	650.0	677.0
Increase in Stocks	16.0	21.3	28.7	13.0	−8.3	24.0	−24.5	−7.1	64.1	11.1	6.7
Private Consumption	1,129.4	1,257.2	1,403.5	1,566.7	1,732.6	1,915.1	2,050.7	2,234.5	2,428.2	2,600.5	2,762.5
Less: Imports[1]	−148.5	−179.1	−208.2	−248.2	−288.1	−310.5	−295.2	−319.8	−388.3	−398.6	−425.4
Gross Domestic Product	1,761.7	1,965.1	2,219.2	2,464.4	2,684.4	3,000.5	3,114.9	3,355.9	3,717.5	3,957.0	4,168.9
Net Factor Income from Abroad	21.1	25.4	30.5	43.8	47.6	52.1	51.2	49.9	47.5	41.2	37.2
Gross National Expenditure = GNP	1,782.8	1,990.5	2,249.7	2,508.2	2,732.0	3,052.6	3,166.0	3,405.7	3,765.0	3,998.1	4,206.1

1. Exports and imports include nonfactor services as well as goods.

SOURCE: IMF-IFS-Y, 1987.

Table 3361

PROVINCIAL LEVEL GDP AND GDP/C IN MEXICO, 1970 AND 1980

PART I. 1970

State (or Territory)	GDP M Pesos	%	Population T	%	GDP/C	Index (Total = 100.0)
Aguascalientes	2,061.0	.5	338.1	.7	6,095.8	69.4
Baja California	11,735.6	2.8	870.4	1.8	13,483.0	153.6

PART II. 1980

State (or Territory)	GDP M Pesos	%	GDP/C	Index (Total = 100.0)
Aguascalientes	25,991	.61	51,629	81.3
Baja California	95,860	2.24	78,225	123.3

Continued in SALA, 24-3361.

Table 3362

GDP AND PER CAPITA GDP AT MARKET PRICES,[1] 19 LR, 1960–86

PART I. GDP

(M 1986 Dollars)

	Country	1960	1970	1980	1984	1985	1986[‡]
A.	ARGENTINA	40,053	60,101	77,394	72,616	69,313	73,261
	Bahamas	~	~	1,779	1,897	1,963	2,003
	Barbados	416	760	896	851	853	893
B.	BOLIVIA	2,822	4,587	7,099	6,412	6,300	6,119
C.	BRAZIL	75,850	128,721	295,983	297,436	322,003	348,407
D.	CHILE	14,077	21,299	27,344	26,177	26,818	28,296
E.	COLOMBIA	11,627	19,365	33,110	35,887	36,760	38,638
F.	COSTA RICA	1,545	2,752	4,764	4,797	4,843	4,987
H.	DOMINICAN REP.	2,468	4,050	7,917	8,739	8,543	8,654
I.	ECUADOR	3,021	4,859	11,401	12,117	12,572	12,790
J.	EL SALVADOR	1,985	3,437	4,723	4,215	4,298	4,343
K.	GUATEMALA	3,766	6,435	11,151	10,601	10,499	10,503
	Guyana	444	622	736	607	612	569
L.	HAITI	1,127	1,221	1,939	1,839	1,859	1,856
M.	HONDURAS	1,224	2,097	3,234	3,326	3,416	3,520
	Jamaica	2,743	4,620	4,203	4,504	4,279	4,373
N.	MEXICO	49,193	96,893	183,604	193,592	198,976	191,506
O.	NICARAGUA	1,405	2,739	2,836	3,052	2,928	2,915
P.	PANAMA	1,297	2,784	4,759	5,228	5,443	5,597
Q.	PARAGUAY	1,694	2,684	6,222	6,696	6,962	6,963
R.	PERU	10,167	16,954	23,809	22,821	23,266	25,252
	Suriname	~	~	1,201	1,177	1,117	1,118
	Trinidad & Tobago	1,601	2,250	3,762	3,321	3,134	2,934
S.	URUGUAY	5,619	6,552	8,820	7,555	7,553	8,029
T.	VENEZUELA	18,981	34,175	51,199	47,919	47,988	49,473
	LATIN AMERICA	253,125	429,957	779,946	783,381	812,298	842,997

Table 3362 (Continued)

GDP AND PER CAPITA GDP AT MARKET PRICES,[1] 19 LR, 1960–86

PART II. PER CAPITA GDP

(1986 Dollars)

	Country	1960	1970	1980	1986[‡]
A.	ARGENTINA	1,943	2,531	2,752	2,361
	Bahamas	~	~	7,941	7,884
	Barbados	1,811	3,169	3,591	3,530
B.	BOLIVIA	857	1,068	1,268	926
C.	BRAZIL	1,049	1,382	2,486	2,525
D.	CHILE	1,853	2,275	2,463	2,306
E.	COLOMBIA	747	926	1,277	1,330
F.	COSTA RICA	1,171	1,595	2,149	1,971
H.	DOMINICAN REP.	717	998	1,432	1,319
I.	ECUADOR	682	815	1,416	1,326
J.	EL SALVADOR	746	971	1,032	892
K.	GUATEMALA	960	1,236	1,613	1,282
	Guyana	733	809	974	714
L.	HAITI	315	289	387	342
M.	HONDURAS	616	774	873	780
	Jamaica	1,631	2,472	1,999	1,869
N.	MEXICO	1,327	1,940	2,734	2,407
O.	NICARAGUA	935	1,390	1,025	862
P.	PANAMA	1,063	1,803	2,434	2,513
Q.	PARAGUAY	953	1,172	1,964	1,829
R.	PERU	979	1,264	1,374	1,250
	Suriname	~	~	3,363	2,767
	Trinidad & Tobago	1,901	2,356	3,349	2,484
S.	URUGUAY	2,214	2,421	3,085	2,738
T.	VENEZUELA	2,384	3,066	3,408	2,762
	LATIN AMERICA	1,223	1,615	2,288	2,140

1. In view of the fact that national series in constant prices have different base years from country to country, their conversion into dollars of a given year—in this instance 1984—was accomplished by multiplying each constant price series by the rate of variation in the implicit deflator of the U.S. gross national product between the year of the constant price series and the year 1984. Each conversion factor is expressed by:

$$\frac{\sum_{k=b-1}^{b+1} GDP_k \, ER_k}{\sum_{k=b-1}^{b+1} GDP_k} \cdot \frac{USD_{1984}}{USD_b}$$

Where "b" represents the base year chosen by the country for the presentation of its constant price national account figures; GDP is the current value of a country's gross domestic product; ER is the reciprocal of the implicit market exchange rate (rf) factor published in the *International Financial Statistics* of the International Monetary Fund; and USD is the U.S. gross national product implicit deflator published in the *Survey of Current Business*.

SOURCE: IDB-SPTF, 1987, Statistical Appendix, table 3.

Table 3363

GROWTH OF GDP AND OF PER CAPITA GDP, 19 LR, 1960–86

(%)

Country	Regional Proportion			Growth of GDP									GDP Per Capita				
					AA-GR		Annual Variation						AA-GR		Annual Variation		
	1960–69	1970–79	1980–86‡	1961–70	1971–80	1961–80	1981	1982	1983	1984	1985	1986‡	1961–80	1981–83	1984	1985	1986‡
A. ARGENTINA	14.8	12.0	9.1	4.1	2.6	3.3	-6.8	-4.6	2.8	2.6	-4.5	5.7	1.8	-4.6	.9	-6.0	4.1
B. BOLIVIA	1.1	1.0	.8	5.0	4.5	4.7	.3	-2.8	-6.6	-.9	-1.7	-2.9	2.0	-5.7	-3.6	-4.4	-5.5
C. BRAZIL	29.9	34.6	38.3	5.4	8.7	7.0	-3.3	.9	-2.5	5.7	8.3	8.2	4.4	-4.1	3.1	5.6	5.6
D. CHILE	5.4	3.9	3.4	4.2	2.5	3.4	5.5	-14.1	-.7	6.3	2.4	5.5	1.4	-5.1	4.6	.7	3.9
E. COLOMBIA	4.5	4.4	4.5	5.2	5.5	5.4	2.3	.9	1.6	3.4	2.4	5.1	2.9	.3	2.1	1.0	3.6
F. COSTA RICA	.6	.6	.6	5.9	5.6	5.8	-2.3	-7.3	2.9	8.0	1.0	3.0	3.1	-4.8	5.7	-1.6	2.7
H. DOMINICAN REP.	.9	1.0	1.1	5.1	6.9	6.0	4.1	1.7	3.9	.4	-2.2	1.3	3.5	.2	-2.4	-4.9	-1.4
I. ECUADOR	1.2	1.4	1.5	4.9	8.9	6.9	3.9	1.2	-2.8	4.0	3.8	1.7	3.7	-2.3	.8	.8	-1.1
J. EL SALVADOR	.8	.8	.5	5.6	3.2	4.4	-8.3	-5.6	.8	2.3	2.0	1.0	1.6	-5.8	1.1	.8	-.9
K. GUATEMALA	1.5	1.5	1.4	5.5	5.7	5.6	.7	-3.5	-2.5	.5	-1.0	0	2.6	-4.6	-2.3	-3.7	-2.8
L. HAITI	.4	.3	.2	.8	4.7	2.7	-2.7	-3.5	.8	.3	1.1	-.2	1.0	-3.2	-.8	-.4	-1.5
M. HONDURAS	.5	.4	.4	5.5	4.4	5.0	1.0	-2.6	1.1	3.5	2.7	3.0	1.8	-3.4	.1	-.5	-.3
N. MEXICO	20.8	22.3	24.4	7.0	6.6	6.8	7.9	-.5	-5.3	3.7	2.8	-3.8	3.7	-2.3	.9	0	-6.4
O. NICARAGUA	.6	.6	.4	6.9	.3	3.6	5.4	-.8	4.6	-1.6	-4.1	-.4	.5	-.4	-4.8	-7.3	-3.7
P. PANAMA	.6	.6	.7	7.9	5.5	6.7	4.2	5.5	.4	-.4	4.1	2.8	4.2	1.1	-2.5	1.9	.7
Q. PARAGUAY	.7	.7	.8	4.7	8.8	6.7	8.7	-1.0	-3.0	3.1	4.0	0	3.7	-1.6	.1	.7	-3.0
R. PERU	4.1	3.6	3.0	5.2	3.5	4.3	3.1	.9	-12.0	4.7	1.9	8.5	1.7	-5.4	2.1	-.6	5.8
S. URUGUAY	1.8	1.2	1.0	1.5	3.0	2.3	1.9	-9.4	-5.9	-1.5	0	6.3	1.7	-5.0	-1.9	-.5	6.3
T. VENEZUELA	7.9	7.5	6.3	6.1	4.1	5.1	-.3	.7	-5.6	-1.2	.1	3.1	1.8	-4.6	-3.9	-2.8	-.1
LATIN AMERICA¹	100.0	100.0	100.0	5.4	6.1	5.8	.5	-.8	-2.9	3.8	3.7	3.8	3.2	-3.4	1.4	1.3	1.4

1. Includes Bahamas, Barbados, Guyana, Jamaica, Suriname, and Trinidad and Tobago.

SOURCE: IDB-SPTF, 1987, table II-6.

Table 3364

TOTAL CONSUMPTION, 19 LR, 1960–86

(M 1986 Dollars)

	Country	1960	1970	1980	1983	1984	1985	1986[‡]
A.	ARGENTINA	8,010	12,744	18,318	10,065	8,993	7,329	8,684
B.	BOLIVIA	430	919	1,043	702	665	639	654
C.	BRAZIL[1]	11,937	27,216	66,415	40,381	41,907	45,892	46,276
D.	CHILE	2,060	4,975	6,531	2,278	3,998	3,734	4,221
E.	COLOMBIA	2,477	3,977	6,509	7,597	7,149	6,309	6,177
F.	COSTA RICA	260	557	1,360	840	932	1,026	1,120
H.	DOMINICAN REP.	244	775	2,004	1,697	1,716	~	~
I.	ECUADOR	596	1,124	3,029	2,031	2,124	2,201	2,220
J.	EL SALVADOR	307	414	592	467	481	455	566
K.	GUATEMALA	406	771	1,276	988	1,048	842	859
L.	HAITI	71	111	339	335	340	316	270
M.	HONDURAS	173	406	808	481	668	631	573
N.	MEXICO	9,274	22,018	51,465	31,853	34,256	38,877	35,292
O.	NICARAGUA	205	466	476	652	658	654	690
P.	PANAMA	221	775	1,122	929	827	760	764
Q.	PARAGUAY	138	332	1,767	1,405	1,341	1,442	1,489
R.	PERU	1,938	2,187	4,039	3,294	3,323	2,867	3,131
S.	URUGUAY	720	694	1,637	773	788	608	645
T.	VENEZUELA	4,062	9,415	14,800	8,133	10,003	10,727	12,068
	LATIN AMERICA[2,3]	45,058	92,340	187,142	117,989	123,823	127,726	125,698

1. Fixed investment only for years 1980–86.
2. The regional totals are not strictly comparable given the lack of complete information
   for some countries for 1960, 1970, 1985, 1986.
3. Includes Bahamas, Barbados, Guyana, Jamaica, Suriname, and Trinidad and Tobago.

SOURCE: IDB-SPTF, 1987, Statistical Appendix, table 4.

Table 3365

GROSS DOMESTIC INVESTMENT, 19 LR, 1960–86

(M 1986 Dollars)

	Country	1960	1970	1980	1983	1984	1985	1986[‡]
A.	ARGENTINA	33,084	47,219	64,400	57,333	60,749	56,840	61,813
B.	BOLIVIA	2,022	3,249	5,668	5,361	5,345	5,355	5,284
C.	BRAZIL[1]	66,462	105,600	236,085	230,256	236,795	254,494	290,773
D.	CHILE	13,171	18,999	22,647	21,321	21,598	21,381	22,197
E.	COLOMBIA	8,987	15,863	27,650	29,109	29,989	30,642	31,561
F.	COSTA RICA	1,380	2,345	3,711	3,252	3,469	3,601	3,751
H.	DOMINICAN REP.	1,975	3,571	6,748	7,338	7,302	~	~
I.	ECUADOR	2,664	4,408	9,523	9,779	9,856	10,131	9,911
J.	EL SALVADOR	1,768	3,094	4,190	3,640	3,785	3,917	4,023
K.	GUATEMALA	3,403	5,474	9,122	8,893	9,004	8,923	9,024
L.	HAITI	943	1,128	1,870	1,665	1,665	1,714	1,743
M.	HONDURAS	957	1,498	2,556	2,518	2,598	2,697	2,826
N.	MEXICO	40,159	76,718	141,644	143,931	148,308	151,232	144,215
O.	NICARAGUA	1,209	2,259	2,900	2,670	2,762	2,719	2,806
P.	PANAMA	1,093	2,102	3,373	3,809	4,156	4,399	4,504
Q.	PARAGUAY	1,574	2,332	4,683	5,428	5,644	5,714	5,824
R.	PERU	7,114	14,074	19,418	17,885	18,022	18,499	21,103
S.	URUGUAY	5,420	6,339	7,722	6,651	6,295	6,436	6,831
T.	VENEZUELA	12,281	22,200	46,584	44,613	42,749	42,871	~
	LATIN AMERICA[2,3]	209,758	344,624	630,189	616,432	630,489	640,923	~

1. Includes change in stocks for years 1980–86.
2. The regional totals are not strictly comparable given the lack of complete information
   for some countries for 1960, 1970, 1985, 1986.
3. Includes Bahamas, Barbados, Guyana, Jamaica, Suriname, and Trinidad and Tobago.

SOURCE: IDB-SPTF, 1987, Statistical Appendix, table 5.

Table 3366

GROSS CAPITAL FORMATION AS A PERCENTAGE OF GDP, 18 L, 1962–83
(% of GDP at Market Prices)

	Country	1962	1965	1970	1975	1976	1977	1978	1979	1980	1981	1982	1983
A.	ARGENTINA	21.31	19.20	20.40	26.57	27.18	27.24	23.91	22.62	22.78	18.20	17.53	~
B.	BOLIVIA	16.44	16.96	17.07	24.44	21.17	20.80	20.00	17.62	13.06	12.20	8.49	~

Continued in SALA, 24-3366.

Table 3367

ESTIMATES OF NATIONAL INCOME,[1] 18 LRC, 1960–80

	Country	Total (M US)							Per Capita (US)						
		1960	1970	1975	1977	1978	1979	1980	1960	1970	1975	1977	1978	1979	1980
A.	ARGENTINA	12,129	23,366	35,227	~	~	~	~	588	984	1388	~	~	~	~
B.	BOLIVIA	339	970	2,334	~	~	~	~	102	226	477	~	~	~	~

Continued in SALA, 24-3367.

Table 3368

ESTIMATES OF NATIONAL DISPOSABLE INCOME,[1] 15 LRC, 1960–80

	Country	Total (M US)							Per Capita (US)						
		1960	1970	1975	1977	1978	1979	1980	1960	1970	1975	1977	1978	1979	1980
B.	BOLIVIA	346	962	2,311	~	~	~	~	104	224	472	~	~	~	~
D.	CHILE	1,752	7,242	4,388	~	~	~	~	231	773	425	~	~	~	~

Continued in SALA, 24-3368.

Table 3369

GROSS PRODUCT PER CAPITA BY ICP AND *ATLAS* [1] METHODS, 16 LC, 1980–85

(United States = 100)

	Economy	1980		1984		1985	
		ICP	*Atlas*	ICP	*Atlas*	ICP	*Atlas*
A.	ARGENTINA	33.5	17.1	27.9	14.0	25.9	13.0
	Austria	75.4	86.6	74.6	58.9	75.5	55.8
	Belgium	82.4	103.9	78.5	55.5	78.3	51.5
B.	BOLIVIA	14.2	4.4	10.0	3.2	9.5	2.9
	Botswana	13.9	8.0	17.8	6.0	18.7	5.1
C.	BRAZIL	29.3	17.2	25.3	11.1	26.4	10.0
	Cameroon	7.9	6.5	9.4	5.2	9.8	4.9
	Canada	101.5	90.3	98.4	85.6	99.8	83.4
D.	CHILE	31.9	20.6	26.9	11.0	26.6	8.8
E.	COLOMBIA	24.8	11.0	23.4	9.1	23.3	8.0
F.	COSTA RICA	27.7	17.3	23.5	7.7	22.8	7.9
	Côte d´Ivoire	12.0	9.5	8.7	4.1	8.7	3.8
	Denmark	85.9	108.4	87.5	72.1	88.3	68.5
H.	DOMINICAN REP.	17.3	9.2	16.0	6.2	15.2	4.9
I.	ECUADOR	22.6	11.8	20.2	7.4	20.0	7.1
J.	EL SALVADOR	12.4	6.3	9.9	4.6	9.8	4.3
	Ethiopia	2.4	.9	2.2	.7	2.0	.7
	Finland	75.5	91.2	77.3	69.5	78.5	66.3
	France	85.4	105.4	82.0	63.1	81.3	58.2
	Germany, Fed. Rep.	89.1	114.1	86.6	71.8	87.4	66.7
	Greece	44.5	36.9	41.9	24.3	42.0	21.6
K.	GUATEMALA	20.3	9.7	16.3	7.7	15.4	7.6
M.	HONDURAS	10.6	5.5	8.8	4.5	8.7	4.5
	Hong Kong	62.4	47.0	72.3	41.0	70.9	37.9
	Hungary	40.4	16.7	41.8	13.3	41.0	11.8
	India	5.0	2.1	5.3	1.7	5.4	1.5
	Indonesia	9.6	4.4	9.7	3.6	9.6	3.2
	Ireland	47.9	46.7	47.7	32.0	46.8	29.5
	Israel	59.4	40.9	55.8	32.8	55.1	30.0
	Italy	68.0	60.3	64.5	41.4	64.7	39.8
	Japan	73.4	77.9	79.0	68.5	81.1	69.1
	Kenya	5.6	3.5	4.9	2.0	4.8	1.8
	Korea, Rep. of	22.5	13.6	27.3	13.8	27.9	13.3
	Luxembourg	92.8	131.9	86.6	84.9	87.4	81.6
	Madagascar	5.0	3.2	3.8	1.7	3.7	1.5
	Malawi	3.7	1.6	3.1	1.2	3.0	1.0
	Mali	3.0	1.7	2.4	.9	2.3	.9
	Morocco	10.5	8.1	9.8	4.3	9.8	3.7
	Netherlands	81.4	102.5	75.5	61.4	75.5	56.0
	Nigeria	7.8	8.8	5.3	4.8	5.2	4.6
	Norway	99.0	117.1	100.4	89.9	101.5	84.7
	Pakistan	9.6	2.7	10.0	2.4	10.3	2.3
P.	PANAMA	27.9	14.6	26.4	12.7	26.4	12.3
Q.	PARAGUAY	18.6	12.6	16.6	7.0	16.5	5.7
R.	PERU	21.9	9.6	17.9	6.6	17.5	5.9
	Philippines	15.2	6.3	13.2	4.2	12.1	3.7
	Poland	37.7	- -	33.4	13.6	33.2	12.9
	Portugal	33.4	20.8	31.4	12.7	31.7	12.0
	Senegal	6.0	4.3	5.7	2.4	5.6	2.3
	Spain	55.5	48.2	52.4	28.6	52.2	26.6
	Sri Lanka	10.7	2.3	11.7	2.3	11.7	2.3
	Tanzania	3.1	2.4	2.6	1.9	2.5	1.6
	Tunisia	17.4	11.8	17.4	8.2	17.6	7.4
	United Kingdom	72.1	81.3	71.2	55.3	72.3	51.2
	United States	100.0	100.0	100.0	100.0	100.0	100.0
S.	URUGUAY	37.2	29.6	28.9	12.4	28.4	10.1
T.	VENEZUELA	47.4	33.6	37.2	22.4	35.7	19.0
	Yugoslavia	35.3	27.9	33.3	14.6	32.7	12.6
	Zambia	6.4	5.5	5.3	3.1	5.2	2.4
	Zimbabwe	7.8	6.4	7.5	4.9	7.7	4.0
	UNITED STATES (US)	11,450	11,650	15,330	15,540	16,160	16,400

1. *Atlas* refers to the World Bank method of calculating GNP per capita.

a. ICP values for 1980 are actual Phase IV results; for other years they are extrapolated from
the 1980 values. *Atlas* estimates are based on the current *Atlas* method applied to current
data and are GNP per capita. ICP values relate to GDP per capita.

SOURCE: WB-WDR, 1987, page 270.

Table 3370

REAL GDP FORECAST, 6 L, 1985–92

(PC)

	Country	1985	1986	1987	1988	1989	1990	1991	1992
A.	ARGENTINA	-3.5	5.5	1.5	2.8	2.6	1.6	2.4	3.1
C.	BRAZIL	8.3	7.1	-2.5	2.7	4.8	3.1	5.1	4.9
D.	CHILE	1.8	5.7	4.7	3.9	4.8	2.5	3.0	3.4
E.	COLOMBIA	2.4	4.5	4.0	4.2	3.9	2.6	5.2	4.1
N.	MEXICO	2.8	-3.7	2.6	3.7	.9	3.2	4.2	4.8
T.	VENEZUELA	.3	3.1	2.5	2.6	1.9	1.8	2.7	2.3

SOURCE: Wharton Econometric Forecasting Associates, "World Economic Outlook,"
April 1987.

Table 3371

MEXICO ALTERNATIVE GDP FORECAST, 1983–92

(PC)

	1983	1984	1985	1986	1987	1988	Azteca Plan[1] 1989	1990	1991	1992
Alternative 1	-5.3	3.7	2.8	-3.7	2.2	3.6	.9	3.2	4.0	4.5
Alternative 2	-5.3	3.7	2.8	-3.7	1.4	2.9	-4.7	2.1	3.0	3.5
Alternative 3	-5.3	3.7	2.8	-3.7	.9	2.3	-2.5	2.2	3.1	3.7

1. Azteca Plan applies only to Alternative 1.

SOURCE: *CIEMEX-WEFA: Mexican Economic Outlook*, May 1987, tables 5.1, 12.1, 12.3.

Table 3372

LATIN AMERICA ECONOMIC AND INDUSTRIAL EXPANSION
AND RETROCESSION, 19 LR, 1950–83

	Country	Gross National Income Total 1950–80	1980–83	Industrial 1950–80	1980–83	Industrial Retrocession[1] Industrial Product	Industrialization Degree
A.	ARGENTINA	3.2	-3.2	3.8	-4.5	1971	1960
B.	BOLIVIA	3.4	-5.5	4.4	-6.2	1975	1978
C.	BRAZIL	7.1	-2.0	8.4	-4.5	1978	1968
D.	CHILE	3.6	-3.4	3.1	-6.1	1967	Before 1950
E.	COLOMBIA	5.1	1.2	6.0	-1.0	1980	1961
F.	COSTA RICA	6.5	-3.8	7.8	-7.1	1976	1973
H.	DOMINICAN REP.	5.9	3.2	6.9	3.3	1983	1970
I.	ECUADOR	6.2	.8	6.9	1.3	1981	1982
J.	EL SALVADOR	4.5	-5.4	5.4	-8.7	1969	1961
K.	GUATEMALA	5.0	-1.7	6.1	-3.7	1979	1968
L.	HAITI	2.2	#	3.5	2.9	1981	1983
M.	HONDURAS	4.4	-.5	7.3	#	1980	1981
N.	MEXICO	6.6	1.0	7.4	-1.0	1980	1970
O.	NICARAGUA	4.4	3.0	6.8	.3	1974	1977
P.	PANAMA	5.1	3.4	7.6	.1	1980	1961
Q.	PARAGUAY	5.2	1.5	5.5	.5	1980	1967
R.	PERU	4.6	-2.8	5.5	-6.1	1973	Before 1960
S.	URUGUAY	2.2	-4.8	2.8	-10.0	1971	1950
T.	VENEZUELA	5.9	-.4	7.2	-.6	1981	1980
	LATIN AMERICA	5.6	-.9	6.5	-3.1	1979	1966

1. Year in which the 1983 figure had been reached.

SOURCE: *Problemas de la Industria Latinoamericana en la Face Crítica*
(Santiago: Cepal, 1986).

Table 3373

LATIN AMERICA ECONOMIC EXPANSION AND INDUSTRIALIZATION, 19 LR, 1950–83

| | | | Industrialization in the Long Run | | | | | Recent Deindustrialization | | | |
| | | | Product Growth | | Degree of Industrialization (%) | | | Product Growth | | Degree of Industrialization (%) |
	Country	Period	Total	Industrial	1950	Final Year	Period	Total	Industrial	1983
A.	ARGENTINA	1950–74	3.6	4.9	23.1	31.2	1974–83	.0	-1.9	26.2
B.	BOLIVIA	1950–80	3.5	4.4	12.6	16.3	1980–83	-5.5	-6.2	15.9
C.	BRAZIL	1950–73	7.2	8.8	19.7	27.6	1973–83	4.3	3.4	25.3
D.	CHILE	1950–72	4.1	5.2	21.5	27.5	1972–83	.7	-2.0	20.4
E.	COLOMBIA	1950–73	5.2	6.9	16.1	23.6	1973–83	3.8	1.8	19.4
F.	COSTA RICA	1950–78	6.8	8.4	13.7	21.2	1978–83	-1.2	-3.7	18.7
H.	DOMINICAN REP.	1950–71	5.6	7.2	13.9	18.9	1971–83	5.7	5.4	18.3
I.	ECUADOR	1950–82	6.0	6.8	17.6	22.5	1982–83	-3.5	-5.6	22.0
J.	EL SALVADOR	1950–76	5.2	6.7	13.7	19.9	1976–83	-2.2	-5.4	15.8
K.	GUATEMALA	1950–80	4.9	6.1	12.0	16.7	1980–82	-1.3	-3.7	15.9
L.	HAITI	1950–83	2.0	3.5	7.9	12.5	#	#	#	12.5
M.	HONDURAS	1950–81	4.3	7.1	6.7	15.3	1981–82	-1.0	-1.5	15.2
N.	MEXICO	1950–79	6.5	7.5	19.4	25.2	1979–83	2.8	1.0	23.5
O.	NICARAGUA	1950–80	4.4	6.7	11.5	22.5	1980–83	3.0	.3	20.8
P.	PANAMA	1950–69	6.4	10.0	6.7	12.7	1969–83	5.0	2.9	9.6
Q.	PARAGUAY	1950–73	3.9	4.6	14.7	17.0	1973–83	7.1	6.1	15.4
R.	PERU	1950–76	5.0	6.3	18.7	25.5	1976–83	-.2	-2.5	21.7
S.	URUGUAY	1950–79	2.1	2.8	21.9	26.8	1979–83	-2.3	-7.0	21.9
T.	VENEZUELA	1950–80	5.9	7.2	12.1	17.4	1980–83	-.4	-.6	17.3
	LATIN AMERICA	1950–73	5.6	6.9	19.2	25.2	1973–83	3.5	2.6	23.2

SOURCE: *Problemas de la Industrial Latinoamericana en la Face Crítica*
(Santiago: Cepal, 1986).

Table 3374

MEXICO GROSS FORMATION OF CAPITAL BY TYPES OF ASSETS
(B Pesos, at 1970 Consumer Prices)

Year	Total	Gross Formation of Fixed Capital	Construction	Machinery and Equipment	Change in Stock
1960	56.1	38.6	23.2	15.4	17.5
1961	54.6	39.0	32.1	15.9	15.6
1962	54.3	39.8	24.6	15.2	14.5
1963	61.1	45.1	28.1	17.0	16.0
1964	74.7	54.9	32.7	22.2	19.8
1965	75.8	57.1	32.4	24.7	18.7
1966	80.1	62.6	36.8	25.8	17.5
1967	89.1	69.9	41.4	28.5	19.2
1968	94.9	76.7	44.4	32.3	18.2
1969	97.1	82.0	48.5	33.5	15.1
1970	101.0	88.7	50.8	37.9	12.3
1971	96.0	87.1	49.9	37.2	8.9
1972	106.1	97.8	55.8	42.0	8.3
1973	122.3	112.2	63.1	49.1	10.1
1974	143.6	121.1	66.7	54.4	22.5
1975	150.9	132.3	71.7	60.6	18.6
1976	147.4	132.9	74.6	58.3	14.5
1977	146.9	124.0	72.6	51.4	22.9
1978	164.5	142.8	82.2	60.6	21.7
1979	193.4	171.7	92.9	78.8	21.7
1980	236.0	197.4	104.6	92.8	38.6
1981	272.8	226.4	116.4	110.0	46.4
1982	194.5	190.3	110.5	79.8	4.2
1983	146.0	137.2	88.5	48.7	8.8
1984	157.1	144.8	91.5	53.3	12.3
1985	178.3	154.0	94.8	59.2	24.3

SOURCE: NAFINSA-MV, April 20, 1987.

Part XI: Development of Data

CHAPTER 34

PROFESSIONAL EXPERTISE AND MEXICAN

MODERNIZATION: SOURCES, METHODS,

AND PRELIMINARY FINDINGS

By

David E. Lorey

James W. Wilkie, David Lorey, and Enrique Ochoa, eds., *Statistical Abstract of Latin America*, vol. 26 (Los Angeles: UCLA Latin American Center Publications, University of California, 1988).

PROFESSIONAL EXPERTISE AND MEXICAN MODERNIZATION: SOURCES, METHODS, AND PRELIMINARY FINDINGS

One of the explicit goals of the Mexican Revolution has been to educate competent professionals—doctors, teachers, engineers, businessmen, lawyers, economists, advanced researchers—so that Mexico can join the modern world and participate in it to Mexican advantage. This goal was voiced at the very inception of "institutionalized" revolution.[1] Since that time, the concern with supplying professional expertise to society has vied for preeminence with the other main goal of the Mexican university system—satisfying the demand for inexpensive educational opportunities for all Mexicans. More recently, higher education support agencies such as ANUIES (Asociación Nacional de Universidades e Institutos de Enseñanza Superior) and CONACYT (Consejo Nacional de Ciencia y Tecnología) have emphasized the production of professionals as the more pressing of the two goals.[2] In general, an increasing number of observers have come to view the creation of a solid superstructure of skilled professionals as a social and economic aim of paramount importance for a modern Mexico.[3]

Given the concern with the role of higher education and its product in Mexico's modernization effort, it is surprising that little study has been devoted to the Mexican system's output of individuals equipped with professional skills. Scholars have avoided this aspect of the university system principally because the quantitative data concerning professionals and professional expertise are generally sketchy and inconsistent over time. Because of a lack of well-formulated approaches to the data that do exist, the basic quantitative dimensions of professional skill development remain unknown.

This study assesses the long-term successes and failures of the Mexican attempt to produce professional expertise for modernization by exploring the available quantitative data in four main ways: (1) it outlines the data and proposes a methodology for approaching them; (2) using time series, it delineates the historical results of the Mexican attempt to produce competent professionals from 1928 to the present in the context of Mexican modernization strategies; (3) it examines data on the relationship between professionals and Mexican political society; (4) it contrasts the Mexican experience with professional education challenges and responses with the experiences of the United States and three Latin American countries.

To describe and analyze trends in the history of Mexican professional education, I develop three new statistical indicators: professional degrees granted, professional degrees registered, and *egresados*[4] of professional fields in Mexico from 1928 to 1984. Part I is devoted to a discussion of the general database and the construction and use of the three indicators.

In Part II, I place the patterns of Mexican professional preparation in historical perspective and analyze significant shifts in professional skills development in the context of twentieth-century policy trends.

In Part III, several common assumptions about the relationship between professional training and the Mexican elite are critiqued by examining cross-sectional as well as time-series data. In addition, the education of Mexican professionals in the United States is quantified and discussed.

In Part IV, a few of the similarities and differences between the problems of professional supply in Mexico and the United States are outlined in order to focus attention on the issue of geographical distribution of professional skills. This section also addresses the question of whether the Mexican case is typical of Latin American experience with professional education by briefly examining the professional profiles of Brazil, Bolivia, and Venezuela.

Part I. Sources and Methodology

The lack of easily manipulated data on Mexico's higher education system has led to an emphasis on theoretical issues in the secondary literature, particularly on political and sociological aspects of Mexican professional training. Roderic

AUTHOR'S NOTE: This study is part of a larger work in progress which comprehensively describes and analyzes professional training in twentieth-century Mexico. The author would like to thank James W. Wilkie, E. B. Lorey, Aída Mostkoff, and Enrique Ochoa for their comments on drafts of the paper. All graphics were produced by the author with Microsoft Chart on an Apple Macintosh, and were prepared for publication on an Apple Laserwriter.

[1] See, for example, Portes Gil (1964: 587 and passim). Although primarily concerned with political aspects of university autonomy, which he granted in 1929, Portes Gil shows frequent concern for the number and quality of professionals produced and the impact of their preparation on Mexican society.

[2] See, for example, ANUIES (1979) and CONACYT (1978).

[3] For discussion of the two major goals of the Mexican university system, their conflicting aspects, and their relation to issues of university autonomy, see Rangel Guerra (1979), who views Mexico as slipping behind in research and technological development because of broad access enrollment policies of the university, and Castrejón Diez (1979), who perceives an elitist university system and calls for increases in popular access to higher education.

[4] For the definition of *egresado*, see the discussion of this indicator in Part I below.

Camp (1980) and Peter H. Smith (1979), for example, have discussed the role of higher educational backgrounds in the formation of Mexico's political elite. Peter S. Cleaves's prominent work (1985) concerns itself with Mexican professionals in the context of the place of professionals in "Latin society." These sociological studies do not directly approach the historical or pressing current issues of Mexico's continuing need for a diverse range of professional skills for modernization and the difficulties of their supply.[5]

Studies of available quantitative data are almost entirely lacking. One source (García Sánchez and Hernández, 1977) bases its conclusions on student enrollment data for 1959–75, and analyzes aggregate degree data for the thirty-year period 1945–75. This kind of quantitative approach cannot be very enlightening because (1) the Mexican dropout rate is exceedingly high and thus enrollment figures extremely misleading, and (2) the development of Mexican society and economy in the 1945–75 period is too complex to be dealt with in aggregate terms.[6] Trends of the period must be examined and compared with those of the 1930s.

A few scholars have addressed the quantitative data in useful ways. Víctor Urquidi and Adrian Lajous Vargas (1967), for example, have analyzed higher education gains and shortcomings during the López Mateos administration (1958–64). Working with preliminary data from the Bank of Mexico, Urquidi and Lajous Vargas voiced concern that the future needs of Mexican society for highly trained professionals could not be met without significant modification of higher education programs.

In general, the small number of useful quantitative approaches results not from an absolute dearth of data, but primarily from the lack of data consistent over the long term. The methodology for keeping track of professionals and the development of professional skills has changed in several important ways during the period covered in this essay. Important subsectors of professionals have been included in different major categories at different points in time, and data have frequently been published in aggregate statistical tables that cannot reflect the large and small changes in the professional picture in the twentieth century.

This essay consolidates data and attempts to make data consistent over time in order to place the concerns of Urquidi and Lajous Vargas in the long-term context of Mexico's twentieth-century modernization effort. The data, and idiosyncrasies in the data, are critiqued before trends apparent in them are discussed.

The Data

Mexican census data reveal some of the most basic dimensions of professional growth (as shown in Part II below). They cannot, however, provide exact information on changing professional capabilities in Mexican society over time. Above all, the census gives us data on how people classify themselves according to two very broad census categories—area of economic activity and level of occupation (from professional manager to non-wage laborer). The data indicate what professional-level jobs are being performed, but do not reflect actual application of professional training in specific fields.

For more detailed coverage of shifts in the development of specific professions, data on degrees that can be disaggregated to reflect career-field choices and the availability of professional expertise in Mexican society must be consulted. The longest series of such data—"professional degrees granted"—comes for the most part from the *Anuario Estadístico* published by Mexico's Dirección General de Estadística and runs from 1900 to 1971.[7]

I focus here on the 1928–84 period. It is during the 1930s that professional education takes its place in the modernization effort as defined by the ruling party. The data on degrees granted are presented below by presidential administration to help define correlations between presidential development strategies and the development of professional skills in the period.

The tables on degrees granted were discontinued in the *Anuario Estadístico* after 1971.[8] Between 1972 and 1977, when consistent data on egresados became available, a gap, representing the Echeverría years, exists. I have attempted to fill this gap with unpublished data on degrees registered with the Dirección General de Profesiones (DGP).[9]

Once a degree is granted, Mexican law requires that it be registered with the DGP before an individual can be employed. In practice, an employer may or may not require registration. Some fields, and even some university professors, are more likely to encourage degree registration than others. Nonetheless, degrees registered data reflect certain realities of the job market with some accuracy because registration indicates actual employment, or expectation of employment in the near future.

The third series that is useful in attempting to gauge the supply of professionals in Mexican society is the ANUIES statistical yearbook data on egresados of all professional

---

[5] Two excellent studies, Levy (1980) and Mabry (1982), explicitly address political issues—particularly the historical conflicts between the "autonomous" university system and the Mexican state. Both works also implicitly critique the conflict between the two main goals of the higher education system outlined above.

[6] García Sánchez and Hernández do present some of their data in disaggregated form, showing the evolution of licentiate, master's, and doctoral thesis theme concentrations at UNAM (Universidad Nacional Autónoma de México) and IPN (Instituto Politécnico Nacional) between 1947 and 1975 in five-year periods.

[7] These data were originally collected by James W. Wilkie and were organized into tabular form with indexes and percentage change calculations by Michael Hammond.

[8] There are some inconsistent aggregate data in later editions of *Anuario Estadístico*.

[9] Registration with the DGP is more helpful in finding employment in some professions than in others. See the discussion of this indicator in Part II below. For a discussion of distortions arising from the fact that certain careers can be followed without registration (even without a degree), see the analysis of egresados data.

fields. An egresado has finished all the necessary course work and has only to complete the final requirement, generally a thesis, to obtain the degree. The number of egresados, then, indicates the number of highly skilled persons available for employment in the professional fields.

Each of these three indicators based on career field preparation—professional degrees granted, professional degrees registered, and egresados—presents a different aspect of evolving professional training and skill development in Mexico. All three indicators are intended to determine the number of persons active or available for employment in a given professional area.

The changing methods of accumulating data on professionals can be interpreted as a response to the changing requirements for measuring the supply of skilled professionals. Over time, neither the number of degrees granted nor the number of degrees registered has continued to accurately indicate the general level of professional preparation of Mexican society. The number of egresados has been increasingly widely adopted as an indicator of professional preparation that is independent of employment trends in the professional fields.

Relationships among the three indicators can be defined in overlapping years. I have carried forward the data on degrees registered from 1977 so as to overlap with the ANUIES data, giving a basis for comparison of the two indicators over time. The data on egresados and degrees registered discussed below, for example, show that for approximately every ten engineering egresados in 1980, one person registered an engineering degree with the DGP.[10] The ratios for the other fields can be likewise estimated. Ratios of egresados, *titulados*, and *registrados* calculated using different sources for various career areas and various years are presented in Appendix B.

Whereas these kinds of comparisons give us an approximate idea of the relationships among the three categories at a given time, use of the ratios to extrapolate either forward or backward in time is almost certainly misleading. The ratios have not remained constant over time and, more importantly, the problem of double– and triple–counting is not easily solved. In many cases, egresados of professional fields eventually earn the degree, and may later register that degree with the DGP. That there is no way to determine with accuracy how many egresados become registered titulados, or over what period of time, means that each series must be used more or less on its own and attention must be focused on trends rather than on numbers. Why professionals do not find it desirable, or necessary, to earn the formal degree, or to register it especially in certain fields, is discussed in more depth in Part II below.

The three indicators discussed here also represent different levels of professional preparation. The degrees granted data include both licentiate degrees and terminal professional degrees from the higher secondary level (*nivel medio*), while both degrees registered and egresados data refer to training at the licentiate level.[11]

We can use the business degrees granted category in the year 1971 as an example of the differences between these two levels. In 1971 business degrees at both secondary and university levels made up 42.3 percent of all degrees, but commercial degrees granted at the middle level alone made up 37.7 percent of all degrees, leaving the share held by licentiate business degrees at 4.6 percent. Seventy-five percent of middle level commercial degrees are granted to women. In contrast, licentiate business degrees make up 21 percent of all licentiate degrees and 84 percent are given to men.

Clearly, then, at least two different levels of professional training are represented in the data: a basic professional level and a highly trained professional level. Unfortunately, 1971 is one of the few years where the degrees granted data can be disaggregated to show the relationships between middle level and higher level training. Because this essay studies long-term changes in Mexico's overall professional skill profile, it must work at the aggregate level with the different levels of professional training and employment represented by the degrees granted data.[12]

The data do not allow us to determine the exact number of persons actually practicing a given profession at a certain level at a specific point in time. The three indicators I employ here, and especially the trends apparent in them, are extremely useful as indicators of the long-term development of professional expertise in Mexico over time. Together, they provide a way to gauge Mexico's professional preparedness for the demands of the modern world.

Part II. The Professional Makeup of Mexican Society and Professional Skill Development, 1900–84

Published census data on occupational distribution from 1900 to 1980 provide a useful primary gauge of the changing influence of professionals in Mexican society. The dramatic increase in the visibility of professionals in Mexico during the first three quarters of this century is apparent in the census data presented in figure 34:1.[13] Professionals increased from an insignificant 1 percent of the economically active population (EAP) in 1900 to almost 7 percent of EAP

---

[10] Figures 34:9 and 34:2.

[11] For a listing of professional fields included under the various headings used in Parts II and III and in the charts, see Appendix A. All three series refer to both public and private universities.

[12] For discussion of different levels of professional employment, see Petricioli and Reynolds (1967), who define two levels, and Davis (1967), who defines four. See also the discussion in Part II below.

[13] Source abbreviations used in the figures are explained in the References.

by 1980.[14] The growth since the 1930 census has been particularly strong and steady, with average jumps of more than 1 percent per decade.

For the years 1950–70, it is possible to define in the census data the relationship of certain basic types of professions to others. Although "service" professionals have increased as a percentage of EAP (figure 34:2), they have declined relative to other professional groupings, notably "commercial" professionals, in the period (figure 34:3).[15] At the same time, the combined portion of service and commercial professionals as a share of all professionals has declined. Clearly, Mexican society is becoming increasingly diverse in its professionalized sectors.

The census data outline some of the basic dimensions of the growth of the importance of professional skills in Mexican society, but tell little about specific career fields. "Service" and "commercial" categories, for example, are extremely broad—"service" professionals include various health professionals and teachers at all school levels.

For more detailed coverage of shifts in the training of professionals, I turn to data that can be organized to display career field choices and the availability of professionals over time. Data on professional degrees granted are graphed in figure 34:4.

Until the 1940s, little differentiation in trends among the various degrees is apparent. Since the census data indicate a jump of at least 1 percent between the 1930 and 1940 census years, and since figure 34:5 shows little differentiation in growth of the three most important fields in the 1928–40 period, we can assume that the growth was in areas of traditional professional concentration.

Two dramatic changes occurred between 1940, the beginning of Mexico's modern industrial growth and economic consolidation, and 1970. First, the absolute number of degrees granted in the categories graphed has increased very rapidly since the mid-1940s.[16] Second, this growth has occurred primarily in business, teaching, and, to a lesser extent, the health professions.[17] In law, the most tradition-bound profession in Mexico, the number of degrees, although remaining substantial, increased only slightly from 1928 to 1970.

Figure 34:6 shows the post–1940 evolution of the four most important professional fields in more detail, adding data on engineering fields, which grew rapidly in absolute terms after 1940. Much of the post-1940 growth in professionalism seen in the census data appears to have taken place in the nontraditional fields of business and engineering.

The changing percentage shares of the five most important degrees granted in the 1929–70 period are shown in figure 34:7. From the 1929–34 period through the 1941–46 presidency of Avila Camacho, the four most important degrees steadily slipped as a share of all degrees as professional preparation became more diverse.

Most striking in figure 34:7 is the meteoric rise in the number of business degrees granted after the 1941–46 period resulting in the displacement of teaching as the dominant degree category.[18] Business degrees rose from 15 percent of all degrees in the 1941–46 period to a high of more than 50 percent by 1959–64. From the 1947–52 period into the 1970s, business remained the single most important area of expertise produced by the Mexican system.

Even with the increased importance of business training, the data indicate that the overall diversity of professional preparation has continued to increase since the early 1950s. Since the 1953–58 period, there has been a general decline of the four most important fields as a share of all degrees.

The data on degrees granted are presented by presidential administration in the charts in order to show correlations between presidential development strategies and the preparation of skilled professionals in the 1929–70 period. The greatly increased attention to business skills after 1941 fits well with our conception of the shift from the Cárdenas presidency and a socially revolutionary era to the beginning of Mexico's industrial revolution and governmental emphasis on economic expenditure.[19] By the time of what James W. Wilkie calls the "balanced revolution" ideology of the late 1950s and early 1960s, we see the gradual decline of business relative to the other three fields.

In turning to discussion of the 1970–76 administration of Luis Echeverría, we move from data on titulados to data on degrees registered (registrados). Absolute data on degrees registered from 1970 through 1984 are presented by field in figures 34:8 and 34:9.[20] The data have been extended beyond 1976 to make possible comparisons with the egresado data discussed below.

---

[14] Although there were changes in census methodology in 1940 and 1980, I have reconciled the series and the basic trend discussed here is unaffected.

[15] "Service" and "commercial" are the official census designations; only in the 1970 census are the categories disaggregated. I have reorganized the data to make them consistent over time.

[16] Figure 34:19 shows that these changes have more than kept pace with population growth.

[17] In general, the charts show only the four or five "most important" fields. These fields are both numerically most significant and most dynamic over time.

[18] Business was listed as a category for the first time in 1941; the various business and commercial degrees had been included in the "other" category before this date. A similar shift between "other" and "business" categories was made in 1948. I have adjusted the data to smooth the sudden transition from 1947 to 1948 by including a percentage (determined by trends in the two categories) of "other" degrees in the "business" category in previous years.

[19] For an analysis of shifts in government expenditure, see Wilkie (1978).

[20] Data for engineering degrees have been partially estimated.

Figure 34:1

MEXICAN PROFESSIONALS AS PERCENT OF EAP, 1900–80

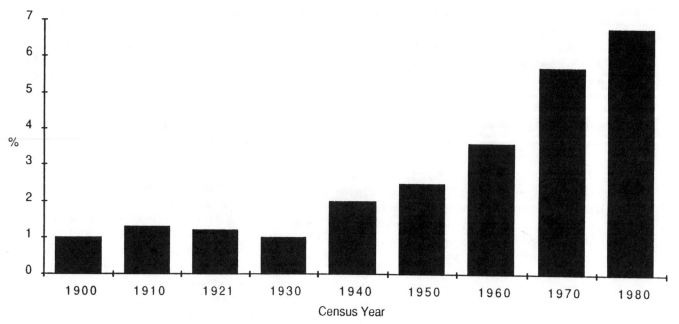

SOURCE: Census.

Figure 34:2

SERVICE PROFESSIONALS AS PERCENT OF EAP, 1950–80

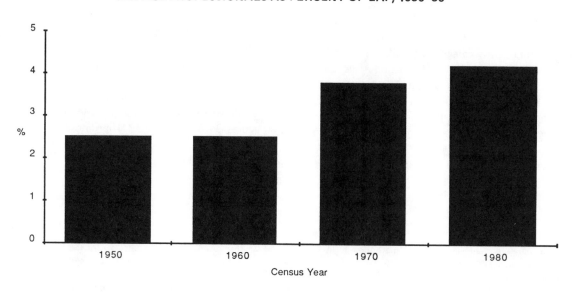

SOURCE: Census.

Figure 34:3

SERVICE AND COMMERCIAL PROFESSIONALS AS PERCENT OF ALL PROFESSIONALS, 1950–70

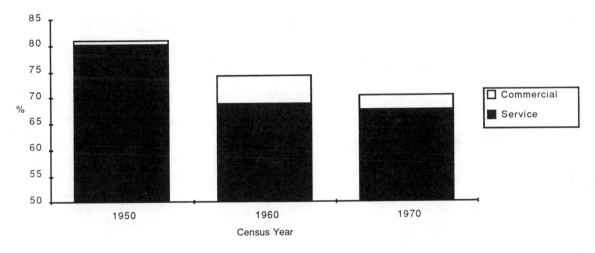

SOURCE: Census.

Figure 34:4

PROFESSIONAL DEGREES GRANTED, FOUR FIELDS, 1928–71

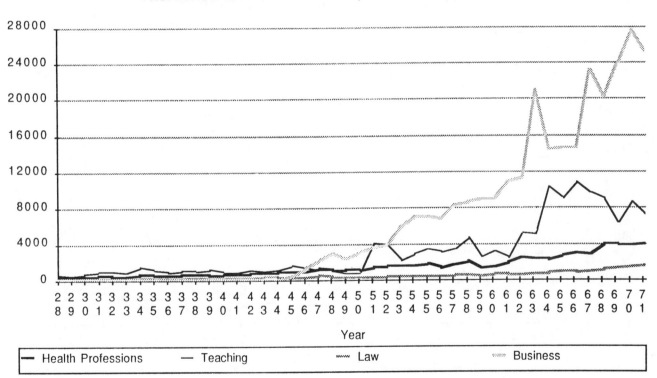

SOURCE: AE.

Figure 34:5

PROFESSIONAL DEGREES GRANTED, THREE FIELDS, 1928–40

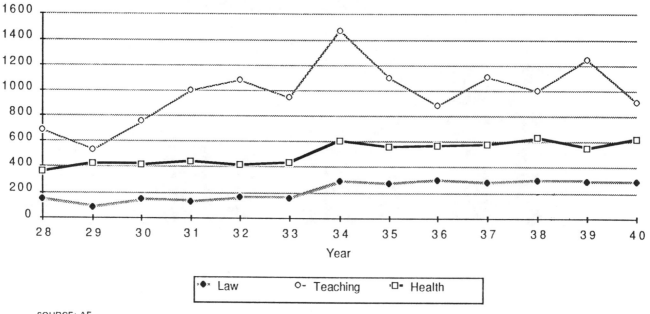

SOURCE: AE.

Figure 34:6

PROFESSIONAL DEGREES GRANTED, FIVE FIELDS, 1941–71

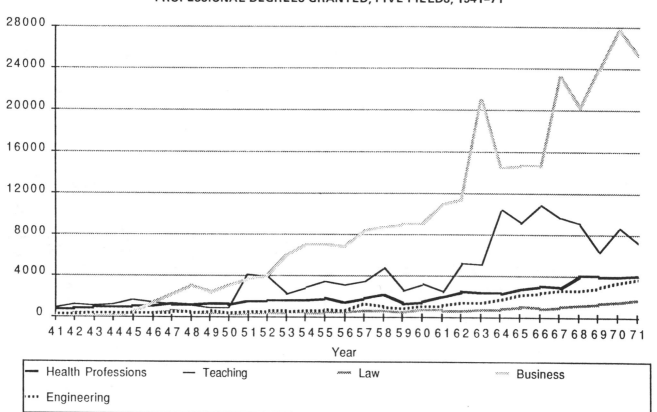

SOURCE: AE.

Figure 34:7

PERCENT SHARE, PROFESSIONAL DEGREES GRANTED, FIVE FIELDS, 1929–70

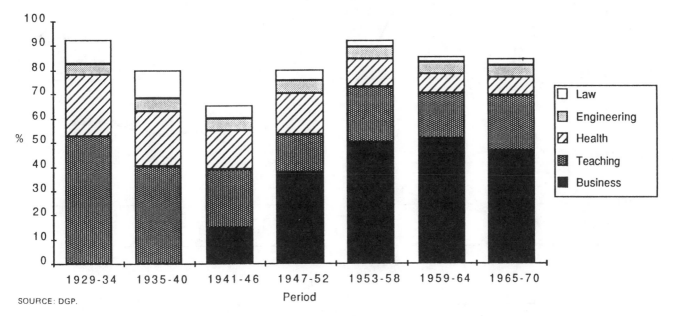

SOURCE: DGP.

Degrees in teaching and health professions were by far the most frequently registered degrees in this period (figure 34:8) and the absolute number of degrees registered for primary teaching and health fields has increased markedly since 1970. Likewise, the number of degrees registered in engineering, law, business, economics, and advanced research fields (M.A./Ph.D.) has increased, although their numbers are far fewer (figure 34:9). Because registration is most necessary for work in government agencies, and since health professionals and teachers are the most numerous of government-employed professionals, this differential is not surprising. The registration of law degrees seems to be in line with the granting of law degrees: lawyers, because they are also frequently government employees, if not because they are inherently more concerned with legal form, would tend to register their degrees.

The relative importance over time of six principal professional degrees registered in the 1970s and early 1980s is shown in figures 34:10 and 34:11. With the exception of business, all degrees experienced an expansion of registrations in the late 1970s and early 1980s. Teaching and law have become less important relative to other fields. The share of engineering degrees registered, although rising quickly in the early 1970s, has fallen steadily since 1976. The share of degrees registered in economics and business has remained fairly constant throughout the period. There are signs of the same general increase in diversity in professional fields noted in the degrees granted data, as the share of these five degrees has steadily decreased.

During the early 1970s President Echeverría brought into government professional groups that had been ignored by the political process for decades even as their numbers had been growing. Along with directly encouraging growth in technical education, Echeverría's inclusion of a wide range of professionals in his administration must be credited with stimulating interest in professional education in general. This stimulus to the training of skilled professionals is apparent in the increase in the number of registrations of professional degrees, compared to the number of degrees granted in previous periods.

The most consistent indicator of educational system output of skilled professionals for the post-Echeverría period is the number of egresados of the various career fields. Figure 34:12 graphs absolute data for the five most important egresado fields for 1977 to 1982. The figure shows a steady rise in law, medicine, teaching, business, and engineering egresados over the six-year period. Teaching egresados have been growing in number faster than egresados in the other categories.

The five fields of law, health, teaching, business, and engineering have retained their respective shares of total egresados over the period 1977–82, as shown in figure 34:13.[21] Teaching egresados have been gaining slightly,

[21] Urquidi and Lajous Vargas (1967) show that this distribution has not always been so stable. In the early 1960s health professions were a low 13 percent, business a high 27 percent (compared with the 1977–84 data).

Figure 34:8

PROFESSIONAL DEGREES REGISTERED, 1970–84, PART I

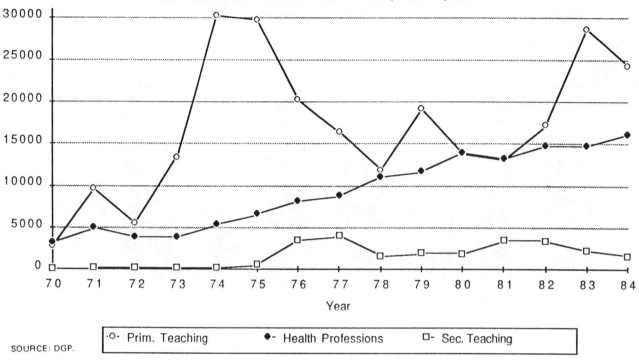

SOURCE: DGP.

Figure 34:9

PROFESSIONAL DEGREES REGISTERED, 1970–84, PART II

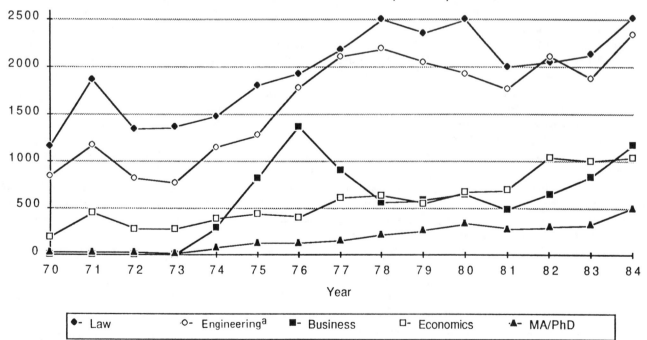

a. Data for engineering partially estimated.

SOURCE: DGP.

Figure 34:10

PERCENT SHARE OF PROFESSIONAL DEGREES REGISTERED, 1972–84, PART I

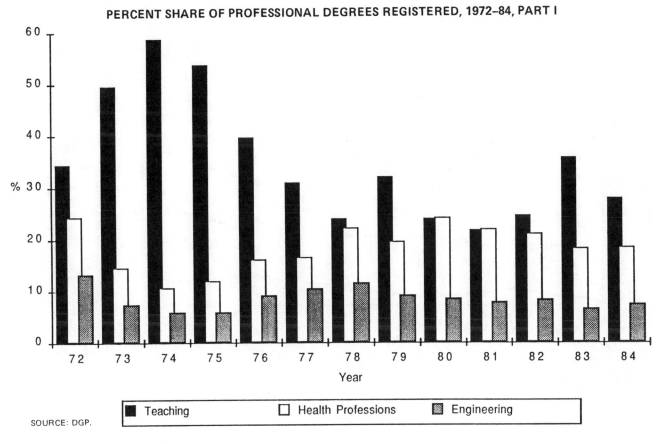

SOURCE: DGP.

| ■ Teaching | □ Health Professions | ▨ Engineering |

Figure 34:11

PERCENT SHARE OF PROFESSIONAL DEGREES REGISTERED, 1972–84, PART II

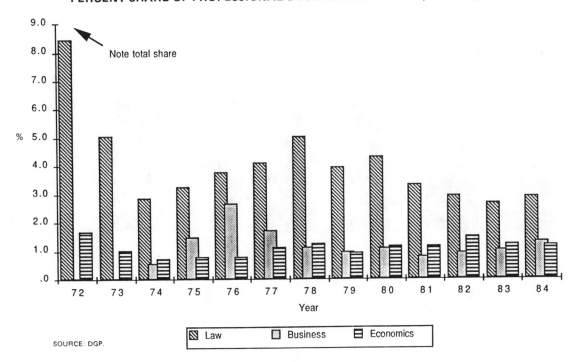

Note total share

SOURCE: DGP.

| ▨ Law | ▨ Business | ▤ Economics |

Figure 34:12

EGRESADOS, FIVE FIELDS, 1977–82

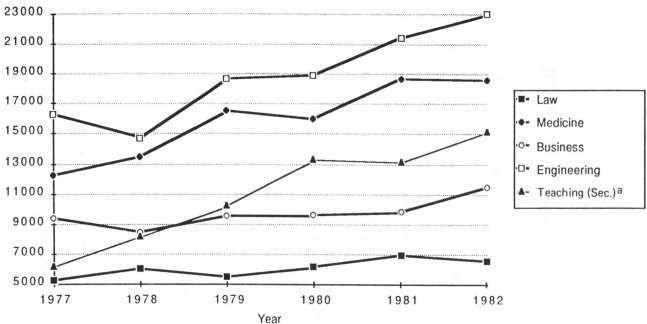

a. Teaching estimated for 1977 and 1978.

SOURCE: ANUIES, AE.

Figure 34:13

PERCENT SHARE OF EGRESADOS, FIVE FIELDS, 1977–82

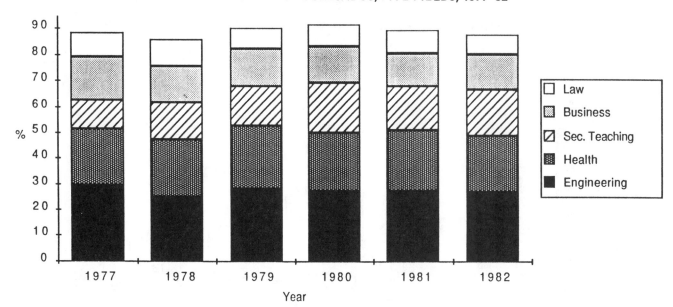

SOURCE: ANUIES, AE.

from 11 percent in 1977 to 18 percent in 1982. The declining overall share of the five egresado categories again indicates increasing diversity, although the data indicate that the rate of increasing diversity has slowed compared with earlier periods.

Comparing the degrees registered data with the egresados data, we note in all fields that the number of egresados exceeds the number of degrees registered in the years for which we have overlapping data. In business and engineering, egresados exceed titulados by many times.[22] Four non-mutually exclusive interpretations of the gap suggest themselves.

First, professionals with business management or engineering training are able to find work without holding a formal degree. The growing practice of hiring in Mexico based on entrance-to-employment examinations, in both public and private sectors, makes a degree increasingly less important for obtaining certain kinds of work (especially in the business and engineering fields, where such exams are common). This practice would tend to support the first interpretation.[23]

Second, the gap between the number of registered degrees and the number of egresados may indicate that overemphasis on high-level training in these areas has led to saturation of the market for these skills and abandonment of the career by professional hopefuls who feel they cannot find employment even with a degree. Development strategies that have been based on technical and financial paths to modernization may have stimulated the education of professionals that the system cannot absorb.

Third, it is possible that the increasing centralization of decision making in Mexican government since the 1970s has restricted the market for certain professional skills in the public sector.[24] In this interpretation, student career choices respond in part to employment opportunities in the decentralized and parastatal sectors, expanding through the 1960s but contracting after 1975.[25]

Fourth, it is clear that in many professions egresados fill the demand for middle-level expertise while titulados (persons holding the degree) or persons with graduate education (M.A. or Ph.D.) occupy more demanding and more rewarding positions. Blanca Petricioli and Clark Reynolds point out in regard to the training of Mexican economists, for example, that egresados frequently make up the pool of secretaries, clerks, compilers of data, and other auxiliary workers for both private firms and government agencies. More qualified economics titulados, those that Petricioli and Reynolds characterize as having "sufficient command of theory and technique to take raw data and turn it to the testing of hypo-

theses of relevance to general theory and specific policy,"[26] are the source of Mexico's professional economists.[27]

The different methods adopted by Mexican agencies for tracking professional skill development provide hints about the changing training and social role of professionals. For example, the current concern over qualitative norms in the Mexican higher education system is a logical result of changes seen in the data presented here. As manifested in the discrepancy between egresados and registered degrees, formal titles appear to be becoming less important as employment is increasingly dependent on entrance-level examination performance. Employers have at least partially taken over the job of ascertaining, and thus to some extent maintaining, quality in professional education in Mexico.

In summary, the three indicators of trends in professional education utilized in this study make it possible to identify important shifts in professional training emphasis for the period 1928–84 which coincide with the evolving development strategies of Mexican presidential coalitions. Social, economic, and balanced phases of the Revolution are revealed in the shifting emphases of professional education. The most striking changes are manifested in the rise to preeminence of business skills after 1940 and the more balanced profile of professional preparation that characterized the 1960s, as the importance of business was tempered by the growth of other dynamic professional fields such as engineering.

On the whole the professional education system appears responsive to the changing development environments created by Mexican presidents.[28] The series analyzed here indicate, however, that the modernization strategies of Mexican presidents themselves deserve further analysis and critique. The data clearly highlight excesses produced in professional fields during the course of these changing strategies. Comparison of the different methodologies for tracking professional skill training indicates one long-term distortion: the historical emphasis of the Mexican system on a few professional fields, particularly those related to a narrow economic conception of modernization, rather than on the overall quality or balance of professional capabilities produced.[29]

---

[22] See Appendix B for some ratios between egresados, titulados, and registrados.

[23] Failure rate for four public sector qualifying exams are given in Appendix C.

[24] On defining this centralizing trend, see Hanson (1977).

[25] See Newell and Rubio (1984).

[26] Petricioli and Reynolds (1967: 15).

[27] Petricioli and Reynolds suggest that it would be both beneficial and cost effective to invest in upgrading economics egresados to titulados, as there exists a need for more highly trained economists while at the same time there is a surplus of egresados for low-paying auxiliary roles. Davis (1967), in regard to technical training, however, sees a growing demand for auxiliary-level technicians in the industrial sector and suggests that technical training be expanded at the middle, rather than at the upper, level.

[28] Development "environments" may be more important than specific development policies. See Latapí's analysis of Echeverría's policies (1980).

[29] This distortion is hardly peculiar to Mexico, however; it lies at the center of the 1986–87 controversies over university reform in France, Italy, and Spain, for example. See *The Nation* (April 11, 1987).

Part III. Professionals and the Mexican Political Elite

I have suggested that historical changes in emphasis of Mexican professional training are intimately linked to the twentieth-century progression of Mexican modernization strategies. The data analyzed above show that, regardless of ruling party rhetoric, such strategies have focused on the growth of business and finance in attempting to propel Mexico into the modern world. In applications that are more structural, cross-sectional data shed light on political and social realities related to the general process of this modernization.

As one example of political analysis to which degree data can be applied, the different types of degrees held by PAN (Partido Acción Nacional) and PRI (Partido Revolucionario Institucional—the official government party) members show (figure 34:14) the social makeup of the governing party and the main opposition group and provide clues to their bases of support. We can see PAN's conservatism reflected in the predominance of legal training, a preparation in continuous decline since 1928. Historically, the PRI appears to have a reasonable claim to being a more "popular" party than the PAN—almost one-third of its party members hold no degree at all. Finally, it must be noted that business training, the most dynamic field in the above data, is almost twice as common in PRI as in PAN ranks.

This type of structural analysis can be expanded to reflect on social issues more directly related to professional education. For example, it is widely believed, both in Mexico and abroad, that professional preparation in Mexico has as its chief aim the acquisition of positions of political power, that professional training is in fact thinly disguised political apprenticeship. This hypothesis can be tested by comparing the data discussed in Part I with data on the educational backgrounds of Mexico's political elite.[30]

Data on the professional preparation of college educated leaders from 1925 to 1976 by presidential administration are graphed in figure 34:15.[31] Legal training, even though much reduced in importance by the 1970s, accounted for at least half of all professional preparation among the Mexican political elite throughout the period. Representation of both engineering and medical expertise has fluctuated greatly from one administration to another, but the two fields seem to remain on average about equally important among elite groups over time. The steady growth of economics training is noteworthy, increasing by over six times during the period. As in all the data on career preparation discussed above, we see increasing professional skill diversity in elite backgrounds over time.

If we compare these data on elite backgrounds (figure 34:15) with the data on professional fields discussed above (figure 34:7), we see little correlation between career paths

chosen by Mexican students and the professional backgrounds of persons in positions of political power. Certainly the importance of legal training declines over time in both charts, but economics is not an important field in figure 34:7, and the business field is absent from figure 34:15. Medical degrees appear to be holding their own in the political arena (although they fluctuate from administration to administration), but, as we have seen, their share of the total degrees has been declining.

If it were the case that Mexican students chose certain professional careers because of perceived political returns, we would expect to see a much greater interest in law from 1928 to the present. Instead, much of the post-1940 change in professional study has been away from fields well represented in the elite, that is, away from law and medicine, in favor of business and technical fields not at all well represented among the elite.

A related conception of Mexican professional education holds that many Mexicans, particularly those belonging to the highest echelon of Mexico's political pyramid, are educated abroad in their specialties, particularly in the United States. But my research indicates that the number of Mexicans studying in the United States is very small compared with the number trained domestically.[32]

Career fields studied by Mexican students in the United States are shown in figure 34:16. The number of Mexicans studying in all fields is increasing rapidly. Percent shares for the different career fields are supplied in figure 34:17 which can be compared with the data in figures 34:7 and 34:15 above. Business, engineering, and physical and life sciences are the most important fields studied by Mexican students in the United States, with business and education growing markedly in importance during the period. Interest in engineering fields has been declining, while interest in agricultural and health professions has remained stable.

Field choices made by Mexican students in the United States appear to be of two kinds. There is a concentration in the most rapidly growing fields in Mexico, business and engineering, and there is a concentration in professional areas in which Mexico does not show strong development according to the data discussed above, natural and social sciences. The data do not suggest that Mexican students in the United States pursue the professional careers typical of Mexico's political elite: United States universities do not appear to serve as a springboard to the top of Mexico's political pyramid.[33]

---

[30] For a discussion of defining Mexico's political elite, see Camp (1980). Camp's definition is adopted here.

[31] The data are from Camp (1980).

---

[32] Generally, the number of Mexican students enrolled in United States universities is less than half of 1 percent of egresados of Mexican universities.

[33] The study of economics by Mexicans in the United States may be an exception to this rule. Degrees in economics earned in the United Staes may be increasing at the same time that economics backgrounds are increasingly common in Mexico's professional makeup and political elite (see figures 34:7 and 34:15); but the field is hidden in the "social science" category in the IIE data graphed in figures 34:16 and 34:17.

Figure 34:14

DEGREES OF PAN AND PRI MEMBERS, 1935–73

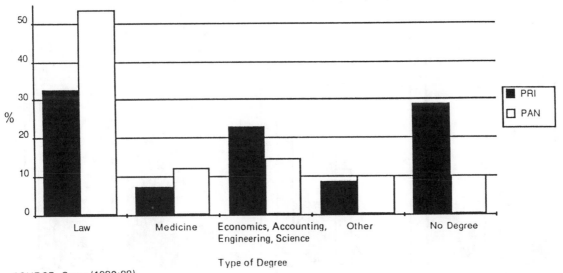

SOURCE: Camp (1980:88).

Figure 34:15

DEGREES EARNED BY COLLEGE-EDUCATED LEADERS, 1935–76

(%)

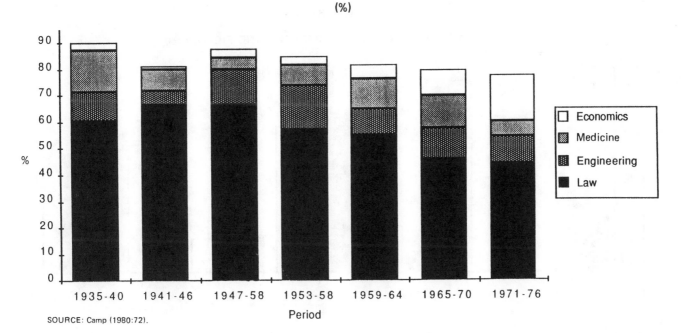

SOURCE: Camp (1980:72).

Figure 34:16

MEXICAN STUDENTS IN U.S. BY FIELD, 1960–75

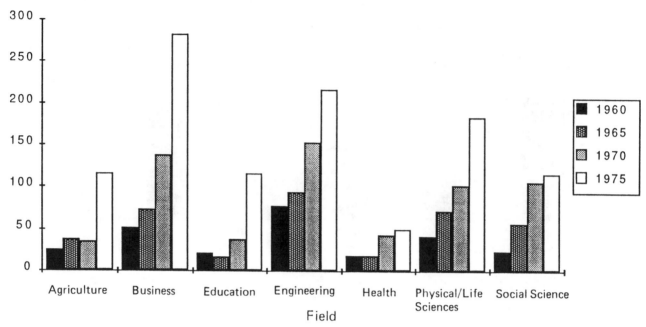

SOURCE: IIE, *Open Doors*.

Figure 34:17

MEXICAN STUDENTS IN U.S., BY PERCENT AND FIELD, 1960–75

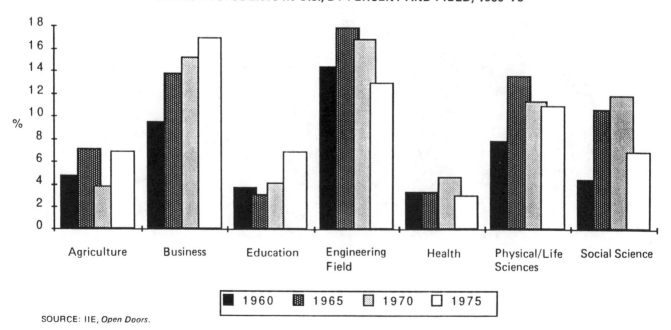

SOURCE: IIE, *Open Doors*.

Similarity in career field choices in Mexico and the United States holds true also for the microcosm of Mexican students at the University of California, Los Angeles (UCLA), according to unpublished data I have collected at UCLA's Office of International Students and Scholars.[34] It is interesting to note, and will prove worthy of consideration in further investigation, that Mexicans, both at United States universities in general and at UCLA specifically, select different areas of study at United States universities than do "Latin American" students in general. The example of Mexican students suggests that, although frequently grouped together, visiting students of different Latin American nationalities probably choose markedly different careers.

Data from both Mexico and the United States indicate that the Mexican professional training system is not structured to respond to the political aspirations of students. Rather, choices seem to be based mainly on student perceptions of future employment opportunities in the Mexican public and private economic systems.[35]

Part IV. Comparisons with the United States, Bolivia, Brazil, and Venezuela

Every year Mexico produces tens of thousands of business professionals for the private sector as well as many doctors who most likely will not practice medicine for significant parts of their professional careers (figures 34:12 and 34:15). A brief comparison of the Mexican data discussed above with similar data from the United States and three Latin American countries will shed light on the overall achievement of Mexico's attempt to supply its modernization effort with individuals equipped with professional skills.

The United States

The changing percent shares of the most important professional degrees granted in the United States, 1940 to 1980, are shown in figure 34:18 (the United States counterpart of figure 34:7). The most important professions in both countries are the same: business, teaching, engineering, health, and law. But two differences are particularly noteworthy. First, whereas business degrees make up less than 20 percent of all United States degrees granted in 1970, in Mexico they represent roughly half of all degrees in that year. Second, the total share of the six most important professions in the United States is a little more than half that of the five most important Mexican professions.[36]

Whereas Mexican advanced degrees per capita have increased greatly since 1930 (as seen in figure 34:19), the United States boasts more advanced degrees per capita, and the number of degrees per capita has increased much more rapidly in the United States than in Mexico over time.[37] The comparison of these two data sets gives some idea of the relative density of professionals in the two countries: approximately one of every 1,000 Mexicans receives an advanced degree each year, whereas one in every 200 United States citizens receives one. While a few degrees dominate the Mexican professional arena, professional degrees are much less significant per capita in Mexico than they are in the United States.

At first glance, then, it appears that the United States is far better off than Mexico, with regard to diversity and density of skilled professionals. But these per capita data tell us little about their geographic distribution.

The general concentration of professionals in the more developed areas of Mexico is shown in figure 34:20. Here we see that Mexico City and other highly urbanized areas attract much more than their share of professionally skilled persons. Differences in literacy and educational attainment among Mexican regions are small in comparison with differences between high-level manpower and capacities for increasing that manpower.[38]

We have seen that Mexico is producing many health professionals every year, but also that medical doctors make up a significant part of Mexico's political elite. The high visibility of medical doctors in the elite groups is surprising in view of the limited availability of quality health care in many rural areas of Mexico. While Mexico says it has 50,000 unemployed doctors at the present time, more than 100,000 of Mexico's less developed population centers, where roughly 10 million people reside, suffer from complete lack of quality health care.[39]

It is not commonly noted that the United States has the same problem of professional skill concentration in developed areas, if more in structure than in dimension. Regarding health professionals, it has been estimated that the United States will have a "surplus" of 70,000 physicians by 1990,[40] yet geographical distribution of health care professionals is extremely skewed, apparently to the detriment of rural and poor inhabitants, as in Mexico. The state of California serves as an excellent example: while San Francisco County boasts 6.2 doctors for every 1,000 inhabitants and

---

[34] The UCLA data are for enrollment.

[35] Undoubtedly, student choices also depend partially on student and parent conceptions of social status associated with both the different careers and the level of study. See Latapí (1980).

[36] Three degree levels are represented in the United States data: B.A., M.A., and Ph.D. or other doctorate.

---

[37] Of course, the United States has had the advantage of a slowing population growth rate. Note that the data in figure 34:19 refer to degrees granted in a given year, not total degrees, per 100,000 population.

[38] Myers (1965:32). For a study of maldistribution of professional expertise, see the study of social work developed by Harris Rivera (1984).

[39] Jaime Martuscelli, Subsecretario de Salud, in *La Opinión* (Los Angeles), September 14, 1986.

[40] "The Physician Glut," *California Physician*, October 1984, p. 12.

Figure 34:18

PERCENT SHARE, U.S. PROFESSIONAL DEGREES
GRANTED, SIX FIELDS, 1940–80

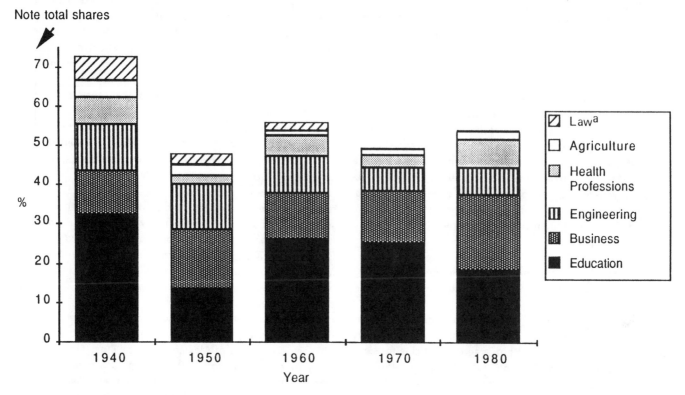

a. Law degrees less than 1% in 1970 and 1980.

SOURCE: DES, BSE.

Figure 34:19

MEXICAN AND U.S. DEGREES GRANTED, 1930–70

(PHTI)

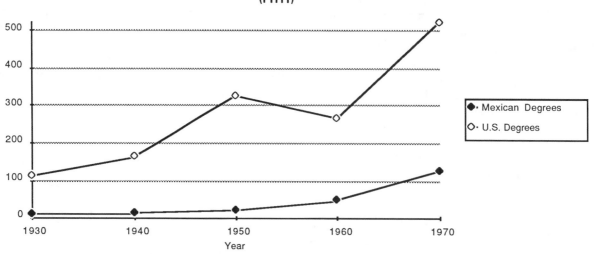

SOURCE: Mexico: Census; U.S.: HSUS, 1960 and SAUS, 1973.

Figure 34:20

STOCK OF "HIGH-LEVEL MANPOWER," SELECTED STATES, 1960

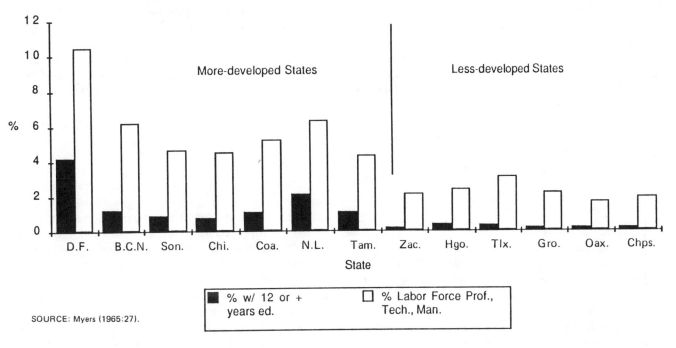

SOURCE: Myers (1965:27).

Figure 34:21

UNIVERSITY GRADUATES, BY FIELD, 4 L, 1984

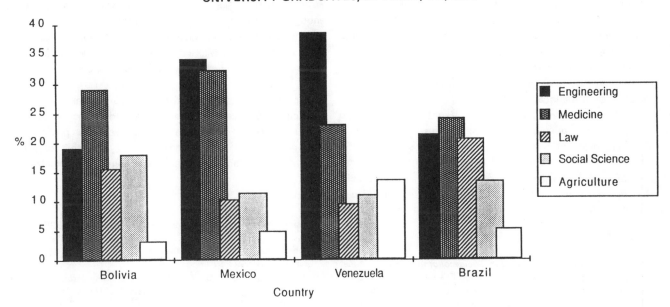

SOURCE: UNESCO-SY, 1984.

Los Angeles County 2.5, Modoc County (a northern rural county) has only .23 physicians per 1,000—one doctor per 4,348 inhabitants.[41]

The distribution of basic professions—medicine, teaching, agricultural engineering—to all geographic regions and all levels of society is as important as the per capita production of professionals, and must be recognized as a crucial ingredient of modernization. Mexico's "highly developed" northern neighbor closely resembles Mexico, frequently classified as an "under" or "sub" developed country, in the uneven geographic distribution of at least one key area of professional expertise. The problem, then, is not specific to Mexico and does not appear to be unique to "developing" countries.

Bolivia, Brazil, and Venezuela

It will prove useful for broader comparative purposes to examine the degree to which the experiences of other Latin American countries parallel that of Mexico—can we define a "Latin American" experience with respect to the preparation of professionals? Figure 34:21 reveals that there is in fact a great deal of variance in the production of professionals among the four Latin American countries graphed for the year 1984. Brazil is representative of a highly developed Latin American nation, Venezuela illustrates the situation in a country "blessed," like Mexico, with oil, and Bolivia is an example of a poorer Latin American country.

Brazil and Bolivia show professional skill development profiles which are more evenly balanced between career fields than those for Mexico and Venezuela. Both Brazil and Bolivia have high relative proportions of doctors and social scientists.[42] Venezuela, by most measurements the least agricultural of the four nations, shows the greatest development of agricultural expertise. Even at state universities in Mexico's most agricultural states, the importance of professional training in agriculture falls far below agriculture's importance in the local economy.[43]

Compared with Mexico and Venezuela, Brazil and Bolivia display greater diversity in professional expertise. The percentage of the four most important study areas in these two countries accounts for a little more than 80 percent of professional fields whereas in Mexico and Venezuela, the four most important areas constitute more than 95 percent.[44] In Mexico engineers and doctors share the dominant

position; in Venezuela, engineers alone claim a 38 percent share of all professional fields.[45]

We cannot speak, apparently, of a simple, one-dimensional Latin American experience with professional preparation. Rather, each country's experience is related, like Mexico's, to national development strategies and distinct historical progressions of social, economic, and political interactions. Also, as shown in Part II above, professionals must be seen in their proper social and political context, which undoubtedly differs markedly from country to country.[46]

Conclusions

The data analyzed here suggest that there is a disparity between Mexico's preparation for the management needs of a modernizing economy and the low production and maldistribution of infrastructure expertise needed for full and balanced development of the human and natural resources of the country. The Mexican higher education system is more responsive to certain needs of Mexican society, in general those of expanding business and financial sectors, than to other, perhaps more basic, social needs.[47] The uneven development of the professions inherently favors the development of Mexico City and other highly developed regions of Mexico, exacerbating a situation revealed in the data on the geographic distribution of health professionals.

Mexico needs well-trained doctors, teachers, and agricultural engineers as well as high-level economic *técnicos*, not only in the largest urban centers and most developed areas, but also in less populated and less developed areas as well. While the data suggest that the Mexican system is responsive enough to be able to shift to an emphasis on the production of infrastructure modernization skills, distribution of these skills to all areas of Mexico is a problem for which Mexican history does not indicate a great deal of flexibility.

Increased government support for certain professional career fields, especially if expressed through grants and other financial assistance, might encourage study of neglected areas and relieve problems of balance and diversity in professional training. But the extra funds necessary for this long-term investment are lacking at the present time. Historically, the

---

[41] California Medical Association, *Socioeconomic Report*, June 1981, p. 5. Large California-based health care organizations such as Kaiser Permanente Medical Care Program and Maxicare consider a ratio of 1 doctor to 800 health plan members more than sufficient for meeting patient needs.

[42] Note, however, that because of incomparable systems for teacher training, the very important teaching category included in data for titulados, registrados, and egresados is not considered here.

[43] Castrejón Diez (1979:176).

[44] All these percentage shares are high compared to the United States; cf. figure 34:18.

---

[45] Business is not considered as a separate area in this UNESCO data; thus, the percentage shares cited here should not be compared with the percentage share data on Mexican and United States skill areas discussed in Part I above.

[46] As also suggested in Part II, professional training *abroad* may have very different proportions and effects in the different Latin American countries.

[47] It must also be noted that advanced research, especially in social sciences and humanities, has been neglected in Mexico. CONACYT (El Consejo Nacional de Ciencia y Tecnología) reported that in 1986 Mexico could claim only 23 researchers per 100,000 population, a proportion inferior to those in Cuba, Argentina, Uruguay, Chile, Venezuela, and Brazil (reported in "Muy bajo índice de investigadores," *La Opinión* [Los Angeles], December 9, 1986).

Mexican government has been slow to spend on higher education the extra amounts necessary to significantly modify or upgrade the system.

The current financial restrictions on the Mexican government make it easier to propose solutions for the problem of distribution than for that of infrastructure skill development. Two possibilities suggest themselves that probably would not be prohibitively costly and could produce short-term payoffs. First, further decentralization of professional training, an education policy aim of the de la Madrid government, could help spread professional expertise.[48] Second, professionals could be directed into less specialized fields than those they currently pursue. In the United States doctors trained as general practitioners have naturally tended to settle in less developed areas of the country, where their general skills are more in demand.[49] Decentralization and generalization of training could have the added benefit of stimulating interest in expertise needed in areas less developed than Mexico's central region and areas of urban concentration, thus naturally tending to resolve gradually the distortions of the production problem.

The data also indicate that Mexico must raise the general level of competence of the professionals produced by the education system in order to meet employer demands for expertise. In the fall of 1986 Mexico appeared to be responding to this pressing issue of qualitative norms. In September the rector of UNAM put into motion a plan that shifted university policy to an emphasis on more stringent exam requirements, the gradual removal of the "automatic pass" from preparatory to professional level, and the raising of course and field standards.[50]

In February 1987, however, the reforms were rescinded after a nineteen-day student strike. Students demanded a primary role in the reform process, and forced the formation of a congress including a powerful student lobby to debate issues of declining quality and the university's social responsibilities. It remains to be seen whether this congress will take the necessary measures to shore up UNAM's reputation and capability.[51]

The Mexican case reveals two major, yet largely unrecognized, factors in the country's twentieth-century development effort: the skewed proportions of skilled professional's produced by the system of higher education and their uneven geographical distribution. I suggest that both distortions are the result of attempts to emulate the highly developed economies of Western societies and the simultaneous, perhaps consequent, neglect of the public health, educational, and agricultural foundations of those economies.

Creating a balanced professional skill pool in Mexico will involve orienting professional education to infrastructural modernization needs and the broad distribution of professional skills. That the pressing need for this orientation has been ignored in the past may be due in large measure to the modernization environments supported by Mexican presidents. Although these strategies have been couched, at least in part, in the social-revolutionary rhetoric of Mexico's ruling coalitions, they have in reality emphasized economic growth over balanced development of human and natural resources. Because the professional education trends presented here reflect Mexico's modernization effort at the basic level of success over the long term, rather than the level of rhetoric and propaganda, analyzing and understanding them are essential to the study of twentieth-century Mexico.

[48] Most professionals already receive their first years of professional training in their home states. See King (1972).

[49] This process has been catalyzed too by medical training which increasingly emphasizes social and ethical aspects of health profession practice.

[50] UNAM, *Modificaciones académicas en la UNAM*, and *Proceso*, September 19, 1986, pp. 16–17.

[51] Another response to the crisis of quality is the increasing role of private universities in training Mexican professionals, especially professionals in business and engineering fields. Universities such as the Iberoamericana also appear to be becoming important as centers for the training of Mexican elites (*Proceso*, March 31, 1986).

Appendix A

PROFESSIONAL FIELDS REPRESENTED IN DEGREE CATEGORIES

Degrees Granted (1929–71)

Business	Accounting, business administration, commerce (including higher secondary after 1965)
Health	Medical and dental surgery, nursing
Teaching	Primary and secondary teaching
Law	Licentiate in law
Engineering	Civil, chemical, agricultural, all others

Degrees Registered (1971–84)

Business	Business administration
Health	Medical and dental surgery, nursing
Teaching	Primary school teaching
Law	Licentiate in law
Engineering	Civil, chemical, agricultural, all others

Egresados (1977–82)

Business	Business administration, marketing, sales, accounting
Health	Medical and dental surgery, nursing
Teaching	Secondary teaching
Law	Licentiate in law
Engineering	Civil, chemical, agricultural, all others

Appendix B

RATIOS OF EGRESADOS, TITULADOS, AND REGISTRADOS

I. Ratio of Egresados to Titulados, 1967
(Titulados = 1)

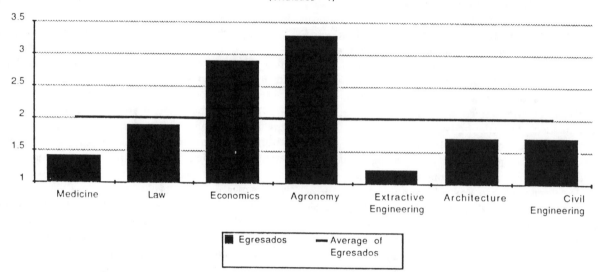

SOURCE: UNAM, AE, 1967.

II. Ratio of Egresados and Registrados to Titulados, 1971
(Titulados = 1)

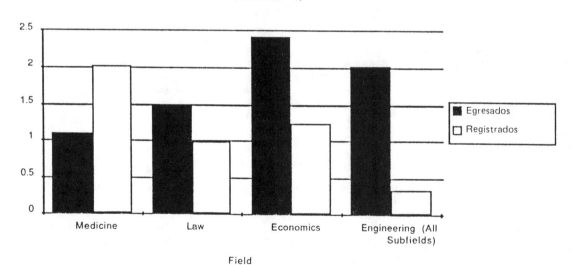

Field

SOURCE: ANUIES, *La enseñanza superior en México, 1971*; DGP.

Appendix C

FAILURE RATE FOR PUBLIC SECTOR QUALIFYING EXAMINATIONS

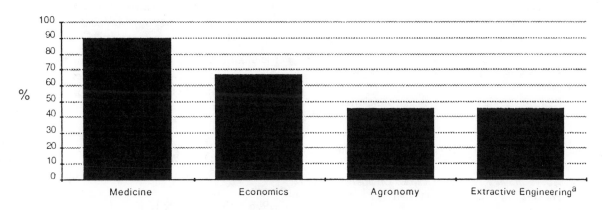

a. For extractive engineering: 10% failure at PEMEX; 80% at IMP.

SOURCE: ANUIES, *La enseñanza superior en México, 1970-76*; UNAM, AE

References

Primary Statistical Sources

AE — Dirección General de Estadística, *Anuario estadístico*, various years

ANUIES, AE — Asociación Nacional de Universidades e Institutos de Enseñanza Superior, *Anuario estadístico*, various years

Census — Decennial Census, Dirección General de Estadística, México, D.F.

DGP — Dirección General de Profesiones, unpublished data

Other Statistical Sources

BSE — U.S. Department of Education, *Biennial Survey of Education*, various years

DES — U.S. Department of Education, *Digest of Education Statistics*, various years

HSUS — *Historical Statistics of the United States*, various years, 1960

IIE — Institute of International Education, *Open Doors*, various years

SAUS — *Statistical Abstract of the United States*, various years, 1973

UNESCO — *Statistical Yearbook*, 1984

Additional Sources

ANUIES
1979 *Planeación de la educación en México*. México, D.F.

California Medical Association
1981 *Socioeconomic Report* (June).

California Physician
1984 "The Physician Glut" (June).

Camp, Roderic A.
1976 *Mexican Political Biographies, 1935-1975*. Tucson: University of Arizona Press.
1980 *Mexico's Leaders: Their Education and Recruitment*. Tucson: University of Arizona Press.

Castrejón Diez, Jaime
1979 *La educación superior en México*. México, D.F.: Editorial Edicol.

Cleaves, Peter S.
1985 *Las profesiones y el Estado: El caso de México*. México, D.F.: El Colegio de México.

CONACYT
1978 *Programa Nacional de Ciencia y Tecnología, 1978-1982*. México, D.F.: Consejo Nacional de Ciencia y Tecnología.

Davis, Russell G.
1967 *Scientific, Engineering and Technical Education in Mexico*. New York: Education and World Affairs.

García Sánchez, Francisco, and Leonicio Hernández
1977 *Educación superior, ciencia y tecnología en México, 1945-1975: Un diagnóstico de la educación superior y de la investigación científica y tecnológica en México*. México, D.F.: Secretaría de Educación Pública.

Hanson, James A.
1977 "Federal Expenditure and 'Personalism' in

Mexican 'Institutional' Revolution." In James W. Wilkie, ed., *Money and Politics in Latin America.* Los Angeles: UCLA Latin American Center Publications.

Harris Rivera, Yolanda Aguirre
1984   *Características socioacadémicas de las escuelas de trabajo social en la República Mexicana.* México, D.F.: Universidad Nacional Autónoma de México.

Hinojosa, Oscar
1986   "La universidad privada escala posiciones como provedora de funcionarios." *Proceso* (March 31), pp. 6–11.

King, Richard G., Alfonso Rangel Guerra, David Kline, and Noel F. McGinn
1972   *Nueve universidades mexicanas: Un análisis de su crecimiento y desarrollo.* México, D.F.: ANUIES.

La Opinión (Los Angeles)
1986   "Muy bajo índice de investigadores" (December 9).

Latapí, Pablo
1980   *Análisis de un sexenio de educación en México, 1970–1976.* México, D.F.: Editorial Nueva Imagen.

Levy, Daniel C.
1980   *University and Government in Mexico: Autonomy in an Authoritarian System.* New York: Praeger.

Mabry, Donald J.
1982   *The Mexican University and the State: Student Conflicts, 1910–1971.* College Station: Texas A&M University Press.

Martuscelli, Jaime
1986   In *La Opinión* (Los Angeles), September 14.

Myers, Charles Nash
1965   *Education and National Development in Mexico.*

Princeton, N.J.: Industrial Relations Section, Dept. of Economics, Princeton University.

Newell G., Roberto, and Luis Rubio F.
1984   *Mexico's Dilemma: The Political Origins of Economic Crisis.* Boulder, Colo.: Westview Press.

Petricioli, Blanca, and Clark W. Reynolds
1967   *The Teaching of Economics in Mexico.* Occasional Report 1. New York: Education and World Affairs.

Portes Gil, Emilio
1964   *Autobiografía de la Revolución Mexicana: Un tratado de interpretación histórica.* México, D.F.: Instituto Mexicano de Cultura.

Proceso
1986   September 29.

Rangel Guerra, Alfonso
1979   *La educación superior en México.* México, D.F.: El Colegio de México, Jornadas 86.

Smith, Peter H.
1979   *Labyrinths of Power: Political Recruitment in Twentieth-Century Mexico.* Princeton, N.J.: Princeton University Press.

UNAM (Universidad Nacional Autónoma de México)
Modificaciones académicas en la UNAM.

Urquidi, Víctor, and Adrián Lajous Vargas
1967   *Educación superior, ciencia y tecnología en el desarrollo económico de México.* México, D.F.: El Colegio de México.

Wilkie, James W.
1967   *The Mexican Revolution: Federal Expenditure and Social Change since 1910.* Berkeley and Los Angeles: University of California Press.

CHAPTER 35

FROM ECONOMIC GROWTH
TO ECONOMIC STAGNATION
IN MEXICO:
STATISTICAL SERIES FOR UNDERSTANDING
PRE- AND POST-1982 CHANGE

By
JAMES W. WILKIE

James W. Wilkie, David E. Lorey, and Enrique Ochoa, eds., *Statistical Abstract of Latin America*, vol. 26 (Los Angeles: UCLA Latin American Center Publications, University of California), 1988.

FROM ECONOMIC GROWTH TO ECONOMIC STAGNATION IN MEXICO

What statistical series can be developed to understand the meaning of Mexico's sustained economic growth prior to 1982 and subsequent economic stagnation? Although numerous statistical series are produced in Mexico to help observers probe Mexico's economic history, most are problematic for several reasons. They cover only a short time span, are dispersed among many sources, and are not presented consistently or with conceptual clarity. The purpose of this chapter is to develop statistical series to interpret the meaning of Mexico's pre- and post-1982 economic stagnation.

Having elsewhere generated long-term series for such factors as Mexico's GDP,[1] devaluations of the peso,[2] public expenditure,[3] real value of the peso as related to real merchandise trade balance,[4] real M_2 money supply,[5] and socioeconomic class structure,[6] here I treat the following topics:

Finance
    Change in money supply (M_1)
    Exchange rates
    Commercial bank deposits
    Mexican stock market boom and bust
    Public sector deficits and debt
Prices
    GDP deflator and Mexico City wholesale prices
    Macro price index for Mexico
    Comparison of consumer price indexes
    Bortz worker cost of living index
    Consumer price index
Production
    Industry
        Manufacturing
        Selected categories
        Vehicles produced

Foreign Income
    Revenues accruing to Mexico and shares by category
    Income from tourism and agriculture
    Major export commodity shares
    Trade in oil
    In-bond plants
    Mexico trade with United States
    U.S. trade with Mexico
    Six most important U.S. trading partners

These series are not exhaustive but illustrate the kinds of materials that need to be generated on a long-term basis.

With regard to the economic growth for which Mexico became famous in the 1960s and 1970s (see figure 35:1), the country's real GDP made gains every year between the Great Depression and the Crisis of the 1980s. From 1933 through 1981 no negative rate of GDP marred the record. GDP registered gains of 8 percent or more in 1936, 1941, 1944, 1950, 1954–55, 1960, 1963–64, 1968, 1972–73, and 1978–81. When these gains are averaged with occasional lows (1938, 1940, and 1953 when increases fell below 2 percent), the average gain of GDP was 6.3 percent yearly prior to 1982. Yet for the years from 1982 through 1986 Mexico has seen the following change in GDP: –.5, –5.2, 3.5, 2.4, –3.8. If GDP for 1987 does not show a negative growth rate and reaches the 1.1 percent projected,[7] observers will be pleasantly surprised. How can we account for the very different results for GDP before and after 1982?

Finance

A major cause of the 1980s decline in GDP to a negative growth rate (averaging –.7 between 1982 and 1986) has been the government's recent failure to control the money supply, a control that had been an article of faith in the governments that came to power out of the Revolution of 1910. The control arose because those new governments were determined to restore the country to a sound financial footing in order to rebuild a country where civil wars had destroyed economic stability and the value of money during the civil wars of the mid-1910s.

With relative order restored to politics and economy by 1920, the Mexican government sought to achieve long-term monetary stability that would provide the framework of trust required to induce the private sector (foreign as well as domestic) to reinvest. Achievement of stability was not immediately possible. Table 3500, which shows volatility

[1] See my study titled "Six Ideological Phases: Mexico's 'Permanent Revolution' Since 1910," in James W. Wilkie, ed., *Society and Economy in Mexico*, Statistical Abstract of Latin America Supplement 10 (Los Angeles: UCLA Latin American Center Publications, University of California, forthcoming), Introduction. (Henceforth cited as SALA-SEM).

[2] Ibid.

[3] "Changes in Mexico Since 1895: Central Government Revenue, Public Sector Expenditure, and National Economic Growth," in SALA 24, chapter 34.

[4] "Mexico's 'New' Financial Crisis of 1982 in Historical Perspective," SALA 22, pp. vii–xviii.

[5] Ibid. (M_2 money supply includes currency, coin, checking accounts, and quasi money.)

[6] "Quantifying the Class Structure of Mexico, 1895–1970," in SALA 21, chapter 35 (coauthored with Paul D. Wilkins).

[7] SALA-SEM, table 1, except projection for 1987 from Mexico-NAFINSA-MV, Jan. 1, 1988.

Figure 35:1

YEARLY CHANGE IN MEXICO GDP, 1896–1986

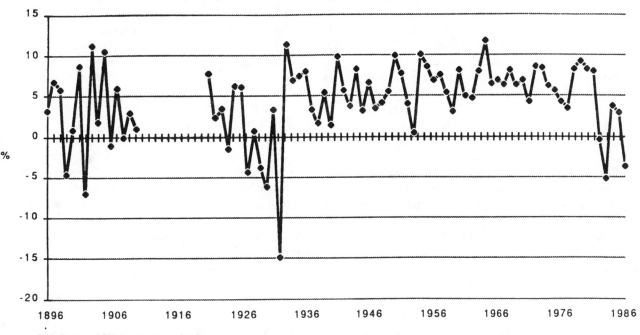

SOURCE: SALA-SEM, Introduction, table 1.

in the percentage change of M_1 (currency, coin, and checking accounts) since 1926, suggests that monetary stability was not easy to attain. Owing to rebellions by generals (who did not want to give up the prerogatives won during battles of the teens) and by lay Catholic rightists (who perceived the new government as anticlerical and antireligious), the government could not keep the money supply on a healthy course, and change in M_1 ranged from −8.9 in 1927 to 28.4 the following year. After permitting minor growth of about 4 percent in 1929 and 1930, the government reduced the money supply by 60.2 percent in 1931, contributing to the depth of Mexico's economic depression in 1932.

The drastic restriction of M_1 complicated the government's development schemes, calling into serious question the credentials of the "revolutionary government" which claimed to be rebuilding the country. President Pascual Ortiz Rubio's decision to decrease the money supply reduced the peasantry to a barter economy. Protest within the general population was matched in the Official Party of the Revolution (founded in 1929 as the Partido de Revolución Nacional to provide peaceful transition of presidential power). The monetary contraction of 1931 contributed significantly to the rise of Lázaro Cárdenas to the presidency of Mexico at the end of 1934. Although Cárdenas rejected the austerity program espoused by Ortiz Rubio (as well as by Plutarco Elías Calles, the strongman of Mexico whom Cárdenas exiled in 1936), he was cautious in his monetary policy. The yearly increase in the money supply during his period in office (1935–40) averaged 12.8 percent.

That the Official Party of the Revolution showed restraint in increasing the money supply may seem contradictory to the revolutionary process, but for the 44 years from 1925 (when the recording of consistent monetary data began) through 1972 the government maintained a steady monetary course in order to institutionalize "revolution" (i.e., change) to make it orderly and predictable. Thus, growth in M_1 rose above 30 percent only in 1932 (to make up for the contraction of 1931), 1942, 1943 (to expand Mexico's industrial production needed by the U.S. effort for World War II), and 1950 (at the onset of the Korean War's stimulus to the Mexican economy). Otherwise M_1 growth exceeded 20 percent in only three years, and never after 1944.

The policy of stable growth in M_1 was abandoned by President Luis Echeverría Alvarez (LEA), who during his term from 1970 to 1976 believed that the economic growth of Mexico had been distorted by the policy of past governments of protecting the peso's relationship to the dollar at the expense of alienating the masses, to whom economic growth had not trickled down. Once LEA unleashed the presses to print money, the process could not be stopped. Between 1973 and 1976, M_1 increased from 19 to 23 percent yearly. Matters were complicated in 1973 when OPEC dramatically raised petroleum prices, spurring Mexico to capitalize on its own neglected source of "black gold."

Under President José López Portillo (JLP), who governed from 1976 to 1982, Mexico took on greater debt to develop the country's economy, a process that had begun in the 1960s and now was hastened by the need to develop the economy around oil exploration, processing, and export. To keep GDP growing at unprecedentedly high rates (averaging 8.4 percent between 1978 and 1981—see figure 35:1), JLP increased M_1 supply at rates into the thirtieth percentile.

When JLP turned over the presidency to Miguel de la Madrid Hurtado (MMH) for the period from 1982 to 1988, the rate of increase in M_1 was 43.5 percent, and reached into the fifties by 1984. In November 1987, the rate reached 139 percent. MMH's rates dwarfed the pre-1982 high of 38.4 percent in 1950.

These post-1982 changes in M_1 influenced the worth of the peso vis-à-vis the U.S. dollar, but not all at once because even as LEA unleashed M_1 supply, he insisted on maintaining the exchange rate. Only after tremendous pressure built as the population shifted from pesos to dollars did the impact of the increase in M_1 become evident. With an ever increasing number of pesos in circulation, inflation took hold in Mexico (discussed below), and persons in all walks of life decided to buy dollars as an inexpensive hedge against inflation.

Table 3501 assembles the peso's average worth for each year from 1900 to 1987, a time span that can be divided into three periods.

The first period was one of relative peso stability, lasting 76 years after 1900. Between 1910 and 1931 the dollar bought about 2 pesos, except for 1914–16. During that civil war–period the peso rose to 3.30 in 1914, 11.15 (a devaluation of 70.4 percent) in 1915, and 23.83 in 1916. Between 1932 and 1937 the peso fell back to the range of 3–4 to the dollar, rising to about 5 after the nationalization of the foreign-owned oil industry in 1938. The rate of 5 pesos to the dollar held until 1948, leveling at 8.5 from 1949 through 1953. After transition in 1954, the peso was pegged at 12.50 to the dollar for the next 21 years, 1955–75.

The second period for the peso was one of tension. President Luis Echeverría (LEA) overvalued the peso and held it at 12.50 to the dollar through 1975. In 1976, LEA devalued the peso in order to stop the flight of money, encouraged by the onset of the oil boom and the rise in oil prices. From 1977 through 1981 President José López Portillo (JLP) held the overvalued peso in the low 20s to the dollar, a policy which had disastrous results beginning in 1982.

The third period for the peso began in 1982 when JLP realized that he could not continue to overvalue the peso at the expense of making Mexico's exports prohibitively expensive on the world market. To stem the flight of capital, JLP let the peso float from 12.50 to 15 to the dollar, making Mexico's dollar debts more costly to repay and reducing the value of oil sales abroad. The deepening economic crisis, sparked in 1982 by the country's inability to repay its foreign debt, saw the peso decline in average value to 150 per dollar in 1983 and to 637 pesos per dollar by 1986 (a devaluation by 1986 of 98 percent from the years of stability when the peso stood at 12.50 to the dollar).

JLP's legacy for MMH was to nationalize the private commercial banking system and legally to convert the dollar

accounts therein into peso accounts, further damaging the image of the peso. The nationalized banks suspended payments on the foreign debt (thus saving the Mexican private sector from bankruptcy) and then orchestrated repayment over longer terms. But the peso slide against the dollar could not be stopped. With the collapse of the peso and the nationalization of the commercial banks, investors in Mexico were reluctant to put their funds into those two systems. The real inflow of pesos to the banks had already fallen from March 1982 by 12.4 percent prior to the bank nationalization on September 1, 1982 (see figure 35:2 and table 3502, part I.) During the nine months after the nationalization, real inflow declined nearly 25 percent, but regained minimal amounts on deposit thereafter through February 1985, after which decline began again. The banks experienced 26 consecutive months of fall in inflow (reaching an annual rate of −15.4 percent in October 1986) before seeing small positive gains in May, June, and August of 1987. (See table 3502, part II.)

Trying to reverse this negative trend in bank deposits and to restore private confidence in the banking system, MMH decided to reduce the Mexican government's 100 percent hold over this nationalized sector. In early 1987 the private sector was permitted to repurchase 34 percent of the banks' stock.[8]

Further, the government initiated a campaign to justify the nationalization of the banks and to point out the efficiencies gained. The government argued that because their number was reduced the banks did not add to the size of the parastate sector, which MMH was reducing. For example, Mexico's commercial banks handle over 36 million accounts, almost 5 million more in 1987 than in 1982; at the same time banking personnel increased only 1 percent yearly between 1982 and 1986.[9]

Yet such arguments fail to take into account the severe shortage of banking facilities for the masses. For example, in 1984 I found that in San Cristóbal de las Casas it was rarely possible for Indians to change U.S. tourist dollars into pesos at the banks because the banks labored under a dire shortage of pesos. (U.S. tourists in need of pesos could at least recur to travel agencies and buy pesos—with discounted dollars.)

Given the problematic state of affairs for banking, investors turned to the Mexican stock exchange (BMV) as a place of refuge and hope. Money flowed into the BMV even as the stock exchange index showed mixed results from March to June 1984 when results showed a small loss in stock values. (See table 3503.) In mid-1984 the index gained about 38 percent before falling back by less than half that figure at the end of January 1985. The first half of 1985 showed a strong gain at the outset, then balanced to minimal

---

[8] For information on the sale of bank stocks, see Mexico-BANAMEX-RESM, March 1987, p. 43.

[9] This positive view was enunciated by the Banco Nacional de México in Mexico-BANAMEX-RESM, July 1987, pp. 198–199.

Table 3500

CHANGE IN MEXICO M$_1$ MONEY SUPPLY,[1] 1926–87

(12-Month Average)

Year	PC	Year	PC	Year	PC
1926	16.2	1947	–.6	1968	12.3
1927	–8.9	1948	13.8	1969	12.6
1928	28.4	1949	11.2	1970	11.3
1929	4.5	1950	38.4[a]	1971	8.1
1930	4.3	1951	11.7	1972	13.5
1931	–60.2	1952	4.2	1973	22.8
1932	31.3	1953	10.9	1974	19.2
1933	15.4	1954	11.9	1975	21.5
1934	13.8	1955	19.6	1976	22.3
1935	7.9	1956	11.2	1977	26.6
1936	23.9	1957	6.7	1978	37.2
1937	5.9	1958	6.6	1979	31.4
1938	10.8	1959	13.1	1980	31.1
1939	19.8	1960	12.1	1981	36.8
1940	20.2	1961	6.0	1982	43.5
1941	19.8	1962	8.3	1983	44.1
1942	37.8	1963	14.0	1984	53.2
1943	52.7	1964	19.8	1985	53.7
1944	23.8	1965	9.0	1986	51.3
1945	6.9	1966	8.4	1987	90.8[b]
1946	–2.2	1967	10.1		

1. M$_1$ = currency, coin, and checking accounts held by the public. For absolute data on M$_1$ and M$_2$, see SALA, 22-2.

a. Shift from Bank of Mexico calculations to IMF calculations; Bank of Mexico datum for 1950 is 37.6 percent.

b. With regard to single-month rates, BDM calculations show that November 1987 reached 139.1 percent—the highest such rate in decades.

SOURCE: 1926–49, calculated from Mexico-BDM-IE-AH, 1983, p. I-H-1;
1950–56, IMF-IFS-Y, 1980, p. 56;
1957–58, IMF-IFS-Y, 1985, p. 82;
1959–82, IMF-IFS-Y, 1987, pp. 90–91;
1983–86, IMF-IFS, February 1988;
1987, *El Mercado de Valores*, Feb. 15, 1988.

gains through June. From that point the index soared, gaining 126 percent by the end of 1985. The rapid pace slowed through April 1986, then soared 269 percent by December. During 1987 gains continued: another 109 percent by March, followed by 249 percent through September. In this big run-up of values, the index went from an April 1986 average of 12,802 (the low point prior to its big runup) to an average of 343,545 by its peak month, September 1987—a gain of 2,586 percent.

Much of the BMV gain was fueled by the return to Mexico of capital that had fled abroad between the mid-1970s and the mid-1980s. By 1987 a flood of dollars was returning to take advantage of the increasingly favorable peso exchange rate and the dramatic rise in stock values on the BMV. The BMV was especially attractive to investors speculating on quick profits. As the fastest rising bull market in the world, the BMV was selling at 22 times earnings, compared with 4.5 a year earlier.[10] As the value of stocks on the BMV ridiculously outpaced inflation, by early October 1987 the BMV found itself more overvalued than Wall Street.

When the U.S. stock market collapsed on October 19, 1987, and the crash of markets internationally followed, the BMV went into a dramatic decline. By November the BMV average had fallen 66.9 percent to 113,628 (see table 3503, part I). From its peak for an individual day, the BMV fell by 70.4 percent from October 6 to December 15 (table 3503, part II.)

Hence the Mexican government moved to establish a fund to buy unsold stocks,[11] and the private sector awoke to several realizations. Not only would government purchase of

[10] *Forbes Magazine*, Aug. 10, 1987, p. 134.

[11] Dan Williams, "Mexico Moves to Prop Up Falling Market," *Los Angeles Times*, Nov. 11, 1987.

Table 3501

DOLLAR VALUE OF THE MEXICAN PESO, 1900–87

(12-Month Average)

PART I. FREE RATE,[1] 1900–75

Year	Market Price	Year	Market Price	Year	Market Price	Year	Market Price
1900	2.06	1919	1.99	1938	4.52	1957	12.50
1901	2.11	1920	2.01	1939	5.18	1958	12.50
1902	2.39	1921	2.04	1940	5.40	1959	12.50
1903	2.38	1922	2.05	1941	4.86	1960	12.50
1904	1.99	1923	2.06	1942	4.85	1961	12.50
1905	2.02	1924	2.07	1943	4.85	1962	12.50
1906	1.99	1925	2.03	1944	4.85	1963	12.50
1907	2.01	1926	2.07	1945	4.85	1964	12.50
1908	2.01	1927	2.12	1946	4.85	1965	12.50
1909	2.01	1928	2.08	1947	4.85	1966	12.50
1910	2.01	1929	2.08	1948	5.74	1967	12.50
1911	2.01	1930	2.12	1949	8.01	1968	12.50
1912	2.01	1931	2.43	1950	8.65	1969	12.50
1913	2.08	1932	3.17	1951	8.65	1970	12.50
1914	3.30	1933	3.53	1952	8.65	1971	12.50
1915	11.15	1934	3.60	1953	8.65	1972	12.50
1916	23.83	1935	3.60	1954	11.34	1973	12.50
1917	1.91	1936	3.60	1955	12.50	1974	12.50
1918	1.81	1937	3.60	1956	12.50	1975	12.50

PART II. FREE AND CONTROLLED RATES,[2] 1976–87[a]

Year	Free[3]	Controlled[4]
1976	15.43	
1977	22.57	
1978	22.77	
1979	22.81	
1980	22.95	
1981	24.51	
1982	56.40	57.44
1983	150.30	120.09
1984	185.19	167.83
1985	310.17	256.87
1986	637.38	611.77
1987	1,405.76	1,378.18

1. The so-called "free" or "market" rate has been subject to support by the Banco Central and/or manipulation by "dirty floats" wherein the rate is in reality a regulated rate. Since 1982 the free rate is used for non-foreign trade transactions. The free rate has not always meant free convertibility of pesos to dollars, for example, for a time beginning in 1982 residents of Mexico's interior could buy no more than 1,500 dollars yearly per person and residents in the border area could purchase no more than 1,500 dollars per month.

2. The controlled rate, established in 1982, is used for most import-export transactions, and it cannot be used for private investments, debt payments, or tourist exchange transactions.

3. IMF-IFS, line "wf" for 1980–82; line "xf" since 1983.
4. For 1982, Nacional Financiera; since 1983, line "wf" in IMF-IFS.

a. Calculations by the Banco de México and Nacional Financiera may differ slightly from IMF calculations used here. With regard to 1986, for example, the Banco de México figures are 637.8754 and 611.3529 (see *Indicadores Económicos*, October 1987, p. IV-9).

SOURCE: 1900–1975, Mexico-INEGI-EHM, II, 810-811; *El Mercado de Valores*, Feb.15, 1988, and IMF-IFS, March 1988.

Figure 35:2

BALANCE OF TOTAL INFLOW TO
MEXICAN COMMERCIAL BANKS
JANUARY 1982–JUNE 1984

(Billions of Real Pesos of 1978)

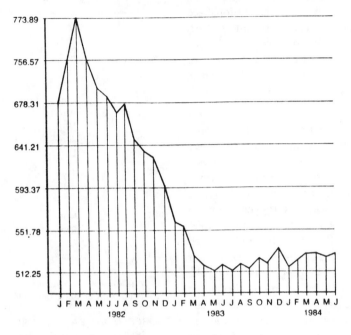

Source: Mexico-BANAMEX-RESM, July, 1984, p. 253.

Table 3502

CONFIDENCE IN MEXICAN COMMERCIAL
BANKING SYSTEM, 1982–84

PART I. RATE OF REAL INFLOW OF PESOS, SAMPLE MONTHS, BEFORE AND AFTER NATION-ALIZATION OF PRIVATE BANKS

Year	Month	Balance in Billions of Real 1978 Pesos[1]	Real PC[2]	Index Aug. 1982 Equals 100
1982	Jan.	678.31	**	100
	Mar.	773.89	14.1	114
	Aug.	678.31	−12.4	100
1983	May	512.25	−24.5	76
	Dec.	532.00	3.9	78
1984	June	527.00	2.9	78

1. Data do not represent accumulated change but levels reached at sample months.
2. Real percentage change from given month to given month (excluding intervening months).

a. Visual estimation from figure 35:1.

SOURCE: Extracted from graphic presentation in figure 35:1.

PART II. ANNUALIZED REAL PRECENTAGE CHANGE IN INFLOW OF PESOS TO BANKS, 1984–87

Month	1984	1985	1986	1987
Jan.	~	4.2	−15.8	−7.4
Feb.	~	.8	−15.0	−5.3
March	−.4	−1.2	−12.7	−.1
April	2.6	−1.6	−13.9	−.2
May	3.4	−1.4	−14.1	1.4
June	2.8	−3.4	−14.8	3.2
July	5.6	−6.1	−13.4	−.7
Aug.	6.5	−10.3	−14.2	1.2
Sep.	5.1	−8.6	−15.2	−.9
Oct.	4.4	−8.9	−15.4	−2.2
Nov.	5.9	−10.9	−9.6	~
Dec.	5.5	−12.9	−9.5	~
Average[1]	3.5	−5.2	−13.6	1.0

1. Arithmetic average of amounts given.

SOURCE: Mexico-BANAMEX-RESM, Mar. 1985; Dec. 1985; Feb. 1986; May 1986; Jan./Feb. 1987; Jul. 1987; Jan. 1988.

unsold stocks involve implicit nationalization of many firms, but also the financial loss to the government would be tremendous and would not be sustainable especially in light of the rising public sector deficit, rate of inflation, and pressure on the peso. Although this plan to buy unsold stocks did not come to fruition (and may have been aimed at channeling investments from the BMV into the nationalized banks), the result was a panic to change pesos into dollars. The government had attempted without success to devalue gradually rather than all at once, but on November 17 was forced to decree a 22 percent devaluation of the peso in order to protect the country's reserves; and by January 1, 1988, the peso stood at 2,240 to the dollar.[12]

   The fall of the peso, drop in bank deposits, and collapse of stock exchange values together with the rise in money supply were interlinked with public sector deficit spending in Mexico. The financial deficit had been firmly established in the late 1960s, President Gustavo Díaz Ordaz having borrowed money abroad to finance the difference between outgo and income. (See table 3504, part I, column A.) LEA doubled the financial deficit to 10 percent before he turned over office to JLP in 1976. Under JLP the deficit declined at first but in the end reached 17.6 percent, precipitating the nationalization of the banks. MMH could not bring the financial deficit much below 9 percent before he felt forced to expend money to spur the lagging economy, especially after the 1985 earthquake that destroyed much of Mexico City. By 1987 the financial deficit surpassed 17 percent.

   MMH, arguing in defense of his expenditure policy that he was trapped under the weight of accumulated interest payments on debts contracted prior to his administration, pointed to the primary economic deficit as the series revealing his true effort to resolve the country's financial problems. The primary economic deficit, which subtracts interest payments from the financial deficit, shows that MMH ran surpluses, not deficits, during his first five years in office. (See table 3504, part I, column B.) During three of those years the primary economic surplus was over 5 percent of GDP.

   MMH also argued that yet a third aspect of the deficit, the operational deficit, needs to be understood. (See table 3504, part I, column C.) Even if interest payments are counted because they are indeed due and payable now, however, the operational deficit redefines matters to exclude the inflationary part of interest payments. The operational deficit reveals the real extent of change in public indebtedness. According to this view, the real debt share of GDP was zero or decreasing in four of MMH's five years in office

Table 3503

MEXICAN STOCK EXCHANGE INDEX, 1984-88

PART I. VALUE FOR KEY MONTHS, 1984-87

Year	Month Avg.	Index	PC
1984	Mar.	3,350	**
	Apr.	2,885[a]	−13.9
	May	3,282[b]	13.7
	June	3,172[a]	−3.4
	Sept.	4,366[b]	37.6
1985	Jan.	3,710[a]	−15.0
	Apr.	4,819[b]	30.2
	May	4,597[a]	−4.6
	June	4,957	7.8
	Dec.	11,197	125.9
1986	Jan.	14,204[b]	26.9
	Apr.	12,802[a]	−9.9
	Dec.	47,101	267.9
1987	Mar.	98,524	109.2
	Sept.	343,545[b]	248.7
	Oct.	200,018	−41.8
	Nov.	113,628	−43.2

a. Low point prior to run-up of index.
b. High point prior to decline in index.

SOURCE: Mexico-BANAMEX-RESM, Mar. and Dec. 1985; Mar. 1986; Jan./Feb. 1987; Jan. 1988.

PART II. SPECIFIC DATES FOR INDEX VALUES, 1987-88

Year	Date	Index
1987	Oct. 6 (peak)	373,216
	Dec. 15	110,627
1988	Jan. 22	140,402

SOURCE: *Wall Street Journal*, Jan. 25, 1988; *Uno Más Uno*, Dec. 16, 1987; *MV*, Dec. 7, 1987.

through 1987, less borrowing having been required because of the effort to reduce public expenditures.[13]

   Analysis of the deficits in relation to the public sector foreign debt is complicated by at least four considerations. First, nominally the debt grew 1,281 percent between 1970 and 1982 and then only 28 percent through MMH's first four years, 1983-86; but in real terms the debt grew 376 percent from 1970 to 1982 and then 26 percent through 1986 (calculated from table 3504, part II.) Second, although interest was paid on smaller amounts, loan commissions, rates of interest, and schedule of payments were higher (especially in the 1970s); although the loan amounts are now higher, the terms are better. Third, because the debts must

---

[12] Devaluation figures are from SALA-SEM, Introduction, table 2 (part I); the rate for January 1, 1988, is from SALA-SEM, Introduction, table 2, part III.

[13] On the definition of the three deficits, see Mexico-NAFINSA-MV, Jan. 1, 1988, pp. 24-29.

Table 3504

MEXICO PUBLIC SECTOR DEFICITS AND FOREIGN DEBT, 1965–87

PART I. THREE VIEWS OF THE DEFICIT

% of GDP; Minus = Surplus

Year	A. Financial[1]	B. Primary Economic[2]	C. Operational (Real Deficit)[3]
1965	.9	0	.7
1966	1.2	.3	.8
1967	2.4	.9	2.0
1968	2.2	.8	1.6
1969	2.2	.7	1.9
1970	3.8	1.5	2.8
1971	2.5	.5	1.4
1972	4.9	2.4	3.5
1973	6.9	3.8	2.7
1974	7.3	4.0	3.3
1975	10.0	6.5	7.1
1976	9.9	4.9	4.6
1977	6.7	2.3	2.9
1978	6.7	2.4	3.6
1979	7.6	2.9	3.9
1980	7.9	3.2	3.6
1981	14.7	8.4	10.1
1982	17.6	7.6	5.5
1983	9.0	−4.4	−1.2
1984	8.7	−4.9	−.3
1985	10.0	−3.6	0
1986	16.3	−1.7	1.9
1987[†]	17.4	−5.0	−.9

PART II. PUBLIC SECTOR FOREIGN DEBT,[1] 1970–87

Year	A. Foreign Debt (M US)	B. U.S. Export Price Index (1980 = 100)	C. Real Foreign Debt (M US) (A/B)
1970	4,262.8	38.2	11,159
1971	4,545.8	39.4	11,538
1972	5,064.6	40.7	12,444
1973	7,070.4	47.4	14,917
1974	9,975.0	60.5	16,488
1975	14,449.0	67.6	21,374
1976	19,600.2	69.9	28,040
1977	22,912.1	72.4	31,647
1978	26,264.3	77.4	33,933
1979	29,757.2	88.1	33,777
1980	33,812.8	100.0	33,813
1981	52,960.6	109.2	48,499
1982	58,874.2	110.4	53,328
1983	62,556.2	111.6	56,054
1984	69,377.9	113.1	61,342
1985	72,080.1	112.2	64,820
1986	75,350.9	112.5	66,979
1987[a]	78,964.8	118.7	66,525

1. For other types of analysis, see Samuel Schmidt's articles on Mexico's foreign debt in SALA 22 (chapter 39) and SALA 23 (chapter 40).

a. Sept.

SOURCE: A, 1970–85, Mexico-NAFINSA-EMC, 1986, p. 271.
1986,   Mexico-NAFINSA-MV, Dec. 28, 1987.
B, IMF-IFS-Y, 1987, p. 698–699; IMF-IFS, Feb. 1988, p. 523.

1. Financial deficit indicates the total financing needed to cover gap between outlay and income of the public sector. (The public sector includes the central government plus parastate agencies.)
2. The primary economic deficit (financial deficit less interest payments on debts contracted in past) indicates the autonomous financial effort made each year to overcome budgetary problems caused by the disequilibria of expenditures in previous years.
3. The operational deficit (financial deficit less the inflationary component of interest payments on the debt) indicates the real change in public indebtedness each year.

SOURCE: Mexico-NAFINSA-MV, Jan. 1, 1988, p. 24.

be repaid in dollars that have become more expensive to buy with devalued pesos, Mexico's cycles of inflation/devaluation compromise repayment. Fourth, MMH's view of the operational deficit may be overly sanguine. Inflation is indeed part of the deficit problem, but it also requires that money be generated to meet the deficit. Generation of money (either through borrowing or increase in M_1) stimulates inflation and also adds to the debt.

Prices

Inflation in Mexico can be examined from a number of vantage points: consumer cost of living, worker cost of living, wholesale prices, and the GDP deflator. Several are linked here to formulate what I call macro and micro price indexes for Mexico.

The only index of inflation going back to 1900 and through all but four years of the civil war period is the wholesale price series for Mexico City, compiled by the Dirección General de Estadística (DGE). The DGE series, given in table 3505, column B, ended in 1976 when it began to show more inflation than the Bank of Mexico (BDM) wholesale price index for Mexico City, presented in column C. In 1975 the former (at 475.9) was 19 percent higher than the latter (400.0).[14]

The BDM wholesale price index for Mexico City dates back only to 1939. It was quite similar to the DGE index through the mid-1940s and then diverged during the 1950s.

After 1977 there is only one index to compare with the BDM wholesale price index, that is, the BDM's GDP deflator which converts the GDP from nominal to real terms by deducting for inflation. By 1985 the difference between the wholesale and GDP deflator indexes was 22.2 percent,[15] the wholesale price index understating inflation. The problem with the government's use of the wholesale prices to express inflation is that the wholesale price index is more oriented toward daily life of the people than is the GDP deflator, which contains prices for such broad categories as government and industrial activity that became so important after the manufacturing revolution got under way in Mexico during the 1940s. The BDM wholesale price index underweights or ignores such items as the cost of services, housing, and transport that influence daily life, thus understating inflation.

The BDM's GDP deflator (given in table 3505, column A), then, reveals the most realistic statement of inflation in Mexico. Through the mid-1940s it was essentially the same as the DGE wholesale price index for Mexico City, after which

it was somewhat higher or lower. The BDM's GDP deflator does not cover the ten years beginning in 1911 and ending in 1920, when the country's economy was disorganized by civil war.

To take advantage of the more complete early coverage by the DGE wholesale price index and the clearer recent measurement of inflation by the GDP deflator, I link the two here at the year 1965, when the two indexes intersected for the last time, the GDP deflator definitively surpassing the level of inflation shown in the DGE index. This linked index is denominated the macro price index and is presented in table 3506.

The macro price index shows that inflation in Mexico approximately doubled for medium intervals in the following years after 1910: 1943, 1950, and 1959. The index then trebled for short intervals as follows: 1976, 1981, 1983, and 1986. This quickening pace of inflation has changed social outlooks in Mexico beginning in 1976.

Several indexes are available to assess specifically the extent of inflation for consumers and workers. First, table 3507 creates what I call the micro price index, which links the DGE food price index to the BDM consumer price index (CPI). Second, table 3508 gives the Bortz worker cost of living index (WCOLI). This innovative index is based upon Jeffrey Bortz's independent scholarly research into DGE unpublished and published data. Because the Bortz index has not been carried forward since 1975 or linked to any other index, one of its main uses is to assess the impact of inflation on the period for which the index exists, 1939–75. From this view, workers experienced ascending inflation as follows: 1950s (10.9 percent), 1960s (23.0), and 1940s (31.6 percent.)

As an independent analysis of prices, Bortz's WCOLI is also useful for assessing the validity of nine price indexes for Mexico available for varying time spans (see table 3509). Having converted all of the indexes in table 3509 to the same base year (1975), we can see that at the five-year benchmark years sampled there is a remarkable similarity between all of the indexes. The Bortz WCOLI (column E) is almost the same as the micro price series (column C). Although some years differ in the complete series for both (cf. tables 3507 and 3508), I see the Bortz series as validating the use of the micro index since 1930 for long-term analysis.

The BDM series on CPI (table 3509, column A) seems to seriously understate inflation and, in any case, is too short for serious analysis. It seems to be the series most influenced by the BDM's monetarist view that would downplay inflation in order to limit its psychological impact on price increases.

The micro price index links BDM data for years since 1950 with DGE food price data for years prior to 1950. Considered separately, the two indexes closely parallel each other all the way into the 1970s when the DGE food price index was terminated. The DGE index was for Mexico City as was the BDM index through 1967, after which it became a national index.

---

[14] This percentage change is calculated horizontally between the indexes for 1976, not vertically within each index. The equation for this calculation is $(475.9/400) - 1 \times 100$.

[15] The equation for this horizontal calculation for 1985 is $(15,147.7/12,392.9) - 1 \times 100$.

Table 3505

COMPARATIVE PRICE INDEXES FOR MEXICO, 1900–86[a]

(1950 = 100)

Year	A. BDM GDP Deflator[1]	B. DGE Mexico City Wholesale Prices[2]	C. BDM Mexico City Wholesale Prices[3]	Year	A. BDM GDP Deflator[1]	B. DGE Mexico City Wholesale Prices[2]	C. BDM Mexico City Wholesale Prices[3]
1900	11.3	12.0	**	1945	65.0	67.0	64.0
1901	14.0	14.7	**	1946	82.8	78.5	73.6
1902	14.3	15.0	**	1947	88.9	80.1	77.6
1903	14.3	15.0	**	1948	91.0	85.0	83.2
1904	13.8	14.7	**	1949	95.0	90.0	91.2
1905	15.5	16.3	**	1950	100.0	100.0	100.0
1906	15.3	16.2	**	1951	119.7	120.6	124.0
1907	15.3	15.9	**	1952	129.1	132.5	128.0
1908	15.7	16.6	**	1953	128.1	135.2	126.6
1909	16.8	17.6	**	1954	141.9	145.6	137.6
1910	19.5	20.7	**	1955[b]	160.0	168.0	156.0
1911	**	19.6	**	1956	170.8	178.3	164.0
1912	**	19.4	**	1957	181.5	189.3	170.4
1913	**	19.2	**	1958	192.3	198.0	178.4
1914	**	**	**	1959	200.0	200.8	180.0
1915	**	**	**	1960	209.2	212.3	188.8
1916	**	**	**	1961	212.3	214.2	191.2
1917	**	**	**	1962	220.0	217.2	194.4
1918	**	43.3	**	1963	220.0	221.2[c]	195.2
1919	**	34.6	**	1964	224.6	228.4	204.0
1920	**	36.3	**	1965[d]	244.6	237.3	208.0
1921	31.9	33.1	**	1966	255.4	239.6	210.4
1922	26.2	27.8	**	1967	256.9	239.7	216.0
1923	27.7	29.8	**	1968	263.1	243.9	220.8
1924	26.0	28.5	**	1969	273.8	246.8	226.4
1925	27.7	30.0	**	1970	303.1	258.2	240.0
1926	27.3	29.4	**	1971	320.0	265.3	248.8
1927	26.0	28.7	**	1972	340.0	276.5	255.2
1928	26.0	27.6	**	1973	384.6	332.9	296.0
1929	26.2	27.5	**	1974	472.3	418.9	362.4
1930	26.8	28.0	**	1975	546.2	475.9	400.0
1931	23.5	24.7	**	1976	652.3	550.3	489.6
1932	21.0	22.5	**	1977	850.8	**	691.2
1933	22.2	23.9	**	1978	993.8	**	800.2
1934	22.9	24.7	**	1979	1,195.4	**	946.4
1935	23.3	24.9	**	1980	1,538.5	**	1,177.5
1936	25.4	26.4	**	1981	1,958.5	**	1,463.5
1937	31.2	31.3	**	1982	3,155.4	**	2,284.7
1938	32.9	32.7	**	1983	6,063.1	**	4,737.6
1939	33.3	33.6	32.0	1984	9,809.2	**	8,070.6
1940	34.8	33.8	32.8	1985	15,147.7	**	12,392.9
1941	35.6	35.9	35.2	1986	~	**	22,734.1
1942	39.0	39.7	38.4				
1943	45.9	47.5	46.4				
1944	61.2	60.9	56.8				

1. Used as part of macro price index developed in table 3506.
2. Used as part of macro price index developed in table 3506; index had 32 items prior to 1929 and 50 thereafter.
3. This 210-item wholesale price index for Mexico City should not be confused with BDM's 32-item wholesale price index for Mexico City which was suspended in 1979.

a. Base years in various sources converted to 1950 = 100; this conversion of bases may yield minor statistical differences because of rounding.
b. Difference of .7 where sources are linked.
c. Later DGE revision = 220.5.
d. Year at which DGE and BDM indexes are linked to create the macro index given in table 3506.

SOURCE: BDM's GDP deflator index through 1954 is from Leopoldo Solís *La Realidad Económica Mexicana Retrovisión y Perspectivas* (México, D.F.: Siglo XXI, 1981), p. 92; 1955 through 1979 from IMF-IFS-Y, 1984; 1980 through 1986 from IMF-IFS-Y, 1987. For theoretical discussion, see IMF-IFS, Supplement 2 (1981), p. ii.

DGE's wholesale price index through 1963 from James W. Wilkie, *The Mexican Revolution: Federal Expenditure and Social Change Since 1910* (Berkeley: University of California Press, 1970), pp. 20–23; and 1964 through 1976 from James W. Wilkie, *La Revolución Mexicana (1910–1976): Gasto Federal y Cambio Social* (México, D.F.: Fondo de Cultura Económica, 1978), p. 350.

BDM's wholesale price index is from Mexico-BDM-IE-AH, II, 1983, p. III-H-II; 1980 through 1988 from IMF-IFS-Y, 1987.

Table 3506

MACRO PRICE INDEX FOR MEXICO,[1] 1900–86

(1950 = 100)

Year	Prices	Year	Prices
1900	12.0	1945	67.0
1901	14.7	1946	78.5
1902	15.0	1947	80.1
1903	15.0	1948	85.0
1904	14.7	1949	90.0
1905	16.3	1950	100.0
1906	16.2	1951	120.6
1907	15.9	1952	132.5
1908	16.6	1953	135.2
1909	17.6	1954	145.6
1910	20.7	1955	168.0
1911	19.6	1956	178.3
1912	19.4	1957	189.3
1913	19.2	1958	198.0
1914	**	1959	200.8
1915	**	1960	212.3
1916	**	1961	214.2
1917	**	1962	217.3
1918	43.3	1963	221.2
1919	34.6	1964	228.4
1920	36.3	1965[a]	244.6
1921	33.1	1966	255.4
1922	27.8	1967	256.9
1923	29.8	1968	263.1
1924	28.5	1969	273.8
1925	30.0	1970	303.1
1926	29.4	1971	320.0
1927	28.7	1972	340.0
1928	27.6	1973	384.6
1929	27.5	1974	472.3
1930	28.0	1975	546.2
1931	24.7	1976	652.3
1932	22.5	1977	850.8
1933	23.9	1978	993.8
1934	24.7	1979	1,195.4
1935	24.9	1980	1,538.5
1936	26.4	1981	1,956.9
1937	31.3	1982	3,155.4
1938	32.7	1983	6,063.1
1939	33.6	1984	9,809.2
1940	33.8	1985	15,147.7
1941	35.9	1986	~
1942	39.7		
1943	47.5		
1944	60.9		

1. Links DGE's wholesale price index through 1964 with BDM's GDP
deflator index since 1965.

a. Linkage point.

SOURCE: See table 3505.

Table 3507

MICRO PRICE INDEX FOR MEXICO,[1] 1930–86

(1975 = 100)

Year	Index	Year	Index
1930	4.8	1960	43.9
1931	4.3	1961	44.6
1932	3.6	1962	45.1
1933	3.5	1963	45.4
1934	3.4	1964	46.5
1935	3.5	1965	48.2
1936	3.8	1966	50.2
1937	4.9	1967	51.7
1938	5.6	1968	52.9
1939	5.9	1969	54.0
1940	6.3	1970	56.7
1941	6.6	1971	59.7
1942	7.2	1972	62.7
1943	9.6	1973	70.3
1944	13.7	1974	87.0
1945	15.4	1975	100.0
1946	18.2	1976	115.9
1947	18.5	1977	149.5
1948	18.7	1978	175.5
1949	19.6	1979	207.5
1950	21.4[a]	1980	261.9
1951	24.1	1981	335.2
1952	27.6	1982	532.6
1953	27.1	1983	1,074.6
1954	28.5	1984	1,779.0
1955	33.0	1985	2,806.3
1956	34.6	1986	5,226.3
1957	36.3		
1958	40.8		
1959	41.9		

1. Links DGE food price index for Mexico with BDM's consumer
price index.

a. Year of linkage.

SOURCE: 1930–1949, DGE Food Price Index for Mexico City in
Mexico-NAFINSA-EMC, 1981, p. 229.

1950–   BDM consumer price index (for Mexico City
through 1967, then for nation) in IMF-IFS-Y,
1980 and 1987. The IMF notes (IMF-IFS,
Feb. 1988, p. 353) that this BDM index covers
172 commodities and services in the entire
country, base 1978. The weights and selected
items are based on a national income and
expenditure survey conducted in 1963. In
1979 the weights were modified on the basis
of national accounts data, and the coverage
of the index was increased from 7 to 16 towns.
See also, BDM-IE-AH, 1983, p. III-H-4.

Table 3508

BORTZ WORKER COST OF LIVING INDEX FOR MEXICO CITY,[1] 1939–75

(1975 = 100)

Year	Index[2]	Year	Index[2]
1939	5.0	1958	43.2
1940	5.5	1959	45.8
1941	6.0	1960	47.9
1942	7.4	1961	48.3
1943	9.4	1962	49.9
1944	13.1	1963	50.0
1945	15.1	1964	52.1
1946	19.2	1965	53.1
1947	20.7	1966	55.0
1948	20.8	1967	53.8
1949	22.0	1968	56.2
1950	22.9	1969	55.4
1951	27.1	1970	59.0
1952	30.2	1971	61.3
1953	29.4	1972	67.0
1954	33.5	1973	72.2
1955	36.6	1974	88.1
1956	38.4	1975	100.0
1957	40.2		

1. Based on published and unpublished data compiled by Mexico's DGE; contains 47 items, including rent, electricity, charcoal, food, clothing, bus transport, beer, and cigarettes.

2. Column E in table 3509.

a. Base converted from 1939 = 100.

SOURCE: Jeffrey Bortz, *Industrial Wages in Mexico City, 1939–1975* (New York: Garland, 1987), table I-3.

To summarize my view on price indexes and their meaning, the macro price index is the most effective to measure inflation since 1900. It is easily updated with data published by the IMF, which utilizes the BDM deflator of GDP. The micro price index is useful for examining consumer prices since 1930, and is easily updated with the BDM's CPI published by IMF. The Bortz WCOLI is important for studying the impact of inflation on laborers from 1939 to 1975. All of the indexes show that inflation was a minor problem for the pre-1976 years compared with later years, relatively speaking. Since 1982 the situation has been increasingly serious for Mexico's population.

Production

How have indexes of production fared in Mexico in the changing context of finance and prices? To answer this question, let us develop long-term measures of industrial activity, including construction and manufacturing. The manufacturing index can be examined in a case example for autos, buses, and trucks since 1950, and it can be traced back to 1900.

Manufacturing for the period 1900–39 is shown in table 3510. From 1900 the index rose to 3.8, a figure that was not reached again until 1922 after peace was restored to the country. The low point of the index came in 1914—2.6, or a 32 percent decline compared with 1910. The index doubled between 1922 and 1939. During that period the low came in 1933 when manufacturing fell almost 14 percent compared to the 1930s high for the century.

The index for manufacturing continues in table 3511 (column B) at 1939, the point of linkage for this NAFINSA series. From 1939 manufacturing doubled by each of the following years: 1951, 1960, 1969, 1980. The index (1970 = 100) reached a high of 213.2 in 1981 before falling to a post-1982 low of 192 in 1983—a loss of almost 10 percent. Results since 1983 have been mixed.

Turning to the index for total industrial activity since 1939 (table 3511, column A), we find that it parallels very closely the index for manufacturing. (Industry includes mining, petroleum and petrochemicals, construction, electricity, and manufacturing of food, textiles and clothing, forest products, chemicals, non-metal materials, and metallurgy). Because its trends are so close to those of manufacturing, then, we can use manufacturing as a proxy for understanding total industrial activity back to 1900. These indexes have diverged since 1982, but the loss to 1983 was also about 10 percent for total industry as it was for manufacturing.

Construction grew at a different pace. (See table 3511, column C). It doubled by the following years after 1939: 1948, 1955, 1964, 1975. Growth of construction then slowed to 40 percent by its index high of 203.1 in 1981. It then fell by 22 percent to a low in 1983, subsequently showing mixed results.

The serious decline since 1982 in some Mexican industrial goods has been offset somewhat by the performance of other goods, as shown in table 3512. Production of crude oil, rods, television sets, household appliances, and car engines declined through 1986. Electrical production and chemical fibers made big gains (23 and 15 percent, respectively), but other products remained at the 1982 output level or slightly above it (steel ingots, cement, beer).

The production of vehicles within the industrial sector is interesting because the total number rose steadily after 1950 up to 1982, with three exceptions. Table 3513 shows a downturn after the Korean War (not seen in the above production indexes) and a sharp decline after the Vietnam War ended in 1975. (There was no decline after 1973 when the United States pulled out of Vietnam, perhaps because the United States continued to send supplies). Since the high unit production of 1981 (597,118 vehicles), units produced fell dramatically by 1986, the low point in the post-1982 years. The percentage declines for the three periods were 10, 21, and 54. The automotive industry's breakthrough for developing a domestic market came in 1962 when the government prohibited the import of new and used vehicles

Table 3509

COMPARISON OF MEXICO CONSUMER PRICE INDEXES (CPI AND MICRO), WORKER COST OF LIVING INDEXES (WCOLI), AND MACRO PRICE INDEX, FIVE-YEAR INTERVALS, 1930–85

(1975 = 100)[a]

	A.	B.	C.	D.	E.	F.	G.	H.	I.
Year	BDM CPI Mexico City	BDM CPI Nation	Micro Index[1,2]	DGE Food Mexico City[2]	Bortz WCOLI Mexico City	DGE Food and Clothes Mexico City	DGE Food Mexico City	DGE WCOLI Mexico City	Macro Index[3]
1930			4.8	4.8					5.1
1935			3.5	3.5				3.8	4.6
1940			6.3	6.3	5.5	4.8		5.5	6.2
1945			15.4	15.4	15.1	13.9		11.5	12.3
1950			21.4	21.4	22.9	22.8	19.4	19.3	18.3
1955			33.0	35.7	36.6	41.1	32.5	29.7	30.8
1960			43.9	43.2	47.9	50.4	42.0	39.5	38.9
1965			48.2	47.8	53.1	56.3	45.9	43.3	44.8
1970	56.6	56.7	56.7	57.2	58.9	57.1	53.1	51.5	55.5
1975	100.0	100.0	100.0	100.0	100.0	100.0	100.0	100.0	100.0
1980	255.6	261.9	261.9						281.7
1985	2,625.2	2,806.3	2,806.3						2,773.3

1. Through 1967 for Mexico City, then for nation.
2. Series does not predate 1930.
3. Through 1964 for Mexico City, then for GDP deflator of national GDP.

a. Varying bases converted here to 1975 = 100.

SOURCE: A, Mexico-BDM-IE, May 1987.
B, Ibid.
C, See table 3507.
D, DGE data in Mexico-NAFINSA-ECM, 1981, p. 229.
E, See table 3508.
F, DGE data in Mexico-INEGI-EHM, II, p. 767.
G, Ibid., pp. 745–746.
H, DGE data from Source D, above.
I, See table 3506.

and required that 60 percent of the content of each vehicle be made in Mexico, compared with 20 percent prior to 1962.

The Mexican government could not always enforce the 60 percent local content requirement, but beginning with the Auto Decree of 1977 it limited further investment except for export production. Multinational auto companies, which continued to hold 100 percent of the shares in their enterprises, could expand to the extent that they export vehicles made with an increased share of local parts. For the first time, in 1985 Mexico had a worldwide trade surplus in motor vehicles, about 500 million dollars.[16] Ironically this surplus came from the collapse of the domestic market owing to inflation. The decline of the peso spurred exports, which previously had not been very salable with an overvalued currency.

[16] On the auto decrees of 1962 and 1977, see James P. Womack, "Prospects for the U.S.–Mexican Relationship in the Motor Vehicle Sector," in Cathryn L. Thorup et al., eds., *The United States and Mexico: Face to Face with New Technology* (New Brunswick, N.J.: Transaction Books, 1987), pp. 110–116.

Foreign Income

The income earned by Mexico from abroad is given in table 3514, which covers benchmark years during the period from 1950 to 1986. It includes the total and major components such as tourism to Mexico, border transactions with the United States, the in-bond industry, and exports of petroleum, cotton, coffee, shrimp, and sugar. These eight categories are the most significant but are not all-inclusive.

Shares of Mexico's total income for the eight categories are presented in table 3515 (which excludes outgo). Cotton was the main export from 1950 through 1974; in 1975 it was overtaken by petroleum. Whereas cotton's maximum percentage of foreign income was near 23 percent for the years sampled, petroleum reached 48 percent as long as oil prices remained high and the peso was overvalued—with a world shortage of oil it behooved Mexico to sell its oil in overvalued pesos to bring in maximum dollars.

With regard to the second most important export shown in table 3515, sugar declined in importance after 1978 because of the mismanagement of Mexico's national

Table 3510

INDEX OF MANUFACTURING PRODUCTION
IN MEXICO, 1900–39[a]

(1970 = 100)

Year	Index	Year	Index
1900	2.6	1920	3.0
1901	2.7	1921	2.9
1902	2.8	1922	4.0
1903	3.0	1923	4.5
1904	3.1	1924	4.8
1905	3.3	1925	4.9
1906	3.4	1926	5.5
1907	3.5	1927	5.0
1908	3.6	1928	5.3
1909	3.8	1929	5.6
1910	3.8	1930	5.9
1911	3.6	1931	7.0
1912	3.0	1932	5.1
1913	3.4	1933	4.7
1914	2.6	1934	7.0
1915	3.1	1935	6.8
1916	2.8	1936	7.8
1917	2.6	1937	8.2
1918	2.4	1938	8.4
1919	3.1	1939	9.0

a. Data for 1939–49 in this series do not exactly match series given in table 3511, e.g., datum here for 1939 is 9.0 but 11.1 in table 3511.

SOURCE: Gonzalo Robles series quoted in Mexico-NAFINSA-EMC, 1981, p. 155.

sugar policy, which did not provide adequate incentives for private reinvestment as internal sugar demand rose, especially after the mid-1960s. Suddenly, Mexico had to import sugar, an export product for which it had been famous in the past. As late as 1950, 7 percent of Mexico's foreign income came from sugar, a decline from bygone days when sugar was a pride of Mexico.[17]

The complexity of foreign income shares can also be seen in table 3515. Through 1970 Mexico's earnings from tourism and border transactions with the United States together accounted for a greater share of exports than did exports from the maquiladora (in-bond) industry, petroleum, cotton, and coffee. By the 1980s, petroleum exports had risen to over 48 percent of Mexico's foreign revenues. This pattern of oil dominance did not hide absolute gains for non-oil products. Rather, owing to a generalized slowdown in the world economy in the early 1980s, demand and prices fell for non-oil income at the same time that peso devaluations had disrupted Mexico's border transactions with the

[17] On the sugar collapse, see Roberto Barajas Sánchez, "Situación de la Industria Azucarera en México," Mexico-BNCE-CE, March 1986, pp. 221–225.

United States—loss of liquidity meant that the intertwined Mexican–U.S. border economy suffered. Tourism to Mexico would increase absolutely but would spend fewer dollars after the devaluations of the 1980s.

The share of foreign income from border transactions had surpassed cotton by 1955, and was not surpassed by tourism until 1985 (see table 3515), when the border economy collapsed along with the value of the peso. Between 1950 and 1986 foreign revenues from tourism threatened to exceed revenues from agriculture, doing so in two of the sample years, 1980 and 1985 (see table 3516).

Concerning exports, table 3517 shows that Mexico was not a monoexport economy until the rise of oil in the late 1970s. Five export products provided balance, with shrimp attaining the same share in the 1960s as petroleum, which illustrates the diversity of development. Yet shrimp farming would eventually bring down the price of that product and reduce its dollar income. Coffee declined as a "Coke" generation in the United States turned to colas, undercutting Mexico's income. Further, the importance of cotton had declined absolutely and in percentage terms as synthetic fabrics won acceptance, and as other countries in the Third World began to contribute to a cotton glut.

Mexico's oil trade is shown in table 3518. Exports increased 62 percent the year after nationalization of the foreign-owned industry in 1938 even though the United States and England reduced their purchases in protest against the loss of their property. Apparently Mexico turned to Europe to make sales during the period 1939–41, but after the United States entered World War II that market declined. Oil exports did not recover until 1947, reaching a peak in 1955 which was offset by increasing imports of refined oil. The favorable balance of trade held up through 1970, but from 1971 to 1974 Mexico had a negative trade balance. Reorganization of the Mexico oil company (PEMEX) coincided with the run-up of oil prices by OPEC countries in the early 1970s, and Mexico made major new oil discoveries to replace the oil fields that had been exhausted. Since 1975 Mexico has been a net oil exporter.

PEMEX has been criticized for letting oil imports approach the level of exports between 1947 and 1970, but that performance had fortunate results. With efficient PEMEX management and honest labor unions working in the field, ironically Mexico would have pumped and exported oil at the low prices then prevailing. Mexico would not have been in a position to capitalize on the increase in the price of OPEC oil after 1973. For example, the real price of Venezuelan oil went from 4 to 5 dollars of 1980 during the 1950s and 1960s to 16 dollars per barrel by 1974. (See table 3231, above). In 1981 the real price of Venezuela's OPEC oil exceeded 29 dollars, which drove up Mexican oil prices.

With the decline in oil price (nominal and real) after 1982, oil's share of Mexico's foreign income fell from 48 percent in 1985 to 26 percent in 1986 (see table 3515). The

Table 3511

INDUSTRIAL PRODUCTION INDEXES IN MEXICO, 1939–86

(1970 = 100)

	A.	B.	C.		A.	B.	C.
Year	Total Industry[1]	Manufacturing	Construction	Year	Total Industry[1]	Manufacturing	Construction
1939	13.5	11.1	6.5	1963	53.7	52.8	54.6
1940	13.5	11.8	7.4	1964	61.9	61.3	63.8
1941	14.1	12.6	9.2	1965	66.2	66.5	62.8
1942	14.8	13.8	9.9	1966	72.0	72.7	71.9
1943	15.5	14.6	10.0	1967	78.0	77.3	81.2
1944	15.9	15.9	12.2	1968	85.2	84.9	87.2
1945	17.0	16.9	13.3	1969	92.6	92.3	95.4
1946	17.0	17.2	15.0	1970	100.0	100.0	100.0
1947	17.5	17.3	12.4	1971	102.2	103.9	88.0
1948	18.0	18.0	13.9	1972	112.4	114.0	99.2
1949	18.9	18.7	16.8	1973	124.7	126.0	113.6
1950	20.8	20.4	20.2	1974	133.7	134.0	121.3
1951	22.7	22.7	22.4	1975	140.7	140.7	128.4
1952	24.6	24.4	23.9	1976	148.2	147.8	134.4
1953	24.4	23.9	24.4	1977	152.0	153.1	127.3
1954	25.7	25.6	25.7	1978	167.9	168.1	143.0
1955	28.7	28.3	30.4	1979	186.9	185.9	161.8
1956	31.6	31.4	33.2	1980	204.1	199.3	181.7
1957	35.2	35.1	36.6	1981	221.6	213.2	203.1
1958	37.7	37.2	36.4	1982	217.9	207.1	192.9
1959	40.2	40.1	38.4	1983	200.3	192.0	158.2
1960	44.6	43.7	44.9	1984	209.1	201.2	163.6
1961	46.7	46.1	44.7	1985	219.7	212.0	187.8
1962	49.0	48.2	47.6	1986	200.4	192.2	159.8

1. Total Industrial Index includes mining, petroleum and petrochemicals, construction, electricity, and manufacturing (food, textiles and clothing, forest products, chemicals, non-metal materials, and metallurgy).

SOURCE: 1939–69, Mexico-NAFINSA, EMC, 1981, pp. 153–154;
1970–84, Mexico-NAFINSA, EMC, 1986, p. 140;
1985–86, Mexico-BANAMEX-RESM, December 1987,
p. 427, and February 1988, p. 99.

Table 3512

PRODUCTION LEVELS OF SELECTED MEXICAN GOODS, 1982–86

(12-Month Averages, 1981 = 100)

Year	Extracted Crude	Electricity	Steel Ingots	Rods	Cement	Chemical Fibers	Car Engines	Television Sets	Household Appliances	Beer
1982	119	107	92	90	107	97	78	81	101	96
1983	116	110	91	84	95	105	48	53	83	84
1984	121	117	98	89	103	112	60	49	72	90
1985	119	125	95	80	113	116	77	70	81	99
1986	108	132	93	85	110	112	57	76	79	102

SOURCE: Mexico-BANAMEX-RESM, May 1987, p. 105.

Table 3513

VEHICLES PRODUCED IN MEXICO, 1950–86

(N)

Year	Total	Autos[1]	Buses and Trucks[2]	Year	Total	Autos[1]	Buses and Trucks[2]
1950	21,575	10,384	11,191	1970	189,986	133,218	56,768
1951	46,081	21,833	24,248	1971	211,393	153,412	52,274
1952	47,987	20,687	27,300	1972	229,791	160,005	57,981
1953	35,709	13,791	21,918	1973	285,568	200,147	66,786
1954	33,380	13,325	20,055	1974	350,947	248,255	85,421
1955	32,275	12,405	19,870	1975	356,624	237,118	119,506
1956	39,387	13,134	26,253	1976	324,979	212,549	112,430
1957	41,106	18,297	22,809	1977	280,813	187,637	93,176
1958	38,955	20,373	18,582	1978	384,127	242,519	141,608
1959	51,118	27,159	23,959	1979	444,426	280,049	164,377
1960	49,807	28,121	21,686	1980	490,006	303,056	186,950
1961	62,563	39,524	23,039	1981	597,118	355,497	241,621
1962	66,637	40,801	25,836	1982	472,637	300,579	172,058
1963	74,515	48,841	25,673	1983	285,485	207,137	78,348
1964	98,435	65,869	32,566	1984	357,998	244,704	113,294
1965	103,584	70,242	33,342	1985	398,192	246,960	151,232
1966	117,764	84,673	33,091	1986	272,168	169,567	102,601
1967	126,210	88,327	37,883				
1968	144,186	102,679	41,507				
1969	165,126	113,553	51,573				

1. Carrying up to 10 passengers.
2. Carrying more than 10 passengers.

SOURCE: Mexico-INEGI-EHM, II, p. 527; except 1971–74 from Mexico-NAFINSA-EMC, 1981, p. 174; and 1985–86 from Mexico-NAFINSA-MV, Mar. 2, 1987, p. 235.

Table 3514

MEXICO TOTAL FOREIGN REVENUE, 1950–86

(M US)

Category and Source	1950	1955	1960	1965	1970	1975	1980	1985	1986
Total Income (A)[1]	994.1	1,329.0	1,444.0	2,062.6	3,254.5	7,134.8	24,947.3	30,774.4	24,265.4
Tourism (A)[2]	110.9	118.1	139.4	245.0	415.0	800.1	1,671.2	1,719.7	1,791.7
Border Transactions (A)[3]	121.9	261.7	366.0	499.5	1,050.1	1,924.7	3,722.1	1,180.6	1,191.7
Maquila Industry (B)	0	0	0	0	82.9[a]	332.4	771.0	1,267.5	1,285.1
Petroleum (C)	34.6	48.0	24.0	40.0	40.0	2,906.3	10,441.3	14,766.6	6,307.2
Cotton (D)[4]	138.7	229.9	157.9	212.2	123.8	174.1	315.5	75.7	6.2
Coffee (D)[5]	44.7	104.1	71.7	73.0	86.1	185.0	446.6	450.1	814.3
Shrimp (D)[6]	6.8	15.0	34.1	44.1	58.9	118.6	348.1	296.6	359.0
Sugar (D)	68.7	57.8	58.0	73.1	97.4	162.2	0	0	0

1. Includes categories not listed here.
2. Excludes border tourism.
3. Excludes tourism beyond the border region; includes border crossings.
4. Cotton was the main export from 1950 through 1974; in 1975 it was surpassed by petroleum.
5. Coffee vied with sugar as the second most important export through 1972, after which sugar dropped out of contention.
6. Shrimp surpassed sugar in importance in 1979.
7. Sugar exports ended in 1979.

a. First year for which data are available on the maquiladora (in-bond) industry, legally allowed beginning in 1966.

SOURCE: A, Mexico-BDM-IE, AH, II, 1983, and Mexico-BDM-IE, May 1987.

B, Sergio Rivas F., "La Industria Maquiladora en México: Realidades y Falacias," Mexico-BNCE-CE, November 1985, p. 1081, except data for 1985 from Secretaría de Hacienda y Crédito Público, "Economic and Financial Statistics, Data Book," Mexico, D.F., mimeo., May 31, 1987, p. 17.

C, Through 1975 calculated from IMF-IFS-Y, 1987; since 1976 from Source A, above. Conversions to dollars are with exchange rate given in SALA, 26-3501.

D, Through 1975 calculated from IMF-IFS-Y, 1980; thereafter data are calculated from IMF-IFS-Y, 1986, and IMF-IFS, April and November 1987. Conversions to dollars are with exchange rate given in SALA, 26-3501.

Table 3515

SHARES OF MEXICO FOREIGN REVENUE, 1950–86

(%)

Category	1950	1955	1960	1965	1970	1975	1980	1985	1986
Tourism	11.1	8.9	9.7	11.9	12.8	11.2	6.7	5.6	7.4
Border Transactions	12.3	19.7	25.4	24.2	32.3	30.0	14.9	3.8	4.9
Maquila Industry	0	0	0	0	2.5	4.7	2.6	4.1	5.3
Petroleum	3.5	3.6	1.7	1.9	1.2	40.7	41.9	48.0	26.0
Cotton	14.0	22.6	10.9	10.3	3.8	2.4	1.3	.2	0
Coffee	5.0	7.8	5.0	3.5	2.6	2.6	1.8	1.5	3.4
Shrimp	.7	1.1	2.4	2.1	1.8	1.7	1.4	1.0	1.5
Sugar	6.9	4.3	4.0	3.5	3.0	2.3	0	0	0

SOURCE: Calculated from table 3514.

Table 3516

MEXICO FOREIGN REVENUE FROM TOURISM AND GREATER AGRICULTURAL SECTOR,[1] SELECTED YEARS, 1950–86

(M US)

Year	Tourism	Agriculture
1950	110.9	253.2
1955	118.1	415.1
1960	139.4	389.2
1965	245.0	580.5
1970	415.0	614.9
1975	800.1	814.8
1980	1,671.2	1,527.9
1985	1,719.7	1,408.9
1986	1,690.0	2,098.4

1. Agriculture, livestock, beekeeping, fishing, and forestry.

SOURCE: Tourism is from table 3514; agriculture is from Mexico-NAFINSA-EMC, 1977, p. 401 (through 1975); Mexico—BDM-IE-AH, II, 1983, and Mexico-BDM-IE, May 1987.

loss of the country's formerly high income from oil meant that JLP could not stem the pressure on the overvalued peso that had been building since 1976.

In spite of the general decline of the Mexican economy since 1982, a bright spot has been the rapid growth of the in-bond industry, an aspect of the Official Party's policy since 1982 for restructuring Mexican industry, based on exporting industrial goods.

The idea for the in-bond or maquiladora industry dates from 1965 when Octaviano Campos Salas, Secretary of Industry and Commerce, traveled to the Far East where he observed U.S.-owned plants that assembled goods for the U.S. market.[18] Campos Salas, who sought to stimulate growth in the underdeveloped north of Mexico, realized that establishment of such plants in Mexico would be attractive to U.S. firms because of their close proximity to the United States. For Mexico, the plants could generate employment opportunities on the border following the U.S. termination in 1964 of its Bracero Program (under which Mexican workers had been able to enter the United States and remain temporarily with work permits). Campos Salas learned that U.S. assembly plants could operate profitably abroad because of U.S. tariff code regulations,[19] which exempted from duty certain imports to the United States.

The U.S. tariff code's schedule 806.30 (implemented in 1930 and amended in 1956), requires payment of U.S. taxes only on the foreign value added (labor, overhead, and profits) to any metal product whose form may be changed abroad and returned to the United States for further processing. This code schedule was originally intended to facilitate the processing of metal items in Canada during emergencies or breakdowns at U.S. manufacturing plants across the border from Detroit.

A second regulation in the U.S. tariff code (implemented in 1963 and revised in 1966) provided under schedule 807 that no duty be levied on the value of any component or raw material originating in the United States and sent to a foreign site for assembly, where additional processing is required in the United States. Firms using this schedule have produced such goods as electronic items, office equipment, engines, auto tail lights and spare parts, sewing machines, textiles, and clothing.

[18] For an early view of the maquiladora industry, see Lacy H. Hunt II, "Industrial Development on the Mexican Border," in *Business Review* (Federal Reserve Bank of Dallas), Feb. 1970, pp. 3–12.

[19] This discussion of the U.S. tariff code is based on Alicia Colin, "Japanese Investment in Mexico's Maquiladora Industry," paper submitted to my graduate Seminar in Recent Latin American History at UCLA, Spring Quarter, 1987.

Table 3517

MEXICO MAJOR EXPORT COMMODITIES AS SHARE OF MEXICO TOTAL EXPORTS,[1] FIVE-YEAR INTERVALS, 1950–85

(%)

Commodity	1950	1955	1960	1965	1970	1975	1980	1985
Petroleum	6.0	6.5	2.7	3.6	2.7	15.8	63.1	66.6
Cotton	26.1	29.3	20.6	18.9	8.8	5.9	2.0	.4
Sugar[2]	12.9	7.4	7.6	6.5	6.9	5.5	0	0
Coffee	8.4	13.3	9.4	6.5	6.1	6.3	2.9	2.4
Shrimp	1.3	1.9	4.5	3.9	4.5	4.0	2.2	1.6

1. Exports are only a part of the foreign income given in table 3514.
2. On the loss of sugar exports after 1978, see Roberto Barajas Sánchez, "Situación de la Industria Azucarera en México," Mexico-BNCE-CE, March 1986, pp. 221–225.

SOURCE: IMF-IFS-Y, 1980 and SALA, 26-2402.

By June 1966 the Mexican government established the Programa de Industrialización Fronteriza, which allowed U.S. companies to establish wholly owned subsidiaries within a twelve-mile border zone. U.S. companies could move equipment and materials duty free into and out of Mexico merely by posting a bond to insure that the maquiladora imports would only be temporary—hence the name "in-bond" industry.

The concept "maquiladora" has much history. The term itself comes from the Spanish word *maquila*, meaning the toll charged by the miller or lord of the manor for processing another's grain, flour, or oil.[20] Today maquiladora, or often maquila, is a generic term for firms that process by assembling or transforming components. Or it can be said that the maquiladora is an economic unit for the production of goods or services based upon the importation of raw materials and equipment for processing in Mexico. Sometimes the maquila industry is called "production sharing" or "twin plant industry" (which would involve labor-intensive plants on the Mexican side and complementary capital-intensive plants on the U.S. side),[21] but the latter term is usually erroneously applied because most of the foreign, non-Mexican plants are not located near the border or even in the Western Hemisphere.

Because the modern maquiladora industry demonstrated immediate prospects for success in providing jobs,

paying Mexican taxes, and stimulating the entire economy, by 1967 Mexico abolished the twelve-mile limit on in-bond location, which has allowed maquiladora industries to locate throughout the country. By 1972 and 1977, the Mexican government codified the in-bond industry as independent of the Border Industrialization Program, but only about 10 percent of maquiladora operations have yet located in the interior.

To translate maquila to mean "in-bond" is becoming increasingly inexact. In 1983 Mexico allowed in-bond companies to sell part of their products in Mexico as long as they have a 15 percent Mexican content. Maquilas located in the interior are permitted to sell up to 40 percent of such goods in the country; maquilas on the border currently face a 10 to 20 percent limit on their sales within Mexico.

With the decline of the peso, foreign investors have seen since 1985 their international exchange buy or rent more plants and equipment and to pay more workers in Mexico at costs highly favorable to other countries. The number of factories rose steadily, reaching more than 400 by the late 1970s and more than 600 by the early 1980s. Then came the big gains of 1985 and 1986, reaching into the 700s and 900s, respectively. The number of employees increased to more than 100,000 in 1979 and to 124,000 one year later, doubling by 1986. (See table 3519). In the meantime, in only one year, 1982, was there a decline in the number of maquiladora employees.

The U.S.–Mexican Trade Relationship

As Mexico confronts change in the areas of finance, prices, production, and foreign income, it is important to point out the constancy of the Mexico–United States trade relationship since the late 1960s. (See table 3520.) Although registered trade (imports plus exports) with the United States prior to World War II stood in the 60 percents, from 1940

[20] On the term "maquila," see *Simon and Schuster's International Dictionary* (1973), p. 1337; María Moliner, *Diccionario de Uso del Español* (1986), p. 343; Real Academia Española, *Diccionario de la Lengua Española* (1984), p. 874.
[21] On generic and economic definitions of the term "maquila," see Norris C. Clement and Stephen R. Jenner, *Location Decisions Regarding Maquiladora/In-Bond Plants Operating in Baja California, Mexico* (San Diego: San Diego State University, 1987), pp. 5–19.

Table 3518

MEXICO OIL TRADE, 1938–85

(T Barrels)

Year	Exports			Imports[1]		
	Crude	Refined	Total	Crude	Refined	Total
1938	3,799	5,196	8,995	0	123	123
1939	8,576	5,958	14,534	0	136	136
1940	8,561	4,265	12,826	0	151	151
1941	7,563	7,855	15,418	0	567	567
1942	1,373	4,717	6,090	0	459	459
1943	1,343	4,382	5,725	0	212	212
1944	655	4,229	4,884	0	261	261
1945	2,432	5,695	8,127	0	414	414
1946	3,302	5,926	9,228	0	972	972
1947	6,742	7,168	13,910	0	2,178	2,178
1948	7,185	5,933	13,118	0	2,547	2,547
1949	7,183	6,942	14,125	0	2,703	2,703
1950	12,183	4,318	16,501	0	3,754	3,754
1951	13,721	3,137	16,858	0	4,729	4,729
1952	9,325	5,995	15,320	0	3,062	3,062
1953	3,484	11,864	15,348	0	3,983	3,983
1954	4,630	18,640	23,270	0	7,286	7,286
1955	6,106	19,727	25,833	0	10,545	10,545
1956	6,617	17,105	23,722	38	10,324	10,362
1957	4,037	11,989	16,026	1,358	10,260	11,618
1958	676	10,966	11,642	717	5,869	6,586
1959	112	13,158	13,270	11	6,005	6,016
1960	1,100	6,447	7,547	0	3,704	3,704
1961	6,683	8,476	15,159	0	3,713	3,713
1962	7,158	11,230	18,388	0	1,758	1,758
1963	7,138	11,580	18,718	145	2,142	2,287
1964	7,621	9,545	17,166	577	2,606	3,183
1965	4,800	15,045	19,845	0	1,255	1,255
1966	0	17,057	17,057	0	3,525	3,525
1967	0	17,984	17,984	0	3,624	3,624
1968	0	16,094	16,094	0	3,619	3,619
1969	0	16,263	16,263	0	8,652	8,652
1970	0	22,413	22,413	0	9,312	9,312
1971	0	17,079	17,079	672	17,088	17,760
1972	0	9,448	9,448	10,776	16,291	27,067
1973	0	8,699	8,699	23,613	24,156	47,769
1974	5,804	6,659	12,463	6,557	16,016	22,573
1975	34,382	2,568	36,950	0	18,152	18,151
1976	34,470	1,220	35,690	0	9,285	9,286
1977	73,736	1,652	75,388	0	3,466	3,465
1978	133,247	673	133,920	0	10,616	10,617
1979	194,485	3,701	198,186	0	9,877	9,875
1980	302,957	17,543	320,019	0	5,429	5,428
1981	400,778	24,206	424,985	0	3,705	3,704
1982	544,614	15,357	559,972	0	3,017	3,016
1983	561,005	30,752	591,757	0	6,347	6,347
1984	558,004	40,944	598,948	0	12,111	12,111
1985	524,943	49,413	574,356	0	19,377	19,377

1. Cf. Mexico-NAFINSA-EMC, 1986, p. 193, which gives much higher
   import figures.

SOURCE: Mexico-INEGI-EHM, II, P. 698, revised with data in Mexico,
Petróleos Mexicanos, *Anuario Estadístico*, 1985 (published in 1986),
pp. 116, 121–122.

Table 3519

MEXICO IN-BOND INDUSTRY, 1970–87

Year	Factories (N)	Employees (T)
1970	120[a]	20[a]
1974	455	76
1975	454	67
1976	448	74
1977	443	78
1978	457	91
1979	540	111
1980	620	124
1981	605	130
1982	585	123
1983	600	173
1984	672	202
1985	760	218
1986	900	255
1987	1,005	308

a. Excludes factories and employees not in the border states.

SOURCE: SALA-MB, p. 53; Sergio Rivas F., "La Industria Maquiladora en México," Mexico-BNCE-CE, November 1985, pp. 1074 and 1076; Mexico-BANAMEX-RESM, December 1986, p. 502; "Lloyds Economic Report," December 1987, p. 3.

Table 3520

MEXICO TRADE WITH THE UNITED STATES AS SHARE OF MEXICO WORLD TRADE,[1] SAMPLE YEARS, 1901–85

Year	Percent	Year	Percent
1901[a]	67.2	1963	66.9
1910[a]	68.1	1967	60.3
1932	64.7	1970	62.6
1936	60.2	1973	60.6
1940	85.1	1976	62.4
1943[b]	88.1	1978	64.3
1947	83.7	1980	66.5
1950	85.4	1981	60.8
1952	80.9	1982	56.0
1953[c]	75.1	1983	58.9
1957	72.2	1984	59.6
1960	68.0	1985	60.0

1. Trade (imports plus exports), excluding CIF and FOB factors; no data for years from 1912 to 1931.

a. Fiscal year.
b. Highest percentage for all years since 1901, regardless of sample.
c. Beginning in 1953 includes border trade.

SOURCE: Through 1984: Calculated from Mexico-INEGI-EHM, I, pp. 665-669.
            1985:   Calculated from Mexico-NAFINSA-EMC, 1986, pp. 322–323 and 335.

Table 3521

U.S. TRADE WITH MEXICO AS SHARE OF TOTAL U.S. TRADE,[1] 1940–86

Year	Percent	Year	Percent
1940	2.6	1965	3.6
1941	3.3	1966	3.5
1942	2.5	1967	3.4
1943	2.3	1968	3.4
1944	2.7	1969	3.3
1945	3.6	1970	3.5
1946	5.0	1971	3.2
1947	4.4	1972	3.8
1948	3.9	1973	4.1
1949	3.8	1974	4.1
1950	4.0	1975	4.0
1951	4.1	1976	3.6
1952	4.2	1977	3.5
1953	3.8	1978	4.0
1954	3.9	1979	4.7
1955	4.1	1980	6.0
1956	3.8	1981	6.4
1957	4.0	1982	6.0
1958	4.4	1983	5.6
1959	3.6	1984	5.5
1960	3.6	1985	5.8
1961	3.8	1986	4.9
1962	3.7		
1963	3.6		
1964	4.0		

1. Trade = imports plus exports.

SOURCE: USDC-SCB, various issues; and USBD-SA, various issues.

into the Korean War period the figure reached into the 80 percents (see figure 35:3). With the end of the Korean War in July 1953, and through the rest of the 1950s, Mexico's trade with its northern neighbor fell into the 70 percents. Since the 1960s, the 60 percent figures have held, except for the years from 1982 through 1984 when Mexico's downturn reduced its U.S. trade to the high 50 percents, the low of 56 percent coming in 1982.

Mexico has had difficulty convincing its major trading partner to treat seriously trade relations between the two countries. Whereas U.S. trade is vital to Mexico, for Washington the importance to the U.S. economy of trade with Mexico has never seemed significant as a percentage of U.S. total trade. Even during World War II, the Mexico share of U.S. trade was below 3.3 percent (see table 3521). That figure reached 5 percent in 1946 and then through 1978 fell to the 3 to 4 percent level. In 1979, when the United States was fighting OPEC domination of world petroleum markets, Mexico's oil shipments to the United States increased, to more than 5 percent of U.S. imports. The peaks came in 1981 (6.4 percent) and in 1980 and 1982 (6.0 percent).

Figure 35:3

MEXICO TRADE WITH THE UNITED STATES, AS SHARE OF MEXICO WORLD TRADE, SAMPLE YEARS, 1901–85

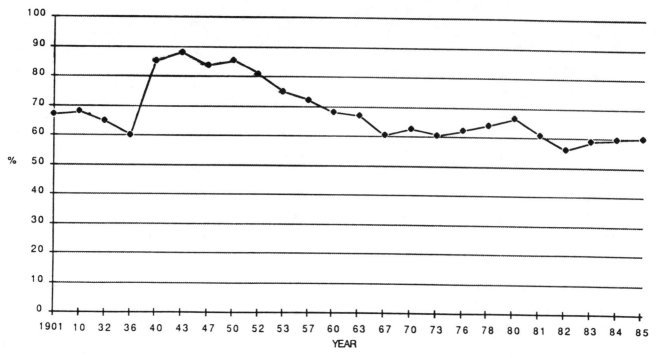

SOURCE: Table 3520.

Table 3522

SIX MOST IMPORTANT U.S. TRADING PARTNERS,[1]
SELECTED YEARS, 1955–85

Country	Percent						Rank				
	1955	1960	1970	1980	1985		1955	1960	1970	1980	1985
Mexico	4.1	3.6	3.5	6.0	5.8		4	6	5	3	3
Japan	4.0	7.3	12.7	11.1	15.9		5	2	2	2	2
Canada	21.9	19.0	24.2	16.9	22.6		1	1	1	1	1
United Kingdom	5.8	7.0	5.7	4.8	4.6		2	3	4	5	5
West Germany	3.6	6.1	7.1	4.9	5.1		6	4	3	4	4
Other	4.3[a]	4.3[a]	3.2[b]	2.8[c]	3.6[d]		3[a]	5[a]	6[b]	6[c]	6[d]

a. Venezuela.
b. Italy.
c. France.
d. Taiwan.

SOURCE: USDC-SCB, various issues; and USBC-SA, various issues.

Mexico's position among U.S. trading partners shows some interesting patterns (see table 3522). In 1955 Mexico ranked fourth in U.S. trade (imports plus exports), but fell to sixth and fifth in 1960 and 1970, respectively. During the world energy crisis from 1973 through 1981, Mexico, with its oil, became the third most important U.S. trading partner in 1980. With added absolute income from the United States, Mexico assured its overall position as the third most important U.S. trading partner. Even though the oil crisis seemingly had passed by 1982, Mexico has retained its third position (but not its high 1981 percentage of U.S. exports) for several interrelated reasons. Significant U.S. and Japanese business has moved to Mexico in order to take advantage of lower energy, labor, and transportation costs in relation to the U.S. market, which is within easy reach of Mexico's developing in-bond northern border industry.

With regard to Japan, Mexico's main competitor for trade with the United States, in 1955 the two countries stood almost even, each with about 4 percent of U.S. trade, far behind Canada's number one trading position. By 1960 Mexico had lost in the race with Japan, which enjoyed the comparative advantage of having its industry totally destroyed in World War II and replaced in the decade after 1945 with state-of-the-art equipment and methods. Meanwhile, Mexico could not afford to do much beyond maintaining its old industrial plant which had worn down under the full-capacity production needed to help win World War II for the Allies.

Although Mexico could not compete with the U.S.–Canadian economic relationship (which has been enhanced by a common language, similar legal and commercial systems, and equivalent high standards of living as well as abundant energy and comparatively low-cost transport access to industry in the northeastern United States), Mexico has been able to compete with the United Kingdom and West Germany, each of which formerly held third place instead of Mexico. Mexico was able to compete because it did not seek to export manufactures so much as to sell its raw materials on the world market. By 1985 Mexico's 5.8 percent of U.S. trade was far behind Canada's 23.6 percent.

Concluding Analysis

Looking back at the economic trends depicted here in statistical series, the intertwined patterns seen in finance, prices, production, and foreign income reveal contradictions in Mexican policy, especially under president Luis Echeverría Alvarez and José López Portillo. Because those contradictions led up to the 1982 shift from economic growth to economic stagnation in Mexico, we can marvel that Mexico's economic growth held up as long as it did.

The huge increase in foreign debt in the 1970s, undertaken with the excuse after 1975 of expanding the infrastructure needed to ship ever greater quantities of oil and gas abroad and to provide cheap energy to its industrial plants in Mexico, and the simultaneous overvaluing of the peso meant that many Mexicans (who were increasingly nervous about the value of the peso) could easily shift their pesos into dollars.

With double-digit inflation in 1976, the peso began to slip from its long standard of 12.50 to the dollar, much to the consternation of LEA. It seems a joke from our vantage point today that on the basis of his record of a strong currency at home and a "strong" anti-imperialist position abroad LEA hoped to become U.N. secretary-general. At one point in his term, he even suggested that, given the twenty-year stability in the Mexican currency, the peso should replace the unstable dollar as the world's reserve money. Too, even as he increased the M_1 money supply he believed that he could hold the peso at 12.50 to the dollar, maintaining the confidence of investors as well as enabling the country to import the machinery needed to produce for the Mexican market.

The problems of the peso mounted under JLP during his presidency from 1976 to 1982.[22] Although the peso was stabilized in the late 1970s, it still remained overvalued as inflation averaged nearly 22 percent between 1977 and 1979. The peso was permitted to lose only .6 percent and 6.4 percent in the years 1980 and 1981, respectively, when consumer prices rose more than 26 percent in 1980 and 28 percent in 1981. In 1982, as pressure built to devalue the peso, JLP claimed that he would defend the peso "like a dog,"[23] plotting to defeat Mexico's "traitors" who were converting their pesos by the billions into dollars. But JLP was forced to raise the average valuation of the peso from 22.75 in 1977 to 56.40 in 1982, a 60 percent devaluation compared with the 256 percent inflation over which he presided.[24]

Moreover, as JLP transferred the presidency to Miguel de la Madrid in 1982, average yearly inflation more than doubled and the peso declined by 56 percent compared with 1981 (cf. tables 3507 and 3501). De la Madrid made the decision to shift to a standard of undervaluing the peso—in 1983 he devalued it by 62.5 percent, the first time since 1955 that devaluation exceeded the rate of inflation. By devaluing at a steady rate greater than inflation (except in 1984 when 65 percent inflation justified more than an 18 percent devaluation), De la Madrid made it impossible for most Mexicans to buy dollars. Whereas Mexicans were encouraged to stay at home, foreign investors and tourists

---

[22] For the relationship of inflation to devaluation, see SALA-SEM, Introduction, table 2, part I.

[23] Quoted in Alan Riding, *Distant Neighbors: A Portrait of the Mexicans* (New York: Knopf, 1984), p. 215.

[24] Devaluation and inflation do not involve one-to-one relationships because in the former case the percentage change is limited to 100 percent and in the latter case the percentage change is unlimited. For example, inflation of 233 percent would require a 70 percent devaluation in order to maintain parity.

were encouraged to enter. The decline of the peso was highlighted by its passing the 1,400 rate per dollar in 1987. (Apart from the average rate, by the end of 1987 the peso hit 2,270.) With an undervalued peso, Mexico's private sector could compete abroad and the restructuring of the economy has become government policy since 1982.

Although implicit and explicit restructuring is salubrious to eliminate the many contradictions leading to the post-1982 economic stagnation,[25] it will be costly for many activities for which devaluation is not a favorable option. Trade is vital for the economics on both sides of the border, but with the decline of the peso, Mexico's border businesses have found their ability to buy U.S. inputs crippled. Also, credit has been restricted in Mexico in order to divert cash

---

[25] On restructuring, see my "Six Ideological Phases," in SALA-SEM, Introduction.

into paying the foreign debt, hence the decline in border transactions (shown in tables 3514 and 3515). If the U.S.-Mexican border seemed to be the temporary loser in the traditional two-way transactions wherein citizens buy each other's goods, the benefits to the maquila industry may provide a new stimulus to the border as well as to the interior of Mexico. Too, where border transactions for Mexico were often offset by Mexican purchases in the United States, the growing maquila industry may yield higher net foreign income to Mexico.

As shown by the many interlocking patterns discussed here, Mexico's problems are complex and will require new policies depending upon such factors as the world price of oil and the government's ability to restore faith in its banking system. In the meantime, if future presidents attempt to defend inoperable policy "like a dog," Mexico will face an even more complex future.

INDEX

Consumption, 26-3000, 3340 to 3360, 3364, 3510; cement, 26-1631; energy, 26-1902, 1907, 1908, 1916, 1918, 1926, 1928; fats, 26-823; fertilizer, 26-209, 210; fish, 26-822; food, 26-824; milk, 26-2207; newspapers and newsprint, 26-500; protein, 26-825

Cooperatives, 26-1424

Copper, 26-1706, 1803, 1821, 2400 to 2404, 2463, 2704, 2717, 3228, 3237; refined, 26-1706

Copra, 26-2108, 3228

Corn. *See* Maize

Corporate business activity, 26-2635, 2900 to 2911

Cost of living, 26-3200 to 3223, 3502, 3507

Cotton, 26-1707, 1708, 2109, 2400 to 2404, 2474 to 2476, 2709, 2714, 2716, 3228, 3238; lint, 26-2109, 2466; U.S., 26-2465; woven, 26-1707; yarn, 26-1708

Cottonseed, 26-2110

Cows; milk products, 26-2204, 2205, 2207

Creditors, 26-2804, 2809, 2823, 2824. *See also* Loans; Public debt

Crime, 26-1340 to 1342; alien 1518

Criminals. *See* Crime

Cropland. *See* Land, crop

Crops: production, 26-1715, 1716, 2102 to 2118; trade, 26-2417 to 2420, 2422 to 2426, 2428 to 2431, 2433 to 2436, 2439 to 2445, 2448 to 2453

Cultivation, 26-202, 203

Currency, 26-3339. *See also* Money

Dairy products, 26-1702, 2204 to 2207, 2407, 2421, 2521 to 2541, 3228

DDT. *See* Pesticides

Deaths, 26-124, 708 to 713; by earthquakes, 26-124; principal causes, 26-711, 713; by sex, 26-713

Debts. *See* Foreign debt; Loans; Private debt; Public debt

Defense, 26-1203, 1204, 1322, 1323, 3010, 3011, 3337

Democracy, 26-1000, 1003

Demography, 26-100, 600 to 674

Density, 26-100, 627 to 648, 663

Dentists, 26-800, 806, 815

Deportations, 26-1518

Deserts, 26-127

Development (land), 26-209

Development (plans), 26-3000

Development (scientific research), 26-924 to 926

Development (projects), tropical land, 26-207

Diet. *See* Calories; Fats; Protein

Diptheria, 26-714. *See also* Disease

Direct foreign investment. *See* Investment

Disease, 26-711, 713 to 717, 808

Distance. *See* Aviation

Distribution of income. *See* Income

Divisions, civil, 26-101 to 120, 627 to 648

Divorce, 26-719

Doctors. *See* Physicians

Dollars: exchange rate, 26-3103, 3104 to 3130, 3503, 3504; measure of GDP, 26-3362; purchasing power, 26-2552, 3324; value of SDR, 26-3102

Dwellings. *See* Households

Dysentery, 26-706, 713, 715. *See also* Disease

EAP (Economically Active Population), 26-849, 850, 1300, 1309 to 1312, 1315, 1316, 1324

Earthquakes. *See* Deaths

ECLA (U.N., Economic Commission for Latin America), 26-2547 to 2549, 2700, 2730, 3227, 3300 to 3321, 3324

Economic activity, 26-1327, 1328, 3300 to 3374

Economic class. *See* Class

Economic characteristics. *See* Economic activity

Economic growth, 26-3000 to 3060, 3300 to 3374. *See also* GDP; GNP; Industry, output

Economic indicators, 26-1820, 2700 to 2730

Economic regions. *See* Regions

ECR (Extended Caribbean Region), 26-649, 2609

Education, 26-800, 801, 900 to 926, 1208, 1209, 1322, 1323, 1513; adult, 26-916; attainment, 26-906; Catholic, 26-1100; college, 26-800; compulsory, 26-905; dropout rate, 26-902; duration, 26-905; enrollment, 26-800, 901, 908 to 912, 916 to 918; entrances ages, 26-903; expenditure, 26-918, 922, 923, 1209, 3010, 3011; field of study, 26-912 to 913; financial period, 26-921; higher, 26-901, 904, 906, 908, 911 to 913, 916, 923, 925; history of enrollment by country, 26-915; immigrants, 26-1513; intermediate, 26-908, 923; library, 26-919, 920; literacy, 26-800, 900, 901; military, 26-1208, 1209; personnel, 26-907 to 911, 917, 918, 925, 1322, 1323; pre-primary, 26-905, 906, 908, 923; primary, 26-800, 904 to 906, 908, 910, 916, 923; private, 26-909; public, 26-922, 923; research, 26-924 to 926; rural, 26-900, 904; secondary, 26-800, 904, 905, 906, 908, 916, 923; special, 26-918; specialties, 26-912, 913; urban, 26-900, 906

Egg, 26-2407, 2521 to 2541

Elections, 26-1002, 1006 to 1056, 3400 to 3430, 3500; absenteeism, 26-1030; by political party, 26-1006, 1012 to 1016, 1019, 1021, 1024 to 1029, 1031 to 1054; by province, 26-1012, 1024, 1025, 1029 to 1031, 1034; congressional, 26-1006, 1013 to 1016, 1020, 1027, 1036 to 1037, 1049, 1050, 1053, 1054, 1056; presidential, 26-1006 to 1008, 1010, 1012, 1015, 1019, 1021 to 1029, 1035, 1037, 1038, 1041 to 1044, 1048 to 1052, 1054, 1055. *See also* Politics

Electricity, 26-1311, 1624, 1625, 1700, 1900, 1906, 1925 to 1930, 2908 to 2910, 3325; installed capacity and projections, 26-1929, 1930

Employees. *See* Employment

Employment, 26-1300 to 1334, 1400, 1717, 1820, 2911 to 2928, 3000; by sector, 26-1304, 1317, 1820; temporary workers, 26-1506. *See also* EAP; Income; Wages

Energy, 26-1900 to 1931, 2851, 2852; biomass, 26-1900, 1901; commercial, 26-1902 to 1908; geothermal, 26-1900, 1924. *See also* Electricity; Gas; Petroleum

Engineers, 26-805, 924 to 926

Enrollment, student. *See* Education; Students

Enrollment history, 26-915

Exchange rates, 26-3100 to 3130, 3501

Ex-Im Bank (Export-Import Bank of the United States), 26-2820, 2821

Expenditure: advertising, 26-514; as share of GDP, 26-1205; by U.S. majority-owned foreign affiliates, 26-2908; functional analysis of, 26-3010; GDP, 26-3338, 3340 to 3360; government, 26-921, 1200, 1204, 3008 to 3012, 3018 to 3037, 3338; housing, 26-3010; military, 26-1200, 1203 to 1205, 1209, 3010, 3011; on public education, 26-922, 923, 3010, 3011; on public health, 26-3011; on research and development, 26-926; social, 26-3011

Exports, 26-1201, 1820, 2209, 2210, 2400 to 2408, 2410, 2411, 2413 to 2418, 2420, 2422 to 2427, 2429, 2431, 2434, 2436, 2438, 2439, 2441, 2442, 2444 to 2453, 2455 to 2459, 2460, 2462 to 2466, 2468, 2471, 2473, 2474, 2476, 2478, 2500 to 2541, 2543, 2548 to 2550, 2552, 2553, 2556, 2600, 2602, 2604 to 2607, 2609, 2612 to 2635, 2700 to 2720, 2722, 2728 to 2747, 2808, 2830, 3000, 3114 to 3119, 3122, 3124, 3125, 3128 to 3130, 3227, 3229 to 3231, 3338, 3340 to 3360, 3509, 3517; as share of GDP, 26-2473; as principal commodities, 26-2400, 2401; intra-regional, 26-2603 to 2609; share in value of world, 26-2600; share of public debt, 26-2808. *See also* Trade

Falkland Islands. *See* Wars

Family planning, 26-827 to 832. *See also* Birth control

FAO (U.N. Food and Agriculture Organization), 26-200, 204, 1001

Fats, 26-823, 2521 to 2541, 3228